The Reader's Adviser

The Reader's Adviser
14th EDITION
Marion Sader, Series Editor

Volume 1
The Best in Reference Works, British Literature, and American Literature
David Scott Kastan and Emory Elliott, Volume Editors

Books About Books • Bibliography • Reference Books: General • Reference Books: Literature • Medieval Literature • Renaissance Literature • Shakespeare • Restoration and Eighteenth-Century Literature • The Romantic Period • The Victorian Period • Modern British and Irish Literature • British Literature: Popular Modes • Early American Literature: Beginnings to the Nineteenth Century • Early Nineteenth-Century American Literature • Middle to Late Nineteenth-Century American Literature • Early Twentieth-Century American Literature • Middle to Late Twentieth-Century American Literature • Modern American Drama • American Literature: Some New Directions • American Literature: Popular Modes

Volume 2
The Best in World Literature
Robert DiYanni, Volume Editor

Introduction to World Literature • Hebrew Literature • Yiddish Literature • Middle Eastern Literatures • African Literatures • Literature of the Indian Subcontinent • Chinese Literature • Japanese Literature • Korean Literature • Southeast Asian Literatures • Greek Literature • Latin Literature • Italian Literature • French Literature • Spanish Literature • Portuguese Literature • German Literature • Netherlandic Literature • Scandinavian Literatures • Russian Literature • East European Literatures • Latin American Literatures • Canadian Literature • Literature of the Caribbean • Australian Literature • New Zealand Literature • Comparative Literature

Volume 3
The Best in Social Sciences, History, and the Arts
John G. Sproat, Volume Editor

Social Sciences and History: General Reference • Anthropology • Economics • Geography • Political Science • Psychology • Sociology • Education • World History • Ancient History • European History • African History • Middle Eastern History • History of Asia and the Pacific • United States History • Canadian History • Latin American History • Music and Dance • Art and Architecture • Mass Media • Folklore, Humor, and Popular Culture • Travel and Exploration

THE
Reader's Adviser®

14th EDITION

Volume 3

The Best in Social Sciences,
History, and the Arts

John G. Sproat, Volume Editor

Marion Sader, Series Editor

R. R. Bowker®
A Reed Reference Publishing Company
New Providence, New Jersey

Published by R. R. Bowker
A Reed Reference Publishing Company
Copyright © 1994 by Reed Publishing (USA) Inc.

International Standard Book Numbers
0-8352-3320-0 (SET)
0-8352-3321-9 (Volume 1)
0-8352-3322-7 (Volume 2)
0-8352-3323-5 (Volume 3)
0-8352-3324-3 (Volume 4)
0-8352-3325-1 (Volume 5)
0-8352-3326-X (Volume 6)
International Standard Serial Number 0094-5943
Library of Congress Catalog Card Number 57-13277

The paper used in this publication meets the minimum requirements
of American National Standard for Information Sciences—Permanence
of Papers for Printed Library Materials, ANSI Z39.48-1984.

ISBN 0 - 8352 - 3320 - 0

9 780835 233200

Contents

Preface

Libraries are busy places and rarely is there time for the reader and the librarian to sit down, discuss and analyze the reader's book problem, direct his interest or locate the book he wants. . . . In answer to this demand readers' advisers are appearing on many library staffs.
—JENNIE M. FLEXNER

When Jennie M. Flexner, founder of the New York Public Library's famous Reader's Advisory service, wrote those words in *Library Journal* in 1938, R. R. Bowker's own *Reader's Adviser* had already been a Baedeker for overwhelmed library patrons for nearly a generation. Known then as *The Bookman's Manual*, it had, as its name suggests, actually been conceived, not by a librarian, but by a bookseller, Bessie Graham. Graham's first edition, published in 1921, was based on an enormously popular bookselling course she had recently taught at the William Penn Evening High School in Philadelphia. Just over 400 pages, that first *Bookman's Manual* was intended to give novice book retailers a basic inventory of essential in-print titles, both to stock and to recommend to customers. (It did, admittedly, fail to mention Shakespeare—a shortcoming that so appalled Mildred C. Smith, the young Bowker employee who had been asked to organize Graham's material, that more than four decades later, as editor of *Publishers Weekly*, Smith still vividly recalled the omission.) Not surprisingly, however, *The Bookman's Manual* was quickly adopted by librarians facing much the same task with their own patrons—and through 13 editions the work, in its various guises, has been successfully matching good books with grateful readers for more than 70 years.

Because of its roots in bookselling, *The Reader's Adviser* has always been far more than a guide to "the classics"—those time-honored treasures that, as Mark Twain once insisted, "everybody talks about but nobody reads." From the very first edition, its chapters reflected current literary, social, and political trends, embracing not only such mainstream categories as "Great Names in English Poetry" and "Essays and Letters" but also, as befitted the new era of universal suffrage, "American Fiction—Contemporary *Men* Writers" and "American Fiction—Contemporary *Women* Writers." Modern British authors experienced the same sexual differentiation in the second edition, published three years later, by which time Shakespeare had returned from exile and books on such extraliterary subjects as "Nature," "Music," and "Travel" had also been added.

Throughout the 1920s and 1930s, *The Bookman's Manual* continued to grow explosively—so much so that, by the time Bessie Graham bid farewell to her "lifework" (as she called it in her preface to the fifth edition of 1941), it had nearly doubled in size. "I commend its future editions to my unknown successor," she wrote, "and take leave of a task that holds only pleasant associations for me now that I pass 'Out of the stress of the doing, Into the peace of the done.' " Sadly, the United States's entry into World War II would soon interrupt that peace as well as the arrival of "future editions."

With the war near an end in June 1945, Bowker's Mildred Smith recommended Hester R. Hoffman, a bookseller with nearly 30 years' experience at the Hampshire Bookshop in Northampton, Massachusetts, to compile the next peacetime edition of Graham's *The Bookman's Manual*. Unfortunately, Hoffman's start was frustrated by more than a wartime paper shortage; Bowker's proposal reached her (as she later put it) while she was "lying flat in a room in a South Boston Hospital recovering from, of all things, a broken neck." Undaunted by her predicament, by the dearth of current titles on publishers' lists, and even by her typesetter's utter lack of foreign accents for the chapter on French literature, she succeeded in pulling together the sixth edition of *The Bookman's Manual* by 1948. The war, though, had taken its toll: despite a seven-year hiatus between editions, Hoffman's first effort was 62 pages *shorter* than Graham's last.

As the 1950s unfolded and the nuclear age cast a lengthening shadow, Hester Hoffman strove to keep *The Bookman's Manual* at the forefront of breaking literary and nonliterary events worldwide. A new chapter on science in the seventh edition of 1954 helped readers make sense of the profound legacy of such diverse theorists as Einstein and Freud. Thanks to Russian literature editors Helen Muchnic and Nicolai Vorobiov, anyone searching for contemporary Soviet novelists could have discovered the great Boris Pasternak (then known in the West only as a poet) fully three years before *Doctor Zhivago* made him an international sensation. In the eighth edition of 1958, the chapter on bibles updated readers who were eager to learn more about one of the seminal discoveries in Judeo-Christian history: a tattered collection of Hebrew and Aramaic parchments, concealed in pottery jars in caves near Qumran, that soon became known as the Dead Sea Scrolls.

Renamed *The Reader's Adviser and Bookman's Manual*, in 1960, the work continued to grow precipitously—struggling to reward the newfound postwar affluence, leisure, and cosmopolitan curiosity of American readers. With the baby boom at that time came a publishing boom, and, as Americans opened the New Frontier, they hungered for books about everything from rockets and space travel to parapsychology to segregation and the South. Indeed, just a glimpse of the new reading lists added during this heady and tumultuous era recaptures a time when readers were discovering ideas, arts, peoples, and places as perhaps they never had discovered before. There were books on the North American Indian and the opening of the West, Soviet history and policy, and the Civil War (as it reached its centenary); there were books by authors from Africa, Japan, China, India, Latin America, and, at long last, black America, as well as books about the lively arts of jazz, cinema, children's theater, and, yes, McLuhan's "cool medium," television.

By 1968, when Winifred F. Courtney guided the eleventh edition to press, one volume could no longer hold it all: It took two. The twelfth edition, published from 1974 to 1977, then blossomed to three volumes. As Bowker's own *Books in Print* continued to document a book market that was all but doubling in size every 10 years (from 245,000 titles in 1967 to 750,000 in 1987), the thirteenth edition, published in two installments, in 1986 and 1988, swelled to five volumes (plus a separately bound index). *The Reader's Adviser*, which always had been a reference tool built on the contributions of subject specialists, now had become virtually an encyclopedia—requiring separate editors for the set, for the individual volumes, for the sections . . . and even for the chapters!

As little as today's *Reader's Adviser* may resemble Bessie Graham's once modest *Bookman's Manual*, the work still adheres to tradition. More than ever the essential starting point for anyone who is setting out to read about the world of literary, artistic, philosophical, or scientific endeavor, the work's individual volumes are designed to carry users from the general to the specific—from overarching reference guides, critical histories, and anthologies about a genre or a field to the lives and works of its leading exemplars. As always, booksellers, reference and acquisitions librarians, lay readers, teachers, academics, and students alike can readily use it to identify the best of nearly everything available in English in the United States today, from the poetry of the ancients to Renaissance philosophy to meditations on the ethics of modern medicine.

Choosing what to include and what to leave out is never easy. As specialists, the volume and chapter editors know their field's most noted and popular figures, current and historic, and the body of literature on which the reputations of those individuals stand. Although I have asked each editor, when possible, to revise an "out of vogue" author's profile and bibliography rather than simply to eliminate it, paring is inevitable with any new edition. Then, too, the mere availability of an author's work can play its own editorial role. Although it is customary to list only titles published as books and (according to the latest monthly release of *Books in Print* on CD-ROM) currently for sale in the United States, exceptions are made for invaluable out-of-print works deemed likely to appear in the stacks of an established, modest-sized municipal library.

Revisions to the fourteenth edition have been judicious. Most noticeably, the set itself is longer and has a larger trim size—up from 6″ x 9″ to 7″ x 10″—to give the pages a more open look. As the heart of *The Reader's Adviser*, the bibliographies have been more extensively annotated than ever before, and the lists of "books by" that accompany each profiled author in Volumes 1 and 2 are now helpfully subcategorized into genres (fiction, nonfiction, poetry, plays, etc.). Furthermore, ISBNs have been added to the usual bibliographic data (again, drawn from the latest monthly release of *Books in Print* on CD-ROM) of publisher, price, and year of publication. In addition, on the sensible assumption that the author profiles preceding bibliographies should be a tantalizing appetizer for the entrée to come, the editors have done their best to season them all with rich, lively biographical detail. Finally, the reader should be aware that not all in-print editions of a work are necessarily listed but, rather, only those editions selected because of their quality or special features.

Another change in this edition is the addition of a "Chronology of Authors" section before the alphabetical arrangement of profiled authors in each chapter—a complement to the chronology that appears at the outset of each volume and a quick and easy means of placing each chapter's profiled entrants in historical perspective. Finally, to boost *The Reader's Adviser's* reference utility, the subject index of each volume has been greatly expanded, and the chapters on "Books about Books," "General Bibliography," and "General Reference" (which were previously split between Volumes 1 and 2) have been brought together and now appear at the beginning of Volume 1.

Of course, much about this new edition of *The Reader's Adviser* remains uniquely similar to the previous edition. The six-volume organization begun with the thirteenth edition continues: Volume 1 encompasses general reference works and American and British literature; Volume 2, world literature in translation; Volume 3, the social sciences, history, and the arts; Volume 4, the literature of philosophy and world religions; and Volume 5, the literature of science, technology, and medicine. Similarly, Volume 6 incorporates the name, title, and subject indexes of each of the previous volumes. Also retained are convenient cross-references throughout, which guide inquiring readers to related authors, chapters, sections, or volumes. A "see" reference leads the reader to the appropriate volume and chapter for information on a specific author. "See also" refers the reader to additional information in another chapter or volume. Within any sections of narrative, the name of an author who appears as a main listing in another chapter or volume is printed in large and small capital letters. If the chapter cross-referenced is to be found in a different volume from the one being consulted, the volume number is also given. Furthermore, to make basic research easier, the annotated bibliographies accompanying profiled individuals separately list works "by" and "about" those authors.

To assure that all volumes of the fourteenth edition are compiled concurrently and arrive together, I have relied on the contributions of countless authorities. Special thanks are due to both *The Reader's Adviser's* team of volume editors and the chapter contributors, whose names are listed in each volume. The book production experts at Book Builders Incorporated directed the almost Herculean task of coordinating the 110 chapters by 120 authors through numerous editing and production stages; to everyone's satisfaction, the system succeeded, as the reader can affirm from a glance at these six volumes. In particular, I must recognize Book Builders' Lauren Fedorko, president and guiding spirit, for her unfailing good spirits and intelligent decisions; Diane Schadoff, editorial coordinator; and Paula Wiech, production manager. Many thanks to them and their staffs for the extra hours and care that they lavished on our "magnum opus." Very special appreciation is due to Charles Roebuck, managing editor *extraordinaire*, whose concerns for accuracy, detail, and style made perfection almost attainable. Charles's contributions are countless, and much of the success of this edition is due to his tact and diplomacy in managing many people, many deadlines, and many pages of manuscript. Here at Bowker, I am especially grateful to my assistant, Angela Szablewski, who has had the monumental responsibility of coordinating all stages of the books' production.

In her 1938 article, Ms. Flexner wrote that "libraries are made up of good, old books as well as good, new books." In agreement with her view, I have continued in the *Reader's Adviser* tradition by including in this new fourteenth edition titles that are timeless, as well as those that are timely; the aim is to provide the user with both a broad and a specific view of the great writings and great writers of the past and present. I wish you all satisfaction in your research, delight in your browsing, and pleasure in your reading.

Marion Sader
Publisher
Professional & Reference Books
R.R. Bowker
September 1993

Contributing Editors

Aurora B. Arbena, LATIN AMERICAN HISTORY
Instructor in Spanish, TriCounty Technical College, Pendleton, South Carolina

Joseph L. Arbena, LATIN AMERICAN HISTORY
Professor of History, Clemson University

Robert H. Babcock, CANADIAN HISTORY
Professor of History, University of Maine

Thomas Barth, POLITICAL SCIENCE
Professor of Political Science, University of Wisconsin at Eau Claire

Donald O. Case, SOCIAL SCIENCE AND HISTORY: GENERAL REFERENCE
Associate Professor, Graduate School of Library and Information Science, University
of California at Los Angeles

Gary E. Clayton, ECONOMICS
Professor of Economics and Finance, Northern Kentucky University

Robert O. Collins, AFRICAN HISTORY
Director and Professor of History, University of California, Santa Barbara, Washington
Center

Florence L. Denmark, PSYCHOLOGY
Robert Scott Pace Professor and Chair, Psychology Department, Pace University,
New York

Suzanne Eggleston, MUSIC AND DANCE
Reference Librarian, Sterling Memorial Library Reference Department, Yale University

Harry Eiss, FOLKLORE, HUMOR, AND POPULAR CULTURE
Associate Professor of English, Eastern Michigan University

Mounir A. Farah, MIDDLE EASTERN HISTORY
Past President, Middle East Outreach Council; Senior Lecturer in Social Sciences,
Western Connecticut State University

Pericles B. Georges, ANCIENT HISTORY
Assistant Professor of History, Lake Forest College

Charles R. Goeldner, TRAVEL AND EXPLORATION
Professor of Marketing and Tourism, University of Colorado

David L. Hicks, WORLD HISTORY
Associate Professor of History, New York University

Judith Holliday, ART AND ARCHITECTURE
Fine Arts Library Librarian, Cornell University

Michael F. Keating, THE MASS MEDIA
Associate Professor; Communications, Film and Video Department; City College of
New York

Michael A. Keller, MUSIC AND DANCE
Director of Libraries, Stanford University

W. Dean Kinzley, HISTORY OF ASIA AND THE PACIFIC
Associate Professor of History, University of South Carolina

Rita Smith Kipp, ANTHROPOLOGY
Professor of Anthropology, Kenyon College

Richard J. Kraft, EDUCATION
Professor of Education, University of Colorado at Boulder

Wendy A. Miller, SOCIAL SCIENCE AND HISTORY: GENERAL REFERENCE
Reference Librarian, Santa Monica Public Library, Santa Monica, California

Arthur Mitchell, EUROPEAN HISTORY
Professor of History, University of South Carolina (Salkehatchie Campus)

Roger A. Salerno, SOCIOLOGY
Associate Professor of Sociology, Pace University, New York

W. Randy Smith, GEOGRAPHY
Associate Professor of Geography, Ohio State University

John G. Sproat, VOLUME EDITOR, UNITED STATES HISTORY
Distinguished Professor Emeritus of History, University of South Carolina

Abbreviations

abr.	abridged
A.D.	in the year of the Lord
annot(s).	annotated, annotator(s)
B.C.	before Christ
B.C.E.	before the common era
B.P.	before the present
Bk(s)	Book(s)
c.	circa
C.E.	of the common era
Class.	Classic(s)
coll.	collected
comp(s).	compiled, compiler(s)
ed(s).	edited, editor(s), edition(s)
fl.	flourished
fwd.	foreword
gen. ed(s).	general editor(s)
ill(s).	illustrated, illustrator(s)
intro.	introduction
Lit.	Literature
o.p.	out-of-print
Pr.	Press
pref.	preface
pt(s).	part(s)
repr.	reprint
rev. ed.	revised edition
Ser.	Series
Supp.	Supplement
trans.	translated, translator(s), translation
U. or Univ.	University
Vol(s).	Volume(s)

Throughout this series, publisher names are abbreviated within bibliographic entries. The full names of these publishers can be found listed in Volume 6, the Index to the series.

Chronology of Authors

Main author entries appear here chronologically by year of birth. Within each chapter, main author entries are arranged alphabetically by surname.

1. Social Sciences and History: General Reference

2. Anthropology

Morgan, Lewis Henry. 1818–1881

Maine, Sir Henry Sumner. 1822–1888

Tylor, Sir Edward Burnett. 1832–1917

Frazer, Sir James George. 1854–1941

Boas, Franz. 1858–1942

Kroeber, Alfred L. 1876–1960

Radcliffe-Brown, A. R. 1881–1955

Malinowski, Bronislaw. 1884–1942

Sapir, Edward. 1884–1939

Benedict, Ruth. 1887–1948

Bloomfield, Leonard. 1887–1949

Herskovits, Melville Jean. 1895–1963

Murdock, George P. 1897–1985

Redfield, Robert. 1897–1958

Whorf, Benjamin L. 1897–1941

White, Leslie Alvin. 1900–1975

Firth, Raymond. 1901–

Mead, Margaret. 1901–1978

Evans-Pritchard, E. E. 1902–1973

Lévi-Strauss, Claude. 1908–

Lewis, Oscar. 1914–1970

Turner, Victor Witter. 1920–1983

Douglas, Mary. 1921–

Geertz, Clifford. 1926–

Harris, Marvin. 1927–

3. Economics

Smith, Adam. 1723–1790

Malthus, Thomas Robert. 1766–1834

Ricardo, David. 1772–1823

Mill, John Stuart. 1806–1873

Marx, Karl Heinrich. 1818–1883

Engels, Friedrich. 1820–1895

Jevons, William Stanley. 1835–1882

George, Henry. 1839–1897

Marshall, Alfred. 1842–1924

Clark, John Bates. 1847–1938

Pareto, Vilfredo. 1848–1923

Wicksell, Knut. 1851–1926

Veblen, Thorstein. 1857–1929

Webb, Beatrice. 1858–1943

Webb, Sidney. 1859–1947

Commons, John Rogers. 1862–1945

Fisher, Irving. 1867–1947

Mitchell, Wesley Clair. 1874–1948

Keynes, John Maynard. 1883–1946

Schumpeter, Joseph Alois. 1883–1950

Knight, Frank Hyneman. 1885–1962

Hansen, Alvin. 1887–1975

Viner, Jacob. 1892–1970

Hayek, Friedrich August von. 1899–1992

Kuznets, Simon Smith. 1901–1985

Neumann, John von. 1903–1957

Robinson, Joan. 1903–1983

Hicks, Sir John Richard. 1904–1989

Leontief, Wassily. 1906–
Galbraith, John Kenneth. 1908–
Myrdal, Gunnar. 1908–1987
Boulding, Kenneth. 1910–
Stigler, George Joseph. 1911–1991
Friedman, Milton. 1912–
Samuelson, Paul Anthony. 1915–
Klein, Lawrence Robert. 1920–
Arrow, Kenneth Joseph. 1921–
Becker, Gary Stanley. 1930–

4. Geography

Humboldt, Alexander von.
1769–1859
Ritter, Karl. 1779–1859
Guyot, Arnold. 1807–1884
Mackinder, Halford John, Sir.
1861–1947
Bowman, Isaiah. 1878–1950
Sauer, Carl Ortwin. 1889–1975
Gottmann, Jean. 1915–
Robinson, Arthur. 1915–
Meinig, Donald W. 1924–
Berry, Brian J. L. 1934–
Brown, Lawrence A. 1935–
Ward, David. 1935–
Jordan, Terry G. 1938–
Scott, Allen J. 1938–
Bourne, Larry S. 1939–
Johnston, Ronald J. 1941–

5. Political Science

Plato. 428–347 B.C.
Machiavelli, Niccolò. 1469–1527
Hobbes, Thomas. 1588–1679
Locke, John. 1632–1704
Montesquieu, Charles de Secondat,
Baron de la Brede et de.
1689–1755
Rousseau, Jean Jacques. 1712–1778
Burke, Edmund. 1729–1797
Jefferson, Thomas. 1743–1826
Bentham, Jeremy. 1748–1832
Madison, James. 1751–1836
Tocqueville, Alexis Charles Henri
Clérel de. 1805–1859
Bryce, James. 1838–1922

Merriam, Charles E. 1874–1963
Laski, Harold J. 1893–1950
Lippmann, Walter. 1899–1974
Lasswell, Harold D. 1902–1978
Key, V. O., Jr. 1908–1963
Almond, Gabriel Abraham. 1911–
Easton, David. 1917–
Lipset, Seymour Martin. 1922–

6. Psychology

Wundt, Wilhelm. 1832–1920
James, William. 1842–1910
Hall, G(ranville) Stanley.
1844–1924
Ladd-Franklin, Christine.
1847–1930
Pavlov, Ivan Petrovich. 1849–1936
Freud, Sigmund. 1856–1939
Binet, Alfred. 1857–1911
Calkins, Mary. 1863–1930
Washburn, Margaret. 1871–1939
Watson, John B(roadus).
1878–1958
Hull, Clark L(eonard). 1884–1952
Horney, Karen. 1885–1952
Hollingworth, Leta. 1886–1939
Tolman, Edward. 1886–1959
Lewin, Kurt. 1890–1947
Piaget, Jean. 1896–1980
Wechsler, David. 1896–1981
Allport, Gordon W(illard).
1897–1967
Klineberg, Otto. 1899–1992
Erikson, Erik H(omburger). 1902–
Rogers, Carl. 1902–1987
Lorenz, Konrad. 1903–1989
Skinner, B(urrhus) F(rederic).
1904–1990
Tinbergen, Nikolaas. 1907–
Anastasi, Anne. 1908–
Miller, Neal E(dgar). 1909–

7. Sociology

Comte, Auguste. 1798–1857
Spencer, Herbert. 1820–1903
Booth, Charles. 1840–1916
Tönnies, Ferdinand. 1855–1936

Adams, Henry. 1838–1918

Roosevelt, Theodore. 1858–1919

Turner, Frederick Jackson.
1861–1932

Du Bois, W(illiam) E(dward)
B(urghardt). 1868–1963

Becker, Carl L(otus). 1873–1945

Beard, Charles A(ustin). 1874–1948

Beard, Mary R(itter). 1876–1958

Morison, Samuel Eliot. 1887–1976

Schlesinger, Arthur M(eier).
1888–1965

Webb, Walter Prescott. 1888–1963

Nevins, Allan. 1890–1971

Bemis, Samuel Flagg. 1891–1973

De Voto, Bernard. 1897–1955

Catton, Bruce. 1899–1978

Commager, Henry Steele. 1902–

Bridenbaugh, Carl. 1903–1992

Kennan, George F(rost). 1904–

Miller, Perry. 1905–1963

Woodward, C(omer) Vann. 1908–

Potter, David M(orris). 1910–1971

Current, Richard N(elson). 1912–

Stampp, Kenneth M(ilton). 1912–

Boorstin, Daniel J(oseph). 1914–

Franklin, John Hope. 1915–

Handlin, Oscar. 1915–

Hofstadter, Richard. 1916–1970

Morgan, Edmund S(ears). 1916–

Schlesinger, Arthur M(eier), Jr.
1917–

Burns, James MacGregor. 1918–

Degler, Carl N(eumann). 1921–

Williams, William Appleman.
1921–1986

Bailyn, Bernard. 1922–

Leuchtenburg, William E(dward).
1922–

Genovese, Eugene D(ominick).
1930–

McPherson, James M(unro). 1936–

16. Canadian History

Garneau, François-Xavier.
1809–1866

Groulx, Lionel. 1878–1967

Innis, Harold Adams. 1894–1952

Creighton, Donald. 1902–1979

Morton, William Lewis. 1908–1980

Cook, G. Ramsay. 1931–

Hamelin, Jean. 1931–

17. Latin American History

Garcilaso de la Vega.
c.1540–c.1616

Prescott, William H(ickling).
1796–1859

Bolton, Herbert E(ugene).
1870–1953

Tannenbaum, Frank. 1893–1969

Cosío Villegas, Daniel. 1898–1976

Arciniegas, Germán. 1900–

Freyre, Gilberto. 1900–1987

James, C(yril) L(ionel) R(obert).
1901–1989

Hanke, Lewis U(lysses). 1905–

Cline, Howard F(rancis).
1915–1971

Scobie, James R(alston).
1929–1981

18. Music and Dance

Tallis, Thomas. c.1505–1585

Monteverdi, Claudio. 1567–1643

Purcell, Henry. 1659–1695

Vivaldi, Antonio. 1678–1741

Bach, Johann Sebastian. 1685–1750

Handel, George Frideric.
1685–1759

Noverre, Jean-Georges. 1727–1810

Haydn, Franz Joseph. 1732–1809

Mozart, Wolfgang Amadeus.
1756–1791

Beethoven, Ludwig van. 1770–1827

Schubert, Franz. 1797–1828

Bellini, Vincenzo. 1801–1835

Berlioz, Hector. 1803–1869

Hensel, Fanny. 1805–1847

Bournonville, August. 1805–1879

Mendelssohn, Felix. 1809–1847

Chopin, Frédéric. 1810–1849

Schumann, Robert. 1810–1856

Liszt, Franz. 1811–1886

Verdi, Giuseppe. 1813–1901

Wagner, Richard. 1813–1883
Gounod, Charles. 1818–1893
Schumann, Clara. 1819–1896
Bruckner, Anton. 1824–1896
Smetana, Bedřich. 1824–1884
Foster, Stephen. 1826–1864
Borodin, Alexander. 1833–1887
Brahms, Johannes. 1833–1897
Mussorgsky, Modest. 1839–1881
Tchaikovsky, Peter Ilich.
    1840–1893
Dvořák, Antonin. 1841–1904
Grieg, Edvard. 1843–1907
Rimsky-Korsakov, Nikolay.
    1844–1908
Fauré, Gabriel. 1845–1924
Janáček, Leoš. 1854–1928
Elgar, Sir Edward. 1857–1934
Puccini, Giacomo. 1858–1924
Mahler, Gustav. 1860–1911
Debussy, Claude. 1862–1918
Strauss, Richard. 1864–1949
Jaques-Dalcroze, Émile. 1865–1950
Sibelius, Jean. 1865–1957
Satie, Erik. 1866–1925
Joplin, Scott. 1868–1917
Diaghilev, Serge. 1872–1929
Scriabin, Aleksandr. 1872–1915
Vaughan Williams, Ralph.
    1872–1958
Caruso, Enrico. 1873–1921
Rachmaninoff, Sergey. 1873–1943
Ives, Charles Edward. 1874–1954
Schoenberg, Arnold. 1874–1951
Ravel, Maurice. 1875–1937
Duncan, Isadora. 1878–1927
Laban, Rudolf. 1879–1958
St. Denis, Ruth. 1879–1968
Bartók, Béla. 1881–1945
Pavlova, Anna. 1881–1931
Stravinsky, Igor. 1882–1971
Webern, Anton von. 1883–1945
Berg, Alban. 1885–1935
Kern, Jerome. 1885–1945
Rubinstein, Artur. 1887–1982
Nijinsky, Vaslav. 1890–1950

Nijinska, Bronislava. 1891–1972
Porter, Cole. 1891–1964
Prokofiev, Sergei. 1891–1953
Shawn, Ted. 1891–1972
Graham, Martha. 1894–1991
Hindemith, Paul. 1895–1963
Humphrey, Doris. 1895–1958
Massine, Léonide. 1896–1979
Thomson, Virgil. 1896–1989
Gershwin, George. 1898–1937
Anderson, Marian. 1899–1993
Astaire, Fred. 1899–1987
Ellington, Edward Kennedy.
    1899–1974
Armstrong, Louis. 1900–1971
Copland, Aaron. 1900–1990
Rodgers, Richard. 1902–1979
Ashton, Sir Frederick. 1904–1988
Balanchine, George. 1904–1983
Basie, William. 1904–1984
Horowitz, Vladimir. 1904–1989
Waller, "Fats". 1904–1943
Tippett, Sir Michael. 1905–
Baker, Josephine. 1906–1975
Shostakovich, Dmitri. 1906–1975
Carter, Benny. 1907–
Kirstein, Lincoln. 1907–
Wilder, Alec. 1907–1980
Carter, Elliott. 1908–
Limón, José. 1908–1972
DeMille, Agnes George. 1909–
Tudor, Antony. 1909–1987
Barber, Samuel. 1910–1981
Ulanova, Galina. 1910–
Rogers, Ginger. 1911–
Cage, John. 1912–1992
Britten, Lord Benjamin. 1913–1976
Holiday, Billie. 1915–1959
Sinatra, Frank. 1915–
Harrison, Lou. 1917–
Bernstein, Leonard. 1918–1990
Robbins, Jerome. 1918–
Cunningham, Merce. 1919–
Fonteyn, Dame Margot. 1919–1991
Parker, Charlie. 1920–1955
Xenakis, Iannis. 1922–

Callas, Maria. 1923–1977
Berio, Luciano. 1925–
Boulez, Pierre. 1925–
Davis, Miles. 1925–1991
Coltrane, John. 1926–1967
Fosse, Bob. 1927–1987
Price, Leontyne. 1927–
Stockhausen, Karlheinz. 1928–
Sills, Beverly. 1929–
Charles, Ray. 1930–
Joffrey, Robert. 1930–1988
Sondheim, Stephen. 1930–
Taylor, Paul. 1930–
Ailey, Alvin. 1931–1989
Pavarotti, Luciano. 1935–
Brown, Trisha. 1936–
Glass, Philip. 1937–
Nureyev, Rudolph. 1939–1993
Domingo, Plácido. 1941–
Tharp, Twyla. 1941–
Feld, Eliot. 1942–
Carreras, José. 1946–
Martins, Peter. 1946–
Baryshnikov, Mikhail. 1948–
Lloyd Webber, Andrew. 1948–
Morris, Mark. 1956–

19. Art and Architecture
Leonardo da Vinci. 1452–1519
Dürer, Albrecht. 1471–1528
Michelangelo Buonarroti.
    1475–1564
Raphael. 1483–1520
Titian. c.1487–1576
Cellini, Benvenuto. 1500–1571
Palladio, Andrea. 1508–1580
Brueghel the Elder, Pieter.
    c.1525–1569
Rubens, Peter Paul. 1577–1640
Bernini, Gianlorenzo. 1598–1680
Velazquez, Diego Rodriguez de Sil-
    va. 1599–1660
Rembrandt Harmensz van Rijn.
    1606–1669
Wren, Sir Christopher. 1632–1723
Reynolds, Sir Joshua. 1723–1792
Gainsborough, Thomas. 1727–1788

Goya y Lucientes, Francisco José
    de. 1746–1828
Turner, Joseph Mallord William.
    1775–1851
Constable, John. 1776–1837
Manet, Edouard. 1832–1883
Richardson, Henry Hobson.
    1836–1886
Cézanne, Paul. 1839–1906
Monet, Claude. 1840–1926
Rodin, Auguste. 1840–1917
Renoir, Pierre Auguste. 1841–1919
Cassatt, Mary. 1845–1926
Gauguin, Paul. 1848–1903
Van Gogh, Vincent. 1853–1890
Sullivan, Louis. 1856–1924
Wright, Frank Lloyd. 1867–1959
Matisse, Henri. 1869–1954
Picasso, Pablo. 1881–1973
Gropius, Walter. 1883–1969
Mies van der Rohe, Ludwig.
    1886–1969
Le Corbusier. 1887–1965
O'Keeffe, Georgia. 1887–1986
Aalto, Alvar. 1898–1976
Moore, Henry Spencer. 1898–1986
Kahn, Louis I(sadore). 1901–1974
Pollock, Jackson. 1912–1956
Warhol, Andy. 1930?–1987

20. The Mass Media
Pulitzer, Joseph. 1847–1911
Riis, Jacob A(ugust). 1849–1914
Tarbell, Ida. 1857–1944
Cocteau, Jean. 1889–1963
Dreyer, Carl. 1889–1968
Lippmann, Walter. 1889–1974
Lang, Fritz. 1890–1976
Renoir, Jean. 1894–1979
Hawks, Howard. 1896–1977
Capra, Frank. 1897–1991
Eisenstein, Sergei. 1898–1948
Luce, Henry R(obinson).
    1898–1967
Buñuel, Luis. 1900–1983
Paley, William S(amuel).
    1901–1990

Liebling, A(bbott) J(oseph).
  1904–1963
Huston, John. 1906–1987
Visconti, Luchino. 1906–1976
Murrow, Edward R(oscoe).
  1908–1965
Salisbury, Harrison. 1908–1993
Kurosawa, Akira. 1910–
McLuhan, Marshall. 1911–1980
Antonioni, Michelangelo. 1912–
Cronkite, Walter. 1916–
Bergman, Ingmar. 1918–
Fellini, Federico. 1920–
Rohmer, Eric. 1920–
Kubrick, Stanley. 1928–
Godard, Jean-Luc. 1930–
Malle, Louis. 1932–
Truffaut, François. 1932–1984
Polanski, Roman. 1933–
Allen, Woody. 1935–
Fassbinder, Werner. 1946–1982

21. Folklore, Humor, and Popular Culture

Grimm, Jacob. 1785–1863
Grimm, Wilhelm. 1786–1859
Thoms, William John. 1803–1885
Campbell, John Francis of Islay.
  1822–1855
Child, Francis J(ames). 1825–1896
Krohn, Julius. 1835–1888
Lang, Andrew. 1844–1912
Frazer, Sir James George.
  1854–1941
Jacobs, Joseph. 1854–1916
Krohn, Kaarle. 1863–1933
Hamilton, Edith. 1867–1963
Rogers, Will. 1879–1935
Barbeau, Charles Marius.
  1883–1969
Thompson, Stith. 1885–1976
Randolph, Vance. 1892–1980
Graves, Robert. 1895–1985
Campbell, Joseph. 1904–1986
Lomax, Alan. 1915–
Dorson, Richard M. 1916–1981
Opie, Peter. 1918–1982

Opie, Iona. 1923–
Browne, Ray. 1922–

22. Travel and Exploration

Polo, Marco. 1254?–1324?
Columbus, Christopher. 1446–1506
Vespucci, Amerigo. 1451–1512
Hakluyt, Richard. 1552–1616
Cook, Captain James. 1728–1779
Clark, William. 1770–1838
Park, Mungo. 1771–1806
Lewis, Meriwether. 1774–1809
Borrow, George. 1803–1881
Kinglake, Alexander. 1809–1891
Livingstone, David. 1813–1873
Dana, Richard Henry, Jr.
  1815–1882
Burton, Sir Richard. 1821–1890
Stanley, Sir Henry Morton.
  1841–1904
Slocum, Joshua. 1844–1909
Peary, Robert E(dwin). 1856–1920
Roosevelt, Theodore. 1858–1919
Scott, Robert Falcon. 1868–1912
Amundsen, Roald. 1872–1928
Stefansson, Vilhjalmur. 1879–1962
Freuchen, Peter. 1886–1957
Byrd, Richard E(velyn). 1888–1957
Lawrence, T(homas) E(dward).
  1888–1935
Morton, H(enry Canova) V(ollam).
  1892–1979
Stark, Freya. 1893–
Gunther, John. 1901–1970
Lindbergh, Charles A(ugustus).
  1902–1974
Snow, Edward. 1902–1982
Van der Post, Laurens. 1906–
Michener, James A(lbert). 1907–
Cousteau, Jacques-Yves. 1910–
Harrer, Heinrich. 1912–
Heyerdahl, Thor. 1914–
Hillary, Sir Edmund. 1919–
Matthiessen, Peter. 1927–
Aldrin, Edwin Eugene, Jr. 1930–
Theroux, Paul. 1941–
Ride, Sally. 1951–
Earle, Sylvia. 1955–

Introduction

Dynamic fields such as the social sciences, history, and the arts have undergone dramatic changes since the publication of the thirteenth edition of *The Reader's Adviser* in 1986. In addition to the emergence of new theories, new trends, and other changes driven by recent scholarship and interpretations, these fields have experienced an explosion of research and study, resulting in the publication of a great deal of new work. Volume 3 of the fourteenth edition of *The Reader's Adviser* has attempted to reflect these changes and to provide readers with the most current and useful materials in these fields.

This volume differs from its predecessor in a number of ways. One of the most obvious improvements is its revised organization, which provides a more useful breakdown of social science and history chapters. Unlike the previous edition, in which the social science disciplines were grouped within one chapter, this edition provides separate chapters on anthropology, economics, political science, psychology, and sociology, with each receiving greater attention and undergoing considerable expansion. Added to this list is a chapter on geography, a subject area that was not covered in the previous edition. Education was a separate chapter in the previous edition, and it remains so in this edition. To aid readers in searching out specific subjects and titles within the social sciences, each chapter is further subdivided into categories that reflect significant research and writing of recent years. In several instances, these categories reflect the growing worldwide interest in such issues as the environment, comparative cultures, gender factors, the communications and information revolutions, and the inevitable effects of a rapidly shifting nationalistic and geographic landscape.

Another organizational change is evident in the history chapters. In this edition, several new history chapters have been added, and others have been reorganized to reflect recent developments in both scholarship and the actual condition of the world. Technological changes, in particular, have put historical relationships in a vastly different perspective from that which prevailed even a few decades ago. The Middle East, Africa, Asia, Europe, Canada, and Latin America—areas with unique and complex histories—now all merit separate chapters for the first time. The British Isles are now properly considered an integral part of Europe rather than a separate and lonely outpost on its periphery; therefore, the chapter on British history that appeared in the previous edition has been incorporated here within a more comprehensive chapter on European history. World history remains a specialized category in its own right, unrestricted by national boundaries or chronologies and focusing on world civilization in general, the philosophy and writing of world history, and on such broad transnational issues as war and peace. Ancient history also remains separate (as it was in the thirteenth edition) and focuses on the roots of Western civilization in ancient Greece and Rome. In the chapter on United States history, chronological divisions and special topics have been updated to reflect recent scholarship. As with the social sciences, the various chapters on history reflect the need to temper, not supplant, the Eurocentrism of traditional scholarship, and efforts have been made to include works of a more balanced nature and individuals from different genders and backgrounds. In this respect, all of the chapters in this volume recognize the inevitable multicultural character of knowledge relating to humankind.

A third section of this volume includes chapters on music and dance; art and architecture; the mass media; and folklore, humor, and popular culture (revised to include a new focus on the growing field of popular culture); and travel and exploration. All of these chapters have been updated to reflect current scholarship and to include new information, books, and profiles.

Each chapter in this volume has been compiled by an expert in the field, and the collective professional skill, diligence, and thoroughness of these scholars will be readily apparent. The chapters reflect not merely an updating of material from the previous edition but, in addition, a rethinking and reconceptualization of the subject matter. Because a wealth of new material is published continuously on the subjects presented in this volume, it is naturally impossible to include *everything* of merit. However, readers may be assured that the contributing editors have selected materials with intelligence and discrimination and that their contributions are informative, responsible, and reliable. It therefore can be said with a great degree of confidence that the current volume reflects the "best" in the social sciences, history, and the arts.

John G. Sproat

The Reader's Adviser

PART ONE

SOCIAL SCIENCES
AND HISTORY

CHAPTER 1

Social Sciences and History: General Reference

Donald O. Case and Wendy A. Miller

Let it be stressed again that the historian and the social scientist have often been the same person, and this will probably increasingly be the case in the future.
—PETER LASLETT, "History and the Social Sciences," *International Encyclopedia of the Social Sciences*

The social sciences are those fields that study human behavior at the level of the individual, the group, and the society, and are concerned with people and their cultures, with the structure and activities of human collectives, and with the interaction of human beings and their physical environment. Although philosophies and methods differ across the social science disciplines, in general social scientists aim to describe, explain, interpret, and predict human behavior. In doing so, some social scientists apply the methods of the physical sciences, including experimental manipulation and observation. Others employ a more interpretive and historical approach. Often social scientists use both approaches to some degree, since extremes of either objectivity or subjectivity both contain problems.

While there is a fair degree of consistency about what are considered to be the main topics and concerns of the social sciences, the question of which disciplines fall under the heading of social science is open to disagreement. History, for example, is considered by some to be a social science and by others to be one of the humanities. Some social scientists consider all history to be "social history," whether historians call it that or not. Given that some of the social sciences have been around for a century or longer, many of its practitioners are now able to use longitudinal—historical—data in their studies. The very availability of longitudinal data has encouraged social scientists to be less present-oriented and has resulted in an accumulation of social studies that are historically grounded. A parallel development among social scientists has been an increasing acceptance and adoption of qualitative methods, including the interpretive style used by most historians.

Similarly, there has been a steady growth in the use of social science data, theories, and methodologies among current historians. An increasing number of historians have been drawn to the use of social statistics collected over the last several centuries by governments and businesses and, more recently, by polling organizations. Although more controversial, some historians have been attracted to economic, political, sociological, and psychological theories that might be used to interpret historical evidence and events. All of these trends have led to lively debate and, it is hoped, to fruitful cross-fertilization.

There is only partial consensus about which disciplines constitute the "core" of the social sciences. In terms of age of each discipline, history, economics, and political science have been considered to be seminal. Yet other disciplines that emerged during the nineteenth century, such as sociology, anthropology, and psychology, are more commonly associated with the "social sciences" in the minds of the general public. Psychology, in particular, far outweighs the other disciplines in number of practitioners and probably also in general influence.

Other social science disciplines cluster around the aforementioned "core" set. All of these "peripheral" fields make use of, and contribute to, the knowledge of the other social sciences. Some of the peripheral disciplines include professional fields, such as law, education, business, and social work. Others are academic disciplines, such as philosophy, linguistics, communication, geography, and the various area studies and ethnic and gender studies programs that have seen the most growth within both the social sciences and history.

The literature of the social sciences presents the reader with many challenges. The topics covered in the various disciplines overlap heavily and are fragmented into a number of subtopics. Research findings tend to be both scattered and noncumulative. Confirmations and refutations of findings are common, as are minor variations in methods or in the population or time frame studied. Journals, which account for roughly one-half of the material cited in social science literature, tend not to be as highly specialized as those in the other sciences. History departs from this generalization, however, with heavier use of monographs and unpublished materials.

The result is that one must be prepared to search across disciplines, to follow citations, and to use a wide variety of materials. As reflected in a number of investigations, information-seeking social scientists tend to make heavy use of current journals; some use of monographs, reports, proceedings, and statistical sources; and little use of indexing and abstracting services. In contrast, historians may make little use of journal literature, some use of monographs, and rely primarily on unpublished documents such as are found in archives. For these reasons, bibliographic research in both the social sciences and history is fascinating, difficult, and different.

This chapter begins by considering the social science disciplines of anthropology, economics, geography, political science, psychology, and sociology. History is treated as a separate yet overlapping area, with its own listing of general reference sources. For history, as for the social sciences, sources are divided by format—dictionaries and encyclopedias; handbooks and guides; indexes and abstracts; bibliographies; and atlases, directories, and yearbooks. In addition, the sections on the social sciences and history each include their own listing of guides and texts on methodology. Given the high proportion of North American writings and the difficulty of reviewing equivalent sources for all of the world's regions and countries, the emphasis in all sections is on North American sources.

SOCIAL SCIENCES

Dictionaries and Encyclopedias

Gould, Julius, and W. J. Kolb. *UNESCO Dictionary of the Social Sciences.* Free Pr. 1964 $49.95. ISBN 0-02-917490-2. In a page or two each, defines about 1,000 basic concepts used in social science research, with each entry explained at several different levels of specificity. Dated, but still useful.

Kuper, Adam, and Jessica Kuper, eds. *The Social Science Encyclopedia*. Routledge 1989 $75.00. ISBN 0-7102-0008-0. Includes more than 700 entries, most one to four pages in length, describing problems, theories, methods, and scholars in social sciences. Alphabetical, no subject index. Good source of references for further reading.

Mitchell, Geoffrey Duncan. *A New Dictionary of the Social Sciences*. Aldine de Gruyter 1979 $42.95. ISBN 0-202-30285-7. Short and mostly sociological. Covers about 300 terms, with brief definitions, notes about historical usage, and citations for further reading. Includes some biographies. No longer new, but still very useful.

Seligman, E. R. A., and Alvin Johnson. eds. *Encyclopaedia of the Social Sciences*. 15 vols. Macmillan 1930–35 o.p. Classic "comprehensive and unifying publication" commissioned by 10 social science organizations. Lengthy introductory chapter covers the meaning, development, and status of social sciences country by country. Although prepared 60 years ago, it remains extremely useful, particularly for its 4,000 biographies of persons relevant to the social sciences. Strongest in the fields of economics and history.

Sills, David L., ed. *International Encyclopedia of the Social Sciences*. 11 vols. Fr. & Eur. 1977 $495.00. ISBN 0-8288-8232-0. *Biographical Supplement*. Free Pr. 1979 $95.00. ISBN 0-02-895690-7. The most comprehensive subject encyclopedia of the field, now rather dated. Signed topical articles on generic concepts, theories, and methods in the social sciences. Together with the *Supplement*, offers over 800 biographies.

Handbooks and Guides

Herron, Nancy L., ed. *The Social Sciences: A Cross-Disciplinary Guide to Selected Sources*. Libs. Unl. 1989 $36.00. ISBN 0-87287-725-6. A short guide to about 800 sources, some described at considerable length. Includes brief introductions to 11 different fields, including "communication" and "statistics and demographics." Easy-to-use format.

Li, Tze-chung. *Social Science Reference Sources*. Greenwood 1990 $75.00. ISBN 0-313-25539-3. Very comprehensive, including about 2,200 sources, with particularly good coverage of the core disciplines and the various "area studies" and good essays on the nature of the social sciences and their literatures. Uneven quality in annotations and indexing.

McInnis, Raymond G., ed. *Social Science Research Handbook*. Garland 1985 o.p. Useful guide to research methods and materials in the social sciences.

Webb, William H., and others. *Sources of Information in the Social Sciences: A Guide to the Literature*. ALA 3rd rev. ed. 1986 $70.00. ISBN 0-8389-0405-X. Classic text (since 1964) covering both reference and original sources in the core fields, with a lengthy, useful commentary on the primary literature of each field. With coverage of more than 8,000 items, it is the most comprehensive guide of its type.

Indexes and Abstracts

Applied Social Sciences Index and Abstracts. UNIPUB 1987–present. Practice- and policy-oriented bimonthly international index, with about 80 percent of the materials referenced English or American. Main strengths are 150-word abstracts and a system of linked index terms. More than 500 journals from 16 countries are indexed.

Brown, Samuel R., ed. *Finding the Source in Sociology and Anthropology: A Thesaurus-Index to the Reference Collection*. Greenwood 1987 $49.95. ISBN 0-313-25263-7. Bibliography of 586 nonannotated entries under four broad subject headings— general, social sciences, sociology, and anthropology—with a "thesaurus-index" that makes it easy to search by multiple subject headings.

Public Affairs Information Service Bulletin. Pub. Aff. Inf. Factual, statistical, and policy-oriented literature in the social sciences. Partially indexes more than 1,400 periodicals. Particularly strong coverage of reports, government documents, and conference proceedings. Relatively easy to use.

Social Sciences Citation Index. Institute for Scientific Information 1969–present. Three-part index (Source, Citation, and Permuterm Subject) that covers 1,500 journals. Invaluable for tracing social science references and for "subject searches" using an author's name. Appears three times per year.

Social Sciences Index. 1974–present. Wilson Vol. 19 1975–84 $190.00. ISBN 0-685-05425-X. Quarterly subject and author index that goes back to 1916. Covers about 350 periodicals, with recent emphasis on psychology material.

Statistical Abstract of the United States 1992: The National Data Book. 1878–present. Bernan Pr. 1992 ed. $39.00. ISBN 0-89059-006-0. Prime source of summarized statistics about the population, health, education, criminal justice system, and government of the United States. Annual.

Bibliographies

International Bibliography of the Social Sciences. Routledge Chapman & Hall 1987 $110.00. ISBN 0-422-81110-6. Selective guide to books, reports, and articles that is published annually under four separate titles, each with a new ISBN—Sociology, Economics, Political Science, and Social and Cultural Anthropology. Covers 28,000 items per year and indexes 1,000 periodicals.

A London Bibliography of the Social Sciences, Twenty-fourth Supplement, 1989 Volume XLVII. Mansell 1990 $180.00. ISBN 0-7201-2034-9. Reviews titles added during 1989 to British libraries of International Law and Political and Economic Science. Documents in many languages arranged by subject and referenced. Familiarity with special subject headings helpful. Annual.

Atlases, Directories, and Yearbooks

Burek. *Encyclopedia of Associations.* 3 vols. Gale 1992 $295.00. ISBN 0-8103-7622-9. Annual that lists more than 21,500 organizations under 18 subject categories. Very useful for direct contact with social science associations.

Rogers, Alisdair. *Atlas of Social Issues.* Facts on File 1990 $16.95. ISBN 0-8160-2024-8. Short discussions of 28 global issues, each covered in about two pages of maps, graphs, drawings, and printed explanations. Vivid, but not deep, analysis.

UNESCO, Social Science Documentation Center. *World Directory of Social Science Institutions.* UNESCO 1985 o.p. Lists about 2,000 active organizations and includes details about staff, activities, and publications. Includes index to organization names and acronyms.

Methods of Social Research

Bavsell, R. Barker. *Advanced Research Methodology: An Annotated Guide to Sources.* Scarecrow 1991 $84.50. ISBN 0-8108-2355-1. Describes tables of contents of more than 400 books, summarizes over 2,200 articles, and reviews methods.

Berelson, Bernard. *Content Analysis in Communications Research.* Hafner 1971 $22.95. ISBN 0-02-841210-9. Still the best source of advice on content analysis.

Campbell, Donald T., and Julian C. Stanley. *Experimental and Quasi-Experimental Designs for Research.* HM 1966 $19.96. ISBN 0-395-30787-2. Analyzes the logic and methods of experimentation and applies them to other methods as well.

Dillman, Don A. *Mail and Telephone Survey: The Total Design Method.* Wiley 1978 $49.95. ISBN 0-471-21555-4. A definitive source for ways of increasing return rates.

Foreman, E. K. *Survey Sampling Principles.* Dekker 1991 $125.00. ISBN 0-8247-8407-3. An introduction to the principles of survey sampling as they are applied in practice.

Kerlinger, Frederick N. *Foundations of Behavioral Research.* HarBraceJ 1986 $52.00. ISBN 0-03-041761-9. Popular general textbook.

Kish, Leslie. *Survey Sampling*. Wiley 1965 $59.95. ISBN 0-471-48900-X. The definitive reference source for anything to do with sampling and statistical inference.

Krueger, Richard A. *Focus Groups: A Practical Guide for Applied Research*. Sage 1988 $38.00. ISBN 0-8039-3186-7. A basic explanation of the history and application of group interviewing techniques.

Miller, Delbert C. *Handbook of Research Design and Social Measurement*. Sage 1991 $35.00. ISBN 0-8039-4219-2. Popular guide to all types of research methods, mostly aimed at the sociologist. Useful for advice on sampling, statistical analysis, instrument design, scale construction, interviewing, and survey administration.

Miller, P. M. *A Dictionary of Social Science Methods*. Wiley 1984 o.p. Provides definitions and examples of various methods, designs, instruments, and statistical tests. Little emphasis on "how to do it."

Rossi, Peter, and others, eds. *Handbook of Survey Research*. Academic Pr. 1983 $49.95. ISBN 0-12-598227-5. Useful reference source on all aspects of survey design and administration.

Tufte, Edward R. *Envisioning Information*. Graphics Pr. 1990 $48.00. ISBN 0-9613921-1-8. A stunning book demonstrating how data may be understood or misunderstood, depending on how it is depicted. Follows up on author's earlier book, *The Visual Display of Quantitative Information* (Graphics Press, 1983).

Webb, Eugene J., and Donald T. Campbell. *Nonreactive Measures in the Social Sciences*. HM 1981 o.p. An update of the authors' classic text, *Unobtrusive Measures* (Rand, 1966). Classic discussion of how to collect data without causing reactive bias among those observed.

HISTORY

Dictionaries and Encyclopedias

Brewer, Annie, ed. *Biography Almanac*. Gale 1981 o.p. Comprehensive reference guide to more than 20,000 famous people from biblical times to the present, as found in over 300 readily available sources.

Cook, Chris. *Dictionary of Historical Terms*. P. Bedrick Bks. 1990 $34.95. ISBN 0-87226-331-2

Dunan, Marcel, ed. *Larousse Encyclopedia of Modern History*. Hamlyn Pub. Group UK 1972 o.p. General historical encyclopedia covering the period from the sixteenth century to the present. Includes information on people, events, the arts, technology, and so on.

Ganjoo, Satish. *Dictionary of History*. S. Asia 1990 $33.50. ISBN 81-7041-237-4

Grun, Bernard. *The Timetables of History: A Horizontal Linkage of People and Events*. S & S Trade 3rd rev. ed. 1991 $35.00. ISBN 0-671-74919-6. Unique topical coverage of world history from 5000 B.C. to the present, with important events and developments listed under literature and theater; religion, philosophy, and learning; visual arts; music; science, technology, and growth; and daily life.

Langer, William L., ed. and comp. *An Encyclopedia of World History*. HM 1973 $44.00. ISBN 0-395-13592-3. Chronologically arranged history of humankind from the Paleolithic era to the present day. Contains information on important people, places, and events. A detailed index is included.

Merriam-Webster Editorial Staff. *Webster's New Biographical Dictionary*. Merriam-Webster Inc. 1988 $24.95. ISBN 0-87779-543-6. Covers in brief, with pronunciations, more than 40,000 individuals, chiefly from English-speaking countries.

A Record of World Events. Longman UK o.p. An annual compendium of information on important events occurring throughout the world; arranged by country.

Teed, Peter. *Dictionary of Twentieth Century History: 1914–1990*. OUP 1993 $30.00. ISBN 0-19-211676-2. International survey with more than 2,000 entries.

Weiner, Philip P., ed. *Dictionary of the History of Ideas*. 5 vols. Scribner 1980 $75.00. ISBN 0-684-16418-3. Lengthy and far-ranging articles for the serious reader, useful for discovering origins of concepts from many fields, including philosophy, religion, and literature. Detailed indexing makes this an excellent source.

Handbooks and Guides

Benjamin, Jules R. *A Student's Guide to History*. St. Martin 5th ed. 1990 $12.70. ISBN 0-312-03168-8

Cheney, C. R., ed. *Handbook of Dates for Students of History*. Boydell & Brewer 1970 $19.00. ISBN 0-901050-10-5

Dollar, Charles M., and Richard J. Jensen. *Historian's Guide to Statistics: Quantitative Analysis and Historical Research*. HR&W Schl. Div. 1971 o.p. Useful for advice on ways to analyze and present numerical data in works of history.

Fritze, Ronald H. *Reference Sources in History: An Introductory Guide*. ABC-Clio 1990 $49.00. ISBN 0-87436-164-8. Very useful book for researchers and others looking for materials.

Poulton, Helen J., and Marguerite S. Howland. *The Historian's Handbook: A Descriptive Guide to Reference Works*. U. of Okla. Pr. 1972 $17.95. ISBN 0-8061-1009-0. A guide to sources of information, mostly general reference works, by format—almanacs, dictionaries, encyclopedias, yearbooks, and so on.

Indexes and Abstracts

America: History and Life. ABC-CLIO 1964–present. Complicated four-part index for United States and Canadian history from prehistory to the present. One part indexes 2,000 serials three times per year; a second reviews semiannually; a comprehensive third combines dissertations with articles and books annually; a fourth adds author, title, and subject indexing annually.

Historical Abstracts. 2 vols. ABC-CLIO 1955–present. Pt. 1 *1450–1914*. Pt. 2 *1914–present*. Quarterly indexing and abstracting service for world history, excepting U.S. and Canadian history. Covers about 2,000 journals in 40 languages and since 1980 includes citations to books and dissertations. Good author and subject indexing.

Humanities Index. 1974–present. Wilson 1974–85 $190.00. ISBN 0-685-48364-9. Quarterly that includes fair coverage of periodicals in history, with subject and author indexes to about 350 periodicals in a familiar format.

Index to Social Sciences and Humanities Proceedings, 1979–. Institute for Scientific Information. Quarterly publication that indexes proceedings in six ways: subject, key word, sponsor, author/editor, meeting location, and corporate name.

Bibliographies

Kinnell, Susan B., ed. *Bibliographies in History Journals: A Comprehensive Index to Bibliographies in History Journals Published Worldwide*. 2 vols. ABC-CLIO 1988 $175.00. ISBN 0-87436-521-X. "Bibliographies in history journals and dissertations covering the United States and Canada" indexed in the first volume and all other countries in the second. The most extensive source currently available.

———, ed. *Historiography: An Annotated Bibliography of Journal Articles, Books, and Dissertations*. 2 vols. ABC-CLIO 1987 $175.00. ISBN 0-87436-168-0. Covers writings about historians, history as a profession, the nature of historical research, and the writing of history itself.

Atlases, Directories, and Yearbooks

Hunter, Brian, ed. *The Statesman's Year-Book 1991–1992*. St. Martin 1991 $75.00. ISBN 0-312-06497-7. Extremely useful for quick information on recent history and social, political, and economic background of countries. Alphabetically arranged country descriptions and chronology of events from April of one year through May of the next, supplemented with bibliographies. Good indexing. Easy to use.

Shepherd, William R. *Shepherd's Historical Atlas*. B&N Imports 1980 o.p. Four thousand years of human history in detailed, colored maps. Excellent index of place names.

Wheeler, Mary B., ed. *Directory of Historical Organizations in the United States and Canada*. AASLH 1990 $79.95. ISBN 0-942063-05-8. Excellent for locating associations, societies, and archives throughout North America.

Wiener, Philip, ed. *Directory of the History of Ideas*. 5 vols. Scribner 1973 o.p. Provides detailed, comprehensive coverage of movements, concepts, people, and so on. The fifth volume is an index volume.

Methods of Historical Research

Barzun, Jacques. *Clio and the Doctors: History, Psycho-History, and Quanto-History*. U. Ch. Pr. 1989 repr. of 1974 ed. $14.95. ISBN 0-226-03851-3. A series of critical essays by a prominent historian on the use of social science theories and methods in history.

———. *The Modern Researcher*. HM 1992 $24.45. ISBN 0-395-64494-1. For many years the most popular introductory text on historical methods. Also useful for fields other than history.

Bloch, Marc. *The Historian's Craft*. Random 1964 $6.95. ISBN 0-394-70512-2. Essays by an influential historian on observation, criticism, analysis, and causation.

Brundage, Anthony. *Going to the Sources: A Guide to Historical Research and Writing*. Harlan Davidson 1989 $32.50. ISBN 0-88295-865-8. Brief introduction to the writing of history, with particular emphasis on sources of evidence.

Fischer, David H. *Historians' Fallacies: Toward a Logic of Historical Thought*. HarpC 1970 $12.00. ISBN 0-06-131545-1. Not a methods text per se. Ways to advance a historical argument well-illustrated in anecdotes of the failings of dozens of noted scholars.

Furay, Conal, and Michael J. Salevouris. *The Methods and Skills of History: A Practical Guide*. Harlan Davidson 1988. ISBN 0-88295-851-8. A beginners' guide to historical research, in a workbook format.

Gottschalk, Louis. *Understanding History: A Primer of Historical Method*. Knopf 1969 $10.00. ISBN 0-394-30215-X. A classic discussion of the purposes, evidence, and methods of historical investigation.

McCoy, F. N. *Researching and Writing in History: A Practical Handbook for Students*. U. CA Pr. 1974 $10.95. ISBN 0-520-02621-7. A step-by-step guide to researching and writing. Good, although dated, discussion of reference sources.

Nugent, Walter T. K. *Creative History*. Lippincott 1973 $2.95. ISBN 0-397-47286-2. Fifteen short chapters on philosophy, sources, inference, objectivity, quantification, and narration in history.

Shafer, Robert Jones, and others, eds. *A Guide to Historical Method*. Wadsworth Pub. 1980. ISBN 0-534-10825-3. Provides overview of values and philosophy underlying history and indicates how to define a topic, find evidence, take notes, analyze quantitative and qualitative data, and communicate findings. Includes brief section on indexes, catalogs, and bibliographies. For the beginner.

CHAPTER 2

Anthropology

Rita Smith Kipp

Now the mass of learned and transmitted motor reactions, habits, techniques,
ideas, and values—and the behavior they induce—is what constitutes *culture*.
—ALFRED L. KROEBER, *Anthropology*

Anthropology—the science of humanity—is by far the most comprehensive of
the social sciences in what it sets out to study. It is concerned with people
anywhere in the world and throughout historical time; it is interested in such
seemingly mundane matters as cooking pots and such abstract and symbolic
matters as language and religion; it studies human biology and evolution, as
well as cultural change in the present.

What gives anthropology the degree of unity it has is a concern for culture
and how it is transmitted. Anthropological archaeologists try to reconstruct past
cultures from the artifacts unearthed in excavations. Specialists in anthropological linguistics focus on the structure and history of languages and on the
patterns of language use. Physical anthropologists, who study human biology in
the past and in the present, understand the human organism as unique in its
dependence on culture and on the way it has evolved in response to a cultural
environment. Applied anthropologists work in a wide variety of fields—designing seats for automobiles, analyzing skeletal remains for purposes of crime
detection, and adding their expertise to development projects, education, and
the health professions.

Cultural anthropologists, or ethnologists, have traditionally studied non-
Western peoples, especially preliterate peoples. Using a research method called
participant observation, anthropologists live among such a group for an
extended period of time, learn the language, observe what people do and say,
and engage them in what seems to be informal conversation. From this
experience of fieldwork, anthropologists write ethnographies, interpretations of
life as it is lived in particular places. While fieldwork remains the primary
source of anthropological data, it is as likely to occur in urban as in remote
settings today; as the peoples they study have become literate, ethnologists
increasingly utilize written materials to understand them and their histories.

Working with ethnographies and archaeological data, anthropologists also
compare cultures and construct theories about human adaptation or about
various aspects of culture and language.

REFERENCE WORKS

Gacs, Ute, and others, eds. *Women Anthropologists: A Biographical Dictionary*. Greenwood 1988 $55.00. ISBN 0-313-24414-6. Contains signed biographies (each 4-6

pages) of 58 anthropologists from the past 100 years. Includes bibliographies, index, and two appendixes.

Kemper, Robert V., and John F. S. Phinney. *The History of Anthropology: A Research Bibliography*. Garland 1977 o.p. A useful bibliography of mainly secondary sources.

Kibee, Josephine Z. *Cultural Anthropology: A Guide to Reference and Information Sources*. Libs. Unl. 1991 o.p. A valuable guide to 12 subfields of anthropology, visual anthropology, and anthropology and the humanities.

Levinson, David, ed. *Encyclopedia of World Cultures*. G.K. Hall 1991– $800.00 set. ISBN 0-8161-1840-X. Projected to be 10 volumes when finished, this series is expected to include more than 1,500 cultural groups, with signed entries.

Library-Anthropology Resource Group Staff. *International Dictionary of Anthropologists*. Ed. by Christopher Winters. Garland 1991 $75.00. ISBN 0-8240-5094-0. Detailed profiles of over 725 contributors to the field of anthropology.

Seymour-Smith, Charlotte, ed. *Dictionary of Anthropology*. Macmillan 1987 $45.00. ISBN 0-8161-8817-3. Contains almost 1,000 entries for terms and concepts used in cultural and social anthropology. Cross references and selected bibliography.

Smith, Margo L., and Yvonne M. Damien, eds. *Anthropological Bibliographies: A Selected Guide*. Redgrave Pub. Co. 1981 o.p. Many annotated entries, arranged both by region and by topic.

Weeks, John M. *Introduction to Library Research in Anthropology*. Westview 1991 $27.50. ISBN 0-8133-7454-5. Overview of anthropological literature.

Winick, Charles. *Dictionary of Anthropology*. Greenwood 1970 repr. of 1956 ed. $55.50. ISBN 0-8371-2094-2. An indispensable word finder, from *à dos rabattu* to *zygomatic arch*.

HISTORIES AND SURVEYS

Brew, J. O., ed. *One Hundred Years of Anthropology*. HUP 1968 $22.00. ISBN 0-674-63900-6. Useful histories of four subfields of anthropology.

Leaf, Murray J. *Man, Mind, and Science: A History of Anthropology*. Col. U. Pr. 1983 $37.00. ISBN 0-231-04618-9. Takes the discipline back to its philosophical foundations.

Service, Elman R. *A Century of Controversy*. Acad. Pr. 1985 $53.00. ISBN 0-12-637380-9. Covers only ethnology, focusing on kinship, totemism, and economic theory.

Siegel, Bernard J., ed. *Annual Review of Anthropology*. 21 vols. Annual Reviews 1972–present. $41.00–44.00. ISBN 0-8243-1921-4. Review articles on current thinking and research, each with a comprehensive bibliography.

Silverman, Sydel, ed. *Totems and Teachers: Perspectives on the History of Anthropology*. Col. U. Pr. 1981 $19.50. ISBN 0-231-05087-9. Essays by students of Boas, Kroeber, Malinowski, Benedict, White, and Redfield.

Spencer, Frank, ed. *A History of American Physical Anthropology, 1930–1980*. Acad. Pr. 1982 $49.95. ISBN 0-12-656660-7. Articles cover forensic anthropology, paleontology, primate studies, and human biology.

Stocking, George W., Jr. *Race, Culture, and Evolution: Essays in the History of Anthropology*. U. Ch. Pr. 1982 $16.95. ISBN 0-226-77494-5. Anthropology's premier historian of science critically reviews Boas, Tylor, and early French anthropology.

———, ed. *Functionalism Historicized: Essays on British Social Anthropology*. Vol. 2. U. of Wis. Pr. 1984 $25.00. ISBN 0-299-09900-8. Insightful essays analyzing the beginnings of functionalist theory in the work of Durkheim, Radcliffe-Brown, and Robertson Smith.

METHODOLOGY AND ISSUES

Bernard, H. Russell. *Research Methods in Cultural Anthropology*. Sage 1988 $39.95. ISBN 0-8039-2977-3. Comprehensive treatment of research methodology with examples of quantitative and statistical techniques. Includes index and bibliography.

Brim, John A., and David H. Spain. *Research Design in Anthropology: Paradigms and Pragmatics in the Testing of Hypotheses.* Irvington 1982 $7.95. ISBN 0-8290-0583-8. Scientific emphasis on building replicability into field projects.

Clifford, James, and George E. Marcus, eds. *Writing Culture: The Poetics and Politics of Ethnography.* U. CA Pr. 1986 $42.50. ISBN 0-520-05652-3. Postmodernist examination of ethnography as a genre.

Emerson, Robert M., ed. *Contemporary Field Research: A Collection of Readings.* Waveland Pr. 1988 $13.95. ISBN 0-88133-342-5

Harris, Marvin. *Cultural Materialism: The Struggle for a Science of Culture.* Random 1980 $15.00. ISBN 0-394-74426-8. Argues the advantages of cultural materialism compared with contending theoretical approaches.

Hodgen, Margaret T. *Anthropology, History, and Cultural Change.* U. of Ariz. Pr. 1974 $8.50. ISBN 0-8165-0451-2. Advocates reducing disciplinary division between history and anthropology.

Manganaro, Marc, ed. *Modernist Anthropology: From Fieldwork to Text.* Princeton U. Pr. 1990 $47.00. ISBN 0-691-06046-1. Essays relating current perspectives on anthropology to the literary-cultural movement of Modernism.

Murdock, George P., Clellan S. Ford, Alfred E. Hudson, Raymond Kennedy, Leo W. Simmons, and W. M. Whiting. *Outline of Cultural Materials.* HRAF Manuals Ser. HRAFP 5th rev. ed. 1982 $25.00. ISBN 0-87536-654-6. A classification of topics typically covered in ethnographies.

Naroll, Raoul, and Ronald Cohen, eds. *A Handbook of Method in Cultural Anthropology.* Col. U. Pr. 1973 o.p. Chapters on fieldwork, categorization, and comparison. Bibliographies are included.

Nencel, Lorraine, and Peter Pels, eds. *Constructing Knowledge: Authority and Critique in Social Science.* Sage 1991 $55.00. ISBN 0-8039-8401-4. Collection focusing on recent critical approaches to the theory and practice of anthropology.

Pelto, Pertti J., and Gretel H. Pelto. *Anthropological Research: The Structure of Inquiry.* Cambridge U. Pr. $18.95. ISBN 0-521-29228-X. Standard text covering participant observation, sampling, and theory building.

Pitt, David C. *Using Historical Sources in Anthropology and Sociology.* Irvington repr. of 1972 ed. ISBN 0-8290-0587-0. Brief introduction to kinds of historical sources available and guidelines for reading them critically, with Samoa provided as a case study.

Poggie, John J., Jr., ed. *Anthropological Research: Process and Application.* State U. NY Pr. 1992 $59.50. ISBN 0-7914-1001-3. Reviews principles for conducting scientific anthropological research.

Stocking, George W., Jr., ed. *Observers Observed: Essays on Ethnographic Fieldwork.* U. of Wis. Pr. 1985 $25.00. ISBN 0-299-09454-5. Gives a sense of how fieldwork has changed and developed, with essays on Boas, Malinowski, and others.

ANTHROPOLOGICAL ARCHAEOLOGY

Anthropologists share an interest in archaeology with scholars in other disciplines, such as history, classics, and art, but anthropological archaeologists cover a broader range of prehistoric societies than do these other disciplines, often investigating the remains of very small societies that left no written records and no monumental architecture. In studying a prehistoric community, anthropological archaeologists aim to reconstruct its total way of life, examining not only the tools and other artifacts it left behind but also microscopic pollens and associated animal bones that reveal the environment and diet. They study the placement of buildings and other structures in relation to each other and to the landscape in order to learn how the society was organized and how work was performed. Burials and the grave goods associated with the dead reveal clues about social status and beliefs about an afterlife.

Anthropological archaeology expands the time of anthropological theory, providing a window on cultural evolution. Paleoarchaeologists examine the very earliest evidence of culture, found in Africa and dating back more than two million years. Other archaeologists study the emergence of the world's great civilizations, searching for answers as to why state-level polities, intensive agriculture, and writing arose in several locations around the world—including China, Mesopotamia, and central Mexico—starting around 10,000 years ago. Still other archaeologists deepen our knowledge of history, searching for the traces of everyday life as it was lived in medieval England or colonial Jamestown.

Binford, Lewis R., ed. *Debating Archaeology*. Acad. Pr. 1989 $49.95. ISBN 0-12-100045-1. A collection on theoretical controversies of the last two decades.

Childe, Vera G. *Progress and Archaeology*. Greenwood 1971 repr. of 1944 ed. $35.00. ISBN 0-8371-4779-4. Concludes that archaeologists can measure progress only through technological change but that the social consequences of cultural evolution do not represent progress.

Clark, Grahame. *Aspects of Prehistory*. U. CA Pr. 1970 $45.00. ISBN 0-520-01584-3. A very brief but useful introduction to world prehistory.

Gibbon, Guy. *Anthropological Archaeology*. Col. U. Pr. 1984 $41.50. ISBN 0-231-05662-1. Research strategies for archaeology both as culture history and as social science.

Hodder, Ian. *Reading the Past: Current Approaches to Interpretation in Archaeology*. Cambridge U. Pr. 1991 $12.95. ISBN 0-521-40957-8. An interpretive, humanistic approach to archaeology.

Isaac, Glynn L. *The Archaeology of Human Origins*. Ed. by Barbara Isaac. Cambridge U. Pr. 1990 $65.00. ISBN 0-521-36573-2. A useful collection of 18 papers on early hominid diet and technologies, by a highly respected paleoanthropologist.

McIntosh, Jane. *The Practical Archaeologist*. Facts on File 1988 $24.95. ISBN 0-8160-1400-0. Methods, findings, and history of archaeology; beautiful illustrations.

Renfrew, Colin. *Archaeology and Language*. Cambridge U. Pr. 1990 $18.95. ISBN 0-521-38675-6. Searches for origins of Indo-European speakers

——. *Approaches to Social Archaeology*. HUP 1984 $28.95. ISBN 0-674-04165-8. Asks what kinds of generalizations are possible in archaeology, especially those about culture change.

Taylor, Walter W. *A Study of Archaeology*. Center Archaeo 1983 $8.00. ISBN 0-88104-009-6. Criticizes historical reconstructions of cultural sequences in favor of trying to discover past ways of life.

Thomas, Julian. *Rethinking the Neolithic*. Cambridge U. Pr. 1991 $54.50. ISBN 0-521-40377-4. Based on research in southern Britain, suggests food production was not as important an economic innovation as scholars had supposed.

Trigger, Bruce G. *A History of Archaeological Thought*. Cambridge U. Pr. 1990 $69.95. ISBN 0-521-32878-0. Covers Soviet as well as classical archaeology.

Weaver, Muriel P. *Aztecs, Maya, and Their Predecessors: Archaeology of Mesoamerica*. Acad. Pr. 1981 $49.00. ISBN 0-12-785936-5. A handy synthesis covering the entire Mesoamerican region.

CULTURE AND ACCULTURATION

"It's the mark of a mature science that it no longer knows what its subject matter is," wrote the English philosopher of science, ALFRED NORTH WHITEHEAD (1861–1947) (see Vol. 4). Anthropologists have thought and written much about culture, the central concept of their discipline, yet they do not all use the term in exactly the same way. Anthropological archaeologists often use the phrase "material culture" to denote humanly made objects; like ALFRED L. KROEBER, whose epigram introduces this chapter, many anthropologists include *behavior* within their definition. Others contend that culture does not consist of objects and behavior but of ideas, values, and beliefs that shape behavior and human products. Regardless of how anthropologists define culture, they learn about other cultures through the study of constructed objects and observable behavior, and, above all, through attention to the words people use. From such tangible data, anthropologists infer how people categorize, evaluate, and understand the world in which they live.

The cultures of the world have always been in a constant state of change. There are no "pure" cultures unaffected by borrowing and outside influences. In all societies, small and large, fads and fashions come and go. Traders, adventurers, and travelers spread new ideas, and return home with knowledge, objects, and ideas from other places. Satellite communication and mass media now link the entire globe. More than simply a mutual sharing, however, the borrowing or adoption of new cultural elements often occurs under conditions of conquest and inequality. Sometimes people want to emulate those they perceive to be rich and powerful. At other times, people resist taking on the culture of those who are oppressing them, constructing a self-conscious ethnicity and harking back to "traditions" (some of them newly minted) that they hope to preserve.

Bateson, Gregory. *Naven: A Survey of the Problems Suggested by a Composite Picture of the Culture of a New Guinea Tribe Drawn from Three Points of View*. Stanford U. Pr. 1958 $42.50. ISBN 0-8047-0519-4. A fascinating analysis of ritual, gender, and psychology.

Fernandez, James W., ed. *Beyond Metaphor: The Theory of Tropes in Anthropology*. Stanford U. Pr. 1991 $39.50. ISBN 0-8047-1940-3. Presents metaphor as an organizational device in cultures.

Geertz, Clifford. *Interpretation of Cultures*. Basic 1977 $16.00. ISBN 0-465-09719-7. Influential essays on the methodology of interpretive approaches.

Harris, Marvin. *Cannibals and Kings*. Random 1991 $11.00. ISBN 0-679-72849-X. Argues that material necessity is the motor of cultural evolution.

Huizinga, Johan. *Homo Ludens: A Study of the Play Element in Culture*. Beacon Pr. 1955 $13.95. ISBN 0-8070-4681-7. Engagingly written thesis that humans are more than rational beings.

Kaplan, David, and Robert A. Manners. *Culture Theory*. Waveland Pr. 1986 o.p. A brief but profound elucidation of the discipline's central concept.

Redfield, Robert. *The Little Community and Peasant Society and Culture*. U. Ch. Pr. 1989 $18.95. ISBN 0-226-70670-2. Peasants viewed first as an isolated social form and then as part of complex societies.

――――. *The Primitive World and Its Transformations*. Cornell Univ. Pr. 1957 $8.95. ISBN 0-8014-9028-6. Describes the "urban revolution" as marked by a distinct moral order and world view.

Sahlins, Marshall. *Culture and Practical Reason*. U. Ch. Pr. 1978 $9.95. ISBN 0-226-73361-0. Points out the limits of materialist theory for analyzing the symbolic world.

Sapir, Edward. *Selected Writings of Edward Sapir: Language, Culture, and Personality*. Ed. by David G. Mandelbaum. U. CA Pr. 1949 $49.95. ISBN 0-520-01115-5. By one of the founders of American linguistics.

Steward, Julian H. *Theory of Culture Change: The Methodology of Multilinear Evolution*. U. of Ill. Pr. 1972 repr. of 1955 ed. $12.95. ISBN 0-252-00295-4. Scientific materialist explanations presented as a corrective to older theories of evolution.

Tylor, E. *Primitive Culture*. 2 vols. Gordon Pr. 1973 $600.00. ISBN 0-87968-091-1. Best known for its evolutionary depiction of religion.

White, Leslie A. *The Evolution of Culture*. McGraw 1959 o.p. Argues that energy capture is the key to cultural evolution.

――――. *The Science of Culture: A Study of Man and Civilization*. FS&G 1969 o.p. Emphasis on symbol use as the distinctively human characteristic.

CULTURE AND PERSONALITY

Some—perhaps most—anthropologists assume the psychic unity of humanity; that is, they assume that humans everywhere have the same perceptual, cognitive, and affective aptitudes. Other anthropologists leave open the question of psychic unity, trying to discover the degree to which the cultural environment shapes a psychological process such as memory or an emotional state such as anger. This is a debate about whether culture overlays people like a veneer, constraining and directing basic human proclivities, or pervades and alters human experience to such a degree that cross-cultural psychology is difficult if not impossible.

Studies in psychological anthropology sometimes draw from Freudian theory and sometimes proceed eclectically from a number of different theoretical traditions. Because the early years of life are so formative, these studies often examine early childhood experiences to discern when the attitudes and personalities of adults first begin to take shape. More than a way of understanding individual psychodynamics, psychoanalytic theory also provides an interpretive framework for viewing cultural phenomena such as myths and rituals, assuming that these collective products reflect personal struggles within culturally specific kinds of families or ways of socializing children.

Bateson, Gregory. *Steps to an Ecology of the Mind*. Aronson 1988 repr. of 1972 ed. $40.00. ISBN 0-87668-950-0. Wide-ranging, stimulating essays on the double bind, schizophrenia, and cybernetics.

Benedict, Ruth. *Patterns of Culture*. HM 1989 repr. of 1961 ed. $9.70. ISBN 0-395-50088-5. Argues that cultures elaborate some character traits at the expense of others.

Hsu, Francis L. *Rugged Individualism Reconsidered: Essays in Psychological Anthropology*. U. of Tenn. Pr. 1983 $42.50. ISBN 0-87049-370-1. Links violence in American culture to the cult of the individual.

LeVine, Robert A., ed. *Culture and Personality: Contemporary Readings*. Aldine de Gruyter 1974 $26.95. ISBN 0-202-01122-4. Articles on diverse topics, including psychological universals, socialization, and the life course in different cultures.

Lévi-Strauss, Claude. *Savage Mind*. U. Ch. Pr. 1968 $13.95. ISBN 0-226-47484-4. Explores the ubiquity of dialectical thinking.

Mead, Margaret. *Growing Up in New Guinea*. Morrow 1975 $13.45. ISBN 0-688-07989-X. One of the first anthropological studies of child care practices.

Parsons, Talcott. *Social Structure and Personality*. Free Pr. 1964 $3.45. ISBN 0-02-924840-X. Views on American psychology from a prominent social theorist.

Schwartz, Theodore, Geoffrey White, and Catherine A. Lutz, eds. *New Directions in Psychological Anthropology*. Cambridge U. Pr. 1992 $54.95. ISBN 0-521-41592-6. Essays on cognition, subjectivity, and the body, recognizing that even small societies are internally diverse.

Stigler, James W., Richard Shweder, and Gilbert H. Herdt, eds. *Cultural Psychology: The Chicago Symposia on Human Development*. Cambridge U. Pr. 1990 $69.95. ISBN 0-521-37154-6. Discredits the assumption of psychic unity.

Whiting, Beatrice B., and Carolyn P. Edward. *Children of Different Worlds: The Formation of Social Behavior*. HUP 1992 $16.95. ISBN 0-674-11617-8. Part of a longitudinal study of 134 children in 6 cultures.

Whiting, John W., and Irvin L. Child. *Child Training and Personality: A Cross-Cultural Study*. Greenwood 1984 repr. of 1953 ed. $41.50. ISBN 0-313-24387-5. Statistical correlations link childhood experiences to cultural forms.

ECONOMIC ANTHROPOLOGY

Peoples everywhere have to produce food and other survival requirements; anthropologists are interested in how they do so, from the tools and energy sources they command to the ways in which they organize themselves to accomplish given tasks. Everywhere, too, people devise ways of moving and transferring goods and of claiming goods and services from other people; anthropologists study economic distribution as a way of understanding how power operates in different societies.

Traditionally, cultural anthropologists worked in societies where money was absent or of little consequence, and where labor and goods changed hands because persons owed each other particular kinds of service or things by virtue of how they were related. Concepts that explain economic behavior in money economies (such as supply and demand) did not go very far in these settings when it came to determining who gave and who received labor and goods. Increasingly, anthropologists study people who work for wages at least some of the time or who sell what they produce for money. The demands of community and family, based on the ethnic of a premoney economy, sometimes conflict with new imperatives to educate one's children or to acquire expensive status symbols.

Chayanov, A. V. *The Theory of Peasant Economy.* Ohio St. U. Pr. 1991 repr. of 1966 ed. $59.50. ISBN 0-8142-0566-6. Develops a theory of household economic behavior based on Russian peasants in the 1920s.

Dalton, George. *Economic Anthropology and Development: Essays on Tribal and Peasant Economies.* Basic 1971 o.p. Frequently cited essays.

Durrenberger, E. Paul, ed. *Chayanov Peasants, and Economic Anthropology.* Acad. Pr. 1984 $41.00. ISBN 0-12-225180-6. How Chayanov's theory applies in various ethnographic settings.

Firth, Raymond. *Primitive Polynesian Economy.* Shoe String 1975 repr. of 1965 ed. o.p. Tikopia's political economy, from food production to labor and distribution.

Herskovits, Melville. *Economic Anthropology.* Knopf 1952 o.p. For many years the standard introductory text on the subject.

Mauss, Marcel. *Gift: Form and Reason for Exchange in Archaic Societies.* Norton 1990 $9.95. ISBN 0-393-30698-4. Sets out the social basis of economies without money.

Meillassoux, C., ed. *Maidens, Meal, and Money.* Trans. by Felicity Edholm. Cambridge U. Pr. $19.95. ISBN 0-521-22902-2. Argues that older men control the labor and produce of women and younger men in lineage societies.

Polanyi, Karl, and others, eds. *Trade and Market in the Early Empires: Economies in History and Theory.* Macmillan 1957 o.p. Reciprocity, redistribution, and market exchange delineated and explained.

Sahlins, Marshall. *Stone Age Economics.* Aldine de Gruyter 1972 $41.95. ISBN 0-202-01098-8. Applies the mode-of-production concept and economic theories to primitive economies.

Strathern, Marilyn. *The Gender of the Gift: Problems with Women and Problems with Society in Melanesia. Studies in Melanesian Anthropology:* No. 6. U. CA Pr. 1988 $47.50. ISBN 0-520-06423-2. Radical theoretical reevaluation of some assumptions and concepts basic to exchange theory.

ETHNOLOGY

Studies of particular cultures and societies produce an expanding body of literature from which anthropologists may draw comparisons and make generalizations. Anthropologists may amass hundreds of cases in which they seek the correlations of traits. Do male initiation rituals at puberty correlate with high levels of warfare? Do religions of ancestor worship cluster in societies marked by unilineal kinship? Cross-cultural correlations such as these provide a sense of the probabilities of our finding certain customs in association; more than that, they point toward the functional and logical relationships that characterize human societies past and present.

Many comparisons within anthropology are less systematic, however. Anthropologists usually carry out their research on one culture, but they read the ethnographies produced by others working in the same region; they also study regional history and geography. In this way, scholars working in the same region develop a sense of the variations within it, and perhaps of the historical relationships among the different peoples there. Other ethnological comparisons disregard regional boundaries altogether, asking whether, for example, pastoral peoples, regardless of where they live, exhibit commonalities. Still others might compare, again without regard to region, matrilineal societies or those influenced by Buddhism.

Firth, Raymond W. *Elements of Social Organization.* 3rd ed. *Josiah Mason Lectures Ser.* Greenwood 1981 repr. of 1961 ed. $65.00. ISBN 0-313-22745-4. Develops a theoretical framework emphasizing choice and process.

Fox, Robin. *The Red Lamp of Incest: An Inquiry into the Origins of Mind and Society.* U. of Notre Dame Pr. 1983 $10.95. ISBN 0-268-01620-8. Offers a biosocial synthesis to explain an almost uniquely human taboo.

Friedl, Ernestine. *Women and Men: An Anthropologist's View.* Waveland Pr. 1984 repr. of 1975 ed. $8.95. ISBN 0-88133-040-X. Examines gender in foraging and horticultural societies.

Kroeber, Alfred L. *Configurations of Culture Growth.* U. CA Pr. 1944 $35.00. ISBN 0-520-00669-0. Compares the growth curves of several great civilizations.

Lee, Richard B., and Irven Devore, eds. *Man the Hunter.* Aldine de Gruyter 1968 $26.95. ISBN 0-202-33032-X. Papers from a symposium on foraging peoples detailing the importance of gathering in their economies.

Lévi-Strauss, Claude. *Structural Anthropology.* Vol. 1. Basic 1974 $18.00. ISBN 0-465-09516-X. Vol. 2. Trans. by Monique Layton. U. Ch. Pr. 1983 $17.95. ISBN 0-226-47491-7. Essays on the history of anthropology, kinship, and the interpretation of myths.

Martin, M. Kay, and Barbara Voorhies. *Female of the Species.* Col. U. Pr. 1975 $21.00. ISBN 0-231-03876-3. Examines gender relations in societies classified according to techno-economic type.

Murdock, George P. *Social Structure.* Free Pr. 1965 $16.95. ISBN 0-02-922290-7. Tests hypotheses about kinship against statistical correlations.

Sahlins, Marshall D., and Elman R. Service, eds. *Evolution and Culture.* U. of Mich. Pr. 1960 $12.95. ISBN 0-472-08776-2. Theoretical essays suggesting laws of cultural evolution paralleling those of biological evolution.

Schneider, David. M., and Kathleen Gough, eds. *Matrilineal Kinship.* U. CA Pr. 1974 $11.95. ISBN 0-520-02529-6. A major compendium on matrilineal descent, with a useful introduction.

Wolf, Eric R. *Europe and the People without History.* U. CA Pr. 1982 $45.00. ISBN 0-520-04459-2. Presents European discovery and colonialism as elements of a world system.

EVOLUTION

Most anthropologists agree that culture is the definitive mark of the human. No other species is quite so dependent on learning for its survival, and no other species has evolved in relation to a cultural environment. Although a long-term evolutionary trend toward greater learning can be seen throughout the animal kingdom, culture has become humanity's primary method of adaptation. Furthermore, it is not possible to account for human evolution without knowing how the cultural environment has shaped our physical being. For example, our upper respiratory tract (specialized for speaking) has evolved in relation to language, and our dexterous hands (specialized for making and using tools) have evolved along with tools of greater and greater refinement.

The biological evolution of the human species has not stopped. In comparison with cultural evolution, however, it proceeds at a snail's pace. Using primarily cultural means, humans have moved to occupy environmental niches that are as diverse as the earth itself. More than simply a proliferation of diversity, the long-term evolution of culture also exhibits a direction or a tendency. Over time, polities and societies have grown larger, more centralized, and more internally heterogeneous. This did not occur everywhere or at the same rate, nor has it been without cycles of rise and collapse in specific locales. Most explanations for this evolutionary tendency point to population pressures, which exacerbate competition for resources and give rise to hierarchical power structures encompassing ever greater numbers of people.

Clark, W. E. *The Fossil Evidence for Human Evolution: An Introduction to the Study of Paleoanthropology.* Ed. by Bernard G. Campbell. U. Ch. Pr. 3rd rev. ed. 1979 $16.00. ISBN 0-226-10937-2. Photographs accompany a classic exposition of major prehuman and early human fossils.

Donovan, Stephen K., ed. *Mass Extinctions: Processes and Evidence.* Col. U. Pr. 1991 $24.50. ISBN 0-231-07091-8. Essays summarizing the present state of knowledge about mass extinction processes.

Fabian, A.C., ed. *Origins.* Cambridge U. Pr. 1989 $24.95. ISBN 0-521-35189-8. Essays delivered as part of the Darwin College Lecture Series addressing the origins of the universe, the solar system, complexity, human life, social behavior, society, and language.

Gould, Stephen J. *Ontogeny and Phylogeny.* HUP 1977 $30.50. ISBN 0-674-63940-5. Argues that human evolution has been retarded, and traces the history of the axiom that ontogeny recapitulates phylogeny.

Grant, Verne. *The Evolutionary Process.* Col. U. Pr. 1991 $52.00. ISBN 0-231-07324-0. Comprehensive and critical review of modern evolutionary theory.

Huxley, Julian. *Evolution: The Main Synthesis.* Paul & Co. Pubs. 1974 o.p. Darwinian theory wedded with Mendelian genetics to produce the modern theory of evolution.

Lopreato, Joseph. *Human Nature and Biocultural Evolution.* Unwin Hyman 1984 $34.95. ISBN 0-04-573017-2. Seeks behavioral predispositions important in human adaptations.

Roe, Anne, and George G. Simpson, eds. *Behavior and Evolution.* Bks. Demand repr. of 1958 ed. $141.80. ISBN 0-8357-7105-9. Essays on several topics, including the genetic basis of behavior and the evolution of learning.

Ross, Robert M., and Warren D. Allmon, eds. *Causes of Evolution: A Paleontological Perspective.* U. Ch. Pr. 1991 $65.00. ISBN 0-226-77823-4. Broad sampling of paleontological research.

Sahlins, Marshall D., and Elman R. Service, eds. *Evolution and Culture.* U. of Mich. Pr. 1960 $12.95. ISBN 0-472-08776-2. Deduces laws of cultural evolution from laws of biological evolution.

Stearns, Stephen C. *The Evolution of Life Histories.* OUP 1992 $29.95. ISBN 0-19-857741-9. Introduction to life history evolution discussing the major research findings and analytical tools used within the areas of population biology, ecology, and evolutionary biology.

Steward, Julian H. *Theory of Culture Change: The Methodology of Multilinear Evolution.* U. of Ill. Pr. 1972 repr. of 1955 ed. $12.95. ISBN 0-252-00295-4. A materialist view of cultural evolution.

Warren, Leonard, ed. *New Perspectives on Evolution.* Wiley 1991 $54.95. ISBN 0-471-56068-5. Collection of papers providing an overview of current thinking about evolution, emphasizing the contributions of such fields as molecular biology and immunology.

White, Leslie A. *The Evolution of Culture.* McGraw 1959 o.p. Emphasizes the capture of energy through technology as the key element.

KINSHIP AND CASTE

In many of the societies anthropologists study, kinship is the primary basis of social organization. The composition of living and work groups, the ownership and inheritance of property, claims to leadership or special forms of knowledge—all of these and more depend on the way people define who their kin are and what are the rights and duties of kinship. It is not simply that people in small-scale societies may keep track of or know more relatives than people who live in complex modern societies. Rather, where kinship is the primary basis of social organization, virtually all interaction, even that between neighbors, friends, or strangers, may be cast in an idiom of metaphoric kinship.

True caste societies are relatively rare. In these, a person is consigned at birth to a social or racial category, with little possibility of altering the designation. Castes are usually endogamous (requiring marriage within the group), and occupations are often hereditary. Even so, the relative status of a caste may change over time. In contemporary India, the best example of a caste society, class and caste have become somewhat separate systems of stratification; a person may belong to a relatively low caste but be well-to-do, or, conversely, a high-caste Brahman may be very poor.

Barnes, J. A. *Three Styles in the Study of Kinship.* U. CA Pr. 1972 $45.00. ISBN 0-520-01879-6. Compares George Murdock, Meyer Fortes, and Claude Lévi-Strauss.

Collier, Jane F., and Sylvia J. Yanagisako, eds. *Gender and Kinship: Essays Toward a Unified Analysis.* Stanford U. Pr. 1987 $47.50. ISBN 0-8047-1366-9. Questions biological assumptions implicit in standard kinship analyses.

Dollard, John. *Caste and Class in a Southern Town.* U. of Wis. Pr. 1989 repr. of 1937 ed. $39.75. ISBN 0-299-12130-5. Race relations (before the civil rights movement), analyzed as a caste system, with a foreword by Daniel P. Moynihan.

Dumont, Louis. *Homo Hierarchicus: The Caste System and Its Implications.* Trans. by Basia Gulati. U. Ch. Pr. rev. ed. 1981 $36.00. ISBN 0-226-16962-6. Examines the ethos and ethic of caste in India, and compares it with Western values of equality and individualism.

Evans-Pritchard, Edward. *Kinship and Marriage among the Nuer.* OUP 1990 repr. of 1951 ed. $37.00. ISBN 0-19-823104-0. Introduction by Wendy James. A central and key volume in his trilogy on the Nuer, linking descent structure to locality and to the politics and religion described in the other two volumes.

Firth, Raymond. *We, the Tikopia: A Sociological Study of Kinship in Primitive Polynesia.* Stanford U. Pr. abr. ed. 1963 repr. of 1936 ed. $57.50. ISBN 0-8047-1201-8. A comprehensive ethnography written around the topics of kinship and family, with a preface by Bronislaw Malinowski.

Geertz, Hildred, and Clifford Geertz. *Kinship in Bali.* U. Ch. Pr. 1978 repr. of 1975 ed. $11.95. ISBN 0-226-28516-2. How the quest for status drives cross-cousin marriage and the formation of endogamous patrilines.

Leach, Edmund R., ed. *Aspects of Caste in South India, Ceylon and North West Pakistan.* Cambridge Papers in Social Anthropology: No. 2. Cambridge U. Pr. 1971 $17.95. ISBN 0-521-07729-X. Introductory essay on the meaning of caste.

Lévi-Strauss, Claude. *Elementary Structures of Kinship*. Ed. by Rodney Needham. Beacon Pr. 1969 repr. of 1968 ed. $19.95. ISBN 0-8070-4669-8. An evolutionary depiction of marriage rules as different kinds of social glue.

Malinowski, Bronislaw. *Sex and Repression in Savage Society*. U. Ch. Pr. 1985 $12.95. ISBN 0-226-50287-2. One of the first ethnographies to focus on family life.

Murdock, George P. *Social Structure*. 1949. Free Pr. 1965 $16.95. ISBN 0-02-922290-7. Many different hypotheses tested against cross-cultural correlations.

Radcliffe-Brown, A. R., and Daryll Forde, eds. *African Systems of Kinship and Marriage*. 1950. Routledge Chapman and Hall 1987 $19.95. ISBN 0-7103-0234-7. Exemplifies the structural-functionalist era in anthropology.

Rivers, William H. *Kinship and Social Organization: Together with the Genealogical Method of Anthropological Enquiry*. London School of Economics. Monographs on Social Anthropology: No. 34. Bks. Demand repr. of 1968 ed. $32.50. ISBN 0-485-19534-8. A founding text in the study of kinship, with commentaries by Raymond Firth and David M. Schneider.

Schneider, David M. *A Critique of the Study of Kinship*. U. of Mich. Pr. 1984 $34.50. ISBN 0-472-10051-3. Debunks genealogy as the universal basis of kinship in favor of culturally specific meanings.

Schneider, David M., and Kathleen Gough, eds. *Matrilineal Kinship*. U. CA Pr. 1974 o.p. The major compendium of studies on this topic, with an especially useful introduction.

Trautman, Thomas R. *Lewis Henry Morgan and the Invention of Kinship*. U. CA Pr. 1987 $39.95. ISBN 0-520-05849-6. An in-depth analysis of the development of Morgan's "kinship project."

Trawick, Margaret. *Notes on Love in a Tamil Family*. U. CA Pr. 1990 $45.00. ISBN 0-520-06636-7. Illustrates abstractions about kinship and marriage with scenes from daily life in a large extended family.

Young, Michael, and Peter Willmott. *Family and Kinship in East London*. Routledge 1986 $35.00. ISBN 0-7102-0914-2. Working-class neighborhood in 1955 with wider kinship networks than sociologists had expected.

LANGUAGE

Anthropologists study language because it is so central to culture. While it is sometimes necessary to rely on interpreters or to use a lingua franca, most cultural anthropologists try to learn and function in the local language where they conduct research. In many cases the language of fieldwork is a relatively minor or obscure tongue, not the sort offered in any university curriculum, so cultural anthropologists study descriptive linguistics to equip themselves to learn a language on their own. Historical linguistics is also of use to anthropologists and archaeologists, because it enables them to compare two languages in order to judge how far back in time both shared a common ancestor. Such comparisons help determine the origins and movements of peoples in prehistoric times. In living societies subtle differences of pronunciation or vocabulary often correlate with significant social differences, such as gender, class, or neighborhood.

Above all, it is impossible to understand people's ideas, values, and beliefs except through a careful attention to their language. "The worlds in which different societies live are distinct worlds, not merely the same world with different labels attached," asserted BENJAMIN L. WHORF, arguing that language shapes people's views of time and of material realities. The challenge facing anthropology is, as E. E. EVANS-PRITCHARD noted, the challenge of translation. The anthropologist must learn first to think in the terms of another culture, and then to write about that culture in the terms of his or her own language.

Boas, Franz. *Handbook of the American Indian Languages*. 4 vols. Rprt. Serv. 1988 $225.00. ISBN 0-7812-5040-4. Boas's introduction distinguishes race from language and sets out the assumptions behind the descriptive research of the early twentieth century.

Bloomfield, Leonard. *Language*. U. Ch. Pr. 1984 $17.95. ISBN 0-226-06067-5. The standard introduction for two generations of students, with a foreword by Charles Hockett.

Burling, Robbins. *Patterns of Language: Structure, Variation, Change*. Acad. Pr. 1992 $24.95. ISBN 0-12-144920-3. Comprehensive introduction to linguistics including extensive information on lexicon, phonology, and syntax.

Chomsky, Noam. *Aspects of the Theory of Syntax*. MIT Pr. 1965 $10.95. ISBN 0-262-53007-4. Presents linguistics as a branch of cognitive psychology.

———. *Syntactic Structures. Janua Linguarum Ser. Minor: No. 4*. Mouton 1978 $12.95. ISBN 0-89925-090-4. A revolutionary reordering of analytical priorities, placing grammar at the center of analysis.

Goffman, Erving. *Forms of Talk. Conduct and Communication Ser*. U. of Pa. Pr. 1981 $39.95. ISBN 0-8122-1112-X. Five papers on the theatricality of all speaking, even speaking to oneself.

Greenberg, Joseph H., Charles A. Ferguson, and Edith Moravcsik, eds. *Universals of Human Language*. 4 vols. Stanford U. Pr. 1978 $199.50. ISBN 0-8047-1012-0. A massive sifting of the evidence for universals at all linguistic levels.

Gumperz, John J., ed. *Language and Social Identity. Studies in Interactional Sociologistics 2*. Cambridge U. Pr. 1983 $17.95. ISBN 0-521-28897-5. Perceptive essays about communication breakdowns and ethnic stereotyping.

Harris, Zellig. *Language and Information*. Col. U. Pr. 1988 $27.50. ISBN 0-231-06662-7. Series of lectures on the formal theory of language structure.

Heller, Monica, ed. *Codeswitching: Anthropological and Sociolinguistic Perspectives*. Mouton 1988 $78.70. ISBN 0-89925-412-8. Examines code-switching—the phenomenon of switching from the linguistic system of one language or dialect to that of another—as a form of language contact.

Hymes, Dell. *Pidginization and Creolization of Languages: Proceedings*. Cambridge U. Pr. 1974 $27.95. ISBN 0-521-09888-2. A theoretical analysis of the origins of pidgins and creoles and of their relevance for linguistic theory.

Kristeva, Julia. *Language: The Unknown: An Initiation into Linguistics*. Col. U. Pr. 1989 $47.50. ISBN 0-231-06106-4. A broad, yet somewhat difficult overview of linguistics with a strong philosophical emphasis.

Labov, William. *Sociolinguistic Patterns. Conduct and Communication Ser*. U. of Pa. Pr. 1973 $19.95. ISBN 0-8122-7657-4. Frequently cited essays on language change, especially sound shifts associated with class aspirations and neighborhood solidarity.

Lakoff, George, and Mark Johnson. *Metaphors We Live By*. U. Ch. Pr. 1981 $9.95. ISBN 0-226-46801-1. Argues that metaphors are essential to the way we think, not merely poetic flourishes.

Sapir, Edward. *Selected Writings of Edward Sapir in Language, Culture, and Personality*. Ed. by David G. Mandelbaum. U. CA Pr. 1949 $49.95. ISBN 0-520-01115-5. Classic essays on language and the status of linguistics as a science.

Wolf, George. *New Departures in Linguistics*. Garland 1992 $33.00. ISBN 0-8240-6102-0. Essays offering the results of recent research in several different branches of modern linguistics, including syntax, semantics, and feminist linguistic theory.

MODERN SOCIETIES

It is difficult, if not impossible, to find any societies in the world that are totally isolated. In this sense, all of the societies that anthropologists study today are modern societies; this is also true of anthropology done in the past. The first generation of anthropologists who did fieldwork were seldom the first outsiders to arrive on the scene; usually they followed in the wake of colonial officers, traders, or missionaries. Even so, anthropologists often succumbed to romantic tendencies, ignoring the vast sea of change in which both they and their subjects were awash. Today more and more anthropologists, rather than giving the impression that they are describing the timeless traditions of untouched primitives, examine how people imitate, resist, rethink, and create modernity.

At the same time that anthropologists have been meeting modernity in the outback, they have begun to realize that the "tribal" exists in their own backyards. Modern societies are, if anything, more diverse than the forms they displace, and anthropology has been forged out of the study of diversity. Although research in urban or suburban settings offers the possibility of using newspaper archives and other historical sources, as well as standard research formats such as the interview or the questionnaire, most anthropologists still use these to supplement participant observation. They try to blend in with and observe interaction in some "exotic" setting, such as a classroom, a racetrack, a hospital emergency room, and even, in one case, the U.S. Congress. There they do what anthropologists do in any fieldwork setting: They listen carefully to the terms people use to talk about their experiences and observe closely to see how work is organized and order is maintained; later they write an ethnography based on their experiences.

Banton, Michael, ed. *Social Anthropology of Complex Societies.* Routledge Chapman and Hall 1968 $15.95. ISBN 0-422-72520-X. Essays on the theory of anthropological research in modern settings.

Barth, Fredrik. *Ethnic Groups and Boundaries.* Little 1969 o.p. Deals with how ethnic identities are marked and how they persist.

Benedict, Ruth. *The Chrysanthemum and the Sword: Patterns of Japanese Culture.* HM 1989 $8.95. ISBN 0-395-50075-3. Introduction by Ezra Vogel. Clarifies the linked values of hierarchy and obligation that bind Japanese society together.

Bourdieu, Pierre. *Distinction: A Social Critique of the Judgement of Taste.* Trans. by Richard Nice. HUP 1984 $39.95. ISBN 0-674-21280-0. A cultural analysis of the symbols of class distinctions.

Clifford, James. *The Predicament of Culture: Twentieth Century Ethnography, Literature, and Art.* HUP 1988 $34.95. ISBN 0-674-69842-8. Essays on identity, the history of anthropology in France, museums, and the dilemmas of the postmodern era.

Davis, Allison, Burleigh B. Gardner, and Mary R. Gardner. *Deep South: A Social Anthropological Study of Caste and Class.* CAAS Community Classics Ser. Vol. 1. UCLA CAAS 1988 $25.95. ISBN 0-934934-26-6. Foreword by Claudia Mitchell-Kernan. Useful descriptions of a lower-class white family, of the relations between poor whites and poor blacks, and between the middle class and the poor.

Gorer, Geoffrey, and John Rickman. *People of Great Russia: A Psychological Study.* Norton 1962 $3.25. ISBN 0-393-00112-1. Another culture-at-a-distance study of the World War II era.

Kondo, Dorinne K. *Crafting Selves: Power, Gender, and Discourses of Identity in a Japanese Workplace.* U. Ch. Pr. 1990 $55.00. ISBN 0-226-45043-0. Young women's concepts of self forged in a dynamic of power relations.

Levy, Robert I. *Tahitians: Mind and Experience in the Society Islands.* U. Ch. Pr. 1975 repr. of 1973 ed. $17.95. ISBN 0-226-47607-3. Examines adoption, suicide, and shame in Christian Tahiti.

Nash, June. *We Eat the Mines and the Mines Eat Us: Dependency and Exploitation in Bolivian Tin Mines.* Col. U. Pr. 1992 $45.00. ISBN 0-231-08050-6. Covers family and community life, as well as labor conflicts.

Ong, Aihwa. *Spirits of Resistance and Capitalist Discipline: Factory Women in Malaysia.* State U. NY Pr. 1987 $59.50. ISBN 0-88706-380-2. Young women's spirit possession reveals society's ambivalence about their new economic power.

Weatherford, J. McIver. *Tribes on the Hill: The United States Congress—Rituals and Realities*. Greenwood rev. ed 1985 $18.95. ISBN 0-89789-072-8. The unspoken rules of protocol in congressional activities.

Willis, Paul. *Learning to Labor: How Working Class Kids Get Working Class Jobs*. Col. U. Pr. 1981 repr. of 1978 ed. $16.50. ISBN 0-231-05357-6. Rebellious peer groups socialize British boys to remain in the working class.

RELIGION

The belief in supernatural beings or powers is virtually universal, as is the idea of a soul, although the specific content of these beliefs varies widely. Ancestor veneration, petitions to the gods, the hallowing of sacred truths, and such magical practices as sorcery or malevolent witchcraft all fall within the purview of religion as anthropologists study it. The tribal religions of small-scale societies are often so interwoven with the rest of life that anthropologists who set out to study politics, kinship, the healing arts, or other topics find themselves studying religion as well. Almost everywhere, too, these tribal religions face pressures from the expansive world religions, especially Islam, Christianity, and Buddhism. In competition with these faiths that claim universal truth, tribal religions often appear at a disadvantage because of their decentralized leadership and their lack of a textual tradition.

"No religions are false; all religions are true," was EMILE DURKHEIM's famous dictum, by which he meant that religious conceptions are true to the lived experiences of the people who hold them. Lacking the texts and emphasis on doctrines of the world religions, tribal religions reveal their truths through rituals and in the practices of everyday life. Through the study of ritual symbolism, anthropologists gain insight into how a particular conception of unseen reality is made real in a behavioral enactment. In the study of everyday life in communities and families, anthropologists discern the social and psychological experiences that confirm the truth of certain conceptions of supernatural power and order.

Banton, Michael, ed. *Anthropological Approaches to the Study of Religion*. Routledge Chapman and Hall 1968 $15.95. ISBN 0-422-72510-2. Formative theoretical essays by Geertz, Spiro, and others.

Bloch, Maurice, and Jonathan Parry, eds. *Death and the Regeneration of Life*. Cambridge U. Pr. 1982 $15.95. ISBN 0-521-27037-5. Explores symbolism of fertility and rebirth that often marks funerals worldwide.

Durkheim, Émile. *The Elementary Forms of the Religious Life*. 1912. Trans. by Joseph W. Swain. Free Pr. 1965 $14.95. ISBN 0-02-908010-X. Drawing on an analysis of aboriginal ritual, it reveals the social basis of religion everywhere.

Frazer, James G., ed. *The Golden Bough*. 13 vols. St. Martin 1969 repr. of 1890 ed. $450.00. ISBN 0-312-33215-7. Circuitous quest for rituals and beliefs relating to priestly kings.

Geertz, Clifford. *Islam Observed: Religious Development in Morocco and Indonesia*. U. Ch. Pr. 1971 repr. of 1968 ed. $6.95. ISBN 0-226-28511-1. Discusses how Islam varies in two very different cultural settings.

———. *The Religion of Java*. U. Ch. Pr. 1976 repr. of 1960 ed. $14.95. ISBN 0-226-28510-3. A rich ethnography of the variety in Javanese religious expressions.

Jules-Rosette, Bennetta, ed. *The New Religions of Africa*. Modern Sociology Ser. Ablex Pub. 1979 $45.00. ISBN 0-89391-014-7. Explores the millenarian movements and independent churches spawned by missions.

Malinowski, Bronislaw. *Magic, Science and Religion and Other Essays*. Greenwood 1992 repr. of 1948 ed. $48.50. ISBN 0-313-24687-4. Introduction by Robert Redfield.

Contains some of his classic essays, including one on the role of myth and another on the spirits of the dead in the Trobriand Islands.

Obeyesekere, Gananath. *Medusa's Hair: An Essay on Personal Symbols and Religious Experience*. U. Ch. Pr. 1984 $9.95. ISBN 0-226-61601-0. Sri Lankan ascetics examined through a Freudian lens.

Rappaport, Roy A. *Ecology, Meaning and Religion*. North Atlantic 1988 $12.95. ISBN 0-938190-27-X. Insightful theoretical essays on the adaptational significance of ritual.

Spiro, Melford E. *Burmese Supernaturalism*. Bks. Demand repr. of 1967 ed. $84.00. ISBN 0-8357-8901-2. Describes spirit beliefs and witchcraft in a Buddhist society.

Turner, Victor. *The Ritual Process: Structure and Anti-Structure*. Symbol, Myth and Ritual Ser. Cornell Univ. Pr. 1977 $9.95. ISBN 0-8014-9163-0. Studies of solidarity forged in liminal moments, with pictures.

SOCIAL STRUCTURE

Social structure, following RAYMOND FIRTH, refers to the formal or official social entities, whether these be corporate lineages, chiefly hierarchies, class or caste divisions, age sets, or gender divisions. The study of social organization—that is, the study of who actually lives with whom, who marries whom, how property and power actually devolve, and so on—inevitably reveals that the messy realities of everyday life do not neatly coincide with structural ideals.

The tribal societies that past generations of anthropologists described as "egalitarian" are, in fact, power systems in which certain persons—usually the elders and men—have the advantage over others. More than simply an ideology for rationalizing forms of dominance, however, social structures can also be "good to think," as CLAUDE LÉVI-STRAUSS once said of that socioreligious form called totemism. Women, children, young men, and those older men marginal to a particular power order may be no less committed (or resigned) to it than those who gain the most from it. However unjust or unsavory gender oppression or a class system may appear from our perspective, anthropologists studying social structures try to understand how certain conceptions of order come to seem both inevitable and appropriate from the perspective of those living in accordance with them.

Collier, Jane F. *Marriage and Inequality in Classless Societies*. Stanford U. Pr. 1988 $35.00. ISBN 0-8047-1365-0. Examines the ways in which marriage perpetuates social inequalities, even within traditionally egalitarian societies.

Crompton, Rosemary, and Michael Mann. *Gender Stratification*. Blackwell Pubs. 1986 $17.95. ISBN 0-7456-0168-5. Considers the problem gender poses for stratification theorists.

Firth, Raymond W. *Elements of Social Organization*. Josiah Mason Lecture Ser. Greenwood 1981 repr. of 1961 ed. $65.00. ISBN 0-313-22745-4. Develops a framework emphasizing choice and process.

Fortes, Meyer. *Time and Social Structure and Other Essays*. London School of Economics Monographs on Social Anthropologist: No. 40. Humanities 1970 $38.50. ISBN 0-485-19540-2

Kelly, Raymond C. *Etoro Social Structure: A Study in Structural Contradiction*. U. of Mich. Pr. 1977 $16.00. ISBN 0-472-08502-6. Depicts a social system as a product of two conflicting principles of order.

Kertzer, David L., and Keith Jennie, eds. *Age and Anthropological Theory*. Cornell Univ. Pr. 1984 $13.95. ISBN 0-8014-9258-0. How aging is affected by different sociocultural settings.

McNall, Scott G. and others, eds. *Bringing Class Back In: Contemporary and Historical Perspectives*. Westview Pr. 1991 $52.50. ISBN 0-8133-1049-0. Essays on class structure, class formation, and class power, conflict, and struggle.

Marias, Julian. *The Structure of Society*. U. of Ala. Pr. 1986 $23.95. ISBN 0-8173-0181-X. Highly recommended analysis of social structure offering new insights into several long-standing problems.

Murdock, George P. *Social Structure*. Free Pr. 1965 $16.95. ISBN 0-02-922290-7. Tests hypotheses about kinship against cross-cultural correlations.

Radcliffe-Brown, Alfred R. *Structure and Function in Primitive Society*. Free Pr. 1965 $19.95. ISBN 0-02-925630-5. Classic essays on structural-functionalist theory.

Rosaldo, Michelle Z., and Louise Lamphere, eds. *Woman, Culture, and Society*. Stanford U. Pr. 1974 $45.00. ISBN 0-8047-0850-9. Influential essays on gender theory and on gender in particular ethnographic settings.

Sahlins, Marshall D. *Social Stratification in Polynesia. American Ethnological Society Monographs*: No. 29. AMS Pr. 1988 repr. of 1958 ed. $34.50. ISBN 0-404-62028. Compares political economies of many Polynesian societies.

Todd, Emmanuel. *The Explanation of Ideology: Family Structures and Social Systems*. Blackwell Pubs. 1985 $45.00. ISBN 0-631-13724-6. Theorizes that present social structures reflect particular family structures.

Van Gennep, Arnold. *Rites of Passage*. Trans. by Monika B. Vizedon and Gabrielle L. Caffee. U. Ch. Pr. 1961 $6.95. ISBN 0-226-84849-3. Delineates universal stages of rituals focused on birth, marriage, death, and other transitions.

Wilson, Monica. *Good Company: A Study of Nyakyusa Age-Villages*. Greenwood 1987 $55.00. ISBN 0-313-23972-X. Ethnography of an African people who live in villages segregated by age.

Young, Frank W. *Initiation Ceremonies: A Cross-Cultural Study of Status Dramatization*. Macmillan. ISBN 0-672-60615-1. Psychogenic and social functions of adolescent initiations in 54 different societies.

TRIBAL SOCIETIES

The topics that anthropology investigates—religion, economics, politics, and so on—are the same ones that scholars in other disciplines study, but the setting in which anthropologists have traditionally worked, tribal societies, often makes the substance of anthropological investigations very different from those in other fields. The phenomenon of "the market," for example, is quite different in the case of an economist talking about international commodities futures from that of an anthropologist trying to figure out how goods move through a weekly market in highland Sumatra. Analyzing an election in a polity of 10 million requires a different approach from studying the exercise of power in a chiefdom of 100,000. Aside from the small scale of tribal societies, the various spheres of life may not be as easily isolated from each other. For this reason, anthropological research in tribal societies tends to be more holistic than other scholarship, meaning that the study of one topic inevitably runs into others. For example, a study of economic life reveals its organization to be based on kinship, or a thesis about religion requires attention to chiefly powers.

Chagnon, Napoleon. *Yanomamo: The Fierce People*. HarBraceJ 1993 $13.50. ISBN 0-03-062328-6. An ethnography of an Amazonian people, popular in university courses.

Driver, Harold E. *Indians of North America*. U. Ch. Pr. 2nd rev. ed. 1969 $25.00. ISBN 0-226-16466-7. A standard source on Native American prehistory and culture.

Evans-Pritchard, Edward E. *Nuer: A Description of the Modes of Livelihood and Political Institutions of a Nilotic People*. OUP 1940 $15.95. ISBN 0-19-500322-5. A classic ethnography of cattle pastoralists.

Firth, Raymond. *We, the Tikopia: A Sociological Study of Kinship in Primitive Polynesia*. Stanford U. Pr. 1963 repr. of 1936 ed. $57.50. ISBN 0-8047-1202-6. A comprehensive and exemplary ethnography, with a preface by Bronislaw Malinowski.

Fortune, R. F. *Sorcerers of Dobu: The Social Anthropologist of the Dobu Islanders of the Western Pacific*. Waveland Pr. 1989 repr. of 1932 ed. $10.95. ISBN 0-8047-1201-8. Used by Ruth Benedict to illustrate a paranoid culture pattern.

Kuper, Hilda. *The Swazi: A South African Kingdom*. HarBraceJ 1986 $13.50. ISBN 0-03-070239-0. A description of ritual and the exercise of power.

Leach, E. R. *Political Systems of Highlands Burma: A Study of Kachin Social Structure. Monograph on Social Anthropology*: No. 44. Humanities 1954 $25.00. ISBN 0-485-19644-1. Argues against the structural-functionalist notion of equilibrium.

Malinowski, Bronislaw. *Argonauts of the Western Pacific*. Waveland Pr. 1984 repr. of 1961 ed. $13.50. ISBN 0-88133-084-1. A famous ethnography detailing the kula ring, a regional exchange of shell valuables; preface by James Frazer.

Morgan, Lewis H. *League of the Iroquois*. 2 vols. Rprt. Serv. repr. of 1922 ed. $150.00. ISBN 0-7812-5160-5. Still the best study of the Iroquois.

Nadel, Siegfried. *Black Byzantium: The Kingdom of Nupe in Nigeria*. Gordon Pr. 1976 $59.95. ISBN 0-8490-1510-3. An impressive ethnography of the kingdom of Nupe in Nigeria.

Rosaldo, Michael Z. *Knowledge and Passion. Cambridge Studies in Cultural Systems*. Cambridge U. Pr. 1980 $16.95. ISBN 0-521-29562-9. Gets inside the heads of Philippine headhunters by close attention to the words they use to talk about emotions and motivations.

Turnbull, Colin M. *The Forest People*. Peter Smith 1988 $19.75. ISBN 0-8446-6333-6. Romantic but well-written ethnography on the Ituri pygmies of Africa's rainforest.

CHRONOLOGY OF AUTHORS

Morgan, Lewis Henry. 1818–1881
Maine, Sir Henry Sumner. 1822–1888
Tylor, Sir Edward Burnett. 1832–1917
Frazer, Sir James George. 1854–1941
Boas, Franz. 1858–1942
Kroeber, Alfred L. 1876–1960
Radcliffe-Brown, A. R. 1881–1955
Malinowski, Bronislaw. 1884–1942
Sapir, Edward. 1884–1939
Benedict, Ruth. 1887–1948
Bloomfield, Leonard. 1887–1949
Herskovits, Melville Jean. 1895–1963

Murdock, George P. 1897–1985
Redfield, Robert. 1897–1958
Whorf, Benjamin L. 1897–1941
White, Leslie Alvin. 1900–1975
Firth, Raymond. 1901–
Mead, Margaret. 1901–1978
Evans-Pritchard, E. E. 1902–1973
Lévi-Strauss, Claude. 1908–
Lewis, Oscar. 1914–1970
Turner, Victor Witter. 1920–1983
Douglas, Mary. 1921–
Geertz, Clifford. 1926–
Harris, Marvin. 1927–

BENEDICT, RUTH. 1887–1948

Born in New York City, American anthropologist Ruth Benedict was educated at Vassar College and Columbia University (Ph.D., 1923). Benedict taught English literature before turning to the social sciences; she also wrote poetry. A student of FRANZ BOAS at Columbia University, she taught for many years at Columbia, where she was tardily made a professor in 1948. Most of her fieldwork was with American Indians, and the two books that brought her fame—*Patterns of Culture* (1934) and *The Chrysanthemum and the Sword* (1946)—are largely about cultures that she knew only secondhand. *The Chrysanthemum and the Sword* is a brilliant reconstruction of Japanese culture on the basis of wartime interviews with Japanese people who had been living in the United States for several decades, but it has been criticized for describing nearly dead patterns of Japanese social behavior. Benedict helped expand the scope of anthropology to include the importance of the role of culture.

BOOKS BY BENEDICT

An Anthropologist at Work: Writings of Ruth Benedict. Ed. by Margaret Mead. Greenwood 1977 repr. of 1966 ed. $57.50. ISBN 0-8371-9576-4. Both an intellectual biography and the record of the friendship between Mead and Benedict.
The Chrysanthemum and the Sword: Patterns of Japanese Culture. 1946. HM 1989 $9.95. ISBN 0-395-50075-3
Patterns of Culture. 1934. HM 1989 repr. of 1961 ed. $9.70. ISBN 0-395-50088-5. Three examples to illustrate the idea that cultures exhibit an internal consistency.
Race: Science and Politics. 1940. Greenwood 1982 repr. of 1950 ed. $38.50. ISBN 0-313-23597-X. Popularized the concept of racism.
Showers. Reiman Assocs. 1980 $7.98. ISBN 0-89821-030-5. Introduction by Carol Wolf.
Tales of the Cochiti Indians. Gordon Pr. 1976 $59.95. ISBN 0-8490-2729-2
Zuñi Mythology. 2 vols. AMS Pr. 1969 repr. of 1935 ed. $70.00. ISBN 0-404-50571-6. Argues that myths provide an outlet for repressed feelings.

BOOKS ABOUT BENEDICT

Caffrey, Margaret M. *Ruth Benedict: Stranger in This Land.* U. of Tex. Pr. 1989 $14.95. ISBN 0-292-74655-5. More objective than the biography by Mead.
Mead, Margaret. *Ruth Benedict.* Col. U. Pr. 1978 $40.00. ISBN 0-231-03519-5. Written by Benedict's close friend and most famous student.
Modell, Judith. *Ruth Benedict: Patterns of a Life.* U. of Pa. Pr. 1983 o.p. A more objective interpretation of Benedict than the biography by Margaret Mead.

BLOOMFIELD, LEONARD. 1887–1949

Leonard Bloomfield, an American professor of Germanic languages, created the field of linguistics as a branch of science. In studying such non-Western languages as Tagalog, spoken in the Philippines, he realized the futility of trying to fit all languages into the format of Latin grammar in the common practice in his time. He then went on to discover the principles of language itself; his book *Language* (1933) integrated the field for the first time. He was one of the founders of the Linguistic Society of America, and he wrote an article for the first issue of its journal in which he explained the need for a society for the new discipline.

BOOKS BY BLOOMFIELD

An Introduction to the Study of Language. 1914. Benjamins North Am. 1983 repr. of 1914 ed. $69.00. ISBN 90-272-1891-9. Introduction by Joseph F. Kess. Covers the nature and origins of language, its physical and mental bases, and the forms of linguistic change.
Language. 1933. U. Ch. Pr. 1984 $17.95. ISBN 0-226-06067-5. With a foreword by Charles Hockett; set the tone of American linguistics for two generations.
A Leonard Bloomfield Anthology. Ed. by Charles F. Hockett. Bks. Demand repr. of 1970 ed. $152.00. ISBN 0-685-44464-3. Contains more than 60 of his short publications, plus a chronological bibliography of his major works and 2 critical essays about his work by others.

BOOK ABOUT BLOOMFIELD

Hall, Robert A., Jr. *A Life for Language: A Biographical Memoir of Leonard Bloomfield.* Benjamins North Am. 1990 $29.00. ISBN 1-55619-350-5. A readable and engaging portrait of a reticent man who revealed himself to very few people during his lifetime.

BOAS, FRANZ. 1858–1942

Franz Boas, a German-born American anthropologist, became the most influential anthropologist of his time. He left Germany because of its antiliberal and anti-Semitic climate. As a Columbia University professor for 37 years (1899–1936), he created both the field of anthropology and the modern concept of culture. Both directly and through the influence of such students as RUTH BENEDICT, MELVILLE J. HERSKOVITS, ALFRED L. KROEBER, and MARGARET MEAD, he set the agenda for all subsequent American cultural anthropology. Boas is the author of hundreds of scientific monographs and articles.

BOOKS BY BOAS

Anthropology and Modern Life. 1928. Greenwood 1984 repr. of 1962 ed. $39.75. ISBN 0-313-24370-0. Introduction by Ruth Bunzel.
Contributions to the Ethnology of the Kwakiutl. 1925. AMS Pr. repr. of 1925 ed. $37.50. ISBN 0-404-50553-8. Contains a description of the potlatch.
A Franz Boas Reader: The Shaping of American Anthropology, 1883–1911. Ed. by George W. Stocking, Jr. U. Ch. Pr. 1989 $21.00. ISBN 0-226-06243-0. A useful collection by a perceptive historian of science.
General Anthropology. Johnson Repr. repr. of 1938 ed. $17.00. ISBN 0-384-04860-9. Textbook for university courses.
Handbook of the American Indian Languages. 4 vols. Rprt. Serv. 1988 repr. of 1911 ed. $225.00. ISBN 0-7812-5040-4. Introduction distinguishes race from language.
The Mind of Primitive Man. 1911. Greenwood 1983 repr. of 1963 ed. $59.50. ISBN 0-313-24004-3. Argues for the psychic unity of humanity—that human minds everywhere employ the same faculties.
Primitive Art. 1927. Peter Smith 1962 $19.25. ISBN 0-8446-1695-8. Beautiful line drawings of the art of the Northwest Coast.

BOOKS ABOUT BOAS

Silverman, Sydel, ed. *Totems and Teachers: Perspectives on the History of Anthropology.* Col. U. Pr. 1981 $32.00. ISBN 0-231-05086-0. A collection of eight essays, including one by Alexander Lesser on Boas.
Stocking, George W., Jr. *Race, Culture, and Evolution: Essays in the History of Anthropology.* U. Ch. Pr. 1982 $16.95. ISBN 0-226-77494-5. Analyzes Boas's use of the culture concept in the context of an era when race was used to explain behavioral differences.

DOUGLAS, MARY. 1921–

Born in Italy, Mary Douglas was educated at Oxford University and began her career as a civil servant in 1943. Her first field research was carried out in what was then the Belgian Congo, and she taught at Oxford and the University of London before moving to the United States in 1977. *Purity and Danger* (1966) is a brilliant essay about the logic of pollution beliefs, suggesting that ideas about dirt and disorder outline and reinforce particular social orders. Her other essays exploring the implicit meanings of cultural symbols follow a similar Durkheimian format. Her recent interests have turned to analysis of risk behavior and cross-cultural attitudes about food and alcohol.

BOOKS BY DOUGLAS

How Institutions Think. Syracuse U. Pr. 1986 $12.95. ISBN 0-8156-0206-5. Raises the question of collective consciousness.
Implicit Meanings: Essays in Anthropology. Routledge 1978 $13.95. ISBN 0-7100-0047-2. Some of her most famous essays on symbolism and myth.

Natural Symbols: Explorations in Cosmology. 1973. Pantheon 1982 $9.60. ISBN 0-394-71105-X. Suggests why societies select certain aspects of the body as significant.
Purity and Danger. 1966. Routledge 1966 o.p.
Risk and Blame: Essays in Cultural Theory. Routledge 1992 $29.95. ISBN 0-7486-03230-9. Explores why certain warnings about danger resonate and others do not.

BOOK ABOUT DOUGLAS

Peacock, James. *Consciousness and Change: Symbolic Anthropology in Evolutionary Perspective.* Blackwell Pubs. 1979 $15.95. ISBN 0-631-19950-0. An evolutionary treatise that extrapolates from Douglas's theories about marginal phenomena and from her division of societies into a group-grid typology.

EVANS-PRITCHARD, E. E. 1902–1973

E. E. Evans-Pritchard, a British anthropologist, was the leader of the fieldwork-based social anthropology that flourished in the United Kingdom in the years following World War II. He believed that anthropological knowledge is based on detailed ethnographic and historical research, and his studies of three African societies—the Azande, the Sanusi, and the Nuer—provided the basis for much of his theoretical work. His study of Nuer religion was the first scholarly study to present the religious beliefs of a preliterate people as having a theological significance comparable to the religious thought of more complex societies.

BOOKS BY EVANS-PRITCHARD

African Political Systems. Ed. by M. Fortes. Routledge Chapman & Hall 1987 $19.95. ISBN 0-7103-0245-2. Influential essays on states and stateless societies.
Nuer: A Description of the Modes of Livelihood and Political Institutions of a Nilotic People. 1940. OUP 1940 $15.95. ISBN 0-19-500322-5. Shows the centrality of cattle and kin.
Nuer Religion. 1956. OUP 1956 $15.95. ISBN 0-19-874003-4
The Political System of the Anuak of the Anglo-Egyptian Sudan. AMS repr. of 1940 ed. $27.50. ISBN 0-404-12041-5
Social Anthropology. Greenwood 1987 $43.75. ISBN 0-313-24680-7. Argues that anthropology is more akin to history than science.
Witchcraft, Oracles, and Magic among the Azande. 1937. Ed. by Eva Gillies. OUP 1937 o.p. Discusses witchcraft as a moral system and as a way of explaining what Westerners relegate to chance.

BOOKS ABOUT EVANS-PRITCHARD

Beattie, J. H., ed. *Studies in Social Anthropology: Essays in Memory of E. E. Evans-Pritchard by His Former Oxford Colleagues.* Ed. by R. G. Lienhardt. OUP 1975 o.p. A collection of essays, over half of which deal with African societies, by prominent British anthropologists.
Douglas, Mary. *Edward Evans-Pritchard.* Viking Penguin 1980 o.p. A thematic treatment of his work, placing it in the context of the debates of his day.

FIRTH, RAYMOND. 1901–

Raymond Firth, a New Zealand-born English anthropologist, was BRONISLAW MALINOWSKI's successor at the London School of Economics. In 1928 he first visited the tiny island of Tikopia in the Solomons, and his monograph *We, the Tikopia* (1936) established his fame. A devoted student of Malinowski, he established no school of anthropological thought, but his productive scholarship and academic statesmanship won him an important reputation in social anthropology.

BOOKS BY FIRTH

Elements of Social Organization. 1951. Greenwood 1981 repr. of 1961 ed. $65.00. ISBN 0-313-22745-4. Emphasizes the importance of choice and process.

Malay Fishermen: Their Peasant Economy. 1946. Norton 1975 repr. of 1966 ed. $4.95. ISBN 0-393-00775-8. Describes the organization of small-scale fishing and marketing.

Social Change in Tikopia: Restudy of a Polynesian Community after a Generation. 1959. Macmillan 1959 o.p. Compares a baseline of 1929 with what he found in 1952, covering primarily economy, kinship, and politics.

We, the Tikopia: A Sociological Study of Kinship in Primitive Polynesia. 1936. Stanford U. Pr. repr. of 1936 ed. 1963 $57.50. ISBN 0-8047-1201-8. Preface by Bronislaw Malinowski.

The Work of the Gods in Tikopia. 1940. Humanities 1967 $48.50. ISBN 0-485-19501-1. On religious life and ritual.

BOOK ABOUT FIRTH

Freedman, Maurice, ed. *Social Organization: Essays Presented to Raymond Firth.* Intl. Spec. Bk. 1967 repr. of 1898 ed. $35.00. ISBN 0-7146-1059-3. Essays on kinship, religion, economy, and social change by Firth's most illustrious British students.

FRAZER, SIR JAMES GEORGE. 1854–1941

James George Frazer was a British social anthropologist, folklorist, and classical scholar who taught for most of his life at Trinity College, Cambridge. Greatly influenced by EDWARD BURNETT TYLOR's *Primitive Culture*, published in 1871, he wrote *The Golden Bough* (1890), a massive reconstruction of the whole of human thought and custom through the successive stages of magic, religion, and science. *The Golden Bough* is regarded by many today as a much-loved but antiquated relic, but, by making anthropological data and knowledge academically respectable, Frazer made modern comparative anthropology possible.

BOOK BY FRAZER

The Golden Bough. 1890–1915. 13 vols. St. Martin 1969 repr. of 1890 ed. $450.00. ISBN 0-312-33215-7. Available in a number of abridged editions.

BOOKS ABOUT FRAZER

Ackerman, Robert. *J. G. Frazer: His Life and Work.* Cambridge U. Pr. 1987 $54.95. ISBN 0-521-34093-4. Exhaustive biography.

Vickery, John B. *The Literary Impact of the Golden Bough.* Princeton U. Pr. 1973 $62.50. ISBN 0-691-06243-9. Focuses on Frazer's influence on Yeats, Eliot, Lawrence, and Joyce.

GEERTZ, CLIFFORD. 1926–

Clifford Geertz, an American anthropologist, is known for his studies of Islam in Indonesia and Morocco and for his studies of the peasant economy of Java. But he is also the leading exponent of an orientation in the social sciences called "interpretation." Social life, according to this view, is organized in terms of symbols whose meaning we must grasp if we are to understand that organization and formulate its principles. Interpretative explanations focus on what institutions, actions, customs, and so on, mean to the people involved. What emerges from studies of this kind are not laws of society, and certainly not statistical relationships, but rather interpretations, that is to say, understanding. Geertz taught for 10 years at the University of Chicago; since 1970 he has been at

the Institute for Advanced Study in Princeton, New Jersey, where he is the
Harold F. Linder professor of social science.

BOOKS BY GEERTZ

Agricultural Involution: The Processes of Ecological Change in Indonesia. 1963. U. CA Pr.
  1963 $12.95. ISBN 0-520-00459-0. Argues that wet rice cultivation led to Java's
  overpopulation.
Interpretation of Cultures. 1973. Basic 1977 $16.00. ISBN 0-465-09719-7. Influential
  essays on the theory and methodology of interpretation.
Islam Observed: Religious Development in Morocco and Indonesia. 1968. U. Ch. Pr. 1971
  repr. of 1968 ed. $6.95. ISBN 0-226-28511-1. Compares Islam in two very different
  cultural settings.
Local Knowledge: Further Essays in Interpretative Anthropology. 1983. Basic 1985 $15.00.
  ISBN 0-465-04162-0. Questions the value of statistical comparisons.
Negara: Theatre-State in 19th Century Bali. Princeton U. Pr. 1980 $14.95. ISBN 0-691-
  00778-0. Suggests that states are as much matters of symbolism and pomp as of force
  and power.
*Peddlers and Princes: Social Development and Economic Change in Two Indonesian
  Towns.* 1963. U. Ch. Pr. 1968 repr. of 1963 ed. $9.95. ISBN 0-226-28514-6. Shows the
  effects of colonialism and independence in Java.
The Religion of Java. 1960. U. Ch. Pr. 1976 repr. of 1960 ed. $14.95. ISBN 0-226-28510-3.
  Describes three varieties of Javanese religious life.
Works and Lives: The Anthropologist As Author. Stanford U. Pr. 1989 $29.95. ISBN 0-8047-
  1428-2. Examines the writings of some well-known anthropologists.

HARRIS, MARVIN. 1927–

Marvin Harris is an American anthropologist who was educated at Columbia
University, where he spent much of his professional career. Beginning with
studies on race relations, he became the leading proponent of cultural
materialism, a scientific approach that seeks the causes of human behavior and
culture change in survival requirements. His explanations often reduce to
factors such as population growth, resource depletion, and protein availability.
A controversial figure, Harris is accused of slighting the role of human
consciousness and of underestimating the symbolic worlds that humans create.
He writes in a style that is accessible to students and the general public,
however, and his books have been used widely as college texts.

BOOKS BY HARRIS

Cannibals and Kings: The Origins of Cultures. 1977. Random 1991 $11.00. ISBN 0-679-
  72849-X. Episodes in cultural evolution illustrating how humans have coped with
  population growth and resource depletion.
Cultural Materialism: The Struggle for a Science of Culture. 1979. Random 1980 $15.00.
  ISBN 0-394-74426-8. Attacks contemporary theories in anthropology that compete
  with materialism.
Culture, People, and Nature: An Introduction to General Anthropology. HarpC 1990
  $43.00. ISBN 0-06-042697-7. A best-selling text.
Death, Sex, and Fertility: Population Regulation in Pre-Industrial and Developing Societies.
  (coauthored with Eric B. Ross). 1987. Col. U. Pr. 1990 $34.00. ISBN 0-231-06270-2.
  An evolutionary comparison of how societies keep or fail to keep population under
  control.
Our Kind: Who We Are, Where We Came From and Where We Are Going. HarpC 1990
  $12.00. ISBN 0-06-091990-6. A whirlwind tour, starting with prehuman origins, that
  deals with current ecological crises and ends with a call for a single world polity.
Patterns of Race in the Americas. 1964. Greenwood 1980 $39.75. ISBN 0-313-22359-9.
  Material and institutional arrangements explain race relations in Latin America.

The Rise of Anthropological Theory: A History of Theories of Culture. 1968. HarpC 1990
    $49.50. ISBN 0-690-70322-8. Materialist theory seen as the culmination of anthropol-
    ogy as a discipline.
Town and Country in Brazil. 1956. *Columbia Univ. Contributions to Anthropology Ser.* Vol.
    37. AMS Pr. 1969 $32.50. ISBN 0-404-50587-2. A study of urbanization, class, and
    race based on fieldwork in 1950–51.
Why Things Don't Work: The Anthropology of Daily Life. S&S Trade 1987 $9.95 ISBN 0-
    671-63577-8. Social ills, such as pornography and crime, blamed on the hyperindus-
    trial economy of the modern world.

BOOK ABOUT HARRIS

Sahlins, Marshall. *Culture and Practical Reason.* U. Ch. Pr. 1978 $9.95. ISBN 0-226-
    73361-0. Critical of materialist theory.

HERSKOVITS, MELVILLE JEAN. 1895–1963

Melville Jean Herskovits, an American anthropologist who was a student of
FRANZ BOAS at Columbia University, became a leading student of acculturation
and an outstanding teacher at Northwestern University, where he founded the
first U.S. program in African Studies in 1951. He did work in Surinam, Haiti,
Trinidad, and Brazil, but his major research was on African blacks and the
forced relocation of their culture to the New World. He studied religion, music,
and folklore, and was particularly interested in how culture influences the arts.

BOOKS BY HERSKOVITS

Acculturation: The Study of Culture Contact. 1938. Peter Smith 1938 o.p. A classic text.
The American Negro: A Study in Racial Crossing. 1928. Greenwood 1985 repr. of 1928 ed.
    $39.75. ISBN 0-313-24795-1. A new physical type, blending black, white, and Indian
    racial stocks.
Dahomey, An Ancient West African Kingdom. 1938. 2 vols. Bks. Demand repr. of 1967 ed.
    Vol. 1 $117.00. ISBN 0-317-10789-5. Vol. 2 $118.00. ISBN 0-317-10790-9. One of the
    best descriptions of an African kingdom.
The Human Factor in Changing Africa. 1962. Random 1962 o.p. A historical treatment
    that begins with prehistory and ends with the era of independence.
The Myth of the Negro Past. 1941. Beacon Pr. 1990 repr. of 1941 ed. $16.00. ISBN 0-8070-
    0905-9. How African origins can be seen in social institutions, family organization,
    religion, art, and language.

BOOK ABOUT HERSKOVITS

Simpson, George E. *Melville J. Herskovits.* Col. U. Pr. 1973 o.p. A brief, unrevealing
    memoir, but an excellent summary of Herskovits's intellectual contributions on a
    variety of subjects, plus some critical commentaries.

KROEBER, ALFRED L. 1876–1960

Alfred L. Kroeber was an American anthropologist whose life was cotermi-
nous with the development of American anthropology. His 1902 Ph.D. from
Columbia University was the first ever awarded. His book *Anthropology*, first
published in 1923, was the only textbook of its time, and it was enormously
influential among students, scholars, and the general public. The 1948 edition
has the subtitle *Race, Language, Culture, Psychology, Prehistory*, indicating the
range of his interests and his contributions. His concept of "cultural configuration" was influential; his notion of culture as "superorganic" was controversial
as well. Much of his research was carried out in California, and he taught at the
University of California, Berkeley, for most of his professional life.

BOOKS BY KROEBER

Anthropology: Culture Patterns and Processes. 1923. HarBraceJ 1963 $9.95. ISBN 0-15-607805-8.

Configurations of Culture Growth. 1944. U. CA Pr. 1944 $35.00. ISBN 0-520-00669-0. Long-term patterns of cultural development in great Old World civilizations.

Handbook of the Indians of California. 1925. Scholarly 1972 repr. of 1925 ed. $95.00. ISBN 0-403-00369-5. A regional survey, giving priority to religion and ideology.

Yurok Myths. U. CA Pr. 1975 $11.95. ISBN 0-520-03639-5. A collection of myths organized by the names of storytellers who recounted them, with a commentary on the whole collection by Alan Dundes.

BOOKS ABOUT KROEBER

Driver, Harold E. *The Contribution of A. L. Kroeber to Culture Area Theory and Practice.* Ind. U. Pr. 1962 o.p. Provides history and theory of attempts to classify cultures by region.

Kroeber, Theodora. *Alfred Kroeber: A Personal Configuration.* U. CA Pr. 1970 $9.95. ISBN 0-520-03720-0. An insightful, skillfully written biography by Kroeber's wife.

LÉVI-STRAUSS, CLAUDE. 1908–

Claude Lévi-Strauss, a French anthropologist, was the founder of structural anthropology. This theoretical position assumes that there are structural propensities in the human mind that lead unconsciously toward categorization of physical and social objects, hence such book titles as *The Raw and the Cooked* (1964) and such expositions of his work by others as *The Unconscious in Culture* and *Elementary Structures Reconsidered.* According to Lévi-Strauss, the models of society that scholars create are often dual in nature: status-contract (MAINE): *Gemeinschaft-Gesellschaft* (TÖNNIES); mechanical-organic solidarity (DURKHEIM); folk-urban (REDFIELD); universalism-particularism (PARSONS); and local-cosmopolitan (MERTON). Lévi-Strauss's writings—some of which have been described by CLIFFORD GEERTZ as "theoretical treatises set out as travelogues"—have been enormously influential throughout the scholarly world. George Steiner has described him, along with FREUD (see also Vol. 5) and MARX (see also Vol. 4), as one of the major architects of the thought of our times.

BOOKS BY LÉVI-STRAUSS

Elementary Structures of Kinship. 1949. Ed. by Rodney Needham. Beacon Pr. 1969 repr. of 1968 ed. $19.95. ISBN 0-8070-4669-8. Stimulating argument about the social consequences of different types of marital exchange.

From Honey to Ashes, Vol. 2: Mythologiques. Trans. by John Weightman and Doreen Weightman. U. Ch. Pr. 1990 $13.00. ISBN 0-685-48382-7. South American myths on themes of food and animals.

The Origin of Table Manners, Vol. 3: Mythologiques. Trans. by John Weightman and Doreen Weightman. U. Ch. Pr. 1990 $19.95. ISBN 0-226-47493-3. Mythic depictions of food and eating reveal a concern to protect the purity of the eater.

The Raw and the Cooked, Vol. 1: Mythologiques. 1964. Trans. by John Weightman and Doreen Weightman. U. Ch. Pr. 1990 $21.00. ISBN 0-685-48381-9. South American myths arranged around metaphors of music.

Savage Mind. 1962. U. Ch. Pr. 1968 $13.95. ISBN 0-226-4784-4. Argues that dialectical thinking is pervasive.

Structural Anthropology. Vol. 1. 1958. Basic 1974 $18.00. ISBN 0-465-09516-X. Introduction by C. Arensberg.

Structural Anthropology. Vol. 2. Trans. by Monique Layton. U. Ch. Pr. 1983 $17.95. ISBN 0-226-47491-7. Essays on kinship and myth.

Totemism. 1962. Beacon Pr. 1963 $11.95. ISBN 0-8070-4671-X. An example of structuralism applied to a social phenomenon.

Tristes Tropiques. 1955. Trans. by Joachin Neugroschel. Basic 1992 $24.94. ISBN 0-465-0925-7. Personal memoir of travels in South America.

The View from Afar. U. Ch. Pr. 1992 $14.95. ISBN 0-226-47474-7. Collection of essays encompassing more than 40 years of cultural analysis.

The Way of the Masks. Trans. by Sylvia Modelski. U. of Wash. Pr. 1988 $16.95. ISBN 0-295-96636-X. Study of the Swaihwe tribal masks and their societal and cross-cultural significance.

BOOKS ABOUT LÉVI-STRAUSS

Badcock, C. R. *Lévi-Strauss: Structuralism and Sociological Theory.* Holmes & Meier 1976 $14.95. ISBN 0-8419-0258-5. A skeptical examination of Lévi-Strauss's methodology, from a sociological point of view.

Korn, Francis. *Elementary Structures Reconsidered: Lévi-Strauss on Kinship.* U. CA Pr. 1973 $39.95. ISBN 0-520-02476-1. Highly critical of Lévi-Strauss's seminal work on kinship and marriage.

Leach, Edmund. *Claude Lévi-Strauss.* U. Ch. Pr. 1989 $9.95. ISBN 0-226-46968-9. One of the most useful brief introductions to Lévi-Strauss.

LEWIS, OSCAR. 1914–1970

Oscar Lewis, an American anthropologist, was renowned for his studies of poverty in Mexico and Puerto Rico and for his controversial concept of "the culture of poverty." After graduating from Columbia University, where he studied under RUTH BENEDICT, FRANZ BOAS, and MARGARET MEAD, his first major book, *Life in a Mexican Village* (1951), was a restudy of ROBERT REDFIELD's village of Tepoztlán, which reached a number of conclusions opposed to those reached by Redfield. Much of the controversy over the culture of poverty disappeared when Lewis labeled it a subculture; ironically, reactionaries have used the concept to blame the poor for their poverty, whereas Lewis believed the poor to be victims. Many of his books are based on tape recordings of family members, a technique in which Lewis was a pioneer.

BOOKS BY LEWIS

The Children of Sanchez. 1961. Random 1979 $16.00. ISBN 0-394-70280-8. A sequel to *Five Families.*

Five Families: Mexican Case Studies in the Culture of Poverty. 1959. Basic 1975 $17.00. ISBN 0-465-09705-7. Argues that poverty is reproduced and mediated by culture.

La Vida: A Puerto Rican Family in the Culture of Poverty—San Juan and New York. 1966. Irvington 1983 repr. of 1966 ed. o.p. A Puerto Rican family epic with a novelistic quality.

Life in a Mexican Village: Tepoztlán Restudied. 1951. Peter Smith 1951 o.p. Critical of Redfield's previous study.

MAINE, SIR HENRY (JAMES) SUMNER. 1822–1888

Henry Sumner Maine, a lecturer on jurisprudence at Oxford and Cambridge universities, was the founder of anthropological jurisprudence, the study of the legal system of ancient societies. In his first and classic work, *Ancient Law* (1861), he contrasted early societies, in which social relations are dominated by status (familylike relations), with complex societies, in which social relations are dominated by contract (obligations arising from the free agreement of individuals). He also distinguished between the law of tort and the law of crime: In the former, individuals are wronged; in the latter, the state is wronged. His enduring contribution to the social sciences is his formulation of the concept of ideal polar types and his use of them for the comparative analysis of social phenomena.

BOOKS BY MAINE

Ancient Law: The Connection with the Early History of Society and Its Relation to Modern Ideas. Peter Smith 1861 $13.25. ISBN 0-8446-0784-3.

Lectures on the Early History of Institutions: A Sequel to Ancient Law. 1875. W. S. Hein 1987 repr. of 1888 ed. $48.50. ISBN 0-89941-562-8. Deals with the Greek and Roman classic world as forerunners of European civilization.

BOOKS ABOUT MAINE

Cocks, Raymond. *Sir Henry Maine: A Study in Victorian Jurisprudence.* Cambridge U. Pr. 1989 $54.95. ISBN 0-521-35343-2. Not a biography, but a learned account of Maine's intellectual contributions.

Grant Duff, M. E. *Sir Henry Maine: A Brief Memoir of His Life.* Ed. by Whitley Stokes. Rothman 1979 repr. of 1892 ed. $35.00. ISBN 0-8377-0609-2. Only a fraction of the book contains a biographical memoir; the remainder records some of Maine's speeches.

MALINOWSKI, BRONISLAW. 1884–1942

Bronislaw Malinowski, a Polish-born British anthropologist, was a major force in transforming nineteenth-century speculative anthropology into an observation-based science of humanity. His major interest was in the study of culture as a universal phenomenon and in the development of fieldwork techniques that would both describe one culture adequately and at the same time make systematic cross-cultural comparisons possible. He is considered to be the founder of the functional approach in the social sciences, which involves studying not just what a cultural trait appears to be but what it actually does for the functioning of society. Although he carried out extensive fieldwork in a number of cultures, he is most famous for his research among the Trobrianders, who live on a small island off the coast of New Guinea.

BOOKS BY MALINOWSKI

Argonauts of the Western Pacific: An Account of Native Enterprise and Adventure in the Archipelagoes of Melanesian New Guinea. 1922. Waveland Pr. 1984 repr. of 1961 ed. $13.50. ISBN 0-88133-084-1. Preface by James Frazer. Based on two years of field research, a landmark general ethnography containing a description of an inter-island exchange of valuables.

A Diary in the Strict Sense of the Term. Stanford U. Pr. 1989 $45.00. ISBN 0-8047-1706-0. Revealing self-portrait in a field journal, with an introduction by Raymond Firth.

The Dynamics of Culture Change. 1945. Ed. by Phyllis M. Kaberry. Greenwood 1976 repr. of 1961 ed. $35.00. ISBN 0-8371-8216-6. Thirteen essays dealing with Africa.

Magic, Science and Religion and Other Essays. Greenwood 1984 repr. of 1948 ed. $48.50. ISBN 0-313-24687-4. Some of Malinowski's best-known essays.

A Scientific Theory of Culture. 1944. U. of NC Pr. 1990 repr. of 1944 ed. $14.95. ISBN 0-8078-4283-4. Posits a set of universal functions that all cultures serve for individuals.

Sex and Repression in Savage Society. 1927. U. Ch. Pr. 1985 $12.95. ISBN 0-226-50287-2. Argues that there is no Oedipal conflict in a matrilineal society.

The Sexual Life of Savages in North-Western Melanesia: An Ethnological Account of Courtship, Marriage, and Family Life among the Natives of the Trobriand Islands, British New Guinea. 1929. Routledge 1982 $22.50. ISBN 0-7100-6659-7. Sensational title for a pedestrian account of marriage and family life.

BOOKS ABOUT MALINOWSKI

Ellen, Roy, and others, eds. *Malinowski Between Two Worlds: The Polish Roots of an Anthropological Tradition.* Cambridge U. Pr. 1989 $49.95. ISBN 0-521-34566-9. Examines the impact of Malinowski's native Poland on his anthropological works, and vice versa.

Firth, Raymond, ed. *Man and Culture: An Evaluation of the Work of Bronislaw Malinowski.* Routledge 1957 o.p. A comprehensive examination of Malinowski's work.

Spiro, Melford E. *Oedipus in the Trobriands.* Transaction Pubs. 1992 $19.95. ISBN 1-56000-627-7. Disputes Malinowski's assertion that there is no Oedipus complex in the Trobriands.

MEAD, MARGARET. 1901–1978

Margaret Mead, an American anthropologist, was for most of her life the most illustrious curator at the American Museum of Natural History in New York. She was famed not only as an anthropologist but also as a public figure, a popularizer of the social sciences, and an analyst of American society. While at Columbia University, she was a student of FRANZ BOAS, whose teaching assistant, RUTH BENEDICT, became one of Mead's closest colleagues and friends; after Benedict's death, Mead became her first biographer and the custodian of her field notes and papers. Mead's early research in Samoa led to her bestselling book, *Coming of Age in Samoa* (1928); it also led, after her death, to a well-publicized attack on her work by the Australian anthropologist Derek Freeman. Her importance was not damaged by his book; in fact, there is probably a greater awareness today of the important role that she played in twentieth-century intellectual history as an advocate of tolerance, education, civil liberties, world peace, and the worldwide ecumenical movement within Christianity. She was an active and devout Episcopalian throughout her life. On January 6, 1979, she was posthumously awarded the Presidential Medal of Freedom, the nation's highest civilian honor.

BOOKS BY MEAD

And Keep Your Powder Dry: An Anthropologist Looks at America. 1937. Ayer facsimile ed. repr. of 1942 ed. $18.00. ISBN 0-8369-2416-9. Mead turns a clinical and critical eye on her own culture.

Balinese Character: A Photographic Analysis. (coauthored with Gregory Bateson.) 1942. NY Acad. Sci. 1962 o.p. Substantiates assertions about Balinese character with beautiful photographic evidence.

Blackberry Winter: My Earlier Years. 1972. Peter Smith $24.50. ISBN 0-317-60065-6. A flattering autobiography of Mead's early life.

Coming of Age in Samoa. 1928. Peter Smith 1971 $22.50. ISBN 0-8446-2571-X. Attributes a happy adolescence to sexual freedom and lack of responsibilities.

Cooperation and Competition among Primitive Peoples. 1937. Peter Smith enl. ed. $13.25. ISBN 0-8446-2570-1. Exemplifies Mead's efforts to teach the general public the lessons of anthropology.

Growing up in New Guinea. 1930. Morrow 1975 $13.45. ISBN 0-688-07989-X. One of the first studies of socialization in a non-Western setting.

People and Places. 1959. o.p. A book geared toward young people.

Sex and Temperament in Three Primitive Societies. 1935. Morrow 1971 $10.45. ISBN 0-688-06016-1. Controversial depiction of societies that seem to reverse Western gender roles.

Soviet Attitudes Toward Authority: An Interdisciplinary Approach to Problems of Soviet Character. 1951. Greenwood 1979 repr. of 1951 ed. $39.75. ISBN 0-313-21081-0.

Survey conducted by a team of anthropologists, psychologists, and political scientists.

BOOKS ABOUT MEAD

American Anthropological Association. *In Memoriam Margaret Mead 1901–1978*. Am. Anthro. Assn. 1980 $20.00. ISBN 0-317-66301-1. Eulogistic essays describing Mead's contributions to oceanic ethnography, to women's studies, and to psychological anthropology.

Freeman, Derek. *Margaret Mead and Samoa: The Making and Unmaking of an Anthropological Myth*. HUP 1983 $29.95. ISBN 0-674-54830-2. A critical restudy of Mead's first research experience.

Holmes, Lowell D. *Quest for the Real Samoa: The Mead-Freeman Controversy and Beyond*. Greenwood 1986 $47.95. ISBN 0-89789-110-4. Examines the historical controversy between Mead and Freeman over Mead's work in Samoa.

Howard, Jane. *Margaret Mead: A Life*. Fawcett 1985 $4.95. ISBN 0-449-20836-2. Not an entirely flattering portrait of a flamboyant character.

Schwartz, Theodore, ed. *Socialization as Cultural Communication: Development of a Theme in the Work of Margaret Mead*. U. CA Pr. 1976 $37.50. ISBN 0-520-03061-3. One biographical and one analytical essay about Mead, plus a number of papers by leaders in the field of psychological anthropology.

MORGAN, LEWIS HENRY. 1818–1881

Lewis Henry Morgan, an American lawyer, studied, lived with, and was eventually adopted by the Iroquois Indians in New York State; this experience made him a self-taught anthropologist who went on to make substantial contributions to the field. His evolutionary theory of the family has been largely abandoned, but his *Ancient Society* (1877) became a classic in Marxist literature. Its account of how culture had actually evolved was the best available during the mid-nineteenth century. Although KARL MARX (see also Vol. 4) died before he was able to write a planned book about Morgan, FRIEDRICH ENGELS (see also Vol. 4) wrote *The Origin of the Family: Private Property and the State* in 1884 largely on the basis of Morgan's work. Morgan was also the first to publish a treatise on Australian kinship.

BOOKS BY MORGAN

Ancient Society. 1877. Gordon Pr. 1974 repr. of 1877 ed. $150.00. ISBN 0-87968-630-8. Outlines the stages of cultural evolution.

The Indian Journals, Eighteen Fifty-Nine to Sixty-Two. Ed. by Leslie A. White and Clyde Walton. Bks. Demand repr. of 1959 ed. $67.30. ISBN 0-317-29147-5. Accounts of Morgan's field trips to the West, with valuable line illustrations and 16 color plates.

League of the Iroquois. 1851. 2 vols. Rprt. Serv. 1993 repr. of 1922 ed. $150.00. ISBN 0-7812-5160-5. Still the best ethnography of the Iroquois.

BOOKS ABOUT MORGAN

Resek, Carl. *Lewis Henry Morgan: American Scholar*. Midway Repr. Ser. U. Ch. Pr. 1974 repr. of 1960 ed. o.p.

Stern, Bernhard J. *Lewis Henry Morgan: Social Evolutionist*. Russell 1967 repr. of 1931 ed. o.p. Classic biography of Morgan.

Trautman, Thomas R. *Lewis Henry Morgan and the Invention of Kinship*. U. of CA Pr. 1987 $39.95. ISBN 0-520-05849-6. In-depth analysis of the development of Morgan's "kinship project."

MURDOCK, GEORGE P. 1897–1985

George P. Murdock, an American anthropologist, studied both sociology and anthropology at Yale University under Albert G. Keller, who had been William

Graham Sumner's most important student. The card file that Sumner used in preparing his famous *Folkways*, published in 1906, became Keller's, and under Murdock's guidance it ultimately became the basis for the Human Relations Area Files, a major database in the field of anthropology. Murdock's interest in cross-cultural analysis led to a number of books and to the journal *Ethnology*, which he founded in 1962. He taught at Yale University until 1960, when he went to the University of Pittsburgh, from which he retired in 1973.

BOOKS BY MURDOCK

Atlas of World Cultures. U. of Pittsburgh Pr. 1981 $18.95. ISBN 0-8229-3432-9. Some 600 societies coded for several dozen features.

Culture and Society: Twenty-Four Essays. U. of Pittsburgh Pr. 1965 o.p. Covers the relationship of anthropology to sociology, kinship, and the theory of cross-cultural comparisons.

Ethnographic Bibliography of North America. 5 vols. HRAFP 1975 $35.00. Organized by region and tribe, without annotations.

Outline of Cultural Materials. 1938. HRAFP 5th rev. ed. 1982 $25.00. ISBN 0-87536-654-6. Gives the topics or categories that ethnographers often cover.

Outline of World Cultures. 1954. HRAFP 1983 6th rev. ed. 1983 $25.00. ISBN 0-87536-664-3. Classifies the cultures of the world, in outline format.

Social Structure. 1949. Free Pr. 1965 $16.95. ISBN 0-02-922290-7. Tests hypotheses about kinship against cross-cultural correlations.

BOOK ABOUT MURDOCK

Goodenough, Ward H., ed. *Explorations in Cultural Anthropology: Essays in Honor of George Peter Murdock.* McGraw 1964 o.p. Wide-ranging essays on topics of ecology, kin terms, warfare, and archaeology.

RADCLIFFE-BROWN, A. R. 1881–1955

A. R. Radcliffe-Brown, an English anthropologist, by his example and his teaching helped establish social anthropology as a generalizing, theoretical discipline in both the United Kingdom and the United States. His application of the ideas of system theory to primitive societies led to a revolution in the analysis of interpretation of social relations. He was educated in Cambridge, but he spent most of his working life abroad: in Cape Town, Sydney, Chicago, Yenching, São Paulo, and Alexandria (Egypt). At all of these universities, he held teaching positions, as well as at Cambridge, Oxford, London, Birmingham, and Manchester—certainly something of a record, and a tribute to his fame. His only extended fieldwork was in the Andaman Islands and northwestern Australia. His genius was in applying theoretical ideas about social structure to the interpretation of the social behavior of primitive tribes.

BOOKS BY RADCLIFFE-BROWN

African Systems of Kinship and Marriage. Routledge Chapman and Hall 1987 $19.95. ISBN 0-7103-0234-7. Essays exploring unilineal descent.

The Andaman Islanders. 1922. Macmillan 1964 o.p. Suggests that ritual inculcates sentiments supporting the social order.

The Social Organization of Australian Tribes. 1931. Macmillan 1948 o.p. Analyzes the marriage classes of aboriginal Australia.

Structure and Function in Primitive Society. 1952. Free Pr. 1965 $19.95. ISBN 0-02-925630-5. Classic essays in structural-functional theory.

BOOK ABOUT RADCLIFFE-BROWN

Kuper, Leo. *The Social Anthropology of Radcliffe-Brown*. Routledge 1977 o.p. Papers by
followers of Radcliffe-Brown, which display the unity of his theoretical approach.

REDFIELD, ROBERT. 1897–1958

Robert Redfield, an American anthropologist, carried out early in his career a
study of Tepoztlán, an Aztec community near Mexico City. This led to his first
position at the Carnegie Institution in Washington, D.C. During the next 16
years he carried out research in Yucatán and Guatemala. Based on HENRY
SUMNER MAINE's contrast between status and contract, and on FERDINAND
TÖNNIE's contrast between *Gemeinschaft* and *Gesellschaft*, he developed a set of
ideas about folk culture, little communities, and Little and Great Traditions that
have been enormously influential. In 1927 he joined the faculty of the University
of Chicago, where he was dean of the social science division from 1934 to 1946.

BOOKS BY REDFIELD

Chan Kom: A Mayan Village. (coauthored with Alfonso Villa Rojas). Bks. Demand repr. of
1962 ed. $61.50. ISBN 0-317-20695-8. A classic study of the basic folk culture in a
village in eastern Yucatán.
The Folk Culture of Yucatán. 1941. Gordon Pr. 1976 $59.95. ISBN 0-8490-1848-X. Four
villages described as points along a folk-urban continuum.
The Folk Society. Irvington 1991 repr. of 1967 ed. $1.00. ISBN 0-8290-2622-3. Sets out the
traits of a folk-urban continuum.
The Little Community and Peasant Society and Culture. 1955–56. U. Ch. Pr. 1989 $18.95.
ISBN 0-226-70670-2. Peasants treated first as isolated communities and then as part
of a larger society.
The Primitive World and Its Transformations. 1953. Cornell Univ. Pr. 1957 $8.95. ISBN 0-
8014-9028-6. Argues that urban society brings a new moral order and world view.
Tepoztlán, a Mexican Village: A Study of Folk Life. 1930. *Midway Repr. Ser*. U. Ch. Pr. 1973
repr. of 1930 ed. o.p. One of the first studies of a peasant community by an American
anthropologist.
A Village That Chose Progress: Chan Kom Revisited. 1950. U. Ch. Pr. 1962 o.p.
Incorporates Weber's ideas on the importance of religion in social change.

BOOK ABOUT REDFIELD

Lewis, Oscar. *Life in a Mexican Village: Tepoztlán Restudied*. U. of Ill. Pr. 1963 repr. of
1951 ed. o.p. Critical of Redfield's interpretation.

SAPIR, EDWARD. 1884–1939

Edward Sapir, an American anthropologist, was one of the founders of both
modern linguistics and the field of personality and culture. He wrote poetry,
essays, and music, as well as scholarly works. MARGARET MEAD noted that "it was
in the vivid, voluminous correspondence with [Edward Sapir] that [RUTH
BENEDICT's] own poetic interest and capacity matured." In the field of
linguistics, Sapir developed phonemic theory—the analysis of the sounds of a
language according to the pattern of their distribution—and he analyzed some
10 American Indian languages. In cultural anthropology, he contributed to
personality-and-culture studies by insisting that the true locus of culture is in
the interactions of specific individuals and in the meanings that the participants
abstract from these interactions.

BOOKS BY SAPIR

The Collected Works of Edward Sapir. (coedited with William Bright). 16 vols. Vol. VII: *Wishram Texts and Ethnography.* Mouton 1990 $103.00. ISBN 3-11-012328-2. Exemplifies Sapir's talents as a field linguist.

Language: An Introduction to the Study of Speech. 1921. HarBraceJ 1955 $7.95. ISBN 0-15-648233-9. Successfully presents linguistic science without technical jargon.

Selected Writings of Edward Sapir in Language, Culture, and Personality. Ed. by David G. Mandelbaum. U. CA Pr. 1949 $49.95. ISBN 0-520-01115-5. The most influential of Sapir's theoretical essays, on the nature of language, on culture, on culture and personality, and on Semitic and Indo-European languages.

BOOKS ABOUT SAPIR

Darnell, Regna. *Edward Sapir: Linguist, Anthropologist, Humanist.* U. CA Pr. 1990 $42.50. ISBN 0-520-06678-2. A comprehensive and balanced biography, interweaving Sapir's life and scholarly achievements, with an excellent bibliography.

Koerner, Konrad. *Edward Sapir: Appraisals of His Life and Work.* Benjamins North Am. 1984 $53.00. ISBN 90-272-4518-5. Excellent introduction to Sapir's life and works, with an excellent bibliography.

Spier, Leslie, A. Irving Hallowell, and Stanley S. Newman, eds. *Language, Culture, and Personality: Essays in Memory of Edward Sapir.* Greenwood 1983 $45.50. ISBN 0-313-24183-X. Essays on the classification of Native American languages, culture change, and socialization, plus a frequently cited essay by Sapir's collaborator, Benjamin Whorf.

TURNER, VICTOR WITTER. 1920–1983

Victor Turner was born in Scotland and educated in England. He began his career as a research officer with the Rhodes-Livingstone Institute in northern Rhodesia. Best known for his ethnographic studies of ritual and social process among the Ndembu, Turner also produced significant theoretical insights about rites of passage, the psychology of healing, conflict management, the importance of drama and play, and the theory of symbolic interpretation. He spent much of his career at universities in the United States and was among the leading figures in the turn to symbolic interpretation that marked American anthropology during the 1960s and 1970s.

BOOKS BY TURNER

The Anthropology of Performance. PAJ Pubns. 1986 $12.95. ISBN 1-55554-001-5. Essays on film, the Brazilian Carnival, and the biological bases of religious experience.

Dramas, Fields, and Metaphors: Symbolic Action in Human Society. 1972. Cornell Univ. Pr. 1975 $12.95. ISBN 0-8014-9151-7. Essays explaining the creative potential of metaphors forged in transitional moments.

The Drums of Affliction. 1965. OUP 1965 o.p. Describes how the Ndembu cure illness and misfortune attributed to ancestor spirits.

The Forest of Symbols: Aspects of Ndembu Ritual. 1966. Cornell Univ. Pr. 1970 $25.00. ISBN 0-8014-0432-0. Classic essays on the theory of symbolic analysis, color symbolism, and healing rites.

From Ritual to Theatre: The Human Seriousness of Play. PAJ Pubns. 1982 $11.95. ISBN 0-933826-17-6. Exploratory essays on social drama and dramatic ritual inspired by experimental theater of the early 1970s.

Image and Pilgrimage in Christian Culture: Anthropological Perspectives. (coedited with Edith Turner). Col. U. Pr. 1978 $41.00. ISBN 0-231-04286-8. Pilgrimages from four different areas viewed as rites of passage.

Revelation and Divination in Ndembu Ritual. Cornell Univ. Pr. 1975 $12.95. ISBN 0-685-01226-3. Reprints of two early essays published in Africa as monographs, "Chihamba the White Spirit" and "Ndembu Divination."

The Ritual Process: Structure and Anti-Structure. 1969. Cornell Univ. Pr. 1977 $9.95.
ISBN 0-8014-9163-0. A collection of essays about classification, liminal states, and
communitas.

Schism and Continuity in an African Society. 1957. Manchester Univ. Pr. 1957 o.p.
Analyzes the social tensions that lead to fission in small communities.

BOOK ABOUT TURNER

Blazing the Trail: Way Marks in the Exploration of Symbols. Ed. by Edith Turner. *The
Anthropology of Form and Meaning Ser.* U. of Ariz Pr. 1992 $32.50. ISBN 0-8165-
1291-4. Essays by Turner on Freud, pilgrimage, and sacrifice, and a biographical
essay by Edith Turner on her husband.

TYLOR, SIR EDWARD BURNETT. 1832–1917

Edward Burnett Tylor, an English anthropologist, was a self-taught Victorian
liberal who, in effect, became the founder of British anthropology. He is famous
for the first scientific definition of culture—that complex whole which includes
knowledge, belief, art, morals, law, custom and any other capabilities and habits
acquired by man as a member of society." He developed both the concept of
cultural survival and a theory of animism, which he believed to be religion in its
minimal, most primitive, and therefore broadest form. From 1883 to 1909, Tylor
was connected with Oxford University and its University Museum.

BOOKS BY TYLOR

Anthropology: An Introduction to the Study of Man and Civilization. 1881. Appleton 1907
o.p. Quaint line drawings illustrates a general text dealing with race, language, and
culture.

The Origins of Culture. Peter Smith 1986 $18.00. ISBN 0-685-12151-8. Part 1 of his
magnum opus, *Primitive Culture*, begins with the first anthropological definition of
"culture" and goes on to explain the utility of the survival concept for evolutionary
reconstructions.

Religion in Primitive Culture. Peter Smith $18.75. ISBN 0-8446-0946-3. Introduction by
Paul Radin. Part 2 of the original *Primitive Culture*, posits with the origin of religion
in the universal concept of the human soul and describes the world view called
"animism" with copious examples.

BOOK ABOUT TYLOR

Burrow, John W. *Evolution and Society: A Study in Victorian Social Theory.* Cambridge
U. Pr. 1966 o.p.

WHITE, LESLIE ALVIN. 1900–1975

Leslie White, an American anthropologist, studied psychology at Columbia
University before earning a Ph.D. in anthropology at the University of Chicago in
1927. He taught at the University of Buffalo and from 1927 to 1930 was curator
of anthropology at the Buffalo Museum of Science. White spent most of his
professional career at the University of Michigan from 1930, and is best known
as a theorist of culture and evolution. In the context of an era that had rejected
discussions of cultural evolution, White revived the respectability of the
approach with essays that were later published in 1959 as *The Evolution of
Culture.* The prime mover of cultural evolution, in his theory, is the increasing
capacity to harness energy. White also stressed the unique human ability to use
symbols; in *The Science of Culture* (1949), he proposed the term "culturology"
to designate the analysis of symbols as a distinct phenomenon.

BOOKS BY WHITE

The Evolution of Culture: The Development of Civilization to the Fall of Rome. McGraw 1959 o.p.
The Science of Culture. Grove Pr. 1949 o.p.

BOOK ABOUT WHITE

Dole, Gertrude E., and Robert L. Carniero, eds. *Essays in the Science of Culture in Honor of Leslie A. White.* 1960. Crowell o.p. Articles on Japanese religion and Australian marriage classes, with a complete bibliography of White's publications.

WHORF, BENJAMIN L. 1897–1941

Benjamin L. Whorf, an American linguist, was throughout his life an employee of the Hartford Fire Insurance Company; linguistics was his hobby. Nevertheless, he received a Social Science Research Council fellowship, and he took courses with EDWARD SAPIR and others at Yale University. According to George L. Trager, "Whorf's monument," the Sapir-Whorf hypothesis, can be stated as follows: "Language *is* culture, culture is stated in language; language mediates action, action is described in language." His continuing influence derives from the basic truth and value of this seemingly "trivial" assertion.

BOOK BY WHORF

Language, Thought and Reality: Selected Writings of Benjamin Lee Whorf. Ed. by John B. Carroll. MIT Pr. 1956 $10.95. ISBN 0-262-73006-5. Often cited for its thesis that language shapes a people's world view.

BOOK ABOUT WHORF

Hoijer, Harry, ed. *Language in Culture: Conference on the Interrelations of Language and Other Aspects of Culture.* U. Ch. Pr. 1958 o.p. Frequently cited papers from a conference on the relationship of language and thought, where the Whorf hypothesis claimed center stage.

CHAPTER 3

Economics

Gary Clayton

"... economics is necessary, not merely for the support of economists, but
for the development and perhaps even for the survival of science in general
and the civilization that supports it ... (economics) is significant ... not
merely because it investigates an important slice of life in the marketplace,
but because the phenomena which emerge in a relatively clear and
quantitative form in the marketplace are also found in virtually all other
human activities."

—KENNETH BOULDING, *Beyond Economics*

Economics is a social science that examines the way in which people cope with
the fundamental problem of scarcity. Economists argue that scarcity is at the
heart of economics, because people's wants are seemingly unlimited, while the
resources needed to satisfy those wants—land, labor, and capital—are limited.
Economics is generally regarded as a social science, because it is the study of
the way we behave, individually as well as collectively, as we go about the
business of "doing the best we can with what we've got."

To a certain extent, scarcity tends to be a relative term, because some people
may be satisfied with fewer things, or have fewer wants, than others. In general,
however, the amount of goods and services that most people would *like* to have
is much greater than the things they will actually be able to earn and consume.
The problem of scarcity gives economics a certain degree of universality:
Scarcity is a problem that has been with us in the past, is present in all societies,
and will be with us for the foreseeable future.

Another central theme in economics is efficiency: It makes sense to use our
scarce resources as effectively as possible. Efficiency has its own requirements;
economists have had to devise decision-making methodologies, such as cost-
benefit analysis, input-output studies, and marginal analysis, to use as guides to
efficient decision making. Economists have also had to develop methods of
measurement—national income accounts, price indicators, unemployment
statistics, and the like—in order to determine if progress is actually being made.

Economics, like many of the harder sciences, is a science with propositions
and testable hypotheses. This is so because people, on average and in the
aggregate, tend to conform to statistical rules and the laws of probability. As a
result, a considerable amount of work in economics has involved formulating
and testing propositions, as well as developing the mathematical tools needed to
test and verify them.

Finally, economics is an evolutionary science, because economists are
dealing with an ever-growing body of understanding regarding the complex
problems of society. The great economic historian, JACOB VINER, recognized as
much when he claimed that "economics is whatever economists do." Above all
else, however, economics is an immensely interesting science, because it is the

study of ourselves and of the way we act and react as we go about the business of our everyday lives.

REFERENCE WORKS

There are three types of useful reference works listed below. The first type includes dictionaries and handbooks that define terms and concepts. The second type includes statistical sources, series, and databases, along with those works that explain how statistics are to be used and interpreted. The third type provides brief biographical sketches of the major figures in the field.

Aliber, Robert Z. *The Handbook of International Financial Management.* Dow Jones-Irwin 1989 $55.00. ISBN 1-55623-019-2. Reference work with an emphasis on "why" and "how" questions; includes sections on global financial markets, tax structures and laws, and managerial decision making.

Bickers, Kenneth N., and Robert M. Stein. *Federal Domestic Outlays, 1983–1990: A Data Book.* M. E. Sharpe 1991 $45.00. ISBN 0-87332-840-X. Historical analysis of expenditures during the Reagan and Bush years; covers distribution of federal funds to congressional districts, states, and regions.

Blaug, Mark. *Great Economists Before Keynes: An Introduction to the Lives and Works of the One Hundred Great Economists of the Past.* Cambridge U. Pr. 1989 $17.95. ISBN 0-521-36741-7. Brief biographical profiles of early theorists; includes short discussion of their major works and major influences.

———. *Great Economists Since Keynes: An Introduction to the Lives and Works of One Hundred Modern Economists.* Cambridge U. Pr. 1989 $17.95. ISBN 0-521-36742-5. A total of 100 short profiles of economists who achieved prominence since Keynes; features photographs, short biographies, synopsis of works.

Breit, William, and Roger W. Spencer, eds. *Lives of the Laureates: Ten Nobel Economists.* MIT Pr. 1990 $19.95. ISBN 0-262-02308-3. Autobiographical accounts of Nobel Laureates in economics: Lewis, Klein, Arrow, Samuelson, Friedman, Stigler, Tobin, Modigliani, Buchanan, and Solow.

Clayton, Gary E., and Martin G. Giesbrecht. *A Guide to Everyday Economic Statistics.* McGraw 1992 $8.75. ISBN 0-07-011327-0. Brief, lucid explanations of 35 common statistical terms.

Downs, John, and Jordan Goodman. *Finance and Investment Handbook.* Barron 1990 $29.95. ISBN 0-8120-6188-8. Handbook of 2,500 terms; includes sections on how to read financial pages of newspapers, and financial reports of companies.

Eatwell, John, and others, eds. *The New Palgrave: A Dictionary of Economics.* Groves Dict. Music 1987 $750.00. ISBN 0-935859-10-1. Four-volume encyclopedia, with 1,900 articles, including 700 biographies. Outstanding reference source for the professional or library.

Freeman, Michael. *Atlas of the World Economy.* S&S Trade 1991 $40.00. ISBN 0-13-050741-5. Depicts relatively recent changes—most from 1950 to 1985—in the world's economy, based mostly on United Nations statistics. Topics include income, industry, agriculture, trade, labor, energy, and population demographics. Excellent combination of maps, graphs, charts, and brief textual explanations.

Frumkin, Norman. *Guide to Economic Indicators.* M. E. Sharpe 1990 $35.00. ISBN 0-87332-521-4. Provides detailed review of major statistical measures and economic indicators.

Pass, Christopher, and others. *The Harper Dictionary of Economics.* HarpC 1993 $25.00. ISBN 0-06-271504-6. A total of 1,700 entries; subjects include Keynesian economics, monetarism, theories of value, and the stock market.

Pearce, David W. *The MIT Dictionary of Modern Economics.* MIT Pr. 1992 $40.00. ISBN 0-262-16132-X. Authoritative reference containing approximately 2,800 entries covering economic concepts, institutions, schools of thought, and important economists.

The 1993 Handbook of World Stock and Commodity Exchanges. Blackwell Pubs. 1993
   $265.00. ISBN 0-631-18888-6. Guide to world stock and commodity exchanges;
   includes indices on market performance.

HISTORIES AND SURVEYS OF ECONOMIC THOUGHT

Histories of economic thought deal with the people, events, and ideas that
shaped the discipline. Some of the works below focus on the entire field, others
on prominent individuals that influenced its evolution. All will give the reader a
better idea of the current range of issues that are important in economics.

Bell, John Fred. *A History of Economic Thought.* Krieger 1980 repr. of 1967 ed. $49.50.
   ISBN 0-89874-065-7. Comprehensive, classic work on development of economic
   thought from Greeks to mathematical economists of neoclassical school.

Blaug, Mark. *Economic Theory in Retrospect.* Cambridge U. Pr. $24.95. ISBN 0-521-
   31644-8. Standard reference work on history of economic thought from mercantilism to Keynes. Focuses on theory and the comparative contributions of economists.

———, ed. *The History of Economic Thought.* Ashgate Pub. Co. 1990 $89.95. ISBN 1-
   85278-191-2. Collection of 21 papers by contemporary economists on their peers:
   Baumol on Say and Mill, Patinkin on Friedman, and so on; covers the last 40 years,
   with emphasis on the 1970s and 1980s.

Breit, William, and Roger L. Ransom. *The Academic Scribblers: American Economists in
   Collision.* HR&W 1971 o.p. Traces the development of ideas of American economists
   since Marshall and Keynes.

Clayton, Gary E., and James Brown. *Economics: Principles and Practices.* Glencoe 1988
   $39.95. ISBN 0-02-823048-5. Provides institutional and descriptive coverage of
   economic systems, business behavior, economic markets, labor and government,
   financial institutions, the world economy.

Coleman, D. C., ed. *Revisions in Mercantilism.* Methuen 1969 o.p. Eight papers on
   mercantilism in England, France, and Germany, by Heckscher, Judges, Viner,
   Coleman, and others. Balanced presentation and extremely readable.

Gherity, James A. *Economic Thought: A Historical Anthology.* Random 1965 o.p. Broad
   selection of writings from St. Thomas Aquinas through Wicksell; contains some
   individual economist profiles.

Giesbrecht, Martin Gerhard. *The Evolution of Economic Society.* W. H. Freeman 1972
   o.p. Delightful account of the development of economic thought from primitive
   societies to the neoclassical school of economics; written from a historical
   perspective in an easy, fluid style.

Heilbroner, Robert. *The Worldly Philosophers: The Lives, Times and Ideas of the Great
   Economic Thinkers.* S&S Trade 1987 $10.95. ISBN 0-671-63318-X. Lively, entertain-
   ing survey of lives and ideas of great economic thinkers from Adam Smith to
   Schumpeter. The first book anyone should read if he or she is new to economics.

Homan, Paul T. *Contemporary Economic Thought.* Ayer 1928 $21.50. ISBN 0-8369-
   0546-6. Contains thoughtful chapters on the life, times, writings, and influence of
   early economists.

Keynes, John Maynard. *Essays in Biography.* Horizon Pr. AZ 1951 o.p. Fifteen essays on
   the work and lives of politicians and economists, including Malthus, Marshall, and
   Jevons; observations based on direct acquaintance.

Mun, Thomas. *England's Treasure by Forraign Trade.* Kelley 1986 repr. of 1664 ed.
   $19.50. ISBN 0-678-06274-9. Classic mercantilist work argues that surplus of exports
   over imports is the source of wealth, but also contends that a favorable balance of
   trade with every nation is not required.

Oser, Jacob, and Stanley Brue. *The Evolution of Economic Thought.* Dryden Pr. 1988
   $33.00. ISBN 0-15-525003-5. Surveys the development of economics for mercantil-
   ism to the Chicago economists Friedman, Stigler, and Becker.

Roll, Eric. *A History of Economic Thought*. Faber & Faber 1992 $24.95. ISBN 0-571-16553-2. Standard reference covering the period from the Old Testament to the neoclassical economists and Keynes.

Samuelson, Paul. *Economics*. McGraw 1989 $38.68. ISBN 0-07-054786-6. Covers macroeconomics, microeconomics, international and global economics; Keynesian in nature, this book is by America's first Nobel Laureate in economics.

Schumpeter, Joseph A. *History of Economic Analysis*. OUP 1954 $29.95. ISBN 0-19-504185-2. Monumental survey and summary of economic history and the contributions of over 1,500 writers; with 1,260 pages containing nearly one million words.

————. *Ten Great Economists from Marx to Keynes*. OUP 1965 o.p. Profiles life and work of Marx, Walras, Menger, Marshall, Bohm-Bawerk, Pareto, Taussig, Fisher, Mitchell, and Keynes.

Spiegel, Henry William. *The Growth of Economic Thought*. Duke 1991 $29.95. ISBN 0-8223-0973-4. Comprehensive text and reference on the development of economic thought from classical Greece to the beginnings of the modern econometric movement.

————, ed. *The Development of Economic Thought, Great Economists in Perspective*. Wiley 1966 o.p. Classic reader on the writing of great economists by great economists, including Marx on the Physiocrats, Veblen on Marx, and Mitchell on Veblen.

Spiegel, Henry William, and Warren J. Samuels. *Contemporary Economists in Perspective*. Jai Pr. 1983 $105.00. ISBN 0-89232-347-7. Second classic reader on economists by economists has articles on 38 prominent economists in the post–World War II period.

Stigler, George J. *Essays in the History of Economics*. U. Ch. Pr. 1965 o.p. Fourteen historical essays on topics from utility theory to Fabian socialism; a modern classic renowned for its clear and uncluttered style of exposition.

METHODOLOGY AND ISSUES

Methodological problems have a rich history in economics. Much of the early work was generated by concerns over the appropriate focus and legitimate concerns of economics. Even now the issue has not been fully resolved, and so the reader might want to consult a collection of modern reading on the subject to sample the diversity.

Boulding, Kenneth E. *Economics as a Science*. U. Pr. of Amer. 1988 $18.25. ISBN 0-8191-7100-X. Short essays devoted to economics as a political science, a social science, a mathematical science, and so on.

Caldwell, Bruce J., ed. *The Philosophy and Methodology of Economics*. Ashgate Pub. Co. 1993 $379.95. ISBN 1-85278-385-0. Extensive collection of 66 scholarly articles from the classics to modern developments. Topics include economics and biology, constitutional economics, hermeneutics, and assessments; many articles are not available elsewhere.

Friedman, Milton. *Essays in Positive Economics*. U. Ch. Pr. 1966 $9.00. ISBN 0-226-26403-3. Collection of previously published essays on such topics as methodology in economics, welfare theory, and monetary policy.

Georgescu-Roegen, Nicholas. *Entropy Law and the Economic Process*. HUP 1971 $14.95. ISBN 0-674-25781-2. Offers "bioeconomic" view of economic growth: that production is subject to law of entropy and that economic growth will eventually end as finite energy and resources are used up.

Keynes, John Neville. *The Scope and Method of Political Economy*. Kelley 1986 repr. of 1917 ed. $39.50. ISBN 0-678-00010-7. Written by the father of John Maynard Keynes, this starting point for reading in economic methodology covers methodological approaches of leading neoclassical writers.

Knight, Frank H. *On the History and Method of Economics*. U. Ch. Pr. 1956 o.p. Collection of 11 previously published essays covering historical and methodological issues such as statics and dynamics and the business cycle; articles date from the 1920s through the 1950s.

Koopmans, Tjalling C. *Three Essays on the State of Economic Science*. Kelley 1991 repr. of 1957 ed. $29.50. ISBN 0-678-01397-7. Three classic essays on the allocation of resources and the price system; a methodological argument about constructing economic knowledge over time, and the interaction of tools, problems, and techniques.

Leontief, Wassily. *Input-Output Economics*. OUP 1986 $26.00. ISBN 0-19-503527-5. Collection of 11 previously published essays; includes interesting discussions of methodology and examples of input-output applications to disarmament and foreign trade.

Machlup, Fritz. *Economic Semantics*. Transaction Pubs. 1990 $19.95. ISBN 0-88738-836-1. Classic collection of 16 previously published essays on economic methodology, semantic issues in value theory, and macro policy.

————. *Methodology of Economics and Other Social Sciences*. Acad. Pr. 1978 $75.00. ISBN 0-12-464550-X. Impressive collection of 26 essays dealing with such topics as verification of operationalism, comparisons between natural and social sciences, and methodological approaches of several different economists.

Morgenstern, Oskar. *On the Accuracy of Economic Observations*. Bks. Demand repr. of 1963 ed. $87.40. ISBN 0-8357-8972-2. Appeals for greater awareness of possible errors in published statistics, with entertaining examples of inconsistencies; useful for anyone who generates or uses economic statistics.

Robbins, Lionel. *An Essay on the Nature and Significance of Economic Science*. Macmillan 1932 o.p. Raises the methodological issue of normative versus descriptive economics.

AGRICULTURE, NATURAL RESOURCES, AND ENVIRONMENTAL ECONOMICS

Historically, agriculture has been concerned with the production of food and related products. In recent years the focus has broadened to include all natural resources, and the scope of economics has expanded to consider efficient use of the environment, not just the traditional factors of production.

Bormann, Herbert F., and Stephen R. Kellert, eds. *Ecology, Economics, Ethics: The Broken Circle*. Yale U. Pr. 1992 $30.00. ISBN 0-300-04976-5. Analysis of global environmental issues; focuses on interconnections of ecology, economics, and ethics.

Daly, Herman E., and Kenneth N. Townsend, eds. *Valuing the Earth: Economics, Ecology, Ethics*. MIT Pr. 1992 $18.95. ISBN 0-262-54068-1. Classic and recent essays arguing that economic growth on a planet of finite resources cannot be physically or economically sustained.

Dornbusch, Rudiger, and James Poterba, eds. *Global Warming: Economic Policy Responses*. MIT Pr. 1991 $32.50. ISBN 0-262-04126-X. Essays on the economic effects of global warming, summarizing current thinking on the topic; coverage includes countries likely to be most affected by climate change, the use of economic incentives to reduce emissions, and prospects for international cooperation.

Gabor, D., and others. *Beyond the Age of Waste: A Report to the Club of Rome*. Pergamon 1981 $56.00. ISBN 0-08-027303-3. Emphasizes finite limits of nonrenewable resources and the consequences for growth; addresses some flaws in the Club of Rome report, *The Limits of Growth*, especially neglect of technology.

Goodman, David, and Michael Redclift, eds. *The International Farm Crisis*. St. Martin 1989 o.p. Sixteen essays on the structural crisis due to global dissemination of an agro-industrial model, whose adoption led to the shift from the food shortages of the

1970s to the overproduction of the 1980s. Tropics, subtropics, and non-Western nations are not covered.

Hanley, Nick, and Clive Splash. *Cost-Benefit Analysis and the Environment*. Elgar 1992 o.p. Examines the applications of cost benefit analysis to acid rain and global warming.

Manne, Alan, and Richard Richels. *Buying Greenhouse Insurance: The Economic Costs of CO_2 Emission Limits*. MIT Pr. 1992 $25.00. ISBN 0-262-13280-X. Develops a model for determining the costs of limiting carbon dioxide emissions; contains region-by-region estimates of the costs required for an international agreement.

Meadows, Donella H., and others. *Beyond the Limits: Confronting Global Collapse, Envisioning a Sustainable Future*. Chelsea Green Pub. 1992 $19.95. ISBN 0-930031-55-5. Updates the predictions and scenarios in *The Limits of Growth*, published 20 years earlier. Concludes that renewable resources are being consumed beyond sustainable rates and that a sustainable future society based on quality rather than quantity is possible.

_____. *The Limits of Growth*. Signet Books 1974 o.p. Study of future conditions given current rates of growth.

Oates, Wallace E., ed. *The Economics of the Environment*. Ashgate Pub. Co. 1992 $149.95. ISBN 1-85278-360-5. Broad collection of 35 scholarly essays; includes classic articles on the theory of environmental regulation, design and implementation of policy, measurement of costs and benefits, enforcement of policies, and economics of conservation.

Schramm, Gunter, and Jeremy J. Warford, eds. *Environmental Management and Economic Development*. Johns Hopkins 1989 $24.95. ISBN 0-8018-3950-5. Collection of 11 essays on economic development and environmental protection; topics include poverty, development, environmental protection, and forest and water resources.

Schultz, Theodore W. *Transforming Traditional Agriculture*. Ayer 1976 repr. of 1964 ed. $21.00. ISBN 0-405-07792-0. Nobel Prize winner argues that rural farmers in developing nations behave rationally when they resist innovation because of uncertain returns and discriminatory government policies.

Ward, Barbara, and Rene Dubos. *Only One Earth: The Care and Maintenance of a Small Planet*. Norton 1983 $5.95. ISBN 0-393-30129-X. Unofficial report to the United Nations Conference on the Human Environment. Discusses problems of technology, costs of pollution, policies for growth, and strategies for survival.

BUSINESS ADMINISTRATION AND BUSINESS ECONOMICS

Some areas of economics are especially appropriate for the manager. Some topics are applied, such as the application of game theory and other decision-making methodologies. Other topics are conceptual, such as those involving ethical issues and entrepreneurship. Still others involve a combination of conceptual analysis and application, such as with mergers, acquisitions, and takeovers.

Baumol, William J. *Economic Theory and Operations Analysis*. P-H 1977. ISBN 0-13-227132-X. Noted for the unification of economics and operations analysis; features practical applications of economic concepts.

Brams, Steven J. *Negotiation Games: Applying Game Theory to Bargaining and Arbitration*. Routledge 1990 $49.50. ISBN 0-415-90337-8. Application of game theory techniques to business situations; requires only modest knowledge of algebra and probability.

Burrough, Bryan, and John Helyar. *Barbarians at the Gate: The Fall of RJR Nabisco*. HarpC 1990 $22.95. ISBN 0-06-016172-8. Engaging and compelling behind-the-scenes account of the largest takeover in the history of Wall Street, written by *Wall Street Journal* reporters who followed the story.

Casson, Mark, ed. *Entrepreneurship*. Elgar 1990 $139.95. ISBN 1-85278-209-9. Extensive collection of scholarly essays on all aspects of entrepreneurship; coverage ranges from classic and seminal articles to results of new studies.

Chandler, Alfred D. *The Visible Hand: The Managerial Revolution in American Business*. MIT Pr. 1977 $35.00. ISBN 0-674-94051-2. History of the rise of modern managerial capitalism written from perspective of an insider; argues that the visible hand of management has superseded the invisible hand of market coordination.

Cyert, Richard, and James March. *A Behavioral Theory of the Firm*. Blackwell Pubs. 1992 $29.95. ISBN 0-631-17451-6. Classic work in organizational theory, intended for economists, social psychologists, organizational theorists, and managers.

Dertouzos, M. L., R. K. Lester, and R. M. Solow. *Made in America*. MIT Pr. 1989 $24.95. ISBN 0-262-04100-6. Identifies what is best in American and international industrial practice; sets out five national priorities for regaining the productive edge.

Glazer, Myron P., and Penina M. Glazer. *The Whistleblowers: Exposing Corruption in Government and Industry*. Basic 1990 $9.95. ISBN 0-465-09174-1. Examines the economic impact of whistleblowing on both the whistle blower and the company.

Hoffmann, M., R. Frederick, and E. Petry. *The Ethics of Organizational Transformation: Mergers, Takeovers, and Corporate Restructuring*. Greenwood 1989 $50.00. ISBN 0-89930-391-9. From a conference on business ethics, this work focuses on employee interests, stockholder welfare, plant closings, and insider trading.

Lichtenberg, Frank R. *Corporate Takeovers and Productivity*. MIT Pr. 1992 $29.95. ISBN 0-262-12164-6. Having studied hundreds of corporate takeovers in the 1970s and 1980s, the author concludes that restructuring contributes to higher productivity and increased international competitiveness.

Sharpe, William F. *Introduction to Managerial Economics*. Col. U. Pr. 1973 $43.00. ISBN 0-231-03693-0. Brief introduction to microeconomic elements of interest to business managers, including value and demand, revenue and profit, time and risk, cost of inputs and outputs. Written by a Nobel Prize-winning economist.

Simon, Herbert A. *Administrative Behavior*. Free Pr. 1976 $29.95. ISBN 0-02-929000-7. Nobel Prize-winning author's major work arguing that economic behavior is bounded by the costs of obtaining information, and that maximization is seldom possible because of the abundance of alternatives.

BUSINESS CYCLES AND FLUCTUATIONS

Business cycle literature is concerned with efforts to recognize the earliest contributors to the field, to document and provide measures of aggregate economic activity, to analyze and explain the underlying causes and sequences of events, and, finally, to predict future business activity. During the 1960s and 1970s, there was a tendency to talk about "fluctuations" rather than cycles—a change based on the optimistic belief that economies could be managed in a way that would break the periodic ups and downs of economic activity. However, the experience of the 1980s and 1990s has shown that this is not the case, and so the term "business cycles" is back in use.

Barro, Robert J., ed. *Modern Business Cycle Theory*. HUP 1989 $35.00. ISBN 0-674-57860-0. Collection of articles focusing on rational expectations and the business cycle.

Burns, Arthur F., and Wesley Mitchell. *Measuring Business Cycles*. Natl. Bur. Econ. Res. 1946 $35.00. ISBN 0-87014-085-X. Monumental classic on statistical series and "reference cycles" that marked the single turning point in total economic activity; a landmark in the field of business cycle measurement.

Clark, John J., and Morris Cohen, eds. *Business Fluctuations, Growth, and Economic Stabilization: A Reader*. Random 1963 o.p. Comprehensive reader in field of business cycles and stabilization with selections covering virtually every major writer in the field; a classic reference volume.

Hall, Thomas E. *Business Cycles: the Nature and Causes of Economic Fluctuations*. Greenwood 1990 $39.95. ISBN 0-275-93085-8. Concise, lucid, and current survey of business cycles.

Mitchell, Wesley Claire. *Business Cycles and Their Causes*. Porcupine Pr. 1989 $12.95. ISBN 0-87991-262-6. Identifies various economic processes at work during periods of economic expansion and contraction, and suggests techniques for identifying leads, lags, and turning points in business cycle activity.

Moore, Geoffrey H. *Leading Indicators for the 1990s*. Busn. One Irwin 1990 $25.00. ISBN 1-55623-258-6. Report on Columbia University's efforts to develop better leading and lagging indicators; summarizes some of the most current work being done in the area.

Reijnders, Jan Long. *Long Waves in Economic Development*. Ashgate Pub. Co. 1990 $59.95. ISBN 1-85278-339-7. Examines the impact of long waves on the process of economic development. An excellent historical review.

Schumpeter, Joseph A. *Essays: On Entrepreneurs, Innovations, Business Cycles and the Evolution of Capitalism*. Transaction Pubs. 1989 $19.95. ISBN 0-88738-764-0. Essays focusing on four main Schumpeterian themes: economic theory and the business cycle; evolution of capitalism; relationship of economic theory, economic history, and the real economy; and Marxism and economic sociology.

Temin, Peter, ed. *Inside the Business Enterprise: Historical Perspectives on the Use of Information*. U. Ch. Pr. 1991 $43.00. ISBN 0-226-79202-1. Collection of articles exploring the link between modern economic theory and recent business history. Focuses on role of imperfect and asymmetric information in the operation of firms, and examines the internal workings of the American firm.

Valentine, Lloyd M. *Business Cycles and Business Forecasting*. SW Pub. 1990. ISBN 0-538-80575-7. Outstanding and comprehensive text on business cycles; clearly written for the specialist and general reader alike.

Zarnowitz, Victor. *Business Cycles*. U. Ch. Pr. 1992 $70.00. ISBN 0-226-97890-7. Study on theories and evidence, history and measurement, cyclical indicators, and forecasting by a leading researcher in the field.

CAPITALISM AND THE ACCUMULATION OF CAPITAL

Capitalism refers to an economic system based on private ownership of the factors of production. Historically, capitalistic economies have shown remarkable growth and have accumulated much wealth, but the change is not without cost. Accordingly, those who write about capitalism tend to see it quite differently—with viewpoints ranging from unadulterated admiration to disgust and revulsion. Some writers attribute a religious influence to the rise of capitalism, while others, such as KARL MARX, recognized the dynamics of the capitalistic system but saw within it the seeds of its own destruction.

Ahmad, Syed. *Capital in Economic Theory*. Ashgate Pub. Co. 1991 $98.95. ISBN 1-85278-201-3. Scholarly treatise on modern capital theory that explores commonalties to different approaches; provides a synthesis of contributions to the field.

Baran, Paul A., and Paul M. Sweezy. *Monopoly Capital: An Essay on the American Economic and Social Order*. Monthly Rev. 1968 $10.00. ISBN 0-85345-073-0. Highly regarded modern classic that extends Marx's model of competitive capitalism to monopoly capitalism.

Dobb, Maurice H. *Studies in the Development of Capitalism*. Intl. Pubs. Co. 1964 $3.95. ISBN 0-7178-0197-7. Marxist view of the evolution of capitalism, which argues that the development of capitalism resulted in the emergence of a propertyless class of wage earners.

Feldstein, Martin. *Inflation: Tax Rules and Capital Formation*. U. Ch. Pr. 1983 $33.00. ISBN 0-226-24085-1. Collection of 14 papers published between 1975 and 1981 by a leading expert in the field.

Heilbroner, Robert L. *The Making of Economic Society*. P-H 1993 $23.00. ISBN 0-13-555186-2. Delightful, lucid discussion of the evolution of economic society from antiquity to modern times, with a new section on the downfall of communism.
————. *The Nature and Logic of Capitalism*. Norton 1986 $8.95. ISBN 0-393-95529-X. Searching, thoughtful analysis of capitalism, described as a system of class domination and mass acquiescence, with the drive for power sublimated into the desire to accumulate capital.

Hughes, Jonathan. *The Vital Few: The Entrepreneur and American Economic Progress*. OUP 1986 $11.95. ISBN 0-19-504038-4. Study of entrepreneurs and their contributions to the American economy from colonial times to the 1930s; portraits include William Penn, Brigham Young, Eli Whitney, Henry Ford, and E. H. Harriman.

Kanth, Rajani K. *Capitalism and Social Theory*. M. E. Sharpe 1992 $49.95. ISBN 1-56324-069-6. Examines the relationship between theory of wealth and theory of power; written in a Marxian tradition.

Kuznets, Simon. *Capital in the American Economy: Its Formation and Financing*. Ayer 1975 repr. of 1961 ed. $48.50. ISBN 0-405-07596-0. Monumental study in capital formation by the second American economist to win the Nobel Prize; covers the period from the Civil War to the 1950s. A classic work dealing with savings, methodological problems, sources of data, trends.

Marx, Karl. *Capital, Vol. 1—A Critique of Political Economy*. Trans. by Ben Fowkes. Viking Penguin 1992 $14.95. ISBN 0-14-044568-4. *Capital, Vol. 2—The Process of Circulation of Capital*. Ed. by Friedrich Engels. Intl. Pubs. Co. 1985 $7.50. ISBN 0-7178-0622-7. *Capital, Vol. 3—The Process of Capitalist Production As a Whole*. Ed. by Friedrich Engels. Intl. Pubs. Co. 1984 $8.95. ISBN 0-7178-0623-5. Discusses the process of capital formation and the fatal flaws that will lead to the decline and collapse of capitalism.

Pack, Spencer J. *Capitalism as a Moral System*. Ashgate Pub. Co. 1991 $49.95. ISBN 1-85278-442-3. Argues that modern supporters of capitalism and laissez-faire have overlooked Adam Smith's reservations about the system, and that Smith was not a dogmatic defender of capitalism. Attempts to dispel other misconceptions about Smith's beliefs.

Romano, Richard, and Melvin Leiman. *Views on Capitalism*. Glencoe 1970 o.p. Examines different perspectives on capitalism. Contains useful overview of works by and selections from conservatives (including Hayek and Friedman), liberals (such as Mill, Keynes, and Galbraith), and radicals (among them Marx, Engels, Veblen, and Harrington).

Rueschemeyer, D., E. H. Stephens, and J. D. Stephens. *Capitalist Development and Democracy*. U. Ch. Pr. 1992 $45.00. ISBN 0-226-73142-1. Historical and comparative analysis of the interplay between capitalism and democracy.

Solow, Robert M. *Capital Theory and the Rate of Return*. Elsevier 1963 o.p. Somewhat advanced work in capital theory, which argues that the determination of the rate of return on capital is critical, not the measurement of capital itself.

Tawney, Richard H. *Religion and the Rise of Capitalism*. Peter Smith 1954 $12.75. ISBN 0-8446-1446-7. Classic study on the development of religious thought and its relation to social and economic questions.

Weber, Max. *The Protestant Ethic and the Spirit of Capitalism*. Peter Smith 1984 $20.50. ISBN 0-8446-6118-X. Argues that the spread of Calvinism in post-Reformation Europe was responsible for new attitudes towards the pursuit of wealth, a motivating force in the development of capitalism.

COMPARATIVE ECONOMIC SYSTEMS

Historically, literature on comparative economic systems has tended to compare the main types of economic systems—capitalism, communism, and socialism—along with a number of case studies of countries with particularly interesting economic histories. With the collapse of the Soviet Union and the rejection of communism in the Eastern European countries, however, much of the new literature deals with the transition from a command economy to a capitalistic, market-based economy.

Blanchard, Olivier, and others. *Reform in Eastern Europe.* MIT Pr. 1991 $8.95. ISBN 0-262-52181-4. Describes attempts by new governments of Eastern Europe to move from centrally planned economies to free-market economies. Identifies major policy choices and discusses what will and will not work.

Carson, Richard L. *Comparative Economic Systems.* M. E. Sharpe 1990 $60.00. ISBN 0-877332-583-4. Standard text describing various economic systems; covers socialism and capitalism, with special attention to Hungary, China, and the former Yugoslavia.

Galbraith, John Kenneth. *Capitalism, Communism and Coexistence: From the Bitter Past to a Better Prospect.* HM 1988 $17.45. ISBN 0-395-47316-0. Dialogue between Galbraith and the noted Soviet economist Stanislav Menshikov on superiority of their respective economic systems. Discusses problems caused by Leninist systems in the Soviet Union and China.

Gold, Thomas B. *State and Society in the Taiwan Miracle.* M. E. Sharpe 1986 $15.95. ISBN 0-87332-399-8. Examines the transformation of Taiwan's economy from the seventeenth century to today; focuses on social structures and values, industrialization, and international influences.

Harrington, Michael. *Socialism: Past and Future.* NAL-Dutton 1989 $9.95. ISBN 0-452-26504-5. Examines the history of socialism and socialism in the third world. Argues that socialism is the best hope for human freedom and justice in the coming century.

Heilbroner, Robert. *Marxism: For and Against.* Norton 1980 $7.95. ISBN 0-393-95166-9. Explores the lingering fascination with Marx in modern times.

Hewett, Ed. A. *Reforming the Soviet Economy.* Brookings 1988 $36.95. ISBN 0-8157-3604-5. Comprehensive and readable study of Gorbachev and the Soviet economy; examines policy prescriptions for conversion to a market economy.

Ito, Takatoshi. *The Japanese Economy.* MIT Pr. 1991 $39.95. ISBN 0-262-09029-5. Introduction to the Japanese economy that uses standard economic concepts to compare Japan with the United States. Compares the two countries in terms of economic performance, underlying institutions, and government policies.

Kornai, Janos. *Growth, Shortage and Efficiency: A Microdynamic Model of the Socialist Economy.* U. CA Pr. 1983 $40.00. ISBN 0-520-04901-2. Noted Hungarian economist argues that planned shortages of consumer goods can be used as an alternative to the Western concept of the market-clearing equilibrium price.

Mises, Ludwig W. von. *Socialism: An Economic and Sociological Analysis.* Yale U. Pr. 1951 o.p. Argues that the lack of a price mechanism means that a socialist society can never allocate efficiently.

Peck, Merton J., and Thomas J. Richardson, eds. *What is to Be Done?* Yale U. Pr. 1991 $28.00. ISBN 05466-1. Collection of essays dealing with the transition of the former Soviet Union from a centrally planned economy to a market economy.

Robinson, Joan. *An Essay on Marxian Economics.* Porcupine Pr. 1991 $12.95. ISBN 0-87991-270-7. One of the best books on Marxian economics ever written; highly recommended.

Sinn, Gerlinde, and Hans-Werner Sinn. *Jumpstart: The Economic Unification of Germany.* MIT Pr. 1993 $24.95. ISBN 0-262-19327-2. Nontechnical account of the economic ramifications of German unification by well-known German economists.

Szekely, Istvan, and David N. G. Newbery, eds. *Hungary: An Economy in Transition.* Cambridge U. Pr. 1993 $54.95. ISBN 0-521-44018-1. Collection of papers discussing Hungary's transition to a market economy; discusses privatization, financial and legal systems, taxation, labor markets, and social safety nets.

Zwass, Adam. *Market, Plan, and State: The Strengths and Weaknesses of the Two World Economic Systems.* M. E. Sharpe 1987 $55.00. ISBN 0-87332-396-3. Provides a global assessment of socialism versus capitalism; descriptive and well written.

ECONOMIC DEVELOPMENT, TECHNOLOGICAL CHANGE, AND GROWTH

Literature on economic development, change, and growth encompasses both the successes of the developed nations and the failures of the developing nations. This is a rich and fertile area for economists, and the reasons attributed to economic growth or lack thereof range from the distribution of natural resources to ideology.

Altvater, and others. *The Poverty of Nations: A Guide to the Debt Crisis—From Argentina to Zaire*. Humanities 1991 o.p. Discusses the evolution of the international debt crisis, and deals with the crisis as one of the urgent problems faced by all economies, not just developing ones.

Boulding, Kenneth E. *The World As a Total System*. Sage 1985 $35.00. ISBN 0-8039-2443-7. Discusses the evolution of the world toward a single economic, cultural, and communications system.

Denison, Edward F. *Accounting for United States Economic Growth, 1929–1969*. Brookings 1974 $14.95. ISBN 0-8157-1803-9. Examines determinants of U.S. growth, expanding on earlier findings that 23 percent of U.S. growth resulted from the growth of education.

Feldstein, Martin, ed. *The American Economy in Transition*. U. Ch. Pr. 1982 $17.95. ISBN 0-226-24081-9. Collection of 27 papers delivered at a 1980 conference. Eclectic topics include evolution of financial markets, trends in international trade, and the changing structure of industry.

Grossman, Gene M., and Elhanan Helpman. *Innovation and Growth in the Global Economy*. MIT Pr. 1991 $16.95. ISBN 0-262-57097-1. Argues that economic growth can be achieved by focusing on technological innovation rather than capital accumulation.

Heilbroner, Robert L. *An Inquiry Into the Human Prospect: Updated and Reconsidered for the Nineteen Nineties*. Norton 1991 $8.95. ISBN 0-393-96185-0. Provocative predictions on the future of humanity in the face of rapid population growth, the presence of obliterative weapons, dwindling resources, and international tensions.

Hirschman, Albert O. *The Strategy of Economic Development*. Yale U. Pr. 1961 o.p. Influential work that rejects a "balanced" approach to economic development by developing nations; argues for unbalanced growth with a focus on key industries.

Johnson, Harry G. *Economic Policies toward Less Developed Countries*. Allen & Unwin 1967 o.p. Blueprint for progress based on existing trade, political setting, international aspects, and policy obstacles.

Kalecki, Michal. *Essays on Developing Economies*. Humanities Pr. 1976 o.p. Collection of 11 previously published articles and essays on the problems of underdeveloped nations; includes case studies on Israel, India, Cuba, and Bolivia.

Kuznets, Simon. *Economic Development, the Family and Income Distribution: Selected Essays*. Cambridge U. Pr. 1989 $65.95. ISBN 0-521-34384-4. Excellent survey of Nobel Laureate's work consists of 11 essays on such topics as population structure, developing countries, and demographic change.

———. *Economic Growth of Nations*. Belknap Pr. 1971 o.p. Discusses levels and variability of growth rates, growth of production, sectorial shares of product, and taxes; coverage includes several European countries, Japan, the United States, Canada, and Australia.

———. *Modern Economic Growth*. Yale U. Pr. 1966 o.p. Explains why modern economic growth has spread to such a limited proportion of the total world population. Presents a general framework for growth incorporating population growth, births, deaths, migration, movement away from agriculture, distribution of income.

Lewis, W. Arthur. *The Theory of Economic Growth*. Allen & Unwin 1955 o.p. Classic, influential text on economic development of developing nations. Postulated that the existence of traditional rural sectors would provide an unlimited supply of labor for more advanced sectors.

Malthus, Thomas Robert. *An Essay on the Principle of Population*. Viking Penguin 1983 $6.95. ISBN 0-14-043206-X. Famous argument that, because population grows at an exponential rate and resources at a geometric rate, the world is headed for subsistence conditions.

Meade, James E. *A Neo-Classical Theory of Economic Growth*. Greenwood 1982 repr. of 1962 ed. $39.75. ISBN 0-313-23965-7. Nobel Laureate's scholarly treatise incorporating dynamic equilibrium growth in a static classical economic system.

Mittelman, James H. *Out from Underdevelopment: Prospects for the Third World*. St. Martin 1988 o.p. Lively text analyzing the problems of economic development in radical terms inspired by the Marxian tradition; argues for setting limits to exploitation, less reliance on global capitalism, and a strong reliance on political will.

Rostow, Walt W. *The Stages of Economic Growth: A Non-Communist Manifesto*. Cambridge U. Pr. 1991 $47.50. ISBN 0-521-40070-8. Somewhat simplified analysis of economic growth occurring in separate and identifiable stages; argues that the global model applies to all countries.

ECONOMIC HISTORY

The primary focus of economic history is on narratives of events that are economic in nature—panics, crises, development of technology, revolutions—rather than on theories that purport to explain how economic systems operate. The titles listed below represent only a small fraction of this rich and absorbing literature.

Capie, Forrest H., ed. *Major Inflations in History*. Ashgate Pub. Co. 1991 $159.95. ISBN 1-85278-402-4. Discusses the characteristics and sources of major inflations prior to 1950.

Commons, John R. *A Documentary History of American Industrial Society*. 10 vols. Ed. by Ulrich B. Phillips and others. AMS Pr. 1988 repr. of 1910 ed. $920.00. ISBN 0-404-20330-2. Describes stages of industrial development and the evolution of labor movement starting with the plantation and the frontier.

Fogel, Robert W., and Stanley L. Engerman. *Time on the Cross: The Economics of American Negro Slavery*. U. Pr. of Amer. 1985 $20.75. ISBN 0-8191-4331-6. Controversial thesis that American slavery was so profitable and efficient that only a cataclysmic event such as the Civil War could end it.

Friedman, Milton. *The Great Contraction, 1929–1933*. Nat. Bur. Econ. Res. 1963 $6.95. ISBN 0-685-03492-5. Reprint of Chapter 7 from *Monetary History of the United States*, exploring the depth and persistence of the Great Depression. Blames the severity of the depression on errors in Federal Reserve System policies.

Galbraith, John Kenneth. *The Great Crash of 1929*. HM 1988 $8.70. ISBN 0-395-47805-7. Riveting historical account of the causes and consequences of the stock market crash of 1929 and the ensuing depression.

Josephson, Matthew. *The Robber Barons*. HarBraceJ 1962 $10.95. ISBN 0-15-676790-2. Classic study of the Rockefellers, Morgans, Vanderbilts, and others who seized economic power after the Civil War.

Kindleberger, Charles P. *Manias, Panics, and Crashes*. Basic rev. ed. 1989 $15.00. ISBN 0-465-04404-2. Historical survey and critical appraisal of financial crises from the South Sea Bubble of 1720 to the Great Depression of the 1930s. Argues the need for an international lender of last resort.

Lopez, Robert S. *The Commercial Revolution of the Middle Ages, 950–1350*. Cambridge U. Pr. 1976 o.p. Comprehensive account of medieval economic structure and the birth of the commercial revolution, which led to the development of modern Europe.

Mun, Thomas. *England's Treasure by Forraign [sic] Trade*. Kelley 1986 repr. of 1664 ed. $19.50. ISBN 0-678-06274-9. Classic mercantilist work that argues that a surplus of exports over imports is the source of wealth; but was also one of the first books to argue that a favorable balance of trade with every nation is not required so long as the total exports of a country exceeded its imports.

Neal, Larry. *The Rise of Financial Capitalism: International Capital Markets in the Age of Reason*. Cambridge U. Pr. 1991 $39.95. ISBN 0-521-38205-X. Argues that a sophisticated and smoothly functioning economic system existed from the mercantilist period of the mid-1700s through the Common Market.

Santino, Jack. *Miles of Smiles, Years of Struggle: Stories of Black Pullman Porters*. U. of Ill. Pr. 1989 $21.95. ISBN 0-252-01591-6. A very interesting annotated oral history of the African American sleeping car porters in which the porters tell their own story of their contributions to the labor movement.

Stein, Herbert. *Presidential Economics: The Making of Economic Policy from Roosevelt to Reagan and Beyond*. Am. Enterprise 1988 $12.75. ISBN 0-8447-3656-2. Lucid examination of events, policies, and personalities that shaped the American economy.

Tawney, Richard H. *Religion and the Rise of Capitalism*. Peter Smith 1954 $12.75. ISBN 0-8446-1446-7. Classic study on the development of religious thought and its relation to social and economic developments; excellent treatment of the medieval period, Luther, Calvin, the Church of England, and Puritanism.

Taylor, George Rogers. *The Transportation Revolution, 1815–1860*. M. E. Sharpe 1977 $16.95. ISBN 0-87332-101-4. Comprehensive history that deals not only with transportation in early America, but also manufacturing, foreign trade, banking, and finance.

Webb, Sidney. *English Poor Law History*. 3 vols. Longman 1927–30 o.p. Comprehensive and detailed account of the British Poor laws, their history, problems, and suggestions for improvement.

———. *The History of Trade Unionism*. Longman 1894 o.p. Classic account of the history of trade unions in England; the best historical account of the topic ever written.

Weber, Max. *The Protestant Ethic and the Spirit of Capitalism*. Peter Smith 1984 $20.50. ISBN 0-8446-6118-X. How Calvinism, which produced new attitudes toward the pursuit of wealth, encouraged the development of capitalism.

FINANCIAL ECONOMICS

Financial economics is a sweeping term that views the financial system as one of the mechanisms that helps keep a complex economy functioning. It includes the financial markets, investments, and institutions that assist in the transfer of savings to investors.

Bernstein, Peter L. *Capital Ideas: The Improbable Origins of Modern Wall Street*. Free Pr. 1992 $24.95. ISBN 0-02-903011-0. Lively and entertaining description of ideas that shaped modern finance.

Blair, Margaret M., ed. *The Deal Decade: What Takeovers and Leveraged Buyouts Mean for Corporate Governance*. Brookings 1993 $39.95. ISBN 0-8157-0946-3. Discusses the impact of takeovers, leveraged buyouts, junk bonds, and recapitalization on the relationship between corporate management and the financial markets.

Chernow, Ron. *The House of Morgan: An American Banking Dynasty and the Rise of Modern Finance*. Atlantic Pr. 1990 $29.95. ISBN 0-87113-338-5. Ambitious, well-researched history of an American banking dynasty; provides an engrossing account of four generations of Morgans and their financial empire.

Greider, William. *Secrets of the Temple: How the Federal Reserve Runs the Country*. S&S Trade 1987 $24.95. ISBN 0-671-47989-X. Fascinating, highly praised account of the inside workings of the Federal Reserve System; exceptional coverage of the struggle between capitalists and politicians.

Lorie, J. H., P. Dodd, and M. H. Kimpton. *The Stock Market: Theories and Evidence*. Irwin 1984 $31.95. ISBN 0-256-01917-7. Delightful survey of recent scientific research on the stock market and related investments. Deals with the behavior of the market, the valuation of securities, and portfolio theory.

Markowitz, Harry M. *Portfolio Selection: Efficient Diversification of Investments*. Blackwell Pubs. 1991 $36.95. ISBN 1-55786-108-0. Nobel Prize winner's advanced text, which proposes that investors diversify portfolios on the basis of mean and variance (return and risk), a cornerstone of modern investment theory.

Mayer, Martin. *The Greatest Ever Bank Robbery: The Collapse of the Savings and Loan Industry*. Macmillan 1992 $12.95. ISBN 0-02-012620-4. Engrossing description of the thrift industry failure in the 1980s; traces causes to the relaxation of bank safety standards, political clout of industry, and profits made by vested interests.

———. *Stealing the Market: How the Giant Brokerage Firms, with the Help of the SEC, Stole the Stock Market from Investors*. Basic 1992 $23.00. ISBN 0-465-05362-9. Solid account of how the stock market discriminates against the small investor.

Pizzo, S., M. Fricker, and Paul Muolo. *Inside Job: The Looting of America's Savings and Loans*. HarpC 1991 $10.95. ISBN 0-06-098600-X. Entertaining, factual description of how hometown savings and loans were looted in the 1980s.

Schwager, Jack. *The New Market Wizards: Conversations with America's Top Traders*. Harper Busn. 1993 $22.50. ISBN 0-88730-587-3. Investment advice from professionals on institutional managers, personal portfolios, futures markets, and market instruments.

Sharpe, William F., and Gordon J. Alexander. *Investments*. P-H 1989 $52.00. ISBN 0-13-504382-4. Popular text coauthored by Nobel Laureate Sharpe; covers security markets, valuation of riskless and risky securities, portfolio analysis, capital asset pricing, modern portfolio theory, bonds, stocks, warrants, futures, more.

Stewart, James B. *Den of Thieves*. S&S Trade 1991 $25.00. ISBN 0-671-63802-5. Engrossing story of the insider trading scandals involving Michael Milken, Ivan Boesky, Martin Siegel, and Dennis Levine; written by a Pulitzer Prize winner and *Wall Street Journal* editor.

White, Lawrence J. *The S&L Debacle: Public Policy Lessons for Bank and Thrift Regulation*. OUP 1991 $24.95. ISBN 0-19-506733-9. Clear, concise discussion of S&L failures in the 1980s.

HEALTH, EDUCATION, AND WELFARE

Economists have long understood the value of education as an investment in human capital. Health has emerged recently as a critical issue because of the way it affects productivity, and health care issues are critical because of the cost. Welfare deals with economic efficiency as well as humanitarian issues. Additional titles on welfare can also be found in the section "Poverty, Discrimination, and Distribution of Income."

Aaron, Henry J., and William B. Schwartz. *The Painful Prescription: Rationing Health Care*. Brookings 1984 $28.95. ISBN 0-8157-0034-2. Guide to health care choices and sacrifices; offers suggestions on how to control health care costs.

Becker, Gary S. *Human Capital: A Theoretical and Empirical Analysis with Special Reference to Education*. U. Ch. Pr. 1983 $14.95. ISBN 0-226-04109-3. Examines how investment in people as a factor of production affects earnings and rates of return. Makes use of government statistics on age, education, sex, and race.

———. *A Treatise on the Family*. HUP enl. ed. 1991 $45.00. ISBN 0-674-90698-5. Update of 1981 edition, with new supplements on effects of human capital investment on the division of labor, intergenerational transmission of wealth, and intergenerational mobility.

Blaug, Mark, ed. *The Economic Value of Education*. Ashgate Pub. Co. 1992 $149.95. ISBN 1-85278-542-X. Collection of 27 scholarly essays on the economic value of education; covers human capital theory, the efficiency of schooling and economic development, and the political economy of schooling.

Culyer, A. J., ed. *The Economics of Health*. Ashgate Pub. Co. 1991 $199.95. ISBN 1-85278-1769-9. Two-volume collection of scholarly articles by leading authorities; articles discuss the value of health, influences on health, the demand for health care, the supply of health care, and the evaluation of health care systems.

Dean, Edwin, ed. *Education and Economic Productivity*. Ballinger 1984 o.p. Excellent guide to the role of education in fostering productivity.

Marmor, T. R., J. L. Mashaw, and P. L. Harvey. *America's Misunderstood Welfare State: Persistent Myths, Enduring Realities*. Basic 1990 $22.95. ISBN 0-465-00122-X. Asks if America's social welfare programs are "taking a bum rap." Also examines the origin, purpose, and operation of social security, public assistance, and medical care.

Schultz, Theodore W. *The Economic Value of Education*. Col. U. Pr. 1963 $29.00. ISBN 0-231-02640-4. Discussion of the costs and benefits of education, augmented by federal government statistics.

———. *Investing in People: The Economics of Population Quality*. U. CA Pr. 1981 $27.50. ISBN 0-520-04787-7. Nobel Laureate's rejection of the traditional argument that physical limitations of space, energy, and cropland are decisive constraints to human betterment; argues instead for improvement in quality of population.

Wolfe, John R. *The Coming Health Care Crisis: Who Will Pay for Care for the Aged in the 21st Century?* U. Ch. Pr. 1993 $22.50. ISBN 0-226-90515-2. Assesses current health care problems and programs and long-term care innovations, including HMOs, reverse annuity mortgages, and mandatory public insurance.

INDUSTRIAL ORGANIZATION

Industrial organization deals with the structure of industry. In particular, it deals with the definitions that are used to define an industry, the criteria used to classify firms into industries, and the characteristics and behaviors of firms in those industries. Since many industrial structures involve monopolies and other forms of organization that restrict competition, government regulation and the economics of regulation are also relevant concerns.

Bain, Joe. *Barriers to New Competition: Their Character and Consequences in Manufacturing Industries*. Kelley 1992 repr. of 1956 ed. $39.50. ISBN 0-678-01467-1. One of the first studies to measure barriers of entry into an industry. Treats barriers as having a predictable effect on the conduct and performance of industrial firms.

Baumol, William J., and Sue A. Blackman. *Perfect Markets and Easy Virtue: Business Ethics and the Invisible Hand*. Blackwell Pubs. abr. ed. 1991 $24.95. ISBN 1-55786-248-6. Three lectures dealing with such topics as contestable markets, business ethics, and social policies designed to aid the invisible hand; includes a lengthy listing of Baumol's publications.

Baumol, William J., and others. *Contestable Markets and the Theory of Industrial Structure*. Dryden Pr. rev. ed. 1988 $28.00. ISBN 0-15-513911-8. Drawing heavily on previously published articles, this work on organizational theory examines large, multiproduct enterprises.

Fellner, William. *Competition Among the Few: Oligopoly and Similar Market Structures*. Kelley 1965 repr. of 1949 ed. $37.50. ISBN 0-678-00042-5. Classic, definitive survey of oligopoly theory, bilateral monopoly, and cartels.

Kahn, Alfred E. *The Economics of Regulation: Principles and Institutions*. MIT Pr. 1988 $31.00. ISBN 0-262-6152-3. Classic work on the principles underlying regulatory theory and practice.

Kuenne, Robert E. *The Economics of Oligopolistic Competition: Price and Nonprice Rivalry*. Blackwell Pubs. 1992 $74.95. ISBN 1-55786-301-6. New theory of oligopoly, with advantages over game theory approaches; allows multiobjective optimization by firms, soluble by nonlinear programming techniques.

Magat, Wesley A., and W. Kip Viscusi. *Informational Approaches to Regulation*. MIT Pr.
 1992 $32.50. ISBN 0-262-13277-X. Explores the influence on consumer behavior of
 risk labeling on hazardous household chemicals and pesticides.

Robinson, Joan. *The Economics of Imperfect Competition*. Macmillan 1933 o.p. Classic
 work that introduced the theory of monopolistic competition.

Stigler, George. *The Organization of Industry*. U. Ch. Pr. 1983 $13.95. ISBN 0-226-77432-5.
 Classic text on industrial organization; covers such topics as competition, monopoly,
 and antitrust policy.

Train, Kenneth E. *Optimal Regulation: The Economic Theory of Natural Monopoly*. MIT
 Pr. 1991 $40.00. ISBN 0-262-20084-8. Synthesis of 20 years of theory on the
 regulation of natural monopoly.

Triffin, Robert. *Monopolistic Competition and General Equilibrium Theory*. HUP 1940 o.p.
 Classic early survey focuses on the work of Chamberlin, Robinson, Stackelberg, and
 Pareto.

Williamson, Oliver E., ed. *Industrial Organization*. Ashgate Pub. Co. 1990 $109.95. ISBN
 1-85278-164-5. Collection of 23 classic articles on the topic; contains broad coverage
 of foundations, organization, and strategic behavior.

INTERNATIONAL ECONOMICS

The benefits and gains from trade have been the historical mainstays of
international economics. After World War II, however, attention began to shift
from the benefits of cooperation to the benefits of integration—as evidenced by
the popularity and success of the European Economic Community. The fall of
communism in Eastern Europe makes the issue of international economic
integration as important as ever, and the subject appears with increasing
frequency in the literature.

Blanchard, Olivier, and others. *Reform in Eastern Europe*. MIT Pr. 1991 $8.95. ISBN 0-
 262-52181-4. Describes attempts by new governments of Eastern Europe to move
 from centrally planned to free-market economies.

Bulmer, Simon, and Andrew Scott, eds. *European Integration: The State of the Art*.
 Blackwell Pubs. 1993 $24.95. ISBN 0-631-19039-2. Collection of papers on the recent
 past, present, and future evolution of European integration.

Caves, Richard E. *Trade and Economic Structure, Models and Methods*. HUP 1960 $22.50.
 ISBN 0-674-89881-8. Classic historical survey of international trade from the
 classical period to the 1960s; a standard reference work.

Feldstein, Martin. *The United States in the World Economy*. U. Ch. Pr. 1988 $24.95. ISBN
 0-226-24078-9. Collection of 28 conference papers on subjects including competition
 between the United States and Latin America, innovations in financial markets, and
 farm policies.

Ito, Takatoshi. *The Japanese Economy*. MIT Pr. 1991 $39.95. ISBN 0-262-09029-5. Uses
 standard economic concepts to compare Japan with the United States in terms of
 economic performance, underlying institutions, and government policies.

Johnson, Harry G. *Aspects of the Theory of Tariffs*. HUP 1971 $30.50. ISBN 0-674-04991-8.
 Previously published journal articles offer advanced treatment of tariff theory and
 related issues from the 1950s and 1960s.

Julius, DeAnne. *Global Companies and Public Policy: The Growing Challenge of Foreign
 Direct Investment*. Coun. Foreign 1990 $14.95. ISBN 0-87609-083-8. Discusses how
 the flow of direct investment has outstripped the growth of world trade.

Kindleberger, Charles P. *The International Economic Order: Essays on Financial Crisis
 and International Public Goods*. MIT Pr. 1988 $37.50. ISBN 0-262-11138-1. Collection
 of 16 previously published papers from the 1980s on subjects including bank
 failures, international financial markets, and the European community.

———. *Multinational Excursions*. MIT Pr. 1984 $30.00. ISBN 0-262-11092-X. Eclectic
 selection of 20 assorted readings, from book reviews to congressional testimony.

Lake, David A. *Power, Protection and Free Trade: International Sources of U.S. Commercial Strategies.* Cornell Univ. Pr. 1990 $12.95. ISBN 0-8014-9753-1. Argues that national trade policy should take advantage of current economic realities, rather than relying so much on abstract economic analysis and domestic politics.

Lustig, Nora, Barry P. Bosworth, and Robert Z. Lawrence, eds. *North American Free Trade.* Brookings 1992 $28.95. ISBN 0-8157-5316-0. Collection of six essays examining the effects on the United States of the North American Free Trade Agreement (NAFTA) between Canada, Mexico, and the United States.

Meade, James E. *The Theory of Customs Unions.* Greenwood 1980 repr. of 1955 ed. $35.00. ISBN 0-313-22379-3. Brief, classic treatise by the Nobel Prize winner on the theory and benefits of customs unions.

————. *The Theory of International Economic Policy: Vol. II, Trade and Welfare.* OUP 1955 o.p. Classic reference work for international trade theorists that reviews arguments for trade controls and puts forth a "theory of the second best."

Ohlin, Bertil. *Interregional and International Trade.* HUP 1967 o.p. Classic work by the Nobel Prize winner, first published in 1933, explaining how distribution of productive resources determines international trade patterns.

Rolfe, Sidney E., and James L. Burtle. *The Great Wheel: The World Monetary System, a Reinterpretation.* Random 1974. ISBN 0-8129-0378-1. Survey of the world of international finance, explaining failure of the system of fixed rates agreed to at Bretton Woods.

Sinn, Gerlinde, and Hans-Werner Sinn. *Jumpstart: The Economic Unification of Germany.* MIT Pr. 1993 $24.95. ISBN 0-262-19327-2. Nontechnical account by a well-known German economist, with policy recommendations based on economic reasoning, not politics.

Tinbergen, Jan. *Shaping the World Economy: Suggestions for an International Economic Policy.* Kraus 1962 $10.00. ISBN 0-527-02836-3. Lays the groundwork for international cooperation among advanced industrial countries and developing nations, to be implemented through the United Nations.

Triffin, Robert. *Our International Monetary System: Yesterday, Today and Tomorrow.* Random 1968 o.p. Outstanding historical survey of the international payments mechanism in the pre-1971 floating rate period.

LABOR AND DEMOGRAPHIC ECONOMICS

With the decline of unionism in the United States, the field of labor economics has focused more on the changing nature of the work force and less on the study of the union struggle for labor equality. The study of labor economics now also includes structural and demographic characteristics, such as the size, growth, density, distribution, and even aging of the work force.

Abraham, Katharine G., and Susan N. Houseman. *Job Security in America.* Brookings 1993 $28.95. ISBN 0-8157-0076-8. Examines German experiences with unemployment insurance, job training, and employment-related health care as a guide for U.S. policy makers; useful and informative comparison of job security and related issues.

Bawden, Lee D., and Felicity Skidmore, eds. *Rethinking Employment Policy.* Urban Inst. 1989 $28.75. ISBN 0-87766-458-7. Collection of essays on employment and unemployment by economists from the Urban Institute; includes chapters on job training, protective legislation, and the internationalization of labor markets.

Bluestone, I., R. Montgomery, and J. Owen, eds. *The Aging of the American Work force: Problems, Programs, Policies.* Wayne St. U. Pr. 1990 $19.95. ISBN 0-8143-2174-7. Collection of 28 papers about the aging of the workforce; topics are varied, interesting, and readable.

Bognanno, Mario F., and Morris M. Kleiner, eds. *Labor Market Institutions and the Future Role of Unions.* Blackwell Pubs. 1992 $19.95. ISBN 1-55786-342-3. Collection of articles examining the changing role of unions in the United States during last 40 years. Topics include constraints due to government regulations, the decline of union representation, and labor relations policies of businesses.

Burtless, Gary, ed. *A Future of Lousy Jobs?* Brookings 1990 $31.95. ISBN 0-8157-1180-8. Collection of essays by labor economists analyzing the distribution of jobs and wages over the past 20 years and forecasting future changes; excellent coverage of labor markets and wage inequality.

Commons, John R. *History of Labor in the United States.* 4 vols. Kelley 1966 repr. of 1918 ed. $195.00. ISBN 0-678-00142-1. History and rationale of labor's quest for class equality and dignity under capitalism

Edwards, Richard. *Rights at Work: Employment Relations in the Post-Union Era.* Brookings 1993 $26.95. ISBN 0-8157-2104-8. Argues for common ground between union and management advocates, and discusses such changes in the workplace as mandatory early notification of plant closings, greater rights for disabled workers, and increased protection for older workers.

Kerr, Clark, and Paul D. Staudohar, eds. *Economics of Labor in Industrial Society.* Jossey-Bass 1986 $39.95. ISBN 1-55542-013-3. Approximately 100 excerpts from labor economics literature tracing the evolution of the labor movement.

Kosters, Marvin H. *Workers and Their Wages: Changing Patterns in the United States.* Am. Enterprise 1991 $27.50. ISBN 0-8447-3747-X. Discusses structural, economic, and demographic changes and their effect on wages; also considers the impact of international trade and trade laws, and wage differences between African Americans and whites.

Lozano, Beverly. *The Invisible Work Force: Transforming American Business with Outside and Home-based Workers.* Free Pr. 1989 $19.95. ISBN 0-02-919442-3. Explores the growing phenomenon of a home-based labor force; considers characteristics, benefits, disadvantages, and wage trends.

Pencavel, John. *Labor Markets under Trade Unionism: Employment, Wages, and Hours.* Blackwell Pubs. 1991 $49.95. ISBN 1-55786-077-7. Summarizes recent employment, wages, and hours and sets agenda for future scholarly research.

Solow, Robert M. *The Labor Market as a Social Institution.* Blackwell Pubs. 1990 $21.95. ISBN 1-55786-086-6. A Nobel laureate views the labor market as a social institution; examines implications for economic policy in the United States and Western Europe.

Stark, Oded. *The Migration of Labor.* Blackwell Pubs. 1991 $54.95. ISBN 1-55786-030-0. Relates the process of development to migration behavior.

Ulman, Lloyd, Barry Eichengreen, and William T. Dickens, eds. *Labor and an Integrated Europe.* Brookings 1993 $36.95. ISBN 0-8157-8682-4. Collection of papers discussing the increased mobility of labor due to the integration of the European Economic Community; focuses on problem areas of bargaining, work rules, training programs, and the repercussions for labor markets elsewhere.

Wise, David A., ed. *The Economics of Aging.* U. Ch. Pr. 1989 $56.00. ISBN 0-226-90295-1. Collection of papers on a broad spectrum of aging issues, including housing, living arrangements, family support, labor force participation, and retirement.

LAW AND ECONOMICS

The legal system is an important part of the economies of most free world countries. Contract law is used to ensure that all parties to an agreement carry out their sides of the bargain. Constitutional law has a bearing on economics and economic policy, because it may set limits on what can and cannot be done. Economic analysis has even been applied to legal penalties to see if they adequately reflect the damage caused by illegal economic behaviors. Finally, the economic consequences of some activities or structures—such as monopolies—are such that laws have been created to govern or regulate such activities.

Adams, Walter, and James W. Brock. *Antitrust Economics on Trial: A Dialogue on the New Laissez-Faire*. Princeton U. Pr. 1991 $29.95. ISBN 0-691-04291-8. Discusses the role of antitrust policy in a market economy; presented as a dialogue in a courtroom setting. An interesting, balanced presentation that should appeal to the general reader.

Bebchuk, Lucian Arye, ed. *Corporate Law and Economic Analysis*. Cambridge U. Pr. 1990 $38.36. ISBN 0-521-36054-4. Short collection of scholarly articles that use economic analysis to analyze key issues in corporate law.

Bork, Robert H. *The Antitrust Paradox: A Policy at War with Itself*. Basic 1980 o.p. Describes antitrust as an area in crisis, because the Supreme Court has, without adequate explanation, inhibited or destroyed many useful businesses and practices.

Breit, William, and Kenneth G. Elzinga. *Antitrust Penalty Reform: An Economic Analysis*. Am. Enterprise 1986 $14.00. ISBN 0-8447-3600-7. Uses cost-benefit analysis to analyze the penalties imposed after public prosecution; written by leading experts in the field.

Brock, James W., and Kenneth G. Elzinga. *Antitrust, the Market, and the State: The Contributions of Walter Adams*. M. E. Sharpe 1991 $39.95. ISBN 0-87332-854-X. Collection of 16 articles on the philosophy of law and economics, the U.S. Constitution and the market economy, and issues in capitalism.

Hirsch, Werner Z. *Law and Economics: An Introductory Analysis*. Acad. Pr. 1988 $49.95. ISBN 0-12-349481-8. Examines the relationship between economic principles and law, with discussion of landlord-tenant, zoning, tort, contract, and criminal law.

Jackson, John. *The World Trading System: Law and the Policy of International Economic Relations*. MIT Pr. 1989 $17.95. ISBN 0-262-60021-8. Introduction to the legal aspects of international trade.

Larner, Robert J., and James W. Meehan, eds. *Economics and Antitrust Policy*. Greenwood 1989 $49.95. ISBN 0-89930-386-2. Multiauthored text that includes discussions of monopoly, merger policies in the 1970s and 1980s, antitrust laws, and vertical price restraints.

McKay, John P., and others. *Industrial Development and the Social Fabric*. Vol. 3 *Law, Economics and Public Policy*. Jai Pr. 1984 $73.25. ISBN 0-89232-396-5. Introduces the field of law and economics; examines the economics of property rights, public choice theory, and critical legal studies. Employs analytical tools to analyze the relationship between legal institutions and the character of economic life.

Posner, Richard A. *Economic Analysis of Law*. Little 1986 $36.00. ISBN 0-316-71438-0. Relates economic theory to, among other things, common law, public regulation of markets, and income distribution.

Weaver, Suzanne. *Decision to Prosecute: Organization and Public Policy in the Antitrust Division*. MIT Pr. 1977 $30.00. ISBN 0-262-23085-2. Study of the Antitrust Division in the U.S. Department of Justice; discusses its sense of history, attention given to policy, regulations, and decisions to prosecute.

MACROECONOMICS AND FISCAL POLICY

Macroeconomics deals with the economics of the whole—as in the entire economy versus an individual or a firm. Fiscal policies are policies that normally involve federal spending or taxation, or both, to affect the allocation of resources and the distribution of output. As such, fiscal policies are designed to deal with inflation, unemployment, stagflation, productivity, economic growth, and economic stability. Fiscal policies can also take the form of regulation, but they do not deal with actions involving the supply of money or the cost of credit.

Block, Fred L. *Postindustrial Possibilities: A Critique of Economic Discourse*. U. CA Pr. 1990 $37.50. ISBN 0-520-06988-9. Controversial but scholarly argument that the core of neoclassical economics has been weakened by the shift to a service economy and the adoption of computer automation.

Haberler, Gottfried. *Problem of Stagflation: Reflections on the Microfoundations of Macroeconomic Theory and Policy.* Am. Enterprise 1985 $12.50. ISBN 0-8447-3578-7. Examines the policy prescriptions of Keynesians, monetarists, and the school of rational expectations as they apply to the stagflation of the 1970s; argues that demand-oriented and supply-side policies can complement each other.

Hailstones, Thomas J., ed. *Viewpoints on Supply-Side Economics.* P-H 1983 $30.00. ISBN 0-8359-8386-2. Examines doubts about Keynesian policies, fiscal effects of supply-side economics, supply-side control of inflation, Reaganomics, and problems with supply-side policies.

Heilbroner, Robert, and Peter Bernstein. *The Debt and the Deficit: False Alarms and Real Possibilities.* Norton 1989 $12.95. ISBN 0-393-02752. Challenges the conventional view that the federal debt saps U.S. economic strength, arguing that it helps finance growth

Hoover, Kevin D., ed. *New Classical Macroeconomics.* Ashgate Pub. Co. 1992 $489.95. ISBN 1-85278-571-1. Extensive three-volume collection of 86 scholarly articles on such topics as general equilibrium, the effectiveness of government policy, econometric applications, monetary theory, business cycles, and economic growth.

Johnson, Harry G. *On Economics and Society: Selected Essays.* HUP 1982 $11.95. ISBN 0-674-04991-8. Twenty-one essays on topics ranging from the Keynesian revolution to the distribution of income.

Krugman, Paul. *The Age of Diminished Expectations: U.S. Economic Policy in the 1990s.* MIT Pr. 1992 $10.95. ISBN 0-262-61078-7. Examines the impact of the Gulf War, trade deficits, and the budget deficit on what is described as a wealthy nation that fails to live up to its promise.

Leijonhufvud, Axel. *On Keynesian Economics and the Economics of Keynes.* OUP 1968 o.p. This scholarly and controversial revisionist treatise on Keynes argues that Keynesian economics is disequilibrium economics.

Modigliani, Franco. *The Debate Over Stabilization Policy and Other Macroeconomic Issues.* Cambridge U. Pr. 1986 $49.95. ISBN 0-521-26790-0. Four lectures, delivered in 1977 and previously unpublished; topics include aggregate demand and the control of inflation, Keynesian and monetarist stabilization policies, monetary mechanics and financial structure, and accumulation of wealth.

Reich, Robert B., and Ira C. Magaziner. *Minding America's Business: The Decline and Rise of the America Economy.* HarBraceJ 1982 o.p. Authors advocate such measures as federal loan guarantees, tax credits, R&D subsidies, and retraining programs to increase productivity.

Schelling, Thomas C. *Micromotives and Macrobehavior.* Norton 1978 $9.95. ISBN 0-393-09009-4. Explains why behavior of aggregates is more than the simple sum of individual behaviors; both serious and whimsical examples are applied to the social problems of segregation and distribution of income.

Schumacher, E. F. *Small is Beautiful: Economics As If People Mattered.* Borgo Pr. 1991 $25.00. ISBN 0-8095-9115-4. Criticizes conventional economic theory as too scientific; having lost sight of people's spirit, it measures only their low-grade behavior.

Stein, Herbert. *The Fiscal Revolution in America.* Am. Enterprise rev. ed. 1990 $16.50. ISBN 0-8447-3737-2. Delightful chronicle of radical change, from Hoover to Kennedy; deemphasizes a balanced budget in favor of increased government spending to promote stability and growth.

Tobin, James. *Asset Accumulation and Economic Activity: Reflections on Contemporary Macroeconomic Theory.* U. Ch. Pr. $5.95. ISBN 0-226-80502-6. Nobel Laureate's short collection of previously unpublished lectures on the real balance effect, expectations and stabilization policies, government deficits, and capital accumulation.

――――. *Essays in Economics, Vol 1: Macroeconomics.* MIT Pr. 1987 $67.50. ISBN 0-262-20062-7. Collection of 24 essays on macroeconomic theory, economic growth, and monetary and fiscal policy.

――――. *Policies for Prosperity: Essays in a Keynesian Mode.* Ed. by Peter M. Jackson. Brookings 1989 $50.00. ISBN 0-8157-8486-4. Over 40 policy-oriented essays for general readers and economists alike, with titles that include "Does Fiscal Policy Matter?" and "Yes, Virginia, There Are Laffer Curves."

Weintraub, Sidney. *Our Stagflation Malaise: Halting Inflation and Unemployment.* Greenwood 1981 $39.00. ISBN 0-89930-005-7. Urges a corporate tax-based incomes policy in order to slow the rate of inflation.

MATHEMATICAL AND QUANTITATIVE METHODS

Mathematics has long been a useful tool for economists. Some problems, such as general equilibrium, game theory, and input-output analysis, are difficult to solve without extensive applications of mathematics. As a result, the field of econometrics—the merger of statistical and quantitative techniques with economic tools—soon evolved and proved its value to the profession. The selections below explain the nature of these quantitative methods and provide illustrations of their use.

Brock, W. A., D. A. Hsieh, and B. LeBaron. *Nonlinear Dynamics, Chaos, and Instability.* MIT Pr. 1991 $32.50. ISBN 0-262-02329-6. Explains new statistical methods useful for testing for chaos in data sets. Discusses how the principles of chaos theory can be applied to economics and finance, the changing structure of stock market returns, and foreign exchange.

Debreu, Gerard. *Mathematical Economics: Twenty Papers of Gerard Debreu.* Cambridge U. Pr. 1986 $54.95. ISBN 0-521-23736-X. Highly mathematical collection of papers, some never before published, on advanced microeconomic topics by a Nobel Prize winner. Includes discussions of social equilibrium existence theorems, limit theorems, and preference orderings.

———. *The Theory of Value: An Axiomatic Analysis of Economic Equilibrium.* Yale U. Pr. 1972 $8.95. ISBN 0-300-01559-3. Rigorous, mathematical treatment of general equilibrium theory. Deals with an explanation of commodity prices resulting from competition in a private economy and the role of prices in an optimal state of equilibrium.

Fudenberg, Drew, and Jean Tirole. *Game Theory.* MIT Pr. 1991 $37.50. ISBN 0-262-06141-4. Advanced text covering noncooperative theory principles, strategic form games, Nash equilibria, subgame perfection, repeated games, and games with incomplete information; has applications to both economics and political science.

Harvey, A. C. *The Econometric Analysis of Time Series.* MIT Pr. 1990 $49.50. ISBN 0-262-08189-X. Focuses on statistical aspects of model building.

Kennedy, Peter. *A Guide to Econometrics.* MIT Pr. 1992 $30.00. ISBN 0-262-11160-8. Popular text characterized by intuitive approach that minimizes technical detail. Coverage includes econometric specification, time series, robust estimation, calculation of variances, and asymptotics.

Klein, Lawrence R., and W. Welfe. *Advanced Lectures in Econometrics.* Elsevier 1984 $37.50. ISBN 0-444-86676-0. Covers model structures, simulations, validations, and dynamic analysis; a highly quantitative work.

Leontief, Wassily. *Input-Output Economics.* OUP 1986 $26.00. ISBN 0-19-503527-5. Collection of 11 previously published essays; an excellent and generally nonquantitative introduction to input-output models. Also contains interesting chapters on methodology and the application of input-output models to disarmament and foreign trade.

Luce, R. Duncan, and Howard Raiffa. *Games and Decisions: Introduction and Critical Survey.* Wiley 1967 o.p. Classic, comprehensive survey of game theory analysis and related decision-making models.

Neumann, John von, and Oskar Morgenstern. *Theory of Games and Economic Behavior.* Princeton U. Pr. 1980 $85.00. ISBN 0-691-04183-0. Difficult but standard reference in the field; introduced zero-sum games to economics.

Ostaszewski, Adam. *Mathematics in Economics.* Blackwell Pub. 1993 $54.95. ISBN 0-631-18055-9. Rigorous application of mathematics to economic problems. Coverage includes sets and numbers, matrices and vectors, discrete variables, functions, Eigenvalues and Eigenvectors, limits and their uses, and much more.

Samuelson, Paul. *Foundations of Economic Analysis.* HUP Economic Studies: No. 80. enl. ed. 1983 $34.95. ISBN 0-674-31301-1. Mathematical treatment of economic theories and principles; revised doctoral dissertation of first U.S. Nobel Laureate in economics.

Tinbergen, Jan. *World Security and Equity.* Ashgate Pub. Co. 1990 $41.95. ISBN 1-85278-187-4. Terse, advanced econometric model of two-world (East-West and North-South) and three-world (includes China and developing nations) trade models by a Nobel Prize-winning economist.

Zeckhauser, Richard, ed. *Strategy and Choice.* MIT Pr. 1991 $37.50. ISBN 0-262-24033-5. Essays on game theory by scholars in economics, psychology, philosophy, and political science.

MICROECONOMICS

Microeconomics deals with the decision making of small units, such as individuals and firms. Traditionally, welfare and utility theory have dominated the study of microeconomics. Production, motivation, decision making, and conflict resolution are also part of this literature.

Baumol, William J. *Welfare Economics and the Theory of the State.* HUP 1969 o.p. Comprehensive overview of welfare theory, including discussions of external economies and economic theory of the state.

Frisch, Ragnar. *New Methods of Measuring Marginal Utility.* Porcupine Pr. 1978 repr. of 1932 ed. $25.00. ISBN 0-87991-863-2. Early attempt by first Nobel Laureate in economics to measure utility; long since rejected, but of historical interest.

———. *Theory of Production.* Rand McNally 1965 o.p. Classic microeconomic text.

Hirschman, Albert O. *Exit, Voice and Loyalty: Responses to Decline in Firms, Organizations and States.* HUP 1970 $7.95. ISBN 0-674-27660-4. Examines individuals' reactions to organizational decline, including "exiting" (leaving) and "voicing" (trying to change events), plus complications of loyalty that explain a wide range of behavior in firms and other organizations.

Kuenne, Robert E., ed. *Microeconomics.* Ashgate Pub. Co. 1990 $329.95. ISBN 1-85278-307-9. Three-volume collection of 54 classic articles in microeconomics; includes such topics as methodology, consumer decision making, price strategies in alternative market structures, monopolistic competition, market adjustments, and social welfare.

Mishan, E. J. *Welfare Economics: Ten Introductory Essays.* Random 1969 o.p. Standard reference by one of the leading writers in field.

Schelling, Thomas C. *The Strategy of Conflict.* HUP 1960 $10.95. ISBN 0-674-84031-3. Lucid, classic work in the bargaining theory literature.

Scitovsky, Tibor. *The Joyless Economy: The Psychology of Human Satisfaction.* OUP rev. ed. 1992 $29.95. ISBN 0-19-507346-0. Provocative, incisive attack on the "rational individual" assumption of economists; argues that individuals crave novelty and variety and that some economic activity is motivated by other than the traditional satisfaction of wants.

Shackle, George L. S. *Expectations in Economics.* Hyperion Conn. 1990 repr. of 1952 ed. $22.00. ISBN 0-88355-816-5. Ingenious attempt to incorporate uncertainty, or "surprise" functions, into micro foundations of economics.

Stigler, George. *The Theory of Price.* Macmillan 1987. ISBN 0-02-417400-9. Classic advanced microeconomic text.

Zeckhauser, Richard, ed. *Strategy and Choice*. MIT Pr. 1991 $37.50. ISBN 0-262-24033-5. Collection of essays on game theory by scholars in economics, psychology, philosophy, and political science.

MONETARY ECONOMICS AND POLICY

Monetary policy deals with the actions and institutions that affect the supply of money and the cost of credit. Some classic studies have dealt with the history of money and the role it has played in the economy. Other works have focused on how the supply of money and the cost of credit can be used as tools to promote economic stability and growth. The Federal Reserve System and those who manage it play a key role, because they have the power to conduct monetary policy.

Brunner, Karl, and A. Meltzer. *Monetary Economics*. Blackwell Pubs. 1989 $45.00. ISBN 0-631-16335-2. Collection of papers on such topics as monetary policy, the Federal Reserve, and monetary policy reform.

Burns, Arthur F. *Reflections of an Economic Policy Maker: Speeches and Congressional Statements, 1969–1978*. Am. Enterprise 1978 $27.25. ISBN 0-8447-3333-4. Partial collection of speeches, pronouncements, and personal philosophies by a former chairman of the Federal Reserve; offers rare insight into monetary policy decisions at the highest level.

Friedman, Milton. *Dollars and Deficits*. P-H 1968 o.p. Collection of the author's best writings on the role and importance of money; topics include inflation, monetary policy, the balance of payments and exchange rates, and the role of an independent monetary authority.

_____. *The Great Contraction, 1929–1933*. Nat. Bur. Econ. Res. 1963 $6.95. ISBN 0-685-03492-5. Explores the depth and persistence of the Great Depression of the 1930s; blames the severity of the depression on errors in Federal Reserve System policies.

Glasner, David. *Free Banking and Monetary Reform*. Cambridge U. Pr. 1989 $32.50. ISBN 0-521-36175-3. Argues for the return to free banking wherein banks would have the power to issue their own notes; the proposal is set in the context of historical performance of the U.S. banking system.

Hicks, John R. *A Market Theory of Money*. OUP 1989 $36.00. ISBN 0-19-828724-0. Analyzes the role of money in markets, money and finance, monetary problems, and policies.

Kettl, Donald F. *Leadership at the Fed*. Yale U. Pr. 1988 $13.00. ISBN 0-300-04363-5. Examines the Federal Reserve's power in the economic policy arena; extensively researched and intended for a broad audience.

Laidler, David E. *The Demand for Money: Theories, Evidence, and Problems*. HarpC 1992 $26.00. ISBN 0-06-501098-1. Extremely comprehensive yet eminently readable text.

Mayer, Thomas. *Elements of Monetary Policy*. Random 1968 o.p. Short primer on goals, tools, strengths, and weaknesses of monetary policy; provides an excellent introduction for the general reader.

_____, ed. *Monetary Theory*. Ashgate Pub. Co. 1990 $72.95. ISBN 1-85278-180-7. Collection of 20 classic articles.

Patinkin, Don. *Money, Interest, and Prices: An Integration of Monetary and Value Theory*. MIT Pr. 1989 $52.50. ISBN 0-262-16114-1. Monumental work, scholarly and difficult for beginners.

Pierce, James L. *The Future of Banking*. Yale U. Pr. 1991 $25.00. ISBN 05058-5. Reviews the banking crisis of the 1980s and 1990s; suggests ideas for reform of the banking system.

POVERTY, DISCRIMINATION, AND THE
DISTRIBUTION OF INCOME

Economists have long been concerned with the problems of poverty, discrimination, and the distribution of income because of the implications these issues have for the economic goals of efficiency and equality. There is less agreement, however, about how to deal with these issues. The works below were selected because they offer a wide range of views, descriptions, and solutions.

Auletta, Ken. *The Underclass.* Random 1983 $7.95. ISBN 0-394-71388-5. Examines why most efforts to solve the problems of the underclass are expensive and only partially successful.

Brittain, John A. *The Inheritance of Economic Status.* Bks. Demand 1977 $49.80. ISBN 0-317-20776-8. Explores the effects of family economic status on educational attainment and the income level of children.

Cherry, Robert. *Discrimination: Its Economic Impact on Blacks, Women, and Jews.* Free Pr. 1989 $35.00. ISBN 0-669-20418-8. Examines the role of discrimination in the distribution of income; discusses the economic status of minority groups.

Gilder, George. *Wealth and Poverty.* Bantam 1982 $5.95. ISBN 0-553-26305-6. Supply-side description of poverty and suggestions for curtailing it.

Harrington, Michael. *The New American Poverty.* Viking Penguin 1985 $8.95. ISBN 0-14-008112-7. Focus on poverty and social programs in the 20 years following President Johnson's War on Poverty.

————. *The Other America.* Viking Penguin 1971 $7.95. ISBN 0-14-021308-2. Portrait of poverty in the United States, from New York's Bowery to the fruit orchards of the west coast.

Kuznets, Simon. *Economic Development, the Family and Income Distribution: Selected Essays.* Cambridge U. Pr. 1989 $65.95. ISBN 0-521-34384-4. Collection of 11 articles dealing with economic growth, population structure, less developed countries, demographic change, and related topics. An excellent survey of the Nobel Laureate's work.

Myrdal, Gunnar. *The Challenge of World Poverty: A World Anti-Poverty Program in Outline.* Pantheon 1970 o.p. Based on 1969 lectures at Johns Hopkins University; covers agriculture, population, education, trade, capital movements, foreign aid, and other policies to reduce world poverty.

Osberg, Lars, ed. *Economic Inequality and Poverty.* M. E. Sharpe 1991 $39.95. ISBN 0-87332-528-1. Collection of articles focusing on the concepts and measurement of poverty, the concentration of wealth, and the implication for social issues; intended for a broad audience.

Rodgers, Harrell, Jr. *Poor Women, Poor Families: The Economic Plight of America's Female-Headed Households.* M. E. Sharpe 1990 $35.00. ISBN 0-87332-594-X. Explores the problem of poverty, in particular the growth of poverty among female-headed households; reviews state-level social welfare programs.

Schultz, Theodore W. *The Economics of Being Poor.* Blackwell Pubs. 1993 $39.95. ISBN 1-55786-320-2. Nobel Laureate discusses the economics of acquiring skills and knowledge, investment in the quality of population, and the increasing economic importance of human capital.

Sen, Amartya K. *Poverty and Famines: An Essay on Entitlements and Deprivation.* OUP 1981 $18.95. ISBN 0-19-828463-2. Argues that famines in developing nations are caused not by droughts or floods but by lack of access to an existing food supply.

Ward, Barbara. *The Rich Nations and the Poor Nations.* Norton 1962 $5.95. ISBN 0-393-00746-4. Popular and passionately written early study about the rich and poor nations; discusses the economics and politics of development.

Wilson, William Julius. *The Truly Disadvantaged: The Inner City, the Underclass, and Public Policy.* U. Ch. Pr. 1987 $19.95. ISBN 0-226-90130-0. Compelling portrait of the deteriorating economic and social condition of poor urban blacks. Recommends a comprehensive social agenda to improve the life chances of the truly disadvantaged.

PUBLIC ECONOMICS

Public economics deals primarily with the role of government and public finance. Individual issues involve public choice, economic efficiency, and the politician's quest for equity, and the appropriate mix of taxation and expenditure. It is one of the newer fields in economics and offers some interesting literature.

Atkinson, A. B., ed. *Modern Public Finance*. Ashgate Pub. Co. 1991 $219.95. ISBN 1-85278-153-X. Contains 43 classic articles on taxation and public spending, the effects of taxes on households and firms, the theory of public goods and public expenditures, the theory of tax reform, the national debt, and fiscal policy.

Baumol, William J. *Superfairness: Applications and Theory*. MIT Pr. 1986 $32.50. ISBN 0-262-02234-6. Bridges the gap between economists' concept of efficiency and politicians' concern for equity.

Blinder, Alan S. *Hard Heads, Soft Hearts; Tough-Minded Economics for a Just Society*. Addison-Wesley 1987 $17.95. ISBN 0-201-11504-2. Describes why economists generally agree on policy, while "politically correct" implementation by politicians results in policy failure.

Brown, C. V., and Peter Jackson. *Public Sector Economics*. Blackwell Pubs. 1990 $29.95. ISBN 0-631-16208-9. Leading text on the relationship between public expenditure and the behavior of individuals, households, and firms.

Buchanan, James M., and Gordon Tulloch. *The Calculus of Consent: Logical Foundations of Constitutional Democracy*. U. of Mich. Pr. 1962 $16.95. ISBN 0-472-06100-3. Explores why rational individuals will accept a constitution from government that restricts individual actions.

Downs, Anthony. *An Economic Theory of Democracy*. HarpC 1990 $26.50. ISBN 0-06-041750-1. Influential work in public choice theory that relates political phenomena to the behavior of voters who respond to the "cost" of obtaining information about candidates and parties.

Maier, Mark H. *The Data Game: Controversies in Social Science Statistics*. M. E. Sharpe 1991 $45.00. ISBN 0-89332-588-5. Discusses the collection and interpretation of public data and the use of statistics to justify public policies; promotes a rather skeptical view of validity and the use of data.

Melman, Seymour. *The Permanent War Economy: American Capitalism in Decline*. S&S Trade 1985 $9.95. ISBN 0-671-60643-3. Controversial work alleging that the modern defense industry weakens the economy's ability to produce profits.

Minarik, Joseph J., ed. *Making America's Budget Policy: From the 1980s to the 1990s*. M. E. Sharpe 1990 $42.50. ISBN 0-87332-573-7. Collection of essays describing the evolution of federal budget policy and tax reform during the 1980s.

Mishan, E. J. *Cost Benefit Analysis*. Unwin Hyman 1988 $24.95. ISBN 0-04-445092-3. Definitive exposition of cost benefit methodology, with examples ranging from the simple to the advanced.

Musgrave, Richard A., and Peggy B. Musgrave. *Public Finance in Theory and Practice*. McGraw 1989 $36.68. ISBN 0-07-044127-3. Updates definitive text of the 1960s, *The Theory of Public Finance*. Includes a greater focus on institutional aspects of government.

Rowley, Charles K., ed. *Public Choice Theory*. Elgar 1993 $399.95. ISBN 1-85278-160-2. Extensive collection of 74 scholarly articles; topics include voting behavior, interest groups, the characteristics of political equilibrium, the role of the executive and the judiciary, the bureaucracy, and constitutional economic policy.

Stein, Herbert, and Murray Foss. *An Illustrated Guide to the American Economy*. Am. Enterprise 1991 $39.95. ISBN 0-8447-3800-X. Examines various myths about the

American economy, such as the idea that the United States is falling behind Japan and that the U.S. taxes and spends more or less than other nations.

Tucker, William. *The Excluded Americans: Homelessness and Housing Policies*. Regnery Gateway 1990 $24.95. ISBN 0-89526-551-6. Analysis of housing economics as applied to the homeless; very readable and excellent review of public housing policies and their economic consequences.

Vanek, Jaroslav. *The Participatory Economy: An Evolutionary Hypothesis and Strategy for Development*. Cornell Univ. Pr. 1971 $38.50. ISBN 0-8014-9148-7. Proposes a participatory economy, with producer and consumer cooperatives sharing production and distribution decisions.

Wolf, Charles. *Markets or Governments: Choosing Between Imperfect Alternatives*. MIT Pr. 1990 $11.95. ISBN 0-262-73092-8. Suggests a framework parallel to the market to analyze the shortcomings of government. Compares market and nonmarket alternatives and other issues in public finance and public choice.

CHRONOLOGY OF AUTHORS

Smith, Adam. 1723–1790
Malthus, Thomas Robert. 1766–1834
Ricardo, David. 1772–1823
Mill, John Stuart. 1806–1873
Marx, Karl Heinrich. 1818–1883
Engels, Friedrich. 1820–1895
Jevons, William Stanley. 1835–1882
George, Henry. 1839–1897
Marshall, Alfred. 1842–1924
Clark, John Bates. 1847–1938
Pareto, Vilfredo. 1848–1923
Wicksell, Knut. 1851–1926
Veblen, Thorstein. 1857–1929
Webb, Beatrice. 1858–1943
Webb, Sidney. 1859–1947
Commons, John Rogers. 1862–1945
Fisher, Irving. 1867–1947
Mitchell, Wesley Clair. 1874–1948
Keynes, John Maynard. 1883–1946
Schumpeter, Joseph Alois. 1883–1950

Knight, Frank Hyneman. 1885–1962
Hansen, Alvin. 1887–1975
Viner, Jacob. 1892–1970
Hayek, Friedrich August von. 1899–1992
Kuznets, Simon Smith. 1901–1985
Neumann, John von. 1903–1957
Robinson, Joan. 1903–1983
Hicks, Sir John Richard. 1904–1989
Leontief, Wassily. 1906–
Galbraith, John Kenneth. 1908–
Myrdal, Gunnar. 1908–1987
Boulding, Kenneth. 1910–
Stigler, George Joseph. 1911–1991
Friedman, Milton. 1912–
Samuelson, Paul Anthony. 1915–
Klein, Lawrence Robert. 1920–
Arrow, Kenneth Joseph. 1921–
Becker, Gary Stanley. 1930–

ARROW, KENNETH JOSEPH. 1921– (NOBEL PRIZE 1972)

Kenneth Arrow, an American economist, is known for his contributions to mathematical economics. Educated at City College of New York and Columbia University, he has taught at Stanford and Harvard universities. He was awarded the Nobel Prize (jointly with SIR JOHN RICHARD HICKS) for his work in welfare economics and the theory of social choice.

The possibility of a theory of social choice—collective choice based on the preferences of individuals—has intrigued economists for some time. Arrow's Ph.D. thesis, published as *Social Choice and Individual Values* (1951), was the seminal work in the field of social choice theory and showed the impossibility of deriving efficient group outcomes based on the aggregate of rational individual preferences. In a later book, *Social Choice and Multicriterion Decision-Making* (1986), which was coauthored with Herve Raynaud, Arrow dealt with additional decision criteria and alternatives in a search for efficient group outcomes.

Despite the importance of these two works, the general reader may find them somewhat difficult and abstruse.

The work of most general equilibrium economists like Arrow is seldom well known outside the economics profession. Even so, Arrow's range of interests extends far beyond the straightforward mathematical treatment of economics. For example, he is an outspoken advocate of the decontrol of oil prices.

BOOKS BY ARROW

Collected Papers of Kenneth J. Arrow, Vol. 1 *Social Choice and Justice.* Belknap Pr. 1983 $25.00. ISBN 0-674-13760-4. Vol. 2 *General Equilibrium.* HUP 1983 $30.00. ISBN 0-674-13761-2. Vol. 3 *Individual Choice under Certainty and Uncertainty.* Belknap Pr. 1984 $30.00. ISBN 0-674-13762-0. Vol. 4 *The Economics of Information.* Belknap Pr. 1984 $30.00. ISBN 0-674-13763-9. Vol. 5 *Production and Capital.* Belknap Pr. 1985 $35.00. ISBN 0-674-13777-9. Vol. 6 *Applied Economics.* Belknap Pr. 1985 $30.00. ISBN 0-674-13778-7

General Competitive Analysis. Advanced Textbooks in Economics: Vol. 12. Elsevier 1977 $44.00. ISBN 0-7204-0750-8. Advanced, highly quantitative text dealing with markets, prices, and equilibrium.

Petroleum Price Regulation: Should We Decontrol? (coauthored with Joseph P. Kalt). Am. Enterprise 1979 o.p. Short essay booklet arguing that the decontrol of petroleum prices is preferable to controls, even if the impact will be uneven.

Public Investment, the Rate of Return and Optimal Fiscal Policy. (coauthored with Mordecai Kurz). Bks. Demand $62.00. ISBN 0-685-12279-4. Highly quantitative treatment of the topic that includes coverage of methodological issues, methods of optimization over time, and optimal investment policy with imperfect capital markets.

Social Choice and Individual Values. Yale U. Pr. 1970 $8.95. ISBN 0-300-01364-7

Social Choice and Multicriterion Decision-Making (coauthored with Herve Raynaud). MIT Pr. 1986 o.p.

BOOKS ABOUT ARROW

Breit, William, and Roger W. Spencer, eds. *Lives of the Laureates: Ten Nobel Economists.* MIT Pr. 1990 $19.95. ISBN 0-262-02308-3. Includes an interesting and informative chapter covering Arrow's life, influences, and works.

Heller, W. P., R. M. Starr, and D. A. Starrett. *Social Choice and Public Decision Making: Essays in Honor of Kenneth Arrow.* Cambridge U. Pr. 1986 $49.95. ISBN 0-521-30454-7. Collection of 32 essays on aspects of Arrow's work, including social choice, public sector decision making, general equilibrium, and micro foundations of macro. Contains a brief biographic section.

Spiegel, Henry W., and Warren J. Samuels. *Contemporary Economists in Perspective.* Jai Pr. 1984 o.p. Appraisals by leading economists on the contributions of 38 other leading economists; chapter on Arrow relates his work to that of others and places him in historical perspective.

BECKER, GARY STANLEY. 1930– (NOBEL PRIZE 1992)

Gary Stanley Becker is an American economist known for his efforts to extend economic analysis to social problems, especially those involving race and gender discrimination, crime and punishment, and the formation and dissolution of families. The essence of his contribution is that human behavior is rationally based on self-interest and the economic incentives of the marketplace.

Cost-benefit analysis is central to Becker's analysis of social phenomena. The following statement, made shortly after he received the Nobel Prize in 1992, illustrates the approach: "The number of children a couple has depends on the costs and benefits of child rearing. . . . Couples tend to have fewer children when the wife works and has a better-paying job, when subsidies and tax deductions for dependents are smaller, when the cost of educating and training children rises, and so forth." Likewise, Becker argues that "couples divorce when they no longer believe they are better off by staying married."

Becker's ability to analyze social issues from a uniquely economic perspective has generated a substantial following. His work has influenced a broad range of educators, scholars, and government officials, and is helping to popularize and demystify the central tenets of economic theory. Becker, who studied at Princeton University and the University of Chicago, is currently a professor of economics at the University of Chicago and a fellow of the Hoover Institution. He has received numerous awards, including the prestigious John Bates Clark award from the American Economic Association in 1967.

BOOKS BY BECKER

The Economic Approach to Human Behavior. U. Ch. Pr. 1978 $15.95. ISBN 0-226-04112-3. Collection of journal articles, some mathematical, covering discrimination, law and politics, irrational behavior, marriage, fertility and the family, and social interactions.

The Economics of Discrimination. U. Ch. Pr. rev. 2nd ed. 1971 $8.95. ISBN 0-226-04116-6. This expanded doctoral dissertation is a rigorous, occasionally mathematical, treatment of discrimination.

Human Capital: A Theoretical and Empirical Analysis with Special Reference to Education. U. Ch. Pr. 1983 $14.95. ISBN 0-226-04109-3. Formal study of investment in people as a factor of production.

A Treatise on the Family. HUP 1981 $27.50. ISBN 0-674-90696-9. Examines how the laws of supply and demand and other economic incentives affect the decision to have children.

A Treatise on the Family. HUP enl. ed. 1991 $45.00. ISBN 0-674-90698-5. Earlier edition updated, with new supplements on human capital investment, intergenerational transmission of wealth, and intergenerational mobility.

BOOK ABOUT BECKER

Shackleton, J. R., and Gareth Locksley. *Twelve Contemporary Economists.* Wiley 1981 o.p. Chapter on Becker by Shackleton includes a brief biography and an examination of his contributions to economics.

BOULDING, KENNETH E. 1910–

Kenneth Boulding is one of the most prolific, provocative, and highly regarded economists of our time. Born in England, he received his M.A. at Oxford University and moved to the United States in 1937. Since then he has authored or coauthored over two dozen books and has taught at a number of leading universities; currently he is affiliated with the Institute of Behavioral Science at the University of Colorado.

In an early essay, "Is Economics Necessary?" Boulding argued that economics is important "not merely because it investigates an important slice of life in the marketplace, but because the phenomena which emerge . . . in the marketplace are also found in virtually all other human activities." Many of his works are extensions of this theme. As a result, his writings cover an astonishing variety of topics, ranging from ecology to religion, to name just two. His pioneering efforts to apply economic concepts to the areas of social conflict, peace, and disarmament have established him as one of the founders of the school of conflict resolution.

Boulding's early work, *Economic Analysis* (1941), is regarded as a classic overview and survey of the field. Many of his other works, including *A Reconstruction of Economics* (1950) and *Conflict and Defense* (1962), were once required reading for graduate students in economics. Others, such as *Beyond Economics* (1968) and *Economics as a Science* (1970), are collections of shorter essays covering such diverse topics as politics, social justice, and ethical problems, and are intended for a broader audience. *The Image* (1956), a theory of human behavior based on perceptions of the world, has received critical praise from all quarters and is perhaps his best-known work among noneconomists.

Boulding has received nearly every significant award or recognition in the field of economics, and he has been the recipient of 25 honorary degrees from universities around the world. In his spare moments, he enjoys poetry, sketching, and watercolor painting.

BOOKS BY BOULDING

Beyond Economics: Essays on Society, Religion, and Ethics. U. Mich. Pr. 1968 $11.95. ISBN 0-472-06167-4.

Collected Papers of Kenneth E. Boulding. 6 vols. Bks. Demand Vol. 2 $134.70. ISBN 0-8357-5525-8. Vol. 3 $160.00. ISBN 0-8357-5526-6. Vol. 4 $160.00. ISBN 0-8357-5527-4. Vol. 5 $113.90. ISBN 0-8357-5528-2. Vol. 6 $160.00. ISBN 0-8357-5529-0

Conflict and Defense: A General Theory. U. Pr. of Amer. 1988 $23.75. ISBN 0-8191-7112-3. Reviews and develops static and dynamic models of conflict, with theoretical models for conflict resolution.

Ecodynamics: A New Theory of Societal Evolution. Sage 1978 $38.00. ISBN 0-8039-0945-4. Applies the tenets of evolutionary theory, economics, and other sciences to developmental processes in human knowledge.

Economic Analysis. HarpC 1966 o.p. Comprehensive treatment of microeconomic concepts, including price theory, exchange, elasticity, cost curves, consumption, and forms of competition. Macroeconomic topics include index numbers and aggregates, national income accounting, money and the financial system, dynamic growth models, and the role of government.

Economics As a Science. U. Pr. of Amer. 1988 $18.25. ISBN 0-8191-7100-X

The Economics of Human Betterment. State U. NY Pr. 1985 $49.50. ISBN 0-87395-925-6. Surveys the search for understanding of human betterment examined in writings from Marx to Keynes.

Evolutionary Economics. Sage 1981 $32.00. ISBN 0-8039-1648-5. Concepts of ecological interaction and mutation applied to economics.

The Image: Knowledge in Life and Society. U. Mich. Pr. 1956 $12.95. ISBN 0-472-06047-3

The Organizational Revolution: A Study in the Ethics of Economic Organization. Greenwood 1984 repr. of 1953 ed. $57.50. ISBN 0-313-24371-9. Examines the nature, causes, and effects of the organizational revolution, with case studies from organized labor, agriculture, and business.

A Preface to Grants Economics: The Economy of Love and Fear. Greenwood 1981 $39.95. ISBN 0-275-90586-1. Discusses the microeconomic theory of grants.

A Reconstruction of Economics. Wiley 1967 o.p. Advanced treatment of both microeconomics, including price theory, preference, production, inventory, expectations and consumption, and the macroeconomic concepts of capital and income, distribution, money and interest, and debt and government.

Toward a New Economics: Critical Essays on Ecology, Distribution and Other Themes. Ashgate Pub. Co. 1992 $69.95. ISBN 1-85278-568-3. Collection of 22 essays on diverse topics, including an autobiography and discussions of space as a factor of production and the economics of pride and shame.

The World As a Total System. Sage 1985 $35.00. ISBN 0-8039-2443-7. Sequel to
    Ecodynamics that describes the evolution of world into a single economic, cultural,
    and communications system.

BOOKS ABOUT BOULDING

Kerman, Cynthia Earl. *Creative Tensions: The Life and Thought of Kenneth Boulding.*
    U. Mich. Pr. 1974 o.p. Flattering yet objective biography of Boulding from birth to
    1970, written by a family friend and former secretary.
Silk, Leonard. *The Economists.* Basic 1974 o.p. Chapter on Boulding includes a short
    biography and a nontechnical description of his professional work.

CLARK, JOHN BATES. 1847–1938

John Bates Clark was the first American to gain an international reputation as
an economist. In 1885 he and two colleagues, Richard Ely and Henry Carter
Adams, organized a group that became the American Economic Association.
Clark served as its third president, and the organization now bestows one of its
highest awards, the John Bates Clark Medal, in his honor.

Born in Providence, Rhode Island, Clark graduated from Amherst College
and then studied economics at Heidelberg and Zurich universities. After his
return to the United States, he married and took a position at Carleton College,
where he befriended an unpopular but promising undergraduate named
THORSTEIN VEBLEN. During his stay at Carleton, Clark contracted a severe illness
that was to sap his strength for the rest of his life, forcing him to organize
carefully all of his activities. Despite this handicap, Clark managed to produce
an important series of works over the next few decades.

In 1881 Clark moved to Smith College, where he published his first work, *The
Philosophy of Wealth* (1885), a volume based on a series of articles on economic
theory and contemporary business organizations originally published in *The
New Englander* magazine. His second important work, *Capital and Its Earnings*
(1888), advanced many propositions of modern capital theory, including the
view that capital "transmutes" itself from one machine to another as old
machines wear out during the production of newer ones. After a brief stint at
Amherst, Clark went to Columbia University in 1895, where he taught until
1923. His third and most important book, *The Distribution of Wealth* (1899), is
recognized as the first American economic work in pure theory. It is noted for
its discussion of statics versus dynamics, economic terms introduced by Clark.

Clark also published *The Control of Trusts: An Argument in Favor of Curbing
the Power of Monopoly by a Natural Method* (1901), which argued for limited
government intervention to restore competition. A revision, jointly published
with and largely revised by his son, appeared in 1912 and offered a stronger case
for antitrust policy. The 1912 edition (revised in 1914) was important because it
conferred academic respectability on antitrust activity. In the final years of his
life, Clark became involved in the peace movement.

BOOKS BY CLARK

Capital and Its Earnings. Ed. by Richard P. Brief. Garland 1988 $25.00. ISBN 0-8240-
    6123-3
The Control of Trusts. Kelley 1971 repr. of 1914 ed. $29.50. ISBN 0-678-00606-7
The Distribution of Wealth: A Theory of Wages, Income and Profits. Kelley 1965 repr. of
    1899 ed. $45.00. ISBN 0-678-00078-6
The Philosophy of Wealth: Economic Principles Newly Formulated. Kelley 1967 repr. of
    1887 ed. $29.50. ISBN 0-678-00274-4

BOOKS ABOUT CLARK

Blaug, Mark, ed. *Harold Hotelling, 1895–1973, Lionel Robbins, 1898–1984, Clark Warburton, 1896–1979, John Bates Clark, 1847–1938, and Ludwig von Mises, 1881–1973.* Ashgate Pub. Co. 1992 $94.95. ISBN 1-85278-504-7. Collection of previously published journal articles includes several on the life and contributions of Clark.

Everett, John Rutherford. *Religion in Economics: A Study of John Bates Clark.* Porcupine Pr. 1982 repr. of 1946 ed. $27.50. ISBN 0-8799-866-7. Contains a biography of Clark as well as essays on religion.

Hollander, Jacob H. *Economic Essays Contributed in Honor of John Bates Clark.* Ayer facs. ed. 1967 repr. of 1927 ed. $20.00. ISBN 0-8369-0399-4. Seventeen essays on the life, methodology, and writings of Clark, including a bibliography.

Homan, Paul T. *Contemporary Economic Thought.* Ayer facs. ed. 1928 $21.50. ISBN 0-8369-0546-6. A lengthy and instructive chapter deals with Clark's life, times, and contributions.

Spiegel, H. W., ed. *The Development of Economic Thought.* Wiley 1966 o.p. Includes an article on Clark by his son and noted economist, John Maurice Clark.

COMMONS, JOHN ROGERS. 1862–1945

John R. Commons was an American economist, educator, and social investigator who believed strongly in the ideal of human equality. He is regarded as an "institutionalist" because of his interest in how institutions—trade unions, governments, and businesses—evolved and interacted in a capitalistic system. As a labor economist, he developed a theory of labor struggle in which the collective actions of unions would lead to human betterment without the dire consequences of a Marxist revolution.

Commons studied at Oberlin College and Johns Hopkins University. His interest in real-world institutions began when he joined the typographers' union as a student. Later, while teaching at Wesleyan, he often discussed current issues with his students and took them on field trips to examine issues firsthand. The administration, preferring someone more interested in textbook problems, terminated his position after one year.

Undaunted, Commons took a chair of sociology at Syracuse University, where he developed the theory that owners of private property use their power to encroach on the rights and welfare of others. The wealthy benefactors at Syracuse, uncomfortable with this analysis, withdrew their financial support for the chair. Commons then spent several years working on various government commissions before he joined the faculty of the University of Wisconsin in 1904. There, in conjunction with his students, he published his classic 11-volume *Documentary History of American Industrial Society* (1910). It was followed by his best-known work, the *History of Labor in the United States* (1918), which chronicled the role of unions working for equality of the "economic classes" of workers and owners.

BOOKS BY COMMONS

A Documentary History of American Industrial Society. 10 vols. Ed. by Ulrich B. Phillips and others. AMS Pr. repr. of 1910 ed. $920.00. ISBN 0-404-20330-2. Describes the stages of industrial development and the evolution of the labor movement, starting with the plantation and the frontier.

History of Labor in the United States. 4 vols. Kelley 1966 repr. of 1918 ed. $195.00. ISBN 0-678-00142-1. A history and rationale of labor's quest for equality and dignity.

Institutional Economics: Its Place in Political Economy. Transaction Pubs. 1990 $24.95. ISBN 0-88738-797-7. Discusses money, banking, labor, and the corporation.

Legal Foundations of Capitalism. Kelley 1974 repr. of 1924 ed. $45.00. ISBN 0-678-
   00897-3. Traces the evolution of the legal foundations of capitalism back to the
   English merchant class and its collective bargaining with the monarchy.
Myself: The Autobiography of John R. Commons. U. of Wis. Pr. 1963 $5.95. ISBN 0-299-
   02924-7. Personal reflections on life and events that influenced the development of
   Commons's institutional point of view.

BOOKS ABOUT COMMONS

Blaug, Mark, ed. *Wesley Mitchell (1874–1948), John Commons, Clarence Ayers.* Ashgate
   Pub. Co. 1992 $89.95. ISBN 1-85278-496-2. Collection of previously published
   articles includes several on the life and works of Commons.
Samuels, Warren J., ed. *Institutional Economics.* 3 vols. Gower Pub. Co. 1988 o.p.
   Volumes One and Two contain several articles on Commons' methodology and work
   as an institutionalist.
Somers, Gerald G., ed. *Labor Management and Social Policy: Essays in the John R.
   Commons Tradition.* Bks. Demand 1963 $82.50. ISBN 0-8357-6770-1. Includes
   biographical references as well as labor history and economic theories of Commons
   and his approach to public policy.
Spiegel, H. W., ed. *The Development of Economic Thought.* Wiley 1966 o.p. Contains a
   short biographical and analytical essay, "Perlman on Commons."

ENGELS, FRIEDRICH. 1820–1895

Friedrich Engels is perhaps best remembered as the confidant, colleague, and
benefactor of KARL MARX. Born into a Calvinist family that owned fabric mills in
the Rhineland and had business interests in Manchester, England, Engels joined
the family business at age 16; he never had a formal university education.
Despite his family's industrial background, Engels was sympathetic to the
poverty of the working masses. At age 18 he published an attack on industrial
poverty, and later joined the Hegelian movement that so influenced Marx and
bothered conservative Prussian authorities. Engels first met Marx in 1842, while
Marx was editor of a radical newspaper in Cologne. However, they did not
establish their lifelong friendship until they met again in Paris two years later.

Engels published several works related to economics, the first of which,
Outlines of a Critique of Political Economy (1844), attempted to reconcile
Hegelian philosophy with the principles of political economy. His second book,
The Condition of the Working Class in England (1845), was a damning
description and condemnation of the poverty generated by the Industrial
Revolution. Engels also coauthored three major works with Marx, the most
important being the *Communist Manifesto* (1948). Engels also wrote several
historical works, which are more important to historians than to economists.
These include *The Peasant War in Germany* (1850), *Germany: Revolution and
Counter-Revolution* (1851), and *The Origin of the Family, Private Property and
the State* (1884). In general, these works are more descriptive than theoretical,
and they closely parallel Marx's views on industrialization and class struggle.

In addition to being a friend of Marx, Engels was his prime benefactor for a
number of years. During their early years in London, beginning in 1849, the
Marx family was nearly destitute, and it was only through the generosity of
Engels that they prevailed. Engels was also responsible for the publication of
Marx's *Das Kapital.* Before his death, Marx was only able to complete the first
volume of this work, and so Engels edited and arranged for the publication of
the last two volumes after Marx's death.

Engels was an engaging and thoughtful writer. It was perhaps his great
fortune and misfortune that he was connected so closely to Marx. On the one

hand, he was responsible for bringing much of Marx's work to fruition in his role as benefactor and editor. On the other hand, the shadow of Marx eclipsed some of the exposure that Engels's own ideas and contributions might have had.

BOOKS BY ENGELS

The Communist Manifesto. (coauthored with Karl Marx). Viking Penguin 1985 $3.50. ISBN 0-14-044478-5

The Condition of the Working Class in England: From Personal Observation and Authentic Sources. Academy Chi. Pubs. 1984 $10.00. ISBN 0-89733-137-0. Riveting description of the exploitation of the English working class. An influential book in the history of Marxist literature.

Germany: Revolution and Counter-Revolution. Ed. by Eleanor Marx. Bks. Demand repr. of 1969 ed. $42.40. ISBN 0-685-20782-X

The Origin of the Family, Private Property, and the State. Viking Penguin 1986 $9.95. ISBN 0-14-044465-3

The Peasant War in Germany. Intl. Pubs. Co. 1966 $2.75. ISBN 0-7178-0152-7

BOOKS ABOUT ENGELS

Carver, Terrell. *Engels.* OUP 1983 $6.95. ISBN 0-19-287548-5. Brief biographical survey and critical analysis of Engels's work; evaluates Engels as a journalist, communist, revolutionary, Marxist, scientist.

Henderson, W. O. *The Life of Friedrich Engels.* Cass 1976 o.p. Comprehensive, exhaustive account of Engels and his relationship with Marx.

Hunley, J. D. *The Life and Thought of Friedrich Engels: A Reinterpretation.* Yale U. Pr. 1991 o.p. Argues that Marx and Engels were in fundamental agreement; rejects the dichotomists, who detect a schism. (Rejection of this schism is important because the dichotomist argument is used by repressive Marxist societies to downplay the humanistic elements of Marx's writings.)

Marcus, Steven. *Engels, Manchester, and the Working Class.* Norton 1985 $6.95. ISBN 0-393-30237. Retraces Engels's visit to Manchester to put *Conditions of the Working Class* in historical perspective.

FISHER, IRVING. 1867–1947

Irving Fisher was an American economist best noted for his work in the fields of statistics, monetary theory, interest, and capital. He spent most of his life at Yale University, first as a student and later as a member of the faculty. A prolific writer, he produced nearly 30 books and hundreds of scientific papers. He was also a reformer—prohibitionist, pacifist, and nutritionist—by way of his best-selling book, *How to Live* (1915).

Fisher's business ventures included a profitable system of card-index filing, which he designed and sold. He was, however, less successful as a forecaster. One week before the infamous stock market crash of 1929, he proclaimed that the U.S. economy was on a "permanently high plateau." During the ensuing crash, he lost most of the fortune he had earned on his filing system.

One of Fisher's lasting contributions was his classic *Making of Index Numbers* (1927), which attempted to develop a theory that would be statistically operative. Another was his theory of a "real" rate of interest. His *Rate of Interest* (1907), and its extensive revision, which appeared as *The Theory of Interest* (1930), offered an explanation of capitalism that made the rate of interest dependent on productivity, time preference, risk, and uncertainty. The latter, according to JOSEPH SCHUMPETER, "teaches us, as does no other work I know, how to satisfy the requirements of both the specialist and the general reader without banishing mathematics to footnotes or appendices. A final, and perhaps most important, contribution was the quantity theory of money expression,

which is used to link changes in the quantity of money to changes in the price
level.

Much of Fisher's work was truly pioneering. His concern with a stable price
level was based as much on a sense of fairness to debtors and creditors as it was
on a desire to avoid the "dance of the dollar"—otherwise known as the business
cycle.

BOOKS BY FISHER

The Making of Index Numbers. Kelley 1967 repr. of 1927 ed. $49.50. ISBN 0-678-00319-X
Mathematical Investigations in the Theory of Value and Price Appreciation and Interest.
     Kelley 1991 repr. of 1892 ed. $29.50. ISBN 0-678-01456-6. Doctoral dissertation
     presents general equilibrium system.
The Purchasing Power of Money. Kelley 1985 repr. of 1922 ed. $45.00. ISBN 0-678-
     00011-5. Develops quantity theory of money and recommends ways to ensure stable
     prices.
The Theory of Interest. Kelley 1986 repr. of 1930 ed. $45.00. ISBN 0-678-00003-4

BOOKS ABOUT FISHER

Allen, Robert Loring. *Irving Fisher: A Biography.* Blackwell Pubs. 1993 $39.95. ISBN 1-
     55786-305-9. Well-researched, comprehensive study of Fisher's life and influence.
Fellner, William, ed. *Ten Economic Studies in the Tradition of Irving Fisher.* Wiley 1967
     o.p. Contains a biographical essay and several others based directly on Fisher's
     contributions.
Fisher, Irving Norton. *My Father, Irving Fisher.* Comet Pr. 1956 o.p. Interesting and
     informative biography that views the life of Fisher's father as an American success
     story.
Schumpeter, Joseph A. *Ten Great Economists From Marx to Keynes.* OUP 1951 o.p.
     Contains an excellent chapter on the theoretical contributions of Fisher; his
     contributions as a social philosopher, "economic engineer," and teacher.

FRIEDMAN, MILTON. 1912– (NOBEL PRIZE 1976)

Milton Friedman is an influential, conservative American economist most
closely associated with the University of Chicago and the school of thought
known as monetarism. His writings have covered an extraordinary variety of
topics, many of them set forth in his early classic, *Capitalism and Freedom*
(1962). Its major theme is "the role of competitive capitalism . . . as a system of
economic freedom and a necessary condition for political freedom." This text,
written for a nonacademic audience, includes proposals that range from
opposition to agricultural subsidies to advocacy of vouchers for public schools.
Despite the fact that Friedman's ideas were radical departures from the
prevailing wisdom, the power of his arguments was such that many of his
proposals have actually come to fruition. The general public is probably most
familiar with Friedman through his short editorials that appeared in *Newsweek*
from 1968 to 1982, the best of which were published in *Bright Promises, Dismal
Performances: An Economist's Protest* (1983).

Friedman's academic contributions in the area of monetary history—his
Monetary History of the United States, 1867–1960 (1963) and his *Monetary
Statistics of the United States: Estimates, Sources, Methods* (1970), both
coauthored with Anna Schwartz—are the definitive works on the growth of the
money supply and its relationship to inflation. The former also provides an
excellent discussion of the consequences of Federal Reserve System actions (or
lack thereof) during the Great Depression of the 1930s.

Friedman has been most influential in his unwavering support of monetarism—the proposition that the quantity of money matters because of its impact on the overall state of the economy. While this may not seem like a novel proposal today, it was regarded as almost heresy during the post-Keynesian 1950s and 1960s, when economists were trying to fine-tune the economy by using such fiscal stimuli as tax credits, automatic stabilizers like unemployment insurance, and various federal spending programs. Friedman claims that the Federal Reserve System should let the money supply grow at a constant rate to avoid destabilizing shocks to the economy. His views attracted a number of adherents, and the school of monetarism soon rivaled the Keynesians of a few decades earlier. It was for his efforts in demonstrating the importance of money and the complexities of stabilization policy that Friedman was awarded the Nobel Prize.

Books by Friedman

Bright Promises, Dismal Performance: An Economist's Protest. HarBraceJ 1983 $6.95. ISBN 0-15-614161-2

Capitalism and Freedom: With a New Preface. U. Ch. Pr. 1963 $8.95. ISBN 0-226-26401-7

Essays in Positive Economics. U. Ch. Pr. 1966 $9.00. ISBN 0-226-26403-3. Collection of previously published essays on methodology in economics, welfare theory, monetary policy, and flexible exchange rates.

Free to Choose: A Personal Statement. 1980. (coauthored with Rose Friedman). HarBraceJ 1990 $7.95. ISBN 0-15-633460-7. Stresses the importance of individual freedom and the superiority of the free market over government programs to remedy social ills.

The Great Contraction, 1929–1933. (coauthored with Anna Schwartz). Nat. Bur. Econ. Res. 1963 $6.95. ISBN 0-685-03492-5. Reprint of Chapter 7 from *Monetary History of the United States,* exploring the depth and persistence of the Great Depression; Friedman blames the severity of the depression on errors in Federal Reserve System policies.

The Essence of Friedman. Ed. by Kurt R. Leube. Hoover Inst. Pr. 1987 $44.95. ISBN 0-8179-8661-8. Selected essays gathered in honor of Friedman's seventy-fifth birthday; volume includes a short biography and bibliography of Friedman's publications.

Monetary History of the United States. 1867–1960. (coauthored with Anna Schwartz). Princeton U. Pr. 1963 $40.00. ISBN 0-685-03494-1

Monetary Mischief: Episodes in Monetary History. HarBraceJ 1992 $19.95. ISBN 0-15-162042-3. Examines the role of money backed by gold and silver versus current fiat money backed by faith in government; historical impact of U.S. bimetallism.

Monetary Statistics of the United States: Estimates, Sources, Methods. (coauthored with Anna Schwartz). Col. U. Pr. 1970 $31.00. ISBN 0-87014-210-0

The Optimum Quantity of Money and Other Essays. Aldine de Gruyter 1969 $42.95. ISBN 0-202-06030-6. Collection of previously published journal articles on topics related to monetary theory; provides an overview of Friedman's views on monetary policy.

Theory of the Consumption Function. Princeton U. Pr. 1957 $30.50. ISBN 0-691-04182-2. Presents an alternative theory of the consumption function based on the permanent income hypothesis.

Books about Friedman

Breit, William, and Roger W. Spencer, eds. *Lives of the Laureates: Ten Nobel Economists.* MIT Pr. 1990 $19.95. ISBN 0-262-02308-3. Contains an interesting and informative chapter concerning Friedman's evolution as an economist and his views on what an economist has to do to get the Nobel Prize.

Butler, Eamonn. *Milton Friedman.* Universe 1985 $16.50. ISBN 0-87663-476-5. Restates Friedman's main positions on inflation, monetary policy, unemployment, and lags in business cycles.

Frazer, William. *Power and Ideas: Milton Friedman and the Big U-Turn*. 2 vols. Gulf-Atlan
   Pub. 1988 $70.00 set. ISBN 0-9619206-0-2. Vol. I *The Background* $35.00. ISBN 0-
   9619206-0-2. Vol II *The U-Turn* $35.00. ISBN 0-685-22793-6. Considers the novelty
   and uniqueness of Friedman's work in light of the prevailing economic wisdom of
   the 1920s and 1930s. Credits Friedman for his unprecedented impact on the change
   in the direction of economic thought.
Raynack, Elton. *Not So Free to Choose: The Political Economy of Milton Friedman and
   Ronald Reagan*. Greenwood 1986 $45.00. ISBN 0-275-92363-0. Views Friedman as an
   ideologue whose work is often simplistic when stripped of jargon, and cavalier in its
   treatment of history.
Wood, John Cunningham, and Ronald N. Woods, eds. *Milton Friedman: Critical
   Assessments*. 4 vols. Routledge 1990 $525.00. ISBN 0-415-02005-0. Comprehensive
   1,600-page work containing 134 previously published articles, both pro and con,
   dealing with Friedman's theories and positions. The most extensive collection of
   critical assessments of his works.

GALBRAITH, JOHN KENNETH. 1908–

John Kenneth Galbraith, a Canadian-born American economist, is perhaps
the most widely read economist in the world. Educated at the University of
Toronto and the University of California, he held several high government
positions during World War II, coauthored John F. Kennedy's inaugural
address, served as ambassador to India during the Kennedy administration, and
taught economics at Harvard University.

Galbraith's views on economics are both unconventional and refreshing. In
general, he rejects the conventional, general-equilibrium wisdom of the
neoclassical economists, as well as the Keynesian propositions of more recent
times. He has been described by one reviewer as "the iconoclast of the
American Establishment" and by another as "the leading antitheoretical
theorist of our time." In his classic work, *American Capitalism: The Concept of
Countervailing Power* (1952), Galbraith argued that large industrial organizations were a permanent part of the modern postdepression economy, because
modern technology required large amounts of capital. Large size was not to be
feared, however, because the economic power of these organizations would be
held in check by countervailing power. As for policy, Galbraith held that the
appropriate role of government should be to make sure that countervailing
organizations did develop; this view ran counter to the conventional position,
which said that antitrust policies should be used to break up the large firms.

Another major work, *The Affluent Society* (1958) portrays a nation with an
increasing abundance of private goods and a declining public sector: deteriorat-
ing educational systems, roads, parks, and medical facilities. Social balance,
according to Galbraith, could be restored only with increased government
expenditures, a spending revolution led by the "new class" of the educated and
affluent. In *The New Industrial State* (1967), Galbraith maintained that there is
no inherent limit to corporate size because of modern technology. Large
entities are governed by technostructures—groups of upper-level administrators and technicians—whose primary concern is preservation of their own
decision-making authority; they work to replace the market with planning,
putting a premium on growth over profitability. This description contrasted
starkly with the modern view of the corporation, which holds that management
should be dedicated to maximizing shareholder wealth.

The most definitive statement of Galbraith's views appears in *Economics and
the Public Purpose* (1973), in which he introduced the concept of the planning
system as an alternative to the market system. The latter, with power residing in

a small number of very large firms, results in uneven economic development that shortchanges the weak. Galbraith advocates government intervention on behalf of the weak sectors of the economy—public housing, transportation, health care—to supply the overall coordination needed in the absence of a self-regulating market mechanism.

BOOKS BY GALBRAITH

The Affluent Society. HM 1984 o.p.

American Capitalism: The Concept of Countervailing Power. HM rev. ed. 1956 o.p.

Capitalism, Communism and Coexistence: From the Bitter Past to a Better Prospect (coauthored with Stanislav Menshikov). HM 1988 $17.45. ISBN 0-395-47316-0. Dialogue between Galbraith and noted economist of the former Soviet Union on the superiority of their respective economic systems.

Economics and the Public Purpose. HM 1973 o.p.

Economics in Perspective: A Critical History. HM 1988 $19.95. ISBN 0-395-35572-9. Argues that Keynesian economics no longer applies to the modern, industrial structure, and that government and industry need to develop consensus in setting economic policy.

The Great Crash of 1929. HM 1988 $8.70. ISBN 0-395-47805-7. Riveting historical account of the stock market crash of 1929 and the Great Depression of the 1930s.

A Life in Our Times: Memoirs. HM 1981 $16.45. ISBN 0-395-30509-8. Witty, entertaining, boastful, name-dropping reflections on acquaintances and events.

The New Industrial State. HM 1985 $19.95. ISBN 0-395-38991-7

A Theory of Price Control: The Classic Account. HUP 1952 $12.50. ISBN 0-674-88170-2. A description and defense of price controls during World War II; argues that they will be needed again in a modern economy dominated by large, powerful organizations.

The Voice of the Poor: Essays in Economics and Political Persuasion. HUP 1983 $10.95. ISBN 0-674-94295-7. Series of lectures criticizing the development of heavy industry rather than education in developing countries.

BOOKS ABOUT GALBRAITH

Bowles, Samuel, and others, eds. *Unconventional Wisdom, Essays in Honor of John Kenneth Galbraith.* HM 1989 $24.45. ISBN 0-395-49179-7. Collection of 22 papers, some previously published, on a wide range of topics; includes two especially interesting biographical essays.

Friedman, Milton. *From Galbraith to Economic Freedom.* Institute of Economic Affairs 1977 o.p. A leading conservative economist evaluates arguments of the leading liberal economist with respectful but biting commentary.

Hession, Charles H. *John Kenneth Galbraith and His Critics.* NAL-Dutton 1972 o.p. Attempts to clarify what Galbraith has written. Provides assessments of Galbraith's critics and Galbraith as a critic.

Lamson, Peggy. *Speaking of Galbraith: A Personal Portrait.* Ticknor & Fields 1991 $21.45. ISBN 0-89919-913-5. About Galbraith as a writer, social activist, and public servant; written by a longtime friend.

Okroi, Loren J. *Galbraith, Harrington, Heilbroner: Economics and Dissent in an Age of Optimism.* Princeton U. Pr. 1988 $37.50. ISBN 0-691-07771-1. Attributes Galbraith's success to his treatment of economics in a social and historical context.

Sharpe, M. E. *John Kenneth Galbraith and the Lower Economics.* IASP 1973 o.p. A Galbraith admirer disagrees with many of his conclusions and analyses.

GEORGE, HENRY. 1839–1897

Henry George, an American economist, enjoyed an adventurous life. His early education in Philadelphia was largely self-acquired from library books, and at age 16 he signed up as a sailor on a cargo ship bound for Calcutta. He spent two years in India and then returned to California to prospect for gold. Failing to strike it rich, he eventually drifted into journalism and wrote columns for the *San Francisco Times*.

George's exposure to poverty in India, and the poverty he experienced before he became a successful journalist, heightened his concern for the plight of the masses. He left the *San Francisco Times* to become an investigative reporter for the rival *Daily Evening Post*; when the *Post* was sold, he took a job as a gas meter inspector. During this period he studied economics and stumbled on the one idea that made him famous.

The essence of George's idea, as spelled out in *Progress and Poverty* (1879), was that land, and the rent derived from it, is the source of wealth. On this assumption George based his radical solution for the eradication of poverty—the abolition of all taxes in the country and their replacement by a single tax on land. This proposition was so revolutionary that George was unable to find a publisher until he agreed to pay for the printing plates out of his own pocket. *Progress and Poverty* was received with contempt by the establishment, but it was a runaway bestseller.

George became an instant celebrity. "Single tax" clubs sprang up all over the United States and Europe, especially Great Britain. The Labor party asked George to run for mayor of New York City; he came in second but ahead of an up-and-coming Republican named THEODORE ROOSEVELT. George wrote several other books, none of which reached the stature of *Progress*, and died during the strain of a second political race. His philosophy of a single tax proved to have lasting appeal and even today has many adherents.

BOOKS BY GEORGE

Complete Works. 10 vols. AMS Pr. repr. of 1911 ed. $325.00 set. $32.50 ea. ISBN 0-404-02800-4. Individual volumes cover such topics as wages and capital, population and subsistence, and the distribution of wealth.
Progress and Poverty. Schalkenbach 1985 $4.00. ISBN 0-911312-58-7
Protection or Free Trade. Schalkenbach 1991 $12.00. ISBN 0-911312-83-8. Passionate argument for free trade and abolition of protectionism. Historical examples of intervention are used to support the arguments.
Science of Political Economy. Schalkenbach 1992 repr. of 1898 ed. $12.00. ISBN 0-911312-51-X

BOOKS ABOUT GEORGE

Andelson, Robert U. *Critics of Henry George: A Centenary Appraisal of their Strictures on Progress and Poverty*. AUP 1979 o.p. Collection of 27 articles presenting arguments of George's most significant critics.
De Mille, Anna G. *Henry George, Citizen of the World*. Greenwood 1972 repr. of 1950 ed. $45.00. ISBN 0-8371-5575-4. Biography by his daughter; comprehensive, definitive, and highly recommended.
Geiger, George R. *The Philosophy of Henry George*. Hyperion Conn. 1975 repr. of 1933 ed. $36.00. ISBN 0-88355-220-5. A lengthy and passionate defense of George. Includes a biographical chapter and offers philosophical, moral, social, and religious arguments for George's position.
Rose, Edward J. *Henry George*. NCUP 1968 $10.95. ISBN 0-8084-0003-7. Acquaints the modern reader with the life and ideas of George and presents him as the most influential non-Marxist spokesperson of the left.

HANSEN, ALVIN. 1887–1975

Alvin Hansen is best remembered as the American economist who brought the Keynesian revolution to America. Born in a small rural community in South Dakota, he received his early education in a one-room schoolhouse, then studied at Yankton College and the University of Wisconsin. After teaching at Brown University, he went on to the University of Minnesota and then to Harvard University.

In 1927 Hansen published his classic *Business-Cycle Theory*, a comprehensive survey of business cycle theories and theorists. The waste and despair of the Great Depression affected him greatly, and he became an ardent supporter of Keynesian economics. His *Full Recovery or Stagnation?* (1938) analyzed the Great Depression, especially the premature termination of the recovery in 1937. Other publications, including *Fiscal Policy and Business Cycles* (1941) and *Business Cycles and National Income* (1951), argued the Keynesian proposition that unemployment was caused by a failure of private investment. Hansen's popular *Guide to Keynes* (1953), with its paragraph-by-paragraph dissection of the *General Theory*, was often assigned to graduate students to be read along with the classic text.

Hansen served as a consultant to, and shaped the form of, the current Social Security system. He was also instrumental in the formulation of the Full Employment Act of 1946 and the creation of the President's Council of Economic Advisers. He was elected president of the American Economic Association in 1967 and taught as a visiting professor at universities around the world after he retired from Harvard University. When he received the prestigious Walker Medal on his eightieth birthday, James Tobin observed that, for Alvin Hansen, "economics was a science for the service of mankind."

BOOKS BY HANSEN

The American Economy. McGraw 1957 o.p. Comprehensive overview of the U.S. economy based on an earlier series of lectures.

Business Cycles and National Income. Norton 1964 o.p. Outstanding historical survey of business cycles from early to modern times.

Business-Cycle Theory: Its Development and Present Status. Hyperion Conn. 1980 repr. of 1927 ed. $18.50. ISBN 0-88355-884-X

Full Recovery or Stagnation? Norton 1938 o.p.

A Guide to Keynes. McGraw 1953 o.p.

Monetary Theory and Fiscal Policy. Greenwood 1983 repr. of 1949 ed. $39.75. ISBN 0-313-23736-0. Keynesian argument for fiscal policy as a stimulus during recessionary periods.

Postwar American Economy: Performance and Problems. Norton 1964 $.95. ISBN 0-393-00236-5. Brief survey of four postwar recessions between 1948 and 1963.

BOOK ABOUT HANSEN

Metzler, Lloyd. *Income, Employment and Public Policy: Essays in Honor of Alvin Hansen.* Norton 1948 o.p. Collection of 16 essays on a variety of topics.

HAYEK, FRIEDRICH AUGUST VON. 1899–1992 (NOBEL PRIZE 1974)

Austrian-born economist, political philosopher, and psychologist Friedrich von Hayek is best remembered today for both his contributions to economic theory and his opposition to socialism. Economics was one of Hayek's early interests; while serving as an artillery officer on the Italian front in 1917, he read an economics text to pass the time. In 1918 he left the army and enrolled at the University of Vienna, where he received degrees in both law and economics. While at the university, he helped organize an influential group of young scholars, who became known as the "Vienna Circle." In 1927 Hayek became one of the founders of the Austrian Economic Society and the Austrian Institute of Business Cycle Research, where he served as director.

In 1929 Hayek published his classic *Monetary Theory and the Trade Cycle*, which argued that the business cycle is caused by an increase in credit or monetary stimulus. In the same year, he became a lecturer at the University of Vienna; by 1932 he had accepted a professorship at the London School of Economics. While in London, Hayek published two of his most important, and largely theoretical, books on capital theory, *Profits, Interest, and Investment* (1939) and *The Pure Theory of Capital* (1941).

After having established a solid reputation as an economist, Hayek became an outspoken and highly effective critic of both nationalism and socialism. Hayek argued that there was a division of knowledge in economic society and that all individuals were in possession of incomplete bits of knowledge that could be put to beneficial use. In a capitalistic society, the price system was the mechanism that "communicated information" and helped to allocate resources efficiently. Socialism, on the other hand, required centralized decision making. The problem, according to Hayek, was that there was no way for individuals to communicate information to a centralized authority so that planners could organize it for efficient decision making. At the same time, hard-line socialists opposed decentralization because it threatened their power. His most famous book, *The Road to Serfdom* (1945), was dedicated to "socialists of all parties" and condemned socialism in all its forms. The book was panned by socialists, praised by antisocialists, generally distorted by critics and admirers alike, and became a runaway bestseller.

In 1950 Hayek left London for the University of Chicago, where he remained for the next 12 years as a professor of moral and social sciences. Although he continued to teach some economics, his work focused more on historical, legal, and methodological issues. In 1962 Hayek went to Freiburg University in West Germany and then to the University of Salzburg from 1968 to 1977. While at Salzburg, in 1974, he was awarded the Nobel Prize in economics (jointly with GUNNAR MYRDAL) for his pioneering analysis of the interdependence of economic, social, and institutional phenomena.

BOOKS BY HAYEK

A Conversation with Friedrich A. von Hayek: Science and Socialism. Am. Enterprise 1979 o.p. Short, nontechnical examination of the topic "Was Socialism a Mistake?"

The Counter-Revolution of Science: Studies on the Abuse of Reason. Liberty Fund 1980 $9.00. ISBN 0-913966-66-5. Sixteen essays presenting an overview of the progressive abuse of reason under socialism, followed by the decay of reason under totalitarianism.

Individualism and Economic Order. U. Ch. Pr. 1980 $19.95. ISBN 0-226-32089-8. Collection of 12 essays, many previously published, ranging from methodological issues to interstate federalism; "not intended for popular consumption," according to the author's preface, but representative of his work.

Monetary Theory and the Trade Cycle. Trans. by N. Kaldor and H. M. Croome. Kelley 1966 repr. of 1937 ed. $22.50. ISBN 0-678-00176-6

Prices and Production. Kelley 2nd rev. & enl. ed. 1967 repr. of 1935 ed. $27.50. ISBN 0-685-02797-X

The Pure Theory of Capital. U. Ch. Pr. 1975 $27.00. ISBN 0-226-32081-2

The Road to Serfdom. U. Ch. Pr. 1956 $19.95. ISBN 0-226-32078-2

BOOKS ABOUT HAYEK

Hicks, John. "The Hayek Story" in *Critical Essays in Monetary Theory.* OUP 1967 o.p. Describes Hayek as the leading character in the drama of the 1930s.

Machlup, Fritz, ed. *Essays on Hayek*. NYU Pr. 1976 o.p. Collection of seven articles about Hayek, with a selected list of Hayek's books in English. Introduction by Milton Friedman.

Romano, Richard, and Melvin Leiman. *Views on Capitalism*. Glencoe 1970 o.p. College reader on different perspectives on capitalism; contains useful overview of, and selections from, *Road to Serfdom*.

Shackleton, J. R., and Gareth Locksley. *Twelve Contemporary Economists*. Wiley 1981 o.p. Chapter on Hayek, by Norman Barry, is titled "Restating the Liberal Order: Hayek's Philosophical Economics."

Wood, John C., and Ronald Woods. eds. *Friedrich A. Hayek: Critical Assessments*. 4 vols. Routledge 1991 $525.00. ISBN 0-415-04659-9. Comprehensive collection of 96 previously published articles.

HICKS, SIR JOHN RICHARD. 1904–1989 (NOBEL PRIZE 1972)

John Richard Hicks, one of the leading economic theorists of the twentieth century, was born in Leamington Spa, England, and graduated from Oxford University. He taught at the London School of Economics, Manchester, and Oxford. Knighted in 1964, he was the first Englishman to be awarded the Nobel Prize (jointly with KENNETH ARROW) for his work on general equilibrium and welfare economics. His writings covered a broad range of topics, including labor and wages, value, capital, trade cycle theory, and economic history.

Hicks's first book, *The Theory of Wages* (1932), was an institutional history of labor economics in Britain that analyzed wages under conditions of supply and demand in a competitive market. His second book, *Value and Capital: An Inquiry into Some Fundamental Principles of Economic Theory* (1939), was a monumental effort that firmly established his reputation among economists. It dealt with an elaboration of value theory and general equilibrium theory that required a considerable amount of persistence to digest. A well-known economist who reviewed the book concluded that it cost him more effort per page than any volume in economics he had ever read.

In 1937 Hicks published "Mr. Keynes and the Classics," a famous journal-length review article of *General Theory of Employment, Interest and Money* by JOHN MAYNARD KEYNES. By working with a two-sector model, Hicks introduced the now-famous IS-LM curves that are central to macroeconomic textbooks. His *Social Framework: An Introduction to Economics* (1942) was a popular economics textbook in the early postwar years. His *Contribution to the Theory of the Trade Cycle* (1950), a multiplier-accelerator model of business cycles, also enjoyed modest success.

When *Capital and Growth* was published in 1965, Hicks tried to provide a theory of growth that featured a microeconomic foundation of macroeconomics. Afterward, when a flaw was discovered in the exposition, Hicks published *Capital and Time: A Neo-Austrian Theory* (1973), which incorporated time into the analysis. His *Theory of Economic History* (1969) gave the market a special role in the development of economic history. This rather short work was highly regarded by Hicks, and he is said to have wished that his Nobel Prize had been awarded for this book rather than for his earlier efforts. However, *Economic History* received very little attention from economists and somewhat critical reviews from economic historians.

Hicks also wrote in a number of other areas, especially in the field of monetary economics. His work is not easily summarized, but the majority of his efforts, aside from *Value and Capital*, have a literary elegance and clarity that deservedly earned him the title of being "an economist's economist."

BOOKS BY HICKS

Capital and Time: A Neo-Austrian Theory. OUP 1987 $49.95. ISBN 0-19-828179-X

Collected Essays on Economic Theory. Vol. 1: Wealth and Welfare. HUP 1981 $37.00.
ISBN 0-674-13741-8. Thirteen previously published papers on the theory of value,
welfare, measurement of capital, valuation of social income, and consumer surplus.

Collected Essays on Economic Theory. Vol. 2: Money, Interest, and Wages. HUP 1982
$37.00. ISBN 0-674-13742-6. Collection of 24 previously published papers include
several appraisals of other economists.

Collected Essays on Economic Theory. Vol. 3: Classics and Moderns. HUP 1983 $37.00.
ISBN 0-674-13743-4. Collection of 32 previously published articles on classical and
postclassical economists, international trade, and mathematical economics.

Economic Perspectives: Further Essays on Money and Growth. OUP 1977 o.p.
Nine previously published essays that appeared between 1965 and 1977, focusing on economic growth, theory of money, inflation expectations, and capital
controversies.

A Market Theory of Money. OUP 1989 $36.00. ISBN 0-19-828724-0. Analyzes the role of
money in markets, money and finance, monetary problems and policies. Contains a
mixture of economic history, history of thought, and history of economic analysis.

Theory of Economic History. OUP 1969 $11.95. ISBN 0-19-881163-2

Value and Capital: An Inquiry into Some Fundamental Principles of Economic Theory.
OUP 1946 $16.95. ISBN 0-19-828269-9

BOOKS ABOUT HICKS

Hamouda, O. F. *John R. Hicks: The Economist's Economist.* Blackwell Pubs. 1993 $39.95.
ISBN 1-55786-065-3. Scholarly, comprehensive analysis providing valuable guidance
to Hicks's works based on his own insights.

Helm, Dieter, ed. *The Economics of John Hicks.* Blackwell Pubs. 1984 $19.95. ISBN 0-
631-13616-9. Lengthy biographical introduction on Hicks, plus additional selections
by him.

Wood, John C., and Ronald N. Woods. *Sir John Hicks: Critical Assessments.* 4 vols.
Routledge 1988 $499.00. ISBN 0-415-01272-4. Comprehensive collection of 95
previously published articles. Includes a biographical article from the 1979
International Encyclopedia of Social Sciences and other biographical material.

JEVONS, WILLIAM STANLEY. 1835–1882

William Stanley Jevons was an English logician, economist, and statistician.
Born in Liverpool, he was the ninth child of a well-to-do family. His father was
an iron merchant, and his mother was a noted banker, historian, and art
collector. Jevons entered University College London to study chemistry and
mathematics but left in 1853 to take a position as assayer at a new mint in
Australia. After six years there, he returned to London to complete his
education.

Jevons devoted much of his time to what he called "combinational logic," a
form of symbolic logic popular at the time. He wrote *Pure Logic* (1863) and also
developed a logic machine now recognized as the forerunner of the modern
computer. One of his first major economic works was *A Serious Fall in the Value
of Gold* (1863), in which he virtually invented the concept of a price index so
that he could compare the change in the value of gold over time. It was followed
by *The Coal Question* (1865), an examination of the depletion of existing coal
reserves that would eventually drive up the price of coal and thereby affect
Britain's industrial dominance. The book was an immediate success, and the
resulting "coal panic" led to the appointment of a royal commission on coal.

In *The Solar Period and the Price of Corn* (1875), Jevons hypothesized that
recurring periods of expanding and contracting business activity might some-

how be linked to sunspot activity. Specifically, he argued that overall economic activity was affected by conditions in agriculture and that "the success of the harvest in any year certainly depends upon the weather. . . . If this weather depends in any degree upon the solar period, it follows that the harvest and the price of grain will depend more or less on the solar period, and will go through periodic fluctuations in periods of time equal to those sunspots." Jevons's idea was ridiculed at the time, but economists now credit him with recognizing the recurrent nature of the business cycle, as well as attempts to correlate business fluctuations with other phenomena. Considering the importance of agriculture at the time, and the correlation actually observed between sunspot activity and the success of the harvests, his theory cannot be completely ruled out.

Jevons's last complete book, *The State in Relation to Labor* (1882), was an attempt to set forth a generalized treatment of economic policy. His *Methods of Social Reform* (1883), published after his death, spelled out his philosophy that government should help enforce contracts but interfere with their terms only if they were negotiated by parties of unequal strength. Jevons's impressive scholarly contributions were cut short by his untimely death at age 47 while swimming during a family holiday.

BOOKS BY JEVONS

The Coal Question. Ed. by A. W. Flux. 3rd rev. ed. Kelley 1965 repr. of 1906 ed. $45.00. ISBN 0-678-00107-3
Methods of Social Reform. Kelley 1965 repr. of 1883 ed. $39.50. ISBN 0-678-00108-1
The Papers and Correspondence of William Stanley Jevons. 7 vols. Ed. by R. D. Collison-Black. Kelley 1972–81 $195.00 set. ISBN 0-678-07017. Vol. 1 *Bibliography and Personal Journal.* ISBN 0-678-07012-1. Vol. 2 *Correspondence, 1850–1862.* ISBN 0-678-07011-3. Vol. 3 *Correspondence, 1863–1872.* ISBN 0-333-10253-3. Vol. 4 *Correspondence, 1873–1878.* ISBN 0-333-19977-4. Vol. 5 *Correspondence, 1879–1882.* ISBN 0-333-19978-2. Vol. 6 *Lectures on Political Economy, 1875–1876.* ISBN 0-333-10258-4. Vol. 7 *Papers on Political Economy.* ISBN 0-333-19979-0
The State in Relation to Labour. Kelley 1968 repr. of 1910 ed. $29.50. ISBN 0-678-00434-X
The Theory of Political Economy. Kelley 1965 repr. of 1957 ed. $39.50. ISBN 0-678-00084-0

BOOKS ABOUT JEVONS

Gherity, James A. *Economic Thought: A Historical Anthology.* Random 1965 o.p. Contains a brief biography of Jevons, an article on Jevons's place in the history of economic thought, and a brief paper by Jevons on mathematics and the theory of political economy.
Keynes, John Maynard. *Essays in Biography.* Horizon Pr. 1951 o.p. Delightful biographical essay on Jevons includes personal observations on his life, times, and economic writings.
Schabas, Margaret. *A World Ruled by Number: William Stanley Jevons and the Rise of Mathematical Concepts.* Princeton U. Pr. 1990 o.p. Overview of Jevons and his work. Includes chapters on logic and scientific method, mathematical theory of economics, reactions to Jevons by his contemporaries, and his contributions to the profession.
Wood, John C., ed. *William Stanley Jevons: Critical Assessments.* 3 vols. Routledge 1988 $525.00. ISBN 0-415-00387-3. Comprehensive collection of 75 previously published articles on the life and work of Jevons.

KEYNES, JOHN MAYNARD. 1883–1946

John Maynard Keynes, an English economist, is regarded as the most important and influential economist of the twentieth century, if not of all time.

A brilliant child, he wrestled with the economic meaning of interest before he was 5 years old. He excelled both as a student and as a member of the debating team at Eton. His reputation at King's College at Cambridge University was such that he was invited to weekly breakfasts with economist A. C. Pigou, and even ALFRED MARSHALL begged him to become a professional economist. He was elected president of the Union, the most important nongovernmental debating society in the world, and his close friends included the intellectual members of the Bloomsbury group. Keynes was described as a phenomenon—and all of this took place before he graduated from Cambridge.

After graduating in 1905, Keynes took a civil service post in India. Bored with his job, he resigned and returned to Cambridge to teach. In 1912 he assumed the editorship of the *Economic Journal*, the leading journal in Britain at the time, continuing in the post for 33 years. His first major book, *Indian Currency and Finance* (1913), was an immediate success. He took part in the Paris Peace Conference as a representative of the Treasury. Later he held several other government advisory posts, served as a director of the Bank of England, and was president of an insurance company. In addition, Keynes was a noted patron of the arts and married the most beautiful and popular ballerina of his era. As if this weren't enough, he managed to amass a small fortune by investing in stocks and foreign currencies in his spare time.

At the Paris Peace Conference, Keynes became so dismayed by the harsh terms imposed on Germany in the Treaty of Versailles that he resigned in anger several days before the treaty was signed. He then wrote *The Economic Consequences of the Peace* (1919), which outlined the folly of the treaty. Being a man of many interests, Keynes next took a brief break from economics to publish *A Treatise on Probability* (1921), which BERTRAND RUSSELL (see Vols. 4 and 5) described as "impossible to praise too highly." Keynes's *A Tract on Monetary Reform* (1923) was a rather technical book that questioned the value of the gold standard over a managed paper currency. *A Treatise on Money* (1930), which explored the business cycle, was followed by *Essays in Persuasion* (1931) and *Essays in Biography* (1933).

The General Theory of Employment, Interest and Money, published in 1936, was Keynes's crowning achievement, and it took the world by storm. According to Keynes, the economy could be thought of as being divided into consumer, investment (or business), government, and foreign sectors. This was hardly a novel idea, but Keynes went on to postulate the exact nature of expenditures in each sector, especially the spending patterns of the consumer sector, which he portrayed by using a graph he called a "consumption function." He reasoned that fluctuations in total economic activity could be traced to instability in the business sector, which had a multiplier effect on the rest of the economy.

The relationship specified in *The General Theory* were tantalizing to economists, because they could be tested and empirically verified. Subsequent research largely confirmed Keynes's propositions. Soon governments, including that of the United States, began to develop a set of national income accounts to provide estimates of gross national product and national income. *The General Theory* was also popular because it offered policy prescriptions to help deal with the problems of depression, recession, and unemployment. Today the term "Keynesian" is used to describe individuals or policies that use taxation and government spending to affect aggregate economic performance.

BOOKS BY KEYNES

The Collected Writings of John Maynard Keynes. 30 vols. Ed. by Donald Moggridge. Cambridge U. Pr. 1992 $1,395.00. ISBN 0-521-30766-X

The Economic Consequences of the Peace. Viking Penguin 1988 $10.95. ISBN 0-14-011380-0

Essays in Biography. Horizon Pr. 1951 o.p. Fifteen outstanding essays on work and lives of politicians and economists, including Jevons and Malthus.

General Theory of Employment, Interest and Money. HarBraceJ 1965 $9.95. ISBN 0-15-634711-3

A Treatise on Money. 2 vols. AMS Pr. repr. of 1930 ed. $75.00. ISBN 0-404-15000-4

BOOKS ABOUT KEYNES

Blaug, Mark. *John Maynard Keynes: Life, Ideas, Legacy.* St. Martin 1990 $29.95. ISBN 0-312-04890-4. Includes conversations with leading economists and the life and ideas of Keynes.

Clarke, Peter. *The Keynesian Revolution in the Making, 1924–36.* OUP 1990 $28.00. ISBN 0-19-820219-9. Historical account of events that influenced Keynes's thinking, as opposed to his economic theories.

Harrod, Roy. *The Life of John Maynard Keynes.* Norton 1983 $14.95. ISBN 0-393-30024-2. Comprehensive, lengthy, and definitive look at Keynes and his work.

Heilbroner, Robert. *The Worldly Philosophers: The Lives, Times and Ideas of the Great Economic Thinkers.* S&S Trade 1987 $10.95. ISBN 0-671-63318-X. Lively and entertaining chapter on Keynes is titled "The Sick World of John Maynard Keynes."

Hillard, John, ed. *J. M. Keynes in Retrospect: The Legacy of the Keynesian Revolution.* Ashgate Pub. Co. 1988 $49.95. ISBN 1-85278-012-6. Collection of 10 articles in honor of the fiftieth anniversary of *The General Theory.* Includes articles on the Keynesian revolution in retrospect and the current use of Keynesian approaches.

Schumpeter, Joseph A. *Ten Great Economists From Marx to Keynes.* OUP 1965 o.p. Contains an excellent biographical chapter on Keynes that also analyzes his theoretical contributions.

Wood, John C. *John Maynard Keynes: Critical Assessments.* 4 vols. Croom Helm UK 1983 o.p. Comprehensive collection of 150 previously published articles on the life and work of Keynes. Contains a brief biography in the overview section and 14 other biographical articles.

KLEIN, LAWRENCE ROBERT. 1920– (NOBEL PRIZE 1980)

Lawrence Klein is an American economist and educator. He received the first Ph.D. granted in economics by MIT, in 1944, and taught at several colleges and universities before joining the faculty of the Wharton School at the University of Pennsylvania. His Nobel Prize was awarded for his work developing econometric models—computer simulations of aggregate economic activity—to forecast economic trends.

Klein was not the first to work on econometric models, but he was the first to combine theoretical models with modern statistics and the power of modern computers on such a massive scale. His first model, designed when he was 24 and described in *An Econometric Model of the United States, 1929–52* (1955), provides a concise and detailed account of the 20 equations that make up the model. The model gained fame when it correctly predicted that the U.S. economy would not slip back into depression after the end of World War II. Today, the model has over 1,000 equations, representing virtually all sectors of the economy; it is constantly being updated with new data as they become available. The model is used to forecast macroeconomic trends in output and unemployment, as well as industry-level outcomes, such as the production of steel or the demand for energy.

Klein is not well known outside the profession because of the mathematical nature of econometric modeling. His work, however, is more accessible than might be thought. The general reader will find *An Introduction to Econometric*

Forecasting and Forecasting Models (1980)—a text dealing with forecasting objectives, resources and structure, model specifications, and appraisal of success—one of the least technical and best introductions to the topic.

BOOKS BY KLEIN

Advanced Lectures in Econometrics. (coauthored with W. Welfe). Elsevier 1984 $37.50. ISBN 0-444-86676-0. Advanced lectures in econometrics dealing with model structures, simulations, validations, and dynamic analysis; highly quantitative.

An Econometric Model of the United States, 1929–52. (coauthored with A. S. Goldberger). Wiley 1955 o.p.

Economic Theory and Econometrics. Ed. by Jaime Marquez. U. of Pa. Pr. 1985 $58.95. ISBN 0-8122-7937-9. Collection of 33 previously published scholarly articles on econometric methodology, econometrics and economic theory, and applied econometrics.

The Economics of Supply and Demand. Johns Hopkins 1983 $24.00. ISBN 0-8018-3095-8. Collection of seven loosely connected essays dealing with supply and demand from a supply-side perspective.

An Introduction to Econometric Forecasting and Forecasting Models. (coauthored with Richard M. Young). Heath 1980 o.p.

A Textbook of Econometrics. P-H 1974 o.p. Classic text on econometric methods.

BOOK ABOUT KLEIN

Breit, William, and Roger W. Spencer, eds. *Lives of the Laureates: Ten Nobel Economists.* MIT Pr. 1990 $19.95. ISBN 0-262-02308-3. Autobiographical accounts of ten Nobel Laureates in economics. Includes a short, readable, chapter by Klein on his life and his efforts to establish the mathematical method in economics.

KNIGHT, FRANK HYNEMAN. 1885–1962

American economist Frank Knight was best known for his theoretical work on the profits earned by entrepreneurs. Knight was the eldest of 11 children born to deeply religious parents in southern Illinois. As an adult, he was known for challenging prevailing economic doctrines. This penchant for questioning the existing order, however, was revealed much earlier. While attending church at age 14 or 15, Knight and his siblings were required to sign pledges binding them to attend church services for the rest of their lives. As soon as they returned home, Knight built a fire behind the barn and demanded that everyone burn these pledges on the grounds that, since they were made under duress, they could not be binding.

Knight received his education at Milligan College, the University of Tennessee, and Cornell University. He taught at Cornell, the University of Iowa, and the University of Chicago, where he remained from 1927 until 1958. Knight's most famous book is *Risk, Uncertainty and Profit* (1921). In it, he attempted to explain why a firm could earn profits under conditions of perfect competition, even though accepted theory argued that equilibrium was incompatible with the existence of profits. To address this problem, he introduced the distinction between risk and uncertainty. Risk involves situations in which the probability of an outcome can be estimated (such as the chance of dying at a certain age, of a labor force going on strike, and so on). If the probability of an outcome could be estimated, then the firm could protect itself in a number of ways, such as by acquiring insurance. Uncertainty, however, involves situations in which the outcome cannot possibly be predicted (such as the introduction of a new and vastly superior product by a close competitor). Since rapid economic change involves uncertainty, Knight reasoned that the profits earned by competitive firms must be a reward for uncertainty, rather than risk. This was, and still is, regarded as a superior explanation of profit, and it marks Knight's most important contribution to the field of economics. Another important contribution involved Knight's attack on the concept of a production period in the theory of capital formation. The concept is somewhat esoteric and mostly of interest to theoretical economists, but it should be noted that Knight's criticism was sufficiently powerful to remove the concept from the literature.

Knight viewed economics as part of a larger whole that involved consensus and rational discussion, and resulted in a liberal society based on individual freedoms. Because of this, his interests extended to morality, ethics, and philosophy. In 1950 Knight was honored with the presidency of the American Economics Association, and in 1957 he received the Walker Medal, the association's highest award.

BOOKS BY KNIGHT

The Ethics of Competition and Other Essays. Ayer facs. ed. 1935 $18.75. ISBN 0-8369-1088-5. Collection of articles dealing with ethics and competition, economic psychology and values, marginal utility, statics and dynamics, cost of production over long and short periods, and value and interest.

Freedom and Reform. Liberty Fund 1982 $14.00. ISBN 0-86597-004-1

On the History and Method of Economics. U. Ch. Pr. 1956 o.p. Collection of 11 essays published from the 1920s through the 1950s discussing historical and methodological issues in economics, statics and dynamics, the business cycle, and other topics.

Risk, Uncertainty and Profit. Kelley 1964 repr. of 1921 ed. $39.50. ISBN 0-678-00031-X

BOOKS ABOUT KNIGHT

Blaug, Mark. *Frank Knight, 1885–1972, Henry Simmons, 1899–1946 and Joseph Schumpeter, 1883–1950.* Ashgate Pub. Co. 1992 $139.95. ISBN 1-85278-500-4. Ten previously published journal articles about methodology, social economics, uncertainty and rational action, religion and economic policy, market power, and comparisons with John R. Commons; includes some biographical material.

Samuels, W. J., ed. *Research in the History of Economic Thought and Methodology, Vol. I.* Ed. by W. J. Samuels. Jai Pr. 1983 $63.50. ISBN 0-89232-328-0. Contains an excellent article, "Frank Hyneman Knight and the History of Economic Thought," by R. S. Howey.

————. *Research in the History of Economic Thought and Methodology, Vol. VIII.* Ed. by W. J. Samuels. Jai Pr. 1986 $63.50. ISBN 0-89232-678-6. Includes an article titled "Frank Knight Before Cornell: Some Light on the Dark Years," by D. Dewey.

KUZNETS, SIMON SMITH. 1901–1985 (NOBEL PRIZE 1971)

Simon Kuznets was the second American economist, after PAUL SAMUELSON, to win the Nobel Prize in economics. The award was made in honor of his work on modern economic growth, but his contributions of decades earlier involved some of the earliest attempts to define and measure components of national income. In fact, the entire thrust of Kuznets's professional life as an economist involved the collection of statistical series in one sense or another.

Kuznets was born in the Ukrainian city of Kharkov and served for a brief period as head of a Soviet statistical office. He then emigrated to the United States, where he studied economics at Columbia University. He was recruited by the National Bureau of Economic Research (NBER) to conduct studies on national income. Kuznets's association with the NBER lasted from 1927 through 1961, and he also held faculty positions at the University of Pennsylvania, Johns Hopkins University, and Harvard University.

Kuznets's earliest work, in the 1930s, included a number of studies and NBER reports on national income and its composition, capital formation, fluctuation in production and prices, and seasonal variations in industrial figures. When KEYNES published his *General Theory* in 1936, Kuznets was one of the first to have the statistical data needed to test and substantiate his propositions concerning the spending patterns of the consumer sector. Kuznets is also credited with the discovery of a building construction cycle of 16–22 years, now known as a "Kuznets cycle."

His later work focused on economic growth. His classic *Capital in the American Economy: Its Formation and Financing* (1961) was a monumental study of the period from the Civil War to the 1950s, and dealt with the importance of savings, methodological problems, and sources of data. His most popular work, and the one recognized by the Nobel Prize, was *Modern Economic Growth* (1966), which explained why modern economic growth has spread to such a limited proportion of the total world population. *Toward a Theory of Growth* (1968) developed a systematic theory of growth based on such factors as urbanization, industrialization, and social and political structures. Interestingly enough, the modern economic growth that Kuznets found in all of his studies transcended political structures, occurring in socialistic, communistic, and capitalistic economies.

BOOKS BY KUZNETS

Capital in the American Economy: Its Formation and Financing. Ayer 1975 repr. of 1961 ed. $48.50. ISBN 0-405-07596-0

Economic Change: Selected Essays in Business Cycles, National Income and Economic Growth. Greenwood 1983 repr. of 1953 ed. $49.50. ISBN 0-313-24007-8. Collection of two new and nine previously published essays on business cycle theory, economic trends, national income, welfare, and international economic differences.

Economic Development, the Family and Income Distribution: Selected Essays. Cambridge U. Pr. 1989 $65.95. ISBN 0-521-34384-4. Collection of 11 previously published papers dealing with economic growth, population structure, developing countries, demographic change, and the size-age structure of families.

Economic Growth and Structure. Norton 1965 o.p. Twelve essays on the theory of growth, population change, regional economic trends, and underdeveloped nations; that originally appeared during the 1950s and 1960s.

Economic Growth of Nations. Belknap Pr. 1971 o.p. Discusses levels and variability of growth rates in several European countries as well as Japan, the United States, Canada, and Australia.

Modern Economic Growth. Yale U. Pr. 1966 o.p.

Toward a Theory of Growth. Norton 1968 o.p.

BOOK ABOUT KUZNETS

Williamson, Jeffery G. *Inequality, Poverty, and History: The Kuznets Memorial Lectures of the Economic Growth Center.* Blackwell Pubs. 1991. o.p. Four lectures that review and extend Kuznets's work; includes a short biography.

LEONTIEF, WASSILY. 1906– (NOBEL PRIZE 1973)

Wassily Leontief is a Russian-born American economist and educator. After graduating from the University of Berlin, he worked briefly as a research associate with the (U.S.) National Bureau of Economic Research, where he did preliminary work on what is now known as an input-output model. He taught at Harvard University and then at New York University, where he founded the Institute for Economic Analysis. His Nobel Prize in 1973 was awarded for his work on input-output studies.

Input-output analysis is a technique for determining how various sectors of the economy interact. Leontief's first input-output table consisted of a 44-sector model of the U.S. economy arranged in the form of a matrix, with columns and rows for each of the sectors. When purchases in a column are added, the result is the total amount of resources, or "inputs," required by the sector. Sales, or "outputs," in any given row represent the output of the sector. The value of the model is that it provides an overall picture of interdependencies among sectors, so that economists can determine how changes in one sector will affect performance in other sectors. The methodology is described in great detail in Leontief's classic *Input-Output Economics* (1966); a more specific application of the methodology can be found in his *Future Impact of Automation on Workers* (1986). The latter explores worker displacement by computer-based automation in U.S. manufacturing, office work, and education and health care industries.

Today input-output models have a broad following, with some containing as many as 1,000 sectors. Leontief's models are used by the Pentagon, the World Bank, the United Nations, and over 30 countries for budgeting and economic prediction. Numerous other specialized applications of the model have been used in waste disposal management, pollution control, and even world disarmament.

BOOKS BY LEONTIEF

Essays in Economics: Theories, Theorizing, Facts and Policies. Transaction Pubs. 1985 $22.95. ISBN 0-87855-993-0. Collection of 31 previously published articles on a wide range of topics, including world economics, mathematics, Marx, Keynes, and capital transfers; the common theme is the structure, use, and misuse of economic theory.

The Future Impact of Automation on Workers. (coauthored with Faye Duchin). OUP 1985 $36.00. ISBN 0-19-503623-9

Input-Output Economics. OUP 1986 $26.00. ISBN 0-19-503527-5. Collection of 11 previously published essays on such topics as methodology, examples of input-output applications to disarmament, and foreign trade. An excellent nonquantitative introduction to input-output models.

The Structure of the American Economy, Nineteen Nineteen to Nineteen Thirty-Nine: An Empirical Application of Equilibrium Analysis. M. E. Sharpe 1976 $65.00. ISBN 0-87332-087-5. Expanded reprint of 1951 edition, which covered 1919–29. Coverage includes discussions of input-output, theoretical schemes, data and variables, structural changes, and empirical studies of interrelationships over time in the U.S. economy.

Studies in Structure of American Economy: Theoretical and Empirical Explorations in Input-Output Analysis. M. E. Sharpe 1976 $65.00. ISBN 0-87332-086-7. Summary of advances made during the Harvard Research Project on input-output analysis; includes changes in technical production coefficients and a lengthy exposition of interregional theory.

BOOKS ABOUT LEONTIEF

Shackleton, J. R., and Gareth Locksley. *Twelve Contemporary Economists.* Wiley 1981 o.p. Contains a chapter, "Wassily Leontief: Input-Output Analysis and Economic Planning," by Martin Cane.

Silk, Leonard. *The Economists.* Basic 1974 o.p. Includes 40-page chapter on Leontief titled "Wassily Leontief: Apostle of Planning." In addition to biographical information, provides a description of input-output analysis and a discussion of Leontief's place in economic history.

MALTHUS, THOMAS ROBERT. 1766–1834

Thomas Robert Malthus was born to a wealthy family near Surrey, England. His father, the eccentric Daniel Malthus, was friends with both DAVID HUME (see Vol. 4) and JEAN-JACQUES ROUSSEAU (see also Vol. 4). Malthus was educated privately at home and, at age 13, began two years of study in residence with Richard Graves, a Protestant minister near Bath. He excelled in history, classics, and fighting. In a letter to Daniel Malthus on the progress of his son, Graves stated that young Thomas "loves fighting for fighting's sake, and delights in bruising. . . ." In 1783 Malthus enrolled in a religious academy for Protestant dissenters; when it failed the same year, he became the private student of a radical Unitarian minister. At age 18, he enrolled at Jesus College, Cambridge, where he studied mathematics and the classics. He graduated from Cambridge in 1788 and became an ordained minister in the Church of England in 1791.

Malthus and his father frequently discussed the issues of the day. When the elder Malthus became fascinated with the utopian philosophy of the popular William Godwin, which preached a vision of peace, prosperity, and equality for all, the younger Malthus expressed his doubts in a manuscript intended only for his father. His father suggested that it be published, however, and so *An Essay on the Principle of Population As It Affects the Future Improvement of Society* appeared in 1798. The book was an instant success. Well written, it argued that population tended to grow at a geometric (exponential) rate, whereas the resources needed to support the population would only grow at an arithmetic (linear) rate. Eventually, society would not have the resources to support its population, and the result would be misery, poverty, and a subsistence standard of living for the masses. *An Essay on the Principle of Population* thrust Malthus into the public eye and dealt such a lethal blow to utopian visions that economics was soon called "the dismal science."

In 1805 Malthus became the first person in England to receive the title of political economist when he was appointed professor of history and political economy at the East India College. In 1811 he met DAVID RICARDO, and the two soon became lifelong friends and professional rivals. In 1820 Malthus published *Principles of Political Economy*, a sometimes obscure but far-reaching treatment of economics that advocated a form of national income accounting, made advances in the theory of rent, and extended the analysis of supply and demand.

Today, Malthus is more remembered for his views on population than for his views on economics. Even so, his other achievements have not gone unnoticed. JOHN MAYNARD KEYNES paid the ultimate tribute when he wrote: "If only Malthus, instead of Ricardo, had been the parent stem from which nineteenth-century economics proceeded, what a much wiser and richer place the world would be to-day!"

BOOKS BY MALTHUS

An Essay on the Principle of Population. Viking Penguin 1983 $6.95. ISBN 0-14-043206-X
The Principles of Political Economy, Considered with a View to Their Practical Application. Kelley 1986 repr. of 1836 ed. $45.00. ISBN 0-678-00038-7

BOOKS ABOUT MALTHUS

Heilbroner, Robert. *The Worldly Philosophers: The Lives, Times and Ideas of the Great Economic Thinkers.* S&S Trade 1987 $10.95. ISBN 0-671-63318-X. Lively and entertaining survey of Malthus and Ricardo, their lives and writings, and the competition between the two; also investigates economic conditions of the times.
Keynes, John Maynard. *Essays in Biography.* Horizon Pr. 1951 o.p. Contains a biographical essay, "Robert Malthus: the First of the Cambridge Economists," with personal observations not found elsewhere.
Turner, Michael, ed. *Malthus and His Time.* St. Martin 1986 $29.95. ISBN 0-312-50942-1. Collection of 15 essays from a 1980 conference on Malthus; focus is on various aspects of his writings and theory rather than biographical background.

Winch, Donald. *Malthus*. OUP 1987 $6.95. ISBN 0-19-287652-X. Short, critical essay examines Malthus as a demographer and political scientist.

MARSHALL, ALFRED. 1842–1924

Alfred Marshall, an English economist, is widely regarded as the founder of the neoclassical school of economics. This school of thought, which followed the classical economists (SMITH, RICARDO, and MILL, among others), gave a more balanced role to supply and demand as determinants of price, took more of an interest in the role of money, and greatly extended the role of marginal analysis.

Marshall was born near London. His father, a clerk at the Bank of England, wanted his son to become a clergyman, but young Alfred was more interested in mathematics. After graduating from St. John's College at Cambridge, he lectured there for several years. When he married one of his former students in 1877, he had to leave Cambridge because of the celibacy requirements in force at the time. Marshall taught at University College, Bristol, and then at Oxford University, before returning to Cambridge in 1884 (the celibacy requirement having been lifted).

Marshall did not publish extensively, but one book was outstanding. His *Principles of Economics*, the first of a planned two-volume work, appeared in 1890. An instant success, it established Marshall as one of the world's leading economists. Its strength lay in its comprehensiveness and the degree to which it incorporated previous developments, along with Marshall's own observations, in a seamless fashion. The book was full of now familiar terms, such as consumer surplus, long- and short-run analysis, and external economies.

The second volume, intended to cover the topics of foreign trade, money, trade fluctuations, and taxation, was never published because of Marshall's failing health and his penchant for exhaustive revision. He did, however, publish a less comprehensive volume, *Industry and Trade* (1919). A final volume, *Money, Credit and Commerce* (1923), was less ambitious and less creative.

Despite his frail health, which troubled him throughout his career, Marshall lived to the ripe old age of 81. His stature was such that he is credited with founding a "Cambridge school of economics," and his few publications forever changed the world of economics.

BOOKS BY MARSHALL

Industry and Trade. Macmillan 1919 o.p. Factual and historical discussion of trends in the British and international economies; regarded by many as Marshall's second most important work.

Memorials of Alfred Marshall. Ed. by A. C. Pigou. Kelley 1925 $49.50. ISBN 0-678-00197-9. Contains 20 selections by Marshall as well as biographical articles by Keynes, Edgeworth, Fay, and Pigou.

Money, Credit and Commerce. Kelley 1991 repr. of 1923 ed. $39.50. ISBN 0-678-01463-9

Principles of Economics. Porcupine Pr. 1982 $28.95. ISBN 0-87997-051-8

Pure Theory of Foreign Trade and the Pure Theory of Domestic Values. Kelley 1975 repr. of 1897 ed. $15.00. ISBN 0-678-01194-X. Contains four theoretical appendices intended for a separate volume on international trade.

BOOKS ABOUT MARSHALL

Homan, Paul T. *Contemporary Economic Thought*. Ayer facs. ed. 1928 $21.50. ISBN 0-8369-0546-6. Contains a chapter on the life, times, influences, and economic writings of Marshall.

Kerr, Clark. *Marshall, Marx and Modern Times*. Cambridge U. Pr. 1969 o.p. Based on lectures at Cambridge in 1968, analyzing the two as opposing prophets representing contrary views of economic evolution.

Keynes, John Maynard. *Essays in Biography*. Horizon Pr. 1951 o.p. Contains a delightful biographical essay on Marshall, with personal observations on life, times, and works of Marshall not found elsewhere.

Reisman, David. *The Economics of Alfred Marshall*. St. Martin 1986 $39.95. ISBN 0-312-23430-9. Interesting reader that contains interpretative chapters on supply and demand, economies of size, diseconomies, market structures, distribution, land, labor, and capital; intended to be read along with Marshall's *Principles*.

Schumpeter, Joseph A. *Ten Great Economists from Marx to Keynes*. OUP 1965 o.p. Contains an excellent chapter on Alfred Marshall, focusing on his ideas and contributions and his stature in the profession.

Spiegel, H. W., ed. *The Development of Economic Thought*. Wiley 1966 o.p. Contains a 16-page biographical chapter on Marshall by the noted economic historian Jacob Viner.

Wood, John C., ed. *Alfred Marshall: Critical Assessments*. 4 vols. Longwood Pr. 1982 o.p. Comprehensive collection of 121 previously published and 2 new articles appearing since 1887. Contains a biographical summary in the volume overview.

MARX, KARL HEINRICH. 1818–1883

German social scientist, economic historian, and revolutionary, Karl Marx was born in Trier, Germany, to a family descended from a long line of Jewish rabbis. His father, however, renounced the Jewish faith and embraced Christianity in order to further his legal practice. In 1835 Marx entered the University of Bonn to study law and, the following year, went to the University of Berlin, where he came under the influence of GEORGE HEGEL (see also Vol. 4). Political turmoil at Berlin forced him to complete his studies at the University of Jena, where he received a doctorate with a thesis on post-Aristotelian Greek philosophy.

Marx was unable to get a university appointment in Prussia because of the political climate there and his involvement with the Hegelians. As a result, he went to Cologne and took a position as editor of a liberal newspaper. When the paper ran into trouble with the authorities and was closed down, Marx went to Paris, where he edited another short-lived newspaper, joined socialist and radical groups, and began a lifelong friendship with FRIEDRICH ENGELS (see also Vol. 4). Paris, however, soon found Marx's views to be too extreme, and he was forced to leave in 1844. From Paris, Marx and Engels moved to Brussels, where Marx began studying economic history. The two friends joined the Communist League and wrote its declaration, the *Manifesto of the Communist Party* (1848). When revolution broke out in Europe the same year, Marx went back to Paris and then to Cologne, where he founded yet another influential newspaper that attacked the Prussian autocracy. When the revolution subsided in 1849, however, the government closed down this newspaper as well. In protest, Marx printed the last issue in red and then fled to London, where he spent the rest of his life in exile.

Marx's years in London were marked by extreme poverty. Unable to find work, he and his wife and three children lived in a two-room slum apartment. Only small gifts and loans from Engels enabled the family to survive. As a result, Marx observed firsthand the Industrial Revolution, with its extremes of wealth and poverty. Not surprisingly, he viewed industrialization as a systematic exploitation of the working class. His views on the subject were put forth in *Das Kapital* (1867), which predicted that capitalism would destroy itself and be replaced by communism. Marx's theory was based on the accepted classical economic doctrines of the period. For example, he embraced DAVID RICARDO's labor theory of value and expanded it to show how surplus value—the value added by a worker in excess of the wage needed for that worker's subsistence—could arise. Marx borrowed the idea of subsistence wage from THOMAS MALTHUS, although he argued that it would occur for other reasons. He also embraced competition and used it in a way to explain the recurrent business cycles of the day. When Marx died in London in 1883, only the first volume of *Das Kapital* had appeared. It was left to Engels to edit and arrange for the publication of the other two.

Marx's writings had only a limited impact on society at the time, and the revolution and fall of capitalism that he so painstakingly predicted never happened. Ironically, Marxism did take hold many years later in the agrarian economies of Russia and China—economies that lacked the industrialization that was to exploit the masses and bring about communism.

BOOKS BY MARX

Capital. Vol. 1 *A Critique of Political Economy.* Trans. by Ben Fowkes. Viking Penguin 1992 $14.95. ISBN 0-14-044568-4

Capital. Vol. 2 *The Process of Circulation of Capital.* Ed. by Friedrich Engels. Intl. Pubs. Co. 1985 $7.50. ISBN 0-7178-0622-7

Capital. Vol. 3 *The Process of Capitalist Production as a Whole.* Ed. by Friedrich Engels. Intl. Pubs. Co. 1984 $8.95. ISBN 0-7178-0623-5

Communist Manifesto. (coauthored with Friedrich Engels). 1848. Viking Penguin 1985 $3.50. ISBN 0-14-044478-5

Poverty of Philosophy. Intl. Pubs. Co. 1992 $6.95. ISBN 0-7178-0701-0

BOOKS ABOUT MARX

Berlin, Isaiah. *Karl Marx: His Life and Environment.* OUP 1978 $9.95. ISBN 0-19-520052-7. Scholarly appraisal of Marx's life, views, and influences. Covers his work as a journalist, propagandist, political strategist, economic theorist.

Heilbroner, Robert. *The Worldly Philosophers: The Lives, Times and Ideas of the Great Economic Thinker.* S&S Trade 1987 $10.95. ISBN 0-671-63318-X. Contains a chapter titled "The Inexorable World of Karl Marx" that covers his life, times, writings, and influence.

———. *Marxism: For and Against.* Norton 1980 $7.95. ISBN 0-393-95166-9. Explores the lingering fascination with Marx, arguing neither for nor against him.

Robinson, Joan. *An Essay on Marxian Economics.* Porcupine Pr. 1991 $12.95. ISBN 0-87991-270-7. One of the best books on Marxian economics ever written. Discovers elements of Keynesian theory in Marx's writings.

Schumpeter, Joseph A. *Ten Great Economists from Marx to Keynes.* OUP 1965 o.p. Contains a 70-page chapter, "The Marxian Doctrine," that covers all aspects of Marx—as a prophet, sociologist, economist, and as a teacher; a searching and thoughtful appraisal.

Sweezy, Paul M. *Theory of Capitalist Development.* Monthly Rev. 1968 $12.00. ISBN 0-85345-079-X. Scholarly appraisal that is highly recommended.

Wilson, Edmund. *To the Finland Station.* FS&G 1972 $14.95. ISBN 0-374-51045-8. Excellent biography of Marx and Engels that reads like a novel.

Wood, John C. *Karl Marx's Economics: Critical Assessments.* 4 vols. Croom Helm UK 1987 $595.00. ISBN 0-7099-5221-X. Comprehensive collection of 150 previously published articles dealing with such topics as the transformation problem, value judgments in *Capital*, labor heterogeneity, alienation, the young Marx, and Marxian analysis. Includes a brief biography in the overview section.

MILL, JOHN STUART. 1806–1873

John Stuart Mill was a writer, philosopher, social scientist, and humanist with broad-ranging interests. He was born in London and educated privately by his father, James Mill, the noted economist and philosopher. At age 17, he became a clerk for the East India Company and remained there until 1858, when he retired from a post as chief examiner. A leading intellectual of the period, Mill wrote extensively; he also directed the *London and Westminster Review* (1834–1840) and served as a member of Parliament (1865–1868).

Even though he had no formal schooling, Mill's education was intensive. He received constant tutoring from his father and was so busy with his studies that he had no idea that his life was out of the ordinary. Life was not without some excitement, however. At the age of 16, he was arrested and spent a night in jail for distributing birth control literature to the poor in the City of London. He had a nervous breakdown in his early twenties, and, by the time he was 24, he had fallen in love with the attractive, intelligent, and sensitive Harriet Taylor, who, unfortunately, was already married. Undaunted by this impediment, Harriet Taylor and John Stuart Mill began a relationship that lasted for 20 years. Harriet refused to divorce her husband, but she moved away from him so that she could see more of Mill. Over the years they wrote to each other and traveled and lived together. Eventually, in 1849, John Taylor died, and two years later, Mill and Harriet Taylor were married. Unfortunately, her health had begun to decline by then, and she died seven years later in 1858. Heartbroken, Mill bought a house near the cemetery in Avignon where she was buried so that he could be nearby.

Mill's most important work in economics was his two-volume *Principles of Political Economy* (1848). This work offered a sweeping and comprehensive survey of economics, and it argued persuasively that the focus of economics should be on production instead of distribution. The implications of Mill's argument were enormous, because it meant that society could do whatever it pleased with the commodities produced by people's labor. In essence, Mill made the distribution of output a social and moral question, not something determined by natural laws. The distribution of wealth was no longer the province of the business and commercial class or of other vested interests that earned profits; it was now the responsibility of the politicians or of society in general.

One of Mill's last books was his provocative *Subjection of Women* (1869), which rejected the common view that the inferior status of women was due to any natural inferiority. Instead, he argued that women would be much more interesting if they were genuinely independent of, and equal with, men. He no doubt had Harriet in mind when he wrote *Subjection*, and when he died he was buried next to her in Avignon.

BOOKS BY MILL

Autobiography of John Stuart Mill. Col. U. Pr. 1960 $15.50. ISBN 0-231-08506-0. Published without alterations or omissions from the original manuscript at Columbia University.

On Liberty. Viking Penguin 1982 $5.95. ISBN 0-14-043207-8

Principles of Political Economy. 1848. Ed. by Donald Winch. Viking Penguin 1986 $9.95. ISBN 0-14-043260-4

The Subjection of Women. 1869. Prometheus Bks. 1986 $4.95. ISBN 0-87975-335-8

A System of Logic. Ibis Pub. VA 1986 $31.95. ISBN 0-935005-29-3

Utilitarianism. Prometheus Bks. $4.95. ISBN 0-87975-376-5

BOOKS ABOUT MILL

Blaug, Mark. *Economic Theory in Retrospect.* Cambridge U. Pr. 1985 $24.95. ISBN 0-521-31644-8. Standard text and reference work on the history of economic thought from mercantilism to Keynes. Focuses on theory, comparative contributions of economists, with a separate chapter on Mill.

Hollander, Samuel. *The Economics of John Stuart Mill.* U. of Toronto Pr. 1985 $95.00. ISBN 0-8020-5671-7. Scholarly and exhaustive analysis of Mill and his works. Contains two chapters on methodology and the scope and method of Mill's works and nine additional chapters covering all aspects of Mill's economic writings.

Packe, Michael St. John. *The Life of John Stuart Mill.* Secker & Warburg 1954 o.p. Comprehensive and definitive biography, based in part on newly released personal papers.

Robson, John M. *The Improvement of Mankind: The Social and Political Thought of John Stuart Mill.* Bks. Demand 1968 $76.50. ISBN 0-317-26963-1. Scholarly biography of Mill that examines the influence of Jeremy Bentham, Mill's mental crisis as young man, and his life with Harriet Taylor.

Romano, Richard, and Melvin Leiman. *Views on Capitalism.* Glencoe 1970 o.p. Examines various perspectives on capitalism. Contains useful overview of, and selections from, Mill's major works.

MITCHELL, WESLEY CLAIR. 1874–1948

Wesley Clair Mitchell was an American economist. Born in Illinois, he studied at the University of Chicago under THORSTEIN VEBLEN and taught at Columbia University. As Veblen's student he developed an "institutional" view of the economy based on his belief that financial factors, especially corporate profits, are the driving force in industry. Director of the National Bureau of Economic Research (NBER) for 25 years, he devoted his life to the study of business cycles.

Mitchell is regarded by many as the greatest of the business-cycle analysts. His first major work, *Business Cycles* (1913), identified various economic processes at work during periods of economic expansion and contraction, and suggested techniques for identifying leads, lags, and turning points. This work, along with *Measuring Business Cycles* (1946), which he coauthored with Arthur Burns, set the standard for determining business-cycle turning points in U.S. economic history. Most of the business-cycle indicator terminology used today is a direct result of Mitchell's work. Mitchell's last work, *What Happens During Business Cycles: A Progress Report* (1951), was an early but incomplete effort to construct a dynamic, self-generating theory of business cycles.

Marshall's legacy to the profession was enormous. Such is the reputation of the NBER's work on business cycles that even the U.S. Department of Commerce defers to it for the dating of cycle turning points.

BOOKS BY MITCHELL

Business Cycles. U. CA Pr. 1913 o.p.

Business Cycles and Their Causes. Porcupine Pr. 1989 $12.95. ISBN 0-87991-262-6. Update and rerelease of theoretical portion of *Business Cycles.*

Measuring Business Cycles. (coauthored with Arthur Burns). NBER 1946 o.p.

Types of Economic Theory: From Mercantilism to Institutionalism. 2 vols. Ed. by J. Dorfman. Kelley 1969 $79.00. ISBN 0-678-00234-7. Transcribed lecture notes from Mitchell's course at Columbia; includes historical origins of economic theories related to particular legal, social, and political events.

What Happens During Business Cycles: A Progress Report. NBER 1951 o.p.

BOOKS ABOUT MITCHELL

Blaug, Mark, ed. *Wesley Mitchell (1874–1948), John Commons, Clarence Ayers.* Ashgate Pub. Co. 1992 $89.95. ISBN 1-85278-496-2. Collection of previously published articles.

Homan, Paul T. *Contemporary Economic Thought.* Ayer facs. ed. 1928 $21.50. ISBN 0-8369-0546-6. Contains a thoughtful chapter on life, times, writings, and influence of Mitchell.

Mitchell, L. S. *Two Lives: The Story of Wesley Clair Mitchell and Myself.* S&S Trade 1953 o.p. Biography written by Mitchell's wife reveals his personal side.

Schumpeter, Joseph A. *Ten Great Economists from Marx to Keynes.* OUP 1965 o.p. Profiles the life and work of famous economists; contains a moving chapter about Mitchell written at the time of his death.

MYRDAL, (KARL) GUNNAR. 1908–1987 (Nobel Prize 1974)

Swedish-born economist Gunnar Myrdal achieved international recognition for his studies of the economic plight of minorities and underdeveloped nations. After earning a doctorate in economics from Stockholm University in 1927, Myrdal went to the United States as a Rockefeller fellow. Upon his return to Sweden in 1930, he became interested in politics and was elected to the Swedish Parliament in 1935. In subsequent years, he held a number of government posts and was appointed executive secretary of the United Nations Economic Commission for Europe from 1947 to 1957. He was also a professor of economics at Stockholm University from 1933 to 1950 and again from 1960 to 1967.

Myrdal's book *Monetary Equilibrium*, published in 1931, introduced the *ex ante* and *ex post* concepts that proved to be a useful way to distinguish between economic anticipations and actual outcomes. Another important work, *The Political Element in the Development of Economic Theory* (1930), raised methodological questions concerning the relevance and application of narrowly defined economic assumptions to the general problems of society. According to Myrdal, economists should bring all relevant knowledge to bear on a problem, even if it involves concepts and ideas from other disciplines.

The general public became acquainted with Myrdal through *An American Dilemma: The Negro Problem and Modern Democracy* (1944). In this work, Myrdal argued that the inferior economic status of African Americans was the result of political and sociological factors, such as prejudice and discrimination, as well as such economic factors as health and education. Two later works, *Economic Theory and Underdeveloped Regions* (1957) and *Asian Drama* (1968), dealt with living standards, economic planning, social attitudes, and political democracy.

One of Myrdal's main economic ideas is cumulative causation, which states that small and seemingly unrelated events have a cumulative effect in raising or lowering living standards—in essence a virtuous or vicious circle of events. In 1974 Myrdal received the Nobel Prize (jointly with Friedrich von Hayek) for his pioneering work in the theory of money and economic fluctuations and his analysis of the interdependence of economic, social, and international phenomena.

Books by Myrdal

An American Dilemma: The Negro Problem and Modern Democracy. 2 vols. Pantheon repr. of 1945 ed. $5.95. ea. ISBNs 0-394-73042-9, 0-394-73043-7

Asian Drama: An Inquiry Into the Poverty of Nations. 3 vols. TCFP-PPP 1968 o.p.

The Challenge of World Poverty: A World Anti-Poverty Program in Outline. Pantheon 1970 o.p. Based on 1969 lectures at Johns Hopkins. Covers such topics as agriculture, population, education, trade, capital movements, foreign aid, and other policies to reduce world poverty.

Economic Theory and Under-developed Regions. HarpC 1957 o.p.

Monetary Equilibrium. 1931. Kelley 1965 repr. of 1939 ed. $29.50. ISBN 0-678-00092-1

The Political Element in the Development of Economic Theory. 1930. Transaction Pubs. 1990 $19.95. ISBN 0-88738-827-2. Based on lectures delivered in 1928; contains a critical historical account of political influence on the evolution of economic thought and discussion of politics and ideology, economic liberalism, theory of public finance, and the role of economics in politics.

BOOKS ABOUT MYRDAL

Jackson, Walter A. *Gunnar Myrdal and America's Conscience: Social Engineering and Racial Liberalism, 1938–1987.* U. of NC Pr. 1990 o.p. Focus on Myrdal as a political intellectual confronting the American conscience on the issue of race. Also examines the influence of Myrdal on other intellectuals.

Southern, David W. *Gunnar Myrdal and Black-White Relations: The Use and Abuse of "An American Dilemma." 1944–1969.* La. State U. Pr. 1987 $40.00. ISBN 0-8071-1302-6. Examines how Myrdal's ideas shaped racial perceptions and events from 1944 through the 1960s.

PARETO, VILFREDO. 1848–1923

The controversial economist and sociologist Vilfredo Pareto was born in Paris, the son of an Italian father and a French mother. When Pareto was 3, the family returned to Italy, and at age 16 he entered the Polytechnic Institute of Turin. While a student at the Institute, he published his first paper in mathematics, and he graduated from there with degrees in mathematics, physical sciences, and engineering. In 1875 Pareto was appointed general manager of a nearly bankrupt iron works company, and he spent the next few years trying to raise capital for the company and visiting other iron works. By 1890 Pareto had tired of management, and he left the company so that he could study economics. He became extremely interested in this field and devoted all of his energies to it. His first writings on the subject appeared between 1892 and 1912, and in 1893 he accepted the chair of political economy at the University of Lausanne.

Pareto is credited with several important theoretical advances in economics. First, he showed that utility did not have to be measurable in order for the economy to reach the theoretical concept of general equilibrium. Second, he improved on accepted general equilibrium equations to specify the now standard equilibrium conditions for the consumer side of the economy. Third, he specified the requirements for an optimal allocation of resources—a condition now termed "Pareto optimality." A final contribution, known as "Pareto's Law," dealt with the distribution of income, stating that 80 percent of the income was earned by only 20 percent of the people. Also called the 80/20 rule, Pareto's Law seems to apply to a number of other situations as well, such as in the assertion that 80 percent of all highway accidents are caused by 20 percent of the drivers or 80 percent of worker tardiness and absenteeism is caused by 20 percent of the employees.

Virtually all of Pareto's contributions in economics are summed up in his masterful *Manual of Political Economy* (1909), which even today is regarded as a milestone in the development of economic theory. Shortly after the publication of the *Manual*, Pareto turned his interests to sociology and human behavior, and he continued to exert influence among scholars in those fields as well. Often frustrated by the inefficiency he observed in Italian government, Pareto feuded with the Italian authorities throughout most of his career. In later life he is thought to have leaned toward fascism as a result of early, favorable impressions of Benito Mussolini.

BOOK BY PARETO

Manual of Political Economy. 1909. Ed. by Alfred N. Page. Trans. by Ann Schweir. Kelley
   1969 $45.00. ISBN 0-678-00881-7

BOOKS ABOUT PARETO

Cirillo, Renato. *The Economics of Vilfredo Pareto.* Int. Spec. Bk. 1979 $28.50. ISBN 0-
   7146-3108-6. Systematic study gleaned from Pareto's many writings, some of them
   not primarily economic in nature. Covers Pareto's life and economic theories,
   welfare economics, laws of income distribution, utility theory, and general equilibrium theory.
Placido, Bucolo, ed. *The Other Pareto.* St. Martin 1980 $36.00. ISBN 0-312-58955-7.
   Explores Pareto's apparent support of fascism in Italy, and the relationship of
   Pareto's ideas to shifting political allegiances.
Powers, Charles. *Vilfredo Pareto. Matters of Sociological Theory Ser.* Sage 1987 $34.95.
   ISBN 0-685-12103-8. Personal profile and overview of Pareto as sociologist;
   examines why he left economics for sociology.

RICARDO, DAVID. 1772–1823

Born in London, David Ricardo was the third child in a family of at least 17
children. His father, a Dutch Jew, was a successful stockbroker who had moved
to London in 1760. Ricardo did not have the typical classical education afforded
the children of other wealthy families, but his father supplied him with tutors,
and he spent three years in an exclusive Jewish school in Amsterdam. At age 14
he began working in his father's brokerage business. Ricardo learned the
brokerage trade well, and he would have been regarded as a rousing success by
his family had he not married a Quaker and joined the Unitarian church,
causing an estrangement from his father. His abilities as a stockbroker,
however, were such that he quickly found other employment. Before long, he
had amassed a small fortune, and, by his early forties, he was able to retire and
devote time to his new interest, economics.

In 1809 Ricardo published his first article, which dealt with the price of gold
and the value of the British pound. This was followed by a popular pamphlet,
The High Price of Bullion, a Proof of the Depreciation of Bank Notes (1810), in
which he argued that the excess production of paper bank notes depreciated
their value. The House of Commons became so alarmed by Ricardo's argument
that it formed a committee to examine the high price of bullion and issued the
famous and controversial Bullion Report. During the bullion controversy,
Ricardo developed two interesting friendships. The first was with JOHN STUART
MILL, who took it upon himself to review Ricardo's manuscript and help him
develop his literary skills. The second was with THOMAS MALTHUS, who would
debate topics with Ricardo in order to help him to clarify his positions.
Although Ricardo and Malthus often took opposing positions on many public
issues, their differences never got in the way of their lifelong friendship.

The events of the period had a strong influence on Ricardo's economic
theories. England at this time was divided into two competing and hostile
groups—the industrialists with their factories and the landed aristocracy who
resented the new-found riches of the industrialists. The industrialists wanted
low grain prices so that wages could be kept low; the landed aristocracy wanted
high prices and high profits on the sale of their grain. The landowners, who held
a majority in Parliament, passed the infamous Corn Laws. These laws established a sliding import tax on grain, thereby setting artificially high prices for
grain in England. Ricardo saw the economic problem in terms of a distribution

of income, a view expressed forcibly in his *Principles of Political Economy and Taxation* (1817). According to Ricardo, workers received wages for their efforts, capitalists earned profits, and landowners received rent for the use of their land. Landowners, however, were unaffected by the pressure of competition and the growth of population, so only they would benefit from future growth.

In addition to Ricardo's contributions to the theory of rent and the distribution of income, he also developed a labor of value, supported free trade, and championed laissez faire. He argued for minimal taxation, the retirement of the national debt, and the abolition of relief policies for the poor on the grounds that it distorted the labor market.

Ricardo died suddenly from an ear infection in 1823, barely 14 years after his article on the bullion controversy. Even so, his theories had a lasting impact on the field of economics and on English economic policies. According to JOHN MAYNARD KEYNES, "Ricardo conquered England as completely as the Holy Inquisition conquered Spain."

BOOKS BY RICARDO

Minor Papers on the Currency Question. Ayer 1809–23 $19.00. ISBN 0-405-10624-6
The Principles of Political Economy and Taxation. C. E. Tuttle 1911 $6.95. ISBN 0-460-87125-0

BOOKS ABOUT RICARDO

Blaug, Mark. *David Ricardo (1772–1823).* Ashgate Pub. Co. 1991 $79.95. ISBN 1-85278-476-8. Comprehensive, scholarly discussion focusing on selected topics, such as full employment, population and wages, and Ricardo's relationship with Mill.

Heilbroner, Robert. *The Worldly Philosophers: The Lives, Times, and Ideas of the Great Economic Thinkers.* S&S Trade 1987 $10.95. ISBN 0-671-63318-X. Contains an excellent short chapter on Malthus and Ricardo.

Hollander, J. H. *David Ricardo: A Centenary Estimate.* AMS Pr. 1982 repr. of 1910 ed. $24.50. ISBN 0-404-61186-9. Brief, scholarly summary of Ricardo's life and impact.

Hollander, Samuel. *The Economics of David Ricardo.* Bks. Demand 1979 $160.00. ISBN 0-8357-3779-9. Comprehensive and authoritative analysis. Includes Ricardo's views on profits, theory of value, allocation mechanism, capital, employment and growth, money and banking, international trade, law of markets, and theory of public policy.

Stigler, George J. *Essays in the History of Economics.* U. Ch. Pr. 1965 o.p. Contains short essay, "The Ricardian Theory of Value and Distribution," that provides a sketch of Ricardo's work to define value and distribution theory; compares Ricardo's arguments to those of his contemporaries.

Weatherall, David. *David Ricardo.* Kluwer Ac. 1976 $42.50. ISBN 90-247-1865-1. Interesting and informative biographical study focusing on Ricardo's life and times and the influences on his life and work.

Wood, John C. *David Ricardo: Critical Assessments.* 4 vols. Routledge Chapman & Hall 1985 $495.00. ISBN 0-7099-2777-0. Extensive collection of 110 previously published articles about Ricardo's life and economic thought; includes a biographical introduction.

ROBINSON, JOAN (MAURICE). 1903–1983

British economist Joan Robinson was widely recognized for her work in monopolistic competition and capital theory. Born Joan Maurice in Chamberley, Surrey, she was educated at Girton College, Cambridge. In 1926 she married Austin Robinson, a Cambridge economist. In 1931 Joan Robinson received an appointment at Cambridge, and she remained there until 1971, succeeding her husband as a professor of economics in 1965.

Robinson's most famous work, *The Economics of Imperfect Competition* (1933), was intended to bridge the gap between the two main types of market structures in economics—perfect competition and monopoly. Her solution was to propose a type of industry structure called monopolistic competition in which an industry would have a number of small producers, each behaving as if it were monopolistic even though its actions affected, and were affected by, the actions of its competitors. The concept of monopolistic competition, which was also proposed by Harvard economist Edward Chamberlin at the same time, was a major advance in the field of economics. Both Robinson and Chamberlin spent years defending and distinguishing their versions of the concept. Most treatments of the topic today involve elements of both, although purists give a slight edge to Chamberlin.

Robinson was one of the early champions of the Keynesian revolution with her *Introduction to the Theory of Employment* (1937). She also wrote the classic, *Essay on Marxian Economics*, in which she pointed out many of the pre-Keynesian concepts in MARX's *Das Kapital*. Her works *The Rate of Interest and Other Essays* (1953) and *The Accumulation of Capital* (1956) attempted to develop a Keynesian approach to long-run equilibrium growth. At about the time that these were written, she thought she had discovered a flaw in the accepted theory of capital, which launched the acrimonious "Cambridge controversies" debate, so named because it involved both Cambridge University in England and Harvard University in Cambridge, Massachusetts. Much later in her career, Robinson rebelled against the prevailing economic theories that relied on comparative static analysis, and she presented her views in *Economic Philosophy* (1962), *Economics—An Awkward Corner* (1966), and *An Introduction to Modern Economics* (1973). Toward the end of her career, she became increasingly radical, expressing admiration for the economic systems of China under MAO TSE-TUNG (see Vol. 2), and North Korea under Kim-Sung. Few economists followed her lead, however, and despite her early reputation, she finished her career on the fringes of mainstream economics.

BOOKS BY ROBINSON

The Accumulation of Capital. 1956. Porcupine Pr. 1986 $45.00. ISBN 0-87991-266-9
Economic Philosophy. Aldine 1962 o.p.
Economics: An Awkward Corner. Pantheon 1966 o.p.
The Economics of Imperfect Competition. Macmillan 1933 o.p.
An Essay on Marxian Economics. Porcupine Pr. 1991 $12.95. ISBN 0-87991-270-7
An Introduction to Modern Economics. (coauthored with J. Eatwell). McGraw 1973 o.p.
Introduction to the Theory of Employment. Macmillan 1937 o.p.
The Rate of Interest and Other Essays. Hyperion Conn. 1986 repr. of 1952 ed. $19.00.
    ISBN 0-88355-959-5

BOOKS ABOUT ROBINSON

Rima, Ingrid H., ed. *The Joan Robinson Legacy.* M. E. Sharpe 1991 $37.50. ISBN 0-87332-
    611-3. Collection of 17 essays on the intellectual legacy of Robinson, her contribu-
    tions to economics and her role as a neoclassical economist.
Shackleton, J. R., and Gareth Locksley. *Twelve Contemporary Economists.* Wiley 1981
    o.p. Contains a chapter on Robinson, with a brief biography and an examination of
    monopolistic competition, capital and value theory, and other topics in a nontechni-
    cal manner.
Triffin, Robert. *Monopolistic Competition and General Equilibrium Theory.* HUP 1940 o.p.
    Classic early survey on monopolistic competition and other forms of imperfect
    competition; focus on the work of Chamberlin, Robinson, Stackelberg, Pareto;
    excellent comparison of Robinson and Chamberlin.

Turner, Marjorie S. *Joan Robinson and the Americans*. M. E. Sharpe 1989 $39.95. ISBN 0-87332-533-8. Discusses the life, times, and contributions of Robinson; coverage of Cambridge controversies, theoretical contributions.

SAMUELSON, PAUL ANTHONY. 1915– (NOBEL PRIZE 1970)

Paul Samuelson was the first American recipient of the Nobel Prize in economics. Born in Indiana, he did his undergraduate work at the University of Chicago and earned a Ph.D. at Harvard University, where he studied with ALVIN HANSEN. He taught for several decades at M.I.T.

Samuelson's first major work was *Foundations of Economic Analysis* (1947), a mathematical treatment of economic theory and principles. Later he made extensive contributions to professional journals in virtually all areas of economic theory. Often he would be the first to offer a mathematical proof of a proposition when most other economists could sense it only intuitively. In 1948 he published the first edition of *Economics*, one of the most successful and influential college texts of our time. It provided an extremely comprehensive treatment of Keynesian economics and microeconomic principles, and played an important part in educating a generation of economists.

Despite Samuelson's role in providing mathematical refinements for economic theory, he has always maintained a public posture, welcoming opportunities to share his views. He was an economic adviser to President John F. Kennedy and wrote a popular column for *Newsweek* from 1966 to 1981. He has generally favored an interventionist approach in policy matters, especially when it has involved using the tax system to battle poverty, fight inflation, or balance the budget.

One of the world's most respected economists, Samuelson is responsible for rewriting considerable parts of economic theory. He has, in several areas, achieved results that rank among the classic theorems in economics.

BOOKS BY SAMUELSON

Collected Scientific Papers of Paul Samuelson. 5 vols. MIT Pr. 1966–78 $70.00 ea. ISBNs 0-262-19021-4, 0-262-19022-2, 0-262-19080-X, 0-262-19167-9, 0-262-19251-9
Economics from the Heart: A Samuelson Sampler. Ed. by Maryann O. Keating. HarBraceJ 1983 $4.95. ISBN 0-15-627551-1. Approximately 100 selected *Newsweek* editorials on various topics.
Economics. McGraw 1989 $38.68. ISBN 0-07-054786-6.
Foundations of Economic Analysis. 1947. HUP enl. ed. 1983 $34.95. ISBN 0-674-31301-1

BOOKS ABOUT SAMUELSON

Breit, William, and Roger W. Spencer, eds. *Lives of the Laureates: Ten Nobel Economists*. MIT Pr. 1990 $19.95. ISBN 0-262-02308-3. Includes an account of Samuelson's life that discusses his evolution as an economist and how the Nobel Prize affected his life.
Brown, Cary E. *Paul Samuelson and Modern Economic Theory*. McGraw 1983 o.p. Ten original essays outlining Samuelson's theoretical contributions in the areas of welfare economics, consumption theory, general equilibrium and stability, international trade, financial economics, monetary policy, fiscal policy, and macroeconomics; includes his own essay "Economics in a Golden Age."
Feiwel, George R,, ed. *Samuelson and Neo-Classical Economics*. Recent Economic Thought Ser. Kluwer Ac. 1982 $49.50. ISBN 0-89838-069-3. Collection of 24 papers leading economists delivered in 1980. Offers critical evaluation of Samuelson's contemporary economic theory and discusses such topics as production and dynamic analysis, trade theory, welfare, and neoclassical synthesis; includes four vignettes of Samuelson as a man and scholar.

Linder, Marc. *The Anti-Samuelson*. 2 vols. Urizen Books 1977 o.p. Unfailingly critical treatment of Samuelson's *Economics* text as a "bourgeois" work; offers chapter-by-chapter rebuttal from a Marxist perspective.

Silk, Leonard. *The Economists*. Basic 1974 o.p. Includes a 44-page chapter titled "Paul Anthony Samuelson: Enfant Terrible Emeritus" that provides a short biography of his life, education and training: a nontechnical description of professional work; and a discussion of his place in economic history.

Wood, John C., and Ronald N. Woods, eds. *Paul A. Samuelson: Critical Assessments*. Routledge 1989 $495.00. ISBN 0-415-02002-6. Comprehensive collection of previously published articles about Samuelson's life and contributions; includes a biographical section.

SCHUMPETER, JOSEPH ALOIS. 1883–1950

Joseph Schumpeter, an American economist of Czech origin, is regarded by many as the second most important economist of the twentieth century after JOHN MAYNARD KEYNES. He was a complex man and a brilliant student versed in mathematics, history, philosophy, and economics.

Schumpeter was born in Moravia, at the time part of the Austro-Hungarian empire. He was educated at the University of Vienna and Columbia University. Schumpeter's first marriage took place in 1907 and lasted for several years before being formally dissolved. Later, while teaching in Bonn, he became so attracted to his porter's 12-year-old daughter Annie that he obtained permission to educate and then marry her when she came of age. During this period he served first as Austrian minister of finance and then as president of a prestigious investment bank in Vienna. It failed, and, a year after his marriage, Annie and her child died in childbirth. Schumpeter, devastated by these events, left Austria to join the faculty at Harvard University, where he remained until his death.

In 1912 Schumpeter published his *Theory of Economic Development*, which argued that the accepted general equilibrium models of the time had room for neither change nor profit, even though both were necessary for growth to take place. In his view, the entrepreneurs are responsible for a process of sustained change as they develop new products and try new ways of using inputs in search of temporary monopoly profits. Despite the work's importance, it was not available in English until 1934, on the eve of the Keynesian revolution. Schumpeter refined and expanded his theory of economic dynamics in the monumental two-volume work, *Business Cycles: A Theoretical, Historical and Statistical Analysis of the Capitalist Process*. This work maintained that periods of business growth resulted from the clustering of innovations which in turn were copied by "swarms" of imitators who set off wavelike expansion in business activity. Unfortunately, the book appeared in 1939, three years after Keynes's *General Theory*, and so never received the attention it deserved.

In 1942 Schumpeter published *Capitalism, Socialism and Democracy*, which dealt with the "creative destruction" inherent in capitalism. New processes and methods of production, wrote Schumpeter, were continually replacing older ones. The result was material progress, but progress that would eventually be taken for granted and even resented by people dissatisfied with the dislocations caused by growth; the end result would be the demise of capitalism and rise of socialism as governments increasingly took control of the means of production. Schumpeter's last major work was his *History of Economic Analysis* (1954), which is widely regarded as one of the best intellectual histories written about any social science.

It is perhaps ironic that Schumpeter never developed a following that could be described as a "Schumpeterian" school of thought. One reason is that much of his work is descriptive rather than prescriptive; Keynes had a solution for the problems of the 1930s, but Schumpeter rarely provided policy advice. Secondly, Schumpeter's work often seems to have an undercurrent of fatalism (which some attribute to the loss of his beloved Annie), with his predictions forecasting the death of capitalism. Finally, there was the question of timing: of his major books, one appeared just before and the other immediately after Keynes's *General Theory*.

BOOKS BY SCHUMPETER

Business Cycles: A Theoretical, Historical and Statistical Analysis of the Capitalist Process. Porcupine Pr. 1989 $24.95. ISBN 0-87991-263-4

Capitalism, Socialism, and Democracy. 1942. Peter Smith 1983 $24.50. ISBN 0-8446-6027-2

Essays: On Entrepreneurs, Innovations, Business Cycles and the Evolution of Capitalism. Transaction Pubs. 1989 $19.95. ISBN 0-88738-764-0. Essays revealing major Schumpeterian themes such as economic theory and the business cycle; the evolution of capitalism; the relationship of economic theory, economic history and the real economy; and Marxism and economic sociology.

History of Economic Analysis. OUP 1954 $29.95. ISBN 0-19-504185-2. Monumental survey and summary of economic history and contributions of over 1,500 writers; with 1,260 pages containing one million words.

Ten Great Economists from Marx to Keynes. OUP 1965 o.p. Profiles of the life and work of Marx, Walras, Menger, Marshall, Bohm-Bawerk, Pareto, Taussig, Fisher, Mitchell, and Keynes.

Theory of Economic Development: An Inquiry into Profits, Capital, Credit, Interest and the Business Cycle. HUP 1934 $16.50. ISBN 0-674-87990-2

BOOKS ABOUT SCHUMPETER

Allen, Robert L. *Opening Doors: The Life and Work of Joseph Schumpeter.* 2 vols. Transaction Pubs. 1990 $439.95 set. ISBN 0-88738-381-5. Vol. 1 *Europe* $69.95. ISBN 0-88738-362-9. Vol. 2 *America* $39.95. ISBN 0-88738-380-7. Solid biography and analysis of Schumpeter's complex personality; respectful, candid, and sensitive.

Blaug, Mark, ed. *Frank Knight, 1885–1972, Henry Simmons, 1899–1946, and Joseph Schumpeter, 1883–1950.* Ashgate Pub. Co. 1992 $139.95. ISBN 1-85278-500-4. Collection of 29 previously published articles, 16 of them devoted to Schumpeter.

Clemence, Richard V., and Francis S. Doody. *The Schumpeterian System.* Kelley 1966 repr. of 1950 ed. $19.50. ISBN 0-678-00136-7. Description and assessment of Schumpeter's vision of a capitalistic process, with an emphasis on innovations and the clustering of innovations. Written by two former students of Schumpeter.

Harris, Seymour E., ed. *Schumpeter, Social Scientist.* Ayer facs. ed. 1951 $24.50. ISBN 0-8369-1138-5. Collection of 20 outstanding essays by leading economists, with superb coverage of the man and his works, his economics, and his role as a sociologist.

Swedberg, Richard. *Schumpeter: A Biography.* Princeton U. Pr. 1991 $24.95. ISBN 0-691-04296-9. Comprehensive and insightful biography and evaluation of Schumpeter's work in light of the declining popularity of Keynes. Examines central themes in his life and the influence of Max Weber.

Wood, John C., ed. *Joseph A. Schumpeter: Critical Assessments.* 4 vols. Routledge 1991 $660.00. ISBN 0-415-05668-3. Comprehensive collection of previously published articles on Schumpeter's life and contributions.

SMITH, ADAM. 1723–1790

Adam Smith was one of the foremost philosophers and personalities of the eighteenth century. As a moral philosopher, Smith was concerned with the observation and rationalization of behavior. His encyclopedic description and insightful analysis of life and commerce in English society established him as an economist at a time when economics was not a recognized discipline. Today he is recognized as the father of the classical school of economics that included THOMAS MALTHUS, DAVID RICARDO, and JOHN STUART MILL. Smith's major work, *The Wealth of Nations* (1776), was the single most important economics treatise to appear up to that time. Although significant works on economics preceded *The Wealth of Nations*, it was truly the first of its kind.

Smith was born in Kirkcaldy, on the east coast of Scotland. He completed high school at age 14 and enrolled at Glasgow University in the same year. After graduating from Glasgow in 1740, he traveled 400 miles on horseback to study at Oxford University, where he remained until 1746. His education at Oxford, however, was not what one might expect. Oxford at that time was not the citadel of learning that it became in later years. As a result, Smith provided much of his own instruction while enjoying the vast resources of Oxford's library. Such independent work was not without peril; he was almost expelled when school officials found a copy of DAVID HUME's (see Vol. 4) *Treatise of Human Nature* in his possession. Aside from the lack of instruction, Smith was unhappy on a personal level. He was unpopular with the English students, as were all Scots at the time, and he suffered varying degrees of harassment. He also developed a nervous tic, a shaking of the head, that remained with him for the rest of his life. Oxford did little for Smith while he was there, and it ignored him long after he became famous. When Smith received an honorary doctorate in 1762, it was from Glasgow University rather than Oxford. In 1746 Smith returned to Scotland and proceeded to give a series of public lectures in Edinburgh. These were followed by an appointment at Glasgow University. Smith was a popular teacher at Glasgow, despite his notorious absentmindedness and idiosyncratic behavior. He never could remember to wear a hat or a coat or carry an umbrella, and he was often observed walking about waving his cane while talking animatedly with himself.

Smith's first book, *The Theory of Moral Sentiments* (1759), was a treatise on the formation of moral judgments by men who acted primarily in their own self-interest. It became an immediate success. Five years after it was published, he left Glasgow to take a well-paid position as tutor to a young English duke who was about to take the customary grand tour of Europe. During his travels, he met and shared ideas with the philosopher VOLTAIRE (see Vols. 2 and 4), the French economist François Quesnay, and the American scientist and statesman BENJAMIN FRANKLIN (see Vol. 1). While on tour, Smith began work on a manuscript on political economy. This work appeared some years later as *The Wealth of Nations*. A tour de force, the book argued that the wealth of a country was the sum of the goods produced and consumed by its people, not the monetary wealth, gold, and treasures owned by the nobility. It also argued that society was guided as if an "invisible hand" directed the selfish interests of individuals toward actions that were in the collective interest of everyone. This process tended to be self-regulating. Competition and the profit motive combined to force producers to offer better products at lower prices and to allocate the factors of production to those activities favored by consumers. *The Wealth of Nations* addressed numerous other issues as well, including the division of labor, the determinants of price, the origins of value, the benefits of international trade, and even economic growth. Oddly enough, *The Wealth of Nations* was not well received at first. In time, however, it found an audience, especially among the merchant and manufacturing classes who found in it a moral justification for the enormous energies that society was devoting to commerce and trade.

Adam Smith remained a bachelor his entire life. Several weeks before he died in early 1790, he supervised the destruction of all of his manuscripts except for the *Theory of Moral Sentiments, The Wealth of Nations,* and several other works that had been published as *Essays on Philosophical Subjects.* He died quietly and contentedly at the age of 67.

BOOKS BY SMITH

Essays on Philosophical Subjects. Liberty Fund Glasgow ed. 1982 $7.50. ISBN 0-86597-023-8

The Theory of Moral Sentiments. 1759. Ibis Pub. VA 1986 $24.95. ISBN 0-935005-66-8

The Wealth of Nations. 1776. McGraw 1985 $9.64. ISBN 0-07-554596-9. Contains useful introduction by Max Lerner.

BOOKS ABOUT SMITH

Campbell R. H., and A. S. Skinner. *Adam Smith.* St. Martin 1985 $13.95. ISBN 0-312-00424-9. Scholarly, yet interesting and informative biography of Smith intended to acquaint readers with the man and his works.

Glahe, Fred R,, ed. *Adam Smith and the Wealth of Nations: 1776–1976 Bicentennial.* Bks. Demand repr. of 1978 ed. $47.40. ISBN 0-8357-5505-3. Eight delightful essays on Smith's lasting contributions.

Heilbroner, Robert. *The Worldly Philosophers: The Lives, Times and Ideas of the Great Economic Thinkers.* S&S Trade 1987 $10.95. ISBN 0-671-63318-X. Entertaining and informative discussion of Smith and his impact on the profession.

Hollander, S. *The Economics of Adam Smith.* Bks. Demand 1973 $93.90. ISBN 0-8357-8108-9. Scholarly commentary on the economic theories and positions of Smith that makes extensive use of direct quotations.

Rae, John. *The Life of Adam Smith.* Kelley 1895 o.p. Classic, scholarly biography with an invaluable introduction by Jacob Viner.

Viner, Jacob. *Guide to John Rae's Life of Adam Smith.* Kelley 1965 $12.95. ISBN 0-678-00749-7. Outstanding introduction to Smith, originally published as an introduction to John Rae's book.

Wood, John C. *Adam Smith: Critical Assessments.* 4 vols. Croom Helm UK 1983–84 o.p. Comprehensive collection of 150 previously published articles about Smith's life and work; includes a brief biographical overview and 13 biographical articles.

STIGLER, GEORGE JOSEPH. 1911–1991 (NOBEL PRIZE 1982)

George Stigler was an American economist whose staunch support of the price system and competitive market forces made him one of the leading proponents of the "Chicago school" of economics. He was educated at the University of Washington, Northwestern University, and the University of Chicago. He taught at several universities, including Columbia University and the University of Chicago.

Stigler's early interest was in the history of economic thought. His *Essays in the History of Economics* (1964), covering topics from utility theory to Fabian socialism, is a modern classic renowned for its clear, uncluttered style. His other classic work, *The Theory of Price* (1946), is a microeconomic text dealing with consumer behavior, prices, costs and production, monopoly, cartels, and the distribution of income.

Stigler was well known for his interest in government regulation of public utilities and its impact on the consumer. His numerous studies led him to conclude that the regulator often becomes an advocate of, and spokesperson for, the industry, a development that tends to dilute the effectiveness of regulation. Regulation, in the long run, tends to weaken competition to the point where "it is of regulation that the consumer must beware." Stigler was awarded the Nobel Prize for his work on government regulation and the structure of industry.

BOOKS BY STIGLER

The Citizen and the State: Essays on Regulation. U. Ch. Pr. 1977 $9.95. ISBN 0-226-77429-5. Collection of previously published essays on the theory, process, and practice of regulation.

The Economist as Preacher and Other Essays. U. Ch. Pr. 1984 $20.00. ISBN 0-226-77430-9. Essays on ethics, sociology, and the history of science, economic thought, and quantitative studies.

Essays in the History of Economics. 1964. U. Ch. Pr. 1965 o.p. Fourteen historical essays on topics from utility theory to Fabian socialism; a modern classic noted for its clear and uncluttered style of exposition.

The Essence of Stigler. Ed. by Kurt R. Leube and others. Hoover Pr. 1986 o.p. Collection of 23 essays by Stigler presented in honor of his seventy-fifth birthday. Covers Stigler's contributions to economics, political economy, industrial organization, and economic thought; four short articles on Stigler's wit.

Memoirs of an Unregulated Economist. Basic 1990 $9.95. ISBN 0-465-04442-5. Part memoir, part scholarly reflection on the influence of academicians on economic policy. Recounts Stigler's personal conviction that antitrust legislation is an ineffective way to fight monopolies.

The Organization of Industry. U. Ch. Pr. 1983 $13.95. ISBN 0-226-77432-5. Classic text on industrial organization, covering such topics as competition, monopoly, market behavior, and antitrust policy.

The Theory of Price. Macmillan 1987. ISBN 0-02-417400-9

BOOK ABOUT STIGLER

Breit, William, and Roger W. Spencer, eds. *Lives of the Laureates: Ten Nobel Economists.* MIT Pr. 1990 $19.95. ISBN 0-262-02308-3. Chapter by Stigler discusses his life work, and examines the influence of his training and work on the problems and methods of economic research.

VEBLEN, THORSTEIN (BUNDE). 1857–1929

Thorstein Bunde Veblen was an American economist and social scientist best known for challenging the economic theories of his time. He rejected the neat logic and natural laws of his contemporaries, asserting instead that economic order was evolutionary and that this evolution was strongly influenced by institutions such as labor unions, business organizations, schools, and even churches. In so doing, Veblen laid the basis for what is now known as the institutional school of economics.

Veblen was often described as being an aloof and isolated, albeit gifted, misfit. His sense of isolation was established early; he was born on a farm in rural Wisconsin to immigrant Norwegian parents. English was spoken only as a second language in the tight-knit Norwegian community and Veblen did not perfect his use of the language until he entered college. A voracious reader with a distinct aversion to farm work, he was sent to nearby Carleton College to study for the Lutheran ministry. While at Carleton, Veblen alienated some of the faculty with inflammatory and agnostic writings, and, although he graduated in 1880, it was without the divinity degree that would have enabled him to teach at one of the many small religious colleges of the time. After graduate work at Johns Hopkins University and Yale University, he returned to his parents' home, where he spent the next seven years relaxing, reading, and doing odd jobs. In 1888 he married Ellen Rolfe, much to the dismay of her uncle who happened to be the president of Carleton College. During this period, Veblen had little luck finding a job, even with the benefit of his wife's and her uncle's connections. Finally, at the age of 34, Veblen went to Cornell University to seek a teaching position. Despite his frontier appearance—corduroy trousers and coonskin cap—he was given a one-year teaching assignment. The next year he joined the faculty at the University of Chicago, where he taught until 1906. While at the University of Chicago, he wrote two of his most important works, *The Theory of the Leisure Class* (1899) and *The Theory of Business Enterprise* (1904).

The Theory of the Leisure Class was an insightful, if not contemptuous, analysis of the excess consumption and wasteful behavior of the wealthy. Veblen contended that the modern quest for the accumulation of money, and its lavish display, was derived from the predatory barbarian practice of seizing goods and wealth without work. In *The Theory of Business Enterprise*, he described the heads of corporate enterprises as saboteurs of the economic system—people interested only in the financing of production rather than the process of production. This was a radical view, but Veblen was writing during the period when the "robber barons" seemed obsessed by the profits that could be made from stock flotations, bond issues, and other complex financial deals.

Veblen's notorious womanizing cost him his position with the University of Chicago in 1906. He moved on to Stanford University, then the University of Missouri, and finally to the New School for Social Research in New York, where he taught briefly before retiring to a small rustic cabin in California. Divorced from his wife in 1911, he remarried in 1914, but his second wife was institutionalized shortly after for psychological problems.

Veblen was one of the most provocative economists of his time, but his ideas were such that he attracted few disciples. Even so, economists have come to recognize the importance of institutions and their impact on economic behavior. Additional testament to the influence of his work is the fact that many of the terms he coined are in wide use today, among them *conspicuous consumption*, the *leisure class*, and *cultural lag*.

BOOKS BY VEBLEN

Absentee Ownership and Business Enterprise in Recent Times. Kelley 1964 repr. of 1923 ed. $39.50. ISBN 0-678-00048-4. Deals with how the industrial revolution, led by engineers who hold the power of production, takes control of industry from absentee corporate owners for the benefit of the masses.

Engineers and the Price System. Transaction Pubs. 1983 $18.95. ISBN 0-87855-915-9. Describes the evolution of modern industrial society, in which vested interests of absentee business owners is replaced by a guild of engineers dedicated to efficient production.

Imperial Germany and the Industrial Revolution. Greenwood 1984 repr. of 1939 ed. $59.75. ISBN 0-313-23495-7. Discusses how latecomers to industrialization, such as Germany, benefit from the latest technologies, unfettered by obsolete capital stock.

Inquiry into the Nature of Peace. Kelley 1964 repr. of 1917 ed. $37.50. ISBN 0-678-00051-4. Considers the importance of technology and industry to modern warfare, the destabilizing role of the business system, and mutual "competitive preparedness" as a penultimate stage of peace.

The Theory of Business Enterprise. 1904. Transaction Pubs. 1978 $9.95. ISBN 0-87855-699-0

The Theory of the Leisure Class. 1899. Transaction Pubs. 1991 $19.95 ISBN 1-56000-562-9

BOOKS ABOUT VEBLEN

Dorfman, Joseph. *Thorstein Veblen and His America*. Kelley 1972 repr. of 1934 ed. $45.00. ISBN 0-678-00007-7. Definitive work on the life and works of Veblen, showing how political, economic, and social forces shaped his thinking.

Dowd, Douglas F., ed. *Thorstein Veblen: A Critical Reappraisal—Lectures and Essays Commemorating the Hundredth Anniversary of Veblen's Birth.* Greenwood Pr. 1977 repr. of 1958 ed. $35.00. ISBN 0-8371-9714-7. Collection of papers evaluating the life, times, and contributions of Veblen.

Duffus, Robert L., and William M. Duffus. *The Innocents at Cedro: A Memoir of Thorstein Veblen and Some Others.* Kelley 1972 repr. of 1944 ed. $27.50. ISBN 0-678-00885-X. Entertaining personal portrait by a 19-year-old boy who lived with Veblen for a year at Cedro Cottage, near Stanford, in the last years of his life.

Homan, Paul T. *Contemporary Economic Thought.* Ayer facs. ed. 1928 $21.50. ISBN 0-8369-0546-6. Contains a thoughtful chapter on the life, times, writings, and influence of Veblen.

Qualey, Carlton C., ed. *Thorstein Veblen: The Carleton College Veblen Seminar Essays.* Col. U. Pr. 1968 $40.00. ISBN 0-231-03111-4. Collection of five essays published in the one-hundredth year of Carleton College. Topics include the future of American capitalism, business in Veblen's America, theology of Veblen, background on Veblen's economic thought, recollections of Veblen.

Spiegel, H. W., ed. *The Development of Economic Thought.* Wiley 1966 o.p. Includes an essay on Veblen by Wesley Clair Mitchell, his friend and student.

Tilman, Rick. *Thorstein Veblen and His Critics, 1891–63: Conservative, Liberal and Radical Perspectives.* Princeton U. Pr. 1992 $39.50. ISBN 0-691-04286-1. Examines how critics perceived Veblen; contains sections on conservative, liberal and radical critics.

VINER, JACOB. 1892–1970

Jacob Viner was a Canadian-born American economist who was educated at McGill University and Harvard University. His teaching career included posts at the University of Chicago and Princeton. Viner's publications covered a remarkable range of subjects, with major contributions in the fields of cost and production, international economics, and the history of economic ideas. According to one authority, Viner was "quite simply the greatest historian of economic thought that ever lived."

In a relatively short journal article published in 1921, Viner anticipated the concept of monopolistic competition that Edward H. Chamberlin and JOAN ROBINSON later made famous. He also developed a model of oligopoly pricing that still stands as the standard textbook explanation for infrequent price changes in oligopolistic industries. Viner also popularized the current textbook presentation of marginal cost and marginal revenue analysis used to find the profit-maximizing quantity of production.

Viner would have been an economist of the first order on the basis of these accomplishments alone, but his contributions in the field of international trade were greater. His doctoral dissertation and first book, *Dumping: A Problem in International Trade* (1923), which dealt with the issue of disposing of large quantities of goods at artificially low prices, was an immediate success. His second book, *Canada's Balance of International Payments, 1900–1913* appeared a year later. His most famous work, however, was his *Studies in the Theory of International Trade* (1937), a history of international economics. According to some critics, this work placed economics on a new footing by working out misunderstandings and clarifying the main lines of advance within the field. A subsequent book, *The Customs Union Issue* (1950), was the definitive statement on common markets and free-trade areas.

Viner's interest in later life was the impact of medieval theological writings on the history of economic ideas. One contribution was his indispensable introduction to John Rae's *Life of Adam Smith*, the standard Smith biography. Another, *The Role of Providence in the Social Order* (1972), explored the extraordinary power of theology on economics during the seventeenth and eighteenth centuries. Viner's *Religious Thought and Economic Society* (1978) is an unfinished intellectual history of the Scholastics, the Jansenists, the Jesuits, and the early Calvinists.

The recipient of a number of honorary degrees, he perhaps is best remembered for his wit, clarity of exposition, and the meticulous care and accuracy that marked his high standard of scholarship.

BOOKS BY VINER

The Customs Union Issue. Kramer 1950 o.p.

Dumping: A Problem in International Trade. Reprints of Economic Classics Ser. Kelley 1991 repr. of 1923 ed. $39.50. ISBN 0-678-01398-5

Essays on the Intellectual History of Economics. Ed. by Douglas A. Irwin. Princeton U. Pr. 1991 $49.50. ISBN 0-691-04266-7. Collection of 19 previously published lectures and articles on such topics as economics and freedom, Adam Smith, and John Stuart Mill; includes a section on review articles and commencement addresses; contains 30-page overview and biographical chapter.

Guide to John Rae's Life of Adam Smith. Kelley 1965 $12.95. ISBN 0-678-00749-7

International Trade and Economic Development. 1952. Clarendon Pr. o.p. Attack on post-World War II "big-push" theories of economic development.

Religious Thought and Economic Society: Four Chapters of an Unfinished Work. Ed. by Jacques Melitz and Donald Winch. Duke 1978 $22.50. ISBN 0-8223-0398-1

The Role of Providence in the Social Order: An Essay in Intellectual History. 1972. Princeton U. Pr. 1976 $11.95. ISBN 0-691-01990-8

Studies in the Theory of International Trade. Kelley 1965 repr. of 1937 ed. $49.50. ISBN 0-678-00122-7

VON NEUMANN, JOHN (JOHANN). 1903–1957

John von Neumann was a Hungarian-born American mathematician with a minor interest in economics. He earned a degree in mathematics from the University of Budapest and one in chemical engineering from the Hochschule in Zurich. He moved to the United States in 1930 and three years later joined the Institute for Advanced Study at Princeton, where he was the youngest member of the small but select group that included ALBERT EINSTEIN (see Vol. 5) and ENRICO FERMI (see Vol. 5).

Von Neumann founded the branch of economics known as game theory. He published a seminal paper on the subject in 1928 and later collaborated with Oskar Morgenstern in developing and expanding it. Game theory analyzes individual choice in situations of risk, where the participants do not control or know the probability distributions of all variables on which the outcome of their acts depends.

In 1944, von Neumann and Morgenstern published their classic *Theory of Games and Economic Behavior*, which achieved immediate prominence because it dealt with bargaining strategies under conditions of conflict. Game theory was applied to a number of situations, such as wage negotiations between unions and management. It was also popular with the Pentagon, which used it to model superpower confrontations that reflected outcomes based on the selection of various military options.

Game theory was only one of von Neumann's many interests. In 1943 he worked on the Manhattan Project and was instrumental in developing the atomic bomb. He also helped develop ENIAC, the first electronic computer. Because of his work with the atomic bomb, he received a presidential appointment to the Atomic Energy Commission in 1955. In 1957, at the age of 53, his illustrious career ended when he died tragically of bone cancer.

BOOKS BY VON NEUMANN

Collected Works. 6 vols. Ed. by A. W. Traub. Franklin 1961–63 $1,670.00. ISBN 0-08-009566-6. Vol. 1 *Logic, Theory of Sets and Quantum Mechanics.* Vol. 2 *Operators, Ergodic Theory and Almost Periodic Functions in a Group.* Vol. 3 *Rings of Operators.* Vol. 4 *Von Neumann Collected Works.* Vol. 5 *Von Neumann Collected Works.* Vol. 6 *Theory of Games, Astrophysics, Hydrodynamics and Meteorology.*

Theory of Games and Economic Behavior. (coauthored with Oskar Morgenstern). 1944. Princeton U. Pr. 1980 $85.00. ISBN 0-691-04183-0. Classic, but difficult, work presenting a detailed account of game theory as it developed over a 15-year period. Includes numerous applications to strategy, economics, and social theory.

BOOKS ABOUT VON NEUMANN

Aspray, William. *John von Neumann and the Origins of Modern Computing.* MIT Pr. 1990 $37.50. ISBN 0-262-01121-2. Surveys the history and evolution of modern computers and the role of von Neumann.

Dore, Mohammed, ed. *John von Neumann and Modern Economics.* OUP 1989 $69.00. ISBN 0-19-828554-X. Collection of 12 essays on von Neumann's growth models; covers historical perspectives, dynamics of game theory, and reformulations of game theory. Includes a brief biographical sketch in the foreword.

WARD, BARBARA (LADY JACKSON). 1914–1981

[SEE Chapter 9 in this volume.]

WEBB, SIDNEY. 1859–1947 and WEBB, BEATRICE. 1858–1943

Sidney and Beatrice Webb, English labor historians and social reformers, were a remarkable couple who had a profound influence on the social thought and political institutions of Great Britain. Their work was largely responsible for the popularity of the Fabian socialists and the repeal of the dreaded British poor laws; it also promoted widespread activities on behalf of the British labor movement and inspired key parts of the British Labor party's social program. The Webbs published some 45 books and numerous pamphlets, and founded the influential weekly, *New Statesman.*

Beatrice, born to a wealthy London family with extensive business dealings, saw the Industrial Revolution and its political aftermath as a chapter of her family history. To prepare for an early article describing working-class poverty in London, she took tailoring lessons so that she could pose as a "plain trouser hand" to get a firsthand view of the sweatshop industry of the period. Sidney's concern for the labor movement grew out of his early interest in socialism. The Fabian Society, which he joined, was founded in 1884 and named after the Roman general Quintus Fabius Maximus Cunctator, known as "the delayer" because of his holding tactics. The Fabians believed that socialism would develop in a democratic society by peaceful and evolutionary means rather than by revolution, as predicted by KARL MARX (see also Vol. 4).

By the time of their marriage in 1892, Sidney and Beatrice were intensely committed to the study of the trade union movement; they spent part of their honeymoon in Dublin in order to review the records of Irish trade societies. The result of their efforts was the *History of Trade Unionism* (1894), which virtually marked the beginning of the academic study of labor and industrial relations. It was followed by *Industrial Democracy* (1897), which portrayed unions as beneficial to the industrial movement because they established minimum working standards that would lead to the eventual well-being of society. Both works provided a history and rationale for the British labor movement— something that had been virtually ignored by academics up to that time. Other books dealt with English local government, the poor laws, the cooperative movement, and a broad range of labor issues.

The Webbs believed strongly that facts alone would be sufficient to reveal the truth, and that socialism would evolve if the truth were known. This belief led them to establish the London School of Economics, which has no restrictions on the doctrinal purity of staff or faculty.

BOOKS BY SIDNEY WEBB

The Consumers' Cooperative Movement. 1912 o.p. Debunks the common belief that consumer cooperatives were established for the benefit and profit of consumers. Also provides a detailed history and description of the movement.

English Poor Law History. 3 vols. Longman 1927–30 o.p. Comprehensive and detailed account of the British poor laws—their history and problems. Also includes suggestions for improvement.

History of English Local Government. 11 vols. Intl. Spec. Bk. 1963. Vol. 1 $32.50. ISBN 0-7146-1372-X. Vol. 2 o.p. Vol. 3 o.p. Vol. 4 $30.00. ISBN 0-7146-1374-6. Vol. 5 $35.00. ISBN 0-7146-1375-4. Vols. 6–10 o.p. Vol. 11 $30.00. ISBN 0-7146-1380-0. Monumental history of local governments from the medieval period to the early 1920s. Discusses the relationship of government to the common people.

The History of Trade Unionism. Longman 1894 o.p.

Industrial Democracy. Longman 1897 o.p.

Socialism in England. Ashgate Pub. Co. 1986 $52.95. ISBN 0-566-05144-3. Historical account of the development of socialism in England, from early times to the present.

BOOKS BY BEATRICE WEBB

My Apprenticeship. AMS Pr. repr. of 1926 ed. $27.50. ISBN 0-404-14045-9

The Diary of Beatrice Webb. Ed. by Norman MacKenzie and Leanne MacKenzie. Vol. 1 *Glitter Around and Darkness Within,* 1873–1892. Belknap Pr. 1982 $30.95. ISBN 0-674-20287-2. Vol. 2 *All the Good Things of Life.* HUP 1983 o.p. Vol. 3 *The Power to Alter Things, 1905–1924.* HUP 1984 $30.95. ISBN 0-674-20289-9. Vol. 4 *The Wheel of Life, 1924–1943.* Belknap Pr. 1984 $30.95. ISBN 0-674-20286-4. Personal and literary account of events and influences in the lives of Beatrice and Sidney Webb. Contains justifications for socialism and discourses on social history.

BOOKS BY SIDNEY AND BEATRICE WEBB

English Poor Law History. 3 vols. Longman 1927–30 o.p. Comprehensive, detailed account of the English poor laws—their history and problems; also includes suggestions for improvement.

Industrial Democracy. Longman 1897 o.p.

BOOKS ABOUT SIDNEY AND BEATRICE WEBB

Cole, Margaret I., ed. *The Webbs and Their Work.* Greenwood 1985 repr. of 1949 ed. $47.50. ISBN 0-313-24677-7. Collection of articles by contemporaries of the Webbs.

Nord, Deborah E. *The Apprenticeship of Beatrice Webb.* Cornell Univ. Pr. 1989 $12.95. ISBN 0-8014-9609-8. Study of the early years of Beatrice Webb's life and literary record. Concludes that *My Apprenticeship,* while a historical record, is also a fiction.

Radice, Lisanne. *Beatrice and Sidney Webb: Fabian Socialists.* St. Martin 1984 o.p. First full-length biography of the Webbs. Covers their Victorian apprenticeship, their courtship and marriage, their politics, writings, and other aspects of their life.

Spiegel, H. W., ed. *The Development of Economic Thought.* Wiley 1966 o.p. Classic reader on the writing of great economists by great economists. Chapter titled "Tawney on the Webbs" was written by the noted economist Richard Tawney.

Stigler, George J. *Essays in the History of Economics*. U. Ch. Pr. 1965 o.p. Contains a short
but illuminating essay titled "Bernard Shaw, Sidney Webb, and the Theory of Fabian
Socialism" that places the Webbs and their work in historical perspective.

WICKSELL, KNUT. 1851–1926

Knut Wicksell, Sweden's most important economist, was born in Stockholm
as the youngest of six children. A quiet and sensitive boy, he was strongly
affected by his mother's death when he was 7 and his father's death eight years
later. At age 15, he became a devout member of the Swedish Lutheran Church
and devoted himself to the study of mathematics. In 1871, after only two years of
study, he earned a degree in mathematics, physics, and astronomy. Eventual
doubts about his faith, along with a severe emotional crisis in 1874, ended his
religious period. He then became a freethinker and outspoken critic of religion,
rejecting all forms of ceremony, including baptism, confirmation, and even
marriage.

While still studying mathematics, Wicksell came across a popular book that
turned his attention to social issues, and he began to deliver lectures and
publish editorials on alcoholism, prostitution, and birth control. The very
mention of these topics was largely taboo, but Wicksell was soon attracting
large audiences. By the early 1880s, he was receiving speaker fees for as many
as 10 appearances per week.

In the 1880s Wicksell's interest shifted to economics, which he studied in
Germany and Austria. He met his future wife, Anna, while in Germany, but only
proposed a common-law marriage on the grounds that he opposed the pomp
and circumstance of a formal wedding. Returning to Stockholm in 1890,
Wicksell took up journalism and lecturing as a source of income. His opposition
to a longer military draft and support for unilateral disarmament in 1892 made
him as controversial as ever. His first important work, *Value, Capital and Rent*,
appeared in 1893. It was followed by *Studies in the Theory of Public Finance*
(1896), which pioneered the application of marginal utility to public-sector
problems. Both were submitted as part of the requirements for a doctorate in
economics, and in 1886 Wicksell received the degree *magna cum laude*. He
could not, however, obtain a professorship in economics because economics
was taught only by law faculties and Wicksell did not have a law degree. After
two more years of study, he earned an undergraduate law degree. Meanwhile he
published another major work, *Interest and Prices: A Study of the Causes
Regulating the Value of Money* (1898). Not until 1904, when Wicksell was 53, did
he finally secure the teaching position that had eluded him so long.

Wicksell's most famous works, *Lectures on Political Economy I* (1901) and
Lectures on Political Economy II (1906), dealt with extensions and improvements of his earlier theories on capital growth and the causes of inflation. These
two works remain the fullest expression of his theories. Wicksell's stature was
such that he is credited with establishing a "Stockholm school" of economic
thought that later included Bertil Ohlin and GUNNAR MYRDAL.

BOOKS BY WICKSELL

Interest and Prices: A Study of the Causes Regulating the Value of Money. 1898. Trans. by
B. F. Kahn. Kelley 1965 repr. of 1936 ed. $29.50. ISBN 0-678-00086-7. Argues that
changes in the price level relate to interest rates and returns on capital assets.
Lectures on Political Economy. 1901, 1906. 2 vols. Ed. by Lionel Robbins. Trans. by E.
Classen. Kelley 1967 repr. of 1934 ed. $50.00. ISBN 0-678-06520-9
Selected Papers on Economic Theory. Ed. by Erik Lindhal. Kelley 1969 repr. of 1958 ed.
$3.50. ISBN 0-678-00493-5

Value, Capital and Rent. 1893. Trans. by S. H. Frowein. Kelley 1970 repr. of 1954 ed. $29.50. ISBN 0-678-00652-0. Scholarly synthesis of marginal utility and marginal productivity theories of Jevons, Menger, and Marshall.

BOOKS ABOUT WICKSELL

Gardlund, Torsten. *The Life of Wicksell.* Almqvist & Wicksell SW 1958 o.p. Biographical account of Wicksell's childhood in Stockholm, including his early schooling and major influences. Discusses his work in a chronological and historical context.

Myrdal, Gunnar. *Monetary Equilibrium.* Kelley 1965 repr. of 1939 ed. $29.50. ISBN 0-678-00092-1. Condensed series of lectures on Wicksell's treatment of monetary theory and general equilibrium analysis.

Uhr, Carl G. *The Economic Doctrines of Knut Wicksell.* U. CA Pr. 1960 o.p. Systematic account and evaluation of Wicksell's theoretical contributions. Includes a synopsis of contributions, including the theory of value, marginal productivity, and theory of capital.

CHAPTER 4

Geography

W. Randy Smith

> . . . Geography, in particular, studies the spatial sections of the earth's surface, of the world . . . seeking to describe, and to interpret, the differences among its parts, as seen at any one time. This field it shares with no other branch of science; rather it brings together in this field parts of many other sciences.
>
> —RICHARD HARTSHORNE, *The Nature of Geography*

Technically, "geography" is derived from two words: *geo* (the earth) and *graph* (writing). Thus, geography is "writing about the earth." It is more appropriate, however, to define it as a distinctive way of thinking about and analyzing the world.

Geography is a discipline that asks two primary questions. The first is "Where are things located?" This emphasizes description and identifies geographic or spatial patterns on the earth's surface. Maps are the hallmark of this component of geography. After specific distributions are located on a map, the next question is "*Why* are they located there?" The emphasis shifts from description to explanation and to the processes that produced the spatial patterns on the maps. These same two questions are asked about two branches of geography—one focusing on the earth's physical features, such as landforms, climate, soils, and vegetation, and the other stressing human characteristics, such as population, economy, and culture.

As an academic subject, geography's "classical period" dates from the late 1700s to the early 1800s and to European geographers, notably CARL RITTER and ALEXANDER VON HUMBOLDT. In their detailed overviews of particular regions, these geographers sought not just to focus on factual compilations but also to draw generalizations about geographic distributions. They addressed both the concept of region—a part of the earth's surface with its own distinctive characteristics—and the concept of relationships between the physical and human environments within the region.

Much of what we see in modern geography, however, is rooted in the twentieth century. Although there continues to be interest in the detailed study of specific regions, that work has been supplemented with "systematic" or "topical" geography. Selected topics, such as climate, economy, population, or urbanization, are examined and the geographic characteristics of each are studied without necessarily focusing on a particular region.

The relevance of, and balance between, the regional and systematic approaches to geography are articulated most clearly in two important position statements by Richard Hartshorne, whose two books *The Nature of Geography: A Critical Survey of Current Thought in Light of the Past* (1939) and *Perspective on the Nature of Geography* (1959), are the starting points for any discussion of approaches to modern geography.

A major development occurred in geographic research in the 1960s, when quantitative methods—the use of mathematical models and statistical techniques—were adopted. Combined with the widespread use of computers, these methods permitted geographers to collect, store, and analyze large sets of data about either specific regions or topical areas. This methodological revolution helped develop "scientific geography" and promoted a positivist approach to the subject by which hypotheses were developed and tested. Today, a substantial component of research and publication in geography is quantitative and analytical in nature, especially in physical geography and in selected areas of human geography (urban and economic geography, most notably).

For some, however, this change resulted in a geography that was too abstract. Beginning with David Harvey's *Explanation in Geography* (1969), which addressed different methodological issues for scientific geography, considerable attention was given over the next two decades to alternative philosophies that gave greater emphasis to the role of the individual or groups of individuals, or to understanding how a broad range of physical, political, cultural, and economic forces affect, and are affected by, geographic distributions.

Although this rich history of philosophical and methodological development over the past two centuries has produced a discipline that is diverse in content and approach, geographic research can be classified into three main traditions: the man-land tradition, which stresses the interrelationship between the physical environment and human activity; the regional studies tradition, which emphasizes the need to divide the world into manageable areas of study and to explain how a region functions or "works"; and the spatial analysis tradition, in which selected topics, such as urbanization or transportation, are studied in detail, with data gathered and analyzed, models developed, hypotheses tested, and predictions possibly included. The rapid development of the spatial analysis tradition has led to a more recent movement to reevaluate the extent to which explanation can be achieved through this approach and a call for broadening the tradition to include other methods of investigation.

By the mid-1980s, a set of annotated bibliographies and overview statements had appeared that showed the complexity of topics in, and approaches to, geography and that set the foundation on which current work has been built. Examples include *A Geographical Bibliography for American Libraries* (1985), edited by Chauncy D. Harris, and the important overviews in *Geography in America* (1989) by Gary L. Gaile and Cort J. Willmott. A large set of major research journals also has developed that includes research papers and reviews covering the full spectrum of geographic topics. Among them are the *Annals of the Association of American Geographers*, *The Professional Geographer*, *Geographical Review*, *Geographical Analysis*, *Progress in Human Geography*, *Progress in Physical Geography*, and journals associated with professional associations in individual countries, such as *The Canadian Geographer* or *Transactions of the Institute of British Geographers*.

By the late 1980s, two additional important activities in geography had begun. One activity focused on new data sets—from, for example, the census or satellite imagery—and on computer technology that permitted the development of geographic information systems (GIS). Computer mapping of physical and human phenomena holds considerable potential for showing the interrelationships between and among features of the earth's surface.

The other activity represents a major advance in geographic education. Efforts are underway to revitalize geography as an academic subject in the precollegiate (K–12) education system. Professional geographers have teamed up with classroom teachers in order to develop materials that introduce five major concepts, or themes, of geography—location, place, human-environmental interaction, movement, and region. These themes are developed most fully in a work by Susan Wiley Hardwick and Donald G. Holtgrieve, *Patterns on Our Planet: Concepts and Themes in Geography* (1990). What lies ahead is research on how students best learn about spatial relationships, with implications for how the relationships should be taught.

Unlike other social sciences, geography as a research discipline traditionally has been characterized more by publications in major referreed journals than by book-length manuscripts. The books listed in this chapter represent examples of books in various subfields that serve as a starting point for further investigation and include ample references to research papers and other books in the discipline.

REFERENCE, SURVEYS, AND COLLECTIONS

Bennett, Robert J., and Richard J. Chorley. *Environmental Systems: Philosophy, Analysis, and Control.* Princeton U. Pr. 1978 $125.00. ISBN 0-691-08217-0. Emphasizes the links between physical and human systems and shows the relevance of quantitative and other approaches.

Boyer, Rick. *Places Rated Almanac: Your Guide to Finding the Best Places to Live in America.* P-H 1989 $16.95. ISBN 0-13-677006-1. Contains 333 metropolitan areas.

Brewer, James G. *The Literature of Geography: A Guide to Its Organisation and Use.* Linnet Bks. 1978 o.p.

Dickenson, Robert E., and Osbert Howarth. *The Making of Geography.* Greenwood 1976 o.p. Helpful starting point for geographic work prior to this century; presented chronologically.

Dunbar, Gary S., ed. *Modern Geography: An Encyclopedic Survey.* Garland 1990 $50.00. ISBN 0-8240-5343-5. Approximately 400 signed entries, covering 1890 to the present; contains definitions of major terms and concepts.

Gaile, Gary L., and Cort J. Willmott. *Geography in America.* Macmillan 1989 ISBN 0-675-20648-0. The most recent overview of the subfields of modern geography, with a synthesis of major research activities and a detailed bibliography in each chapter.

Hardwick, Susan Wiley, and Donald G. Holtgrieve. *Patterns on Our Planet: Concepts and Themes in Geography.* Macmillan 1990. ISBN 0-675-21052-6. First major book to develop substantively the "five themes" of geography; particularly important for the new geography education movement.

Harris, Chauncy D., ed. *A Geographical Bibliography for American Libraries.* Assn. Am. Geographers 1985 $25.00. ISBN 0-89291-193-X. Outstanding annotated bibliography of journals and books in all the subfields of modern geography. Can be updated with materials in Gaile and Wilmott.

Hartshorne, Richard. *The Nature of Geography: A Critical Survey of Current Thought in Light of the Past.* Assn. Am. Geographers. Greenwood 1977 repr. of 1939 ed. $41.50. ISBN 0-8371-9328-1. Classic analysis of the field of geography and the appropriate methods for its distinctive focus on spatial relationships.

———. *Perspective on the Nature of Geography.* Assn. Am. Geographers. St. Martin 1987 $45.00. ISBN 0-317-62296-X. Follow-up to the discussion of the author's earlier work in light of new methodological advances and debates.

Harvey, David. *Explanation in Geography.* Routledge Chapman & Hall 1969 o.p. Important book for discussing the positivist philosophy for "scientific geography." Led to extended debate within human geography about appropriate approaches to explanation.

Johnston, Ronald J. *Geography and Geographers: Anglo-American Human Geography since 1945.* Routledge Chapman & Hall 1983 o.p. Survey of human geography highlighting different subfields and debates on philosophy and methodology.

_____. *Philosophy and Human Geography: An Introduction to Contemporary Approaches.* Routledge Chapman & Hall 1983 o.p. Introductory overview of positivist, humanistic, and structuralist approaches to human geography.

Kish, George. *A Source Book in Geography.* HUP 1978 $40.00. ISBN 0-674-82270-6. Collection of geographical writings up to the classical period of the early eighteenth century.

Lee, David R. *Women and Geography: A Comprehensive Bibliography.* Florida Atlantic Univ. 1986 updated by supplements, 1988–90.

Ley, David, and Marwyn S. Samuels, eds. *Humanistic Geography: Prospects and Problems.* Methuen 1978 o.p. Collection of papers developing the humanistic approach to geography.

Peet, Richard. *Radical Geography: Alternative Viewpoints on Contemporary Social Issues.* Methuen 1977 o.p. Collection of papers that brought Marxist perspectives to issues in geographic research.

Perkins, C. R., and R. B. Parry. *Information Sources in Cartography.* K. G. Saur 1990 $96.00. ISBN 0-408-02458-5. Thirty chapters with references; in five parts with detailed indexes.

Small, R. J., and Michael W. Witherick, eds. *A Modern Dictionary of Geography.* Routledge Chapman & Hall 1989 $45.00. ISBN 0-340-49318-6. Update of the 1986 edition; contains 2,000 entries, 1,135 illustrations and maps. Good for the nonspecialist.

Thomas, G. Scott. *The Rating Guide to Life in America's Small Cities.* Prometheus Bks. 1990 $16.95. ISBN 0-87975-600-4. Lifestyle factors for 219 metropolitan areas, such as climate, education, health care, and housing.

METHODOLOGY AND ISSUES

Geographic inquiry is characterized by a wide variety of methods. Early research focused on field observations, use of secondary sources, and the production of simple hand-drawn maps to show spatial distributions of selected phenomena. More recent scientific geography continues to use fieldwork, particularly in physical geography and in selected aspects of human geography. At the same time, however, there has been a growing trend toward the use of other data sources and methods. Data from national censuses, from private and public agencies, and from satellite imagery, for example, have provided the modern geographer with a wealth of information for analysis. If data are unavailable in these forms, researchers can collect their own through surveys and interviews. Overall, there remains a strong empirical orientation to research in geography. Most important, data analysis in geography has adopted advanced quantitative methods in which most professional geographers now have background training at some level. Drawing on work in mathematics and statistics, geographers' analyses range from simple summary statistics to advanced regression-analysis techniques, from sophisticated time-series analyses to models of spatial interaction.

Barber, Gerald M. *Elementary Statistics for Geographers.* Guilford Pr. 1988 $39.95. ISBN 0-89862-777-X. Covers descriptive statistics, univariate statistics, and statistical relationships between two variables.

Boots, B., and A. Getis. *Spatial Point Pattern Analysis.* Sage Pub. 1988 o.p. Part of a series of brief overviews of statistical methods for selected geographic topics.

Clark, W.A.V., and P.L. Hosking. *Statistical Methods for Geographers.* Wiley 1986 $49.95. ISBN 0-471-81807-0. Excellent introduction to probability, statistical inference, and regression analysis.

Griffith, Daniel, and others. *Statistical Analysis for Geographers*. P-H 1990 $47.00. ISBN 0-13-844184-7. Written from the human and physical geographical perspectives. Treats both descriptive and inferential statistics.

Haining, Robert. *Spatial Data Analysis in the Social and Environmental Sciences*. Cambridge U. Pr. 1990 $69.95. ISBN 0-521-38416-8. Describes and evaluates methods for spatial analysis in order to show what is available, how different techniques relate to one another, and to illustrate what can be achieved. Complete coverage.

Norcliffe, Glen B. *Inferential Statistics for Geographers*. Hutchinson 1977 o.p. Introduction to statistical inference, nonparametric and parametric methods; includes many geographic examples.

CARTOGRAPHY AND GEOGRAPHIC INFORMATION SYSTEMS

Prominent geographers, such as ARTHUR ROBINSON and Waldo Tobler, led cartography as an academic subject in directions other than simple map production. With theoretical development in cartographic communication models, map symbolization, and cognitive research, cartography now is strongly quantitatively oriented and more strongly applied than in earlier years. National and international projects have emerged to ensure cartographic data quality and to develop data transfer standards.

Over the past decade, geographic information systems (GIS) has developed rapidly as a subfield. As noted by Gaile and Willmott, "A GIS implements the processes required to convert geographic data into more useful information. Geographic data must be systematically gathered, spatially registered, stored, analyzed, generalized, retrieved, and displayed. Geographic information systems represent the integration of all of these separate operations into a single automated environment." With advances in computer hardware and software, GIS is a rapidly changing and ever more technically sophisticated field. An important tool for geographers, it has remarkable potential for use in the various substantive fields of geography to show the relationships between variables at scales ranging from the global to the city block. It also has the potential to be a valuable tool in policy development for agencies that deal with physical and/or human environment.

Antenucci, John C., and others. *Geographic Information Systems: A Guide to the Technology*. Van Nos. Reinhold. 1991 $59.95. ISBN 0-442-00756-6. Discusses numerous aspects. Topics range from geographical databases, data sources, system configuration, system implementation, and design philosophies and methodologies, to the technology's history and legal issues.

Burrough, P. A. *Principles of Geographical Information Systems for Land Resources Assessment*. OUP 1987 $39.95. ISBN 0-19-854592-4. Treats the principles and applications of geographical information systems as they apply to environmental sciences.

Huxhold, William E. *An Introduction to Urban Geographic Information Systems*. OUP 1991 $49.95. ISBN 0-19-506535-2. Intended as a first exposure to geographic information systems for students of urban geography as well as urban studies.

Mossman, Jennifer, ed. *Encyclopedia of Geographic Information Sources*. Gale 4th ed. 1986 $105.00. ISBN 0-8103-0410-4. Comprehensive and wide-ranging. More than 11,000 current citations, discusses nearly 400 major cities, states, and regions in the United States. Focuses on business, economic, and financial sources as well as geographic.

Peuquet, Donna J., and Duane F. Marble. *Introductory Readings in Geographic Information Systems*. Taylor & Francis 1990 $149.50. ISBN 0-85066-856-5. The first major overview on the new field of geographic information systems.

Robinson, Arthur H. *The Look of Maps: An Examination of Cartographic Design.* U. of Wis. Pr. 1952 $20.00. ISBN 0-299-00950-5. Early work by a leading researcher in cartography, consisting of 10 research papers that helped set the agenda for research for many years.

Robinson, Arthur H., and Barbara Bartz Petchenik. *The Nature of Maps: Essays toward Understanding Maps and Mapping.* U. Ch. Pr. 1976 o.p. Collection of papers on the cognitive aspects of cartography.

Robinson, Arthur H., and others. *Elements of Cartography.* Wiley 5th ed. 1984 $51.95. ISBN 0-471-09877-9. Major text in cartography. Introduced computer-assisted cartography into several chapters.

HUMAN GEOGRAPHY

The human population of the earth has evolved with its own distinctive geography. Population distribution, culture, and economic activities vary geographically across the earth's surface. Geographers study these phenomena, attempting to understand past and current patterns, and, in some cases, to predict future distributions. Four main subfields—cultural geography, economic geography, political geography, and urban geography—can be highlighted. Though not exhaustive, this list accounts for a large proportion of geographic research.

Cultural Geography

Culture, which refers to the way of life of people in particular parts of the world, traditionally has included analyses of language, religion, types of economy, and most important within geography, the relationship between the population and the physical environment it inhabits. This branch of geography has developed considerably from the research of CARL ORTWIN SAUER, who produced a pioneering work on the spread of agricultural systems and emphasized a more humanistic geography. Past efforts to draw broad generalizations about large culture regions now are supplemented with a more process-oriented approach that shows the interaction between humans, their culture, and their landscape in more localized settings. Much of the field of historical geography, given the methods of analysis adopted, can be linked to this subfield, and outstanding regional analyses have been produced, the best of which include work on the historical geography of North America by DONALD W. MEINIG.

Ehrlich, Paul R. *Population Bomb.* Ballantine 1986 $4.50. ISBN 0-345-33834-0. Controversial book updated.

Gesler, Wilbert M. *The Cultural Geography of Health Care.* U. of Pittsburgh Pr. 1991 $39.95. ISBN 0-8229-3664-X. Health care interpreted in terms of regional, ecological, evolutionary, diffusionist, and materialist perspectives on culture.

Jordan, Terry G., and Lester Rowntree. *The Human Mosaic: A Thematic Introduction to Cultural Geography.* HarpC 1990 $15.95. ISBN 0-06-043460-0. Review of concepts of culture, including culture regions and cultural diffusion as they apply to language, religion, and economic systems.

Haupt, Arthur, and Thomas T. Kane. *The Population Handbook.* Population Ref. 1985 $5.00. ISBN 0-917136-09-8. Introduction to basic measures of population.

Norton, William. *Explorations in the Understanding of Landscape: A Cultural Geography.* Greenwood 1989 $42.95. ISBN 0-313-26494-5. Offers an evaluation of cultural geography and its central concept, landscape.

Rubenstein, James M. *The Cultural Landscape: An Introduction to Human Geography*. West Pub. 1983 $49.25. ISBN 0-314-69674-1. Detailed examination of cultural elements, with related contemporary issues that emerge from them.

Zelinsky, Wilbur. *The Cultural Geography of the United States*. P-H 1992 $22.67. ISBN 0-13-194424-X. Discusses role of geography in shaping the people and destiny of the United States.

Economic Geography

Although, to some, economy is a part of cultural geography, its complexity and importance to the modern world have resulted in its development as a large and important subfield of its own—one with a strong quantitative and analytical orientation. National and regional economies can be divided into three main sectors—the primary sector (agriculture, mining, forestry, fishing), the secondary sector (manufacturing and construction), and the tertiary sector (the distribution of goods and services). Geographers and other social scientists have developed models to help explain the geographic distributions of these activities. Examples include classical models for agricultural land use, manufacturing location, and the location of service towns. Today, however, classical models have been revised substantially, and, as local, national, and international economies restructure in the latest stage of global capitalism, their relevance is open to debate. The result has been a more deconcentrated geographic pattern of some economic activities. Explaining these changes has meant detailed research on the changing relationship of capital and labor, on stages in the development of firms, and on the roles of high technology and research and development.

Within this field, a rapidly growing area is the study of development. Because not all parts of the world have followed, or will follow, the same path to development that occurred in North America and Europe, geographers and other social scientists have studied the impact of "dependency" relationships created during the colonial period but not yet broken economically. They also have studied the relevance of the work of KARL MARX (see also Vol. 4) in understanding the uneven development of the modern world.

Dicken, Peter. *Global Shift: The Internationalization of Economic Activity*. Guilford Pr. 1992 $30.00. ISBN 0-89862-488-6. Solid analysis of late twentieth-century global changes tied to transnational corporations, nation states, and technological change.

Dicken, Peter, and Peter E. Lloyd. *Location in Space: Theoretical Perspectives in Economic Geography*. HarpC 1990 $60.50. ISBN 0-06-041677-7. Classic text on theories and methods of analysis in economic geography.

Fotheringham, A. Stuart, and Morton E. O'Kelly. *Spatial Interaction Models: Formulations and Applications*. Kluwer Ac. 1989 $81.50. ISBN 0-7923-0021-1. Practical guide to spatial interaction modeling that focuses on spatial flows and has strong theoretical and applied relevance. Part of "Studies in Operational Regional Science" series.

Hartshorn, Truman A., and John W. Alexander. *Economic Geography*. P-H 1988 $48.00. ISBN 0-13-225160-4. Excellent overview of the main research themes in economic geography.

Knox, Paul, and John Agnew. *The Geography of the World Economy*. Routledge Chapman & Hall 1989 $21.95. ISBN 0-7131-6517-0. Focuses on contemporary patterns of economic geography with more attention given to historical processes and regional interdependence than to mathematical modeling.

Kodras, Janet, and John Paul Jones, eds. *Geographic Dimensions of United States Social Policy*. Routledge Chapman & Hall 1990 o.p. Good recent account of the spatial dimensions of policy implications of such topics as homelessness, the medically vulnerable, and African American female-headed households.

Sayer, Andrew, and Richard Walker. *The New Social Economy: Reworking the Division of Labor*. Blackwell Pubs. 1992. ISBN 1-55786-280-X. Analysis of recent reorganizations of the division of labor in households, corporations, and multinational networks.

Taaffe, Edward J., and Howard L. Gauthier. *A Geography of Transportation*. P-H 1973 o.p. Remains the single best overview of concepts and methods in this important subfield of economic geography. A new edition is presently being prepared.

Political Geography

This subfield, which has a long tradition in geography, involves a better understanding of the linkages between political processes and geographic areas at all scales—local, state, and international. Historically, in addition to a descriptive orientation, the field has had well-established areas of investigation, ranging from studies of boundary disputes to the links between territorial organization and power relationships to patterns of voting behavior. But over the past two decades, a new political geography has emerged that focuses more heavily on the theoretical development of the relationship between politics and space. Moreover, methodological concern that positivist approaches to political geography could not help explain such issues as social deprivation, poverty, and gender inequity has resulted in adoption of a more historical orientation that stresses the impact of the capitalist world economy and the uneven development that results from it. Marxist thought has played a central role in this work. There also has been substantial interest in political geography at the local, metropolitan scale of analysis. Included are studies of neighborhood conflict and broad urban social movements. In general, this work stresses the importance of the production and reproduction of places at all scales on the earth's surface.

Agnew, John A. *Place and Politics: The Geographical Mediation of State and Society*. Routledge Chapman & Hall 1987 $55.00. ISBN 0-04-320177-6. Excellent example of modern political geography by one of its best writers and analysts.

Archer, J. Clark, and Peter J. Taylor. *Section and Party: A Political Geography of American Presidential Elections from Andrew Jackson to Ronald Reagan*. Bks. Demand repr. of 1981 ed. $74.10. ISBN 0-8357-3529-X. Good example of electoral geography through rigorous modern spatial analysis tradition.

Cox, Kevin R. *Conflict, Power, and Politics in the City: A Geographic View*. McGraw 1973 o.p. Brings political geography clearly to the modern city; a scale of analysis that to this point had not been addressed as fully.

Harvey, David. *The Limits to Capital*. U. Ch. Pr. 1982 $24.95. ISBN 0-226-31954-7. Landmark book on the geography of capitalism and the role of Marx's work in its interpretation.

Taylor, Peter J., and J. W. House, eds. *Political Geography: Recent Advances and Future Directions*. B&N Imports 1984 $50.00. ISBN 0-389-20493-5. Coedited by one of the most prolific writers in the field at a time when political geography was developing new directions.

Urban Geography

Approximately one-half of the world's population lives in urban areas. In fact, in some regions more than three-quarters of the population is urban. As a result, urban areas have become a focus for geographic research and publication. Generally, these areas are studied at two scales—"urban systems, or interurban, analysis," in which cities are studied in the aggregate as a national or regional set and broad geographic characteristics are analyzed; and "intraurban analysis," in which geographic distributions of land use and population within cities are analyzed. In the second scale, the current emphasis is on central city versus suburban distinctions. This distinctive local geography has considerable applied or policy relevance, and geographers have contributed substantially to the field of urban planning.

Brown, Lawrence A. *Place, Migration, and Development in the Third World: An Alternative View*. Routledge 1991 o.p. Detailed conceptual and empirical analysis of population movements and the relationship to economic development; focused primarily on Latin America.

Brunn, Stanley D., and Jack Williams. *Cities of the World: World Regional Urban Development*. HarpC 1993 $42.50. ISBN 0-06-041028-0. Collection of essays on urban development and urban policy in all of the continental regions of the world.

Cadwallader, Martin. *Migration and Residential Mobility: Macro and Micro Approaches*. U. of Wis. Pr. 1992 $18.95. ISBN 0-299-13494-6. Analysis by a leading researcher of migration from region to region and within cities in highly developed countries. Theory, empirical analysis, and models used.

Hartshorn, Truman A. *Interpreting the City: An Urban Geography*. Wiley 1992 $52.95. ISBN 0-471-88750-1. Leading text that covers both the inter- and intraurban scales of analysis. Particular attention given to North American cities.

Ward, David. *Cities and Immigrants: A Geography of Change in Nineteenth-Century America*. OUP 1971 $13.95. ISBN 0-19-501284-4. The single best overview of the historical development of the geography of American cities.

REGIONAL GEOGRAPHY

Regional study has a long tradition in geography and is done on many scales. There exist numerous overviews of regions at the global scale; many of which categorize the world into "more developed" and "less developed" parts and highlight similarities and differences between and among continentally sized regions, usually examining the various subfields of physical and human geography for each region. Detailed books also exist on each of the continental regions and on many of the world's nearly 200 political states. At each of these scales, a debate ensues as to whether the approach should be a regional inventory or survey, as was the case in most regional overviews until the past decade, or whether a more systematic approach should be taken, in which the models and theories of each of the subfields of geography are addressed in turn. The latter approach stresses generalization more than a particularistic approach.

Regional analysis can be done on a much more localized scale as well, highlighting regions within countries or individual cities. Over the past two decades, there has been an increase in regional study at this scale, notably for North America and Latin America.

Almost all good work in regional geography is derived from singly or jointly authored books. Collections of papers by sets of authors are uncommon.

Agnew, John. *The United States in the World Economy: A Regional Geography*. Cambridge U. Pr. 1987 $49.95. ISBN 0-521-30410-5. Examines the changing dialectic between local interests and conflict and the wider mechanisms, economic and social, which shape the world system.

Birdsall, Stephen S., and John W. Florin. *Regional Landscapes of the United States and Canada*. Wiley 1992 $37.50. ISBN 0-471-61646-X. Good example of a detailed overview of a particular world region; includes both systematic topical and subregional approaches.

Congdon, Peter, and Peter Batey. *Advances in Regional Demography: Forecasts, Information, Models.* St. Martin 1989 $55.00. ISBN 1-85293-046-2. An interdisciplinary approach to the study of population change at local and regional levels.

de Blij, Harm J., and Peter O. Muller. *Geography: Regions and Concepts.* Wiley 1992 $40.00. ISBN 0-471-57275. The single best introduction to geography and the regional approach, with chapters devoted to each region of the world, each with a detailed bibliography relevant to the given region.

Gaile, Gary L., and Cort J. Willmott. *Geography in America.* Macmillan 1989. ISBN 0-675-20648-0. Provides references for books on Africa, Latin America, Asia, the former Soviet Union and eastern Europe, and Canada.

Harris, Chauncy D., ed. *A Geographical Bibliography for American Libraries.* Assn. Am. Geographers 1985 $25.00. ISBN 0-89291-193-X. Identifies all major works for each continental region.

Jackson, Richard H., and Lloyd E. Hudman. *World Regional Geography: Issues for Today.* Wiley 1990 $49.95. ISBN 0-471-50633-8. Describes how and why geographic factors create broad global contrasts.

Meinig, Donald W. *The Shaping of America: A Geographical Perspective on 500 Years of History.* Vol. 1: *Atlantic America, 1492–1800.* Yale U. Pr. 1986 $50.00. ISBN 0-300-03548-9. Geographic perspective on the early development of the United States by the researcher widely regarded as one of the best historical geographers. Distinctive approach to studying a region.

PHYSICAL GEOGRAPHY

The earth's physical environment has its own changing geography. The physical features of the earth developed long before there was a human population. In general, the physical environment is composed of four main spheres, each of which is studied by geographers and is a subfield of physical geography. One is the lithosphere, the earth's surface, with its landform patterns. The lithosphere provides the soil base and contains the mineral resources used by the human population. Geographers who study this sphere focus on geomorphology. A second sphere is the atmosphere, the gaseous envelope above the lithosphere within which processes of day-to-day weather and long-term climate occur. Geographers who study this sphere focus on climatology. A third sphere is the hydrosphere, which refers to the water on the earth's surface. Research in hydrology stresses the importance of water for food supply and transportation and its impact on the atmosphere and lithosphere. The fourth sphere is the biosphere, the living things on the earth's surface— plants and animals, including humans.

Considerable attention in research is being given today to climatology and biogeography. In climatology, current work focuses on modeling, in quantitative terms, atmospheric dynamics. Some research occurs at the global scale on long-term climatic change and some occurs at the local level, as climatologists examine the impact of the local urban environment on atmospheric dynamics. In biogeography, the emphasis is on the changing ranges, or geographic regions, of plants and animals over time and at different geographic scales— local, regional, national, and global. For some researchers, the emphasis is on vegetation dynamics and the impact, for example, of such natural disasters as fire or volcanic activity. For other researchers the emphasis is on the interaction of the human population with the environment. Included are such topics as tropical deforestation or the spread of population into fragile environments—mountain, desert, or polar regions, for example.

Ballard, Robert D. *Exploring Our Living Planet.* Ed. by Jonathan B. Tourtellot. Natl. Geog. 1983 $21.95. ISBN 0-87044-397-6. Illustrations of various physical features of the planet.

Bradshaw, Michael. *An Introduction to Physical Geography.* Mosby Yr. Bk. 1992 $46.95. ISBN 0-8016-0298-X

Cox, C. B. and P. D. Moore. *Biogeography: An Ecological and Evolutionary Approach.* Blackwell Sci. 1993 $34.95. ISBN 0-632-01332-X. Discusses how ecology, geography, geology, evolutionary history, and economic anthropology integrate to produce the patterns of distribution of life.

Fellows, Donald K. *Our Environment: An Introduction to Physical Geography.* Wiley 1985 $41.95. ISBN 0-471-88193-7

Linacre, Edward. *Climate Data and Resources.* Routledge 1992 $75.00. ISBN 0-415-05702-7. Covers each of the basic climatic parameters and illustrates the statistical handling of information, as well as instruments and measurements, methods of analysis, and applications of climatalogical data.

Lutgens, Frederick K., and Edward J. Tarbuck. *The Atmosphere: An Introduction to Meteorology.* P-H 1992 $49.00. ISBN 0-13-051467-5. Detailed introduction to the study of atmospheric processes; includes temperature, precipitation, severe storms, air pollution, and global climatic change.

McIntyre, Michael P., and others. *Physical Geography.* Wiley 1991 $41.95. ISBN 0-471-62017-3. Popular introduction to physical geography. Emphasizes the interrelationship of people and the environment and stresses the global patterns of physical geography.

McKnight, Tom L. *Physical Geography: A Landscape Appreciation.* P-H 1992 $48.00. ISBN 0-13-667171-3. Thorough overview of the concepts and methods of analysis used by geographers to study the different spheres of the physical environment.

Strahler, Alan H., and Arthur N. Strahler. *Modern Physical Geography.* Wiley 4th ed. 1992 $40.00. ISBN 0-471-53392-0. Overview by two leading researchers in physical geography that often is seen as the standard to which other books are compared.

CHRONOLOGY OF AUTHORS

Humboldt, Alexander von. 1769–1859
Ritter, Karl. 1779–1859
Guyot, Arnold. 1807–1884
Mackinder, Halford John, Sir. 1861–1947
Bowman, Isaiah. 1878–1950
Sauer, Carl Ortwin. 1889–1975
Gottmann, Jean. 1915–
Robinson, Arthur. 1915–

Meinig, Donald W. 1924–
Berry, Brian J. L. 1934–
Brown, Lawrence A. 1935–
Ward, David. 1935–
Jordan, Terry G. 1938–
Scott, Allen J. 1938–
Bourne, Larry S. 1939–
Johnston, Ronald J. 1941–

BERRY, BRIAN J. L. 1934–

Currently Founders Professor at the University of Texas, Brian Berry received his doctoral degree from the University of Washington in 1958. In the 1960s he helped lead the quantitative revolution in geography. As a faculty member at the University of Chicago, he served as dissertation supervisor to numerous students who later became productive research faculty and leaders in the discipline throughout the United States and Canada.

Berry's pioneering work in urban geography added methodological rigor and empirical dimensions to the analysis of established concepts. He was particularly influential in developing "factorial ecology" as a means of understanding the social geography of cities. His work in retail geography is well known also, particularly through *The Geography of Market Centers and Retail Distribution* (1967). He helped document and analyze the population turnaround—sunbelt and nonmetropolitan growth in the 1970s. More broadly, Berry helped define research directions in urban systems analysis and in the geography of development.

BOOKS BY BERRY

America's Utopian Experiments: Communal Havens From Long-Wave Crises. U. Pr. of New Eng. 1992 $40.00. ISBN 0-87451-589-0. Part of the *Nelson Rockefeller Series in Social Science and Public Policy*. Examines social movements and collective settlements in the United States particularly.

City Classification Handbook: Methods and Applications. (ed.) Bks. Demand 1972 $101.50. ISBN 0-317-09217-0. Excellent collection showing the latest methods for urban and economic analysis, particularly for urban areas.

Commercial Structure and Commercial Blight: Retail Patterns and Processes in the City of Chicago. U. Ch. Pr. 1963 o.p. Good example of early analytical work on urban retail structure, with Chicago as the example.

Comparative Urbanization: Divergent Paths in the Twentieth Century. St. Martin 1981 o.p. Rare example of effort to show changes in the urbanization process in different global regions.

Contemporary Urban Ecology. (coauthored with John D. Kasarda). Macmillan 1977 o.p. Important book for both geography and sociology. Examines urban social structure in different development contexts.

Geographic Perspectives on Urban Systems. (coauthored with Frank Horton). P-H 1970 o.p. First effort to show the modern city as a system of economic and demographic attributes.

Long-Wave Rhythms in Economic Development and Political Behavior. Johns Hopkins 1991 $49.50. ISBN 0-8018-4035-X. Recent work that examines short-term and long-term inflationary and deflationary growth cycles.

Market Centers and Retail Location: Theory and Applications. (coauthored with John B. Parr). P-H 1988 $46.00. ISBN 0-13-556184-1. Updated version of Berry's classic 1967 study on the quantitative and theoretical work in retail geography.

BOURNE, LARRY S. 1939–

One of Canada's leading research geographers, Larry S. Bourne was a student of BRIAN BERRY at the University of Chicago, where he received his Ph.D. in 1968. Through the 1970s and early 1980s, he served as director of the Center for Urban and Community Studies at the University of Toronto. In this position Bourne oversaw the publication of numerous discussion papers and books that documented the details of the urbanization process in Canada. The methods and concepts utilized were adopted in studies in other regional contexts.

Bourne has researched the urbanization process on both the inter- and intraurban scales. His early work on private redevelopment of central cities was a landmark study on that topic.

His work on Canada was supplemented with broader research themes, such as the geography of housing, and through the International Geographical Union's Commission on Settlement Systems, his comparative work on urban systems. One of his current projects is a soon-to-be-published book on the social geography of Canada.

BOOKS BY BOURNE

Geography of Housing. Routledge Chapman & Hall 1981 o.p. Detailed overview of theoretical developments in the subfield of the residential structure of cities. Includes discussion of the role of government.

Internal Structure of the City: Readings on Urban Growth, Form, and Policy. OUP 1982
$25.00. ISBN 0-19-503032-X. Updated edition of 1971 classic collection of papers on
a variety of topics on the geography of the modern city, including retail structure,
residential land use, and transportation.

*Private Redevelopment of the Central City: Spatial Processes of Structural Change in the
City of Toronto.* Bks. Demand 1967 $58.10. ISBN 0-7837-0392-9. One of the first
analyses of the processes associated with private redevelopment in a major
metropolitan center. Established the base for Bourne's later interest in the
geography of housing.

Urban Systems: Strategies for Regulation. OUP 1975 $15.95. ISBN 0-19-874055-7. Useful
example of comparative work at the urban systems scale. Highlights urban policies
in Britain, Sweden, Canada, and Australia.

Urbanization and Settlement Systems: International Perspectives. (coauthored with R.
Sinclair). OUP 1984 $49.95. ISBN 0-19-823243-8. Collection of papers comparing
trends in urbanization of more than 20 countries.

BOWMAN, ISAIAH. 1878–1950

Isaiah Bowman was born in Ontario, Canada, and educated at Harvard and
Yale universities. While attending Yale, he led the first South American Yale
expedition. It was an adventure that greatly influenced his later contributions to
the field of geography. In 1911 Bowman served as geographer-geologist on
another Yale expedition, this time to Peru. That same year, he published his
book *Forest Physiography*, which offered the first in-depth study of the relief,
climate, vegetation, and soils of the United States. The geography of the United
States continued to interest him throughout his career. He was especially
interested in what he called the "Pioneer fringe," the area between early
America's wilderness and civilization. In 1931 he published a book called *The
Pioneer Fringe*, the first of a series on world frontier areas.

In 1915 Bowman became the director of the American Geographical Society.
At that time, the Society was a small, relatively unknown organization, but
under Bowman's direction, it became a highly respected center for geographic
research and scholarship. One of the things Bowman did was to initiate a 25-
year study by the Society to map the region known as Hispanic America. At the
end of World War I, Bowman traveled to the Versailles peace conference as
President Woodrow Wilson's territorial adviser to help draw the postwar
boundaries of European nations. During World War II, he was once again a
territorial adviser, this time for the United States State Department. From 1935
to 1948, he was president of Johns Hopkins University, which renamed its
geography department in his honor. A member and officer of many geographic
and related clubs, boards, associations, and groups, he was considered one of
the greatest modern authorities on political geography.

BOOKS BY BOWMAN

The Andes of Southern Peru. 1916. Greenwood 1968 $35.00. ISBN 0-8371-0025-9
Desert Trails of Atacama. 1924. Ayer repr. of 1924 ed. $18.50. ISBN 0-404-00964-6
Limits of Land Settlement: A Report on Present-Day Possibilities. 1937. Ayer repr. of 1937
ed. $24.50. ISBN 0-8369-0233-5
The Pioneer Fringe. 1931. Ayer repr. of 1931 ed. $38.50. ISBN 0-8369-5828-4

BOOK ABOUT BOWMAN

Martin, Geoffrey J. *The Life and Thought of Isaiah Bowman.* Shoe String 1980 $29.50.
ISBN 0-208-01844-1. Informative biography emphasizing Bowman's major contribution to the understanding and appreciation of United States geography; includes a
bibliography and index.

BROWN, LAWRENCE A. 1935–

One of a group of geographers trained in quantitative methods in the 1960s, Lawrence A. Brown received his Ph.D. in 1965 from Northwestern University. Most of his career since then has been spent as professor at Ohio State University, which has one of the leading research and graduate programs in modern geography.

Brown's early work focused on the dynamics of modern cities, and his research on intraurban migration remains among the most often cited in this broadly interdisciplinary subject. Throughout the 1970s his research focused more closely on the geographic spread of innovations. The last of the three books he produced based on this research, *Innovation Diffusion: A New Perspective* (1981), was particularly well received because it shifted attention from the demand for innovations to their supply.

By the 1980s, Brown's work had extended to focus on the process of economic and demographic development, particularly as it relates to Latin America. He developed a paradigm for the interrelationships between migration and economic development. His current work is on the spatial aspects of settlement system evolution in Latin America.

BOOKS BY BROWN

Diffusion Processes and Location: A Conceptual Framework and Bibliography. Regional Sci. Res. Inst. 1968 $10.00. ISBN 1-55869-026-3. Dissertation research on the diffusion process from a geographic perspective. Built on earlier work by other geographers, economists, and regional scientists.

Innovation Diffusion: A New Perspective. Methuen 1981 o.p. Well-received book that put the emphasis on supply as opposed to demand considerations.

Place Migration and Development in the Third World: An Alternative View with Particular Reference to Population Movements, Labor Market Experiences, and Regional Change in Latin America. Routledge 1991 o.p. Detailed analysis at both conceptual and empirical levels of development processes in selected countries of Latin America. Excellent example of the use of appropriate statistical methods for this type of analysis.

GOTTMANN, JEAN. 1915–

Jean Gottmann, one of geography's most widely known writers, received his undergraduate degree in France in 1932. In 1968 he completed his M.A. at Oxford University and received his doctorate at the University of Paris two years later. Through just a few books, Gottmann has developed a set of concepts and generalizations to help understand the geography of the human landscape and has made substantial contributions in three main areas. First, his text on the geography of Europe, through several editions, remains a classic in regional geography. Second, he introduced and developed what are now fundamental concepts in modern geography—the concept of "megalopolis," especially as it applies to the northeastern United States, and the concept of "center and periphery," now known as core and periphery. Third, he addressed the growing importance of modern telecommunications in city development and examined the "transactional city." Currently Gottmann is professor emeritus at Oxford University.

BOOKS BY GOTTMANN

Center and Periphery: Spatial Variations in Politics. (ed.) Sage 1980 o.p. Based on papers from a Paris symposium of the International Political Science Association. Focuses on the spatial polarization of the world at different scales.

Geography of Europe. HR&W 4th ed. 1969 o.p. Classic regional geography of Europe. Includes discussion of the systematic fields of geography for all of the subregions of the continent.

Megalopolis: The Urbanized Northeastern Seaboard of the United States. Twentieth Century Fund 1961 o.p. Introduced and developed the concept of megalopolis and applied it to the region from Boston to Washington, D. C.

BOOK ABOUT GOTTMANN

Patten, John, ed. *The Expanding City: Essays in Honor of Professor Jean Gottmann*. Acad. Pr. 1983 $101.00. ISBN 0-12-547250-1. Set of papers on the changing nature of urban areas in the late twentieth century.

GUYOT, ARNOLD. 1807–1884

Born in Switzerland, Arnold Guyot completed his doctorate in 1825 and then spent six weeks in the Alps observing the ways in which ice moved in the mountains. He became the first to formulate laws regarding the movement of glaciers and other ice structures. Guyot became a professor of history and physical geography in Germany, but in 1848 he was persuaded by his friend LOUIS AGASSIZ (see Vol. 5) to come to the United States to live and work.

After arriving in the United States, Guyot taught at Lowell Technological Institute in Massachusetts and then at Princeton University. Turning his attention to mountain ranges in the United States, he was responsible for the development of topographical maps of the Appalachian and Catskill ranges in eastern North America. It was his research that led to the establishment of the U.S. Weather Bureau, now known as the National Weather Service, which still keeps Americans informed of weather conditions.

Among the books Guyot wrote about his observations was *Earth and Man* (1849), which theorizes about Earth's evolution and the place human beings hold in that evolution. He also wrote many geography textbooks for use at the college level. Today, the term *guyot*, in his honor, is used to refer to sea mountains with flat tops.

BOOKS BY GUYOT

Earth and Man: Lectures on Comparative Physical Geography in Its Relation to the History of Mankind. 1849. Ayer 1970 $20.00. ISBN 0-405-02669-2

The Influence of Geography Upon the History of Mankind. 1855. 2 vols. Trans. by C. C. Felton. Found. Class. Repr. 1986 $189.75. ISBN 0-89901-275-2

HUMBOLDT, (FRIEDRICH HEINRICH) ALEXANDER VON. 1769–1859

Baron Alexander von Humboldt was born in Berlin, Germany. During his early school years, he studied such subjects as geology, biology, metallurgy, and mining, and his main interest was in nature and other lands.

In 1796 Humboldt traveled to the German Alps, where he measured the atmospheric pressure, humidity, and oxygen content of the air. Shortly after, in 1799, he was granted permission by the Spanish king to explore Spain's mysterious holdings in the Americas. For the next five years, he and his companion, Aimé Bonplaud, explored the region that is now Venezuela, Cuba, Colombia, Peru, Ecuador, and Mexico. While in the Andes, he fell prey to mountain sickness, which led him to become the first person to explain that the sickness was caused by a lack of oxygen. During these travels, he and Bonplaud collected 60,000 plant specimens; mapped the area; and studied its climates, bodies of water, wildlife, and minerals. The findings of this exhaustive adventure were published in a 23-volume series, *Voyage de Humboldt et Bonplaud* (1805–34).

In 1829, at the invitation of the Russian government, Humboldt made an expedition to Russia and Siberia, categorizing, observing, and recording as he went. One of the results of this expedition was a 5-volume work, *Kosmos* (1845–62), in which he tried to combine the vague ideals of the eighteenth century with the exact scientific requirements of his own.

Considered one of the founders of modern geography, Humboldt showed geographers that there was more to the study of geography than the shape of Earth and its regions. He gave them a system of geographic inquiry, he was the first to draw an isothermal map, studied tropical storms and volcanoes, and pioneered the field of terrestrial magnetism. Equally important, he was responsible for one of the first examples of international scientific cooperation, which led to the formation of a system of meteorological stations throughout Russia and Great Britain. During one of his many expeditions, he measured the temperature of the current with which his ship sailed from Lima, Peru, to Acapulco, Mexico. Later this current was named the Humboldt Current in his honor.

BOOKS BY HUMBOLDT

Aspects of Nature in Different Lands and Different Climates. 1850. Trans. by Mrs. Sabine. AMS Pr. 1970 $32.00. ISBN 0-404-03385-7

Island of Cuba. 1856. Trans. by J. S. Thrasher. Greenwood 1969 $35.00. ISBN 0-8371-2627-4

Personal Narrative of Travels to Equinoctial Regions of America During the Years 1799–1804. 1851. 3 vols. Trans. by Thomasina Ross. Ayer 1969 $60.00. ISBN 0-405-08642-3

Political Essay on the Kingdom of New Spain. 1811. 4 vols. Trans. by John Black. AMS Pr. $9.95. ISBN 0-404-03450-0

BOOK ABOUT HUMBOLDT

von Hagen, Victor Wolfgang. *South America Called Them; Explorations of the Great Naturalists: La Condamine, Humboldt, Darwin, Spence.* AMS Pr. 1949 $49.50. ISBN 0-404-20278-0. Critical interpretation of von Humboldt's explorations in South America.

JOHNSTON, RONALD J. 1941–

Currently vice-chancellor at the University of Essex in the United Kingdom, Ronald Johnston was trained in geography in the United Kingdom and in Australia, countries that have a strong tradition of geography as an academic subject. Since receiving his Ph.D. in 1967, he has become one of the most prolific writers in human geography. Both his books and his research articles cover a broad spectrum, including statistical methods, detailed empirical and theoretical work in political and economic geography, and overviews of philosophical and methodological debates in modern geography. His work includes both introductory syntheses and in-depth regional or systematic topics.

BOOKS BY JOHNSTON

The American Urban System: A Geographical Perspective. St. Martin 1982 $15.35. ISBN 0-312-03125-4. Very different approach to the study of urbanization in the United States that gives considerable attention to the political/historical context for urban development.

Geography and Geographers: Anglo-American Human Geography since 1945. Routledge Chapman & Hall 1991 $19.95. ISBN 0-340-51755-7. Good example of Johnston's efforts to document and analyze philosophical and methodological debates within geography over the past four decades. Important starting point for someone wanting an overview of the broad nature of the discipline.

Geography and the State: An Essay in Political Geography. St. Martin 1982 o.p. Middle-of-the-road argument for the need to develop a theory of the state in geography.

Multivariate Statistical Analysis in Geography: A Primer on the General Linear Model. Longman 1978 o.p. Introduction to modern quantitative methods in geographic research. Particularly helpful for introductory students at the college level.

Political, Electoral and Spatial Systems: An Essay in Political Geography. OUP 1979 o.p. Empirical work that contrasts the U. S. and U. K. political systems. Part of a tradition in political geography that focuses on electoral geography.

JORDAN, TERRY G. 1938–

Currently the W. P. Webb Professor in the Department of Geography at the University of Texas in Austin, Terry G. Jordan received his Ph.D. from the University of Wisconsin in 1965 and was part of the strong tradition in historical geography there. Over the past 20 years, he has produced a set of books that combine the best traditions in cultural geography. In these works he has included both cultural landscape features, such as building types, and more broadly relevant historical topics, such as ethnicity.

Jordan, who has served as president of the Association of American Geographers, also has brought his expertise to general texts in cultural geography.

BOOKS BY JORDAN

The American Backwoods Frontier: An Ethnic and Ecological Interpretation. (coauthored with Matti Kaups). Johns Hopkins 1992 repr. of 1989 ed. $22.95. ISBN 0-9-8018-4375-8. Excellent work on pioneer life and ethnicity in the Delaware, New York, New Jersey region.

American Log Buildings: An Old World Heritage. U. of NC Pr. 1985 $24.95. ISBN 0-8078-1617-5. Thorough analysis of building type.

The European Culture Area: A Systematic Geography. HarpC 1990 $65.50. ISBN 0-06-043467-8. Good example of regional geography from a cultural perspective on a region with remarkable cultural diversity.

The Human Mosaic: A Thematic Introduction to Cultural Geography. (coauthored with Lester Rowntree). HarpC 1990 $56.50. ISBN 0-06-043481-3. Useful example of how cultural geography can be synthesized and presented in introductory manner. Nontraditional approach that reflects changes in geography in the 1960s and 1970s.

Texas Graveyards: A Cultural Legacy. U. of Tex. Pr. 1982 $11.95. ISBN 0-292-78070-2. Analysis that ties features of the cultural landscape to social life and customs of the region.

MACKINDER, SIR HALFORD JOHN. 1861–1947

From an early age, John Mackinder was interested in the history of the countryside where he lived in England. He attended Oxford University, but, since geography was not an academic subject, he took classes in the subject closest to it that he could find—natural history. After completing his education, he began to research and explore his nation, eventually publishing *Britain and the British Seas* (1902), which is still considered a definitive work.

Mackinder's interest and experience led to a position as professor of geography at Oxford, a position he used to create a renewed interest in geography. He also was responsible for making geography an academic subject. An explorer as well as a teacher, Mackinder became the first European to climb Mount Kenya, Africa's second highest mountain. From 1903 to 1908, Mackinder served as director of the London School of Economics. In 1909, he became a member of Parliament, where he remained a member until 1922, at which time he went on to hold other government posts. In 1920, he was knighted.

Mackinder was a supporter of geopolitics—a belief that political developments are directly related to geographic space. Like other geopolitical theorists, he emphasized the role geography played in international relations. Mackinder acknowledged that in the past the sea powers had been dominant in the world. But he believed that, with the coming of railroads, that power had switched to land and that Eurasia had become the world's "heartland." And, in his view, "Who rules the Heartland . . . commands the world." Those in power in Great Britain and the United States paid little attention to this theory, which he discussed in his work entitled *Democratic Ideas and Reality* (1919). But the theory was very convincing to a German geopolitician named Karl Haushofer, whose writings impressed Germany's ruler, Adolf Hitler. Hitler ultimately made the theory part of his master plan of world domination and used it to justify German expansion.

BOOKS BY MACKINDER

Britain and the British Seas. 1902. *British Heritage Ser.* Greenwood 1970 $25.00. ISBN 0-8371-2754-8
Democratic Ideas and Reality. 1919. Greenwood 1981 $38.50. ISBN 0-313-23150-8

BOOKS ABOUT MACKINDER

Blouet, Brian. *Halford Mackinder: A Biography.* Texas A & M Univ. Pr. 1987 $21.50. ISBN 0-89096-292-8. Well-written and researched biographical study.
Parker, W. H. *Mackinder: Geography as an Aid to Statecraft.* OUP 1982 $39.95. ISBN 0-19-823235-7. Discussion of Mackinder's geopolitical theories.

MEINIG, DONALD W. 1924–

Donald W. Meinig is the Maxwell Research Professor in the Department of Geography at Syracuse University. Over the past two decades, he has become one of the world's most prolific and best historical geographers. Since receiving his Ph.D. in 1953 from the University of Washington, he has focused his research on the historical geography of North America and its various subregions. From his work on the Southwest from Texas to the Columbia River Valley, and through his ongoing three-volume project on the broad epochs of American historical development, Meinig's work is critically praised for showcasing vividly the interrelationships between geography and history.

BOOKS BY MEINIG

The Great Columbia Plain: A Historical Geography. U. of Wash. Pr. 1968 o.p. Detailed analysis of the development of an important corridor of settlement in the Northwest.
Imperial Texas: An Interpretive Essay in Cultural Geography. U. of Tex. Pr. 1968 $10.95. ISBN 0-292-73807-2. Good example to show the linkages between historical and cultural geography.
The Interpretation of Ordinary Landscapes: Geographical Essays. (ed.) OUP 1979 $19.95. ISBN 0-19-502536-9. Nine essays that show how landscapes can be evaluated from a historical, cultural, geographic perspective.
The Shaping of America: A Geographical Perspective on 500 Years of History. Vol. 1: *Atlantic America 1492–1800.* Yale U. Pr. 1986 $50.00. ISBN 0-300-03548-9. Widely regarded as the best geographic interpretation of the historical development of the first main stage in North American settlement.

Southwest: Three Peoples in Geographical Change 1600–1970. OUP 1971 $15.95. ISBN 0-19-501289-5. The single best overview of the historical development of this distinctive culture region.

RITTER, KARL. 1779–1859

Born in Quedlinburg, Germany, Karl Ritter is considered the founder of modern scientific geography. A keen observer of the world around him, Ritter was very aware of the relationships between things in his immediate vicinity. As a geographer, he expanded this idea to encompass the study of relationships over the entire earth.

In 1817 Ritter published the first volume of his monumental *Die Erdkunde* (*General Comparative Geography*). (A total of 19 volumes were eventually published between 1817 and 1859, all dealing with Africa and Asia.) This work, which stresses the relation between man and his natural environment, had a great impact on the geographic thinking of the time and led to Ritter's appointment as professor of geography at the University of Berlin, the first appointment of its kind in Germany. Because *Die Erdkunde* was the first work to deal with large regions of the Earth, Ritter has often been called the founder of regional geography.

Ritter made it a point not only to practice geography but also to define and prescribe the nature and scope of the field. He attempted to define a new, more scientific geography in which spacial relationships were better understood. He also emphasized the importance of history, and he wanted to avoid a geography that consisted merely of unrelated facts. In his own work, Ritter tended to focus primarily on humankind and its relation to geography. He believed that a reciprocal relationship existed between humans and earth, and this approach tended to foster the growth of environmentalism in geography, that is, the influence of the environment on human activities.

Unlike his adventurous contemporary ALEXANDER VON HUMBOLDT, Ritter confined his own fieldwork to Europe, relying on the observations and records of others for information on other regions. Despite this limitation, it was Ritter who established definitions for the field of geography for years to come.

BOOK BY RITTER

The Comparative Geography of Palestine and the Sinaitic Peninsula. 4 vols. Greenwood 1969 $19.50. ISBN 0-8371-0638-9

ROBINSON, ARTHUR. 1915–

Arthur Robinson is arguably the century's most well-known and respected researcher in cartography. Currently the L. Martin Professor Emeritus of Cartography at the University of Wisconsin, his research activities have helped bring a theoretical orientation to what too many believed was simply a practical tool for geographers. Whether through his classic introductory text in cartography, his handbook on mapping terms, or his book on the "nature of maps," Robinson has helped redefine cartographic communication. By the late 1980s, his world map projection—the "Robinson projection"—had been widely adopted throughout the world as the best example of a map of the world that minimized continental distortions, particularly in the polar regions.

BOOKS BY ROBINSON

Cartographic Innovations: An International Handbook of Mapping Terms to 1900. (coedited with Helen M. Wallen). Map Collection Pubs. 1987 o.p. Important addition to the growing body of work on historical cartography.

Choosing a World Map: Attributes, Distortions, Classes, Aspects. American Congress on
   Surveying and Mapping 1988 o.p. Helpful practical and theoretical guide for
   mapping decision-making.
Early Thematic Mapping in the History of Cartography. U. Ch. Pr. 1982 $39.95. ISBN 0-
   226-72285-6. Useful interpretation of the development of "thematic maps." Important, given its relationship to the development of thematic or topical geography.
Elements of Cartography. Wiley 5th ed. 1984 $51.95. ISBN 0-471-09877-9. Standard text
   for introductory cartography.
The Nature of Maps: Essays Toward Understanding Maps and Mapping. (coauthored with
   Barbara Bartz Potchenik). U. Ch. Pr. 1976 o.p. Collection of papers that helped
   highlight theoretical ideas about cartography.

SAUER, CARL ORTWIN. 1889–1975

Born in Missouri and educated at the University of Chicago, Carl Sauer led a
varied professional life. Among other things, he was a teacher, did fieldwork in
geography and other subjects, and worked for such corporations as Rand
McNally. Sauer believed that, because human beings have an enormous and far-
reaching impact on Earth, the study of history and other disciplines would serve
to enhance people's geographic understanding. For this reason, he studied such
diverse subjects as archaeology and sociology. He was especially interested in
the origins of agriculture and in whether the earliest crops bred and grown
were seed or root crops.

Sauer is credited with the development and modernization of geographical
field resource techniques. Together with Wellington Jones, he provided
geographers in the midwestern United States with the tools they needed to
observe and map the physical and cultural aspects of that region. These
techniques came to be used successfully in such projects as the Tennessee
Valley Authority. Sauer was also interested in the American Southwest and in
Mexico and produced works on those areas. One of the most notable of these
was *Pueblo Sites in Southeastern Arizona* (1930).

BOOKS BY SAUER

Aboriginal Population of Northwestern Mexico. 1935. AMS Pr. $11.50. ISBN 0-404-15670-3
Geography of the Ozark Highland of Missouri. 1920. AMS Pr. 1970 $17.50. ISBN 0-404-
   05562-1
Land and Life: A Selection from the Writings of Carl Ortwin Sauer. 1950. Ed. by John
   Leighly.. U. CA Pr. 1982 $37.50. ISBN 0-520-04762-1
Man in Nature: America Before the Days of the White Man. New World Writing Ser. Turtle
   Isl. Foun. 1975 $17.50. ISBN 0-913666-01-7
The Road to Cibola. 1932 AMS Pr. $14.50. ISBN 0-404-15669-X
Selected Essays: 1963–1975. Ed. by Bob Callahan. Turtle Isl. Foun. 1981 $19.95. ISBN 0-
   913666-45-9
Sixteenth-Century North America: The Land and the People as Seen by Europeans. U. CA
   Pr. 1971 $9.95. ISBN 0-520-02777-9

SCOTT, ALLEN J. 1938–

As part of the group of geographers trained at Northwestern University in the
1960s, Allen J. Scott helped lead the quantitative movement. His use of
mathematical models in spatial allocation analysis was well received. Now as
professor of geography at the University of California in Los Angeles, Scott has,
over the past two decades, helped define a new geography that combines
rigorous statistical methods with efforts to develop broader social theory. His
work on modern industrial location has been highly influential to a new
generation of urban, economic, and political geographers.

BOOKS BY SCOTT

Combinatorial Programming, Spatial Analysis, and Planning. Methuen 1971 o.p. Good example of the use of mathematical models, particularly as they relate to urban and regional planning.

An Introduction to Spatial Allocation Analysis. Assn. Am. Geographers 1971 o.p. Methods book that focuses on interaction—transportation—processes.

Metropolis: From Division of Labor to Urban Form. U. CA Pr. 1988 $37.50. ISBN 0-520-06078-4. Outgrowth of earlier research that focuses on the role of labor in urban industrial development.

Production, Work, Territory: The Geographical Anatomy of Industrial Capitalism. (coedited with M. Storper). Routledge Chapman & Hall 1986 $60.00. ISBN 0-04-338126-X. Excellent work on the implications of capitalism in economic history and on regional economic disparities.

The Urban Land Nexus and the State. Pion 1980 o.p. Important book on the linkages between urban and political geography.

Urbanization and Urban Planning in a Capitalist Society. (coedited with Michael Dear). Routledge Chapman & Hall 1981 $19.95. ISBN 0-416-74650-0. Important, well-cited collection of papers on the urbanization process and planning practices.

WARD, DAVID. 1935–

Currently vice-chancellor for academic affairs and professor of geography at the University of Wisconsin at Madison, David Ward received his Ph.D. in 1963 from the University of Wisconsin. He was one of a large number of Wisconsin students who, throughout the 1960s and 1970s, led a major research thrust in historical geography, much of which had a solid theoretical and analytical orientation.

Over the past two decades, Ward has published a set of important books on North America, particularly its cities. His *Cities and Immigrants* (1971), historical geography at its best, set a research agenda for scholars for more than a decade after its publication. Although some of this research relates to broad themes relevant to the evolution of the human landscape, it also includes detailed examinations of selected cities, notably Boston and New York.

BOOKS BY WARD

Cities and Immigrants: A Geography of Change in Nineteenth Century America. OUP 1971 $13.95. ISBN 0-19-501284-4. Excellent analysis, using primary and secondary sources, of the evolution of the urban landscape of the United States. Examines the concept of core and periphery in historical context and analyzes the impact of manufacturing and immigration on American cities.

Geographic Perspectives on America's Past: Readings on the Historical Geography of the United States. (ed.) OUP 1979 $10.95. ISBN 0-19-502353-6. Collection of papers including such topics as westward expansion and urbanization.

The Landscape of Modernity: Essays on New York City 1900–1940. (coauthored with Oliver Zunz). Russell Sage 1992 $35.95. ISBN 0-87154-900-X. Examination of planning efforts in the early twentieth century, including discussion of the central business district.

Poverty, Ethnicity, and the American City, 1840–1925: Changing Conceptions of the Slum and Ghetto. Cambridge U. Pr. 1989 $54.95. ISBN 0-521-25783-2. Detailed historical examination of the urban poor, slums, and other social conditions.

CHAPTER 5

Political Science

Thomas Barth

The study of politics is the study of influence and the influential. The science
of politics states conditions; the philosophy of politics justifies preferences.
. . . The influential are those who get the most of what there is to get.
—HAROLD LASSWELL, *Politics: Who Gets What, When, How*

Although the study of politics is ancient (Aristotle described politics as the
"queen of the sciences"), the modern discipline of political science is usually
dated from the latter half of the nineteenth century, when the focus became
more scholarly and scientific.

Some university departments of political science are called departments of
government, and government is the major focus in political science, which is
the social science that examines "the authoritative allocation of values in a
society." Thus, political scientists study both the structures and processes of
government and the behavior of the actors in those processes. The study of
political science is focused frequently on theories and descriptions of governmental institutions and on the state, while its analytical attention generally is
devoted to power relationships among classes, groups, and nations.

Attention is given to political values (democracy, order, liberty, security,
equality), to political institutions and processes (legislatures, executives,
administrative agencies, courts), and to political behavior (voting patterns,
decision making, acquiring political opinions). This focus on values, institutions
and processes, and behavior leads to a wide variety of research and a range of
approaches.

Traditional divisions of the field include political theory, comparative politics,
international relations, American government, public policy, and public law.
The research methods used in political science are common generally to the
social sciences. Indeed, much has been borrowed from sociology, psychology,
economics, and even history.

Since the 1940s the emphasis in political science has been on empirical
studies of behavior and of efforts at quantification of behavioral patterns. Survey
research, case studies, and structural-functional analysis have dominated the
field. This has led to a tension between those committed to the discipline as a
"science" and those interested in "values." Efforts to bridge this division
include attempts at building theory from empirical studies that will incorporate
the role of values in political life. At the same time, traditional political thought,
such as that appearing in the work of PLATO, ARISTOTLE (see also Vols. 2 and 4),
LOCKE, and MACHIAVELLI, and modern doctrine, such as found in *The Federalist
Papers* and the *Communist Manifesto*, enjoy a rekindled curiosity.

The list of readings is divided into works of reference and methodology,
histories and surveys of political science as a field, and 15 topics that political
scientists have studied in some detail.

REFERENCE AND METHODOLOGY

Bernstein, Robert A., and James A. Dyer. *An Introduction to Political Science Methods.* P-H 1991. ISBN 0-13-489071-X. Discusses political science methodology and research techniques.

Findling, John E. *Dictionary of American Diplomatic History.* Greenwood 1989 $49.95. ISBN 0-313-26024-9. Coverage to mid-1988. Lists biographies of more than 500 persons and descriptions or definitions of more than 500 terms, ranging from *crises* to *catchwords*. Includes appendixes and an index.

Greenstein, F. I., and N. W. Polsby. *The Handbook of Political Science.* 8 vols. Addison-Wesley 1975 o.p. An extremely useful, encyclopedic survey of the entire field.

Holler, Frederick L. *The Information Sources of Political Science.* ABC-CLIO 1986 $89.50. ISBN 0-87436-375-6. A detailed inventory of reference sources, both printed and computerized, in political science and related social sciences and humanities. Greatly expanded since the first edition in 1971, this fourth edition includes over 1,750 reference works, with critical annotations. Includes subject, author, title, and typology indexes.

Johnson, Janet Buttolph, and Richard A. Joslyn. *Political Science Research Methods.* Congr. Quarterly 1991 $30.95. ISBN 0-87187-556-X. Provides a basic introduction to political science along with sample illustrative case studies.

Paxton, John, ed. *The Statesman's Yearbook World Gazetteer.* St. Martin 1991 $49.95. ISBN 0-312-05597-8. The most up-to-date gazetteer in print, providing detailed statistics on major geographical locations for political scientists.

Taylor, Charles L., and others. *World Handbook of Political and Social Indicators.* 2 vols. Yale U. Pr. 1983 o.p. Compilation of social and political indicators; an essential source book for political research and statistical analysis.

Weisberg, Herbert F., and others. *An Introduction to Survey Research and Data Analysis.* Scott F. 1989 $24.50. ISBN 0-673-39764-5. Methodological discussion of social research and statistical analysis; focuses on various methods of statistical analysis.

York, Henry E. *Political Science: A Guide to Reference and Information Sources.* Libs. Unl. 1990 $38.00. ISBN 0-87287-794-9. Includes annotations for 805 sources, mostly English-language, from 1980–87. Covers bibliographies, directories, handbooks, and so on.

HISTORIES AND SURVEYS

Birch, Anthony H. *The Concepts and Theories of Modern Democracy.* Routledge 1993 $59.95. ISBN 0-415-09107-1

Brecht, Arnold. *Political Theory: The Foundations of Twentieth Century Political Thought.* Bks. Demand repr. of 1959 ed. $115.00. ISBN 0-3170-9452-1. Examines the history of political science, focusing on its methodological development.

Crick, Bernard. *The American Science of Politics: Its Origin and Conditions.* Greenwood 1982 $43.75. ISBN 0-313-2369658. Traces the history of political science in the United States.

Easton, David. *The Political System: An Inquiry into the State of Political Science.* U. Ch. Pr. 1981 o.p. An influential classic.

O'Sullivan, Noel. *The Structure of Modern Ideology. Critical Perspectives on Social and Political Theory.* Ashgate Pub. Co. 1989 $49.95. ISBN 1-85278-036-3. A collection of "highly recommended" essays that explores the ambiguities intrinsic to the concept of ideology, which itself remains central to much social, scientific, and philosophical debate.

Somit, Albert, and Joseph Tanenhaus. *Development of American Political Science: From Burgess to Behavioralism.* Irvington 1982 o.p. Discusses political-science teaching and study methods in the United States.

White, Stephen K. *Political Theory and Postmodernism.* Cambridge U. Pr. 1991 $12.95. ISBN 0-521-40948-9. Examines the contribution of postmodern thinking to political thought. Remarkably free of unexplained jargon and written with an evident clarity and serious engagement.

Wolin, Sheldon S. *Politics and Vision: Continuity and Innovation in Western Political Thought.* Little 1960 o.p. Analyzes the development of political science as a separate discipline.

CIVIL LIBERTIES AND CIVIL RIGHTS

Bodenhamer, David J. *Fair Trial: Rights of the Accused in American History.* OUP 1991 $24.95. ISBN 0-19-505559-4. One of the brief but excellent *Bicentennial Essays on the Bill of Rights Series.*

Curry, Thomas J. *The First Freedoms: Church and State in America to the Passage of the First Amendment.* OUP 1987 $14.95. ISBN 0-19-505181-5. Excellent examination of church-state relations from colonial times to passage of the Bill of Rights.

Curtis, Michael K. *No State Shall Abridge: The Fourteenth Amendment and the Bill of Rights.* Duke 1986 $29.95. ISBN 0-8223-0599-2. Essential to understanding how the Fourteenth Amendment has come to make parts of the Bill of Rights applicable to the states.

Ely, James W., Jr. *The Guardian of Every Other Right: A Constitutional History of Property Rights.* OUP 1991 $32.00. ISBN 0-19-505564-0. Another of the *Bicentennial Essays*; argues for the centrality of property rights in relation to other liberties.

Garvey, John H., and Frederick Schauer. *The First Amendment: A Reader.* West Pub. 1992 $20.00. ISBN 0-314-00775-X. A splendid collection of well-edited, scholarly articles on First Amendment issues.

Nieman, Donald G. *Promises to Keep: African Americans and the Constitutional Order, 1776 to the Present.* OUP 1991 $29.95. ISBN 0-19-505560-8. One of the *Bicentennial Essays*; summarizes the ambivalent relationship between African Americans and the Constitution.

Van Alstyne, William W. *First Amendment: Cases and Materials.* Foundation Pr. 1991 $35.95. ISBN 0-88277-879-X. Outstanding collection of Supreme Court decisions and other materials on the First Amendment.

Walker, Samuel. *In Defense of American Liberties: A History of the ACLU.* OUP 1990 $29.95. ISBN 0-19-504539-4. A lively history, with riveting accounts of many important legal struggles.

Whitebread, Charles H., and Christopher Slobogin. *Criminal Procedure: An Analysis of Cases and Concepts.* Foundation Pr. 1986 $39.95. ISBN 0-88277-326-7. A comprehensive examination of the law on criminal process.

COMPARATIVE POLITICAL IDEOLOGIES

Apter, David E., ed. *Ideology and Discontent.* Macmillan 1964 o.p. Discusses political psychology and the concept of ideology; examines the national socialist movements of the mid-twentieth century.

Arendt, Hannah. *The Origins of Totalitarianism.* Peter Smith 1983 $22.50. ISBN 0-8446-5994-0. Examines imperialism and antisemitism in totalitarian regimes.

Bell, Daniel. *The End of Ideology.* HUP 1988 repr. of 1960 ed. $29.95. ISBN 0-674-25229-2. A reprint of the 1965 revision. With a new afterword.

Carew Hunt, R. N. *The Theory and Practice of Communism.* Geoffrey Bles rev. ed. 1957 o.p. Traces the history of communism, focusing on the worldwide political influence of Marx and Engels.

Carr, Edward H. *The Romantic Exiles: A Nineteenth-Century Portrait Gallery.* MIT Pr. 1981 $10.95. ISBN 0-262-53040-6. Examines anarchism and anarchists in nineteenth-century Russia.

Cole, G. D. H. *A History of Socialist Thought.* 5 vols. St. Martin 1953–60 o.p. Examines the roots of socialism in the industrial revolution and traces its development to the socialist state of the 1950s.

Dolbeare, Kenneth M., and Linda J. Metcalf. *American Ideologies Today: Shaping the New Politics of the 1990s.* McGraw 1992 $15.16. ISBN 0-07-017411-3. Explores the history of ideological thought in the United States in the twentieth century; analyzes the development of the political right and left in American politics.

Hann, E. M., ed. *Socialism: Ideals, Ideologies, and Local Practice.* Routledge 1993 $27.50. ISBN 0-415-08322-2. Edited papers on socialism and cross-cultural studies presented at a conference at the University Centre in Cambridge.

Heywood, Andrew. *Political Ideologies: An Introduction.* St. Martin 1992 $45.00. ISBN 0-312-07514-6. A comprehensive survey of contemporary ideologies. Includes a useful glossary of authors and terms.

Hobsbawm, Eric J. *Revolutionaries.* NAL-Dutton 1975 o.p.

Lane, Robert E. *Political Ideology.* Macmillan 1967 o.p. Discusses the concept of ideology with a focus on democracy and the concept of liberty.

Lipset, Seymour M. *Political Man: The Social Bases of Politics.* Johns Hopkins 1981 repr. of 1966 ed. $15.95. ISBN 0-8018-2522-9. Analysis of democracy in the United States; examines politics, government, and the two-party system, tracing its history and party influence at polling places.

Love, Nancy S. *Dogmas and Dreams: Political Ideologies in the Modern World.* Chatham Hse. Pubs. 1991 $19.95. ISBN 0-934540-84-5. Investigates the ideology of the political right and left.

Mannheim, Karl. *Ideology and Utopia: An Introduction to the Sociology of Knowledge.* HarBraceJ 1955 $12.95. ISBN 0-15-643955-7. Combination of past writings by the author; a good introduction to the concept of ideology.

Mosca, Gaetano. *The Ruling Class.* 1891. Greenwood 1980 repr. of 1939 ed. $45.50. ISBN 0-313-22617-2. Examines the concept of social class with the keen eye of a political scientist.

Neumann, Franz L. *Behemoth: The Structure and Practice of National Socialism, 1933–1944.* Hippocrene Bks. 1963 o.p. Discusses the National Socialist movements in Italy and Germany and their effect on the society and culture.

Pennock, J. Roland, ed. *Anarchism: Nomos XIX.* Ed. by John W. Chapman. NYU Pr. 1978 o.p. Traces the history of anarchism and famous anarchists in history; examines the philosophy and its roots in the idea of utopia.

Proudhon, Pierre J. *What Is Property?* Gordon Pr. 1972 $300.00. ISBN 0-8490-1287-2. A classic statement of the philosophy of anarchism, first published in French in 1876.

Rejai, Mostafa. *Political Ideologies: Comparative Approach.* M. E. Sharpe 1991 $39.95. ISBN 0-87332-806-X. Analyzes and evaluates nationalism, fascism, Marxism, Leninism, guerrilla communism, and democracy.

Schumpeter, Joseph A. *Capitalism, Socialism, and Democracy.* 1942. Peter Smith 1983 $24.50. ISBN 0-8446-6027-2. Discussion of the major eco-political systems of the twentieth century.

Skidmore, Max J. *Ideologies: Politics in Action.* HB Coll. Pubs. 1993. ISBN 0-15-500149-3. Investigates the history of the political philosophy of the right and left and the role of ideology in their respective histories.

Sorel, Georges. *Reflections on Violence.* AMS Pr. repr. of 1914 ed. $27.50. ISBN 0-404-56165-9. Examines social conflict in modern political systems; focuses on violence linked to union strikes and lockouts.

Stankiewicz, W. J. *In Search of Political Philosophy: Ideologies at the Close of the Twentieth Century.* Routledge 1993 $59.95. ISBN 0-415-08874-7

Wilson, Richard W. *Compliance Ideologies: Rethinking Political Culture.* Cambridge U. Pr. 1992 $44.95. ISBN 0-521-41581-0. Comparative analysis of political culture conceptualized as compliance ideologies that legitimize systems of institutional control.

Wittfogel, Karl A. *Oriental Despotism: A Comparative Study of Total Power.* Elliots Bks. 1957 $79.50. ISBN 0-685-45661-7. Traces the development of despotism in Asian society through the historiography of Oriental civilization; examines the role of despotism in oriental politics.

COMPARATIVE POLITICAL SYSTEMS

Almond, Gabriel, and Sidney Verba. *The Civic Culture Study, 1959–1960*. ICPSR 1974. ISBN 0-89138-065-5. A landmark work on the relationship between political culture and a democratic political system.

———. *The Civic Culture Revisited*. Russell Sage 1989 $42.95. ISBN 0-8039-6560-9. A reexamination based on a review of more recent research in five countries of original study.

Dalton, Russell J. *Citizen Politics: Public Opinion and Political Parties in the United States, United Kingdom, France and West Germany*. Chatham Hse. Pubs. 1988 $18.95. ISBN 0-934540-44-6. Compares the elements of political mobilization. Solid comparative-politics study.

Dalton, Russell J., and Manfred Kuechler, eds. *Challenging the Political Order: New Social and Political Movements in Western Democracies*. OUP 1990 $38.00. ISBN 0-19-520833-1. A good collection of essays on the development and impact of the peace movement, the environmental movement, and other movements.

Heidenheimer, Arnold. *Comparative Public Policy: The Politics of Social Change in America, Europe and Japan*. St. Martin 1989 $24.00. ISBN 0-312-00493-1. Examines policies on health, education, and housing, among others.

Inglehart, Ronald. *Culture Shift in Advanced Industrial Society*. Princeton U. Pr. 1989 $55.00. ISBN 0-691-07786-X. Continues his long-term examination of postmaterialist culture in advanced industrial society.

Wiarda, Howard, ed. *New Directions in Comparative Politics*. Westview 2nd rev. ed. 1991 $18.95. ISBN 0-8133-0996-4. Examines various theories and approaches.

CONSTITUTIONALISM AND FEDERALISM

Ackerman, Bruce. *We The People: Vol. 1 Foundations*. Belknap Pr. 1991 $24.95. ISBN 0-674-94840-8. First of three projected volumes; examines the unique role of the Constitution in American politics.

Beard, Charles A. *An Economic Interpretation of the Constitution of the United States*. 1913. Free Pr. 1965 $10.95. ISBN 0-02-902030-1. Classic study reveals the financial stake of the framers in the Constitution that they wrote.

Bowen, Catherine Drinker. *Miracle at Philadelphia: The Story of the Constitutional Convention, May to September 1787*. Little 1986 $18.95. ISBN 0-316-10387-0. A detailed account of the Federal Convention in Philadelphia that produced the U.S. Constitution; focuses on the central figures, debates, and compromises that made the Constitution a reality.

Ducat, Craig R., and Harold W. Chase. *Constitutional Interpretation*. West Pub. 1992 $40.00. ISBN 0-314-93456-1. A superior collection of cases, excerpts, and text materials on the distribution of powers and individual rights and liberties in the Constitution.

Farber, Daniel A., and Suzanna Sherry. *A History of the American Constitution*. West Pub. 1989 $26.75. ISBN 0-314-56768-2. Using Madison's notes on constitutional convention as a base, the authors add other historical sources, extending coverage to the Civil War amendments.

Hamilton, Alexander, James Madison, and John Jay. *The Federalist Papers*. Ed. by Clinton Rossiter. NAL-Dutton 1961 $15.95. ISBN 0-451-62541-2. Indispensable to an understanding of the intent of the framers of the Constitution; arguably the only significant American contribution to political philosophy.

Kammen, Michael. *The Origins of the American Constitution: A Documentary History.* Viking Penguin 1986 $8.95. ISBN 0-14-008744-3. The best collection of documents from the period; includes the Articles of Confederation.

Kelly, Alfred H., and others. *The American Constitution: Its Origins and Development.* 2 vols. Norton 1971 Vol. 1 $18.95. ISBN 0-393-96056-0. Vol. 2 $18.95. ISBN 0-393-96119-2. A good, lively constitutional history from the founding of the English colonies to the present.

Levy, Leonard W. *Original Intent and the Framers' Constitution.* Macmillan 1988 $19.95. ISBN 0-02-918791-5. Provocative examination of approaches to constitutional interpretation and problems of determining the framers' intent.

Levy, Leonard W., and Dennis J. Mahoney, eds. *The Framing and Ratification of the Constitution.* Macmillan 1987 $19.95. ISBN 0-317-62103-3. Reviews the major controversies and compromises at the convention.

Levy, Leonard W., and others, eds. *Encyclopedia of the American Constitution.* 2 vols. Macmillan 1990 $175.00. ISBN 0-02-918695-1. Contains more than 2,000 entries pertaining to the doctrinal concepts, specific judicial decisions, important people, and historical periods in American constitutional development.

McDonald, Forest. *Novus Ordo Seclorum: The Intellectual Origins of the Constitution.* U. Pr. of KS 1985 $29.95. ISBN 0-7006-0284-4. A very readable examination of the intellectual setting of the Constitutional Convention.

McIlwain, Charles Howard. *Constitutionalism: Ancient and Modern.* Cornell Univ. Pr. 1958 $8.95. ISBN 0-8014-9010-3. Explores the meaning of constitutionalism over time.

Tribe, Laurence H. *American Constitutional Law.* Foundation Pr. 1991 $45.00. ISBN 0-88277-601-0. A refreshing treatise on constitutional law, written out of strong convictions and a generally liberal bent.

Urofsky, Melvin I. *Documents of American Constitutional and Legal History.* McGraw 1989. Vol. 1 $15.95. ISBN 0-07-557092-0. Vol. 2 $15.50. ISBN 0-394-38580-2. A very useful collection of documents and cases.

DEMOCRATIC THEORY AND PRACTICE

Berns, Walter. *In Defense of Liberal Democracy.* Am. Enterprises 1984 $18.25. Discusses the concepts of democracy and liberty and their practice in the United States.

Botwinick, Aryeh. *Postmodernism and Democratic Theory.* Temple U. Pr. 1993. ISBN 0-8772-997-X. Discusses the idea of postmodernism and skepticism in the context of political science; attempts to analyze modernity in the context of democracy.

Chomsky, Noam. *Deterring Democracy.* Hill & Wang 1992 $15.00. ISBN 0-374-52349-5. Critical look into U.S. foreign relations from 1989 to the present; examines alleged unethical practices of the U.S. government.

Dahl, Robert A. *Preface to Democratic Theory.* U. Ch. Pr. 1963 $6.00. ISBN 0-226-13426-1. Traces the historical foundations of democracy in the politics and government of the United States.

Deetz, Stanley A. *Democracy in an Age of Corporate Colonization.* State U. NY Pr. 1992 $54.50. ISBN 0-7914-0863-9. Discusses corporate domination in public decision making and reclaiming the politics of personal identity.

Diamond, Larry, and Marc F. Plattner, eds. *The Global Resurgence of Democracy.* Johns Hopkins 1993 $50.00. ISBN 0-8018-4564-5. Compilation of articles, originally published in the *Quarterly Journal,* discussing democracy and world politics from 1989 to the present.

Downs, Anthony. *An Economic Theory of Democracy.* 1965 HarpC 1990 $26.50. ISBN 0-06-041750-1. Discusses the economic influences in voting and the role these influences have in political parties; also examines economic influences in public administration.

Fishkin, James S. *Democracy and Deliberation: New Directions for Democratic Reform.* Yale U. Pr. 1992 $17.95. ISBN 0-300-5161-1. Suggests halting electoral apathy by using a televised computer model.

Friedrich, Carl J. *Constitutional Government and Democracy: Theory and Practice in Europe and America.* 1937. Blaisdale 1968 o.p. Traces the development of constitutions in the United States and Europe; contrasts the goals of constitutional government with actual practice.

Fuller, Graham. *The Democracy Trap.* NAL-Dutton 1992 $20.00. ISBN 0-525-93371-9. The prospect of democracy facing an altered political landscape worldwide.

Goldfarb, Jeffrey C. *After the Fall: The Pursuit of Democracy in Central Europe.* Basic 1993 $15.00. ISBN 0-465-00081-9. Theorizes on the demarcation of left- and right-wing ideologies in Central Europe and the ensuing political condition that remains.

Golding, Sue. *Gramsci's Democratic Theory: Contributions to a Post-Liberal Democracy.* U. of Toronto Pr. 1992. $45.00. ISBN 0-8020-7674-2. Examines the contributions of Antonio Gramsci to the field of political science and to modern theories of democracy.

Kornhauser, William. *The Politics of Mass Society.* Macmillan 1959 o.p. Analyzes the politics of modern totalitarian and democratic societies.

Lindsay, A. D. *The Modern Democratic State.* 1943. OUP 1959 o.p. Critical look into the operations of the modern democratic state, focusing on American politics.

Mayo, Henry B. *An Introduction to Democratic Theory.* OUP 1960 o.p. Interesting survey of modern democratic thought and ideology.

Novak, Michael. *The Spirit of Democratic Capitalism.* 1982. Madison Bks. UPA 1991 $27.95. ISBN 0-8191-7822-5. Critical overview of the moral and ethical aspects of democratic capitalism and their impact on economics.

Pereira, Luiz C., and others. *Economic Reforms in New Democracies: A Socio-Democratic Approach.* Cambridge U. Pr. 1992. ISBN 0-521-43259-6. Traces the development of democracy in South America and analyzes the mixed economies of that region and Southern Europe.

Sanders, Arthur. *Victory: How a Progressive Democratic Party Can Win and Govern.* M. E. Sharpe 1992 $42.50. ISBN 1-56324-087-4. Examines practices and political strategies of the U.S. Democratic party.

Sartori, Giovanni. *Democratic Theory.* Greenwood 1973 repr. of 1962 ed. $65.00. ISBN 0-8371-6545-8. Examines the philosophy behind democratic theory and compares the modern and ancient aspects of it.

Schumpeter, Joseph A. *Capitalism, Socialism and Democracy.* HarpC 1962 $12.00. ISBN 0-06-133008-6. General overview of the philosophies of capitalism, socialism, and democracy and their place in modern political history.

Tocqueville, Alexis de. *Democracy in America.* Trans. by Phillips Bradley. 2 vols. 1835–40. Random 1954. Vol. 1 $7.95. ISBN 0-394-70110-0. Vol. 2 $7.95. ISBN 0-394-70110-9. Famous survey of democratic politics and government and social conditions in the United States.

ELECTORAL POLITICS

Beck, Paul Allen, and Frank J. Sorauf. *Party Politics in America.* Scott F. 1987 $30.50. ISBN 0-673-39750-5. The leading text on political parties.

Campbell, Angus, and others. *The American Voter.* 1960 U. Ch. Pr. 1980 $28.00. ISBN 0-206-09254-2. The classic study of voting behavior.

Gant, Michael M., and Norman L. Luttbeg. *American Electoral Behavior, 1952–1988.* Peacock MI 1990 $22.00. ISBN 0-87581-346-1. An excellent summary of the research on voting behavior.

Ginsberg, Benjamin, and Martin Shefter. *Politics by Other Means: The Declining Importance of Elections in America.* Basic 1991 $19.95. ISBN 0-465-05960-0. A counterargument to the assumption that elections are important in the United States.

Jamieson, Kathleen Hall, and David S. Birdsell. *Presidential Debates: The Challenge of Creating an Informed Electorate.* OUP 1988 $25.00. ISBN 0-19-505539-X. A good analysis of the contribution of debates to elections.

Longley, Lawrence D., and Alan G. Braun. *The Politics of Electoral College Reform.* Bks. Demand repr. of 1972 ed. $61.90. ISBN 0-8357-8277-8. Still the major review of the persistence of the Electoral College in presidential elections.

Miller, Warren E. *Without Consent: Mass-Elite Linkages in Presidential Politics.* U. Pr. of Ky. 1988 $20.00. ISBN 0-8131-0550-1. Examines the relationship of national convention delegates to public opinion.

Niemi, Richard G., and Herbert F. Weisberg. *Controversies in Voting Behavior.* Congr. Quarterly $25.95. ISBN 0-87187-706-6. An excellent collection of state-of-the-art behavior studies.

Piven, Frances Fox, and Richard A. Cloward. *Why Americans Don't Vote.* Pantheon 1989 $9.95. ISBN 0-685-37789-X. A fine analysis of causes and importance of nonvoting in the United States.

Sabato, Larry J. *PAC Power: Inside the World of Political Action Committees.* Norton 1985 $15.95. ISBN 0-393-01857-1. A major investigation of the impact of interest groups on elections and government.

Salmore, Barbara G. *Candidates, Parties, and Campaigns.* Congr. Quarterly 1989 $18.95. ISBN 0-87187-484-9. A first-rate description of modern American election campaigns.

Shafer, Byron E. *Bifurcated Politics: Evolution and Reform in the National Party Convention.* HUP 1988 $29.95. ISBN 0-674-07256-1. The premier analysis of contemporary national nominating conventions.

Sorauf, Frank J. *Money in American Elections.* Scott F. 1988 $18.00. ISBN 0-673-39784-X. A summary of campaign-finance practice, law, and effects.

Wayne, Stephen J. *The Road to the White House 1992: The Politics of Presidential Elections.* St. Martin 1991 $16.70. ISBN 0-312-05195-6. A good summary of the presidential election process.

INTERNATIONAL RELATIONS

Art, Robert J., and Seyone Brown. *U.S. Foreign Policy: The Search for a New Role.* Macmillan 1992. ISBN 0-02-303941-8. Essays exploring the decision-making process, broad contemporary issues, and regional policies.

Bishop, William W., Jr. *International Law: Cases and Materials.* Little 1971 $45.00. ISBN 0-316-09664-4. Excellent, if dated, collection.

Bledsoe, Robert, and Boleslaw Boczek. *The International Law Dictionary.* ABC-CLIO 1987 $56.50. ISBN 0-87436-406-X. A highly useful basic source.

Boulding, Kenneth E. *Three Faces of Power.* Russell Sage 1989 $41.95. ISBN 0-8039-3862-4. Offers a general theory of power.

Buzan, Barry. *People, State and Fear: An Agenda for International Security in the Post-Cold War Era.* Lynne Rienner 1991 $66.95. ISBN 1-55587-282-4. A theoretical analysis of security and the state.

Dougherty, James E., and Robert L. Pfaltzgraff, Jr. *Contending Theories of International Relations: A Comprehensive Study.* HarpC 1990 $34.50. ISBN 0-06-041706-4. A basic review of various schools of global political analysis.

Haas, Ernst B. *Beyond the Nation-State: Functionalism and International Organization.* Stanford U. Pr. 1964 $60.00. ISBN 0-8047-0186-5. Traces the history, structure, and politics of the International Labor Organization.

Henkin, Louis, and others. *International Law: Cases and Materials.* West Pub. 1987 $42.95. ISBN 0-314-30405-3. The best current casebook.

Levi, Werner. *Contemporary International Law: A Concise Introduction.* Westview 1990 $78.00. ISBN 0-8133-1094-6. General survey of international law with a focus on recent trends.

Nye, Joseph S., Jr. *Bound to Lead: The Changing Nature of American Power*. Basic 1990 $19.95. ISBN 0-465-00743-0. Introduces the idea of "soft" power and explores how interdependence limits military power.

Riker, William H. *The Theory of Political Coalitions*. Greenwood 1984 repr. of 1962 ed. $55.00. ISBN 0-313-24299-2. Utilizes political-science methodology in his approach to the concept of coalitions.

Rosenau, James N. *Turbulence in World Politics: A Theory of Change and Continuity*. Greenwood 1990 $55.00. ISBN 0-691-02308-5. An important contribution by a leading authority.

Rothgeb, John M., Jr. *Defining Power: Influence and Force in the Contemporary International System*. St. Martin 1992. ISBN 0-312-08682-2. A comprehensive review of different perspectives on definitions and techniques of power.

Sharp, Gene. *The Politics of Nonviolent Action*. Porter Sargent 1974 Pt. 1 $3.95. ISBN 0-87558-070-X. Pt. 2 $4.95. ISBN 0-87558-071-8. Pt. 3 $5.95. ISBN 0-87558-072-6. Presents his basic theory of power from a nonviolent perspective.

Spero, Joan E. *The Politics of International Economic Relations*. St. Martin 1991 $35.00. ISBN 0-312-04063-6. A good introduction to what is likely to be the major playing field of the future.

LAW AND SOCIETY

Abraham, Henry J. *The Judicial Process: An Introductory Analysis of the Courts of the U.S., England, and France*. OUP 1993 $19.95. ISBN 0-19-50680-7. An impressive description of judicial process, structures, and concepts. Regrettably, this edition condenses what had been a superb bibliography.

Friedman, Lawrence M. *American Law: An Introduction*. Norton 1985 $19.95. ISBN 0-393-95251-7. Discussion of law and the legal system in the United States; surveys famous cases and laws.

Gilmore, Grant. *The Ages of American Law*. Yale U. Pr. 1977 $27.00. ISBN 0-300-01951-3. Compilation of addresses, essays, and lectures that trace the history of law in the United States.

Hall, Kermit. *The Magic Mirror: Law in American History*. OUP 1989 $16.95. ISBN 0-19-504460-6. A very readable history of law in the United States.

Hall, Kermit L., and others, eds. *The Oxford Companion to the Supreme Court of the United States*. OUP 1992 $45.00. ISBN 0-19-505835-6. Essentially an encyclopedia of U.S. Supreme Court personnel, cases, and practices.

Lasser, William. *The Limits of Judicial Power: The Supreme Court in American Politics*. U. of NC Pr. 1988 $34.95. ISBN 0-8078-1810-0. Argues that the U.S. Supreme Court has more enduring power than is often thought.

McCloskey, Robert G. *The American Supreme Court*. U. Ch. Pr. 1961 $10.95. ISBN 0-226-55675-1. Classic analysis of the role and limits of the U.S. Supreme Court in American history to 1960.

O'Brien, David M. *Storm Center: The Supreme Court in American Politics*. Norton 1993 $19.95. ISBN 0-393-96350-0. An incisive look at the practices and politics of the U.S. Supreme Court.

Pound, Roscoe. *Masonic Jurisprudence*. Kessinger Pub. 1992 repr. of 1924 ed. $12.95. ISBN 1-56459-048-8. Reappearance of a classic.

Skolnick, Jerome H. *Justice without Trial: Law Enforcement in Democratic Society*. Wiley 1975 o.p. Still the best examination of the role of police.

Stone, Julius. *Social Dimensions of Law and Justice*. W. W. Gaunt 1971 repr. of 1966 ed. $85.00. ISBN 0-912004-01-0. Examines the concept of sociological jurisprudence and traces its history.

Stumpf, Harry P. *American Judicial Politics*. HarBraceJ 1988 $27.00. ISBN 0-15-502340-3. Good coverage of federal and state courts and legal processes.

Stumpf, Harry P., and John H. Culver. *The Politics of State Courts*. Longman 1992 $22.95. ISBN 0-8013-0051-7. Focuses on structures and processes in state courts.

LEGISLATIVE BEHAVIOR

Fenno, Richard F., Jr. *Home Style: House Members in Their Districts.* Scott F. 1987 $20.00. ISBN 0-673-39440-9. A powerful explanation of politics in the U.S. Congress, exploring relationships of representatives and their constituents.

Fiorina, Morris P. *Congress: Keystone of the Washington Establishment.* Yale U. Pr. 1989 $25.00. ISBN 0-300-04640-5. Provocative argument on causes and consequences of iron triangles. Places blame on the U.S. Congress.

Kingdon, John W. *Congressmen's Voting Decisions.* U. of Mich. Pr. 1989 $15.95. ISBN 0-472-06401-0. Analyzes various forces that shape how representatives vote.

Mayhew, David R. *Congress: The Electoral Connection.* Yale U. Pr. 1974 $10.00. ISBN 0-300-01809-6. Pioneering statement of thesis that the principal motive for representatives' behavior is desire for reelection.

Rosenthal, Alan. *Governors and Legislatures: Contending Powers.* Congr. Quarterly 1990 $18.95. ISBN 0-87187-545-4. One of the most comprehensive and coherent studies of state legislative politics.

Wahlke, John C., and others. *The Legislative System.* Wiley 1962 o.p. A classic on legislative behavior, still quoted.

POLICY PLANNING AND FORMULATION

Anderson, James E., and others. *Public Policy and Politics in America.* Brooks-Cole 1984 $25.95. ISBN 0-534-03094-7. General overview of formulation and content of contemporary American public policies.

Jones, Charles O. *An Introduction to the Study of Public Policy.* Brooks-Cole 1984 $18.95. ISBN 0-534-03093-9. An overview of the stages of the policy-making process, with diverse cases illustrating each stage.

Polsby, Nelson W. *Political Innovation in America: The Politics of Policy Initiation.* Yale U. Pr. 1984 $27.50. ISBN 0-300-03089-4. Investigates changes in the government and politics of the United States from 1945–1989.

Pressman, Jeffrey, and Aaron Wildavsky. *Implementation.* U. CA Pr. 1984 $45.00. ISBN 0-520-05232-3. An in-depth case study of the problems of implementing an economic development program in Oakland, California.

Wildavsky, Aaron. *Speaking Truth to Power: The Art and Craft of Policy Analysis.* Transaction Pubs. 1987 $19.95. ISBN 0-88738-697-0. A realistic and irreverent view of "discipline" of policy analysis. Problems of resources, dogma, rhetoric, and political interaction and their impact on programs and policy.

THE PRESIDENCY

Bailey, Harry, and Jay Shafritz. *The American Presidency: Historical and Contemporary Perspectives.* Brooks-Cole 1988 $22.95. ISBN 0-534-10464-9. An extensive collection of articles by well-known scholars on the presidency.

Barber, James D. *The Presidential Character: Predicting Performance in the White House.* P-H 1992 $15.95. ISBN 0-13-718123-X. Expanded version of the author's theory of presidential performance and typology of presidential character. In-depth case studies.

DiClerico, Robert E., ed. *Analyzing the Presidency.* Dushkin Pub. 1990 $13.95. ISBN 0-87967-815-1. Classic readings that provide counterpoint to several conventional approaches in presidential scholarship.

Jamieson, Kathleen. *Packaging the Presidency: A History and Criticism of Presidential Campaign Advertising.* OUP 1992 $35.00. ISBN 0-19-507298-5. Historical analysis of tactics and strategies in presidential races.

Koenig, Louis W. *The Chief Executive.* HarBraceJ 1986 $16.50. ISBN 0-15-506674-9. Concerned with the effectiveness of a "diminished presidency" balanced against democratic values and a republican form of government.

Neustadt, Richard. *Presidential Power and the Modern Presidents: The Politics of Leadership from Roosevelt to Reagan.* Free Pr. 1990 $22.95. ISBN 0-02-922795-X. An extended version of Neustadt's thesis that the power of the presidency is the power to persuade.

Schlesinger, Arthur M., Jr. *The Imperial Presidency.* HM 1989 $12.70. ISBN 0-395-51561-0. Argues for a strong presidency that is effective at problem solving but is balanced by strong democratic control.

Wayne, Stephen. *The Road to the White House 1992: The Politics of Presidential Elections.* St. Martin 1991 $23.00. ISBN 0-312-06883-2. Focuses on process and politics of presidential selection.

PUBLIC ADMINISTRATION

Downs, Anthony. *Inside Bureaucracy.* Scott F. 1967 $23.00. ISBN 0-673-39432-8. A theoretical analysis of the internal and external environment of bureaus and the politics and process of decision making. A classic.

Peters, B. Guy. *The Politics of Bureaucracy.* Longman 1989 $20.95. ISBN 0-8013-0066-5. Role of public bureaucracy and institutional politics in policy making. Strong comparative flavor (Europe, Kenya, Japan, among others) throughout.

Shafritz, Jay M., and Albert C. Hyde. *Classics of Public Administration.* Brooks-Cole 1992 $21.95. ISBN 0-534-17310-1. An extensive collection of major thinkers and key works in all aspects of public administration.

Simon, Herbert A. *Administrative Behavior.* Macmillan 1976 $13.95. ISBN 0-02-929000-7. A classic.

Stillman, Richard J., Jr. *Public Administration: Concepts and Cases.* HM 1992 $28.00. ISBN 0-395-59015-9. Combination approach to key concepts with essential readings, articles, and complementary cases.

Waldo, Dwight. *The Administrative State: A Study of the Political Theory of American Public Administration.* Holmes & Meier 1984 $15.95. ISBN 0-8419-0886-9. Critical look at public administration in the United States.

Wildavsky, Aaron. *The New Politics of the Budgetary Process.* HarpC 1991 $23.00. ISBN 0-673-52179-6. Investigates the politics behind the U.S. budget and explores the allotment of money to various federal programs.

PUBLIC OPINION

Adorno, T. W., and Else Frenkel-Brunswik. *The Authoritarian Personality.* Norton 1983 $12.95. ISBN 0-393-30042-0. A groundbreaking study of the sources of prejudice.

Asher, Herbert. *Polling and the Public.* Congr. Quarterly 1991 $16.95. ISBN 0-87187-603-5. A basic introduction to the conduct and analysis of polls.

Barner-Barry, Carol, and Robert Rosenwein. *Psychological Perspectives on Politics.* Waveland Pr. 1991 $17.95. ISBN 0-88133-619-X. Summarizes major findings of studies of political psychology and attitudes.

Graber, Doris A. *Mass Media and American Politics.* Congr. Quarterly 1988 $19.95. ISBN 0-87187-475-X. A leading authority's description of how the mass media influence political perspectives.

Hess, Robert D., and Judith V. Torney. *The Development of Political Attitudes in Children.* Aldine Pub. 1967 o.p. The classic study of political socialization of children.

Lippmann, Walter. *Public Opinion.* 1922. Transaction Pubs. 1990 $21.95. ISBN 0-88738-861-2. Provocative discussion of the relationship between public opinion and democracy.

McClosky, Herbert, and John Zaller. *The American Ethos: Public Attitudes Toward Capitalism and Democracy.* HUP 1985 $14.95. ISBN 0-674-02331-5. Examines the relationship between values of the public and influence of the elite.

Milburn, Michael A. *Persuasion and Politics: The Social Psychology of Public Opinion.* Brooks-Cole 1991 $12.95. ISBN 0-534-15948-6. Explores the psychological bases of political opinions.

Stimson, James A. *Public Opinion in America: Moods, Cycles, and Swings.* Westview 1991 $52.00. ISBN 0-8133-1166-7. Offers explanations for moods and trends in American public opinion.

Verba, Sidney, and Norman H. Nie. *Participation in America: Political Democracy and Social Equality.* U. Ch. Pr. 1987 $16.95. ISBN 0-226-85296-2. The most influential study of public participation in American politics.

Yankelovich, Daniel. *Coming to Public Judgment: Making Democracy Work in a Complex World.* Syracuse U. Pr. 1991 $16.95. ISBN 0-8156-0254-5. A major pollster examines the conflict between public and expert opinion.

STATE AND LOCAL GOVERNMENT

Adrian, Charles R., and Michael R. Fine. *State and Local Politics.* Nelson-Hall 1991 $30.95. ISBN 0-8304-1285-9. A basic introduction and overview.

Elliot, Jeffrey M. *The State and Local Government Political Dictionary.* ABC-CLIO 1988 $55.00. ISBN 0-87436-417-5. Defines 290 concepts and terms, arranged alphabetically within 11 topical chapters. Includes an index.

Gray, Virginia, and others. *Politics in the American States: A Comparative Analysis.* Scott F. 1990 $35.50. ISBN 0-673-52013-7. Most important recent research usually winds up in these articles.

Harrigan, John J. *Political Change in the Metropolis.* Scott F. 1988 $37.00. ISBN 0-673-39848-X. Best work on metro-government; it stays current.

Jewell, Malcolm E., and David M. Olson. *Political Parties and Elections in American States.* Brooks-Cole 1988 $17.95. ISBN 0-534-10594-7. Analysis of the electoral system and party influence at the polls.

Kane, Joseph Nathan. *Facts About the States.* Wilson 1989 $55.00. ISBN 0-8242-0407-7. Presents basic data related to 50 states, the District of Columbia, and Puerto Rico, including geographic, economic, political, and cultural facts. Includes bibliographies and comparative tables.

Moulder, Evelina. *The Municipal Year Book, 1992.* Intl. City-Cty Mgt. 1992 $77.50. ISBN 0-8732-967-5. Yearly publication of facts and information.

Rosenthal, Alan. *Governors and Legislatures: Contending Powers.* Congr. Quarterly 1990 $18.95. ISBN 0-87187-545-4. Analyzes the dynamics of states' legislative actions in policy making and budget setting.

Sabato, Larry. *Goodbye to Goodtime Charlie: The American Governorship Transformed.* Bks. Demand $67.90. ISBN 0-8357-3829-9. Definitive analysis of the changed role of state governors.

Walker, David B. *Toward a Functioning Federalism.* Scott F. 1987 $19.50. ISBN 0-673-39487-5. Traces the history of federalism in the United States and examines the relationship between state and federal government.

Wright, Deil S. *Understanding Intergovernmental Relations.* Brooks-Cole 1988 $22.95. ISBN 0-534-09012-5. First-rate look at theory of intergovernmental relations and federalism.

WAR AND PEACE

Brown, Seyom. *The Causes and Prevention of War.* St. Martin 1987 $39.95. ISBN 0-312-00473-7. Examines literature of human aggression and the role of state violence along with ideas for ending war.

Fischer, Dietrich. *Preventing War in the Nuclear Age.* Rowman 1984 $41.25. ISBN 0-8476-7342-1. Presents a theoretical argument on how to achieve peace and common security.

Kainz, Howard P., ed. *Philosophical Perspectives on Peace: An Anthology of Classical and Modern Sources.* Ohio U. Pr. 1986 $39.95. ISBN 0-8214-0849-6. Examines various approaches to securing peace.

Kennedy, Paul. *The Rise and Fall of the Great Powers: Economic Change and Military Conflict from 1500 to 2000.* Random 1987 $24.95. ISBN 0-394-54674-1. Analyzes the relationship between great-power status, excessive military spending, and economic decline.

Richardson, Lewis F. *Arms and Insecurity: A Mathematical Study of the Causes and Origins of War.* Ed. by Nicolas Rashevsky and Ernesto Trucco. Bks. Demand repr. of 1960 ed. $83.80. ISBN 0-8357-5742-5

———. *Statistics of Deadly Quarrels.* Ed. by Quincy Wright and C. C. Lienau. Boxwood 1960 $45.00. ISBN 0-910286-10-8. Richardson was a meteorologist, and these two books, first published in 1960 after his death, represent his attempt to understand war as weather is understood. Antiquated but fascinating.

Singer, J. D., ed. *The Correlates of War.* Free Pr. 1979 $29.95. ISBN 0-02-928960-2. Statistically based study of war.

Small, Melvin, and J. David Singer. *Resort to Arms: International and Civil Wars, 1816–1980.* Bks. Demand repr. of 1982 ed. $97.00. ISBN 0-8357-8510-6. Statistical history of conflicts.

Wright, Quincy. *A Study of War.* U. Ch. Pr. 1983 $22.00. ISBN 0-226-91001-6. A classic.

CHRONOLOGY OF AUTHORS

Plato. 428–347 B.C.
Machiavelli, Niccolò. 1469–1527
Hobbes, Thomas. 1588–1679
Locke, John. 1632–1704
Montesquieu, Charles de Secondat, Baron de la Brede et de. 1689–1755
Rousseau, Jean Jacques. 1712–1778
Burke, Edmund. 1729–1797
Jefferson, Thomas. 1743–1826
Bentham, Jeremy. 1748–1832
Madison, James. 1751–1836

Tocqueville, Alexis Charles Henri Clérel de. 1805–1859
Bryce, James. 1838–1922
Merriam, Charles E. 1874–1963
Laski, Harold J. 1893–1950
Lippmann, Walter. 1899–1974
Lasswell, Harold D. 1902–1978
Key, V. O., Jr. 1908–1963
Almond, Gabriel Abraham. 1911–
Easton, David. 1917–
Lipset, Seymour Martin. 1922–

ALMOND, GABRIEL ABRAHAM. 1911–

Born in Rock Island, Illinois, American political scientist Gabriel Almond was educated at the University of Chicago. During World War II, he was associated with the Office of War Information and also with the War Department in Europe. Since the war, he has served on the faculties of several universities, including Princeton University, Yale University, and Stanford University. He has also been visiting professor at the University of Tokyo and the University of Belo Horizonte in Brazil as well as a consultant to the U.S. Department of State and the U.S. Air Force. Almond is most noted for his work in comparative politics and comparative political systems. He is the author and coauthor of several landmark books, including *The Civic Culture: Political Attitudes and Democracy in Five Nations* (1963), a seminal piece in the field (coauthored with Sidney Verba). Among Almond's other well-known works are *The Politics of Developing*

Areas (1960) and *Comparative Politics: A Developmental Approach* (1966). A member of the National Academy of Sciences, the American Academy of Arts and Sciences, and the American Political Science Association, Almond received the James Madison Award in 1972 for his work in the field.

BOOKS BY ALMOND

The Civic Culture: Political Attitudes and Democracy in Five Nations. Bks. Demand repr. of 1963 ed. $149.80. ISBN 0-8357-3844-2

The Civic Culture Revisited. Russell Sage 1989 repr. of 1980 ed. $42.95. ISBN 0-8039-3559-9. Survey of political participation in society, political culture, and political psychology.

Comparative Politics: A Developmental Approach. Little 1966 o.p. Surveys politics and government in underdeveloped areas.

Comparative Politics: System, Process, and Policy. Little 1978 o.p. Argues for a comparative governmental approach focusing on developing countries and their politics and governments.

The Politics of the Developing Areas. Bks. Demand repr. of 1960 ed. $164.20. ISBN 0-8357-2929-X. A comparative approach to the political ideologies of developing countries.

ARISTOTLE. 384–322 B.C.

[SEE Chapter 10 in this volume.]

AUGUSTINE. 354–430

[SEE Volume 4.]

BENTHAM, JEREMY. 1748–1832

A very bright child, Jeremy Bentham was born in London, the son of an attorney. He was admitted to Queen's College, Oxford, at age 12 and graduated from there in 1763. An English reformer and political philosopher, Bentham spent his life supporting countless social- and political-reform measures and trying as well to create a science of human behavior. He advocated a utopian welfare state and designed model cities, prisons, schools, and so on, to achieve that goal. He defined his goal as the objective study and measurement of passions and feelings, pleasures and pains, will and action. The principle of "the greatest happiness of the greatest number," set forth in his *Introduction to the Principles of Morals and Legislation*, governed all of his schemes for the improvement of society, and the philosophy he devised, called utilitarianism, set a model for all subsequent reforms based on scientific principles.

BOOKS BY BENTHAM

A Fragment on Government. 1776. Ed. by F. C. Montague. Greenwood 1980 repr. of 1931 ed. $38.50. ISBN 0-313-22323-8. Commentaries on English law that explain his philosophy of political science and constitutional law.

An Introduction to the Principles of Morals and Legislation. 1780. Ed. by J. Lafleur. *Lib. of Class. Ser.* Hafner 1948 $10.95. ISBN 0-02-841200-1

The Rationale of Judicial Evidence, Specially Applied to English Practice. 1827. Ed. by David Berkowitz and Samuel Thorne. *Class. of Eng. Legal History in the Modern Era Ser.* 5 vols. Garland 1979 o.p. Explores jurisprudence in England and discusses the validity of evidence in law.

The Theory of Legislation. Rothman 1987 repr. of 1931 ed. $47.50. ISBN 0-8377-1947-X. Traces the history of civil and criminal law.

The Works of Jeremy Bentham: Published under the Superintendence of His Executor, John Bowing. Scholarly 1976 repr. of 1838–43 ed. o.p. Collected works covering Bentham's writings on law and political science.

BOOKS ABOUT BENTHAM

Atkinson, Charles M. *Jeremy Bentham, His Life and Work*. AMS Pr. repr. of 1905 ed. $8.50. ISBN 0-404-00416-4. Complete portrait of Bentham's life, family, work, influences, creeds and aims, and politics.

Campos-Boralevi, Lea. *Bentham and the Oppressed*. De Gruyter 1984 $52.00. ISBN 3-11-009974-8. Explores the political and social views of Bentham by focusing on social and political problems faced by oppressed classes of society.

Hart, Herbert L. *Essays on Bentham: Studies in Jurisprudence and Political Theory*. OUP 1982 $55.00. ISBN 0-19-825348-6. Biographical and critical studies of Bentham and his views of jurisprudence and politics.

Mack, Mary Peter. *Jeremy Bentham*. Heinemann Ed. 1962 o.p. Historiographic probe into the life and work of Jeremy Bentham; surveys his ideas of law and government.

Rosen, Frederick. *Jeremy Bentham and Representative Democracy: A Study of the Constitutional Code*. OUP 1983 o.p. An analysis of Bentham's conceptions of constitutional law.

Rosenblum, Nancy L. *Bentham's Theory of the Modern State*. HUP 1978 $18.50. ISBN 0-674-06665-0. Argues that Bentham's views on legislation and his acceptance of diversity in politics signalize his modernity.

Steintrager, James. *Bentham*. Cornell Univ. Pr. 1977 o.p. Focuses on Bentham's ideas on the philosophy of law and discusses the idea of utilitarianism.

Stephen, Leslie. *The English Utilitarians: Jeremy Bentham, James Mill, John Stuart Mill*. 3 vols. Peter Smith $24.00. ISBN 0-8446-1422-X. Explores the utilitarian philosophy through a focused look at the philosophy of Bentham and John Stuart Mill.

BRYCE, JAMES. 1838–1922

Born in Belfast and educated at Trinity College, Oxford, James Bryce was a lawyer, writer, and member of Parliament. He also served as his country's ambassador to the United States from 1907 to 1913. Bryce achieved fame primarily for his book *The American Commonwealth* (1888). His aim was to produce the first substantial description of U.S. democracy, covering not only the constitutional structure but also state and local government, the party system, public opinion, and social institutions. TOQUEVILLE's *Democracy in America* was in one sense his model, but Bryce deliberately avoided Tocqueville's speculative method and concentrated more on detailed description and also on some prescription. "Law," he noted, "will never be strong or respected unless it has the sentiment of the people behind it." *The American Commonwealth* became the first textbook on U.S. government and, along with Tocqueville's book, one of the most notable to have ever been written about the United States.

BOOKS BY BRYCE

The American Commonwealth. 3 vols. AMS Pr. repr. of 1888 ed. $150.00. ISBN 0-404-03770-4

The Holy Roman Empire. 1864. AMS Pr. repr. of 1913 ed. $28.50. ISBN 0-404-14516-7. Based on a prize-winning essay written at Oxford University.

Modern Democracies. 1921. 2 vols. Arden Lib. 1983 repr. of 1924 ed. o.p. Examines the idea of democracy and theories of political science.

Studies in History and Jurisprudence. Essay Index Repr. Ser. 2 vols. Ayer 1968 repr. of 1901 ed. $44.00. ISBN 0-8369-0261-0. Historical survey of law and jurisprudence with a focus on the history of Roman and English Law; explores the development of the concept of a constitution.

BOOKS ABOUT BRYCE

Brooks, Robert C., ed. *Bryce's American Commonwealth: Fiftieth Anniversary*. Macmillan 1939 o.p. Compilation of papers and essays on the work of James Bryce, many focusing on his methodology.

Fisher, Herbert A. *James Bryce*. 2 vols. Greenwood repr. of 1927 ed. $30.50. ISBN 0-8371-4797-2. Discursive but noted for its lively style.

BURKE, EDMUND. 1729–1797

Edmund Burke, Irish statesman and political writer, was born in Dublin and educated at a Quaker boarding school and at Trinity College, Dublin. Although he studied law, he soon abandoned that for writing. Burke is renowned for his theory of social order, his advocacy of conservative politics, and his sustained hostility to the French Revolution. He contrasted the French Revolution with social and political change in Great Britain, where he believed the existing order is peacefully altered when it conflicts with the extension of human freedom. "All government—indeed every human benefit and enjoyment, every virtue, and every prudent act," he said in his *Second Speech on Conciliation with America*, "is founded on compromise and barter." A member of Parliament for almost 30 years, Burke vigorously opposed the policies of King George III and advocated the emancipation of the American colonies. With his vast knowledge, great imagination, and passionate sympathies, he ranks as one of Britain's foremost political thinkers. His political thought has become the basis of modern British conservatism.

BOOKS BY BURKE

Letters, Speeches and Tracts on Irish Affairs. Ed. by Matthew Arnold. AMS Pr. repr. of 1881 ed. $45.00. ISBN 0-404-13802-0. A collection of works dealing with the politics, government, and the Catholic Church in eighteenth-century Ireland.
A Philosophical Enquiry into the Origin of Our Ideas of the Sublime and Beautiful. 1757. OUP 1990 $7.95. ISBN 0-19-281807-4. His only strictly theoretical work; with an introduction by Adam Phillips. Examines the ideas of aesthetics in the early 1800s.
Reflections on the Revolution in France. Prometheus Bks. 1988 $7.95. ISBN 0-87975-411-7. Originally published in 1790, setting off a furious controversy.
The Works of Edmund Burke. 12 vols. Rprt. Serv. 1987 repr. of 1899 ed. $895.00. ISBN 0-7812-0439-9. This 12-volume collection of the works of Burke explores his political philosophy and the politics and government of Great Britain.

BOOKS ABOUT BURKE

Bryant, Donald C. *Edmund Burke and His Literary Friends*. Folcroft 1939 $22.00. ISBN 0-8414-0168-3. The latter included Samuel Johnson and Oliver Goldsmith.
Cameron, David. *The Social Thought of Rousseau and Burke: A Comparative Study*. U. of Toronto Pr. 1973 o.p. Comparative look at the philosophy of Rousseau and Burke.
Canavan, Francis. *Edmund Burke: Prescription and Providence*. Carolina Acad. Pr. 1988 $24.95. ISBN 0-89089-307-1. Bibliographic investigation into the life and work of Edmund Burke; explores his political and social philosophy.
————. *The Political Reason of Edmund Burke*. Duke 1960 o.p.
Cone, Carl B. *Burke and the Nature of Politics*. 2 vols. U. Pr. of Ky. 1957–64 o.p. Examines the work of Burke in relation to other English political scientists.
Fasel, George. *Edmund Burke*. Twayne's Eng. Authors Ser. G. K. Hall 1983 o.p. Introduction to Burke's life and work.
Graubard, Stephen R. *Burke, Disraeli, and Churchill: The Politics of Perseverance*. Bks. Demand repr. of 1961 ed. $68.00. ISBN 0-8357-7479-1. Compares the political theory and careers of Burke, Disraeli, and Churchill.
Kirk, Russell. *Edmund Burke: A Genius Reconsidered*. Sugden 1986 $8.95. ISBN 0-317-30086-5. Well-written biography of Burke.
MacCunn, John. *Political Philosophy of Burke*. Russell Sage repr. of 1913 ed. 1965 $8.00. ISBN 0-8462-0616-1. Examines Burke's ideas on politics, government, and law.

EASTON, DAVID. 1917–

Political scientist David Easton was born in Toronto, Ontario, and was educated at the University of Toronto and Harvard University. A professor of political science at the University of Chicago since 1955, Easton has also served as a fellow at the Center for Advanced Study in the Behavioral Sciences and a consultant to the Brookings Institution. The author of a number of important works, he is probably best known for *The Political System: An Inquiry into the State of Political Science* (1953). In both his work and writing, Easton is concerned primarily with the study of political science as a discipline, focusing on political theory and the importance of the field. A member of the National Academy of Sciences and the American Political Science Association, he has received honorary degrees from McMaster University and Kalamazoo College.

BOOKS BY EASTON

A Framework for Political Analysis. P-H 1965 o.p. Analyzes political trends and ideas and discusses Easton's theory of political science.

The Political System: An Inquiry into the State of Political Science. 1953. Knopf 1971 o.p.

A System Analysis of Political Life. U. Ch. Pr. 1979 $8.95. ISBN 0-226-18016-6. Explains his theory of political psychology and discusses methodology for political-science research.

A Systems Approach to Politics. 1965. Purdue U. Pr. 1965 o.p.

HOBBES, THOMAS. 1588–1679

Thomas Hobbes was born in Malmesbury, the son of a wayward country vicar. He was educated at Magdalen Hall, Oxford, and was supported during his long life by the wealthy Cavendish family, the Earls of Devonshire. Traveling widely, he met many of the leading intellectuals of the day, including FRANCIS BACON (see Vol. 4), GALILEO GALILEI (see Vol. 4), and RENÉ DESCARTES (see Vols. 4 and 5). As a philosopher and political theorist, Hobbes established—along with, but independently of, Descartes—early modern modes of thought in reaction to the scholasticism that characterized the seventeenth century. Because of his ideas, he was constantly in dispute with scientists and theologians, and many of his works were banned. His writings on psychology raised the possibility (later realized) that psychology could become a natural science, but his theory of politics is his most enduring achievement. In brief, his theory states that the problem of establishing order in society requires a sovereign to whom people owe loyalty and who in turn has duties toward his or her subjects. His prose masterpiece *Leviathan* (1651) is regarded as a major contribution to the theory of the state. In his vigorous old age, Hobbes enjoyed tennis and spirited argumentation.

BOOKS BY HOBBES

De Cive or the Citizen. Ed. by Sterling P. Lamprecht. 1642. Greenwood 1982 repr. of 1949 ed. $38.50. ISBN 0-313-23659-3. Explains the idea of and need for authority in governmental systems.

The Elements of Law: Natural and Politic. Ed. by Ferdinand Tönnies. 1650. Biblio Dist. 2nd rev. ed. 1969 $35.00. ISBN 0-7146-2540-X. Argues for his interpretation of natural law and analyzes politics through that view.

Leviathan. Ed. by C. B. MacPherson. 1651. Viking Penguin 1981 $5.95. ISBN 0-14-043195-0. Philosophical tract that discusses the origins and uses of government.

BOOKS ABOUT HOBBES

Bowle, John. *Hobbes and His Critics: A Study in Seventeenth Century Constitutionalism.* Biblio Dist. 1969 repr. of 1951 ed. o.p. Critical examination of Hobbes's contributions to political science.

Gauthier, David P. *Logic of Leviathan: The Moral and Political Theory of Thomas Hobbes.* OUP 1969 o.p. Critical look at Hobbes's *Leviathan* and the moral and political philosophy expressed within it.

Goldsmith, M. M. *The Political Philosophy of Hobbes: The Rationale of the Sovereign State.* Col. U. Pr. 1966 o.p. A historical look at Hobbes's political and social theory, focusing on his views of sovereignty and authority.

Hinnant, Charles H. *Thomas Hobbes: A Reference Guide.* G. K. Hall 1980 $35.00. ISBN 0-8161-8173-X. A bibliographic overview of Hobbes's works.

Strauss, Leo. *Political Philosophy of Hobbes: Its Basic and Its Genesis.* Trans. by Elsa M. Sinclair. U. Ch. Pr. 1984 $12.95. ISBN 0-226-77705-7. Historical overview of the development of Hobbes's thought.

Von Leyden, W. *Hobbes and Locke: The Politics of Freedom and Obligation.* St. Martin 1982 $25.00. ISBN 0-312-38824-1. Discusses the contrasting ideas of liberty, authority, and duty of Hobbes and Locke and explores their conflicting views of political science.

JEFFERSON, THOMAS. 1743–1826

Thomas Jefferson, the third president of the United States, was the premier philosopher of American democracy. His "Summary View of the Rights of British America," written in 1774, was one of the earliest denials of the right of the British Parliament to legislate for the American colonies. He was the principal author of the Declaration of Independence, which is based on LOCKE's (see also Vol. 4) doctrine of the rights of man; this origin of the Declaration helped transform the first great colonial revolt of modern times into the first great democratic revolution. Jefferson wrote the Virginia Statute for Religious Freedom; as the nation's first secretary of state, he made important contributions to the law of nations and ordered the first census of the U.S. population; he conceived, planned, designed, and supervised in every detail the founding and construction of the University of Virginia; and when the British burned Washington, D.C., in the War of 1812, his personal library became the foundation of the Library of Congress. He also found time to devise the American system of decimal coinage, compile a dictionary of Indian dialects, and invent the storm window. Jefferson died at his home, Monticello, on July 4, 1826, the fiftieth anniversary of the Declaration of Independence.

BOOKS BY JEFFERSON

The Complete Jefferson. Ed. by Saul K. Padover. *Select Bibliographies Repr. Ser.* Ayer repr. of 1943 ed. $56.00. ISBN 0-8369-5027-5. A compilation of Jefferson's writings on politics and government; examines the role of the individual in society.

Political Writings of Thomas Jefferson. Ed. by Edward Dumbauld. Bobbs 1955 o.p. Selections of Jefferson's writings focusing on the role of government and its impact on individual liberty.

The Portable Thomas Jefferson. Ed. by Merrill D. Peterson. Viking Penguin 1977 $7.95. ISBN 0-14-015080-3. Compilation of Jefferson's ideas on politics, society, and the role of government.

Writings. Ed. by Merrill D. Peterson. Library of America 1984 $30.00. ISBN 0-940450-16-X

BOOKS ABOUT JEFFERSON

Becker, Carl L. *The Declaration of Independence: A Study in the History of Political Ideas.* Random 1958 $6.95. ISBN 0-394-70060-0. Traces the role of politics and government in the Revolutionary War era, culminating in the Declaration of Independence.

Boorstin, Daniel J. *The Lost World of Thomas Jefferson.* U. Ch. Pr. 1981 $12.95. ISBN 0-226-06496-4. Traces the development of American philosophical thought through an investigation of Jefferson's life and works.

Brodie, Fawn M. *Thomas Jefferson: An Intimate History.* Bantam 1975 $5.95. ISBN 0-553-25443-X. Looks at Jefferson's life, with a special focus on his presidency and the role of Sally Hemings in his life.

Malone, Dumas. *Jefferson and His Time.* 6 vols. Little 1948–81 $25.00 ea. ISBNs 0-316-54472-8, 0-316-54473-6, 0-316-54469-8, 0-316-54467-1, 0-316-54465-5, 0-316-54463-9. The definitive biography.

Padover, Saul K. *Jefferson.* Arden Lib. 1982 repr. of 1942 ed. $50.00. ISBN 0-8495-4415-7. Examines Jefferson's major accomplishments.

Peterson, Merrill D. *The Jefferson Image in the American Mind.* OUP 1960 o.p. Examines Jefferson's influence on American political thought.

———. *Thomas Jefferson and the New Nation: A Biography.* OUP 1970 $19.95. ISBN 0-19-501909-1

KEY, V. O., JR. 1908–1963

V. O. Key, Jr., an American political scientist, played a central role in the behavioral movement within American political science, that is, the study not of how the political system is supposed to function, but of how politicians, civil servants, and voters actually behave. His pioneering text, *Politics, Parties, and Pressure Groups* (1942), discusses the interest groups that contend for power, the roles of the party system and the electorate, the use of force and violence, the uses of pecuniary sanctions, and the role of education as a form of political control. His *Southern Politics* (1949) is based on both the analysis of local election returns and interviews with politicians and observers; in subsequent books, he pioneered in the use of survey research data in the study of politics. As both teacher and government consultant, he was noted for his unpretentiousness and concern for students and colleagues.

BOOKS BY KEY

American State Politics: An Introduction. 1956. Greenwood 1983 repr. of 1965 ed. $38.50. ISBN 0-313-24246-1. Examines the state governmental system of the United States and analyzes its relation and impact on the federal government.

Politics, Parties, and Pressure Groups. 1942. HarpC 1964 o.p.

A Primer of Statistics for Political Scientists. T. Y. Crowell 1954 o.p. Explains political science statistical research and analysis.

Public Opinion and American Democracy. Knopf 1961 o.p. Investigates the role of public opinion on the political and electoral process.

The Responsible Electorate: Rationality in Presidential Voting, 1936–1960. Ed. by Milton C. Cummings, Jr. HUP 1966 o.p. Epitomizes Key's ability to extract meaning from statistics.

Southern Politics in State and Nation. 1949. U. of Tenn. Pr. 1984 $29.95. ISBN 0-87049-434-1. With an introduction by Alexander Heard.

LASKI, HAROLD J. 1893–1950

Born in Manchester, England, and educated at New College, Oxford, the British political scientist and Labor party leader Harold Laski taught history at Harvard University from 1916 to 1920. At that time, he returned to England to teach at the London School of Economics and Political Science, where he remained until his death. His name and the London School became almost synonymous terms in the minds of many, particularly students from the United States and from Asia and Africa, who learned from Laski the political knowledge necessary to overthrow their British rulers. A brilliant lecturer, he espoused a modified form of Marxism while holding a strong belief in individual freedom. Laski was a prolific writer and an active Socialist politician as well as a sensitive commentator on British and U.S. political institutions. Oddly, the letters that he exchanged during a period of 19 years with his American friend, Justice OLIVER WENDELL HOLMES (see Vol. 1), published in two volumes in 1953, are read and appreciated more widely today than any of his books.

BOOKS BY LASKI

Authority in the Modern State. Shoe String 1968 repr. of 1919 ed. $37.50. ISBN 0-208-00460-2. Analyzes the power of the church in modern state government.

Democracy in Crisis. AMS Pr. repr. of 1933 ed. $19.25. ISBN 0-404-03882-4. Examines the strengths and weaknesses of representative government.

The Foundations of Sovereignty, and Other Essays. Essay Index Repr. Ser. Ayer repr. of 1921 ed. $18.00. ISBN 0-8369-0607-1. Articles exploring the concept of sovereignty as it applies to modern state government.

A Grammar of Politics. 1925. Elliots Bks. 1925 o.p. Reversed his earlier position attacking the all-powerful sovereign state, now terming it "the fundamental instrument of society."

Holmes-Laski Letters: The Correspondence of Mr. Justice Holmes and Harold J. Laski, 1916–1935. (coauthored with Oliver W. Holmes). Ed. by Mark DeWolfe Howe. 2 vols. HUP 1953 o.p. With a foreword by Felix Frankfurter. Compilation of correspondence revealing their views on American jurisprudence.

Liberty in the Modern State. 1930. Kelley rev. ed. 1949 $25.00. ISBN 0-678-03166-5. An analysis of liberty in modern political systems.

Reflections on the Constitution: The House of Commons, the Cabinet [and] the Civil Service. 1951. Manchester Univ. Pr. 1962 o.p. Examines the parliamentary system of Great Britain and traces its development.

Reflections on the Revolution of Our Time. Biblio Dist. 1968 repr. of 1943 ed. $25.00. ISBN 0-7146-1564-1. Discusses world politics from 1933 to 1945 and probes the influence of World War II in modern politics.

BOOKS ABOUT LASKI

Deane, Herbert A. *The Political Ideas of Harold J. Laski.* Shoe String 1972 repr. of 1955 ed. $37.50. ISBN 0-208-01234-6. Critical but fair analysis of Laski's inconsistencies as a political thinker.

Magid, Henry M. *English Political Pluralism: The Problem of Freedom and Organization.* AMS Pr. repr. of 1941 ed. o.p. A look at Laski's views on autonomy and freedom and their relation to political pluralism in Great Britain.

Martin, Kingsley. *Harold Laski, 1893–1950: A Biographical Memoir.* Viking Penguin 1953 o.p. Traces the life and work of Laski.

LASSWELL, HAROLD D. 1902–1978

Harold D. Lasswell was the wunderkind of American political science. Beginning in his twenties, he attempted through his writings to develop a theory about the individual and society that draws on and illuminates all of the social sciences. When he enrolled in the University of Chicago at age 16, he had already read widely such writers as KANT (see Vol. 4) and FREUD (see also Vol. 5). His doctoral dissertation was published in 1927 as *Propaganda Technique in the World War*, a major work in the development of communications research. He created a phrase that set the agenda for communications research for a generation: "Who says what to whom with what effect?" After World War II, he moved to Yale Law School, where he introduced a generation of law students to the social sciences. He believed that the creation of what he called "the policy sciences" was his greatest achievement; the book by that title that he edited with Daniel Lerner in 1951 is still widely read today.

BOOKS BY LASSWELL

The Language of Politics: Studies in Quantitative Semantics. 1949. MIT Pr. 1965 o.p. Examines the terminology of political science and how semantics influences political ideology.

The Policy Sciences: Recent Developments in Scope and Method. (coauthored with Daniel Lerner). 1951. Stanford U. Pr. 1968 o.p. Compilation of addresses, essays, and lectures that examines political science developments and theories.

Politics: Who Gets What, When, and How. 1936. Peter Smith $21.75. ISBN 0-8446-1277-4. A probe into the proper methods of political-science inquiry.

Psychopathology and Politics. 1930. U. Ch. Pr. 1977 repr. of 1960 ed. $18.95. ISBN 0-226-46919-0. With an introduction by Fred I. Greenstein. Examines the concept of personality and politics, focusing on psychology and pathology in political-science research.

World Handbook of Political and Social Indicators. (coauthored with Bruce M. Russett and others). Yale U. Pr. 1964 o.p. Guide to tools and methods for comparative political research.

World Politics and Personal Insecurity. 1935. Macmillan 1965 o.p. Examines world politics from a social-psychology perspective.

BOOKS ABOUT LASSWELL

McDougall, Derek. *Harold D. Lasswell and the Study of International Relations.* U. Pr. of Amer. 1985 $32.75. ISBN 0-8191-4296-4. Analyzes Lasswell's work, focusing on his contribution to international relations.

Rogow, Arnold A., ed. *Politics, Personality and Social Science in the Twentieth Century: Essays in Honor of Harold D. Lasswell.* U. Ch. Pr. 1969 $27.50. ISBN 0-226-72399-2. First full-scale effort to deal fully with the unusual scope of Lasswell's work.

LENIN (born VLADIMIR ILYICH ULYANOV). 1870–1924

[SEE Chapter 9 in this volume.]

LIPPMANN, WALTER. 1899–1974

Walter Lippmann, an American political journalist, dominated political journalism in the United States from World War I almost until his death. In his last year as a student at Harvard University, he was an assistant to the philosopher GEORGE SANTAYANA (see Vol. 4). He read extensively in FREUD (see also Vol. 4) and was in every sense an "intellectual" journalist. His *Public Opinion* (1922) became the intellectual anchor for the study of public opinion, and it is widely read today. He came close in this book to questioning whether citizens can possibly make rational, democratic decisions. The source of the difficulty is not our irrationality but the inherent nature of the modern system of mass communication; information must be condensed into brief slogans. These slogans become stereotypes, a concept that Lippmann brilliantly analyzed prior to its acceptance by psychologists. As a political columnist, he wrote on many topics, particularly on foreign relations, and he held a position of prestige in Washington's press corps that has never been matched. Alastair Buchan wrote in 1974 that Walter Lippman was "the name that opened every door."

BOOKS BY LIPPMANN

The Cold War: A Study in U.S. Foreign Policy. HarpC 1947 o.p. Traces U.S. foreign relations and politics during the Cold War period.

A Preface to Morals. 1929. Macmillan 1952 o.p. Lippmann's understanding of morals and
  ethics and their role in politics.
A Preface to Politics. 1913. U. of Mich. Pr. 1962 o.p. Examines the role of politics in
  American government.
Public Opinion. 1922. Macmillan 1965 $12.95. ISBN 0-02-919130-0

BOOKS ABOUT LIPPMANN

Blum, D. Steven. *Walter Lippmann: Cosmopolitanism in the Century of Total War.* Cornell
  Univ. Pr. 1984 $22.50. ISBN 0-8014-1676-0. Traces the development of Lippmann's
  political philosophy through an examination of his research.
Steel, Ronald. *Walter Lippmann and the American Century.* Little 1980 $22.50. ISBN 0-
  316-81190-4. Standard biography of Lippmann and his contributions to political
  journalism.

LIPSET, SEYMOUR MARTIN. 1922–

American political theorist and sociologist Seymour Lipset was born in New
York City and educated at City College of New York and Columbia University.
Lipset has taught at a number of universities, including the University of
Toronto, Columbia University, the University of California at Berkeley, Harvard
University, and Stanford University. A senior fellow at the Hoover Institution, he
is also a member of the International Society of Political Psychology, the
American Political Science Association, and the American Academy of Science.
Lipset maintains that contemporary democracy is flawed; nevertheless, he
believes that it is still "the good society itself in operation." Applying both
political science and sociological approaches to political systems, he supports a
trend to replace political ideology with sociological analysis. Among Lipset's
many works are *Political Man: The Social Bases of Politics* (1960), *Class, Status,
and Power* (1953), and *Revolution and Counterrevolution* (1968). He has also
contributed articles to a number of magazines, including *The New Republic,
Encounter,* and *Commentary.* Lipset has received a number of awards for his
work, including the MacIver Award in 1962, the Gunnar Myrdal Prize in 1970,
and the Townsend Harris Medal in 1971.

BOOKS BY LIPSET

Class, Status, and Power. 1953. Free Pr. 1953 o.p.
The First New Nation: The U.S. in Historical and Comparative Perspective. Norton 1979
  $9.95. ISBN 0-393-00911-4. Analyzes the characteristics of American civilization by
  tracing its history and comparing it to other societies.
Political Man: The Social Bases of Politics. Johns Hopkins 1981 repr. of 1961 ed. $15.95.
  ISBN 0-8018-2522-9
Revolution and Counterrevolution. Transaction Pubs. 1987 $19.95. ISBN 0-88738-694-6.
  Compilation of addresses, essays, and lectures on revolution and its role in political
  change.
Social Mobility in Industrial Society. 1959. Transaction Pubs. 1991 $21.95. ISBN 1-56000-
  606-4

LOCKE, JOHN. 1632–1704

English philosopher John Locke was born in Wrington, Somerset, and was
educated at Westminster School and Christ Church College, Oxford. His
influence can hardly be overestimated. A founder of the Enlightenment in
England and France, Locke believed that a person's mind at birth is like a blank
tablet and that almost all knowledge is gained from experience. From the point
of view of political science, Locke's major work is *Two Treatises of Government*
(1690), which contains a loosely presented theory of government and an

analysis of the relationship of the individual to the state. He stressed that the origin of the state is a mutual contract among individuals and that the members of society may resist government when they judge that its actions violate the terms of the social contract. In addition, he challenged the idea of the divine right of kings and said that a government should exist only with the consent of the governed. Through his political ideas and his doctrine of the rights of man, he was one of the intellectual fathers of the American and French revolutions. In writing the Declaration of Independence, THOMAS JEFFERSON (see also Vol. 1) used many of Locke's ideas, including the belief that a government must protect its citizens' natural right to life, liberty, and property. His philosophy was influential in the thought of such persons as VOLTAIRE (see Vols. 1 and 4) and GEORGE BERKELEY (see Vol. 4), and his psychology—what he called "human understanding"—is reflected in nineteenth- and twentieth-century psychological theory.

BOOKS BY LOCKE

The Correspondence of John Locke. Ed. by E. S. Beer. OUP 1976–1989. Vol. 1 *Letters 1–461.* $115.00. ISBN 0-19-8243960. Vol. 2 *Letters 462–848.* $129.00. ISBN 0-19-8245599. Vol. 3 *Letters 849–1241.* $125.00. ISBN 0-19-824560-2. Vol. 4 *Letters 1242–1701.* $135.00. ISBN 0-19-824561-0. Vol. 5 *Letters 1702–2198.* $135.00. ISBN 0-19-824562-9. Vol. 6 *Letters 2199–2664.* $135.00. ISBN 0-19-824563-7. Vol. 7 *Letters 2665–3286.* $135.00. ISBN 0-19-824564-5. Vol. 8 *Letters 3287–3648.* $115.00. ISBN 0-19-824565-3. Part of the *Clarendon Edition of The Works of John Locke Ser.,* which is projected to number 35 volumes and promises to be the definitive collection.
Drafts for the Essay Concerning Human Understanding and Other Philosophical Writings. Ed. by Peter Nidditch and G. A. Rogers. OUP 1990 $98.00. ISBN 0-19-824545-9. Traces the development of Locke's theory of knowledge as well as other philosophical perspectives.
An Essay Concerning Human Understanding. 1690. NAL-Dutton 1989 $9.95. ISBN 0-452-00941-3. Presents Locke's theory of human knowledge and discusses the proper methods of education.
Locke on Money. Ed. by Patrick Hyde Kelly. 2 vols. OUP 1991. Vol. 1 $118.00. ISBN 0-19-8245467. Vol. 2 $95.00. ISBN 0-19-8248377. Examines Locke's views on money and currency and their role in seventeenth-century Great Britain.
A Paraphrase and Notes on the Epistles of St. Paul. 2 vols. OUP 1988. Vol. 1 $98.00. ISBN 0-19-8248016. Vol. 2 $89.00. ISBN 0-19-8248067. With an introduction by Arthur W. Wainwright.
Some Thoughts Concerning Education. Ed. by John W. Yoltan and Jean Yoltan. OUP 1989 $92.00. ISBN 0-19-824582-3. Presents his views on moral education; elaborates the methods he believes will provide an individual with a moral education.
Two Treatises of Government. 1690. Ed. by Peter Haslett. *Cambridge Texts in History of Politcal Thought Ser.* Cambridge U. Pr. 1988 $49.95. ISBN 0-521-35448-X
The Works of John Locke. 10 vols. Adlers Foreign Bks. repr. of 1823 ed. $700.00. ISBN 3-511-02600-8. Collected works encompassing all of Locke's political, social, and epistemological work.

BOOKS ABOUT LOCKE

Aaron, Richard I. *John Locke.* OUP 1971 o.p. Traces the development of Locke's political philosophy.
Cranston, Maurice. *John Locke: A Biography.* Ed. by J. P. Mayer. *European Political Thought Ser.* Ayer 1979 repr. of 1957 ed. $34.50. ISBN 0-403-11690-X. Complete biography beginning with his childhood and education and covering his works and later years.
Dunn, John. *The Political Thought of John Locke: An Historical Account of the Argument of the Two Treatises of Government.* Cambridge U. Pr. 1983 $19.95. ISBN 0-521-

27139-8. Locates the roots of Locke's political thought in his theological commitment to Calvinism.

Grant, Ruth W. *John Locke's Liberalism.* U. Ch. Pr. 1987 $24.95. ISBN 0-226-30607-0. Particularly good treatment of *The Second Treatise* and the concepts of contract and political obligation.

MACHIAVELLI, NICCOLÒ. 1469–1527

Niccolò Machiavelli was an Italian political and military theorist, civil servant, historian, playwright, and poet who lived during the Golden Age of Florence, and whose major work, *The Prince* (1513), is dedicated to Lorenzo de' Medici, the ruler of Florence. In *The Prince* Machiavelli sought to discern an order in the nature of political activity itself, not in some external cause. He examined politics in a modern, detached, and rational manner, analyzing the ways in which power is gained and held. He demonstrated the soundness of certain political precepts by using a kind of calculus to test them. Precisely because of the objectivity of his descriptions of the political process and of how power is obtained and held, Machiavelli is often thought of as a kind of evil adviser of princes, and Machiavellianism has come to mean a political doctrine that denies the relevance of morality in political affairs and holds that craft and deceit are justified in pursuing and maintaining political power; that is, opportunism is all. But these precepts do not describe Machiavelli as a person. He described the corrupt state of Florence, but he was not corrupt himself. He was critical of the popes and their political activities but, according to at least some scholars, died a Christian. He is controversial to this day, but he is viewed by many as a forerunner of the Enlightenment and as the first modern political scientist.

BOOKS BY MACHIAVELLI

The Art of War. 1521. Trans. by Peter Whitehorne. AMS Pr. repr. of 1560 ed. $45.00. ISBN 0-404-51951-2. Advocates the concept of a national army based on conscription and traces the development of weaponry and its use in warfare.

The Discourses. 1517. Ed. by Bernard Crick. Viking Penguin 1984 $6.95. ISBN 0-14-044428-9. Outlines Machiavelli's republican principles.

The Portable Machiavelli. Ed. by Peter Bondanella and Mark Musa. Viking Penguin 1979 o.p. Compilation of Machiavelli's political and other writings.

The Prince. 1532. Trans. by Peter Bondanella and Mark Musa. OUP 1984 $2.50. ISBN 0-19-281602-0

BOOKS ABOUT MACHIAVELLI

Christie, Richard, and others. *Studies in Machiavellianism. Social Psychology Ser.* Acad. Pr. 1970 o.p. Series of essays on the political philosophy of Machiavelli.

de Grazia, Sebastian. *Machiavelli in Hell.* Princeton U. Pr. 1990 $49.50. ISBN 0-691-00861-2. A scholarly intellectual biography showing the relationship between Machiavelli's life experiences and his ideas.

Mansfield, Harvey C., Jr. *Machiavelli's New Modes and Orders: A Study of the "Discourses on Livy."* Cornell Univ. Pr. 1979 o.p.

Pitkin, Hanna F. *Fortune Is a Woman: Gender and Politics in the Thought of Niccolò Machiavelli.* U. CA Pr. 1984 $45.00. ISBN 0-520-04932. Analyzes Machiavelli's views on women and their relation to his political philosophy.

Ridolfi, Roberto. *The Life of Niccolò Machiavelli.* 1954. U. Ch. Pr. 1963 o.p. Sympathetic biography of a real man in a historical environment.

Strauss, Leo. *Thoughts on Machiavelli.* U. Ch. Pr. 1984 $19.95. ISBN 0-226-77704-9. Overview of Machiavelli's life and work.

MADISON, JAMES. 1751–1836

James Madison, the fourth president of the United States, was born at Port Conway, Virginia. He was raised on a large family farm, called Montpelier, which remained his home throughout his life. After receiving a boarding school education, he entered the College of New Jersey (now Princeton University), from which he graduated in 1771. In 1776 Madison was elected a delegate to the Virginia Revolutionary Convention, where he was a strong advocate of religious freedom. He then became a Virginia legislator. As delegate to the Constitutional Convention of 1787, he became the chief architect of the U.S. Constitution and, later, of the Bill of Rights. Madison served in the first Congress from 1789 to 1797, rising to the position of speaker of the house. In 1801 he became secretary of state in the administration of THOMAS JEFFERSON, and in 1809 he was elected president.

Madison's insights on the nature of politics and the operations of government are as relevant today as they were in his time. His journals provide our principal source of knowledge about the Constitutional Convention of 1787. He also shared the authorship of *The Federalist Papers* (1787–88), arguably the most significant American contribution to political theory, with Alexander Hamilton and John Jay. His insights into political behavior (such as Federalist paper number 10 on the subject of factions) and the nature of government (Federalist papers numbers 39 and 51 on the allocation of power) continue to be useful for those who seek to write constitutions for new governments today.

BOOKS BY MADISON

The Complete Madison: His Basic Writings. Ed. by Saul K. Padover. Kraus repr. of 1953 ed. $48.00. ISBN 0-527-60300-7. Comprehensive edition of Madison's writings.

The Federalist Papers. 1787–88. (coauthored with Alexander Hamilton and John Jay). Ed. by Isaac Kramnick. Viking Penguin 1987 $7.95. ISBN 0-14-044495-5

Journal of the Federal Convention. Ed. by E. H. Scott. Ayer repr. of 1893 ed. $33.00. ISBN 0-8369-5381-9. Provides a firsthand account of the Constitutional Convention; useful for a study of U.S. constitutional history.

Notes of Debates in the Federal Convention of 1787. Norton 1987 $14.95. ISBN 0-393-30405-1. Madison's notes on the Constitutional Convention of 1787, reflecting the process of debate and compromise and revealing the roles of individual participants.

The Papers of James Madison. Ed. by Robert A. Rutland and others. 17 vols. U. Pr. of Va. Vol. 1 1987 $37.50. ISBN 0-8139-1093-5. Vol. 2 1992 $50.00. ISBN 0-8139-1345-4. Vols. 3–10 o.p. Vol. 11 1977 $37.50. ISBN 0-8139-0739-X. Vol. 12 1979 $37.50. ISBN 0-8139-0803-5. Vol. 13 1981 $37.50. ISBN 0-8139-0861-2. Vol. 14 1983 $37.50. ISBN 0-8139-0955-4. Vol. 15 1985 $47.50. ISBN 0-8139-1059-5. Vol. 16 1989 $45.00. ISBN 0-8139-1212-1. Vol. 17 1991 $47.50. ISBN 0-8139-1288-1. Collection of Madison's writing, especially revealing of his political philosophy.

The Virginia Report of 1799–1800, Touching the Alien and Sedition Laws. Da Capo 1970 repr. of 1850 ed. $35.00. ISBN 0-306-71860-X

BOOKS ABOUT MADISON

Brant, Irving. *The Fourth President: The Life of James Madison*. Macmillan 1970 o.p. A condensation of the masterful six-volume biography.

Hunt, Gaillard. *Life of James Madison*. Russell Sage 1968 repr. of 1902 ed. o.p. Examines Madison's role in the development of American political theory and government.

Ketcham, Ralph. *James Madison: A Biography*. U. Pr. of Va. 1990 repr. of 1971 ed. $17.95. ISBN 0-8139-1265-2. Well-researched biography of Madison.

Koch, Adrienne. *Jefferson and Madison: The Great Collaboration*. U. Pr. of Amer. 1987 repr. of 1964 ed. $43.50. ISBN 0-8191-5875-5. Examines parallels in the thought and political views of Jefferson and Madison.

Miller, William L. *The Business of May Next: James Madison and the Founding*. U. Pr. of
Va. 1992 $24.95. ISBN 0-8139-1368-3. Examines the history of the U.S. Constitution
and Madison's role in its creation.

MERRIAM, CHARLES E. 1874–1963

Charles E. Merriam, an American political scientist, is generally regarded as
the father of the behavioral movement in political science. He spent most of his
career at the University of Chicago and played an active role in Chicago reform
politics. He was also dedicated to interdisciplinary research and was a major
founder of the Social Science Research Council in 1923. He was a member of
the presidential committee that produced the monumental *Recent Social
Trends in the United States* in 1933; during the Roosevelt administration, he
took part in the work of several influential committees and boards.

BOOKS BY MERRIAM

The History of American Political Theories. Repr. in Government and Political Science Ser.
Gordon Pr. $59.95. ISBN 0-8490-0317-2
Non-Voting: Causes and Methods of Control. (coauthored with Harold F. Gosnell.) U. Ch.
Pr. 1924 o.p. A pioneering work in the use of statistics.
Political Power: Its Composition and Incidence. McGraw 1934 o.p. Carries into the
twentieth century Tocqueville's vision of American democracy as the best hope for
governing humankind.
Primary Elections: A Study of the History and Tendencies of Primary Election Legislation.
1908. (coauthored with Louise Overacker). U. Ch. Pr. rev. ed. 1928 o.p.

BOOKS ABOUT MERRIAM

Karl, Barry D. *Charles E. Merriam and the Study of Politics*. U. Ch. Pr. 1975 $22.50. ISBN
0-226-42519-3. Focuses on Merriam as both entrepreneur and "moralizing nationalist."
White, Leonard, ed. *The Future of Government in the United States: Essays in Honor of
Charles E. Merriam.* U. Ch. Pr. 1942 o.p.

MILL, JOHN STUART. 1806–1873

[SEE Chapter 3 in this volume.]

MONTESQUIEU, CHARLES DE SECONDAT, BARON DE LA BREDE ET DE. 1689–1755

Charles de Secondat, Baron de la Brède et de Montesquieu, French
philosopher and political theorist, is viewed variously as the most important
precursor of sociology, as the father of modern historical research, and as the
first modern political scientist. In *The Persian Letters* (1721), which was an
immediate publishing success, he depicted France as seen by two imaginary
Persians and thus demonstrated the possibility for objectivity that he demonstrated 27 years later in *The Spirit of the Laws* (1748), his masterpiece. On the
surface, *The Spirit* is a treatise on law, but it also describes every domain
affecting human behavior and raises questions of philosophical judgment about
the merits of various kinds of legislation. It describes three types of government
and their principles: Virtue is the principle of republics; honor, of monarchies;
and fear, of despotism. With these "ideal types" as starting points, he proceeded
to analyze legislation and the state in great detail. He made comparison the
central method of his political science and thus directed the focus of inquiry
from Europe to all societies in the world. His direct influence on the social
sciences has been profound.

BOOKS BY MONTESQUIEU

The Persian Letters. 1721. Viking Penguin 1973 $8.95. ISBN 0-14-044281-2
The Spirit of the Laws. 1748. Cambridge U. Pr. 1989 $59.95. ISBN 0-521-36183-4

BOOKS ABOUT MONTESQUIEU

Richter, M., ed. *The Political Theory of Montesquieu.* Cambridge U. Pr. 1977 o.p.
Discussion of Montesquieu's political and social views.
Shackleton, Robert. *Montesquieu: A Critical Biography.* Ed. by David W. Carrithers. OUP
1961 o.p. Notable biography analyzing Montesquieu's contributions to political
theory and historical research.

PLATO. 428–347 B.C.

Plato has been described as the founder of political theory and sociology and
as the greatest thinker of all time. The facts of his life are disputed by scholars,
and most of his books are in the form of Socratic dialogues, in which SOCRATES
(see Vol. 4) is the main speaker and the superior intellect. It was the tragic death
of Socrates in 399 B.C. that seems to have turned his student Plato into an
author. Much of Plato's political diagnosis is concerned with the causes of
political degeneration in the Greek city-states, from hereditary kingship, the
rule of one, to aristocracy, the rule of the few, to democracy, the rule of the
many. In *The Republic* (370–360 B.C.), democracy is shown to lead only too
easily to a final stage of decay: the rule of the ruthless demagogue who makes
himself the tyrant of the city. Plato's solution to this cycle—his political
program—is to arrest all social change and return to the patriarchic state.
Fundamentally, many scholars believe, Plato's political philosophy is authoritarian and hostile to democratic ideas. This conclusion is hotly debated today, but
all scholars agree that his influence has been immeasurable. As Karl R. Popper,
a scholar critical of Plato, has asserted: "Western thought, one might say, has
been either Platonic or anti-Platonic, but hardly ever non-Platonic."

BOOKS BY PLATO

The Laws. History of Ideas in Ancient Greece Ser. Ayer 1976 repr. of 1921 ed. $97.50.
ISBN 0-405-07327-5
Portable Plato. Ed. by Scott Buchanan. Viking Penguin 1977 $7.95. ISBN 0-14-015040-4.
Collection of Plato's writings; includes *Symposium, Phaedo,* and the *Republic.*
The Republic. 2 vols. Ed. by James Adams. Cambridge U. Pr. Vol. 1 $70.00. ISBN 0-521-
05963-1. Vol. 2 $85.00. ISBN 0-521-05964-X
Works of Plato. 5 vols. AMS Pr. repr. of 1804 ed. $290.00. ISBN 0-404-16360-2.
Comprehensive collection of Plato's work.

BOOKS ABOUT PLATO

Crossman, R. S. *Plato Today.* Ed. by E. B. England. Unwin Hyman 1963 o.p. Examines
Plato's ideas about democracy and his relevance to democratic thought today;
analysis of the Republic and the ideas of fascism.
Koyre, Alexandre. *Discovering Plato.* Trans. by Leonora C. Rosenfeld. Bks. Demand repr.
of 1960 ed. $32.00. ISBN 0-317-09006-2. Introductory survey of Plato's work and
ideas; examines several important works.
Popper, Karl R. *The Open Society and Its Enemies.* 2 vols. Princeton U. Pr. 1966 $15.95.
ISBN 0-691-01968-1. Investigates Plato's ideas on politics and government and his
views on the nature of man.
Strauss, Leo. *The Argument and the Action of Plato's Laws.* U. Ch. Pr. 1983 o.p. Discussion
of the *Republic* and Plato's ideas of democracy. With a foreword by Joseph Cropsey.
Wilson, John F. *The Politics of Moderation: An Interpretation of Plato's "Republic."* U. Pr.
of Amer. 1984 $45.50. ISBN 0-8191-4017-1

ROUSSEAU, JEAN JACQUES. 1712–1778

Jean Jacques Rousseau was a Swiss philosopher and political theorist who lived much of his life in France. Many reference books describe him as French, but he generally added "Citizen of Geneva" whenever he signed his name. He presented his theory of education in *Émile* (1762), a novel, the first book to link the educational process to a scientific understanding of children; Rousseau is thus regarded as the precursor, if not the founder, of child psychology. "The greatest good is not authority, but liberty," he wrote, and in *The Social Contract* (1762) Rousseau moved from a study of the individual to an analysis of the relationship of the individual to the state: "The art of politics consists of making each citizen extremely dependent upon the polis in order to free him from dependence upon other citizens." This doctrine of sovereignty, the absolute supremacy of the state over its members, has led many to accuse Rousseau of opening the doors to despotism, collectivism, and totalitarianism. Others say that this is the opposite of Rousseau's intent, that the surrender of rights is only apparent, and that in the end individuals retain the rights that they appear to have given up. In effect, these Rousseau supporters say, the social contract is designed to secure or to restore to individuals in the state of civilization the equivalent of the rights they enjoyed in the state of nature. Rousseau was a passionate man who lived in passionate times, and he still stirs passion in those who write about him today.

Books by Rousseau

The Confessions of Jean Jacques Rousseau. Trans. by John M. Cohen. *Penguin Class. Ser.* Viking Penguin 1953 $5.95. ISBN 0-14-044033-X. An intensely personal autobiography.
Émile. 1762. Trans. by Allan Bloom. Basic 1979 $14.95. ISBN 0-465-01931-5
The Social Contract. 1762. Darby Pub. 1980 repr. of 1893 ed. $35.00. ISBN 0-89987-716-8

Books about Rousseau

Chapman, John W. *Rousseau: Totalitarian or Liberal.* AMS Pr. 1956 $16.50. ISBN 0-404-51589-4. Analyzes the intent of Rousseau's political philosophy.
Durkheim, Emile. *Montesquieu and Rousseau: Forerunners of Sociology.* U. of Mich. Pr. 1960 o.p. Two essays, originally written in 1892 (Montesquieu) and 1918 (Rousseau). In the latter, the preeminent sociologist praises Rousseau for his recognition of social forces in shaping the individual. With a foreword by H. Peyre.
Masters, Roger D. *The Political Philosophy of Rousseau.* Bks. Demand $126.90. ISBN 0-685-44420-1. Discusses Rousseau's contributions to the field of political science.
Miller, James. *Rousseau: Dreamer of Democracy.* Yale U. Pr. 1984 $30.00. ISBN 0-300-03044. Examines Rousseau's political idealism and his ideas on democracy.

TOCQUEVILLE, ALEXIS CHARLES HENRI CLÉREL DE. 1805–1859

French writer and politician Alexis de Tocqueville was born in Verneuil to an aristocratic Norman family. He entered the bar in 1825 and became an assistant magistrate at Versailles. In 1831 he was sent to the United States to report on the prison system. This journey produced a book called *On the Penitentiary System in the United States* (1833), as well as a much more significant work called *Democracy in America* (1835–40), a treatise on American society and its political system. Of all the commentaries on American government and politics by foreign visitors, none have been as perceptive and influential as those of Tocqueville. Indeed, many political scientists regard *Democracy in America* as the best analysis ever written of the social roots of American political arrangements. Active in French politics, Tocqueville also wrote *Old Regime and the Revolution* (1856), in which he argued that the Revolution of 1848 did not constitute a break with the past but merely accelerated a trend toward greater centralization of government. Tocqueville was an observant Catholic, and this has been cited as a reason why many of his insights, rather than being confined to a particular time and place, reach beyond to see a universality in all people everywhere.

BOOKS BY TOCQUEVILLE

Democracy in America. 1835–40. Ed. by Phillips Bradley. Knopf 1945 $49.50. ISBN 0-394-42186-8

Old Regime and the French Revolution. 1856. Ed. by J. P. Mayer and A. P. Kerr. Doubleday 1955 $7.95. ISBN 0-385-09260-1. Effects of the Revolution of 1848.

On the Penitentiary System in the United States. (coauthored with Gustave de Beaumont). 1833. Kelley 1970 repr. of 1833 ed. $59.50. ISBN 0-678-00670-9

BOOKS ABOUT TOCQUEVILLE

Boesche, Roger. *The Strange Liberalism of Alexis de Tocqueville.* Cornell Univ. Pr. 1987 $34.50. ISBN 0-8014-1964-6. An attempt to interpret Toqueville in the context of the nineteenth century.

Drescher, Seymour. *Dilemmas of Democracy: Tocqueville and Modernization.* Bks. Demand repr. of 1968 ed. $79.00. ISBN 0-317-26641-1. Analysis of Tocqueville's theory of democracy and its relation to modern democratic thought.

Goldstein, Doris S. *Trial of Faith: Religion and Politics in Tocqueville's Thought.* Elsevier 1975 $39.00. ISBN 0-685-15413-0. Examines the religious and political aspects of Tocqueville's thought.

Herr, Richard. *Tocqueville and the Old Regime.* Princeton U. Pr. 1962 o.p.

Jardin, Andre. *Tocqueville: A Biography.* Trans. by Lydia Davis. FS&G 1984 $35.00. ISBN 0-374-27836-9. An authoritative biography.

Lamberti, Jean-Claude. *Tocqueville and the Two Democracies.* HUP 1989 $50.00. ISBN 0-674-89435-9. Tocqueville seen in the context of the France and United States of his day.

Lively, Jack. *The Social and Political Thought of Alexis de Tocqueville.* OUP 1962 o.p.

Mayer, Jacob B. *Alexis de Tocqueville: A Biographical Study in Political Science.* Ayer 1979 repr. of 1972 ed. $14.00. ISBN 0-405-11716-7. Explores the contributions of Tocqueville to political theory through an analysis of his writings.

Reeves, Richard. *American Journey: Traveling with Tocqueville in Search of "Democracy in America."* S&S Trade 1982 $15.95. ISBN 0-671-24746-8. Recapitulating the earlier journey, the author stresses parallels and differences between Tocqueville's time and our own.

Zetterbaum, Marvin. *Tocqueville and the Problem of Democracy.* Bks. Demand 1967 $30.00. ISBN 0-318-35031-9. Analysis of Tocqueville's ideas on democracy and his criticisms of it.

CHAPTER 6

Psychology

Florence L. Denmark

The mind is at every stage a theatre of simultaneous possibilities.
—WILLIAM JAMES, *The Principles of Psychology*

Psychology as the search to understand human mind and behavior is very ancient, but the modern science of psychology began in the last quarter of the nineteenth century with WILLIAM WUNDT. He established the first psychology laboratory and trained students from all over the world in the new discipline. From Wundt's founding until the early twentieth century, psychology was subjective in orientation, concerned with the study of consciousness, using introspection (self-observation of mental events) as its major experimental method. In the early decades of this century, the subjective view of psychology was challenged by JOHN B. WATSON and other behaviorists, who insisted that, in order to be a science, psychology had to use the scientific method, and that required objective observation. Since each mind is necessarily private and accessible to only one person, the mind cannot be scientifically observed. They proposed instead to investigate behavior, public actions that can be objectively observed and recorded.

Until the middle of the twentieth century, behaviorism was the dominant position in American psychology. In its most extreme form, it discounted not only the importance but also the existence of mental life. In the work of such neobehaviorists as EDWARD TOLMAN and CLARK L. HULL, however, mental life was acknowledged, though considered qualitatively similar to overt behavior. Thus, there was (and is) a radical difference in psychology between those who held that psychology is the science of mind and those who maintained that it is the science of behavior. The psychoanalysis of SIGMUND FREUD (see also Vol. 5), for example, belongs to the first category and the radical behaviorism of B. F. SKINNER to the second. Where Freud laid supreme importance on the unconscious, seeing it as directing much of overt behavior, and claimed that only by probing this hidden entity could people's actions be understood, Skinner claimed just the opposite—that the laws that govern overt behavior are the same as those that govern mental events and that, if one knows the former, one will automatically know the latter.

The dominance of behaviorism began to wane during the late 1950s and 1960s, partly because it did not yield the understanding that the early behaviorists had promised. There had always been some psychologists who believed that the discipline should study *both* mind and behavior—indeed, that it could not claim to be a complete science unless it did so—and they became more numerous during the second half of the twentieth century. Still, the problem of integrating the two areas remains, and psychology does not yet have a paradigm—a philosophical and theoretical framework that establishes the fundamental nature of the field and that the majority of all psychologists subscribe to.

Despite this failure to establish a paradigm, psychology is a major academic discipline in its own right and has made enormous strides as a descriptive and interpretive discipline. It has yielded a variety of theoretical systems that have greatly enlarged our understanding of ourselves. It is the only one of the social sciences that focuses on the individual, offering rich insights into personality, individual development, intelligence, perception, learning, motivation, cognition, and aggression. The subfield of social psychology focuses on that area where psychology and sociology overlay; it studies the individual as a member of a social group and groups as influenced by the individual personality traits of their members. Physiological psychology studies the role of various organs in the body in different psychological phenomena (the role of the brain in memory, for example). Applied psychology studies ways in which psychology can solve problems; one of its branches, engineering psychology, is concerned mainly with the relationship between humans and machines and how productivity can be improved through better training and better machines. Clinical psychology and counseling psychology are concerned with the mental health or happiness of individuals.

HISTORY OF THE FIELD

Boring, Edwin G. *A History of Experimental Psychology*. P-H 2nd ed. 1950 $60.00. ISBN 0-13-390039-8. Classic history of experimental psychology by a pioneer in the field.
————, ed. *A History of Psychology in Autobiography*. Ed. by Gardner Lindzey. 8 vols. Stanford U. Pr. 1989 $52.50. ISBN 0-8047-1492-4. Autobiographical essays by leading psychologists who discuss the discipline, its history, and their personal and professional relation to it.
Evans, Rand B., and others, eds. *The American Psychological Association: A Historical Perspective*. Am. Psychol. 1992 $40.00. ISBN 1-55798-136-1. Documents the Association's evolution in response to intellectual, cultural, political, and economic developments.
Foucault, Michel. *Madness and Civilization: A History of Insanity in the Age of Reason*. Random 1988 $11.00. ISBN 0-679-72110-X. History of debates on insanity in Europe from the eighteenth century on, showing how notions of normality and madness were constructed.
Hergenhahn, B. R. *An Introduction to the History of Psychology*. Brooks-Cole 1992. ISBN 0-534-16812-4. Examines how cultural factors have influenced philosophical speculation on the mind by the Greeks, Renaissance scholars, and present-day psychologists.
Koch, Sigmund, and David E. Leary, eds. *A Century of Psychology As Science*. Am. Psychol. 1992 $49.95. ISBN 1-55798-171-X. Compendium of ideas from the first 100 years of psychological science.
Leahy, Thomas. *History of Modern Psychology*. P-H 1990 $40.00. ISBN 0-13-388521-6. Sets the field in a broad historical and social context that illuminates its role in modern society.
MacLeod, Robert B. *The Persistent Problems in Psychology*. Duquesne 1975 o.p.
Miller, George A., and Robert Buckhout. *Psychology: The Science of Mental Life*. HarpC 2nd ed. 1973 o.p. Examines the work of major contributors in defining the field and what psychologists do.
Murphy, Gardner, and Joseph K. Kovach. *Historical Introduction to Modern Psychology*. HarBraceJ 3rd ed. 1972 o.p. A history of the discipline from its antecedents in seventeenth-century Europe to the present.

Puente, A., J. Matthews, and C. Brewer, eds. *Teaching Psychology in America: A History*. Am. Psychol. 1992 $59.95. ISBN 1-55798-181-7

Rieber, R. W., and Kurt Salzinger, eds. *The Roots of American Psychology: Historical Influences and Implications for the Future*. NY Acad. Sci. 1977 $22.00. ISBN 0-89072-037-1

Smith, Samuel. *Ideas of the Great Psychologists*. HarpC 1983 o.p.

Watson, Robert I. *Basic Writings in the History of Psychology*. OUP 1979 $29.95. ISBN 0-19-502443-5. A collection of seminal articles on the human mind and its workings from Galileo to B. F. Skinner.

_____. *The Great Psychologists from Aristotle to Freud*. HarpC 4th ed. 1978 o.p. Discusses the works of psychologists from Aristotle to Freud.

SURVEYS OF THE FIELD

Annual Review of Psychology. Ed. by Lyman W. Porter and Mark R. Rosenzweig. Vol. 44 Annual Reviews 1993 $43.00. ISBN 0-8243-0244-3. Most recent issue continues the practice of combining regularly scheduled articles with those on timely topics. Reviews developments in various branches of psychology.

Deutsch, Morton. *Theories in Social Psychology*. Basic 1965 $13.95. ISBN 0-465-08435-4. With a foreword by Edwin G. Boring.

Evans, Rand B., and others. *The American Psychological Association: A Historical Perspective*. Am. Psychol. 1992 $40.00. ISBN 1-55798-136-1. Documents the Association's evaluation in response to current sociological developments.

Flanagan, Owen J. Jr. *The Science of the Mind*. MIT Pr. 1991 $15.95. ISBN 0-262-56056-9. New edition of this introduction to cognitive science and the philosophy of psychology brings recent developments in the theory of neuronal group selection and connectionism to bear on various problems connected with consciousness and identity.

Hampden-Turner, Charles. *Maps of the Mind*. Macmillan 1982 $16.95. ISBN 0-02-076870-2. Lively text accompanies illuminative, clearly drawn maps of the mind as depicted in the work of artists, philosophers, and psychologists from T'ai Chi, through Freud, to Martin Luther King Jr.

Kagan, Jerome, and Julius Segal. *Psychology: An Introduction*. HarBraceJ 6th ed. 1988 $42.75. ISBN 0-15-572639-0. Includes detailed coverage of behavior therapy, group approaches, and biological therapies.

Kimble, Daniel P. *Biological Psychology*. HarBraceJ 1992 $48.00. ISBN 0-03-040487-8. Substantially updated new edition.

Koch, Sigmund, and David E. Leary, eds. *A Century of Psychology As Science*. Am. Psychol. 1992 $49.95. ISBN 1-55798-171-X. A compendium of ideas from the first 100 years of psychological science.

Morris, Charles G. *Psychology: An Introduction*. P-H 6th ed. 1988. ISBN 0-13-734450-3. Venerable textbook for introductory college psychology courses.

Rosenberg, Morris, and Ralph H. Turner. *Social Psychology: Sociological Perspectives*. Transaction Pubs. 1990 $24.95. ISBN 0-88738-854-X. This text, by two sociologists, should be compared with a text by a psychologist, such as Morton Deutsch's *Theories in Social Psychology*. Both are sound, but the emphasis is different.

METHODS OF RESEARCH

Allport, Gordon W. *The Use of Personal Documents in Psychological Science*. Kraus repr. of 1942 ed. o.p.

Aronson, E., P. Ellsworth, J. Carlsmith, and M. Gonzales. *Methods of Research in Social Psychology*. McGraw 2nd ed. 1990 $35.43. ISBN 0-07-002466-9. Handily lays out how research is carried out in the various fields of social psychology.

Bakan, David. *On Method: Toward a Reconstruction of Psychological Investigation. Social and Behavioral Sciences Ser.* Bks. Demand repr. of 1974 ed. $51.30. ISBN 0-685-16091-2. Critiques experimental psychology and makes the case for empirical research-based approaches.

Bornstein, Marc H., ed. *Comparative Methods in Psychology. Crosscurrents in Contemporary Psychology Ser.* L. Erlbaum Assocs. 1980 $59.95. ISBN 0-89859-037-X. Various authors discuss psychological differences between humans and animals as well as cross-cultural differences.

Buchanan, Nina K., and John F. Feldhusen, eds. *Conducting Research and Evaluation in Gifted Education.* Tchrs. Coll. 1991 $49.95. ISBN 0-8077-3083-1. Provides a clear and complete explanation of the processes, methods, and tools available for use in studying and evaluating gifted students.

Christensen, Larry B. *Experimental Methodology.* Allyn 5th ed. 1991 $47.00. ISBN 0-205-12726-6. Describes key psychological methods that have lasted through time.

Dieckman, Hans. *Methods in Analytical Psychology: An Introduction.* Trans. by Borris Matthews. Chiron Pubns. 1991 $17.95. ISBN 0-933029-48-9. Written to specify technique in analytical (Jungian) psychotherapy.

Estes, W. K. *Statistical Methods in Psychological Research.* L. Erlbaum Assocs. 1991 $39.95. ISBN 0-8058-0688-1. Covers basic material on probability theory and basic concepts of statistical methods.

Robinson, J., P. Shaver, and L. Wrightsman. *Measures of Personality and Social Psychological Attitudes.* Acad. Pr. 1990 $54.95. ISBN 0-12-590244-1. Handy and exhaustive guide on the most effective use of statistics in psychology; for both professionals and general readers.

Weaver, Donald B., and others. *How to Do a Literature Search in Psychology.* Resource Pr. 1982 o.p. Excellent book on putting together a research project, bibliography, or grant proposal in the field of psychology.

REFERENCE BOOKS

American Psychiatric Association. *Biographical Directory of Fellows and Members.* 1941– Lists American psychiatrists with specialties, training, experience, etc.; geographical index. Latest volume is 1983.

American Psychological Association. *Biographical Directory.* 1970– Triennial publication. The 1981 edition lists 54,000 names of members, with data and geographical index.

Chaplin, J. P. *Dictionary of Psychology.* Dell 2nd rev. ed. 1985 $6.99. ISBN 0-440-31925-0

Corsini, Raymond J. ed. *Concise Encyclopedia of Psychology.* 4 vols. Wiley 1987 $89.95. ISBN 0-471010-68-5. A new, updated edition of the earlier 4-volume *Encyclopedia of Psychology* (1984).

Gregory, R., and O. L. Zangwill, eds. *The Oxford Companion to the Mind.* OUP 1987 $49.95. ISBN 0-19-866124-X. Dictionary approach to the human mind that comprises topical definitions and discussions by more than 100 authorities and scholars.

Lindzey, Gardner, and Elliott Aronson, eds. *The Handbook of Social Psychology.* 2 vols. L. Erlbaum Assocs. Vol. 1 1985 $70.00. ISBN 0-89859-718-8. Vol. 2 1985 $80.00. ISBN 0-89859-719-6. Articles, with bibliographies, on various aspects of social psychology, including theory, methodology, and new areas of research.

O'Connell, Agnes N., and Nancy Felipe Russo, eds. *Women in Psychology: A Bio-Bibliographic Sourcebook.* Greenwood 1990 $55.00. ISBN 0-313-26091-5. Biographies of 36 women prominent in psychology.

Pettijohn, Terry F., ed. *The Encyclopedic Dictionary of Psychology.* Dushkin Pub. 4th ed. 1991 $13.95. ISBN 0-87967-885-2. Provides easy access to substantial representation of the language, institutions, and practices unique to psychology.

Statt, David. *Dictionary of Psychology.* HarpC 1982 o.p. Provides clear, concise definitions of most terms used in different areas of psychology; with illustrations.

Thesaurus of Psychological Index Terms. Am. Psychol. 6th ed. 1991 $65.00. ISBN 1-55798-111-6. Contains some 230 new terms along with additional cross references and scope notes.

Wolman, Benjamin B., ed. *Dictionary of Behavioral Science*. Acad. Pr. 2nd ed. 1989 $59.00. ISBN 0-12-762455-4. New edition covers all fields of the behavioral sciences, including social work, anthropology, education, and human relations.

AGGRESSION

Berkowitz, Leonard. *Aggression: A Social Psychological Analysis*. McGraw 1962 o.p.
_____. *Aggression: Its Causes, Consequences, and Control*. McGraw 1992 $32.50. ISBN 0-07-004883-5. Discusses the social and psychological causes of aggression in the individual and society.

Campbell, Anne. *Men, Women, and Aggression*. Basic 1993 $22.00. ISBN 0-465-09217-9. Finds differences between men and women, affecting how each gender perceives situations.

Dollard, John, and Robert R. Sears. *Frustration and Aggression*. Greenwood 1980 repr. of 1939 ed. $35.00. ISBN 0-313-22201-0. Develops theory of aggression based on frustration and applies it to adolescence, criminality, political movements, and primitive society.

Geen. *Human Aggression*. Brooks-Cole 1991 $20.25. ISBN 0-534-15630-4. Defines aggression and summarizes the prevailing theoretical positions.

Groebel, J., and R. A. Hinde, eds. *Aggression and War: Their Biological and Social Bases*. Cambridge U. Pr. 1989 $16.95. ISBN 0-521-35871-X. Presents the main issues regarding the problem of human aggression, as well as human beliefs about the subject. Contributions range in complexity from the physiological to individual aggression, group conflict, and international war.

Lorenz, Konrad. *On Aggression*. Trans. by Marjorie K. Wilson. HarBraceJ 1974 $9.95. ISBN 0-15-668741-0. Controversial when first published, this is now a classic statement on the aggressive nature and behavior of human beings.

Milavsky, J. Ronald. *Television and Aggression: Results of a Panel Study*. Quantitative Studies in Social Relations Ser. Acad. Pr. 1982 $53.00. ISBN 0-12-495980-6. Exhaustive, somewhat technical study of the long-term impact of television violence on teenage boys.

Montagu, Ashley. *Man and Aggression*. OUP 2nd ed. 1973 o.p. Empirical and theoretical critiques of Lorenz's views on human aggression.

Prentky, R., and V. Quinsey. *Human Sexual Aggression*. NY Acad. Sc. 1988 o.p. Empirical studies by scholars in many disciplines on child molestation and rape, with discussion of legislation and other methods of preventing sexual crimes.

Scott, John P. *Aggression*. U. Ch. Pr. 2nd rev. ed. 1976 o.p. Explains aggression in both animals and humans as being caused by many factors and suggests ways of curbing aggressive behavior.

BIOLOGICAL BASES OF BEHAVIOR

Aronson, Eliot. *The Social Animal*. W. H. Freeman 6th ed. 1991 $29.95. ISBN 0-7167-2165-1. Argues for the relevance of social psychology for understanding contemporary society.

Caplan, David, ed. *Biological Studies of Mental Processes*. MIT Pr. 1980 o.p. Scholars from various science and social science disciplines examine the biological bases of human maturation and intellectual development.

Crawford, C., M. Smith, and D. Krebs, eds. *Sociobiology and Psychology: Ideas, Issues, and Findings*. L. Erlbaum Assocs. 1987 $59.95. ISBN 0-89859-580-0. Intended for general readers who want an introduction to sociobiological thought.

Darwin, Charles R. *The Expression of the Emotions in Man and Animals*. Greenwood 1969 repr. of 1955 ed. $35.00. ISBN 0-8371-2291-0. Fascinating study of the emotional life of animals, the insane, and infants (including Darwin's own baby) written in his erudite Victorian prose style.

Galluscio, Eugene H. *Biological Psychology*. Macmillan 1990. ISBN 0-02-340472-8. Discusses biological mechanisms underlying human behavior.

Goldsmith, T. *The Biological Roots of Human Nature: Forging Links Between Evolution and Behavior*. OUP 1991 $24.95. ISBN 0-19-506288-4. Attempts to clarify many of the issues that nonexperts find confusing about an evolutionary approach to behavior.

Gruter, Margaret. *Law and the Mind: Biological Origins of Human Behavior*. Sage 1991 $22.95. ISBN 0-8039-4046-7. Deals with ethology and its relationship to the origin of the law and of legal systems.

Lorenz, Konrad. *Evolution and Modification of Behavior*. U. Ch. Pr. 1986 repr. of 1965 ed. $9.95. ISBN 0-226-49334-2. Critique of the notion that human beings have innate characteristics and of the psychological theories based on that notion.

_____. *King Solomon's Ring*. Apollo Eds. NAL-Dutton 1991 $3.95. ISBN 0-451-62831-4. Charmingly written and illustrated description of the darker and lighter sides of animal behavior.

Mosekilde, E., and L. Mosekilde, eds. *Complexity, Chaos and Biological Evolution*. Plenum Pub. 1991 $110.00. ISBN 0-306-44026-1. Based on lectures by experts in theoretical biology, morphogenesis, evolution, artificial life, hormonal regulation, and population dynamics.

Nebylitsyn, V. D., and J. A. Gray, eds. *Biological Bases of Individual Behavior*. Acad. Pr. 1972 o.p.

Prothro, Edwin T., and P. T. Teska. *Psychology: A Biosocial Study of Behavior*. Greenwood 1972 repr. of 1950 ed. $35.00. ISBN 0-8371-6215-7. Easy-to-read text for those unfamiliar with the subject but interested in the practical and everyday issues of psychology.

Selye, Hans. *The Stress of My Life: A Scientist's Memoirs*. McGraw 2nd ed. 1978 o.p. Somewhat stiffly written autobiography by a Canadian scientist who was a pioneer in the study of stress.

Tinbergen, Nikolaas. *The Study of Instinct*. OUP 1990 $30.00. ISBN 0-19-857740-0. Chapters cover behavior as a response to stimuli and the neurophysiological bases of innate behavioral patterns in individuals.

Wilson, Edward O. *Sociobiology: The New Synthesis*. HUP 1975 $45.00. ISBN 0-674-81621-8. A rather controversial book by a biologist. Social scientists believe that he oversimplifies the relationship between biology and behavior.

COGNITION

Amsel, A. *Behaviorism, Neobehaviorism, and Cognitivism in Learning Theory: Historical and Contemporary Perspectives*. L. Erlbaum Assocs. 1988 $24.95. ISBN 0-8058-0332-7. Critiques the cognitive revolution in psychology from a neobehaviorist perspective.

Anderson, J. R., and G. H. Bower. *Human Associative Memory*. L. Erlbaum Assocs. 1980 $49.95. ISBN 0-89859-108-2

Bever, Thomas, and others, eds. *Talking Minds: The Study of Language in Cognitive Sciences*. MIT Pr. 1982 o.p. Essays on the relationships among language, thought, speech, and psychological processes.

Cole, Michael, and Barbara Means. *Comparative Studies of How People Think: An Introduction*. HUP 1981 $20.00. ISBN 0-674-15260-3. Theoretical work comparing cognitive processes across cultures.

Festinger, Leon. *A Theory of Cognitive Dissonance*. Stanford U. Pr. 1957 $35.00. ISBN 0-8047-0911-4. Discusses the social influences and causes of pessimism and fear.

Hunt, H. *The Multiplicity of Dreams: Memory, Imagination, and Consciousness*. Yale U. Pr. 1988 $32.00. ISBN 0-300-04330-9. Covers the diverse literature of dreams and assembles it coherently and clearly.

Izard, Carroll E. *Emotions, Cognition, and Behaviour*. Cambridge U. Pr. 1988 $34.95. ISBN 0-521-31246-9. Theoretical contributions on the study of emotions and cognitive processes in many different areas of psychology.

Luria, A. R. *Cognitive Development*. HUP 1976 $8.95. ISBN 0-674-13732-9. A Marxist account of the impact of cultural and socioeconomic factors on cognition and behavior.

Narmour, Eugene. *The Analysis and Cognition of Melodic Complexity*. U. Ch. Pr. 1992 $49.95. ISBN 0-226-56842-3. Constitutes a comprehensive theory of melody founded on psychological research. Extends unique theories of musical perception.

Pick, Herbert L. Jr., and others. *Cognition*. Am. Psychol. Assoc. 1992 $40.00. ISBN 1-55798-165-5. Raises conceptual and metatheoretical questions against a background of relevant empirical investigations.

Roloff, Michael E., and Charles R. Berger. *Social Cognition and Communication*. Bks. Demand repr. of 1982 ed. $85.30. ISBN 0-8357-4850-2. Specialized work that applies social cognition theories to examine inter- and intra-personal communication.

GROUPS

Argyle, Michael. *The Psychology of Interpersonal Behavior*. Viking Penguin rev. ed. 1985 o.p.

Bales, Robert F. *Interaction Process Analysis*. Midway Repr. Ser. U. Ch. Pr. 1951 o.p. Pioneering work on the theory and methods of small group interaction.

Bales, Robert F., and others. *Symlog: A System for the Multiple Level Observation of Groups*. Free Pr. 1979 $45.00. ISBN 0-02-901300-3. Introductory text on the use of symlog—a complex system for the study of groups and group interactions.

Cartwright, Dorwin, and Alvin Zander, eds. *Group Dynamics: Research and Theory*. HarpC 3rd ed. 1968 o.p. Considers how the scientific methods of psychology could be used to improve social life in democracies.

Forsyth, D. *Group Dynamics*. Brooks-Cole 2nd ed. 1990 $52.00. ISBN 0-534-08010-3. Reviews theories and research on inter-group and intra-group dynamics.

Hare, A. Paul. *Handbook of Small Group Research*. Macmillan 2nd ed. 1976 o.p. Explains different methods for applying psychological research to small groups.

Homans, George C. *The Human Group*. Transaction Pubs. 1992 $24.95. ISBN 1-56000-572-6. Attempts to formulate a general theory of social psychology based on the study of small groups.

――――. *Social Behavior: Its Elementary Forms*. HarBraceJ rev. ed. 1974 o.p. Behaviorist approach to the social functioning of both small and large groups.

Mills, Theodore M. *The Sociology of Small Groups*. P-H 2nd ed. 1984. ISBN 0-13-820910-3. Empirical and theoretical essays on the impact of personality, culture, the unconscious, and other factors on small groups.

Power, Margaret. *The Egalitarians, Human and Chimpanzee*. Cambridge U. Pr. 1991 $44.95. ISBN 0-521-40016-3. Discusses natural chimpanzee social organization as highly egalitarian. Author extends her thesis to human foraging societies.

Roethlisberger, F. J., and William J. Dickson. *Management and the Worker: An Account of a Research Program Conducted by Western Electric Co.* HUP 1939 $38.00. ISBN 0-674-54676-8. This study—which found that experimentally changing working conditions had less impact on workers' productivity than the mere fact of being studied and thus "paid attention to" (the so-called Hawthorne effect)—had an enormous impact on the social sciences, virtually creating the field of human relations in industry.

Scherzer, Kenneth A. *The Unbounded Community*. Duke 1992 $34.95. ISBN 0-8223-1228-X. Reveals the complex composition of neighborhoods that defy simple categorization by class or ethnicity.

Tubbs, S. *A Systems Approach to Small Group Interaction.* Random 4th ed. 1992 $21.18. ISBN 0-07-065407-7. Intended as a primary text on group communication; utilizes examples from business organizations.

Whyte, William F. *Street Corner Society: The Social Structure of an Italian Slum.* U. Ch. Pr. 4th ed. 1993 $40.00. ISBN 0-226-89544-0. Readable account of group interaction and social structure of a gang of Italian boys in a large metropolitan area.

Zander, Alvin. *Groups at Work: Unresolved Issues in the Study of Organizations. Social and Behavioral Sciences Ser.* Bks. Demand repr. of 1977 ed. $41.60. ISBN 0-8357-4927-4. Examines the functioning of small groups, drawing examples from business organizations.

INDIVIDUAL DEVELOPMENT

Baltes, Paul B., and K. Warner Schaie, eds. *Life-Span Developmental Psychology: Personality and Socialization.* Acad. Pr. 1973 o.p. Theoretical contributions on the impact of personality, gender, family, and society on individual development.

Blos, Peter. *On Adolescence: A Psychoanalytic Interpretation.* Free Pr. 1966 $19.95. ISBN 0-02-904320-4. Empirical and theoretical discussion of adolescence by a clinical psychoanalyst.

Bower, T. G. *Development in Infancy.* Freeman 2nd ed. 1982 o.p.

Brim, Orville G., Jr., and Jerome Kagan, eds. *Constancy and Change in Human Development.* HUP 1980 $45.00. ISBN 0-674-16625-6. Presents various critiques of the Freudian notion that childhood experiences determine all aspects of adult human behavior.

Elder, Glen H., Jr., ed. *Life Course Dynamics: Trajectories and Transitions, 1968–1980.* Cornell Univ. Pr. 1985 $42.50. ISBN 0-8014-9323-4

Erikson, Erik H. *Childhood and Society.* Norton 1986 $8.95. ISBN 0-393-30288-1. Cross-cultural study of how childhood affects subsequent social behavior among German, Russian, American and Native American children.

_____. *Identity and the Life Cycle.* Norton 1980 o.p. Three of Erikson's early papers focusing on adolescence, showing the origins of his thinking on the relation between life and life-history.

Gottlieb, Gilbert. *The Genesis of Novel Behavior: Individual Development and Evolution.* OUP 1991 $35.00. ISBN 0-19-506893-9. Treats the relationship between the growth of evolutionary ideas and ontogeny and genetics.

Grusec, J., and H. Lytton. *Social Development.* Spr.-Verlag 1992 $49.00. ISBN 0-387-96591-2. Provides an excellent overview of the social development of the young child.

Hall, G. Stanley. *Adolescence: Its Psychology and Its Relations to Physiology, Anthropology, Sociology, Sex, Crime, Religion and Education.* 2 vols. Telegraph Bks. 1981 repr. of 1905 ed. o.p.

Hareven, Tamara K., ed. *Transitions: The Family and the Life Course in Historical Perspectives. Studies in Social Discontinuity Ser.* Acad. Pr. 1978 o.p. Various contributors discuss stability and change within the contemporary Massachusetts family.

Horowitz, Francis D., ed. *Review of Child Development Research.* U. Ch. Pr. 1975 $25.00. ISBN 0-226-35353-2

Hurrelmann, Klaus. *Social Structure and Personality Development.* Cambridge U. Pr. 1988 $44.95. ISBN 0-521-35474-9. Analyzes concepts of human development that underlie the different sociological and psychological theories of personality development.

Kagan, Jerome, and Moss Howard. *From Birth to Maturity.* Yale U. Pr. 1983 o.p. A study of 89 children over a period of time; critiques the notion that childhood experiences influence adult behavior.

Kegan, Robert. *The Evolving Self: Problem and Process in Human Development.* HUP 1982 $10.95. ISBN 0-674-27231-5. Theoretical work on how individuals develop the concept of self and identity.

Lerner, Richard M., ed. *Developmental Psychology: Historical and Philosophical Perspectives.* L. Erlbaum Assocs. 1983 $49.95. ISBN 0-89859-247-X. Important and somewhat specialized papers on the origins, history, and current state of developmental psychology.

Maccoby, Eleanor E., ed. *The Development of Sex Differences.* Stanford U. Pr. 1966 o.p. Articles by biologists and psychologists on the causes and consequences of human sex difference.

Mead, Margaret. *Coming of Age in Samoa.* Morrow 1971 $12.50. ISBN 0-688-30974-7. Classic study of adolescence in an aboriginal society by the well-known anthropologist.

Mussen, P.H. *Carmichael's Manual of Child Psychology.* 2 vols. Wiley 3rd ed. 1970 o.p. Comprehensive account of the contemporary state of child psychology.

Piaget, Jean. *The Language and Thought of the Child.* Humanities 3rd ed. 1962 o.p. Uses a two-tiered model of a child's mind to explain how the young think, speak, and form judgments.

———. *The Moral Judgment of the Child.* Trans. by Marjorie Gabain. Free Pr. 1965 $15.95. ISBN 0-02-925240-7. Clinical investigation and explanation of children's ideas of justice, responsibility, equality, authority, and other moral issues.

Santrock, J. *Adolescence: An Introduction.* Brown & Benchmark 1993. ISBN 0-697-12752-4

INTELLIGENCE AND ARTIFICIAL INTELLIGENCE

Binet, Alfred. *The Psychology of Reasoning.* 1896. Routledge 1901 o.p. Early work on human reasoning based on hypnotic experiments.

Block, N. J., and Gerald Dworkin, eds. *The IQ Controversy.* Pantheon 1976 o.p. Specialized and general readings on the relationship between genetics and intelligence.

Boden, Margaret. *Artificial Intelligence and Natural Man.* Basic 1987 $17.00. ISBN 0-465-00456-3. Survey of the history of artificial intelligence and its relevance to human society.

Cancro, Robert, ed. *Intelligence: Genetic and Environmental Influences.* Saunders 1971 o.p.

Gardner, Howard. *Creating Minds.* Basic 1993 $30.00. ISBN 0-465-01455-0. Discusses Freud, Einstein, and Picasso and the qualitative aspects of "genius."

———. *Frames of Mind: The Theory of Multiple Intelligences.* Basic 1983 $23.50. ISBN 0-465-02508-0. Argues that intelligence cannot be tested since competence is manifold and varies across cultures and skills.

Gould, Stephen J. *The Mismeasure of Man.* Norton 1983 $9.95. ISBN 0-393-30056-0. Critique of existing works on intelligence testing by the well-known scientist; approached from the perspective that environmental factors condition intelligence.

Guilford, Joy P. *The Nature of Human Intelligence. Psychology Ser.* McGraw 1967 o.p.

Jensen, Arthur R. *Bias in Mental Testing.* Free Pr. 1980 $35.00. ISBN 0-02-916430-3. Very technical argument to demonstrate that IQ testing is objective and unbiased.

Kail, Robert V., and J. W. Pellegrino. *Human Intelligence: Perspectives and Prospects.* W. H. Freeman 1985 $15.95. ISBN 0-7167-1689-5. Covers the three main approaches to the study of human intelligence—the psychometric, information-processing, and Piagetian structural developmental approaches.

Klineberg, Otto. *Race Differences.* Greenwood 1974 repr. of 1935 ed. $45.00. ISBN 0-8371-7519-4

Kurzweil, Ray. *Age of Intelligent Machines.* MIT Pr. 1992 $24.95. ISBN 0-262-61079-5. Named Most Outstanding Computer Science Book of 1990.

Loehlin, John C., and J. N. Spuhler. *Race Differences in Intelligence. Psychology Ser.* W. H. Freeman 1975 o.p. Argues that environmental rather than genetic factors determine intelligence.

Rowe, H., ed. *Intelligence: Reconceptualization and Measurement.* L. Erlbaum Assocs. 1991 $49.95. ISBN 0-8058-0942-2

Schank, Roger C., and Peter G. Childers. *The Cognitive Computer: On Language, Learning and Artificial Intelligence.* Addison-Wesley 1985 $17.95. ISBN 0-201-06446-4. Discusses human and machine intelligence and how the latter would change the world.

Simon, Herbert A. *Sciences of the Artificial.* MIT Pr. 2nd ed. 1981 $9.95. ISBN 0-262-69073-X. Argues that psychology is an "artificial" science which can be used to enhance the efficiency of business organizations.

Sternberg, R. *Metaphors of Mind: Conceptions of the Nature of Intelligence.* Cambridge U. Pr. 1990 $47.95. ISBN 0-521-35579-6. Offers a discussion of the wide array of metaphors that researchers have used for intelligence.

LEARNING AND MOTIVATION

Arnold, William J., and Monte M. Page, eds. *Nebraska Symposium on Motivation.* U. of Nebr. Pr. 1968 $27.95. ISBN 0-8032-0610-1. Various contributors discuss recent developments in the psychology of motivation.

Atkinson, John W. *An Introduction to Motivation.* Van Nos. Reinhold 2nd ed. o.p. Argues that motivation is based on achievement rather than needs or emotions.

Bandura, Albert, and R. H. Walters. *Social Learning and Personality Development.* H. Holt & Co. 1963 o.p. Socio-behaviorist explanation of learning and how it modifies human conduct; stresses the role of imitation.

Bower, Gordon H., and Ernest J. Hilgard. *Theories of Learning.* P-H 5th ed. 1981 $50.00. ISBN 0-13-914432-3. Theoretical work on the development of cognitive capacity in infants and the impact of the psychological environment on this process.

Bruner, Jerome S. *On Knowing: Essays for the Left Hand.* HUP 1979 $19.95. ISBN 0-674-63525-6

Dunn, Rita, and others. *The Giftedness in Every Child.* Wiley 1992 $19.95. ISBN 0-471-52803-X. Hopes to help parents identify the giftedness, or talents which each child possesses.

Estes, William K., ed. *Models of Learning, Memory and Choice: Selected Papers.* Greenwood 1982 $45.00. ISBN 0-275-90786-4

Frager, Robert, and James Fadiman. *Maslow's Motivation and Personality.* HarpC 3rd ed. 1990 $31.50. ISBN 0-06-041987-3. Presents a positive view of human nature through a discussion of motivation in terms of basic needs.

Gagné, Robert M. *The Conditions of Learning and Theories of Instruction.* HarBraceJ 1985 $41.25. ISBN 0-03-063688-4. Classic theoretical work on learning.

Hergenhahn, B. *An Introduction to Theories of Learning.* P-H 1988. ISBN 0-13-498569-9

McClelland, David C., and others. *The Achievement Motive. Century Psychology Ser.* Irvington 1985 $42.50. ISBN 0-8290-1167-6. Summarizes the state of research related to the concept of motivation.

———. *The Achieving Society. Social Relations Ser.* Free Pr. 1967 $18.95. ISBN 0-02-920510-7. Interdisciplinary work on the social bases of achievement, the need for which increases with rapid rates of economic growth.

Maslow, A., and R. Frager. *Motivation and Personality.* HarpC 1987 o.p.

Medin, Doug., ed. *The Psychology of Learning and Motivation.* Acad. Pr. 1992 $59.95. ISBN 0-12-543328-X. Contains seven papers examining topics in the field of cognition encompassing learning, conditioning, and memory. Highly detailed and heavily referenced.

Milgram, Stanley. *Obedience to Authority: An Experimental View.* HarpC 1983 $11.00. ISBN 0-06-131983-X. Seeks to explain how and why people willingly obey authority.

Miller, Neal E., and John Dollard. *Social Learning and Imitation*. Greenwood 1979 repr. of 1962 ed. $35.00. ISBN 0-313-20714-3. Combines psychological and other social science methods to examine learning in humans and animals.

Pavlov, Ivan P. *Conditioned Reflexes: An Investigation of the Physiological Activity of the Cerebral Cortex*. Ed. by G. V. Anrep. Dover repr. of 1927 ed. $9.95. ISBN 0-486-60614-7. Revised version of the author's celebrated lectures on conditioned reflexes in dogs.

Piaget, Jean. *Play, Dreams and Imitation in Childhood*. Peter Smith 1988 $19.50. ISBN 0-8446-6320-4

Skinner, B. F. *The Behavior of Organisms: Experimental Analysis*. P-H 1966 o.p. Classic behaviorist text on animal and human behavior.

Smith, Charles P., ed. *Motivation and Pesonality: A Handbook of Thematic Content Analysis*. Cambridge U. Pr. 1992 $ 69.95. ISBN 0-521-40052-X

Spence, Kenneth W., ed. *The Psychology of Learning and Motivation: Advances in Research and Theory*. Acad. Pr. Vol. 1 1967 o.p. Vol. 2 1968. ISBN 0-12-543302-6. Vol. 3. ISBN 0-12-543303-4. Vol. 4 1970. ISBN 0-12-543304-2. Vol. 5 1972. ISBN 0-12-543305-0. Vol. 6 1972. ISBN 0-12-543306-9. Vol. 7 1973. ISBN 0-12-543307-7. Vol. 8 1974. ISBN 0-12-543308-5. Vol. 9 1975. ISBN 0-12-543309-3. Vol. 10 1976. ISBN 0-12-543310-7. Vol. 11 1977 o.p. Vol. 12 1978. ISBN 0-12-543312-3. Vol. 13 1977. ISBN 0-12-543311-5. Vol. 14 1980. ISBN 0-12-543314-X. Annual publication that reviews theoretical and research developments in the field.

Tarde, Gabriel. *The Laws of Imitation*. Peter Smith $13.25. ISBN 0-8446-1442-4

Watson, John B. *Behaviorism*. Norton 1970 repr. of 1930 ed. $9.95. ISBN 0-393-00524-0. Classic and controversial work; argues that observable and verifiable behavior leads to a better understanding of the psyche than speculations on consciousness and the unconscious.

Wilson, Edward O. *Sociobiology: The New Synthesis*. HUP 1975 $45.00. ISBN 0-674-81621-8. Controversial text that argues that human behavior is biologically rather than environmentally determined.

OPINIONS, ATTITUDES, AND BELIEFS

Allport, Gordon W. *The Nature of Prejudice*. Addison 1979 $7.64. ISBN 0-201-00178-0. Classic work on the nature of prejudice.

Allport, Gordon W., and Leo Postman. *The Psychology of Rumor*. Russell 1965 repr. of 1947 ed. o.p. Discusses rumor-mongering and the social and emotional needs this serves.

Duckitt, John. *The Social Psychology of Prejudice*. Greenwood 1992 $49.95. ISBN 0-275-94241-4. Reviews many literatures in an interdisciplinary approach.

Gillet, Richard. *Change Your Mind, Change Your World*. S&S Trade 1992 $11.00. ISBN 0-671-73538-1. Discusses beliefs that influence behavior, moods, relationships, and perceptions.

Hovland, Carl I., and Harold H. Kelley. *Communication and Persuasion: Psychological Studies of Opinion Change*. Greenwood 1982 repr. of 1953 ed. $47.50. ISBN 0-313-23348-9. Examines how and why people change their minds and who influences such changes.

Lewin, Kurt. *Resolving Social Conflicts*. Ed. by Gertrude W. Lewin. Intl. Spec. Bk. 1978 o.p. Analyzes the nature and causes of conflict in the family, factory, and society; argues that psychological methods can help reduce conflict.

Plous, S. *The Psychology of Judgment and Decision Making*. McGraw 1993 $12.75. ISBN 0-07-050477-6. Theoretical discussion of how people make decisions in everyday life.

Zimbardo, P., and M. Leippe. *The Psychology of Attitude Change and Social Influence*. Temple U. Pr. 1991 $44.95. ISBN 0-87722-852-3. Provides a comprehensive summary of experimental research in the field of attitude change and social influence.

PERCEPTION

Arnheim, Rudolf. *Art and Visual Perception: A Psychology of the Creative Eye—The New Version.* U. CA. Pr. 2nd rev. ed. 1974 $37.50. ISBN 0-520-02327-7. Applies gestalt psychology to the study of visual perception and the criticism of art.

Boff, K., L. Kaufman, and J. Thomas, eds. *Handbook of Perception and Human Performance.* 2 vols. Wiley 1986. Vol. 1 *Sensory Processes and Perception.* $125.00. ISBN 0-471-88544-4. Vol. 2 *Cognitive Processes and Performance.* $145.95. ISBN 0-471-82957-9. Encyclopedic coverage of experimental psychology for the professional.

Carterette, Edward C., and Morton P. Friedman, eds. *Handbook of Perception.* 10 vols. Acad. Pr. Vol. 1 1974 $50.00. ISBN 0-12-161901-X. Vol. 2 1974 $81.00 ISBN 0-12-161902-8. Vol. 3. o.p. Vol. 4 o.p. Vol. 5 1975 $81.00. ISBN 0-12-161905-2. Vol. 6 Pt. 1 1978 $81.00. ISBN 0-12-161906-0; Pt. 2 1978 $81.00. ISBN 0-12-161922-2. Vol. 7 1976 $81.00. ISBN 0-12-161907-9. Vol. 8 1978 $81.00. ISBN 0-12-161908-7. Vol. 9 1978 $81.00. ISBN 0-12-161909-5. Vol. 10 1978 $81.00. ISBN 0-12-161910-9

Gibson, James J. *The Senses Considered as Perceptual Systems.* Greenwood 1983 repr. of 1966 ed. $62.50. ISBN 0-313-23961-4

Humphreys, Glyn W., ed. *Understanding Vision.* Blackwell Pubs. 1992. ISBN 0-631-17908-9. Presents current work in computer science, neuropsychology, cognitive science, and artificial intelligence relevant to vision research.

Koffka, Kurt. *Principles of Gestalt Psychology.* HarBraceJ 1967 o.p. Classic and somewhat polemical statement by one of the originators of the field of gestalt psychology.

Kohler, Wolfgang. *Gestalt Psychology.* Norton 1992 repr. of 1970 ed. $10.95. ISBN 0-87140-218-1

Marks, Lawrence, E. *Sensory Processes: The New Psychophysics.* Acad. Pr. 1974 $48.00. ISBN 0-12-472950-9. Explains and theorizes the application of psychophysics to the study of sensory processes.

Rock, Irvin. *The Logic of Perception.* MIT Pr. 1983 $14.95. ISBN 0-262-68045-9

Smith, B., ed. *Foundations of Gestalt Theory.* Philosophia Pr. 1988 $119.00. ISBN 3-88405-060-5. Discussions of the history, explicative potential, and current state of gestalt psychology.

Wade, Nicholas J., and Michael Swanston. *Visual Perception: An Introduction.* Routledge 1991 $59.95. ISBN 0-415-01042-X. Describes the perception of location motion, and object recognition, as well as the machinery of vision.

PERSONALITY

Abramson, Jeffrey. *Liberation and Its Limits: The Moral and Political Thought of Freud.* Free Pr. 1984 $19.95. ISBN 0-02-900210-9. Argues that Freud, despite his critics, was not a rabid individualist but had a notion of community.

Adorno, T. W., and others. *The Authoritarian Personality.* Norton 1983 $12.95. ISBN 0-393-30042-0. Monumental study of prejudice, written after the Holocaust, that seeks to explain the personality traits that characterize fascism, paranoia, and anti-Semitism.

Allport, Gordon W. *Personality: A Psychological Interpretation.* H. Holt & Co. 1937 o.p. Early work aimed at defining the psychology of personality; emphasizes what makes individuals different rather than what they have in common.

———. *Personality and Social Encounter: Selected Essays.* U. Ch. Pr. 1981 repr. of 1960 ed. o.p.

Clark, Margaret S., ed. *Emotion.* Sage 1992 $44.00. ISBN 0-8039-4613-9. Reflects the keen interest in emotional phenomena shown in recent years by U.S. psychology researchers.

Drapela, Victor J. *A Review of Personality Theories.* C. C. Thomas 1987 $26.50. ISBN 0-398-05281-6

Grunbaum, Adolf. *The Foundations of Psychoanalysis: A Philosophical Critique*. U. CA Pr. 1984 $35.00. ISBN 0-520-05016-9. Critiques the clinical credentials of Freud and argues that Freudian psychoanalysis is fatally flawed.

Hall, Calvin S. *A Primer of Freudian Psychology*. NAL-Dutton 1955 $4.99. ISBN 0-451-62625-7. Handy and easy-to-read introduction to the basic concepts of Freudian psychoanalysis.

Josephs, Lawrence. *Character Structure and the Organization of Self*. Col. U. Pr. 1992 $50.00. ISBN 0-231-07312-7. Reviews the psychoanalytic theory of character structure from Freud to Klein to Kohut, and proposes an integrative model of the organization of the self.

Lasswell, Harold D. *Power and Personality*. Greenwood 1976 repr. of 1948 ed. $49.50. ISBN 0-8371-8374-X. Discusses the relation between power and personality in both democratic and authoritarian societies.

Laufer, William S., and James M. Day, eds. *Personality Theory, Moral Development, and Criminal Behavior*. Lexington Bks. 1983 o.p.

Liebert, R., and M. Spiegler. *Personality: Strategies and Issues*. Brooks-Cole 1990 $50.00. ISBN 0-534-12228-0. Examines the four most commonly used strategies in the study of personality.

Lindzey, Gardner, and Martin Manosevitz, eds. *Theories of Personality: Primary Sources and Research*. Krieger 1988 repr. of 1973 ed. $43.50. ISBN 0-89464-254-5. Discusses major ancient and modern theories of human personality, both Eastern and Western.

Murray, H. A. *Explorations in Personality*. Wiley 1938 o.p. Psychoanalytic study of personality based on a research study of young men called "personology."

Rieff, Philip. *Freud: The Mind of the Moralist*. U. Ch. Pr. 3rd ed. 1979 $19.95. ISBN 0-226-71639-2. Witty and well-known work on the cultural importance of Freud and his thought.

Shakow, David, and David Rapaport. *The Influence of Freud on American Psychology*. *Psychological Issues Monographs*. Intl. Univs. Pr. 1964 $35.00. ISBN 0-8236-2656-3. Detailed account of the reception of Freud's ideas in the United States and their impact on the field of psychology and psychoanalysis.

PSYCHOLOGY OF WOMEN

Adler, Leonore L. *Women in Cross-Cultural Perspective*. Greenwood 1991 $47.95. ISBN 0-275-93658-9

Lott, B. *Women's Lives: Themes and Variations in Gender Learning*. Brooks-Cole 1987 $26.75. ISBN 0-534-07440-5. Explores ways in which gender is learned and maintained by girls and women in the United States.

Matlin, Margaret. *The Psychology of Women*. HarBraceJ 1987 $24.75. ISBN 0-03-063409-1

Paludi, Michele A. *The Psychology of Women*. Brown & Benchmark 1992. ISBN 0-697-11499-6.

Sayers, Janet. *Mothers of Psychoanalysis: Helene Deutsch, Karen Horney, Anna Freud, Melanie Klein*. Norton 1991 $24.95. ISBN 0-393-03041-5. Interweaves biography, psychological analysis, and interpretation of each woman's theories.

Schuker, Eleanor, and Nadine Levinson. *Female Psychology*. Analytic Pr. 1991 $59.95. ISBN 0-88163-087-X. Covers more than 2,000 articles, essays, and books from the psychoanalytic literature and related disciplines.

Sherman, J. *On the Psychology of Women: A Survey of Empirical Studies*. C. C. Thomas 1971 o.p.

Sherman, J., and Florence L. Denmark, eds. *The Psychology of Women: Future Directions in Research*. Psych. Dimensions 1979 $59.95. ISBN 0-88437-009-7

Unger, Rhoda K., and M. Crawford. *Women and Gender: A Feminist Psychology*. Temple U. Pr. 1991 $39.95. ISBN 0-87722-897-3. Analyzes the impact of gender at the individual, interpersonal, and cultural levels.

Unger, Rhoda K., and Florence L. Denmark, eds. *Woman: Dependent or Independent Variable?* Psych. Dimensions 1975 $39.95. ISBN 0-88437-000-3

CHRONOLOGY OF AUTHORS

Wundt, Wilhelm. 1832–1920
James, William. 1842–1910
Hall, G(ranville) Stanley. 1844–1924
Ladd-Franklin, Christine. 1847–1930
Pavlov, Ivan Petrovich. 1849–1936
Freud, Sigmund. 1856–1939
Binet, Alfred. 1857–1911
Calkins, Mary. 1863–1930
Washburn, Margaret. 1871–1939
Watson, John B(roadus). 1878–1958
Hull, Clark L(eonard). 1884–1952
Horney, Karen. 1885–1952
Hollingworth, Leta. 1886–1939
Tolman, Edward. 1886–1959

Lewin, Kurt. 1890–1947
Piaget, Jean. 1896–1980
Wechsler, David. 1896–1981
Allport, Gordon W(illard). 1897–1967
Klineberg, Otto. 1899–1992
Erikson, Erik H(omburger). 1902–
Rogers, Carl. 1902–1987
Lorenz, Konrad. 1903–1989
Skinner, B(urrhus) F(rederic).
   1904–1990
Tinbergen, Nikolaas. 1907–
Anastasi, Anne. 1908–
Miller, Neal E(dgar). 1909–

ALLPORT, GORDON W(ILLARD). 1897–1967

Gordon W. Allport, the chief founder of the psychological study of personality and the informal dean of American psychologists during his lifetime, was born in Montezuma, Indiana. He came East to study at Harvard University, and, while doing social work as an undergraduate, discovered that, in order to help people deal effectively with their problems, he needed a lifelike psychology of human personality. Developing a full-bodied theory of personality that would do justice to the attitudes, values, and traits of the unique individual life became his goal. After graduating from Harvard in 1919, he studied in Germany and traveled in Europe. At the age of 22, he managed a meeting with SIGMUND FREUD (see also Vol. 5) in Vienna, at which Freud mistook his nervous attempt to strike up a conversation by relating an incident he had just witnessed on a train for a confession of his own childhood trauma. This helped convince Allport that depth psychology often erred in slighting manifest motives in favor of probing the unconscious for hidden motives.

When he returned to the United States in 1924, Allport was appointed to a teaching position at Harvard, where he remained for most of his career. His research on attitudes, values, religion, group conflict, and prejudice, as well as his extensive writings on what he called an "open system" of personality, are quoted extensively in the contemporary literature of psychology.

BOOKS BY ALLPORT

The Nature of Prejudice. 1954. Addison-Wesley 1979 $12.45. ISBN 0-201-00179-9. Explores the role of prejudice in social interactions and suggests ways in which it might be eliminated.

Personality: A Psychological Interpretation. H. Holt & Co. 1937 o.p. Allport's introductory work on personality.

Personality and Social Encounter: Selected Essays. U. Ch. Pr. 1981 repr. of 1960 ed. o.p. This collection illustrates Allport's idea of the dynamic personality that is shaped by its environment.

The Psychology of Rumor. (coauthored with Leo Postman). Russell 1965 repr. of 1947 ed. o.p. Examines the way in which rumors develop; based on clinical studies.

The Use of Personal Documents in Psychological Science. Kraus repr. of 1942 ed. o.p. Traces the psychological use of personal documents from its emergence to its establishment as a method in its own right.

BOOKS ABOUT ALLPORT

Evans, Richard I. *Dialogue with Gordon Allport.* Greenwood 1981 $39.95. ISBN 0-275-90615-9. This dialogue with psychologist Evans serves as a good introduction to Allport's ideas.

————. *Gordon Allport: The Man and His Ideas.* NAL-Dutton 1971 o.p.

ANASTASI, ANNE. 1908–

Anne Anastasi is an American psychologist who has achieved a worldwide reputation as an authority on psychological testing, especially the evaluation and interpretation of intelligence testing, "culture-free" testing, and the methodological problems of test development. She is also noted for her proposed resolution of the long-standing nature-nurture controversy in psychology, stating that they are mutually influencing interactions. She has advanced the development of psychology as a quantitative behavioral science and made highly significant contributions to our knowledge about psychological traits and the experiential and environmental influences on development. In 1972 Anastasi became the third woman to be elected president of the American Psychological Association; she was honored with the organization's Gold Medal Award in 1984. President Ronald Reagan presented her with the National Medal of Science in 1987 in recognition of her numerous scientific achievements.

BOOKS BY ANASTASI

Differential Psychology. Macmillan 1958 o.p. Anastasi's major work on the reasons for the wide variety of human behavior.

Fields of Applied Psychology. McGraw 1979 $36.25. ISBN 0-07-001602-X

Psychological Testing. Macmillan 6th ed. 1989. ISBN 0-02-303020-8. Anastasi explains the workings of psychological tests and offers ways in which their results should be interpreted.

BINET, ALFRED. 1857–1911

Alfred Binet, a French psychologist, is best known for his applied research on intelligence. He initially worked on pathological psychology, which was the major psychological specialty in France, writing on such topics as hysteria. In 1891, however, he turned to experimental psychology and established it as a subdiscipline. In 1905, at his suggestion, the Ministry of Education considered setting up special classes for mentally abnormal children. In order to determine which children could not profit from normal instruction, Binet and Theodore Simon proposed a series of 30 intelligence tests. These tests were immediately successful and assured Binet's fame. A subsequent refinement of the tests by Lewis M. Terman, the Stanford-Binet Intelligence Scale, is still in use today. Binet was one of the originators of the questionnaire method. He also studied the psychology of arithmetic prodigies and chess players and pioneered the study of small groups.

BOOKS BY BINET

Alterations of Personality. 1892. Trans. by Helen G. Baldwin. Greenwood 1977 repr. of 1896 ed. $75.00. ISBN 0-313-26944-0

On Double Consciousness. Open Court 1899 o.p. Series of articles that looks at states of double consciousness and double personality in hysterical subjects.
The Psychology of Reasoning. 1896. Routledge 1901 o.p.

BOOKS ABOUT BINET

Pollock, R. H., and Margaret J. Brenner, eds. *The Experimental Psychology of Alfred Binet.* Springer 1969 o.p.
Wolf, Theta H. *Alfred Binet.* U. Ch. Pr. 1973 $20.00. ISBN 0-226-90498-9. Authoritative biography of the founder of scientific psychology in France.

CALKINS, MARY (WHITON). 1863–1930

Mary Whiton Calkins, an American psychologist and philosopher, is best known for her system of self-psychology and her invention of the paired-association experimental technique for studying memory, which is still taught in research classes today. Calkins attended Smith College, where she studied philosophy and the classics, and then taught Greek at Wellesley College. After she became interested in psychology, she managed to gain access to Harvard University's psychology seminars and laboratory, but, although her professors considered her a brilliant student, she was denied a Ph.D. by the university solely because she was a woman. Undeterred, she pursued her psychological investigations as a faculty member of Wellesley, where in 1891 she founded one of the earliest psychological laboratories in the United States. Calkins challenged the then dominant doctrine that the empirical study of human psychology should be confined to elemental sensations, emotions, and images. Her personalistic theory of the self posited that each person possesses a complex, unitary, and unique self that is obviously present in conscious experience. She spent 40 productive years at Wellesley and became the first woman president of the American Psychological Association.

BOOKS BY CALKINS

Essays, Principles, Dialogues: With Selections from Other Writings. Scribner 1929 o.p. A collection that examines the possibility of an idealistic philosophy existing in the modern age.
The Good Man and the Good: An Introduction to Ethics. 1918. AMS Pr. 1975 $24.50. ISBN 0-404-59090-X

BOOKS ABOUT CALKINS

O'Connell, Agnes N., and Nancy F. Russo, eds. *Women in Psychology.* Greenwood 1990 $55.00. ISBN 0-313-26091-5
Puente, Antonio E., Janet R. Matthews, and Charles L. Brewer, eds. *Teaching Psychology in America: A History.* Am. Psychol. 1992 $59.95. ISBN 1-55798-181-7

ERIKSON, ERIK H(OMBURGER). 1902–

Erik H. Erikson, a German-born American psychologist and psychoanalyst, developed theories concerning the sequence of human development that have had an impact on clinical psychoanalysis, ethics, history, literature, child care, and the emerging interdisciplinary study of the life course. Erikson began as an art student, but after undergoing psychoanalysis by ANNA FREUD (see Vol. 5) in Vienna in 1927, he turned to the field of psychology. According to Erikson's life-cycle theory, first published in *Childhood and Society* (1950), there are eight developmental stages, which are biologically determined but environmentally shaped: infancy, early childhood, play age, school age, adolescence, young adulthood, mature adulthood, and old age. Each of these stages is associated with a particular crisis that the individual must successfully resolve in order to proceed normally to the next stage—for example, identity versus confusion in adolescence. The concept of the identity crisis is now firmly embedded in psychiatric theory. Erikson also studied the relationship between a person's life and the times in which he or she lives; and his historical-biographical studies of LUTHER (see Vol. 4), and GANDHI (see Vol. 4) are outstanding products of this inquiry. For 30 years, Erikson taught at Harvard University.

BOOKS BY ERIKSON

Childhood and Society. 1950. Norton 1986 $8.95. ISBN 0-393-30288-1

Gandhi's Truth: On the Origins of Militant Nonviolence. 1969 Norton 1970 $5.95. ISBN 0-393-00741-3. Historical-biographical study of the great Indian leader Mohandas Gandhi.

Identity and the Life Cycle. 1959. Norton 1980 $4.95. ISBN 0-393-00949-1. Erikson outlines his major theories on identity and self-knowledge.

Insight and Responsibility. Norton 1964 $8.95. ISBN 0-393-09451-0

Themes of Work and Love in Adulthood. (coedited with Neil J. Smelser). HUP 1980 $24.95. ISBN 0-674-87750-0

Toys and Reasons: Stages in the Ritualization of Experience. Norton 1977 o.p. Explores the relationship between childhood play and political imagination.

Young Man Luther. 1958. Norton 1962 $5.95. ISBN 0-393-00170-9. Erikson puts forth his theory of identity crisis in the context of the young Luther and his times.

BOOKS ABOUT ERIKSON

Coles, Robert. *Erik Erikson: The Growth of His Work.* Da Capo 1987 $12.95. ISBN 0-306-80291-0. Intellectual biography that looks at the psychological and historical research and the ethical reflections of Erikson as clinician.

Evans, Richard I. *Dialogue with Erik Erikson: And Reactions from Ernest Jones.* Greenwood 1981 $38.50. ISBN 0-275-90613-2.

Gross, Francis L., Jr. *Introducing Erik Erikson: An Invitation to His Thinking.* U. Pr. of Amer. 1987 $17.50. ISBN 0-8191-5789-9. A plain-spoken introduction to Erikson's work, with emphasis on his *Childhood and Society.*

Roazen, Paul. *Erik H. Erikson: The Power and Limits of a Vision.* Free Pr. 1976 $15.95. ISBN 0-02-926450-2. Comprehensive examination of all of Erikson's writings, covering criticisms of his views of femininity and his responses to those criticisms.

Stevens, Richard. *Erik Erikson: An Introduction.* St. Martin 1983 $10.95. ISBN 0-312-25811-9. Comprehensive introduction to Erikson's psychoanalytic thought that explains and examines different aspects of his theories.

FREUD, SIGMUND. 1856–1939

Sigmund Freud was the founder of psychoanalysis, simultaneously a theory of personality, a therapy, and an intellectual movement. He was born into a middle-class Jewish family in Freiburg, Moravia, now part of Czechoslovakia, but then a city in the Austro-Hungarian Empire. At the age of 4, he moved to Vienna, where he spent nearly his entire life. In 1873 he entered the medical school at the University of Vienna and spent the following eight years pursuing a wide range of studies, including philosophy, in addition to the medical curriculum. After graduating, he worked in several clinics and went to Paris to study under Jean-Martin Charcot, a neurologist who used hypnosis to treat the symptoms of hysteria. When Freud returned to Vienna and set up practice as a clinical neurologist, he found orthodox therapies for nervous disorders ineffective for most of his patients, so he began to use a modified version of the hypnosis he had learned under Charcot. Gradually, however, he discovered that it was not necessary to put patients into a deep trance; rather, he would merely encourage them to talk freely, saying whatever came to mind without self-censorship, in order to bring unconscious material to the surface, where it could be analyzed. He found that this method of free association very often evoked memories of traumatic events in childhood, usually having to do with sex. This discovery led him, at first, to assume that most of his patients had actually been seduced as children by adult relatives and that this was the cause of their neuroses; later, however, he changed his mind and concluded that his patients' memories of childhood seduction were fantasies born of their childhood sexual desires for adults. (This reversal is a matter of some controversy today.) Out of this clinical material he constructed a theory of psychosexual development through oral, anal, phallic and genital stages.

Freud considered his patients' dreams—and his own—to be "the royal road to the unconscious." In *The Interpretation of Dreams* (1900), perhaps his most brilliant book, he theorized that dreams are heavily disguised expressions of deep-seated wishes and fears and can give great insight into personality. These investigations led him to his theory of a three-part structure of personality: the id (unconscious biological drives, especially for sex), the superego (the conscience, guided by moral principles), and the ego (the mediator between the id and superego, guided by reality).

Freud's last years were plagued by severe illness and the rise of Nazism, which regarded psychoanalysis as a "Jewish pollution." Through the intervention of the British and U.S. governments, he was allowed to emigrate in 1938 to England, where he died 15 months later, widely honored for his original thinking. His theories have had a profound impact on psychology, anthropology, art, and literature, as well as on the thinking of millions of ordinary people about their own lives.

Freud's daughter ANNA FREUD (see Vol. 5) was the founder of the Hampstead Child Therapy Clinic in London, where her specialty was applying psychoanalysis to children. Her major work was the *The Ego and the Mechanisms of Defense* (1936).

BOOKS BY FREUD

Abstracts of the Standard Edition of the Complete Psychological Works of Sigmund Freud. Ed. by Carrie L. Rothgeb. Intl. Univ. Pr. 1973 $70.00. ISBN 0-8236-0030-0. Abstracts of each paper presented in the Standard Edition with editorial notes.

The Basic Writings of Sigmund Freud. Ed. by A. A. Brill. Random 1977 $19.95. ISBN 0-394-60400-8. A collection of six of Freud's major works, including *Totem and Taboo* and *The Interpretation of Dreams.*

The Standard Edition of the Complete Psychological Works of Sigmund Freud. Trans. and ed. by James Strachey. 24 vols. Norton 1976 $895.00. ISBN 0-393-01128-3. All of Freud's psychological writings plus an autobiographical study.

Studies on Hysteria. (coauthored with Joseph Breuer). Basic 1982 $17.00. ISBN 0-465-08274-2. The work that laid the groundwork for Freud's theory of catharsis; examines psychosexual factors and infantilism, the importance of dreams and unconscious symbolism.

Three Essays on the Theory of Sexuality. 1905. Trans. by James Strachey. Basic 1982 $17.00. ISBN 0-465-08276-9. The development, aberrations, and transformations of the sexual instinct.

BOOKS ABOUT FREUD

Abramson, Jeffrey. *Liberation and Its Limits: The Moral and Political Thought of Freud.* Free Pr. 1984 $19.95. ISBN 0-02-900210-9

Bettelheim, Bruno. *Freud and Man's Soul.* Random 1984 $6.95. ISBN 0-394-71036-3. Demonstrates how English translations of Freud's writings have distorted some of the central concepts of psychoanalysis, causing misunderstanding and misuse of psychoanalysis in America.

Dilman, Ilham. *Freud and the Mind.* Blackwell Pubs. 1984 $45.00. ISBN 0-631-13529-4. Full-scale philosophical treatment of Freud's conception of the mind and of the limits of the individual's autonomy.

Freeman, Lucy, and Herbert S. Strean. *Freud and Women.* Continuum 1987 $10.95. ISBN 0-8044-5374-8. Exploration of Freud's important relationships with women, whom he both idealized and feared, loved and hated.

Fromm, Erich. *The Greatness and Limitations of Freud's Thought.* NAL-Dutton 1981 $5.95. ISBN 0-452-00958-8. Stimulating critique of Freud's contributions to modern thought, showing how his greatest discoveries were distorted by Freud's own public and private premises.

Gay, Peter. *Freud: A Life for Our Time.* Norton 1988 $24.50. ISBN 0-393-02517-9. Complete biography of Freud, drawing on a vast store of unpublished documents, with an integration of the case histories and technical papers.

———. *Freud, Jews, and Other Germans: Masters and Victims in Modernist Culture.* OUP 1979 $30.00. ISBN 0-19-502258-0

Hale, Nathan G., Jr. *Freud and the Americans: The Origins and Foundation of the Psychoanalytic Movement in America, 1876–1918.* OUP 1971 $27.50. ISBN 0-19-501427-8. Analysis of why America embraced Freud's psychoanalytic theories and techniques more warmly than any other country did.

Hall, Calvin S. *A Primer of Freudian Psychology.* NAL-Dutton 1955 $4.99. ISBN 0-451-62625-7

Jahoda, Marie. *Freud and the Dilemmas of Psychology.* U. of Nebr. Pr. 1981 repr. of 1977 ed. o.p.

Jones, Ernest. *The Life and Work of Sigmund Freud.* 3 vols. Basic 1953–1957 $80.00. ISBN 0-465-04015-2. The standard biography. Volume I covers the formative years and the great discoveries, 1856–1900; Volume 2, the years of maturity, 1902–1919; and Volume 3, the last phase, 1919–1939.

Malcolm, Janet. *In the Freud Archives.* Random 1985 $9.00. ISBN 0-394-72922-6

Marcus, Steven. *Freud and the Culture of Psychoanalysis: Studies in the Transition from Victorian Humanism to Modernity.* Norton 1987 $7.70. ISBN 0-393-30410-8. Assesses Freud as an exemplary late Victorian and as a pivotal figure in the creation of modern thought and culture.

Masson, Jeffrey Moussaieff. *The Assault on Truth: Freud's Suppression of the Seduction Theory.* FS&G 1984 $16.95. ISBN 0-374-10642-8. Highly controversial exposé of the origins of psychoanalysis, based on letters and other new information discovered at the Freud Archives and in Europe.

Rieff, Philip. *Freud: The Mind of the Moralist.* U. Ch. Pr. 3rd ed. 1979 $19.95. ISBN 0-226-71639-2

Schellenberg, James A. *Masters of Social Psychology: Freud, Mead, Lewin, and Skinner.* OUP 1978 $7.95. ISBN 0-19-502622-5. Short biographies of Freud, Mead, Lewin, and Skinner that show the kinds of experiences that led them to formulate their individual approaches.

Sears, Robert R. *Survey of Objective Studies of Psychoanalytic Concepts. Social Science Research Council Bulletin.* Greenwood 1979 repr. of 1943 ed. $39.75. ISBN 0-313-21249-X

Shakow, David, and David Rapaport. *Influence of Freud on American Psychology. Psychological Issues Monographs.* Intl. Univ. Pr. 1964 $35.00. ISBN 0-8236-2656-3. A retrospective that compares Freud's influence to Darwin's on the intellectual life of the nineteenth century.

Sulloway, Frank J. *Freud, Biologist of the Mind: Beyond the Psychoanalytic Legend.* Basic 1979 $23.50. ISBN 0-465-02559-5. A comprehensive intellectual biography that treats Freud within the context of the history of science.

HALL, G(RANVILLE) STANLEY. 1844–1924

The American psychologist G. Stanley Hall received a Ph.D. in psychology from Harvard University, the first person in the United States to be granted this newly established degree. He is more important as an organizer and administrator than as an original thinker in psychology, although he did much to advance the study of childhood and adolescence. The first of many Americans to study under WILHELM WUNDT at Heidelberg, he also studied at Bonn and Berlin. Hall then became a professor of psychology at Johns Hopkins University, where in 1884 he opened the first university psychology laboratory in the United States. Three years later, he helped found the *American Journal of Psychology*. In 1889 he became the first president of Clark University, as well as a professor of psychology. He was one of the first Americans to teach FREUD's (see also Vol. 5) views, and Freud's visit to the United States in 1906 was at Hall's invitation.

BOOKS BY HALL

Adolescence: Its Psychology and Its Relations to Physiology, Anthropology, Sociology, Sex, Crime, Religion and Education. 2 vols. Telegraph Bks. 1981 repr. of 1905 ed. o.p. Hall's premise is that the developing individual repeats the development of the human species from primitive to advanced.

Life and Confessions of a Psychologist. Ed. by Walter P. Metzger. Ayer repr. of 1923 ed. $48.50. ISBN 0-405-10008-6

Senescence: The Last Half of Life. Family in Amer. Ser. Ayer 1972 repr. of 1922 ed. $29.00. ISBN 0-405-03860-7

BOOK ABOUT HALL

Ross, Dorothy. *G. Stanley Hall: The Psychologist as Prophet.* U. Ch. Pr. 1972 $25.00. ISBN 0-226-72821-8. Examines Hall's life in the context of American intellectual and social history.

HOLLINGWORTH, LETA. 1886–1939

Leta Anna Stetter Hollingworth, an American psychologist, received her Ph.D. in clinical psychology from Columbia University. She was a primary contributor to scientific stringency in the teaching of psychology. Her most important work, however, was her empirical research refuting widely held views on sex differences that allegedly impaired women's intelligence and her research disproving some of the myths of social Darwinism—in particular, the variability hypothesis, or the idea that the high status of humankind was based on the greater variability of human beings compared to other species. In addition, Hollingworth contributed to child psychology and education with her innovative studies of gifted children and adolescents.

BOOKS BY HOLLINGWORTH

Gifted Children. Macmillan 1926 o.p. Based on author's research with "special opportunity classes" in a New York public school.

The Psychology of Adolescence. Appleton 1928 o.p.

The Psychology of Subnormal Children. Macmillan 1920 o.p.

HORNEY, KAREN (DANIELSEN). 1885–1952

Karen Danielsen Horney was a German-born American psychiatrist and psychoanalyst. Educated at the universities of Freiburg, Göttingen, and Berlin, she practiced in Europe until 1932, when she moved to the United States. Initially, she taught at the New York Psychoanalytic Institute, but with others broke away in 1941 to found the American Institute for Psychoanalysis.

Horney took issue with several orthodox Freudian teachings, including the
Oedipus complex, the death instinct, and the inferiority of women. She thought
that classical psychoanalytic theory overemphasized the biological sources of
neuroses. Her own theory of personality stressed the sociological determinants
of behavior and viewed the individual as capable of fundamental growth and
change.

BOOKS BY HORNEY

Neurosis and Human Growth: The Struggle Toward Self-Realization. Norton 1991 $10.95.
ISBN 0-393-30775-1

The Neurotic Personality of Our Time. 1937. Norton 1965 $4.95. ISBN 0-393-00742-1.
Discusses the role of society in causing neurosis.

New Ways in Psychoanalysis. 1939. Norton 1964 $3.95. ISBN 0-393-00132-6. A critical
reevaluation of psychoanalytic theories from a feminist perspective.

Our Inner Conflicts: A Constructive Theory of Neurosis. 1945. Norton 1992 $7.95. ISBN 0-
393-30940-1. Four possible solutions to conflict are offered: moving toward people,
moving against people, moving away from people, and moving toward realization of
an idealized image of the self.

Self-Analysis. Norton 1942 o.p. How individuals can analyze themselves, although
"severe neuroses belong in the hands of experts."

BOOKS ABOUT HORNEY

Quinn, Susan. *A Mind of Her Own: The Life of Karen Horney.* Addison-Wesley 1988
$12.45. ISBN 0-201-15573-7. Full-scale biography with photographs, using new
material and unpublished diaries.

Westkott, Marcia. *The Feminist Legacy of Karen Horney.* Yale U. Pr. 1988 $12.00. ISBN 0-
300-04204-3. Interpretation of Horney's work as a historically based psychoanalysis
of women; provides a major contribution to contemporary feminist thought.

HULL, CLARK L(EONARD). 1884–1952

Clark L. Hull, an American psychologist, rose from a harsh rural life in
upstate New York and an early bout with poliomyelitis that left him partially
paralyzed to an outstanding career in American psychology. His behaviorist
theory of learning set the agenda for learning theory research in the decades
preceding and following World War II.

The first part of Hull's career was spent at the University of Wisconsin, where
he carried out research on the measurement and prediction of achievement. In
1928 he moved to Yale University's Institute of Human Relations, where he
began to formalize his mechanistic theory of learning behavior. In a series of
experiments, he reduced the more complex types of learning to simple
reinforced stimulus-response events. He also showed that there is a quantitatively definable goal gradient in learning—that is, the closer an action is to contact
with a desired object, or goal, the more it is reinforced by that goal. Hull was
convinced that this work would lead to a unified theory of behavior, a goal few
now believe is possible. His research, however, established the pattern for
logical theory construction, which has been applied in many fields.

BOOKS BY HULL

Aptitude Testing. World 1928 o.p. Designed to be a general handbook for those engaged
in the measurement of aptitude.

A Behavior System. Greenwood 1974 repr. of 1952 ed. o.p.

Mathematico-Deductive Theory of Rote Learning: A Study in Scientific Methodology.
(coauthored with others). Greenwood repr. of 1940 ed. o.p.

Principles of Behavior: An Introduction to Behavior Theory. Appleton 1943 o.p. Hull
outlines his reasons for proposing that the study of behavior should be regarded as a
natural science.

JAMES, WILLIAM. 1842–1910

The philosopher-psychologist William James was a member of an exceptional
American family. He was the brother of the novelist HENRY JAMES (see Vol. 1)
and the diarist ALICE JAMES (see Vol. 1), and the son of Henry James, Sr., a
Swedenborgian writer and lecturer and friend of prominent intellectuals on
both sides of the Atlantic. William benefited immensely from the lively
intellectual atmosphere at home and frequent family travel to Europe, where he
received a sporadic education in various German, Swiss, French, and English
schools. Following a failed attempt to become a painter, he entered Harvard
University in 1861 and, after several interruptions for travel and recovery from
nervous disorders, received a medical degree in 1869.

Finding himself unsuited to the practice of medicine, he accepted a position
on the Harvard faculty, where he spent the rest of his career teaching, at various
times, physiology, psychology, and philosophy. There he also set up the first
psychological laboratory in the United States in 1875, the same year that
WILLIAM WUNDT established in Germany the only other psychology laboratory in
the world. In contrast to Wundt, however, James did not believe that mental life
could accurately be broken down into discrete ideas, sensations, and emotions;
rather, he thought that it is a "stream of consciousness," a flowing unity of
integrated events. This holistic view of experience anticipated Gestalt
psychology.

James never carried out much psychological research himself, but his classic
treatise *The Principles of Psychology* (1890) displays a thorough grasp of
European psychological literature and a remarkable ability to describe and
illuminate psychological problems and experiences in ways that are both
interesting and relevant to people's lives. Its chapter on the self is considered
one of the classics of psychological literature. His *Talks to Teachers on
Psychology* (1899) did much to stimulate the field of educational psychology,
and his *Varieties of Religious Experience* (1900), an intensive study of the
psychology of conversion and mystical experiences, is still widely read today.

BOOKS BY JAMES

Pragmatism: A New Name for Some Old Ways of Thinking. 1907. Prometheus Bks. 1990
$7.95. ISBN 0-87975-633-0. James's classic contribution to the body of philosophic
literature.

The Principles of Psychology. 1890. HUP 1983 $22.50. ISBN 0-674-70625-0

Talks to Teachers on Psychology: And to Students on Some of Life's Ideals. 1899. Norton
1958 $8.95. ISBN 0-393-00165-2

The Varieties of Religious Experience: A Study in Human Nature. 1903. Liguori Pubns.
1992 $8.95. ISBN 0-89243-509-7. Classic, pioneering study of psychology of religion;
with an introduction by Eugene Kennedy.

The Will to Believe. 1897. *Works of William James Ser.* HUP 1979 $34.95. ISBN 0-674-
95281-2. With an introduction by Edward H. Madden. Examination of how and why
people hold to their systems of belief.

BOOKS ABOUT JAMES

Barzun, Jacques. *A Stroll with William James.* HarpC 1983 $25.00. ISBN 0-226-03865-3.
An erudite but gracefully written examination of James's thought, friendships and
associations, and deep influence on his own times and ours.

Bjork, Daniel W. *William James: The Center of His Vision*. Col. U. Pr. 1988 $35.00. ISBN 0-231-05674-5. Imaginative biography that integrates James's life and thought, using previously unpublished diaries, notebooks, letters to his wife, and family correspondence.

Brennan, Bernard P. *William James. Twayne's United States Authors Ser.* NCUP 1968 $10.95. ISBN 0-8084-0005-3. Accessible explanation of James's critical thought, including some biographical material.

Edie, James M. *William James and Phenomenology. Studies in Phenomenology and Existential Philosophy Ser.* Ind. U. Pr. 1987 $9.95. ISBN 0-253-20419-4. Complete analysis of James's influence and involvement in phenomenology, the philosophical study of occurrences and facts directly perceived by the senses.

Myers, Gerald E. *William James: His Life and Thought*. Yale U. Pr. 1986 $19.95. ISBN 0-300-04211-6. Critical analysis of James's writing on consciousness, time, space, perception, memory, thought, morality, and so on, using fresh biographical information to illuminate his ideas.

Suckiel, Ellen Kappy. *The Pragmatic Philosophy of William James*. U. of Notre Dame Pr. 1982 $19.95. ISBN 0-268-01548-1. Analysis of James's pragmatism as a systematic worldview.

Taylor, Eugene, ed. *William James on Exceptional Mental States: The 1896 Lowell Lectures*. U. of Mass. Pr. 1984 $13.95. ISBN 0-87023-451-X. In eight lectures James examines the psychology of the subconscious and its role in the social sphere.

Wilshire, Bruce. *William James and Phenomenology: A Study of "The Principles of Psychology."* AMS Pr. repr. of 1968 ed. $24.00. ISBN 0-404-15226-0

KLINEBERG, OTTO. 1899–1992

Otto Klineberg, a Canadian-born American psychologist, was trained as a psychiatrist at McGill University in Montreal, Canada, before he earned his Ph.D. in psychology at Columbia University in 1927. There he became a research associate of FRANZ BOAS, and his first fieldwork was among Indian children. Klineberg was very much an international social scientist, both substantively through his work on race and international tensions and organizationally through his long association with UNESCO. He helped organize the World Federation for Mental Health and later served as its president, and he was an unofficial ambassador for the social sciences in many countries. But probably his most enduring research is contained in *Negro Intelligence and Selective Migration* (1935), which demonstrated through carefully controlled studies that the I.Q. scores of southern African American children improved when they moved to the North, and hence that environment, not race, is the determinant of lower I.Q. scores among African American children. This research was introduced to the Supreme Court in the deliberations that led to the famous 1954 decision on school desegregation, *Brown v. Board of Education.*

BOOKS BY KLINEBERG

The Human Dimension in International Relations. Holt 1964 o.p.

Negro Intelligence and Selective Migration. Greenwood 1975 repr. of 1935 ed. $35.00. ISBN 0-8371-7771-5

Race Differences. Greenwood 1974 repr. of 1935 ed. $49.75. ISBN 0-8371-7519-4. Klineberg cites his research to refute claims of the existence of any racial hierarchy.

Tensions Affecting International Understanding: A Survey of Research. Social Science Research Council 1950 o.p. Explores the development of national and racial stereotypes and ways in which they can be combated.

LADD-FRANKLIN, CHRISTINE. 1847–1930

Christine Ladd-Franklin was an American psychologist best known for her work on vision. Although she earned a Ph.D. from Johns Hopkins University in 1882, it was not granted to her for more than 40 years because of the university's longstanding policy of not conferring degrees on women. This experience impelled her to campaign for equal access to education for women. Ladd-Franklin formulated her theory of color vision while teaching at Johns Hopkins and Columbia universities, where her interest in mathematics extended to the investigation of the horopter—the locus of all points in the field of vision that fall on corresponding parts in the two retinas. Her experimental work in color vision extended the hypothesis of the German physiologist Ewald Hering regarding color perception in that it demonstrated that black-white vision is the most primitive form of color vision. She continued to develop this theory for four decades.

BOOK BY LADD-FRANKLIN

Colour and Colour Theories. Ayer repr. of 1929 ed. $20.00. ISBN 0-405-05143-3

LEWIN, KURT. 1890–1947

Kurt Lewin was born and educated in Germany and much influenced by the school of Gestalt psychology (the study of responses to whole psychological and physiological events) prominent in that country during the 1920s. One of the many intellectuals driven into exile by the rise of Nazism, he came to the United States in 1932. Although he conducted research in such diverse fields as cognition, motivation, and group behavior, he maintained a consistent theoretical position requiring an interdisciplinary approach, which he came to call "field theory." The term derives from the premise that events are determined by forces acting on them in an immediate field rather than by forces acting at a distance. Perhaps the most widely known of Lewin's concepts is that of "psychological lifespace," which refers to the totality of events or facts that determine the behavior of an individual at a given time. For example, the unconscious structures that a therapist uncovers in working with a patient are said to be active in the present, not just replicas of past realities and reactions.

Lewin gradually became interested in social psychology. His concept of "social space," the interaction of political, economic, cultural, and physical events, led to work in group dynamics and the formation of the National Training Laboratories. First held in Bethel, Maine, the summer after Lewin's death, these training sessions for leadership roles are sponsored today by the National Institute for Applied Behavioral Science and have become a major link between people in the behavioral sciences and those in the professions and industry.

BOOKS BY LEWIN

A Dynamic Theory of Personality. 1935. McGraw 1955 o.p. A series of reprints of the papers most fundamental to Lewin's system.

Field Theory in Social Science. Ed. by Dorwin Cartwright. Greenwood 1975 repr. of 1951 ed. $48.50. ISBN 0-8371-7236-5. Examines Lewin's work concerning the philosophy of science and principles in research fields.

Frustration and Aggression: An Experiment with Young Children. (coauthored with Robert Barker and Tamara Dembo). U. of Iowa Pr. 1941 o.p.

Principles of Topological Psychology. Johnson Repr. 1969 repr. of 1936 ed. o.p.

Resolving Social Conflicts. Ed. by Gertrud W. Lewin. Intl Spec. Bk. 1978 o.p.

Books about Lewin

Leeper, Robert W. *Lewin's Topological and Vector Psychology: A Digest and a Critique.*
U. of Ore. Pr. 1943 o.p.

Marrow, Alfred J. *The Practical Theorist: The Life and Work of Kurt Lewin.* Bks. Demand
repr. of 1977 ed. $79.80. ISBN 0-317-28352-9. Biography written by a friend and
colleague with an intimate knowledge of Lewin's work.

Schellenberg, James A. *Masters of Social Psychology: Freud, Mead, Lewin, and Skinner.*
OUP 1978 $7.95. ISBN 0-19-502622-5. Short biographies that show the kinds of
experiences that led Freud, Mead, Lewin, and Skinner to formulate their different
approaches.

LORENZ, KONRAD. 1903–1989 (Nobel Prize 1973)

Konrad Lorenz, an Austrian zoologist, is included in this chapter because his
specialty, the biological origins of social behavior, is of major interest to
psychologists. Lorenz pioneered in the direct study of animal behavior and was
the founder of modern ethology (the study of animals in their natural
surroundings). He received the Nobel Prize for physiology in 1973 for his
research on instinctive behavior patterns and on imprinting—the process
through which an animal very early in life acquires a social bond, usually with
its parents, that enables it to become attached to other members of its own
species. His major book, *On Aggression* (1963), was attacked by many anthropologists, psychologists, and sociologists, who maintained that Lorenz's claim that
aggression is inborn means that it cannot be controlled; his supporters
countered that Lorenz never stated that inborn traits could not be changed.
Lorenz's work continues to play a key role in this contemporary version of the
nature-nurture debate.

Books by Lorenz

Behind the Mirror: A Search for a Natural History of Human Knowledge. 1973. Trans. by
Ronald Taylor. HarBraceJ 1978 $7.95. ISBN 0-15-611776-2. Lorenz charts his
lifelong search for the history of human cognitive development.

Evolution and Modification of Behavior. 1961. U. Ch. Pr. 1986 $9.95. ISBN 0-226-49334-2

King Solomon's Ring. 1952. Peter Smith 1988 $23.75. ISBN 0-8446-6309-3. Illustrations
by the author enliven the text, which is written sensitively but without anthropo-
morphic overtones.

On Aggression. 1963. Trans. by Marjorie K. Wilson. HarBraceJ 1974 $9.95. ISBN 0-15-
668741-0

MILLER, NEAL E(DGAR). 1909–

Neal Edgar Miller, an American psychologist, produced the first demonstration of trial-and-error learning caused by electrical stimulation of the brain. He
also studied the motivational effects of chemical brain stimulation, as well as
the effects of instrumental learning on visceral responses and the possible role
of such learning in normal homeostasis, disease, and therapy. Miller was
educated at the University of Washington, Stanford University, and Yale
University. He later joined the faculty of Rockefeller University and collaborated
with John Dollard of Yale University to research the role of imitation in
learning. The two investigators' experiments led them to relate learning to such
psychological problems as conflict, displacement of aggression, and emotional
stress.

Miller has served as president of the American Psychological Association and
the Society for Neuroscience. He has received the APA Gold Medal Award for
scientific accomplishments and the National Medal of Science.

BOOKS BY MILLER

Frustration and Aggression. (coauthored with J. Dollard and L. Dobb). Greenwood 1980 repr. of 1939 ed. $35.00. ISBN 0-313-22201-3. Report on studies showing that aggression follows from frustration.
Graphic Communication and the Crisis in Education. NEA 1957 o.p.
Social Learning and Imitation. 1941. Greenwood 1979 repr. of 1962 ed. $35.00. ISBN 0-313-20714-3

PAVLOV, IVAN PETROVICH. 1849–1936 (NOBEL PRIZE 1904)

Ivan Petrovich Pavlov, a Russian physiologist and psychologist, demonstrated, by his 62 years of active research, one model of the research career: making a major discovery by studying more and more about less and less. He first studied the neural mechanisms of blood circulation and digestion; then the mechanisms of digestion; and finally salivation. His studies of salivation led to his discovery of the conditioned reflex: a dog trained to associate feeding with the sounding of a bell would salivate when the bell was sounded, even though no food was made available.

He received the Nobel Prize in 1904 for his work on the processes of digestion, but it was his further experiments in the operation of the conditioned reflex that made him an important figure in psychology. His work has had its greatest impact on behavioral psychologists, who concern themselves primarily with observable relationships between measurable stimuli and behavioral responses in human beings as well as in animals. They quickly saw that Pavlov's objective techniques could be used to establish laws of behavior, especially in the area of learning. Thus, Pavlov's concept of the conditioned reflex has become an important feature of learning theory.

BOOKS BY PAVLOV

Conditioned Reflexes: An Investigation of the Psychological Activity of the Cerebral Cortex. Ed. by G. V. Anrep. Dover repr. of 1927 ed. $9.95. ISBN 0-486-60614-7
Lectures on Conditioned Reflexes. 1923. *Classics in Psychology Ser*. St. Martin repr. of 1927 ed. o.p. With an introduction by Jeffrey Gray. Talks summing up 25 years of objective study of the higher nervous activity of animals.

BOOKS ABOUT PAVLOV

Babkin, Boris P. *Pavlov: A Biography*. U. Ch. Pr. 1975 o.p.
Gray, Jeffrey A. *Ivan Pavlov. Modern Masters Ser*. Viking Penguin 1981 o.p. Concise account of Pavlov's life and works.
Wells, Harry K. *Ivan P. Pavlov: Toward a Scientific Psychology and Psychiatry*. Intl. Pubs. Co. 1956 o.p. Introduction to teachings of Pavlov that are pertinent to psychology and psychiatry.

PIAGET, JEAN. 1896–1980

Jean Piaget, a Swiss psychologist, whose original training was in the natural sciences, spent much of his career studying the psychological development of children, largely at the Institut J. J. Rousseau at the University of Geneva, but also at home, with his own children as subjects. The impact of this research on child psychology has been enormous, and Piaget is the starting point for those seeking to learn how children view numbers, how they think of cause-and-effect relationships, or how they make moral judgments.

Piaget found that cognitive development from infancy to adolescence invariably proceeds in four major stages from infancy to adolescence: sensorimotor, preoperational, concrete operational, and formal operational. Each of these stages is marked by the development of cognitive structures, making possible the solution of problems that were impossible earlier and laying the foundation for the cognitive advances of the next stage. He showed that rational adult thinking is the culmination of an extensive process that begins with elementary sensory experiences and unfolds gradually until the individual is capable of dealing with imagined concepts, that is, abstract thought. By learning how children comprehend the world and how their intellectual processes mature, Piaget contributed much to the theory of knowledge as an active process in which the mind transforms reality. Put simply, Piaget described children from a perspective that no one before had seen.

BOOKS BY PIAGET

The Child's Conception of the World. 1926. Littlefield 1975 $14.95. ISBN 0-8226-0213-X. Piaget traces five stages of childhood development in an attempt to ascertain what conceptions children form naturally.

The Development of Thought: Equilibration of Cognitive Structures. Trans. by Arnold Rosin. Viking Penguin 1977 o.p.

The Essential Piaget. Ed. by Howard E. Gruber and J. Jacques Voneche. Basic 1982 $23.95. ISBN 0-465-02064-X

The Language and Thought of the Child. 1923. Humanities 1962 o.p. Piaget employs his clinical method to examine how children develop both objective and symbolic thought.

The Moral Judgment of the Child. 1932. Macmillan 1985 $19.95. ISBN 0-02-925230-X. Examines the psychological relations between children and adults and between children and other children; based on questions posed to schoolchildren.

Play, Dreams and Imitation in Childhood. 1946. Norton 1962 $9.95. ISBN 0-393-00171-7

Psychology of the Child. (coauthored with Barbel Inhelder). Trans. by Helen Weaver. Basic 1969 $14.00. ISBN 0-465-01500-3

BOOKS ABOUT PIAGET

Décarie, Thérèse G. *Intelligence and Affectivity in Early Childhood: An Experimental Study of Jean Piaget's Object Concept and Object Relationships.* Intl. Univs. Pr. 1966 $27.50. ISBN 0-8236-2720-9. Experimental study of children up to two years of age that attempts to derive testable hypotheses from the theories of Piaget and the Freudian ego psychologists.

Evans, Richard I. *Jean Piaget: The Man and His Ideas.* NAL-Dutton 1973 o.p. Dialogue with Piaget plus illuminating articles by David Elkind and others.

Furth, Hans G. *Piaget and Knowledge: Theoretical Foundations.* Psychology Ser. U. Ch. Pr. 1981 $7.50. ISBN 0-226-27420-9. Analysis of Piaget's basic theoretical positions in order to clarify psychological problems, with an introduction by Piaget.

Gardner, Howard. *The Quest for Mind: Piaget, Lévi-Strauss, and the Structuralist Movement.* U. Ch. Pr. 2nd ed. 1981 $24.00. ISBN 0-226-28331-3

Ginsburg, Herbert, and Sylvia Opper. *Piaget's Theory of Intellectual Development.* P-H 1988 $13.50. ISBN 0-13-763001-6. Interprets Piaget's theories and provides a concise introduction to Piaget's basic ideas and findings concerning children's intellectual development.

Inhelder, Barbel, ed. *Piaget and His School: A Reader in Developmental Psychology.* Springer-Verlag 1976 o.p. Collection of studies (1960–1970) of the Geneva School of Psychology influenced by Piaget, with an introduction by Piaget.

Piattelli, Palmarini Massimo, ed. *Language and Learning: The Debate Between Jean Piaget and Noam Chomsky.* HUP 1980 $16.50. ISBN 0-674-50941-2. A critical inventory of research strategies regarding the foundations of language and the development of cognitive structures.

Pulaski, Mary Ann Spencer. *Understanding Piaget: An Introduction to Children's Cognitive Development.* HarpC 1980 $15.45. ISBN 0-06-013454-2. Lucid and thorough introduction to Piaget's studies of cognitive development.

Richmond, P. G. *An Introduction to Piaget*. Basic 1971 o.p.
Schwebel, Milton, and Jane Raph. *Piaget in the Classroom*. Basic 1973 o.p.

ROGERS, CARL. 1902–1987

Carl Rogers was an American psychologist who earned worldwide recognition for originating and developing the humanistic movement in psychotherapy, which has influenced all fields of psychology. Originally trained in Freudian techniques, he later rejected them because of what he saw as an arrogant attitude of omniscience on the part of the classical psychoanalyst. His own clinical work led him to believe that every individual consists of two systems: the organism—the person's entire range of experience, both conscious and unconscious; and the self—the ideas, values, and perceptions that the person is aware of having. There is often a serious split between the two, because people experience what Rogers called conditional positive regard as children, or affection dependent upon conforming to parental standards, and this leads them to deny or to distort their own perceptions. Rogers' client-centered therapy concentrated on giving people unconditional positive regard and support in discovering and expressing their true feelings.

Rogers spent 24 years teaching at Ohio State University, the University of Chicago, and Wisconsin University. While at Wisconsin, he became so disenchanted with the constrictive rules for obtaining a Ph.D. and the rigid structure of graduate school education that he left academia to foster the encounter group movement at the Western Behavioral Science Institute and later at the Center for the Studies of the Person, which he founded. He devoted the last 15 years of his life to applying his person-centered approach to politics by training groups in conflict resolution, leadership, and policy making. An abiding interest was the reduction of interracial and international tensions.

Books by Rogers

Becoming Partners: Marriage and Its Alternatives. Delacorte 1972 o.p. Using interviews with American couples as basic material, Rogers examines relationships between men and women in a nonacademic manner.
Client-Centered Therapy: Its Current Practice, Implications, and Theory. HM 1951 o.p. Rogers's exposition of his theory that each person is of unique worth and capable of self-understanding and self-direction and the kind of therapy that can help people achieve this realization.
Freedom to Learn: A View of What Education Might Become. Merrill 1969 o.p.

Books about Rogers

Evans, R. *Carl Rogers: The Man and His Ideas*. NAL-Dutton 1975 o.p.
Kirschenbaum, Howard, and Valerie L. Henderson. *A Carl Rogers Reader*. HM 1989 $12.70. ISBN 0-395-48357-3
_____. *Carl Rogers: Dialogues*. HM 1989 $9.70. ISBN 0-395-48345-5
Thorne, Brian. *Carl Rogers. Key Figures in Counselling and Psychotherapy Ser*. Sage 1992 $39.95. ISBN 0-8039-8462-6

SKINNER, B(URRHUS) F(REDERIC). 1904–1990

B. F. Skinner, an American behavioral psychologist, is known for his many contributions to learning theory. His *Behavior of Organisms* (1938) reports his experiments with the study of reflexes. *Walden Two* (1949), a utopian novel, describes a planned community in which positive rather than negative reinforcers serve to maintain appropriate behavior; the novel stimulated the founding of some experimental communities. In *Beyond Freedom and Dignity*

(1971), Skinner attempted to show that only what he called a technology of behavior could save democracy from the many individual and social problems that plague it. (An early example of this technology is the so-called Skinner box for conditioning a human child.)

A teacher at Harvard University from 1948 until his retirement, Skinner was for some the model of the objective scientist, for others the epitome of the heartless behaviorist who would turn people into automatons.

BOOKS BY SKINNER

The Analysis of Behavior: A Program for Self-Instruction. (coauthored with James G. Holland). McGraw 1961 $30.77. ISBN 0-07-029565-4
The Behavior of Organisms: Experimental Analysis. 1938. P-H 1966 o.p.
Particulars of My Life. NYU Pr. 1985 o.p. Skinner's autobiographical work covering his early years.
Verbal Behavior. P-H 1957 $46.00. ISBN 0-13-941591-2. Skinner's complex exposition of the ways in which verbal skills are acquired and shaped by environment.
Walden Two. 1949. Macmillan 1976. ISBN 0-02-411510-X

BOOKS ABOUT SKINNER

Carpenter, Finley. *The Skinner Primer: Behind Freedom and Dignity.* Free Pr. 1985 $14.95. ISBN 0-02-905900-3. Balanced critique of Skinner's major theories.
Dews, Peter B., ed. *Festschrift for B. F. Skinner. Century Psychology Ser.* Irvington 1977 $39.00. ISBN 0-89197-497-0
Sagal, Paul T. *Skinner's Philosophy.* U. Pr. of Amer. 1981 $9.75. ISBN 0-8191-1433-2. Presentation of Skinner's work and thought; a good introduction to *Beyond Freedom and Dignity.*
Schellenberg, James A. *Masters of Social Psychology: Freud, Mead, Lewin, and Skinner.* OUP 1978 $7.95. ISBN 0-19-502622-5. Short biographies of Freud, Mead, Lewin, and Skinner that show the kinds of experiences that led them to formulate their varied approaches.

TINBERGEN, NIKOLAAS. 1907– (NOBEL PRIZE 1973)

Nikolaas Tinbergen, a Dutch zoologist, with the Austrian biologist KONRAD LORENZ founded the field of modern ethology—the study of animals in their natural surroundings. The two men shared the Nobel Prize for physiology and medicine with KARL VON FRISCH (see Vol. 5) in 1973.

Convinced of the sterility of much contemporary comparative and experimental psychology, and appalled at the far-reaching generalizations made by psychologists on the basis of observations of a few species of caged rodents, Tinbergen set out to study a few highly specific problems in animal behavior: the nature of the stickleback's courtship, the stimuli causing a young herring gull to beg for food, and the reasons gulls bother to remove empty eggshells from their nests. His influential book *The Study of Instinct* (1951) had a tremendous impact on the development of ethology. Ethologists believe that instinct is a motivational basis for human behavior as well as for animal behavior and hence that ethological studies have valid human applications. Tinbergen is particularly concerned that human beings are in danger of losing their ability to adapt because of the very rapid changes taking place in contemporary society. He thinks there is much we can learn from close study of animal adaptation.

BOOKS BY TINBERGEN

The Animal in Its World: Explorations of an Ethologist, 1932–1972. 2 vols. HUP Vol. 1 1972 $10.95. ISBN 0-674-03724-3. Vol. 2 1976 $9.95. ISBN 0-674-03728-6

Curious Naturalists. U. of Mass. Pr. rev. ed. 1984 $14.95. ISBN 0-87023-456-0
The Herring Gull's World. Lyons & Burford 1989 repr. of 1960 ed. $14.95. ISBN 1-55821-049-0. With an introduction by Konrad Lorenz.
Social Behavior in Animals: With Special Reference to Vertebrates. Chapman & Hall 1990 $22.50. ISBN 0-412-36920-6
The Study of Instinct. OUP 1990 $30.00. ISBN 0-19-857740-0

TOLMAN, EDWARD (CHACE). 1886–1959

Edward Chace Tolman was a neobehaviorist who received his Ph.D. from Harvard University in 1915. As a graduate student, he had traveled to Germany and met Kurt Koffka, who introduced him to Gestalt psychology. His own theory of behavior, which he presented in *Purposive Behavior in Animals and Men* (1932), focused on molar (whole) behavioral units and on the purposive nature of behavior; both of these emphases clearly diverged from classical behaviorism and showed the influence of Gestalt principles on Tolman's thinking. One of Tolman's most important contributions to experimental psychology was that of the intervening variable, a concept that made it possible to operationalize unobservable states, such as hunger, and thus scientifically to scrutinize them. His research on learning theory stimulated investigation and made a substantial impact on cognitive psychology.

BOOKS BY TOLMAN

Behavior and Psychological Man. U. CA Pr. 1951 o.p.
Drives Toward War. Appleton 1942 o.p.
Purposive Behavior in Animals and Men. 1932. U. CA Pr. 1951 o.p.

WASHBURN, MARGARET (FLOY). 1871–1939

Margaret Floy Washburn, an American psychologist, was one of the first women to receive an advanced degree in psychology in the United States. Because she was allowed by Columbia University to enroll only as a "hearer," she moved to Cornell University, where she studied with E. B. Titchener and received a Ph.D. in 1894. Washburn established a psychology laboratory at Vassar College, where she wrote her classic text on comparative psychology, *The Animal Mind* (1908). Her motor theory of consciousness, which stated that consciousness results from a certain balance between excitation and inhibition in a motor discharge, attempted to reconcile the introspective and behavioral approaches to psychology.

BOOKS BY WASHBURN

The Animal Mind: A Textbook of Comparative Psychology. 1908. Macmillan o.p.
Movement and Mental Imagery: Outlines of a Motor Theory of the Complexer Mental Processes. Ayer repr. of 1916 ed. $18.00. ISBN 0-405-05168-9

WATSON, JOHN B(ROADUS). 1878–1958

John B. Watson, an American psychologist, was the founder of behaviorism, an enormously influential orientation that had an impact on sociology and political science as well as psychology. His own early research was experimental, in animal psychology and in child behavior, but in 1913 he published a startling polemical paper entitled "Psychology as a Behaviorist Views It." In it he enunciated the doctrine that psychology is strictly the science of behavior. Mentalistic concepts, images, the study of consciousness, and introspection must all be abandoned, he said, to be replaced by the objective observation of the organism's response to controlled stimuli.

Watson taught for 12 years at Johns Hopkins University, where he founded a laboratory for animal experimentation and did the research and writing on which his reputation rests. Then a sensational divorce in 1920 forced him to leave the academic world for a career in advertising. He later published a semipopular book, *Behaviorism* (1925), which made him the second best-known psychologist of his time (after Freud). For many people, Watson's claims that there are no hereditary traits and that behavior consists of learned habits constituted the core of psychology. There are no pure behaviorists in the social sciences today, but Watson's work—which led, for example, to the use of rooms with one-way glass walls for studying behavior—survives in many direct and indirect ways.

BOOKS BY WATSON

Behavior: An Introduction to Comparative Psychology. H. Holt & Co. 1914 o.p. Calls for the use of animals as subjects in psychological studies.
Behaviorism. 1925. Norton 1970 repr. of 1930 ed. $9.95. ISBN 0-393-00524-0. In this manifesto for the broader public, Watson argues that human behavior can be studied objectively and scientifically.
Psychology from the Standpoint of a Behaviorist. Classics of Psychology and Psychiatry Ser. Pinter 1983 repr. of 1919 ed. o.p.

WECHSLER, DAVID. 1896–1981

David Wechsler, a Romanian-born American psychologist, is noted for his work on intelligence testing. After receiving his Ph.D. from Columbia University in 1925, he developed a number of intelligence tests, including the Bellevue-Wechsler I (1939), the Bellevue-Wechsler II, or Army Wechsler (1942), the Wechsler Intelligence Scale for Children (1949), and other scales for adults and for preschoolers. Wechsler introduced the concept of the Deviation Quotient— computing IQ by considering the individual's mental ability in comparison with that of the average individual the same age. His definition of intelligence as the "global capacity to act purposefully, to think rationally, and to deal effectively with the environment" emphasized that intelligence is multifaceted. His tests, internationally known and used, have stimulated further exploration of the concept of intelligence. Wechsler received the Distinguished Professional Contribution Award from the American Psychological Association in 1967.

BOOKS BY WECHSLER

Measurement of Adult Intelligence. Williams & Wilkins 1964 o.p.
The Range of Human Capacities. Williams & Wilkins 1935 o.p.

WUNDT, WILHELM. 1832–1920

Wilhelm Wundt, a German psychologist, was the founder of experimental psychology. He was trained in medicine at Heidelberg and became a physiologist, but he soon began collecting data on behavior as well as on structure. In 1873 he published his *Principles on Physiological Psychology*. This book of 870 pages eventually became three volumes totaling 2,317 pages in the sixth edition of 1908–1911. These six editions were, in effect, the history of experimental psychology's first 40 years. From 1875 until 1910, Wundt taught at Leipzig. There he established the world's first psychology laboratory (1875) and founded its first journal of psychology (1881). Wundt's laboratory research concentrated on two topics: (1) sensation and perception and (2) the measurement of reaction times. To study these, he used the technique of introspection, in which human subjects reported exactly what they experienced upon being presented with a stimulus (e.g., light). Despite the primitive conditions of this early laboratory remarkably little that Wundt did has been totally rejected, and the research he conducted created the basic character of modern experimental psychology.

BOOKS BY WUNDT

Ethics: An Investigation of the Facts and Laws of the Moral Life. 1886. 3 vols. Macmillan 1908–11 o.p.

Lectures on Human and Animal Psychology. 1864–65. Greenwood repr. of 1894 ed. $75.00. ISBN 0-313-26945-9

Outlines of Psychology. Scholarly repr. of 1896 ed. $39.00. ISBN 0-403-00038-6

Principles of Physiological Psychology. 1873. Macmillan 1905 o.p.

BOOK ABOUT WUNDT

Rieber, Robert W. *Wilhelm Wundt and the Making of a Scientific Psychology.* Plenum 1980 o.p. Volume of essays that examines Wundt from a historical perspective and provides an account of his work as one of the founders of experimental psychology.

CHAPTER 7

Sociology

Roger A. Salerno

> Sociology is not an impossible science, but it is a very difficult one. It has progressed by disengaging the web of everyday belief, not all at once but little by little, as one taken-for-granted assumption after another has been questioned and replaced. As was once said of philosophy, sociology is like rebuilding a boat, plank by plank, while floating on it in the middle of the ocean.
> —Randall Collins and Michael Makowsky, *The Discovery of Society*

Sociology, the study of social relationships and institutions, is among the youngest social science disciplines. Since its inception, it has been continually struggling to define itself. Although sociology has aimed to be an all-inclusive social science, its lack of boundaries has often made it the subject of intense scholarly criticism. Nevertheless, sociologists have tended to keep their focus broad.

The roots of sociology are to be found in social philosophy, modernity, and the European Enlightenment. Although the French social philosopher AUGUSTE COMTE (see also Vol. 4) is credited with having formulated this study and given it a name and a direction in the early nineteenth century, it was not until the efforts of EMILE DURKHEIM and MAX WEBER several decades later that the discipline took on a more substantial form. Both men made careful studies of the societies in which they lived, setting in motion a wave of sociological research.

As a discipline, sociology is often viewed as an intellectual response to market capitalism, industrialization, urbanization, and the social inequities these forces brought about in mid-nineteenth-century Europe. These dynamic changes gave sociology not only a focus for study but also a particularly Western European bias.

Those who first devised the formal aspects of sociology assumed that science could and would be utilized to better understand the social world and to address its problems. European social philosophers, especially HEGEL (see also Vol. 4), were quite influential in directing the discipline's early course, giving it a decidedly rationalist emphasis. There was a general belief on the part of the founding sociologists that sociology would help to create a new utopia predicated on reason and the methods of science. Gradually, however, the works of KARL MARX (see also Vol. 4) added another dimension. Radical social theory, which emphasized economic hegemony and class distinctions, stimulated much more critical sociology. For Marx and the sociologists influenced by him, society seemed to be characterized by a continuous struggle between weak and strong, poor and rich.

By the twentieth century, sociology had developed a variety of perspectives and modes of scholarly inquiry. The field borrowed from economics, politics, and psychology in formulating its own unique brand of theory. In the early

1900s, sociology in Great Britain and the United States became utilitarian and pragmatic. The Chicago School, which emerged at the University of Chicago in the 1920s under the direction of ROBERT PARK, focused on studies of urban social change: the dynamics of race relations, the marginalization of immigrants, and the social isolation and depersonalization of city living.

World War II and its aftermath gave sociologists the opportunity to work with governments in designing programs and policies to address important social problems. Thus, sociological studies, for the most part, became more empirical. On the other hand, the war also encouraged the development of a more critical sociology as a response to the horrors which had taken place in Nazi Germany. A group of German exiles who were affiliated with what had become known as the Frankfurt School took up such postwar issues as authoritarianism, individual repression, and alienation. This wave of critical inquiry, however, was displaced by others by the early 1970s.

As a discipline that has had to keep pace with its times, sociology has undergone numerous intellectual and theoretical transmutations. Since social reality is never a constant, sociology has assumed varied forms, subject to myriad philosophical, political, and ideological biases that have made the discipline suspect to those who looked to it for definitive, objective answers to complex social questions.

Sociology has never lost its connection to philosophy. It continues to be represented by numerous schools of thought ranging from the positivistic to the existential. Today the theoretical trend in sociology combines Marxism, Freudianism, and poststructural linguistic theory.

However, the more eminent theorists writing today, including JÜRGEN HABERMAS and ANTHONY GIDDENS, have been highly critical of the new intellectual trends in sociological scholarship. They view postmodernism as intellectually self-indulgent, narcissistic, and nihilistic—a road leading to nowhere.

For most sociologists, what separates their field from all the rest is their belief that the social environment should remain the most important focus of attention. By and large, they view the individual as a social construction incapable of human meaning and existence without a socially generated culture. Although one group of sociologists, the sociobiologists, contends that genetic composition has critical social consequences, the vast majority of sociologists view biology as merely one contributing factor.

The subject matter of sociology is exceedingly rich. Whether we look at criminal behavior, human sexuality, religion, women's issues, socialization, race and ethnicity, or the many other concerns that confront our society today, sociology has provided us with many unique insights. The following reading lists present us with a starting point for developing a better understanding of both the discipline itself and its subject matter.

HISTORY AND SURVEYS OF THE FIELD

Aron, Raymond. *Main Currents in Sociological Thought.* 2 vols. Doubleday 1989 $8.95 ea.
  Vol. 1 *Montesquieu, Compte, Marx, Tocqueville, the Sociologists, and the Revolution of 1848.* ISBN 0-385-08804-3. Vol. 2 *Durkeim, Pareto, & Weber.* ISBN 0-385-01976-9.
  Aron's famous lectures at the Sorbonne on the history of sociology and sociological theory.

Bottomore, Tom. *The Frankfurt School and Critical Theory*. Routledge Chapman & Hall $10.95. ISBN 0-85312-468-X. The Frankfurt Institute for Social Research originated so-called critical theory, which stresses the subjective, political role of sociology.

Bulmer, Martin. *The Chicago School of Sociology: Institutionalization, Diversity, and the Rise of Sociological Research*. ISBN 0-226-08005-6. Account of how American sociology first developed its tradition of empirical research.

Collins, Randall, and Michael Makowsky. *The Discovery of Society*. McGraw 1988 ISBN 0-07-553754-8. History of sociological thought, with an emphasis on the lives and work of classical theorists.

Coser, Lewis A. *Masters of Sociological Thought: Ideas in Historical and Social Context*. HarBraceJ 1977 $42.75. ISBN 0-15-555130-2. A survey of classical and contemporary sociologists and their theories.

––––––. *Refugee Scholars in America: Their Impact and Their Experiences*. Yale U. Pr. 1984 $38.00. ISBN 0-300-03193-9

Encyclopedia of Sociology. 3 vols. Macmillan 1991 $340.00. ISBN 0-02-897051-9. A survey of the discipline's central ideas, concepts, and theories.

Gouldner, Alvin. *The Coming Crisis of Western Sociology*. Basic 1970 o.p. Critical survey of the last hundred years of Western sociology.

Inkeles, Alex, Ralph Turner, W. R. Scott, and Judith Blake, eds. *Annual Review of Sociology*. 18 vols. Annual Reviews 1975–present. Vol. 18 1992 $49.00. ISBN 0-8243-2218-5

Jary, David, and Julia Jary. *The Harper Collins Dictionary of Sociology*. HarpC 1992 $13.00. ISBN 0-06-461036-5. Comprehensive dictionary of basic ideas, schools of thought, and sociologists.

Madge, John H. *Origins of Scientific Sociology*. Free Pr. 1967 $16.95. ISBN 0-02-919710-4. Very readable review of major developments in social research.

Schwendinger, Herman, and Julia Schwendinger. *The Sociologists of the Chair*. Basic 1974 o.p. Comprehensive, radical history of the intellectual and ideological roots of American sociology and its European influences.

Smelser, Neil J., ed. *Handbook of Sociology*. Sage 1988 $89.95. ISBN 0-8039-2665-0. Collection of essays examining historical trends and developments.

Smith, Dennis. *The Chicago School: A Liberal Critique of Capitalism*. St. Martin 1988 $14.95. ISBN 0-312-003862-2. Surveys the ideology and theories of the Chicago School.

Swingewood, Alan. *A Short History of Sociological Thought*. St. Martin 1981 $39.95. ISBN 0-312-06735-6

METHODS OF RESEARCH

Aiken, Leona, and Stephen G. West. *Multiple Regression*. Sage 1991 $34.00. ISBN 0-8039-36052-2. Good reference book for those working on multivariate prediction research projects.

Bailey, Kenneth D. *Methods of Social Research*. Free Pr. 1987 $32.95. ISBN 0-02-901450-6. Basic introduction to both quantitative and qualitative methods.

Blumer, Herbert. *Symbolic Interactionism: Perspective and Method*. U. CA Pr. 1986 $11.95. ISBN 0-520-05676-0

Durkeheim, Emile. *The Rules of Sociological Method*. 1895. Free Pr. 1982 $14.95. ISBN 0-02-907940-3. Asserts that the scientific method is applicable to the study of society and can help discover "social facts" underlying all human relations.

Lazarsfeld, Paul F., and others, eds. *The Language of Social Research: A Reader in the Methodology of Social Research*. Free Pr. 1965 o.p.

AGE AND AGING

Binstock, Robert H., and Linda George, eds. *Handbook of Aging and the Social Sciences*. Acad. Pr. 1990 $74.95. ISBN 0-12-099190-X. New topics addressed here include mortality and morbidity, social psychological states, illness behavior in later life, and comparative study of old age pensions.

Birren, James, and Ethel Shanas. *Handbook of the Psychology of Aging*. Acad. Pr. 1991 $34.95. ISBN 0-12-10128-6. Intended to serve as a definitive reference. Incorporates recent developments in research.

Brubaker, Timothy H., ed. *Family Relationships in Later Life*. Sage 1990 $46.00. ISBN 0-8039-3321-5

Eckert, Kevin. *The Unseen Elderly: A Study of Marginally Subsistent Hotel Dwellers*. 1980. SDSU Pr. 1980 $37.50. ISBN 0-916304-47-7. A study of single-room-occupancy hotel dwellers in downtown San Diego.

Golant, Stephen M. *Housing America's Elderly*. Sage 1992 $24.00. ISBN 0-8039-4764-X. An examination of how the aged are housed.

Hess, Beth B., and Elizabeth W. Markson. *Aging and Old Age: An Introduction to Social Gerontology*. Macmillan 1980 o.p.

Kelley, Patricia, and Maggie Callanan. *Final Gifts: Understanding the Special Awareness, Needs and Communications of the Dying*. Poseidon Pr. 1992 $21.00. ISBN 0-671-70006-5. Acute observations and astute advice from two hospice nurses who have cared for the dying.

Kertzer, D. L., and Jennie Keith, eds. *Age and Anthropological Theory*. Cornell Univ. Pr. 1984 $39.95. ISBN 0-8014-1567-5

Quill, Timothy E. *Death and Dying: Making Choices and Taking Charge*. Norton 1993 $21.95. ISBN 0-393-03448-8. One physician's redefining of medicine's role in cases of terminal illness. A humane, honest, and sympathetic outlook.

Riley, Matilda W., and others. *Aging and Society*. 3 vols. Russell Sage. Vol. 1 *An Inventory of Research Findings*. 1968 $55.00. ISBN 0-87154-718-X. Vol. 2 *Aging and the Professions*. 1969 $40.00. ISBN 0-87154-719-8. Vol. 3 *A Sociology of Age Stratification*. 1972. ISBN 0-87154-720-1

Rubinstein, Robert L., Janet Kilbridge, and Sharon Nagy. *Elders Living Alone: Frailty and the Perception of Choice*. Aldine de Gruyter 1992 $35.95. ISBN 0-202-36083-0. A study of the single elderly and their struggle to maintain independence.

AIDS, HEALTH CARE, AND DISABLING CONDITIONS

Baldwin, Steve, and John Hattersley, eds. *Mental Handicap: Social Science Perspectives*. Routledge 1990 $55.00. ISBN 0-415-00596-5. Examines the treatment and care of the mentally challenged.

Bailey, Eric J. *Urban African American Health Care*. U. Pr. of Amer. 1991 $49.00. ISBN 0-8191-8276-1. Case studies of African-American health care in two cities, Detroit and Houston.

Fee, Elizabeth, and Daniel Fox, eds. *AIDS: The Making of a Chronic Disease*. U. CA Pr. 1992 $45.00. ISBN 0-520-07778-4. Collection of essays dealing with the social and political issues centering on AIDS.

Garbarino, James, Patrick Brookhauser, and others. *Special Children–Special Risks: The Maltreatment of Children with Disabilities*. Aldine de Gruyter 1987 $44.95. ISBN 0-202-36045-8. Discusses the abuse of handicapped children and the ways to protect them.

Gupta, Sunil, and Tessa Boffin, eds. *Ecstatic Antibodies: Resisting the AIDS Mythology*. Unwin Hyman 1990 $44.95. ISBN 1-85489-005-0. Examination of the AIDS crisis and its relationship to notions of gender, family, nation, race, and diversity.

Levine, Paula L., John Bruhn, and N. Turner. *The Psychosocial Aspects of AIDS: An Annotated Bibliography*. Garland 1990 $75.00. ISBN 0-8240-5835-6. Analyzes the social dimensions of AIDS epidemic, including epidemiology and AIDS prevention and awareness programs.

Luske, Bruce. *Mirrors of Madness: Patrolling the Psychic Boarders*. Aldine de Gruyter 1990 $39.95. ISBN 0-202-30422-1. Impact of the mentally ill on those who care for them.

Patton, Cindy. *Inventing AIDS*. Routledge 1990 $42.50. ISBN 0-415-90256-8. Examines peoples' attitudes about AIDS and the types of public policies developed to address this health problem.

Wertz, Dorothy C., ed. *Research in the Sociology of Health Care*. Vol. 2 Jai Pr. 1981 $63.50. ISBN 0-89232-199-7. Vol. 6 Jai Pr. 1987 $63.50. ISBN 0-89232-834-7. Reports on research dealing with the sociology of health care.

ART, LITERATURE, AND INTELLECTUAL LIFE

Ben-David, Joseph, and Terry Nicholas Clark, eds. *Culture and Its Creators*. U. Ch. Pr. 1977 $30.00. ISBN 0-226-04222-7. Includes essays by 13 leading social scientists.

Coser, Lewis A., and others. *Books: The Culture and Commerce of Publishing*. U. Ch. Pr. 1985 $16.95. ISBN 0-226-11593-3. A brilliant sociological analysis of the book publishing industry.

Eagleton, Terry. *Marxism and Literary Criticism*. U. CA Pr. 1976 $9.95. ISBN 0-520-03243-8. Short introduction to Marxist literary criticism.

Escarpit, Robert. *The Sociology of Literature*. Trans. by E. Pick. Intl. Spec. Bk. 1971 $32.50. ISBN 0-7146-2729-1

Foster, Hal. *Recordings: Art, Spectacle, Cultural Politics*. Bay Pr. 1985 $16.95. ISBN 0-941920-03-8. Critical essays on contemporary art and its relation to a rapidly changing society.

Ghirardo, Diane, ed. *Out of Site: A Social Criticism of Architecture*. Bay Pr. 1991 $16.95. ISBN 0-941920-19-14. Essays on the sociology of architecture in modern society.

Gouldner, Alvin W. *The Future of Intellectuals and the Rise of the New Class*. OUP 1982 o.p. Describes the rise of a new intellectual class and the ideology supporting it, with close attention to the role of communications technology.

Hauser, Arnold. *The Social History of Art*. 4 vols. Random 1985 $6.95 ea. Vol. 1 *Prehistoric Times Ancient-Oriental Urban Cultures Greece and Rome Middle Ages*. ISBN 0-685-09925-3. Vol. 2 *Renaissance Mannerism and Baroque*. ISBN 0-685-09926-1. Vol. 3 *Rococco Classicism and Romanticism*. ISBN 0-685-09927-X. Vol. 4 *Naturalism Impressionism and the Film Age*. ISBN 0-685-09928-8

Sennett, Richard. *The Conscience of the Eye*. Knopf 1992 $9.95. ISBN 0-394-30878-2. Examines urban life and culture by looking at its art, architecture, and literature.

Shils, Edward. *The Intellectuals and the Powers: And Other Essays*. U. Ch. Pr. 1972 o.p. Collection of essays dealing with intellectuals of various sorts—their work, institutions, and societal relations.

Wallis, Brian, ed. *If You Lived Here...The City in Art, Theory, and Social Activism*. Bay Pr. 1991 $16.95. ISBN 0-941920-18-6. Documents the current crisis in urban housing and discusses how artists have tried to bring about change.

Znaniecki, Florian. *The Social Role of the Man of Knowledge*. Transaction Pubs. 1985 $19.95. ISBN 0-88738-642-3. Introduction by Lewis A. Coser.

COLLECTIVE BEHAVIOR

Allport, Gordon W., and Leo Postman. *The Psychology of Rumor*. Russell 1965 repr. of 1947 ed. o.p. Using an experimental research method, authors examine the nature of rumor, its function, its circulation, and its results.

Argyle, Michael. *Cooperation: The Basis of Sociability*. Routledge 1991 o.p. Examines the origins of cooperation and how it is manifest in all social relations.

Cantril, Hadley. *The Invasion from Mars*. Bks. Demand repr. of 1940 ed. $64.80. ISBN 0-7837-1947-7. Fascinating study of reaction to Orson Welles radio program describing an invasion of Martians.

Kornhauser, William. *The Politics of Mass Society*. Macmillan 1959 o.p. Examines differences in mass tendencies and pluralistic tendencies in modern society and attempts to show how pluralism supports liberal democracy.

Le Bon, Gustave. *The Crowd*. Cherokee 1982 repr. of 1895 ed. $9.95. ISBN 0-87797-168-4. Recalls recent college graduate's travels from North Carolina to South Dakota en route to Pacific Coast.

McPhail, Clark. *The Myth of the Madding Crowd*. Aldine de Gruyter 1991 $44.95. ISBN 0-202-30424. After analyzing major theories of crowd behavior, the author theorizes that there is a life cycle of human gatherings and a taxonomy of collective behavior.

Ortega y Gasset, José. *The Revolt of the Masses*. 1932. Trans. by Anthony Kerrigan. U. of Notre Dame Pr. 1984 $25.95. ISBN 0-268-01609-7. Introduction by Saul Bellow. Analysis of ways in which social and technological advances of the nineteenth century gave rise to twentieth-century political movements intent on destroying the conditions that fostered them.

Rose, Jerry. *Outbreaks*. Free Pr. 1981 $16.95. ISBN 0-02-926790-0

Shibutani, Tamotsu, ed. *Human Nature and Collective Behavior: Papers in Honor of Herbert Blumer*. Transaction Pubs. 1973 repr. of 1970 ed. $5.95. ISBN 0-087855-581-1. Essays on various aspects of collective behavior and social psychology involving symbolic interactionist research techniques.

Smelser, Neil J. *Theory of Collective Behavior*. Free Pr. 1962 o.p.

Turner, Ralph, and Lewis Killian. *Collective Behavior*. P-H 1972 $26.95. ISBN 0-13-140682-5. Diverse essays on speculative, historical, and quantitative studies on collective behavior and its forms and attributes.

COMMUNICATIONS, FILM, AND TELEVISION

Bogart, Leo. *The Age of Television: A Study of Viewing Habits and the Impact of Television on American Life*. Continuum o.p. Thorough analysis of the history, content, audience habits, and advertisers of the commercial television medium.

_____. *The Press and Public: Who Reads What, Where, and Why in American Newspapers*. Erlbaum 1981 $29.95. ISBN 0-8058-0432-3. Examination of how the newspaper industry deals with social and technological changes that threaten its survival.

Compaine, Benjamin. *Understanding New Media: Trends and Issues in Electronic Distribution of Information*. Harper Busn. 1984 $32.00. ISBN 0-88410-977-1

Coser, Lewis A., and others. *Books: The Culture and Commerce of Publishing*. U. Ch. Pr. 1985 o.p.

DeFleur, Melvin L., and Sandra J. Ball-Rokeach. *Theories of Mass Communication*. Longman 1989 $24.95. ISBN 0-582-99870-0

Dennis, Everett. *Basic Issues in Mass Communication*. Longman 1991 o.p.

_____. *Of Media and People*. Sage 1992 $16.95. ISBN 0-8039-4747-X. Individuals who work in the media and current trends of media consolidation.

Field, Harry, and Paul F. Lazarsfeld. *The People Look at Radio*. Ayer 1976 repr. of 1946 ed. $16.00. ISBN 0-405-07675-4

Gitlin, Todd. *Inside Prime Time*. Pantheon 1985 $17.00. ISBN 0-394-73787-3. Examines the people who create prime-time television.

_____. *The Whole World Is Watching*. U. CA Pr. 1980 $35.00. ISBN 0-520-03889-4. Looks at how the mass media made and unmade the "new left" of the 1960s.

Herman, Edward S., and Noam Chomsky. *Manufacturing Consent: The Political Economy of the Mass Media*. Pantheon 1988 $14.95. ISBN 0-679-72034-0. Argues that the popular news media are controlled by an elite.

Lazarsfeld, Paul F. *Radio and the Printed Page: An Introduction to the Study of Radio and Its Role in the Communication of Ideas*. Ayer 1971 repr. of 1940 ed. $25.50. ISBN 0-405-03575-6

_____. *Radio Listening in America: The People Look at Radio Again*. Ed. by Lewis A. Coser and Walter W. Powell. *Perennial Works in Sociology Ser*. Ayer 1979 repr. of 1948 ed. $15.00. ISBN 0-405-12100-8

McLuhan, Marshall. *Understanding Media: The Extensions of Man*. NAL-Dutton 1973 $4.50. ISBN 0-451-62196-3

Qualter, Terence H. *Advertising and Democracy in the Mass Age*. St. Martin 1991 $45.00. ISBN 0-312-06507-8. Examines the problems inherent in mass society and mass media advertising.

Riggins, Stephen. *Ethnic Minority Media*. Sage 1992 $42.95. ISBN 0-8039-47232. Analyzes the impact of minority media on ethnic and cultural cohesion.

Shearer, Benjamin F., and Marilyn Huxford, eds. *Communications and Society: A Bibliography on Communications Technologies and Their Social Impact*. Greenwood 1983 $35.00. ISBN 0-313-23713-1

Steiner, Gary A. *The People Look at Television*. Knopf 1963 o.p.

Tannenbaum, Percy H., ed. *The Entertainment Functions of Television*. L. Erlbaum Assocs. 1980 $39.95. ISBN 0-89859-013-2

Wolfenstein, Martha, and Nathan Leites. *Movies: A Psychological Study*. Atheneum 1970 repr. of 1950 ed. o.p.

CONFLICT AND CONFLICT RESOLUTION

Coleman, James S. *Community Conflict*. Free Pr. 1957 o.p. Community controversy in relation to selected public policy issues.

Collins, Randall. *Conflict Sociology: Toward an Explanatory Science*. Acad. Pr. 1975 o.p.

Coser, Lewis A. *The Functions of Social Conflict*. Macmillan 1964 $13.95. ISBN 0-02-906810-X. Study of the positive aspects of social conflict and its uses in enhancing social relations.

Dahrendorf, Ralf. *Class and Class Conflict in Industrial Society*. Stanford U. Pr. 1959 $45.00. ISBN 0-8047-0560-7

Herman, Edward S., and Gerry O'Sullivan. *The "Terrorism" Industry: The Experts and Institutions that Shape Our View of Terror*. Pantheon 1990 $14.95. ISBN 0-679-72559-8. Contends that multinational industries have created an artificial perception of terrorism to manipulate support for increased military spending while cloaking their own terrorist acts.

Lewin, Kurt. *Resolving Social Conflicts*. Ed. by Gertrud W. Lewin. Spec. Bk. 1978 o.p. Collection of essays written between 1935 and 1946 that deal with the individual in the group, group dynamics, and group psychology.

Powell, Walter W., and Richard Robbins, eds. *Conflict and Consensus: A Festschrift in Honor of Lewis A. Coser*. Free Pr. 1984 $29.95. ISBN 0-02-925400-0

Raiffa, Howard. *The Art and Science of Negotiation*. HUP 1982 $12.50. ISBN 0-674-4813-X

Short, James F., Jr., and Marvin E. Wolfgang, eds. *Collective Violence*. Am. Acad. Pol. Soc. Sci. 1970 $15.95. ISBN 0-87761-129-7. Collection of essays by various authors dealing with diverse aspects of national and international violence.

Simmel, Georg. *Conflict and the Web of Group Affiliations*. 1908. Free Pr. 1955 $12.95. ISBN 0-02-928840-1

Van der Dennen, Johan M. G., and Vincent S. Falger. *Sociobiology and Conflict*. Chapman & Hall 1990 $89.50. ISBN 0-412-33770-3. An international team of researchers tries to explain violence and conflict as products of human evolution.

Varoufakis, Yanis. *Rational Conflict*. Blackwell Pubs. 1991 o.p. A critical review of the rationalist argument that human conflict can be scientifically predicted.

CRIME, DEVIANCE, AND SOCIAL CONTROL

Bedau, Hugo A., ed. *The Death Penalty in America*. OUP 1982 $12.95. ISBN 0-19-502987-9

Cashmore, E. Ellis, and Eugene McLaughlin, eds. *Out of Order? The Policing of Black People*. Routledge 1991 $15.95. ISBN 0-415-03726-3. Looks at police-community relations in black communities in the United States and Britain.

Cavadino, Michael, and James Dignan. *The Penal System: An Introduction*. Sage 1992 $55.00. ISBN 0-8039-8343-3. Examination of the British penal system.

Foucault, Michel. *Discipline and Punish: The Birth of the Prison*. Random 1979 $11.00. ISBN 0-394-72767-3. Examines how physical and mental control have been used on individuals to ensure compliance and maintain order.

_____. *Madness and Civilization: A History of Insanity in the Age of Reason*. Random 1988 $11.00. ISBN 0-679-72110-X. Examines the concept of madness and how it has changed between 1500 and 1800.

Goffman, Erving. *Asylums*. Doubleday 1961 $10.95. ISBN 0-0385-00016-2

Johnston, Les. *The Rebirth of Private Policing*. Routledge 1992 o.p. Historical and social analysis of private and public policing.

Hirschi, Travis. *Causes of Delinquency*. U. CA Pr. 1969 o.p.

Holmes, Ronald M., and James DeBuger. *Serial Murder*. Sage 1987 $38.00. ISBN 0-8039-2840-8. Historical examination of serial murders and their perpetrators.

Kadish, Sanford H., ed. *Encyclopedia of Crime and Justice*. 4 vols. Macmillan 1983 $375.00. ISBN 0-02-918110-0. An interdisciplinary and scholarly approach to the study of criminal behavior and society's responses.

Kuper, Leo. *Genocide: Its Political Use in the Twentieth Century*. Yale U. Pr. 1982 $35.00. ISBN 0-300-03120-3

Mokhiber, Russell. *Corporate Crime and Violence*. Sierra 1989 $16.00. ISBN 0-87156-608-7. Case studies of corporate violence against the environment, communities, and individuals.

Morris, Allison. *Women, Crime and Criminal Justice*. Blackwell Pubs. 1987 $45.00. ISBN 0-631-15444-2. Study of women's criminality and how the stereotypical conception of women's roles affects responses to them in the criminal justice system.

Riedel, Marc. *Stranger Violence: A Theoretical Inquiry*. Garland 1992 $35.00. ISBN 0-8153-0094-8. The first comprehensive study of stranger violence; includes statistics and theoretical analysis.

Sellin, Thorsten. *Culture, Conflict, and Crime*. Kraus repr. of 1938 ed. o.p.

Silberman, Charles E. *Criminal Violence, Criminal Justice*. Random 1980 $9.95. ISBN 0-394-74147-1. Gripping report on continuing causes of crime in the United States.

Stinchcombe, Arthur L. *Crime and Punishment: Changing Attitudes in America*. Social and Behavioral Science Ser. Bks. Demand repr. of 1980 ed. $49.70. ISBN 0-8357-6898-8

Sutherland, Edwin H. *White Collar Crime*. Greenwood 1983 repr. of 1961 ed. $43.75. ISBN 0-313-24227-5. Foreword by Donald Cressey.

Tunnell, Kenneth. *Choosing Crime*. Nelson-Hall 1992 $17.95. ISBN 0-8304-1242-5. Deals with various theories of criminal behavior.

Vold, George B. *Theoretical Criminology*. OUP 1985 $29.95. ISBN 0-19-503616-6

ENVIRONMENT, TECHNOLOGY, AND POPULATION

Bean, Lee L., Geraldine Mineau, and D. Anderson. *Fertility Change on the American Frontier*. U. CA Pr. 1990 $42.50. ISBN 0-520-06633-2. Sociohistorical study of U.S. demographic changes.

Bogue, Donald J. *The Population of the United States: Historical Trends and Future Projections*. Free Pr. 1989 $137.50. ISBN 0-02-904700-5. Good bibliographies, charts, graphs, and tables.

Bonner, Raymond. *At the Hand of Man: Peril and Hope for Africa's Wildlife*. Knopf 1993 $24.00. ISBN 0-679-40008-7. An important exploration into the wider ramifications of Western animal rights activists' over-zealousness and exclusive focus on animals. An examination into a mindset that extends to all environmental issues.

Brown, Phil, and Edwin J. Mikkelsen. *No Safe Place: Toxic Waste, Leukemia, and Community Action*. U. CA Pr. 1990 $24.95. ISBN 0-520-07034-8. Community action by people living near toxic waste sites.

Bullard, Robert D., ed. *Confronting Environmental Racism*. South End Pr. $40.00. 1993 ISBN 0-89608-447-7. Leading scholars and activists contend that governments discriminate against minority communities in disposing of toxic waste.

Canter, David, David Stea, and M. Krampen. *Ethnoscapes: Transcultural Studies in Action and Place.* 2 vols. Ashgate Pub. Co. 1987. Vol. 1 *New Directions in Environmental Participation.* $54.95. ISBN 0-566-05570-8. Vol. 2 *Environmental Policy Assessment.* $58.00. ISBN 0-566-05569-4. Examines citizen participation in environmental planning.

Gore, Al. *Earth in the Balance: Ecology and the Human Spirit.* NAL-Dutton 1993 $13.00. ISBN 0-452-26935-0. Bold initiatives for change in Vice President Gore's compelling primer.

Menard, Scott, and Elizabeth Moen. *Perspectives on Population.* OUP 1987 $29.95. ISBN 0-19-504190-9. A comprehensive reader that covers basic population issues from a variety of perspectives.

Petersen, William, and Renée Petersen. *Dictionary of Demography.* 2 vols. Greenwood 1986 $150.00. ISBN 0-313-24134-1. Fifty-seven international contributing scholars and statesmen.

Ross, John A., ed. *International Encyclopedia of Population.* 2 vols. Macmillan 1982. ISBN 0-02-927430-3. A useful and authoritative general reference.

Shabecoff, Philip. *A Fierce Green Fire: The American Environmental Movement.* Hill & Wang 1993. ISBN 0-8090-8459-7. Wide-ranging survey of the U.S. environmental tradition; by a former veteran *New York Times* correspondent.

Sitarz, Daniel, ed. *Agenda Twenty-one: The Earth Summit Strategy to Save Our Planet.* Nova Pub. IL 1993 $24.95. ISBN 0-935755-11-X. Comprehensive in its scope and resulting from a massive global effort. An abridged edition of the 900 page U.N. document. Highly recommended for all readers.

FAMILY AND MARRIAGE

Aker, Loren E., and others. *AIDS-Proofing Your Kids.* Beyond Words Pub. 1992 $8.95. ISBN 0-941831-72-8. Practical guide written by three Ph.D's. Critical social issues are discussed, as well as general sex education.

Barrett, Michele, and Mary McIntosh. *The Anti-Social Family.* Routledge Chapman & Hall 1991 $16.95. ISBN 0-86091-545-X. A radical feminist response to the myths of familialism; calls for a return to family values.

Becker, Gary S. *A Treatise on the Family.* HUP 1991 $45.00. ISBN 0-674-90698-5

Bernard, Jessie. *The Future of Marriage.* Yale U. Pr. 1982 $15.00. ISBN 0-300-02853-9

Cherlin, Andrew. *Marriage, Divorce, Remarriage.* HUP 1992 $12.95. ISBN 0-674-55082-X

Clapp, Genevieve. *Divorce and New Beginnings: An Authoritative Guide.* Wiley 1992 $14.95. ISBN 0-471-52631-2. Directed to divorced couples, non-custodial parents, single parents, and childless couples. Drawn from nearly 400 sources.

Coontz, Stephanie. *The Way We Never Were: American Families and the Nostalgia Trap.* Basic 1992 $27.00. ISBN 0-465-00135-1. A reassessment of the true nature of families in the United States and how family structures have evolved.

Dym, Barry, and Michael L. Glenn. *Couples: Exploring and Understanding the Cycles of Intimate Relationships.* HarpC 1993 $20.00. ISBN 0-06-016713-0. An attempt to codify and define various stages in intimate relationships in order to overcome stagnancy.

Goldscheider, Frances K., and Linda Waite. *New Families, No Families? Studies in Demography Ser.* U. CA Pr. 1991 $34.95. ISBN 0-520-07222-7. Reviews the changes taking place in the form and functions of American families.

Goode, William J. *The Family.* P-H 1982 $15.95. ISBN 0-13-30762-1

Greteman, James. *Creating a Marriage.* Paulist Pr. 1993 $6.95. ISBN 0-8091-3393-8. Beautifully and poetically written.

Henderson, Ronald W., ed. *Parent-Child Interaction: Theory, Research and Prospects.* Acad. Pr. 1981 $65.00. ISBN 0-12-340620-X

Henslin, James M., ed. *Marriage and Family in a Changing Society.* Free Pr. 1985 $15.95. ISBN 0-02-914870-7

Muller, Ann. *Parents Matter*. Naiad Pr. 1987 $9.95. ISBN 0-930044-91-6. An intelligent study on parents of gay and lesbian children.

Newberger, E., and R. Bourne. *Unhappy Families*. Mosby Yr. Bk. 1989 $29.95. ISBN 0-88416-504-3. Examines the causes, consequences, and possible cures for abuse.

Olkin, Sylvia K. *Positive Parenting Fitness*. Avery Pub. 1992 $12.95. ISBN 0-89529-481-8. Interesting and readable. An alternative approach using established yoga techniques and natural nutrition.

Weitzmann, Lenore J. *The Divorce Revolution: The Unexpected Social and Economic Consequences for Women and Children in America*. Free Pr. 1985 $29.95. ISBN 0-02-934710-6

Whyte, Martin King. *Dating, Mating and Marriage*. Aldine de Gruyter 1990 $49.95. ISBN 0-202-30415-9. Traces changing American patterns of dating, courtship, and marriage.

Worth, Cecilia. *The Birth of a Father*. McGraw 1988 $8.95. ISBN 0-07-071875-3. Pregnancy and birth from a male perspective. Informative, valuable, and virtually unprecedented.

GENDER

Barnes, Ruth, and Joanne B. Eicher, eds. *Dress and Gender*. Berg Pubs. 1993 $65.00. ISBN 0-85496-720-6. Collection of essays on the gender significance of clothing in various cultures at various times.

Bernard, Jessie. *The Female World*. Free Pr. 1981 $14.95. ISBN 0-385-07305-4

Bradley, Harriet. *Men's Work, Women's Work*. U. of Minn. Pr. 1989 $44.95. ISBN 0-1866-1814-3. An examination of the sex-typing of work and how women's occupations have varied with place, culture, and era.

Butler, Judith. *Gender Trouble: Feminism and the Subversion of Identity*. Routledge 1989 $32.95. ISBN 0-415-90042-5. Views gender as primarily a product of power relationships.

Crompton, Rosemary, and Michael Mann, eds. *Gender and Stratification*. Blackwell Pubs. 1986 $49.95. ISBN 0-7456-0167-7. Analyzes the relationships among gender, social power, and advantage.

Davidson, Nicholas, ed. *Gender Sanity: The Case Against Feminism*. U. of PA Pr. 1989 o.p. A conservative response to feminist ideals and philosophy.

Easthope, Antony. *What A Man's Gotta Do: The Masculine Myth in Popular Culture*. Unwin Hyman 1990 $34.95. ISBN 0-04-445739-1. Examines masculinity in Western society, especially how the media represent its emphasis on denial of feminine side.

Klein, Ethel. *Gender Politics*. HUP 1984 $20.00. ISBN 0-674-34196-1

Rossi, Alice S., ed. *Gender and the Life Course*. Aldine de Gruyter $43.95. ISBN 0-202-30311-X

Shaver, Philip, and Clyde Hendrex. *Sex and Gender*. Sage 1987 $42.95. ISBN 0-8039-2929-3. Collection of essays on various gender issues.

Walczak, Yvette. *He and She: Men in the Eighties*. Routledge 1990 $49.95. ISBN 0-415-00514-0. In interviews, 51 men discuss how they consider themselves to be different from women.

Williams, Christine L. *Gender Differences at Work*. U. CA Pr. 1989 $22.50. ISBN 0-520-06373-2. A study of men and women working in nontraditional occupations.

HUMAN SEXUALITY

Carter, Angela. *The Sadeian Woman: An Ideology of Pornography*. Pantheon 1988 $8.95. ISBN 0-394-75893-5. A feminist analysis of Sade and the role of power in sexual relations.

Foucault, Michel. *The History of Sexuality: The Care of the Self, Volume III*. Random 1984 $7.95. ISBN 0-394-74115. Eroticism in Golden Age of Rome and the moral reflections of Plutarch, Seneca, and others.

———. *The History of Sexuality: An Introduction, Volume I*. Random 1976 $9.00 ISBN 0-679-72469-9. Traces the history of human sexuality, self-identity, and power.

———. *The History of Sexuality: The Uses of Pleasure, Volume II*. Random 1984 $8.95. ISBN 0-394-75122-1. Examines ancient Greek texts on eroticism and the connection between Western morality and regulation of sexual behaviour.

Gullotta, Thomas P., Gerald Adams, and R. Montemayor, eds. *Adolescent Sexuality*. Sage 1992 $42.95. ISBN 0-8039-4772-0. Papers that explore such issues as adolescent pregnancy, homosexuality, and gender.

Humphreys, Laud. *The Tearoom Trade: Impersonal Sex in Public Places*. Aldine de Gruyter 1975 $39.95. ISBN 0-202-30282-2. Unorthodox study of anonymous male homosexual encounters in public restrooms.

Ruse, Michael. *Homosexuality*. Blackwell Pubs. 1988 $19.95. ISBN 0-631-17553-9. Looks at past and present theories and attitudes about homosexuality.

Turner, Bryan S. *The Body and Society*. Blackwell Pubs. o.p. Advocates the integration of the body into sociological discussion.

INTERACTION

Barber, Bernard. *The Logic and Limits of Trust*. Rutgers U. Pr. 1983 $27.50. ISBN 0-8135-1002-3

Blau, Peter M. *Exchange and Power in Social Life*. Transaction Pubs. 1986 $14.95. Analysis of the complex social processes and interpersonal relations that govern social structures, dependence, competition, and conflict.

Blumer, Herbert. *Symbolic Interactionism: Perspective and Method*. P-H 1969 $21.95. ISBN 0-88738-628-8. A collection of Blumer's writings on this topic.

Fischer, Claude S. *To Dwell among Friends: Personal Networks in Town and City*. U. Ch. Pr. 1982 $35.00. ISBN 0-226-25138-1. Research on the residents of 50 California cities; reveals how people form social networks.

Gambetta, Diego. *Trust: Making and Breaking Cooperative Relations*. Blackwell Pubs. 1988 $38.95. ISBN 0-318-49987-8. Collection of essays dealing with the social and intellectual attributes and purpose of trust.

Mead, George H. *Mind, Self, and Society: From the Standpoint of a Social Behaviorist*. 1934. Ed. by Charles W. Morris. o.p. U. Ch. Pr. 1967 $30.00. Presents Mead's "Me-I" model to explain the formation of self-identity.

Perrucci, Robert, and Harry R. Porter, eds. *Networks of Power*. Aldine de Gruyter 1990 $39.95. ISBN 0-202-30342-X. Analysis of power using innovative research methodologies.

INTERGROUP RELATIONS

Allport, Gordon W. *The Nature of Prejudice*. 1954. Addison-Wesley 1979 $5.95. ISBN 0-201-00179-9. Classic work on nature of prejudice. Preface by Thomas Pettigrew.

Apostle, Richard A., and Marijean Suelzle. *The Anatomy of Racial Attitudes*. U. CA Pr. 1983 $42.50. ISBN 0-520-4719-2

Campbell, Angus. *White Attitudes toward Black People*. Inst. Soc. Res. 1971 $8.00. ISBN 0-87944-006-6. Analysis of data from the Survey Research Center on white attitudes toward African Americans between the years 1964 and 1970.

Clark, Kenneth B. *Dark Ghetto: Dilemmas of Social Power*. HarpC 1965 $10.00. Classic study of the African-American ghetto in the United States and the social, psychological, educational, and economic problems associated with urban ghetto life.

Coleman, James S. *Equality of Educational Opportunity.* 2 vols. Ed. by Lewis A. Coser and Walter W. Powell. *Perennial Works in Sociology Ser.* Ayer 1975 repr. of 1966 ed. $49.95. ISBN 0-905-12088-5

Eisenstadt, Shmuel N. *The Absorption of Immigrants.* Greenwood 1975 repr. of 1954 ed. o.p.

Farley, Reynolds. *Blacks and Whites: Narrowing the Gap? Social Trends in the United States Ser.* HUP 1984 $22.95. ISBN 0-674-07631-1. Assessment of the gains of African Americans as a result of the civil rights struggles of the 1960s and 1970s.

Freyre, Gilberto. *The Masters and the Slaves.* Knopf 1964 o.p. Study of the formation and disintegration of patriarchal society in Brazil starting from the sixteenth century.

James, Daniel. *Illegal Immigration: An Unfolding Crisis.* U. Pr. of Amer. 1991 $42.00. ISBN 0-8191-8404-7. Examination of illegal immigration in the United States, with an emphasis on Mexico.

Myrdal, Gunnar. *An American Dilemma.* 1944. Harper 1962 o.p. A monumental study of blacks in American life, conducted by an eminent Swedish economist.

Pettigrew, Thomas F. *The Sociology of Race Relations: Reflection and Reform.* Free Pr. 1980 $19.95. ISBN 0-02-925710-9

Pettigrew, Thomas F., and others. *Prejudice. Dimensions in Ethnicity Ser.* HUP 1982 $6.95. ISBN 0-674-70063-5

Portes, Alejandro, and Ruben G. Rimbaut. *Immigrant America: A Portrait.* U. CA Pr. 1990 $11.95. ISBN 0-520-07038-0. A comprehensive examination of recent American immigration.

Portes, Alejandro, and Robert L. Bach. *Latin Journey: Cuban and Mexican Immigrants in the United States.* U. CA Pr. 1985 $57.00. ISBN 0-520-05003-7

Quinley, Harold E., and Charles Y. Glock. *Anti-Semitism in America.* Transaction Pubs. 1983 $15.95. ISBN 0-87855-940-X. Based on a 15-year nationwide research project; the authors document the nature, extent, and characteristics of anti-Semitism in the United States.

Selznick, Gertude J., and Stephen Steinberg. *The Tenacity of Prejudice: Anti-Semitism in Contemporary America.* Greenwood 1979 repr. of 1969 ed. $49.75. ISBN 0-313-20965-0. This study, based on a sample of over 2,000 cases, assesses the sources, nature, and extent of anti-Semitism during the 1940s and 1950s.

MODERNIZATION AND SOCIAL CHANGE

Alexander, Jeffrey C., and Piotr Sztompka, eds. *Rethinking Progress.* Routledge Chapman & Hall 1990 $55.00. ISBN 0-04-445753-7. Critical assessments of the notion of progress by American and European contributors.

Campbell, Colin. *The Romantic Ethic and the Spirit of Modern Consumerism.* Blackwell Pubs. 1989 $16.95. ISBN 0-631-16941-5. A scholarly look at the relationship between the romantic movement and modern consumer society.

Giddens, Anthony. *Modernity and Self-Identity.* Stanford U. Pr. 1991 $35.00. ISBN 0-847-1943-8. Calls upon Foucault, Goffman, Lasch, and Freud, among others, to discuss experiences of self in the period of high modernity, which is often conceived as a culture of risk.

Lash, Scott, and Jonathan Friedman, eds. *Modernity and Identity.* Blackwell Pubs. 1991 $64.95. ISBN 0-631-17585-7. Essays by social critics and philosophers on the ideas of modernity and individualism.

Nisbet, Robert. *The Making of Modern Society.* NYU Pr. 1987 $45.00. ISBN 0-8147-5761-8

Riesman, David. *The Lonely Crowd: A Study of the Changing American Culture.* Yale U. Pr. 1973 repr. of 1950 ed. $14.00. ISBN 0-300-00193-2. Study of the individualistic drive transformed into the will to conform.

Sennett, Richard. *The Fall of Public Man.* Norton 1992 $10.95. ISBN 0-393-30879-0

ORGANIZATIONS

Barnard, Chester I. *The Functions of the Executive.* HUP 1968 $11.95. ISBN 0-674-32803-5. Classic analysis of the role executives should perform; written by a former CEO of Bell Telephone. Introduction by K. R. Andrews.

Blau, Peter M. *The Dynamics of Bureaucracy.* U. Ch. Pr. 1973 $6.95. ISBN 0-226-05726-7

Cyert, Richard M., and J. G. March. *A Behavioral Theory of the Firm.* P-H 1963 o.p.

Festinger, Leon, and others. *When Prophecy Fails: A Social and Psychological Study of a Modern Group That Predicted the Destruction of the World.* HarpC 1964 $12.00. ISBN 0-06-131132-4

Glaser, William A., and David L. Sills, eds. *The Government of Associations.* Bedminster Pr. 1966 o.p.

Goffman, Erving. *Asylums: Essays on the Social Situation of Mental Patients and Other Inmates.* Doubleday 1961 $10.95. ISBN 0-385-00016-2

Harrison, Michael I. *Diagnosing Organizations.* Sage 1987 $19.95. ISBN 0-8039-2626-X. Explains how to diagnose organizational problems.

Hassard, John, and Denis Pym. *The Theory and Philosophy of Organizations.* Routledge 1990 $49.95. ISBN 0-415-00428-4. A critical analysis of contemporary organizational theory.

March, James G., ed. *Handbook of Organizations.* Rand McNally 1965 o.p. Reference book with chapters by various authors; deals with all aspects of organizations, including their structure, influence, growth, development, and dynamics.

March, James G., and Herbert A. Simon. *Organizations.* Blackwell Pubs. 1993 $30.45. ISBN 0-631-18361-X. Analysis of various schools of organizational theory, with particular emphasis on behaviorist and cognitive perspectives.

McWhinney, Will. *Paths of Change: Strategic Choices for Organizations and Society.* Sage 1992 $38.00. ISBN 0-8139-3930-2. Strategies for resolving complex societal issues and effecting change.

Melvin, Patricia Mooney, ed. *American Community Organizations: A Historical Dictionary.* Greenwood 1986 $55.00. ISBN 0-313-24053-1. Documents the history of grass-roots community organizations and action.

Merton, Robert K., and others, eds. *A Reader in Bureaucracy.* Free Pr. 1965 $22.95. ISBN 0-02-921070-4

Sayer, Derek. *Capitalism and Modernity: An Excursus on Marx and Weber.* Routledge 1991 $15.95. ISBN 0-415-01728-9. An assessment of the ideas of Marx and Weber on modernity and its relation to capitalism.

Selznick, Philip. *TVA and the Grass Roots: A Study of Politics and·Organization.* U. CA Pr. 1979 $37.50. ISBN 0-520-03979-3. Comprehensive case study of the "grass-roots" origins and local planning mechanisms that helped to create, manage, and direct policy for the TVA during the early 1940s.

Sills, David L. *The Volunteers: Means and Ends in a National Organization.* Ed. by Harriet Zuckerman and Robert K. Merton. *Dissertations on Sociology Ser.* Ayer 1980 repr. of 1957 ed. $28.50. ISBN 0-405-12994-7. Study of voluntary associations in the United States, with particular reference to how these organizations are transformed by their membership.

Sills, David L., C. P. Wolf, and Vivien B. Shelanski, eds. *Accident at Three Mile Island: The Human Dimensions.* Westview 1981 $12.50 o.p. Articles dealing with various human factors involved in the Three Mile Island nuclear accident of March 1979.

Simon, Herbert A. *Administrative Behavior.* Macmillan 1976 $29.95. ISBN 0-02-928970-X. Classic study of the process of decision making in complex organizations, and the factors that influence this process.

Smith, Constance, and Anne Freedman. *Voluntary Associations: Perspectives on the Literature.* HUP 1972 $17.95. ISBN 0-674-94310-4

Weber, Max. *The Theory of Social and Economic Organization.* Trans. by Talcott Parsons. Free Pr. 1947 $17.95. ISBN 0-02-934920-06

POSTMODERNISM

Baudrillard, Jean. *America*. Trans. by C. Turner. Verso 1989 $13.95. ISBN 0-86091-978-1. Views the United States as the quintessential postmodern society.

_____. *Jean Baudrillard: Selected Writings*. Ed. by M. Poster. Stanford U. Pr. 1988 $32.50. ISBN 0-8047-1478-9. Selections from Baudrillard's more popular works that provide a basic introduction to his ideas. Includes an introduction by M. Poster.

_____. *The Mirror of Production*. Trans. by M. Poster. Telos Pr. 1975 $9.50. ISBN 0-914386-06-9. Advances a new theory of semiotics based on a revision of Marx's ideas on commodification and Baudrillard's idea of symbolic exchange.

Bauman, Zygmunt. *Imitations of Postmodernity*. Routledge 1992 $16.95. ISBN 0-415-06750-2. Examines the roots of postmodernity in themes related to self and society.

Derrida, Jacques. *The Other Heading: Reflections on Today's Europe*. Ind. U. Pr. 1992 $19.95. ISBN 0-253-31693-6. Brilliant and respected French philosopher and leading deconstructionist examines the changes in Europe.

_____. *The Post-Card: From Socrates to Freud and Beyond*. U. Ch. Pr. 1987 $19.95. ISBN 0-226-14322-8. Postmodern "re/de construction" of canonical works through time.

Eagleton, Terry. *The Ideology of the Aesthetic*. Blackwell Pubs. 1990 $49.95. ISBN 0-631-16301-8. Traces the relationship between aesthetics and political interest from the Enlightenment through postmodernism.

_____. *Ideology: An Introduction*. Routledge Chapman & Hall 1991 $17.95. ISBN 0-86091-538-7. Analyzes and redefines conceptions of ideology confronting mainstream postmodern thought.

Game, Ann. *Undoing the Social: Towards a Deconstructive Sociology*. U. of Toronto Pr. 1991 $18.95. ISBN 0-8020-6897-9. Attempts to redefine the role of sociological inquiry in light of current feminist and postmodernist thought.

Harvey, David. *The Condition of Postmodernity: An Inquiry into the Origins of Social Change*. Blackwell Pubs. 1989 $49.95. ISBN 0-631-16294-1. A comprehensive analysis of postmodernity and its cultural and social implications.

Lash, Scott. *The Sociology of Postmodernism*. Routledge 1990 $14.95. ISBN 0-415-04785-4. Assesses the differences between modernism and postmodernism.

Lyotard, Jean-Francois. *The Postmodern Condition: A Report on Knowledge*. Trans. by G. Bennington and B. Massumi. U. of Minn. Pr. 1984 $12.95. ISBN 0-8166-1173-4. A definition of "postmodern" based on the works of Freud, Marx, De Saussure, Nietzsche, and others.

Meisel, Perry. *The Myth of the Modern*. Yale U. Pr. 1987 $30.00. ISBN 0-300-03946-8. Critique of major British writers in a postmodernist light.

POVERTY AND SOCIAL CLASS

Burton, C. Emory. *The Poverty Debate: Politics and the Poor in America*. Greenwood 1992 $47.95. ISBN 0-313-28594-2. Excellent overview of both conservative and liberal arguments.

Duncan, Cynthia M. *Rural Poverty in America*. Greenwood 1992 $49.95. ISBN 0-86569-013-8. Interdisciplinary outlook on poverty in rural America.

Funicello, Theresa. *The Tyranny of Kindness*. Grove-Atlitic 1993 $23.00. ISBN 0-87113-543-4. Having been on welfare in New York City for four years, the author cites her firsthand knowledge in explicating reform.

Huston, Aletha C., ed. *Children in Poverty: Child Development and Public Policy*. Cambridge U. Pr. 1992 $14.50. ISBN 0-521-39162-8. In light of the increase in poverty among children, the authors detail reasons for, and effects of, this crisis.

Katz, Michael. *The Undeserving Poor*. Pantheon 1989 $15.95. ISBN 0-679-72561-X. A social history of poverty and welfare in the United States.

Kozol, Jonathan. *Savage Inequalities*. Crown Pub. Group 1991 $20.00. ISBN 0-517-58221-X. Examines public schools across the United States and shows how poor children are condemned to receiving an inferior education.

Mead, Lawrence M. *The New Politics of Poverty*. Basic Bks. 1992 $25.00. ISBN 0-465-05962-7. Blames the poverty level since 1960 on a breakdown of the work ethic.

Newman, Katherine S. *Falling from Grace: The Experience of Downward Mobility in the American Middle Class*. Free Pr. 1988 $29.95. ISBN 0-02-923121-3. A study of the impact of downward social mobility on American families.

Pivin, Frances Fox, and Richard A. Cloward. *Regulating the Poor: The Functions of Public Welfare*. Random 1972 $9.00. ISBN 0-394-71743-0. Analyzes how welfare policies have been used to control the behavior of the poor.

Ryan, William. *Blaming the Victim*. Random 1976 $7.96. ISBN 0-394-72226-4. Shows how Americans prefer to blame poverty on its victims rather than on societal inequality.

RACE AND ETHNICITY

Chrisman, Robert, and Robert Allen, eds. *Court of Appeal: The Black Community Speaks Out on the Racial and Sexual Politics of Thomas vs. Hill*. Ballantine 1992 $9.00. ISBN 0-345-38136-X. Major figures in the African American community write on issues of gender, race, and politics in light of the Clarence Thomas Supreme Court nomination.

Glasgow, Douglas G. *The Black Underclass*. Vin. 1981 $10.00. ISBN 0-394-74725-9. Why thousands of African Americans remain part of an underclass, despite welfare and antipoverty programs.

Hooks, Bell. *Race and Representation*. South End Pr. 1992 $30.00. ISBN 0-89608-434-5. The image of people of color among white supremacists.

Jaimes, M. Annette, ed. *The State of Native America: Genocide, Colonization and Resistance*. South End Pr. 1992 $40.00. ISBN 0-89608-425-6. Essays by noted Native Americans on the five-hundredth anniversary of Columbus's first voyage to the Americas.

Lemann, Nicholas. *The Promised Land: The Great Black Migration and How It Changed America*. Knopf $24.95. ISBN 0-394-56004-3. A study of the consequences of African American migration from the rural South to the urban North.

Perlmatter, Philip. *Divided We Fall*. Iowa St. U. Pr. 1992 $44.95. ISBN 0-8138-0644-5. Lengthy history of prejudice in the United States.

Sigelman, Lee, and Susan Welch. *Black Americans' Views of Racial Inequality: The Dream Deferred*. Cambridge 1991 $24.95. ISBN 0-521-40015-5. Issues of race and inequality viewed from an African American standpoint.

Tyler, Bruce M. *From Harlem to Hollywood*. Garland 1992 $39.00. ISBN 0-8153-0814-0. Examines the Harlem Renaissance in the 1940s and its broader ramifications.

Wilson, William Julius. *The Declining Significance of Race*. U. Ch. Pr. 1980 $9.95. ISBN 0-226-90129-7

RELIGION

Baer, Hans A., and Merrill Singer. *African-American Religion in the 20th Century*. U. of Tenn. Pr. 1992 $32.95. ISBN 0-87049-746-4. An outstanding contribution to the theoretical interpretation and typological classification of African American religious groups in relation to social changes.

Berger, Peter. *The Sacred Canopy: Elements of a Sociological Theory of Religion*. Doubleday 1990 repr. of 1967 ed. $8.95. ISBN 0-385-07305-4

Durkheim, Emile. *The Elementary Forms of the Religious Life*. 1912. Trans. by J. Swain. Free Pr. 1965 $14.95. ISBN 0-02-908010-X

Guthrie, Stewart E. *Faces in the Clouds: A New Theory of Religion*. OUP 1993 $30.00. ISBN 0-19-506901-3. Drawing upon cognitive science, experimental psychology, and anthropology, Guthrie attempts to explain the human "will to religion."

Hammond, Philip E., ed. *The Sacred in a Secular Age; Toward Revision in the Scientific Study of Religion*. U. CA Pr. 1985 $47.50. ISBN 0-520-05342-7

Herberg, Will. *Protestant, Catholic, Jew: An Essay in American Religious Sociology*. U. Ch. Pr. 1983 $11.95. ISBN 0-226-32734-5

Hume, David. *Writing on Religion*. Open Court 1992 $7.50. ISBN 0-8126-9112-1. An important treatise on the modern conceptions of religion.

Milbank, John. *Theology and Social Theory*. Blackwell Pubs. 1991 $64.95. ISBN 0-631-14573-7. Reviews the relationship between social theory and theology, from Plato to Baudrillard.

Niebuhr, H. Richard. *The Social Sources of Denominationalism*. Peter Smith 1984 $20.00. ISBN 0-8446-6150-3

Watt, William Montgomery. *Muslim-Christian Encounters*. Routledge 1991 $49.95. ISBN 0-415-05410-9. A historical view of Muslim and Christian encounters and misunderstandings, with some suggestions of ways to overcome the latter.

Weber, Max. *The Protestant Ethic and the Spirit of Capitalism*. 1904–05. Trans. by T. Parsons. Routledge Chapman & Hall 1989 $14.95. ISBN 0-04-331101-6. Introduction by A. Giddens.

———. *Sociology of Religion*. Trans. by E. Fischoff. Beacon Pr. 1964 $15.00. ISBN 0-8070-4193-5

SCIENCE

Aronowitz, Stanley. *Science as Power*. U. of Minn. Pr. 1990 $39.95. ISBN 0-8166-1658-2. A reassessment of science as a social force; includes proposals for a more humane science.

Barber, Bernard. *Science and the Social Order*. Greenwood 1978 repr. of 1952 ed. $45.00. ISBN 0-313-20356-3. Foreword by Robert K. Merton. Examination of the nature and organization of science in the United States and its role in maintaining the social order.

Barber, Bernard, and others. *Research on Human Subjects: Problems of Social Control in Medical Experimentation*. Russell Sage 1973 $29.95. ISBN 0-87154-090-8

Ben-David, Joseph. *The Scientist's Role in Society: A Comparative Study with a New Introduction*. U. Ch. Pr. 1984 $20.00. ISBN 0-226-04227-8. Cross-cultural, sociological, and historical analysis of the role of the scientist, and a study of the organization of scientific work.

Cole, Jonathan R., and Stephen Cole. *Social Stratification in Science*. U. Ch. Pr. 1973 o.p.

Crane, Diana. *Invisible Colleges: Diffusion of Knowledge in Scientific Communities*. U. Ch. Pr. 1988 $14.95. ISBN 0-226-11856-8. Argues that small groups of highly productive scientists control the development and growth of scientific knowledge in their respective fields.

Ellul, Jacques. *Technological Society*. Random 1967 $9.00. ISBN 0-394-70390-1. Introduction by Robert K. Merton.

Fischhoff, Baruch. *Acceptable Risk*. Cambridge U. Pr. 1984 $16.95. ISBN 0-521-27892-9

Gieryn, Thomas, ed. *Science and Social Structure: A Festschrift for Robert K. Merton*. NY Acad. Sci. 1980 $17.00. ISBN 0-89766-043-9. Essays on sociology of science in honor of leading scholar in field.

Haraway, Donna J. *Simians, Cyborgs, and Women: The Reinvention of Nature*. Routledge 1990 $55.00. ISBN 0-415-90386-6. Essays examining the nature/culture split in Western societies and a feminist analysis of the symbolic role of the cyborg in literature and science.

Kuhn, Thomas S. *The Structure of Scientific Revolutions. Foundations of the Unity of Science Ser*. U. Ch. Pr. 1970 $19.95. ISBN 0-226-45803-2. A book that transformed how science as an institution is studied.

Mannheim, Karl. *Essays on the Sociology of Knowledge*. Ed. by Paul Kecskemeti. OUP 1952 o.p. Essays by the founder of the sociology of science, first published between 1923 and 1929.

Merton, Robert K. *The Sociology of Science: Theoretical and Empirical Investigations*. Ed. by Norman W. Storer. U. Ch. Pr. 1979 $19.95. ISBN 0-226-52092-7

Merton, Robert K., and Jerry Gaston, eds. *The Sociology of Science in Europe.* 1975. *Perspectives in Sociology* S. Ill. U. Pr. 1977 o.p.

Nelkin, Dorothy. *Controversy: Politics of Technical Decisions. Focus Eds.* Sage 1992 $46.00. ISBN 0-8039-4466-7. Presentation of 13 cases involving public decisions that impacted the safety and welfare of the population.

_____. *Science as Intellectual Property: Who Controls Scientific Research.* Free Pr. 1983 $15.95. ISBN 0-685-08671-2

Perrow, Charles. *Normal Accidents: Living with High Risk Technologies.* Basic 1985 $17.50. ISBN 0-465-05142-1. Assessment of accidents in high-tech industries and a critical evaluation of risk assessment techniques.

Price, Derek J. de Solla. *Big Science, Little Science.* Col. U. Pr. 1986 o.p.

Shils, Edward. *The Intellectuals and the Powers: And Other Essays.* U. Ch. Pr. 1972 o.p.

Spiegel-Rosing, Ina, and Derek J. de Solla Price, eds. *Science, Technology and Society: A Cross Disciplinary Perspective.* Sage 1977 o.p.

Winner, Langdon. *Autonomous Technology: Technics out of Control as a Theme in Political Thought.* MIT Pr. 1977 $12.95. ISBN 0-262-73049-9. Philosophical, historical, and political examination of the control of technology.

Zuckerman, Harriet. *Scientific Elite: Nobel Laureates in the United States.* Free Pr. 1979 $10.95. ISBN 0-02-935880-9. Study of the lives and work of American Nobel Prize winners.

SOCIAL CLASS

Berberoglu, Berch. *The Legacy of an Empire: Economic Decline and Class Polarization in the United States.* Greenwood 1992 $39.95. ISBN 0-275-93792-5. Develops a class-based theory of the decline of the U.S. economy.

Dohrenwend, Bruce P., and Barbara S. Dohrenwend. *Social Status and Psychological Disorder: A Causal Inquiry. Personality Processes Ser.* Wiley 1969 o.p. A cross-cultural examination of the relationship between social mobility and psychological disorders.

Domhoff, G. William. *The Power Elite and the State.* Aldine de Gruyter $49.95. ISBN 0-202-30372-1. How the power elite controls public policy.

Duncan, Otis Dudley, and others. *Socioeconomic Background and Achievement. Studies in Population.* Academic Pr. 1972 o.p. Investigation of factors such as education, occupation, race, and family and how they affect social mobility in the United States.

Featherman, David L., and Robert M. Hauser. *Opportunity and Change. Studies in Population.* Acad. Pr. 1978 o.p.

Jencks, Christopher. *Inequality: A Reassessment of the Effect of Family and Schooling in America.* HarpC 1973 o.p. Study based on empirical data that shows how equal educational opportunity does not produce a greater degree of social mobility.

Kohn, Melvin L., and Carmi Schooler. *Work and Personality: An Inquiry into the Impact of Social Stratification.* Ablex Pub. 1983 $55.00. ISBN 0-89391-121-6

Lipset, Seymour M., and Reinhard Bendix. *Social Mobility in Industrial Society: A Study of Political Sociology.* Transaction Pubs. 1991 $21.95. ISBN 0-56000-606-4

Quirk, William J., and Bridwell, R. Randall. *Abandoned: The Betrayal of the American Middle Class Since World War II.* Madison Bks. UPA 1992 $21.95. ISBN 0-8191-8459-4. Indictment of the nation's cultural elite.

Sewell, William H., and Robert M. Hauser, eds. *Schooling and Achievement in American Society. Studies in Population.* Acad. Pr. 1976 $52.00. ISBN 0-12-637860-6. Collection of 15 papers dealing with quality education and socioeconomic achievement.

Verba, Sidney, and Gary Orren. *Equality in America: The View from the Top.* HUP 1985 $28.00. ISBN 0-674-25960-2. Historical analysis of social, economic, and political equality in America, with a particular emphasis on leadership.

Zweingenshaft, Richard L., and William G. Domhoff. *Blacks in the White Establishment?* Yale U. Pr. 1991 $29.50. ISBN 0-300-04788-6. A study of what happened to the young impoverished minority students who took part in the War on Poverty program.

SOCIAL MOVEMENTS

D'Emilio, John. *Sexual Politics, Sexual Communities: The Making of a Homosexual Minority in the United States, 1940–1970*. U. Ch. Pr. 1984 $10.95. ISBN 0-226-14266-3. Historical review of homosexual politics and identity, including a study of gay and lesbian collective action for social change since World War II.

Echols, Alice. *Daring to Be Bad: Radical Feminism in America, 1967–1975*. U. of Minn. Pr. 1989 $14.95. ISBN 0-8166-1787-2. An intellectual and social account of the origins of radical feminism.

Freeman, Jo, ed. *Social Movements of the Sixties and Seventies*. Longman 1982 o.p.

Mauss, Armand L. *Social Problems as Social Movements*. HarpC 1975 o.p.

Piven, Frances F., and Richard A. Cloward. *Poor People's Movements: Why They Succeed, How They Fail*. Random 1978 $7.96. ISBN 0-394-72697-9. Historical examination of organized and unorganized political expressions of the poor, since the Depression of the 1930s, to bring about social and welfare reform.

Scott, Alan. *Ideology and the New Social Movements*. Routledge Chapman & Hall 1990 $17.95. ISBN 0-04-301276-9-0. Examines the theoretical positions underlying collective action.

Skocpol, Theda. *States and Social Revolutions*. Cambridge U. Pr. 1979 $16.95. ISBN 0-521-29499-1

Smelser, Neil J. *Theory of Collective Behavior*. Macmillan 1962 o.p.

Zald, Mayer N., and John D. McCarthy. *The Dynamic of Social Movements: Resource Mobilization, Social Control, and Tactics*. Little 1979 o.p.

SOCIAL STRUCTURE

Blau, Peter M. *Inequality and Heterogeneity: A Primitive Theory of Social Structure*. Free Pr. 1977 $27.95. ISBN 0-02-903660-7

——, ed. *Approaches to the Study of Social Structure*. Macmillan 1975 o.p.

Burt, Ronald. *Toward a Structural Theory of Action: Network Models of Social Structure, Perception and Action*. Quantitative Studies in Social Relations Ser. Acad. Pr. 1982 $53.00. ISBN 0-12-147150-0

Calhoun, Craig. *Habermas and the Public Sphere*. MIT Pr. 1992 $45.00. ISBN 0-262-03183-3. Some 20 interdisciplinary articles on social and political theory. Celebrates Habermas's work.

Colomy, Paul. *The Dynamics of Social Systems*. Sage 1992 $25.95. ISBN 0-8039-8760-9. An examination of the fundamental elements of social systems and how they relate to social conflict and change.

Coser, Lewis A., ed. *The Idea of Social Structure: Papers in Honor of Robert K. Merton*. HarBraceJ 1975 o.p.

Giddens, Anthony. *The Consequences of Modernity*. Stanford U. Pr. 1990 $10.95. ISBN 0-8047-1891-1. Notions of modernity and its effect on sociological discourse.

——. *The Constitution of Society: Outline of the Theory of Structuration*. U. CA Pr. 1985 $15.95. ISBN 0-520-05728-7

Gomez, M. Guillermo L. *Dynamic Probabilistic Models and Social Structure*. Kluwer Ac. 1992 $137.00. ISBN 0-7923-1713-0. Study of socioeconomic problems arising in processes of development and growth.

Kohn, Melvin L., and Kazimierz M. Slomcynski. *Social Structure, Work, and Personality*. Blackwell Pubs. 1990 $39.95. ISBN 0-55786-018-1. Presents results and insights on the relationship between social structure and personality.

Lienhardt, Samuel. *Social Networks: A Developing Paradigm*. Acad. Pr. 1977 $45.00. ISBN 0-12-442450-3

Merton, Robert K. *Social Theory and Social Structure*. Free Pr. 1968 $32.95. ISBN 0-02-921130-1. Systematic outline of the theoretical foundations of functional sociology.

——. *Sociological Ambivalence and Other Essays*. Free Pr. 1976 $19.95. ISBN 0-02-921120-4

Parsons, Talcott. *The Social System.* 1951. Free Pr. 1964 $22.95. ISBN 0-02-924190-1
⸻. *The Structure of Social Action.* 1937. 2 vols. Free Pr. 1967 Vol. 1 $14.95. ISBN 0-02-924240-1. Vol. 2 $21.95. ISBN 0-02-924250-9. Positivistic approach to understanding human social action that draws heavily from social and economic theory.

SOCIALIZATION

Brim, Orville G., Jr. *Socialization after Childhood: Two Essays.* Wiley 1966 o.p.
Denzin, Norman K. *Childhood Socialization: Studies in the Development of Language, Social Behavior, and Identity.* Social and Behavioral Science Ser. Bks. Demand repr. of 1977 ed. $62.30. ISBN 0-685-16289-3. Through use of the symbolic interactionist perspective, these studies reveal how lives of children are shaped by social interaction with parents and caretakers.
Goslin, David A. *Handbook of Socialization Theory and Research.* HM 1969 o.p. Collection of articles dealing with the theory of socialization from various psychological and sociological perspectives.
Handel, Gerald, ed. *Childhood Socialization.* Aldine de Gruyter 1988 $49.95. ISBN 0-202-30335-7. A collection of studies dealing with the agencies of socialization and the ways in which individuals are enculturated and accepted into society.
Hess, Beth B., and Elizabeth W. Markson. *Aging and Old Age: An Introduction to Social Gerontology.* Macmillan 1980 o.p.
Hyman, Herbert H. *Political Socialization: A Study in the Psychology of Political Behavior.* Macmillan 1969 o.p.
Rose, Peter I., ed. *Socialization and the Life Cycle.* St. Martin 1979 $21.35. ISBN 0-312-73800-5
Rosow, Irving. *Socialization to Old Age.* U. CA Pr. 1975 $10.95. ISBN 0-520-03417-1. Assesses socialization of the elderly and concludes that the elderly in America are not effectively socialized.

URBAN AND COMMUNITY LIFE

Gottman, Jean. *Megalopolis: The Urbanized Northeastern Seaboard of the United States.* Kraus repr. 1961 o.p. Classic study of the social and economic integration of cities in the northeastern region of the United States.
Jacobs, Jane. *Cities and the Wealth of Nations: Principles of Economic Life.* Random 1985 $12.50. ISBN 0-394-72911-0. Study of the competition between cities for industrial resources and jobs.
Jankowski, Martin Sanchez. *Islands in the Street.* U. CA Pr. 1991 $24.95. ISBN 0-520-07264-2. Having lived and worked with urban gangs he studied, the author shows how gang members view themselves and others.
Lofland, L. *A World of Strangers: Order and Action in Urban Public Space.* Waveland Pr. 1985 repr. of 1973 ed. $11.95. ISBN 0-88133-136-8. Study of the history, role, and social aspects of strangers in the urban environment.
Logan, John, and Harvey Molotch. *Urban Fortunes.* U. CA Pr. 1987 $42.50. ISBN 0-520-05577-2. A neo-Marxist assessment of urban patterns of growth and decline.
Mumford, Lewis. *The City in History: Its Origins, Its Transformations and Its Prospects.* HarBraceJ 1968 repr. of 1961 ed. $21.95. ISBN 0-15-618035-9. Classic study of the origins and physical and socioeconomic development of world cities from ancient to modern times.
⸻. *The Culture of Cities.* Greenwood 1981 repr. of 1970 ed. $52.50. ISBN 0-313-22746-2. Historical examination of the impact of urbanization on the transformation of culture.
Park, Robert E. *City.* Heritage of Sociology Ser. U. Ch. Pr. 1984 repr. of 1967 ed. o.p. Introduction by Morris Janowitz.

Sennett, Richard. *Uses of Disorder: Personal Identity and City Life*. Norton $8.95. ISBN 0-393-30909-6. Argues that America's quest for a "purified community" should be counteracted by encouraging urban diversity and disorder.

————. *Conscience of the Eye: The Design and Social Life of Cities*. Knopf 1990 $24.45. ISBN 0-394-57104-5

Sjoberg, Gideon. *Preindustrial City: Past and Present*. Free Pr. 1965 $14.95. ISBN 0-02-928980-7

Stein, Maurice R. *The Eclipse of Community: An Interpretation of American Studies*. Princeton U. Pr. 1971 o.p.

Timberlake, Michael. *Urbanization in the World Economy*. Studies in Social Discontinuity Acad. Pr. 1985 $50.00. ISBN 0-12-691290-4. Represents the efforts of 15 U.S. social scientists to apply the world systems perspective to urbanization.

Weber, Max. *The City*. 1921. Free Pr. 1966 $22.95. ISBN 0-02-934200-7. Essays on ancient and medieval occidental cities.

Wilson, Elizabeth. *The Sphinx in the City*. U. CA Pr. 1992 $35.00. ISBN 0-520-07850-0. Examines the notion of order and chaos in cities and how male-dominated planning ensures urban order.

Zukin, Sharon. *Landscapes of Power: From Detroit to Disney World*. U. CA Pr. 1991 $24.95. ISBN 0-520-07221-9. Examines the ways in which communities are constructed by political and economic power.

UTOPIANISM AND COMMUNES

Berger, Bennett. *Survival of a Counterculture: Ideological Work and Everyday Life among Rural Communards*. U. CA Pr. 1981 $12.95. ISBN 0-520-04950-0

Bestor, Arthur. *Backwoods Utopia*. U. of Pa. Pr. 1971 o.p.

Cummings, Michael S., and Nicholas Smith. *Utopian Studies II*. UPA 1989 $34.50. ISBN 0-8191-7304-5. Collection of essays on utopian issues, from classical utopian ideas to more modern utopian thinking.

Erasmus, Charles J. *In Search of the Common Good: Utopian Experiments Past and Future*. Macmillan 1977 $24.95. ISBN 0-02-909630-8

Kanter, Rosabeth M. *Commitment and Community: Communes and Utopias in Sociological Perspective*. HUP 1972 $25.50. ISBN 0-674-14575-5

Kumar, Krishnan. *Utopianism*. U. of Minn. Pr. 1991 $29.95. ISBN 0-8166-1974-3. Views utopia as a bounded Western concept.

Moore, Sally F., and Barbara G. Myerhoff, eds. *Symbol and Politics in Communal Ideology: Cases and Questions*. Symbol, Myth and Ritual Ser. Cornell Univ. Pr. 1975 o.p.

Zablocki, Benjamin. *Alienation and Charisma: A Study of Contemporary American Communes*. Macmillan 1980 o.p.

WOMEN AND WOMEN'S ISSUES

Banks, Olive. *Faces of Feminism: A Study of Feminism as a Social Movement*. Blackwell Pubs. 1986 repr. of 1982 ed. $16.95. ISBN 0-631-14945-7. A history of the women's movement in the United States and England from 1840 to the present.

Benjamin, Jessica. *The Bonds of Love: Psychoanalysis, Feminism, and the Problem of Domination*. Pantheon 1988 $16.00. ISBN 0-394-75730-3. Examines the psychological and social place of domination in gender and human relations.

Blee, Kathleen M. *Women of the Klan: Racism and Gender in the 1920s*. U. CA Pr. 1991 $12.00. ISBN 0-520-07876-4. By examining relationship of gender and racism, the author reveals female passivity as a myth.

Buijs, Gina, ed. *Migrant Women: Crossing Boundaries and Changing Identities*. Berg Pubs. 1993 $59.95. ISBN 0-85496-729-X. An examination of how immigration has forced some women to change their culture and self-identity in order to gain greater autonomy.

Davis, Angela. *Women, Race and Class*. Random 1983 $10.00. ISBN 0-394-71351-6. A study of the racial and class bias in the women's movement from abolitionist days to the present.

Faludi, Susan. *Backlash: The Undeclared War Against American Women*. Crown Pub. Group 1991 $24.00. ISBN 0-517-57698-8. Discusses current attacks on women's rights.

Fraser, Nancy. *Unruly Practices: Power, Discourse and Gender in Contemporary Social Theory*. U. of Minn. Pr. 1989 $34.95. ISBN 0-8166-1777-5. An integration of feminist and poststructuralist theory aimed at constructing a theory of late-capitalist political culture.

Kitzinger, Celia. *The Social Construction of Lesbianism*. Sage 1988 $45.00. ISBN 0-8039-8116-3. Survey and analysis of research dealing with male and female homosexuality, with particular emphasis on the latter.

Matteo, Sherrie, ed. *American Women in the Nineties*. NE U. Pr. 1992 $14.95. ISBN 1-55553-151-2. Critical women's issues addressed in 13 academic essays.

O'Barr, Jean, and Mary Wyer, eds. *Engaging Feminism*. U. Pr. of Va. 1992 $12.95. ISBN 0-8139-1387-X. Critiques on women's studies, teaching, and higher education.

Sampselle, Carolyn M., ed. *Violence Against Women*. Hemisphere Pub. 1991 $39.50. ISBN 1-56032-217-9. Articles by researchers in nursing, medicine, law, and social sciences.

Watson, G. Llewellyn. *Feminism and Women's Issues, 1974 to 1986*. 2 vols. Garland 1989 $200.00. ISBN 0-8240-5543-8. Excellent reference for materials on feminism and women's issues.

WORK

Blau, Peter M., and Otis D. Duncan. *The American Occupational Structure*. Free Pr. 1978 repr. of 1967 ed. $15.95. ISBN 0-02-903670-4

French, John R. P., Jr., and others. *Career Change in Midlife: Stress, Social Support and Adjustment*. Inst. Soc. Res. 1983 $15.00. ISBN 0-87944-290-5

Fuentes, Annette, and Barbara Ehrenreich. *Women in the Global Factory*. South End Pr. 1983 $5.00. ISBN 0-89608-198-2. Examines the lives of women who work in free trade zones from New York City sweatshops to Mexico's border factories.

Jackall, Robert, and Henry M. Levin, eds. *Worker Cooperatives in America*. U. CA Pr. 1984 $12.95. ISBN 0-520-05941-4

Pahl, R. E., ed. *On Work: Historical, Comparative and Theoretical Approaches*. Blackwell Pubs. 1988 $49.95. ISBN 0-631-15761-1. A collection of articles dealing with the various sociological aspects of work, including issues related to gender, politics, and ideology.

CHRONOLOGY OF AUTHORS

Comte, Auguste. 1798–1857
Spencer, Herbert. 1820–1903
Booth, Charles. 1840–1916
Tönnies, Ferdinand. 1855–1936
Veblen, Thorstein. 1857–1929
Durkheim, Emile. 1858–1917
Simmel, Georg. 1858–1918
Mead, George Herbert. 1863–1931
Thomas, W(illiam) I(saac). 1863–1947
Cooley, Charles H(orton). 1864–1929
Park, Robert Ezra. 1864–1944
Weber, Max. 1864–1920

Michels, Robert. 1876–1936
Ogburn, William Fielding. 1886–1959
Sorokin, Pitirim A. 1889–1968
Lynd, Robert S. 1892–1970
Mannheim, Karl. 1893–1947
Frazier, E(dward) Franklin. 1894–1962
Lynd, Helen Merrell. 1894–1982
Wirth, Louis. 1897–1952
Myrdal, Gunnar. 1898–1987
Blumer, Herbert. 1900–1987
Lazarsfeld, Paul F(elix). 1901–1976

Wirth, Louis. 1897–1952
Myrdal, Gunnar. 1898–1987
Blumer, Herbert. 1900–1987
Lazarsfeld, Paul F(elix). 1901–1976
Parsons, Talcott. 1902–1979
Bernard, Jessie. 1903–
Taeuber, Conrad. 1906–
Taeuber, Irene B. 1906–1974
Riesman, David. 1909–
Merton, Robert K(ing). 1910–
Nisbet, Robert A. 1913–
Shils, Edward. 1915–
Mills, C(harles) Wright. 1916–1962
Garfinkel, Harold. 1917–
Janowitz, Morris. 1919–1988
Bell, Daniel. 1919–

Gouldner, Alvin. 1920–1980
Bottomore, Thomas B. 1920–
Goffman, Erving. 1922–1983
Wrong, Dennis H. 1923–
Coleman, James S(amuel). 1926–
Bellah, Robert N(eelly). 1927–
Gans, Herbert J. 1927–
Abu-Lughod, Janet L(ippman). 1928–
Berger, Peter L(udwig). 1929–
Habermas, Jürgen. 1929–
Wallerstein, Immanuel. 1930–
Wilson, William Julius. 1935–
Lofland, Lyn. 1937–
Giddens, Anthony. 1938–
Fischer, Claude S. 1948–
Sennett, Richard. 1948–

ABU-LUGHOD, JANET L(IPPMAN) 1928–

Janet L. Abu-Lughod is an American sociologist who specializes in social change and urbanization in the developing world. She was educated at the universities of Chicago and Massachusetts. She began her career as an urban planner and research consultant to organizations dealing with community development issues and housing problems. As an academic, she taught at the University of Cairo and Smith College before moving to Northwestern University. Currently she teaches sociology at the New School for Social Research in New York, where she continues to conduct research on urban problems.

BOOKS BY ABU-LUGHOD

Before European Hegemony: The World System A.D. 1250–1350. OUP 1991 repr. of 1989 ed. $15.95. ISBN 0-19-506774-6. A sociohistorical account of urbanization in Europe and the Middle East during the Middle Ages.
Changing Cities: Urban Sociology. HarpC 1991 $45.00. ISBN 0-06-040138-9. An introductory text dealing with world urbanization.
Rabat: Urban Apartheid in Morocco. Princeton U. Pr. 1981 $57.50. ISBN 0-691-05315-4. A study of racial segregation in a Moroccan city.
Third World Urbanization. (Coedited with Richard Hay, Jr.) Routledge Chapman & Hall 1980 $12.95. ISBN 0-416-60141-3. A collection of essays and research papers on urbanization in the developing world.

BELL, DANIEL. 1919–

Daniel Bell, an American sociologist, studied at City College and Columbia University. As a journalist he was an editor of *Fortune* magazine and later served on several presidential committees. His work as chairman of the American Academy of Arts and Sciences' Commission on the Year 2000 led to the publication of a collection of futuristic essays and discussions by some of the finest minds of the century. His teaching career included posts at Chicago, Columbia, and Harvard universities.

In Bell's best-known book, *The Coming of Post-Industrial Society* (1976), he analyzed the emerging role of information technology in the West. He was among the first scholars to realize that the production of information and knowledge would eclipse manufacturing in the developed world. Bell will be most remembered for his groundbreaking work in social change. He contended that new theories and models of decision making had to be devised to address the issues presented by an information-based society.

BOOKS BY BELL

The Coming of Post-Industrial Society: A Venture in Social Forecasting. Basic 1976 $17.00. ISBN 0-465-09713-8. A look at the changes taking place in the nature of modern economies; includes proposals for forecasting change.

Cultural Contradictions of Capitalism. Basic 1978 $16.00. ISBN 0-465-09727-8. Inherent in modern capitalism, Bell claims, are tensions between what he calls "axial principles" (equality, self-expression, and the like) and universal citizenship; such tensions should be viewed as challenges.

The End of Ideology. HUP 1988 repr. of 1960 ed. $14.95. ISBN 0-674-25230-6. Argues that left-right ideological dichotomy is over and that professionalization of work will bring an end to labor-management antagonism.

BOOKS ABOUT BELL

Brick, Howard. *Daniel Bell and the Decline of Intellectual Radicalism.* U. of Wis. Pr. 1986 $30.00. ISBN 0-299-10550-4. Focuses on the intellectual and ideological transformation of Bell from outspoken socialist to mainstream liberal.

Liebowitz, Nathan. *Daniel Bell and the Agony of Modern Liberalism.* Greenwood 1985 $42.95. ISBN 0-313-24279-8. A study of Bell's intellectual life and his theoretical influences.

BELLAH, ROBERT N(EELLY). 1927–

Robert N. Bellah, an American sociologist, received his Ph.D. from Harvard University in 1955 and now teaches at the University of California at Berkeley. He is best known for his work on community and religion. Although he has written on religions in non-Western cultures, he has focused much of his research on the notion of "civil religion" in the West.

To Bellah, American society confronts a moral dilemma whereby communalism competes with individualism for domination. His most important book, *Habits of the Heart* (1985), dealt with the American character and the decline of community. Bellah holds that the radical split between knowledge and commitment is untenable and can result only in a stunted personal and intellectual growth. He argues for a social science guided by communal values.

BOOKS BY BELLAH

The Good Society. Random 1992 $13.00. ISBN 0-679-73359-0. A follow-up to *Habits of the Heart*, which suggests ways in which social institutions can be made to work for the common good.

Habits of the Heart: Individualism and Commitment in American Life. HarpC 1986 repr. of 1985 ed. $13.00. ISBN 0-06-097027-8. A survey of American attitudes and values related to family and civil life; based on extensive research.

BERGER, PETER L(UDWIG). 1929–

Peter L. Berger is a Viennese-born American sociologist educated at Wagner College and the New School for Social Research. He teaches at Boston University and directs the Institute for the Study of Economic Culture. Berger's work has focused on the sociology of knowledge, the sociology of economics, and the sociology of religion. His closest collaborator has been his wife, Brigitte Kellner Berger, who coauthored several volumes with him and has been a central influence on his work.

Berger is perhaps best known for *The Social Construction of Reality* (1967), which he wrote with Thomas Luckmann. In this book, considered one of the most important works on the sociology of knowledge written in the twentieth century, the authors make a case for humanistic sociology that views human reality as socially constructed. They propose that sociological knowledge can best be achieved through a continuing conversation with history and philosophy.

BOOKS BY BERGER

The Capitalist Revolution: Fifty Propositions About Prosperity, Equality and Liberty. Basic 1988 $10.95. ISBN 0-465-00868-2. Examines how capitalism revolutionalized modern life by creating hyper-individualism.

An Invitation To Sociology: A Humanistic Perspective. Doubleday 1963 $8.95. ISBN 0-385-06529-9. An introduction to the discipline and its unique way of looking at social life.

The Sacred Canopy: Elements of a Sociological Theory of Religion. Doubleday 1990 $8.95. ISBN 0-385-07305-4. Examines the relationship between the sociology of knowledge and the sociology of religion in modern, secularized society.

The Social Construction of Reality: A Treatise in the Sociology of Knowledge. (Coauthored with Thomas Luckmann). Doubleday 1967 $8.95. ISBN 0-385-05898-5. Discusses the social acquisition of knowledge and the construction of reality as a social process.

BERNARD, JESSIE. 1903–

A pioneer American feminist sociologist, Jessie Bernard conducted groundbreaking research in the area of gender roles and the changing character of the family. She studied with PITIRIM A. SOROKIN at the University of Minnesota and received her Ph.D. from Washington University in 1935. Bernard began her sociological career as a promoter of social positivism but later became an outspoken feminist. She is perhaps best known for her work on gender roles and the future of relationships between men and women.

BOOKS BY BERNARD

The Female World. Free Pr. 1981 $14.95. ISBN 0-02-903060-9. Celebrates women's unique strengths and differences and discusses the transcendence of prescribed sex roles.

The Future of Marriage. Yale U. Pr. 1982 $13.95. ISBN 0-300-02853-9. Contends that husbands and wives inhabit different, unique worlds.

BLUMER, HERBERT. 1900–1987

Herbert Blumer, an American sociologist, received his Ph.D. from the University of Chicago, where he taught for many years before becoming professor of sociology at the University of California at Berkeley. A student of GEORGE MEAD, ROBERT PARK, and W. I. THOMAS, Blumer laid much of the intellectual foundation for symbolic interaction theory. Most of his work was published after his death. Nevertheless, he is remembered for his influence on his students—one of whom was ERVING GOFFMAN—and for his humanistic approach to social science.

BOOKS BY BLUMER

Critiques of Research in Social Sciences: An Appraisal of Thomas and Znaniecki's The Polish Peasant in Europe and America. Transactions Pubs. 1979 $14.95. ISBN 0-87855-694-X. A panel discussion on a classic study.

Industrialization as an Agent of Social Change: A Critical Analysis. Edited by David Maines and Thomas Morrione. Aldine de Gruyter 1990 $39.95. ISBN 0-202-30411-6. A collection of essays, published posthumously, dealing with social organization and industrialization from an interactionist perspective.

Symbolic Interactionism: Perspective and Method. U. CA Pr. 1986 $11.95. ISBN 0-520-05676-0. A collection of Blumer's writings on the process and method of symbolic interaction and its relation to empirical study.

BOOKS ABOUT BLUMER

Baugh, Kenneth. *The Methodology of Herbert Blumer: Critical Interpretation and Repair. ASA Rose Monograph Ser.* Cambridge U. Pr. 1990 $32.95. ISBN 0-521-38246-7. A critical interpretation of Blumer's method, comparing it with Goffman's perspective and other interactionist theories.

Hammersley, Martyn. *The Dilemma of Qualitative Method: Herbert Blumer and the Chicago Tradition.* Routledge 1990 $16.95. ISBN 0-415-01772-6. A review of the qualitative methodology proposed by Blumer and other Chicago theorists in an attempt to give life to a nonquantitative social research.

BOOTH, CHARLES. 1840–1916

Charles Booth was a British social reformer and social scientist who was also a wealthy shipowner and industrialist. His monumental 17-volume classic, *The Life and Labour of the People of London, 1890–1900* (1889–91), based on an enormous amount of statistical and descriptive data, revealed—to cite just one finding that has a modern ring—that 30 percent of the people of London were "below the line of poverty." He was a methodological and sociological precursor of ROBERT EZRA PARK and the Chicago School of urban studies, and all subsequent community studies owe something to his work.

BOOK BY BOOTH

The Life and Labour of the People of London, 1890–1900. 1889–91. 17 vols. AMS Pr. repr. of 1904 ed. $502.50. ISBN 0-404-00940-9

BOTTOMORE, THOMAS B. 1920–

Thomas B. Bottomore is a British sociologist whose work centers on issues of class, labor, social theory, and ideology. Educated at the London School of Economics, he taught for much of his career at the University of Sussex in Brighton. He has contributed extensively to Marxist sociology, having written and edited several volumes dealing with MARX's (see also Vol. 4) sociological thought. Bottomore has stressed the notion that his role as a sociologist is to enhance our understanding of our social world, while his role as a scholar-activist is to make that world more just.

BOOKS BY BOTTOMORE

Classes in Modern Society. Unwin Hyman 1991 o.p. An overview to the study of social class in modern societies, with some analysis of the failure of totalitarian socialism in Eastern Europe.

A Dictionary of Marxist Thought. Blackwell Pubs. 1992 $24.95. ISBN 0-631-1802-6. Defines and explains various Marxist concepts, ideas, and theories.

Interpretations of Marx. Blackwell Pubs. 1989 $45.00. ISBN 0-631-15255. A collection of essays by several scholars, including Lukas, Habermas, Schumpeter, Althusser, and Bottomore himself, dealing with Marx's work.

Political Sociology. U. of Minn. Pr. 1993 $34.95. ISBN 0-8166-2324-4. A survey of important issues in the field of political sociology.

Sociology As Social Criticism. Pantheon 1974 o.p. Essays dealing with conservative versions of sociology and radical attempts to develop more progressive approaches.

COLEMAN, JAMES S(AMUEL). 1926–

James S. Coleman is an American sociologist who has focused much of his work on mathematical sociology. His areas of interest have been social conflict, collective decision making, and the sociology of education. He received his Ph.D. from Columbia University in 1955 and subsequently taught at Johns Hopkins University.

Coleman is best known for heading a commission charged by the federal government with investigating the lack of educational opportunities for minorities in public schools. The document produced by the commission, *Equity of Educational Opportunity* (1966), is better known as the Coleman Report. It indicated that student achievement has more to do with family background and peer environment than with school resources. The Coleman Report became the basis for the institution of student busing to achieve racial integration in public schools. The report remains controversial, and its findings and methods have been challenged by social scientists from a variety of political perspectives.

BOOKS BY COLEMAN

The Asymmetric Society. Syracuse U. Pr. 1982 $14.95. ISBN 0-8156-0174-3. Based on a series of lectures given by the author at Syracuse University, these essays deal with a variety of concerns, ranging from perceptions of society to the raising of children.
Community Conflict. Free Pr. 1957 $7.95. ISBN 0-02-906480-5. An assessment of community controversy in relation to selected public policy issues.
Equality and Achievement in Education. Westview 1990 $41.00. ISBN 0-8133-7791-9. Analyzes the social forces that generate educational inequality along racial lines, together with an examination of desegregation policies.
Equity of Educational Opportunity. U.S. Gov. Printing Office 1966 o.p. More commonly referred to as the Coleman Report.
Foundations of Social Theory. HUP 1990 $39.50. ISBN 0-674-31225-2. Attempts to integrate social thought and theory by examining social action in social systems.

COMTE, AUGUSTE. 1798–1857

Auguste Comte was a French philosopher and moralist who, in 1838, first used the term "sociology." Although his influence is universally acknowledged, his many books are not widely read today. What lives is the name of a core social science discipline and Comte's insight that sociology as a science would develop within the framework of a general reorientation of human thought—a reorientation that characterizes modern industrial society.

Comte was interested in the stability of societies: how they change (social dynamics) and how they maintain equilibrium (social statics). As a functionalist, he promoted the philosophy of positivism. He believed that the motivations behind human behavior could be the object of empirical study. Although he never engaged in such studies himself, he had great faith that science could be used to solve social problems. Like his mentor, Saint-Simon, he envisioned a time when scientists, the priests of the future, would guide the world toward peace and harmony.

BOOKS BY COMTE

General View of Positivism. 1848. *Reprints in Sociology Ser.* Irvington 1971 $39.50. ISBN 0-697-00214-4. A series of lectures on positivism, dealing with such topics as art, women, and the worship of humanity.

Introduction to Positive Philosophy. Hackett 1988 $4.25. ISBN 0-87220-050-7. Describes the primary elements, concepts, and ideology that characterize positivism and its method.

System of Positive Polity. 1851–54. 4 vols. Longman 1875–77 o.p.

BOOKS ABOUT COMTE

Hawkins, Raymond. *Auguste Comte and the United States 1816–1853. Harvard Studies in Romance Languages* Vol. 2 Kraus 1936 $15.00. ISBN 0-527-0109-6. A history of the importance of positivism in the United States; includes discussion of the movement's American proponents and critics.

Levy-Bruhl, Lucien. *The Philosophy of Auguste Comte.* Gordon Pr. 1976 $59.95. ISBN 0-8490-2430-7. Traces the social, historical, and intellectual origins of Comte's philosophy.

Marvin, Francis S. *Comte: The Founder of Sociology.* Russell 1965 repr. of 1936 ed. o.p.

Pickering, Mary. *Auguste Comte: An Intellectual Biography.* Vol. 1 Cambridge U. Pr. 1993 $49.95. ISBN 0-521-43405-X. A study of the social and intellectual life of the founder of sociology.

Thompson, Kenneth. *Auguste Comte: The Foundation of Sociology.* Wiley 1975 o.p. A discussion of Comte's sociology and its impact on Spencer, Mill, and Durkheim.

COOLEY, CHARLES H(ORTON). 1864–1929

Charles H. Cooley, an American sociologist, was born in Ann Arbor, Michigan, where he spent most of his life. He did little empirical research, but his writings on the individual and the group, particularly on how the sense of self develops through social interaction (the "looking-glass self," he called it), had an enormous influence on all subsequent social psychology.

Cooley was an early (1897) critic of Sir FRANCIS GALTON's (see Vol. 5) notions about the biological inheritance of genius. His work, which is considered interactionist in its perspective, was influenced by the work of WILLIAM JAMES. Cooley contended that people gain an impression of themselves only by participating in society. Their perceptions of others' reactions to the "self" presented in such interactions guide individuals in developing and modifying their personalities. And things that people imagine about one another become ultimate facts.

BOOKS BY COOLEY

Human Nature and the Social Order. 1902. *Social Science Classic Ser.* Transaction Pubs. 1983 $21.95. ISBN 0-87855-918-3. A classic work on the process of social communication that argues that every society produces its own unique social structure. Includes an introduction by Phillip Reiff.

Social Organization: A Study of the Larger Mind. 1909. *Social Sciences Classic Ser.* Transaction Pubs. 1983 $21.95. ISBN 0-87855-918-3. Focuses on the major ways in which societies and cultures are formed and how they operate. Introduction by Phillip Reiff.

Social Process. 1918. Southern Illinois U. Pr. 1966 o.p. Introduction by R. C. Hinkle.

Sociological Theory and Social Research. Kelley repr. of 1930 ed. o.p. Papers written between 1894 and 1929. Introduction by Roger C. Angell.

BOOK ABOUT COOLEY

Jandy, Edward D. *Charles Horton Cooley: His Life and His Social Theory.* Octagon 1969 repr. of 1942 ed. $19.00. ISBN 0-37941-99-8. An intellectual biography of Cooley, focusing on his social theory; includes an extensive bibliography.

DU BOIS, W.E.B. 1868–1963

[SEE Chapter 15 in this volume.]

DURKHEIM, EMILE. 1858–1917

Emile Durkheim, French sociologist, is, with MAX WEBER, one of the two principal founders of modern sociology. (Although they were near contemporaries, they seem not to have known of each other.) Durkheim became a professor of sociology at the Sorbonne, where he founded and edited the very important journal *L'Année Sociologique*. He is renowned for the breadth of his scholarship; for his studies of primitive religion; for creating the concept of *anomie* (normlessness); for his study of the division of labor; and for his insistence that sociologists must use sociological (e.g., rates of behavior) rather than psychological data. His *Suicide* (1897) is a major sociological classic that is still read today, not so much for its data, which are limited and out of date, but for the brilliance of his analysis of suicide rates and other data that had been initially obtained for administrative rather than scientific purposes. Durkheim's notion of community—his view that religion forms the basis of all societies—had a profound impact on the course of community studies. His work continues to influence new generations of sociologists.

BOOKS BY DURKHEIM

The Division of Labor in Society. 1893. Trans. by W. D. Hall. Macmillan text ed. 1984 $10.95. ISBN 0-685-10064-2
Durkheim and the Law. St. Martin 1983 o.p.
The Elementary Forms of the Religious Life. 1912. Trans. by Joseph W. Swain. Free Pr. 1965 $14.95. ISBN 0-02-908010-X. Introduction by Robert Nisbet.
Primitive Classification. 1903. Trans. by Rodney Needham. U. Ch. Pr. 1967 $3.95. ISBN 0-226-17334-8
Professional Ethics and Civic Morals. Routledge 1992 $16.95. ISBN 0-415-06225-X. Characterizes the state as the ultimate moral force.
The Rules of Sociological Method. 1895. Macmillan $14.95. ISBN 0-02-908500-4. Asserts that the scientific method is applicable to the study of society and that it can help us discover "social facts" underlying all human relations.
Suicide. 1897. Free Pr. 1966 $27.95. ISBN 0-02-908650-7. The first empirical sociological study; examines religion and commitment as correlates of suicide.

BOOKS ABOUT DURKHEIM

Hamilton, Peter. *Emile Durkheim: Critical Assessments*. 3 vols. Routledge 1990 $550.00. ISBN 0-415-01742. A comprehensive assessment of Durkheim's life and work, including analyses that have become sociological classics in their own right.
Mestrovic, Stjepan. *The Coming Fin de Siècle*. Routledge 1991 $55.00. ISBN 0-415-04838-9. An analysis of the modernist and postmodernist implications of Durkheim's ideas.
Nisbet, Robert. *The Sociology of Emile Durkheim*. OUP 1974 o.p. Presents an overview of Durkheim's major works, particularly his sociological method and how his ideas relate to modern social thought.
Pearce, Frank. *The Radical Durkheim*. Unwin Hyman 1989 $16.95. ISBN 0-0445270-5. A Marxist reappraisal of Durkheim's theories that challenges the notion that he was inherently conservative and positivistic.
Pickering, W. S. *Durkheim's Sociology of Religion*. Routledge 1984 $65.00. ISBN 07100-9298-9. A critical appraisal of Durkheim's last book that provides a systematic treatment of its content and its relation to his other works.
Wolff, Kurt H., ed. *Emile Durkheim, 1858–1917: A Collection of Essays, with Translations and a Bibliography*. Ayer repr. 1979 $38.00. ISBN 0-405-12130-X. Essays by outstanding scholars, including Talcott Parsons and Lewis Coser, dealing with topics ranging from Durkheim's personal life to the various influences on his work.

FISCHER, CLAUDE S. 1948–

Claude Fischer is a French-born American sociologist. He received his Ph.D. from Harvard University and currently teaches sociology at the University of California at Berkeley. Most of Fischer's work focuses on urban society. He has written extensively on structural changes in modern society and has researched social networks and the displacement of traditional territorially based communities by new communities of human association. Fischer is also interested in the impact of technology on social relations and social institutions; most recently, he has investigated the social history of the telephone.

BOOKS BY FISCHER

America Calling: A History of the Telephone to 1940. U. CA Pr. 1992 $25.00. ISBN 0-520-07933-7. Examines the sociohistorical roots of the telephone and its impact on the structure of society.
To Dwell Among Friends. U. Ch. Pr. 1982 $19.95. ISBN 0-226-25138-1. Research conducted among residents of 50 northern California communities revealing how people form social networks.

FRAZIER, E(DWARD) FRANKLIN. 1894–1962

E. Franklin Frazier, born in Baltimore, Maryland, attended Harvard University and received his Ph.D. in sociology from the University of Chicago. He taught at Howard University from 1934 until his death and was the first African American to be elected president of the American Sociological Association. Frazier focused much of his research on the African American family. He was also interested in intercultural relations and the impact of cultural diversity on social organization and structure. He is perhaps best known for his groundbreaking work on the rise of the African American middle class.

BOOKS BY FRAZIER

Black Bourgeoisie. Free Pr. 1965 $12.95. ISBN 0-2-908660-4. An analysis of the behavior, values, and social isolation of the African American middle class in the United States.
The Negro Family in the United States. U. Ch. Pr. 1966 $13.95. ISBN 0-226-26141-7. Traces the struggle of African Americans to maintain stable family forms despite social adversity.

BOOK ABOUT FRAZIER

Platt, Anthony. *E. Franklin Frazier Reconsidered.* Rutgers U. Pr. 1991 $27.95. ISBN 0-8135-1631-5. The first comprehensive biography of Frazier to trace his personal, intellectual, and political development.

GANS, HERBERT J. 1927–

Herbert Gans is a German-born American sociologist who was educated at the University of Chicago and the University of Pennsylvania. Active in urban planning and housing at the beginning of his career, he taught planning and sociology at Columbia Teachers College and subsequently at Columbia University. He is best known for his work on American communities, including *The Urban Villagers* (1962)—a study of Boston's West End—and *The Levittowners* (1967). He has focused much of his research on the American middle class.

BOOKS BY GANS

The Levittowners. Col. U. Pr. 1967 $18.00. ISBN 0-231-05571-4. A case study of social organization in a post-World War II suburb.

Middle American Individualism. Free Pr. 1988 $19.99. ISBN 0-02-911251-6. A study of the values, norms, and mores of the American working class.

The Urban Villagers. Free Pr. 1992 repr. of 1962 ed. $12.95. ISBN 0-02-911240-0. A study of the social structure of working-class Italian Americans in Boston during the 1950s.

GARFINKEL, HAROLD. 1917–

Harold Garfinkel received his Ph.D. from Harvard University in 1952. He is known primarily as the founder of "ethnomethodology," which focuses on how social actors create and understand the bases of their actions. As a phenomenologist, he has attempted to discover the properties that underlie human communication and social relations. Each actor is seen as creating his or her own social reality based on personal interpretation of the so-called rules that govern relationships. He is a strong advocate of the interactionist perspective in sociology.

BOOK BY GARFINKEL

Studies in Ethnomethodology. 1967. Blackwell Pubs. 1985 $16.95. ISBN 0-7456-0005-0. Proposes a new method of sociological investigation and analysis based on expected patterns of everyday behavior.

GIDDENS, ANTHONY. 1938–

Anthony Giddens, a British sociologist, was educated at Hull, the London School of Economics, and Cambridge, and is a fellow of King's College, Cambridge. His interests have been varied, but they tend to focus on questions related to the macro-order. Much of his theoretical writing deals with stratification, class, and modernity. Although he has concentrated on dynamic issues of social structure, he has also examined how social psychological concerns are part of this broader order of human relations.

BOOKS BY GIDDENS

Capitalism and Modern Social Theory. Cambridge U. Pr. 1971 o.p. Analyzes the work of Marx, Durkheim, and Weber, emphasizing their methods as well as their intellectual similarities and differences.

Contemporary Critique of Historical Materialism. U. CA Pr. 1987 $39.50. ISBN 0-520-04535-1. A critical examination of both functionalism and historical materialism as sociological perspectives.

Modernity and Self-Identity. Stanford U. Pr. 1991 $35.00. ISBN 0-8047-1943-8. Examines how the problems associated with development of individual identity in modern society relate to the condition of modernity itself.

Social Theory and Modern Sociology. Stanford U. Pr. 1987 $39.50. ISBN 0-8047-13553. A collection of essays on theoretical and practical issues confronting sociology; includes critiques of Goffman, Gouldner, and Habermas.

BOOKS ABOUT GIDDENS

Bryant, Christopher, and David Jary, eds. *Giddens' Theory of Structuration: A Critical Appreciation.* Routledge 1990 $59.95. ISBN 0-415-00796-8. A critical look at Giddens's theory of structuration.

Craib, Ian. *Anthony Giddens.* Routledge 1992 $49.95. ISBN 0-415-07072-4. An introduction to Giddens's theories and a critical appraisal of his work.

GOFFMAN, ERVING. 1922–1983

Erving Goffman, an American sociologist, received his Ph.D. from the University of Chicago. He is known for his distinctive method of research and writing. He was concerned with defining and uncovering the rules that govern social behavior down to the minutest details. He contributed to interactionist theory by developing what he called the "dramaturgical approach," according to which behavior is seen as a series of mini-dramas. Goffman studied social interaction by observing it himself—no questionnaires, no research assistants, no experiments. The title of his first book, *The Presentation of Self in Everyday Life* (1959), became one of the themes of all of his subsequent research. He also observed and wrote about the social environment in which people live, as in his *Total Institutions*. He taught his version of sociology at the University of Pennsylvania; he died during the year in which he served as president of the American Sociological Association.

BOOKS BY GOFFMAN

Asylums: Essays on the Social Situation of Mental Patients and Other Inmates. Doubleday 1961 $9.95. ISBN 0-385-00016-2. Examines the "total institution" of the mental hospital and how patients and staff define themselves through their interactions.
Behavior in Public Places. Free Pr. 1966 $14.95. ISBN 0-02-911940. Deals with how people "frame" themselves in interpersonal public ritual.
The Presentation of Self in Everyday Life. 1959. Doubleday $9.00. ISBN 0-385-09402-7. Outlines his theory of "dramaturgy" and the "situational-self."
Stigma. 1963. S & S Trade 1986 $6.95. ISBN 0-671-62244-7. Explores strategies used by stigmatized persons to deal with rejection.

BOOKS ABOUT GOFFMAN

Burns, Tom. *Erving Goffman.* Routledge 1992 $49.95. ISBN 0-415-06492-9. A detailed review of Goffman's intellectual and social influences and his various contributions to sociology.
Ditton, Jason, ed. *The View from Goffman.* St. Martin 1980 $27.50. ISBN 0-312-84598-7. Essays on Goffman's work written by sociologists, ranging from Lyn Lofland to Randall Collins.

GOULDNER, ALVIN. 1920–1980

Alvin Gouldner was an American sociologist who received his Ph.D. from Columbia University. He was founder and editor of *Transaction*, and early in his career he worked for the American Jewish Committee. Later he taught for many years at Washington University in St. Louis. Gouldner firmly believed in what he called "reflexive" sociology, meaning that sociologists should examine their own beliefs just as they review the beliefs of others. He called to task those who would attempt to make the study of society more empirical and scientific, claiming that the major significance of social theory is its ideology. Gouldner, frequently condemned by his contemporaries as a radical, is best remembered for his contributions to the intellectual history of sociology, the history of Western ideas, and complex organizations.

BOOKS BY GOULDNER

The Coming Crisis of Western Sociology. Avon 1970 o.p. A critical examination of the intellectual traditions in sociological thought, with particular focus on the place of values in the discipline.
The Dialectic of Ideology and Technology. OUP 1982 $8.95. ISBN 0-19-503064-8. Traces the emergence of a new class based on a new technological order.
The Future of Intellectuals and the Rise of the New Class. OUP 1982 o.p. Studies the rise of a new intellectual class and the ideology supporting it, with close attention paid to the role of communications technology in modern society.

HABERMAS, JÜRGEN. 1929–

Jürgen Habermas is a German sociologist who studied at the universities of Göttingen, Zurich, and Bonn. He taught at Frankfurt am Main, Marburg, and Heidelberg before becoming professor of philosophy at the University of Frankfurt. His works, widely translated, have made him one of the most influential social theorists of our time.

Habermas is considered by some to be an intellectual heir to MAX WEBER and what has been called the Frankfurt School. His work has centered mainly on the role of communication and technology in changing patterns of social relations, human activity, and values. An outspoken advocate of the Enlightenment and a champion of reason, he has also cautioned that the technical rationality associated with modern capitalism often functions as ideology and may stand in the way of human progress.

BOOKS BY HABERMAS

Communication and the Evolution of Society. 1976. Trans. by T. McCarthy. Beacon Pr. 1979 $16.00. ISBN 0-8070-1513-X. Five essays dealing with such topics as communication theory, moral development, social evolution, and law and legitimation.
Knowledge and Human Interest. 1968. Trans. by J. Shapiro. Beacon Pr. $15.00 1972. ISBN 0-8070-1541-5. A defense of rationality and a discussion of means for achieving human knowledge, with a particular emphasis on communication.
Legitimation Crisis. 1973. Trans. by T. McCarthy. Beacon Pr. 1975. ISBN 0-8070-1521-0. An examination of the tendency toward crises in advanced capitalist societies.
The New Conservatism: Cultural Criticism and the Historians' Debate. Trans. and ed. by S. Nicholsen. MIT Pr. 1991 $14.95. ISBN 0-262-58107-8. Commentaries on recent conservatism in Germany, the rise of the Christian Democrats, and the trivialization of the Nazi era.
Theory and Practice. 1971. Trans. by J. Vietrel. Beacon Pr. 1973 $14.00. ISBN 0-8070-1527-X. Explores the role of reason in connecting theory and praxis.

BOOKS ABOUT HABERMAS

Braaten, Jane. *Habermas's Critical Theory of Society.* SUNY Pr. 1991 $44.50. ISBN 0-7914-0759-4. A general survey of his social theories.
Brand, Arie. *The Force of Reason: An Introduction to Habermas' Theory of Communicative Action.* Unwin Hyman 1990 $7.95. ISBN 0-04-370190-6. Designed to help students prepare for reading Habermas's theory of communicative action; a useful guide and summary.
Holbub, Robert C. *Jürgen Habermas: Critic in the Public Sphere.* Routledge 1991 $45.00. ISBN 0-415-02208-8. Examines Habermas's disagreements with current intellectuals and philosophers.
Keat, Russell. *The Politics of Social Theory: Habermas, Freud and the Critique of Positivism.* Blackwell Pubs. 1981 $9.00. ISBN 0-0226-42876-1. A powerful critique of Habermas and the Frankfurt School. Finds fault with Habermas's underlying assumptions, particularly his use of psychoanalytic thought.
White, Stephen K. *The Recent Work of Jürgen Habermas.* Cambridge U. Pr. 1988 $42.95. ISBN 0-521-34360-7. Focuses on an analysis of Habermas's thoughts and theories after the publication of *Knowledge and Human Interest* in 1968.

JANOWITZ, MORRIS. 1919–1988

Morris Janowitz was an American sociologist educated at the University of Chicago. As a student of many Chicago School theorists, he was most interested in the process of communication and its role in establishing a sense of community. Prejudice was another lifelong interest. During World War II, Janowitz worked as a propaganda analyst for the U.S. Department of Justice. He is best known for *The Community Press in An Urban Setting* (1980), his early study of the role of newspapers in establishing a sense of community. This work combined his interest in the press as an agent of solidarity with his concern about the perpetuation of prejudice.

BOOKS BY JANOWITZ

The Community Press in an Urban Setting. U. Ch. Pr. 1980 $12.00. ISBN 0-226-39318. Deals with the role played by the local press in fostering community consensus.
The Professional Soldier. 1952. Free Pr. 1961 $16.95. ISBN 0-02-916170-3. A classic study of attitudes and morale of the American military elite; based on extensive interviews.
Social Change and Prejudice. (coauthored with Bruno Bettelheim). 1950. Free Pr. 1964 $24.95. ISBN 0-02-903480-9. Examines prejudice among veterans and the role of social institutions in fostering prejudice.

LAZARSFELD, PAUL F(ELIX). 1901–1976

Paul F. Lazarsfeld was a Viennese-born American mathematician, psychologist, and sociologist who immigrated to the United States in 1933. In Vienna he had established an applied social research center, which became a model for others in the United States; the most famous product of the Vienna center is *Marienthal* (1933) a pioneering study of unemployment in an Austrian village. In the United States, Lazarsfeld became director of a Rockefeller Foundation-supported study of the impact of radio; through this study, communications research was established as a field of social science inquiry. In 1937 Lazarsfeld founded a research center, which became the Bureau of Applied Social Research at Columbia University; he taught at Columbia from 1940 until 1969.

Lazarsfeld's research areas included mass communications, voting, latent structure analysis, mathematical models, the history of quantitative research, and the analysis of survey data. His major goal was to find intellectual convergences between the social sciences and the humanities, between concept formation and index construction, and between quantitative and qualitative research. His enthusiasm and originality had an enormous impact on colleagues and students; an annual evening lecture and reception at Columbia provided an opportunity for them to share both vivid memories and current experiences.

BOOKS BY LAZARSFELD

The Academic Mind: Social Scientists in a Time of Crisis. (coauthored with Wagner Thielens, Jr.). Ed. by Walter P. Metzger. Ayer 1977 repr. of 1958 ed. $35.50. ISBN 0-405-10006
Continuities in the Language of Social Research. Macmillan 1972 o.p.
The Language of Social Research: A Reader in the Methodology of Social Research. 1955. Macmillan 1965 o.p.
Marienthal: The Sociography of an Unemployed Community. 1933. Aldine de Gruyter 1971 o.p.
The People's Choice: How the Voter Makes Up His Mind in a Presidential Campaign. 1944. Bks. Demand $58.30. ISBN 0-685-20795-1. Deals with the steps taken by voters in choosing candidates.
Personal Influence: The Part Played by People in the Flow of Mass Communications. (coauthored with Elihu Katz). 1955. Macmillan 1964 o.p.
Qualitative Analysis: Historical and Critical Essays. Allyn 1972 o.p.
Radio and the Printed Page: An Introduction to the Study of Radio and Its Role in the Communication of Ideas. 1940. Ayer 1971 $25.00. ISBN 0-405-03575-6. An examination of the accomplishments of radio research.
Radio Research, 1941. Ayer 1941 $26.00. ISBN 0-405-12101-6
Voting: A Study of Opinion Formation in a Presidential Campaign. U. Ch. Pr. 1954 o.p.

The Varied Sociology of Paul F. Lazarsfeld. Ed. by Patricia L. Kendall. Col. U. Pr. 1982 $63.00. ISBN 0-231-05122-0. Introduction by James S. Coleman.

BOOK ABOUT LAZARSFELD

Merton, Robert K., and others, eds. *Qualitative and Quantitative Social Research: Papers in Honor of Paul F. Lazarsfeld.* Macmillan 1979 $29.95. ISBN 0-02-920930-7

LOFLAND, LYN. 1937–

Lyn Loffland is an American sociologist who received her Ph.D. from the University of California at San Francisco. She worked as a social worker early in her professional career and later taught sociology at the University of California at Davis. She is best known for her work on the study of human relations in urban society. Her now classic study, *A World of Strangers* (1973), stressed the importance of spatial arrangements for human communication and interaction in cities.

BOOK BY LOFLAND

A World of Strangers. Waveland Pr. 1985 repr. of 1973 ed. $11.95. ISBN 0-88133-136-8. A study of the history, role, and social aspects of strangers in the urban environment.

LYND, ROBERT S. 1892–1970, and LYND, HELEN MERRELL. 1894–1982

Robert S. Lynd and Helen Merrell Lynd, American sociologists, became renowned for their pioneering studies of the small city of Muncie, Indiana, which they called Middletown. Not since TOCQUEVILLE's *Democracy in America* has there been such a careful analysis of daily life in an American community. The research in Middletown won Robert Lynd a professorship at Columbia University and Helen Lynd one at Sarah Lawrence College. In the 1970s, Middletown was restudied by a team of sociologists led by Theodore Caplow.

BOOK BY ROBERT S. LYND

Knowledge for What? The Place of Social Science in American Culture. 1939. U. Pr. of New Eng. $14.95. ISBN 0-8195-6170-3. An assessment of the role of social science in creating social change and improving social conditions.

BOOKS BY ROBERT S. LYND AND HELEN MERRELL LYND

Middletown. HarBraceJ 1959 $12.95. ISBN 0-15-659550-8. An intensive examination of an American community and its people's ways of life, values, and ideals.
Middletown in Transition: A Study in Cultural Conflicts. HarBraceJ 1982 ISBN 0-15-6595508. Using the original *Middletown* findings as base-line data, the authors reexamine the community 10 years later.

BOOKS ABOUT ROBERT S. LYND AND HELEN MERRELL LYND

Caplow, Theodore, and others. *All Faithful People: Change and Continuity in Middletown's Religion.* Bks. Demand 1983 $19.50. ISBN 0-7837-2972-3
_____. *Middletown Families: Fifty Years of Change and Continuity.* U. of Minn. Pr. 1982 $14.95. ISBN 0-8166-1435-0

MANNHEIM, KARL. 1893–1947

Karl Mannheim, a Hungarian-born German sociologist, taught at the Universities of Heidelberg and Frankfurt until 1933, when the coming of the Nazis to power forced him to find refuge at the University of London. His major fields of inquiry were the sociology of knowledge and the sociology of intellectual life. His masterpiece, *Ideology and Utopia* (1936), asserts that there are two types of knowledge: true knowledge based on science and knowledge based on social class. Ideas are of two types: "Utopian" ideas support underprivileged groups, while "ideologies" support privileged groups.

Mannheim, studying the trend toward increasing centralization, believed that modern society is dominated by large, powerful, impersonal organizations; as they consolidate, they will be controlled by powerful elites. He urged that, since this trend is inevitable, power should rest in the hands of unbiased intellectuals. He hoped that planning by trained social scientists could preserve and foster democracy. Mannheim's pioneering work in the sociology of knowledge had relatively little direct influence on contemporary research, but his bringing the concept of ideology to the attention of sociologists was of consequential importance.

BOOK BY MANNHEIM

Ideology and Utopia. 1936. Trans. by L. Wirth and E. Shils. Harvest Bks. 1955 $12.95. ISBN 0-15643955-7. Deals with the uncertainty associated with modernity as it relates to the relativity of truth and values and the role of the intellectual in bridging and synthesizing human ideologies.

BOOKS ABOUT MANNHEIM

Loader, Colin. *The Intellectual Development of Karl Mannheim.* Cambridge U. Pr. 1985 ISBN 0-521-26567-3. Looks at Mannheim's theories of culture, politics, and planning, and their relation to modern thought and human action.

Rempel, Warren F. *The Role of Value in Karl Mannheim's Sociology of Knowledge.* The Hague 1965 o.p. A critical study of Mannheim's whole range of sociological thought.

MARX, KARL. 1818–1883

[SEE Chapter 9 in this volume.]

MEAD, GEORGE HERBERT. 1863–1931

George Herbert Mead, an American social psychologist, taught at the University of Chicago for his entire career. The task he set for himself was to explain how humans learn to think in abstractions, become self-conscious, and behave purposefully and morally. He contended that these attributes rest on language and are acquired and maintained through group life. Social psychology, for Mead, was the study of regularities in individual behavior that result from participation in groups.

Mead was very much influenced by pragmatist philosophers, especially JOHN DEWEY (see also Vol. 4) and CHARLES H. COOLEY. He was something of a cult figure during and after his lifetime; he published no books, and his posthumous books were reconstructed from his notes and from the notes of students. He was a man far ahead of his time, and many of the concepts he developed at the turn of the century are widely accepted today: the selective nature of perception, cognition through linguistic symbols, role playing, decision processes, reference groups, and socialization through participation in group activities.

BOOKS BY MEAD

George Herbert Mead on Social Psychology. U. Ch. Pr. 1964 $13.95. ISBN 0-226-51665-2. A collection of essays explaining Mead's concept of personality as a product of human interaction.

Mind, Self, and Society. U. Ch. Pr. 1967 $11.95. ISBN 0-226-51668-7. Presents Mead's "Me-I" model to explain the formation of self-identity.

Movements of Thought in the Nineteenth Century: George H. Mead. Ed. by M. Moore. 1936 U. Ch. Pr. 1950 o.p. Early writings on Schilling, Hegel, Marx, and others.

Selected Writings George Herbert Mead. Ed. by Andrew Reck. Bobbs U. Ch. Pr. 1981
$10.95. ISBN 0-226-57671-7. A collection of papers, reviews, and other writings on
such topics as social reform, ethics, and aesthetics.

BOOKS ABOUT MEAD

Petras, Peter. *George Herbert Mead: Essays on His Social Philosophy.* Tchrs. Coll. Pr. 1968
o.p. Essays dealing with both the theoretical content of Mead's work and applied
versions of his pragmatism.
Schellenberg, James A. *Masters of Social Psychology: Freud, Mead, Lewin and Skinner.*
OUP 1978 o.p.

MERTON, ROBERT K(ING). 1910–

Robert K. Merton, an American sociologist, has had a major impact on almost
all branches of sociology, as well as on contemporary intellectual life. After
undergraduate work at Temple University, he studied with TALCOTT PARSONS and
PITIRIM SOROKIN at Harvard University. Since 1941 he has been associated with
Columbia University. Three of his interests are the study of social structure,
structural-functional analysis, and the sociology of science.

Many of Merton's concepts have become central to sociological research
today. "The unanticipated consequences of purposive social action" calls
attention to the difference between the intent and the consequences of social
behavior. "The self-fulfilling prophecy" explains how the beliefs of others about
individuals or groups lead these individuals or groups to act as the others have
prophesized. The "Matthew effect" points out that, in science, recognition tends
to accrue to those who already have it, a phenomenon that may both penalize
individuals and frustrate the diffusion of new ideas. "Obliteration by incorpora-
tion" is a pattern of success in science and scholarship in which a person's work
becomes so widely accepted that his or her identity is often not mentioned.
Merton, the leader of an active tradition of empirical research in the sociology
of science and scientists, is frequently referred to as "the dean of American
sociology."

BOOKS BY MERTON

A Reader in Bureaucracy. (coauthored with George Reader and Patricia Kendall). Free
Pr. 1965 $19.95. ISBN 0-02-921070-4
Science, Technology and Society in Seventeenth Century England. 1938. Fertig 1970 o.p.
A look at the social, cultural, and economic forces involved in the rise of modern
science and technology.
On the Shoulders of Giants. 1965. Harvest Bks. 1967 $4.95. ISBN 015-688781-X. Playful
treatment of scientific discoveries.
Social Theory and Social Structure. 1949. Free Pr. 1968 $29.95. ISBN 0-8371-5226-7. A
systematic outline of the theoretical foundations of functional sociology.
Sociological Ambivalence and Other Essays. Free Pr. 1976 $16.95. ISBN 0-02-921120-4.
Includes the title essay and several others covering a broad range of conceptual
territory.
Sociological Ideas and Social Facts. Blackwell Pubs. 1989 $24.95. ISBN 0-631-15727-1.
Classic essays on various topics, plus personal recollections of Parsons, Lazarsfeld,
Gouldner, and others.
The Sociology of Science. U. Ch. Pr. 1979 $15.95. ISBN 0-226-52092-7
The Student Physician. 1957. Bks. Demand $93.00. ISBN 0-8357-9179-3. Examines how
medical education forms the social behavior and culture of the medical profession.

BOOK ABOUT MERTON

Sztompka, Piotr. *Robert K. Merton's Social Theory.* St. Martin 1986 $11.95. ISBN 0-312-
68739-7. The first complete intellectual profile of Merton discusses his social theory,
his method of structural and functional analysis, and his sociology of science.

MICHELS, ROBERT. 1876–1936

Robert Michels was a German sociologist who spent the last 10 years of his life in Italy. In the English-speaking world, he is most famous for his book *Political Parties* (1911), in which he formulated the problem of the oligarchic tendencies of organizations. "He who says organization," he asserted, "says oligarchy." But political parties, he believed, are less oligarchic than single-purpose organizations concerned with specific reforms or with technical problems. An important study of the International Typographical Union, *Union Democracy* by SEYMOUR M. LIPSET, Martin A. Trow, and James S. Coleman (1956), has been said by some scholars to challenge many of Michels's findings about organizations. Rather, by pointing out the essential characteristics of a democratic trade union, this book confirms Michels's thesis. Michels also wrote about democracy, socialism, revolution, class conflict, trade unionism, mass society, nationalism, imperialism, and intellectuals, and he made intensive studies of the politics of the working class.

BOOKS BY MICHELS

First Lectures in Political Sociology. Trans. by Alfred de Grazia. *Perspectives in Social Inquiry Ser.* Ayer repr. 1974 o.p.
Political Parties: A Sociological Study of the Oligarchical Tendencies of Modern Democracy. 1911. Macmillan 1966 o.p. Introduction by Seymour M. Lipset.

BOOK ABOUT MICHELS

Coser, Lewis A. *Masters of Sociological Thought: Ideas in Historical and Social Context.* HarBraceJ 1977 $42.75. ISBN 0-15-555130-2. Classical and contemporary sociologists and their theories, including Michels.

MILLS, C(HARLES) WRIGHT. 1916–1962

C. Wright Mills, an American sociologist, was one of the most controversial social scientists of the mid-twentieth century. He considered himself a rebel against both the academic establishment and American society in general, and he rarely tried to separate his radical ideas from his teaching and writing. Irving Louis Horowitz summarized much of Mills's ideas in the subtitle of his biography of him: *An American Utopian.* Mill's most traditional sociological study is *The Puerto Rican Journey.* His most direct attack on his colleagues in sociology is *The Sociological Imagination* (1959) (which he found left much to be desired). His most ideological work is *The Power Elite* (1956), an attempt to explain the overall power structure of the United States. Mills thought that the dominant "value-free" methodology of American sociology was an ideological mask, hiding values that he did not share. According to his younger colleague IMMANUEL WALLERSTEIN, Mills was essentially a utopian reformer who thought that knowledge properly used could bring about a better society.

BOOKS BY MILLS

The Power Elite. 1956. Oxford U. Pr. 1956 $13.95. ISBN 0-19-50068-0. Examines the lives and power of corporate executives, military leaders, politicians, and journalists, and concludes that there is a small elite group of men who control the major decisions of national import.
The Sociological Imagination. 1959. Oxford U. Pr. 1967 $7.95. ISBN 0-19-500751-4. An intellectual call to sociological study and analysis as a means of dealing with the most pressing issues of the day.

White Collar. Oxford U. Pr. 1951. $30.00. ISBN 0-19-500024-2. A post–World War II
examination of the new and growing middle class. Mills looks at its diversity as well
as the social and psychological issues it confronts.

BOOKS ABOUT MILLS

Aptheker, Herbert. *The World of C. Wright Mills.* Kraus 1960 $24.00. ISBN 0-52703003-1.
Examines the strengths and weaknesses of Mills's ideas on power elites, poverty,
mass society, democracy, and other topics.
Horowitz, Irving. *C. Wright Mills: An American Utopian.* Free Pr. 1983 $29.95. ISBN 0-02-
914970-3. An intellectual and social biography of Mills, with a focus on his evolution
as a scholar.
Tilman, Rick. *C. Wright Mills: A Native Radical and His American Intellectual Roots.* Pa.
St. U. Pr. 1984 $27.50. ISBN 0-271-00360-X

MYRDAL, GUNNAR. 1898–1987 (NOBEL PRIZE 1973)

Gunnar Myrdal, a Swedish economist, gained fame in American sociology for
An American Dilemma (1944), the report of a large-scale Carnegie Corporation-
supported study of the status of African Americans in American life. (He was
awarded the Nobel Peace Prize in 1973; his wife, Alva, a sociologist, received it
in 1982). Myrdal was selected by Carnegie to direct the study of African
Americans because he was from "a non-imperialist country with no background
of discrimination of one race against another." He arrived in the United States
in September 1938 and soon acquired as collaborators nearly all of the
luminaries of American social science, from FRANZ BOAS to W. I. THOMAS to
MARGARET MEAD. The massive report and a large number of complementary
books cannot, of course, be easily summarized. The title refers to Myrdal's
conclusion that the black problem does not concern blacks; rather, the problem
is how to guide individual Americans in reconciling their Christian principles
with their behavior and attitudes in their dealings with blacks. The study
remains a classic of large-scale, organized research, although the extent to
which it contributed to improvements in the status of African Americans in
American society is difficult to determine.

BOOKS BY MYRDAL

Against the Stream: Critical Essays on Economics. 1973. Random 1974 o.p.
An American Dilemma. Vols. 1 and 2. Pantheon 1975 o.p. One of the most comprehensive
studies of the problem of American race relations at mid-century.
Asian Drama: An Inquiry into the Poverty of Nations. 3 vols. Kraus 1968 o.p.
Beyond the Welfare State: Economic Planning and Its International Implications.
Greenwood 1982 $38.50. ISBN 0-313-23697-6. Promotes the need for economic and
social planning in wealthy Western nations.

NISBET, ROBERT A. 1913–

Robert Nisbet, an American sociologist, received his doctorate from the
University of California at Berkeley and taught at Columbia University before
moving to the University of California at Riverside. Known for his fine
scholarship and conservative ideology, Nisbet has been a consultant to such
groups as the American Enterprise Institute and has been a libertarian
promoter of cultural pluralism. Nisbet has done considerable work in researching the history and development of Western sociological thought. His areas of
personal interest have also included the classical social theorists, modernization and social thought, and community and society.

BOOKS BY NISBET

Conservatism: Dream and Reality. U. of Minn. Pr. 1986 $12.95. ISBN 0-8166-1526-8.
   Examines the development of conservatism from the late eighteenth century to the
   present.
The Making of Modern Society. NYU Pr. 1987 $45.00. ISBN 0-8147-576-8. Essays on a
   variety of issues, including pieces on Vico, Turgot, Rousseau, and Tocqueville, as
   well as the notion of citizenship.
The Quest for Community. 1953 I.C.S. Pr. 1990 $10.95. ISBN 1-53815-058-7. Deals with
   the growing centralization of power and other dangers to individual liberty.
Sociology as an Art Form. OUP 1976 $6.95. ISBN 0-19-502103-7. Looks at the relationship
   between themes in literature and those in sociology.
Twilight of Authority. OUP 1975 o.p. Analyzes the decline of political community and the
   corruption of twentieth-century Western culture.

OGBURN, WILLIAM FIELDING. 1886–1959

William Fielding Ogburn, an American sociologist, was a professor at the
University of Chicago for most of his career. His research into social change,
especially its quantitative measurement, lives today in the field of social
indicators. Ogburn also created the concept of culture lag to describe how one
facet of culture gets out of phase with the others. The most common illustration
is that technology develops while the necessary social institutions to control it
lag behind. During the 1920s, Ogburn was appointed by President Hoover as
chairman of a presidential commission to study social change; its massive
report, *Recent Social Trends in the United States*, was published in 1933. It is
said that when President-elect Franklin D. Roosevelt took a cruise on Vincent
Astor's yacht prior to his inauguration, the page proofs of this book were his
major serious reading. Ogburn's many students, particularly Otis Dudley
Duncan and Albert J. Reiss, Jr., carried on and extended his interest in the
quantitative study of social and cultural change.

BOOKS BY OGBURN

Recent Social Trends in the United States. 2 vols. 1933. Ayer 1979 repr. of 1933 ed. o.p.
   Although the President's Research Committee on Social Trends is listed as the
   author of this book, Ogburn was, in fact, the editor. Foreword by Herbert Hoover.
Social Change: With Respect to Culture and Original Nature. 1922. Peter Smith 1964 repr.
   of 1950 ed. o.p.
William F. Ogburn on Culture and Social Change: Selected Papers. Ed. by Otis Dudley
   Duncan. *History of Sociology Ser*. U. Ch. Pr. 1964 o.p.

PARK, ROBERT EZRA. 1864–1944

Robert Ezra Park, an American sociologist, is credited with making American
sociology more empirical and less theoretical than its European counterpart.
He was a leading figure in the so-called Chicago School of sociology. The
department of sociology at the University of Chicago trained a large number of
sociologists in the 1920s and 1930s; it emphasized the study of crime and of
urban neighborhoods. Park's students made Chicago into a "social laboratory."
They went out into its streets to look at their physical and social surroundings
and then produced outstanding monographs on the conditions of urban life.
Park coauthored with Ernest W. Burgess the most influential text in sociology of
the time. With his student R. D. McKenzie, he adapted the concepts of animal
ecology to the study of the city: invasion, succession, dominance, and so on.
They coined the term "human ecology" and published a number of now-famous

maps of Chicago, showing by means of concentric circles the morphology of the city's growth.

BOOKS BY PARK

The City. (coauthored with Ernest Burgess and Roderick McKenzie). 1925. U. Ch. Pr. 1984 $14.95. ISBN 0-226-64608-4. Essays by Park defining human ecological approach to the study of society.

Collected Papers of Robert Ezra Park. 3 vols. Ed. by Everett C. Hughes, and others. Macmillan 1950–55 o.p. Papers dealing with a broad range of Park's ideas, from human ecology to race relations.

BOOKS ABOUT PARK

Lyman, Stanford M. *Militarism, Imperialism, and Racial Accommodation.* U. of Ark. Pr. 1992 $30.00. ISBN 1-55728-219-6. An analysis of some of Park's earlier writings, including his Congo papers and his views on war and race.

Matthews, Fred. *Quest for An American Sociology.* McGill-Queens U. Pr. 1977 o.p. A biography of Park focusing on his work at the University of Chicago.

PARSONS, TALCOTT. 1902–1979

Talcott Parsons, an American sociologist, introduced MAX WEBER to American sociology and became himself the leading theorist of American sociology after World War II. His *Structure of Social Action* (1937) is a detailed comparison of ALFRED MARSHALL, EMILE DURKHEIM, Max Weber, and VILFREDO PARETO. Parsons concluded that these four scholars, coming from contrasting backgrounds and from four different countries, converged, without their knowing of the others, on a common theoretical and methodological position that he called "the voluntaristic theory of action." Subsequently, Parsons worked closely with the anthropologists Clyde Kluckhohn, Elton Mayo, and W. Lloyd Warner, and the psychologists GORDON W. ALLPORT and HENRY A. MURRAY, to define social, cultural, and personality systems as the three main interpenetrative types of action organization. He is widely known for his use of four pattern variables for characterizing social relationships: affectivity versus neutrality, diffuseness versus specificity, particularism versus universalism, and ascription versus achievement.

BOOKS BY PARSONS

Essays in Sociological Theory. 1949. Free Pr. 1964 $18.95. ISBN 0-02-924030-1

The Evolution of Societies. Ed. by Jackson Toby. P-H 1977 o.p.

Family, Socialization, and Interaction Process. Macmillan 1955 o.p.

The Social System. 1951. Free Pr. 1964 $22.95. ISBN 0-02-924190-1

Sociological Theory and Modern Society. Free Pr. 1967 $35.00. ISBN 0-02-924200-2

The Structure of Social Action. 2 vols. Free Pr. 1967 Vol. 1 $14.95 ISBN 0-02-924240-1 Vol. 2 $21.95. ISBN 0-02-924250-1

Toward A General Theory of Action. (coauthored with Edward Shils). HarpC 1962 o.p. A collection of essays by Parsons, Shils, and others that attempts to develop a unified theory of social science.

BOOKS ABOUT PARSONS

Black, Max, ed. *The Social Theories of Talcott Parsons: A Critical Examination.* S. Ill. U. Pr. 1976 repr. of 1961 ed. $9.95. ISBN 0-8093-0759-6

Bourricaud, François. *The Sociology of Talcott Parsons.* Trans. by Arthur Goldhammer. U. Ch. Pr. 1984 $12.50. ISBN 0-226-06756-4

Hamilton, Peter, ed. *Talcott Parsons. Key Sociologists Ser.* Routledge Chapman & Hall 1983 $8.95. ISBN 0-85317439-6

Holton, Robert J., and Bryan Turner. *Talcott Parsons on Economy and Society.* Routledge 1989 $15.95. ISBN 0-415-03292-3. A collection of essays dealing with the issues and problems inherent in Parson's theory of social action.

Loubser, Jan J., and others, eds. *Explorations in General Theory in Social Science: Essays in Honor of Talcott Parsons.* 1976 2 vols. Free Pr. 1976 Vol. 1 o.p. Vol. 2 $95.00. ISBN 0-02-919360-5

RIESMAN, DAVID. 1909–

David Riesman, an American sociologist, was educated at Harvard University. He trained as a lawyer, and served as law clerk to Justice Louis Brandeis before practicing law in Boston and New York. Later he became interested in the study of contemporary American society. His book *The Lonely Crowd*, published in 1950, became an instant bestseller. Readers saw in its descriptions of "inner-directed" versus "other-directed" social types insightful descriptions of themselves and their neighbors. He has subsequently written extensively on American higher education. In the field of sociology, he is known as the major exponent of qualitative analysis—of learning about the whole through careful and detailed interviews with individuals. He is currently Henry Ford II emeritus professor of sociology at Harvard University.

BOOKS BY RIESMAN

Abundance for What? Transaction Pubs. 1992 ISBN 1-56000-599-8. Essays about affluence and its consequences in the West.

The Lonely Crowd: A Study of the Changing American Culture. Yale U. Pr. 1961 ISBN 0-300-00193-2. A classic examination of social character patterns that developed in American society during the mid-twentieth century.

SENNETT, RICHARD. 1948–

Richard Sennett is an American sociologist who received his doctorate from Harvard University. He currently teaches at New York University. During his academic career, he has concentrated on the social dynamics of cities and the history of urban thought. Among his special interests are architecture, urban design, art, and literature. Much of his writing has dealt with the relinquishment of public life and community; Sennett sees this trend as the result of important sociohistorical forces that he has helped to identify in his work.

BOOKS BY SENNETT

The Conscience of the Eye: The Design and Social Life of Cities. Knopf 1990 $24.95. ISBN 0-394-57104-5. Using art, history, literature, and social theory, the author describes how urban dwellers have become more isolated over time.

The Fall of Public Man. 1974. Norton 1992 $10.95. ISBN 0-393-30879-0. Contends that public life has been eclipsed by private interests.

The Uses of Disorder: Personal Identity and City Life. 1970. Norton 1992 $8.95. ISBN 0-393-30909-6. Argues that Americans' quest for a "purified community" should be counteracted by encouraging urban diversity and disorder.

SHILS, EDWARD. 1915–

Edward Shils, an American sociologist, is a professor at both the University of Chicago and King's College, Cambridge. The editors of a Festschrift prepared in his honor note that he has been a pioneer in clearing up the logical confusion over the concept of ideology and in exploring the role of intellectuals in contemporary life. Shils's work on the institutionalization of sociology as an academic discipline has been fundamental to all discussions of this question.

His interest in sociological concepts has been valuable in analyzing political and cultural leadership and societal cohesion. These concepts include his interpretation of "charisma," his own concepts of "center" and "periphery," and his revision of the term "mass society." Shils also introduced into sociology the concept of "scientific community," now central to the sociology of science. He is the founding editor of *Minerva*, a major journal in the field of higher education and the sociology of knowledge generally.

BOOKS BY SHILS

The Academic Ethic. U. Ch. Pr. $7.95. ISBN 0-226-75330-1

The Calling of Sociology: And Other Essays on the Pursuit of Learning. U. Ch. Pr. 1980 $27.50. ISBN 0-226-75323-9

Center and Periphery: Essays in Macro Sociology. Vol. 2. U. Ch. Pr. 1975 o.p.

The Constitution of Society. Vol. 2 U. Ch. Pr. $30.00. ISBN 0226-75327-1. Essay topics include mass society, center and periphery, charisma, tradition, and intellectuals.

The Intellectuals and the Powers: And Other Essays. U. Ch. Pr. 1972 o.p.

Remembering the University of Chicago: Teachers, Scientists & Scholars. U. Ch. Pr. 1991 $24.95. ISBN 0-226-75335-2. Personal reflections, particularly about Chicago School theorists.

Tradition. U. Ch. Pr. $11.95. ISBN 0-226-75326-3. An assessment of the place of tradition in social life and its importance in holding society together.

SIMMEL, GEORG. 1858–1918

Georg Simmel, a German sociologist, was a brilliant scholar who wrote about many aspects of human existence but never developed a systematic theory. He lectured at Berlin University for many years but was never given a permanent position because of his Jewish origins, his nonprofessorial brilliance, and what some took to be his destructive intellectual attitude. He is remembered in the United States for a number of insightful essays on such topics as the social role of the stranger and the nature of group affiliation. His book on conflict formed the basis of Lewis A. Coser's *The Functions of Social Conflict*, one of the classics of American sociology.

BOOKS BY SIMMEL

Georg Simmel on Individuality and Social Form. Trans. by D. Levine. U. Ch. Pr. 1972 $17.95. ISBN 0-226-75776-5

Georg Simmel On Women, Sexuality and Love. Trans. by G. Oakes. Yale U. Pr. 1984 $11.00. ISBN 0-300-03934-4

The Philosophy of Money. Ed. by D. Frisby. Trans. by T. Bottomore. Routledge 1990 $19.95. ISBN 0-415-04641-6. Simmel's ideas of the social, philosophical, and cultural significance of money in modern societies.

Schopenhauer and Nietzsche. Trans. by H. Loiskondl. U. Ill. Pr. 1991 $15.95. ISBN 0-252-06228-0

The Sociology of Georg Simmel. Ed. and trans. by K. Wolff. 1964. Free Pr. $12.95. ISBN 0-02-92890-3. A collection of Simmel's work, including his more important essays.

BOOKS ABOUT SIMMEL

Frisby, David. *Simmel and Since.* Routledge 1992 $49.95. ISBN 0-415-00975-8. A reevaluation of Simmel, assessing his ideas on such issues as urban life and modernity.

_____. *Sociological Impressionism: A Reassessment of Georg Simmel's Social Theory.* 1981. Routledge 1991 $16.95. ISBN 0-415-05795-7. A critical appraisal of Simmel's work and its relationship to modern social thought.

SOROKIN, PITIRIM A. 1889–1968

Pitirim A. Sorokin, a Russian-born American sociologist, wrote extensively on such subjects as the sociology of knowledge, the sociology of art, political sociology, social stratification, and methodology. A scholar of enormous learning, he attempted to analyze the processes of social organization, disorganization, and reorganization—all within a panoramic view of history that stressed periodic fluctuation as the heart of social change.

Sorokin moved to the United States in 1922 after he was banned from the Soviet Union because of his opposition to the Bolshevik regime; during the revolution of 1917, he had been a member of the Constituent Assembly, the private secretary of Prime Minister Kerensky, and the editor of a newspaper. In the United States, he taught at the University of Minnesota and then at Harvard University. His *Social and Cultural Dynamics* (1937–41), contains his sociological interpretation of history. His *Fads and Foibles of Modern Sociology and Related Sciences* (1956) is a comprehensive methodological critique of the quantification and formalization of sociocultural phenomena that he believed characterized sociology in the United States.

BOOKS BY SOROKIN

Fads and Foibles of Modern Sociology and Related Sciences. Greenwood 1976 repr. of 1956 ed. $45.00. ISBN 0-8371-8733-8. Examines nonscientific elements in sociology and related disciplines.

A Long Journey: The Autobiography of Pitirim A. Sorokin. NCUP 1963 $22.95. ISBN 0-8084-0203. Story of Sorokin's life, from his Russian peasant roots to his role during the revolution to his emergence in the United States as the first chairman of the sociology department at Harvard University.

Social and Cultural Dynamics. 4 vols. 1937–41. Bedminster Pr. 1962 o.p.

BOOKS ABOUT SOROKIN

Cowell, Frank R. *History, Civilization and Culture: An Introduction to the Historical and Social Philosophy of Pitirim A. Sorokin*. Hyperion Conn. 1979 repr. of 1950 ed. o.p.

Tiryakian, Edward A., ed. *Sociocultural Theory, Values, and Sociocultural Change: Essays in Honor of Pitirim A. Sorokin*. Macmillan 1963 o.p.

SPENCER, HERBERT. 1820–1903

Herbert Spencer, an English philosopher-scientist, was—with the anthropologists EDWARD BURNETT TYLOR and LEWIS HENRY MORGAN—one of the three great cultural evolutionists of the nineteenth century. A contemporary of CHARLES DARWIN (see Vol. 5), he rejected special creation and espoused organic evolution at about the same time. He did not, however, discover, as did Darwin, that the mechanism for evolution is natural selection. He was immensely popular as a writer in England, and his *The Study of Sociology* (1873) became the first sociology textbook ever used in the United States. With the recent revival of interest in evolution, Spencer may receive more attention than he has had for many decades.

BOOKS BY SPENCER

An Autobiography. 1904. Watts 1926 o.p.

The Evolution of Society: Selections from Herbert Spencer's "Principles of Sociology." Ed. by Robert L. Carniero. Bks. Demand $77.00. ISBN 0-685-23867-9

The Principles of Psychology. 1855. Gregg Intl. Pub. ISBN 0-576-29155-2

Social Statics. 1850. Schalkenbach 1970 $7.00. ISBN 0-911312-33-1

The Study of Sociology. 1873. U. of Mich. Pr. 1961 o.p. Introduction by Talcott Parsons.

BOOKS ABOUT SPENCER

Peel, J. D. *Herbert Spencer*. Ashgate Pub. Co. 1992 $59.95. ISBN 0-7512-0094-8. Well-researched and fascinating biography.

Wiltshire, David. *The Social and Political Thought of Herbert Spencer*. OUP 1978 $32.00. ISBN 0-19-821873-7. Very scholarly analysis of Spencer's sociological theories and method, as well as an examination of his political thought.

TAEUBER, CONRAD. 1906– , and IRENE B. TAEUBER, 1906–1974

Irene B. Taeuber and Conrad Taeuber were leading figures in American demography for nearly 50 years. For most of her life, Irene Taeuber worked at the Library of Congress in Washington, D.C., and was also a staff member of the Office of Population Research, Princeton University. Her major interest was in the demography of East Asia, and her masterpiece *The Population of Japan* has been widely acclaimed as the best volume on the demography of one country ever produced. Conrad Taeuber was one of the able professionals attracted to Washington in the early days of the Roosevelt administration; he served in the Department of Agriculture from 1935 to 1946, at the United Nations from 1946 to 1951, and at the Bureau of the Census from 1951 to 1973, where he was associate director and the major architect of the 1960 and 1970 censuses, *The Changing Population of the United States* and *People of the United States in the Twentieth Century*. Together, their work went far toward establishing demography as a scientific discipline and as a source of information crucial to modern government.

BOOKS BY CONRAD TAEUBER AND IRENE TAEUBER

The Changing Population of the United States. Wiley 1958 o.p.

The People of the United States in the Twentieth Century. Government Printing Office 1971 o.p.

BOOK BY IRENE TAEUBER

The Population of Japan. Princeton U. Pr. 1958 o.p.

THOMAS, W(ILLIAM) I(SAAC). 1863–1947

W. I. Thomas, an American sociologist, received his Ph.D. from the University of Chicago after studying at the universities of Berlin and Göttingen. He published several important books on a variety of subjects, but he probably would not have become famous had he not written *The Polish Peasant in Europe and America* (1984), a study of the Americanization of Polish immigrants to the United States at the turn of the century. Coauthored with Florian Znaniecki, a Polish sociologist who helped him interpret Polish culture, this massive two-volume work became a classic example of how such personal documents as letters and diaries can be combined with interviews to study social change. Ten years after its publication, in a journal article, Thomas used the phrase "If men define situations as real they are real in their consequences"—a phrase extensively quoted to this day in order stress the importance of perception over reality in people's lives.

BOOKS BY THOMAS

The Polish Peasant in Europe and America. (coauthored with Florian Znaniecki) 2 vols. 1918–1920. U. Ill. Pr. 1984 $29.95. ISBN 0-2520-1090-6. A study of the transformation and Americanization of Polish immigrants at the turn of the century.

Social Behavior and Personality: Contributions of W. I. Thomas to Theory and Social Research. Ed. by Edmund H. Volkart. Greenwood 1981 repr. of 1951 ed. $99.50. ISBN 0-313-22778-0. Foreword by Donald Young.

The Unadjusted Girl, with Cases and Standpoints for Behavior Analysis. 1923. Patterson Smith $18.00. ISBN 0-7585-026-X

W. I. Thomas on Social Organization and Social Personality. Ed. by Morris Janowitz. Heritage of Sociology Ser. U. Ch. Pr. 1966 o.p.

TOCQUEVILLE, ALEXIS DE. 1805–1859

[SEE Chapter 5 in this volume.]

TÖNNIES, FERDINAND. 1855–1936

Ferdinand Tönnies, a German sociologist, was a major figure in Germany at the turn of the century. Tönnies, GEORG SIMMEL, Werner Sombart, and MAX WEBER founded the German Sociological Society. Tönnies was president from 1909 until 1933, when he was dismissed from all of his positions by the Nazis. His fame rests largely on his first book, *Gemeinschaft und Gesellschaft*, published in 1887, which went through seven editions in German and was published in English in 1957 as *Community and Society*. According to Tönnies, social clubs and religious sects, for example, result from mutual sympathy, habit, or common belief; these involve *Gemeinschaft*-like social relationships. Business and political organizations, on the other hand, are intended by their members to be means to specific ends; these involve *Gesellschaft*-like relationships. This typology is closely related to others: status-contract (HENRY SUMNER MAINE); rural-urban; organic-mechanical solidarity (EMILE DURKHEIM); folk-urban (ROBERT REDFIELD); and particularism-universalism (TALCOTT PARSONS).

BOOK BY TÖNNIES

Community and Society. 1887. Transaction Pubs. 1988 $17.95. ISBN 0-88738-750-0. Introduction by John Samples.

VEBLEN, THORSTEIN. 1857–1929

Thorstein Veblen, an American economist and sociologist, was an unorthodox teacher who had a troubled domestic life. Accordingly, he never held an academic position for long. For a few years during the early 1920s, he was one of the "big four" on the faculty of the New School for Social Research; the others were JOHN DEWEY, James Harvey Robertson, and WESLEY C. MITCHELL. In 1926 he retired to a cabin in California, where he died in obscurity and poverty three years later. He published a remarkable series of books, all which were critical of the major institutions of American society; it was said of him that he was the last man who knew everything. His fame today rests largely on *The Theory of the Leisure Class* (1899), an analysis of the latent functions of "conspicuous consumption" and "conspicuous waste" as symbols of upper-class status and as competitive methods of enhancing individual prestige.

BOOKS BY VEBLEN

Engineers and the Price System. Transaction Pubs. 1983 $18.95. ISBN 0-87855-915-9. Introduction by Daniel Bell.

The Higher Learning in America. Transaction Pubs. 1992 $21.95. ISBN 1-56000-600-5

The Portable Veblen. Ed. by Max Lerner. Viking Penguin 1958 o.p.

The Theory of the Leisure Class. Kelley repr. of 1899 ed. $39.50. ISBN 0-678-01455-8

BOOKS ABOUT VEBLEN

Dorfman, Joseph. *Thorstein Veblen and His America*. Kelley repr. of 1934 ed. $45.00. ISBN 0-678-00007-7

Duffus, Robert L. *The Innocents at Cedro: A Memoir of Thorstein Veblen and Some Others*. Kelley repr. of 1944 ed. $27.50. ISBN 0-678-00885-X

Riesman, David. *Thorstein Veblen: A Critical Interpretation.* Continuum 1975 repr. of 1960 ed. o.p.

WALLERSTEIN, IMMANUEL. 1930–

Wallerstein studied at Columbia University, where he received his Ph.D. in 1959. His work has focused primarily on what he calls "world systems theory," which deals with the socioeconomic dynamics of global dependence and interdependence. As Wallerstein sees it, the wealthy nations of the world control and manipulate the destinies of weaker nations and keep them dependent. The world system is an outcome of historic global, political, and ideological forces leading to Western hegemony.

BOOKS BY WALLERSTEIN

The Capitalist World Economy. Cambridge U. Pr. 1979 $18.95. ISBN 0-521-29358-8. Essays summarizing the basic ideas of world system theory.

The Modern World System I: Capitalist Agriculture and the Origins of the European World Economy in the 16th Century. Acad. Pr. 1974 $9.00. ISBN 0-12-785920-9. Traces the emergence of a modern world economic system to the sixteenth-century mercantilist policies of France, England, and the Netherlands.

The Modern World System II: Mercantilism and the Consolidation of the European World Economy. Acad. Pr. 1980 $27.00. ISBN 0-12-785924. Carries the history of the world economic system up to the eighteenth century.

The Modern World System III: The Second Era of Great Expansion of the Capitalist World Economy 1730–1840. Acad. Pr. 1988 $49.00. ISBN 0-12-785925-X

Politics of the World Economy: The States, the Movements and the Civilizations. Cambridge U. Pr. 1984 $14.95. ISBN 0-521-27760-4

Transforming the Revolution: Social Movement and the World System. Monthly Review $35.00. ISBN 0-85345-807-3

Unthinking Social Science: The Limits of Nineteenth Century Paradigms. Blackwell Pubs. 1991 $47.95. ISBN 0-7456-0876-0

WEBER, MAX. 1864–1920

Max Weber, a German political economist, legal historian, and sociologist, had an impact on the social sciences that is difficult to overestimate. According to a widely held view, he was the founder of the modern way of conceptualizing society and thus the modern social sciences. His major interest was the process of rationalization, which characterizes Western civilization—what he called the "demystification of the world." This interest led him to examine the three types of domination or authority that characterize hierarchical relationships: charismatic, traditional, and legal. It also led him to the study of bureaucracy; all of the world's major religions; and capitalism, which he viewed as a product of the Protestant ethic. With his contemporary, the French sociologist EMILE DURKHEIM—they seem not to have known each other's work—he created modern sociology.

BOOKS BY WEBER

Ancient Judaism. 1917–19. Free Pr. 1967 $16.95. ISBN 0-02-934130-2

Basic Concepts in Sociology. Greenwood 1962 $35.00. ISBN 0-8371-2146-9

The City. Ed. and trans. by D. Martindale and G. Neuwirth. Free Pr. 1966 $19.95. ISBN 0-02-934200-7. Essays on ancient and medieval occidental cities.

The Protestant Ethic and the Spirit of Capitalism. 1930. Unwin Hyman 1989 $14.95. ISBN 0-04-331101-6. Classic study stressing the connection between Protestant asceticism and the growth of European capitalism.

Religion in China. Free Pr. 1968 $19.95. ISBN 0-02-934440-9

Sociology of Religion. Trans. by E. Fischoff. Beacon Pr. 1964 $15.00. ISBN 0-8070-4193-9

Theory of Social and Economic Organization. Ed. and trans. by T. Parsons. Free Pr. 1964 $17.95. ISBN 0-02-834920-6. Weber's thoughts on authority, power, commerce, politics, and methods of social science.

BOOKS ABOUT WEBER

Bendix, Reinhard. *Max Weber: An Intellectual Portrait*. U. CA Pr. 1978 o.p. One of the best studies of Weber's intellectual life.

Holton, Robert J., and Bryan Turner. *Max Weber on Economy and Society*. Routledge 1989 $37.50. ISBN 0-415-02916-3. An outline and interpretation of Weber's key sociological concerns, including his basic theories on religion, economics, power, and class.

Sayer, Derek. *Capitalism and Modernity: An Excursus on Marx and Weber*. Routledge 1990 $15.95. ISBN 0-415-01728-9. A discussion of how these two thinkers viewed capitalism and modernity.

WILSON, WILLIAM JULIUS. 1935–

William Julius Wilson, an American sociologist, received his Ph.D. from Washington State University in 1966 and teaches at the University of Chicago. His scholarly work, written from both historical and sociological perspectives, has concentrated on the condition of African Americans living in inner cities, especially the underclass. He stresses urban divisions separating the middle class from the poor.

BOOKS BY WILSON

The Declining Significance of Race. U. Ch. Pr. 1981 $9.95. ISBN 0-0226-90129-7. Describes the economic and social divisions within African American communities.

Power, Racism and Privilege: Race Relations in Theoretical and Sociohistorical Perspectives. Free Pr. $15.95. ISBN 0-02-935580-X. Examines race relations in South Africa and the United States, with special attention to the institutionalization of racism.

The Truly Disadvantaged: The Inner City, the Underclass and Public Policy. 1987. U. Ch. Pr. 1990 $12.95. ISBN 0-226-90131-9. Argues that the underclass has developed its own unique, self-perpetuating subculture.

WIRTH, LOUIS. 1897–1952

Louis Wirth was a German-born American sociologist who spent most of his career at the University of Chicago. Like other members of the Chicago School, he was instrumental in linking social theory to planning and action. His studies on cities in general and on Chicago in particular helped lay the foundation for social planning and policy making in the United States. Wirth was instrumental in generating funding for academic projects that supported social amelioration, and his work in race relations helped improve conditions for minorities before the civil rights movement of the 1950s and 1960s. As a man of erudition, Wirth not only introduced the English-speaking world to the works of important German social scientists like KARL MANNHEIM, but also furthered a more theoretical approach to cities and their problems. His essay "Urbanism as a Way of Life" became a landmark of modern urban sociological theory and established a research agenda for generations of sociologists to come.

BOOKS BY WIRTH

The Ghetto. 1928. *Midway Reprint Ser.* U. Ch. Pr. 1982 $14.95. ISBN 0-226-90252-8. Historical treatment of the Jewish European ghetto, together with a study of Chicago's Jewish ghetto.

Louis Wirth on Cities and Social Life. 1964 Ed. by Albert J. Reiss, Jr. *Heritage of Sociology Ser.* U. Ch. Pr. 1982 $15.00. ISBN 0-226-90242-0. Collected papers on community and social planning; includes the article "Urbanism as a Way of Life."

BOOK ABOUT WIRTH

Salerno, Roger. *Louis Wirth: A Bio-bibliography.* Greenwood Pr. 1987 $42.95. ISBN 0-31-25473-7. An extensive biographical essay and comprehensive annotated bibliography.

WRONG, DENNIS H. 1923–

Educated at the University of Toronto and Columbia University (from which he received his Ph.D. in 1956), Wrong teaches at New York University. He is interested especially in social change and social psychology. Much of his work has been an attempt to better understand human nature and its relationship to the structure of society. He contends that sociologists and social psychologists have failed to free themselves from their own perspectives and have thus been unable to gain a truly dialectical vision of human nature.

BOOKS BY WRONG

Population & Society. McGraw 1977 repr. of 1961 ed. $7.88. ISBN 0-07553676-5. Deals with the history of population growth, mobility, and social change, with particular emphasis on the psychological determinants of change.

Skeptical Sociology. Col. U. Pr. 1976 $49.00. ISBN 0-231-04014-8. A collection of essays on such issues as stratification, power, and the "oversocialized conception of man."

CHAPTER 8

Education

Richard J. Kraft

> I believe that all education proceeds by the participation of the individual in the social consciousness of the race.
> —JOHN DEWEY, *Dewey on Education*

> If an unfriendly foreign power had attempted to impose on America the mediocre educational performance that exists today, we might well have viewed it as an act of war . . . We have, in effect, been committing an act of unthinking, unilateral educational disarmament.
> —U.S. DEPT. OF EDUCATION, *A Nation at Risk*

Education and public schooling have long held an almost sacred place in the hearts of Americans. Schools were seen as the best hope for millions to move out of rural poverty and urban ghettoes and achieve middle-class status. For large numbers of citizens, the American schools did exactly that. They took immigrants from all over the world and gave them literacy, numeracy, values, and skills to survive in the factories of an industrialized society. Revisionist historians have pointed out the not-so-hidden curriculum of the school: to keep the young out of the labor market, teach middle-class values, sort people into jobs and social classes—maybe even to prepare a docile work force. Nevertheless, there is no doubt that public schools did serve as a way out of poverty for millions. In spite of debates between "progressive" followers of JOHN DEWEY and "basics" educators, and in spite of the fact that many parents preferred parochial schools, there was still a broad consensus on the importance and necessity of supporting a high-quality public school system to which most citizens would send their children.

With the coming of the postindustrial information era, however, schools have come under increasing fire for not preparing the current generation for the realities of the twenty-first century. A so-called crisis in education has dominated the national agenda and the news since the early 1980s.

A Nation at Risk, a 1983 U.S. Department of Education study (and the source of the quotation introducing this chapter), is still the best-known and perhaps most influential report from among the hundreds of local, state, and national documents that followed it. It used metaphors from war and sports to urge the United States to avoid further educational "disarmament" and to "defeat" our competitors around the world, particularly the Japanese, by strengthening our science and math education. Calls for excellence drowned out much of the earlier debate on equality of opportunity. Only with the publication of Jonathan Kozol's *Savage Inequalities* in 1991 did the nation again turn seriously to the massive failures of our inner cities to provide quality education, to say nothing of a safe learning environment. The gap between majority and minority achievement continued to be significant. Graduation rates from high school continued to average between 73 and 75 percent nationally, with many cities falling at or below the 50-percent mark. With local property taxes still providing major financial support for schools and regularly scheduled votes for school boards and bond issues, education is perhaps closer to the people than almost any other governmental activity. Calls for greater accountability and higher quality were heard in Congress, state legislatures, and communities all over the country.

The first wave of school reform, beginning in the early 1980s, was characterized by top-down mandates of longer school years, more student and teacher testing, a narrowing of the curriculum, and higher graduation requirements; it did not appear to have a significant impact on such indicators as student attendance, achievement as measured by standardized examination, graduation rates, or such social pathologies of youth as substance abuse. A second wave of school reform, beginning in the late 1980s and continuing to the present, has emphasized reforms at the local level. Authentic assessment, with its emphasis on actual performance on "real world" tests, has replaced some of the emphasis on standardized examinations. New coalitions of the right and left are building around the need for greater choice and options for students, parents, and teachers in a wider variety of public and private schools than has been traditional in American educational history. The middle-school movement—with its emphasis on interdisciplinary studies, on teams of teachers working with small groups of students, and on social skills as well as academic achievement for the early adolescent—has all but replaced the more traditional junior high school.

It is difficult to reach agreement on what should be done to improve public schooling, because education is a topic about which almost everyone has an opinion and on which many consider themselves to be experts. Almost everyone attends school for many years and can expound on the successes and failures of education from a personal perspective. In addition, much of the research in the field has been subjective and lacking in rigor. Through medical research, a consensus rapidly develops on the best treatments for disease; engineers and scientists use generally accepted mathematical formulas and scientific methods. Only in the past two decades, however, has educational research begun to develop objective standards in determining the best pedagogical practices, organizational structures, and teaching materials.

Even with these gains, the debate over education continues and is likely to do so for decades to come. Among its issues are these: whole word versus phonics in reading instruction; mainstreaming children with special needs; the advisability of a local, state, or nationally developed curriculum and standardized examinations; homogeneous versus heterogeneous grouping of students, particularly as it affects the gifted and talented; vocational training versus general education in comprehensive secondary schools; and public and/or private choice or voucher systems. Other unresolved questions include equality of opportunity for minority students, particularly in poor urban or rural areas; the effects of day care and Head Start on the emotional lives and intellectual achievement of young children; the perceived decline in ethics, morality, and behavior of children and young people and the role of the school in combating it; the rise in substance abuse, suicide, tenn pregnancy, and other social pathologies; the improvement of teacher quality through better certification and testing; bilingual and multicultural education; and the reform of schools through bottom-up, site-based decisionmaking instead of top-down state and federal mandates.

Although primary and secondary schools in the United States have been under nearly constant attack, the American higher educational system generally has been considered to be the best in the world. Most major research universities are found in the United States; exceptional private undergraduate colleges are numerous; and state-run four-year and community colleges have made higher education accessible to a large percentage of the population. However, cutbacks in state funding and federally backed loans and scholarships, together with steadily rising costs, have made higher education an increasingly difficult goal for many poor and minority students. How the United States maintains both high quality and access for all qualified students will be a major challenge to this sector of our educational system for years to come.

With hundreds of books being published each year in the field of education, it is a formidable task to select from among the best of the past. The following bibliography has two parts. The first consists of books on education that are of interest to and appropriate for the educated layperson or professional educator. The second lists college-level or in-service titles that are most appropriate for school and college teachers and administrators. A few important works from throughout our educational history have been included, but most of the books are from 1983 to 1993.

BIBLIOGRAPHY

Works of Interest to the Educated Lay Public

Adler, Mortimer J. *The Paideia Proposal: An Educational Manifesto.* Macmillan 1984 $5.95. ISBN 0-02-064100-1. The author, as spokesman for a consortium of education experts called the Paideia group, advocates—among other things—a basic curriculum for all students that would offer no electives except in foreign language studies.

Avrich, Paul. *The Modern School Movement: Anarchism and Education in the United States.* Princeton U. Pr. 1980 $25.00. ISBN 0-691-10094-2. "Avrich's immensely engaging book . . . brings back to life the marvelously rich and vivid personalities associated with the education experiment . . . [of] the Modern School Movement" (Alan Ryan, *Times Literary Supplement*).

Barth, Roland S. *Run School Run.* HUP 1980 $22.95. ISBN 0-674-78036-1. Written by an elementary school principal, who relates his experiences in encouraging pluralistic education in the schools.

Beauchamp, Edward R., ed. *Windows on Japanese Education.* Greenwood 1991 $56.95. ISBN 0-313-26243-8. Why and how the Japanese succeed in schooling their children.

Bellah, Robert N., Richard N. Madsen, William M. Sullivan, Ann Swidler, and Steven M. Tipton. *Habits of the Heart: Individualism and Commitment in American Life.* HarpC repr. of 1985 ed. $13.00. ISBN 0-06-097027-8. Considered by many to be the most persuasive description of American society in the late twentieth century. Though not directly a book on education, its implications for schooling in the United States are profound because it discusses the tension between the desire for individual freedom and the need to build community.

Bloom, Allan. *The Closing of the American Mind.* S&S Trade 1988 $10.95. ISBN 0-671-65715-1. A critique of American higher education and how it has failed to meet the needs of individual students and society.

Bloom, Benjamin S. *All Our Children Learning: A Primer for Parents, Teachers, and Other Educators.* McGraw 1982 $6.95. ISBN 0-07-006121-1. ". . . a fine book [that] should be read by everyone interested in understanding more about how children learn and how we should teach them" (B. M. Caldwell, *Harvard Educational Review*).

Boyer, Ernest L. *High School: A Report on Secondary Education in America.* HarpC 1985 $13.00. ISBN 0-06-091224-3. "This book is an important contribution to the coming educational policy debate of the 1980s; beyond that, it is a powerful and well-articulated vision of what secondary education can be" (*Choice*).

Cahn, Steven M. *Education and the Democratic Ideal.* Nelson-Hall 1979 o.p. "The intention of the author is to present a coherent, thorough, and sound philosophy of higher education. He effectively achieves this. . . . Although the examples are drawn from higher education, the message is applicable to any educational level" (J. J. Groark, *Library Journal*).

Carrol, Deborah. *Good News: How Sharing the Newspaper with Your Children Can Enhance Their Performance in School.* Viking Penguin 1993 $8.50. ISBN 0-14-017039-1. Proves that newspapers can be valuable tools to better the skills learned in school. Details dozens of reading, math, and social studies activities.

Coleman, James S., and Thomas Hoffer. *Public and Private High Schools: The Impact of Communities.* Basic 1987 $21.95. ISBN 0-465-06767-0. Using data from a large study of achievement in public and private high schools, the authors conclude that even when race, ethnicity, socioeconomic, and family factors are accounted for, students at private schools, particularly Catholic parochial ones, achieve at a higher level than their counterparts in the public schools.

Coles, Robert. *The Call of Stories: Teaching and the Moral Imagination.* HM 1989 $8.70. ISBN 0-395-52815-1. Written by a professor of child psychiatry at Harvard, this book links a love of literature with a concern for morality.

———. *Children of Crisis: A Study of Courage and Fear.* Little 1967 $19.95. ISBN 0-316-15154-8. Interviews reveal how desegregation struggles affected both black and white children.

College Handbook, 1993. College Bd. 1992 $19.00. ISBN 0-87447-431-0. Definitive guide and reference to colleges across the United States.

Comer, James P., and Alvin Poussaint. *Raising Black Children.* NAL-Dutton 1992 $12.00. ISBN 0-452-26839-7. By two African American psychiatrists, this is an indispensable book for parents of African American children and for teachers or other professionals attempting to meet the needs of African American children in today's society.

Commager, Henry S. *The Commonwealth of Learning.* HarpC 1968 o.p.

Coombs, Philip H. *The World Crisis in Education: A View from the Eighties.* OUP 1985 $16.95. ISBN 0-19-503503-8. Follow-up of an earlier work by a leading educational planner; deals with the quantitative and qualitative aspects of educating the world's 5 billion people.

Crawford, James. *Hold Your Tongue: Bilingualism and the Politics of "English Only."* Addison-Wesley 1992. ISBN 0-201-55044-X. Journalist's well-reasoned, impassioned argument opposed to making English the official language of the United States; also deals with such critical issues as bilingualism, cultural unity, and immigration.

D'Souza, Dinesh. *Illiberal Education: The Politics of Race and Sex on Campus.* Random 1992 $12.00. ISBN 0-679-73857-6. Polemic directed against "political correctness," affirmative action, multicultural activism, and gender wars in American higher education.

Duke, Daniel L. *Teaching: The Imperiled Profession.* State U. NY Pr. 1984 $49.50. ISBN 0-87395-788-1. Examines not only contemporary issues but also the rewards and frustrations of the teaching profession.

Ekins, Paul. *A New World Order: Grassroots Movements for Global Change.* Routledge 1992 $74.50. ISBN 0-415-07115-1. Examines major problems facing the world today—war, poverty, the environment, and human rights violations—with implications for educational systems.

Estell, Doug, and others. *Reading Lists for College-Bound Students.* P-H 1993 $10.00. ISBN 0-671-84712-0. What is being read at top college campuses.

Finn, Chester E., Jr., and others, eds. *Against Mediocrity: The Humanities in America's High Schools.* Holmes & Meier 1984 $29.50. ISBN 0-8419-0944-X. With a foreword by William J. Bennett. A frank appraisal of the conditions of the humanities in the schools; provides suggestions on what can be done to teach humanities disciplines. Concentrates primarily on secondary schools.

First, Joan M. *New Voices: Immigrants in U.S. Public Schools.* NCAS 1991 repr. of 1988
ed. $14.95. ISBN 1-880002-01-9. Research and policy report that documents the
experiences of recent immigrants who have radically changed the face of U.S. public
schooling.

Gardner, Howard. *Multiple Intelligences: The Theory in Practice.* Basic 1993 $30.00. ISBN
0-465-01821-1. Details research evidence for an expansion of our conception of
intelligence; has begun to influence schools, which now are seeking ways to develop
musical, spatial, kinesthetic, interpersonal, and intrapersonal intelligences rather
than concentrating to such a large extent on logico-mathematical and linguistic
ones.

Gardner, John W. *Excellence: Can We Be Equal and Excellent Too?* Norton repr. of 1984
ed. $6.95. ISBN 0-393-30377-2. Revision of Gardner's 1961 work, examining the
social contexts that promote or stifle excellence and the role of schools in this
process.

Garms, Walter I., James W. Guthrie, and L. C. Pierce. *School Finance: The Economics
and Politics of Public Education.* P-H 1978 $27.95. ISBN 0-13-793315-0. "Stimulating
and controversial, . . . the book is worth thoughtful reading by concerned laymen in
spite of a few technical chapters" (*Library Journal*).

Gilligan, Carol. *In a Different Voice: Psychological Theory and Women's Development.*
HUP 1982 $20.00. ISBN 0-674-44543-0. Classic work on how psychology and society
have "persistently and systematically misunderstood women—their motives, their
moral commitments, the course of their psychological growth and their special view
of what is important in life."

Goodlad, John I. *What Schools Are For. Foundation Monograph Ser.* Phi Delta Kappa
1979 $5.50. ISBN 0-87367-422-7. "An exceptionally readable and potentially helpful
book. . . . [It] is a book in praise of the American dream of a common school, but,
instead of calling us to quick action, Goodlad speaks of the need for thoughtful
dialogue" (N. V. Overly, *Phi Delta Kappan*).

Gould, Stephen Jay. *The Mismeasure of Man.* Norton repr. of 1981 ed. $9.95. ISBN 0-393-
30056-0. Presents the "disastrous" history of psychometrics and the resulting
historical racism that continues to plague society and schools.

Hazen, Robert M., and James Trefill. *Science Matters: Achieving Scientific Literacy.*
Doubleday 1991 $12.00. ISBN 0-385-26108-X. Suggestions for improving our
scientific literacy, not only in schools but throughout society as well.

Heath, Shirley Brice. *Ways with Words: Language, Life and Work in Communities and
Classrooms.* Cambridge U. Pr. 1983 $69.95. ISBN 0-521-27319-6. This classic work
compares two communities, one white and one African American; deep cultural
differences in the way children use words are carefully documented and beautifully
described.

Holland, Dorothy C., and Margaret A. Eisenhart. *Educated in Romance: Women,
Achievements, and College Culture.* U. Ch. Pr. 1992 $11.95. ISBN 0-226-34944-6.
Women and higher education.

Holt, John. *How Children Learn.* Delacorte rev. ed. 1983 $9.95. ISBN 0-440-55051-3.
Concludes that education at its best avoids intruding on children's natural desire to
learn.

Illich, Ivan. *Deschooling Society. World Perspective Ser.* HarpC 1989 $9.00. ISBN 0-06-
132086-2. A discussion of issues that are raised when people embrace the hypothesis
that society can be deschooled. Develops criteria and goals to bring about an "Age of
Leisure."

Kearns, David T., and Denis D. Doyle. *Winning the Brain Race.* ICS Pr. 1991 $10.95. ISBN
1-55815-166-4. Calls on the business community to become involved in educational
reform.

Kerr, Clark. *The Uses of the University.* HUP 1963 $10.95. ISBN 0-674-93171-8. Assesses
the changing nature and role of higher education.

Kidder, Tracy. *Among School Children.* Avon 1990 $11.00. ISBN 0-380-71089-7. This
bestseller tells of the author's nine months observing a fifth-grade classroom in
Massachusetts.

Kirp, David L. *Learning by Heart: AIDS and Schoolchildren in America's Communities.* Rutgers U. Pr. 1989 $30.00. ISBN 0-8135-1596-0. Chronicles how eight communities dealt with the struggles over whether to admit children with AIDS into their schools; deals not only with the politics of this issue, but also with such topics as homosexuality, death, deviance, and blame as played out in schools and society.

Kohl, Herbert. *Basic Skills: A Guide for Parents and Teachers on the Subjects Most Vital to Education.* Bantam 1984 o.p.

_____. *Basic Skills: A Plan for Your Child, A Program for All Children.* Little 1982 o.p. Defines five basic skills (language ability, problem solving, scientific understanding, use of the imagination, and an understanding of group process) and proposes a program for implementing them in public education.

Kozol, Jonathan. *Illiterate America.* NAL-Dutton 1986 $10.00. ISBN 0-452-26203-8. Raises the specter of tens of millions of Americans who are functionally illiterate and incapable of meaningful participation in the modern economy; the author not only indicts schools but also offers many practical suggestions for improvement.

_____. *Savage Inequalities: Children in America's Schools.* Crown Pub. Group 1991 $20.00. ISBN 0-517-58221-X. Devastating critique of the disparities in education, particularly as they affect children of the poor and minority populations in America's inner cities.

Lerner, Allan W., and B. Kay King. *Continuing Higher Education: The Coming Wave.* Tchrs. Coll. 1992 $36.00. ISBN 0-8077-3197-8. New role of higher education in the 1990s.

Lickona, Thomas. *Educating for Character: How Our Schools Can Teach Respect and Responsibility.* Bantam 1991 $22.50. ISBN 0-553-07570-5. Captures the practical aspects of dealing with values and issues of character in the classroom. Other books might be better on the theory of ethics, but few give more practical advice for teachers.

Lightfoot, Sara L. *The Good High School: Portraits of Character and Culture.* Basic 1985 $16.00. ISBN 0-465-02696-6. Descriptions of two inner-city high schools, two upper-middle-class high schools, and two elite preparatory schools based on interviews and observations. All schools are judged excellent, but each succeeds in different ways.

Loeffler, Margaret H. *Montessori in Contemporary American Culture.* Heinemann Ed. 1992 $20.00. ISBN 0-435-08709-6. Record of a 1990 symposium that describes the adaptations of the Montessori method to America; provides useful insight into the history and the method.

McCarthy, Martha M. *Public School Law: Teachers' and Students' Rights.* Allyn 1992 $48.00. ISBN 0-205-13500-5. A well-organized and relatively nontechnical account of the legal foundations of American public education. Foreword by Alexander Kern.

Nathan, Joe. *Free to Teach: Achieving Equity and Excellence in Schools.* Pilgrim OH 1991 $16.95. ISBN 0-8298-0905-8. An assistant principal describes his own experiences and presents ideas for educational program innovation and policy reforms.

National Council on Education Standards and Testing. *Raising Standards for American Education.* USGPO 1992 o.p. Provided much of the impetus for putting standards into place to help measure the National Goals for Education developed in the 1980s; represents efforts of many political figures and educational leaders of both political parties and differing educational philosophies.

Neill, A. S. *Summerhill: A Radical Approach to Child Rearing.* PB 1977 o.p. A controversial and radical text on the raising of children in a fictional school called Summerhill.

O'Neil, Robert M. *Classrooms in the Crossfire: The Rights and Interests of Students, Parents, Teachers, Administrators, Librarians and the Community.* Ind. U. Pr. 1981 o.p. A balanced, clear analysis of the current increase in attacks on the public school curriculum, textbooks, and libraries.

Papert, Seymour. *Mindstorms: Children, Computers, and Powerful Ideas.* Basic 1993 $13.00. ISBN 0-465-04674-6. Examines the use of computers in the classrooms and urges expansion of their use, especially for those with "mathophobia."

Postman, Neil. *Teaching as a Conserving Activity*. Dell 1987 $4.95. ISBN 0-440-38486-9. Proposes an idea-centered educational program that includes the study of history, standard English, and the philosophies of science and religion.

Postman, Neil, and Charles Weingartner. *Teaching as a Subversive Activity*. Dell 1987 $4.95. ISBN 0-440-38485-0. Bestseller and major influence on the radical educational reforms attempted in the 1970s.

Ravitch, Diane. *The Schools We Deserve: Reflections on the Educational Crises of Our Time*. Basic 1985 $16.00. ISBN 0-465-07234-8. Conservative critique of American schooling in the late twentieth century, written from a historical perspective.

_____. *The Troubled Crusade: American Education, 1945–1980*. Basic 1985 $17.00. ISBN 0-465-08757-4. A well-documented survey that takes into account the numerous political, racial, and cultural issues influencing schools during the post–World War II period.

Roedell, Wendy C., Nancy E. Jackson, and Halbert B. Robinson. *Gifted Young Children*. Ed. by Abraham J. Tannenbaum. *Perspectives on Gifted and Talented Education Ser*. Tchrs. Coll. 1980 $8.95. ISBN 0-8077-2587-0. "This information would be useful to parents of precocious preschoolers, to directors of early childhood education programs, and to school districts interested in providing appropriate differentiated education to gifted students throughout their school careers" (M. C. Rhodes, *Phi Delta Kappan*).

Rossman, Parker. *The Emerging Worldwide Electronic University: Information Age Global Higher Education*. Greenwood 1992 $42.95. ISBN 0-313-27927-6. Cites evidence that the "growing use of electronic tools for teaching, learning, and research constitutes an emerging worldwide electronic university."

Schorr, Lisbeth B., with Daniel Schorr. *Within Our Reach: Breaking the Cycle of Disadvantage*. Doubleday 1989 $9.95. ISBN 0-385-24244-1. Details successful innovative programs around the country—parent education, home-based nursing, magnet schools, and others—that meet the needs of our most vulnerable children.

Schultz, Fred. *Annual Editions: Education 93–94*. Dushkin Pub. 1993 $11.95. ISBN 0-56134-197-5. Provocative collection of the year's best popular articles on education. Recent compendiums have included, in addition to annual Gallup poll on education, articles on international comparisons, morality and values, classroom management, and special-needs children.

Sewall, Gilbert T. *Necessary Lessons: Decline and Renewal in American Schools*. Free Pr. 1983 $27.95. ISBN 0-02-929030-9. "*Newsweek*'s education editor critically evaluates the current state of America's schooling, beset as it is with academic and attitudinal problems" (Shirley L. Hopkinson, *Library Journal*).

Silberman, Charles E. *Crisis in the Classroom: The Remaking of American Education*. Vin. 1971 o.p. Highly influential and readable work, which set the tone for much of the experimentation in education in the 1970s and perhaps contributed to the backlash "back to basics" movement of the 1980s.

Spitzberg, Irving J. *Creating Community on College Campuses*. State U. NY Pr. 1992 $57.50. ISBN 0-7914-1005-6. Role of community in the educational processes on college campuses.

Taylor, Denny, and Catherine Dorsey-Gaines. *Growing Up Literate: Learning from Inner-City Families*. Heinemann Ed. 1988 $17.50. ISBN 0-435-08457-7. Ethnographic, family, and racial issues related to inner-city African American children and families.

U.S. National Commission on Excellence in Education. *A Nation at Risk: The Imperative for Educational Reform*. USGPO 1983 o.p. This committee report, which stirred considerable debate, defines problems and solutions in American educational curricula, standards, basic skills, teacher preparation and the teaching profession, educational leadership, and fiscal support.

William T. Grant Foundation Commission on Work, Family, and Citizenship. *The Forgotten Half: Pathways to Success for America's Youth and Young Families*. William T. Grant 1988 o.p. This report, though not technically on education, has been very influential, especially in reminding people that at least half of all young people in the United States never will graduate from college.

Williams, Frederick, and Victoria Williams. *Microcomputers in Elementary Education: Perspectives on Implementation.* Wadsworth Pub. 1984 o.p. Based upon on-site investigations of 12 elementary schools and the issues surrounding their implementation of computers and how they are being used.

Young, Margaret W., ed. *Youth and America's Future: A Special Report on Youth, Embodying Research Analysis and Recommendations.* 2 vols. Omnigraphics Inc. 1989 $95.00. ISBN 0-55888-814-4. Comprises 21 documents prepared initially for the William T. Grant Foundation Commission on Work.

Works of Interest to the Professional Educator

Adams, Anthony, and Esnor Jones. *Teaching Humanities in the Microelectronic Age.* Taylor & Francis 1983 $25.00. ISBN 0-335-10196-8. This is not a how-to manual, but rather a collection of essays that explore the issues surrounding the introduction and use of computers in the language arts curriculum.

Adams, Marilyn Jager. *Beginning to Read: Thinking and Learning about Print.* MIT Pr. 1990 $32.50. ISBN 0-262-01112-3. Excellent introduction to a theoretical understanding of how children learn to read and find meaning.

Altbach, Philip G., ed. *Comparative Higher Education Abroad: Bibliography and Analysis.* Interbk. Inc. 1976 $5.50. ISBN 0-89192-222-9. Includes an essay that surveys the historical, political, and international comparative nature of higher education.

Anderson, Richard, Elfrieda H. Hiebert, Judith A. Scott, and Ian A. G. Wilkinson. *Becoming a Nation of Readers.* Natl. Inst. of Educ. 1985 o.p. One of the first major national reports on curriculum.

Arnove, Robert F., Philip G. Altbach, and Gail P. Kelly, eds. *Emergent Issues in Education: Comparative Perspectives.* State U. NY Pr. 1992. ISBN 0-7914-1031-5. Excellent introduction to the field of comparative education; includes research-based articles, essays on issues of major international importance, and topics of specific concern in both First and Third World countries.

Atlas, James. *Battle of the Books: What It Takes to Be Educated in America.* Norton 1990 $17.95. ISBN 0-393-03413-5. Carefully outlines the debate in higher education over canons and curriculum.

Atwell, Nancie. *In the Middle: Writing, Reading and Learning with Adolescents.* Boynton Cook Pubs. 1987 $24.95. ISBN 0-86709-164-9. Examines how an eighth-grade teacher turned "reluctant readers into voracious ones." Teachers will appreciate the practical advice, and laypersons will find the book helpful as well.

Banks, James. *Teaching Strategies for the Social Studies.* Longman 1990 $38.95. ISBN 0-8013-0472-5. Scholarly yet practical guide for teachers of social studies, written by perhaps the nation's leading authority on multicultural education.

Barth, Roland. *Improving Schools from Within.* Jossey-Bass 1990 $26.95. ISBN 1-55542-215-2. Former school administrator contends that genuine reform must come from below or within the schools, not be forced from above.

Beaty, Janice. *Preschool: Appropriate Practices.* HB Coll. Pubs. 1992. ISBN 0-03-047524-4. Excellent resource for preschool teachers and directors and for parents wishing to know more about quality education for young children.

Bowen, James. *A History of Western Education.* 3 vols. St. Martin. Vol. 1 *The Ancient World—Orient and Mediterranean 2000 B.C.–A.D. 1054.* 1972 $27.50. ISBN 0-312-38710-5. Vol. 2 *Civilization of Europe, Sixth to Sixteenth Century.* 1975 $30.00. ISBN 0-312-58795-8. Vol. 3 *The Modern West, Europe and the New World.* 1981 $35.00. ISBN 0-312-38780-6. "Bowen's three-volume work supersedes all previous histories of Western education" (*Choice*).

Bowles, Samuel, and Herbert Gintis. *Schooling in Capitalist America: Educational Reform and the Contradictions of Economic Life.* Basic 1976 $16.00. ISBN 0-465-09718-9. Classic leftist critique of the role American schools have played in the development of the economy and in the preparation for the world of work.

Bruner, Jerome S. *The Relevance of Education. Norton Lib.* Norton 1971 o.p. A collection of essays written from 1964 to 1970, during the time that the "youth culture" was emerging.

Chastain, Kenneth. *Developing Second-Language Skills: Theory and Practice.* HB Coll. Pubs. 1988 $16.00. ISBN 0-15-517619-6. Basic text for new or practicing teachers who work with immigrant or other children whose second language is English.

Chubb, John E., and Terry M. Moe. *Politics, Markets and America's Schools.* Brookings 1990 $34.95. ISBN 0-8157-1409-2. Details an extensive research project that led the authors to conclude that school choice, public or private, is a significant factor in the academic success of students.

Churgin, Jonah R. *The New Woman and the Old Academy: Sexism and Higher Education.* Libra 1979 $15.00. ISBN 0-87212-076-7. "In three parts, Churgin deals successfully with the problems women face in society today, the particular manifestations of these problems on the college campus, and the beneficial effects of affirmative action for both men and women" (*Choice*).

Cremin, Lawrence A. *American Education: The Colonial Experience, 1607–1783.* HarpC o.p.

———. *American Education: The National Experience, 1783–1876.* HarpC 1980 o.p. With the volume above, the first two of a planned three-volume comprehensive history.

———. *Traditions of American Education.* Basic 1979 $11.00. ISBN 0-465-08684-5. In this series of published lectures, the complexity of the U.S. educational system is put in a historical framework.

Darder, Antonia. *Culture and Power in the Classroom: A Critical Foundation for Bicultural Education.* Greenwood 1991 $13.95. ISBN 0-89789-239-9. An excellent introduction to the issues surrounding bilingual and bicultural education.

Duschl, Richard A., and Richard S. Hamilton, eds. *Philosophy of Science, Cognitive Psychology, and Educational Theory and Practice.* State U. NY Pr. 1992 $57.50. ISBN 0-7914-1053-6. Raises fundamental issues of teaching science from very different perspectives.

Edelsky, Carole, Bess Altwerger, and Barbara Flores. *Whole Language: What's the Difference.* Heinemann Ed. 1991 $10.95. ISBN 0-435-08537-9. Introduces parents and professionals to an important movement in reading and writing theory.

Education Index. 8 vols. Wilson $175.00 ea. ISBN 0-685-22246-2. Comprehensive guide to more than 250 educational periodicals.

Eisenhart, Margaret, and Hilda Borko. *Designing Classroom Research.* Allyn 1993 o.p. Summarizes the wide range of methodologies for conducting classroom research and discusses the pitfalls.

Eisner, Elliot W. *The Educational Imagination: On the Design and Education of School Programs.* Macmillan 1985. ISBN 0-02-332110-5. "This seminal work in curriculum theory effectively challenges most of the conventional wisdom of current educational thinking" (*Choice*).

Fetterman, David M. *Excellence and Equality: A Qualitatively Different Perspective on Gifted and Talented Education.* State U. NY Pr. 1988 $59.50. ISBN 0-88706-641-0. Examines over 30 programs for gifted and talented children in California; also gives a case study of a "model" midwestern program and an overview of international approaches.

Fuller, R. Buckminster. *R. Buckminster Fuller on Education.* Ed. by Peter H. Wagschal and Robert D. Kahn. U. of Mass. Pr. 1979 $11.95. ISBN 0-87023-204-5. A collection of essays by an ardent critic of American education. He argues for increased and more innovative uses of technology as an educational medium.

Garibaldi, Antoine, ed. *Black Colleges and Universities: Challenges for the Future.* Greenwood 1984 $47.95. ISBN 0-295-91163-2. Fifteen papers addressing the current and future roles for African American colleges.

Gearhart, Bill R., Mel W. Weishahn, and Carol J. Gearhart. *The Exceptional Students in the Regular Classroom.* Mayfield Pub. 1988 $40.95. ISBN 0-87484-793-7. Introduces the regular classroom teacher to students with special needs, who now are being mainstreamed.

Giamatti, A. Bartlett. *The University and the Public Interest.* Atheneum 1981 o.p. The late president of Yale University explores "such topics as private universities, the federal government, language, athletics, power and politics, and teachers. Although each is a self-contained piece, the refreshing writing style, vocabulary, and relationship to the theme tie them into an intellectually stimulating volume" *(Choice).*

Giroux, Henry A. *Schooling and the Struggle for Public Life: Critical Pedagogy in the Modern Age.* U. of Minn. Pr. 1988 $39.95. ISBN 0-8166-1706-6. Leading critical theorist deals with the role schools play in citizenship education and in perpetuating existing power relationships in society.

Glass, Gene V., and Kenneth D. Hopkins. *Statistical Methods in Education and Psychology.* P-H 1984. ISBN 0-13-844944-9. Widely used text for teaching basic statistics in schools of education and psychology departments.

Graves, Donald H. *Build a Literate Classroom.* Heinemann Ed. 1991 $12.50. ISBN 0-435-08488-7. Discusses practical ways for teachers to improve literacy in their classrooms.

Greene, Maxine. *Landscapes of Learning.* Tchrs. Coll. 1978 $17.95. ISBN 0-8077-2534-X. The author's essays delve into emancipatory education, social issues as they affect pedagogy, artistic-aesthetic concerns, and the predicaments of women.

Grossman, Pamela L. *The Making of a Teacher: Teacher Knowledge and Teacher Education.* Tchrs. Coll. 1990 $38.95. ISBN 0-8077-3048-3. Examines how teacher preparation can be improved, based on research on teaching and teacher education.

Gutek, Gerald L. *American Education in a Global Society: Internationalizing Teacher Education.* Longman 1992 $17.56. ISBN 0-8013-0530-6. An introduction to the field of international and comparative education, with detailed descriptions of six national systems: United Kingdom, Russia and the Commonwealth of Independent States, Mexico, Japan, China, and Nigeria.

Gutmann, Amy. *Democratic Education.* Princeton U. Pr. 1987 $12.95. ISBN 0-691-07736-3. Tightly reasoned philosophical defense of the liberal tradition in education; examines the historical background for many of the issues facing schools, such as equality of opportunity, professionalism, parental choice, creationism, and the purposes of education at the various levels.

Hallahan, Daniel P., and James M. Kauffman. *Exceptional Children: Introduction to Special Education.* P-H 1990. ISBN 0-13-293333-0. Provides teachers with an excellent understanding of children with special needs.

Hawkridge, David G. *New Information Technology in Education.* Johns Hopkins 1983 o.p. Interesting and informative reading that surveys the new information technologies, how they are being used for learning (preschool through adult education), the social, economic, and educational problems that arise with their use, and forecasts for the future.

Hoffman, Nancy, ed. *Woman's "True" Profession: Voices from the History of Teaching.* Feminist Pr. 1981 $9.95. ISBN 0-912670-72-X. Excerpts from autobiographies, letters, diaries, oral histories, and other primary sources provide insights into the experiences and personal lives of classroom teachers between 1830 and 1920.

Hofstadter, Richard, and Wilson Smith. *American Higher Education: A Documentary History.* 2 vols. U. Ch. Pr. 1961 $35.00. ISBN 0-226-34814-8

Holland, Dorothy C., and Margaret A. Eisenhart. *Educated in Romance: Women, Achievement, and College Culture.* U. Ch. Pr. 1990 $19.95. ISBN 0-226-34943-8. Anthropological study of college women documents social and other pressures that lead them toward being "educated for romance," rather than toward academic or other goals; also looks at the interplay of race and gender.

Houle, Cyril O. *Patterns of Learning: New Perspectives on Life Span Education. Higher Education Ser.* Jossey-Bass 1984 $39.95. ISBN 0-87589-597-2. Successfully highlights an eclectic group of individuals (sixteenth-century Frenchman Michel de Montaigne, Henry David Thoreau, Billy Graham, to name a few) and educational methods (for example, travel and oratory) to show the complex nature of education as a lifelong activity.

Hunter, Madeline. *Mastery Teaching*. Tip Pubns. 1982 $10.95. ISBN 0-935567-09-7. This small volume—along with accompanying videotapes and personal presentations of Professor Hunter—has had a powerful effect on classroom teaching behavior. Hunter's techniques are both praised and condemned by educational professionals, but there is no denying the impact of her ideas on thousands of classrooms.

Jackson, Philip W. *Life in Classrooms*. Tchrs. Coll. 1990 repr. of 1968 ed. $15.95. ISBN 0-8077-3034-3. Offers keen insights into students and teachers and what actually occurs in the classroom; one of the most influential books in the field of educational research.

Joyce, Bruce, and Marsha Weil. *Models of Teaching*. P-H 1992 $49.95. ISBN 0-205-15578-3. Classic and best text on the wide array of options for classroom instruction; describes how the various models can be implemented in the classroom at all age levels.

Kliebard, Herbert. *Forging the American Curriculum*. Routledge 1991 $47.50. ISBN 0-415-90468-4. Collection of essays by America's best-known curriculum theorist and historian puts current debates into perspective.

———. *The Struggle for the American Curriculum: 1893–1958*. Routledge 1987 $13.95. ISBN 0-7102-1363-8. The best history of the curriculum debates that occurred in the earlier decades of this century.

Knowles, Malcolm M. *Self-Directed Learning: A Guide for Learners and Teachers*. Cambridge Bk. 1988. ISBN 0-8428-2215-1. A classic work that establishes a rationale for self-directed learning experiences and then provides a framework for implementing the ideas.

Liston, Daniel P., and Kenneth M. Zeichner. *Teacher Education and the Social Conditions of Schooling*. Routledge 1991 $39.95. ISBN 0-415-90071-9. One of the more perceptive works on the current status and future possibilities of the process of training teachers.

McKay, Sandra Lee, and Sau-ling Cynthia Wong. *Language Diversity*. Heinle & Heinle 1988 $22.95. ISBN 0-8384-2706-5. Based on the premise that linguistic diversity is a "valuable national resource," this work deals with a wide range of issues facing ESL professionals who work with linguistic minorities in the United States.

Madaus, George F., Peter W. Airasian, and Thomas Kellaghan. *School Effectiveness: A Reassessment of the Evidence*. McGraw 1980 o.p. Discusses the concepts and issues that emerged following the 1960s' federally based educational reform efforts.

The Mathematical Association Staff (UK). *Math Talk*. Heinemann Ed. 1987 $12.50. ISBN 0-435-08307-4. British attempt to deal with the crisis in mathematics achievement.

Meier, Kenneth J., and Joseph Stewart, Jr. *The Politics of Hispanic Education*. State U. NY Pr. 1991 $59.50. ISBN 0-7914-0507-9. Focuses on educational discrimination against America's fastest growing minority.

Morris, Richard J., and Burton Blatt. *Special Education: Research and Trends*. Pergamon 1986 o.p. Essays on a wide range of issues, including assessment, early intervention, behavior modification, learning disabilities, behavior disorders, language research, and sensory impairments.

Morris, Robert C. *Reading, Writing and Reconstruction: The Education of Freedmen in the South, 1861–1870*. U. Ch. Pr. 1981 $28.00. ISBN 0-226-53978-8. A comprehensive history of the contributions of religious and secular organizations and the government toward schooling of the freedmen.

Nachtigal, Paul M., ed. *Rural Education: In Search of a Better Way. Educational Ser.* Westview 1982 o.p. "The editor . . . led a team of observers in on-site visits of 13 different [rural education] programs. . . . The results are reported by the observers in a case-study format written in a free-flowing journalistic [style] . . . [that is] easy to read" (*Choice*).

Nodelman, Perry. *The Pleasures of Children's Literature*. Longman 1992 $19.95. ISBN 0-8013-0219-6. Excellent text on helping teachers gain a solid understanding of the field of children's literature.

Ogbu, John U. *Minority Education and Caste: The American System in Cross-Cultural Perspective*. Acad. Pr. 1978 o.p. The author, an anthropologist born in Nigeria, argues that lower school performance of African Americans is tied to the myths and stereotypes perpetuated by the U.S. system of racial stratification.

Ornstein, Allan C., and Daniel U. Levine. *Foundations of Education.* HM 1993 o.p. Covers in detail and depth a wide range of social, political, historical, economic, and professional issues facing schools in the 1990s.

Orr, Eleanor Wilson. *Twice as Less: Black English and the Performance of Black Students in Mathematics and Science.* Norton 1989 $15.95. ISBN 0-393-02392-3. Attempts to summarize the issues surrounding the use of Black English and its effects on the performance of students in science and mathematics. Although its findings and positions are not universally accepted, the book has raised important issues in the educational community.

Ortiz, Flora I. *Career Patterns in Education: Women, Men and Minorities in Public School Administration.* Greenwood 1982 $29.95. ISBN 0-03-059223-2. Using the public school as a framework, this study explores the interaction of organizations and the individuals in them.

Parsons, Talcott, and Gerald Platt. *The American University.* HUP 1973 $30.50. ISBN 0-674-02970-8. "Not only is its senior author America's most influential sociologist, but the volume provides one of the very few efforts to place the university in its societal context" *(Choice).*

Passmore, John. *The Philosophy of Teaching.* HUP 1980 o.p. "There is nothing he discusses which he does not illuminate" (Kenneth Minogue, *Times Literary Supplement).*

Perkinson, Henry J. *Since Socrates: Studies in the History of Western Educational Thought.* Longman 1980 o.p. A historical survey of significant trends in educational philosophy and thought.

Pusey, Nathan M. *American Higher Education, 1945–1970: A Personal Report.* HUP 1978 $17.00. ISBN 0-674-02425-7. A former president of Harvard University presents a readable account of the quantitative and qualitative changes in higher education from the postwar boom to the 1970s reevaluation.

Reutter, Edmund E., Jr. *The Supreme Court's Impact on Public Education.* Phi Delta Kappa 1982 $9.00. ISBN 0-87367-784-6. "Up to date and comprehensive, the book summarizes the decisions of the Supreme Court that directly affect or have had substantial effect on public education policies and procedures. . . . Reutter's writing [is to be admired] for its precision and its freedom from legal and educational argot" (Robert E. Phay, *Phi Delta Kappan).*

Rice, F. Philip. *The Adolescent: Development, Relationships and Culture.* Allyn 1992. ISBN 0-205-14125-0. A comprehensive, research-based, but highly readable text on all aspects of adolescent development.

Sanders, Jo, and Mary McGinnis. *Computer Equity in Math and Science.* Scarecrow 1991 $19.95. ISBN 0-8108-2368-3. For mathematics and science educators.

Santrock, John W., and Steven R. Yussen. *Child Development: An Introduction.* Brown & Benchmark 1989. ISBN 0-697-11057-5. An excellent text for teachers of preschool, primary, and intermediate children.

Shapiro, H. Svi, and David E. Purpel, eds. *Critical Social Issues in American Education: Toward the 21st Century.* Longman 1992 $25.56. ISBN 0-8013-0950-6. Examines capitalism, social justice, inequality, and other issues facing schools today.

Shore, Kenneth. *The Special Education Handbook: A Comprehensive Guide for Parents and Educators.* Warner Bks. 1988 $9.95. ISBN 0-446-38664-2. Good introduction for both laypeople and educational professionals on such important issues as evaluation, individualized education programs, and the partnership of schools and parents in the education of special children. Contains an excellent glossary, checklists, and other practical information.

Slavin, Robert E. *Educational Psychology: Theory into Practice.* P-H 1990. ISBN 0-13-237751-9. Highly accessible text, scholarly yet filled with practical information for teachers and parents.

Spanos, William. *The End of Education: Toward Posthumanism*. U. of Minn. Pr. 1992
$24.95. ISBN 0-8166-1955-7. Examines events and intellectual ideas of the twentieth
century and offers a new perspective.

Spring, Joel. *The American School: 1642–1985*. Longman 1986 $21.95. ISBN 0-582-
28571-2. Rather than being a dry recounting of facts, this book takes a social-
historical perspective in dealing with such topics as the role of religion in schools,
the role of women in schools and society, debates over educational equality, and the
nature of power relationships as they have affected schooling throughout American
history.

Strike, Kenneth A., and Kieran Egan, eds. *Ethics and Educational Policy. International
Lib. of the Philosophy of Education*. Routledge 1978 o.p. This collection of well-
written, insightful essays addresses the aims of education from elementary school to
higher education.

Strike, Kenneth A., and Jonas F. Soltis. *The Ethics of Teaching*. Tchrs. Coll. 1992 $11.95.
ISBN 0-8077-3141-2. Scholarly yet understandable philosophical text for teachers,
concentrating on the wide range of ethical issues facing the profession today.

Taylor, John F. A. *The Public Commission of the University: The Role of the Community of
Scholars in an Industrial, Urban, and Corporate Society*. NYU Pr. 1981 o.p. "A
provocative study . . . Taylor's well-penned volume represents a timely and valuable
contribution to the literature regarding the commission of American universities"
(*Educational Studies*).

Tiedt, Pamela, and Iris M. Tiedt. *Multicultural Teaching: A Handbook of Activities,
Information, and Resources*. Allyn 1989 $33.00. ISBN 0-205-12214-0. Practical guide
for infusing multicultural content into the curriculum in all subjects and at all grade
levels.

Tukagi, Dana Y. *The Retreat from Race: Asian Admissions and Racial Politics*. Rutgers U.
Pr. 1993 $35.00. ISBN 0-8135-1913-6. Top university admissions and issues of race.
University policy and politics of admissions are examined.

Tyack, David B. *The One Best System: A History of American Urban Education*. HUP 1974
$27.50. ISBN 0-674-63780-1. Excellent analysis by a new revisionist historian of
education; concentrates on the decision-making processes and organization of urban
public schools during the 1960s and early 1970s.

Van Scotter, Richard D., John D. Haas, Richard J. Kraft, and James D. Schott. *Social
Foundations of Education*. P-H 1990. ISBN 0-13-816992-6. Introduces students of
education to the wide range of educational foundations, in addition to confronting
issues of race, gender, international education, and educational futures.

Vierra, Andrea, and Judith Pollack. *Reading Educational Research*. Gorsuch Scarisbrick
1988 $28.00. ISBN 0-89787-522-0. Scholarly text that provides the professional
educator with a basic understanding of educational research.

CHRONOLOGY OF AUTHORS

Mann, Horace. 1796–1859
Barnard, Henry. 1811–1900
Washington, Booker T(aliaferro).
   1856–1915
Dewey, John. 1859–1952
Montessori, Maria. 1870–1952
Kilpatrick, William Heard. 1871–1965

Thorndike, Edward L(ee). 1874–1949
Piaget, Jean. 1896–1980
Hutchins, Robert M(aynard).
   1899–1977
Goodlad, John I. 1920–
Freire, Paulo. 1921–
Sizer, Theodore. 1932–

BARNARD, HENRY. 1811–1900

Born in Hartford, Connecticut, Henry Barnard was educated at Yale
University. Barnard supported legislation to provide for better schools in

Connecticut and, in doing so, copied HORACE MANN's earlier reforms in Massachusetts. He later instituted educational reforms in Rhode Island as well, and he started several school libraries there.

After various academic appointments, including one as president of St. John's College in Annapolis, Maryland, Barnard became the first U.S. commissioner of education (1867–70). In this position, he was influential in shaping the future direction of the U.S. Office of Education. He initiated numerous reforms and promoted the importance of education (not just schools) through federally sponsored experimentation, research, and scholarship and the collection and dissemination of educational statistics and information.

Barnard's emphasis on a need to create common school districts throughout the United States was based on his strong belief in public education and the notion that schools should foster moral education and temper social unrest. In addition to his books, which cover a wide range of educational issues and concerns, Barnard was the founder and editor of a widely read journal, *The American Journal of Education* (1855–82).

BOOKS BY BARNARD

Henry Barnard on Education. Ed. by John S. Brubacher. Russell Sage 1965 repr. of 1931 ed. o.p.

Reformatory Education: Papers on Preventive, Correctional and Reformatory Institutions and Agencies in Different Countries. Folcroft 1978 o.p.

BOOKS ABOUT BARNARD

Downs, Robert B. *Henry Barnard. World Leaders Ser.* G. K. Hall 1977 o.p.

Lannie, Vincent P. *Henry Barnard: American Educator.* Tchrs. Coll. 1974 o.p. A brief biography of educator Henry Barnard; includes his correspondence with Horace Mann and various reports.

MacMullen, Edith N. *In the Cause of True Education: Henry Barnard and Nineteenth-Century School Reform.* Yale U. Pr. 1991 $37.50. ISBN 0-300-04809-2. The first full-scale critical biography.

Neuman, A. R. *Dr. Barnard as I Knew Him. Educational Ser.* Norwood repr. of 1914 ed. o.p.

Thursfield, Richard E. *Henry Barnard's American Journal of Education.* AMS Pr. repr. of 1945 ed. $28.50. ISBN 0-404-61303-9. Investigates the tremendous contributions of Henry Barnard's *American Journal of Education* in the development of American education.

DEWEY, JOHN. 1859–1952

John Dewey, a native of Vermont, was educated at the University of Vermont and Johns Hopkins University. He is known as the foremost authority on progressive education in the United States. In 1899 he published his revolutionary *School and Society*, which set forth his view of education as a process whereby people learn to solve problems more effectively. "Progressive" schools, embodying his concept of learning while experiencing—that is, becoming involved in the process of knowledge, as opposed to mere book learning and rote reproduction of the words of the teacher—burgeoned in this country in the 1920s. Taking field trips, making model cities and villages, using dramatization, and freer classrooms with movable furniture are just a few of the elements by which Dewey's view of education as personal inquiry is still pursued in education today.

Logic: The Theory of Inquiry (1938), published when he was nearly 80, is Dewey's major philosophical work. He made his field the whole of human experience, including politics and psychology, following eagerly wherever the spirit of inquiry might lead him. Dewey accepted American democracy completely and believed that democracy is a primary ethical value.

Dewey taught at the Universities of Michigan and Minnesota before moving to the University of Chicago in 1894. While at Chicago, he initiated reform movements in educational theory and methods, testing many of them in the university's high school. In 1904 Dewey became professor of philosophy at Columbia University, where he remained until his retirement in 1930.

Dewey also was active in a number of other areas. He was a founder of the New School for Social Research (New York City) and helped organize New York City's first teachers' union. He was also a charter member of the American Civil Liberties Union.

Books by Dewey

The Child and the Curriculum (and *The School and Society*). U. Ch. Pr. 1956 $12.00. ISBN 0-226-14394-5

A Common Faith. Yale U. Pr. 1934 $6.95. ISBN 0-300-00069-3. Considers the role of religion in society and the relationship between religion and the supernatural.

Democracy and Education: An Introduction to the Philosophy of Education. Free Pr. 1966 $13.95. ISBN 0-02-907370-7. Attempts to detect and state the ideas implied in a democratic society and to show how these ideas can be applied to problems in education.

The Early Works of John Dewey, 1882–1898. Ed. by Jo Ann Boydston. 5 vols. S. Ill. U. Pr. Vol. 1 *Collected Essays and Leibniz's New Essays Concerning the Human Understanding.* 1969 $22.50. ISBN 0-8093-0349-3. Vol. 2 *Psychology.* 1967 $22.50. ISBN 0-8093-0282-9. Vol. 3 *Collected Essays and Outline of a Critical Theory of Ethics.* 1969 $22.50. ISBN 0-8093-0402-3. Vol. 4 *Collected Essays and the Study of Ethics.* 1971 $22.50. ISBN 0-8093-0496-1. Vol. 5 *Collected Essays.* 1972 $22.50. ISBN 0-8093-0540-2. A chronological presentation of the published works of John Dewey, written from 1882 to 1898, during his formative period.

Education Today. Ed. by Joseph Ratner. Greenwood repr. of 1940 ed. $65.00. ISBN 0-8371-2550-2. The classic work of Dewey's philosophy of education; explores his conception of learning as a social procress.

Experience and Education. Peter Smith 1983 $17.50. ISBN 0-8446-5961-4. Dewey's most concise statements of his ideas about the needs, the problems, and possibilities of education.

Experience and Nature. Open Court 1971 $7.50. ISBN 0-87548-097-7. A controversial philosophical work that considers the relationship between nature and the human condition.

How We Think: A Restatement of the Relation of Reflective Thinking to the Educative Process. Prometheus Bks. 1991 $10.95. ISBN 0-87975-701-9

Human Nature and Conduct. S. Ill. U. Pr. 1988 $14.95. ISBN 0-8093-1437-1

The Later Works of John Dewey, 1925–1953. 12 vols. Ed. by Jo Ann Boydston and others. S. Ill. U. Pr. Vol. 1 *1925.* 1981 $25.00. ISBN 0-8093-0986-6. Vol. 2 *1925–1927.* 1984 $32.50. ISBN 0-8093-1131-3. Vols. 3–4 o.p. Vol. 5 *1929–1930.* 1984 $35.00. ISBN 0-8093-1162-3. Vol. 6 *1931–1932.* 1985 $37.50. ISBN 0-8093-1199-2. Vol. 7 *1932.* 1985 $37.50. ISBN 0-8093-1200-X. Vol. 8 o.p. Vol. 9 *1933–1934.* 1986 $30.00. ISBN 0-8093-1265-4. Vol. 10 *Art as Experience.* 1987 $32.50. ISBN 0-8093-1266-2. Vol. 11 *Essays and Liberalism and Social Action.* 1987 $40.00. ISBN 0-8093-1267-0. Vol. 12 *Logic: The Theory of Inquiry.* 1986 $45.00. ISBN 0-8093-1268-9. A multivolume collection of the written works of John Dewey; covers the years from approximately 1925 to 1953.

Logic: The Theory of Inquiry. Irvington 1982 repr. of 1938 ed. $49.50. ISBN 0-89197-831-3

The Middle Works of John Dewey, 1899–1924. 15 vols. Ed. by Jo Ann Boydston. S. Ill. U. Pr. 1976–1983. Vol. 1 *Collected Articles and "The School and Society" and "The Educational Situation."* 1976 $22.50. ISBN 0-8093-0753-7. Vol. 2 *Essays on Logical*

Theory, 1902–1903. 1976 $22.50. ISBN 0-8093-0754-5. Vol. 3 *Essays on the New Empiricism, 1903–1906.* 1977 $22.50. ISBN 0-8093-0775-8. Vol. 4 *Essays on Pragmatism and Truth, 1907–1909.* 1977 $22.50. ISBN 0-8093-0776-6. Vol. 5 *Essays on Ethics, 1908.* 1978 $30.00. ISBN 0-8093-1139-9. Vol. 6 *1910–1911.* 1979 $30.00. ISBN 0-8093-0835-5. Vol. 7 *1912–1914.* 1979 $22.50. ISBN 0-8093-0881-9. Vol. 8 *1915.* 1979 $27.50. ISBN 0-8093-0882-7. Vol. 9 *1916.* 1980 $25.00. ISBN 0-8093-0933-5. Vol. 10 *1916–1917.* 1980 $27.50. ISBN 0-8093-0934-3. Vol. 11 *1918–1919.* 1982 $27.50. ISBN 0-8093-1003-1. Vol. 12 *1920.* 1982 $25.00. ISBN 0-8093-1004-X. Vol. 13 *1921–1922.* 1983 $32.50. ISBN 0-8093-1083-X. Vol. 14 *1922.* 1983 $25.00. ISBN 0-8093-1084-8. Vol. 15 *1923–1924.* 1983 $27.50. ISBN 0-8093-1085-6. Includes Dewey's publications from 1899 to 1924; his works in both logic and social philosophy are discussed more fully than works from his early years.

Moral Principles in Education. S. Ill. U. Pr. 1975 repr. of 1909 ed. $9.95. ISBN 0-8093-0715-4. Examines the place and the role of ethical and moral principles in educational training.

The School and Society. S. Ill. U. Pr. 1980 $9.95. ISBN 0-8093-0967-X. Introduction by Joe R. Burnett.

BOOKS ABOUT DEWEY

Bernstein, Richard J. *John Dewey.* Ridgeview 1981 repr. of 1966 ed. $30.00. ISBN 0-917930-35-5. A sympathetic and comprehensive statement of Dewey's intellectual vision; enables the reader to evaluate his contribution to philosophic inquiry and American thought.

Geiger, George R. *John Dewey in Perspective.* Greenwood 1974 repr. of 1958 ed. $35.00. ISBN 0-8371-7094-X

Gouinlock, James. *John Dewey's Philosophy of Value.* Humanities 1972 o.p.

Hickman, Larry A. *John Dewey's Pragmatic Technology.* Ind. U. Pr. 1992 $29.95. ISBN 0-253-32747-4. Comprehensive canvass of Dewey's intellectual processes.

Hook, Sidney. *John Dewey: An Intellectual Portrait.* Greenwood repr. of 1939 ed. $19.75. ISBN 0-8371-3951-1

Nathanson, Jerome. *John Dewey: The Reconstruction of the Democratic Life.* Continuum 1967 $45.00. ISBN 0-8371-3951-1

Paringer, William A. *John Dewey and the Paradox of Liberal Reform.* State U. NY Pr. 1990 $57.50. ISBN 0-7914-0253-3. Critique of Dewey from the perspective of critical theory.

Roth, Robert J. *John Dewey and Self-Realization.* Greenwood 1978 repr. of 1963 ed. o.p.

Westbrook, Robert B. *John Dewey and American Democracy.* Cornell Univ. Pr. 1991 $29.95. ISBN 0-8014-2560-3. Thorough and instructive treatment.

Williams, Robert B. *John Dewey: Recollections.* U. Pr. of Amer. 1982 o.p. A collection of personal reminiscences about Dewey.

Zeltner, Philip M. *John Dewey's Aesthetic Philosophy.* Humanities 1975 o.p.

FREIRE, PAULO. 1921–

Paulo Freire is one of the most widely read educational philosophers and practitioners in the world today, except in the United States, where he remains relatively unknown to many in the educational community as well as the general public. Freire received international acclaim and notoriety with his first and best-known work, *Pedagogy of the Oppressed,* first published in English in 1970. His teachings draw much of their inspiration from a Marxist critique of society; for this reason he was forced into exile from his native Brazil in 1964, and his works were banned in many developing nations. His pedagogy for adult literacy has been implemented successfully in several African nations and has been the basis for literacy crusades in Nicaragua and other Latin American countries. His philosophical approach to education forms the basis for much of the critical theory work in education now taking place in the United States, Europe, and developing nations.

BOOKS BY FREIRE

Education for Critical Consciousness. Continuum 1973 $9.95. ISBN 0-8264-0007-8. Two of the author's essays carrying the central message that one can know only to the extent that one "problematizes" the natural, cultural, and historical reality in which he or she is placed.

Learning to Question: A Pedagogy of Liberation. (coauthored with Antonio Faundez). Continuum 1989 $16.95. ISBN 0-8264-0509-6. A "spoken book," taking the author's experiences in Africa and Latin America and applying them to specific themes and/or concepts.

Literacy: Reading the Word and the World. (coauthored with Donaldo Macedo). Greenwood 1987 $45.00. ISBN 0-89789-125-2

A Pedagogy for Liberation: Dialogues on Transforming Education. (coauthored with Ira Shor). Greenwood 1986 $42.95. ISBN 0-89789-104-X. A long discussion on the questions that teachers ask most about education. Covers an agenda of real issues raised by teachers.

Pedagogy of the Oppressed. Continuum 1993 $10.95. ISBN 0-8264-0611-4. Radical theory of education that evolved from the author's work with illiterate adults in developing nations.

The Politics of Education: Culture, Power, and Liberation. Greenwood 1984 $42.95. ISBN 0-89789-042-6. Collected writings compiled to stimulate more discussion of current major issues in education. Provides a solid basis for a comprehensive and critical theory of pedagogical struggle.

BOOKS ABOUT FREIRE

McLaren, Peter, and Peter Leonard, eds. *Paulo Freire: A Critical Encounter.* Routledge 1993 $49.95. ISBN 0-415-03859-2

Schipani, Daniel S. *Conscientization and Creativity: Paulo Freire and Christian Education.* U. Pr. of Amer. 1984 $49.50. ISBN 0-8191-3881-9. Explores why the "Freire method" has been so successful and how his contribution can inform Christian educations. An interdisciplinary study written primarily for people interested in Christian education.

GOODLAD, JOHN I. 1920–

John Goodlad was born in British Columbia, Canada, and educated at the University of British Columbia and the University of Chicago. A former dean of the graduate school of education at the University of California at Los Angeles, he is currently a professor of education at the University of Washington. Goodlad has written more than 20 books and hundreds of articles on education. Among his best-known works are *The Ecology of School Renewal* (1987) and *A Place Called School: Prospects for the Future* (1984). A major figure in the educational reform movements that began in the 1980s, he has been a leading figure in the field of teacher education for the past 30 years. In addition to his teaching and writing, Goodlad directs the state Partnerships for Educational Renewal throughout the United States, and he also is active in many educational organizations and educational task forces.

BOOKS BY GOODLAD

The Development of a Conceptual System for Dealing with Problems of Curriculum and Instruction. U. CA Pr. 1966 o.p.

The Dynamics of Educational Change. McGraw 1975 o.p. An excellent work focusing on the process and dynamics of educational change and improvement. Based on the premise that schools, under certain conditions. can become much more vital than they currently are.

The Ecology of School Renewal. U. Ch. Pr. 1987 $23.00. ISBN 0-226-60144-7

The Nongraded Elementary School. 1959. Tchrs. Coll. repr. of 1959 ed. $18.95. ISBN 0-8077-2845-4. Classic text relating critical ideas for today's school reform movement; considers the practice and effectiveness of nongradedness, individualized instruction, and the "open classroom."

A Place Called School: Prospects for the Future. 1984. McGraw 1984 $15.95. ISBN 0-07-23627-5

Teachers for Our Nation's Schools. 1990. Jossey-Bass 1990 $26.95. ISBN 0-55542-270-5

HUTCHINS, ROBERT M(AYNARD). 1899–1977

Robert Hutchins wrote widely about education and is best known for his support of liberal education, which he believed "prepares the young for anything that may happen; it has value under any circumstances. . . . It gets them ready for a lifetime of learning. It connects man with man. It introduces all men to the dialogue about the common good of their own country and of the world community. It frees their mind of prejudice. It lays the basis of practical wisdom." He believed that the increasing complexities of civilization did not justify any modification in this approach. "The more technological the society," he says in *The Learning Society* (1968), "the less *ad hoc* education can be. The reason is that the more technological the society is, the more rapidly it will change and the less valuable *ad hoc* education will become. It now seems safe to say that the best practical education is the best theoretical one."

After serving as dean of Yale Law School in 1929, Hutchins became (at age 29) president and in 1949 chancellor of the University of Chicago, remaining there until 1951. During this period, he and MORTIMER ADLER (see Vol. 4) introduced the Great Books program into the Chicago curriculum. They believed that the best education is achieved through reading and understanding the great minds of the past. Later he became associate director of the Ford Foundation and president of the Fund for the Republic. In the latter post, Hutchins faced the oppressive climate for free expression brought about by McCarthyism, but he saw to it that the fund's projects included studies of the federal loyalty-security program, of political blacklisting in the entertainment industries, and of the nature of communism in the United States. He retired as the chief executive officer of the Center for the Study of Democratic Institutions in Santa Barbara, California, a "community of scholars" under the aegis of the Ford Foundation.

BOOKS BY HUTCHINS

The Conflict in Education in a Democratic Society. Greenwood 1972 repr. of 1953 ed. $38.50. ISBN 0-8371-5693-9. Proposes that the chaos now found in the philosophy of education is a result of the turmoil in philosophy in general.

The Higher Learning in America. Greenwood 1979 repr. of 1962 ed. $35.00. ISBN 0-313-20713-5. A consideration of the external conditions under which American education operates, the particular difficulties faced by universities, what general education is, and what a university might be.

No Friendly Voice. Greenwood 1962 repr. of 1936 ed. $62.50. ISBN 0-8571-0490-4

Saint Thomas and the World State. Marquette 1949 $7.95. ISBN 0-87462-114-3

The University of Utopia. U. Ch. Pr. 1964 o.p. A frank discussion of the hazards to education in the United States; proposes methods to overcome those dangers and a standard by which to measure aims and accomplishments.

BOOKS ABOUT HUTCHINS

Ashmore, Harry S. *Unseasonable Truths: The Life of Robert Maynard Hutchins.* Little 1989
    $27.50. ISBN 0-316-05396-1. Written by a Pulitzer Prize-winning journalist.
Cohen, Arthur A., ed. *Humanistic Education and Western Civilization: Essays for Robert
    M. Hutchins. Essay Index Repr. Ser.* Ayer repr. of 1964 ed. $15.00. ISBN 0-8369-
    8150-2. A collection of essays, prepared in honor of Robert Hutchins's sixty-fifth
    birthday, examines the role of education in the world.
Dzuback, Mary A. *Robert M. Hutchins: Portrait of an Educator.* U. Ch. Pr. 1991 $24.95.
    ISBN 0-226-17710-6. Documents Hutchins's university careers at both Yale and the
    University of Chicago.
Mayer, Milton. *Robert Maynard Hutchins: A Memoir.* U. CA Pr. 1993. ISBN 0-520-07091-7.
    Edited from 900 pages of a working draft left by Mayer.

KILPATRICK, WILLIAM HEARD. 1871–1965

William Heard Kilpatrick's friendship with JOHN DEWEY strongly influenced
his work as a teacher-educator, particularly his numerous books on educational
philosophy. Kilpatrick promoted the principles of progressive education when
discussing the need for curriculum reform in U.S. schools. As an alternative to
the teaching of traditional subjects—which he saw as disjointed—he originated
the project method of education.

Kilpatrick earned A.B. and A.M. degrees from Mercer University, where he
taught mathematics and served as the university's acting president from 1903 to
1938. He completed his doctorate at Columbia University. From 1909 to 1938,
Kilpatrick taught at Teachers College. He also helped found Bennington College
in Vermont.

BOOKS BY KILPATRICK

Dutch Schools of New Netherland and Colonial New York. Ayer 1969 repr. of 1912 ed.
    $16.00. ISBN 0-405-01431-7. A collection of older works focusing on the author's
    research of seventeenth- and early eighteenth-century Dutch schools in the Nether-
    lands, New Netherlands, and New York.
Education for a Changing Civilization. Ayer 1972 repr. of 1926 ed. $10.00. ISBN 0-405-
    03709-0. Three education lectures delivered to the Luther Laflin Kellogg Foundation
    at Rutgers University in 1926.
Foundations of Method: Informed Talks on Teaching. Ayer 1972 repr. of 1925 ed. $19.00.
    ISBN 0-405-03710-4
Intercultural Attitudes in the Making: Parents, Youth Leaders and Teachers at Work.
    (coauthored with William Van Til). Ayer repr. of 1947 ed. $19.00. ISBN 0-8369-
    2776-1. Aims to give better insight into the processes by which the attitudes of
    children and adolescents are actually shaped. Designed primarily for teachers and
    school officials.
Montessori System Examined. Ayer 1971 repr. of 1914 ed. $8.00. ISBN 0-405-03609-4

BOOK ABOUT KILPATRICK

Bertrand Russell, A. S. Neill, Homer Lane, W. H. Kilpatrick: Four Progressive Educators.
    Macmillan 1968 o.p.

MANN, HORACE. 1796–1859

Born in Franklin, Massachusetts, and educated at Brown University, Horace
Mann is considered the founder of U.S. public education because of his
pioneering educational leadership. Although trained as a lawyer, he became
interested in education while he was a member of the Massachusetts legislature.
As a legislator, he promoted the lyceum movement, which resulted in a series of
key legislative acts that often are considered the basis for the public educational

system. When the Massachusetts Board of Education was established in 1837, Mann was appointed its secretary. Under his leadership the state mandated a minimum school year, raised teachers' salaries, and allocated state funds to improve school buildings and equipment. The spread of public schools led to a need for teachers, and, in response, Mann founded the first state normal schools in the United States.

From 1848 to 1853, Mann served in the U.S. House of Representatives. In 1852 he became the first president of Antioch College, a position he held until 1859. While at Antioch, he demonstrated the advantages of coeducation and did much to raise the standards of the college. Mann's ground-breaking work influenced education at various levels throughout the United States.

BOOKS BY MANN

Lectures on Education. Ayer 1969 repr. of 1855 ed. $17.00. ISBN 0-405-01437-6

Letters of Horace Walpole, Earl of Oxford, to Sir Horace Mann. 2 vols. Arden Lib. 1979 repr. of 1843 ed. o.p.

Slavery: Letters and Speeches. Black Heritage Lib. Collection Ser. Ayer 1969 repr. of 1851 ed. $24.50. ISBN 0-405-00643-8.

BOOKS ABOUT MANN

Hinsdale, Burke A. *Horace Mann and the Common School Revival in the United States.* Somerset Pub. repr. of 1898 ed. $39.00. ISBN 0-403-08928-X. A lengthy commentary on the role that Horace Mann played in the development of public schools in America.

Melby, Ernest O. *The Education of Free Man.* Greenwood 1977 $35.00. ISBN 0-8371-9501-7

Morgan, Joy E. *Horace Mann: His Ideas and Ideals. Educational Ser.* Norwood repr. of 1936 ed. o.p. A brief introduction to both the life and writings of Horace Mann; for all who are interested in learning the significance of universal free public education.

Sawyer, Ken K. *Horace Mann.* Chelsea Hse. 1993 $17.95. ISBN 0-7910-1741-9. Examines Mann's life and work.

MONTESSORI, MARIA. 1870–1952

Maria Montessori, an Italian educator who was the first woman doctor granted a degree in Italy, has been well known in the field of childhood education since the early 1900s. Dissatisfied with the educational methods of her time, she developed her own theories in systematic fashion. The Montessori Method, as it became known, allows each child to develop at his or her own pace through the manipulation of materials. The teacher's role is to provide the materials and then act as a supervisor and a guide. This and other concepts of hers have had considerable influence on modern education.

Montessori first worked with retarded children, then classified as "untrainable," most of whom she succeeded in teaching to read and write. She established a number of Houses of Children in Italy devoted to providing new opportunities for underprivileged children. Recent U.S. efforts in this direction have led to a strong revival of interest in her work, and Montessori's methods also have been expanded to children beyond the preschool years.

BOOKS BY MONTESSORI

The Absorbent Mind. Dell 1969 $9.95. ISBN 0-440-55056-4. Illustrates the unique mental powers of the young child that enables the child to develop all of the characteristics of the human personality.

The Advanced Montessori Method. 2 vols. Schocken. Vol. 1 1989 o.p. Vol. 2 *Materials for Educating Elementary School Children.* 1989 $2.95. ISBN 0-8052-0927-1. Concerns the education of children aged 7–11.

The Child in the Family. Avon 1970 o.p. A study that considers the child as a personality separate from the adult; proposes a method of providing a nurturing environment for the developing child.

Collected Works. Gordon Pr. 1973 $500.00. ISBN 0-87968-894-7

The Discovery of the Child. Ballantine 1986 $5.95. ISBN 0-345-33656-9

Dr. Montessori's Own Handbook. 1914. Schocken 1988 $8.95. ISBN 0-8052-0921-2. Examines Montessori's insights and methods for rearing and working with children.

The Montessori Method: The Education of Children from Three to Six. Educational Ser. Schocken 1988 $4.00. ISBN 0-8052-0922-0

Pedagogical Anthropology. 3 vols. Fourd Class. Reprints 1984 $327.75. ISBN 0-8990-160-8

The Secret of Childhood: A Book for All Parents and Teachers. 1936. Trans. by Barbara B. Carter. N. Montessori 1983 repr. of 1978 ed. $14.95. ISBN 0-86131-375-5. Work highlighting the contribution that children can give to humanity.

BOOKS ABOUT MONTESSORI

Blessington, John P. *Let My Children Work.* Doubleday 1975 o.p. An interesting and conversational work dealing with change and formal education, relating the author's own frank observations and suggestions as an educator.

Kramer, Rita. *Maria Montessori: A Biography.* U. Ch. Pr. 1988 $14.38. ISBN 0-201-09227-1. The definitive biography of Montessori's life.

Lillard, Paula P. *Montessori: A Modern Approach.* Schocken 1988 $8.95. ISBN 0-8052-0920-4. An excellent introduction to Montessori's work and methods; aims to inspire readers to learn as much as they can about the educator's contributions and to improve upon them.

O'Connor, Barbara. *Mammolna: A Story about Maria Montessori.* Carolrhoda Bks. 1992 $10.95. ISBN 0-87614-743-0. Of special interest to those directly involved with Montessori schools.

Packard, Rosa C. *The Hidden Hinge.* R. C. Packard 1977 $10.00. ISBN 0-8190-0074-4

Pollard, Michael. *Maria Montessori.* Morehouse Pub. 1990 $7.95. ISBN 0-8192-1539-2

PIAGET, JEAN. 1896–1980

Jean Piaget's research into, and writings about, the developmental psychology of children have had a profound impact on education, particularly on early childhood and elementary educational programs and methods of instruction. Through extensive and systematic observations of children, he identified four distinct stages of intellectual development: sensorimotor, preoperation, concrete operational, and formal operational.

Piaget was a Swiss scientist, who published his first paper (dealing with albino sparrows) at age 10. He completed a doctorate in natural science at the University of Neuchâtel, Switzerland, in 1918. In addition to teaching at a number of Swiss and French universities, Piaget codirected the institute of J. J. Rousseau in Geneva (1933–80) and helped found the International Center on Genetic Epistemology in 1954. He also contributed to the fields of zoology, philosophy, religion, sociology, and mathematics.

BOOKS BY PIAGET

Adaptation and Intelligence: Organic Selection and Phenocopy. Trans. by Steward Eames. U. Ch. Pr. 1982 $11.00. ISBN 0-226-66777-4

Biology and Knowledge: An Essay on the Relations between Organic Regulations and Cognitive Processes. Trans. by Beatrix Walsh. U. Ch. Pr. 1971 o.p. Provides a specific program by which acquired adaptations can in some cases be hereditarily "fixed"; also presents Piaget's own biological experiments supporting his theory.

The Child and Reality: Problems of Genetic Psychology. Trans. by Arnold Rosin. Beekman Pubs. 1973 o.p.

The Child's Conception of Number. Based upon the hypothesis that the child's conception of number is closely related to the development of logic. Records experiments investigating classes, relations, and numbers as cognitive domains.

The Child's Conception of Physical Causality. Norton 1981 repr. of 1930 ed. $8.95. ISBN 0-393-00057-5

The Child's Conception of the World. Littlefield 1975 repr. of 1929 ed. $14.95. ISBN 0-8226-0213-X. An investigation into the conceptions of the world that a child forms at different stages of development. Closely examines the child's notion of reality.

Genetic Epistemology. Trans. by Eleanor Duckworth. Norton 1971 repr. of 1970 ed. $5.95. ISBN 0-393-00596-8. Discusses through analysis of children's thinking how we learn to perceive and to organize what we experience.

Judgment and Reasoning in the Child. Littlefield 1976 repr. of 1966 ed. $9.95. ISBN 0-8226-0205-9

Language and Thought of the Child. Humanities o.p. A study in child logic, specifically answering the question "What are the needs that a child tries to satisfy when he or she talks?"

The Origins of Intelligence in Children. Trans. by Margaret Cook. Intl. Univs. Pr. 1966 o.p. A groundbreaking study organizing the development of intelligence into six successive stages, beginning with the use of reflexes and arriving at deduction, invention, and language.

Play, Dreams and Imitation in Childhood. Peter Smith 1988 $19.50. ISBN 0-8446-6320-9. The third in a series devoted to the early years of a child's development. The gap between sensory-motor activity prior to representation and the operational forms of thought are bridged.

The Psychology of Intelligence. Littlefield 1976 repr. of 1966 ed. $9.95. ISBN 0-8226-0222-9. Outlines the author's view based on the formation of operations and its place among others that have been put forward.

BOOKS ABOUT PIAGET

Almy, Millie, and others. *Young Children's Thinking: Studies of Some Aspects of Piaget's Theory.* Bks. Demand repr. of 1966 ed. $42.00. ISBN 0-317-10467-5. A comprehensive study dealing with the intellectual development of children; depends heavily on the classic work of Piaget.

Bringuier, Jean-Claude. *Conversations with Jean Piaget.* Trans. by Basia M. Gulati. U. Ch. Pr. 1989 $11.95. ISBN 0-226-07505-2. Author's various talks with Piaget in 1969 and 1975.

Elkind, David. *Child Development and Education: A Piagetian Perspective.* OUP 1976 $18.95. ISBN 0-19-502069-3

Forman, George E., and David S. Kuschner. *The Child's Construction of Knowledge: Piaget for Teaching Children.* Natl. Assn. Child Ed. repr. of 1977 ed. $6.00. ISBN 0-912674-92-X. A personal work of the author's thoughts and experiences, highlighting the constructivism in Piaget's epistemology and providing a useful pedagogical tool for teachers of preschool children.

Furth, Hans G. *Knowledge As Desire: An Essay on Freud and Piaget.* Col. U. Pr. 1990 $14.50. ISBN 0-231-06459-4. Seeks to provide a "Freudian-Piagetian synthesis."

Furth, Hans G., and Harry Wachs. *Thinking Goes to School: Piaget's Theory in Practice with Additional Thoughts.* OUP 1974 $12.95. ISBN 0-19-501927-X. A series of activities and games providing a general foundation to help the child deal successfully with specific academic subjects. Written for those concerned with the successful development of children.

Modgil, Sohan, and Celia Modgil. *Jean Piaget: Consensus and Controversy.* Greenwood 1982 $55.00. ISBN 0-275-90862-3

SIZER, THEODORE. 1932–

American educator Theodore Sizer was born in New Haven, Connecticut, and was educated at Yale and Harvard universities. He has served as headmaster of Phillips Academy, dean of the Graduate School of Education at Harvard, and is currently professor of education and chairman of the Coalition of Essential Schools at Brown University. For over 25 years, Sizer has been one of the leading critics of American education in the United States, endorsing structural and curricular reform in order to improve the public schools. In addition to being the author of numerous books, he also has written for a number of journals, including *Saturday Review* and *Psychology Today*.

BOOKS BY SIZER

The Age of the Academies. 1964. Tchrs. Coll. 1964 o.p. A study of the uniqueness and significance of the academy movement irrespective of its effect on the development of public education.

Horace's Compromise: The Dilemma of the American High School. 1984. HM 1992 $9.70. ISBN 0-395-61158-X. An analysis of the problems facing schools; based on interviews and observations at 15 high schools across the country.

Horace's School: Redesigning the American High School. 1992. HM 1993 $9.95. ISBN 0-395-65973-6. Urges increased teacher involvement in curriculum development and efforts at educational reform.

Moral Education: Five Lectures. 1970. HUP 1970 $4.95. ISBN 0-674-58661-1. Coedited with Nancy F. Sizer and Joseph M. Gustafson.

Places for Learning, Places for Joy: Speculations on American Schooling. 1973. HUP 1973 $14.50. ISBN 0-674-66985-1. Presents the author's views on reform and change in the American educational system.

Religion and Public Education. 1967. HM 1967 o.p. A collection of papers by renowned authors with regard to the place of religion in public schools. Attempts to increase the reader's understanding of the relationship between religion and schooling.

Secondary Schools at the Turn of the Century. 1964. Greenwood 1976 repr. of 1964 ed. $45.00. ISBN 0-8371-8972-1. Examines the findings of *Report of the Committee on Secondary School Studies*, compiled at the turn of the century.

SKINNER, B(URRHUS) F(REDERIC). 1904–1990

[SEE Chapter 6 in this volume.]

THORNDIKE, EDWARD L(EE). 1874–1949

Educational psychologist and author of the intelligence test bearing his name, Edward L. Thorndike also is known for his work in educational statistics. He studied under WILLIAM JAMES (see also Vol. 4) at Harvard University and carried out experiments on animal intelligence with some chickens that he kept in the basement of James's house—his landlady having refused to let him keep them in his room. Thorndike's first papers were on "The Psychology of Fishes" and "The Mental Life of Monkeys" When he received his doctorate from Columbia University in 1898, the statistical treatment of test results in psychology was experimental. He became an instructor in genetic psychology at Teachers College in 1899. He believed that "everything that exists exists in quantity" and could be measured as a key to scientific progress in education. He devised scales for measuring excellence in reading, English composition, handwriting, and drawing, as well as intelligence tests for various grade levels. The former dean of Teachers College James E. Russell said of him: "His service to pedagogical procedure has revolutionized educational administration." Thorndike's "Law of Effect," which had its origin in his early tests on animals, was strengthened by his later experiments on human learning. He concluded that the important factors in learning are repetition and reward. His techniques of animal experimentation and his methods of psychological measurement were important advances in U.S. psychology before World War I, and he often is thought of as the founder of modern educational psychology.

BOOKS BY THORNDIKE

Education. Educational Ser. Norwood repr. of 1912 ed. o.p.
Educational Psychology. Ayer repr. of 1913 ed. $44.00. ISBN 0-405-01484-8
Fundamentals of Learning. AMS Pr. repr. of 1932 ed. $28.50. ISBN 0-404-06429-9
Human Learning. Johnson Repr. repr. of 1931 ed. $15.00. ISBN 0-384-60360-2. A series of lectures outlining fundamental facts and principles of human learning.
Man and His Works. Essay and General Lit. Index Repr. Ser. Assoc. Faculty Pr. 1969 repr. of 1943 ed. o.p.
Notes on Child Study. Classics in Child Development Ser. Ayer repr. of 1975 ed. o.p.
The Psychology of Wants, Interests and Attitudes. Psychology Ser. Johnson Repr. repr. of 1935 ed. o.p.
Selected Writings from a Connectionist's Psychology. Greenwood repr. of 1949 ed. $35.00. ISBN 0-8371-2570-7

BOOK ABOUT THORNDIKE

Joncich, Geraldine. *The Sane Positivist: A Biography of Edward L. Thorndike.* Wesleyan Univ. Pr. 1968 o.p. A lengthy intellectual, historical biography of Thorndike.

WASHINGTON, BOOKER T(ALIAFERRO). 1856–1915

Booker T. Washington was born into slavery in Virginia. (His mother was a mulatto slave on a plantation, and his father was a white man.) He overcame his slave heritage, however, and became a leading educator of African Americans. After graduating from, and teaching at, Hampton Normal and Industrial Institute, he was chosen to found the coeducational Tuskegee Normal and Industrial Institute in Alabama.

Between 1880 and 1915, Washington expanded Tuskegee from two buildings to more than 100 buildings, with a faculty of 200 and an enrollment exceeding 1,500 students. He held strong beliefs about the dignity of manual labor and the need for African Americans to work hard rather than fight segregation, and he promoted these principles in his highly regarded speeches and writings. His accommodationist stance was opposed by more militant leaders, especially W. E. B. DuBois, but, given the extreme racism of the time, Washington's approach probably accomplished more than confrontation would have done. Highly respected both as an educator and as a spokesperson for African Americans, he was granted honorary degrees from Harvard and Dartmouth.

BOOKS BY WASHINGTON

The Booker T. Washington Papers. 14 vols. Ed. by Louis R. Harlan and others. U. of Ill. Pr. 1989 $495.00. ISBN 0-252-01152-X. The autobiographical writings of Booker T. Washington. Includes bibliographies and a cumulative index.
The Negro in the South: His Economic Progress in Relation to His Moral and Religious Development. Carol Pub. Group 1970 $6.50. ISBN 0-685-03375-9. Traces the economic development of African Americans in the South. Includes a bibliography.
Up from Slavery. Rprt. Serv. 1991 repr. of 1901 ed. $69.00. ISBN 0-7812-8403-1. The autobiography of Booker T. Washington, from childhood to his founding of the Tuskegee Institute to his later years.

BOOKS ABOUT WASHINGTON

Denton, Virginia L. *Booker T. Washington and the Adult Education Movement.* U. Press Fla. 1993 $34.95. ISBN 0-8130-1182-5

Harlan, Louis R. *Booker T. Washington.* Vol. 1 *The Making of a Black Leader, 1856–1901.* OUP 1972 $39.95. ISBN 0-19-501596-7. Follows the life of Booker T. Washington from birth to the plateau of his power and influence in 1901.

———. *Booker T. Washington.* Vol. 2 *The Wizard of Tuskegee, 1901–1915.* OUP 1986 $39.95. ISBN 0-19-503202-0. A biographical study of the complex figure of Booker T. Washington. Recounts the struggles of the African American middle class during his generation.

Hawkins, Hugh. *Booker T. Washington and His Critics. Problems in Amer. Civilization.* Heath 1974 $8.50. ISBN 0-669-87049-8

McKissack, Patricia, and Frederick McKissack. *Booker T. Washington: Leader and Educator.* Enslow 1992 $12.95. ISBN 0-89490-314-4. Brief, informative, and educational.

Meier, August. *Negro Thought in America, 1880–1915: Racial Ideologies in the Age of Booker T. Washington.* U. of Mich. Pr. 1963 $18.95. ISBN 0-472-06118-6. Traces the development of African American thought and philosophy in America from 1880 to 1915. Attention given to institutional development in the African American community during this time.

CHAPTER 9

World History

David L. Hicks

> History is the science of men in time . . . [and] the only true history . . . is
> universal history.
> —Marc Bloch, *The Historian's Craft*

Rarely have these words of the great French historian Marc Bloch been heeded. Indeed, outside of medieval European chronicles (called "universal" out of ignorance) very few modern universal or "world" histories have been written. The reason is quite simple—very few modern historians feel competent in more than a relatively narrow field, such as Latin American history, or European history, or Chinese history.

This does not mean, however, that a handful of writers, some of whom considered themselves historians, did not have a worldwide historical impact. One such writer was KARL MARX. A gifted interpreter of the past in the context of nineteenth-century thought, his dialectical materialism, rooted in his belief that history is subject to immutable laws, has been perhaps the single most influential idea throughout the world during the last 150 years. Less well known is the imperial theory of the American naval historian ALFRED THAYER MAHAN. His explanation of Britain's worldwide dominion as deriving from and depending on sea power convinced Theodore Roosevelt in the United States, Kaiser Wilhelm in Germany, and the emperor and his military advisers in Japan to build big navies to rival Britain's. The results can be seen in two world wars.

Today there are no Marxs or Mahans writing such profoundly influential "world history." There are, however, a number of lesser lights, trying to escape the parochialism and particularism of much current historiography. And given the widespread movement in all intellectual fields to tear down ethnic and cultural boundaries, there are bound to be more in the future.

The focus of this chapter is on world history in general and with individuals who have had, in some way, a worldwide impact. Thus, among the individuals included are LENIN, STALIN, SPENGLER, and TOYNBEE. The actions of the former have dramatically influenced world events, and the writings of the former have dealt primarily with universal themes and issues. Not included are individuals whose impact has been more narrowly focused on a particular country or region. Discussion of the history of specific world regions and the historians whose work focuses on those regions is found in other chapters within this volume. Also not included in this chapter are general reference works that focus on history as a discipline; those are to be found in Chapter 1 of this volume.

REFERENCE WORKS

Historians are only slowly learning to broaden their horizons. As a result, many of the atlases, encyclopedias, bibliographies, and "how to" books listed below and on the following pages are Eurocentric and treat specific areas and countries rather than the world as a whole.

Adams, Simon, and others. *Illustrated Atlas of World History.* Random 1992 $13.00. ISBN 0-679-82465-0. Excellent introduction to the subject, with simple and apt explanations.

Alder, D. D., and G. M. Linden, eds. *Teaching World History: Structural Inquiry Through a Historical-Anthropological Approach.* Soc. Sci. Ed. 1976 o.p. Reasonably successful attempt to approach world history from a new, though somewhat trendy, angle.

Atlas of World History. Hammond Incorporated Eds. Hammond 1990 $11.95. ISBN 0-679-82465-0. The standard, but out-of-date as soon as published.

Aufricht, Hans. *Guide to League of Nations Publications.* AMS Pr. repr. of 1951 ed. $32.50. ISBN 0-404-00418-0

Bibliographies in History Journals: A Comprehensive Index to Bibliographies in History Journals Published World-Wide. 2 vols. ABC-CLIO 1988 $175.00. ISBN 0-87436-521-X. The only up-to-date guide of its kind.

Boehm, Eric H., and others, eds. *Historical Periodicals Directory.* 4 vols. *Clio Periodicals Directories Ser.* ABC-CLIO 1984 $95.00 ea. ISBNs 0-87636-018-8, 0-87436-019-6, 0-87436-020-X, 0-87436-021-8. Comprehensive source of up-to-date information on journals and selected serial publications.

Boia, Lucian, ed. *Great Historians from Antiquity to 1800: An International Dictionary.* Greenwood 1989 $65.00. ISBN 0-313-24517-7. Signed articles are arranged by country; each covers life, contributions, bibliography of historians.

Bramwell, A. *Atlas of Twentieth-Century World History.* HarpC 1991 $29.95. ISBN 0-06-016009-8. Elaborate effort. As up-to-date as any other contemporary atlas.

Catchpole, Brian. *A Map History of the Modern World.* Heinemann Ed. 1982 o.p.

Chambers Atlas of World History. St. Mut. 1980 o.p. A convenient handbook of easy-to-read maps that trace the historical development of world cultures and nations.

Cook, C., ed. *Dictionary of Historical Terms.* P. Bedrick Bks. 1991 $14.95. ISBN 0-87226-241-3. Limited to terms familiar to westerners, particularly English-speakers.

Demographic Yearbook. Ed. by the United Nations. UN 1988 $110.00. ISBN 92-1-051072-0. Comprehensive collection of useful statistics. This edition features the results of varying population censuses.

East, W. Gordon. *Geography Behind History.* Norton 1967 $9.95. ISBN 0-393-00419-8. Good theoretical introduction for students.

Foreign Affairs 50-Year Index, 1922–1972. Ed. by Robert J. Palmer. Bowker 1973 o.p. Reference work with over 2,000 book reviews that shed light on the last 50 years of international relations.

Glenisson, A., and M. K. Keul. *International Bibliography of the Historical Sciences.* K. G. Saur 1991 $155.00. ISBN 3-598-20411-6. The standard guide, but only a start for serious students.

Gould, Julius, and W. J. Kolb. *UNESCO Dictionary of the Social Sciences.* Macmillan 1964 $49.95. ISBN 0-02-917490-2

Green, D. Brooks. *Historical Geography: A Methodological Portrayal.* Rowman 1991 $49.50. ISBN 0-8476-7666-8. Truly useful guide for both students and professionals.

Guide to the Sources of the History of Nations. Ed. by the International Council on Archives Staff. 3rd ser. Vol. 7 K. G. Saur 1987 $67.00. ISBN 3-598-21482-0. Standard guide.

International Encyclopedia of the Social Sciences Biographical Supplement. Ed. by David L. Sills. Free Pr. $95.00. ISBN 0-02-895690-7. Multivolume work with an exhaustive range of topical and biographical articles.

Israel, Fred L., ed. *Major Peace Treaties of Modern History 1967–1979*. Chelsea Hse. 1969 $65.00. ISBN 0-87754-126-4. Text of treaties from Westphalia (1648) to Tashkent (1966).

Judge, H., and R. Blake, eds. *Oxford Illustrated Encyclopedia: World History from the Earliest Times*. 2 vols. OUP 1988 $85.00. ISBN 0-19-869161-0. Very attractive and informative book for the lay reader.

Kinnell, S. K., ed. *People in World History: An Index to Biographies in History Journals and Dissertations Covering All Countries of the World Except Canada and the U.S.* 2 vols. ABC-CLIO 1989 $185.00. ISBN 0-87436-550-6. Quite thorough. Complete to date of publication.

Langer, William L., ed. *An Encyclopedia of World History*. HM 1973 $44.00. ISBN 0-395-13592-3. Limited largely to political subjects.

National Geographic Society. *National Geographic Atlas of the World*. Natl. Geog. 1990 $59.95. ISBN 0-87044-398-4. Attractive and easy-to-use selection of maps; capitalizes on the expertise of the National Geographic Society.

New Encyclopedia of World History in Convenient Tabulated Form for the Benefit of Students, Professors, Writers, Editors, Politicians, Speakers and Researchers. Ed. by the Research Associates Staff. Am. Inst. Psych. 1990 $287.75. ISBN 0-89266-689-7. Unusual and useful compilation of worldwide events and dates that facilitates comparative history.

Norton, William. *Historical Analysis in Geography*. Wiley 1984 $16.95. ISBN 0-582-30104-1. Practical student text.

Palmer, Alan. *The Penguin Dictionary of Modern History, 1789–1945*. Viking Penguin 1984 o.p.

Pearcy, G. Etzel, and Elvyn A. Stoneman. *Handbook of New Nations*. T. Y. Crowell 1968 o.p.

Rider, K. J. *The History of Science and Technology: A Select Bibliography*. Oryx 1970 o.p.

Rogers, A. Robert. *The Humanities: A Selective Guide to Information Sources*. Libs. Unl. 1980 o.p.

Shepherd, William R. *Shepherd's Historical Atlas*. HarpC 1973 repr. of 1964 ed. o.p. Classic atlas by one of the first historians of the expansion of Europe.

Voight, M., and J. Treyz, comps. *Books for College Libraries*. 6 vols. ALA 1988 $600.00. ISBN 0-839-3353-X. A recommended core collection of books on world history and related subjects for undergraduate libraries.

Wagar, W. Warren. *Books in World History: A Guide for Teachers and Students*. Ind. U. Pr. repr. of 1973 ed. $48.00. ISBN 0-8357-7347-7. A helpful bibliography for the student; provides abstracts of significant books in the field.

White, Carl M. *Sources of Information in the Social Sciences: A Guide to the Literature*. ALA 1973 o.p. A valuable reference guide for the field.

Wiener, Philip P., ed. *Dictionary of the History of Ideas*. 5 vols. Scribner 1980 o.p. Presents an outline of the major developments and accomplishments of the human mind.

World Resources 1986. A Report by the World Resources Institute and the International Institute for Environment and Development. Basic 1986 o.p. A wealth of useful statistics.

SURVEYS AND GENERAL WORKS

For generations historians have been trained to be wedded to the study of single nations or regions. As a result, there are very few adequate, let alone good, "world histories." And the better of these are collaborative efforts. Some of those available are listed below, together with the less useful world histories that are really histories of Europe with the rest of the world tacked on. Also included are the rare efforts by a single historian to do it all. For the present, readers interested in discovering the newest methods and subjects of history must continue to refer to the studies of individual nations and regions.

Abu-Lughad, Janet L. *Before European Hegemony: The World System, 1250–1350.* OUP 1991 $13.95. ISBN 0-19-506774-6. Brilliant study of commerce from the Eastern end. A model for the writing of "world history."

Brower, D. R. *The World in the Twentieth Century: The Age of Global War and Revolution.* P-H 1988. ISBN 0-13-965526-03. One of the best attempts to escape Eurocentrocism in a text.

Burns, Edward M., and Philip L. Ralph. *World Civilizations.* 2 vols. in 1 Norton 1982 $22.95. ISBN 0-393-95517-6

Cornwell, R. D. *World History in the Twentieth Century.* Longman 1981 $24.80. ISBN 0-582-33074-2. A highly readable general outline of world history in the twentieth century; includes numerous maps and photographs.

Freeman-Grenville, G. S. *A Chronology of World History: A Calendar of Principal Events from 300 B.C. to A.D. 1976.* Rowman 1978 o.p.

Frolov, I. *Global Problems of Civilization.* South Asia Bks. 1989 $16.00. ISBN 0-8364-2527-8

Garraty, J., and P. Gay, eds. *The Columbia History of the World.* Col. U. Pr. 1990 $9.95. ISBN 0-317-99661-4. More sound than substance. Useful but disappointing given the quality of the editors and authors.

Geiger, Theodore. *The Conflicted Relationship: The West and the Transformation of Asia, Africa and Latin America.* Atlantic Policy Studies Ser. McGraw 1967 o.p. Examines the main economic, political, and sociocultural elements in the relationships among the Western nations and Asia, Africa, and Latin America.

Goff, Richard, and others. *The Twentieth Century: A Brief Global History.* McGraw 1990 $21.43. ISBN 0-07-023536-8

Greaves, R., and others. *Civilizations of the World: The Human Adventure.* HarpC 1990 $42.25. ISBN 0-06-047302-9. Good text, well-organized and illustrated. Shows that historians are beginning to catch on to what "world history" consists of.

Grigg, David B. *The Agricultural Systems of the World: An Evolutionary Approach.* Cambridge U. Pr. 1974 $29.95. ISBN 0-521-09843-2. Describes the chief characteristics of the major agricultural regions of the world and how they came into being.

Jones, E. L. *Growth Recurring: Economic Change in World History.* OUP 1988 $55.00. ISBN 0-19-828300-8. Excellent example of how economic historians are ahead of their colleagues in thinking in global terms.

Keay, J. *History of World Exploration.* BDD Promo Bk. 1991 $28.98. ISBN 0-7924-5325-5. Informative, but tries to cover too much.

McKay, John P. *A History of World Societies.* HM 1991 $52.36. ISBN 0-395-47293-8. One of the better attempts at a true world history.

McNeill, William H. *The Rise of the West: A History of the Human Community.* U. Ch. Pr. 1991 $19.95. ISBN 0-226-56141-0. A pioneering attempt to present Western history in a world setting.

Palmer, Robert R., and Joel Colton. *A History of the Modern World.* Knopf 1991 $54.50. ISBN 0-679-41014-7. Classic college history texts. Readable survey useful to general readers.

Rao, B. V. *Concise Book of World History.* Apt. Bks. 1988 o.p. An Indian historian's view of global history.

Roberts, J. M. *The Pelican History of the World.* Viking Penguin 1988 $11.95. ISBN 0-14-022785-7. Competent survey.

Shafer, Boyd C. *Europe and the World in the Age of Expansion.* 10 vols. U. of Minn. Pr. 1974–84 o.p. Could be an exception to the rule that world histories must be superficial.

Smith, J. *Essentials of World History.* Barron 1988 $9.95. ISBN 0-8120-0637-2. Brief, reasonably competent survey.

Stavrianos, Leften. *A Global History: The Human Heritage.* P-H 1983 $20.95. ISBN 0-13-357152-1. Explores the main trends in world history from a global perspective.

Upshur, Jiu-Hwa L., and others. *World History*. 2 vols. West Pub. 1991 $35.50. ea. ISBNs 0-314-79266-X, 0-314-79267-8. Perhaps the most innovative and successful attempt to present an integrated, comparative history of the world in a single text.

THE WRITING AND PHILOSOPHY OF HISTORY

The selections that follow represent only a fraction of the many works on the meaning and purpose of history and on how to do research and write on a historical subject. Their titles and pretensions notwithstanding, all take their ideas and methods from the Western historical tradition that dates from the Italian Renaissance. From that time until the later nineteenth century, historians wrote mostly about past politics in the hope that knowledge of past political history would encourage European governing élites of later generations to act wisely in the future. In the last 100 years, however, political history has gone out of style, overshadowed first by economic history, then by social history, and most recently, by the history of popular culture. Although such theories of literary criticism as "deconstruction" have found their way into the thought of philosophers of history, works on the writing and philosophy of history have reflected but have not been slaves to these trends. The works listed here include those that discuss all branches of contemporary historical writing.

Aron, Raymond. *Introduction to the Philosophy of History: An Essay on the Limits of Historical Objectivity*. 1938. Trans. by George J. Irwin. Greenwood 1976 repr. of 1961 ed. o.p. A complex inquiry into the meaning of history; questions whether a universally valid science of history is possible.

Barzun, Jacques. *Clio and the Doctors: History, Psycho-History, and Quanto-History*. U. Ch. Pr. 1989 $14.95. ISBN 0-226-03851-3. Largely negative view of a distinguished elder among historians about some of the "new history."

Barzun, Jacques, and Henry F. Graff. *The Modern Researcher*. HM 1992 $24.45. ISBN 0-395-64494-1. Concentrates on historical research.

Becker, Carl L. *Everyman His Own Historian: Essays on History and Politics*. Times Bks. 1972 o.p. A small classic.

Benjamin, Jules R. *A Student's Guide to History*. St. Martin 1990 $12.70. ISBN 0-312-03168-8. Contains an extremely useful bibliography of reference works and excellent advice on research and writing.

Berkhofer, Robert F., Jr. *A Behavioral Approach to Historical Analysis*. Macmillan 1971 o.p. Encourages historians to approach their subject by including the basic social sciences in their approach.

Brundage, A. *Going to the Sources: A Guide to Historical Research and Writing*. Harlan Davidson 1989 $32.50. ISBN 0-88295-865-8. Excellent recent handbook. Particularly good for advanced undergraduates.

Burke, Peter, ed. *New Perspectives on Historical Writing*. Pa. St. U. Pr. 1992 $32.50. ISBN 0-271-00827-X. Very stimulating and useful anthology for both students and professional historians.

Cantor, Norman F., and Richard I. Schneider. *How to Study History*. Harlan Davidson $7.95. ISBN 0-88295-709-0. As good as any of its kind.

Carr, Edward H. *What Is History?* Random 1967 $4.95. ISBN 0-394-70391-X. Reflections on history by a leading historian of the Russian Revolution.

Cohen, Morris R. *The Meaning of Human History*. Open Court 1968 $11.95. ISBN 0-87548-101-9. Cohen's most significant work; argues for an interdisciplinary approach to the study of history.

Daniels, Robert. *Studying History: How and Why*. P-H 1981 $12.95. ISBN 0-13-858738-8. Useful methodological handbook.

Dray, W. H. *On History and Philosophies of History*. E. J. Brill 1989 $77.25. ISBN 90-04-09000-2. Eurocentric, but excellent analyses of the ideas included.

Fischer, David H. *Historian's Fallacies: Toward a Logic of Historical Thought*. HarpC 1970 $12.00. ISBN 0-06-131545-1. Philosophical work that attempts to shed light on the nature of history.

Fukuyama, F. *The End of History and the Last Man*. Free Pr. 1992 $24.95. ISBN 0-02-910975-2. Controversial, but stimulating. A worthwhile book with which to be familiar.

Furedi, F. *Mythical Past—Elusive Future: An Introduction to Historical Sociology*. Paul & Co. Pubs. 1992 $45.00. ISBN 0-7453-0530-X. Excellent and much-needed introduction to a subject that puzzles many more-traditional historians.

Gay, Peter. *Style in History*. Norton 1989 $7.95. ISBN 0-393-30558-9. Pleasurable reading for the adult interested in the history of historical thought.

Gellner, E. *Plough, Sword, and Book: The Structure of Human History*. U. Ch. Pr. 1990 $14.95. ISBN 0-226-28702-5. Serious, if not always successful, attempt at a very difficult subject.

Ginzburg, G. *Clues, Myths, and the Historical Method*. Trans. by John and Anne Tedeschi. Johns Hopkins 1989 $35.00. ISBN 0-8018-3458-9. What and how historians should study by a guru of popular cultural history.

Himmelfarb, G. *The New History and the Old*. HUP 1987 $24.95. ISBN 0-674-61581-6. Conservative historian's defense of traditional history and historical methodology.

Howard, M. *The Lessons of History*. Yale U. Pr. 1991 $27.50. ISBN 0-300-04728-2. Reflections of a most distinguished historian on history.

Hughes, H. Stuart. *History as Art and as Science: Twin Vistas on the Past*. History and Historiography Ser. U. Ch. Pr. $9.95. ISBN 0-226-35916-6. An enlightening collection of five lectures outlining Hughes's approach to historical study.

Iggers, G. G., and H. T. Parker. *International Handbook of Historical Studies: Contemporary Research and Theory*. Greenwood 1980 $55.00. ISBN 0-313-21367-4. Useful and interesting. Title promises more than the contents deliver.

Jarausch, K. H., and K. A. Hardy. *Quantitative Methods for Historians: A Guide to Research Statistics*. U. of NC Pr. 1991 $37.50. ISBN 0-8078-1947-6. Indispensable tool for historians using quantitative methodology.

Kaye, H. J. *The Education of Desire: Marxists and the Writing of History*. Routledge 1992 $45.00. ISBN 0-415-90587-7. Balanced treatment of the subject for what has been called the post-Marxist world.

Le Roy-Ladurie, Emmanuel. *The Territory of the Historian*. Trans. by Ben Reynolds and Sian Reynolds. U. Ch. Pr. 1979 repr. of 1973 ed. o.p. Thoughts of one of the most prestigious modern historians.

Lewis, Bernard. *History Remembered, Recovered, Invented*. Princeton U. Pr. 1975 o.p. Defines three types of history: traditional, discovery and analysis of historical data by academic scholarship, and construction of history for a particular end.

Lifton, Robert J., and Eric Olson, eds. *Explorations in Psychohistory: The Wellfleet Papers of Erik Erikson, Robert Jay Lifton and Kenneth Kenniston*. S&S Trade 1975 o.p. Collection of papers by distinguished thinkers. Important and potentially influential contribution in the emergence of psychohistory.

Meyerhoff, Hans, ed. *The Philosophy of History in Our Times*. Garland 1985 o.p. Very useful anthology; the only one of its kind.

Offen, K., and others, eds. *Writing Women's History: International Perspectives*. Ind. U. Pr. 1991 $37.50. ISBN 0-0253-34160-4. Important, pioneering work.

Plumb, J. H. *The Death of the Past*. Humanities 1978 o.p. A collection of essays and an intellectual autobiography that combine to give an illuminating picture of the historian at work.

Pok, A., ed. *A Selected Bibliography of Modern History*. Greenwood 1992 $55.00. ISBN 0-313-27231-X. Bibliography of *world* history.

Poplasen, Ilija. *The World History Made in the Present*. MIR PA 1986 $20.00. ISBN 0-935352-20-1. Interesting, different approach to history and historiography.

Rowse, A. L. *The Use of History*. History and Historiography Ser. Garland 1985 o.p. A great Elizabethan historian philosophizes.

Shafer, Robert J., ed. *A Guide to Historical Method*. Wadsworth Pub. 1980 $15.50. ISBN 0-534-10825-3

Stoianovich, Traian. *French Historical Method: The "Annales" Paradigm*. Cornell Univ. Pr. 1976 o.p. The "Annales" School has had worldwide influence.

Thompson, J. W. *A History of Historical Writing*. 2 vols. Peter Smith o.p. The most thorough study of modern European historiography.

Toynbee, Arnold J. *A Study of History*. 12 vols. OUP 1961. Vols. 1–6 o.p. Vols. 7–10 $65.00. ISBN 0-19-519689-9. Vol. 11 $36.50. ISBN 0-19-215223-8. Vol. 12 $25.00. ISBN 0-19-500197-4. Toynbee's classic; presents his challenge-response theory of history.

Young, Robert D. *White Mythologies: Writing, History, and the West*. Routledge 1991 $74.50. ISBN 0-415-05371-4. Much-needed study that is informative without being strident.

WAR AND PEACE IN THE MODERN WORLD

Included here are books on various aspects of war and diplomacy, and representative studies of efforts, particularly since World War II, to advance the cause of world peace. Until now, few serious studies have been published that take into account, let alone analyze, the consequences for world peace of the fragmentation of the Soviet Union and the collapse of Communist rule in the nations of eastern Europe. Although the end of the Cold War and the dangerous rivalry between the United States and the Soviet Union have changed fundamentally the problems of peace-keeping, it will take a while for the experts to invent new theories and recommendations.

Adamthwaite, Anthony. *The Lost Peace: International Relations in Europe, 1918–1939*. St. Martin 1981 $25.00. ISBN 0-312-49882-9

Albrecht-Carrié, Rene. *A Diplomatic History of Europe: Since the Congress of Vienna*. HarpC 1973 o.p. Characterized by sound scholarship and carefully drawn conclusions.

Allison, Graham T. *Essence of Decision: Explaining the Cuban Missile Crisis*. Scott F. 1987 $22.00. ISBN 0-673-93412-3

Baer, George W. *Test Case: Italy, Ethiopia and the League of Nations*. Hoover Inst. 1977 o.p. Scholarly study of a subject too often overlooked.

Baker, Paul R. *The Atomic Bomb: The Great Decision*. H. Holt & Co. 1976 o.p. Excellent collection of articles pro and con.

Baldwin, Hanson W. *Battles Lost and Won: Great Campaigns of World War II*. Avon 1967 o.p. Popular, readable, accurate, and useful. By a noted war correspondent.

_____. *World War I: An Outline History*. HarpC 1962 o.p. An overview of the First World War with special emphasis on the concept of total war.

Blumenson, Martin. *The Patton Papers*. 2 vols. HM 1972–74 $35.00–$39.50 ea. ISBNs 0-395-12706-8, 0-395-18498-3

Boeman, J. S. *Peace, from War to War*. MA-AH Pub. 1991 $42.50. ISBN 0-89126-170-2. Interesting attempt to understand why "peace" has never been permanent.

Bradley, J. *War and Peace since 1945*. East Eur. Quarterly 1989 $36.00. ISBN 0-88033-964-0. Excellent review of the Cold War period, to be forgiven for failing to foresee its end.

Brock-Utne, B. *Feminist Perspectives on Peace and Peace Education*. Pergamon 1989 $43.00. ISBN 0-08-036568-X. Fresh point of view about peace and how to teach it. Now becoming a bit out-of-date.

Brown, S. *The Causes and Prevention of War*. St. Martin 1987 $39.95. ISBN 0-312-12532-1. Interesting and original study that asks all the right questions and answers most of them well.

Calvocoressi, Peter, and Guy Wint. *Total War: Causes and Courses of the Second World War*. Pantheon 1989 $39.95. ISBN 0-394-57811-2. A comprehensive volume that includes new information from government archives.

Cancian, F. M., and J. W. Gibson, eds. *Making War-Making Peace: The Social Foundations of Violent Conflict*. Wadsworth Pub. 1990. ISBN 0-534-12348-1. Valuable theoretical study, much of it valid for analyzing the "little" wars of this post-Cold War period.

Carlton, E. *War and Ideology*. Routledge 1990 $49.95. ISBN 0-415-04157-0. Excellent historical treatment of the subject.

Carr, Edward H. *International Relations between the Two World Wars, 1919–1939*. St. Martin 1969 $22.50. ISBN 0-312-42315-2

Chamberlain, Neville. *In Search of Peace. Essay Index Repr. Ser.* Ayer repr. of 1939 ed. $18.00. ISBN 0-8369-2274-3

Collier, Basil. *The Second World War: A Military History*. Peter Smith $19.00. ISBN 0-8446-4724-1

Cooper, S. E. *Patriotic Pacifism: Waging War on War in Europe, 1815–1914*. OUP 1991 $39.95. ISBN 0-19-505715-5. Brilliant study from the post-Marxian point of view of nineteenth-century anti-war ideas and movements.

Craig, William. *Enemy at the Gates*. Ballantine 1974 $1.95. ISBN 0-345-25885-1. Vivid and detailed account of the struggle. Heavily researched.

Davis, Lynn E., and others. *The Cold War Begins: Soviet-American Conflict over Eastern Europe*. Princeton U. Pr. 1974 o.p. Examines the origins of the Cold War in the postwar struggle over the future of Eastern Europe.

De Landa, M. *War in the Age of Intelligent Machines*. Zone Bks. 1989 $32.95. ISBN 0-942299-75-2. Slightly superficial overview.

Dunnigan, J. F., and A. Bay. *A Quick and Dirty Guide to War*. Morrow 1991 $14.50. ISBN 0-688-10033-3. To be read for grim amusement and wisdom.

Dupuy, T. N. *The Evolution of Weapons and Warfare*. Da Capo 1990 $13.95. ISBN 0-306-80384-4. Insightful overview of the subject.

Eisenhower, John S. *The Bitter Woods: A Comprehensive Study of the War in Europe*. Putnam Pub. Group 1969 o.p. Superb study of the German and Allied commands during the European campaign of World War II with emphasis on the Battle of the Bulge.

Falls, Cyril. *The Great War, 1914–1918*. Capricorn Bks. 1961 o.p. Classic study of World War I.

Feis, Herbert. *Churchill, Roosevelt, Stalin: The War They Waged and the Peace They Sought*. Princeton U. Pr. 1967 $89.00. ISBN 0-691-01050-1. Necessary reading for those who wish to study the foreign diplomacy of the Roosevelt period and the interactions of Roosevelt, Churchill, and Stalin.

Fellman, M. *Inside War*. OUP 1990 $9.95. ISBN 0-19-506471-2. Examines the use of guerilla warfare in wartime, including during the Civil War.

Fischer, Fritz. *Germany's Aims in the First World War*. Norton 1968 o.p.

———. *War of Illusions: German Policies from 1911 to 1914*. Trans. by Marion Jackson. Norton 1975 o.p. An exhaustive description of German policy before World War I and its effect on German society.

———. *World Power or Decline: The Controversy over Germany's Aims in the First World War*. Trans. by Lancelot L. Farrar and others. Norton 1974 o.p.

Folks, H. *The Human Costs of War*. Gordon Pr. 1990 $79.95. ISBN 0-8490-4053-1. Bleakly thorough reminder, very well done.

Freedman, Lawrence. *The Evolution of Nuclear Strategy*. St. Martin 1989 $39.95. ISBN 0-312-02817-2. A detailed and critical history of official and unofficial attempts to construct a plausible nuclear strategy.

Fuller, John F. *The Conduct of War, 1789–1961: A Study of the Impact of the French, Industrial and Russian Revolutions on War and Its Conduct*. Da Capo 1992 repr. of 1961 ed. $14.95. ISBN 0-306-80467-0

Fussell, Paul. *The Great War and Modern Memory*. OUP 1975 $10.95. ISBN 0-19-502171-1. Brilliant study on how World War I is remembered—and forgotten.

Gimbel, John. *The Origins of the Marshall Plan.* Stanford U. Pr. 1976 $27.50. ISBN 0-8047-0903-3. Argues persuasively that the Marshall Plan was intended to make German economic recovery politically acceptable in the U.S. and Europe.

Goldstein, J. S. *Long Cycles: Prosperity and War in the Modern Age.* Yale U. Pr. 1988 $19.95. ISBN 0-300-04112-8. Important study that lays to rest many of the clichés about war's economic benefits.

Greenfield, Kent R. *American Strategy in World War II: A Reconsideration.* Greenwood 1979 repr. of 1963 ed. $35.00. ISBN 0-313-21175-2. An official history of the U.S. Army and its Air Forces during World War II.

Groebel, J., and R. A. Hinde, eds. *Aggression and War: Their Biological and Social Bases.* Cambridge U. Pr. 1990 $15.95. ISBN 0-521-35871-X. Diverse articles with those on social "bases" more successful than others.

Gulick, Edward V. *Europe's Classical Balance of Power: A Case History of the Theory and Practice of One of the Great Concepts of European Statecraft.* Greenwood 1982 $55.00. ISBN 0-313-23350-0

Haas, J., ed. *The Anthropology of War.* Cambridge U. Pr. 1990 $49.50. ISBN 0-521-38042-1. Numerous articles that are at best tentative in their often questionable conclusions.

Harris, A., and Y. King, eds. *Rocking the Ship of State: Towards a Feminist Peace Politics.* Westview 1989 $58.00. ISBN 0-8133-0710-4. Worthwhile collection. Includes several articles that set forth the feminist position with vigor and intelligence.

Hicks, D., ed. *Education for Peace: Issues, Principles, and Practice in the Classroom.* Routledge 1988 $17.95. ISBN 0-205-13603-6. Excellent one-of-a-kind teachers' handbook.

Hillgruber, Andreas. *Germany and the Two World Wars.* Trans. by William C. Kirby. HUP 1981 $6.95. ISBN 0-674-35522-6. A short, concise analysis of the German share of responsibility for the two World Wars.

Jackson, William. *Overlord: Normandy, 1944.* Ed. by Christopher Dowling. *Politics and Strategy of the Second World War Ser.* U. of Delaware Pr. 1979 $18.50. ISBN 0-87413-161-8. Book on tactics and strategy by a distinguished military historian.

Joll, James. *The Origins of the First World War.* Longman 1984 $17.95. ISBN 0-582-49016-2. Wide-ranging analysis of the historical forces at work in prewar Europe and the ways in which historians have attempted to explain them.

Keegan, John. *The Face of Battle.* Viking Penguin 1983 $9.95. ISBN 0-14-004897-9. War viewed in an entirely new way through the battles of Agincourt, Waterloo, and the Somme.

———. *Six Armies in Normandy: From D-Day to the Liberation of Paris.* Viking Penguin 1983 $8.95. ISBN 0-14-005293-3

Kohl, Wilfrid L. *French Nuclear Diplomacy.* Princeton U. Pr. 1971 $58.00. ISBN 0-691-07540-9. Study of the origins of nuclear policy under the Fourth French Republic and further developments under the Fifth Republic.

La Feber, Walter. *America, Russia, and the Cold War.* McGraw 1992 $11.95. ISBN 0-07-035853-2. Examines the cold war from both sides and shows how the domestic policies of both nations influenced foreign policy.

Langhorne, Richard. *The Collapse of the Concert of Europe, 1890–1914.* St. Martin 1981 $22.50. ISBN 0-312-14723-6. Deals with diplomacy in the decades before World War I.

Lewin, Ronald. *The War on Land: The British Army in World War II.* Morrow 1970 o.p.

Liddell Hart, Basil H. *History of the First World War.* Cassell 1970 o.p.

———. *History of the Second World War.* Putnam Pub. Group 1980 $17.95. ISBN 0-399-50445-1. With the *History of the First World War,* a masterwork by this century's most distinguished military historian.

Luttwak, E. N. *Strategy: The Logic of War and Peace.* HUP 1987 $10.95. ISBN 0-647-83996-X. Unusually successful attempt by a distinguished analyst to see the big picture.

Mandelbaum, Michael. *The Nuclear Question.* Cambridge U. Pr. 1980 $37.95. ISBN 0-521-29614-5. Insightful study of U.S. atomic weapon policy and nuclear diplomacy.

Manwaring, M. G., ed. *Uncomfortable Wars: Toward a New Paradigm of Low-Intensity Conflict.* Westview 1990 $24.95. ISBN 0-8133-8081-2. Extremely thoughtful start to the study of what will almost certainly be the wars of the future.

Midlarsky, M. I., ed. *Handbook of War Studies.* Unwin Hyman 1989 $49.95. ISBN 0-8133-8081-2

Milward, Alan S. *War, Economy and Society, 1939–1945.* U. CA Pr. 1977 $14.95. ISBN 0-520-03942-4

Morris, A. J. *The Scaremongers: The Advocacy of War and Rearmament, 1896–1914.* Routledge 1984 o.p. Looks at the role certain British journalists played in England's entry into World War I.

Nicolson, Harold. *Peacemaking 1919.* Peter Smith 1984 o.p. A comprehensive diplomatic history of treaty-making at the end of World War I.

Okerstrom, D., and S. J. Morgan, eds. *The Peace and War Reader.* Allyn 1992 $22.00. ISBN 0-205-13603-5. Up-to-date judicious selection covering a variety of topics.

Pipes, Richard. *U.S.-Soviet Relations in the Era of Détente: A Tragedy of Errors,* Westview 1981 o.p. A collection of eight essays that formed the basis for conservative thinking on Soviet policy.

Pogue, Forrest C. *George C. Marshall.* Viking Penguin 1989 $12.95. ISBN 0-14-011909-4. Exemplary biography, thoroughly researched and judicious in its conclusions.

Prins, Gwyn, ed. *The Nuclear Crisis Reader.* Random 1984 o.p.

Puri, Rashimi-Sudha. *Gandhi on War and Peace.* Greenwood 1986 $47.95. ISBN 0-275-92303-7. Thoughtful and relevant selection of Mohandas Gandhi's writings.

Quester, George H. *Nuclear Proliferation: Breaking the Chain.* U. of Wis. Pr. 1981 $32.50. ISBN 0-299-08604-6. Examines the ways in which international politics has exploited the possibility of nuclear proliferation.

Rapaport, A. *The Origins of Violence: Approaches to the Study of Violence.* Paragon 1989 $39.95. ISBN 0-943852-47-1. Highly theoretical, but of some use to the layperson.

———. *Peace: An Idea Whose Time Has Come.* U. of Mich. Pr. 1992 $29.95. ISBN 0-472-10315-6. Good early attempt to weigh the benefits and the risks of the new world political situation.

Remak, J. *The Origins of the Second World War.* P-H 1976 o.p.

Rommel, Erwin. *Rommel Papers.* Ed. by Basil H. Liddell Hart. *Quality Pap. Ser.* Da Capo 1982 repr. of 1953 ed. $14.95. ISBN 0-306-8015-7-4. Skillfully edited memoirs that fully reveal the "Desert Fox."

Rotberg, R. I., and T. K. Rabb, eds. *The Origin and Prevention of Major Wars.* Cambridge U. Pr. 1989 $12.95. ISBN 0-521-37955-5. Collection of historical essays, most of them quite solid.

Rudney, R., ed. *Peace Research in Western Europe: A History Guide.* Access Sec. Info. Serv. 1989 $4.00. ISBN 1-878597-05-1. Brief but remarkably complete compilation.

Scott, Harriet F., and William F. Scott. *The Armed Forces of the USSR.* Westview $22.50. ISBN 0-8133-0887-9. Analysis of the development and organization of the Soviet armed forces.

Seabury, P. *War: Ends and Means.* Basic 1990 $11.75. ISBN 0-465-09068-6

Sherwin, Martin J. *A World Destroyed.* Random 1987 $13.00. ISBN 0-394-75204-X. Traces the ways in which Truman's wartime atomic policies produced fateful consequences for the future of international relations.

Smith, G., ed. *How It Was in the War.* Trafalgar 1991 $39.95. ISBN 1-85745-363-6. Personal accounts. Strong stuff.

Strahan, Hew. *European Armies and the Conduct of War.* Allen & Unwin 1983 o.p. Tells how European armies rationalized their experience of military campaigns and so prepared their plans and doctrines.

Toland, John. *Battle: The Story of the Bulge.* NAL-Dutton 1982 o.p.

———. *The Last One Hundred Days.* Bantam 1990 $6.95. ISBN 0-553-28640-4. The dramatic story of the 100 days between Yalta and the fall of Berlin.

———. *Rising Sun: The Decline and Fall of the Japanese Empire: 1936–1945.* Random 1970 o.p. Emminently readable and informative account of World War II from the Japanese point of view.

Tunney, Christopher. *Biographical Dictionary of World War II*. St. Martin 1973 o.p. Includes more than 400 short biographies of the major participants of World War II.
Uldricks, Teddy J. *Diplomacy and Ideology: The Origins of Soviet Foreign Relations, 1917–1930*. Sage 1979 o.p.
Walters, F. P. *The League of Nations*. OUP 1965 o.p. The standard account.
Watt, Donald C. *Too Serious a Business: European Armed Forces and the Coming of the Second World War*. U. CA Pr. 1991 $10.95. ISBN 0-393-30815-4. Examines the role of the European armed forces and the approach of World War II.
Werth, Alexander. *Russia at War*. Carroll & Graf 1984 $17.95. ISBN 0-88184-084-X. An excellent history of the war years in Russia by an author who was there at the time.
Wright, Gordon. *The Ordeal of Total War, 1939–1945*. HarpC 1968 $13.00. ISBN 0-06-131408-0. Focuses on the impact of World War II on European politics and society.
Young, Peter. *Short History of World War Two, 1939–1945*. *Apollo Eds*. T. Y. Crowell 1972 o.p. Useful, but sometimes lacking in significant detail.

CHRONOLOGY OF AUTHORS

Herder, Johann Gottfried. 1744–1803
Hegel, Georg Wilhelm Friedrich. 1770–1831
Marx, Karl. 1818–1883
Mahan, Alfred Thayer. 1840–1914
Croce, Benedetto. 1866–1952
Lenin, Vladimir Ilyich (Ulyanov). 1870–1924
Trotsky, Leon. 1879–1940
Stalin, Joseph (Vissarionovich). 1879–1953

Spengler, Oswald. 1880–1936
Toynbee, Arnold J(oseph). 1889–1975
Kohn, Hans. 1891–1971
Braudel, Fernand. 1902–1985
Aron, Raymond. 1905–1983
Arendt, Hannah. 1906–1975
Ward, Barbara. 1914–1981
McNeill, William H(ardy). 1917–

ARENDT, HANNAH. 1906–1975

Born in Hanover, Germany, Hannah Arendt received her doctorate from Heidelberg University in 1928. A victim of naziism, she fled Germany in 1933 for France, where she helped with the resettlement of Jewish children in Palestine. In 1941, she emigrated to the United States. Ten years later she became an American citizen. Arendt held numerous positions in her new country—research director of the Conference on Jewish Relations, chief editor of Schocken Books, and executive director of Jewish Cultural Reconstruction in New York City. A visiting professor at several universities, including the University of California, Columbia, and the University of Chicago, and university professor on the graduate faculty of the New School for Social Research, in 1959 she became the first woman appointed to a full professorship at Princeton. She also won a number of grants and fellowships. In 1967 she received the Sigmund Freud Prize of the German Akademie für Sprache und Dichtung for her fine scholarly writing.

Arendt was well equipped to write her superb *The Origins of Totalitarianism* (1951) which David Riesman called "an achievement in historiography." In his view, "such an experience in understanding our times as this book provides is itself a social force not to be underestimated." Arendt's study of Adolf Eichmann at his trial—*Eichmann in Jerusalem* (1963)—part of which appeared originally in *The New Yorker*, was a painfully searching investigation into what made the Nazi persecutor tick. In it, she states that the trial of this Nazi illustrates the "banality of evil." In 1968, she published *Men in Dark Times*,

282 THE READER'S ADVISER

which includes essays on Hermann Broch, Walter Benjamin, and BERTOLT BRECHT (see Vol. 2), as well as an interesting characterization of Pope John XXIII.

BOOKS BY ARENDT

Between Past and Future: Eight Exercises in Political Thought. 1961. Viking Penguin 1977 $10.00. ISBN 0-14-004662-3. Best for analyzing Arendt's thought.
Crises of the Republic. HarBraceJ 1972 $10.95. ISBN 0-15-623200-6. Collection of essays summing up much of the author's political thought.
Eichmann in Jerusalem: A Report of the Banality of Evil. 1963. Viking Penguin 1977 $10.00. ISBN 0-14-004450-7. A profound and well-documented analysis of the issues and the historical background of the Adolf Eichmann trial.
The Human Condition. U. Ch. Pr. 1970 $13.95. ISBN 0-226-02593-4. Startling and profound interpretation of recent history.
Men in Dark Times. HarBraceJ 1970 $8.95. ISBN 0-15-658890-0
On Revolution. Greenwood 1982 repr. of 1963 ed. $38.50. ISBN 0-313-23493-0. Insightful historical and political examination of the three great revolutions of modern times: the American, French, and Russian revolutions.
On Violence. 1969. HarBraceJ 1970 $5.95. ISBN 0-15-669500-6. Reflections on a century of wars and revolution; examines the nature and causes of violence.
The Origins of Totalitarianism. 1951. HarBraceJ 1973 $14.95. ISBN 0-15-670153-7. Arendt's most profound and characteristic work.

BOOKS ABOUT ARENDT

Bradshaw, L. *Acting and Thinking: The Political Thought of Hannah Arendt.* U. of Toronto Pr. 1989 $45.00. ISBN 0-8020-2625-7. Good, solid academic analysis, with several new insights into *The Origins of Totalitarianism.*
Conovan, M. *Hannah Arendt: A Reinterpretation of Her Political Thought.* Cambridge U. Pr. 1992 $54.95. ISBN 0-521-41911-5. Too recent for serious comment, but based on the author's reputation should be considered a major reevaluation.
Isaac, J. C. *Arendt, Camus and Modern Rebellion.* Yale U. Pr. 1992 $30.00. ISBN 0-300-05203-0. Comparative study of some of the more controversial views of Arendt and some of her contemporaries.
Nordquist, J., ed. *Hannah Arendt: A Bibliography.* Ref. Rsch. Serv. 1989 $15.00. ISBN 0-937855-26-X. Complete with annotations and critical comments.

ARON, RAYMOND. 1905–1983

Raymond Aron was a French political scientist, economist, and philosopher who was several times a visiting professor in the United States. He commented regularly and influentially on social and political topics and current issues in the conservative French newspaper *Le Figaro,* in books and on radio, and as a teacher at *L'école pratique des hautes études* in Paris. Because of his consistent opposition to Marxism and his admiration and respect for the United States, Aron was perhaps not so highly regarded as French intellectuals of the Left. But he was always a voice for reason and moderation at a time when his critics were often strident and ineffectual.

BOOKS BY ARON

The Century of Total War. Greenwood 1981 repr. of 1954 ed. $45.00. ISBN 0-313-22852-3. Historical survey of World War I and World War II, concentrating on the technological advances of warfare.
Democracy and Totalitarianism. U. of Mich. Pr. 1990 $42.95. ISBN 0-472-09451-3. Together with *The Century of Total War,* contains most of Aron's seminal thought. Introduction by R. Pierce.

German Sociology. Ed. by L. A. Coser and W. W. Powell. Trans. by M. and T. Bottomore. Ayer 1979 repr. of 1964 ed. $13.00. ISBN 0-405-12083-4. A historical interpretation.

The Great Debate: Theories of Nuclear Strategy. Trans. by E. Powel. Greenwood 1981 repr. of 1964 ed. $45.00. ISBN 0-313-22851-5. Dated now, but illustrative of Aron's moderate views.

In Defense of Decadent Europe. U. Pr. of Amer. 1984 o.p. Written for a French audience; an elucidation on the nature of political and economic freedom.

Philosophy of History. Beacon Pr. 1961 o.p.

Politics and History. Ed. by M. B. Conant. Transaction Pubs. 1984 $18.95. ISBN 0-87855-944-7. A summing up.

BRAUDEL, FERNAND. 1902–1985

Perhaps the most admired and respected European historian of the present generation, Fernand Braudel, through his unique interests and methodology, made the *Annales* school of history the most influential of all contemporary schools of history. His monumental *The Mediterranean and the Mediterranean World in the Age of Philip II* (1949) was the first attempt to study a historic period (the sixteenth century) and an area (the lands bordering the Mediterranean Sea) in their totality, from climatic conditions to social structures, from ethnic origins to trade routes. This work was written from memory while he was detained in a German prison camp. His work has inspired dozens of younger historians, the best of whom trained under him at *L'école pratique des hautes politiques* in Paris, of which he was director.

BOOKS BY BRAUDEL

Afterthoughts on Materialism and Capitalism. Trans. by P. M. Ranum. Johns Hopkins 1977 $8.95. ISBN 0-8018-2217-3. Addenda to Braudel's three-volume *Civilization and Capitalism, Fifteenth to Eighteenth Century.*

Civilization and Capitalism, Fifteenth to Eighteenth Century. 3 vols. Trans. by S. Reynolds. U. CA Pr. 1992. ISBN 0-520-08116-1. Best introduction to the author's theories and methods of history. A mine of data, but limited by Braudel's strong preconceptions.

The Identity of France. 2 vols. Trans. by S. Reynolds. HarpC. Vol. 1 *History and Environment.* 1990 $12.00. ISBN 0-06-091643-5. Vol. 2 *People and Production* 1992 $17.00. ISBN 0-06-092142-0. Braudel's preconceptions as applied to his native land.

The Mediterranean and the Mediterranean World in the Age of Philip II. 2 vols. Trans. by S. Reynolds. 2nd rev. ed. HarpC 1977. Vol. 1 $19.00. ISBN 0-06-090566-2. Vol. 2 $18.95. ISBN 0-06-09567-0. The work that made Braudel famous and influenced a generation of young historians.

On History. Trans. by S. Mathews. U. Ch. Pr. 1982 $9.95. ISBN 0-220-07151-0. Sums up the views that shaped *Annales* in the half century since World War II.

Out of Italy: 1450–1650. Trans. by S. Reynolds. Abbeville Pr. 1991 $50.00. ISBN 2-08013-500-7. Documents the explosion of cultural achievements during the years of the Italian renaissance.

The Perspective of the World: Civilization and Capitalism, Vol. III. HarpC 1986 $22.50. ISBN 0-06-091296-0. Last volume of Braudel's controversial work.

CROCE, BENEDETTO. 1866–1952

The most famous of the Italian anti-Fascists during the Mussolini period, Benedetto Croce served as a senator, then a minister of education, and after 1943, a leader of the Liberal party. He was one of the most respected and influential philosopher-historians of the first half of the twentieth century. Although his most important work was in philosophy, continuing and modifying the Hegelian Idealist tradition in a uniquely Italian way, he also wrote on major works of literature. His critical analysis of SHAKESPEARE (see Vol. 1) won him the admiration of both British and American Shakespearian scholars. As a historian, he wrote on several periods and subjects in Italian history, perhaps most notably on his native Naples, where he lived most of his life.

BOOKS BY CROCE

Historical Materialism and the Economics of Karl Marx. Transaction Pubs. 1981 $34.95. ISBN 0-87855-695-8. Brilliant critique from the idealist perspective.

The History of Aesthetics as the Science of Expression. 2 vols. Gloucester Art 1991 $287.60. ISBN 0-86650-310-2

The History of the Theory of the Beautiful. Gloucester Art 1984 $298.00. ISBN 0-86650-109-6

The Irrationality of History and the Tragedy of Mankind. Am. Inst. Psych. 1991 $327.00. ISBN 0-89920-249-7

Marxism and the Philosophy of History. Found. Class. Reprints 1986 $117.75. ISBN 0-89901-292-2. An intellectual annihilation of the Marxist theory of history.

The Philosophy of History. Found. Class. Reprints 1983 $127.75. ISBN 0-89901-128-4. Analysis and modification of Hegelian historical idealism. Difficult for readers not grounded in philosophy.

Proust and the Psychology of Decadence in History. Am. Inst. Psych. 1989 $317.00. ISBN 0-8047-0950-5

BOOKS ABOUT CROCE

Bosanquet, B. *Croce's Aesthetic.* Gordon Pr. 1974 $59.95. ISBN 0-87968-969-2. Standard analysis of this aspect of Croce's philosophy, using his literary interpretations.

Carr, H. W. *Time and History in Contemporary Philosophy with Special Reference to Bergson and Croce.* Gordon Pr. 1974 $59.95. ISBN 0-8490-2750-0. Technical study contrasting the intuitionism of the one with the neo-idealism of the other.

Collingwood, R. G. *The Idea of History.* Ed. by T. M. Knox. OUP 1946 $11.95. ISBN 0-19-500205-9. Treats the essentials of Croce's philosophy as he applied it to thinking and writing about history.

De Gennaro, Angelo A. *Philosophy of Benedetto Croce: An Introduction.* Citadel Pr. 1961 $1.50. ISBN 0-8065-0080-8. For students, the best brief and understandable explanation of Croce's philosophy.

Roberts, D. D. *Benedetto Croce and the User of Historicism.* U. CA Pr. 1987 $42.50. ISBN 0-520-05904. Highly technical study. Most useful to theorists of historical causation.

HEGEL, GEORG WILHELM FRIEDRICH. 1770–1831

Born the son of a government clerk in Stuttgart, Germany, George Wilhelm Friedrich Hegel received his education at Tübingen in theology. At age 35, after serving some years as a tutor, he became professor at the University of Jena. In 1808 he took a position as rector of a *Gymnasium* at Nuremberg, where he remained for the next eight years. A professorship at Heidelberg followed and then a professorship at Berlin. Arguably the most influential philosopher of the nineteenth century, Hegel's lectures—most notably at the University of Berlin from 1818 to his death—deeply influenced not only philosophers and historians but generations of political activists of both the Right and Left, champions of the all-powerful nation-state on the one hand and KARL MARX on the other. His lectures at Berlin were the platform from which he set forth the system elaborated in his writings.

At the heart of Hegel's philosophy is his philosophy of history. In his view, history works in a series of dialectical steps—thesis, antithesis, synthesis. His whole system is founded on the great triad—the Idea as thesis, Nature as antithesis, and the Spirit as synthesis. The Idea is God's will; Nature is the material world, including man; Spirit is man's self-consciousness of the Idea, his coming to an understanding of God's will. The formation over time of this consciousness is History.

Spirit does not exist in the abstract for Hegel, but is comprehended in "peoples," cultures, or civilizations, in practice *states*. Hegelian Freedom is only possible in organized states, where a National Spirit can be realized. This National Spirit, a part of the World Spirit, is realized in History largely through the actions of World Historical Individuals, heroes such as Napoleon, who embody that Spirit. A profound misunderstanding of this doctrine led many German intellectuals to subvert it into a narrow, authoritarian nationalism that glorified the "state" as an end in itself.

Although Hegel saw his philosophy as universal, applicable throughout the world, the focus and inspiration of his thought was European. And in his own even smaller world, he was content to support and work for the Prussian state, which he believed to be the highest development of history up to that time.

BOOKS BY HEGEL

The Essential Writings. Ed. by F. G. Weiss. HarpC 1977 $13.00. ISBN 0-06-131831-0. The best way to get an overview of Hegel's philosophical ideas.

The Philosophy of History. Trans. by J. Sibree. Prometheus Bks. 1990 $9.95. ISBN 0-87975-631-4. Hegelian conceptions of the history of the Greeks, Romans, and German peoples; outlines his larger philosophical principles.

BOOKS ABOUT HEGEL

Caird, Edward. *Hegel.* AMS Pr. repr. of 1883 ed. $22.50. ISBN 0-004-01362-7. Standard biography of the German philosopher-historian.

Inwood, M. J. *Hegel.* Routledge 1984 $13.95. ISBN 0-7100-9509-0. Short account that includes the most recent thinking.

Perkins, Robert L., ed. *History and System: Hegel's Philosophy of History.* State U. NY Pr. 1984 $59.50. ISBN 0-87395-814-4. Contains fresh insights but is rather technical for the lay reader.

Plant, R. *Hegel.* Blackwell Pubs. 1984 $8.95. ISBN 0-631-13334-8. Good biography for students.

Wilkins, Burleigh T. *Hegel's Philosophy of History.* Cornell Univ. Pr. 1974 $28.50. ISBN 0-8014-0819-9. Excellent explication of Hegel's thought.

HERDER, JOHANN GOTTFRIED. 1744–1803

By far the most influential of the eighteenth-century's proto-Romantic philosophers of world history, Johann Herder was a Protestant pastor who spent much of his life serving and sermonizing the Weimar court. Born in East Prussia, he was educated in theology at Königsberg. Partly as a reaction against the linear, rationalistic history of the Enlightenment and partly as a consequence of his own Pietistic religious beliefs, he came to view world history in terms of a myriad of separate cultures, or *Volker*, each derived from common ancestors but each developing and evolving in its own way and each possessing its own special and inestimable genius. For Herder, history consisted of the story of individual culture, or *Volk*, and the tragedies of history occurred when one *Volk* subjugated another or was removed from its own unique geographic and climatic environment, or *Klima*. Herder's philosophy of history was welcomed by all those *Volker* who believed themselves oppressed or subjugated, most notably the ethnic groups of the Russian and Austro-Hungarian empires, and his views became a principal justification for nineteenth-century cultural nationalism.

Books by Herder

Reflections on the Philosophy of the History of Mankind. Bks. Demand $111.60. ISBN 0-
    8357-7007-9. His masterwork explains his major thesis on the nature of historical
    developments.

Books about Herder

Koepke, Wulf. *J. G. Herder.* Macmillan 1987 $26.95. ISBN 0-8057-6634-0. A standard
    biography.
Meuller-Vollmer, Kurt, ed. *Herder Today.* De Gruyter 1990 $121.00. ISBN 3-11-011739-8.
    Examines the newest interpretations of Herder's work.

KENNAN, GEORGE F(ROST). 1904–

[See Chapter 15 in this volume.]

KOHN, HANS. 1891–1971

Known as "one of the great teachers of our day," Hans Kohn received his
doctorate from the German University in his native city of Prague. Taken
prisoner by the Russians in World War I, he was sent to Turkestan and Siberia,
where he witnessed the Russian Revolution and Civil War. Afterward he settled
in Jerusalem and wrote several books on the history and politics of the Middle
East. In 1931 he came to the United States, and in 1934, after a period of
lecturing at the New School for Social Research in New York, became professor
of modern European history at Smith College. In 1949 he went to City College,
New York, where he was made emeritus professor in 1962. Kohn's work, *Living
in a World Revolution: My Encounters with History* (1964), is a highly personal
book in which he discusses the impact on himself and on western civilization of
two world wars, the Russian Revolution, and the dissolution of European
colonialism. An earlier work, *The Idea of Nationalism* (1944), had established
him as the outstanding authority on the problem of nationalism.

Books by Kohn

The Age of Nationalism: The First Era of Global History. Greenwood 1976 repr. of 1962 ed.
    $39.95. ISBN 0-8371-9087-8. The author's classic statement of his ideas.
Nationalism and Imperialism in the Hither East. Fertig 1932 $45.00. ISBN 0-86527-139-9.
    Remains a useful study.
Revolutions and Dictatorships. Ayer 1939 $25.50. ISBN 0-8369-1145-8. Work, published at
    the outbreak of World War II, that made Kohn's reputation.

LENIN, VLADIMIR ILYICH (ULYANOV). 1870–1924

Born Vladimir Ilyich Ulyanov in the Russian trading center of Simbirsk, the
son of middle-class parents, Lenin's early training was in law. After his older
brother's 1887 execution for involvement in a plot against Tsar Alexander III,
the teenage Lenin dedicated himself entirely to revolutionary causes. Jailed and
exiled several times to Siberia for these activities, in 1900 he went to live in
London, where he headed the Bolshevik revolutionary party. He returned to his
homeland at the time of the abortive revolution of 1905, but in 1907 again went
abroad, writing and speaking in Marxist terms to promote the uprising of the
Russian working classes. At the outbreak of the 1917 revolution he left
Switzerland, where he had been living, and returned to Russia. With the victory
of the Bolsheviks over the Kerensky government, Lenin assumed the powerful
post of chairman of the Council of People's Commissars. By now also chairman
of the Communist party, he played the major role in suppressing the Christian

churches, establishing the Third International, and laying the groundwork for Communist control of what was for many decades the Soviet Union.

BOOKS BY LENIN

The Communist Interpretation of the Philosophy of Karl Marx. 2 vols. Am. Classical Coll. Pr. 1983 $187.50. ISBN 0-89266-423-1. Indispensable to understanding the theories and ideology behind the Bolshevik party.

Complete Collected Works. 45 vols. Imported Pubns. 1980 o.p. 45 volumes that span from his earliest writings to his death.

Dictatorships and the Passage from Capitalism to Communism. 2 vols. Ins. Econ. Finan. 1987 $277.50. ISBN 0-86722-149-6. Lenin applies a Marxist forecast to the economic and political future.

Economic Thought and the Problem of the Unity of the World. 2 vols. Inst. Econ. Pol. 1987 $257.50. ISBN 0-86722-152-6

Imperialism, The Highest Stage of Capitalism. 1916. China Bks. 1975 repr. of 1965 ed. $3.95. ISBN 0-8351-0113-4. Brilliant look at the European nations' greed and exploitation overseas in the years before World War I.

Letters of Lenin. Ed. and trans. by E. Hill and D. Mudie. Hyperion Conn. 1973 repr. of 1937 ed. $32.40. ISBN 0-88355-045-8

Selected Works. 3 vols. Imported Pubns. 1977 o.p.

State and Revolution: Marxist Teachings about the Theory of the State and the Tasks of the Proletariat in the Revolution. 1917. Greenwood 1978 repr. of 1935 ed. $35.00. ISBN 0-313-20351-2. Brilliant and fascinating primer for Communist revolutionaries.

What Is To Be Done? 1902. Viking Penguin 1990 $7.95. ISBN 0-14-018126-1. Lenin's program for creating and using a disciplined party to lead the revolution.

BOOKS ABOUT LENIN

Clark, R. W. *Lenin.* Borg. Pr. 1991 $27.00. ISBN 0-8095-9128-6. Balanced, unbiased biography, entirely up-to-date in its sources.

Pomper, P. *Lenin, Trotsky and Stalin: The Intelligentsia and Power.* Col. U. Pr. 1990 $47.50. ISBN 0-231-06906-5. Well-conceived study of the background to the power struggles of the 1920s.

Resnick, Abraham. *Lenin: Founder of the Soviet Union.* Childrens 1987 $18.60. ISBN 0-516-03260-7. Easy-to-read life of Lenin targeted for a young audience.

Service, R. *Lenin: A Political Life.* Vol. 2 *Worlds in Collision.* Ind. U. Pr. 1991 $39.95. ISBN 0-253-33325-3. Judicious biography that is becoming standard.

MAHAN, ALFRED THAYER. 1840–1914

The greatest U.S. military historian and one of the most influential of all nineteenth-century historians, Alfred Thayer Mahan was the son of an instructor at West Point. The younger Mahan, however, attended Annapolis and embarked on a naval career seeing duty in the South Atlantic and Gulf of Mexico against the Confederacy. He taught briefly at Annapolis, but spent most of his academic career at the newly founded Naval War College in Newport, Rhode Island, where he eventually served as president. His lectures at the college formed the basis for his two major works, *The Influence of Sea Power upon History, 1660–1783*, published in 1890, and *The Influence of Sea Power upon the French Revolution and Empire, 1793–1812*, published two years later. These works attributed the dominance of Great Britain in world politics during the eighteenth and nineteenth centuries to its invincible navy. His ideas were picked up by THEODORE ROOSEVELT in the United States, by Admiral von Tirpitz in Germany, and by Admiral Togo in Japan, and used to justify the building of large U.S., German, and Japanese fleets. Indeed, Mahan was assigned some of the blame for the naval race before World War I. Mahan wrote other books on sea power as well as biographies of Horatio Nelson and David Farragut. He was a founder of the Navy League and fought throughout his life for a Panama Canal.

BOOKS BY MAHAN

The History and Management of Ocean Warfare: A Critique of Major Naval Contemporary Combats. Inst. Econ. Pol. 1987 repr. of 1903 ed. $277.00. ISBN 0-86722-142-9

The Influence of Sea Power on the French Revolution and Empire. 1892. 2 vols. Scholarly 1898 $33.00. ISBN 0-403-00193-5

The Influence of Sea Power upon History, 1660–1783. 1890. Dover 1987 repr. of 1894 ed. $11.95. ISBN 0-486-25509-3. Famous and influential text making the case for a strong navy.

The Interest of America in Sea Power, Present and Future. Ayer repr. of 1897 ed. $21.00. ISBN 0-8369-5583-8. Sets forth all the arguments that greatly influenced world leaders.

Life of Nelson, the Embodiment of the Sea Power of Great Britain. 2 vols. in 1. Scholarly 1899 $26.00. ISBN 0-403-00076-9. Still stands up well as a strictly military biography.

Mahan on Naval Strategy: Selections from the Writings of Rear Admiral Alfred Thayer Mahan. Naval Inst. 1991 $32.95. ISBN 1-55750-556-X. Excellent selection. Plenty of grist for the mill of anyone but the specialist. Introduction by J. B. Hattendorf.

Major Operations of the Navies in the War of American Independence. Greenwood 1969 $35.00. ISBN 0-8371-1002-5. Discusses the battles in technical detail with little wider context.

A Military and Historical Analysis of the Great Wars of the 17th and 18th Centuries. 2 vols. Inst. Econ. Pol. repr. of 1895 ed. $277.00. ISBN 0-86722-100-3. Preparatory work for *The Influence of Sea Power upon History.*

The Panama Canal and the Sea Power in the Pacific. Inst. Econ. Pol. 1983 repr. of 1913 ed. $217.00. ISBN 0-86722-027-9. Offers the naval justification for the canal.

BOOKS ABOUT MAHAN

Livezey, William E. *Mahan on Sea Power.* U. of Okla. Pr. 1986 $18.95. ISBN 0-8061-1918-7. Still the best exposition of Mahan's thought.

Turk, R. W. *The Ambiguous Relationship: Theodore Roosevelt and Alfred Thayer Mahan.* Greenwood 1987 $42.95. ISBN 0-313-25644-6. A most interesting study of the naval theorist's influence on the president.

McNEILL, WILLIAM H(ARDY). 1917–

Born in Canada, William H. McNeill was chairman of the Department of History at the University of Chicago and one of the editors of the *Readings in World History Series* published by Oxford University Press. His one-volume *A World History*, which gives equal space to Asia and the West, was greeted as a work of major importance by such recognized historians as ARNOLD TOYNBEE, HANS KOHN, Geoffrey Bruun, Stringfellow Barr, and John Barkham.

Toynbee has acclaimed McNeill's *The Rise of the West*, which took nine years to write, as "the most lucid presentation of world history in narrative form that I know." It won the 1963 National Book Award for history and the Gordon J. Laing Prize of the University of Chicago.

BOOKS BY McNEILL

The Age of Gunpowder Empires: 1450–1800. Am. Hist. Assn. 1989 $6.00. ISBN 0-87229-043-3. McNeill has made military matters and European expansion overseas a special interest.

Arnold J. Toynbee: A Life. OUP 1989 $30.00. ISBN 0-19-505863-1. Solid biography that shows that McNeill understands Toynbee.

A History of the Human Community. P-H 1989. ISBN 0-13-391301-5. Latest and best of the author's several books that try to cover world history. As good as any "text" in English.

Plagues and People. Peter Smith 1992 $19.50. ISBN 0-8446-6492-8. Fascinating attempt to explain great chunks of much of world history in terms of disease.

Polyethnicity and National Unity in World History. U. of Toronto Pr. $10.95. ISBN 0-8020-6643-7. Far-ranging essay on ethnic groups and nationalism.

Population and Politics since 1750. U. Pr. of Va. 1990 $15.00. ISBN 0-8139-1257-1. Explains history by demography.

The Pursuit of Power: Technology, Armed Force and Society since A.D. 1000. U. Ch. Pr. 1984 $12.95. ISBN 0-226-56158-5. Brilliant analysis of the transformation of European armies and navies and the political, social, and economic effects to the nineteenth century.

The Rise of the West: A History of the Human Community. 1963. U. Ch. Pr. 1991 $19.95. ISBN 0-226-56141-0. Reprint, with some changes, of the classic—indeed the first—respectable world history.

Venice: The Hinge of Europe: 1081–1797. 1974. U. Ch. Pr. 1986 $18.95. ISBN 0-226-56149-6. A more specific case study that is not as successful as the author's broader, more synthetic works.

MARX, KARL. 1818–1883

German philosopher and revolutionary, Karl Marx was a scholar and polemicist of broad interests who may be categorized as an economist, as a sociologist, even as a philosopher. But first and foremost he was a historian—and a very good one. Using his own version of Hegelian dialectic, he formulated a theory of history that explained society and humankind's place in it from the beginning of recorded time to his own day. Most of the theory he worked out while in political exile, first in Paris, then in Brussels, and finally in London, where he worked at the British Museum and observed Britain's industrialization with a critical eye.

Like GEORG HEGEL, Marx considered his historical theories universally applicable although he derived them exclusively from a study of Europe. Also like Hegel, his history is deterministic, a history that evolves dialectically, phase by phase, according to a theses-antithesis-synthesis pattern. But for Marx the driving force is an inanimate economic process, and every dialectical phase is characterized by its mode of production, the way people satisfy their material needs at that time. Hence, "dialectical materialism." One of two components of the mode of production is productive relations, the relationships between the people engaged in producing material goods, the most important of which is that between the owners of the means of production—land, machinery—and the workers who use them. This relationship divides all known human societies into classes, into slave and master, peasant and landlord, proletarian and capitalist. The mode of production and the class conflict it creates, the economic "substructure," give form and character to the social, political, and cultural "superstructure" at any given time and place in human history. For Marx, this process was determined with absolute, indeed "scientific," certainty. And, of course, it would continue beyond his own time, until the "victory of the proletariat" finally eliminated class conflict.

The impact of Marx and Marxism resounded throughout the world. The Marxist explanation of World History has and still does make sense to many political activists and historians. While pure Marxist theory has ceased to be a major historical methodology, most contemporary historians have been influenced by it in their thinking about the past.

BOOKS BY MARX

Capital. 1867–1894. Ed. by Frederick Engels. Regal Pubn. 1992 repr. of 1906 ed. $49.00.
    ISBN 1-877767-76-X. Detailed analysis of how dialectical materialism works to
    produce capitalism and how capitalism will give way to socialism.
The Civil War in France. C. H. Kerr 1934 $19.95. ISBN 0-88286-035-6. Vindication of the
    Paris Commune of 1870.
Communist Manifesto. 1848. With Frederick Engels. Viking Penguin 1985 $3.50. ISBN 0-
    14-044478-5. The classic volume that lays down the guiding principles for worldwide
    communism.
Early Writings. Trans. by R. Livingston and G. Benton. Viking Penguin 1992 $9.95. ISBN
    0-14-044574-9. Essays that span from Marx's views on the Jewish question to the rise
    of socialism.
The Eighteenth Brumaire of Louis Bonaparte. Intl. Pubs. Co. 1963 $4.95. ISBN 0-394-
    72005-9. Brilliant historical synthesis. The how and why of Napoleon III's rise to
    power.
The Portable Karl Marx. Viking Penguin 1983 $9.95. ISBN 0-14-015096-X. Excellent
    selection of Marx's most influential writings.
Poverty of Philosophy. Intl. Pubs. Co. 1992 $6.95. ISBN 0-7178-0701-0. Marx's attack on
    nineteenth-century French social theorist Pierre Proudhon.

BOOKS ABOUT MARX

Althusser, L. *Montesquieu, Rousseau and Marx: Politics and History.* Routledge 1982
    $14.95. ISBN 0-902308-96-3. Traces certain of Marx's ideas from the Enlightenment.
Appelbaum, R. P. *Karl Marx.* Sage 1988 $39.95. ISBN 0-8039-2579-4. Solid biography that
    takes into account all the newest ideas and research.
Arineri, S. *Social and Political Thought of Karl Marx.* Cambridge U. Pr. 1970 $54.95. ISBN
    0-521-04070-X. Good, well-balanced treatment of Marx's social and political thought.
Berlin, I. *Karl Marx: His Life and Environment.* OUP 1978 $9.95. ISBN 0-19-520052-7.
    Seminal work when first published. One of the most perceptive biographies even
    today.
Bottomore, T., ed. *Interpretations of Marx.* Blackwell Pubs. 1988 $75.00. ISBN 0-631-
    15255-5. Indispensable for understanding Marx, particularly the history of the
    development of his thought.
Brewer, A. *Marxist Theories on Imperialism: A Critical Survey.* Routledge 1991 $66.00.
    ISBN 0-415-04468-5. A survey and reassessment of Marx's theories of imperialism
    and the evolution of capitalism.
Cohen, G. A. *Karl Marx's Theory of History: A Defence.* Princeton U. Pr. 1980 $39.50. ISBN
    0-691-07175-6. Lively and almost convincing attempt to make history subject to the
    bonds of dialectic.
Conway, D. *A Farewell to Marx: An Outline and Appraisal of His Theories.* Viking Penguin
    1987 $6.95. ISBN 0-14-022365-7. Excellent and pleasantly down-to-earth summary of
    Marx's ideas. Especially good for students new to the subject.
Elser, J., ed. *Karl Marx: A Reader.* Cambridge U. Pr. 1986 $12.95. ISBN 0-521-29705-2.
    Especially thoughtful anthology. Excellent for students to get at the meat of Marx.
Katz, C. T. *From Feudalism to Capitalism: Marxian Theories of Class Struggle and Social
    Change.* Greenwood 1989 $42.95. ISBN 0-313-26423-6. Good, clear, sympathetic
    exposition of Marx's "laws" of history.
Miller, R. W. *Analyzing Marx: Morality, Power and History.* Princeton U. Pr. 1984 $47.00.
    ISBN 0-691-06613-2. Develops a more political interpretation of Marxist thought in
    the field of human relations.
Shaw, W. H. *Marx's Theory of History.* Stanford U. Pr. 1978 $27.50. ISBN 0-8047-1059-7.
    Perhaps the best, and certainly the easiest to understand, exposition of Marx's
    theory.

NEHRU, JAWAHARLAL. 1889–1964

[SEE Chapter 14 in this volume.]

SPENGLER, OSWALD. 1880–1936

German historian and philosopher Oswald Spengler studied at the universities of Munich, Berlin, and Halle. Although originally trained in the natural sciences and mathematics, he read widely in history, philosophy, and literature.

In 1918, Spengler published the first volume of his two-volume master work, *The Decline of the West* (1918–1922). Written during World War I, when Spengler was living in extreme poverty in Munich, the work has as its theme the rise and decline of civilization. Spengler, who believed that present occidental civilization had reached its period of decadence and was about to be conquered by the Mongolian people of Asia, revised his work in the period of despair following the war, and the 1923 edition brought him wealth and fame. Because of his dislike of "non-Aryan" peoples and his belief in the ideal of obedience to the state he was popular with the Nazis when they first sought power. But when he refused to participate in their anti-Semitic activities, he was ostracized. Although allowed to stay in Germany and to keep his property, the last years of his life were spent under the cloud of official disfavor.

BOOKS BY SPENGLER

The Decline of the West. 1918–1922. 2 vols. Knopf 1945 $80.00. ISBN 0-394-42178-7. Traces world history from the development of cities and cultures, the rise of states, and the impact of political and economic life.

The Hour of Decision. Trans. by C. F. Atkinson. AMS Pr. repr. of 1934 ed. $27.50. ISBN 0-404-16988-0. Prophetic analysis of events in the early 1930's in Germany; predicted war in 1934.

The Problem of World History and the Destiny of Mankind. 2 vols. Inst. Econ. Pol. 1987 $189.75. ISBN 0-86722-159-3

World History: The Destiny-Idea and the Causality-Principle. Found. Class. Reprints 1984 $137.95. ISBN 0-89901-176-4

BOOKS ABOUT SPENGLER

Fischer, K. D. *History and Prophecy: Oswald Spengler and the Decline of the West.* P. Lang Pubs. 1989 $30.95. ISBN 0-8204-1071-3. Competent but very academic study.

Hughes, H. Stuart. *Oswald Spengler.* Transaction Pubs. 1991 $18.75. ISBN 1-56000-576-9. Splendid analysis by a distinguished historian of ideas that sets Spengler in his intellectual context.

STALIN, JOSEPH (VISSARIONOVICH). 1879–1953

Born Josif Vissarionovich Dzhugashvili to humble parents in Gori, Georgia, Joseph Stalin first became interested in Marxism while he was studying for the priesthood. Those studies ended abruptly with his expulsion for revolutionary activities aimed at the overthrow of the tsar. After various periods of arrest and escape or imprisonment, he became a follower of LENIN. Between 1903 and 1913, he wrote revolutionary material. Around 1913 he took the name Stalin, "man of steel." An editor of the embryo Communist paper *Pravda*, in 1917 he took charge of the newspaper and began his rise to power in the Communist party, eventually becoming the leading member of the triumvirate that ruled the U.S.S.R. after Lenin's death. During the period of his dictatorship, which followed, many of his former comrades perished in purges he initiated.

During World War II, after Nazi Germany broke the mutual nonaggression agreement it had signed with Russia, Stalin joined the Allies. During and after the Allied victory he met with the other Allied leaders—Churchill, Roosevelt, and Truman—at the Teheran, Yalta, and Potsdam conferences. His postwar takeover of the countries of eastern Europe helped launch the cold war.

At his death, Stalin received the funeral of a state hero and was buried next to Lenin in Moscow's Red Square. In 1961, after Nikita Khrushchev had denounced him and his policies, his body was moved to the cemetery for heroes near the Kremlin Wall. In March 1969, about two years after Stalin's daughter Svetlana Alliluyeva caused a sensation when she abandoned the U.S.S.R. and her family to seek haven in the United States, *Pravda* began issuing excerpts from the new novel *They Fought for Their Country* by Mikhail Sholokhov, which imply that Stalin was unaware of the activities of his secret police in pursuing the purges of the 1930s. Svetlana also produced a work on her father—*Twenty Letters to a Friend: A Memoir.* In it she cast new light on Stalin's private life and her mother's suicide. She refrains from expressing active hostility to her father and believes that he was to some extent deceived by Beria, chief of his secret police. Of the many biographical studies of Stalin, however, one of the most fascinating is that by LEON TROTSKY. In the introduction to the 1967 edition, Bertram D. Wolfe writes: "In all literature there is no more dramatic relationship between author and subject. . . . It is like Robespierre doing a life of Fouche, Kurbsky of Ivan the Terrible, Muenzer of Martin Luther."

BOOKS BY STALIN

The Great Patriotic War of the Soviet Union. 1945. Greenwood 1970 repr. of 1945 ed. $38.50. ISBN 0-8371-2559-6. Collection of radio addresses, speeches, and writings that Stalin gave in the early stages of World War II.

The October Revolution: A Collection of Articles and Speeches. AMS Pr. repr. of 1934 ed. $16.50. ISBN 0-404-15372-0. Survey of Stalin's thinking on the direction and purpose of the October Revolution.

Stalin on China: A Collection of Five Writings on the Chinese Question. Hyperion Conn. 1977 repr. of 1951 ed. $15.00. ISBN 0-88355-392-9. Stalin's thoughts on China's approach to the construction of a Communist state.

Works. 1952–1955. 3 vols. Ed. by R. H. McNeal. Hoover Inst. 1967 o.p. Three-volume survey of Stalin's thought on a variety of subjects.

BOOKS ABOUT STALIN

Adams, A. E. *Stalin and His Times.* Waveland Pr. 1986 $10.95. ISBN 0-88133-250-X. Standard biography for students.

Bullock, A. *Hitler and Stalin: Parallel Lives.* Knopf 1992 $34.50. ISBN 0-394-58601-8. Brilliant, necessarily controversial, comparative study by the distinguished biographer of Hitler.

Chapman, D. *Stalin: Man of Steel.* Longman 1988 $11.64. ISBN 0-582-85749-X. Good biography for the nonexpert.

Daniels, R. V. *Trotsky, Stalin and Socialism.* Westview 1991 $41.50. ISBN 0-8133-1223-X. Interesting study of conflicting ideas. A bit sympathetic to Trotsky.

De Jonge, A. *Stalin.* Morrow 1987 $15.00. ISBN 0-688-07291-7. Solid, standard, not very lively biography.

Deutcher, Isaac. *Stalin: A Political Biography.* OUP $17.95. ISBN 0-19-500273-3. A slightly dated classic study still valuable for its analysis of Stalin's *Works.*

Hoobler, T., and D. Hoobler. *Joseph Stalin.* Chelsea Hse. 1985 $17.95. ISBN 0-87754-576-6. Good young people's biography.

Krushchev, N. S. *Anatomy of Terror.* Greenwood 1979 repr. of 1956 ed. $35.00. ISBN 0-313-21218-X. Relates the horrifying truth about Stalin's reign.

Marrin, A. *Stalin: Russia's Man of Steel.* Viking Penguin 1988 $14.95. ISBN 0-670-82102-0. High-quality study for young people that examines Stalin's life and political career.

Matlock, J. F. *An Index to the Collected Works of J. V. Stalin.* Kraus 1955 $29.00. ISBN 0-8115-3800-1

McNeal, R. H. *Stalin: Man and Ruler.* NYU Pr. 1988 $40.00. ISBN 0-8147-5443-0. Excellent popular biography.

Rapoport, L. *Stalin's War Against Jews: The Doctor's Plot and the Soviet Solution.* Free Pr. 1990 $22.95. ISBN 0-02-925821-9

Slusser, R. M. *Stalin in October: The Man Who Missed the Revolution.* Johns Hopkins 1987 $40.00. ISBN 0-8018-3457-0. Interesting and detailed study of Stalin's activities during the October Revolution.

Spriano, P. *Stalin and the European Communists.* Trans. by J. Rothchild. Routledge 1985 $29.95. ISBN 0-86091-103-9. Important study by an Italian scholar of Europe's ambivalent Communists.

TOYNBEE, ARNOLD J(OSEPH). 1889–1975

A native of Great Britain, Oxford-educated Arnold J. Toynbee was a prolific scholar who had a varied and interesting political and academic career. He served in the British foreign office during both world wars and was a delegate to the 1919 Paris Peace Congress. From 1925 to 1955, he held the position of director of studies at the Royal Institute of International Affairs and was professor of history at the University of London during approximately the same time. Toynbee was always a controversial historian who made sweeping generalizations about history that were often criticized by other scholars. Of himself, he wrote: "What I am trying to do is explain to Western people that they are only a small minority of the world—the great world is Asia and Africa— outside the West."

Among Toynbee's publications are *East to West: A Journey round the World* (1958), a collection of world portraits of contemporary affairs and conditions in ancient settings, and *Between Oxus and Jumna* (1961), an unsurpassed travel guide to a little-known, rugged area encompassing Afghanistan, western Pakistan, and northwest India. But his major work is without doubt his *A Study of History* (1934–1961), his investigation into the growth and decay of civilizations, which took him 40 years of steady labor. In this work Toynbee examines all of recorded history and concludes that each civilization is subject to a cycle of early struggle, growth, and then decline. Rather than revise all the volumes of this monumental work, he decided to correct errors and refute his critics, in the twelfth volume of the set, *Reconsiderations* (1961)

At age 80, Toynbee was still going strong and continuing to work a seven-day week. "I suppose that one day I might stop, and if I stopped I might suddenly crumple," he said. "It is very important to keep going."

BOOKS BY TOYNBEE

Between Oxus and Jumna. Bks. Demand o.p.

Change and Habit: The Challenge of Our Time. Bks. Demand $60.00. ISBN 0-317-29814-3

Christianity and Civilization. Pendle Hill 1947 $3.00. ISBN 0-87574-039-1. The essence of Toynbee's theory of historical causation.

Hellenism: The History of a Civilization. Greenwood repr. of 1959 ed. 1981 $35.00. ISBN 0-313-22742-X. Shows how good a historian Toynbee really was when working in his special field.

Mankind and Mother Earth: A Narrative History of the World. OUP 1976 $39.95. ISBN 0-19-215257-2. Interesting attempt, but very old-fashioned in its approach and conclusions.

A Study of History. 12 vols. OUP Vols. 1–6 1961 o.p. Vols. 7–10 OUP 1954 $65.00. ISBN 0-19-519689-9. Vol. 11 *Historical Atlas and Gazetter.* 1959 $36.50. ISBN 0-19-215223-8. Vol. 12 *Reconsiderations.* 1961 $25.00. ISBN 0-19-500197-4

A Study of History. 10 vols. Abbr. ed. by D. C. Somervell. OUP Vols. 1–6 1987 $14.95. ISBN 0-19-505080-0. Vols. 7–10 1987 $14.95 ISBN 0-19-505081-9. The best way to get at Toynbee's purpose and thought.

BOOKS ABOUT TOYNBEE

Neilson, F. *Toynbee's Study of History*. Revisionist Pr. 1979 $49.95. ISBN 0-685-96644-5. Not entirely sympathetic critical analysis.

Ortega y Gasset, J. *An Interpretation of Universal History*. Trans. by M. Adams. Norton 1984 $7.95. ISBN 0-393-00751-0. Brilliant, but tells more about Ortega's thought than Toynbee's.

Rabinowitz, O. K. *Arnold Toynbee on Judaism and Zionism: A Critique*. Beekman Pubs. 1975 $25.00. ISBN 0-8464-0149-9

TROTSKY, LEON. 1879–1940

Leon Trotsky was born Lev Davidovich Bronshteyn, the son of a prosperous Jewish farmer in the Ukraine. Sent to Odessa for his secondary-school education, he became a member of a Marxist circle in 1896. Imprisoned many times, he escaped from exile in Siberia in 1902 by using the name of a jailer called Trotsky on a false passport. During World War I, he lived in Switzerland, France, and New York City, where he edited the newspaper *Novy Mir (New World)*. In 1917, after the overthrow of Tsar Nicholas II, he went back to Russia and joined LENIN in the first, abortive, July Revolution of the Bolsheviks. A key organizer of the successful October Revolution, he was People's Commissar for Foreign Affairs in the Lenin regime. But antagonism developed between him and JOSEPH STALIN during the Civil War of 1918–20, and after Lenin's death Stalin exiled him. Trotsky fled across Siberia to Norway, France, and finally Mexico, carrying with him source material on his experiences in the revolution. In Mexico he began working on the biography of his bitter enemy Stalin in a heavily barred and guarded home in Coyoacan. He realized he was racing against time and was able to complete 7 of the 12 chapters before a member of the Soviet secret police managed to work his way into the household by posing as a convert to Trotskyism. An attempt made on Trotsky's life in May 1940 was unsuccessful. Two months later another attempt was made. This one was successful—Trotsky was killed with a pickax at the desk where he was writing "Stalin," and the manuscript was spattered with its author's blood. The construction of the remaining five chapters was accomplished by the translator Charles Malamuth, from notes, worksheets, and fragments. Malamuth's translation of the initial chapters had been completed and checked by Trotsky before his death.

A ruthless, energetic, and messianic visionary, Trotsky inspired both confidence and mistrust among those around him. In his later years, he was the focus of communists opposed to Stalin. A writer of power and venom, he was an advocate of permanent world revolution.

BOOKS BY TROTSKY

Case of Leon Trotsky: Report of Charges Made Against Him in the Moscow Trials. Pathfinder NY 1968 repr. of 1937 ed. $70.00. ISBN 0-87348-037-6. Trotsky responds to treason accusations made against him.

Diary in Exile, 1935. HUP 1976 $18.50. ISBN 0-674-91006-0. Excerpts from a diary that Trotsky kept from February to September 1935 during his second exile to France and his move to Norway.

History of the Russian Revolution. 1932. Anchor Found. 1980 $35.00. ISBN 0-913460-83-4. Trotsky's masterwork. Essential to understanding the revolution.

My Life. 1930. Pathfinder NY 1970 $25.95. ISBN 0-87348-143-7. Autobiography written in 1929 that focuses on the second period of the Soviet revolution, Lenin's illness, and the beginning of the campaign against him.

The Permanent Revolution: Results and Prospects. Labor Pubns. Inc. 1992 $18.95. ISBN 0-929087-55-0. The best source for Trotsky's revolutionary theories.

Portraits, Political and Personal. Ed. by G. Breitman and G. Saunders. Pathfinder NY $45.00. ISBN 0-87348-504-1. Trotsky on his friends. Ideal for understanding Trotsky's mind.

Russian Revolution: The Overthrow of Czarism and the Triumph of the Soviets. 1932. Doubleday Abbr. ed. 1959 $9.95. ISBN 0-385-09398-5. Excellent condensation. Ideal for students.

Third International after Lenin. 1930. Pathfinder NY 1970 $24.95. ISBN 0-87348-185-2

Writings of Leon Trotsky. 14 vols. Pathfinder NY $350.00. ISBN 0-87348-730-3. Fourteen-volume collection that traces Trotsky's fortunes from the early days of the revolution to his time in exile.

Books about Trotsky

Alexander, R. J. *International Trotskyism, 1929–1985: A Documented Analysis of the Movement.* Duke 1991 $165.00. ISBN 0-8223-0975-0. Indispensable to the serious student of worldwide Communist revolutionary history.

Callinicos, A. *Trotskyism.* U. of Minn. Pr. 1990 $11.95. ISBN 0-8166-1905-0. Short and insightful. Ideal for students.

Deutscher, I. *The Profit Outcast: Trotsky, 1929–1940.* OUP 1980 $35.00. ISBN 0-19-281066-9. Brilliant study by a distinguished historian.

Knei-Paz, B. *The Social and Political Thought of Leon Trotsky.* OUP 1978 $29.95. ISBN 0-19-827234-0. The standard, detailed analysis.

Molyneux, J. *Leon Trotsky's Theory of Revolution.* St. Martin 1981 $25.00. ISBN 0-312-47994-8. Scholarly examination of Trotsky's political thought and philosophy.

Shanchez Salazar, L. A., and J. Gorkin. *Murder in Mexico.* Hyperion Conn. 1978 repr. of 1950 ed. $23.50. ISBN 0-88355-049-0. Details and speculation about Trotsky's assassination.

Sinclair, L. *Trotsky: A Bibliography.* Ashgate Pub. Co. 1989 $169.95. ISBN 0-85967-820-2. Definitive, in all languages.

TUCHMAN, BARBARA W(ERTHEIM). 1912–1989

[SEE Chapter 11 in this volume.]

WARD, BARBARA (LADY JACKSON). 1914–1981

British-born Barbara Ward was educated at the Sorbonne and Oxford, where she took first-class honors in philosophy, politics, and economics. In 1939 she joined the staff of the *Economist*, becoming foreign editor the following year. For four years, beginning in 1946, she served as a governor of the British Broadcasting Company. In the years that followed she was Carnegie Fellow and Visiting Scholar at Harvard, Albert Schweitzer Professor at Columbia, and a member of the Pontifical Commission of Justice and Peace.

An outstanding authority on world political, social, and economic issues, Barbara Ward has written many books for the general reader. In her *Five Ideas That Change the World* (1959) the ideas are nationalism, industrialism, colonialism, communism, and internationalism. In another work, *India and the West* (1961), she defined the urgency of India's desperate economic requirements and outlined a specific program for their accomplishment. Of it Edward Weeks wrote in the *Atlantic*: "Ward's new book . . . is in many respects the most important she has ever written. The qualities which she brings to her writing—her gift for historical analysis, her explanation of difficult economic problems, and her reasonable faith in the initiative of the free world—were never more needed."

The Rich Nations and the Poor Nations (1962), which President Lyndon Johnson remarked "excites and inspires me" and Adlai Stevenson found "exceedingly important," was described in the *New York Times Book Review* by Eric F. Goldman as "wondrously lucid, richly informed and trenchantly argued, tough-minded but never failing to assume that intelligence and will can move human society forward."

BOOKS BY WARD

Five Ideas That Change the World. Norton 1959 $6.95. ISBN 0-393-09438-3. Examination of the impact that nationalism, industrialism, colonialism, communism, and internationalism have had on world history.
The Home of Man. Norton 1976 $8.95. ISBN 0-393-06420-4
Interplay of East and West: Points of Conflict and Cooperation. Norton 1962 $1.25. ISBN 0-393-00162-8
Progress for a Small Planet. 1962. Norton 1979 $14.95. ISBN 0-393-01277-8. She sees some hope in her last years.
Rich Nations and Poor Nations. Norton 1962 $5.95. ISBN 0-393-00746-4. Well-reasoned plea for developed nations to help developing nations.

CHAPTER 10

Ancient History

Pericles Georges

> I shall rest content if my words are judged useful by those who want to understand clearly these events of the past, which in accordance with human nature will necessarily repeat themselves at some future time and in much the same ways.
>
> —Thucydides 1.22

Although periods of history do not, in actual fact, have unequivocal beginnings or endings, most historians agree that the period commonly referred to as "ancient history" commences with the beginning of written records and ends in A.D. 476 with the fall of the Roman Empire of the West. In practice, however, some of these same historians include in their studies of ancient history the long period of prehistory before there were written records.

The study of ancient history, like that of any time distant from our own, involves a perpetual contest between the sense of the familiar and the sense of the alien. The Egyptians created a civilization that evolved into a rich, powerful, and united nation—a civilization that lasted for several thousand years. Egypt, which enjoyed the longest period of union and independence of any nation in the ancient world, influenced and intrigued many. The Greeks also created a civilization—one that in a relatively short period of time became one of the bases of all Western civilization. No other nation the size of Greece can boast such a profusion of contributions: in government, rule by the people, the first democratic constitution, and the first study of written government; in science, the scientific method and the basic rules of geometry; in philosophy, new ways of thinking; in the arts, tragedy, comedy, new styles of architecture, and magnificent sculpture; and, most important, a belief in the freedom and worth of the individual. Nor can the Roman legacy to Western civilization be ignored. Rome itself became a model for many European cities, and from the Roman system of law came the idea that there should be the same justice for all, an idea that helped shape the legal tradition of the Western world.

The ancient Greeks and Romans created much of our whole way of thinking—about good and evil, about war and peace, and about almost every other matter affecting human beings. At a more pedestrian level, they ate and drank, earned livings, raised families, died. In short, they shared the basic experiences of daily life with people of all times. At the same time, their economy was primitive and their technology more so. Only free male citizens had full rights. Slavery was standard. Pagan religion involved a relationship to the world that we of the modern industrial state find difficult to view or to enter into sympathetically. All of this—that which is familiar and that which is strange or alien in or about the world of the ancients—has been recaptured and brought to life by historians such as those whose works are listed on the following pages.

REFERENCE WORKS

Shatzman, Avi-Yonah, and Israel Shatzman. *Illustrated Encyclopedia of the Classical World*. HarpC 1975 o.p. Composed of 2,300 articles, covering themes, persons, and places of Greek and Roman history; index included.

Bowder, Diana, ed. *Who Was Who in the Roman World*. Cornell Univ. Pr. 1980 o.p. Historiography of the individuals who shaped the history of the Roman Empire.

Broughton, T. R. S. *Magistrates of the Roman Republic*. 3 vols. Scholars Pr. GA 1974 $44.95–$65.00. ISBNs 0-89130-706-0, 0-89130-812-1, 0-89130-811-3. An exhaustive annual listing of Rome's magistrates from the beginning of the Republic to the principate of Augustus, with full references to the sources and modern discussions.

The Cambridge Ancient History. 12 vols. Ed. by I. E. Edwards and others. Cambridge U. Pr. 1927–1992 $34.50–$160.00 ea. Massive and detailed reference work, with chapters by authorities on different periods and subjects and with extensive bibliographies. Not unified, and the quality of the sections varies greatly, but the only work of its scope in English. Treats the ancient Near East and Egypt in great detail. Vols. 1 and 2 cover prehistory and the ancient Near East; vols. 3–12 cover Greece and Rome.

Classical Scholarship. A Biographical Encyclopedia. Garland Reference Library of the Humanities. Ed. by Ward W. Briggs and William M. Calder III. Garland 1990 $110.00. ISBN 0-8240-8448-9. Discusses some 50 scholars active from 1977 to 1986 in signed essays, each accompanied by illustrations.

Hammond, N. G. L., and H. H. Scullard, eds. *Oxford Classical Dictionary*. OUP 1970 $55.00. ISBN 0-19-869117-3. Entries on all aspects of classical antiquity.

Kenney, E. J., ed. *Latin Literature*. HUP 1979 $55.00. ISBN 0-674-51295-2. Analysis and criticism of Latin literature.

Stillwell, Richard, ed. *The Princeton Encyclopedia of Classical Sites*. Bks. Demand repr. of 1976 ed. $160.00. ISBN 0-8357-7559-3. In need of updating but still the single most comprehensive reference guide to the archeological sites of the ancient world. Includes excellent bibliography.

Talbert, Richard J. *Atlas of Classical History*. Routledge 1989 $18.95. ISBN 0-415-03463-9. Perhaps the best inexpensive reference atlas. Covers Greek and Roman history from Troy and Knossos to the Roman Empire.

GENERAL WORKS

Bengtson, Hermann. *Introduction to Ancient History*. Trans. by R. I. Frank and F. D. Gilliard. U. CA Pr. 1976 $45.00. ISBN 0-520-03150-4. Translation of a standard German introductory manual for students. Very substantial bibliography about the ancient historians and ancient history.

Bickerman, Elias J., and Morton Smith. *The Ancient History of Western Civilization*. HarpC 1976 o.p. Very readable brief survey from prehistory to late antiquity.

Finley, Moses I. *Politics in the Ancient World*. Cambridge U. Pr. $7.95. ISBN 0-521-275570-9. Important comparative study of the nature of political life in the Greek city-states and in Rome under the institutions of the free Republic.

Grant, Michael, and Rachel Kitzinger, eds. *Civilization of the Ancient Mediterranean: Greece and Rome*. 3 vols. Scribner 1988 $195.00. ISBN 0-684-17594-0. Contains 100 signed articles arranged by subject, covering the period from 1000 B.C. to the fifth century A.D. Includes bibliographies, a chronology, and an index.

Harvey, Paul. *The Oxford Companion to Classical Literature*. 1937. OUP 1989 $45.00. ISBN 0-19-866121-5. Provides useful information on the forms, structure, and content of ancient classical literature.

The Oxford History of the Classical World. 2 vols. Ed. by J. Boardman, J. Griffin, and O. Murray. OUP 1986 $21.50 ea. Vol. 1 *Greece and the Hellenistic World*. Vol. 2 *The Roman World*. ISBNs 0-19-282165-2, 0-19-282166-0. Series of highly informative chapter-essays by specialists that address the history and the intellectual and artistic heritage of Mediterranean antiquity. Well illustrated; very useful bibliographies.

Ste.-Croix, G. E. M. de. *The Class Struggle in the Ancient Greek World: From the Archaic Age to the Arab Conquest*. Cornell Univ. Pr. 1981 $79.50. ISBN 0-8014-9597-0. Investigates social life and customs in ancient Greece and the class distinctions that existed.

Snowden, Frank M., Jr. *Before Color Prejudice: The Ancient View of Blacks*. HUP 1991 $12.95. ISBN 0-674-06381-3. Examines race relations in the ancient world.

————. *Blacks in Antiquity: Ethiopians in the Greco-Roman Experience*. HUP 1970 $11.95. ISBN 0-674-07626-5. Probes the impact of black art and civilization on ancient Greece and Rome.

Starr, Chester G. *A History of the Ancient World*. OUP 1991 $32.50. ISBN 0-19-506629-4. Well-balanced, somewhat detailed treatment covering from the Paleolithic period to the end of antiquity.

Trump, D. H. *The Prehistory of the Mediterranean*. Yale U. Pr. 1980 o.p. Surveys the history of the Mediterranean region before the rise of the classical Greek and Roman civilizations.

SOURCES AND DOCUMENTS

In the distant past, when historians said "no document, no history," they meant precisely that. In more recent years, the meaning has changed as the term "document" has been expanded to include many kinds of documentary sources, from ancient literary works to kitchen midden. Such traditional documents as letters, treaties, and chronicles continue to provide rare insights into the distant past. At the same time, much valuable information has been and will continue to be gleaned from such sources as coins, weapons, ornaments, utensils, jewelry, inscriptions, and remains of ancient art. The books listed here provide an introduction to some of these sources and to what one can learn from them.

Austin, Michel M. *The Hellenistic World from Alexander to the Roman Conquest: A Selection of Ancient Sources in Translation*. Cambridge U. Pr. 1981 $29.95. ISBN 0-521-22829-8. Analyzes the history of Greek Hellenistic civilization using firsthand accounts.

Bagnall, Roger, and Peter Derow. *Greek Historical Documents: The Hellenistic Period*. Scholars Pr. GA 1981 $15.95. ISBN 0-89130-496-7. Compilation and analysis of primary source materials from the period of about 325 B.C. to 146 B.C.

Burnstein, Stanley M. *The Hellenistic Age from the Battle of Ipsos to the Death of Kleopatra VII*. Cambridge U. Pr. 1985 $19.95. ISBN 0-521-28158-X. The next best thing to original source documents.

Crawford, Michael, ed. *Ancient Greece and Rome. Sources of History Ser.* Cambridge U. Pr. 1984 $22.95. ISBN 0-521-24782-9. Contributions on literature, epigraphy, archaeology, and numismatics. Shows how the ancient historian uses evidence to write history.

Crawford, Michael, and David Whitehead. *Archaic and Classical Greece: A Selection of Ancient Sources in Translation*. Cambridge U. Pr. 1983 $85.00. ISBN 0-521-22775-5. Fine collection of primary source documents from the Archaic and Classical periods.

Fornara, Charles W., and E. Badian, eds. *Translated Documents of Greece and Rome: Archaic Times to the End of the Peloponnesian War*. Vol. 1. Trans. by Charles W. Fornara. Johns Hopkins 1977 o.p. Traces the history of ancient Greek civilization through the writings of ancient historians.

Harding, Phillip. *From the End of the Peloponnesian War to the Battle of Ipsus*. Cambridge U. Pr. 1985 $54.95. ISBN 0-521-23435-2. Strictly literal, line for line translations.

Lewis, Naphtali. *Greek Historical Documents*. 2 vols. Samuel-Stevens 1971–74 o.p. A documentary history of ancient Greece; traces the rise and fall of Greek civilization.

Lewis, Naphtali, and Reinhold Meyer, eds. *Roman Civilization*. 2 vols. Col. U. Pr. 1990 $125.00. ISBN 0-231-07054-3. The most extensive collection of translated sources, inscriptions, papyri, and literary works.

Reynolds, L. D., and N. G. Wilson. *Scribes and Scholars: A Guide to the Transmission of Greek and Latin Literature*. OUP 1991 $89.00. ISBN 0-19-872145-5. An introduction to the history of texts. Helps the reader understand how the works of the ancient historians are preserved and what sorts of problems may be encountered in their texts.

Sherk, Robert K. *Rome and the Greek East to the Death of Augustine*. Cambridge U. Pr. 1984 $54.95. ISBN 0-521-24995-3

Turner, E. G. *Greek Papyri: An Introduction*. OUP 1932 ed. $29.95. ISBN 0-19-814841-0. The best introduction in English to the papyri and their contents, both literary and documentary. Lovingly detailed and lively in account.

Wickersham, John, and Gerald Verbrugghe. *Greek Historical Documents: The Fourth Century B.C.* Samuel-Stevens 1973 o.p. Mostly translations of Greek inscriptions.

ANCIENT CIVILIZATIONS OF WESTERN ASIA AND EGYPT

Aldred, Cyril. *The Egyptians. Ancient Peoples and Places Ser*. Thames Hudson 2nd rev. ed. 1987 $11.95. ISBN 0-500-27345-6. A standard, readable history of ancient Egypt.

Aubet, Maria E. *The Phoenicians and the West: Politics, Colonies and Trade*. Cambridge U. Pr. $59.95. ISBN 0-521-41141-6. The only detailed study on the trans-Mediterranean commerce of the Phoenician cities from Sidon to Carthage, on which the whole of this civilization rested.

Cook, J. M. *The Persian Empire*. 1983 o.p. Fundamental account marked by masterly use of literary and archeological evidence for the Achaemenid State.

Crawford, Harriet. *Sumer and the Sumerians*. Cambridge U. Pr. 1991 $44.95. ISBN 0-521-38175-4. Fresh and accessible overview (3800–2000 B.C.) based on current evidence.

Edwards, I. E. *The Pyramids of Egypt*. Viking Penguin 1975 $4.95. ISBN 0-14-022549-8. Investigates the construction of the pyramids and the various periods in which they were built.

Emery, Walter B. *Archaic Egypt*. Viking Penguin 1961 o.p. Basic history of the earliest Egyptian dynasties; focuses on the people and their culture.

Erman, Adolf, ed. *The Ancient Egyptians: A Source Book of Their Writings*. Peter Smith 1971 o.p. A survey of ancient Egypt through an analysis of primary source documents.

Frankfort, Henri, and others. *Before Philosophy*. Viking Penguin 1949 o.p. Explores the religious heritage and practices of ancient cultures.

Gardiner, Alan H. *Egypt of the Pharoahs: An Introduction*. OUP 1966 $14.95. ISBN 0-19-500267-9. Examines the power and authority of Egypt's pharaohs during different dynastic periods.

Gurney, O. R. *The Hitties*. Viking Penguin 1954 o.p. Traces the history of the Hittite empire from their origin in Asia minor to their fall at the hands of conquering Assyrians.

Hallo, William W., and William Kelly Simpson. *The Ancient Near East: A History*. HarpC 1971 $20.00. ISBN 0-15-502755-7. General survey of the civilizations of Asia Minor up to 622 B.C.

James, T. G. H., ed. *Excavating in Egypt: The Egypt Exploration Society, 1882–1982*. U. Ch. Pr. 1984 $14.95. ISBN 0-226-39192-2. Examines the history of archaeological exploration in ancient Egypt and the significant findings between 1882 and 1982.

Lichtheim, Miriam. *Ancient Egyptian Literature*. 3 vols. U. CA Pr. 1973–1980 $11.95–$37.50. ISBNs 0-520-02899-6, 0-520-03615, 0-520-03882-7. Analysis of ancient Egyptian literature and its importance to history.

Mallowan, M. E. L. *Early Mesopotamia and Iran*. McGraw 1965 o.p. Analysis of the archaeological finds in the region of Iraq and Iran and what they reveal about the region's history.

Mellaart, James. *Catal Huyuk: A Neolithic Town in Anatolia*. McGraw 1967 o.p. Discusses the archaeological findings from the Catal Huyuk mound in Turkey; analyzes the neolithic culture of the region as revealed by these excavations.

Renfrew, Colin. *Archaeology and Language: The Puzzle of Indo-European Origins*. Cambridge U. Pr. 1990 $18.95. ISBN 0-521-38675-6. Compares and contrasts the languages of Europe and those of early Indo-European civilizations; a historiographic survey of language.

Roux, G. *Ancient Iraq*. Viking Penguin rev. ed. 1976 $9.95. ISBN 0-14-020828-3. A history of Mesopotamian civilization through archaeological evidence as well as ancient writings.

Sulimirski, T., ed. *The Cambridge History of Iran*. Vol. 2 Cambridge U. Pr. 1985 o.p. The most detailed single source for every aspect of Achaemenid history and civilization.

Trigger, B. G., and others. *Ancient Egypt: A Social History*. Cambridge U. Pr. 1983 $9.95. ISBN 0-521-24080-8. Illuminating survey of life in dynastic Egypt from a number of perspectives.

GREECE AND THE HELLENIC WORLD

Andrewes, Antony. *The Greeks*. Norton 1978 repr. of 1967 ed. $9.95. ISBN 0-393-00877-0. Interesting survey of Greek civilization from the Archaic period to 146 B.C.; focuses on culture and customs.

Bosworth, A. B. *Conquest and Empire: The Reign of Alexander the Great*. Cambridge U. Pr. 1990 $15.95. ISBN 0-521-40679-X. The sanest account in English of the phenomenon of Alexander. Extensive bibliography on other recent but less accessible research on Philip, Alexander, and the rise of the Macedonian kingdom.

Cartledge, Paul. *Agesilaos and The Crisis of Sparta*. Johns Hopkins 1987 $62.50. ISBN 0-8018-3505-4. Deeply researched account of fourth-century Greek history from a Spartan perspective. Provides admirable description of Spartan society and institutions in the Classical age.

Davies, J. K. *Democracy and Classical Greece. Fontana History of the Ancient World Ser.* Stanford U. Pr. 1978 $12.95. ISBN 0-8047-1226-3. Explores the democratic tradition of ancient Athens and its impact on Greek society.

Ehrenberg, Victor. *From Solon to Socrates: Greek History and Civilization during the 6th–5th Centuries B.C.* Routledge 1973 $18.95. ISBN 0-415-04024-8. Discusses the politics and government of the ancient Greeks.

―――. *The Greek State*. Methuen 2nd ed. 1974 o.p. Critical look at the Greek city-state and the concept of the *polis*.

Fine, John V. A. *The Ancient Greeks: A Critical History*. HUP 1983 $18.95. ISBN 0-674-03314-0. Mainly political narrative.

Finley, M. I. *The Ancient Greeks: An Introduction to Their Life and Thought*. Viking Penguin 1977 $9.95. ISBN 0-14-055223-5. Traces the customs, traditions, and philosophy of ancient Greece.

―――. *The World of Odysseus*. Viking Penguin rev. ed. 1979 repr. of 1978 ed. $6.95. ISBN 0-14-020570-5. Investigates the Greek civilization as revealed in the works of Homer.

Fitzhardinge, L. F. *The Spartans. Ancient Peoples and Places Ser.* Thames Hudson 1980 o.p. A look at the city-state of Sparta; examines the customs and lives of the warrior Spartans.

Fornara, C. W., and L. J. Samons, *Athens from Cleisthenes to Pericles*. U. CA Pr. 1991 $29.95. ISBN 0-520-06923-4. A thought-provoking essay on Athens' internal political development in the fifth century.

Forrest, W. G. *A History of Sparta 950–192 B.C.*, Norton 1980 $7.95. ISBN 0-393-00481-3. Short and sparsely documented but extremely acute, with an excellent short bibliography.

Godolphin, Francis R. B., ed. *The Greek Historians.* 2 vols. Random 1942 o.p. Complete translations, with introduction and notes, of Herodotus, Thucydides, Xenophon, and Arrian.

Greek Political Oratory. Trans. by A. N. W. Saunders. Viking Penguin 1978 $6.95. ISBN 0-14-044223-5. Compilation of addresses and speeches from ancient Greeks; analyzes the customs, beliefs, and politics of the Greeks as revealed in these primary source documents.

Hammond, N. G. *A History of Greece to 322 B.C.* OUP 1986 $29.95. ISBN 0-19-873095-0. Compendious one-volume history that gives helpful citations to the ancient evidence. Marred by uncritical use of evidence; should be used with caution.

Hornblower, Simon. *The Greek World, 478-323 B.C.* Routledge 1983 $13.95. ISBN 0-416-74990-9. Careful, lucid, and intelligent account with valuable notes and critical bibliography.

Jeffery, Lillian H. *Archaic Greece: The City-States c.700–500 B.C.* St. Martin 1976 o.p. Examines the development of the earliest Greek city-states.

Jones, A. H. *The Greek City from Alexander to Justinian.* OUP 1979 repr. of 1940 ed. $32.50. ISBN 0-19-814842-9. Discusses municipal government from the Hellenistic age to the Byzantine empire; surveys the towns and cities of that period.

Meiggs, Russell. *The Athenian Empire.* OUP 1979 $36.00. ISBN 0-19-814843-7. Discusses the politics and government of Athens during the period of its greatest power and influence.

Murray, Oswyn. *Early Greece. Fontana History of the Ancient World Ser.* Stanford U. Pr. 1980 $12.95. ISBN 0-8047-1185-2. Surveys the development of Greek civilization during the Archaic period.

Ober, Josiah. *Mass and Elite in Democratic Athens: Rhetoric, Ideology, and the Power of the People.* Princeton U. Pr. 1989 $16.95. ISBN 0-691-09443-8. Best single work on how the classical Athenian democracy worked in practice. Valuable bibliography.

Rostovtzeff, Mikhail. *The Social and Economic History of the Hellenistic World.* 3 vols. OUP 1986 $198.00. ISBN 0-19-814230-7. Detailed but readable account. Extensively annotated and illustrated.

Snodgrass, Anthony M. *Archaic Greece: The Age of Experiment.* U. CA Pr. 1981 $13.95. ISBN 0-520-04373-1. Analyzes Greek civilization during the Archaic period to determine the roots of classical civilization.

Vermeule, Emily T. *Aspects of Death in Early Greek Art and Poetry.* U. CA Pr. 1979 $14.95. ISBN 0-520-04404-5. Investigates the portrayal of death in the art of ancient Greece; discusses what this reveals about Greek civilization.

――――. *Greece in the Bronze Age.* U. Ch. Pr. 1972 $17.95. ISBN 0-226-85354-3. Survey of Greek culture during the Bronze Age.

Walbank, F. W. *The Hellenist World. Fontana History of the Ancient World Ser.* HUP 1981 $9.95. ISBN 0-674-38725-7. The best survey in English of political, social, and cultural developments from Alexander to the Roman conquest of the Hellenistic East.

Webster, T. B. L. *Athenian Culture and Society.* U. CA Pr. 1973 o.p. Focuses on the customs, culture, and people of ancient Athens during its Golden Age.

ROME AND THE ROMAN EMPIRE

Barnes, T. D. *Constantine and Eusebius.* HUP 1981 $46.50. ISBN 0-674-16530-6. Balanced, thorough, comprehensive treatment of the first Christian emperor and his biographer.

Bowersock, G. W. *Julian the Apostate.* HUP 1978 $14.50. ISBN 0-634-48881-4. Interesting biography of emperor Julian of Rome.

Brown, Peter. *Power and Persuasion in Late Antiquity: Towards a Christian Empire.* U. of Wis. Pr. 1992 $45.00. ISBN 0-299-13340-0. Sensitive, original, deeply learned study of the infiltration of Christian bishops, monks, theologians, and ecclesiastical politicians into the courts and minds of the emperors after Constantine. Notes alone are first-rate guide to best recent research on the later Empire.

———. *The World of Late Antiquity: 150–750.* History of European Civilization Lib. Norton 1989 $9.95. ISBN 0-393-95803-5. Brilliant evocation of the transformation of the Roman Empire into Byzantium and the civilization of the Middle Ages.

Brunt, P. A. *Social Conflicts in the Roman Republic.* Norton 1974 $6.95. ISBN 0-393-00586-0. Analytical historical essay on causes of the eventual collapse of the Republic, by leading student of the question.

Cary, M., and H. H. Scullard. *A History of Rome.* St. Martin 1976 $40.00. ISBN 0-312-38395-9. Best of the textbook histories.

Gibbon, Edward. *The Decline and Fall of the Roman Empire.* Ed. by Moses Hadas. Fawcett 1987 $4.95. ISBN 0-449-30056-0. Classic survey of the history of ancient Roman civilization.

Gruen, E. S. *The Hellenistic World and the Coming of Rome.* 2 vols. U. CA Pr. 1984 $70.00. ISBN 0-520-04569-6. Exhaustive examination of the evidence for Roman relations with the Greeks. Tries to show that Greek attempts to enlist Romans in their quarrels helped draw the Romans into war with the Greek states and kingdoms.

———. *The Last Generation of the Roman Republic.* U. CA Pr. 1974 $65.00. ISBN 0-520-02238-6. Offers a penetrating, but controversial, diagnosis of the fall of the Republic, emphasizing the institutional continuities and the normal course of politics through most of the period, rather than the lurid careers of Pompey and Caesar.

Heurgon, J. *The Rise of Rome to 264 B.C.* U. CA Pr. 1973 $37.50. ISBN 0-520-01795-1. Outstanding essay on the expansion of Rome from its origins to the domination of Italy and the eve of the conflict with Carthage.

Kaegi, Walter E. *Byzantium and the Decline of Rome.* Princeton U. Pr. 1968 o.p. Surveys the history of the Roman Empire from A.D. 204 to 476; analyzes the relationship between Rome and Byzantium.

Laistner, M. M. W. *The Greater Roman Historians.* U CA Pr. 1947 $29.00. ISBN 0-520-03365-5. Historiographic survey of the Roman Empire through the work of various Roman historians.

Lewis, Naphtali. *Life in Egypt under Roman Rule.* OUP 1986 $9.95. ISBN 0-19-814872-0. Traces the history of ancient Egypt during the Ptolemaic period.

Millar, Fergus. *The Emperor in the Roman World.* Aspects of Greek and Roman Life Ser. Cornell U. Pr. 1977 $75.00. ISBN 0-8014-1058-4. Analyzes imperial power and authority in the Roman Empire.

———, ed. *The Roman Empire and Its Neighbors.* Holmes & Meier 2nd ed. 1981 $49.50. ISBN 0-8419-0711-0. Analyzes the relationships among Rome, its colonies and provinces, and the lands outside the empire.

Ogilvie, R. M. *Early Rome and the Etruscans.* 1976 o.p. Good introduction to the subject.

Rostovtzeff, Mikhail. *The Social and Economic History of the Roman Empire.* 2 vols. Ed. by P. M. Fraser. OUP 1957 o.p. Discusses economic and social conditions within the Roman Empire.

Scullard, H. H. *From the Gracchi to Nero: A History of Rome from 133 B.C. to A.D. 87* Routledge 1991 $19.95. ISBN 0-415-02527-3. Standard critical account of the crucial transitional era of the Roman state from aristocratic republic to universal monarchy.

———. *History of the Roman World 753–146 B.C.* Routledge 1991 $18.95. ISBN 0-415-05915-1. Up-to-date narrative account of Rome through the conquest of the Mediterranean.

Syme, Ronald. *The Roman Revolution.* Oxford Pap. Ser. OUP 1939 $16.95. ISBN 0-19-881001-6. The decisive work about Augustus and his times. Highly critical account of power politics in the late Republic. Fundamental for all subsequent discussions.

Wells, Colin. *The Roman Empire.* Fontana History of the Ancient World Ser. Stanford U. Pr. 1984 $42.50. ISBN 0-8047-1237-9. Good, general overview of the history of the Roman Empire; analyzes reasons for its decline.

SUPPLEMENTARY TOPICAL READING LISTS

Agriculture, Science, and Technology

Burford, Alison. *Craftsmen in Greek and Roman Society*. Cornell U. Pr. 1972 o.p.
Discusses the art and artisans of ancient Greece and Rome; traces the development
of craftmanship in both civilizations.

Casson, Lionel. *Ships and Seamanship in the Ancient World*. Bks. Demand repr. of 1971
ed. $155.80. ISBN 0-7837-0564-6. Examines the maritime accomplishments and
innovations of the ancient world.

Isager, Signe, and Erik Skydsgaard. *Ancient Greek Agriculture: An Introduction*.
Routledge 1992 $59.95. ISBN 0-415-00164-1. The latest descriptive and theoretical
work. Puts forth the thesis that, given the primitive state of Greek agricultural
technology, the long-held belief that farming was the basis of the economy of the
city-state should be revised.

Oleson, John P. *The History of Bronze Age, Greek and Roman Technology*. Garland 1986
$83.00. ISBN 0-8240-8677-5. Well chosen entries, with informative and critical
annotations.

Phillips, E. D. *Greek Medicine*. Cornell U. Pr. 1973 o.p. Discusses medicine and medical
innovations of ancient Greece.

Scarborough, John. *Roman Medicine. Aspects of Greek and Roman Life Ser*. Ed. by H. H.
Scullard. Cornell U. Pr. 1970 o.p. Looks at medicine and medical treatment in
ancient Rome.

White, K. D. *Greek and Roman Technology. Aspects of Greek and Roman Life Ser*. Cornell
Univ. Pr. 1983 $48.95. ISBN 0-8014-1439-3. A history of technology of ancient Greece
and Rome, focusing on the impact of technology of society and economics.

———. *Roman Farming. Aspects of Greek and Roman Life Ser*. Ed. by H. H. Scullard.
Cornell U. Pr. 1970 o.p. Surveys the farming techniques of ancient Rome and the
impact of these techniques on agriculture and economics.

———, trans. *Country Life in Classical Times*. Cornell U. Pr. 1977 $29.95. ISBN 0-8014-
1014-9. Examines rural life in ancient Rome and compares it to life in the cities;
utilizes sources from classical literature.

Archaeology

Archaeology has played an important role in the study of ancient history.
While some knowledge of ancient civilizations has been gained through
studying documents, the number of surviving documents is not that great. Much
of our understanding of these ancient cultures comes from the study of
archaeological remains uncovered at ancient sites.

Biers, William R. *The Archaeology of Greece: An Introduction*. Cornell U. Pr. 1981 o.p.
General overview of important archaeological findings in ancient Greece and what
these reveal about Greek civilization.

Boardman, John. *The Greeks Overseas: Their Early Colonies and Trade*. Thames Hudson
rev. ed. 1982 o.p. Discusses the trade relations between the Greek city-states and
their colonies throughout the Mediterranean region.

Hodder, Ian. *Reading the Past: Current Approaches to Interpretation in Archaeology*.
Cambridge U. Pr. 1991 $12.95. ISBN 0521-40957-8. Controversial critique of
archaeologists' assumptions and practices.

Kraus, T., and L. von Matt. *Pompeii and Herculaneum: The Living Cities of the Dead*. 1975
o.p. Examines the archaeological finds of Pompeii and Herculaneum, the two cities
destroyed by the eruption of Vesuvius in A.D. 79, and discusses what these findings
reveal about Roman civilization.

MacDonald, William L. *The Architecture of the Roman Empire*. Yale U. Pr. 1982 $18.95.
ISBN 0-300-02819-9. Looks at Roman architecture and building techniques.

McKay, Alexander G. *Houses, Villas and Palaces in the Roman World*. Cornell U. Pr. 1975 o.p. Examines the domestic architecture of ancient Rome and analyzes Roman life based on their homes.

MacKendrick, Paul. *The Greek Stones Speak: The Story of Archaeology in Greek Lands*. Norton 1983 $24.95. ISBN 0-393-01463-0. An interesting history of archaeology in ancient Greece; analyzes a number of significant findings.

———. *The Mute Stones Speak: The Story of Archaeology in Italy*. Norton 1983 $12.95. ISBN 0-393-30119-2. A companion to the author's *The Greek Stones Speak*; discusses the archaeological finds of ancient Italy.

———. *Romans on the Rhine: Archaeology in Germany*. Funk and Wagnalls 1970 o.p. Another of MacKendrick's interesting books on archaeology, this time focusing on archaeological finds of Roman antiquities in the Rhine Valley. Examines the history of Roman settlements in that region.

Morgan, Catherine. *Athletes and Oracles: The Transformation of Olympia and Delphi in the Eighth Century B.C.* Cambridge U. Pr. 1990 $47.95. ISBN 0-521-37451-0. Indispensible synthesis of the archaeological evidence for Olympia and Delphi's growth to importance from local origins at the dawn of the Greek Archaic age.

Morris, Ian. *Burial and Ancient Society: The Rise of the Greek City-State*. Cambridge U. Pr. 1990 $18.95. ISBN 0-521-38738-8. Synthesis of the archaeological indications for the creation of common institutions and cults among groups of villages at the end of the Greek Dark Age.

Pallottino, Massimo. *The Etruscans*. Trans. by J. Cremona. Ind. U. Pr. rev. ed 1975 o.p. Examines the history and culture of the Etruscans, the most developed civilization in Italy before the founding of Rome; analyzes their customs, traditions, and beliefs.

Randsberg, Klaus. *The First Millenium A.D. in Europe and the Mediterranean: An Archaeological Essay*. Cambridge U. Pr. 1991 $54.95. ISBN 0-521-39504-6. Presents the material and archaeological record of the transformation of the Western Roman Empire under the impact of the barbarian invasions.

Richardson, Emeline. *The Etruscans: Their Art and Civilization*. U. Ch. Pr. 1976 o.p. Broad survey based on artistic and archaeological remains. Numerous plates.

Sear, Frank. *Roman Architecture*. Cornell U. Pr. 1983 $19.95. ISBN 0-8014-9245-9. Investigates the architecture of Rome and its aesthetics.

Woodhead, Peter. *Keyguide to Information Sources in Archaeology*. Mansell 1985 $36.00. ISBN 0-7201-1753-3. General description of archaeological research with annotated bibliography of reference sources, arranged by subject. Indexes included.

Law

Berger, Adolf. *Encyclopedic Dictionary of Roman Law*. Amer. Philosophical Society 1953 o.p. A history of Roman law in dictionary format.

Buckland, W. W. *Roman Law and Common Law: A Comparison in Outline*. Rev. by F. H. Lawson. Cambridge U. Pr. 1952 o.p. Examines the influence of Roman law on modern common law.

Buckland, W. W., and Arnold D. McNair. *A Text-Book of Roman Law from Augustus to Justinian*. Rev. by Peter Stein. Cambridge U. Pr. 1981 o.p. Standard English textbook, with great detail and full citation of the ancient texts.

Cohen, Edward E. *Ancient Athenian Maritime Courts*. Princeton U. Pr. 1973 o.p. Discusses the maritime laws of ancient Athens and what these reveal about Greek culture and society.

Crook, J. A. *Law and Life of Rome: 90 B.C. to A.D. 212*. Cornell U. Pr. 1984 $14.95. ISBN 0-8014-9273-4. Examines Roman law and courts and their relationship to Roman life and society.

Daube, David. *Roman Law*. Col. U. Pr. 1969 $17.50. ISBN 0-85224-051-1. Public lectures, distinguished for sharp observation, unusual perspectives, and great wit.

Frier, Bruce W. *Landlords and Tenants in Imperial Rome*. Princeton U. Pr. 1980 o.p. Examines the legal relationship between the landlord and tenant in ancient Rome.

Gardner, Jane F. *Being a Citizen in Ancient Rome.* Routledge 1993 $49.95. ISBN 0-415-00154-1. Study of the legal rights inherent in Roman citizenship.

Jolowicz, H. F., and Barry Nicholas. *Historical Introduction to the Study of Roman Law.* Bks. Demand repr. of 1972 ed. $138.50. ISBN 0-317-07947-6. Traces the history of Roman law and jurisprudence.

Lintott, Andrew. *Judicial Reform and Land Reform in the Roman Republic: A New Edition, with Translation and Commentary, of the Laws from Urbino.* Cambridge U. Pr. 1992 $95.00. ISBN 0-521-40374-1. Critical discussion of land reform legislation of ancient Rome.

MacDowell, Douglas M. *The Law in Classical Athens. Aspects of Greek and Roman Life Ser.* Cornell U. Pr. 1978 $13.95. ISBN 0-685-01221-2. Examines jurisprudence in the Athenian city-state and its relationship to democracy.

Nicholas, Barry. *Introduction to Roman Law. Clarendon Law Ser.* OUP 1962 $12.95. ISBN 0-19-876063-9. General survey of jurisprudence in the Roman Empire; analyzes courts and legal procedures.

Sherwin-White, A. N. *The Roman Citizenship.* OUP 1973 $38.00. ISBN 0-19-814847-X. In many respects a civic history of Rome. Full discussion of the definition and distribution of Roman citizenship in its various forms from the early period to the universal grant of citizenship in A.D. 211.

Numismation

Carson, Robert. *Coins of the Roman Empire.* Routledge 1990 $199.50. ISBN 0-415-01591-X. The culmination of the author's life's work as Keeper of Coins and Medals at the British Museum.

Foss, Clive. *Roman Historical Coins.* Trafalgar 1990 $65.00. ISBN 0-900652-97-7

Kent, J. P. *Roman Coins.* Abrams 1978 o.p. A look at Roman history through an examination of coins.

Kraay, Colin. *Archaic and Classical Greek Coins. Lib. of Numismatics.* S. J. Durst 1990 $80.00. ISBN 0-685-36400-3. Traces the history of design of ancient Greek coins; discusses what these coins reveal about Greek history.

Morkholm, Otto. *Early Hellenistic Coinage from the Accession of Alexander to the Peace of Apamaea (336–188 B.C.).* Cambridge U. Pr. 1991 $95.00. ISBN 0-521-39504-6. First full study on this corpus, with copious illustrations. Important contribution to Hellenistic studies.

Philosophy, Religion, Education

Brown, Peter. *Augustine of Hippo: A Biography.* U. CA Pr. 1967 o.p. Classic study of Augustine's life, thought, and environment.

Ferguson, John. *The Religions of the Roman Empire. Aspects of Greek and Roman Life Ser.* Cornell U. Pr. 1970 $11.95. ISBN 0-8014-9311-0. Traces the history of religion in ancient Rome and discusses the various deities that were worshipped.

Fox, R. L. *Pagans and Christians.* Knopf 1987 $45.00. ISBN 0-394-55495-7. Brilliant, highly readable account of Graeco-Roman religion and religious life in the age when Christianity overtook paganism in the Mediterranean world.

Gruen, Erich S. *Culture and National Identity in Republican Rome.* Cornell U. Pr. 1993 $37.50. ISBN 0-8014-2759-2. Masterly and original investigation of the cultural impact of Greece on the Romans.

Liebeschuetz, J. *Continuity and Change in Roman Religion.* OUP 1979 $79.00. ISBN 0-19-814822-0. Analyzes the development and evolution of religion in the Roman Empire.

MacMullen, Ramsay. *Paganism in the Roman Empire.* Yale U. Pr. 1981 $13.00. ISBN 0-300-02984-5. Sympathetic attempt to understand paganism in its own terms.

Marrou, H. I. *History of Education in Antiquity.* U. of Wis. Pr. 1982 $14.95. ISBN 0-299-08814-6. Examines the educational methods used by the ancient Greeks and Romans and discusses the role of education in these societies.

Momigliano, Arnaldo. *Alien Wisdom: The Limits of Hellenization*. Cambridge U. Pr. 1990 $15.95. ISBN 0-521-38761-2. Masterly essay on Greek and Roman views of the foreigner and the terms on which foreigners were admitted into the societies of classical antiquity.

Vlastos, Gregory. *Socrates, Ironist and Moral Philosopher*. Cornell U. Pr. 1992 $57.50. ISBN 0-8014-2551-4. Accessible and profound. Best and latest word on Socrates' thought and personality by the leading modern interpreter.

Zaidman, Louise B., and Pauline S. Pantel. *Religion in the Ancient Greek City*. Cambridge U. Pr. $54.95. ISBN 0-521-41262-5. Looks at the role of religion in the Greek city-state and discusses the various deities worshipped.

Society, Economy, and Trade

Austin, Michel M., and Pierre Vidal-Naquet. *Economic and Social History of Ancient Greece: An Introduction*. U. CA Pr. 1978 $13.95. ISBN 0-520-04267-0. Mostly literary ancient sources in translation with extensive annotation and commentary.

Carcopino, Jerome. *Daily Life in Ancient Rome: The People and the City at the Height of the Empire*. Trans. by E. O. Lorimer. Ed. by Harry T. Rowell. Yale U. Pr. 1960 $14.00. ISBN 0-300-00031-6. Interesting account of life in ancient Rome; focuses on the customs and beliefs of the common people.

Cartledge, Paul, and others, eds. *Nomos: Essays in Athenian Law, Politics, and Society*. Cambridge U. Pr. 1991 $54.95. ISBN 0-521-38761-2. Spectrum of views on aspects of classical Athenian life that together provide an overview on the state of Athenian studies today. Includes copious and up-to-date bibliographies.

Finley, Moses I. *The Ancient Economy*. U. CA Pr. 1985 $13.95. ISBN 0-520-05452-0. Highly readable and argumentative account emphasizing the primitive characteristics of the ancient economy and the centrality of agriculture.

Frank, Tenney, ed. *An Economic Survey of Ancient Rome*. 6 vols. Octagon 1972 o.p. Massive compilation, arranged by region, of evidence about the economic life of the Roman Empire. Numerous translated documents and lists of economic data.

Garland, Robert. *The Greek Way of Death*. Cornell U. Pr. 1987 $31.95. ISBN 0-8014-1823-2. Focuses on Greek funeral rites and customs.

_____. *The Greek Way of Life*. Cornell U. Pr. 1990 $48.95. ISBN 0-8014-2335-X. Richly anecdotal account of individual life in the Greek world, from childhood to old age.

Garnsey, Peter. *Famine and Food Supply in the Graeco-Roman World. Responses to Risk and Crisis*. Cambridge U. Pr. 1989 $16.95. ISBN 0-521-37585-1. Analysis of food production and supply in ancient Greece and Rome and how those societies responded to conditions of famine.

Garnsey, Peter, and Richard Saller. *The Roman Empire: Economy, Society and Culture*. U. CA Pr. 1987 $45.00. ISBN 0-520-06066-0. Outstanding and accessible account of the structure and fabric of Roman civilization using the best recent methodologies.

Gelzer, M. *The Roman Nobility*. OUP 1969 o.p. The classic exposition of the workings of Roman aristocratic politics in the Republican period.

Hands, A. R. *Charities and Social Aid in Greece and Rome*. Cornell U. Pr. 1968 o.p. Traces the public welfare system of the ancient Greeks and Romans.

Harris, H. A. *Sport in Greece and Rome. Aspects of Greek and Roman Life Ser*. Ed. by H. H. Scullard. Cornell U. Pr. 1972 $28.95. ISBN 0-8014-0718-4. Traces the history of various sports of the ancient Romans and Greeks.

Hopkins, K. *Conquerors and Slaves*. Cambridge U. Pr. 1978 o.p. Essays on the economic and human exploitation of Rome's defeated victims.

Humphreys, S. C. *The Family, Women and Death*. U. of Mich. Pr. 1983 $36.50. ISBN 0-472-08163-2. Essays on domestic life in classical Greece, with a new introduction on recent scholarship.

Lewis, Naphtali. *Life in Egypt under Roman Rule*. OUP 1983 $9.95. ISBN 0-19-814872-0. Examines the social, economic, and political conditions of Egypt during Roman rule.

MacMullen, Ramsay. *Enemies of the Roman Order: Treason, Unrest, and Alienation in the Empire.* Bks. Demand repr. of 1966 ed. $102.60. ISBN 0-7837-1717-2. Analysis of various resistance movements against the central government of the Roman Empire.

_____. *Roman Social Relations, 50 B.C. to A.D. 284.* Yale U. Pr. 1974 $12.00. ISBN 0-300-02702-8. Overview of Roman social categories and social disciplines by a first-rate social historian.

Meeks, Wayne A. *The First Urban Christians: The Social World of the Apostle Paul.* Yale U. Pr. 1984 $14.00. ISBN 0-300-03244-7. Analysis of the Pauline letters in terms of our knowledge of contemporary society.

Ste. Croix, G.E.M. de *The Class Struggle in the Ancient Greek World.* 1981 $79.50. ISBN 0-8014-1442-3. Monumental and already-classic study by a leading British Marxist scholar of the exploitation of the many by the few in the ancient world. Said to be the only history of antiquity ever written from the point of view of the lower classes.

Sallares, Robert. *The Ecology of the Ancient Greek World.* Cornell Univ. Pr. 1992 $75.00. ISBN 0-8014-2615-4. Deals with human beings and the landscape in the ancient Mediterranean: historical population biology.

Saller, R. P. *Personal Patronage under the Early Empire.* Cambridge U. Pr. 1982 $54.95. ISBN 0-521-23300-3. Important study of the cement of Roman social relations.

War, Peace, and Diplomacy

Adcock, Frank E. *Diplomacy in Ancient Greece.* Cornell U. Pr. 1975 o.p. Examines the foreign relations between the Greeks and other Mediterranean states.

_____. *The Greek and Macedonian Art of War.* U. CA Pr. 1974 $9.95. ISBN 0-520-00005-6. Comparative study of the art and science of the military and military strategy in Macedonia and the Greek city-states.

Anderson, J. K. *Military Theory and Practice in the Age of Xenophon.* U. CA Pr. 1970 o.p. Explores the history of military art and science in Greece during the fourth and fifth centuries B.C.

Campbell, J. B. *The Emperor and the Roman Army.* OUP 1984 o.p. Analysis of the structure and organization of the Roman army and the role of the emperor.

Connolly, P. *Greece and Rome at War.* P-H 1981 $30.00. ISBN 0-13-364976-8. A military history of ancient Greece and Rome; examines key wars and battles.

Engels, Donald W. *Alexander the Great and the Logistics of the Macedonian Army.* U. CA Pr. 1978 $12.95. ISBN 0-520-4272-7. Biographic look at Alexander the Great and his genius as a military leader.

Garlan, Yvon. *War in the Ancient World.* 1975 o.p. Wide-ranging discussion by a leading French scholar.

Hanson, Victor D. *The Western Way of War: Infantry Battle in Classical Greece.* OUP 1989 $9.95. ISBN 0-394-57188-6. Splendid evocation of the realities of war for the citizen soldier of classical Greece. Already a classic and the best single work on the subject for the general reader. Excellent bibliography.

Harris, William V. *War and Imperialism in Republican Rome, 327–70 B.C.* OUP 1979 o.p. Brilliant analysis of the cultural and economic motives that led the Romans to make constant war until they had conquered all the powers and peoples on their horizons.

Keppie, L. *The Making of the Roman Army.* Balsford 1984 o.p. Solid general study.

Luttwak, Edward N. *The Grand Strategy of the Roman Empire: From the First Century A.D. to the Third.* Johns Hopkins 1977 $12.95. ISBN 0-8018-2158-4. Explores the goals of military strategy during Rome's Imperial age; focuses on the expansion of the empire and the consequences of that expansion.

MacMullen, Ramsay. *Soldier and Civilian in the Later Roman Empire.* HUP 1963 $15.00. ISBN 0-674-81690-0. Essential reading on relations between the military and civilian worlds of imperial Rome in the age of the barbarian invasions.

Rich, J., and G. Shipley. *War and Society in the Greek World.* Routledge 1993. ISBN 0-415-06643-3. Essays from Homer to Alexander, with up-to-date bibliography.

_____, eds. *War and Society in the Roman World.* Routledge 1993. ISBN 0-415-06644-1. Companion to *War and Society in the Greek World.*

Watson, G. R. *The Roman Soldier. Aspects of Greek and Roman Life Ser.* Cornell U. Pr. 1969 $38.95. ISBN 0-8014-0519-X. Deals with the life of Roman soldiers and the militaristic subculture of imperial Rome.

Yadin, Yvon. *The Art of Warfare in Biblical Lands.* 1963 o.p. Standard work by an author who was both a general and an archaeologist.

Women, the Family, and Sexuality

Cameron, Averil, and Amelie Kuhrt. *Images of Women in Antiquity.* Wayne St. U. Pr. 1983 $19.95. ISBN 0-8143-1763-4. Examines the status and role of women of antiquity to A.D. 500.

Dover, K. J. *Greek Homosexuality.* HUP 1978 $12.95. ISBN 0-674-36270-5. An analysis of homosexuality in Greece as seen through its literature and art.

Hallett, Judith P. *Fathers and Daughters in Roman Society.* Princeton U. Pr. 1984 o.p. Deals with women and social condition in Rome; examines the societal role of women in Roman culture.

Halperin, D. M. *One Hundred Years of Homosexuality and Other Essays on Greek Love.* Routledge 1992 $39.95. ISBN 0-415-90097-2. Wide-ranging essays by a leading scholar. Aims to explain Greek sexual practices in their own cultural context.

Halperin, D. M., and others, eds. *Before Sexuality: The Construction of Erotic Experience in the Ancient Greek World.* Princeton U. Pr. 1991 $69.50. ISBN 0-691-03538-5. Diverse collection of essays on sex in Greek myth, the Greek city, and the Greek home. Brings together in the notes much of the recent work done in this newly popular field.

Lacey, W. K. *The Family in Classical Greece. Aspects of Greek and Roman Life Ser.* Cornell U. Pr. 1984 $14.95. ISBN 0-8014-9274-2. Analyzes family relationships in ancient Greece; discusses marriage and marriage practices.

Lefkowitz, Mary R., and Maureen B. Fant, eds. *Women's Life in Greece and Rome.* Johns Hopkins rev. ed. 1989 $38.50. ISBN 0-8018-4474-6. Collection of ancient sources in translation.

Pomeroy, Sarah B. *Goddesses, Whores, Wives and Slaves: Women in Classical Antiquity.* Schocken 1976 o.p. Historiographic look at the history of women to the year A.D. 500; examines their various roles and conditions.

Rabinowitz, Nancy S., and Amy Richlin, eds. *Feminist Theory and the Classics.* Routledge 1993 $49.95. ISBN 0-415-90645-8. Essays on the newest wave in classical scholarship.

Winkler, John J. *The Constraints of Desire: The Anthropology of Sex and Gender in Ancient Greece.* Routledge 1992 $47.50. ISBN 0-415-90122-7. Brilliant but biased ideological attack on "phallocratic" Greek customs by an author whose stance is frankly "feminist, anthropological, pro-lesbian."

CHRONOLOGY OF AUTHORS

Herodotus. c.484–425 B.C.
Thucydides. c.460–400 B.C.
Xenophon. c.434?–c.355? B.C.
Aristotle. 384–322 B.C.
Polybius. c.200–c.118 B.C.
Cicero, Marcus Tullius. 106–43 B.C.
Caesar, Julius. 100–44 B.C.
Sallust. 86–35 B.C.
Diodorus Siculus. ?–c.21 B.C.
Livy. c.59 B.C.–A.D. 17
Josephus, Flavius. 37–95

Dio Chrysostom. c.40–c.112
Plutarch. c.46–c.125
Tacitus, Cornelius. c.56–c.120
Pliny the Younger. c.61–c.112
Suetonius. c.69–c.140
Appian. c.85–90?
Arrian. c.95–c.175
Dio Cassius. c.150–after 229
Ammianus Marcellinus. c.330–395
Procopius. c.500–c.565

AMMIANUS MARCELLINUS. c.330–395

Born into a good family in Antioch, the megalopolis and intellectual center of Roman Asia, Ammianus used his education and his position in society to secure a military career under the emperors Constantius II, Julian "the Apostate," and the unfortunate Valens. After he retired from the military, he wrote a political and military history of imperial Rome covering the period from A.D. 96 to 378, thus picking up where TACITUS left off and ending in his own day with the defeat and death of the emperor Valens at Hadrianopolis (Edirne). Of the original 31 books that made up the history, only the last 18, which concern the 25-year-period 335–378, have survived from antiquity. The lost 13 books, then, which spanned a period of some 150 years, must have been far less detailed than the meticulously reported material that survives. When he wrote his history in retirement at Rome, Ammianus was in touch with the leading senatorial literary circle around Symmachus. He wrote his work for this audience in Latin, although his native language was Greek. Much of what he wrote reflects his opportunities to observe events as a high-ranking officer attached to a unit of the imperial bodyguard. He saw service from Gaul to the Mesopotamian frontier.

Ammianus's work is written in an extremely rhetorical style in excellent, although sometimes artificial, Latin that owes much to his wide reading in major Latin authors, including CICERO, LIVY, SALLUST, and TACITUS. His history remains our major source for the brief and dramatic reign of Julian, whom Ammianus admired. It also continues to be a prime source for the rest of the important period that his surviving work covers, a time when the first Christian emperors were establishing their authority while defending the frontiers of the empire from new barbarian incursions.

Ammianus shared the catholic temper of later pagan antiquity. Although not a Christian himself, he was tolerant of the new religion and admired the probity and simplicity of provincial bishops. As a native Greek, his ambition to impress the senatorial aristocracy of Latin-speaking Rome is a symptom of the future Byzantine orientation of the empire. The Christian and Greek-speaking Byzantines chose a Roman identity, as did Ammianus, a bilingual Greek servant of Roman emperors.

BOOK BY AMMIANUS

Roman History. 3 vols. Trans. by J. C. Rolfe. *Loeb Class. Lib.* HUP $15.50 ea. Well-translated edition of Ammianus's political and military history of Rome.

BOOKS ABOUT AMMIANUS

Den Boeft, J., and others. *Philological and Historical Commentary on Ammianus Marcellinus.* Benjamins North Am. 1987 $63.00. ISBN 90-6980-012-8. Useful reference work.

Elliot, T. G. *Ammianus Marcellinus and Fourth Century History.* 1983 o.p. Explores the significance of Ammianus's history.

Matthews, John. *The Roman Empire of Ammianus.* Johns Hopkins 1990 $60.00. ISBN 0-8018-3965-3. The best study in English of the historian and his times, with up-to-date bibliography.

Rike, R. L. *Apex Omnium: Religion in the Res Gestae of Ammianus.* U. CA Pr. 1987 $35.00. ISBN 0-520-05858-5. Study of Ammianus's personal faith and his response to the new religion of Christianity. Reflects the contradictions and compromises of a public life in a transitional age.

Seager, Robin. *Ammianus Marcellinus: Seven Studies in His Language and Thought.* U. of
Mo. Pr. 1986 $22.00. ISBN 0-862-0495-3. Series of essays on Ammianus, his language,
and his historical method.
Syme, Ronald. *Ammianus and the Historia Augusta.* OUP 1968 o.p.

APPIAN (APPIANUS). c.85–90?

Born probably in the reign of Domitian (81–96), Appian was an Alexandrian
Greek who rose to high imperial office under Antoninus Pius (137–61). He
wrote a history of Rome's wars from the founding of Rome to the reign of
Trajan, arranged ethnographically. Of the 24 original "books"—papyrus rolls of
standard length—written in Greek, 16 have survived essentially complete.
Appian was not an original historian but a derivative and pedestrian narrator
who understood only imperfectly the institutions of the former Republic about
which he wrote. However, he used some good sources for his work, making it of
great value to modern scholars. This is particularly true of his *Civil Wars*,
describing the last convulsions of the Republic and the rise of Octavian.

BOOK BY APPIAN

Roman History. 4 vols. Trans. by H. E. White. *Loeb Class. Lib.* HUP $15.50 ea. Useful
edition of Appian's works on Roman history.

ARISTOTLE. 384–322 B.C.

Not a historian but a philosopher who wrote works of direct relevance to
historians of today, Aristotle's lifetime bridged the world of the classical city and
that of the Hellenistic monarchies. At the academy, he was by far the greatest of
PLATO's (see also Vol. 4) students, but his interests—unlike those of Plato—
tended less toward metaphysics than toward science and its methods. A leading
example is his *Politics*, an unsentimental examination of the forms of the state
and their permutations in the Greek world. The constitutional histories of some
158 cities were researched for this treatise, probably by Aristotle's students. Of
these constitutions, only one survives, the *Constitution of Athens*, written on
papyrus. It was not recovered until 1888. Both the *Politics* and the *Constitution
of Athens* are of the greatest importance for Athenian history and Greek political
institutions. (See also Volume 4 for more on Aristotle.)

BOOKS BY ARISTOTLE

Aristotle's Constitution of Athens. Ayer repr. of 1912 ed. $25.00. ISBN 0-405-04857-2.
Examination of Athenian politics, government, and law.
The Complete Works of Aristotle: The Revised Oxford Translation. 2 vols. Princeton U. Pr.
1984 $79.00. ISBN 0-691-109950-2. Comprehensive collection of Aristotle's writings;
covers the theory of man, politics, law, art, and so on.
The Politics. Ed. by Stephen Everson. Cambridge U. Pr. 1988 $37.95. ISBN 0-521-35449-8.
His concept of politics and its various facets.

BOOKS ABOUT ARISTOTLE

Barnes, Jonathan. *Aristotle.* OUP 1982 $7.95. ISBN 0-19-287581-7. Short introduction to
the philosophy and science of Aristotle by a modern master.
Jaeger, Werner. *Aristotle.* OUP 1948 o.p. Basic history of Aristotle's development as a
philosopher.
Lloyd, G. E. *Aristotle: Growth and Structure of His Thought.* Cambridge U. Pr. 1968
$54.95. ISBN 0-521-09456-9. Analyzes the development of Aristotle's philosophy
from his early to his later works.

Rhodes, P. J. *A Commentary on the Aristotelian Athenaion Politeia.* OUP 1981 $115.00.
ISBN 0-19-814004-5. Examines Aristotle's political thought and its influence on later
writers.

ARRIAN (FLAVIUS ARRIANUS). c.95–c.175

Historian, philosopher, and general, Arrian was born into a wealthy Greek
family in Asia Minor. For six years, from 131 to 137, he served as governor of
Cappadocia under the emperor Hadrian. It was during this time that he
successfully drove back invading Alans. Arrian wrote several geographical and
historical works, including the *Indica*, an account of a voyage to India. He also
edited the discourses of the philosopher Epictetus. He is best known, however,
as author of the *Anabasis*. A much praised and valuable account of the life of
Alexander the Great, it is based on the writings of Ptolemy I and Aristobulus,
two of Alexander's generals, and is modeled on XENOPHON's *Anabasis*.

BOOKS BY ARRIAN

The Anabasis of Alexander, Indica. 2 vols. Trans. by P. A. Brunt and E. Iliff Robson. *Loeb
Class. Lib.* HUP $15.50 ea. Arrian's history of the campaigns of Alexander the Great
from 356–323 B.C., and his account of the people of India.
The Campaigns of Alexander. Trans. by Aubrey de Selincourt. Rev. by J. R. Hamilton.
Viking Penguin 1976 $9.95. ISBN 0-14-044253-7. Useful edition of Arrian's history of
the conquests of Alexander.

BOOK ABOUT ARRIAN

Stadter, Philip A. *Arrian of Nicomedia.* U. of NC Pr. 1980 $32.50. ISBN 0-8078-1364-8.
Well-written biography of Flavius Arrianus; analyzes his significance as a historian
and philosopher.

CAESAR, JULIUS (GAIUS JULIUS CAESAR). 100–44 B.C.

Born into a noble family that had fallen from influence, Julius Caesar secured
his future by allying himself early in his life with the popular general and
senator, Gaius Marius. Although his refusal to divorce his wife Cordelia led him
to flee Rome for a period, the political and military campaigns he conducted
upon his return both renewed and increased his prominence. With Senators
Crassus and Pompey, he formed the First Triumvirate in 60 and 59 B.C., and for
the next 10 years served as governor of several Roman provinces. His decision
to assume the position of Roman consul led to war, to an encounter in Egypt
with Cleopatra, and ultimately to his position as dictator of Rome. His
increasing popularity and power, brought about by the numerous reforms he
initiated, led to his assassination by a group of conspirators who feared he
would try to make himself king.

Caesar left posterity his accounts of his campaigns in Gaul (modern France)
and against his rival Pompey. Although self-serving in the extreme, they
nevertheless provide an immensely valuable historical source for the last years
of the Republic. His works mirror his character. He was an individual of
outstanding genius and versatility: a brilliant soldier, a stylist whose lucidity
reflects his clarity of vision, an inspiring leader, and a personality of hypnotical-
ly attractive charm. But the verdict of antiquity rests upon his single, altogether
Roman, flaw—he could not bear to be the second man in the state. To preserve
his position, he made war on his political enemies and brought down the
Republic. Then, as he was incapable of restoring the republican regime, which
had furnished his political contemporaries with a sense of freedom, power, and
self-respect, he was stabbed to death by his own friends.

BOOKS BY CAESAR

The Civil War. 2 vols. Ed. by J. M. Carter. David Braun 1991 $49.95. ISBN 0-85668-461-9. Account of the Roman civil war during the period from 49–48 B.C.

The Conquest of Gaul. Trans. by S. A. Handford. Viking Penguin 1983 $7.95. ISBN 0-14-044433-5. Introduction by Jane F. Gardner. Description of the Roman conquest of Gauls.

BOOKS ABOUT CAESAR

Adcock, F. E. *Caesar as Man of Letters.* 1956. Shoe String 1969 o.p. Focuses on Caesar's importance as a historian.

Gelzer, Matthias. *Caesar, Politician and Statesman.* HUP 1968 $11.95. ISBN 0-674-09001-2. Best single-volume study of Caesar in English.

Yavetz, Zvi. *Julius Caesar and His Public Image.* Cornell U. Pr. 1983 $34.50. ISBN 0-8014-1440-7. Study of Caesar's dictatorship.

CICERO, MARCUS TULLIUS. 106–43 B.C.

Cicero was not a historian but a politician, orator, and the author of numerous philosophical works. Of his extensive writings, 58 speeches, several essays, and 925 personal letters survive. His large collection of letters, which were never meant to be published, reveal both his personality and his times. Together the letters and his other works and speeches provide the most intimate and detailed evidence for contemporary events and for the social and intellectual climate of the Roman aristocracy of Cicero's generation.

Although Cicero's works place him at the center of the study of his times at Rome, in his own lifetime he was rather at the margins of power. A born seeker of civility and consensus, he lived at a time when the great warlords CAESAR and Pompey, and their enemies in the Senate, valued neither. Cicero aroused himself to save the Republic only after it had been lost. He hoped that Octavian and Marc Antony, the rivals for supreme power after Caesar's assassination, would destroy each other. To this end he supported Octavian against Antony, whom he vilified in a series of public speeches. But when the two rivals joined forces and drew up a list of enemies to be murdered, Cicero was among those on the list. He was beheaded by a henchman of Antony's, and his head and hands hung from the speakers' rostrum in the Forum.

BOOKS BY CICERO

Cicero. 17 vols. *Loeb Class. Lib.* HUP o.p. Comprehensive edition of Cicero's writings.

Letters to Atticus. 3 vols. HUP $15.50 ea. Compilation of correspondence between Cicero and Roman businessman and writer Titus Atticus.

The Murder Trials. Trans. by Michael Grant. Hippocrene Bks. 1986 $16.95. ISBN 0-88029-075-7. Accounts of various murder trials of ancient Rome; includes forensic orations.

Selected Letters. Trans. by D. R. Shackleton-Bailey. Viking Penguin 1986 $9.95. ISBN 0-14-044458-0. Various correspondences to Latin writers.

Selected Political Speeches. Trans. by Michael Grant. Viking Penguin 1977 $6.95. ISBN 0-14-044214-6

Selected Works. Trans. by Michael Grant. Viking Penguin 1960 $8.95. ISBN 0-14-044099-2. Includes political and legal speeches, as well as some philosophical writings.

BOOKS ABOUT CICERO

Bailey, D. R. Shackleton. *Cicero.* 1971 o.p. Jewel-like presentation in both style and sense by the greatest student of Cicero's letters.

Stockton, David. *Cicero, a Political Biography.* OUP 1988 $37.50. ISBN 0-19-872033-5.
Excellent assessment of Cicero's career in public life.

DIO CASSIUS (CASSIUS DIO COCCEIANUS). c.150–after 229

Born of a leading Asiatic Greek family, Dio pursued a distinguished senatorial
career at Rome and in 229 was consul with the emperor Septimius Severus. He
wrote a history of Rome from its origins to the year of his consulship,
considerable parts of which survive either in full or in epitomes by later
authors. Dio's deep experience of life in imperial circles gives value to his work
as the narrative approaches his own time. The whole of the surviving portions,
however, preserve republican historical traditions of value, reflecting, in
particular, LIVY's lost books on the end of the Republic and the Triumviral
Period, from 68 to 30 B.C.

BOOK BY DIO CASSIUS

Roman History. Ed. by J. W. Rich. David Brown 1991 $49.95. ISBN 0-85668-383-3.
Competent translation of Dio Cassius's history of Rome.

BOOK ABOUT DIO CASSIUS

Millar, F. *Cassius Dio.* OUP 1964. o.p. Scholarly look at the life and work of Dio Cassius.
Analyzes his account of Roman history.

DIO CHRYSOSTOM. c.40–c.112

Dio was not a historian but an orator and philosophical writer from a wealthy
Greek family of Asia Minor. His speeches, however, present a great deal of
information about the society of his times.

BOOK BY DIO CHRYSOSTOM

Discourses. 5 vols. Trans. by J. W. Cohoon and H. L. Crosby. *Loeb Class. Lib.* HUP Pr.
$15.50 ea.

BOOK ABOUT DIO CHRYSOSTOM

Jones, C. P. *The Roman World of Dio Chrysostom. Loeb Class. Monographs Ser.* HUP 1978
$27.00. ISBN 0-674-77915-0. Evocation of the social and intellectual milieu of a
leading Greek orator of the Roman Empire.

DIODORUS SICULUS. ?–c.21 B.C.

Sicilian historian Diodorus Siculus was the author of a world history in 40
papyrus "books." The work focused on the non-Greek world, including Egypt,
Mesopotamia, and India, and on the Greeks and Romans from the earliest times
to CAESAR's conquest of Gaul. The value of this work, of which about one-third
survives, lies far less in itself than in its reflection of the lost historians that it
summarizes. In a few cases, such as the reign of Philip II of Macedon, it is the
major source for an important period of history. Diodorus's work is the chief
surviving example of a genre of potted history that became increasingly
necessary and popular in later antiquity among newly risen provincials who
needed to acquaint themselves in a hurry with the past of the civilization they
had joined.

BOOK BY DIODORUS

Diodorus of Sicily. 12 vols. Trans. by C. H. Oldfather and others. *Loeb Class. Lib.* HUP
1933–67 o.p. Complete edition of Diodorus's history of Sicily.

BOOK ABOUT DIODORUS

Sacks, Kenneth. *Diodorus Siculus and the First Century.* Princeton U. Pr. 1990 $31.50. ISBN 0-691-03600-4. Examines the life and work of Diodorus Siculus in the context of his time.

HERODOTUS. c.484–425 B.C.

Herodotus was the inventor of universal history. Often called the Father of History, his histories are divided into nine books named after the nine muses. A native of Halicarnassus on the coast of Asia Minor (modern Bodrum, Turkey), he traveled extensively, writing lively descriptions of the lands he saw and the peoples he encountered.

Herodotus set out to relate the story of the conflict of the Greeks of his own time against the "barbarian" Asiatic empire of Achaemenid Persia. His long narrative, titled by modern convention *The Histories*, begins with the earliest traditions he believed reliable. It ends with a highly colored account of the defeat of the Persian emperor Xerxes and his immense army of slaves by a much smaller number of Greeks fighting to preserve their freedom.

Herodotus wrote history, but his methods and assumptions were not those of a modern historian, and his work was unjustly rejected by his successor THUCYDIDES as factually highly unreliable and full of inappropriate romance. By his own admission, Herodotus retold the stories of other peoples without necessarily believing them all. This allowed him total artistic freedom and control to create a picture of the world that corresponded entirely to his own view of it. The result is a picture of Herodotus's world that is also a picture of his mind and, therefore, of many other Greek minds during the period known as "late Archaic."

During this period, the Greek mind was dominated by reason, the domain of the first philosophers and the observant and thoughtful medical theorists of the Hippocratic school. Traditional beliefs in the gods of HOMER (see Vols. 2 and 4) and in their Oracles, especially the Oracle at Delphi, also dominated during this period.

The literary genius of Herodotus consisted in the art of the storyteller. The stories he chose to tell, and the order in which he told them, provide his readers with a total view of his world and the way in which the will of the gods and the ambitions of humans interacted to produce what is known as *history*. For this reason the ancient critic LONGINUS (see Vol. 2) justly called Herodotus "the most Homeric of all authors." Like Homer, Herodotus strove to understand the world *theologically*—a goal that makes his work difficult for the reader to understand at first.

But, in place of Homer's divine inspiration, Herodotus used his eyes and ears and wrote not poetry but prose. Rejecting what is commonly known as *myth*, he accepted instead "oral tradition" about remembered events. For example, although he believed that the Trojan War had been fought, he could not investigate it beyond what the poets had said. In his view this "ancient history" of the Greeks and the peoples of Asia was not like contemporary history, because the heroes of old who had created it were beings of a different and superior order who had had a different, direct, and personal relationship with the gods. In recognizing this distinction, Herodotus defined for all time the limits of the historian's discipline.

BOOKS BY HERODOTUS

Histories. Trans. by Aubrey de Selincourt. Viking Penguin 1954 $5.95. ISBN 0-14-044034-8. Highly regarded edition of Herodotus's histories.

The History. Trans. by David Grene. U. Ch. Pr. 1988 $9.95. ISBN 0-226-32772-8.
   Superlative translation, insightful commentary.
The Persian Wars. Trans. by George R. Rawlinson. McGraw 1964 $6.95. ISBN 0-07-
   553640-4. *The Histories* with a different title.

BOOKS ABOUT HERODOTUS

Drews, R. *The Greek Accounts of Eastern History.* The Center for Hellenic Studies 1973
   o.p. On Herodotus and his predecessors.
Evans, J. A. *Herodotus. Twayne's World Authors Ser.* G. K. Hall 1982 o.p. Profile of
   Herodotus for the general reader.
_____. *Herodotus, Explorer of the Past: Three Essays.* Princeton U. Pr. 1991 $24.95. ISBN
   0-691-06871-2. Studies by a leading scholar of Herodotus of imperialism, individuals,
   and oral tradition in *The Histories.*
Gould, John. *Herodotus.* St. Martin 1989 $24.95. ISBN 0-312-02855-5. A reliable
   introduction.
Hartog, François. *The Mirror of Herodotus.* Trans. by Janet Lloyd. U. CA Pr. 1988 $52.50.
   ISBN 0-520-05487-3. Brilliant structural analysis of the subtexts of Herodotus's
   outlook on Greeks versus other peoples, which has revolutionized scholarly readings
   of *The Histories.*
Immerwahr, Henry R. *Form and Thought in Herodotus.* Scholars Pr. GA 1983 $27.00.
   ISBN 0-89130-478-9. Original scholarly treatment of Herodotus and his work.
Lang, Mabel. *Herodotean Narrative and Discourse.* HUP 1984 $20.00. ISBN 0-674-
   38985-9. Examines Herodotus's work in relation to the oral tradition of Greece, and
   discusses his narrative style.
Lateiner, Donald. *The Historical Method of Herodotus.* U. of Toronto Pr. 1989 $19.95.
   ISBN 0-8020-7684-X. Exhaustive exploration of Herodotus's compositional methods
   and ideas concerning historical causation. Reflects the most recent scholarship.
   Largely excludes Herodotus's metaphysical aims.

JOSEPHUS, FLAVIUS. 37–95

A member of a wealthy priestly family in Judea, Josephus was a Pharisee
originally named Joseph ben Matthias. An active supporter of anti-Roman
activity, he became governor of Galilee, a post he held with honor and valor
until Galilee was taken by the Romans in A.D. 67. He won the favor of the Roman
general Vespasian, whose name—Flavius—he took as his own and through
whose patronage he later became a Roman citizen. Although often criticized for
becoming a supporter of Rome, in his work *Against Apion* he passionately
defends Jewish religion and culture.

Josephus wrote both in Greek and in Hebrew. His writings are neither
remarkably fine representatives of classical culture nor the product of deep
learning in Jewish literature and history. They do, however, tell the reader a
great deal not known from other sources. *The Jewish War* (75–79), based to a
great extent on what Josephus himself saw, heard, and experienced, describes
the tragic events of the Jewish revolt against Rome. *Antiquities of the Jews* (93)
covers the history of the Jews from creation to the war with Rome, with special
attention given to the Maccabees and the dynasty of Herod.

BOOKS BY JOSEPHUS

The Jewish War. Trans. by G. A. Williamson. Ed. by E. Mary Smallwood. Viking Penguin
   1984 $7.95. ISBN 0-14-044420-3. Investigation of the history of the Jews from 168
   B.C. to A.D. 135; analyzes the Jewish rebellion of A.D. 66–73.
Works. 9 vols. Trans. by H. Thackery and others. Ed. by E. H. Warmington. *Loeb Class.
   Lib.* o.p.

BOOK ABOUT JOSEPHUS

Rajak, Tessa. *Josephus: The Historian and His Society*. Ed. by E. H. Warmington. Fortress Pr. 1984 o.p. Critical look at Josephus's life and work and how it reflects Jewish society of the period.

LIVY (TITUS LIVIUS). c.59 B.C.–A.D. 17

Very little is known about the life of Livy (Titus Livius) other than that he was born in Patavium (modern-day Padua) and lived most of his life in Rome. It is clear from his writings that he was familiar with ancient Greek and Latin literature and was, in fact, influenced by CICERO (see also Vols. 2 and 4).

Although Livy produced several works on philosophy and literary criticism, his masterpiece and life work of 40 years was his *History of Rome*, which covers a vast sweep of Rome's history from its origins to Livy's own time. Of the original 142 books that made up the work, only 35 are extant—Books 1–10 and 20–45—which treat the years 753–293 B.C. and 218–167 B.C. Fragments of others, however, do remain, and summaries exist of all but one. When he wrote the history, Livy, who extolled the virtues of discipline, piety, and patriotism, believed that Rome was in a state of decline and moral decay. Wealth and luxury, he wrote, had led to "the dark dawning of our modern day, when we can neither endure our vices nor face the remedies needed to cure them."

According to modern standards, Livy was neither an impressive nor critical historian. He perpetuated many inaccuracies. This, however, does not greatly minimize the value of his writing. His acumen lay in his vibrant style, his keen eye for character, and his gift for dramatic composition.

BOOKS BY LIVY

The Early History of Rome. Trans. by Aubrey de Selincourt. Rev. by Robert Ogilvie. Viking Penguin 1960 $4.95. ISBN 0-14-044104-2. Contains Books 1–5.
Rome and Italy. Trans. by Betty Radice. Viking Penguin 1982 $5.95. ISBN 0-14-044388-6. Contains Books 6–10.
Rome and the Mediterranean. Trans. by Henry Bettenson. Viking Penguin 1976 $6.95. ISBN 0-14-044318-5. Contains Books 31–45.
The War with Hannibal. Trans. by Aubrey de Selincourt. Viking Penguin 1965 $6.95. ISBN 0-14-044145-X. Contains Books 21–30.

BOOK ABOUT LIVY

Lake, E., and F. Porter. *Livy: Hannibal the Scourge of Rome. Selections from Book XXI*. Focus Info. Gr. 1984 repr. of 1934 ed. $14.95. ISBN 0-86292-131-7. Discusses Livy's history of the Carthaginian general who tried to conquer Rome.

PLINY THE YOUNGER (GAIUS PLINIUS CAECILIUS SECUNDUS). c.61–c.112

Northern Italian-born and orphaned at an early age, [Gaius Plinius Caecilius Secundus]—Pliny the Younger—was adopted by his uncle, the naturalist PLINY THE ELDER (see also Vol. 5). First a student and then a practitioner of law, he served Rome in a variety of official capacities, including senator, consul, and governor of Bithynia in Asia Minor. As governor he corresponded with the emperor Trajan on such issues as the treatment of Christians, whom Pliny viewed as superstitious and harmless.

Pliny is best known for his letters, which probably were written for publication. Published in 10 books (100–112), the letters are a valuable source of historical information about the personal, financial, and political life of a wealthy and cultured upper-class Roman of the early Roman Empire. Books I through IX incorporate letters addressed to friends, whereas Book X consists of Pliny's correspondence with Trajan.

BOOK BY PLINY THE YOUNGER

The Letters of the Younger Pliny. Trans. by Betty Radice. Viking Penguin 1963 $6.95. ISBN 0-14-044127-1. An edition of selected letters, including many on law and politics.

PLUTARCH. c.46–c.125

Considered by many the most important Greek writer of the early Roman period, Plutarch was a member of a well-to-do Greek family, a chief magistrate, a priest at Delphi, and an exceptionally well-read individual. His philosophical views were based on those of PLATO (see Vol. 4) and, although a Greek, he esteemed the achievements and attributes of the Romans.

By the time Plutarch's works were published for the first time in the eleventh century, some had already been lost. He wrote innumerable essays on philosophical, historical, political, religious, and literary subjects, 78 of which survive today and are known collectively as the "Moralia." He is known primarily, however, for his *Parallel Lives of Greeks and Romans*, which consists of 50 biographies—23 of prominent Greeks, 23 of Roman leaders, and 4 separate lives—accompanied at intervals by short comparative essays. Although historical information is included in the work, Plutarch wrote it originally to inspire emulation in youth, so the emphasis is on character, moral choice, and anecdote. Sir Thomas North's 1579 translation into English of *Parallel Lives* became an important source for WILLIAM SHAKESPEARE (see Vol. 1), which he used for three plays, *Julius Caesar, Antony and Cleopatra*, and *Coriolanus*.

BOOKS BY PLUTARCH

The Age of Alexander: Nine Greek Lives. Trans. by Ian Scott-Kilvert. Viking Penguin 1973 $7.95. ISBN 0-14-044286-3. Selections from Plutarch's *Lives*, focusing on leaders during the Hellenistic age.

The Fall of the Roman Republic: Six Roman Lives. Trans. by Rex Warner. Viking Penguin 1954 $8.95. ISBN 0-14-044084-4. Additional biographies from the *Lives*, of the Roman period.

The Makers of Rome: Nine Lives by Plutarch. Trans. by Ian Scott-Kilvert. Viking Penguin 1965 $8.95. ISBN 0-14-044158-1

Plutarch's Lives. Trans. by John Dryden. Random 1977 $20.00. ISBN 0-394-60407-5. Complete edition of *Parallel Lives*; includes accounts of the lives of Coriolanus, Fabius Maximus, Macellus, Cato the Elder, Tiberius Gracchus, Gaius Gracchus, Sertorius, Brutus, and Mark Anthony.

The Rise and Fall of Athens: Nine Greek Lives. Trans. by Ian Scott-Kilvert. Viking Penguin 1960 $7.95. ISBN 0-14-044102-6. Biographies of Greek leaders from the Classical period; provides an account of the rise and fall of Athens.

BOOKS ABOUT PLUTARCH

Russell, D. A. *Plutarch. Class. Life and Letters Ser.* Ed. by John S. White. Biblio Dist. 1979 o.p. Discusses Plutarch's narrative style in his biographies.

Stadter, Philip A. *Plutarch's Historical Methods: An Analysis of the Mulierum Virtues. Loeb Class. Lib.* HUP 1965 o.p. Analysis of one of Plutarch's essays, focusing on his historical method.

POLYBIUS. c.200–c.118 B.C.

Polybius was a well-educated Greek politician who witnessed, participated in, and wrote of the rise and triumph of the Roman Empire. As a result of years spent as a hostage in Rome, he came to admire that empire and its institutions and became friendly with many eminent Roman statesmen. Under the patronage of the Scipios, an ancient and powerful Roman patrician family, Polybius wrote a 40-book history that covers the Mediterranean world from before 200 B.C. to 146 B.C. and includes general discussions on such topics as the purpose of history writing and the principles of the Roman state. Of the 40 books, only the first five have survived intact, with portions of the others in excerpts. Polybius's presentation is solemn, analytical, and without rhetoric. The style of the meticulously researched work, however, has been criticized for its moralizing tone and overwhelming amount of detail.

BOOKS BY POLYBIUS

Histories. Trans. by Mortimer Chambers. Ed. by E. Badian. Irvington 1986 repr. of 1966 ed. $29.50. ISBN 0-8290-2014-4. Contains complete extant books of Polybius's history of the ancient Mediterranean world.

The Rise of the Roman Empire. Trans. by Ian Scott-Kilvert. Viking Penguin 1980 $8.95. ISBN 0-14-044362-2. Good translation of Polybius's history of Rome and Greece; analysis of the Punic wars.

BOOK ABOUT POLYBIUS

Walbank, F. W. *A Historical Commentary on Polybius.* 3 vols. Ed. by E. Badian. OUP Vol. 1 o.p. Vol. 2 1982 repr. of 1967 ed. $130.00. ISBN 0-19-814173-4. Vol. 3 1979 $145.00. ISBN 0-19-814011-8. Examines the narrative style of Polybius and his analyses of history.

PROCOPIUS. c.500–c.565

Born in Caesarea in Palestine and trained in law, Procopius had a distinguished military and official career. He accompanied Byzantine general Belisarius on his campaigns in North Africa, Syria, and Italy and for a time served as prefect of Constantinople, where he is thought to have lived until his death. Procopius wrote two very different histories of his time—*Procopius' History of His Own Time* and *Secret History of Procopius.* The former is an official and military history covering primarily the wars against the Goths, Vandals, and Persians. The latter is an unofficial, anecdotal, and scurrilous court chronicle that became the source of scandals attributed to the empress Theodora. Procopius also authored a six-book work, *On Buildings,* devoted to buildings erected by the emperor Justianian. Collectively, his works are a major source of knowledge of the reign and times of Justinian.

BOOKS BY PROCOPIUS

Secret Wars. Trans. by Richard Atwater. U. of Mich. Pr. 1961 $7.95. ISBN 0-472-08778-2. Foreword by A. E. Bouk.

Works. 7 vols. Trans. by H. B. Ewing. *Loeb Class. Lib.* HUP o.p.

BOOK ABOUT PROCOPIUS

Evans, J. A. *Procopius.* Irvinton 1972 $17.95. ISBN 0-8290-1748-8

SALLUST (GAIUS SALLUSTIUS CRISPUS). 86–35 B.C.

Roman historian and politician [Gaius Sallustius Crispus], known as Sallust, was a tribune of the people and a praetor. In 50 B.C., after being expelled from the Senate supposedly for adultery, he showed his support for JULIUS CAESAR by participating in his African campaign and by serving as his governor in Numidia (modern-day Algeria). Charged with extortion upon his return to Rome, he retreated from public life and retired to literary pursuits. His first work, *Catilina* (43–42 B.C.), recounts the suppression of Catiline's conspiracy to seize power. His next work, *Jugurtha* (41–40 B.C.), focuses on the frailties of the Roman aristocracy during the war against the Numidian king Jugurtha. Sallust's *Histories*—his last work—devoted to the history of Rome, survives only in fragments and probably covers the period from 78 to 67 B.C. In his literary pursuits, which tend to be inaccurate and strongly biased, Sallust distinguished himself more for his terse and direct style than for substance.

BOOKS BY SALLUST

The Jugurthine War (and *The Conspiracy of Catiline*). Trans. by S. A. Handford. Viking Penguin 1964 $9.95. ISBN 0-14-044132-8. Competent translation of Sallust's account of the war between the Numidian king Jugurtha and the Roman army.

Sallust. Trans. by J. C. Rolfe. *Loeb Class. Lib.* HUP 1921 o.p. A scholarly, early edition of Sallust; contains an analysis of the orations and letters from histories.

BOOKS ABOUT SALLUST

Earl, D. C. *The Political Thought of Sallust*. Cambridge U. Pr. 1961 o.p. Critical look at Sallust's political philosophy and its impact on his writings.

Syme, Ronald. *Sallust*. U. CA Pr. 1974 repr. of 1964 ed. $59.95. ISBN 0-520-01246-1. Readable biography of Sallust; focuses on his life, work, and historical bias.

SUETONIUS (GAIUS SUETONIUS TRANQUILLUS). c.69–c.140

Gaius Suetonius Tranquillus—Suetonius—was born on the north coast of Africa. Although he held a variety of official positions under emperors of the first and early second centuries, he achieved no distinction in such pursuits. However, some of those positions, such as the one as an imperial secretary under the emperor Hadrian, provided him access to documents of great use to him as a writer. Suetonius is best known as a biographer. Most of his c.113 work, *De Viris Illustribus (On Illustrious Men)*, which consists of 34 biographies of Roman writers, has been lost. But his *Lives of the Caesars* (c.121) survives, distinguished more for its encyclopedic compilation of detail than for critical historical inquiry. The racy, often scandalous, biographies of JULIUS CAESAR and of Rome's first 11 emperors, from Augustus to Domitian, inspired two well-known works by the British poet and novelist ROBERT GRAVES (see also Vol. 1)—*I, Claudius* (1934) and *Claudius the God* (1934).

BOOKS BY SUETONIUS

Lives of the Caesars. 2 vols. *Loeb Class. Lib.* HUP $15.50 ea. ISBNs 0-674-99035-8, 0-674-99042-0. Competent edition of Suetonius's *Lives*.

The Twelve Caesars. Trans. by Robert Graves. Viking Penguin 1957 $8.95. ISBN 0-14-044072-0. Edition noted for its translation by Robert Graves.

BOOKS ABOUT SUETONIUS

Baldwin, B. *Suetonius: The Biographer of the Caesars*. Coronet Bks. 1983 $87.50. ISBN 0-317-46477-9

Wallace-Hadrill, Andrew. *Suetonius: The Scholar and His Caesars*. Yale U. Pr. 1984 $27.50. ISBN 0-300-03000-2. Critical examination of Suetonius's work, focusing on its narrative style.

TACITUS, CORNELIUS. c.56–c.120

Tacitus was a Roman senator who survived the terror launched among the Roman aristocracy by the emperor Domitian to rise to prominence and become first suffect consul and later proconsul of Asia. His historical works, which originally covered the first century of the empire from the accession of Tiberius to the assassination of Domitian, are an indictment of the emperors and of the senatorial aristocracy under imperial autocracy. They remain the fundamental sources of imperial history in this period. The embarrasing paradox of Tacitus's success under a "bad" emperor appears to have had an effect on his works, whose tone may have struck contemporaries as a defense of his prominence under a despot.

Tacitus is thus often thought to have nursed a nostalgia for the Republic and the free nobility of its senatorial order. However, his attitude is less genuinely backward-looking than occupied with the contemporary moral and political problems of aristocratic honor. In *The Annals*, which survives only in part, he examines palace politics under the Julio-Claudians. The unspoken questions that occupy this examination are those of the possibilities of uncompromised and dignified service under despotism, and the opportunities therein to mitigate its evil. These themes emerge into daylight in *The Agricola*, his laudatory biography of his father-in-law, the Roman general who conquered Britain. The work portrays Agricola as a straightforward military man who preserved his integrity and the admiration of his contemporaries under the emperor Domitian, even though his greatest achievements went unrewarded.

Tacitus was a trained advocate, and fundamental to his outlook is his prosecutorial purpose. He states the case against the emperors and others who attract his unfavorable judgment. This bias can be difficult for the reader to overcome. But Tacitus also played by the rules of advocacy. He appears to bring to light facts unfavorable to his case in order to interpret them according to the necessities of his argument. His lawyerly honesty thereby allows the historian to dissect the facts from their matrix in order to use them in reconstructing a historical account of the first century of the empire which is more balanced, if inevitably less committed, than that of Tacitus.

BOOKS BY TACITUS

The Agricola and the Germania. Trans. by Hugh Mattingly. Viking Penguin 1971 $5.95. ISBN 0-14-044241-3. An account of the life of Gnaeus Julius Agricola, Tacitus's father-in-law; noted for its elevated style and dramatic force.

The Annals of Imperial Rome. Trans. by Michael Grant. Viking Penguin 1956 $7.95. ISBN 0-14-044060-7. Explores the history of the first Caesars and of Rome under their reign.

The Histories. Trans. by Kenneth Wellesley. Viking Penguin 1976 $6.95. ISBN 0-14-044150-6. Traces the history of Rome during the reign of the Flavians.

BOOKS ABOUT TACITUS

Martin, R. *Tacitus*. U. CA Pr. 1981 $47.50. ISBN 0-520-04427-4. Sound overview containing much good sense.

Mellor, Ronald. *Tacitus*. Routledge 1992 $25.00. ISBN 0-415-90665-2. Challenging interpretation by an excellent scholar.

Syme, Ronald. *Tacitus*. 2 vols. OUP 1980 $145.00. ISBN 0-19-814327-3. Comprehensive look at the life and work of Tacitus.

THUCYDIDES. c.460–400 B.C.

Born into a family of Athens's old nobility claiming descent from the Homeric hero Ajax of Salamis, Thucydides pursued a political career under Pericles and served as a general in the Great Peloponnesian War of 431–404 B.C. His subsequent exile for failure to prevent a Spartan takeover of an Athenian colony in Thrace enabled him to observe the war from both sides. In his history of the war, he examines the policies and motives of the people involved with a calculated rationality that nevertheless conveys great passion. Although his narrative style is lucid and astringent, the language of the speeches that he gives his protagonists is some of the most difficult, yet rhetorically powerful, Greek from any period of antiquity. The work is deeply serious in tone. As Thucydides tells his readers at the beginning of the work, it contains nothing of entertainment value. He meant it, as he says, to be not simply a set-piece written for the delectation of an audience, but a "possession for ever."

As HERODOTUS was the inventor of universal history, Thucydides was the inventor of the analytical historical monograph. He wrote in conscious contrast to Herodotus, whose work is full of entertaining fable and romance. While Herodotus wrote about the past by using all manner of traditions gleaned in his travels, Thucydides considered only contemporary history to be reliable and writes as an interrogator and witness of contemporary men and events.

The gods, too, are absent from Thucydides's work, which scrutinizes human motivations as the exclusive business of history. The most powerful intellectual influences visible are the fully rational method of description and prognosis developed by the Hippocratic physicians and the tools of logical analysis and verbal argument then being forged by the Sophists. Behind these, however, lay a sense of tragedy. The history of Thucydides possesses the rhythm of a Sophoclean drama of reversal of fortune in which Athens falls from the pinnacle of imperial success and brilliance into political corruption, ruthless and amoral imperial aggression, and finally utter defeat and disaster. Athens's imperial hubris leads to its nemesis at the hands of Sparta, a conservative and landlocked state that had been powerless at the beginning of the war to inflict significant harm on the Athenians.

Thucydides's work is unfinished. It ends abruptly in midsentence during a discussion of the events of the year 411 B.C. It was continued to the end of the war by XENOPHON. Although very much the intellectual inferior of Thucydides, Xenophon managed by imitation to infuse this part of his *Hellenica*(his continuation to 362 B.C. of the history of Thucydides) with an elevation absent in the rest of his work.

Until relatively recently, scholars took Thucydides at his word as an objective writer. More recently it has been recognized that his work skillfully promotes a patriotic and political argument, written in the climate of postwar recriminations. He presents Athens's empire as a natural consequence of the position of that city-state in the Greek world and the Athenian leader Pericles as Athens's greatest statesman, a leader who had governed Athens and preserved the empire with a firm and intelligent hand.

Thucydides wanted to persuade his readers that Pericles was not the villain who destroyed Athens, that the blame fell to the politicians who came after him and pandered to the most extreme ambitious of the common citizens, the politicians who were the ultimate arbiters of policy in Athens's democracy. Some modern historians remain persuaded by Thucydides's portrait of Pericles and the Athenian democracy, but others argue from Thucydides's own testimony that Pericles led Athens into an unnecessary war in the belief that the opportunity had arrived to advance Athenian domination over the whole of the Greek world.

BOOK BY THUCYDIDES

The Peloponnesian War. Modern Lib. College Ed. Ser. Trans. by Terry Wick. McGraw 1982 $7.88. ISBN 0-07-554377-9

BOOKS ABOUT THUCYDIDES

Allison, June W. *Power and Preparedness in Thucydides*. Johns Hopkins 1989 $24.00. ISBN 0-8018-3821-5. Study of Thucydides' attention to preparation and foresight in the practice of war and politics.

Connor, W. Robert. *Thucydides*. Princeton U. Pr. 1987 $15.95. ISBN 0-691-10239-2. Scholarly biography of Thucydides and critical look at his history of the Peloponnesian War.

Finley, John H., Jr. *Three Essays on Thucydides*. Loeb Class. Monographs Ser. Bks. Demand repr. of 1967 ed. $57.50. ISBN 0-7837-3863-3. Compilation of previously published material on Thucydides, focusing on his views of Pericles.

Gomme, A. W., and others. *A Historical Commentary on Thucydides*. 5 vols. OUP 1956–81 $95.00. ISBN 0-19-814198-X. The standard work in English.

Hornblower, Simon. *A Commentary on Thucydides*. Vol. 1, Bks. I–III. OUP 1991 $120.00. ISBN 0-19-814880-1. Useful supplement to Gomme's *Historial Commentary*. Contains up-to-date bibliography.

———. *Thucydides*. Johns Hopkins 1987 $32.50. ISBN 0-8018-3259-1. Straightforward general study that perpetuates many older views.

Hunter, Virginia J. *Past and Process in Herodotus and Thucydides*. 1981 $44.50. ISBN 0-691-3556-3. Illuminating comparative study that stresses the underlying commonalties between the very different approaches of the two historians.

Ostwald, Martin. *Anarke in Thucydides*. Scholars Pr. GA 1988 $17.95. ISBN 1-55540-279-8. Study of necessity versus human freedom of action in Thucydides' history.

Parry, Adam. *Logos and Ergon in Thucydides*. 1981 $26.95. ISBN 0-405-14045-2. Far-reaching essay on word and action, thought and deed, appearance and reality, in the thought of Thucydides.

Pouncey, Peter. *The Necessities of War: A Study of Thucydides' Pessimism*. Bks. Demand repr. of 1980 ed. $55.40. ISBN 0-8357-8965-9. Argues that Thucydides's account of Pericles is basically sound.

Rawlings, Hunter R., III. *The Structure of Thucydides' History*. Bks. Demand repr. of 1981 ed. $76.20. ISBN 0-8357-7898-3. Critical analysis of Thucydides's work and its historical accuracy.

Westlake, H. D. *Studies in Thucydides and Greek History*. 1988 o.p. Series of essays on Thucydides and his role as a historian.

XENOPHON. c.434?–c.355? B.C.

Xenophon's life and personality is better known to us, perhaps, than that of any other Greek who lived before Alexander the Great. Much of his considerable output of historical writing and essays is frankly or implicitly autobiographical. He reveals himself as one of those many Athenians and other Greeks who turned to autocratic political models, including admiration of Persia, after the excesses of the Athenian democracy led to disaster in the Peloponnesian War. He also reveals himself as much more than a literary man and a critic of his times. A gentleman adventurer and something of a professional soldier, he followed in turn the philosopher SOCRATES (see Vol. 4), the Persian prince Cyrus the Younger, and the Spartan king Agesilaus, all of whom he wrote about with an air of close personal knowledge. His works include the autobiographical *Anabasis*, an account of his service with a mercenary Greek army that marched from Mesopotamia to the Black Sea after the defeat and death of the younger Cyrus. It provides the most detailed single perspective on the military practices and military mentality of Xenophon's age. His *Hellenica*, by contrast, is an impersonal continuation to the end of the Peloponnesian War of the work of THUCYDIDES and a patchy memoir that concentrates on Sparta's fortunes until the definitive end of its power in 362 B.C.

Xenophon's other major works are the *Cyropaedia* and the rambling Socratic dialogues known as the *Memorabilia*. The *Cyropaedia* is a fictional idealization of the career of Cyrus the Great, the only great conqueror known to the Greeks before Alexander. Often regarded merely as a novel, it is a species of a priori historical reconstruction. A retrojection of the military science and political values of the day into a largely unknown Persia of the past, it is intended to explain Cyrus's success on rational principles. The *Memorabilia* and the Socratic *Apology* that comes down with them contain nothing of philosophical value but are thought by some scholars to offer a possible corrective to PLATO's (see Vol. 4) altogether too Platonic Socrates.

Xenophon had a conventional and second-rate mind, but he is a valuable resource because of his mediocrity. He enables us to make contact with an ordinary intellect from a world that often seems dominated by geniuses.

BOOKS BY XENOPHON

Complete Works. 7 vols. *Loeb Class. Lib.* HUP 1914–1925 o.p.
A History of My Times. Trans. by Rex Warner. Viking Penguin 1979 $9.95. ISBN 0-14-044175-1
The Persian Expedition. Trans. by Rex Warner. Viking Penguin 1949 o.p.

BOOKS ABOUT XENOPHON

Anderson, J. K. *Xenophon. Class, Life and Letters Ser.* Biblio Distr. 1979 o.p. Well-written biography, focusing on the significance of his work.
Hirsch, S. W. *The Friendship of the Barbarians: Xenophon and the Persian Empire.* U. Pr. of New Eng. 1985 $30.00. ISBN 0-87451-322-7. Biographical account of the relationship between Xenophon and Cyrus the Younger.

CHAPTER 11

European History

Arthur Mitchell

The study of history is said to enlarge and enlighten the mind. Why? Because,
as I conceive, it gives it a power of judging of passing events, and of all events,
and a conscious superiority over them, which before it did not possess.
—John Henry Newman

The influence of European civilization is apparent around the world. People of
European descent control the Americas and Australia and are scattered around
the fringes of Africa and Asia. Although Europe's direct control of Africa and
Asia has ended, European models of organization, culture, and thought remain
powerful examples in most of the world. European civilization in this century
has been convulsed with social and nationalist conflict, but it still retains its
energy and creativity in science, in technology, in culture, and in political
institutions. Most of the rest of the world has had to react and respond to
European achievement.

In geographic terms, Europe is not a continent, but a relatively small
extension of the Eurasian land mass, the great "world island." Yet it is defined
geographically—north to south from the Arctic Sea to the Mediterranean, and
east to west from the Ural Mountains to the Atlantic seaboard—and recognized
as a single civilization, though one strongly divided along linguistic/nationalist
lines. This is readily apparent in interpretation of history; the great schools of
thought about the past are generally delimited by national groupings. The
nineteenth-century historian Jacob Burckhardt once defined historical studies
as contemplation based upon the sources. The results of this contemplation,
however, are clearly conditioned by where it is done.

Since the end of World War II, Europeans have been bridging their divisions
through the European Economic Community, which is fostering social and
political as well as economic integration. The collapse of the Soviet bloc in
recent years has increased the likelihood of further unity.

GENERAL STUDIES AND REFERENCE WORKS

Aldcroft, Derek H. and Richard Rodger. *Bibliography of European Economic and Social
History.* Manchester U. Pr. 1984 $69.95. ISBN 0-7190-3492-2. Covers 1700 to 1939
and cites more than 6,0000 books, articles, and reports.
American Historical Association. *American Historical Association Guide to Historical
Literature.* Macmillan 1961 o.p. Selective annotated bibliography arranged in broad
subject and county groups, each done by a specialist. Valuable, but needs updating.
Anderson, Bonnie S., and Judith P. Zinsser. *A History of Their Own: Women in Europe
from Prehistory to the Present.* HarpC 1989 $16.00. ISBN 0-06-091452-1. Good general
survey of a subject of increasing interest.

Artz, Frederick B. *Intellectual History of Europe from St. Augustine to Marx: A Guide*. Gordon Pr. 1973 $59.95. ISBN 0-8490-0412-8. Excellent outline on the emergence of the European mind.

Barr, Stringfellow. *The Pilgrimage of Western Man*. Greenwood 1974 $35.00. ISBN 0-8371-6152-5. Highly readable text written in the grand manner by a grand old man.

Bridenthal, Renate, and Claudia Koonz. *Becoming Visible: Women in European History*. HM 1987 $29.95. ISBN 0-395-41950-6. Well-researched and insightful study of the role of females in the European spectrum.

Clebsch, William. *Christianity in European History*. OUP 1979 $13.95. ISBN 0-19-502472-9. Penetrating study of the role of religion in European development.

Cook, Christopher, and John Stevenson. *Longman Handbook of Modern European History, 1763–1985*. Longman 1987 $22.95. ISBN 0-582-48584-3. Coverage of Europe in the broad sense, including events in Russia, the Balkans, and Scandinavia. Presents chronological, statistical, and tabular information, with biographies of important persons, a glossary of terms, and a subject bibliography.

DeRougemont, Denis. *Love in the Western World*. Schocken 1990 $12.95. ISBN 0-8052-0950-6. Intellectual tour de force on love that goes back to the troubadors.

Durant, Will, and Ariel Durant. *The Lessons of History*. S&S Trade 1968 $17.95. ISBN 0-671-41333-3. Readable examination of various aspects of civilization.

Foucault, Michel. *History of Sexuality, Vol. 1*. Random 1990 $10.00. ISBN 0-679-72469-9. Necessary reading about a subject that historians long neglected.

Frey, Linda, Marsha Frey, and Joanne Schneider. *Women in Western European History: A Select Chronological, Geographical, and Topical Bibliography from Antiquity to the French Revolution*. Greenwood 1984 $85.00. ISBN 0-313-22859-0

Greer, Thomas H., and Gavin Lewis. *A Brief History of the Western World*. HarBraceJ 1992 $25.00. ISBN 0-15-505552-6. Widely used one-volume text with clear, concise narrative.

Hook, Sidney. *The Hero in History: A Study in Limitation and Possibility*. Transaction Pubs. 1991 $29.95. ISBN 0-88738-428-5. Fascinating examination of myth and leadership originally published in 1943.

Kennedy, Paul. *The Rise and Fall of the Great Powers: Economic Change and Military Conflict from 1500 to 2000*. Random 1987 $24.95. ISBN 0-394-54674-1. Lengthy and thought-provoking investigation of how major powers drive themselves to bankruptcy in the pursuit of greater glory.

Jones, Eric L. *The European Miracle: Environments, Economies and Geopolitics in the History of Europe and Asia*. Cambridge U. Pr. 1987 $39.50. ISBN 0-521-33670-8

Kranzberg, Melville, and Carroll Pursell. *Technology in Western Civilization*. 2 vols. OUP 1967 o.p. Provides insight into the reasons Westerners have excelled in the development of technology.

Langer, William L. *The New Illustrated Encyclopedia of World History*. Abrams 1975 $44.00. ISBN 0-395-13592-3. This newest 2-volume edition of a standard reference work includes world developments through 1970 and adds a chapter on "the Recent Period" addressing space exploration and scientific-technical advances. Text is same as 1972 edition except for correction of errors and additions of illustrations.

Lindemann, Albert S. *A History of European Socialism*. Yale U. Pr. 1983 $45.00. ISBN 0-300-02797-4. Concise and balanced history of the ideological rival to capitalism.

Mackinder, Halford. *The Geographical Pivot of History*. 1904 o.p. Declares, contrary to Mahan's thesis, that the force that controls eastern Europe dominates the heartland of the "world island."

McNeill, William H. *The Rise of the West*. U. Ch. Pr. 1991 $19.95. ISBN 0-226-56141-0. Difficult but insightful worldview. A book to chew on, small bites at a time. Winner of the 1964 National Book Award.

Matossian, Mary K. *Poisons of the Past: Molds, Epidemics, and History*. Yale U. Pr. 1989 $25.00. ISBN 0-300-03949-2. Explores the role of infectious diseases in human affairs.

Mitchell, Brian. *European Historical Statistics, 1750–1970*. Col. U. Pr. 1979 $34.50. ISBN 0-231-04569-7. A volume of historical economic statistics covering the years 1840 to 1954.

Mosse, George L. *The Culture of Western Europe: The Nineteenth and Twentieth Centuries*. Westview 1988 $22.95. ISBN 0-8133-0623-X. Valuable survey of cultural traditions.

Mosse, George, and others, eds. *Europe in Review: Reading and Sources*. Rand McNally 1962 o.p. Examines how societies have confronted modern warfare and the political consequences of that confrontation.

Muller, Herbert J. *The Uses of the Past*. OUP 1957 o.p. Collection of articles that is required reading for anyone interested in what civilization is all about.

Ortega y Gasset, José. *An Interpretation of Universal History*. Norton 1984 $7.95. ISBN 0-393-00751-0. Engaging romp from classical times to early modern European history. Puts Arnold Toynbee's theories under the microscope.

Palmer, R. R., and Joel Colten. *A History of the Modern World*. Knopf 1991 $54.50. ISBN 0-679-41014-7. This will be a standard work for many years to come.

Quigley, Carroll. *The Evolution of Civilizations: An Introduction to Historical Analysis*. Liberty Fund 1979 $20.00. ISBN 0-913966-56-8. Interesting look at universal patterns of development.

Roach, John. *A Bibliography of Modern History*. Bks. Demand repr. of 1968 ed. $103.00. ISBN 0-8357-7197-0. Relatively short but useful compilation.

Stearns, Peter N. *The Face of Europe*. Forum Pr. IL 1977 $7.95. ISBN 0-88273-400-8. Excellent short treatment of a large subject.

Stromberg, Roland N. *European Intellectual History since 1789*. P-H 1990. ISBN 0-13-291998-2. Standard work on the role of ideas in shaping what Europeans did to themselves and to the world.

Toynbee, Arnold. *A Study of History*. OUP 1946 $25.00. ISBN 0-19-500198-2. Classic volume that outlines Toynbee's "challenge-response" philosophy of history.

Walford, Albert John. *Walford's Guide to Reference Material*. Vol. 2. 4th ed. Lib. Assoc. 1982 o.p.

Williams, E. Neville. *The Facts on File Dictionary of European History, 1485–1789*. Facts on File 1980 o.p. Entries on important people and subjects; emphasis is on political history.

FOUNDATIONS OF EUROPEAN CIVILIZATION

European civilization was the next to last of the great civilizations to be established; Islamic civilization followed a bit later. Europe's foundations rest on the tripod of Christianity, the Greco-Roman heritage, and the energy and ambition of the barbarian peoples.

Because Christianity was an import, with roots in the western fringe of Asia, the Europeans escaped the difficult task of forging a comprehensive developed religion for themselves. Nor did they have to create a religious structure; they simply borrowed the great model of organization of the Roman Empire and applied it to the church. Where Europe did contribute to this religion was in theology—the formulation of a body of thought about Christian beliefs.

The Greco-Roman heritage was also fundamental in the emergence of Europe. The incredible creative range of the ancient Greeks is seen in their work in philosophy, science, mathematics, architecture, and political institutions. The Romans took everything they could from the Greeks, broadened and refined it, added some ideas of their own, and then developed a massive empire that ringed the Mediterranean and flowed northward to the natural boundaries of the Rhine, the Alps, and the Danube. The Romans left a permanent mark on Europe; even today there is a north-south gradient, with southern Europe more cosmopolitan, tolerant, and worldly, and northern Europe narrower and more ethnocentric.

The Germanic barbarians were the third leg of the tripod. They put an end to the declining "classical" civilization of the Greeks and Romans, and in the process inflicted enormous physical damage and substantially disrupted economic and political arrangements that had existed for centuries. After the destruction of the Roman Empire, Europe went through a tumultuous period— the so-called Dark Ages—while these energetic, strong, and ambitious barbarians groped their way toward the formation of a new civilization.

The first Europeans to put together the combination of Christianity, Greco-Roman learning, and barbarian creativity were the Irish. Ireland's geographic distance from the center of disorder was an undoubted advantage. In this relatively tranquil land the arrival of Christianity, and with it the Greco-Roman heritage, had a profound impact, transforming a preliterate pastoral society into one that devoted enormous amounts of energy and intelligence to cultural interpretation, education, and literacy. The Irish demonstrated the possibilities of building a new, European civilization on the three legs of the tripod.

Initially, however, the most that could be achieved was the establishment of small, semistable, local economic and political units. Political organization on a larger scale was still beyond the capacity of the Europeans, who were divided not only by the north-south cultural gradient but also by a multiplicity of languages. Unlike Chinese or Islamic civilization, Europe was marked from the beginning by great cultural, ethnic, and linguistic diversity. Although the European languages can be grouped in four major families—Romance (or Latin–based), Germanic, Slavic, and Celtic—the many languages in vernacular use have constituted a serious barrier to the formation of cultural and political unity. In terms of historical knowledge, these languages have limited mutual understanding, particularly of the smaller groups of peoples of Europe. Charlemagne's vast Holy Roman Empire dissolved after his death in the early ninth century, and out of it came several regions loosely affiliated by language, custom, and culture. No other centralized state would develop until the sixth century.

Bark, W. C. *Origins of the Medieval World.* Stanford U. Pr. 1958 $25.00. ISBN 0-8047-0513-5. Excellent introduction to the beginnings of a distinctive European civilization.

Barraclough, Geoffrey. *The Crucible of Europe: The Ninth and Tenth Centuries in European History.* U. CA Pr. 1976 $10.95. ISBN 0-520-03118-0. A major study of this formative period.

Bieler, Ludwig. *Ireland and the Culture of Early Medieval Europe.* Ashgate Pub. Co. 1980 $83.95. ISBN 0-86078-211-5

Dawson, Christopher. *The Making of Europe.* 1957 o.p. Emphasizes Christianity as the dominant force in the formation of European civilization.

Duby, Georges. *The Early Growth of the European Economy.* Cornell Univ. Pr. 1978 $9.95. ISBN 0-8014-9169-X. Discussion of the economy by a leading French medievalist.

Herrin, Judith. *The Formation of Christendom.* Princeton U. Pr. 1989 $18.95. ISBN 0691-00831-0. Examines the role of religion in the formation of European civilization.

Lewis, A. R. *Emerging Medieval Europe.* 1967 o.p. Extensive examination of social and economic development.

Lewis, Bernard. *The Arabs in History.* HarpC 1960 $11.00. ISBN 0-06-131029-8. Relates the story of Arab stimulation of Europe.

Moss, Henry S. *The Birth of the Middle Ages, 395–814.* Greenwood 1980 $55.00. ISBN 0-313-22708-X. An English historian's examination of the origins of medieval Europe.

Pirenne, Henri. *Mohammed and Charlemagne.* B & N Imports 1983 $17.95. ISBN 0-389-20134-0

Roesdahl, Else. *The Vikings.* Viking Penguin 1991 $24.95. ISBN 0-7139-9048-1. Examines the paradox of violence and destruction, creativity and construction that characterized the Vikings.

Sullivan, Richard E. *Heirs of the Roman Empire.* Cornell Univ. Pr. 1960 $7.95. ISBN 0-8014-9854-6. Readable account of the period of transition.

MEDIEVAL EUROPE

It was on the modest base of manorialism, with its provision of a stable food supply and a slowly growing agricultural productivity, that the new European civilization was built. Its first great achievement was the establishment of a single unifying religion for the whole of Europe. Despite this accomplishment, the east-west division between right thought and right action that went back to the Greeks and the Romans worked its way into Christian theology and the European mind. Also dividing east and west was the issue of authority in the church. In western Europe the pope emerged as the acknowledged head of the church after the collapse of the western empire in the fifth and sixth centuries. In the Eastern Mediterranean and the Balkans, however, the Byzantine empire survived until the fifteenth century, and there religious and political authority were concentrated in the person of the emperor. Thus there was state control of religion in the east, while in the west the church remained largely independent of political domination. Over the centuries popes strenuously resisted attempts by emerging political entities to take control of the church, and secular rulers just as strenuously resisted attempts by popes to take control of their affairs. From exposure to frequent controversies between church and state, people in the west developed the idea that diversity of opinion was normal and legitimate, and this idea later became the basis of freedom of speech. In the East the Byzantine model of centralized authority prevailed, and the idea that there could be only one official point of view became strongly established.

By the year 1100 Europe had become a powerful entity in the world, largely because of the steady rise in its agricultural productivity. With an expanding food supply, it was possible to shift human resources out of basic food production and into other activities—hence the rise of towns and cities. These emerging urban centers permitted people to acquire a wider range of experience. Where the countryside was feudal, traditional, and communal, the towns were free of feudal control, innovative, and individualistic. With the removal of the old conservative restraints came the unleashing of the greatest source of human achievement—the energy, creativity and ambition of the individual.

Large political units had also been permanently established by 1100. The medieval kingdom was based on a common language; a delimited area claimed by people who spoke that language; an economic foundation in an expanding, efficient agricultural system and dynamic towns; and political leadership provided by a collection of families, one of which formed a dynasty. Political development was uneven. Some peoples developed substantial medieval kingdoms; others did not. More than half a dozen kingdoms took shape in this period in the east (Poland and Russia), the north (Sweden and Denmark), along the Danube (Austria), and on the west coast (France and England). The Italians and most of the Germans, however, did not unite politically until modern times.

Two political units—England and Russia—emerged in unique geographic conditions. The fact that England was situated on an island was the governing factor in its rise. Once the other peoples in Britain, and then in Ireland, had been subordinated, England created a superior navy and used control of the seas as its primary means of defense. Russia, on the other hand, was locked in a land mass next to the nomadic lands of Asia. This was an advantage in that it permitted Russia to develop unmolested by powerful neighbors, and a disadvantage in that it kept the country relatively isolated.

As Europe matured economically and politically, it also grew intellectually with the establishment of universities and the flowering of medieval theology. Medieval theology gave commanding consideration to the matter of logic in religion, borrowing the natural philosophy of the Greeks and examining the Christian religion by its standards. It was THOMAS AQUINAS (born in 1225 A.D. in southern Italy) who wove together Greek philosophy and the faith of Christianity to demonstrate that the religion was logical. Also during this period the first substantial literature in the vernacular emerged; THE SONG OF ROLAND (see Vol. 2), written in medieval French, dates to about 1200.

Perhaps the most important European achievement during this period, however, was in technology. Why technology develops in one place and not in another is not an easy thing to determine. Perhaps it is such a complex matter that there is relatively no simple explanation, because, in fact, high human achievement has occurred in all kinds of places, barring the most severe environments. In any case, by 1100 Europe had experienced substantial technological development and was poised to take the lead in a variety of areas, from agricultural machinery and metallurgy to employment of wind and water power to the construction of large buildings. Some likely factors explaining this lead in technology are the religious influence, which inspired the new civilization's first great buildings, the cathedrals; the splendid physical remains of the Roman Empire—roads, bridges, fortresses, and aqueducts that even in a state of decay aroused admiration and a desire to emulate; and the varied climate and topography, which encouraged a range of agriculture and had a bracing effect on the mind.

According to WILLIAM H. MCNEILL, in his magisterial study The Rise of the West, European civilization by 1100 had developed three distinctive characteristics: the rapid assimilation of outside techniques and ideas, extensive rationalization of human effort, and broad participation in a variety of activities. The result was a more productive mobilization of human and natural resources than anywhere else.

Bloch, Marc. Feudal Society. 2 vols. U. Ch. Pr. 1964. Vol. 1 $8.95. ISBN 0-226-05978-2. Vol. 2 $7.95. ISBN 0-226-05979-0. Comprehensive study of the subject.

Bourke, Vernon J. The Pocket Aquinas. PB 1991 $5.95. ISBN 0-671-73991-3. Representative sections reflect every aspect of Aquinas's thought and philosophy; includes a biographical introduction.

Brooke, Christopher, and Rosalind Brooke. Popular Religion in the Middle Ages. Thames Hudson 1985 $10.95. ISBN 0-500-27381-2. Examines the religious aspirations, hopes, fears, and doctrines of lay people in Western Christendom.

DeRougemont, Denis. Love in the Western World. Schocken 1990 $12.95. ISBN 0-8052-0985-6

Duckett, Eleanor S. Gateway to the Middle Ages: Monasticism. U. of Mich. Pr. 1988 $34.50. ISBN 0-472-09051-8. Important study of the role of religious congregations in the organization and mobilizaton of European energies and capacities.

Ferguson, Chris D. *Europe in Transition: The 12th Century Renaissance in Europe.* Garland 1989 $26.00. ISBN 0-8240-3722-7. Brief introduction to the early Renaissance in Europe.

Gies, Frances, and Joseph Gies. *Women in the Middle Ages.* HarpC 1979 $6.95. ISBN 0-06-464037-X. Contains narrative and quotations from primary sources.

Gimpel, Jean. *The Medieval Machine: The Industrial Revolution of the Middle Ages.* Viking Penguin 1977 $7.95. ISBN 0-14-004514-7. Examines closely the industrial life and institutions of the Middle Ages.

Haskins, Charles Homer. *The Rise of Universities.* Cornell Univ. Pr. 1957 $6.95. ISBN 0-8014-9015-4. An account of the origin and nature of the earliest medieval universities.

Heer, Friedrich. *The Medieval World: Europe 1100 to 1350.* NAL-Dutton 1964 $5.95. ISBN 0-451-62542-0. An illustrated overview of medieval life and civilization.

Hollister, C. Warren. *Medieval Europe: A Short History.* McGraw 1990 $11.40. ISBN 0-07-557141-2. Presents medieval civilization clearly and concisely.

Holmes, Urban T. *Daily Living in the Twelfth Century.* Greenwood 1980 $45.00. ISBN 0-313-22796-9. Interesting and revealing examination of ordinary people in the 1100s.

Huizinga, Johan. *The Waning of the Middle Ages.* Doubleday 1954 $8.95. ISBN 0-385-09288-1. Insightful and highly readable treatment of the end of the first great period of European evolution.

Lawrence, C. H. *Medieval Monasticism.* Longman 1989 $19.95. ISBN 0-582-01727-0. Traces Western monasticism from its fourth-century origins in Egypt to the various forms of religious life in the Middle Ages.

Lewis, Bernard. *The Arabs in History.* HarpC 1960 $11.00. ISBN 0-06-131029-8. A great book that is required reading for European history—and for today's world.

Lyon, H. R. *The Middle Ages: A Concise Encyclopedia.* Thames Hudson 1989 $39.95. ISBN 0-500-25103-7

Mundy, J. H. *Europe in the High Middle Ages, 1150–1309.* Longman 1991 $24.95. ISBN 0-582-49395-1. Highly rated survey of the subject.

Neillands, Robin. *The Hundred Years War.* Routledge 1991 $15.95. ISBN 0-415-07149-6. Account of the on-again, off-again conflict that helped to forge the identities of the first two great European peoples—the French and the English.

Newhall, Richard A. *The Crusades.* Paperbook Pr. Inc. 1991 $2.25. ISBN 1-877891-03-7. Succinct account of the movement that brought about sweeping changes at home.

Ozment, Steven E. *The Age of Reform, 1250–1550.* Yale U. Pr. 1980 $17.00. ISBN 0-300-02760-5. Deals with the intellectual and religious currents that characterized the period.

Painter, Sidney. *Medieval Society.* Paperbook Pr. Inc. 1991 $2.25. ISBN 1-877891-06-1. Contains concrete, brief accounts of daily existence, with emphasis on technological development.

Peters, Edward. *Inquisition.* U. CA Pr. 1989 $12.95. ISBN 0-520-06630-8. An intellectual history that examines the true nature of the Inquisition and the ways it has been perceived.

Phillips, J. R. S. *The Medieval Expansion of Europe.* OUP 1988 $15.95. ISBN 0-19-289123-5

Pirenne, Henri. *Medieval Cities: Their Origins and the Revival of Trade.* Princeton U. Pr. 1952 $10.95. ISBN 0-691-00760-8. Classic treatment of the development of European urbanism.

———. *Economic and Social History of Medieval Europe.* HarBraceJ 1956 $5.95. ISBN 0-15-627533-3

Power, Eileen, and M. Poston. *Medieval Women.* Cambridge U. Pr. 1976 $12.95. ISBN 0-521-09946-3. Excellent collection of articles about the rise of women in an age when "birth determines nothing."

Powers, Eileen. *Medieval People.* HarpC 1971 $7.95. ISBN 0-06-463253-9. Revised and enlarged edition of a valuable study.

Rorig, Fritz. *The Medieval Town.* U. CA Pr. 1967 $12.95. ISBN 0-520-01579-7. Important study of an often neglected aspect of medieval life and times.

Russell, Burton J. *Witchcraft in the Middle Ages*. Cornell Univ. Pr. 1984 $39.95. ISBN 0-8014-0697-8. Chronicles witchcraft in the context of the Catholic Church and views the phenomenon in light of the instability of institutions.

Strayer, Joseph R. *Western Europe in the Middle Ages: A Short History*. Waveland Pr. 1991 $12.95. ISBN 0-88133-624-6. Clear, balanced account of the period and how it affected the region and its populations.

Tierney, Brian, and Sidney Painter. *Western Europe in the Middle Ages: 300–1475*. McGraw 1982 $34.00. ISBN 0-07-554402-4. Excellent general treatment of an important period in Europe's history.

Tuchman, Barbara W. *A Distant Mirror: The Calamitous Fourteenth Century*. Ballantine 1987 $14.00. ISBN 0-345-34957-1. A highly-readable account of the effects of the Black Plague on fourteenth-century society.

White, Lynn, Jr. *Medieval Technology and Social Change*. OUP 1962 $8.95. ISBN 0-19-500266-0

Ziegler, Philip. *The Black Death*. HarpC 1971 $11.00. ISBN 0-06-131550-8. Account of the fourteenth-century plague that wiped out one-third of Europe's population; a horrible story vividly told.

THE RENAISSANCE

The Renaissance was the first full flowering of European civilization. It marked the transition from a medieval worldview to a modern one—and oddly enough, this great change was stimulated by models of antiquity. The enthusiastic interest in classical art, literature, architecture, philosophy, and Roman republican government in fourteenth- and fifteenth-century Italy spread throughout most of Europe and produced something vastly different from both antiquity and the Middle Ages. It was the art historian JACOB BURCKHARDT who, in the nineteenth century, first brought the wonders of this age to the attention of the modern world. Although his work contains oversimplifications, in sweep and majesty his account has no superior.

Since Italy was the center of the classical Roman world, it is fitting that the Renaissance started there. By the fifteenth century several Italian city-states had reached a level of wealth sufficient to afford extravagance in art, literature, and architecture. They combined this extravagance with a commitment to humanism, individualism, secularism, cosmopolitanism, and learning. The great principle that birth determines nothing about a person has galvanized creative energy and ambition in the hearts and minds of millions of people ever since. The sweeping Italian achievements set the agenda for European civilization at the time and ever since.

How do historians account for this staggering demonstration of European power? William H. McNeill provides a succint explanation: Due to the rise of individualism, Europeans were aggressive, forceful, and ruthlessly determined. In addition, they had developed a capacity for disciplined group action, which included the training of animals for warfare. They had clear superiority in weapons. Finally, they unwittingly subjected their Amerindian hosts to the ravages of Eurasian infectious diseases, to which the latter had no immunity. The Europeans had begun the process of world domination.

Aston, Margaret. *The Fifteenth Century*. HarBraceJ 1968 o.p. An outstanding short book.

Berenson, Bernard. *Italian Painters of the Renaissance*. Cornell Univ. Pr. 1980 $13.95. ISBN 0-8014-9195-9. An exposition by the acknowledged authority on the subject.

Boccaccio, Giovanni. *The Decameron*. NAL-Dutton 1982 $5.95. ISBN 0-451-62134-4. Lively, earthy tales circa 1350. Well worth reading, especially for those wanting to gain the flavor of the period.

Bouwsma, William J. *Venice and the Defense of Republican Liberty.* U. CA Pr. 1968 $13.95. ISBN 0-520-00151-6. Focuses on the origins of European republicanism.

Brown, Howard M. *Music in the Renaissance.* P-H 1976 $31.00. ISBN 0-13-608497-4. A lively treatment of theory and performance.

Brucker, Gene A. *The Civic World of Early Renaissance Florence.* Bks. Demand 1977 $45.00. ISBN 0-8357-2612-6. Prize-winning treatment of the rise of Florence.

Burckhardt, Jacob. *The Civilization of the Renaissance in Italy.* Viking Penguin 1990 $9.95. ISBN 0-14-044534-X. Difficult but rewarding reading. Based on lectures from the 1860s, so should be read in conjunction with recent scholarship.

Burke, Peter. *Popular Culture in Early Modern Europe.* Ashgate Pub. Co. 1988 $19.95. ISBN 0-7045-0596-7. Well done survey of the subject.

Cellini, Benvenuto. *Autobiography.* Viking Penguin 1956 $6.95. ISBN 0-14-04409-6. The story of his life and times by a renowned Renaissance artist; according to Goethe, a work from which one learned more than from the historians of the sixteenth century.

Donaldson, Peter S. *Machiavelli and Mystery of State.* Cambridge U. Pr. 1992 $16.95. ISBN 0-521-43790-3. Brilliant analysis that should be consulted after reading Machiavelli.

Ferguson, Wallace K. *The Renaissance in Historical Thought.* AMS Pr. repr. of 1948 ed. $32.50. ISBN 0-404-14887-5. Valuable examination of the wide-ranging influence of the Italian miracle.

Machiavelli, Niccolo. *The Prince.* NAL-Dutton 1952 $2.50. ISBN 0-451-62755-5. Sixteenth-century literary masterpiece that addresses political theory and power.

McCarthy, Mary. *The Stones of Florence.* HarBraceJ 1987 $49.95. ISBN 0-317-64159-X. The famed essayist, novelist, and critic lends her gifts to a lively description of the city.

———. *Venice Observed.* HarBraceJ 1963 $7.95. ISBN 0-15-693521-X. A wonderful travelog that illuminates the dynamic life of this city.

McNeill, William H. *Venice: The Hinge of Europe, 1081–1797.* U. Ch. Pr. 1986 $18.95. ISBN 0-226-56149-6. Read anything written by this excellent historian.

Maclean, Ian. *The Renaissance Notion of Women.* Cambridge U. Pr. 1983 $14.95. ISBN 0-521-27436-2

Miskimin, Harry. *The Economy of Early Renaissance Europe, 1300–1460.* Cambridge U. Pr. 1975 o.p. Best short survey of economic development during the earlier stages of the Renaissance.

Murray, Peter, and Linda Murray. *The Art of the Renaissance.* Thames Hudson 1985 $12.95. ISBN 0-500-20008-4

Pirenne, Henri. *Early Democracies in the Low Countries.* Norton 1971 o.p. Examines medieval urban life and the origin and nature of the medieval town.

Sellery, George C. *Renaissance: Its Nature and Origin.* U. of Wis. Pr. 1962 $5.95. ISBN 0-299-00644-1. Penetrating study of the renewal of the European world.

Tracy, James D. *Erasmus: The Growth of a Mind.* Coronet Bks. 1972 o.p. Inside the mind of the great humanist.

THE REFORMATION

The Reformation demonstrated the power of centrifugal forces within European civilization. Europe was diverse in language, and thus in culture. The effort to maintain one system of religious belief and organization had already broken down along the east-west gradient. In the sixteenth century there came another break, this time along the north-south gradient—the successor states to the Roman world versus the Germanic north. To read the works of the German theologian and reformer MARTIN LUTHER (see Vols. 2 and 4) is to realize the deep resentment of northerners about their exploitation at the hands of Rome. Of course, there was a truly religious dimension to the upheaval—enforced uniformity of belief and organization versus freedom of conscience in both. The immediate results of the Reformation, however, did not include religious freedom but rather the seizure of church property by kingdoms and other political entities in northern Europe and, more importantly, state control of religion. In the Catholic Counter-Reformation the state was also called in as an ally, thus increasing its influence in the church.

The longer-term effects of the Reformation did include the revolutionary idea of freedom of conscience. The French-born reformer JOHN CALVIN (see Vol. 4) is probably best known for his doctrine of predestination, but it was his concept of individual conscience and responsibility that made a creative and liberating force in the parts of Europe to which Calvinism spread.

Bainton, Roland. *The Age of the Reformation*. Krieger 1984 $9.50. ISBN 0-89874-736-8. Short, useful history of a large and complicated subject by an expert on the period.

Bouwsma, William J. *John Calvin, a Sixteenth Century Portrait*. OUP 1989 $12.95. ISBN 0-19-505951-4. Best recent biography of the founder of radical Protestantism.

Collison, Patrick. *The Elizabethan Puritan Movement*. OUP 1990 $24.95. ISBN 0-19-822298-X

Davidson, Nicholas S. *The Counter-Reformation*. Blackwell Pubs. 1987 $8.95. ISBN 0-631-14874-4. Short treatment of the Catholic reaction to the Reformation and the Church's successful efforts to turn the tide.

Delumeau, J. *Catholicism between Luther and Voltaire*. 1977 o.p. An excellent broad view of a period during which the Catholic Church went from being on the defensive to taking the offensive.

Elton, G. R. *Reform and Reformation England, 1509–1558*. HUP 1977 $30.50. ISBN 0-674-75245-7. Treats the intertwining of religion with politics during the reigns of three Tudor monarchs: the Catholic-turned-Protestant Henry VIII, his Protestant son Edward VI, and his Catholic daughter Mary I.

Elton, G. R., ed. *The Reformation*. Cambridge U. Pr. 1990 $49.50. ISBN 0-521-34536-7. Volume 2 of the *New Cambridge Modern History*.

Erikson, Eric. *Young Man Luther*. Norton 1962 $5.95. ISBN 0-393-00170-9. The first psychohistory; deals with the early life of Martin Luther.

Muller, Herbert J. *Religion and Freedom in the Modern World*. U. Ch. Pr. 1965 $1.50. ISBN 0-226-5415-5. Succinct treatment of two major themes of European history that are rooted in the Reformation.

Scribner, R. W. *The German Reformation*. Humanities 1986 $8.95. ISBN 0-391-03362-X. Excellent treatment of the beginnings of religious reform.

Spinka, Matthew. *John Hus: A Biography*. Greenwood 1978 $42.50. ISBN 0-313-21050-0. Good biography of the fourteenth-century Czech religious reformer who was an important forerunner of the Protestant Reformation.

Stephens, W. P. *Zwingli: An Introduction to His Thought*. OUP 1992 $49.95. ISBN 0-19-826329-5. Presents the thinking and philosophy of the revolutionary Swiss Protestant.

Weber, Max. *The Protestant Ethic and the Spirit of Capitalism*. HarpC 1985 $8.95. ISBN 0-00-302070-3. Classic analysis that should be read by anyone interested in the relationship between religion and the rise of capitalism.

Zagorin, Peter. *Rebels and Rulers*. 2 vols. Cambridge U. Pr. 1982 $59.95 ea. Vol. 1 *Society, States and Early Modern Revolutions: Agrarian and Urban Rebellions*. ISBN 0-521-24473-0. Vol. 2 *Provincial Rebellions: Revolutionary Civil Wars, 1560–1660*. ISBN 0-521-24472-2. Two-volume work that examines the general and historical problem of revolution and the civilization of early modern Europe.

EUROPEAN EXPANSION AND EXPLORATION

In the fifteenth century, Europe went from being invaded by outsiders to exploring and exploiting the outside world and from being the attacked to being the attacker. The major reason for this shift was that by then Europeans had developed the capacity for stability, organization, and discipline. The Renaissance had unleashed the great force of individualism and the pursuit of fame, fortune, and adventure followed.

The extraordinary and almost unparalleled feat of the Spaniards in carving out a great empire in the western hemisphere within a few decades after CHRISTOPHER COLUMBUS's voyages began an era in which Europeans ranged the maritime world, exploring here, attacking there, and colonizing elsewhere. There was a great deal of mutual borrowing between them and the peoples they encountered, but the advantage clearly lay with the Europeans because they were taking freely what they wanted, while the host peoples were having European ideas and patterns imposed on them.

The Europeans justified their oppressive actions on two grounds: that it was the function of a superior society to rule others and that they were bringing Christianity to the heathen. In fact, what they were doing was engaging in a mad scramble for the natural wealth of the Western Hemisphere. This crazed drive for wealth was responsible for the revival of slavery, which had disappeared from Europe in medieval times, and the massive subordination of indigenous peoples to European overlords. It also precipitated the greatest mass movement of people in history.

There was no turning back. The enormous power and influence that Europeans achieved during the sixteenth century throughout the maritime world has become a permanent factor in the world and has been maintained despite the successful campaigns of Asians and Africans to overthrow their European overlords in the twentieth century.

Boxer, C. R. *The Dutch Seaborne Empire, 1600–1800*. Viking Penguin 1989 $8.95. ISBN 0-14-021-660-6. A revealing treatment of a great maritime people.

Cipolla, Carlo. *Guns, Sails and Empires*. Sunflower U. Pr. 1985 $7.95. ISBN 0-89745-071-X. Good study of how technology fostered overseas expansion.

Davies, Nigel. *Voyages to the New World*. U. of NM Pr. 1985 $10.95. ISBN 0-8263-0880-5. Clear examination of pre-Columbian contacts with the Western Hemisphere.

Davis, David B. *The Problem of Slavery in Western Culture*. OUP 1988 $14.95. ISBN 0-19-505639-6. The best study of this vital subject.

Davis, Ralph. *The Rise of the Atlantic Economies*. Cornell Univ. Pr. 1973 $14.95. ISBN 0-8014-9143-6

Elliott, J. H. *The Old World and New, 1492–1650*. Cambridge U. Pr. 1992 $7.95. ISBN 0-521-42709-6. Deals with the impact of America on early modern Europe.

Gibson, Charles. *Spain in America*. HarpC 1967 $10.00. ISBN 0-06-133077-9. Examines the ways in which Hispanic and Native cultures have interacted in Latin American societies.

Hale, John R. *Renaissance Exploration*. Norton 1972 $7.95. ISBN 0-393-00635-2. Brief, stimulating study of the first wave of exploration.

Lach, Donald F. *Asia in the Making of Europe*. Vol. 2. U. Ch. Pr. 1978 $60.00. ISBN 0-226-46751-1. (See also Vol. 1 1965 o.p.) Engrossing exposition of the impact of Asia on Europeans as they explored and colonized that part of the world.

Ley, Charles D. *Portuguese Voyages, 1498–1663*. Gordon Pr. 1977 $59.95. ISBN 0-8490-2459-5. Great saga beginning with Vasco da Gama's voyage to the Indies.

McAlister, Lyle N. *Spain and Portugal in the New World: 1492–1700*. U. of Minn. Pr. 1984 $44.95. ISBN 0-8166-1218-8

Morison, Samuel E. *The European Discovery of America: The Northern Voyages*. OUP 1971 $39.95. ISBN 0-19-501377-8. Covers the entire field of New World discovery.

———. *The European Discovery of America: The Southern Voyages*. OUP 1974 $39.95. ISBN 0-19-501823-0

Pagden, Anthony. *European Encounters with the New World: From the Renaissance to Romanticism*. Yale U. Pr. 1993 $25.00. ISBN 0-300-05285-5. European intellectual responses to the reality of the Western Hemisphere.

Parry, J. H. *The Age of Reconnaissance: Discovery, Exploration and Settlement*. U. CA Pr. 1982 $12.95. ISBN 0-520-04235-2. Historical writing at its best.

Schaeffer, Dagmar. *Portuguese Exploration to the West and the Formation of Brazil: 1450–1800*. J. C. Brown 1988 $15.00. ISBN 0-916617-33-5

SEVENTEENTH CENTURY

Freed from the restrictions of the religion-dominated philosophy of the Middle Ages and the constraints of a monolithic church, the European mind probed deeply into the areas of science, mathematics, and secular philosophy. Thus began the dramatic exploration of the laws of nature and the intellectual quest for origins, meaning, and purpose that inevitably extended to the political realm. From a rational-scientific standpoint, traditional government, based on the principle of inherited political authority, was an absurd proposition.

The English Revolution of the seventeenth century grappled with the issues of freedom of religion and the principle of representative government, although the Puritan Oliver Cromwell could not, or would not, make these beliefs the foundation of his Commonwealth. Still, the English led the way in self-government. Why were they the pioneers? The island theory could be applied here: The nation's defenses depended on a powerful navy, and this expensive necessity forced English kings to content themselves with relatively small armies that proved insufficient to quell spontaneous popular political and religious revolt. Since the king could not command, he had to rule with the cooperation of the representatives of a variety of groups. The result was the rise of Parliament and the beginnings of self-government in the English towns.

The Dutch were the next people to develop self-government—and initially they went further than the English. As in England, superior naval defenses were a key factor in protecting revolutionary religious and political developments in The Netherlands, but the country had an additional advantage—a small, cohesive population that was disinclined to court disaster in the form of continuing communal divisions based on religion. Hence the Dutch became the first people in Europe to practice religious toleration—a hallmark of democratic rule. Finally, as a newly independent state, the Netherlands had no deeply entrenched traditional political authority. The prosperous and vigorous Dutch republic established in the seventeenth century lasted almost two centuries.

Braudel, Fernand. *The Mediterranean and the Mediterranean World in the Age of Philip II*. HarpC 1992 $40.00. ISBN 0-06-015958-8. A large two-volume work that surveys the forces governing life in the sixteenth-century Mediterranean.

Doyle, William. *The Ancien Régime*. Humanities 1986 $8.95. ISBN 0-391-03412-X. Clear treatment of traditional European government and society.

Hill, Christopher. *The Century of Revolution: 1603–1714*. Norton 1982 $19.95. ISBN 0-393-30016-1. Broadly Marxist interpretation of the British upheavals.

Koenigsberger, H. G. *Early Modern Europe, 1500–1789*. Longman 1987 $34.95. ISBN 0-582-49401-X. Traces the transition of Europe from a medieval to a modern society.

Mainstone, Madeleine, and Rowland Mainstone. *The Seventeenth Century*. Cambridge U. Pr. 1981 $11.95. ISBN 0-521-29376-6

Wilson, Charles. *The Dutch Republic and the Civilization of the Seventeenth Century*. McGraw 1968 o.p. Short, lively treatment of a great people in their great age.

THE RISE OF SCIENCE AND THE ENLIGHTENMENT

During the seventeenth and eighteenth centuries, Europe experienced a massive increase in scientific knowledge. Through observation, research, and hypothesis, European scientists demonstrated that there were laws of nature that produced a rational, integrated, and harmonious world. This growing body of evidence had profound social and political implications.

If the world was governed by natural laws, should these apply to human society? Do all human beings have some basic natural rights? Was legally binding social inequality an artificial construct that should be eliminated? To the growing middle class—educated, articulate, and ambitious—the answer to all these questions was *yes*. Armed with the disciplined rationalism of RENÉ DESCARTES (see Vols. 4 and 5), the bourgeoisie of France set out to reformulate government and society based on the principles of natural law.

Becker, Carl L. *Heavenly City of the Eighteenth-Century Philosophers.* Yale U. Pr. 1932 $9.95. ISBN 0-300-00017-0. A study that has stood the test of time.

Berlin, Isaiah. *The Age of Enlightenment.* Ayer 1956 $17.00. ISBN 0-8369-1822-3. Broad survey of European intellectual development of the period by a masterful historian.

Bennett, Jonathan. *Locke, Berkeley, Hume: Central Themes.* OUP 1971 $19.95. ISBN 0-19-875016-1. Important study of three of the great British minds of the period.

Butterfield, Herbert. *The Rise of Science and the Enlightenment.* Free Pr. 1965 o.p. Out of print for the moment but needs to be read.

Cassirer, Ernst. *The Philosophy of the Enlightenment.* Princeton U. Pr. 1951 $14.95. ISBN 0-691-01963-0

Chartier, Roger. *Cultural History: Between Practices and Representations.* Cornell Univ. Pr. 1988 $34.50. ISBN 0-8014-2223-X

Cranston, Maurice. *Philosophers and Pamphleteers: Political Theorists of the Enlightenment.* OUP 1986 $13.95. ISBN 0-19-289289-8

Gay, Peter. *The Enlightenment: An Interpretation.* 2 vols. Norton 1977. Vol. 1 *The Rise of Modern Paganism.* $13.95. ISBN 0-393-00870-3. Vol. 2 *The Science of Freedom.* $15.95. ISBN 0-393-00875-4

Horowitz, Asher. *Rousseau, Nature and History.* U. of Toronto Pr. 1987 $19.95. ISBN 0-8020-5681-4

Houston, R. A. *Literacy in Early Modern Europe: Culture and Education, 1500–1800.* Longman 1988 $17.95. ISBN 0-582-55266-4

Jacob, Margaret C. *Living the Enlightenment: Freemasonry and Politics in Eighteenth Century Europe.* OUP 1991 $16.95. ISBN 0-19-507051-8

Pascal, Blaise. *Pensées.* Viking Penguin 1966 $7.95. ISBN 0-14-044171-9. A French philosopher's insights into eternity.

EIGHTEENTH CENTURY

During the eighteenth century, Europeans consolidated the control they exerted in various parts of the world, advanced their knowledge in science and technology, and created highly centralized political entities. These achievements were accompanied by a series of wars that spanned the century.

The continuing European achievements in technology and science helped to breach the walls of traditional political and religious authority. The confidence gained from making such great strides in these areas carried over to the political and social realms. Armed with a wonderful new body of scientific and technical knowledge, social-political reformers grew bolder and more insistent on breaking with the old ways. Contemporary commentators and historians came down on both sides of the widening gap, some adhering to tradition, and others seeking a new and freer society.

Behrens, C.B.A. *The Ancien Régime.* Norton 1989 $9.95. ISBN 0-393-95801-9. Stimulating study of how the European world was run before the French decided to revolutionize it in 1789.

Black, Jeremy. *Eighteenth Century Europe, 1700–1789.* St. Martin 1990 $16.95. ISBN 0-312-04010-5. Broad-based study of the European world up to the great upheaval of the French Revolution.

Darnton, Robert. *The Literacy Underground of the Old Régime.* HUP 1982 o.p. Very readable collection of articles that delve into the seeds of intellectual change.

Deane, Phyllis. *The First Industrial Revolution, 1750–1850.* Cambridge U. Pr. 1980 $15.95. ISBN 0-521-29609-9. Good study of the origins of industrialization.

DeVries, J. *Economy of Europe in an Age of Crisis: 1600–1750.* Cambridge U. Pr. 1976 $14.95. ISBN 0-521-29050-3

Doyle, William. *Old European Order, 1660 to 1800.* OUP 1978 $22.50. ISBN 0-19-913131-7. Broad survey by an expert on the subject.

Durant, Will, and Ariel Durant. *The Age of Reason Begins.* S&S Trade 1961 $29.95. ISBN 0-671-01320-3. Readable, stimulating exploration of the intellectual development of European civilization.

Gershoy, Leo. *From Despotism to Revolution, 1763–1783.* Greenwood 1983 repr. of 1944 ed. o.p. Excellent older account of the shifting political tides of the later eighteenth century.

Industrial Revolutions and After. Vol. 6. *Cambridge Economic History of Europe.* Cambridge U. Pr. 1965 o.p. Essential history of the beginnings of European industrialization in the eighteenth century.

Jacob, Margaret C., and Wijinand Mijhardt, eds. *The Dutch Republic in the Eighteenth Century: Decline, Enlightenment and Revolution.* Cornell Univ. Pr. 1992 $41.50. ISBN 0-8014-2624-3

Kraus, Michael. *The Atlantic Civilization: Eighteenth Century Origins.* Peter Smith 1949 o.p. Fine study of the development of the trans-Atlantic civilization that emerged in this period.

McKay, Derek, and H. M. Scott. *The Rise of the Great Powers: The Great Powers and European State Systems, 1648–1815.* Longman 1983 $18.95. ISBN 0-582-48554-1. Examines the diplomatic history of the first seventy-five years of the era of European nation states.

Mahan, Alfred T. *The Influence of Sea Power on History.* Little 1970 $24.95. ISBN 0-316-54382-9. Highly influential book, first published in 1890, about the control of the sea in wartime. Cites the domination of the British navy in the seventeenth and eighteenth centuries as a major reason for Great Britain's subsequent status as a world power.

Snyder, Louis L. *The Age of Reason.* Krieger 1979 $9.50. ISBN 0-88275-907-8. Good general treatment of the era.

Starobinski, Jean. *Jean-Jacques Rousseau: Transparency and Obstruction.* U. Ch. Pr. 1988 $19.95. ISBN 0-226-77128-8. Great biography of the most important French political theorist of the ages.

Treasure, Geoffrey. *The Making of Modern Europe, 1648 to 1780.* Routledge Chapman & Hall 1985 $16.95. ISBN 0-416-72370-5. A general history that discusses the intellectual revolution of the age, and the idea of enlightened absolutism.

Wilson, Arthur M. *Diderot.* OUP 1972 $45.00. ISBN 0-19-501506-1. National Book Award winner that explores the world of the great French encyclopedist.

REVOLUTIONARY EUROPE

When revolution exploded in France in the late eighteenth century, the European world shook. France was the acknowledged center of European culture, learning, and power. When the old mold was broken there with the motto "Liberty, Equality, Fraternity," no amount of vigorous effort could fully fit it back together again. The Revolution's unleashing of the common people was a dynamic but destructive introduction to the power of mass mobilization for a popular program. The French Revolution also demonstrated the limitations of such a program, for the old world and ways could not be completely swept away by slogans and popular enthusiasm.

Europe's greater revolution—industrial—came afterward in the early nineteenth century, just in time to avert a demographic catastrophe. Industrialization resulted in massive urbanization and a consequent drop in the birthrate, and the demographic threat subsided, though Europe still needed the safety valve of emigration to the Americas—which absorbed 50 million Europeans over the next century.

Best, Geoffrey, ed. *The Permanent Revolution: The French Revolution and Its Legacy.* U. Ch. Pr. 1989 $24.95. ISBN 0-226-04427-0. Stimulating collection of articles about the effects of the great upheaval in the center of European civilization.

Bonaparte, Napoleon. *Napoleon's Memoirs.* Dufour 1986 $19.95. ISBN 0-948166-10-X. Interesting self-revelation by the man who dominated Europe physically for a short time and psychologically for quite a bit longer.

Caldwell, Ronald J. *The Era of the French Revolution: A Bibliography of the History of Western Civilization, 1789–1799.* Garland 1985 ISBN 0-8240-8794. Topical listing of over 42,000 books, articles, etc.

Connelly, Owen. *The French Revolution and the Napoleonic Era.* HarBraceJ 1991 $15.50. ISBN 0-03-053329-5. A standard work by a master historian.

———. *Blundering to Glory: Napoleon's Military Campaigns.* Scholarly Res. Inc. 1992 $12.95. ISBN 0-8420-2375-5. Focuses on the emperor as a military scrambler, master of the broken play. Winner of Outstanding Academic Book Award, *Choice* magazine.

Deane, Seamus. *The French Revolution and Enlightenment in England, 1789–1832.* HUP 1988 $27.50. ISBN 0-674-32240-1. An intellectual treat by an Irish writer of note.

Delderfield, R. F. *Napoleon's Marshals.* Madison Bks. UPA 1980 $8.95. ISBN 0-8128-6055-1. A must book for fans of military history.

Furet, François, and Mona Ozouf, eds. *A Critical Dictionary of the French Revolution.* Trans. by Arthur Goldhammer. HUP 1989 $85.00. ISBN 0-674-17728-2. A summary of contemporary scholarship presented as a collection of essays arranged by topics such as Events, Actors, Institutions, Ideas, and Historians. Includes indexes and illustrations.

Gershoy, Leo. *The French Revolution.* Paperbook Pr. Inc. 1991 $2.25. ISBN 1-877891-05-3. Fine study of the upheaval of a nation and its people.

Kafker, Frank A., and James M. Laux. *The French Revolution: Conflicting Interpretations.* Krieger 1989 $23.50. ISBN 0-89464-247-2. Presents all sides of opinion on the great explosion.

Lefebvre, Georges. *The Coming of the French Revolution.* Princeton U. Pr. 1989 $37.50. ISBN 0-691-05112-7. Examines the ways in which class distinctions were largely irrelevant in the overthrow of the monarchy.

Markham, Felix. *Napoleon and the Awakening of Europe.* Collier Bks. 1965 o.p. A biography of Napoleon that also examines democratic movements throughout Europe.

Roberts, J. M. *The French Revolution.* OUP 1978 $12.95. ISBN 0-19-289069-7. Balanced, scholarly study by a noted British historian.

Rude, Charles. *The Crowd in History: A Study of Popular Disturbances in France and England, 1730–1848.* Greenwood 1986 $65.00. ISBN 0-313-25168-1

———. *The French Revolution: Its Causes, Its History and Its Legacy after Two Hundred Years.* Grove Pr. 1991 $12.95. ISBN 0-8021-3272-3. Covers all the bases exceptionally well.

Thompson, J. M. *Napoleon Bonaparte*. Blackwell Pubs. 1988 $29.95. ISBN 0-631-16414-6.
Brief British version of events in the life of the French ruler.

NINETEENTH CENTURY

The social and political effects of the economic upheaval known as the
Industrial Revolution reshaped the European world. Uprooted from village and
farm, people became conditioned to industrial, urban living. Political and
cultural rootlessness, popular politics, and uniformity of experience were the
consequences. These undoubtedly were the causes of the growth of nationalism,
which was second only to industrialization as a dominant force in nineteenth-
century Europe. Political leaders embarked on a quest for national greatness
through the conquest and humiliation of neighbors.

Two other ideologies also emerged in this century. One was liberalism, which
came as an adjunct to capitalist economics and became the pervading ideology
of the century. Liberalism stood for individual freedom—politically and
economically—limited but constitutional government, and rule by law. Pulsing
underneath and then overtaking liberalism was the doctrine of democracy
bequeathed by the French Revolution. The other ideology was Marxism.
Socialistic alternatives to harsh nineteenth-century capitalism had been proposed for decades before becoming a mighty eruption under the intellectual
force and polemics of the German economist and social philosopher KARL MARX
(see also Vol. 4). His searing indictments of the brutality of raw capitalism and
the hypocrisy of liberalism badly frightened the property-owning classes. The
whole system of modern European politics is largely a reaction to his
thundering threats and prophecies.

As early industrialization gave rise to mass production, however, the common
people increasingly benefited. Mass consumption, glorification of the nation
and state, political ideology, and the wonders of science and technology began
to take the place of traditional beliefs, including religious beliefs. By the late
nineteenth century European imperialism dominated Africa and much of Asia,
as well as other places. European achievements in technology, industry,
organization, education, and culture far exceeded those of other civilizations.

Anderson, M. S. *The Ascendancy of Europe, 1815–1914*. Longman 1986 $22.95. ISBN 0-
582-49386-2. Stimulating study of the great age of European power.

Arblaster, Anthony. *Rise and Decline of Western Liberalism*. Blackwell Pubs. 1986 $16.95.
ISBN 0-631-14618-0. Broad survey of the dominant ideology of this century.

Artz, Frederick B. *Reaction and Revolution, 1814–1832*. HarpC 1963 o.p. Classic study of
the swing of the political pendulum.

Barzun, Jacques. *Berlioz and His Century: An Introduction to the Age of Romanticism*.
U. Ch. Pr. 1982 $14.95. ISBN 0-226-03861-0. Very readable and important study of
major figures in shaping the thought of the period.

Chadwick, Owen. *The Secularization of the European Mind in the Nineteenth Century*.
Cambridge U. Pr. 1990 $10.95. ISBN 0-521-39829-0. Relates how science, technolo-
gy, nationalism, and ideology crowded out religion in the 1800s.

Clausewitz, Karl von. *On War*. Viking Penguin 1982 $5.95. ISBN 0-14-044427-0. Classic
examination of the art and science of warfare, in which the author declares that the
object of warfare is peace.

Craig, Gordon A. *Europe, 1815–1914*. HarBraceJ 1972 $22.50. ISBN 0-03-089194-9.
Standard work in its field.

DeRuggiero, Guido. *History of European Liberalism*. Peter Smith 1977 $19.00. ISBN 0-
8446-1970-1. Classic study originally published in 1927 with translation by R. C.
Collingwood.

Epstein, Klaus. *Genesis of German Conservatism*. Princeton U. Pr. 1975 $26.95. ISBN 0-691-10030-6

Eyck, Erich. *Bismarck and the German Empire*. Norton 1964 $9.95. ISBN 0-393-00235-7. Attempts to determine the German leader's place in history.

Flinn, Michael W. *The European Demographic System: 1500–1820*. Johns Hopkins 1985 $11.95. ISBN 0-8018-3155-5. Revealing study of the population boom that, even with the safety valve of emigration to the Americas, threatened to overwhelm Europe.

Hayes, Carleton J. *A Generation of Materialism, 1871–1900*. Greenwood 1983 $48.50. ISBN 0-313-24082-5. Essential reading.

Hobsbawm, Eric J. *The Age of Empire*. Random 1989 $14.00. ISBN 0-679-72175-4. Survey of the near-conquest of the world by European imperialism, by the leading British historian on the subject.

Honeyman, Katrina, and Jordan Goodman. *Gainful Pursuits: The Making of Industrial Europe, 1600–1914*. Routledge Chapman & Hall 1988 $19.95. ISBN 0-7131-606-1. Traces the history of industrial Europe from the beginning of the seventeenth century to the outbreak of the first World War.

Kennedy, Paul M. *The Rise and Fall of British Naval Mastery*. Humanities 1986 $17.50. ISBN 0-948660-5. Examines the importance to the world of British naval supremacy over three centuries.

Kissinger, Henry. *A World Restored: Metternich, Castlereagh and the Problems of Peace, 1812–1822*. HM 1973 $11.70. ISBN 0-395-17229-2. Focuses on the struggle to restore the new "old order" after the Congress of Vienna.

Kohn, Hans. *Nationalism and Realism, 1852–1879*. Krieger 1968 $9.50. ISBN 0-442-00096-0. A brief but incisive look at the charming monster of nationalism by a great German historian.

Langer, William L. *European Alliances and Alignments, 1871–1890*. Greenwood 1977 $45.50. ISBN 0-8371-9518-7. Valuable study of how the nations of Europe began to line up for World War I in the next century.

Lindemann, Albert S. *History of European Socialism*. Yale U. Pr. 1984 $18.00. ISBN 0-300-03246-3. Clear treatment of the rise of the alternative to capitalism.

Olsen, Donald J. *The City as a Work of Art: London, Paris and Vienna*. Yale U. Pr. 1986 $50.00. ISBN 0-300-02870-9. Imaginative and perceptive contribution to European urban history.

Olson, James, and others, eds. *Historical Dictionary of European Imperialism*. Greenwood 1991 $99.50. ISBN 0-313-26257-8. Brief descriptive essays on the last five hundred years of European imperialism.

Pollard, S. *Peaceful Conquest: The Industrialization of Europe, 1760–1970*. OUP 1981 $17.95. ISBN 0-19-877095-2. Excellent account of the rise to dominance of European technology.

Seaman, L. C. *Victorian England: Aspects of English and Imperial History, 1837–1901*. Routledge Chapman & Hall 1973 $15.95. ISBN 0-416-77550-0. Detailed discussion of England and the world during the reign of Victoria.

Stansky, Peter. *Gladstone: A Progress in Politics*. Norton 1981 $8.95. ISBN 0-393-00037-0. Good short biography of the venerable British statesman.

Talmon, J. R. *Romanticism and Revolt*. Norton 1979 $9.95. ISBN 0-393-95081-6. Looks into the cult of nationalism and the myth of revolution.

Taylor, Arthur J. P. *Bismarck, the Man and the Statesman*. Random 1967 $8.00. ISBN 0-394-70387-1. Lively account of the life and times of the "Iron Chancellor" by a valued historian.

Williams, Raymond. *Culture and Society, 1780 to 1950*. Col. U. Pr. 1983 $17.50. ISBN 0-231-05701-6

Wilson, Edmund. *To the Finland Station*. FS&G 1972 $14.95. ISBN 0-374-51045-8. Good writing on the lives of Marx, Engels, and Lenin by one of America's foremost authors.

TWENTIETH CENTURY

The first European civil war of the twentieth century forged totalitarianism by demonstrating that nations could assume total control over their people through the power of nationalistic propaganda and the organization of mass mobilization. Two decades after the devastation of World War I, Europe regrouped its forces and began another bout of general warfare accompanied by the systematic extermination of "surplus" groups of people. The grip of totalitarian ideology was not fatally broken by the defeat of the Nazis, for there were still the Communists. The Soviet state, established in 1917 while much of the rest of the world made war on one another, extended its control to eastern Europe in the wake of World War II. Eventually, however, the communist movement foundered on its poor economic performance.

Today Europe is undergoing a period of transition in which both communism and old-time capitalism matter less and less. The disintegration of the violent revolutionary form of socialism, however, does not mean that social democratic policies and principles are dead. Indeed, the "mixed" economies of Europe have demonstrated extraordinary energy, creativity, and productivity since World War II.

In the postwar period Europeans reluctantly shed the burden of imperialism and concentrated their energies on creating an economic, political, and social union among themselves. The expanding European Economic Community is a testimony to the success of the economic part of this movement toward unity. Political and social unity have proved much harder to accomplish, though after centuries of ethnocentrism Europeans—especially younger Europeans—seem determined to break down barriers of language and nationalism. From the Atlantic to the Urals, from the Arctic to the Mediterranean, European peoples are coming together in peace, freedom, cooperation, and democracy.

In the broadest perspective, the role of the United States in twentieth-century Europe has been to act as the unwitting but constructive counterweight to European excess. In the two great military crises of the century, the United States intervened to prevent German domination of the Continent, and the ravages of ideological extremes have been muted by the American values of freedom, equality, opportunity, and self-government. American industrial power has acted as an impetus to foster economic growth throughout Europe as well. America's model and experience have, in part, inspired European unity, popular culture, and the development of human resources in the last half of the twentieth century.

General Works

Arendt, Hannah. *On Revolution.* Viking Penguin 1977 $7.95. ISBN 0-14-021681-2. Brilliant analysis of the revolutionary impulse in this century.

Barzini, Luigi. *The Europeans.* Viking Penguin 1984 $9.95. ISBN 0-14-007150-4. Lively personal reflections on the major national groups of Europe.

Gilbert, Felix. *End of the European Era: 1890 to the Present.* Norton 1991 $14.95. ISBN 0-393-96059-5. Relatively short text that provides a chronology of the events of this century.

Kohr, Leopold. *The Breakdown of Nations.* NAL-Dutton 1978 o.p. Argues that small units or bigger, international entities are necessary because the modern nation-state has become so powerful that it cannot resist an inevitable drive for expansion and aggression.

Mandell, Richard. *Sport: A Cultural History*. Col. U. Pr. 1986 $47.50. ISBN 0-231-05470-X. By far the best study of the activity that has become a mega-business in the late twentieth century and whose only rival is popular commercial music.

Mitchell, Brian R. *European Historical Statistics, 1750 to 1970*. Col. U. Pr. 1979 $34.50. ISBN 0-231-04569-7. Read this to get your bearings, then proceed to narratives.

Pick, Daniel. *War Machine: The Rationalization of Slaughter in the Modern Age*. Yale U. Pr. 1993 $30.00. ISBN 0-300-05417-3. The author's thesis is that relentless techno-logical progress and the power of the military-industrial complex risk turning international conflict into sophisticated games played by high-precision automata.

Europe: 1900–1920

Ferro, Marc. *The Great War, 1914–1918*. Dorset Pr. 1990 $17.95. ISBN 0-88029-449-3. Excellent treatment of the war from a European perspective.

Fussell, Paul. *The Great War and Modern Memory*. OUP 1975 $10.95. ISBN 0-19-502171-1. Responses and reflections on World War I.

Hobson, John A. *Imperialism*. 1902. U. of Mich. Pr. 1965 $15.95. ISBN 0-472-06103-8. At the turn of the century, the author predicted that imperialism would inevitably lead to warfare among the imperialists.

Hughes, H. Stuart. *Consciousness and Society: The Reorientation of European Social Thought: 1890–1930*. Random 1961 $7.95. ISBN 0-394-70201-8. The best in intellec-tual and cultural history of this period or any other.

Keegan, John. *The Face of Battle*. Viking Penguin 1983 $9.95. ISBN 0-14-004897-9. Deals with how war, particularly that of the years 1914 through 1918, was experienced by those who actually participated in the battles.

Lewis, Jane. *Women and Social Action in Victorian and Edwardian England*. Stanford U. Pr. 1991 $42.50. ISBN 0-8047-1905-5. Traces the roots of the welfare state to the charity work undertaken by middle-class women as an extension of their family responsibilities.

Pettigrew, Jane. *An Edwardian Childhood*. Little 1992 $25.00. ISBN 0-8212-1915-4. Popular and idealistic portrait of childhood during the first decade of the twentieth century in England.

Pick, Daniel. *Faces of Degeneration: Aspects of a European Disorder, 1848–1918. Ideas in Context Ser.* Cambridge U. Pr. 1989 $49.95. ISBN 0-521-36021-8

Service, Robert. *The Russian Revolution, 1900–1927*. Longman 1986 $8.95. ISBN 0-391-03405-7. Popular western views of the events compared to the historical record.

Stone, Norman. *Europe Transformed, 1878–1919*. HUP 1984 $12.50. ISBN 0-674-26923-3. Chronicles the long-term social changes that led to the English Civil War.

Taylor, Edmund. *The Fall of the Dynasties: The Collapse of the Old Order, 1905–1922*. Doubleday 1990 $19.95. ISBN 0-88029-390-X. Well-told tale of the overthrow of monarchies in Russia, Austria-Hungary, and Germany in the wake of defeat in World War I.

Tuchman, Barbara. *The Proud Tower*. Bantam 1983 $6.95. ISBN 0-553-25602-5. Masterful treatment of the achievement, pride, and pomposity that enveloped Europe before World War I.

———. *The Guns of August*. Bantam 1982 $6.95. ISBN 0-553-25401-4. Vivid, gripping account of the trench warfare and military barrages that gripped Europe during one month—August 1918.

Vincent, David, and Andrew Miles, eds. *Building European Society: Occupational Change and Social Mobility in Europe, 1840–1940*. St. Martin 1993 $69.95. ISBN 0-7190-3499-X

Wolfe, Bertram. *Three Who Made a Revolution*. Madison Bks. UPA 1986 $14.95. ISBN 0-8128-6212-0. Biographical history of three Russian leaders—Trotsky, Lenin, and Stalin.

Europe: 1920–1945

Borowski, Tadeusz. *This Way for the Gas, Ladies and Gentlemen.* Viking Penguin 1976 $8.95. ISBN 0-1400-4114-1. Memoir of life inside an extermination camp in Poland.

Bullock, Alan. *Hitler and Stalin: Parallel Lives.* Knopf 1992 $34.95. ISBN 0-394-58601-8. Detailed and revealing contrast of the two great dictators at different stages of their lives.

Carr, Edward H. *International Relations between the Two World Wars: 1919–1939.* St. Martin 1969 $22.50. ISBN 0-312-42315-2. Standard work on the convoluted diplomacy that led to a new general war.

Conot, Robert E. *Justice at Nuremberg.* Carroll & Graff 1984 $12.95. ISBN 0-88184-032-7. Revealing examination of the Nazi leaders on trial.

Deutscher, Isaac. *Stalin: A Political Biography.* OUP $17.95. ISBN 0-19-500273-3. Follows the development of Stalin's political career and personal character; quite appropriate for the general reader.

Feis, Herbert. *Churchill, Roosevelt and Stalin: The War They Waged and the Peace They Sought.* Princeton U. Pr. 1967 $85.00. ISBN 0-691-05607-2. An analysis of the wartime methods and aims of the Allied leaders.

Fromm, Erich. *Escape from Freedom.* Avon 1976 $5.99. ISBN 0-380-01167-0. An exposition on why some people prefer commands to choices.

Greenberg, Allan C. *Artists and Revolution: Dada and the Bauhaus, 1917–1925.* Bks. Demand 1980 $77.50. ISBN 0-8357-1080-7. Excellent and well-written study of artistic and cultural innovation in Weimar Germany.

Jones, Larry E. *German Liberalism and the Dissolution of the Weimar Party System, 1918–1933.* U. of NC Pr. 1988 $50.00. ISBN 0-8078-1764-3. Deals with the failure of German liberalism in the 1920s and the reasons that failure led to world tragedy.

Kitchen, Martin. *Europe between the Wars: A Political History.* Longman 1988 $37.95. ISBN 0-528-01741-6. Examines the peace settlement of World War I and the economic and social problems of the interwar years.

Lafore, Laurence. *The End of the Glory: An Interpretation of the Origins of World War II.* Lippincott 1970 o.p. Lively treatment of people and events but without much interpretation.

Martel, Gordon, ed. *Origins of the Second World War Reconsidered: The A.J.P. Taylor Debate After Twenty-Five Years.* Routledge Chapman & Hall 1986 $19.95. ISBN 0-04-940085-1

Mosse, George L. *Masses and Man: Nationalist and Fascist Perceptions of Reality.* Wayne St. U. Pr. 1987 $16.95. ISBN 0-8143-1895-9. Serious examination of the phenomena of rabid nationalism and the glorification of violence.

Northedge, F. S. *League of Nations: Its Life and Times, 1920–1946.* Holmes & Meier 1986 $47.50. ISBN 0-8419-1065-0. Relates the sad story of the failure of the first world body.

Rubenstein, Richard L. *The Cunning of History: The Holocaust and the American Future.* HarpC 1987 $10.00. ISBN 0-06-132068-4. Brief, searing survey of the mechanism of mass murder.

Ryan, Cornelius. *The Longest Day.* Ulverscroft 1977 o.p. Fascinating narrative that portrays D-Day—the Allied invasion of Normandy in 1944—in all its exciting detail.

Schapiro, J. Salwyn. *Liberalism and the Challenge of Fascism.* Hippocrene Bks. 1964 $26.00. ISBN 0-374-97087-4. Penetrating examination of a challenge not met.

Shirer, William L. *The Rise and Fall of the Third Reich.* Fawcett 1991 $7.99. ISBN 0-449-21977-1. Excellent narrative written by an American journalist who was on the scene.

Smith, Denis Mack. *Mussolini: A Biography.* Random 1983 $16.95. ISBN 0-394-71658-2. Good biography of the founder of fascism by an authority on modern Italy.

Sontag, Raymond J. *A Broken World, 1919–1939.* HarpC 1972 $13.00. ISBN 0-06-131651-2. Detailed narrative of the period that led up to another European catastrophe.

Spengler, Oswald. *The Decline of the West*. OUP 1991 $35.00. ISBN 0-19-506751-7. Wide-ranging and startling exposition of the precarious position of Europe. Influential in the interwar period in spite of being clouded by racism.

Stern, J. P. *Hitler: The Führer and the People*. U. CA Pr. 1988 $10.95. ISBN 0-520-02952-6. Riveting exploration of Hitler's appeal to the German people.

Taylor, A.J.P.. *Origins of the Second World War*. Macmillan 1983 $12.95. ISBN 0-689-70658-8. Presents the controversial thesis that Hitler was not solely to blame for the war.

Wilmot, Chester. *The Struggle for Europe*. Greenwood 1972 $43.00. ISBN 0-8371-5711-0. Lively treatment of World War I by a British journalist who was in the middle of it.

Young, Desmond. *Rommel: The Desert Fox*. Morrow 1987 $11.20. ISBN 0-688-06771-9. Best biography of the legendary German general.

Europe Since 1945

Althusser, Louis. *For Marx*. Routledge Chapman & Hall 1985 $16.95. ISBN 0-902308-79-3. A stimulating defense of Marxist ideology. A work that demands response and reaction.

Ambrosius, Gerald, and William Hubbard. *Social and Economic History of Twentieth-Century Europe*. HUP 1989 $19.95. ISBN 0-674-81341-3

Ardagh, John. *Germany and the Germans*. Viking Penguin 1992 $12.00. ISBN 0-14-014340-8. Fine study of a dynamic, creative people who once again dominate Europe.

Boggs, Carl, and David Plotke, eds. *Politics of Eurocommunism: Socialism in Transition*. South End Pr. 1980 $16.00. ISBN 0-89608-051-X. Study of the modified Marxist ideology that may experience a revival in Europe.

Brock, Peter. *Folk Cultures and Little People: Aspects of National Awakening in East Central Europe*. Col. U. Pr. 1992 $35.00. ISBN 0-88033-243-3

Darwin, John. *End of the British Empire: The Historical Debate*. Blackwell Pubs. 1991 $42.95. ISBN 0-631-16427-8. Various explanations about what happened to the greatest of modern empires.

Deacon, Bob. *The New Eastern Europe: Social Policy Past, Present and Future*. Sage 1992 $19.95. ISBN 0-8039-8439-1

Denitch, Bogdar. *End of the Cold War: European Unity, Socialism and the Shift in Global Power*. U. of Minn. Pr. 1990 $29.95. ISBN 0-8166-1872-0. Wide-ranging examination of today's changing world.

Dockrill, M. L. *The Cold War, 1945–1963*. Humanities 1988 $8.95. ISBN 0-391-03592-4. Short treatment of the great postwar rivalry between the United States and the Soviet Union from Yalta to the test-ban treaty.

Emerson, Michael. *What Model for Europe?* MIT Pr. 1988 $22.50. ISBN 0-262-05036-6. Survey of alternative paths in the development of European unity.

Gillingham, John. *Coal, Steel and the Rebirth of Europe, 1945–1955*. Cambridge U. Pr. 1991 $45.00. ISBN 0-521-40059-7. Prize-winning story of the critical first stage of western European economic integration.

Goodman, S. F. *European Community*. St. Martin 1991 $29.95. ISBN 0-312-04882-3. Important study of emerging European unity.

Hess, Gary R., ed. *America and Russia: From Cold War Confrontation to Coexistence*. *Problem Studies in Amer. History Ser.* Harlan Davidson 1973. ISBN 0-88295-743-0

Hogan, Michael, ed. *The End of the Cold War: Its Meaning and Implications*. Cambridge U. Pr. 1992 $44.95. ISBN 0-521-43128-X. Articles by leading historians and political analysts about the significance of the recent revolution in eastern Europe.

Holland, R. F. *European Decolonization, 1918–1981: An Introductory Survey*. St. Martin 1985 $29.95. ISBN 0-312-27060-7. Lengthy examination of the crumbling of European imperialism.

Johnson, Paul. *Intellectuals*. HarpC 1990 $12.00. ISBN 0-06-091657-5. Lively treatment of the role of intellectuals by a prolific British writer.

Kaiser, Robert G. *Why Gorbachev Happened: His Triumphs and His Failures*. S&S Trade 1992 $14.00. ISBN 0-671-77878-1

Kramer, Jane. *Unsettling Europe*. Viking Penguin 1990 $8.95. ISBN 0-14-012898-0. Examines the problem of refugees and illegal immigrants in contemporary Europe.

Laqueur, Walter. *Europe since Hitler: The Rebirth of Europe*. Viking Penguin 1982 $10.95. ISBN 0-14-021411-9. Lengthy discussion of the revival of Europe by a noted historian.

Medvedev, Roy, and Zhores A. Medvedev. *Khrushchev: The Years in Power*. Norton 1975 $7.95. ISBN 0-393-00879-7. Objective view of the Soviet leader by two Russian opponents of the Communist system.

Mosse, George L. *Fallen Soldiers: Reshaping the Memory of the World Wars*. OUP 1990 $24.95. ISBN 0-19-506247-7

Paterson, William, and Stephen Padgett. *A History of Social Democracy in Postwar Europe*. Longman 1991 $46.95. ISBN 0-582-49173-8

Pfeil, Fred. *Another Tale to Tell: Essays on Postmodern Culture*. Routledge Chapman & Hall 1990 $45.00. ISBN 0-86091-992-7

Schmitt, Hans A. *European Union: From Hitler to DeGaulle*. Krieger 1969 $8.95. ISBN 0-686-47388-4. Short history of the bumpy road to economic and political integration.

Schumacher, E. F. *Good Work*. HarpC 1979 o.p. Asserts the need for human-scale technology and an innovative form of productive ownership.

Sevan-Schreiber, Jean Jacques. *The American Challenge*. Avon 1978 $1.65. ISBN 0-380-01016-X. Wonderfully alarmist 1967 tome on the danger that the Americans would take over everything in Europe.

Simons, Thomas W. *End of the Cold War*. St. Martin 1990 $16.95. ISBN 0-312-04536-0. Good study of the end of the long-standing rivalry between the superpowers and their allies.

Smith, Tony, ed. *The End of European Empire: Decolonization after World War II*. Heath 1975. ISBN 0-669-93195-0. Collection of primary documents by Asian and African historians and the participants of decolonization.

Solzhenitsyn, Aleksandr. *Gulag Archipelago*. Vol. 1. HarpC 1991 $16.00. ISBN 0-06-092102-1. Grim, moving tale of survival in the Soviet labor camps by a leading Soviet dissident.

Treverton, Gregory. *Europe and America Beyond Two Thousand*. NYU Pr. 1990 $25.00. ISBN 0-685-48111-5. Looks forward to the continuation of the great relationship that has borne so much good fruit.

Wegs, J. Robert. *Europe Since 1945: A Concise History*. St. Martin 1990 $21.35. ISBN 0-312-00972-0. Third edition of a standard work on postwar European history.

THE JEWS OF EUROPE

The Jews and European civilization have been intertwined from the beginning. There was, in fact, a substantial Jewish presence along the Mediterranean rim before European civilization developed. As Europe became Christianized, however, Jews were restricted. In contrast, after the Islamic conquest of Iberia beginning in the early seventh century, Jews in that area were granted wide autonomy, and flourished economically, culturally, and intellectually. The European reconquest of Iberia in the fifteenth century resulted in a diaspora of Jews who refused to convert to Christianity. In this great northeastern movement, a small number eventually found their way to the Netherlands, where a policy of religious toleration gave them safe haven, but a far larger number settled in Poland. In 1334 the Polish state granted special status to Jews, and by the nineteenth century the great majority of Jews were concentrated in eastern Europe.

The idea of universal rights that came out of the French Revolution was spread by Napoleon throughout much of western Europe. Thus, wherever French power was imposed, the Jews gained civil equality. Elsewhere in western Europe governments removed remaining constraints on Jews later in the nineteenth century. Eastern Europe, on the other hand, which did not experience the liberating force of the French Revolution and remained essentially feudal, continued to ghettoize its Jewish populations to varying degrees.

Civil equality presented the Jews of western Europe with the opportunity to assimilate and this was the route most of them followed. In 1897 Theodore Herzl (1860–1904) presented an alternative—Zionism, a separate state for the Jews where they could live a fully Jewish religious and cultural life. Very few Jews actively supported him, although there was a trickle of Jewish migration to Palestine starting at the turn of the century. Much more attractive to European Jews was the United States; in the period 1889–1920, one million immigrated to America. The majority, however, went to neither land but remained in Europe.

When World War I started, European Jews loyally supported their country of birth, although the British government attempted to gain Zionist support outside of Britain by issuing the Balfour Declaration, which declared in favor of the formation of a Jewish homeland. In the interwar period, the position of western European Jews was made difficult by the large influx of eastern European Jews into the region. When the Nazis, with their aggressive racism, gained power in Germany in the 1930s, they pursued a vigorous policy of expulsion and, later, extermination of the country's Jewish population. Wherever the Germans conquered or "annexed" countries through World War II, they organized a system of extermination of Jews. With the exceptions of Denmark and the Netherlands, governments—sometimes reluctantly, sometimes eagerly—handed over their Jewish populations to the Nazis. By the end of the war 6 million of Europe's 10 million Jews had been murdered.

Galvanized by shock and guilt, most European governments supported the establishment in 1948 of the state of Israel in the former British mandate of Palestine. Today about three million Jews remain in Europe, more than half of them in the Soviet Union, but the great intellectual and cultural Jewish communities of Europe no longer exist.

Adler, Jacques. *The Jews of Paris and the Final Solution: Communal Response and Internal Conflicts, 1940–1944.* OUP 1989 $16.95. ISBN 0-19-504306-5. Relates the agony of the French Jews, whose sacrifice is commemorated in the Jewish Museum in Paris.

Arendt, Hannah. *Eichmann in Jerusalem: A Report of the Banality of Evil.* 1963. Viking Penguin 1977 $10.00. ISBN 0-14-004450-7. The author covered the trial for *The New Yorker* and the series of articles in that magazine form the bulk of this book.

Aschheim, Steven E. *Brothers and Strangers: The East European Jew in German and German-Jewish Consciousness, 1800–1923.* U. of Wis. Pr. 1982 o.p. Excellent insight into German and German-Jewish ideology.

Baron, Salo W. *A Social and Religious History of the Jews.* 18 vols. Col. U. Pr. $65.00 ea. ISBN 0-231-08852-3. A masterpiece, still incomplete, by the greatest living historian of the Jews.

Bein, Alex. *Theodor Herzl: A Biography of the Founder of Modern Zionism.* Trans. by Maurice Samuel. Atheneum 1970 o.p. Good biography of the main founder of Zionism.

Bettelheim, Bruno. *The Informed Heart: Autonomy in a Mass Age.* Avon 1971 $3.95 o.p.

Bridger, David, and Samuel J. Wolk. *The New Jewish Encyclopedia.* 1925. Behrman 1962 o.p. Concise encyclopedia with definitions concerning Jewish religion and liturgy, places, and people in Jewish history.

Byrnes, R. F. *Antisemitism in Modern France.* Fertig 1969 o.p. Very interesting study of anti-Semitism in twentieth-century France.

Chesler, Evan R. *The Russian Jewry Reader.* Anti-Defamation League o.p.

Cuddihy, John Murray. *The Ordeal of Civility: Freud, Marx, Levi-Strauss, and the Jewish Struggle with Modernity.* Basic 1974 o.p. "Analyzes Jewish assimilation in post-18th-century Europe and America as a subcultural microcosm of the general global process of modernization" (*Library Journal*).

Davidowicz, Lucy S., ed. *The Golden Tradition: Jewish Life and Thought in Eastern Europe.* Schocken 1984 $15.95. ISBN 0-8052-0768-6. "For the excellence of the selections and the high qualtiy of the translation, this book is highly recommended" (*Library Journal*).

———. *A Holocaust Reader.* Behrman 1976 o.p.

Deutscher, Isaac. *The Non-Jewish Jew and Other Essays.* Alyson 1982 o.p. An expert on Soviet affairs analyzes the question of being a Jew.

Edwards, John. *The Jews in Christian Europe, 1400–1700.* Routledge 1988 $35.00. ISBN 0-415-00864-6. Broad view of a fringe people in the "middle period."

Eisenberg, Azriel. *Jewish Historical Treasures.* Bloch Publishing 1969 o.p. "From nearly four millennia of Jewish history the author has chosen . . . objects, artifacts, manuscripts, and instruments with the purpose of illuminating Jewish life through the ages" (*Library Journal*).

Eisenstadt, S. N. *Jewish Civilization: The Jewish Historical Experience in a Comparative Perspective.* State U. NY Pr. 1992 $74.50. ISBN 0-7914-1096-X. Unique comparative study about the European "outsiders."

Finkelstein, Louis, ed. *The Jews.* 3 vols. Schocken 1970–71 o.p. A classic collection of Jewish thought, focusing on the meaning of Jewish history and culture.

Friedlander, Henry, and Sybil Milton, eds. *The Holocaust: Ideology, Bureaucracy and Genocide.* Kraus 1981 o.p. Selected essays on anti-Semitism and the Nazi genocide.

Friesel, Evyatar. *Atlas of Modern Jewish History.* OUP 1990 $55.00. ISBN 0-19-505393-1

Graetz, Heinrich. *The Structure of Jewish History and Other Essays.* Ktav o.p. Contains the essential arguments of the nineteenth-century nationalist Jewish historian.

Greenberg, Louis. *The Jews in Russia: The Struggle for Emancipation.* 2 vols. AMS Pr. repr. of 1965 ed. $27.50. ISBN 0-404-09023-0. Pursues the roots of the Jewish bund in Russian society in the late nineteenth century.

Heller, Celia S. *On the Edge of Destruction: Jews of Poland between the Two World Wars.* Schocken 1987 $8.95. ISBN 0-8052-0651-5. Story of a great community facing the rise of violent anti-Semitism, with the fate of total annihilation before it.

Hertzberg, Arthur. *French Enlightenment and the Jews.* Col. U. Pr. 1990 $18.50. ISBN 0-231-07385-2. An original, enduring work on a favorite source of controversy.

———, ed. *The Zionist Idea: A Historical Analysis and Reader.* Macmillan 1972 $17.00. ISBN 0-689-70093-8

Hilberg, Raoul. *The Destruction of the European Jews.* Holmes & Meier 1985 $99.50. ISBN 0-8419-0910-5. Although his views on the passivity of European Jewry in the face of destruction are controversial, Hilberg's work remains unequaled as the definitive history of the Holocaust.

Hyman, Louis. *The Jews of Ireland from Earliest Times to the Year 1910.* Irish Academic Pr. 1972 o.p.

Hyman, Paula. *The Emancipation of the Jews of Alsace: Acculturation and Tradition in the Nineteenth Century.* Yale U. Pr. 1991 $29.95. ISBN 0-300-04986-2. The remarkable story of how the Prussian administration liberated the Jews of Alsace when the area was incorporated in the united Germany of 1871.

———. *From Dreyfus to Vichy: The Transformation of French Jewry, 1906–1939.* Col. U. Pr. 1979 o.p. Probing study of the French Jewish community in the decades before the Holocaust that gives special attention to the relations between native Jews and immigrants.

Israel, Jonathan I. *European Jewry in the Age of Mercantilism, 1550–1750.* OUP 1989 $24.95. ISBN 0-19-821136-8. Study is divided into three separate periods and discusses the changing role of Jews in European affairs in each.

Kaplan, Chaim A. *A Scroll of Agony: The Warsaw Diary of Chaim A. Kaplan.* Trans. by Abraham Katsh. Macmillan 1981 o.p. Chronicles daily life in the Warsaw Ghetto, giving the reader a sense of immediacy often missing from general histories.

Katz, Jacob. *From Prejudice to Destruction: Anti-Semitism, 1700–1933.* HUP 1980 $30.50. ISBN 0-674-32505-2. The main theme of this well-informed overall study is how anti-Semitism gained enough widespread power and acceptance to allow the Holocaust to occur.

———. *Out of the Ghetto: The Social Background of Jewish Emancipation, 1770–1870.* Schocken 1973 $14.00. ISBN 0-8052-0601-9. Political and intellectual survey of the transformations in Jewish society structured mainly around the comparison of conditions in Germany and France.

Kochan, Lionel. *Jews, Idols and Messiahs: The Challenge from History.* Blackwell Pubs. 1990 $42.95. ISBN 0-631-15477-9

Laqueur, Walter. *A History of Zionism.* H. Holt & Co. 1972 o.p. "An extremely important book that could be qualified as unique" (*Journal of Modern History*).

Levin, Nora. *The Jews in the Soviet Union Since 1917.* NYU Pr. 1990. 2 vols. $200.00 ea. ISBNs 0-8147-5051-6, 0-8147-5052-4. Comprehensive history of the Jewish community under the Soviets.

———. *While Messiah Tarried: Jewish Socialist Movements, 1871–1917.* Schocken 1977 $24.50. Examines the history of three movements: the Jewish Bund in pre-revolutionary Russia, Jewish labor movement in the United States, and Socialist Zionism in Europe.

McCagg, William O. *Jewish Nobles and Geniuses in Modern Hungary. East European Monographs.* East European Quarterly 1973 o.p. Portrays notable Jews in eighteenth and nineteenth century Hungary, and examines their roles as part of a larger historical and social context.

Marrus, Michael R. *The Politics of Assimilation: The French Jewish Community at the Time of the Dreyfus Affair.* OUP 1980 o.p. Examines the reluctance of the French Jewish community to recognize the anti-Semitic significance of the Dreyfus affair.

Marrus, Michael R., and Robert O. Paxton. *Vichy France and the Jews.* Basic 1981 o.p. The thesis of this study is that of all the German-occupied countries in World War II, France was the most willing to comply with the Nazi program to destroy the Jews.

Memmi, Albert. *The Liberation of the Jew.* Trans. by Judy Hyun. Viking Penguin 1967 o.p. A Tunisian Jew examines the problems of being Jewish in the modern world.

Mendelsohn, Ezra. *The Jews of East Central Europe between the World Wars.* Ind. U. Pr. 1983 $35.00. ISBN 0-253-33160-9. A concise study of the changes undergone by the Jewish communities of Poland, Hungary, Czechoslovakia, Rumania, and the Baltic States, as well as the changes in Jewish-gentile relations.

———. *Zionism in Poland: The Formative Years, 1915–1926.* Bks. Demand 1982 $103.70. ISBN 0-7837-3324-0. Studies the social and political history surrounding the rise of Zionism in post-World War I Poland, and examines it as a product of the uniquely Jewish and Polish milieu.

Mendes-Flohr, Paul R., and Jehuda Reinharz. *The Jews in the Modern World: A Documentary History.* OUP 1980 $37.50. ISBN 0-19-502631-4. Collection of over 250 primary source documents; essential to the study of Jewish history from 1649 to the present.

Meyer, Michael A. *The Origins of the Modern Jew: Jewish Identity and European Culture in Germany, 1749–1824.* Wayne St. U. Pr. 1972 repr. of 1967 ed. o.p. A detailed study on the early period of Jewish emancipation in Germany that examines the interaction between Jewish thought and the Enlightenment.

———, ed. *Ideas of Jewish History. Lib. of Jewish Studies.* Wayne St. U. Pr. 1987 $15.95. ISBN 0-8143-1951-3. The selections in this anthology, many of them appearing for the first time in English, cover a broad spectrum of Jewish attitudes toward history.

Michaelis, Meir. *Mussolini and the Jews: German-Italian Relations and the Jewish Question in Italy, 1922–1945.* OUP 1978 $95.00. ISBN 0-19-822542-3. Interesting study of the Jews in Italy under Mussolini.

Mosse, George L. *Germans and Jews*. Fertig 1984 o.p. A collection of essays investigating the intellectual background of German and Jewish ideologies and the attempts to establish a German-Jewish dialog.

———. *Toward the Final Solution: A History of European Racism*. Fertig 1978 $40.00. ISBN 0-86527-941-1. A concise account of the roots and history of racism in Europe from the eighteenth century to the Holocaust.

Mosse, George, and Bela Vago, eds. *Jews and Non-Jews in Eastern Europe, 1918–1945*. Transaction Pubs. 1974 $15.95. ISBN 0-87855-155-7. Essays representing a variety of viewpoints on Jewish-gentile relations, with most of the authors examining the topic in a sociopolitical context.

Niewyk, Donald L. *The Jews in Weimar Germany*. La. St. U. Pr. 1980 o.p. The first major study of the Jewish community in Germany and German-Jewish relations during the years immediately leading up to the Holocaust.

Parkes, James W. *The Jew in the Medieval Community*. Hermon 1976 $13.95. ISBN 0-87203-060-1. A study of the social, legal, and religious position of the Jews in the Middle Ages, including several important primary documents.

Polonsky, Antony, and others. *The Jews in Poland*. Blackwell Pubs. 1986 $39.95. ISBN 0-631-14857-4. A collection of essays covering a broad range of Polish-Jewish history.

Poppel, Stephen M. *Zionism in Germany, 1897–1933: The Shaping of a Jewish Identity*. Jewish Publication Society 1977 o.p. A social history that examines the German Zionist movement and the cultural climate that produced it, focusing on how Zionism helped to forge a new identity for German Jews.

Porath, Jonathan D. *Jews in Russia: The Last Four Centuries*. United Syn. Bk. 1973 $3.75. ISBN 0-8381-0220-4

Reinharz, Jehuda. *Fatherland or Promised Land: The Dilemma of the German Jews, 1893–1914*. U. of Mich. Pr. 1975 o.p. An analysis of the ideological struggle within the Jewish community in Germany prior to World War I.

Reitlinger, Gerald. *The Final Solution*. A. S. Barnes 1961 o.p. Excellent book on the Jews, Hitler, and the Holocaust.

Rothenberg, Joshua. *The Jewish Religion in the Soviet Union*. Ktav 1971 o.p. Examines the situation of Jews and Judaism in the former Soviet Union, focusing on the period of the late 1960s.

Rubenstein, Richard. *The Cunning of History: the Holocaust and the American Future*. HarpC 1987 $10.00. ISBN 0-06-132068-4. Short but gripping examination of the murder machine of the Nazis and their various associates.

———. *After Auschwitz: History, Theology and Contemporary Judaism*. Johns Hopkins 1992 $48.50. ISBN 0-8018-428-0. A necessary retrospective view of the ramifications of the Holocaust.

Sachar, Howard M. *The Course of Modern Jewish History*. Delacorte 1977 $12.95. ISBN 0-385-28172-2. Authoritative one-volume work that offers a long, detailed survey of the period from the French Revolution to the birth of Israel.

Sanders, Ronald. *The High Walls of Jerusalem: A History of the Balfour Declaration and the Birth of the British Mandate for Palestine*. H. Holt & Co. 1983 o.p. A chronological study of English policy toward Jewish nationalism and an examination of the origins of the British declaration of Zionist sympathy.

Sartre, Jean-Paul. *Anti-Semite and Jew*. Schocken 1967 o.p. Sartre's controversial work is a psychological analysis of the attitudes of anti-Semites and Jews; takes the position that anti-Semitism is not just a "Jewish problem."

Schleunes, Karl A. *The Twisted Road to Auschwitz: Nazi Policy toward German Jews, 1933–1939*. U. of Ill. Pr. o.p. Holds that the Holocaust was only one of several possible outcomes of Nazi policy toward the "Jewish problem."

Scholem, Gershom. *On Jews and Judaism in Crisis: Selected Essays*. Ed. by Werner J. Dannhauser. Schocken 1989 $12.95. ISBN 0-8052-0954-9

Schorske, Carl. *Fin-de-Siècle Vienna: Politics and Culture*. Random 1980 $16.95. ISBN 0-394-74478-0. Seven separate studies on Vienna at the turn of the century—politics and culture including a study of Jews and anti-Semitism.

Snyder, Louis L. *The Dreyfus Case: A Documentary History.* Rutgers U. Pr. 1973 o.p. The standard study.

Sokolow, Nahum. *History of Zionism, 1600–1918.* 2 vols. Ktav 1969 $59.50. ISBN 0-87068-107-9. Although broad in scope, this fundamental work contains much information essential to understanding the early development of Jewish nationalism.

Stein, Leonard. *The Balfour Declaration.* Humanities 1983 repr. of 1961 ed. o.p. A conclusive history of the origins of the Balfour Declaration that examines British interests in the Middle East and English-Zionist relations from the 1830s on.

Steiner, Jean Francis. *Treblinka.* New Amer. Pr. 1968 $5.99. ISBN 0-451-62566-8. Best-selling account of the abortive prisoners' revolt in the infamous concentration camp. Introduction by Terrence Des Pres.

Tal, Uriel. *Christians and Jews in Germany: Religion, Politics, and Ideology in the Second Reich, 1870–1914.* Trans. by Noah J. Jacobs. Cornell Univ. Pr. 1975 o.p. Looks at the period from the establishment of the German empire to World War I, and analyzes the ideological foundation of Christian anti-Semitism and its growth as a powerful political force.

Weizmann, Chaim. *Trial and Error: The Autobiography of Chaim Weizmann.* Greenwood 1972 repr. of 1949 ed. $35.00. ISBN 0-8371-6166-5. Focuses on the political life of the liberal first president of Israel.

Wertheimer, Jack. *Unwelcome Strangers: East European Jews in Imperial Germany.* OUP 1987 $45.00. ISBN 0-19-504893-8. Study of the large migration from the east that inflamed German anti-Semitism during the late nineteenth century.

Wiesel, Elie. *Jews of Silence: A Personal Report on Soviet Jewry.* Schocken 1987 $8.95. ISBN 0-8052-0826-7

————. *Legends of Our Time.* Schocken 1982 $12.00. ISBN 0-8052-0714-7

Weisenthal, Simon. *The Murderers among Us: The Simon Wiesenthal Memoirs.* Ed. by Joseph Wechsberg. 1967. Bantam 1973 o.p. Memoirs of a man who dedicated himself to tracking down Nazi war criminals, 900 of whom he brought to justice.

Wilson, Stephen. *Ideology and Experience: Anti-Semitism in France at the Time of the Dreyfus Affair.* Fairleigh Dickinson 1982 o.p. Examines French anti-semitism and the Dreyfus Affair within the context of the social crises occuring within the nation.

Yahil, Leni. *The Holocaust: The Fate of European Jewry, 1932–1945.* OUP 1990 $39.95. ISBN 0-19-504522-X. A full examination of the mass-murder machine from its origins.

THE BRITISH ISLES: ENGLAND, SCOTLAND, WALES, AND IRELAND

Until the twentieth century, the writing of British history was generally constructed around a limited number of themes. These included the struggle for popular rights, usually through the courts and Parliament, against arbitrary monarchy; the cause of English religious liberty against continental, and especially papal, absolutism; and the Anglo-Saxon proclivity toward local free and democratic practices in spite of the imposition of the Norman yoke of despotism. Like all popular historical consciousness, this approach was filled with contradictions. For instance, it was the greatly strengthened monarchy of the sixteenth century that broke the religious link with Rome. Furthermore, both conservatives defending an existing order and radical reformers seeking change would try to shroud themselves with the Anglo-Saxon cloak, the former as champions of tradition and the latter as the radical restorers of ancient liberties.

This approach to history, which was perfected in the nineteenth century, when the writing of history became professionalized, has been labeled the "Whig Interpretation of History." In his work *The Whig Interpretation of History,*

Herbert Butterfield defined the approach as "the tendency in many historians to write on the side of Protestants and Whigs, to praise revolutions, provided they have been successful, to emphasize certain principles of progress in the past and to produce a story which is the ratification if not the glorification of the present."

In the twentieth century, there has been a substantial shift away from the Whig school of history, which most recent historians view as simplistic and partisan. The ideology of socialism provided a new perspective for viewing the British past. There have been Marxist or socialist analyses of the Reformation and the Industrial Revolution by EDWARD PALMER THOMPSON and others. In addition, extensive interest has developed in social history, that is, the examination of the lives of ordinary people rather than the great figures of an era. As these social historians are influenced by the issues of their times and present times, there are many studies of women, of sexual behavior, and of leisure activities, and proportionately fewer of kings and generals.

The writing of the history of Ireland has followed a somewhat different path. It began in the fourth century A.D., when Christianity took root in Ireland and communities of scribes and scholars began recording Irish sagas from early Celtic times. This scholarly activity continued until about 1200. Then, during the centuries-long contest between the British and Irish for control of Ireland, little history was written within the country except by a few of the English settlers, from an Anglo-Irish perspective. In the nineteenth century a completely different interpretation was provided by Irish nationalists, many of them writing in exile. Later in the century the Irish literary revival greatly stimulated interest in early Irish history.

The sustained, violent, and ultimately successful movement for independence produced mostly nationalist hagiographies on one side and counterblasts on the other. There was very little in the way of professionally written history before the formation of the Irish Historical Society in the 1930s. By that time a cadre of scholars—T. W. Moody, R. Dudley Edwards, R. B. McDowell, J. C. Beckett, and others—were prepared to examine the recent history of the country without polemics. Their numbers were augmented gradually by young people entering the profession. Beginning in the 1960s, the number of persons writing Irish history increased dramatically with the influx of scholars from the United States, England, and elsewhere who tackled a range of hitherto neglected subjects. The result was a massive increase in the number of books published on Irish history in Britain and the United States as well as in Ireland.

The eruption of sectarian conflict in Northern Ireland in 1968 forced historians of Ireland to reconsider many of their assumptions. Obviously there was a determined group of people in the northeastern part of the country who would no longer suffer systematic discrimination and separation from the Republic of Ireland. Had Irish historians taken too nationalist an approach to Irish history? This was the position of the "revisionists," but it was rejected by many others and remains controversial. The other event that has greatly affected the writing of Irish history in recent times was the entrance of Ireland into the European Community in 1973. This stimulated some historians to look at the history of the Irish people in the context of northwest Europe.

The history of Scotland has been inextricably linked with that of Great Britain since 1746, when the last Scottish revolt was crushed. That year marked the end of centuries of conflict, during which the Scots struggled to maintain their independence from their southern neighbor. Scotland's own history might be said to begin in A.D. 844, when Kenneth MacAlpin became King of the Scots and established the first United Kingdom in Scotland. For the next several hundred years, Scotland advanced in many ways: agriculture and trade prospered, roads and bridges were built, and Scottish culture flourished. During this time, relations between Scotland and England were often strained, although for some periods the two countries maintained an uneasy peace. In 1603 James VI of Scotland inherited the English throne, thus joining the two kingdoms under one monarch. With the death of Queen Anne, the last Stuart monarch, in 1714, many Highland Scots remained loyal to the Stuarts and allied behind James Edward Stuart, the pretender to the throne. This precipitated a series of rebellions that continued until 1746, when Bonnie Prince Charlie was defeated by the British at Culloden Moor. Although a part of Great Britain today, Scotland has preserved much of its rich heritage and customs.

Like Scotland, Wales is today a part of Great Britain, having been united with its eastern neighbor since 1536, and its history since that time has been linked to that of Great Britain. The history of the nation before that time was, also like Scotland, the story of a struggle to maintain independence. Conflicts between Wales and England existed for centuries. English domination of the nation began in 1071, when William the Conqueror declared himself lord of Wales and gave borderlands to Norman barons. These barons soon controlled most of central and southern Wales. English control expanded in the 1200s, when Edward I of England placed northern Wales directly under English control. In 1301 Edward I bestowed the title Prince of Wales on his son, and since that time all English monarchs have given that title to their oldest son. Despite attempts at rebellion at various times, England was able to maintain its control until, finally, in 1536, King Henry VIII formally joined the two countries under a single government by the first Act of Union. After some boundary changes and other adjustments, the union was finalized in 1543 with the passage of the second Act of Union. Despite the centuries of English domination and control, the Welsh people have kept alive their own language, literature, and traditions, and they take great pride in their heritage.

England

REFERENCE WORKS

Altholz, Josef L. *Victorian England, 1837–1901. Bibliographical Handbooks of the Conference on British Studies.* Cambridge U. Pr. 1970 o.p. Convenient reference guide for students and scholars; broadly representative of the various aspects of Victorian England.

Altschul, Michael. *Anglo-Norman England, 1066–1154. Bibliographical Handbooks of the Conference on British Studies.* Bks. Demand 1969 $23.00. ISBN 0-8357-548-2. A comprehensive bibliography covering all aspects of printed materials about Anglo-Norman England.

Brown, Lucy M., and Ian Christie. *Bibliography of British History, 1789–1851.* OUP 1977 $125.00. ISBN 0-19-822390-0. A comprehensive survey of available primary sources and reference works dealing with the years 1789–1851.

Butler, David E., and Gareth Butler, eds. *British Political Facts, 1900–1985.* St. Martin 1986 $45.00. ISBN 0-312-10467-7. A sourcebook of statistics on English life from 1900 to 1985.

Chaloner, W. H., and R. C. Richardson. *Bibliography of British Social and Economic History.* Manchester Univ. Pr. 1984 o.p. A bibliographical guide; chronologically divided into three sections.

Cook, Chris, and David Waller, eds. *The Longman Guide to Sources in Contemporary British History.* Longman 1994 ISBN 0-582-20971-4

Cook, Christopher, and John Stevenson. *British Historical Facts, 1688–1760*. St. Martin 1988 $45.00. ISBN 0-312-02106-2. Lists all those who held high political, military, judicial, or administrative office, with basic information on the institutions which they served. Other volumes, now out of print, cover 1603–88, 1760–1830, and 1830–1900.

Cook, Christopher, and John Stevenson. *Longman Atlas of Modern British History: A Visual Guide to British Society and Politics, 1700–1970*. Longman 1978 o.p.

Darby, H. C., ed. *A New Historical Geography of England after 1600*. Cambridge U. Pr. 1978 $70.00. ISBN 0-521-31037-7. An illustrated account of the geography of England from the arrival of the Anglo-Saxons to 1900.

———. *A New Historical Geography of England before 1600*. Cambridge U. Pr. 1978 o.p.

Falkus, Malcolm, and John Gillingham, eds. *Historical Atlas of Britain*. Continuum 1981 o.p.

Freeman-Grenville, G. S. *Atlas of British History*. Rowman 1979 o.p.

Fryde, E. B., ed. *Handbook of British Chronology*. Royal Historical Society 1986 $50.00. ISBN 0-86193-106-8. Standard work, now updated from the second edition (1961).

Graves, Edgar B., ed. *A Bibliography of English History to 1485*. OUP 1975 $135.00. ISBN 0-19-822391-9. A systematic survey of printed materials relating to the political, constitutional, social, and economic history of England.

Hanham, H. J., ed. *Bibliography of British History, 1851–1914*. OUP 1976 $155.00. ISBN 0-19-822389-7. Lists major works of value to the student, with a selection of biographies and autobiographies.

Havighurst, A. F. *Modern England: 1901–1984. Bibliographical Handbooks of the Conference on British Studies*. Cambridge U. Pr. 1988 $54.95. ISBN 0-521-30974-3. A bibliographical handbook of primary and secondary sources published from 1901 to 1970.

Jordan, Gerald, ed. *British Military History: Military History Bibliographies*. Garland 1988 ISBN 0-8240-8450-0. A supplement to Robin Higham's *Guide to the Sources of British Military History*; coverage to 1984.

Kanner, Barbara, ed. *The Women of England from Anglo-Saxon Times to the Present: Interpretive Bibliographical Essays*. Shoe String 1979 o.p. Bibliographical essays exploring the English female experience as revealed in published historical accounts.

Kelly, Rosemary. *A World of Change: Britain in the Early Modern Age, 1450–1700*. Dufour 1988 $12.95. ISBN 0-8590-540-5

Kenyon, J. P., ed. *A Dictionary of British History*. Madison Bks. UPA 1983 $20.00. ISBN 0-8128-2910-7. Short but well-done reference work.

Levine, Mortimer, ed. *Bibliographical Handbook on Tudor England: 1485–1603. Bibliographical Handbooks of the Conference on British Studies*. Cambridge U. Pr. 1968 o.p. A handy guide to works relating to the Tudor period; fairly extensive coverage.

Mitchell, Brian R., and Phyllis Deane. *Abstract of British Historical Statistics*. Cambridge U. Pr. 1962 o.p.

Mitchell, Sally, ed. *Victorian Britain: An Encyclopedia*. Garland 1988 $125.00. ISBN 0-8240-1513-4. Signed articles alphabetically arranged; includes bibliographies.

Pargellis, Stanley, and D. J. Medley. *Bibliography of British History: The Eighteenth Century, 1714–1789*. Rowman 1977 repr. of 1951 ed. o.p. This reference work is more concerned with source material than with secondary literature.

Rasor, Eugene L.. *British Naval History Since 1815*. Garland 1990 $90.00. ISBN 0-8240-7735-0. Covers naval and maritime history since 1815.

Read, Conyers, ed. *Bibliography of British History: Tudor Period, 1485–1603*. Rowman 1978 repr. of 1959 ed. o.p. A systematic survey of print material concerning the history of Tudor England.

Smith, George. *Dictionary of National Biography from the Earliest Times to 1900*. Ed. by Stephen Leslie and Sidney Lee. 22 vols. OUP 1882–1953 Supp. 1 $1,100.00 ISBN 0-19-865101-5. With supplements to 1980. One of the most important reference works.

Stevenson, Bruce, comp. *Reader's Guide to Great Britain: A Bibliography*. Bowker 1977 o.p.

Treasure, Geoffrey. *Who's Who in British History*. St. James Pr. 1988–90 o.p. Biographical essays in chronological arrangement; contains charts, maps, glossary, and subject index.

Wilkinson, B. *The High Middle Ages in England, 1154–1377. Bibliographical Handbooks of the Conference on British Studies*. Cambridge U. Pr. 1978 o.p.

GENERAL HISTORIES

Beresford, M. W., and J.K.S. St. Joseph. *Medieval England: An Aerial Survey. Cambridge Air Studies*. Cambridge U. Pr. 1979 o.p. Collection of photographs that illustrate various aspects of England's settlement history.

Bossy, John. *The English Catholic Community, 1570–1850*. OUP 1976 o.p. Examines the English Catholic community within the larger context of English history.

Checkland, Sydney. *British Public Policy, 1776–1939: An Economic and Social Perspective*. Cambridge U. Pr. 1985 $69.95. ISBN 0-521-24596-6. Discusses the evolution of the British state from the late eighteenth century to the outbreak of World War II.

Clarkson, Leslie A. *Death, Disease and Famine in Pre-Industrial England*. St. Martin 1975 o.p.

Cockburn, J. S. *Crime in England*. Princeton U. Pr. 1977 o.p.

Dickinson, W. Croft. *Scotland from the Earliest Times to 1603*. Ed. by Archibald A. Duncan. OUP 1977 $69.00. ISBN 0-19-822453-2. A readable general history that chronicles the ancient kingdom of Scotland.

Duncan, A. A. *Scotland: The Making of the Kingdom. Edinburgh History of Scotland Ser.* St. Mut. 1986 $75.00. ISBN 0-901824-83-6

Flinn, M. W. *British Population Growth, 1700–1850. Studies in Economic and Social History*. Humanities 1970 o.p.

Girouard, Mark. *Life in the English Country House: A Social and Architectural History*. Yale U. Pr. 1978 $45.00. ISBN 0-300-02273-5

——. *The Return to Camelot: Chivalry and the English Gentleman*. Yale U. Pr. 1981 $20.00. ISBN 0-300-02739-7

Haigh, Christopher, ed. *The Cambridge Historical Encyclopedia of Great Britain and Ireland*. Cambridge U. Pr. 1985 ISBN 0-521-25559-7. Signed articles arranged by chronological period.

Harvie, Christopher. *Scotland and Nationalism: Scottish Society and Politics, 1707–1977*. St. Mut. 1986 $35.00. ISBN 0-317-89988-0. Examines the nationalist movement in Scotland and its impact on relations with Great Britain.

Kanner, Barbara, ed. *The Women of England from Anglo-Saxon Times to the Present: Interpretive Bibliographical Essays*. Shoe String 1979 o.p.

Kearney, Hugh F. *The British Isles: A History of Four Nations*. Cambridge U. Pr. 1989 $29.95. ISBN 0-521-33420-9. Fresh, balanced work that gives full attention to the Welsh, Scots, and Irish.

Keir, David L. *Constitutional History of Modern Britain since 1485*. Norton 1967 o.p.

Kellas, James G. *Modern Scotland: The Nation since 1870*. Unwin Hyman o.p. An overview focusing on those institutions that are peculiarly Scottish.

Knowles, David. *The Religious Orders in England*. 3 vols. Cambridge U. Pr. 1948–1979 o.p.

Lawrence, Clifford H., ed. *The English Church and the Papacy in the Middle Ages*. Fordham 1965 o.p.

Lloyd, T. O. *The British Empire, 1558–1983. Short Oxford History of Modern World*. OUP 1984 $19.95. ISBN 0-19-873025-X. Examines the major trends effecting the British Empire from the beginning of British expansionism to the decline of colonialism.

Lyon, Bryce. *A Constitutional and Legal History of Medieval England*. Norton 1980 o.p. Summarizes the best modern scholarly opinion on the problems concerning English medieval institutions.

Norman, E. R. *Church and Society in England, 1770–1970: A Historical Survey*. OUP 1976 o.p. Presentation by an orthodox churchman.

O'Farrell, P. J. *England and Ireland since 1800*. OUP 1975 o.p. Study of conflicting national attitudes.

Pelling, Henry. *A History of British Trade Unionism.* Sheridan 1987 $45.00. ISBN 0-333-44285-7. An account of the domestic and foreign policy of Labor administrations, with an examination of their leaders.

Pinchbeck, Ivy, and Margaret Hewitt. *Children in English Society.* U. of Toronto Pr. 1973 o.p.

Webb, Robert K. *Modern England: From the Eighteenth Century to the Present.* HarpC 1980 $32.00. ISBN 0-06-046974-9. One of the best histories of modern England.

Wrigley, E. A. *The Population History of England, 1541–1871: A Reconstruction. Studies in Social and Demographic History.* HUP 1982 $76.00. ISBN 0-674-69007-9

PRE-1066

The Anglo-Saxon Chronicle. Ed. by G. N. Garmonsway. C. E. Tuttle 1991 $7.95. ISBN 0-460-87038-6. Fundamental narrative source of early English history, consisting of annals composed in various monasteries, done in earnest during King Alfred's reign (871–899) and continuing until the end of King Stephen's reign. Taken as a whole, it is the first history of a western nation in its own language.

Ashe, Geoffrey. *Kings and Queens of Early Britain.* Methuen 1984 o.p. Chronicles the lives of England's rulers from the earliest legendary kings to Alfred the Great.

Barlow, Frank. *The English Church, 1000–1066: A Constitutional History.* Shoe String 1963 o.p. Examines the constitutional history of the English church in the period before Gregorian reform.

Birley, Anthony. *The People of Roman Britain.* U. CA Pr. 1980 $49.95. ISBN 0-520-04119-4

Blair, P. H. *An Introduction to Anglo-Saxon England.* Cambridge U. Pr. 1977 $74.95. ISBN 0-521-21650-8. A general introduction to the history of England from the latter part of the Roman occupation to the beginning of the Norman era.

———. *Roman Britain and Early England, 55 B.C. to A.D. 871.* Norton 1966 $8.95. ISBN 0-393-00361-2. A very good book at an old-fashioned price.

Brooke, Christopher. *From Alfred to Henry III, 871–1272.* Norton 1966 $8.95. ISBN 0-393-00362-0

Duckett, Eleanor S. *Alfred the Great: The King and His England.* U. Ch. Pr. 1958 $8.95. ISBN 0-226-16779-8. Excellent study of one of the first kings of a united English people.

Frere, Sheppard. *Britannia: A History of Roman Britain.* Routledge Chapman & Hall 1987 $55.00. ISBN 0-7102-1215-1. Carefully researched and well-organized update of earlier research on Roman Britain.

Laing, Lloyd. *Celtic Britain. Britain before the Conquest Ser.* Scribner 1979 o.p. Traces the Celtic civilization in relation to the European Iron Age.

Laing, Lloyd, and Jennifer Laing. *Anglo-Saxon England. Britain before the Conquest Ser.* Academy Ch. Pubs. 1983 o.p. Traces the establishment of the Anglo-Saxons in Britain and their evolution into the English.

Loyn, H. R. *The Vikings in Britain.* St. Martin 1977 o.p. Describes the Viking period of raid and settlement and its impact on England from 954 to 1100 A.D.

Richmond, I. A. *Roman Britain.* Viking Penguin 1978 $5.95. ISBN 0-14-020315-X

Stenton, Frank M. *Anglo-Saxon England.* Gordon Pr. 1977 $79.95. ISBN 0-8490-1430-X

Thomas, Charles. *Celtic Britain.* Thames Hudson 1986 $22.50. ISBN 0-500-02107-4. Illustrated history focusing on the achievements of the Celts in the fifth and sixth centuries.

Whitelock, Dorothy. *The Beginnings of English Society.* Viking Penguin 1952 o.p. An account of English life up to the Norman conquest.

NORMAN AND ANGEVIN ENGLAND, 1066–1216

Barlow, Frank. *The Feudal Kingdom of England: 1042–1216.* Longman 1988 $18.95. ISBN 0-582-49504-0. Part of a 10-volume series that provides a readable narrative of the history of England.

Brown, R. Allen. *Normans and the Norman Conquest.* Longwood 1985 $36.00. ISBN 0-85115-427-1. Stresses the importance of the Norman conquest in the formation of English medieval society.

Denny, Norman, and Josephine Filmer-Sankey. *The Bayeux Tapestry: The Norman Conquest, 1066.* Merrimack 1984 o.p. Dedicated to the tapestry that celebrates the Norman conquest of England.

Gibson, Margaret. *Lanfranc of Bec.* OUP 1978 o.p. Perceptive study of the archbishop of Canterbury, who was a close associate and ally of William the Conqueror.

Holt, James C. *Magna Carta and the Idea of Liberty.* Krieger 1982 $9.50. ISBN 0-89874-47-1. A collection of studies on the people and documents that shaped the history of the Middle Ages.

Howarth, David. *Ten Sixty Six: The Year of the Conquest.* Viking Penguin 1981 $5.95. ISBN 0-14-005850-8. Describes the year 1066 from the varying points of view of the people who lived through it.

Jones, Thomas M. *The Becket Controversy.* Wiley 1970 o.p. Analysis of the twelfth-century church-state clash that continues to intrigue scholars, poets, and playwrights.

Knowles, David. *Thomas Becket.* Stanford U. Pr. 1971 $18.50. ISBN 0-8047-0766-9

Powicke, F. M. *Thirteenth Century, 1216–1307.* OUP 1962 $49.95. ISBN 0-19-821708-0

Stenton, Doris M. *English Justice between the Norman Conquest and the Great Charter, 1066–1215.* Bks. Demand 1964 $62.50. ISBN 0-317-28293-X. A description of English society in the Middle Ages; drawn largely from contemporary sources.

———. *English Society in the Early Middle Ages, 1066–1307.* Viking Penguin 1952 $5.95. ISBN 0-14-020252-8

Warren, W. L. *Henry II.* Eng. Monarchs Ser. U. CA Pr. 1973 $15.95. ISBN 0-520-03494-5. Biography of one of the greatest kings of England.

———. *King John.* U. CA Pr. 1978 $14.95. ISBN 0-520-03643-3. Biography of Henry II's son, who was forced by his barons to sign the Magna Carta.

THE LATER MIDDLE AGES, 1216–1485

Barber, Richard. *The Life and Campaigns of the Black Prince.* St. Martin 1986 $29.95. ISBN 0-312-48382-1. The royal warrior who fought in the Hundred Years War.

Bolton, J. L. *The Medieval English Economy, 1150–1500.* Rowman & Littlefield Univ. Lib. Rowman 1980 o.p.

Chancellor, John. *The Life and Times of Edward I.* Kings and Queens of England Ser. Biblio Dist. 1981 o.p. Good introduction to the great lawgiver and summoner of Parliaments in the late thirteenth century.

Dobson, R. B. *The Peasants' Revolt of Thirteen Eighty One.* Humanities 1986 $15.00. ISBN 0-333-25505-4. Argues that the peasants' courage was better than their cause.

Fowler, Kenneth, ed. *Hundred Years War.* St. Martin 1971 o.p.

Goodman, Anthony. *The Wars of the Roses: Military Activity and English Society, 1452–1497.* Routledge 1990 $16.95. ISBN 0-415-05264-5. Treats the struggle for the throne of England in the fifteenth century and the effect it had on the English people.

Griffiths, Ralph A. *The Reign of Henry VI.* U. CA Pr. 1981 $50.00. ISBN 0-520-04356-1. Biography of the last Lancastrian king.

Hallam, Elizabeth, ed. *The Plantagenet Encyclopedia: An Alphabetical Guide to 400 years of English History.* Grove Weidenfeld 1990 $32.95. ISBN 0-8021-1289-7. Covers English history roughly from the mid-1100s to the death of Richard III in 1485; lavishly illustrated dictionary of short entries, identifying people, places, and subjects.

Hatcher, John. *Plague, Population and the English Economy, 1348–1530.* Studies in Economic and Social History. Humanities 1977 $9.95. ISBN 0-332-21292-2

Holmes, George A. *The Estates of the Higher Nobility in Fourteenth-Century England.* AMS Pr. repr. of 1957 ed. $28.50. ISBN 0-404-18570-3

Keen, Maurice. *The Outlaws of Medieval Legend.* Studies in Social History. Routledge Chapman & Hall 1987 $15.95. ISBN 0-7102-1203-8. Examines the Robin Hood legend and the concept of the medieval outlaw to show how they may be representative of commoners' social concerns.

Kendall, Paul M., ed. *Richard III: The Great Debate.* Norton 1992 $10.95. ISBN 0-393-00310-8. A different look at the villainously regarded monarch of the late fifteenth century.

Lander, J. R. *Government and Community: England, 1450–1509. New History of England Ser.* HUP 1980 $30.50. ISBN 0-674-35793-0

Myers, A. R. *England in the Late Middle Ages.* Viking Penguin 1952 $5.95. ISBN 0-14-020234-X. Blends social and political history to examine the rapid development of the later Middle Ages.

Power, Eileen E. *The Wool Trade in English Medieval History.* Greenwood 1987 repr. of 1941 ed. $38.50. ISBN 0-313-25656-X

Prestwich, Michael. *The Three Edwards: War and State in England, 1272–1377.* St. Martin 1980 $27.50. ISBN 0-312-80251-X. A coherent account of how England responded to the pressures of war and the part played in the process by three kings.

Senior, Michael. *The Life and Times of Richard II.* Ed. by Antonia Fraser. *Kings and Queens of England Ser.* Biblio Dist. 1981 o.p.

Ziegler, Philip. *Black Death.* HarpC 1971 repr. of 1969 ed. o.p. Discussion by an eminent scholar of the causes and influence of the fourteenth-century plague.

TUDOR PERIOD, 1485–1603

Andrews, Kenneth R. *Trade, Plunder and Settlement: Maritime Enterprise and the Genesis of the British Empire, 1480–1630.* Cambridge U. Pr. 1985 $54.50. ISBN 0-521-25760-3. Explores the causes for and early years of British imperialism.

Bernard, G. W. *War, Taxation, and Rebellion in Early Tudor England: Henry VIII, Wolsey and the Amicable Grant of 1525.* St. Martin 1986 $32.50. ISBN 0-312-85611-3. A careful study of a single grant of 1525 is a vehicle for surveying many aspects of Henry VIII's reign.

Bindoff, S. T. *Tudor England.* Vol. 5. Viking Penguin 1950 $5.95. ISBN 0-14-020212-9

Chambers, Jonathan D. *Population, Economy, and Society in Pre-Industrial England. Oxford Pap. Ser.* OUP 1972 o.p. Explores the way population change influences the economy during periods of advance and stagnation. Introduction by W. A. Armstrong.

Cressy, David. *Literacy and the Social Order.* Cambridge U. Pr. 1980 $44.95. ISBN 0-521-22514-0. Relates the effects of the introduction of the printing press on education and the social-class structure.

Cross, Claire. *Church and People, 1450–1600. Fontana Lib. of Eng. History.* Humanities 1976 o.p. Discussion of an era when religion and politics were inseparable.

Dickens, Arthur G. *The English Reformation. Fabric of British History Ser.* Schocken 1968 o.p. Examines a large area of mid-Tudor England to show the impact of the Reformation on a regional society.

Duffy, Eamon. *The Stripping of the Altars: Traditional Religion in England, 1400–1580.* Yale U. Pr. 1992 $45.00. ISBN 0-300-05342-8. Presents a powerful argument that Catholicism in England at the time of the state takeover was neither decadent nor decayed but a strong and vigorous tradition.

Dwyer, Frank. *Henry VIII. World Leaders—Past and Present Ser.* Chelsea Hse. 1988 $17.95. ISBN 0-87759-530-8. Well-detailed and readable account of Henry VIII's life and time. Includes chronologies and bibliographies.

Edwards, R. Dudley. *Church and State in Tudor Ireland: A History of Penal Laws against Irish Catholics, 1534–1603.* Russell Sage 1972 repr. of 1935 ed. o.p. Analysis of the traditional conflict in Ireland, where the Reformation existed only on the surface, under the Tudors.

Elton, G. R. *England under the Tudors.* Routledge Chapman & Hall 1974 $19.95. ISBN 0-416-70690-8. Chronicles the achievements of the House of Tudor from 1485 to 1603.

Fritze, Ronald H., ed. *Historical Dictionary of Tudor England, 1485–1603.* Greenwood 1991 $85.00. ISBN 0-313-26598-4. Almost 300 entries, ranging from 250 to 2,000 words each, discussing people, events, laws, institutions, and special topics related to sixteenth-century England.

Greenblatt, Stephen J. *Sir Walter Raleigh: The Renaissance Man and His Roles.* Yale U. Pr. 1973 o.p.

Guth, De Lloyd J., and John W. McKenna. *Tudor Rule and Revolution.* Cambridge U. Pr. 1983 $69.95. ISBN 0-521-24841-8

Hexter, J. H. *Reappraisals in History: New Views on History and Society in Early Modern Europe.* U. Ch. Pr. 1979 o.p. Significant critique of prevailing historical interpretations.

Hoskins, W. G. *The Age of Plunder: The England of Henry VIII, 1500–1547. Social and Economic History of England Ser.* Longman 1976 o.p. A social and economic history that examines the reign of King Henry VIII.

Jordan, W. K. *Edward VI, The Young King: The Protectorship of the Duke of Somerset.* HUP 1968 $35.00. ISBN 0-674-23965-2

Levine, Mortimer. *Tudor Dynastic Problems, 1462–1571. Historical Problems: Studies and Documents.* Unwin Hyman 1973 o.p. Focuses on problems that were the key to much of what happened in this period.

Loades, David. *The Mid-Tudor Crisis, 1545–1565.* St. Martin 1992 $39.95. ISBN 0-312-08370-X. A revisionist historical account of the period. Loades challenges the notion of "crisis," insisting on the strength of English institutions during the interludes of Edward VI and Mary I.

——. *The Reign of Mary Tudor: Politics, Government and Religions in England, 1553–1558.* St. Martin 1979 o.p. Centers around the attempt by Queen Mary to undo the Reformation.

MacCaffrey, Wallace. *The Shaping of the Elizabethan Regime.* Princeton U. Pr. 1971 $47.00. ISBN 0-691-05168-2. Focuses on the central personalities of the age; special attention is paid to issues of foreign and domestic policy.

Martin, T. W., *Religious Radicals in Tudor England.* Hambledon Press 1989 $55.00. ISBN 1-85285-006-X. Argues that the Reformation was the result of popular spiritual desires, as well as of acts of state, for upper-division graduate students and above.

Mattingly, Garrett. *The Armada.* HM o.p. History told in the grand style.

Read, C. *Lord Burghley and Queen Elizabeth.* Knopf 1960 o.p. Focuses on Elizabeth I and her chief minister, their personal relationship and public policy.

Ridley, Jasper, *The Tudor Age.* Overlook Pr. 1990 $29.95. ISBN 0-87951-405-1. A topical overview of sixteenth-century England aimed at the general reader.

Routh, C. R., ed. *Who's Who in Tudor England. Who's Who in British History Ser.* St. James Pr. 1991 $45.00. ISBN 1-55862-133-4. An excellent reference for teachers of upper-division undergraduates and beginning graduate students in Tudor history. Should be noted that the entries show a strong Protestant bias and that there are very few entries on women.

Scarisbrick, J. J. *Henry VIII.* U. CA Pr. 1968 o.p. Explores the personal domestic events of Henry's life, as well as the political affairs in which he was involved.

Smith, Lacey B. *Elizabeth Tudor: Biography of a Queen.* Little 1977 $9.95. ISBN 0-316-80153-4. This biography combines psychological insight with solid scholarship to present a clear picture of the queen.

Smith, Ralph Bernard. *Land and Politics in the England of Henry VIII.* OUP 1970 o.p. Treats what some schools of historical thought regard as the central issue of the Tudor era—the relationship between land and politics.

Stone, Lawrence. *The Family, Sex and Marriage in England, 1500–1800.* HarpC 1983 $13.00. ISBN 0-06-131979-1. Outstanding work of English social history.

Van Cleave Alexander, Michael. *The First of the Tudors: A Study of Henry VII and His Reign.* Rowman 1980 o.p.

Wernham, R. B. *Before the Armada: The Emergence of the English Nation, 1485–1588.* Norton 1972 o.p. Describes and explains the growth of England's foreign policy during the Tudor period.

Williams, Penly. *The Tudor Regime.* OUP 1979 $22.50. ISBN 0-19-822678-0

STUART PERIOD, 1603–1714

Ashley, Maurice, *The English Civil War.* St. Martin 1991 $29.95. ISBN 0-312-05198-0. Surveys the long-term and immediate causes of the war and traces its course.

Bergerson, David M. *Royal Family, Royal Lovers.* U. of Mo. Pr. 1991 $27.50. ISBN 0-8262-0783-9. Biography of James I. Provides a pivot for examining the various members of his extended family; draws extensively on primary materials.

Childs, John. *The Army, James II and the Glorious Revolution.* St. Martin 1981 $27.50. ISBN 0-312-04949-8

Coward, Berry. *The Stuart Age. A History of England Ser.* Longman 1980 $21.95. ISBN 0-582-48833-8

Fletcher, A. J. *The Outbreak of the English Civil War.* NYU Pr. 1981 o.p. Examines the numerous religious and political issues that led to the English Civil War.

Fletcher, Anthony. *Reform in the Provinces: The Government of Stuart England.* Yale U. Pr. 1986 $40.00. ISBN 0-300-03673-6. A revisionist account, analyzing the evolution and operation of local government in the Stuart era and altering, rejecting, or reorienting views propounded in earlier works.

Fraser, Antonia. *Cromwell.* Knopf 1973 o.p. A lively biography of the driven Protector.

Gardiner, Samuel R. *Cromwell's Place in History. Select Bibliographies Reprint Ser.* Ayer 1897 $15.00. ISBN 0-8369-5044-5

Greaves, Richard L.. *Saints and Rebels: Seven Nonconformists in Stuart England.* Mercer Univ. Pr. 1985 $18.95. ISBN 0-86554-136-1. Presents the life stories and times of seven Puritan men, linking religious men with political causes.

Gregg, Edward. *Queen Anne.* Routledge 1984 o.p. Excellent study of a distracted ruler.

Hibbard, Caroline M. *Charles I and the Popish Plot.* U. of NC Pr. 1983 o.p. Examines the role that anti-Catholic feeling played in the outbreak of the English Civil War.

Hibbert, Christopher. *Cavaliers and Roundheads: The English at War 1642–1649.* Macmillan 1993 $27.50. ISBN 0-684-19557-7. A narrative history of the English civil war concentrating on the actions rather than the causes of the war.

Hill, C. P., ed. *Who's Who in Stuart Britain. Who's Who in British History Ser.* St. James Pr. 1990 $45.00. ISBN 1-55862-132-6. Inclusive reference work on important figures in Stuart England; recommended for academic libraries that support courses in the English history of the period.

Hunt, William. *The Puritan Moment: The Coming of Revolution in an English County.* HUP 1985 $12.50. ISBN 0-674-73904-3. Examines the English Civil War by focusing on the county of Essex and the impact of Puritanism.

Jones, James Rees. *Country and Court: England, 1658–1714. New History of England Ser.* HUP 1978 $28.00. ISBN 0-674-17525-5. General history that takes contemporary areas of research and inquiry into account.

_____. *The Revolution of 1688 in England. Revolutions in the Modern World Ser.* Norton 1973 o.p. Uniquely intelligent treatment of the event that parallels 1776 in Anglo-American constitutional liberalism.

Kenyon, J. P. *The Popish Plot.* St. Martin 1972 o.p. Analysis of the anti-Catholic paranoia that helped found the Whig party.

_____. *Stuart England.* Viking Penguin 1978 $5.95. ISBN 0-14-022552-8

Kishlansky, Mark A. *The Rise of the New Model Army.* Cambridge U. Pr. 1979 $32.50. ISBN 0-521-22751-8. Study of the revolutionary army of the parliamentary-Puritan cause.

Manning, Brian. *The English People and the English Revolution, 1640–1649.* Holmes & Meier 1976 o.p. History of the English Civil War that refutes the idea that it was primarily a dispute among the ruling classes.

Miller, John. *James II: A Study in Kingship.* Wayland Pr. 1978 o.p. A study of failure.

Peck, Linda L. *Court Patronage and Corruption in Early Stuart England.* Routledge 1990 $55.00. ISBN 0-04-942195-6. Analyzes patronage and corruption in early Stuart England in terms of the rhetoric used by contemporaries.

Riley, P. W. *The Union of England and Scotland: A Study in Anglo-Scottish Politics of the Eighteenth Century.* Rowman 1978 o.p.

Smuts, R. Malcolm. *Court Cultures and the Origins of a Royalist Tradition in Early Stuart England.* U. of Pa. Pr. 1987 $44.95. ISBN 0-8122-8039-3. Indicates that cultural attitudes of the court were shared by a wider circle of aristocrats than courtiers, rejecting the view that there were two antagonistic cultures in Caroline England; recommended for specialists in the field.

Thirsk, Joan. *The Restoration. Problems and Perspectives in History.* Longman 1975 o.p. Account of the return of the Stuart monarchy after Cromwell's defeat.

Trevor-Roper, Hugh. *From Counter-Reformation to Glorious Revolution.* U. Ch. Pr. 1992 $29.95. ISBN 0-226-81230-8. A collection of essays by a renowned Cambridge historian revolving around religious controversies in Britain.

Walzer, Michael. *The Revolution of the Saints: A Study in the Origins of Radical Politics.* HUP 1982 o.p. Study of the ultimate in revolutionary fanaticism: the belief that only the "saved" should rule.

Wedgwood, Cicely V. *King's Peace.* Macmillan 1969 o.p. This and *The King's War* (o.p.), *Thomas Wentworth, First Earl of Stafford: A Revaluation* (o.p.), and *The Trial of Charles I* (o.p.) remain the standard account of the English Civil War and the reign of Charles I.

Weston, Corinne, and Janelle R. Greenberg. *Subjects and Sovereigns: The Grand Controversy over Legal Sovereignty in Stuart England.* Cambridge U. Pr. 1981 $59.95. ISBN 0-521-23272-4. Explains the two conflicting political theories that were used by pamphleteers of the time to justify and condemn the English Civil War.

Willson, D. H. *King James VI and I.* Jonathan Cape 1956 o.p. Celebrated biography of "the wisest fool in Christendom."

Woolf, D. R., *The Idea of History in Early Stuart England.* U. of Toronto Pr. 1990 $50.00. ISBN 0-8020-5862-0. Studies the works of individual historians and the themes that connect them.

Woolrych, Austin. *Commonwealth to Protectorate.* OUP 1982 o.p. History of constitutional evolution under Cromwell.

Worden, B. *The Rump Parliament, 1648–1653.* Cambridge U. Pr. 1974 o.p. A detailed, scholarly examination of the rise and fall of the Rump Parliament.

Zagorin, Perez. *The Court and the Country: The Beginning of the English Revolution.* Atheneum 1971 o.p. Examines the specific factors that engendered the revolt against King Charles I.

Zaller, Robert. *The Parliament of 1621: A Study in Constitutional Conflict.* U. CA Pr. 1971 o.p. Analysis of the Parliament that wanted to support the Protestants in the Continental war, curb and control royal expenditures, and impeach Lord Chancellor Francis Bacon.

HANOVERIAN PERIOD, 1717–1837

Anstey, Roger, and A. P. Antippas. *The Atlantic Slave Trade and British Abolition, 1760–1810. Cambridge Commonwealth Ser.* Humanities 1975 o.p. Focuses on the effort to curb one of the horrors of European expansion.

Ayling, Stanley. *The Elder Pitt: Earl of Chatham.* McKay 1976 o.p. Appraisal of the maker of the British empire.

Brock, Michael. *The Great Reform Act.* Ed. by Joel Hurstfield. Humanities 1974 o.p. Brief treatment of the first step toward the democratization of Britain.

Browning, Reed. *The Duke of Newcastle.* Yale U. Pr. 1975 o.p. Biography of one of the great Whig patrons and political managers under George II.

Cannon, John, ed. *The Whig Ascendancy: Colloquies on Hanoverian England.* St. Martin 1981 $25.00. ISBN 0-312-86761-1

Chambers, Jonathan D., and Gordon E. Mingay. *The Agricultural Revolution.* David & Charles 1975 o.p. Study of the transformation that enabled Britain to feed a greatly expanded population.

Christie, Ian R., and Benjamin W. Labaree. *Empire or Independence, 1760–1776: A British American Dialogue.* Norton 1977 o.p. British and U.S. examination of the prelude to the American Revolution.

Colley, Linda. *Britons: Forging the Nation, 1707–1837.* Yale U. Pr. 1992 $35.00. ISBN 0-300-5737-7. Lively, extensive account of how the English and Scots formed a political union.

Cookson, J. E. *Lord Liverpool's Administration: The Crucial Years, 1815–1822.* Shoe String 1975 o.p. Investigates an administration beset by an insane king, a rakish regent, the threat of revolution, and a prime minister who was more leader and head of government than the king's servant.

Cunningham, Hugh. *Leisure in the Industrial Revolution, 1780–1880.* St. Martin 1980 o.p. Explores the early notions of leisure time and how it was shaped by the demands of industrial production

Dann, Uriel. *Hanover and Britain, 1740–1760.* St. Martin 1991 $65.00. ISBN 0-7185-1352-5

Deane, Seamus. *The French Revolution and Enlightenment in England, 1789–1832.* HUP 1988 $25.00. ISBN 0-674-32240-1. Broad-ranging exposition by an Irish literary critic.

Derry, John W. *Castlereagh.* British Political Biography Ser. St. Martin 1976 o.p. Biography of a major statesman of the Congress of Vienna era. Examines the American Revolution within the context of mid-eighteenth century British politics.

———. *English Politics and the American Revolution.* St. Martin 1977 o.p.

Dickinson, H. T. *Liberty and Property: Political Ideology in Eighteenth Century Britain.* Holmes & Meier 1978 o.p.

———. *Walpole and the Whig Supremacy.* Men and Their Times Ser. Verry 1973 o.p. Study of the first prime minister and the man who guaranteed Whig ascendancy and the heritage of the Glorious Revolution.

Emsley, Clive. *British Society and the French Wars, 1793–1815.* Rowman 1979 o.p. Explores the social effects of the fighting between Great Britain and revolutionary and Napoleonic France.

Goodwin, Albert. *The Friends of Liberty: The English Democratic Movement in the Age of the French Revolution.* HUP 1979 o.p. View of a movement inevitably regarded as subversive, especially when England was at war with revolutionary France.

Hibbert, Christopher. *George IV: Prince of Wales, 1752–1811.* HarpC 1972 o.p.

———. *George IV: Regent and King, 1811–1830.* HarpC 1974 Vol. 2 o.p. Biography of the rakish and unpleasant son of the religious and dutiful George III.

Himmelfarb, Gertrude. *The Idea of Poverty: England in the Early Industrial Age.* Knopf 1983 $24.50. ISBN 0-394-53062-4

Kronenberger, Louis. *The Extraordinary Mr. Wilkes.* Doubleday 1974 o.p. The radical demagogue of the 1760s and 1770s.

McMahon, Marie P. *The Radical Whigs, John Trenchard and Thomas Gordon: Libertarian Loyalists to the New House of Hanover.* U. Pr. of Amer. 1990 $34.00. ISBN 0-8191-7677-3

Marcus, Geoffrey. *Heart of Oak: A Survey of British Sea Power in the Georgian Era.* OUP 1975 o.p.

Marshall, Dorothy. *Eighteenth Century England, 1714 to 1784.* History of England Ser. Longman 1975 o.p.

Marshall, P. J. *East India Fortunes: The British in Bengal in the Eighteenth Century.* OUP 1976 o.p. Examines how men made their fortunes in eighteenth-century Bengal and how their exploits affected British expansion.

Mingay, Gordon E. *English Landed Society in the Eighteenth Century.* U. of Toronto Pr. 1963 o.p.

———. *The Gentry: The Rise and Fall of a Ruling Class.* Themes in British Social History. Longman 1976 o.p.

O'Brien, Conor C. *The Great Melody: A Thematic Biography of Edmund Burke.* U. Ch. Pr. 1992 $34.95. ISBN 0-226-61650-9. Fresh, provocative look at the founder of modern conservatism.

O'Gorman, Frank. *Voters, Patrons and Parties: The Unreformed Electorate of Hanoverian England 1734–1837.* OUP 1989 $89.00. ISBN 0-19-820056-0. Startlingly brilliant revision of the role of the electorate in English politics before the great reform bill of 1832.

Peters, Marie. *Pitt and Popularity: The Patriot Minister and London Opinion during the Seven Years War.* OUP 1980 o.p. Examines Pitt's career and how he used nationalistic sentiment to bolster his political career.

Rosenheim, James M. *The Townshends of Raynham.* U. Pr. of New Eng. 1989 $40.00. ISBN 0-8195-5217-8. Examines lives and political careers of the first and second Viscount Townshend, showing how the English aristocracy came to dominate the kingdom in the eighteenth century. Important study of the transition in the Restoration and early Hanoverian England.

Rudé, George. *Hanoverian London, 1714–1808. History of London Ser.* U. CA Pr. 1971 o.p. A general history that weaves together the life and history of London over the span of one hundred years.

Semmel, Bernard. *The Methodist Revolution.* Basic 1973 o.p. Relates the enormous social, economic, and political implications of the Protestant movement.

Speck, W. A. *Stability and Strife: England, 1714–1760. New History of England Ser.* HUP 1977 $17.00. ISBN 0-674-83347-3

Summerson, John. *Georgian London.* Trafalgar 1993 $29.95. ISBN 0-7126-5036-9

Thomas, Peter D. *Lord North. British Political Biography Ser.* St. Martin 1975 $25.00. ISBN 0-312-49860-3. Biography of George III's prime minister during the American Revolution.

Treasure, Geoffrey., ed. *Who's Who in Early Hanoverian England.* St. James Pr. 1992 $45.00. ISBN 1-55862-136-9

Ward, Adolphus W. *Great Britain and Hanover: Some Aspects of the Personal Union.* Haskell 1969 $48.95. ISBN 0-8383-0252-1

VICTORIAN PERIOD, 1837–1901

Altick, Richard D. *Victorian People and Ideas.* Norton 1974 $10.95. ISBN 0-393-09376-X. Interesting and perceptive glimpses of the age.

Blake, Robert. *Disraeli.* Univ. Paperbks. 1969 o.p. Model of what a critical biography should be.

Briggs, Asa. *Age of Improvement, 1783 to 1867. History of England Ser.* Longman 1959 o.p. Pace-setting general history of the period.

_____. *Victorian People.* U. Ch. Pr. 1975 $15.95. ISBN 0-226-07488-9. Classic study of prominent personalities in the period from 1851 to 1867.

Brundage, Anthony. *The Making of the New Poor Laws: The Politics of Inquiry, Enactment, and Implementation, 1832–1839.* Rutgers U. Pr. 1978 o.p. Provides insights on a rational but heartless welfare system.

Childs, Michael J. *Labour's Apprentices: Working-Class Lads in Late Victorian and Edwardian England.* U. of Toronto Pr. 1992 $44.95. ISBN 0-7735-0915-1. Studies adolescent English males of the period as well as their broader social and historical contexts.

Conacher, J. B. *The Peelites and the Party System, 1846–52. Lib. of Politics and Society Ser.* Shoe String 1972 $32.50. ISBN 0-208-01268-0. The breakaway conservatives who would form coalitions with the Whigs.

Cook, Christopher. *A Short History of the Liberal Party, 1900–1975.* Merrimack 1984 o.p.

Curtis, L. Perry, Jr. *Apes and Angels: The Irishman in Victorian Caricature.* Ayer 1924 $18.00. ISBN 0-8369-3309-5

Emy, H. V. *Liberals, Radicals and Social Politics, 1892–1914.* Cambridge U. Pr. 1973 o.p. Traces liberalism's move from laissez-faire to collectivism.

Ensor, Robert C. *England, 1870 to 1914.* OUP 1986 $59.00. ISBN 0-19-821705-6. Reprint of a standard work of the period.

Farwell, Byron. *The Great Anglo-Boer War.* Norton 1990 $12.95. ISBN 0-393-30659-3

Fergusson, Thomas G. *British Military Intelligence, 1870–1914: The Develoment of a Modern Intelligence Organization.* U. Pubns. Amer. 1984 o.p. Annotated citations to selected studies that examine the major social, political, cultural, and economic currents of twelfth-century Europe.

Freeden, Michael. *The New Liberalism: An Ideology of Social Reform.* OUP 1978 o.p. Assessment of turn-of-the-century collectivist liberalism.

Gallagher, J. A. *The Decline, Revival and Fall of the British Empire.* Cambridge U. Pr. 1982 o.p. Revisionist history of British imperialism.

Hamer, D. A. *Liberal Politics in the Age of Gladstone and Roseberry: A Study in Leadership and Policy.* OUP 1972 o.p. Examines the philosophies and strategies of the leading liberal politicians in the years 1867 to 1905.

Holcombe, Lee. *Victorian Ladies at Work: Middle Class Working Women in England and Wales, 1850–1914*. Shoe String 1973 o.p. Study of women who challenged the confinements of their era.

Jones, Raymond A. *The British Diplomatic Service, 1815–1914*. Humanities 1983 o.p. Integrates the history of the diplomatic service in the nineteenth century into the overall development of the Victorian civil service.

Joyce, Patrick. *Work, Society, and Politics: The Culture of the Factory in Later Victorian England*. Ashgate Pub. Co. 1992 $59.95. ISBN 0-7512-0008-5. Traces the rise of factory production and the creation of a factory proletariat in later Victorian England.

Kidd, Alan J., and Ken Roberts, eds. *City, Class, and Culture: Studies of Cultural Formation and Social Policy in Victorian Manchester*. St. Martin 1988 $49.95. ISBN 0-7190-1768-8. A collection of essays that illuminate middle-class ideology as reflected in social policy and cultural aspects of Victorian Manchester.

Kirk, Neville. *The Growth of Working-Class Reformism in Mid-Victorian England. The Working Class in European History Ser*. U. of Ill. Pr. 1985 $34.95. ISBN 0-252-01223-2. Deals with the nature and significance of the decline of radicalism and the growing emphasis upon reform by industrial workers in Victorian Britain.

Laqueur, Thomas W. *Religion and Respectability: Sunday Schools and English Working Class Culture, 1780–1850*. Bks. Demand 1976 $81.10. ISBN 0-8357-8302-2. Explores the role of Sunday school in shaping the feelings and desires of working people at the time.

LeMay, G. H. *The Victorian Constitution*. St. Martin 1979 $27.50. ISBN 0-312-84145-0

Lewis, Jane. *Women and Social Action in Victorian and Edwardian England*. Stanford U. Pr. 1991 $42.50. ISBN 0-8047-1905-5. Uses the lives and work of five women to illuminate late-nineteenth- and early-twentieth-century approaches to philanthropy.

Lyons, F. S. *Charles Stewart Parnell*. OUP 1977 o.p. Definitive biography of the constitutional nationalist Irish leader.

MacDonagh, Oliver. *Early Victorian Government, 1830–1870*. Holmes & Meier 1977 $32.50. ISBN 0-8419-0304-2. Decisive analysis, setting the premises for other historians.

———. *Ireland: The Union and Its Aftermath*. Allen & Unwin 1977 o.p. Develops the fundamental questions for other historians.

Magnus, Philip. *Gladstone*. NAL-Dutton 1964 o.p. Superb biography of the great Victorian politician.

Mingay, Gordon E. *Rural Life in Victorian England*. Holmes & Meier 1978 o.p.

Mitchell, Sally, ed. *Victorian Britain: An Encyclopedia*. Garland 1988 $125.00. ISBN 0-8240-1513-4. Useful and readable reference work.

Moore, David C. *The Politics of Deference: A Study of the Mid-Nineteenth Century English Political System*. B & N Imports 1977 o.p. Examination of the willingness of most English people to be ruled by those judged to be their "betters."

Pakenham, Thomas. *The Boer War*. Avon 1992 $15.00. ISBN 0-380-72001-9. Chronicles the last imperial war using firsthand, largely unpublished accounts of contemporaries.

Paz, D. G. *Popular Anti-Catholicism in Mid-Victorian England*. Stanford U. Pr. 1992 $42.50. ISBN 0-8047-1984-5. A well-researched work that illustrates and confirms the popularity of anti-Catholic action and sentiment in mid-Victorian England.

Pelling, Henry. *Popular Politics and Society in Late Victorian Britain*. Humanities 1979 o.p.

Robbins, Keith. *The Eclipse of a Great Power: Modern Britain, 1870–1975*. Longman 1983 o.p.

Roberts, David. *Paternalism in Early Victorian England*. Rutgers U. Pr. 1979 $50.00. ISBN 0-8135-0868-1. Traces the development of paternalism from a social ideal to social remedy.

Royle, Edward. *Radicals, Secularists and Republicans: Popular Freethought in Britain, 1866 to 1915*. Rowman 1980 o.p. Examines the history of secularism as an expression of popular dissent.

Saville, John. *Eighteen Forty-Eight: The British State and the Chartist Movement.* Cambridge U. Pr. 1987 $59.95. ISBN 0-521-33341-5. Description by an expert of the encounter between the great popular movement and the established order of government and society.

Smith, Roger. *Trial by Medicine: The Insanity Defense in Victorian England.* Col. U. Pr. 1981 $33.00. ISBN 0-85224-407-X

Thomis, Malcolm I. *Responses to Industrialization: The British Experience, 1780–1850.* Shoe String 1976 o.p. Examines to what extent those living at the time of the Industrial Revolution were aware of the significance of the changes taking place.

Thompson, Edward P. *The Making of the English Working Class.* Random 1966 $25.00. ISBN 0-394-70322-7

Thompson, F. M. *The Rise of Respectable Society: A Social History of Victorian Britain.* HUP 1988 $34.95. ISBN 0-674-77285-7. Engaging and probing examination of Victorian social conditioning. Classic Marxist account of the birth and early development of the British working class and its organizations.

Thornton, A. P. *The Imperial Idea and Its Enemies: A Study in British Power.* St. Martin 1985 $29.95. ISBN 0-312-40989-3. Provocative examination of British imperialism and its outspoken opponents.

Townshend, Charles. *Political Violence in Ireland: Government and Resistance since 1848.* OUP 1984 $65.00. ISBN 0-19-821753-6

Ward, John T. *Chartism.* Humanities 1973 o.p. Study of the first mass political movement in England.

Young, George M. *Portrait of an Age: Victorian England.* OUP 1977 $49.00. ISBN 0-19-212961-9

Zedner, Lucio. *Women, Crime, and Custody in Victorian England.* OUP 1992 $72.00. ISBN 0-19-820264-4. Deals with crime trends, penal theory, and perceptions of women and the links between them in Victorian England.

Ziegler, Philip. *Melbourne.* Atheneum 1982 o.p. Biography of Victoria's first prime minister.

THE TWENTIETH CENTURY

Bartlett, C. J. *A History of Postwar Britain, 1945–74.* Longman 1977 o.p.

Bedarida, François. *A Social History of England, 1851–1975.* Routledge 1991 $17.95. ISBN 0-415-01614-2. Description and critical assessment of the evolution of modern English society.

Beer, Samuel H. *Modern British Politics: Parties and Pressure Groups in the Collectivist Age.* Norton 1982 repr. of 1965 ed. $9.95. ISBN 0-393-00952-1. Explores the rise of collectivism from the late nineteenth century to the early 1960s.

Branson, Noreen. *Britain in the Nineteen Twenties.* Ed. by Eric J. Hobsbawm. *History of British Society Ser.* U. of Minn. Pr. 1976 o.p. A social history focusing on the labor and popular movements of the day.

Burnham, Peter. *The Political Economy of Postwar Reconstruction.* St. Martin 1970 $49.95. ISBN 0-312-03075-4. Rebuts the thesis that U.S. hegemony after World War II forced a British "capitulation" to an American strategy for a new international system that impaired Britain's chances for postwar recovery.

Cannadine, David. *The Decline and Fall of the British Aristocracy.* Yale U. Pr. 1990 $40.00. ISBN 0-300-04761-4. "Blockbuster" study of the downfall of the nobility. Winner of the 1990 Lionel Trilling Book Award.

Churchill, Winston S. *Memoirs of the Second World War.* HM 1990 $34.00. ISBN 0-395-52226-5

Cook, Christopher. *Age of Alignment: Electoral Politics in Britain, 1922–1929.* U. of Toronto Pr. 1975 o.p. Traces the decline of the Liberal Party, focusing on changes in the party from 1920 to 1924.

Cowling, Maurice. *The Impact of Hitler: British Politics and British Policy, 1933–1940. Cambridge Studies in the History and Theory of Politics.* U. Ch. Pr. 1977 o.p. Examines the effect Hitler had on British politics and foreign policy.

_____. *Impact of Labour, Nineteen Twenty to Nineteen Twenty Four: The Beginning of Modern British Politics.* Cambridge U. Pr. 1971 o.p. Examines the emergence of the Labor Party, focusing on the letters and diaries of the politicians who played major roles.

Dangerfield, George. *The Strange Death of Liberal England, 1910–1914.* Capricorn 1961 o.p. Vivid description of the excitement caused by militant workers, women, and Irish nationalists just before the "Great War."

Darby, Phillip. *Three Faces of Imperialism: British and American Approaches to Asia and Africa, 1870–1970.* Yale U. Pr. 1987 $30.00. ISBN 0-300-03748-1. Revealing comparative study of how the Americans and British viewed and practiced imperialism.

Davies, Andrew. *Leisure, Gender, and Poverty: Working-class Culture in Salford and Manchester, 1900–1939. Themes in Twentieth Century Ser.* Taylor & Francis 1992 $95.00. ISBN 0-335-15638-X. Examines the voluntary or involuntary leisure time of the working class in English industrial cities. Emphasizes the different experiences of men and women, and the youth culture.

Eatwell, Roger. *The Labour Governments, 1945–1951.* Trafalgar 1979 o.p.

Farnsworth, Susan H. *The Evolution of British Imperial Policy During the Mid-nineteenth Century.* Garland 1992 $97.00. ISBN 0-8153-0474-9. Details critical developments in Britain during the mid-nineteenth century focusing on the challenges faced by Imperialist leaders of the period.

Gilbert, Bentley B. *Britain since 1918.* St. Martin 1980 $23.50. ISBN 0-312-09876-6. Solid account of social change in Great Britain after World War I.

Gorst, Tony, Lewis Johnman, and W. Scott Lucas. *Postwar Britain, 1945–1964.* St. Martin 1989 $47.50. ISBN 0-86187-760-8. Articles encompassing themes such as political, economic, and social trends in postwar Britain.

Grigg, John. *The People's Champion, 1902–1911.* U. CA Pr. 1979 $55.00. ISBN 0-520-03634-4. A comprehensive biography of the British leader at the zenith of his achievement.

_____. *The Young Lloyd George.* U. CA Pr. 1978 repr. of 1973 ed. $52.00. ISBN 0-520-02677-2. Discusses the significance of Lloyd-George's formative days as a politician to his subsequent career.

Harkness, David. *Northern Ireland since Nineteen Twenty.* Irish Bk. Ctr. 1983 o.p. Chronological account of the history of devolved government in Northern Ireland, with an epilogue on later developments; especially suitable for the general reader.

Harrison, Brian. *Separate Spheres: The Opposition to Woman Suffrage in Britain.* Holmes & Meier 1978 o.p. Seeks to understand the women's suffrage movement by studying its opponents.

Havighurst, Alfred F. *Britain in Transition: The Twentieth Century.* U. Ch. Pr. 1979 $10.00. ISBN 0-226-31968-7. Narrative account of British decline, from the high point of Victorian imperialism to social disintegration in the Thatcher years; for the general reader.

Hill, Michael. *The Welfare State in Britain: A Political History since 1945.* Ashgate Pub. Co. 1993 $69.95. ISBN 1-85278-436-9. Traces the development of social-welfare programs and their opponents.

Howell, David. *British Social Democracy: A Study in Development and Decay.* St. Martin 1980 $28.50. ISBN 0-312-10536-3

Jones, Barry, and Michael Keating. *Labour and the British State.* OUP 1985 $36.00. ISBN 0-19-876187-2. Deals with the historical evolution of the Labor Party from the angle of the party's formulation of a theory of the state.

Kennedy, Paul. *The Realities behind Diplomacy: Background Influences on British External Policy, 1865–1980.* Routledge Chapman & Hall 1981 $37.95. ISBN 0-04-902005-6. Fairly specialized account of the forces that shaped and influenced modern British foreign policy.

_____. *The Rise of the Anglo-German Antagonism: 1860–1914.* Humanities 1987 $22.50. ISBN 0-948660-06-6

Koss, Stephen. *Nonconformity in Modern British Politics.* Shoe String 1975 o.p. A mainly parliamentary history of the decline in importance of religion in British politics.

Lee, J. M. *The Churchill Coalition, 1940–1945*. Shoe String 1980 $29.50. ISBN 0-208-01880-8. Examines the policies and dynamics of the bipartisan government that ruled Britain during World War II.

Lloyd, T. O. *Empire to Welfare State: English History, 1906–1976. Short Oxford History of the Modern World Ser.* OUP 1986 $62.00. ISBN 0-19-822135-5. Examines the relationship between the decline of British power overseas and the parallel increase in democratic participation inside the country in the twentieth century.

Louis, William R. *The Brittish Empire in the Middle East, 1945–1951: Arab Nationalism, the United States, and Postwar Imperialism.* OUP 1984 $55.00. ISBN 0-19-822489-3

Marwick, Arthur. *British Society since 1945. Pelican Social History of Britain Ser.* Allen Lane 1984 $15.95. ISBN 0-317-00889-7. Social history of postwar Britain, focusing on the rise and fall of the Labor Party.

Meacham, Standish. *A Life Apart: The English Working Class, 1890–1914*. HUP 1977 $18.50. ISBN 0-674-53075-6. Traces the various patterns of English working class consciousness before World War I.

Moore, Roger. *The Emergence of the Labour Party, 1880–1924*. Humanities 1978 o.p. A socioeconomic analysis of the emergence of the British Labor Party and how it replaced the Liberals as the alternative to the Conservatives.

Morgan, Kenneth O. *Consensus and Disunity: The Lloyd George Coalition Government, 1918 to 1922*. OUP 1979 $79.00. ISBN 0-19-822497-4. Discusses Lloyd-George's post-1918 coalition government in the context of changes in the socioeconomic situation and national psyche of Britain.

——. *Wales in British Politics, Eighteen Sixty Eight to Nineteen Twenty Two*. Humanities 1980 o.p. Deals with the nature and failure of Welsh nationalist politics, analysed in the wider British context.

Pelling, Henry. *A Short History of the Labour Party*. St. Martin 1977 o.p. Brief account of the birth, struggles, successes, and failures of the Labor Party as seen through the policies and personalities of its leaders.

Phillips, Gregory D. *The Diehards: Aristocratic Society and Politics in Edwardian England*. HUP 1979 $20.00. ISBN 0-674-20555-3. Looks at that section of the Edwardian aristocracy who unsuccessfully resisted attempts to dilute the parliamentary power of the House of Lords.

Ponting, Clive. *1940: Myth and Reality*. I. R. Dee 1993 $24.95. ISBN 0-929587-68-5. Deals with the confusion of and misinformation collected and disbursed by the British government during the crisis year as revealed in recent research.

Porter, Bernard. *The Lion's Share: A Short History of British Imperialism, 1850–1970*. Longman 1984 $18.95. ISBN 0-582-49387-0. Readable, amusing, yet scholarly view of the rise and fall of British imperialism.

Ramsden, John. *The Age of Balfour and Baldwin, 1902–1940. History of the Conservative Party Ser.* Longman 1978 o.p. Discusses the origins, evolution, and functioning of the Conservative Party.

Rowland, Peter. *David Lloyd George: A Biography*. Macmillan 1976 o.p. Monumental, yet somewhat dispassionate, biography of the British leader.

Sampson, Anthony. *The Changing Anatomy of Britain*. Random 1983 o.p. Ideal introduction for the layperson and very useful for the scholar as well.

Sked, Alan, and Christopher Cook. *Post War Britain: A Political History. Penguin Nonfiction Ser.* Viking Penguin 1985 o.p. Readable account of the governments and policies of postwar British prime ministers.

Taylor, Alan J. P. *English History, 1914–1945*. OUP 1992 $16.95. ISBN 0-19-285268-X. Unrivaled study that is completely divorced from nationalistic cant, yet idiosyncratic.

Thomas, Hugh. *Suez*. HarpC 1967 o.p. Interesting narrative of the British and French debacle in Egypt in 1956.

Thompson, Paul. *The Edwardians: The Remaking of British Society*. Academy Chi. Pubs. 1985 $10.00. ISBN 0-89733-144-3. Oral history of Edwardian England, based on interviews with 500 people of all classes.

Wiener, Martin. *English Culture and the Decline of the Industrial Spirit, 1850–1980*. Cambridge U. Pr. 1981 o.p. Explores England's ambiguous relationship with modern industrial society.

Young, Hugo. *Iron Lady*. FS&G 1990 $14.95. ISBN 0-374-52251-0. Full critical examination of Margaret Thatcher, the "Iron Lady" who dominated British politics and government for a dozen years.

Scotland

Barrow, Geofrey W. *Kingship and Unity: Scotland, 1000 to 1306 A.D.* Col. U. Pr. 1989 $15.00. ISBN 0-85224-643-9. Engrossing story of the emergence of the Scottish state.

_____. *Robert Bruce and the Community of the Realm of Scotland*. Col. U. Pr. 1988 $40.00. ISBN 0-85224-539-4. Dramatic story of the preservation of an independent Scotland.

Black, Jeremy. *Culloden and the Forty Five*. St. Martin 1991 $35.00. ISBN 0-312-05197-2. Moving narrative concerned with the end of independent Scotland.

Donaldson, Gordon, ed. *The Faith of the Scots*. Trafalgar 1991 $39.95. ISBN 0-7134-6052-0. Interesting history of religion in Scotland since 1500.

_____. *Scottish Historical Documents*. B & N Imports 1970 o.p.

_____. *Who's Who in Scottish History*. B & N Imports 1973 o.p. Contains the usual brief biographical sketches of major and minor figures in Scottish history.

Donnachie, Ian, and George Hewitt. *A Companion to Scottish History: From the Reformation to the Present*. Facts on File 1990 $27.50. ISBN 0-8160-2398-0. Excellent introduction to the Scots.

Erickson, Carolly. *Bonnie Prince Charlie*. Morrow 1989 $19.95. ISBN 0-688-06087-0. Latest and well-written biography of the last of the Stuarts.

Fraser, Antonia. *Mary, Queen of Scots*. Delacorte 1978 o.p. Bedtime reading at its best. A full biography of the ill-starred monarch.

Fry, Michael. *Patronage and Principle: A Political History of Modern Scotland*. Macmillan 1987 $39.90. ISBN 0-08-035063-1. A study of Scotland's distinctive political history from 1832.

Fry, Plantagenet, and Fiona S. Fry. *The House of Stuart*. Routlege Chapman & Hall 1982 $25.00. ISBN 0-7100-9100-3. Fine history of a great Scottish dynasty.

Grant, Alexander. *Independence and Nationhood: Scotland, 1306–1469*. Col. U. Pr. 1991 $20.00. ISBN 0-7486-0273-9. Examines the Scottish quest to maintain its independence in this period; seen in the wider context of political developments in Europe.

Grant, Isabel. *The Economic History of Scotland*. AMS Pr. repr. of 1934 ed. $22.50. ISBN 0-404-14799-2. The standard, if now somewhat dated, economic history of Scotland.

Harvie, Christopher. *No Gods and Precious Few Heros: Scotland, 1914–1980*. Bks. Demand 1981 $48.00. ISBN 0-685-15765-2. Popular history of the country since 1914.

Lee, Maurice, Jr. *The Road to Revolution: Scotland under Charles I, 1625–37*. U. of Ill. Pr. 1985 $29.95. ISBN 0-252-01136-8

MacKenzie, William C. *The Highlands and Isles of Scotland: A Historical Survey*. AMS Pr. 1937 $26.45. ISBN 0-404-14682-1. A requirement in Scottish history—a trip to the highlands and islands.

Maclean, Fitzroy. *A Concise History of Scotland*. Thames Hudson 1983 $11.95. ISBN 0-500-27224-7. Brief, chronological account of major developments in Scottish history.

Magnusson, Magnus, and Graham White. *The Nature of Scotland*. Trafalgar 1992 $45.00. ISBN 0-86241-333-8

Mitchison, Rosalind, and Peter Roebuck, eds. *Economy and Society in Scotland and Ireland, 1500–1939*. Humanities 1988 $55.00. ISBN 0-85976-171-1. Valuable collection of articles comparing the development of these two countries.

Wales

Davies, Charlotte A. *Welsh Nationalism in the Twentieth Century: The Ethnic Option and the Modern State*. Greenwood 1989 $39.95. ISBN 0-275-93116-1. Investigates the cross currents in the quest for a modern Welsh identity.

Fishlock, Trevor. *Talking of Wales: A Companion to Wales and the Welsh*. Academy Chi. Pubs. 1978 $6.00. ISBN 0-586-04555-4. Good general introduction to the people and their land.

Jones, Gareth E. *Modern Wales: A Concise History, 1485 to 1979*. Cambridge U. Pr. 1985 $47.50. ISBN 0-521-28414-5. A Welsh chronology—from Henry Tudor to Richard Burton.

Llewellyn, Richard. *How Green Was My Valley*. Macmillan 1940 o.p. Popular romantic novel about the life and tribulations of Welsh coal miners during bad economic times.

Morgan, Kenneth O. *Rebirth of a Nation: Wales, 1880–1980*. OUP 1981 o.p. Excellent history of the country in the nineteenth century.

Rosser, David. *A Dragon in the House*. St. Mut. 1987 $40.00. ISBN 0-86383-357-8. Fire-breathing history of life in twentieth-century Wales.

Smith, David, ed. *A People and a Proletariat: Essays in the History of Wales, 1780–1980*. Pluto Pr. 1980 o.p. Examination of the effects of industrialization on southern Wales.

Thomas, David, ed. *Wales: A New Study*. Trafalgar 1977 $24.95. ISBN 0-7153-7414-1. Looks at the economic geography of Wales—land use, agriculture, industry, tourism, and so on.

Thomas, W. S. *Stuart Wales*. St. Mut. 1989 $39.00. ISBN 0-86383-439-6. Examines the dramatic changes in Wales following legislation by the Stuarts aimed at integrating the nation within the British union.

Walker, David. *Medieval Wales*. Cambridge U. Pr. 1990 $42.95. ISBN 0-521-32317-1. Introductory account of the political and cultural clashes in medieval Wales.

Williams, Glanmor. *Recovery, Reorientation and Reformation: Wales, 1415–1642*. OUP 1987 $89.00. ISBN 0-19-821733-1. History of Wales before and after it was incorporated into the British union.

Williams, Gwyn A. *The Welsh in Their History*. Routledge Chapman and Hall 1982 o.p. Looks at the history of Wales through the eyes of its people.

Ireland

REFERENCE WORKS AND GENERAL HISTORIES

Bartlett, Thomas, and others. *Irish Studies: A General Introduction*. B & N Imports 1988 $16.25. ISBN 0-389-20806-X

Cullen, Louis M. *An Economic History of Ireland since 1660*. Trafalgar 1991 $29.95. ISBN 0-7134-5808-9. Excellent and brief economic history of Ireland.

DePaor, Liam. *The Peoples of Ireland: From Prehistory to Modern Times*. U. of Notre Dame Pr. 1990 $15.95. ISBN 0-268-01590-2. Comprehensive look at the history, interaction, immigration, and emigration of the various groups of people that made Ireland.

Doherty, J. E., and D. J. Hickey. *A Chronology of Irish History since 1500*. B & N Imports 1989 $42.50. ISBN 0-389-20895-7. Straightforward chronological account of the main events in Irish history; for the general reader.

Edwards, Ruth Dudley. *An Atlas of Irish History*. B & N Imports 1981 o.p. Easy-to-read maps, information, and statistics of the political, economic, social and cultural geography of Ireland.

Foster, Roy F. *Modern Ireland, 1600–1972*. Viking Penguin 1990 $15.95. ISBN 0-14-012510-8. Non-anglocentric account of modern Irish political history.

Kee, Robert. *Ireland: A History*. Little 1982 $19.95. ISBN 0-316-48506-3

McCaffrey, Lawrence J. *Ireland: From Colony to Nation State*. P-H 1979. ISBN 0-13-506188-1. Brief history of the trials and tribulations of modern Irish nationalism.

Moody, T. W., and F. X. Martin, eds. *The Course of Irish History*. Dufour $25.95. ISBN 0-85342-710-0

Mitchell, Arthur, and Padraig O. Snoddaigh, eds. *Irish Political Documents, 1896–1916.* Intl. Spec. Bk. 1989 $35.00. ISBN 0-7165-2422-8

————. *Irish Political Documents, 1916–1949.* Intl. Spec. Bk. 1985 $39.50. ISBN 0-7165-0588-6

Ranelagh, John. *Ireland: An Illustrated History.* OUP 1981 $39.95. ISBN 0-19-520261-9. Readable overview of Irish history; for the general reader.

PREHISTORY TO 1800

Bieler, Ludwig. *Ireland and the Culture of Early Medieval Europe.* Ashgate Pub. Co. 1986 $83.95. ISBN 0-86078-211-5. Excellent study by an art historian of the Irish contribution to the formation of European civilization.

Canny, Nicholas. *Kingdom and Colony: Ireland in the Atlantic World, 1560–1800.* Johns Hopkins 1988 $28.00. ISBN 0-8018-3603-4. Concerned with Ireland as a stepping stone in English expansionism.

Connolly, S. J. *Religion, Law and Power: The Making of Protestant Ireland, 1660–1760.* OUP 1992 $92.00. ISBN 0-19-820118-4. Probing study of the effort to consolidate the English interest in Ireland.

Dolley, Michael. *Anglo-Norman Ireland, 1100–1318.* Macmillan 1972 o.p. Examination of the half-conquest of Ireland by the Normans.

Elliott, Marianne. *Wolfe Tone: Prophet of Irish Independence.* Yale U. Pr. 1990 $40.00. ISBN 0-300-04637-5. Excellent biography by the leading scholar of Franco-Irish relations in the revolutionary period.

Ellis, Peter B. *Hell or Connaught: Cromwellian Colonization of Ireland, 1652–1660.* Dufour 1988 $13.95. ISBN 0-85640-404-7. Well-told tale of the mass transfer of the "natives" to the barren west coast of Ireland.

Harbison, Peter. *Pre-Christian Ireland: From the First Settlers to the Early Celts.* Thames Hudson 1988 $24.95. ISBN 0-500-02111-0

Hughes, Kathleen. *Church and Society in Ireland, A.D. 400–1200.* Ashgate Pub. Co. 1987 $91.95. ISBN 0-86078-206-9

McDowell, Robert Brendan. *Ireland in the Age of Imperialism and Revolution, 1760–1801.* OUP 1979 o.p. Panoramic view of the country in the late eighteenth century.

O'Connell, Maurice. *Irish Politics and Social Conflict in the Age of the American Revolution.* Greenwood 1976 $30.00. ISBN 0-8371-8758-3. Masterful exposition of Irish politics and society from Lexington to Yorktown.

Pakenham, Thomas. *The Year of Liberty: The Story of the Great Rebellion of 1798.* P-H 1970 o.p. Thorough account of the Irish rebellion prior to the British-imposed union treaty; discussed in the context of the French revolution.

SINCE 1800

Bell, J. Bowyer. *The Gun in Politics: An Analysis of Irish Violence, 1916–1986.* Transaction Pubs. 1991 $19.95. ISBN 1-56000-566-1. Expert examination of sectarian and communal violence.

Brown, Terence. *Ireland: A Social and Cultural History, 1922 to the Present.* Cornell Univ. Pr. 1985 $42.50. ISBN 0-8014-1731-4

Caulfield, Malachy. *The Easter Rebellion.* Greenwood 1975 $35.00. ISBN 0-8371-7507-0. Balanced and exciting narrative of the six-day revolt that shook the Irish world.

Garvin, Tom. *The Evolution of Irish Nationalist Politics.* Holmes & Meier 1981 $44.75. ISBN 0-8419-0741-2. Brilliant analysis of the leaders of the national independence movement.

Hammond, J. L. *Gladstone and the Irish Nation.* Greenwood 1974 $45.00. ISBN 0-8371-7665-4. Comprehensive analysis of Gladstone's efforts to improve political conditions in Ireland.

Hopkinson, Michael. *Green against Green: A History of the Irish Civil War.* St. Martin 1988 $39.95. ISBN 0-312-02448-7. Scholarly history of the 1922–23 conflict between nationalists.

Ireland, John deCourcy. *Ireland and the Irish in Maritime History*. Ir. Bks. Media 1986 $25.00. ISBN 0-907606-28-8. Revealing study by Ireland's leading maritime historian.

Kearney, Richard, ed. *Across the Frontiers: Ireland in the 1990s*. DuFour 1989 $40.00. ISBN 0-86327-210-X

Larkin, Emmet. *The Roman Catholic Church and the Creation of the Modern Irish State, 1878–1886*. Bks. Demand 1975 $109.00. ISBN 0-317-29437-7. One of several books on Ireland and Catholicism by the expert in the field.

Lee, Joseph J. *Ireland: 1912–1985, Politics and Society*. Cambridge U. Pr. 1990 $79.95. ISBN 0-521-26648-3. Monumental, engrossing, and provocative. The best thing written in Ireland since the Book of Kells.

Longford, Lord, and T. P. O'Neill. *DeValera*. HM 1971 o.p. Definitive biography of the dominant Irish political figure of the first half of this century.

Lyons, Francis S. L. *Ireland Since the Famine*. 1973 o.p. Authoritative and encyclopedic study of Ireland since the 1840s that offers a clear, balanced, and extensive chronology of the country's recent history.

McDonagh, Oliver. *The Emancipist: Daniel O'Connell, 1830–1847*. St. Martin 1989 $35.00. ISBN 0-312-03711-2. Moving study of the last years of the Emancipator.

Miller, Kerby. *Emigrants and Exiles: Ireland and the Irish Exodus to North America*. OUP 1988 $13.95. ISBN 0-19-505187-4. Full treatment of the fate of millions of Irish people.

Murphy, Cliona. *The Women's Suffrage Movement and Irish Society in the Early Twentieth Century*. Temple U. Pr. 1989 $34.95. ISBN 0-87722-636-9. Lively but scholarly history of early feminism, Irish-style.

O'Malley, Ernie. *On Another Man's Wound*. Ir. Bks. Media 1979 $13.95. ISBN 0-947962-31-X. Arresting personal account of an Irish freedom fighter. Originally published in 1936 in the United States as *Army Without Banners*.

Pakenham, Frank. *Peace by Ordeal: The Negotiation of the Anglo-Irish Treaty, 1921*. Trafalgar 1993 $19.95. ISBN 0-7126-9835-3

Ward, Margaret. *Unmanageable Revolutionaries: Women and Irish Nationalism*. Branden Pub. Co. 1983 o.p. A history of the often thorny relationship between the women's and nationalist movements in Ireland.

Woodham-Smith, Cecil. *The Great Hunger: Ireland, 1845–1849*. HarpC 1982 o.p. Great historical work on the Famine.

NORTHERN IRELAND

Arthur, Paul, and Keith Jeffry. *Northern Ireland since 1968*. Blackwell Pubs. $34.95. ISBN 0-631-16141-4. Objective treatment of the area since the eruption of large-scale sectarian conflict.

Bew, Paul, Peter Gibbon, and Henry Patterson. *The State in Northern Ireland, 1921–72: Political Forces and Social Classes*. St. Martin 1979 o.p. Examines the political and social forces that created a sectarian government.

Mansergh, Nicholas. *The Unresolved Question: The Anglo-Irish Settlement and its Undoing, 1912–72*. Yale U. Pr. 1991 $40.00. ISBN 0-300-05069-0. Probing study by a great historian of the relations between the two islands.

Miller, David. *Queen's Rebels: Ulster Unionism in Historical Perspective*. o.p. Penetrating study of the attitudes, values, and perceptions of the northern unionists.

O'Malley, Padraig. *Uncivil Wars: Ireland Today*. Beacon Pr. 1991 $16.95. ISBN 0-8070-0215-1. Interesting treatment of the conflict in the north during the last quarter century.

Stewart, Anthony. *The Narrow Ground*. Faber & Faber 1977 o.p. Historical examination of the closed world of the northern unionists.

FRANCE

In the general matter of European civilization, France has been the leader and the model, with its intellectual life, culture, art, and organization acting as stimulants to the rest of Europe. In the writing of history, the French have made two great contributions—one in the eighteenth century and the other in the twentieth century. In the eighteenth century, DIDEROT (see Vol. 4) and the other encyclopedists described the past in secular and rationalist terms, making a mighty break from religious and literary interpretations of the past. In the twentieth century, the *Annales* school of history, based on the ideas of Marc Bloch, Lucien Febvre, and FERNAND BRAUDEL, wrote history from an inclusive perspective. Braudel declared that this was an approach to the past "whose scope would extend to embrace all the sciences of man—to the 'globality' of all the human sciences." Thus the history of a particular period would go far beyond the usual political chronology to include social, cultural, economic, and intellectual conditions of the time. In contrast to the German developmental model of history, the *Annales* school emphasizes organizations and structures and gives society and culture greater weight than politics. It places far more importance on collective actions and ideas than on individuals. The narrow specialist is lost in this wide, wide world of "total" history.

Ambler, John S., ed. *The French Welfare State: Surviving Social and Ideological Change.* NYU Pr. 1991 $45.00. ISBN 0-8147-0599-5

Anderson, R. D. *France, 1870–1914: Politics and Society.* Routledge 1984 $9.95. ISBN 0-7102-0175-3. An excellent survey. Analyzes political developments in the third French republic in their social context.

Ashley, Maurice. *Louis the Fourteenth and the Greatness of France.* Free Pr. 1965 $12.95. ISBN 0-02-901080-2

Beauroy, Jacques, and others. *The Wolf and the Lamb: Popular Culture in France from the Old Regime to the Twentieth Century.* Anma Libri 1977 o.p. Leading literary critics, historians, ethnographers, and others discuss French popular culture from the vantage point of their own disciplines.

Bernstein, Samuel. *French Political and Intellectual History.* Transaction Pubs. 1983 o.p.

Briggs, Robin. *Early Modern France, 1560–1715.* OUP 1977. ISBN 0-19-289040-9. Incorporates scholarship that modified many of the older views of this period.

Cerny, Philip G. *Social Movements and Protest in France.* St. Martin 1982 $25.00. ISBN 0-312-73310-0

Cobb, Richard. *French and Germans, Germans and French: A Personal Interpretation of France under Two Occupations.* U. Pr. of New Eng. 1983 $14.95. ISBN 0-87451-318-9. Lively personal account by a former American soldier on the relations between French civilians and their German occupiers during the two world wars.

Crozier, Brian. *De Gaulle.* Scribner 1974 o.p. Good biography, critical of De Gaulle.

De Bertier Sauvigny, Guillaume, and David H. Pinkney. *History of France.* Trans. by James Friguglietti. Forum Pr. IL 1983 $29.95. ISBN 0-88273-426-1

DeGaulle, Charles. *The Complete War Memoirs of Charles DeGaulle, 1940–1946.* Da Capo 1984 $14.95. ISBN 0-306-80227-9. The great Frenchman's magisterial recollections.

Derfler, Leslie. *The Third French Republic, 1870–1940.* Krieger 1982 $9.50. ISBN 0-89874-480-6

Farrier, Susan E. *The Medieval Charlemagne Legend: An Annotated Bibliography.* Garland 1992 $83.00. ISBN 0-8240-0949-5. Destined to become a standard reference on a major topic of medieval studies.

Frears, J. R. *France in the Giscard Presidency.* Unwin Hyman 1981 o.p. Compares the Giscard presidency and democratic institutions in France to the British and U.S. systems.

Goodwin, Albert. *The French Revolution.* Hutchinson 1984 o.p. Perhaps the most readable and understandable book on the revolution for the nonexpert.

Goubert, Pierre. *The Ancien Regime: French Society, 1600–1750.* Trans. by Steve Cox. HarpC 1974 o.p. Explains the French Revolution as a conflict between the poor and the rich, rather than the more common view of a conflict between an emerging capitalist bourgeoisie and the old aristocracy.

————. *The Course of French History*. Routledge 1991 $16.95. ISBN 0-415-06671-9. Very useful outline history.

Hanley, David L, A. P. Kerr, and Neville H. Waites. *Contemporary France: Politics and Society since 1945*. Routledge Chapman & Hall 1984 $17.95. ISBN 0-7102-0360-8. Discusses the development of the postwar French political system in its economic and social context.

Horne, Alistair. *The French Army and Politics, 1870–1970*. Bedrick Bks. 1984 o.p. Overview of the sometimes harmonious, sometimes combative relationship between the French military and politicians.

————. *A Savage War of Peace: Algeria, 1954–1962*. Viking Penguin 1987 $12.95. ISBN 0-14-010191-8

Hughes, Judith M. *To the Maginot Line: The Politics of French Military Preparations in the 1920's*. HUP 1971 $20.00. ISBN 0-674-89310-7. Examines the failure of the French state, following its defeat in World War I, to anticipate and prepare for further conflict with Germany.

Hunt, Lynn. *The Family Romance of the French Revolution*. U. CA Pr. 1992 $20.00. ISBN 0-520-07741-5. Difficult yet fascinating book that explores the "collective unconscious images of the familial order" underlying revolutionary beliefs.

————. *Politics, Culture and Class in the French Revolution*. U. CA Pr. 1984 $37.50. ISBN 0-520-05204-8

Kedward, H. R. *Resistance in Vichy France*. OUP 1978 o.p. Detailed study of French resistance fighters and what motivated them.

Kuisel, Richard F. *Capitalism and the State in Modern France: Renovation and Economic Management in the Twentieth Century*. Cambridge U. Pr. 1981 o.p. Discusses state economic policy in the early twentieth century.

Lefebvre, Georges. *Coming of the French Revolution*. Trans. by Robert R. Palmer. Princeton U. Pr. 1989 $39.50. ISBN 0-691-05112-7. Excellent account of the French aristocracy and how its actions led to the French Revolution.

————. *Napoleon from 18 Brumaire to Tilsit, 1799–1807*. Col. U. Pr. 1969 $52.50. ISBN 0-231-02558-0. First volume of the classic biography of Napoleon.

————. *Napoleon from Tilsit to Waterloo, 1807–1815*. Trans. by J. E. Anderson. Col. U. Pr. 1969 $53.00. ISBN 0-231-03313-3. Second volume of the classic biography of Napoleon.

Lichtheim, George. *Marxism in Modern France*. Col. U. Pr. 1968 $17.50. ISBN 0-231-08584-2. Discusses French Communist party ideology and politics in the context of the cold war.

Micaud, Charles A. *French Right and Nazi Germany, 1933–1939*. Octagon 1964 o.p. Examines the evolution of French foreign policy against a backdrop of pan-Germanism and Hitler.

Mousnier, Roland E. *The Institutions of France under the Absolute Monarchy, 1598–1789: Society and the State*. Trans. by Brian Pearce. U. Ch. Pr. repr. of 1974 ed. $55.00. ISBN 0-226-54327-7. Discusses the political and social changes among the aristocracy in prerevolutionary and revolutionary France.

Neale, J. E. *The Age of Catherine de Medici*. Merrimack 1978 o.p. Brief, accessible account of Catherine's reign.

Northcutt, Wayne, ed. *Historical Dictionary of the French Fourth and Fifth Republics, 1946–1990*. Greenwood 1992 $45.00. ISBN 0-313-26356-6. A comprehensive reference work.

————. *Mitterand: A Political Biography*. 1993. Holmes & Meier $34.95. ISBN 0-8419-1295-5. Traces the shifts in Mitterand's policies and positions, particularly in relation to de Gaulle's Fifth Republic.

Paxton, Robert O. *Vichy France: Old Guard and New Order, 1940–1944*. Col. U. Pr. 1982 $53.00. ISBN 0-231-05426-2. Claims that those French who collaborated with the Nazis did so to preserve national stability.

Pickles, Dorothy. *The Fifth French Republic*. Greenwood 1976 $38.50. ISBN 0-8371-8544-0. In-depth examination of De Gaulle's controversial constitution in its postwar context.

Sobel, Robert. *French Revolution: A Concise History and Interpretation.* Peter Smith $11.00. ISBN 0-8446-0922-6. Brief account of the main events of the French Revolution; for the general reader.

Talbott, John. *The War without a Name: France in Algeria, 1954–1962.* Knopf 1980 o.p. Discusses the Algerian war of independence through the eyes of French participants.

Thompson, J. M. *Louis Napoleon and the Second Empire.* Col. U. Pr. 1983 o.p. The standard biography of Napoleon Bonaparte's nephew.

_____. *Robespierre.* Blackwell Pubs. $34.95. ISBN 0-631-15504-X. Lively, revealing biography of the revolutionary leader.

Tint, Herbert. *France since 1918.* St. Martin 1980 $25.00. ISBN 0-312-30315-7

Williams, Philip M., and Martin Harrison. *Politics and Society in De Gaulle's Republic.* Greenwood 1979 $35.00. ISBN 0-313-21085-3

Wright, Gordon. *France in Modern Times.* Norton 1987 $19.95. ISBN 0-393-95582-6. A standard text that focuses on the evolution of the modern French social and political systems.

_____. *In Command of France: French Foreign Policy and Military Planning, 1933–1940.* HUP 1978 $25.50. ISBN 0-674-44536-8. Discusses the foreign and military policies that led to France's easy defeat at the hands of the Nazis.

Zeldin, Theodore. *France, 1848–1945: Anxiety and Hypocrisy.* OUP 1981 $10.95. ISBN 0-19-285106-3. A thorough survey, with extremely useful bibliographies.

GERMANIC EUROPE: AUSTRIA, GERMANY, SWITZERLAND

Austria's rich and culturally diversified past has provided fertile ground for historical study. Two thousand years ago, the Celts ventured into this land at the geographic epicenter of Europe, and were followed by Huns, Goths, and Lombards. The Romans considered the Danube the empire's frontier. Charlemagne later claimed the region, as did the Magyars before Rudolph I took the area for the House of Hapsburg in 1218. The Hapsburgs governed central Europe's largest political entity for over six centuries, recapturing southern Germany for Catholicism, halting the Turkish invasion of Europe at the gates of Vienna, and propagating Western European culture in East-Central Europe and the Balkans.

After 1800, however, Austria floundered. First the Prussians achieved hegemony in Germanic Europe, then the Hungarians demanded equal partnership in a dual monarchy. The Austrian-Hungarian Empire was able to impose a thin veneer of charming baroque uniformity on polyglot dominions, but after World War I the victorious Allies whittled the vanquished Hapsburg Empire down into a modest-sized German Catholic nation.

Since 1919 Austria has weathered political instability in the interwar era, annexation by Hitler, Russian invasion, and four-power occupation. In 1955 it emerged as an autonomous neutral state and in later years became a prosperous east-west link.

Germany has not only made much of Europe's history, it has also contributed greatly to the writing of it. It was a German—Leopold von Ranke—who in the early nineteenth century laid the foundations of the historical profession by insisting that history must be based on an assessment of evidence, particularly the written record, and that the ability to shift and judge this evidence must be developed by training and education. He and his associates developed a graduate school system based on the idea that philosophy is the foundation of historical studies. They reasoned that one could not understand the past unless one could think clearly and logically, and that required training in philosophy, especially in the great German philosophical triumvirate—KANT (see Vol. 4), GOETHE (see Vol. 2), and HEGEL (see Vol. 4).

German professional historians like von Ranke, JOHANN FICHTE (see Vol. 4), and Heinrich von Treitschke used German philosophy to justify German hegemony in Europe. The pronounced nationalist bent of their books and lectures, when combined with romantic ideas about the innate greatness of the German folk, armed Germans with a powerful sense of mission. History, backed by philosophy, was on their side!

By 1900 Germany was leading Europe in science, engineering, technology, industry, and military power. Its defeat in the first great European war of this century left many Germans stunned. The revival of strong German nationalism in the postwar period was, in part, a rejection of the liberal Weimar Republic's decision to surrender in the face of military defeat in 1918. History and philosophy, the Germans believed, had not let them down; their leaders had. The Nazi party's great appeal was based on its claim to grasp these historical and philosophical truths and its promise that it had the leadership to gain Germans their rightful place in the world. The Nazis' mixture of fiery rhetoric, a philosophy of German natural superiority, and criminal leadership led the country to destruction, and German historians have been digging out of the intellectual and moral ruins ever since. Yet, as the century draws to a close, Germany once again leads Europe in technology, organization, and industry.

Switzerland is a clear demonstration of how geographic conditions can govern a nation's history. About two-thirds of its people are culturally and linguistically German, a quarter are French, a small number are Italian, and a tiny population high up in the Alps speaks Romansh (a Latin-based dialect). Despite this diversity, one nationality emerged in the Swiss Alpine retreat.

Swiss separatism began in 1291, when several cantons, or local units, formed a defensive alliance. After centuries of struggle against the Hapsburgs of Austria and continuing political consolidation, Switzerland received international recognition as an independent nation in 1648. A constant policy of neutrality in European wars has allowed the Swiss to concentrate their resources on educational and economic development. Even bitter religious controversy growing out of the Reformation did not destroy Swiss unity or democracy.

Austria

Bridge, F. R. *The Hapsburg Monarchy among the Great Powers, 1815–1918*. Berg Pubs. 1991 $59.95. ISBN 0-85496-307-3. Study of the last, and probably greatest, century of the polyglot state.

Crankshaw, Edward. *The Hapsburgs: Portrait of a Dynasty*. Viking Penguin 1971 o.p. Great history of a great dynasty.

Cronin, Audrey K. *Great Power Politics and the Struggle over Austria, 1945–1955*. Cornell Univ. Pr. 1986 $32.50. ISBN 0-8014-1854-2

Gruber, Helmut. *Red Vienna: Experiment in Working-Class Culture, 1919–1934*. OUP 1991 $29.95. ISBN 0-19-506914-5. History of social and political innovation by Vienna's Social Democrats.

Herzstein, Robert E. *Waldheim: The Missing Years*. Arbor House 1988 o.p. Remarkable investigation into the hidden wartime activities of the former president of Austria.

Hofmann, Payl. *The Viennese: Splendour, Twilight and Exile*. Doubleday 1989 $10.95. ISBN 0-385-23975-0. Study of the people of the historic city on the Danube.

Johnston, William M. *The Austrian Mind: An Intellectual and Social History, 1848–1938*. U. CA Pr. 1976 o.p. A treat for those with cultural and intellectual interests.

MacDonald, Mary. *The Republic of Austria, 1918–1934; A Study in the Failure of Democratic Government.* OUP 1946 o.p. Probing examination of the dynamics of Austrian domestic politics.

Morton, Frederic. *A Nervous Splendour: Vienna 1888–89.* Viking Penguin 1980 $8.95. ISBN 0-14-005667-X

Rickett, Richard. *A Brief Survey of Austrian History.* IBD Ltd. 1983 $24.25. ISBN 3-85367-001-6. A useful guide.

Schmidt, Elfriede. *Nineteen Thirty-Eight . . . and the Consequences.* Ariadne CA 1992 $27.50. ISBN 0-929497-34-1

Schorske, Carl E. *Fin-de-Siècle Vienna: Politics and Culture.* Random 1980 $16.95. ISBN 0-394-74478-0

Seward, Desmond. *Metternich: The First European.* Viking Penguin 1991 $24.95. ISBN 0-670-82600-6

Sully, Melanie. *A Contemporary History of Austria.* Routledge 1990 $48.50. ISBN 0-415-01928-1

Zeman, Z. A. B. *The Break-up of the Hapsburg Empire, 1914–1918.* OUP 1961 o.p.

Germany

Abraham, David. *The Collapse of the Weimar Republic: Political Economy and Crisis.* Holmes & Meier 1986 $45.00. ISBN 0-8419-1083-9. Explains Nazism as emerging from a conflict between organized industrial and agricultural forces as well as between capital and labor, which led to a situation that paralyzed democratic forces.

Baker, Kendall L., and others. *Germany Transformed: Political Culture and the New Politics.* HUP 1981 o.p. Study of postwar Germany's democracy.

Bendersky, Joseph W. *A History of Nazi Germany.* Nelson-Hall 1984 o.p. Concise but thematically comprehensive history of Nazi Germany; for the general reader.

Bracher, Karl D. *The German Dictatorship: The Origins, Structure, and Effects of National Socialism.* H. Holt & Co. 1972 o.p. Comprehensive study of Nazism, explained in terms of the German penchant for authoritarianism.

Bullock, Alan. *Hitler: A Study in Tyranny.* HarpC 1964 o.p. The authoritative and easy-to-read biography of Hitler.

Carr, Edward H. *German-Soviet Relations Between the Two World Wars, 1919–1939.* Greenwood 1980 repr. of 1951 ed. $39.75. ISBN 0-313-24117-1. The standard work on the most important European relationship.

Carsten, Franz L. *Reichswehr and Politics: 1918–1933.* OUP 1966 o.p. Particularly illuminating work on the German army in the 1920s.

Childs, David, ed. *Honecker's Germany.* Unwin Hyman 1985 $49.95. ISBN 0-04-354031-7

Craig, Gordon A. *Germany, 1866–1945.* OUP 1978 $19.95. ISBN 0-19-502724-8. Typically comprehensive history of modern Germany in the *Oxford Modern History Series.*

Detwiler, Donald S., ed. *World War Two German Military Studies.* 10 pts. in 23 vols. Garland 1979 o.p.

Eyck, Eric. *Bismarck and the German Empire.* Norton 1964 o.p. Elegant, yet acerbic account of the Weimar republic by an active participant in its politics.

———. *A History of the Weimar Republic.* Macmillan 1970 $3.95. ISBN 0-689-70218-3

Feuchtwanger, E. J., ed. *Upheaval and Continuity: A Century of German History.* U. of Pittsburgh Pr. 1974 o.p. German scholars detail different aspects of twentieth-century German politics and history.

Fischer, Fritz. *Germany's Aims in the First World War.* Norton 1968 o.p.

Gay, Peter. *Freud, Jews and Other Germans: Masters and Victims in Modernist Culture.* OUP 1979 $30.00. ISBN 0-19-502258-0. Using the German Jew as metaphor for modernity, discusses the relationship between German culture and the modernist movement.

———. *Weimar Culture: The Outsider as Insider.* Greenwood 1981 $55.00. ISBN 0-313-22972-4. Extremely perceptive analysis by a distinguished scholar.

Gimbel, John. *The American Occupation of Germany: Politics and the Military, 1945–1949.* Stanford U. Pr. 1968 $39.50. ISBN 0-8047-0667-0

Henderson, W. O. *The Rise of German Industrial Power, 1834–1914*. U. CA Pr. 1976 o.p. The origin and rise to prominence of German industrial might, seen in its sociopolitical context.

Hiden, John. *Germany and Europe, 1919–1939*. Longman 1993 repr. of 1978 ed. $19.95. ISBN 0-582-08722-8

Hiden, John, and John Farquharson. *Explaining Hitler's Germany: Historians and the Third Reich*. Trafalgar 1989 $29.95. ISBN 0-7134-6257-4. Stimulating and revealing investigation of mass criminality by a "civilized" people.

Hildebrand, Klaus. *The Foreign Policy of the Third Reich*. U. CA Pr. 1983 $12.95. ISBN 0-520-02528-8. Brief account of the foreign policy of Nazi Germany; for the general reader.

Hiscocks, Richard. *The Adenauer Era*. Greenwood 1976 repr. of 1966 ed. o.p. The Adenauer era, seen in the demoralized context of postwar Germany.

Hitler, Adolf. *Mein Kampf*. Trans. by Ralph Manheim. HM 1973 $10.70. ISBN 0-395-08362-1. Should be read by anyone wanting to understand the Nazi era.

Holborn, Hajo. *A History of Modern Germany*. 3 vols. Princeton U. Pr. 1982 $16.95 ea. ISBN 0-691-00795-0. Covers the period from the late fifteenth century to the end of World War II with grace and superb scholarship.

Keithly, David. *The Collapse of East German Communism: The Year the Wall Came Down, 1989*. Greenwood 1992 $47.95. ISBN 0-275-94261-9

Kohn, Hans. *The Mind of Germany*. HarpC 1960 o.p.

Laqueur, Walter. *Weimar: A Cultural History*. Putnam Pub. Group 1976 o.p. Readable account of Weimar Germany, which is viewed as having the first truly modern culture.

McCauley, Martin. *The German Democratic Republic Since 1945*. St. Martin 1986 $14.95. ISBN 0-312-32554-1. Chronology of the democratic regime forced on the Germans by their conquerors.

Mosse, George L. *The Crisis of German Ideology: Intellectual Origins of the Third Reich*. Schocken 1981 $12.75. ISBN 0-8052-0669-8. Explains how the ideas of national socialism were deeply embedded and institutionalized in Germany from the nineteenth century on.

————. *The Nationalization of the Masses: Political Symbolism and Mass Movements in Germany from the Napoleonic Wars through the Third Reich*. Fertig 1975 $40.00. ISBN 0-86527-140-2

Nettl, J. P. *Rosa Luxemburg*. OUP 1966 o.p. Standard biography.

Prittie, Terence. *Willy Brandt: Portrait of a Statesman*. Schocken 1974 o.p. Good biography, though somewhat uncritical.

Ritter, Gerhard. *The Sword and the Scepter: The Problem of Militarism in Germany*. Trans. by Heinz Norden. 4 vols. U. of Miami Pr. 1988. Vol. 1 *The Prussian Tradition*. $25.00. ISBN 0-945726-18-X. Classic, detailed historical analysis of Prussian/German militarism from 1740.

Ryder, A. J. *Twentieth-Century Germany: From Bismarck to Brandt*. Col. U. Pr. 1976 $26.50. ISBN 0-231-08350-5. Useful survey with good bibliographies.

Schoenbaum, David. *Hitler's Social Revolution: Class and Status in Nazi Germany, 1933–1939*. Norton 1980 $10.95. ISBN 0-393-00993-9. Examines how the Third Reich and German society influenced each other.

Scribner, R. W. *Popular Culture and Popular Movements in Reformation Germany*. Hambledon Press 1988 $55.00. ISBN 0-907628-81-8. Broad view of the life and times of the German common people in the age of Luther.

Shirer, William L. *The Berlin Diary: The Journal of a Foreign Correspondent, 1934–1941*. Viking Penguin 1979 o.p. A gripping account of the journalist's experiences during Germany's descent to war.

Smith, Bradley F. *Reaching Judgment at Nuremberg: The Untold Story of How the Nazi War Criminals Were Judged*. New Amer. Pr. 1979 o.p. The most balanced assessment of the war-crime trials.

Snyder, Louis L. *Encyclopedia of the Third Reich*. Paragon Hse. 1988 $16.95. ISBN 1-55778-144-3. How the political monster worked—and thrived.

Speer, Albert. *Inside the Third Reich.* Macmillan 1981 $14.95. ISBN 0-02-037500-X. The psychologically revealing memoirs of a man who was a high-ranking Nazi.

Stern, Fritz. *Dreams and Delusions: The Drama of German History.* Knopf 1987 $19.95. ISBN 0-394-55995

———. *Dreams and Delusions: National Socialism in the Drama of the German Past.* Random 1989 $10.95. ISBN 0-394-75772-6

Stern, J. P. *Hitler: The Führer and the People.* U. CA Pr. 1975 $10.95. ISBN 0-520-02952-6. Probing examination of the appeal of Hitler and the Nazis to many Germans.

Taylor, Alan J. P. *The Course of German History: A Survey of the Development of Germany Since 1815.* Capricorn 1962 o.p.

Turner, Henry A., Jr. *Germany—from Partition to Reunification.* Yale U. Pr. 1992 $35.00. ISBN 0-300-05345-2. Original title—*The Two Germanies Since 1945: East and West.* Reviews major shifts in political structure since mid-century.

Weinberg, Gerhard L. *The Foreign Policy of Hitler's Germany: Diplomatic Revolution in Europe, 1933–1936.* U. Ch. Pr. 1970 o.p. Provides a subtle, thorough analysis of the role of diplomacy during the Nazi era.

———. *The Foreign Policy of Hitler's Germany: Starting World War II, 1937–1939.* U. Ch. Pr. 1980 $44.00. ISBN 0-226-88511-9

Wolfe, Nancy T. *Policing a Socialist Society: The German Democratic Republic.* Greenwood 1992 $55.00. ISBN 0-313-26530-5. A nonpolitical study of the criminal justice system of the German Democratic Republic.

Switzerland

Bonjour, Edgar, and others, eds. *A Short History of Switzerland.* Greenwood 1985 repr. of 1952 ed. $52.50. ISBN 0-313-24675-0

Gilliard, Charles. *A History of Switzerland.* Greenwood 1978 $35.00. ISBN 0-313-20529-9

Luck, J. Murray. *History of Switzerland: From Before the Beginnings to the Days of the Present.* SPOSS 1985 $36.00. ISBN 0-930664-06-X

Luck, J. Murray, and others, eds. *Modern Switzerland.* SPOSS 1978 $22.00. ISBN 0-930664-01-9. A broad-based look at Switzerland's points of distinction as well as its unique problems.

Schmid, Carol L. *Conflict and Consensus in Switzerland.* U. CA Pr. 1981 $37.50. ISBN 0-520-04079-1

Segalman, Ralp. *The Swiss Way of Welfare: Lessons for the Modern World.* Greenwood $45.00. ISBN 0-275-92044-5. A detailed description of why their methods work better than ours in preventing welfare dependency.

Soloveytchik, George. *Switzerland in Perspective.* Greenwood 1982 repr. of 1954 ed. $47.50. ISBN 0-313-23363-2

NORTHERN EUROPE: SCANDINAVIA AND THE LOW COUNTRIES

The Germanic people living in small maritime units on the northern fringe of Europe did not figure in the emerging Europe until the ninth century, when, driven partly by overpopulation and limited resources, they burst upon the scene. Sweeping down the rivers of eastern Europe, the Swedish Rus established the first political entity in what was to become Russia; sailing out into the Atlantic, the Norwegians went from Iceland to Greenland and beyond— archeological evidence has confirmed a Viking presence in Newfoundland and Nova Scotia in the 1100s. A combination of Vikings from Norway and Denmark descended on Ireland, Britain, northern France, and, later, Sicily, southern Italy, and Greece. Initially a destructive force, the Vikings became founders of urban communities and traders after the adoption of Christianity, countermeasures by other countries, and cultural assimilation put an end to their aggressiveness.

During the medieval period Norway, Sweden, and Denmark achieved political integration under Danish leadership. In 1523, however, Sweden became a separate kingdom and over the next two centuries expanded into northern Germany, Finland, and Russia. Defeat at the hands of a northern alliance in the early 1700s put an end to this dynamic movement. A century later Scandinavia experienced territorial realignments as a result of the Napoleonic wars; Finland was transferred to Russia, while Sweden gained Norway. In 1905, in a remarkably peaceful and constitutional process, Norway became an independent state. Finland achieved independence during the Russian Revolution.

The Scandinavians avoided involvement in the first European war of this century, but in the second, Denmark and Norway were occupied by the Germans, while Sweden maintained neutrality with a tilt toward Germany and Finland allied itself outright with Germany in a fruitless effort to regain territory seized by Russia in 1939–40. In 1944 Iceland declared independence. After World War II, cold war pressures divided Scandinavia, with Denmark, Iceland, and Norway joining NATO, and Sweden and Finland remaining unaligned. The European drive toward economic union also split the region: so far only Denmark has joined the European Community. Since the 1930s domestic politics in the region have been dominated by socialist parties, which have forged mixed economies in all the Scandinavian countries and provided high living standards and comprehensive social welfare services for the Scandinavian peoples.

The Netherlands and Belgium—the Low Countries—were originally populated by Germanic people. During the medieval period, several small political units formed in the area, but the chief entity was the town, based on manufacturing, principally cloth weaving and trade. Unrestrained by feudalism, these prosperous towns developed pioneering forms of representative government.

In the late fifteenth century, the Low Countries were nominally inherited by the royal family of Austria, and this Hapsburg connection led to Spanish rule. But with the adoption of Calvinism in the northern area in the mid-1500s, resistance to the Spaniards was based on religion, as well as on ethnicity and the desire to preserve the autonomy of the developing institutions of self-government. With the support of England, the Dutch people rose up in revolt in the 1560s and became independent as the United Provinces of the Netherlands in 1581, while the southern region remained under Hapsburg control. The seventeenth-century Dutch Republic was one of the most dynamic and creative political entities in history. It was the first stable European republic and the first European nation to practice religious toleration. The Dutch made great contributions to European civilization in science, philosophy, political theory, and the arts. They also began a massive program of commercial development in this century; Dutch shipping dominated the north Atlantic Ocean and Dutch explorers ranged over the world. This period of expansion was checked by the growing powers England and France, however, and by 1700 the Netherlands had been reduced to secondary status in European affairs. At the Congress of Vienna at the end of the Napoleonic wars in 1815, the Netherlands was saddled with a hereditary monarchy (though it did retain representative government) and lost its South African Cape colony to Britain, though it held unto the Dutch East Indies, which became the hub of a commercial empire. It was also forced into union with the southern territory, but due to religious, ethnic, and historical differences, this region emerged as the independent nation of Belgium in 1830. By international agreement Belgium became a nonaligned buffer zone between Britain, France, and an emerging Germany. This status did not prevent the Belgians from joining in the European scramble for overseas territory; beginning in 1885, they carved out a huge colony in west-central Africa.

In the first general European war of this century, Belgium was occupied by Germany, while the Netherlands remained neutral. In the second war both countries suffered German occupation. After the war the tide of anticolonialism forced the Dutch out of the East Indies and the Belgians out of the natural resource–rich Congo. In the postwar period, the people of the Low Countries— including the grand duchy of Luxembourg—became the innovators of European integration, forging a common economic unit among themselves (Benelux) in 1948 and helping to found the European Steel and Coal Community in 1953 and the European Common Market in 1957. The Netherlands and Belgium also joined NATO, the European defensive military alliance formed with American leadership in 1949.

Today the Netherlands is a progressive, prosperous, tolerant society. Belgium, however, has experienced considerable economic difficulties in the last 20 years, along with a linguistic-ethnic conflict between the French-speaking Walloons and the Dutch-speaking Flemings. Nonetheless, because of its tradition of neutrality and central location, Belgium has considerable international prominence. Its capital city, Brussels, is the headquarters of NATO as well as the capital of the expanding European Community.

Surveys and General Works

Arneson, Ben A. *The Democratic Monarchies of Scandinavia.* Greenwood 1975 repr. of 1949 ed. $35.00. ISBN 0-8371-7485-6

Derry, Thomas. *A History of Scandinavia: Norway, Sweden, Denmark, Finland and Iceland.* U. of Minn. Pr. 1979 $17.95. ISBN 0-8166-0936-5

Eyck, F. Gunther. *The Benelux Countries: An Historical Survey.* Van Nos. Reinhold 1959 o.p.

Foote, Peter G., and D. M. Wilson. *The Viking Achievement: The Society and Culture of Early Medieval Scandinavia.* St. Martin 1990 $35.00. ISBN 0-312-03510-1. Addresses a vast selection of significant topics in Viking culture.

Hovde, B. J. *Scandinavian Countries, 1720–1865.* 2 vols. Assoc. Faculty Pr. 1948 o.p. An intriguing look at the origins of the modern social order.

Ingstad, Helge. *Westward to Vinland: The Discovery of Pre-Columbian Norse House-Sites in North America.* St. Martin 1969 o.p. A popular account of the author's archaeological expeditions in Newfoundland; anecdotal and informative.

Kossmann, Ernst H. *The Low Countries, 1780–1940.* OUP 1978 $89.00. ISBN 0-19-882108-8. Compares the histories of the Belgian and Dutch peoples along political lines.

Logan, F. Donald. *The Vikings in History.* Unwin Hyman 1991 $19.95. ISBN 0-04-446040-6. Offers fresh insight into Europe's encounter with this northern people.

Nordstrom, Byron J., ed. *Dictionary of Scandinavian History.* Greenwood 1986 $85.00. ISBN 0-313-22887-6. A succinct, highly readable reference work covering one thousand years of history; includes about 400 signed entries, with bibliographies.

Pirenne, Henri. *Early Democracies in the Low Countries.* Norton 1963 o.p. A lively and learned discussion of how the development of towns impacted political and social life. In this book, first published in 1910, the great Belgian historian examines one of the birthplaces of representative government.

Turville-Petre, E. Gabriel. *The Heroic Age of Scandinavia*. Greenwood 1976 repr. of 1951 ed. $35.00. ISBN 0-8371-8128-3

Vexler, Robert L. *Scandinavia: Denmark, Norway, Sweden, 1319–1974: A Chronology and Fact Book*. Oceana 1977 o.p.

Scandinavia

DENMARK

Anderson, Robert T. *Denmark: Success of a Developing Nation*. Transaction Pubs. 1975 $29.95. ISBN 0-87073-738-4. Points up Denmark's impressive record of improving living standards over a century.

Birch, John H. *Denmark in History*. Gordon Pr. 1976 $59.95. ISBN 0-8490-1707-6. Danelaw, Danegeld, and more.

Desmond, S. *The Soul of Denmark*. Gordon Pr. 1977 $59.95. ISBN 0-8490-2632-6

Johansen, Hans C. *The Danish Economy in the Twentieth Century*. St. Martin 1986 $39.95. ISBN 0-312-00373-0

Jones, W. Glyn. *Denmark: A Modern History*. Routledge 1986 $57.50. ISBN 0-7099-1468-7

Miller, Kenneth E. *Denmark: A Troubled Welfare State*. Westview 1991 $40.00. ISBN 0-8133-0834-8

FINLAND

Alapuro, Risto. *State and Revolution in Finland*. U. CA Pr. 1988 $39.95. ISBN 0-520-05813-5. Story of the struggle for Finnish independence after 1918.

Edelsward, L. M. *Sauna as Symbol: Society and Culture in Finland*. P. Lang Pubs. 1991 $46.00. ISBN 0-8204-1396-2. Bracing look at contemporary Finnish society.

Engman, Max, and David Kirby, eds. *Finland: People, Nation State*. Ind. U. Pr. 1989 $40.00. ISBN 0-253-32067-4. Remarkable story of Finnish democracy.

Deullmann, Stephan. *Epic of the Finnish Nation*. Gordon Pr. 1977 $59.95. ISBN 0-8490-1780-7

Singleton, Fred. *A Short History of Finland*. Cambridge U. Pr. 1990 $44.95. ISBN 0-521-32275-8. An up-to-date explanation of this land.

ICELAND

Byock, Jesse L. *Medieval Iceland: Society, Sagas and Power*. U. CA Pr. 1988 $39.95. ISBN 0-520-05420-2. A fascinating, original attempt to integrate cultural legacy with social reality.

Durrenberger, E. Paul. *The Dynamics of Medieval Iceland: Political Economy and Literature*. U. of Iowa Pr. 1992 $19.95. ISBN 0-87745-388-8

Guthmundsson, Barthi. *The Origin of the Icelanders*. U. of Nebr. Pr. 1967 $18.95. ISBN 0-8032-0063-3

Jones, Gwyn. *The Norse Atlantic Saga: Being the Norse Voyages of Discovery and Settlement to Iceland, Greenland, America*. OUP 1986 $11.95. ISBN 0-19-285160-8

Magnusson, Arthur A. *Sphinx: Iceland and the Icelanders from the Settlement to the Present*. McGill CN o.p.

Tomasson, Richard F. *Iceland: The First New Society*. U. of Minn. Pr. 1980 $19.50. ISBN 0-8166-0913-6

NORWAY

Derry, Thomas. *A Short History of Norway*. Greenwood 1979 $35.00. ISBN 0-313-21467-0. Provides a comprehensive introduction to Norwegian history.

Fiske, Arland O. *The Best of the Norwegian Heritage*. N. Amer. Heritage Pr. 1990 $9.95. ISBN 0-942323-12-2

Gjerset, Knut. *History of the Norwegian People*. AMS Pr. repr. of 1932 ed. $57.50. ISBN 0-404-02818-7. Classic narrative of a people.

Koht, Halvdan, and Sigmund Skard. *Voice of Norway*. AMS Pr. repr. of 1944 ed. $24.00. ISBN 0-404-03769-0

Lindgren, Raymond E. *Norway-Sweden: Union, Disunion and Scandinavian Integration.* Greenwood 1979 repr. of 1959 ed. $38.50. ISBN 0-313-21043-8

Olsen, Johna P., ed. *Organized Democracy: Political Institutions in a Welfare State—The Case of Norway.* OUP 1983 $20.00. ISBN 82-00-06442-5. A provocative analysis of the friction that results when political theory and governmental practices are incongruent.

SWEDEN

Anderson, Ingvar. *A History of Sweden.* Greenwood 1975 $35.00. ISBN 0-8371-8044-9. Point of departure for the study of this country.

Gordon, Raoul, ed. *Sweden: Its People and Industry.* Gordon Pr. 1976 $25.00. ISBN 0-8490-2719-5

Gustavson, Carl G. *The Small Giant: Sweden Enters the Industrial Era.* Ohio U. Pr. 1986 $27.95. ISBN 0-8214-0825-9. The remarkable story of Swedish industrial development.

Kirby, David. *Northern Europe in the Early Modern Period: The Baltic World, 1492–1772.* Longman 1990 $39.95. ISBN 0-582-00410-1. Details the rise of Sweden to domination of the Baltic area.

Milner, Henry. *Sweden: Social Democracy in Practice.* OUP 1990 $45.00. ISBN 0-19-827714-8. Depicts the future as present in a modern industrial society.

Roberts, Michael. *The Swedish Imperial Experience, 1560–1718.* Cambridge U. Pr. 1984 $18.95. ISBN 0-521-27889-9. Study of Sweden as an early superpower by the leading English-language historian of that country.

The Low Countries

BELGIUM

Hutchinson, Walter. *Belgium, the Glorious.* Gordon Pr. 1977 $222.95. ISBN 0-8490-1486-7

Mallinson, Vernon. *Belgium.* Greenwood 1970 o.p.

Pirenne, Henri. *Belgian Democracy: Its Early History.* AMS Pr. repr. of 1915 ed. $20.00. ISBN 0-404-05057-3

Simonet, Henri. *Belgium in the Postwar Period: Partner and Ally.* CSI Studies 1981 $1.95. ISBN 0-89206-033-6

THE NETHERLANDS

Barnouw, Adriaan. *The Making of Modern Holland: A Short History.* Unwin Hyman 1948 o.p.

Boxer, C. R. *The Dutch Seaborne Empire, 1600–1800.* Viking Penguin 1989 $8.95. ISBN 0-14-021600-6. The remarkable story of a small group of people who created a great empire.

Du Plessis, Robert S. *Lille and the Dutch Revolt: Urban Stability in the Era of Revolution, 1500–1582. Studies in Early Modern History.* Cambridge U. Pr. 1991 $64.95. ISBN 0-521-39415-5. A thorough study of sixteenth century Lille, based on primary and other sources.

Geyl, Pieter. *The Revolt of the Netherlands, 1555–1609.* B & N Imports 1980 o.p. One of the many works by the master Dutch historian of this century.

Huizinga, Johan. *Dutch Civilization in the Seventeenth Century and Other Essays.* Continuum 1968 o.p. Eloquent and thoughtful ideas on Dutch history and the practice of history.

Jacob, Margaret C., and Wijnand W. Mijnhardt, eds. *The Dutch Republic in the Eighteenth Century: Decline, Enlightenment, and Revolution.* Cornell Univ. Pr. 1992 $42.95. ISBN 0-8014-2624-3. Sixteen essays analyzing various aspects of Dutch Society prior to the revolution.

Kuietenbrouwer, Maarten. *The Netherlands and the Rise of Modern Imperialism: Colonies and Foreign Policy, 1870–1902.* Berg Pubs. 1991 $75.00. ISBN 0-85496-681-1. Attempts to place Dutch imperialism in the larger context of Western Imperialism.

Lambert, Audrey M. *The Making of the Dutch Landscape: An Historical Geography of the Netherlands.* Acad. Pr. 1985 $100.00. ISBN 0-12-434645-6. Study of the Van Dykes.

Marshall, Sherrin D. *The Dutch Gentry, Fifteen Hundred to Sixteen-Fifty: Family, Faith, and Fortune.* Greenwood 1987 $55.00. ISBN 0-313-25021-9. Argues that Dutch society during this period was structurally closer to modern Europe than those in other countries.

Newton, Gerald. *The Netherlands: An Historical and Cultural Survey, 1795–1977.* Westview 1978 o.p. Treats the important but often-overlooked period of the Decline.

Schama, Simon. *The Embarrassment of Riches: An Interpretation of Dutch Culture in the Golden Age.* Knopf 1987 $39.95. ISBN 0-394-51075-5. A series of essays dealing with the way of life during the Dutch Republic's heyday of the sixteenth century.

Shetter, William Z. *The Pillars of Society: Six Centuries of Civilization in the Netherlands.* Nijhoff 1971 o.p.

Smit, P., and J. W. Smit, eds. *The Netherlands: A Chronology and Fact Book.* Oceana 1973 $8.50. ISBN 0-379-16301-2

Van Deursen, A. Th. *Plain Lives in a Golden Age: Popular Culture, Religion, and Society in Seventeenth-Century Holland.* Cambridge U. Pr. 1991 $74.95. ISBN 0-521-36785-9. A history of how the common people of the Netherlands lived between 1572 and 1648, a period that includes the Golden Age.

Wilson, Charles. *The Dutch Republic and the Civilization of the Seventeenth Century.* McGraw 1968 o.p.

SOUTHERN EUROPE: ITALY, PORTUGAL, SPAIN

Italy was one of the last countries in Europe to establish a unified independent state. A major impediment was the control of central Italy by the Roman Catholic church. Despite this lack of nationhood, Italian achievement was great. The Renaissance originated in the Italian peninsula, the dynamic city-states in northern Italy taught the European world about secularism, popular education, political theory, and humanism, and Italian explorers led the way in overseas expeditions. Political disentity, however, left the Italians vulnerable to invasion, first by the Germans, then the Spaniards and the French. The Renaissance statesman and political philosopher NICCOLÒ MACHIAVELLI (see also Vol. 4) urged Italians to unite to throw off the foreign yoke, but it was not until the nineteenth century that Italian nationalists, led by Giuseppe Mazzini, Count Cavour, and Giuseppe Garibaldi, succeeded in accomplishing that goal.

The new state created in 1870, facing the daunting task of developing a modern infrastructure in a country that had seriously fallen behind much of Europe, decided to finance this work through the seizure of church lands and other properties, which led to a breach between church and state that was not mended until 1929. The new Italian government also sought colonies, principally to relieve the pressure of overpopulation through emigration. However, the colonies established in east Africa and in Libya and Rhodes proved unsuitable for large-scale settlement, so most Italian emigrants went to the United States, Brazil, and Argentina instead.

Italy played an opportunistic role in the first European war of this century, joining the Allies in 1915 and acquiring the South Tyrol, Trieste, and Istria as its rewards. In the immediate postwar period, the country was riven by political and social conflict, which ended when conservative forces rallied behind the Fascist Benito Mussolini, who took power in 1922. Over the next 20 years, the Italian people experienced one-party rule, nationalistic bombast, and involvement in the second European war—this time on the losing side. For two years, the Italian penninsula was a major battleground.

Since 1946 Italy has been a republic with a representative form of government nearly continuously run by the Christian Democratic party. This monopoly of power resulted in widespread public corruption, the scope of which only became apparent in 1992. Despite these problems Italy has experienced rapid reconstruction since the war, and today it has a gross national product that is the fifth largest in the world. The creative abilities of the Italian people are still evident, not only in industry and technology, but also in the arts and literature.

The Iberian peninsula was a core province of the Roman Empire, and like many other provinces was flooded by Germanic tribes as the empire collapsed. Within three centuries Islamic forces from north Africa took control of most of the area. These Moors created a tolerant, prosperous, dynamic society, but throughout the medieval period the struggle for control continued. By 1492 the Christian forces had prevailed and proceeded to expel all Muslims and Jews who refused to convert to Christianity. Two united kingdoms were formed—Portugal and Spain.

The Portuguese had actually established an independent kingdom in 1139, long before the Spaniards, and slowly conquered the western portion of the peninsula. To shore up its minority position in Iberia, Portugal entered into a commercial treaty with England in 1294, and this Anglo-Portuguese alliance presisted for centuries. The Portuguese were also explorers long before the Spaniards. In the 1270s they began moving down the coast of Africa, and it was Vasco DeGama, not CHRISTOPHER COLUMBUS, who in 1498 found the long-sought water route to India. The Portuguese followed up this feat by exploring and colonizing lands in Africa and Asia and establishing themselves in South America in Brazil, which became the largest Latin American nation in area and population.

Spain became a single political entity in 1492, with the union of Isabella of Castile and Ferdinand of Aragon. The Spaniards, led at first by Italian explorers, swept into the new world and within 40 years had conquered the three great developed societies in the Americas. The result was the first great European empire, which brought Spain tremendous wealth and dominance in Europe. The country did not remain the European dominant power for long, however; failure to effectively invest the new wealth, public extravagance, and a series of wars dissipated the Spanish advantage. Spain did manage, under Phillip II in 1580, to annex Portugal, but the Portuguese regained their independence in 1640. In the mid-1600s, both Iberian states declined in status to secondary European powers, although they did successfully resist other European powers' attempts to seize their colonial possessions. The radical French Revolution and French occupation of Spain and Portugal for a few years at the beginning of the nineteenth century produced a reactionary nationalist movement in both countries and started an era of political turbulence that spanned the century. Beginning in the 1820s, both countries lost most of their colonial possessions to independence fighters, though Spain retained Cuba, Puerto Rico, and the Philippines until these islands were seized by the United States in 1898.

Portugal and Spain entered the twentieth century politically and economically backward. Portugal began the process of political modernization in 1910 with the overthrow of the monarchy and the creation of a republic. In the mid-1920s, however, the country was taken over by a military junta and was shackled by conservative, authoritarian regimes until the mid-1970s. In Spain the feudal form of government was toppled in 1931 and a democratic republic was established, but within a few years ideological conflicts brought on a civil war in which the fascist side, with the active support of Nazi Germany and Fascist Italy, the Catholic church, and "nationalists" defeated the republican-socialist side. The conservative dictatorship of Francisco Franco lasted until 1975. Today Portugal and Spain are liberal democratic states with stable governments. Both nations belong to the European Community and are pursuing economic development vigorously after their long decline.

Italy

Abulafia, David. *Italy, Sicily and the Mediterranean, 1100–1400*. Ashgate Pub. Co. 1987 $87.95. ISBN 0-86078-198-4. A broad view of the development of the Renaissance.

Barzini, Luigi. *The Italians*. Atheneum 1977 $9.95. ISBN 0-689-70540-9. Entertaining, insightful examination of his own people by the author of *The Europeans*.

Beales, D. *The Risorgimento and the Unification of Italy*. Longman 1982 o.p. Argues vigorously that the relationship between the nationalist movement and the unification was anything but obvious.

Blackmer, Donald L. *Unity in Diversity: Italian Communism and the Communist World. Studies in Communism, Revisionism and Revolution*. MIT Pr. 1968 $40.00. ISBN 0-262-02030-0. Explores the Italian party's balancing act between its domestic interests and international loyalties.

Blackmer, Donald L., and Sidney Tarrow, eds. *Communism in Italy and France*. Princeton U. Pr. 1975 $75.00. ISBN 0-691-08724-5. Comparative perspectives on the local and international attributes of the Communist party.

Bosworth, Richard. *Italy and the Approach of the First World War*. St. Martin 1984 o.p. Explains how domestic politics translated into Italian foreign policy.

Cannistraro, Philip V., ed. *Historical Dictionary of Fascist Italy*. Greenwood 1982 $85.00. ISBN 0-313-21317-8. The most comprehensive source of information on political and social topics related to the Fascist era in Italy.

Clark, Martin. *Modern Italy, 1871–1982*. Longman 1984 $20.95. ISBN 0-582-48362-X. Discusses the difficult relationship between state and society since unification.

de Grand, Alexander J. *Italian Fascism: Its Origins and Development*. U. of Nebr. Pr. 1982 o.p. Compares Fascist ideology with its political reality, and seeks their reconciliation.

Delzell, Charles F. *Italy in the Twentieth Century*. Amer. Historical Association 1981 o.p. Compare this biography to that of Denis Mack Smith.

Fermi, Laura. *Mussolini*. U. Ch. Pr. 1966 $13.00. Probes the complex and contradictory personality of the dictator who wished to be known as a "monolith."

Frischauer, Paul. *Garibaldi, The Man and the Nation*. London Pub. 1935 o.p. Outstanding biography of the great nationalist leader.

Hughes, Serge. *The Fall and Rise of Modern Italy*. Greenwood 1983 repr. of 1967 ed. $52.50. ISBN 0-313-23737-9. A serious attempt to unify theoretically the precarious politics of this century.

Kogan, Norman. *A Political History of Post-War Italy: From the Old to the New Center Left*. Greenwood 1983 $40.95. ISBN 0-275-91029-6. Charts the major economic and political trends since World War II.

LaPalombra, Joseph. *Democracy, Italian Style*. Yale U. Pr. 1987 $35.00. ISBN 0-300-03913-1. Lively investigation into the labyrinth of Italian political life.

Mack Smith, Denis. *Italy: A Modern History*. U. Mich. Pr. 1969 $29.95. ISBN 0-472-07051-7. Presents the failure of Italian politics in this century as the flipside of its great success a century earlier.

Machiavelli, Niccolo. *Florentine Histories*. Princeton U. Pr. 1969 $29.95. ISBN 0-472-07051-7. History of his home town by the father of *realpolitik*.

Noether, Emiliana P. *Seeds of Italian Nationalism, 1700–1815*. AMS Pr. repr. of 1951 ed. $14.00. ISBN 0-404-51570. Seeks the origins of this distinctly modern movement in traditional Italian culture.

Sarti, Roland. *Fascism and the Industrial Leadership in Italy, 1919–1940: A Study in the Expansion of Private Power under Fascism.* U. CA Pr. 1971 o.p. Discusses the unusual combination of strategy and chance that gave industrialism greater control.

Seton-Watson, Christopher. *Italy from Liberalism to Fascism, 1870–1925.* Methuen 1967 o.p. A standard work on a period of dialectical political change.

Villari, Luigi. *Italian Life.* Gordon Pr. 1976 $59.95. ISBN 0-8490-2087-5. A look inside the realities of Italy by a fine historian.

Wiskemann, Elizabeth. *Italy since 1945.* St. Martin 1972 o.p. Explores the effects of politics on society.

Portugal

Boxer, C. R. *From Lisbon to Goa, 1500–1750: Studies in Portuguese Maritime Enterprise.* Ashgate Pub. Co. 1984 $89.95. ISBN 0-86078-142-9. Well-told tale of a nation of mariners.

Bruneau, Thomas C. *Politics and Nationhood: Post-Revolutionary Portugal.* Greenwood 1984 $31.95. ISBN 0-275-91298-1. Informative study of the country since the ending of the dictatorship.

DeOlivera, Marques Antonia H. *Henry of Portugal.* 2 vols. Col. U. Pr. 1972 o.p. Massive biography of the prince who plotted Portuguese exploration.

Diffie, Bailey W., and George D. Winius. *Foundations of the Portuguese Empire, 1415–1850.* U. of Minn. Pr. 1977 $39.95. ISBN 0-8166-0782-6

Graham, Lawrence S., and Harry M. Makler, eds. *Contemporary Portugal: The Revolution and Its Antecedents.* U. of Tex. Pr. 1979 $27.50. ISBN 0-292-71047. Range of articles on the efforts to create a new Portugal.

Kaplan, Marion. *The Portuguese: The Land and Its People.* Viking Penguin 1992 $27.50. ISBN 0-670-82364-3. Very good introduction to the subject.

Ley, Charles D. *Portuguese Voyages, 1498–1663.* Gordon Pr. 1977 $59.95. ISBN 0-8490-2459-5. Sweeping narrative about the people who found the water route to India and went on from there.

Livermore, Harold U. *A New History of Portugal.* Eyre & Spottiswood 1970 o.p.

Machado, Diamantino P. *The Structure of Portuguese Society: The Failure of Fascism.* Greenwood 1991 $47.95. ISBN 0-275-93784-4. Stimulating look inside Portuguese society by a Portuguese scholar.

Kay H. *Salazar and Modern Portugal.* Scribner 1973 o.p. Good biography of the man who held political control for nearly 50 years.

Spain

Alba, Victor. *Transition in Spain from Franco to Democracy.* Trans. by Barbara Lotito. Transaction Pubs. 1978 o.p. An animated account of Spain's peculiar political history.

Beevor, Antony. *The Spanish Civil War.* Bedrick Bks. 1983 o.p.

Carr, Raymond. *Spain, 1808–1975.* OUP 1982 $35.00. ISBN 0-19-822128-2. The standard history of the period in English.

Carr, Raymond, and Juan P. Fusi. *Spain: Dictatorship to Democracy.* Unwin Hyman 1981 o.p.

Castro, Americo. *The Spaniards: An Introduction to Their History.* Trans. by Willard F. King and Selma Margaretten. U. CA Pr. 1985 $55.00. ISBN 0-520-05469-5. A challenging, theoretical approach to topics in social history.

Chapman, Charles E. *A History of Spain Founded on the Historia de España y de la Civilización Española of Rafael Altamira.* Darby Pub. repr. of 1938 ed. o.p. An impressively comprehensive account of Spanish history.

Collins, Roger. *The Basques.* Blackwell Pubs. 1987 $39.95. ISBN 0-6311-3478-6. Good account of a pre-Indo-European people and their struggle for self-government.

_____. *Early Medieval Spain: Unity in Diversity, 400–1000.* St. Martin 1983 $35.00. ISBN 0-312-22464-8. A vivid description of the formative years of the Iberian Peninsula.

Elliott, J. H. *Imperial Spain, 1469–1716*. Viking Penguin 1990 $9.95. ISBN 0-14-013517-0. A good general survey of social and economic developments in Spain at the height of its power.

Harrison, Joseph. *An Economic History of Modern Spain*. Holmes & Meier 1978 o.p. Examines an underdeveloped Spain in the context of its more successful capitalist neighbors.

Harvey, L. P. *Islamic Spain, 1250 to 1500*. U. Ch. Pr. 1990 $47.00. ISBN 0-226-31960-1. Revealing story of the final period of Moorish control of Iberia.

Herr, Richard. *An Historical Essay on Modern Spain*. U. CA Pr. 1974 $13.95. ISBN 0-520-02534-2. A subtle analysis of the complex processes of political change under Franco.

———. *Spain. Modern Nations in Historical Perspective Ser*. P-H 1971 o.p.

Jackson, Gabriel. *Spanish Republic and the Civil War, 1931–1939*. Princeton U. Pr. 1965 $19.95. ISBN 0-691-00757-8. A well-balanced study.

Kamen, Henry. *Concise History of Spain*. Scribner 1973 o.p.

———. *Inquisition and Society in Spain in the Sixteenth and Seventeenth Centuries*. Ind. U. Pr. 1985 $35.00. ISBN 0-253-22775-5. Excellent examination of the infamous religious organization and its consequences.

Lynch, John. *Bourbon Spain: Seventeen Hundred to Eighteen Hundred Eight*. Blackwell Pubs. 1989 $39.95. ISBN 0-631-14576-1. An expert looks at the last days of the *ancien régime* in Spain.

———. *Spain under the Habsburgs*. 2 vols. NYU Pr. 1984 o.p.

Mitchell, David. *The Spanish Civil War*. Watts 1983 o.p.

O'Callaghan, Joseph F. *A History of Medieval Spain*. Cornell Univ. Pr. 1983 o.p. The definitive narrative history of medieval Spain and Portugal.

Payne, Stanley G. *Falange: A History of Spanish Fascism*. Stanford U. Pr. 1961 o.p. The best study of Spain's Fascist party.

———. *A History of Spain and Portugal*. 2 vols. U. of Wis. Pr. 1973 o.p.

———. *Spanish Revolution. Revolutions in the Modern World Ser*. Norton 1969 o.p.

Thomas, Hugh. *Spanish Civil War*. HarpC 1977 o.p. Provocative and well-informed study.

Vilar, Pierre. *Spain: A Brief History*. Pergamon 1977 $7.75. ISBN 0-08-021461-4. Good short treatment of a great nation.

Wishaw, B., and E. M. Wishaw. *Arabic Spain*. Gordon Pr. 1974 $59.95. ISBN 0-87968-652-9

EASTERN EUROPE

The first important factor in the history of eastern Europe is the dominating presence of the Slavs, who arrived in the region around 500 B.C. and today are the largest group there. The second is that the region lies between two great, powerful nations—Germany and Russia.

The Slavic people who penetrated the farthest west were the Czechs. They came under German domination in the seventeenth century, but, by the nineteenth century, the Czech territory of Bohemia was part of Austria. The disintegration of the Austrian-Hungarian empire after World War I gave the Czechs the opportunity to form an independent state with the Slovaks, and this was the only eastern European nation to maintain a system of representative government in the interwar period. With the acquiescence of France and Britain, however, Nazi Germany destroyed the Czechoslovak state in 1938–39, and Bohemia once again came under German control, while Slovakia was allowed nominal independence.

The land that is now Hungary was settled in the ninth century by the Magyars, who came from beyond the Urals and spoke a Finno-Ugric language. The kingdom the Magyars established lasted until 1526, when it was overwhelmed by the Turks. Subsequently, Hungary came under the control of Austria, but vigorous Hungarian nationalism persuaded the Austrians to enter into a unique arrangement in 1867—the joint monarchy of Austria-Hungary. As a result, Hungary participated in the 1914–18 war on the side of the Central states, whose defeat resulted in Hungary's loss of the large territory of Transylvania to Rumania and the formation of a democratic republic. As elsewhere in eastern Europe, however, an authoritarian regime soon emerged.

In the early medieval period, Poland was the powerful state in eastern Europe. The unified Polish kingdom that emerged in the tenth century at various times incorporated modern-day Lithuania, Belarus, and Ukraine. The rise of Prussia and Russia, coupled with political devisiveness and a lack of natural barriers to invasion, resulted in the extinction of the Polish state. The Congress of Vienna handed over most of Poland to Russia, and Polish efforts to regain independence in the 1830s and 1860s were suppressed by Russian force.

A new Polish state emerged in the wake of the Russian Revolution and the defeat of Germany in 1918. This democratic republic failed to stimulate significant social and economic development and was replaced by a military dictatorship in 1926. The country remained in this arrested political state until the joint German and Russian conquest in 1939.

The area of eastern Europe that is now Rumania was once part of the Roman Empire, and the Rumanians are the only people in eastern Europe who have a Latin-based language. Rumania became an independent kingdom very late in history—in 1878. As a participant in World War I on the winning side, Rumania gained Transylvania from Hungary in the postwar division of spoils. After prolonged political turbulence, a military dictatorship was established in 1940.

All of the peoples of eastern Europe were drawn into World War II—the Hungarians, Slovakians, and Rumanians as allies of Germany, and the Czechs and Poles as German subjects. The Russian conquest and occupation of the area in 1944–45 resulted in the rise to power of Communist parties in all of these countries, which proceeded to nationalize industry and, in most countries, collectivize agriculture. The resentment of Communist hegemony grew into resistance in the 1950s. Backed by the Catholic church and U.S. financial assistance, the Poles managed to edge away from total Communist control beginning in 1956. In Hungary that same year there was a revolution against Communist rule. A liberal, non-Communist government was formed, but a few weeks later the Soviet army invaded the country and brutally suppressed the revolution. Czechoslovakia made its first attempt to escape from monolithic communism and Russian control in 1968, when Czech leaders proposed to establish "socialism with a human face," meaning that political and economic diversity would be encouraged. Again, the Soviet army crushed the liberal forces. In Rumania there was a drift away from Soviet domination beginning in the mid-1960s, and this was sufficient to gain Rumania substantial U.S. financial aid. The country remained strongly Communist, however.

After dramatic changes were initiated in the Soviet Union by the reformist government of Mikhail Gorbachev in the mid-1980s, the disintegration of Communist governments in eastern Europe was inevitable. In Poland the Catholic church, headed by a Polish pope, and Solidarity, an independent trade union, were the forces that brought about the collapse of the Communist regime and the creation of a system of representative government. The other countries of the region soon followed suit, Rumania most dramatically and violently, and Czechoslovakia most peacefully. The peoples of eastern Europe are now in the process of exploring the parameters of capitalism and popular government.

Surveys and General Works

Jones, Christopher. *Soviet Influence in Eastern Europe: Political Autonomy and the Warsaw Pact*. Greenwood 1981 $42.95. ISBN 0-275-90657-4

Kann, Robert A., and Zdenek V. David. *The Peoples of the Eastern Hapsburg Lands, 1526–1918*. U. of Wash. Pr. 1984 $35.00. ISBN 0-295-96095-7. A systematic survey of regional, rather than national, historical themes.

Kaser, M. C., and E. A. Radice. *The Economic History of Eastern Europe, 1919–1975*. 3 vols. OUP 1984 Vol. 1 $79.00. ISBN 0-19-828446-6. Vol. 2 $98.00. ISBN 0-19-828445-4. Vol. 3 $69.00. ISBN 0-19-828446-2. Presents extensive, systematic documentation of the economic transformations sweeping this region since World War I.

Okey, Joseph. *Eastern Europe, 1740–1985: Feudalism to Communism*. U. of Minn. Pr. 1986 $15.95. ISBN 0-8166-1561-6

Rothchild, Joseph. *East Central Europe between the Two World Wars*. U. of Wash. Pr. 1990 $17.50. ISBN 0-295-95357-8. Offers a valuable comparative perspective on the political climate in the interwar years.

———. *Return to Diversity: A Political History of East Central Europe since World War II*. OUP 1990 $27.95. ISBN 0-19-504574-2. An engaging trek through the major political developments up to very recent times.

Staar, Richard F. *Communist Regimes in Eastern Europe*. Hoover Inst. Pr. 1988 $11.95. ISBN 0-8179-8812-2. An up-to-date introduction to primary source materials.

Czechoslovakia: The Czech Republic and Slovakia

Havel, Vaclav. *Disturbing the Peace*. Random 1991 $11.00. ISBN 0-679-73402-3. Narrative of the campaign to overthrow communism by the person who became head of state after it was accomplished.

Korbel, Josef. *Twentieth Century Czechoslovakia: The Meaning of Its History*. Col. U. Pr. 1977 $43.58. ISBN 0-231-03724-4. Good general account of the creation of an independent state.

Krejci, Jaroslav. *Czechoslovakia at the Crossroads of European History*. St. Martin 1990 $29.50. ISBN 1-85043-194-9. Moving account of the collapse of communism in Czechoslovakia.

Krystutek, Zdenek. *The Soviet Regime in Czechoslovakia*. East Eur. Quarterly 1981 $50.50. ISBN 0-914710-75-3. Story of the ultimate futility of imposing a regime on a hostile people.

Valenta, Jiri. *Soviet Intervention in Czechoslovakia, 1968: Anatomy of a Decision*. Johns Hopkins 1991 $35.00. ISBN 0-8018-4297-2. History of the brutal effort of the Soviets to maintain control of eastern Europe.

Wolchik, Sharon L. *Czechoslovakia in Transition: Politics, Economy and Society*. St. Martin 1992 $17.50. ISBN 0-86187-408-0. Survey of the short history of post-Communist Czechoslovakia.

Zinner, Paul E. *Communist Strategy and Tactics in Czechoslovakia, 1918–1948*. Greenwood 1976 $38.50. ISBN 0-8371-8550-5. History of a minor party that rode to power on the back of the Russian army.

Hungary

Balogh, Sandor, and Jakob Sandor. *The History of Hungary after the Second World War, 1944–1948*. Intl. Spec. Bk. 1986 $14.95. ISBN 963-13-2434-6. Account of the transition to communism in the aftermath of Soviet occupation.

Barany, George. *Stephen Szechenyi and the Awakening of Hungarian Nationalism, 1791–1841*. Princeton U. Pr. 1968 o.p.

Hanak, Peter, ed. *One Thousand Years: A Concise History of Hungary.* Intl. Spec. Bk. 1991 $19.95. ISBN 963-13-3367-1. The best book for a general overview.

Hoensh, Jorg. *A History of Modern Hungary, 1867–1986.* Longman 1988 $34.95. ISBN 0-582-01484-0. A conscientiously even-handed work focusing on social and economic history.

Michener, James. *Bridge at Andau.* Random 1957 $19.95. ISBN 0-394-41778-X. The story of the 1956 revolt against communism, told by a master storyteller.

Richet, Xavier. *The Hungarian Model.* Cambridge U. Pr. 1989 $49.95. ISBN 0-521-34314-3. Illuminating picture of how the Hungarians moved away from the Soviet economic model.

Poland

Bromke, Adam. *The Meaning and Uses of Polish History.* East Eur. Quarterly 1987 $34.50. ISBN 0-88033-109-7

Davies, Norman. *God's Playground: A History of Poland.* 2 vols. Col. U. Pr. $45.00. ISBN 0-231-04327-9

Kaminski, Bartlomie. *The Collapse of State Socialism: The Case of Poland.* Princeton U. Pr. 1991 $39.50. ISBN 0-691-07880-7. An in-depth study of how politics and economics interrelate, in this case to destroy each other.

Karski, Jan. *The Great Powers and Poland, 1919 to 1945.* U. Pr. of Amer. 1985 $75.25. ISBN 0-8191-4398-7. An exhaustive investigation of how the Great Powers dominated Polish politics and eventually determined Poland's fate.

Lopinski, Maciej, and others. *Konspiva: Solidarity Underground.* U. CA Pr. 1990 $24.95. ISBN 0-520-06131-4. Edited transcripts of taped interviews with seven prominent solidarity activists, detailing the attempt to set up underground networks after the organization was banned in 1981.

Ludwikowski, Rett. *Continuity and Change in Poland.* Cath. U. Pr. 1992 $39.95. ISBN 0-8132-0743-6. Detailed history of Polish conservatism.

Michnik, Adam. *The Church and the Left.* U. Ch. Pr. 1992 $24.95. ISBN 0-226-52424-8. Michnik justifies the alliance of the Catholic church and Polish dissidents in their opposition to Communist rule.

Pogonowski, Iwo. *Poland: An Historical Atlas.* Hippocrene Bks. 1989 $27.50. ISBN 0-87052-742-8. Pictorial perspectives on political events of significance to the Polish national character.

Walesa, Lech. *The Struggle and the Triumph: An Autobiography.* Arcade Pub. Inc. 1992 $24.95. ISBN 1-55970-149-8. His own story—from shipyard electrician to president of free Poland.

Romania

Bechr, Edward. *Kiss the Hand You Cannot Bite: The Rise and Fall of the Ceausecus.* Random 1991 $22.50. ISBN 0-679-40128-8. Fascinating story of megalomania.

Castellan, Georges. *A History of the Romanians.* East Eur. Quarterly $46.50. ISBN 0-88033-154-2. Good general survey by a leading historian of eastern Europe.

Georgescu, Vlad. *The Romanians: A History.* Ohio St. U. Pr. 1991 $49.50. ISBN 0-8142-0511-9. Broad-based survey of a people who speak a romance language in a sea of Slavic tongues.

THE BALKANS AND GREECE

After the fall of the western Roman Empire, the eastern branch, which had been separated since A.D. 395, lasted for another thousand years. The Byzantine Empire, named after the Greek city of Byzantium on the Bosporus, was Greek in language and culture. This powerful entity had to contend not only with incursions by western European Crusaders but, also, more importantly, with Slavs pressing down from the Balkans, Arabs surging across the Mediterranean, and Turks threatening from the past. Before it was finally overwhelmed by Turkish forces in 1453, the Byzantine state managed to spread Christianity and Byzantine political traditions to the Balkans and much of eastern Europe, including Russia.

The Turks went on to conquer Greece and the Balkans and twice reached the walls of Vienna. Turkish domination continued until the nineteenth century. With western European assistance, Greece attained independence in 1820, and after a series of wars Turkish control was effectively ended in the Balkans in the late nineteenth century. An independent Serbia emerged in 1882; Bulgaria achieved a wide measure of autonomy in 1878 and full independence in 1908.

Warfare, largely directed against the remaining Turkish territory but also between the Balkan states, erupted in the area in 1910. At the end of the conflict Turkey held only a small area of European territory, while Greece gained Crete, Thessaly, and much of Macedonia, and the independent state of Albania was formed. Continuing nationalist rivalries in the region ignited the first general European war in 1914, which led to further political realignment in the region. Combining the Roman Catholic Croats and Slovenes, the eastern Orthodox Serbs and the Muslims of Bosnia, a kingdom of Yugoslavia was formed in 1918. Greece attempted to seize territory in Asia Minor from Turkey, but was repulsed. In the interwar period governments in the region alternated between representative institutions and military dictatorships, with the latter the norm by the eve of World War II.

During that war Germany occupied almost the entire area, though the occupation was resisted by popular forces, generally led by Communists. Russian occupation of Bulgaria and Yugoslavia led to the establishment of Communist governments in both countries, as well as in Albania. Greece experienced civil war between Communist and non-Communist forces in the immediate postwar period, which galvanized the United States to take a strong role in this region, providing substantial financial military assistance to the non-Communist Greek forces. It also provided vital assistance to Yugoslavia when it broke out of the Soviet orbit in 1948. In the 1960s Greece became embroiled in a violent dispute with Turkey concerning the status of the island of Cyprus, two-thirds of whose population is Greek. The dispute continues, though far less violently.

The collapse of communism in the late 1980s led to the creation of some form of representative government in most of the Balkan states. It also resulted in the disintegration of Yugoslavia and terrible ethnic violence among the Serbs, Croats, and Muslims.

The Balkans

SURVEYS AND GENERAL WORKS

Augustinos, Gerasimos, ed. *Diverse Paths to Modernity in Southeastern Europe: Essays in National Development*. Greenwood 1990 $42.95. ISBN 0-313-26670-0. Valuable collection of articles on recent developments in the Balkans.

Castellan, Georges. *History of the Balkans from Mohammed the Conquerer to Stalin*. Col. U. Pr. 1991 $56.00. ISBN 0-88033-222-0. Comprehensive history of a diverse region with great scope.

Jelavich, C., and B. Jelavich. *The Establishment of the Balkan National States, 1804–1920*. U. of Wash. Pr. 1977 o.p. Focuses on the development of disruptive Balkan nationalism in the wake of Turkish retreat.

Poulton, Hugh. *The Balkans: Minorities and States in Conflict*. Paul & Co. Pubs. 1991 $49.95. ISBN 1-873194-25-0. Studies the pressures faced by various ethnic minorities in Greece, Bulgaria, Albania and Yugoslavia, pressures often emanating from the governments of those nations.

Ristelhueber, Rene. *History of the Balkan Peoples*. Irvington 1978 repr. of 1971 ed. $47.50. ISBN 0-8290-0176-X

Sforza, Carlo. *Fifty Years of War and Diplomacy in the Balkans*. AMS Pr. repr. of 1940 ed. $16.50. ISBN 0-404-05757-8. Historical survey concentrating on the life of Serbian statesman Nicola Pashich.

Stoianovich, Traian. *Between East and West, The Balkan and Mediterrean Worlds: Economies and Societies: Traders, Towns and Households*. Caratzas 1991 $85.00. ISBN 0-89241-502-9

Sugar, Peter F. *Southeastern Europe under Ottoman Rule, 1354–1804*. U. of Wash. Pr. 1977 $17.50. ISBN 0-295-96033-7. Revealing examination of the background to the modern Balkans.

ALBANIA

Biberaj, Elez. *Albania: A Socialist Maverick*. Westview 1990 $43.00. ISBN 0-8133-0513-6. Examines Albania's maverick behavior within the international Communist system and its rigid domestic policy.

Pano, Nicholas. *Albania*. Col. U. Pr. 1989 $47.50. ISBN 0-86187-392-0. A general study praising the post-World War II government for maintaining Albania's boundaries and independence, but points out that efforts to reform have been less successful.

BULGARIA

Brown, James F. *Bulgaria under Communist Rule*. Greenwood o.p. Indispensible to understanding Bulgaria's current situation, this well-researched volume examines the problems faced by Bulgaria's Communist leadership.

Crampton, R. J. *Bulgaria, 1878–1918: A History*. East Eur. Quarterly $60.00. ISBN 0-88033-029-5. Narrative history tracing the economic and social development of Bulgaria from its independence to the end of World War II.

————. *A Short History of Modern Bulgaria*. Cambridge U. Pr. 1987 $44.95. ISBN 0-521-25340-3

Kolar, Walter W. *Culture and History of the Bulgarian People: Their Bulgarian and American Parallels*. Tamburitza 1981 $10.00. ISBN 0-936922-04-4. A compilation of papers, including those of several noted scholars, presented at a 1980 symposium on Bulgarian folk arts.

McIntyre, Robert J. *Bulgaria: Politics, Economics and Society*. St. Martin 1987 $49.00. ISBN 0-86187-398-X. An introduction to the Bulgarian political system and Bulgarian society that notes the effects of limited reforms.

YUGOSLAVIA, SERBIA

Cohen, Lenard J. *Broken Bonds: The Rise and Fall of Yugoslavia*. Westview 1993 $24.50. ISBN 0-8133-8030-8. Excellent short account of recent history.

Djilas, Aleska. *The Contested Country: Yugoslav Unity and Communist Revolution, 1919–1953*. HUP 1991 $34.95. ISBN 0-674-16698-1. Examines the origins of the Communist Yugoslav federation, and the ultimately unstable ideological foundations upon which it was built.

Djilas, Milovan, *Memoir of a Revolution*. HarBraceJ 1973 o.p. An idealistic Communist's encounter with party discipline and state control.

Gow, James. *Legitimacy and the Military: The Yugoslav Crisis*. St. Martin 1992 $45.00. ISBN 0-312-07209-0. Aims to put the current civil war in Yugoslavia into context by examining the important role of the Yugoslav People's Army in the breakup.

Laffan, R. G. *The Serbs: Guardians of the Gate*. Dorset Pr. 1990 $17.95. ISBN 0-88029-413-2. The bitter history of the Serbian people.

Pavlowitch, Steven K. *The Improbable Survivor: Yugoslavia and Its Problems, 1918–1988*. Ohio U. Pr. 1990 $14.95. ISBN 0-8142-0505-4

Phillips, John. *Yugoslav Story, 1843–1983*. St. Mut. 1987 $113.00. ISBN 0-317-54519-1. Provides a broad picture of the development of the multi-ethnic state.

Schiffman, Ruth. *Josip Broz Tito*. Chelsea Hse. 1987 $17.95. ISBN 0-87754-443-3. Meticulously detailed biography of the Yugoslav leader from his leadership of the partisan army to his achievements as head of state.

Singleton, Fred. *A Short History of the Yugoslav Peoples*. Cambridge U. Pr. 1985 $18.95. ISBN 0-521-17485-0. An excellent introduction by an expert.

Greece

Augustinos, Gerasimos. *The Greeks of Asia Minor: Confession, Community and Ethnicity in the Nineteenth Century*. Kent St. U. Pr. 1992 $39.00. ISBN 0-87338-459-8

Clogg, Richard. *A Concise History of Greece*. Cambridge U. Pr. 1992 $44.95. ISBN 0-521-37228-3

Robinson, Cyril. *A History of Greece*. Routledge 1957 $16.50. ISBN 0-423-71290-X. Standard work about a people who have the longest history in one place.

Theodoracopulos, Taki. *The Greek Upheaval: Kings, Demagogues and Bayonets*. Caratzas 1978 $20.00. ISBN 0-89241-080-9. A study of Greece in the modern era since 1967.

Woodhouse, C. M. *Modern Greece: A Short History*. Faber & Faber 1992 $12.95. ISBN 0-571-16122-7. Succinct and readable work tracing Greek history from A.D. 1320 to the end of the military junta in 1974.

———. *Struggle for Greece, 1941–1949*. Beekman Pubs. 1979 $34.95. ISBN 0-8464-0042-1. A largely military analysis that studies this belligerent period by breaking it into three phases.

RUSSIA, THE EURASIAN REPUBLICS, AND THE BALTIC STATES

Russian historical studies have a long and rich history despite concerted efforts by both czarist and Communist governments to inhibit or manipulate scholarship. Widespread foreign interest in Russia is primarily a more recent development.

Russian historical works have their origins in the Byzantine-influenced efforts of the Kievan era. The histories of the day follow Greek precedent in both style and structure in an effort to provide objective analysis and offer instruction for the future. More commonplace were the chronicles of the time, the most acclaimed of which are *The Chronicle of Nestor* in the eleventh century and the *Chronicle of Novgorod* (1016–1471). A rich selection of hagiography is also evident in early Kievan times.

The Tatar yoke, Muscovite regime's relative cultural isolation from the West and constant political instability retarded Russian historical efforts. The great debate in the later Romanov era—whether Russia should accelerate its feeble modernization program or follow its own Slavonic tradition—involved many historical issues. Westerners and Slavophiles alike mustered historical data in their ideological warfare and in the process awakened all Russian scholarship. Nikolai Danilevsky's *Russia and Europe* was a monumental effort of the day that influenced both OSWALD SPENGLER and ARNOLD TOYNBEE (see also Vol. 4). Probably the greatest of the nineteenth century historians, Vasili Klyuchevsky, emphasized economic and bureaucratic institutions rather than individual rulers.

The October Revolution had a profound influence on the study of Russian history. Interest in Russian history in all its aspects rose in the West, but a militant Marxist dogma was the order of the day in Russia. Mikhail Pokrovsky headed the ranks of early Soviet historians who emphasized class struggle, the abuse of the masses by the czarist state, and a diminished role of the nationalities. By the mid-1930s, Pokrovsky was in disrepute with the Kremlin. Russia's unique national traditions became the vogue, and JOSEPH STALIN's agenda necessitated historical sanction.

Post-Stalin Soviet historical studies were cautiously granted more latitude. With *glasnost* came a loosening of restraints, permitting widespread interaction with western historians for the first time. If democracy succeeds, a torrent of new assessments of the Soviet era can be expected.

General Works

Abraham, Richard, and Lionel Kochan. *The Making of Modern Russia*. St. Martin 1984 $29.95. ISBN 0-312-50-703-8. An updated version of Kochan's 1962 work; takes the narrative beyond 1945 and contains increasing emphasis on the twentieth century.

Billington, J. H. *The Icon and the Axe: An Interpretive History of Russian Culture*. Random 1970 $20.00. ISBN 0-394-70846. Impressionistic, probing, provocative view of Russian cultural history with considerable emphasis on religious and intellectual activity.

De Mowbray, Stephen. *Key Facts in Soviet History*. G. K. Hall 1990 $40.00. ISBN 0-8161-1820-5. Covers the years between 1917 and June 1941; for nonspecialists.

Fitzpatrick, Sheila, and Lynne Viola, eds. *A Researcher's Guide to Sources on Soviet Social History in the 1930's*. M. E. Sharpe 1989 $55.00. ISBN 0-87332-497-8. Guide to information and sources on Soviet history in the 1930s by an author who has written several books on the Soviet Union in the 1920s and 1930s.

Hilden, John and Patrick Salmon. *The Baltic Nations and Europe: Estonia, Latvia & Lithuania in the 20th Century*. Longman 1991 $39.95. ISBN 0-582-08246-3. A concise history of the Baltic states in the modern period from the end of World war I to 1990.

Jackson, George, ed. *Dictionary of the Russian Revolution*. Greenwood 1989 $75.00. ISBN 0-313-21131-0. Contains 300 signed articles, covering 1898–1922.

Jelavich, Barbara. *Russian's Balkan Entanglements, 1806–1914*. Cambridge U. Pr. 1991 $43.00. ISBN 0-521-40126-7. Examines the reason for Russian involvement in the Balkan peninsula and the five wars arising from Russian entanglement.

Kline, George L. *Religious and Anti-Religious Thought in Russia*. Bks. Demand 1968 $47.30. ISBN 0-317-09813-6. With religious freedom prevailing, this work merits additional attention.

Kliuchevskii, Vasilii O. *A History of Russia*. 5 vols. Russell Sage 1911–1931. o.p. A solid overview by one of the most popular Russian university professors of all time.

Mclean, Fitzroy. *All the Russians*. Smithmark 1990 $29.98. ISBN 0-8317-0278-8. Survey of Russian history from the first Slavic settlements to Gorbachev's presidency. Offers a useful cultural overview of 22 major nationalities.

Miller, Donald E., and Lorna Touryar Miller. *Survivors: An Oral History of the Armenian Genocide*. U. CA Pr. 1993 $25.00. ISBN 0-520-07984-1. Gripping interviews with survivors of Turkish genocide policies in Armenia. A gruesome account of the mass murders of a million Armenians.

Naarden, Bruno. *Socialist Europe and Revolutionary Russia*. Cambridge U. Pr. 1992 $64.95. ISBN 0521-41473-3. Analyzes images of late tsarist and early Marxist Russia by a European socialist.

Nichols, Robert L., and Theofanis G. Stavrou, eds. *Russian Orthodoxy under the Old Regieme*. U. of Minn. Pr. 1978 $8.95. ISBN 0-8166-0847-4. Sweeping study of Greek orthodoxy in tsarist Russia.

Palmer, Francis H. *Russian Life in Town and Country*. Ayer 1970 repr. of 1901 ed. $17.00. ISBN 0-405-03056-8. Useful social survey of daily life c.1900.

Pares, Bernard. *A History of Russia*. Knopf 1953 $42.50. ISBN 0-404-15122-1. Comprehensive work that covers the Russian epoch from the earliest times to 1947, emphasizing social and economic conditions.

Rauch, George Von. *The Baltic States: Estonia, Latvia, Lithuania—The Years of Independence 1917–1940*. U. CA Pr. 1974 $24.75. ISBN 0-520-026004. A relatively objective history that views the three states as part of a single Baltic whole. Also looks at the social, economic, and diplomatic concerns of each country.

Riasanousky, Nicholas V. *A History of Russia*. OUP 1984 $39.95. ISBN 0-19-5033655. Comprehensive history of Russia with a heavy emphasis on its geographic and cultural foundations.

Salisbury, Harrison E. *Russia*. Atheneum 1965 $3.25. ISBN 0-689-10239-9. Very succinct outline of Russia's rise from a primitive nation to superpower status. Analyzes key historical figures, ethnic makeup, and geographic factors shaping Russia's history.

Vernadsky, George. *Kievan Russia*. Yale U. Pr. 1953 $16.00. ISBN 0-300-01647-6. Definitive work on the formative era of Russian history by one of the best-received scholars in Russian history.

Wieczynski, Joseph L. *The Russian Frontier: The Impact of Borderlands upon the Course of Early Russian History*. Bks. Demand 1992 $32.40. ISBN 0-8357-3143-X. Serves as excellent background to the nationalities problem. Discusses the role of the everchanging frontiers.

The Tsarist Era

Alexander, John T. *Emperor of the Cossacks: Pugachev and the Frontier Jacquerie, 1773–1775*. Coronado Pr. 1975 o.p. A chronologically organized military history of Pugachev's rebellion.

Barratt, Glynn R. *Voices in Exile: The Decembrist Memoirs*. McGill CN 1974 o.p. A sampling of memoirs written by some of the key personalities behind the Decembrist movement.

Golden, Frank. *Russian Expansion to the Pacific 1641–1850*. Peter Smith 1975 o.p.

Hare, Richard. *Portraits of Russian Personalities Between Reform and Revolution*. Greenwood 1975 $49.75. ISBN 0-8371-8063-5. Personality sketches of pivotal political and cultural figures during a crucial era.

Kliuchevskii, Vasilii O. *The Rise of the Romanovs*. St. Martin 1970 o.p. Monumental work imperative for any library, by one of the titans of Russian scholarship.

Presniakov, K. U. *Tsardom of Muscovy*. Academic Intl. 1991 $10.00. ISBN 0-87569-090-4. Survey of the Muscovite era from Ivan to Peter.

Robinson, Geroid T. *Rural Russia under the Old Regime: A History of the Landlord Peasant World and a Prologue to the Peasant Rebellion of 1917*. U. CA Pr. 1967 $12.95. ISBN 0-520-01075-2. A classic survey of the period from the emancipation of the serfs to the revolution.

Seton-Watson, Hugh. *Russian empire 1801–1917*. OUP 1967 $12.50. ISBN 0-19-822103. Standard work on the late Russian empire. Focuses on political and diplomatic events.

Solzhenitsyn, Aleksandr I. *August 1914*. Viking Penguin 1992 $15.00. ISBN 0-14-007122-9. Masterful account of the Russian debacle on the Eastern front.

Summer, Benedict H. *Peter the Great and the Emergence of Russia*. Macmillan 1951 o.p. Reliable account of Russia's dynamic reformer.

Thompson, Gladys S. *Catherine the Great and the Expansion of Russia*. Ed. by A. L. Rowse. Greenwood 1985 o.p. The best-known work on an illustrious tsarina.

The Soviet Era

Andrew, Christopher, and Oleg Gordievsky. *KGB*. HarpC 1992 $12.80. ISBN 0-06-092109-9. A peek into the Kremlin's elite and elusive police state by a former KGB agent and a historian.

Arrich, Paul, ed. *The Anarchists in the Russian Revolution. Documents of Revolution Ser.* Greenwood 1980 $35.00. ISBN 0-313-22571-0. A compilation of primary source documents, several of them appearing for the first time in English, covering many aspects of Russian anarchy.

Bialer, Seweryn, ed. *Stalin and His Generals: Soviet Military Memoirs of World War II.* Westview 1984 o.p. Classic study of the Soviet Union in World War II that presents a composite picture of Stalin and the Red Army inner circle.

Bradley, John. *Allied Intervention in Russia, 1917–1920.* U. Pr. of Amer. 1984 o.p. Interesting account of America's diplomatic and military debacle.

Breslaver, George W. *Five Images of the Soviet Future. Policy Papers in International Affairs Ser.* U. CA Pr. 1978 $5.50. ISBN 0-87725-504-0. An interesting study despite the fact that current events have made predictions of the USSR's future rather useless.

Carr, William H. *The Russian Revolution from Lenin to Stalin, 1917–1929.* Macmillan 1979 $16.95. ISBN 0-02-905140-1. A single-volume permutation of Carr's monumental fourteen-volume *A History of Soviet Russia,* condensed and revamped for popular consumption.

Chamberlain, William Henry. *The Russian Revolution.* 2 vols. G&D o.p. A time-honored standard work.

Conquest, Robert. *The Great Terror—Stalin's Purge of the Thirties.* Macmillan 1973 $13.95. ISBN 0-19-507132-8. Highly readable account of Stalin's bloodchilling effort to eradicate all potential dissent.

Deutscher, Issac. *The Prophet Armed.* OUP 1980 o.p. The standard work on Trotsky's early career, which is followed by *The Prophet Unarmed* (1921–29) and *The Prophet Outcast* (1929–40).

Ferror, Marc. *October 1917.* Routledge 1980 o.p. Studies the various groups involved in the revolution and their role in the formation of the Soviet state.

Fischer, Louis. *The Road to Yalta: 1944–45.* HarpC 1972 o.p. Definitive story of the Yalta Conference, with an emphasis on the key players of the time: Churchill and Stalin.

Graves, William S. *America's Siberian Adventure 1918–20.* Ayer 1971 $19.00. ISBN 0-405-03083-5. A study of U.S. intervention in the Russian Civil War, first published in 1931.

Haimson, Leopold. *The Making of Three Russian Revolutionaries: Voices from the Menshivik Past.* Cambridge U. Pr. 1988 $49.50. ISBN 0-521-26325-5. Interviews with the Menshivik revolutionaries Lydia Dan, Boris Nicolaevsky, and George Denike, with an introduction on Menshevism and the evolution of the Russian intelligentsia.

Homberger, Eric. *John Reed and the Russian Revolution: Uncollected Articles Letters and Speeches on Russia.* St. Martin 1992 $49.95. ISBN 0-312-06891-3. Fascinating collection of materials from America's leading player in the drama of the October Revolution.

Hughes, Gwyneth, and Simon Welfare. *Red Empire—The Forbidden History of the USSR.* St. Martin 1991 $29.95. ISBN 0-312-65295-2. Spinoff from a British television series, with hundreds of photographs and a fast-paced text. Not for the Russian specialist but vivid, punchy, and entertaining.

Katkov, George. *Russia 1917—The February Revolution.* Greenwood 1979 $65.00. ISBN 0-313-20932-4. An in-depth study, written from a rather western standpoint, that places special emphasis on German intervention in the war.

———. *Russia 1917: The Karnilov Affair: Kerensky and the Breakup of the Russian Army.* Longman 1980 $65.00. ISBN 0-582-49101-0. A detailed examination of the conflict between Kornilov and Kerensky.

Keenan, George. *Soviet-American Relations 1917–20.* Princeton U. Pr. 1990 $14.95. ISBN 0-691-00847-7. The latest edition of an expansive, two-volume study by a former U.S. ambassador to Russia.

Kerensky, Alexander. *Prelude to Bolshevism.* Haskell 1972 $75.00. ISBN 0-8383-1422-8. Memoirs of the ill-fated provisional government's chief executive.

Khruschev, Nikita S. *Khruschev Remembers: The Last Testament.* Ed. by Strobe Talbot. Little 1971 o.p. Autobiography centering on Kruschev's activities in the 1930s as Stalin's point man in the Ukraine.

Klose, Kevin. *Russia and the Russians: Inside the Closed Society.* Norton 1984 $17.50. ISBN 0-393-01786-9. Interviews with Soviet dissidents. Accounts are set in context of Russian labor camp, creating a polemic of the cold war.

Larina, Anna. *This I Can Not Forget: The Memoirs of Nikolai Bukharin's Widow*. Norton 1990 $24.95. ISBN 0-404-15122-1. The ordeals of a woman who spent two decades in the gulag for being married to recently "rehabilitated" Nikolai Bukharin.

Lincoln, W. Bruce. *Red Victory: A History of the Russian Civil War*. Touchstone Bks. 1991 $14.95. ISBN 0-671-73286-2. A military history of the war between the Red and White armies.

Meduedev, Roy. *The October Revolution*. Col. U. Pr. 1985 $18.50. ISBN 0-231-04591-3. A Marxist analysis of the Bolshevik Revolution.

Moynahan, Brian. *Comrades: Russia in Revolution 1917–1992*. Little 1992 $24.95. ISBN 0-316-58698-6. A readable history that uses narrative to detail the events in the lives of the key figures of revolutionary Russia.

Noue, Alec. *An Economic History of the USSR*. Viking Penguin 1990 $8.95. ISBN 0-14-013972-9. A well-written study that examines how politics always took precedence over economics throughout the history of the Soviet Union.

Pasternak, Boris. *Doctor Zhivago*. Buccaneer Bks. 1991 $36.95. ISBN 0-8996-6839-9. Great historical novel.

Paulou, Dmitrii V. *Leningrad Nineteen Forty-One: The Blockade*. Bks. Demand $52.50. ISBN 0-317-09259-6. The definitive discussion of one of World War II's titanic battles.

Pearson, Michael. *The Seated Train: Lenin's Eight-Month Journey from Exile to Power*. Putnam Pub. Group 1975 o.p. Delightful and vivid account of Lenin's famed passage through Germany after the tsar's fall.

Pipes, Richard. *History of the Russian Revolution*. Knopf 1990 $39.50. ISBN 0-394-50241-8. A comprehensive account of the tumultuous revolutionary period and the sorrows it inflicted upon the Russian people.

Porter, Cathy. *Women in Revolutionary Russia*. Cambridge U. Pr. 1987 $6.50. ISBN 0-521-31969-2. Very brief sketch of women's role in revolutionary times.

Raleigh, Donald J., ed. *A Russian Civil War Diary: Alexis v. Babine in Saratov 1917–1922*. Duke 1988 $6.95. Revealing, observant case study of a region racked by fraticidal warfare.

Reed, John. *Ten Days That Shook the World*. Intl. Pubs. Co. 1989 $6.95. ISBN 0-7178-0200-0. An American Bolshevist's eyewitness account of the Russian Revolution.

Sakharov, Andrei. *Progress, Coexistence and Intellectual Freedom*. Norton 1968 o.p. The former Soviet Union's most famous dissident voices his opinions on the democratization of the Communist system.

Salisbury, Harrison E. *The 900 Days: The Siege of Leningrad*. Avon 1970 o.p. Well-researched, expansive account that places the siege in a rich historical context by including background far beyond the siege itself.

Schapiro, Leonard. *The Russian Revolutions of 1917: The Origins of Modern Communism*. Basic 1984 $9.95. ISBN 0-465-07155-4. Analyzes seeds of revolution, focusing on prominent personalities.

Serge, Victor. *Memoirs of a Revolutionary*. Trans. by Peter Sedgewick. Writers & Readers 1984 o.p. Written by a dissident revolutionary, this book provides lots of material on contemporaries of the period.

Solzhenitsyn, Aleksander I. *The Gulag Archipelago*. Trans. by Thomas P. Whitney. 3 vols. HarpC Vol. 1 1974 $16.00. ISBN 0-06-092102-1. Vol. 2 1992 $10.00. ISBN 0-685-52544-9. Vol. 3 1992 $16.00. ISBN 0-06-092104-8. One of Russia's greatest authors, himself a veteran of the Gulag correctional labor camps, exposes the true nature of the Soviet system during Stalin's regime.

Tucker, Robert C. *Stalin as Revolutionary 1879–1929: A Study in History and Personality*. Norton 1973 o.p. A thorough biography that utilizes psychoanalysis to delve into Stalin's mind, creating a complete and frightening picture of the tyrant.

Ulam, Adam Bruno. *Stalin: The Man and His Era*. Viking Penguin 1973 o.p. Although utilizing a conventional approach, this well-authored work is still considered one of the best biographies of Stalin available.

White, Stephen. *New Directions in Soviet History*. Cambridge U. Pr. 1991 $54.95. ISBN 0-521-41376-1. Essays on a variety of topics by scholars from both sides of the Atlantic. Subject matter covered starts in the 1920s.

The Post-Soviet Era

d'Encoussee, Helene C. *The End of the Soviet Empire—The Triumph of the Nations*. Basic 1993 $23.00. ISBN 0-465-09812. Timely work on the disintegration of central authority and the reemergence of ethnic nation-states.

James, Donald. *The Fall of the Russian Empire*. NAL-Dutton 1992 $5.99. ISBN 0-451-13462-1. Timely survey of the turbulent events of 1991.

Laquer, Walter. *The Long Road to Freedom: Russia and Glasnost*. Scribner 1989 $21.95. ISBN 0-684-19030-3. *Glasnost* under scrutiny. Useful, if somewhat dated, guide to a transitional period.

Lewis, Moshe. *The Gorbachev Phenomena: A Historical Interpretation*. U. CA Pr. 1991 $22.50. ISBN 0-520-07428-9. Probing monograph that may need revision of its final chapter.

Remnick, David. *Lenin's Tomb: The Last Days of the Soviet Empire*. Random 1993 $25.00. ISBN 0-679-42376-1. Journalistic vignettes of individual reactions to the former Soviet Union's disclosure of its sinister past.

Richards, Susan. *Epics of Everyday Life: Encounters in a Changing Russia*. Viking Penguin 1991 $22.95. ISBN 0-670-82743-6. Glimpse at the everyday affairs of ordinary citizens in a diarylike tone. An observant, detailed view of a nation unraveling.

Sakharov, Andrei. *From Gorky to Moscow and Beyond*. Knopf 1990 $19.95. ISBN 0-685-38880-8

Smith, Hedrick. *The New Russians*. Random 1990 $24.95. ISBN 0-394-58190-3. Surveys changes under Gorbachev and obstacles to greater reform.

CHRONOLOGY OF AUTHORS

Macaulay, Thomas Babington. 1800–1859

Burckhardt, Jacob. 1818–1897

Froude, James A(nthony). 1818–1894

Lecky, W(illiam) E(dward) H(artpole). 1838–1903

Pirenne, Henri. 1862–1935

Hammond, John L., 1872–1949 and Hammond, Barbara. 1873–1962

Churchill, Winston Spencer. 1874–1965

Trevelyan, George Macaulay. 1876–1962

Guerard, Albert L(eon). 1880–1959

Durant, Will(iam), 1885–1981 and Durant, Ariel. 1898–1981

Vernadsky, George. 1887–1973

Namier, Lewis B(ernstein). 1888–1960

Taylor, A(lan) J(ohn) P(ercivale). 1906–

Plumb, J(ohn) H(arold). 1911–

Hill, Christopher. 1912–

Tuchman, Barbara W(ertheim). 1912–1989

Bullock, Alan. 1914–

Trevor-Roper, Hugh R(edwald). 1914–

Hobsbawm, Eric J. 1917–

Stone, Lawrence. 1919–

Elton, Geoffrey R(udolph). 1921–

Thompson, Edward Palmer. 1924–

ARENDT, HANNAH. 1906–1975

[SEE Chapter 9 in this volume.]

ARON, RAYMOND (CLAUDE). 1905–

[SEE Chapter 9 in this volume.]

BRAUDEL, FERNAND. 1902–1985

[SEE Chapter 9 in this volume.]

BULLOCK, ALAN. 1914–

A fellow of St. Catherine's College, Oxford University, and a former administrator of the university, Alan Bullock established himself as a historian with the publication of his biography of Hitler, *Hitler: A Study in Tyranny* (1952). Although he had the advantage of being the first person to write a scholarly study of the German leader, his work remains one of the best, if not *the* best, biography of the dominant political personality of the first half of the twentieth century.

Bullock also produced a major work in British history, *The Life and Times of Ernest Bevin* (1960–1983), a three-volume biography of the British transport-union leader and foreign secretary. He also has written a number of books on broad themes and was cogeneral editor of the *Oxford History of Modern Europe*. His latest work, *Hitler and Stalin: Parallel Lives* (1992) compares the two great dictators at different stages of their lives.

BOOKS BY BULLOCK

Has History a Future? U. Pr. of Amer. 1977 $9.50. ISBN 0-8191-5846-1

Hitler: A Study in Tyranny. 1952. HarpC 1991 repr. of 1971 ed. $14.00. ISBN 0-06-092020-3. An impressive attempt to provide a comprehensive narrative biography of this exceptionally powerful dictator.

Hitler and Stalin: Parallel Lives. Random 1993 $20.00. ISBN 0-679-72994-1. Compares the lives of twentieth-century Europe's two worst dictators, yielding a new perspective on evil; an absorbing masterpiece of historical exposition and biographical art.

The Liberal Tradition. 1956 o.p.

The Life and Times of Ernest Bevin. Vol. 1 1960. Vol. 2 1967. Vol. 3 1983 o.p. Studies the extraordinary character and career of the union leader and high-ranking politician.

Natalia Ginzberg: Human Relationships in a Changing World. Women's Ser. Berg Pubs. 1991 $59.95. ISBN 0-85496-178-X. Carefully presented and well-documented introduction to Ginberg's works.

The Past and the Future. U. Pr. of Amer. 1982 $9.50. ISBN 0-8191-5871-2

BURCKHARDT, JACOB (CHRISTOPH). 1818–1897

Born into a well-to-do Swiss family, Jacob Burckhardt studied at the University of Berlin. He went on to teach history and art history at the University of Basel, where he remained for most of his professional life. His lecture notes, in fact, formed the basis of several of his published works.

Burckhardt is universally recognized as one of the greatest historians of the nineteenth century and the greatest historian of the Italian Renaissance. In his major works, he developed the branch of history known as *Kulturgeschichte*— "history of culture." He believed that each age had its own pattern of culture and brilliantly demonstrated his cultural interpretation of history to contemporaries whose interest had traditionally been in purely political history. In the best-known and most influential of his works, *Die Kultur der Renaissance in Italien* (*The Culture of the Renaissance in Italy*) (1860), he defined the Italian Renaissance as the beginning of modern times and its protagonists as the first modern men. Though questioned and modified by later historians, particularly by medievalists, Burckhardt's definition remains generally valid today.

BOOKS BY BURCKHARDT

The Age of Constantine the Great. 1853. Trans. by Moses Hadas. U. CA Pr. 1983 $12.95. ISBN 0-520-04680-3. Treats the fascinating era of transition between the ancient and the medieval world.

The Architecture of the Italian Renaissance. Ed. by Peter Murray. U. Ch. Pr. 1987 $24.95. ISBN 0-226-08049-8. A dense and masterful reference work covering architectural as well as decorative art.

The Cicerone: An Art Guide to Painting in Italy for the Use of Travellers and Students. 1855. Ed. by Sydney J. Freedberg. *Connoisseurship Criticism and Art History Ser.* Garland 1979 o.p. A history of Italian art, mainly during the Renaissance.

The Civilization of the Renaissance in Italy. Viking Penguin 1990 $9.95. ISBN 0-14-644534-X

History of Greek Culture. Trans. by Palmer Hilty. Continuum 1963 o.p.

Reflections on History (Force and Freedom). 1905. Liberty Fund 1979 $15.00. ISBN 0-913966-37-1

CHURCHILL, WINSTON SPENCER 1874–1965 (NOBEL PRIZE 1953)

Prime minister of Great Britain from 1940 to 1945 and again from 1951 to 1955, Winston Churchill was one of his country's most notable statesmen, as well as a writer of British history. During World War II, he rallied the British people against the Nazis. As a foresighted statesman, he worked with President Franklin D. Roosevelt of the United States to produce a global strategy that served as a basic framework for peace in the postwar world. As an author, he produced a six-volume series, *The Second World War* (1948–53), for which he received the Nobel Prize for literature in 1953. In recognition of Churchill's achievements, the British Crown bestowed on him a knighthood in 1953 and the U.S. Congress made him an honorary U.S. citizen in 1963.

A graduate of the Royal Military College at Sandhurst, Churchill served with the British army in Cuba, India, and the Sudan. In 1899 he gave up his military career to enter politics. Defeated for a seat in Parliament, he went to South Africa, where he served as a war correspondent in the Boer War and also took part in the fighting there. Returning to Great Britain as a military hero, he became a member of Parliament in 1900 and served thereafter in the cabinet under several prime ministers. As lord of the admiralty, Churchill readied the British navy for both world wars. Prior to World War II, Churchill was one of the few influential voices in England who warned of the Nazi menace. When Prime Minister Neville Chamberlain resigned in 1940, the task of providing Great Britain with wartime leadership fell to Churchill. He also foresaw the cold war and was the first to call the symbolic separation between the Western and Communist countries the "Iron Curtain."

All of Churchill's books about his own experiences are intensely self-centered and partisan. On the other hand, he wrote in a lively, interesting style.

BOOKS BY CHURCHILL

Great Contemporaries. 1937. Norton 1991 $22.50. ISBN 0-393-02961-7. Contains brief, eminently readable essays on important turn-of-the-century European statesmen around the turn of the century; probably his best book.

A History of the English-Speaking Peoples. 1956–58. 4 vols. Dodd 1956–58 o.p.

Liberalism and the Social Problem. British History Ser. Haskell 1972 repr. of 1909 ed. o.p.

Memoirs of the Second World War: Chartwell Edition. 1948–53. HM 1990 $34.00. ISBN 0-395-52262-5

My Early Life: A Roving Commission. Shoe String 1989 $37.50. ISBN 0-85052-257-9

While England Slept: A Survey of World Affairs, 1932–1938. Ayer 1982 repr. of 1938 ed.
o.p.

BOOKS ABOUT CHURCHILL

Gilbert, Martin. *Churchill: A Life.* H. Holt & Co. 1991 $35.00. ISBN 0-8050-0615-X
Jablousky, David. *Churchill, the Great Game and Total War.* Intl. Spec. Bk. 1991 $35.00.
ISBN 0-7146-3367-4. A penetrating interpretation of the development of this larger-
than-life character and his career.
Jefferys, Kevin. *The Churchill Coalition and Wartime Politics, 1940–1945.* St. Martin 1991
$49.95. ISBN 0-7190-2559-1. An astute analysis of political manipulation in action.
Lewin, Ronald. *Churchill As Warlord.* Madison Bks. UPA 1982 $10.95. ISBN 0-8128-
6099-3. An even-handed analysis of Churchill's leadership during World War II;
addresses his great achievements as well as his glaring errors.
Neilson, Francis. *Churchill's War Memoirs.* Revisionist Pr. 1979 $25.00. ISBN 0-87700-
275-4

CROCE, BENEDETTO. 1866–1952

[SEE Chapter 9 in this volume.]

DURANT, WILL(IAM) (JAMES), 1885–1981 and DURANT, ARIEL. 1898–1981

American historian and essayist Will Durant was born in North Adams,
Massachusetts. He earned his undergraduate degree at St. Peter's College in
New Jersey and went on to earn a Ph.D. in philosophy in 1917 from Columbia
University. While teaching at the libertarian Ferrer Modern School in New
York, he had as a pupil a young woman named Ada Kaufman, whom he later
called Ariel. She became his wife—and his coauthor.

In 1917 Durant published his first work, his doctoral dissertation, *Philosophy
and the Social Problem.* In 1926 he published another work, *The Story of
Philosophy.* The following year, he began writing the comprehensive history of
civilization on which he was to spend much of the next 30 years of his life, the
massive *Story of Civilization.* By the time the seventh volume was published in
1961, ARIEL DURANT's diligent assistance on the project had earned her title-page
recognition as coauthor.

The Durants made several world tours to visit the countries they treated in
their history and received countless honorary degrees. In 1968 they received the
Pulitzer Prize for *Rousseau and Revolution,* the tenth and final volume of their
story. Explaining why they stopped at this point in history, they wrote: "We find
ourselves exhausted on reaching the French Revolution. We know that this
event did not end history, but it ends us."

The Durants brought popular history to the intelligent lay reader, a fact that
Orville Prescott noted: "To introduce and to popularize is not less worthy an
enterprise than to unearth some hitherto unknown facts or to present some new
and controversial theory. Many professional historians believe that it is, and
some have looked down their noses at the Durants. The truth is that the art of
history includes both kinds of writing and needs both. The scholar who delves
into obscure archives is essential; without him ignorance would prevail. But the
writer who can make history available to the general reader is necessary too"
(*Saturday Review*).

BOOKS BY THE DURANTS

Interpretations of Life. 1970. S&S Trade 1976 o.p. Includes essays on Faulkner,
Hemingway, O'Neill, Pound, Sartre, Mann, and Kafka.

The Lessons of History. S&S Trade 1968 $17.95. ISBN 0-671-41333-3. "A modest,
balanced and helpful statement of the beliefs and values that have resulted from the
Durants' immersion in historical investigation these many years. Here are their
fairmindedness, their respect for human dignity, their exaltation of reason, their
horror of bigotry and their faith in education as the clue to the betterment of the
human condition" (*N.Y. Times*).

The Pleasures of Philosophy. S&S Trade $15.95. ISBN 0-671-58110-4. Endeavors to
provide a consistent philosophy of life.

Renaissance. S&S Trade 1953 $29.95. ISBN 0-671-61600-5

Rousseau and Revolution. S&S Trade 1967 $35.00. ISBN 0-671-63058-X

The Story of Civilization. 10 vols. S&S Trade 1935 o.p.

ELTON, GEOFFREY R(UDOLPH). 1921–

English historian Geoffrey Elton was born in Germany but educated at the
University of London. In 1967 he became professor of constitutional history at
Cambridge University. A scholar of Tudor administrative history, his studies
have emphasized the development of modern governmental machinery, under
the direction of Thomas Cromwell, as the central feature of the Tudor era. He
has written many excellent works, a recent one being *The English* (1992).

BOOKS BY ELTON

England Under the Tudors. Routledge Chapman & Hall 1974 $19.95. ISBN 0-416-70690-8.
A detailed interpretation of political events of defining importance to that government and that age.

The English. Blackwell Pubs. 1992 $24.95. ISBN 0-631-17681-0

Essays on Tudor and Stuart Politics and Government: Papers and Review, 1973–1981.
Cambridge U. Pr. 1983 $74.95. ISBN 0-521-24893-0

Maitland. Yale U. Pr. 1985 $20.00. ISBN 0-300-03528-4

Policy and Police: The Enforcement of the Reformation in the Age of Thomas Cromwell.
Cambridge U. Pr. 1985 $19.95. ISBN 0-521-31309-0. An excellent elaboration of how
governmental principles translated into social practice.

The Parliament of England, 1559–1581. Cambridge U. Pr. 1986 $64.95. ISBN 0-521-
32835-7

Reform and Renewal: Thomas Cromwell and the Common Weal. Cambridge U. Pr. 1973
$13.95. ISBN 0-521-09809-2. Portrays Cromwell in an unconventionally positive light
as a complex mind and a serious promoter of reform.

The Reformation. Vol. 2. *New Cambridge History of Modern Europe.* Cambridge U. Pr.
1990 $54.50. ISBN 0-521-34536-7

Return to Essentials: Reflections on the Present State of Historical Study. Cambridge U. Pr.
1991 $29.95. ISBN 0-521-41098-3

The Tudor Constitution: Documents and Commentary. 1960. Cambridge U. Pr. 1982
$89.95. ISBN 0-521-24506-0

The Tudor Revolution in Government. 1953. Cambridge U. Pr. 1959 o.p. Searches for the
new principles involved in government under Henry VIII and through Cromwell.

FROUDE, JAMES A(NTHONY). 1818–1894

English historian James Froude studied at Oxford University, where for a time
he fell under the influence of the religiously motivated Oxford movement.
Eventually he left Oxford and went to London, where he formed a close
friendship with THOMAS CARLYLE (see Vol. 1). A vigorous Protestant nationalist,
Froude was sympathetic to Henry VIII but highly critical of Elizabeth I. Among
the best known of Froude's many works is his 12-volume *The History of England
from the Fall of Wolsey to the Defeat of the Spanish Armada* (1856–70). Written
in a style that was both refined and fluent, it represented the first detailed
account of this period of English history.

The Divorce of Catherine of Aragon. AMS Pr. repr. of 1891 ed. $31.50. ISBN 0-404-02626-5. A thorough, unsensational treatment of the subject.

The Earl of Beaconsfield. Select Bibliographies Repr. Ser. Ayer repr. of 1890 ed. o.p. A reverential biography seeking to reflect the Earl's private life and character as well as his public image.

English in Ireland in the Eighteenth Century. AMS Pr. repr. of 1881 ed. $90.00. ISBN 0-404-02640-0

English in the West Indies; or The Bow of Ulysses. Greenwood repr. of 1888 ed. o.p. Attempts to account for England's position and prospects in this colony.

History of England from the Fall of Wolsey to the Defeat of the Spanish Armada. 1856–70. 12 vols. AMS Pr. repr. of 1870 ed. $540.00. ISBN 0-404-02650-8

The Life and Letters of Erasmus and the Unknown Historical Significance of the Protestant Reformation. Am. Class. Coll. Pr. 1984 $147.55. ISBN 0-89266-469-X. Lectures discussing points of interest in Erasmus's letters; also contains largely abridged versions of selected letters.

Oceana; or England and Her Colonies. Black Heritage Lib. Collection Ser. Ayer repr. of 1886 ed. $18.75. ISBN 0-8369-9096-X. A gentlemanly account of the author's travels, acquaintances, and experiences.

Thomas Carlyle: A History of His Life in London, 1834–1881. Scholarly 1971 repr. of 1881 ed. $59.00. ISBN 0-403-00191-9

Thomas Carlyle: A History of the First Forty Years of His Life. Rprt. Serv. 1992 $150.00. ISBN 0-7812-7489-3

BOOKS ABOUT FROUDE

Burrow, John W. *A Liberal Descent: Victorian Historians and the English Past.* Cambridge U. Pr. 1983 $59.95. ISBN 0-521-20479-4

Dunn, Waldo H. *Froude and Carlyle: A Study of the Froude-Carlyle Controversy.* Assoc. Faculty Pr. 1969 repr. of 1933 ed. o.p. An extensive, impartial investigation into whether Froude's biography of Carlyle was indeed slanderous.

Goetzman, Robert. *James Anthony Froude: A Bibliography of Studies. Reference Lib. of the Humanities.* Garland 1977 o.p.

GUERARD, ALBERT L(EON). 1880–1959

Born and educated in France, Albert Guerard came to the United States as a college teacher of French in 1906 and did much to interpret the civilization of his native land. He wrote many excellent volumes that combine erudition and "esprit" with literary elegance. His *France in the Classical Age* has long been a classic. His autobiography, *Personal Equation* (1948), is out of print, as is his *Testament of a Liberal* (1956).

BOOKS BY GUERARD

French Civilization in the Nineteenth Century. History of French Civilization Ser. Gordon Pr. 1972 repr. of 1918 ed. $59.95. ISBN 0-8490-0197-8. An amusing though opinionated survey of political and cultural events.

French Civilization from Its Origins to the Close of the Middle Ages. Cooper Sq. repr. of 1921 ed. $35.00. ISBN 0-8154-0298-8

HAMMOND, JOHN L., 1872–1949 and HAMMOND, BARBARA. 1873–1962

The Hammonds were early twentieth-century British radical historians. Their committed research indicted oligarchic exploitation of the peasantry, the worker, and the artisan on the eve of and during the Industrial Revolution.

BOOKS BY JOHN L. HAMMOND

Gladstone and the Irish Nation. Shoe String 1964 repr. of 1938 ed. o.p.

The Skilled Labourer, 1760–1832. Longman 1979 o.p.

The Village Labourer, 1760–1832: A Study in the Government of England before the Reform Bill. A. Sutton Pub. 1989 $12.00. ISBN 0-86299-345-8. A pioneering work of social history that documents the impact of the Industrial Revolution on a segment of the working people of England.

BOOKS BY THE HAMMONDS

Lord Shaftesbury. Shoe String 1969 $35.00. ISBN 0-208-00215-4
The Rise of Modern Industry. Haskell 1974 $75.00. ISBN 0-4383-1795-2
The Town Labourer, 1760–1832: The New Civilization. Peter Smith 1967 $11.25. ISBN 0-8446-2197-8

HILL, CHRISTOPHER. 1912–

Master of Balliol College, Oxford University, Christopher Hill is a neo-Marxist whose work examines the role of economic factors in the events of the seventeenth century. He places particular emphasis on the grievances and treatment of the poorer and outcast sectors of society.

BOOKS BY HILL

The Century of Revolution, 1603–1714. Norton 1982 $19.95. ISBN 0-393-01573-4
Change and Continuity in Seventeenth-Century England. HUP 1975 $25.00. ISBN 0-674-10765-9. Looks at changes in social attitudes, the law, religion, and relations between town and country before and during the English revolution.
English Revolution, 1640. Beekman Pubs. 1966 o.p. Three essays by Marxist historians on Cromwell's revolution, contemporary interpretations of it, and its impact on the poet Milton's work.
The Experience of Defeat: Milton and Some Contemporaries. Viking Penguin 1984 o.p. Discusses the thoughts of those who considered the restoration of the English monarchy a defeat; main focus is on Milton.
God's Englishman: Oliver Cromwell and the English Revolution. HarpC 1972 $12.50. ISBN 0-06-131666-0. Excellent biography of Cromwell for the general reader; focuses on his political and military career.
Good Old Cause: English Revolution of 1640–1660. Intl. Spec. Bk. 1983 $32.50. ISBN 0-7146-1483-1. Various contributors discuss the causes, course, and consequences of the English revolution.
Intellectual Origins of the English Revolution. OUP 1980 $21.00. ISBN 0-19-8226-35-7. Examines the role played by religious dissent and dissenters in Cromwell's revolution.
Some Intellectual Consequences of the English Revolution. U. of Wis. Pr. 1980 o.p. Examines some of the negative consequences and paths not taken in the English revolution.
The World Turned Upside Down. Viking Penguin 1984 $5.95. ISBN 0-14-055147-6. Discusses the ideas of ordinary Englishmen—the Diggers, Levellers, etc.—during the revolution and how they attempted to look after their interests.

HOBSBAWM, ERIC J. 1917–

Eric Hobsbawm is a neo-Marxist historian of the Industrial Revolution who pays particular attention to the inequities toward the lower classes, especially in law and politics.

BOOKS BY HOBSBAWM

Age of Capital, 1848–1875. NAL-Dutton 1984 $4.95. ISBN 0-452-00696-1. Second volume of his *History of Civilization*; deals with imperialism and the expansion of untrammeled capitalism across the globe.
Age of Revolution, 1789–1848. NAL-Dutton 1964 $5.95. ISBN 0-451-62720-2.

Bandits. Pageant of History Ser. Delacorte 1969 o.p. An account of social banditry across ages and cultures; for the general reader.

Captain Swing: A Social History of the Great English Agricultural Uprising of 1830. (coauthored with George Rudé). Norton 1975 $8.95. ISBN 0-393-00793-6. Attempts to recreate the mental world of the nineteenth-century English farm laborer.

Industry and Empire. Vol. 3 in *Pelican Economic History of Britain.* Viking Penguin 1970 $7.95. ISBN 0-14-020898-4. An economic history of Britain since 1750; examines the intimate nexus between industry and empire.

The Invention of Tradition. (coedited with Terence Ranger). Cambridge U. Pr. 1992 $10.95. ISBN 0-521-43773-3. An important work in which various authors demonstrate how tradition is often a modern creation and not as ancient as its proponents claim.

Peasants in History: Essays in Honour of Daniel Thorner. 1980 o.p. Contributors discuss peasant conditions in different periods of Scottish, Indian, Russian, and Chinese history.

Primitive Rebels. Norton 1965 $7.95. ISBN 0-393-00328-0. Deals with political activities and consciousness of rebels not usually written about—peasants, shepherds, bandits, and illiterate laborers.

Revolutionaries. New Amer. Pr. 1975 o.p. Examines the theory and practice of Marxist revolution from Russia to Vietnam, Marx to Che Guevara.

KOHN, HANS. 1891–1971

[SEE Chapter 9 in this volume.]

LECKY, W(ILLIAM) E(DWARD) H(ARTPOLE). 1838–1903

British historian W. E. H. Lecky was born in Ireland. A foremost Victorian Whig-liberal, he gained major recognition as a literary historian for his encyclopedic study of eighteenth-century England and Ireland, *History of England in the Eighteenth Century* (1878–90). A combination of social and political history, the eight-volume work is a reflection of his own political beliefs.

BOOKS BY LECKY

Democracy and Liberty. Liberty Fund 1981 repr. of 1896 ed. o.p. Random comments on political events of the day; not as theoretical as the title would suggest. Introduction by William Murchinson.

Historical and Political Essays. Essay Index Repr. Ser. Ayer repr. of 1908 ed. o.p.

History of England in the Eighteenth Century. 1878–90. 7 vols. AMS Pr. repr. of 1893 ed. $210.00. ISBN 0-404-03930-8. Comprehensive treatment of all major aspects of English civilization from a Victorian liberal perspective.

History of European Morals from Augustus to Charlemagne. European Sociology Ser. Ayer 1975 $66.00. ISBN 0-405-06518-3

History of Ireland in the Eighteenth Century. 5 vols. AMS Pr. repr. of 1893 ed. $57.50. ISBN 0-405-06518-3. For years the standard history of Ireland; this work is rather dated today.

Leaders of Public Opinion in Ireland. Europe 1815–1945 Ser. 2 vols. Da Capo 1973 repr. of 1903 ed. $79.50. ISBN 0-306-70574-5. Essays on Swift, O'Connell, and other influential Irish figures.

MACAULAY, THOMAS BABINGTON. 1800–1859

Leicestershire-born Thomas Babington Macaulay studied at Cambridge University and in 1826 began a legal career. In 1830, with his election to Parliament, he embarked on another course, this time in government, which eventually included several more terms as a member of Parliament, a stint as a paymaster, and a number of years as secretary of war. In Parliament he quickly gained recognition as a Whig orator. Meanwhile, his association with the East India Company took him to India for several years, during which time he sought to reform the Indian educational system and create a legal code for the colony. In 1857 Macaulay assumed the title of Baron of Rothley.

When he was still in his mid-twenties, Macaulay became a regular contributor to the Edinburgh *Review*. He continued to write while in public office. From 1849 to 1861, he published his greatest work—a five-volume history covering the years 1685 to 1702. Titled *The History of England from the Accession of James the Second*, it is the classic statement of Whig history: the celebration of the Glorious Revolution for preserving the constitutional foundations on which English liberty developed. Although the work proved to be a great success, praised for its narrative style and extensive research, it was not without criticism. Claiming that the author's Whig and Protestant bias was evident in the work, some have faulted it for its lack of objectivity.

BOOKS BY MACAULAY

History of England from the Accession of James II. Ed. by C. H. Firth. 6 vols. 1849–61. AMS Pr. repr. of 1915 ed. $425.00. ISBN 0-404-04110-8. A classic Whig (liberal) interpretation of English history; though dated, an impressive read.
Napoleon and the Restoration of the Bourbons. Col. U. Pr. 1977 $35.50. ISBN 0-231-04376-7. Fragment of his unfinished history of France; a historical and theoretical account of Napolean's political career.

BOOKS ABOUT MACAULAY

Bryant, Arthur. *Macaulay.* B & N Imports 1979 $26.50. ISBN 0-06-490761-9. Popular, anecdotal, and somewhat simplistic biography of Macaulay.
Firth, C. H. *Commentary on Macaulay's "History of England."* Biblio Dist. 1964 o.p.
Roberts, Sydney C. *Lord Macaulay: The Pre-Eminent Victorian.* Arden Lib. 1978 repr. of 1927 ed. o.p.

NAMIER, LEWIS B(ERNSTEIN). 1888–1960

Born in Poland, Lewis Namier was educated in England at the London School of Economics and Oxford University. In 1931 he accepted a professorship at Manchester University, where he remained for more than 20 years. An active Zionist, he served for several years as political secretary of the Jewish Agency for Palestine. Knighted in 1952, as a historian Namier specialized in studies of eighteenth-century English political and diplomatic history, setting the pattern for later studies in that and other eras. For his major work, *Structure of Politics at the Accession of George III* (1929), he prepared detailed biographical studies of individual members of several Parliaments as a method of studying mid-eighteenth-century England. He concluded that the underlying motives behind political action were especially familial and oligarchic connections and the quest for position and place, rather than great events and issues. His method came to be called Namierism in his honor. Although criticized by some scholars, it led other historians and scholars to reevaluate much of English history.

BOOKS BY NAMIER

Conflicts: Studies in Contemporary History. Ayer repr. of 1942 ed. o.p. Collected essays, written during World War II, on war and democracy in Europe.
England in the Age of the American Revolution. St. Martin 1974 o.p. Analyzes British politics in the late eighteenth century.

Europe in Decay, 1936–40. 1950. Peter Smith $11.75. ISBN 0-8446-1322-3. On the rise of Hitler as seen in the wider European context.

Facing East: Essays on Germany, the Balkans, and Russia in the Twentieth Century. Gannon 1947 o.p. Essays on nationalism and anti-Semitism in modern Eastern Europe.

In the Margin of History. Ayer repr. of 1939 ed. $18.00. ISBN 0-8369-0050-2. A disparate collection of his writings on T. E. Lawrence, Napolean, anti-Semitism, Israel, foreign affairs, and so forth.

Personalities and Powers. Greenwood 1974 o.p. Collected essays and book reviews on modern British politics.

Skyscrapers, and Other Essays. Ayer repr. of 1931 ed. $14.50. ISBN 0-8369-0734-5. A lively collection of his journalism on topics including Trotsky, Zionism, and skyscrapers.

Structure of Politics at the Accession of George III. 1929. St. Martin 1957 o.p. Excellent study of the membership of the British Parliament at the time of King George III.

Vanished Supremacies. Ayer repr. of 1958 ed. $12.50. ISBN 0-8369-5195-6. Collected essays on modern European history.

PIRENNE, HENRI. 1862–1935

Belgian-born historian Henry Pirenne spent most of his professional life as professor of history at the University of Ghent. During World War I, he was a leader of Belgian passive resistance and spent several years as a hostage of the Germans. As a historian Pirenne centered his attention on the urban development of the Low Countries during the medieval period. In *Medieval Cities,* published in 1925, he argues that medieval urban development grew out of regional fortresses. With the economic revival beginning in the tenth century, city and town life expanded. These communities created their own laws, allowing the development of individual freedoms.

Pirenne is best remembered, however, for the "Pirenne thesis" about the foundations of European civilization, which he put forth in his 1937 work *Mohammed and Charlemagne.* The thesis is that the great event that pushed Europeans into the formation of their own civilization was not the collapse of the Roman Empire in the fifth century but the Islamic conquest of much of the Mediterranean.

BOOKS BY PIRENNE

Bibliography of History of Belgium. 1899–1932. Coronet Bks. repr. of 1931 ed. $67.50. ISBN 0-317-46438-8

Early Democracies in the Low Countries. Norton 1971 o.p.

Economic and Social History of Medieval Europe. 1936. HarBraceJ 1956 $5.95. ISBN 0-15-627533-3. The best brief social and economic history of Europe from the end of the Roman Empire to the mid-fifteenth century.

Medieval Cities: Their Origins and the Revival of Trade. 1925. Princeton U. Pr. 1952 $10.95. ISBN 0-691-00760-8. Argues that invasions from the east and the closure of trade routes led to the decline of medieval European cities.

Mohammed and Charlemagne. 1937 o.p. Highly controversial argument that the collapse of Western civilization in the Middle Ages was caused by the spread of Islam.

BOOK ABOUT PIRENNE

Havighurst, Alfred F. *The Pirenne Thesis.* Heath 1976 $8.50. ISBN 0-669-94680-X

PLUMB, J(OHN) H(AROLD). 1911–

British-born and educated historian John Plumb received his B.A. in 1933 from the University of London and his Ph.D. three years later from Cambridge

University. After eight years as a research fellow at Cambridge, he became a member of the faculty and in 1966 professor of modern English history. During the same period and in the 1970s, he was a visiting professor in the United States at Columbia and at New York University. Plumb is the definitive authority on England's first prime minister, Robert Walpole, about whom he wrote a two-volume biography. Plumb presents a balanced study of the era of Whig supremacy and the earlier Hanoverian period, 1714–60. In addition to authoring books, Plumb has edited a number of multivolume works and has published numerous articles and book reviews. Says Crane Brinton, "Plumb writes firmly and well in the British academic tradition of his master, G. M. TREVELYAN" (*N.Y. Herald Tribune*).

BOOKS BY PLUMB

England in the Eighteenth Century, 1714–1815. 1950. Viking Penguin 1951 $5.95. ISBN 0-14-020231-5. Brief but comprehensive history of England in the eighteenth century; for the general reader.
The English Heritage. Forum Pr. 1978 o.p.
Georgian Delights: The Pursuit of Happiness. Little 1980 o.p.
Growth of Political Stability in England, 1675–1725. Humanities 1967 $18.50. ISBN 0-333-23061-2. Argues that the steady expansion of the parliamentary electorate resulted in the continuing political stability in England after the revolution.
Men and Centuries. Greenwood 1979 repr. of 1963 ed. $45.00. ISBN 0-313-20868-9
Sir Robert Walpole. 1956–60. 2 vols. Kelley repr. of 1961 ed. o.p. The standard biography of the man often called Britain's first prime minister.
Studies in Social History. Ayer repr. of 1955 ed. $22.00. ISBN 0-8369-1063-X. Essays on aspects of English social history in the last four centuries; somewhat dated.

STONE, LAWRENCE. 1919–

Stone teaches history at Princeton University. With his semi-Marxist perspective, he examines class relationships and ambitions as explanatory factors in sixteenth- and seventeenth-century English history.

BOOKS BY STONE

The Causes of the English Revolution. HarpC 1972 $11.00. ISBN 0-06-131678-4. Looks at the socioeconomic changes in England in the early part of the seventeenth century that led to the revolution.
Crisis of the Aristocracy, 1558–1641. OUP 1965 $75.00. ISBN 0-19-821314-X. An important study of economic and social change among the aristocracy in the shadow of Cromwell's revolution.
Family and Fortune: Studies in Aristocratic Finance in the Sixteenth and Seventeenth Centuries. OUP 1973 o.p. Studies the impact of social and economic change on the financial histories of several leading aristocratic families in seventeenth-century England.
The Family, Sex and Marriage in England, 1500–1800. HarpC 1983 $13.00. ISBN 0-06-131979-1. Classic, comprehensive study of practices and attitudes toward sex, marriage, and the family among all classes of the English population over three centuries.
An Open Elite? England, 1540–1880. OUP 1986 $14.95. ISBN 0-19-285149-7
The Past and the Present. Routledge Chapman & Hall 1987 $49.95. ISBN 0-7102-1253-4. Various writings on historiography and the emergence of modernity in Western Europe.

TAYLOR, A(LAN) J(OHN) P(ERCIVALE). 1906–

British historian A.J.P. Taylor studied at Oxford University and in 1938 became a fellow of Magdalen College. Interested chiefly in diplomatic and central European history, he is a prolific and masterful writer. Fritz Stern wrote of him and his *The Struggle for Mastery in Europe, 1848–1918* (1954) in the *Political Science Quarterly:* "There is something Shavian about A. J. P. Taylor and his place among academic historians; he is brilliant, erudite, witty, dogmatic, heretical, irritating, insufferable, and withal inescapable. He sometimes insults and always instructs his fellow-historians, and never more so than in his present effort to reinterpret the diplomatic history of Europe from 1848 to the end of the First World War. . . . After a brilliant introduction, in which he defines the balance of power and assesses the relative and changing strength of the Great Powers, Mr. Taylor presents a chronological survey, beginning with the diplomacy of war, 1914–1918. . . . [He] writes on two levels. He narrates the history of European diplomacy and compresses it admirably into a single volume. Imposed upon the narrative is his effort to probe the historical meaning of given actions and conditions. . . . He has a peculiar sense of inevitability, growing out of what he regards the logic of a given development, as well as a delicate feeling for live options and alternatives. Mr. Taylor suggests that fear, not aggression, was the dominant impulse of pre-war diplomacy."

The Origins of the Second World War (1961), again controversial and lively, starts from the premise (in Taylor's words) that "the war of 1939, far from being premeditated, was a mistake, the result on both sides of diplomatic blunders." The *New Statesman* said of it: "Taylor is the only English historian now writing who can bend the bow of Gibbon and MACAULAY. [This is] a masterpiece: lucid, compassionate, beautifully written in a bare, sparse style, and at the same time deeply disturbing."

Several of Taylor's other works also received high praise. Among these were *Bismarck, the Man and the Statesman* (1955), in which he exonerated Bismarck; *Hapsburg Monarchy, 1809–1914*, a survey of the era; and *English History, 1919–1945*, a volume in the *Oxford History of England Series*, greeted by the *N.Y. Review of Books* as "an astonishing tour de force."

BOOKS BY TAYLOR

Bismarck: The Man and the Statesman. 1955. Random 1967 o.p.

The Course of German History. 1945. Putnam Pub. Group 1962 o.p. A study of modern German history and what made the nation different from the rest of Europe.

English History, 1914–1945. OUP 1992 $16.95. ISBN 0-19-285268-X. Part of the Oxford series, this comprehensive work looks at the parallel development of empire and the welfare state in early twentieth-century Britain.

The First World War: An Illustrated History. Putnam Pub. Group 1988 $8.95. ISBN 0-399-50260-2. Illustrated history of major developments in World War I; for the general reader.

From Napoleon to Stalin: Comments on European History. AMS Pr. repr. of 1950 ed. o.p. Various essays on political change in modern Europe.

From Sarajevo to Potsdam. History of European Civilization Lib. HarBraceJ 1966 o.p. The political thoughts and opinions of both ordinary people and their leaders during the two world wars.

Germany's First Bid for Colonies, 1884–1885: A Move in Bismarck's European Policy. Norton 1970 repr. of 1938 ed. $1.25. ISBN 0-393-00530-5. On Germany's role in the late nineteenth-century scramble for Africa.

The Origins of the Second World War. Macmillan 1983 $12.95. ISBN 0-689-70658-8. Account of the political developments that led to World War II; for the general reader.

The Struggle for Mastery in Europe: 1848–1918. History of Modern Europe Ser. OUP 1954 o.p. Study of European diplomacy and the major developments of the period.

Contains absorbing accounts of the policies and ambitions of individual powers and diplomats, the changing diplomatic alignments, and the crises and wars of the time.
The War Lords. Viking Penguin 1979 $6.95. ISBN 0-14-004638-0

THOMPSON, EDWARD PALMER. 1924–

Thompson is a contemporary neo-Marxist. He has studied especially the development of a working-class consciousness in the early years of the Industrial Revolution.

BOOKS BY THOMPSON

Albion's Fatal Tree: Crime and Society in Eighteenth-Century England. (coauthored with others). Pantheon 1976 $11.20. ISBN 0-394-73085-2
Customs in Common: Studies in Traditional Popular Culture. New Press NY 1992 $29.95. ISBN 1-56584-003-8
Making of the English Working Class. Random 1966 $25.00. ISBN 0-394-70322-7. Classic, eminently readable Marxist account of the birth and early development of the British working class and its organizations.
Whigs and Hunters. Pantheon 1976 o.p. A study of the eighteenth century, focusing on the Black Act that decreed the death penalty for petty criminal acts, including cutting trees and deer stalking.
William Morris: Romantic to Revolutionary. Stanford U. Pr. 1988 $19.95. ISBN 0-8047-1509-2. A comprehensive, readable biography of the English social reformer, poet, and artist who founded the Socialist League.

TREVELYAN, GEORGE MACAULAY. 1876–1962

The grandnephew of THOMAS MACAULAY, and son of British historian and politician Sir George Otto Trevelyan, George Macaulay Trevelyan is probably the most widely read twentieth-century historian of Britain. Educated at Cambridge University in 1927 he became professor there of modern history, a position he held until 1940, when he became Master of Trinity College. Following that, he became chancellor of Durham University, a position he held until 1957.

Trevelyan wrote in the liberal tradition, concentrating to a great extent on eighteenth- and nineteenth-century England. He was a firm believer in the development of literary style in historical writing and spoke out against "scientific" history. In addition to his many works on England, he received high praise for the three-volume extended study of Garibaldi, published in 1907, 1909, and 1911.

BOOKS BY TREVELYAN

Early History of Charles James Fox. AMS Pr. repr. of 1880 ed. $45.00. ISBN 0-404-06524-4
England in the Age of Wycliffe. AMS Pr. repr. of 1900 ed. $34.50. ISBN 0-404-56677-4. The state of English society, politics, and religion at the end of the medieval period and the beginning of the modern age.
England under Queen Anne. 3 vols. AMS Pr. repr. of 1930–34 ed. $149.50. ISBN 0-404-20263-2. Perhaps the best modern account of England in this period; scholarly but readable.
England under the Stuarts. 1907. Routledge 1966 $19.95. ISBN 0-416-69240-0. Excellent political, social, and cultural history of England in the Stuart period.
The English Revolution, 1688–1689. 1938. OUP 1965 o.p. Somewhat dated but popular account of what he calls "the sensible revolution."
English Social History: A Survey of Six Centuries, Chaucer to Queen Victoria. 1942. McKay 1965 o.p. Celebrated account of "English people's history with the politics left out" from the age of Chaucer to that of Victoria; rather dated today.

Grey of Fallodon: Being the Life of Sir Edward Grey. AMS Pr. repr. of 1937 ed. o.p.
Life of John Bright. Greenwood 1971 $49.75. ISBN 0-8371-4552-X. The official biography
    of the champion of the English middle class in the nineteenth century.
Lord Grey of the Reform Bill: Being the Life of Charles, Second Earl Grey. 1920.
    Greenwood 1971 $38.50. ISBN 0-8371-4553-8. The official biography of the Whig
    Prime Minister who abolished the slave trade and curbed the powers of the House of
    Lords.

TREVOR-ROPER, HUGH R(EDWALD). 1914–

Regius professor of modern history at Oxford University since 1957, Hugh
Trevor-Roper is a meticulous researcher and an eloquent and prolific writer.
His books cover all of British history from medieval to contemporary days. His
The Last Days of Hitler (1947) is considered a classic.

BOOKS BY TREVOR-ROPER

Catholics, Anglicans and Puritans: Seventeenth Century Essays. U. Ch. Pr. 1988 $27.50.
    ISBN 0-226-81228-6. Essays on aspects of English intellectual and religious history
    before and after the Puritan revolution.
The European Witch Craze in the Sixteenth and Seventeenth Centuries and Other Essays.
    HarpC 1969 o.p.
From Counter-Reformation to Glorious Revolution. U. Ch. Pr. 1992 $29.95. ISBN 0-226-
    81230-8. Collected essays on European history between the English revolution and
    the Thirty Years War.
Historical Essays. 1956. Gannon 1966 o.p.
The Last Days of Hitler. 1947. U. Ch. Pr. 1992 $9.95. ISBN 0-226-81224-3. Account of the
    last days of Hitler based on the author's experience working for British intelligence;
    for the general reader.
Plunder of the Arts in the Seventeenth Century. Trans-Atl. Phila. 1972 $8.75. ISBN 0-500-
    55002-6
Renaissance Essays. U. Ch. Pr. 1989 $22.50. ISBN 0-226-81227-8. Essays on such
    renaissance intellectual and cultural figures as Thomas More, Erasmus, and
    Maximilian.
The Rise of Christian Europe. 1966. Norton 1989 $9.95. ISBN 0-393-95802-7. Readable
    history of Europe from the dark ages to the Renaissance.

TROTSKY, LEON. (pseud. of Lev Davydovich Bronstein). 1879–1940

[SEE Chapter 9 in this volume.]

TUCHMAN, BARBARA W(ERTHEIM). 1912–1989

American historian and journalist Barbara Tuchman was the daughter of
Maurice Wertheim, a New York banker, art collector, and founder of the
Theatre Guild, and granddaughter of Henry Morgenthau, Sr. Without an
academic title or advanced degree, Tuchman became a prize-winning writer of
history. Among her first books were *The Lost British Policy* (1938), *Bible and
Sword* (1956), and *The Zimmerman Telegram* (1958). *The Guns of August* (1962),
a dramatic retelling of the events of the first 30 days of World War I, became a
runaway bestseller and won the Pulitzer Prize in 1963. Of her earlier book on
the same subject, the *N.Y. Times* said: "The value and importance of her book
lies in her brilliant use of well known materials, her sureness of insight, and her
competent grasp of a complicated chapter of diplomatic history." Tuchman
won a second Pulitzer Prize in 1972 for *Stillwell and the American Experience in
China, 1911–1945* (1971). The book carefully examines the shaping of America's
foreign policy in China over a 35-year period. *A Distant Mirror* (1978), another
popular work, began as a study of the bubonic plague in medieval Europe but

turned into a detailed account of fourteenth-century France and its parallels to the present. Among her later works is the best-selling *The March of Folly: From Troy to Vietnam* (1984), an examination of the human penchant for war. This work looks closely at historical events that were mismanaged by governments and investigates the results of those errors. Tuchman's histories, noted for their narrative style and believable portrayals of historic figures, were intended to be comprehensible to the average reader and, as a result, many of her works became bestsellers. She has thus helped popularize history for the general reader rather than write for the academic specialist.

BOOKS BY TUCHMAN

Bible and Sword: England and Palestine from the Bronze Age to Balfour. Ballantine 1984 $14.00. ISBN 0-345-31427-1

A Distant Mirror: The Calamitous Fourteenth Century. Ballantine 1980 $45.00. ISBN 0-394-40026-7. Granted that the fourteenth century is a most difficult period to deal with, this book is still particularly disappointing in that it neglects Italy, where the Renaissance was just beginning, almost entirely.

The First Salute: A View of the American Revolution. Knopf 1988 $22.95. ISBN 0-394-55333-0. On the American Revolution and its significant impact on Europe.

The Guns of August. Bantam 1982 $6.95. ISBN 0-553-25401-4. A military history of the Western front in World War I.

The March of Folly: From Troy to Vietnam. Ballantine 1985 $12.00. ISBN 0-345-30823-9. The "folly" is war. An interesting approach through case histories, but too often the facts take second place to the overall preconception.

Notes from China. Macmillan 1972 $6.95. ISBN 0-02-074800-0. Poignant travelogue of her journey through China during Nixon's famous 1972 visit; contains her notes of discussions with ordinary people plus the essay, "What if Mao came to Washington in 1945?"

Practicing History: Selected Essays. Knopf 1981 $16.50. ISBN 0-394-52086-6. Reflections on own previous work and on Henry Kissinger, the Holocaust, Japan, Vietnam, etc.

The Proud Tower. Macmillan 1966 $60.00. ISBN 0-02-620300-6. Examines the state of politics in Western Europe and the United States before World War I in order to explain its underlying causes.

Stilwell and the American Experience in China, 1911–1945. Macmillan 1971 $60.00. ISBN 0-02-620290-5. U.S. relations with China and the rest of Asia in the early twentieth century as seen through the career of this famous general who served in Asia.

The Zimmerman Telegram. 1958. Macmillan 1966 $14.95. ISBN 0-02-620320-0. Detailed study of the course of events that led to U.S. intervention in World War I.

VERNADSKY, GEORGE. 1887–1973

Professor Emeritus George Vernadsky of Yale University was a Russian émigré who settled in the United States and became one of the foremost historians on the subject of his native land. His life, he said, fell into three periods. The first was his youth in Moscow, taking his degree from the University of Moscow, teaching Russian history at the University of Petrograd (1914–17) in the stimulating intellectual atmosphere of the former St. Petersburg, and finally, studying and teaching in the Urals and Crimea, where, he said, even the revolution did not unduly disturb the universities. His second period was seven years in exile, spent teaching in Constantinople, Athens, Prague, and Paris. In 1927, invited to Yale, he came to the United States and remained in New Haven, first as a research associate in history and then as professor of Russian history, for the rest of his academic career. Gradually he produced a monumental body of work on Russian history. "While the transition from one span of my life to another was more or less painful," he said, "the more I think of the course of my life, the more I find that in many respects I should be grateful to Fate for this tortuous path, since it gave me the variety and richness of experience, and since in each of the three paths I was fortunate to meet so many kind and congenial friends."

Vernadsky's major work is the five-volume *A History of Russia* (1943–69). Planned as a collaboration between Vernadsky and Michael Karpovich of Harvard University, it was originally intended to run to nine volumes, but Karpovich's death in 1959 ended the possibility of his doing the later sections, and no further volumes appeared. Nevertheless, for the period it covers—to the time of the Renaissance and Reformation in Europe—it is the definitive work. Vernadsky's shorter *A History of Russia* (1961) brings the history of Russia up to the nuclear age.

BOOKS BY VERNADSKY

A History of Russia: Ancient Russia. Bks. Demand repr. of 1943 ed. $110.30. ISBN 0-8357-5469-3. Preface by Michael Karpovich. For a long time the standard history of medieval and modern Russia; now dated. "It is impossible within the limits of a review to suggest all the ideas, outlooks, insights which 'Ancient Russia' provides. . . . Despite the remoteness of the centuries treated, the reader will find insights of every kind into the Russia of our day. And all who are interested in Russian history will recognize in 'Ancient Russia' a notable achievement of scholarship and interpretation" (*N.Y. Herald Tribune*).

Kievan Russia. 1948. Yale U. Pr. 1973 $16.00. ISBN 0-300-01647-6. "This volume is an outstanding contribution to the understanding of an important period of Russian history. It is bound to have a marked influence on Western opinion about the year in Russian history it treats in such a masterly manner" (*Saturday Review*).

The Mongols and Russia. Yale U. Pr. 1953 o.p. "A volume distinguished by mature scholarship and based on thorough research and keen synthesis . . ." (*Saturday Review*).

Russia at the Dawn of the Modern Age. Yale U. Pr. 1959 o.p. "The moment one begins to read a careful, scholarly history of Russia, such as the great work which Professor Vernadsky has in progress, the superficiality of so many of our current concepts about Russia becomes apparent" (*Saturday Review*).

The Tsardom of Moscow, 1547–1682. 2 vols. Bks. Demand 1969 Pt. 1 $125.00. ISBN 0-317-10883-2. Pt. 2 $102.50. ISBN 0-317-10884-0. "Vernadsky is the most prolific student of Russian history in the United States, past or present, and he richly deserves our gratitude for the remarkable erudition and energy he has consistently brought to his writings" (S. H. Baron, *American Historical Review*).

A History of Russia. Yale U. Pr. rev. ed. 1961 $18.00. ISBN 0-300-00247-5

Medieval Russian Laws. (ed.) 1947. Hippocrene Bks. o.p.

Lenin: Red Dictator. AMS Pr. repr. of 1931 ed. o.p. A very critical, unsympathetic, and biased political biography of the leader of the Russian Revolution.

CHAPTER 12

African History

Robert O. Collins

There wasn't any history in Africa, as far as I'd ever been taught. Perhaps one should find out.

—BASIL DAVIDSON, *The Black Man's Burden*

The perception held by scholars and the general international community that Africa had no discernible history has been thoroughly discredited by the past two generations of historical research and writing. Although in the fifth century B.C. HERODOTUS (see also Vol. 4), the "father of history," had written of dynastic Egypt and the lands beyond the borders of Egypt called Nubia, with the decline of the Roman Empire Europe displayed little interest in the external world outside its own borders. The far-flung Muslim empire sealed off Africa from Europe but preserved the ancient learning and produced its own sophisticated scholarship. Arab travelers roamed deep into Africa, generating rich accounts of the expansive Sudanic African empires of Ghana, Mali, and Songhay, which flourished roughly in succession from the eighth to the fifteenth centuries. Some Arab travelers followed the ancient trade routes along the Sabaean Lane, which stretched from the city-states of East Africa to southern Arabia, Persia, India, and beyond. From their accounts came descriptions of African states of the East African littoral that lay on the periphery of the evolving states in the interior of West, Central, and Southern Africa.

Although our historical understanding of the West African coastal kingdoms begins in the 1400s with the Portuguese expeditions seeking to circumnavigate the continent, for centuries little attempt was made at a historical synthesis. In the latter half of the nineteenth century, European colonial rule produced its historians of Africa. However, their orientation was primarily imperial, emphasizing the conquest and its justification more than the past of their African subjects. Exceptions were few, unsystematic, and not completely reliable. Of greater importance was the information collected by European administrators. Intended primarily to enable them to rule their African subjects more effectively, the information they accumulated about African societies and their past proved to be of great value to historians.

Prior to World War II, Americans had displayed little interest in Africa and none in the African past. World War II dramatically changed this complacency. Both in Europe and in the United States, African studies became a major component of the curriculum and research in major universities and in various branches of government. In Europe a revitalized interest paralleled that in the United States with the expansion of African studies in Great Britain at the University of London School of Oriental and African Studies (SOAS), in France at the Sorbonne, and in Belgium at the Académie Royale des Sciences d'Outremer. In the United States, where one-tenth of the population were of

African descent, considerable sums of money were appropriated by the U.S. Congress and supplemented by funds from private foundations for African Studies. To administer these initiatives, numerous African Studies centers were established in a number of universities. The various departments of history in these universities that had an African focus, symbolized by their African centers, soon attracted a coterie of students who would study the African past. This academic organization was not confined to the United States; a similar organization occurred in Great Britain, France, and Belgium.

The result of the infusion of resources from the U.S. federal government and foundations clearly could not be ignored by the universities themselves. Whether or not they had a designated African Studies Center, they responded by making funds available to establish faculty positions in African history. This was not accomplished without difficulty. The international community of historians was skeptical of accepting the history of the African peoples, the explication of which did not fit the traditional methodology practiced by professional historians. Many shared the opinion expressed by University of Oxford Regius Professor of History HUGH TREVOR-ROPER that "Perhaps, in the future, there will be some African history to teach. But at present there is none or very little: There is only the history of the Europeans in Africa. The rest is largely darkness. . . . And darkness is not a subject for history." These historians believed that the history of a people resided only in the written word. Gradually, throughout the 1950s and 1960s, this archaic perception of the study of Africa's past began to change. The new generation of historians was prepared to accept new methodologies, such as oral traditions, archaeology, anthropology, and linguistics, in order to piece together the history of African culture. The work of these new historians could not be dismissed or ignored by even the most narrow of traditionalists; nor could social change in society, particularly in the United States among the African American communities whose origins had been Africa. In addition, the coming of independence to the former African colonies of Europe revitalized in Africa itself a search for, and recognition of, the African past. Throughout Africa, from Khartoum to Cape Town and from Free Town to Addis Ababa, departments of history in the newly established universities immersed themselves in the study of their own history. The dismissal of African history by Professor Trevor-Roper has now proven false. By thorough research and balanced presentation, African historians of every ethnic persuasion have established their case for the integrity of African history.

REFERENCE WORKS

Ajayi, J. F. A., and Michael Crowder, eds. *Historical Atlas of Africa*. Longman 1985 o.p. A thorough atlas of Africa through its evolution in time.

Collins, N. Mark, Jeffrey A. Sayer, and Caroline Harcourt. *The Conservation Atlas of Tropical Forests: Africa*. S&S Trade 1992 $85.00. ISBN 0-13-175332-0. Unmatched by other recent books. Highly recommended for academic libraries and for public libraries with collection interests in Africa or world environmental issues.

Coquery-Vidrovitch, Catherine. *Africa: Endurance and Change South of the Sahara*. Trans. by David Maisel. U. CA Pr. 1988 $50.00. ISBN 0-520-05679-5. One of the most comprehensive and best-written books about the social, economic, and political changes in Africa.

Crowder, Michael. *The Cambridge History of Africa, 1940–1975*. Vol. 8. Cambridge U. Pr. 1985 $130.00. ISBN 0-685-08824-3

Crowder, Michael, and Roland Oliver, eds. *An Encyclopaedia of Africa.* 1983 o.p. A useful source for checking factual information on African history.

Davidson, Basil. *Africa in History.* Macmillan 1992 $15.00. ISBN 0-2-042791-3. Excellent reference for undergraduates and the general reader.

Fage, J. D. *An Atlas of African History.* Hutchison rev. ed. 1978 o.p. For the more general reader; not as thorough as the *Historical Atlas* by Ajayi and Crowder.

Gailey, Harry A., Jr. *The History of Africa in Maps.* Denoyer-Geppert 1979 o.p. An easy-to-use historical atlas.

Holt, P. M., Ann K. S. Lambton, and Bernard Lewis, eds. *The Cambridge History of Islam.* 2 vols. Cambridge U. Pr. 1970 o.p. The authoritative history of Islam, with several chapters dealing exclusively with Africa south of the Sahara.

Oliver, Roland, and Brian Fagan. *Africa in the Iron Age.* Cambridge U. Pr. 1975 $54.95. ISBN 0-521-09900-5. A synthesis of recent research on the Early Iron Age by an archaeologist and a historian working in collaboration.

Oliver, Roland, and J. D. Fage, eds. *The Cambridge University History of Africa.* 8 vols. Cambridge U. Pr. 1975–86 o.p. Still the standard reference work for African history. Some essays dated. The standard for other multivolume histories because of the evenness of the editing and the rich source of materials.

Otchere, Freda E. *African Studies Thesaurus: Subject Headings for Library Users.* Greenwood 1992 $75.00. ISBN 0-313-27437-1. For specialized libraries of African studies. Useful reference, especially with regard to Library of Congress subject headings.

Shillington, Kevin. *History of Africa.* St. Martin 1989 $49.95. ISBN 0-312-03179-3. Written from an African perspective. Emphasizes developments affecting ordinary, everyday lives.

UNESCO. *General History of Africa.* Ki-Zerbo, G., and others, eds. 8 vols. UNIPUB. Vol. 1 *Methodology and African Prehistory.* 1980 $41.00. ISBN 92-3-101707-1. Vol. 2 *Ancient Civilizations of Africa.* 1980 $41.00. ISBN 92-3-101708-X. Vol. 3 *Africa from the Seventh to Eleventh Century.* 1988 $35.00. ISBN 92-3-101710-1. Vol. 4 *Africa from the Twelfth to Sixteenth Century.* 1984 $35.00. ISBN 92-3-101710-1. Vol. 5 *Africa from the Sixteenth to Eighteenth Century.* 1988 $45.00. ISBN 92-3-101711-X. Vol. 6 *The Nineteenth Century until 1880.* 1990 $35.00. ISBN 92-3-101712-8. Vol. 7 *Africa under Colonial Domination.* 1990 o.p. Vol. 8 *Africa since the Ethiopian War, 1935–1975.* 1990 o.p. A massive publication largely by African scholars, with an enormous amount of information. Can be used as a ready reference, although many essays are uneven.

SURVEYS AND GENERAL WORKS

Abubakar, Ahmad. *Africa and the Challenge of Development: Acquiescence and Dependency vs. Freedom and Development.* Greenwood 1989 $42.95. ISBN 0-275-93221-4. An examination of Africa's economic future.

Austin, Ralph. *Africa in Economic History.* Heinemann 1987 o.p. A comprehensive survey of African economic history for the general reader.

Betts, Raymond F., ed. *The Scramble for Africa. Problems in European Civilization.* Heath 1972 o.p. A handy reader for those interested in the partition of Africa; primarily a classroom text.

Bohannan, Paul, and Philip D. Curtin. *Africa and Africans.* Waveland Pr. 1988 $14.95. ISBN 0-8813-347-6. An excellent book for the neophyte in African history.

Bullwinkle, Davis A., ed. *Africa's Women: A General Bibliography 1976–1985.* Greenwood 1989 $49.95. ISBN 0-313-26607-7. Over 4,100 original English-language works on all subjects by African women.

Chilcote, Ronald H. *Portuguese Africa.* P-H 1967 o.p. A general work on the history of Portuguese Africa designed for classroom use and for the public reader.

Clark, J. Desmond, and Steven A. Brandt, eds. *From Hunters to Farmers.* 1984. U. CA Pr. ISBN 0-520-04574-2. The most thorough account of Africa during the Iron Age.

Curtin, Philip D., and others. *African History*. Longman 1978 $23.95. ISBN 0-582-64663-4. Probably the best general text, covering all of Africa from the late Stone Age to the end of the colonial era.

————. *Image of Africa: British Ideas and Action, 1780–1850*. Bks. Demand repr. of 1964 ed. $145.10. ISBN 0-8357-6772-8. Using British sources, the author demonstrates how British ideas about Africans and their country underwent fundamental changes in the late eighteenth and nineteenth centuries.

Davidson, Basil. *Africa in History: Themes and Outlines*. Macmillan rev. ed. 1974 $11.95. ISBN 0-02-031260-1. Outlines the basic themes for the general reader.

————. *Africa in Modern History: The Search for a New Society*. Allen Lane 1978 o.p. The author attempts to justify by historical examples policies undertaken by the independent African states.

————. *The African Genius: An Introduction to Social and Cultural History*. Little 1970 $10.95. ISBN 0-316-17432-7. A stimulating, well-written book on African cultural history for the general reader.

————. *Discovering Africa's Past*. Longman 1978 o.p. A general work in which the author justifies Africa's past.

————. *Modern Africa*. Longman 1989 $18.95. ISBN 0-582-01900-1. A journalistic discourse on independent Africa.

Fage, J. D. *A History of Africa*. Unwin Hyman 1989 $65.00. ISBN 0-04-445388-4. A competent general text designed for classroom use or for the general reader.

Flint, J. E. *A History of Africa*. 1978 o.p. A general survey for classroom use or for the general reader.

Gailey, Harry A., Jr. *The History of Africa*. 2 vols. Krieger 1980 repr. of 1972 ed. Vol. 1 $17.50. ISBN 0-89874-032-0. Vol. 2 o.p. A straightforward text for the general reader and for classroom use.

Gann, L. H., and Peter Duignana, eds. *Colonialism in Africa, 1870–1960*. 5 vols. Cambridge U. Pr. Vol. 1 *History and Politics of Colonialism, 1870–1914*. 1969 $87.50. ISBN 0-521-07373-1. Vol. 2 *History and Politics of Colonialism, 1914–1960*. 1970 $84.50. ISBN 0-521-07732-X. Vol. 3 1971 $79.95. ISBN 0-521-07844-X. Vol. 4 *The Economics of Colonialism*. 1975 $120.00. ISBN 0-521-08641-8. Vol. 5 *Bibliography*. 1974 $99.95. ISBN 0-521-07859-8. A massive collaborative work that covers colonialism in Africa thoroughly.

————. *Colonialism in Africa, 1969–1975*. o.p. Contains many excellent chapters by leading authorities.

Gifford, Prosser, and W. R. Louis, ed. *Decolonization and African Independence*. Yale U. Pr. 1988 $60.00. ISBN 0-300-04070-7. Perhaps the most thorough study of decolonization and the policies that arose from it.

————. *The Transfer of Power in Africa: Decolonization, 1940–60*. Yale U. Pr. 1982 o.p. A series of important essays on decolonization for the well-informed reader.

Greenberg, Joseph H. *The Languages of Africa, 1963*. Ind. U. Pr. o.p. The most influential analysis of African languages and their relationship with one another; not for the general reader.

Hallett, Robin. *Africa since 1875. History of the Modern World Ser*. Ann Arbor 1974 o.p. A competent survey.

————. *Africa to 1875. History of the Modern World Ser.* Ann Arbor 1974 o.p. Well-written survey of African history from the early period to the nineteenth century.

Harris, Eddy. *Native Stranger: A Black American's Journey into the Heart of Africa*. Random 1993 $12.00. ISBN 0-679-74232-8. Harris's magnificent recounting of the year he spent traveling through Africa.

Hull, Richard. *African Cities and Towns before the European Conquest*. Norton 1977 $10.95. ISBN 0-393-05581-7. An excellent book, well written and perceptive, intended for the informed lay reader.

July, Robert W. *A History of the African People*. Waveland Pr. 1985 $22.95. ISBN 0-88133-631-9. Suffers from the author's attempt to cover too much.

————. *Precolonial Africa: An Economic and Social History*. Scribner 1975 o.p. A survey for the general reader of Africa before the colonial period.

Lovejoy, Paul. *Transformations in Slavery: A History of Slavery in Africa*. Cambridge U. Pr. 1983 $42.50. ISBN 0-521-24369-6. A powerful and thoughtful work on slavery in Africa in distinction to the trans-Atlantic slave trade.

Miers, Suzanne, and Igor Kopytoff, eds. *Slavery in Africa: Historical and Anthropological Perspectives*. U. of Wis. Pr. 1977. ISBN 0-299-07330-0. An important series of essays for the specialist on the evolution and development of slavery in Africa; should be consulted together with the work of Paul Lovejoy.

Ogot, B. A., ed. *War and Society in Africa*. Intl. Spec. Bk. 1972 $30.00 $17.50. ISBN 0-7146-4009-3. Deals with African rivalries before the coming of the Europeans.

Oliver, Roland, and Anthony Atmore. *Africa since 1800*. Cambridge U. Pr. 1981 o.p. A general survey of Africa in the nineteenth and twentieth centuries; designed for classroom use.

———. *The African Middle Ages*. Cambridge U. Pr. 1981 $16.95. ISBN 0-521-29894-6

Pakenham, Thomas. *The Scramble for Africa*. Random 1991 $31.50. ISBN 0-394-51576-5. A brilliant, readable account of the scramble for Africa by the European powers.

Penrose, Ernest Francis, ed. *European Imperialism and the Partition of Africa*. Intl. Spec. Bk. 1975 $35.00. ISBN 0-7146-3058-6. Focuses on the politics of empire building by European powers during the nineteenth century.

Rake, Alan. *Who's Who in Africa? Leaders for the Nineteen Nineties*. Scarecrow 1992 $59.50. ISBN 0-8108-2557-0. A new biographical source on Africa's political leaders.

Robinson, Ronald, and John Gallagher. *Africa and the Victorians*. St. Martin 1961 o.p. An exciting, well-written account of the partition of Africa, which the authors contend revolved around the competition for the Nile Valley.

Rodney, Walter. *How Europe Underdeveloped Africa*. Howard U. Pr. 1992 $14.95. ISBN 0-88258-105-8. Regarded as one of the most important books on African history. Explains the lack of development in Africa. A starting point for an ongoing debate, despite the author's Marxist methodology.

Strong, Polly. *African Tales: Folklore of the Central African Republic*. Telcraft Bks. 1992 $10.95. ISBN 1-878893-15-7. An important cultural information source.

Yeoman, Guy. *Africa's Mountains of the Moon: Journeys to the Snowy Sources of the Nile*. Universe 1989 $35.00. ISBN 0-87663-697-0. An abundantly illustrated narrative account of a 1987 expedition to study mountain flora. Excellent botanical illustrations.

NORTH AFRICA AND THE SAHEL

Abun-Nasr, J. M. *A History of the Maghrib*. Bks. Demand repr. of 1975 ed. $108.00. ISBN 0-317-26070-7. The most comprehensive, readable history of North Africa.

Adams, W. Y. *Nubia: Corridor to Africa*. Princeton U. Pr. 1977 $75.00. ISBN 0-691-09370-9. Majesterial history of Nubia that demonstrates its links between dynastic Egypt and Africa.

Bevan, Edwyn. *A History of Egypt under the Ptolemaic Dynasty*. 1927 o.p. Remains the standard general account of Egypt under the rule of the Greeks.

Bovill, Edward W., and Robin Hallett. *Golden Trade of the Moors*. OUP rev. ed. 1970 o.p. Deals with an important phase in the history of the Sudan.

Carver, Norman F., Jr. *North African Villages: Morocco, Nigeria, and Tunisia*. Documan 1989 $29.95. ISBN 0-932076-08-4

Collins, R. O. *The Southern Sudan, 1883–1898*. Yale U. Pr. 1962 o.p. The history of the Southern Sudan during the upheavals caused by the rise of the Mahdist State.

Fuglestad, F. *A History of Niger, 1850–1960*. Cambridge U. Pr. 1983 o.p. Describes European penetration up the river and rivalries among Africans and Europeans and among Europeans themselves.

Hasan, Y. F. *The Arabs and the Sudan*. 1967 o.p. A standard work on the Arab penetration and settlement of Christian Nubia.

Hill, Richard. *Egypt in the Sudan, 1820–81*. Greenwood repr. of 1959 ed. ISBN 0-313-25116-9. The authoritative one-volume account in English of nineteenth-century Egypt.

Holt, P. M. *The Mahdist State in the Sudan, 1881–98*. Clarendon Pr. 1958 o.p. A scholarly study of the Mahdiyya, founded by the Mahdi in the early 1880s.

———. *The Mahdist State in the Sudan*. Clarendon Pr. 1970 o.p. A revision that incorporates new material on our understanding of the Mahdist State.

Holt, Peter M. *Egypt and the Fertile Crescent, 1516–1922: A Political History*. Cornell Univ. Pr. 1969 $15.95. ISBN 0-8014-9079-0. A survey of Egypt and the Levant, with passing references to the Sudan.

Holt, P. M., and M. W. Daly. *A History of the Sudan*. Longman 1988 $17.50. ISBN 0-582-00406-3. A survey for the general reader of the history of the Sudan.

Miers, Suzanne, and Igor Kopytoff, eds. *The White Nile*. Humanities 1980 $42.50. ISBN 0-485-19553-4. A history of the Upper Nile Basin in the Sudan and Uganda whence flows the White Nile; excellent reading.

Miller, E. Willard, and Ruby M. Miller. *The Third World—North Africa: A Bibliography*. Vance Biblios. 1990 $8.75. ISBN 0-7920-0681-X

Robinson, David. *The Holy War of Umar Tal*. Clarendon Pr. o.p. A marvelous piece of historical writing, well researched and presented for both the general reader and the scholar. About al-Hajj Umar, who established the Tukolor Empire in the nineteenth-century Western Sudan.

Sanderson, G. N. *England, Europe and the Upper Nile*. Edinburgh U. Pr. 1965 o.p. A thorough description and analysis of the European struggle for the Upper Nile. Readable but detailed for the general reader.

Simon, Reeva, ed. *The Middle East and North Africa: Essays in Honor of J. C. Hurewitz*. Col. U. Pr. 1990 $58.00. ISBN 0-231-07148-5. A collection of essays related to the history and politics of the Middle East and Africa. Compiled in honor of a prominent researcher and writer in the field.

Vatikiotis, P. J. *The History of Egypt*. Johns Hopkins 1986 o.p. A standard general history of Egypt.

WEST AND CENTRAL AFRICA

Anstey, Roger. *The Atlantic Slave Trade and British Abolition 1760–1810*. Macmillan 1975 o.p. A balanced survey of the trans-Atlantic trade. Includes a history of the Abolitionist movement from original sources.

Ajayi, J. F. A., and Michael Crowder, eds. *History of West Africa*. 3 vols. 1974–1986. Longman o.p. A standard text for the study of West Africa, but too detailed for the general reader.

Biebuck, Daniel P. *The Arts of Central Africa: An Annotated Bibliography*. G. K. Hall 1987 $49.00. ISBN 0-8161-8601-4. Citations for 1,920 authors. Comprehensive, thorough, and detailed reference.

Birmingham, David, and Phyllis M. Martin, eds. *History of Central Africa*. 2 vols. 1983 o.p. The standard text for the history of Central Africa; for classroom use and for the general reader.

Bovill, Edward W., and Robin Hallett. *The Golden Trade of the Moors*. OUP 1968 o.p. A bit dated, but remains the classic study of old African trade centering on the great city of Timbuktu.

Cassell, Abayomi. *Liberia: History of the First African Republic*. 2 vols. Irvington 1984 o.p. The standard work for the general reader on the history of Liberia.

Collins, R. O. *King Leopold, England and the Upper Nile, 1899–1909*. Bks. Demand repr. of 1968 ed. $69.00. ISBN 0-8357-9376-1. A history of King Leopold's efforts to acquire access to the Nile Valley.

Crowder, Michael, and Roland Oliver, eds. *The Story of Nigeria*. Faber & Faber 1978 o.p. A summary history of the country from ancient times to independence.

———. *West Africa: An Introduction to Its History*. Longman 1977 $14.95. ISBN 0-582-60005-0. A brief history, with the principal themes of West Africa's past; for secondary and university students.

———. *West Africa under Colonial Rule*. Northwestern U. Pr. 1968 o.p. A history for the general reader who is interested in an overall view of West Africa.

———. *West African Resistance: The Military Response to Colonial Occupation*. Holmes & Meier 1971 o.p. Details aspects of the African struggle against colonialism.

Curtin, Philip D. *The Atlantic Slave Trade: A Census*. U. of Wis. Pr. 1972 $12.95. ISBN 0-299-05404-7. An important work that has revised our understanding of the numbers of Africans transported to the New World.

Davidson, Basil. *The African Slave Trade*. Little rev. ed. 1988 $11.95. ISBN 0-316-17458-6. The best general description of the nature of the trans-Atlantic slave trade.

Delavignette, R. *Freedom and Authority in French West Africa*. Bks. Demand 1968 repr. of 1950 ed. $43.00. ISBN 0-8357-3026-3. Although dated, the best summary of the French colonial past and presence in West Africa.

Fage, J. D. *A History of West Africa: An Introductory Survey*. Ashgate Pub. Co. 1992 $55.95. ISBN 0-7512-0102-2. A general survey for the inexperienced reader; somewhat dated.

Flint, J. E. *Sir George Goldie and the Making of Nigeria*. OUP 1960 o.p. An excellent biography of Goldie, who was the single most important individual in the forging of the British presence in the Niger.

Forde, C. Daryll, and P. M. Kaberry, eds. *West African Kingdoms in the Nineteenth Century*. OUP 1967 o.p. Extremely useful in understanding the African background of modern African history.

Fyfe, Christopher. *A History of Sierra Leone*. Ashgate Pub. Co. 1992 $123.95. ISBN 0-7512-0086-7. The best comprehensive history of Sierra Leone; for the ambitious reader.

Gailey, Harry A., Jr. *A History of the Gambia*. Praeger 1965 o.p. The best overall history of the Gambia.

Gemery, Henry A., and Jan S. Hogendorn, eds. *The Uncommon Market: Essays in the Economic History of the Atlantic Slave Trade*. Academic Pr. 1979 o.p. A series of important essays on the economic controversies of the trans-Atlantic slave trade; for the informed reader.

Gray, R., and David Birmingham, eds. *Pre-Colonial African Trade*. OUP 1970 o.p. The standard work on precolonial long-distance trade before the coming of the Europeans, with particular emphasis on Central Africa.

Hargreaves, J. D. *The End of Colonial Rule in West Africa: Essays in Contemporary History*. B & N Imports 1979 o.p. A series of thoughtful essays for the specialist on decolonization in West Africa.

———. *Prelude to the Partition of West Africa*. St. Martin 1963 o.p. The standard account of the period immediately leading up to the partition of Africa. For the specialized reader. Should be read in conjunction with the author's volumes on the partition.

———. *West Africa, the Former French States*. P-H 1967 o.p. A companion work to that of Delavignette, giving a lucid account of the independent states of French West Africa.

———. *West Africa Partitioned*. 2 vols. Vol. 1 *The Loaded Pause, 1885–89*. Macmillan 1974 o.p. Vol. 2 *Elephants and the Grass*. U. of Wis. Pr. 1985 $35.00. ISBN 0-299-09990-3. A majesterial account of the partition of West Africa but limited in time; for the knowledgeable reader.

Herskovits, M. J. *Dahomey: An Ancient African Kingdom*. 2 vols. Northwestern U. Pr. 1967 o.p. The standard history of the king of Dahomey by a distinguished American anthropologist.

Hodgkin, Thomas. *Nigerian Perspectives*. 1975 o.p. An excellent anthology from sources up to 1900.

Hopkins, A. G. *An Economic History of West Africa*. *Economic History of the Modern World Ser.* Col. U. Pr. 1973 o.p. The first work by an economic historian to establish the basis of African economic history firmly in the precolonial period.

Kalck, Pierre. *Historical Dictionary of the Central African Republic*. Trans. by Thomas O'Toole. Scarecrow 1992 $32.50. ISBN 0-8108-2521-X. Identifies people, events, and places of significance. Includes maps and an historical overview.

Kanya-Forstner, A. S.. *The Conquest of the Western Sudan*. 1969 o.p. Covers a rather specialized subject, but important for understanding the success of French imperialism in West Africa.

Kirk-Greene, A., and Douglas Rimmer. *Nigeria since 1970: A Political and Economic Outline*. Holmes & Meier 1981 $29.95. ISBN 0-8419-0721-9. Covers two decades of Nigerian history.

Langer, W. L. *The Diplomacy of Imperialism*. Knopf rev. ed. 1951 o.p. A majesterial work that has lasted many years as the standard work on European imperialism in West Africa.

Last, Murray. *Sokoto Caliphate*. Humanities 1967 o.p. Explains the dynamics of the dominant precolonial state in northern Nigeria.

Levtzion, N. *Ancient Ghana and Mali*. Holmes & Meier repr. of 1974 ed. $29.50. ISBN 0-8419-0432-4. Very concise, authoritative study of the western part of the region.

Lewis, I. M., ed. *Nationalism in the Horn of Africa*. 1983 o.p. Essays on the principal issues in the Horn of Africa. Background reading for the general reader.

Liebenow, J. G. *The Evolution of Privlages*. Cornell Univ. Pr. 1969 o.p. The standard cultural history of Liberia. For the general reader and for scholarly reference.

MacGaffey, Wyatt. *Modern Kongo Prophets: Religion in a Plural Society*. Bks. Demand repr. of 1983 ed. $78.30. ISBN 0-685-23906-3. Studies the Kimbanguist movement and its setting.

————. *Religion and Society in Central Africa: The Bakongo of Lower Zaire*. U. Ch. Pr. 1986 $45.00. ISBN 0-226-50029-2. Second major study by the leading interpreter of Central African religion.

Markovitz, I. L. *Leopold Sedar Senghor and the Politics of Negritude*. Atheneum 1969 o.p. One of the best accounts of the life and times of the man who dominated the literary and political life of Senegal during the latter colonial period.

Newbury, C. *The Western Slave Coast and Its Rulers*. Greenwood 1983 repr. of 1961 ed. $43.75. ISBN 0-313-23967-3. A study of European trade and administration among the Yoruba and Adja-speaking peoples of southwestern Nigeria, southern Dahomey, and Togo.

Perham, Margery. *Lugard*. 2 vols. o.p. Comprehensive biography of one of Britain's most ambitious empire builders and the founder of Nigeria.

Rodney, Walter. *A History of the Upper Guinea Coast, 1545–1800*. Monthly Rev. repr. of 1970 ed. $10.00. ISBN 0-85345-546-5. Demonstrates the tragic effect of the vigorous slave trade on the Upper Guinea Coast during the period of Portuguese domination.

Sarno, Louis. *Song from the Forest: My Life among the Ba-Benjelle Pygmies*. HM 1993 $22.45. ISBN 0-395-61331-0. An encounter between an American and the pygmies in Central Africa.

Slade, Ruth. *King Leopold's Congo*. Greenwood 1974 repr. of 1962 ed. o.p. A study of Belgian policy during the decades before World War II.

Smith, Robert. *Kingdoms of the Yoruba*. U. of Wis. Pr. 1988 $39.75. ISBN 0-299-11604-2. An excellent survey of a country overshadowed by its neighboring giant, South Africa.

Vansina, Jan. *Kingdoms of the Savanna*. U. of Wis. Pr. 1968 $14.95. ISBN 0-299-03664-2. Central Africa during the period before European colonization. Deals with the emergence of states to the south of the Congo forest.

————. *Paths Through the Rainforest: Toward a History of Political Tradition in Equatorial Africa*. U. of Wis. Pr. 1990 o.p. Principally for scholars, this important work has laid to rest the long-standing controversy on how the Bantu managed to make their way through the great tropical rainforest of Zaire.

Wilks, Ivor. *Asante in the Nineteenth Century*. Cambridge U. Pr. 1989 $94.95. ISBN 0-521-20463-1. Majesterial work on the Asante kingdom of the modern-day Republic of Ghana. Long and detailed but would appeal to those interested in West Africa and Ghana in particular.

EAST AFRICA

Bennett, G. *Kenya: A Political History*. OUP 1963 o.p. A general survey of the history of Kenya during colonial rule but dated, with little on independent Kenya.

Coupland, Reginald. *East Africa and Its Invaders*. OUP 1983 o.p. Still the standard work on Asian and European imperialism in East Africa.

_____. *The Exploitation of East Africa*. St. Mut. 1967 $35.00. ISBN 0-89771-008-8. A study of one aspect of European colonialism.

Greenfield, Richard. *Ethiopia*. Praeger 1965 o.p. A standard and general account of the peoples and history of Ethiopia for the general reader.

Hancock, Graham, ed. *African Ark: People and Ancient Cultures of Ethiopia and the Horn of Africa*. Abrams 1990 $65.00. ISBN 0-8109-1902-8. Focuses on an area sheltering an astonishing variety of landscapes and human societies.

Huxley, Elspeth. *White Man's Country*. 1953 o.p. A well-written account of the life and times of Baron Hugh Cholmodeley Delamere and of pioneer life, politics, and government in Kenya.

Iliffe, John. *A Modern History of Tanganyika*. Cambridge U. Pr. 1979 $37.50. ISBN 0-521-29611-0. The most comprehensive history of Tanganyika (Tanzania) but long and detailed for the general reader.

Ingham, K. *The Making of Modern Uganda*. Greenwood repr. of 1958 ed. $38.50. ISBN 0-313-23114-1. A general survey that is dated and without much new information.

Kenyatta, Jomo. *Facing Mount Kenya*. Random 1962 $5.76. ISBN 0-394-70210-7. A classic exposition of the Kikuyu point of view.

Lewis, I. M. *The Modern History of Somaliland*. Weidenfeld & Nicolson 1965 o.p. Deals with both the Italian and the British territories. The standard work on Somalia by its leading British scholar.

Low, D. Anthony, and R. Cranford Pratt. *Buganda and British Overrule, 1900–1955*. OUP 1960 o.p. An important study of imperial history in Uganda, suited to an informed reader.

Marcus, Harold G. *The Life and Times of Menelik II, 1844–1913*. Clarendon Pr. 1975 o.p. A well-researched study of the most famous of all Ethiopian emperors.

Moorehead, Alan. *The Blue Nile*. HarpC 1962 o.p. Wonderfully researched and written history of Ethiopia and the Sudan centered around the theme of one of the major tributaries of the Nile.

Mungeam, G. H. *British Rule in Kenya*. Clarendon Pr. 1968 o.p. A dated but very readable survey for the general reader.

Nurse, Derek, and Thomas Spear. *The Swahili*. U. of Pa. Pr. 1985 $20.00. ISBN 0-8122-7928-X. A scholarly study that covers the period from 800 to 1500. Offers a revisionist view of the origin of the Swahili people and their culture.

Ogot, B. A., and J. A. Kieran. *History of the Southern Luo*. East African Publishing House 1967 o.p. A specialized monograph important for its clarification of the migration of the Luo people.

_____, eds. *Zamani: A Survey of East African History*. Humanities 1974 o.p. A series of essays designed for the general reader. Updates the more authoritative *Oxford History of East Africa* and presents East Africa's history in more readable form for classroom use.

Oliver, Roland. *Sir Harry Johnston and the Scramble for Africa*. Chatto and Windus 1959 o.p. A biography of one of Britain's leading imperialists, who was instrumental in the British acquisition of much of tropical Africa.

Oliver, Roland, and Gervase Mathew, eds. *History of East Africa, Vol. 1*. OUP 1962 o.p. The first volume in the authoritative *Oxford History of East Africa*. Out of date but still useful as a reference.

Oxford History of East Africa. 3 vols. Clarendon Pr. 1963–1976 o.p. The authoritative work, though not for the general reader except as a reference.

Parkin, David. *The Sacred Void: Spatial Images of Work and Ritual among the Giriama of Kenya*. Cambridge U. Pr. 1991 $54.50. ISBN 0-521-40466-5. Rich study into the religious ideas and practices of the Giriama society.

Powells, Randall L. *Horn and Crescent: Cultural Change and Traditional Islam on the East African Coast 800–1900*. Cambridge U. Pr. 1987. ISBN 0-521-323308-8. Examines a localized form of Islam unique to, and developed by, isolated East African coastal towns.

Rosberg, Carl G., and John Nottingham. *The Myth of Mau Mau*. Praeger 1966 o.p. The standard explanation for the movement in Kenya known as Mau Mau.

Sellassie, Sergew Hable. *Ancient and Medieval Ethiopian History*. 1972 o.p. Provides a useful survey of the main sources.

Strandes, Justus. *The Portuguese Period in East Africa*. East African Publishing House o.p. The definitive work of the history of the Portuguese in East Africa.

Tamrat, Taddesse, and Roland Oliver, eds. *The Cambridge History of Africa*. 1977. Vol. 3. ISBN 0-521-20981-1. Provides the best introduction to the medieval history of Ethiopia and the Horn of Africa.

SOUTHERN AFRICA

Birmingham, David, and Martin Birmingham. *Trade and Conflict in Angola*. OUP 1966 o.p.

Bley, Helmut. *South-West Africa under German Rule*. 1971. o.p. The definitive work on the history of German rule in what now is known as Namibia.

Clarence-Smith, Gervase. *The Third Portuguese Empire, 1825–1975: A Study in Economic Imperialism*. Manchester Univ. Pr. 1985 o.p. A detailed exposition of the later Portuguese empire in Africa.

Crocker, Chester A. *High Noon in Southern Africa: Making Peace in a Rough Neighborhood*. Norton 1993 $29.95. ISBN 0-393-03432-1. Memoir of a former assistant secretary of state's effort to bring peace to southern Africa.

Davenport, T. R. *South Africa: A Modern History*. U. of Toronto Pr. 1991 $60.00. ISBN 0-8020-5940-6. A standard text for the general reader on the history of South Africa.

de Kiewiet, C. W. *A History of South Africa: Social and Economic*. OUP 1941 o.p. Dated, but still the best general survey of the economic history of South Africa.

Denoon, Donald, and Balaam Nyeko. *Southern Africa since 1800*. Longman 1984 $18.95. ISBN 0-582-72707-3. A solid, generally sound survey.

Hammond, R. J. *Portugal and Africa, 1815–1910*. Stanford U. Pr. 1966 $47.50. ISBN 0-8047-0296-9. A competent but critical analysis of Portuguese rule during the nineteenth century.

Hancock, W. K. *Smuts*. 2 vols. Cambridge U. Pr. 1962 o.p. A great biography by a great historian.

Isaacman, Allen F. *Mozambique: The Africanization of a European Institution, the Zambezi Prazeros, 1750–1902*. U. of Wis. Pr. 1972 o.p. A detailed and informative study of the African Portuguese Prazeros in Mozambique. More for the specialist than for the general reader.

Isaacman, Allen F., and Barbara Isaacman. *Mozambique: From Colonialism to Revolution, 1900–82*. Westview 1983 o.p. The most comprehensive work on the later years of Portuguese rule in Mozambique leading to revolution and decolonization.

Levinson, Orde. *The African Dream: Visions of Love and Sorrow: The Art of John Huafangejo*. Thames Hudson 1993 $14.95. ISBN 0-500-27682-X. Introduction by Nelson Mandela.

Macmillan, W. M. *Bantu, Boer and Briton*. Greenwood 1979 repr. of 1936 ed. $35.00. ISBN 0-313-20906-5. The most thoughtful and descriptive study of the complex relationships and history of the South African peoples.

Mandela, Nelson. *Nelson Mandela Speeches 1990: Intensify the Struggle to Abolish Apartheid*. Pathfinder NY 1990 $5.00. ISBN 0-87348-545-5. Introduction by Greg McCartan.

Marcum, J. *The Angolan Revolution*. MIT Pr. 1969 $45.00. ISBN 0-262-13048-3. A scholarly and authoritative account of the history of Angola during the period of decolonization.

Mason, Philip. *The Birth of a Dilemma: Conflict and Settlement of Rhodesia.* Greenwood repr. of 1958 ed. o.p. Focuses on relations between the races during European conquest and settlement of Rhodesia.

Miller, Joseph. *Kings and Kinsmen: Early Mbundu States in Angola.* OUP 1976 o.p. A rather specialized monograph on early states in Angola before and during the Portuguese, but well researched and written.

Morris, D. R. *The Washing of the Spears.* S&S Trade 1986 $21.45. ISBN 0-671-63108-X. The story of the Zulu nation.

Omer-Cooper, J. D. *History of Southern Africa.* Heinemann Ed. 1987 $22.50. ISBN 0-435-0800-5. A history from a black, as well as white, perspective.

———. *The Zulu Aftermath.* Northwestern U. Pr. 1966 o.p. Still the standard text on the Mfecane, the crushing of African peoples by the Zulu during their diaspora of the 1820–30s.

Paton, Alan. *Hofmeyr.* OUP 1964 o.p. The majesterial biography of one of the great Afrikaner leaders in South Africa.

Rotberg, Robert I. *The Founder: Cecil Rhodes and the Pursuit of Power.* OUP 1990 $16.95. ISBN 0-19-506668-5. The definitive biography of the man whose ideology and wealth did so much to change the history of Southern Africa.

Shillington, K. *History of Southern Africa.* Longman 1988. ISBN 0-582-58521-X. A comprehensive, general survey for the general reader.

Sillery, Anthony. *Botswana: A Short Political History.* HarpC 1974 o.p. An excellent, clearly written summary.

Thompson, Leonard. *A History of South Africa.* Yale U. Pr. 1992 $15.00. ISBN 0-300-05135-2. The best single-volume history of South Africa. For the advanced student.

———. *The Unification of South Africa, 1902–10.* Clarendon Pr. 1960 o.p. The standard work on the complex history of the unification of South Africa following the Boer War.

Vail, Leroy, ed. *The Creation of Tribalism in Southern Africa.* U. CA Pr. 1988 $50.00. ISBN 0-520-06284-1. An important contribution to a complex and seminal issue, treated in depth and without jargon.

Vieira, Sergio, William G. Martin, and Immanuel Wallerstein. *How Fast the Wind: Southern Africa, 1975–2000.* Africa World 1992 $49.95. ISBN 0-86543-307-0. An impressive assembly of data detailing the internal relationships of the region and the impact of the global economy.

Walker, E. A. *The Great Trek.* A. C. Black 1934 o.p. Still stands as the standard history of the Great Trek for the general reader and scholar alike.

Who's Who of Southern Africa, 1991–92. Intl. Pubns. Serv. 1991 $130.00. ISBN 0-620-15974-X. A comprehensive directory of influential persons of Southern Africa.

Wilson, Monica, and Leonard M. Thompson, eds. *A History of South Africa to 1870.* Westview 1983 o.p. Originally published as Vol. 1 of *The Oxford History of South Africa.*

———. *The Oxford History of South Africa: South Africa, 1870–1966.* OUP 1971 o.p. An excellent, in-depth work that examines the history and peoples of South Africa from 1870–1966.

CHRONOLOGY OF AUTHORS

Davidson, Basil Risbridger. 1914–
Curtin, Philip de Armond. 1922–
Diop, Chiekh Anta. 1923–1986
Oliver, Roland Anthony. 1923–

Meillassoux, Claude. 1925–
Ajayi, Jacob Festus Ade. 1929–
Vansina, Jan. 1929–
Rodney, Walter. 1942–1980

AJAYI, JACOB FESTUS ADE. 1929–

Internationally recognized African historian, Jacob Festus Ade Ajayi, son of Chief E. Ade Ajayi, was born in Nigeria and educated at University College, Ibadan; University College, Leicester; and the University of London, from which he received his B.A. and Ph.D. Ajayi soon became one of the most influential historians of Africa through his numerous publications, academic administrative positions, and awards. A prolific writer, he published four major works on Africa during the early 1960s—*Milestones in Nigerian History* (1962); *A Thousand Years of West African History* (1964); *Yoruba Warfare in the Nineteenth Century*, which he coauthored with R. S. Smith (1964); and his best-known work, *Christian Missions in Nigeria: The Making of a New Elite* (1965). These were followed by other writings that appeared in both historical journals and books. Most were concerned with the history of West Africa, and many were produced in collaboration with Michael Crowder. Included among his literary credits is editorship of *Africa in the Nineteenth Century until the 1880's*, the seventh volume in the massive UNESCO *General History of Africa*.

Ajayi's contribution to African history was paralleled by a long academic and administrative career. He was professor of history at the University of Ibadan from 1963 until 1989, when he retired as Professor Emeritus. During that same period, he served in several major administrative posts at the university, including dean of the Faculty of Arts and assistant to the vice-chancellor. From 1972 to 1978, he also served as vice-chancellor at the University of Lagos. From 1984 to 1988, he was pro-chancellor at Ondo State University, Ado-Ekiti. Equally important has been Ajayi's contribution to African historical studies as a member and officer of numerous organizations, committees, and councils, including the United Nations University Council; the National Archives Committee of Nigeria; the National Antiquities Committee; the Executive Council of the International African Institute, London; and the Historical Society of Nigeria.

BOOKS BY AJAYI

Christian Missions in Nigeria: The Making of a New Elite. Northwestern U. Pr. 1965 o.p.
Covers the beginning of the movement to re-establish Christianity in Nigeria, from 1841–1891, when the success of missionary efforts was associated with the creation of a Christian-educated middle class.

History of West Africa. Longman 1985 o.p. Coauthored with Michael Crowder. Covers the vast changes that have taken place over the past two hundred years of West Africa's history, from the reform movements of the early 1800s to the emergence of independent states. The essential reference work for students of West African history.

Topics in West African History. Longman 1986 $18.95. ISBN 0-582-58504-X. Coauthored with Adu Boahen and Michael Tidy.

CURTIN, PHILIP DE ARMOND. 1922–

Born in Philadelphia, Pennsylvania, Philip de Armond Curtin was educated at Swarthmore College and at Harvard University, from which he received a Ph.D. in history in 1953. That same year he joined the Swarthmore faculty as an instructor and assistant professor. In 1956 he moved on to the University of Wisconsin at Madison, where he remained for 14 years. During that time he was chair of the Wisconsin University Program in Comparative World History, the Wisconsin African Studies Program, and, for five years, Melville J. Herskovits Professor. In 1975 he joined the department of history at Johns Hopkins University, where he is still in residence. At both Wisconsin and Johns Hopkins, he has been instrumental not only in assisting a generation of younger scholars but also in shaping the study of the African past by the many graduate students who came to study under his tutelage.

In addition to holding Guggenheim fellowships in 1966 and 1980 and being a senior fellow of the National Endowment for the Humanities, Curtin has taken a leadership role in various organizations, including the African Studies Association, the International Congress of Africanists, and the American Historical Association. He also has gained recognition for his influential books on African history, including *The Image of Africa* (1964), *Africa Remembered* (1967), and *The Atlantic Slave Trade: A Census* (1969). In the latter, he demonstrated that the number of Africans who reached the New World during the centuries of the trans-Atlantic slave trade had been highly exaggerated. This conclusion, which has had widespread influence in understanding the nature of the Atlantic slave trade and its impact both in Africa and in the Americas, has created controversy among those historians who continue to accept the traditional numbers of Africans transported and those who concur with Curtin's conclusions. Nonetheless, his conclusions have now become widely accepted by scholars who are concentrating on slavery in the Americas as well as by those who are concentrating on the nature of slavery in Africa.

BOOKS BY CURTIN

Africa and the West: Intellectual Responses to European Culture. U. of Wis. Pr. 1972 $35.00. ISBN 0-299-06121-3

African History (edited with others). Longman 1978 $23.95. ISBN 0-582-64663-4. A well-regarded text.

Africa Remembered: Narratives by West Africans from the Era of the Slave Trade. 1967. U. of Wis. Pr. 1968 $14.95. ISBN 0-299-04284-7

The Atlantic Slave Trade: A Census. 1969. U. of Wis. Pr. 1972 $12.95. ISBN 0-299-05404-1. Authoritative history of the trans-Atlantic slave trade.

Cross-Cultural Trade in World History. Studies in Comparative World History. Cambridge U. Pr. 1984 $13.95. ISBN 0-521-26931-8. Examination of trade and exchange across cultural lines; considers similarities and differences.

Death by Migration: Europe's Encounter with the Tropical World in the Nineteenth Century. Cambridge U. Pr. 1989 $47.95. ISBN 0-521-37162-7. A quantitative study of the high mortality rates among European soldiers caused by their encounters with the tropics during colonization.

Economic Change in Precolonial Africa: Senegambia in the Era of the Slave Trade. Bks. Demand repr. of 1975 ed. $114.50. ISBN 0-7837-1655-9

Economic Change in Precolonial Africa: Supplementary Evidence. Bks. Demand repr. of 1975 ed. $44.10. ISBN 0-7837-1656-7

The Image of Africa: British Ideas and Action, 1780–1850. 1967. Bks. Demand repr. of 1964 ed. $145.10. ISBN 0-8357-6772-8. An excellent history tracing British thought on West Africa from 1780 to 1850. Shows how early ideas were formed and integrated with Western thought.

The Rise and Fall of the Plantation Complex: Early Atlantic History. Cambridge Studies in Comparative World History. Cambridge U. Pr. 1990 $44.95. ISBN 0-521-37475-8. Essays on the role that slavery played in the development of the economic and political structures of South America.

Two Jamaicas: The Role of Ideas in a Tropical Colony, 1830–1865. Greenwood 1968 repr. of 1955 ed. $41.50. ISBN 0-8371-0055-0. An excellent examination of the social conditions in Jamaica from 1830 to 1865.

DAVIDSON, BASIL RISBRIDGER. 1914–

Basil Risbridger Davidson, who has done more than any other single writer or historian to remove the stereotype of "Darkest Africa" for the general public, began his journalistic career as a member of the editorial staff of *The Economist* in 1938. That assignment was interrupted by World War II, during which Davidson served in the British army with distinction, receiving the Military Cross, the U.S. Bronze Star, and the Jugoslav Zasluge za Narod for his service in the Balkans, North Africa, and Italy. After being demobilized from the service, Davidson returned to journalism, first as the diplomatic correspondent of *The Star* and then as the Paris correspondent of *The Times*. He went on to become chief foreign lead writer and then special correspondent for the *New Statesman*, special correspondent for the *Daily Herald*, and lead writer for the *Daily Mirror*. As a journalist he published numerous works of fiction—*Highway Forty* (1949), *Golden Horn* (1952), *The Rapids* (1955), *Lindy* (1958), *The Andrassy Affair* (1966)—and nonfiction—*Partisan Picture* (1946), *Germany from Potsdam to Partition* (1948), *Daybreak in China* (1953). Most of these were the outcome of his wartime experiences and subsequent career in journalism.

During these years Davidson took an increasing interest in the African past. This interest brought him to the University of Ghana as a visiting professor in 1964 and as professor in 1965. By then he had become completely engrossed in Africa, particularly in its relatively unknown history. Since that time he has devoted himself to the discovery of that history. He published his first work on Africa, *Report on Southern Africa*, in 1952. A host of other publications followed. His work has been characterized not only by his sympathy for Africa and for the Africans but also by the explication of the African past with a combination of the thoroughness of an investigative reporter and a style that has made his books popular with a large international audience. Although some of Davidson's earlier conclusions have been revised by later scholarly research, this in no way has diminished his influence on giving legitimacy to the history of Africa. His readable elucidation of African history has brought him many honors and awards over the years. His most effective exposition of the African past, however, may have been as author and narrator of a popular eight-part television documentary of Africa's history that aired in 1984. His most reflective thoughts on his research and writing on the African past may be found in his latest book, *The Black Man's Burden: Africa and the Curse of the Nation State* (1992).

BOOKS BY DAVIDSON

Africa in History. Macmillan rev. ed. 1992 $15.00. ISBN 0-02-042791-3. Traces the major themes of African historical development from ancient times to the present.

Africa in History: Themes and Outlines. 1968. Macmillan 1974 $11.95. ISBN 0-02-031260-1

African Civilization Revisited: From Antiquity to Modern Times. Africa World 1990 $39.95. ISBN 0-86543-123-X. Includes source materials from western, eastern, and southern Africa, with an emphasis on pre-nineteenth-century times.

The African Genius: An Introduction to Social and Cultural History. Little 1970 $10.95. ISBN 0-316-17432-7. A summary of the ideas, social systems, religions, moral values, magical beliefs, arts, and metaphysics of Africans. Emphasis is on tropical peoples and traces their cultural development from the past to present times.

Black Man's Burden: Africa and the Curse of the Nation State. Random 1992 $24.00. ISBN 0-8129-1998-X. Essays on the nature of the African experience in the postcolonial era. Argues that the instability of African nations in general can be attributed to the flawed model of the nation-state imposed by European colonizers.

Black Star: A View of the Life and Times of Kwame Nkrumah. 1974. Westview 1989 $35.00. ISBN 0-8133-0928-X. A timely biography of a renowned figure in postcolonial African history.

Can Africa Survive? Arguments Against Growth without Development. Little 1974 $9.95. ISBN 0-316-17434-3. Argues that, despite economic growth within Africa, there has not been real development. The author contends that development can only occur when existing economic and governing structures are replaced with new ones.

The Fortunate Isles. Africa World 1989 $11.95. ISBN 0-86543-121-3. A useful account of Cape Verde's history.

Ghana: An African Portrait. 1976. Aperture 1976 $30.00. ISBN 0-912334-65-7. A pictorial survey of Ghana, offering a complex overview of the diversity and beauty of the land.

A History of West Africa, 1000–1800. Ed. by F. A. Bush and J. F. Ade Ajayi. *The Growth of African Civilisation Ser.* Longman 1977 $17.95. ISBN 0-582-60340-4. A comprehensive historical survey of West Africa from 1000–1800. Includes an excellent bibliography and data tables.

Let Freedom Come: Africa in Modern History. Little 1979 $10.95. ISBN 0-316-17437-8. A history of modern twentieth-century Africa focusing on the development of African political ideas and practices.

Lost Cities of Africa. Little 1988 $10.95. ISBN 0-316-17431-9. A general description of the history of African life south of the Sahara. Includes a detailed bibliography.

Modern Africa: A Social and Political History. Longman 1989 $18.95. ISBN 0-582-01900-1. Presents the history of modern Africa in an all-African overview of events, trends, ideas, dates, and movements between 1914 and 1985.

No Fist Is Big Enough to Hide the Sky: The Liberation of Guinea Bissau and Cape Verde. *Africa Ser.* Humanities 1969 $27.50. ISBN 0-905762-93-2. The story of the revolutionary armed struggle of Guinea-Bissau and Cape Verde for liberation from Portugal.

The People's Cause: A History of Guerrillas in Africa. *Longman Studies in African History.* Bks. Demand $57.80. ISBN 0-8357-6590-3. Examines the tradition of guerrilla warfare in the pre-colonial period and analyzes the development of forms of struggle against European colonialism in parts of Africa during the twentieth century. Considers the strategy and tactics used by guerrilla groups.

Scenes from the Anti-Nazi War. Monthly Rev. 1981 $6.50. ISBN 0-85345-588-0

DIOP, CHIEKH ANTA. 1923–1986

One of Africa's most recognized historians, Chiekh Anta Diop was born in Dioubel, Senegal, and received his Litt. D. in France. Founder of two political parties in Senegal and of the first carbon-14 dating laboratory in Africa, he is remembered for his efforts to prove that black people played a much greater role in the history of civilization than is generally acknowledged. The World Festival of Negro Arts honored Diop as the black intellectual who had exercised the most fruitful influence in the twentieth century toward the discovery of the African past. Despite his many accomplishments and honors, he is best known for his historical writings, particularly *Nations Negroes et Culture* (*Black Nations and Culture*), published in 1955. The principal theme of this seminal work is that the ancient Egyptians, extremely advanced in science and culture, were black. Variations of this theme later appeared in *L'Unité Culturelle de l'Afrique Noire: Domaines du Patriarcat et du Matriarcat dans l'Antique Classique* (1959), a translation of which was published in 1962 as *The Cultural Unity of Negro Africa: The Domain of Patriarchy and of Matriarchy in Classical Antiquity.*

Books by Diop

The African Origin of Civilization: Myth or Reality. 1955. Ed. and trans. by Mercer Cook. L. Hill Bks. 1974 $11.95. ISBN 1-55652-072-7. An important book that argues that Western civilization finds its origins in Africa through Egypt, a recurrent theme in African historiography.

Black Africa: The Economic and Cultural Basis for a Federated State. L. Hill Bks. 1987 $7.95. ISBN 1-55652-061-1. A brief study of the economic conditions and the civilization of sub-Saharan Africa. Includes a bibliography.

Civilization or Barbarism: An Authentic Anthropology. Ed. by Harold J. Salemson and Marjolijn DeJager. Trans. by Yas-Lengi Meema Ngemi. 1991 $35.00. ISBN 1-55652-049-2. A summation and expansion of *Precolonial Black Africa* and *The African Origin of Civilization*. Attempts to prove the primacy of African culture by offering evidence that ancient Egypt was a black society.

The Cultural Unity of Black Africa. 1959. Third World 1987 $14.95. ISBN 0-88378-049-6. Examines the role and relationships between men and women in Africa in classical antiquity.

Precolonial Black Africa. Trans. by Harold J. Salemson. L. Hill Bks. 1987 $16.95. ISBN 1-55652-088-3. A comparative study of the political and social systems of Europe and black Africa, from antiquity to the formation of modern states.

MEILLASSOUX, CLAUDE. 1925–

Historical anthropologist Claude Meillassoux was born in Roubaix, France, and educated in part at the Institute of Political Studies in Paris. In addition to his diploma from the institute, he earned a B.A. from the Faculty of Law and Economics in Paris, an M.A. from the University of Michigan, and a Ph.D. from the University of Paris. Before embarking upon a scholarly career, he worked in a factory, in advertising, and as an interpreter. In 1957 he became an assistant in the Practical School of Higher Studies in Paris, a position he held until 1964. At that point in time, he became a research fellow at the National Center of Scientific Research, also in Paris. Recognized for his firmly radical political convictions, Meillassoux is regarded as one of the most influential historical anthropologists and is noted for his contributions toward understanding the complex institution of slavery within Africa itself. He is best known for his theory of slavery in Africa, as expressed in his 1975 work, *L'Esclavage en Afrique Pré-coloniale* (*Slavery in Pre-colonial Africa*). Meillassoux's recent research, particularly *The Anthropology of Slavery: The Womb of Iron and Gold* (1991), has had an enormous influence on discerning a theory of slavery in Africa.

BOOKS BY MEILLASSOUX

The Anthropology of Slavery: The Womb of Iron and Gold. U. Ch. Pr. 1991 $49.95. ISBN 0-226-51911-2. A neo-Marxist philosophical analysis of slavery.

Maidens, Meal, and Money. Cambridge U. Pr. 1981 $19.95. ISBN 0-521-29708-7

Urbanization of an African Community. AMS Pr. 1988 repr. of 1968 ed. $30.00. ISBN 0-404-62943-1

OLIVER, ROLAND ANTHONY. 1923–

Born in Srinagar, Kashmir, the son of a British army major and his wife, Roland Anthony Oliver has been recognized as the leading British historian of Africa. Educated at Stowe and King's College, Cambridge University, he served in the Foreign Office from 1942 to 1945, at which time he left to complete his graduate studies at Cambridge on an R. V. Smith research studentship. In 1948 he became lecturer at the University of London School of Oriental and African Studies, a position he held until 1958, when he became reader in African History. In 1964 he was appointed the first professor of the history of Africa at the University of London, where he remained until his retirement in 1986.

Oliver's long tenure at the University of London and his numerous publications made him one of the leading academic protagonists for the study of the African past both in the United Kingdom and internationally. A whole generation of American, European, and African students passed through the School of Oriental and African Studies at the University of London under his tutelage, strongly influenced by him. Professionally very active and the principal academic spokesman for the study of African history, he received numerous honors, including Francqui professor at the University of Brussels and visiting professor at Northwestern and Harvard universities. Among his many publications is *A Short History of Africa*, which he coauthored with J. D. Fage in 1962 and which has probably been the most widely used text in schools and universities. His most massive contribution, however, was the general editorship of the eight-volume *Cambridge History of Africa* (1975–86). He shared the editorship with J. D. Fage, with whom he also edited for many years *The Journal of African History*, the leading journal in the field and by far the most influential in shaping African historiography.

BOOKS BY OLIVER

Africa in the Iron Age. (coauthored with Brian M. Fagan). Cambridge U. Pr. 1975 $54.95. ISBN 0-521-20598-0. An interesting account of the period of African history from 500 B.C. to A.D. 1400, referred to today as the Iron Age.

The African Experience. 1991. HarpC 1992 $23.00. ISBN 0-06-435850-X. Oliver's seminal work. A reflective work that discusses a set of themes chosen for their significance for the continent as a whole. Arranged chronologically, the work reflects the teaching and research of the author over his lifetime.

The African Middle Ages, Fourteen Hundred to Eighteen Hundred. (coauthored with A. E. Atmore). Cambridge U. Pr. 1981 $16.95. ISBN 0-521-29894-6. Compact chronicle of the history of Africa from 1400–1800; the dominant sources of evidence examined are literary and traditional.

A Short History of Africa. (coauthored with J. D. Fage). Facts on File 1989 $29.95. ISBN 0-8160-2089-2. Draws on the full range of literature about Africa as well as archaeological findings, oral traditions, language relationships, and societal institutions.

RODNEY, WALTER. 1942–1980

Walter Rodney was born in British Guiana (now Guyana) and educated in England. He taught African history at the University College of the West Indies at Mona, Jamaica, until 1968, when his Marxist views were deemed subversive and he was forced to leave. He spent the next four years teaching at the University of Dar es Salaam, Tanzania. He then returned to his home in Guyana as chair of the department of history at the University of Guyana. When his position was revoked under pressure from the government, he assumed leadership of the Working People's Alliance. His leadership was cut short by a car-bomb explosion that took his life on June 13, 1980. By then Rodney had achieved an international reputation, not only for his scholarship, but also for his vigorous advocacy for the rights of African Americans throughout the world.

Rodney's Marxist writings denounce capitalism and imperialism for the destruction they brought upon African American societies. His expulsion from Jamaica had resulted from his 1967 work, *West Africa and the Atlantic Slave Trade* and the series of lectures he published in 1969 as *The Grounding with My Brothers*. In 1970 he published *A History of the Upper Guinea Coast, 1545–1800*, in which he raised new questions about the nature of African societies and their impact on the Atlantic slave trade. Despite Rodney's critics, the book was clearly an important contribution to the history of Africa. His most influential work, however, was *How Europe Underdeveloped Africa* (1972). Written from an African perspective, this Marxist interpretation of colonialism and imperialism in Africa has insured Rodney's place in the writing of the African past.

BOOKS BY RODNEY

A History of the Guyanese Working People 1881–1905. Johns Hopkins 1981 $42.00. ISBN 0-8018-2428-1

A History of the Upper Guinea Coast 1545–1800. 1970. Monthly Rev. repr. of 1980 ed. $10.00. ISBN 0-85345-546-5. The historiography of the Upper Guinea coast, focusing on the period from 1545–1800, when the society of the region was still free of profound European influence.

How Europe Underdeveloped Africa. 1972. Howard U. Pr. 1982 $9.95. ISBN 0-88258-096-5. Rodney blames Africa's underdevelopment on European colonialism and imperialism, the exploitation of which can only be dissolved by a break with the international capitalist system.

VANSINA, JAN. 1929–

Belgium-born and educated, Jan Vansina is known internationally for his many contributions to social anthropology and to African history. Currently a professor at the University of Wisconsin at Madison, he received his Ph.D. in modern history from the University of Leuven in 1957, during which time he was a research scholar at the International Center for African Research in Belgium. That same year he became director of the center, a position he held for the next several years. After serving for some time as professor of history and anthropology, he joined the University of Wisconsin at Madison as the Vilas Research Professor. He has held concurrent positions as visiting lecturer at the University of Lovanium, Leopoldville, and at Northwestern University and as visiting professor and then professor at the University of Lovanium, Kinshasha. Vansina is one of the foremost pioneers in the development of techniques and methods in the history of culture that employ the use of oral traditions in the search for the African past. Although he was not the first scholar to use oral traditions in African history, he was the first scholar to evolve a rational methodology—one that has become the standard adopted by Africanists in many disciplines for using oral data. The evolution of Vansina's rational methods for the most effective use of oral traditions is reflected in his many publications, the most recent of which is *Paths in the Rainforest: Towards a History of Political Tradition in Equatorial Africa* (1990). In this work he has successfully resolved a question that has long perplexed historians of Africa—how the Bantu peoples passed from their origins in the Niger-Benue region through the great tropical rainforests of Zaire to the savanna lands to the south, where they proliferated throughout eastern, central, and southern Africa.

BOOKS BY VANSINA

Art History in Africa. Longman 1984 $18.95. ISBN 0-582-64368-6

The Children of Woot: A History of the Kuba Peoples. U. of Wis. Pr. 1978 $35.00. ISBN 0-299-07490-0. A fascinating history of the Kuba culture of Zaire; examines their society, neighbors, kingdoms, major markets, and old trade routes to the West.

Habitat, Economy, and Society in the Central African Rainforests. Berg Pubs. 1992 $6.50. ISBN 0-85496-733-8

L'Evolution du Royaume Rwanda des Origines a 1900. Academie Royale des Sciences d'Outre-Mer, Memoires Ser.: Vol. 26, No. 2. Johnson Repr. repr. of 1962 ed. $12.00. ISBN 0-384-63959-3

Kingdoms of the Savanna. U. of Wis. Pr. 1968 $14.95. ISBN 0-299-3664-2. A political history of Central Africa, limited to the savannas north of the Zambesi and south of the equatorial forest. Traces the development of the major states in the area and examines how they influenced surrounding peoples.

Oral Tradition as History. 1961. U. of Wis. Pr. 1985 $12.95. ISBN 0-299-10214-9. Examines the various forms of oral traditions within their historical context.

Paths in the Rainforests: Towards a History of Political Tradition in Equatorial Africa. U. of Wis. Pr. 1990 $40.00. ISBN 0-299-12570-X. A brilliant introduction to 5,000 years of African equatorial history.

The Tio Kingdom of the Middle Congo, 1880–1892. Bks. Demand repr. of 1973 ed. $158.10. ISBN 0-8357-6976-3. A comprehensive chronicle of the Eastern Batéké, or Tio society, of the Middle Congo in Africa from 1880–1892.

CHAPTER 13

Middle Eastern History

Mounir A. Farah

> History is a science of fine principles, manifold uses, and noble purpose. It
> informs us about the people, the characters of nations, the lives of prophets,
> the kingdoms and policies of kings. . . . [Historians] require many sources
> and varied knowledge; they also require keen judgment and careful scrutiny
> to lead them to the truth.
>
> —IBN KHALDUN, *al-Muqaddimah*

Historians intensely argue and at times disagree over the meaning and
interpretation of many key events and developments in the history of the Middle
East—that area of north Africa and southwest Asia extending from Libya on the
west to Afghanistan on the east. They are in agreement, however, regarding the
importance and impact on the world of Middle Eastern history and civilization.
The effects of this civilization can be seen clearly in South Asia, Southeast Asia,
Central Asia, Africa, and Europe, particularly in southeastern Europe and
Iberia. From the 700s through the 1300s, the Islamic states, which were rooted
in the Middle East, dominated vast areas of the world, from the borders of China
in the east to the Atlantic Coast in the west.

Most historians divide Middle Eastern history into four major periods. The
first, the Ancient Period, extends from the beginnings of civilization to A.D. 622
and encompasses such kingdoms and empires as the ancient Egyptians, the
Babylonians, the Hittites, the Israelites, the Persians, and the Greek, Roman,
and Byzantine provinces in the Middle East. The second, the Medieval Period,
extends from 622 to 1453 and is the period during which the Arabs, under the
banner of Islam, established their vast empire and Islamic civilization and
Arabic and Persian cultures reached their zenith. The year 622, when
MUHAMMAD (see Vol. 4) and a number of his followers migrated from Makkah
(Mecca) to take refuge in Madinah (Medina), marks the beginning of the Islamic
calendar. The year 1453 marks the fall of Constantinople and the beginning of
the Ottoman Empire, which lasted through World War I.

The third period of Middle Eastern history, the Early Modern Period, extends
from 1453 to 1918, the year World War I ended. Until the seventeenth century
the Ottoman Empire, which controlled the eastern Mediterranean and much of
North Africa and the Balkans, was powerful and nearly invincible. Two other
Islamic empires—those of the Safavids of Persia and the Moguls of India—also
reached their height during the seventeenth century. In the eighteenth and
nineteenth centuries, the Islamic empires declined as parts of the Middle East
came under European control. The fourth major period, the Contemporary
Period, began in 1918 and extends to the present. The history of this period
revolves around three main themes—the struggle for independence from
colonial rule, the Arab-Israeli conflict that has periodically erupted into full-
scale war, and the process of economic and social development.

Early Middle East historians wrote chronicles of events and the exploits of famous rulers, often running into long and detailed volumes, such as AL-TABARI'S *Ta'rikh ar-Rusul wa-al-Muluk* (History of the Prophets and the Kings). Later, another historian, IBN KHALDUN, made the writing of history into an organized discipline, relating events to social and economic factors. Many historians who followed him were influenced by his work and organized their own accounts of events in a true historical fashion. Still later, during the late nineteenth and early twentieth centuries, European historians assumed the leadership in writing about the history of the Middle East. Although their writings contributed a good deal to the West's understanding and appreciation of Islamic civilization, in recent years they have come under much criticism by Middle East historians for presenting Islamic civilization from a Western perspective, marked by all the prejudices that the West held against Islam for many centuries.

Until the twentieth century, American interest in Middle Eastern history was generally confined to the Ancient Period, for two reasons. The first was American fascination with pharaonic Egypt after the ancient hieroglyphic language was deciphered in the early 1800s; and the second was the intense interest by Christian denominations in the United States, particularly the Congregationalists and Presbyterians, in the Middle East as the cradle of Christianity. The first American missionaries arrived in the Middle East in 1820 with the intent of converting its populations before the Second Coming of Christ, which they believed was imminent. Nevertheless, American writing about the region continued to focus on the Ancient Period.

During World War I the United States did not declare war on Turkey, although Turkey was an ally of Germany but, instead, supported relief work in the region. After the war some American historians wrote about the Medieval Period of Middle Eastern history, and a few universities—most notably Harvard, Princeton, and the universities of Chicago and Michigan—expanded their Middle Eastern studies (often called "Oriental" or "Near Eastern" studies) to the Early Modern Period. The 1960s saw a rapid growth in these centers and the development of several others, in part because of the availability of federal funds for area studies.

GENERAL REFERENCE WORKS AND SURVEYS

Adams, Michael. ed. *The Middle East*. Facts on File 1987 $45.00. ISBN 0-8160-1268-7. Overview by 41 scholars, giving basic information on each country (e.g., statistics, essays, etc.); includes subject index.

Antonius, George. *The Arab Awakening: The Story of the Arab National Movement*. Intl. Bk. Ctr. 1969 $24.95. ISBN 0-86685-000-7. Discusses the rise of Arab nationalism during World War I.

Ashtor, Eliyahu. *The Medieval Near East: Social and Economic History*. S. Mut. 1978 o.p. Some of the author's articles written between 1949 and 1977 are reprinted here in the original English, French, or Italian.

Ayalon, Ami, ed. *Middle East Contemporary Survey*. Westview 1992 $99.00. ISBN 0-8133-1449-6

Bailey, Betty J. *From the Beginning: Resources and Guide for the Middle East Study*. Friendship Pr. 1992 $6.95. ISBN 0-377-00241-0

Barakat, Halim. *The Arab World: Society, Culture, and State*. U. CA Pr. 1993. ISBN 0-520-07907-8. Interesting sociopolitical treatise on the Arab world.

Beaumont, Peter, and others. *The Middle East: A Geographical Study*. Beekman Pubs. 1988 $60.95. ISBN 0-8464-1510-0. A very detailed study of area geography, climate, and demographics, with country-specific details.

Berger, Morroe, ed. *The Arab World Today*. Hippocrene Bks. 1980 repr. of 1962 ed. o.p. Discusses economic and political conditions in various Arab states and examines their governments as of the early 1960s.

———. *The New Metropolis in the Arab World*. Hippocrene Bks. 1973 $20.00. ISBN 0-374-90609-2. Surveys various cities and towns in the Arab nations and advocates planned, humane urbanization in the Middle East.

Bickerton, Ian J., and Carla L. Klausner. *A Concise History of the Arab-Israeli Conflict*. P-H 1990 $19.93. ISBN 0-13-173634-5. Well documented overview of the Arab-Israeli conflict.

Brown, L. Carl, ed. *From Medina to Metropolis: Heritage and Change in the Near Eastern City*. Darwin Pr. 1973 $24.95. ISBN 0-87850-006-5. A collection of papers presented at the "Urban Planning and Urban Prospects in the Near East and North Africa" conference at Princeton in 1970.

Bulliet, Richard, ed. *Encyclopedia of the Modern Middle East*. 4 vols. Macmillan 1994 $70.00. ISBN 0-02-897061-6. Major, comprehensive resource on Middle Eastern region.

Carter, Jimmy. *The Blood of Abraham: Insights into the Middle East*. HM 1985 o.p. The former U.S. president's work on Arabia and the Levant, arranged by country, with chronologies, maps, and official instruments.

Clarke, J.I., and W.B. Fisher. *Populations of the Middle East and North Africa: A Geographical Approach*. Holmes & Meier 1972 o.p. Scholarly articles on Middle East demographics.

Congressional Quarterly, Inc. *Middle East: U.S. Policy, Israel, Oil and the Arabs*. Congr. Quarterly 7th ed. 1991 $25.95 ISBN 0-87187-630-2. A short encyclopedia-style work arranged by topic and country, with an emphasis on politics.

Cook, M.A., ed. *Studies in the Economic History of the Middle East: From the Rise of Islam to the Present Day*. OUP 1970 o.p.

Costello, V.F. *Urbanization in the Middle East*. Urbanization in Developing Countries Ser. Cambridge Pr. 1977 o.p. Short but dense consideration of the subject.

Curtis, Michael, ed. *The Middle East: A Reader*. Transaction Pubs. 1986 $34.95. ISBN 0-88738-101-4. A collection of essays from *The Middle East Review* covering a range of topics.

Davis, E. *Challenging Colonialism: Bank Misr and Egyptian Industrialization, 1920–1941*. Princeton U. Pr. 1982 $37.50. ISBN 0-691-07640-5. Brief examination of Egyptian industrial development up to World War II.

Eickelman, Dale P. *The Middle East*. P-H 1989. ISBN 0-13-582289-0

Fallon, N. *Middle East Oil Money and Its Future Expenditure*. Taylor & Francis 1976 o.p. In-depth examination of Middle East oil profits and how they were used in the mid-1970s.

Freedman, Robert O., ed. *The Middle East since Camp David*. Westview 1984 o.p. Collection of essays written from different perspectives on the Middle East political situation.

———. *Soviet Policy toward the Middle East since 1970*. Praeger 1978 o.p. A detailed account of Soviet policy in the Middle East from Nasser's death up to Sadat's visit to Israel.

Gardner, J. Anthony. *The Iraq-Iran War: A Bibliography*. GK Hall 1989 $56.00. ISBN 0-8161-8997-8. More than 500 annotated citations to books, articles, films, etc., arranged topically under broad headings, focusing on the 1980–1987 conflict.

Glassman, Jon D. *Arms for Arabs: The Soviet Union and War in the Middle East*. Johns Hopkins 1976 $35.00. ISBN 0-8018-1747-1. Descriptive analysis of Israeli-Arab conflicts through the 1973 war with concentration on the role played by the Soviet Union in arming Middle East nations, Egypt in particular.

Glubb, John Bagot. *A Short History of the Arab People*. Madison Bks. UPA 1970 $25.00. ISBN 0-8128-1351-0.

Golan, Galia. *Yom Kippur and After. Soviet and East European Studies.* Cambridge U. Pr.
1977 o.p. An assessment of the impact of the Yom Kippur War on Soviet Middle East
policy.

Gresh, Alain, and Dominique Vidal. *An A–Z of the Middle East.* Trans. by Bob Cumming.
Humanities 1990 $49.95. ISBN 0-86232-880-2. A short encyclopedia in dictionary
form; appendix contains official instruments and documents.

Haddad, George M. *Revolutions and Military Rule in the Middle East: Egypt, Sudan,
Yemen.* Speller $14.95. ISBN 0-8315-0061-1. A very detailed account of each
country's modern political history.

Harrow, Leonard. *From the Lands of Sultan and Shah.* Interlink Pub. 1990 $34.95. ISBN
0-905906-60-8

Hentsch, Thierry. *Imagining the Middle East.* Paul & Co. Pubs. 1992 $38.95. ISBN 1-
895431-13-1

Hershlag, Z.Y. *Introduction to the Modern Economic History of the Middle East.*
Humanities 1980 repr. of 1964 ed. o.p. Detailed examination of Middle East economy
until World War I and of economic and social changes in the interwar period.

Herzog, Chaim. *The Arab-Israeli Wars.* Random 1983 $15.00. ISBN 0-394-71746-5.
Analysis of the Arab-Israeli conflict by a former president of Israel.

Hitti, Philip K. *History of the Arabs.* St. Martin 1970 $32.00. ISBN 0-312-37520-4. Survey
of the civilizations of Arabia and their history.

———. *Islam and the West: A Historical Cultural Survey.* Krieger 1979 $9.50. ISBN 0-
88275-787-3. Lectures delivered in 1967 on Islamic religion, state, and culture.

———. *A Short History of the Near East.* Van Nos. Reinhold 1966 o.p. The best survey
available for the general reader.

Hourani, Albert. *Arabic Thought in the Liberal Age, 1798–1939.* Cambridge U. Pr. 1983
$21.95. ISBN 0-54-27423-0. A good short survey of Arab thought during this period.

———. *A History of the Arab Peoples.* Warner Bks. 1992 $14.99. ISBN 0-446-39392-4.
Comprehensive study of Arab civilization and culture.

Irani, George. *The Papacy and the Middle East.* U. of Notre Dame Pr. 1986 $10.95. ISBN
0-268-01582-1. Deals with Vatican diplomacy in the modern Middle East.

Issawi, Charles, ed. *The Economic History of the Middle East: A Book of Readings. Midway
Repr. Ser.* U. Ch. Pr. 1976 o.p. Prints primary sources on ninteenth-century Middle
East economy and development.

———. *An Economic History of the Middle East and North Africa. Economic History of the
Modern World Ser.* Col. U. Pr. 1984 $17.50. ISBN 0-231-08377-7. From the author's
lectures at Columbia and Princeton; short and specific coverage.

Jacoby, Neil H. *Multinational Oil: A Study in Industrial Dynamics. Studies of the Modern
Corporation Ser.* Macmillan 1974 $22.95. ISBN 0-02-915990-3. A detailed examina-
tion of economic aspects of the international oil market.

Karpat, Kemal H., ed. *Political and Social Thought in the Contemporary Middle East.*
Greenwood 1982 $49.95. ISBN 0-275-90834-8. A comprehensive collection of works
by Middle East scholars.

Khouri, Fred J. *The Arab-Israeli Dilemma.* Syracuse U. Pr. 1976 $17.95. ISBN 0-8156-
2340-2. A historian looks at the troubled relationship between Muslims and Jews in
the Middle East since 1917.

Landen, Robert G. *The Emergence of the Modern Middle East: Selected Readings.* Van
Nos. Reinhold 1970 o.p. Primary-source documents on modernization in the Middle
East; useful for students.

Lapidus, Ira M. *A History of Islamic Societies.* Cambridge U. Pr. 1988 $64.95. ISBN 0-521-
22552-3. A study of Arab-Islamic civilization from the 600s to the 1980s.

Lenczowski, George. *The Middle East in World Affairs.* Cornell Univ. Pr. 1980 $49.95.
ISBN 0-8014-1273-0. Comprehensive text on Middle East politics from 1914 to the
late 1970s.

Lerner, Daniel. *The Passing of Traditional Society.* Free Pr. 1964 o.p. A study of the
industrial development of the Middle East that includes attitude surveys done in six
countries.

Levy, Reuben. *A Baghdad Chronicle. Studies in Islamic History.* Porcupine Pr. 1978 repr. of 1929 ed. o.p. A history of the city that is comprehensive but a bit dated.

Lippman, Thomas W. *Islam: Politics and Religion in the Muslim World.* Foreign Policy 1982 $40.00. ISBN 0-87124-075-0

Mack, John E. *A Prince of Our Disorder: The Life of T.E. Lawrence.* Little 1978 $15.00. ISBN 0-316-54232-6. Uses the life story of the British soldier-adventurer T.E. Lawrence to examine the role of the British in the Middle East during World War I.

Mansfield, Peter. *The Middle East: A Political and Economic Survey.* OUP 1980 o.p. A fairly detailed area survey arranged by country.

———. *The Ottoman Empire and Its Successors.* St. Martin 1973 $29.25. ISBN 0-312-59010-5

Middle East and North Africa. Omnigraphics Inc. 1992 $265.00. ISBN 1-55888-782-2. The 38th edition of an excellent resource for officials; includes a general survey and information on individual countries and regional organizations.

Middle East Organizations in Washington, D.C. Middle East Institute 1989 $9.00. ISBN 0-916808-34-3. Directory of 135 services, agencies, research centers, etc.

Mitchell, Richard P. *An Annotated Bibliography on the Modern History of the Near East.* Ctr. for Northeast and North African Studies 1980 o.p. A short annotated bibliography, mostly for educators.

Mostyn, Trevor, and Albert Hourani, eds. *The Cambridge Encyclopedia of the Middle East.* Cambridge U. Pr. 1988 $55.00 ISBN 0-521-32190-5. Short, dense encyclopedia arranged by peoples, histories, cultures, countries, foreign policies, and economics; with maps.

Otto-Dorn, Katharina. *The Art and Architecture of the Islamic World.* U. CA Pr. 1990 $65.00. ISBN 0-520-04325-1

Owen, Roger. *Middle East in the World Economy, 1800–1914.* Routledge Chapman & Hall 1987 $25.00. ISBN 0-416-03272-9

Perry, Glenn E. *The Middle East: Fourteen Islamic Centuries.* P-H 1991 $20.00. ISBN 0-13-584459-2. A good, short college survey with extensive bibliography.

Pfeiffer, Charles C., and Howard F. Vos. *The Wycliffe Historical Geography of the Bible Lands.* Moody 1967 o.p.

Polk, William R. *The Arab World (The United States and the Arab World). Amer. Foreign Policy Lib.* HUP 1991 $14.95. ISBN 0-674-04320-0. Analysis of the history of Arab-U.S. relations.

———. *The Arab World Today.* HUP 1991 $14.95. ISBN 0-674-04320-0. A lengthy general survey text.

Rosof, Patricia J., and others. *The Middle East and North Africa: Medieval and Modern History.* Haworth Pr. 1983 $32.95. ISBN 0-917724-65-3

Said, Edward W. *Orientalism.* Random 1979 $12.00. ISBN 0-394-74067-X. A modern classic detailing the history of Western attitudes toward the East.

Shavit, David. *The United States in the Middle East: A Historical Dictionary.* Greenwood 1988 $75.00. ISBN 0-313-25341-2. One-paragraph entries provide information about people, institutions, and events, followed by bibliographic references.

Sherbiny, Nalem A. *Arab Oil: Impact on Arab Countries and Global Implications.* Ed. by Mark A. Tessler. Greenwood 1976 $49.95. ISBN 0-275-90251-X. Analysis of how the petroleum industry affects Arab and world economics with a discussion of Middle East business and trade practices.

Shwadran, Benjamin. *The Middle East, Oil, and the Great Powers.* Transaction Pubs. 1973 $19.95. ISBN 0-87855-157-3. Detailed and comprehensive study of oil's impact on different areas of the Middle East.

Spencer, William. *Global Studies: Middle East.* Dushkin Pub. 1992 $12.95. ISBN 1-56134-074-X

Tibi, Bassam. *Conflict and War in the Middle East, 1967–1991.* St. Martin 1992 $39.95. ISBN 0-312-08405-6. Refreshing analysis of the major wars of the Middle East since 1967. Informative and theoretically sophisticated.

Tilman, Seth P. *The United States and the Middle East.* Ind. U. Pr. 1982 $35.00. ISBN 0-253-36172-9. Examines the aims of American diplomacy in the Middle East.

Vatikiotis, P.J. *Conflict in the Middle East*. Allen & Unwin 1971 o.p. A broad survey of the
   political situation in the Middle East in the early 1970s.
Vita, Finzi Claudio. *Mediterranean Valleys: Geological Change in Historical Times*.
   Cambridge U. Pr. 1969 o.p. A short but detailed examination of the impact of changes
   in Mediterranean streams upon their valleys.
Westrute, Bruce C. *The Arab Bureau: British Policy in the Middle East, 1916–1920*. Pa. St.
   U. Pr. 1992 $35.00. ISBN 0-271-00794-X. Reassessment of the Arab Bureau's
   personnel and accomplishments in the light of recently revealed secret Foreign
   Office documents, personal papers, and Bureau reports.
Wiet, Gaston. *Baghdad: Metropolis of the Abbasid Caliphate*. Trans. by Seymour Feiler.
   Bks. Demand repr. of 1971 ed. $36.00. ISBN 0-8357-9720-1. A brief history of the city.
Young, Hubert W. *The Independent Arab*. AMS Pr. repr. of 1933 ed. $35.00. ISBN 0-404-
   56335-X. Historical survey of Iran and the Arabian Peninsula during World War I
   that makes use of personal narratives of British citizens living in the Middle East.

ISRAEL AND JEWISH HISTORY

The ancient Hebrews came to the land of Canaan (which corresponds vaguely
to the area later called Palestine) during the early part of the second millennium
B.C. and founded the united monarchy of Israel. After the death of King
Solomon in the late tenth century, the kingdom split into a northern half
(Israel) and a southern half (Judah). The Assyrians conquered the north in the
eighth century B.C. and the Babylonians conquered the south and destroyed the
Temple in Jerusalem during the sixth century, capturing many of Judah's elite
and taking them into exile in Babylon. After the fall of Babylon to the Persians,
the descendants of these captives, now called Jews, were allowed to return to
Jerusalem, and many of them did so. Eventually the land came under Greek,
then Roman, rule. After a Jewish revolt against Roman rule failed in A.D. 69, the
Romans destroyed what remained of Jewish self-government and dispersed
much of the population.

For almost 2,000 years, the Jews of the Diaspora lived in numerous places
around the world, some of them converting to Christianity or Islam. Those who
remained loyal to Judaism often had to endure discrimination and persecution
in medieval and modern Europe, which culminated in the Holocaust, the
murder of 6 million Jews that took place under Nazi rule during the early 1940s.

The movement to establish a national state for the Jews, which began in the
nineteenth century, grew in strength after World War II. Palestine, the home of
the ancient Hebrew state, was selected as the site of that state and, with the
permission of the British government, which then ruled Palestine under an
international mandate, hundreds of thousands of Jews came to Palestine
seeking a refuge and a home. By 1947 nearly one-third of the population of
Palestine consisted of Jews who had recently migrated and others who had lived
there for generations. These settlers set about improving the land with irrigation
works and other projects and modernizing their ancient homeland.

When the British withdrew in 1948, the United Nations partitioned Palestine
between Jews and Muslim and Christian Palestinians, and Jews declared the
establishment of the State of Israel. Because non-Jewish Palestinians opposed
an exclusively Jewish state in Palestine, conflict between them and the Jewish
population broke out; as a result, many Palestinians became refugees. Arab
armies from neighboring states declared war on Israel, and the first of five wars
between Israel and its Arab neighbors broke out. In the third war, in 1967,
Israel acquired Arab territories that are greater in size than the original State of

Israel. About 93 percent of the inhabitants of these territories are Muslim and Christian Palestinians who continue to resist Israeli occupation.

Since its establishment, Israel has faced major challenges, the foremost of which has been concluding peace agreements with its Arab neighbors. In 1979 the Israeli and Egyptian governments signed a peace treaty obligating Israel to return the Sinai, which it had occupied since 1967, to Egypt. Since 1991, Israel has entered into direct negotiations with other Arab countries, as well as with the Palestinians, to try to reach a peaceful settlement of long-standing issues of land, peace, and sovereignty.

The other two major challenges that Israelis have faced are the absorption of Jewish immigrants from around the world (the Jewish population of Israel has increased nearly fivefold since 1948, mostly from immigration) and an enormous military burden. Both challenges have proved to be highly costly, but Israel has received substantial foreign aid, especially from the United States, and regular contributions from Jewish communities around the world.

Bain, Kenneth R. *The March to Zion: United States Policy and the Founding of Israel.* Tex. A & M Univ. Pr. 1980 $24.50. ISBN 0-89096-076-3. Reviews U.S. policy toward the creation of the State of Israel during Truman's presidency.

Beilin, Yossi. *Israel: A Concise Political History.* St. Martin 1993 $35.00. ISBN 0-312-09124-9. A political history of Israel from prestate origins in the nineteenth century until the present.

Beinin, Joel. *Was The Red Flag Flying There?* U. CA Pr. 1990 $45.00. ISBN 0-520-07035-6. A Marxist interpretation of the Arab-Israeli conflict.

Bell, J. Bowyer. *Terror out of Zion: The Fight for Israeli Independence, 1929–1949.* University MT 1984 repr. of 1979 ed. o.p. An examination of the Zionist and Palestinian underground movements during this period.

Ben Gurion, David, ed. *The Jews in Their Land.* Doubleday 1974 o.p. Presents the continuous story of the Jewish people within Israel.

Berler, Alexander. *New Towns in Israel.* Transaction Pubs. 1970 $24.95. ISBN 0-87855-174-3

Chamish, Barry. *The Fall of Israel.* Trafalgar 1993 $34.95. ISBN 0-86241-355-9. A rare and candid portrayal of Israeli shortcomings.

Dayan, Moshe. *Breakthrough: A Personal Account of the Egypt-Israel Peace Negotiation.* Knopf 1981 o.p. Detailed account of the 1977–78 Egypt-Israeli peace negotiations by a participant.

———. *Diary of the Sinai Campaign.* Greenwood 1979 repr. of 1967 ed. $35.00. ISBN 0-313-20928-6. Dayan's personal account of the 1965 war with the Arabs.

Elazar, Daniel J., and Janet Aviad. *Religion and Politics in Israel: The Interplay of Judaism and Zionism.* Am. Jewish Comm. 1981 $2.50. ISBN 0-87495-033-3

Evenari, Michael, and Nephtali Tadmor. *The Negev: The Challenge of a Desert.* HUP 1982 $40.50. ISBN 0-674-60672-8. Summary of over two decades of scientific study of the habitability of the Negev desert.

Feldman, Lily G. *The Special Relationship between West Germany and Israel.* Routledge Chapman & Hall 1984 $44.95. ISBN 0-04-327068-9. Reveals the intricacies of German-Israeli policy relations.

Fernea, Elizabeth W., and Mary E. Hocking. *The Struggles for Peace: Israelis and Palestinians.* U. of Tex. Pr. 1992 $35.00. ISBN 0-292-76541-X. Analyzes conflict resolution in the Middle East peace process.

Freedman, Robert O. *Israel in the Begin Era.* Greenwood 1982 $55.00. ISBN 0-275-90795-3. A look at Menachem Begin's Likud government.

———. *World Politics and the Arab-Israeli Conflict.* Pergamon 1979 o.p. A multidimensional examination of Arab-Israeli relations.

Friedman, Thomas L. *From Beirut to Jerusalem.* FS&G 1991 $25.00. ISBN 0-374-15895-9. Focuses on the Lebanese civil war and the Israeli invasion of Lebanon.

Gayron, Daniel. *Israel after Begin*. State U. NY Pr. $64.00. ISBN 0-7914-0367-X. Assesses the impact of the invasion of Lebanon on Israel.

Harkabi, Yehoshafat. *Israel's Fateful Hour*. HarpC 1988 $10.95. ISBN 0-06-091613-3. Examines Israel's security and its relations with the Palestinians.

Herzog, Chaim. *The War of Atonement, October 1973*. Little 1975 o.p. Describes the 1973 Yom Kippur War and its implications.

Hopkins, I.W. *Jerusalem: A Study in Urban Geography*. Ed. by Charles F. Pfeiffer. *Baker Studies in Biblical Archaeology*. 1970 o.p.

Horowitz, Dan, and Moshe Lissak. *Origins of the Israeli Polity: Palestine under the Mandate*. Trans. by Charles Hoffman. U. Ch. Pr. 1979 $24.00. ISBN 0-226-35366-4. A political and social history of the Jewish community in Palestine before the establishment of the State of Israel.

Jamison, D.M. *The Israeli People*. Shepherd Pub. 1993 $11.95. ISBN 1-882749-00-6. Includes many family charts and geneologies.

Katz, Samuel M. *Israel Versus Jibril: The Twenty-Year War Against a Master Terrorist*. Paragon Hse. 1993 $24.95. ISBN 1-55778-433-7. Arresting account by an Israeli-American military historian.

Kedourie, Elie, and Sylvia G. Haim, eds. *Palestine and Israel in the Nineteenth and Twentieth Centuries*. Intl. Spec. Bk. 1982 $39.50. ISBN 0-7146-3121-3. Deals with the economic and social history of Palestinians and Israelis.

Kollek, Teddy, and Moshe Pearlman. *Jerusalem: A History of Forty Centuries*. Random 1968 o.p. An in-depth history of Jerusalem.

Krausz, Ernest, ed. *Politics and Society in Israel*. Transaction Pubs. 1984 $29.95. ISBN 0-685-42645-9. A sociological view of political life in Israel.

Kutcher, Arthur. *The New Jerusalem: Planning and Politics*. MIT Pr. 1974 o.p. Takes a look at city planning schemes in Jerusalem and their impact on the landscape.

Leon, D. *Kibbutz: New Way of Life*. Franklin 1969 $87.00. ISBN 0-08-013356-8. Provides an introduction to the largest of four national federations of communal settlements in Israel.

Morris, Benny. *The Birth of the Palestinian Refugee Problem, 1947–1949*. Cambridge U. Pr. 1987 $16.95. ISBN 0-521-33889-1. A well-documented history of the origins of the problem.

Neff, Donald. *Warriors Against Israel*. Amana Bks. 1988 $19.95. ISBN 0-915597-59-4. Account of the Yom Kippur/Ramadan War of 1973.

———. *Warriors at Suez*. Amana Bks. 1987 $9.95. ISBN 0-915597-58-6. Deals with the Suez crisis and war of 1956.

———. *Warriors for Jerusalem*. Amana Bks. 1988 $9.95. ISBN 0-915597-57-8. Account of the Six-Day War of 1967.

Orni, Efraim, and Elisha Ofrat. *Geography of Israel*. Phila. o.p. Presents the geology, morphology, climate, population, history, and economy of Israel.

Parfitt, Tudor. *Journey to the Vanished City: The Search for a Lost Tribe of Israel*. St. Martin 1993 $22.95. ISBN 0-312-08829-9. Examines claims of the Lemba of South Africa who believe themselves to be the legendary lost tribe of Israel.

Peretz, Don. *The Intifada*. Westview 1990 $53.50. ISBN 0-8133-0859-3. Chronicles the Palestinian resistance to the Israeli occupation of the West Bank.

Reinharz, Jehuda. *Chaim Weizmann: The Making of a Zionist Leader*. OUP 1987 $35.00. ISBN 0-19-505069-X. A detailed account of Weizmann's life.

Roberts, Samuel J. *Survival or Hegemony? The Foundations of Israeli Foreign Policy*. Bks. Demand 1974 $43.80. ISBN 0-317-41684-7. An analysis of the historical roots of Israel's foreign policy.

Sachar, Howard M. *A History of Israel: From the Rise of Zionism to Our Time*. Knopf 1979 $19.95. ISBN 0-394-73679-6. Chronicles Israel's political and ideological development and growth as a nation.

Safran, Nadav. *United States and Israel*. Amer. Foreign Policy Lib. HUP 1963 o.p.

Schiff, Ze'ev, and Ehud Ya'ari. *Israel's Lebanon War*. Trans. by Ina Freidman. S&S Trade 1984 o.p. Focuses on the politics behind the Israel-Lebanon War.

———. *The Palestinian Uprising—Israel's Third Front.* S&S Trade 1990 o.p. Examines the Intifada and its effect on Israel.

Weizman, Ezer. *The Battle for Peace.* Bantam 1981 o.p. A personal account of the Israel-Egypt peace negotiations.

ISLAMIC CULTURE AND NATIONS

Founded by the prophet Mohammed in the seventh century A.D., the religion of Islam is one of the world's major religions, with close to one billion followers spread throughout the world. The greatest concentration of the religion's followers, known as Muslims, are found in the Middle East, North Africa, South Asia (most notably Pakistan and Bangladesh), and South East Asia (Indonesia in particular). For its adherents, Islam is more than a religion; it is also a way of life, permeating most, if not all, aspects of culture and society.

Islam began among the Arabic peoples of the Middle East. Shortly after its founding, these people swept across the Middle East and moved both east and west, conquering Persia, Egypt, northern Africa, and even much of the Iberian Peninsula (Portugal and Spain). They brought their religion and their culture with them, establishing a widespread empire that reached its pinnacle of power and achievement at a time when Europe was mired in its so-called Dark Ages. Islamic civilization at this time was rich in art, science, and philosophy. Contacts between Europeans and Muslims were few at first, particularly because of their religious differences. In time, however, Muslim learning spread to western Europe, most notably through Islamic centers in Spain. Indeed, much of the subsequent development of Western Europe during its renaissance owes some debt to Islamic civilization and its achievements, particularly its translation and preservation of scientific findings and texts from earlier times. Islamic Arabs made important contributions in astronomy, mathematics, art, and literature; they share with the Byzantines the credit for preserving the great books and learning of ancient Greece and Rome.

As the Islamic empire spread, it began to lose much of its unity as far-flung regions become virtually independent under local rulers. In time, this led to a decline in political power by the dominant Arab Muslims. What emerged instead was a vast area in which Islamic religion was embraced by different ethnic groups, speaking different languages and following their own local customs. The past hundred years have brought about many changes in the Islamic world. During this time, Muslim regions under European colonial control have gained their independence, resulting in more than forty independent nations. Ethnic and national feelings often have been as important as religion in causing independence movements and in deciding the borders of these new nations. Nevertheless, religion is still a very important part of these countries, and Islam remains the dominant force in most of them.

The Muslim countries of today have a variety of governments. In some, such as Saudi Arabia and Iran, traditional Islamic rules and customs are strictly enforced by the government. In others, such as Turkey and Albania, there is a great deal of separation between religion and the state. Muslim nations also differ widely in their ethnic composition and history. Indonesia and Pakistan, for example, are very differently ethnically and historically from each other, and both are very different from such north African nations as Morocco and Algeria. Yet despite the differences dividing Muslim nations today, Islam continues to act as a common heritage that helps unite Muslims throughout the world.

Islamic Culture

Abdalati, Hammudah. *The Family Structure in Islam*. Am. Trust Pubns. 1976 $8.50. ISBN 0-685-00342-6. A comprehensive but overgeneralized work on Muslim familial relations.

Afzal-Ur-Rehman. *Economic Doctrines of Islam*. 4 vols. Kazi $39.50. ISBN 0-935782-81-8

Ahmed, Ziauddin, and others. *Money and Banking in Islam*. New Era Pubns. MI 1983 $9.95. ISBN 0-939830-27-2. Collection of articles by Saudi economists on monetary structure and banking practices in Islamic culture.

Akhtar, Shabbir. *A Faith for All Seasons: Islam and the Challenge of the Modern World*. I. R. Dee 1991 $28.50. ISBN 0-929587-54-5. Author argues for the modernization of Islam.

Ali, Abdullah. *The Spirit and the Future of Islam*. Inst. Econ. Pol. 1983 2 vols. $287.00. ISBN 0-86722-051-1. A comprehensive but somewhat dated history of Islam and its prospects in the modern world.

Ali, Ameer. *Spirit of Islam*. S. Asia 1990 repr. of 1923 ed. $18.50. ISBN 81-85395-91-8

Anderson, Norman. *Islam in the Modern World*. InterVarsity 1990 $22.99. ISBN 0-8308-5458-4

Ashraf, Syed A. *Islam*. Ed. by W. Owen Cole. *World Religions Ser*. Dufour 1992 $14.95. ISBN 1-871402-10-7

Bannerman, Patrick. *Islam in Perspective: A Guide to Islamic Society*. Routledge 1989 $35.00. ISBN 0-415-01015-2

Bosworth, C. E., ed. *The Encyclopedia of Islam* E. J. Brill 1992 $37.25. ISBN 90-04-09591-8. Later volumes of the Lewis *Encyclopedia;* detailed and comprehensive.

Boulares, Habib. *Islam: The Fear and the Hope*. Humanities 1990 $45.00. ISBN 0-86232-944-2. A defense of Islam and its separation from politics by a former minister of culture and information of Tunisia.

Brett, Michael, and Werner Forman. *The Moors: Islam in the West*. Merrimack River 1984 o.p. A coffee table book with glossy pages and breathtaking photos, but not for the scholar.

Bukhsh, S. K. *The Renaissance of Islam*. Kazi 1981 $29.00. ISBN 0-933511-39-6

Cameron, Averil, and Lawrence Conrad, eds. *Byzantine and Early Islamic Near East*. Darwin Pr. 1992 $29.95. ISBN 0-87850-080-4. Discusses basic texts required to understand the transition from Byzantine to Islamic culture.

Charnay, J. P. *Islamic Culture and Socio-Economic Change. Social, Economic and Political Studies of the Middle East*. Humanities 1981 o.p. Vol. IV of *Social, Economic, and Political Studies of the Middle East:* a short, general work.

Christopher, John B. *The Islamic Tradition. Major Traditions in World Civilization Ser*. HarpC 1972 o.p. A brief introductory volume to the series.

Dawasha, Adeed, ed. *Islam in Foreign Policy*. Cambridge U. Pr. 1985 $34.50. ISBN 0-521-25815-4. Contains 12 short articles by prominent scholars covering the foreign policies of different countries; follows and complements Piscatori's *Islam in the Political Process*.

Denny, Frederick. *An Introduction to Islam*. Macmillan 1993. ISBN 0-02-328519-2. An introductory text for college students.

Dessouki, Ali. *Islamic Resurgence in the Arab World*. Greenwood 1982 $42.95. ISBN 0-275-90781-3. Theory and case studies by social scientists on the Islamic revival in Arab countries.

Donaldson, Dwight M. *The Shi'ite Religion: A History of Islam in Persia and Irak*. AMS Pr. repr. of 1933 ed. $49.50. ISBN 0-404-18959-8. A detailed history of Shi'ism in Persia and Iraq.

Esposito, John L. *Islam: The Straight Path*. OUP 1992 repr. of 1990 ed. $15.95. ISBN 0-19-507472-6. A short college survey text, expanded in 1992.

———. *Women in Muslim Family Law. Contemporary Issues in the Middle East Ser*. Syracuse U. Pr. 1982 $13.95. ISBN 0-8156-2278-3. A brief general study of women's status in Islamic law.

Farah, Caesar E. *Islam*. Barron 1987 $10.95. ISBN 0-8120-3799-5

Geertz, Clifford. *Islam Observed: Religious Development in Morocco and Indonesia.* U. Ch. Pr. 1971 $6.95. ISBN 0-226-28511-1. Very short, dense work on Indonesian and Moroccan Islam.

Gibb, H.A.R., and J. H. Kramers, eds. *Shorter Encyclopedia of Islam.* Cornell Univ. Pr. 1957 $89.95. ISBN 0-8014-0150-X. Contains all the articles in the *Encyclopedia of Islam* that relate to Islam as a religion; very dense.

Glasse, Cyril. *The Concise Encyclopedia of Islam.* Harper SF 1991 repr. of 1989 ed. $24.95. ISBN 0-06-063126-0. Good handbook with maps and chronology but not for the serious scholar; contains articles of moderate length, with cross-references, in alphabetical order.

Hitti, Philip K. *Islam: A Way of Life.* Regnery Gateway 1971 o.p.

Holt, Peter M., and others, eds. *Cambridge History of Islam.* 2 vols. Cambridge U. Pr. 1970 o.p.

Hopwood, Derek. *Middle East and Islam: A Bibliographical Introduction.* Intl. Pub. Co. 1972 o.p. A comprehensive bibliography.

Hourani, Albert. *Arabic Thought in the Liberal Age, 1798–1939.* Cambridge U. Pr. 1983 $21.95. ISBN 0-521-27423-0. Political history of Arab countries during this era.

———. *Minorities in the Arab World.* AMS Pr. repr. of 1947 ed. $18.50. ISBN 0-404-16402-1. Discusses the various minority groups dispersed throughout the Arab world, focusing on their treatment under the Islamic system.

Hughes, Thomas P. *A Dictionary of Islam.* 2 vols. Gordon Pr. 1980 $199.95. ISBN 0-8490-3121-4. Very old (1895) dictionary with Arabic pronounciation guide and illustrations.

Israeli, R., ed. *Islam in Asia: Southeast and East Asia.* Westview 1984 o.p.

Issawi, Charles. *The Arab World's Legacy.* Darwin Pr. 1981 $14.95. ISBN 0-87850-040-5. Analysis of the history of various Arab civilizations and their heritage for modern Middle East nations.

Keddie, Nikki R., ed. *Scholars, Saints and Sufis: Muslim Religious Institutions Since 1500.* U. CA Pr. 1972 $11.95. ISBN 0-520-03644-1. Essays by scholars on Islamic religious institutions.

Khalidi, Tarif. *Classical Arab Islam: The Heritage and Culture of the Golden Age.* Darwin Pr. 1984 o.p. A short work on Islam's foundations based on the author's lectures at University of Michigan in 1978.

Khan, Mohammad S. *Islam: Social and Economic Structure.* S. Asia 1989 $17.00. ISBN 81-7024-265-7

Khumayni, Ruh A. *Islam and Revolution: Writings and Declarations of Imam Khomeini.* Trans. by Hamid Algar. Routledge Chapman & Hall 1985 $24.50. ISBN 0-7103-0098-0. Some writings and speeches of Khomeini; meant as an introduction to his thought, but very detailed.

Khuri, Raif. *Modern Arab Thought: Channels of the French Revolution to the Arab East.* Ed. by Charles Issawi. Trans. by Ihsan Abbas. Kingston Pr. 1983 $29.00. ISBN 0-940670-16-X. Discussion of Arabian history and intellectual life that probes the influence of the French Revolution on modern Arab thought.

Levy, Reuben. *The Social Structure of Islam.* Cambridge U. Pr. 1957 o.p. Sociological study of Islamic religion and culture.

Lewis, Bernard. *Islam and the West.* OUP 1993 $25.00. ISBN 0-19-507619-2. Eleven eclectic essays concerning the 1400-year-long rivalry between Christendom and Islam.

———. *The Muslim Discovery of Europe.* Norton 1982 $12.95. ISBN 0-393-30233-4. A good history of Arab-Western relations from an Arab perspective.

———. *Race and Colour in Islam.* Hippocrene Bks. 1980 o.p. A short examination of racial prejudice in Islamic cultures.

Lewis, Bernard, and others, eds. *Encyclopedia of Islam.* 5 vols. Humanities 1960–78 o.p. Four volumes with supplement; very comprehensive but somewhat traditionally Western biased.

Lewis, I. M., ed. *Islam in Tropical Africa.* Ind. U. Pr. 1980 $10.95. ISBN 0-253-28514-3.

Mernissi, Fatima. *Islam and Democracy: Fear of the Modern World*. Addison-Wesley 1993. ISBN 0-201-60883-9. Argues that Islam has been perverted by Arab leaders who want to deny their people democracy.

Moon, Ross A. *About Islam*. NW Pub. 1992 $7.95. ISBN 1-800416-19-0. Fascinating in-depth examination of Islamic religion that explains what behavior is appropriate for believers.

Morey, Robert A. *Islam Unveiled: The True Desert Storm*. Scholars Pr. GA 1991 $9.95. ISBN 0-9629394-0-4

Nasr, Seyyed H. *Traditional Islam in the Modern World*. Routledge Chapman & Hall 1989 $19.95. ISBN 0-7103-0332-7. A fairly detailed examination of Islamic traditions and how they fit into modern life.

Netton, Ian R. *A Popular Dictionary of Islam*. Humanities 1992 $18.50. ISBN 0-391-03756-0. A comprehensive general sourcebook for students, scholars, and general readers.

Patai, Raphael. *The Arab Mind*. Macmillan 1983 $16.95. ISBN 0-684-17809-5. "In 16 chapters Patai discusses a number of topics, among them Arab child rearing practices, Bedouin ethos, sexual behavior, the role of Islam and of the Arabic language . . . Arab unity and the Arab's reactions to and relations with the West" (*Choice*).

Patwardhan, Vinayak N., and William J. Darby. *The State of Nutrition in the Arab Middle East*. Vanderbilt U. Pr. 1972 o.p. Examines dietary deficiencies and their effects on health in the Arab world.

Piscatori, James P., ed. *Islam in the Political Process*. Cambridge U. Pr. 1983 $18.95. ISBN 0-521-27434-6. Contains 12 short articles by prominent scholars on different Islamic countries; the product of a conference.

Planhol, Xavier De. *World of Islam*. Cornell Univ. Pr. 1959 $10.95. ISBN 0-8014-9830-9. A very short general survey of the geography of Islamic countries; translated from the French.

Rahman, Fazlur. *Islam and Modernity: Transformation of an Intellectual Tradition*. U. Ch. Pr. 1984 $10.95. ISBN 0-226-70284-7. Product of a short research project at University of Chicago examining the modernization of Islam.

Roberts, Robert. *The Social Laws of the Qoran*. Humanities 1990 $12.50. ISBN 0-391-03661-0

Rodinson, Maxime. *Islam and Capitalism*. Trans. by Brian Pearce. U. of Tex. Pr. 1978 o.p. A sociological perspective on the relationship between Islam and capitalism.

Said, Edward W. *Covering Islam*. Pantheon 1993 $12.00. ISBN 0-394-74808-5. The acknowledged master examines media and expert influence on Western perspectives of Islam.

Siddigri, A. H. *The Islamic Concept of Religion and Its Revival*. Kazi 1981 $19.00. ISBN 1-56744-091-6. A short theological work by an adherent.

Trimingham, J. Spencer. *The Influence of Islam upon Africa*. Intl. Bk. Ctr. 1980 $40.00. ISBN 0-86685-539-6. A compact history of Islam in Africa.

_____. *Islam in East Africa*. Ayer 1980 repr. of 1964 ed. $24.00. ISBN 0-8369-9270-9. A brief, dense examination of East African Islam.

Udovitch, A. L., ed. *Islamic Middle East, 700–1900: Studies in Economic and Social History*. Darwin Pr. 1981 o.p. Author's work in a Princeton research seminar in 1974.

Islamic Nations

EGYPT

Since ancient times, Egypt has played a key role in Middle Eastern history. The Egyptians produced one of the most important of ancient civilizations, but, after thousands of years of self-rule, the country was conquered and ruled by a succession of foreigners: Assyrians, Persians, Greeks, Romans, and Byzantines. Then, in the seventh century A.D. Muslim Arabs conquered Egypt and incorporated it into a rapidly growing Muslim empire. Eventually, Arabic became the spoken language of the Egyptians and Islam the majority religion. For about 400 years, Egypt was part of the Ottoman Empire, although, for much of that time, Egyptian rulers ran the country without much direct interference from Istanbul, the Ottoman capital.

Europeans had long had a geopolitical interest in Egypt, but with the completion of the Suez Canal—built by the French in 1869 but soon controlled by the British—that interest intensified. During the 1880s the British assumed effective control of Egyptian politics, and, when Turkey sided with Germany during World War I, Egypt was declared a kingdom independent of Ottoman rule, though the British continued to dominate the country's economy and politics. After military officers overthrew the Egyptian king in 1952, the new government, under the leadership of Gamal Abdul Nasser, reached an agreement with the British that resulted in the latter's full withdrawal from the Suez Canal.

Two major issues that have occupied the Egyptian government in recent decades have been relations with Israel and economic development. After four wars, Egypt signed a peace treaty with the Jewish state in 1979, but economic development remains an enormous challenge in the face of a rapidly growing population with rising expectations.

Abdel-Fadil, M. *Development, Economic Distribution and Social Change in Rural Egypt, 1952–1970.* Cambridge U. Pr. 1976 o.p.

Abu-Lughod, Janet. *Cairo: 1001 Years of the City Victorious.* Princeton U. Pr. 1971 o.p. Traces the social and physical history of Cairo.

Aliboni, R., and others. *Egypt's Economic Potential.* Croom Helm 1984 o.p. An assessment of the future impact on Egypt of major transformations in its economy in recent years.

al-Sadat, A. *In Search of Identity: An Autobiography.* HarpC 1978 o.p. Excellent autobiography by the president of Egypt who started the peace process with Israel.

al-Sayyid-Marsot, Afaf L. *Egypt's Liberal Experiment, 1922–1936.* U. CA Pr. 1977 o.p. A sociopolitical history of Egypt.

Baker, Raymond W. *Egypt's Uncertain Revolution under Nasser and Sadat.* HUP 1978 $20.00. ISBN 0-674-24154-1

Beaucour, Ferrard, and others. *The Discovery of Egypt.* Trans. by Bambi Ballard. Abbeville Pr. 1993 $50.00. ISBN 2-08013-506-6. Unparalleled glimpse of Egypt through the eyes of artists, scientists and scholars.

Berque, Jacques. *Egypt.* Faber & Faber 1972 o.p.

Bowie, Robert R. *Suez, 1956. International Crisis and the Role of Law Ser.* OUP 1974 o.p. A study of the 1956 Suez crisis in a series that examines the role of international law in international crises.

Budge, Ernest A. *A Short History of the Egyptian People.* Norwood 1980 o.p.

Dykstra, Darrell I. *Egypt in the Nineteenth Century: The Impact of Europe upon a Non-Western Society.* UM Ctr. MENAS 1979 $5.00. ISBN 0-932098-15-0

Freiberger, Steven Z. *Dawn over Suez: The Rise of American Power in the Middle East, 1953–1957.* I. R. Dee 1992 $26.50. ISBN 0-929587-83-9. Focuses on how the Suez War increased U.S. power in the Middle East.

Ghosh, Amitav. *In an Antique Land.* Knopf 1993 $23.00. ISBN 0-394-58368-X. A review of a seldom-studied subject: Indian-Egyptian relations.

Gilsenan, Michael. *Saint and Sufi in Modern Egypt: An Essay in the Sociology of Religion. Monographs in Social Anthropology.* OUP 1973 o.p.

Goldschmidt, Arthur, Jr. *Modern Egypt: The Formation of a Nation State.* Westview 1989 $59.00. ISBN 0-86531-182-X. A well-written general history of modern Egypt.

Grimal, Nicolas. *History of Ancient Egypt.* Trans. by Ian Shaw. Blackwell Pubs. 1992 $34.95. ISBN 0-631-17472-9. An in-depth history of Egypt.

Harik, Iliya F. *Political Mobilization of Peasants: A Study of an Egyptian Community.* Ind. U. Pr. 1974 o.p. Highlights a village's response to Egypt's revolutionary movement.

Harris, Christina. *Nationalism and Revolution in Egypt: The Role of the Muslin Brother-hood.* Hyperion Conn. 1987 repr. of 1964 ed. $26.00. ISBN 0-8305-0034-0. Deals with the relationship between the fundamentalist Muslim Brotherhood and the Government of the Revolution in Egypt.

Heikal, Mohamed. *The Sphinx and the Commissar: The Rise and Fall of Soviet Influence in the Arab World.* HarpC 1979 o.p. An analysis of Egyptian relations with the Soviet Union.

Holt, Peter M. *Egypt and the Fertile Crescent, 1516–1922: A Political History.* Cornell Univ. Pr. 1969 $15.95. ISBN 0-8014-9079-0. Examines internal developments in Egypt from the heyday of the Ottoman Empire to its decline.

————, ed. *Political and Social Change in Modern Egypt: Historical Studies from the Ottoman Conquest to the United Arab Republic.* OUP 1968 o.p. Covers Egyptian history and politics from the Ottoman conquest to the formation of a United Arab Republic.

Hussein, Mahmoud. *Class Conflict in Egypt, 1945–1970.* Trans. by Alfred Ehrenfeld and others. Monthly Rev. 1973 o.p. A study of the class struggle in Egypt.

Landes, David S. *Bankers and Pashas: International Finance and Economic Imperialism in Egypt.* HUP 1980 $14.95. ISBN 0-674-06165-9. A detailed account of nineteenth-century financial operations in Egypt.

Lyons, Robert. *Egyptian Time.* Doubleday 1992 $50.00. ISBN 0-385-42104-4

Mabro, Robert. *The Egyptian Economy, 1952–1972. Economies of the World Ser.* OUP 1974 o.p. Provides a brief review of economic developments in Egypt during this 20-year period.

————. *The Industrialization of Egypt, 1939–1973: Policy and Performance.* OUP 1976 o.p. Examines industrial policies and their implementation in Egypt from World War II through the early 1970s.

Macleod, Arlene. *Accommodating Protest: Working Women, the New Veiling, and Change in Cairo.* Col. U. Pr. 1993 $14.00. ISBN 0-231-07281-3. Based on 28 lower-middle class households and interviews with about 60 working women.

Richmond, John. *Egypt, 1798–1952: Her Advance toward Modern Identity.* Col. U. Pr. 1977 $43.00. ISBN 0-231-04296-5. Outlines Egypt's history from Napoleon's invasion in the late eighteenth century to the Free Officers' Revolution in the mid-twentieth century.

Roberts, Paul N. *River in the Desert.* Random 1993 $25.00. ISBN 0-679-42104-1

Shoukri, Ghali. *Egypt: Portrait of a President—Sadat's Road to Jerusalem.* Biblio Dist. 1982 o.p. A critical review of Egyptian affairs from Nasser's death in 1970 to Sadat's assassination in 1981.

Vatikiotis, P. J. *The Egyptian Army in Politics.* Greenwood 1975 repr. of 1961 ed. $49.75. ISBN 0-8371-6473-7

————. *Nasser and His Generation.* St. Martin 1978 o.p. An account of Nasser's life in the context of the ideas and politics of his generation.

Waterbury, John. *The Egypt of Nasser and Sadat: The Political Economy of Two Regimes. Princeton Studies on the Near East.* Princeton U. Pr. 1983 $68.00. ISBN 0-691-07650-2. Studies the role of public policy in the economic and social development of Egypt during the regimes of Abu Nasser and Anwar Sadat.

Wheelock, Keith. *Nasser's New Egypt. Foreign Policy Research Institute Ser.* Greenwood 1975 repr. of 1960 ed. $49.75. ISBN 0-8371-8233-6. An analysis of Gamal Abdel Nasser's military regime in Egypt.

IRAN

Iran, which was known as Persia until modern times, has had a notable history for more than 2,500 years. In the sixth and fifth centuries B.C., its ancient empire stretched from the western border of the Indian subcontinent to the Mediterranean Sea and western Egypt. After a short period of Greek control, initiated by Alexander the Great in the late fourth century B.C., the Persians reestablished their kingdom and maintained their independence until the seventh century A.D., expanding into central Asia and, at times, into the Fertile Crescent. In that century Persia was conquered by the Muslim Arabs and incorporated into the Islamic empire. In time the Persian people converted to Islam, becoming strong advocates of the faith and contributed immensely to Islamic civilization.

With the decline of the Islamic empire, the Persians assumed virtual independence and, by the sixteenth century, had reestablished a separate kingdom, which in the following century grew into a prosperous empire under the Safavids, who ruled from 1501 to 1722 and established Shi'a Islam as the state religion. During Europe's imperialistic expansion throughout the nineteenth century, the British and the Russians vied for control of Persia. Neither was able to defeat the other, so, at the beginning of the twentieth century, the two powers agreed to divide the country into a British sphere of influence in the south and a Russian sphere in the north, leaving the middle area as a neutral buffer zone.

Oil has greatly affected Iran's history during the past 50 years. The country has been a major oil exporter since the 1950s and the rapid rise in oil prices during the 1970s provided Iran's ruler, Shah Mohammad Reza Pahlavi, with vast sums of money, much of which he spent on weapons and construction in the city of Tehran in an attempt to restore the glory of ancient Persia. Only a minority of the population shared in this oil wealth, and, as dissatisfaction with the Shah's rule grew, he became repressive.

In 1979 an Islamic revolution overthrew the monarchy and brought the religious leader Ayatollah Ruhollah Khomeini to power. Khomeini and his successors built an Islamic state that has imposed religious standards and values on the country's social and political institutions. Shortly after the revolution, war broke out between Iran and Iraq; it lasted for about 10 years, and both countries paid dearly in lives and resources. Iran is now in the process of trying to rebuild its economy and mend fences with the Western countries that it had antagonized after the revolution.

Amirsadeghi, Hossein, ed. *Twentieth-Century Iran*. Holmes & Meier 1977 $45.00. ISBN 0-8419-0325-5. Chronicles changes and developments within Iran from 1900 to 1976.

Barth, Frederik. *Nomads of South Persia: The Basseri Tribe of the Khamseh Confederacy*. Waveland Pr. 1986 $9.50. ISBN 0-8813-207-0. A detailed observation of the society and culture of Iran's Basseri nomads.

Bill, James. *The Eagle and the Lion*. Yale U. Pr. 1988 $37.00. ISBN 0-300-04097-0. Examines present-day U.S.-Iranian relations.

Bonnie, Michael E., and Nikki R. Keddie, eds. *Continuity and Change in Modern Iran*. State U. NY Pr. 1981 o.p. Traces the tensions and opposition movements that ignited the 1978–79 revolution in Iran.

Cambridge History of Iran. 7 vols. Cambridge U. Pr. 1968–91. Vol. 1 1968 $105.00. ISBN 0-521-06935-1. Vol. 2 1985 o.p. Vol. 3 1983 $180.00. ISBN 0-521-24699-7. Vol. 4 1975 $110.00. ISBN 0-521-20093-8. Vol. 5 1968 $105.00. ISBN 0-521-06936-X. Vol. 6 1986 $130.00. ISBN 0-521-20094-6. Vol. 7 1991 $135.00. ISBN 0-521-20095-4. A comprehensive history of Iran.

Elwell-Sutton, L. P. *Persian Oil: A Study in Power Politics*. Greenwood 1975 repr. of 1955 ed. $21.50. ISBN 0-88355-288-4

Farmaian, Sattareh F. *Daughter of Persia*. Crown Pub. Group 1992 $22.00. ISBN 0-517-58697-5. Author's account of her life in Iran and the West.

Fesharaki, Fereidun. *The Development of the Iranian Oil Industry: International and Domestic Aspects*. Praeger 1976 o.p. A study of the development of the oil industry in Iran that focuses on the National Iranian Oil Company's role.

Fischer, Michael M. *Iran: From Religious Dispute to Revolution. Harvard Studies in Cultural Anthropology.* HUP 1980 $10.95. ISBN 0-676-46617-9. Centers on the role religious education plays in molding character in Iran and investigates how this role is changing.

Hasan-Ibn-Hasan, Fasa'l. *A History of Persia under Quajar Rule.* Trans. by Herbert Busse. Col. U. Pr. 1973 $61.00. ISBN 0-231-03197-1. A detailed history of the province of Fars while under Qajar rule from 1789 to 1883.

Hooglund, Eric J. *Land and Revolution in Iran, 1960–1980. Modern Middle East Ser.* U. of Tex. Pr. 1982 $19.95. ISBN 0-292-74633-4. Investigates the relationship between the land reform program initiated in Iran in 1962 and the 1978 mass opposition movement to the shah's rule.

Irving, Clive. *Crossroads of Civilization: Three Thousand Years of Persian History.* B & N Imports 1979 o.p. A concise history of Persia up to the Iranian Revolution of 1978–79.

Ismael, Tareq Y. *Iraq and Iran: Roots of Conflict. Contemporary Issues in the Middle East Ser.* Syracuse U. Pr. 1982 o.p. Examines the historical, legal, and ideological origins of the war between Iran and Iraq.

Issawi, Charles. *Economic History of Iran, 1800–1914.* Ed. by William R. Polk. *Publications of the Ctr. for Middle Eastern Studies.* U. Ch. Pr. 1971 $27.00. ISBN 0-226-38606-6. An interesting study of Iran's economic history during this period.

Katouzian, Homa. *The Political Economy of Modern Iran: Despotism and Pseudo-Modernism.* NYU Pr. 1981 $20.00. ISBN 0-8147-4578-4. Analyzes social and economic change in modern Iran up to the overthrow of the shah.

Keddie, Nikki R. *Religion and Politics in Iran: Shi'ism from Quietism to Revolution.* Yale U. Pr. 1984 $13.00. ISBN 0-300-03245-5. Traces religeopolitical conditions in Iran from pre-Islamic times to the present.

Keddie, Nikki R., and Yann Richard. *Roots of Revolution: An Interpretive History of Modern Iran.* Yale U. Pr. 1981 $40.00. ISBN 0-300-02606-4. A comprehensive study of modern Iranian history and politics.

Kordi, Gohar. *An Iranian Odyssey.* Consort Bk. Sales 1993 $13.95. ISBN 1-85242-213-0

Koury, Enver M., and Charles G. MacDonald, eds. *Revolution in Iran: A Reappraisal.* Inst. of Middle Eastern & North African Affairs 1982 o.p. Assesses the nature of the Iranian Revolution and its implications.

Looney, Robert E. *Economic Origins of the Iranian Revolution.* Pergamon 1982 $80.00. ISBN 0-08-025950-2. Identifies the economic origins of the 1978–79 Iranian Revolution.

Moaddel, Mansoor. *Class, Politics, and Ideology in the Iranian Revolution.* Col. U. Pr. 1992 $37.50. ISBN 0-231-07866-8. Analyzes the Iranian Revolution from a sociological perspective.

Moshiri, Farrokh. *The State and Social Revolution in Iran: A Theoretical Perspective.* P. Lang Pubs. 1985 $28.85. ISBN 0-8204-0149-8. Analysis of the intertwining of Islam and politics in the past and present state of Iran; describes the Iranian political system.

Purser, B. H., ed. *The Persian Gulf.* Springer-Verlag 1973 o.p. Scientific and geological survey of the Persian Gulf.

Ramazani, Rouhollah K. *Iran's Foreign Policy, 1941–1973: A Study of Foreign Policy in Modernizing Nations.* U. Pr. of Va. 1975 $40.00. ISBN 0-8139-0594-X. Analysis of Iranian foreign relations during this period with the Arab nations and the West.

Sanasarian, Eliz. *Women's Rights Movement in Iran: Mutiny, Appeasement, and Repression from 1900 to Khomeini.* Greenwood 1982 $38.50. ISBN 0-275-90894-1. Survey of the twentieth-century Iranian women's rights movement that concludes feminism has failed in Iran.

Siddique, Kaukab. *Islamic Revolution: The Iranian Experiment.* Ed. by Nadrat Naeem. Am. So. Ed. & Rel. 1984 o.p. Describes the various sects of Islam and examines the roles religion has played in the various conflicts between Muslims.

Sykes, Perry. *A History of Persia.* Gordon Pr. 1976 $69.95. ISBN 0-8490-1982-6. Historiography of Persia; examines the various cultural shifts in the area, its economy, its politics, and among its people.

Tahir-Kheli. *The Iran-Iraq War: Old Conflicts, New Weapons.* Greenwood 1983 $47.95. ISBN 0-275-91088-1. Compilation of essays, lectures, and addresses on the Iran-Iraq War of 1980–88.

Vaziri, Mostafa. *Iran as Imagined Nation.* Paragon Hse. 1993 $46.95. ISBN 1-55778-573-2

Wilber, Donald N. *Iran Past and Present: From Monarchy to Islamic Republic.* Princeton U. Pr. 9th ed. 1981 o.p. Examines the political evolution of Iran from the reign of the sultans to the triumph of Khomeini.

IRAQ

The earliest known codifications of laws and some of the most ancient city-states in history developed in Mesopotamia, the land between the Tigris and the Euphrates rivers that constitutes modern Iraq. These city-states grew into kingdoms, and the kingdoms into empires in ancient times. For centuries this cradle of civilization was a battleground between the Persians and the Byzantines. In the seventh century A.D., when it was conquered by Islamic forces from Arabia, its inhabitants welcomed the newcomers as deliverers from constant wars. Soon the majority of them converted to Islam, and, in the middle of the eighth century, the center of the vast Islamic empire moved to Iraq, where the city of Baghdad was built as the capital of the empire. Baghdad was at its height during the ninth and tenth centuries. Later it suffered numerous invasions, the most devastating of which was by the Mongols in the middle of the thirteenth century.

Iraq came under British influence during the first half of the twentieth century. Its oil reserves made it important to the West, and Iraq was invited into anti-Communist Western alliances in the early 1950s. A few years after a military coup overthrew the government in 1958, the country came under the rule of the Ba'th party, which quickly moved to suppress other political parties.

In 1979 the Iraqi dictator Saddam Hussein, feeling threatened by the revolutionary Islamic leaders in neighboring Iran, who were calling for the overthrow of his secular government, seized on a border dispute as a reason for invading Iran. In the ensuing decade-long war between the two countries, Iraq's oil-rich economy suffered a severe decline. In 1990, after making peace with Iran, Saddam Hussein invaded the neighboring country of Kuwait, whose oil-based investment fund exceeded all of Iraq's debts, and annexed it. This aroused the opposition of the West, and in 1991 a multinational force, led by the United States and sanctioned by the United Nations, ousted the Iraqis from Kuwait and destroyed much of Iraq's military power and economic infrastructure. Iraq is still under an UN-trade embargo that is severely hampering its efforts to rebuild after these two devastating wars.

Adams, Robert McC. *Land behind Baghdad: A History of Settlement on the Diyala Plains.* U. Ch. Pr. 1965 $63.50. ISBN 0-685-15601-X. Identifies the environmental and human forces that have shaped the Diyala plains of Iraq.

al-Khalil, Samir. *Republic of Fear: The Inside Story of Saddam's Iraq.* Pantheon 1991 $12.95. ISBN 0-679-73502-X. Searing account of life in Iraq under Saddam.

al-Marayati, Abid A. *Diplomatic History of Modern Iraq.* Speller 1961 $9.95. ISBN 0-8315-0108-1. Reviews the events and experiences that led Iraq to participate in the League of Nations and, later, the U.N.

Batatu, John. *The Old Social Classes and the Revolutionary Movements of Iraq: A Study of Iraq's Old Landed and Commercial Classes and Its Communists, Ba'thists and Free Officers. Princeton Studies on the Near East.* Princeton U. Pr. 1979 $55.00. ISBN 0-

691-02198-8. A three-part study of landowners, communists, Ba'thists, and Free Officers in Iraq.

Blair, Arthur H. *At War in the Gulf*. Tex. A & M Univ. Pr. 1992 $9.95. ISBN 0-89096-507-2. Follows the Gulf War from Iraq's invasion of Kuwait to Saddam Hussein's surrender.

David, Charles-Philippe, and others. *Foreign Policy Failure in the White House*. U. Pr. of Amer. 1993 $46.50. ISBN 0-8191-9075-6

Finnie, David H. *Shifting Lines in the Sand*. HUP 1992 $29.95. ISBN 0-674-80639-5. An examination of the historical origins of Iraq's claims to Kuwait.

Ghareeb, Edmund. *The Kurdish Question in Iraq. Contemporary Issues in the Middle East Ser*. Bks. Demand 1981 $63.20. ISBN 0-7837-1195-6. A study of the Kurds in Turkey and Iraq that focuses on Iraq's attempts to achieve a political understanding with the Kurds since 1968.

Ismael, Tareq Y. *Iraq and Iran: Roots of Conflict. Contemporary Issues in the Middle East Ser*. Syracuse U. Pr. 1982 o.p. Examines the historical, legal, and ideological origins of the war between Iran and Iraq.

Langley, Kathleen M. *The Industrialization of Iraq. Middle Eastern Monographs Ser*. HUP o.p. Follows the growth of industry in Iraq; investigates charges that industrialization was impeded under Iraq's Hashemite regime.

Longrigg, Stephen H. *Iraq, 1900–1950. Arab Background Ser*. Int. Bk. Ctr. 1968 o.p.

Marr, Phebe. *The Modern History of Iraq*. Westview 1991 $17.95. ISBN 0-8133-1328-7. Examines the history of Iraq from the 1920s to the present, analyzing its role as an Arab nation.

Penrose, Edith, and E. F. Penrose. *Iraq: Economics, Oil and Politics. Nations of the Modern World Ser*. Westview 1978 o.p. Examination of the past and present interrelationship of oil economics and politics in Iraq, plus a descriptive history of the country's modernization.

Purser, B. H., ed. *The Persian Gulf*. Springer-Verlag 1973 o.p. Scientific and geological survey of the Persian Gulf.

Roux, Georges. *Ancient Iraq*. Viking Penguin 1993 $13.00. ISBN 0-14-012523-X. Surveys the politics, culture, and economic history of Mesopotamia from prehistorical times to the Christian era.

Tahir-Kheli. *The Iran-Iraq War: Old Conflicts, New Weapons*. Greenwood 1983 $47.95. ISBN 0-275-91088-1. Compilation of essays, lectures, and addresses on the Iran-Iraq War of 1980–88.

Timmerman, Kenneth R. *The Death Lobby: How the West Armed Iraq*. HM 1991 $21.95. ISBN 0-395-59305-0. Examines how Western businesses and governments helped Iraq amass a formidable arms arsenal.

SAUDI ARABIA AND THE ARABIAN PENINSULA

As home of the holiest Islamic sites and a possessor of the world's largest oil reserves, Saudi Arabia has a special place in Islamic and world politics and economics. The country is vast but, with the exception of the western region and a few oases, is almost entirely desert. Nevertheless, urban life, trade, and skilled crafts were known on the Arabian Peninsula long before the coming of Islam in the seventh century A.D., although the majority of its people were nomads, called Bedouins. When Muhammad preached the new religion of Islam in the seventh century, he was resisted at first, then recognized as a prophet and a political leader who could unify Arabia. He established the rule of Islamic law, and after his death in 632, the Muslims began their historic conquest.

Although the political centers of the Islamic empire moved out of Arabia in subsequent centuries, the region has remained important for religious and geopolitical reasons. During World War I, the British promised to support an independent Arab state if the Arabs would rise up against Turkey but failed to keep the promise when the war ended. During the 1920s and 1930s, the Saudi clan took control of most of Arabia, including the holy cities of Makkah (Mecca) and Madinah (Medina), and declared the head of the clan king. Thus the nation of Saudi Arabia was born. With the discovery of oil in the 1950s and the vast wealth it brought over the next few decades, the country was transformed into a modern state. The Saudi government has used some of this wealth to assist developing countries, but much of it has been spent in Saudi Arabia or has been invested in the world market.

The Arabian Peninsula includes several countries besides Saudi Arabia: Yemen, Oman, the United Arab Emirates, Qatar, Bahrain, and Kuwait. Most of these countries were under British control until the late 1950s or early 1960s, when they gained independence. Combined, they have the second largest oil reserve in the world.

Demir, Soliman. *The Kuwait Fund and the Political Economy of Arab Regional Development.* Greenwood 1976 $49.95. ISBN 0-275-90247-1. Examines the role of Kuwaiti money in the development of other Arab nations.

el-Mallakh, Ragaei. *Economic Development and Regional Cooperation: Kuwait. Publications of the Ctr. for Middle Eastern Studies.* U. Ch. Pr. 1968 o.p. Account of Kuwaiti relations with the West that focuses on the impact of foreign policy on domestic economics.

Fenelon, K. G. *The United Arab Emirates: An Economic and Social Survey.* Bks. Demand 1976 $42.50. ISBN 0-685-16374-1. Examines the social and economic conditions of the UAE, paying particular attention to the unequal distribution of wealth and power.

Graham, Douglas F. *Saudi Arabia Unveiled.* Kendall-Hunt 1991 $13.95. ISBN 0-8403-6461-X. Revealing study of the history, people, culture, and royalty of Saudi Arabia.

Hawley, Donald. *Oman and Its Renaissance.* Intl. Bk. Ctr. 1980 $60.00. ISBN 0-86685-519-X. Probes the history, culture, and people of one of the republics of the United Arab Emirates.

———. *The Trucial States.* Irvington 1971 $14.95. ISBN 0-8290-0454-8. History of the United Arab Emirates that examines each of the various republics.

Holden, David, and Richard Johns. *The House of Saud: The Rise and Rule of the Most Powerful Dynasty in the Arab World.* H. Holt & Co. 1981 o.p. Saudi Arabian history that focuses on the Saud dynasty.

Hopwood, Derek, ed. *The Arabian Peninsula: Society and Politics. Studies on Modern Asia and Africa.* Allen & Unwin 1972 o.p. Compilation of addresses, essays, and lectures on the Arabian Peninsula produced by a seminar held by the Center of Middle Eastern Studies.

Kostiner, Joseph. *The Making of Saudi Arabia.* OUP 1993 $39.95. ISBN 0-10-507440-8. Discusses the evolution from tribal society to the present Saudi monarchy.

Lindsey, Gene. *Saudi Arabia.* Hippocrene Bks. 1991 $19.95. ISBN 0-87052-998-6. Historiography of Saudi Arabia; examines the people, their culture, and their government.

Mauger, Thierry. *The Ark of the Desert.* Routledge Chapman & Hall 1991 $49.95. ISBN 0-7103-0436-6. Examines the social practices and customs of the nomadic Bedouins of Saudi Arabia.

Pesce, Angelo. *Jiddah: Portrait of an Arabian City.* St. Mut. 1977 o.p. Discusses the history of the city of Jiddah in Saudi Arabia and its position in the modern Arab world.

Rashid, Nasser I., and Esber I. Shaheen. *Saudia Arabia and the Gulf War.* Intl. Inst. Tech. 1992 $22.95. ISBN 0-940485-01-X. Narrative account of the events that led to the Gulf War plus in-depth analysis of the threat the Iraqi invasion of Kuwait presented to Saudi Arabia and its effect on the U.N. decision to use force.

Wenner, Manfred W. *Modern Yemen, 1918–1966. Studies in Historical and Political Science.* Johns Hopkins 1967 $34.50. ISBN 0-8018-0668-2. Historiography of the Republic of Yemen that discusses its people, places, and social customs.

———. *The Yemen Arab Republic: Development and Change in an Ancient Land.* Westview 1991 $43.00. ISBN 0-89158-774-8. Survey of the land, people, and civilization that gave rise to today's Republic of Yemen.

Zahlan, Rosemarie S. *Making of the Modern Gulf States*. Routledge Chapman & Hall 1989 $16.95. ISBN 0-04-445293-4. Describes how the modern Gulf states arose, with emphasis on the role played by British occupation.

TURKEY

Modern Turkey emerged during the 1920s. Until World War I, Turkey was part of the Ottoman Empire, which lasted four and a half centuries. Although the Turks dominated most of the empire's political and military institutions, the state was more Islamic than national until 1909, when the Young Turks took control of the government and tried to impose a purely Turkish national character on all of its subjects. After Turkey's defeat in World War I, foreign forces invaded the country and attempted to divide it, but, under the leadership of Kemal Ataturk, the Turkish forces were able to expel the foreigners and establish the new state of Turkey. Ever since then, Turkey has maintained a republican form of government. It remained neutral during World War II but joined Western alliances after the war. The history of Turkey before World War I may be found most easily under the subject headings "Ottoman Turkey" and "Ottoman history."

Ahmad, Feroz. *The Making of Modern Turkey*. Routledge 1993 $55.00. ISBN 0-415-07835-0. Discussion of Turkish politics and government from 1909 to the present; examines the role of the Ordu.

Alderson, Anthony D. *The Structure of the Ottoman Dynasty*. Greenwood 1982 repr. of 1956 ed. $62.50. ISBN 0-313-22522-2. Survey of Turkish history from 1288 to 1918 that traces the Ottoman Empire from its beginnings to its fall.

Bailey, Frank E. *British Policy and the Turkish Reform Movement: A Study in Anglo-Turkish Relations, 1826–1853*. Fertig 1970 repr. of 1942 ed. $45.00. ISBN 0-86527-019-8. Examines the foreign and commercial relations between Turkey and Great Britain during an interesting period in the nineteenth century.

Bisbee, Eleanor. *The New Turks: Pioneers of the Republic, 1920–1950*. Greenwood 1975 repr. of 1951 ed. $35.00. ISBN 0-8371-7868-1. Analysis of the founding of modern Turkey after World War I and its history through 1950.

Cawlor, Eric. *Looking for Osman*. Random 1993 $11.00. ISBN 0-679-73822-3. A journalist analyzes social, political, and economic conditions in modern Turkey.

Celik, Zeyneb. *The Remaking of Istanbul*. U. CA Pr. 1993 $25.00. ISBN 0-520-08239-7

Constas, Dimitre, ed. *The Greek-Turkish Conflict in the 1990s*. St. Martin 1991 $59.95. ISBN 0-312-04887-4. Edited lectures and essays on the struggle between Greeks and Turks for control of the island of Cyprus in recent decades.

Davis, P. H., ed. *Flora of Turkey and the East Aegean Islands*. 10 vols. Col. U. Pr. 1956–79 $125.00 ea. Scientific look at the flora of Turkey and the Aegean Islands off Greece and Turkey.

Ferrier, J. P. *Caravan Journeys and Wandering in Persia, Afghanistan, Turkistan, and Beloochistan*. Gregg Intl. repr. of 1857 ed. $230.00 ISBN 0-576-03350-2. A nineteenth-century writer's account of a journey through the Near East and encounters with various nomadic desert tribes.

Findley, Carter V. *Bureaucratic Reform in the Ottoman Empire: The Sublime Porte, 1789–1922*. Princeton U. Pr. 1980 $65.50. ISBN 0-691-05288-3. Survey of Turkish politics and government; during this period that concentrates on the role of the Turkish bureaucracy.

Furcher, Erik. *Turkey: A Modern History*. St. Martin 1993 $49.95. ISBN 1-85043-614-2

Geyikdaqi, Mehmet Y. *Political Parties in Turkey: The Role of Islam*. Greenwood 1984 $27.95. ISBN 0-275-91167-5. Analysis of the influence of Islam on Turkish politics that specifically treats various political parties in Turkish government.

Hasluck, F. W. *Christianity and Islam under the Sultans*. 2 vols. Hippocrene Bks. repr. of 1929 ed. o.p. Description of the relations between Christianity in Turkey during this period; includes a discussion of Turkish folklore and its role in religion.

Hirsch, Eva. *Poverty and Plenty on the Turkish Farm: An Economic Study of Turkish Agriculture in the 1950s. Modern Middle East Ser.* Col. U. Pr. 1970 o.p. Discussion of the agrarian economy with an analysis of agricultural income and its distribution.

Howard, Harry N. *Turkey, the Straits, and U.S. Foreign Policy. Middle East Institute Sponsor Ser.* Johns Hopkins 1975 $45.00. ISBN 0-8018-1590-8. "An excellent, serious, well-documented analysis of US involvement with and interest in the historic Turkish straits" (*Library Journal*).

Issawi, Charles. *The Economic History of Turkey, 1800–1914. Publications of the Ctr. for Middle Eastern Studies.* U. Ch. Pr. 1981 o.p. Historiography of the economy of Turkey from the early nineteenth century to World War I.

Kent, Marian, ed. *The Great Powers and the End of the Ottoman Empire.* Allen & Unwin 1984 o.p. Examines Turkish foreign policy vis-à-vis Europe from 1871 to 1945.

Kinross, Lord. *The Ottoman Centuries: The Rise and Fall of the Turkish Empire.* Morrow 1979 $15.45. ISBN 0-688-08093-6. Genealogical survey of Turkish history from 1288 to 1918 that examines the role the Ottoman Empire played in Turkish development.

Kortepeter, C. Max. *Ottoman Imperialism during the Reformation.* NYU Pr. 1974 o.p. Focuses on Ottoman expansion in Eastern Europe and the Black Sea region.

———. *The Ottoman Turks: Nomad Kingdom to World Empire.* Isis Pr. CA 1991 o.p. Fifteen essays on Ottoman-Turkish history and society.

Lewis, Bernard. *The Emergence of Modern Turkey. Royal Institute of International Affairs Ser.* OUP 1968 $15.95. ISBN 0-19-500344-6. Survey of twentieth-century Turkish history emphasizing political, social, and economic development.

———. *Studies in Classical and Ottoman Islam (7th–16th Centuries).* St. Mut. 1980 o.p. Compares the classical idea of Islam with the Ottoman Empire's view: historiography of Islam from the seventh to the sixteenth century.

Mansfield, Peter. *The Ottoman Empire and Its Successors.* St. Martin 1973 $18.70. ISBN 0-312-58975-1. The history of Turkey from the late Ottoman Empire (1801) until 1927.

Paine, Suzanne. *Exporting Workers: The Turkish Case.* Cambridge U. Pr. 1974 o.p. Examines both the economic conditions in Turkey from 1918 to the 1970s that encouraged emigration and the experiences of Turkish immigrant workers in Europe.

Settle, Mary L. *Turkish Reflections: A Biography of a Place.* S&S Trade 1992 $10.00. ISBN 0-671-77997-4. Reminiscence on Turkey, its people, and its culture by a foreigner.

Shaw, S. J. *History of the Ottoman Empire and Modern Turkey.* 2 vols. Cambridge U. Pr. 1977. Vol. 1 $27.95. ISBN 0-521-29163-1. Vol. 2 $34.95. ISBN 0-521-29166-6. Historiography of Turkey, including political, social, and economic evolution, from the Ottoman Empire (1288–1918) to the development of the modern nation (1918–1960).

Vucinich, W. S. *The Ottoman Empire: Its Record and Legacy.* Krieger 1979 $9.50. ISBN 0-88275-785-7. Examines the history and political, social, and religious legacy of the Ottoman Empire.

Webster, D. E. *The Turkey of Ataturk: Social Process in the Turkish Reformation.* AMS Pr. repr. of 1939 ed. $20.00. ISBN 0-404-56333-3

Weiker, Walter F. *The Modernization of Turkey from Ataturk to the Present Day.* Holmes & Meier 1981 $45.00. ISBN 0-8419-0503-7. Analysis of Turkish politics and government and their impact on economic conditions from 1909 to 1980.

OTHER STATES AND PEOPLES

The other major countries of the Middle East are found in the northern region, an area that used to be called Greater Syria. These nations are Syria, Lebanon, and Jordan. Civilization in the northern region can be traced back more than 7,000 years. It became prosperous and powerful in the third millennium B.C., and Syria's capital, Damascus, is perhaps the oldest continually inhabited city in the world. The coastal area was inhabited in ancient times by peoples known as Canaanites and Phoenicians; the latter developed the first known phonetic alphabet and were famous traders who crisscrossed the seas. In the interior, the Aramaeans dominated overland trade. The area was ruled successively by Persians, Greeks, and Romans before the rise of Islam, when Greater Syria became part of the Islamic empire. From the sixteenth to the twentieth centuries, the region was ruled by the Ottoman Empire. Then, during World War I, Syrian leaders revolted against the Ottomans, and, after the war ended, they declared the independence of Greater Syria at a specially convened congress in Damascus. France and Great Britain intervened, however, and divided the country into four states: Palestine and Trans-Jordan, ruled by Britain; Lebanon and Syria, ruled by France. After World War II, four countries in the area emerged as independent states: Israel, Syria, Lebanon, and Jordan. The majority of Palestinians who live outside of Israel and the occupied territories reside in the latter three countries.

Beginning in the 1970s, Lebanon endured a tragic civil war that lasted for nearly 15 years and is now reconstructing its economy. Jordan, a constitutional monarchy ruled by a Hashemite king (the Hashemites are descendants of the prophet Muhammad), has developed quite rapidly in recent decades, despite its lack of natural resources and its entanglement in the Arab-Israeli conflict. Syria, the largest and most populous of the four states, became a parliamentary democracy upon independence, but a military coup in 1949 overthrew the elected government. The government changed hands several times until 1970, when Hafez Asad assumed power. Syria opposed Iraq's invasion of Kuwait and supported the campaign to oust Saddam Hussein's forces from the oil-rich country.

In addition to these major nations, a number of other small nations are found in the Middle East. These include Kuwait, Yemen, Oman, Qatar, Bahrain, and the United Arab Emirates. These smaller states, many ruled by hereditary rulers, also have a rich Islamic heritage. Their importance today lies in the great reserves of oil found beneath them. Although not located in the Middle East, the Islamic nation of Afghanistan lies just to the east. It also has a long, rich history and, in more recent years, has been notable for its civil war and Soviet involvement in it.

al-Mushin Mad'a, al-Mud'aj. *Yemen in Early Islam*. Paul & Co. Pubs. 1991 $50.00. ISBN 0-86372-102-8. Examines the role Yemen played in the early Islamic community.

Bosworth, Clifford E. *The Later Ghaznavids*. Mazda Pubs. 1977 $19.95. ISBN 0-231-04428-3. Examines the Ghaznavid tribe of Afghanistan and Iran and details the history of Afghanistan and India.

Bradsher, Henry S. *Afghanistan and the Soviet Union*. Duke 1985 $39.95. ISBN 0-8223-0556-9. Examines foreign relations between Afghanistan and the Soviet Union and the Soviet occupation of the country between 1979 and 1989.

Castle, Wilfrid T. *Syrian Pageant: The History of Syria and Palestine, 100 B.C. to A.D. 1945*. Gordon Pr. 1977 $59.95. ISBN 0-8490-2716-0

Clements, Frank A. *Kuwait*. ABC-CLIO 1985 $50.00. ISBN 0-903450-99-2

Deonna, Laurence. *Yemen*. Three Continents 1991 $32.00. ISBN 0-89410-710-0

Dresch, Paul. *Tribes, Government, and History of Yemen*. OUP 1990 $98.00. ISBN 0-19-827331-2

Dupree, Louis. *Afghanistan*. Princeton U. Pr. 1973 $26.95. ISBN 0-691-00023-9. Historiography of Afghanistan and its people that analyzes the political, social, and economic conditions before the Soviet occupation.

el-Fathaly, Omar I., and Monte Palmer. *Political Development and Social Change in Libya*. Lexington Bks. 1980 o.p.

Fletcher, Arnold. *Afghanistan: Highway of Conquest*. Greenwood 1982 repr. of 1965 ed. o.p. Examines the history of Afghanistan in light of its strategic location; discusses the various wars and conquests of the Afghani people.

Gall, Sandy. *Behind Russian Lines: An Afghan Journal.* St. Martin 1984 $35.00. ISBN 0-312-07260-0. A look at the Soviet occupation of Afghanistan by a journalist who traveled through the war-torn country in 1981.

Hanson, Diania. *Postwar Kuwait—The Middle East.* Landmark TX 1991 $19.95. ISBN 0-9629852-0-1

Hart, Alan. *Arafat: A Political Biography.* Ind. U. Pr. 1984 $39.95. ISBN 0-253-32711-3. Detailed look at Arafat and the Palestine Liberation Organization (PLO).

Ismael, Jacqueline S. *Kuwait: Dependency and Class in a Rentier State.* U. Press Fla. 1993 $19.95. ISBN 0-8130-1186-8

Loizos, Peter. *The Greek Gift: Politics in a Cypriot Village.* St. Martin 1975 o.p. History of Cyprus that examines political, social, and economic conditions on the island.

Longrigg, Stephen H. *Syria and Lebanon under French Mandate.* Hippocrene Bks. 1972 $29.00. ISBN 0-374-95088-1. Analysis of political, social, and economic conditions in Syria and Lebanon under French rule.

Miller, Donald E., and Lorna Touryan. *Survivors: An Oral History of the Armenian Genocide.* U. CA Pr. 1993. ISBN 0-520-07984-1. A political and social history of the Armenian people.

Newell, Nancy P., and Richard S. Newell. *The Struggle in Afghanistan.* Cornell Univ. Pr. 1982 o.p. Surveys Afghanistan during the Soviet occupation (1979–89); examines the Afghanis' long experience of war and conquest.

Nikolaos, Van Dam. *The Struggle for Power in Syria: Sectarianism, Regionalism and Tribalism in Politics, 1961–1978.* St. Martin 1979 o.p. Analysis of two decades of Syrian politics with special emphasis on the political power of minorities.

Porter, Jadranka. *Under Siege in Kuwait.* HM 1991 $8.70. ISBN 0-395-60580-6. Discusses the situation of the Kuwaiti people during the Iraqi occupation.

Quandt, William B. *The Politics of Palestinian Nationalism.* U. CA Pr. 1973 $37.50. ISBN 0-520-02336-6. Examines Palestinian nationalism and the political movements it has given rise to, particularly the Fedayeen.

Said, Edward W. *The Question of Palestine.* Random 1992 $11.00. ISBN 0-679-73988-2. Examines overall Israel-Arab relations with focus on the Palestinian Arabs living in the occupied territories and their quest for an independent state.

Seale, Patrick. *Assad: The Struggle for the Middle East.* U. CA Pr. 1989 $35.00. ISBN 0-520-06667-7. Deals with Syrian politics during the 1970s and 1980s.

Vatikiotis, P.J. *Politics and the Military in Jordan: A Study of the Arab Legion, 1921–1957.* Biblio NY 1967 o.p. Analysis of the development of Jordan's military and the role it played in Jordanian politics from the 1920s to the late 1950s.

Wai, Dunstan M., ed. *The Southern Sudan: The Problem of National Integration.* Intl. Spec. Bk. 1973 $29.50. ISBN 0-7146-2985-5. Genealogy of the Sudan that focuses on its history; contains an analysis of the 1955–1972 civil war.

CHRONOLOGY OF AUTHORS

Al-Tabari. c.839–923
Ibn Khaldun, Abd al-Rahman. 1332–1406
Hitti, Philip Khuri. 1886–1978
Gibb, Hamilton. 1895–1971

Hourani, Albert. 1916–1993
Inalcik, Halil. 1916–
Lewis, Bernard. 1916–
Peters F(rancis) E(dward). 1927–
Said, Edward. 1935–

AL-TABARI (ABU JA'FAR MUHAMMAD IBN JABIR AL-TABARI). c.839–923

Persian-born al-Tabari is one of the most prolific historians of medieval and Islamic history. A teacher of law, in his youth he traveled in Iraq, Syria, and Egypt to collect written materials and to record oral traditions. Eventually, he settled and remained in Baghdad, residing there during turbulent times in the history of the Abbasid Caliphate. It was in that city that he wrote his most famous work, *Ta'rikh ar-Rusul wa-al-Muluk (History of the Prophets and the Kings)*, a multivolume compendium in which he condensed the vast knowledge and traditions of preceding generations. The work traced history from creation to A.D. 915. Historians often have used al-Tabari's history as an important source in their writings about Islamic history before A.D. 915. Because he did not explore or speculate on causes of events, his history is essentially an extensive chronology of events that occurred in each year of the period. Most of what he wrote about took place in the central Islamic lands. Al-Tabari's work became so popular that it was soon translated into Persian.

BOOKS BY AL-TABARI

History of al-Tabari. State U. NY Pr. Vol. 3 Trans. by W. M. Brinner. 1991 $44.50. ISBN 0-7914-0687-3. Vol. 6 Trans. by W. M. Watt and M. V. McDonald. 1987 $57.50. ISBN 0-88706-344-6. Vol. 9 Trans. by I. K. Poonawala. 1990 $59.50. ISBN 0-88706-692-5. Vol. 12 Trans. by Y. Friedmann. 1991 $59.50. ISBN 0-7914-0733-0. Vol. 13 Trans. by G. Juynboll. 1989 $44.50. ISBN 0-88706-8766. Vol. 19 Trans. by C. E. Bosworth. 1991 $57.50. ISBN 0-7914-0040-9. Vol. 21 Trans. by M. Fishbein. 1990 $54.50. ISBN 0-7914-0221-5. Vol. 23 Trans. by M. Hinds. 1990 $49.50. ISBN 0-88706-721-2. Vol. 24 Trans. by D. S. Powers. 1989 $44.50. ISBN 0-7914-0073-5. Vol. 27 Trans. by J. A. Williams. 1985 $44.50. ISBN 0-7914-0625-3. Vol. 33 Trans. by C. E. Bosworth. 1991 $57.50. ISBN 0-7914-0493-5

GIBB, HAMILTON (ALEXANDER ROSSKEEN). 1895–1971

Hamilton Gibb was born in Alexandria, Egypt, and was educated at Edinburgh University and London University. After serving in the Royal Field Artillery during World War I, he became a professor of Arabic at the University of London and at Oxford University. Later he taught at Harvard (1955–64). He was a founder of Fuad I Academy of Arabic Languages in Cairo and director of the Center for Middle Eastern Studies from 1957 to 1966. Author of several works on Arab history, culture, and literature, and editor of *The Encyclopedia of Islam* (1960), a standard work, Gibb was one of the finest Islamic scholars of his generation. He wrote of Islam, he said, as a Christian "engaged in a common spiritual enterprise."

BOOKS BY GIBB

The Arab Conquests in Central Asia. AMS Pr. repr. of 1923 ed. $16.00. ISBN 0-404-02718-0
Arabic Literature: An Introduction. o.p.
Islamic Society in the West (coauthored with Harold Bowen). o.p.
The Life of Saladin. o.p.
Modern Trends in Islam. o.p.
Shorter Encyclopedia of Islam E. J. Brill 1991 repr. of 1953 ed. $63.00. ISBN 90-04-00681-8. Relates particularly to the religion and law of Islam.
Studies in Contemporary Arabic Literature. o.p.

HITTI, PHILIP KHURI. 1886–1978

Born in Lebanon, Philip K. Hitti was educated at the American University of Beirut and at Columbia University in New York. He received his Ph.D. in history from Columbia in 1915, two years after he had settled in the United States. In 1925, following a number of years of teaching at Columbia and at American University of Beirut, he accepted an appointment at Princeton University, where he remained until his retirement in 1954. He became the first director of Princeton's Near Eastern Studies Program.

Hitti translated, wrote, and lectured extensively about the Arab world and Islamic civilization. A leading authority in the United States on Arabic and Islamic studies, he promoted and popularized Arabic studies in American educational institutions for nearly half a century. His most famous work is *History of the Arabs*, published in 1937, today considered a standard in the field.

BOOKS BY HITTI

Capital Cities of Arab Islam. Bks. Demand 1973 $46.00. ISBN 0-317-42319-3. Genealogy of the chief cities and towns of Arab Islam.

History of the Arabs. 1937. St. Martin 10th ed. 1970 $32.00. ISBN 0-312-37520-4

Islam: A Way of Life. Regnery Gateway 1971 o.p. Discusses the religion and culture of Islam; a look into the traditions of a civilization built on religion.

Islam and the West: A Historical Cultural Survey. Krieger 1979 $9.50. ISBN 0-88275-787-3. Examines relations between the Islamic East and the Christian West and contrasts these two civilizations' cultural and religious ideals.

A Short History of the Arabs. Regnery Gateway 1956 $7.50. ISBN 0-89526-982-1. Examines the customs, traditions, and peoples that created Arabic civilization.

HOURANI, ALBERT. 1916–1993

Distinguished historian and interpreter, Albert Hourani grew up in Manchester, England, with his parents, who had immigrated from Lebanon. He was educated in London and at Magdalen College of Oxford University. During his academic career, he traveled to the Middle East frequently and lectured widely at major universities and conferences in the United States.

A renowned scholar and professor of Middle Eastern history, he served as director of the Middle East Center at St. Antony's College, Oxford University—a center that he helped to found in 1958. Hourani's *A History of the Arab Peoples* (1991), a single-volume work that chronicles the story of Arab civilization, has been hailed as one of the most definitive works on the subject. In the words of Roy Mottahedeh of Harvard University, "Albert Hourani's *A History of the Arab Peoples* offers, in beautifully clear English, a study that supersedes all earlier treatments. . . . It is fair but never afraid to take a point of view. To write such a sound work, ranging over centuries and topics, is an astonishing feat."

BOOKS BY HOURANI

Arabic Thought in the Liberal Age, 1798–1939. Cambridge U. Pr. 1983 $21.95. ISBN 0-521-27423-0. A discussion of politics and government in the Middle East during the period known as the Liberal Age.

Europe and the Middle East. U. CA Pr. 1980 $45.00. ISBN 0-520-03742-1. Compilation of addresses, essays, and lectures on the Middle East and Europe, Islam and Christianity; examines the role of religion in politics in Arab nations.

A History of the Arab Peoples. Warner Bks. 1992 $14.99. ISBN 0-446-39392-4

Minorities in the Arab World. AMS Pr. 1947 $18.50. ISBN 0-404-16402-1. Discussion of the various minorities in Arab nations and the role they have played in these nations' politics and history.

IBN KHALDUN, ABD AL-RAHMAN. 1332–1406

Called the Father of the Philosophy of History and the Father of Sociology, Ibn Khaldun is considered the first and one of the greatest philosophers of history. Born in Muslim Spain and educated in Tunis, he served as a judge and a secretary in the service of rulers in both Spain and North Africa. In 1382 he moved to Egypt, where he became chief judge of Cairo and a lecturer at the Azhar Mosque University. In 1400 he accompanied the Egyptians on their campaign against the Mongol warrior Tamerlane and played a role in the arrangements for the surrender of Damascus. Ibn Khaldun gained much recognition for his seven-volume work on universal history, *Kitab al-Ibar (Book of Lessons)*. In the work, focused mostly on the Muslim world, Ibn Khaldun attempts to treat history as a science. He made his most important contribution in the first part of the work, *Muqaddimah (The Introduction)*, in which he outlines his philosophy of history, analyzing causes of events and setting social, geographic, and economic contexts for historical changes.

BOOKS BY IBN KHALDUN

The Muqaddimah. Abr. ed. by N.J. Dowood, based on Rosenthal's translation. Princeton U. Pr. 1967 $14.95. ISBN 0-691-01754-9.
The Muqaddimah. 3 vols. Trans. by Franz Rosenthal. Princeton U. Pr. 2nd ed. 1967 $190.00. ISBN 0-691-09797-6

INALCIK, HALIL. 1916–

A prominent scholar in Middle Eastern history for nearly half a century, Halil Inalcik was born in Istanbul, Turkey, and received his Ph.D. from the University of Ankara in 1942. He taught at his alma mater from 1943 to 1972, when he accepted a professorship in Middle Eastern history at the University of Chicago, where he currently is professor emeritus. An authority on the Ottoman-Turkish period, particularly in the field of social and economic history, Inalcik lectures widely at major universities and international conferences and has written numerous articles and books in both Turkish and English.

BOOKS BY INALCIK

The Ottoman Empire: Conquest, Organization, and Economy. Ashgate Pub. Co. 1970 o.p. Examines the economic organization of the empire from its beginnings in 1288 to its demise in 1918.
The Ottoman Empire: The Classical Age 1300–1600. Caratzas 2nd ed. 1989 $50.00. ISBN 0-89241-388-3. Discusses Turkish history during the two periods that make up the Classical Period: 1288–1453 and 1453–1683.
Studies in Ottoman Social and Economic History. Ashgate Pub. Co. 1985 $89.95. ISBN 0-86078-162-3. Scrutinizes the social and economic effects of Ottoman rule from 1288 to 1918.

LEWIS, BERNARD. 1916–

Born in London, Bernard Lewis grew up in England. In 1974 he immigrated to the United States and eight years later became a U.S. citizen. A distinguished scholar of Middle Eastern history and a prolific writer, his education includes a *diplôme des études semitiques* from the University of Paris and a Ph.D. from the University of London, where he taught for 25 years before coming to Princeton in 1974. Most recently he has served as professor at the Institute of Advanced Studies and the Department of Near Eastern Studies at Princeton. As a visiting professor, he lectured at a number of notable universities in Europe and the United States.

BOOKS BY LEWIS

Arabs in History. OUP 1993 $20.00. ISBN 0-19-285258-2. Analysis of history and civilization of the Arabian Peninsula.
The Assassins: A Radical Sect in Islam. OUP 1987 $9.95. ISBN 0-19-520550-2. A fascinating study of the radical sect of assassins known as the Ismailites.
The Emergence of Modern Turkey. OUP 2nd ed. 1968 $15.95. ISBN 0-19-500344-6. A study of the origins of modern Turkey.

Islam and the Arab World: Faith, People, Culture. (ed. & trans.) Knopf 1976 o.p. Examines Islamic culture and art and the civilization that produced them.

Istanbul and the Civilization of the Ottoman Empire. U. of Okla. Pr. 1972 $9.95. ISBN 0-8061-1060-0. Origins and history of the capital and principal city of Turkey.

The Jews of Islam. Princeton U. Pr. 1987 $42.50. ISBN 0-691-05419-3. Probes the relations of Jews and Muslims in the Arab nations.

The Muslim Discovery of Europe. Norton 1985 $12.95. ISBN 0-393-30233-4

The Political Language of Islam. U. Ch. Pr. 1988 $9.95. ISBN 0-226-47693-6. Compiled from lectures given at the University of Chicago.

Race and Slavery in the Middle East. OUP 1992 $10.95. ISBN 0-19-505326-5. Describes the Middle Eastern slave trade in former times and the modern practice of slavery and its connection with race.

Semites and Anti-Semites. Norton 1987 $7.95. ISBN 0-393-30420-5. Analysis of anti-Semitism in the Arab nations.

PETERS, F(RANCIS) E(DWARD). 1927–

The American scholar F. E. Peters is professor of classics and history at New York University and chairs the university's Department of Near Eastern Languages and Literature. He was educated at St. Louis University and received his Ph.D. in Oriental Studies from Princeton University in 1961. Peters has written about classical civilizations in the Middle East and Near Eastern urbanism, and about the religion and culture of Islam, especially during the Early Period.

BOOKS BY PETERS

Allah's Commonwealth. 1974 o.p.

Aristotle and the Arabs. 1968 o.p.

The Children of Abraham: Judaism, Christianity, Islam. Princeton U. Pr. 1983 $12.95. ISBN 0-691-02030-2

Jersulem: The Holy City. Princeton U. Pr. 1985 $45.00. ISBN 0-691-07300-7. Remarkably objective history up to 1838. Focuses on historical events and the major religious sites.

SAID, EDWARD. 1935–

Born in Jerusalem and educated at Victoria College in Cairo and at Princeton and Harvard universities, Edward Said has taught at Columbia University since 1963 and has been a visiting professor at Harvard and Johns Hopkins University. He has had an unusual dual career as a professor of comparative literature, a recognized expert on the novelist and short story writer JOSEPH CONRAD, (see Vol. 1) and as one of the most significant contemporary writers on the Middle East, especially the Palestinian question and the plight of Palestinians living in the occupied territories.

Although he is not a trained historian, his *Orientalism* (1978) is one of the most stimulating critical evaluations of traditional Western writing on Middle Eastern history, societies, and literature. In the controversial *Covering Islam* (1981), he examined how the Western media have biased Western perspectives on the Middle East. A Palestinian by birth, Said has sought to show how Palestinian history differs from the rest of Arabic history because of the encounter with Jewish settlers and to present to Western readers a more broadly representative Palestinian position than they usually obtain from Western sources.

Said is presently Old Dominion Foundation Professor in the Humanities at Columbia, editor of *Arab Studies Quarterly*, and chair of the board of trustees of the Institute of Arab Studies. He is a member of the Palestinian National Council as well as the Council on Foreign Relations in New York.

BOOKS BY SAID

After the Last Sky: Palestinian Lives. Pantheon 1986 $20.00. ISBN 0-394-74469-1. Poetic and powerful book focusing on a theme of exile. Something beyond the daily headlines.

Blaming the Victims: Spurious Scholarship and the Palestinian Question. Routledge Chapman & Hall 1988 $50.00. ISBN 0-86091-887-4. Addresses the politics and demographics of the Arab-Isaeli conflict.

Covering Islam. Pantheon 1993 $12.00. ISBN 0-394-74808-5

Orientalism. Random 1979 $12.00. ISBN 0-394-74067-X

The Question of Palestine. Random 1980 ISBN 0-8129-0832-5

CHAPTER 14

History of Asia and the Pacific

W. Dean Kinzley

It is because the Far-East holds up the mirror to our civilization—a mirror that like all mirrors gives us back left for right—because by her very oddities, as they strike us at first, we truly learn to criticize, examine, and realize our own way of doing things, that she is so interesting. It is in this that her great attraction lies.

—PERCIVAL LOWELL, *Choson*

Until at least the mid-twentieth century, Western studies of Asian and Pacific history were narrowly conceived. Writers often focused on exotic, distinctive, or simply weird behaviors or artifacts. Peculiarities were representative and exoticism the norm. The region existed as an alternative universe outside the usual or normal range of historical experience. If the region was considered part of a broader history, it was only as the object of European ambition, expansion, or selfless civilizing efforts.

World War II and events surrounding it forced Western historians and writers to begin to look at Asian and Pacific society and history differently. The immediate concern became to understand the origins of war in the Pacific. At the same time, the growth of anticolonial movements in India, Indonesia, and Indochina, as well as emerging Nationalist and Communist movements in China and Korea, also encouraged scholars to begin to take the region seriously. The unfolding midcentury catastrophic events in Asia gave rise to new interest in understanding its history and character. Since about the 1970s, the emphasis has shifted from seeking the causes of destruction and failure to explaining growth and success. The emergence of Japan as an economic superpower, the explosive growth of the region's newly industrialized countries (NICs), and the beginnings of economic revitalization in China and India have led scholars to explore the roots of these developments. Thus, while the focus of recent Western scholarship on Asian history and society has changed, recognition of its importance has not only remained but also has expanded.

It would probably be unhelpful, misleading, and certainly unwise to proffer specific themes developed in the historiography on the region. Its breadth and diversity make such an effort impossible. Nevertheless, a few general observations may be appropriate. First, a critical theme in Asian and Pacific history has been—and remains—the issue of modern nation building. How did Asian societies respond to European intrusions and challenges? How were political and social institutions reformulated to establish or retain independence and national sovereignty? How did the new states seek to fit themselves into their own traditions and into the world community? Questions such as these underlie, for example, JOHN KING FAIRBANK's *The Great Chinese Revolution, 1890–1985* (1986), Charles F. Keyes's *Thailand: Buddhist Kingdom as Modern Nation-State* (1987), and the work of many other scholars of the region.

A second theme that emerges in the writings on numerous countries in the region is the issue of social and ethnic diversity and conflict. The ongoing struggles in the countries of South Asia have been and remain a major concern driving historical scholarship. The less obvious problems of ethnicity in China and Southeast Asia have also informed historical writing, as in David Joel Steinberg's *The Philippines: A Singular and a Plural Place* (1982). The clash between European and indigenous peoples in Australia and the South Pacific is, not surprisingly, a major undercurrent in historical writing on that broad area.

A third theme is economic organization and action. How have local and regional economies functioned and changed? How and in what ways have the political and economic spheres intersected? How has contemporary economic activity and behavior been shaped by traditional practices and ideas? Questions of this sort have been especially prominent in historical writing over the last 25 years as Western writers have sought to explain Asian economic success.

This list of themes is certainly not exhaustive, but it does suggest the range of concerns that has been driving the work of writers of Asian and Pacific history since World War II. These themes move away from exoticism and toward issues that underlie Western history itself. In the same way, the analytical tools to write Asian history are those also used by students of Western history. Thus, in the last 15 years, both social and cultural history have been prominent. More recently still, women's history and gender studies are apparent in historical work on Asia and the Pacific. Just as Asia has come to be seen as a major actor in an interconnected global community, Western-language writing on Asian and Pacific history has come out from behind the door of exoticism and difference to join the dialogue on the human past and thus the meaning of our collective present.

REFERENCE WORKS

Association for Asian Studies. *Cumulative Bibliography of Asian Studies, 1941–1965.* 4 vols. G. K. Hall 1970 $445.00. ISBN 0-8161-0805-6. Covers books and articles and includes a four-volume author bibliography and a four-volume subject bibliography.
————. *Cumulative Bibliography of Asian Studies, 1966–1970.* G. K. Hall 1973 o.p. Consists of a three-volume author bibliography and a four-volume subject bibliography.
Bibliography of Asian Studies. 1977. Bks. Demand repr. of 1980 ed. $160.00. ISBN 0-8357-7177-6. Basic resource that covers all areas of Asia. Published annually as a separate volume since 1970 but currently about five years behind. Volumes come with membership in the Association for Asian Studies and accompany the *Journal of Asian Studies.*
Embree, Ainslie T. *Encyclopedia of Asian History.* 4 vols. Macmillan 1988 $360.00. ISBN 0-684-18619-5. Impressive new reference tool prepared under the auspices of the Asia Society. Includes signed articles by scholars, bibliographies, and a topical index.
Fenton, Thomas P., and Mary J. Heffron, eds. and comps. *Asia and the Pacific: A Directory of Resources.* Orbis Bks. 1986 $12.95. ISBN 0-88344-528-X. Directory listing books, organizations, periodicals, pamphlets, articles, and so on, that aim to promote reform. Includes indexes.
Historical and Cultural Dictionaries of Asia. Scarecrow 1972–76 o.p. Separate volumes covering each country; entries cover topics and personal names.
Nunn, G. Raymond, ed. *Asia Reference Works: A Selected Annotated Guide.* Wilson 1980 repr. of 1971 ed. o.p.

Shavit, David. *The United States in Asia: A Historical Dictionary.* Greenwood 1990 $75.00. ISBN 0-313-26788-X. Short articles with bibliographies; topical index. Does not include the Middle East.

Wint, Guy. *Asia: A Handbook.* Greenwood 1966 o.p.

SURVEYS AND GENERAL WORKS

Davenport-Hines, R.P.T., and Geoffrey Jones, eds. *British Business in Asia Since 1860.* Cambridge U. Pr. 1989 $64.95. ISBN 0-521-33527-2. Essays that survey British economic activities in various states in Asia.

Esposito, John L., ed. *Islam in Asia: Religion, Politics, and Society.* OUP 1987 $15.95. ISBN 0-19-504082-1. Essays on the nature and social place of Islam in various Asian countries.

Farmer, Edward L., and others. *Comparative History of Civilizations in Asia.* 2 vols. Westview 1986 $26.95 ea. ISBNs 0-8133-0354-0, 0-8133-0356-7. Workmanlike study of countries and regions from Egypt to Japan. Detailed treatment but not analytically well developed. Satisfactory as a general introduction.

Mabbet, Ian, ed. *Patterns of Kingship and Authority in Traditional Asia.* Routledge Chapman & Hall 1985 o.p. Essays on the differing role and character of the traditional sovereign in various states in Asia.

Pye, Lucian W. *Asian Power and Politics: The Cultural Dimensions of Authority.* HUP 1985 $14.95. ISBN 0-674-04979-9. Focuses on the distinctiveness of the various Asian cultural values.

Welty, Paul T. *The Asians: Their Heritage and Their Destiny.* HarpC 1976 o.p.

EAST ASIA

In this chapter East Asia refers to China, Japan, and Korea. These countries are bound in their relationship to the classic China-centered world and the effort to redefine that world in the nineteenth century. There is a substantial body of writing that seeks to clarify the relationship among these countries. How have Japan and Korea been influenced by their larger neighbor? How have the various countries sought to maintain their separate identities and cultures? Why have the modern destinies of these countries been so dramatically different? While trying to answer such questions, writers on East Asia have also sought to show that, despite the powerful ties that bind these countries one to the other, each differs profoundly from the other.

Reference Works

Abraham, Roberta. *Bibliography on Technology and Social Change in China and Japan.* Committee on Technology and Social Change in Foreign Cultures. Iowa St. U. Pr. 1974 $12.00. ISBN 0-945271-21-2. Useful reference tool focused on a topic important to contemporary writers and scholars.

Koh, Hesung Chun. *Korean and Japanese Women: An Analytic Bibliographical Guide.* Greenwood 1982 o.p.

O'Neill, Hugh B. *Companion to Chinese History.* Facts on File 1987 $27.50. ISBN 0-87196-841-X. Provides basic information on several hundred topics and people. Chronology covering 1506–1985. Does not include indexes.

Silberman, Bernard S. *Japan and Korea: A Critical Bibliography.* Greenwood 1962 $49.75. ISBN 0-313-23594-5. Good starting place.

Surveys and General Works

Boyle, John H. *China and Japan at War. 1937–1945: The Politics of Collaboration.* Stanford U. Pr. 1972 $49.50. ISBN 0-8047-0800-2. Focuses on the politics of the second Sino-Japanese War.

Conroy, Hilary. *The Japanese Seizure of Korea, 1868–1910: A Study of Realism and Idealism in International Relations.* U. of Pa. Pr. 1960 o.p. Influential analysis of forces leading to the colonization of Korea.

DeBary, William Theodore. *East Asian Civilizations: A Dialogue in Five Stages.* HUP 1988 $9.95. ISBN 0-674-22406-X. Broad synthesis of East Asian development and the influence of China and Chinese ideas.

DeVos, George A., and Takao Sofue, eds. *Religion and Family in East Asia.* U. CA Pr. 1986 $16.95. ISBN 0-520-05762-7. Wide-ranging essays on the social implications of religious thought in the East Asian region.

Fairbank, John K., and others. *East Asia: Tradition and Transformation.* HM rev. ed. 1989 $50.36. ISBN 0-395-45023-3. Classic American text on the region.

Goodman, Grant K., ed. *Japanese Cultural Policies in Southeast Asia During World War 2.* St. Martin 1991 $39.95. ISBN 0-312-05243-X. Five essays on Japanese activities in Southeast Asian countries intended to secure dominance.

Hanley, Susan B., and Arthur P. Wolf, eds. *Family and Population in East Asian History.* Stanford U. Pr. 1985 $45.00. ISBN 0-8047-1232-8. Stimulating and important volume using contemporary demographic methodologies.

Iriye, Akira. *After Imperialism: The Search for a New Order in the Far East, 1921–1931.* Imprint Pubns. 1990 $15.95. ISBN 1-879176-00-9. Important study of the effort to reestablish stability in Asia following World War I.

———, ed. *The Chinese and Japanese: Essays in Political and Cultural Interactions.* Princeton U. Pr. 1980 $55.00. ISBN 0-691-03126-6. Essays on a variety of topics linking China and Japan.

Iriye, Akira, and Warren Cohen, eds. *American, Chinese, and Japanese Perspectives on Wartime Asia, 1931–1949.* Scholarly Res. Inc. 1990 $40.00. ISBN 0-8420-2347-X. Essays by scholars from several Asian countries offering differing views of the war years.

Jansen, Marius B. *Japan and China: From War to Peace, 1894–1972.* Rand McNally 1975 o.p. Excellent survey of the dynamic relationship among Northeast Asian countries.

———. *The Japanese and Sun Yat-sen.* HUP 1954 o.p. Still the best treatment of the links between Japan and China's revolutionary movement.

Kim, Key-Hiuk. *The Last Phase of the East Asian World Order: Korea, Japan, and the Chinese Empire, 1860–1882.* U. CA Pr. 1979 $47.50. ISBN 0-520-03556-9. Deals with the struggle to create a new diplomatic regime in Northeast Asia.

Lebra, Joyce, ed. *Japan's Greater East Asia Co-Prosperity Sphere in World War II: Selected Readings and Documents.* OUP 1975 o.p. A useful collection and analysis of material related to Japanese control of various Asian countries.

Lee, Chong-sik. *Japan and Korea: The Political Dimension.* Hoover Inst. Pr. 1985 $24.95. ISBN 0-8179-8181-0. A general treatment of political dialogue from 1945 to the present.

Lensen, George Alexander. *Balance of Intrigue: International Rivalry in Korea and Manchuria, 1884–1899.* UH Pr. 1982 o.p. A study of the complex struggles among the various powers over this region.

McCoy, Alfred W., ed. *Southeast Asia Under Japanese Occupation.* Southeast Asia Studies. Yale U. Pr. 1980 $14.00. ISBN 0-938692-08-0. Essays on conditions in the several countries controlled by Japan.

McKnight, Brian E. *Law and the State in Traditional East Asia: Six Studies on the Sources of East Asian Law.* UH Pr. 1987 $20.00. ISBN 0-8248-0838-X. Solid studies of Chinese law or the influence of Chinese law on other Asian countries.

Moulder, Frances V. *Japan, China and the Modern World Economy: Toward a Reinterpretation of East Asian Development.* Cambridge U. Pr. 1977 o.p. A controversial study of the effects of imperialism on Asian modern development.

Myers, Ramon H., and Mark R. Peattie, eds. *The Japanese Colonial Empire, 1895–1945.* Princeton U. Pr. 1984 $21.95. ISBN 0-691-10222-8. Centers on the state and conduct of colonial administration throughout Asia.

Newell, William H., ed. *Japan in Asia.* Singapore Univ. Pr. 1981 o.p. Seven essays on the World War II period.

Rozman, Gilbert. *The East Asian Region: Confucian Heritage and Its Modern Adaptation.* Princeton U. Pr. 1991 $29.95. ISBN 0-691-05597-1. Essays on the presence and place of Confucian ideas and tradition in modern Asia.

Scalapino, Robert A. *The Politics of Development: Perspectives on Twentieth Century Asia.* HUP 1989 $19.95. ISBN 0-674-68757-4. Broad and thoughtful analyses of forces leading toward development in Asia.

Woodside, Alexander B. *Vietnam and the Chinese Model—A Comparative Study of Nguyen and Ch'ing Civil Government in the First Half of the Nineteenth Century.* HUP 1971 $14.00. ISBN 0-674-93721-X. An important study of an important topic.

China

Western writing on China has a long and rich tradition. From MARCO POLO forward, the size and grandeur of China and its history have fascinated Western travelers and writers. Much of the early writing focused on the splendor of the Chinese imperial tradition. By the nineteenth century, this perspective was nearly reversed as foreigners saw China as a backward, bankrupt, and barbarous relic. Since World War II, historical writing on China has undergone real growth, as writers sought to understand the roots of the People's Republic of China, its relationship to the traditional Chinese order, and the historical forces that led first to the weakening and ultimately to the collapse of that order. This renaissance has resulted in a richly textured body of writing on Chinese history using Chinese language sources that has demonstrated the diversity of both the traditional and the more modern society. Scholarship on women, workers, and minorities has served to break down the image of an undifferentiated imperial system, with the result that China and the Chinese appear both more human and more real.

REFERENCE WORKS

Berton, Peter, and Eugene Wu. *Contemporary China: A Research Guide.* Hoover Inst. Pr. 1967 o.p. Contains 2,226 entries of books, periodicals, and theses published mainly after 1949 in Communist China and after 1945 in Taiwan.

Ebrey, Patricia B., ed. *Chinese Civilization and Society: A Sourcebook.* Free Pr. 1981 $18.95. ISBN 0-02-908760-0

Goodrich, L. Carrington, and Chaoying Fang, eds. *Dictionary of Ming Biography 1368–1644.* 2 vols. Col. U. Pr. 1976 $191.00. ISBN 0-685-62034-4. A trove of important and interesting tidbits of facts.

Hook, Brian, ed. *The Cambridge Encyclopedia of China.* Cambridge U. Pr. 1991 $49.50. ISBN 0-521-35594-X. Nicely illustrated encyclopedia that provides basic information about Chinese history and culture up to the 1980s.

Hsieh, Chiao-min. *Atlas of China.* McGraw 1973 o.p. A useful guide.

Hucker, Charles O. *China: A Critical Bibliography.* U. of Ariz. Pr. 1962 o.p.

Hummel, Arthur W. *Eminent Chinese of the Ch'ing Period.* Gordon Pr. 1976 repr. of 1943 ed. $75.00. ISBN 0-8490-1761-0. Older title that remains a valuable resource.

Kaplan, Frederic M., and others, eds. *Encyclopedia of China Today.* Eurasia Pr. 1991 $29.95. ISBN 0-932030-11-4. A comprehensive guide to the People's Republic of China that includes chronologies, maps, charts, a glossary, and an annotated bibliography.

MacKerras, Colin. *The Cambridge Handbook of Contemporary China.* Cambridge U. Pr. 1991 $40.00. ISBN 0-521-38342-0

Needham, Joseph. *Science and Civilization in China*. 6 vols. Cambridge U. Pr. Magisterial study of the totality of the scientific tradition. Vol. 1. *Introductory Orientations*. 1956 $84.95. ISBN 0-521-05799-X. Vol. 2. *History of Scientific Thought*. 1991 $130.00. ISBN 0-521-05800-7. Vol. 3. *Mathematics and Sciences of the Heavens and the Earth*. 1959 $185.00. ISBN 0-521-05801-5. Vol. 4. *Physics and Physical Technology: Part 1 Physics*. 1962 $110.00. ISBN 0-521-05802-3. Vol. 4. *Physics and Physical Technology: Part 2 Mechanical Engineering*. 1991 $150.00. ISBN 0-521-05803-1. Vol. 4. *Physics and Physical Technology: Part 3 Civil Engineering and Nautics*. 1971 $185.00. ISBN 0-521-07060-0. Vol. 5. *Chemistry and Chemical Technology: Part 1 Paper and Printing*. 1985 $120.00. ISBN 0-521-08690-6. Vol. 5. *Chemistry and Chemical Technology: Part 2 Spagyrical Discovery and Invention*. 1974 $120.00. ISBN 0-521-08571-3. Vol. 5. *Chemistry and Chemical Technology: Part 3 Spagyrical Discovery and Invention*. 1976 $120.00. ISBN 0-521-21028-3. Vol. 5. *Chemistry and Chemical Technology: Part 4 Spagyrical Discovery and Invention*. 1980 $150.00. ISBN 0-521-08573-X. Vol. 5. *Chemistry and Chemical Technology: Part 5 Spagyrical Discovery and Invention*. 1983 $130.00. ISBN 0-521-08574-8. Vol. 5. *Military Technology: The Gunpowder Epic*. 1987 $130.00. ISBN 0-521-30358-3. Vol. 6. *Biology and Biological Technology: Part 1 Botany*. 1986 $130.00. ISBN 0-521-08731-7. Vol. 6. *Biology and Biological Technology: Part 2 Agriculture*. 1984 $130.00. ISBN 0-521-25076-5.

O'Neill, Hugh B. *Companion to Chinese History*. Facts on File 1987 $27.50. ISBN 0-87196-841-X. Provides basic information on several hundred topics and people. Chronologically arranged to cover the years 1506–1985.

Skinner, G. William, ed. *Modern Chinese Society, an Analytical Bibliography*. 3 vols. Stanford U. Pr. 1972–1973 Vol. 1 $75.00. ISBN 0-8047-0751-0. Vol. 2 $75.00. ISBN 0-8047-0752-9. Vol. 3 $55.00. ISBN 0-8047-0753-7. Remains an important reference tool.

Twitchett, Denis, and John K. Fairbank, eds. *The Cambridge History of China*. 15 vols. Cambridge U. Pr. 1978–1991 $110.00–165.00 ea. Vol. 1 ISBN 0-521-24327-0. Vol. 2 o.p. Vol. 3 ISBN 0-521-21446-7. Vol. 4–5 o.p. Vol. 6 ISBN 0-521-24331-9. Vol. 7 ISBN 0-521-24332-7. Vol. 8–9 o.p. Vol. 10 ISBN 0-521-21447-5. Vol. 11 ISBN 0-521-22029-7. Vol. 12 ISBN 0-521-23541-3. Vol. 13 ISBN 0-521-24338-6. Vol. 14 ISBN 0-521-24336-X. Vol. 15 ISBN 0-521-24337-8

Wu Yuan-li, ed. *China: A Handbook*. Greenwood 1973 o.p. A general guide to Chinese history, society, and culture.

SURVEYS AND GENERAL WORKS

Adshead, S.A.M. *China in World History*. St. Martin 1988 $37.50. ISBN 0-312-00506-7. An ambitious study that seeks to place China in an integrated global history.

Bonavia, David. *The Chinese*. Viking Penguin 1989 $7.95. ISBN 0-14-010479-8

Chang, K. C. *Food in Chinese Culture: Anthropological and Historical Perspectives*. Yale U. Pr. 1981 $15.95. ISBN 0-300-02759-1. An important book on an important topic.

Chao, Kang. *Man and Land in Chinese History*. Stanford U. Pr. 1986 $37.50. ISBN 0-8047-1271-9. An ambitious study of Chinese economic history.

Clayre, Alasdair. *The Heart of the Dragon*. HM 1985 o.p.

Clubb, O. Edmund. *Twentieth-Century China*. Col. U. Pr. 1978 $22.50. ISBN 0-231-04519-0

Cohen, Paul A., and Merle Goldman. *Ideas across Cultures: Essays on Chinese Thought in Honor of Benjamin I. Schwartz*. HUP 1990 $28.00. ISBN 0-674-44225-3. Ten essays that assay major axial moments in Chinese intellectual tradition.

deBary, William Theodore, and others, eds. *Sources of Chinese Tradition*. 2 vols. Col. U. Pr. 1964. Vol. 1 $19.50. ISBN 0-231-08602-4. Vol. 2 $18.00. ISBN 0-231-08603-2. Excerpts from the writings of Chinese philosophers and others. Includes numerous important historical documents.

Ebrey, Patricia B., and James L. Watson, eds. *Kinship Organization in Late Imperial China, 1000–1940*. U. CA Pr. 1986 $52.50. ISBN 0-520-05416-4. Essays that demonstrate the historical evolution and regional diversity of Chinese kinship organization.

Elvin, Mark. *Pattern of the Chinese Past.* Stanford U. Pr. 1973 $42.50. ISBN 0-8047-0826-6. A stimulating and influential study of China's social and economic development.

Fairbank, John King. *China: A New History.* Belknap Pr. 1992 o.p. Offers an overview of China's illustrious past.

———. *China: Tradition and Transformation.* HM rev. ed. 1989 $32.76. ISBN 0-395-49692-6. A popular college text.

Freedman, Maurice, ed. *Family and Kinship in Chinese Society.* Stanford U. Pr. 1970 $35.00. ISBN 0-8047-0713-8. A good general study of family organization.

Huang, Ray. *China: A Macro History.* M. E. Sharpe 1988 $24.95. ISBN 0-87332-452-8. An interesting interpretive essay that encapsulates Chinese history and compares it to European development.

Hucker, Charles. *China's Imperial Past.* Stanford U. Pr. 1975 $45.00. ISBN 0-8047-0887-8. A good summary of Chinese history.

Rawski, Thomas G., and Lillian M. Li, eds. *Chinese History in Economic Perspective.* U. CA Pr. 1992 $45.00. ISBN 0-520-07068-2. Essays that consider the evolution of China from the seventeenth century to today from an economic point of view.

Schram, Stuart R., ed. *Foundation and Limits of State Power in China.* Coronet Bks. 1987 $42.50. ISBN 962-201-370-8. A collection of essays that seeks to show the institutional connections between China's imperial and postimperial periods.

Spence, Jonathan D. *Chinese Roundabout: Essays in History and Culture.* Norton 1992 $24.95. ISBN 0-393-03355-4. Essays that cover a broad spectrum of topics relevant to Chinese life and times.

Sullivan, Michael. *The Arts of China.* U. CA Pr. 1984 $47.50. ISBN 0-520-04917-9. The best and most accessible analysis of China's artistic tradition.

Van Slyke, Lyman P. *Yangtze: Nature, History, and the River.* Addison-Wesley 1988 $14.95. ISBN 0-201-08894-0. A very readable treatment of the nature of life along one of China's great rivers; contains useful discussion of major themes.

Waldron, Arthur. *The Great Wall of China: From History to Myth.* Cambridge U. Pr. 1990 $44.95. ISBN 0-521-36518-X. A fascinating discussion of the place of the Great Wall in China's history and thought.

CHINA TO 1900

Bodde, Derk. *Chinese Thought, Society, and Science: The Intellectual and Social Background of Science and Technology in Pre-modern China.* UH Pr. 1991 $38.00. ISBN 0-8248-1334-0. Large-scale examination of the factors that supported and hindered the growth of science in China.

Chaffee, John W. *The Thorny Gates of Learning in Sung China: A Social History of Examinations.* Cambridge U. Pr. 1985 o.p. A narrative on the social meaning of the bureaucratic examination system.

Cleary, Thomas. *The Essential Tao.* HarpC 1992 $18.00. ISBN 0-06-250162-3. A useful introduction to Taoism, incorporating the teachings of Chuang Tzu and the *Tao Te Ching.*

Crossley, Pamela Kyle. *Orphan Warriors: Three Generations and the End of the Qing World.* Princeton U. Pr. 1990 $39.50. ISBN 0-691-05583-1. A fascinating social and cultural history of the people who controlled China's last dynasty.

Davis, Richard L. *Court and Family in Sung China, 960–1279: Bureaucratic Success and Kinship Fortunes for the Shih of Min-chou.* Duke 1986 $39.95. ISBN 0-8223-0512-7. An important study of the intersection of state and society.

Eastman, Lloyd E. *Family, Fields, and Ancestors: Constancy and Change in China's Social and Economic History.* OUP 1988 $34.00. ISBN 0-19-505269-2. A good general study of local and social history of the late imperial period.

Ebrey, Patricia B. *Confucianism and Family Rituals in Imperial China: A Social History of Writing about Rites.* Princeton U. Pr. 1991 $27.50. ISBN 0-691-03150-9. Explores the connection between Confucianism and Chinese society from antiquity to late imperial China.

Fairbank, John K. *The Great Chinese Revolution, 1800–1985.* HarpC 1986 $10.00. ISBN 0-06-039076-X. An account of the movement of change that has been evolving since the 1800s in China.

———, ed. *The Cambridge History of China, Vol. 10: Late Ch'ing. 1800–1911. Part 1.* Cambridge U. Pr. 1978 $140.00. ISBN 0-521-21447-5

Gernet, Jacques. *China and the Christian Impact: A Conflict of Cultures.* Trans. by Janet Lloyd. Cambridge U. Pr. 1985 $64.95. ISBN 0-521-26681-5. One of the most important works on a new scholarly interest in the intellectual struggle between Chinese thought and Christianity.

———. *Daily Life in China on the Eve of the Mongol Invasion, 1250–1276.* Trans. by H. M. Wright. Stanford U. Pr. 1962 $10.95. ISBN 0-8047-0720-0. Filled with interesting details about the Chinese and their culture.

Hansen, Valerie. *Changing Gods in Medieval China, 1127–1276.* Princeton U. Pr. 1990 $37.50. ISBN 0-691-05559-9. An illuminating study of popular religion.

Hao Yen-p'ing. *The Commercial Revolution in Nineteenth Century China.* U. CA Pr. 1986 $55.00. ISBN 0-520-05344-3. An important recent study.

Hartman, Charles. *Han Yu and the T'ang Search for Unity.* Princeton U. Pr. 1986 $65.00. ISBN 0-691-06665-5. Deals with political as well as literary and intellectual history.

Henricks, Robert G., trans. *Lao-Tzu: Tao Te Ching: A New Translation Based on the Recently Discovered Ma-Wang-Tui Texts.* Ballantine 1989 $19.95. ISBN 0-345-34790-0. A new translation rendered from the two oldest manuscripts yet discovered.

Hymes, Robert P. *Statesmen and Gentlemen: The Elite of Fu-Chou, Chiang-Hsi in Northern and Southern Sung.* Cambridge U. Pr. 1986 $59.95. ISBN 0-521-30631-0. An important study of the social history of the Sung dynasty in China.

Keightley, David N. *The Origins of Chinese Civilization.* U. CA Pr. 1983 $55.00. ISBN 0-520-04229-8. A bit technical in places but an indispensable source.

Kuhn, Philip A. *Soulstealers: The Chinese Sorcery Scare of 1768.* HUP 1990 $29.95. ISBN 0-674-82151-3. Uses a bizarre incident to examine the broader social and political character of China's last dynasty. Fascinating reading.

Liu, Kwang-Ching, ed. *Orthodoxy in Late Imperial China.* U. CA Pr. 1990 $47.50. ISBN 0-520-06542-5. A collection of essays that seeks to illuminate the character of the orthodox intellectual and ideological system in the latter years of imperial history.

McMullen, David. *State and Scholars in T'ang China.* Cambridge U. Pr. 1988 $64.95. ISBN 0-521-32991-4. Treats schools, scholarship, and state control over intellectual orthodoxy.

Mote, Frederick W., and Denis Twitchett, eds. *The Cambridge History of China. Vol. 7: The Ming Dynasty, 1368–1644. Part 1.* Cambridge U. Pr. 1988 $130.00. ISBN 0-521-24332-7. Considered to be the standard reference work, the 15-volume Cambridge series details Chinese history from 221 B.C. to present times. Volume 7 provides a standard political history of the Ming period.

Murray, Dian H. *Pirates of the South China Coast, 1790–1810.* Stanford U. Pr. 1987 $35.00. ISBN 0-8047-1376-6. An interesting social history of pirates, piracy, and outcast society in China.

Naquin, Susan, and Evelyn S. Rawski. *Chinese Society in the Eighteenth Century.* Yale U. Pr. 1987 $30.00. ISBN 0-300-03848-8. Ambitious synthesis on the social history of late imperial China.

Ronan, Charles E., and Bonnie B. C. Oh, eds. *East Meets West: The Jesuits in China, 1582–1773.* Loyola 1988 $19.95. ISBN 0-9294-0572-0. Nine essays that consider a variety of aspects of Jesuit links between Europe and China.

Rossabi, Morris. *Khublai Khan: His Life and Times.* U. CA Pr. 1987 $29.95. ISBN 0-520-05913-1. A useful biography of the Mongol emperor most important for China.

Rowe, William T. *Hankow: Commerce and Society in a Chinese City, 1796–1889.* Stanford U. Pr. 1984 $47.50. ISBN 0-8047-1204-2. A good summary of Ch'ing dynasty social history, as well as an important case study of one urban area.

Schwartz, Benjamin. *The World of Thought in Ancient China.* Belknap Pr. 1985 $30.50. ISBN 0-674-96190-0. Major synthesis of the roots of China's intellectual tradition.

Skinner, G. William. *The City in Late Imperial China*. Stanford U. Pr. 1977 $75.00. ISBN 0-8047-0892-4. Essays that chart the transformation and character of China's cities.

Spence, Jonathan D. *The Death of Woman Wang*. Viking Penguin 1979 $8.95. ISBN 0-14-005121-X. Fiction based on official provincial histories, a local official's memoirs, and several modern short stories.

―――. *The Memory Palace of Matteo Ricci*. Viking Penguin 1984 $9.95. ISBN 0-14-008098-8. A fascinating study of one of the most influential Jesuits in China.

Taylor, Rodney L. *The Religious Dimensions of Confucianism*. State U. NY Pr. 1990 $57.50. ISBN 0-7914-0311-4. Draws together various elements of the Confucian tradition within a religious context.

Twitchett, Denis, ed. *The Cambridge History of China, Vol. 3. Sui and T'ang, 580–906 A.D. Part 1*. Cambridge U. Pr. 1979 $150.00. ISBN 0-521-21446-7. Ten lengthy essays primarily concerned with the political character of the new and enlarged state created by the Sui and T'ang dynasties.

Twitchett, Denis, and Michael Loewe, eds. *The Cambridge History of China, Vol. 1. The Ch'in and Han Empires, 221 BC–AD 220*. Cambridge U. Pr. 1986 $140.00. ISBN 0-521-24327-0. An authoritative account of the first two imperial dynasties.

von Glahn, Richard. *The Country of Streams and Grottoes: Expansion, Settlement, and the Civilizing of the Sichuan Frontier in Song Times*. Harvard U. Pr. 1987 $24.00. ISBN 0-674-17543-3. An important addition to understanding the expansion of the Chinese empire.

Wakeman, Frederick Jr. *The Great Enterprise: The Manchu Reconstruction of Imperial Order in Seventeenth-Century China*. 2 vols. U. CA Pr. 1985 $90.00. ISBN 0-520-04804-0. A major study of empire and state building.

―――. *Strangers at the Gate: Social Disorder in South China, 1839–1861*. U. CA Pr. 1966 o.p. Still an important and readable source on social breakdown in late imperial China.

Wright, Mary C. *The Last Stand of Chinese Conservatism*. Stanford U. Pr. 1957 $49.50. ISBN 0-8047-0475-9. Older but still important and influential study of China's response to imperialism.

MODERN CHINA

Bergere, Marie-Claire. *The Golden Age of the Chinese Bourgeoisie, 1911–1937*. Trans. by Janet Lloyd. Cambridge U. Pr. 1990 $64.95. ISBN 0-521-32054-2. A major study filled with fascinating detail on the growth of China's business community and its evolving clash with various state powers.

Billingsley, Phil. *Bandits in Republican China*. Stanford U. Pr. 1988 $42.50. ISBN 0-8047-1406-1. Links early twentieth-century banditry with broad social dislocation and peasant economic difficulties.

Ch'en, Yung-Fa. *Making Revolution: The Communist Movement in Eastern and Central China, 1937–1945*. U. CA Pr. 1986 $70.00. ISBN 0-520-05002-9. Large-scale examination of political and social action under Japanese occupation.

Clark, Paul. *Chinese Cinema: Culture and Politics Since 1949*. Cambridge U. Pr. 1987 $54.95. ISBN 0-521-32638-9. The best general treatment of contemporary Chinese film. Masterfully relates film to the larger social context.

Davin, Delia. *Woman-Work: Women and the Party in Revolutionary China*. OUP 1976 o.p. Interesting treatment of women and employment during the revolutionary period.

Dietrich, Craig. *People's China: A Brief History*. OUP 1986 $38.00. ISBN 0-19-503688-3. A readable introductory synthesis of scholarship on the People's Republic of China.

Dirlik, Arif. *The Origins of Chinese Communism*. OUP 1989 $14.95. ISBN 0-19-505454-7. An important reevaluation of Communist ideology in China.

Dirlik, Arif, and Maurice Meisner, eds. *Marxism and the Chinese Experience*. M. E. Sharpe 1989 $47.50. ISBN 0-87332-515-X. Essays that seek to show what socialism and communism mean in a Chinese context.

Dittmer, Lowell. *China's Continuous Revolution: The Post-Liberation Epoch, 1949–1981*. U. CA Pr. 1987 $40.00. ISBN 0-520-06599-9. Important study of a shifting ideological struggle in China since 1949.

Duara, Pransenjit. *Culture, Power, and the State: Rural North China, 1900–1942*. Stanford U. Pr. 1988 $42.50. ISBN 0-8047-1445-2. An important study that evaluates the impact on local communities of twentieth-century state building.

Eastman, Lloyd. *The Abortive Revolution: China Under Nationalist Rule, 1927–1937*. HUP 1974 $18.00. ISBN 0-674-00176-1. An important study of the brief period of Republican dominance.

———. *Seeds of Destruction: Nationalist China in War and Revolution*. Stanford U. Pr. 1984 $37.50. ISBN 0-8047-1191-7. Traces the Nationalists from the Japanese occupation until the revolution.

Eng, Robert Y. *Economic Imperialism in China: Silk Production and Exports, 1861–1932*. Inst. of East Asian Studies. U. CA Pr. 1987 $7.50. ISBN 0-912966-85-8. Discusses China's efforts to enter international trade and the impediments placed in its way by the imperialist powers.

Esherick, Joseph. *Reform and Revolution in China: The 1911 Revolution in Hunan and Hubei*. U. CA Pr. 1976 $15.95. ISBN 0-520-05734-1. An important study of the Republican Revolution.

Esherick, Joseph W., and Mary Backus Rankin, eds. *Chinese Local Elites and Patterns of Dominance*. U. CA Pr. 1990 $59.95. ISBN 0-520-06763-0. Essays that seek to bridge the gap between history and social science by carefully examining what has changed and what has not changed in modern China.

Fairbank, John K., ed. *The Cambridge History of China, Vol. 12: Republican China 1912–1949, Part 1*. Cambridge U. Pr. 1983 $165.00. ISBN 0-521-23541-3

Fairbank, John K., and Albert Feuerwerker, eds. *The Cambridge History of China, Vol. 13: Republican China 1912–1949, Part 2*. Cambridge U. Pr. 1986 $145.00. ISBN 0-521-24338-6

Fairbank, John K., and K. C. Liu, eds. *The Cambridge History of China, Vol. 11: Late Ch'ing 1800–1911, Part 2*. Cambridge U. Pr. 1978 $140.00. ISBN 0-521-22029-7. Ten essays on the final years of the Ch'ing dynasty and the revolution of 1911.

Friedman, Edward, and others. *Chinese Village, Socialist State*. Yale U. Pr. 1991 $35.00. ISBN 0-300-04655-3. Evaluates the evolving relationship between local society and the emerging Communist state.

Garver, John W. *Chinese-Soviet Relations 1937–1945: The Diplomacy of Chinese Nationalism*. OUP 1988 $39.95. ISBN 0-19-505432-6. Shows that Sino-Soviet relations reflected the Nationalist struggle between Joseph Stalin on one side and Mao Zedong and Chiang K'ai-shek on the other.

George, Alexander L. *The Chinese Communist Army in Action: The Korean War and Its Aftermath*. Col. U. Pr. 1967 $17.00. ISBN 0-231-08595-8.

Gittings, John. *China Changes Faces: The Road from Revolution 1949–1989*. OUP 1989 $29.95. ISBN 0-19-215887-2. A useful and balanced introduction to Chinese history since the revolution.

Goldman, Merle. *China's Intellectuals: Advise and Dissent*. HUP 1981 $22.00. ISBN 0-674-11970-3. Deals with the clashing positions of the state and intellectual leaders.

Harding, Harry. *China's Second Revolution: Reform After Mao*. Brookings Institution. 1987 $14.95. ISBN 0-8157-3461-1. A useful evaluation of the decade of change following Mao's death.

Hartford, Kathleen, and Steven M. Goldstein, eds. *Single Sparks: China's Rural Revolution*. M. E. Sharpe 1989 $17.95. ISBN 0-87332-753-5. Five essays on local dimensions of revolutionary action during the 1930s and 1940s.

Heng, Liang, and Judith Shapiro. *Son of the Revolution*. Random 1984 $10.00. ISBN 0-394-72274-4. Beautifully written account of life during the Chinese Cultural Revolution.

Hershatter, Gail. *The Workers of Tianjin, 1900–1949*. Stanford U. Pr. 1986 $39.50. ISBN 0-8047-1318-9. An important study of working-class life and culture before 1949.

Honig, Emily. *Sisters and Strangers: Women in the Shanghai Cotton Mills, 1919–1949*. Stanford U. Pr. 1986 $39.50. ISBN 0-8047-1274-3. A fascinating social history.

Houn, Franklin W. *Short History of Chinese Communism: Completely Updated*. P-H 1973 o.p.

Hsiao, K. C. *Modern China and the New World: K'ang Yu-Wei, Reformer and Utopian, 1858–1927.* U. of Wash. Pr. 1975 $40.00. ISBN 0-295-95385-3. An important investigation of a key modern figure and the intellectual transformation at the end of dynastic history.

Hsiung, James Chieh. *Ideology and Practice: The Evolution of Chinese Communism.* Greenwood 1970 o.p. A useful introduction to the ideas of the Chinese Communist party.

Hsu, Immanuel C. Y. *The Rise of Modern China.* OUP 1990 $36.00. ISBN 0-19-505867-4. Good introductory treatment of major events from 1600 to the present.

Huang, Philip C. C., and others. *Chinese Communists and Rural Society, 1927–1934.* U. CA Pr. 1978 o.p. An illuminating treatment of the changing Communist connection to rural communities and peasants.

Jacobsen, C. G. *Sino-Soviet Relations since Mao: The Chairman's Legacy.* Greenwood 1981 $39.95. ISBN 0-275-90652-3

Johnson, Chalmers A. *Peasant Nationalism and Communist Power: The Emergence of Revolutionary China, 1937–1945.* Stanford U. Pr. 1962 $32.50. ISBN 0-8047-0073-7. A still influential discussion about the rise of Communist power, focusing on the role of the Japanese occupation.

Karnow, Stanley. *Mao and China: A Legacy of Turmoil.* Viking Penguin 1990 $10.95. ISBN 0-14-013417-4

Levenson, J. R. *Confucian China and Its Modern Fate.* 3 vols. U. CA Pr. 1968 $49.95. ISBN 0-520-00737-9. A powerful and influential work dealing with intellectual life and communism in China.

———. *Liang Ch'i-ch'ao and the Mind of Modern China.* HUP 1965 o.p. A classic study of the movement toward the intellectual transformation of modern China.

Li, Lillian M. *China's Silk Trade: Traditional Industry in the Modern World, 1842–1937.* HUP 1981 $21.00. ISBN 0-674-11962-2. Focuses on the effects of international trade on silk production and on China's larger economy.

Link, Perry, and others, eds. *Unofficial China: Popular Culture and Thought in the People's Republic.* Westview 1989 $48.00. ISBN 0-8133-0923-9. A rich and textured study of popular culture; a useful starting place for understanding modern China.

Lyons, Thomas P. *Economic Integration and Planning in Maoist China.* Col. U. Pr. 1987 $61.00. ISBN 0-231-06542-6. Seeks to show the effort to establish national and local economic self-reliance.

MacFarquhar, Roderick, and John K. Fairbank, eds. *The Cambridge History of China, Vol. 14: The Emergence of Revolutionary China: 1949–1965.* Cambridge U. Pr. 1987 $110.00. ISBN 0-521-24336-X

———. *The Cambridge History of China, Vol. 15: The People's Republic.* Cambridge U. Pr. 1992 $120.00. ISBN 0-521-24337-8

Madsen, Richard P. *Morality and Power in a Chinese Village.* U. CA Pr. 1984 $40.00. ISBN 0-520-05925-5. A major study of modern Chinese cultural values and their articulation with the Communist state.

May, Ernest R., and John K. Fairbank, eds. *America's China Trade in Historical Perspective.* HUP 1986 $25.00. ISBN 0-674-03075-3. Nine essays on various aspects of the trade relationship between the two nations. Contains useful case studies.

Meisner, Maurice. *Marxism, Maoism, and Utopianism: Eight Essays.* U. of Wis. Pr. 1982 $10.95. ISBN 0-299-08420-5. Provides thoughtful observations on the nature of modern China's political culture.

Ono Kazuko. *Chinese Women in a Century of Revolution, 1850–1950.* Ed. by Joshua Fogel. Stanford U. Pr. 1989 $35.00. ISBN 0-8047-1496-7. A useful introductory history of modern Chinese women. Especially good up to the 1911 revolution.

Pye, Lucian. *The Mandarin and the Cadre: China's Political Culture.* Ctr. for Chinese Studies 1989 $12.50. ISBN 0-89264-083-9. An excellent synthesis of China's political values.

Rankin, Mary Backus. *Elite Activism and Political Transformation in China: Zhejiang Province, 1865–1911.* Stanford U. Pr. 1986 $39.50. ISBN 0-8047-1321-9. An important new assessment of the 1911 revolution and its origins.

Riskin, Carl. *China's Political Economy: The Quest for Development Since 1949*. OUP 1988 $21.00. ISBN 0-19-877090-1. A general history of China's economic policies since the Communist revolution.

Scalapino, Robert A., and George T. Yu. *Modern China and Its Revolutionary Process: Recurrent Challenges to the Traditional Order 1850–1920*. U. CA Pr. 1985 $75.00. ISBN 0-520-05030-4. Large-scale synthesis of scholarship on the emergence of revolutionary sentiment and practice in China.

Schrecker, John E. *The Chinese Revolution in Historical Perspective*. Greenwood 1991 $47.95. ISBN 0-313-27485-1. Seeks to evaluate China's revolutionary century from the 1890s to the present.

Schwartz, Bejamin I. *In Search of Wealth and Power: Yen Fu and the West*. HUP 1964 $22.00. ISBN 0-674-44651-8. Still among the best studies of the intellectual reconstruction of China.

———, ed. *Reflections on the May Fourth Movement: A Symposium*. HUP 1972 $11.00. ISBN 0-674-75230-9. A useful collection of essays.

Sheridan, James. *China in Disintegration: The Republican Era in Chinese History*. Free Pr. 1977 $18.95. ISBN 0-02-928610-7. Traces the overall history of China from 1911 to 1949.

Shue, Vivienne. *Peasant China in Transition*. U. CA Pr. 1980 $49.95. ISBN 0-520-03734-0. A good account of the initial transformations that China underwent after 1949.

Snow, Edgar. *Red Star Over China*. Bantam 1978 repr. of 1938 ed. $6.95. ISBN 0-553-26239-4. A classic account of the emergence of Communist power by an American journalist who was close to the party leadership.

Spence, Jonathan D. *The Search for Modern China*. Norton 1990 $29.95. ISBN 0-393-027098-2. An excellent general history that covers the period from the early 1600s to recent times.

Strand, David. *Rickshaw Beijing: City People and Politics in the 1920s*. U. CA Pr. 1989 $40.00. ISBN 0-520-06311-2. An account of urban life and the threat to the public sphere by warlords and revolutionary pressure.

Stross, Randall E. *The Stubborn Earth: American Agriculturalists on Chinese Soil, 1898–1937*. U. CA Pr. 1986 $25.00. ISBN 0-520-05700-7. Focuses on the checkered history of some American efforts to reform Chinese agricultural practices.

Teng Ssu-yu, and others, eds. *China's Response to the West*. HUP 1954 $10.95. ISBN 0-674-12025-6. A useful collection of primary documents related to China's meeting with the West.

Wakeman, Frederic. *The Fall of Imperial China*. Free Pr. 1975 $12.95. ISBN 0-02-933690-2. Among the best capsule histories of the end of imperial Chinese history.

Wang, James C. *Contemporary Chinese Politics: An Introduction*. P-H 1991 $28.00. ISBN 0-13-174442-9

Wasserstrom, Jeffrey N. *Student Protests in Twentieth-Century China: The View from Shanghai*. Stanford U. Pr. 1991 $45.00. ISBN 0-8047-1881-4. Examines the place and importance of student protest movements, one of the most visible forms of opposition to the state.

Wilber, C. Martin. *The Nationalist Revolution in China, 1923–1928*. Cambridge U. Pr. 1983 o.p.

Wilson, Dick. *The Long March, 1935: The Epic of Chinese Communism's Survival*. Viking Penguin 1982 $7.95. ISBN 0-14-006113-4. A useful account of a near-mythic event.

Wolf, Margery, and Roxane Witke, eds. *Women in Chinese Society*. Stanford U. Pr. 1974 $37.50. ISBN 0-8047-0874-6. An important early study of the role of women in China.

Yang, Benjamin. *From Revolution to Politics, Chinese Communists on the Long March*. Westview 1990 $43.50. ISBN 0-8133-7672-6. A detailed treatment of the Long March that disputes the heroic quality usually attributed to it. Contains a useful evaluation of political debate along the march.

Japan

The growth in scholarship and interest in Japan since World War II has been astonishing. Initially this growth was fueled by wartime interest in the Western enemy in the Pacific. Writers and scholars hoped to explain why the small island nation of Japan would launch a destructive war against most of the world. What had been the source of militarist zeal? What kinds of forces supported military expansion? How had the constitutional state of Japan so distorted the Western models on which they had based their modern development? These questions led writers to look at the nature and character of Japan's 1889 constitution and the political structure that supported it, at the continuities of the earlier military elite in the new modern state, and at the expansionist zeal of Japan's modern leaders.

In time, Japan's economic growth and its leadership in the world economy shifted the historical focus. How had the Japanese economy grown so rapidly? How and to what extent was that growth supported by traditional cultural norms? To what extent has Japan's economic activity followed Western models? This interest in Japan's rapid economic growth and role in the global economy has given rise to unusually broad enthusiasm for business and labor history, comparative economic development, and political economy. At the same time, this economic interest has supported enquiries into the social and cultural history of cities, social relationships, and gender. As a result, Western writing on Japanese history has grown remarkably sophisticated in an incredibly short period of time.

REFERENCE WORKS

Asada, Sadao. *Japan and the World, 1853–1952: A Bibliographic Guide to Japanese Scholarship in Foreign Relations*. Col. U. Pr. 1989 $59.00. ISBN 0-231-06690-2. Important entry point into Japanese scholarship.

Catalogue of Books in English on Japan, 1945–1981. Comp. by The Japan Foundation 1986 o.p. Lists some 9,000 books published between 1945 and 1981 in humanities, social sciences, art, and history. Classified arrangement with author and title indexes.

Dower, John W. *Japanese History and Culture from Ancient to Modern Times: Seven Basic Bibliographies*. Weiner Pub. Inc. 1986 $39.95. ISBN 0-910129-20-7. Especially useful for twentieth-century materials; includes primary sources on the U.S. occupation of the island nation.

Grilli, Peter, ed. *Japan in Film: A Comprehensive Catalogue of Documentary and Theatrical Films on Japan in the United States*. Japan Soc. 1984 $15.00. ISBN 0-913304-20-4. An excellent annotated guide to films on Japan.

Hunter, Janet E. *Concise Dictionary of Modern Japanese History*. U. CA Pr. 1984 $55.00. ISBN 0-520-04390-1. Good starting place for readers with little familiarity with Japan.

Kodansha Encyclopedia of Japan. 9 vols. Kodansha 1983 $780.00. ISBN 0-87011-620-7. The most complete guide to numerous places, individuals, and events, with over 10,000 entries. Includes excellent thematic articles written from a Japanese perspective.

Perren, Richard, comp. *Japanese Studies from Pre-History to 1990: A Bibliographical Guide*. Manchester Univ. Pr. 1992 $29.50. ISBN 0-7190-2458-7. A useful reference guide.

Shulman, Frank J. *Japan*. ABC-CLIO 1985 $139.50. ISBN 1-85109-074-6. Provides 1,615 annotated entries for books, arranged topically and emphasizing titles published during the 1970s and 1980s. Includes indexes.

Wray, William D. *Japan's Economy: A Bibliography of its Past and Present*. Weiner Pub. Inc. 1989 $39.95. ISBN 0-910129-79-7. An excellent, well-organized bibliography on economic and business history.

SURVEYS AND GENERAL WORKS

Beasley, W. G. *The Modern History of Japan*. St. Martin 1981 o.p.

Benedict, Ruth F. *The Chrysanthemum and the Sword: Patterns of Japanese Culture*. HM 1989 $9.95. ISBN 0-395-50075-3. A famous and controversial analysis based on World War II-era studies by the U.S. Office of War Information.

Bernstein, Gail Lee, and Haruhiro Fukui, eds. *Japan and the World: Essays in Japanese History and Politics*. St. Martin 1988 $45.00. ISBN 0-312-01145-8. A collection of 13 essays on a wide variety of topics.

Cortazzi, Hugh. *The Japanese Achievement*. St. Martin 1990 $35.00. ISBN 0-312-04237-X. A rather old-fashioned but attractively written general history of Japan.

Hall, John W. *Japan: From Prehistory to Modern Times*. Dell 1970 $12.95. ISBN 0-385-28478-0. Strong institutional history; best on the period before 1900.

Hane, Mikiso. *Japan: A Historical Survey*. Scribner 1972 o.p. Emphasizes social development and social history.

Kitagawa, Joseph M. *On Understanding Japanese Religion*. Princeton U. Pr. 1987 $16.95. ISBN 0-691-10229-5. A collection of 18 articles by the dean of Japanese religious studies. Provides important insights.

Morris, Ivan. *The Nobility of Failure: Tragic Heroes in the History of Japan*. H. Holt & Co. 1976 $14.95. ISBN 0-374-52120-4. Ten essays drawn together around the theme of heroic failure. An interesting and important contribution to the cultural history of Japan.

Reischauer, Edwin O., and Albert M. Craig. *Japan: Tradition and Transformation*. HM rev. ed. 1989 $35.96. ISBN 0-395-25814-6. Widely used college text.

Sansom, George B. *Japan: A Short Cultural History*. Stanford U. Pr. rev. ed. 1952 $55.00. ISBN 0-8047-0952-1. General treatment of Japan's multifaceted cultural character.

Singer, Kurt. *Mirror, Sword and Jewel: The Geometry of Japanese Life*. Kodansha 1981 $6.25. ISBN 0-87011-460-3. A fascinating study of Japanese life by a longtime resident.

Smith, Robert J. *Japanese Culture: Tradition, Self, and the Social Order*. Cambridge U. Pr. 1984 $13.95. ISBN 0-521-31552-2. An anthropological study of the intersection of traditional and contemporary life.

Varley, H. Paul. *Japanese Culture: A Short History*. UH Pr. 1984 $12.95. ISBN 0-8248-0927-0. Emphasizes artistic and cultural dimensions of Japanese development.

PREMODERN JAPAN

Bellah, Robert N. *Tokugawa Religion: The Values of Pre-industrial Japan*. Free Pr. 1957 $11.95. ISBN 0-02-90260-9. A classic study that tries to demonstrate the emergence of a functional analogue to Protestantism in Tokugawa Japan.

Berry, Mary Elizabeth. *Hideyoshi*. HUP 1982 $14.00. ISBN 0-674-39026-1. The best biography of the powerful warrior who united all Japan during the sixteenth century.

Boxer, Charles R. *The Christian Century in Japan, 1549–1650*. U. CA Pr. 1951 o.p. Although general interpretations are dated, this remains an important source on early Christianity in Japan.

Collcutt, Martin. *Five Mountains: The Rinzai Zen Monastic Institution in Medieval Japan*. HUP 1980 $25.00. ISBN 0-674-30497-7. Focuses on the creation and structure of Zen religious organizations.

Dore, Ronald P. *Education in Tokugawa Japan*. U. CA Pr. 1965 o.p. Classic study of the expansion of education and its role in preparing Japan for modernity.

Duus, Peter. *Feudalism in Japan*. McGraw 1975 $12.28. ISBN 0-07-553625-0. Brief but useful introduction to the period of warrior dominance in Japan.

Elison, George. *Deus Destroyed: The Image of Christianity in Early Modern Japan*. HUP 1974 $14.00. ISBN 0-674-19962-6. Focuses on the challenging intellectual dimensions of Japan's sixteenth and seventeenth-century engagement with Christianity.

Elison, George, and Bardwell L. Smith, eds. *Warlords, Artists, and Commoners: Japan in the Sixteenth Century*. UH Pr. 1981 $14.00. ISBN 0-8248-1109-7. Eleven essays on the social and cultural implications of sixteenth-century warrior dominance.

Farris, William Wayne. *Population, Disease and Land in Early Japan, 645–900*. HUP 1985 $20.00. ISBN 0-674-69031-1. A good but challenging analysis of the rigors of early Japanese life.

Frederic, Louis. *Daily Life in Japan in the Age of the Samurai, 1185–1603*. Praeger 1972 o.p. Focuses on the actual conduct of living in early Japan.

Hall, John W. *Government and Local Power in Japan, 500 to 1700: A Study Based on Bizen Province*. Princeton U. Pr. 1981 o.p. A major study of the institutional connections of local and national levels of government.

———, ed. *The Cambridge History of Japan, Volume 4: Early Modern Japan*. Cambridge U. Pr. 1991 $99.50. ISBN 0-521-22355-5. Essays primarily on the Tokugawa period.

Hall, John W., and others, eds. *Japan Before Tokugawa: Political Consolidation and Economic Growth, 1500 to 1650*. Princeton U. Pr. 1981 $57.50. ISBN 0-691-05308-1. Deals with land control, urbanization, and the general economic transformation.

———. *Japan in the Muromachi Age*. U. CA Pr. 1976 $14.95. ISBN 0-520-03214-4. Essays on the cultural and political dimensions of the period of struggle leading to Tokugawa consolidation.

———. *Medieval Japan: Essays in Institutional History*. Yale U. Pr. 1974 o.p. Writings on the creation and operation of the earliest coherent structures of warrior power.

———. *Studies in the Institutional History of Early Modern Japan*. Princeton U. Pr. 1968 $57.50. ISBN 0-691-03071-5. A collection of previously published and new essays on the establishment and governance of Japan's Tokugawa era.

Hanley, Susan B., and Kozo Yamamura. *Economic and Demographic Change in Preindustrial Japan, 1600–1868*. Princeton U. Pr. 1978 o.p. Emphasizes the stability of the preindustrial population and the steady but slow growth of the economy.

Hurst, G. Cameron. *Insei: Abdicated Sovereigns in the Politics of Late Heian Japan, 1086–1185*. Col. U. Pr. 1976 o.p. Examines the evolving civil government by looking at the transformation taking place within the imperial household.

Jannetta, Ann Bowman. *Epidemics and Mortality in Early Modern Japan*. Princeton U. Pr. 1987 $30.00. ISBN 0-691-05484-3. Offers the first serious look at epidemic disease in Tokugawa Japan and its effect on the population.

Keene, Donald. *The Japanese Discovery of Europe: Honda Toshiaki and Other Discoverers, 1720–1830*. Stanford U. Pr. rev. ed. 1969 $35.00. ISBN 0-8047-0668-9. Considers the emerging awareness of, and response to, Westerners and Western ideas.

Koschmann, J. Victor. *The Mito Ideology: Discourse, Reform, and Insurrection in Late Tokugawa Japan*. U. CA Pr. 1986 $40.00. ISBN 0-520-05768-6. Examines the emergence of new ideas that challenged Tokugawa orthodoxy.

McMullin, Neil. *Buddhism and the State in Sixteenth-Century Japan*. Princeton U. Pr. 1985 $60.00. ISBN 0-691-07291-4. Examines the political role of Buddhist monasticism.

Mass, Jeffrey P. *Court and Bakufu in Japan: Essays in Kamakura History*. Yale U. Pr. 1982 $40.00. ISBN 0-300-02653-6. A collection of studies on the shape and character of Japan's first military government.

Mass, Jeffrey P., and William Hauser, eds. *The Bakufu in Japanese History*. Stanford U. Pr. 1985 $35.00. ISBN 0-8047-1278-6. A somewhat loose collection of essays focusing on the linkage between central and peripheral power in the various structures of warrior governance.

Morris, Ivan. *The World of the Shining Prince: Court Life in Ancient Japan*. Viking Penguin 1972 o.p. Examines the life of the aristocratic court described in Lady Murasaki Shikibi's *The Tale of Genji*.

Najita, Tetsuo. *Visions of Virtue in Tokugawa Japan*. U. Ch. Pr. 1987 $37.50. ISBN 0-226-56804-0. Focuses on the transformation of Neo-Confucianism in Tokugawa Japan to support the idea of merchant political activity.

Nosco, Peter, ed. *Confucianism and Tokugawa Culture*. Princeton U. Pr. 1984 $17.95. ISBN 0-691-00839-6. Essays trace the evolving ideological character of the Tokugawa-era state.

Ooms, Herman. *Tokugawa Ideology: Early Constructs, 1570-1680*. U. Ch. Pr. 1985 $17.95. ISBN 0-691-00838-8. Shows the complex interplay of indigenous and externally generated ideas that went into the creation of the Tokugawa ideological system.

Pearson, Richard. *Ancient Japan*. Braziller 1992 $80.00. ISBN 0-8076-1282-0. Catalog of recent show. An excellent treatment of the present state of archaeological understanding of ancient Japan.

Sansom, George B. *A History of Japan*. 3 vols. Stanford U. Pr. 1958–1963. Chronicles Japanese development and growth from early times to the mid-1800s.

Smith, Thomas C. *The Agrarian Origins of Modern Japan*. Stanford U. Pr. 1959 $32.50. ISBN 0-8047-0530-5. Focuses on early emerging market economies and their impact.

Suzuki, Daisetz T. *Zen and Japanese Culture*. Princeton U. Pr. 1959 $14.95. ISBN 0-691-01770-0. Includes chapters on swordsmanship, Confucianism, poetry, the tea ceremony, and attitudes toward nature.

Toby, Ronald P. *State and Diplomacy in Early Modern Japan: Asia in the Development of the Tokugawa Bakufu*. Princeton U. Pr. 1983 $39.50. ISBN 0-8047-1951-9. Seeks to break down the stereotype of Tokugawa isolation by showing Japan's links with Asia.

Totman, Conrad. *Politics in the Tokugawa Bakufu, 1600–1853*. U. CA Pr. 1988 $15.95. ISBN 0-520-06313-9. The best general study of the institutional structure of the Tokugawa political world.

Vlastos, Stephen. *Peasant Protests and Uprising in Tokugawa Japan*. U. CA Pr. 1986 $37.50. ISBN 0-520-04614-5. Views protests as related to growing demands for political participation.

Wilson, William Scott, ed. and trans. *Ideals of the Samurai: Writings of Japanese Warriors*. Ohara Pubns. 1982 o.p. Translations from warrior-family codes from about 1250 to 1600.

Yamamura, Kozo, ed. *The Cambridge History of Japan, Volume 3: Medieval Japan*. Cambridge U. Pr. 1990 $110.00. ISBN 0-521-22354-7. Covers the entire range of medieval Japan in a probing, analytical fashion.

Yazaki, Takeo. *Social Change and the City in Japan: From Earliest Times through the Industrial Revolution*. Japan Pubns. USA 1968 o.p. Remains among the best treatments of long-term urban development.

MODERN JAPAN

Bartholomew, James R. *The Formation of Science in Japan: Building a Research Tradition*. Yale U. Pr. 1989 $35.00. ISBN 0-300-04261-2. A good general study of academic and organizational science.

Beasley, W. G. *The Meiji Restoration*. Stanford U. Pr. 1972 $60.00. ISBN 0-8047-0815-0. A broad and general study of the revolution that created modern Japan. Gives much weight to Western intrusion.

_____. *The Rise of Modern Japan*. St. Martin 1990 $14.95. ISBN 0-312-04077-6. General history that is somewhat weighted toward traditional politics and foreign-policy concerns.

Berger, Gordon M. *Parties Out of Power in Japan, 1931–1941*. Princeton U. Pr. 1977 o.p. Shows that party politicians continued to be influential despite growing militarism.

Bernstein, Gail Lee, ed. *Recreating Japanese Women, 1600–1945*. U. CA Pr. 1991 $40.00. ISBN 0-520-07015-1. The first substantial collection of important essays on Japanese women in history.

Bordon, William S. *The Pacific Alliance: The United States Foreign Economic Policy and Japanese Trade Recovery, 1947–1955*. U. of Wis. Pr. 1984 o.p. Shows the self-interested role of U.S. economic policy toward postwar Japan.

Bowen, Roger W. *Rebellion and Democracy in Meiji Japan: A Study of Commoners in the Popular Rights Movement*. U. CA Pr. 1980 $15.95. ISBN 0-520-05230-7. Shows how commoners absorbed and acted upon new democratic principles.

Burks, Ardath W., ed. *The Modernizers: Overseas Students, Foreign Employees, and Meiji Japan*. Westview 1984 o.p. Essays on learning from the West.

Cole, Robert E. *Japanese Blue Collar: The Changing Tradition*. U. CA Pr. 1971 $13.95. ISBN 0-520-02354-4. Among the best sources for understanding recent working-class behavior.

Collier, Basil. *Japan at War: An Illustrated History of the War in the Far East, 1931-45*. Hippocrene Bks. 1977 o.p.

Cook, Haruko Taya, and Theodore F. Cook. *Japan at War: An Oral History*. New Press NY 1992 $27.50. ISBN 1-56584-014-3. A vast compilation of stories of ordinary Japanese people during World War II.

Crowley, James B. *Japan's Quest for Autonomy: National Security and Foreign Policy, 1930–1938*. Princeton U. Pr. 1968 o.p. An important study of Japan's prewar understanding of foreign policy and its role in shaping the nation's military policies.

Dore, Ronald P. *British Factory, Japanese Factory: The Origins of National Diversity in Employment Relations*. U. CA Pr. 1973 $14.95. ISBN 0-520-02495-8. An important case study that compares the organization and operation of large firms in Britain and in Japan.

Dower, John W. *Empire and Aftermath: Yoshida Shigeru and the Japanese Experience, 1878–1954*. HUP 1979 $14.00. ISBN 0-674-25126-1. A political biography of Japan's first important post-World War II prime minister.

_____. *War Without Mercy: Race and Power in the Pacific War*. Pantheon 1986 $15.00. ISBN 0-394-75172-8. Argues that racial stereotyping was important in shaping World War II in the Pacific.

_____, ed. *Origins of the Modern Japanese State: Selected Writings of E. H. Norman*. Pantheon 1975 o.p. An important work that reprints several of Norman's classic studies of the emergence of modern Japan.

Duus, Peter. *The Cambridge History of Japan, Volume 6: The Twentieth Century*. Cambridge U. Pr. 1988 $89.50. ISBN 0-521-22357-1. Primarily devoted to the years up to World War II.

Fletcher, Miles. *The Search for a New Order: Intellectuals and Fascism in Prewar Japan*. U. of NC Pr. 1982 o.p. Discusses intellectual adaptations to, and support of, an authoritarian state.

Francks, Penelope. *Technology and Agricultural Development in Pre-War Japan*. Yale U. Pr. 1982 $45.00. ISBN 0-300-02927-6. An important study of rural development and its connection to the emerging industrial economy.

Garon, Sheldon. *The State and Labor in Modern Japan*. U. CA Pr. 1988 $42.50. ISBN 0-520-05983-2. Focuses on the intersection of labor policy and political reform.

Gluck, Carol. *Japan's Modern Myths: Ideology in the Meiji Period*. Princeton U. Pr. 1985 $16.95. ISBN 0-691-00812-4. An important study of the emergence and evolution of new ideological constructs of the modern state.

Gordon, Andrew. *The Evolution of Labor Relations in Japan: Heavy Industry, 1853–1955*. HUP 1985 $14.00. ISBN 0-674-27131-9. Demonstrates that evolving systems of labor relations were not simply imposed from above but were a product of intense negotiations between managers and workers.

_____. *Labor and Imperial Democracy in Prewar Japan*. U. CA Pr. 1991 $37.50. ISBN 0-520-06783-5. Examines the intersection of labor problems and political development.

Hane, Mikiso. *Peasants, Rebels, and Outcasts: The Underside of Modern Japan*. Pantheon 1982 $10.95. ISBN 0-394-71040-1. Extended quotations from, and analysis of, those Japanese left behind by the nation's rapid modern development.

_____. *Reflections on the Way to the Gallows: Rebel Women in Prewar Japan*. U. CA Pr. 1988 $27.50. ISBN 0-520-06259-0. Lengthy translations from the writings of a variety of prewar radical women.

Hardacre, Helen. *Shinto and the State, 1868–1988*. Princeton U. Pr. 1989 $29.50. ISBN 0-691-02052-3. Discusses the creation of Shinto as a modern state-led phenomenon.

Havens, Thomas. *Valley of Darkness: The Japanese People and World War Two*. U. Pr. of Amer. 1986 $17.75. ISBN 0-8191-5495-4. Deals with the social meaning of war in Japan.

Hirschmeier, Johannes. *The Origins of Entrepreneurship in Meiji Japan*. HUP 1964 o.p. Views entrepreneurship as emerging from traditional warrior values.

Hirschmeier, Johannes, and Tsunehiko Yui. *The Development of Japanese Business, 1600–1980*. Unwin Hyman 1981 o.p. A good general business history.

Huber, Thomas M. *The Revolutionary Origins of Modern Japan.* Stanford U. Pr. 1981 $35.00. ISBN 0-8047-1048-1. Argues that the Meiji Restoration was a revolutionary struggle between new kinds of social class groupings.

Ienaga, Saburo. *The Pacific War, 1931–1945.* Pantheon 1978 $13.00. ISBN 0-394-73496-3. An excellent general history of World War II from the Japanese perspective.

Iriye, Akira. *The Origins of the Second World War in Asia and the Pacific.* Longman 1987 $17.95. ISBN 0-582-49349-8. A good introductory history.

Irokawa, Daikichi. *The Culture of the Meiji Period.* Ed. and trans. by Marius Jansen. Princeton U. Pr. 1985 o.p. Examines the cultural and social implications of the new Meiji state.

Jansen, Marius B. *The Cambridge History of Japan, Volume 5: The Nineteenth Century.* Cambridge U. Pr. 1989 $95.00. ISBN 0-521-22356-3

Jansen, Marius B., and Gilbert Rozman, eds. *Japan in Transition: From Tokugawa to Meiji.* Princeton U. Pr. 1986 $18.95. ISBN 0-691-10245-7. Essays that treat the restructuring of Japan during the years immediately following the Meiji Restoration.

Johnson, Chalmers. *Miti and the Japanese Miracle: The Growth of Industrial Policy, 1925–1975.* Stanford U. Pr. 1982 $42.50. ISBN 0-8047-1128-3. Evaluates the role of the state in economic development by looking at the agency most responsible for economic planning.

Jones, Hazel J. *Live Machines: Hired Foreigners and Meiji Japan.* Univ. of British Columbia Pr. 1980 o.p. The most complete study of foreign specialists hired to assist the new state after 1868.

Kinmonth, Earl. *The Self-Made Man in Meiji Japanese Thought: From Samurai to Salary Man.* U. CA Pr. 1981 o.p. Emphasizes the emergence of modern business and economic ideology.

Kinzley, W. Dean. *Industrial Harmony in Modern Japan: The Invention of a Tradition.* Routledge 1991 $49.95. ISBN 0-415-05167-3. Examines the evolving ideology of labor-management relations.

Large, Stephen S. *Organized Workers and Socialist Politics in Interwar Japan.* Cambridge U. Pr. 1981 o.p. Attributes the failures of organized labor to weaknesses of the leadership.

Lewis, Michael. *Rioters and Citizens: Mass Protest in Imperial Japan.* U. CA Pr. 1990 $42.00. ISBN 0-520-06642-1. A detailed study of the Rice Riots of 1919.

Lifton, Robert J., and others. *Six Lives, Six Deaths: Portraits from Modern Japan.* Yale U. Pr. 1979 $40.00. ISBN 0-300-02266-2. Psychohistories of six important modern individuals.

Lockwood, William W. *The Economic Development of Japan: Growth and Structural Change, 1868–1938.* Princeton U. Pr. rev. ed. 1969 o.p. Although somewhat dated, remains among the best general treatments of modern economic development.

Marshall, Byron. *Capitalism and Nationalism in Prewar Japan: Ideology of the Business Elite, 1868–1941.* Stanford U. Pr. 1967 $25.00. ISBN 0-8047-0325-6. Links the growth of authoritarianism to the failure of businessmen to develop a clear justification for capitalism and profit.

Maruyama, Masao. *Thought and Behavior in Modern Japanese Politics.* OUP 1963 o.p. Pioneering essays on nationalism and fascism in Japan.

Minear, Richard. *Victor's Justice: The Tokyo War Crimes Trial.* Princeton U. Pr. 1971 o.p. A critical study of the Allied war crimes trials.

Minichiello, Sharon. *Retreat from Reform: Patterns of Political Behavior in Interwar Japan.* UH Pr. 1984 $18.00. ISBN 0-8248-0778-2. Demonstrates the shallowness of the post-World War I political reform impulse.

Miyoshi, Masao. *As We Saw Them: The First Japanese Embassy to America.* U. CA Pr. 1979 $35.00. ISBN 0-520-03767-7. Discusses Japan's first official visit to the West in 1860.

Myers, Ramon H., and Mark R. Peattie, eds. *The Japanese Colonial Empire, 1895–1945.* Princeton U. Pr. 1984 $21.95. ISBN 0-691-10222-8. Essays on the administration of Japanese colonial holdings primarily in Korea and Taiwan.

Najita, Tetsuo. *Japan: The Intellectual Foundations of Modern Japanese Politics*. U. Ch. Pr. 1980 $8.95. ISBN 0-226-56803-2. An important interpretive treatment of bureaucracy and Japanese politics.

Najita, Tetsuo, and J. Victor Koschmann, eds. *Conflict in Modern Japanese History: The Neglected Tradition*. Princeton U. Pr. 1982 $65.00. ISBN 0-691-05364-2. Essays showing that Japanese development has been neither smooth nor harmonious.

Nakamura, Takafusa. *Economic Growth in Prewar Japan*. Univ. of Tokyo Pr. 1982 $45.00. ISBN 0-300-02451-7. A general history of Japan's economic growth.

———. *The Postwar Japanese Economy: Its Development and Structure*. Univ. of Tokyo Pr. 1981 $30.00. ISBN 0-86008-284-9. One of the most lucid and complete studies of Japan's economic development since World War II.

Ohkawa, Kazushi, and Henry Rosovsky. *Japanese Economic Growth: Trend Acceleration in the Twentieth Century*. Stanford U. Pr. 1973 $39.50. ISBN 0-8047-0833-9. Econometric study of Japan's modern economic transformation.

Oka, Yoshitake. *Five Political Leaders of Modern Japan*. Univ. of Tokyo Pr. 1985 o.p. Includes thoughtful analyses of key political figures.

———. *Konoe Fumimaro: A Political Biography*. Trans. by Shumpei Okamoto and Patricia Murray. Univ. of Tokyo Pr. 1983 o.p. The best available biography of the key wartime leader.

Patrick, Hugh, ed. *Japanese Industrialization and Its Social Consequences*. U. CA Pr. 1976 o.p. An important collection of essays that discusses the other side of economic success.

Pyle, Kenneth B. *The Making of Modern Japan: An Introduction*. Heath 1977 $10.50. ISBN 0-669-84657-0. A very compact, accessible treatment of Japan's modern development.

———. *The New Generation in Meiji Japan: Problems in Cultural Identity*. Stanford U. Pr. 1969 $25.00. ISBN 0-8047-0697-2. An important discussion of the emerging clash between modernity and tradition.

Robins-Mowry, Dorothy. *Hidden Sun: Women of Modern Japan*. Westview 1983 o.p. A good general treatment of social conditions and the role of women in Japan.

Roden, Donald J. *Schooldays in Imperial Japan: A Study in the Culture of a Student Elite*. U. CA Pr. 1980 $47.50. ISBN 0-520-03910-6. Treats the structure and patterns of elite education and its connection to the state.

Rosenstone, Robert A. *Mirror in the Shrine: American Encounters with Meiji Japan*. HUP 1988 $25.00. ISBN 0-674-57641-1. Deals with the impact of Japan on the lives of three important American visitors.

Schaller, Michael. *The American Occupation of Japan: The Origins of the Cold War in Asia*. OUP 1985 $30.00. ISBN 0-19-503626-3. An interesting revisionist study.

Seidensticker, Edward. *Low City, High City: Tokyo from Edo to the Earthquake*. HUP 1991 $14.95. ISBN 0-674-53939-7. A fascinating general history of Tokyo and how it changed with the development of modern society.

———. *Tokyo Rising: The City Since the Great Earthquake*. HUP 1991 $14.95. ISBN 0-674-89461-8. Continues the Tokyo story into World War II and the years that followed.

Shillony, Ben-Ami. *Politics and Culture in Wartime Japan*. OUP 1982 $19.95. ISBN 0-19-820260-1. One of the first studies to discuss politics and life in Japan during World War II.

Sievers, Sharon L. *Flowers in Salt: The Beginnings of Feminist Consciousness in Modern Japan*. Stanford U. Pr. 1983 $32.50. ISBN 0-8047-1382-0. Deals with the period from the end of the nineteenth century to the early years of the twentieth century.

Smethurst, Richard J. *Agricultural Development and Tenancy Dispute in Japan, 1870–1940*. Princeton U. Pr. 1986 $65.00. ISBN 0-691-05468-1. A controversial study that seeks to show that rural conditions were improving during this period.

———. *A Social Basis for Prewar Japanese Militarism: The Army and the Rural Community*. U. CA Pr. 1974 $52.50. ISBN 0-520-02552-0. Shows how the army mobilized and controlled local communities.

Smith, Robert J., and Ella Lury Wiswell. *The Women of Suye Mura.* U. Ch. Pr. 1982 $13.95. ISBN 0-226-76345-5. An anthropological study based on fieldwork done during the 1930s.

Smith, Thomas C. *Native Sources of Japanese Industrialization, 1750–1920.* U. CA Pr. 1988 $40.00. ISBN 0-520-05837-2. A collection of important previously published essays on the roots of economic development.

Toland, John. *The Rising Sun: The Decline and Fall of the Japanese Empire, 1936–1945.* Bantam 1982 $7.95. ISBN 0-553-26435-4. An approachable, detailed general history of World War II in the Pacific.

Totten, George O. *The Social Democratic Movement in Prewar Japan.* Yale U. Pr. 1966 o.p. An important general treatment of political and social opposition movements.

Tsurumi, E. Patricia. *Factory Girls: Women in the Thread Mills of Meiji Japan.* Princeton U. Pr. 1990 $29.95. ISBN 0-691-03138-X. The most complete discussion of women in the early textile industry.

Umegaki, Michio. *After Restoration: The Beginning of Japan's Modern State.* NYU Pr. 1988 $50.00. ISBN 0-8147-8552-2. Discusses the uncertain beginnings of the building of Japan's modern state.

Ward, Robert E., and Sakamoto Yoshikazu, eds. *Democratizing Japan: The Allied Occupation.* UH Pr. 1987 $31.00. ISBN 0-8248-0883-5. Essays on various elements of the occupation of Japan after World War II.

Waswo, Ann. *Japanese Landlords: The Decline of a Rural Elite.* U. CA Pr. 1977 $42.50. ISBN 0-520-03217-9. An important study of the dominant rural class and its transformation.

Westney, D. Eleanor. *Imitation and Innovation: The Transfer of Western Organizational Patterns to Meiji Japan.* HUP 1987 $27.50. ISBN 0-674-44437-X. Looks at several areas in which Western organizational systems were borrowed and adapted.

White, James W., and others, eds. *The Ambivalence of Nationalism: Modern Japan between East and West.* U. Pr. of Amer. 1990 o.p. A collection of essays that seeks to show the Japanese sense of place in the modern world.

Wray, Harry, and Hilary Conroy, eds. *Japan Examined: Perspectives on Modern Japanese History.* UH Pr. 1983 $12.95. ISBN 0-8248-0839-8. Numerous brief essays that are set up as a debate on major themes in modern history.

———. *Pearl Harbor Reexamined: Prologue to the Pacific War.* UH Pr. 1990 $22.50. ISBN 0-8248-1235-2. Many brief essays that take up major issues surrounding the beginnings of World War II in the Pacific.

Wray, William D. *Managing Industrial Enterprise: Cases from Japan's Prewar Experience.* HUP 1989 $25.00. ISBN 0-674-54770-5. Nine essays on business history.

Yamamura, Kozo. *Economic Policy in Postwar Japan: Growth versus Economic Democracy.* U. CA Pr. 1967 o.p. A good early study of the movement toward development.

Korea

During different periods of its history, Korea has been dominated by its two powerful neighbors, China and Japan, as a result of its peninsular location between those two nations. Despite such influence, the country has maintained its unique culture and society. In the twentieth century, the country has undergone a major transformation as a result of cold war ideologies, emerging after World War II as a divided nation. While much postwar writing focused on the divisions between North and South Korea, there is increasing interest in Korean culture and the remarkable economic gains of The Republic of Korea (South Korea). As cold war tensions ease, writings about the two nations that make up the Korean peninsula may focus increasingly on Korean society and culture and on the two nations' responses to, and interaction with, the contemporary world, especially the growing economic dominance of Pacific Rim nations.

REFERENCE WORKS

Aepli, Martine. *Korea*. Routledge Chapman & Hall 1990 $49.50. ISBN 0-7103-0367-X. A general overview of Korean history, culture, and society.

Center for Korean Studies Staff. *Korean Studies*. UH Pr. 1977 $13.50. ISBN 0-8248-0560-7. A series of studies on various aspects of Korean culture and history.

Hazard, B. H., ed. *Korean Studies Guide*. Greenwood 1975 repr. of 1954 ed. $38.50 ISBN 0-8371-7662-X. A general compilation of materials on Korea.

Hoare, James, and Susan Pares. *Korea: An Introduction*. Routledge Chapman & Hall 1988 $12.95. ISBN 0-7103-0299-1. Informative introduction to the life, history, and institutions of Korea, tracing the peninsula's history from earliest times to the present.

Steenson, Gary. *Coping With Korea*. Blackwell Pubs. 1987 $29.95. ISBN 0-631-15622-4. An introduction to the country's history, culture, and attractions.

Yonhap News Agency Staff. *Korea*. Western Pubns. Serv. 1992 $30.00. ISBN 89-7433-005-9. A helpful handbook of facts and statistics on the Korean society and economy.

SURVEYS AND GENERAL WORKS

Eckert, Carter, and others. *Korea Old and New: A History*. HUP 1990. ISBN 0-9627713-0-9. A detailed survey.

Grayson, James H. *Korea: A Religious History*. OUP 1990 $74.00. ISBN 0-19-826186-1. Looks at the history of Korea from a religious perspective, examining its impact on Korean life and society.

Henthorn, William E. *History of Korea*. Free Pr. 1974 $19.95. ISBN 0-02-914610-0

Hoare, James, and Susan Pares. *Korea: An Introduction*. Routledge Chapman & Hall 1988 $12.95. ISBN 0-7103-0299-1. An informative introduction to the life, history, and institutions of South Korea.

Howe, Russel W. *The Koreans: Passion and Grace*. HarBraceJ 1988 $12.95. ISBN 0-15-647185-X. A detailed examination of Korean culture, including extensive information on religious practices and ancient traditions.

Nahm, Andrew C. *Introduction to Korean History and Culture*. Hollym Intl. 1992 $29.95. ISBN 0-930878-07-8. An interesting study focusing on Korean culture and society.

_____. *Korea: Tradition and Transformation: A History of the Korean People*. Hollym Intl. 1988 $44.50. ISBN 0-930878-56-6. Perhaps the best synthesis of Korean history from antiquity to the present.

Osgood, Cornelius. *The Koreans and Their Culture*. Bks. Demand repr. of 1951 ed. $108.80. ISBN 0-8357-9523-3. Examines Korean culture and its place within the broader culture of East Asia.

Steinberg, David I. *The Republic of Korea: Economic Transformation and Social Change*. Westview 1988 $41.00. ISBN 0-86531-720-8. A concise, comprehensive survey examining recurring social and historical themes within Korean development.

Stone, I. F. *The Hidden History of the Korean War, 1950–1951. A Non-Conformist History of Our Times Ser.* Little 1988 $8.95. ISBN 0-316-81770-8

MODERN KOREA

Byoung-Lo, Philo Kim. *Two Koreas in Development: A Comparative Study of Principles and Strategies of Capitalist and Communist Third World Development*. Transaction Pubs. 1991 $32.95. ISBN 0-88738-437-4. Comparison of the divergent patterns of socioeconomic development of North and South Korea from 1945–88. Provides a comprehensive overview of Korean historical development.

Clark, Donald N. *Christianity in Modern Korea*. U. Pr. of Amer. 1986 $22.50. ISBN 0-8191-5384-2. Acknowledges the growing influence of Korean Christianity through an analysis of church development over the last 50 years and current church-state relations.

Eckert, Carter J. *Offspring of Empire: The Koch'ang Kims and the Colonial Origins of Korean Capitalism*. U. of Wash. Pr. 1991 $40.00. ISBN 0-295-97065-0. Highly innovative work, detailing Japan's role in furthering modern Korean economic expansion.

Lee, Manwoo. *The Odyssey of Korean Democracy: Korean Politics, 1987–1990*. Greenwood 1990 $42.95. ISBN 0-275-93660-0. The most up-to-date survey of contemporary South Korean politics. A superb analysis of South Korea's democratic transition.

Rees, Davis. *Short History of Modern Korea*. Hippocrene Bks. 1988 $16.95. ISBN 0-87052-575-1. A concise, comprehensive history focusing on the post–World War II years.

Ridgway, Matthew B. *The Korean War*. Doubleday 1967 o.p. An intelligent assessment by a leading participant.

Robinson, Michael E. *Cultural Nationalism in Colonial Korea, 1920–1925*. U. of Wash. Pr. 1989 $30.00. ISBN 0-295-96600-9. A historical analysis of the Korean nationalist movement.

Yoo, Yushin. *The Making of Modern Korea*. Golden Pond Pr. 1990 $24.95. ISBN 0-942091-03-5. Account of Korean national development focusing on educational, economic, and social changes since World War II.

SOUTH ASIA

While South Asia consists of a number of nations, including Pakistan, Bangladesh, and Sri Lanka, India is at the center of the region and of South Asian history. The political divisions that make up the region and define its nations are of relatively recent origin, and separate studies of these offshoots on the subcontinent are correspondingly small. Studies of the whole of South Asia are essentially concerned with what could be called Greater India, which would include all of the newer political entities (India, Pakistan, Bangladesh, and Sri Lanka) under the larger Indian umbrella. A. L. Basham's classic study, *The Wonder That Was India*, is the best example of this approach. South Asian scholarship, however, is also very concerned with the region's evolving interaction with outside powers, first Arab and then European. Much of the writing on South Asian history, therefore, focuses on the nature of Indian confrontation with the outside world and how and in what kinds of ways the area has coped with that challenge.

Reference Works

Dutt, Ashok K. *Atlas of South Asia*. Westview 1987 $19.95. ISBN 0-8133-0045-2. Surveys the region's history, politics, society, culture, and so on, via text, charts, and maps. Arranged topically.

Pearson, J. D., ed. *South Asian Bibliography: A Handbook and Guide*. Humanities 1979 o.p. A comprehensive bibliography of bibliographies and general reference materials.

Robinson, Francis, ed. *The Cambridge Encyclopedia of India, Pakistan, Bangladesh, Sri Lanka, Nepal, Bhutan and the Maldives*. Cambridge U. Pr. 1989 $55.00. ISBN 0-521-33451-9. A compendium of social science and humanistic information on South Asia presented in this intelligent volume.

Schwartzberg, Joseph E., and others, eds. *A Historical Atlas of South Asia*. OUP 1992 $250.00. ISBN 0-19-506869-6. More comprehensive edition prepared under the auspices of the Association for Asian Studies.

Sukhwal, B. L. *South Asia: A Systematic Geographic Bibliography*. Scarecrow 1974 o.p. An unannotated but extensive bibliography on matters pertaining to South Asian geography.

General Works

Basham, A. L. *A Cultural History of India*. OUP 1984 $34.50. ISBN 0-19-561520-4. General essays on the cultural developments of the subcontinent.

_____. *The Wonder That Was India: A Survey of the History and Culture of the Indian Subcontinent before the Coming of the Muslims.* Merrimack River 1983 o.p. A classic text.

Chaudhuri, K. N. *Trade and Civilization in the Indian Ocean: An Economic History from the Rise of Islam to 1750.* Cambridge U. Pr. 1985 $54.95. ISBN 0-521-24226-6. A stimulating discussion of the commercial unity of an Indian Ocean trade zone.

Spate, O.H.K., and A.T.A. Learmonth. *India and Pakistan: A General and Regional Geography.* South Asia Bks. 1967 $64.00. ISBN 0-8364-2603-7. Older but still useful introduction.

India

Much of the historical writing on India concentrates on two main themes. The first theme is the character of British colonial rule. Writers have examined the means by which British power inserted itself; how Indian cultural and social life responded to British domination; and how regional, religious, and ethnic differences were cultivated or exacerbated by the British presence. The second theme is an extension of the first and revolves around such questions as: What were the sources of the Indian independence movement? How did Nationalist ideas grow and prosper? What were the sources and nature of the partition that separated Pakistan from India?

Historical scholarship on Indian history prior to the colonial period is richly varied, with much emphasis on ethnic and regional differences and on early contacts between Indian peoples and various outsiders. Nevertheless, there is a strong tendency in histories of the earlier period to demonstrate the strength, the grandeur, and the independence of early India in contrast to what would come later. It is in the history of the later, less happy, periods, however, that the writing of India has become most fully developed.

REFERENCE WORKS

Bhattacharya, Sachchidananda. *A Dictionary of Indian History.* Greenwood 1972 $58.50. ISBN 0-8371-9515-2. An extensive dictionary of European and Indian individuals important in Indian life and history.

Chopra, Pran Nath. *Encyclopedia of India.* S. Asia. 1992 $1750.00. ISBN 0-8364-2750-5. The most, and perhaps only, detailed encyclopedia of India. Written by prominent Indian scholars. Examines history, people, government, education, culture, languages, literature, economic life, and places of interest. Also considers physical, religious, and social aspects of life. Bibliographies, chronologies, and indexes. Authoritative and up-to-date.

Davies, C. Collin. *An Historical Atlas of the Indian Peninsula.* OUP 1959 $5.95. ISBN 0-19-635139-1

Kurian, George Thomas. *Historical and Cultural Dictionary of India.* Scarecrow 1976 o.p. Brief but useful entries in a general dictionary of Indian life and history.

Mehra, Parshotam. *A Dictionary of Modern Indian History, 1707–1947.* OUP 1987 $38.00. ISBN 0-19-561552-2. Includes some 400 essay-type entries with a select chronology and detailed index. Arranged alphabetically, the entries cover places, events, people, and so on. Includes bibliographies, appendixes, and a glossary.

GENERAL WORKS

Ballhatchet, Kenneth, and John Harrison, eds. *The City in South Asia: Pre-Modern and Modern.* Humanities 1980 o.p. Useful essays about the urban character of South Asia during different periods.

Chaitanya, Krishna. *Arts of India: Architecture, Sculpture, Painting, Music, Dance and Handicraft.* S. Asia 1987 $80.00. ISBN 81-7017-209-8. A concise summary of the great traditions of Indian art.

Embree, Ainslie T., and Stephen Hay, eds. *Sources of Indian Tradition.* 2 vols. Col. U. Pr. 1988. Vol. 1 $59.50. ISBN 0-231-06650-3. Vol. 2 $58.00. ISBN 0-231-06414-4. A collection of documents and writings crucial in the history of India.

Grewal, J. S. *The Sikhs of the Punjab.* Cambridge U. Pr. 1990 $34.50. ISBN 0-521-26884-2. A thoughtful and informative general history of the Sikhs from the fifteenth century to present times.

Guy, John, and Deborah Swallow. *Arts of India: 1550–1990.* Trafalgar 1992 $39.95. ISBN 1-85177-022-4. A highly recommended study of the arts of premodern India. Includes an overview of present museum collections.

Heesterman, J. C. *The Inner Conflict of Tradition: Essays in Indian Ritual, Kingship, and Society.* U. Ch. Pr. 1985 $14.95. ISBN 0-226-32299-8. A challenging but important book on the nature of social and political value in Indian history and culture.

Herman, A. L. *A Brief Introduction to Hinduism: Religion, Philosophy and Ways of Liberation.* Westview 1991 $38.50. ISBN 0-8133-8109-6. A brilliant overview of the three major strands of Hinduism.

Ludden, David. *Peasant History in South India.* Princeton U. Pr. 1985 $55.00. ISBN 0-691-05456-8. An important work that seeks to study the last 1,000 years of Indian history from the perspective of the peasantry.

Majumdar, R. C., and P. N. Chopra. *Main Currents of Indian History.* Sterling 1988 $22.50. ISBN 81-207-0770-2

Wolpert, Stanley. *India.* U. CA Pr. 1991 $24.95. ISBN 0-520-07217-0. An accessible general study of Indian history and culture.

————. *A New History of India.* OUP 1989 $37.00. ISBN 0-19-505636-1. Among the best general histories of India and its peoples.

THE PRECOLONIAL ERA

Blake, Stephen P. *Shahjahanabad: The Sovereign City in Mughal India, 1639–1739.* Cambridge U. Pr. 1991 $49.95. ISBN 0-521-39045-1. A history of the great Mughal city. Links urban character to the nature of the state and makes comparisons with other major Asian cities.

Boxer, C. R. *Portuguese India in the Mid-Seventeenth Century.* OUP 1980 o.p. Among the most accessible of Boxer's many important works on Portugal's Asian empire.

Disney, A. R. *Twilight of the Pepper Empire: Portuguese Trade in Southwest India in the Early Seventeenth Century.* HUP 1978 $18.50. ISBN 0-674-91429-5. A solid history of Portuguese trade and its institutional weaknesses in India.

Pearson, M. N. *The Portuguese in India.* Cambridge U. Pr. 1988 $39.95. ISBN 0-521-25713-1. An account of the social, economic, and religious interaction between the Portuguese and Indians from the sixteenth century onwards.

Raychaudhuri, Tapan, and Irfan Habib, eds. *The Cambridge Economic History of India, Vol. 1: c.1200–c.1750.* Cambridge U. Pr. 1982 $110.00. ISBN 0-521-22692-9. Essays on various key themes of India's precolonial economic history.

Stein, Burton. *Peasant State and Society in Medieval South India.* OUP 1980 $12.95. ISBN 0-19-561830-0. A complex but important general study of early rural life and its intersection with the building of the state.

Streusand, Douglas E. *The Formation of the Mughal Empire.* OUP 1989 $16.95. ISBN 0-19-562490-4. An ambitious attempt to reinterpret the Mughal state.

Subrahmanyam, Sanjay. *The Political Economy of Commerce: Southern India, 1500–1650.* Cambridge U. Pr. 1990 $64.95. ISBN 0-521-37180-5. Focuses on the indigenous structures of trade relationships into which European traders plunged.

THE COLONIAL ERA

Arnold, David. *Police Power and Colonial Rule: Madras, 1859–1947.* OUP 1986 $28.00. ISBN 0-19-561-893-9. A study of the growth of state power over time.

Ballhatchet, Kenneth. *Race, Sex, and Class Under the Raj: Imperial Attitudes and Policies and Their Critics, 1793–1905.* St. Martin 1980 o.p. A social history of the Raj and its attitudes.

Bayly, C. A. *The Raj: India and the British 1600–1947.* Antique Collect. 1990 $95.00. ISBN 1-855140-26-8. A catalog of major exhibitions at London's National Portrait Gallery that includes nine focused and thoughtful essays on the Raj.

————. *Rulers, Townsmen, and Bazaars: North Indian Society in the Age of British Expansionism.* Cambridge U. Pr. 1983 o.p. Major social history of India under colonialism. Shows middle- and lower-class life thoroughly connected to local culture.

Borthwick, Meredith. *The Changing Role of Women in Bengal, 1849–1905.* Princeton U. Pr. 1984 $57.50. ISBN 0-691-05409-6. A richly textured study that demonstrates the collective weakness of women in the later years of the Raj.

Embree, Ainslie T. *Charles Grant and British Rule in India.* AMS Pr. 1962 $10.00. ISBN 0-404-51606-8. A study of the influential and powerful official of the East India Company.

Fisher, Michael H. *A Clash of Cultures.* Riverdale Co. 1987 $35.00. ISBN 0-913215-27-9. A study of the social and political character of the most important of the post-Mughal states and its relationship with the British.

Fox, Richard. *Lions of the Punjab: Culture in the Making.* U. CA Pr. 1985 $45.00. ISBN 0-520-05491-1. Focuses on the cultural changes within the Sikh community and its response to the British.

Gupta, Narayani. *Delhi Between Two Empires, 1803–1931. Society, Government, and Urban Growth.* OUP 1981 o.p. A well-written and extremely engaging urban history.

Irving, Robert Grant. *Indian Summer: Lutyens, Baker, and Imperial Delhi.* Yale U. Pr. 1982 o.p. An attractive book on the construction and character of Britain's new colonial capital.

Metcalf, Barbara Daly. *Islamic Revival in British India: Deoband, 1860–1900.* Princeton U. Pr. 1982 $45.00. ISBN 0-691-05343-X. Study of the institutional character of Muslim leadership and their enlarged and changed role in South Asian Muslim society.

Metcalf, Thomas R. *An Imperial Vision: Indian Architecture and Britain's Raj.* U. CA Pr. 1989 $45.00. ISBN 0-520-06235-3. Argues that British power took shape in colonial architecture, which in turn reinforced British dominance.

O'Hanlon, Rosalind. *Caste, Conflict and Ideology: Mahatma Jotirao Phule and Low-Caste Protest in Nineteenth-Century Western India.* Cambridge U. Pr. 1985 $59.95. ISBN 0-521-26615-7. A finely wrought biography of a key leader and chief ideological architect of nonelite protest movements.

Oldenburg, Veena Talwar. *The Making of Colonial Lucknow, 1856–1877.* Princeton U. Pr. 1984 $11.95. ISBN 0-19-562473-4. A fascinating and balanced study of the British role in shaping and inventing Lucknow.

Pemble, John. *The Raj, the Indian Mutiny, and the Kingdom of Oudh, 1801–1859.* Farleigh Dickinson 1978 $35.00. ISBN 0-8386-2092-2. An account of major forces during a critical time in India's history.

Tomlinson, B. R. *The Political Economy of the Raj, 1914–1947: The Economics of Decolonization in India.* Macmillan 1979 o.p. A study of the changes that British India was forced to undergo after 1913.

MODERN INDIA—THE MOVE TOWARD INDEPENDENCE AND BEYOND

Baker, Christopher John. *An Indian Rural Economy, 1880–1955: The Tamiland Countryside.* OUP 1984 $65.00. ISBN 0-19-821572-X. A useful economic history of the Madras region that seeks to connect rural life to the urban community.

Bardhan, Pranab. *The Political Economy of Development in India.* Blackwell Pubs. 1984 $34.95. ISBN 0-631-13544-8. A brief but thought-provoking evaluation of the state and character of Indian economic activity and development.

Brass, Paul R. *The New Cambridge History of India: The Politics of India Since Independence.* Cambridge U. Pr. 1990 $15.95. ISBN 0-521-39651-4. A good one-volume synthesis of a tumultuous period.

Brown, D. M. *The Nationalist Movement: Indian Political Thought from Randade to Bhave.* Peter Smith 1962 o.p. An older but still useful introduction to Indian political thought.

Brown, Judith M. *Gandhi: Prisoner of Hope*. Yale U. Pr. 1990 $29.95. ISBN 0-300-05125-5. The most comprehensive and detailed biography of Gandhi presently available.
———. *Modern India: The Origins of an Asian Democracy*. OUP 1984 $55.00. ISBN 0-19-913124-4. A useful introduction to the history of modern India.

Chakrabarty, Dipesh. *Rethinking Working-Class History: Bengal 1890–1940*. Princeton U. Pr. 1989 $39.50. ISBN 0-691-05548-3. A study of the Bengal jute industry and its workers. An important study of earlier cultural practices in the new economic order.

Das, M. N. *Partition and Independence of India*. Humanities 1983 o.p.

Frankel, Francine R. *India's Political Economy, 1947–1977*. Princeton U. Pr. 1978 o.p. A useful introduction to the political evolution of India after independence.

Galanter, Marc. *Law and Society in Modern India*. Ed. by Rajeev Dhavan. OUP 1989 $32.50. ISBN 0-19-562294-4. A collection of previously published essays that show the connection of social norms and legal structure.

Gordon, Leonard A. *Brothers against the Raj: A Biography of Indian Nationalists, Sarat and Subhas Chandra Bose*. Col. U. Pr. 1990 $65.00. ISBN 0-231-07442-5. An important double biography of the brothers who together played important, if very different, roles in the independence movement.

James, Josef, ed. *Art and Life in India: The Last Four Decades*. S. Asia 1989 $26.00. ISBN 81-7018-567-X

Jones, Kenneth W. *The New Cambridge History of India: Socio-Religious Reform Movements in British India*. Cambridge U. Pr. 1990 $39.95. ISBN 0-521-24986-4. A good general study of religious-based reform movements from the nineteenth into the twentieth century.

Low, D. A. *Congress and the Raj: Facets of the Indian Struggle, 1917–47*. S. Asia 1977 $24.00. ISBN 0-8364-0007-0. Essays on numerous topics relating to independence and nationalist movements.

Mahajan, V. D. *History of Modern India 1919–1982*. 2 vols. Coronet Bks. 1983 $77.50. ISBN 0-685-14075-X

Markovits, Claude. *Indian Business and Nationalist Politics, 1931–1939: The Indigenous Capitalist Class and the Rise of the Congress Party*. Cambridge U. Pr. 1985 $54.95. ISBN 0-521-26551-7. A useful discussion of businessmen and business pressures for change.

Nanda, B. R. *Gokhale, Gandhi and the Nehrus: Studies in Indian Nationalism*. St. Martin 1974 o.p. Rather old-fashioned but still useful introductions to the major figures in the Nationalist movement.

Ray, Rajat Kanta, ed. *Entrepreneurship and Industry in India, 1800–1947*. OUP 1992 $24.95. ISBN 0-19-562806-3. Essays on the evolution of the Indian economy.

Rudolph, Lloyd I., and Susanne H. Rudolph. *The Modernity of Tradition: Political Development in India*. U. Ch. Pr. 1984 $16.00. ISBN 0-226-73137-5. Argues that many of the characteristics and problems of India that are identified as traditional are instead recent products of the state- and nation-building process.

Sarkar, Sumit. *Modern India, 1885–1947*. Macmillan 1983 $14.00. ISBN 0-8364-1236-2. A good introduction to the modern period of India.

Spear, Percival. *The Oxford History of Modern India, 1740–1975*. OUP 1978 $13.95. ISBN 0-19-561076-8. The standard and still useful general history of modern India.

Srinivas, M. N. *Social Change in Modern India*. U. CA Pr. 1966 o.p. A useful investigation of the structure and character of the caste system.

Wiser, William H., and Charlotte Vially Wiser. *Behind Mud Walls, 1930–1960*. With a sequel: *The Village in 1970*. U. CA Pr. rev. ed. 1971 $32.50. ISBN 0-520-02093-6. A classic study and description of traditional Indian village life.

Bangladesh

Ahmed, Rafiuddin, ed. *Religion, Nationalism and Politics in Bangladesh*. S. Asian 1990 o.p. Essays on the political cultures of Bangladesh from a regional perspective.

Baxter, Craig, and Syedur Rahman. *Historical Dictionary of Bangladesh.* Scarecrow 1989 $22.50. ISBN 0-8108-2177-X. Includes a chronology, an introduction, 70 pages of alphabetical listings, and 3 appendixes.

Chakravarty, S. R., and Virendra Narain, eds. *Bangladesh.* 2 vols. Nataraj Bks. 1986 $12.50 ea. *Vol. 1: History and Culture. Vol. 2: Domestic Policies.*

Rājjāka, Moḥ Ābadura. *Bangladesh: A Select General Bibliography.* Razzaque 1987 o.p. A topical listing of 1,000 books, with indexes.

Wright, Dennis. *Bangladesh: Origins and Indian Ocean Relations, 1971–75.* Apt Bks. 1988 $17.95. ISBN 81-207-0839-3. The most scholarly analysis to date of the emergence and early history of Bangladesh as a nation-state.

Pakistan

Ahmad, Viqar, and Rashid Amjad. *The Management of Pakistan's Economy, 1947–1982.* OUP 1984 o.p. A general introduction to the general contours of Pakistani economic activity since the Partition.

Ahmed, Abkar S. *Religion and Politics in Muslim Society: Order and Conflict in Pakistan.* Cambridge U. Pr. 1983 $59.95. ISBN 0-521-24635-0. Study of one Pakistani region and the role of religious leaders in shaping political decisions and action.

Burki, Shahid Javed. *Historical Dictionary of Pakistan.* Scarecrow 1991 $35.00. ISBN 0-8108-2411-6. Useful general dictionary of people, institutions, and events important in Pakistani life and history.

Damodar, Singhat. *Pakistan: The Modern Nations in Historical Perspective.* Asia Bk. Corp. 1972 $9.95. ISBN 0-13-648469-7

Gilmartin, David. *Empire and Islam, Punjab and the Making of Pakistan.* U. CA Pr. 1988 $40.00. ISBN 0-520-06249-3. Focuses on the changing ideas about state and society in the Punjab and the importance of Islam in the mediation of these ideas.

Jalal, Ayesha. *The Sole Spokesman: Jinnah, the Muslim League, and the Demand for Pakistan.* Cambridge U. Pr. 1985 $59.95. ISBN 0-521-24462-5. Highly critical of Jinnah and his policies in the creating of Pakistan.

Taylor, David D. *Pakistan.* ABC-CLIO 1990 $70.00. ISBN 1-85109-081-9. Lists about 800 English-language books; also contains several articles, topically arranged and annotated. Includes indexes and a chronology.

Weiss, Anita M. *Culture, Class, and Development in Pakistan: The Emergence of an Industrial Bourgeoisie in Punjab.* Westview 1991 $33.00. ISBN 0-8133-7910-5. Considers the cultural factors in the rise of a bourgeoisie in Pakistan since 1947.

Wilcox, Wayne A. *Pakistan: The Consolidation of a Nation.* Col. U. Pr. 1963 o.p. Focuses on the politics and government of the nation.

Wolpert, Stanley A. *Jinnah of Pakistan.* OUP 1984 $30.00. ISBN 0-19-503412-0. A good biography of the leader of modern Pakistan.

Zakaria, Rafiq. *Women and Politics in Islam: The Trial of Benazir Bhutto.* Apex Pr. 1990 $21.50. ISBN 0-945257-24-4

Sri Lanka

Bandarage, Asoka. *Colonialism in Sri Lanka: The Political Economy of the Kandyan Highlands, 1833–1866.* Mouton 1983 $104.00. ISBN 90-279-3080-5. Deals with the social meaning of colonial plantation economies.

de Silva, K. M. *Sri Lanka: A Survey.* UH Pr. 1977 $25.00. ISBN 0-8248-0568-2. A good, brief introduction to Sri Lanka after independence.

Manor, James. *The Expedient Utopian: Bandaranaike and Ceylon.* Cambridge U. Pr. 1990 $59.95. ISBN 0-521-37191-0. A political biography of a major postindependence leader.

Moore, Mick. *The State and Peasant Politics in Sri Lanka.* Cambridge U. Pr. 1985 $59.95. ISBN 0-521-26550-9. Argues that there is a general lack of articulation of peasant interests in the island's political culture.

Peebles, Patrick. *Sri Lanka: A Handbook of Historical Statistics.* G. K. Hall 1982 o.p. A useful guide.

Samaraweera, Vijaya. *Sri Lanka.* ABC-CLIO 1987 $40.50. ISBN 1-903450-33-X. An annotated list of books, government publications, and so on, organized alphabetically; includes author, title, and subject index.

Tambiah, S. J. *Sri Lanka: Ethnic Fratricide and the Dismantling of Democracy.* U. Ch. Pr. 1986 $19.95. ISBN 0-226-78951-9. A thoughtful but impassioned discussion of the tradition of ethnic struggle and its political and social meaning.

SOUTHEAST ASIA

Made up of at least 11 countries between India to the west and China to the north and east, Southeast Asia covers a broad area and has a very large population base. Nevertheless, its giant neighbors have had a much larger place in Western concepts of Asia. The idea of a unified Southeast Asia is itself a relatively recent concept dating only from the end of World War II. With the exception of Thailand, all of the countries in the region have been subject to colonial domination from at least the nineteenth century and into the twentieth century. Much of the historical writing both on the region as a whole and on individual countries has been concerned with colonialism and its legacy. Studies of more recent periods have focused on how the countries of the region interact with one another and with the outside world as individual states and as members of the Association of Southeast Asian Nations (ASEAN). There is, for example, a large body of writing on the Vietnam War. James Olson's *Dictionary of the Vietnam War* (1987) is a good place to begin to uncover this substantial body of work.

Reference Works

ASEAN: A Bibliography, 1981–85. Ed. by Patricia Lim Pui Huen, and others. Inst. SE Asian Studies 1988 o.p. A basic bibliography, listing over 6,300 books, articles, papers, and other materials in all languages. Arranged topically, with an author index.

Bixler, Paul. *Southeast Asia: Bibliographic Directions in a Complex Area.* Choice Pubns. 1972 o.p. A useful basic bibliography, with illuminating introductory essays on the region and on individual countries.

Jeffrey, Robin, ed. *Asia—The Winning of Independence.* St. Martin 1981 $27.50. ISBN 0-312-05614-1. Essays on the growth and success since 1945 of nationalist movements in the various former colonies of Southeast Asia.

Johnson, Donald Clay, and others, eds. *Southeast Asia: A Bibliography for Undergraduate Libraries.* Bro-Dart Publishing 1970 o.p. A good basic bibliography graded for importance and centrality.

Nevadomsky, Joseph-John, and Alice Li. *Chinese in Southeast Asia: A Selected and Annotated Bibliography of Publications in Western Languages, 1960–1970.* Center for South and Southeast Asia Studies. U. CA Pr. 1970 o.p. A useful and well-constructed guide.

Tregonning, Kennedy G. *Southeast Asia: A Critical Bibliography.* Bks. Demand 1969 $29.90. ISBN 0-318-34750-4. A useful, annotated, and thoughtful bibliography.

Surveys and General Works

Cady, John Frank. *Southeast Asia: Its Historical Development.* McGraw 1964 o.p. A general introductory look at the region.

Chandler, Glen, and others, eds. *Development and Displacement: Women in Southeast Asia.* Center of Southeast Asian Studies. Monash University 1988 $14.00 o.p.

A somewhat disjointed but useful introduction to women's place in the development of the region.

Hall, Daniel George Edward. *A History of South-East Asia*. St. Martin 1981 $24.95. ISBN 0-312-38641-9. A basic and still useful general history of the area.

Longmire, R. A. *Soviet Relations with South-East Asia: An Historical Survey*. Routledge Chapman & Hall 1989 $65.00. ISBN 0-7103-0343-2. A general treatment of Soviet relations with the region from 1945 to the 1990s.

McVey, Ruth T. *Southeast Asian Transitions: Approaches through Social History*. Yale U. Pr. 1978 o.p. Essays that seek understanding of general Southeast Asian history by looking closely at local history and developments.

Marten, Gerald G. *Traditional Agriculture in Southeast Asia: A Human Ecology Perspective*. Westview 1986 $70.00. ISBN 0-8133-7026-4. Useful essays on the variety of agricultural patterns in the region.

O'Connor, Richard A. *A Theory of Indigenous Southeast Asian Urbanism*. Inst. SE Asian Studies 1983 o.p. Treats the development of cities in the region and the effect of Western intrusion.

Reid, Anthony. *Southeast Asia in the Age of Commerce, 1450–1680, Volume 1: The Lands Below the Winds*. Yale U. Pr. 1988 $12.95. ISBN 0-300-04750-9. A major study of the entire region as it began to be populated with European traders and conquerors.

Steinberg, David Joel, ed. *In Search of Southeast Asia: A Modern History*. UH Pr. rev. ed. 1987 $18.50. ISBN 0-8248-1110-0. An important collection of essays on the modern history of the region and its various countries.

Suwannathat-Pian, Kobkua. *Thai-Malay Relations: Traditional Intra-regional Relations from the Seventeenth to the Early Twentieth Centuries*. OUP 1989 $35.50. ISBN 0-19-588892-8. Shows historical linkages of the states and the changing role of Britain in the interchange.

Burma

Cady, John Frank. *A History of Modern Burma*. Cornell Univ. Pr. 1958 $54.95. ISBN 0-8014-0059-7. Early general history that remains useful.

Cheng, Siok-hwa. *The Rice Industry of Burma, 1852–1940*. Univ. of Malaya 1968 o.p. Studies the production and trade of rice when Burma was the world's largest exporter.

Gyi, Maung Maung. *Burmese Political Values: The Socio-Political Roots of Authoritarianism*. Greenwood 1983 $42.95. ISBN 0-275-90993-X. An important study of Burmese political culture.

Lieberman, Victor B. *Burmese Administrative Cycles: Anarchy and Conquest, c.1580–1760*. Princeton U. Pr. 1984 $50.00. ISBN 0-691-05407-X. An important history of political development before British colonial rule.

Lintner, Bertil. *The Rise and Fall of the Communist Party in Burma*. Cornell Univ. Pr. 1990 $10.00. ISBN 0-87727-123-2. Half-century history of the party from 1939.

Maung, Mya. *The Burma Road to Poverty*. Greenwood 1991 $59.95. ISBN 0-275-93613-9. A personal and thoughtful analysis of the contemporary collapse of Burma.

Myint, Ni Ni. *Burma's Struggle Against British Imperialism, 1885–1895*. The Universities Pr. 1983 o.p. A detailed, thoughtful treatment of Burmese actions and policies responding to the British.

Steinberg, David I. *Burma: A Socialist Nation of Southeast Asia*. Westview 1982 o.p. A brief but useful introduction to Burma.

Taylor, Robert H. *The State in Burma*. UH Pr. 1988 $32.00. ISBN 0-8248-1141-0. An incisive study of the history and character of the state system's expansion of authority over civil society.

Trager, Frank N. *Burma, From Kingdom to Republic: A Historical and Political Analysis*. Praeger 1966 o.p. A richly documented general history.

Trager, Helen Gibson. *Burma Through Alien Eyes: Missionary Views of the Burmese in the Nineteenth Century*. Greenwood 1966 o.p. Focuses on missionary obfuscations and the general confusion of Westerners in Burma.

Thailand

Bitz, Ira. *A Bibliography of English-language Source Materials on Thailand in the Humanities, Social Sciences, and Physical Sciences.* Am. Univ. Pr. 1968 o.p. The most comprehensive earlier bibliography.

Ingram, James. *Economic Change in Thailand 1850–1970.* Stanford U. Pr. rev. ed. 1971 $42.50. ISBN 0-8047-0782-0. Emphasizes the role of international market forces in the shaping of Thailand's economic development.

Keyes, Charles F. *Thailand: Buddhist Kingdom as Modern Nation-State.* Westview 1987 $54.00. ISBN 0-86531-138-2. The best recent introduction to Thailand's history, society, and culture.

Nuechterlein, Donald Edwin. *Thailand and the Struggle for Southeast Asia.* Cornell Univ. Pr. 1965 o.p. An important study of Thailand's foreign policy from 1932 to 1960.

Riggs, Fred W. *Thailand: The Modernization of a Bureaucratic Policy.* East-West Ctr. 1966 o.p. Strongest on Thailand's place in comparative public administration.

Siffin, William J. *The Thai Bureaucracy: Institutional Change and Development.* East-West Ctr. 1966 o.p. Good background and evaluation of the role of Buddhism in administration.

Suehiro, Akira. *Capital Accumulation in Thailand, 1855–1985.* The Centre for East Asian Cultural Studies 1989 $34.66. ISBN 4-89656-105-8. A highly detailed and systematic business history arguing that conflicts between internal technocratic groups have shaped Thailand's capitalist growth.

Terwiel, B. J. *Through Travellers' Eyes: An Approach to Early Nineteenth Century Thai History.* Editions Duang Kamol 1989 o.p. Discussion of the nature of state and society in nineteenth-century Thailand based on contemporary travel accounts.

Thrombley, Woodworth G., and William J. Siffin, eds. *Thailand: Politics, Economy and Socio-cultural Setting; A Selective Guide to the Literature.* Ind. U. Pr. 1972 $24.50. ISBN 0-404-15297-X. A useful guide for introductory readers.

Wyatt, David K. *Thailand: A Short History.* Yale U. Pr. 1984 $40.00. ISBN 0-300-03054-1. An excellent one-volume history that tends to concentrate on traditional political development.

Xuto, Somsakdi. *Government and Politics of Thailand.* OUP 1987 $65.00. ISBN 0-19-582657-4. Essays by five political scientists on the history and character of Thai political life.

Vietnam, Cambodia, and Laos

Ablin, David A., and Marlowe Hood, eds. *The Cambodian Agony.* M. E. Sharpe 1987 $17.95. ISBN 0-87332-754-3. Essays on important aspects of Cambodia from the late 1950s to the 1980s.

Butler, Deborah A. *American Women Writers on Vietnam: Unheard Voices.* Garland 1990 $40.00. ISBN 0-8240-3528-3. Lists and annotates almost 800 items published between 1954 and 1987. Includes an index.

Buttinger, Joseph. *A Dragon Defiant: A Short History of Vietnam.* Greenwood 1972 o.p. A useful general history that is especially helpful on Vietnam's earlier relations with China and on domestic arrangements before the French.

Chandler, David P. *The Tragedy of Cambodian History: Politics, War, and Revolution Since 1945.* Yale U. Pr. 1991 $35.00. ISBN 0-300-04919-6. A superb, balanced narrative history.

Duong, Pham Cao. *Vietnamese Peasants Under French Domination, 1861–1945.* U. Pr. of Amer. 1985 $23.50. ISBN 0-8191-4715-X. Indispensable reference for those interested in the period of French control and the modern history of Vietnam.

Khanh, Huynh Kim. *Vietnamese Communism, 1925–1945.* Cornell Univ. Pr. 1982 $14.95. ISBN 0-8014-9397-8. Argues that the national liberation line and the shape of the party itself were a result of indigenous forces.

Lockhart, Greg. *Nation in Arms: The Origins of the People's Army of Vietnam*. Unwin Hyman 1991 $38.95. ISBN 0-04-301294-9. Focuses on the origins and organization of the army that defeated the French and fought the United States to a standoff.

McConnell, Scott. *Leftward Journey: The Education of Vietnamese Students in France, 1919–1939*. Transaction Pubs. 1989 $34.95. ISBN 0-88738-238-X. Traces the lives and ideas of young Vietnamese nationalists studying abroad.

Marr, David G. *Vietnamese Anti-Colonialism, 1885–1925*. U. CA Pr. 1971 $37.50. ISBN 0-520-04278-6. Centers on the development of Vietnamese literature and political thought in response to French colonialism.

Olson, James S. *Dictionary of the Vietnam War*. Greenwood 1988 $65.00. ISBN 0-313-24943-1. A useful dictionary, chronology, and bibliography.

Sage, William W., comp. *Laos: A Bibliography*. Inst. SE Asian Studies 1986 o.p. An extensive listing, mostly in English language, of materials published between 1975 and 1984; arranged topically, with indexes.

Smith, Richard Bernard. *Vietnam and the West*. Cornell Univ. Pr. 1971 o.p. Discusses French challenges to indigenous culture and the Vietnamese response.

Smith, Roger. *Cambodia's Foreign Policy*. Cornell Univ. Pr. 1965 o.p. A good treatment of foreign policy issues after 1954.

Stuart-Fox, Martin, and Mary Kooyman. *Historical Dictionary of Laos*. Scarecrow 1992 $35.00. ISBN 0-8108-2498-1. A comprehensive listing of historically significant people, places, and movements. Includes an extensive bibliography.

Tai, Hue-Tam Ho. *Radicalism and the Origins of the Vietnamese Revolution*. HUP 1992 $34.95. ISBN 0-674-74612-0. Concentrates on the 1920s and 1930s in search of the core of nationalist and revolutionary fervor.

Thayer, Carlyle A. *War by Other Means: National Liberation and Revolution in Vietnam, 1954–1960*. Unwin Hyman 1989 $24.95. ISBN 0-04-370187-6. Analysis of a crucial period in Vietnamese history.

Woodside, Alexander B. *Community and Revolution in Modern Vietnam*. HM 1976 o.p. Thoughtful and useful discussion that analyzes Vietnamese history from about 1900 to 1970 in terms of community, revolution, and several other themes.

Zasloff, Joseph J., and Leonard Unger. *Laos: Beyond the Revolution*. St. Martin 1991 $45.00. ISBN 0-312-04486-0. Essays on the politics, economics, social conditions, and foreign policy of Laos.

Indonesia

Abeyasekere, Susan. *Jakarta: A History*. OUP rev. ed. 1990 $16.95. ISBN 0-19-588947-9. A lively history of Indonesia's largest and, in many ways, most contradictory city.

Booth, Anne, and others, eds. *Indonesian Economic History in the Dutch Colonial Era*. Southeast Asian Studies. Yale U. Pr. 1990 $30.00. ISBN 0-938692-42-9. A somewhat loose but still useful collection of essays on a variety of themes about the period of Dutch control.

Cribb, Robert. *Historical Dictionary of Indonesia*. Scarecrow 1992. ISBN 0-8108-2542-2

Dahm, Bernard. *History of Indonesia in the Twentieth Century*. Greenwood 1971 o.p. Survey of critical turning points in the nation's modern history.

Frederick, William H. *Visions and Heat: The Making of the Indonesian Revolution*. Ohio U. Pr. 1989 $17.95. ISBN 0-8214-0906-9. Traces the revolutionary years in Surabaya of the 1930s and early 1940s. A useful addition to urban and revolutionary history.

Kahin, Audrey R., ed. *Regional Dynamics of the Indonesian Revolution: Unity from Diversity*. UH Pr. 1985 $25.00. ISBN 0-8248-0982-3. A collection of essays that looks at the revolution in Indonesia beyond the central stage of Java.

Stoler, Ann Laura. *Capitalism and Confrontation in Sumatra's Plantation Belt, 1870–1979*. Yale U. Pr. 1985 $30.00. ISBN 0-300-03189-0. An important study of the political economy of Sumatran development through a prism of gender and ethnicity.

MALAYSIA, SINGAPORE, AND BRUNEI DARUSSALAM

Andaya, Barbara Watson, and Leonard Y. Andaya. *A History of Malaysia*. St. Martin 1982 $16.95. ISBN 0-312-38121-2. Among the best one-volume studies of Malaysia and the Malay antecedents.

Dancz, Virginia H. *Women and Party Politics in Peninsular Malaysia*. OUP 1987 $32.50. ISBN 0-19-58289-2. A straightforward study of women's political action since World War II.

Gullick, J. M. *Malaysia: Economic Expansion and National Unity*. Westview 1981 o.p. A good book; especially strong in social and cultural areas of growth.

_____. *Malay Society in the Late Nineteenth Century: The Beginnings of Change*. OUP 1987 $49.95. ISBN 0-19-588850-2. A major study that identifies real ruptures in earlier social practice and ideology. Difficult in places but a substantial contribution.

Hill, R. D. *Rice in Malaya: A Study in Historical Geography*. OUP 1977 o.p. A fascinating history of rice cultivation in Malaya and how it developed and expanded.

Leake, David, Jr. *Brunei: The Modern Southeast Asian Islamic Sultanate*. McFarland & Co. 1989 $29.95. ISBN 0-89950-434-5. A crusty but approachable brief history of the tiny sultanate.

Milne, R. S., and Diane K. Mauzy. *Malaysia: Tradition, Modernity, and Islam*. Westview 1986 o.p. Essays on various themes in Malaysian history and society. Contains a well-written introduction.

_____. *Singapore: The Legacy of Lee Kuan Yew*. Westview 1990 $43.50. ISBN 0-8133-0407-5. An excellent introduction to Singapore and its political and cultural life.

Mulliner, K., and Lian The-Mulliner, eds. *Historical Dictionary of Singapore*. Scarecrow 1991 $32.50. ISBN 0-8108-2504-X. Identifies such things as people, events, and places with maps, a chronology, and political data.

Ongkili, James P. *Nation Building in Malaysia, 1946–1974*. OUP 1985 $55.00. ISBN 0-19-582574-8. A survey of Malaysian political evolution.

Pelzer, Karl. *West Malaysia and Singapore: A Selected Bibliography*. HRAFP 1971 $25.00. ISBN 0-87536-235-4. Useful starting place with more than 4,000 citations.

Quah, Stella R. *Singapore*. ABC-CLIO 1988 $52.50. ISBN 1-85109-071-1. Contains listings of English-language works, published between 1980 and 1988, dealing with Singapore.

Roff, William R. *The Origins of Malay Nationalism*. Yale U. Pr. 1967 o.p. A pioneering study.

Stubbs, Richard. *Hearts and Minds in Guerilla Warfare: The Malayan Emergency, 1948–1960*. OUP 1989 $29.95. ISBN 0-19-588942-8. A broadly based analysis of these years of crisis. Key reference on this era of state building.

Trocki, Carl. *Opium and Empire: Chinese Society in Colonial Singapore, 1800–1910*. Cornell Univ. Pr. 1990 $39.95. ISBN 0-8014-2390-2. A fascinating treatment of efforts to control the opium trade and the growth of Chinese social leadership.

Turnbull, C. Mary. *A History of Malaysia, Singapore, and Brunei*. Paul and Co. Pubs. 1989 $19.95. ISBN 0-04-364025-7. A broad, general history that is an excellent starting place.

Wang, Gungwu, ed. *Malaysia: A Survey*. Greenwood 1964 o.p. Useful essays intended to provide background for contemporary events.

Winstedt, Sir Richard Olof. *The Malays: A Cultural History*. Routledge 1966 o.p. A classic study of the cultural contours of traditional Malay cultures.

Philippines

Anderson, Gerald H., ed. *Studies in Philippine Church History*. Cornell Univ. Pr. 1969 o.p. Essays on many aspects of religious history.

Corpuz, Onofre D. *The Philippines*. P-H 1966 o.p. A well-written introductory study.

Doeppers, Daniel F. *Manila, 1900–1941: Social Change in a Late Colonial Metropolis*. Southeast Asia Studies. Yale U. Pr. 1984 $14.00. ISBN 0-938692-06-2. A challenging, worthwhile study of Manila during the American period.

Friend, Theodore. *Between Two Empires: The Ordeal of the Philippines, 1929–1946*. Yale U. Pr. 1965 o.p. Among the best early studies of the clash between the United States and Japan in the Philippines.

May, Glenn Anthony. *Battle for Batangas: A Philippine Province at War*. Yale U. Pr. 1991 $30.00. ISBN 0-300-04850-5. An important study of the Philippine-American War from the perspective of one local province.

Paredes, Ruby R., ed. *Philippine Colonial Democracy*. Southeast Asian Studies. Yale U. Pr. 1988 $15.00. ISBN 0-938692-34-8. Essays on the political character of Philippine control from the last two decades of Spanish rule through World War II.

Phelan, John Leddy. *The Hispanization of the Philippines: Spanish Aims and Filipino Responses, 1565–1700*. U. of Wis. Pr. 1959 o.p. An important study of the mixing of Philippine cultures.

Rafael, Vicente L. *Contracting Colonialism: Translation and Christian Conversion in Tagalog Society Under Spanish Rule*. Cornell Univ. Pr. 1988 $27.95. ISBN 0-8014-2065-2. An insightful treatment of Spanish activities in the early Philippines.

Steinberg, David Joel. *Philippine Collaboration in World War II*. U. of Mich. Pr. 1967 o.p. An excellent treatment of a sensitive subject.

———. *The Philippines: A Singular and a Plural Place*. Westview rev. ed. 1990 $47.50. ISBN 0-8133-0766-X. A well-written and engaging brief study of Philippine life from a historical perspective.

AUSTRALIA, NEW ZEALAND, AND PACIFIC ISLAND NATIONS

Australia, New Zealand, and the island nations of the Pacific make up a very heterogeneous grouping. What tends to distinguish and connect these nations is that they are neither Asian nor Western. They represent relatively recent political constructions that emerged out of European explorations of the Pacific and the subsequent domination by Europeans of the sparsely populated islands they found there. Much of the historical writing on these countries is about this movement of domination and settlement and about the interaction with indigenous peoples. This approach, most conspicuous in discussions about the Maori in New Zealand, is an important feature of historical writing on the Pacific Island nations. More recently, historical treatment of the place and evolution of aboriginal peoples in Australia has achieved new prominence. In general, historical writing on these countries has employed the new historical tools of social and cultural history to look at the complexities of the region and the individual countries that make it up. Thus, in the studies of this region, as in so many others, there are important recent works on gender, ethnic diversity, and cultural negotiation.

General Works

Bassett, Jan. *The Concise Oxford Dictionary of Australian History*. OUP 1987 o.p. Contains about 550 short articles about Australia, covering a wide range of topics.

Beaglehole, J. C. *The Exploration of the Pacific*. Stanford U. Pr. 1966 $42.50. ISBN 0-8047-0310-8. An older, interesting, and useful study.

———. *The Life of Captain James Cook*. Stanford U. Pr. 1974 $55.00. ISBN 0-8047-0848-7. A classic biography of the principal European explorer of the region.

Bellwood, Peter. *Man's Conquest of the Pacific: The Prehistory of Southeast Asia and Oceania*. HarpC 1978 o.p. The most comprehensive and authoritative work on this general theme.

Jackson, H. R. *Churches and People in Australia and New Zealand, 1860–1930*. Unwin Hyman 1987 A$19.94. ISBN 0-86861-698-2. A useful introduction to the church history of the region.

Sinclair, Keith. *Tasman Relations: New Zealand and Australia, 1788–1988*. Auckland U. Pr. 1987 NZ$49.95. ISBN 1-86940-018-6. Essays on the historical character and relations between the two states, based for the most part on the assumption that the two are more similar than different.

Australia

Bolton, Geoffrey, ed. *The Oxford History of Australia*. 5 vols. OUP Vol. 1 o.p. Vol. 2 *Colonial Australia 1770–1860*. 1992 $45.00. ISBN 0-19-554610-5. Vol. 3 *Glad Confident Morning, 1860–1900*. 1989 $45.00. ISBN 0-19-554611-3. Vol. 4 *1901–1942*. 1987 $38.00. ISBN 0-19-554612-1. Vol. 5 *1942–88, The Middle Way*. 1990 $39.95. ISBN 0-19-554613-X. The most recent general treatment, with writing by five separate authors.

Broome, Richard. *Aboriginal Australians: Black Responses to White Dominance, 1788–1980*. Unwin Hyman 1982 A$13.95. ISBN 0-86861-051-8. An important survey of Australian race relations.

Buckley, Ken, and Ted Wheelwright. *No Paradise for Workers: Capitalism and the Common People in Australia, 1788–1914*. OUP 1988 A$19.95. ISBN 0-19-554622-9. A critical treatment of the nature and character of Australian economic development.

Clark, C.M.H. *History of Australia*. 6 vols. Melbourne Univ. Pr. 1971–1987. Vol. 1 1971 $37.50. ISBN 0-522-84008-6. Vols. 2–4 o.p. Vol. 5 $37.50. ISBN 0-522-84223-2. Vol. 6 o.p. A magisterial study of the whole of Australian history.

Crowley, Frank, ed. *A New History of Australia*. Holmes & Meier 1975 $49.50. ISBN 0-8419-6100-X. Useful essays, somewhat dated, on the nation's general history.

Deacon, Desley. *Managing Gender: The State, The New Middle Class and Women Workers, 1830–1930*. OUP 1989 $24.95. ISBN 0-19-554817-5. The first general study of the relationship between state, gender, and class in the formative period of Australian history.

Docherty, James C. *Historical Dictionary of Australia*. Scarecrow 1992 $35.00. ISBN 0-8108-2613-5

Dyster, Barrie, and David Meredith. *Australia in the International Economy in the Twentieth Century*. Cambridge U. Pr. 1990 $69.95. ISBN 0-521-33496-9. The most recent and comprehensive modern economic history of Australia and its place in the global economy.

Grey, Jeffrey. *A Military History of Australia*. Cambridge U. Pr. 1990 $54.95. ISBN 0-521-36659-3. An excellent new study of military life and culture that blends traditional military concerns with new social interests of military historians.

Kingston, Beverley. *My Wife, My Daughter, and Poor Mary-Ann: Women and Work in Australia*. Nelson-Hall 1975 $9.95. ISBN 0-17005-212-5. Among the first important studies of women's history from a feminist perspective.

Matthews, Jill Julius. *Good and Mad Women: The Historical Construction of Femininity in Twentieth Century Australia*. Unwin Hyman 1984 A$14.95. ISBN 0-86861-665-6. An important study of modern gender relations.

Millar, T. B. *Australia in Peace and War: External Relations, 1788–1977*. ANU Pr. 1978 o.p. The best general study of Australian foreign affairs.

Sinclair, W. A. *The Process of Economic Development in Australia*. Cheshire Pub. 1976 o.p. A useful general treatment of Australian economic growth.

New Zealand

Belich, James. *The Victorian Interpretation of Racial Conflict: The Maori, the British, and the New Zealand Wars*. U. of Toronto Pr. 1990 $37.50. ISBN 0-7735-0750-7. Important study of the major struggles between the white settlers and the Maori. A useful evaluation of the early conflict over the founding of modern New Zealand.

Easton, Brian. *Social Policy and the Welfare State in New Zealand*. Unwin Hyman 1980 $19.95. ISBN 0-86861-393-2. Focuses on the state management of social issues in the modern state.

Fairburn, Miles. *The Ideal Society and Its Enemies: The Foundations of Modern New Zealand, 1850–1900.* Auckland Univ. Pr. 1989 $32.95. ISBN 0-86940-028-3. An important social history of the establishment of modern New Zealand, focusing on the centrality of individuality and separateness of life.

McLauchlan, Gordon, ed. *The Illustrated Encyclopedia of New Zealand.* D. Bateman 1989 o.p. ISBN 1-86953-007-1. Contains articles current through the mid-1980s, and a chronology through 1988. Presents a popular and comprehensive view of all areas of interest.

Oliver, W. H., ed. *The Oxford History of New Zealand.* Oxford U. Pr. 1981 $34.95. ISBN 0-19-558063-X. Essays on the whole of New Zealand history.

Sinclair, Keith. *A Destiny Apart: New Zealand's Search for National Identity.* Unwin Hyman 1986 o.p. A history of New Zealand nationalism up to 1940.

———. *The Oxford Illustrated History of New Zealand.* Oxford U. Pr. 1990 $35.00. ISBN 0-19-558209-8. A beautifully illustrated general history of New Zealand.

Oceania

Bellwood, Peter. *The Polynesians.* Thames Hudson 1987 $10.95. ISBN 0-500-27450-9. A solid introductory history of the region.

Bennett, Judith A. *The Wealth of the Solomons: A History of a Pacific Archipelago, 1800–1978.* UH Pr. 1987 $35.00. ISBN 0-8248-1078-3. A solid general history of the archipelago.

Corris, Peter. *Passage, Port and Plantation: A History of the Solomon Islands Labour Migration, 1870–1914.* Melbourne Univ. Pr. 1973 $22.95. ISBN 0-522-84056-7. A historical ethnography of Solomon Islanders' labor migration to Australia.

Craig, Robert D., and Frank P. King, eds. *Historical Dictionary of Oceania.* Greenwood 1981 $85.00. ISBN 0-313-21060-8. A good general dictionary of people, organizations, and events in Oceania and its history.

Crocombe, Ron. *The South Pacific: An Introduction.* Univ. of South Pacific Pr. 1987 $10.00. Especially useful for the period of decolonization and after.

Daws, Gavan. *Shoal of Time. A History of the Hawaiian Islands.* UH Pr. 1974 o.p. General history of Hawaii from Captain Cook to statehood. Seeks to balance discussion of European and Hawaiian influences.

Fry, Gerald. *Pacific Basin and Oceania.* ABC-CLIO 1987 $55.00. ISBN 1-85109-015-0. Lists 1,178 English-language books and articles covering the period from 1975 to 1985, arranged by topic and annotated. Includes an index.

Hempenstall, Peter J. *Pacific Islanders Under German Rule.* ANU Pr. 1978 $29.00. ISBN 0-080-32901-2. A thoughtful, detailed study of twentieth-century colonial administration in the Pacific.

Hezel, Francis X. *The First Taint of Civilization: A History of the Carolina and Marshall Islands in Pre-Colonial Days, 1521–1885.* UH Pr. 1983 $30.00. ISBN 0-8248-0840-1. Attractively written and interesting history of the early contact and impact that tends to center on the Europeans.

Lyons, Martin. *The Totem and the Tricolor: A Short History of New Caledonia since 1774.* Univ. of New South Wales Pr. 1986 $9.95. ISBN 0-86840-122-6. A brief but useful history of this South Pacific archipelago.

MacDonald, Barry. *Cinderellas of the Empire: Towards a History of Kiribati and Tuvalu.* ANU Pr. 1982 A$29.00. ISBN 0-08-329591-4. A brief study of these small islands and their intersection with European powers.

Morrell, W. P. *Britain in the Pacific Islands.* OUP 1960 o.p. Still the most wide-ranging and authoritative work on nineteenth-century Pacific Islands history.

Newbury, Colin. *Tahiti Nui: Change and Survival in French Polynesia 1767–1945.* UH Pr. 1980 $25.00. ISBN 0-8248-0630-1. A study of Tahiti and surrounding islands, which, the author argues, have long been connected through a complex market network.

Sahlins, M. *Historical Metaphors and Mythical Realities: Structure in the Early History of the Sandwich Islands Kingdom.* U. of Mich. Pr. 1981 $11.95. ISBN 0-472-02721. A major study of Cook's fatal voyage to the Hawaiian islands.

———. *Islands of History.* U. Ch. Pr. 1985 $22.50. ISBN 0-226-73358-0. Essays on Pacific Islands culture and history focusing primarily on the Hawaiian Islands.

Scarr, Deryck. *Fiji: A Short History.* Unwin Hyman 1984 o.p. Treats the history, politics, and government of the island over time.

Segal, Gerald, ed. *Political and Economic Encyclopedia of the Pacific.* St. James Pr. 1990 $85.00. ISBN 1-55862-033-8. Includes signed articles on countries, people, and a variety of topics, emphasizing post-1945 developments.

CHRONOLOGY OF AUTHORS

Sansom, Sir George B(ailey).
  1883–1965
Nehru, Jawaharlal. 1889–1964
Fairbank, John King. 1907–1991
Reischauer, Edwin O(ldfather).
  1910–1990

Smith, Thomas C. 1916–
Barnett, A(rthur) Doak. 1921–
Embree, Ainslie T(homas). 1921–
Spence, Jonathan D(ermott). 1936–

BARNETT, A(RTHUR) DOAK. 1921–

Born in Shanghai, political scientist and educator Arthur Doak Barnett spent much of his early life in China. After receiving an M.A. from Yale University in 1942 and a Ph.D. in 1947, he began a career as a journalist, working as the China and Southeast Asia correspondent for the *Chicago Daily News* from 1947 to 1950 and again from 1952 to 1955. He also worked in the region in various positions for the U.S. State Department and served on the American Universities Field Staff. Since 1961 Barnett has held various posts at Columbia University, Johns Hopkins University, and the Brookings Institution, as well as numerous positions on Chinese and international studies organizations. In 1989 he became professor emeritus, John Hopkins School of Advanced International Studies.

Barnett has been one of the best-known experts in the United States on China. Widely consulted on issues relating to foreign policy and U.S. relations with China, his work is a major source for understanding the evolving complexity of the People's Republic of China.

BOOKS BY BARNETT

Cadres, Bureaucracy, and Political Power in Communist China. 1967. Col. U. Pr. 1967 $54.00. ISBN 0-231-03035-5. A clear and forceful analysis of the Chinese Communist party and the state system it ran.

China after Mao: With Selected Documents. 1967. Princeton U. Pr. 1967 $9.95. ISBN 0-691-00000-X. Based on a lecture series at Princeton.

China and the Major Powers in East Asia. 1977. Brookings 1978 $15.95. ISBN 0-8157-0823-8. The new geo-political role of China.

China's Economy in Global Perspective. Brookings 1981 $39.95. ISBN 0-8157-0827-0. Examines the post-Mao internationalizing economic initiatives.

Communist China: The Early Years, 1949–1955. 1964. Greenwood 1964 o.p. Remains a useful collection of articles on the early People's Republic of China.

The FX Decision: Another Crucial Moment in U.S.-China-Taiwan Relations. Studies in Defense Policy. 1981. Brookings 1981 $7.95. ISBN 0-8157-0827-0. On the delicate negotiations between the three countries on defense issues. An important case study.

The Making of Foreign Policy in China: Structures and Process. 1985. Westview 1985 o.p. An important analysis of the agents of Chinese policy making.

EMBREE, AINSLIE T(HOMAS). 1921–

Born and educated through a B.A. degree in Nova Scotia, Canada, Ainslie T. Embree received an M.A. from Union Theological Seminary in 1947. He then went to India, where he taught history at Indore Christian College for a decade. In 1958 he emigrated to the United States, where two years later he received his Ph.D. from Columbia University. The remainder of his professional career has been spent at Columbia and at Duke universities. A naturalized citizen of the United States since 1965, he has served as a member of the Council on Foreign Relations and as a counselor for cultural affairs in the American Embassy in New Delhi.

A past president of both the Association of the American Institute of Indian Studies and the Association of Asian Studies, Embree has produced a number of major works. Recently he served as editor in chief of the four-volume *Encyclopedia of Asian History* (1988), a major new reference tool for Asia. Embree's work has been important in illuminating India's tortuous path from colonial domination to cultural and political independence. His work on the individual, religious, and cultural meaning of modernity in India has been very influential.

BOOKS BY EMBREE

Charles Grant and British Rule in India. AMS Pr. 1962 $10.00. ISBN 0-404-51606-8. A study of the East India Company official who, in the latter years of the eighteenth century and the first years of the nineteenth century was involved in more arenas of British control of India than anyone else.

The Hindu Tradition. Ed. 1966. Random 1976 $7.16. ISBN 0-394-71702-3. Reproduction and evaluation of crucial literary and religious Hindu texts.

Imagining India: Essays on Indian History. OUP 1989 o.p. An important collection of earlier essays on various topics, the most important of which center on the Raj.

India in Eighteen Fifty-Seven: The Revolt Against Foreign Rule. S. Asia 1987 $21.00. ISBN 81-7001-027-6. Contemporary discussions and analysis of the first Indian assault on British control.

India's Search for National Identity. 1971. S. Asia 1988 $14.00. ISBN 81-7001-032-2. Important discussion of India's struggle with modernity.

Utopias in Conflict: Religion and Nationalism in Modern India. U. CA Pr. 1990 $22.50. ISBN 0-520-06866-1. Treats the clashing religious conflicts in South Asia.

FAIRBANK, JOHN KING. 1907–1991

Born in South Dakota, John King Fairbank attended local public schools for his early education. From there he went on first to Exeter, then the University of Wisconsin, and ultimately to Harvard, from which he received his B.A. degree summa cum laude in 1929. That year he traveled to Britain as a Rhodes Scholar. In 1932 he went to China as a teacher and after extensive travel there received his Ph.D. from Oxford University in 1936. Between 1941 and 1946, he was in government service—as a member of the Office of Strategic Services, as special assistant to the U.S. ambassador to China, and finally as director of the U.S. Information Service in China. Excepting those years, beginning in 1936, Fairbank spent his entire career at Harvard University, where he served in many positions, including Francis Lee Higginson Professor of History and director of Harvard's East Asian Research Center.

Fairbank, who came to be considered one of the world's foremost authorities on modern Chinese history and Asian-West relations, was committed to reestablishing diplomatic and cultural relations with China. He was also committed to the idea that Americans had to become more conversant with

Asian cultures and languages. In his leadership positions at Harvard and as president of the Association for Asian Studies and the American Historical Association, he sought to broaden the bases of expertise about Asia. At the same time, he wrote fluidly and accessibly, concentrating his work on the nineteenth century and emphasizing the relationship between China and the West. At the same time, his writings placed twentieth-century China within the context of a changed and changing global order. It was precisely this understanding that led him to emphasize the reestablishment of American links with China. More than anyone else, Fairbank helped create the modern fields of Chinese and Asian studies in America. His influence on American understanding of China and Asia has been profound.

BOOKS BY FAIRBANK

China: A New History. HUP 1992 $27.95. ISBN 0-074-11670-4. Fairbank's final, magisterial overview of the totality of China's past.

China Perceived: Images and Policies in Chinese American Relations. 1974. Random 1976 $11.95. ISBN 0-674-11651-8

China: Tradition and Transformation. (coauthored with Edwin O. Reischauer). HM rev. ed. 1989 $32.76. ISBN 0-395-49692-6. The newest edition of a widely used college textbook.

Chinabound: A Fifty Year Memoir. 1982. HarpC 1982 $29.95. ISBN 0-06-039005-0. A breezy self-portrait of Fairbank's life and the development of Chinese studies in America.

China's Response to the West: A Documentary Survey, 1839–1923. 1954. (coauthored with T'eng Ssu-y'u). Atheneum 1975 $8.95. ISBN 0-689-70194-2. A collection of Chinese documents selected to show China's responses to Westerners.

Ch'ing Administration: Three Studies. 1960. (coauthored with T'eng Ssu-y'u). HUP 1960 $5.00. ISBN 0-674-12700-1. A study of the bureaucratic system of the last Chinese dynasty.

East Asia: Tradition and Transformation. 1972. (coauthored with Albert M. Craig and Edwin O. Reischauer). HM rev. ed. 1989 $50.36. ISBN 0-395-45023-3. A classic American text on Asia.

The Great Chinese Revolution, 1800–1985. 1986. HarpC 1986 $10.00. ISBN 0-06-039076-X. Seeks to place contemporary China in the movement for change that has evolved since the nineteenth century.

Modern China: A Bibliographical Guide to Chinese Works 1898–1937. 1950. (coauthored with Kwang-Ching Liu). HUP 1950 o.p. Significant and important catalog of the extensive Chinese language holdings at Harvard University.

The Missionary Enterprise in China and America. Studies in American East Asian Relations. HUP 1974 $28.00. ISBN 0-674-57655-1. A collection of essays that considers varied characteristics of American missionary activity in China.

Trade and Diplomacy on the China Coast: The Opening of the Treaty Ports, 1842–1854. 1954. Stanford U. Pr. 1953 $18.95. ISBN 0-8047-0648-4. A detailed treatment of early foreign intervention in China.

BOOKS ABOUT FAIRBANK

Cohen, Paul A., and Merle Goldman, comps. *Fairbank Remembered.* HUP 1992 $12.95. ISBN 0-674-29153-0. Recollections by former students and colleagues.

Evans, Paul M. *John Fairbank and the American Understanding of Modern China.* Blackwell Pubs. 1988 $24.95. ISBN 0-631-15853-7. A fair and full biography of Fairbank as academic empire builder and as a major influence on America's engagement with Asia.

NEHRU, JAWAHARLAL. 1889–1964

The son of an attorney and journalist, Jawaharlal Nehru, architect of India's freedom and prime minister from independence in 1947 until his death in 1964, wrote widely on Indian nationalist activities. Educated at Harrow and Cambridge, after reading for the bar in 1912 he returned to India and served on the High Court of Allabahad. In 1919 he joined Mohandas K. Gandhi's movement. In 1942 he succeeded Gandhi as leader of the National Congress party. Imprisoned in 1921 for actions in protest of British rule, he spent most of the next 25 years in jail serving one term after another. During one stretch of imprisonment in the early 1930s, he passed the time by writing letters to his young daughter—who years later would become prime minister in her own right—about humankind's whole history—enough letters to fill a 1,000-page volume, published as *Glimpses of World History* (1936). It "retains all of Nehru's philosophical reflections about history, with enough glimpses to illustrate the main course of development in both East and West and their relations today" (*N.Y. Times*).

Much loved and often criticized, Nehru, nurtured by his long periods of contemplation and inaction in prison, was at once revolutionary, philosopher, and practical politician. He was perhaps the last great example of the leader who through experience and training—and great literary ability—understood equally and interpreted the ancient East and modern West.

BOOKS BY NEHRU

An Autobiography: Centenary Edition. OUP 1989 $19.95. ISBN 0-19-562361-4. A self-portrait revealing in personal terms much about the last years of the British Raj and the struggle for Indian independence.

A Bunch of Old Letters: Written Mostly to Jawaharlal Nehru, and Some Written by Him. Asia Pub. Hse. 1960 o.p. Mostly letters on matters of domestic political concern from the years leading up to independence.

Discovery of India. OUP 1990 $19.95. ISBN 0-19-562394-0. Essentially a plea for Indian independence.

Glimpses of World History: Centenary Edition. OUP 1989 $22.50. ISBN 0-19-562396-7

Independence and After. 1950. *Essay Index Repr. Ser*. Ayer repr. of 1950 ed. $26.50. A panoramic history of the subcontinent about which Nehru wrote while imprisoned in 1944.

India's Foreign Policy. Asia Bk. Corp. 1985 repr. of 1961 ed. $34.95. ISBN 0-940500-94-9. Demonstrates clearly the wise moderation of Nehru's view of the world.

India's Quest: Being Letters on Indian History. Asia Pub. Hse. 1967 o.p. Letters to his daughter on Indian history, written mostly during the 1930s.

Jawaharlal Nehru: An Anthology. Ed. by S. Gopal. OUP 1980 $36.00. ISBN 0-19-561342-2. Excellent introduction to all aspects of Nehru's thought.

Mahatma Gandhi. Asia Pub. Hse. 1966 o.p. An appealing and intimate biography.

Nehru on World History. Ed. by Saul K. Padover. 1942. Ind. U. Pr. 1962 o.p. Selection of writings on history.

Selected Works of Jawaharlal Nehru. Ed. by S. Gopal. 10 vols. S. Asia 1972–78 $12.75–$16.00 ea. A collection of some of the extensive writings of Nehru on Indian history and society.

Speeches, 1946–1964. 5 vols. Verry o.p. The most extensive but still incomplete collection of Nehru's speeches.

BOOKS ABOUT NEHRU

Akbar, M. J. *Nehru: The Making of India*. Viking Penguin 1990 $9.95. ISBN 0-14-010083-0. Puts Nehru at the cultural center of change following independence.

Benudhar, Pradham. *The Socialist Thought of Jawaharlal Nehru*. S. Asia 1974 o.p. A study of Nehru's ideas on political economy.

Butler, Lord C. H. *Jawaharlal Nehru*. Cambridge U. Pr. 1967 $1.95. Looks at Nehru's life and accomplishments.

Chakraborty, A. K. *Jawaharlal Nehru's Writings*. South Asia 1981 $15.00. Critical review of Nehru's major writings and important themes and issues.

Chhibber, V. N. *Jawaharlal Nehru: Man of Letters*. Verry 1970 o.p. On Nehru as intellectual leader and historian.

Copeland, Ian. *Jawaharlal Nehru of India, 1889–1964. Leaders of Asia Ser*. Univ. of Queensland Pr. 1980 $3.00. Comprehensive account of Nehru's life and times.

Darbari, J., and R. Darbari. *Commonwealth and Nehru*. Humanities 1984 o.p. On Nehru's political role in independence and his links with British leaders.

Edwardes, Michael. *Nehru: A Pictorial Biography*. Viking Penguin 1963 o.p. This portrait based in part on material supplied by Nehru's family includes many pictures never before printed.

Gopal, Ram. *The Mind of Jawaharlal Nehru*. Apt Bks. 1980 $3.95.

―――. *Trials of Jawaharlal Nehru*. Biblio 1964 $24.00. Examines the personal and political challenges faced by Nehru.

Haksar, P. N., ed. *Nehru's Vision of Peace and Security in a Nuclear Age*. S. Asia 1988 $34.00. ISBN 0-317-93110-5. Well-argued and fair analysis.

Patil, V. T., ed. Studies on Nehru. Apt Bks. 1987 $45.00. ISBN 81-207-0624-2. Contains all that is essential for the student to know about Nehru.

Range, Willard. *Jawaharlal Nehru's World View: A Theory of International Relations*. U. of Ga. Pr. 1961 o.p. Analyzes Nehru's published writings, speeches, and interviews.

Seton, Marie. *Panditji: A Portrait of Jawaharlal Nehru*. Taplinger 1967 o.p. The author, observing Nehru from the standpoint of an admiring family friend, "is very self-consciously a Boswell" (*N.Y. Times*).

Sharma, J. S. *Jawaharlal Nehru: A Descriptive Biography*. Coronet 1969 $30.00. ISBN 0-685-13783-X. Good, reliable, but somewhat worshipful biography.

REISCHAUER, EDWIN O(LDFATHER). 1910–1990

Edwin O. Reischauer was born in Japan in 1910, the son of Protestant educational-missionary parents, founders of Japan's first school for the deaf. After being educated in Japanese and American schools, he received his B.A. from Oberlin College in 1931 and his M.A. from Harvard in 1932. Four years later he received a Ph.D. in Far Eastern Languages from Harvard. In 1938 he joined the faculty at Harvard, where he rose to the position of professor and acted for an extensive period as director of the Harvard-Yenching Institute. His academic career was interrupted by World War II, during which he served as an intelligence officer in the U.S. Army, and he held civilian posts first in the War Department and later in the Department of State. In 1961 he again took leave from Harvard to accept a position for which he had been hand-picked by President John F. Kennedy—ambassador to Japan. The Japanese accepted him as one of their own; one editorial writer welcomed him by writing that he was well informed about Japan, "having no equal among foreigners on that point." Another remarked how satisfying it would be to "write an editorial and know that the American Ambassador will actually be able to read it."

Reischauer was a prolific writer and an energetic speaker who saw his role as introducing Japan to America. In his writings and in his activities in other media such as film, he was committed to reaching as broad an audience as possible. At Harvard he led in training the first generation of true American scholars of Japan. As U.S. ambassador to Japan, however, his role became reversed as he sought to educate Japanese about America and Americans. In the wake of the war in the Pacific, Reischauer hoped to show Americans and Japanese that the two countries could and should be close allies and friends. His assessment of Japan's history emphasized the nonrevolutionary character of its modern history and its outward-looking development. In his view Japanese war and aggression were aberrations in a long emerging liberal tradition. His positivist interpretation has been a leading influence in defining America's postwar vision of Japan.

BOOKS BY REISCHAUER

Beyond Vietnam: The United States and Asia. 1967. Knopf 1967 o.p. Important statement seeking to reestablish the central role of Japan in Asian policy and positively reorient America's Asia policy.

East Asia: Tradition and Transformation. (coauthored with Albert M. Craig and John King Fairbank). 1973. HM rev. ed. 1989 $50.36. ISBN 0-395-45023-3. Revised edition of the classic Asian history textbook.

Ennin's Travels in T'ang China. 1955. Bks. Demand $89.30. ISBN 0-317-11321-6. Author's dissertation published as a book. Focuses on Japan's early embrace and interpretation of Buddhism and relationship with China.

Japan: The Story of a Nation. 1970, 1981. Knopf 1991 $29.45. ISBN 0-394-58527-5. Very general popular history that is accessible and attractively written.

Japan: Tradition and Transformation. (coauthored with Albert M. Craig). HM rev. ed. 1989 $35.96. ISBN 0-395-25814-6. A well-established college textbook on Japan.

The Japanese Today: Change and Continuity. 1988. HUP 1988 $25.00. ISBN 0-674-47181-4. Seeks to explain Japan's modern success story.

My Life Between Japan and America. 1986. HarpC 1986 $22.50. ISBN 0-060-39054-9. A self-portrait of the author's life as soldier, scholar, and diplomat.

SANSOM, SIR GEORGE B(AILEY). 1883–1965

Born in London in 1883, George B. Sansom went on to serve in the great British diplomatist scholar tradition. As a youngster, he was educated at a lycée in France. Later he attended Giessen and Marburg universities. In the years following 1903, he held various posts in the consular and diplomatic service of Great Britain, from the early 1920s to 1940 serving as a key adviser in the British embassy in Tokyo. During this time, he amassed a great amount of knowledge about Japanese history and culture, and during and after World War II he acted in numerous advisory positions on Pacific affairs. Following the war he became Professor of Japanese studies at Columbia University and from 1949 to 1955 was director of the East Asian Institute.

Sansom's dense but attractively written work on the great sweep of Japanese history influenced two generations of readers and students. In particular, his *Japan: A Short Cultural History* (1931) was the first text of choice for both the generation before and the generation after the war. His grand histories were the first in Western languages to draw heavily on the extensive historical literature in Japanese, and many of the questions he first raised more than a half century ago remain of critical interest today. Sansom's work continues to be of interest for the richness of writing and the quality of insight.

BOOKS BY SANSOM

A History of Japan to 1334. Stanford U. Pr. 1958 $49.50. ISBN 0-8047-0522-4. Emphasizes the rich and complex texture of early Japan.

A History of Japan, 1334–1615. Stanford U. Pr. 1961 $49.50. ISBN 0-8047-0524-0. Remains the broadest study of the consolidation of warrior power.

A History of Japan, 1615–1867. Stanford U. Pr. 1963 $35.00. ISBN 0-8047-0527-5. A sympathetic treatment of the emergence of early modern Japan.

Japan: A Short Cultural History. Stanford U. Pr. rev. ed. 1952 $55.00. ISBN 0-8047-0952-1. A general treatment of the religious, artistic, and general cultural character of Japan's long history.

The Western World and Japan. 1950. Knopf 1965 o.p. One of the best studies of the interaction between the Western world and Japan from the fifteenth to the nineteenth centuries.

SMITH, THOMAS C. 1916–

Born in Colorado, Thomas C. Smith received his B.A. from Santa Barbara College in 1938 and his Ph.D. from Harvard University in 1948. He has served as professor of Japanese and East Asian history first at Stanford University and then at the University of California, Berkeley.

Smith's work on the emergence of modern Japan has been among the most influential and has done much to shape Western understanding of the cultural and social meaning of modernity in Japan. Additionally, Smith has profoundly affected the ways in which the connection between rural communities and industrial growth is perceived.

Books by Smith

The Agrarian Origins of Modern Japan. Stanford U. Pr. 1959 $32.50. ISBN 0-8047-0530-5. Concerns emerging market economies in early modern Japan and how they shaped Japan's modern growth.

Nakahara: Family Farming and Population in a Japanese Village. Stanford U. Pr. 1977 $25.00. ISBN 0-8047-0928-9. One of the first studies to employ demography to understand Japan's movement toward modernity.

Native Sources of Japanese Industrialization, 1750–1920. U. CA Pr. 1988 $40.00. ISBN 0-520-05837-2. A collection of essays on a variety of topics concerning Japanese industrialization.

Political Change and Industrial Development in Japan: Government Enterprise, 1868–1880. Stanford U. Pr. 1955 $19.50. ISBN 0-8047-0469-4. Examines the role of the state in modern economic development.

SPENCE, JONATHAN D(ERMOTT). 1936–

Jonathan D. Spence was born in England and received his B.A. from Cambridge University. In 1966 he received his Ph.D. from Yale University and has been a professor of Chinese history there since that time. Spence has won a variety of major fellowships and has served as visiting professor at Belfast's Queens University, Princeton University, and Beijing University. He employs a distinctive writing and historical style, weaving together various kinds of materials to fashion new forms of historical narrative. The best examples of his unique style are *The Death of Woman Wang* (1979) and *The Memory Palace of Matteo Ricci.* In his works, Spence provides a uniquely accessible vision of late imperial China. His writings have won numerous awards and prizes. *The Gate of Heavenly Peace* (1982) won two awards—the Los Angeles Times Book Award and the Henry D. Vursell Memorial Award of the American Academy-Institute of Arts and Letters.

Books by Spence

Chinese Roundabout: Essays in History and Culture. Norton 1992 $24.95. ISBN 0-393-03355-4. A collection of short pieces on various topics from Chinese food to opium addiction.

The Death of Woman Wang. Viking Penguin 1979 $8.95. ISBN 0-14-005121-X. A powerful fusion of official histories of a Chinese province, the memoirs of a local magistrate, and several contemporary short stories create a compelling example of reality-based fiction.

Emperor of China: Self-Portrait of K'ang-Hsi. Random 1988 $8.95. ISBN 0-679-72074-X. Splices together contemporary accounts of the K'ang-Hsi emperor to create a kind of autobiography.

The Gate of Heavenly Peace: The Chinese and Their Revolution, 1895–1980. Viking Penguin 1982 $10.95. ISBN 0-14-006279-3. Recent Chinese history through the eyes of Chinese writers and artists.

The Question of Hu. Knopf 1988 $19.95. ISBN 0-394-57190-8. Focuses on the travel of one Chinese to Europe in the eighteenth century.

The Search for Modern China. Norton 1990 $29.95. ISBN 0-393-027098-2. Covers the period from the early seventeenth century to the late twentieth century. One of the best new general histories of modern China.

To Change China: Western Advisers to China, 1620–1960. Viking Penguin 1980 $9.95. ISBN 0-14-005528-2. Studies the evolving place of Westerners in China.

Ts'ao Yin and the K'ang-Hsi Emperor, Bondservant and Master. Yale U. Pr. 1988 $40.00. Uses the life of an imperial servant to illuminate the institutions he served.

CHAPTER 15

United States History

John G. Sproat

> History is a tangled skein that one may take up at any point, and break when
> one has unravelled enough; but complexity precedes evolution.
> —HENRY ADAMS, *The Education of Henry Adams*

The most significant development in the writing of U.S. history in recent years is
the rediscovery of complexity. Subjects that only a few decades ago seemed
beyond the bounds of inquiry are now commonplace, and the literature of
American history today teems with works on a wondrous variety of subjects that
go beyond "conventional" inquiries into political, economic, and cultural
behavior and institutions—small towns and large cities, the environment and
natural resources, the poor and the disabled, prisons, churches, sexual
behavior, women and children and families, medical practices. No aspect of the
human experience is beyond the scrutiny of the historian. As a result,
knowledge of the American past is becoming deeper and more diversified.

As Michael Kammen notes, this explosion of knowledge means that history is
becoming "more responsive to the pluralistic and increasingly egalitarian
society in which it functions." History is growing more cosmopolitan, recognizing not only the interdependence of societies and nations but also of "past,
present, and future prospects." American historians have made great strides in
utilizing methodologies ordinarily associated with the social sciences and
mathematics and in integrating those techniques with more traditional descriptive and narrative history. The "line" between quantitative and narrative
historians is increasingly blurred, and such writers as Alice Kessler-Harris,
JAMES M. McPHERSON, WILLIAM E. LEUCHTENBURG, Leon F. Litwack, Elizabeth
Fox-Genovese, and Eric Foner demonstrate in their works the integration of
innovation with tradition.

Among the arenas in which innovation is most apparent are local and public,
or applied, history. Particularist studies of towns and ecologies, for example,
steadily feed into larger perspectives, while public history, with its oral
interviews and emphasis on preservation and reconstruction of documents and
artifacts, sharpens awareness that the past belongs to everyone.

Organizationally, this chapter provides an introduction to U.S. historical
research and coverage arranged by historical period, beginning with the
colonial period (1606–1763) and ending with the modern period (1945 to the
present). This arrangement allows the reader or researcher to get a sense of the
ebb and flow of history as well as to approach the study of history from a more
structured perspective. Writings on selected specific topics, such as foreign
policy, ethnicity, and politics, are included in supplementary reading lists.
Selected major historians are briefly profiled, and writings by and about them
are listed immediately afterward.

In addition to the works cited in this chapter, special mention should be made of two important indexes that can be used to become further acquainted with the work of U.S. historians—*Writings on American History* and *America: History and Life*. Both are indispensable reference tools. For additional information regarding the writings and careers of U.S. historians, consult *American Historians, 1607–1865* (1984) and *Twentieth-Century American Historians* (1983), both edited by Clyde N. Wilson. Two major research journals, the *Journal of American History* and the *American Historical Review*, should also be consulted, not only for their scholarly articles, but also for their extensive book reviews, historical film and video critiques, and notes sections. These journals provide a convenient way to keep up with developments and publications in the field of American history.

REFERENCE WORKS

Given the wealth of reference material on U.S. history, this section does not presume to be all-inclusive. It includes only a representative overview of the kinds of materials available to scholars and general readers alike. The section is subdivided into four categories: "General Reference Works," "Encyclopedias and Dictionaries," "Bibliographies," and "Documentary Histories." The U.S. Government Printing Office publishes the *Public Papers of the Presidents of the United States* and can provide a small catalog of this series.

GENERAL REFERENCE WORKS

Adams, James T., ed. *Atlas of American History*. Scribner 2nd rev. ed 1985 $65.00. ISBN 0-684-18411-7. Updated version of the celebrated atlas first published in 1943. Detailed black-and-white maps of all regions and periods of American history.

Biographical Directory of the United States Congress, 1774–1989. USGPO 1989 $82.00. ISBN 0-16-006384-1. Short, concise, objective sketches of all members of Congress; a section on officers of the executive branch and cabinet members from Washington to Bush; and a chronological listing by state of legislators from the First to the Ninety-fourth Congress.

Biographical Directory of the United States Executive Branch, 1774–1989. Ed. by Robert Sobel. Greenwood 3rd rev. ed. 1990 $75.00. ISBN 0-313-26593-3. Patterned on preceding publication. Includes brief sketches of presidents, heads of state, and cabinet officers.

Bureau of the Census Staff, U.S. Dept. of Commerce, ed. *Statistical Abstract of the United States*. USGPO 1992 $19.95. ISBN 1-878753-08-8. Statistics on the social, political, and economic condition of the United States. Published annually from 1879 to the present.

Cappon, Lester J. *Atlas of Early American History: The Revolutionary Era, 1760–1790*. Princeton U. Pr. 1975 $250.00. ISBN 0-691-0463404. Well-designed atlas. Most complete work of its kind.

Carrington, Henry B. *Maps and Charts of the American Revolution*. Ayer 1974 repr. of 1877 ed. $35.00. ISBN 0-405-05540-4. Excellent complement to narrative histories of the revolution.

Chatfield, Charles. *The American Peace Movement: Ideals and Activism*. Macmillan 1992 $24.95. ISBN 0-8057-3851-7. Well-written and analytical historical narrative, devoid of jargon. Will be the definitive work in this area for years to come.

Congressional Quarterly, Inc. Staff. *Guide to Congress*. Congr. Quarterly 1982 $110.00. ISBN 0-87187-239-0. Most authoritative source for finding out how Congress works.

———. *Guide to U.S. Elections*. Congr. Quarterly 1985 $114.00. ISBN 0-87187-339-7. Most detailed and reliable volume on election statistics.

———. *Guide to the U.S. Supreme Court*. Congr. Quarterly 1989 $169.00. ISBN 0-685-33558-5. Informative narratives on the origins, history, and development of the court, with appropriate statistics and dates.

DeGregorio, William A. *The Complete Book of U.S. Presidents*. Barricade Bks. 1989 $29.95. ISBN 0-942637-17-8. A wealth of information about the lives and careers of the presidents.

Ebony Pictorial History of Black America. 4 vols. Ed. by Lerone Bennett, Jr. Johnson Repr. 1971 o.p. Complete history of African Americans with more than 1,000 illustrations.

Franklin, John Hope, and August Meier, eds. *Black Leaders of the Twentieth Century*. U. of Ill. Pr. 1983 $11.95. ISBN 0-252-00939-8. Includes essays on major figures, past and recent.

Freidel, Frank, and Richard Showman, eds. *Harvard Guide to American History*. 2 vols. in 1. HUP rev. ed. 1974 $20.00. ISBN 0-674-37555-6. Comprehensive and very useful guide. Includes practical suggestions on research, writing, and publishing.

Friedman, Leon, and Fred L. Israel, eds. *The Justices of the United States Supreme Court, 1789–1991*. 5 vols. Chelsea Hse. 1992 $350.00. ISBN 0-7910-1377-4. Information on all the justices, including major decisions and contributions to the court.

Goehlert, Robert U., and Fenton S. Martin. *Congress and Law-Making: Researching the Legislative Process*. ABC-CLIO 1989 $39.50. ISBN 0-87436-509-0. Concise introduction to congressional publications and the tools for researching the legislative process. Also discusses secondary source material.

———. *The Presidency: A Research Guide*. ABC-CLIO 1985 $49.50. ISBN 0-87436-373-X. Extensive guide to primary and secondary sources for studying the presidency.

Gustafson, Milton O., ed. *The National Archives and Foreign Relations Research*. Ohio U. Pr. 1974 o.p. Useful guide to diplomatic history.

Hacker, Andrew, and Lorrie Millman, eds. *U.S.: A Statistical Portrait of the American People*. Viking Penguin 1983 $8.95. ISBN 0-14-006579-2. Statistical compendium. Data and narrative together provide a unique picture of the United States.

Hotten, John Campden, ed. *The Original Lists of Persons of Quality: Emigrants, Religious Exiles, Political Rebels, Serving Men Sold for a Term of Years, Apprentices . . . and Others Who Went from Great Britain to the American Plantations, 1600–1700*. Genealog. Pub. 1986 repr. of 1874 ed. o.p. Extraordinary compendium of more than 11,000 names.

Kane, Joseph N. *Facts about the Presidents*. Wilson 1989 $45.00. ISBN 0-8242-0774-2. Useful compendium of factual data.

———. *Facts about the States*. Wilson 1989 $55.00. ISBN 0-8240-0407-7. Useful compendium of information about the states.

Leidy, W. Philip. *A Popular Guide to Government Publications*. Col. U. Pr. 1976 $63.00. ISBN 0-231-04019-9. Bibliographical data for a selected list of government publications.

Lester, DeeGee. *Roosevelt Research: Collections for the Study of Theodore, Franklin, and Eleanor*. Praeger 1992 $55.00. ISBN 0-313-27204-2. Very useful guide to a major political "dynasty."

Linden-Ward, Blanche, and Carol H. Green. *American Women in the 1960s*. Macmillan 1992 $55.00. ISBN 0-8057-9905-2. Impressive complexity, scope, and seriousness.

Long, E. B., and Barbara Long. *The Civil War Day by Day: An Almanac, 1861–1865*. Da Capo 1985 $19.95. ISBN 0-306-80255-4. Unique record of the war and its course.

Morehead, Joe, and Mary Fetzer. *Introduction to United States Government Information Sources*. Libs. Unl. 1992 $32.50. ISBN 1-56308-066-4. Best introduction to accessing and using federal government documents.

Notable Americans: What They Did from 1620 to the Present. Gale 1992 $155.00. ISBN 0-8103-6967-2. Good tool for finding basic information about the most important figures in American history.

Parsons, Elsie C., ed. *North American Indian Life*. Dover 1993 repr. of 1922 ed. $10.95. ISBN 0-486-27377-6. Activities, customs, and beliefs of 23 tribes. Essays by authoritative anthropologists.

Peirce, Neal, and Jerry Hagstrom. *The Book of America: Inside the 50 States Today*. Warner Bks. 1984 $27.50. ISBN 0-393-01639-0. Lively and colorful compendium of information and maps on political, social, and economic aspects of major cities and regions.

Poulton, Helen, and Marguerite S. Howland. *The Historian's Handbook: A Descriptive Guide to Reference Works*. U. of Okla. Pr. 1972 $17.95. ISBN 0-8061-1009-0. Useful research tool.

Prucha, Francis P. *Handbook for Research in American History: A Guide to Bibliographies and Other Reference Works*. U. of Nebr. Pr. 1987 $10.95. ISBN 0-8032-87194. Essential, inexpensive, and highly useful.

Raimo, John, ed. *Biographical Directory of American Colonial and Revolutionary Governers, 1607–1789*. Meckler 1980 $125.00. ISBN 0-313-28133-5. Brief sketches and bibliographical information on all governors up to 1789.

Sabin, Joseph, and others, eds. *Dictionary of Books Relating to America from Its Discovery to the Present Time*. 1869–92, 1928–36. 29 vols in 2. Scarecrow 1966 $325.00. ISBN 0-8108-0033-0. Huge compendium of useful references.

Schlesinger, Arthur M., Jr., ed. *The Almanac of American History*. Putnam Pub. Group 1984 o.p. Covers events in American history from A.D. 986 through 1982. Arranged in five historical periods—986–1787, 1788–1865, 1866–1900, 1901–1945, and 1945–1982.

Sloan, Irving J. *The Blacks in America, 1492–1977: A Chronology and Fact Book*. Oceana 4th rev. ed. 1977 $8.50. ISBN 0-379-00524-7. A basic tool for research on African Americans.

Smith, Jessie C., ed. *Notable Black American Women*. Gale 1992 $75.00. ISBN 0-8103-8350-0. Useful guide with informative entries.

Statistical Abstract of the United States, 1878–present. USGPO 112th ed. 1992 $19.95. ISBN 1-878753-08-0. This outstanding compendium is a boon to librarians and researchers. Data are from government and private sources. Reviewed and evaluated annually.

Tuleja, Thaddeus F. *American History—One Hundred Nutshells*. Fawcett 1992 $8.00. ISBN 0-449-90346-X. Quick-reference guide that is authoritative and unassuming.

U.S. Congress. *The Congressional Directory*. 1809–present. USGPO 1987–88 $20.00. ISBN 0-685-43877-5

U.S. Government Manual. 1935–present. Bernan Pr. 1991 $23.00. ISBN 0-89059-001-X. Indispensable tool that lists and describes the functions of all departments of the federal government, their divisions, bureaus, commissions and services. Revised annually.

Urdang, Laurence, ed. *The Timetables of American History*. S&S Trade 1983. $20.00. ISBN 0-671-25246-1. Chronological arrangement of history from A.D. 1000 to 1980, including some events happening outside of North America. Lists developments under history and politics, the arts, science and technology, and miscellaneous.

Utter, Jack. *American Indians: Answers to Today's Questions*. Natl. Woodlands Pub. 1993 $21.95. ISBN 0-9628075-3-2. Painstakingly researched, amply researched, comprehensive index, bibliography with 422 references, and 9 appendices.

Whitnah, Donald R., ed. *Government Agencies*. Greenwood 1983 $67.95. ISBN 0-313-22017-4. Encyclopedic volume providing historical sketches of origins and organization of all major departments and agencies of the federal government.

Who Was Who in America. 12 vols. Marquis 1993 $767.50. ISBN 0-8379-0222-3. Profiles over 122,000 notable figures in American history. With index volume.

Who's Who in America 1994. 3 vols. Marquis 1993 $429.95. ISBN 0-8379-0151-0

Who's Who in American Politics 1993–94. 2 vols. Bowker 14th ed. 1993 $225.00. ISBN 0-8352-3285-9. Lists 26,000 decision makers whose politics, policies, and conduct shape our nation.

Yanak, Ted, and Pam Cornelison. *The Great American History Fact-Finder*. HM 1993 $24.95. ISBN 0-395-65992-2. More than 200 entries. Solid addition to the general survey library.

ENCYCLOPEDIAS AND DICTIONARIES

Beers, Henry P. *The American Revolution: An Encyclopedia*. 2 vols. Ed. by Richard L. Blanco. Garland 1993 $175.00. ISBN 0-8240-5623-X. Comprehensive, with an emphasis on military history.

Boatner, Mark M., III. *The Civil War Dictionary*. Random 1991 $18.00. ISBN 0-679-73392-2. Includes illustrations, maps, and diagrams.

_____. *Encyclopedia of the American Revolution*. McKay 1980 $9.98. ISBN 0-679-50440-0. Concise fact book, providing information on individuals, events, and places.

Carruth, Gorton, and others, eds. *The Encyclopedia of American Facts and Dates*. HarpC 8th rev. ed. 1987 $35.00. ISBN 0-06-181143-2. Includes large number of well-indexed events in American history, ranging from about A.D. 1000 through 1986, and arranged in four topical columns that cover, roughly, politics, the arts, science/technology/philosophy, and social/daily life.

Concise Dictionary of American History. Scribner 1983 $95.00. ISBN 0-684-17321-2. Best single-volume dictionary of a general nature relating to U.S. history.

Current, Richard N., and others, eds. *Encyclopedia of the Confederacy*. 4 vols. S&S Trade 1993 $355.00. ISBN 0-13-275991-8. Superb compendium of information, ranging from legends and anecdotes to biographies and interpretive essays. An ideal reference work.

DeConde, Alexander. *Encyclopedia of American Foreign Policy: Studies of the Principal Movements and Ideas*. 3 vols. Scribner 1978 o.p. Factual information plus conceptual and theoretical essays.

Faragher, John Mack, ed. *Encyclopedia of Colonial and Revolutionary America*. Facts on File 1990 $50.00. ISBN 0-8160-1744-1. Comprehensive one-volume quick reference that covers a wide range of topics.

Findling, John E. *Dictionary of American Diplomatic History*. Greenwood 1989 $59.25. ISBN 0-313-26024-9. Excellent starting place for basic information.

Foner, Eric, and John Garraty, eds. *The Reader's Companion to American History*. HM 1991 $35.00. ISBN 0-395-51372-3. One-volume encyclopedia containing short factual entries, longer interpretive essays, and biographies, cross-referenced to one another. Emphasizes cultural and social aspects of history. Fascinating reading.

Gale, Robert L. *The Gay Nineties in America: A Cultural Dictionary of the 1890s*. Praeger 1992 $75.00. ISBN 0-313-27819-9. Lively guide to a colorful and critical period.

Greene, Jack P., ed. *Encyclopedia of American Political History*. 3 vols. Scribner 1984 $250.00. ISBN 0-684-17003-5. Very useful reference for political history.

Greene, Jack P., and J. R. Pole, eds. *The Blackwell Companion to the American Revolution*. Blackwell Pubs. 1991 $50.00. ISBN 0-55786-244-3. Authoritative articles by experts on the revolution.

Hine, Darlene Clark, ed. *Black Women in American History: From Colonial Times through the Nineteenth Century*. *Black Women in United States History Ser*. Carlson Pub 1993 $195.00. ISBN 0-9926019-14-7. An exceptional source of information, skillfully edited.

_____, *Black Women in American History: The Twentieth Century*. *Black Women in United States History Ser*. 4 vols. Carlson Pub. 1990 $275.00. ISBN 0-926019-15-5. An exceptional source of information, skillfully edited.

Hirschfelder, Arlene, and Paulette Molin. *The Encyclopedia of Native American Religions*. Facts on File 1992 $40.00. ISBN 0-8160-2017-5. Extensive coverage. Useful in any religion curriculum or Native American studies.

Johnson, John W., ed. *Historic U.S. Court Cases, 1690–1990: An Encyclopedia*. Garland 1993 $125.00. ISBN 0-8240-4430-4. Valuable compendium, comprising in effect a legal history.

Ketz, Louise B., ed. *Dictionary of American History.* 7 vols. Scribner 1976 $348.00. ISBN 0-684-13856-5. Exceptionally comprehensive, with over 6,000 signed entries covering concepts, terms, places, and events in American history.

Levy, Leonard W., and others, eds. *Encyclopedia of the American Presidency.* S&S Trade 1993 $295.00. ISBN 0-13-275983-7. Useful and reliable compendium.

Lowery, Charles D., and John E. Marszalek, eds. *Encyclopedia of African-American Civil Rights: From Emancipation to the Present.* Praeger 1992 $59.95. ISBN 0-313-25011-1. Useful guide to a major and persistent movement in U.S. history.

Maisel, L. Sandy, ed. *Political Parties and Elections in the U.S.: An Encyclopedia.* Garland 1993 $150.00. ISBN 0-7975-2. Important and useful information for those interested in political history.

Martin, Michael, and Leonard Gelber. *Dictionary of American History.* 1978. Dorset Pr. 1990 $19.95. ISBN 0-88029-431-0. Lively and interesting dictionary useful to general readers and scholars.

Miller, Randall, and John D. Smith, eds. *Dictionary of Afro-American Slavery.* Greenwood 1988 $95.00. ISBN 0-313-23814-6. Good introduction to the subject.

Morris, Richard B., and others, eds. *Encyclopedia of American History.* HarpC 1982 o.p. Excellent reference work for a general audience.

Neely, Mark E., Jr. *The Abraham Lincoln Encyclopedia.* Da Capo 1984 $18.95. ISBN 0-306-80209-0. A gold mine of information and facts about Lincoln.

Plano, Jack C., and Milton Greenberg, eds. *The American Political Dictionary.* H. Holt & Co. 1989 $16.50. ISBN 0-03-022932-4. Clear and precise definitions for political terms and jargon.

Porter, Glenn, ed. *Encyclopedia of American Economic History.* 3 vols. Scribner 1980 $250.00. ISBN 0-684-16271-7. Covers all aspects of U.S. economic history. Volume 1 contains an excellent historiography.

Roller, David C., and Robert Twyman, eds. *The Encyclopedia of Southern History.* La. State U. Pr. 1979 $95.00. ISBN 0-8071-0575-9. In-depth essays on institutions and customs peculiar to the South.

Shavit, David. *The United States in Latin America: A Historical Dictionary.* Praeger 1992 $75.00. ISBN 0-313-27595-5. Revealing guide to U.S. interest and involvement.

Voorhees, David William, ed. *Concise Dictionary of American History.* Scribner 1983 $60.00. ISBN 0-684-17321-2. One-volume version of the *Dictionary of American History*, produced by shortening some articles and eliminating others.

Wilson, Charles Reagan, and William Ferris, eds. *Encyclopedia of Southern Culture.* U. of NC Pr. 1989 $69.96. ISBN 0-8078-1823-2. A splendid volume organized around 24 thematic sections. Covers every aspect of southern life and culture.

BIBLIOGRAPHIES

Bataille, Gretchen M. *Native American Women: A Bibliographic Dictionary.* Garland 1992 $40.00. ISBN 0-05267-6. Groundbreaking work on a long-neglected subject.

Beers, Henry P. *Bibliographies in American History, 1942–1978: Guide to Materials for Research.* 2 vols. Res. Publns. CT 1982 $275.00. ISBN 0-89235-038-5. A bibliography of bibliographies listing 11,700 items.

Blanco, Richard L. *The War of the American Revolution: A Selected Annotated Bibliography of Published Sources.* Garland 1983 $64.00. ISBN 0-8240-9171-X. Excellent guide to major writings and other sources.

Burke, Robert E., and Richard Lowitt, comps. *The New Era and the New Deal, 1920–1940. Goldentree Bibliographies in Amer. History Ser.* Harlan Davidson 1981 $19.95. ISBN 0-88295-581-0. Excellent coverage of the economics, politics, and social developments of the era.

Burns, Richard Dean, ed. *Guide to American Foreign Relations since 1700.* ABC-CLIO 1982 o.p. Best and most comprehensive bibliography and historiography on U.S. foreign policy and diplomacy.

Cassara, Ernest, ed. *History of the United States of America: A Guide to Information Sources*. Gale 1977 $68.00. ISBN 0-8103-1266-2. Good place to begin research on any aspect of the American past.

Church, Elihu Dwight. *Catalog of Books Relating to the Discovery and Early History of North and South America*. Comp. by G. W. Cole. Peter Smith repr. of 1907 ed. $24.00. ISBN 0-8446-1113-1. Older compilation that is still useful.

Cronon, E. David, and Theodore D. Rosenof, comps. *The Second World War and the Atomic Age, 1940–1973. Goldentree Bibliographies in Amer. History Ser.* Harlan Davidson 1975 $13.95. ISBN 0-88295-538-1. Excellent source for research on post–World War II history.

Donald, David, comp. *The Nation in Crisis, 1861–1877. Goldentree Bibliographies in Amer. History Ser.* Harlan Davidson 1969 $6.95. ISBN 0-88295-511-X. Comprehensive bibliography on the era of sectional conflict.

Dornbusch, Charles E., comp. *Military Bibliography of the Civil War*. 1861–1872. 4 vols. NY Pub. Lib. 1987–1989. Vol. 1 $35.00. ISBN 0-87104-117-0. Vol. 2 $30.00. ISBN 0-87104-504-4. Vol. 3 $25.00. ISBN 0-87104-514-1. Vol. 4 $40.00. ISBN 0-685-51647-4. Most comprehensive directory of writings on and about the Civil War.

Evans, Charles. *American Bibliography*. 1903–34. 13 vols. in 1. Scarecrow 1967 $42.00. ISBN 0-9446-1173-5. Classic bibliographical source for early American history.

Fenton, Martin S., and Robert U. Goehlert, eds. *The American Presidency: A Bibliography*. Congr. Quarterly 1987 $95.00. ISBN 0-87187-415-6. Most current and comprehensive bibliography on the presidency.

Ferguson, E. James, comp. *Confederation, Constitution, and Early National Period, 1781–1815. Goldentree Bibliographies in Amer. History Ser.* Harlan Davidson 1975 $12.95. ISBN 0-88295-534-9. Especially strong on economics and politics of the post-Constitution period.

Gephart, Ronald E. *Revolutionary America, 1763–1789: A Bibliography*. USGPO 1984 $38.00. ISBN 0-16-003970-3. Includes political, economic, and social histories. Good bibliography of the period.

Goehlert, Robert U., and John R. Sayre. *The United States Congress: A Bibliography*. Free Pr. 1981 o.p. Comprehensive listing that covers the origins, history, and workings of Congress. Useful to both scholars and interested laypersons.

Grim, Richard E., ed. *Historical Geography of the United States and Canada: A Guide to Information Sources*. Gale 1982 o.p. Good introduction to the literature of historical geography.

Hall, Kermit L. *A Comprehensive Bibliography of American Constitutional and Legal History, 1896–1979*. 5 vols. Kraus 1984 $650.00. ISBN 0-527-37408-3. Huge bibliography, with more than 18,000 citations on American constitutional history.

Hall, Kermit L., ed. *Comprehensive Bibliography of American Constitutional and Legal History: Supplement, 1980–1987*. Kraus 1991 $155.00. ISBN 0-527-37414-8

Jackson, Rebecca. *The 1960s: An Annotated Bibliography of Social and Political Movements in the United States*. Praeger 1992 $49.95. ISBN 0-313-27255-7. Interesting collection of works and annotations on a milestone decade.

Johannsen, Robert W., ed. *Democracy on Trial*. U. of Ill. Pr. 1988 $34.95. ISBN 0-252-01478-2. Fifty-five documents illustrate the depth of the crisis posed by the Civil War.

Leary, William M., and Arthur S. Link, eds. *The Progressive Era and the Great War, 1896–1920. Goldentree Bibliographies in Amer. History Ser.* Harlan Davidson 1978 $23.95. ISBN 0-88295-575-6. Useful basic bibliography with many biographic citations.

Maurer, David J., ed. *U.S. Politics and Elections: A Guide to Information Sources. Amer. Government and History Information Guide Ser.* Gale 1978 o.p. Covers important political figures as well as events.

Miller, Elizabeth W., and May Fisher, comps. *The Negro in America: A Bibliography*. HUP rev. ed. 1970 $12.50. ISBN 0-674-60702-3. Selective scholarly bibliography compiled for the American Academy of Arts and Sciences. Topically arranged, with extensive annotations.

Mitterling, Philip I. *U.S. Cultural History: A Guide to Information Sources. Amer. Government and History Information Ser.* Gale 1980 o.p. Includes popular culture as well as the fine arts.

Nevins, Allan, and others. *Civil War Books: A Critical Bibliography.* 2 vols. Broadfoot 1984 repr. of 1967 ed. $60.00. ISBN 0-916107-09-4. Listing of important titles published for the U.S. Civil War Centennial Commission.

Salem, Dorothy C., ed. *African American Women: A Bibliographic Dictionary.* Garland 1993 $55.00. ISBN 0-8240-9782-3. A very up-to-date guide.

Shaw, Ralph, and Richard H. Shoemaker, comps. *American Bibliography, 1801–1819.* Scarecrow 1983 $45.00. ISBN 0-8108-1607-5. A preliminary checklist and geographical index.

Shy, John, comp. *The American Revolution. Goldentree Bibliographies in Amer. History Ser.* Harlan Davidson 1972 o.p. Short work that is still useful.

Smith, Dwight L., ed. *Afro-American History: A Bibliography.* ABC-CLIO 1981 o.p.

Tingley, Donald F. *Social History of the United States: A Guide to Information Sources. Amer. Government and History Information Guide Ser.* Gale 1979 o.p. Good introduction to the enormous increase in the literature of the social sciences.

DOCUMENTARY HISTORIES

Adler, Mortimer J., and Charles Van Doren, eds. *The Annals of America.* 24 vols. Encyclopaedia Brittanica 1976 $549.00. ISBN 0-87827-199-6. Original source materials arranged chronologically by specific periods in American history from 1493 to 1973. Topics index and bibliography provided in two-volume *Conspectus.*

Aptheker, Herbert. *A Documentary History of the Negro People in the United States.* 4 vols. Carol Pub. Group. Vol. 1 *From Colonial Times Through the Civil War.* 1989 repr. of 1962 ed. $14.95. ISBN 0-8065-0168-5. Vol. 2 *From the Reconstruction Years to the Founding of the NAACP.* 1989 repr. of 1964 ed. $14.95. ISBN 0-8065-0168-5. Vol. 3 *1932–1945.* 1974 $17.50. ISBN 0-8065-0438-2. Vol. 4 *From the Beginning of the New Deal to the End of the Second World War.* 1990 repr. of 1974 ed. $14.95. ISBN 0-8065-1007-2. "Still an important source book" (*Choice*).

Bailyn, Bernard, and N. Garrett, eds. *Pamphlets of the American Revolution, 1750–1776.* HUP 1965 o.p. Excellent collection of firsthand materials on the Revolution.

Berlin, Ira, and others. *Free at Last: A Documentary History of Slavery, Freedom, and the Civil War.* New Amer. Pr. 1993 $25.00. ISBN 1-56584-015-1. One-volume selection from the Freedmen and Southern Society Project's *Freedom: A Documentary History of Emancipation.* A major encounter with the American past.

Commager, Henry Steele, and Milton Cantor, eds. *Documents of American History, Vol. I: To 1898.* P-H 1990 $41.00. ISBN 0-13-217274-7. Valuable collection of major documents of the period.

Hofstadter, Richard, and Michael Wallace, eds. *American Violence: A Documentary History.* Random 1971 o.p. Collection of annotated documents on violence in America.

Johnson, Donald B., comp. *National Party Platforms, 1840–1976.* 2 vols. U. of Ill. Pr. 6th rev. ed. 1978 $64.95. ISBN 0-252-00692-5. Very useful collection for those interested in politics and political history.

Levy, Peter B., ed. *Documentary History of the Modern Civil Rights Movement.* Praeger 1992 $55.00. ISBN 0-313-27233-6. Very useful compendium of information.

Miller, Perry, and Thomas H. Johnson, eds. *The Puritans: A Sourcebook of Their Writings.* 2 vols. HarpC 1938 o.p. Excellent firsthand introduction to Puritan culture.

Morris, Richard B. *Basic Documents in American History.* Krieger 1980 $9.50. ISBN 0-89874-839-9. Useful short compendium of basic documents.

Peckham, Howard Henry. *Historical Americans: Books from Which Our Early History Is Written.* U. of Mich. Pr. 1980 $12.95. ISBN 0-472-06320-0. Fascinating study of the major publications of the colonial and early national periods.

Scott, Donald M., and Bernard Wishy, eds. *America's Families: A Documentary History*. HarpC 1981 o.p. Includes documents, letters, and excerpts from monographs on such topics as courtship, marriage, and child rearing.

Washburn, Wilcomb E., comp. *The American Indian and the United States: A Documentary History*. 4 vols. Greenwood 1973 o.p. Source material on the historic relationship between Native Americans and the federal government.

Willis, George, ed. *The American Curriculum*. Greenwood 1992 $65.00. ISBN 0-313-26730-8. What has been taught in American schools and the reasons for their selection. Comprehensive documentary sources.

SURVEYS AND GENERAL WORKS

Readers have access to a great variety of histories of the United States, ranging from relatively straightforward school or college textbooks to highly interpretive and sometimes controversial accounts for a wider public. While some histories reflect a well-defined perspective—sectional, economic, ethnic, cultural—others focus on a particular chronological period—the colonial era, the Gilded Age, modern America—and a few offer truly magisterial overviews of the entire national experience. Some are somberly scholarly in tone, others journalistically light. Treatments range from multivolume narratives to brief, quickly digested summaries.

Adams, James Truslow, ed. *Album of American History*. Scribner rev. ed. 1983 $225.00. ISBN 0-684-16846-0. The nation's history told in photographs and illustrations.

Bailey, Thomas A., and David M. Kennedy. *The American Pageant: A History of the Republic*. Heath 1991 $30.50. ISBN 0-669-21050-1. Clear, lively, and often witty narrative history.

Bailyn, Bernard A., and others. *The Great Republic: A History of the American People*. 2 vols. Heath 1992. ISBNs 0-669-20986-4, 0-669-20987-2. One of the best textbooks. Readable and entertaining.

Blum, John M., and others. *The National Experience: A History of the United States*. 2 vols. HarBraceJ 1992. Pt. 1 *A History of the U.S. to 1877*. $34.00. ISBN 0-15-565657-0. Pt. 2 *A History of the U.S. since 1865*. $34.00. ISBN 0-15-565658-9. Authoritative and well-written text by six distinguished senior historians—Edmund S. Morgan, Kenneth M. Stampp, C. Vann Woodward, William S. McFeeley, Arthur M. Schlesinger, Jr., and Blum.

Boorstin, Daniel J. *The Americans*. 3 vols. Random $109.90. ISBN 0-394-49588-8. Highly informative account of the American experience from the first days of English settlement.

Burns, James MacGregor. *The American Experiment*. 3 vols. Knopf. Vol. 1 *The Vineyard of Liberty*. 1982 $39.00. ISBN 0-394-50546-8. Vol. 2 *The Winds of Democracy*. 1985 $30.00. ISBN 0-394-51275-8. Vol. 3 *The Crossroads of Freedom*. 1989 $35.00. ISBN 0-394-51276-6. Superb general history that covers the period from the ratification of the Constitution to recent times.

Brinkley, Alan. *The Unfinished Nation: A Concise History of the American People*. Knopf 1993 $40.00. ISBN 0-679-42548-9. Refreshing new interpretation by a gifted historian and writer.

Carroll, Peter N., and David W. Noble. *The Free and the Unfree: A New History of the United States*. Viking Penguin 1988 $8.95. ISBN 0-14-022827-6. Good survey, with special attention paid to the Europeanization of America and the condition of minority groups.

Cashman, Sean Dennis. *African-Americans and the Quest for Civil Rights, 1900–1990*. NYU Pr. 1993 $15.00. ISBN 0-8147-1441-2. Good as both a visual history and a narrative.

Cooke, Alistair. *Alistair Cooke's America*. Knopf 1977 $24.95. ISBN 0-394-73449-1. "A panoramic book, traveling fast and high, and the view it gives of our land and the people below is exhilarating" (*Atlantic*).

Cooper, William J., Jr., and Thomas E. Terrill. *The American South: A History*. Knopf 1990 $50.00. ISBN 0-394-58948-3. First new comprehensive history of the South in more than 40 years.

Current, Richard N., and T. Harry Williams. *American History: A Survey*. 2 vols. Knopf 1988 $22.95 ea. ISBNs 0-685-13227-7, 0-685-13228-5. Well-written and straightforward narrative useful to both the scholar and the layperson.

Davidson, Marshall B. *The Drawing of America: Eyewitnesses to History*. Abrams 1983 o.p. A visual history of the United States with more than 300 illustrations.

Degler, Carl N. *Out of Our Past: The Forces That Shaped America*. HarpC 1983 $15.00. ISBN 0-06-131985-6. Beautifully crafted and very readable interpretive history based on major themes in the nation's past.

Evans, Sara M. *Born for Liberty: A History of Women in America*. Free Pr. 1989 $24.95. ISBN 0-02-902990-2. First-rate chronicle of womanhood in the American past. Beautifully written and full of fresh insights.

Franklin, John Hope, and Alfred A. Moss, Jr. *From Slavery to Freedom: A History of Negro Americans*. Knopf 1988 $19.91. ISBN 0-394-37013-9. Classic survey of the African American experience. Thorough, judicious, and interesting.

Garraty, John A. *A Short History of the American Nation*. 2 vols. HarpC 1992 $18.50. ISBNs 0-06-500742-5, 0-06-500743-3. Brief, thoughtful, and judicious history of the nation.

Garraty, John A., and the eds. of *American Heritage*. *The American Nation*. 2 vols. HarpC 1990 $35.50 ea. ISBNs 0-06-042243-2, 0-06-042244-0. Panoramic view of the nation's past. Well written and amply illustrated. Introduction by Roger Butterfield.

Grob, Gerald N., and George A. Billias. *Interpretations of American History*. 2 vols. Free Pr. 1982. Vol. 1 $12.95. ISBN 0-02-912690-8. Vol. 2 $11.95. ISBN 0-685-01678-1. Excellent survey of U.S. historiography that includes all major schools of thought and methodologies.

Johnson, Thomas H., ed. *The Oxford Companion to American History*. OUP 1966 $39.95. ISBN 0-19-500597-X. Comprehensive and authoritative.

Jordan, Winthrop D., and Leon F. Litwack. *The United States*. 2 vols. in 1. P-H 1991 $35.00. ISBN 0-13-933524-2. Widely used successor to Hofstadter, Miller, and Aaron, *A History of the United States* (1957). Authors are prize-winning historians—Jordan, the National Book Award and the Bancroft and Parkman prizes in 1968, and Litwack, the Pulitzer and Parkman prizes and the American Book Award in 1980.

Kerber, Linda K., and Jane Sherron De Hart. *Women's America: Refocusing the Past*. OUP 1991 $45.00. ISBN 0-19-506261-2. The American experience in the perspective of women's roles and contributions.

LaFeber, Walter, and Nancy Woloch. *The American Century*. Random 1979. ISBN 0-394-34193-7. Panoramic survey of the twentieth century. Strong on foreign affairs.

Link, Arthur S., and others. *The American People: A History*. Brandywine Press 1980 $16.95. ISBN 0-9603726-0-1. Comprehensive and thoughtful, with special attention devoted to ethnic and racial factors.

Link William A., and Arthur S. Link. *American Epoch: A History of the United States since 1900*. McGraw 1992 $25.95. ISBN 07-037951-3. Excellent survey of the United States in the twentieth century.

Marcus, Greil. *Lipstick Traces: A Secret History of the Twentieth Century*. 1989. HUP 1990 $14.95. ISBN 0-674-535810-2. "A bold blending of anecdote, personal confession and cultural analysis. . . . A coruscatingly original piece of work, vibrant with the energy of the bizarre happenings it maps out" (Terry Eagleton, *N.Y. Times Book Review*).

Morison, Samuel Eliot. *The Oxford History of the American People*. 3 vols. NAL-Dutton 1972. Vol. 1 $5.95. ISBN 0-451-62600-1. Vol. 2 $4.95. ISBN 0-451-62408-4. Vol. 3 $4.95. ISBN 0-451-62446-7. Very readable general history from prehistoric times to the assassination of John Fitzgerald Kennedy.

Morrison, Samuel Eliot, Henry Steele Commager, and William E. Leuchtenburg. *The Growth of the American Republic.* 2 vols. OUP 1980. Vol. 1 $29.95. ISBN 0-19-502593-8. Vol. 2 $29.95. ISBN 0-19-502594-6. A classic survey, still one of the best.

Nevins, Allan, and Henry Steele Commager. *A Short History of the United States.* Knopf 1991 $4.95. ISBN 0-671-62992-1. Concise historical survey.

Norton, Mary Beth, and others. *A People and A Nation: Brief Edition.* HM 1991. ISBN 0-395-47302-0. Thorough and lively account.

Patterson, James T. *America in the Twentieth Century: A History.* HarBraceJ 1988 $23.00. ISBN 0-15-502264-4. Clear and vivid history of modern America that emphasizes political developments.

Perry, Lewis. *Intellectual Life in America: A History.* U. Ch. Pr. 1989 $14.95. ISBN 0-226-66101-6. Balanced and readable intellectual history.

Quint, Howard H., and others, eds. *Main Problems in American History.* 2 vols. Wadsworth Pub. 1988 o.p. Excellent collection of essays on major issues of the past.

Rhodes, James Ford. *History of the United States from the Compromise of 1850 to the McKinley-Bryan Campaign of 1896.* 1893–1919. 9 vols. Rprt. Serv. rev. ed. 1991 repr. of 1928 ed. $675.00. ISBN 0-7812-6039-6. A classic older interpretation, still distinguished by the quality of the writing.

Sellers, Charles, and others. *A Synopsis of American History.* I. R. Dee 1992 $28.25. ISBN 0-929587-76-6. Authoritative brief survey.

Thernstrom, Stephan. *A History of the American People.* 2 vols. HarBraceJ 1989 $21.00 ea. ISBNs 0-15-536533-9, 0-15-536534-7. Good introductory survey. Discusses significant economic, political, social, and intellectual developments.

Tindall, George B., with David E. Shi. *America: A Narrative History.* 2 vols. Norton 1992 $16.95 ea. ISBNs 0-393-96149-4, 0-393-96151-6. Well-written narrative with a keen eye to dramatic events and characters.

Williams, George W. *The History of the Negro Race in America from 1619 to 1880.* Amer. Negro: His History and Lit. Ser. 2 vols. Ayer 1968 repr. of 1883 ed. Vol. 1 $32.50. ISBN 0-88143-100-1. Vol. 2 $37.50. ISBN 0-88143-101-X. "A monument in American historiography" (C. Vann Woodward, *Saturday Review*).

Zinn, Howard. *A People's History of the United States.* HarpC 1980 $12.00. ISBN 0-06-090792-4. Written from the perspective of those who were exploited. A unique approach, well crafted.

ON WRITING U.S. HISTORY

American Foreign Relations: A Historiographical Review. Contributions in Amer. History Ser. P-H 1981 $43.00. ISBN 0-313-21061-6. Analysis of historiographical trends and methodologies in diplomatic history. A good introduction to the subject.

Bailey, Thomas A., and David M. Kennedy. *The American Spirit: United States History as Seen by Contemporaries.* 2 vols. Heath 1991 $15.00 ea. ISBNs 0-669-21472-8, 0-669-21473-6. Provides individual perspectives on the American experience.

Belz, Herman, and others, eds. *To Form a More Perfect Union.* U. Pr. of Va. 1992 $35.00. ISBN 0-8139-1343-8. Philosophic and political theoretical origins of the Constitution.

Benson, Lee. *Turner and Beard: American Historical Writing Reconsidered.* Greenwood 1980 repr. of 1960 ed. o.p. Interesting analysis of two early-twentieth-century influences.

Brugger, Robert J. *Our Selves/Our Past: Psychological Approaches to American History.* Johns Hopkins 1981 $15.95. ISBN 0-8018-2381-X. Reveals the wide range of research in the field of psychohistory.

Cunliffe, Marcus. *In Search of America: Transatlantic Essays, 1951–1990.* Contributions in Amer. History Ser. Greenwood 1991 $55.00. ISBN 0-313-27712-5. European perspective of America.

Davidson, James West, and Mark Lytle. *After the Fact: The Art of Historical Detection.* McGraw 1992 $20.20. ISBN 07-554971-9. Fascinating exercises in historical "detective" work. An excellent introduction to the craft.

Davis, Kenneth C. *Don't Know Much About History: Everything You Need to Know About American History but Never Learned.* Avon 1991 $10.95. ISBN 0-380-71251-0. Witty compendium of information and "disinformation" about American history.

Fitzgerald, Frances. *America Revised: History Schoolbooks in the Twentieth Century.* Vin. 1980 $3.95. ISBN 0-394-74439-X. Perceptive analysis of American history textbooks. Constructively critical of both content and writing.

Fogel, Robert W., and G. R. Elton. *Which Road to the Past? Two Views of History.* 1983. Yale U. Pr. 1984 $10.00. ISBN 0-300-03278-1. Dialogue comparing the "traditional" and the "scientific" schools of historical inquiry.

Gardner, James B., and George R. Adams, eds. *Ordinary People and Everyday Life: Perspectives on the New Social History.* Amer. Assoc. for State and Local History 1983 o.p. A useful anthology focusing on local and regional history.

Gay, Peter. *A Loss of Mastery: Puritan Historians in Colonial America.* Bks. Demand repr. of 1966 ed. $44.00. ISBN 0-685-23585-8. Includes analyses of William Bradford, Cotton Mather, and Jonathan Edwards.

Hanke, Lewis, ed. *Guide to the Study of United States History Outside the U.S., 1945–1980.* 5 vols. Kraus 1985 $418.00. ISBN 0-527-36717-6. "New sources and fresh perspectives" on U.S. history by foreign scholars. Contains essays and annotated bibliography of 3,100 books, articles, and dissertations published abroad.

Higham, John. *Writing American History: Essays on Modern Scholarship.* Bks. Demand repr. of 1972 ed. $54.30. ISBN 0-317-27824-X. Incisive analysis and critique of methodologies and philosophies.

Hofstadter, Richard. *The Progressive Historians: Turner, Beard, Parrington.* U. Ch. Pr. 1979 $14.00. ISBN 0-226-34818-0. In-depth study of the three highly influential historians.

Kammen, Michael, ed. *The Past Before Us: Contemporary Historical Writing in the United States.* Cornell Univ. Pr. 1982 o.p. Excellent collection of essays on changes and trends in recent historical research.

Lyons, Oren. *Exiled in the Land of the Free.* Clear Light 1992 $24.95. ISBN 0-940666-15-4. Excellent reinterpretation of the founding of the United States in light of the recently acknowledged role of the Native American in establishing the Constitution. Foreword by Peter Matthiessen; preface by Senator Daniel K. Inouye.

Kraus, Michael, and David D. Joyce. *The Writing of American History.* U. of Okla. Pr. 1990 $39.50. ISBN 0-8061-1519-X. From the Norse voyages to writings since World War II.

McMahon, Robert J., *Major Problems in the History of the Vietnam War. Major Problems in Amer. History Ser.* Heath 1990 o.p. Balanced collection of essays and documents that provide a good introduction to the war and to problems in interpreting it.

Malone, Michael P., ed. *Historians and the American West.* U. of Nebr. Pr. 1983 $28.50. ISBN 0-8032-3071-0. Important survey and essays on the historiography of the West.

Moody, J. Carroll, and Alice Kessler-Harris, eds. *Perspectives on American Labor History: The Problem of Synthesis.* N. Ill. U. Pr. 1990 $28.50. ISBN 0-87580-15-1. Experts in labor history consider problems of research and analysis in their field.

Neustadt, Richard E., and Ernest R. May. *Thinking in Time: The Uses of History for Decision Makers.* Free Pr. 1988 $27.95. ISBN 0-02-927790-0. Thought-provoking study of history's actual and potential influence in the centers of power.

Novick, Peter. *That Noble Dream: The "Objectivity Question" and the American Historical Profession.* Cambridge U. Pr. 1988 $64.95. ISBN 0-521-3438-3. Thoughtful discussion and analysis of a persistent problem for students and writers of history.

Robertson, James Oliver. *American Myth, American Reality. Amer. Century Ser.* 1980. Hill & Wang 1982 $10.95. ISBN 0-8090-0152-7. Fascinating exploration of myths in the American experience, how they differ from those of other societies, and how they reflect reality.

Steffen, Jerome O., ed. *The American West: New Perspectives, New Dimensions.* U. of Okla. Pr. 1981 $10.95. ISBN 0-8061-1744-3. Essays suggesting new methodologies and the need for research on environment, demography, and behavior. Reflective of a new attention to western history.

_____. *Comparative Frontiers: A Proposal for Studying the American West*. U. of Okla. Pr. 1980 $19.95. ISBN 0-8061-1617-X. Examines major approaches and methodologies that have been used to study the American frontier.

Trachtenberg, Alan. *Reading American Photographs: Images as History from Mathew Brady to Walker Evans*. Hill & Wang 1989 $25.00. ISBN 0-8090-8037-0. Interesting discussion of the intelligent use of supplementary and complementary visual materials.

Turner, Frederick Jackson. *The Frontier in American History*. U. of Ariz. Pr. 1985 $16.95. ISBN 0-8169-0946-8. Essays elaborating on Turner's views concerning the frontier.

Vecsey, Christopher T., and Robert W. Venables, eds. *American Indian Environments: Ecological Issues in Native American History*. Bks. Demand repr. of 1980 ed. $63.80. ISBN 0-8357-3120-0. Collection covering such topics as environment, natural resources, and cultural relationships to the land.

Woodward, C. Vann, ed. *The Comparative Approach to American History*. Basic 1980 o.p. Useful essays by able historians, testing the uniqueness of American history by comparing it with other national experiences.

Ziff, Larzer. *Writing in the New Nation*. Yale U. Pr. 1991 $25.00. ISBN 0-300-05040-2. A thoroughly New Historicist hypothesis.

COLONIAL PERIOD, 1606–1763

Colonial history has benefited measurably from the growing interest in social and cultural history. Recent studies look at the social and demographic structure of local communities and cultures both as a means of reconstructing the lives and societies of ordinary people and as a means of piecing together a more authentic mosaic of colonial society generally. Native American and African American histories and women's studies add substance to this effort.

Allen, David Grayson. *In English Ways: The Movement of Societies and the Transferral of English Local Law and Custom to Massachusetts Bay in the Seventeenth Century*. Bks. Demand repr. of 1981 ed. $90.20. ISBN 0-7837-0286-8. Important study of the transit of civilization from the Old World to the New.

Axelrod, Alan. *Chronicle of the Indian Wars: From Colonial Times to Wounded Knee*. P-H 1993 $25.00. ISBN 0-671-84650-7. Informative and thought-provoking chronicle of Native Americans and the land that was once their home.

Bonomi, Patricia. *A Factious People: Politics and Society in Colonial New York*. Col. U. Pr. 1971 o.p. Class and ethnic tensions in the middle colonies.

_____. *Under the Cope of Heaven: Religion, Society, and Politics in Colonial America*. OUP 1986 $39.95. ISBN 0-19-504118-6. First-rate study of religion in early America, noting the interrelation of revivalism and democratic tendencies.

Boyer, Paul S., and Stephen Nissenbaum. *Salem Possessed*. HUP 1974 $9.95. ISBN 0-674-78526-6. The witchcraft episode in the perspective of social and cultural change.

Breen, T. H. *Puritans and Adventurers: Changes and Persistence in Early America*. OUP 1980 $43.95. ISBN 0-19-503207-1. Essays on colonial Massachusetts and Virginia examining the differences between two kinds of societies developing simultaneously.

Bushman, Richard L. *King and People in Provincial Massachusetts*. 1985. U. of NC Pr. 1992 $17.95. ISBN 0-8078-4398-9. Comprehensive and significant history of pre-revolutionary Massachusetts.

Demos, John. *Entertaining Satan: Witchcraft and the Culture of Early New England*. HUP 1982 $35.00. ISBN 0-19-503131-8. The best place to begin a study of the Salem witchcraft episode. Winner of 1983 Bancroft Prize.

Fagan, Brian M. *The Great Journey*. Thames Hudson 1987 $19.95. ISBN 0-500-28515-7. Fascinating study by an archaeologist of pre-Columbian migrations to and within the New World.

Fischer, David Hackett. *Albion's Seed: Four British Folkways in America. America: A Cultural History Vol. I*. OUP 1989 $39.95. ISBN 0-19-503794-4. Imaginative and creative exploration of American cultural roots. Part of a projected general cultural history of the United States.

Fitzhugh, William. *William Fitzhugh and His Chesapeake World, 1676–1701.* Ed. by Richard Beale Davis. U. Pr. of Va. 1963 o.p. Well-edited letters of a major figure in Potomac society, covering a great variety of commercial, professional, and personal subjects.

Friedenberg, Daniel M. *Life, Liberty, and the Pursuit of Land.* Prometheus Bks. 1992 $27.95. ISBN 0-87975-722-1. Argues that the prime force behind the colonization of the New World, the Revolutionary War, the extradition of the Native American, and the ratification of the Constitution was the desire to own land for political and economic power.

Godbeer, Richard. *The Devil's Dominion: Magic and Religion in Early New England.* Cambridge U. Pr. 1992 $24.95. ISBN 0-21-40329-4. Superb study of the relation between religion and witchcraft among the Puritans.

Goodfriend, Joyce D. *Before the Melting Pot: Society and Culture in Colonial New York City, 1644–1730.* Princeton U. Pr. 1992 $35.00. ISBN 0-691-04794-4. A perceptive social history that focuses on ethnic relations.

Greene, Jack P. *Pursuits of Happiness: The Social Development of the Early Modern British Colonies and the Formation of American Culture.* U. of NC Pr. 1988 $34.95. ISBN 0-8078-18-4-6. Fine study of social conditions in the colonies, noting the great diversity.

Green, Jack P. and J. R. Pole, eds. *Colonial British America: Essays in the New History of the Modern Early Era.* Johns Hopkins 1984 $16.95. ISBN 0-8018-3555-9. Informative essays on the revolutionary and confederation periods.

Gura, Philip F. *A Glimpse of Sion's Glory: Puritan Radicalism in New England, 1620–1660.* Wesleyan Univ. Pr. 1984 $40.00. ISBN 0-8195-5095-7. Emphasis on the pluralistic and dynamic aspects of Puritanism, plus an interesting analysis of Separatists, Quakers, Anabaptists, and other radicals.

Hall, David D. *Worlds of Wonder, Days of Judgment: Popular Religious Beliefs in Early New England.* Knopf 1989 $29.95. ISBN 0-394-50108-X. Outstanding study of religious life and customs in everyday New England.

Hall, David D., and David Grayson Allen, eds. *Seventeenth-Century New England.* Colonial Soc. of Massachusetts 1984 o.p. Excellent collection of essays on a wide range of topics that include diet, popular culture, magic, and daily life.

Hall, David D., John M. Murrin, and Thad W. Tate, eds. *Saints and Revolutionaries: Essays on Early American History.* Norton 1984 $27.50. ISBN 0-393-01751-6. Interesting essays on various aspects of colonial life.

A History of the American Colonies Series. 13 vols. Kraus Intl. *Colonial Delaware.* Ed. by John A. Munroe. 1978 $35.00. ISBN 0-527-18711-9. *Colonial Massachusetts.* Ed. by Benjamin Labaree. 1979 $35.00. ISBN 0-527-18714-3. *Colonial Connecticut.* Ed. by Robert S. Taylor. 1979 $35.00. ISBN 0-527-18710-0. *Colonial Maryland.* Ed. by Aubrey C. Land. 1981 $35.00. ISBN 0-527-18713-5. *Colonial New Hampshire.* Ed. by Jere R. Daniell. 1982 $35.00. ISBN 0-527-18715-1. *Colonial South Carolina.* Ed. by Robert H. Weir. 1983 $35.00. ISBN 0-527-18721-6. *Colonial Virginia.* Ed. by Thad W. Tate and others. 1986 $35.00. ISBN 0-527-18722-4. *Colonial Georgia.* Ed. by Kenneth Coleman. 1976 $35.00. ISBN 0-527-18712-7. *Colonial Pennsylvania.* Ed. by Joseph E. Illick. 1976 $35.00. ISBN 0-527-18719-4. *Colonial New York.* Ed. by Michael Kammen. 1975 $35.00. ISBN 0-527-18717-8. *Colonial Rhode Island.* Ed. by Sidney V. James. 1975 $35.00. ISBN 0-527-18720-8. *Colonial New Jersey.* Ed. by John E. Pomfret. 1973 $35.00. ISBN 0-527-18716-X. *Colonial North Carolina.* Ed. by Hugh T. Lefler and William S. Powell. 1973 $35.00. ISBN 0-527-18718-6. Individual volumes on all original colonies by eminent colonial historians.

Hoffer, Peter C. *Law and People in Colonial America.* Johns Hopkins 1992 $14.95. ISBN 0-8018-4507-3. Examines how the American colonists adapted English law and transformed it into a unique American system.

Hofstadter, Richard. *America at 1750: A Social Portrait.* Random 1973 $7.95. ISBN 0-393-71795-3. Engrossing study of social conditions during the colonial period.

Karlsen, Carol F. *The Devil in the Shape of a Woman: Witchcraft in Colonial New England*. Norton 1989 $12.95. ISBN 0-679-72184-3. Fascinating inquiry into the place of superstition in colonial life.

Kolodny, Annette. *The Land Before Her: Fantasy and Experience of American Frontiers, 1630–1860*. U. of NC Pr. 1984 $34.95. ISBN 0-8078-1571-3. Rich and detailed study of women's writings about the frontier, including travel diaries and novels.

Kulikoff, Alan. *Tobacco and Slaves: The Development of Southern Cultures in the Chesapeake, 1680–1800*. U. of NC Pr. 1986 $34.95. ISBN 0-8078-1671-X. Important study of a major plantation industry and culture in early America.

Main, Jackson Turner. *Society and Economy in Colonial Connecticut*. Princeton U. Pr. 1985 $45.00. ISBN 0-691-047261-X. Detailed analysis of wealth, position, and standard of living of workers and professionals.

May, Henry F. *The Enlightenment in America*. OUP 1976 $14.95. ISBN 0-19-502367-6. Outstanding study of intellectual trends in the eighteenth century. Winner of the Beveridge Award.

Middlekauff, Robert R. *The Mathers: Three Generations of Puritan Intellectuals, 1596–1728*. OUP 1971 $7.95. ISBN 0-19-502115-0. An important work that places the highly influential and controversial Puritan oligarchy in reasonable historical perspective.

Morgan, Edmund S. *American Slavery, American Freedom: The Ordeal of Colonial Virginia*. Norton 1976 $9.95. ISBN 0-393-90156-2. Beveridge Award winner. Presents theory of racism.

———. *The Puritan Dilemma: The Story of John Winthrop*. Scott F. 1987 $13.00. ISBN 0-673-39347-X. Treats the first governor of the Massachusetts Bay Colony and how he deals with a major ethical dilemma.

Moseley, James G. *John Winthrop's World: History as a Story/The Story as History. History of Amer. Thought and Culture*. U. of Wis. Pr. 1993 $42.50. ISBN 0-299-13530-6. Compelling biography that places Winthrop in historical context as a leader and man.

Nash, Gary B. *Red, White, and Black: The Peoples of Early America*. P-H 1982. ISBN 0-13-769786-4. Brilliant original approach to colonial history focusing on the interactions of three cultures.

Rice, Kym S. *Early American Taverns: Entertainment of Friends and Strangers*. Fraunces Tavern 1983 $16.95. ISBN 0-9616495-0-9. Lavishly illustrated and lively history of taverns throughout the colonies, covering such aspects as food, innkeepers, drink, and entertainment.

Rutman, Darrett B., and Anita H. Rutman. *A Place in Time: Middlesex County Virginia, 1650–1750*. Norton 1986 $11.95. ISBN 0-393-30318-7. An engaging social history, with an important analysis of individual and community interrelations.

Spruill, Julia Cherry. *Women's Life and Work in the Southern Colonies*. Norton 1972 $10.95. ISBN 0-393-00662-X. Classic study of life and customs in colonial America.

Stick, David. *Roanoke Island: The Beginning of English America*. U. of NC Pr. 1983 $16.95. ISBN 0-8075-1554-3. Readable and generally reliable popular account of the first English attempts at settlement in the New World.

Van Dusen, Albert E., ed. *Adventures for Another World: Jonathan Trumble's Commonplace Book*. Connecticut Hist. Soc. 1983 $5.95. ISBN 0-940748-87-8. Repository of random observations and thoughts, revealing much of the flavor and feeling of early New England.

Vaughan, Alden T. *American Genesis: Captain John Smith and the Founding of Virginia. Lib. of Amer. Biography*. Scott F. 1987 $13.00. ISBN 0-673-39355-0. Concise, informative biography.

Webb, Stephen. *1676: The End of American Independence*. Bks. Demand repr. of 1984 ed. $128.60. ISBN 0-7837-1735-0. Provocative argument that English authority was undermined by Bacon's Rebellion and the Indian wars long before the Revolution itself.

Winslow, Ola E. *Meetinghouse Hill, 1630–1783*. Norton 1972 $2.95. ISBN 0-393-00632-8. Superb social history of a central institution in early New England life.

Wood, Forrest G. *The Arrogance of Faith: Christianity and Race in America from the Colonia Era to the Twentieth Century.* NE U. Pr. 1991 repr. of 1990 ed. $16.95. ISBN 1-55553-096-6. Extensive critique of how the Bible has been used to justify slavery and promote racial divisions in society. An important study, strongly grounded in historical fact.

Wood, Peter. *Black Majority: Negroes in Colonial South Carolina from 1670 through the Stono Rebellion.* Norton 1975 $9.95 ISBN 0-393-00777-4. Important reminder of demographic and social realities in a southern colony. Winner of 1974 Beveridge Award.

REVOLUTION AND THE NEW NATION, 1763–1815

Important new studies of the American Revolution, including those by Gordon Wood, Robert Middlekauf, and Sylvia Frey, highlight the recent historiography of this period of U.S. history. These studies join a corpus of work that both broadens and deepens our understanding of this pivotal event in the American past. Along with works marking the bicentennial of the Constitution, readers have available refreshing new information on the demography, politics, social structure, economic pursuits, and cultural activities of the first generation of the Republic.

Alden, John R. *The American Revolution, 1775–1783. New Amer. Nation Ser.* HarpC 1954 $11.00. ISBN 0-06-133011-6. Reliable and readable general survey.

———. *George Washington: A Biography. Southern Biography Ser.* La. State U. Pr. 1984 $24.95. ISBN 0-8071-1153-8. Good brief biography of the first U.S. president.

Appleby, Joyce. *Capitalism and a New Social Order: The Republican Vision of the 1790s.* NYU Pr. 1984 $30.00. ISBN 0-8147-0851-2. Original and thought-provoking study of the Jeffersonian Republican party from 1792 to 1828.

Bailyn, Bernard. *Faces of the Revolution: Personalities and Themes in the Struggle for American Independence.* Knopf 1990 $29.95. ISBN 0-394-49895-X. Introduces the people and issues of a crucial period in America's early history.

———. *The Ideological Origins of the American Revolution.* HUP 1967 $21.00. ISBN 0-674-4430-4. Pulitzer and Bancroft Prize-winning (1968) argument concerning the role of "Radical Whig" ideology in the struggle for independence.

———. *The Ordeal of Thomas Hutchinson.* HUP 1974 $27.00. ISBN 0-674-64160-4. Pulitzer Prize-winning biography (1975) of the unpopular governor of the Massachusetts Bay Colony.

Banning, Lance. *The Jeffersonian Persuasion: Evolution of a Party Ideology.* Cornell Univ. Pr. 1978 $36.00. ISBN 0-8014-1151-3. Development of republican government and democratic ideas.

Becker, Carl. *The Declaration of Independence: A Study in the History of Political Ideas.* Vin. 1958 $6.95. ISBN 0-394-70060-0. Analysis of the structure, drafting, and philosophy of the Declaration.

Bennett, Lerone, Jr. *Before the Mayflower: A History of Black America.* Viking Penguin rev. ed. 1984 $10.95. ISBN 0-14-007214-4. Good treatment of African American conditions and contributions during the colonial and revolutionary periods.

Bonomi, Patricia U., ed. *Party and Political Opposition in Revolutionary America.* Sleepy Hollow Pr. 1980 o.p. Useful essays, a number of which challenge traditional views about party politics and tactics.

Bonwick, Colin. *The American Revolution.* U. Pr. of Va. 1991 $35.00. ISBN 0-8139-1346-2. Lucid, brief history, capped off with a well-annotated bibliography.

Bowen, Catherine Drinker. *Miracle at Philadelphia.* Little 1986 $18.45. ISBN 0-316-10378-0. Popular and reliable depiction of the Constitutional Convention based on James Madison's records.

Bridenbaugh, Carl. *Cities in Revolt: Urban Life in America, 1743–1776.* OUP 1971 o.p. Focuses on the role of urban centers during the period of the Revolution.

————. *Early Americans*. OUP 1981 $30.00. ISBN 0-19-502788-4. Fascinating anthology on little-known events and individuals during colonial times.

————. *The Spirit of '76: The Growth of American Patriotism Before Independence*. OUP 1974 o.p. Argues that Americans were a "nation" before 1776.

Brodie, Fawn. *Thomas Jefferson: An Intimate History*. Bantam 1981 $6.95. ISBN 0-553-27335-3. Controversial psychobiography.

Brown, Roger H. *The Republic in Peril, 1812*. 1964. Norton 1971 $7.95. ISBN 0-393-00578-X. "A major revision of thinking about the War of 1812" (*Library Journal*).

Countryman, Edward. *The American Revolution*. Ed. by Eric Foner. *Amer. Century Ser.* Hill & Wang 1985 $9.95. ISBN 0-8090-0162-4. Concise and thought-provoking interpretive history.

Crow, Jeffrey J., and Larry E. Tise, eds. *The Southern Experience in the American Revolution*. U. of NC Pr. 1978 o.p. Important essays examining the social and political effects of the Revolution on the southern colonies.

Cunningham, Noble E., Jr. *In Pursuit of Reason: The Life of Thomas Jefferson*. *Southern Biography Ser.* La. State U. Pr. 1987 $24.95. ISBN 0-8071-1375-1. Excellent one-volume biography.

Doerflinger, Thomas M. *A Vigorous Spirit of Enterprise: Merchants and Economic Developments in Revolutionary Philadelphia*. U. of NC Pr. 1986 $39.95. ISBN 0-8078-1653-1. Bancroft Prize–winning study of the critical role of the mercantile class in the revolutionary era.

Foner, Eric. *Tom Paine and the American Revolution*. OUP 1976 $13.95. ISBN 0-19-502182-7. Fine study of the master propagandist of the Revolution.

Fowler, William M., Jr., and Wallace Coyle, eds. *The American Revolution: Changing Perspectives*. NE U. Pr. 1979 o.p. Noteworthy essays that explore such lesser-known groups in the era as Native Americans and African Americans.

Frey, Sylvia. *Water from the Rock: Black Resistance in a Revolutionary Age*. Princeton U. Pr. 1991 $35.00. ISBN 0-691-04784-7. Excellent study of African American reaction to the movement for independence.

Gelb, Norman. *Less Than Glory*. Putnam Pub. Group 1984 o.p. A popular history emphasizing the lesser-known, sometimes seamy aspects of the American Revolution.

Greene, Jack P., comp. *The American Revolution: Its Character and Limits*. 1959. Greenwood 1979 repr. of 1968 ed. $65.00. ISBN 0-313-20930-8. Collection of noteworthy essays, with comments, on the aims, successes, and unresolved problems of the era.

Hawke, David F. *Everyday Life in Early America*. *Everyday Life in Amer. Ser.* 1988. HarpC 1989 $11.00. ISBN 0-06-091251-0. Interesting, readable social history.

Hibbert, Christopher. *Redcoats and Rebels: The American Revolution Through British Eyes*. Norton 1990 $29.95. ISBN 0-393-02895-X. Interesting and readable military history of the Revolution from the British perspective.

Hoadley, John F. *Origins of American Political Parties, 1789–1803*. U. Pr. of Ky. 1986 $24.00. ISBN 0-8131-1562-0. Solid overview of the development of parties.

Hoffman, Ronald, and Peter J. Albert. *Arms and Independence: The Military Character of the American Revolution*. Bks. Demand repr. of 1984 ed. $63.80. ISBN 0-8357-5744-7. Analytical study of the military events of the Revolution in relation to society and concepts of warfare.

Hyneman, Charles S., and Donald S. Lutz. *American Political Writing during the Founding Era, 1760–1805*. 2 vols. Liberty Pr. 1983 $50.00. ISBN 0-86597-038-6. Good collection of political writings with noteworthy introductions.

Isaac, Rhys. *The Transformation of Virginia, 1740–1790*. Norton 1988 $12.95. ISBN 0-8078-1489-X. Superb study of social life and customs in colonial Virginia. Winner of 1983 Pulitzer Prize in history.

Kammen, Michael. *A Machine That Would Go of Itself: The Constitution in American Culture*. Knopf 1986 o.p. "A comprehensive cultural history of the Constitution that shows how it has become revered by the American public" (Tindall and Shi, *America: A Narrative History*).

————. *Sovereignty and Liberty. History of Amer. Thought and Culture Ser.* U. of Wis. Pr. 1988 $25.00. ISBN 0-299-11730-8. Discourses on the Constitution and American culture.

Lavender, David. *The Way to the Western Sea: Lewis and Clark Across the Continent.* HarpC 1988 $22.95. ISBN 0-06-015982-0. Detailed and readable account of the explorations.

Lewis, Jan. *The Pursuit of Happiness: Family and Values in Jefferson's Virginia.* 1983. Cambridge U. Pr. 1985 $42.95. ISBN 0-521-25306-3. Interesting account of the role the Virginia gentry played in public life, including politics, commerce, and religion, between 1750 and 1830.

McDonald, Forrest. *Alexander Hamilton: A Biography.* Norton 1982 $11.75. ISBN 0-393-30048-X. Excellent, readable examination of the man and his times.

————. *Novus Ordo Seclorum: The Intellectual Origins of the Constitution.* U. Pr. of KS 1985 $29.95. ISBN 0-7006-0284-4. Solidly researched and thoughtful treatise on the Constitution.

Maier, Pauline. *The Old Revolutionaries: Political Lives in the Age of Samuel Adams.* Norton 1990 $10.95. ISBN 0-393-30663-1. Perceptive study of the evolution of revolutionary thought.

Martin, James Kirby. *In the Course of Human Events: An Interpretive Exploration of the American Revolution.* Harlan Davidson 1979 $14.95. ISBN 0-88295-794-5. Good summary of recent research and writing on the revolutionary era.

Middlekauff, Robert. *The Glorious Cause: The American Revolution, 1763–1789.* OUP 1985 $39.95. ISBN 0-19-502921-6. Superb narrative history of the revolutionary era and its momentous events.

Miller, John C. *The Federalist Era, 1789–1800. Amer. Nation Ser.* HarpC 1963 $11.00. ISBN 0-06-133027-2. A balanced, authoritative treatment.

Morgan, Edmund S. *The Birth of the Republic, 1763–1789.* U. Ch. Pr. rev. ed. 1992 $25.00. ISBN 0-226-53756-0. Excellent introduction to the era of the American Revolution.

————. *The Genius of George Washington.* Norton 1982 $6.95. ISBN 0-303-00060-5. Good study of the American leader.

————. *Inventing the People: The Rise of Popular Sovereignty in Europe and America.* Norton 1989 $9.95. ISBN 0-393-30623-2. A nontraditional view of Whig history.

Morris, Richard B. *The Forging of the Union, 1781–1789. New Amer. Nation Ser.* HarpC 1988 $8.95. ISBN 0-06-091424-6. Excellent overview of the Confederation period.

————. *The Peacemakers: The Great Powers and American Independence.* NE U. Pr. 1983 repr. of 1965 ed. $37.50. ISBN 0-930350-35-9. Notable account of the negotiations and deliberations that produced the Treaty of Paris, ending the war. Winner of the 1965 Bancroft Prize.

————. *Witnesses at the Creation: Hamilton, Madison, Jay, and the Constitution.* NAL-Dutton 1989 $4.00. ISBN 0-451-62686-9. Discusses the role of the three men in the formulation of the Constitution.

Nash, Gary B. *The Urban Crucible: Social Change, Political Consciousness, and the Origins of the American Revolution.* HUP rev. ed. 1986 $38.00. ISBN 0-674-93058-4. Excellent study of mercantile and urban influences on the course of the Revolution.

Norton, Mary Beth. *The British-Americans: The Loyalist Exiles in England, 1774–1789.* Little 1972 o.p. Examination of the fate of loyalist Americans who remained in England.

Quarles, Benjamin. *The Negro in the American Revolution.* Norton 1973 $8.95. ISBN 0-393-00674-3. Thoroughly documented account of the African American contribution. Includes an excellent guide to sources.

Robinson, Donald L. *Slavery in the Structure of American Politics, 1765–1820.* Norton 1979 o.p. Includes discussion of the near-fatal flaw in the Constitution—its implicit sanction of slavery.

Rutland, Robert A. *James Madison and the Search for Nationhood.* Lib. Congress 1981 $18.00. ISBN 0-8444-0363-6. Excellent introduction to the leaders and culture of the Jeffersonian era. Incorporates letters, paintings, and illustrations.

Schaffer, Arthur. *To Be an American: David Ramsay and the Making of American Consciousness.* U. of SC Pr. 1991 $39.95. ISBN 0-87249-718-6. Useful insights into the process of Americanization in the revolutionary era.

Schlesinger, Arthur M. *The Birth of the Nation: A Portrait of the American People on the Eve of Independence.* HM 1981 $11.70. ISBN 0-395-31675-8. Summary and discussion of the traits and characteristics that helped shape American history. Introduction by Arthur M. Schlesinger, Jr.

Shy, John W. *A People Numerous and Armed: Reflections on the Military Struggle for American Independence.* U. of Mich. Pr. rev. ed. 1990 $14.95. ISBN 0-472-06431-2. Excellent social and military history.

Smith, Page. *A New Age Now Begins: A People's History of the American Revolution.* 2 vols. Viking Penguin 1984 $31.90. ISBN 0-14-095354-X. Good overview of the founding of the nation.

Stites, Frances N. *John Marshall: Defender of the Constitution.* Ed. by Oscar Handlin. *Lib. of Amer. Biography.* 1981. Scott F. 1987 $13.00. ISBN 0-673-39353-4. For the general reader, an excellent introduction to the great Chief Justice of the Supreme Court.

Stuart, Reginald C. *War and American Thought: From the Revolution to the Monroe Doctrine.* Bks. Demand repr. of 1982 ed. $70.80. ISBN 0-7837-0314-7. Explores the early debate about the proper role of diplomacy and military force in a democracy.

Tuchman, Barbara W. *The First Salute: A View of the American Revolution.* Ballantine 1988 $11.95. ISBN 0-345-33667-4. Splendid narrative of conditions leading to the triumph of the revolutionary cause.

Ward, Christopher. *The War of the Revolution.* 2 vols. Macmillan 1952 o.p. Excellent military history, noteworthy for its detail and clear maps.

Wills, Gary. *Cincinnatus: George Washington and the Enlightenment.* Doubleday 1984 o.p. Perceptive and stimulating biography focusing on the image of Washington as citizen-soldier-hero.

———. *Inventing America: Jefferson's Declaration of Independence.* Random 1979 $5.95. ISBN 0-394-72735-5. One of the best and most thorough analyses of the Declaration ever written.

Wood, Gordon S. *The Creation of the American Republic, 1776–1787.* U. of NC Pr. 1969 $45.00. ISBN 0-8078-1104-1. "One of the half dozen most important books ever written about the American Revolution" (*N.Y. Times*). Winner of the 1970 Bancroft Prize.

———. *The Radicalism of the American Revolution.* Random 1992 $15.00. ISBN 0-679-40493-7. A subtle and brilliant interpretation, arguing that the Revolution was the most radical and far-reaching event in American history. Winner of the 1993 Pulitzer Prize for history.

Young, Alfred F., ed. *The American Revolution: Explorations in the History of American Radicalism.* N. Ill. U. Pr. 1976 $12.00. ISBN 0-87580-519-1. Social aspects and effects of the Revolution.

MIDDLE PERIOD, 1815–1850

Recent historical studies of the "middle period" share the general trend toward opening up a broader understanding of the diversity of the American experience. Although slavery has been a major concern of historians for the past quarter of a century, new studies of the subject have put enslaved African Americans into better perspective by relating them to free blacks and Native Americans. Studies such as Charles Joyner's *Down by the Riverside* (1984) convey a poignant sense of the actual everyday lives of enslaved persons, while Catherine Clinton and others bring understanding to the role of women in the cataclysmic events of the midcentury. Among the most significant trends in recent historiography is a new perception of the effects of the settlement of the

West, not only on national development, but also on Native Americans and on the land itself.

Bartlett, Irving H. *Daniel Webster.* Norton 1981 $8.95. ISBN 0-393-00996-3. Solidly researched and gracefully written biography, emphasizing Webster's role as national politician.

Bauer, K. Jack. *The Mexican War, 1846–1848.* U. of Nebr. Pr. 1993 $16.95. ISBN 0-8032-6107-1. Evenhanded history of the conflict.

Berlin, Ira. *Slaves Without Masters: The Free Negro in the Antebellum South.* OUP 1992 $10.95. ISBN 0-19-502905-4. Thorough analysis of the status, ideas, and life of free blacks in the antebellum South.

Blassingame, John W. *The Slave Community: Plantation Life in the Antebellum South.* OUP rev. ed. 1979 $13.95. ISBN 0-19-502563-6. Important study of acculturation and accommodation in plantation life, based heavily on memoirs of former enslaved persons.

Bleser, Carol K. R. *The Hammonds of Redcliffe.* OUP 1987 $29.95. ISBN 0-19-502920-8. Revealing look into the lives and minds of a slaveholding family.

Clinton, Catherine. *The Plantation Mistress: Woman's World in the Old South.* Pantheon 1984 $11.95. ISBN 0-394-72253-1. Excellent study of plantation life from the female perspective.

Cochran, Thomas C. *Frontiers of Change: Early Industrialism in America.* OUP 1981 $12.95. ISBN 0-19-503284-5. How industrialization shaped American society in the years from the American Revolution to the Civil War.

Coit, Margaret L. *John C. Calhoun: American Portrait. Southern Classics Ser.* U. of SC Pr. 1991 $49.95. ISBN 0-87249-774-7. Pulitzer Prize–winning biography of 1950 with new introduction by Clyde N. Wilson.

Cross, Whitney R. *The Burned-Over District.* Hippocrene Bks. 1981 $31.50. ISBN 0-374-91932-1. The extraordinary story of revivalist religion in antebellum America.

Curry, Leonard P. *The Free Black in Urban America, 1800–1850: The Shadow of a Dream.* U. Ch. Pr. 1986 $27.50. ISBN 0-226-13125-4. Plight of free blacks struggling against poverty and abuse.

Davidson, Basil. *Black Mother: The African Slave Trade.* Little rev. ed. 1981 o.p. Important study of the African beginnings of the slave trade.

Davis, David Brion. *The Problem of Slavery in the Age of Revolution, 1770–1823.* Cornell Univ. Pr. 1975 $15.95. ISBN 0-8014-9156-8. Profound study of the rise and development of antislavery thought. Winner of the National Book Award, the Bancroft Prize, and the Beveridge Award.

De Voto, Bernard. *Across the Wide Missouri. Amer. Heritage Lib. Ser.* AMS Pr. 1988 repr. of 1947 ed. $94.50. ISBN 0-404-20079-6. Second book of a trilogy that offers a vigorous account of the lands and peoples of the West. Winner of the 1948 Pulitzer Prize.

Eaton, Clement. *The Growth of Southern Civilization, 1790–1860.* HarpC 1961 o.p. Thorough, readable study of the antebellum South useful as background for understanding contemporary and subsequent conditions and problems in the region.

Elkins, Stanley M. *Slavery: A Problem in American Institutional and Intellectual Life.* U. Ch. Pr. 1976 $13.95. ISBN 0-226-20477-4. Provocative exploration of the psychological aspects of American slavery.

Faragher, John M. *Sugar Creek: Life on the Illinois Prairie.* Yale U. Pr. 1986 $32.00. ISBN 0-300-03545-4. Readable and evocative account.

Faust, Drew Gilpin. *A Sacred Circle: The Dilemma of the Intellectual in the Old South, 1840–1860.* U. of Pa. Pr. 1986 $17.95. ISBN 0-8122-1229-0. Important study of an increasingly beleaguered society.

Feldberg, Michael. *The Turbulent Era: Riot and Disorder in Jacksonian America.* OUP 1980 $9.95. ISBN 0-19-502678-0. Skillful examination of the history and reasons for the prevalence of urban violence.

Ford, Lacy K. *Origins of Southern Radicalism: The South Carolina Upcountry, 1800–1860*. OUP 1991 $14.95. ISBN 0-19-506961-7. Superb study of the interaction of economic, political, and social factors.

Formisano, Ronald P. *The Transformation of Political Culture: Massachusetts Parties, 1790s–1840s*. OUP 1983 $35.00. ISBN 0-10-503124-5. Important work for understanding early parties throughout the young republic.

Fox-Genovese, Elizabeth. *Within the Plantation Household: Black and White Women in the Old South. Gender and Amer. Culture Ser*. U. of NC Pr. 1988 $37.50. ISBN 0-8078-1808-9. Superb treatment of a fascinating human relationship in the antebellum South.

Freehling, Alison G. *Drift Toward Dissolution: The Virginia Slavery Debate of 1831–1832*. La. State U. Pr. 1982 $40.00. ISBN 0-8071-1035-3. Shows the broad geographical, class, and demographic implications of the critical debate.

Freehling, William W. *Prelude to Civil War: The Nullification Controversy in South Carolina, 1816–1836*. OUP 1992 $12.95. ISBN 0-19-507681-8. Masterly analysis of slavery's profound influence in southern politics. Bancroft Prize winner.

Friedman, Lawrence J. *Gregarious Saints: Self and Community in American Abolitionism, 1830–1870*. Cambridge U. Pr. 1982 o.p. Socio-psychological history of abolitionism, focusing on emotional and personal motives of the movement's leaders.

Fry, Gladys-Marie. *Night Riders in Black Folk History*. U. of Ga. Pr. 1991 $14.95. ISBN 0-8203-1338-6. Important examination of techniques used to keep enslaved persons "in their place" and maintain social order.

Genovese, Eugene D. *Roll, Jordan, Roll: The World the Slaves Made*. Random 1976 $16.95. ISBN 0-394-71652-3. Bancroft Prize winner. Study of enslaved persons and their masters in the South.

———. *The World the Slaveholders Made: Two Essays in Interpretation*. Random 1976 $16.95. ISBN 0-394-71652-3. Compares slavery in the Americas and analyzes and interprets George Fitzhugh's proslavery argument.

Goetzmann, William H. *Exploration and Empire: The Explorer and the Scientist in the Winning of the American West*. Norton 1978 $16.95. ISBN 0-393-00881-9. Important reminder of the deliberate nature of westward expansion. Winner of 1967 Pulitzer Prize.

Hawke, David F. *Nuts and Bolts of the Past: A History of American Technology, 1776–1860*. HarpC 1988 o.p. Good overview of a critical aspect of early American industrial development.

Hofstadter, Richard. *Anti-Intellectualism in American Life*. Random 1966 $14.95. ISBN 0-394-70317-0. Delves into American intellectual fears and self-doubt. Winner of the 1964 Pulitzer Prize for general nonfiction.

Jackson, Donald Gale. *Gold Dust*. Knopf 1980 $17.95. ISBN 0-394-40046-1. Detailed and comprehensive popular account of the California gold rush.

Johannsen, Robert W. *To the Halls of Montezuma: The Mexican War in the American Imagination*. OUP 1988 $13.95. ISBN 0-19-504981-0. Illuminating treatment of a controversial war.

Joyner, Charles. *Down by the Riverside: A South Carolina Slave Community. Blacks in the New World Ser*. U. of Ill. Pr. 1984 $29.95. ISBN 0-252-01058-2. Evocative and delightfully readable study of slave life in the Waccamaw Neck area of South Carolina.

Kolchin, Peter. *American Slavery, 1619–1877*. Hill & Wang 1993 $9.95. ISBN 8090-1555-4. Good brief survey.

Kushma, John J., and Stephen E. Maizlish, eds. *Essays on American Antebellum Politics, 1840–1860*. Tex. A & M Univ. Pr. 1982 $19.50. ISBN 0-89096-136-0. Essays using new methodologies to explore the nature of politics.

Lerner, Gerda. *The Grimké Sisters from South Carolina: Rebels Against Slavery. Studies in the Life of Women Ser*. Schocken 1967 $11.96. ISBN 0-8052-0321-4. Superb study of a southern abolitionist family.

Litwack, Leon F. *North of Slavery: The Negro in the Free States, 1790–1860.* 1961. U. Ch. Pr. 1965 $11.95. ISBN 0-226-48586-2. Revealing account of African American life in the antebellum North.

McCoy, Drew. *The Last of the Fathers: James Madison and the Republican Legacy.* Cambridge U. Pr. 1989 $34.95. ISBN 0-521-36407-8. Fine study of Madison's thought and influence.

Merk, Frederick, and Lois B. Merk. *Manifest Destiny and Mission in American History: A Reinterpretation.* Greenwood 1983 $41.50. ISBN 0-313-23844-8. A classic treatment, essential to an understanding of westward expansion and the Mexican War.

Oakes, James. *The Ruling Race: A History of American Slaveholders.* Vin. 1983 $10.36. ISBN 0-394-71639-6. Important study contending that most slaveholders were more democratic than authoritarian.

Oates, Stephen B. *The Fires of Jubilee: Nat Turner's Fierce Rebellion.* NAL-Dutton 1983 $3.95. ISBN 0-451-623308-8. Very readable study of a critical event in the history of slavery and the South.

Pease, William H., and Jane H. Pease. *The Web of Progress: Private Values and Public Styles in Boston and Charleston, 1828–1843.* U. of Ga. Pr. 1991 $18.00. ISBN 0-8203-1390-4. Two cities as focal points of emerging sectionalism.

Perry, Lewis, and Michael Fellman, eds. *Antislavery Reconsidered: New Perspectives on the Abolitionists.* La. State U. Pr. 1979 $10.95. ISBN 0-8071-0889-8. Essays discussing recent investigations of abolitionism and its effects.

Peterson, Merrill. *The Great Triumvirate: Webster, Clay, and Calhoun.* OUP 1987 $35.00. ISBN 0-19-503877-0. First-rate study of antebellum statecraft.

Remini, Robert V. *Andrew Jackson.* HarBraceJ 1969 $6.00. ISBN 0-06-080132-8. Excellent introduction to Jackson, which may lead the reader to Remini's monumental three-volume biography: *Andrew Jackson and the Course of American Empire, 1767–1821* (1977), *Andrew Jackson and the Course of American Freedom, 1822–1832* (1981), and *Andrew Jackson and the Course of American Democracy, 1833–1845* (1984).

Rogin, Michael P. *Fathers and Children: Andrew Jackson and the Subjugation of the American Indian.* Transaction Pubs. 1991 $19.95. ISBN 0-88738-886-8. Thought-provoking psychological interpretation of Jackson's policy toward Native Americans.

Sellers, Charles G. *The Market Revolution: Jacksonian America, 1815–1846.* OUP 1991 $35.00. ISBN 0-19-503889-4. Important socioeconomic study.

Slotkin, Richard. *Regeneration through Violence: The Mythology of the American Frontier, 1600–1860.* U. Pr. of New Eng. 1973 $22.95. ISBN 0-8195-6034-0. A significant perspective on westward expansion.

Smith, Page. *The Nation Comes of Age: A People's History of the Ante-Bellum Years.* Viking Penguin 1990 $16.95. ISBN 0-14-012260-5. Focuses on the economic system, rise of the arts, and other new forces that shaped modern America in the pre–Civil War years.

Stampp, Kenneth M. *The Peculiar Institution: Negro Slavery in the Ante-Bellum South.* Vin. 1989 $10.00. ISBN 0-679-72307-2. Important discussion of slavery in America.

Stansell, Christine. *City of Women: Sex and Class in New York City, 1789–1860.* Knopf 1986 $30.00. ISBN 0-394-51534-X. Penetrating analysis of women in New York City during the Jacksonian era.

Stanton, William B. *The Leopard's Spots: Scientific Attitudes toward Race in America, 1815–1859.* U. Ch. Pr. 1982 $16.95. ISBN 0-226-77124-5. Fascinating study of scientific and pseudo-scientific obsessions with race.

Starobin, Robert, ed. *Blacks in Bondage: Letters of American Slaves.* 1974. Wiener Pub. Inc. 1988 $9.95. ISBN 0-910129-87-8. Writings in which enslaved persons reveal their innermost feelings about their condition.

Stegner, Wallace E. *The Gathering of Zion: The Story of the Mormon Trail.* U. of Nebr. Pr. 1992. ISBN 0-8032-9213-9. A unique aspect of westward expansion, related by a master storyteller.

Unruh, John D., Jr. *The Plains Across: The Overland Emigrants and the Trans-Mississippi West, 1840–1860.* U. of Ill. Pr. 1982 $14.95. ISBN 0-252-00968-1. Comprehensive descriptive study of the westward movement.

Wallace, Anthony F. C. *The Long, Bitter Trail: Andrew Jackson and the Indians.* Hill & Wang 1993 $7.95. ISBN 0-8090-1552-8. The Trail of Tears set in revealing historical context.

Walters, Ronald G. *American Reformers, 1815–1860.* Amer. Century Ser. Hill & Wang 1978 $10.00. ISBN 0-8090-0130-6. Excellent introduction to such early movements as pacifism, utopianism, and temperance.

Watson, Harry L. *Liberty and Power: The Politics of Jacksonian America.* Hill & Wang 1990 $25.00. ISBN 0-8090-6546-0. Important study of Jacksonian democracy.

Wiebe, Robert. *The Opening of American Society: From the Adoption of the Constitution to the Eve of Disunion.* Knopf 1984 o.p. Excellent account of democratization in Jacksonian America.

Wyatt-Brown, Bertram. *Southern Honor: Ethics and Behavior in the Old South.* OUP 1982 $35.00. ISBN 0-19-503310-8. Original and wide-ranging study of culture and society in the Old South.

SECTIONAL CONFLICT, 1850–1877

Events in and around the Civil War continue to dominate the interest of historians. JAMES M. MCPHERSON's superb histories of the sectional conflict and war and Eric Foner's fresh study of Reconstruction bring together much of the recent research on the conflict and its aftermath, while books such as Leon Litwack's *Been in the Storm So Long: The Aftermath of Slavery* (1979) and the extraordinary documentary history *Freedom* shed light on special aspects. The role of women in American life in general, and in the war years in particular, also draws the attention of able historians.

Beringer, Richard, and Herman Hattaway. *Why the South Lost the Civil War.* U. of Ga. Pr. 1991 $19.95. ISBN 0-8203-1396-3

Berlin, Ira, and others, eds. *Freedom: A Documentary History of Emancipation, 1861–1867.* Cambridge U. Pr. 1983–92. Vol. 1 1986 $59.95. ISBN 0-521-22979-0. Vol. 2 1983 $59.95. ISBN 0-521-22984-7. Vol. 3 1991 $54.95. ISBN 0-521-39493-7. Vol. 4 1992. ISBN 0-521-41742-2. Monumental ongoing documentary series based on the Freedom and Southern Society Project (Freedmen's Bureau Papers) at the University of Maryland.

——. *Slaves No More: Three Essays on Emancipation and the Civil War.* Cambridge U. Pr. 1992 $44.95. ISBN 0-521-43102-6. Important essays by members of the Freedom and Southern Society Project.

Bernstein, Iver. *The New York City Draft Riots: Their Significance for American Society and Politics in the Age of the Civil War.* OUP 1989 $35.00. ISBN 0-19-505006-1. Study of the draft riots that became vicious race riots and of their consequences.

Bleser, Carol K. R., ed. *Secret and Sacred: The Diaries of James Henry Hammond, a Southern Slaveholder.* OUP 1988 $29.95. ISBN 0-19-505308-7. An extraordinary record, skillfully edited and annotated. Fascinating reading.

Bogue, Allan G. *The Earnest Men: Republicans of the Civil War Senate.* Cornell Univ. Pr. 1981 $49.95. ISBN 0-8014-1357-5. Analysis of Radical Republicanism, depicting the differences and distinctiveness of leading legislators.

Bremner, Robert H. *The Public Good: Philanthropy and Welfare in the Civil War Era.* Knopf 1980 o.p. Documents the shifts in philanthropic and reform movements from the notion of prevention to melioration.

Brown, Richard D. *Modernization: The Transformation of American Life, 1600–1865.* Amer. Century Ser. Waveland Pr. 1988 repr. of 1976 ed. $9.95. ISBN 0-88133-362-X. The socioeconomic forces many historians believe underlay the sectional conflict.

Carter, Dan T. *When the War Was Over: The Failure of Self-Reconstruction in the South, 1865–1867*. La. State U. Pr. 1985 $9.95. ISBN 0-8071-1204-6. Excellent history of the first two critical years of Reconstruction.

Catton, Bruce. *Centennial History of the Civil War*. 1961–1965. 3 vols. o.p. Engrossing, readable account of the forces that led to war, the conduct of the war, and the events that resulted from it.

Channing, Steven A. *Crisis of Fear: Secession in South Carolina*. Norton 1974 $9.95. ISBN 0-393-00730-0. Study of the movement toward secession driven by fear of emancipation.

Chesnut, Mary Boykin Miller. *Mary Chesnut's Civil War*. Ed. by C. Vann Woodward. Yale U. Pr. 1981 $45.00. ISBN 0-300-02459-2. Civil War diaries of the wife of a Confederate cabinet member. Winner of 1982 Pulitzer Prize for biography.

Clinton, Catherine, and Nina Silber. *Divided Houses: Gender and the Civil War*. OUP 1992 $29.95. ISBN 0-19-507407-6. Instructive study of a neglected aspect of Civil War history.

Commager, Henry Steele, ed. *The Blue and the Gray: The Story of the Civil War as Told by Participants*. 1950. 2 vols. NAL-Dutton 1973. Vol. 1 $5.99. ISBN 0-451-62778-4. Vol. 2 $5.90. ISBN 0-451-62640-0. Superb collection of firsthand accounts and observations.

Cooper, William J., Jr. *Liberty and Slavery: Southern Politics to 1860*. Knopf 1983 $17.95. ISBN 0-394-53289-9. Informed study of the unique course of southern politics.

Cox, LaWanda. *Lincoln and Black Freedom: A Study in Presidential Leadership*. Blacks in the New World Ser. 1981. U. of Ill. Pr. 1985 $10.95. ISBN 0-252-01173-2. Stimulating inquiry into Lincoln's options and obstacles in confronting emancipation.

Craven, Avery O. *The Coming of the Civil War*. U. Ch. Pr. 1966 $14.50. ISBN 0-226-11894-0. An older interpretation that is still useful.

Current, Richard N. *The Lincoln Nobody Knows*. 1958. *Amer. Century Ser*. Hill & Wang 1964 $9.95. ISBN 0-8090-0059-8. Skillful and sensitive treatment of Lincoln and his views.

Delbanco, Andrew, ed. *The Portable Abraham Lincoln*. Viking Penguin 1993 $25.00. ISBN 0-670-84088-2. Useful popular compendium.

Donald, David. *Charles Sumner and the Coming of the Civil War*. U. Ch. Pr. 1961 o.p. Sophisticated and persuasive psychobiography. Awarded the Pulitzer Prize in 1961.

Douglass, Frederick. *My Bondage and My Freedom*. *Amer. Biography Ser*. 1972 repr. of 1855 ed. $89.00. ISBN 0-7812-8111-3. "The classic fugitive slave narrative and one of the classics of American autobiography" (C. Vann Woodward, *Saturday Review*).

Drago, Edmund L. *Black Politicians and Reconstruction in Georgia*. U. of Ga. Pr. 1992 $17.95. ISBN 0-8203-1438-2. Present edition contains a new preface about recent research. Widely hailed.

DuBois, Ellen C. *Feminism and Suffrage: The Emergence of an Independent Women's Movement in America, 1848–1869*. Cornell Univ. Pr. 1978 $8.95. ISBN 0-8014-9182-7. Major study of the beginnings of an important element in the women's movement.

Du Bois, W. E. B. *Black Reconstruction, 1860–1880*. *Studies in Amer. Negro Life*. Macmillan 1972 $16.95. ISBN 0-689-70063-6. Pioneer revisionist history.

Durden, Robert F. *The Self-Inflicted Wound: Southern Politics in the Nineteenth Century*. U. Pr. of Ky. 1985 $16.00. ISBN 0-8131-0307-X. Critical and fair examination of a sometimes puzzling phenomenon.

Faust, Drew Gilpin. *The Creation of Confederate Nationalism: Ideology and Identity in the Civil War South*. 1988. La. State U. Pr. 1990 $6.96. ISBN 0-8071-1606-8. Excellent study of the Confederate problem of "national identity."

Fehrenbacher, Don E. *The Dred Scott Case: Its Significance in American Law and Politics*. OUP 1978 $45.00. ISBN 0-19-502403-6. New and fresh interpretation of the famous Supreme Court case that preceded the Civil War.

Foner, Eric. *Politics and Ideology in the Age of the Civil War*. OUP 1980 $8.95. ISBN 0-19-502926-7. Sophisticated examination of the political climate of opinion during the sectional crisis.

————. *Reconstruction: America's Unfinished Revolution, 1863–1877*. New Amer. Nation Ser. HarpC 1988 $29.95. ISBN 0-06-015851-4. Superb reinterpretation of the period, incorporating scholarship of the past half-century. Winner of the Bancroft Prize and the Parkman Award.

Foote, Shelby. *The Civil War: A Narrative*. 3 vols. in 1. Random 1986 $72.00. ISBN 0-394-74913-8. A "recapitulation of both sides of the Civil War which weaves together political issues, military strategy, and the personalities of contemporaries" (*Booklist*).

Frassanito, William A. *Gettysburg: A Journey in Time*. 1975. Scribner 1976 $17.95. ISBN 0-684-14696-7. Successful combination of history and photography, conveying a vivid sense of the battle and its victims.

Fredrickson, George. *The Inner Civil War: Northern Intellectuals and the Crisis of the Union*. 1965. HarpC 1968 o.p. Superb study of the "collective trauma" of northern intellectuals.

Freehling, William W. *The Road to Disunion Vol I: Secessionists at Bay, 1776–1854*. OUP 1990 $30.00. ISBN 0-19-505814-3. Exhaustive and original study of the South's constitutional and political journey along the road to secession.

Hagerman, Edward. *The American Civil War and the Origins of Modern Warfare: Ideas, Organization, and Field Command*. 1988. Midlands Bks. 1992 $37.50. ISBN 0-253-30546-2. The Civil War as the first modern war.

Hanchett, William. *The Lincoln Murder Conspiracies*. U. of Ill. Pr. 1983 $29.95. ISBN 0-252-01046-9. Fascinating examination of myths and realities.

Hattaway, Herman, and Archer Jones. *How the North Won: A Military History of the Civil War*. U. of Ill. Pr. 1983 $39.95. ISBN 0-252-00918-5. Good overview of the fighting.

Hess, Earl J. *Liberty, Virtue, and Progress: Northerners and Their War for Union*. NYU Pr. 1988 $35.00. ISBN 0-8147-3451-0. Good study of northern thought and emotions.

Kunhardt, Philip B., and others. *Lincoln, An Illustrated Biography*. Knopf 1992 $50.00. ISBN 0-679-40862-2. An extraordinary photographic study, featuring 900 illustrations.

Lankford, Nelson D., ed. *An Irishman in Dixie: Thomas Conolly's Diary of the Fall of the Confederacy*. U. of SC Pr. 1988 $24.95. ISBN 0-87249-555-8. Excellent firsthand commentary on events, places, and people.

Linderman, Gerald F. *Embattled Courage: The Experience of Combat in the American Civil War*. Free Pr. 1989 $24.95. ISBN 0-02-919760-0. Important narrative of battlefield experiences.

Litwack, Leon F. *Been in the Storm So Long: The Aftermath of Slavery*. 1979. Vin. 1980 $15.95. ISBN 0-394-74398-9. "As a comprehensive study of the coming of freedom, Litwack's book has no rival" (C. Vann Woodward, *N.Y. Review of Books*). Winner of the 1980 Pulitzer Prize and the American Book Award.

McFeely, William S. *Grant: A Biography*. 1981. Norton 1982 $14.95. ISBN 0-393-30046-3. A model biography. Awarded the Pulitzer Prize in 1982.

McGlynn, Frank, and Seymour Drescher, eds. *The Meaning of Freedom*. U. of Pittsburgh Pr. 1992 $44.95. ISBN 0-8229-3695-X. Eleven essays on the state of African Americans after emancipation. Very academic and scholarly in tone.

McPherson, James M. *Battle Cry of Freedom: The Civil War Era*. Ed. by C. Vann Woodward. *Oxford History of the United States*. OUP 1988 $39.95. ISBN 0-19-503863-0. Winner of the 1988 Pulitzer Prize. "This new volume . . . should become a standard general history of the Civil War period—it's one that will stand up for years to come" (*Kirkus Reviews*).

————. *The Negro's Civil War: How American Negroes Felt and Acted during the War for the Union*. 1982. Ballantine 1988 $10.00. ISBN 0-345-37120-8. Examination and analysis of African American sentiments and reactions.

————. *Ordeal by Fire: The Civil War and Reconstruction*. Knopf 1982 $29.95. ISBN 0-685-62839-9. Study of the social, economic, and political changes brought on by the war.

McWhiney, Grady, and Perry D. Jamieson. *Attack and Die: Civil War Military Tactics and the Southern Heritage.* U. of Ala. Pr. 1982 $12.50. ISBN 0-8173-0229-8. How battlefield tactics failed to keep up with technological innovations.

Massey, Mary Elizabeth. *Ersatz in the Confederacy: Shortages and Substitutes on the Southern Homefront. Southern Classics Ser.* U. of SC Pr. 1993 $14.95. ISBN 0-87249-877-8. Unique study of life in the South during the war enhanced by Barbara L. Bellows's appreciation of the author in her introduction.

Myers, Robert Manson, ed. *Children of Pride: A True Story of Georgia and the Civil War.* 1972. Yale U. Pr. 1987 $20.00. ISBN 0-300-04053-9. Extraordinary and expertly edited collection of letters of a large and prominent Georgia family. Winner of the National Book Award and Fletcher Pratt Award for 1972 as best nonfiction book on the Civil War.

Neely, Mark E., Jr. *The Fate of Liberty: Abraham Lincoln and Civil Liberties.* OUP 1992 $11.95. ISBN 0-19-508032-7. Winner of the 1992 Pulitzer Prize.

Nevins, Allan. *The Ordeal of the Union.* 1947–71. 4 vols. Macmillan 1992 $25.00 ea. ISBNs 0-02-035441-X, 0-02-035442-8, 0-02-035443-6, 0-02-035445-2. Classic narrative history.

Oates, Stephen B. *Abraham Lincoln: The Man Behind the Myth.* 1984. HarpC 1985 $10.00. ISBN 0-452-00939-1. Excellent one-volume biography that explodes many myths and misconceptions.

———. *To Purge This Land with Blood: A Biography of John Brown.* U. of Mass. Pr. 1984 $16.95. ISBN 0-87023-458-7. Brown's early years, when misfortunes and personal problems helped to shape his character and foreshadow his later actions.

Paludan, Philip S. *"A People's Contest": The Union at War, 1861–1865. New Amer. Nation Ser.* HarpC 1989 $9.95. ISBN 0-06-091607-9. Best treatment of the North at war.

———. *Victims: A True Story of the Civil War.* U. of Tenn. Pr. 1981 $19.95. ISBN 0-97049-316-7. Case study of Union soldiers massacred on suspicion of guerrilla activities. A human story of war atrocities.

Potter, David M. *The Impending Crisis, 1848–1861. New Amer. Nation Ser.* HarpC 1977 $13.00. ISBN 06-131929-5. Excellent overview of the sectional conflict.

———. *The South and the Sectional Conflict.* La. State U. Pr. 1968 $12.95. ISBN 0-8071-0201-6. Essays on the South plus a review of relevant historical literature.

Powell, Lawrence N. *New Masters: Northern Planters during the Civil War and Reconstruction.* Yale U. Pr. 1980 $35.00. ISBN 0-300-02217-4. Important study of northerners who settled in the South after the war.

Quarles, Benjamin. *The Negro in the Civil War. Quality Paperback Ser.* 1969. Da Capo 1989 $12.95. ISBN 0-669-06428-9. One of the first accounts of the "invisible soldiers" of the war.

Randall, James G., and David Donald. *The Civil War and Reconstruction.* Heath 2nd rev. ed. 1969 $21.00. ISBN 0-669-06428-9. Still useful, although largely superseded by McPherson.

Ransom, Roger L. *Conflict and Compromise: The Political Economy of Slavery, Emancipation, and the American Civil War.* Cambridge U. Pr. 1989 $44.95. ISBN 0-521-32343-6. Forceful reminder of the complex nature of the sectional crisis.

Roark, James L. *Masters without Slaves: Southern Planters in the Civil War and Reconstruction.* Norton 1978 $9.95. ISBN 0-393-00901-7. How former masters adjusted—or failed to adjust—to their new roles.

Roland, Charles P. *The Confederacy. History of Amer. Civilization Ser.* 1960. U. Ch. Pr. 1962 $11.95. ISBN 0-226-72451-4. Good account of the government and its trials.

Rose, Willie Lee. *Rehearsal for Reconstruction.* 1964. OUP 1976 $14.95. ISBN 0-19-519882-4. Parkman Award–winning account of the Port Royal experiment in South Carolina during the war.

Rosengarten, Theodore. *Tombee: Portrait of a Cotton Planter.* McGraw 1988 $12.95. ISBN 0-07-053821-2. Fine firsthand account of the postwar South.

Royster, Charles. *The Destructive War: William Tecumseh Sherman, Stonewall Jackson, and the Americans.* Knopf 1991 $29.00. ISBN 0-394-52485-3. Powerful recounting of the real nature of the war.

Sandburg, Carl. *Lincoln: The Prairie Years and the War Years*. HarBraceJ 1974 $19.95. ISBN 0-15-602611-2. Enduring and appealing study of Lincoln before and during his presidency.

Saum, Lewis O. *The Popular Mood of Pre–Civil War America. Contributions in Amer. Studies*. Greenwood 1980 $38.50. ISBN 0-313-21056-X. Good estimate of prewar public opinion, in which despair seems to prevail over optimism.

Smith, Page. *Trial by Fire: A People's History of the Civil War and Reconstruction*. 1982. Viking Penguin 1990 $20.00. ISBN 0-14-012261-3. Popular narrative history that conveys the drama of the era.

Stampp, Kenneth M. *America in 1857: A Nation on the Brink*. 1990. OUP 1992 $14.94. ISBN 0-19-503902-5. Probing study of the year during which the forces leading to the Civil War took shape.

_____. *And the War Came: The North and the Secession Crisis, 1860–61*. Greenwood 1980 repr. of 1950 ed. $35.00. ISBN 0-313-22566-4. Unemotional analysis of the crisis and the factors that contributed to it.

Stewart, James B. *Holy Warriors: The Abolitionists and American Slavery*. Hill & Wang 1976 $8.95. ISBN 0-8090-0123-3. Excellent account of antislavery sentiment and action in the prewar North.

Sutherland, David E. *The Expansion of Everyday Life, 1860–1876. Everyday Life in Amer. Ser.* HarpC 1990 $8.95. ISBN 0-06-091639-7. Good reading, especially about life during the Civil War years.

Thomas, Benjamin P. *Abraham Lincoln, A Biography*. 1952. Modern Lib. 1979 repr. of 1965 ed. $13.95. ISBN 0-394-60468-7. Superb one-volume portrait of the American leader.

Thomas, Emory N. *The Confederate Nation, 1861–1865. New Amer. Nation Ser.* HarpC 1981 $12.00. ISBN 0-06-131965-1. Comprehensive, clear, and well-documented account that explains the Confederacy in terms of southern nationalism.

_____. *Travels to Hallowed Ground: A Historian's Journey to the American Civil War*. U. of SC Pr. 1987 $22.95. ISBN 0-87249-477-2. Evocative personal commentary on the war and its legacies.

Ward, Geoffrey C., Ric Burns, and Ken Burns. *The Civil War: An Illustrated History*. Knopf 1990 $30.00. ISBN 0-394-56285-2. Excellent visual history that grew out of the Burns's very successful television series on the war.

Wiley, Bell I. *Confederate Women. Contributions in Amer. History Ser.* Greenwood 1975 $39.95. ISBN 0-8376-7534-8. Sensitive account of the role of women in the southern cause.

_____. *The Life of Billy Yank*. 1943. La. State U. Pr. 1971 $9.95. ISBN 0-8071-0476-0. Superb collection of personal observations on the war by Union soldiers, combined with exciting narrative based on extensive research.

_____. *The Life of Johnny Reb*. 1943. La. State U. Pr. 1971 $9.95. ISBN 0-8071-0475-2. Compelling collection of personal observations by those who fought on the Confederate side, accompanied by a very readable narrative.

Williams, T. Harry. *Lincoln and His Generals*. 1952. McGraw 1967 $6.95. ISBN 0-07-553705-2. Compelling study of Lincoln's wartime military leadership.

PRELUDE TO WORLD POWER, 1877–1920

Once a relatively neglected aspect of U.S. history, this period is undergoing extensive examination and reconsideration by historians. Based on new research and perceptions, an entire new history of the West is emerging, finding a place for women and African Americans and reassessing the cultures of Native Americans. In the best of this work, traditional interpretations are integrated with the new findings rather than arbitrarily discarded, and an exciting new synthesis is emerging. In social history, the American Social History Project— the legacy of the late Herbert G. Gutman—brings readers such rewarding studies as *Who Built America? Working People and the Nation's Economy, Politics, Culture, and Society* (1989). Historians of American foreign policy, meanwhile, look upon the late nineteenth century as an important period of preparation, in effect, for the explosion of activity that came with the presidencies of THEODORE ROOSEVELT and Woodrow Wilson.

Ayers, Edward L. *The Promise of the New South: Life After Reconstruction.* OUP 1992 $30.00. ISBN 0-19-503756-1. Impressive new assessment of the South in the late nineteenth century.

Berwanger, Eugene H. *The West and Reconstruction.* U. of Ill. Pr. 1981 $29.95. ISBN 0-252-00868-5. Role of the West in postbellum development, a generally neglected aspect of Reconstruction.

Bleser, Carol, ed. *In Joy and in Sorrow: Women, Family, and Marriage in the Victorian South, 1830–1900.* OUP 1992 $13.95. ISBN 0-19-506048-2. Revelations of a different "New South." Instructive and valuable.

Brown, Dee. *Bury My Heart at Wounded Knee: An Indian History of the American West.* 1971. H. Holt & Co. 1991 $27.95. ISBN 0-8050-1045-9. Readable and popular history that presents the Native American perspective of the settling of the "last frontier."

Clements, Kendrick A. *The Presidency of Woodrow Wilson.* Amer. Presidency Ser. U. Pr. of KS 1992 $29.95. ISBN 0-7006-0523-1. Thoughtful and persuasive brief study.

Coffman, Edward M. *The War to End All Wars: The American Military Experience in World War I.* 1968. U. of Wis. Pr. 1986 $12.50. ISBN 0-299-10964-X. The best treatment of American involvement in the fighting.

Cooper, John Milton, Jr. *The Warrior and the Priest.* HUP 1983 $12.95. ISBN 0-674-94751-7. Comparison of Theodore Roosevelt and Woodrow Wilson.

Cronon, William. *Nature's Metropolis: Chicago and the Great West.* Norton 1992 $15.95. ISBN 0-393-30873-1. Superb reassessment of westward expansion that focuses on the interplay between Chicago and its immense hinterland. Winner of the 1992 Bancroft Prize.

Cronon, William, and others, eds. *Under an Open Sky: Rethinking America's Western Past.* Norton 1992 $35.00. ISBN 0-393-02993-X. Essays delineating a "new history" of the American West.

Crunden, Robert M. *Ministers of Reform: The Progressives' Achievement in American Civilization, 1889–1920.* U. of Ill. Pr. 1986 $12.95. ISBN 0-252-01167-8. Major study of the Progressive movement and its achievements.

Dick, Everett. *The Sod-House Frontier, 1854–1890.* Bks. Demand repr. of 1989 ed. $160.00. ISBN 0-8357-6601-2. A nonromanticized view of life on the northern plains.

Foster, Gaines M. *Ghosts of the Confederacy: Defeat, the Lost Cause, and the Emergence of the New South, 1865–1913.* OUP 1988 $13.95. ISBN 0-19-505420-2. Good study of the interplay of myth and reality.

Garner, John S., ed. *The Company Town: Architecture and Society in the Early Industrial Age.* OUP 1992 $39.95. ISBN 0-10-5070027-5. Interesting study of good intentions too often gone awry.

Goodwyn, Lawrence. *Democratic Promise: The Populist Movement in America.* OUP 1976 $35.00. ISBN 0-19-501996-2. Highly favorable assessment of populism as a genuinely radical movement.

Gould, Lewis L. *The Presidency of Theodore Roosevelt.* Amer. Presidency Ser. U. Pr. of KS 1991 $29.95. ISBN 0-7006-0435-9. Thoughtful and persuasive brief study.

———. *Reform and Regulation: American Politics from Roosevelt to Wilson.* McGraw 1986 $13.16. ISBN 0-07-554946-8. Excellent overview of political developments in the early twentieth century.

Gutman, Herbert G. *Work, Culture, and Society in Industrializing America.* Vin. 1977 $7.96. ISBN 0-394-72251-8. Major new perspective on the relation of traditional values to the workplace in a changing society.

Hofstadter, Richard. *The Age of Reform: From Bryan to FDR.* Knopf 1955 $16.95. ISBN 0-394-41442-X. A social and political history focused on the progressive tradition. Winner of the 1956 Pulitzer Prize.

Jeffrey, Julie Roy. *Frontier Women: The Trans-Mississippi West, 1840–1880. Amer. Century Ser.* Hill & Wang 1979 $9.95. ISBN 0-8090-0141-1. Lively history of women in the westward migration. Written for general readers.

Jensen, Richard. *The Winning of the Midwest: Social and Political Conflict, 1888–1896.* U. Ch. Pr. 1971 o.p. Excellent study of electoral and cultural politics in the critical decade of the 1890s.

Karnow, Stanley. *In Our Image: America's Empire in the Philippines.* Ballantine 1990 $14.95. ISBN 0-345-32816-7. Winner of the Pulitzer Prize in 1990.

Kennedy, David M. *Over Here: The First World War and American Society.* OUP 1980 $12.95. ISBN 0-19-503209-8. Account of how the war changed the old order and shaped the new.

La Feber, Walter. *The New Empire: An Interpretation of American Expansion, 1860–1898.* 1963. Cornell Univ. Pr. 1967 $12.95. ISBN 0-8014-9048-0. Thoroughly documented and persuasively argued Beveridge Award-winning study.

Leckie, William H. *The Buffalo Soldiers: A Narrative of the Negro Cavalry in the West.* 1967. U. of Okla. Pr. 1975 $12.95. ISBN 0-8061-1244-1. An important story well related.

Limerick, Patricia. *The Legacy of Conquest: The Unbroken Past of the American West.* Norton 1988 $11.95. ISBN 0-393-30497-3. Major reinterpretation of western history. Engagingly written but lacking the "happy ending" of older studies.

Limerick, Patricia, and others, eds. *Trails: Toward a New Western History.* U. Pr. of KS 1991 $12.95. ISBN 0-7006-0501-0. Further elebration of a new perspective on the West.

Link, Arthur S. *Woodrow Wilson: Revolution, War, and Peace.* Harlan Davidson 1979. ISBN 0-88295-798-8. A sympathetic account of Wilson's positions in foreign affairs.

———, ed. *Woodrow Wilson and a Revolutionary World, 1913–1921.* U. of NC Pr. 1982 $29.95. ISBN 0-8078-1529-2. Includes useful essays on Wilson's role in international affairs.

Link, Arthur S., and Richard L. McCormick. *Progressivism. Amer. History Ser.* Harlan Davidson 1983 $6.95. ISBN 0-88295-814-3. Concise and readable overview of the Progressive era with a useful review of the literature on the subject.

McClymer, John F. *War and Welfare: Social Engineering in America, 1890–1925. Contributions in Amer. History.* Greenwood 1980 $42.95. ISBN 0-313-21129-9. Details the rise of social experts in the United States and evaluates their influence and impact on society.

McCullough, David. *The Path between the Seas: The Creation of the Panama Canal, 1870–1914.* S&S Trade 1978 $12.95. ISBN 0-671-24409-4. Lively, very readable history of the canal, with attention to its effects on diplomacy and domestic politics. National Book Award winner.

McMath, Robert. *American Populism: A Social History, 1877–1900.* Hill & Wang 1992 $8.95. ISBN 0-374-52264-2. A balanced view, well expressed.

McMillen, Neil R. *Dark Journey: Black Mississippians in the Age of Jim Crow.* U. of Ill. Pr. 1989 $14.95. ISBN 0-252-06156-X. Outstanding study of one Deep South state that sheds light on other parts of the South as well.

Murphy, Paul L. *World War I and the Origin of Civil Liberties in the United States. Essays in Amer. History.* Norton 1980 $9.95. ISBN 0-393-95012-3. Argues that the idea of civil liberties as a policy concern stems from domestic problems during the war.

Nash, George H. *The Life of Herbert Hoover: The Engineer, 1874–1914.* Norton 1983 $25.00. ISBN 0-393-01634-X. Fine study of Hoover's early life as an engineer and businessman.

Nelson, Wilson E. *The Roots of American Bureaucracy, 1830–1900.* HUP 1982 $8.00. ISBN 0-674-77945-2. Traces the growth and development of the U.S. bureaucracy, which it views as an outgrowth of a pluralist society.

O'Toole, G.J.A. *The Spanish War: An American Epic, 1898.* Norton 1986 $11.95. ISBN 0-393-30304-7. Lively and readable history of the "unnecessary war."

Pringle, Elizabeth Allston. *A Woman Rice Planter. Southern Classics Ser.* U. of SC Pr. 1992 repr. of 1913 ed. $16.95. ISBN 0-87249-826-3. Extraordinary insights into

Southern life after the Civil War. Enhanced by Charles Joyner's sensitive introduction.

Reps, John W. *The Forgotten Frontier: Urban Planning in the American West before 1890*. U. of Mo. Pr. 1982 $27.00. ISBN 0-8262-0351-5. An aspect of city planning that reveals how extensive the movement was in the United States.

Schaffer, Ronald. *America in the Great War: The Rise of the War Welfare State*. OUP 1991 $27.95. ISBN 0-19-504903-9. Important assessment of the far-reaching effects of modern war.

Schlereth, Thomas J. *Victorian America: Transformations in Everyday Life, 1876–1915*. *Everyday Life in Amer. Ser*. HarpC 1991 $30.00. ISBN 0-06-016218-X. Excellent overview of social change in the Gilded Age.

Smith, Henry Nash. *Virgin Land: The American West as Symbol and Myth*. HUP 1950 $9.95. ISBN 0-674-93955-7. Bancroft Prize–winning study of the cultural and intellectual significance of the West in American life.

Sproat, John G. *"The Best Men": Liberal Reformers in the Gilded Age*. 1968. U. Ch. Pr. 1982 o.p. "[R]equired reading for the Gilded Age . . . a fine addition to nineteenth-century historiography" (Willie Lee Rose, *Journal of Southern History*).

Teaford, Jon C. *The Unheralded Triumph: City Government in America, 1870–1900*. Johns Hopkins 1984 $16.95. ISBN 0-8018-3063-X. Important revisionist study that notes the successes of nineteenth-century cities in solving economic and social problems.

Trask, David F. *The War with Spain in 1898*. *Wars of the United States Ser*. Macmillan 1981 $39.95. ISBN 0-02-932950-7. Most complete and satisfactory study of the war.

Urofsky, Melvin I. *Louis D. Brandeis and the Progressive Tradition in America*. *Lib. of Amer. Biography*. 1980. Scott F. 1987 $13.00. ISBN 0-673-39354-2. Good introduction to the subject intended for the general reader.

Wagenknecht, Edward. *American Profile, 1900–1909*. U. of Mass. Pr. 1982 $35.00. ISBN 0-87023-350-5. Delightful overview of the decade, with chapters on art, music, books, popular entertainment, and personalities.

Wiebe, Robert H. *The Search for Order, 1877–1920*. Hill & Wang 1966 $10.95. ISBN 0-8090-0104-7. Thoughtful and readable overview of the period, emphasizing the struggle to rationalize change.

Williamson, Joel. *The Crucible of Race*. OUP 1984 $35.00. ISBN 0-19-503382-5. A major reinterpretation of race relations in the South after emancipation.

Woodward, C. Vann. *Origins of the New South, 1877–1913*. *History of the Amer. South Ser*. 1951. La. State U. Pr. rev. ed. 1971 $37.50. ISBN 0-8071-0009-9. Superb study of the South after Reconstruction.

———. *The Strange Career of Jim Crow*. OUP 3rd rev. ed. 1974 $8.95. ISBN 0-19-501805-2. Classic, valuable work on black-white relations in the United States.

DEPRESSION AND GLOBAL WAR, 1920–1945

Histories of the interwar years continue to illuminate the many social and cultural changes experienced by the United States and to probe and analyze the sweeping economic consequences of the Great Depression and the New Deal. With World War II now half a century into history, retrospectives and new studies of its causes, course, and consequences attract both historians and readers.

Agee, James, and Walker Evans. *Let Us Now Praise Famous Men*. 1960. HM 1989 $24.95. ISBN 0-395-48901-6. Superb written and photographic depiction of the Great Depression.

Ambrose, Stephen E. *Eisenhower: Soldier and President*. S&S Trade 1991 $16.00. ISBN 0-671-74758-4. Excellent biography. Based on the author's more detailed two-volume study.

Badger, Anthony J. *The New Deal: The Depression Years, 1933–1940*. Hill & Wang 1989 $19.95. ISBN 0-8090-7260-2. Good overview of the period and its moods.

Banks, Ann, ed. *First-Person America*. 1980. Norton 1991 $10.95. ISBN 0-393-30781-6. Enjoyable oral history derived from interviews conducted by the Federal Writers Project between 1938 and 1942.

Blum, John Morton. *V Was for Victory: Politics and American Culture during World War II*. HarBraceJ 1977 $10.95. ISBN 0-15-603628-3. Solid history of events on the homefront.

Brinkley, Alan. *Voices of Protest: Huey Long, Father Coughlin, and the Great Depression*. Vin. 1983 $12.00. ISBN 0-394-71628-0. National Book Award winner. "An important work of historical analysis . . . alive with details and quotations and eminently readable" (*Los Angeles Times Book Review*).

Brinkley, David. *Washington Goes to War*. Knopf 1988 $18.95. ISBN 0-394-51025-9. Veteran journalist's reflections on a provincial city's emergence as a world capital.

Buchanan, A. Russell, ed. *The United States and World War Two: Military and Diplomatic Documents. Documents History of the U.S. Ser.* U. of SC Pr. 1972 o.p.

Campbell, D'Ann. *Women at War with America: Private Lives in a Patriotic Era*. HUP 1984 $25.00. ISBN 0-674-95475-0. Study of women during World War II based on a number of interesting primary sources.

Clausen, John A. *American Lives: Looking Back at the Children of the Great Depression*. Free Pr. 1993 $22.95. ISBN 0-02-905535-0. In-depth profiles illustrating the author's theory that choices made in our youth are the ultimate determinant of the future.

Cole, Wayne S. *Roosevelt and the Isolationists, 1932–1945*. U. of Nebr. Pr. 1983 $37.50. ISBN 0-8032-1410-3. Centers on FDR's political struggle to develop a response to the world crisis.

Conklin, Paul. *The New Deal. The Amer. History Ser.* Harlan Davidson 1992. ISBN 0-88295-889-5. Excellent synthesis of the New Deal and its historiography. A good introduction to the subject.

Cook, Blanche Wiesen. *Eleanor Roosevelt: Volume One, 1884–1933*. Viking Penguin 1993 $27.50. ISBN 0-14-009460-1. Major study of one of the century's most significant women.

Costello, John. *The Pacific War*. Morrow 1982 $17.95. ISBN 0-688-01620-0. Overview of the war against Japan that sets the conflict in historical context.

Craven, Wesley F., and James L. Cate. *The Army Air Forces in World War II*. Ed. by James Gilbert. 7 vols. Ayer 1979 repr. of 1948 ed. $294.00. ISBN 0-405-12135-0

Daniel, Pete. *Standing at the Crossroads: Southern Life Since 1900*. Hill & Wang 1986 $14.95. ISBN 0-8090-8821-5. Perceptive commentary on social and cultural change in the South.

Daniels, Roger. *Prisoners without Trial: Japanese Americans in World War II. Critical Issues Ser.* Hill & Wang 1993 $7.95. ISBN 0-8090-1553-6. Concise, authoritative account of internment and its aftermath and effects.

Dower, John W. *War without Mercy: Race and Power in the Pacific War*. Pantheon 1987 $15.00. ISBN 0-394-75172-8. Powerful inquiry into the racial ideas on both sides in the war against Japan.

Eliot, Thomas H. *Recollections of the New Deal: When the People Mattered*. Ed. by John Kenneth Galbraith. NE U. Pr. 1992 $24.95. ISBN 1-55553-134-2. Absorbing firsthand accounts of people and events.

Fass, Paula S. *The Damned and the Beautiful: American Youth in the 1920's*. OUP 1977 $12.00. ISBN 0-19-502492-3. The lifestyle, political interests, and culture of college youth during a decade of change.

Feis, Herbert. *Road to Pearl Harbor: The Coming of the War between the United States and Japan*. Bks. Demand repr. of 1950 ed. $99.40. ISBN 0-7837-3874-9

Gaddis, John L. *The United States and the Origins of the Cold War, 1941–1947. Contemporary History Ser.* Col. U. Pr. 1972 $54.00. ISBN 0-231-03289-7. Balanced and authoritative Bancroft Prize–winning history.

Green, Harvey. *The Uncertainty of Everyday Life, 1915–1945. Everyday Life in Amer. Ser.* HarpC 1992 $28.00. ISBN 0-06-016396-1. Most recent volume in an excellent social history series.

Greenberg, Cheryl. *Or Does I Explode: Black Harlem in the Great Depression.* OUP 1991 $38.00. ISBN 0-19-505868-2. The decade after the Harlem Renaissance and the resulting conflictual crisis at all levels.

Gregory, Ross. *America 1941: A Nation at the Crossroads.* Free Pr. 1989 $27.00. ISBN 0-02-912801-3. Poignant retrospective of America on the eve of war.

Heinrichs, Waldo H. *Threshold of War: Franklin D. Roosevelt and American Entry into World War II.* OUP 1988 $30.00. ISBN 0-19-504424-X. Important evaluation of interplay between foreign policy and domestic politics.

Honey, Maureen. *Creating Rosie the Riveter: Class, Gender, and Propaganda during World War II.* U. of Mass. Pr. 1984 $27.50. ISBN 0-87023-443-9. Good study of the shifting image of women during the war and postwar years.

Kee, Robert. *1939: In the Shadow of War.* Little 1984 o.p. Colorful re-creation of a single year using newspaper reports, photographs, cartoons, and advertisements.

Klehr, Harvey. *The Heyday of American Communism: The Depression Decade.* Basic 1984 o.p. Authoritative history of the party and its influence in interwar years.

Larrabee, Eric. *Commander-in-Chief: Franklin D. Roosevelt, His Lieutenants and Their War.* Touchstone Bks. 1988 $16.95. ISBN 0-671-66382-8. Important history of relations between Washington and the battlefronts.

Leuchtenburg, William E. *Franklin D. Roosevelt and the New Deal, 1932–1940.* New Amer. Nation Ser. HarpC 1963 $10.00. ISBN 0-07-133025-6. Excellent synthesis by a historian well versed in the New Deal era. Winner of 1964 Bancroft Prize.

Louchheim, Katie, ed. *The Making of the New Deal: The Insiders Speak.* HUP 1983 $22.00. ISBN 0-674-54345-7. Enjoyable and revealing reminiscences of 24 New Dealers.

Lowitt, Richard. *The New Deal and the West.* Amer. West in the 20th-Century Ser. Ind. U. Pr. 1984 $34.95. ISBN 0-253-34005-5. Surveys the impact of the New Deal on the West, especially in developing and conserving natural resources.

McElvaine, Robert S., ed. *Down and Out in the Great Depression: Letters from the "Forgotten Man."* U. of NC Pr. 1983 $10.00. ISBN 0-8078-4099-8. Close look at how the Depression affected ordinary people.

Miller, Nathan. *F.D.R.: An Intimate History.* U. Pr. of Amer. 1991 $16.95. ISBN 0-8191-8061-0. "The definitive popular Roosevelt biography" (*Library*).

O'Neill, William. *A Democracy at War: America's Fight at Home and Abroad in World War II.* Free Pr. 1993 $24.95. ISBN 0-02-923678-9. Different perspective on the war, pointing out in reasoned terms the failures in mobilization, production, and diplomacy.

Perrett, Geoffrey. *Days of Sadness, Years of Triumph, 1939–1945.* 1973. U. of Wis. Pr. 1985 $14.95. ISBN 0-299-10394-3. Well-documented, perceptive examination of America at war, focusing on the homefront.

———. *There's a War to Be Won: The United States Army in World War II.* Random 1991 $29.50. ISBN 0-394-57831-7. Entertaining and informative military and social history.

Prange, Gordon W. *At Dawn We Slept: The Untold Story of Pearl Harbor.* 1981. Viking Penguin rev. ed. 1991 $35.00. ISBN 0-670-84074-2. A lively and authoritative account, rich in detail and anecdotes.

Prange, Gordon W., and others. *Miracle at Midway.* 1982. Viking Penguin 1983 $12.95. ISBN 0-14-006814-7. Brilliant account of the decisive engagement in the Pacific war.

Romasco, Albert U. *The Politics of Recovery: Roosevelt's New Deal.* OUP 1983 $24.95. ISBN 0-19-503248-9. Good combination of political and economic history.

Rosengarten, Theodore. *All God's Dangers: The Life of Nate Shaw.* 1974. Vin. 1989 $12.95. ISBN 0-679-72761-2. Beautifully edited, compelling, and revealing autobiography of an African American sharecropper in the South. Winner of the National Book Award.

Schlesinger, Arthur M., Jr. *The Age of Roosevelt.* 1957–60. 3 vols. HM o.p. Well-constructed history of the period from the twenties through the New Deal.

Sherwin, Martin J. *A World Destroyed: Hiroshima and the Origins of the Arms Race.* 1975. Vin. 1987 $13.00. ISBN 0-394-75204-X. Important history of the atom bomb, the decision to use it, and the consequences.

Spector, Ronald. *Eagle Against the Sun: The American War with Japan.* Macmillan Wars of the U.S. Ser. 1984. Vin. 1985 $13.00. ISBN 0-394-74101-3. Excellent one-volume history of the Pacific war that covers both sides in the conflict well.

Stock, Catherine M. *Main Street in Crisis.* U. of NC Pr. 1992 $37.50. ISBN 0-8078-2011-3. Study of the "Old Middle Class" and the emergence of the "New" middle class after the Great Depression.

Tateishi, J., ed. *And Justice for All: An Oral History of the Japanese-American Detention Camps.* Random 1984 $19.95. ISBN 0-394-52955-3. Moving oral history of a tragic domestic consequence of World War II.

Terkel, Studs. *"The Good War": An Oral History of World War Two.* Pantheon 1984 $19.95. ISBN 0-304-53103-5. Evocative and fascinating oral history that conveys the personal side of the war. Winner of the 1985 Pulitzer Prize for general nonfiction.

———. *Hard Times: An Oral History of the Great Depression.* 1970. Pantheon 1986 $12.00. ISBN 0-394-74691-0. Superb re-creation of a dramatic period in American history.

Toland, John. *Infamy: Pearl Harbor and Its Aftermath.* 1982. Berkley Pub. 1991 $5.95. ISBN 0-429-09040-X. A revisionist history that blames Roosevelt for not preventing the Japanese attack on Pearl Harbor.

Ware, Susan. *Beyond Suffrage: Women in the New Deal.* HUP 1981 $24.95. ISBN 0-674-06921-8. Explores the ambivalent role women played in the New Deal.

Weigley, Russell F. *Eisenhower's Lieutenants: The Campaign of France and Germany, 1944–1945.* Ind. U. Pr. 1981 $39.95. ISBN 0-253-13333-5. A study of military leadership that encompasses the entire military strategy in Western Europe.

Weiss, Nancy J. *Farewell to the Party of Lincoln: Black Politics in the Age of FDR.* Princeton U. Pr. 1983 $15.95. ISBN 0-691-10151-5. Penetrating study of a critical shift in political allegiances.

Wyman, David. *The Abandonment of the Jews: America and the Holocaust, 1941–1945.* Pantheon 1986 $16.00. ISBN 0-394-74077-7. Searing study of a failure of leadership and conscience. Massively documented.

Wynn, Neil. *The Afro-American and the Second World War.* 1976. Holmes & Meier 1979 $37.50. ISBN 0-8419-0232-1. Important account of African American participation in the military.

MODERN AMERICA, 1945–THE PRESENT

Histories of recent developments in the United States touch every aspect of politics, diplomacy, and life. The demise of the cold war brings retrospectives and evaluations of America's role in the world. Legacies of the civil rights movement, the progress of feminism, and the multiplication of urban and ecological problems all command the attention of historians and readers.

Abernethy, Glenn, and others. *The Carter Years: The President and Policy Making.* St. Martin 1984 o.p. Essays on the major themes, accomplishments, and failings of the Carter presidency.

Berman, Larry. *Planning a Tragedy: The Americanization of the War in Vietnam.* Norton 1983 $8.95. ISBN 0-393-95326-2. Focuses on failures of intelligence and flawed planning.

Bernard, Richard M., and Bradley R. Rice. *Sunbelt Cities: Politics and Growth since World War II.* U. of Tex. Pr. 1983 $14.95. ISBN 0-292-77580-6. Multidisciplinary analysis of the politics, planning, economics, and urban history of sunbelt metropolitan centers.

Branch, Taylor. *Parting the Waters: America in the King Years, 1954–63.* Touchstone Bks. 1989 $14.94. ISBN 0-671-68742-5. Monumental history of the civil rights movement and its charismatic leader. Part one of projected two-volume study. Winner of 1989 Pulitzer Prize.

Bremner, Robert H., and Gary W. Reichard, eds. *Reshaping America: Society and Institutions, 1945–1960. Studies in Recent Amer. History.* Ohio St. U. Pr. 1982 $31.50. ISBN 0-8142-0308-6. Covers such themes as feminism, rural society, children and the state, and other trends.

Brinkley, Douglas. *Dean Acheson: The Cold War Years, 1953–71.* Yale U. Pr. 1992 $35.00. ISBN 0-300-04773-8. Balanced study of a powerful figure in Cold War diplomacy.

Cambell, Colin, and others. *The Bush Presidency: First Appraisals.* Chatham Hse. Pubs. 1991 $25.00. ISBN 0-934540-90-X. Bush's politics and its relationship to the governmental system.

Cannon, Lou. *President Reagan: The Role of a Lifetime.* S&S Trade 1991 $24.95. ISBN 0-671-54294-X. "All of Reagan's friends and foes will find this book indispensable" (John Chancellor, NBC News).

Caro, Robert A. *The Years of Lyndon Johnson, Vol. I: The Path to Power.* Knopf 1984 $29.95. ISBN 0-394-49973-5. "A powerful, absorbing, at times awe-inspiring, and often deeply alarming story . . . of one of this century's authentically great politicians" (Alan Brinkley, *Boston Sunday Globe*).

———. *The Years of Lyndon Johnson, Vol. II: Means of Ascent.* Knopf 1990 $24.95. ISBN 0-394-52835-2. Caro writes "with the narrative passion and the unique gift for making us grasp the way the world really works" (Publisher).

Carroll, Peter N. *It Seemed Like Nothing Happened: The Tragedy and Promise of America in the 1970s.* 1982. Rutgers U. Pr. 1990 $15.00. ISBN 0-8135-1538-6. Superb social and political history of the decade, noting fierce conflict between traditional values and new alternative ideas.

Carter, Jimmy. *Turning Point: A Candidate, a State, and a Nation Come of Age.* Thorndike Pr. 1993. ISBN 1-56054-772-3. Sensitive and revealing presidential memoir, one of the best of its genre.

Chafe, William H. *The Unfinished Journey: America Since World War II.* OUP 1991 $38.00. ISBN 0-19-5-6626-X. Vibrant and incisive chronicle of recent U.S. history. Superb overview of the period.

Conkin, Paul. *Big Daddy from the Pedernales: Lyndon Baines Johnson. Twayne's Twentieth-Century Amer. Biography Ser.* Twayne 1986 $26.95. ISBN 0-8057-7762-8. As much a thought-provoking history of the times as a lucid biography of its subject.

Cook, Blance Wiesen. *The Declassified Eisenhower: A Startling Reappraisal of the Eisenhower Presidency.* Viking Penguin 1984 $8.95. o.p. "More than a biography, [this book] is a rethinking of postwar American history" (*Village Voice*).

Dallek, Robert. *Lone Star Rising: Lyndon Johnson and His Times, 1908–1960.* OUP 1992 $30.00. ISBN 0-19-505435-0. Judicious treatment of a complicated man, taking him to the eve of his presidency.

Divine, Robert A. *Eisenhower and the Cold War.* OUP 1981 $29.95. ISBN 0-19-502823-6. Eisenhower as a "hands on" executive in foreign affairs.

Donovan, Robert J. *Conflict and Crisis: The Presidency of Harry S Truman, 1945–1948.* Norton 1979 $11.95. ISBN 0-393-00924-6. Clear and informative narrative of Truman's first term.

———. *Tumultuous Years: The Presidency of Harry S Truman, 1949–1953.* Norton 1984 $9.95. ISBN 0-303-30164-8. Comprehensive study of Truman's second term.

Fairclough, Adam. *To Redeem the Soul of America: The Southern Christian Leadership Council and Martin Luther King, Jr.* U. of Ga. Pr. 1987 $17.95. ISBN 0-8203-0938-9. Sensitive account of the nonviolent resistance movement.

Ferrell, Robert H. *Harry S Truman and the Modern American Presidency. Lib. of Amer. Biography.* Scott F. 1987 $13.00. ISBN 0-673-393376-2. Good brief biography.

Firestone, Bernard J., and Alexej Ugrinsky, eds. *Gerald R. Ford and the Politics of Post-Watergate America.* Greenwood 1992 $125.00. ISBN 0-313-28009-6. The road to normality in the uproar of Watergate and Vietnam.

Fitzgerald, Frances. *Fire in the Lake: The Vietnamese and the Americans in Vietnam.* 1972. Vin. 1989 $14.00. ISBN 0-679-72394-3. Superb study of a tangle of political deception and human misery. National Book Award and Bancroft Prize winner, 1973.

Flynn, George Q. *The Draft, 1940–1973*. U. Pr. of KS 1993 $45.00. ISBN 0-7006-0586-X. Study of a major instrument of social change in the modern United States.

Freedman, Lawrence, and Efraim Karsh. *The Gulf Conflict, 1990–1991*. Princton U. Pr. 1993 $29.95. ISBN 0-691-08527-3. Well-researched and reasonably balanced account of the war with Iraq.

Gaddis, John Lewis. *The United States and the End of the Cold War: Implications, Reconsiderations, Provocations*. OUP 1992 $24.95. ISBN 0-19-505201-3. Thoughtful review of past events and future possibilities.

Garrow, David J. *Bearing the Cross: Martin Luther King, Jr., and the Southern Christian Leadership Conference*. Morrow 1986 $22.95. ISBN 0-688-04794-7. Pulitzer Prize–winning (1987) biography and study of the nonviolent resistance movement.

Gilbert, James. *Another Chance: Postwar America, 1945–1968*. Temple U. Pr. 1981 $29.95. ISBN 0-87722-224-X. Good overview, that covers the cultural and social scenes as well as political developments.

Gosnell, Harold Foote. *Truman's Crises: A Political Biography of Harry S Truman. Contributions in Political Science*. Greenwood 1980 $36.95. ISBN 0-313-21273-2. Detailed and comprehensive biography that emphasizes Truman's role in foreign affairs.

Greenstein, Fred I. *The Hidden-Hand Presidency: Eisenhower as Leader*. Basic 1984 $16.00. ISBN 0-465-02951-5. Portrays Eisenhower as an activist president and model modern leader.

Halberstam, David. *The Best and the Brightest*. 1972. McKay rev. ed. 1992 $29.50. ISBN 0-679-41062-7. Scathing critique of American policy in Vietnam. One of the most influential books of the period.

Hamby, Alonzo. *Liberalism and Its Challengers: From FDR to Bush*. OUP 1992 $39.95. ISBN 0-19-507029-1. Good perspective on the postwar period, successfully blending domestic and foreign concerns.

Hamilton, Nigel. *JFK: Reckless Youth*. Random 1993 $30.00. ISBN 0-679-41216-6. Controversial account of Kennedy's early years that reveals much about his home life, indiscriminate affairs, and health.

Herring, George C. *America's Longest War: The United States and Vietnam, 1950–1975*. 1979. Knopf 1986 $14.00. ISBN 0-07-554795-3. Balanced, comprehensive history of the war. The best introduction to the subject.

Hodgson, Godfrey. *America in Our Time: From World War II to Nixon—What Happened and Why*. Random 1978 $12.76. ISBN 0-394-72517-4. Engaging history by a perceptive British journalist.

Isaacson, Walter. *Kissinger, A Biography*. S&S Trade 1992 $30.00. ISBN 0-671-66323-2. Provocative, readable biography of a controversial diplomat.

Jezer, Marty. *The Dark Ages: Life in the United States, 1945–1960*. South End Pr. 1982 $25.00. ISBN 0-89608-128-1. Popular survey of the post–World War II years that focuses on the political and social events that led to the changes and unrest of the 1960s.

Johnpoll, Bernard K., and Lillian Johnpoll. *The Impossible Dream: The Rise and Demise of the American Left. Contributions in Political Science*. Greenwood 1981 $42.95. ISBN 0-313-22488-9. Comprehensive and interesting survey of radicalism since the early nineteenth century.

Karnow, Stanley. *Vietnam: History*. 1984. Viking Penguin 1991 $30.00. ISBN 0-670-84218-4. Popular narrative written to accompany the public television series on the Vietnam War.

Kattenburg, Paul M. *The Vietnam Trauma in American Foreign Policy, 1945–1975*. Transaction Pubs. 1980 $9.95. ISBN 0-87855-903-5. Reasoned explanation by a veteran foreign service officer of how the United States became involved in Vietnam.

Kaufman, Burton I. *The Presidency of James Earl Carter, Jr.* U. Pr. of KS 1993 $29.95. ISBN 0-7006-0572-X. Balanced, thorough history of a troubled presidency.

Kearns, Doris. *Lyndon Johnson and the American Dream*. New Amer. Pr. 1977 o.p. An interesting psychobiography. Written for a general audience.

Kissinger, Henry. *White House Years*. Little 1979 o.p. Insights into the politics of the Nixon White House and the making of foreign policy. Winner of the 1980 National Book Award.

Kutler, Stanley I. *The American Inquisition: Justice and Injustice in the Cold War*. Hill & Wang 1982 $6.95. ISBN 0-8090-0157-8. Judicious treatment of domestic reaction and overreaction to the Cold War. Winner of the 1988 American Bar Association Silver Gavel Award.

————. *The Wars of Watergate: The Last Crisis of Richard Nixon*. 1990. Norton 1992 $15.95. ISBN 0-393-30827-8. "Overall this study is, and will remain, the standard book on the 'underside' of the Nixon presidency for the foreseeable future" (*American Historical Review*).

Leuchtenburg, William E. *In the Shadow of FDR: From Harry Truman to Ronald Reagan*. Cornell Univ. Pr. 2nd rev. ed. 1989 $35.95. ISBN 0-8014-2341-4. Splendid political history.

Levering, Ralph B. *The Cold War, 1945–1972*. Amer. History Ser. 1983. Harlan Davidson 1988 $7.95. ISBN 0-88295-858-5. Concise and scholarly history that stresses the interaction between domestic and foreign affairs.

Lincoln, C. Eric, ed. *Martin Luther King, Jr.: A Profile*. Hill & Wang rev. ed. 1985 $10.95. ISBN 0-374-52152-2. Useful introduction to the man, his work, and his influence.

McCullough, David. *Truman*. S&S Trade 1992 $30.00. ISBN 0-671-45654-7. Massive biography rich in detail and anecdotes. Winner of the 1993 Pulitzer Prize for biography.

Maclear, Michael. *The Ten Thousand Day War: Vietnam, 1945–1975*. Avon 1982 $10.95. ISBN 0-380-60970-3. Informative popular history of the war.

Manchester, William R. *The Death of a President, November 1963*. HarpC 1988 $15.00. ISBN 0-06-091531-5. Detailed and responsible account of the assassination of John Fitzgerald Kennedy.

————. *The Glory and the Dream: A Narrative History of America, 1932–1972*. Little 1974 $35.00. ISBN 0-316-54496-5. Compelling narrative of a 40-year period of extraordinary change in American life.

Martin, Ralph G. *A Hero for Our Time: An Intimate Story of the Kennedy Years*. Random 1984 $5.95. ISBN 0-449-20604-1. Lively, revealing account that focuses on Kennedy's personal life.

Matusow, Allen J. *The Unraveling of America: A History of Liberalism in the 1960s*. New Amer. Nation Ser. HarpC 1986 $12.00. ISBN 0-06-132058-7. Comprehensive and critical overview of the era.

Messer, Robert L. *The End of an Alliance: James F. Byrnes, Roosevelt, Truman, and the Origins of the Cold War*. Bks. Demand repr of 1982 ed. $82.10. ISBN 0-7837-0307-4. Incisive look at personal rivalries and foreign policy.

Mosley, Leonard. *Dulles: A Biography of Eleanor, Allen, and John Foster Dulles and Their Family Network*. Dial 1978 o.p. Three powerful players in the Cold War years and their extraordinary influence in shaping history.

Norman, Elizabeth. *Women at War: The Story of Fifty Military Nurses Who Served in Vietnam*. U. of Pa. Pr. 1990 $15.95. ISBN 0-8122-1317-3. Extraordinary accounts of the all-too-often unrecognized military nurses.

Oates, Stephen B. *Let the Trumpet Sound: The Life of Martin Luther King, Jr.* 1982. NAL-Dutton 1988 $5.99. ISBN 0-451-62350-9. Concise and sensitive biography.

O'Neill, William L. *American High: The Years of Confidence, 1945–1960*. Free Pr. 1989 $11.95. ISBN 0-02-923679-7. Well-written and spirited account of the early post–World War II years.

————. *Coming Apart: An Informal History of America in the 1960s*. Times Bks. 1974 $10.95. ISBN 0-8129-6223-0. Good general history of the decade, especially the counterculture.

Paglia, Camille. *Sexual Personae*. Yale U. Pr. 1990 $37.00. ISBN 0-300-04396-1. An important, if not controversial, figure in the "feminist" movement.

Paterson, Thomas G. *On Every Front: The Making and Unmaking of the Cold War*. Norton rev. ed. 1992 $22.95. ISBN 0-393-03060-1. Critical, well-researched, excellent interpretive history of the Cold War.

Powers, Richard Gid. *Secrecy and Power: The Life of J. Edgar Hoover*. Free Pr. 1988 $27.95. ISBN 0-02-925060-9. "Based on new material, this superb biography makes clear how Hoover became Public Hero number one and at the same time reveals the dark side of the man and the sinister aspects of his nearly 50-year dictatorship of the FBI" (*Publishers Weekly*).

Sitkoff, Harvard. *The Struggle for Black Equality, 1954–1992*. Amer. Century Ser. Hill & Wang rev. ed. 1993 $10.95. ISBN 0-374-52356-8. Excellent concise history of the civil rights movement.

Strober, Gerald S., and Deborah H. Strober. *"Let Us Begin Anew": An Oral History of Kennedy as President*. HarpC 1993 $25.00. ISBN 0-06-016720-3. Fascinating glimpses of the inner White House during the Kennedy years.

Terry, Wallace. *Bloods: An Oral History of the Vietnam War by Black Veterans*. Ballantine 1985 $5.95. ISBN 0-345-31197-3. "These men faced a special test of patriotism and no one seemed to know or care. These are voices that should be heard" (*San Diego Tribune*).

U.S. News and World Report staff. *Triumph Without Victory: The Unreported History of the Persion Gulf War*. Random 1992 $24.50. ISBN 0-8129-1948-3. Important journalistic account of the war.

Viorst, Milton. *Fire in the Streets: America in the 1960s*. Touchstone Bks. 1981 $14.95. ISBN 0-671-42814-4. Focuses on the social unrest and movements of the decade. Good character studies.

White, Theodore. *America in Search of Itself: The Making of the President, 1956–1980*. 1983. Warner Bks. 1988 $9.95. ISBN 0-446-37098-3. Popular history of presidential campaigns and elections by a well-known journalist and commentator.

_____. *Breach of Faith: The Fall of Richard Nixon*. Dell 1975 o.p. Sensitive account of the politics of manipulation and the consequences.

Willenson, Kim, with the correspondents of *Newsweek*. *The Bad War: An Oral History of the Vietnam War*. NAL-Dutton 1987 $8.95. ISBN 0-452-26063-9. "A fascinating, well-organized compendium of diverse opinions and often emotional judgments" (*Library Journal*).

Wills, Garry. *Nixon Agonistes: The Crisis of the Self-Made Man*. 1969. Cherokee 1990 repr. of 1970 ed. $34.95. ISBN 0-87797-198-6. Perceptive and very readable study of a deeply complex president and a troubled nation.

_____. *Reagan's America*. 1985. Viking Penguin 1988 $10.00. ISBN 0-14-010557-3. "For efforts to find Mr. Reagan's 'place in history,' this book is indispensable" (C. Vann Woodward, *N.Y. Times Book Review*).

Woodward, Bob, and Carl Bernstein. *All the President's Men*. S&S Trade 1987 $9.95. ISBN 0-671-64644-3

_____. *The Final Days*. 1976. Touchstone Bks. 1989 $8.95. ISBN 0-671-69087-6. Moment-by-moment account of Nixon's last days in office, by the investigative reporters who uncovered the Watergate scandal.

Young, Marilyn B. *The Vietnam Wars, 1945–1990*. HarpC 1991 $25.00. ISBN 0-06-016553-7. Superb history of the conflict. Meticulously documented, analytically perceptive, and highly readable.

SUPPLEMENTARY READING LISTS

Books in these lists either do not fit neatly into the chronological listings or are of a general nature within broad subject categories. A wide variety of topics is addressed—the arts and entertainment; philosophy and religion; popular culture; urban and rural history; African American, Native American, and other ethnic histories; women's history and family history; education; the making and conduct of foreign policy; histories of business, labor, and economic institutions; politics and political culture; constitutional and legal history; and environmental history. The books listed reflect the breadth of research in which historians are engaged and the growing volume of literature on these topics. Most of the books are both serious scholarly studies and interesting and enjoyable reading.

The Declaration of Independence, the Constitution, and the Federalist Papers

Cooke, Jacob E., ed. *The Federalist*. 1961. U. Pr. of New Eng. 1982 $19.95. ISBN 0-8195-6077-4. Definitive text of the classic by Hamilton, Madison, and Jay, with the question of disputed authorship discussed in a learned introduction. Vital for scholarly reference.

Documentary History of the Constitution of the United States of America, 1786–1870: Derived from Records, Manuscripts, and Rolls Deposited in the Bureau of Rolls and Library of the Department of State. 5 vols. Johnson Repr. 1966 repr. of 1894 ed. o.p. Definitive source of firsthand information on the writing and implementation of the Constitution.

Dumbauld, Edward. *The Declaration of Independence and What It Means Today*. Bks. Demand repr. of 1968 ed. $52.00. ISBN 0-317-27970-X. Interesting history and commentary.

Farrand, Max, ed. *The Records of the Federal Convention of 1787*. 3 vols. Yale U. Pr. 1986. Vol. 1 $50.00. ISBN 0-300-00447-8. Vol. 2 $50.00. ISBN 0-300-00448-6. Vol. 3 $17.00. ISBN 0-300-00082-0. Reprinted exactly from originals and presented in chronological sequence.

Jensen, Merrill. *The Making of the American Constitution*. Krieger 1979 $9.50. ISBN 0-88275-904-3. Good narrative history.

Kelly, Alfred H., and Winfred A. Harbison. *The American Constitution: Its Origins and Development*. 1948. 2 vols. Norton 1991 $18.95 ea. ISBNs 0-393-96056-0, 0-393-96119-2. A classic history that is thorough and straightforward.

Main, Jackson Turner. *The Antifederalists: Critics of the Constitution, 1781–1788*. 1961. Norton 1974 $9.95. ISBN 0-393-00760-X. "First-rate scholarship" (*Library Journal*).

Rutland, Robert Allen. *The Birth of the Bill of Rights, 1776–1791*. 1955. NE U. Pr. 1991 $35.00. ISBN 1-55553-111-3. Straightforward and informative.

_____. *The Ordeal of the Constitution: The Antifederalists and the Ratification Struggle of 1787–1788*. 1966. NE U. Pr. 1983 repr. of 1966 ed. $35.00. ISBN 0-930350-51-0. Valuable account of the struggle for ratification. Sheds light on the nature and thought of opponents of ratification.

Shapiro, Martin, ed. *The Constitution of the United States and Related Documents*. Harlan Davidson 1966 $3.25. ISBN 0-88295-025-8

Political and Constitutional History

Adams, Willi Paul. *The First American Constitutions: Republican Ideology and the Making of the State Constitutions in the Revolutionary Era*. Trans. by Rita Kimber and Robert Kimber. U. of NC Pr. 1980 $39.95. ISBN 0-8078-1388-5. Extends research on constitutional history by examining the evolution of state constitutions.

Bailey, Thomas A. *The Pugnacious Presidents: White House Warriors on Parade*. Free Pr. 1980 o.p. A novel history of the presidency that is enjoyable and informative.

Bailyn, Bernard. *The Origins of American Politics*. Random 1970 $4.76. ISBN 0-394-70865-2. Three essays in which the author expresses his views on the American Revolution and its heritage.

Barone, Michael. *Our Country: The Shaping of America from Roosevelt to Reagan*. Free Pr. 1990 $32.95. ISBN 0-02-901861-7. Good overview of recent political history.

Beard, Charles. *An Economic Interpretation of the Constitution of the United States.* Free Pr. 1986 $27.95. ISBN 0-02-902470-6. A classic interpretation of the Constitution.

Bennett, David H. *The Party of Fear: From Nativist Movements to the New Right in American History.* U. of NC Pr. 1988 $32.50. ISBN 0-8078-1772-4. Fascinating and disturbing study of paranoia as an element in American politics.

Bensel, Richard Franklin. *Yankee Leviathan: The Origins of Central State Authority in America, 1859–1877.* Cambridge U. Pr. 1991 $59.95. ISBN 0-521-39136-9. Important study of the expansion of federal authority during the sectional crisis.

Berger, Raoul. *Impeachment: The Constitutional Problems. Studies in Legal History.* HUP 1973 $12.95. ISBN 0-674-44476-0. Useful commentaries on a thorny aspect of American constitutionalism.

Berkowitz, Edward D. *America's Welfare State: From Roosevelt to Reagan.* Johns Hopkins 1991 $38.95. ISBN 0-8018-4127-5. Well-researched and interesting study of the expansion of political horizons.

Bickel, Alexander M. *The Supreme Court and the Idea of Progress.* Yale U. Pr. 1978 o.p. Presentation of the Supreme Court as a key factor in shaping the political environment.

Black, Earl, and Merle Black. *The Vital South: How Presidents Are Elected.* HUP 1992 $29.95. ISBN 0-674-94130-6. Persuasive analysis of southern politics in the modern era.

Boller, Paul F. *Presidential Anecdotes.* 1981. OUP $24.95. ISBN 0-19-502915-1. Enjoyable, lively, and amusing compendium.

———. *Presidential Campaigns.* OUP 1985 $24.95. ISBN 0-19-503420-1. Concise and informative accounts for the general reader.

Bunzel, John H. *Anti-Politics in America: Reflections on the Anti-Political Temper and Its Distortions of the Democratic Process.* Greenwood 1979 repr. of 1967 ed. $45.00. ISBN 0-313-20834-4. Thought-provoking commentary on the political process.

Christensen, Terry. *Reel Politics: American Political Movies from "Birth of a Nation" to "Platoon".* Blackwell Pubs. 1987 $24.95. ISBN 0-631-15844-8. Fascinating survey that reveals much about both movie-making and politics.

Clarke, James W. *American Assassins: The Darker Side of Politics.* Princeton U. Pr. 1982 o.p. A critically important, if also unpleasant, aspect of American political history.

Congressional Quarterly, Inc. *The Supreme Court: Justice and the Law.* Congr. Quarterly 1983 o.p. Concise guide to the development of the Court—its major decisions and most influential justices.

Crispell, Kenneth, and Carlos F. Gomez. *Hidden Illness in the White House.* Duke 1988 $29.95. ISBN 0-8223-0839-8. Another unpleasant aspect of politics, skillfully handled.

Diggins, John P. *The Lost Soul of American Politics: Virtue, Self-Interest, and the Foundations of Liberalism.* U. Ch. Pr. 1986 $23.95. ISBN 0-226-14877-7. Interesting history of American political thought in the first century of the Republic.

Ferrell, Robert H. *Ill-Advised: Presidential Health and Public Trust.* U. of Mo. Pr. 1992 $19.95. ISBN 0-8262-0864-9. Judicious history of presidential incapacity, its effects, and its implications.

Gans, Herbert J. *Middle American Individualism: Political Participation and Liberal Democracy.* OUP 1991 repr. of 1988 ed. $27.95. ISBN 0-19-507217-0. Informed commentary on subtle conflicts between individualism and democracy.

Gardner, Gerald. *The Mocking of the President: A History of Campaign Humor from Ike to Ronnie.* Wayne St. U. Pr. 1988 $29.95. ISBN 0-8143-2056-2. Enjoyable study of an indispensable element of American politics.

Garraty, John A., ed. *Quarrels That Have Shaped the Constitution.* HarpC 1988 $13.00. ISBN 0-06-132084-6. Major Supreme Court cases illuminating the nature of the document.

Gienapp, William E. *The Origins of the Republican Party, 1852–1856.* OUP 1988 $16.95. ISBN 0-19-505501-2. Solidly researched political history. Likely the definitive work on the subject.

Goldman, Ralph M. *Search for Consensus: The Story of the Democratic Party*. Temple U. Pr. 1979 $34.95. ISBN 0-87722-152-9. Covers intraparty struggles, the rise and fall of leaders, and grass-roots organization.

Green, David E. *Shaping Political Consciousness: The Language of Politics in America from McKinley to Reagan*. Cornell Univ. Pr. 1992 $32.50. ISBN 0-8014-2029-6. Interesting study of political oratory.

Hertsgaard, Mark. *On Bended Knee: The Press and the Reagan Presidency*. FS&G 1988 $22.50. ISBN 0-374-25197-5. Critical study of what the author sees as the failures of the press in dealing with presidential politics.

Hofstadter, Richard. *The American Political Tradition and the Men Who Made It*. Knopf 1973 $24.95. ISBN 0-394-48880-6. Essays that focus on individuals instrumental in the formation of American political thought.

——. *The Paranoid Style in American Politics and Other Essays*. 1965. U. Ch. Pr. 1979 $5.95. ISBN 0-226-34817-2. Essays on some pervasive forces in U.S. politics.

Holt, Michael F. *Political Parties and American Political Development from the Age of Jackson to the Age of Lincoln*. La. State U. Pr. 1992 $35.00. ISBN 0-8071-1728-5. Important study of parties and cultural politics.

Kelley, Robert L. *The Cultural Patterns in American Politics: The First Century*. U. Pr. of Amer. 1981 $22.00. ISBN 0-8191-1825-7. Good analysis of the influence of religion and ethnicity in politics.

Ladd, Everett, Jr., and Charles D. Hadley. *Transformation of the American Party System: Political Coalitions from the New Deal to the 1970s*. Norton 1975 $6.95. ISBN 0-393-09203-8. Expert analysis of political trends in the mid-twentieth century.

Lasch, Christopher. *The New Radicalism in America, 1889–1963: The Intellectual as a Social Type*. Norton 1986 repr. of 1965 ed. $8.95. ISBN 0-393-30319-5. Critical assessment of radical political thought in the modern age.

McDonald, Forrest. *We the People: The Economic Origins of the Constitution*. 1958. Transaction Pubs. 1992 $21.95. ISBN 1-56000-574-2. Careful and convincing refutation of the Beard economic interpretation.

Murphy, Bruce A. *The Brandeis/Frankfurter Connection: The Secret Political Activities of Two Supreme Court Justices*. OUP 1982 $30.00. ISBN 0-19-503122-9. Dual biography with new insights into the personal and political relationship between two of the most important justices.

Murphy, Paul L. *The Constitution in Crisis Times, 1918–1969*. HarpC 1971 o.p. Excellent study of the Supreme Court and the Constitution in times of stress and change.

Murray, Robert K., and Tim H. Blessing. *Greatness in the White House: Rating the Presidents, Washington through Carter*. Pa. St. U. Pr. 1988 $10.00. ISBN 0-271-00659-5. Interesting survey based on a poll of members of the historical profession on their estimates of the presidents.

Padover, Saul K., and Jacob W. Landynski. *The Living U.S. Constitution*. NAL-Dutton 1983 $4.95. ISBN 0-451-62174-3. Well-written commentary on the evolution of the documenmt.

Pessen, Edward. *The Log Cabin Myth: The Social Backgrounds of the Presidents*. Yale U. Pr. 1986 $12.00. ISBN 0-300-03754-6. Excellent study of myths, realities, and élites.

Pole, J. R. *The Pursuit of Equality in American History*. U. CA Pr. 1993 $35.00. ISBN 0-520-07987-6. Thoughtful and persuasive study.

Ross, Shelley. *Fall from Grace: Sex, Scandal, and Corruption in American Politics from 1702 to the Present*. Ballantine. 1988 $10.00. ISBN 0-345-35381-1. Lively and entertaining history of past and recent political figures' misdeeds.

Schlesinger, Arthur M., Jr. *The Imperial Presidency*. HM 1989 $12.70. ISBN 0-395-51561-0. Survey of the use and misuse of presidential power over the years.

——, gen. ed. *History of U.S. Political Parties*. 4 vols. Chelsea Hse. 1981 repr. of 1973 ed. $200.00. ISBN 0-87754-134-5

Storing, Herbert J., and Murray Dry, eds. *The Complete Anti-Federalist*. 7 vols. U. Ch. Pr. 1981 $175.00. ISBN 0-226-77573-9. Massive collection of the writings of the Anti-Federalists.

Sundquist, James. *Politics and Policy: The Eisenhower, Kennedy, and Johnson Years.* Brookings 1968 $29.95. ISBN 0-8157-8222-5. Excellent study of politics and public policy during the 1960s.

Theoharis, Athan. *The Boss: J. Edgar Hoover and the Great American Inquisition.* Temple U. Pr. 1988 $27.95. ISBN 0-87722-532-X. Thoroughly researched indictment of Hoover's persecution of political dissenters.

Wills, Garry. *Explaining America: The Federalist.* Viking Penguin 1982 o.p. Controversial interpretation that argues that "virtue" was the most important concept set forth in the papers.

————. *Inventing America: Jefferson's Declaration of Independence.* Random 1979 $11.16. ISBN 0-394-72735-5. Argues that Jefferson's ideas were based on Scottish moral philosophy rather than on John Locke.

Woodward, Bob, and Scott Armstrong. *The Brethren.* Avon 1981 $5.95. ISBN 0-380-52183-0. Critical look inside the Burger Court.

Woodward, C. Vann, ed. *Responses of the Presidents to Charges of Misconduct.* Delacorte 1974 o.p. Compendium of executive misbehavior from the first presidency through the thirty-sixth.

Diplomacy and Foreign Relations

Ambrose, Stephen E. *Rise to Globalism: American Foreign Policy since 1938.* Viking Penguin 4th rev. ed. 1985 $7.95. ISBN 0-14-022622-2. Clear, concise, and reliable history of U.S. foreign affairs in the period.

Bailey, Thomas A. *A Diplomatic History of the American People.* P-H 1980 $50.00. ISBN 0-13-214726-2. A classic in its field.

Berman, William C. *William Fulbright and the Vietnam War: The Dissent of a Political Realist.* Kent St. U. Pr. 1988 $24.00. ISBN 0-87338-351-6. Dissent by a high-ranking U.S. senator during the Vietnam crisis. An enlightening episode.

Black, George. *The Good Neighbor: How the United States Wrote the History of Central America and the Caribbean. A New Look History.* Pantheon 1988 $12.95. ISBN 0-394-75965-6. Vivid, disturbing, well-illustrated study of U.S. adventurism in the area.

Clements, Kendrick A. *Woodrow Wilson, World Statesman.* Twayne 1987 $26.95. ISBN 0-8057-7756-3. Concise and thoughtful estimate of Wilson and his foreign policies.

Crabb, Cecil V. Jr., *The Doctrines of American Foreign Policy: Their Meaning, Role, and Future.* La. State U. Pr. 1982 $12.95. ISBN 0-8071-1060-4. Careful analysis of the origin of U.S. foreign policy and assessment of its successes and failures.

Crabb, Cecil V., Jr., and Pat M. Holt. *Invitation to Struggle: Congress, the President and Foreign Policy. Politics and Public Policy Ser.* Congr. Quarterly 1988 $19.95. ISBN 0-87187-478-4. A look at who formulates and implements foreign policy, using case studies to illuminate the process.

Dallek, Robert. *The American Style of Foreign Policy: Cultural Politics and Foreign Affairs.* OUP $10.95. ISBN 0-19-506205-1. Penetrating study of the relationship between domestic concerns and foreign policy.

DeConde, Alexander. *Ethnicity, Race, and American Foreign Policy.* NEU. Pr. 1992 $32.50. ISBN 1-55553-133-4. Balanced study of some critical factors in the shaping of foreign policy.

Divine, Robert A. *Second Chance: The Triumph of Internationalism in America during World War II.* 1967. Atheneum 1971 o.p. "A first-rate history of the international organization movement and its effect upon American foreign policy before and during World War II" (*Library Journal*).

Dobbs, Charles M. *The Unwanted Symbol: American Foreign Policy, the Cold War and Korea, 1945–1950.* Bks. Demand repr. of 1981 ed. $65.80. ISBN 0-685-23370-7. How Korea became the symbol of anticommunism during the early years of the Cold War.

Dulles, Foster Rhea. *American Policy toward Communist China, 1949–1969.* Harlan Davidson 1972 $12.95. ISBN 0-88295-728-7. Solid, well-written history of a stormy relationship.

Gaddis, John L. *The Long Peace: Inquiries into the History of the Cold War*. OUP 1989 repr. of 1987 ed. $30.00. ISBN 0-19-504336-7. Interesting analysis of the relative international stability produced by the Cold War.

———. *Russia, the Soviet Union, and the United States: An Interpretive History*. McGraw 1978 $12.44. ISBN 0-07-557258-3. Good survey of the major international relation of the twentieth century.

———. *The United States and the End of the Cold War: Implications, Reconsiderations, Provocations*. OUP 1992 $24.95. ISBN 0-19-505201-3. Intelligent analysis of the problems and possibilities of the new peace.

Gardner, Lloyd C. *Approaching Vietnam: From World War II through Dienbienphu, 1941–1954*. Norton 1989 $22.50. ISBN 0-393-02540-3. Useful work that traces the steps that led the United States into the quagmire of Vietnam.

———. *A Covenant with Power: America and World Order from Wilson to Reagan*. OUP 1986 $14.95. ISBN 0-19-504009-0. Critical analysis of America's emergence and development as a world power.

———, ed. *Redefining the Past: Essays in Diplomatic History in Honor of William Appleman Williams*. Oreg. St. U. Pr. 1986 $29.95. ISBN 0-87071-348-5. Group of essays that demonstrate the influence of the unconventional and controversial Williams.

Glennon, Michael J. *Constitutional Diplomacy*. Princeton U. Pr. 1991 $45.00. ISBN 0-691-07842-4. Examines the lack of involvement on the part of Congress and the Judiciary in foreign policy making.

Hunt, Michael H. *Ideology and United States Foreign Policy*. Yale U. Pr. 1988 repr. of 1987 ed. $11.00. ISBN 0-300-04369-4. Careful inquiry into a critical aspect of American attitudes and policies.

Jones, Howard. *"A New Kind of War": America's Global Strategy and the Truman Doctrine in Greece*. OUP 1989 $38.00. ISBN 0-19-504581-5. Penetrating analysis of a critical moment in the emergence of the global Cold War.

———. *Dawning of the Cold War: The U.S. Quest for Order*. U. of Ga. Pr. 1991 $35.00. ISBN 0-8203-1265-7. Important revisionist interpretation of events after World War II, casting U.S. actions in a new light.

———. *Union in Peril: The Crisis Over British Intervention in the Civil War*. U. of NC Pr. 1992 $34.95. ISBN 0-8078-2048-2. Solid study of a critical situation in the midst of the Civil War.

Kegley, Charles W., Jr., and Eugene R. Wittkopf. *American Foreign Policy: Patterns and Process*. St. Martin 1991 $30.65. ISBN 0-312-03656-6. Good overview of the U.S. foreign policy decision-making process.

Kennan, George F. *American Diplomacy, 1900–1950*. U. Ch. Pr. rev. ed. 1985 $7.95. ISBN 0-226-43147-9. Collection of well-written essays about the topic.

Kissinger, Henry A. *American Foreign Policy: A Global View*. 1982. Ashgate Pub. Co. 1983 $10.00. ISBN 0-9971-902-54-0. Succinct expression of Henry Kissinger's views in the 1980s.

Kwitny, Jonathan. *Endless Enemies: The Making of an Unfriendly World*. Viking Penguin 1986 $9.95. ISBN 0-14-008093-7. Well-documented and hard-hitting argument that U.S. foreign policy often defeats its own best interests.

LaFeber, Walter. *America, Russia, and the Cold War, 1945–1992*. McGraw 1992 $11.95. ISBN 0-07-035853-2. Superb concise survey of the roots and course of the Cold War.

———. *The American Age: United States Foreign Policy at Home and Abroad Since 1750*. Norton 1989 $19.95. ISBN 0-393-95611-3. First-rate survey that relates foreign policy to domestic concerns and developments and to events abroad.

———. *Inevitable Revolutions: The United States in Central America*. Norton 1984 $18.95. ISBN 0-393-01787-7. Thoughtful discourse on a perennial problem in United States diplomacy.

———. *The Panama Canal: The Crisis in Historical Perspective*. OUP rev. ed. 1990 $30.00. ISBN 0-19-505930-1. Dispassionate treatment of the controversies regarding the building, status, and ultimate disposition of the canal.

Leckie, Robert. *The Wars of America*. HarpC 1992 $50.00. ISBN 0-06-016831-5. "A splendidly dramatic and fascinating panoramic narrative, and probably as good a popular access to the wars of America and the men who led them and fought them, all in a single volume" (*N.Y. Times*).

Levin, N. Gordon. *Woodrow Wilson and World Politics: America's Response to War and Revolution*. OUP 1968 $14.95. ISBN 0-19-500803-0. Important critique of the Wilsonian world view and its legacies. Winner of the 1969 Bancroft Prize.

May, Ernest R., ed. *American Cold War Strategy: Interpreting NSC 68*. St. Martin 1993 $35.00. ISBN 0-312-09445-0. Essays evaluating one of the most powerful instruments of the Cold War.

―――. *Imperial Democracy: The Emergence of America as a Great Power*. Imprint Pubns. 1991 $15.95. ISBN 1-879176-04-1. Masterly synthesis of diplomatic and political history for the general reader as well as the specialist.

―――. *The "Lessons" of the Past: The Use and Misuse of History in American Foreign Policy*. OUP 1973 $8.95. ISBN 0-19-501890-7. Thoughtful consideration of the political manipulation of scholarship.

Mayers, David. *George Kennan and the Dilemmas of United States Foreign Policy*. 1988. OUP 1990 $12.95. ISBN 0-19-506318-X. Biography of a leading American diplomat and shaper of foreign policy.

Millet, Allan R. *Semper Fidelis: The History of the United States Marine Corps. Macmillan Wars of the United States Ser*. 1980. Free Pr. 1982 $35.00. ISBN 0-02-921590-0. Institutional history depicting the corps as a complex organization.

Millet, Allan R., and Peter Maslowski. *For the Common Defense: A Military History of the United States, 1607–1983*. Free Pr. 1984 $27.95. ISBN 0-02-921580-3. Straightforward informative military history.

Miscamble, Wilson D. *George F. Kennan and the Making of American Foreign Policy, 1947–1950. Princeton Studies in International History and Politics*. Princeton U. Pr. 1992 $35.00. ISBN 0-691-08620-6. Keen analysis of the containment policy and its author.

Paterson, Thomas G. *On Every Front: The Making and Unmaking of the Cold War. Norton Essays in Amer. History*. 1979. Norton rev. ed. 1992 $24.95. ISBN 0-393-03060-1. Clear explanation of the "bewildered, baffled, and breathless" world in which the Cold War took shape.

Perret, Geoffrey. *A Country Made by War: From the Revolution to Vietnam—The Story of America's Rise to Power*. Random 1989 $22.50. ISBN 0-394-55398-5. Excellent single-volume history of the nation's considerable military experience.

Ranelagh, John. *The Agency: The Rise and Decline of the CIA*. 1986. S&S Trade 1987 $17.00. ISBN 0-671-63994-3. "The best comprehensive history of the CIA. . . . A fine book" (*Foreign Affairs*).

Sick, Gary. *All Fall Down: America's Tragic Encounter with Iran*. 1985. Viking Penguin 1986 $9.95. ISBN 0-14-008837-79. Superb chronicle of the hostage crisis, with an authoritative explanation of its causes.

Smith, Gaddis. *Morality, Reason, and Power: American Diplomacy in the Carter Years*. Hill & Wang 1986 o.p. Balanced and thoughtful treatment of a largely misunderstood foreign policy.

Tucker, Robert W. *The Radical Left and American Foreign Policy. Studies in International Affairs*. Bks. Demand repr. of 1971 ed. $42.00. ISBN 0-317-55519-7. Reasoned critique of the "revisionist" school of Cold War history.

Tucker, Robert W., and David C. Hendrickson. *Empire of Liberty: The Statecraft of Thomas Jefferson*. OUP 1990 $24.95. ISBN 0-19-506207-8. Superb study of Jeffersonian foreign policy.

Unger, Sanford J., ed. *Estrangement: America and the World*. OUP 1985 $30.00. ISBN 0-19-503707-3. Essays on America's position in the world by a distinguished group of historians and other experts. A Carnegie Endowment book.

Weeks, William Earl. *John Quincy Adams and American Global Empire*. U. Pr. of Ky. 1992 $29.00. ISBN 0-8131-1779-8. "Like much good history, this book uses the story of a single event to reveal a great deal about the era in which it took place—and something about our own times as well" (*Library Journal*).

Williams, T. Harry. *The History of American Wars from 1745 to 1918*. 1981. La. State U. Pr. 1985 $12.95. ISBN 0-8071-1234-8. Deservedly popular military history.

Williams, William Appleman. *The Tragedy of American Diplomacy, 1900–1950*. Norton rev. ed. 1988 $9.95. ISBN 0-393-30493-0. Volume that, in effect, established the "revisionist" school of diplomatic history.

Economic History

Bilstein, Roger E. *Flight in America: From the Wrights to the Astronauts*. Johns Hopkins 1987 $15.95. ISBN 0-8018-3561-5. Exciting story of a major modern industry.

Brody, David. *Workers in Industrial America: Essays on the Twentieth Century Struggle*. OUP 1993 $35.00. ISBN 0-19-504503-2. Major studies of industrial workers and their efforts to organize.

Bruchey, Stuart. *Enterprise: The Dynamic Economy of a Free People*. HUP 1990 $49.50. ISBN 0-674-25745-6. Informed discussion by a distinguished business historian.

Carosso, Vincent P. *The Morgans: Private International Bankers, 1854–1913*. Harvard Studies in Business History. HUP 1987 $69.95. ISBN 0-674-58729-4. Impressive study of a banking house that played a major role in developing the U.S. economy.

Conkin, Paul K. *Prophets of Prosperity: America's First Political Economists*. Bks. Demand repr. of 1980 ed. $90.30. ISBN 0-685-23879-2. Interesting introduction to the major economists of the early Republic.

Corn, Joseph J. *The Winged Gospel: America's Romance with Aviation, 1900–1950*. OUP 1983 $28.00. ISBN 0-19-5-3356-8. Story of the remarkable growth of an industry and social institution.

Cortada, James W. *Before the Computer: IBM, NCR, Burroughs, and Remington Rand and the Industry They Created, 1865–1956*. Princeton Studies in Business and Technology. Princeton U. Pr. 1993 $55.00. ISBN 0-685-55383-3. Authoritative study of a major twentieth-century industry.

Fogel, Robert W., and Stanley L. Engerman. *Time on the Cross: The Economics of American Negro Slavery*. 1973. U. Pr. of Amer. 1985 $20.75. ISBN 0-8191-4331-6. Highly controversial quantitative study of slavery that set off a spirited debate among historians.

Frazier, E. Franklin. *Black Bourgeoisie: The Rise of a New Middle Class in the United States*. 1962. Free Pr. 1965 $14.95. ISBN 0-02-910580-3. Landmark in African American studies.

Galambos, Louis, and Joseph Pratt. *The Rise of the Corporate Commonwealth: U.S. Business and Public Policy in the Twentieth Century*. Basic 1988 $19.95. ISBN 0-465-07028-0. Well-written and authoritative account.

Gartman, David. *Auto Slavery*. Rutgers U. Pr. 1986 $45.00. ISBN 0-8135-1181-X. Discusses the automotive industry and its growth and development as a function of economic stresses.

Genovese, Eugene D. *The Political Economy of Slavery: Studies in the Economy and Society of the Slave South*. 1967. Vin. 1989 $4.95. ISBN 0-8195-6208-4. Essays in a doctrinaire Marxist vein.

Goldin, Claudia. *Understanding the Gender Gap: An Economic History of American Women*. OUP 1990 $14.95. ISBN 0-19-507270-7. Long-neglected story, well told.

Gutman, Herbert G. *Power and Culture: Essays on the American Working Class*. Ed. by Ira Berlin. New Press NY 1992 $29.95. ISBN 1-56584-010-0. Important collection of essays by the most influential American exponent of the "new social history."

Harris, William H. *The Harder We Run: Black Workers since the Civil War*. OUP 1982 $14.95. ISBN 0-19-502941-0. The problems and frustrations of black workers in industrializing America.

Hoerr, John P. *And the Wolf Finally Came: The Decline of the American Steel Industry*. Social and Labor History Ser. U. of Pittsburgh Pr. 1988 $39.95. ISBN 0-8229-3572-4. Pointed account of a major economic national failure.

Hughes, Thomas P. *American Genesis: A Century of Invention and Technological Enthusiasm*. 1989. Viking Penguin 1990 $12.95. ISBN 0-14-009741-4. Interesting chronicle of people and events that contributed mightily to American economic development.

Hurt, R. Douglas. *The Dust Bowl: An Agricultural and Social History*. Nelson-Hall 1981 $27.95. ISBN 0-88229-541-1. Engaging account of a unique phenomenon in U.S. history.

Jacoway, Elizabeth, and David R. Colburn, eds. *Southern Businessmen and Desegregation*. La. State U. Pr. 1982 $37.50. ISBN 0-8071-0893-6. Important essays based heavily on oral histories. Show how and why community leaders accommodated to racial change.

Klebaner, Benjamin J. *American Commercial Banking: A History. Evolution of Amer. Business Ser.* Macmillan 1990 $26.95. ISBN 0-8057-9804-8. Good study of a critical element in the nation's economic development.

Kulikoff, Allan. *The Agrarian Origins of American Capitalism*. U. Pr. of Va. 1992 $49.50. ISBN 0-8139-1388-8. Well-researched and persuasive study.

Lamoreaux, Naomi. *The Great Merger Movement in American Business, 1895–1904*. Cambridge U. Pr. 1988 $14.95. ISBN 0-521-35765-9. Details the emergence of the supercorporations at the turn of the century.

Litwack, Leon F., ed. *The American Labor Movement*. 1962. S&S Trade 1986 o.p. Union manifestoes, personal testimonies, editorials, labor laws, and songs brought together as a vivid record of labor and antilabor activity in American history.

Long, Priscilla. *Where the Sun Never Shines: A History of America's Bloody Coal Industry*. Paragon Hse. 1989 $24.95. ISBN 1-55778-224-5. Fascinating history of a vital and dangerous industry and its workers.

McCusker, John J., and Russell R. Menard. *The Economy of British America, 1607–1789*. 1985. U. of NC Pr. 1991 $18.95. ISBN 0-8078-4351-2. First-rate examination of colonial economic life. Important for understanding the movement toward independence.

Mandell, Lewis. *The Credit Card Industry: A History. Evolution of Amer. Business Ser.* Macmillan 1990 $26.95. ISBN 0-8057-9810-2. Good account of how the ubiquitous "plastic" achieved such spectacular success.

Marchand, Roland. *Advertising the American Dream: Making Way for Modernity, 1920–1940*. U. CA Pr. 1985 $47.50. ISBN 0-520-05253-6. Skillful analysis of social content in advertising during the 1920s and 1930s.

Markusen, Ann, and others. *The Rise of the Gunbelt: The Military Remapping of Industrial America*. OUP 1991 $38.00. ISBN 0-19-506648-0. Revealing study of extraordinary demographic, economic, social, and cultural changes resulting from the arms race.

Patterson, James T. *America's Struggle against Poverty, 1900–1980*. 1981. HUP 1986 $12.95. ISBN 0-674-03122-9. Excellent account of government attempts to alleviate economic distress.

Perkins, Edwin J. *The Economy of Colonial America*. 1980. Col. U. Pr. 1988 $40.50. ISBN 0-231-06338-5. Good basic survey of the colonial economy and its major problems.

Peterson, Richard H. *The Bonanza Kings: The Social Origins and Business Behavior of Western Mining Entrepreneurs, 1870–1900*. 1971. U. of Okla. Pr. 1991 $10.95. ISBN 0-8061-2389-3. Well-told story of a unique and sometimes colorful group of entrepreneurs.

Prude, Jonathan. *The Coming of Industrial Order: Town and Factory Life in Rural Massachusetts, 1810–1860*. 1983. Cambridge U. Pr. 1985 $16.95. ISBN 0-521-31396-1. Important treatment of industrialization as a process rather than as an event and good analysis of nonunionized workers.

Rae, John B. *The American Automobile Industry. Evolution of Amer. Business Ser.* 1984. Macmillan 1985 $22.95. ISBN 0-8057-9803-X. Good account of the early years of a major industry.

Ransom, Roger L. *Conflict and Compromise: The Political Economy of Slavery, Emancipation, and the American Civil War*. Cambridge U. Pr. 1989 $44.95. ISBN 0-521-32343-6. Strong reminder of the complex nature of the sectional crisis.

Ransom, Roger L., and Richard Sutch. *One Kind of Freedom: The Economic Conse-quences of Emancipation.* Cambridge U. Pr. 1977 o.p. First-rate examination of weaknesses in the postwar southern economy and the resulting human costs.

Rosenberg, Emily S. *Spreading the American Dream: American Economic and Cultural Expansion, 1890–1945.* Amer. Century Ser. Hill & Wang 1982 $9.95. ISBN 0-8090-0146-2. Good popular account of the U.S. drive to export its technological and consumer-oriented society.

Salvatore, Nick. *Eugene V. Debs: Citizen and Socialist. The Working Class in Amer. History Ser.* U. of Ill. Pr. 1982 $29.95. ISBN 0-252-00967-3. First-rate biography and winner of the Bancroft Prize for 1983.

Sklar, Martin J. *The Corporate Reconstruction of American Capitalism, 1890–1916: The Market, the Law, and Politics.* Cambridge U. Pr. 1988 $64.95. ISBN 0-521-30921-2. Brilliant analysis of a critical turn in the nation's economic and financial history.

Stewart, James. *Den of Thieves.* S&S Trade 1992 $12.00. ISBN 0-671-79227-X. Tells of the rise and fall during the 1980s of the biggest insider trading ring in Wall Street history. Updated version.

Strasser, Susan. *Never Done: A History of American Housework.* Pantheon 1982 $13.56. ISBN 0-394-70841-5. Excellent account of women as "homemakers" in a changing economy and society.

_____. *Satisfaction Guaranteed: The Making of the American Mass Market.* Pantheon 1989 $24.95. ISBN 0-394-55292-X. Traces the development of the great American consumer society.

Thernstrom, Stephen. *The Other Bostonians: Poverty and Progress in the American Metropolis, 1880–1970. Studies in Urban History.* HUP 1973 $25.50. ISBN 0-674-04495-6. Model quantitative economic history and winner of the Bancroft Prize in 1974.

Thomas, Gordon, and Max Morgan. *The Day the Bubble Burst: A Social History of the Wall Street Crash of 1929.* Viking Penguin 1980 o.p. Uses a nice combination of oral histories and other primary sources to create a lively account of the financial crisis that heralded the Great Depression.

Wall, Joseph Frazier. *Alfred I. Du Pont: The Man and His Family.* OUP 1990 $35.00. ISBN 0-19-504349-9. Biography that offers insights into a major industry and extraordinary social scene.

Zunz, Olivier. *Making America Corporate, 1870–1920.* U. Ch. Pr. 1990 $24.95. ISBN 0-226-99459-7. Good general account of the rise of big business.

Environmental History

Cranz, Galen. *The Politics of Park Design: A History of Urban Parks in America.* MIT Pr. 1982 $15.95. ISBN 0-262-53084-8. Well-written and organized account of the political and historical development of parks since 1850.

Cronon, William. *Changes in the Land: Indians, Colonists, and the Ecology of New England.* Amer. Century Ser. Hill & Wang 1983 $9.95. ISBN 0-8090-0158-6. Sophisticated study of the dynamic relationship between people and the physical world over time. A model environmental history.

Dick, Everett. *The Lure of the Land: A Social History of the Public Lands from the Articles of Confederation to the New Deal.* U. of Nebr. Pr. 1970 $40.00. ISBN 0-8032-0725-5. Basic social history of the nation's public domain.

Dunlap, Thomas R. *Saving America's Wildlife.* 1988. Princeton U. Pr. 1991 $35.00. ISBN 0-691-04750-2. History of the conservation movement and its opposition.

Egerton, Frank N., III, ed. *History of American Ecology: An Original Anthology.* Ayer 1978 $36.50. ISBN 0-405-10399-9. Essays illuminating the rise of ecological concerns plus an excellent bibliography on the subject.

Fox, Stephen R. *John Muir and His Legacy: The American Conservation Movement.* Little 1981 $29.95. ISBN 0-316-29110-2. History of the conservation movement and a biography of America's first great preservationist.

Hays, Samuel P. *Beauty, Health, and Permanence: Environmental Politics in the United States, 1955–1985. Studies in Environment and History.* 1987. Cambridge U. Pr. 1989 $19.95. ISBN 0-521-38928-3. Important assessment of modern environmentalism.

_____. *Conservation and the Gospel of Efficiency: The Progressive Conservation Movement, 1890–1920.* HUP 1959 $9.95. ISBN 0-674-16501-2. Perceptive study of the Progressive approach to conservation.

Kolodny, Annette. *The Land Before Her: Fantasy and Experience of the American Frontiers, 1630–1860.* U. of NC Pr. 1984 $34.95. ISBN 0-8078-1571-3. Imaginative re-creation based on literary sources that reveals gender-based conceptions of the frontier and wilderness.

Mazmanian, Daniel, and David Morell. *Beyond Superfailure: America's Toxic Policy for the 1990s.* Westview 1992 $16.95. ISBN 0-8133-1467-4. Chronicles the history of toxic disasters and successful cleanups. Intelligent suggestions for future preventative measures.

Merchant, Carolyn. *The Death of Nature: Women, Ecology, and the Scientific Revolution.* 1980. Harper SF 1990 $12.00. ISBN 0-06-250595-5. Women in science as pioneers in ecology and in developing a philosophy of nature.

_____. *Ecological Revolutions: Nature, Gender, and Science in New England.* U. of NC Pr. 1989 $37.50. ISBN 0-8078-1858-5. Good study of relations between Native Americans, white settlers, and the environment.

Mitchell, Lee Clark. *Witnesses to a Vanishing America: The Nineteenth-Century Response.* Princeton U. Pr. 1987 $44.50. ISBN 0-691-06461-X. Consequences of the interaction of white settlers, Native Americans, and the environment.

Mitman, Gregg. *The State of Nature: Ecology, Community, and American Social Thought. Science and Its Conceptual Foundation Ser.* U. Ch. Pr. 1992 $58.00. ISBN 0-216-53236-4. Thoughtful treatment of ecology in broad social and ideological perspectives.

Nash, Roderick F. *The Rights of Nature: A History of Environmental Ethics.* U. of Wis. Pr. 1989 $35.00. ISBN 0-299-11840-1. Excellent introduction to human ecology in the context of "nature's rights."

_____. *Wilderness and the American Mind.* 1967. Yale U. Pr. 1982 $15.00. ISBN 0-300-02910-1. Myths and realities in the American contact with the environment.

_____, comp. *American Environmentalism: Readings in Conservation History.* 1976. McGraw 1990 $14.90. ISBN 0-07-046059-0. Readings that collectively constitute a good overview of thinking on the subject.

Petulla, Joseph M. *American Environmental History: The Exploitation and Conservation of Natural Resources.* 1977. Macmillan 1988. ISBN 0-675-20885-8. Good introduction and survey.

Renehan, Edward J., Jr. *John Burroughs: An American Naturalist.* Chelsea Green Pub. 1992 $24.95. ISBN 0-930031-59-8. Fine biography of an environmental advocate who influenced Theodore Roosevelt.

Rosenkrantz, Barbara Gutman, comp. *American Habitat: A Historical Perspective.* Free Pr. 1973 o.p. Useful collection of primary and secondary source materials.

Runte, Alfred. *National Parks: The American Experience.* 1979. U. of Nebr. Pr. 1987 $25.00. ISBN 0-8032-3878-9. Excellent history that argues that parks were established to serve cultural rather than biological purposes.

Sale, Kirkpatrick. *The Green Revolution: The Environmental Movement, 1962–1992.* Hill & Wang 1993 $7.95. ISBN 0-8090-1551-X. Overview of recent surge of interest in environmentalism among scholars as well as the general public.

Stilgoe, John R. *Common Landscape of America, 1580 to 1845.* 1982. Yale U. Pr. 1983 $19.00. ISBN 0-300-03046-0. Imaginative study that analyzes physical spaces as conscious cultural creations.

Udall, Stewart I. *The Quiet Crisis and the Next Generation.* 1963. Gibbs Smith Pub. 1991 $12.95. ISBN 0-87905-334-8. Early ecological warning by a former U.S. secretary of the interior.

White, Richard. *"It's Your Misfortune and None of My Own": A History of the American West*. U. of Okla. Pr. 1991 $39.95. ISBN 0-8061-2366-4. Spirited narrative history that incorporates findings of recent research.

————. *Land Use, Environment, and Social Change: The Shaping of Island County, Washington*. 1980. U. of Wash. Pr. 1991 $14.95. ISBN 0-295-97143-6. Case study illustrating the importance of Native American history and concerns in environmental matters.

Worster, Donald, ed. *The Ends of the Earth: Perspectives on Modern Environmental History. Studies in Environment and History*. Cambridge U. Pr. 1989 $47.95. ISBN 0-521-34365-8. Cambridge U. Pr. 1989 $47.95. ISBN 0-521-34365-8. Reflections on the environment from a variety of perspectives.

————. *Nature's Economy: A History of Ecological Ideas. Studies in Environment and History*. 1977. Cambridge U. Pr. 1985 $49.95. ISBN 0-521-26792-7. First-rate overview.

————. *Rivers of Empire: Water, Aridity, and the Growth of the American West*. 1985. OUP 1992 $12.95. ISBN 0-19-507806-3. Focus on water as the lifeblood of an entire region and economy.

————. *Under Western Skies: Nature and History of the American West*. OUP 1992 $27.50. ISBN 0-19-505820-8. Excellent study of human geography and ecology.

History and Social Change

Altherr, Thomas L. *Procreation or Pleasure? Sexual Attitudes in American History*. Krieger 1983 $10.50. ISBN 0-89874-609-4. Provocative inquiry into a generally neglected aspect of social history.

Anderson, Margo J. *The American Census: A Social History*. Yale U. Pr. 1988 $13.00. ISBN 0-300-04709-6. Examines one of the great sources of historical information.

Barnouw, Erik. *Documentary: A History of the Non-Fiction Film*. 1983. OUP 2nd rev. ed. 1992 $10.95. ISBN 0-19-507898-5. Useful and interesting history for specialists and for general readers.

————. *Tube of Plenty: The Evolution of American Television*. 1975. OUP 2nd rev. ed. 1990 $39.95. ISBN 0-19-506483-6. Authoritative and readable history of television with commentary on its cultural and social influence.

Bartlett, Richard. *The New Country: A Social History of the American Frontier, 1776–1890*. 1974. OUP 1976 $19.95. ISBN 0-19-502021-9. Good history of the frontier as an arena of social change.

Baughman, James L. *The Republic of Mass Culture: Journalism, Broadcasting, and Film Making in America Since 1945. Amer. Moment Ser.* Johns Hopkins 1992 $38.95. ISBN 0-8018-4276-X. Examines the extraordinary explosion of mass media and its cultural consequences.

Boorstein, Daniel. *The Image: A Guide to Pseudo-Events in America*. 1962. Macmillan 1971 $10.95. ISBN 0-689-70280-9. Probing inquiry into the nature of American society, culture, and national characteristics.

Bordley, James, III, and A. McGehee Harvey. *Two Centuries of American Medicine, 1776–1976*. Saunders 1976 $72.50. ISBN 0-7216-1873-1. Descriptive history, with special emphasis on the period since 1946.

Brown, Howard. *Familiar Faces, Hidden Lives: The Story of Homosexual Men in America Today*. HarBraceJ 1989 $8.95. ISBN 0-15-630120-2. Explores the history of gay subculture in America.

Burnham, John C. *Bad Habits: Drinking, Smoking, Taking Drugs, Gambling, Sexual Misbehavior and Swearing in American History*. NYU Pr. 1992 $35.00. ISBN 0-8147-1187-1. An illustrated history of vice in America.

Burns, Stewart. *Social Movements of the 1960s: Searching for Democracy*. Macmillan 1990 $25.95. ISBN 0-8057-9737-8. Good history "from the bottom up" that examines civil rights, the New Left, and feminism as movements for social change.

Cory, Donald W. *The Homosexual in America: A Subjective Approach*. Ayer repr. of 1951 ed. $20.00. ISBN 0-405-07365-8

Curry, Richard O., and Lawrence B. Goodheart, eds. *American Chameleon: Individualism in Trans-National Context.* Kent St. U. Pr. 1991 $35.00. ISBN 0-87388-443-1. "A fascinating exploration of the diversity of historical meanings of a concept that is probably more identifyingly American than any one can think of" (Carl Degler).

Dawley, Alan. *Struggles for Justice: Social Responsibility and the Liberal State.* HUP 1991 $27.95. ISBN 0-685-48479-3. Excellent survey of the period 1890–1940, incorporating new labor, social, and gender history.

D'Emilio, John, and Estelle F. Freedman. *Intimate Matters: A History of Sexuality in America.* 1988. HarpC 1989 $12.00. ISBN 0-06-091550-1. Unusual history of, among other things, how sexual matters moved from the privacy of the bedroom to the exposure of mass culture.

Faderman, Lillian. *Odd Girls and Twilight Lovers: A History of Lesbian Life in Twentieth-Century America.* Viking Penguin 1992 $12.00. ISBN 0-14-017122-3. Well-done history of a long-hidden aspect of American life.

Filene, Peter. *Him/Her/Self: Sex Roles in Modern America.* Johns Hopkins 1986 $38.00. ISBN 0-8018-2893-7. Fascinating examination of the confusion of sex roles in America.

Fischer, David Hackett. *Growing Old in America.* OUP rev. ed. 1978 $9.95. ISBN 0-19-502366-8. Outstanding study of a timely subject. Enhanced by a fine bibliographic essay.

Grob, Gerald. *Mental Illness and American Society, 1875–1940.* Princeton U. Pr. 1983 $63.00. ISBN 0-691-08332-0. Interesting social history of the evolution of mental hospitals and the profession of psychiatry.

Grover, Kathryn, ed. *Dining in America, 1850–1900.* U. of Mass. Pr. 1987 $25.00. ISBN 0-87023-573-7. Unusual and entertaining social history.

Guttmann, Allen. *A Whole New Ball Game: An Interpretation of American Sports.* U. of NC Pr. 1988 $12.95. ISBN 0-8078-4220-6. Good history of a central part of American social life.

Hook, J. N. *Family Names: How Our Surnames Came to America.* Macmilian 1983 $8.95. ISBN 0-685-46244-7. Enjoyable history of surnames and how they fared in a New World setting.

Horowitz, Helen Lefkowitz. *Campus Life: Undergraduate Cultures from the End of the Eighteenth Century to the Present.* Knopf 1987 $24.95. ISBN 0-394-54997-X. Splendid chronicle of campus social and cultural life through the years.

Jackson, Kenneth T. *Crabgrass Frontier: The Suburbanization of America.* OUP 1985 $30.00. ISBN 0-19-503610-7. Winner of the 1986 Bancroft Prize.

Jones, Jacqueline. *The Dispossessed: America's Underclasses from the Civil War to the Present.* Basic 1992 $25.00. ISBN 0-465-00127-0. Ambitious and largely successful effort to chronicle the history of the "inarticulate and invisible."

Kasson, John F. *Amusing the Million: Coney Island at the Turn of the Century.* Amer. Century Ser. Hill & Wang 1978 $9.95. ISBN 0-8090-0133-0. Delightful social history of America's most famous amusement park and beach.

Katzman, David J., and William H. Tuttle, Jr., eds. *Plain Folk: The Life Stories of Undistinguished Americans.* U. of Ill. Pr. 1982 $24.95. ISBN 0-252-00884-7. Interesting forays into the life histories of ordinary people.

Lasch, Christopher. *Haven in a Heartless World: The Family Besieged.* 1977. Basic 1979 $14.00. ISBN 0-465-02884-5. Reasoned discourse on the deterioration of family relationships in modern America.

Lender, Mark Edward, and James Kirby Martin. *Drinking in America.* 1982. Free Pr. rev. ed. 1987 $14.95. ISBN 0-02-918570-X. Fascinating history of the use, misuse, and abuse of alcoholic beverages.

Levine, Bruce, and others, eds. *Who Built America? Working People and the Nation's Economy, Politics, Culture, and Society.* 2 vols. Pantheon 1989 $20.00 ea. ISBNs 0-679-72699-3, 0-679-73022-2. Extraordinary social history, rich in detail and gracefully written. Product of the American Social History Project founded by the late Herbert G. Gutman.

Ling, Peter J. *America and the Automobile: Technology, Reform, and Social Change, 1893–1923*. St. Martin 1990 $59.95. ISBN 0-7190-2636-9. Good account of the early years of the automobile age.

Lingeman, Richard. *Small Town America: A Narrative History, 1620 to the Present*. HM 1981 o.p. Rich and engrossing history of an integral part of the American experience.

Lystra, Karen. *Searching the Heart: Women, Men, and Romantic Love in Nineteenth-Century America, 1830–1900*. OUP 1989 $30.00. ISBN 0-19-505817-8. Excellent treatment of an absorbing subject.

Magdol, Edward, and John L. Wakelyn, eds. *The Southern Common People: Studies in Nineteenth-Century Social History*. Contributions in Amer. History Ser. Greenwood 1980 $49.95. ISBN 0-313-21403-4. Informative essays on everyday life in the 1800s.

Michaels, Walter Benn. *The Gold Standard and the Logic of Naturalism: American Literature at the Turn of the Century*. U. CA Pr. 1987 $37.50. ISBN 0-520-05981-6. Superb historical literary criticism that uses the works of Dreiser, Norris, and others to analyze the pervasiveness of the market in American social thought.

Mintz, Steven, and Susan Kellogg. *Domestic Revolutions: A Social History of American Family Life*. Free Pr. 1989 $12.95. ISBN 0-02-921290-1. Good general history of social conditions in the United States.

Morgan, H. Wayne. *Drugs in America: A Social History, 1800–1980*. 1981. Syracuse U. Pr. 1982 $12.95. ISBN 0-8156-2282-1. Important contribution to the growing literature on drugs in American society.

Musto, David F. *The American Disease: Origins of Narcotic Control*. Bks. Demand 1987 $95.70. ISBN 0-8357-8018-X. Important study that places a major current social and health concern in historical context.

Pivar, David J. *Purity Crusade: Sexual Morality and Social Control, 1868–1900*. Contributions in Amer. History Ser. Greenwood 1973 $38.50. ISBN 0-8371-6319-6. Significant and extensive examination of the social-purity movement.

Ravitch, Diane. *Troubled Crusade: American Education, 1945–1980*. 1983. Basic 1985 $19.95. ISBN 0-465-08756-6. Chronicle in historical context of the various problems and reform movements facing the U.S. educational system.

Riley, Glenda. *Divorce: An American Tradition*. OUP 1991 $24.95. ISBN 0-19-506123-1. Fascinating inquiry into the history of a pervasive social phenomenon in America.

Robertson, James Oliver, and Janet C. Robertson. *All Our Yesterdays: A Century of Family Life in an American Small Town*. HarpC 1993 $30.00. ISBN 0-06-019017-5. Change and its effects on the lives and fortunes of individuals and families.

Rothman, Ellen K. *Hands and Hearts: A History of Courtship in America*. 1984. HUP 1987 $9.95. ISBN 0-674-37160-7. Interesting scholarly history of courtship from 1770 to 1920.

Simon, Kate. *Fifth Avenue: A Very Special History*. HarBraceJ 1979 o.p. Delightful history of the families and buildings associated with the famous New York City thoroughfare.

Sklar, Robert. *Resisting Images: Essays on Cinema and History*. Temple U. Pr. 1990 $44.95. ISBN 0-87722-731-4. Interesting comments on the relation between visual images and historical realities.

Starr, Paul. *The Social Transformation of American Medicine*. 1982. Basic 1984 $17.00. ISBN 0-465-07935-0. Analyzes the rise of the medical profession and the change of medicine into an industry in the twentieth century.

Stilgoe, John R. *Borderland: Origins of the American Suburb, 1820–1939*. 1988. Yale U. Pr. 1990 $18.95. ISBN 0-300-04866-1. Engaging social history replete with attractive drawings and photographs.

Wilkinson, Rupert. *American Tough: The Tough-Guy Tradition and American Character*. Contributions in Amer. Studies. Greenwood 1984 $42.95. ISBN 0-313-23797-2. Intriguing exploration of the "macho" mystique.

Gender, Race, and Ethnicity

Abzug, Robert H., and Stephen E. Maizlish, eds. *New Perspectives on Race and Slavery in America: Essays in Honor of Kenneth M. Stampp*. U. Pr. of Ky. 1986 $24.00. ISBN 0-8131-1571-X

Alba, Richard D., ed. *Ethnicity and Race in the U.S.A.: Toward the Twenty-First Century*. 1984. Routledge 1988 $13.95. ISBN 0-415-00772-0. Significant volume of papers presented in 1984 at a major conference on race and ethnicity.

Banner, Lois. *Women in Modern America: A Brief History*. 1978. HB Coll. Pubs. 1984 $20.00. ISBN 0-15-596196-9. Reliable, comprehensive history that is well suited to both general readers and specialists.

Berkhofer, Robert F., Jr. *The White Man's Indian: Images of the American Indian from Columbus to the Present*. 1978. Random 1979 $8.75. ISBN 0-394-72794-0. Important scrutiny of white attitudes—often leading to actions—toward Native Americans.

Berry, Mary E., and John W. Blassingame. *Long Memory: The Black Experience in America*. OUP 1982 $39.95. ISBN 0-19-502909-7. History of the African American experience in the United States that takes a thematic approach, covering such topics as family and education.

Catlin, George. *Letters and Notes on the Manners, Customs and Conditions of the North American Indian*. 1844. 2 vols. Dover 1973 $8.95 ea. ISBNs 0-486-22118-0, 0-486-22119-9. "Catlin's 'letters'—traveler's accounts sent to Eastern newspapers—are as vividly descriptive as his famous portraits of Western chiefs" (*Library Journal*).

Cell, John W. *The Highest Stage of White Supremacy: The Origins of Segregation in South Africa and the American South*. Cambridge U. Pr. 1982 $59.95. ISBN 0-521-24096-4. Comparative history at its best, shedding light on the two societies and on the larger general subject of racism.

Chafe, William H. *The American Woman: Her Changing Social, Economic, and Political Roles, 1920–1970*. 1972. OUP 1974 $10.95. ISBN 0-19-501785-4. Sensitive study of feminism as it evolved into its contemporary manifestation.

Clinton, Catherine. *The Other Civil War: American Women in the Nineteenth Century*. Hill & Wang 1984 $8.95. ISBN 0-8090-0156-X. Good account of the first wave of feminism.

Cott, Nancy F., and Elizabeth H. Pleck, eds. *A Heritage of Her Own: Toward a New Social History of American Women. Families, Work, and Feminism in Amer. Ser.* S&S Trade 1980 $11.95. ISBN 0-317-05160-1. Essays reflecting wide-ranging research in all disciplines in women's studies.

Debo, Angie. *A History of the Indians of the United States. Civilization of Amer. Indians Ser.* 1970. U. of Okla. Pr. 1984 $16.95. ISBN 0-8061-1888-1. "An outstanding student of American Indian history has here synthesized her almost 50 years' research" (*Choice*).

Degler, Carl N. *At Odds: Women and the Family in America from the Revolution to the Present*. OUP 1980 $14.95. ISBN 0-19-502934-8. Comprehensive history of U.S. women over a period of 200 years.

Deloria, Vine, Jr. *Custer Died for Your Sins: An Indian Manifesto*. 1969. U. of Okla. Pr. 1988 $12.95. ISBN 0-8061-2129-7. Important discourse on the wrongs done to Native Americans and the differences between their problems and those of other minorities.

Donaldson, Gary A. *The History of African-Americans in the Military: Double V*. Krieger 1991 $15.50. ISBN 0-89464-514-5. Interesting chronicle of segregation, frustration, resistance, and heroism.

Duberman, Martin Baum. *Paul Robeson: A Biography*. 1989. Knopf 1990 $24.95. ISBN 0-394-52780-1. Superb biography of a great talent and outspoken advocate of racial justice.

Durham, Philip, and Everett L. Jones. *Negro Cowboys*. 1965. U. of Nebr. Pr. 1983 $9.95. ISBN 0-8032-6560-3. Fascinating story of the more than 5,000 African Americans who rode the ranges of America from Texas to Montana.

Edmunds, R. David, ed. *American Indian Leaders: Studies in Diversity*. U. of Nebr. Pr. 1980 $8.95. ISBN 0-8032-6705-3. Collection of 12 biographies showing the richness and variety of leadership roles among Native Americans.

Finkelman, Paul A., ed. *Race, Law, and American History, 1700–1990: The African-American Experience*. 10 vols. Garland 1992 o.p. Anthology of scholarly articles dealing with the critical aspect of race relations in U.S. history.

Forbes, Jack D. *Africans and Native Americans: The Language of Race and the Evolution of Red-Black Peoples*. U. of Ill. Pr. 1993 $14.95. ISBN 0-252-06321-X. Study of intermarriage and other relations between the two groups.

Franklin, John Hope. *Race and History: Selected Essays, 1938–1988*. La. State U. Pr. 1990 $29.95. ISBN 0-8071-1547-9. Essays reflecting the author's long-term study of race as a factor in the American experience.

Fredrickson, George M. *The Arrogance of Race: Historical Perspectives on Slavery, Racism, and Social Inequality*. U. Pr. of New Eng. 1988 $35.00. ISBN 0-8195-5177-5. Thoughtful essays on the centrality of race and ethnicity in the American experience.

Garcia, Mario T. *Mexican Americans: Leadership, Ideology, and Identity, 1930–1960*. Yale U. Pr. 1991 $17.95. ISBN 0-300-04984-6. Focuses on political leadership and roles in government.

Gatewood, Willard B. *Aristocrats of Color: The Black Elite, 1880–1920*. 1989. Ind. U. Pr. 1990 $39.95. ISBN 0-252-32552-8. Treats the social life and customs of a select group of African Americans in a difficult period.

Ginzberg, Lori D. *Women and the Work of Benevolence: Morality, Politics, and Class in the Nineteenth-Century United States*. 1990. Yale U. Pr. 1992 $12.00. ISBN 0-300-05254-5. "Her questions about the intersections of gender, morality, class, and politics will remain significant for years to come" (*American Historical Review*).

Goldfield, David. *Black, White, and Southern: Race Relations and Southern Culture, 1940 to the Present*. La. State U. Pr. 1991 $12.95. ISBN 0-8071-1682-3. Capable overview of the impact of the civil rights movement on the modern South.

Grossman, James R. *Land of Hope: Chicago, Black Southerners, and the Great Migration*. U. Ch. Pr. 1990 $14.95. ISBN 0-226-30995-9. Emphasizes the human aspects of the exodus from the South to the cities of the North.

Gutman, Herbert G. *The Black Family in Slavery and Freedom, 1750–1925*. 1976. Random 1977 $20.00. ISBN 0-394-72451-8. An "exciting, important, and humane book . . . [by] one of the most original and creative minds in the historical profession" (David H. Donald, publisher's note).

Hagan, William T. *American Indians. The Chicago History of Amer. Civilization Ser*. U. Ch. Pr. 1993 $13.95. ISBN 0-226-31237-2. Brief, vivid discourse on the tragic and unequal clash of the Native American nations and the rising United States.

Harding, Vincent. *The Other Revolution. Afro-Amer. Culture and Society Monographs*. Center for Afro-Amer. Studies 1981 o.p. Traces the course of the African American struggle in the United States from its African roots to the civil rights marches.

———. *There Is a River: The Black Struggle for Freedom in America*. 1981. HarBraceJ 1992 $19.95. ISBN 0-15-189342-X. History of black radicalism in the United States by a prominent African American intellectual.

Harlan, Louis R. *Booker T. Washington*. OUP Vol. 1 1972 $39.95. ISBN 0-19-501596-7. Vol. 2 1986 $39.95. ISBN 0-19-503202-0. Splendid biography still in process. Winner of the Bancroft and Beveridge prizes in 1983.

Hernton, Calvin. *Sex and Racism in America*. 1966. Doubleday 1992 $10.00. ISBN 0-385-42433-7. Fascinating study of fears, follies, myths, and realities in race relations.

Hill, Herbert, and James E. Jones, Jr., eds. *Race in America: The Struggle for Equality*. U. of Wis. Pr. 1993 $45.00. ISBN 0-299-13420-2. Massive work of great scope and depth with contributions from leading authorities on the subject.

Howe, Irving. *World of Our Fathers*. Schocken 1989 $14.95. ISBN 0-8052-0928-X

Huggins, Nathan Irvin. *Black Odyssey: The Afro-American Ordeal in Slavery*. 1977. Random rev. ed. 1990 $12.00. ISBN 0-679-72814-7. Eloquent, almost poetic, evocation of the slave experience.

Iorizzo, Luciano J., and Salvatore Mordello. *The Italian-Americans.* Macmillan 1980 $23.95. ISBN 0-8057-8416-0

Jensen, Joan M. *Passage from India: Asian Indian Immigrants in North America.* Yale U. Pr. 1988 $40.00. ISBN 0-300-03846-1. Good study of a growing and often neglected ethnic group in America.

Jones, Jacqueline. *Labor of Love, Labor of Sorrow: Black Women, Work, and the Family from Slavery to the Present.* 1985. Random 1986 $12.95. ISBN 0-394-74536-1. Fine work of scholarship that won the Bancroft Prize in 1986.

Jones, Maldwyn Allen. *American Immigration.* 1960. U. Ch. Pr. 1992 $35.00. ISBN 0-226-40634-2. Concise, readable, and informative overview of the subject.

Jordan, Winthrop D. *White Over Black: American Attitudes Toward the Negro, 1550–1812.* U. of NC Pr. 1968 $50.00. ISBN 0-8078-1055-X. National Book Award–winning dissection of racism in early American history. A monumental work of scholarship.

Josephy, Alvin M., ed. *America in 1492: The World of the Indian Peoples before the Arrival of Columbus.* Random 1992 $17.00. ISBN 0-679-74537-5. Sets the stage for the tragic clash of cultures that ensued.

Kessler-Harris, Alice. *Out to Work: A History of Wage-Earning Women in the United States.* OUP 1982 $30.00. ISBN 0-19-503024-9. Landmark history of women in the workplace.

Kluger, Richard. *Simple Justice: The History of Brown v. Board of Education and Black America's Struggle for Equality.* 1975. Random 1977 $25.00. ISBN 0-394-72255-8. Compelling history of a judicial case that revolutionized race relations in the United States.

Lee, Joann F., comp. *Asian American Experiences in the United States: Oral Histories of First to Fourth Generation Americans from China, the Philippines, Japan, India, the Pacific Islands, Vietnam, and Cambodia.* McFarland & Co. 1991 $24.95. ISBN 0-89950-585-6. Good collection of firsthand accounts that cover the full range of experiences and reactions.

Lemann, Nicholas. *Promised Land: The Great Black Migration and How It Changed America.* Knopf 1991 $24.45. ISBN 0-394-56004-3. Good social history of the twentieth-century migrations.

Lerner, Gerda, ed. *Black Women in White America: A Documentary History.* 1972. Random 1992 $15.00. ISBN 0-679-74314-6. Fine collection of documents from both the North and the South.

————. *The Female Experience: An American Documentary.* 1977. OUP 1992 $14.95. ISBN 0-19-507258-8. Collection that emphasizes social conditions from colonial to modern times.

Levine, Lawrence W. *Black Culture and Black Consciousness.* OUP 1977 $11.95. ISBN 0-19-502374-9. Brilliant study that shows the rich and diverse black culture that existed under slavery and how it has developed and deepened since.

McLaurin, Melton A. *Separate Pasts: Growing Up White in the Segregated South.* U. of Ga. Pr. 1987 $19.95. ISBN 0-8203-0943-5. Poignant personal recollections and historical reflections of a southern historian.

Mageli, Paul. *The Immigrant Experience.* Salem Pr. 1991 $40.00. ISBN 0-89356-671-3. An excellent bibliographic reference emphasizing the continuing role of immigration in U.S. history.

Malcolm X. *The Autobiography of Malcolm X, as Told to Alex Haley.* 1965. Ballantine 1992 $12.00. ISBN 0-345-37671-4. "Extraordinary. A brilliant, painful, important book" (*N.Y. Times*).

Marable, Manning. *Race, Reform, and Rebellion: The Second Reconstruction in Black America, 1945–1982.* 1984. U. Pr. of Miss. 2nd rev. ed. 1991 $35.00. ISBN 0-87805-505-3. Able assessment of the entire civil rights movement.

Marks, Carole. *Farewell—We're Good and Gone: The Great Black Migration. Blacks in the Diaspora Ser.* Ind. U. Pr. 1989 $37.95. ISBN 0-253-33642-2. Sets the record straight about the background, makeup, and nature of the exodus from the South in World War I and the 1920s.

Matthews, Glenna. *"Just a Housewife": The Rise and Fall of Domesticity in America.* OUP 1987 $25.00. ISBN 0-19-503869-2. Important study of a neglected aspect of labor history.

Meier, August, and Elliott Rudwick. *From Plantation to Ghetto.* 1966. Hill & Wang 1976 $10.95. ISBN 0-8090-0122-5. Excellent survey of the African American experience.

Miller, Kerby A. *Emigrants and Exiles: Ireland and the Irish Exodus to North America.* OUP 1985 $39.95. ISBN 0-19-503594-1. Fresh study of a major trans-Atlantic migration and of the conditions that led to it.

Mostwin, Danuta. *The Transplanted Family: A Study of Social Adjustment of the Polish Immigrant after the Second World War.* Ayer 1981 $38.50. ISBN 0-405-13442-8

Munoz, Carlos, Jr. *Youth, Identity, Power: The Chicano Movement.* Routledge Chapman & Hall 1989 $50.00. ISBN 0-86091-197-7. Authoritative chronicle of the Mexican American movement in modern times.

Nabokov, Peter, ed. *Native American Testimony: A Chronicle of Indian-White Relations from Prophecy to the Present, 1492–1992.* Viking Penguin 1993 $15.00. ISBN 0-14-012986-3. Remarkable collection of firsthand materials.

Nugent, Walter. *Crossings: The Great Transatlantic Migrations, 1870–1914.* Ind. U. Pr. 1992 $29.95. ISBN 0-253-34140-X. Concise and readable history of one of the great migrations in human history.

O'Brien, David J., and Stephen S. Fugita. *The Japanese American Experience. Minorities in Modern Amer. Ser.* Ind. U. Pr. 1991 $29.95. ISBN 0-253-34161-7. Good general history.

O'Reilly, Kenneth. *"Racial Matters": The FBI's Secret File on Black America, 1960–1972.* Free Pr. 1989 $29.95. ISBN 0-02-923681-9. Skillfully researched, judicious, and fascinating story of the perversion of law enforcement.

Raines, Howell. *My Soul Is Rested.* 1977. Viking Penguin 1983 $10.00. ISBN 0-14-006753-1. Superb oral history of the civil rights movement.

Rosenberg, Rosalind. *Divided Lives: American Women in the Twentieth Century. Amer. Century Ser.* Hill & Wang 1992 $35.00. ISBN 0-8090-9784-2. Good general history.

Rutledge, Paul J. *The Vietnamese Experience in America. Minorities in Modern Amer. Ser.* Ind. U. Pr. 1992 $29.95. ISBN 0-253-34997-4. Important study of an unforeseen consequence of the Vietnam War.

Ryan, Mary P. *Women in Public: Between Banners and Ballots, 1825–1880.* Johns Hopkins 1990 $30.00. ISBN 0-8018-3908-4. Speculative and stimulating reinterpretation of the relationship between gender and public life.

Salmon, Marylynn. *Women and the Law of Property in Early America.* U. of NC Pr. 1986 $29.95. ISBN 0-8078-1687-6. Important inquiry into the legal status of women, married and single, in the colonies and the early Republic.

Sanders, Ronald. *Lost Tribes and Promised Lands: The Origins of American Racism.* 1978. HarpC 1992 $13.00. ISBN 0-06-097449-4. Search for the roots of modern racism.

Shapiro, Herbert. *White Violence and Black Response from Reconstruction to Montgomery.* U. of Mass. Pr. 1988 $18.95. ISBN 0-87023-578-X. The vivid history—often sordid, always compelling—of violence in race relations in the United States.

Smith, John D., ed. *Racial Determinism and the Fear of Miscegenation Pre-1900.* Garland $71.00. ISBN 0-8153-0979-1

Stannard, David E. *American Holocaust: Columbus and the Conquest of the New World.* OUP 1992 $26.00. ISBN 0-19-507581-1. Stunning account, forcefully argued and thoroughly documented, of the destruction of the native peoples of the Americas by Europeans and white Americans.

Takaki, Ronald T. *Iron Cages: Race and Culture in 19th-Century America.* 1979. OUP 1990 $15.95. ISBN 0-19-506385-6. "A highly individual, discerning and provocative analysis . . . immensely readable" (*Publishers Weekly*).

———. *Strangers from a Different Shore: A History of Asian Americans.* 1989. Viking Penguin 1990 $13.00. ISBN 0-14-013885-4. Imaginative blend of oral history, narrative, and personal recollections, resulting in a portrait of great diversity.

Tolzman, Don H., ed. *The German Immigrant in America.* Heritage 1992 $14.50. ISBN 1-55613-630-7

Tsai, Shih-shan Henry. *The Chinese Experience in America.* Ind. U. Pr. 1986 $29.95. ISBN 0-253-31359-7. Good general account.

Weaver, Jack W., and Lester DeeGee. *Immigrants from Great Britain and Ireland.* Greenwood 1986 $39.95. ISBN 0-313-24342. One of the first works to list unpublished manuscript and archival materials about English, Scottish, Welsh, and Irish settlers in North America.

Weisbrot, Robert. *Freedom Bound: A History of America's Civil Rights Movement.* 1989. NAL-Dutton 1991 $11.00. ISBN 0-452-26553-3. Concise, readable history.

Williamson, Joel. *New People: Miscegenation and Mulattoes in the United States.* 1980. NYU Pr. 1984 $15.00. ISBN 0-8147-9199-9. Discerning study of a complex aspect of American life.

Cultural and Intellectual History

Alexander, Charles C. *Here the Country Lies: Nationalism and the Arts in Twentieth-Century America.* Ind. U. Pr. 1980 $35.00. ISBN 0-2535-15544-4. Interesting study of the influence nationalism has on the arts.

Arrington, Leonard J., and Davis Britton. *The Mormon Experience: A History of the Latter-day Saints.* 1979. U. of Ill. Pr. 1992 $14.95. ISBN 0-252-06236-1. Sound and judicious treatment of a major element in U.S. religious history.

Barth, Gunther. *City People: The Rise of Modern City Culture in Nineteenth-Century America.* OUP 1980 $32.95. ISBN 0-19-502755-8. Good social and cultural history that notes the persistence of ambivalent attitudes about city life.

Boyer, Paul. *By the Bomb's Early Light: American Thought and Culture at the Dawn of the Atomic Age.* 1985. Pantheon 1986 $11.95. ISBN 0-394-74767-4. "The best work yet on the atomic bomb's initial impact on American thought, culture and consciousness" (*Seattle Times*).

———. *When Time Shall Be No More: Prophecy Belief in Modern American Culture. Studies in Cultural History.* HUP 1992 $29.95. ISBN 0-674-95128-Y. Fascinating inquiry into a persistent social and cultural phenomenon.

Bruce, Robert V. *The Launching of Modern American Science.* Cornell Univ. Pr. 1988 $14.95. ISBN 0-8014-9496-6. Winner of the 1988 Pulitzer Prize.

Butler, Jon. *Awash in a Sea of Faith: Christianizing the American People, 1550–1865.* HUP 1990 $29.50. ISBN 0-674-05600-0. Lively revisionist history of early American religion that challenges several mainstream perceptions.

Ceplair, Larry, and Steven Englund. *The Inquisition in Hollywood: Politics in the Film Community, 1930–1960.* U. CA Pr. 1983 $13.95. ISBN 0-520-04886-5. Interesting case study of the relationship between the arts and government.

Clecak, Peter. *America's Quest for the Ideal Self: Dissent and Fulfillment in the 60s and 70s.* 1973. OUP 1983 $17.95. ISBN 0-19-503544-5. Original social history that examines the search for personal fulfillment and concludes that it was largely futile.

Cole, Thomas R. *The Journey of Life: A Cultural History of Aging in America.* Cambridge U. Pr. 1991 $27.95. ISBN 0-521-41020-7. Important addition to the growing body of literature on aging.

Cremin, Lawrence A. *American Education: The Metropolitan Experience, 1876–1980.* HarpC 1988 o.p. Third volume of a major history of education that relates education's colonial beginnings, traces its democratization, and recounts its transformation by urbanization and industrialization.

Curti, Merle. *Human Nature in American Thought: A History.* 1968. U. of Wis. Pr. 1980 $37.50. ISBN 0-299-07970-8. Surveys 400 years of political thought, noting the singular place "human nature" occupies in American perceptions.

Dary, David. *Cowboy Culture: A Saga of Five Centuries.* 1981. U. Pr. of KS 1989 $9.95. ISBN 0-7006-03990-5. Comprehensive history of the cowboy, his origins, and his lifestyle. Intended for the general reader.

Davis, Allen F. *American Heroine: The Life and Legend of Jane Addams.* 1975. Peter Smith 1983 $17.95. ISBN 0-8446-6016-7. "An impressively researched and splendidly written new biography . . . a major contribution both to urban and to intellectual history" (*Times Literary Supplement*).

Davis, David Brion. *From Homicide to Slavery: Studies in American Culture*. OUP 1986 $45.00. ISBN 0-19-505418-0. Essays of remarkable range and depth on such topics as violence, virility, loyalty, and identity.

Denning, Michael. *Mechanic Accents: Dime Novels and Working-Class Culture in America*. Verso 1987 $39.95. ISBN 0-86091-178-0. Study of the reading patterns of the masses and their cultural effects in industrializing America.

Dickstein, Morris. *Gates of Eden: American Culture in the 60s*. 1977. Viking Penguin 1989 $9.95. ISBN 0-14-011617-6. Good introduction to the relationship between culture and populist radicalism.

Erenberg, Lewis A. *Steppin' Out: New York Nightlife and the Transformation of American Culture, 1890–1930. Contributions in Amer. Studies*. Greenwood 1981 $38.50. ISBN 0-313-21342-9. Entertaining and substantial history of mass-consumer culture. For the general reader as well as the scholar.

Fitzgerald, Frances. *Cities on a Hill: A Journey through Contemporary American Cultures*. 1986. S&S Trade 1987 $11.00. ISBN 0-671-64561-7. Interesting survey of lifestyles and community groupings from 1960 to 1980.

Fox, Richard W., and T. Jackson Lears, eds. *The Culture of Consumption: Critical Essays in American History, 1880–1980*. Pantheon 1983 $10.36. ISBN 0-394-71611-6. Six historians explore the meaning, nature, and effects of consumer culture.

Gilbert, James, and others. *The Mythmaking Frame of Mind: Social Imagination and American Culture*. Wadsworth Pub. 1993. ISBN 0-534-19038-3. Essays documenting the variety of influences on the nation's cultural history, including the popular culture of cities, images and rituals, and the role of the marketplace.

Glassberg, David. *American Historical Pageantry: The Uses of Tradition in Early Twentieth Century America*. U. of NC Pr. 1990 $45.00. ISBN 0-8078-1916-6. Explores drama, festivity, and the like as instruments of cultural control.

Graebner, William. *The Age of Doubt: American Thought and Culture in the 1940s*. Macmillan 1990 $26.95. ISBN 0-8057-9061-6. "A splendid read, full of information" (*Choice*).

Hall, Peter Dobkin. *The Organization of American Culture, 1700–1900*. NYU Pr. 1982 $50.00. ISBN 0-8147-3415-4. Traces the rise of a distinctively American national culture.

Halttunen, Karen. *Confidence Men and Painted Women: A Study of Middle-Class Culture in America, 1830–1870. Yale Historical Publications*. 1983. Yale U. Pr. 1986 $13.00. ISBN 0-300-03788-0. Imaginative and provocative study of American culture in the mid-nineteenth century.

Hardison, O. B., Jr. *Disappearing through the Skylight: Culture and Technology in the Twentieth Century*. 1989. Viking Penguin 1990 $14.00. ISBN 0-14-011582-X. Account of the interaction of technology, nature, and human evolution.

Hatch, Nathan O. *The Democratization of American Christianity*. 1989. Yale U. Pr. 1991 $13.95. ISBN 0-300-05060-7. Important study of the impact on religion of democratic forces and an expansionist society.

Holifield, E. Brooks. *The Era of Persuasion: American Thought and Culture, 1521–1680. Amer. Thought and Culture Ser.* Macmillan 1989 $26.95. ISBN 0-8057-9050-0. Intellectual history of psychology and religion in the colonies.

Hollinger, David A., and Charles Capper, eds. *The American Intellectual Tradition: A Source Book*. 2 vols. OUP 1993 $39.95. ea. ISBNs 0-19-507778-4, 0-19-507780-6. Excellent collection.

Huggins, Nathan Irvin. *Harlem Renaissance*. OUP 1971 $15.95. ISBN 0-19-501665-3. Sensitive and thoughtful study of a major African American cultural phenomenon.

Hunter, James Davison. *Culture Wars: The Struggle to Define America*. Basic 1991 $25.00. ISBN 0-465-01533-6. Important study of the continuing clash between modern realities and traditional values.

Huston, Aletha C., and others. *Big World, Small Screen*. U. of Nebr. Pr. 1992 $25.00. ISBN 0-8032-2357-9. Evaluation of television's impact on American audiences. Study by American Psychology Association.

Kaledin, Eugenia. *The Education of Mrs. Henry Adams. Amer. Civilization Ser.* Temple U. Pr. 1982 o.p. Sensitive and perceptive complement to *The Education of Henry Adams*.

Kammen, Michael. *The Mystic Chords of Memory: The Transformation of Tradition in American Culture*. Random 1993 $20.00. ISBN 0-679-74177-1

Kasson, John F. *Rudeness and Civility: Manners in Nineteenth-Century Urban America. Amer. Century Ser.* 1990. Hill & Wang 1992 $22.95. ISBN 0-8090-3470. Entertaining contribution to the cultural history of everyday life.

Jhally, Sut, and Justin Lewis. *Enlightened Racism: The Cosby Show, Audiences, and the Myth of the American Dream*. Westview 1992 $15.95. ISBN 0-8133-1419-4. Based on an extensive study, funded by Bill Cosby himself.

Larson, Gary O. *The Reluctant Patron: The United States Government and the Arts, 1943–1965*. U. of Pa. Pr. 1983 $23.95. ISBN 0-8122-1144-8. Important history of the stormy relationship between the arts and Washington in the postwar period.

Lasch, Christopher. *The Culture of Narcissism: American Life in an Age of Diminished Expectations*. 1979. Norton 1991 $9.95. ISBN 0-393-30738-7. Call for rejection of the self-absorption of recent history in favor of a new politics and social discipline to meet challenges of the future. Winner of the 1980 National Book Award.

————. *The True and Only Heaven: Progress and Its Critics*. Norton 1990 $25.00. ISBN 0-393-02916-6. Work of profound cultural criticism that argues there is a basic incompatibility between democracy and progress.

Lears, T. Jackson. *No Place of Grace: Antimodernism and the Transformation of American Culture, 1800–1920*. 1981. Pantheon 1983 $18.50. ISBN 0-394-50816-5. "Auspicious radical history: cogently argued, crisply written, and alive with intellectual passion" (*Kirkus Reviews*).

Levine, Lawrence W. *Highbrow/Lowbrow: The Emergence of Cultural Hierarchy in America*. HUP 1988 $29.95. ISBN 0-674-39076-8. Innovative history that traces the growing gap between "serious" (highbrow) and "popular" (lowbrow) culture and analyzes the consequences.

————. *The Unpredictable Past: Explorations in American Cultural History*. OUP 1993 $16.95. ISBN 0-19-508297-4. Insightful essays on a variety of subjects by a leading cultural historian and former MacArthur Fellow.

Lewis, David L. *When Harlem Was in Vogue*. 1981. OUP 1989 $13.95. ISBN 0-19-505969-7. First-rate intellectual and social history of Harlem from 1905 to 1935 that captures the spirit and energy of the community.

Marcus, Greil. *Mystery Train: Images of America in Rock 'n' Roll Music*. 1975. NAL-Dutton 1990 $13.00. ISBN 0-452-26712-9. Imaginative history of popular culture as expressed in music.

May, Henry F. *The End of American Innocence: A Study of the First Years of Our Own Time, 1912–1917*. 1959. OUP 1979 $12.95. ISBN 0-19-502528-8. Major reinterpretation of American cultural history in the early twentieth century.

May, Lary. *Screening Out the Past: The Birth of Mass Culture and the Motion Picture Industry*. OUP 1980 $29.95. ISBN 0-19-502762-0. Splendid inquiry into the impact of a major cultural industry.

Newby, I. A. *Plain Folk in the New South: Social Change and Cultural Persistence, 1880–1915*. La. State U. Pr. 1989 $37.50. ISBN 0-8071-1456-1. Important study of social and cultural change among millworkers and sharecroppers.

O'Brien, Michael. *Rethinking the South: Essays in Intellectual History*. Johns Hopkins 1988 $38.50. ISBN 0-8018-3617-4. Essays presenting a revisionist view of southern life and culture before and after the Civil War.

O'Connor, John E., and Martin A. Jackson, eds. *American History/American Film: Interpreting the Hollywood Image*. 1983. Continuum 1988 $12.95. ISBN 0-8044-2672-4. Critical study of the television medium that uses individual program examples as documents or artifacts of the American past.

Pells, Richard H. *The Liberal Mind in a Conservative Age: American Intellectuals in the 1940s and 1950s.* 1985. U. Pr. of New Eng. 1989 $19.95. ISBN 0-8195-6225-4. Interesting overview and analysis of the rise of anticommunism and the retreat of liberalism during the two decades.

————. *Radical Visions and American Dreams: Cultural and Social Thought in the Depression Years.* 1973. U. Pr. of New Eng. $19.95. ISBN 0-8195-6122-3. Good study of the cultural impact of the New Deal.

Peretti, Burton W. *The Creation of Jazz: Music, Race, and Culture in Urban America.* U. of Ill. Pr. 1992 $29.95. ISBN 0-252-01708-0. Relying heavily on oral history, Peretti examines urban history and the jazz subculture beneath it.

Perry, Charles. *The Haight-Ashbury: A History.* Random 1984 $16.95. ISBN 0-394-41098-X. Richly detailed history of the counterculture capital of the 1960s.

Raboteau, Albert J. *Slave Religion: The "Invisible Institution" in the Antebellum South.* OUP 1978 $12.95. ISBN 0-19-502705-1. Excellent study of the institution around which antebellum African American culture developed.

Shi, David E. *The Simple Life: Plain Living and High Thinking in American Culture.* 1985. OUP 1986 $29.95. ISBN 0-19-503457-9. Imaginative history of conflicting forces in American culture—the persistent search for luxury and the preference for simplicity.

Sklar, Robert. *Movie-Made America: A Cultural History of American Movies.* 1975. Vin. 1976 $18.00. ISBN 0-394-72120-9. Impressive study of a major industry and cultural force in the modern United States.

Stein, Stephen J. *The Shaker Experience in America: A History of the United Society of Believers.* Yale U. Pr. 1992 $40.00. ISBN 0-300-05139-5. "Clear and well-researched: an invaluable history for those interested in one of the more fascinating forms of the American religious experience" (*Kirkus Reviews*).

Stevenson, Louise. *The Victorian Homefront: American Thought and Culture, 1860–1880.* *Amer. Thought and Culture Ser.* Macmillan 1991 $28.95. ISBN 0-8057-9058-6. Good overview of the period.

Udelson, Joseph H. *The Great Television Race: A History of the American Television Industry, 1925–1941.* U. of Ala. Pr. 1982 $17.50. ISBN 0-8173-0082-1. History of the development and early influence of television in the United States.

CHRONOLOGY OF AUTHORS

Davis, Jefferson. 1808–1889
Parkman, Francis. 1823–1893
Adams, Henry. 1838–1918
Roosevelt, Theodore. 1858–1919
Turner, Frederick Jackson. 1861–1932
Du Bois, W(illiam) E(dward) B(urghardt). 1868–1963
Becker, Carl L(otus). 1873–1945
Beard, Charles A(ustin). 1874–1948
Beard, Mary R(itter). 1876–1958
Morison, Samuel Eliot. 1887–1976
Schlesinger, Arthur M(eier). 1888–1965
Webb, Walter Prescott. 1888–1963
Nevins, Allan. 1890–1971
Bemis, Samuel Flagg. 1891–1973
De Voto, Bernard. 1897–1955
Catton, Bruce. 1899–1978
Commager, Henry Steele. 1902–
Bridenbaugh, Carl. 1903–1992
Kennan, George F(rost). 1904–

Miller, Perry. 1905–1963
Woodward, C(omer) Vann. 1908–
Potter, David M(orris). 1910–1971
Current, Richard N(elson). 1912–
Stampp, Kenneth M(ilton). 1912–
Boorstin, Daniel J(oseph). 1914–
Franklin, John Hope. 1915–
Handlin, Oscar. 1915–
Hofstadter, Richard. 1916–1970
Morgan, Edmund S(ears). 1916–
Schlesinger, Arthur M(eier), Jr. 1917–
Burns, James MacGregor. 1918–
Degler, Carl N(eumann). 1921–
Williams, William Appleman. 1921–1986
Bailyn, Bernard. 1922–
Leuchtenburg, William E(dward). 1922–
Genovese, Eugene D(ominick). 1930–
McPherson, James M(unro). 1936–

ADAMS, HENRY (BROOKS). 1838–1918

Born in Boston, Massachusetts, American historian and philosophy Henry Brooks Adams was the son of American diplomat Charles Frances Adams. As the Great grandson of John Adams, the second president of the United States, and grandson of John Quincy Adams, the sixth president, Henry Adams always understood that he had a special obligation to his country. Although he trained as an attorney, he was unable to accommodate himself to a political career and made history and travel his occupations instead. Both of these occupations served him well in their separate ways. One masterpiece of writing emerged from Adams's sojourns abroad—*Mont-St.-Michel and Chartres* (1904) a classic study of the unity of art and religion in the middle ages. Another derived from his brief sojourn (1870–1877) as a teacher of medieval history at Harvard University—his monumental nine-volume *History of the United States During the Administrations of Jefferson and Madison* (1889–1891). A third work, *The Education of Henry Adams* (1906), evolved out of his personal life and his efforts to define a basic philosophy of history. One of the most thoughtful of American autobiographies, it won the Pulitzer Prize for autobiography in 1919. In most of his writings, Adams blended well the eye of the worldly observer with the detachment of the scholar.

BOOKS BY ADAMS

Degradation of the Democratic Dogma. 1919. Peter Smith $12.00. ISBN 0-8446-1007-0. Elaboration of the "dynamic theory of history" enunciated in *The Education*, but also a reflection of Adams's doubts about democracy. Introduction by Brooks Adams.

Democracy: An American Novel. 1880. NAL-Dutton 1983 $3.50. ISBN 0-452-00651-1. Adams's opinion of public life in the Gilded Age. Lacking literary merit but interesting as a reflection of the times.

The Education of Henry Adams. 1906. Random 1990 $14.50. ISBN 0-679-73232-2. Neither a true autobiography nor a history, but part philosophy of history and part personal comment on the times, with enduring appeal.

Esther. Ed. by Robert E. Spiller. Schol. Facsimiles 1976 $50.00. ISBN 0-8201-1187-2. Second of Adams's imperfect novels. Strongly reflects Adams's religious doubts.

Henry Adams. Ed. by R. P. Blackmur. HarBraceJ 1980 $19.95. ISBN 0-15-139997-2. Selections from Adams's writings.

Henry Adams, Selected Letters. Ed. by Ernest Samuels. HUP 1992 $29.95. ISBN 0-674-38757-0. Judicious and representative selection of letters from the massive six-volume collection.

History of the United States During the Administrations of Jefferson and Madison. Ed. by Earl Harbert. 1889–91. Rprt. Serv. 1989 repr. of 1889 ed. $79.00. ISBN 0-7812-1440-8. Brilliant constitutional and political chronicle that illuminates individuals and issues and demonstrates a mastery of diplomatic history.

John Randolph of Roanoke. AMS Pr. repr. of 1882 ed. $31.50. ISBN 0-404-50865-0. Solid, readable biography.

Letters to a Niece and Prayer to the Virgin of Chartres. Ed. by Mabel La Farge. Scholarly 1970 repr. of 1920 ed. $29.00. ISBN 0-403-00490-X. Interesting elaborations of familiar themes in Adams's other writings.

Mont-St.-Michel and Chartres. 1904. Viking Penguin 1986 $7.95. ISBN 0-14-039054-5. Masterpiece of travel writing, beautifully evocative of the great shrines it celebrates.

Novels, Mont-Saint-Michel, The Education. Ed. by Ernest Samuels and Jayne N. Samuels. Library of America 1983 $27.50. ISBN 0-940450-12-7. Convenient and worthy collection edited by outstanding experts on Adams.

Tahiti: Memoirs of Arii Taimai. Schol. Facsimiles 1976 repr. of 1901 ed. $50.00. ISBN 0-8201-1213-5. Good reflection of the observant eye of a world traveler.

The United States in 1800. Cornell Univ. Pr. 1955 $7.95. ISBN 0-8014-9014-6. Reprint of the first six chapters of the *History of the United States During the Administrations of Jefferson and Madison.*

BOOKS ABOUT ADAMS

Adams, James Truslow. *Henry Adams.* Scholarly 1970 repr. of 1933 ed. $10.50. ISBN 0-403-00491-8. Good, but somewhat dated, one-volume biography.

Baym, M. I. *French Education of Henry Adams.* Kraus repr. of 1951 ed. o.p. Useful specialized study.

Chalfant, Edward. *His First Life, 1838–1862.* Vol. 1 in *Both Sides of the Ocean: A Biography of Henry Adams.* Shoe String 1982 $39.50. ISBN 0-208-01901-4. A good study of Adams's youthful years.

Condor, John. *Formula of His Own: Henry Adams' Literary Experiment.* U. Ch. Pr. 1970 $8.50. ISBN 0-226-11437-6. Interesting analysis of Adams's idiosyncratic approach to literature as reflected in his two novels.

Contosta, David R. *Henry Adams and the American Experiment.* *Lib. of Amer. Biography.* Little 1980 o.p. Readable concise biography of Adams.

Jordy, William H. *Henry Adams: Scientific Historian.* Elliotts Bks. 1970 o.p. Perhaps the best effort to decipher Adams's complex theory of history.

Kaledin, Eugenia. *The Education of Mrs. Henry Adams.* *Amer. Civilization Ser.* Temple U. Pr. 1982 o.p. Story of the woman in Adams's life, who ended her own life and profoundly affected his.

Levenson, J. C. *The Mind and Art of Henry Adams.* Stanford U. Pr. 1957 $52.50. ISBN 0-8047-0623-9. Outstanding study of the man and his place in history.

Nagel, Paul C. *Descent from Glory: Four Generations of the John Adams Family.* OUP 1983 $30.00. ISBN 0-19-503172-5. Excellent study of the remarkable family of which Henry was a part and which profoundly affected his life.

O'Toole, Patricia. *The Five of Hearts: An Intimate Portrait of Henry Adams and His Friends 1880–1918.* Crown Pub. Group 1990 $25.00. ISBN 0-517-56350-9. Revealing study of Adams's circle of highly influential friends, among them John Hay, Henry Cabot Lodge, and Theodore Roosevelt.

Samuels, Ernest. *Henry Adams.* 3 vols. HUP. Vol. 1 *The Young Henry Adams.* 1948 $28.00. ISBN 0-674-96630-9. Vol. 2 *The Middle Years.* 1958 $33.00. ISBN 0-674-38753-8. Vol. 3 *The Major Phase.* 1964 $40.50. ISBN 0-674-38751-1. Volume 2 won the Bancroft and Parkman prizes in 1959. A majestic achievement, generally considered one of the great biographies of American letters.

BAILYN, BERNARD. 1922–

An innovative and influential historian of early America, Bernard Bailyn has written quantitative studies of the colonial New England economy, probing examinations of the ideological origins of the American Revolution, and penetrating studies of the social and cultural foundations of American education. Bailyn is particularly adept at interweaving social, intellectual, economic, and political factors into coherent narrative history. A pioneer in adapting the new tools of social science to the writing of history, he is also a fine literary stylist.

Bailyn was born in Hartford, Connecticut, and did his undergraduate work at Williams College. He began his teaching career at Harvard University immediately after that university granted him a Ph.D. in 1953, and he remained there until he retired in 1991. During his tenure at Harvard, he was Winthrop Professor, Adams University Professor, and James Duncan Phillips Professor of Early American History. For years Bailyn was editor in chief of the Harvard Library and director of the Charles Warren Center for Studies in American History.

Bailyn has been Pitt Professor at Cambridge University and president of the American Historical Association, and he holds membership in the American Academy of Arts and Sciences and in the British Academy. His writings have earned him the Bancroft Prize, the National Book Award, and two Pulitzers— one in 1968 for *The Ideological Origins of the American Revolution* (1967), which challenges traditional interpretations of the causes of the Revolution, and the other in 1987 for *Voyagers to the West* (1986), which explores reasons for migration to America just prior to the Revolution.

BOOKS BY BAILYN

Education in the Forming of American Society: Needs and Opportunities for Study. 1960. Bks. Demand repr. of 1960 ed. $43.00. ISBN 0-7837-0280-9. Focuses on the influence of the New World environment on traditional European concepts of education.

Faces of Revolution: Personalities and Themes in the Struggle for American Independence. Knopf 1990 $29.95. ISBN 0-394-49895-X. Marvelous introduction to the people and issues of the time.

Glimpses of the Harvard Past. HUP 1986 $19.95. ISBN 0-674-35443-5. Interesting review of a great institution's heritage.

The Ideological Origins of the American Revolution. HUP 1967 $21.00. ISBN 0-674-44300-4. Elegantly written assertion that "Radical Whig" ideology was the critical element in the struggle for independence.

The Intellectual Migration: Europe and America, 1930–1960. (coedited with Donald H. Fleming). 1969. Bks. Demand repr. of 1969 ed. $160.00. ISBN 0-317-09993-0. Essays on the migration and effects of intellectual refugees from nazism and communism.

The New England Merchants in the Seventeenth Century. 1955. HUP 1980 $9.95. ISBN 0-674-61280-9. How family ties interconnected with political, economic, and social forces to help undermine the authority of the Puritan oligarchy.

The Ordeal of Thomas Hutchinson. HUP 1974 $27.00. ISBN 0-674-64160-4. Controversial biography of the Massachusetts Bay Colony governor. Winner of the National Book Award.

The Origins of American Politics. 1968. Random 1970 $4.76. ISBN 0-394-70865-2. Essays that elaborate the author's views on the American Revolution and its heritage.

The Peopling of British North America: An Introduction. 1986. Random 1988 $8.00. ISBN 0-394-75779-3

The Press and the American Revolution. (coedited with John B. Hench). NE U. Pr. 1980 $37.50. ISBN 0-930350-32-4. Collection of representative writings.

Strangers Within the Realm: Cultural Margins of the First British Empire. (coedited with Philip D. Morgan). 1980. U. of NC Pr. 1991 $39.95. ISBN 0-8078-1952-2. Coherent collection of essays dealing with the processes of "anglicization" in the First British Empire.

Voyagers to the West: A Passage in the Peopling of America on the Eve of the Revolution. Knopf 1986 $35.00. ISBN 0-394-51569-2. Pulitzer Prize–winner (1986) that with *Strangers Within the Realm* refutes the view of the frontier as a democratizing environment and puts new emphasis on the trans-Atlantic nature of the early American experience.

BEARD, CHARLES A(USTIN). 1874–1948, and BEARD, MARY R(ITTER). 1876–1958

Indiana-born Charles A. Beard studied at Oxford, Cornell, and Columbia universities, where he taught history and politics for more than a decade. One of the founders of the New School for Social Research, he also served as director of the Training School for Public Service in New York City. A political scientist whose histories were always written from an economic perspective, Beard was an authority on U.S. politics and government. Yet his great survey history, *The Rise of American Civilization*, published in 1927, deals with the whole range of human experience—war, imperialism, literature, art, music, religion, the sciences, the press, and women—as well as politics and economics.

Collaborating with Beard on this and other books was his wife, Mary Ritter Beard. Charles Beard described their coauthorship as a "division of argument." An able historian in her own right, Mary Ritter Beard took a special interest in the labor movement and feminism, subjects on which she produced several works. The Beards's books are scholarly, well written, and often witty, though sometimes a bit ponderous; they stand the test of time well. *The New Yorker* observed of their *Basic History* that it is "perhaps, all in all, the best one-volume history that has ever been written about the United States."

BOOKS BY CHARLES BEARD

America Faces the Future. (ed.) *Essay Index Repr. Ser.* Ayer repr. of 1932 ed. $24.50. ISBN 0-8369-1244-6. One among many volumes of essays, reflecting Beard's wide range of interests and concerns.

An Economic Interpretation of the Constitution of the United States. 1913. Free Pr. 1986 $27.95. ISBN 0-02-902470-6. Landmark study of the Constitution that still commands attention even though its economic interpretation of the founders' motives has been strongly challenged.

Century of Progress. (ed.) *Essay Index Repr. Ser.* Ayer repr. of 1932 ed. $27.50. ISBN 0-8369-1903-3. Volume of essays covering a variety of topics, including inventions and economic conditions.

Devil Theory of War: An Inquiry into the Nature of History and the Possibility of Keeping out of War. Greenwood 1969 repr. of 1936 ed. $35.00. ISBN 0-8371-0300-2. Sets forth Beard's theories of international relations and basic isolationism.

Economic Basis of Politics. Essay Index Repr. Ser. Ayer 3rd rev. ed. repr. of 1945 ed. $17.95. ISBN 0-8369-2535-1. Some of Beard's most significant writings on the economic interpretation of history and politics.

The Future Comes: A Study of the New Deal. (coauthored with George H. Smith). Greenwood 1972 repr. of 1933 ed. $38.50. ISBN 0-8371-5808-7. See *America Faces the Future.*

Industrial Revolution. Greenwood 1969 repr. of 1927 ed. $55.00. ISBN 0-8371-2168-X. Volume of essays covering topics germane to the period.

President Roosevelt and the Coming of the War, 1941: A Study in Appearances and Realities. 1948. Shoe String 1968 o.p. A scathing attack on FDR's foreign policy. Provoked widespread discussion and controversy in the postwar years.

Whither Mankind. (ed.) *Essay Index Repr. Ser.* Ayer repr. of 1928 ed. $24.50. ISBN 0-8369-2344-8. Collection of essays reflecting on the future of the nation and of humanity. Illustrative of Beard's wide-ranging interests.

Written History as an Act of Faith. Tex. Western 1960 o.p. Beard's 1933 presidential address to the American Historical Association, setting forth his philosophy of history. Still very much worth reading.

BOOKS BY MARY BEARD

America through Women's Eyes. (ed.) Rprt. Serv. 1991 repr. of 1933 ed. $109.00. ISBN 0-7812-6000-0. Interesting essays on the social conditions of women in America. A significant document in women's history.

The American Labor Movement: A Short History. Ayer 1969 repr. of 1931 ed. $13.00. ISBN 0-405-02103-8. Important study of labor that emphasizes social conditions and women's roles.

Women as a Force in History: A Study in Traditions and Realities. Persea Bks. 1987 repr. of 1946 ed. $12.95. ISBN 0-89255-113-5. Important early title in women's history.

BOOKS BY CHARLES BEARD AND MARY BEARD

America in Midpassage. 1939. *Rise of Amer. Civilization Ser.* Peter Smith 1966 o.p. Sequel to *The Rise of American Civilization* that focuses on the period from 1918 to 1945.

The Beards' New Basic History of the United States. 1944. Doubleday rev. ed. 1960 o.p.
  Revised edition to which William Beard added the word *New* to the title.
The Rise of American Civilization. 1927. 2 vols. in 1. Macmillan 1964 o.p. Masterly
  synthesis of American history that is still a pleasure to read and ponder.

BOOKS ABOUT CHARLES BEARD

Benson, Lee. *Turner and Beard: American Historical Writing Reconsidered.* Greenwood
  1980 repr. of 1960 ed. o.p. Thoughtful discussion of two master writers of history.
Brown, Robert E. *Charles Beard and the Constitution: A Critical Analysis of "An
  Economic Interpretation of the Constitution."* Greenwood 1979 repr. of 1956 ed.
  $45.00. ISBN 0-313-21048-9. Generally persuasive but sometimes overdrawn indict-
  ment of Beard's methodology and assumptions.
Hofstadter, Richard. *The Progressive Historians: Turner, Beard, Parrington.* U. Ch. Pr.
  1979 o.p. Searching analysis, critical but judicious, that puts Beard in proper
  historical context.
Skotheim, Robert Allen. *American Intellectual Histories and Historians.* Greenwood 1978
  repr. of 1966 ed. $35.00. ISBN 0-313-20120-X. Good assessment of Beard's
  contributions.

BOOKS ABOUT MARY BEARD

Cott, Nancy F., ed. *A Woman Making History: Mary Ritter Beard Through Her Letters.* Yale
  U. Pr. 1991 $17.00. ISBN 0-300-05252-9. Provides a myriad of insights into the
  founder of the field of women's history.
Lane, Anne J., ed. *Mary Ritter Beard: A Sourcebook.* NE U. Pr. 1988 $11.95. ISBN 1-55553-
  029-X. Skillfully edited essays, lectures, and addresses.

BECKER, CARL L(OTUS). 1873–1945

Few historians of the United States have written as well as Carl Becker,
Cornell University's famous professor of modern European history. Becker was
born in Iowa and studied at the University of Wisconsin, where he earned his
Ph.D. in 1907. His broad study, *The Heavenly City of the Eighteenth-Century
Philosophers* (1932), is a classic, as is *The Heavenly City Revisited.* Becker taught
at Dartmouth and the University of Kansas before joining the Cornell faculty in
1917. After his retirement in 1941, he was professor emeritus and university
historian at Cornell. He remains today a model for writers of history, who
admire his economy of words, keen analytical sense, and graceful style. As a
distinguished essayist, practicing historian, and apostle of democracy, Becker
almost always made freedom and responsibility his themes.

BOOKS BY BECKER

The Beginnings of the American People. 1915. Cornell Univ. Pr. 1960 o.p. Superb concise
  history of the colonial period.
The Declaration of Independence: A Study in the History of Political Ideas. Peter Smith
  $18.75. ISBN 0-8446-1619-2. Brilliant analysis of the structure, drafting, and
  philosophy of the Declaration.
Detachment and the Writing of History: Essays and Letters of Carl L. Becker. Ed. by Phil L.
  Snyder. Greenwood 1972 repr. of 1958 ed. $49.75. ISBN 0-8371-6023-5. Small gems
  on historical writing, education, and democracy.
The Eve of the Revolution: A Chronicle of the Breach with England. Rprt. Serv. 1991 repr.
  of 1920 ed. $79.00. ISBN 0-7812-6110-4. Classic study of the events leading to
  independence.
Everyman His Own Historian. Quadrangle 1966 o.p. Elegant statement of Becker's
  philosophy of history.

Freedom and Responsibility in the American Way of Life. Greenwood 1980 repr. of 1945 ed. $35.00. ISBN 0-313-22361-0. Brilliant commentary on some essentials of the American polity.

The Heavenly City of the Eighteenth-Century Philosophers. Storrs Lecture Ser. Yale U. Pr. 1932 $9.95. ISBN 0-300-00017-0. Becker's masterpiece—a superb study of the Enlightenment.

A History of Political Parties in the Province of New York, 1760–1776. 1908. Madison Hse. 1991 $9.95. ISBN 0-685-53540-1. Becker's first book. Still an authoritative study.

How New Will the Better World Be? A Discussion of Post-War Reconstruction. Essay Index Repr. Ser. Ayer repr. of 1944 ed. $20.00. ISBN 0-8369-2482-7. Reflection of Becker's hopes and fears about the post–World War II world.

Progress and Power. AMS Pr. repr. of 1949 ed. $21.50. ISBN 0-404-20023-0. Thoughtful essay on prospects for the world.

Safeguarding Civil Liberty Today. Peter Smith 1949 $11.25. ISBN 0-8446-1064-X. Becker's well-founded concern about civil liberty in the early Cold War years.

The Spirit of '76 and Other Essays. Rprt. Serv. 1991 repr. of 1927 ed. $69.00. ISBN 0-7812-6102-3. Trenchant and readable essays on freedom, politics, the Constitution, and other topics.

BOOKS ABOUT BECKER

Hofstadter, Richard. *The Progressive Historians: Turner, Beard, Parrington.* U. Ch. Pr. o.p. Discusses similarities and differences between Becker and the progressive triumvirate.

Rockwood, Raymond O., ed. *Carl Becker's Heavenly City Revisited.* Shoe String repr. of 1958 ed. $17.50 o.p. Good analysis and appreciation.

Skotheim, Robert Allen. *American Intellectual Histories and Historians.* Greenwood 1978 repr. of 1966 ed. $35.00. ISBN 0-313-20120-X. Good survey that puts Becker in historical perspective.

Strout, Cushing. *The Pragmatic Revolt in American History: Carl Becker and Charles Beard.* Greenwood 1980 repr. of 1966 ed. o.p. Thoughtful evaluation of Becker's work and influence.

BEMIS, SAMUEL FLAGG. 1891–1973

An outstanding authority on the history of U.S. diplomacy, Samuel Bemis taught history at several schools before joining the faculty of Yale University in 1935. In 1945 he became Sterling Professor of Diplomatic History and International Relations at Yale, where he remained until 1960. Bemis, who was born in Worcester, Massachusetts, and received his Ph.D. from Harvard University, won two Pulitzer Prizes, one in history for *Pinckney's Treaty* (1926) and one in biography for *John Quincy Adams* (1949). He served as president of the American Historical Association and was for many years advisory editor for the series *The American Secretaries of State and Their Diplomacy.*

BOOKS BY BEMIS

American Foreign Policy and the Blessings of Liberty, and Other Essays. Greenwood 1975 repr. of 1962 ed. $35.00. ISBN 0-8371-8132-1. Essays reflecting Bemis's strong faith in democracy and the American system.

The American Secretaries of State and Their Diplomacy, 1776–1925. (ed.) 1927. 10 vols. in 5. Cooper Sq. repr. of 1928 ed. o.p. Valuable collection of documents and commentaries on the nation's foreign affairs.

The Diplomacy of the American Revolution. 1935. Greenwood 1983 repr. of 1957 ed. $45.50. ISBN 0-313-24173-2. Judicious and comprehensive history of delicate maneuvering in foreign affairs.

Guide to the Diplomatic History of the United States, 1775–1921. (coauthored with Grace
   Gardner Griffin). 1935. Peter Smith 1959 o.p. Very useful reference tool for anyone
   interested in the history of American foreign policy.
Jay's Treaty: A Study in Commerce and Diplomacy. 1923. Greenwood 1975 repr. of 1962
   ed. $35.00. ISBN 0-8371-8133-X. Definitive study of the 1794 treaty with Great
   Britain, the first international treaty of Washington's presidency.
John Quincy Adams. 2 vols. Greenwood 1980–81 repr. of 1949–1956 ed. o.p. Superb
   biography of the nation's greatest diplomat. Written with authority and grace.
Pinckney's Treaty: America's Advantage from Europe's Distress, 1783–1800. 1926.
   Greenwood 1973 repr. of 1960 ed. $65.00. ISBN 0-8371-6954-2. The subtitle tells the
   theme of this excellent study of American diplomacy in the early Republic.

BOORSTIN, DANIEL J(OSEPH). 1914–

A prolific writer, Daniel Boorstin is the author of numerous scholarly and
popular works in American Studies. In 1959 Columbia University awarded him
its Bancroft Prize for *The Americans: The Colonial Experience* (1958), the first
volume of his trilogy *The Americans.* In 1966 he received the Francis Parkman
Award for the second volume, *The Americans: The National Experience* (1965),
and in 1974 he won the Pulitzer Prize for the third volume, *The Americans: The
Democratic Experience* (1973). Boorstin's wife Ruth has been editor for all of his
books, many of which have been translated into Chinese, Japanese, and various
European languages.

Born in Georgia and raised in Oklahoma, Boorstin received degrees from
Harvard and Yale universities and was a Rhodes Scholar at Balliol College,
Oxford. A member of the Massachusetts Bar, he has been visiting professor of
American History at the Universities of Rome, Puerto Rico, Kyoto, and Geneva.
He was the first incumbent of the chair of American History at the Sorbonne
and Pitt Professor of American History and Institutions at Cambridge. For 25
years, he taught at the University of Chicago. In 1969 Boorstin became director
of the National Museum of History and Technology of the Smithsonian
Institution. In 1973 he became senior historian at the Smithsonian. Boorstin
was appointed Librarian of Congress in 1975 and served in that position with
distinction for 12 years, becoming Librarian Emeritus in 1987.

BOOKS BY BOORSTIN

America and the Image of Europe: Reflections on American Thought. 1960. Peter Smith
   $11.25. ISBN 0-8446-1703-2. Treatise on American national characteristics.
America in Two Centuries: An Inventory. (ed.) 53 vols. Ayer 1976 $3,571.50. ISBN 0-405-
   07666-5. Huge collection on technology and society.
The Americans. 3 vols. Random 1958–73. $109.90. ISBN 0-394-49588-8. "An excellent
   socio-history of the American community. . . . Highly organized, with a wealth of
   material never previously drawn from primary sources" (*Library Journal*).
The American Primer. (ed.) 1966. NAL-Dutton 1968 $9.00. ISBN 0-452-00922-7. Useful
   source of information about the United States and American society.
The Creators: A History of Heroes of the Imagination. Random 1992 $29.95. ISBN 0-394-
   54395-5. Chronicle of humanity's creative spirit in the arts and other areas.
Decline of Radicalism: Reflections of America Today. Random 1969 $5.95. ISBN 0-394-
   42184-1
Democracy and Its Discontents: Reflections on Everyday America. Random 1974 $5.95.
   ISBN 0-394-49146-7. Reflections of a "consensus historian" on social and political
   conditions in modern America.
The Discoverers: A History of Man's Search to Know His World and Himself. Random 1985
   $16.00. ISBN 0-394-72625-1. Chronicle of creativity and imagination in geography,
   the sciences, history, and other fields.

The Discoverers: An Illustrated History of Man's Search to Know His World and Himself. 2 vols. Abrams 1991 $75.00. ISBN 0-8109-3207-5

The Exploring Spirit: America and the World, Then and Now. Random 1976 $6.95. ISBN 0-394-40602-8. Celebration of the American inquisitive and enterprising spirit.

The Genius of American Politics. 1953. U. Ch. Pr. 1958 $8.95. ISBN 0-226-06491-3. Deservedly popular and enduring inquiry into the nature of American politics and constitutionalism.

Hidden History. 1987. Peter Smith 1992 $21.00. ISBN 0-8446-6614-9. Thoughts on the nature of American civilization.

The Image: A Guide to Pseudo-Events in America. 1961. Peter Smith 1984 $23.75. ISBN 0-8446-6122-8. Published earlier as *The Image; or, Whatever Happened to the American Dream.* Probing inquiry into the nature of American society, culture, and national characteristics.

The Lost World of Thomas Jefferson. 1948. U. Ch. Pr. 1981 $12.95. ISBN 0-226-06496-4. Superb study of political philosophy in the early Republic.

BRIDENBAUGH, CARL. 1903–1992

A prolific historian of colonial and revolutionary America, Carl Bridenbaugh was born in Philadelphia and educated at Dartmouth College and Harvard University (Ph.D., 1936). He taught at Massachusetts Institute of Technology and Brown University and from 1945 to 1950 directed the Institute of Early American History and Culture at Williamsburg, Virginia. For the next 12 years, he was Margaret Byrne Professor of United States History at the University of California in Berkeley, a position he left in 1962 to become University Professor at Brown University.

Member of the American Philosophical Society, a fellow of the American Academy of Arts and Sciences, president of the American Historical Association (1962), and recipient of many honors in this country and abroad, Bridenbaugh wrote social and intellectual history in a straightforward, vigorous manner. His *Cities in the Wilderness* (1938) and *Cities in Revolt* (1955) anticipated by many years the urban social history of later scholars. Although these works lack the analytical quality of later studies in that genre, they still stand as models of historical skill and mastery.

BOOKS BY BRIDENBAUGH

Cities in Revolt: Urban Life in America, 1743–1776. 1955. OUP 1971 o.p. Focuses on the importance of urban centers in the coming and course of the American Revolution.

Cities in the Wilderness: The First Century of Urban Life in America, 1625–1742. 1938. OUP 1971 o.p. Exhaustive social history of colonial city life, crammed with fascinating details.

The Colonial Craftsman. 1950. Bks. Demand repr. of 1961 ed. $60.00. ISBN 0-685-15677-X. An appreciation of skilled artisanship in early American society.

Early Americans. OUP 1981 $30.00. ISBN 0-19-502788-4. Essays on various topics illustrating the growth and development of colonial society.

Gentleman's Progress: The Itinerarium of Dr. Alexander Hamilton, 1744. U. of Pittsburgh Pr. 1992 repr. of 1948 ed. $29.95. ISBN 0-8229-3698-4. Classic travel account, superbly interpreted.

Jamestown, 1544–1699. OUP 1980 $40.00. ISBN 0-19-502650-0. "Mr. Bridenbaugh makes very vivid the kind of rag, tag, and bobtail who were our earliest immigrants. . . . His sense of the past is inclusive: he tells of religion and sports and architecture as well as politics and war" (*The New Yorker*).

Mitre and Sceptre: Transatlantic Faith, Ideas, Personalities, and Politics, 1689–1775. 1962. OUP 1967 o.p. Persuasive argument that fear of an Anglican episcopacy in America was an important part of the revolutionary movement.

Myths and Realities: Societies of the Colonial South. Greenwood 1981 repr. of 1952 ed.
$45.00. ISBN 0-313-22770-5. Expert analysis of the three colonial societies of
Chesapeake, the Carolinas, and the Back Settlements.

No Peace Beyond the Line: The English in the Caribbean, 1624–1690. (coauthored with
Roberta Bridenbaugh). OUP 1972 o.p. "[A] conceptual masterpiece, for the
Bridenbaughs successfully weave together the complex economic, social, racial, and
political strands of the story" (*Choice*).

Rebels and Gentlemen: Philadelphia in the Age of Franklin. (coauthored with Jessica
Bridenbaugh). Greenwood 1978 repr. of 1942 ed. $38.50. ISBN 0-313-20300-8.
Persuasive portrait of colonial Philadelphia as one of the great cities of the world and
a center of culture.

Seat of Empire: The Political Role of Eighteenth-Century Williamsburg. Williamsburg rev.
ed. 1958 o.p. Interesting look at a colonial capital.

Silas Downe, Forgotten Patriot: His Life and Writings. 1974. Madison Hse. 1991 $12.95.
ISBN 0-685-53545-2. Chronicle of an early influential Rhode Islander.

The Spirit of '76: The Growth of American Patriotism Before Independence. OUP 1975 o.p.
For the general reader. A bold argument that Americans were already a "nation" by
the time of the Revolution.

Vexed and Troubled Englishmen, 1590–1642. OUP 1968 $29.95. ISBN 0-19-500493-0.
Fascinating catalog of traits and habits of the English generation that formed the first
migration to America.

BURNS, JAMES MACGREGOR. 1918–

Born in Melrose, Massachusetts, James Burns was educated at Williams
College and Harvard University (Ph.D., 1947). In 1941 he began teaching at
Williams, where he remains as Distinguished Professor Emeritus. Although a
political scientist by training, Burns approaches his work with the eye of a
historian. His forté is American political history, as masterfully demonstrated in
his popular biographies of Franklin Roosevelt (*Roosevelt: The Lion and the Fox,*
1956, and *Roosevelt: The Soldier of Fortune,* 1970), and John Kennedy (*John
Kennedy: A Political Profile,* 1959), and in his multivolume history *The American
Experiment.*

Burns's two volumes on the life and work of FDR won him the Pulitzer Prize,
the Parkman Prize, and the National Book Award. The first volume of *The
American Experiment—The Vineyard of Liberty* (1982)—earned him a second
Pulitzer. Not content with merely writing about politics and political history,
Burns has long been active on the national political scene. In 1958 he ran
unsuccessfully for Congress.

BOOKS BY BURNS

The American Experiment, Vol. I: The Vineyard of Liberty. Random 1983 $22.95. ISBN 0-
394-71629-9. "[Burns] writes political history in the grand style, encompassing not
only politics but economic growth, cultural issues, intellectual currents, and
anything else he can get his hands on" (Joel Sibley, *Journal of American History*).

The American Experiment, Vol. II: The Workshop of Democracy. 1985. Random 1986
$23.00. ISBN 0-394-74320-2. Splendid narrative and sharp analysis of the period of
industrial growth and emergence of the United States as a world power.

The American Experiment, Vol. III: The Crosswinds of Freedom. 1989. Vin. 1990 $16.95.
ISBN 0-679-72819-8. Central theme is the decline of political leadership in the
twentieth century. A curious mix of pessimism and optimism.

Cobblestone Leadership: Majority Rule, Minority Power. (coauthored with Marvin L.
Overby). U. of Okla. Pr. 1990 $19.95. ISBN 0-8061-2314-1. Collection of forceful
essays on the failures and prospects for reform of American party government.

Government by the People. (coauthored with others). 1952. P-H 1987. ISBN 0-13-
361684-3. Popular standard survey of American government.

John Kennedy: A Political Profile. 1959. Avon 1961 o.p. First full-length biography of JFK. Superseded in some ways by more recent studies, but still a vivid and exciting narrative.

A People's Charter: The Pursuit of Rights in America. (coauthored with Stewart Burns). Knopf 1991 $29.50. ISBN 0-394-57763-9. Account of the struggle to gain and maintain the people's rights against the state's tendency to curtail them in favor of social stability.

Roosevelt: The Lion and the Fox. 1956. HarBraceJ 1983 o.p. Shrewd, witty, and perceptive political biography focusing on the New Deal years.

Roosevelt: The Soldier of Fortune. HarBraceJ 1970 o.p. Continuation of a highly successful political biography into the war years.

CATTON, (CHARLES) BRUCE. 1899–1978

Bruce Catton was "a journalist turned historian." Born in Michigan, he studied at Oberlin College, which he left to pursue a career in journalism. In 1941 he became a government information specialist and during World War II served on the War Production Board. Out of this came his first book, *War Lords of Washington* (1948). A founding editor of the *American Heritage* magazine from 1954 to 1959, he continued to serve as senior editor thereafter.

Catton made the Civil War his bailiwick and proved himself a master at marshaling an amazing number of facts into highly readable narratives. His story of the last year of the Civil War, *A Stillness at Appomattox* (1953), won both the National Book Award for distinguished nonfiction and the Pulitzer Prize in history in 1954. His three-volume *Centennial History* has been called "the finest type of popular yet factual historical writing" (*Library Journal*). In 1968 Catton was appointed to a three-year term as an honorary consultant in American history by the Library of Congress. During his lifetime he received honorary degrees from some 20 universities.

BOOKS BY CATTON

America Goes to War: The Civil War and Its Meaning to Americans Today. 1958. U. Pr. of New Eng. 1993 $9.95. ISBN 0-8195-6016-2. Thoughtful assessment of the war's place in U.S. history.

American Heritage Picture History of the Civil War. (ed.) 1960. Outlet Bk. Co. 1985 $19.99. ISBN 0-517-38556-2. Outstanding photographic record of the war years with very readable narrative by Catton.

The Army of the Potomac: A Trilogy. 1951–53. 3 vols. Doubleday 1990 $38.85. ISBN 0-385-41689-X. Superb military history, written with understated elegance.

The Civil War. 1971. HM 1985 $10.70. ISBN 0-8281-0305-4. Somewhat different version of the *American Heritage Picture History of the Civil War.*

The Coming Fury. Centennial History of the Civil War, Vol. 1. WSP 1971 o.p. Dramatic narrative of the coming of the war and the first engagements.

Gettysburg: The Final Fury. 1974. Doubleday 1990 $10.95. ISBN 0-385-41145-6. Vivid portrayal of the bloody turning point in the war.

Grant Moves South. 1960. Little 1990 $15.95. ISBN 0-316-13244-6. Second volume in a three-volume biography begun by Lloyd Lewis and taken over by Catton after Lewis's death. Focuses on Grant's campaigns in Tennessee.

Grant Takes Command. 1969. Little 1990 $15.95. ISBN 0-316-13240-3. Third volume in the Grant biography. Follows Grant from the time he takes over the Army of the Potomac to the end of the war.

Never Call Retreat. Centennial History of the Civil War, Vol. 3. Buccaneer Bks. 1991 $31.95. ISBN 0-89966-800-3. Final volume in the series. Carries the war from Fredericksburg to the South's surrender and the death of Lincoln.

Reflections on the Civil War. Ed. by John Leekley. Doubleday 1984 $4.95. ISBN 0-425-10495-8. Selected writings by Catton on the war.

Terrible Swift Sword. Centennial History of the Civil War, Vol. 2. PB 1982 $4.95. ISBN 0-671-44925-7. Traces the people and events leading to the Emancipation Proclamation and McClellan's removal from command of the Union Army.

This Hallowed Ground. Doubleday 1956 $17.95. ISBN 0-385-04664-2. Story of the Union side in the Civil War.

Two Roads to Sumter. (coauthored with William B. Catton). 1963. Peter Smith 1992 $18.50. ISBN 0-8446-6498-7. Reliable and readable history of the secession crisis.

U. S. Grant and the American Military Tradition. Lib. of Amer. Biography. 1954. Scott F. 1987 $13.00. ISBN 0-673-39327-5. Grant as a man, soldier, and president.

Waiting for the Morning Train: An American Boyhood. Wayne St. U. Pr. 1972 $13.95. ISBN 0-8143-1885-1. Author's reminiscences of his youth.

War Lords of Washington. Greenwood repr. of 1948 ed. $35.00. ISBN 0-8371-2149-3. Journalistic chronicle of Washington in World War II.

COMMAGER, HENRY STEELE. 1902–

A native of Pittsburgh, Pennsylvania, who was educated at the University of Chicago, Henry Steele Commager taught history first at New York University and then at Columbia University. Upon his "retirement" from Columbia in 1956, he moved on to Amherst College, where he remains today as Emeritus Professor and Simpson Lecturer. In addition to lecturing at many universities throughout the world, he has been Harmsworth Professor at Oxford University and Pitt Professor at Cambridge University, where he is also an honorary fellow at Peterhouse College. Commager's writings, which are extensive, are deservedly popular with both scholars and general readers and range widely over such topics as education, the Civil War, civil liberties, the Enlightenment, and immigration. Many of his books reflect his keen interest in constitutional history and civil liberties. Commager is also a great documentarian, who is said to consider *Documents of American History* (1934), the 1988 edition of which he coedited with Milton Cantor, to be his most significant contribution.

BOOKS BY COMMAGER

The American Mind: An Interpretation of American Thought and Character since the 1880's. Yale U. Pr. 1950 $16.00. ISBN 0-300-00046-4. Good intellectual history that is both judicious and assertive of the author's views.

The Blue and the Gray: The Story of the Civil War as Told by Participants. (ed.) 1950. 2 vols. Outlet Bk. Co. 1982 $12.98. ISBN 0-517-38379-9. Dramatic, popular, and firsthand history.

Britain through American Eyes. McGraw 1974 o.p. Delightful reflections on the two societies.

Commonwealth of Learning. HarpC 1968 o.p. Bold call for universities to take an active role in reshaping the societies in which they function.

The Defeat of the Confederacy. (ed.) 1964. Krieger $8.50. ISBN 0-442-00071-5. Useful collection of documents.

Documents of American History. (coedited with Milton Cantor). 1934. Vol. 1 (to 1898). P-H 1988 $41.00. ISBN 0-13-217274-7. Enormously useful collection. Currently undergoing extensive re-editing.

The Empire of Reason: How Europe Imagined and America Realized the Enlightenment. OUP 1982 repr. of 1977 ed. $9.95. ISBN 0-19-503062-1. Work culminating Commager's lifelong study of the Enlightenment.

The Era of Reform Eighteen Thirty to Eighteen Sixty. Krieger 1982 $9.50. ISBN 0-89874-498-9. Valuable study of the period.

Fifty Basic Civil War Documents. (ed.) Krieger 1982 repr. of 1965 ed. $9.50. ISBN 0-89874-497-0. Illustrative and useful collection.

Freedom, Loyalty, Dissent. OUP 1954 $19.95. ISBN 0-19-500510-4. Ringing defense of civil liberties written at a time when those liberties were under severe attack in the United States.

Henry Steele Commager's The Story of the Second World War. 1945. Brasseys 1991 $23.95. ISBN 0-08-041066-9. Historian's perspective on a war that had just concluded.

Lester Ward and the Welfare State. Irvington 1967 $49.50. ISBN 0-672-50998-9. Fine study of pioneer American sociologist whose ideas anticipated the New Deal.

Majority Rule and Minority Rights. 1943. Peter Smith $11.25. ISBN 0-8446-1123-9. Thoughtful study in constitutional and legal history.

Noah Webster's American Spelling Book. Tchrs. College Pr. 1963 $7.00. ISBN 0-8077-1176-4. Delightful look at the Americanization of the English language in the early Republic.

Pocket History of the United States. (coauthored with Allan Nevins). 1942. PB 9th rev. ed. 1991 $4.95. ISBN 0-671-62992-1. Perennially popular and useful brief history.

The Spirit of '76: The Story of the American Revolution as Told by Participants. (coauthored with Richard B. Morris). 1958. HarpC 1967 o.p. Still valuable collection of firsthand accounts.

Theodore Parker: Yankee Crusader. 1936. Peter Smith 1982 $11.25. ISBN 0-8446-1884-5. Superb biography of an antebellum reformer and abolitionist.

CURRENT, RICHARD N(ELSON). 1912–

Born in Colorado City, Colorado, Richard Current received his B.A. from Oberlin College and went on to earn an M.S. at the Fletcher School of Law and Diplomacy and a Ph.D. in history (1939) at the University of Wisconsin. He taught at a number of institutions, including Rutgers University, Lawrence College, Mills College, the University of Illinois, and the University of Wisconsin, before becoming Distinguished Professor of American History at the University of North Carolina at Greensboro (1966–1983). Current has also taught in Japan, India, the Netherlands, Australia, Chile, and Germany. He was Harmsworth Professor at Oxford University.

Current's interests are legion, and he has written with authority and verve on subjects ranging from the invention of the typewriter to American diplomacy. Few historians have so skillfully and sensitively probed Abraham Lincoln's racial views and actions as well as Current has in his 1958 work *The Lincoln Nobody Knows.*

BOOKS BY CURRENT

Arguing with Historians: Essays on the Historical and the Unhistorical. U. Pr. of New Eng. 1989 $14.95. ISBN 0-8195-6219-X. Writings on myths and realities regarding a variety of topics, including the Civil War, Reconstruction, and race relations.

Daniel Webster and the Rise of National Conservatism. 1955. Waveland Pr. 1992 $9.95. ISBN 0-88133-653-X. Excellent brief biography that places Webster in good historical perspective.

Lincoln and the First Shot. 1963. Waveland Pr. 1990 $9.00. ISBN 0-88133-498-7. Good account of the complex political maneuvering that preceded hostilities in the Civil War.

The Lincoln Nobody Knows. Greenwood 1980 repr. of 1958 ed. $45.00. ISBN 0-313-22450-1

Lincoln's Loyalists: Union Soldiers from the Confederacy. NE U. Pr. 1992 $21.95. ISBN 1-5553-124-5. Tells the little-known story of recruiting and utilizing Southerners in the Union cause.

Northernizing the South. U. of Ga. Pr. 1983 $18.00. ISBN 0-8203-0666-5. Essays and addresses on a variety of topics pertaining to the South.

Phi Beta Kappa in American Life: The First Two Hundred Years. OUP 1990 $35.00. ISBN 0-19-506311-2. Important contribution to intellectual history.

The Political Thought of Abraham Lincoln. Macmillan 1967. ISBN 0-02-326420-9. Useful analysis.

Secretary Stimson: A Study in Statecraft. 1954. Anchor 1970 o.p. Valuable, brief biography of a major statesman.

Those Terrible Carpetbaggers. 1988. OUP 1989 $35.00. ISBN 0-19-504872-5. First-rate revisionist history that counters a long-held stereotypical view of Reconstruction.

The Typewriter and the Men Who Made It. Post Group 1988 $17.95. ISBN 0-911160-88-4. Fascinating study of a key invention and its roll in American economic and social history.

DAVIS, JEFFERSON. 1808–1889

Jefferson Davis was born in Kentucky but grew up in Mississippi. After graduating from West Point in 1828, he served at frontier military posts and in the Black Hawk War. He resigned from the military in 1835, the same year his bride of three months, who was Zachary Taylor's daughter, died. For the next 10 years, he managed his brother's isolated plantation in Mississippi. In 1845 he married for a second time and entered the world of politics as a member of the U.S. House of Representatives.

Davis's reputation as a historian rests on one work—*The Rise and Fall of the Confederate Government* (1878–81), an account based in large measure on his own intimate experiences. Chosen by the provisional congress as president of the Confederate States of America in 1861, Davis faced criticism throughout his tenure. After Lee surrendered without his approval, Davis was indicted by the federal government for treason. Although he spent several years in prison, he was never brought to trial. In 1867 he was released on bond, and he retired to his estate, Beauvoir, on the Gulf of Mexico in Mississippi. There he wrote *The Rise and Fall* to vindicate the South in general and his presidency in particular.

BOOKS BY DAVIS

The Calendar of the Jefferson Davis Postwar Manuscripts in the Louisiana Historical Association Collection. B. Franklin 1970 repr. of 1943 ed. o.p. Valuable reference guide.

Jefferson Davis, Constitutionalist: His Letters, Papers, and Speeches. 10 vols. Ed. by Dunbar Rowland. AMS Pr. repr. of 1923 ed. $960.00. ISBN 0-404-02000-3. Exhaustive collection of firsthand materials.

Papers of Jefferson Davis. 6 vols. La. State U. Pr. 1971–present. Vol. 1 Haskel M. Monroe, Jr. and James T. McIntosh, eds. $55.00. ISBN 0-8071-0943-6. Vol. 2 McIntosh, ed. $60.00. ISBN 0-8071-0082-X. Vol. 3 McIntosh, ed. $55.00. ISBN 0-8071-0786-7. Vol. 4 Linda L. Crist, ed. $55.00. ISBN 0-8071-1037-X. Vol. 5 Crist, ed. $55.00. ISBN 0-8071-1240-2. Vol. 6 Crist and Mary S. Dix, eds. $60.00. ISBN 0-8071-1502-9

The Rise and Fall of the Confederate Government. 1878–81. 2 vols. Da Capo 1990 $15.95 ea. ISBNs 0-306-80420-4, 0-306-80419-0

BOOKS ABOUT DAVIS

Catton, Bruce, and William B. Catton. *Two Roads to Sumter.* 1963. Peter Smith 1992 $18.50. ISBN 08446-6498-7. Traces Davis's role in the secession crisis.

Davis, Varina. *Jefferson Davis, a Memoir by His Wife.* 2 vols. Nautical & Aviation Publ. Co. of Amer. 1990 $98.00. ISBN 1-877853-05-4

Davis, William C. *Jefferson Davis: The Man and His Hour.* HarpC 1991 $40.00. ISBN 0-06-016706-8. Good biography that sets Davis and his policies in historical perspective.

Eaton, Clement. *Jefferson Davis.* Free Pr. 1979 $15.95. ISBN 0-02-908740-6. Readable, reliable biography.

Escott, Paul D. *After Secession: Jefferson Davis and the Failure of Confederate National-ism.* La. State U. Pr. 1978 $10.95. ISBN 0-8071-1807-9. Critical study that places heavy blame for the Confederate failure on Davis.

Gibson, Ronald. *Jefferson Davis and the Confederacy: Chronology-Documents-Biblio-graphical Aids. Presidential Chronology Ser.* Oceana 1977 $18.00. ISBN 0-379-12095-X. Useful collection of research aids.

Hamilton, Holman. *The Three Kentucky Presidents: Lincoln, Taylor, Davis. Bicentennial Bookshelf Ser.* U. Pr. of Ky. 1978 $10.00. ISBN 0-8131-0246-4. Interesting compari-son of the three American leaders.

Patrick, Rembert. *Jefferson Davis and His Cabinet.* AMS Pr. repr. of 1944 ed. $43.50. ISBN 0-404-20197-0. Thorough study of the Confederate government.

Pollard, Edward A. *Life of Jefferson Davis, with a Secret History of the Southern Confederacy, Gathered behind the Scenes in Richmond. Select Bibliographies Repr. Ser.* Ayer repr. of 1869 ed. $33.00. ISBN 0-8369-5074-7. Interesting as a piece of history in itself.

Ross, Ishbel. *First Lady of the South: The Life of Mrs. Jefferson Davis.* Greenwood 1973 repr. of 1958 ed. $35.00. ISBN 0-8371-6927-5. The only study of Varina Howell Davis, the second wife of Jefferson Davis.

Strode, Hudson. *Jefferson Davis.* 3 vols. HarBraceJ 1955–64 o.p. The most fully documented biography of the Confederate leader.

Woodworth, Steven E. *Jefferson Davis and His Generals: The Failure of Confederate Command in the West.* U. Pr. of KS 1990 $35.00. ISBN 0-7006-0461-8. Critical analysis of a crucial military theater in the war.

DEGLER, CARL N(EUMANN). 1921–

Carl Degler writes history with flair, and his spirited and readable topical history of the United States, *Out of Our Past* (1959), has long been a favorite among college students and general readers. In 1972 another of his works, *Neither Black nor White* (1971), won the Pulitzer Prize in history and the Bancroft Prize and was co-winner of the Beveridge Prize.

Born in Orange, New Jersey, Degler matriculated at Upsala College and received his Ph.D. from Columbia University in 1947. He taught at Hunter College, New York University, and City College of New York before joining the faculty of Vassar College in 1952. Sixteen years later he moved on to Stanford University, where he was Margaret Byrne Professor until his retirement in 1990. In 1973 and 1974 he was Harmsworth Professor at Oxford University. He served as president of the American Historical Association from 1958 to 1986 and the Organization of American Historians from 1979 to 1980.

BOOKS BY DEGLER

At Odds: Women and the Family in America from the Revolution to the Present. OUP 1980 $14.95. ISBN 0-19-502934-8. Splendid social history of struggle and accommodation.

In Search of Human Nature: The Decline and Revival of Darwinism in American Social Thought. 1991. OUP 1992 $24.95. ISBN 0-19-506380-5. Examination of recent controversies between exponents of "nature" and "nurture" in the study of human behavior.

Neither Black Nor White: Slavery and Race Relations in Brazil and the United States. 1971. U. of Wis. Pr. 1986 $12.95. ISBN 0-299-10914-3. Successful and revealing exercise in comparative history.

The New Deal. (ed.) 1970. Wiener Pub. Inc. 1973 $8.95. ISBN 0-317-30664-2. Good selection of views on the New Deal.

The Other South: Southern Dissenters in the Nineteenth Century. 1974. NE U. Pr. 1983 $40.00. ISBN 0-930350-33-2. Useful inquiry into a neglected aspect of Southern history.

Out of Our Past: The Forces That Shaped America. 1959. HarpC 1983 $15.00. ISBN 0-06-131985-6

Place Over Time: The Continuity of Southern Distinctiveness. La. State U. Pr. 1977 o.p. Reflections on social conditions and the place of slavery in Southern history.

DE VOTO, BERNARD (AUGUSTINE). 1897–1955

A Harvard University graduate and impassioned student and teacher of American history and literature, Utah-born Bernard De Voto held faculty positions at Northwestern University and Harvard University. He was also the second editor of the *Saturday Review of Literature* and for many years wrote "The Editor's Easy Chair" column in *Harper's* magazine. At Harvard, De Voto was the editor of the MARK TWAIN (see Vol. 1) manuscripts and produced several works about Twain and his time. He is best known for his trilogy—*The Year of Decision: 1846* (1943), *Across the Wide Missouri* (1947), and *The Course of Empire* (1952). For *Across the Wide Missouri*, he personally traced the western trails first blazed by LEWIS and CLARK. HENRY STEELE COMMAGER called *The Course of Empire*, covering the exploration of the United States to the year 1805, "the largest of the books, largest in conception and in scope, largest, too, in spirit. It is . . . the best book that has been written about the West since Webb's 'Great Plains' and it is the best written book about the West since PARKMAN (see Vol. 1)." Although recent scholarship has changed many perceptions about the West, De Voto's splendid accounts continue to have wide appeal.

BOOKS BY DE VOTO

Across the Wide Missouri. AMS Pr. repr. of 1947 ed. $94.50. ISBN 0-404-20079-6. Panoramic account of the first great official exploration of the Far West.

The Course of Empire. HM 1989 $11.70. ISBN 0-395-51014-7. Superb chronicle of discovery and exploration in North America, with attention to the effects on Native Americans.

Easy Chair. Essay Index Repr. Ser. Ayer repr. of 1955 ed. $20.00. ISBN 0-8369-2433-9. Collection of some of De Voto's always interesting *Harper's* essays.

Forays and Rebuttals. Essay Index Repr. Ser. Ayer repr. of 1936 ed. $27.50. ISBN 0-8369-1604-2. More of De Voto's interesting essays.

The Journals of Lewis and Clark. (ed.) 1953. HM 1973 $10.70. ISBN 0-395-08380-X. Skillfully edited chronicle of the great expedition undertaken by Lewis and Clark.

Mark Twain's America. Greenwood 1978 repr. of 1967 ed. $65.00. ISBN 0-313-20368-7. Fine evocation of mid-nineteenth century America.

The Portable Mark Twain. Outlook Bk. Co. 1985 $6.98. ISBN 0-517-47856-0. Entertaining and useful brief volume.

The Year of Decision: 1846. 1943. HM 1989 $11.70. ISBN 0-395-50079-6. Superb narrative of an extraordinary year of war, exploration, and boundless adventure.

BOOKS ABOUT DE VOTO

Bowen, Catherine Drinker, Edith Mirrielees, Arthur M. Schlesinger, Jr., and Wallace Stegner. *Four Portraits and One Subject: Bernard De Voto.* HM 1963 o.p. Four distinct assessments of De Voto, accompanied by a useful bibliography.

Sawey, Orlan. *Bernard De Voto. Twayne's U.S. Authors Ser.* Irvington 1969 $17.95. ISBN 0-89197-675-2. Good concise biography.

Stegner, Wallace. *The Uneasy Chair: Biography of Bernard De Voto.* Gibbs Smith Pub. 1989 $12.95. ISBN 0-87905-299-6. Splendid biography by another gifted chronicler of the West.

DU BOIS, W(ILLIAM) E(DWARD) B(URGHARDT). 1868–1963

Few writers of American history have led as rich and varied a life as W.E.B. Du Bois. He was born in Great Barrington, Massachusetts, just five years after the Emancipation Proclamation was issued. After earning B.A. degrees from both Harvard and Fisk universities, he studied at the University of Berlin and earned an M.A. and a Ph.D. at Harvard. After teaching briefly at Wilberforce University, he became professor of history and economics at Ohio's Atlanta University. There he established his reputation as an opponent of BOOKER T. WASHINGTON's accommodationist response to racism and wrote *The Souls of Black Folk* (1903) to prove the fallacy of prevailing theories about race and intelligence.

In 1905 Du Bois became a major figure in the Niagara Movement, a crusading effort to end discrimination. Although the effort failed, it paved the way for the founding of the National Association for the Advancement of Colored People (NAACP), an organization in which Du Bois played a major role. He became the NAACP's director of publicity and research and editor of its official organ, *The Crisis*.

Du Bois's interest in Africa was deep and abiding, and in 1919 he organized the first Pan-African Congress meeting in Paris. In 1961, at the age of 90, he moved to Ghana, where he directed the *Encyclopedia Africana* project and became a Ghanaian citizen. He died in Ghana at the age of 93.

Over the years, Du Bois lectured and wrote books, pamphlets, and essays on a myriad of topics, from the slave trade to morals and manners. His influence on the writing of African American history was profound, for his many publications established a foundation upon which other scholars built. Du Bois also wrote several novels and numerous volumes in sociology and economics.

BOOKS BY DU BOIS

Against Racism: Unpublished Essays, Papers, Addresses, 1887–1961. Ed. by Herbert Aptheker. U. of Mass. Pr. 1985 $15.95. ISBN 0-87023-624-5. Good representative collection.

Autobiography: A Soliloquy on Viewing My Life from the Last Decade of Its First Century. Ed. by Herbert Aptheker. Kraus Intl. 1976 $20.00. ISBN 0-527-25262-X

Black Folk Then and Now: An Essay in the History and Sociology of the Negro Race. Kraus Intl. 1975 repr. of 1939 ed. $24.00. ISBN 0-527-25275-1. Major essay on the progress and lack thereof in race relations.

Black North in 1901: A Social Study. Amer. Negro: His History and Lit. Ser. Ayer 1970 repr. of 1901 ed. $9.00. ISBN 0-405-01921-1. Study of African Americans in Boston, New York, and Philadelphia.

Black Reconstruction in America, 1860–1880. 1935. Macmillan 1972 $16.95. ISBN 0-689-70063-6. Pioneer revisionist history that paved the way for all subsequent studies of Reconstruction. Noteworthy especially for recognizing the positive contributions of the freed men and women.

Color and Democracy: Colonies and Peace. Kraus Intl. 1975 repr. of 1945 ed. $10.00. ISBN 0-527-25290-5. Evaluation of the post–World War II world, the fate of colonialism in Africa, and the burgeoning problem of racism.

The Complete Works of W. E. B. Du Bois. 3 vols. Kraus Intl. 1985. Vol. 1 *Creative Writings: A Pageant, Poems, Short Stories and Playlets.* $42.00. ISBN 0-527-25346-4. Vol. 2 *Pamphlets and Leaflets.* $90.00. ISBN 0-527-25348-0. Vol. 3 *Writings in Periodicals.* $42.00. ISBN 0-527-25350-2

The Dusk of Dawn: An Essay toward an Autobiography of a Race Concept. 1940. Transaction Pubs. 1991 $19.95. ISBN 0-87855-917-5. Trenchant analysis of racism.

The Gift of Black Folk. 1924. Kraus Intl. 1975 $21.00. ISBN 0-527-25310-3. An early appreciation of the role African Americans played in the making of the United States.

John Brown. Ed. by E. P. Overholtzer. *American Crisis Biographies.* Intl. Pubs. Co. 1987 $4.95. ISBN 0-7178-0375-9. Still a useful biography of Brown.

Morals and Manners among Negro Americans. Atlanta Univ. Publications Ser. Kraus Intl. repr. of 1914 ed. $15.00. ISBN 0-527-03119-4. Interesting sociocultural study.

The Negro. Kraus Intl. 1975 repr. of 1915 ed. $17.00. ISBN 0-527-25315-4. One of the earliest comprehensive studies of blacks as a race.

The Negro Artisan. Atlanta Univ. Publications Ser. Kraus Intl. repr. of 1902 ed. $16.00. ISBN 0-527-03110-0

Negro in Business. AMS Pr. repr. of 1899 ed. $12.50. ISBN 0-404-00153-X. Report on the Conference on the Study of Negro Problems, concentrating on the problem of employment.

The Philadelphia Negro: A Social Study. 1899. Kraus Intl. 1973 $31.00. ISBN 0-525-25320-0. Focused study on domestic workers in a single community.

Prayers for Dark People. Ed. by Herbert Aptheker. U. of Mass. Pr. 1980 $9.95. ISBN 0-87023-303-3. Fascinating work on prayer books, devotions, services, and the like relating to the African American community.

Quest of the Silver Fleece: A Novel. NE U. Pr. $15.95. ISBN 1-55553-064-8. Good enough to be taken as a serious work of early-twentieth-century American literature.

A Select Bibliography of the Negro American. Atlanta Univ. Publications Ser. Kraus Intl. repr. of 1905 ed. $14.00. ISBN 0-527-03112-7

The Souls of Black Folk. 1903. Kraus Intl. 1973 repr. of 1953 ed. $17.00. ISBN 0-527-25330-8. Major essays ranging in topics from the meaning of progress to Booker T. Washington to sorrow songs.

The Suppression of the African Slave Trade. Harvard Historical Studies. 1898. La. State U. Pr. 1970 $12.95. ISBN 0-8071-0149-4. First title in the *Harvard Historical Series.* Still considered a landmark work on the slave trade.

W. E. B. Du Bois on Sociology and the Black Community. Ed. by Dan S. Green and Edwin D. Driver. 1978. U. Ch. Pr. 1987 $21.00. ISBN 0-326-16762-3. Reflects Du Bois's concern with social conditions.

W. E. B. Du Bois Speaks. 2 vols. Ed. by Philip Foner. Pathfinder NY 1970 $17.95 ea. ISBNs 0-87348-125-9, 0-87348-126-7. Contains tributes to Du Bois from Martin Luther King, Jr., and Kwame Nkrumah.

The World and Africa: An Inquiry into the Part Which Africa Has Played in World History. 1955. Kraus Intl. repr. of 1965 ed. $21.00. ISBN 0-527-25340-5. Reflective of Du Bois's intense interest in Africa, especially during his later years.

BOOKS ABOUT DU BOIS

Aptheker, Herbert. *Annotated Bibliography of Published Writings of W. E. B. Du Bois.* Kraus Intl. 1973 $54.00. ISBN 0-527-02750-2

Broderick, Francis L. *W. E. B. Du Bois: Negro Leader in a Time of Crisis.* Stanford U. Pr. 1959 $35.00. ISBN 0-8047-0558-5. "Applying an easy style and a gift for trenchant analysis to a thorough knowledge of his material Broderick has produced a highly readable and scholarly intellectual biography" (*American Historical Review*).

De Marco, Joseph P. *The Social Thought of W. E. B. Du Bois.* U. Pr. of Amer. 1983 $22.75. ISBN 0-8191-3236-5. Good intellectual history.

Du Bois, Shirley G. *His Day is Marching On: Memoirs of W. E. B. Du Bois.* Okpaku Communications 1971 $15.00. ISBN 0-89388-157-0. Intimate literary portrait of Du Bois by his wife.

————. *Pictorial History of W. E. B. Du Bois.* Johnson Chi. $14.95. ISBN 0-87485-076-2. Interesting and valuable photographic record.

Hawkins, Hugh. *Booker T. Washington and His Critics. Problems in Amer. Civilization Ser.* Heath 1974 $8.50. ISBN 0-669-87049-8. Useful selection fully revealing the gulf between Du Bois and Washington.

Horne, Gerald. *Black and Red: W. E. B. Du Bois and the African-American Response to the Cold War, 1944–1963.* State U. NY Pr. 1985 $19.95. ISBN 0-88706-088-9. Important aspects of both African American and Cold War histories.

Partington, Paul W. *W. E. B. Du Bois: A Bibliography of His Published Writings.* PG Partington 1985 $20.00. ISBN 0-960-2538-3-1. Useful guide to sorting out Du Bois's voluminous writings.

Rampersad, Arnold. *Art and Imagination of W. E. B. Du Bois*. Schocken 1990 $14.95.
  ISBN 0-8052-0985-9. An appreciation of Du Bois the literary artist.
Tuttle, William M., Jr., comp. *W. E. B. Du Bois. Great Lives Observed Ser*. P-H 1973 $2.45.
  ISBN 0-13-220889-X. Good collection of perspectives on Du Bois.

FRANKLIN, JOHN HOPE. 1915–

A native of Oklahoma and the son of an attorney who practiced before the
U.S. Supreme Court, John Hope Franklin has had a distinguished career as
teacher, scholar, and historian of the African American experience in the United
States. A Phi Beta Kappa graduate of Fisk University who took his Ph.D. at
Harvard University in 1941, Franklin has taught or been visiting lecturer at a
dozen institutions in the United States and abroad and holds honorary degrees
from a great many more. After serving as professor and department chair at
Brooklyn College and the University of Chicago, he assumed simultaneously
two positions at Duke University—James B. Duke Professor in the Humanities
and Professor of Legal History in the Law School. He has been president of the
American Historical Association, the Organization of American Historians, the
Southern Historical Association, and the American Studies Association. He also
is a founding member of the Black Academy of Arts and has served on the U.S.
Commission for UNESCO and the Committee on International Exchange of
Scholars.

Franklin's scholarly contributions are many. His comprehensive history *From
Slavery to Freedom* (1947) is in its sixth edition and is generally acknowledged
to be the basic survey of African American history. His other writings, which
also have been well received, explore various aspects of America's racial and
regional history, all with balance, sensitivity, and integrity.

BOOKS BY FRANKLIN

Black Leaders of the Twentieth Century. (coauthored with August Meier). U. of Ill. Pr.
  1982 $29.95. ISBN 0-252-00870-7. Useful collection of biographical essays.
The Emancipation Proclamation. Doubleday 1963 o.p. Lucid and detached history and
  analysis of the document, including its antecedents and legacy.
The Free Negro in North Carolina, 1790–1860. 1943. Norton 1971 $2.25. ISBN 0-393-
  00579-8. Franklin's first work of scholarship. Solidly researched and significant.
From Slavery to Freedom: A History of American Negroes. (coauthored with Alfred A.
  Moss, Jr.). 1947. Knopf 1987 $37.00. ISBN 0-394-56362-X. Franklin's classic survey
  of the history and struggles of African Americans.
George Washington Williams, A Biography. 1985. U. Ch. Pr. 1987 $24.95. ISBN 0-226-
  26083-6. Splendid biography of an influential African American educator.
The Militant South, 1800–1961. 1956. HUP rev. ed. 1970 $25.50. ISBN 0-674-57450-8.
  Interesting exploration of the South's "fighting spirit," important for understanding
  the region's history.
Race and History: Selected Essays, 1938–1988. 1989. La. State U. Pr. 1990 $29.95. ISBN 0-
  8071-1547-9. Essays reflecting a scholar's lifetime study of race as a factor in the
  American experience.
Racial Equality in America. U. Ch. Pr. 1976 o.p. The 1976 Jefferson Lectures in the
  Humanities on civil rights and the African American experience.
Reconstruction after the Civil War. History of Amer. Civilization Ser. 1961. U. Ch. Pr. 1962
  $12.95. ISBN 0-226-26076-3. Balanced and forceful history augmented by an
  excellent bibliography.
A Southern Odyssey—Travelers in the Antebellum North. La. State U. Pr. 1976 $32.50.
  ISBN 0-8071-0161-3. Revealing look at conflicting perspectives before the Civil War.

BOOK ABOUT FRANKLIN

Anderson, Eric, and Alfred A. Moss, Jr., eds. *The Facts of Reconstruction: Essays in Honor of John Hope Franklin*. La. State U. Pr. 1991 $29.95. Essays on topics in southern and African American history, with an appreciation and bibliography.

GENOVESE, EUGENE D(OMINICK). 1930–

Born in Brooklyn, New York, Eugene Genovese was educated at Brooklyn College and Columbia University, where he received his Ph.D. in 1959. He has taught at Rutgers University, at Sir George Williams University in Montreal, at the University of Rochester, and has been visiting professor at several universities. He has served as Pitt Professor of American History at Cambridge University and is now Distinguished Scholar in Residence at the University Center in Georgia.

An erudite, unconventional, and often unpredictable Marxist, Genovese has forced historians of the Old South—and especially of slavery—to think in new ways about important questions. Ranging over a multitude of topics, his work is concerned mainly with the relationship between economic factors, social conditions, and culture. Shunning ideological rigidity, Genovese often challenges doctrinaire Marxist interpretations with sharp questions and perceptions of his own. Of his best-known work, *Roll, Jordan, Roll* (1974), David Brion Davis wrote: "Genovese's great gift is his ability to penetrate the minds of both slaves and masters, revealing not only how they viewed themselves and each other, but also how their contradictory perceptions interacted" (*N.Y. Times Book Review*).

BOOKS BY GENOVESE

Debates on American History. (coauthored with Forrest McDonald). Brandywine 1983 $3.95. ISBN 0-686-98000-X. Lively intellectual exchanges between two strong wills.
From Rebellion to Revolution: Afro-American Slave Revolts in the Making of the Modern World. 1979. La. State U. Pr. 1992 $9.95. ISBN 0-8071-1768-4. Brief, assertive book that argues that slave revolts, especially after the 1791 Haitian rebellion, were concerned as much with overthrowing a social system as with gaining freedom.
The Fruits of Merchant Capital: Slavery and Bourgeois Property in the Rise and Expansion of Capitalism. (coauthored with Elizabeth Fox-Genovese). OUP 1983 $35.00. ISBN 0-19-503157-X. "This is an exciting book . . . brilliant, witty, difficult, polemical, cantankerous, and important" (Peter Kolchin, *Journal of American History*).
In Red and Black: Marxian Explorations in Southern and Afro-American History. 1971. U. of Tenn. Pr. 1984. $32.50. ISBN 0-87049-428-7. Essays emphasizing, among other things, the persistence of human factors in the enslaved person-master relationship.
Plantation, Town, and County: Essays on the Local History of American Slave Society. (coedited with Elinor Miller). 1974. Bks. Demand $115.80. ISBN 0-317-09956-6. Slavery examined "from the ground up" in several areas of the South.
The Political Economy of Slavery: Studies in the Economy and Society of the Slave South. 1965. U. Pr. of New Eng. 1989 $18.95. ISBN 0-8195-6208-4. Essays on the Old South in a doctrinaire Marxist vein—"sometimes mechanistic," as the author candidly acknowledged later.
Roll, Jordan, Roll: The World the Slaves Made. 1974. Random 1976 $17.00. ISBN 0-394-71652-2. Bancroft Prize-winning study of slavery.
The Slaveholders' Dilemma: Freedom and Progress in Southern Conservative Thought, 1820–1860. U. of SC Pr. 1991 $19.95. ISBN 0-87249-783-6. Strongly revisionist study of the relationship between political theory and slavery.
The World the Slaveholders Made: Two Essays in Interpretation. 1969. U. Pr. of New Eng. 1988 $16.95. ISBN 0-8195-6204-1. Comparative treatment of slavery in the Americas, plus an analysis and interpretation of George Fitzhugh's proslavery argument.

HANDLIN, OSCAR. 1915–

Born in Brooklyn, New York, Oscar Handlin received his Ph.D. from Harvard University, where he has taught since 1939 and was director of the Center for the Study of the History of Liberty until 1966. From 1979 to 1984, he was director of the university library at Harvard, and, after holding the Charles Warren chair in history for many years, in 1984 he became Charles M. Loeb University Professor.

Handlin, who is a consensus historian and a strong advocate of civil rights, has written extensively on urban history and immigration. He won the Pulitzer Prize in 1952 for *The Uprooted* (1951), his study of immigrants in the eastern cities of America written from the perspective of the immigrant. The son of immigrant parents himself, he made his special field of study the social history of immigrant groups who came to the United States in the nineteenth century from eastern and southern Europe. In *The Americans* (1963), as in others of his books, he dispensed with footnotes, bibliography, and identification of quotations in favor of "unobtrusive" learning. Handlin edited *Children of the Uprooted* (1966), which includes excerpts from various authors on the subject of the "marginality" of immigrants, and collaborated on a number of works with his first wife, Mary, and his second wife, Lillian. On the subject of education, he wrote *The American University as an Instrument of Republican Culture* (1970) and *John Dewey's Challenge to Education: Historical Perspectives on the Cultural Context* (1959).

BOOKS BY HANDLIN

Abraham Lincoln and the Union. (coauthored with Lilian Handlin). *Lib. of Amer. Biography.* 1980. Scott F. 1987 $13.50. ISBN 0-673-39340-2. Brief, dependable biography of the American leader.

Al Smith and His America. *Lib. of Amer. Biography.* 1958. NE U. Pr. $11.95. ISBN 1-55553-021-4. Concise, readable biography of a colorful politician.

American Immigration Collection, Series 1. (ed.) 42 vols. Ayer 1969 $1,493.00. ISBN 0-405-00500-8. Immensely valuable collection of books written on subjects relating to immigration and ethnicity.

The Americans: A New History of the People of the United States. Atlantic Monthly 1963 o.p. Study of the influence of immigration on the American people, from Leif Ericson to 1962.

Boston's Immigrants: A Study of Acculturation. HUP 1959 $12.95. ISBN 0-674-07985-X. First-rate examination of major immigrant groups.

Chance or Destiny: Turning Points in American History. Greenwood 1977 repr. of 1955 ed. $35.00. ISBN 0-8371-9334-6

Children of the Uprooted. (ed.) Braziller 1966 o.p. "In three brief explanatory essays, the editor gives a quick account of types of migration to America and the changing American scene into which the migrants came" (*Library Journal*).

Commonwealth: A Study of the Role of Government in the American Economy, Massachusetts, 1774–1861. HUP 1969 $10.95. ISBN 0-674-14691-6. Model study in political economy.

The Dimensions of Liberty. (coauthored with Mary Handlin). HUP 1961 $16.00. ISBN 0-674-20750-5. Exploration of the concept of liberty in historical context.

Fire-Bell in the Night: The Crisis in Civil Rights. Atlantic Monthly 1964 o.p. Clearly portrays the author's concerns about civil disorders.

John Dewey's Challenge to Education: Historical Perspective on the Cultural Context. Greenwood 1972 repr. of 1959 ed. $38.50. ISBN 0-8371-5602-5. Excellent study of Dewey's theories and their impact.

The Historian and the City. (coedited with John Burchard). MIT Pr. 1966 $8.95. ISBN 0-262-58006-3. Essays on the history and sociology of cities.

Liberty in America, 1600 to the Present. 3 vols. HarpC. Vol. 1 1986 o.p. Vol. 2 1989 o.p.
  Vol. 3 1992 $26.00. ISBN 0-06-39143-X. "Vintage Handlin—feisty, fast paced, written
  with verve—certain to delight some readers, irritate others" (*Journal of American
  History*).
Newcomers: Negroes and Puerto Ricans in a Changing Metropolis. HUP 1959 $14.50.
  ISBN 0-674-62101-8. Regional study of changing demographics and social condi-
  tions.
*This Was America: True Accounts of People and Places, Manners and Customs, as
  Recorded by European Travelers to the Western Shore in the 18th, 19th and 20th
  Centuries.* (ed.) HUP 1949 $38.00. ISBN 0-674-88470-1. Fine collection of travel
  accounts that vividly document the uniqueness of American life.
The Uprooted: The Epic Story of the Great Migrations that Made the American People.
  1951. Little rev. ed. 1973 $10.95. ISBN 0-316-34313-7

BOOK ABOUT HANDLIN

Bushman, Richard L. *Uprooted Americans: Essays to Honor Oscar Handlin.* Little 1979
  o.p. Essays by Handlin's students on aspects of immigration and ethnicity.

HOFSTADTER, RICHARD. 1916–1970

DeWitt Clinton Professor of History at Columbia University from 1959 until
the time of his death, Richard Hofstadter was one of the most influential
historians in post–World War II America. His political, social, and intellectual
histories raised serious questions about assumptions that had long been taken
for granted and cast the American experience in an interesting new light. His
1948 work, *The American Political Tradition*, is an enduring classic study in
political history. His 1955 work, *The Age of Reform*, which still commands
respect among both historians and general readers, won him that year's Pulitzer
Prize. A measure of Hofstadter's standing in literary and scholarly circles is the
honors he received in 1964 for *Anti-Intellectualism in American Life* (1963)—
Pulitzer Prize for general nonfiction, the Ralph Waldo Emerson Prize of Phi
Beta Kappa, and the Sidney Hillman Prize Award. Hofstadter's greatest talent,
however, may have been his ability to order complex events and issues and to
synthesize from them a rational, constructively critical perspective on American
history.

BOOKS BY HOFSTADTER

Academic Freedom in the Age of the College. 1955. Col. U. Pr. 1961 o.p. Important
  contribution to the history of higher education in the early Republic.
The Age of Reform: From Bryan to F.D.R. Knopf 1955 $16.95. ISBN 0-394-41442-X. Classic
  political history that traces the progressive tradition in the twentieth century.
America at 1750: A Social History. Random 1973 $7.95. ISBN 0-394-71795-3. Superb
  study of social conditions in early America.
The American Political Tradition and the Men Who Made It. 1948. Knopf 1973 $24.95.
  ISBN 0-394-48880-6. Forceful essays on a bevy of leaders.
American Violence: A Documentary History. (coedited with Michael Wallace). Vin. 1971
  o.p. Excellent collection of annotated documents on the prevalence and varieties of
  violence in the national experience.
Anti-Intellectualism in American Life. 1963. Random 1966 $14.95. ISBN 0-394-70317-0.
  Profound study of American fears and self-doubt in matters of reason and intellect.
The Development of Academic Freedom in the United States. (coauthored with Walter P.
  Metzger). 1955. Col. U. Pr. 1965 o.p. Important record of intellectual freedom's
  mixed history in American education.
Great Issues in American History: 1865–1981. (coedited with Bernice K. Hofstadter).
  1958. Random 1982 $11.00. ISBN 0-394-70842-3. Collection of judiciously selected
  issues and documentary materials since the Civil War.

Great Issues in American History: From Settlement to Revolution, 1584–1776. (coedited with Clarence L. Ver Steeg). 1958. Random 1969 $12.00. ISBN 0-394-70540-8. Collection of vital issues and documents of the period.

The Idea of a Party System: The Rise of Legitimate Opposition in the United States, 1780–1840. U. CA Pr. 1969 $37.50. ISBN 0-520-01389-1. The Jefferson Lectures, tracing the early development of parties.

The Paranoid Style in American Politics and Other Essays. 1964. U. Ch. Pr. 1979 $5.95. ISBN 0-226-34817-2. Trenchant essays on persistent irrational forces in American politics.

The Progressive Historians: Turner, Beard, Parrington. 1968. U. Ch. Pr. 1979 o.p. Superb study of three historians whose influence in political and social thought goes well beyond the academic world.

The Progressive Movement, 1900–1915. (ed.) P-H 1964 $4.95. ISBN 0-13-730721-3. Well-edited collection of articles by participants in the movement.

Social Darwinism in American Thought. 1953. Beacon Pr. 1992 $15.00. ISBN 0-8070-5503-4. Classic study of a persistent major contradiction in American social thought.

BOOK ABOUT HOFSTADTER

Elkins, Stanley R., and Eric L. McKitrick, eds. *The Hofstadter Aegis, A Memorial.* Knopf 1974 o.p. Some of Hofstadter's essays and lectures, plus an appreciation of his life and career.

KENNAN, GEORGE F(ROST). 1904–

George Kennan's histories range from nineteenth-century Russia to the post–cold war world. In most instances, however, they deal—either directly or indirectly—with the role and influence of the United States in the world. Kennan epitomizes the term "diplomatic historian," for he is a brilliant practitioner of both diplomacy and historical scholarship. After graduating from Princeton University in 1925, he entered the Foreign Service and served in many critical posts during the crisis years of the mid-twentieth century. In 1933 he helped reopen the U.S. embassy in Moscow after long-delayed recognition of the Soviet Union by the United States. In 1938, as secretary of the American legation in Prague, he watched Hitler's troops occupy the city, and in 1939, when he was assigned to the Berlin embassy, the onset of World War II kept him confined in Germany for six months. After the war, Kennan's expertise on Russia made him a leading figure in U.S. diplomacy. He helped to implement the Marshall Plan and served in Moscow, first as chief aide and then briefly as ambassador. In 1953 he left the Foreign Service and joined the Institute for Advanced Studies at Princeton. He has also taught at the University of Chicago and at Oxford University. In 1961 he emerged briefly from official retirement to serve as U.S. ambassador to Yugoslavia.

Within the limitations of his official roles, Kennan has been and remains today a vocal and intelligent critic of U.S. foreign policy. In 1947 his article for *Foreign Affairs*, signed "Mr. X", recommended a policy of containment toward the Soviet Union, which he later charged was badly misconstrued by U.S. policymakers. During the Vietnam War, he called the Johnson administration's policy "a massive miscalculation and error . . . for which it is hard to find any parallels in our history." Over the years, Kennan has authored a number of works on history, diplomacy, and foreign relations. Two of his books, *Russia Leaves the War* (1956) and *Memoirs, 1925–1950* (1967), have won the Pulitzer Prize and the National Book Award.

Books by Kennan

American Diplomacy, 1900–1950. 1951. U. Ch. Pr. rev. ed. 1985 $7.95. ISBN 0-226-43147-9. Gracefully written essays that established the author's reputation as a major historian of American foreign policy as well as of Russia and the Soviet Union.

Around the Cragged Hill: A Personal and Political Philosophy. Norton 1992 $22.95. ISBN 0-393-03411-9. Both a memoir and a provocative commentary on the "troublesome nature of people and nations and the ameliorating power and glory of religion" (*N.Y. Times*)

The Decline of Bismarck's European Order: Franco-Russian Relations, 1875–1890. Princeton U. Pr. 1979 $19.95. ISBN 0-691-00784-5. First-rate study of diplomatic maneuvering in late nineteenth-century Europe.

The Fateful Alliance: France, Russia, and the Coming of the First World War. Pantheon 1984 o.p. Good example of Kennan's extraordinary erudition as a diplomatic historian.

From Prague After Munich: Diplomatic Papers, 1938–1940. Princeton U. Pr. 1968 $14.95. ISBN 0-691-01063-3. An "invaluable eyewitness account and analysis of the dismemberment and destruction of a nation as recorded by a particularly knowledgeable, articulate and sensitive observer" (*N.Y. Times*).

Memoirs, 1925–1963. 1967–72. 2 vols. Pantheon 1983. Vol. 1 $18.00. ISBN 0-394-71624-8. Vol. 2 $15.95. ISBN 3-394-71626-4. "A remarkably candid, beautifully written and utterly fascinating intellectual career autobiography of a distinguished diplomat and scholar" (*N.Y. Times*).

The Nuclear Delusion. Pantheon 1983 $8.95. ISBN 0-394-71318-4. Reasoned discussion of the nuclear stalemate.

Russia and the West under Lenin and Stalin. NAL-Dutton 1961 $5.99. ISBN 0-451-62460-2. Detached and authoritative analysis of Soviet foreign policy.

Russia, the Atom and the West. Greenwood 1974 repr. of 1958 ed. $48.50. ISBN 0-8371-7394-9. Trenchant critique of atomic diplomacy at the height of the Cold War.

Sketches from a Life. Pantheon 1990 $12.95. ISBN 0-679-72877-5. Remarkably candid, often poignant, commentaries on Kennan's life and times, derived largely from his private diaries.

Soviet-American Relations, 1917–1920. 1956–58. 2 vols. Princeton U. Pr. 1990 $26.95. ISBNs 0-691-00841-8, 0-691-00847-7. Masterly history of a critical period in twentieth-century history.

Books about Kennan

Encounters with Kennan: The Great Debate. Intl. Spec. Bk. 1979 $30.00. ISBN 0-7146-3132-9. Kennan and his critics and defenders engaging in a spirited examination of his views and writings.

Gellman, Barton. *Contending with Kennan: Toward a Philosophy of American Power.* Greenwood 1985 $42.95. ISBN 0-275-91737-1. Good appraisal of the philosophy underlying Kennan's political and historical writings.

Hertz, Martin F., ed. *Decline of the West? George Kennan and His Critics.* Georgetown Pr. 1978 $34.50. ISBN 0-89633-018-4. Good discussion of Kennan's diplomacy and scholarship.

Hixson, Walter F. *George F. Kennan: Cold War Iconoclast. Studies in Contemporary History.* Col. U. Pr. 1989 $44.00. ISBN 0-231-06894-8. Critical evaluation asserting that Kennan bears some responsibility for the international developments he later deplored.

Mayers, David A. *George Kennan and the Dilemmas of United States Foreign Policy.* OUP 1988 $12.95. ISBN 0-19-506318-X. Intellectual biography that sorts out the rights and wrongs and presents Kennan as a human being.

Miscamble, Wilson D. *George F. Kennan and the Making of American Foreign Policy.* Princeton U. Pr. 1992 $35.00. ISBN 0-691-08620-6. Keen analysis of the containment policy and its author.

LEUCHTENBURG, WILLIAM E(DWARD). 1922–

Born in Ridgewood (Queens), New York, William Leuchtenburg is currently William Rand Kenan, Jr. Professor of History at the University of North Carolina at Chapel Hill. He was educated at Cornell University and at Columbia University, from which he received his Ph.D. in 1951. After teaching briefly at Smith College and Harvard University, he began a 30-year tenure on the faculty at Columbia, where he became De Witt Clinton Professor of American History in 1971. He has served as president of the Organization of American Historians, the Society of American Historians, and most recently (1991) the American Historical Association. He has also been Harmsworth Professor at Oxford University.

Leuchtenburg is an expert on twentieth-century U.S. political history, especially the era of the New Deal. His book *Franklin D. Roosevelt and the New Deal, 1932–1940* (1963) won both the Bancroft and Parkman prizes.

BOOKS BY LEUCHTENBURG

A Concise History of the American Republic. (coauthored with Samuel Eliot Morison and Henry Steele Commager). OUP rev. ed. of *The Growth of the American Republic* 1983 $49.95. ISBN 0-19-503179-2. Balanced and readable survey of the American experience.

Franklin D. Roosevelt and the New Deal, 1932–1940. New Amer. Nation Ser. HarpC 1963 $10.00. ISBN 0-06-133025-6. The best one-volume synthesis of the New Deal.

In the Shadow of FDR: From Harry Truman to Ronald Reagan. 1983. Cornell Univ. Pr. rev. ed. 1989 $35.95. ISBN 0-8014-2341-4. Legacies of the New Deal examined. Political history in best sense of the term—informed, judicious, and lively.

The Nineteen Eighty-Four Election in Historical Perspective. Baylor Univ. Pr. 1986 $4.50. ISBN 0-918954-45-2. Informed reflections of a political historian.

The Perils of Prosperity, 1914–32. History of Amer. Civilization Ser. U. Ch. Pr. 1958 $9.95. ISBN 0-226-47369-4. Highly readable and reliable survey of America in the era of World War I and its aftermath.

Political Parties. (ed.) *Great Contemporary Issues Ser.* Ayer 1977 $25.00. ISBN 0-405-09866-9. Useful commentaries on political history and the political system.

A Troubled Feast: American Society Since 1945. 1973. Scott F. rev. ed. 1987 $20.00. ISBN 0-673-39343-7. Fine survey of recent American history. Written with verve and authority.

MCPHERSON, JAMES M(UNRO). 1936–

James McPherson was born in Valley City, North Dakota. After an undergraduate education at Gustavus Adolphus College, he studied history with C. VANN WOODWARD at Johns Hopkins University and received his Ph.D. in 1963. He began teaching at Princeton University in 1962 and is now George Henry Davis '86 Professor of American History there.

Concerned from the start of his career with race relations and the history of African Americans, McPherson produced books of distinction in those areas before turning to his brilliant histories of the Civil War and Reconstruction. Perhaps the most distinguishing characteristic of those histories is their skillful integration of African American history into the larger narrative of the sectional conflict. His Pulitzer Prize-winning work of 1988, *Battle Cry of Freedom: The Civil War Era,* drew this accolade from the *New York Times Book Review*: "It is the best one-volume treatment of its subject I have ever come across. It may actually be the best ever published. . . . This is historical writing of the highest order."

BOOKS BY MCPHERSON

The Abolitionist Legacy: From Reconstruction to the NAACP. Princeton U. Pr. 1975 o.p. Good exercise in tracing continuity in history.

Abraham Lincoln and the Second American Revolution. 1991. OUP 1992 $17.95. ISBN 0-19-505542-X. "[S]lim volume of short essays that go right to the heart of the meaning of the war and Abraham Lincoln's role in it" (Frederick Allen, *N.Y. Times Book Review*).

The Anti-Slavery Crusade in America. (coedited with William L. Katz). 70 vols. Ayer 1970 $1,120.00. ISBN 0-405-00600-4. Comprehensive collection of source materials.

Battle Chronicles of the Civil War. (ed.) 6 vols. Macmillan 1989 $325.00. ISBN 0-02-920661-8. Comprehensive collection of military history.

Battle Cry of Freedom: The Civil War Era. C. Vann Woodward, ed. *Oxford History of the United States, Vol. VI.* OUP 1988 $39.95. ISBN 0-19-503863-0. Skillful synthesis of military and political history in a lucid narrative with a fresh interpretation.

Blacks in America: Bibliographic Essays. (ed.) Doubleday 1971 o.p. Useful guide to writings on African Americans.

Marching Toward Freedom: Blacks in the Civil War, 1861–1865. 1967. Facts on File 1990 $16.95. ISBN 0-8160-2337-9. Solid and reliable chronicle of African American participation in the war.

The Negro's Civil War: How American Negroes Felt and Acted During the War for the Union. 1965. Ballantine 1991 $10.00. ISBN 0-345-37120-8. Revealing examination and analysis of African American attitudes and actions.

Ordeal by Fire: The Civil War and Reconstruction. McGraw 1981 $29.95. ISBN 0-685-02389-8. Best single-volume history of the war and its aftermath, lucidly written and comprehensive in coverage.

Region, Race, and Reconstruction: Essays in Honor of C. Vann Woodward. (coedited with J. Morgan Kousser). OUP 1982 $29.95. ISBN 0-19-503075-3. Writings by McPherson and other former students of Woodward.

Why the Confederacy Lost. (coedited with Gabriel S. Boritt). OUP 1992 $19.95. ISBN 0-19-507405-X. Essays by McPherson and others probing the question in the title and the concomitant one of why the Union won.

MILLER, PERRY (GILBERT EDDY). 1905–1963

Born and educated in Chicago, Perry Miller received his Ph.D. from the University of Chicago in 1931. From that year until his death, he taught at Harvard University. Working with such source materials as diaries and letters, he studed the literature and culture of New England in the colonial and early national eras. His books, and especially his most popular work, *The New England Mind* (1939–53), radically altered the old stereotypical view of Puritan life as dreary and uninvolved with worldly matters and did much to create renewed interest in the Puritanism of early New England. As Granville Hicks wrote, "He respected the Puritans as thinkers, and he regarded them more highly than he did their successors who moderated their teachings" (*Saturday Review*).

A professor of American literature, Miller wrote critical essays and compiled anthologies of early American poetry and prose. One work, *The Life of the Mind in America*, published posthumously in 1965, won the 1966 Pulitzer Prize in history. All of Miller's works were informed by a keen sense of history and reminded students of American civilization of how much the Puritans and the Transcendentalists shaped the national culture.

BOOKS BY MILLER

American Puritans: Their Prose and Poetry. (ed.) 1956. Col. U. Pr. 1982 $18.00. ISBN 0-231-05419-X. Fine collection of the most important writings.

American Thought: The Civil War to World War I. (ed.) H. Holt & Co. 1954 o.p. Good
   material on the intellectual history of the period.
American Transcendentalists: Their Prose and Poetry. (ed.) 1957. Johns Hopkins 1981 o.p.
   Excellent collection of writings on early-nineteenth-century American literature.
Errand into the Wilderness. HUP 1956 $10.95. ISBN 0-674-26155-0. Delightful, yet erudite
   essays, mostly on religion in early America.
Jonathan Edwards. Amer. Men of Letters Ser. Greenwood 1973 repr. of 1949 ed. $35.00.
   ISBN 0-8371-6551-2. Splendid biography of the great Puritan divine.
The Life of the Mind in America: From the Revolution to the Civil War. 1965. Harvest Bks.
   1970 $12.95. ISBN 0-15-651990-9. Profound and somewhat ironic. Intended as part
   of a fuller study Miller did not live to complete.
Major Writers in America. (ed.) 1962. HarBraceJ abr. ed. 1966 $27.00. ISBN 0-15-
   554602-3. Useful compendium.
Nature's Nation. HUP 1967 $24.95. ISBN 0-674-60550-0. Essays of Miller's later years,
   often sharply critical in tone, dealing with religion and the philosophy of nature.
The New England Mind. 2 vols. 1939–53. HUP 1983 $13.95 ea. ISBNs 0-674-61301-5, 0-
   674-61306-6. Brilliant intellectual history that examines the theology of New
   Englanders in the 1600s and traces its evolution.
The Raven and the Whale: The War of Words and Wits in the Era of Poe and Melville.
   Greenwood 1973 repr. of 1956 ed. $45.50. ISBN 0-8371-6707-8. Important aspects of
   the American Renaissance.
Religion and Freedom of Thought. (coauthored with others). *Essay Index Repr. Ser.* Ayer
   repr. of 1954 ed. $10.00. ISBN 0-8369-2199-2. Thoughtful essays on a sensitive
   subject.
Transcendentalists: An Anthology. (ed.) HUP 1950 $16.95. ISBN 0-674-90333-1. Excellent
   selection of writings.

MORGAN, EDMUND S(EARS). 1916–

   Born in Minneapolis, Minnesota, Edmund Morgan spent most of his youth in
Cambridge, Massachusetts, and was educated at the Belmont Hill School,
Harvard, and the London School of Economics. He received his Ph.D. from
Harvard in 1942 and three years later began his teaching career at the University
of Chicago. From there he moved first to Brown University and then to Yale,
where he became Sterling Professor in 1965 and emeritus in 1986.
   Morgan's historical writings greatly enhance our understanding of such
complex aspects of the American experience as Puritanism, the Revolution, and
the relationship between slavery and racism. At the same time, they captivate
readers in the classroom and beyond. His work is a felicitous blend of rigorous
scholarship, imaginative analysis, and graceful presentation.
   Although sometimes characterized as the quintessential Whig historian, in
reality Morgan transcends simplistic categorization and has done more,
perhaps, than any other historian to open new and creative paths of inquiry into
the meaning of the early American experience.

BOOKS BY MORGAN

American Slavery, American Freedom: The Ordeal of Colonial Virginia. 1975. Norton 1976
   $9.95. ISBN 0-393-09156-2. Important book that argues that the planter elite
   deliberately fostered racism so as to separate "dangerous free whites from
   dangerous slave blacks by a screen of racial contempt."
The Birth of the Republic, 1763–1789. 1956. U. Ch. Pr. 1992 $25.00. ISBN 0-226-53756-0.
   Elegantly written brief narrative of the American Revolution. Ideal introduction to
   the subject.
The Challenge of the American Revolution. 1976. Norton 1978 $10.95. ISBN 0-393-
   05603-1. Judicious and wide-ranging essays on varying aspects of the Revolution.

The Genius of George Washington. 1980. U. Pr. of Amer. 1985 $20.25. ISBN 0-8191-4871-7. Concise, perceptive look at the great Virginian.

The Gentle Puritan: A Life of Ezra Stiles, 1727–1795. 1962. Bks. Demand repr. of 1974 ed. $132.10. ISBN 0-8357-3923-6. Fine biography of a patriot, intellectual, founder of Brown University, and president of Yale University.

Inventing the People: The Rise of Popular Sovereignty in England and America. 1988. Norton 1989 $9.95. ISBN 0-393-30623-2. An "ironic twist to the more standard version of Whig history, for he pivots his explanation for the emergence of popular sovereignty on the notion that it is a fiction" (Joyce Appleby, *Journal of American History*).

The Meaning of Independence: John Adams, George Washington and Thomas Jefferson. 1976. U. Pr. of Va. 1979 $10.00. ISBN 0-8139-0694-6. Morgan at his "humanizing" best, presenting the three founders as men who rose above their times and circumstances.

Prologue to Revolution: Sources and Documents on the Stamp Act Crisis, 1764–1776. (ed.) Norton 1972 $3.95. ISBN 0-393-09424-3. Excellent and useful collection of documents.

The Puritan Dilemma: The Story of John Winthrop. 1958. Scott F. 1987 $13.00. ISBN 0-673-39347-X. Graceful treatment of the central Puritan dilemma of doing right in a world that does wrong, as exemplified in life of Massachusetts Bay Colony's first governor.

The Puritan Family: Religion and Domestic Relations in Seventeenth-Century New England. 1944. Greenwood 1980 repr. of 1966 ed. $38.50. ISBN 0-313-22703-9. Sharp challenge to traditional views about Puritan morality and ethics.

Roger Williams: The Church and the State. 1967. Norton 1987 $6.95. ISBN 0-393-30403-5. Having, in his own words, "misunderstood and misjudged" the man earlier, Morgan pays tribute to Williams's creativity and courage.

The Stamp Act Crisis: Prologue to Revolution. (coauthored with Helen M. Morgan). U. of NC Pr. 1953 o.p. Splendid account of the crisis that generated the constitutional principles underlying the struggle for independence.

Virginians at Home: Family Life in the Eighteenth Century. U. Pr. of Va. 1952 $14.95. ISBN 0-910412-52-9. Account of daily life in colonial Virginia, similar in approach to *The Puritan Family.*

Visible Saints: The History of a Puritan Idea. 1963. Cornell Univ. Pr. 1965 $7.95. ISBN 0-8014-9041-3. Tightly disciplined study of how Puritans handled the delicate matter of church membership.

MORISON, SAMUEL ELIOT. 1887–1976

Samuel Eliot Morison wrote in a lively style with authority and an engaging grace. An accomplished scholar, he had a long association with Harvard University, where he took his Ph.D. in 1912, and taught for many years, serving as the university's official historian and writing a three-volume history of the institution. He also was an accomplished sailor who retired from the navy in 1951 as a rear admiral.

In preparing for his Pulitzer Prize–winning biographies of CHRISTOPHER COLUMBUS and John Paul Jones—*Admiral of the Ocean Sea* (1941) and *John Paul Jones: A Sailor's Biography* (1952)—he took himself out of the study and onto the high seas, where he traced the voyages of his subjects and "lived" their stories insofar as possible. When it came time for the U.S. Navy to select an author to write a history of its operations in World War II, Morison was the natural choice for the task.

A product of the Brahmin tradition, Morison wrote about Bostonians and other New Englanders and about life in early Massachusetts. He was an "American historian" in the fullest sense of the term. He also had a keen appreciation for the larger history of the nation and world—*provincial* is the last word one would use to describe Morison's writing.

BOOKS BY MORISON

Admiral of the Ocean Sea: A Life of Christopher Columbus. Atlantic Monthly 1941 $45.00. ISBN 0-316-58354-5. Excellent biography, challenged in some ways by more recent studies but still a fine read.

Builders of the Bay Colony. AMS Pr. repr. of 1930 ed. $26.45. ISBN 0-404-14741-0. Fine literary portraits of the Puritan oligarchy.

Christopher Columbus, Mariner. 1955. NAL-Dutton 1983 $9.00. ISBN 0-452-00992-8. Brief narrative account that focuses on the great discoverer's seamanship.

Dissent in Three American Wars. (coauthored with others). HUP 1970 o.p. Reminder of the difficulties of achieving consensus in times of crisis.

The European Discovery of America: The Northern Voyages. OUP 1971 $39.95. ISBN 0-19-501377-8. Narrative history of the discovery.

The European Discovery of America: The Southern Voyages. OUP 1974 $39.95. ISBN 0-19-501823-0. With *The Northern Voyages,* constitutes a superb history of the discovery— the capstone of Morison's career.

Founding of Harvard College. HUP 1935 $30.95. ISBN 0-674-31450-6. Account of a major event in early American cultural and intellectual history.

The Great Explorers: The European Discovery of America. OUP 1978 $39.95. ISBN 0-19-502314-5. Condensed from Morison's two earlier volumes on the discovery.

The Growth of the American Republic. (coauthored with Henry Steele Commager and William E. Leuchtenburg). 1930. 2 vols. OUP 1980 $29.95 ea. ISBNs 0-19-502593-8, 0-19-502594-6. Readable and solid survey long held in high esteem.

History of United States Naval Operations in World War II, 1939–1945. 15 vols. Little 1947–62 $375.00. ISBN 0-316-58300-6. Majestic history that covers every phase of the sea war.

The Intellectual Life of Colonial New England. Greenwood 1980 repr. of 1956 ed. $35.00. ISBN 0-313-22032-8. Small gem of intellectual history. Originally titled *The Puritan Pronaos.*

John Paul Jones: A Sailor's Biography. 1952. NE U. Pr. 1985 $14.95. ISBN 0-930350-70-7. One sailor's scholarly and readable appreciation of another.

The Maritime History of Massachusetts: 1783–1860. NE U. Pr. 1979 $35.00. ISBN 0-930350-06-5. Story of the Bay State's heyday as the nation's shipping center.

One Boy's Boston: 1887–1901. NE U. Pr. 1983 repr. of 1962 ed. $12.95. ISBN 930350-49-9. Delightful reminiscence of the author's Beacon Hill-Back Bay childhood.

The Oxford History of the American People. 1927. 3 vols. NAL-Dutton 1972 $4.95–$5.95 ea. ISBNs 0-451-62600-1, 0-451-62408-4, 0-451-62446-7. Morison's own history of the nation.

Portuguese Voyagers to America in the Fifteenth Century. 1940. Octagon 1965 o.p. Good history of seafaring.

The Ropemakers of Plymouth: A History of the Plymouth Cordage Company, 1824–1849. Companies and Men: Business Enterprise in Amer. Ser. Ayer 1976 repr. of 1950 ed. $21.00. ISBN 0-405-08086-7. Story of an industry crucial to maritime commerce.

Sailor Historian. Ed. by Emily Morison Beck. HM 1977 o.p. Some of Morison's reminiscences and observations about history and the sea.

Sources and Documents Illustrating the American Revolution, 1764–1788, and the Formation of the Federal Constitution. (ed.) 1923. OUP 1965 $14.95. ISBN 0-19-500262-8. Excellent collection of documentary materials.

The Story of Mt. Desert Island, Maine. Atlantic Monthly 1960 $15.00. ISBN 0-316-58362-6. Fine history of a favorite locale.

Three Centuries of Harvard, 1636–1936. HUP 1936 $14.95. ISBN 0-674-88891-X. Model of academic institutional history.

The Two-Ocean War: A Short History of the United States Navy in the Second World War. 1963. Atlantic Monthly 1989 $16.95. ISBN 0-316-58352-9. One-volume condensation of the 15-volume history of U.S. World War II naval operations. Concentrates on major battles and campaigns.

Vistas of History. Knopf 1964 o.p. Selected papers, including the noteworthy essay "The Experiences and Principles of an Historian."

BOOK ABOUT MORISON

Skotheim, Robert Allen. *American Intellectual Histories and Historians.* 1960. Greenwood 1978 repr. of 1966 ed. $35.00. ISBN 0-313-20120-X. Perceptive estimate of Morison's contributions.

NEVINS, ALLAN. 1890–1971

Illinois-born Allan Nevins studied at the University of Illinois and went on to make journalism his first career, working for some years as a reporter for several New York newspapers and as an editor of the *Nation.* In 1928 he turned to the world of academia, and for over a quarter of a century he taught and wrote history—first at Cornell University, then at Columbia University. In 1948 he established the first oral history program in the nation at Columbia. In 1958 he "retired" to become a senior research associate at the Huntington Library in California, where he continued his indefatigable research and writing.

One of this century's most prolific historians, Nevins's interests ranged widely—and he wrote biographies of presidents, entrepreneurs, explorers, inventors, and journalists as well as studies of the Civil War, banking, statecraft, and education. His political biographies *Grover Cleveland* (1932) and *Hamilton Fish* (1936) won Pulitzer Prizes. Not always the most discerning critic of his subjects, Nevins nonetheless wrote memorable narrative histories that remain readable and interesting today.

BOOKS BY NEVINS

America Through British Eyes. (ed.) 1948. Peter Smith o.p. Well-edited compilation of divergent and interesting views from 1789 through World War II.

American Press Opinion: Washington to Coolidge. Rprt. Serv. 1991 repr. of 1928 ed. $99.00. ISBN 0-7812-6023-X. Useful survey by a skilled journalist-historian.

American Social History as Recorded by British Travellers. (ed.) Kelley 1969 repr. of 1923 ed. o.p. Complementary volume to *America Through British Eyes.*

The American States during and after the Revolution, 1775–1789. Rprt. Serv. 1992 repr. of 1924 ed. $109.00. ISBN 0-685-54681-0. Good survey of political developments through the Confederation period.

A Century of Political Cartoons. (coauthored with Frank Weitenkampf). Octagon 1991 repr. of 1914 ed. $69.00. ISBN 0-7812-6038-8. Informative and entertaining.

The Diary of George Templeton Strong, 1835–1875. (coedited with Milton H. Thomas). 1952. U. of Wash. Pr. 1987 $35.00. ISBN 0-295-96511-8. Diary packed with information about almost every aspect of life in mid–nineteenth-century New York.

Diary of Philip Hone, 1828–1851. (ed.) Rise of Urban Amer. 2 vols. in 1. Ayer 1970 repr. of 1927 ed. $52.00. ISBN 0-405-02468-1. Fascinating "secret diaries" of a leading New Yorker. Reveals much about life in Jacksonian America.

Emergence of Modern America, 1865–1878. History of Amer. Life Ser. Scholarly 1971 repr. of 1927 ed. $95.00. ISBN 0-403-01127-2. Representative volume in a major undertaking in social history early in the twentieth century.

Evening Post: A Century of Journalism. Russell Sage 1968 repr. of 1922 ed. o.p. Retrospective on a major American newspaper, long defunct, for which Nevins worked as a young reporter.

Ford. Companies and Men: Business Enterprise in Amer. Ser. 3 vols. Ayer 1976 $140.00. ISBN 0-405-08089-1. Conventional but informative study of the man and the industry.

Frémont: Pathmarker of the West. 1928. Rprt. Serv. 1992 $75.00. ISBN 0-7812-5070-6.
    First edition titled *Frémont: The World's Greatest Adventurer.* Standard biography of
    a controversial explorer and soldier.
The Greater City: New York, 1898 to 1948. (coedited with John A. Kraut). Greenwood
    1981 repr. of 1948 ed. $43.75. ISBN 0-313-23072-2. Colorful documentary history of
    the city.
Grover Cleveland: A Study in Courage. 1932. Dodd 1964 o.p. Uncritical but informative
    biography.
Hamilton Fish: The Inner History of the Grant Administration. 1936. Continuum 1957 o.p.
    Prize-winning political biography.
*History of the Bank of New York and Trust Company, 1784–1934. Companies and Men:
    Business Enterprise in Amer. Ser.* Ayer 1976 repr. of 1934 ed. $24.50. ISBN 0-405-
    08088-3. Solid, straightforward history of a major financial institution.
James Truslow Adams: Historian of the American Dream. 1968. Bks. Demand repr. of 1968
    ed. $85.60. ISBN 0-8357-6168-1. Tribute to a leading early-twentieth-century
    historian.
John D. Rockefeller: The Heroic Age of American Enterprise. 2 vols. Kraus Intl. 1976 repr.
    of 1940 ed. $88.00. ISBN 0-527-66800-1. Major biography of a captain of industry,
    later reissued under title *A Study in Power: John D. Rockefeller, Industrialist and
    Philanthropist* (1953), perhaps in response to assertions that original version was too
    uncritical.
The Ordeal of the Union. 1947–71. 8 vols. in 4. Macmillan 1992 $24.95 ea. ISBNs 0-02-
    035441-X, 0-02-035442-8, 0-02-035442-6, 0-02-035445-2. Classic narrative history of
    the sectional conflict and of the age. Winner of National Book Award.
A Pocket History of the United States. (coauthored with Henry Steele Commager). 1942.
    PB 9th rev. ed. 1991 $7.50. ISBN 0-671-62992-1. Perennially popular and useful brief
    history.
The State Universities and Democracy. Greenwood 1977 repr. of 1962 ed. $38.50. ISBN 0-
    8371-9705-8. Assessment of land-grant and other state institutions of higher learning.

PARKMAN, FRANCIS. 1823–1893

Born in Boston to an old and wealthy New England family, Francis Parkman
was raised in an environment that honored patriotism and literary talent, both
of which qualities always informed his histories. Although his work was marred
by anticlerical bias and racial prejudice against Native Americans, few
historians captured better the spirit of adventure and grandeur that marked the
expansion of European-American civilization into the Great West. Kenneth
Rexroth wrote of *France and England in North America* (1865–92) that
"Parkman's history is the story of our heroic age, and, like the *Iliad*, it is the
story of the war between two basic types of personality. It is from this archetypal
struggle that it derives its epic power. As Parkman works his history out in
detail, the personal conflicts of its actors give it the intricacy and ambiguity of a
psychological novel. That this struggle is echoed in the spiritual conflict of the
author gives the book an intimacy and depth beyond that of factual history"
(*Saturday Review*). Of the same book EDMUND WILSON (see Vol. 1) said, "The
clarity, the momentum and color of the first volumes of Parkman's narrative are
among the most brilliant achievements in the writing of history as an art" (*O
Canada*).

Parkman's journals, discovered and published many years after his death,
were started while he was a Harvard undergraduate, determined even then to
write history in spite of poor health and failing eyesight. The early journals
include precise and dramatic descriptions of summer trips from 1841 to 1846 in
the wilds of New England, New York State, Canada, the Northwest, and Europe.
Of particular interest are his notes for *The Oregon Trail*, published in book form

in 1899 as *The California and Oregon Trail* and which he dictated to a cousin after a breakdown in health.

BOOKS BY PARKMAN

France and England in North America. 1865–92. 2 vols. Ed. by David Levin. Library of America 1983 $32.50 ea. ISBNs 0-940450-10-1, 0-940450-11-9. Majestic study of the great imperial struggle for much of North America.

The History of the Conspiracy of Pontiac. 1851. Macmillan o.p. A narrative of the "conspiracy" that offers a brilliant summary of the entire Anglo-French conflict in the New World.

The Jesuits in North America. Corner Hse. 1970 repr. of 1895 ed. $24.00. ISBN 0-87928-016-6. Despite its ambivalent attitude toward Catholicism, goes far in achieving the author's goal to "reproduce an image of the past with photographic clearness and truth."

Journals. Ed. by Mason Wade. 2 vols. in 1. Kraus Intl. 1947 o.p.

La Salle and the Discovery of the Great West. 1889. Random 1990 $9.50. ISBN 0-679-72615-2. An exciting wilderness narrative marred only by over-admiration for La Salle's personality.

Letters. Ed. by Wilbur R. Jacobs. 2 vols. Bks. Demand $54.00–$65.00. ISBNs 0-8357-9730-9, 0-685-07758-6. More than 400 letters that tell a romantic story of Parkman's West.

Montcalm and Wolfe. 1884. Peter Smith o.p. Dramatic narrative of the climactic struggle for North America—the siege and fall of Quebec.

The Oregon Trail: Sketches of Prairie and Rocky Mountain Life. Bks. Demand repr. of 1949 ed. $160.00. ISBN 0-317-42104-2. Notable book of travel and adventure that is less a history than an autobiographical sketch of Parkman's own experiences in following the trail.

The Parkman Reader. Ed. by Samuel Eliot Morison. Little 1955 o.p. Careful selections from Parkman's larger works that give a coherent picture of eary North American colonial history.

Pioneers of France in the New World. Corner Hse. 1970 repr. of 1865 ed. $24.00. ISBN 0-87928-017-4. Focuses on the bitter struggles for survival of the Huguenots in Florida and Champlain in Canada.

Seven Years War: A Narrative Taken from "Montcalm and Wolfe," "The Conspiracy of Pontiac" and "A Half Century of Conflict." Ed. by John McCallum. HarpC 1968 o.p. Good selection and condensation to illustrate the nature of the war.

Works. 20 vols. AMS Pr. repr. of 1902 ed. $770.00. ISBN 0-404-04920-6

BOOKS ABOUT PARKMAN

Doughty, Howard. *Francis Parkman.* HUP 1983 $8.95. ISBN 0-674-31775-0. Good relatively recent biography.

Farnham, Charles H. *The Life of Francis Parkman.* Rprt. Serv. 1991 repr. of 1901 ed. $89.00. ISBN 0-7812-6024-8. Long the standard biography. Still useful in spite of an uncritical estimate.

Jacobs, Wilbur R. *Francis Parkman, Historian as Hero: The Formative Years.* Amer. Studies Ser. U. of Tex. Pr. 1991 $27.50. ISBN 0-292-72467-5. Fine study of Parkman in his youthful years.

Pease, Otis A. *Parkman's History: The Historian as Literary Critic.* Shoe String 1968 repr. of 1953 ed. o.p. Good critical evaluation.

Wade, Mason. *Francis Parkman: Heroic Historian.* Shoe String 1972 repr. of 1942 ed. $47.50. ISBN 0-208-01213-3. An informed and balanced evaluation.

POTTER, DAVID M(ORRIS). 1910–1971

In 1968 Martin Duberman described David Potter as a man who "may be the greatest living historian of the United States. With the additional evidence of this collection of his essays [*The South and the Sectional Conflict*] I'm glad for the chance to say that in print, not least because Potter is little known outside the historical profession, in part because he has written only a few volumes . . . and in part because he has always shied away from self-advertisement" (*N.Y. Times*).

A native southerner, Potter did his undergraduate studies at Emory University and took his Ph.D. at Yale University in 1940. He taught at a number of universities, including Yale from 1942 to 1961 and Stanford from 1961 until his death. He also lectured widely in this country and abroad and served as Harmsworth Professor at Oxford University and Commonwealth Fund Lecturer at London University.

BOOKS BY POTTER

Division and the Stresses of Reunion, 1845–1876. Scott F. 1973 o.p. Good basic history of the sectional conflict.

Eight Issues in American History: Views and Counterviews. (coauthored with Curtis Grant). Scott F. 1966 o.p. Perceptive examination of major crises in the past.

Freedom and Its Iimitations in American Life. Ed. by Don E. Fehrenbacher. Stanford U. Pr. 1976 $15.00. ISBN 0-8047-0933-5. Essays on the sectional conflict and other issues in U.S. history.

History and American Society: The Essays of David Potter. Ed. by Don E. Fehrenbacher. OUP 1973 o.p. Trenchant essays on such topics as historical objectivity, the Turner thesis, women in American history, the nature of nationalism—all displaying the range of Potter's historical curiosity.

The Impending Crisis, 1848–1861. New Amer. Nation Ser. 1976. HarpC 1977 $13.00. ISBN 0-06-131929-5. Balanced and comprehensive overview of the sectional conflict.

Lincoln and His Party in the Secession Crisis. AMS Pr. repr. of 1942 ed. $27.00. ISBN 0-404-14809-3. Intensive analysis of the crisis. Potter's "position as the sworn enemy of hindsight lends a freshness and illumination to the treatment" (*Nation*).

People of Plenty: Economic Abundance and the American Character. 1954. U. Ch. Pr. 1958 $8.95. ISBN 0-226-67633-1. Profound inquiry into the nature of the American national character and what makes American behavior different from that of other peoples.

The South and the Concurrent Majority. Ed. by Don E. Fehrenbacher and Carl N. Degler. La. State U. Pr. 1972 o.p. Fleming Lectures at LSU, analyzing the intellectual and political bases for southern particularism.

The South and the Sectional Conflict. La. State U. Pr. 1968 o.p. Essays of subtle perception seeking the essential nature of the South. Includes valuable review of the historical literature of the region.

ROOSEVELT, THEODORE. 1858–1919

Periodically throughout his extraordinary career, Theodore Roosevelt turned to the writing of history. Energetic about everything he did, he imbued his writing with verve and a strong sense of drama that continues to attract readers today. Born in New York City and educated at Harvard University, he immersed himself in public affairs long before he became President of the United States. A man of many talents, he was, among other things, police commissioner, mayoral candidate, rancher, hunter, explorer, soldier, and governor. His strong sense of history probably influenced his actions more times than not, and certainly he brought to the White House in 1901 an awareness of how much the past conditions the present and informs the future. Roosevelt made history, influenced history, and wrote history.

BOOKS BY ROOSEVELT

Addresses and Presidential Messages, 1902–1904. Kraus Intl. o.p. Both the contents and the introduction by Henry Cabot Lodge are important historical documents.

American Ideals and Other Essays, Social and Political. Scholarly repr. of 1897 ed.
   $17.00. ISBN 0-404-05398-X. Collection of essays that represent Roosevelt's views on
   a variety of matters.
Autobiography. Da Capo 1985 repr. of 1913 ed. $15.95. ISBN 0-306-80232-5. Interesting
   account, influenced more by political considerations than by a historical outlook.
Gouverneur Morris. Rprt. Serv. 1992 repr. of 1898 ed. $89.00. ISBN 0-7182-6128-7. Good
   biography of an early American statesman and diplomat.
Hunting Trips of a Ranchman. 1885. Regnery Gateway 1991 $14.95. ISBN 0-89526-738-1.
   Adventure, plus awareness of environment and history.
Letters of Theodore Roosevelt. 8 vols. Ed. by Elting E. Morison. HUP 1951–54 $75.00.
   ISBN 0-685-02130-0
Maxims. Irvington repr. of 1903 ed. $17.00. ISBN 0-8398-1764-9. Offers Roosevelt's
   opinions on a wide variety of subjects.
*The Naval War of 1812; or The History of the United States Navy during the Last War with
   Great Britain.* Rprt. Serv. 1988 repr. of 1882 ed. $59.00. ISBN 0-7812-0174-8.
   Competent and dramatic account.
The New Nationalism. Peter Smith repr. of 1910 ed. $11.25. ISBN 0-8446-0237-X.
   Roosevelt's "blueprint" for modern America. A major historical document.
Outdoor Pastimes of an American Hunter. Amer. Environmental Studies. Ayer 1970 repr.
   of 1905 ed. $29.00. ISBN 0-405-02687-0. Reflects the "strenuous life" and interest in
   environmental matters.
Presidential Addresses and State Papers. 4 vols. Kraus Intl. repr. of 1905 ed. o.p.
   Introduction by Albert Shaw.
Ranch Life and the Hunting Trail. Amer. Environmental Studies. Ayer 1970 repr. of 1901
   ed. $15.00. ISBN 0-405-02688-9. Elements that went into the making of a dedicated
   conservationist.
Rough Riders. Corner Hse. 1971 repr. of 1899 ed. $22.50. ISBN 0-87928-018-2. Firsthand
   account of the famous cavalry unit.
*Selections from the Correspondence of Theodore Roosevelt and Henry Cabot Lodge,
   1884–1918. Amer. Public Figures Ser.* 2 vols. Rprt. Serv. 1992 repr. of 1925 ed.
   $150.00. ISBN 0-7812-6221-6. Documentation of the close relationship of two
   powerful political leaders, dating from their youthful years.
Strenuous Life: Essays and Addresses. Scholarly repr. of 1902 ed. $39.00. ISBN 0-403-
   00311-3
Thomas Hart Benton. Ed. by John T. Morse. *Amer. Statesmen Ser.* AMS Pr. repr. of 1899
   ed. $34.50. ISBN 0-404-50873-1. Admiring biography of an American artist.
*The Wilderness Hunter: An Account of the Big Game of the United States and Its Chase
   with Horse, Hound and Rifle.* Irvington repr. of 1900 ed. $29.50. ISBN 0-8290-1955-3.
   Further evidence of Roosevelt's love of the wilderness.
The Winning of the West. 4 vols. Ed. by Harvey Wish. Somerset Pub. $295.00. ISBN 0-403-
   04339-5. Main work upon which Roosevelt's reputation as a historian rests.
   Influential, readable, and romanticized.

BOOKS ABOUT ROOSEVELT

Beale, Howard K. *Theodore Roosevelt and the Rise of America to World Power.* 1956.
   Johns Hopkins 1984 $15.95. ISBN 0-8018-3249-7. Excellent account of Roosevelt's
   foreign policy.
Blum, John M. *The Republican Roosevelt.* 1954. HUP 1977 $7.95. ISBN 0-674-76302-5.
   Perceptive overall assessment.
Burton, David H. *The Learned Presidency: Theodore Roosevelt, William Howard Taft,
   Woodrow Wilson.* Fairleigh Dickinson 1987 $27.50. ISBN 0-8386-3313-7. Interesting
   study that deals with literate and intellectual aspects of the three presidents.
Chessman, G. Wallace. *Theodore Roosevelt and the Politics of Power.* 1969. *Library of
   Amer. Biography.* Scott F. 1987 $13.00. ISBN 0-673-39329-1. Careful, clear study of
   Roosevelt the politician.

Collins, Richard H. *Theodore Roosevelt, Culture, Diplomacy, and Expansion: A New View of American Empire.* La. State U. Pr. 1985 $30.00. ISBN 0-8071-1214-3. Reflects recent perspectives on American diplomacy, connecting it with cultural factors.
———. *Theodore Roosevelt's Caribbean: The Panama Canal, the Monroe Doctrine, and the Latin American Context.* La. State U. Pr. 1990 $45.00. ISBN 0-8071-1507-X. Important revision of some traditional views about U.S. Caribbean policy.

Cooper, John Milton. *The Warrior and the Priest: Woodrow Wilson and Theodore Roosevelt.* HUP 1983 $12.95. ISBN 0-674-94751-7. Superb comparative study of two men who profoundly influenced the course of American history.

Cutright, Paul R. *Theodore Roosevelt, the Making of a Conservationist.* U. of Ill. Pr. 1985 $29.95. ISBN 0-252-1190-2. Brings research and thinking about Progressive conservationism up to date.

Dennett, Tyler. *Theodore Roosevelt and the Russo-Japanese War.* Peter Smith 1958 $11.75. ISBN 0-8446-1150-6. Solid study of Roosevelt at his diplomatic best.

Esthus, Raymond A. *Theodore Roosevelt and Japan.* U. of Wash. Pr. 1967 o.p. "A clear and straightforward narrative of a complicated and important period of American diplomatic history" (*Library Journal*).

Friedenberg, Robert V. *Theodore Roosevelt and the Rhetoric of Militant Decency.* Greenwood 1990 $45.00. ISBN 0-313-25448-1. Welcome analysis of Roosevelt's pronouncements, moralisms, and bombast.

Gibson, William M. *Theodore Roosevelt among the Humorists: W. D. Howells, Mark Twain, and Mr. Dooley.* Bks. Demand repr. of 1980 ed. $25.00. ISBN 0-8357-69134-5. Roosevelt as the object of wit, humor, and satire—political and otherwise.

Gould, Lewis L. *The Presidency of Theodore Roosevelt.* U. Pr. of KS 1991 $29.95. ISBN 0-7006-0435-9. Excellent straightforward study of Roosevelt in office.

Hagedorn, Hermann. *The Roosevelt Family of Sagamore Hill.* Macmillan 1954 o.p. Graceful and refreshing account of Roosevelt as a family man.

Harvard University Library: Theodore Roosevelt Collection, Dictionary Catalogue and Shelflist. 5 vols. HUP 1970 $250.00. ISBN 0-670-87775-6. Major collection of source materials.

Hurwitz, Howard L. *Theodore Roosevelt and Labor in New York State, 1880–1900. Columbia Univ. Studies in the Social Sciences.* AMS Pr. repr. of 1943 ed. $18.00. ISBN 0-404-51500-2. Earliest evidence of an always ambivalent attitude toward labor.

McCullough, David G. *Mornings on Horseback.* Touchstone Bks. 1982 $14.95. ISBN 0-671-44754-8. Intimate portrait of the man and president. Winner of the 1983 National Book Award.

Marks, Frederick W., III. *Velvet on Iron: The Diplomacy of Theodore Roosevelt.* U. of Nebr. Pr. 1979 $25.00. ISBN 0-8032-3057-5. Generally balanced and able study.

Miller, Nathan. *Theodore Roosevelt: A Life.* Morrow 1992 $27.00. ISBN 0-688-0678-90. Readable and up-to-date biography.

Morris, Edmund. *The Rise of Theodore Roosevelt.* Ballantine 1980 $12.95. ISBN 0-345-33902-9. Good readable study of Roosevelt during the pre-presidential years.

Mowry, George E. *Theodore Roosevelt and the Progressive Movement.* 1946. Hill & Wang 1960 o.p. Scholarly and critical work emphasizing political concerns.

O'Gara, Gordon C. *Theodore Roosevelt and the Rise of the Modern Navy.* Greenwood 1970 repr. of 1943 ed. $38.50. ISBN 0-8371-1480-2. Excellent treatment of an important aspect of Roosevelt's career.

Pringle, H. F. *Theodore Roosevelt.* 1931. Harvest Bks. 1956 $8.95. ISBN 0-15-688943-9. Pulitzer Prize–winning (1932) biography, outdated in many ways but still very readable.

Sproat, John G. *"The Best Men": Liberal Reformers in the Gilded Age.* 1968. U. Ch. Pr. 1972 o.p. Discusses important early influences on Roosevelt's subsequent political career.

SCHLESINGER, ARTHUR M(EIER). 1888–1965

Arthur Schlesinger was a scholar of great breadth of vision and a significant precursor of the "new social history." Born in Xenia, Ohio, he studied as an undergraduate at Ohio State University and did his graduate work at Harvard University. In 1924, after teaching at Ohio State and at the State University of Iowa, he joined the faculty at Harvard, where he remained for many years and went, in his words, on many "professional pilgrimages to worldwide houses of learning." His volume of essays *New Viewpoints in American History* (1922) was far-reaching in its effects and marked a turning point in the profession's conceptions of research and subject matter. He once said, "In my writing and teaching I have done all I could to disseminate the idea that history should be as inclusive as life itself."

It is a mark of Schlesinger's professional demeanor and vision that in 1965, to recognize Schlesinger's pioneering work in emphasizing women's roles in history and to honor his wife's work in furthering what would one day be called women's studies, Radcliffe College renamed its Women's Archives the Arthur and Elizabeth Schlesinger Library on the History of Women in America.

BOOKS BY SCHLESINGER

The Birth of the Nation: A Portrait of the American People on the Eve of Independence. 1968. HM 1988 $9.95. ISBN 0-317-64564-1. A literary portrait drawn with grace and balance, setting the stage for great events.

The Critical Period in American Religion, 1875–1900. Fortress Pr. 1967 o.p. Perceptive study of major changes underway in the churches.

Colonial Merchants and the American Revolution, 1763–1776. Atheneum 1968 o.p. Trenchant study of an important group in the revolutionary crisis.

History of American Life Series. (coedited with Dixon Ryan Fox). 12 vols. Macmillan 1950 o.p. A superb endeavor that set the stage in many ways for the rich social history of our time.

In Retrospect: The History of a Historian. HarBraceJ 1963 o.p. "A rewarding autobiographical memoir—an engaging causerie, not a reverie" (Charles Poore, *N.Y. Times*).

Learning How to Behave: A Historical Study of American Etiquette Books. Cooper Sq. 1968 repr. of 1946 ed. $30.00. ISBN 0-8154-0201-5. Charming history of social customs.

New Viewpoints in American History. Rprt. Serv. 1991 repr. of 1922 ed. $79.00. ISBN 0-7812-6025-6

Nothing Stands Still: Essays by Arthur M. Schlesinger. HUP 1969 o.p. Worthwhile volume, whose title tells much about the tenor of its contents.

Paths to the Present. AMS Pr. 1963 repr. of 1949 ed. $29.50. ISBN 0-404-20228-4. Reflections on studying, writing, and thinking about history.

Prelude to Independence: The Newspaper War on Britain, 1764–1776. 1938. NE U. Pr. 1980 $13.95. ISBN 0-930350-13-8. Interesting aspect of the revolutionary movement, well related.

The Rise of the City, 1878–1898. History of Amer. Life Ser. Macmillan 1933 o.p. In the context of its time, first-rate social history, intelligently covering the arts, religion, education, and women.

SCHLESINGER, ARTHUR M(EIER), JR. 1917–

Born in Columbus, Ohio, the son of historian parents, Arthur Schlesinger, Jr., graduated from Harvard University in 1938 and became a Henry Fellow at that institution the same year. He began teaching at Harvard in 1946 after serving with the offices of War Information and of Strategic Services. He left Harvard 15 years later to become a special assistant to the president of the United States. In 1966 he was appointed Albert Schweitzer Professor in the Humanities at City

University of New York, a position he still holds. Schlesinger is an accomplished political historian, whose works on Andrew Jackson, Franklin D. Roosevelt, John F. Kennedy, and other leaders are notable for their high literary quality and scholarly integrity. Both *The Age of Jackson* (1945) and *A Thousand Days* (1965), which focuses on the Kennedy presidency, won a Pulitzer Prize, the former for history and the latter for biography. Among the other awards he has received are the National Book Award (1965), the Parkman Prize (1957), the Bancroft Prize (1958), and the Gold Medal of the National Institute of Arts and Letters (1967).

BOOKS BY SCHLESINGER, JR.

The Age of Jackson. 1945. Little 1988 $22.50. ISBN 0-316-77343-3. Important book that is, in effect, an interpretation of democracy's future through an analysis of its past.

The Age of Roosevelt. 3 vols. HM 1957–60. Vol. 1 1988 $11.70. ISBN 0-395-48903-2. Vol. 2 1959 $19.45. ISBN 0-395-08160-2. Vol. 3 1988 $11.70. ISBN 0-395-498904-0. Superb narrative and analytical history of the 1920s, Great Depression, and New Deal.

The Almanac of American History. (ed.) Putnam Pub. Group 1984 o.p. Chronologically arranged coverage of events in American history from the Viking explorations to the early 1980s.

The Bitter Heritage: Vietnam and American Democracy, 1941–1966. 1966. Fawcett rev. ed. 1972 o.p. Disturbing but important inquiry into the antecedents of the crisis of the 1960s.

The Causes of the Civil War: A Note on Historical Sentimentalism. Irvington Repr. Ser. in Amer. History. Irvington 1991 $2.30. ISBN 0-8290-2609-6. Brief but influential contribution to the historical debate on causation.

The Coming to Power: Critical Presidential Elections in American History. (coauthored with Fred L. Israel). Chelsea Hse. 1981 repr. of 1972 ed. $10.95. ISBN 0-87754-217-1. Interesting explorations in political history.

The Crisis of Confidence: Ideas, Power and Violence in America. HM 1969 o.p. Sensitive inquiry into the roots of the domestic disorder of the 1960s.

The Cycles of American History. 1986. HM 1987 $11.70. ISBN 0-395-45400-X. Well-documented argument that reform and reaction—or liberalism and conservatism—run in a cyclical pattern throughout American history.

The Disuniting of America. 1991. Norton 1992 $15.95. ISBN 0-393-03380-5. A historian's reflections on multiculturalism and ethnic diversity in American society.

The History of American Presidential Elections. (coedited with Fred L. Israel). 10 vols. Chelsea Hse. repr. of 1971 ed. o.p. Very useful compendium of information.

The Imperial Presidency. 1973. HM 1989 $12.70. ISBN 0-395-51561-0. Searching inquiry into the use and misuse of presidential power, past and present.

Origins of the Cold War. (ed.) *Irvington Repr. Ser. in Amer. History.* Irvington 1991 $2.60. ISBN 0-8290-2614-2. Good collection of differing views on the topic.

The Politics of Hope. HM 1963 o.p. Compilation taken from essays, articles, speeches, and reviews over a 13-year period.

Robert Kennedy and His Times. 1978. Ballantine 1985 $6.95. ISBN 0-345-324547-8. Admiring biography full of valuable insights into the man and the times.

Robert Kennedy in His Own Words. (ed.) BDD Promo. Bk. 1991 $3.98. ISBN 0-7924-1223-0. Selection of Kennedy's speeches and writings.

Running for President: The Candidates and Their Images. 2 vols. Grove Pr. 1992 $30.00 ea. ISBNs 0-8021-1456-3, 0-8021-1459-8. Fast-paced and informative perspective on campaigning.

A Thousand Days: John F. Kennedy in the White House. Fawcett 1977 repr. of 1965 ed. o.p. Vivid and informative history from an insider's perspective.

The Vital Center: The Politics of Freedom. 1949. Da Capo 1988 $10.95. ISBN 0-306-80323-2. Vigorous affirmation of a rational "middle ground" as the central arena of American politics.

STAMPP, KENNETH M(ILTON). 1912–

A native of Milwaukee, Kenneth Stampp received his Ph.D. from the University of Wisconsin in 1941 and then taught at the University of Arkansas and the University of Maryland. In 1945 he joined the faculty at the University of California at Berkeley, where he is currently Morrison Professor Emeritus of American History. Stampp has served as Harmsworth Professor at Oxford, Commonwealth Lecturer at the University of London, Fulbright Professor at the University of Munich, and visiting professor at Harvard University and Colgate University and Williams College. A past president of the Organization of American Historians, in 1993 he received the Lincoln Prize from the Lincoln and Soldiers Institute of Gettysburg College.

Stampp touched off a revolution in the study of slavery with the publication of *The Peculiar Institution* (1956), which vigorously refutes the long-prevailing Dunning-Phillips interpretation and demolishes a host of myths about the master-slave relationship. His further works on the sectional conflict and its causes established him as a leading authority on that subject as well.

BOOKS BY STAMPP

America in 1857: A Nation on the Brink. 1990. OUP 1992 $29.95. ISBN 0-19-503902-5. Superb examination of a "critical year," when all the forces that would produce the Civil War took unmistakable shape.

And the War Came: The North and the Secession Crisis. Greenwood 1980 repr. of 1950 ed. $35.00. ISBN 0-313-22566-4. Dispassionate examination marked by political realism and a recognition of the interplay among ideals, emotions, and vested interests.

The Causes of the Civil War. (ed.) 1965. Touchstone Bks. 3rd rev. ed. 1992 $10.00. ISBN 0-671-75155-7. Good sampling of views from people who lived through the crisis and historians who have written about it.

The Era of Reconstruction. 1965. Vin. 1967 $7.96. ISBN 0-394-70388-X. Balanced yet forceful synthesis of a controversial period in American history.

The Imperiled Union: Essays on the Background of the Civil War. 1980. OUP 1981 $9.95. ISBN 0-19-502991-7. Trenchant essays, including "The Southern Road to Appomattox," which suggests that many Confederates had inward doubts about their cause and subconsciously welcomed its defeat.

Indiana Politics During the Civil War. Ind. U. Pr. 1978 repr. of 1949 ed. o.p. Economic factors behind the political disputes in the sectional crisis.

The Peculiar Institution: Slavery in the Ante-Bellum South. 1956. Vin. 1989 $10.00. ISBN 0-679-72307-2. Still the book with which to begin a study of chattel slavery in the United States.

Reconstruction: An Anthology of Revisionist Writings. (coedited with Leon F. Litwack). La. State U. Pr. 1969 $12.95. ISBN 0-8071-0138-9. Useful collection of relatively recent research and writing on Reconstruction.

BOOK ABOUT STAMPP

Maizlish, Stephen, and Robert Abzug, eds. *New Perspectives on Race and Slavery in America: Essays in Honor of Kenneth M. Stampp.* U. Pr. of Ky. 1986 $19.00. ISBN 0-8131-1571-X. Includes a biographical sketch of Stampp and an evaluation of his contributions.

TURNER, FREDERICK JACKSON. 1861–1932

Born in Portage, Wisconsin, Frederick Jackson Turner graduated from the University of Wisconsin and in 1890 received his Ph.D. from The Johns Hopkins University. From 1889 to 1910, he taught at Wisconsin University, where he helped build an excellent graduate history program. In 1910 he accepted a chair at Harvard University, where he remained for the next 14 years. In 1927 he became a senior research associate at the Henry E. Huntington Library in San Marino, California.

Turner wrote relatively little, but his 1893 paper on the link between the land and democracy—"The Significance of the Frontier in American History"— affected the course of American scholarship and marked him as one of the most influential and renowned scholars in the profession. The year after his death, his study in sectionalism, *The Significance of Sections in American History*, was awarded the Pulitzer Prize in history. Turner once described U.S. history as "a series of social evolutions recurring in differing geographic basins across a raw continent." He claimed to derive his hypothesis from his early training in medieval history, where he learned about the relationships between people and their environment and saw "the interplay of economic, social and geographic factors in the politics, institutions, ideals and life of a nation and its relations with its neighbors."

Turner's views have always been subject to intense scrutiny and criticism, not least among historians of the American West today. Yet the fact that his hypothesis continues to be tested is testimony to its penetrating influence.

BOOKS BY TURNER

The Character and Influence of the Indian Trade in Wisconsin. AMS Pr. repr. of 1891 ed. $11.50. ISBN 0-404-61070-6. Turner's doctoral dissertation, based on research and firsthand observations in Wisconsin.

Correspondence of the French Ministers to the United States, 1791–1797. (ed.) Da Capo 1971 repr. of 1904 ed. $115.00. ISBN 0-306-71315-2. Careful editing of important documents in diplomatic history.

Early Writings. Ayer repr. of 1938 ed. $19.00. ISBN 0-8369-1054-0

Frederick Jackson Turner's Legacy: Unpublished Writings in American History. Ed. by Wilbur R. Jacobs. U. of Nebr. Pr. 1965 $19.95. ISBN 0-8032-0922-3. Interesting essays and lectures on a variety of topics.

The Frontier in American History. Krieger 1976 repr. of 1920 ed. $23.50. ISBN 0-88275-347-9. Carefully constructed essays elaborating on the "Turner Thesis."

Reuben Gold Thwaites: A Memorial Address. Rprt. Serv. 1991 repr. of 1914 ed. $59.00. ISBN 0-7812-6026-4. Tribute to a friend who, as director of the Wisconsin Historical Society, figured large in Turner's work.

The Rise of the New West, 1819–1829. The Amer. Nation Ser. 1906. Macmillan 1962 o.p. One of the few complete books Turner produced. A felicitous narrative history.

The Significance of the Frontier in American History. 1894. Ed. by Harold P. Simonson. Continuum 1985 $5.95. ISBN 0-8044-6919-9. The central statement of Turner's hypothesis.

The Significance of Sections in American History. 1932. Peter Smith o.p. Carefully constructed essays in which Turner further elaborates his frontier thesis.

BOOKS ABOUT TURNER

Billington, Ray Allen. *Genesis of the Frontier Thesis: A Study in Historical Creativity.* Huntington Lib. 1971 $19.95. ISBN 0-87328-050-4. Sensitive tracing of Turner's developing views.

———. *The Frontier Thesis: Valid Interpretation of American History?* Amer. Problem Studies. 1966. Krieger 1977 $9.50. ISBN 0-88275-586-2. Careful examination of the criticisms and the defense.

Carpenter, Ronald H. *The Eloquence of Frederick Jackson Turner.* Huntington Lib. 1983 $20.00. ISBN 0-87328-078-4. Historiographical study of Turner's work.

Hofstadter, Richard. *The Progressive Historians: Turner, Beard, Parrington.* U. Ch. Pr. 1979 $14.95. ISBN 0-226-34818-0. Study of three historians whose theories, the author considers, strongly influenced American historical thought of the first half of the twentieth century.

Jacobs, Wilbur, and others. *Turner, Bolton, and Webb: Three Historians of the American Frontier.* U. of Wash. Pr. 1979 $5.95. ISBN 0-295-95677-1. Provides a balanced estimate of Turner's contribution.

Taylor, George R., ed. *The Turner Thesis Concerning the Role of the Frontier in American History.* Problems in Amer. Civilization Ser. Heath 3rd ed. 1972 $8.50. ISBN 0-669-81059-2. Full examination of the debate in a well-organized and useful college-level problems book.

WEBB, WALTER PRESCOTT. 1888–1963

A regional historian of imagination and vision, Walter Prescott Webb presented his studies of the frontier, the Great Plains, and his beloved Texas in terms that enhanced the reader's understanding of the entire national experience. Born into a poor East Texas family at a time when the plains were succumbing to the pressure of white civilization, he was a true product of his environment and liked to say that he had begun research on his classical study *The Great Plains* (1931) "when I was four." Trained at the University of Texas, he began teaching there as well in 1918; yet a series of misadventures prevented him from receiving his Ph.D. until 1932. In 1938 he was Harkness lecturer in American history at the University of London and several years later Harmsworth Professor of American history at Oxford University.

Although Webb's work excited controversy and sharp criticism in some quarters, it inspired significant new thinking about the role of regionalism and the environment in the nation's history. In his presidential address to the American Historical Association in 1958, Webb spoke of "History as High Adventure," an apt reflection of his lifelong approach to his work.

BOOKS BY WEBB

Divided We Stand: The Crisis of a Frontierless Democracy. 1937. Hyperion Conn. 1985 repr. of 1944 ed. $18.00. ISBN 0-88355-903-X. Militant defense of regional traits under assault by relentless nationalism.

The Great Frontier. 1952. U. of Nebr. Pr. 1986 $9.95. ISBN 0-8032-9711-4. Ambitious attempt to update the frontier thesis, arguing that the nation's entire cultural fabric was shaped by the commingling of great natural wealth, ample land, and a "manageable" population.

The Great Plains. 1931. U. of Nebr. Pr. 1981 $12.95. ISBN 0-8032-9701-5. Environmental history in the full sense of the term, showing the interrelationship of geography, history, economics, and regional characteristics.

Handbook of Texas. (coedited with H. Bailey Carroll). Tex. St. Hist. Assn. 1952 $65.00. ISBN 0-87611-013-8

History as High Adventure. Pemberton Pr. 1969 o.p. Webb's 1958 presidential address to the American Historical Association.

The Texas Rangers: A Century of Frontier Defense. 1935. U. of Tex. Pr. 1965 $27.95. ISBN 0-292-78110-5. Geography, history, and politics, as they shaped the myths and realities of a legendary frontier institution.

BOOKS ABOUT WEBB

Frantz, Joe B., and others. *Essays on Walter Prescott Webb.* U. of Tex. Pr. 1976 o.p.

Jacobs, Wilbur R., and others. *Turner, Bolton, and Webb: Three Historians of the Frontier.* U. of Wash. Pr. 1979 $5.95. ISBN 0-295-95677-1. Good essay by Frantz.

Shannon, Fred A. *An Appraisal of Walter Prescott Webb's "The Great Plains".* Greenwood 1979 repr. of 1940 ed. $45.00. ISBN 0-313-21211-2. Balanced and insightful.

Tobin, Gregory M. *The Making of a History: Walter Prescott Webb and the Great Plains.* Bks. Demand repr. of 1976 ed. $53.10. ISBN 0-8357-7766-9. Skillful tracing of a masterwork.

WILLIAMS, WILLIAM APPLEMAN. 1921–1986

The leading "revisionist" historian during the years of the cold war, William Appleman Williams played a major role in shaping the perceptions of a generation of young historians. His best-known book, *The Tragedy of American Diplomacy* (1959), established themes he would pursue throughout his career as a writer and a teacher—the contradictions between ideals and "practicality" in the conduct of U.S. foreign policy and the centrality of economic factors in the nation's world outlook. Product of a solidly rural Iowa background and a graduate of the U.S. Naval Academy at Annapolis, Williams nonetheless became a figure of controversy because of his unconventional, often iconoclastic, observations about the American experience and his subjection of capitalism to a searching criticism that borrowed freely from Karl Marx (see Vols. 3 and 4), even as it rejected doctrinaire Marxism.

At a time when most historians subscribed to a generally benevolent view of the nation's past and of its role in world affairs, Williams's freewheeling critiques often irritated the older generation of scholars. Yet they also opened the way for younger historians to break from the "consensus" school of history and enter into previously unexplored pathways to the American past.

Books by Williams

America Confronts a Revolutionary World: 1776–1976. Morrow 1976 o.p. America's evolution from nation to empire, with what the author sees as its unfortunate consequences.

American-Russian Relations, 1781–1947. 1952. Octagon 1971 o.p. Traces the deterioration in relations from friendship to animosity, putting the onus on the expansionist implications of "open door" economic diplomacy in American policy.

The Contours of American History. 1961. Norton 1989 $9.95. ISBN 0-393-30561-9. Free-ranging critique of the American experience, dismissed as an intellectual fraud by some historians, hailed as a challenging new interpretation by others.

Empire as a Way of Life: An Essay on the Causes and Character of America's Present Predicament. OUP 1980 $29.95. ISBN 0-190502766-3. Important elaboration of Williams's controversial views. Marred by some factual errors and an often turgid style.

From Colony to Empire: Essays in the History of American Foreign Policy. (ed.) Bks. Demand repr. of 1972 ed. $129.50. ISBN 0-8357-9895-X

The Great Evasion: An Essay on the Contemporary Relevance of Karl Marx and on the Wisdom of Admitting the Heretic into the Dialogue About America's Future. Quadrangle 1964 o.p. Controversial treatment. Tests the Marxist interpretation without embracing its orthodoxies.

The Roots of the Modern American Empire: A Study of the Growth and Shaping of a Social Consciousness in a Marketplace Society. Random 1969 o.p. The agrarians' search for markets as the earliest stimulus to American expansionism, refined later by industrial and financial interests.

The Shaping of American Diplomacy: Readings and Documents in American Foreign Relations. (ed.) 1956. Rand McNally rev. ed. 1970 o.p. Chapter introductions present the view that economics and ideology are as important as political and military considerations in American diplomatic history.

Some Presidents: Wilson to Nixon. Random 1972 $1.95. ISBN 0-685-04242-1. Views on the continuity of American policy.

The Tragedy of American Diplomacy. 1959. Norton 1988 $9.95. ISBN 0-393-30493-0. Brief but very influential interpretation of American diplomatic history.

Book about Williams

Gardner, Lloyd C., ed. *Redefining the Past: Essays in Diplomatic History in Honor of William Appleman Williams.* Oreg. St. U. Pr. 1986 $29.95. ISBN 0-87071-348-5.

Collection of provocative essays reflecting Williams's influence. Includes biographical sketch and a bibliography.

WOODWARD, C(OMER) VANN. 1908–

One of the world's most distinguished historians, C. Vann Woodward was born in Vanndale, Arkansas, and educated at Emory University and the University of North Carolina, where he received his Ph.D. in 1937. After teaching at Georgia Institute of Technology, the University of Florida, and Scripps College for a time, in 1946 he joined the faculty at The Johns Hopkins University, where he began producing the many young Ph.D.s who have followed him into the profession. In 1961 he became Sterling Professor at Yale University, where he remains today as emeritus professor. He has been the Jefferson Lecturer in the Humanities, Harmsworth Professor at Oxford University, and Commonwealth Lecturer at the University of London. Past president of all the major historical associations, he holds the Gold Medal of the National Academy and Institute of Arts and Letters and is a member of the British Academy and the Royal Historical Society. His honors also include a Bancroft Prize for *Origins of the New South, 1876–1913* (1951) and a 1982 Pulitzer Prize for *Mary Chesnut's Civil War* (1981).

A premier historian of the American South and of race relations in the United States, Woodward studies the South in a way that sheds light on the human condition everywhere. In recent years he has turned his attention increasingly to comparative history.

BOOKS BY WOODWARD

American Counterpoint: Slavery and Race in the North-South Dialogue. OUP 1971 $9.95. ISBN 0-19-503269-1. Informed examination of the stereotypes, myths, and misconceptions that cloud considerations of race and region.

The Burden of Southern History. 1960. La. State U. Pr. rev. ed., 1968 $27.50. ISBN 0-8071-0837-5. Thoughtful, sensitive evaluation of the southern experience with war, defeat, racism, and guilt.

The Comparative Approach to American History. (ed.) Basic 1968 o.p. Collection of essays displaying great virtuousity in applying comparative methods to the study of history.

The Future of the Past. OUP 1989 $30.00. ISBN 0-19-505744-9. Positing history as a "third something" between science and art, further addresses on a comparative basis such topics as race, slavery, and emancipation.

Mary Chesnut's Civil War. (ed.) Yale U. Pr. 1981 $45.00. ISBN 0-300-02459-2. Superb firsthand account by a southern "aristocrat" of conditions in the South during the war. Skillfully edited and annotated.

The Old World's New World. 1991. OUP 1992 $21.95. ISBN 0-19-506451-8. Observations on the European reaction to America over three centuries.

Origins of the New South, 1877–1913. 1951. *History of the South Ser.* La. State U. Pr. 1972 $37.50. ISBN 0-8071-0009-9. Brilliant study of the post-Reconstruction South. Brings a fresh perspective and critical intelligence to the subject.

The Private Mary Chesnut: The Unpublished Civil War Diaries. (coedited with Elizabeth Muhlenfeld). OUP 1985 $12.95. ISBN 0-19-503513-5. Beautifully edited supplement to the earlier Chesnut diaries.

Responses of the Presidents to Charges of Misconduct. (ed.) Delacorte 1974 o.p. Minute examination of executive misbehavior from George Washington through Lyndon Johnson, commissioned by the Impeachment Inquiry Staff of Congress and conducted by 16 historians. Unusual and valuable compendium.

Reunion and Reaction: The Compromise of 1877 and the End of Reconstruction. 1951. OUP 1991 $9.95. ISBN 0-19-506423-2. Concise and incisive examination of the "deal" that ended Reconstruction.

The Strange Career of Jim Crow. OUP 3rd rev. ed. 1974 $8.95. ISBN 0-19-501805-0. Important contribution to the literature on segregation, challenged by some historians, but still a reasoned and humane study.

Thinking Back: The Perils of Writing History. La. State U. Pr. 1986 $14.95. ISBN 0-8071-1304-2. Retrospective essays on a remarkably productive career.

Tom Watson: Agrarian Rebel. U. Pr. of Va. 1982 $35.00. ISBN 0-8139-0952-X. Biography of a southern political leader. Important for an understanding of the connection between populism and racism.

BOOKS ABOUT WOODWARD

Kousser, J. Morgan, and James M. McPherson, eds. *Region, Race, and Reconstruction: Essays in Honor of C. Vann Woodward.* OUP 1982 $29.95. ISBN 0-19-503075-3. Significant essays by some of Woodward's talented former students, together with an appreciation and a bibliography.

Roper, John H. *C. Vann Woodward, Southerner.* U. of Ga. Pr. 1987 $30.00. ISBN 0-8203-0938-8. Balanced study, reasonable in both praise and criticism.

CHAPTER 16

Canadian History

Robert H. Babcock

Canada's historians have all been nationalists of various hues, and sometimes their judgements about what was central to the past and what was peripheral arose as much from divergent conceptions of nationality as from disagreements about interpretations of the same evidence.
—CARL BERGER, *The Writing of Canadian History*

In the view of some historians, Canada lacks many of the more common unifying bonds of other nations. As contemporary economist KENNETH BOULDING informed a group of students in Toronto in 1957, "Canada has no cultural unity, no linguistic unity, no religious unity, no economic unity, no geographic unity. All it has is unity." In part this lack of the more common unifying bonds can be explained by the fact that the New World remnants of the eighteenth-century French and British empires spawned two national outlooks—English Canadian and French Canadian—which have evoked quite different myths about the same historical events. More recently, Canadians have been redefining themselves in the context of an impinging American strategic and commercial empire; indeed, during the twentieth century, Canada has often been overshadowed by its neighbor and long-time ally, the United States. Living in a vast, sparsely settled region that has evolved over four centuries on the fringes of three empires, embracing at least two distinct national perspectives, yet remaining together in one federalized polity, Canadians may be forgiven for their introspection.

Historians have taken it upon themselves to define Canada's identity. During the nineteenth century, FRANÇOIS-XAVIER GARNEAU articulated a nationalist historical vision, defending French Canadian language, culture, and traditions against British assimilation. English Canadians, meanwhile, celebrated an expanding British Empire that their historians told them was firmly rooted in universal liberal democratic principles. By the early twentieth century, British North America had evolved into an autonomous nation within the British Commonwealth. The Canadian identity, however, remained anomalous. French Canadian historians like LIONEL GROULX evoked the heroes of Catholic New France to protect French Canada from the secularizing and assimilating forces of industrial capitalism. World War I stimulated an English Canadian nationalism that found expression in the work of HAROLD ADAMS INNIS and DONALD CREIGHTON. They presented a basic interpretation of Canadian history chronicling the emergence of a unique political economy in the St. Lawrence River and lower Great Lakes basin. This view, however, did not find universal acceptance. WILLIAM LEWIS MORTON and others criticized Innis and Creighton for ignoring the hinterland peoples exploited by the staples economy.

Only within the past 30 years have historians of Canada gradually retreated from a self-appointed task to define the Canadian identity. Influenced by new scholarly fashions, historians like JEAN HAMELIN have chosen to write about communities, regions, ethnic groups, native peoples, families, schools, workers, and a host of circumscribed topics in both linguistic traditions without dramatizing any connections to the nation-state. This concerns historians like RAMSAY COOK, who fear that, by focusing on more limited themes, historians will lose sight of important national perspectives. Craig Brown's words, penned in *Nationalism in Canada* in 1967, still ring true for many:

"Debating nationalism is the great Canadian national pastime. . . . There is no great national hero who cut down a maple tree, threw a silver dollar across the St. Lawrence and then proceeded to lead a revolution and govern the victorious nation wisely and judiciously. There are no great Canadian charters of freedom or independence expressing the collective will of the people. But the search goes on."

This bibliography includes many important works from the overtly nationalist pre-1960 era. Greater overall emphasis, however, is given to studies that cumulatively reflect more recent trends. For the most part, the material is organized either topically or chronologically by the major turning points in Canadian history.

REFERENCE WORKS

The Canadian Encyclopedia. 3 vols. Hurtig 1988 o.p. Up-to-date, illustrated, readable, and authoritative compilation of information on people, places, institutions, groups, and terms.

Granatstein, J. L., and Paul Stevens, eds. *A Reader's Guide to Canadian History 2: Confederation to the Present.* U. of Toronto Pr. 1982 o.p. Eleven essays evaluating literature on politics, foreign policy, social history, and individual provinces.

Halpenny, Frances, and others, eds. *Dictionary of Canadian Biography.* 7 vols. U. of Toronto Pr. Vol. 1 *1000–1700.* 1966 $75.00. ISBN 0-8020-3142-0. Vol. 2 *1701–1740.* 1969 $75.00. ISBN 0-8020-3240-0. Vol. 3 *1741–1770.* 1974 $75.00. ISBN 0-8020-3314-8. Vol. 4 *1771–1800.* 1979 $75.00. ISBN 0-8020-3351-2. Vol. 5 o.p. Vol. 6 *1821–1835.* 1972 $75.00. ISBN 0-8020-3436-5. Vol. 7 *1836–1850.* 1982 $75.00. ISBN 0-8020-3452-7. Scholarly biographies arranged by year of death, with each volume prefaced by essays providing helpful analyses of major themes.

Harris, R. C., and others. *Historical Atlas of Canada.* Vol. 1 *From the Beginning to 1800.* U. of Toronto Pr. 1987 $95.00. ISBN 0-8020-2495-5. Outstanding collection of maps with accompanying essays about the discovery, exploration, and settlement of Canada.

Kerr, Donald, and D. W. Holdsworth, eds. *Historical Atlas of Canada.* Vol. 3 *Addressing the Twentieth Century, 1891–1961.* U. of Toronto Pr. 1990 $95.00. ISBN 0-8020-3448-9. First-rate maps, charts, graphs, and essays chronicling the impact of industrialization, the Depression, and World War II.

Klinck, Carl F., ed. *Literary History of Canada: Canadian Literature in English.* 3 vols. U. of Toronto 1976 o.p. Essays on literature, drama, theology, history, and poetry produced in Canada from the eighteenth century to the present.

Leacy, F. H., ed. *Historical Statistics of Canada.* Statistics Canada 1983 o.p. Provides a wide range of economic, social, and political data from Confederation to the mid-1970s.

Muise, D. A., ed. *A Reader's Guide to Canadian History 1: Beginnings to Confederation.* U. of Toronto Pr. 1982 $14.95. ISBN 0-8020-6442-6. Seven helpful essays evaluating mostly recent literature on New France, Quebec, British North America, the Atlantic Provinces, the North, and Confederation.

Story, Norah. *The Oxford Companion to Canadian History and Literature.* OUP 1967 o.p. Somewhat dated, but still useful, compendium of data on people, places, and themes in Canadian political and cultural history.

Thibault, Claude, comp. *Bibliographia Canadiana.* Longman 1973 o.p. Dated, but still valuable, one-volume guide to the secondary literature in Canadian history and historiography.

Wallace, W. Stewart. *The Macmillan Dictionary of Canadian Biography.* Macmillan 1963 o.p. Useful sketches of Canadian politicians, jurists, doctors, clergy, scholars, authors, explorers, merchants, and many others.

SURVEYS AND GENERAL WORKS

Berger, Carl. *The Sense of Power: Studies in the Ideas of Canadian Imperialism 1867–1914.* U. of Toronto Pr. 1970 $15.95. ISBN 0-8020-6113-3. Argues persuasively that British imperialism was a form of Canadian nationalism.

Bliss, Michael. *Northern Enterprise: Five Centuries of Canadian Business.* Firefly Bks. Ltd. 1987 o.p. Sweeping examination of entrepreneurs, their businesses, and their relations with politicians.

Brown, Craig, ed. *The Illustrated History of Canada.* Firefly Bks. Ltd. 1991 o.p. Up-to-date, well-illustrated chronicle by seven of Canada's leading historians.

Daigle, Jean, ed. *The Acadians of the Maritimes: Thematic Studies.* Centre d'Études Acadiennes 1982 o.p. Fifteen authoritative essays by scholars of Acadian history, geography, demography, economy, politics, and culture.

Easterbrook, W. T., and H. Aitken. *Canadian Economic History.* U. of Toronto Pr. 1988 repr. of 1956 ed. $24.95. ISBN 0-8020-6696-8. Classic survey explaining the effects of nineteenth century staples development. Weak on industrialization.

Easterbrook, W. T., and M. H. Watkins, eds. *Approaches to Canadian Economic History.* Firefly Bks. Ltd. 1967 o.p. Important collection of essays on the staples approach and on the role of the state in the Canadian economy.

Francis, R. Douglas, Richard Jones, and Donald B. Smith. *Origins: Canadian History to Confederation.* 2 vols. H. Holt & Co. Vol. 1 1992 o.p. Vol. 2 *Destinies: Canadian History since Confederation.* 1992 o.p. First and second volumes of the best survey of Canadian history. Controversies surrounding the interpretation of key events delineated by sidebars.

Gagnon, Serge. *Quebec and Its Historians 1840–1920.* Harvest Hse. 1982 o.p. Skillful evaluations of the work of François-Xavier Garneau, Ferland, Sulte, and Lionel Groulx, placed within their cultural contexts.

———. *Quebec and Its Historians: The Twentieth Century.* Montreal: Harvest Hse. 1985 o.p. Five essays exploring such diverse historiographical themes as New France, the Quiet Revolution, and the relationship between ideology and method.

Granatstein, J. L., and Norman Hillmer. *For Better or For Worse: Canada and the United States to the 1990s.* Copp o.p. Best available survey of United States-Canada relations from Confederation to the present. Emphasizes political, economic, and strategic issues.

Grant, George. *Lament for a Nation: The Defeat of Canadian Nationalism.* Firefly Bks. Ltd. 1970 o.p. A brilliant polemic arguing that Canada is doomed to eventual absorption by the United States.

Griffiths, N. E. S., and G. A. Rawlyk, eds. *Mason Wade, Acadia and Quebec: The Perception of an Outsider.* Carleton U. Pr. 1991 o.p. Includes five chapters by Wade on the Acadians and three essays by others assessing the prominent American-born scholar's contributions to the history of French Canada.

Harris, R. Cole, and John Warkentin. *Canada Before Confederation: A Study in Historical Geography.* OUP 1974 o.p. Excellent synthesis. Offers a spatial as well as temporal dimension to Canadian history for the period.

Hartz, Louis, ed. *The Founding of New Societies: Studies in the History of the United States, Latin America, South Africa, Canada, and Australia.* HarBraceJ 1969 repr. of

1964 ed. $6.95. ISBN 0-15-632728-7. Includes Kenneth D. MacRae's "The Structure of Canadian History."

Heron, Craig. *The Canadian Labour Movement: A Short History.* Lorimer 1989 o.p. Valuable interpretation of labor as a social movement.

Hutchinson, Bruce. *The Struggle for the Border.* Ayer repr. of 1955 ed. $25.00. ISBN 0-8369-5601-X. Gripping narrative of efforts by politicians and explorers to carve out the boundary between the United States and Canada.

McNaught, Kenneth. *Pelican History of Canada.* Viking Penguin rev. and updated 1975 $6.95. ISBN 0-14-021083-0. Relates how two traditions, French Canadian and British Loyalist, gradually joined in common hostility to an expansionist United States.

Martin, Chester. *Empire and Commonwealth: Studies in Governance and Self-Government in Canada.* OUP 1929 o.p. Classic Whig interpretation stressing the evolution of British political institutions.

Morton, Desmond. *A Military History of Canada: From Champlain to the Gulf War.* Firefly Bks. Ltd. 1992 o.p. Emphasizes the ways in which war has shaped Canadian society and helped to foster a national identity.

Norrie, Kenneth, and Doug Owram. *A History of the Canadian Economy.* HarBraceJ 1991 o.p. Outstanding interweaving of the staples and quantitative approaches by an economist and a historian.

Palmer, Bryan. *Working-Class Experience: Rethinking the History of Canadian Labour, 1800–1990.* Firefly Bks. Ltd. 1992 o.p. The best survey of labor from the perspective of the new social history. Includes a valuable annotated bibliography.

Prentice, Alison, and others. *Canadian Women: A History.* HarBraceJ 1988 o.p. Vivid, well-integrated synthesis on the history of women from New France to the 1982 Charter of Rights.

Saunders, S. A. *The Economic History of the Maritime Provinces.* Acadiensis 1984 o.p. Originally published in 1939. Argues from the Laurentian perspective that the economic decline of the region was unrelated to Confederation.

Schultz, John, ed. *Writing about Canada: A Handbook for Modern Canadian History.* P-H 1990 o.p. Ten chapters on different kinds of history that survey both what has been done and what still needs to be done.

Taylor, M. Brook. *Promoters, Patriots, and Partisans: The Writing of English Canadian History in the Nineteenth Century.* U. of Toronto Pr. 1989 $40.00. ISBN 0-8020-2683-4. Focuses on regions. Complements Carl Berger's analysis of twentieth-century English Canadian historians.

Winks, Robin W. *The Blacks in Canada: A History.* Yale U. Pr. 1971 o.p. Fine-grained study from the perspective of an American student of Canadian history.

Woodcock, George. *The Canadians.* HUP 1980 $23.50. ISBN 0-674-09335-6. Well-illustrated, gracefully written examination of Canadian history and culture.

TOPICAL WORKS

Diplomatic History

Brebner, J. B. *The North Atlantic Triangle: The Interplay of Canada, the United States and Great Britain.* Firefly Bks. Ltd. 1968 o.p. Originally published in 1945. Masterful interweaving of British, American, and Canadian history from early settlements to World War II.

Clarkson, Stephen. *Canada and the Reagan Challenge.* Lorimer 1982 o.p. Spirited critique of Ronald Reagan's policies toward Canada based on interviews with movers and shakers in Canada and the United States.

Granatstein, J. L. *Marching to Armageddon: Canada and the Great War, 1914–1919.* Lester & Orpen Dennys 1989 o.p. Picture-history of World War I from the perspective of the foot soldiers.

_____. *Canada's War: The Politics of the Mackenzie King Government, 1939–1945*. OUP 1990 $24.95. ISBN 0-8020-6797-2. Emphasizes the ways that King wrestled with political, economic, and ethnic issues on the home front.

Granatstein, J. L., and Robert Bothwell. *Pirouette: Pierre Trudeau and Canadian Foreign Policy*. U. of Toronto Pr. 1990 $35.00. ISBN 0-8020-5780-2. Exhaustive study arguing that Trudeau's foreign policy largely failed.

Jones, Howard. *To the Webster-Ashburton Treaty: A Study in Anglo-American Relations, 1783–1843*. Bks. Demand repr. of 1977 ed. $70.80. ISBN 0-8357-3886-8. Offers new evidence upgrading the reputation of Webster and Ashburton.

Perin, Roberto. *Rome in Canada: The Vatican and Canadian Affairs in the Late Victorian Age*. U. of Toronto Pr. 1990 $45.00. ISBN 0-8020-5854-X. Relates how the failure of Rome to support French Canadian nationalism contributed to the victory of a Protestant, Anglo-Saxon version of Canada's destiny.

Smith, Denis. *Diplomacy of Fear: Canada and the Cold War, 1941–1948*. U. of Toronto Pr. 1988 $18.95. ISBN 0-8020-6684-4. Focuses on the role Soviet espionage in Canada played in pushing an anxious government into the American camp.

Socknat, Thomas. *Witness against War: Pacifism in Canada, 1900–1945*. U. of Toronto Pr. 1987 $40.00. ISBN 0-8020-5704-7. Shows that although influential beyond their numbers, Canadian pacifists were only a cultural island.

Stacey, C. P. *Canada and the Age of Conflict: A History of Canadian External Policies*. 2 vols. U. of Toronto Pr. Vol. 1 *1867–1921*. 1984 $20.95. ISBN 0-8020-6560-0. Vol. 2 *1921–1948—The Mackenzie King Era*. 1981 $22.95. ISBN 0-8020-6420-5. Emphasizes the manner in which changing internal situations dictated the country's reactions to external affairs and stresses the extraordinary influence of the office of prime minister on foreign relations.

Stairs, Denis. *The Diplomacy of Constraint: Canada, the Korean War and the United States*. U. of Toronto Pr. 1974 o.p. Chronicles efforts by Ottawa to moderate the exercise of American power.

Winks, Robin W. *Canada and the United States: The Civil War Years*. Johns Hopkins 1988 repr. of 1960 ed. $30.00. ISBN 0-8191-7116-6. Argues persuasively that the American Civil War was an important turning point for Canadians as well as Americans.

Social History

Adachi, Ken. *The Enemy that Never Was: A History of the Japanese Canadians*. Firefly Bks. Ltd. 1991 o.p. Stresses the unjust evacuation and detention during World War II of 21,000 people, most of them Canadian citizens.

Akenson, Donald H. *The Irish in Ontario: A Study in Rural History*. U. of Toronto Pr. 1984 $39.95. ISBN 0-7735-0430-3. Finds that the Irish in Ontario settled largely in rural rather than urban areas.

Dumont, Micheline, and others. *Quebec Women: A History*. Women's Pr. 1987 o.p. A feminist evaluation of the lives of ordinary women from the time of the early settlements to 1979.

Fingard, Judith. *Jack in Port: Sailortowns of Eastern Canada*. U. of Toronto Pr. 1982 $40.00. ISBN 0-8020-2458-0. Re-creates the boisterous dockside life in Quebec City, Halifax, and Saint John.

McLaren, Angus, and Arlene Tigar McLaren. *The Bedroom and the State: The Changing Practices and Politics of Contraception and Abortion in Canada, 1880–1980*. Firefly Bks. Ltd. 1986 o.p. Shows how dramatic historical shifts in the politics of contraception put current debates in a new context.

Metcalfe, Alan. *Canada Learns to Play: The Emergence of Organized Sport, 1807–1914*. Firefly Bks. Ltd. 1987 o.p. Offers insights into the impact of American and British sports on Canadian pastimes.

Parr, Joy. *The Gender of Breadwinners: Women, Men, and Change in Two Industrial Towns, 1880–1950*. U. of Toronto Pr. 1990 $45.00. ISBN 0-8020-5853-1. Award-winning comparative examination of the effects of gender identities at the workplace.

Prentice, Alison. *The School Promoters: Education and Social Class in Mid-Nineteenth Century Upper Canada.* Firefly Bks. Ltd. 1977 o.p. Account of public schooling as an instrument of middle-class "reform."

Ramirez, Bruno. *On the Move: French-Canadian and Italian Migrants in the North Atlantic Economy, 1860–1914.* Firefly Bks. Ltd. 1991 o.p. Comparative analysis showing that emigration and depopulation originated in both agrarian and commercial economies.

Sangster, Joan. *Dreams of Equality: Women on the Canadian Left, 1920–1950.* Firefly Bks. Ltd. 1990 o.p. Uncovers a feminist element in the political beliefs and practices of radical women reformers.

Trudeau, Pierre Elliott, ed. *The Asbestos Strike.* James Louis & Samuel 1974 o.p. Thorough analysis of the most important precursor to Quebec's Quiet Revolution in the 1960s.

Ward, Peter. *Courtship, Love, and Marriage in Nineteenth-Century English Canada.* U. of Toronto Pr. 1990 $24.95. ISBN 0-7735-0749-3. Fascinating story chronicling the gradual erosion of barriers to the expression of intimacy.

Cultural and Regional History

Barman, Jean. *The West Beyond the West: A History of British Columbia.* U. of Toronto Pr. 1991 $35.00. ISBN 0-8020-2739-3. Readable, up-to-date survey tracing the emergence of a distinct provincial identity.

Bulger, F.W.P., ed. *Canada's Smallest Province: A History of P. E. I.* Chelsea Green Pub. 1991 $16.95. ISBN 0-921054-91-2. Rather uneven collection of essays organized by chronological periods.

Clark, Andrew H. *Three Centuries and the Island: A Historical Geography of Settlement and Agriculture in Prince Edward Island.* Bks. Demand repr. of 1959 ed. $75.00. ISBN 0-317-27978-5. Compendium of data on the interaction of settlement and land use. Pays due attention to political and cultural overtones.

Clark, S. D. *Church and Sect in Canada.* U. of Toronto Pr. 1948 o.p. Applies Frederick Jackson Turner's frontier thesis to the evolution of Canadian religious institutions.

Friesen, Gerald. *The Canadian Prairies: A History.* U. of Toronto Pr. 1984 $21.95. ISBN 0-8020-2513-7. Captivating synthesis of the people and forces shaping the western interior region.

Grant, John W. *A Profusion of Spires: Religion in Nineteenth-Century Ontario.* U. of Toronto Pr. 1988 $30.00. ISBN 0-8020-5798-5. Traces the evolution of denominations with distinctive leaders, institutions, and traditions.

———. *The Church in the Canadian Era: The First Century of Confederation.* McGraw 1972 o.p. Volume 3 of *The History of the Christian Church in Canada.* Emphasizes Christian responses to such national issues as ultramontanism, the social gospel, church union, and secularism.

Harper, J. Russell. *Painting in Canada: A History.* U. of Toronto Pr. 1977 $35.00. ISBN 0-8020-2271-5. Traces the evolution of Canadian painting from its roots in the seventeenth century to today's diverse expressions.

Kallman, Helmut. *A History of Music in Canada, 1534–1914.* U. of Toronto Pr. 1987 $18.95. ISBN 0-8020-6102-8. Surveys four centuries of French Canadian and English Canadian traditions in folk, religious, and secular music.

Kaplan, William. *State and Salvation: The Jehovah's Witnesses and Their Fight for Civil Rights.* U. of Toronto Pr. 1989 $35.00. ISBN 0-8020-5842-6. Details violations of religious liberty by the Canadian government during World War II.

Linteau, Paul-André, René Durocher, and Jean-Claude Robert. *Quebec: A History 1867–1929.* Lorimer. Vol. 1 1983 o.p. Vol. 2 *Quebec Since 1930.* 1991 o.p. Encyclopedic *Annales*-style history of the geography, economy, society, politics, and culture of Quebec since Confederation.

McKillop, A. B. *Contours of Canadian Thought.* U. of Toronto Pr. 1987 $14.95. ISBN 0-8020-5740-3. Eight essays exploring English Canadian ideas, mostly on the relationship between scientific and humanistic values.

MacNutt, W. S. *New Brunswick: A History, 1784–1867.* Macmillan 1963 o.p. Analyzes the interaction between the lumber-based economy and provincial politics up to Confederation.

Moir, John S. *The Church in the British Era: From the British Conquest to Confederation.* McGraw 1972 o.p. Vol. 2 of the *History of the Christian Church in Canada.* Chronicles the growth pangs, rivalries, and regional differences among denominations in British North America.

Palmer, Howard, with Tamara Palmer. *Alberta: A New History.* Firefly Bks. Ltd. 1990 o.p. Well-written survey of the province's demography, economy, and politics from settlement to the 1980s.

Tippett, Maria. *Making Culture: English-Canadian Institutions and the Arts before the Massey Commission.* U. of Toronto Pr. 1990 $40.00. ISBN 0-8020-2743-1. Focuses on the professionalization of cultural activity under private and public patronage from the 1880s to the late 1940s.

Trofimenkoff, Susan M. *The Dream of Nation: A Social and Intellectual History of Quebec.* Macmillan 1982 o.p. Informed interpretation of French Canadian nationalism from seventeenth-century visions of empire to the 1980 referendum.

Westfall, William. *Two Worlds: The Protestant Culture of Nineteenth Century Ontario.* U. of Toronto Pr. 1989 $34.95. ISBN 0-7735-0669-1. Deals with the interconnections between secular and religious spheres in Canada's most Victorian province.

Young, Brian, and John A. Dickinson. *A Short History of Quebec: A Socio-Economic Perspective.* Copp 1988 o.p. An incisive analysis of Quebec from a neo-Marxist perspective.

Zaslow, Morris. *The Northward Expansion of Canada, 1914–1967. Canadian Centenary Ser.* Firefly Bks. Ltd. 1988 o.p. Explores industrial frontiers sweeping across subarctic Canada and assesses their impact on indigenous peoples.

HISTORICAL PERIODS

Discovery, Exploration, and Indigenous Peoples

Brebner, John Bartlet. *The Explorers of North America 1492–1806.* AMS Pr. repr. of 1933 ed. $67.50. ISBN 0-404-20043-5. Well-written survey of the major explorations in Canada, the United States, and Mexico.

Dickason, Olive P. *Canada's First Nations: A History of Founding Peoples from Earliest Times.* U. of Okla. Pr. 1992 $39.95. ISBN 0-7710-2801-6. Up-to-date, well-researched, and sympathetic portrayal of Canada's indigenous peoples.

Fisher, Robin. *Contact and Conflict: Indian-European Relations in British Columbia, 1774–1890.* UBC Pr. 1992 o.p. Prize-winning study of the interaction between west coast aboriginals and the Spanish, Russians, British, and Americans.

Giraud, Marcel. *The Metis in the Canadian West.* 2 vols. Trans. by George Woodcock. UAP 1986 o.p. Largest and most thorough ethnography and history of this people of mixed parentage.

Gough, Barry M. *Distant Dominion: Britain and the Northwest Coast of North America, 1579–1809.* UBC Pr. 1980 o.p. Relates how Britain outmaneuvered Spain to gain control over the lucrative trade in furs with the Far East.

Grant, John Webster. *Moon of Wintertime: Missionaries and the Indians of Canada in Encounters since 1534.* U. of Toronto Pr. 1984 $35.00. ISBN 0-8020-5643-1. Survey concluding that no set of religious beliefs can be imposed on the Indians.

Instad, Helge. *Westward to Vinland: The Discovery of Pre-Columbian Norse House-sites.* St. Martin 1967 $19.95. ISBN 0-87599-136-X. Popular account of the first archeological dig that proved Norse settlement in the New World.

Jaenen, Cornelius J. *Friend and Foe: Aspects of French-Amerindian Cultural Contact in the Sixteenth and Seventeenth Centuries.* Firefly Bks. Ltd. 1976 o.p. Prize-winning analysis of both French and Amerindian viewpoints on their inter-relations.

Miller, J. R. *Skyscrapers Hide the Heavens: A History of Indian-White Relations in Canada.* U. of Toronto Pr. 1991 $20.95. ISBN 0-8020-6869-3. Readable, comprehensive study of Indian-white relations from Jacques Cartier in 1534 to Oka in 1990.

Ray, Arthur. *Indians in the Fur Trade: Their Role as Trappers, Hunters, and Middlemen in the Lands Southwest of Hudson Bay.* U. of Toronto Pr. 1974 $16.95. ISBN 0-8020-2118-2. Authoritative account of the way the fur trade integrated Indians and Europeans and transformed their lives.

Trigger, Bruce. *The Children of Aataentsic: A History of the Huron People to 1860.* U. of Toronto Pr. 1987 $80.00. ISBN 0-7735-0626-8. Exhaustive ethnographic study that focuses on Huron relations with the French.

———. *Natives and Newcomers: Canada's "Heroic Age" Reconsidered.* U. of Toronto Pr. 1985 $39.00. ISBN 0-7735-0594-6. Argues persuasively that indigenous peoples played a significant role in the early development of Canada.

Van Kirk, Sylvia. *"Many Tender Ties": Women in Fur Trade Society in Western Canada, 1670–1870.* U. of Okla. Pr. 1980 $15.95. ISBN 0-920486-06-1. Fascinating study of the evolution of a Métis society and the critical importance of women to the fur trade.

Early Canada and New France

Arsenault, Georges. *The Island Acadians, 1720–1980.* Ragweed 1989 o.p. Illustrated history of Acadians on Prince Edward Island.

Bishop, Morris. *Champlain: The Life of Fortitude.* 1948. Firefly Bks. Ltd. 1963 o.p. Highly readable if over-romanticized portrait of the founder of New France.

Brebner, John Bartlet. *New England's Outpost: Acadia Before the Conquest of Canada.* Rprt. Serv. 1991 repr. of 1927 ed. $79.00. ISBN 0-7812-6367-0. Argues that neutrality was the only option available to the Acadians in the eighteenth century.

Clark, Andrew Hill. *Acadia: The Geography of Early Nova Scotia to 1760.* Bks. Demand repr. of 1968 ed. $122.20. ISBN 0-8357-6000-6. Masterful analysis of the thriving French marshland communities around the Bay of Fundy.

Dechêne, Louise. *Habitants and Merchants in Seventeenth-Century Montreal.* U. of Toronto Pr. 1992 $55.00. ISBN 0-7735-0658-6. Pioneer *Annales*-based reinterpretation of early French settlements.

Eccles, W. J. *Canada Under Louis XIV, 1663–1701. Canadian Centenary Ser.* Firefly Bks. Ltd. 1965 o.p. Gripping account of the expansion of New France from the banks of the St. Lawrence to the interior of North America.

———. *The Canadian Frontier, 1534–1760.* U. of NM Pr. 1983 $13.95. ISBN 0-8263-0705-1. Distinguishes between commercial, religious, settlement, and military frontiers in French Canada.

———. *France in America.* New American Nation Ser. Mich. St. U. Pr. 1990 $17.95. ISBN 0-87013-284-9. Masterfully crafted, provocative interpretation of France in Quebec, the West Indies, and Louisiana.

Frégault, Guy. *Canada: The War of Conquest.* OUP 1969 o.p. Nationalistic assessment decrying France's inept and insufficient support for its colony.

Greer, Allan. *Peasant, Lord, and Merchant: Rural Society in Three Quebec Parishes 1740–1840.* U. of Toronto Pr. 1985 $35.00. ISBN 0-8020-2559-5. Provides an argument for the essential continuity of rural life in Quebec throughout the transition from French to British rule.

Griffiths, Naomi. *The Acadian Deportation: Deliberate Perfidy or Cruel Necessity?* Copp 1969 o.p. Includes a selection of sources in English and in French that shed penetrating light on a complex historical controversy.

———. *The Contexts of Acadian History, 1686–1784.* U. of Toronto Pr. 1992 $39.95. ISBN 0-7735-0883-X. Presents the full sweep of the Acadian past in the context of North American and European realities.

Harris, R. Cole. *The Seigneurial Regime in French Canada: A Geographical Study.* Porcupine Pr. 1980 $45.00. ISBN 0-87991-130-1. Argues that the seigneurial system was largely irrelevant to early Canada and was in decline by the time of the Conquest.

Miquelon, Dale. *Dugard of Rouen: French Trade to Canada and the West Indies, 1729–1770*. U. of Toronto Pr. 1978 o.p. Business history of an important firm involved in the fur trade.

———. *New France 1701–1744: "A Supplement to Europe." Canadian Centenary Ser.* Firefly Bks. Ltd. 1987 o.p. A skillful synthesis. Emphasizes social and economic development without omitting other themes.

Moore, Christopher. *Louisbourg Portraits: Life in an Eighteenth-Century Garrison Town.* Macmillan 1982 o.p. Chronicles how ordinary people lived in France's most important garrison town in Atlantic Canada.

Reid, John G. *Acadia, Maine, and New Scotland: Marginal Colonies in the Seventeenth Century.* U. of Toronto Pr. 1981 o.p. Comparative study of the first tentative colonizing efforts by England, France, and Scotland in the northeast.

Stacey, C. P. *Quebec, 1759: The Siege and the Battle.* Macmillan 1959 o.p. Masterful analysis by a leading military historian of one of the most important battles in North America.

Stanley, George F. G. *New France: The Last Phase, 1744–1760. Canadian Centenary Ser.* Firefly Bks. Ltd. 1968 o.p. Rather pedestrian synthesis that focuses almost exclusively on military events.

Trudel, Marcel. *The Beginnings of New France, 1524–1663. Canadian Centenary Ser.* Firefly Bks. Ltd. 1973 o.p. Lucid and exciting account of the age of French exploration and settlement.

Walsh, H. H. *The Church in the French Era: From Colonization to the British Conquest.* McGraw 1966 o.p. Volume 1 of *A History of the Christian Church in Canada.* Analyzes the differing roles of the Catholic Church during the discovery and settlement of New France.

British North America to 1867

Berton, Pierre. *Flames Across the Border, 1813–1814.* Firefly Bks. Ltd. 1981 o.p. Completes the story of a struggle that confirmed Canadians as a distinct North American people.

———. *The Invasion of Canada, 1812–1813.* Firefly Bks. Ltd. 1980 o.p. Dramatic account of the first part of a war that provided British North Americans with a new sense of identity.

Bolger, F. W. P. *Prince Edward Island and Confederation, 1863–1873.* St. Dunstan's U. Pr. 1964 o.p. Focuses on the political battle for unification with British North America.

Brebner, John Bartlet. *The Neutral Yankees of Nova Scotia: A Marginal Colony During the Revolutionary Years.* Firefly Bks. Ltd. 1969 o.p. Argues that Nova Scotia failed to join the Revolution because its merchants could not throw off British mercantilism.

Brown, Wallace. *The Good Americans: The Loyalists in the American Revolution.* Morrow 1969 o.p. Argues that the Loyalists who left for Canada shared much in common with the Whigs who stayed.

Brown, Wallace, and Hereward Senior. *Victorious in Defeat: The Loyalists in Canada.* Methuen 1984 o.p. Sequel to *The Good Americans.* Surveys the impact of the Loyalists on British North America.

Bumsted, J. M. *Land, Settlement, and Politics on Eighteenth-Century Prince Edward Island.* U. of Toronto Pr. 1987 $37.95. ISBN 0-7735-0566-0. Account of the complex tangle of land and political issues that for decades shaped the life of the colony.

Burt, Alfred. *The United States, Great Britain and British North America from the Revolution to the Establishment of Peace After the War of 1812.* Yale U. Pr. 1940 o.p. Traces the origins of the War of 1812 to British violations of American rights on the high seas.

Careless, J. M. S. *The Union of the Canadas: The Growth of Canadian Institutions, 1841–1857. Canadian Centenary Ser.* Firefly Bks. Ltd. 1967 o.p. Illustrates that the union of Upper and Lower Canada only served to entrench the divisions between French and English Canadians.

Cohen, Marjorie Griffin. *Women's Work, Markets and Economic Development in Nineteenth-Century Ontario*. U. of Toronto Pr. 1988 $40.00. ISBN 0-8020-2651-6. Shows how patriarchal relations modified the pattern of economic development.

Condon, Ann Gorman. *The Envy of the American States: The Loyalist Dream for New Brunswick*. New Ireland Pr. 1984 o.p. Focuses on the determination of Loyalist leaders to develop a society that would inspire the admiration of Whigs in the new American republic.

Craig, Gerald. *Upper Canada: The Formative Years, 1784–1841*. Canadian Centenary Ser. Firefly Bks. Ltd. 1963 o.p. Reveals how out of the clashing of British and American views there emerged a people with distinct traits.

Errington, Jane. *The Lion, the Eagle and Upper Canada: A Developing Colonial Ideology*. U. of Toronto Pr. 1987 $34.95. ISBN 0-7735-0603-9. Undermines the Hartz-Lipset thesis by showing the extent to which elites on both sides of the boundary shared similar values.

Kilbourn, William. *The Firebrand: William Lyon Mackenzie and the Rebellion in Upper Canada*. Clarke, Irwin 1956 o.p. Remarkable evocation of the agrarian leader and his times.

Lanctôt, Gustave. *Canada and the American Revolution 1774–1783*. Clarke, Irwin 1967 o.p. Narrative of the politico-religious drama in Quebec provoked by momentous events nearby.

Lower, A.R.M. *Great Britian's Woodyard: British America and the Timber Trade, 1763–1867*. U. of Toronto Pr. 1973 o.p. Multifaceted analysis of the timber economy that includes both the merchants and the lumberjacks involved in it.

MacKinnon, Neil. *This Unfriendly Soil: The Loyalist Experience in Nova Scotia, 1783–1791*. U. of Toronto Pr. 1986 $34.95. ISBN 0-7735-0596-2. Relates how those who fled New York and Boston to settle in Nova Scotia hoped to prove that the Revolution was a terrible mistake.

MacNutt, W. S. *The Atlantic Provinces: The Emergence of Colonial Society, 1712–1857*. Canadian Centenary Ser. Firefly Bks. Ltd. 1965 o.p. Traces the political evolution of four distinct provinces knit together by imperial policies rather than common goals.

Martin, Ged. *The Durham Report and British Policy: A Critical Essay*. Cambridge U. Pr. 1972 o.p. Revisionist account that downplays the governor general's contribution to the evolution of colonial policy.

———, ed. *The Causes of Confederation*. Acadiensis 1990 o.p. Seven essays examining the motives of supporters and opponents of a federal union.

Neatby, Hinda. *Quebec: The Revolutionary Age, 1760–1791*. Canadian Centenary Ser. Firefly Bks. Ltd. 1966 o.p. Shows that British policies were by-products of events outside the province.

Ouellet, Fernand. *Economic and Social History of Quebec, 1760–1850: Structures and Conjonctures*. Carleton U. Pr. 1980 o.p. *Annales*-based study maintaining that the British conquest had no significant impact on Quebec structures.

———. *Lower Canada, 1791–1840: Social Change and Nationalism*. Canadian Centenary Ser. Firefly Bks. Ltd. 1980 o.p. Award-winning reinterpretation of the origins of French Canadian nationalism.

Pryke, Kenneth. *Nova Scotia and Confederation, 1864–1871*. Bks. Demand 1979 $63.00. ISBN 0-317-55719-X. Argues that the province entered into and remained in Confederation only by default.

Rawlyk, George A. *Nova Scotia's Massachusetts: A Study of Massachusetts-Nova Scotia Relations, 1630–1784*. U. of Toronto Pr. 1973 o.p. Narrative focusing on the two spheres of influence—Great Britain and New England—between which Nova Scotians lived.

Read, Colin. *The Rising in Western Upper Canada, 1837–38: The Duncombe Revolt and After*. Bks. Demand repr. of 1982 ed. $88.20. ISBN 0-8357-6366-8. Important revisionist study of the origins of the Rebellions of 1837.

Rich, E. E. *The Fur Trade and the Northwest to 1857*. Canadian Centenary Ser. Firefly Bks. Ltd. 1967 o.p. Argues that the fur traders played a vital role in making Confederation possible.

Schull, Joseph. *Rebellion: The Rising in French Canada, 1837*. Macmillan 1971 o.p. Well-written narrative focusing on the leaders and skirmishes.

Stewart, Gordon T. *The Origins of Canadian Politics: A Comparative Approach*. UBC Pr. 1986 o.p. Explains brilliantly why Canadian political culture diverged from British and American patterns.

Wade, Mason. *The French Canadians: 1760–1945*. Macmillan 1955 o.p. Chronicles the incessant struggle of a cultural minority to forge a viable national identity.

Waite, P. B. *The Life and Times of Confederation, 1864–1867: Politics, Newspapers, and the Union of British North America*. U. of Toronto Pr. 1962 o.p. Highly readable newspaper-based account of the coming of the union. Emphasizes differing provincial perspectives.

Whitelaw, William Menzies. *The Maritimes and Canada Before Confederation*. AMS Pr. repr. of 1934 ed. $42.50. ISBN 0-404-20287-X. Somewhat dated, but still valuable, study of the political evolution of the three provinces until the mid-nineteenth century. Introduction by P. B. Waite.

Wynn, Graeme. *Timber Colony: A Historical Geography of Early Nineteenth Century New Brunswick*. U. of Toronto Pr. 1980 $25.00. ISBN 0-8020-5513-3. Shows how British industrial capitalism transformed the landscape, economy, and society of a hinterland province.

Confederation and Dominion

Armstrong, Christopher, and H. V. Nelles. *Monopoly's Moment: The Organization and Regulation of Canadian Utilities, 1830–1930*. U. of Toronto Pr. 1988 $47.50. ISBN 0-8020-2671-0. Award-winning revision of traditional views about the relationship of technology and public enterprise to a staples-driven economy.

Avery, Donald. *"Dangerous Foreigners": European Immigrants, Workers, and Labour Radicalism in Canada, 1896–1932*. Firefly Bks. Ltd. 1979 o.p. Portrays immigrants' working conditions and their hostile reception by British Canadians.

Babcock, Robert H. *Gompers in Canada: A Study in American Continentalism before the First World War*. Bks. Demand repr. of 1974 ed. $75.50. ISBN 0-317-27774-X. Award-winning analysis of the consequences of an American labor leader's takeover of the Canadian labor movement.

Berger, Carl. *The Sense of Power: Studies in the Ideas of Canadian Imperialism 1867–1914*. U. of Toronto Pr. 1970 $17.50. ISBN 0-8020-1669-3. Argues that British imperialism became a form of Canadian nationalism.

Brown, R. Craig. *Robert Laird Borden: A Biography*. 2 vols. Macmillan 1975 o.p. Absorbing portrait of a leader during World War I who redefined Canada's status within the empire.

Careless, J. M. S. *Frontier and Metropolis: Regions, Cities and Identities in Canada before 1914*. U. of Toronto Pr. 1989 o.p. Four lectures explaining how metropolitanism modifies the staples approach.

Copp, Terry. *The Anatomy of Poverty: The Condition of the Working Class in Montreal, 1897–1929*. Firefly Bks. Ltd. 1974 o.p. Tells how and why government regulations improved the economic and social conditions of the city's working class only marginally.

Crunican, Paul. *Priests and Politicians: Manitoba Schools and the Election of 1896*. U. of Toronto Pr. 1974 o.p. Explores a key issue in church-state relations, focusing especially on reaction in Quebec.

Dawson, R. M., and H. B. Neatby. *William Lyon Mackenzie King: A Political Biography*. 3 vols. Vol. 1 *1874–1923*. U. of Toronto Pr. 1958 $38.50. ISBN 0-8020-1083-0. Vol. 2 *The Lonely Heights, 1924–1932*. Bks. Demand repr. of 1970 ed. $123.30. ISBN 0-8357-8357-8. Vol. 3 *The Prism of Unity, 1932–1939*. U. of Toronto Pr. 1976 $35.00. ISBN 0-8020-5381-5. Magisterial assessment of Canada's longest-serving prime minister. Based in large part on Mackenzie King's diary.

Flanagan, Thomas. *Louis 'David' Riel: Prophet of a New World.* Bks. Demand repr. of 1983 ed. $56.50 ISBN 0-317-27051-6. Interprets the Métis leader in the context of aboriginal peoples' millenarian religious movements.

Forbes, Ernest. *The Maritime Rights Movement, 1919–27: A Study in Canadian Regionalism.* U. of Toronto Pr. 1979 $29.95. ISBN 0-7735-0321-8. Argues that the region had genuine grievances and cannot be considered a bastion of conservatism.

Gaffield, Chad. *Language, Schooling, and Cultural Conflict: The Origins of the French-Language Controversy in Ontario.* U. of Toronto Pr. 1987 $39.95. ISBN 0-7735-0602-0. Study of the complex demographic patterns and economic trends in Prescott county that mirrored cultural tensions elsewhere in the province.

Graham, Roger. *Arthur Meighen: A Biography.* 3 vols. Vol. 1 *The Door of Opportunity.* Clarke, Irwin 1960 o.p. Vol. 2 *And Fortune Fled.* Clarke, Irwin 1963 o.p. Vol. 3 *No Surrender.* Clarke, Irwin 1965 o.p. Magisterial, occasionally uncritical study of Borden's successor and Mackenzie King's bitter rival.

Granatstein, J. L., and J. M. Hitsman. *Broken Promises: A History of Conscription in Canada.* OUP 1977 o.p. Examines the most important issue dividing Canadians during both World Wars.

Kealey, Gregory S. *Toronto Workers Respond to Industrial Capitalism 1867–1892.* U. of Toronto Pr. 1980 $24.95. ISBN 0-8020-6883-9. Award-winning study of the impact of industrial capitalism on the working class of Canada's major metropolis.

Lupul, Manoly R. *The Roman Catholic Church and the North-West School Question: A Study in Church-State Relations in Western Canada.* Bks. Demand repr. of 1974 ed. $79.10. ISBN 0-8357-3646-6. Draws upon episcopal correspondence to reinterpret an issue that provoked a serious crisis for Prime Minister Laurier.

Macdonald, Norman. *Canada: Immigration and Colonization, 1841–1903.* Macmillan 1966 o.p. Focuses on the reasons for emigration and immigrants' contributions to the development of the nation.

Miller, J. R. *Equal Rights: The Jesuit Estates Act Controversy.* McGill-Queen's U. Pr. 1979 o.p. Explores a major late nineteenth-century episode in the perennial conflict between English Canadians and French Canadians.

Nelles, H. V. *The Politics of Development: Forests, Mines and Hydro-Electric Power in Ontario, 1849–1941.* Macmillan 1974 o.p. Provocative study of the multifaceted and conflicting relationships between the state and resource developers.

Schull, Joseph. *Laurier: The First Canadian.* St. Martin 1965 o.p. A life-and-times study of Canada's first French-Canadian prime minister.

Shortt, S. E. D. *The Search for an Ideal: Six Canadian Intellectuals and Their Convictions in an Age of Transition 1890–1930.* Bks. Demand 1976 $56.50. ISBN 0-685-15846-2. Analyzes the impact of six academics upon the major social questions of their age.

Smith, Goldwin. *Canada and the Canadian Question.* 1891. Bks. Demand repr. of 1971 ed. ISBN 0-8357-6367-6. Argues that geography is destiny and that Canada inevitably will be absorbed by the United States.

Stanley, George. *The Birth of Western Canada.* 1936. U. of Toronto Pr. 1973 $24.95. ISBN 0-8020-6931-2. Projects an inevitable conflict between white settlers and the Métis, or between the plough and the prairie.

————. *Louis Riel.* McGraw 1963 o.p. Portrays the great Métis leader as a tragic, doomed figure.

Traves, Tom. *The State and Enterprise: Canadian Manufacturers and the Federal Government, 1917–31.* U. of Toronto Pr. 1979 $20.00. ISBN 0-8020-5445-5. Asserts that state intervention into the economy was prompted by the competing claims of manufacturers, workers, and farmers.

Zaslow, Morris. *The Opening of the Canadian North, 1870–1914. Canadian Centenary Ser.* Firefly Bks. Ltd. 1971 o.p. Argues that the government sacrificed native interests in a blind pursuit of development policies.

Modern Canada

Abella, Irving M. *None is Too Many: Canada and the Jews of Europe, 1933–1948*. Lester Publishing Ltd. 1991 o.p. Exposes the Canadian government's failure to come to the aid of European Jews.

Berton, Pierre. *The Great Depression, 1929–1939*. Firefly Bks. Ltd. 1990 $29.95. ISBN 0-7710-1270-5. A year-by-year account of the era's events, great and small.

Bothwell, Robert, Ian Drummond, and John English. *Canada since 1945: Power, Politics, and Provincialism*. U. of Toronto Pr. rev. ed. 1989 $139.10. ISBN 0-7837-0537-9. Well-written text surveying postwar Canadian internal and external political and economic affairs.

Clarkson, Stephen, and Christina McCall. *Trudeau and Our Times*. Vol. 1 *The Magnificent Obsession*. McClelland 1991 o.p. Brilliant evaluation of the relationship between leader and those led. Focuses on the last five years of Trudeau's career.

English, John. *Shadows of Heaven: The Life of Lester Pearson*. Vol. I *1897–1948*. Lester & Orpen Dennys 1989 o.p. Examines formative influences in the life of Canada's most important postwar diplomat.

Fowke, Vernon C. *The National Policy and the Wheat Economy*. U. of Toronto Pr. 1957 $80.50. ISBN 0-6851-5758-X. Traces the growth of the wheat staple in the Canadian prairies and the marketing problems it created.

Granatstein, J. L.. *Canada 1957–1967: The Years of Uncertainty and Innovation*. Firefly Bks. Ltd. 1986 o.p. A political and foreign policy analysis of the Diefenbaker and Pearson years.

Horn, Michiel. *The League for Social Reconstruction: Intellectual Origins of the Democratic Left in Canada, 1930–42*. U. of Toronto Pr. 1980 $32.50. ISBN 0-8020-5487-0. Chronicles the history of a group of intellectuals who helped launch the CCF party.

Katz, Michael B. *The People of Hamilton, Canada West: Family and Class in a Mid-Nineteenth-Century City*. HUP 1975 $107.50. ISBN 0-783-7344-7. Pioneering study in quantitative history that explores family, social structure, and transiency.

Neary, Peter. *Newfoundland in the North Atlantic World, 1929–1949*. U. of Toronto Pr. 1988 $34.95. ISBN 0-7735-0668-3. Challenges several stereotypes about the Commission government set up during the 1930s.

Neatby, H. Blair. *The Politics of Chaos: Canada in the Thirties*. U. of Toronto Pr. 1972 o.p. Analyzes the Depression years from the perspective of the provinces.

Newman, Peter C. *Renegade in Power: The Diefenbaker Years*. Firefly Bks. Ltd. 1963 o.p. Racy, anecdotal life-and-times portrait by one of Canada's most widely read journalists.

Simpson, Jeffrey. *Discipline of Power: The Conservative Interlude and the Liberal Restoration*. Personal Library 1980 o.p. The rise and fall of the Joe Clark government during 1979–80, chronicled by a gifted political reporter.

Strong-Boag, Veronica. *The New Day Recalled: Lives of Girls and Women in English Canada, 1919–1939*. U. of Toronto Pr. 1988 o.p. Argues persuasively that winning the vote failed to change the lives of middle-class English-Canadian women.

Thompson, John Herd, and Allen Seager. *Canada, 1922–1939: Decades of Discord*. *Canadian Centenary Ser*. Firefly Bks. Ltd. 1985 o.p. Thoroughly researched, well-written treatment that is sensitive to regional as well as national issues.

Thomson, Dale C. *Louis St. Laurent, Canadian*. Macmillan 1967 o.p. Detailed examination of the political career of Mackenzie King's handpicked successor.

Young, Walter. *The Anatomy of a Party: The National CCF, 1932–61*. Bks. Demand repr. of 1969 ed. ISBN 0-8357-5462-6. Tells how Canada's social democrats created both a party and a movement.

Zaslow, Morris. *The Northland Expansion of Canada, 1914–1967*. *Canadian Centenary Ser*. Firefly Bks. Ltd. 1988 o.p. Emphasizes industrial frontiers, changes among indigenous peoples, and the maturation of the territories.

CHRONOLOGY OF AUTHORS

Garneau, François-Xavier. 1809–1866
Groulx, Lionel. 1878–1967
Innis, Harold Adams. 1894–1952
Creighton, Donald. 1902–1979

Morton, William Lewis. 1908–1980
Cook, G. Ramsay. 1931–
Hamelin, Jean. 1931–

COOK, G. RAMSAY. 1931–

An authority on French Canadian and English Canadian relations, Ramsay Cook was born in Alameda, Saskatchewan. After receiving his undergraduate degree from the University of Manitoba in 1954, he went on to Queen's University for his M.A. He continued his studies at the University of Toronto, from which he earned a Ph.D. in 1960. During the turbulent 1960s, he wrote a series of penetrating essays that brought an encyclopedic knowledge of both French Canadian and English Canadian history to bear on the crisis provoked by Quebec's Quiet Revolution. The essays show how a command of the historical past can enlighten our grasp of the present.

Cook, who shares Pierre Trudeau's vision of a bilingual, bicultural Canada within existing constitutional arrangements, is one of Canada's most distinguished historians. He taught at the University of Toronto and in 1968–69 and 1978–79 was visiting professor of Canadian studies at Harvard University. From 1978 to 1983, he served as Chairman of the Institute for Historical Microreproduction. Currently, Cook is a professor of history at York University. A former editor of the Canadian *Historical Review*, he presently serves as editor of both the Canadian Centenary Series and the *Dictionary of Canadian Biography*.

BOOKS BY COOK

Canada, 1896–1920: A Nation Transformed. (coauthored with Robert Craig Brown). *Canadian Centenary Ser.* Firefly Bks. Ltd. 1974 o.p. A masterful synthesis on one of the most important eras in Canadian history.
Canada and the French-Canadian Question. Macmillan 1966 o.p. Nine essays on nationalism, Confederation, and Quebec.
French-Canadian Nationalism: An Anthology. Macmillan 1969 o.p. Collection of 25 essays by French Canadians, most of them reflecting the ideology of survival; edited by Cook, who also translated many of these essays, making them available in English for the first time.
The Maple Leaf Forever: Essays on Nationalism and Politics in Canada. Macmillan 1971 o.p. ISBN 0-7705-0059-5. Thirteen essays offering diverse historical perspectives on the relationship between Canada's two founding peoples.
Provincial Autonomy: Minority Rights and the Compact Theory, 1867–1921. Queen's Printer 1969 o.p. Argues that the Confederation was not a compact between Canada's two founding peoples.
The Regenerators: Social Criticism in Late Victorian English Canada. U. of Toronto Pr. 1985 $32.50. ISBN 0-8020-5670-9. Prize-winning study of efforts by religious liberals to build the Kingdom of God in urban Canada.

CREIGHTON, DONALD. 1902–1979

Raised in a book-filled Toronto home, Donald Creighton acquired an all-consuming taste for literature. After studying both literature and history at the University of Toronto, he pursued graduate work in European history at Oxford

University. In 1927 he joined the University of Toronto faculty and soon came under the influence of HAROLD INNIS. Abandoning European history, he devoted most of his life to an amplification of the Laurentian—St. Lawrence River-based—interpretation of Canadian history.

By the 1960s Creighton came to be considered Canada's foremost historian by many. His scholarship can be divided roughly into two phases. During the first phase, he focused on the creative role of the post-Conquest Montreal English-speaking merchant community that erected a transcontinental economy along the St. Lawrence river basin. His 1937 work, *The Commercial Empire of the St. Lawrence*, has been compared to a theatrical performance. In the first act, the merchants take over the French fur trade but are thwarted by the American Revolution. In the second act, they reconstruct a staples trading system based on lumber and wheat, only to be frustrated by internal political disturbances. During the third act, these conflicts explode into a shortsighted farmers' rebellion that dooms the merchants' vision.

Early in the second phase of his scholarship, Creighton produced a magisterial biography of the first prime minister of Canada, John A. Macdonald. Told from the subject's perspective, it is the story of a man of sterling character who triumphed over a succession of personal and political obstacles. According to Creighton, Macdonald resurrected the Montreal merchants' continental vision, which they then achieved politically through the 1867 confederation of the British North American provinces.

During the remainder of his career, Creighton, celebrated for the elaboration of the Laurentian interpretation, focused intently on the enemies of the Laurentian vision—especially Mackenzie King and the Liberal party, or domineering Americans caught up in cold war imperialism. Although a staunch nationalist, he expressed pessimism about Canada's long-term chances for survival.

BOOKS BY CREIGHTON

Canada, 1939–1957: The Forked Road. Canadian Centenary Ser. McClelland 1976 o.p. Relates how a willful, petulant Mackenzie King abandoned Britain in order to lead Canada into America's clutches.

The Commercial Empire of the St. Lawrence: A Study in Commerce and Politics. McGraw 1937 o.p.

John A. Macdonald, a Biography. 2 vols. Macmillan. Vol. 1 *The Young Politician.* 1952 o.p. Vol. 2 *The Old Chieftain.* 1955 o.p. Vivid, unforgettable narrative of a leader's heroic struggles to build a new dominion.

The Road to Confederation. The Emergence of Canada: 1863–1867. Greenwood 1976 repr. of 1965 ed. ISBN 0-8371-8435-5. Vivid explanation of how the Fathers of Confederation overcame enormous obstacles to create a vast new nation.

Towards the Discovery of Canada: Selected Essays. Macmillan 1972 o.p. Eighteen essays on various historical themes written between the early 1930s and 1971.

BOOKS ABOUT CREIGHTON

Berger, Carl. *The Writing of Canadian History: Aspects of English-Canadian Historical Writing: 1900–1970.* U. of Toronto Pr. 1986 $35.00. ISBN 0-8020-2546-3. Includes chapter by Carl Berger that exposes the strongly held convictions underlying Creighton's word wizardry.

Klinck, C. F., ed. *Literary History of Canada: Canadian Literature in English.* Vol. 2. U. of Toronto Pr. 1976 o.p. Includes section by William Kilbourn, "The Writing of Canadian History," that stresses Creighton's incomparable literary gifts.

GARNEAU, FRANÇOIS-XAVIER. 1809–1866

Historian, poet, and literary journalist, François-Xavier Gateau was born in Quebec City to a large family too poor to pay for his education. He did receive some education at the Quebec Seminary and, while preparing to become a notary, he read widely in history and literature. Visits to the United States and Europe stirred his interest in reform politics. Still celebrated as the first great French Canadian historian, his work remains the starting point for clerical and secular nationalist historians in his province.

After the British had suppressed the Canadian rebellions in 1837 and unified English-speaking Upper Canada with French-speaking Quebec, Garneau embarked upon the lifelong preparation of a history dedicated to helping his compatriots resist Anglo-Saxon assimilation. Some say he set out to prove false Lord Durham's comment that French Canadians were "without a history and without a literature." Although plagued by ill health, Garneau doggedly assembled source materials from Quebec, New York, and European archives and eventually published his three-volume *Histoire du Canada*, which saw three different editions between 1845 and 1859. The work strongly emphasized French contributions to Canadian culture. Fundamentally nationalist in outlook, this self-taught scholar's interpretation stressed the consequences of the Conquest and dwelt at length on the battles between French Canadian *patriotes* and the British oligarchy. In later editions Garneau toned down his criticisms of the Catholic hierarchy.

BOOK BY GARNEAU

Histoire du Canada depuis sa découverte jusqu'à nos jours. 4 vols. Vol 1 *Napoléon Aubin.* 1845 o.p. Vol. 2 1846 o.p. Vol. 3 *Imprimerie Fréchette et Frère.* 1848 o.p. Vol. 4 *John Lovell.* 1852 o.p.

BOOKS ABOUT GARNEAU

Dictionary of Canadian Biography. Ed. by Jean Hamelin. Vol. 9 1976 $75.00. ISBN 0-8020-3320-2. Includes a fairly lengthy entry on Garneau that presents an integrated assessment of his life and work.

Quebec and Its Historians 1840–1920. Harvest Hse. 1982 o.p. Includes chapter on Garneau by Serge Gagnon in which he views Garneau's nationalism from a class perspective.

GROULX, LIONEL. 1878–1967

A priest and history teacher, Lionel Groulx is considered by some to be the spiritual father of modern Quebec. Trained in theology at Rome, he turned to history in order to inculcate a stronger desire by French Canadians to survive in a sea of Anglo-Saxons. During World War I, he assumed the chair in Canadian history at Laval University's Montreal campus. Sharp conflicts between French Canadians and English Canadians over conscription and language rights doubtless accelerated the evolution of his overtly nationalist perspective. After the war he engaged in historical research and in political activity through the Catholic Action movement.

Groulx picked up FRANÇOIS-XAVIER GARNEAU's nationalist mantle. However, in contrast to Garneau, he idealized New France and projected an overtly religious vision of the past. In his view, God chose French Canadians to resist English assimilation in order to carry out a Catholic Christian mission to civilize the New World. Groulx contrasted the moral superiority of the old French Canadian agrarian way of life with the more secularizing trends of his own times. He ransacked the past to find great men who might provide moral lessons for urban youth. Above all he elevated to historical sainthood Dollard des Ormeaux, the young man who gave his life defending New France against the Iroquois.

Groulx left a legacy that includes an enormous body of writings produced over nearly a half-century of vigorous activity in scholarship and political advocacy. In 1947 he founded the major professional journal in French Canadian history, *Revue d'Histoire de l'Amérique Française* (*Review of the History of French America*), and he helped to prepare a generation of professionally trained historians. His writings provided an ideological framework for the Quiet Revolution in Quebec during the 1960s.

BOOKS BY GROULX

Histoire du Canada depuis la découverte. 2 vols. Fides 1962 o.p. A celebration of French Canada's golden age.

Lendemain de conquête. Bibliotheque Action Française 1920 o.p. Explains why the British Conquest of 1763 is an important turning point.

Nos luttes constitutionnelles. Le Devoir 1916 o.p. Composed at the time of the legal battle by Franco-Ontarians to preserve their rights.

Notre maître le passé. 3 vols. Bibliothèque Action Française 1924-44. o.p. Collection of essays delineating the glories of New France and extracting moral lessons from its history.

Roland-Michel Barrin de La Galissonière 1693-1756. Bks. Demand repr. of 1970 ed. ISBN 0-317-27037-0. Biography of a heroic governor who warned apathetic French officials about the perils facing New France. In English.

BOOKS ABOUT GROULX

Abbé Groulx: Variations on a Nationalist Theme. Copp 1973 o.p. Includes a brief sketch of Groulx and a selection from his writings.

Gagnon, Serge. *Quebec and Its Historians 1840-1920.* Harvest Hse. 1982 o.p. Includes section on Groulx that propounds that his utopianism produced nostalgia rather than a program of political action.

HAMELIN, JEAN. 1931-

Born in Quebec, Jean Hamelin obtained graduate training during the 1950s in Paris, where French scholars such as FERNAND BRAUDEL and Pierre Goubert had begun to redefine the historians' tasks. They composed "total" histories that analyzed long-term changes in social and economic structures, encompassed the lives of ordinary people, and recreated *mentalités*. In his doctoral thesis, Hamelin asked why New France lacked a powerful business class. Rather than employing a clerico-nationalist perspective, he applied the quantitative techniques of his *Annales* mentors and concluded that the entire economy of New France had been seriously flawed.

Hamelin's work failed to persuade some critics. Nonetheless, his emphasis on the primacy of socioeconomic questions and his use of quantitative data have been taken up by many historians in Quebec who challenge the nationalistic interpretations of LIONEL GROULX and his disciples.

BOOKS BY HAMELIN

Économie et société en Nouvelle-France. Presses de l'université Laval 1960 o.p. Pioneering socio-economic history of New France based on quantitative data.

Idéologies au Canada Français, 1850-1900. 3 vols. Presses de l'université Laval 1971 o.p. Essays that examine ideologies in Quebec newspapers, literature, social movements, political parties, and the Church.

Histoire économique du Québec, 1851–1896. (coauthored with Yves Roby). Fides 1971
o.p. Survey of Quebec's economic history that includes an evaluation of the role of
the Church in the industrialization of Quebec.
Les travailleurs québécois, 1851–1896. Presses de l'université du Québec 1973 o.p. Essays
on the trade-union movement and working-class life of Quebec.
Histoire du catholicisme québécois. 3 vols. Boreal Express 1984 o.p. Comprehensive
history of the Catholic Church in Quebec from the Conquest to the 1940s.

BOOK ABOUT HAMELIN

Gagnon, Serge. *Quebec and Its Historians: The Twentieth Century.* Harvest Hse. 1985 o.p.
Includes chapter on the historiography of New France from 1960 to 1974, useful for
gauging the impact on Quebec historians of Hamelin's early work.

INNIS, HAROLD ADAMS. 1894–1952

A lifelong student of political economy, Harold Innis became an internationally prominent social scientist and chief architect of the staples interpretation of
Canadian history. An undergraduate student at McMaster University at the
opening of World War I, Innis volunteered for military service. While in
France, he was seriously wounded. What Innis experienced during the war
contradicted popular beliefs at home that the Canadian identity was a pale
reflection of British imperialism and deepened his nationalist outlook.

After doctoral studies at the University of Chicago, Innis joined the faculty of
the University of Toronto. Rejecting the thesis of American historian FREDERICK
JACKSON TURNER as a key to Canada's history, during the 1920s and 1930s he
articulated the framework for a new Laurentian—St. Lawrence River-based—
interpretation. At any given period, Innis argued, the pattern of Canadian
economic development was based on the physical characteristics of a particular
staple and the methods by which it was extracted and carried to distant markets.

Innis first outlined his ideas in *The Fur Trade in Canada* (1930). Beginning
with an extended discussion of the unique characteristics of the beaver, he then
elaborates upon the importance of indigenous people's harvesting and processing techniques, the fur traders' business methods, and the critical river
transportation routes that fostered a distinctive pattern of development in
Canada over three centuries. In the last chapter, Innis suggests ways that other
staples, such as timber, wheat, and minerals, modified the patterns originally
established during the fur trade. Innis devoted the remainder of his life to
fleshing out these ideas, and toward the end he began to explore the biases
embedded in staples-driven communications systems. Some of his ideas were
taken up and extended by MARSHALL MCLUHAN.

The Laurentian paradigm dominated Canadian history and social science
from the 1930s to the early 1970s. Its influence is still reflected in the work of
Canadian scholars most skeptical about America's cold war leadership. In its
pursuit of less nationalistic themes in Canadian history, the present generation
has not so much revised Innis's work as ignored it.

BOOKS BY INNIS

The Bias of Communications. U. of Toronto Pr. 1951 o.p. Provocative exploration of the
boundaries limiting methods of communication from ancient times to the present.
Introduction by Marshall McLuhan.
The Cod Fisheries: The History of an International Economy. U. of Toronto Pr. rev. ed.
1978 $16.95. ISBN 0-8020-6344-6. Shows how the exploitation of cod has been
closely linked to developments in western Europe and North America.
Essays in Canadian Economic History. Ed. by Mary Q. Innis. Bks. Demand 1979 $110.30.
ISBN 0-8357-3780-2. Indispensable collection of essays on staples-related topics
revealing the range and depth of the author's innovative mind.

The Idea File of Harold Adams Innis. Ed. by William Christian. Bks. Demand repr. of 1980
    ed. ISBN 0-8357-3775-6. Some 1,500 notes revealing Innis's extraordinary range of
    intellectual interests and passions.

BOOKS ABOUT INNIS

Creighton, Donald. *Harold Adams Innis: Portrait of a Scholar.* Bks. Demand repr. of 1978
    ed. ISBN 0-8357-3659-8. Finely crafted memoir by a historian who knew Innis well
    and was strongly influenced by his ideas.
Neill, Robin. *A New Theory of Value: The Canadian Economics of H. A. Innis.* U. of
    Toronto Pr. 1972 o.p. Confirms that Innis went beyond neo-classical theory to place
    social science interpretations on a new ethical foundation.
Patterson, Graeme. *History and Communications.* U. of Toronto Pr. 1990 $40.00. ISBN 0-
    8020-6810-3. Perceptive exploration of the relationship between the ideas of Innis
    and the works of McLuhan.

MORTON, WILLIAM LEWIS. 1908–1980

Born on a Manitoba farm, William Lewis Morton grew up in a political
environment that was simultaneously British, imperial, and western Canadian
in outlook. After completing a degree at the University of Manitoba, he moved
on to Oxford University, where he was a Rhodes scholar. Morton then returned
to Manitoba to teach and write history for more than two decades.

From Morton's standpoint the history of western Canada differed as sharply
from that of eastern Canada as it did from that of the American plains. He
believed that the Canadian west had become a distinct society and that
Manitoba was the most Canadian of all the provinces. While he accepted the
staples interpretation of Canadian history, he criticized it from a prairie
perspective. "Confederation was brought about to increase the wealth of
Central Canada," he wrote, "and until that original purpose is altered, . . .
Confederation must remain an instrument of injustice." (*University of Toronto
Quarterly* XV, April 1946). He believed that perennial gusts of righteous
discontent blowing over the prairies had generated a succession of reform
waves expressed in the Progressive, Social Credit, and CCF political parties.

Toward the end of his career, Morton evolved from a regional to a national
historian, articulating a conservative viewpoint that stressed the importance of
the monarchy, the empire/commonwealth, and parliamentary institutions in
the formation of a dual Canadian identity.

BOOKS BY MORTON

The Canadian Identity. 1961. U. of Toronto Pr. 1962 o.p. Brilliant historical explanation
    of the essential geographical, economic, political, and cultural differences between
    Canada and the United States.
*The Critical Years: The Union of British North America 1857–1873. Canadian Centenary
    Ser.* Firefly Bks. Ltd. 1964 o.p. A perceptive insight into the dual nature of the
    Canadian identity during the drive for Confederation.
Manitoba: A History. U. of Toronto Pr. 1967 o.p. A masterful interweaving of the many
    local, national, and international strands that make the history of Manitoba so
    unique.
The Progressive Party in Canada. U. of Toronto Pr. 1967 o.p. Sympathetic analysis of the
    origins of western political discontent during the World War I era.

BOOK ABOUT MORTON

Berger, Carl, and Ramsay Cook, eds. *The West and the Nation: Essays in Honour of W. L.
    Morton.* Firefly Bks. Ltd. 1976 o.p. An appraisal and celebration of Morton's
    distinguished career as a historian.

CHAPTER 17

Latin American History

Joseph L. Arbena and Aurora B. Arbena

> My imagination, taking flight to the ages to come, is captured by the vision of
> future centuries, and when, from that vantage point, I observe with
> admiration and amazement the prosperity, the splendor, the fullness of life
> which will then flourish in this vast region, I am overwhelmed. I seem to
> behold my country as the very heart of the universe.
> —SIMÓN BOLÍVAR, "The Angostura Address"

The history of the lands now called Latin America, which take in everything in
the Western Hemisphere south of the United States, often has balanced grand
dreams and admirable achievements with intense pessimism and frustrating
failures. For a long time, serious and balanced study of that complex region was
hampered by insufficient language skills and a lack of respect for the region's
culture. The roots of these problems are found in a number of interrelated
factors. One is the Black Legend, which held that Spain and, to a lesser degree,
Portugal had pursued conquest and colonization in a manner that was cruel and
exploitive, with no redeeming value. Another is a virulent spirit of anti-
Catholicism, born in the passions of the Reformation and fueled by Britain's
long wars with Spain. A third is Anglo-American racism that disparaged the
human and cultural qualities of peoples with any degree of Native American or
African (i.e., nonwhite) ancestry. A fourth is an unwillingness to travel to the
tropics. And last is a Eurocentric view that assumed that nothing important
existed or happened outside the non-Iberian European sphere.

In short, until well into the twentieth century, writings on Latin America
derived mainly from either curiosity about the exotic or from concern with the
promotion and defense of European and North American economic and
security interests. It is not surprising that much of the earliest literature in
English on Latin America came from the pens of travelers, many associated with
businesses, scientific expeditions, or the military and diplomatic services. Later,
such scholars as Bernard Moses, HERBERT E. BOLTON, Isaac J. Cox, Charles W.
Hackett, Carlos E. Castañeda, and Arthur P. Whitaker, studying the borderlands—Florida and the old Southwest, Texas and the new Southwest, and
California—were drawn into Spanish and Mexican history. Later, after World
War I, as the historical profession grew within the context of a more
international community, they and other historians began to ask questions
about the grander history of the entire Western Hemisphere. Though based
increasingly on fieldwork, multilingual sources, and broader interpretive
perspectives, much of the emphasis remained on politics, diplomacy, war, and
business.

The last two decades have seen several new orientations in the study of Latin
America. Above all there has been a search for the history and culture of people
traditionally ignored by historians—nonwhites, women, and the poor. This is

history from the bottom up and is presented from the point of view of the very people it attempts to examine. This has led to the elaboration of so-called popular culture—the culture of nonelites—and its relationship to broader power struggles and conflicts over social space. This, in turn, is linked to such paradigms as world-systems analysis, dependency theory, and hegemony theory, all of which are in contrast to both liberal modernization models and classical Marxism. The result has been an enrichment of the factual and analytical content of writings on Latin America's past and present.

Readers who wish to go beyond the titles listed in this chapter or who desire more complete reviews of works cited should consult the major English-language journals in the field: *Hispanic American Historical Review, The Americas, Latin American Research Review, Journal of Latin American Studies, Luso-Brazilian Review, Journal of Inter-American Studies and World Affairs, Bulletin of Latin American Research, Latin American Perspectives, Studies in Latin American Popular Culture*, and *Inter-American Review of Bibliography*. For citations of articles from a wide range of periodicals in English, Spanish, and Portuguese, *Hispanic American Periodicals Index (HAPI)*, with volumes published annually since 1970, is extremely useful.

REFERENCE WORKS

Arbena, Joseph L., comp. *An Annotated Bibliography of Latin American Sports: Pre-Conquest to the Present.* Greenwood 1989 $55.00. ISBN 0-313-25495-8. Cites more than 1,300 books and articles, mainly in English and Spanish, that treat historical and social aspects of physical education, recreation, and sports.

Collier, Simon, and others, eds. *The Cambridge Encyclopedia of Latin America and the Caribbean.* Cambridge U. Pr. 2nd rev. ed. 1992 $55.00. ISBN 0-521-41322-2. The geography, history, and culture of Latin America, including the Caribbean islands, introduced by 75 experts. Useful tables and good illustrations.

Corke, Bettina, ed. *Who Is Who, Government, Politics, Banking and Industry in Latin America.* Decade Media 1992 $95.00. ISBN 0-910365-06-7. Though not truly historical, provides key data on more than 2,000 individuals in 35 Latin American countries who have been influential leaders over the last generation.

Delpar, Helen, ed. *Encyclopedia of Latin America.* McGraw 1974 o.p. Obviously dated, but most of the entries on earlier topics serve as useful introductions.

Grieb, Kenneth J., comp. *Central America in the Nineteenth and Twentieth Centuries: An Annotated Bibliography.* Macmillan 1988 $100.00. ISBN 0-8161-8130-6. Cites more than 5,400 books published in English and Spanish between the early 1800s and about 1980. Includes Belize but not Panama.

———, ed. *Research Guide to Central America and the Caribbean.* U. of Wis. Pr. 1985 $35.00. ISBN 0-299-10050-2. Comprehensive collection, divided into topical essays and descriptions of depositories, that seeks to identify archival resources available to historians regarding Central America and the Caribbean and to indicate future directions for research about the region.

Griffith, Charles C., ed. *Latin America: A Guide to the Historical Literature.* U. of Tex. Pr. 1981 o.p. Dated but well worth consulting for basic sources on older historical topics. Contains both thematic essays and annotated bibliographical listings prepared by 37 scholars.

Grow, Michael. *Scholars' Guide to Washington, D.C., for Latin American and Caribbean Studies.* Rev. by Craig VanGrasstek. W. Wilson Ctr. Pr. 1992 $60.00. ISBN 0-943875-36-6. Extremely helpful in identifying the locations in Washington, D.C., of materials related to Latin America and in explaining how to gain access to them.

Lombardi, Cathryn, and others. *Latin American History: A Teaching Atlas*. U. of Wis. Pr. 1983 $7.95. ISBN 0-299-09714-5. So-called recent statistical maps are dated, but the historical maps remain very useful.

Martin, Dolores Moyano, ed. *Handbook of Latin American Studies*. U. of Tex. Pr. 1988 $65.00. ISBN 0-292-73041-1. Basic bibliographical reference that cites both books and articles in various languages. Published annually through the resources of the Hispanic Division of the Library of Congress.

McNeil, Robert A., and Barbara G. Valk, eds. *Latin American Studies: A Basic Guide to Sources*. Scarecrow 2nd rev. ed. 1990 $42.50. ISBN 0-8108-2236-9. Comprehensive and practical guide to libraries, bibliographies, other print and nonprint sources, specialized information, and research and career development as related to Latin American studies.

Stoner, K. Lynn, ed. *Latinas of the Americas: A Source Book*. Garland 1989 $100.00. ISBN 0-8240-8536-1. Thematic survey by 15 scholars of the most recent research on Latin women in all of the Americas. Includes essays and bibliographical listings.

Thomas, Jack Ray, comp. *Bibliographical Dictionary of Latin American Historians and Historiography*. Greenwood 1984 $55.00. ISBN 0-313-23004-8. Bio-bibliographical sketches of more than 250 Latin Americans, from the Colonial era into the twentieth century, who have written on the history of their countries or regions.

SURVEYS AND GENERAL WORKS

Bethell, Leslie, ed. *The Cambridge History of Latin America: Colonial Latin America*. 5 vols. Cambridge U. Pr. Vol. 1 1985 $99.95. ISBN 0-521-23223-6. Vol. 2 1985 $105.00. ISBN 0-521-24516-8. Vol. 3 1985 $110.00. ISBN 0-521-23224-4. Vol. 4 1986 $95.00. ISBN 0-521-23225-2. Vol. 5 1986 $110.00. ISBN 0-521-24517-6. Eight volumes projected covering Latin America from conquest to the present, each volume containing extensive narrative and interpretive essays by most of the leading scholars in the field. Will be the basic reference work for many years, with essays from each volume also being regrouped for publication as topical or national histories.

Burns, E. Bradford. *Latin America: A Concise Interpretive History*. P-H 5th ed. 1990. ISBN 0-13-526782-X. Popular undergraduate text that is argumentative but reliable.

Crow, John A. *The Epic of Latin America*. U. CA Pr. 3rd ed. 1980 $16.95. ISBN 0-520-03776-6. Sweeping survey of Latin American history written in a basic style for a general audience.

Dealy, Glen Caudill. *The Latin Americans: Spirit and Ethos*. Westview 1992 $44.00. ISBN 0-8133-8225-4. Focuses on certain constants of Latin America's Catholic, "caudillaje" civic life, offering implicit and explicit juxtapositions to Protestant, capitalist society. Argues that the former is a dualistic society that clearly distinguishes between public and private realms. Builds on the author's provocative *The Public Man: An Interpretation of Latin American and Other Catholic Cultures* (1977, o.p.).

Galeano, Eduardo. *Open Veins of Latin America: Five Centuries of the Pillage of a Continent*. Trans. by Cedric Belfrage. Montly Rev. 1973 $10.00. ISBN 0-85354-308-X. Impassioned essay by an articulate Uruguayan intellectual and writer who denounces the way foreigners have oppressed and exploited Latin America since 1492. A minor classic.

Gott, Richard. *Land Without Evil: Utopian Journeys Across the South American Watershed*. Routledge Chapman & Hall 1992 $34.95. ISBN 0-86091-398-8. Contemporary travelogue interwoven with detailed histories of various colonial utopian projects over centuries of strife in South America.

Hopkins, Jack W., ed. *Latin America: Perspectives on a Region*. Holmes & Meier 1987 $39.50. ISBN 0-8419-0917-2. Readable, reliable, and comprehensive introduction to the region's similarities and differences, with chronological and thematic chapters and an appendix on researching about Latin America.

Knight, Franklin W. *The Caribbean: The Genesis of a Fragmented Nationalism.* OUP 2nd rev. ed. 1990 $42.50. ISBN 0-19-505440-7. Analysis of the forces hindering development by promoting decentralization and artificial divisions within the Caribbean. Strong on both the colonial and the postindependence periods.

Richardson, Bonham C. *The Caribbean in the Wider World, 1492–1992: A Regional Geography.* Cambridge U. Pr. 1992 $49.95. ISBN 0-521-35186-3. Demonstrates how the colonization and recolonization of the Caribbean have affected the physical and cultural landscape; explains ways in which Caribbean peoples have reacted to constantly changing external influences. Historical geography at its best.

Rout, Leslie B., Jr. *The African Experience in Spanish America, 1502 to the Present Day.* Cambridge U. Pr. 1976 o.p. Survey of the place of blacks in the Spanish-speaking countries of Latin America. Notes that, although blacks have been treated differently in Spanish America than in North America, their status is not necessarily better or improving. Worth consulting for overview.

Stone, Samuel Z. *The Heritage of the Conquistadors: Ruling Classes in Central America from the Conquest to the Sandinistas.* U. of Nebr. Pr. 1990 $12.95. ISBN 0-8032-9214-7. Emphasizes the continuity of elite families from colonial times to the present within each Central American country and the extensive connections among those families across national boundaries.

Tannenbaum, Frank. *Slave and Citizen: The Negro in the Americas.* Knopf 1946 o.p. Argues that blacks received more respect and better treatment in Latin America than in British North America.

Watson, Alan. *Slave Law in the Americas.* U. of Ga. Pr. 1989 $25.00. ISBN 0-8203-1179-0. Looks to legal codes rather than religion and morality as the determinant factors in an attempt to establish a historical relationship between slavery and race relations.

Watson, Robert G. *Spanish and Portuguese South America During the Colonial Period.* 2 vols. Gordon Pr. 1972 $200.00. ISBN 0-8490-1100-0. Lively account of the rise and fall of the Spanish and Portuguese empires in South America, from the conquistadores to the wars of independence.

Williamson, Edwin. *The Penguin History of Latin America.* Viking Penguin 1992 $35.00. ISBN 0-7139-9076-7. Sweeping, balanced, authoritative survey, from discovery to the present. Good introduction for those who want both detail and interpretation.

Wolf, Eric. *Sons of the Shaking Earth.* U. Ch. Pr. 1962 $12.95. ISBN 0-226-90500-4. One of the most exciting books ever written on what now is called Mexico and Central America. Concentrates on pre-Columbian cultures but provides considerable insight into modern life in Middle America. Valuable despite its age.

Woodward, Ralph L., Jr. *Central America: A Nation Divided.* OUP 2nd rev. ed. 1985 $32.00. ISBN 0-19-503592-5. Concise and detailed study of the isthmus from Guatemala to Panama, including Belize. Highlights continuous tension between centrifugal and centripetal forces in the region and the ongoing problem of outside intervention.

Zea, Leopoldo. *The Role of the Americas in History.* Ed. by Amy A. Oliver. Trans. by Sonja Karsen. Rowman 1992 $49.00. ISBN 0-8476-7721-4. Recent translation of an important work originally published in 1957 by a major Mexican historian and philosopher. Offers a provocative analysis of the cultural differences between Protestant North America and Catholic Latin America.

PRE-COLUMBIAN PEOPLES AND CULTURES

For several centuries most of what was known of pre-Columbian civilizations was based on documents from the 1500s—Spanish chronicles, transcriptions of Native American accounts, a few surviving indigenous documents, and some unscientific ethnographic reports prepared by colonial priests and administrators. Only after the mid-1800s, when John L. Stephens and others rediscovered the Mayan sites of the Mesoamerican Petén, did amateur explorers and trained scholars begin to feel the need for serious study of all pre-Hispanic cultures.

Until relatively recently, progress in understanding those cultures was limited by lack of funds, technology, access, and trained personnel. Still, thanks to support from such groups as the Carnegie Institute; to the pioneering labors of such researchers as George C. Vaillant, J. Alden Mason, Sylvanus G. Morley, and J. Eric S. Thompson; and to the stimulating impact of the widely read volumes by Victor W. von Hagen, by the 1940s, the general geographical and chronological outlines of the major civilizations were taking shape, and interest in the field was growing.

Fortunately, despite the disruption, even destruction, of many sites by criminal grave robbers who sell their precious booty on the black market, the last generation has witnessed an explosion of work on ancient American societies. The continuing discovery of previously unknown and miraculously undamaged sites in both the Mesoamerican and Andean zones and the decipherment of much of the previously unreadable Mayan text has opened new horizons. And the desire on the part of scholars and social activists alike to trace links between pre-European traits and today's indigenous and mestizo cultures has accelerated the effort to define more fully—and at times glorify—the characteristics of pre-Columbian peoples. The titles that follow include some of the more recent efforts by historians and scholars to inform and enlighten the specialist and nonspecialist about these early peoples and cultures.

Bauer, Brian S. *The Development of the Inca State.* U. of Tex. Pr. 1993 $25.00. ISBN 0-292-71563-3. Interdisciplinary, innovative, refreshing study of the Incas.

Bernal, Ignacio. *The Olmec World.* Trans. by Doris Heyden and Fernando Horcasitas. U. CA Pr. 1969 $16.95. ISBN 0-520-02891-0. Introduction by an eminent Mexican scholar to Mesoamerica's oldest known source culture, noted for its colossal sculptures, jade carvings, and contributions to the Mayan and other later civilizations.

Clendinnen, Inga. *Aztecs: An Interpretation.* Cambridge U. Pr. 1991 $29.95. ISBN 0-521-40093-7. The best available study of Aztec society and culture, their integrated nature, and the pervasive presence of the sacred.

Coe, Michael D. *Breaking the Maya Code: The Last Great Decipherment of an Ancient Script.* Thames Hudson 1992 $29.95. ISBN 0-500-05061-9. Important work on how the Mayan script was deciphered.

———. *The Maya.* Thames Hudson 4th rev. ed. 1987 $14.95. ISBN 0-500-27455-X. Standard and well-illustrated introduction by a major scholar in Mesoamerican studies.

Davies, Nigel. *The Ancient Kingdoms of Mexico.* Viking Penguin 1984 $7.95. ISBN 0-14-022232-4. Traces the major stages of civilization in the Mexican area of Mesoamerica: Olmec, Teotihuacán, Toltec, and Aztec.

———. *The Aztec Empire: The Toltec Resurgence.* U. of Okla. Pr. 1987 $39.50. ISBN 0-806-12098-3. Broadly describes Aztec society, noting the importance of Toltec heritage.

Denevan, William H., ed. *The Native Population of the Americas in 1492.* U. of Wis. Pr. 2nd rev. ed. 1992 $45.00. ISBN 0-299-13430-X. Brings the latest evidence to bear on the pivotal problem of estimating the population of the Americas before the Europeans arrived.

Gallenkamp, Charles. *Maya: The Riddle and Rediscovery of a Lost Civilization.* Viking Penguin 3rd rev. ed. 1985 $22.95. ISBN 0-670-80387-1. Discusses how amateurs and professionals over the last century have managed to unearth the mysteries of the Mayan world. Good reading for nonspecialists.

Hammond, Norman. *Ancient Maya Civilization.* Rutgers U. Pr. 1982 $15.00. ISBN 0-8135-0906-8. Perhaps the best-written overview of Mayan history and culture. More detailed than Michael Coe's *The Maya*, but less technical and better organized than the Linda Schele and David Freidel study, *A Forest of Kings*.

Hassig, Ross. *War and Society in Ancient Mesoamerica*. U. CA Pr. 1992 $45.00. ISBN 0-520-07734-2. Examines the methods, purposes, and values of warfare across 3,000 years and numerous societies in the Mesoamerican region.

Houston, S.D. *Reading the Past: Maya Glyphs*. U. CA Pr. 1989 $8.95. ISBN 0-520-06771-1. Brief introduction, accessible to nonspecialists, that provides a succinct description of the form, grammar, and subject matter of Mayan writing and a history of its decipherment.

Marcus, Joyce. *Mesoamerican Writing Systems: Propaganda, Myth, and History in Four Ancient Civilizations*. Princeton U. Pr. 1992 $49.95. ISBN 0-691-09474-8. Interprets many ancient Mesoamerican written sources, whether based on fact or myth, as essentially propagandistic rather than historical.

Métraux, Alfred. *The History of the Incas*. Trans. by George Ordish. Schocken 1970 o.p. Nontechnical survey that, despite its age, remains a useful introduction for nonspecialists to the long sweep of Incan history and society.

Patterson, Thomas C. *The Inca Empire: The Formation and Disintegration of a Pre-Capitalist State*. Berg Pubs. 1992 $16.95. ISBN 0-85496-348-0. Synthesis of recent evidence concerning the forces that both built the Inca state and engendered internal tensions.

Sabloff, Jeremy A. *The Cities of Ancient Mexico: Reconstructing a Lost World*. Thames Hudson 1989 $19.95. ISBN 0-500-05053-8. Focuses on eight ancient communities representing six of Mesoamerica's civilizations. Makes available to a general audience a readable introduction to the origins and evolution of Mesoamerican cultures based on the best of recent scholarship.

Scarborough, Vernon L., and David R. Wilcox, eds. *The Mesoamerican Ballgame*. U. of Ariz. Pr. 1993 $18.95. ISBN 0-8165-1360-0. Elucidates the temporal, spatial, functional, and symbolic aspects of the rubber-ball game throughout greater Mesoamerica, including the southwestern United States.

Schele, Linda, and David Freidel. *A Forest of Kings: The Untold Story of the Ancient Maya*. Morrow 1990 $29.95. ISBN 0-688-07456-1. Reconstructs much of the history of the Petén Maya in the classic period based on recent archeological discoveries and the remarkable translations of Mayan dynastic glyphs. Many illustrations.

THE CONQUEST AND COLONIAL ERA

Alchon, Suzanne Austin. *Native Society and Disease in Colonial Ecuador*. Cambridge U. Pr. 1992 $39.50. ISBN 0-521-40186-0. Examines the relationship between the indigenous peoples of northern Ecuador and diseases, especially those introduced by Europeans in the sixteenth century.

Boxer, C. R. *The Golden Age of Brazil, 1695–1750: Growing Pains of a Colonial Society*. U. CA Pr. 1962 $12.95. ISBN 0-520-01550-9. Now the standard political and economic study of the early Portuguese empire in the New World.

Brading, D. A. *The First America: The Spanish Monarchy, Creole Patriots, and the Liberal State, 1492–1867*. Cambridge U. Pr. 1991 $64.95. ISBN 0-521-39130-X. Impressive volume that pursues, through what is almost a general intellectual history of early Spanish America, the uneven and regionally varied signs of emerging national identity across the Spanish empire.

Burkholder, Mark A., and Lyman L. Johnson. *Colonial Latin America*. OUP 1990 $38.00. ISBN 0-19-504542-4. Comprehensive yet readable survey covering social, economic, and political relations.

Cortés, Hernán. *Letters from Mexico*. Ed. and trans. by Anthony Pagden. Yale U. Pr. 1986 $55.00. ISBN 0-300-03724-4. Rich primary source in which the leader of the Spanish conquest of the Aztec empire justifies his actions to his monarch.

Crosby, Alfred W., Jr. *The Columbian Exchange: Biological and Cultural Consequences of 1492*. Greenwood 1973 $39.95. ISBN 0-8371-5821-4. Now classic analysis of the global impact of the encounter of previously distinct biospheres following the European arrival in America.

Díaz, Bernal. *The Conquest of New Spain*. Trans. by J. M. Cohen. Viking Penguin 1976 $7.95. ISBN 0-14-044123-9. Eyewitness account of the Spanish conquest of the Aztec written, in his old age, by one of Cortez's soldiers.

Hanke, Lewis. *The Spanish Struggle for Justice in the Conquest of America*. U. of Pa. Pr. 1949 o.p. Classic attack on the Black Legend that details the efforts made by church and crown to Christianize the Indians and protect them from bodily harm throughout the sixteenth century. Written by a preeminent historian of Latin America.

Haring, C. H. *The Spanish Empire in America*. HarBraceJ 1963 $7.95. ISBN 0-15-684701-9. Useful introduction to the institutional organization of the Spanish empire.

Las Casas, Bartolomé de. *A Short Account of the Destruction of the Indies*. Trans. by Nigel Griffin. Viking Penguin 1992 $9.95. ISBN 0-14-044562-5. Written by the priest called the Protector of the Indians and first published in 1552, protests the atrocities allegedly committed by the early Spanish colonizers against the native populations.

Lavrin, Asunción, ed. *Sexuality and Marriage in Colonial Latin America*. U. of Nebr. Pr. 1992 $33.00. ISBN 0-8032-2885-6. Ten essays illustrating how resourceful women struggled to maintain themselves and their families within an often forbidding institutional network.

León-Portilla, Miguel, ed. *The Broken Spears: The Aztec Account of the Conquest of Mexico*. Trans. by Lysander Kemp. Beacon Pr. 1992 $13.00. ISBN 0-8070-5501-8. Anthology of accounts written by the Aztecs themselves, detailing their own view of the Spaniards who conquered them and destroyed their main city of Tenochtitlán in the early 1500s. A moving description of an epic event.

Lockhart, James. *Spanish Peru, 1532–1560: A Colonial Society*. U. of Wis. Pr. 1974 $14.95. ISBN 0-299-04664-8. Excellent microstudy, focusing on the period of violence and political confusion in the decades immediately after the conquest of the Incas. Detailed but fascinating, showing the interaction among political, economic, and social forces, and the personalities of the Spanish conquistadores.

McAlister, Lyle N. *Spain and Portugal in the New World, 1492–1700*. U. of Minn. Pr. 1984 $44.95. ISBN 0-8166-1216-1. Narrative and interpretive history of Spanish and Portuguese exploration, settlement, and colonization of the Americas prior to the reform programs of the eighteenth century.

McFarlane, Anthony. *Colombia Before Independence: Economy, Society, and Politics under Bourbon Rule*. Cambridge U. Pr. 1993 $59.95. ISBN 0-521-41641-8

MacLachlan, Colin M., and Jaime E. Rodriquez. *The Forging of the Cosmic Race: A Reinterpretation of Colonial Mexico*. U. CA Pr. 1990 $14.95. ISBN 0-520-04280-8. Revisionist view of the argument that Spain was always an exploitive power that drained colonial resources. Contends that the colonial system developed prosperity and capitalism for both Mexican society and the parent country.

MacLeod, Murdo J. *Spanish Central America: A Socioeconomic History, 1520–1720*. U. CA Pr. 1985 $49.95. ISBN 0-520-05356-7. Classic study of the social and economic structure of colonial Central America. Emphasizes the destructive results of reliance on a single-crop agricultural system.

Padden, R. C. *The Hummingbird and the Hawk: Conquest and Sovereignty in the Valley of Mexico, 1503–1541*. HarpC 1975 $13.00. ISBN 0-06-131898-1. Stirring account of the expansion of the Aztec empire, with an emphasis on the link between violence and religion. In turn, analyzes the role of religion in the Spanish conquest and the clash between two religious systems in the struggle to establish sovereignty after the Aztec defeat.

Robinson, David J., ed. *Migration in Colonial Spanish America*. Cambridge U. Pr. 1990 $49.50. ISBN 0-521-36281-4. Points out that spatial mobility was no less pronounced in colonial Spanish America than was social and ethnic-racial change.

Rouse, Irving. *The Tainos: Rise and Decline of the People Who Greeted Columbus*. Yale U. Pr. 1992 $25.00. ISBN 0-300-05181-6. Covers all four of the Columbus voyages and describes their ecological and demographic impact on the Amerindian communities. A balanced assessment of what the Spaniards did and why.

Sale, Kirkpatrick. *The Conquest of Paradise: Christopher Columbus and the Columbian Legacy*. NAL-Dutton 1991 $14.00. ISBN 0-452-26669-6. Emotional critique of the good and the especially bad aspects of the Columbian legacy, condemning much of what Columbus and his European successors have done to the pre-1492 American "paradise" and its occupants.

Sauer, Carl O. *The Early Spanish Main*. U. CA Pr. 1992 $40.00. ISBN 0-520-01125-2. Classic work in historical geography that first laid out many of the still intriguing questions about the character of Columbus and the impact of the early Spanish on the ecology of the Caribbean region.

Weckmann, Luis. *The Medieval Heritage of Mexico*. Trans. by Frances M. López-Morillas. Fordham U. Pr. 1992 $85.00. ISBN 0-8232-1324-2. Detailed description by a Mexican scholar of the extent to which Mexican colonial society reproduced Spanish medieval institutions and perspectives.

Williams, Eric. *Capitalism and Slavery*. U. of NC Pr. 1944 o.p. Focusing on the West Indies, analyzes the role of slavery in providing capital for the Industrial Revolution and the role of industrial capitalism in destroying the slave system. Written by a prominent historian who worked for the independence of Trinidad and Tobago and became its prime minister in the 1960s.

THE MODERN ERA

Students of post-1810 Latin American history and culture have long been torn between a regional and a national perspective. Is generalizing about Latin America as a whole sufficient to provide an understanding of the historical processes at work within any individual country? Or does the history of a single country allow one to generalize about the region? The debate goes on. Some scholars prefer to offer overviews and generalizations about a vast region that surely is marked internally by both similarities and differences. Others, however, choose to focus on specific countries, convinced that history develops most meaningfully within national boundaries and institutions and that parallels with experiences in other countries are subordinate to unique national experiences. The truth is that even most of the so-called general works tend to cite selected national cases or to admit that not all countries fit any regional pattern except on the grandest theoretical level, whereas many writers on national themes contend that their works represent case studies of broader regional patterns.

Several patterns characterize the long-term production of single-country studies by historians of Latin America: (1) A tendency to focus on the largest countries. Works on Brazil and Mexico dominate the field, with Argentina, Cuba, Chile, and Colombia lagging behind, although ahead of the rest. (2) A move in recent years to search out groups ignored by traditional historians—women, nonwhites, the poor, and the culture they possess and express. (3) Cyclical shifts toward so-called problem areas, those countries suffering pronounced political turmoil and thereby elevating concern, for strategic or humanitarian reasons, in the United States. These include Mexico in the 1910s and 1920s, Argentina in the 1940s, Cuba in the 1960s and 1970s, Chile in the 1970s, and Central America in the 1980s. (4) The appeal of the exceptional personality—nineteenth-century military and political caudillos, Juan and Eva Perón, Fidel Castro, Colombian drug lords—or the dramatic happening, such as the Paraguayan War, the Malvinas (Falklands) War, environmental crises, and natural disasters.

Readers should appreciate that what currently is published and in print might reflect journalistic, policy, and scholarly interests notably different from those of older works now available only in libraries. They should realize also that quality does not always keep pace with quantity.

Regional Studies

Burns, E. Bradford. *The Poverty of Progress: Latin America in the Nineteenth Century*. U. CA Pr. 1980 $32.50. ISBN 0-520-04160-7. Provocatively argues that liberal attempts to bring progress to Latin America in the last century destroyed folk communities and cultures and impoverished more people physically and psychologically than they helped.

Bushnell, David, and Neill Macaulay. *The Emergence of Latin America in the Nineteenth Century*. OUP 1989 $32.50. ISBN 0-19-504463-0. Organized geographically but highlights themes common across the region—state building and constitutional debates, religious questions, social relations, and connections to international economic system.

Cockcroft, James D. *Neighbors in Turmoil: Latin America*. HarpC 1989 o.p. Country-by-country survey of Latin America since independence, emphasizing socioeconomic conflict and alleged foreign intervention and exploitation.

Coleman, Kenneth M., and George C. Herring, eds. *Understanding the Central American Crisis: Sources of Conflict, U.S. Policy, and Options for Peace*. Scholarly Res. Inc. 1991 $13.95. ISBN 0-8420-2383-6. Without ignoring Central America's internal historical sources of conflict, examines the skewed premises that have led the United States to pursue often erroneous and costly policies in the region.

Collier, David, and Ruth Berins Collier. *Shaping the Political Arena: Critical Junctures, the Labor Movement, and Regime Dynamics in Latin America*. Princeton U. Pr. 1991 $75.00. ISBN 0-691-07830-0. Looking at eight countries in a comparative perspective, considers the importance of labor mobilization and control in the evolution of Latin American politics in the twentieth century. Not easy reading.

Dorfman, Ariel. *The Empire's Old Clothes: What the Lone Ranger, Babar, and Other Innocent Heroes Do to Our Minds*. Trans. by Clark Hansen. Pantheon 1983 $9.95. ISBN 0-394-71486-5. Provocative interpretation of the values hidden in foreign—mainly United States—children's comic strips and books and of how these serve to shape attitudes among Latin American audiences for the benefit of capitalist and imperialist interests.

Johnson, John J. *Latin America in Caricature*. U. of Tex. Pr. 1980 $27.50. ISBN 0-292-74626-1. U.S. perceptions of Latin America as expressed in political cartoons.

Kahl, Joseph A. *Three Latin American Sociologists: Gino Germani, Pablo González Casanova, and Fernando Henrique Cardoso*. Transaction Pubs. 2nd ed. 1988 $24.95. ISBN 0-88738-169-3. Summarizes the contributions of three prominent social scientists to the analysis of Latin America in a comparative and global context.

LaFeber, Walter. *Inevitable Revolutions: The United States in Central America*. Norton 2nd rev. ed. 1993 $22.95. ISBN 0-393-03434-8. Attributes most of the recent instability in Central America to long-term internal causes exacerbated by the failure of the United States to accept reasonable and necessary changes, thereby promoting even more radical movements.

Langley, Lester D. *The United States and the Caribbean in the Twentieth Century*. U. of Ga. Pr. 4th ed. 1989 $35.00. ISBN 0-8203-1154-5. Even-handed survey that covers the periods from the Big Stick of the early 1900s to the Panama invasion and the movement toward peace in Central America.

Leonard, Thomas M. *Central America and the United States: The Search for Stability*. U. of Ga. Pr. 1991 $35.00. ISBN 0-8203-1320-3. Admits that Central American countries and the United States often have had conflicting foreign policy goals and that the United States frequently has employed a heavy hand, but does not blame the United States for all of the region's problems.

Lernoux, Penny. *Cry of the People: The Struggle for Human Rights in Latin America; The Catholic Church Conflict with U. S. Policy.* Viking Penguin 1982 $9.95. ISBN 0-14-006047-2. Passionate account of the Roman Catholic church's role in Latin America, especially its increasingly progressive social and political programs and actions; serves as an indictment of the governments of the region and of U.S. foreign policy.

Lynch, Edward A. *Latin America's Christian Democratic Parties: A Political Economy.* Praeger 1993 $45.00. ISBN 0-275-94464-6. Analyzes the interaction between theology and economics in the evolution of a political movement important throughout Latin America over the past generation.

Lynch, John. *Caudillos in Spanish America, 1800–1850.* OUP 1992 $76.00. ISBN 0-19-821135-X. A look at the powerful and colorful figures who brought Spanish American independence and laid the foundations of the early republics.

_____. *The Spanish American Revolutions, 1808–1826.* Norton 2nd ed. 1986 $11.95. ISBN 0-393-95537-0. Sees independence movements after 1808 as a result of the conflict between Spain's new bureaucratic imperialism of the eighteenth century and an emerging national identity in Spanish America. Highlights important regional differences within the Spanish empire.

Madariaga, Salvador de. *Bolívar.* Greenwood 1979 repr. of 1952 ed. $65.00. ISBN 0-313-22029-8. Controversial biography by a renowned Spanish historian that is extremely critical of the Liberator, labeling him a renegade and impugning his character.

Masur, Gerhard. *Simon Bolívar.* U. of NM Pr. rev. ed. 1969 o.p. Probably the best biography of Bolívar ever published in English. Now out of print but worth searching for.

Nunn, Frederick M. *The Time of the Generals: Latin American Professional Militarism in World Perspective.* U. of Nebr. Pr. 1992 $50.00. ISBN 0-8032-3334-5. The leading expert on modern Latin American militaries interprets his subject in a global context. Authoritative and provocative.

Pérez Brignoli, Héctor. *A Brief History of Central America.* Trans. by Ricardo B. De Sawrey and Susana S. De Sawrey. U. CA Pr. 2nd ed. 1989 $45.00. ISBN 0-520-06049-0. Strongly Costa Rican in perspective and devoted almost entirely to the postindependence period. Offers a concise sketch of the major social, political, and economic themes in the region since 1800.

Pike, Frederick B. *The United States and Latin America: Myths and Stereotypes of Civilization and Nature.* U. of Tex. Pr. 1992 $40.00. ISBN 0-292-78523-2. Probes the origins of the stereotypes and myths that have shaped relations between the United States and Latin America, focusing primarily on the distortion that results from a North American tendency to identify its culture as civilized and that of Latin America as primitive.

Rippy, J. Fred. *British Investment in Latin America: 1822–1949.* Ed. by Mira Wilkins. Ayer 1977 repr. of 1959 ed. $20.00. ISBN 0-405-09771-9. Old-fashioned history but still a useful reference.

Schutte, Ofelia. *Cultural Identity and Social Liberation in Latin American Thought.* State U. NY Pr. 1993 $54.50. ISBN 0-7914-1317-9

Skidmore, Thomas E., and Peter H. Smith. *Modern Latin America.* OUP 3rd ed. 1992 $39.95. ISBN 0-19-507648-6. Focuses on the years after 1880, with principal chapters devoted to Argentina, Chile, Brazil, Peru, Mexico, and Cuba, plus short sections on the countries of Central America and the Caribbean. Examines the relationship between economics and politics within an international context.

Smith, Peter H., ed. *Drug Policy in the Americas.* Westview 1992 $54.95. ISBN 0-8133-8239-4. Sees the hemispheric drug situation as both multidimensional and multilateral. A good antidote to simplistic proposals to solve the problems.

Wynia, Gary W. *The Politics of Latin American Development.* Cambridge U. Pr. 3rd ed. 1990 $54.95. ISBN 0-521-38027-8. Refreshing treatment of the interaction of Latin American politics and economics, viewing various political structures as games with particular and specific players and rules.

Individual Countries

ARGENTINA

Adkin, Mark. *Goose Green: A Battle Is Fought to Be Won*. Shoe String 1992 $38.50. ISBN 0-85052-207-2. Presents the British side of the military campaign in the Falklands (Malvinas) War of 1982.

Barnes, John. *Evita, First Lady: A Biography of Eva Perón*. Grove Pr. 1978 $5.95. ISBN 0-8021-5124-8. Entertaining and useful study of a controversial figure.

Collier, Simon. *The Life, Music, and Times of Carlos Gardel*. U. of Pittsburgh Pr. 1986 $24.95. ISBN 0-8229-3535-X. Warm study that examines the talents that helped make the French-born Gardel Latin America's first and possibly greatest superstar of light entertainment. Also analyzes the tango, which Gardel helped popularize and universalize.

Danchev, Alex, ed. *International Perspectives on the Falklands Conflict: A Matter of Life and Death*. St. Martin 1992 $65.00. ISBN 0-312-07189-2. Examination by leading British and Argentine authorities of aspects of the controversy that led to war in 1982, from the relevance of the Falklands' (Malvinas') past to prospects for the future.

Fraser, Nicholas, and Marysa Navarro. *Eva Perón*. Norton 1981 $9.95. ISBN 0-393-30238-5. Balanced analysis, favorable but restrained, of the controversial Evita as person and political force. Probably the best single study available.

Hodges, Donald C. *Argentina's "Dirty War": An Intellectual Biography*. U. of Tex. Pr. 1991 $37.50. ISBN 0-292-70423-2. Offers insight into the ideas that motivated the Argentine military and security forces to terrorize their own people between 1975 and the early 1980s.

Page, Joseph A. *Perón: A Biography*. Random 1983 $25.00. ISBN 0-394-52297-4. The most complete biography of Juan D. Perón through his entire career. Good on the man and his inner circle; less effective in understanding the larger historical and social context.

Scobie, James R. *Argentina: A City and a Nation*. OUP 2nd ed. 1971 $13.95. ISBN 0-19-501480-4. Though now dated, still offers an excellent analysis of how modern Argentina was shaped by the conflicts and compromises between the interests of the agricultural interior and the dominant forces of the capital port city.

Tulchin, Joseph S. *Argentina and the United States: A Conflicted Relationship*. Macmillan 1990 $26.95. ISBN 0-8057-7900-0. Contends that, with a shared sense of moralism, messianism, and exceptionalism, Argentina and the United States are too much alike to avoid confrontation, which Argentina often has pursued in a vain search for international prestige and autonomy.

Wynia, Gary W. *Argentina: Illusions and Realities*. Holmes & Meier 2nd rev. ed. 1992 $18.95. ISBN 0-8419-1296-3. Puts forth the premise that Argentines are an energetic and intelligent people who find it difficult to control their "combative urges" in the political arena and thus fail to achieve prolonged political stability and economic progress.

BOLIVIA

Klein, Herbert S. *Bolivia: The Evolution of a Multi-Ethnic Society*. OUP 2nd ed. 1992 $39.95. ISBN 0-19-505734-1. Explores in Bolivian history the interaction of Western patterns and pre-Columbian traditions that has produced a particular class organization, dual social systems, poverty and exploitation, yet a spirit of independence and creativity.

Malloy, James M., and Eduardo Gamarra. *Revolution and Reaction: Bolivia 1964–1985*. Transaction Pubs. 1988 $29.95. ISBN 0-88738-159-6. Examines the alterations among various authoritarian and democratic models of governance during two unstable decades. Relates the Bolivian case to common regional patterns.

Nash, June. *We Eat the Mines and the Mines Eat Us: Dependency and Exploitation in Bolivian Tin Mines*. Col. U. Pr. 1982 $19.50. ISBN 0-231-04711-8. Sensitive study based on 16 months of fieldwork. Sympathetically portrays the difficult lives of based on 16 months of fieldwork. Sympathetically portrays the difficult lives of Bolivian tin miners and their families, victims of a brutal system of economic exploitation and physical abuse.

Prado Salmón, Gary. *The Defeat of Che Guevara: Military Response to Guerrilla Challenge in Bolivia*. Trans. by John Deredita. Praeger 1990 $47.95. ISBN 0-275-93211-7. Useful and interesting account by a Bolivian military officer who participated in Guevara's capture in 1967.

BRAZIL

Burns, E. Bradford. *A History of Brazil*. Col. U. Pr. 2nd ed. 1980 $87.00. ISBN 0-231-04748-7. Balanced and well-written survey for the years it covers. Good place to start for those who wish to know periodization and long-term trends in Brazilian history.

Lever, Janet. *Soccer Madness*. U. Ch. Pr. 1984 $17.50. ISBN 0-226-47382-1. Tells how soccer functions to help Brazilians overcome their social and regional differences and to promote a greater sense of national identity.

Levine, Robert M. *Vale of Tears: Revisiting the Canudos Massacre in Northeastern Brazil, 1893–1897*. U. CA Pr. 1992 $45.00. ISBN 0-520-07524-2. Exciting reevaluation of a pivotal episode in Brazilian history that provides insights into many aspects of Brazilian society and the problems of the critical northeast region.

Macaulay, Neill. *Dom Pedro: The Struggle for Liberty in Brazil and Portugal, 1798–1834*. Duke 1986 $39.95. ISBN 0-8223-0681-6. Expresses Brazil's struggle for independence and stability through the life of the Portuguese prince who became the nation's first emperor but eventually was forced to abdicate.

Roett, Riordan. *Brazil: Politics in a Patrimonial Society*. Praeger 4th ed. 1992 $55.00. ISBN 0-275-94121-3. Detailed narrative relating how, in the face of international economic pressures and domestic social inequities, Brazil has struggled since the 1940s to find a political system adequate to maintain a reasonable degree of order.

Schneider, Ronald M. *"Order and Progress": A Political History of Brazil*. Westview 1991 $61.00. ISBN 0-8133-1077-6. Looking mainly at the post-1889 years, focuses on the military's search for "order and progress" as the moving force in Brazil's political evolution. Secondarily touches on the Roman Catholic church and propertied elites.

Schwartz, Stuart B. *Slaves, Peasants, and Rebels: Reconsidering Brazilian Slavery*. U. of Ill. Pr. 1992 $34.95. ISBN 0-252-01874-5. Revisionist study that focuses on the role slaves played in shaping both their own lives and the nature of Brazilian slavery.

Skidmore, Thomas E. *Politics in Brazil, 1930–1964: An Experiment in Democracy*. OUP 1986 $19.95. ISBN 0-19-500784-0. Comprehensive and reliable survey of Brazilian politics from the rise of Getulio Vargas to the military coup that ended Brazil's shaky constitutional regime.

———. *The Politics of Military Rule in Brazil, 1964–1985*. OUP 1990 $35.00. ISBN 0-19-503898-3. Traces Brazilian political and economic history under an often divided and unpredictable military regime.

Stone, Roger D. *Dreams of Amazonia*. Viking Penguin rev. ed. 1992 $10.00. ISBN 0-14-017430-3. Moving protest against the development of the Amazonian rain forest by the Brazilian government and allied business interests. Proposes alternatives to current destructive policies.

CHILE

Constable, Pamela, and Arturo Valenzuela. *A Nation of Enemies: Chile under Pinochet*. Norton 1991 $24.95. ISBN 0-393-03011-3. Rich and detailed study that discusses the emergence of the personalist rule of General Pinochet, the effects of the dictatorship on a cross-section of society, and the reasons for the eventual end of military rule.

Drake, Paul W., and Iván Jaksic, eds. *The Struggle for Democracy in Chile, 1982–1990*. U. of Nebr. Pr. 1991 $45.00. ISBN 0-8032-1691-2. Essays concentrating on economic and political developments as Chile moved from the Pinochet dictatorship to renewed democracy.

Loveman, Brian. *Chile: The Legacy of Hispanic Capitalism.* OUP 2nd ed. 1988 $39.95. ISBN 0-19-505219-6. General history of Chile that sees democratic capitalism as the country's most appropriate form of development and emphasizes socioeconomic trends, especially in its analysis of the working class and the poor.

Sater, William F. *Chile and the United States: Empires in Conflict.* U. of Ga. Pr. 1991 $35.00. ISBN 0-8203-1249-5. Argues that conflict between these distant American neighbors has been more common than cooperation because of long tendencies by both to assume a stance of superiority toward one another and to claim a moral right to impose their will on other countries.

Sigmund, Paul E. *The United States and Democracy in Chile.* Johns Hopkins 1993 $38.50. ISBN 0-8018-4580-7. Focusing on the years between the military coup of 1973 and the return of democracy in 1990, finds U.S. influence in Chilean politics to be significant but not decisive.

COLOMBIA

Bergquist, Charles W., and others, eds. *Violence in Colombia: The Contemporary Crisis in Historical Perspective.* Scholarly Res. Inc. 1992 $14.95. ISBN 0-8420-2376-3. Fourteen essays that link Colombia's recent rash of violence less to the drug trade and more to the heritage of La Violencia (The Violence), a period of terror, political banditry, and peasant unrest that plagued the country from the 1940s into the 1960s.

Bushnell, David. *The Making of Modern Colombia: A Nation in Spite of Itself.* U. CA Pr. 1993 $42.00. ISBN 0-520-07802-0. Sweeping survey that notes Colombia's many seeming contradictions and its people's enduring skill at "muddling through."

————. *Santander Regime in Gran Colombia.* Greenwood 1970 repr. of 1954 ed. $35.00. ISBN 0-8371-2981-8. Examines the emergence of the early Colombian republic.

Hartlyn, Jonathan. *The Politics of Coalition Rule in Colombia.* Cambridge U. Pr. 1988 $47.50. ISBN 0-521-34055-1. Highly regarded introduction to the ways by which Colombian elites, through formal and informal cooperation between the Liberal and Conservative parties, generally have maintained political control and order.

Leal, Richard L. *Arrogant Diplomacy: U.S. Policy toward Colombia, 1903–1922.* Scholary Res. Inc. 1987 $35.00. ISBN 0-8420-2287-2. Focuses on the difficult years during which the two countries sought to overcome the legacy of the role of the United States in Colombia's loss of Panama.

Randall, Stephen J. *Colombia and the United States: Hegemony and Interdependence.* U. of Ga. Pr. 1992 $40.00. ISBN 0-8203-1401-3. Contends that some Colombian-U.S. disputes have been worsened by the U.S. failure to understand that Colombians do not see themselves as a weak, insignificant, Third World nation.

Wade, Peter. *Blackness and Race Mixture: The Dynamics of Racial Identity in Colombia.* Johns Hopkins 1993 $58.00. ISBN 0-8018-4458-4. Provocative analysis of the meanings and implications of "blackness" and discrimination across region and class within various cultural realms in a multiethnic society.

COSTA RICA

Biesanz, Richard, and others. *The Costa Ricans.* Waveland Pr. 1988 repr. of 1982 ed. $9.95. ISBN 0-88133-340-9. A bit dated and superficial in places but still a useful introduction for nonspecialists by authors who know and love Costa Rica and its people.

Creedman, Theodore S., ed. *Historical Dictionary of Costa Rica.* Scarecrow 2nd rev. ed. 1991 $42.50. ISBN 0-8108-2215-6. Useful, basic reference covering, however briefly, many aspects of Costa Rican history broadly defined.

Edelman, Marc. *The Logic of the Latifundio: The Large Estates of Northwestern Costa Rica Since the Late 19th Century.* Stanford U. Pr. 1992 $55.00. ISBN 0-804-72044-4. Valuable contribution to understanding specific dimensions of Costa Rican society and the place of the *latifundio* in Latin America.

Winson, Anthony. *Coffee and Democracy in Modern Costa Rica.* St. Martin 1989 $45.00. ISBN 0-312-02521-1. Explains the development of Costa Rica's democracy after

World War II as a function of the unique interaction of a weakened coffee oligarchy and the progressive leadership of a group of enlightened intellectuals and politicians.

CUBA

Balfour, Sebastian. *Castro*. Longman 1990 $26.95. ISBN 0-582-02971-6. Studies the man in his context, looking more at personality and personal style and at how he has been perceived by Cubans over the years.

Benjamin, Jules R. *The United States and the Origins of the Cuban Revolution: An Empire of Liberty in an Age of National Liberation*. Princeton U. Pr. 1992 $35.00. ISBN 0-691-07835-X. Study in the nature of hegemony and its limitations, asserting that U.S. efforts to Americanize Cuba produced many of the forces that led to the revolution of 1959.

Pérez, Louis A., Jr. *Cuba: Between Reform and Revolution*. OUP 1988 $30.00. ISBN 0-19-504587-4. Balanced, comprehensive, readable work by one of the leading experts on modern Cuban history. The best one-volume survey currently available.

_____. *Cuba and the United States: Ties of Singular Intimacy*. U. of Ga. Pr. 1990 $35.00. ISBN 0-8203-1208-8. Comprehensive, sophisticated, readable work that focuses on the simultaneous attraction and repulsion and the mutual but unequal influence in the relationship of Cuba and the United States.

Pérez-López, Jorge F. *The Economics of Cuban Sugar*. U. of Pittsburgh Pr. 1991 $49.95. ISBN 0-8229-3663-1. Though offering limited analysis, provides a comprehensive survey of the literature on Cuban sugar and thus raises many significant questions about a key theme in Cuban history.

Ruiz, Ramón Eduardo. *Cuba: The Making of a Revolution*. Norton 1970 $7.95. ISBN 0-393-00513-5. Very readable interpretation of the Cuban revolution of 1959. Emphasizes long-term historical forces rather than the mere personality of Fidel Castro.

DOMINICAN REPUBLIC

Calder, Bruce J. *The Impact of the Intervention: The Dominican Republic During the U.S. Occupation of 1916–1924*. U. of Tex. Pr. 1984 $30.00. ISBN 0-292-73830-7. Deals with what the United States achieved and failed to achieve during that intervention and the continuing legacy of that event both in Dominican history and in relations between the two countries.

De Galindez, Suarez J. *The Era of Trujillo: Dominican Dictator*. Bks. Demand repr. of 1973 ed. $81.50. ISBN 0-317-28617-X

Palmer, Bruce, Jr. *Intervention in the Caribbean: The Dominican Crisis of 1965*. U. Pr. of Ky. 1989 $28.00. ISBN 0-8131-1691-0. Account and rationale by the general who commanded U.S. forces during the U.S.-led intervention in 1965.

Ruck, Rob. *Tropic of Baseball: Baseball in the Dominican Republic*. Meckler Corp. 1991 $37.50. ISBN 0-88736-707-0. Describes the sociohistorical factors that have produced so many high-quality baseball players in such a small country.

ECUADOR

Martz, John D. *Politics and Petroleum in Ecuador*. Transaction Pubs. 1987 $34.95. ISBN 0-88738-132-4. Analyzes interplay in Ecuadorian politics among global oil companies, nationalistic forces, and the policy orientations of various military and civilian governments.

Schodt, David W. *Ecuador: An Andean Enigma*. Westview 1987 $49.50. ISBN 0-8133-0230-7. A basic, competent, readable survey, with an emphasis on economic forces and their influence in the political arena.

EL SALVADOR

Americas Watch staff. *El Salvador's Decade of Terror: Human Rights Since the Assassination of Archbishop Romero*. Yale U. Pr. 1991 $25.00. ISBN 0-300-04939-0. Description and analysis of the sources of human rights violations during the 1980s, a decade of civil war, noting the inability of the United States to bring effective protection of human rights or often even to admit that violations had occurred. Cautiously optimistic about the future.

Lindo-Fuentes, Héctor. *Weak Foundations: The Economy of El Salvador in the Nineteenth Century, 1821–1898.* U. CA Pr. 1990 $34.95. ISBN 0-520-06927-7. Traces the rise of the coffee elite and its relation to El Salvador's land system, political structure, and international economic dependency.

Parkman, Patricia. *Nonviolent Insurrection in El Salvador: The Fall of Maximiliano Hernández Martínez.* U. of Ariz. Pr. 1988 $28.95. ISBN 0-8165-1062-8. Limited study of the administration of a long-time Salvadoran dictator who was removed in 1944. Somewhat helpful for understanding the country's problems in the 1970s and 1980s.

GUATEMALA

Gleijeses, Piero. *Shattered Hope: The Guatemalan Revolution and the United States, 1944–1954.* Princeton U. Pr. 1992 $45.00. ISBN 0-691-02556-8. Looking mainly at the presidency of Jacobo Arbenz (1951–54), reports favorably on the efforts of the Guatemalan revolution until undermined by U.S. policy.

Jonas, Susanne. *The Battle for Guatemala: Rebels, Death Squads, and U.S. Power.* Westview 1991 $42.00. ISBN 0-8133-7462-6. Considering such domestic factors as political culture, ethnic relations, and gender issues, as well as the international context and the failure of previously tested models, offers a discouraging prognosis for Guatemala's search for order and social justice.

Kinzer, Stephen, and Stephen Schlesinger. *Bitter Fruit: The Untold Story of the American Coup in Guatemala.* Doubleday 1983 $10.95. ISBN 0-385-18354-2. Disturbing account of the CIA-orchestrated coup of 1954 that overthrew the democratically elected government of Jacobo Arbenz and initiated years of repression, corruption, and slaughter in Guatemala.

Woodward, Ralph L., Jr. *Rafael Carrera and the Emergence of the Republic of Guatemala, 1821–1871.* U. of Ga. Pr. 1993 $65.00. ISBN 0-8203-1448-X. Centers on the controversial mixed-blood, conservative leader who was the dominant figure in Guatemala and Central America for decades, seeking domestic progress through traditional means but disturbing his neighbors with frequent interventions.

GUYANA

Singh, Chaitram. *Guyana: Politics in a Plantation Society.* Greenwood 1988 $37.95. ISBN 0-275-92989-2. Brief introduction to the history of the former British colony, with an emphasis on the issues of race, class, economic stagnation, and socialist ideology in recent politics.

HAITI

Bellegarde-Smith, Patrick. *Haiti: The Breached Citadel.* Westview 1989 $43.00. ISBN 0-8133-7172-4. Handsomely produced account, written by a Haitian, and accessible to the general reader. Covers a wide range of political, social, and economic topics.

Diederich, Bernard, and Al Burt. *Papa Doc: Haiti and Its Dictator.* Wiener Pub. Inc. 1991 repr. of 1972 ed. $12.95. ISBN 0-943862-43-4. Focuses on the dominant "black" figure in post-1945 Haitian politics. Exciting reading and useful for understanding the problems that continue to plague this troubled country.

James, C. L. R. *The Black Jacobins: Toussaint l'Ouverture and the San Domingo Revolution.* Random 2nd ed. 1963 $8.95. ISBN 0-394-70242-5. Exciting social history by a West Indian writer and activist focusing on the only successful slave revolt in history, which brought forth a gifted leader and later the troubled country of Haiti.

Plummer, Brenda Gayle. *Haiti and the United States: The Psychological Moment.* U. of Ga. Pr. 1992 $45.00. ISBN 0-8203-1423-4. Deals with the search for common ground, made difficult by disparities in culture and wealth, the dilemma of race, and respective domestic political contexts.

Pratt, Frantz, comp. *Haiti: Guide to the Periodical Literature in English, 1800–1990.* Greenwood 1991 $45.00. ISBN 0-313-27855-5. Lists by topic and without annotations over 5,000 items. Useful for finding information on a country about which so few books are available in English.

HONDURAS

Acker, Alison. *Honduras: The Making of a Banana Republic.* South End Pr. 1988 $30.00. ISBN 0-89608-336-5. Lacking in depth and context, but providing a readable overview of a small country about which little has been written in English.

MacCameron, Robert. *Bananas, Labor and Politics in Honduras: 1954–1963.* Syracuse U. Foreign Comp. 1983 $14.00. ISBN 0-915984-96-2

Peckenham, Nancy, and Annie Street, eds. *Honduras: Portrait of a Captive Nation.* Greenwood 1985 $15.95. ISBN 0-275-91676-X

JAMAICA

Keith, Nelson W., and Novella Z. Keith. *The Social Origins of Democratic Socialism in Jamaica.* Temple U. Pr. 1992 $44.95. ISBN 0-87722-906-6. Using a class analysis, seeks to identify the structural dynamics that have both promoted and limited reform in Jamaica since independence.

Levi, Darrell E. *Michael Manley: The Making of a Leader.* U. of Ga. Pr. 1990 $32.00. ISBN 0-8203-1221-5. Survey of Jamaican political history since the 1960s seen through the career of the longtime leader of the People's National party.

MEXICO

Aguilar Camín, Héctor, and Lorenzo Meyer. *In the Shadow of the Mexican Revolution: Contemporary Mexican History, 1910–1989.* Trans. by Luis Alberto Fierro. U. of Tex. Pr. 1993 $35.00. ISBN 0-292-70446-1. Translation that affords U.S. readers the opportunity to appreciate how Mexican historians view their own recent history.

Anna, Timothy E. *The Mexican Empire of Iturbide.* U. of Nebr. Pr. 1990 $42.50. ISBN 0-8032-1027-2. Well-researched and balanced interpretation of the first Mexican empire (1821–23), headed by the controversial Agustín de Iturbide, who was so important in Mexico's winning independence.

Bauer, K. Jack. *The Mexican War, 1846–1848.* U. of Nebr. Pr. 1992 $16.95. ISBN 0-8032-6107-1. Perhaps the best military history of the Mexican War on both sides.

Beezley, William H. *Judas at the Jockey Club and Other Episodes of Porfirian Mexico.* U. of Nebr. Pr. 1987 $25.00. ISBN 0-8032-1195-3. Entertaining description of the interaction between popular culture and the modernizing values of the elites during the years Porfirio Díaz dominated Mexico (1877–1911).

Benson, Nettie Lee. *The Provincial Deputation in Mexico: Harbinger of Provincial Autonomy, Independence, and Federalism.* U. of Tex. Pr. 1992 $35.00. ISBN 0-292-76531-2. Sees the institution of the provincial deputation as putting Mexico (New Spain) on the road to independence and a strong federalist outlook. A major work by a scholar who influenced much research on Mexican history and who built the magnificent Latin American collection at the University of Texas at Austin.

García Canclini, Néstor. *Transforming Modernity: Popular Culture in Mexico.* Trans. by Lidia Lozano. U. of Tex. Pr. 1993 $27.50. ISBN 0-292-72758-5. Application by a noted Argentine-Mexican anthropologist of his theories of popular culture to a critique of capitalist modernism in the Michoacán region of Mexico.

Hart, John Mason. *Revolutionary Mexico: The Coming and Process of the Mexican Revolution.* U. CA Pr. 1987 $47.50. ISBN 0-520-05995-6. Examines how, in its labor and peasant origins and in its achievement of change in land ownership, Mexico in the 1910s produced something truly revolutionary.

Knight, Alan. *The Mexican Revolution.* 2 vols. Cambridge U. Pr. 1986 $69.95 ea. ISBNs 0-521-24475-7, 0-521-26651-3. Detailed study that combines empirical substance with interpretive skill and a balance between national trends and local variations. Will be the standard study of the 1910–20 upheaval for a long time.

Meyer, Michael C, and William L. Sherman. *The Course of Mexican History*. OUP 4th ed. 1991 $49.95. ISBN 0-19-506599-9. Solid, basic survey that treats social, cultural, political, and economic themes from pre-Columbian times to the present. Provides comprehensive suggestions for further reading.

Raat, W. Dirk. *Mexico and the United States: Ambivalent Vistas*. U. of Ga. Pr. 1992 $45.00. ISBN 0-8203-1456-0. Emphasizing such factors as a disequilibrium of power, a shared border, and distinct cultural roots, considers the interdependent nature of Mexican-U.S. relations in the context of a dynamic world system.

Riding, Alan. *Distant Neighbors: A Portrait of the Mexicans*. Random 1989 $10.00. ISBN 0-679-72441-9. Attempt by a perceptive journalist to understand the complexities of Mexico's present as an outcome of its continuous yet inconsistent past, its mestizo character, and its often conflicting blend of Indian and Spanish, Asian and Western.

Ruiz, Ramón Eduardo. *The Great Rebellion: Mexico, 1905–1924*. Norton 1980 $13.95. ISBN 0-393-95129-4. Enjoyable study that sees the Mexican revolution in more limited political terms.

———. *Triumphs and Tragedy: A History of the Mexican People*. Norton 1992 $29.95. ISBN 0-393-03023-7. Solid, comprehensive, readable survey.

Vázquez, Josefina Zoraida, and Lorenzo Meyer. *The United States and Mexico*. U. Ch. Pr. 1987 $11.95. ISBN 0-226-85205-9. Articulate summary by two prominent Mexican scholars of the often critical view of the ways the United States has treated Mexico since independence.

NICARAGUA

Burns, E. Bradford. *Patriarch and Folk: The Emergence of Nicaragua, 1798–1858*. HUP 1991 $39.95. ISBN 0-674-65796-9. Relates how divisions among the elites and the strength of folk communities made it impossible for Nicaragua to build a minimal nation-state until 1858, when the elites combined sufficiently to crush the threatening power of the folk.

Cabezas, Omar. *Fire from the Mountain: The Making of a Sandinista*. NAL-Dutton 1986 $9.00. ISBN 0-452-26276-3. Memoir that follows a revolutionary's journey to manhood and shows who the Sandinistas are and how they came to power in 1979.

Diederich, Bernard. *Somoza and the Legacy of U.S. Involvement in Central America*. Wiener Pub. Inc. 1989 $12.95. ISBN 0-943862-42-6. Impassioned denunciation of the corrupt and brutal dictatorship of Anastasio Somoza Debayle.

Macaulay, Neill. *The Sandino Affair*. Duke 1985 $14.95. ISBN 0-8223-0696-4. Gripping account of the futile attempts on the part of the United States to capture or kill the Nicaraguan nationalist Augusto César Sandino in the late 1920s, one of the incidents that helped set the stage for the Nicaraguan uprising of the 1970s.

Selser, Gregorio. *Sandino*. Trans. by Cedric Belfrage. Monthly Rev. 1982 $10.00. ISBN 0-85345-559-7. Though lacking depth and some findings of recent scholars, still a useful introduction to Sandino's life, if only because it is one of the few serious biographies available in English.

Walker, Thomas W. *Nicaragua: The Land of Sandino*. Westview 1991 3rd rev. ed. $44.00. ISBN 0-8133-1090-3. The best available general history of Nicaragua and the Sandinista revolution by a knowledgeable author generally sympathetic to the Sandinista cause.

PANAMA

Conniff, Michael L. *Panama and the United States: The Forced Alliance*. U. of Ga. Pr. 1992 $35.00. ISBN 0-8203-1359-9. Views isthmian transportation—and its meaning for Panamanian sovereignty and economics and for U.S. economics and security—as the pivotal issue in U.S. relations with Panama.

Dinges, John. *Our Man in Panama: The Shrewd Rise and Brutal Fall of Manuel Noriega*. Random 1991 $13.00. ISBN 0-8129-1950-5. Incredibly detailed account of the career of the Panamanian strongman taken prisoner and tried by the United States.

Sketches Noriega's complex relationships with the CIA and other U.S. agencies, the drug business, and Fidel Castro. Not a pretty story.

LaFeber, Walter. *The Panama Canal: The Crisis in Historical Perspective.* OUP 1989 $13.95. ISBN 0-19-506192-6. Well-written and comprehensive survey that is highly sympathetic to Panamanian feelings about U.S. colonialist behavior in the isthmus during the twentieth century.

McCullough, David. *The Path between the Seas: The Creation of the Panama Canal, 1870–1914.* S & S Trade 1978 $14.95. ISBN 0-671-24409-4. Highly informative and entertaining book by a superb writer. Covers the diplomatic and technological story of how the canal came to be built by the United States inside an independent Panama.

Zimbalist, Andrew, and John Weeks. *Panama at the Crossroads: Economic Development and Political Change in the Twentieth Century.* U. CA Pr. 1991 $13.95. ISBN 0-520-07311-8. Examines how an economic system heavily dependent on the Canal, the Colón Free Trade Zone, and international banking contributed to social unrest and political instability.

PARAGUAY

Phelps, Gilbert. *Tragedy of Paraguay.* St. Martin 1975 $26.00. ISBN 0-312-81340-6. Moving and relatively balanced account of the controversial career of Paraguayan president Francisco Solano López and the disastrous war that his leadership provoked.

Roett, Riordan, and Richard S. Sacks. *Paraguay: The Personalist Legacy.* Westview 1991 $40.50. ISBN 0-86531-272-9. Succinct summary of Paraguayan history, economics, culture and society, politics and government, and international relations, with an emphasis on the policies and legacy of Alfredo Stroessner's personalist regime (1954–89).

Warren, Harris G. *Paraguay: An Informal History.* Greenwood 1982 repr. of 1949 ed. $65.00. ISBN 0-313-23651-8. Readable survey of Paraguay through the 1940s; one of very few available in English.

PERU

Americas Watch staff. *Peru under Fire: Human Rights Since the Return to Democracy.* Yale U. Pr. 1992 $23.50. ISBN 0-300-05237-5. Charts an increase in human rights violations in Peru over the last decade and criticizes U.S. policy in the face of an escalating civil conflict.

Dobyns, Henry F., and Paul L. Doughty. *Peru: A Cultural History.* OUP 1976 $22.50. ISBN 0-19-502-089-8. Scholarly and comprehensive, yet easy to read, overview of a country with a complex social history.

Mariátegui, José C. *Seven Interpretive Essays on Peruvian Reality.* Trans. by Marjory Urquidi. U. of Tex. Pr. 1988 $11.95. ISBN 0-292-77611-X. Major analysis of the problems of modern Peruvian society by the Marxist thinker who died in 1930, proclaiming the kinship of socialism and Peru's indigenous reform movement. A significant document in Peruvian political and intellectual history.

Palmer, David Scott, ed. *The Shining Path of Peru.* St. Martin 1992 $45.00. ISBN 0-312-06115-3. Considers the origins, ideology, organization, leadership, and social context of Sendero Luminoso (Shining Path), the guerilla movement that has caused so much violence in Peru since its founding in the early 1980s.

Rudolph, James D. *Peru: The Evolution of a Crisis.* Greenwood 1992 $42.95. ISBN 0-275-94146-9. Comprehensive and current political history that emphasizes the twentieth century.

PUERTO RICO

Carr, Raymond. *Puerto Rico: A Colonial Experiment.* NYU Pr. 1984 $40.00. ISBN 0-8147-1389-0. Controversial study that is still the best place to start for an appreciation of the complexity of the relations between the United States and the Commonwealth of Puerto Rico.

Fowlie-Flores, Fay, comp. *Annotated Bibliograhy of Puerto Rican Bibliograhies.* Greenwood 1990 $45.00. ISBN 0-313-26124-5. Good starting point for a study of Puerto Rico. Contains 563 titles organized by topic, with author and subject indexes.

Morales Carrión, Arturo, and others, eds. *Puerto Rico: A Political and Cultural History.* Norton 1983 o.p. Mainly a political history, divided into the Spanish and American periods, but with attention paid to the island's unique cultural heritage and its search for social identity and to the resulting interaction between politics and culture.

TRINIDAD-TOBAGO

Magid, Alvin. *Urban Nationalism: A Study of Political Development in Trinidad.* U. Pr. Fla. 1988 $28.95. ISBN 0-8130-0853-0

Naipaul, V. S. *The Loss of El Dorado.* Random 1984 o.p. Insightful analysis by a prominent author. Good place to start to gain an understanding of the legacy of colonialism in the emergence of modern Trinidad.

Ryan, Selwyn D. *Race and Nationalism in Trinidad and Tobago: A Study of Decolonization in Multiracial Society.* Bks. Demand 1972 $131.30. ISBN 0-317-55731-9

URUGUAY

Gillespie, Charles Guy. *Negotiating Democracy: Politicians and Generals in Uruguay.* Cambridge U. Pr. 1991 $49.50. ISBN 0-521-40152-6. Focusing on Uruguay's political parties, traces the process by which the military agreed to allow the restoration of democracy in the late 1980s.

González, Luis E. *Political Structures and Democracy in Uruguay.* U. of Notre Dame Pr. 1991 $26.95. ISBN 0-268-01589-9. Emphasizing the combination of presidentialism and factionalization, this work examines the sources of Uruguay's political crisis of the 1960s and 1970s and the obstacles to restored democracy after 1984.

VENEZUELA

Ellner, Steve. *Organized Labor in Venezuela, 1958–1991: Behavior and Concerns in a Democratic Setting.* Scholarly Res. Inc. 1993 $40.00. ISBN 0-8420-2443-3. Analyzes the modern Venezuelan labor movement in the context of Venezuela's alleged exceptionalism in the Latin American context. A good case study in labor history and useful in understanding the workings of Venezuelan democracy.

Levine, Daniel H. *Religion and Politics in Latin America: The Catholic Church in Venezuela and Colombia.* Princeton U. Pr. 1981 $15.95. ISBN 0691-02200-3. Emphasizes the variety of opinions and political views within Latin American Roman Catholicism. Especially good on the Venezuelan church.

Lombardi, John V. *Venezuela: The Search for Order, the Dream of Progress.* OUP 1982 $29.95. ISBN 0-19-503013-3. Basic survey of Venezuela's evolution through a long history of instability and poverty to leadership in the democratic world, with a rising standard of living.

Wright, Winthrop R. *Café con Leche: Race, Class, and National Image in Venezuela.* U. of Tex. Pr. 1990 $25.00. ISBN 0-292-71128-X. Using Venezuela as a case study, illuminates the subtleties and complexities of defining race and class in multiethnic Latin America compared to more simplistic North American perceptions.

CHRONOLOGY OF AUTHORS

Garcilaso de la Vega. c.1540–c.1616

Prescott, William H(ickling). 1796–1859

Bolton, Herbert E(ugene). 1870–1953

Tannenbaum, Frank. 1893–1969

Cosío Villegas, Daniel. 1898–1976

Arciniegas, Germán. 1900–

Freyre, Gilberto. 1900–1987

James, C(yril) L(ionel) R(obert). 1901–1989

Hanke, Lewis U(lysses). 1905–1993
Cline, Howard F(rancis). 1915–1971
Scobie, James R(alston). 1929–1981

ARCINIEGAS, GERMÁN. 1900–

Writer and historian Germán Arciniegas was born in Bogotá, Colombia, the son of a Colombian father and a Cuban mother. A skilled observer of society, he has written about Latin American history and culture in numerous books, essays, biographies, and articles in magazines and newspapers all over the Americas.

As a historian, Arciniegas complains that textbooks on history are generally limited to political history, "what government officials and warriors did." He takes pride, on the other hand, in writing "la pequena historia" (the little history), or what MIGUEL DE UNAMUNO Y JUGO (see Vol. 2) called "intrahistoria" (inner history). Thus, most of his work focuses, not on the political history of specific countries, but on the many facets of Latin American culture and society in general, and he has devoted thousands of pages to narratives of common people, common events, and common things. His literary legacy is an excellent point of departure from which to penetrate into the Latin American psyche.

The most controversial aspect of Arciniegas's writing is his treatment of Spain. He is often critical of the conquistadores, the Spanish crown, and the colonial system in general. He is a firm believer in the *Leyenda Negra*, or Black Legend, which holds that the conquistadores killed the Indians, the colonists exhausted the mines, and the Spanish officials did nothing but justify the abuses that they themselves often perpetrated. Even so, he concedes that the people who conquered America were ordinary people, some from the lowest strata of Spanish society, and his descriptions of Spanish expeditions in America enhance the heroic status of many of these anonymous early explorers.

BOOKS BY ARCINIEGAS

Caribbean, Sea of the New World. 1945. Knopf 1946 o.p. Contains a number of anecdotal and entertaining pieces dealing with the people, culture, and society of the Caribbean region.
Latin America: A Cultural History. 1965. Knopf 1967 o.p.
America in Europe: A History of the New World in Reverse. 1975. HarBraceJ 1986 o.p. Argues that the influence of the New World on the Old has been neglected by historians, and tries to remedy that fault.
The State of Latin America. 1952. Knopf 1952 o.p. A series of sociopolitical essays about Latin American society and culture.

BOLTON, HERBERT E(UGENE). 1870–1953

Born in Wilton, Wisconsin, Herbert Bolton became one of the pioneers in Latin American history as well as the history of the southwestern United States. After an apprenticeship as a printer's devil and several years teaching school, Bolton entered the University of Wisconsin to study law. While at the university, however, he came under the influence of historian FREDERICK JACKSON TURNER, and his interest began shifting to history. After receiving a PH.D. in history from the University of Pennsylvania, Bolton taught first at Milwaukee State Normal School and then at the University of Texas.

Bolton's position at the University of Texas became a turning point in his career. Surrounded by evidences of Spanish and Mexican culture, he began to focus his studies and work on the history and culture of Latin America in relation to the United States. His first significant historical work, *Guide to Materials for the History of the United States in the Principal Archives of Mexico* (1913), proved to be a milestone in American historiography and launched him on a career that eventually made him the foremost Latin American historian of his time.

In 1909 Bolton moved to Calfornia, first to Stanford University and then to the University of California at Berkeley, where he remained until his retirement in 1940. It was in California that his ideas matured, particularly his concept of the history of the Americas as a unifying theme in American history. At Berkeley, Bolton launched a new course, "History of the Americas," which became legendary on campus. As professor and chairman of the history department, his influence was enormous, and he attracted thousands of students from all over the country, instilling in them the importance of Latin American history and its role in the history of the American Southwest. Out of his seminars came hundreds of doctoral dissertations and thousands of Masters' theses—an enormous contribution to knowledge from the classroom of one individual. In addition to his influence as a teacher, Bolton also contributed numbers of significant works. Among them are *Spanish Exploration in the Southwest* (1916), *Anza's California Expeditions* (1930), and *History of the Americas* (1935).

For his contributions, Bolton was honored by the king of Spain in 1925, decorated as Comendador de la Real Orden de Isabel la Católica. In 1949 Pope Pius XII named him a Knight of St. Sylvester in recognition of his monumental labors in the history of the Catholic church in America. Bolton also received a Bancroft Prize in 1949 for his distiguished writings in American history.

BOOKS BY BOLTON

Anza's California Expeditions. 1930. 5 vols. Rt. Serv. 1991 repr. of 1930 ed. $375.00. ISBN 0-7812-6337-9

Coronado: Knight of the Pueblos and Plains. 1949. U. of NM Pr. 1990 $15.95. ISBN 0-8263-0007-3

Fray Juan Crespi, Missionary Explorer on the Pacific Coast. 1927. AMS Pr. repr. of 1927 ed. $29.00. ISBN 0-404-01838-6

Guide to Materials for the History of the United States in the Principal Archives of Mexico. 1913. Kraus $45.00. ISBN 0-527-00698-X

History of the Americas. 1935. Greenwood 1980 repr. of 1935 ed. $45.00. ISBN 0-8371-5273-9

Spanish Exploration in the Southwest. 1916. Rt. Serv. 1992 repr. of 1925 ed. $75.00. ISBN 0-7812-5009-9

Texas in the Middle Eighteenth Century: Studies in Spanish Colonial History and Administration. 1915. U. of Tex. Pr. 1970 $10.95. ISBN 0-292-70034-2

BOOKS ABOUT BOLTON

Bannon, John F. *Herbert Eugene Bolton: The Historian and the Man, 1870–1953*. U. of Ariz. Pr. 1978 $15.00. ISBN 0-8165-0557-8. Well-written and researched biography of Bolton, focusing on his contributions to Latin American history.

Hanke, Lewis, ed. *Do the Americas Have a Common History? A Critique of the Bolton Theory*. Knopf 1964 o.p. Series of essays examining Bolton's views of history and the relation between Latin American history and that of the United States.

Jacobs, Wilbur R., and others. *Turner, Bolton, and Webb: Three Historians of the American Frontier*. U. of Wash. Pr. 1979 $5.95. ISBN 0-295-95677-1. Looks at Bolton's role as a pioneer historian of the American Southwest.

CLINE, HOWARD F(RANCIS). 1915–1971

Born in Detroit, Howard Francis Cline received undergraduate and graduate degrees from Harvard University, where he specialized in Mexican history mainly under the direction of historian Clarence Haring. With a special interest in social and ethnic history, having spent a year working in the Mexican Department of Indian Affairs, Cline wrote his doctoral dissertation on social conflict in mid-nineteenth-century Yucatán. He then looked at the larger sweep of Mexican history and the critical decades of the mid-twentieth century. His books on these latter topics were standard reading for a generation of students of Mexican history after World War II and contributed to the growing appreciation in the United States of the importance of Mexico and its history. Like FRANK TANNENBAUM, Cline did much to make the Mexican revolution understandable to a U.S. audience.

From 1952 until his death, Cline served as director of the Hispanic Foundation of the Library of Congress. He also was a prime mover in the 1967 Conference on Latin American History. In this role he inaugurated the publication of various invaluable reference works, including his own two-volume edited survey of Mexican historical studies.

BOOKS BY CLINE

Latin American History: Essays on Its Study and Teaching, 1898–1965. 2 vols. U. of Wis. Pr. 1979 repr. of 1967 ed. $40.00. ISBN 0-299-08190-7. Collection of essays compiled and edited by Cline. Provides a useful introduction to a field just gaining full professional status by the early 1960s.

Mexico: From Revolution to Evolution, 1940–1960. Greenwood 3rd ed. 1981 $38.50. ISBN 0-313-22993-7. Views the decades after Cárdenas (1934–40) as a period of slowdown in Mexico's revolutionary zeal.

The United States and Mexico. 1953. Atheneum rev. ed. 1963 o.p. For many years a standard survey of Mexican history and Mexico's interaction with the United States. Still useful for the pre-1960 period.

COSÍO VILLEGAS, DANIEL. 1898–1976

Typical of Latin American intellectuals of his day, Daniel Cosío Villegas was international in his orientation and multifaceted in his education and career. He studied in Mexico, the United States, England, and France and functioned as economist, banker, diplomat, writer, publisher, teacher, and administrator. He worked for the Mexican government, the United Nations, public and private universities, professional journals, and academic presses.

As a historian Cosío Villegas was especially interested in the political history of Mexico between the 1860s and the 1930s. Although his nine-volume *Historia Moderna de México* (1955–72) never has appeared in English, his research and writing have strongly influenced many North Americans and Mexicans. Although he was a Mexican nationalist and partisan liberal, his work nonetheless set new standards for the exploitation of documents and reasoned analysis. His public service and writings on contemporary issues likewise contributed much to Mexican society in his lifetime. Some consider him the "dean" of modern Mexican historians.

BOOKS BY COSÍO VILLEGAS

American Extremes. Trans. by Américo Paredes. U. of Tex. Pr. 1964 o.p. Collection of 10 essays that reflect the breadth and convictions of the author and provide provocative comments on the United States, the world arena, and Mexican themes.

The United States and Porfirio Díaz. Trans. by Nettie Lee Benson. U. of Nebr. Pr. 1963 o.p.
A model for case studies in diplomatic history, reflecting Mexican nationalistic pride
in what the author considers a rare Mexican diplomatic victory in the nineteenth
century.

FREYRE, GILBERTO (DE MELLO). 1900–1987

Born in Recife, Brazil, the son of a teacher and judge, Gilberto Freyre was
educated at Baylor University in Texas and Columbia University. Considered the
twentieth-century pioneer in studies of northeastern Brazil, he gained international renown for his work tracing the evolution of modern Brazilian society
from its roots in the slaveholding culture of past centuries. Much of Freyre's
work is concerned with relating the socioeconomic development of the
northeastern region of Brazil to the Portuguese-speaking nations of Africa. One
of his basic premises is that the Portuguese were successful in building a
multicultural and multiracial society in South America because of their Afro-
European cultural experience prior to the discovery of Brazil.

Freyre's best-known work is *The Masters and the Slaves* (1933), an account of
the relationship between Brazil's Portuguese colonizers and their African slaves.
The book is praised as one of the outstanding works of Latin American
scholarship and a brilliant analysis of the origin of Brazilian cultural mores and
racial attitudes. In this work, Freyre breaks new ground with his multidisciplin-
ary approach to history in which he emphasizes the small details of everyday
social life as a means of illustrating the broader sweep of historical events.

Freyre's critics have accused him of exaggerating the degree of racial
democracy in Brazil and of ignoring widespread and longstanding discrimination against dark-skinned Brazilians. Despite such criticism, Freyre's work has
helped to demolish old racist myths and to point out the benefits of mestizism.
In doing so, it has helped to revolutionize the Brazilian people's self-image,
encouraging a new sense of pride in cultural diversity and an identity as a
mixed-race nation.

Freyre was twice nominated for the Nobel Prize in literature, and he was
knighted by Queen Elizabeth II in 1971.

BOOKS BY FREYRE

Brazil: An Interpretation. 1945. Greenwood 1980 o.p.
The Mansions and the Shanties. 1936. U. CA Pr. 1986 $15.95. ISBN 0-520-05681-7. Traces
the processes of urbanization and the decline of the rural patriarchal society in
Brazil.
The Masters and the Slaves. 1933. U. CA Pr. 1986 $17.95. ISBN 0-520-05665-5
Order and Progress: Brazil from Monarchy to Republic. 1959. Greenwood 1980 $55.00.
ISBN 0-313-22363-7

GARCILASO DE LA VEGA (EL INCA). 1539–1616

Born in Cuzco, Peru, the son of a Spanish conquistador and an Incan
princess, Garcilaso de la Vega is often considered the first spokesperson for the
South American mestizo. Garcilaso spent much of his youth listening to stories
of the culture and glories of his mother's civilization and the heroics of his
father's conquering comrades. At age 20, after the death of his parents, he
moved to Spain, where he spent the rest of his life. In Spain he served for a time
in the Spanish army, was ordained a priest, and wrote on a variety of subjects.
His account of Hernando de Soto's travels in Florida, *The Florida of the Inca*
(1605), set the stage for his more personal interest in the pre-Hispanic history of
his homeland of Peru. This interest culminated in his masterpiece, *Royal*

Commentaries of the Incas (1609), in which he movingly describes the Inca empire and its conquest by Spain.

A mestizo, Garcilaso wrote a mestizo history in the *Royal Commentaries*, both praising and criticizing his parents' peoples. His work is less true history, in the modern sense, than a memoir or a source on which to build history. His desire to know and understand the past in order to know one's self and one's present reflected a serious historical consciousness and made Garcilaso one of several sixteenth-century chroniclers whose writings began a long Latin American narrative tradition. Their work, with its factual as well as emotional content, continues to enrich the work of students of the Euro-American encounter. Garcilaso was also among the first to appreciate that bicultural encounter from the perspective of the conquered indigenous populations.

BOOKS BY GARCILASO DE LA VEGA

The Florida of the Inca. 1605. Trans. and ed. by John G. and Jeannette Varner. U. of Tex. Pr. 1951 $18.95. ISBN 0-292-72434-9. Focuses on the career of Hernando de Soto and other heroic Spanish conquerors of the New World.

Royal Commentaries of the Incas, and General History of Peru. 2 vols. Trans. by Harold V. Livermore. U. of Tex. Pr. 1966 o.p. The author's classic work, based on extensive reading, lengthy interviews, and childhood memories. A rich source of detail about the Incas both before and after the Spanish conquest of Peru. Includes a foreword by Arnold Toynbee.

BOOKS ABOUT GARCILASO DE LA VEGA

Castanien, Donald Garner. *El Inca Garcilaso de la Vega.* Twayne 1969 o.p. A short, readable introduction to the life and writings of El Inca; enthusiastically favorable toward the subject.

Varner, John G. *El Inca: The Life and Times of Garcilaso de la Vega.* U. of Tex. Pr. 1968 $25.00. ISBN 0-292-78375-2. A balanced study by a scholar who knew his subject well; more detailed and comprehensive than the Castanien work.

HANKE, LEWIS (ULYSSES). 1905–1993

Latin American historian Lewis Hanke was born in Oregon City, Oregon. After receiving undergraduate and graduate degrees at Northwestern University, he taught for several years at the American University in Beirut before returning to the United States to work on a doctoral degree at Harvard University. Upon receiving his Ph.D. in 1936, Hanke founded and published the initial volume of the *Handbook of Latin American Studies.* Since its founding, the *Handbook* has become an indispensable interdisciplinary tool for researchers on Latin America.

A tireless researcher and prolific writer, Hanke consistently stressed the importance of history as a basic key to human self-awareness and global understanding. He revealed his own commitment to history throughout his writings, most conspicuously on Spanish attitudes and behavior toward Indians in colonial Latin America. Hist best-known work, *The Spanish Stuggle for Justice in the Conquest of America* (1949), examines the efforts of Spanish theologians to define and defend the humanity of the indigenous populations of Latin America.

Among Hanke's other works are *The First Social Experiments in America* (1935) and *The Imperial city of Potosi* (1956), both of which anticipated and precipitated the modern analysis of Latin American social history. He also wrote several works on the Spanish missionary Bartolomé de las Casas, including *Bartolomé de las Casas: Bookman, Scholar, and Propagandist* (1952), and

Bartolomé de las Casas in History: Toward an Understanding of the Man and His Work (1974).

Throughout his career, Hanke stuggled to develop Latin American history as a legitimate field of scholarship. It was this determination that led to the founding of the *Handbook*. At the same time, he urged historians to develop intellectual perspectives on a global scale. He maintained that there is a need for U.S. historians to broaden their knowledge of other cultures and for foreign historians to learn more about the United States, because no single history can be properly understood in isolation.

Hanke taught at the University of Texas, Columbia Universtiy, the University of California at Irvine, and the University of Massachusetts, where he was professor emeritus. In addition to his editorship of *The Handbook of Latin American Studies*, he served as president of the American Historical Association, director of the Hispanic Foundation, and member of various historical societies throughout Latin America.

BOOKS BY HANKE

Bartolomé de las Casas in History: Toward an Understanding of the Man and His Work. N. Ill. U. Pr. 1974 $30.00. ISBN 0-87580-025-4

The First Social Experiments in America. Peter Smith 1964 o.p.

The Imperial City of Potosi: An Unwritten Chapter in the History of Spanish America. Nijhoff 1956 o.p.

In Defense of the Indians. N. Ill. U. Pr. 1974 $30.00. ISBN 0-87580-042-4

The Spanish Struggle for Justice in the Conquest of America. U. of Pa. Pr. 1949 o.p.

JAMES, C(YRIL) L(IONEL) R(OBERT). 1901–1989

A native of Trinidad, C. L. R. James grew up in a very respectable middle-class black family steeped in British manners and culture. Although justifiably well-known in the British world as a writer, historian, and political activist, his contributions have been underappreciated in the United States. A student of history, literature, philosophy, and culture, James thought widely and wrote provocatively. He also turned his words into deeds as a journalist, a Trotskyite, a Pan-African activist, a Trinidadian nationalist politican, a university teacher, and a government official.

James was a teacher and magazine editor in Trinidad until the early 1930s, when he went to England and became a sports writer for the *Manchester Guardian*. While in England he became a dedicated Marxist organizer. In 1938 he moved to the United States and continued his political activities, founding an organization dedicated to the principles of Trotskyism. His politics led to his expulsion from the United States in 1953, and he returned to Trinidad, from which he was also expelled in the early 1960s. He spent the remainder of his life in England.

Among James's extensive writings, the two most influential volumes are *Black Jacobins* (1967), a study of the anti-French Dominican (Haitian) slave rebellion of the 1790s, and *Beyond a Boundary* (1963), a remarkable exploration of sport, specifically cricket, as social and political history. Other important works include *A History of Negro Revolt* (1938) and *The Life of Captain Cipriani* (1932). James represents an unusual combination of activist-reformer (even revolutionary) and promoter of the best in art, culture, and gentility.

BOOKS BY JAMES

Beyond a Boundary. 1963. Pantheon 1984 $8.95. ISBN 0-394-722283-3. A classic description of the role of cricket as both a colonizing force in the British West Indies

and as a means by which the suppressed black majority developed a source of
cultural identity and political independence.

Black Jacobins: Toussaint l'Ouverture and the San Domingo Revolution. 1967. Random
1989 $14.00. ISBN 0-679-72467-2. Perhaps the most impassioned explanation of the
1790s black rebellion against the French slave system in today's Haiti.

C.L.R. James Reader. Blackwell Pubs. 1992 $19.95. ISBN 0-631-18495-3. A stimulating
introduction to the breadth and grace of James's extensive writings.

The Life of Captain Cipriani: An Account of British Government in the West Indies. 1932.
Hogarth 1933 o.p. One of the first works to urge full self-determination for West
Indians.

BOOK ABOUT JAMES

Buhle, Paul. *C.L.R. James: The Artist as Revolutionary.* Routledge Chapman & Hall 1988
$35.00. ISBN 0-86091-221-3. A highly sympathetic analysis of the interaction
between James's writings and his political actions and impact.

PRESCOTT, WILLIAM H(ICKLING). 1796–1859

Born into a wealthy family in Salem, Massachusetts, educated at Harvard
University, and virtually blind most of his adult life, William Hickling Prescott
was known for his charm, friendliness, charity, and generosity. After touring
Europe for several years following his 1814 graduation from Harvard, he
returned to Boston to study European history and literature. With the help of
secretaries who read to him and odd mechanical aids, and driven by courage,
patience, and rigorous self-discipline, he challenged his adversity and became a
prolific writer on various topics. He contributed his first piece to the *North
American Review* in 1821. In 1937 he came out with his first major historical
work, *History of the Reign of Ferdinand and Isabella the Catholic*, which quickly
became a great success. The 1904 edition of his collected works required 22
volumes.

In the field of Latin American history, Prescott's monumental works are the
three-volume *History of the Conquest of Mexico* (1843) and the *History of the
Conquest of Peru* (1847). Large, detailed, comprehensive studies rich in
excitement and imagery, they are profusely documented with sources in
numerous languages, reflecting Prescott's commitment to accuracy. Although
these two works reflect a certain Christian bias against the Native Americans
and an Anglo-Saxon bias against the Spanish, Prescott had such high integrity,
love of truth, and admiration for life that all of his characters appear to a degree
heroic.

Even before producing the *Conquest* volumes, Prescott had considered
writing a history of the reign of the Spanish ruler Philip II. He spent the better
part of the rest of his life on that work, *The History of the Reign of Philip the
Second* (1855–58). Only 3 volumes of the 10 he had hoped to produce were
completed. And, in the view of many, they were his weakest contribution.

Although later scholarship has altered many of Prescott's factual and
interpretive assertions, the comprehensiveness of his sources makes his books a
good place to start for researchers even today, just as the quality of his narrative
continues to make his text very good literature. Prescott clearly knew how to
tell a good story. Collectively, his massive surveys earned him the respect of
archivists, historians, writers, and statesmen across Europe and North America.
Prescott was a remarkable human being whose historical legacy continues to
thrill new readers.

BOOK BY PRESCOTT

History of the Conquest of Mexico and History of the Conquest of Peru. Random 1979 $15.95. ISBN 0-685-19921-5

BOOKS ABOUT PRESCOTT

Cline, Howard F., and others, eds. *William Hickling Prescott: A Memorial.* Bks. Demand repr. of 1959 ed. $47.30. ISBN 0-317-42233-2. Assessment of Prescott's legacy by a group of modern scholars.

Darnell, Donald G. *William Hickling Prescott.* Twayne 1975 o.p. Although short, a good introduction to Prescott's life and works.

SCOBIE, JAMES R(ALSTON). 1929–1981

Latin American scholar and historian James Scobie was born in Valparaiso, Chile. The son of an educator and banker, he was educated at Princeton University and Harvard University, receiving his Ph.D. from the latter in 1954. In addition to teaching at Indiana University and the University of California at San Diego, Scobie was active in the Latin American Studies Association and the Pacific Coast Council on Latin American Studies. The primary focus of his work has been Argentina, and his published works include *Argentina: A City and a Nation* (1964), *Revolution on the Pampas* (1964), and *Buenos Aires: From Plaza to Suburb* (1974). Between 1967–69 and 1980–81, Scobie was the advisory editor of the *Latin American Research Review.* He was awarded a Guggenheim fellowship in 1967–68.

BOOKS BY SCOBIE

Argentina: A City and a Nation. 1964. OUP 1971 o.p. Overview of Argentine society and culture, focusing on the primacy of Buenos Aires.

Buenos Aires: From Plaza to Suburb, 1870–1910. 1974. OUP 1978 $17.50. ISBN 0-19-501821-4. Study of Buenos Aires and its power and impact on Argentine society.

Revolution on the Pampas: A Social History of Argentina Wheat, 1860–1910. 1964. U. of Tex. Pr. 1964 o.p.

Secondary Cities of Argentina: The Social History of Corrientes, Salta, and Mendoza. Stanford U. Pr. 1988 $45.00. ISBN 0-8047-1419-3. Multidisciplinary, in-depth study of three medium-sized Argentine cities.

TANNENBAUM, FRANK. 1893–1969

A native of Austria, Frank Tannenbaum migrated to the United States in 1905. In America his concern for land, workers, and human justice led to a long career in journalism, academia, and the promotion of social change. In 1921, following membership in the Industrial Workers of the World and a short prison term for "disturbing the peace"—actually helping the homeless—he graduated Phi Beta Kappa from Columbia College. In 1927 he earned a doctorate in economics from the Brookings Institution. Over the years he served in the U.S. cavalry; traveled extensively, especially in Latin America; championed prison reform; and served as an adviser to the Mexican government. By 1935 he had joined the faculty of Columbia University, from which he retired as professor of Latin American history in 1961. There he trained several generations of students and was instrumental in developing the renowned University Seminar Program.

Tannenbaum's major contributions to scholarly writing on Latin America fall into two categories. One is his work on the post-1910 Mexican revolution, with emphasis on agrarian reform, industrialization, and the pursuit of democracy. The work was widely read on both sides of the Río Grande, winning him friendships and awards among both Mexican leaders and his North American colleagues. The second is his 1947 work *Slave and Citizen*, which raised for a large U.S. audience key questions about the nature of slavery and race relations in the Americas. Although much of the "Tannenbaum thesis" has been refuted by later scholars, Tannenbaum had the imagination to pursue a line of comparative analysis little seen before and to challenge his white compatriots to seek better ways to treat racial minorities.

Perhaps a fitting monument to Tannenbaum's breadth of vision and commitment to expanded education is his *Ten Keys to Latin America* (1962). This prize-winning book, now somewhat outdated and out of print, was for thousands of readers an enjoyable thematic introduction to the essence of Latin American society.

BOOKS BY TANNENBAUM

The Mexican Agrarian Revolution. Shoe String 1968 repr. of 1929 ed., $49.50. ISBN 0-208-00709-1. Sympathetic description of Mexico's effort to achieve social justice through land reform under the constitution of 1917.

Mexico: The Struggle for Peace and Bread. Greenwood 1984 repr. of 1968 ed. $47.50. ISBN 0-313-24453-7. Calls for continued encouragement of the best of Mexico's programs for change.

Peace by Revolution: An Interpretation of Mexico. Ayer repr. of 1933 ed. $26.50. ISBN 0-8369-5996-5. Seeks to explain Mexico's revolutionary path at the beginning of the critical administration of Lázaro Cárdenas, a personal friend of the author.

Slave and Citizen: The Negro in the Americas. Beacon Pr. 1992 repr. of 1947 ed. $11.95. ISBN 0-8070-0913-X. Argues that blacks as slaves or as freemen were more highly regarded as human beings and thus better treated in Latin America than in British North America.

Ten Keys to Latin America. Knopf 1963 o.p. An introduction to Latin America through such themes as race, religion, regionalism, education, politics, and the role of the United States.

Part Two

The Arts and Popular Culture

CHAPTER 18

Music and Dance

Michael A. Keller and Suzanne Eggleston

The trumpet shall be heard high
The dead shall live, the living die,
And Music shall untune the sky!
— JOHN DRYDEN, *A Song for St. Cecilia's Day*

The hills and the sea and the earth dance. The world of man dances in
laughter and tears. . . . and the Creator is well pleased.
—KABIR, 15th-century Indian poet

Music and dance are constants in the human environment. The beginnings of
these arts predate written history. They have served as part of religious,
ceremonial, and work activities, as well as provided aesthetic pleasure. From
the work songs of the pyramid builders to the background elevator music and
the rap music of the present era, music and the movement to its rhythm, or
dance, have been common to every segment of society. For much of history,
however, experiencing a professional performance has been an infrequent
occurrence for most people. Modern technology has radically changed this
situation so that music to suit a wide variety of tastes is readily and
inexpensively available. Radio, television, and home entertainment systems are
pouring forth a continual blanket of music. Nor are people restricted by
location—portable radios and cassette and CD players allow them to enjoy their
favorite sounds everywhere. More people have heard and seen PAVAROTTI on
one television program than have attended all of CARUSO's performances, and
such artists as NUREYEV and BARYSHNIKOV have danced for larger audiences
than NIJINSKY would have dreamed possible.

These technological changes have sparked an interest in the greater understanding of music and dance—in their history, criticism of them, and in the
personalities involved in these two art forms. The titles listed below not only
cover the more traditional forms of opera, classical music, and ballet but also
include jazz, ethnic music and dance, and contemporary music and dance.
Nearly all of the books selected incorporate references to sources and are
replete with bibliographies, indexes, glossaries, illustrations, and other aids to
the reader.

MUSIC

General Reference

Allen, Daniel. *Bibliography of Discographies, Vol. 2: Jazz.* Bowker 1981 $40.00. ISBN 0-
8352-1342-0. Because most of the information here was found buried in monographs

and periodicals, this guide to the literature about jazz recordings is an invaluable reference.

Arnold, Denis, ed. *The New Oxford Companion to Music*. 2 vols. OUP 1983 $135.00. ISBN 0-19-311316-3. Dictionary of terms, titles, people, forms, places, and periods of musical significance. Oriented to the general reader and complete in itself, with a British slant.

ASCAP Biographical Dictionary. Bowker 1980 o.p. Composers and authors licensed by ASCAP completed questionnaires serving as the basis for the approximately 10,000 entries.

Ayre, Leslie. *The Gilbert and Sullivan Companion*. Dodd 1972 o.p. Brief essay on the careers of Gilbert and Sullivan, followed by a dictionary of works, people, places, characters, songs, and favorite lines in their productions. Introduction by Martyn Green.

Bane, Michael. *Who's Who in Rock*. Facts on File 1981 o.p. Crucial facts on the 1,200 most famous individuals and groups in rock and closely related musical genres.

Barlow, Harold, and Sam Morgenstern, eds. *A Dictionary of Musical Themes*. Crown Pub. Group rev. ed. 1989 $24.95. ISBN 0-517-52446-5. Themes of orchestral literature in original keys displayed in musical notation. Introduction by J. Erskine.

————. *A Dictionary of Opera and Song Themes*. Crown Pub. Group 1976 o.p. A list by composer of famous vocal themes.

Block, Adrienne F., and Carol Neuls-Bates, eds. *Women in American Music: A Bibliography of Music and Literature*. Greenwood 1979 $49.95. ISBN 0-313-21410-7. Classical bibliography including abstracts about women in American music.

Brody, Elaine, and Claire Brooke. *The Music Guide to Austria and Germany*. Dodd 1976 o.p. Musical Baedeker, arranged by city, covering guides and services, opera houses and concert houses, concert series, libraries and museums, conservatories and schools, musical landmarks, musical organizations, and the business of music.

————. *The Music Guide to Belgium, Luxembourg, Holland and Switzerland*. Dodd 1977 o.p.

————. *The Music Guide to Great Britain*. Dodd 1976 o.p.

————. *The Music Guide to Italy*. Dodd 1978 o.p.

Brook, Barry S. *Thematic Catalogs in Music: An Annotated Bibliography*. Pendragon NY 1972 $42.00. ISBN 0-918728-02-9. Works covering varied bodies of music by composer(s), manuscript(s), publisher(s), and so on, in systematic order, providing positive identification by reference to musical concepts or themes. Citations in musical notation.

Bull, Storm. *Index to Biographies of Contemporary Composers*. Scarecrow 1987 $65.00. ISBN 0-8108-1930-9. A tabular index to periodical articles and dictionary entries in approximately 185 sources on composers active in the twentieth century up to 1973.

Claghorn, Charles E. *Biographical Dictionary of American Music*. Parker Pub. IL 1973 o.p. Includes entries for American lyricists, librettists, hymnists, and other musicians.

————. *Biographical Dictionary of Jazz*. P-H 1983 o.p. Dictionary of jazz musicians; includes such information as birthdates, family, residence, and career highlights.

Cobbett, Walter Wilson, and Colin Mason, eds. *Cobbett's Cyclopedic Survey of Chamber Music*. 3 vols. OUP 1987 $275.00. ISBN 0-19-318306-4. Dictionary of articles about ensemble music; the chamber musician's standard reference work.

Cohen, Aaron I. *International Encyclopedia of Women Composers*. Bks. Music USA 1987 $130.00 ISBN 0-9617485-2-4. Brief biographical sketches of more than 5,000 women composers, most with lists of works.

Craig, Warren. *Sweet and Lowdown: America's Popular Song Writers*. Scarecrow 1978 $40.00. ISBN 0-8108-1089-1. A biographical dictionary with indexes to song titles and musicals.

Crofton, Ian, comp. *A Dictionary of Musical Quotations*. Schirmer Bks. 1985 $14.95. ISBN 0-02-870622-6. A collection of more than 3,000 notable, often celebrated, utterances by and about music and musicians; organized within almost 300 headings, with indexes.

Davies, John H. *Musicalalia: Sources of Information in Music.* Pergamon 1966 o.p. Excellent book organized by categories of researchers (e.g., listener, singer, collector).

De Lerma, Dominque René. *Bibliography of Black Music* 4 vols. Greenwood. Vol. 1 *Reference Materials.* 1981 $45.00. ISBN 0-313-21340-2. Vol. 2 *Afro-American Idioms.* 1981 $49.95. ISBN 0-313-21344-3. Vol. 3 *Geographical Studies.* 1982 $49.95. ISBN 0-313-23510-4. Vol. 4 o.p. Including more than 100,000 entries in all four volumes, this set is the definitive bibliography on the music of Africa and the African diaspora.

Del Mar, Norman. *The Anchor Companion to the Orchestra.* Doubleday 1987 $19.95. ISBN 0-385-24081-3. Presents essential information about the orchestra and its instruments in a ready-reference style format.

Diamond, Harold J. *Music Criticism: An Annotated Guide to the Literature.* Scarecrow 1979 $25.00. ISBN 0-8108-1268-1. Annotated index to critical and analytical writings about musical compositions drawn from many sources; not comprehensive, but very helpful.

Duckles, Vincent, and Michael A. Keller. *Music Reference and Research Materials: An Annotated Bibliography.* Macmillan rev. ed. 1993 $45.00. ISBN 0-02-870822-9. Describes more than 3,000 music-reference works, principally works covering Western music.

Eisler, Paul E. *World Chronology of Music History.* 6 vols. Oceana 1980 $270.00. ISBN 0-379-16080-3. Entries by year, month, and day for large and small events and achievements in music history.

Fink, Roberts, and Robert Ricci. *The Language of Twentieth-Century Music.* Schirmer Bks. 1975 o.p. Definitions of the basic terms of twentieth-century musical styles: computer and electronic music, film music, jazz, and so on, with a topical listing of terms and bibliographies arranged by style.

Fuld, James J. *The Book of World Famous Music: Classical, Popular and Folk.* Dover 1985 repr. of 1966 ed. $15.95. ISBN 0-486-24857-7. Entries by title include information about compositions, origins, variants, sources, and first and early editions; contains basic historical information about hundreds of well-known melodies. With an introduction providing information about publishing and copyrighting music. The music-reference librarian's secret weapon.

Green, Stanley. *Encyclopedia of the Musical Theatre.* Da Capo 1980 repr. of 1976 ed. $14.95. ISBN 0-306-80113-2. Alphabetical array of short articles on the facts about the most important people, productions, and songs of the musical theater in New York and London. Avoids vaudeville, Gilbert and Sullivan, one-act or one-person shows, and similar genres; includes lists of awards.

———. *The World of Musical Comedy.* Da Capo 1984 repr. of 1980 ed. $22.50. ISBN 0-306-80207-4. Covers the vast, vaguely defined area between opera and vaudeville through a discussion of significant composers.

Griffiths, Paul. *The Thames and Hudson Encyclopaedia of 20th-Century Music.* Thames Hudson 1986 $19.95. ISBN 0-500-23449-3. Provides a basic gazetteer to the confusing world of twentieth-century music. Covers over 500 composers.

Heyer, Anna H. *Historical Sets, Collected Editions, and Monuments of Music.* 2 vols. ALA 1981 $87.50. ISBN 0-8389-0288-X. Covers complete editions of the works of individual composers and major published collections of music. Reveals the wealth of music not ordinarily accessible through library catalogs, but nevertheless in library collections.

Hitchcock, H. Wiley, and Stanley Sadie. *The New Grove Dictionary of American Music.* 4 vols. Macmillan 1986 $695.00. ISBN 0-943818-36-2. Articles on American music, covering musicians, works, events, terms, and numerous special topics, providing information formerly scattered among numerous sources. Easily the most important single reference work on American music.

Hughes, Andrew. *Medieval Music: The Sixth Liberal Art.* U. of Toronto Pr. 1980 $45.00. ISBN 0-8020-2358-4. Classified and annotated bibliography of approximately 2,300 works about medieval music.

International Who's Who in Music and Musician's Directory 1990-91. Intl. Pubns. Serv. 1990 $150.00. ISBN 0-948875-20-8. More than 8,000 biographical entries submitted by the subjects.

Jablonski, Edward. *The Encyclopedia of American Music*. Doubleday 1982 o.p. Essays divided into historical periods in American music covering significant events and developments of each period.

Jacobs, Arthur. *The Penguin Dictionary of Musical Performers*. Viking Penguin 1990 $21.95. ISBN 0-670-80755-9. A listing of thousands of musical performers from the sixteenth century to the present, with information about the major achievements of each.

Julian, John, ed. *A Dictionary of Hymnology: Origin and History of Christian Hymns*. 4 vols. Gordon Pr. 1977 $1,200.00. ISBN 0-8490-1719-X. Systematic, classic reference work.

Kallmann, Helmutt, and others, eds. *Encyclopedia of Music in Canada*. U. of Toronto Pr. 1981 $85.00. ISBN 0-8020-5509-5. Covers activities and contributions of Canadian individuals and music organizations.

Kernfeld, Barry. *The New Grove Dictionary of Jazz*. Groves Dict. Music 1988 $350.00. ISBN 0-935859-39-X. Thorough, scholarly dictionary with all of the apparatus of scholarship on the important subject of jazz at its broadest and most international definition, treating people, places, recording companies, works, events, and ensembles with extensive, signed articles in this first-rate work.

Kinkle, Roger D. *The Complete Encyclopedia of Popular Music and Jazz, 1900–1950*. 4 vols. Crown Pub. Group 1974 o.p. Complex, authoritative work including people who were active before 1950, with the first volume providing a chronological list of important musical works and volumes two and three containing biographies of individuals and groups and providing short discographies; last volume a compendium of lists, indexes, and a brief bibliography.

Krummel, Donald W., and others. *Resources of American Musical History: A Directory of Source Materials from Colonial Times to World War II*. U. of Ill. Pr. 1981 $70.00. ISBN 0-252-00828-6. A bicentennial project listing collections of research materials by city and state.

Kutsch, K. J., and Leo Riemens. *A Concise Biographical Dictionary of Singers, from the Beginning of Recorded Sound to the Present*. Trans. by Harry Earl Jones. Chilton 1969 o.p.

Larkin, Colin, ed. *The Guinness Encyclopedia of Popular Music*. N. Eng. Pub. Assoc. 1992 $295.00. ISBN 1-882267-00-1

LePage, Jane Weiner. *Women Composers, Conductors, and Musicians of the Twentieth Century: Selected Biographies*. 3 vols. Scarecrow. Vol. 1 1980 $32.50. ISBN 0-8108-1298-3. Vol. 2 1983 $35.00. ISBN 0-8108-1597-4. Vol. 3 1988 $35.00. ISBN 0-8108-2082-X. Makes readily available the contributions and accomplishments of some of the gifted women musicians of the twentieth century.

Lewine, Richard, and Alfred Simon. *Songs of the Theater: A Definitive Index to the Songs of the Musical Stage*. Wilson 1984 $78.00. ISBN 0-8242-0706-8. A comprehensive index to more than 17,000 songs from 1,200 Broadway and off-Broadway shows.

McLaren, Jay. *The Encyclopaedia of Gay and Lesbian Recordings*. McLaren 1992 o.p.

Michaelides, Solon. *The Music of Ancient Greece: An Encyclopedia*. Faber & Faber 1978 o.p. Entries on persons, terms, places, and instruments.

Music Industry Directory. Marquis 1983 o.p. Basic information on organizations, competitions and awards, education, resources, performance, management, and commercial aspects of the music industry. Lengthy directory of American music publishers.

Musical Instruments of the World; An Illustrated Encyclopedia. Facts on File 1978 $37.50. ISBN 0-87196-320-5. Descriptions of instruments; copiously illustrated.

Nulman, Mary. *Concise Encyclopedia of Jewish Music*. Feldheim o.p. More than 500 entries, covering all facets of Jewish music.

Parsons, Denys. *The Directory of Tunes and Musical Themes*. Little 1975 o.p. Indexes of more than 14,000 themes; uses the direction of successive pitches in each theme so that one need not know how to read music to identify the origin of the theme.

Randel, Don M. *The New Harvard Concise Dictionary of Music*. HUP 1986 $30.00. ISBN 0-674-61525-5. Biographical information, definitions of terms, and entries on compositions and instruments. The best pocket-size dictionary of music.

_____, ed. *The New Harvard Dictionary of Music*. HUP 1986 $37.50. ISBN 0-674-61525-5. Authoritative entries on terms in music. Brief bibliographies.

Roche, Jerome, and Elizabeth Roche. *A Dictionary of Early Music, from the Troubadours to Monteverdi*. OUP 1981 $27.95. ISBN 0-19-520255-4. Compact work with entries on instruments, forms, terms, and composers from c.1100 to c.1650

Roxon, Lillian. *Rock Encyclopedia*. G&D 1978 o.p. Covers musicians, groups, terms, and concepts; with many discographies.

Sachs, Harvey. *Virtuoso, the Instrumentalist as Superstar*. Thames Hudson 1982 $18.95. ISBN 0-500-01286-5. Short biographies of Niccolo Paganini, Franz List, Anton Rubenstein, Ignace Jan Paderewski, Fritz Kreisler, Pablo Casals, Wanda Landowski, Vladimir Horowitz and Glenn Gould.

Sadie, Stanley, ed. *The New Grove Dictionary of Music and Musicians*. 20 vols. Groves Dict. Music 1980 $2,300.00. ISBN 0-333-23111-2. An encyclopedia about music featuring signed articles about people, terms, instruments, cities and countries, forms and genres, and virtually all facets of the art form. Most articles followed by bibliographies of the most relevant secondary sources, with lists of varying extensiveness following entries on individual composers. Widely accepted as the fundamental music reference work around the world.

_____. *The New Grove Encyclopedia of Musical Instruments*. 3 vols. Macmillan 1984 o.p. Another of the worthy dictionaries emanating from the *New Grove* workshop, giving excellent introductory articles on musical instruments around the world. With articles on non-Western instruments being, in many cases, the first scholarly entries ever composed.

_____. *The Norton / Grove Concise Encyclopedia of Music*. Norton 1988 $40.00. ISBN 0393-02620-5. Originally published as the *Grove Concise Dictionary of Music*, updated with corrections.

Shapiro, Nat, ed. *An Encyclopedia of Quotations about Music*. Da Capo 1981 repr. of 1978 ed. $13.95. ISBN 0-306-80138-8. Aphorisms quoted and identified by name and source and indexed by keywords. Arranged in topical order.

Shaw, Arnold, ed. *Dictionary of American Pop/Rock*. Macmillan 1985 $19.95. ISBN 0-02-872350-3. Concise entries on people, places, terms, titles, and jargon of rock and other popular musical styles.

Shemel, Sidney, and M. William Krasilovsky. *This Business of Music*. Watson-Guptill 1985 o.p. Discussion of business end of the music industry, including contracts, deals, agreements, agents, licensing, records, copyright, payola, performing-rights organizations, foreign rights, arrangements, infringements, sources of information and assistance, and forms and taxation.

Simpson, Claude M. *The British Broadside Ballad and Its Music*. Rutgers U. Pr. 1966 o.p. Analytic survey of the genre arranged by title.

Slonimsky, Nicholas. *Lectionary of Music*. McGraw 1989 $22.95. ISBN 0-07-058222-X. Dictionary of musical terms and phrases, composers, compositions, etc; written by a major music composer.

_____. *Music since 1900*. Schirmer Bks. 1993 $100.00. ISBN 0-02-872418-6. Chronological survey of twentieth-century music up to 1969 with a section quoting documents and letters on musical subjects in the same period. With a glossary.

_____, ed. *Baker's Biographical Dictionary of Musicians*. Schirmer Bks. 1991 $125.00. ISBN 0-02-872415-1. Brief but authoritative entries on musical figures throughout history, including lists of works and occasional short bibliographies. With a preface discussing problems of writing biographies of musicians.

Southern, Eileen. *Biographical Dictionary of Afro-American and African Musicians.* Greenwood 1982 $75.00. ISBN 0-313-21339-9. Short pieces on the professional lives of African American musicians.

Stambler, Irwin, and Grelun Landon. *The Encyclopedia of Folk, Country, and Western Music.* St. Martin 1983 o.p. Long entries on performers, institutions, ensembles. Lists of awards.

Thompson, Kenneth. *St. Martin's Dictionary of Twentieth-Century Composers, 1910–1971.* St. Martin 1973 o.p. Lengthy essays on 32 of the most respected composers of the first half of the twentieth century.

Vinton, John, ed. *The Dictionary of Contemporary Music.* Nal-Dutton 1974 o.p. Covers composers, styles, terms, schools, and instruments of twentieth-century concert music in the Western tradition. Contains many entries on composers based on information supplied by the composers themselves.

Who's Who in American Music: Classical. Bowker 1985 $124.95. ISBN 0-8352-2074-5. Information supplied by the subjects. Geographic and professional classifications and indexes.

Zaimont, Judith Lang, and others, eds. *Contemporary Concert Music by Women: A Directory of the Composers and Their Works.* Greenwood 1981 $39.95. ISBN 0-313-22921-X. Entries include photographs and samples of orthography with classified lists of compositions.

———. *The Musical Woman: An International Perspective, 1986–1990.* Greenwood 1991 $95.00. ISBN 0-313-23589-9. Chronicle of women's achievements in music around the world as composers, conductors, critics, scholars, and entrepreneurs, not as solo performers.

History and Criticism

Abraham, Gerald, *A Hundred Years of Music.* Rprt. Serv. 1993 repr. of 1949 ed. $89.00. ISBN 0-7812-9562-9. Music from Beethoven to Schoenberg.

Abraham, Gerald, and others. *New Oxford History of Music.* 10 vols. OUP. Vol. 1 *Ancient and Oriental Music.* 1957 $95.00. ISBN 0-19-316301-2. Vol. 2 *Early Medieval Music up to 1300.* 1954 $95.00. ISBN 0-19-316302-0. Vol. 3 *Ars Nova and the Renaissance, 1300–1540.* 1960 $95.00. ISBN 0-19-316303-9. Vol. 4 *The Age of Humanism, 1540–1630.* 1968 $95.00. ISBN 0-19-316304-7. Vol. 5 *Opera and Church Music, 1630–1750.* 1975 $95.00. ISBN 0-19316305-5. Vol. 6 *Concert Music, 1630–1750.* 1986 $95.00. ISBN 0-19-316306-3. Vol. 7 *The Age of Enlightenment, 1745–1790.* 1973 $95.00. ISBN 0-19-316307-1. Vol. 8 *The Age of Beethoven, 1790–1830.* 1982 $95.00. ISBN 0-19-316308-X. Vol. 9 *Romanticism, 1830–1890.* 1990 $99.00 ISBN 0-19-316309-8. Vol. 10 *Modern Age, 1890–1960.* 1974 $95.00. ISBN 0-19-316310-1. Lengthy surveys by leading scholars within broad topical areas: "Ancient and Oriental Music"; "The Early Middle Ages to 1300"; "Ars Nova and the Renaissance"; "The Age of Humanism"; "Opera and Church Music"; "Concert Music, 1630–1750"; "The Growth of Instrumental Music"; "The Age of Enlightenment"; "The Age of Beethoven"; "Romanticism"; and "Modern Age."

Adorno, Theodor W. *Introduction to the Sociology of Music.* Trans. by E. B. Ashton. Continuum 1988 $12.95. ISBN 0-8264-0403-0. Contains 12 essays on the social contexts of music espousing a complex philosophical view that incorporates method and substance.

Austin, William W. *Music in the 20th Century, from Debussy through Stravinsky.* Norton 1966 $33.95. ISBN 0-393-09704-8. Provocative history of music in the first two-thirds of the twentieth century; outstanding bibliography.

Barzun, Jacques. *Critical Questions: On Music and Letters, Culture and Biography, 1940–1980.* Ed. by Bea Friedland. U. Ch. Pr. 1984 $22.50. ISBN 0-226-03863-7. An anthology of reprinted articles on a wide variety of subjects aimed at the culturally informed reader.

Bloch, Ernest. *Essays on the Philosophy of Music.* Trans. by Peter Palmer. Cambridge U. Pr. 1985 $69.95. ISBN 0-521-24873-6. Contains "The Philosophy of Music"; "Magic

Rattle, Human Harp"; "Paradoxes and the Pastorale in Wagner's Music"; "The Exceeding of Limits"; and "The World of Man at Its Most Richly Intense in Music." With an introduction by David Drew.

Blum, David. *The Art of Quartet Playing: The Guarneri Quartet in Conversation with David Blum*. Cornell Univ. Pr. 1987 $14.95. ISBN 0-8014-9456-7. A series of interviews with the quartet; arranged by subject and member of the group.

Blum, Stephen, Philip V. Bohlman, and Daniel M. Neuman, eds. *Ethnomusicology and Modern Music History*. U. of Ill. Pr. 1990 $34.95. ISBN 0-252-01738-2. A collection of case studies examining the effects of music and society upon each other, presented within a framework of the need for a universal music history.

Bowers, Jane, and Judith Tick, eds. *Women Making Music: The Western Art Tradition, 1150–1950*. U. of Ill. Pr. 1987 $16.95. ISBN 0-252-01204-6. A solid, well-researched history of female composers.

Brown, Calvin S. *Music and Literature: A Comparison of the Arts*. U. Pr. of New Eng. 1987 $12.00. ISBN 0-87451-402-9. Author compares music and literature and discusses the interactions between them.

Budd, Malcolm. *Music and the Emotions: The Philosophical Theories*. Routledge 1985 $29.95. ISBN 0-7102-0520-1. Investigates the relationship between music and emotions, and discusses how emotions affect one's appreciation and understanding of music.

Bukofzer, Manfred F. *Music in the Baroque Era: From Monteverdi to Bach*. Norton 1947 $23.95. ISBN 0-393-09745-5. Thoughtful survey through style criticism rather than detailed analysis of individual pieces of music; standard history of the period.

Burrows, David L. *Sound, Speech, and Music*. U. of Mass. Pr. 1990 $22.50. ISBN 0-87023-685-7. Argues that vocal sound, and the articulation of thought it makes possible, is the unique key to human evolution.

Caldwell, John. *The Oxford History of English Music*. Vol. 1. OUP 1992 $98.00. ISBN 0-19-816129-8. Traces the history of music in England; includes the scores of famous pieces.

Chase, Gilbert. *America's Music: From the Pilgrims to the Present*. U. Ill. Pr. 1987 $34.95. ISBN 0-252-00454-X. The standard one-volume study of American music since its first publication in 1455; quite readable. Foreword by Richard Crawford and discographical essays by William Brooke.

Cook, Nicholas. *Music, Imagination, and Culture*. OUP 1992 $18.95. ISBN 0-19-816303-7

Crocker, Richard L. *A History of Musical Style*. Dover 1986 repr. of 1966 ed. $14.95. ISBN 0-486-25029-6. Covers the development of Western musical style, stressing the continuity of basic musical principles; particularly strong in earlier periods.

Dahlhaus, Carl. *Esthetics of Music*. Trans. by William W. Austin. Cambridge U. Pr. 1982 $39.95. ISBN 0-521-23508-1. "A systematic and historical survey and critique of the chief esthetic theories about European music" (Translator's introduction).

———. *Nineteenth-Century Music*. Trans. by J. Bradford Robinson. U. CA Pr. 1988 $39.95. ISBN 0-520-05291-9. A well-written dissection of nineteenth-century music, elucidating its origins and historical context.

Dichter, Harry, and Elliot Shapiro. *Early American Sheet Music, 1768–1889*. Dover 1977 o.p. Classic study of music, mostly popular, published on a few "sheets" of paper and widely distributed before the age of the phonograph eclipsed the age of the parlor piano.

Doughtie, Edward. *English Renaissance Song*. Macmillan 1986 $25.95. ISBN 0-8057-6915-3. An examination of the English song's development from the late sixteenth century to the early seventeenth, focusing on the relationship between poetry and song. A scholarly volume, perhaps too dense for the average reader.

Downs, Philip G. *Classical Music: The Era of Haydn, Mozart, and Beethoven*. Norton 1992 $32.95. ISBN 0-393-95191-X. Traces the development of classical music by giving consistent treatment to technical innovations and the careers of great composers.

Einstein, Alfred. *Music in the Romantic Era*. Norton 1947 $24.95. ISBN 0-393-09733-1. History of the romantic movement as manifested in music.

Ember, Ildiko. *Music in Painting: Music as Symbol in Renaissance and Baroque Painting.* St. Mut. 1989 $90.00. ISBN 0-685-34427-4

Engel, Lehman. *The Making of a Musical.* Limelight Edns. 1985 repr. of 1976 ed. $9.95. ISBN 0-87910-049-4. A step-by-step analysis of the elements that comprise a musical show.

Fenlon, Iain, ed. *The Renaissance: From the 1470s to the End of the 16th Century.* P-H 1990. ISBN 0-13-773417-4. Examines the Renaissance period in relation to social, economic, and political circumstances of the time.

Francès, Robert. *The Perception of Music.* Trans. by W. Jay Dowling. L. Erlbaum Assoc. 1987 $69.95. ISBN 0-89859-688-2. The English translation of the classic *La Perception de la Musique,* an extremely well-researched volume for serious scholars only.

Gagne, Cole, and Tracy Caras. *Soundpieces: Interviews with American Composers.* Scarecrow 1982 $32.50. ISBN 0-8108-1474-9. With introductory essays by Nicholas Slonimsky and Gilbert Chase and photographs by Gene Bagnato. Interviews with two dozen contemporary composers in which they discuss how to better understand the "new music."

Gänzl, Kurt. *The British Musical Theatre.* 2 vols. OUP 1986 $145.00. ISBN 0-19-520509-X. Research here not flawless; nevertheless, still the most comprehensive study of British musicals from 1865 to 1985.

Grout, Donald J., and Claude V. Palisca. *A History of Western Music.* Norton 1988 $49.95. ISBN 0-393-95627-X. A history of music styles, techniques, and innovators from the ancient world through the twentieth century.

Hamm, Charles. *Music in the New World.* Norton 1983 $35.95. ISBN 0-393-95193-6. History of the importation, imitation, and synthesis of music in America; references to currently available recordings.

Hanslick, Eduard. *On The Musically Beautiful: A Contribution Towards the Revision of the Aesthetics of Music.* Ed. and trans. by Geoffrey Payzant. Hackett Pub. 1986 $24.50. ISBN 0-87220-015-9. A new translation of the 1891 edition, in which Hanslick furthers his attempt to interpret music as an exact aesthetical science.

Harnoncourt, Nikolaus. *Baroque Music Today: Music as Speech, Ways to a New Understanding of Music.* Ed. by Reinhard G. Pauly. Trans. by Mary O'Neill. Timber 1988 $19.95. Revised collection of essays and lectures sampling the author's wide-ranging reflections on baroque music.

Hazen, Margaret Hindle, and Robert M. Hazen. *The Music Men: An Illustrated History of Brass Bands in America, 1800–1920.* Smithsonian 1987 $22.95. ISBN 0-87474-547-0. Traces the evolution of the American band movement from its origins in the early nineteenth century through the end of World War I; includes profiles of both professional and amateur musicians.

Herndon, Marcia, and Suzanne Ziegler, eds. *Music, Gender, and Culture. Intercultural Music Studies.* C. F. Peters Corp. 1990 o.p. A collection of essays that examine women's music and its relationship to the male musical sphere.

Hitchcock, H. Wiley. *Music in the United States: A Historical Introduction.* P-H 1988 $31.00. ISBN 0-13-608407-9. A history of music in the United States, based largely on primary sources.

Hoppin, Richard H., ed. *Anthology of Medieval Music.* Norton 1978 $12.95. ISBN 0-393-09080-9. An anthology of music scores, chosen as a survey of medieval music forms and styles from Gregorian chants through the polyphony of the late fourteenth century.

Jacob, Gordon. *The Composer and His Art.* Greenwood 1986 repr. of 1955 ed. $45.00. ISBN 0-313-25050-2

Katz, Ruth, and Carl Dahlaus, eds. *Contemplating Music: Source Readings in the Aesthetics of Music.* 3 vols. Pendragon NY 1987–92 $36.00 ea. ISBNs 0-918728-60-6, 0-918728-68-1, 0-945193-04-1

Kerman, Joseph. *Contemplating Music: Challenges to Musicology.* HUP 1985 $20.00. ISBN 0-674-16677-9. Historical and philosophical orientation of the scholarly field of musicology. Intended to be challenging and provocative to scholars; reveals much about the profession for those who might wish to know why and how various attitudes and techniques may have influenced program notes and books about music.

———. *Listen*. Worth 1980 $43.95. ISBN 0-87901-127-0. Essentially a text on music appreciation that includes thumbnail biographies, time lines, and a glossary.

Kingman, Daniel. *American Music: A Panorama*. Macmillan 1990 $29.95. ISBN 0-02-873370-3. A wide survey of American music; investigates several more or less parallel streams of development.

Kivy, Peter. *Sound Sentiment: An Essay on the Musical Emotions, Including the Complete Text of The Corded Shell. The Arts and Their Philosophies*. Temple U. Pr. 1989 $39.95. ISBN 0-87722-6415. Reflections on issues relating to musical expression; revises and comments on earlier work on the subject.

Kramer, Jonathan D. *The Time of Music: New Meanings, New Temporalities, New Listening Strategies*. Macmillan 1988 $42.00. ISBN 0-02-872590-5. Examines various themes and styles in music and challenges the reader with suggestions about new ways to listen to both old and new music.

Lang, Paul H., ed. *Music in Western Civilization*. Norton 1940 $35.95. ISBN 0-393-09428-6. Chronicles the role of music in the making of Western civilization.

Lerner, Alan Jay. *The Musical Theatre: A Celebration*. McGraw 1986 o.p. A history of how musicals were created and developed and how and why they have changed.

Leppert, Richard, and Susan McClary, eds. *Music and Society: The Politics of Composition, Performance, and Reception*. Cambridge U. Pr. 1989 $17.95. ISBN 0-521-37977-6. A collection of essays that raise a series of questions about the extent to which music is or is not autonomous from the impact of society.

Lippman, Edward A., ed. *Musical Aesthetics: A Historical Reader. Aesthetics in Music*. 3 vols. Pendragon Pr. 1986–1990 $73.00 ea. Vol. 1 *From Antiquity to the Eighteenth Century*. ISBN 0-918728-41-X. Vol. 2 *The Nineteenth Century*. ISBN 0-918728-90-8. Vol. 3. *The Twentieth Century*. ISBN 0-945193-10-6

Longyear, Rey M. *Nineteenth-Century Romanticism in Music*. P-H 1988 $31.00. ISBN 0-136-22697-3. A survey of nineteenth-century music; discusses over 150 composers and looks at the key movements in the music of the time.

Lovell, John. *Black Song: The Forge and The Flame, The Story of How the Afro-American Spiritual Was Hammered Out*. Paragon Hse. 1986 $14.95. ISBN 0-913729-53-1

McClary, Susan. *Feminine Endings: Music, Gender, and Sexuality*. U. of Minn. Pr. 1991 $39.95. ISBN 0-8166-1898-4. A collection of essays in feminist music criticism addressing the problems of gender and sexuality in repertoires from the early seventeenth century to contemporary rock and performance art.

McKinnon, James, ed. *Antiquity and The Middle Ages: From Ancient Greece to the 15th Century. Man and Music*. P-H 1990 o.p. A discussion of music from ancient Greece to the fifteenth century, with an emphasis on the context in which different musical forms arose.

———. *Music in Early Christian Literature. Cambridge Readings in the Literature of Music*. Cambridge U. Pr. 1987 o.p. Designed primarily to alleviate the inaccessibility of early Christian references to music in writing.

Mates, Julian. *America's Musical Stage: Two Hundred Years of Musical Theatre. Contributions in Drama and Theatre Studies*. Greenwood 1985 $49.95. ISBN 0-313-23948-7. A history of the American musical stage, with analysis of the interrelationships among different musical stage forms.

Mellers, Wilfrid. *Music in a New Found Land: Two Hundred Years of American Music*. OUP 1987 $12.95. ISBN 0-19-520526-X. Cosmopolitan and selective history of 200 years of American music from Billings and Beiderbeck to Coltrane and Cage.

Meyer, Leonard B. *Style and Music: Theory, History, and Ideology. Studies in the Criticism and Theory of Music*. U. of Pa. Pr. 1989 $46.95. ISBN 0-8122-8178-0. Examines compositional choices made by men and women in relation to their historical and cultural circumstances.

Morgan, Robert P. *Twentieth-Century Music: A History of Musical Style in Modern Europe and America.* Norton 1991 $31.95. ISBN 0-393-95272-X. Looks at developments and currents in twentieth-century music, highlighting important musical innovators.

Newlin, Dika. *Bruckner, Mahler, Schoenberg.* Norton rev. ed. 1993 $79.00. ISBN 0-7812-9582-3. Discussion of the Viennese musical tradition, beginning with mid-nineteenth century Bruckner and ending with mid–twentieth-century Schoenberg; demonstrates the connection between Schoenberg and Mahler and pointing out the necessity of understanding Mahler in order to appreciate Schoenberg.

Page, Christopher. *Voices and Instruments of the Middle Ages: The Sound Picture of Songs in France, 1000–1300.* U. CA Pr. 1986 $39.95. ISBN 0-520-05932-8. A dispassionate assessment of where musical instruments belong in the surviving repertoires of the music of the Middle Ages.

Palisca, Claude V. *Baroque Music.* P-H 1991 $27.33. ISBN 0-13-058496-7. An introduction to Baroque music that provides the reader entry into the most significant aspects of composition through concrete examples.

_____. *Humanism in Italian Renaissance Musical Thought.* Yale U. Pr. 1990 $22.00. ISBN 0-300-04962-5. Documents the debt that Renaissance musical thought owes to the ancient past.

Pauly, Reinhard G. *Music in the Classic Period.* P-H 1988 $31.00. ISBN 0-13-607623-8. An introduction to the music of the Classical period, from its evolution to the transition to Romanticism.

Pendle, Karin, ed. *Women and Music: A History.* Ind. U. Pr. 1991 $27.50. ISBN 0-253-34321-6. A survey of the role of women in music performance, composition, teaching, and patronage from the time of the ancient Greeks to the present.

Peyser, Joan. *Twentieth-Century Music: The Sense Behind the Sound.* Schirmer Bks. 1980 o.p. Introduction by Jacques Barzun.

Plantinga, Leon. *Romantic Music: A History of Musical Style in Nineteenth-Century Europe. The Norton Introduction to Music History.* Norton 1985 $27.95. ISBN 0-393-95196-0. An account of art music in nineteenth-century Europe; incorporates forays into social and intellectual history.

Porter, Andrew. *Musical Events: A Chronicle, 1983–1986.* S&S Trade 1990 $16.95. ISBN 0-671-69656-4. Collection of essays from *The New Yorker.*

_____. *A Musical Season: A Critic from Abroad in America.* Viking Penguin 1974 o.p.

_____. *Music of Three More Seasons, 1977–1980.* Knopf 1981 o.p.

_____. *Music of Three Seasons, 1974–1977.* FS&G 1978 o.p. Works gathered from the Musical Events column of *The New Yorker.*

Pratt, Ray. *Rhythm and Resistance: Explorations in the Political Uses of Popular Music. Media and Society Ser.* Greenwood 1990 $49.95. ISBN 0-275-92624-9. An interpretive exploration of the political uses of popular music from the era of slavery through the present.

Rauchhaupt, Ursula von, ed. *The Symphony.* Thames Hudson 1973 o.p. Anthology of essays about this musical genre and the orchestral organization.

Raeburn, Michael, and Alan Kendall, eds. *Heritage of Music.* 4 vols. OUP 1989 $225.00. ISBN 0-19-520493-X. Vol. 1 *Classical Music and Its Origins.* Vol. 2 *The Romantic Era.* Vol. 3 *The Nineteenth-Century Legacy.* Vol. 4 *Music in the Twentieth Century.*

Raymond, Jack. *Show Music on Record: The First 100 Years.* Smithsonian 1992 $45.00 ISBN 1-56098-151-2. Lists chronologically all commercially issued recordings of show music from the American stage, screen, and television.

Reese, Gustave. *Music in the Middle Ages.* Norton 1940 $37.95. ISBN 0-393-09750-1. A classic standard history of music in the Middle Ages; contains many bibliographic references.

_____. *Music in the Renaissance.* Norton rev. ed. 1959 $37.95. ISBN 0-393-09530-4. A standard history of music from 1350 to c.1650; lavish bibliographic references.

Roche, Jerome. *The Madrigal. Early Music Ser.* OUP 1991 $59.00. ISBN 0-19-313131-5. Discusses the madrigal in terms of its Italianate manifestations and principal offshoots.

Rognoni, Luigi. *The Second Vienna School: Expressionism and Dodecaphony.* Trans. by Robert W. Mann. Riverrun NY 1977 $15.95. ISBN 0-7145-3865-5. Looks at the two opposite and divergent processes that emerge from the Second Vienna School of Music.

Rosen, Charles. *The Classical Style: Haydn, Mozart, Beethoven.* Norton Lib. Norton repr. of 1972 ed. $14.95. ISBN 0-393-00653-0. Focuses on the three giant figures of the period and describes musical conventions, techniques, and vocabulary.

————. *Sonata Forms.* Norton rev. ed. 1988 $19.95. ISBN 0-393-30219-9. Relates the sonata to eighteenth-century social and musical conditions; briefly discusses post–eighteenth-century sonata forms.

Rosselli, John. *Music and Musicians in Nineteenth-Century Italy.* Timber 1991 $29.95. ISBN 0-931340-40-3

Rushton, Julian. *Classical Music: A Concise History from Gluck to Beethoven. World of Art.* Thames Hudson 1986 $11.95. ISBN 0-500-20210-9. Covers the period from the mid-eighteenth century to 1830, showing the main changes in music and musical life.

Sachs, Curt. *The Commonwealth of Art: Style in the Fine Arts, Music and the Dance.* Da Capo 1946 $42.50. ISBN 0-306-79467-5. A major study of history and culture shows how "all arts unite in one consistent evolution to mirror man's diversity in space and time and the fate of his soul" (Introduction).

————. *Rhythm and Tempo: A Study in Music History.* Col. U. Pr. 1988 $61.00. ISBN 0-231-06910-3. Best of a handful of English works on the subject.

————. *The Rise of Music in the Ancient World: East and West.* Norton 1943 o.p. "An exposure to the roots from which the music of the West has grown" (Preface).

Salzman, Eric. *Twentieth-Century Music: An Introduction.* P-H 1988 $31.00. ISBN 0-13-935057-8. Examines the creative development of musical ideas during the last 85 years as understood against and distinct from the past.

Samson, Jim, ed. *The Late Romantic Era: From the Mid-19th Century to World War I.* P-H 1991. ISBN 0-13-524182-0

Scheader, Catherine. *Contributions of Women in Music.* Dillon Pr. 1985 o.p.

Schonberg, Harold C. *The Glorious Ones: Classical Music's Legendary Performers.* Times Bks. 1985 o.p. Examines the lives and works of various Classical music superstars.

Scott, Derek B. *The Singing Bourgeois: Songs of the Victorian Drawing Room and Parlour.* Taylor & Francis 1989 $95.00. ISBN 0-335-15291-0. Looks at English songs from before 1870 and tries to determine their role in nationalism, imperialism, and the dissemination of bourgeois values.

Seaton, Douglass. *Ideas and Styles in the Western Musical Tradition.* Mayfield Pub. 1991 $37.95. ISBN 0-87484-956-X

Shattuck, Roger. *The Banquet Years: The Origins of the Avant-Garde in France, 1885 to World War I.* Ayer repr. of 1968 ed. $28.00. ISBN 0-8369-2826-1. Studies how the fluid state known as "bohemian" crystallized for a few decades into a self-conscious avant-garde movement.

Southern, Eileen. *The Music of Black Americans: A History.* Norton 1983 $18.95. ISBN 0-393-95279-7. An introductory history and guide to the musical contributions of African Americans; includes elements of social, political, and economic history.

Stedman, Preston. *The Symphony.* P-H 1992 $46.00. ISBN 0-13-880055-3. Examines the forces that created the symphony around 1750 and those that shaped it as it accommodated changing norms.

Stevens, John E. *Words and Music in the Middle Ages: Song, Narrative, Dance, and Drama, 1050–1350. Cambridge Studies in Music.* Cambridge U. Pr. 1986 $94.95. ISBN 0-521-24507-9. Studies all manifestations and uses of the monophonic song during the Middle Ages in England and elsewhere.

Strunk, Oliver. *Source Readings in Music History from Classical Antiquity throughout the Romantic Era.* Norton 1950 $24.95. ISBN 0-393-09742-0. Documents crucial to the history of Western music; includes extensive annotations and footnotes to make the contexts clear.

Subotnik, Rose Rosengard. *Developing Variations: Style and Ideology in Western Music*. U. of Minn. Pr. 1991 $39.95. ISBN 0-8166-1873-9. A collection of essays, grouped thematically in categories of ideological criticism, stylistic criticism, and perspectives of Western music history.

Supičič, Ivo. *Music in Society: A Guide to the Sociology of Music*. Sociology of Music. Pendragon NY 1988 $62.00 ISBN 0-918728-35-5. Investigates the sociology of music as an autonomous and specialized discipline.

Swain, Joseph Peter. *The Broadway Musical: A Critical and Musical Survey*. OUP 1990 $30.00. ISBN 0-19-505434-2. Surveys the achievements of the music and drama of the American musical theater.

Tawa, Nicholas E. *A Most Wondrous Babble: American Art Composers, Their Music, and the American Scene, 1950–1985*. Contributions to the Study of Music and Dance. Greenwood 1987 $42.95. ISBN 0-313-25692-6

_____. *Serenading the Reluctant Eagle: American Musical Life, 1925–1945*. Schirmer Bks. 1984 o.p. Strives to develop a fuller understanding of American musical culture from 1925 to 1945 by focusing on composers, audiences, and U.S. social and cultural trends.

Tovey, Donald E. *Chamber Music*. OUP 1989 $10.95. ISBN 0-19-315161-8

_____. *Concertos and Choral Works*. OUP 1989 $12.95. ISBN 0-19-315149-9

_____. *Essays in Musical Analysis*. 6 vols. OUP 1993 rep. of 1944 ed. $79.00. ISBN 0-7812-9671-4. Formative essays on a large number of works in the standard repertory. Essential program notes for the informed concertgoer. Glossary and index in Volume 6.

_____. *Symphonies and Other Orchestral Works*. OUP 1989 $23.95. ISBN 0-19-315146-4

Treitler, Leo. *Music and the Historical Imagination*. HUP 1989 $37.50. ISBN 0-674-59128-3. An examination of how music can be viewed through historical imagination and the significance of that study.

Weiss, Piero, and Richard Taruskin. *Music in the Western World: A History in Documents*. Schirmer Bks. 1984 $21.00. ISBN 0-02-872900-5. Translated historical documents bring music of the Western world into perspective through the words of major music figures and their observers.

Whittall, Arnold. *Romantic Music: A Concise History from Schubert to Sibelius*. Thames Hudson 1987 $12.95. ISBN 0-500-20215-X

Wilder, Alec. *American Popular Song: The Great Innovators, 1900–1950*. Ed. by James T. Maher. OUP 1972 $29.95. ISBN 0-19-501445-6. Surveys the musical distinctions of the American pop song, primarily by following the careers of important song writers.

Wolff, Konrad. *Masters of the Keyboard: Individual Style Elements in the Piano Music of Bach, Haydn, Mozart, Beethoven, Schubert, Chopin, and Brahms*. Ind. U. Pr. 1990 $35.00. ISBN 0-253-365458-2. Using piano scores, this work studies in detail the work of five composers to illuminate some of the inner meaning of their music.

Zaslaw, Neal. ed. *The Classical Era: From the 1740s to the End of the 18th Century*. Man and Music. P-H 1989. ISBN 0-13-136938-5. Examines the social, cultural, and intellectual forces that shaped the development of music from 1740 to 1800.

Zetlin, Mikhail. *The Five: The Evolution of The Russian School of Music*. Ed. and trans. by George Panin. Bks. Demand repr. of 1959 ed. $88.80. ISBN 0-317-09940-X

Music Appreciation

Bamberger, Jeanne Shapiro, Howard Brofsky, Martin Brody and Roland Vazquez. *The Art of Listening: Developing Musical Perception*. HarpC 1988 o.p. With a foreword by Roger Sessions.

Barzun, Jacques, ed. *Pleasures of Music: An Anthology of Writings about Music and Musicians from Cellini to Bernard Shaw*. U. Ch. Pr. 1977 $15.00. ISBN 0-226-03856-4

Downes, Edward. *The New York Philharmonic Guide to the Symphony*. Walker & Co. 1976 o.p. Anthology of program notes for pieces frequently appearing in symphonic programs. Sensitive and supportive but not critical. Cites main themes in musical notation.

Haggin, B. H. *The Listener's Musical Companion*. Ed. and comp. by Thomas Hathaway. OUP 1991 $39.95. ISBN 0-19-506374-0. Provides insight into how to listen to music, how to judge its quality, and how to interpret its meanings.

Kamien, Roger. *Music: An Appreciation*. McGraw 1993 $26.95. ISBN 0-07-034819-7. Provides an approach to perceptive listening and an introduction to musical elements, forms, and styles.

Kerman, Joseph. *Listen*. Worth 1980 $43.95. ISBN 0-87901-127-0. Covers the whole span of Western music, focusing on technique rather than history.

Machlis, Joseph. *The Enjoyment of Music: An Introduction to Perceptive Listening*. Norton 1984 $29.95. ISBN 0-393-95297-5. Classic, dated, but clear introduction to the resources and some principal musical styles of Western music.

McLeish, Kenneth, and Valerie McLeish. *The Listener's Guide to Classical Music: An Introduction to the Great Classical Composers and Their Works*. Macmillan 1992 $30.00. ISBN 0-8161-7369-9. Offers a guide to the huge repertoire of classical music available to the concertgoer and home-listener.

Types of Music

CONTEMPORARY MUSIC

Antokoletz, Elliott. *Twentieth-Century Music*. P-H 1991 $46.67. ISBN 0-13-934126-9. A detailed discussion of twentieth-century musical innovations, with a look at composers from all over the world.

Brindle, Reginald Smith. *The New Music: The Avant-Garde Since 1945*. OUP 1987 $35.00. ISBN 0-19-315471-4. Gives a concise picture of the more adventurous evolutions of music since 1945.

Brown, Peter, and Steven Gaines. *The Love You Make: An Insider's Story of the Beatles*. McGraw 1984 $5.99. ISBN 0-451-16067-3

Dutton, Gregory Battcock. *Breaking the Sound Barrier: A Critical Anthology of the New Music*. S&S Trade 1992 $12.98. ISBN 0-671-74212-4. Thirty essays on the styles characterizing music since 1960.

Griffiths, Paul. *Modern Music: A Concise History from Debussy to Boulez*. World of Art. Thames Hudson 1985 $12.95. ISBN 0-500-20164-1. Originally published as *A Concise History of Avant-Garde Music*.

Martin, William R., and Julius Drossin. *Music of the Twentieth Century*. P-H 1980 o.p. Illustrated look at the cycles of experimentation and consolidation that have characterized twentieth-century music.

Mellers, Wilfrid. *The Twilight of the Gods: The Music of the Beatles*. Viking Penguin 1974 o.p. A study of English rock-and-roll bands that focuses on their unique musical achievements.

Mertens, Wim. *American Minimal Music*. Trans. by J. Hautekiet. Pro-Am Music $12.50. ISBN 0-912483-15-6. Preface by Michael Nyman. Traces the roots of the American repetitive school, and considers the music in light of French libidinal philosophy.

Morgan, Robert P. *Twentieth-Century Music: A History of Musical Style in Modern Europe and America*. Norton 1991 o.p.

Nelson, Havelock, and Michael A. Gonzales. *Bring the Noise: A Guide to Rap Music and Hip-Hop Culture*. Crown Pub. Group 1991 $12.00. ISBN 0-517-58305-4. Definitive early study of a genre that continues to grow in popularity and significance.

Perle, George. *Serial Composition and Atonality: An Introduction to the Music of Schoenberg, Berg, and Webern*. U. CA Pr. 1991 $25.00. ISBN 0-520-07505-6. Technical study that examines post-Schoenbergian 12-tone compositions and the work of the Second Vienna School.

Pollock, Bruce. *When Rock Was Young: A Nostalgic Review of the Top Forty Era*. H. Holt & Co. o.p. Covers the first decade (1955–65) of rock-and-roll.

Salzman, Eric. *Twentieth-Century Music: An Introduction*. P-H 1988 $31.00. ISBN 0-13-935057-8. Engagingly written work that chronicles the great changes and varied richness of the twentieth-century musical experience.

Schwartz, Elliot. *Electronic Music: A Listener's Guide*. Da Capo 1989 repr. of 1975 ed. $29.50. ISBN 0-306-76260-9. Introduction to electronic music through the music itself, including a section of observations by composers of electronic music. With a bibliography, discography, indexes.

Shaw, Arnold. *Honkers and Shouters: The Golden Years of Rhythm and Blues*. Macmillan 1986 $14.95. ISBN 0-02-061740-2. Rhythm and blues as an indigenous African American musical style separate from rock and soul music.

Simms, Bryan R. *Music of the Twentieth Century: Style and Structure*. Schirmer Bks. 1986 $30.00. ISBN 0-02-872580-8. A study of musical culture in the twentieth century, presented through the examination of its outstanding works.

Stambler, Irwin. *Encyclopedia of Pop, Rock, and Soul*. St. Martin 1990 $19.95. ISBN 0-312-04310-4. Lengthy entries on famous artists and groups, with lists of awards.

Straus, Joseph Nathan. *Remaking the Past: Musical Modernism and the Influence of the Tonal Tradition*. HUP 1990 $32.50. ISBN 0-674-75990-7. Develops a critical framework for interpreting the allusions to older music by Stravinsky, Schoenberg, Bartok, Webern, and Berg.

Strickland, Edward. *American Composers: Dialogues on Contemporary Music*. Ind. U. Pr. 1991 $39.95. ISBN 0-253-35498-6. A collection of interviews with important contemporary composers ranging from Keith Jarret to Philip Glass.

Tjepkema, Sandra L. *A Bibliography of Computer Music: A Reference for Composers*. U. of Iowa Pr. $34.95. ISBN 0-87745-110-9. A comprehensive listing of books, articles, dissertations, and papers relating to the use of computers by composers of music.

Watkins, Glenn. *Soundings: Music in the Twentieth Century*. Schirmer Bks. 1987 $36.00. ISBN 0-02-873290-1. A readable and comprehensive overview of twentieth-century music.

Whittall, Arnold. *The Music of Britten and Tippett: Studies in Themes and Techniques*. Cambridge U. Pr. 1990 $64.95. ISBN 0-521-38501-6. A double portrait that illustrates the way in which each composer's work serves to complement and illuminate that of the other.

ETHNIC MUSIC

Blum, Stephen, Philip V. Bohlman, and Daniel M. Neuman, eds. *Ethnomusicology and Modern Music History*. U. of Ill. Pr. 1990 $18.95. ISBN 0-252-06343-0. Collection of essays that examine how the reproduction of music may enhance, support, or undermine the power and authority of particular groups.

Buchner, Alexander. *Folk Music Instruments of the World*. Crown Pub. Group 1972 o.p. An illustrated survey.

Collaer, Paul. *Music of the Americas: An Illustrated Music Ethnology of the Eskimo and American Indian Peoples*. Trans. by Irene R. Gibbons. Praeger 1973 o.p. Covers the music of the indigenous peoples of the New World.

Koskoff, Ellen. *Women and Music in Cross-Cultural Perspective*. Greenwood 1987 $49.95. ISBN 0-313-24314-X

Kunst, Jaap. *Ethnomusicology: A Study of Its Nature, Its Problems, Methods and Representative Personalities to Which Is Added a Bibliography*. Scholarly 1959 $49.00. ISBN 0-403-01608-8. A seminal study.

McAllester, David P., ed. *Readings in Ethnomusicology*. Johnson Repr. 1971 o.p. Contains 23 essays by scholars on notation and classification, history, functionalism, and regional studies.

Malm, William P. *Music Cultures of the Pacific, the Near East and Asia*. P-H 1977 $31.00. ISBN 0-13-607994-6. An introductory work, with definitions of many regional terms.

May, Elizabeth, ed. *Music of Many Cultures: An Introduction*. U. CA Pr. 1980 o.p. Twenty essays written by specialists but intended for the general reader; with a filmography.

Merriam, Alan P. *The Anthropology of Music*. Northwestern U. Pr. 1964 $25.95. ISBN 0-8101-0178-5. Provides a theory and methodology for the study of music as human behavior, based on the fusion of methods of cultural anthropology and ethnomusicology; with an extensive bibliography.

Myers, Helen, ed. *Ethnomusicology*. Norton 1992 $35.00. ISBN 0-393-03377-5. Collection of essays that serves as a basic introduction to the field.

Nettl, Bruno. *The Western Impact on World Music: Change, Adaptation, and Survival*. Schirmer Bks. 1985 $26.00. ISBN 0-02-870860-1. Examines the effects of Western musical culture on the traditions of the non-Western world over the last one hundred years.

Nettl, Bruno, and Philip V. Bohlman, eds. *Comparative Musicology and Anthropology of Music: Essays on the History of Ethnomusicology*. U. Ch. Pr. 1991 $49.95. ISBN 0-226-57408-3. Studies the different ways ethnomusicologists have approached their field of study.

Nettl, Bruno and others. *Excursions in World Music*. P-H 1991. ISBN 0-13-299025-3.

———. *Folk and Traditional Music of the Western Continents*. P-H 1990 $31.00. ISBN 0-13-323247-6. Includes chapters on the music of Latin America by Gerard Behague.

Reck, David B. *Music of the Whole Earth*. Scribner 1977 o.p. An illustrated study of nonart, non-Western music.

Sachs, Curt. *The Wellsprings of Music*. Ed. by Jaap Kunst. Da Capo 1977 $6.95. ISBN 0-306-80073-X. A masterfully woven tapestry of the musical world, placing Western classical music in the fabric of the rest of musical culture.

FILM MUSIC

Bordman, Gerald Martin. *American Musical Theatre: A Chronicle*. OUP 1992 $49.95. ISBN 0-19-507242-1

Evans, Mark. *Soundtrack: The Music of the Movies*. Da Capo 1979 repr. of 1975 ed. $9.95. ISBN 0-306-80099-3. An examination of the way musical scoring contributes to the filmmaking process.

Hemming, Roy. *The Melody Lingers On: The Great Songwriters and Their Movie Musicals*. Newmarket 1988 $29.95. ISBN 0-937858-57-9

Limbacher, James L., ed. *Film Music: From Violins to Video*. Scarecrow 1974 $57.50. ISBN 0-8108-0651-7. Reprinted essays on film music, mostly by film composers; contains a bibliography on film music.

Mast, Gerald. *Can't Help Singin': The American Musical on Stage and Screen*. Overlook Pr. 1987 $24.95. ISBN 0-87951-283-0. Argues for both the artistic and social importance of the genre.

Palmer, Christopher. *The Composer in Hollywood*. M. Boyars Pubs. 1990 $42.00. ISBN 0-7145-2885-4

Prendergast, Roy M. *Film Music: A Neglected Art*. Norton 1992 $10.95. ISBN 0-393-30874-X. "The first attempt at a comprehensive look at the history, aesthetics, and techniques of film music" (Preface).

JAZZ

Balliet, Whitney. *American Musicians: Fifty-Six Portraits in Jazz*. OUP 1986 $35.00. ISBN 0-19-503758-8. A collection of essays, originally appearing principally in *The New Yorker*.

———. *American Singers*. OUP 1979 $21.95. ISBN 0-19-502524-5. Portraits of American popular and jazz singers by one of the most distinguished New York jazz critics.

———. *Barney, Bradley, and Max: Sixteen Portraits in Jazz*. OUP 1989 $22.95. ISBN 0-19-506124-1. Another collection of essays from *The New Yorker*.

———. *Dinosaurs in the Morning: Forty-One Pieces on Jazz*. Greenwood 1978 repr. of 1962 ed. $42.50. ISBN 0-313-20283-4. Anthology of previously published reviews and essays.

———. *Goodbyes and Other Messages: A Journal of Jazz, 1981–1990*. OUP 1991 $22.95. ISBN 0-19-503757-X. A collection of pieces written for *The New Yorker*. Includes recollections on such jazz greats as Charlie Parker and Thelonious Monk.

———. *Night Creature: A Journal of Jazz, 1975–80*. OUP 1981 $21.95. ISBN 0-19-502908-9. Anthology of previously published reviews and essays.

Blesh, Rudi, and Harriet Janis. *They All Played Ragtime*. Oak Pub. 1971 o.p. Definitive history of one of the precursors of jazz.

Bushell, Garvin. *Jazz From the Beginning*. Mark Tucker, ed. U. of Mich. Pr. 1988 $29.95. ISBN 0-472-10098-X. Introduction by Lawrence Gushee. The jazz pioneer recounts his life in music from New York in the 1920s to Africa in the 1960s.

Chilton, John. *Who's Who of Jazz*. Da Capo 1985 $29.50. ISBN 0-306-76271-4. Entries for more than 1,000 jazz musicians born before 1920.

Coker, Jerry. *Listening to Jazz*. P-H 1981 $7.95. ISBN 0-13-537225-9. A basic appreciation text.

Condon, Eddie. *We Called It Music: A Generation of Jazz*. Da Capo 1992 repr. of 1947 ed. $13.95. ISBN 0-306-80466-2. With an introduction by Gary Giddins and narration by Thomas Sugrue.

Dance, Stanley. *The World of Swing*. Da Capo 1979 $10.95. ISBN 0-306-80103-5. Covers big-band jazz of the 1930s and later.

Davis, Francis. *In the Moment: Jazz in the 1980s*. OUP 1986 $24.95. ISBN 0-19-504090-2. Previously published essays.

Feather, Leonard. *The Encyclopedia of Jazz*. Da Capo 1984 repr. of 1950 ed. $19.95. ISBN 0-306-80214-7. Chronology, with brief entries on jazz musicians and composers, with short concluding essays.

_____. *The Encyclopedia of Jazz in the Sixties*. Da Capo 1986 o.p. Foreword by John Lewis. Instructive guide to one of the most important periods in jazz.

_____. *The Encyclopedia Yearbook of Jazz*. Da Capo 1992 repr. of 1956 ed. $29.50. ISBN 0-306-76289-7. Foreword by Benny Goodman.

_____. *The Jazz Years: Earwitness to an Era*. Da Capo 1987 $25.00. ISBN 0-306-79468-3. The recollections of a jazz chronicler.

_____. *The Passion for Jazz*. Da Capo 1990 repr. of 1980 ed. $10.95. ISBN 0-306-80402-6. Examines the ways in which jazz acted as a powerful cultural force throughout the 1970s.

Feather, Leonard, and Ira Gitler. *The Encyclopedia of Jazz in the Seventies*. Da Capo 1987 repr. of 1976 ed. $16.95. ISBN 0-306-80290-2. Introduction by Quincy Jones. Comprehensive reference guide to the key musicians and trends of the decade.

Finn, Julio. *The Bluesman: The Musical Heritage of Black Men and Women in the Americas*. Interlink Pub. 1992 $29.95. ISBN 0-940793-98-9. Illustrated by Willa Woolston. Biographical essays on early players that help trace the roots of this art form.

Friedlander, Lee. *The Jazz People of New Orleans*. Pantheon 1992 $50.00. ISBN 0-679-41638-2. Afterword by Whitney Balliett.

Friedlander, Will. *Jazz Singing: America's Great Voices from Bessie Smith to Bebop and Beyond*. Macmillan 1992 $15.00. ISBN 0-02-080131-9

Giddins, Gary. *Rhythm-a-ning: Jazz Traditional and Innovation in the '80s*. OUP 1986 $24.95. ISBN 0-19-503558-5. Chronicle of the jazz scene in the 1980s taken from the author's *Village Voice* column.

Gioia, Ted. *West Coast Jazz: Modern Jazz in California*. OUP 1992 $24.95. ISBN 0-19-506310-4. Traces the developments and contributions made by California artists between 1945 and 1960.

Gridley, Mark C. *Concise Guide to Jazz*. P-H 1991 $26.67. ISBN 0-13-175092-5

_____. *Jazz Styles: History and Analysis*. P-H 1990 $41.00. ISBN 0-13-507963-2. Chronological introduction to jazz written for those who have no experience with jazz, with clearly presented basic facts about important figures of jazz and their musical contributions.

Hadlock, Richard. *Jazz Masters of the Twenties*. Da Capo 1988 repr. of 1965 ed. $10.95. ISBN 0-306-80328-3. Biographical essays on the most important performers of the 1920s; includes Louis Armstrong, Fats Waller, and Bessie Smith.

Hefele, Bernhard. *Jazz Bibliography: An International Literature on Jazz, Blues, Spirituals, Gospel, and Ragtime Music with a Selected List of Works on the Social and Cultural Background from the Beginning to the Present*. K. G. Saur 1981 $40.00. ISBN 3-598-10205-4. Classified bibliography, providing excellent coverage up to about 1980.

Hodeir, André. *Jazz: Its Evolution and Essence*. Trans. by David Noakes. Da Capo 1975 repr. of 1956 ed. $35.00. ISBN 0-306-70682-2. Classic essay dealing with the principal styles, personalities, and problems of jazz.

Horricks, Raymond. *Profiles in Jazz: From Sidney Bechet to John Coltrane*. Transaction Pubs. 1991 $32.95. ISBN 0-88738-432-3. Collection of the author's profiles from *Crescendo* magazine.

Korall, Burt. *Drummin' Men, The Heartbeat of Jazz, the Swing Years*. Schirmer Bks. 1996 $27.95. ISBN 0-02-870711-7. Foreword by Mel Tormé. Biographical sketches of great jazz drummers; concentrates on the players of the 1920s and 1930s.

Meadows, Eddie S. *Jazz Reference and Research Materials: A Bibliography*. Garland 1981 $56.00. ISBN 0-8240-9463-8. Thorough survey of books and articles on jazz.

Placksin, Sally. *American Women in Jazz: Nineteen Hundred to the Present: Their Words, Lives and Music*. Putnam Pub. Group 1982 o.p.

Rose, Al, and Edmond Souchon. *New Orleans Jazz: A Family Album*. La. State U. Pr. 1984 $19.95. ISBN 0-8071-1173-2. A "who was who" with pictures, including a section on ensembles and a number of illustrated essays.

Rosenthal, David. *Hard Bop: Jazz and Black Music, 1955–1965*. OUP 1992 $23.00. ISBN 0-19-505869-0. A look at what the author considers the golden age of jazz. Explores the transition from be-bop and the decline of the sound.

Russell, Ross. *Jazz Styles in Kansas City and the Southwest*. U. CA Pr. 1982 repr. of 1971 ed. $32.50. ISBN 0-520-04767-2. Discussion of jazz styles in Kansas City, one of the three provincial centers of jazz development between 1920 and 1940, and throughout the Southwest.

Sales, Grover. *Jazz: America's Classical Music*. P-H 1984 $11.95. ISBN 0-13-509118-7. The principles of jazz explicated for the layperson, including good descriptions of the music and the performers.

Schuller, Gunther. *The Swing Era: The Development of Jazz, 1930–1945*. OUP 1989 $35.00. ISBN 0-19-504312-X. Comprehensive volume that traces the swing period from its earliest days to the beginning of the be-bop era; includes over 500 musical examples.

Shapiro, Nat, comp. *Hear Me Talkin' to Ya: The Story of Jazz by the Men Who Made It*. Ed. by Nat Shapiro and Nat Hentoff. Dover 1966 $7.95. ISBN 0-486-21726-4. A wide variety of jazz legends reminisce on their lives and their music.

Simon, George T. *The Big Bands*. Schirmer Bks. rev. ed. 1981 $29.95. ISBN 0-02-872420-8. Foreword by Frank Sinatra. A report on the greatest years of the big bands (1935–1946); focuses on the music and memories of the great players.

Smith, Michael P. *New Orleans Jazz Fest: A Pictorial History*. Pelican 1991 $21.95. ISBN 0-88289-810-8. Foreword by Ben Sandmel.

Stearns, Marshall Winslow. *The Story of Jazz*. OUP 1956 $22.50. ISBN 0-19-501269-0. Classic history of the genre.

Welding, Peter, and Toby Byron, eds. *Bluesland: Portraits of Twelve Major American Blues Masters*. NAL-Dutton 1991 $26.95. ISBN 0-525-3375-1. A well-illustrated collection of essays that profiles blues greats from Blind Lemon Jefferson to Chuck Berry.

Williams, Martin. *The Jazz Heritage*. OUP 1987 $25.00. ISBN 0-19-503611-5. Re-examinations of jazz artists after reissues of some of their recordings. Profiles of jazz artists and some consideration of theoretical matters.

———. *Jazz Masters in Transition, 1957–1969*. Da Capo 1980 repr. of 1970 ed. $32.50. ISBN 0-306-79612-0. Collection of articles from various sources.

———. *The Jazz Tradition*. OUP rev. ed. 1993 $39.95. ISBN 0-19-507815-2. Essays on jazz masters and jazz matters by the producer of acclaimed Smithsonian jazz albums.

———. *Where's the Melody: A Listener's Introduction to Jazz*. Da Capo 1983 repr. of 1966 ed. $8.95. ISBN 0-306-80183-3

NON-WESTERN MUSIC

Berliner, Paul F. *The Soul of Mbira: Music and Traditions of the Shona People of Zimbabwe*. U. Ch. Pr. 1993 $14.95. ISBN 0-226-04379-7. A study of African musical culture from the frame of reference of the *mbira*, the so-called finger piano. A good attempt to break from the colonialist mentality so often found in studies of non-Western music by Westerners.

Encyclopaedia of Indian Music, with Special Reference to the Ragas. Orient Bk. Dist. repr. of 1918 ed. 1986 $35.00. ISBN 81-7030-007-X

Holvik, Leonard C. *Japanese Music: Another Tradition, Other Sounds.* Ed. by Jackson H. Bailey. Earlham College Pr. 1990 $5.00. ISBN 0-9619977-7-X. Excellent introduction to Japan's long and distinguished history of musical culture.

Kaufman, Walter. *Musical References in the Chinese Classics.* Harmonie Pk. Pr. 1976 $30.00. ISBN 0-911772-68-5. Includes essays, translations, and sources of the original Chinese texts.

Lai, T. C., and Robert Mok. *Jade Flute: The Story of Chinese Music.* Schocken 1985 o.p.

Nketia, Joseph H. *The Music of Africa.* Norton 1974 $16.95. ISBN 0-393-09249-6. A survey of the broad musical traditions of Africa, set in their historical, social, and cultural contexts.

Titon, Jeff Todd, ed. *Worlds of Music: An Introduction to the Music of the World's Peoples.* Schirmer Bks. 1992 $32.95. ISBN 0-02-872602-2. Chapters on North America, Africa, Europe, and India, with recorded examples.

Wade, Bonnie C. *Music in India: The Classical Traditions.* Riverdale Co. 1987 $23.00. ISBN 0-913215-25-2. Introduction to the fundamental aspects of two classical Indian traditions, the Hindustani and the Karnatic.

OPERA

Abbate, Carolyn. *Unsung Voices: Opera and Musical Narrative in the Nineteenth Century. Princeton Studies in Opera.* Princeton U. Pr. 1991 $35.00. ISBN 0-691-09140-4

Conrad, Peter. *A Song of Love and Death: The Meaning of Opera.* Poseidon Pr. 1987 $12.00. ISBN 0-671-67263-0. Looks at opera's history to determine how each period makes drama out of music.

DiGaetani, John Louis. *An Invitation to the Opera.* Doubleday 1986 $10.95. ISBN 0-385-26339-2. A well-illustrated introductory history of the art form.

Donington, Robert. *Opera and Its Symbols: The Unity of Words, Music, and Staging.* Yale U. Pr. 1990 $32.00. ISBN 0-300-04713-4. Explores the ways in which opera combines modes of artistic expression to create a unique and powerful experience.

Grout, Donald J., and Hermine Weigel Williams. *A Short History of Opera.* Col. U. Pr. 1988 $49.00. ISBN 0-231-06192-7. A major work that traces the development of music and drama from the lyric theatre of the Greeks to the avant-garde work of the early twentieth century.

Hayter, Charles. *Gilbert and Sullivan.* St. Martin 1987 $21.95. ISBN 0-333-40759-8

Kerman, Joseph. *Opera as Drama.* U. CA Pr. rev. ed. 1988 $10.95. ISBN 0-520-06273-6. A discussion of operas by Monteverdi, Purcell, Mozart, Verdi, Wagner, and Stravinsky, among others, demonstrating that opera is a hybrid art form requiring appreciation and understanding from a number of viewpoints.

Kimbell, David R. B. *Italian Opera.* Cambridge U. Pr. 1991 $59.95. ISBN 0-521-23533-2. A comprehensive history of Italian opera that examines the form in its social context from its origins to the work of Puccini.

Loewenburg, Alfred, ed. *Annals of Opera, 1597–1940.* 2 vols. Riverrun NY 1994. Vol. 1 $99.00. ISBN 0-7145-3657-1. Vol. 2 $105.00. ISBN 0-7145-3777-2. Classic chronological reference to opera, each entry including names of librettist and composer, sources of plot, name of theater and city of first and subsequent productions, and other significant information. No synopses of plots included.

Martin, George W. *The Companion to Twentieth-Century Opera.* Trafalgar 1992 $24.95. ISBN 0-7195-4767-9. Short essays on a variety of operatic subjects, a glossary of operatic terms, and synopses of commonly produced operas.

Moore, Frank L. *Crowell's Handbook of World Opera.* Greenwood 1974 repr. of 1961 ed. $43.00. ISBN 0-8371-68228. Packed with useful information. Introduction by Darius Milhaud.

Orrey, Leslie. *Opera: A Concise History*. Ed. and rev. by Rodney Milnes. Thames Hudson 1987 $11.95. ISBN 0-500-20217-6. An illustrated history tracing the development of the genre throughout the Western world.

Orrey, Leslie, and Gilbert Chase, eds. *The Encyclopedia of Opera*. Scribner 1976 o.p. Approximately 3,000 entries on operas, operatic people, and places particularly relevant to opera today.

Pleasants, Henry. *The Great Singers: From the Dawn of Opera to Our Own Time*. S&S Trade rev. ed. 1985 $6.95. ISBN 0-671-42160-3. Biographical essays of those singers who have made significant contributions to the decisive phases of vocal art.

Rasponi, Lanfranco. *The Last Prima Donnas*. Limelight Edns. 1985 $19.95. ISBN 0-87910-040-0

Robinson, Paul A. *Opera and Ideas: From Mozart to Strauss*. Cornell Univ. Pr. 1986 $11.95. ISBN 0-06-015450-0. Illustrates the ways in which opera embodies the intellectual and cultural currents of its time. Explores the link between the philosophical and the musical.

Traubner, Richard. *Operetta: A Theatrical History*. Doubleday 1983 $16.95. ISBN 0-19-520778-5. An undocumented history of light opera from the 1850s to the 1950s. International scope; illustrated; musical examples; bibliography.

Tuggle, Robert. *The Golden Age of Opera*. H. Holt & Co. 1983 o.p. Covers Metropolitan Opera, its singers, and productions. Foreword by Anthony A. Bliss.

Tyrrell, John. *Czech Opera*. National Traditions of Opera. Cambridge U. Pr. 1988 $54.95. ISBN 0-521-23531-6

CONDUCTORS

Chester, Robert, ed. *Conductors in Conversation: Herbert von Karajan, Sir Georg Solti, Carlo Maria Giulini, Claudio Abbado, Eugene Ormandy, Riccardo Muti, James Levine*. Limelight Edns. 1992 repr. of 1990 ed. $14.95. ISBN 0-87910-156-3

Holmes, J. L. *Conductors on Record*. Greenwood 1982 $55.00. ISBN 0-313-22990-2. Entries include lists of works recorded by each conductor.

Lebrecht, Norman. *The Maestro Myth: Great Conductors in Pursuit of Power*. Carol Pub. Group 1992 $22.50. ISBN 1-55972-108-1. Attacks world-famous, power-hungry conductors for their facades and for placing money over the welfare of orchestras.

LePage, Jane Weiner. *Women Composers, Conductors, and Musicians of the Twentieth Century: Selected Biographies*. 2 vols. Scarecrow. Vol. 1 1980 $32.50. ISBN 0-8108-1298-3. Vol. 2 1983 $35.00. ISBN 0-8108-1597-4. Biographical sketches that trace the careers of significant women in music; includes selected compositions, discographies, and addresses.

Matheopoulous, Helena Maestro. *Encounters with Conductors of Today*. HarpC 1982 o.p. Essays on and interviews with 24 of the best-known musical directors; the von Karajan interview especially long and revealing.

The Music Lover's Literary Companion. Comp. by Dannie Abse and Joan Abse. Parkwest Pubns. 1991 $14.95. ISBN 0-86051-654-7

Unger-Hamilton, Clive, and Peter van der Spek, eds. *The Great Symphonies, The Great Orchestras, The Great Conductors*. Sidgwich & Jackson 1988 o.p. Contributions by Janny de Jong and others.

Wagar, Jeannine. *Conductors In Conversation: Fifteen Contemporary Conductors Discuss Their Lives and Profession*. Macmillan 1991 $29.95. ISBN 0-8161-8996-X

MUSICAL INSTRUMENTS

Boyden, David D. *History of Violin Playing, from Its Origins to 1761 and Its Relationship to the Violin and Violin Music*. OUP 1990 $39.95. ISBN 0-19-816183-2. The definitive study.

Gill, Dominic, ed. *The Book of the Piano*. Cornell Univ. Pr. 1981 $52.50. ISBN 0-8014-1399-0. A book of well-illustrated essays.

————. *The Book of the Violin*. Rizzoli Intl. 1984 o.p. A collection of well-illustrated essays.

Good, Edwin M. *Giraffes, Black Dragons and Other Pianos: A Technological History from Cristofori to the Modern Concert Grand.* Stanford U. Pr. 1982 $42.50. ISBN 0-8047-1120-8. A chronological treatment of the advances, or changes, made on the piano in its various stages of development.

Kehler, George. *The Piano in Concert.* 2 vols. Scarecrow 1982 o.p. Contains 2,000 biographical sketches of important pianists of the nineteenth and twentieth centuries, with chronological lists of composition in their repertories.

Lenz, Wilhelm von. *The Great Piano Virtuosos of Our Time: A Classic Account of Studies with Liszt, Chopin, Tausig, and Henselt.* Ed. by Philip Reder. Da Capo 1973 repr. of 1899 ed. $25.00. ISBN 0-306-70528-1

Loesser, Arthur. *Men, Women and Pianos.* S&S Trade 1964 o.p. Popular account filled with quotations from contemporary sources tracing the history of the piano from its inception to the mid-twentieth century.

Mach, Elyse. *Great Pianists Speak for Themselves.* Dodd 1980 o.p. Essays by the most famous pianists, each preceded with a biographical sketch and a photographic portrait. Introduction by George Solti.

Marcuse, Sibyl. *Musical Instruments: A Comprehensive Dictionary.* Norton rev. ed. 1975 o.p. Brief entries covering instruments of all times and places.

Ratcliffe, Ronald V. *Steinway.* Chronicle Bks. 1989 $40.00. ISBN 0-87701-592-9. Covers musical, technological, business, and cultural history in an ingratiating manner.

Remnant, Mary. *Musical Instruments: An Illustrated History, From Antiquity to the Present.* Timber 1990 $32.95. ISBN 0-931340-23-3. Well-illustrated volume that chronicles the evolution of musical instruments and their uses in performance.

Sachs, Curt. *The History of Western Instruments.* Norton 1940 o.p. Chronologically covers Western and non-Western instruments.

Schwartz, Boris. *Great Masters of the Violin, from Corelli to Stern, Zukerman, and Perlman.* S&S Trade 1983 $24.00. ISBN 0-671-22598-7. Foreword by Yehudi Menuhin. Comprehensive study tracing the careers of great performers and composers from the sixteenth century to the twentieth century.

SINGERS

Balliett, Whitney. *American Singers: Twenty-seven Portraits in Song.* OUP 1988 $27.95. ISBN 0-19-504610-2. Biographical sketches of 12 contemporary popular vocalists.

Breslin, Herbert H., ed. *The Tenors.* Macmillan 1974 o.p. Essays by established opera critics on Richard Tucker, Jon Vickers, Franco Corelli, Placido Domingo, and Luciano Pavarotti.

Celletti, Rodolfo. *The History of Bel Canto.* Trans. by Frederick Fuller. OUP 1991 $59.00. ISBN 0-19-313209-5. Traces Bel Canto singing and the singers who most epitomized the style.

Cowden, Robert H., ed. *Concert and Opera Singers: A Bibliography of Biographical Materials.* Greenwood 1985 $49.95. ISBN 0-313-24828-1

Hemming, Roy, and David Hajdu. *Discovering Great Singers of Classic Pop. Discovering Great Music Ser.* Newmarket 1992 $14.95. ISBN 1-55704-148-2

Hines, Jerome. *Great Singers on Great Singing.* Doubleday 1982 $13.95. ISBN 0-87910-025-7. Interviews with many of the great singers.

Kutsch, K. J., and Leo Riemens. *A Concise Biographical Dictionary of Singers, from the Beginning of Recorded Sound to the Present.* Trans. by Harry Earl Jones. Chilton 1969 o.p. Standard reference tool on the subject.

Mordden, Ethan. *Demented: The World of the Opera Diva.* Watts 1984 o.p. Narrative about the difficulties of being a prima donna.

Pleasants, Henry. *The Great American Popular Singers.* S&S Trade 1985 o.p. Biographical entries.

———. *The Great Singers, from Jenny Lind to Callas and Pavarotti.* S&S Trade rev. ed. 1981 o.p.

Rosselli, John. *Singers of Italian Opera: History of a Profession.* Cambridge U. Pr. 1992 $44.95. ISBN 0-521-41683-3

CHRONOLOGY OF AUTHORS
(Music)

Tallis, Thomas. c.1505–1585
Monteverdi, Claudio. 1567–1643
Purcell, Henry. 1659–1695
Vivaldi, Antonio. 1678–1741
Bach, Johann Sebastian. 1685–1750
Handel, George Frideric. 1685–1759
Haydn, Franz Joseph. 1732–1809
Mozart, Wolfgang Amadeus.
  1756–1791
Beethoven, Ludwig van. 1770–1827
Schubert, Franz. 1797–1828
Bellini, Vincenzo. 1801–1835
Berlioz, Hector. 1803–1869
Hensel, Fanny. 1805–1847
Mendelssohn, Felix. 1809–1847
Chopin, Frédéric. 1810–1849
Schumann, Robert. 1810–1856
Liszt, Franz. 1811–1886
Verdi, Giuseppe. 1813–1901
Wagner, Richard. 1813–1883
Gounod, Charles. 1818–1893
Schumann, Clara. 1819–1896
Bruckner, Anton. 1824–1896
Smetana, Bedřich. 1824–1884
Foster, Stephen. 1826–1864
Borodin, Alexander. 1833–1887
Brahms, Johannes. 1833–1897
Mussorgsky, Modest. 1839–1881
Tchaikovsky, Peter Ilich. 1840–1893
Dvořák, Antonin. 1841–1904
Grieg, Edvard. 1843–1907
Rimsky-Korsakov, Nikolay. 1844–1908
Fauré, Gabriel. 1845–1924
Janáček, Leoš. 1854–1928
Elgar, Sir Edward. 1857–1934
Puccini, Giacomo. 1858–1924
Mahler, Gustav. 1860–1911
Debussy, Claude. 1862–1918
Strauss, Richard. 1864–1949
Sibelius, Jean. 1865–1957
Satie, Erik. 1866–1925
Joplin, Scott. 1868–1917
Scriabin, Aleksandr. 1872–1915
Vaughan Williams, Ralph. 1872–1958
Caruso, Enrico. 1873–1921
Rachmaninoff, Sergey. 1873–1943
Ives, Charles Edward. 1874–1954
Schoenberg, Arnold. 1874–1951
Ravel, Maurice. 1875–1937

Bartók, Béla. 1881–1945
Stravinsky, Igor. 1882–1971
Webern, Anton von. 1883–1945
Berg, Alban. 1885–1935
Kern, Jerome. 1885–1945
Rubinstein, Artur. 1887–1982
Porter, Cole. 1891–1964
Prokofiev, Sergei. 1891–1953
Hindemith, Paul. 1895–1963
Thomson, Virgil. 1896–1989
Gershwin, George. 1898–1937
Anderson, Marian. 1899–1993
Ellington, Edward Kennedy.
  1899–1974
Armstrong, Louis. 1900–1971
Copland, Aaron. 1900–1990
Rodgers, Richard. 1902–1979
Basie, William. 1904–1984
Horowitz, Vladimir. 1904–1989
Waller, "Fats". 1904–1943
Tippett, Sir Michael. 1905–
Shostakovich, Dmitri. 1906–1975
Carter, Benny. 1907–
Wilder, Alec. 1907–1980
Carter, Elliott. 1908–
Barber, Samuel. 1910–1981
Cage, John. 1912–1992
Britten, Lord Benjamin. 1913–1976
Holiday, Billie. 1915–1959
Sinatra, Frank. 1915–
Harrison, Lou. 1917–
Bernstein, Leonard. 1918–1990
Parker, Charlie. 1920–1955
Xenakis, Iannis. 1922–
Callas, Maria. 1923–1977
Berio, Luciano. 1925–
Boulez, Pierre. 1925–
Davis, Miles. 1925–1991
Coltrane, John. 1926–1967
Price, Leontyne. 1927–
Stockhausen, Karlheinz. 1928–
Sills, Beverly. 1929–
Charles, Ray. 1930–
Sondheim, Stephen. 1930–
Pavarotti, Luciano. 1935–
Glass, Philip. 1937–
Domingo, Plácido. 1941–
Carreras, José. 1946–
Lloyd Webber, Andrew. 1948–

ANDERSON, MARIAN. 1899–1993

Marian Anderson was born in Philadelphia. She studied with Giuseppe Boghette and Frank La Forge. An African American contralto, Anderson had successfully performed throughout Europe before ecstatic audiences, yet was refused permission by the Daughters of the American Revolution to sing at Constitution Hall in Washington, D.C., in 1939. The following Easter Sunday, she sang before hundreds at the Lincoln Memorial. In 1955 she became the first African American to perform at the Metropolitan Opera, singing as Ulrica in *Un Ballo in Maschera*. She received many honors, including the American Freedom Medal. She is admired for her artistic integrity.

BOOK ABOUT ANDERSON

Patterson, Charles. *Marian Anderson*. Watts 1988 $13.90. ISBN 0-531-10568-7. An interesting and informative biography; includes a substantial discography.

ARMSTRONG, LOUIS ("SATCHMO"). 1900–1971

Louis Armstrong, or "Satchmo," was one of the most innovative American jazz trumpeters of his era and one of the great ambassadors of American jazz. Armstrong began his career in New Orleans, where, as a young boy, he was a street singer and learned to play the trumpet. In 1922 he moved to Chicago and joined the jazz orchestra of Joe "King" Oliver. He quickly became noted for his improvisational style and raised the importance of solo performances in jazz. By the late 1920s, Armstrong led his own jazz ensemble, called the Louis Armstrong Hot Five, which later became the Hot Seven.

As he gained in popularity, Armstrong made numerous recordings and performed around the world. He had a number of hit records, including "Hello, Dolly" and "Mack the Knife." He also appeared in Broadway shows and in films. His raspy baritone voice and brilliant trumpet playing combined to make an unforgettable musical sound, appreciated worldwide by young and old alike.

BOOKS BY ARMSTRONG

Louis Armstrong: A Self-Portrait. Eakins 1971 o.p. The interview by Richard Meryman.
Satchmo: My Life in New Orleans. Da Capo 1986 $10.95. Introduction by Dan Morgenstern.
Swing That Music. Longman 1936 o.p. Introduction by Rudy Vallee.

BOOKS ABOUT ARMSTRONG

Collier, James Lincoln. *Louis Armstrong, an American Genius*. OUP 1983 $12.95. ISBN 0-19-503727-8
Giddins, Gary. *Satchmo*. Doubleday 1992 $15.00. ISBN 0-385-244290. A hip and insightful biography by the *Village Voice* jazz critic.
Hoskins, Robert. *Louis Armstrong: Biography of a Musician*. Holloway 1980 o.p. Back matter includes filmography and discography.
Jones, Max, and John Chilton. *Louis: The Louis Armstrong Story, 1900–1971*. Da Capo 1988 repr. of 1971 ed. $10.95. ISBN 0-306-80322-6. Authorized biography of Armstrong by a friend and writer about jazz and by a fellow jazz trumpeter.
Pinfold, Mike. *Louis Armstrong, His Life and Times*. Universe 1987 $17.50. ISBN 0-87663-667-9. Illustrated biography that views Armstrong as the greatest single influence in the history of jazz.

BACH, JOHANN SEBASTIAN. 1685–1750

Composer, organist, and the most famous of an illustrious family of German musicians, Johann Sebastian Bach was a master of polyphonic baroque music—a musical form characterized by the use of multiple parts in harmony and by an ornate, exuberant style. Bach's father, Johann Ambrosius, taught his son to play the violin at a very early age. At age 10, after both of his parents died, Bach lived with his brother Johann Christoph, an organist, who taught him to play keyboard instruments. Bach's musical genius, however, soon surpassed his brother's skill. During his lifetime, Bach was known more for his skill as an organist than as a composer. His fame as a composer did not come until years after his death, when his works were "discovered" by the composers FELIX MENDELSSOHN and ROBERT SCHUMANN and published in the 1800s.

Bach served as an organist in the German cities of Arnstadt, Muhlhausen, and Weimar between the years 1703 and 1717. During this time, Bach wrote chorales, cantatas, concertos, preludes, and fugues, primarily for the organ. These works fused Italian, French, and German characteristics with a profound mastery of the contrapuntal technique. While serving as music director at the court of a German prince from 1717 to 1723, Bach wrote many compositions for the clavier and instrumental ensembles. These included preludes, fantasies, toccatas, and dance suites that served as both music instruction and entertainment. Of these works, the best known is the *Well-Tempered Clavier*, a series of preludes and fugues composed in 1722 and 1740.

In his last position as cantor and music director of St. Thomas's Church in Leipzig (1724–50), Bach exerted considerable influence on Lutheran church music. During this period, he composed as many as 300 cantatas, 200 of which have been preserved. After his death at the age of 65, Bach became revered as one of the world's greatest composers, and his compositions are regarded by many as the most sublime music ever composed.

BOOKS ABOUT BACH

David, Hans T., and Arthur Mendel, eds. *The Bach Reader.* Norton rev. ed. 1966 $14.95. ISBN 0-393-00259-4. A collection of documents on Bach's life and music up to the "discovery" of Bach by Mendelssohn and others in the late 1820s.

Forkel, Johann N. *Johann Sebastian Bach: His Life, Art and Work.* Trans. by Charles S. Terry. Da Capo 1970 $42.50. ISBN 0-306-70010-7. First biography of Bach, written in 1749, that claims his preeminence.

Geiringer, Karl, and Irene Geiringer. *Bach.* Little 1979 o.p. A general biography that provides a clear picture of the composer's life and creative process.

BARBER, SAMUEL. 1910–1981

One of America's most accomplished composers, Samuel Barber was born in West Chester, Pennsylvania. He grew up in a musical family—his mother was a pianist, and his aunt, Louise Homer, was a famous opera contralto. Barber began studying piano at the age of 6. By the age of 7, he attempted to write his first composition, a piano piece entitled *Sadness*. At the age of 10, Barber planned a full-length opera.

While attending high school, Barber performed for Harold Randolph, director of the Peabody Conservatory in Baltimore. Randolph advised Barber to devote himself entirely to music and encouraged him to apply to the Curtis Institute, a newly founded school of music. At that institute, Barber studied piano, composition, and singing. In 1928 he received the Bearns Prize for a violin sonata. However, it was not until several years later, when Barber wrote two highly innovative orchestral works, that he became recognized as a composer of considerable worth. The first of these works was *Overture to the School for Scandal* (1933), which brought Barber the Bearns Prize for a second time. The second was *Music for a Scene from Shelley*, a piece inspired by PERCY BYSSHE SHELLEY's (see Vol. 1) *Prometheus Unbound*.

After winning the Prix de Rome, Barber settled in Rome at the American Academy. There he composed his first symphony, the *Symphony in One Movement* (1936), in which he compressed four sections of a traditional symphony into one movement.

While serving in World War II, Barber was commissioned to write a symphony in honor of the U.S. Air Force. Obviously influenced by the war, this piece was considerably more dissonant and astringent than his previous work had been. After being discharged, Barber returned to Capricorn, his home in Mount Kisco, New York. There Barber wrote the major works for which he would be placed first among American composers, including *Concerto for Cello and Orchestra* (1945) and the ballet *Medea* (1946).

By the late 1940s, Barber's style was established. He combined strong lyrical and emotional elements with modern harmonic and rhythmic approaches. Barber's first opera, *Vanessa* (1958), received the Pulitzer Prize in Music. He received a second Pulitzer Prize in Music in 1962 for his *Piano Concerto*.

BOOKS ABOUT BARBER

Broder, Nathan. *Samuel Barber*. Greenwood 1985 repr. of 1954 ed. $45.00. ISBN 0-313-24984-9. The first substantive biography of Barber; covers his career to 1951.

Heyman, Barbara B. *Samuel Barber: The Composer and His Music*. OUP 1992 $45.00. ISBN 0-19-506650-2. An exhaustive historical study that traces Barber's career in light of all of his published and most of his unpublished works.

BARTÓK, BÉLA. 1881–1945

One of the outstanding composers of the twentieth century, Béla Bartók was born in Hungary in 1881. His mother began to teach him piano at the age of 5, and, by the age of 9, he had begun to compose his own music. Between 1899 and 1903, he attended the Academy of Music in Budapest and was appointed professor of piano in 1907.

Bartók's early compositions were complex and not well received by the public. In 1905 he turned his attention to collecting and cataloging the folk music of his native Hungary. With the help of his friend and fellow Hungarian, composer Zoltán Kodály, Bartók produced a series of commentaries, anthologies, and arrangements of the folk music that he had collected. Bartók's interest in folk music had a profound effect on his compositions. The influence is seen in the unadorned power of his music, especially in the rhythmic drive of fast movements and in his use of folk melodies, rhythms, and harmonic patterns.

Throughout his life, Bartók had to struggle to make a living. Yet he refused to teach musical composition, believing that this would inhibit his own composing. Instead, he earned a living teaching piano and performing. During the 1920s he traveled throughout Europe giving piano recitals, and, in 1927 and 1928, he made a concert tour of the United States.

In 1940, after the outbreak of World War II, Bartók left Hungary to settle in the United States, where he continued to perform and compose music. He was supported by patroness Elizabeth Sprague Coolidge. Bartók died of leukemia in 1945. Among his most famous compositions are the *Mikrokosmos* for piano

(1926–27), *Music for Strings, Percussion, and Celesta* (1936), and *Concerto for Orchestra* (1943).

BOOK BY BARTÓK

Essays. Ed. by Benjamin Suchoff. U. of Nebr. Pr. 1992 repr. of 1976 ed. $19.95. ISBN 0-8032-6108-X. Essays demonstrating his broad range of interests.

BOOKS ABOUT BARTÓK

Gillies, Malcolm. *Bartók Remembered.* Norton 1991 $25.95. ISBN 0-393-02971-9. Personal reflections on the composer's personal and musical achievements.

Milne, Hammish. *Bartók.* 1981 $40.00. ISBN 0-8464-3095-2. Comprehensive account of the composer's life and work.

Ránki, György, ed. *Bartók and Kodály Revisited.* Humanities 1987 $35.00. ISBN 963-05-4510-1

Stevens, Halsey. *Life and Music of Béla Bartók.* OUP rev. ed. 1967 o.p. Scholarly examination of Bartók's life and music.

Wilson, Paul. *The Music of Béla Bartók.* Yale U. Pr. 1992 $27.50. ISBN 0-300-05111-5. The most current and comprehensive analysis of Bartók's music.

BASIE, WILLIAM ("COUNT"). 1904–1984

William "Count" Basie was the most famous and long-lived jazz composer identified with the big-band style. Although Basie is known for playing jazz piano, his interest in music began with drums. It was not until Basie received lessons from a local teacher that he concentrated solely on piano.

Early in his music career, Basie played with several groups in Kansas City, New York City, Dallas, and Little Rock, Arkansas. In 1935 Basie returned to Kansas City to work as a solo musician. Later, he joined with a trio before jointly leading the Barons of Rhythm with altoist Buster Smith. Under Basie's leadership, the band broadcast over Station WXBY. From that time Basie was nicknamed "Count." Shortly after the broadcast, Basie embarked on his first national tour.

Throughout the 1940s, the Basie band played in most of the major ballrooms and theaters throughout the United States. From the 1950s until his death, Basie toured worldwide.

Basie's piano style was recognizable by the predominant use of his right hand. In 1981 he received national recognition at the Kennedy Center. He is the composer of such popular classics as "April in Paris," "Jumpin' at the Woodside," "Broadway," and the "One O'Clock Jump."

BOOK BY BASIE

Good Morning Blues: The Autobiography of Count Basie. (coauthored with Albert Murray). D.I. Fine 1985 $10.95. ISBN 0-917657-89-6. Divides Basie's career into two sections—from 1927 to 1950 and from 1951 to 1984.

BOOKS ABOUT BASIE

Dance, Stanley. *The World of Count Basie.* Da Capo 1985 $13.95. ISBN 0-306-80245-7. Examines Basie's music and the sociocultural context in which it was created.

Horricks, Raymond. *Count Basie and His Orchestra, Its Music and Its Musicians.* Greenwood 1972 repr. of 1957 ed. $22.50. ISBN 0-8371-5656-4. Views Basie's orchestra as the major force in the forward progression of the big band in jazz.

BEETHOVEN, LUDWIG VAN. 1770–1827

Ludwig van Beethoven was born in Berlin, where he began studying music at the age of 4 and published his first works at the age of 11. In 1792 he moved to

Vienna and studied briefly with FRANZ JOSEPH HAYDN and Johann Georg Albrechtsberger. His compositions revolutionized music with their dramatic use of harmonic and rhythmic motives. Beethoven was the first major composer to attempt to make a living from compositions without having continuous employment in a noble court or a church. His symphonies, string quartets, and the *Missa Solemnis* compete in importance only with his piano sonatas. Although deafness began to afflict him in 1801, it did not affect his creative genius. His funeral was attended by thousands of admirers.

BOOKS ABOUT BEETHOVEN

Arnold, Denis, and Nigel Fortune, eds. *The Beethoven Reader.* Norton 1971 o.p. Essays by Beethoven specialists striving to fill in gaps in the history and understanding of Beethoven and his music.

Cooper, Barry, ed. *The Beethoven Compendium.* Thames Hudson 1992 $40.00. ISBN 0-500-01523-6

_____. *Beethoven and the Creative Process.* OUP 1990 $75.00. ISBN 0-19-816163-8. A comprehensive view of the way Beethoven composed his music. Examines what his chief compositional goals were and how he achieved them.

Landon, H. C. Robbins, ed. *Beethoven: His Life, Work and World.* Thames Hudson 1993 $40.00. ISBN 0-500-01540-6. An excellent biography that includes a section of portraits and an index of his compositions.

Newman, William S. *Beethoven on Beethoven: Playing His Piano Music His Way.* Norton 1991 $14.95. ISBN 0-393-30719-0. Explores the main interpretive problems confronting the performer, teacher, and student of Beethoven's piano music.

Solomon, Maynard. *Beethoven.* Schirmer Bks. 1979 $16.00. ISBN 0-02-872240-X. Significantly illuminates the composer's psychological development and evolution of his personal relationships and the connections between his life and his music.

_____. *Beethoven Essays.* HUP 1988 $14.95. ISBN 0-674-06379-1. All of Solomon's essays on Beethoven. Contains in-depth studies of psychological, historical, and creative issues; also includes the complete texts of several background papers.

Tovey, Donald F. *A Companion to Beethoven's Pianoforte Sonatas.* AMS Pr. repr. of 1931 ed. $30.00. ISBN 0-404-13117-4. Each sonata is presented with critical and historical information.

Tyson, Alan, ed. *Beethoven Studies II.* OUP 1977 $34.95. ISBN 0-19-315315-7. Essays include biographical, critical, and analytical information on the composer. Investigates sketches and similar source material.

_____. *Beethoven Studies III.* Cambridge U. Pr. 1982 $74.95. ISBN 0-521-24131-6. Third collection of essays, this time with special emphasis on Beethoven's working methods.

Wegeler, Franz Gerhard, and Ferdinand Ries. *Beethoven Remembered: The Biographical Notes of Franz Wegeler and Ferdinand Ries.* Great Ocean 1987 $16.95. ISBN 0-915556-15-4. With a foreword by Christopher Hogwood and an introduction by Eva Badura-Skoda.

Winter, Robert, and Robert Martin, eds. *The Beethoven Quartet Companion.* U. CA Pr. 1994. ISBN 0-520-08211-7

BELLINI, VINCENZO. 1801–1835

Vincenzo Bellini was born in Satania, Sicily. He represented only one generation in a long history of professional musicians. His father, who was an organist for Cantania Cathedral, gave Bellini his first music lessons. Early in his music career, Bellini wrote religious and secular pieces that attracted the attention of the Duchess of Sammartino, who provided funds for Bellini to attend the San Sebastiano Conservatory in Naples. There Bellini completed two masses; *Ismene,* a cantata; a symphony; and his first opera, *Adelson e Salvina* (1825).

Also in 1825 impresario Barbaja commissioned Bellini to write an opera for one of his theaters. Bellini wrote *Bianca e Fernando* (1825). His next opera, *Il Pirata* (1827), foreshadowed characteristics of Bellini's developed style, which are exemplified in *I Capuletti e I Montecchi* (1830), an opera based on SHAKESPEARE'S (see Vol. 1) *Romeo and Juliet*. Bellini's next opera, *La Sonnambula* (1831), represents his first undisputed masterwork. The success of this opera led to another commissioned opera, for which Bellini wrote *Norma* (1831). *Norma* was Bellini's personal favorite and his second critically acclaimed masterpiece. In *Norma*, Bellini attained majestic melodic expressiveness and elegant lyricism, as exemplified in Norma's aria, "Casta Diva." Before Bellini died of intestinal fever, he finished his final opera *I Puritani* (1835). His last two operas are produced regularly by the world's major opera companies.

Bellini is highly regarded as a composer of great melodies in the bel canto style. In addition to his remarkable melodic gifts, Bellini was a powerful dramatist who influenced the direction and evolution of opera.

BOOK ABOUT BELLINI

Orrey, Leslie. *Bellini.* FS&G 1969 o.p. An account of his life and work.

BERG, ALBAN. 1885–1935

Born in Vienna, Austria, Alban Berg received no formal music instruction. His father's death left him in financial trouble. Berg began writing music to support the family. At the age of 18, he tried to commit suicide after a frustrating love affair and a failure on a school examination. As he was emerging from his depression, Berg was introduced by his older brother to ARNOLD SCHOENBERG. His lessons with Schoenberg were his first formal instruction in music. He studied with Schoenberg for six years, in which time he completed a number of works, including a piano sonata, op. 1 (1908); *Four Songs*, op. 2 (1909); and a string quartet, op. 3 (1910).

Berg's first piece independent of Schoenberg was *Five Orchestral Songs*, op. 4 (1912). He completed two more works before the outbreak of World War I—*Four Pieces*, for clarinet and piano, op. 5 (1913), dedicated to Schoenberg, and *Three Orchestral Pieces*, op. 6 (1914). These works represent the way in which Berg assimilated Schoenberg's atonal language and intricate contrapuntal textures but used them in a unique way. Berg brought together in his atonal writing a romantic, intimate approach and a strong, dramatic viewpoint.

After the war, Berg began work on the operatic score for GEORG BÜCHNER's (see Vol. 2) play *Wozzeck*. He had previously written the libretto himself in 1917. He completed the basic score by 1920 and the orchestration by 1921. *Wozzeck* received mixed reviews: Some regarded it as pure genius; others regarded the opera as the ravings of a madman. *Wozzeck* is a highly complex opera; it fuses avant-garde methods with such classical forms as the fugue, suite, march, and symphony.

During the last seven years of his life, Berg labored on *Lulu*, an opera he did not live to complete. Berg wrote the libretto himself, which he adapted from two dramas by FRANK WEDEKIND (see Vol. 2)—*Die Büchse der Pandora* and *Erdgeist*. *Lulu* relies exclusively on the 12-tone system, the row on which the opera is based appearing at the very beginning. When Berg died of blood poisoning brought about by a bee sting, he had only finished the first two acts of *Lulu*, 268 measures of the third act, and the finale.

BOOKS ABOUT BERG

Brand, Juliane, Christopher Hailey, and Donald Harris. *The Berg-Schoenberg Correspondence: Selected Letters*. Norton 1987 $35.00. ISBN 0-393-01919-5. A selection of the correspondence between Arnold Schoenberg and Alban Berg.

Carner, Mosco. *Alban Berg*. Holmes & Meier 1983 $47.50. ISBN 0-8419-1256-4. A full-length study of Alban Berg as man and artist.

Jarman, Douglas. *The Berg Companion*. NE U. Pr. 1990 $40.00. ISBN 1-55553-068-0. Provides information of use to Berg scholars and shows the range of work being done in the field of Berg studies.

————. *The Music of Alban Berg*. U. CA Pr. 1978 $15.95. ISBN 0-520-04954-3. Examines Berg's work, his technique, and the role that tonality and other traditional elements play in his music.

Monson, Karen. *Alban Berg*. HM 1979 o.p. A detailed, extensively researched biography of Alban Berg.

BERIO, LUCIANO. 1925–

Luciano Berio was born in Oneglia, near Genoa, Italy. Music was an intrinsic part of his childhood. His father was his first teacher, instructing him on the organ and piano. At the age of 15, Berio went to the Milan Conservatory, where he studied composition and conducting. After graduation, Berio worked for a short period as a voice coach and conductor in several Italian opera houses and composed several pieces, including *Due Pezzi*, for violin and piano (1951); *Variazioni*, for piano (1952); and *Chamber Music*, for voice, clarinet, cello, and harp, based on poems by JAMES JOYCE (see Vol. 1).

While at the Berkshire Music Center at the Tanglewood Music Center in Lenox, Massachusetts, Berio studied composition with Luigi Dallapiccola. Dallapiccola introduced Berio to the artistic potentials of 12-tone music and serialism. *Variations for Chamber Orchestra* (1953); *Nones*, for orchestra (1954); and *Allelujah 1*, for orchestra (1956) are characterized as controlled serialism. In 1954 Berio returned to Milan, where he founded the Studio di Fonologia Musicale in order to experiment with electronic music. He incorporated electronic sounds into such compositions as *Mutazioni* (1955); *Omaggio a Joyce* (1958), based on Chapter 11 of James Joyce's *Ulysses*; and *Momento* (1958). Berio no longer confined music to pitched sound; he embraced the world of sound and experimented with and used sounds of all kinds in his compositions. *Visage* (1960) was the last piece of music that Berio wrote during this period of experimentation with electronics at his Milan studio.

In 1960 Berio returned to the United States. He taught music at Mills College at Oakland, California, and Harvard University before settling at the Julliard School of Music in New York City.

BOOK BY BERIO

Two Interviews with Rossana Dalmonte and Balint Andras Varga. Ed. and trans. by David Osmond-Smith. M. Boyars Pubs. 1985 o.p. Wide-ranging discussions of Berio's aesthetic views as well as his views on technical matters and the avant-garde musical scene. With a short biography.

BOOK ABOUT BERIO

Osmond-Smith, David. *Berio*. OUP 1991 $21.00. ISBN 0-19-315478-1. An examination of Luciano Berio's musical career.

BERLIOZ, HECTOR. 1803–1869

French composer Hector Berlioz was one of the most influential composers of the romantic period in music. The son of a French physician, Berlioz showed an early aptitude for music and taught himself to perform and compose. For a time, his father indulged this pastime, but in 1821 he sent his son to Paris to study medicine. Although he attended lectures at the medical school there, Berlioz gave most of his attention to music, studying with a private music teacher and composing his own pieces. Finally, in 1826 Berlioz abandoned his medical studies and enrolled at the Paris Conservatory. To support himself, he gave music lessons and wrote articles on music.

While at the Paris Conservatory, Berlioz applied for the Prix de Rome. He entered the contest four times before finally winning the prize in 1830. In that same year, Berlioz completed the *Symphonie Fantastique*, his most ambitious and well-known work. The symphony is a musical description of the dreams of an artist under the influence of opium. Based on *Confessions of an English Opium Eater* by THOMAS DE QUINCEY (see Vol. 1), the symphony is an example of program music—music that represents a story or sequence of ideas. Berlioz developed the genre of program music into a highly regarded art, drawing themes from the works of WILLIAM SHAKESPEARE (see Vol. 1), JOHANN WOLFGANG VON GOETHE (see Vol. 2), LORD BYRON (see Vol. 1), and Théophile Gautier.

Because the unusual nature of his compositions failed to win him much recognition, Berlioz was forced to earn a living as a music critic and music librarian. By the time he was 34 years old, he had established a pattern in his career: Each new musical composition was greeted by a mixture of wild enthusiasm from younger composers and hostility from the entrenched musical establishment. Although he did achieve some measure of fame in later life, Berlioz's genius went largely unrecognized.

Despondent in later years because of a broken marriage and financial problems, Berlioz composed the dramatic symphony *Romeo and Juliet*. His last years were lived in bitterness and loneliness after the death of his second wife and his son. He died in Paris in 1869 after a long illness.

Berlioz has been called the greatest composer of melody since MOZART. He is also recognized as a master of the orchestra, having greatly expanded its expressive range through his profound understanding of individual instruments. Finally, his experimentation with new musical structures and meters freed younger composers from the strict requirements of classical musical forms and opened the way to other musical approaches.

BOOKS BY BERLIOZ

Hector Berlioz: Selections from His Letters, and Aesthetic, Humorous and Satirical Writings. Trans. by William F. Apthorp. Longwood MA 1976 repr. of 1879 ed. $40.00. ISBN 0-89341-018-7

The Life, as Written by Himself in His Letters and Memoirs. Trans. by Katharine F. Boult. AMS Pr. repr. of 1803 ed. $18.00. ISBN 0-404-12865-3. An autobiographical account of Berlioz's life from his letters and memoirs.

Memoirs. Dover 1960 $9.95. ISBN 0-486-21563-6. Comprises Berlioz's travels in Germany, Italy, Russia, and England. An attempt on his part to correct many misstatements printed about him.

New Letters of Berlioz, 1830–1868. Trans. by Jacques Barzun. Greenwood 1974 $22.50. ISBN 0-8371-3251-7. A collection of Berlioz's previously unpublished correspondence.

BOOKS ABOUT BERLIOZ

Barzun, Jacques. *Berlioz and His Century: An Introduction to the Age of Romanticism.* U. Ch. Pr. 1982 $14.95. ISBN 0-226-03861-0. Analysis of the composer's role in the romantic period of music and art.

Holoman, D. Kern. *The Creative Process in the Autograph Musical Documents of Hector Berlioz.* Ed. by George Buelow. Bks. Demand repr. of 1980 ed. $104.60. ISBN 0-685-20832-X. Includes documents, the methods of Berlioz's works, and three examples of these methods.

MacDonald, Hugh. *Berlioz Orchestral Music.* Biblio Dist. 1983 o.p. A comprehensive guide to Berlioz's orchestral music.

Rushton, Julian. *The Musical Language of Berlioz.* Cambridge U. Pr. 1984 $59.50. ISBN 0-521-24279-7. Analysis of the French composer's musical style, including his use of melody, rhythm, and orchestral features.

BERNSTEIN, LEONARD. 1918–1990

Called by many the greatest figure in American music, Leonard Bernstein was a charismatic and controversial conductor, a gifted teacher, an accomplished pianist, and a highly admired composer. As a teacher Bernstein communicated his love for music, whether classical or popular, through his Young People's Concerts, many of which were televised. At the Tanglewood Music Center in Lenox, Massachusetts, he taught many students who are now present-day conductors of American symphony orchestras. As a composer Bernstein is best known for his popular works, including the Broadway musicals *West Side Story* (1958), *Candide* (1956), and *Wonderful Town*; the film score for *On the Waterfront*; and the ballet *Fancy Free* (1958)—all of which were published in the 1950s. However, it was as a conductor with an exuberant, dynamic, and dramatic style that Bernstein captured the attention of the American public.

Born to Russian-Jewish immigrants in Lawrence, Massachusetts, Bernstein started taking piano lessons at the age of 10, using his own allowance to pay for the lessons. He continued his musical studies at the Curtis Institute of Music in Philadelphia, where he quickly displayed his varied talents as a pupil of renowned conductor Fritz Reiner.

At the age of 25, Bernstein became an overnight sensation when he substituted for an ailing conductor during a concert. In 1958, when he was named musical director of the New York Philharmonic, Bernstein became the first native-born American to head a symphony orchestra. His association with the New York Philharmonic lasted until 1969, when he resigned to concentrate on composing.

BOOKS BY BERNSTEIN

Bernstein on Broadway. Astor Bks. $19.95. ISBN 0-911320-01-6

Findings. S&S Trade 1982 o.p. A brilliant self-portrait of Bernstein as both an individual and an artist.

The Joy of Music. S&S Trade 1963 $5.95. ISBN 0-671-39721-4. An adventure in musical understanding based on seven scripts from Bernstein's *Omnibus* television shows and five penetrating essays.

The Unanswered Question: Six Talks at Harvard. HUP 1976 $17.95. ISBN 0-674-92001-5. Six lectures originally prepared for an audience at Harvard University.

BOOKS ABOUT BERNSTEIN

Fluegel, Jane, ed. *Bernstein Remembered.* Carroll & Graf 1991 o.p. Brilliant biography of Bernstein's life and work; includes numerous photographs. With an introduction by Donal Henahan and a preface by Isaac Stern.

Gradenwitz, Peter. *Leonard Bernstein.* St. Martin 1987 $21.95. ISBN 0-85496-510-6. A collection of personal contributions about Bernstein by such notables as Yehudi and Diane Menuhin, Isaac Stern, Lukas Foss, Virgil Thomson, and Abba Eban; includes a bibliography, filmography, and discography.

Peyser, Joan. *Bernstein: A Biography*. Ballantine 1988 $5.95. ISBN 0-345-35296-3. Well-written biography providing an even-handed look at his personal life and creative output.

BORODIN, ALEXANDER. 1833–1887

Born in St. Petersburg, Alexander Borodin was educated at home by private tutors. He excelled in many subjects, including foreign language and science. Without formal instruction, Borodin learned to play the flute and the cello and acquired the rudiments of music theory from textbooks. At the age of 10, Borodin wrote *Helene*, a piano polka inspired by, and dedicated to, his first love. Later, Borodin became an active and productive member of "The Russian Five," the school with which Russian nationalistic music came to full flower. Borodin's main occupation was as a scientist; his music took a lesser role. Even though he described himself as a "Sunday composer," Borodin compiled a respectable body of work, including operas, orchestral and chamber music, and piano and vocal music. Most notable is his unfinished opera *Prince Igor*, from which he extracted the well-known "Polovtsian Dances" for orchestra. Borodin's compositions are noted for their use of rhythmic and orchestral color.

BOOKS ABOUT BORODIN

Figurovskii, Nikolai Aleksandrovich. *Aleksandr Porfirevich Borodin: A Chemist's Biography*. Trans. by Charlene Steinberg and George B. Kauffman. Springer-Verlag 1988 $96.00. ISBN 0-387-17888-0. A biography of Borodin that attempts to close the gaps in previous treatments of his life and accomplishments. Foreword by Martin D. Kamen.

Habets, Alfred. *Borodin and Liszt*. Trans. by Rosa Newmarch. AMS Pr. repr. of 1895 ed. $19.50. ISBN 0-404-12938-2. Vol. 1 *Life and Works of a Russian Composer*. Vol. 2 *Liszt, as Sketched in the Letters of Borodin*.

BOULEZ, PIERRE. 1925–

As a child, Pierre Boulez sang in his church choir. His sister taught him to play the piano at an early age. He received additional training in music from private teachers. Despite his musical aptitude, his parents directed him toward a career in engineering; however, his interest and talent in music eventually won out. After he graduated from the Paris Conservatory in 1945, Boulez continued to study with Olivier Messiaen, one of his teachers at the conservatory. That same year, Boulez completed his first composition, *Three Psalmodies*, for piano, which exhibits an influence of Messiaen's intricate rhythms.

Boulez believed that twentieth-century composers were meant to create a new musical language free from romantic associations. ARNOLD SCHOENBERG's 12-tone system dominated his writing and thinking. In 1946 he wrote a sonata for piano and a sonata for two pianos that used a strict 12-tone row.

Although the 12-tone system greatly influenced Boulez's compositions, he took his music one step further. In 1948 Boulez wrote a second piano sonata that broke the bounds of the 12-tone system. Boulez aimed for the application of the 12-tone technique not only to pitch, as had been previously done, but also to durations, dynamics, and articulation. During the 1950s Boulez continued to experiment with music and sounds, incorporating concrete music. *Polyphonie x*, for 18 instruments (1951), exemplifies this technique. In later years, Boulez also experimented with rearranging the stage of the traditional symphony orchestra. In 1966 Boulez again became the center of controversy when he announced he was severing all connections with the French government and disassociating himself from all its music organizations.

BOOKS BY BOULEZ

Notes of an Apprenticeship. 1968 o.p. The most extensive collection of writings by Boulez
   yet published.
Orientations: Collected Writings. Ed. by Jean-Jacques Nattiez. Trans. by Martin Cooper.
   HUP 1986 $14.95. ISBN 0-674-64375-5. A new translation of Boulez's most crucial
   set of essays.
Stocktakings from an Apprenticeship. Coll. by Paule Thévenin. Trans. by Stephen Walsh.
   OUP 1991 $82.00. ISBN 0-19-311210-8. Contains the ideas and judgments worked out
   by Boulez over a period of 15 years.

BRAHMS, JOHANNES. 1833–1897

A composer, pianist, and conductor, Johannes Brahms was born in Hamburg,
Germany. Possessing a talent that could have taken him in any musical
direction, he chose the piano and composing. He made his debut as a pianist at
the age of 14. In 1853 Brahms met the German composer ROBERT SCHUMANN,
who regarded Brahms as a genius. Schumann and his wife CLARA, a noted
concert pianist, became Brahms's lifelong friends. In 1862 Brahms moved to
Vienna, where his talents as a composer reached full flower. The music of
Brahms shows great respect for the form and structure of eighteenth-century
classicism, yet it also incorporates the romantic style that was typical of the
nineteenth century.

Brahms is considered a giant among nineteenth-century composers of
chamber music and symphonies. Among his 24 published chamber-music
works are a piano trio in B, opus 8 (1854); two string quartets; two piano
quartets; and a piano quintet in F minor, opus 34a (1864). He composed four
great symphonies: *Symphony in C Minor* (finished in 1876 after many years of
work), *Symphony in D Minor* (1877), *Symphony in F Major* (1883), and
Symphony in E Minor (1885). While classic in structure and design, Brahms's
symphonies are romantic in their musical language and sound. Nonetheless,
they exhibit feelings of repose that illustrate a return to discipline and a revival
of order and form, indicative of changes in music to come in the 1900s. Today,
many of the works of Brahms are staples of the concert repertoire.

BOOK BY BRAHMS

The Herzogenberg Correspondence. Music Reprint Ser. Ed. by Max Kalbeck. Trans. by
   Hannah Bryant. Da Capo 1987 repr. of 1909 ed. $45.00. ISBN 0-306-76281-1.
   Contains selections from the 281 extant letters exchanged between Brahms and the
   Herzogenbergs.

BOOKS ABOUT BRAHMS

Latham, Peter. *Brahms.* Biblio Dist. 1975 o.p. A revised biography of Johannes Brahms.
May, Florence. *The Life of Johannes Brahms.* 2 vols. Scholarly 1976 $79.00. ISBN 0-403-
   03630-5. Thorough biography focusing on Brahms's family, music, and concerts.
   Introduction by Ralph Hill.
Schumann, Clara, and Johannes Brahms. *Brahms Letters, 1853–1896.* Ed. by Berthold
   Litzmann. 2 vols. in 1. Hyperion Conn. 1980 repr. of 1927 ed. $45.00. ISBN 0-88355-
   761-4. Compilation of letters between the composer and his friend Clara Schumann.

BRITTEN, LORD BENJAMIN. 1913–1976

Considered the most significant British composer since seventeenth-century
composer HENRY PURCELL, Benjamin Britten excelled in composing series of
songs, operas, and other types of vocal music. Britten was a conscientious
objector in World War II; his *War Requiem* (1962) is a moving tribute to the

victims of war everywhere. The composition, which incorporates parts for soloists, choruses, and orchestra, is based on the Latin text of the Mass for the Dead and verses by WILFRED OWEN (see Vol. 1), a young English soldier killed in World War I. Following its first performance at Coventry Cathedral in Coventry, England, it received worldwide acclaim.

Pursuing a youthful interest in the piano, Britten studied at the Royal College of Music in London. His work drew the favorable attention of critics with the premiere of his *Fantasy Quartet for Oboe and Strings* in 1934. After World War II, Britten devoted himself principally to composing operas. His first operatic work was *Paul Bunyan* (1941), a choral operetta about a lumberjack who likes to sing ballads. Britten's two most successful operas are *Peter Grimes* (1945) and *The Turn of the Screw* (1954). Other operas by Britten include *Rape of Lucretia* (1946), *A Midsummer Night's Dream* (1960), and *Death in Venice* (1973). Using a remarkable sensitivity to text, Britten evolved vocal melodic lines followed by orchestral interludes that punctuate and enhance the dramatic flow of his operas.

BOOKS ABOUT BRITTEN

Brett, Philip, ed. *Benjamin Britten: Peter Grimes*. Cambridge U. Pr. 1983 $18.95. ISBN 0-521-2976-8. A collection of essays for the serious amateur or scholar concerning the history, analysis, and interpretation of this opera.

Britten, Beth. *My Brother Benjamin*. Kensal Pr. UK 1986 o.p.

Evans, Peter. *The Music of Benjamin Britten*. U. of Minn. Pr. 1979 o.p. A review of the composer's entire creative output.

Kennedy, Michael. *Britten*. Biblio Dist. 1981 o.p. Discusses Britten's life and music from childhood through death.

Palmer, Christopher, ed. *The Britten Companion*. Cambridge U. Pr. 1984 $47.95. ISBN 0-521-26121-X. Essays by scholars and critics covering Britten's musical life; based in part on materials in the Britten-Pears Library and Archive.

White, Eric W. *Benjamin Britten: His Life and Operas*. Ed. by John Evans. U. CA Pr. 1983 $14.95. ISBN 0-520-04894-6. Critical biography of the British composer and discussion of his operas.

Whittall, Arnold. *The Music of Britten and Tippett: Studies in Themes and Techniques*. Cambridge U. Pr. 1982 $59.95. ISBN 0-521-23523-5. Compares and contrasts Britten and Tippett from the 1930s on.

BRUCKNER, ANTON. 1824–1896

Anton Bruckner was an Austrian symphonist, choral composer, and organist. His first major work was an *Ave Maria* for seven voices. After hearing a performance of RICHARD WAGNER's *Tannhäuser* in 1863, he became a Wagner disciple. In the last third of his life, he composed nine symphonies and numerous sacred works. He was a devout Roman Catholic and a famous music teacher in Vienna.

BOOK ABOUT BRUCKNER

Watson, Derek. *Bruckner*. Littlefield 1975 $11.50. ISBN 0-8226-0708-5. A vivid account of Bruckner's struggles and achievements in both his personal life and creative career.

CAGE, JOHN. 1912–1992

A modernist composer, John Cage is known for his unusual theories and experimental compositions. Although Cage was interested in music from an early age, it was not until he had completed high school that he became attracted to the creative process in music. Cage studied under, and was influenced by, ARNOLD SCHOENBERG, Henry Cowell, and Adolf Weiss, all of whom encouraged experimentation and innovation.

Cage was also greatly influenced by Edgard Varese's experiments in organized sound and rhythmic patterns and by Henry Cowell's innovations with tone clusters and the drawing of unusual sounds from the piano by manipulating the strings on the soundboard. Under their influence, Cage was drawn to percussion music. In 1936 Cage became a member of the music faculty at Cornish School in Seattle, Washington. There he began his earliest experiments with percussion music by featuring concerts of percussion instruments.

Cage's fascination with percussion led to his inventing the prepared piano, for which Cage attached materials such as metal and wood to a piano's strings, thus simulating the sound of percussion instruments. *Bacchanale* and *Sonatas and Interludes* (1948) are two examples of prepared piano music.

Cage is also known for his "chance" music, which was based on the *I Ching*, or the Chinese *Book of Changes*. Cage used the *I Ching* to develop a prearranged system for all of the materials and means of musical composition. The most complex work in his "chance" method was *Concert for Piano and Orchestra* (1958).

The next stage in Cage's experimentation resulted in audiovisual music, for which he used anything that was audible. For example, *Variations V* (1965), Cage's most daring and innovative audiovisual piece, requires several dancers, a bicycle, electronic equipment, and a screen on which distorted images from television and film clips are flashed.

On his sixty-fifth birthday, Cage was honored in New York City with a retrospective concert.

BOOK BY CAGE

Silence: Lectures and Writings of John Cage. U. Pr. of New Eng. 1961 $16.95. ISBN 0-8195-6028-6. A collection of articles and lectures that reflect his major concerns.

BOOKS ABOUT CAGE

Kostelanetz, Richard, ed. *John Cage: An Anthology.* Da Capo 1991 repr. of 1970 ed. $13.95. ISBN 0-306-80435-2. Monograph about Cage told mostly in the composer's own words.

Revill, David. *The Roaring Silence: A Biography of John Cage.* Arcade Pub. Inc. 1992 $27.95. ISBN 1-55970-166-8. Describes the hows and whys of Cage's music.

CALLAS, MARIA. 1923–1977

An American soprano of Greek parentage, Maria Callas was known as much for her dramatic interpretations of operatic roles as for her singing. Her personal life and her relationships with employers were equally fiery and well publicized.

In 1947 Callas began her real career. She was soon in demand for such roles as Aïda, Isolde, Kundry, and Brünnhilde. Her greatest triumphs, though, were as Norma, Medea, Anne Boleyn, Lucia di Lammermoor, Verdi's Lady Macbeth and Violetta, and Tosca. She was also widely praised for her performance in the movie *Medea*. Growing vocal troubles in the 1960s led to her gradual withdrawal from the stage.

BOOKS ABOUT CALLAS

Meneghini, Giovannibattista. *My Wife Maria Callas.* Trans. by Henry Wisneski. FS&G 1982 o.p. Callas's estranged husband's account of their life together.

Scott, Michael. *Maria Meneghini Callas*. NE U. Pr. 1992 $29.95. ISBN 1-55553-146-6.
Traces the steps by which Callas entered the field and climbed to its heights.
Stassinopoulis, Arianna. *Maria Callas: The Woman Behind the Legend*. Ballantine 1982
o.p. A fascinating account of Callas's personal life and career.

CARRERAS, JOSÉ. 1946–

Born in Barcelona, José Carreras first dreamed, like other boys his age, of playing football and scoring more goals than anyone else. To pass the long, hot days, he spent a great deal of time in the cinema. It was there that he saw for the first time the film *The Great Caruso*, with Mario Lanza in the title role, that Carreras was inspired to take up singing. The next day he began imitating Lanza and noticed that he was able to reproduce almost all of the arias in the film with amazing accuracy. At the age of 8, he entered the Barcelona Conservatory. At the age of 11, Carreras made his debut on stage playing a child in Manuel de Falla's *El Retablo de Maese Pedro*, a part written for a soprano. By his twenty-first birthday, Carreras decided to pursue his true vocation as a tenor.

Carreras is noted for his roles as Alfredo, Pinkerton, Leicester in *Maria Stuarda*, and Edgardo. He has overcome lymphatic leukemia and established a leukemia foundation.

In 1991 the tenors Carreras, PLÁCIDO DOMINGO, and LUCIANO PAVAROTTI teamed up to record *In Concert*, which has sold over 5 million CDs and cassettes worldwide. *In Concert* rose to number one on the U.S. classical music charts for that year. It was also ranked number 43 on Billboard's pop charts, the highest any classical recording has climbed since rock-and-roll dominated album charts in the mid-1960s.

BOOK BY CARRERAS

Singing From the Soul: An Autobiography. YCP Pubns. 1991 $27.95. ISBN 1-878756-89-3.
Carreras's account of his life-threatening bout with leukemia and subsequent events.

CARTER, BENNY. 1907–

Benny Carter began his musical career as an instrumentalist on the piano, trumpet, and alto saxophone. In 1928 this self-taught, African American musician and composer formed his own band for the Arcadia Ballroom in New York City. He left the band in 1931 to become musical director of McKinney's Cotton Pickers.

Later in his career, Carter began arranging for such jazz greats as DUKE ELLINGTON, Teddy Hill, Fletcher Henderson, and Benny Goodman. Late in the 1950s and 1960s, he wrote scores for several national television series, including "M Squad," Alfred Hitchcock's series, and the Chrysler Theater series. Carter also arranged and composed music for films. Films he also appeared in include *Stormy Weather*, *The Snows of Kilimanjaro*, *As Thousands Cheer*, and *Clash by Night*.

BOOK ABOUT BENNY CARTER

Berger, Morrow, and James Patrick Edward. *Benny Carter: A Life in American Music*.
Scarecrow 1982 $49.50. ISBN 0-8108-1580-X. This story of Benny Carter is one of a kind in the now voluminous literature on jazz.

CARTER, ELLIOTT. 1908–

Born in New York City, Elliott Carter revealed a strong aptitude for music before he could read or write. Undecided about his future, Carter majored in English literature at Harvard University. After graduation, he studied piano with

Newton Swift and composition with Nadia Boulanger. In 1936 he wrote articles and reviews for *Modern Music* and served as musical director of the Ballet Caravan from 1937–39.

In 1953 he was awarded the Prix de Rome, and in 1956 he was elected a member of the National Institute of Arts and Letters. From 1960 to 1962, Carter was a professor of composition at Yale University, where he wrote his Pulitzer Prize-winning string quartet.

Carter has been described as a neo-classicist, but such a characterization reveals too little. His works are complex rhythmically; dramatic in the use of harmonies, tonality, and tone clusters; and brilliant in the exploitation of instrumental timbres. Such works as *Sonata for Flute, Oboe, Cello, and Harpsichord* (1952) are enticing, whereas the larger orchestral works, such as the *Double Concerto* and the *Piano Concerto* are sonorous, expansive events. Carter's music is complicated and deep but rewarding to listeners who invest some time in exploring its many facets.

BOOK BY ELLIOTT CARTER

Elliott Carter: In Conversation with Enzo Restagno for Settembre Musica 1989. Trans. by Katherine Silberblatt Wolfthal. Inst. Amer. Music 1991 $15.00. ISBN 0-914678-35-3. Series of conversations between Dr. Enzo Restagno and Elliott Carter as well as 33 of Carter's essays.

BOOKS ABOUT ELLIOTT CARTER

Pollack, Howard. *Harvard Composers: Walter Piston and His Students, from Elliott Carter to Frederic Rzewski*. Scarecrow 1992 $52.50. ISBN 0-8108-2493-0. On Walter Piston and 33 students who studied with him at Harvard.

Rosen, Charles. *The Musical Languages of Elliott Carter*. Lib. Congress 1984 o.p. Includes a guide to Elliott Carter research materials at the Library of Congress Music Division by Morgan Cundiff.

CARUSO, ENRICO. 1873–1921

The eighteenth, and first surviving, child of an Italian worker's family, Enrico Caruso worked to develop his natural ear and singing ability. He achieved international renown and imparted a lasting influence. His sustained bel canto and dramatic expression set the standard for tenors of this century, particularly as seen in his performances of Cavaradossi in *Tosca* and Canio in *Pagliacci*.

BOOK BY CARUSO

How to Sing. London 1913 o.p. Instructs the would-be singer on how to prepare for a singing career.

BOOKS ABOUT CARUSO

Caruso, Dorothy. *Enrico Caruso: His Life and Death*. Greenwood 1987 repr. of 1945 ed. $62.50. ISBN 0-313-25377-3. A biography of Caruso by his widow; includes pictures.

Caruso, Enrico, Jr. *Enrico Caruso: My Father and My Family*. Timber 1990 $39.95. ISBN 0-931340-24-1. Highly personal account by the great singer's own son.

Greenfield, Howard. *Caruso*. Da Capo 1984 $9.95. ISBN 0-306-80215-5. Highly readable account of the life and career of the legendary tenor.

_____. *Caruso: An Illustrated Life*. Trafalgar 1991 $24.95. ISBN 0-94395-544-0. Well-written and straightforward account enhanced by excellent illustrations, period photographs, and several of the tenor's caricatures.

Robinson, Francis. *Caruso: His Life in Pictures*. NY Bramhall House 1957 o.p. Magnificent collection of photographs showing Caruso in 26 of his famous roles and with his celebrated colleagues.

Scott, Michael. *The Great Caruso*. NE U. Pr. 1989 $14.95. ISBN 1-55553-061-3. Shows how the Caruso legend benefited not only from his live performances but from the new technique of sound recording.

CHARLES, RAY. 1930–

Known as a pioneer in soul music, Ray Charles was born in Albany, Georgia. As a child, Charles developed glaucoma, an eye disorder that left him blind. He began playing piano at the age of 3. He learned to compose and arrange music in Braille and to play the piano, clarinet, alto saxophone, organ, and trumpet at the St. Augustine School for Deaf and Blind Children in St. Augustine, Florida. By the time he was in his twenties, Charles had established his own style and original sound. He is credited with almost single-handedly creating soul music by fusing the intensity, inflection, and structures of gospel music, the subject matter of blues, and the horn riffs of jazz.

Throughout the 1980s and 1990s, Charles toured and played to large audiences in the United States and abroad. In 1988 he received the lifetime achievement award from the National Academy of Recording Arts and Sciences. He has also won 11 Grammy awards. "Georgia on My Mind" and "I Can't Stop Loving You" are among his classics.

In addition, Charles has recorded television commercials, many of which he produced himself. His Diet Pepsi advertisement was rated the most memorable commercial of 1991. Charles has also appeared on several television shows, including "Saturday Night Live," "Who's the Boss," and "St. Elsewhere."

BOOK BY CHARLES

Brother Ray: Ray Charles' Own Story. (coauthored with David Ritz). Da Capo 1992 repr. of 1978 ed. $13.95. ISBN 0-306-80482-2

CHOPIN, FRÉDÉRIC. 1810–1849

Born near Warsaw, Poland, of French and Polish parentage, Frédéric Chopin showed a great talent as a pianist from a very young age. He published his first work—a rondo for two pianos—when he was 14 years old and continued to compose exclusively for the piano. From 1826 to 1829, he studied composition at the Warsaw Conservatory. At the age of 19, Chopin left Poland on a concert tour and eventually settled in Paris. There he had a long, stormy, and dependent relationship with the French novelist Amandine-Aurore-Lucile Dupin, better known as GEORGE SAND (see Vol. 1). The dependency in Chopin's personal life and his poor health contrast dramatically with his musical compositions, which require brilliant technique to master their elaborate melodic and harmonic figurations.

Although he never returned to Poland, Chopin continued to reflect in his compositions his love for his native land and his misery at its political misfortunes. His polonaises, and especially his mazurkas, are filled with rhythms and musical elements found in Polish popular music and are among the earliest and best examples of the inspiration that nationalism had on the music of the romantic period. Chopin's principal works are two concertos—the *Concerto in E Minor* (1833) and *Concerto in F Minor* (1836); several sonatas, including the *Sonata in B Flat Minor* (1840) and the *Sonata in B Minor* (1845); 27 études—tone poems based on a single musical motive that concentrate on a specific technical skill; and 24 preludes. Through his piano works, Chopin effectively removed the bonds of symphonic and choral traditions that had restricted the full flowering of the piano as a solo instrument. Interestingly, he disliked playing in public; he concentrated, instead, on teaching and composing. Chopin's innovative and brilliant work came to an early end when he died of tuberculosis at the age of 39.

BOOK BY CHOPIN

Chopin's Letters. Collected by Henryk Opienski. Trans. by E. L. Voynich. Dover 1988 repr. of 1931 ed. $8.95. ISBN 0-486-25564-6. Superbly edited selection of nearly 300 of Chopin's letters; first collection published in English.

BOOKS ABOUT CHOPIN

Liszt, Franz. *Frédéric Chopin.* Trans. by Edward N. Waters. Vienna Hse. 1973 $10.00. ISBN 0-8443-0066-7. Portrait of Chopin by his friend and fellow composer.

Marek, George R., and Maria Gordon-Smith. *Chopin.* HarpC 1978 o.p. A collaborative effort that presents a rich and complete portrait of Chopin.

Walker, Alan, ed. *The Chopin Companion: Profiles of the Man and the Musician.* Norton 1973 repr. of 1967 ed. $7.95. ISBN 0-393-00668-9. Collection of essays by eminent Chopin scholars with discography, bibliography, and chronological catalog.

COLTRANE, JOHN. 1926–1967

A virtuoso jazz tenor saxophonist, John Coltrane was one of the pantheon of jazz improvisers. During the 1960s, Coltrane abandoned be-bop, which made him famous, for open-ended improvisation influenced by African and Indian music. However, some critics believe that Coltrane would have returned to simpler forms of jazz had his career and life not been cut short by cancer. St. John's church in San Francisco was founded in 1971 in honor of Coltrane. Founder Franzo King, now a bishop of the African Orthodox Church, conducts traditional ceremonies mixed with jazz.

Coltrane is considered to be one of the most important jazz musicians in the history of music. His influence remains in the jazz world and even infiltrated the rock world in the music of The Byrds, the Grateful Dead, and Jimi Hendrix.

BOOKS ABOUT COLTRANE

Cole, Bill. *John Coltrane.* Schirmer Bks. 1976 o.p. Examines Coltrane both as a musician and as a religious person.

Simpkins, C. O. *Coltrane: A Biography.* Herndon Hse. o.p. A moving, in-depth account of Coltrane and his music.

Thomas, J. C. *Chasin the Trane: The Music and Mystique of John Coltrane.* Da Capo 1976 $10.95. ISBN 0-306-80043-8. Traces Coltrane's life and career from his childhood through his apprenticeships to its culmination in his classical quartet.

COPLAND, AARON. 1900–1990

Born in Brooklyn, New York, Aaron Copland was inspired by a piano recital that he heard at the age of 13. From that point on, he thought earnestly about a career in music. At the age of 14 he began piano lessons, being taught by one of his sisters. He soon demanded and received more formal training. By 1916 Copland knew that he wanted to be a composer. He was accepted as the first student at the newly established music school for Americans in France. There he studied composition and orchestration with Nadia Boulanger.

Supported early in his career by Serge Koussevitzky, Copland employed folk elements in many of his compositions, among them *Billy the Kid* (1938), *Appalachian Spring* (1945), and *Rodeo* (1942). Copland exerted enormous influence on the development of younger American composers by sponsoring concert series, festivals, artistic colonies, and competitions.

BOOKS BY COPLAND

Copland on Music. Norton 1963 $8.95. ISBN 0-393-00198-9. Contains a selection of occasional pieces about music and musicians written over a span of more than 30 years.

Copland: 1900 through 1942. (coauthored with Vivian Perlis). St. Martin 1987 $12.95. ISBN 0-312-01149-0. Copland's autobiography; covers the years of his coming of age as a composer.

Copland. Since 1943. (coauthored with Vivian Perlis). St. Martin 1989 $29.95. ISBN 0-312-03313-3. Essentially an autobiography interspersed with historical narrative and reminiscences by Copland's associates.

Music and Imagination. HUP 1952 $6.95. ISBN 0-674-58915-7. Provides fascinating insight into the creative process in music.

What to Listen for in Music. McGraw 1988 $17.95. ISBN 0-07-013091-4. Excellent guide for the novice, with a new introduction by William Schuman.

DAVIS, MILES. 1925–1991

Jazz trumpeter and composer, Miles Davis was one of the world's finest and most loved musicians and the most consistent jazz trendsetter in that genre's history. Davis rose to prominence in the 1940s as a member of CHARLIE PARKER's band. He formed his own band years later and hired JOHN COLTRANE as a band member. Davis also provided the platform that brought prominence to Tony Williams and Herbie Hancock. He introduced audiences around the world to jazz, be-bop, modal playing, free-form explorations, and the use of electronics. During his four-decade career, Davis also incorporated into his music elements of pop, rock, classical, and flamenco. Some of his most acclaimed works include *Kind of Blue, Bitches Brew, Miles Ahead, Miles Smiles, Birth of the Cool,* and *In a Silent Way.* The Grammy Award-winning musician died of pneumonia, respiratory failure, and a stroke at the age of 65.

BOOKS ABOUT DAVIS

Carr, Ian. *Miles Davis: A Critical Biography.* Morrow 1982 o.p. A descriptive account of Davis's personal life and his music. With a foreword by Len Lyons.

Cole, Bill. *Miles Davis: A Musical Biography.* Morrow 1974 o.p. Deals with Davis's bands and the people who influenced his music.

Nisenson, Eric. *Round about Midnight: A Portrait of Miles Davis.* Doubleday 1982 o.p. A biography of Davis compiled primarily from interviews.

DEBUSSY, CLAUDE. 1862–1918

The French composer Claude Debussy is regarded as the chief musical figure in the early twentieth-century impressionist school that was centered in Paris. Debussy showed great musical talent at an early age and began studying music at the Paris Conservatory at the age of 10. By the age of 22, he had won the Grand Prix de Rome. Debussy's use of the whole-tone scale in his compositions, which were common to Russian and Asian music, led to expressive harmonies and the achievement of surprising nuances of mood. He also used numerous harsh-sounding harmonies and other new and original compositional techniques and elements. His music, like impressionist painting and poetry, stirs the imagination by its evocation of dreamlike sights and sounds. Because of his revolutionary changes and inventions, Debussy is considered to be one of the most creative and influential forces in the history of music. A list of composers influenced by his work would include nearly every distinguished composer during the first half of the twentieth century.

Prelude to the Afternoon of a Faun (1894), a symphonic poem, is Debussy's famous orchestral work that has been choreographed for ballet and is an example of his use of stunning orchestral coloration. Other outstanding orchestral works are *Nocturnes* (1899) and *La Mer* (*The Sea*) (1905). Among Debussy's impressive piano works are 24 preludes, 12 études, and the *Suite Bergamasque* (1905), which contains the popular "Clair de Lune." Debussy also wrote many individual songs for voice and an opera, *Pelléas et Mélisande* (1892–1902), considered by many to be his masterpiece. Debussy died in Paris of cancer in 1918.

BOOKS BY DEBUSSY

Debussy Letters. Ed. by Francois Lesure and Roger Nichols. Trans. by Roger Nichols. HUP 1987 $27.50. ISBN 0-674-19429-2. Makes available the texts of all Debussy's songs; also includes some letters.

The Poetic Debussy: A Collection of His Song Texts and Selected Letters. Ed. by Margaret G. Cobb. Trans. by Richard Miller. NE U. Pr. 1981 o.p. A comprehensive collection of Debussy's letters to friends and close associates.

BOOKS ABOUT DEBUSSY

Dietschy, Marcel. *A Portrait of Claude Debussy*. Ed. and trans. by William Ashbrook and Margaret G. Cobb. OUP 1990 $65.00. ISBN 0-19-315469-2. Deals entirely with the life of the composer rather than describing or analyzing his music.

Holloway, Robin. *Debussy and Wagner*. Da Capo 1982 repr. of 1979 ed. $19.50. ISBN 0-903873-55-9. Comparative look at the work of Debussy and German composer Richard Wagner.

Wenk, Arthur B. *Claude Debussy and the Poets*. U. CA Pr. 1976 o.p. Examines the influence of contemporary poets, such as Baudelaire, Verlaine, and Mallarmé, on Debussy and his music.

DOMINGO, PLÁCIDO. 1941–

The son of zarzuela singers, Plácido Domingo was born in Madrid, Spain, but lived in Mexico from the age of 7. While in Mexico, Domingo learned piano, conducting, and singing. In 1961 Domingo played his first important tenor role as Alfredo in *La Traviata* in Monterrey, Mexico. Between 1962 and 1965, Domingo was a member of the Israeli National Opera, where he sang 300 performances of 10 operas, most of them in Hebrew. In 1965 Domingo made his American debut as Pinkerton in *Madama Butterfly* at the New York City Opera. In his debut at the Metropolitan Opera House, Domingo played the tenor lead in *Adriana Lecouvreur*.

This lyric tenor has performed throughout the world and is widely regarded as the supreme lyric-dramatic tenor of the late twentieth century. He is known for the many excellent leading roles he has sung in operas, which include *Tosca*, *Aïda*, *Otello*, *Carmen*, and *Tales of Hoffman*. In 1986 Domingo played Otello in Franco Zeffirelli's film version of VERDI's *Otello*. In 1991 the tenors JOSÉ CARRERAS, Domingo, and LUCIANO PAVAROTTI teamed up to record *In Concert*, which has sold over 5 million CDs and cassettes worldwide. *In Concert* rose to number one on the U.S. classical charts for that year. It was also ranked number 43 on Billboard's pop charts, the highest any classical recording has climbed since rock-and-roll dominated album charts in the mid-1960s.

BOOK BY DOMINGO

My First Forty Years. Knopf 1983 o.p. Domingo's account of his personal life and career.

BOOKS ABOUT DOMINGO

Snowman, Daniel. *The World of Plácido Domingo*. McGraw 1985 o.p. An intimate look at
Domingo focusing on his artistic development.

Stefoff, Rebecca. *Plácido Domingo*. Chelsea Hse. 1992 $17.95. ISBN 0-7910-1563-7.
Useful and informative account of Domingo's extraordinary accomplishments and
achievements.

DVOŘÁK, ANTONIN. 1841–1904

Antonin Dvořák is regarded as the greatest composer of the nationalist
movement in what was to become Czechoslovakia. Throughout his childhood,
Dvořák displayed an interest only in music. He left home at the age of 16 to
study composition at the Prague Organ School. Although Dvořák is best known
for his orchestral and chamber music, from the late 1860s he was constantly
engaged in an operatic project. RICHARD WAGNER's musical style highly
influenced Dvořák's operas.

Hymnus for mixed chorus and orchestra (1873) attracted wide attention and
marks the beginning of Dvořák's international fame and influence. In 1875 he
was awarded the Austrian State Prize for *Symphony in E Flat*. In 1884 he was
invited to conduct his *Stabat Mater* in London. He accepted an invitation to
head the National Conservatory in New York in 1892. In America, Dvořák wrote
his celebrated work, his symphony *From the New World* (1893). His peripatetic
career (he traveled extensively) and the honors bestowed on him by numerous
nations are paralleled in his compositions by their cosmopolitan use of national
and folk melodies and the free-flowing new melodies he composed. Dvořák
later returned to Prague and was appointed director of the Prague Conservatory.

BOOKS ABOUT DVOŘÁK

Butterworth, Neil. *Dvořák: His Life and Times*. Paganiniana Pubns. 1981 $14.95. ISBN 0-
87666-580-6. Gives fresh insight into Dvořák's fascinating career as well as his
hobbies.

Clapham, John. *Dvořák*. Riverrun NY 1994 $33.95. ISBN 0-7145-4145-1. Reexamines
commonly held views of the life and work of Dvořák.

Robertson, Alec. *Dvořák*. Little 1977 o.p. A detailed account of Dvořák's life and a critical
examination of his work.

ELGAR, SIR EDWARD. 1857–1934

Born in Broadheath, near Worcester, Edward Elgar received his musical
training from his father, who was an organist at St. George's Roman Catholic
Church in Worcester. At the age of 22, Elgar took a few violin lessons in London
from Adolf Pollitzer and accepted an appointment as bandmaster at the County
Lunatic Asylum in Worcester. In 1882 he was appointed conductor of the
Worcester Amateur Instrumental Society. Three years later he succeeded his
father as organist at St. George's.

During the 1890s, Elgar's work received much success. The production of his
cantata *Scenes from the Saga of King Olaf* in 1896 attracted considerable
attention from the musical public. In 1904 he was knighted.

Elgar received many honorary degrees from English and American universi-
ties. His works include the oratorio *Dream of Gerontius* (1900), the orchestral
Variations on an Original Theme (1899) (more commonly called *Enigma
Variations*), *Violin Concerto* (1910), and *Cello Concerto* (1919).

BOOKS BY ELGAR

Edward Elgar: Letters of a Lifetime. OUP 1991 $71.00. ISBN 0-19-315472-2. Fascinating
documentation of the deep humanity of the composer.

*Edward Elgar, The Windflowers Letters: Correspondence with Alice Caroline Stuart
Wortley and Her Family*. Ed. by Jerrold Northrop Moore. OUP 1989 $72.00. ISBN 0-
19-315473-0. Reveals some of the all-too-flawed inner man behind the glorious,
almost flawed, music.

BOOKS ABOUT ELGAR

Anderson, Robert. *Elgar. The Master Musicians Ser*. Schirmer Bks. 1993 $30.00. ISBN 0-
02-870185-2.

Monk, Raymond, ed. *Elgar Studies*. Scholars Pr. GA 1990 o.p. Analytical, biographical,
textual, and critical essays on Elgar.

Kennedy, Michael. *Portrait of Elgar*. OUP 1987 $16.95. ISBN 0-19-284017-7. Detailed
portrait of Elgar's life and musical career.

Moore, Jerrold Northrop. *Edward Elgar: A Creative Life*. OUP repr. of 1984 ed. $29.95.
ISBN 0-19-284014-2. An examination of Elgar that combines his creative life with his
works.

Redwood, Christopher, ed. *An Elgar Companion*. Sequoia Pub. Inc. 1982 o.p. A standard
and accessible biography of Elgar.

Reed, William H. *Elgar as I Knew Him*. OUP 1989 $12.95. ISBN 0-19-282257-8. Reveals
occurrences and episodes in the life of Elgar as witnessed by the author.

ELLINGTON, EDWARD KENNEDY ("DUKE"). 1899–1974

Jazz pianist, composer, and popular band leader, Edward Ellington was
known as "Duke" to his contemporaries. His skill as a pianist and his popularity
as a band leader are surpassed only by the impressive depth and quality of his
work as a composer. Born in Washington, D.C., Ellington began to study the
piano at the age of 7. He organized his first band, The Duke's Serenaders, at the
age of 18.

In 1923 Ellington moved to New York, where he and his band, The
Washingtonians, performed at nightclubs in Harlem and at the Kentucky Club
in downtown Manhattan. Capitalizing on the popularity of phonographic
recordings, Ellington began to record his performances and reorganized the
band as Ellington's Kentucky Club Orchestra. From 1927 through 1932, he and
his band made frequent radio broadcasts. Soon, Ellington and jazz were
synonymous. Many other musicians attempted to copy Ellington's musical style,
which led to many instrumental innovations in the musical language of jazz.

The range of Ellington's musical compositions is impressive. Many of his
short compositions, including "Mood Indigo" (1930), "Solitude" (1933), and
"Sophisticated Lady" (1933), remain popular staples of jazz instrumentalists
everywhere. His longer works, such as *Creole Rhapsody* (1932); *Black, Brown,
and Beige* (1943), a 50-minute work that told the story of African Americans;
Liberian Suite (1947); *Harlem Nights* (1951); and *Night Creatures* (1955), include
complex orchestration. These works helped shift jazz from the smoky confines
of nightclubs to the sophisticated setting of the concert stage. In addition to
performing in jazz festivals and concert tours in this country and around the
world, Ellington appeared in several films and made many recordings.

BOOKS BY ELLINGTON

Duke Ellington in Person: An Intimate Memoir. (coauthored with Stanley Dance). Da Capo
1979 $11.95. ISBN 0-306-80104-3. Account of Ellington's life and music.

Music Is My Mistress. Da Capo 1976 $13.95. ISBN 0-306-80033-0. Ellington's fascinating account of his life and music.

BOOKS ABOUT ELLINGTON

Dance, Stanley. *The World of Duke Ellington.* Da Capo 1980 repr. of 1970 ed. $10.95. ISBN 0-306-80136-1. A discussion of Ellington's music and times. Foreword by Duke Ellington.

George, Don. *Sweet Man: The Real Duke Ellington.* Putnam Pub. Group 1981 o.p. A detailed yet very readable biography of Duke Ellington.

Rattenbury, Ken. *Duke Ellington, Jazz Composer.* Yale U. Pr. 1993 repr. of 1991 ed. ISBN 0-300-05507-2. An examination of Duke Ellington as a jazz composer and investigates his impact upon the music.

Tucker, Mark. *Ellington: The Early Years.* U. of Ill. Pr. 1990. ISBN 0-252-01425-1. Presents an overview of Ellington's life, beginning with his pre-Cotton Club years.

FAURÉ, GABRIEL. 1845–1924

An accomplished French composer, Gabriel Fauré developed a style that pushed tonality to its limits, while becoming increasingly economical. Many of Fauré's shorter works became and remain popular; however, the true worth of his achievement in song, piano, and chamber music are only gradually being recognized. Fauré also developed a musical idiom all his own that anticipated the procedures of impressionism.

In addition, Fauré was an illustrious teacher. Among his now-famous students were Raul Enesco, Charles Koechlin, Jean Roger-Ducasse, Laparra, Florent Schmitt, Louis Aubert, and Nadia Boulanger.

BOOK ABOUT FAURÉ

Nectoux, Jean Michel. *Gabriel Fauré: A Musical Life.* Cambridge U. Pr. 1991 $79.95. ISBN 0-521-23524-3. An analytical, historical, and aesthetic examination of Fauré and his work.

FOSTER, STEPHEN (COLLINS). 1826–1864

Born in Lawrenceville, Pennsylvania, Stephen Foster became a well-known American composer of many popular songs that are still sung and enjoyed today. As a child, Foster learned to play the flute. At the age of 18, he published his first song, "Open Thy Lattice, Love." In 1846 Foster moved to Cincinnati to work as an accountant for one of his brothers.

During his career, Foster wrote 189 songs, to most of which he wrote both the words and the music. Among his most notable songs are "Old Folks at Home" (or "Swanee Ribber," as it was commonly called), "O Susanna," "My Old Kentucky Home," and "Jeanie with the Light Brown Hair." "Beautiful Dreamer" was the last song he wrote. Foster finished the composition only a few days before his death.

Foster's music was greatly influenced by black minstrel shows. The gentleness of many of Foster's songs was not characteristic of his life. He was constantly in need of money, his marriage was most unhappy, and he died penniless in New York's Bellevue Hospital.

Foster's fame lives on today. Hundreds of reprints of Foster's songs are available, almost all of which have "improved" arrangements.

BOOKS ABOUT FOSTER

Austin, William W. *"Susanna," "Jeanie," and the "Old Folks at Home": The Songs of Stephen C. Foster from His Time to Ours.* U. of Ill. Pr. 1989 $34.95. ISBN 0-252-

01476-6. A ground-breaking exploration of the various meanings of Foster's songs in their social and historical contexts.

Howard, John Tasker. *Stephen Foster, America's Troubadour.* Rprt. Serv. 1993 repr. of 1934 ed. $89.00. ISBN 0-7812-5470-1. Interesting narrative work on Foster's life, with a useful guide to source material.

GERSHWIN, GEORGE. 1898–1937

Jacob Gershvin, George Gershwin's real name, according to his birth registry, began his music career when he was 16 years old by playing piano in music stores to demonstrate new popular songs. He later studied piano with Ernest Hutcheson and Charles Hambitzer in New York and studied harmony with Edward Kilenyi and with Rubin Goldmark. Gershwin was an almost immediate success with his song "Swanee."

Gershwin also studied counterpoint with Henry Cowell and with Joseph Schillinger. Schillinger's influence can be seen in many of Gershwin's pieces, particularly in *Porgy and Bess,* an opera written for black singers using African American musical styles. *Rhapsody in Blue,* for piano and jazz orchestra, is another ground-breaking piece, incorporating jazz and blues sources and idioms in the classical concerto style. His song "I Got Rhythm" has been performed thousands of times in hundreds of ways by jazz musicians. His brother, Ira, wrote the lyrics for many of his songs.

His melodic talent and genius for rhythmic invention are what made Gershwin an important American composer. He died at the age of 38 of a gliomatous cyst in the brain. Every year on the anniversary of his death, Lewisohn Stadium in New York holds a memorial concert.

BOOKS ABOUT GERSHWIN

Armitage, Merle. *George Gershwin: Man and Legend.* Ayer repr. of 1958 ed. $26.50. ISBN 0-8369-8016-6. Consists of articles written about Gershwin by his friends.

Kendall, Alan. *George Gershwin, A Biography.* Universe 1987 o.p. A well-researched record of Gershwin's life and works.

Schwartz, Charles. *Gershwin: His Life and Music.* Da Capo 1979 repr. of 1973 ed. $14.95. ISBN 0-306-80096-9. Focuses on Gershwin's music and his role in twentieth-century music.

GLASS, PHILIP. 1937–

Throughout his childhood and early career, Philip Glass received a relatively traditional and classical training. It was not until he met and studied with Ravi Shankar, Indian sitar virtuoso, that Glass was introduced to the mysterious world of Hindu ragas and modern musical styles. In the late 1960s, Glass formed associations with modern painters and sculptors who strove to obtain maximum effects with a minimum of means. Glass attempted to do the same in his music; he developed a technique of composition that was dubbed "minimalism."

In 1976 the Metropolitan Opera House presented *Einstein on the Beach,* Glass's first opera and the work that placed him and minimalism in music history. In 1986 he approached the Met with an idea for an opera that would commemorate the five-hundredth anniversary of CHRISTOPHER COLUMBUS's arrival in the New World. The Met accepted his proposal, and Glass wrote *The Voyage.*

The Portuguese government has commissioned Glass to write an opera in honor of the nation's sea explorations. The result, *White Raven,* was scheduled to premiere in either Lisbon or Bonn in 1994. It centers on the Portuguese explorer Vasco da Gama, who sailed around the southern tip of Africa and established a maritime route to India.

BOOKS BY GLASS

Music By Philip Glass. Ed. by Robert T. Jones. HarpC 1987 o.p. Glass's own examination
of his life as a composer.
Opera on the Beach. Ed. by Robert T. Jones. Faber & Faber 1988 o.p.

GOUNOD, CHARLES. 1818–1893

Taught primarily by his mother, Charles Gounod became an accomplished French composer and important figure in French music during the latter part of the nineteenth century. In 1837 Gounod won the 2nd Prix de Rome with his cantata *Marie Stuart et Rizzio*. He won the Grand Prix in 1839 with his cantata *Fernand*.

Gounod studied and composed in Rome and Vienna, receiving useful commissions in each city before finally returning to Paris. While his first music was sacred, he is best known for the operas he began to write about 1850. His *Faust* (1859) was such a success that it opened numerous doors for his career and is his best-known work. Gounod only received mild success with his operas written after *Faust*. However, he recaptured his universal acclaim with *Roméo et Juliette* (1867). The last years of his life were again devoted to sacred works, the most important of which was *La Rédemption*, a trilogy. *A Requiem* (1893) was left unfinished. It was arranged by Henri Busser after Gounod's death. One of his most popular settings to religious worlds is *Ave Maria*.

BOOK BY GOUNOD

Autobiographical Reminiscences, with Family Letters and Notes on Music. Trans. by W.
Hely Hutchinson. Da Capo 1970 repr. of 1896 ed. $35.00. ISBN 0-306-71081-1. Story
of the most important events in Gounod's artistic life and their impact on his career.

BOOK ABOUT GOUNOD

Huebner, Steven. *The Operas of Charles Gounod.* OUP repr. of 1990 ed. $24.95. ISBN 0-
19-315329-7. Examines Gounod's influence as an operatic composer.

GRIEG, EDVARD. 1843–1907

Edvard Grieg was a Norwegian composer who began his professional life as a pianist. His mother, an amateur pianist, taught Grieg to play the piano and provided him with his first introduction to music. In 1858 Grieg attended the Leipzig Conservatory, where he studied piano with Plaidy and Wenzel and later with Ignaz Moscheles. He studied theory with E. F. Richter, Robert Papperitz, Moritz Hauptmann, and Carl Reinecke. For most of his early career, Grieg was immersed in the atmosphere of German romanticism. His early works are infused with lyric moods related to these influences.

During the mid-1870s, the Norwegian government granted Grieg an annuity of 1,600 crowns, which enabled him to devote most of his time to composing.

Grieg is known as a nationalistic composer, as he often quoted Norwegian folk songs in his works. The *Peer Gynt Suite*, numerous piano works, and even more vocal-choral compositions remain in the active repertory.

BOOKS BY GRIEG

Edvard Grieg and Frederick Delius: The Correspondence. Ed. by Lionel Carley. Rizzoli
Intl. 1993 $35.00. ISBN 0-7145-2961-3

Grieg, the Writer. B. Kortsen 1972 o.p. A collection of essays and letters compiled by Bjarne Kortsen.

BOOKS ABOUT GRIEG

Benestad, Finn. *Edvard Grieg: The Man and the Artist.* Trans. by William H. Halverson and Leland B. Sateren. U. of Nebr. Pr. 1988 $65.00. ISBN 0-8032-1202-X. Presents an unvarnished view of Grieg and his role in music.
Horton, John. *Grieg.* Dent 1974 o.p. Detailed, extensively researched biography of Grieg.
Schlotel, Brian. *Grieg.* Ariel Music 1986 o.p. A comprehensive guide to virtually all of Grieg's music; helps music lovers rediscover Grieg and his work.

HANDEL, GEORGE FRIDERIC. 1685–1759

Born in Halle in the German state of Saxony, George Frideric Handel was trained as an organist and a composer. As a young man, he traveled to Italy, where he absorbed the Italian style of music and the operatic form. He eventually settled in Great Britain, where he became famous as one of the greatest masters of baroque music.

As a youth, Handel became an accomplished harpsichordist and organist, studied violin and oboe, and became familiar with the music of contemporary German and Italian composers. During his stay in Italy from 1706 to 1710, he composed several operas and oratorios, which helped establish his early success. This success led to an appointment in Germany as musical director to the prince of Hanover. After only a brief stay in Hanover, Handel visited Great Britain in order to stage his opera *Rinaldo.* In 1712 he again returned to Great Britain and decided to make it his permanent residence. Then, in 1714, the prince of Hanover became King George I of England, and Handel enjoyed the patronage of the new royal family of his adopted homeland. He became a naturalized British citizen in 1726.

Handel's musical output was prodigious. He wrote 46 operas, among them *Julius Caesar* (1724) and *Berenice* (1737); 33 oratorios, the most famous of which is the widely celebrated *The Messiah* (1742); 100 Italian solo cantatas; and numerous orchestral works, including 12 grand concertos (1739). In 1751 Handel suffered an impairment to his sight that led to total blindness by 1753. Nonetheless, Handel continued to conduct performances of his works, which strongly influenced British composers for a century after his death in 1759.

BOOK BY HANDEL

Letters and Writings of George Frideric Handel. Ed. by Erich H. Muller. *Select Bibliographies Reprint Ser.* Ayer 1935 $16.00. ISBN 0-8369-5286-3

BOOKS ABOUT HANDEL

Deutsch, Otto. *Handel: A Documentary Biography.* Da Capo 1974 repr. of 1954 ed. $85.00. ISBN 0-306-70624-5. Biography of Handel's life; includes letters, a bibliography, and all important documents.
Flower, Newman. *Handel: His Personality and His Times.* Academy Chi. Pubs. 1972 o.p. Study of the composer focusing on his personality and music as reflections of the baroque period.
Harris, Ellen T. *Handel and the Pastoral Tradition.* OUP 1980 o.p. Assesses the impact of pastoral drama on the music of Handel.
Hogwood, Christopher. *Handel.* Thames Hudson 1988 $14.95. ISBN 0-500-27498-3. Account of the composer including extensive quotations from contemporaneous documents.

HARRISON, LOU. 1917–

Born in Portland, Oregon, Lou Harrison became a composer of the avant-garde. He studied with Henry Cowell and ARNOLD SCHOENBERG, both of whom greatly influenced Harrison's work and plunged him into the crosscurrents of modern music. He has composed for various instruments, including those for orchestra, chamber, and voice.

Harrison was one of the earliest adherents of a small group of American musicians who promoted the music of CHARLES IVES, Carl Ruggles, Edgard Varèse, and Henry Cowell. During the 1960s Harrison sought new sources of sound production. As a result, he organized a percussion ensemble of multitudinous drums and such common noisemakers as coffee cans and flower pots. Harrison traveled to Japan and Korea in order to study modalities and rhythmic structure and has composed music for *gamelan*, an orchestra of Indonesian instruments.

BOOKS BY HARRISON

Joys and Perplexities: Selected Poems of Lou Harrison. Jargon Soc. 1992 o.p.
Music Primer; Various Items About Music to 1970. Peters Corp. NM 1971 o.p.

BOOK ABOUT HARRISON

Garland, Peter, ed. *A Lou Harrison Reader*. Soundings Pr. 1987 o.p. A chronological look at Harrison's musical output and his life.

HAYDN, FRANZ JOSEPH. 1732–1809

Franz Joseph Haydn, born in a little Austrian town near the Hungarian border, was one of the great masters of classical music. Haydn's musical training began at about age 6 and came from an uncle with whom he lived. After serving as a choirboy at St. Stephen's Cathedral in Vienna, which dismissed him when his voice changed, Haydn struggled to earn a living as a teacher and an accompanist. Largely self-taught, Haydn learned counterpoint and received some instruction in composition. An important opportunity came in 1761, when he entered the service of the princes Esterházy, noblemen who were devoted patrons of music and the arts. He remained in their service as a musical director until 1790, at which time he accepted a commission to write and conduct six symphonies in London. After a successful sojourn in London, he returned to Vienna in 1792 and remained there until his death at the age of 77.

Haydn is best known for his symphonies and string quartets, but his sacred works and operas are just as accomplished. He had a significant influence on the music of MOZART and BEETHOVEN, who was one of Haydn's students. On first hearing, Haydn's music seems clear and direct, but it is filled with instrumental brilliance, subtlety, invention, and emotion, all in classical proportions. During his lifetime, Haydn composed an enormous amount of music. He composed more than 100 symphonies, among them the *Farewell Symphony* (1772), the *Surprise Symphony* (1791), and the *Clock Symphony* (1794). He also composed more than 60 string quartets and 50 piano sonatas, as well as numerous operas, songs, and masses.

BOOKS ABOUT HAYDN

Geiringer, Karl, and Irene Geiringer. *Haydn, A Creative Life in Music*. Rprt. Serv. 1993 repr. of 1946 ed. $89.00. ISBN 0-7812-9604-8. Revised biography drawing from present research on Haydn and new letters.

Landon, H. Robbins. *Haydn: Chronicle and Works.* 5 vols. Ind. U. Pr. Vol. 1 *Haydn: The Early Years, 1732–1765.* 1981 o.p. Vol. 2 *Haydn at Eszterhazn 1776–1790.* 1978 o.p. Vol. 3 *Haydn in England 1791–1795.* 1976 $70.00. ISBN 0-253-37003-5. Vol. 4 *Haydn: The Years of "The Creation" 1796–1800.* 1977 $75.00. ISBN 0-253-37004-3. Vol. 5 *Haydn: The Late Years 1801–1809.* 1977 $70.00. ISBN 0-253-37005-1. Comprehensive study of the composer and his music.

Schroeder, David P. *Haydn and the Enlightenment: Audience Reception and the Late Symphonies.* OUP 1990 $55.00. ISBN 0-19-816159-X. Examines the impact of the Austrian Enlightenment on Haydn's work.

HENSEL, FANNY (MENDELSSOHN-BARTHOLDY). 1805–1847

As a member of the Mendelssohn family, Fanny Hensel received an excellent musical education at home.

The sister of Felix Mendelssohn-Bartholdy, six of her songs were published under her brother's name. She also composed piano works and part songs. Her early death was followed shortly by her grieving brother's death.

BOOK BY HENSEL

Letters of Fanny Hensel to Felix Mendelssohn. Ed. by Marcia J. Citron. Pendragon NY 1987 o.p. A collection of the letters of Fanny Hensel to her brother, Felix Mendelssohn, spanning a period of 26 years.

HINDEMITH, PAUL. 1895–1963

Paul Hindemith was a German composer and conductor of great originality. His career began with the study of the violin and the viola, and he held important positions in German ensembles before the Nazi era. Under Hitler's regime, Hindemith experienced difficulties, both artistically and politically. For example, he refused to cease ensemble playing with known Jews. Dr. Joseph Goebbels, Hitler's propaganda minister, accused Hindemith of cultural Bolshevism, and his music fell into official desuetude. Unwilling to compromise, Hindemith began accepting engagements abroad. During the late 1930s, he emigrated to the United States, and in 1946 he became a U.S. citizen.

Hindemith's musical style is uniquely his own. He sought in each piece to find the style, musical vocabulary, and thematic material most suitable for the intended use of the piece. He was immensely prolific and eclectic as a composer, writer, and teacher.

BOOK BY HINDEMITH

A Composer's World: Horizons and Limitations. Peter Smith $17.00. ISBN 0-8446-0697-9. A guide through the working methods of a composer; intended mostly for a general audience.

BOOK ABOUT HINDEMITH

Skelton, Geoffrey. *Paul Hindemith: The Man behind the Music.* Taplinger 1977 o.p. Follows the composer's life from his birth in 1895 to his death in 1963; focuses on his personal life and its effect on his music.

HOLIDAY, BILLIE (ELEANORA). 1915–1959

Billie Holiday, "Lady Day," started singing in Harlem nightclubs when she was 14 years old; she began singing professionally at the age of 15. She was discovered by impresario JOHN HAMMOND and bandleader Benny Goodman in 1933. She appeared in bands with Benny Goodman, COUNT BASIE, Artie Shaw, and others. She also had a successful solo career, giving concerts in the United

States and Europe. Her addiction to narcotics and alcohol brought about her early death at the age of 44. She sang mostly popular tunes of the day with her own unique "bluesy" style. Her recordings are still reissued, and a film based on her life, *Lady Sings the Blues*, starring Diana Ross, was released in 1972.

BOOKS ABOUT HOLIDAY

Burnett, James. *Billie Holiday*. St. Mut. 1984 o.p. A short and very readable account of Holiday's life and career. Selected discography by Tony Middleton.

Chilton, John. *Billie's Blues: The Billie Holiday Story, 1933–1959*. Da Capo 1989 $12.95. ISBN 0-306-80363-1. Presents the life of Holiday and investigates the various contradictions of her life.

O'Meally, Robert G. *Lady Day: The Many Faces of Billie Holiday*. Arcade Pub. Inc. 1991 $29.95. ISBN 1-55970-147-1. Charts Holiday's rise as an artist and provides a critical framework for her music.

White, John. *Billie Holiday, Her Life and Times*. Universe 1987 o.p. Covers Holiday's childhood and her music and assesses the impact of other musicians on her.

HOROWITZ, VLADIMIR. 1904–1989

Vladimir Horowitz, an American pianist of Russian birth, made his public debut at a recital in 1920, which launched his remarkable career. In 1926 he gave a recital in Berlin, his first appearance outside Russia. He then began touring throughout Europe. In 1926 he made his American debut, performing TCHAIKOVSKY's first piano concerto, with the New York Philharmonic. Afterward, he earned the reputation as a piano virtuoso of the highest caliber.

Horowitz played at the White House for President Hoover in 1931. Eleven years later, he became a U.S. citizen. Between 1953 and 1965, Horowitz withdrew from the stage but made numerous recordings. In 1965 he returned to the stage, only to retreat again four years later. In 1978 he again played at the White House, this time for President Carter. This engagement marked the fiftieth anniversary of his U.S. debut. Horowitz is best known for his performances of great romantic piano literature, especially the music of LISZT, TCHAIKOVSKY, CHOPIN, and that of his friend RACHMANINOFF.

BOOK ABOUT HOROWITZ

Plaskin, Glenn. *Horowitz: A Biography of Vladimir Horowitz*. Morrow 1983 o.p. A detailed biography of Horowitz based on personal recollections and interviews with approximately 650 of the pianist's friends and associates.

IVES, CHARLES EDWARD. 1874–1954

Charles Edward Ives was an American composer who learned music at home and then studied it at Yale University. He was a prosperous insurance man, but he continued to compose as an avocation. Ives was profoundly influenced by his father, who was a bandleader of the First Connecticut Heavy Artillery during the Civil War. His *Concord* sonata for piano, *Three Places in New England* for orchestra, and 114 songs are masterpieces featuring many unusual musical elements. Ives was one of the most remarkable American composers, who changed the direction of American music and whose music influenced the new generation of composers.

BOOK BY IVES

Essays before a Sonata, the Majority, and Other Writings. Ed. by Howard Boatwright. Norton 1970 repr. of 1962 ed. $8.95. ISBN 0-393-00528-3. The composer's thoughts on the *Concord* sonata, the work so representative of his highest achievements, the influence of the Concord transcendentalists preceding him, and the American cultural scene that formed his context.

BOOKS ABOUT IVES

Cowell, Henry, and Sidney Cowell. *Charles Ives and His Music*. Da Capo 1981 repr. of 1969 ed. $35.00. ISBN 0-306-76125-4. Authoritative and sympathetic biography of Ives.

Hitchcock, H. Wiley. *Ives*. OUP 1977 o.p. Short critical survey of Ives's work; biographical detail is kept to a minimum.

Perlis, Vivian. *Charles Ives Remembered: An Oral History*. Yale U. Pr. 1974 o.p. A fascinating account of Ives obtained through interviews with people who knew him. Foreword by Aaron Copeland.

Rossiter, Frank. *Charles Ives and His America*. Liveright 1975 o.p. Full biographical study of Ives that considers the composer within his historical context. Deals forthrightly with the most perplexing questions about the composer.

JANÁČEK, LEOŠ. 1854–1928

Leoš Janáček was born in Moravia, part of the Czech Republic. At the age of 10, he was placed at the Augustine monastery in Brno as a chorister. For two years (1872–74), he was a student at Brno Teachers Training College and at the Organ School in Prague, where he studied organ with Skuhersky. He later took lessons in composition with L. Grill at the Leipzig Conservatory. From 1879 to 1880, Janáček studied with Franz Krenn at the Vienna Conservatory. A year later, he returned to Brno, where he conducted the Czech Philharmonic Orchestra. Between 1919 and 1925, Janáček taught at the Conservatory of Brno. Many Czech composers of younger generations were his students.

Janáček began composing music early in his life in many genres, including choral works, orchestral music, chamber music, and piano music. However, it was not until the 1916 production of his opera *Její Pastorkyňa* (*Her Foster Daughter*), known more widely as *Jenůfa*, that his importance as a composer was realized in the music world. Many of Janáček's operas were based on important Russian literary works. *Kát'a Kabanová* (1921) and *From the House of the Dead* (1938) are two such operas. Janáček also believed in the artistic importance of folk songs. He collected a number of folk songs in his native Moravia.

Janáček is considered the most important modern Czech composer. In addition to *Jenůfa*, his works include the symphonic poem *Taras Bulba* (1918) and the *Glagolitic Mass* (1926), a Latin text translated into Czech. During the last two decades of his life, Janáček was highly influenced by French impressionistic music.

BOOKS BY JANÁČEK

Janáček Operas: A Documentary Account. Ed. by John Tyrell. Princeton U. Pr. 1992 o.p. Letters and other writings, chiefly by Janáček.

Janáček's Uncollected Essays on Music. Ed. and trans. by Mirka Zemanova. M. Boyars Pubs. 1992 $18.95. ISBN 0-7145-2951-6. Preface by John Tyrell.

BOOKS ABOUT JANÁČEK

Susskind, Charles. *Janáček and Brod*. Yale U. Pr. 1985 o.p. Deals with friendship and cooperation between Janáček and Max Brod, the man who helped establish his musical career and reputation in Europe. Foreword by Sir Charles Mackerras.

Tausky, Vilem, and Margaret Tausky, eds. *Janáček: Leaves From His Life*. Pro-Am Music 1989 $12.95. ISBN 0-912483-32-6. Janáček's almost playful thoughts on everyday things—natural, human, and artificial. Helps throw light on his music.

JOPLIN, SCOTT. 1868–1917

Scott Joplin learned to play the piano at home, in Texarkana, Arkansas. When he was 17 years old, he went to St. Louis, where he worked playing the piano at a local emporium. In 1899 Joplin achieved success as a ragtime composer with his "Maple Leaf Rag," which he named after a local dance hall, the Maple Leaf Club. Joplin also wrote a ragtime ballet, the *Ragtime Dance* (1902), and a ragtime opera, *A Guest of Honor* (c.1903), but the music is lost. Joplin moved to New York City in 1907, where he continued his career as a teacher and a composer. He wrote another opera, *Treemonisha* (1911). This opera was not a success; however, 60 years later, T. J. Anderson's orchestrated version of the opera renewed interest in Joplin's second and last opera.

During his lifetime, Joplin wrote about 50 piano rags, 2 operas, and a few songs, waltzes, and marches. His fame, however, has come only since the 1970s, due to the reprinting of most of his piano works in an edition by Vera Brodsky Lawrence, published by the New York Public Library. The movie *The Sting* (1974), which used Joplin's music, also brought the composer unprecedented acclaim and popularity that he did not have while he was alive. In 1976 Joplin was posthumously awarded recognition by the Pulitzer Prize committee.

BOOKS ABOUT JOPLIN

Gammond, Peter. *Scott Joplin and the Ragtime Era*. St. Martin rev. ed. 1975 o.p. Discusses Joplin's work in the musical context from which it emerged.

Haskins, James S., and Kathleen Benson. *Scott Joplin*. Doubleday 1978 o.p. Contains the best available information of this still relatively unknown artist.

KERN, JEROME. 1885–1945

Jerome Kern was born in New York. In 1904 he became a pianist and a salesman for a publishing company. With his first song, "How'd You Like to Spoon with Me" (1905), Kern achieved success. His success as a composer came with his musical comedy *The Red Petticoat* (1912). In 1917 Kern produced seven shows on Broadway. He composed more than 60 works for the stage and wrote several motion picture scores. Among his most important musical comedies are *Very Good, Eddie* (1915), *Have a Heart* (1917), *Head over Heels* (1918), *Stepping Stones* (1923), and *Sunny* (1925). *Show Boat* (1927) was his most remarkable score and one of the finest American works of its genre.

BOOKS ABOUT KERN

Bordman, Gerald. *Jerome Kern: His Life and Music*. OUP 1990 repr. of 1980 ed. $12.95. ISBN 0-19-506574-3. Comprehensive account of Kern's life and music aimed at the general reader.

Freedland, Michael. *Jerome Kern*. Stein and Day 1981 o.p. Brief, popular biography of Kern; considers his many works.

LISZT, FRANZ. 1811–1886

A Hungarian composer, conductor, and pianist, Franz Liszt was a child prodigy who began studying piano with his father at the age of 6. At the age of 9, he gave his first public performance and a year later went to Vienna, where he studied with Karl Czerny and Antonio Salieri. By the end of Liszt's life, he was acknowledged as the greatest pianist of his time. One of the foremost musicians of the romantic period, Liszt enthralled audiences with his expressive interpretations and dramatic gestures in a style of playing that greatly influenced the advancement of pianistic techniques.

From about 1822 to 1848, Liszt lived in Paris, where he came under the influence of Niccolo Paganini. Paganini's virtuosity inspired him to accomplish unheard-of feats in piano technique and expression. Between 1848 and 1861, Liszt was musical director for the court at Weimar in Germany, where he conducted performances of many important works, including those of RICHARD WAGNER. After 1861, Liszt spent much time in Rome, where he became a friend of the pope and took minor orders in the Catholic church. The rest of Liszt's life was divided among Rome, Weimar, and Budapest.

Liszt's compositions had an important impact on musical history. Avoiding traditional musical forms, he concentrated on program music. In this vein, "Liebestraume" (c.1850) is perhaps one of his most popular works. Also important are his 19 published *Hungarian Rhapsodies* and the *Sonata in B Minor* (1853). Not to be overlooked in historical importance are Liszt's transcriptions of other composers' works. These transcriptions familiarized a wide audience with major musical works and also demonstrated the piano's potential for interpreting orchestral music. Liszt also wrote books and essays on music, in many ways anticipating the music of the twentieth century.

BOOK BY LISZT

Letters of Franz Liszt. 2 vols. Haskell 1969 repr. of 1894 ed. $79.95. ISBN 0-8383-0307-2. Selections from letters Liszt wrote while touring Europe at the height of his fame. Volume one covers 1828 to 1861; Volume two covers 1862 to his death.

BOOKS ABOUT LISZT

Huneker, James G. *Franz Liszt*. Rprt. Serv. repr. of 1924 ed. $89.00. ISBN 0-7812-9071-6. A somewhat idiosyncratic response to those aspects of Liszt's art and enigmatic personality that intrigue the author; not a full biography.

Searle, Humphrey. *Music of Liszt*. Dover 1966 $6.95. ISBN 0-486-21700-0. Focuses on the significance of the composer's music.

Sitwell, Sacheverell. *Liszt*. Dover 1967 $8.95. ISBN 0-486-21702-7. Portrait of Liszt, beginning with his childhood and ending with the years in Budapest.

Walker, Alan. *Franz Liszt: The Virtuoso Years, 1811–1847*. Cornell Univ. Pr. 1987 $19.95. ISBN 0-8014-9421-4. Traces the composer's career from his beginning as a child prodigy to the peak of his success.

Westerby, Herbert. *Liszt, Composer, and His Piano Works*. Greenwood 1971 repr. of 1936 ed. $35.00. ISBN 0-8371-4365-9. Descriptive and critical analysis of Liszt, written in a popular and concise style.

LLOYD WEBBER, ANDREW. 1948–

In the tradition of his musically talented family, Andrew Lloyd Webber learned to play the piano, violin, French horn and to improvise music, which he did mostly in the form of American musicals. While attending college, Webber wrote his first musical, *The Likes of Us*. At the age of 19, he composed *Joseph and the Amazing Technicolor Dreamcoat*, for which he received considerable success. In this piece Webber combined a biblical subject with rock music, French chansonnettes, and country-western music.

Webber achieved his first commercial success with *Jesus Christ Superstar* (1970–71). This "rock opera" combined another religious theme with jazz and rock music. The Broadway production closed after 720 performances and won seven Tony awards. The record version sold 3 million copies and in 1981 received the Grammy Award for best Broadway-cast album. His other Broadway hit musicals include *Evita* (1978) and *Cats* (1982). He has also composed *Variations* for cello and jazz ensemble and a *Requiem Mass* (1985).

BOOKS ABOUT LLOYD WEBBER

McKnight, Gerald. *Andrew Lloyd Webber*. St. Martin 1984 o.p. Hagiographical treatment of Webber suitable for the general reader.

Walsh, Michael. *Andrew Lloyd Webber: His Life and Works*. Abrams 1989 $39.95. ISBN 0-8109-1275-9. A critical but sympathetic treatment of Webber's life and musicals; illustrated.

MAHLER, GUSTAV. 1860–1911

The last of the great late-romantic composers, Gustav Mahler was born in Austria in 1860. Although born in the Jewish faith, he converted to Catholicism in 1897 but held a more expansive philosophy than either religion offered. Mahler began studying piano, harmony, and composition at the Vienna Conservatory at the age of 15. At the age of 20 he began conducting and held positions at the Budapest Imperial Opera (1880–90), the Hamburg Municipal Theater (1891–97), the Vienna State Opera (1897–1907), the Metropolitan Opera House of New York (1908–10), and the New York Philharmonic (1909–11). As a conductor, Mahler held his orchestras to very high standards, but it was as a composer of symphonies that he is best remembered and revered.

Mahler completed nine symphonies and at his death left one unfinished, which was later completed by another composer. He also wrote five series of songs for solo voices with orchestra. The last of these—*The Song of the Earth* (1908)—was first performed after Mahler's death and is thought by many music experts to be his finest work. In it he expresses feelings of pleasure and foreboding, both of which characterized the mood of the late romantic period. Mahler's work often mixed simplicity with sophistication, lofty ideas with strong feelings, and the grotesque or fantastic with the common and ordinary. While Mahler's symphonies are regarded as the high point of the romantic period, they also include elements that foreshadowed the age to follow, influencing such composers as ARNOLD SCHOENBERG, ALBAN BERG, and ANTON VON WEBERN.

BOOKS BY MAHLER

Mahler's Unknown Letters. Ed. by Herta Blaukopf. Trans. by Richard Stokes. NE U. Pr. 1987 $25.00. ISBN 1-55553-016-8. A collection of Mahler's more interesting letters to musicians and others in the profession.

Selected Letters of Gustav Mahler. Ed. by Knud Martner and Alma Mahler. Trans. by Eithne Wilkins and others. FS&G 1979 o.p. A subjective selection of Mahler's letters made by his wife. Contains letters written after 1877.

BOOKS ABOUT MAHLER

Cooke, Deryck. *Gustav Mahler: An Introduction to His Music*. Cambridge U. Pr. 1980 $10.95. ISBN 0-521-36863-4. Scholarly treatment of the composer's music.

De la Grange, Henry-Louis. *Mahler*. Doubleday 1973 o.p. The standard biography of Mahler.

Mitchell, Donald. *Gustav Mahler: The Early Years*. Ed. by David Mathews. U. CA Pr. 1980 $47.50. ISBN 0-520-04141-0. Comprehensive account of the composer's early life and career; includes an extensively documented bibliography.

MENDELSSOHN, FELIX. 1809–1847

A German composer and conductor whose brief life resulted in many great works, Felix Mendelssohn wrote songs, sonatas, cantatas, organ works, concertos, and symphonies. His first masterpiece, the overture to *A Midsummer Night's Dream*, was produced when he was only 17. His symphonies and incidental music are remarkable in that they were composed by someone so young.

Mendelssohn is also responsible for the revival of interest in BACH's vocal and choral music by having performed the *St. Matthew Passion* in Berlin in 1829.

BOOKS ABOUT MENDELSSOHN

Finson, John W., and R. Larry Todd, eds. *Mendelssohn and Schumann: Essays on Their Music and Its Context.* Duke 1985 $54.95. ISBN 0-8223-0569-0. A collection of essays on one of the more remarkable musical friendships of the nineteenth century.

Radcliffe, Philip. *Mendelssohn.* Biblio Dist. rev. ed. 1976 o.p. The standard biography; well-researched and very readable.

MONTEVERDI, CLAUDIO. 1567–1643

Claudio Monteverdi acquired a mastery of composition at an early age. When he was 15 years old, a collection of his three-part motets were published in Venice. In the early 1600s, Monteverdi turned his attention to opera. His first opera *Orfeo* (1607) is distinguished by Monteverdi's flexible use of music to advance and to comment on the dramatic action.

His genius was in the way in which he expressed human emotion in moving melodies. One biographer has termed Monteverdi "the creator of modern music." He is credited with establishing the foundations of modern opera as drama in music.

BOOKS ABOUT MONTEVERDI

Arnold, Denis. *Monteverdi.* Biblio Dist. rev. ed. 1975 o.p. Popular account of Monteverdi's life and work and his impact on music.

Arnold, Denis, and Nigel Fortune, eds. *Monteverdi Companion.* Norton 1972 o.p.

Redlich, Hans F. *Claudio Monteverdi: Life and Works.* Trans. by Kathleen Dale. Greenwood repr. of 1952 ed. o.p. More of a musical analysis than a complete biography of Monteverdi.

Schrade, Leo. *Monteverdi: Creator of Modern Music.* Da Capo 1979 repr. of 1950 ed. $42.50. ISBN 0-306-79565-5. Views Monteverdi's music, seen in its seventeenth-century cultural context, as incorporating an early modern sensibility.

MOZART, WOLFGANG AMADEUS. 1756–1791

Born in Salzburg, Austria, Wolfgang Amadeus Mozart's life and musical career were fiery but brief. The son of Leopold Mozart, a musician and well-known composer, Wolfgang Mozart was a child prodigy. By the age of 5, he was writing minuets and playing the harpsichord; by the age of 8, he had written his first symphony. Because of his prodigious talent, Mozart's father took him and his sister (who was also an excellent musician) on tour throughout Europe, and he met and performed for several royal courts.

In 1769, at the age of only 13, Mozart was made concertmaster at the court of the Archbishop of Salzburg. By 1781 he had become unhappy in Salzburg and quarrelled with the Archbishop. As a result, he was dismissed from his position and left for Vienna. In 1782, while in Vienna, Mozart married Constanze Weber. Although plagued by troubles, including the deaths of four of his children and his wife's ill health, he composed some of his finest works in Vienna. These included the operas *The Abduction from the Seraglio* (1782) and *Cosi fan tutte* (1790), his famous last three symphonies, several piano concertos, and many other works.

By 1788 Mozart was seriously in debt. One reason was that audiences began finding some of his latest music difficult and stayed away from his concerts. In the summer of 1791, he began suffering from fever and severe headaches. Later that year he fell into a coma and died on December 5, leaving behind his last great work, the *Requiem* mass, which was left unfinished. Because he was so poor, his coffin was dumped into an unmarked pauper's grave, and his place of burial remains unknown.

Mozart's talent as a musician was tremendous. He could compose whole symphonies and operas in his head, needing only to write them out for performance. His gifts as a composer of endless streams of melodies, beautifully harmonized, are astounding. His symphonies and concerti are brilliant; his chamber music, stunning. His operas *Don Giovanni* (1787), *The Magic Flute* (1791), and *The Marriage of Figaro* (1786), are among the best-known and beloved operas performed today. His brief life has produced nearly two centuries of deserved adulation from the trained musician, the music scholar, and unsophisticated listener.

Books about Mozart

Anderson, Emily, ed. and trans. *The Letters of Mozart and His Family*. Norton 1986 $75.00. ISBN 0-393-02248-X. A classic of Mozart scholarship; contains all the extant letters of Mozart and his immediate family.

Biancolli, Louis, ed. *The Mozart Handbook: A Guide to the Man and His Music*. Greenwood 1975 repr. of 1954 ed. $45.00. ISBN 0-8371-8496-7. Comprehensive account of Mozart's life and work; examines his relation to the musical tradition of his age and his impact on later musicians.

Blom, Eric. *Mozart*. Biblio Dist. rev. ed. 1976 o.p. A good, readable introduction to Mozart for the non-specialist.

Deutsch, Otto E. *Mozart: A Documentary Biography*. Stanford U. Pr. 1966 $52.50. ISBN 0-8047-0233-0. Mammoth collection of all the documents (except letters) pertaining to Mozart's life and career; even includes the wedding certificate of his grandparents, newspaper reviews of performances, and so on.

Hildesheimer, Wolfgang. *Mozart*. Trans. by Marion Faber. FS&G 1991 $12.95. ISBN 0-374-52298-7. Comprehensive, somewhat controversial, account of the relationship between Mozart's emotional life and his work.

Landon, Howard C. *Mozart and Vienna*. Schirmer Bks. 1991 $22.50. ISBN 0-02-871317-6. Various eminent critics write on all aspects of Mozart's music.

Landon, Howard C., and Donald Mitchell, eds. *The Mozart Companion*. Greenwood 1981 repr. of 1956 ed. $35.00. ISBN 0-313-23084-6

Stafford, William. *Mozart's Death: A Corrective Survey of the Legends*. Macmillan 1991 o.p.

MUSSORGSKY, MODEST. 1839–1881

Russian composer Modest Mussorgsky was born in Karevo, Russia. Educated for the army, he resigned his commission in 1848 after the onset of a nervous disorder and began studying music. Along with BORODIN and RIMSKY-KORSAKOV, he was one of the first to promote a national Russian style of music.

Mussorgsky first became known for his songs, among them the well-known setting of GOETHE's (see Vol. 2) satirical "Song of the Flea" (1879). His masterpiece, however, is the opera *Boris Godunov* (1874), a wonderful example of his ability to "color" his music. His piano suite *Pictures from an Exhibition* (1874) is also a standard work in the concert repertoire of today.

During the latter part of his life, Mussorgsky sank into chronic alcoholism, and this contributed to an early death. After his death, his friend Rimsky-Korsakov took many of the composer's unfinished pieces and completed or arranged them. Today, the original versions of many of Mussorgsky's works are making a comeback and deserve serious attention.

BOOKS ABOUT MUSSORGSKY

Brown, Malcolm H. *Mussorgsky: In Memoriam, 1881–1981*. UMI Research 1982 o.p.
    Contributors discuss different aspects of Mussorgsky's life and work.
Calvocoressi, M. D. *Mussorgsky*. Ed. by Gerald Abraham. Biblio Dist. rev. ed. 1974 o.p.
    Examines the relationship between Mussorgsky's music and Russian nationalism.
Orlova, Alexandra. *Mussorgsky's Days and Works: A Biography in Documents*. Ed. by
    Malcolm Brown. Trans. by Roy Guenther. UMI Research 1983 o.p. Comprehensive
    collection of documents pertaining to Mussorgsky, including relevant selections
    from his letters.

PARKER, CHARLIE ("BIRD"). 1920–1955

Born in Kansas City, Kansas, Charlie Parker taught himself to play the alto
saxophone, a present from his mother when he was 11 years old. At the age of
15, Parker left school and became a professional musician. In 1939 he moved to
New York. In 1941, as a member of Jay McShann big band, he made his first
recording. He later formed a quartet with Dizzy Gillespie, with whom he
developed a new style of jazz known as be-bop. Parker, however, is commonly
known as the leader of be-bop, because he developed a unique improvising
technique for which he will always be remembered.

BOOKS ABOUT PARKER

Priestly, Brian. *Charlie Parker*. Ed. by John L. Smith. Hippocrene Bks. 1984 o.p. Brief
    account of Parker's life; for the general reader.
Reisner, Robert G., ed. *Bird: The Legend of Charlie Parker*. Da Capo 1975 repr. of 1962 ed.
    $29.50. ISBN 0-306-88069-1
Russell, Ross. *Bird Lives: The High Life and Hard Times of Charlie (Yardbird) Parker*.
    McKay 1973 o.p.

PAVAROTTI, LUCIANO. 1935–

Born in Modena, Italy, Luciano Pavarotti learned to sing as a boy alto in a
church choir and the Chorale Gioacchino Rossini, an amateur group. He began
his career as a school teacher and an insurance salesman, but, after continued
vocal study, he began to sing professionally in 1961. He had been performing for
five years, in Europe, America, and Australia, when he achieved international
fame from his performance as Tonio in *La Fille du régiment* at Covent Garden.
Among his most famous roles are those of Rodolfo in *La Bohème* and Nemorino
in *L'elisir d'amore*.

In 1982 Pavarotti appeared in an unsuccessful film, *Yes, Giorgio*, in which he
plays an opera superstar who pursues an independent female doctor during an
American tour. In 1991 the tenors JOSÉ CARRERAS, PLÁCIDO DOMINGO, and
Pavarotti teamed up to record *In Concert*, which has sold over 5 million CDs
and cassettes worldwide. *In Concert* rose to number one on the U.S. classical
charts for that year. It was also ranked number 43 on Billboard's pop charts, the
highest any classical recording has climbed since rock-and-roll dominated
album charts in the mid-1960s.

BOOKS BY PAVAROTTI

Grandissimo Pavarotti. Doubleday 1986 $40.00. ISBN 0-385-23138-5. Career chronology
    and recorded repertory, photo editing, and captioning by Gerald Fitzgerald.
Pavarotti: My Own Story. (coauthored with William Wright). Doubleday 1981 $13.95.
    ISBN 0-385-15340-6. The tenor tells his own story; a whimsical read.

BOOK ABOUT PAVAROTTI

Pavarotti, Adua, and Wendy Dallas. *Pavarotti: Life with Luciano*. Rizzoli Intl. 1992 $35.00. ISBN 0-8478-1573-0. Special photography by Judith Kovacs, Robin Mathews, and Mirella Ricciardi.

PORTER, COLE. 1891–1964

Cole Porter began his musical career at Yale University, writing songs for college functions and football games, including "Bulldog" and "Bingo Eli Yale." He also took academic courses at Harvard Law School and later at the Harvard School of Music. His first musical comedy in New York City was *See America First* (1916). Porter wrote the words and music for *Can-Can* (1953), *Kiss Me Kate* (1948), and *Silk Stockings* (1955), all of which are distinguished by their sophisticated and engaging songs. His most popular songs include "Night and Day" (1932), "Let's Do It" (1928), and "In the Still of the Night" (1937).

BOOKS BY PORTER

The Complete Lyrics of Cole Porter. Ed. by Robert Kimball. Da Capo 1992 repr. of 1983 ed. $19.95. ISBN 0-306-80482-2. Contains the lyrics and scores of all the musicals; with a useful introduction.
You're The Top: Cole Porter in the 1930s. Koch Intl. 1992 o.p.

BOOKS ABOUT PORTER

Citron, Stephen. *Noel and Cole: The Sophisticates*. OUP 1993 $25.00. ISBN 0-19-508385-7
Eells, George. *The Life That He Led: A Biography of Cole Porter*. Putnam Pub. Group 1967 o.p. Popular biography of Porter.
Howard, Jean. *Travels with Cole Porter*. Abrams 1991 $39.95. ISBN 0-8109-3408-6. Introduction by George Eells.
Kimball, Robert, ed. *The Unpublished Cole Porter*. S&S Trade 1975 o.p.
Schwartz, Charles. *Cole Porter: A Biography*. Da Capo 1979 repr. of 1977 ed. $13.95. ISBN 0-306-80047-7

PRICE, LEONTYNE. 1927–

Leontyne Price was the first African American to have a successful career as a diva in the European operatic tradition. Her performance as Tosca in 1955 created a sensation, partly for this reason, but more for her marvelous voice and ability. She had already been singled out by VIRGIL THOMSON and performed in the premiere of SAMUEL BARBER's *Prayers of Kierkegaard*. She has given wonderful performances as Aïda, Madame Butterfly, Donna Anna, Pamina, and Cleopatra in Barber's *Anthony and Cleopatra*, and also as a concert artist.

Price's honors include 19 Grammy awards, including the Lifetime Achievement Award, numerous honorary doctorates, three Emmy awards, the National Medal of the Arts, and the Presidential Medal of Freedom.

Price recently expanded her talents to include writing. In 1990 she brought the world of opera to young readers with her award-winning retelling of *Aïda*.

BOOK ABOUT PRICE

Lyon, Hugh Lee. *Leontyne Price: Highlights of a Prima Donna*. Vantage 1973 o.p.

PROKOFIEV, SERGEI. 1891–1953

The music of twentieth-century Russian composer Sergei Prokofiev is a sharp mix of traditional and modern elements. His innovative style is characterized by emotional restraint, strong drumlike rhythms, harsh-sounding harmonies, and humor.

Prokofiev was born in the town of Sontzovka, in the Ukraine. His mother, an accomplished pianist, encouraged her young son to play along with her as she practiced. The young Prokofiev showed unusual talent and began composing music at the age of 5. At the age of 13, he entered the St. Petersburg Conservatory, where he studied with some of the finest teachers of the day, including RIMSKY-KORSAKOV. By the time he graduated in 1914, Prokofiev has established himself as a musical innovator.

In 1918 Prokofiev left Russia to appear as a pianist and conductor in Europe and the United States. While in America, he composed his most popular opera, *Love for Three Oranges* (1919), a musical satire of traditional operatic plots and conventions. From 1922 to 1933, Prokofiev lived mostly in Paris, where he composed two ballets, three symphonies, and four concertos.

In 1934 Prokofiev returned to the Soviet Union. Back in his native land, Prokofiev's style mellowed, and he accepted the idea that a state-supported artist must appeal to a wide audience. During the next few years, he composed some of his most popular and best-known pieces, including *Peter and the Wolf* (1936) and *Romeo and Juliet* (1938). Prokofiev won the Stalin Prize during World War II. However, in 1948 Prokofiev and other leading Russian composers were denounced by Soviet Communist party leaders for "antidemocratic tendencies alien to the Soviet people." He returned to favor in the early 1950s and enjoyed great success in the Soviet Union, winning the Stalin Prize a second time. By the year of his death, Prokofiev's music had become well known throughout the world.

BOOK BY PROKOFIEV

Prokofiev by Prokofiev: A Composer's Memoir. Doubleday 1979 o.p. Entertaining and detailed recollections of his childhood and youth.

BOOKS ABOUT PROKOFIEV

Robinson, Harlow Loomis. *Sergei Prokofiev: A Biography.* Paragon Hse. 1988 o.p. Comprehensive look at the twentieth-century Russian composer.

Seroff, Victor. *Sergei Prokofiev: A Soviet Tragedy.* Taplinger 1979 o.p. Sympathetic portrait of Prokofiev tracing both his public and private life.

Shostakovich, Dmitri, and others. *Sergei Prokofiev: Materials, Articles, Interviews.* Imported Pubns. 1978 o.p. Prokofiev in his own words and those of his colleagues, including Dmitri Shostakovich; published in a translation authorized by the Soviet Union.

PUCCINI, GIACOMO. 1858–1924

Giacomo Puccini came from a long line of musicians of local Italian prominence. However, Puccini showed no special interest or talent in music. His mother, in an attempt to keep the family tradition alive, sent Puccini to the Istituto Musicale of Lucca. He progressed rapidly through the program and in the end became a good pianist and organist. He then entered the Milan Conservatory, where he studied music seriously for three years. For his graduation he wrote his first opera *Capriccio sinfonico*, which elicited much praise from the critics.

The subsequent operas of Puccini quickly won esteem and have become part of the standard repertory of the world's leading opera companies. *La Bohème* (1896), *Madama Butterfly* (1904), *Tosca* (1900), *La fanciulla del west* (1910), and *Turandot* (completed posthumously) demonstrate his ability to create an intense psychodrama from the first notes of the first act. He was a true successor to GIUSEPPE VERDI.

BOOKS ABOUT PUCCINI

Ashbrook, William. *The Operas of Puccini.* Cornell Univ. Pr. 1985 $36.50. ISBN 0-8014-9309-9. Meticulous but readable analysis of Puccini's music and methodology.

Carner, Mosco. *Puccini: A Critical Biography.* Holmes & Meier rev. ed. 1992 $59.50. ISBN 0-8419-1326-9. Comprehensive biography of the man and his work; views Puccini as a not-quite-great artist.

Osborne, Charles. *The Complete Operas of Puccini: A Critical Guide.* Da Capo 1983 repr. of 1982 ed. $10.95. ISBN 0-306-80200-7. Guide to Puccini's operas for the music lover. Contains background and biographical information, historical context, and critical discussion of the music.

PURCELL, HENRY. 1659–1695

Born in Westminster, England, Henry Purcell is considered by many experts to be that country's finest native-born composer. Purcell's musical career began at the age of 10, when he joined the choir of London's Chapel Royal, where he remained a member until he was 14 years old. While a choirboy, he was taught to play the organ by his mentor, Dr. John Blow, the chapel's choirmaster and also the organist at Westminster Abbey. In 1677 Purcell was appointed composer for the king's band, and two years later he was named organist at Westminster Abbey, where he remained until his death.

As a composer, Purcell proved to be a master of lyrical melody and of combining it with harmonic invention and counterpoint. Purcell's *Dido and Aeneas* (1689) is regarded by many as the finest opera ever written in English. It shows his skill as a dramatist, contrapuntist, and melodist. The opera also highlights the way in which he was able to incorporate other musical elements, including ones from seventeenth-century English theater, into his own musical style. Among Purcell's many other works are odes for chorus and orchestra, cantatas, songs, anthems, chamber sonatas, and harpsichord suites. Especially notable are *The Fairy Queen* (1692), a masque, or dramatic composition, based on SHAKESPEARE's (see Vol. 1) *A Midsummer Night's Dream;* the music for *King Arthur* (1691), a drama written by JOHN DRYDEN (see Vol. 1); and "Sound the Trumpets," a birthday ode for King James II.

BOOKS ABOUT PURCELL

Westrup, Jack A. *Purcell.* Rprt. Serv. 1993 repr. of 1949 ed. $89.00. ISBN 0-7812-8614-5. Revised by Nigel Fortune.

Zimmerman, Franklin B. *Henry Purcell: His Life and Times*, 1659–1695. U. of Pa. Pr. 1983 o.p. Looks at the composer within the context of seventeenth-century England.

RACHMANINOFF, SERGEY. 1873–1943

Russian-born Sergey Rachmaninoff's early career was as a pianist, but PETER ILICH TCHAIKOVSKY recognized his importance as a conductor and encouraged him to continue composing. At the age of 19, Rachmaninoff wrote *Prelude in C-Sharp Minor*, which became one of his most celebrated pieces throughout the world. By the age of 24, Rachmaninoff had composed the opera *Aleko*. His piano concertos are regarded by many as models of the late-romantic formulation of that genre. His music was eclectic in style, and his belief that music existed to reveal beauty left him opposed to Russian nationalist composers. In 1909 he first traveled to the United States. He became an exile as a result of the Russian Revolution and lived in Switzerland and the United States.

BOOKS ABOUT RACHMANINOFF

Bertensson, Sergei, and Jay Leyda. *Sergei Rachmaninoff: A Lifetime in Music*. NYU Pr.
    1956 o.p. Readable biography of Rachmaninoff focusing on his life and music.
Norris, Geoffrey. *Rakhmaninoff*. Biblio Dist. 1976 o.p.
Piggott, Patrick. *Rachmaninoff*. Faber & Faber 1978 $9.95
Walker, Robert. *Rachmaninoff: His Life and Times*. Paganiniana Pubs. rev. ed. 1981
    $14.95. ISBN 0-87666-582-2

RAVEL, MAURICE. 1875–1937

The French composer Maurice Ravel was the leading exemplar of musical
impressionism. Ravel entered the Paris Conservatory in 1889, where his
teachers included GABRIEL FAURÉ. As a composer, Ravel produced highly
original, fluid music, much of it within the outlines of musical classicism. He
excelled at piano composition and orchestration, and his compositions reveal
many of the musical trends active in Paris after the turn of the century. His
coloristic effects and occasional use of whole-tone scales and tritones place him
with CLAUDE DEBUSSY and the impressionists. Yet the sense of proportion and
the austere aspects of some of his compositions also reflect his interest in, and
reverence for, classical forms of music.

Ravel composed *Pavanne for a Deceased Infant* (1899), the piano work *Jeux
d'eau* (1902), his song cycle *Shéhérazade* (1903), and his *String Quartet* (1903)
while still a student at the conservatory. In subsequent years, Ravel composed
ballets, including *Daphne and Chloé* (1912); symphonic poems, such as *La Valse*
(1920); two operas, *L'Heure espagnole* (1911) and *L'Enfant et les sortilèges*
(9125); and many pieces for piano, violin, and orchestra. His orchestration of
MODEST MUSSORGSKY's *Pictures at an Exhibition* (1922) attracted worldwide
attention and inclusion in the repertoire of major orchestras. Another staple of
major orchestras is Ravel's *Boléro* (1928). Ravel died in Paris following brain
surgery in 1937.

BOOKS ABOUT RAVEL

Demuth, Norman. *Ravel*. Hyperion Conn. 1989 repr. of 1947 ed. $26.00. ISBN 0-88355-
    690-1. Short account of Ravel's life and music; for the general reader.
Myers, Rollo H. *Ravel: His Life and Works*. Greenwood 1973 repr. of 1960 ed. $49.75.
    ISBN 0-8371-6841-4. A detailed account of the life and music of Ravel.
Nichols, Roger. *Ravel*. Biblio Dist. 1977 o.p. Narrative that balances both Ravel's work
    and his personal life.
Orenstein, Arbie. *Ravel: Man and Musician*. Dover 1991 $9.95. ISBN 0-486-26633-8. A
    detailed biography of the French composer and his music.
———, ed. *A Ravel Reader: Correspondence, Articles, Interviews*. Col. U. Pr. 1990 $49.00.
    ISBN 0-231-04962-5. Ravel's selected letters, articles, and interviews on music;
    includes an autobiographical sketch.

RIMSKY-KORSAKOV, NIKOLAY. 1844–1908

One of the great Russian composers of the nineteenth century, Nikolay
Rimsky-Korsakov is known for the excellence of his orchestration. As a music
teacher, Rimsky-Korsakov was of the greatest importance to the development
and maintenance of the traditions of the Russian national school. A prolific
composer, some of his best-known works include *Scheherazade* (1888), *The
Golden Cockerel* (1909), *Snow Maiden* (1882), and *Russian Easter Festival*
overture (1888).

Rimsky-Korsakov made use of both the purely Russian idioms and coloristic oriental melodic patterns. *Scheherazade* is representative of Russian orientalism at its best.

BOOKS BY RIMSKY-KORSAKOV

My Musical Life. Ed. by Carl van Vechten. Trans. by Judah A. Joffe. Faber & Faber 1990 repr. of 1942 ed. $14.95. ISBN 0-571-14245-1. Badly written but brutally frank account of his music and that of his Russian peers.

Reminiscences of Rimsky-Korsakov. Ed. by Florence Jonas. Col. U. Pr. 1985 $77.00. ISBN 0-231-05260-X. Foreword by Gerald Abraham. Encounters with Rimsky-Korsakov, written in diary format by the musician's close friend Vasily Yastrebkev.

RODGERS, RICHARD. 1902–1979

An American composer for the musical theater, Richard Rodgers composed some of the best-loved musicals of this century. He collaborated for 18 years with lyricist Lorenz Hart. Their highly popular musical comedies include *The Girl Friend* (1926), *A Connecticut Yankee* (1927), *Babes in Arms* (1927), and *I Married an Angel* (1938).

After Hart's death in 1943, Rodgers teamed up with Oscar Hammerstein II. Together they wrote such musical classics as *Oklahoma!* (1943), which received a Pulitzer Prize in 1944; *South Pacific* (1949), which received a Pulitzer Prize in 1950; *The King and I* (1951); and *The Sound of Music* (1959). After Hammerstein's death in 1960, Rodgers wrote both the lyrics and music for *No Strings* (1962). Rodgers also wrote music for television shows, including *Victory at Sea* (1952) and *Winston Churchill: The Valiant Years* (1960).

BOOK BY RODGERS

Musical Stages: An Autobiography. Random 1975 o.p. Lively story of his family, life, influences, and musical career.

BOOKS ABOUT RODGERS

Gottfried, Martin. *Rodgers and Hammerstein: The Men and Their Music.* Abrams 1988 o.p.

Marx, Samuel, and Jan Clayton. *Rodgers and Hart: Bewitched, Bothered, and Bedeviled: An Anecdotal Account.* Putnam Pub. Group 1976 o.p. Anecdotal, tragicomic, and entertaining narrative of the collaboration between Rodgers and Hart.

Mordden, Ethan. *Rodgers and Hammerstein.* Abrams 1992 $45.00 ISBN 0-8109-1567-7. The famous musicals are described and discussed for the general reader; includes some great pictures.

Nolan, Frederick. *The Sound of Their Music: The Story of Rodgers and Hammerstein.* Walker & Co. 1978 o.p.

Taylor, Deems. *Some Enchanted Evenings: The Story of Rodgers and Hammerstein.* Greenwood 1972 repr. of 1953 ed. ISBN 0-8371-5414-6. Hagiographical account of the collaboration.

RUBINSTEIN, ARTUR. 1887–1982

Polish-born pianist Artur Rubinstein was especially renowned for his interpretation of the music of his compatriot FRÉDÉRIC CHOPIN. He gave his first public concert at the age of 7 and went on to perform with Joseph Joachim, to study with Ignacy Paderewski, and to play Camille Saint-Saëns's G-minor piano concerto for the composer himself. He performed the music of Spanish and Latin American composers with true understanding, and that of BEETHOVEN, MOZART, SCHUMANN, and BRAHMS with spirit and inspiration.

BOOKS BY RUBINSTEIN

My Many Years. Random 1980 o.p. Entertaining autobiography, written at age 92.
My Young Years [by] Artur Rubinstein. Random 1973 o.p. Concentrates on his childhood, youth, and early career.

SATIE, ERIK. 1866–1925

At the age of 13, Erik Satie went to Paris, where he attended the Paris Conservatory. He soon, however, relinquished his formal and systematic study of music. Early in his career, he played in cabarets in Montmartre. In 1892 he began to produce short piano pieces with eccentric titles, intended to ridicule proponents of both modern and classical music. He was 40 years old when he decided to learn about the techniques of composition.

Although he was dismissed as a serious musician by his contemporaries, Satie greatly influenced French musicians of a younger generation. He became well known as an innovator in the modern idiom after his death.

BOOK ABOUT SATIE

Orledge, Robert. *Satie The Composer*. Cambridge U. Pr. 1990 $70.00. ISBN 0-521-35037-9. Speculative biography of the secretive composer; attempts to discover his motivations and reveal his creative impulses.

SCHOENBERG, ARNOLD. 1874–1951

An American of Austrian birth, Arnold Schoenberg composed initially in a highly developed romantic style but eventually turned to painting and expressionism. At first he was influenced by RICHARD WAGNER and tried to write in a Wagnerian style. He attracted the attention of ALBAN BERG and ANTON VON WEBERN, with whom he created a new compositional method based on using all 12 half-steps in each octave as an organizing principle, the so-called 12-tone technique. His importance to the development of twentieth-century music is incredible, but the music he composed using this new method is not easily accessible to most concertgoers.

BOOKS BY SCHOENBERG

Arnold Schoenberg Correspondence: A Collection of Translated and Annotated Letters Exchanged with Guido Adler, Pablo Casals, Emanuel Feuermann, and Olin Downes. Ed. by Egbert M. Ennulat. Scarecrow 1991 $37.50. ISBN 0-8108-2452-3. The musician's memorable and expressive letters to four professional musicians; written over a period of 50 years.
Arnold Schoenberg Self-Portrait: A Collection of Articles, Program Notes, and Letters by the Composer About His Own Works. Ed. by Nuria Schoenberg Nono. Belmont Music Pub. 1988 o.p.
Style and Idea: Selected Writings of Arnold Schoenberg. Ed. by Leonard Stein. Faber & Faber 1985 $69.95. ISBN 0-520-05286-2. Schoenberg's thoughts on music, politics, and other subjects.

BOOKS ABOUT SCHOENBERG

Leibowitz, Rene. *Schoenberg and His School: The Contemporary Stage of the Language of Music*. Da Capo 1975 repr. of 1949 ed. $5.95. ISBN 0-306-80020-9. Influential work by a French musician on Schoenberg's influence on Western music.
Ringer, Alexander L. *Arnold Schoenberg: The Composer As Jew*. OUP 1990 $58.00. ISBN 0-19-315466-8. Examines the impact of Schoenberg's Jewish heritage and anti-semitism on his work.
Rose, Charles. *Arnold Schoenberg*. Viking Penguin 1975 o.p.

Stuckenschmidt, H. H. *Arnold Schoenberg: His Life, World and Work*. Trans by Humphrey
   Searle. Greenwood 1979 repr. of 1960 ed. ISBN 0-313-20762-3. Comprehensive
   account of the relationship between the musician's life, work, and contemporary
   events.

SCHUBERT, FRANZ. 1797–1828

Franz Schubert was born in Vienna, Austria, the son of a schoolmaster who
was also an amateur cellist. As a boy, he learned to play the piano, violin, and
organ and sang in the church choir. Schubert had an uncommon talent for
melody and soon began to compose his own music. By the age of 17, he had
written his first symphony and many songs, including his first song masterpiece
"Gretchen am Spinnrade" (1814).

In 1814 Schubert began to teach, but he hated teaching and gave up his
position in 1818. From this point on, he lived fairly precariously, earning a
living primarily by giving private music lessons. At the same time, he composed
furiously and constantly, sometimes writing as many as eight songs in a day.
Although he sold many of his songs and piano pieces, he was always short of
money and often relied on the generosity of his friends. His health began to
decline after 1822 as a result of syphilis.

Schubert's brief and difficult life is not reflected at all in his astounding
outpouring of lieder cycles, symphonies, and chamber and church music. His
work shows that he was a poet in music, conveying a wide range of emotions
and meanings through his songs and other pieces. Among his best-known and
most important works are the song cycles *Die schöne Müllerin* (1823) and *Die
Winterreise* (1826), and his Unfinished Symphony (Symphony No. 8) (1822).

BOOKS ABOUT SCHUBERT

Brown, Maurice John Edwin. *Schubert: A Critical Biography*. Da Capo 1988 repr. of 1958
   ed. $12.95. ISBN 0-306-80329-1. Short biography for the general reader; concen-
   trates on the music.
Deutsch, Otto E. *Schubert: A Documentary Biography*. Trans. by Eric Blom. Da Capo 1977
   repr. of 1946 ed. $125.00. ISBN 0-306-77420-8. Comprehensive collection of all the
   documents pertaining to Schubert.
Fischer-Dieskau, Dietrich. *Schubert's Songs: A Biographical Study*. Trans. by Kenneth S.
   Whitton. Limelight Edns. 1984 $17.95. ISBN 0-87910-005-2. On the influences,
   mainly poetic, on Schubert's songs.
Hutchings, Arthur. *Schubert*. Biblio Dist. 1978 o.p. The music of Schubert explained for
   the general reader.

SCHUMANN, CLARA (WIECK). 1819–1896

Clara Schumann, the wife of composer ROBERT SCHUMANN, was born in
Leigzig, Germany. His father, piano teacher Friedrich Wieck, turned her into
one of the most brilliant and renowned concert pianists of her day. She gave her
first major concert when she was only 11 years old, and several of her
polonaises were published the following year.

After their marriage in 1840, Robert and Clara Schumann made several
concert tours throughout Europe. In addition to touring together, Clara
Schumann also made many solo tours. After 1856 she played often for the
Philharmonic Society in London. On her many tours and concerts, she gave
definitive performances of many of her husband's works. Her own compositions
include work for the piano and vocal songs.

BOOK BY CLARA SCHUMANN

Letters of Clara Schumann and Johannes Brahms, 1853–1896. Ed. by Berthold Litzmann. Hyperion Conn. 1979 o.p. Selected and abridged correspondence between the two famous musicians, their friends, and collaborators.

BOOKS ABOUT CLARA SCHUMANN

Chissel, Joan. *Clara Schumann, A Dedicated Spirit: A Study of Her Life and Work.* Taplinger 1983 o.p. Interesting account of Schumann's personal life, her talent and career, and the effect of her gender on her work.

Litzmann, Berthold. *Clara Schumann: An Artist's Life, Based on Material Found in Diaries and Letters.* 2 vols. Trans. and abr. by Grace E. Hadow. Da Capo 1979 repr. of 1913 ed. $95.00. ISBN 0-306-79528-5. Vivid biography of Schumann based on personal knowledge plus letters and other documents. With an introduction by Elaine Brody.

Reich, Nancy B. *Clara Schumann: The Artist and the Woman.* OUP 1989 $13.95. ISBN 0-19-282648-4. Discusses the impact that being a woman in a man's world had on Schumann's work.

Schumann, Ferdinand. *Reminiscences of Clara Schumann from the Diary of Her Grandson Ferdinand Schumann.* Musical Scope Pub. 1973 o.p.

SCHUMANN, ROBERT. 1810–1856

Born in Zwickau, Germany, Robert Schumann hoped early in his career to become a piano virtuoso. That dream was shattered in 1832, however, when he sustained permanent injury to his right hand while using a finger-strengthening device that he had invented. Thereafter, he devoted his energies to composition. His first compositions, the Toccata, Paganini studies, and Intermezzi, were published in 1833. A year later, he founded and edited *Neue Leipzige Zeitschrift für Musik,* a music magazine that became influential in its support of romanticism.

Schumann's attachment to Clara Wieck (the future CLARA SCHUMANN), the daughter of his piano teacher, was frowned upon by her disapproving father, who considered Schumann unsuitable. Despite this opposition, the two were married in 1849. The Schumanns made several concert tours together, with Clara performing the premieres of many of Robert's works.

Schumann is especially noted for his cycles of piano music, particularly *Papillons* (1829-31), *Carnaval* (1834-35), and *Phantasiestücke* (1837). His works are marked by imaginative power, with beautiful melodies and harmonies, and they embody the romantic spirit that prevailed at the time.

During the latter part of his life, Schumann worked as an orchestral conductor in Dresden and Düsseldorf. In 1854 his health began to decline and he was plagued by symptoms of mental illness that had recurred throughout his life. That same year, fearing for his sanity, he threw himself into the Rhine river. He was rescued by fishermen and taken to an asylum, where he died two years later.

BOOKS ABOUT ROBERT SCHUMANN

Finson, Jon W. *Robert Schumann and the Study of Orchestral Composition.* OUP 1989 $49.95. ISBN 0-19-313213-3. Provides an in-depth analysis of Schumann's First Symphony.

Fischer-Dieskau, Dietrich. *Robert Schumann Words and Music: The Vocal Compositions.* Trans. by Reinhard G. Pauly. Timber 1988 $28.95. ISBN 0-931340-06-3. Unique perspective from a singer who has performed many if not most of these compositions.

Macy, Sheryl. *Two Romantic Trios: A Sextet of Extraordinary Musicians.* Allegro OR 1991 $12.95. ISBN 0-9627040-0-8. Shows us the passionate lives of six romantic composers, including Robert and Clara Schumann.

SCRIABIN, ALEKSANDR. 1872–1915

Aleksandr Scriabin received his musical education from his aunt. At the age of 12, he began piano lessons. He entered the Moscow Conservatory in 1898 as a student of Safanov. In 1899 Safanov conducted Scriabin's first orchestra piece, *Reverie,* in Moscow. He also conducted Scriabin's first symphony in 1901.

Scriabin was profoundly influenced during his early years by CHOPIN, LISZT, and WAGNER, but he soon developed his own style. Scriabin was a genuine innovator of harmony.

BOOKS ABOUT SCRIABIN

Baker, James M. *The Music of Alexander Scriabin.* Yale U. Pr. 1986 $50.00. ISBN 0-300-03337-0. Deals with the transition to atonality in Scriabin's work; a rather specialized work.

Macdonald, Hugh. *Skryabin.* OUP 1978 o.p..

Scholezer, Boris de. *Scriabin: Artist and Mystic.* Trans. by Nicolas Slonimsky. U. CA Pr. 1987 $37.50. ISBN 0-520-04384-7. Introductory essays by Marina Scriabine. Somewhat difficult work on the impact of mysticism on Scriabin's work; by his philosopher friend.

SHOSTAKOVICH, DMITRI. 1906–1975

A child of Tsarist Russia and the Russian Revolution, Dmitri Shostakovich was born in St. Petersburg. Throughout his entire life, Shostakovich suffered from the effects of a childhood of malnutrition and disease. Despite such deprivation, he became a composer of powerful and advanced music. After studying music at the Leningrad Conservatory between 1919 and 1925, Shostakovich presented his *First Symphony* in 1925 to critical acclaim. In subsequent years he wrote 14 more symphonies, always attempting to follow the Communist party prescription to portray "Socialist Realism." For his efforts, however, Shostakovich was alternately reviled and hailed by the leadership of the Soviet Union. On his sixtieth birthday, he was finally honored as a Hero of Socialist Labor.

Of his 15 symphonies, only the *Fifth Symphony* (1937) and the *Tenth Symphony* (1953) have gained a prominent place in concert repertoires. The *Fifth Symphony* is a masterpiece of symphonic composition and follows traditional symphonic construction in its movements. In the *Tenth Symphony,* Shostakovich introduced musical elements that he also incorporated into other compositions, notably the fifth and eighth string quartets and his concertos for violin and cello. Shostakovich wrote ballets, such as *The Golden Age* (1930). Many of his other works were also choreographed as ballets. He also composed an opera, *Lady Macbeth of the District of Mtsensk* (1930–32). Although it was condemned by Soviet authorities, who considered it full of "Western decadence," it enjoyed some success outside the Soviet Union. Shostakovich's music is remarkably consistent in style, technique, and emotional content.

BOOKS BY SHOSTAKOVICH

Sergei Prokofiev: Materials, Articles, Interviews. (coauthored with others). Imported 1978 o.p.

Shostakovich: About Himself and His Times. Imported 1981 o.p. Shostakovich's articles reprinted by a Russian publisher and translated into English.

Testimony: Memoirs of Dmitri Shostakovich. Ed. by Solomon Volkov. Trans. by Antonina
W. Bouis. Limelight Edns. 1984 repr. of 1979 ed. $15.95. ISBN 0-87910-021-4. The
review by Laurel Fay in the *Russian Review,* October 1980, raises some questions
about this work's authenticity.

BOOKS ABOUT SHOSTAKOVICH

Kay, Norman. *Shostakovich.* OUP 1972 o.p. Scholarly biography of the notable Russian
composer.
MacDonald, Ian. *The New Shostakovich.* NE U. Pr. 1990 $30.00 ISBN 1-55553-089-3.
Biography of the socialist musician seen within the context of changing political
times in the Soviet Union.

SIBELIUS, JEAN. 1865–1957

Finnish composer Jean Sibelius personified Finnish nationalism and, through
his involvement with Norse mythology and nature, heavily influenced the
development of Scandinavian music. Sibelius studied in Helsinki, Berlin, and
Vienna, returning to Finland in the early 1890s to compose the *Kullervo*
Symphony (1892), based on the Finnish epic *Kalevala.* Shortly thereafter,
Sibelius wrote *En Saga,* or "a legend," one of his most remarkable pieces.
Finlandia (1899) became the musical symbol of Finland in the wars and political
struggles with Germany and the Soviet Union. Sibelius ceased to compose
music after 1927. His symphonies and tone poems are heard frequently and are
valued for their unique sonorities and formal logic.

BOOKS ABOUT SIBELIUS

Abraham, Gerald. *The Music of Sibelius.* Da Capo 1975 repr. of 1947 ed. $29.50. ISBN 0-
306-70716-0. Contributors discuss various aspects of Sibelius's work.
Burnett James, David. *The Music of Jean Sibelius.* Fairleigh Dickinson 1983 $29.50. ISBN
0-8386-3070-7
———. *Sibelius.* Omnibus Pr. 1989 $27.95. ISBN 0-8464-3069-X.
Dahlstrom, Fabian. *The Works of Jean Sibelius.* Sibelius-Seura 1987 o.p.
Ekman, Karl. *Jean Sibelius, His Life and Personality.* Trans. by Edward Birse. Rprt. Serv.
1992 repr. of 1938 ed. $79.00. ISBN 0-7812-9491-6. Forward by Ernest Newman.
Readable biography that focuses on the personality more than the music.
Tawaststjerna, Erik. *Sibelius.* Trans. by Robert Layton. U. CA Pr. 1976 $55.00. ISBN 0-
520-03014-1. Covers the years 1865 through 1905. The mammoth, standard biogra-
phy.

SILLS, BEVERLY. 1929–

Born in Brooklyn, New York, Beverly Sills began her career at the age of 3,
when she sang on the radio under the nickname "Bubbles." The following year
she joined a Saturday morning children's program. Then, at the age of 7, she
sang in a movie. By the time she was 10 years old, Sills played a part on the
radio show "Our Gal Sunday."

In 1947 Sills began her operatic career, appearing for the first time as
Frasquita in *Carmen.* An American soprano noted for her voice, virtuosity, and
intelligence, she also served as an excellent administrator of the New York City
Opera. She sang American and avant-garde roles as well as standards and is
remembered for her roles as Cleopatra in *Giulio Cesare* by HANDEL, Lucia di
Lammermoor, Elizabeth in *Roberto Devereux,* Anna Bolena, Elvira in *I puritani,*
and Maria Stuarda.

Sills also actively campaigns on behalf of the handicapped and disadvantaged;
she has been active in the March of Dimes since 1971.

BOOKS BY SILLS

Beverly: An Autobiography (coauthored with Lawrence Linderman). Bantam 1987 $4.95.
ISBN 0-553-26647-0. A fun, poignant, autobiography.
Bubbles: A Self-Portrait. Macmillan 1976 $13.95. ISBN 0-685-73303-30. An anecdotal,
richly illustrated account; deals mostly with her younger days and early career.

SINATRA, FRANK. 1915–

A native of Hoboken, New Jersey, Frank Sinatra is an American icon and
singer of popular American songs. Although he originally wanted to be a
sportswriter, listening to Bing Crosby and BILLIE HOLIDAY inspired Sinatra to
become a singer. Like many of his contemporaries, Sinatra never learned to
read music, but he had a natural talent for singing and for entertainment.
Sinatra stirred young female fans of the World War II era to fainting frenzy at
his performances. The media dubbed Sinatra "Swoonlight Sinatra." Sinatra still
sings to large, sold-out audiences throughout the world. His music is reissued
on CDs and rereleased in new collections.

Sinatra also has had a respectable acting career. He won an Academy Award
for Best Supporting Actor in *From Here to Eternity* (1953).

BOOK BY SINATRA

Paintings: A Man and His Art. Random 1991 $34.50. ISBN 0-394-58297-7. Introduction by
Tina Sinatra.

BOOKS ABOUT SINATRA

Adler, Bill. *Sinatra, The Man and the Myth: An Unauthorized Biography.* New Amer. Pr.
1987 o.p.. A critical but objective biography of Sinatra.
Doctor, Gary L. *The Sinatra Scrapbook.* Carol Pub. Group 1991 $15.95. ISBN 0-8065-
1250-4
Kelley, Kitty. *His Way: The Unauthorized Biography of Frank Sinatra.* Bantam 1987 $5.99.
ISBN 0-553-26515-6. Contains all the possible dirt on "Ol' Blue Eyes"; little wonder
he tried to prevent its publication.
Ridgway, John. *The Sinatrafile.* John Ridgway 1977 o.p.
Sayers, Scott, and Ed O'Brien. *Sinatra, the Man and His Music: The Recording Artistry of
Francis Albert Sinatra, 1939–1992.* Tx. St. Direct. 1992 $23.97. ISBN 0-934367-24-8
Sinatra, Nancy. *Frank Sinatra, My Father.* PB 1986 $4.50. ISBN 0-671-62508-X

SMETANA, BEDŘICH. 1824–1884

Czech composer Bedřich Smetana was born in Litomyšl and educated in
Prague. From 1856 to 1869, he conducted for the Philharmonic Orchestra in
Göteborg, Sweden. After his return to Prague, he opened a music school and
then, in 1866, became conductor of the new National Theatre, where his own
operas were first performed. Overwork destroyed Smetana's health, and in 1874
he became totally deaf. He continued to compose, however, until he suffered a
mental breakdown in 1883.

Smetana is known for the intense national character of his compositions.
Among his best-known works are the opera *The Bartered Bride* (1866), six
symphonic works entitled *Má Vlast* (1874), and the string quartet *Aus meinem
Leben*, the latter two composed while he was deaf.

BOOK BY SMETANA

Bedřich Smetana: Letters and Reminiscences. Ed. by Frantisek Bartos. Trans. by Daphne
Rusbridge. Artia 1955 o.p.

BOOKS ABOUT SMETANA

Clapham, John. *Smetana*. Octagon Bks. 1972 o.p. Short biography with an emphasis on
music; a part of the *Master Musician Series*
Large, Brian. *Smetana*. Da Capo 1985 repr. of 1970 ed. $49.50. ISBN 0-306-76243-9.
Fairly detailed biography with a genealogical tree in the appendix

SONDHEIM, STEPHEN. 1930–

Stephen Sondheim was born in New York and studied music at Williams
College, where he wrote the lyrics and music for two college shows. Sondheim
also studied at Princeton University with Milton Babbit. He received recognition for writing lyrics for LEONARD BERNSTEIN's *West Side Story* (1957) and
success as a lyricist-composer with *A Funny Thing Happened on the Way to the
Forum* (1962). However, his next musical, *Anyone Can Whistle* (1964), was
unsuccessful. The production of *Company* (1970) again established Sondheim
as a major composer and lyricist on Broadway. Sondheim's other productions
include *Follies* (1971); *A Little Night Music* (1973), wherein its leading song,
"Send in the Clowns," was awarded a Grammy in 1976; and *Sunday in the Park
with George* (1983), a musical inspired by George Seurat's famous painting "A
Sunday Afternoon on the Island of La Grande Jatte." His music and plays have
won him three Tony Awards, a Grammy Award, the New York Drama Critics
Circle Best Musical Award, and the Pulitzer Prize.

BOOKS ABOUT SONDHEIM

Gordon, Joanne Lesley. *Art Isn't Easy: The Achievement of Stephen Sondheim*. S. Ill. U. Pr.
1990 $39.95. ISBN 0-8093-1407-X
———. *Art Isn't Easy: The Theater of Stephen Sondheim*. Da Capo 1992 repr. of 1990 ed.
$16.95. ISBN 0-306-80468-9. Contains criticism and interpretations of Sondheim's
musicals; arranged by work
Gottfried, Martin. *Stephen Sondheim*. Abrams 1993. ISBN 0-8109-3844-8

STOCKHAUSEN, KARLHEINZ. 1928–

A German composer and educator, Karlheinz Stockhausen became involved
with the electronic studio of the West German Radio in Cologne in 1953. He has
been a pioneer of "time music," using controlled improvisation, adding
direction as an element of music by placing performers and electronic devices
around the hall in which his music is performed, projecting images on screens
as part of the performance, and involving the participation of the audience. His
music is highly complex, dissonant, and full of changing instrumental colors,
free rhythms, and percussive effects. His lectures and performances have
attracted huge audiences, and he has been awarded membership in the Berlin
Academy of Arts and the American Academy and Institute of Arts and Letters,
among others.

BOOKS BY STOCKHAUSEN

Conversations with Stockhausen. (coauthored with Mya Tannenbaum). Trans. by David
Butchart. OUP 1988 $26.00. ISBN 0-19-315467-6. Very short series of interviews
conducted between November 1979 and April 1991.
Stockhausen on Music: Lectures and Interviews. Comp. by Robin Maconie. M. Boyers
Pubs. 1989 $27.50. ISBN 0-7145-2887-0. Fairly small collection of lectures and
interviews by the composer on his life and music
Towards a Cosmic Music. Trans. by Tim Nevill. Element MA 1989 $15.95. ISBN 1-85230-
084-1. Small selection of the composer's articles on music and music theory.

Books about Stockhausen

Cott, Jonathan. *Stockhausen: Conversations with the Composer.* S&S Trade 1973 o.p. Various interviews between the author and the composer from February and September 1971.

Harvey, Jonathan. *The Music of Stockhausen: An Introduction.* U. CA Pr. 1975 o.p. Introductory guide to the composer's music, with an introduction by the composer himself.

Maconie, Robin. *The Works of Karlheinz Stockhausen.* OUP 1990 $74.00. ISBN 0-19-315477-3. Foreword by Karlheinz Stockhausen.

STRAUSS, RICHARD. 1864–1949

The celebrated German conductor and post-romantic composer Richard Strauss completed his first work, *Polka in C,* at the age of 6. Success as a composer came at the age of 17, with his first major work, *Symphony in D Minor,* closely followed by his *Violin Concerto* two years later and his *Symphony in F Minor* a year after that. A turning point in Strauss's life came when he was introduced to the philosophical, literary, and musical depth of the works of RICHARD WAGNER and FRANZ LISZT. For some time thereafter, he devoted himself to producing tone poems. These tone poems, especially *Macbeth* (1890), *Till Eulenspiegels lustige Streiche* (1895), *Don Juan* (1889, revised 1891), and *Tod und Verklärung* (1891), are rich tapestries of musical themes and harmonic complexity. Strauss's musical innovations seemed unorthodox and shocking when they were first introduced, but they now seem commonplace after years of being imitated.

Strauss leaped into worldwide fame as a composer of opera with the first performance of *Salome* (1905). Thereafter, the powers of depiction and characterization that he had used in creating symphonic poems were used almost exclusively in the production of operas. After *Salome* came *Elektra* (1909) and *Der Rosenkavalier* (1911), the latter considered Strauss's operatic masterpiece. During his lifetime, Strauss composed a total of 15 operas and 2 ballets, as well as many orchestral works, chamber music, piano pieces, and arrangements of other works. On his death at the age of 85, the world mourned the loss of his multifaceted genius. He is considered to be one of the last of the German romantics.

Books by Strauss

A Confidential Matter: The Letters of Richard Strauss and Stefan Zweig, 1931–1935. Bks. Demand repr. of 1977 ed. $38.50. ISBN 0-685-23497-5. Foreword by Edward E. Lowinsky. Letters between Strauss and Zweig, with Strauss's "Die Schweigsame Frau" (in English) in the appendix

A Working Friendship: The Correspondence between Richard Strauss and Hugo von Hofmannsthal. Trans. by Hans Hammelmann and Ewald Osers. Vienna Hse. 1974 repr. of 1961 ed. $17.50. ISBN 0-8443-0050-0. A complete edition of the Strauss-von Hofmannsthal letters from 1900 to the time of von Hofmannsthal's death in 1929

Recollections and Reflections. Trans. by L. J. Lawrence. Greenwood 1974 repr. of 1953 ed. $45.00. ISBN 0-8371-7366-3

Books about Strauss

Hartman, Rudolf. *Richard Strauss: The Staging of His Operas and Ballets.* OUP 1981 $75.00. ISBN 0-19-520251-1. Scholarly discussion of the production and staging of the composer's operas and ballets.

Schuh, Willi. *Richard Strauss: A Chronicle of the Early Years, 1864–1898.* Trans. by Mary Whittall. Cambridge U. Pr. 1982 o.p. Focuses on the early life and musical development of Strauss.

STRAVINSKY, IGOR. 1882–1971

The Russian composer Igor Stravinsky, considered to be one of the greatest composers of the twentieth century, was born in 1882 near St. Petersburg. Stravinsky began piano lessons at the age of 9. He had little interest in a career in music, however, until 1902, when he was introduced to RIMSKY-KORSAKOV while studying law at the University of St. Petersburg. For the next three years, he studied composition with Rimsky-Korsakov.

In 1909 the ballet impresario SERGE DIAGHILEV heard a performance of one of Stravinsky's symphonic works and commissioned him to compose three ballets for his Ballets Russes in Paris. These three pieces—*The Firebird* (1910), *Pétrouchka* (1911), and *The Rite of Spring* (1913)— established Stravinsky as the foremost musical innovator in his use of syncopated and irregular rhythms and harsh-sounding harmonies.

After World War I, Stravinsky settled in France. The Russian Revolution of 1917 and the Communist dictatorships that followed kept him away from his native land until 1962. In France, Stravinsky's association with Diaghilev continued until the impresario's death in 1929. During this time, the composer adopted a simpler musical style, inspired by the classical composers of the eighteenth century. One of the first indications of this interest in classical music was heard in his ballet *Pulcinella* (1920). Stravinsky's interest in classical forms influenced his music for over 30 years.

Stravinsky moved to the United States in 1939 and became an American citizen in 1945. His continued interest in ballet resulted in an association with the Russian-born choreographer GEORGE BALANCHINE and his New York City Ballet company, for whom Stravinsky wrote several works. In addition, Stravinsky composed a variety of other works, including several operas, the most famous of which is *The Rake's Progress* (1951). During the mid-1950s, Stravinsky became interested in serialism. The use of serialism in his later works resulted in highly structured and concise compositions, such as his choral composition *Threni* (1958). A unique and unpredictable composer, Stravinsky never founded a specific school of composition. Nevertheless, his work has had a great influence on many modern composers.

BOOKS BY STRAVINSKY

Conversations with Igor Stravinsky. (coauthored with Robert Craft). U. CA Pr. 1980 o.p. A series of short interviews.

Dialogues. (coauthored with Robert Craft). 1968. U. CA Pr. 1982 o.p. A series of personal interviews with Robert Craft

Expositions and Developments. (coauthored with Robert Craft). U. CA Pr. 1981 o.p. One lengthy interview on musical composition.

Igor Stravinsky: An Autobiography. Rprt. Serv. 1992 repr. of 1936 ed. $69.00. ISBN 0-7812-9472-X. A short and fascinating autobiography.

Memories and Commentaries. (coauthored with Robert Craft). U. CA Pr. 1981 o.p.

Poetics of Music in the Form of Six Lessons. HUP 1970 o.p. Preface by G. Seferis. A short introduction to music appreciation through the composer's self-examination of music and musical forms.

Stravinsky Petrushka. Ed. by Charles Hamm. Norton 1967 o.p.

Stravinsky, Selected Correspondence. Ed by Robert Craft. 3 vols. Knopf 1982–85. o.p. $35.00. Comprehensive selection of the composer's letters.

BOOKS ABOUT STRAVINSKY

Craft, Robert. *Stravinsky: Glimpses of A Life*. St. Martin 1992 $22.95. ISBN 0-312-08896-5

Haimo, Ethan, and Paul Johnson, eds. *Stravinsky Retrospectives*. U. of Nebr. Pr. 1987 $55.00. ISBN 0-8032-2335-8. Seven articles by composers and scholars on Stravinsky's work.

Horgan, Paul. *Encounters with Stravinsky: A Personal Record*. Wesleyan Univ. Pr. rev. ed. 1989 $14.95. ISBN 0-8195-6215-7. Biography written by Stravinsky's close friend.

Libman, Lillian. *Music at the Close: Stravinsky's Last Years, a Personal Memoir*. Beekman Pubs. 1972 $27.95. ISBN 0-8464-0659-4. Focuses on the later life and works of the composer.

Pasler, Jann, ed. *Confronting Stravinsky: Man, Musician, and Modernist*. U. CA Pr. 1986 $62.50. ISBN 0-520-06466-6. A collection of articles about Stravinsky and his work by critics, artists, theoreticians, and composers.

Stravinsky, Theodore. *Catherine and Igor Stravinsky*. Boosey & Hawkes 1973 $15.00. ISBN 0-85162-008-6. Personalized account of the life of the composer and his wife.

Stravinsky, Vera, and Robert Craft. *Stravinsky: In Pictures and Documents*. S&S Trade 1979 o.p. Illustrated presentation of the composer including primary source documents.

Van den Toorn, Pieter C. *The Music of Igor Stravinsky*. Yale U. Pr. 1983 o.p. Comprehensive discussion and analysis of the composer's music.

White, Eric W. *Stravinsky: The Composer and His Works*. U. CA Pr. 1980 $15.95. ISBN 0-520-03985-8. Short biography with a lengthy register of works providing copious information and a description of each work; includes appendixes of documents, arrangements, bibliographic sources.

TALLIS, THOMAS. c.1505–1585

Thomas Tallis was an English organist and composer who served as gentleman of London's Chapel Royal from the reign of Henry VIII into the reign of Elizabeth I. His compositions include 3 masses, 52 motets and other Latin-texted works, and more than 20 English anthems. His most famous composition is *Spem in aluim* (1567) for a 40-part choir. One of his themes was used by RALPH VAUGHAN WILLIAMS in a beautiful set of variations.

Tallis was among the first composers to set English words to music for rites of the Church of England. He is most revered for his great contrapuntal skill.

BOOK ABOUT TALLIS

Doe, Paul. *Tallis*. OUP 1976 o.p. An exceedingly short examination of Tallis's work.

TCHAIKOVSKY, PETER ILICH. 1840–1893

One of Russia's greatest composers, Peter Ilich Tchaikovsky was born in Votkinsk, Russia. He received a good early education; his instructors included a French governess and a music teacher. When he was 10 years old, the family moved to St. Petersburg, and Tchaikovsky continued his studies, although his musical talent did not seem particularly great. Nevertheless, he continued to study music and graduated from the St. Petersburg Conservatory in 1865. From there he went on to teach theory and composition at the Moscow Observatory from 1866 to 1877. A generous allowance from a wealthy patroness allowed Tchaikovsky to devote time to his own composition without financial worries. His first successful composition was *Romeo and Juliet* (1869), a fantasy overture in which Tchaikovsky used the sonata form, adapting it to the demands of the Shakespearean play and its characters. Soon after Tchaikovsky's short marriage in 1877 ended, he quit the observatory to devote all of his time to composition. In the years that followed, he wrote his most popular and well-known works.

In all, Tchaikovsky wrote nine operas, six symphonies, many songs and short piano pieces, three ballets, three string quartets, and other works, including suites and symphonic poems. The operas *Eugene Onegin* (1879) and *Queen of Spades* (1890) were both adapted from stories by ALEKSANDR PUSHKIN (see Vol. 2). Among Tchaikovsky's best-known works are his last three symphonies—No. 4 in F minor (1877); No. 5 in E minor (1888); No. 6 in B minor, also known as the *Pathétique* (1893); and his three ballets—*Swan Lake* (1877), *Sleeping Beauty* (1889), and *The Nutcracker* (1892). Tchaikovsky's music is richly orchestrated, of great emotional intensity, and reflects the composer's melancholy nature and fatalism.

BOOKS BY TCHAIKOVSKY

Letters to His Family: An Autobiography. Ed. by Percy M. Young. Trans. by Galina von Meck. Madison Bks. UPA 1982 $12.95. ISBN 0-8128-6167-1

Tchaikovsky: A Self-Portrait. Comp. by Alexandra Orlova. Trans. by R. M. Davison. OUP 1990 $55.00 ISBN 0-19-315319-X. Foreword by David Brown.

To My Best Friend: Correspondence Between Tchaikovsky and Nadezhda von Meck, 1876–1878. Ed. by Edward Garden and Nigel Gotteri. Trans. by Galina von Meck. OUP 1993 $55.00. ISBN 0-19-816158-1

BOOKS ABOUT TCHAIKOVSKY

Brown, David. *Tchaikovsky: The Crisis Years.* 2 vols. Norton 1979–83 o.p. An in-depth biography; divided into early and late periods.

Garden, Edward. *Tchaikovsky.* Biblio Dist. 1973 o.p.

Kendall, Alan. *Tchaikovsky: A Biography.* Trafalgar 1988 o.p.. A fairly general biography that provides a good introduction to the composer.

Poznansky, Alexander. *Tchaikovsky: Quest for the Inner Man.* Schirmer Bks. 1991 $39.95. ISBN 0-02-871885-2. An in-depth biography that sometimes engages in over-analysis.

Volkoff, Vladimir. *Tchaikovsky: A Self-Portrait.* Taplinger 1975 o.p. A general biography based on quotations by or about the composer.

Wiley, Roland J. *Tchaikovsky's Ballets: Swan Lake, Sleeping Beauty, Nutcracker.* OUP 1985 $75.00. ISBN 0-19-315314-9. Detailed look at and analysis of the composer's three popular ballets.

THOMPSON, VIRGIL. 1896–1989

The musical development of this American composer and critic received much of its force from his association with GERTRUDE STEIN (see Vol. 1) in Paris during the 1920s. Gertrude Stein wrote the libretto for *Four Saints in Three Acts* (1934), which soon became an American classic. It is a masterpiece of contrast, treating the buffa-like plot with hymnlike seriousness. In 1940 Thomson was appointed music critic of the *New York Herald-Tribune.* Then in 1948 he received the Pulitzer Prize for his score for the motion picture *Louisiana Story.* Finally, in 1983 he was awarded the sixth annual Kennedy Center Honor for lifetime achievement. Thomson's music and prose are subtle, humorous, and well crafted, but beneath it all there resides a profound philosophy.

BOOKS BY THOMSON

American Music since 1910. H. Holt & Co. 1971 o.p.

The State of Music 1939. Greenwood 1974 repr. of 1939 ed. o.p. The composer's thoughts on being a composer in the twentieth century.

Virgil Thomson. Da Capo 1977 $6.95. ISBN 0-306-80081-0. A comprehensive autobiography focusing on events and anecdotes of Thomson's life; contains less on his music.

A Virgil Thomson Reader. HM 1981 o.p. A selection of writings about music by one of the wisest and wittiest of the composer-critics. Includes two interviews and a bibliography of Thomson's writings. Introduction by John Rockwell.

TIPPETT, SIR MICHAEL. 1905–

Sir Michael Tippett was educated entirely in England. He has been very involved with political and social events but has maintained his well-developed neoromantic style of composition. For example, his oratorio *A Child of Our Time* (1939–41) was inspired by the case of a Jewish boy, who in 1938 assassinated a member of the German embassy in Paris. Tippett also possesses a fine literary gift; he writes the librettos for his operas and oratorios. He is an inheritor of the best British tradition of composing understandable but deeply emotional music.

BOOKS BY TIPPETT

Abundance of Creation: An Artist's Vision of Creative Peace. Housmans 1975 o.p.
Those Twentieth Century Blues: An Autobiography. Trafalgar 1993 $39.95. ISBN 0-09-175307-4

BOOKS ABOUT TIPPETT

Bowen, Meirion. *Michael Tippett.* Universe 1982 o.p. A very short biography with some commentary on the composer's work
Kemp, Ian. *Tippett: The Composer and His Music.* Da Capo 1985 $39.50. ISBN 0-903873-23-0. A short biography followed by commentary; arranged by periods of the composer's life.
Lewis, Geraint, ed. *Michael Tippett, O. M.: A Celebration.* Pro-Am Music 1985 $39.95. ISBN 0-85936-140-3
Matthews, David. *Michael Tippett: An Introductory Story.* Faber & Faber 1980 o.p.
White, Eric W. *Tippett and His Operas.* Da Capo 1981 repr. of 1979 ed. $25.00. ISBN 0-306-76111-4. Preface by Andrew Porter. A short commentary on the operas; arranged by work.
Whittall, Arnold. *The Music of Britten and Tippett: Studies in Themes and Techniques* Cambridge U. Pr. 1982 $59.95. ISBN 0-521-23523-5. Commentary on the works of the two composers, arranged chronologically by work.

VAUGHAN WILLIAMS, RALPH. 1872–1958

English composer Ralph Vaughan Williams was born in Down Ampney, Gloucestershire. An early aptitude for music was encouraged by his parents, and he studied at the Royal College of Music in London as well as in Paris and Berlin.

Vaughan William's music is essentially English in character, making him the first truly national composer since the sixteenth century. He is especially in touch with the English choral tradition. His first major success was *Sea Symphony* (1910), a choral piece set to words by WALT WHITMAN (see Vol. 1). His interest in choral music contributed to his becoming a leader in the English folk-song movement, and he was an enthusiastic collector of traditional folk songs. In his own work, Vaughan Williams often combined folk melodies with modern harmonies, creating a very distinctive style.

Among his orchestral music, the most notable are the beautiful *Fantasia on a Theme by Thomas Tallis* (1909), *London Symphony* (1914), *Pastoral Symphony* (1922), and *Sinfonia Antarctica* (1952), a tribute to the explorer ROBERT FALCON SCOTT. Other well-known works include the ballad opera *Hugh the Drover* (1911–14) and the opera *The Pilgrim's Progress* (1948–49). He has also composed works for the ballet, for the stage, and for films.

BOOKS ABOUT VAUGHAN WILLIAMS

Douglas, Roy. *Working with Vaughan: The Correspondence of Ralph Vaughan Williams and Roy Douglas.* British Library 1988 o.p.

Mellers, Wilfrid. *Vaughan Williams and The Vision of Albion.* Pimlico 1991 o.p.

Moore, Jerrold Northrop. *Vaughan Williams, A Life in Photographs.* OUP 1992 $49.95. ISBN 0-19-816296-0

Williams, Ursula. *R.V.W.: A Biography of Ralph Vaughan Williams.* OUP 1993 $23.00. ISBN 0-19-282082-6. A comprehensive biography with a chronology and short bibliography.

VERDI, GIUSEPPE. 1813–1901

Giuseppe Verdi, Italy's foremost operatic composer, was born in Le Roncale in northern Italy. The son of an innkeeper, his musical career began with lessons from a local church organist and continued with a teacher in the nearby town of Busseto. Despite a rejection by the Milan Conservatory in 1832 because he did not have enough technical skill as a composer, Verdi remained in Milan to study with a private teacher. While in Milan, he became interested in opera, which he saw performed at La Scala, Milan's famous opera house. Between 1839 and 1893, Verdi composed 26 operas.

Verdi's career as an operatic composer was firmly established with the appearance of *Rigoletto* in 1851. This was quickly followed by *Il trovatore* and *La traviata*, both produced in 1853. His reputation as a leading composer of opera was further enhanced with *Aïda*, which he was commissioned to compose for the opening of the Suez Canal in 1869. Because Verdi did not complete the opera until 1871, *Rigoletto* was performed instead. *Aïda*'s premiére was held at the opera house in Cairo in 1871. Except for his *Messa da Requiem* (1874), a few other sacred texts, a few songs, and a string quartet, all of Verdi's published works were written for the operatic stage.

In his operas Verdi found a formula that worked, and he used it consistently. Each opera had four parts—either four acts or three acts with a prologue. The second and third acts ended with important ensemble finales. The third act almost always had a big duet, and the fourth almost always opened with a meditative solo, usually sung by the heroine. Constantly striving for refinement of drama and technique, Verdi brought Italian opera to its highest perfection and greatest renown.

BOOK BY VERDI

Verdi: The Man in His Letters. Rprt. Serv. 1988 repr. of 1942 ed. $49.00. ISBN 0-7812-0099-7

BOOKS ABOUT VERDI

Baldini, Gabriele. *The Story of Giuseppe Verdi.* Cambridge U. Pr. 1980 $54.95. ISBN 0-521-22911-1. Comprehensive biography that also discusses Verdi's music. Introduction by Julian Budden.

Budden, Julian. *The Operas of Verdi.* 3 vols. OUP rev. ed. Vol. 1 *From Oberto to Rigoletto.* 1978 $60.00. ISBN 0-19-520030-6. Vol. 2 *From Il Trovatore to La Forza Del Destino.* 1978 $65.00. ISBN 0-19-520068-3. Vol. 3 *From Don Carlos to Falstaff.* 1992 $22.50. ISBN 0-19-816263-4. Comprehensive, scholarly treatments of Verdi's operas.

————. *Verdi.* Biblio Dist. 1985 o.p. Traces Verdi's development as an artist from humble beginnings to his discovery of an individual voice.

Busch, Hans, trans. *Verdi's Aïda: The History of an Opera in Letters and Documents.* Bks. Demand repr. of 1978 ed. $180.00. ISBN 0-7837-2974-X. Looks at the development of the opera *Aïda* through primary source documents.

————. *Verdi's Otello and Simon Boccanegra in Letters and Documents.* 2 vols. OUP 1988 $135.00. ISBN 0-19-313207-9. Foreword by Julian Budden.

Conati, Marcello, ed. *Encounters with Verdi.* Trans. by Richard Stokes. Cornell Univ. Pr. 1984 $33.50. ISBN 0-8014-9430-3. Vivid portrait of Verdi, based on 50 eyewitness accounts by his contemporaries. Foreword by Julian Budden.

Kimbell, David R. *Verdi in the Age of Italian Romanticism.* Cambridge U. Pr. 1981 o.p. Critical study of Verdi and his role in the romantic period of Italian music.

Martin, George. *Verdi: His Music, Life and Times.* Da Capo 1979 $49.50. A detailed treatment of Verdi's life and work; includes lists and descriptions.

Osborne, Charles. *Verdi: A Life in The Theatre.* Fromm Intl. Pub. 1989 repr. of 1987 ed. $11.95. ISBN 0-88064-106-1. A fairly detailed biography, with a bibliography and a list of Verdi's works.

Walker, Frank. *The Man Verdi.* U. Ch. Pr. 1982 repr. of 1962 ed. $9.95. ISBN 0-226-87132-0. Biography of the personality and life of the great composer.

Weaver, William, ed. *Verdi: A Documentary Study.* Thames Hudson 1977 o.p. Tells the story of Verdi through letters, photographs, and other primary source documents.

Weaver, William, and Martin Chusid, eds. *The Verdi Companion.* Norton 1988 $10.95. ISBN 0-393-30443-4. Examines Verdi's work from various points of view.

VIVALDI, ANTONIO. 1678–1741

Antonio Vivaldi entered the priesthood, taking the tonsure in 1693 and Holy Orders in 1703. He devoted his early years to writing operas. A prolific composer, Vivaldi also wrote chamber works, sacred works, and concertos. He often used material from his operas in his concertos, and vice versa. Although his operas are respectable, his greatness lies in his superb instrumental works. *The Four Seasons* (1725) is a work of genuine genius, but his prolixity apparently did not permit him to recapitulate this quality often. Vivaldi's works were well known and have been used as the basis of numerous works by other composers, including JOHANN SEBASTIAN BACH.

BOOKS ABOUT VIVALDI

Booth, John. *Vivaldi.* Beekman Pubs. 1990 $27.95. ISBN 0-8464-3078-9

Kolneder, Walter. *Antonio Vivaldi, Documents of His Life and Works.* Trans. by Kurt Michaelis. C. F. Peters 1982 o.p. Translated from German, into which the author had translated some of Vivaldi's written work.

————. *Antonio Vivaldi: His Life and Work.* Trans. by Bill Hopkins. Rprt. Serv. repr. of 1970 ed. $49.00. ISBN 0-685-14840-8. U. CA Pr. Well-researched examination of the composer's work, with a brief biographical introduction.

WAGNER, RICHARD. 1813–1883

Richard Wagner, one of the most influential German composers, was born in Leipzig in 1813. His stepfather brought the world of the theater into Wagner's life, and it fascinated him. As a youth, he began studying musical composition and wrote a number of pieces. His professional music career began in 1833 with an appointment as chorusmaster of the Würzburg Theater. This was followed by several positions producing operas—his own and those of other composers. After success with his opera *Rienzi* in 1842 and *The Flying Dutchman* in 1843, Wagner became director of the opera at Dresden. During his stay there, he wrote *Tannhäuser* (1845) and *Lohengrin* (1846–48). Political troubles in Germany in 1848 forced Wagner to leave Dresden and flee to Switzerland, where he remained for several years. While in exile, Wagner wrote a series of essays about opera and also began work on *The Ring of the Nibelung,* a cycle of four musical dramas based on ancient Germanic folklore. Among the other notable operas Wagner wrote are *Tristan und Isolde* (1857–59), *Die Meister-*

singer von Nürnberg (1862–67), and *Parsifal* (1882). In 1870, following a series of love affairs, Wagner married Cosima, FRANZ LISZT's daughter.

Wagner wrote both music and libretto for all his operas. Calling these operas "music-dramas," he sought to achieve a complete union between music and drama. In so doing, he created a new operatic form and transferred the center of the operatic world from Italy to Germany. In 1876 Wagner opened the Festival Theater in Bayreuth, which was dedicated to the preservation of his operas.

Wagner's operatic music is highly dramatic and builds to amazing climaxes. His work symbolizes the synthesis of all of the arts in opera—the dramatic content and the scenery as well as the music—and had a great influence on all operatic composers who came after him. Especially significant was Wagner's view of opera as drama, with all components working in harmony. Equally significant was his use of continuous music throughout the opera, with the orchestra maintaining continuity within the divisions of the drama.

BOOKS BY WAGNER

Family Letters of Richard Wagner. Trans. by William Ashton Ellis. U. of Mich. Pr. rev. ed. 1992 $49.50. ISBN 0-472-10292-3. Introduction and notes by John Deathridge. Contains most of the composer's letters to his family, including some fragmentary correspondence.

My Life. Ed. by Mary Whittall. Trans. by Andrew Gray. Da Capo 1980 repr. of 1960 ed. $40.00. ISBN 0-405-13075-9 A comprehensive autobiography through 1864.

The Ring of the Nibelung. Trans. by Andrew Porter. Norton 1977 $17.50. ISBN 0-393-02200-5 Contains the German text and English translation (side by side) of the libretto of the famous four operas.

Selected Letters of Richard Wagner. Ed. and trans. by Stewart Spencer and Barry Millington. Norton 1988 $35.00. ISBN 0-393-02500-4. Brings together some 500 of Wagner's most important and revealing letters.

BOOKS ABOUT WAGNER

Aberbach, Alan David. *The Ideas of Richard Wagner: An Examination and Analysis of His Major Aesthetic, Political, Economic, Social, and Religious Thoughts: New Addendum, The Ring of the Nibelung, an Interpretative Guide.* U. Pr. of Amer. rev. ed 1988 $44.50. ISBN 0-8191-6855-6

Digaetani, John L., ed. *Penetrating Wagner's Ring: An Anthology.* Da Capo 1983 $49.50. ISBN 0-306-76205-6. A comprehensive collection of primary sources and scholarly articles analyzing Wagner's *Ring* cycle.

Gregor-Dellin, Martin. *Richard Wagner: His Life, His Work, His Century.* 2 vols. Trans. by J. Maxwell Brownjohn. HarBraceJ 1983 o.p. A lengthy biography of Wagner, with a fairly comprehensive bibliography.

Hodson, Phillip. *Who's Who in Wagner: An A to Z Look at His Life and Work.* Macmillan 1984 o.p. Information about people, places, and ideas central to Wagner's life and works.

James, David B. *Wagner and the Romantic Disaster.* Hippocrene Bks. 1983 o.p.

Kropfinger, Klaus. *Wagner and Beethoven: Richard Wagner's Reception of Beethoven.* Trans. by Peter Palmer. Cambridge U. Pr. 1991 $54.95. ISBN 0-521-34201-5. A brief but in-depth analysis of Beethoven's influence on Wagner.

Large, David C., and William Weber, eds. *Wagnerism in European Culture and Politics.* Cornell Univ. Pr. 1984 $16.95. ISBN 0-8014-9283-1

McCreless, Patrick P. *Wagner's Siegfried: Its Drama, History, and Music.* Ed. by George Buelow. UMI Research 1982 o.p. A short but in-depth analysis of *Siegfried.*

Magee, Elizabeth. *Richard Wagner and the Nibelungs.* OUP 1991 $55.00. ISBN 0-19-816190-5. A short work about Wagner's research and composition of the *Ring* cycle.

Mann, Thomas. *Pro and Contra Wagner*. Trans. by Allan Blunden. U. Ch. Pr. 1985 o.p. A
    good collection of Mann's writings on Wagner and his work.
Millington, Barry, ed. *The Wagner Compendium: A Guide to Wagner's Life and Music*.
    Schirmer Bks 1992 $35.00. ISBN 0-02-871359-1. Comprehensive and detailed, with
    analysis and criticism by prominent scholars.
Newman, Ernest. *The Wagner Operas*. Princeton U. Pr. 1991 $19.95. ISBN 0-691-02716-1
Osborne, Charles. *Richard Wagner and His World*. Scribner 1977 o.p. Traces Wagner's
    life through hardship, debt, political exile, and long artistic frustration to his
    eventual success as a composer.
————. *The World Theater of Wagner: A Celebration of 150 Years of Wagner Productions*.
    Macmillan 1982 o.p. Study of a great variety of productions of Wagner's operas in
    theaters around the world.
Rather, L. J. *Reading Wagner: A Study in the History of Ideas*. La. State U. Pr. 1990 $35.00.
    ISBN 0-8071-1557-6
Skelton, Geoffrey. *Richard and Cosima Wagner: Biography of a Marriage*. HM 1982 o.p.
Westernhagen, Curt von. *Wagner: A Biography, 1813–1833*. Trans. by Mary Whittall.
    Cambridge U. Pr. 1981 $27.95. ISBN 0-521-28254-3. Concentrates equally on
    biography and musical work.

WALLER, "FATS" (THOMAS WRIGHT). 1904–1943

"Fats" Waller was a great jazz pianist, playing "stride" piano lightly and
brilliantly. He began as a recording artist and composed music for several
Broadway shows, including *Keep Shufflin'* (1928) and *Hot Chocolates* (1929). He
was always an entertaining performer, live and in films. His song "Ain't
Misbehavin'" became the title song of a popular retrospective revue of his
works in 1978.

BOOKS ABOUT WALLER

Kirkeby, W. T., ed. *Ain't Misbehavin': The Story of Fats Waller*. Da Capo 1975 repr. of 1966
    ed. $8.95. ISBN 0-306-80015-2
Machlin, Paul S. *Stride, The Music of Fats Waller*. Twayne 1985 o.p.
Vance, Joel. *Fats Waller: His Life and Times*. Robson Books 1988 o.p. A short, general
    biography; suitable for a general audience.
Waller, Maurice, and Anthony Calabrese. *Fats Waller*. Schirmer Bks. 1977 o.p. Foreword
    by Michael Lispskin.

WEBERN, ANTON VON. 1883–1945

Perhaps the most severe of the Second Viennese School of composers, Anton
Webern studied musicology but quickly became a follower of ARNOLD
SCHOENBERG. Schoenberg, ALBAN BERG, and Webern are known as the Vienna
Trinity.

During Hitler's regime, Webern's music was banned as a manifestation of
"cultural Bolshevism" and "degenerate art." After the Anschluss in 1938, his
works could no longer be published. He died on September 15, 1945, when he
was accidentally shot by an American soldier. After his death, Webern's music
increasingly influenced modern composers. Jazz composers have claimed the
use of his ideas of tone color. His remaining works are practically gossamer in
their adherence to the most rigid interpretation of the rules for compositions
using 12 tones.

BOOKS ABOUT WEBERN

Bailey, Kathryn. *The Twelve-Note Music of Anton Webern: Old Forms in a New Language*.
    Cambridge U. Pr. 1991 $74.95. ISBN 0-521-39088-5

Kolneder, Walter. *Anton Webern: An Introduction to His Works*. Trans. by Humphrey Searle. Greenwood 1982 repr. of 1968 ed. $38.50. ISBN 0-313-23342-X
Moldenhauer, Hans, and Demar Irvine, eds. *Anton von Webern: Perspectives*. Da Capo 1978 repr. of 1966 ed. $32.50. ISBN 0-306-77518-2
Moldenhauer, Hans, and Rosaleen Moldenhauer. *Anton von Webern: A Chronicle of His Life and Work*. Knopf 1979 o.p.

WILDER, ALEC. 1907–1980

Alec Wilder was an American composer who wrote both serious and popular music. He composed short operas and chamber music, including the *Suite for String Orchestra*. He composed and arranged band music for Benny Goodman and Jimmy Dorsey, among others. His songs were performed by such singers as FRANK SINATRA and Judy Garland and include "It's So Peaceful in the Country" and "The Lady Sings the Blues." He also composed film scores and children's songs.

BOOKS BY WILDER

Alec Wilder (1907–1980): An Introduction to the Man and His Music. Margun Music 1991 o.p.
American Popular Song: The Great Innovators, 1900–1950. Ed. by James T. Maher. OUP 1972 $29.95. ISBN 0-19-501445-6. With an introduction by the editor and a foreword by Gene Lees. A comprehensive wide-ranging look at early songwriters.
Letters I Never Mailed. Little 1975 o.p.

BOOKS ABOUT WILDER

Balliet, Whitney. *Alec Wilder and His Friends: The Words and Sounds of Marian McPartland, Mabel Mercer, Marie Marcus, Bobby Hackett, Tony Bennett, Ruby Braff, Bob and Ray, Blossom Dearie, and Alec Wilder*. Da Capo 1983 repr. of 1974 ed. $25.00. ISBN 0-306-76153-X. Illustrated by Geoffrey James. Ten short portraits of the musicians.
Demsey, David, Ronald Prather, and Judith Bell. *Alec Wilder: A Bio-Bibliography*. Greenwood 1993 $55.00. ISBN 0-313-27820-2. A short biography, with a comprehensive bibliography.

XENAKIS, IANNIS. 1922–

Iannis Xenakis is an avant-garde Greek composer who attempts to apply mathematical constructs to musical composition, such as using the theory of sets, symbolic logic, and probabilistic calculus. He was the founder and director of the Centre d' Études Mathematiques et Automatiques Musicales in Paris and at the Center for Mathematical and Automated Music at Indiana University, where he served on the faculty from 1967 to 1972. In this age of technology, his work captivates many other composers and may prove to be one of the formative generators of compositional technique in the late twentieth century.

BOOKS BY XENAKIS

Arts, Sciences, Alloys: The Thesis Defense of Iannis Xenakis Before Olivier Messiaen, Michel Ragon, Olivier Revault d'Allonnes, Michel Serres, and Bernard Teyss'edre. Trans. by Sharon Kanach. Pendragon Pr. 1985 o.p.
Formalized Music: Thought and Mathematics in Composition. Indiana U. Pr. 1992 $48.00. ISBN 0-945193-24-6. Number six in the *Harmonologia Series;* an interesting work on the philosophy and mathematics of musical composition.

BOOKS ABOUT XENAKIS

Bois, Mario. *Iannis Xenakis, The Man and His Music: A Conversation with the Composer and a Description of His Works.* Greenwood 1980 repr. of 1967 ed. $42.50. ISBN 0-313-22415-3

Matossian, Nouritza. *Xenakis.* Pro-Am Music 1991 $19.95. ISBN 0-912483-35-0. A short biography concentrating on Xenakis's music.

DANCE

General Reference

Cobbett-Steinberg, Steven, ed. *The Dance Anthology.* NAL-Dutton 1980 $10.95. ISBN 0-452-25702-6. Essays and articles on a variety of themes by some of the most thoughtful writers on the dance, many of whom are choreographers, dancers, and musicians; with chronologies, dance family trees, and a guide to dance literature.

Cohen-Stratyner, Barbara Naomi. *Biographical Dictionary of Dance.* Schirmer Bks. 1982 o.p. Profiles 2,900 dancers in classical and popular dance. Contains lists of works and bibliographies.

Copeland, Roger, and Marshall Cohen. *What Is Dance: Readings in Theory and Criticism.* OUP 1983 $29.95. ISBN 0-19-503217-9. A widely diversified collection of good writings about dance, examining fundamental questions of dance aesthetics.

The Encyclopedia of Dance and Ballet. Ed. by Mary Clarke and David Vaughan. Putnam Pub. Group 1977 o.p.

Hawkins, Alma. *Moving from Within: A New Method for Dance Making.* A capella Bks. 1991 $12.95. ISBN 1-55652-139-1

Hayes, Elizabeth. *Dance Composition and Production.* Princeton Bk. Co. 1993 $16.95. ISBN 0-87127-188-5

Koegler, Horst. *The Concise Oxford Dictionary of Ballet.* OUP 1982 $29.95. ISBN 0-19-311330-9. Crisp entries on all aspects of ballet (people, works, companies, terms, and ethnic and social dancing), including modern dance. Occasional bibliographies.

Kraus, Richard G., Sarah Chapman Hilsendager, and Brenda Dixon. *History of the Dance in Art and Education.* P-H 1991. ISBN 0-13-389362-6

Lawson, Joan. *The Principles of Classical Dance.* Knopf 1980 o.p. Photographs accompanying brief explications of the rules of movement for ballet. Photographs by Anthony Crickmay.

McDonagh, Don. *The Complete Guide to Modern Dance.* Doubleday 1976 o.p. Brief entries on major figures in modern dance, with analyses of the most characteristic of their productions. End papers show "extended choreographic families in a single graphic representation."

Raffe, W. G., and M. E. Purdon. *Dictionary of the Dance.* A. S. Barnes 1975 o.p. Covers all periods and places with entries on terms, genres, locations, costumes, sets, and themes. No biographical materials, but contains a bibliography and geographical and subject indexes.

Sharp, Harold, and Marjorie Z. Sharp. *Index to Characters in the Performing Arts* 2 pts. Scarecrow 1966–73 $17.50–$45.00. ISBNs 0-8108-0486-7, 0-8108-0605-3. Identifies characters, lists creative persons, and gives dates and places of first performances.

The Simon and Schuster Book of the Ballet. S&S Trade 1980 o.p. Chronological, illustrated catalog of ballets. Introduction by Mario Psai.

Van Zile, Judy A. *Dance in India: An Annotated Guide to Source Materials.* Asian Music Pub. 1973 $7.50. ISBN 0-913360-06-6. Comprehensive listing of source materials in English.

Wilson, G.B.L. *A Dictionary of Ballet.* Theatre Arts Bks. 1971 o.p. Covers Western dance with very brief entries on persons, dances, and terms.

History and Criticism

Anderson, Jack. *Ballet and Modern Dance: A Concise History*. Princeton Bk. Co. 1992 $16.95. ISBN 0-87127-172-9. Remarkable, insightful short history of Western theatrical dance since the Renaissance. Includes a select bibliography and a collection of short profiles of people and companies cited in the book.

Au, Susan. *Ballet and Modern Dance: A Concise History*. Thames Hudson 1988 $11.95. ISBN 0-500-20219-2

Buckle, Richard. *Buckle at the Ballet: Selected Ballet Writings*. Atheneum 1980 o.p. Collected articles from 1959 to 1975 of the ballet critic for the *Sunday Times* (London), arranged by subject and indexed.

Cass, Joan. *Dancing Through History*. P-H 1993 $24.00. ISBN 0-13-204389-0. General history of all genres of dance.

Clarke, Mary, and Pam Thomas. *A History of Dance*. Outlet Bk. Co. 1981 o.p. Authoritatively covers dance around the world and all periods rather briefly. Copiously illustrated.

Cohen, Selma J. *Next Week, Swan Lake: Reflections on Dance and Dances*. U. Pr. of New Eng. 1986 $14.95. ISBN 0-8195-6110-X. Concerned with the identity of certain works, genres, and dance itself. Reviews historic, dramatic, stylistic, and personal problems of the art. Focuses on Western concert dance.

Croce, Arlene. *Going to the Dance*. Knopf 1982 o.p. Articles collected from this most perceptive critic's writing in *The New Yorker* from the previous five years.

First Steps in Modern Ballet: The Technique, Practice, Origins, Great Names, and the Most Famous Names in Modern Ballet. Parramón Ediciones 1986 o.p.

Haskell, Arnold L. *Balletomania: Story of an Obsession*. AMS Pr. repr. of 1934 ed. $19.50 ISBN 0-404-03154-4. Story of a personal odyssey to achieve a depth of understanding that can be described as intoxicating. Annotated after nearly four decades of more experience as a dance critic and followed by new pieces on recent developments.

Kerner, Mary. *Barefoot to Balanchine: How to Watch Dance*. Doubleday 1991 $9.95. ISBN 0-385-26436-4

Kirstein, Lincoln. *Dance: A Short History of Classic Theatrical Dancing*. Princeton Bk. Co. 1987 $17.95. ISBN 0-87127-019-6. Dated, but thorough, history of the Western dance tradition.

McDonagh, Don. *The Rise and Fall and Rise of Modern Dance*. A. capella Bks. 1990 $14.95. ISBN 1-55652-089-1. An account of 1960s modern dance; arranged by choreographer.

Martin, John. *Introduction to the Dance*. Dance Horizons o.p. A consideration of the dance in history and society, intending to awaken or verbalize responses to dance as a means of communication; considered a classic.

Nevell, Richard. *A Time to Dance: American Country Dancing from Hornpipes to Hot Hash*. St. Martin 1977 o.p.

Novack, Cynthia Jean. *Sharing the Dance: Contact Improvisation and American Culture*. U. of Wis. Pr. 1990 $30.00. ISBN 0-299-12440-1. Historical work on dance improvisation with emphasis on anthropological aspects.

Reynolds, Nancy, and Susan Reimer-Torn. *Dance Classics: A Viewer's Guide to the Best-Loved Ballets and Modern Dance*. A. capella Bks. 1991 $29.95. ISBN 1-55652-109-X

Robertson, Allen. *The Dance Handbook*. Macmillan 1990 $25.00 ISBN 0-8161-9095-X

Sachs, Curt. *World History of the Dance*. Trans. by Bessie Schoenberg. Norton 1963 o.p. A comprehensive text on dance history; a bit dated.

Sawyer, Elizabeth. *Dance with the Music: The World of the Ballet Musician*. Cambridge U. Pr. 1986 ISBN 0-521-26502-9. A short but in-depth work on the interplay between music and ballet.

Siegel, Marcia B. *The Tail of the Dragon: New Dance, 1976–82*. Duke 1991 $39.95. ISBN 0-8223-1156-9. Reviews of modern-dance performances in the United States.

Teck, Katherine. *Music for the Dance: Reflections on a Collaborative Art. Contributions to the Study of Music and Dance*. Greenwood 1989 $69.95. ISBN 0-313-26376-0

Terry, Walter. *How to Look at Dance*. Morrow 1982 o.p. Covers all styles of art and popular dance. Photographs by Jack Vartoogian and Linda Vartoogian.
———. *I Was There: Selected Dance Reviews and Articles, 1936–1976*. Princeton Bk. Co. 1978 o.p. The best writings of the American dean of dance critics.
Twentieth-Century Dance in Britain: A History of Major Dance Companies in Britain. Princeton Bk. Co. 1985 $17.95. ISBN 0-903102-85-4

Ballet

Balanchine, George, and Jeffrey Bairstow. *Balanchine's Complete Stories of the Great Ballets*. Doubleday 1977 o.p. Basic facts, plot summaries, and notes on approximately 450 ballets, with brief concluding essays and a glossary.
Beaumont, Cyril. *Ballets of Today: Being a Second Supplement to the Complete Book of Ballets*. Putnam Pub. Group 1954 o.p. Description of ballets, followed by short critical commentary.
———. *Ballets Past and Present: Being a Third Supplement to the Complete Book of Ballets*. Putnam Pub. Group 1955 o.p. Description of ballets as in *Ballets of Today*.
———. *Complete Book of Ballets: A Guide to the Principal Ballets of the Nineteenth and Twentieth Centuries*. Putnam Pub. Group 1938 o.p. Classic work featuring summaries of the plots and basic facts of the most famous ballets.
Clarke, Mary. *The Ballet Goer's Guide*. Knopf 1981 o.p.
Clarke, Mary and Clement Crisp. *Ballet: An Illustrated History*. Viking Penguin 1993 $30.00. ISBN 0-241-13068-9
———. *Ballet Art from the Renaissance to the Present*. Crown Pub. Group 1978 o.p. Study of images of ballet in art.
Guest, Ivor. *Adventures of a Ballet Historian, an Unfinished Memoir*. Dance Horizons 1982 o.p. Includes a bibliography of works by this prolific writer of dance books.
———. *The Dancer's Heritage: A Short History of Ballet*. Dancing Times 1988 o.p.
Lawson, Joan. *A Ballet-Maker's Handbook: Sources, Vocabulary, Styles*. Routledge Chapman & Hall 1991 $18.95. ISBN 0-87830-017-1
Lee, Carol. *An Introduction to Classical Ballet*. L. Erlbaum Assocs. 1983 $29.95. ISBN 0-89859-279-8. A dry, but solid, work on the historical and technical foundations of classical ballet. Intended for the developing professional but worth attention by the serious balletomane.

American Dance

Mazo, Joseph H. *Prime Movers: The Makers of Modern Dance in America*. Princeton Bk. Co. 1983 $15.95. ISBN 0-916622-27-4
Novack, Cynthia Jean. *Sharing the Dance: Contact Improvisation and American Culture*. U. of Wis. Pr. 1990 $14.95. ISBN 0-299-12444-4
Roan, Carol. *Clues to American Dance*. Starrhill Pr. 1993. ISBN 0-913515-83-3
Siegel, Marcia B. *The Shapes of Change: Images of American Dance*. U. CA Pr. 1985 $12.00. ISBN 0-520-04203-4
Stearns, Marshall, and Jean Stearns. *Jazz Dance: The Story of American Vernacular Dance*. Schirmer Bks. 1979 o.p. Deals with American dancing that is formed to and with the rhythms of jazz.

Ethnic Dance

Emery, Lynne Fauley. *Black Dance in the United States from 1619 to Today*. Ayer 1988 $39.00. ISBN 0-88143-074-9. Comprehensive study of the dance forms of African Americans. A scholarly but readable work replete with quotations, footnotes, and an extensive bibliography.
Ness, Sally Ann. *Body, Movement, and Culture: Kinesthetic and Visual Symbolism in a Philippine Community*. U. of Pa. Pr. 1992 $39.95. ISBN 0-8122-3110-4
Royce, Anya P. *The Anthropology of Dance*. Ind. U. Pr. 1977 o.p. Explores the meanings and symbolisms of dance in general and of ethnic and tribal groups in particular.

Zoete, Beryl de, and Walter Spies. *Dance and Drama in Bali*. OUP 1983 o.p. Classic exposition of Balinese dance, revealing the important and recurring links between drama and dance.

Dance Companies

Barnes, Clive. *Inside American Ballet Theatre*. Da Capo 1983 o.p. Annotated photographic essay. Introduction by Justin Colin.

Bland, Alexander. *The Royal Ballet: The First Fifty Years*. Doubleday 1981 o.p. History of the ballet company that began as the Sadler's Wells Ballet.

Cameron, Judy, photographer. *The Bolshoi Ballet*. HarpC 1975 o.p. Introduction by Walter Terry.

Castle, Kate. *Ballet Company*. Covent Garden 1985 o.p.

Crickmay, Anthony. *A Portrait of the Royal Ballet*. M. O'Mara Bks. 1988 o.p.

Doeser, Linda. *Ballet and Dance: The World's Major Companies*. St. Martin 1978 o.p. Descriptions of dance companies from all over the world. Focuses on European, Russian, and American companies.

Fraser, John. *Private View: Behind the Scenes with Baryshnikov's American Ballet Theatre*. Bantam 1988 $19.50. ISBN 0-553-35451-5

Garafola, Lynn. *Diaghilev's Ballet Russe*. OUP 1992 repr of 1989 ed. $17.95. ISBN 0-19-507604-4

Gregory, John, and Alexander Ukladnikov. *Leningrad's Ballet: Maryinsky to Kirov*. Seven Hills Bk. Dists. 1991 $18.95. ISBN 0-9511069-6-5. Introduction to the history, traditions, and life of the famous Kirov Ballet Company.

Grigorovich, Y., and V. Vanslov. *Bolshoi Ballet*. Paganiniana Pubns. 1984 $39.95. ISBN 0-86622-043-7

Jessel, Camilla. *Life at the Royal Ballet School*. Routledge Chapman & Hall 1985 $15.95. ISBN 0-416-30191-6

Leibovitz, Annie. *American Ballet Theatre: The First Fifty Years*. Dewynters PLC 1989 o.p.

Newman, Barbara. *Striking a Balance: Dancers Talk about Dancing*. Limelight Edns. 1992 $17.95. ISBN 0-87910-154-7. Transcribed conversations with ballet dancers.

Walker, Katherine Sorley. *DeBasil's Ballets Russes*. Atheneum 1983 o.p. Chronicle of the Ballet Russe de Monte Carlo, with extensive appendixes.

———. *The Royal Ballet: A Picture History*. Threshold Bks. UK 1986 o.p.

White, Joan, ed. *Twentieth-Century Dance in Britain: A History of Major Dance Companies in Britain*. Princeton Bk. Co. 1985 $17.95. ISBN 0-903102-85-4

Choreographers

Hastings, Baird. *Choreographer and Composer*. Twayne 1983 o.p. Modern history of the complementary roles of the chief creators of dance. Discusses working relationships and the creative process.

Nijinska, Bronislava. *Bronislava Nijinska: Early Memoirs*. Duke 1992 $18.95 ISBN 0-8223-1295-6. First paperback printing of the work originally published by Holt, Rinehart, and Winston in 1981.

Osumare, Halifu. *Black Choreographers Moving: A National Dialogue*. Expansion Arts 1991 o.p.

Perces, Marjorie, Ana M. Forsythe, and Cheryl Bell. *The Dance Technique of Lester Hornton*. Princeton Bk. Co. 1992 $24.95. ISBN 0-87127-164-8. Includes reminiscences by Hornton's former students, a brief biography of the choreographer, and detailed descriptions of Hornton's movements. Recommended for modern dance practitioners.

Rogosin, Elinor. *The Dance Makers: Conversations with American Choreographers*. Walker & Co. 1980 o.p. A dozen interviews with legendary and budding choreographers.

Souritz, Elizabeth. *Soviet Choreographers in the 1920s*. Duke 1990 $29.95. ISBN 0-8223-0952-1. Uses Russian archival material, theater literature, and reminiscences of performers, designers, and choreographers to describe the period and its influence on the development of American ballet.

Warren, Larry. *Anna Sokolow: The Rebellious Spirit.* Princeton Bk. Co. 1991 $29.95. ISBN 0-87127-162-1. Provides a critical reevaluation of the importance of Sokolow's contributions to modern dance with regard to the political, social, and artistic environment of the 1930s.

Winearls, Jane. *Choreography, The Art of the Body: An Anatomy of Expression.* Princeton Bk. Co. 1990 o.p.

CHRONOLOGY OF AUTHORS
(Dance)

Noverre, Jean-Georges. 1727–1810
Bournonville, August. 1805–1879
Jaques-Dalcroze, Émile. 1865–1950
Diaghilev, Serge. 1872–1929
Duncan, Isadora. 1878–1927
Laban, Rudolf. 1879–1958
St. Denis, Ruth. 1879–1968
Pavlova, Anna. 1881–1931
Nijinsky, Vaslav. 1890–1950
Nijinska, Bronislava. 1891–1972
Shawn, Ted. 1891–1972
Graham, Martha. 1894–1991
Humphrey, Doris. 1895–1958
Massine, Léonide. 1896–1979
Astaire, Fred. 1899–1987
Ashton, Sir Frederick. 1904–1988
Balanchine, George. 1904–1983
Baker, Josephine. 1906–1975
Kirstein, Lincoln. 1907–

Limón, José. 1908–1972
DeMille, Agnes George. 1909–1993
Tudor, Antony. 1909–1987
Ulanova, Galina. 1910–
Rogers, Ginger. 1911–
Robbins, Jerome. 1918–
Cunningham, Merce. 1919–
Fonteyn, Dame Margot. 1919–1991
Fosse, Bob. 1927–1987
Joffrey, Robert. 1930–1988
Taylor, Paul. 1930–
Ailey, Alvin. 1931–1989
Brown, Trisha. 1936–
Nureyev, Rudolph. 1939–1993
Tharp, Twyla. 1941–
Feld, Eliot. 1942–
Martins, Peter. 1946–
Baryshnikov, Mikhail. 1948–
Morris, Mark. 1956–

AILEY, ALVIN, JR. 1931–1989

African American dancer, choreographer, teacher, and director Alvin Ailey was born in Texas. He trained in New York under MARTHA GRAHAM, DORIS HUMPHREY, Charles Weidman, and Hanya Holm while dancing and acting in Broadway and off-Broadway shows.

In 1958 Ailey founded the Alvin Ailey Dance Theatre, the first multiracial modern-dance troupe. He performed his breakthrough piece *Blues Suite* with the company that same year. His most famous dance, *Revelations* (1960), a mournful and celebratory story of religious spirit, became the company's signature piece. With these and other pieces, Ailey demonstrated to a skeptical public that modern dance could be terrific entertainment, and his company became hugely popular.

In 1965 Ailey retired from dancing in order to devote his time and energy to choreography and to directing his company. Ailey's work has been widely performed by a number of other modern dance companies as well, and he choreographed for such companies as the Joffrey Ballet and the American Ballet Theater. His choreography is direct and often topical, reflecting his observations of the body language of urban blacks as well as the contrasting rhythms of rural life. In addition to *Revelations,* other well-known works are *Creation of the World* (1961) and *At the Edge of the Precipice* (1983).

BOOKS ABOUT AILEY

Kerensky, Oleg. *The World of Ballet.* Coward-McCann 1970 o.p.
Probosz, Kathilyn Solomon. *Alvin Ailey, Jr.* Bantam 1991 $3.50. ISBN 0-553-15930-5

ASHTON, SIR FREDERICK. 1904–1988

Born in Guayaquil, Ecuador, of English parents, Sir Frederick Ashton was raised in Peru. It was there, in Lima, that he became interested in dance when he saw ANNA PAVLOVA perform when he was 14 years old. Ashton pursued his interest in dance in England, studying with LEONIDE MASSINE and Marie Rambert, who commissioned his first choreographed work, *A Tragedy of Fashion,* in 1926. After a year of dancing in America under the direction of BRONISLAVA NIJINSKA, he returned to England and helped found the Ballet Club, which became Ballet Rambert. During this time, he partnered and created roles for a variety of ballerinas. In 1935 he joined the Vic-Wells Ballet as a dancer and choreographer, remaining there as the company developed into the Royal Ballet. He became one of the company's artistic directors in 1948 and then director in 1963.

Ashton was perhaps the best-loved and most influential contemporary British dancer and choreographer. Incredibly prolific, he created more than 60 works, many of which form the basic repertoire of the Royal Ballet today. These include such works as *La Fille Mal Gardee* (1960), *Marguérite and Armand* (1963), *A Month in the Country* (1979), and *Rhapsody* (1980). In addition to his work in ballet, Ashton also choreographed musicals and collaborated with both BENJAMIN BRITTEN and VIRGIL THOMSON. In 1962 he was knighted and made Chevalier of the Legion d'Honneur.

BOOKS ABOUT ASHTON

Dominic, Zoe. *Frederick Ashton: A Choreographer and His Ballets.* Regnery Gateway 1973 o.p.
Macaulay, Alastair. *Some Views and Reviews of Ashton's Choreography.* National Resource Centre for Dance 1987 o.p.
Vaughan, David. *Frederick Ashton and His Ballets.* Knopf 1977 o.p. Synopses of ballets and transcriptions of choreographic notes of the great British choreographer.

ASTAIRE, FRED. 1899–1987

Fred Astaire was the greatest popular dancer of his time. He made his debut at the age of 7 accompanied by his older sister Adele on the vaudeville Keith-Orpheum circuit. The brother-sister team made their Broadway debut in *Over the Top* (1916). For more than a decade, they performed in musicals on Broadway and in London, including GEORGE GERSHWIN's *Lady Be Good* (1925).

An extraordinary tap, theater, and ballroom dancer, Astaire soon turned his attention to film, in which he became accessible to millions. His first picture was with Joan Crawford in *Dancing Lady* in 1933. That same year, Astaire teamed up with GINGER ROGERS in *Flying Down to Rio.* As the most successful dance team in films, Astaire and Rogers made numerous pictures, including *Top Hat* (1935), *Swing Time* (1936), and *Shall We Dance* (1937). During his successful film career, Astaire also danced with Rita Hayworth, Eleanor Powell, and Cyd Charisse. Astaire's dancing displayed incredible technical skill and sophistication.

Books about Astaire

Giles, Sarah. *Fred Astaire*. Doubleday 1988 $30.00. ISBN 0-385-24741-9
Mueller, John. *Astaire Dancing*. Outlet Bk. Co. 1985 $24.99. ISBN 0-517-06075-2
Thomas, Bob. *Astaire: The Man, the Dancer*. St. Martin 1985 $3.95. ISBN 0-312-90037-6

BAKER, JOSEPHINE. 1906–1975

Josephine Baker was an African American dancer who became enormously popular in New York and Paris from the mid-1920s to the mid-1950s. She began her career as a singer and dancer in 1921 in a chorus revue, the Sissle and Blake musical comedy *Shuffle Along*, and appeared in the revue of the Plantation Club in New York in 1924. She first performed in Paris at the Thêâtre des Champs-Elysées in *La Revue Nègre* in 1925 and from that date was a hit on both sides of the Atlantic. Her costumes were especially revealing, and her lifestyle affected a liberation long before that term became popular in America during the late 1960s. During her successful career, she appeared in films, theater, and on television.

Book by Baker

Josephine. (coauthored with Jo Bouillon and Mariana Fitzpatrick). Paragon Hse. 1988 $9.95. ISBN 1-55778-108-7

Books about Baker

Hammond, Bryan and Patrick O'Connor. *Josephine Baker*. Little 1991 $24.95. ISBN 0-8212-1860-3
Rose, Phyllis. *Jazz Cleopatra*. Random 1990 $13.00. ISBN 0679-73133-4
Schroeder, Alan. *Josephine Baker*. Chelsea Hse. 1991 $17.95. ISBN 0-7910-1116-X

BALANCHINE, GEORGE. 1904–1983

Russian-born dancer and choreographer George Balanchine is considered one of the major figures in twentieth-century ballet. Born in St. Petersburg of Georgian heritage, Balanchine studied ballet at the school of the Imperial Theatre. His first piece was choreographed while he was still a student there. After graduating from the school, he studied at the Petrograd Conservatory and formed his own dance company. Balanchine's innovations troubled authorities, however, and he defected while on a European tour with the Soviet State Dancers. After his defection, he worked with Sergei Diaghilev in Paris and choreographed several ballets for Diaghilev's Russian Ballet, including *La Pastorale* (1925), *The Trimph of Neptune* (1926), and two of his masterpieces, *Apollo* (1928) and *The Prodigal Son* (1929).

When Diaghilev died in 1929, Balanchine worked for various companies before forming Les Ballets Russe de Monte Carlo in 1932. Then, in 1934, he was invited to the United States, where he formed the School of American Ballet in New York City. The first ballet he choreographed in America, *Serenade* (1934), became the signature piece of the company. After World War II, the American Ballet company disbanded and Balanchine directed a small dance company known as the Ballet Society. In 1948 this small company became the New York City Ballet, and Balanchine became its guiding light.

Under Balanchine's creative genius and leadership, the New York City Ballet emerged as one of the premier dance companies in the United States. He created nearly 100 works of great variety for the company, including *Agon* (1957), *Stars and Stripes* (1958), *Symphony in C* (1959), *Theme and Variations* (1960), *Ballo della Regina* (1978), *Davidsbundlertanze* (1980), and *Mozartiana*

(1981). The company, along with its ballet school, the School of American Ballet, has been a vital force in American ballet, producing distinctive dancers and works. In 1993 the New York City Ballet presented a major retrospective of Balanchine's works.

BOOKS ABOUT BALANCHINE

Buckle, Richard. *George Balanchine: Ballet Master.* Random 1988 $29.95. ISBN 0-394-53906-0

Kirstein, Lincoln. *Portrait of Mr. B: Photographs of George Balanchine with an Essay.* Viking Penguin 1984 o.p. Includes photographs and essays, by Jonathan Cott and Edwin Denby, from 1904 to 1983. Foreword by Peter Martins.

Kirstein, Lincoln, and Martha Swope. *Union Jack—the New York City Ballet.* Eakins 1977 $9.95. ISBN 0-87130-047-8

Maiorano, Robert, and Valerie Brooks. *Balanchine's Mozartiana: The Making of a Masterpiece.* Freundlich 1985 $17.95. ISBN 0-88191-013-9. Balanchine at work.

Mason, Francis. *I Remember Balanchine.* Doubleday 1992 $25.00. ISBN 0-385-26610-3

Taper, Bernard. *Balanchine.* U. CA Pr. 1987 $15.00. ISBN 0-520-06059-8

Volkov, Solomon. *Balanchine's Tchaikovsky: Interviews with George Balanchine.* Trans. by Antonina W. Bouis. Doubleday 1992 $11.00. ISBN 0-385-42387-X

BARYSHNIKOV, MIKHAIL. 1948–

Born in Riga, Latvia, Mikhail Baryshnikov is one of the twentieth-century's most exciting and popular dancers. After initial training at the Riga Choreography School, Baryshnikov began his career in Leningrad with the famed Kirov Ballet. In 1974, while on tour in Canada, he defected and immediately began dancing for the National Ballet of Canada and then the American Ballet Theatre in the United States. His amazing talent, matchless technique, and dynamic style soon made him an international star, rivaling his compatriot RUDOLPH NUREYEV.

Much in demand, Baryshnikov has worked with a number of choreographers, including GEORGE BALANCHINE, JEROME ROBBINS, FREDERICK ASHTON, and modern choreographer TWYLA THARP, whose *Push Comes to Shove* (1976) has become a sort of signature piece for the dancer. A number of roles have been created especially for him, including Frederick Ashton's last important work, *Rhapsody* (1980).

In 1980 Baryshnikov became artistic director of the American Ballet Theatre, but he left the company in 1989 to pursue other opportunities, including experimenting in modern dance with MARK MORRIS, one of America's most important young choreographers. In addition to his work in ballet and modern dance, he has also appeared in several films, including *The Turning Point* (1977), *White Knights* (1985), and *Dancers* (1987). Not yet retired from dancing, Baryshnikov has focused more on modern dance than ballet in recent years.

BOOKS ABOUT BARYSHNIKOV

Aria, Barbara. *Misha! The Mikhail Baryshnikov Story.* St. Martin 1989 $16.95. ISBN 0-312-02610-2

France, Charles E., and Martha Swope. *Baryshnikov.* Abrams 1980 $16.95. ISBN 0-8109-2225-8

Fraser, John, and Eve Arnold. *Private View: Behind the Scenes with American Ballet.* Bantam 1988 o.p.

Smakov, Gennady. *Baryshnikov: From Russia to the West.* FS&G 1981 o.p.

Swope, Martha. *Baryshnikov at Work.* Knopf 1978 $22.95. ISBN 0-394-73587-0

BOURNONVILLE, AUGUST. 1805–1879

The son of a famous French dancer and choreographer, August Bournonville was born in Copenhagen and trained for the dance with the Royal Danish Ballet. In 1826 he moved to Paris to study at the Paris Opera but returned to Denmark two years later. The rest of his career was spent at the Royal Danish Ballet as dancer, choreographer, and director. He created more than 60 dances for the company, utilizing techniques and subjects he had learned in both Paris and Denmark. Among his surviving works, the most well known include *Valdemar* (1835), *La Sylphide* (1836), *The Fisherman and His Bride* (1842), *Napoli* (1842), *Far from Denmark* (1860), and *From Siberia to Moscow* (1876).

Bournonville's choreography employs a great amount of dancing "en pointe." It also is noted for its precise technique, romantic style, bourgeois values, and equality of the sexes. Dance historians consider him to be one of the most important, if not the most important, choreographers of the nineteenth century.

BOOK BY BOURNONVILLE

My Theatre Life. Trans. by Patricia McAndrew. Wesleyan Univ. Pr. 1979 o.p. Autobiography of the nineteenth-century ballet choreographer and impresario.

BOOKS ABOUT BOURNONVILLE

Jurgensen, Knud A., and Ann H. Guest. *The Bournonville Heritage: A Choreographic Record, 1829–1875; Twenty Unknown Dances in Labanotation.* Princeton Bk. Co. 1990 $100.00. ISBN 1-85273-025-0

Ralov, Kirsten. *The Bournonville School.* Bks. Demand 1979 $34.30. ISBN 0-8357-7370-1.

BROWN, TRISHA. 1936–

Postmodern choreographer Trisha Brown was born in Aberdeen, Washington. She began studying dance locally as an adolescent and continued her studies while attending Mills College. After graduation she taught for two years at Reed College, participating in summer workshops on dance and improvisation.

In 1960 Brown moved to New York and studied with Robert Dunn at the MERCE CUNNINGHAM studio. Dunn's classes produced a group of dancers and choreographers who formed the Judson Dance Theater, among them Simone Forti, Yvonne Rainer, Steve Paxton, David Gordon, Lucinda Childs, Meredith Monk, and Brown. At Judson, Brown created a number of dance roles and also choreographed her own works, including *Trillium* (1962), *Lightfall* (1963), *Chanteuse Excentrique Americaine* (1963), *Rulegame 5* (1965), and *A String* (1966).

In 1968 Brown began creating "equipment pieces," dances that involved the use of external support systems, such as moving up a wall (*Planes*, 1968). She has since added other variations in her dances: accumulation pieces in which each dancer takes turns adding to a system of gestures, sounds, or words; and dances based on the formation of lines by performers using props or their own bodies (*Locus*, 1975; *Solo Olos*, 1976; and *Line Up*, 1977). Brown now choreographs for her own group, Trisha Brown and Dancers.

CUNNINGHAM, MERCE. 1919–

American dancer, teacher, and choreographer and a celebrated soloist in the MARTHA GRAHAM Dance Company from 1940 to 1955, Merce Cunningham participated in the third-generation development of modern dance. Born in

Centralia, Washington, he began his career in the second-generation period of the American modern-dance theater under the tutelage of Martha Graham. He later became a creator and choreographer of his own dances and in 1950 established his own dance company.

Through the Merce Cunningham Dance Company, Cunningham taught his students to follow new paths of creativity—to choreograph dances to avant-garde musical compositions, to be free of spatial restraints, to replace a strong central focus with a random approach to choreographic patterns, and to devise dances that could be viewed from any angle. Working with American composer JOHN CAGE as musical director, Cunningham taught his students to experiment with dances that used electronic and other newly developed forms of music. His best-known works include *Suite by Chance* (1952), a work in which a toss of the dice determines the structure, and *Symphonie Pour un Homme Seul* (1952). Both reveal the spare, expressive style that is the Cunningham hallmark.

BOOKS BY CUNNINGHAM

Changes: Notes on Choreography. Ed. by Frances Starr. Ultramarine Pub. o.p. Typograph-ically difficult book that gives a unique view of the creative impulse in modern dance.

The Dancer and the Dance: Merce Cunningham in Conversation with Jacqueline Lesschaeve 1985. (coauthored with Jacqueline Lesschaeve). Ed. by Henry Nathan. M. Boyars Pubs. 1985 $27.50. ISBN 0-7145-2809-9

BOOKS ABOUT CUNNINGHAM

Anderson, Jack, and Richard Kostelanetz. *Merce Cunningham: Dancing in Space and Time, Essays 1944–1992.* A. cappella Bks. 1992 o.p.

Klosty, James, ed. *Merce Cunningham.* Limelight Edns. 1987 $19.95. ISBN 0-87910-055-9. Contains 15 essays by composers, dancers, and other artists who worked with Cunningham. Interspersed with candid photographs of the Merce Cunningham Dance Company.

Sontag, Susan, Richard Francis, and others. *Cage Cunningham Johns: Dancers on a Plane.* Knopf 1990 $49.50. ISBN 0-394-58847-9

DEMILLE, AGNES GEORGE. 1909–1993

Choreographer and ballet and theater dancer Agnes George DeMille began her career as a concert dancer in 1927. Perhaps her most famous characteriza-tion was her *Ballet Class after Dègas*, portraying an opera dancer of the late nineteenth century. DeMille danced and choreographed in London with the Rambert Company and the company of ANTONY TUDOR. She staged the London production of COLE PORTER's *Nymph Errant* in 1933, followed quickly by *Oklahoma!*, in which her deliberately limited range of steps unified characters, time, and place. She later choreographed *Carousel, Brigadoon, Paint Your Wagon,* and *Gentlemen Prefer Blondes,* among others. *Rodeo,* with music by AARON COPLAND, is among the ballets she has created. DeMille is highly respected, not only for her art, but also for her leadership and finesse as a spokesperson for the arts.

BOOK ABOUT DEMILLE

DeMille, Agnes G. *Dance to the Piper and Promenade Home: A Two-part Autobiography.* Da Capo 1982 $10.95. ISBN 0-306-80161-2

DIAGHILEV, SERGEI. 1872–1929

The famed Russian impresario Sergei Diaghilev was born in Novgorod. Although he studied law and obtained a degree in that field, his real love was the arts. Rather than pursue law, he became editor of an arts magazine, *Mir Iskousstva* (*World of Art*), in 1898. He also organized exhibitions of Russian art and concerts of Russian music. In 1911 Diaghilev founded the Ballet Russe de Diaghilev, which maintained its headquarters in Monte Carlo. The company toured Europe and overseas for 20 years, exposing audiences to the genius and talent of VASLAV NIJINSKY, LEONIDE MASSINE, and GEORGE BALANCHINE, who all worked for the company at one time. Artists Leon Bakst and PABLO PICASSO and composers ERIK SATIE and IGOR STRAVINSKY also played important roles in the success of Diaghilev's Ballet Russe.

An avant-gardist of the first order, Diaghilev strove to develop new sounds and sights that were distinct from traditional fare, and the luminaries he worked with helped him achieve that goal. At the same time, he is credited with bringing traditional Russian ballet to Europe and the United States. As an impresario he combined ruthlessness with charm. He was also a catalyst, unleashing the genius and talent of others and allowing them to create their finest works of art.

BOOKS ABOUT DIAGHILEV

Buckle, Richard. *Diaghilev*. Atheneum 1979 o.p.
Garafola, Lynn. *Diaghilev's Ballets Russes*. OUP 1989 $35.00. ISBN 0-19-505701-5
Haskell, Arnold, and Walter W. Nouvel. *Diaghileff: His Artistic and Private life*. Da Capo 1977 $9.95. ISBN 0-306-80085-3
Lifar, Serge. *Serge Diaghilev: His Life, His Work, His Legends*. Da Capo 1976 $32.50. ISBN 0-306-70839-6
MacDonald, Nesta. *Diaghilev Observed*. Princeton Bk. Co. 1975 $69.95. ISBN 0-903102-14-5
———. *Diaghilev Observed by Critics in England and the United States, 1911–1929*. Dance Horizons 1975 o.p. Transmits contemporaneous accounts of Diaghilev's performances and activities. Arranged chronologically and by performance.

DUNCAN, ISADORA. 1878–1927

A native of San Francisco, Isadora Duncan was known as an innovator and a first-generation pioneer of modern dance. A modernist whose lifestyle became even more visible and well known than her dancing, she was a feminist and lived her life as the legend it became.

Duncan's dancing was bold and innovative. She danced barefoot, often to the music of BEETHOVEN, WAGNER, and Gluck—music that was not originally intended as an accompaniment for the dance. Her costume was an adaptation of a Greek tunic, embellished with several colored shoulder scarves. Using natural flowing movements that emanated from her wrist, she weaved and whirled to express the emotions prompted by the music. Although Duncan established schools in Berlin, Paris, Moscow, and London, her dance technique was so improvisational, abstract, and personal that her many imitators were largely unsuccessful. They lacked her daring and dynamic personality. Duncan's accidental death in Paris was a tragedy mourned by the entire dance world.

BOOKS BY DUNCAN

Art of the Dance. Ed. by Sheldon Chevey. Routledge Chapman & Hall 1969 $19.95. ISBN 0-87830-005-8
Isadora Speaks. City Lights 1981 $5.95. ISBN 0-87286-133-3

My Life. Rprt. Serv. 1991 $79.00. ISBN 0-7812-8115-6. Autobiography, once considered
scandalous, lays bare aspects of the life and crusade of the artist in her advocacy of
serious modern dance.

BOOKS ABOUT DUNCAN

Desti, Mary. *The Untold Story: The Life of Isadora Duncan, 1921–1927*. Da Capo 1981
repr. of 1929 ed. $35.00. ISBN 0-306-76044-4
Loewenthal, Lillian. *The Search for Isadora: The Legend and the Legacy of Isadora
Duncan*. Princeton Bk. Co. 1992 $26.95. ISBN 0-87127-179-6
Schneider, Ilya I. *Isadora Duncan: The Russian Years*. Da Capo 1981 repr. of 1968 ed.
$6.95. ISBN 0-306-80142-6

FELD, ELIOT. 1942–

Dancer, choreographer, and director Eliot Feld was born in New York City.
He received his early ballet training at the School of American Ballet and
appeared in the title role of GEORGE BALANCHINE's *The Nutcracker* in its first
season in 1954. As a child he also performed in the musical *Sandhog* and with
the Pearl Lang Company while attending the High School of Performing Arts.

In 1963 Feld joined the American Ballet Theater and danced with that
company until 1970. While with the company, he choreographed three noted
works: *Harbinger* (1967), *At Midnight* (1967), and *Intermezzo* (1969). In 1969 he
formed his own company, the American Ballet Company, which made its debut
at the Spoleto Festival in Italy performing his *Cortège Burlesque* (1969) and
Meadow Lark (1968). Other notable works he created for his company include
The Consort (1970) and *The Gods Amused* (1971).

Following the dissolution of the American Ballet Company, Feld formed a
new company in 1974, The Eliot Feld Ballet. This company is one of the more
successful small dance companies in New York; it performed regularly at The
Public Theater until 1979 and has since found a permanent home at the Joyce
Theater.

FONTEYN, DAME MARGOT. 1919–1991

Born in Reigate, England, Margot Fonteyn (the stage name of Margaret
Hookham) is thought by many critics to have been the best British dancer of the
mid-twentieth century. Fonteyn began her career as a snowflake in a production
of *The Nutcracker* with the Vic-Wells Ballet in 1931. She remained with this
company, which later became the Royal Ballet, for her entire career. In 1935
she performed her first important role with the company as the lead in a revival
of FREDERICK ASHTON's *Rio Grande*. She created many roles with Ashton,
including *Le Baiser de la Fee* (1935), *The Haunted Ballroom* (1939), *Symphonic
Variations* (1946), and *The Fairy Queen* (1946). Fonteyn eventually became the
Royal Ballet's foremost prima ballerina. Especially notable was her partnering
with RUDOLPH NUREYEV during a creative partnership that became legendary. An
expressive, versatile performer, Fonteyn was the first ballerina of international
status developed by a British ballet school and company.

BOOK BY FONTEYN

Margot Fonteyn: Autobiography. Knopf 1976 o.p.

BOOK ABOUT FONTEYN

Stewart, Rachel. *Margot Fonteyn. Profiles Ser*. Trafalgar $11.95. ISBN 0-237-60033-1

FOSSE, BOB (ROBERT LOUIS). 1927–1987

Dancer, choreographer, and director Bob Fosse was born in Chicago, Illinois, the son of a vaudeville entertainer. As a teenager and a young man, Fosse performed in vaudeville, burlesque, and nightclubs. By the age of 23 he had made his Broadway debut in the musical revue *Dance Me a Song*. His first major success as a choreographer came with the witty "Steam Heat" number he created for *The Pajama Game* (1954). From that time on, he was much in demand as a choreographer, working on such shows as *Damn Yankees* (1955), *Bells Are Ringing* (1956), *Redhead* (1959), *How to Succeed in Business without Really Trying* (1961), *Little Me* (1963), *Sweet Charity* (1966), *Pippin* (1973), and *Dancing* (1978). Fosse also provided choreography for and directed the film versions of *Sweet Charity* and *Cabaret* (1972), and he choreographed, directed, and wrote the screenplay for the movie *All That Jazz* (1979). For his work, Fosse was honored with six Tony awards, an Oscar, and an Emmy.

Books about Fosse

Gottfried, Martin. *All His Jazz: The Life and Death of Bob Fosse*. Bantam 1990 $24.95. ISBN 0-553-0738-X
Grubb, Kevin B. *Razzle Dazzle: The Life and Work of Bob Fosse*. St. Martin 1991 $16.95. ISBN 0-312-05502-1

GRAHAM, MARTHA. 1894–1991

Not only is Martha Graham correctly identified as a pioneer of modern-dance, but also she must be termed the progenitor of modern dancers and modern-dance companies. More than 35 of her students and dancers have become noted choreographers or directors of dance companies.

Born in Pittsburgh, Pennsylvania, Graham trained in Los Angeles at the Denishawn School founded by RUTH ST. DENIS and TED SHAWN and danced with the Denishawn Company until 1926, when she made her independent debut in New York City. Her early work, such as *Lamentation* (1930), made a great contribution to the American Constructivist movement and to the development of modern dance. During the 1930s, Graham was influenced by Native American life and mythology, and this influence was evident throughout her career in such works as *Two Primitive Canticles*, *Primitive Mysteries*, *Ceremonials*, and *Appalachian Spring* (1958). Much of her work also reflects the early American pioneer spirit and is based on historical characters. This influence can be seen as the inspiration for such works as *American Provincials*, *Frontier* (1935), and *American Document*.

Graham used her own dance company not only as a showcase for her work but also to train dancers in her own method, which was to give physical substance to emotions and to use every aspect of the body and mind—movement, breathing, and muscular control—to dramatic purpose. Through the Martha Graham School of Contemporary Dance, her method of training has been widely adopted in dance schools and college dance programs throughout the world.

Book by Graham

The Notebook of Martha Graham. HarBraceJ 1973 o.p.

Books about Graham

Armitage, Merle. *Martha Graham: The Early Years*. Da Capo 1978 repr. of 1937 ed. $25.00. ISBN 0-306-79504-3

DeMille, Agnes. *Martha: The Life and Work of Martha Graham*. Random 1992 $15.00.
ISBN 0-679-74176-3
McDonagh, Don. *Martha Graham*. Greenwood 1974 o.p. First extensive biography.
Terry, Walter. *Frontiers of Dance: The Life of Martha Graham*. Crowell 1975 o.p.

HUMPHREY, DORIS. 1895–1958

A pioneer of modern dance, Doris Humphrey was born in Oak Park, Illinois.
Humphrey began dancing at the age of 8 and began a career as a teacher of
ballroom dance in Chicago in 1913. In 1917 she moved to Los Angeles, where
she worked with the Denishawn Company. She remained with this company
until 1927, dancing in the early "music visualizations" *Sedon Arabesque* (1917)
and *Sonata Pathetique* (1922) and choreographing her own first work, *Tragica*,
in 1920.

In 1927 Humphrey left the Denishawn Company with her dance partner
Charles Weidman and went to New York, where they formed their own
company the following year. The company performed for 16 years until arthritis
forced Humphrey to retire from dancing, at which time the company disbanded. During that time she also originated the Julliard Dance Theatre and ran
the Summer School of Dance at Bennington College (1934–42). She also
choreographed highly original works during this period, including *The Shakers*
(1931), *Theatre Piece* (1935), and *With My Red Fires* (1936). These works helped
build the foundation for the philosophy of modern dance.

After her retirement, Humphrey continued to choreograph for a number of
companies, including one founded by one of her most talented students, JOSÉ
LIMÓN. One of the works she created for the Limón company, *Day on Earth*, is
considered by many to be one of the quintessential works for modern dance.
She also served as artistic director of the Limón company from 1946 until her
death. Humphrey's book *The Art of Making Dances* (1959) is a rigorous work still
used by those who work in modern and postmodern dance.

BOOKS BY HUMPHREY

The Art of Making Dances. Princeton Bk. Co. 1991 repr. of 1959 ed. $14.95. ISBN 0-87127-
158-3
Doris Humphrey: The Collected Works. Dance Notation Bureau 1978 $125.00. ISBN 0-
932582-00-1

BOOK ABOUT HUMPHREY

Siegel, Marcia B. *Days on Earth: The Dance of Doris Humphrey*. Yale U. Pr. 1987 $35.00.
ISBN 0-300-03856-9

JAQUES-DALCROZE, ÉMILE. 1865-1950

Born in Vienna, Émile Jaques-Dalcroze was a composer whose gift of dance
arose from exercises he devised to teach rhythm by translating sounds into
physical movements. This technique became known as the Dalcroze method, or
eurhythmics. He educated many followers, who, in turn, have passed his
methods on through many generations. There are Dalcroze schools around the
globe.

BOOK BY DALCROZE

Eurhythmics, Art and Education. Ayer repr. of 1930 ed. o.p.

Book about Dalcroze

Findlay, Elsa. *Rhythm and Movement: Applications of Dalcroze Eurhythmics.* Sumy-Birchard 1971 $12.95. ISBN 0-87487-078-X

JOFFREY, ROBERT. 1930–1988

Born Abdullah Jaffa Bey Khan in Seattle, Washington, choreographer and dance-company director Robert Joffrey was the son of an Afghani immigrant and an Italian-born mother. Joffrey began studying ballet at the age of 8. In 1948 he moved to New York City, where he studied with Alexandra Fedorova and at George Balanchine's School of American Ballet. Joffrey's short performance career began in Seattle in 1949, with a solo concert of his own works, and continued through 1952, with performances with Roland Petit's Ballets de Paris (1949) and the May O'Donnell Concert Group (1950–52). From 1950 to 1955, he taught at New York's High School of the Performing Arts.

More interested in choreographing and directing than in performing, Joffrey formed his first small dance company, the Robert Joffrey Ballet Concert, in 1954. In 1956 he formed the Robert Joffrey Ballet with childhood friend Gerald Arpino as collaborator, choreographer, and codirector. This company became known as the City Center Joffrey Ballet in 1966, and its name was later changed to the Joffrey Ballet.

The Joffrey Ballet has become one of America's major ballet companies, producing works by Joffrey himself, Arpino, and revivals of works by a number of artists, including Frederick Ashton and Leonide Massine. The company is noted for its eclectic repertoire, drawing upon the classics, new works, and fusions of modern dance and ballet. Joffrey's own most notable works include *Pas des Dèéses* (1954), *Gamelan* (1962), *Astarte* (1967), *Remembrances* (1973), *Beautiful Dreamer* (1975), and *Postcards* (1980). Joffrey also worked extensively as an opera choreographer, particularly during the 1960s at the New York City Opera. Among the operas he staged are Carlisle Floyd's *Susannah* (1959), Douglas Moore's *The Wings of the Dove* (1961), and Marc Blitzstein's *Regina* (1959). Since Joffrey's death in 1988, the Joffrey Ballet has continued to perform, most notably with annual concerts in New York and Los Angeles.

Book about Joffrey

Horosko, Manan, and Judith Kupersmith. *The Dancer's Survival Manual: Everything You Need to Know About Being a Dancer . . . Except How to Dance.* HarpC 1987 $10.95. ISBN 0-06-096199-6

KIRSTEIN, LINCOLN. 1907–

Lincoln Kirstein first became involved in dance as a spectator and then moved to writing about dance, an occupation that he has continued throughout his life.

Kirstein is considered by many to be the American authority on dance. He contributed more than any other contemporary American toward the development of theatrical dance in the United States. He is also credited with bringing Japanese theater to the United States.

During the 1930s and 1940s, Kirstein founded and directed numerous ballet schools and companies, including the School of American Ballet, New York (1934), the American Ballet (1935), the Ballet Caravan (1936), and the Ballet Society (1946). He was also the founding director of *The Dance Index.*

BOOKS BY KIRSTEIN

Ballet: Bias and Belief. Princeton Bk. Co. $39.95. ISBN 0-817127-133-8. Introduction by Nancy Reynolds.
Quarry: A Collection in Lieu of Memoirs by Lincoln Kirstein. Twelve Trees Pr. 1986 $35.00. ISBN 0-942642-27-9

LABAN, RUDOLF. 1879–1958

Born in Slovakia, Rudolf Laban was the inventor of the dance-notation system. Laban is celebrated because of his unique dance-notation system, which not only conveys notions of shape and direction but also of movement and energy levels needed to perform the movements. Labanotation, or Kinetographic Laban, or Effort/Shape notation, is used not only for dance notation but also for kinesthetic studies in psychological treatments, as well as industrial-efficiency studies. Ironically, Laban is thought to have been an important European modern dancer, though little research has been done to document this.

BOOKS BY LABAN

Laban's Principles of Dance and Movement Notation. (coauthored with Rod Lange). Princeton Bk. Co. 1975 $14.95. ISBN 0-7121-1648-6
A Life for Dance: The Autobiography of Rudolf Laban. Princeton Bk. Co. 1975 $19.95. ISBN 0-7121-1231-6

BOOKS ABOUT LABAN

Hutchinson, Ann. *Labanotation: The System of Analyzing and Recording Movement.* Routledge Chapman & Hall rev. ed. 1970 $17.95. ISBN 0-87830-527-0
Ullmann, Lisa. *A Vision of Dynamic Space, Rudolf Laban.* Taylor & Francis 1984 $31.00. ISBN 1-85000-008-5

LIMÓN, JOSÉ (ARCADIO). 1908–1972

José Limón, whom many consider to be the greatest performer in the history of modern dance, was born in Culiacán, Mexico. As a dancer and choreographer, he greatly expanded the repertoire of modern dance with works exploring the human character and its strengths and weaknesses. He had an extraordinary ability to communicate with the audience, and his stage presence imbued any movement, from the tiniest gesture to the grandest action, with riveting power.

Limón came to the United States as a young man to study art. In 1930, however, he began studying dance with DORIS HUMPHREY and Charles Weidman and became one of the leading dancers of their company. In 1945 he formed his own dance company, with Humphrey as artistic director. His first major work, *The Moor's Pavane* (1949), expressed magnificently the jealousy, rage, and remorse of SHAKESPEARE's (see Vol. 1) Othello within the context of dance. Much of Limón's choreography derived from natural gesture and was intended to express human dignity, grandeur, and nobility. He drew his themes from history, literature, and religion. His works were also characterized by a well-defined structure and form. In addition to *The Moor's Pavane*, his most celebrated works include *La Malinche* (1949), *Exiles* (1950), *Emperor Jones* (1956), *The Apostate* (1959), *A Choreographic Offering* (1962), and *The Winged* (1966).

The 1950s and 1960s were Limón's most prolific period as a choreographer, and he continued dancing until 1969. His dance company, The José Limón

Dance Company, survived the death of its founder in 1972 and continues to perform within the United States and around the world.

MARTINS, PETER. 1946–

At 6 feet 2 inches, Peter Martins towers over most of his dance contemporaries. He is one of a few tall dancers who can project grace and elegance in the classical body line. Born in Copenhagen, Denmark, Martins began studying dance at the Royal Danish Ballet School when he was 8 years old. By the age of 20, he had become a principal dancer with the Royal Danish Ballet, dancing roles in many of the works created for the company by the great choreographer AUGUST BOURNONVILLE.

In 1967 Martins came to the attention of GEORGE BALANCHINE when he filled in for one of the New York City Ballet's dancers at the Edinburgh Festival. Three years later, after several guest appearances with the company, he emigrated to the United States and joined the New York City Ballet. Among the first roles created for Martins by Balanchine were in *Stravinsky Violin Concerto* (1972) and the *Duo Concertant* (1972). Martins danced with ballerina Kay Mazzo in both productions, and the pair became one of the most exciting dance partnerships of the decade.

Martins retired from dancing in 1983 in order to devote his energy full time to choreography. That same year, however, Balanchine died, and Martins stepped into his place at the New York City Ballet, sharing the directorship of the company with JEROME ROBBINS. In the years since, he has struggled to maintain Balanchine's high standards for the company. Among his recent successes has been a thorough revival of the Balanchine reportory, including many of the lesser-known works. Martin's son Nilas is also a dancer with the New York City Ballet.

BOOKS BY MARTINS

Far From Denmark. (coauthored with Robert Cornfield). Little 1982 o.p.
Peter Martins. (coauthored with Martha Swope and Arthur Todd). Princeton Bk. Co. 1975 o.p.

BOOK ABOUT MARTINS

Caras, Steven. *Peter Martins, Prince of the Dance.* Abrams 1986 o.p. Introduction by Francis Mason.

MASSINE, LÉONIDE. 1896–1979

Russian dancer and choreographer Léonide Massine was born in Moscow and studied at the ballet school of the Imperial Theatres in St. Petersburg. During the early years of DIAGHILEV's Ballet Russe, Massine became a principal dancer with the company and also choreographed a number of works, including *Parade* (1917) and *La Boutique fantasque* (1919). After the breakup of the Ballet Russe, Massine worked occasionally in America before settling in Europe, where he worked for such companies as Sadler's Wells and Ballets des Champs Elysées. In addition to his work on the stage, he appeared in the two noted ballet films *The Red Shoes* (1948) and *The Tales of Hoffman* (1950).

As both a dancer and choreographer, Massine employed facial and body gestures from vaudeville, the circus, and the cinema. His choreographic ideas are so much a part of ballet today that they seem almost old-fashioned. During the height of his creative powers in the 1930s, Massine was lauded as the greatest choreographer in Europe.

BOOK BY MASSINE

Massine on Choreography: Theory and Exercises in Composition. Faber & Faber 1977 o.p.

MORRIS, MARK. 1956–

Born in Seattle, Washington, dancer and choreographer Mark Morris became interested in music and dance at an early age and was encouraged to pursue these interests by his parents. He began studying dance at the age of 8 and quickly absorbed the rudiments of flamenco, folk, modern dance, and ballet. By his early teens, he was already choreographing short pieces for his dancing-school recitals. Following graduation from high school, Morris traveled through Europe, settling for a time in Madrid, where he continued his training in Spanish dance. He left Spain in 1975, however, because of his dislike for the homophobia of the Franco regime and the furtiveness of gay life in Madrid. Upon returning to the United States, he settled in New York, where he performed briefly with the Eliot Feld Ballet and as a guest dancer with a number of dance companies.

In 1981 Morris formed his own company, the Mark Morris Dance Group. One of the most gifted choreographers in modern dance, Morris has produced a number of notable works for his company, including *Castor and Pollux* (1981), *Songs That Tell a Story* (1982), *O Rangasayee* (1984), *Sonata for Clarinet and Piano* (1988), *Fantasy* (1988), and *Strict Songs* (1988). Morris's taste in music is eclectic, and he has choreographed works to an unusually wide range of compositions, from baroque to punk rock. Especially unique to Morris is the straightforward "gayness" of some of his works. He often abandons gender-determined roles as well, having both men and women share partnering responsibilities and sometimes having dancers of the same sex partner each other. Typical of his more recent works is their complex choreographic structure, the musical detail, and their tongue-in-cheek humor.

NIJINSKA, BRONISLAVA. 1891–1972

Bronislava Nijinska was a Russian-born ballet dancer and choreographer. She was the daughter of two ballet dancers. Nijinska was enrolled in the Imperial Ballet School in St. Petersburg with her brother VASLAV NIJINSKY. Her teachers were Enrico Cecchetti, Mikhail Fokine, and Nicholai Legat. She joined SERGE DIAGHILEV's Ballet Russe in 1909 and from that time on danced important roles in *Le Carnival, L'Après-midi d'un Faune, Pétrouchka, Les Sylphides,* and *Prince Igor.* For Diaghilev she choreographed *Les Noces, Le Train Bleu,* and *Romeo et Julliette,* the only woman to do so. Later she created the dances for Max Reinhardt's American film *A Midsummer Night's Dream.* Renowned for her timeless abstractions, she choreographed works for a number of international companies through the 1960s.

BOOK BY NIJINSKA

Bronislava Nijinska: Early Memoirs. Duke 1992 $18.95. ISBN 0-8223-1295-6

BOOK ABOUT NIJINSKA

Van Norman Baer, Nancy. *Bronislava Nijinska: A Dancer's Legacy.* Fine Arts Mus. 1986 $14.95. ISBN 0-88401-048-1

NIJINSKY, VASLAV. 1890-1950

Considered by many to be the greatest male dancer of the twentieth century, Vaslav Nijinsky danced for only 12 years. Born in Kiev, Nijinsky began his studies in Moscow and continued them at the Imperial Ballet School in St. Petersburg. His first appearance was at the Maryinski Theatre. Introduced to Western audiences as a principal dancer with DIAGHILEV's Ballet Russe, he became enormously popular. His prodigious technical skills, coupled with intelligence, style, and bearing, made him the most famous dancer of his time. He also had an instinctive sense of theater and a talent with make-up, enabling him to create a whole gallery of characters and stage personae. One of his most notable roles with the Ballet Russe was that of Petrouchka in IGOR STRAVINSKY's ballet of the same name. Although he choreographed only a few works, two in particular were both revolutionary and masterworks—*L'Après-midi d'un Faune* (1912) and *La Sacre du Printemps* (1913).

Interned in Hungary during the early years of World War I, Nijinsky rejoined the Ballet Russe after the war. He suffered a mental breakdown in 1917, however, and was diagnosed as a paranoid schizophrenic. His career cut tragically short by insanity, he spent the remainder of his life in retirement in England and Switzerland. Despite his brief career, he has become a legendary figure in the world of dance.

BOOKS ABOUT NIJINSKY

Krasovskaya, Vera. *Nijinsky*. Trans. by John E. Bowlt. Schirmer Bks. 1979 o.p. Literary, not scientific, biography.

Nijinsky, Romola. *The Diary of Vaslav Nijinsky*. U. CA Pr. 1968 $9.95. ISBN 0-520-00945-2

———. *Last Years of Nijinsky*. AMS Pr. 1968 repr. of 1952 ed. $16.00. ISBN 0-404-04775-0

Whitworth, Geoffrey. *Art of Nijinsky*. Ayer repr. of 1913 ed. $20.00. ISBN 0-405-09073-0

NOVERRE, JEAN-GEORGES. 1727–1810

Jean-Georges Noverre was a French theorist of ballet and choreography. Connected through his teachers, Jean-Denis Dupré and Louis Dupré, he performed at the court of Frederick the Great in Berlin in 1745 and became ballet master in Marseilles around 1748. Noverre also performed and created works for London audiences. Noverre developed many of the principles that govern ballet to the present day. He was also the first to advocate reform in stage costumes. He is credited with creating *ballet d'action*. He is best remembered now for his *Letters on Dancing and Ballet* (1760), in which he describes the responsibilities of a ballet master, addresses theories of dance, and offers practical advice on staging, acoustics, and stage architecture.

BOOK BY NOVERRE

Letters on Dancing and Ballet. Princeton Bk. Co. 1966 $14.95. ISBN 0-87127-006-4

NUREYEV, RUDOLPH. 1939–1993

Rudolph Nureyev was one of the most widely recognized ballet stars of the twentieth century. Born in Siberia, Nureyev trained first as a folk dancer and then studied ballet at the Leningrad Choreographic School. He danced with the Kirov Ballet until 1961, when he defected to the West while on tour, the first of the modern defections that plagued the Kirov Ballet. Granted political asylum in Paris, Nureyev became a member of Le Grand Ballet du Marquis de Cuevas. Nureyev's independence and fiery temperament were not well suited to a single company, however, and he began to appear as a guest artist with many of the most prominent dance companies of the world. His brilliant dancing and electrifying stage presence captivated audiences everywhere.

In 1962 Nureyev made his debut at Covent Garden dancing with the Royal Ballet star MARGOT FONTEYN. The two went on to become one of the most renowned partnerships in dance during the 1960s and 1970s. During the 1980s, Nureyev began to dance less, and in 1983 he became the director of the Paris Opera Ballet. While there, he caused a stir on numerous occasions as a result of rather daring programming decisions. Passionately committed to his art, Nureyev would not retire from dancing completely. He continued to perform throughout the 1980s and early 1990s, despite criticism that he was becoming too old and that his technique was suffering. In 1993 Nureyev showed signs of grave illness, and he died that same year as a result of AIDS. With his death, the dance world lost one of its most brilliant performers.

BOOK BY NUREYEV

Nureyev: An Autobiography with Pictures. NAL-Dutton 1963 o.p.

BOOK ABOUT NUREYEV

Barnes, Clive. *Nureyev.* Helene Obolensky Ent. 1982 $35.00. ISBN 0-9609736-2-1

PAVLOVA, ANNA. 1881–1931

Anna Pavlova was a child star; she was considered to be the superb lyricist of her generation. She was inspired to become a ballet dancer after seeing a performance of *Sleeping Beauty* at the Maryinski Theatre. She attended the Imperial School in St. Petersburg and worked with Mikhail Fokine before SERGE DIAGHILEV engaged Pavlova for the debut season of the Ballets Russes. Pavlova achieved ballerina status in 1906. One year later, Fokine devised *The Dying Swan* for Pavlova. After leaving Diaghilev's company, Pavlova formed her own troupe and toured worldwide for more than 20 years.

Pavlova died suddenly of pneumonia just before her fiftieth birthday. In 1936 Pavlova's husband made a film, *The Immortal Swan,* about his wife's life and career. Many consider Pavlova to have been the definition of the perfect female dancer. She inspired a love of dance in everyone who saw her, including FREDERICK ASHTON, who became interested in dance after he saw Pavlova in Lima, Peru, when he was 14 years old.

BOOKS ABOUT PAVLOVA

Lazzarini, John, and Roberta Lazzarini. *Pavlova: Repertoire of a Legend.* Schirmer Bks. 1980 o.p. An annotated photographic biography.
Money, Keith. *Anna Pavlova: Her Life and Art.* Knopf 1982 o.p. Extensive; includes translations of newspaper and journal articles.
Franks, A. H., ed. *Pavlova: A Collection of Memoirs.* Da Capo 1981 repr. of 1956 ed. $6.95. ISBN 0-306-80149-3

ROBBINS, JEROME. 1918–

Choreographer, theatrical director, and dancer Jerome Robbins was born in New York City. He began his career during the 1940s dancing with the American Ballet Theatre and in Broadway musicals. His first major roles for the American Ballet Theatre were in the productions *Helen of Troy* and *Romeo and Juliet.* After four years dancing with the company, he decided to focus on choreography, and *Fancy Free* (1944) was his first major work.

In 1949 Robbins joined the New York City Ballet, dancing in several BALANCHINE ballets and choreographing 9 ballets in 10 years. During that time he also worked on a variety of Broadway shows, including his first, *On the Town* (1944) (which was derived from the popular *Fancy Free*), *The King and I* (1951), *Peter Pan* (1954), and the hugely successful *West Side Story* (1957). Other Broadway successes included *Gypsy* (1959) and *Fiddler on the Roof* (1964).

Robbins returned to New York City Ballet in 1969 when he choreographed *Dances at a Gathering* for the company. Since that time he has remained with the company, adding his own works to the repertory and serving as joint ballet master and codirector with Peter Martins after the death of George Balanchine in 1983. The works he has created for New York City Ballet combine classical ballet with more earthy folk styles. In addition to *Dances at a Gathering*, his most well-known ballet works include *The Goldberg Variations* (1971), *Watermill* (1972), *Piano Concerto in G* (1975), and *Glass Pieces* (1983). Robbins won two Oscars in 1961 for the film version of *West Side Story*.

BOOK BY ROBBINS

Jerome Robbins Broadway. H. Leonard Pub. Corp. 1990 $12.95. ISBN 0-88188-829-X

ROGERS, GINGER. 1911–

A dancer in American theater and film as well as an actress, Ginger Rogers began her career in vaudeville, which led to engagements in Broadway shows. She co-starred in George Gershwin's *Girl Crazy* (1930), and that role led to Hollywood contracts. Blessed with a comedic gift and the willingness to engage it, Rogers played opposite Fred Astaire, offsetting his sophisticated presentation while matching his dancing skill. Among the many films in which she starred are *Gay Divorcee*, *Top Hat*, *Kitty Foyle*, and *Monkey Business*.

BOOK BY ROGERS

Ginger: My Story. HarpC 1991 $22.00. ISBN 0-06-018308-X

BOOK ABOUT ROGERS

Dickens, Homer C. *The Films of Ginger Rogers.* Carol Pub. Group 1975 $14.00. ISBN 0-8065-0496-X

ST. DENIS, RUTH. 1879–1968

Ruth St. Denis (originally Ruth Denis) was born in Somerville, New Jersey, the daughter of an inventor and farmer. At an early age, she began performing in vaudeville and became known for exotic and colorful Eastern dances. In 1914 she married dancer Ted Shawn and, a year later, the two founded a dance school and company known as Denishawn in Los Angeles. The company toured the United States until 1931, when St. Denis and Shawn separated and the company folded. After this breakup, St. Denis continued dancing well into her eighties.

In her work, St. Denis was strongly influenced by the theories of French theoretician and singing teacher Francois Delsarte and the American producer and playwright David Belasco. Her works are characterized by exoticism, richness, and magnificence. It has been suggested by some critics that she adopted elements of foreign cultures and incorporated them in her dances with no particular comprehension of either the cultures or the place of the abstracted elements.

BOOK BY ST. DENIS

Ruth St. Denis: An Unfinished Life. AMS Pr. repr. of 1939 ed. $42.50. ISBN 0-404-18075-2. Autobiographical, but with substantial material on the precursors of modern dance.

BOOK ABOUT ST. DENIS

Shelton, Suzanne. *Divine Dancer: A Biography of Ruth St. Denis.* Doubleday 1981 o.p.

SHAWN, TED. 1891–1972

Born in Kansas City, Missouri, dancer and director Ted Shawn originally studied theology and had no thought of becoming a dancer. After suffering from diphtheria, however, he took up dancing in order to strengthen his legs. While in New York City in 1914, Shawn met dancer RUTH ST. DENIS, and the two were married shortly after. The next year, Shawn and St. Denis founded Denishawn, a dance school and company that became well known throughout the United States. Hollywood studios often looked to Denishawn for dance talent, and the school offered a varied curriculum of dance classes, from ballet to Eastern dance, throughout the country. The collaboration of Shawn and St. Denis produced a dancing style that amalgamated a kind of exhibitionistic ballroom style with Greek and Asian influences.

After Shawn and St. Denis separated in 1931, Shawn moved to a farm in Massachusetts and formed a small dance company called Ted Shawn and His Men Dancers. The company toured the United States until 1941, presenting a variety of works, many of which were inspired by Native American culture and others of which were influenced by modernist dance from Germany that focused on themes associated with power, force, and energy. Later in the 1940s, Shawn's farm became the home of Jacob's Pillow, a summer dance school and festival.

BOOK ABOUT SHAWN

Terry, Walter. *Ted Shawn: Father of American Dance.* Dial 1976 o.p.

TAYLOR, PAUL. 1930–

Modern dancer and choreographer Paul Taylor was born in Wilkinsburg, Pennsylvania. As a youth, Taylor excelled in sports and entered Syracuse University in 1947 on a swimming scholarship. His interest changed to dance, however, and in 1952 he entered the Julliard School, where he studied modern dance with MARTHA GRAHAM, DORIS HUMPHREY, and JOSÉ LIMÓN and ballet with ANTONY TUDOR and Margaret Craske.

Taylor began his professional career in 1953, dancing with the Martha Graham company, where he created such roles as Aegisthus in *Clytemnestra* (1958) and Hercules in *Alcestis* (1960). He also performed in works by other noted choreographers, including Charles Weidman, MERCE CUNNINGHAM, and GEORGE BALANCHINE, who created a special solo for him in his ballet *Episodes* (1959).

Taylor began choreographing his own work in 1954 and formed the Paul Taylor Dance Company that same year. Since that time, he has created numerous works for his company. Some of his best-known dances are *Aureole* (1962), *Esplanade* (1975), *Runes* (1975), *Cloven Kingdom* (1976), *Big Bertha* (1970), *Airs* (1978), and *Arden Court* (1981). One of the most productive, imaginative, and musical choreographers of his generation, Taylor is known for his use of a wide variety of movement styles and the rare sense of humor displayed in many of his dances. Taylor retired from dancing in the 1970s but has continued to devote all of his talent and energy to his very popular dance company.

BOOK BY TAYLOR

Private Domain. Knopf 1987 $22.95. ISBN 0-394-51683-4

THARP, TWYLA. 1941–

Modern dancer and choreographer Twyla Tharp was born in Portland, Indiana. As a child, Tharp was an accomplished musician, dancer, and athlete. In the early 1960s, she went to New York City to study dance, and she performed with the Paul Taylor Dance Company from 1963 to 1965. Then, in 1965, she formed her own small company, focusing her efforts on choreographing severe modern-dance works.

As both a dancer and a choreographer, Tharp is noted for her ability to create dance with a popular appeal without losing integrity or depth. Although her first works were rather somber and highly structured in style, her later works have often captured a more whimsical note. *Eight Jelly Rolls* (1971), for example, delighted audiences with its dancing set to the jazz piano music of "Jelly Roll" Morton. Other enormously popular works include *Coupe* (1973), a piece set to music by the Beach Boys, and *Push Comes to Shove* (1976), which was choreographed for the ballet star MIKHAIL BARYSHNIKOV.

In addition to creating works for her own company, Tharp has created commissioned pieces for a number of other dance companies, for films, and for nondancers in such other entertainment fields as ice-skating and sports. These works include *Bach Partita* (1984), created for American Ballet Theatre, *When We Were Very Young* (1980) and *The Catherine Wheel* (1983), created for Broadway, and dance numbers created for the films *Hair* (1979) and *White Knights* (1985).

BOOK BY THARP

Push Comes to Shove: An Autobiography. Bantam 1992 $24.50. ISBN 0-553-07306-0. An illuminating self-portrait of this important choreographer; describes a dancer's struggle for artistic and personal growth.

TUDOR, ANTONY. 1909–1987

British dancer and choreographer Antony Tudor was born in London and worked in a city meat market while studying dance with the Polish-born British ballerina Marie Rambert. In 1930 he became stage manager of Rambert's Ballet Club, which provided him with not only financial security but also the opportunity to continue his training and perform with the company. Tudor's first choreographed works were created for the Ballet Club, including *Cross Garter'd* (1931), *Lilac Garden* (1936), and *Dark Elegies* (1937).

During the early 1940s, American choreographer AGNES DE MILLE persuaded Tudor to move to New York City, where he became staff choreographer for the Ballet Theatre (known as the American Ballet Theatre since 1956). Among his triumphs with the company were *Romeo and Juliet* and *Pillar of Fire*. After 10 years with the Ballet Theatre, Tudor devoted his time primarily to teaching at the Metropolitan Opera Ballet School and the Julliard School of Music. He continued, however, to be a guest artist with both the American Ballet Theatre and the Royal Swedish Ballet.

Tudor's choreographic talent resulted in a number of memorable works for the American Ballet Theatre in the 1960s, including *Echoing of Trumpets* (1963) and *Shadowplay,* and again in the 1970s with *The Leaves Are Fading* (1975) and *The Tiller in the Fields* (1978). Tudor's impact is often compared with that of FREDERICK ASHTON and GEORGE BALANCHINE. Although his choreographic output was small compared with these and other artists, he is considered by many to be one of the great choreographers of the twentieth century.

BOOKS ABOUT TUDOR

Percival, John. *Antony Tudor.* 2 vols. Dance Perspectives 1963 o.p.
Permutter, Donna. *Shadowplay: The Life of Antony Tudor.* Viking Penguin 1991 $24.95. ISBN 0-670-83937-X

ULANOVA, GALINA. 1910–

A Russian ballerina, Galina Ulanova studied in St. Petersburg and made her debut in *Les Sylphides* with the Kirov Ballet. In 1944 she joined the Bolshoi Ballet and became the leading ballerina of the Soviet Union, a four-time winner of the Stalin Prize, and recipient of the Lenin Prize in 1957. Ulanova is best known for the prima ballerina roles in *Swan Lake, Raymonda, Don Quixote,* and *Giselle,* the latter being her best-known role through the release of a film in the United States. She retired from dancing in 1962 but continued to teach at the Bolshoi. Many critics consider her the leading ballerina of the mid-twentieth century.

BOOK BY ULANOVA

The Making of a Ballerina. Foreign Languages Pub. Hse. o.p.

BOOK ABOUT ULANOVA

Kahn, Albert E. *Days with Ulanova: An Intimate Portrait of the Legendary Russian Ballerina.* Ayer 1980 $49.50. ISBN 0-8369-9297-0

CHAPTER 19

Art and Architecture

Judith Holliday

> A sheet of paper so shocks me that as soon as it is on the easel I am forced to scrawl on it with charcoal or pencil, or anything else, and the process gives it life.
>
> —ODILON REDON, *Artists on Art*

The enormous increase in writing on art and in illustrated art books is a phenomenon of the twentieth century. It reflects not only the central role of art in the human experience but also a growing interest in past beauty, a critical concern with the varied, fast-changing, and often problematic art of the present, and a wondering about the future. Everything we see and touch is to some degree art: a table, a picture, a house, an entire city. It started with cave drawings, but it will not end with skyscraper design. Art books existed in antiquity: in Greece, in Rome, and in China. In the Western world, writing on art started in earnest with the Italian Renaissance (although the medieval scholastics had much to say about beauty). A particularly rich literature developed on architecture (LEON BATTISTA ALBERTI (see Vol. 2), who also wrote magnificently on painting and sculpture; SEBASTIANO SERLIO; ANDREA PALLADIO; GIACOMO BAROZZI DA VIGNOLA). With the advent of sophisticated printing techniques, as engraving and etching replaced the more simple woodcut, the book with illustrations took over. Often the book on art was itself a work of art. The eighteenth century was particularly rich in art publications of the most elaborate kind. The nineteenth century witnessed the rise of new graphic techniques, lithography above all, followed by the great breakthrough into photography. All of this resulted in a vast new literature in the arts. Great encyclopedias and their more modest cousins, dictionaries, came into being. Pattern books and how-to books—with deep roots in the past—appeared in great numbers, with all the new styles, materials, and techniques they could now offer. The nineteenth century also saw the beginning of art history as a discipline and as a branch of art literature—art not as a present-day activity, but as a treasure of the past, a key to the past, a historic phenomenon.

Art theory is another branch of art literature. What is art all about? Why art? What is great art? And, for that matter, what is bad art? Closely related to art theory is art criticism, particularly in the twentieth century, where a history of contemporary art is of necessity also a critique and a selection. The biography of artists is another important category of art literature, with a tradition going back to Giorgio Vasari and the Renaissance.

Architecture stands somewhat apart, because it is both an art and a utilitarian pursuit; some buildings may not be art, but all must be structurally sound. The books on architecture listed in this chapter deal with architecture primarily as an art; titles on architectural engineering are not included, although, of course, most books on architecture contain some practical elements—as does the very first of all such treatises, by the Roman Vitruvius in the first century B.C.

The literature on the decorative arts—furniture, glass, metalwork, and so on—also stresses practical considerations. Titles in this field are listed separately from painting and sculpture. Although the list is by no means exhaustive, most of the basic books are included, as well as many of those dealing with a specific area, such as furniture design. In this literature, theory and criticism seem less central, and many of the publications are directed toward the amateur, the lover of art objects, and the collector.

The books listed in this chapter are more than a cross-section. They represent a broad selection of the most important books encompassing *all* of the arts—painting, sculpture, architecture, the graphic arts, and decoration—as well as those on the specifics of theory, history, style, country, and social background: criticism as well as practice. The most comprehensive history of art in the English language is the *Pelican History of Art*. Each volume is by a different eminent author and deals with a different specific subject; for example, *Architecture: 19th and 20th Centuries*, by Henry-Russell Hitchcock, or *Art and Architecture in Italy, 1600–1800*, by Rudolf Wittkower. These volumes are not listed individually. A good art library should have all of them. For current periodical literature, see the *Art Index*.

ART

General Reading List

Alperson, Philip, ed. *The Philosophy of the Visual Arts*. OUP 1992 $29.95. ISBN 0-19-505975-1

Arnheim, Rudolf. *Art and Visual Perception: A Psychology of the Creative Eye*. U. CA Pr. 2nd rev. ed. 1974 $37.50. ISBN 0-520-02327-7. Explains the dynamics of perception, focusing on the complex relationship between the eye and the creative mind.

Arntzen, Etta, and Robert Rainwater. *Guide to the Literature of Art History*. ALA 1981 $32.50. ISBN 0-8389-0263-4. The most comprehensive bibliography of art literature available; a highly scholarly tool.

The Art Index: A Cumulative Author and Subject Index to a Selected List of Fine Arts Periodicals and Museum Bulletins. Wilson 1929–present. Issued quarterly with annual cumulations. Vols. 1–8 1929–1953 $190.00 ea. ISBN 0-685-22229-2. Vols. 9–28 1953–1985 $225.00 ea. ISBN 0-685-22230-6. Vols. 29–34 1986–1992. ISBN 0-685-22231-1. Available in paper copy, CD-ROM, and on-line through WILSONLINE. The basic periodical index for art research.

Clark, Kenneth. *What Is a Masterpiece?* Thames Hudson 1992 $7.95. ISBN 0-500-27206-9. Noted critic defines "masterpiece" for the layman and discusses common characteristics of selected masterworks.

Cleaver, Dale G. *Art: An Introduction*. HB Coll. Pubs. 1988 $35.25. ISBN 0-15-503434-0. General introduction for the novice to the visual arts; examines a variety of genres.

Covert, Nadine, ed. *Art on Screen: A Directory of Films and Videos about the Visual Arts*. G. K. Hall 1992 $35.00. ISBN 0-8161-0538-3. Catalogues documentaries on visual arts and high-quality feature films on art-related subjects. A useful reference for educators.

De la Croix, Horst, and others. *Gardner's Art Through the Ages*. HB Coll. Pubs. 1990 $54.75. ISBN 0-15-503769-2. The most useful of the older general surveys. Revised many times.

Dreyfuss, Henry. *Symbol Sourcebook: An Authoritative Guide to International Graphic Symbols*. Van Nos. Reinhold 1984 $29.95. ISBN 0-442-21806-0. Identifies hundreds of graphic symbols of the sort used to direct traffic, indicate restrooms, and so on. Proposes increased use of these symbols.

Ehrenzweig, Anton. *The Hidden Order of Art: A Study in the Psychology of Artistic Imagination.* U. CA Pr. 1967 $14.95. ISBN 0-520-03845-2. A study in the psychology of artistic imagination.

Elsen, Albert E. *Purposes of Art: An Introduction to the History and Appreciation of Art.* HB Coll. Pubs. 1981 $41.25. ISBN 0-03-049766-3. Basic introductory text, organized by theme rather than chronology. Attempts to increase the readers appreciation of art.

Encyclopedia of World Art. 17 vols. J. Heraty Assocs. 1961–1987 Vols. 1,6,7,9,16,17 $100.00 ea. Vols. 2-5, 8, 10-15 o.p. Vol. 16 and 17 are supplements. The most comprehensive and far-ranging encyclopedia in the arts.

Fichner-Rathus, Lois. *Understanding Art.* P-H 1991 $38.50. ISBN 0-13-932203-5

Gombrich, E. H. *The Story of Art.* P-H 15th rev. ed. 1989 $44.67. ISBN 0-13-849852-0. One of the most learned and sophisticated general texts.

Gowling, Lawrence. *The Encyclopedia of Visual Art.* 10 vols. P-H 1989 $279.00. ISBN 0-85229-187-6. Volume 1 is a history of art; Volume 2 is a biographical dictionary of artists that is international in scope and richly illustrated.

Hall, James. *Dictionary of Subjects and Symbols in Art.* HarpC 1979 $14.00. ISBN 0-06-430100-1. Explains classical and Christian themes to enhance the layperson's understanding of art from the Renaissance onward.

Hartt, Frederick. *Art: A History of Painting, Sculpture, Architecture.* P-H 1993 $27.95. ISBN 0-13-047374-X. Sets forth a chronological survey of American and European art; separate section on Asian art.

Hauser, Arnold. *The Social History of Art.* 4 vols. Random 1957–58 $12.95 ea. ISBNs 0-394-70114-3, 0-394-70115-1, 0-394-70116-X, 0-394-70117-8. Treats economic and social forces that have shaped the history of art.

Hobbs, Jack A. *Art in Context.* HB Coll. Pubs. 1990 $35.25. ISBN 0-15-503472-3. Teaches the layperson to look at art in its social and historical context.

Holt, Elizabeth. *A Documentary History of Art.* 3 vols. Vol. 1 *The Middle Ages and the Renaissance.* Princeton U. Pr. 1981 $16.95. ISBN 0-691-00333-5. Vol. 2 *Michelangelo and the Mannerists—the Baroque and the Eighteenth Century.* Princeton U. Pr. 1983 $16.95. ISBN 0-691-00344-0. Vol. 3 *From the Classicists to the Impressionists: Art and Architecture in the Nineteenth Century.* Yale U. Pr. 1986 $55.00. ISBN 0-300-03358-3. A selection of original texts.

Honour, Hugh. *The Visual Arts: A History.* P-H 1991 $46.67. ISBN 0-13-950494-X. A particularly fine survey.

Hudson, Kenneth, and Ann Nicholls, eds. *The Directory of Museums and Living Displays.* Groves Dict. Music 1986 $195.00. ISBN 0-943818-17-6. Lists museums worldwide with a brief description of their contents. Does not assess quality or importance.

Janson, H. W. *History of Art.* Abrams 1991 $55.00. ISBN 0-8109-3401-9. Among the most usable and widely used one-volume texts.

Jobes, Gertrude. *Dictionary of Mythology, Folklore and Symbols.* 3 vols. Scarecrow 1961 $99.50. ISBN 0-8108-2036-6. Includes African, Asian, and Islamic material as well as classical, Christian, and Western legends.

Lucie-Smith, Edward. *Art and Civilization.* Abrams 1993 $60.00. ISBN 0-8109-1924-9. Discusses and places various art forms in the historic development of Western Civilization.

——. *The Thames and Hudson Dictionary of Art Terms.* Thames Hudson 1988 $12.95. ISBN 0-500-20222-2. While not exhaustive, gives succinct explanations of key terms.

Mayer, Ralph. *The HarperCollins Dictionary of Art Terms and Techniques.* HarpC 1992 $25.00. ISBN 0-06-271518-6. Explains technical terms describing materials, mediums, tools, and processes employed by artists.

Murray, Peter, and Linda Murray. *Dictionary of Art and Artists.* Viking Penguin rev. ed. 1984 $8.95. ISBN 0-14-051133-4. A highly useful small volume.

Official Museum Directory, 1994. Bowker 1993 $185.00. ISBN 0-8352-3372-3. Published in cooperation with the American Association of Museums; lists over 7,000 institutions, including information on exhibits, special collections, and personnel. Annually updated and basic for a library.

Osborne, Harold. *The Oxford Companion to Art.* OUP 1970 $49.95. ISBN 0-19-866107-X. Clear, concise discussions of artists, schools of art, and themes. A good place to turn when puzzled by a term.

The Oxford Dictionary of Art. Ed. by Ian Chilvers and Harold Osborne. OUP 1988 $49.95. ISBN 0-19-866133-9. More than 300 new entires in this descendant of the Osborne work (above).

The Pelican History of Art. Yale U. Pr. 1953 o.p. The most comprehensive history of art and architecture published in English, with each volume by a different author on a different subject.

Piper, David, ed. *Looking at Art: An Introduction to Enjoying the Great Paintings of the World.* McGraw 1984 $23.30. ISBN 0-07-554784-8. Guides the reader beyond recognition and familiarity into the realm of enjoyment.

Saff, Donald, and Deli Sacilotto. *Printmaking: History and Process.* HB Coll. Pubs. 1978 $40.00. ISBN 0-03-085663-9. Technical, yet readable, step-by-step discussion of the making of famous prints.

Thames and Hudson Dictionary of Art and Artists. Ed. by Herbert Read and Nikos Stangos. Thames Hudson 1988 $19.95. ISBN 0-685-19584-9. Useful small volume, particularly well illustrated.

Wölfflin, Heinrich. *Principles of Art History: The Problem of the Development of Style in Later Art.* Dover 1950 $5.95. ISBN 0-486-20276-3. An influential book on the basic pairs of concepts in Western art, such as painterly versus linear, sculptural versus planar, etc.

Woodhead, Peter, and Jeoffrey Stansfield. *Keyguide to Information Sources in Museum Studies.* Cassell 1989 $55.00. ISBN 0-7201-2025-X. Overview of museum studies and its literature. Includes bibliography, selected organizations, and indexes.

Special Aspects

Arnason, H. H. *History of Modern Art: Painting, Sculpture, Architecture, Photography.* Rev. and updated by Daniel Wheeler. P-H 1986 $46.95. ISBN 0-13-390360-5. Traces the beginning of modern art from the invention of photography and the rise of impressionism through abstractionism. Well illustrated.

Baigell, Matthew. *Dictionary of American Art.* HarpC 1980 $12.00. ISBN 0-06-430078-1. Brief discussions of American artists with an emphasis on their stylistic development and artistic achievement rather than biographical detail.

Berenson, Bernard. *Italian Painters of the Renaissance. Landmarks in Art History Ser.* 2 vols. Found Class. 1980 repr. of 1897 ed. $327.75. ISBN 0-89901-070-9. A list of the principal artists and their works by the famous connoisseur and master attributor.

Boardman, John. *Greek Art. World of Art Ser.* Thames Hudson rev. ed. 1985 $12.95. ISBN 0-500-20194-3. Focuses on Greek art and architecture from the ninth century B.C. to the Roman conquest. Stresses the importance of studying the mediocre as well as the great.

Boas, Franz. *Primitive Art.* Dover 1955 repr. of 1927 ed. $7.95. ISBN 0-486-20025-6. Dismisses the notion of the primitive mind. Argues that primitive and modern minds differ only in the degree of knowledge of the objective world, and that aesthetic pleasure is universal.

Brown, Milton W., and others, eds. *American Art, Painting, Sculpture, Architecture, Decorative Arts.* Abrams 1979 $55.00. ISBN 0-8109-0658-9. Wide-ranging, richly illustrated; by several major scholars.

Burt, Eugene C. *Erotic Art: An Annotated Bibliography with Essays.* Macmillan 1989 $50.00. ISBN 0-8161-8957-9. Worldwide coverage of seven geographic/chronological sections, each with an introductory essay. Cites 318 twentieth-century artists, with entries for both scholarly and popular works.

Carpenter, Rhys. *Greek Sculpture*. U. Ch. Pr. 1971 o.p. Traces sculptural development of Greek sculpture from the rigid "Egyptian" style naturalism of the fifth century B.C. Discusses the search for the ideal and the conflict between real and ideal.

Chadwick, Whitney. *Women, Art and Society*. World of Art Ser. Thames Hudson 1989 $24.95. ISBN 0-500-18194-2. Discusses women's role both as artistic creator and subject. Written from a postmodern feminist perspective.

Coomaraswamy, Ananda K. *History of Indian and Indonesian Art*. Dover 1985 repr. of 1927 ed. $9.95. ISBN 0-486-25005-9. By a leading scholar responsible for teaching generations of students to see more in Indian art than the exotic.

Craven, Roy C. *Indian Art: A Concise History*. World of Art Ser. Thames Hudson 1985 $11.95. ISBN 0-500-20146-3. Short beginner's guide focusing on Indian art prior to British colonization.

Crowe, Joseph A., G. B. Cavalcaselle, and Douglas Langston. *A History of Painting in Italy, Umbria, Florence, and Siena from the Second to the Sixteenth Century*. 6 vols. AMS Pr. repr. of 1914 ed. $245.00. ISBN 0-404-01920-X. The first and still usable comprehensive survey in English.

Denvir, Bernard. *The Thames and Hudson Encyclopedia of Impressionism*. Thames Hudson 1990 $11.95. ISBN 0-500-20239-7. A concise compendium of information, with illustrated entries, chronology (1855–90), and bibliography.

Feest, Christian F. *Native Arts of North America*. World of Art Ser. Thames Hudson 1985 $11.95. ISBN 0-500-20179-X. Argues that all North American indigenous art had a practical use, though sometimes this use was ceremonial.

Findlay, James, comp. *Modern Latin American Art: A Bibliography*. Art Reference Collection Ser. Greenwood 1983 $55.00. ISBN 0-313-23757-3. Arranged by geographical areas. Many references are to works in Spanish or German.

Goldman, Shifra M. *Arte Chicano: A Comprehensive Annotated Bibliography of Chicano Art, 1965–1981*. U. CA Pr. 1985 $25.50. ISBN 0-918520-09-6. Includes 2,500 annotated editions and a list of 2,200 Chicano artists.

Hamilton, George H. *Nineteenth and Twentieth Century Art: Painting, Sculpture, Architecture*. P-H 1971 $46.95. ISBN 0-13-622639-6. Historical survey from the classicism of the mid-eighteenth century through post-World War II trends. Includes many fine illustrations.

Hartt, Frederick. *History of Italian Renaissance Art: Painting, Sculpture, Architecture*. Abrams 1987 $55.00. ISBN 0-8109-1163-9. Good introductory text; discusses many individual works in some depth. Beautifully illustrated.

Hunter, Sam, and John Jacobus. *Modern Art*. Abrams 1992 $55.00. ISBN 0-8109-3609-7. Historical approach to modern art; attempts to discuss representational works in some depth rather than cover everything. Includes various works from the 1990s.

Jeffrey, Ian. *Photography: A Concise History*. World of Art Ser. Thames Hudson 1985 $19.95. ISBN 0-500-18187-X. Historical survey of trends in photography's first 130 years through an examination of the works of leading photographers.

Karpel, Bernard, ed. *Arts in America: A Bibliography*. 4 vols. Smithsonian 1979–80 o.p. One of the most comprehensive in the field; includes film, theater, photography, dance, graphic arts, and architecture.

Lee, Sherman. *A History of Far Eastern Art*. Abrams 1982 $55.00. ISBN 0-8109-1080-2. Rich in illustrations.

Livingston, Alan. *Thames and Hudson Encyclopedia of Graphic Design and Designers*. World of Art Ser. Thames Hudson 1992 $12.95. ISBN 0-500-20259-1

Lucie-Smith, Edward. *Movements in Art since 1945*. World of Art Ser. Thames Hudson rev. ed. 1985 $11.95. ISBN 0-500-20197-8. Claims most postwar art does not measure up to the great works of the past.

Madsen, Stephen. *Sources of Art Nouveau*. Da Capo 1976 $10.95. ISBN 0-306-80024-1. Examines the how and why of the Art Nouveau style; stresses its asymmetrical nature and the unique emphasis on curved lines.

Moholy-Nagy, Laszlo. *Vision in Motion.* Theobald 1947 $21.50. ISBN 0-911498-00-1. The pioneer Bauhaus painter-photographer's statement "on the interrelatedness of art and life"—a major modern document.

Murray, Linda. *High Renaissance and Mannerism: Italy, the North and Spain 1500–1600. World of Art Ser.* Thames Hudson 1985 $11.95. ISBN 0-500-20162-5. Defines mannerism as an artistic style that flourished between 1520 and 1590. Explores how mannerist style violated certain classical canons.

Newhall, Beaumont. *History of Photography: From 1839 to the Present.* Museum Mod. Art 5th rev. ed. 1982 $27.95. ISBN 0-87070-38-1. First published as a catalog for a 1937 exhibition at the Museum of Modern Art. Updated to include some postwar works.

Osborne, Harold, ed. *The Oxford Companion to Twentieth Century Art.* OUP 1988 $22.50. ISBN 0-19-282076-1. Useful guide to modern and contemporary art; examines a number of works in some depth.

Panofsky, Erwin. *Early Netherlandish Painting.* 2 vols. HarpC 1971 $30.00 ea. ISBNs 0-06-430002-1, 0-06-430003-X. The most scholarly and authoritative work on the subject.

Rawson, Philip. *The Art of Southeast Asia: Cambodia, Vietnam, Thailand, Laos, Burma, Java, Bali. World of Art Ser.* Thames Hudson 1990 $11.95. ISBN 0-500-20060-2. Organized by regions that correspond to old kingdoms. Discusses art in general from the prehistoric period through the fourteenth century.

Read, Herbert. *A Concise History of Modern Painting. World of Art Ser.* Thames Hudson 1985 $11.95. ISBN 0-500-20141-2. Readable overview of modern painting from impressionism through the 1950s.

Rewald, John. *The History of Impressionism.* Museum of Mod. Art 1990 $29.95. ISBN 0-8109-6036-2. Written in a lively and engaging manner; includes many high-quality illustrations.

Rice, David Talbot. *Art of the Byzantine Era. World of Art Ser.* Thames Hudson 1985 $11.95. ISBN 0-500-20004-1. General overview of Byzantine art and architecture; well illustrated.

_____. *Islamic Art. World of Art Ser.* Thames Hudson 1985 $11.95. ISBN 0-500-20150-1. Illustrated survey of Islamic art; takes the reader beyond the "seeming sameness" to an appreciation of the unique qualities of the Islamic masterworks.

Selz, Peter. *Art in Our Times: A Pictorial History 1890–1980.* HB Coll. Pubs. 1981 $26.75. ISBN 0-15-503473-1. Discusses the political, social, and economic conditions within which the many illustrated works were created.

Sieveking, Ann. *Cave Artists. Ancient People and Places Ser.* Thames Hudson 1979 $19.95. ISBN 0-500-02092-2. Helps the reader appreciate the naturalistic qualities of paleolithic art; frankly admits that we will never know "inner meaning" due to remoteness in time.

Stanley-Baker, Joan. *Japanese Art. World of Art Ser.* Thames Hudson 1984 $11.95. ISBN 0-500-20192-7. An illustrated historical survey of Japanese art; a good introductory work.

Strong, Donald. *Roman Art.* Ed. by Roger Ling, and others. Yale U. Pr. 1992 repr. of 1972 ed. $25.00. ISBN 0-300-05293-6. Historical survey of Roman art from its founding through the fifth century A.D. Contends that key developments were initiated by patrons rather than artists.

Tregear, Mary. *Chinese Art. World of Art Ser.* Thames Hudson 1985 $19.95. ISBN 0-500-18178-0. Insightful outline of major trends in Chinese art from the neolithic period to modern times. Half of the text is devoted to illustrations.

Wheeler, Mortimer. *Roman Art and Architecture. World of Art Ser.* Thames Hudson 1985 $12.95. ISBN 0-500-20021-1. Traces the development of Roman art from its Greek and Etruscan roots to art that emerged in imperial territories. A short but well-written general work.

Willett, Frank. *African Art. World of Art Ser.* Thames Hudson 1985 $12.95. ISBN 0-500-20237-X. One of the best surveys.

Zarnecki, George. *Art of the Medieval World: Architecture, Sculpture, Painting and the Sacred Arts.* P-H 1976 $40.95. ISBN 0-13-047514-9. A synthesis of medieval art by a leading scholar who has written extensively on aspects of both Romanesque and Gothic art.

Biography

Canaday, John. *Lives of the Painters.* 4 vols. Norton 1969 $75.00. ISBN 0-393-04231-6. One of the most comprehensive works available.

Cummings, Paul, ed. *Dictionary of Contemporary American Artists.* St. Martin 1988 $75.00. ISBN 0-312-00232-7. Nine hundred entries, including 87 new artists.

Davis, Lenwood G., and Janet L. Sims. *Black Artists in the United States: An Annotated Bibliography of Books, Articles, and Dissertation on Black Artists, 1779–1979.* Greenwood 1980 $42.95. ISBN 0-313-22082-4

Emmanuel, Muriel, and others, eds. *Contemporary Artists.* St. Martin 1983 $75.00. ISBN 0-312-16643-5. Contains brief biographies, critical discussions of work, and lists of publications and exhibitions of over 1,000 contemporary artists.

Fielding, Mantle. *Dictionary of American Painters, Sculptors and Engravers.* Rev. ed. by Genevieve Doran. Modern Bks. 1975 repr. of 1926 ed. $17.50. ISBN 0-913274-03-8. Biographical data on 1,200 American artists; includes minimal discussion of their work.

Harris, Ann S. *Women Artists: Fifteen Fifty to Nineteen Fifty.* Knopf 1977 $24.95. ISBN 0-394-73326-6. Contains biographies, lists of publications and exhibitions, and brief critical discussions of the work of approximately 600 contemporary photographers.

Held, Michael, and others, eds. *Contemporary Photographers.* St. Martin 1982 $70.00. ISBN 0-312-16791-1

Naylor, Colin, ed. *Contemporary Artists.* St. James Pr. 1989 $135.00. ISBN 0-912289-96-1
——, ed. *Contemporary Photographers.* St. James Pr. 1988 $135.00. ISBN 0-912289-79-1. Highly recommended. One hundred new entries.

Podro, Michael. *The Critical Historians of Art.* Yale U. Pr. 1984 $13.00. ISBN 0-300-03240-4. On the major art historians and their writings.

Rubinstein, Charlotte S. *American Women Artists: From Early Indian Times to the Present.* Avon 1982 $15.95. ISBN 0-380-61101-5. Discusses the work of women artists, from the basketwork of native women to contemporary performance art. An authoritative work on a traditionally overlooked subject.

Vasari, Giorgio. *Lives of the Most Eminent Painters, Sculptors, and Architects.* 10 vols. AMS Pr. repr. of 1915 ed. $750.00. ISBN 0-404-09730-8. One of the great source books of Italian Renaissance art, with ever-fresh biographies of most of the great masters.

ARCHITECTURE

General Reading List

Copplestone, Trewin, ed. *World Architecture: An Illustrated History from the Earliest Times.* Crescent Bks. 1981 o.p. A monumental, beautifully illustrated survey.

Fletcher, Banister. *History of Architecture.* Ed. by J. C. Palmes. Macmillan 1975. ISBN 0-684-14207-4. A richly illustrated basic text.

Harris, Cyril M. *Dictionary of Architecture and Construction.* McGraw 1992 $59.50. ISBN 0-07-02688-6. An excellent work on technical terms.

Hatje, Gerd, ed. *Encyclopedia of Modern Architecture.* Abrams 1964 o.p. A useful one-volume survey, international in scope.

Jordan, Robert F. *A Concise History of Western Architecture.* HB Coll. Pubs. 1969 $21.50. ISBN 0-15-512950-3. Historical survey from ancient Greece to modern times. Stresses the practical purpose and the effect of severe, practical limitations on art.

Kostof, Spiro. *A History of Architecture: Settings and Rituals.* OUP 1985 $65.00. ISBN 0-19-503472-4. The basic textbook for the study of architectural history.

Nuttgens, Patrick J. *The Story of Architecture.* P-H 1983 $36.95. ISBN 0-13-850131-9. Studies various buildings, primitive to postmodern, to explain the reasons for a particular architectural style or construction.

Pevsner, Nikolaus, John Fleming, and Hugh Honour. *The Penguin Dictionary of Architecture.* Viking Penguin 1991 $12.00. ISBN 0-14-051241-1. Biographical as well as historical, with less emphasis on technical terms. Of great all-around use.

Rasmussen, Steen E. *Experiencing Architecture.* MIT Pr. 1962 $8.95. ISBN 0-262-68002-5. A good introduction to the theory of architectural appreciation.

Sharp, Dennis. *Illustrated Encyclopedia of Architects and Architecture.* Watson-Guptill 1991 $39.95. ISBN 0-8230-2539-X. Includes brief biographies of leading architects and illustrations of their works, as well as entries on buildings, architectural styles, and so on.

Summerson, John. *The Classical Language of Architecture.* MIT Pr. 1966 $6.95. ISBN 0-262-69012-8. The most lucid explanation of the so-called orders and the classical tradition they represent.

Trachtenberg, Marvin. *Architecture, from Prehistory to Post-Modernism.* P-H 1991 $44.95. ISBN 0-13-044702-1. Good, basic survey. More than 1,000 illustrations.

Special Aspects

Benevolo, Leonardo. *History of Modern Architecture.* 2 vols. MIT Pr. 1977 $35.00. ISBN 0-262-52046-X

Blumenson, John C. *Identifying American Architecture: A Pictorial Guide to Styles and Terms, 1600–1945.* AASLH 1981 $11.95. ISBN 0-910050-50-3. A pictorial guide to styles and terms, with a foreword by Nikolaus Pevsner.

Bussagli, Mario. *Oriental Architecture I: India, Indonesia, Indochina. History of World Architecture Ser.* Rizzoli Intl. 1988 $29.95. ISBN 0-8478-1056-9. Introduces the westerner to Indian and Indonesian architecture through a survey of temples built before A.D. 1000.

————. *Oriental Architecture II: China, Korea, Japan. History of World Architecture Ser.* Rizzoli Intl. 1989 $29.95. ISBN 0-8478-1055-0. Contains separate chapters on Chinese and Korean temples and palaces built before the seventeenth century and Japanese civic, residential, and religious architecture.

Curtis, William J. R. *Modern Architecture since 1900.* P-H 1983 $35.95. ISBN 0-13-586669-3. Balanced overview that avoids advocating any particular school of architecture.

Fitch, James Marsten. *Historic Preservation: Curatorial Management of the Built World.* U. Pr. of Va. 1990 $14.95. ISBN 0-8139-1272-5. Examines the problems faced by the architectural curator.

Giedion, Sigfried. *Space, Time and Architecture: The Growth of a New Tradition.* HUP 1967 o.p. The most influential book on the development of modern architecture.

Grodecki, Louis. *Gothic Architecture. History of World Architecture Ser.* Rizzoli Intl. 1985 o.p.

Guidoni, Enrico. *Primitive Architecture. History of World Architecture Ser.* Rizzoli Intl. 1987 $29.95. ISBN 0-8478-0797-5. General introduction to primitive architecture, with reference to 200 examples drawn from around the world.

Hamlin, Talbot. *Greek Revival Architecture in America.* Dover repr. of 1944 ed. $11.95. ISBN 0-486-21148-7. Theorizes that the Greek revival style represented America's turning away from its colonial roots toward a culture compatible with democracy.

Heyden, Doris, and Paul Gendrop. *Pre-Columbian Architecture of Mesoamerica. History of World Architecture Ser.* Rizzoli Intl. 1988 o.p. Introduces the reader to the structures built by indigenous peoples of Central America and Mexico.

Hitchcock, Henry-Russell. *American Architectural Books: A List of Books, Portfolios, and Pamphlets on Architecture and Related Subjects Published in America before 1895.* Ed. by Adolf K. Placzek. *Architectural and Decorative Arts Ser.* Da Capo 1976 repr. of 1946 ed. $29.50. ISBN 0-306-70742-X. A comprehensive bibliography of architecture books published in America up to 1895.

Hoag, John D. *Islamic Architecture. History of World Architecture Ser.* Rizzoli Intl. 1987 $29.95. ISBN 0-8478-0796-7. Extracts unifying principles from a great diversity of Islamic architecture.

Jordy, William H., and William H. Pierson. *American Buildings and Their Architects.* 4 vols. OUP 1986. Vol. 1 *The Colonial and Neo-Classical Styles.* $17.95. ISBN 0-19-504216-6. Vol. 2 *Technology and the Picturesque: The Corporate and the Early Gothic Styles.* $16.95. ISBN 0-19-504217-4. Vol. 3 *Progress and Academic Ideals at the Turn of the Twentieth Century.* $18.95. ISBN 0-19-504218-2. Vol. 4 *The Impact of European Modernism in the Mid-Twentieth Century.* $18.95. ISBN 0-19-504219-0

Kaufmann, Emil. *Architecture in the Age of Reason: Baroque and Post Baroque in England, Italy and France.* Dover 1968 repr. of 1955 ed. $8.95. ISBN 0-486-21928-3

Kubach, Han Erich. *Romanesque Architecture. History of World Architecture Ser.* Rizzoli Intl 1988 repr. of 1975 ed. $29.95. ISBN 0-8478-0920-X. Traces the development of the style and examines regional differences.

Lloyd, Seton, and Hans Wolfgang Muller. *Ancient Architecture: Mesopotamia and Egypt. History of World Architecture Ser.* Rizzoli Intl. 1986 $29.95. ISBN 0-8478-0692-8. Well-illustrated treatment of the architecture of these two ancient regions; each author discusses one region.

Mango, Cyril. *Byzantine Architecture. History of World Architecture Ser.* Rizzoli Intl. 1985 $29.95. ISBN 0-8478-0615-4. Distinguished from other studies by its inclusion of nonecclesiastical works.

Martin, Roland. *Greek Architecture. History of World Architecture Ser.* Rizzoli Intl. 1988 $29.95. ISBN 0-8478-0968-4

Middleton, Robin, and David Watkin. *Neoclassical and Nineteenth-Century Architecture. History of World Architecture Ser.* 2 vols. Rizzoli Intl. 1987 $29.95 ea. ISBNs 0-8478-0850-5, 0-8478-0851-3. Discusses the development from neoclassicism through Gothic revival to the dawn of modernism, within a social and political context.

Morrison, Hugh. *Early American Architecture: From the First Colonial Settlement to the National Period.* Dover 1987 $14.95. ISBN 0-486-25492-5. Explores colonial, regional differences in style and discusses the thirteen original colonies, as well as California and the Southwest; describes the emergence of a national style.

Murray, Peter. *Renaissance Architecture. History of World Architecture Ser.* Rizzoli Intl. 1988 $29.95. ISBN 0-8478-0474-7. Scholarly discussion of the masterpieces, but assumes the reader has a general familiarity with the period. Illustrations include architectural drawings.

Nabokov, Peter. *Native American Architecture.* OUP 1988 $65.00. ISBN 0-19-503781-2. Authoritative and well-illustrated work on a neglected subject.

Norberg-Schulz, Christian. *Baroque Architecture. History of World Architecture Ser.* Rizzoli Intl. 1986 $29.95. ISBN 0-8478-0693-6. Scholarly analysis of "the last great universal style." Shows common elements in diverse works.

———. *Late Baroque and Rococo Architecture. History of World Architecture Ser.* Rizzoli Intl. 1985 $29.95. ISBN 0-8478-0475-5. Deals with the evolution of Baroque into the Rococo.

Palladio, Andre. *The Four Books of Architecture.* 1570. Ed. by Isaac Ware. Dover 1960 repr. of 1738 ed. $13.95. ISBN 0-486-21308-0. One of the great books of classic architecture, with rich illustrations derived from the English edition of 1738.

Pevsner, Nikolaus. *Outline of European Architecture.* Viking Penguin 1950 $14.95. ISBN 0-14-020109-2. The best-written and most fundamental book on the subject.

Poppeliers, John. *What Style Is It?: A Guide to American Architecture.* Preservation Pr. 1984 $8.95. ISBN 0-89133-116-6. A slim, easily portable volume, ideal for use by the tourist.

Roth, Leland M. *A Concise History of American Architecture*. HarpC 1980 $22.50. ISBN 0-06-430086-2. Good introduction to the subject; discusses and illustrates more than 300 examples.

Ruskin, John. *The Seven Lamps of Architecture*. Dover 1989 $8.95. ISBN 0-486-26145-X. The manifesto of Victorian architecture.

Sharp Dennis. *Illustrated Encyclopedia of Architects and Architecture*. Watsun-Guptill 1991 $39.95. ISBN 0-8230-2539-X. Some 300 biographical entries and 400 well-selected illustrations.

_____. *Twentieth Century Architecture: A Visual History*. Facts on File rev. ed. 1991 $65.00. ISBN 0-8160-2438-3. Excellent reference. Well illustrated, with a good index.

Smith, G. E. Kidder. *The Architecture of the United States*. 3 vols. Doubleday 1981 o.p. One of the most comprehensive guides to buildings and structures throughout the United States; with numerous illustrations.

Tafuri, Manfredo, and Francesco Dal Co. *Modern Architecture*. History of World Architecture Ser. 2 vols. Rizzoli Intl. 1987 $29.95 ea. ISBNs 0-8478-0760-6, 0-8478-0761-4

Vitruvius. *The Ten Books on Architecture*. Trans. by Morris H. Morgan. Dover 1960 $7.95. ISBN 0-486-20645-9. Written in the first century A.D. by a Roman architect, a book that has remained the main source for thinking about Greco-Roman architecture; with hundreds of later editions in all major languages.

Ward-Perkins, J. B. *Roman Architecture*. History of World Architecture Ser. Rizzoli Intl. 1988 $29.95. ISBN 0-8478-0972-2

Whiffen, Marcus. *American Architecture since 1780: A Guide to the Styles*. MIT Pr. rev. ed. 1992 $25.00. ISBN 0-262-23164-6. Believes architectural styles are best studied at their "zenith."

Wittkower, Rudolf. *Architectural Principles in the Age of Humanism*. St. Martin 1988 $35.00. ISBN 0-312-02082-1. Originally published in 1949, a learned treatise that has remained an influential interpretation of Renaissance architecture and its ideas.

Biography

Morgan, Ann L. *Contemporary Architects*. St. James Pr. 1987 $135.00. ISBN 0-912289-26-0. Provides short biographies of over 600 world architects; includes bibliographies of books by and about them and lists of their major architectural works.

Placzek, Adolf K. *Macmillan Encyclopedia of Architects*. 4 vols. Macmillan 1982 $400.00. ISBN 0-02-925000-5. The most comprehensive biographical work across the ages, with thorough essays on all of the major architects.

Pro File: The Official Directory of the American Institute of Architects. Archimedia 1983 o.p.

Travis, Jack. *African-American Architects in Current Practice*. Princeton Arch. 1992 $19.95. ISBN 1-878271-38-5. Short topical essays and autobiographical sketches by over 30 contemporary African American architects.

Williamson, Roxanne K. *American Architects and the Mechanics of Fame*. U. of Tex. Pr. 1991 $35.00. ISBN 0-292-75121-4. A study of more than 60 architects and their subsequent patterns of success.

Withey, Henry F., and Elsie Rathburn Withey. *Biographical Dictionary of American Architects (Deceased)*. New Age 1956 o.p. In spite of some inaccuracies, the most detailed listing of American architects, especially minor ones.

DECORATIVE ARTS

The term "decorative arts" is generally used to mean a type of art that is useful as well as beautiful. Whereas fine art objects, such as paintings and sculpture, are created primarily to be looked at and admired, decorative art objects, such as furniture, ceramics, rugs, glassware, and the like, are created to be used as well as admired. Over time, of course, decorative art objects often function more like fine art objects as people collect them for their beauty. This is particularly true of decorative arts from earlier periods, which become highly valued, not only for their beauty, but also for their age, rarity, and historical significance.

Bingham, Don, and Joan Bingham. *Tuttle Dictionary of Antiques and Collectible Terms.* C. E. Tuttle 1992 $19.95. ISBN 0-8048-1756-1. Defines over 4,000 terms. Pocket-size; excellent for use at auctions, galleries, and open markets.

Boger, Louise, and H. Batterson Boger. *Dictionary of Antiques and the Decorative Arts.* Scribner 1979 o.p.

The Encyclopedia of Arts and Crafts: The International Arts Movement, 1850–1920. Ed. by Gillian Naylor and others. Dutton 1989 $39.95. ISBN 0-525-24804-8. A handbook, with eight chapters by specialists, that contains illustrations, biographies, chronology, and an index.

Evans, Joan. *Pattern: A Study of Ornament in Western Europe from 1180 to 1900.* 2 vols. Da Capo 1976. Vol. 1 $9.95. ISBN 0-306-80040-3. Vol. 2 $9.95. ISBN 0-306-80041-1. A scholarly survey.

Fleming, John, and Hugh Honour. *The Penguin Dictionary of Decorative Arts: New Edition.* Viking Penguin 1990 $40.00. ISBN 0-670-82047-4. With 600 new subject entries and 67 new color plates. Highly recommended for academic and large public libraries; replaces the 1977 edition.

Hamlin, A. D. *A History of Ornament: Ancient and Medieval.* Hollowbrook 1985 $85.00. ISBN 0-89341-360-7. Still one of the most scholarly surveys in English.

Herman, Lloyd. *Art that Works: The Decorative Arts of the Eighties Crafted in America.* U. of Wash. Pr. 1990 $50.00. ISBN 0-295-96937-7. Places contemporary American crafts in the social and cultural context of the past 100 years.

Jones, Owen. *Grammar of Ornament.* 1856. Van Nos. Reinhold 1982 $19.95. ISBN 0-685-16811-5. The greatest nineteenth-century illustrated album on ornament.

Lewis, Philippa. *Dictionary of Ornament.* Pantheon 1986 o.p. Includes 1,020 entries, including styles and people's names.

Michael, George. *The Basic Book of Antiques and Collectibles.* Chilton 1992 $17.95. ISBN 0-87069-649-1. Covers a wide range. Written by a seasoned antique collector.

Osborne, Harold, ed. *The Oxford Companion to the Decorative Arts.* OUP 1985 $22.50. ISBN 0-19-281863-5. Unsigned articles and lengthy bibliography. Covers such arts as ceramics, textiles, woodworking, typography, and jewelry.

Ware, Dora, and Maureen Stafford. *An Illustrated Dictionary of Ornament.* St. Martin 1975 o.p.

Wills, Geoffrey, comp. *A Concise Encyclopedia of Antiques.* Van Nos. Reinhold 1975 o.p.

Ceramics and Glassware

Barber, Edwin. *The Pottery and Porcelain of the United States and Marks of American Potters.* Wallace-Homestead o.p.

Battie, David. *Sotheby's Concise Encyclopedia of Glass.* Little 1990 $60.00. ISBN 0-316-08374-7. Traces the 4,000-year history of glass. Includes brilliant color photographs from collections worldwide.

Cameron, Elisabeth. *Encyclopedia of Pottery and Porcelain, 1800-1960.* Facts on File 1986 $35.00. ISBN 0-8160-1225-3. Worldwide coverage with entries of varying lengths.

Camusso, Lorenzo, and Sandro Bortone, eds. *Ceramics of the World: From Four Thousand B.C. to the Present.* Abrams 1992 $95.00. ISBN 0-8109-3175-3. An international survey spanning the entire history of ceramics.

Chaffers, William. *Marks and Monograms on European and Oriental Pottery and Porcelain.* 1965. Borden 1983 $39.95. ISBN 0-87505-067-1. The basic reference tool.

Fournier, Robert. *Practical Illustrated Dictionary of Pottery-Diccionario Ilustrado de Alfareria Practica*. Fr. & Eur. 1981 $49.95. ISBN 0-8288-1425-2

Kampler, Fritz, and Klaus G. Beye. *Glass: A World History*. New York Graphic Society 1966 o.p. The story of 4,000 years of fine glassmaking.

Mehlman, Felice. *Phaidon Guide to Glass*. P-H 1983 $6.95. ISBN 0-13-662015-9

Newman, Harold, and George Savage. *An Illustrated Dictionary of Ceramics*. Thames Hudson 1985 $14.95. ISBN 0-500-27380-4

Penny, Barbara, and others. *American Ceramics: The Collection of Everson Museum of Art*. Rizzoli Intl. 1989 repr. of 1988 ed. $75.00. ISBN 0-8478-1025-9. The comprehensive catalog for the Everson Museum, the front-runner in the promotion of twentieth-century American ceramics.

Phillips, George. *Concise Introduction to Ceramics*. Van Nos. Reinhold 1991 $44.95. ISBN 0-442-00890-2. An introduction for those working in materials science.

Tait, Hugh. *Glass: Five Thousand Years*. Abrams 1991 $60.00. ISBN 0-8109-3361-6. A global and chronological history of hot-worked glass.

Furniture

Aronson, Joseph. *The Encyclopedia of Furniture*. Crown 1965 $27.50. ISBN 0-517-03735-1. Alphabetical arrangement of short articles, with 1,400 illustrations.

Edwards, Ralph. *The Dictionary of English Furniture*. 3 vols. Antique Collect 1986 $175.00. ISBN 1-85149-037-X

Fiell, Charlotte, and Peter Fiell. *Modern Furniture Classics since 1945*. AIA Pr. 1991 $49.95. ISBN 1-55835-040-3. A complete visual history of furniture design since 1945.

Fine Woodworking Editors. *The Best of Fine Woodworking: Modern Furniture Projects*. Ed. by John Kelsey. Taunton 1991 $14.95. ISBN 0-942391-91-8

Gloag, John. *A Short Dictionary of Furniture*. Allen & Unwin 1976 o.p. Contains 1,767 terms used in Britain and America.

Haywood, Helene, ed. *World Furniture: An Illustrated Survey*. Outlet Bk. Co. 1988 $29.99. ISBN 0-517-35150-1. A massive, richly illustrated world survey.

Jobe, Brock, and others. *American Furniture with Related Decorative Arts, 1660–1830: The Milwaukee Art Museum and the Layton Art Collection*. Ed. by Gerald W. Ward. Hudson Hills 1992 $85.00. ISBN 1-55595-068-X. Complete photographic documentation of 189 images.

Mang, Karl. *History of Modern Furniture*. Abrams 1979 $35.00. ISBN 0-8109-1066-7

Nutting, Wallace. *Furniture Treasury*. 3 vols. Macmillan 1949. Vols. 1 and 2 (one vol.) $75.00. ISBN 0-02-590980-0. Vol. 3 $35.00. ISBN 0-02-591040-X. A standard set.

Payne, Christopher, ed. *Sotheby's Concise Encyclopedia of Furniture*. HarpC 1989 $49.95. ISBN 0-06-016141-8. Chronological arrangement with index to names and styles; good color illustrations.

Ward, Gerald, ed. *Perspectives on American Furniture*. Norton 1989 $29.95. ISBN 0-393-02654-X. A collection of scholarly essays.

White, Tony, and Bruce Robertson. *Furniture and Furnishings*. 2 vols. TAB Bks. 1991 $12.95. ISBN 0-8306-1832-5. Over 900 clear line drawings. More than 1,500 entries.

Illustrated Books and Manuscripts

De Hamel, Christopher. *History of Illustrated Manuscripts*. Godine 1986 $45.00. ISBN 0-87923-631-0

Harthan, John. *The History of the Illustrated Book: The Western Tradition*. Thames Hudson 1981 $60.00. ISBN 0-500-23316-0

———. *Illuminated Manuscripts*. Stemmer Hse. 1984 $14.95. ISBN 0-88045-019-3

Morgan, N. J. *Early Gothic Manuscripts*. 2 vols. OUP. Vol. 1 *Part I, 1190–1250*. 1982 $95.00. ISBN 0-19-921026-8. Vol. 2 *Part II, 1250–1285*. 1988 $125.00. ISBN 0-905205-5-3. Comprehensive study on English illuminated manuscripts of the Middle Ages.

Parker, Muriel. *Illuminated Letter Designs in the Historical Style of the 13th and 15th Centuries*. Stemmer Hse. 1986 $5.95. ISBN 0-88045-082-7

Ward, Gerald W. *The American Illustrated Book in the Nineteenth Century*. U. Pr. of Va. 1988 $35.00. ISBN 0-912724-17-X. A distinguished collection of papers contributing to both the history of prints and the art of the book.

Weinberger, Norman S. *Encyclopedia of Comparative Letterforms for Artists and Designers*. Art Direction Book 1971 $32.75. ISBN 0-910158-01-0

Weitzman, Kurt, and George Galavaris. *The Monastery of Saint Catherine at Mount Sinai*. Princeton U. Pr. 1990 $175.00. ISBN 0-691-03602-2. An excellent, scholarly catalog devoted in part to the oldest preserved Greek monastic library, as well as its unique collection of icons.

Metal Arts

Brett, Vanessa. *The Sotheby's Directory of Silver: 1600–1940*. Sotheby Pubns. 1986 $57.50. ISBN 0-85667-193-2

Cherry, John. *Goldsmiths*. U. of Toronto Pr. 1992 $18.95. ISBN 0-8020-7711-0. A finely illustrated survey of craftsmanship in the Middle Ages.

Ebert, Katherine. *Collecting American Pewter*. Scribner 1973 o.p.

Hill, Gerard, ed. *Faberge and the Russian Master Goldsmiths*. H. L. Levin 1989 $75.00. ISBN 0-88363-889-4. An examination of the distinctly Russian styles of gold and jewelry crafts.

Glanville, Philippa, and Jennifer F. Goldsborough. *Women Silversmiths, 1685–1845*. Natl. Museum Women 1990 $34.95. ISBN 0-940979-11-X. Highlights the careers of 36 women silversmiths and their roles in a traditionally "gentleman's" profession.

Kovel's American Silver Marks. Crown Pub. Group 1989 $40.00. ISBN 0-517-56882-9. A guide for collectors and dealers. Includes working dates, location, marks. Over 10,000 silversmiths listed.

Youngs, Susan, ed. *The Work of Angels: Masterpieces of Celtic Metalwork, 6th–9th Centuries A.D. U. of Tex. Pr. 1989 $27.95. ISBN 0-292-79058-9. A strong introductory work on this overlooked but important domain of metalwork.*

Rugs and Textiles

Barber, E. J. *Prehistoric Textiles: The Development of Cloth in the Neolithic and Bronze Ages with Special Reference to the Aegean*. Princeton U. Pr. 1991 $69.50. ISBN 0-691-03597-0. Early textiles and their manufacture.

Colchester, Chloe. *The New Textiles*. Rizzoli Intl. 1991 $45.00. ISBN 0-8478-1418-1. High fashion, fine art, and craft textiles in the twentieth century.

Eiland, Murray L. *Oriental Rugs: A New Comprehensive Guide*. Bulfinch Pr. 1982 $70.00. ISBN 0-8212-1127-7. Index and color illustrations

Jerde, Judith. *Encyclopedia of Textiles*. Facts on File 1992 $45.00. ISBN 0-8160-2105-8. A good one-volume reference work for the general reader.

Mawell, Robyn. *Tradition, Trade and Transformation: Southeast Asian Textiles*. OUP 1990 $135.00. ISBN 0-19-553186-8. A cultural examination of Southeast Asian textiles and their important role in cultural life.

Schoeser, Mary, and Kathleen Dejardin. *French Textiles: From 1760–present*. Trafalgar 1992 $75.00. ISBN 1-85669-006-7. A study of both the industrial and social history of French textiles over a 200-year period.

The Macmillan Atlas of Rugs and Carpets. Ed. by David Black. Macmillan 1985 $29.95. ISBN 0-02-511120-5. Around the world with rugs! Includes glossary, bibliography, and index.

Weibel, Adele C. *Two Thousand Years of Textiles*. Hacker 1972 repr. of 1952 ed. o.p.

ARTISTS, ARCHITECTS, AND THEIR WORK

The reader who wishes to learn about an individual artist will naturally start with his or her biography. Biographies may be either by contemporaries, such as Giorgio Vasari or Ascanio Condivi or MICHELANGELO, or by the more critical and systematic authors of later times. Not infrequently an artist will write (or, so to speak, invent) his or her own biography: autobiography is an ancient and honored branch of art literature. Beyond the autobiographical, the writing of great artists on their art—and on art in general—is of prime importance. It may be noted that some artists and architects are also articulate and prolific writers; others, apart from what they express through their art, are almost silent. As a result, it should be noted that this chapter, unlike others, may include profiles of individuals who have not written any books. Michelangelo wrote superb poetry; REMBRANDT, hardly a word; FRANK LLOYD WRIGHT wrote reams; H. H. RICHARDSON, nothing. Some, particularly modern artists, have written extensively about their theories or programs for society; some have defined ideologies; others act like tongue-tied artisans. Some write extraordinary diaries (DÜRER, for example); others produced wonderfully revealing letters, such as VAN GOGH.

What else should one look for? Records of the artist's work—complete records if possible. It should be remembered that some artists were masters in several media, such as Michelangelo: supreme architect, sculptor, painter. Book selection must reflect that. And to be of use to the reader, a book must represent the artist's work pictorially: Excellence of reproduction in an art book is an important consideration, although it cannot be conveyed on a catalog card or in a bibliographic entry. A catalog of an artist's entire oeuvre, or a major part of it, with annotations, datings, ascriptions, and so on, is called a *catalogue raisonné*. Where available, such a catalog constitutes a basic element in the literature on a given artist. However, many of those recording the works of European masters are not in English, and are therefore not included in the following bibliography.

Evaluation, criticism, and reappraisal are other areas in the literature on artists. So are aesthetic analysis and even description of images—although, here, an illustration is indeed worth a thousand words. There are, too, the books that put an individual artist into the context of his or her time and those that deal with special aspects of the artistic process. Further, for most great masters, there are books on major works, such as the many books on Michelangelo's Sistine Chapel or the works on Picasso's *Guernica*.

While not all the categories mentioned are covered for each profiled artist, they should provide a framework to guide the readers in their selections. Exhibition catalogs are also valuable for special studies. Some are important scholarly tools; some are ephemeral; others cover only certain aspects or certain collections. Therefore, exhibition catalogs are not listed here for general use.

Forty artists and architects were chosen for inclusion here. All are of the first rank or near it. The selection was focused first on the towering figures of the Italian Renaissance—Michelangelo, LEONARDO, and TITIAN—together with some of the great artists of the sixteenth and seventeenth centuries in other Western countries in the persons of DÜRER and VELAZQUEZ; then the Netherlands represented by the great figures of REMBRANDT and RUBENS and the fascinating BRUEGHEL. Somewhat lesser artists command interest because of their colorful writing: CELLINI was included on this basis. The great time of the eighteenth century in England is represented by bibliographies on WREN, REYNOLDS, and GAINSBOROUGH; early nineteenth-century England, the time of the great romantic poets, is represented by CONSTABLE and TURNER. Then come the moderns: the great impressionists, from MANET and MONET, to the great triad CEZANNE, GAUGUIN, and VAN GOGH, and on to MATISSE and PICASSO. The leading architects of modernism are also listed: LE CORBUSIER, MIES VAN DER ROHE, AALTO, and KAHN, as are the three master architects who made U.S. architecture so exciting—RICHARDSON, SULLIVAN, and WRIGHT.

It is remarkable how vast a literature some artists and architects have around them. On others, there is often surprisingly little from which to choose; they may still have to wait for reevaluation or rediscovery. Many more monographs need to be written. Art literature, art criticism, and indeed art biography are fields that are in full development.

CHRONOLOGY OF AUTHORS

Leonardo da Vinci. 1452–1519
Dürer, Albrecht. 1471–1528
Michelangelo Buonarroti. 1475–1564
Raphael. 1483–1520
Titian. c.1487–1576
Cellini, Benvenuto. 1500–1571
Palladio, Andrea. 1508–1580
Brueghel the Elder, Pieter. c.1525–1569
Rubens, Peter Paul. 1577–1640
Bernini, Gianlorenzo. 1598–1680
Velazquez, Diego Rodriguez de Silva. 1599–1660
Rembrandt Harmensz van Rijn. 1606–1669
Wren, Sir Christopher. 1632–1723
Reynolds, Sir Joshua. 1723–1792
Gainsborough, Thomas. 1727–1788
Goya y Lucientes, Francisco José de. 1746–1828
Turner, Joseph Mallord William. 1775–1851
Constable, John. 1776–1837
Manet, Edouard. 1832–1883

Richardson, Henry Hobson. 1836–1886
Cézanne, Paul. 1839–1906
Monet, Claude. 1840–1926
Rodin, Auguste. 1840–1917
Renoir, Pierre Auguste. 1841–1919
Cassatt, Mary. 1845–1926
Gauguin, Paul. 1848–1903
Van Gogh, Vincent. 1853–1890
Sullivan, Louis. 1856–1924
Wright, Frank Lloyd. 1867–1959
Matisse, Henri. 1869–1954
Picasso, Pablo. 1881–1973
Gropius, Walter. 1883–1969
Mies van der Rohe, Ludwig. 1886–1969
Le Corbusier. 1887–1965
O'Keeffe, Georgia. 1887–1986
Aalto, Alvar. 1898–1976
Moore, Henry Spencer. 1898–1986
Kahn, Louis I(sadore). 1901–1974
Pollock, Jackson. 1912–1956
Warhol, Andy. 1930?–1987

AALTO, ALVAR. 1898–1976

Alvar Aalto is considered the father of modernism in Scandinavia. Born in Kuortane, Finland, Aalto's reputation as an architect has spread far beyond the bounds of his native country, where he built the majority of his work. He is perhaps Finland's greatest architect and certainly one of the major figures of twentieth-century architecture.

In his early career, beginning in 1923, Aalto built in a typical Scandinavian style, relying heavily on native materials—timber in Finland's case—and produced such masterworks as the Library at Viipuri (1927–35), the Paimio Sanitarium, and the Villa Mairea. In 1932 he invented the process for making bent wood furniture. After World War II, his work began to be noticed internationally as he developed his own singular style, and he built some of his finest works, the Finlandia Concert Hall in Helsinki and his only building in the United States, the Baker Dorms at the Massachusetts Institute of Technology (1947–49). His style is based on irregular and asymmetric forms (with many curved walls and single-pitched roofs) and a highly imaginative use of natural materials. Aalto is also known for the design of several classic styles of chairs, tables, and glassware.

BOOKS ABOUT AALTO

Dunster, David. *Alvar Aalto: An Academy Architectural Monograph.* St. Martin 1984 $19.95. ISBN 0-312-02150-X

Pearson, Paul D. *Alvar Aalto and the International Style.* Watson-Guptill 1989 $27.50. ISBN 0-8230-0174-1. Explores the relationship of Aalto's work to the international style.

Quantrill, Malcolm. *Alvar Aalto: A Critical Study.* New Amsterdam Bks. 1989 repr. of 1982 ed. $30.00. ISBN 0-941533-35-2. Assesses Aalto's development in terms of the Finnish national romantic movement and the modern movement in architecture.

Schildt, Goran. *Alvar Aalto: The Mature Years.* Rizzoli Intl. 1991 $50.00. ISBN 0-8478-1329-0. Discusses the artist's personal life from World War II until his death.

BERNINI, GIANLORENZO. 1598–1680

Sculptor and architect, Bernini was the formative master of the Roman baroque. Son of a fine sculptor, his own originality and power soon became evident. He ceased to treat marble as a block and concentrated on the multiplicity of viewpoints from which a figure could be experienced. The drama and richness of his sculpture—in marble, stucco, and stone—is extraordinary. Subsequent neoclassicist critics disapproved of him, but his fame has returned and will endure.

Bernini was also one of baroque Rome's greatest architects. He created the mighty square and colonnades in front of St. Peter's and the baldacchino in the basilica. In addition, he was a painter and writer of note. Of a tempestuous temperament, he was deeply religious. The mystical-sensuous *Ecstasy of St. Theresa* is among his most famous sculptures.

BOOKS ABOUT BERNINI

Chantelou, Paul Freart de. *Diary of the Cavaliere Bernini's Visit to France.* Ed. by Anthony Blunt. Trans. by Margery Corbett. Princeton U. Pr. 1985 $68.00. ISBN 0-691-04028-1. A contemporary account of Bernini's visit to France to work for Louis XIV.

Harris, Ann Sutherland, ed. *Selected Drawings of Gian Lorenzo Bernini.* Dover 1977 $7.50. ISBN 0-486-23525-4. Contains a balanced, representative selection.

Hibbard, Howard. *Bernini.* Viking Penguin 1966 $7.95. ISBN 0-14-020701-5. A general account of Bernini's sculpture, with some discussion of his architecture.

Perlove, Shelley. *Bernini and the Idealization of Death: The Blessed Ludovica Albertoni and the Altieri Chapel.* Pa. St. U. Pr. 1990 $32.50. ISBN 0-271-00684-6. Illuminates Bernini's contribution to the chapel and interprets the nature of the experience reflected in the work.

Wittkower, Rudolf. *Gian Lorenzo Bernini: The Sculptor of the Roman Baroque.* Cornell Univ. Pr. 3rd rev. ed. 1981 $72.50. ISBN 0-8014-1430-X. The most complete and scholarly study of Bernini's sculpture.

BRUEGHEL THE ELDER, PIETER. c.1525–1569

Born in the village of Bruegel, near Breda, Pieter Brueghel was the founder and greatest figure of an extraordinary family of Flemish painters. Because of his realistic subject matter, he is often called the "Peasant" Brueghel. His son, Pieter II (c.1564–1638), who made numerous copies of his father's great paintings, is called the "Hell" Brueghel; another son, Jan (1568–1625), carries the name "Velvet" Brueghel. Pieter Brueghel, himself no peasant, but a learned humanist who had traveled to France and—significantly—to Renaissance Italy, is famous for his stark peasant scenes. These include dramatic pictures of historical events, such as the terrible *Massacre of the Innocents*, which is believed to depict the Spanish atrocities in the Netherlands. He was also a great painter of landscapes, into which he put scenes of peasant life (*Ice Skating*) or of mythological events (*The Fall of Icarus*).

BOOKS ABOUT BRUEGHEL

Delevoy, Robert L. *Bruegel*. Rizzoli Intl. 1991 $25.00. ISBN 0-8478-1349-5. A well-illustrated survey of Brueghel's life.

Gibson, Walter S. *Bruegel. World of Art Ser*. Thames Hudson 1985 $19.95. ISBN 0-500-18159-4. A survey of Brueghel's drawings and paintings considered in the context of the society in which he worked.

Hughes, Robert, ed. *The Complete Paintings of Bruegel*. Abrams 1970 o.p.

Klein, H. Arthur, ed. *Graphic Worlds of Peter Bruegel the Elder: Reproducing 64 Engravings and a Woodcut after Designs by Peter Bruegel the Elder*. Dover 1963 $9.95. ISBN 0-486-21132-0

Stechow, Wolfgang. *Bruegel Masters of Art*. Abrams 1990 $22.95. ISBN 0-8109-3103-6. Concise edition of the original 1970 publication. Includes numerous color illustrations with annotations.

CASSATT, MARY. 1845–1926

While other women of the late nineteenth century were making a name for themselves as reformers, educators, and writers, Pittsburgh-born Mary Cassatt was becoming an important American painter. Born into a wealthy family, Cassatt went to Paris as a tourist, became interested in art, and stayed to become an important Impressionist painter. Cassatt's work, influenced more by her French contemporaries than by artists in the United States, was little appreciated in the United States before World War I. Today, however, her work is well represented in the United States in important museums, galleries, and private collections.

Cassatt painted vigorously, using bright colors and displaying a charming simplicity, using oils and pastels, and etching dryprints and color prints. Her favorite subject, motherhood, was displayed in several versions of *Mother and Child*. One version hangs in the Metropolitan Museum of Art in New York City and another in the Museum of Fine Arts in Boston. In 1893 she painted a mural, *Modern Woman*, for the women's building at the Chicago World's Fair. Another outstanding example of her work, painted in 1894, is *La Toilette*, which was exhibited in Paris. Cassatt is the only American whose works have often been exhibited with other outstanding Impressionists, such as French painters Edgar Degas and EDOUARD MANET.

BOOK BY CASSATT

The Mary Cassatt Datebook. Hudson Hills 1988 o.p.

BOOKS ABOUT CASSATT

Bullard, E. John. *Mary Cassatt, Oils and Pastels*. Watson-Guptill 1984 $16.95. ISBN 0-8230-0570-4. A biography that includes numerous color prints of her work.

Cain, Michael. *Mary Cassatt. American Women of Achievement Ser*. Chelsea Hse. 1989 $17.95. ISBN 1-55546-647-8. An illustrated biography that details Cassatt's contributions to American art.

Matthews, Nancy M., and Barbara S. Shapiro. *Mary Cassatt: The Color Prints*. Abrams 1989 $39.95. ISBN 0-8109-1049-7. Technical and artistic impact of Cassatt's color prints. Written by established scholars and curators.

Meyer, Susan E. *Mary Cassatt*. Abrams 1990 $19.95. ISBN 0-8109-3154-0. Artfully designed and filled with high-quality reproductions.

CELLINI, BENVENUTO. 1500–1571

A native of Florence, Italy, Benvenuto Cellini was one of the best-known artisans of his time. Though trained as a goldsmith, he also achieved fame as a sculptor; one of his best-known works is a sculpture of the Greek hero Perseus holding the head of Medusa. Yet today, Cellini may be more famous for his autobiography than for his statue of *Perseus*. His autobiography has been called the most unflinching in all literature. His unhesitating confession of hate, theft, murder, and sensuality has sometimes seemed shocking. The story of his many dishonorable adventures reads like a picaresque novel, but this colorful nonfiction text is a valuable picture of its time. The manuscript of Cellini's autobiography was circulated for more than 150 years before it was printed in 1730. During that time it was frequently copied, and many different texts of it still exist today.

BOOKS BY CELLINI

The Autobiography of Benvenuto Cellini. Random 1985 $12.95. ISBN 0-394-60528-4
Treatises of Benvenuto Cellini on Goldsmithing and Sculpture. Trans. by C. R. Ashbee. Dover 1966 $6.95. ISBN 0-486-21568-7

CÉZANNE, PAUL. 1839–1906

Paul Cézanne, who was one of the most influential and powerful painters of the postimpressionist phase, led the way to twentieth-century cubism and abstract art. He was born in Aix-en-Provence, the son of a prosperous banker. It was his close friend, the novelist ÉMILE ZOLA (see Vol. 2), who steered him to art and persuaded him to study in Paris. He was at first closely allied with his fellow painters, Pissarro and other impressionists, but gradually drew apart from them in his painstaking and dedicated search for a new style. In 1886 he retired to Provence, where, because he was financially independent, he could totally concentrate on his art. The careful balance of tones, building form with color into almost geometrical (indeed, almost cubist) compositions, distinguishes his work. A firm grounding in the great French classical tradition turned him away from the romantic and impressionist toward the abstract art of the future. Cézanne, particularly in his later years, was a solitary man, not an intellectual, and he wrote very little. His watercolors are often as masterful as his oil paintings.

BOOKS BY CÉZANNE

A Cézanne Sketchbook: Figures, Portraits, Landscapes and Still Lives. Dover 1985 repr. of 1951 ed. $5.95. ISBN 0-486-24790-2
Paul Cézanne, Letters. Ed. by John Rewald. Trans. by Seymour Hacker. AMS Pr. repr. of 1941 ed. $49.50. ISBN 0-404-20053-2. Provides great insight into the artist's work; includes numerous letters to Émile Zola.

BOOKS ABOUT CÉZANNE

Badt, Kurt. *The Art of Cézanne*. Hacker 1985 repr. of 1965 ed. $50.00. ISBN 0-87817-302-1. Focuses on Cézanne's watercolor techniques, symbolism, and historical position and significance.

Fry, Roger. *Cézanne: A Study of his Development*. U. Ch. Pr. 1989 $32.50. ISBN 0-226-26644-3. First major work on Cézanne in English, by a famous British critic.

Gowing, Lawrence. *Cézanne, the Early Years, 1859–1872*. Abrams 1988 $45.00. ISBN 0-8109-1048-9. A well-illustrated catalog, with annotations by a major Cézanne scholar.

Longstreet, Stephen, ed. Drawings of Cézanne. Borden 1964 $10.95. ISBN 0-87505-001-8.

Mack, Gerstle. *Paul Cézanne*. 1935. Paragon Hse. 1989 $14.95. ISBN 1-55778-214-8. A biographical account focusing more on Cézanne's personal life than on his art.

Rewald, John. *Cézanne: A Biography*. Abrams 1986 $75.00. ISBN 0-8109-0775-5. A well-illustrated biography by an important scholar.

_____. *Paul Cézanne: The Watercolors—A Catalogue Raisonné*. New York Graphic Society 1984 o.p. Includes an authoritative selection of the artist's watercolors. Compiled by a leading scholar.

Rubin, William. *Cézanne: The Late Work*. Museum of Mod. Art 1977 $55.00. ISBN 0-87070-278-5. A catalog of a major Cézanne exhibition.

Schapiro, Meyer. *Paul Cézanne. The Library of Great Painters Ser*. Abrams 1962 $49.50. ISBN 0-8109-0052-1. Consists chiefly of colored plates with commentaries.

CONSTABLE, JOHN. 1776–1837

Born at East Bergholt in Suffolk, John Constable left home in 1799 to study art at the Royal Academy schools in London. Together with J.M.W. TURNER, Constable was one of the two greatest English landscape painters of the nineteenth century. It was his deep love of nature ("The sound of water . . . willows, old rotten planks . . . I love those things. These scenes made me a painter") that inspired him: Changing clouds, trees, rivers, the effect of light and atmosphere were his lifelong inspiration. But he was also a master of careful formal composition, which he developed from his many wonderfully spontaneous sketches, and of a fresh and loose technique, which influenced the French impressionists. His life was relatively uneventful: He was financially secure, became successful, and kept at his work with remarkable concentration. He is distinguished from Turner by a certain restraint in both his subject matter and his technique. Although successful during his lifetime, Constable's popularity did not peak until 1890, long after his death, when more of his works became known to the public.

Book by Constable

John Constable's Correspondence. 6 vols. Ed. by R. B. Beckett. *Suffolk Records Society*. Boydell & Brewer 1962–68 o.p.

Books about Constable

Cormack, Malcolm. *Constable*. Cambridge U. Pr. 1986 $75.00. ISBN 0-521-32353-3. A major work.

Fleming-Williams, Ian, and Leslie Parris. *The Discovery of Constable*. Holmes & Meier 1984 o.p.

Parris, Leslie. *Constable: Pictures from an Exhibition*. U. of Wash. Pr. 1992 $20.00. ISBN 1-85437-072-3. The catalog of an exhibition at the Tate Gallery in London, featuring Constable's landscapes.

Rosenthal, Michael. *Constable*. Thames Hudson 1987 $11.95. ISBN 0-500-20211-7. A good, basic introduction.

Taylor, Basil. *Constable Paintings, Drawings and Watercolors*. St. Mut. 1975 o.p.

Walker, John. *John Constable. The Library of Great Painters Ser*. Abrams 1991 $22.95. ISBN 0-8109-3171-0. Consists chiefly of color illustrations with commentaries.

DÜRER, ALBRECHT. 1471–1528

Albrecht Dürer was the commanding figure of the German Renaissance. Born in Nuremburg, the son of a goldsmith, he was apprenticed at age 15 to a painter and printmaker, from whom he learned the precision of detail that is one of the hallmarks of his great art, both in his woodcuts and in his drawings (*The Hare* is a famous example). As a young man, he traveled widely throughout Germany and also to Italy, where he was profoundly affected by the emerging art of the High Renaissance, of which he became the primary exponent in the North. He settled in Nuremburg, which he left in 1520 on a trip to the Netherlands, the diaries of which are among the most interesting documents in the history of art. Besides being a fine painter, Dürer was one of the greatest graphic artists of all time. He left behind more than 350 woodcuts, 100 engravings, and approximately 900 drawings and watercolors. As a humanist artist of his time, he was also deeply concerned with art theory and wrote treatises on measurement, fortification, proportion, and on artistic theory itself.

BOOK BY DÜRER

Albrecht Dürer: Sketchbook of His Journey to the Netherlands, 1520–21. Praeger 1971 o.p. With extracts from his diary.

BOOKS ABOUT DÜRER

Dodgson, Campbell. *Albrecht Dürer: Engravings and Etchings.* Da Capo 1967 $35.00. ISBN 0-306-70976-7. Reprint of 1926 edition.

Hutchison, Jane Campbell. *Albrecht Dürer: A Biography.* Princeton U. Pr. 1990 $24.95. ISBN 0-691-03978-X. A scholarly study emphasizing Dürer's life rather than his art.

Kurth, Willi, ed. *The Complete Woodcuts of Albrecht Dürer.* Dover 1963 $10.95. ISBN 0-486-21097-9

Panofsky, Erwin. *The Life and Art of Albrecht Dürer.* Princeton U. Pr. 1955 $29.95. ISBN 0-691-00303-3. Among the most important contributions to the extensive Dürer literature.

Smith, Alistair, trans. *The Complete Paintings of Dürer.* Abrams 1968 o.p. Stunning high-quality color reproductions of all the artist's known paintings.

Strauss, Walter L., ed. *The Complete Engravings, Etchings, and Drypoints of Albrecht Dürer.* Dover 1972 $10.95. ISBN 0-486-22851-7

———, ed. *The Human Figure: The Complete "Dresden Sketchbook."* Dover 1972 repr. of 1905 ed. $10.95. ISBN 0-486-21042-1

Strieder, Peter. *Albrecht Dürer, Paintings, Prints, Drawings.* Trans. by Nancy M. Gordon and Walter L. Strauss. Abaris Bks. 1990 $95.00. ISBN 0-89835-057-3. A well-rounded, extensively illustrated investigation.

Wölfflin, Heinrich. *Drawings of Albrecht Dürer.* 1923. Dover 1970 $8.95. ISBN 0-486-22352-3

GAINSBOROUGH, THOMAS. 1727–1788

Thomas Gainsborough was perhaps the greatest painter of eighteenth-century England. He came from a simpler, more provincial background than his famous rival SIR JOSHUA REYNOLDS. His masters were the Dutch landscape painters of the seventeenth century, rather than those of the Italian Renaissance whom Reynolds adored. Gainsborough was a superb portraitist, with an impeccable technique and a warm sympathy for his sitters. The *Blue Boy*, currently held at the Huntington Library in San Marino, California, is his most popular painting. His lifelong love, however, was landscape painting, rather than portraiture, and here he led the way to the nineteenth century.

BOOK BY GAINSBOROUGH

Letters. Ed. by Mary Woodall. NY Graphic Society. 1963 o.p.

BOOKS ABOUT GAINSBOROUGH

Cormack, Malcolm. *The Paintings of Thomas Gainsborough*. Cambridge U. Pr. 1992 $40.00. ISBN 0-521-38241-6. An up-to-date introduction with an essay and 75 plates.

Hayes, John T. *The Landscape Paintings of Thomas Gainsborough: A Critical Text and Catalogue Raisonné*. 2 vols. Cornell Univ. Pr. 1982 $150.00. ISBN 0-8014-1528-4. The most comprehensive study of Gainsborough available.

Lindsay, Jack. *Gainsborough: His Life and Art*. Academy Ch. Pubs. 1983 $7.95. ISBN 0-586-05613-0. A reliable biography, with only a few illustrations.

GAUGUIN, PAUL. 1848–1903

Paul Gauguin, together with VINCENT VAN GOGH and PAUL CÉZANNE, was one of the great masters of postimpressionism. His life story, prototypical of the artist-rebel, was the subject of films and novels, such as *The Moon and Sixpence* by W. SOMERSET MAUGHAM (see Vol. 1). Born in Paris, Gauguin spent his youth with his Peruvian mother's family in Peru and went to sea as a 16-year-old. He then became a stockbroker in Paris, painting only in his spare time. His early paintings were in the impressionist style. In 1883 he broke with his bourgeois life and eventually separated from his family. In 1888 he visited Van Gogh in Arles—with disastrous results. In 1891 he went to Tahiti. Apart from a short return to Paris, he spent the rest of his life in the South Sea Islands, suffering from poverty, poor health, and recurring struggles with the colonial authorities. In his art, Gauguin sought to return to nature and truth. Inspired by the islanders among whom he was living, he covered his canvases with stark forms, rhythmic patterns, and strong color, going far beyond naturalistic representation. Through this, his influence on modern art was powerful. His book *Noa Noa* (1894–1900) is a moving account of his thoughts and life.

BOOKS BY GAUGUIN

Gauguin's Letters from the South Seas. Dover 1992 repr. of 1923 ed. $4.95. ISBN 0-486-027137-4

The Intimate Journals of Paul Gauguin. Routledge Chapman & Hall 1985 $14.95. ISBN 0-7103-0105-7. Despite the disclaimer, this is not a book written for publication; it was intended to shock and amuse readers.

Noa Noa: The Tahitian Journal. Dover 1985 repr. of 1919 ed. $3.95. ISBN 0-486-24859-3. Reveals how the artist was overcome by the beauty of Tahiti and its people; shows Gauguin's concerns about their exploitation.

Paul Gauguin: Letters to his Wife and Friends. Ed. by Maurice Malingue. Trans. by Henry J. Stenning. AMS Pr. repr. of 1949 ed. $30.00. ISBN 0-404-20106-7. Letters that primarily reveal the downside of the artist's life; documents his problems with his family, finances, and health.

The Writings of a Savage. Ed. by Daniel Guerin. Paragon Hse. 1990 $12.95. ISBN 1-55778-272-5. A selection of excerpts from Gauguin's writings.

BOOKS ABOUT GAUGUIN

Brettell, Richard, and others. *The Art of Paul Gauguin*. Bulfinch Pr. 1988 o.p. A richly illustrated presentation of Gauguin and his work.

Gauguin's South Seas. Universe 1992 $16.95. ISBN 0-87663-633-4. Mostly illustrations, with brief commentaries.

Goldwater, Robert. *Gauguin*. Library of Great Painters Ser. Abrams 1972 $49.50. ISBN 0-8109-0137-4. Consists mostly of color plates with commentaries.

———. *Gauguin*. Masters of Art Ser. Abrams 1983 $22.95. ISBN 0-8109-0983-9. A concise edition of the above.

Leymarie, Jean. *Gauguin: Watercolors, Pastels, Drawings*. Rizzoli Intl. 1989 $25.00. ISBN 0-8478-1050-X. A well-illustrated survey.

Thomson, Belinda. *Gauguin. World of Art Ser.* Thames Hudson 1987 $11.95. ISBN 0-500-20220-6. A good, basic introduction to the life and art of Gauguin.

GOYA Y LUCIENTES, FRANCISCO JOSÉ DE. 1746–1828

Francisco José de Goya y Lucientes was the great Spanish painter and graphic artist whose fame rests not only on his superb painterly abilities but also on the darkness and drama of the subject matter he recorded. REMBRANDT's powerful influence is easily observed. Born in Saragossa, he settled in Madrid in 1774. His early paintings are lively, cheerful, and almost rococo in feeling (e.g., his tapestry cartoons in the Prado). In 1789 Goya was appointed official court painter—a position once held by DIEGO VELAZQUEZ, whom he admired and emulated.

In 1794 Goya became deaf, and his mood changed profoundly. He began to draw and etch. The *Caprichos* (1796–98), aquatinted etchings which date from that period, present satirical, grotesque, and nightmarish scenes. His famous, unsparingly realistic *Family of King Charles IV* (Critics still wonder how he got away with it) was painted in 1800. When Spain was taken over by Napoleon in 1808, a terrible civil war ensued. Goya, torn between his Francophile liberalism and his Spanish patriotism, more than all else hated the cruelties of war. The 65 etchings that comprise *Los Desastres de la Guerra* are among the most moving antiwar documents in all art. Fourteen large mysterious murals, the so-called *Black Paintings*, were painted toward the end of Goya's life. He spent his last years in Bordeaux, in voluntary exile from the Spanish Bourbon regime.

BOOKS ABOUT GOYA

Gudiol, José. *Goya. Masters of Art Ser.* Trans. by Priscilla Muller. Abrams 1985 $22.95. ISBN 0-8109-0992-8. Mostly illustrations with commentaries by a preeminent Goya scholar.

Harris, Tomas. *Goya: Lithographs and Engravings.* 2 vols. A. Wofsy Fine Arts 1983 repr. of 1964 ed. $225.00. ISBN 0-915346-72-9. Volume 2 contains the catalogue raisonné.

Perez Sanchez, Alfonso E. *Goya.* Trans. by Alexandra Campbell. H. Holt & Co. 1990 $29.95. ISBN 0-8050-1444-6. A well-illustrated summary of Goya's life and work.

Perez Sanchez, Alfonso E., and Eleanor A. Sayre. *Goya and the Spirit of Enlightenment.* BDD Promo. Bks. 1989 $39.98. ISBN 0-7924-4827-8. The catalog of an important exhibition, showing the relationship between Goya and the Enlightenment.

Salas, Xavier de. *The Drawings of Goya in the Prado Museum. Master Draftsman Ser.* Trans. and ed. by Stephen Longstreet. Borden 1969 $10.95. ISBN 0-87505-010-7

GROPIUS, WALTER. 1883–1969

Walter Gropius, as leader of the famous Bauhaus, as teacher, and as designer, was a dominant figure in twentieth-century architecture. Born in Berlin to a family with a great architectural tradition (his father was an architect), he strove—in the years after World War I—to bring architecture into harmony with the new industrial age and with the social needs of the times. Gropius was one of the founders of the *Deutsche Werkbund* (1907), whose aim was the modern design of everyday objects. In 1919 he became director of the Weimar School of Design, which he reorganized and renamed the Bauhaus; its goal was to educate designers who would create functional, rational, and socially responsive architecture and objects of art for daily use. In 1925 the Bauhaus moved to Dessau, where, for its new quarters, Gropius designed buildings in a clean, functional, highly innovative style. The Bauhaus was suppressed by the Nazis in 1933, and Gropius fled to England in 1934. There he practiced architecture with the architect Maxwell Fry. In 1937 he came to the United

States, where he headed the highly influential department of architecture at Harvard University until 1952. A firm and articulate believer in teamwork, Gropius founded the Architects Collaborative, which designed a number of buildings, including the U.S. Embassy in Athens and the Pan American Building (now the MetLife Building) in New York City. Working with a team of young architects, Gropius designed the Harvard Graduate Center. He also wrote several books, among them *The Scope of Total Architecture* (1952). As a teacher, lecturer, and writer, as well as an architect, Gropius had an enormous influence on a whole generation of American architects.

BOOKS BY GROPIUS

Apollo in the Democracy. Trans. by Ise Gropius. McGraw 1968 o.p.
New Architecture and the Bauhaus. 1935. MIT Pr. 1965 $7.95. ISBN 0-262-57006-8. Gropius's seminal work.
The Scope of Total Architecture. 1952. Macmillan 1962 o.p. Gropius's own statements on the totality of modern architecture.

BOOKS ABOUT GROPIUS

Giedon, Sigfried. *Walter Gropius*. Dover 1992 repr. of 1952 ed. $17.95. ISBN 0-486-27118-8
Issacs, Reginald. *Gropius: An Illustrated Biography of the Creator of Bauhaus*. Bulfinch Pr. 1991 $40.00. ISBN 0-8212-1753-4. Written by a longtime friend and colleague.
Wingler, Hans. *Bauhaus: Weimar, Dessau, Berlin, Chicago*. MIT Pr. 1969 o.p. The most comprehensive volume, not only on Gropius, but also on the teachings and activities of the famous and influential Bauhaus in its various locations.

KAHN, LOUIS I(SADORE). 1901–1974

Louis Kahn, a pioneer of functionalist architecture, was born in Estonia but came with his family to the United States at the age of 4. A graduate of the University of Pennsylvania, he taught at Yale University from 1947 to 1957, during which time he became known for his addition to the Yale University Art Gallery (1951–53). This work, along with his design for the Richards Medical Research Building in Philadelphia (1957–61), gained him wide recognition. Kahn's international reputation as a major force in contemporary architecture came with his designs for the Salk Institute Laboratories in La Jolla, California (1959–65), the Kimbell Art Museum in Fort Worth, Texas, (1872) and the Paul Mellon Center for British Studies at Yale University (1969–72). From 1957 until his death, Kahn returned to his alma mater, the University of Pennsylvania, to teach. While there, he helped to start the so-called Philadelphia school of modernism. Kahn's designs, though simple, are powerfully compex and subtle at the same time.

BOOK BY KAHN

What Will Be Has Always Been: The Words of Louis I. Kahn. Rizzoli Intl. 1985 $35.00. ISBN 0-8478-0607-3

BOOKS ABOUT KAHN

Latour, Alessandra. *Louis I. Kahn: Writings, Lectures, Interviews*. Rizzoli Intl. 1991 $50.00. ISBN 0-8478-1356-8
Lobell, John. *Between Silence and Light: Spirit in the Architecture of Louis I. Kahn*. Shambhala Pubns. 1979 $15.95. ISBN 0-394-73687-7. Poetic fragments of the architect's words, edited with feeling by a disciple; accompanied by photographs of key buildings.
Loud, Patricia C. *The Art Museums of Louis I. Kahn*. Duke 1989 $60.00. ISBN 0-8223-0989-0. An illustrated account of three museums designed by Kahn.

LE CORBUSIER (pseud. of Charles Edouard Jeanneret-Gris). 1887–1965

Le Corbusier is considered by many to be the leading architect of modern architecture. Born of Swiss parentage near Geneva, but a lifelong Parisian by choice, he started his practice in 1922. In 1923 he published his startling manifesto of what he called "the aesthetics of modern life," *Vers une architecture (Towards a New Architecture)*. Le Corbusier worked first at simplifying and liberating house design through the revolutionary use of new materials—particularly, reinforced concrete—and new technical ideas for mass production, which he applied in the so-called Dom-Ino and the Citrohan House. In his widely influential book *La Ville Radieuse (The Radiant City)* (1935), he laid down his urban planning ideas: a city of high-rise buildings set among trees and grass. His designs for large building groups proved to be as influential as his domestic designs had been. These include the famous housing project in Marseilles (the *Unité d'Habitation*), his League of Nations project in Geneva (unexecuted), and, toward the end of his life, the startling designs for the capital city of Punjab, Chandigarh. He also participated—controversially—in the designs for the U.N. headquarters in New York.

In his last years, Le Corbusier turned away from the geometry and pure logic of his first designs and adopted sculptural and dramatic forms, as in Chandigarh. The almost mystical complexities of Le Corbusier's Pilgrim Church of Ronchamps in the French Jura opened another chapter in the history of twentieth-century architecture.

BOOKS BY LE CORBUSIER

The City of Tomorrow and Its Planning. Trans. by Frederick Etchells. Dover 1987 repr. of 1929 ed. $8.95. ISBN 0-486-25332-5. Impassioned plea for city planning; views a European city as "strangled by the picturesque" and on the verge of being overtaken by chaos.

The Decorative Art of Today. Trans. by James Dunnett. MIT Pr. 1987 $32.00. ISBN 0-262-12118-2. Denounces art deco style; proposes wholesale whitewashing of residential interiors and exteriors.

Journey to the East. Trans. by Ivan Zaknic. MIT Pr. 1987 $13.95. ISBN 0-262-62068-5. Written as a young man but published posthumously; documents the profound effect that sites, especially the Parthenon, had on the artist.

Le Corbusier Sketchbooks. 4 vols. MIT Pr. 1981–82 o.p. Shows Le Corbusier as a painter and master of drawing; with notes by Françoise de Franclieu.

Moduor I and II. Trans. by Peter de Francia and Anna Bostock. HUP 1980 $15.95. ISBN 0-674-58102-4. Book I proposes replacing the metric system with an innovative measurement system based on the mathematics of the human body. Book II replies to criticism of the first volume and expands or modifies earlier views.

The Radiant City (La Ville Radieuse). 1935. Trans. by Pamela Knight. Viking Penguin 1967 o.p. One of the most influential books on modern architecture.

Towards a New Architecture. Trans. by Frederick Etchells. Dover 1986 repr. of 1936 ed. $8.95. ISBN 0-486-25023-7. One of the world's most influential books about modern architecture.

BOOKS ABOUT LE CORBUSIER

Benton, Tim. *The Villas of Le Corbusier 1920–1930.* Yale U. Pr. 1991 repr. of 1987 ed. $29.95. ISBN 0-300-04935-8. Explores the conflicts experienced by Le Corbusier as the fees for designing luxury villas became his principal source of revenue.

Brooks, H. Allen, ed. *Le Corbusier.* Princeton U. Pr. 1987 $19.95. ISBN 0-691-00278-9. A collection of essays about the master by prominent scholars.

Gardiner, Stephen. *Le Corbusier.* Da Capo 1988 repr. of 1972 ed. $10.95. ISBN 0-306-80337-2. One of the few biographies of Le Corbusier in English.

Guiton, Jacques, ed. *The Ideas of Le Corbusier: On Architecture and Urban Planning.* Braziller 1981 $10.95. ISBN 0-8076-1005-4. Puts ideas that are "bewildering from the point of the rigid rationalist" in a condensed and orderly form.

Jencks, Charles. *Le Corbusier and the Tragic View of Architecture.* HUP 1974 $20.00. ISBN 0-674-51860-8. A standard work on Le Corbusier.

Palazzollo, Carlo, and Riccardo Vio, eds. *In the Footsteps of Le Corbusier.* Rizzoli Intl. 1991 $29.95. ISBN 0-8478-1219-7. A useful collection of essays.

Papadaki, Stamo, ed. *Le Corbusier: Architect, Painter, Writer.* Macmillan 1948 o.p. An important early book.

Walden, Russell, ed. *The Open Hand: Essays on Le Corbusier.* MIT Pr. 1977 o.p. Scholars discuss diverse matters, such as the artist's fliration with facism, his approval of the design of New Delphi, and his dedication to harmony and order.

LEONARDO DA VINCI. 1452–1519

Often called the Universal Man, this towering genius in science, engineering, aeronautics, technology—in fact, in almost all human pursuits—was also one of the world's greatest painters, as well as a sculptor, an architect, and a town planner. Born in Vinci, Leonardo was apprenticed as a 14-year-old to the sculptor-painter Andrea Verrocchio in Florence. In 1482 he went to Milan as a military engineer, sculptor, and architect, and remained there for 17 years. While in Milan, he designed the crossing tower of the Milan cathedral and, among many other works, painted *The Last Supper* (1496–97), a mural in the Church of Santa Maria delle Grazie; this is one of his greatest creations and a major accomplishment of Western art. During these creative years in Milan, da Vinci also composed his *Treatise on Painting* (1489–1518) and filled his ever-fascinating notebooks.

In 1499, after the fall of his patron Lodovico Sforza, da Vinci returned to Florence. The *Mona Lisa* (1503–06) dates from that period. After a short and unsuccessful time in Rome (1513–16), he settled in France under the patronage of Francis I. He died in Amboise at the age of 67. A supposedly lost manuscript of da Vinci's was rediscovered at the National Library in Madrid in 1965 and published in 1974.

Books by Leonardo da Vinci

Codex Atlanticus: A Facsimile of the Restored Manuscript. 12 vols. Johnson Repr. o.p. A vast publishing venture, beautifully reproducing Leonardo's greatest manuscript.

Leonardo on Painting. Ed. by Martin Kemp. Yale U. Pr. 1989 $37.00. ISBN 0-300-04542-5

The Madrid Codices of Leonardo da Vinci. Trans. by Ladislao Reti. McGraw 1974 $400.00. ISBN 0-07-037194-6. Leonardo's rediscovered codex, long considered lost; a work of major importance.

The Notebooks of Leonardo da Vinci. Ed. by Irma A. Richter. OUP 1982 $5.95. ISBN 0-19-281538-5

Books about Leonardo da Vinci

Clark, Kenneth. *Leonardo da Vinci.* Viking Penguin 1989 $14.95. ISBN 0-14-022707-5. Introduction to the life and work of the world-renowned artist.

Freud, Sigmund. *Leonardo da Vinci and a Memory of his Childhood.* Norton 1990 $5.95. ISBN 0-393-00149-0. Reconstructs the emotional life of the artist's early childhood years.

————. *Leonardo da Vinci, a Study in Psychosexuality.* Random 1955 $6.00. ISBN 0-394-70132-1. Examines Leonardo's curiosity as a form of sexual inquisitiveness left unsatisfied since childhood.

Goldscheider, Ludwig. *Leonardo da Vinci: Life and Work, Paintings and Drawings.* 1943. New York Graphic Society 1967 o.p. This classic includes a biography, da Vinci's letters, other documents concerning him, a chronology, and a bibliography. Reproduces all Leonardo's paintings and 80 drawings.

Hart, Ivor B. *The Mechanical Investigations of Leonardo da Vinci.* Greenwood 1982 repr. of 1963 ed. $48.50. ISBN 0-313-23489-2. Deals with yet another interest of the original "Renaissance Man"—aeronautics.

Kemp, Martin, and Jane Roberts. *Leonardo da Vinci.* Yale U. Pr. 1989 $25.00. ISBN 0-300-04563-8. A catalog of an exhibition held at the Hayward Gallery, London.

———. *The World of Leonardo da Vinci.* Kelley repr. of 1962 ed. o.p. "This interesting book will long remain a standard work on Leonardo as scientist and engineer" (*N.Y. Times*).

Leonardo da Vinci, Engineer and Architect. U. Pr. of New Eng. 1987 o.p. Catalog of an exhibition held at the Montreal Museum of Fine Arts.

Philipson, Martin, ed. *Leonardo da Vinci: Aspects of the Renaissance Genius.* Braziller 1966 o.p. Includes 13 studies on Leonardo, including ones by Bernard Berenson, Herbert Read, George Sarton, Kenneth Clark, and K. R. Eissler.

Wasserman, Jack. *Leonardo da Vinci. Library of Great Painters Ser.* Abrams 1975 $49.50. ISBN 0-8109-0262-1. Mostly color plates with commentaries.

———. *Leonardo da Vinci. Masters of Art Ser.* Abrams 1984 $22.95. ISBN 0-8109-1285-6. A concise edition of the above.

MANET, EDOUARD. 1832–1883

Edouard Manet was one of the founders of impressionism and of the new naturalism in painting. With pictures like the *Absinthe Drinkers* and the famous *Déjeuner sur l'Herbe*—a naked woman picnicking in the woods with three fully dressed men—he caused a storm of criticism. In 1863, together with his friends MONET, RENOIR, Sisley, and Pissarro, he led the influential *Salon des Refusés* (Salon of the Rejected), which ushered in the new style of impressionism. Strongly influenced by the Venetian Renaissance masters Giorgione and TITIAN, but even more by the Spanish tradition of VELAZQUEZ and GOYA, he was thoroughly aware of the traditions of the past. Yet he was one of the great innovators in painting, in subject matter as well as in technique.

Manet's later years were marred by ill health. For him, official recognition came too late; he died at the age of 51, a disappointed man. Among his later great paintings are *In the Conservatory* and *The Bar at the Folies-Bergères.*

BOOKS ABOUT MANET

Cachin, Francoise, and others. *Manet, 1832–1883.* Abrams 1983 $49.50. ISBN 0-87099-357-3. Catalog of a major exhibition celebrating the centennial of Manet's death.

Courthion, Pierre. *Manet. Library of Great Painters Ser.* Abrams 1959 $49.50. ISBN 0-8109-0260-5. Color plates with commentaries.

Hamilton, George Heard. *Manet and His Critics.* Yale U. Pr. 1986 $12.95. ISBN 0-300-03759-7. A study of the criticism of Manet by his contemporaries.

Richardson, John. *Manet. Phaidon Color Library Ser.* Watson-Guptill 1989 $19.95. ISBN 0-8230-3000-8. Mostly color plates.

Wilson-Bareau, Juliet, ed. *Manet by Himself.* Bulfinch Pr. 1991 $60.00. ISBN 0-8212-1842-5. The artist's correspondence and conversations shed light on his most important works, which are beautifully reproduced.

MATISSE, HENRI. 1869–1954

Next to PICASSO, Matisse is probably the greatest and most versatile artist of modernism. His long career embraced most of the currents of postimpressionist art, in all of which he created highly personal works of remarkable beauty and subtlety.

Born in Picardie, France, Matisse came to Paris as a youth to study law, but soon began to study painting under such conventional masters as Bouguereau. Later, he moved to impressionism and fell under the influence of CÉZANNE; soon after, he was using pure color in the style that characterized the *Fauves* (*The Wild Beasts*), an innovative school of art whose leading master he became. Subsequently, Matisse went through an expressionist phase, during which he was much affected by African and Near Eastern art. In that period, flat decorative patterns in brilliant colors predominated in his work, such as *La Danse* and *La Musique*.

In 1914 Matisse went to live on the Riviera, where he remained for the rest of his long life. Here his great series of *Odalisques* occupied him until the 1930s. His last major work was the decoration of a convent chapel at Venice. Matisse was also a book illustrator of originality, a highly individual sculptor, and a creator of extraordinary paper cutouts, in which he composed pictures using pieces of brightly colored paper. Despite severe arthritis, Matisse worked until his death at the age of 85. In 1992 a major exhibition of his works was held at the Museum of Modern Art in New York City; the extraordinarily large attendance only confirmed his place as one of the greatest French painters of the twentieth century.

BOOKS ABOUT MATISSE

Elderfield, John. *The Cut-outs of Henri Matisse*. Braziller 1978 $17.95. ISBN 0-8076-0886-6. Explores Matisse's self-described "drawing with scissors" and the works he produced with this technique.

———. *Henri Matisse, a Retrospective*. Abrams 1992 $75.00. ISBN 0-8109-6116-4. A catalog of an important exhibition.

———. *Matisse in the Collection of the Museum of Modern Art*. Abrams 1990 $14.95. ISBN 0-8109-6050-8. An overview of Matisse's entire career and oeuvre explored through MOMA's collection.

Gowing, Lawrence. *Matisse*. World of Art Ser. Thames Hudson 1985 $19.95. ISBN 0-500-18171-3. An illustrated biography.

Jacobus, John. *Henri Matisse*. Abrams 1973 $49.50. ISBN 0-8109-0277-X. Mostly color illustrations with commentaries.

Noel, Bernard. *Matisse*. Masters of Modern Art Ser. Trans. by Jane Brenton. Universe 1987 $10.95. ISBN 0-87663-523-0. A small-format introduction to Matisse.

Schneider, Pierre. *Matisse*. Trans. by Bridget S. Romer. Rizzoli 1984 $110.00. ISBN 0-8478-0546-8. An important, major study of the artist and his work.

Watkins, Nicholas. *Matisse*. OUP 1985 $60.00. ISBN 0-19-520464-6. A well-illustrated biography.

MICHELANGELO BUONARROTI. 1475–1564

Michelangelo was one of the greatest artists the human race has produced. As sculptor, painter, and architect, he personified the climax of the Italian High Renaissance, as well as its transition to mannerism and the baroque.

Michelangelo was born near Florence in 1475, to the noble but poor family of Buonarroti. He was trained as a fresco painter by the great Ghirlandaio but soon turned to sculpture. The lovely *Pietá* in St. Peter's in Rome is one of his earliest masterpieces; the *David* in Florence came soon after. In 1505 Michelangelo went to Rome, where he worked for Pope Julius II, a powerful and tempestuous patron of the arts who asked the artist to design a vast tomb with 40 figures. The project, with which the artist struggled for years, was gradually cut down until only the majestic *Moses* and the two *Slaves* remained. For Michelangelo, this was one of the great tragedies of his life. It was, however, Julius II who commissioned him to paint the vast cycle of frescoes on the ceiling of the Sistine Chapel—one of the greatest works ever created by human hand, done entirely by Michelangelo alone, working under incredible difficulties, literally lying on his back on a high scaffold for years (1508–12). Many years later (1536), he added the huge dramatic fresco of the *Last Judgment* on the altar wall of the same chapel. In Florence he created the Medici Chapel with the famous sculptured figures of *Day* and *Night*, *Dawn* and *Evening*. In 1547, at the age of 72, he became chief architect of the incomplete church of St. Peter's in Rome, on which he worked tirelessly until his death in 1564 at the age of 89; the basilica's mighty dome is his creation. In his later years, Michelangelo also wrote sublime poetry, into which he poured the innermost heart of a lonely, melancholy, and intensely religious genius.

BOOK BY MICHELANGELO

Complete Poems and Selected Letters of Michelangelo. Trans. by Creighton Gilbert. Princeton U. Pr. 1980 $14.95. ISBN 0-691-00324-6. Poems express the artist's intense self-criticism; letters reveal the impossible standards he set for others. Interesting reading.

BOOKS ABOUT MICHELANGELO

Condivi, Ascanio. *The Life of Michelangelo*. 2 vols. Trans. by Fanny E. Bunnett. Greenwood repr. of 1900 ed. o.p. Together with Vasari's *Lives*, the main contemporary source.

De Tolnay, Charles Q., ed. *Michelangelo*. 7 vols. Princeton U. Pr. 1969–1975. Vol. 1 $125.00. ISBN 0-691-03858-9. Vol. 2 $115.00. ISBN 0-691-03856-2. Vol. 3 $125.00. ISBN 0-691-03854-6. Vol. 4 $125.00. ISBN 0-691-03857-0. Vol. 5 $125.00. ISBN 0-691-03855-4. Vol. 6 $89.00. ISBN 0-691-03853-8. Vol. 7 $90.00. ISBN 0-691-03876-7. One of the most comprehensive works on the artist.

_____. *Michelangelo: Sculptor-Painter-Architect*. Princeton U. Pr. 1975 $24.95. ISBN 0-691-00337-8. A one-volume condensation of the great seven-volume scholarly work.

De Vecchi, Pierluigi. *Michelangelo*. Trans. by Alexander Campbell. H. Holt & Co. 1992 $35.00. ISBN 0-8050-1790-9. An overview with color illustrations.

Grimm, Herman F. *Life of Michelangelo*. 2 vols. Gordon Pr. 1972 $200.00. ISBN 0-8490-0533-7. One of the greatest biographies.

Hartt, Frederick. *Michelangelo*. *Masters of Art Ser*. Abrams 1984 $22.95. ISBN 0-8109-1335-6. Attractively illustrated look at the artist's work.

_____. *Michelangelo*. *Library of Great Painters Ser*. Abrams 1964 $49.50. ISBN 0-8109-0299-0

Hibbard, Howard. *Michelangelo*. HarpC 1985 $10.95. ISBN 0-06-430148-6. Illustrated introduction to all areas of Michelangelo's career.

Hirst, Michael. *Michelangelo and his Drawings*. Yale U. Pr. 1988 $50.00. ISBN 0-300-04391-0. Discussion of more than 600 surviving drawings.

Liebert, Robert S. *Michelangelo: A Psychoanalytic Study of His Life and Images*. Yale U. Pr. 1983 $45.00. ISBN 0-300-02793-1. Written by a psychoanalyst.

Murray, Linda. *Michelangelo*. *World of Art Ser*. Thames Hudson 1984 $22.95. ISBN 0-500-20174-9. Explores a life of nearly 90 years of "continuous creativity."

Seymour, Charles, ed. *Michelangelo, the Sistine Chapel Ceiling: Illustrations, Introductory Essay, Backgrounds and Sources, Critical Essays*. Norton 1972 $12.95. ISBN 0-393-09889-3. Focuses on the artist's famous paintings in the Vatican's Sistine Chapel.

Summers, David. *Michelangelo and the Language of Art*. Princeton U. Pr. 1981 $25.50. ISBN 0-691-10097-7. Discusses how the artist's intellectual framework and the concepts of Renaissance thought influenced his life.

MIES VAN DER ROHE, LUDWIG. 1886–1969

Mies van der Rohe, a founder of modern architecture, was the great master of steel-and-glass construction. Born in Aachen, Germany, he soon became a leading force in the experimental architecture in the restless period after 1918. He designed revolutionary expressionist glass skyscrapers, which, however, were never built. A classic rationalism then took over Mies's work: the German Pavilion for the Barcelona Exhibition of 1929 (now destroyed) is the most famous example of his geometrical, unadorned design, which revealed all of its component parts.

In 1930 Mies built the fine Tugendhat house in Brno, Czechoslovakia. He was director of the Bauhaus from 1930 until it was closed by the Nazis in 1933. He emigrated to the United States in 1937 and there began a second great career: His prototypical skeleton-frame skyscrapers include the Lake Shore Drive Apartments in Chicago (1948–50) and, most famous of them all, the Seagram Building in New York City (1957–58). Mies remained in the United States for the rest of his life. Two of Mies's sayings have become almost proverbial: "Less is more" and "God is in the detail."

BOOKS ABOUT MIES VAN DER ROHE

Mies van der Rohe: European Works. Architectural Monographs Ser. 11. St. Martin 1986 $45.00. ISBN 0-312-53214-8

Schulze, Franz. *Mies van der Rohe: A Critical Biography.* U. Ch. Pr. 1989 $39.95. ISBN 0-226-74059-5. Discusses the architect's life in Germany, his association with the Bauhaus, his flight from Nazi Germany, and the great success he achieved in the United States.

Tegethoff, Wolf. *Mies van der Rohe: The Villas and Country Houses.* Trans. by Russell M. Stockman. Museum of Mod. Art 1985 $75.00. ISBN 0-262-20050-3. Discusses the first half of Mies's career, when he concentrated his energies on residential design and the creation of modern furniture that was later widely copied.

Zukowsky, John. *Mies Reconsidered: His Career, Legacy, and Disciples.* Rizzoli Intl. 1986 $22.50. ISBN 0-8478-0771-1. Explores Meis's influence on the work of his students.

MONET, CLAUDE. 1840–1926

Claude Monet was probably the greatest painter of the impressionist group and, throughout his long life, its most unswerving representative. He was devoted to the representation of visual impressions, of light and color, rather than sharp forms in dramatic compositions. He spent little time studying the old masters, but he worked with Courbet, admired MANET, and was aware of TURNER and of Japanese art. He lived much of his life in poverty, becoming known only gradually. He liked to paint series—or variations—on the same theme, like the *Poplars*, the *Haystacks*, and *Rouen Cathedral*.

In 1883 Monet settled at Giverny, where he made himself an elaborate garden. He spent the rest of his life there, and it was there that he painted—again and again—his famous *Waterlilies*. The almost abstract patterns of his late works, completed as blindness was setting in, anticipate abstract expressionism.

BOOKS ABOUT MONET

Gordon, Robert. *Monet.* Abrams 1989 $34.95. ISBN 0-8109-8091-6. An excellent introduction to Monet's life and work.

Kendall, Richard, ed. *Monet by Himself: Paintings, Drawings, Pastels, Letters.* Bulfinch Pr. 1990 $55.00. ISBN 0-8212-1766-6. Reproductions of selected works along with contemporaneous correspondence.

Seitz, William C. *Claude Monet. Library of Great Painters Ser.* Abrams 1960 $49.50. ISBN 0-8109-0326-1. Color plates with commentaries.

———. *Claude Monet.* Abrams 1982 $22.95. ISBN 0-8109-134-0. A concise edition of the above.

Tucker, Paul Hayes. *Monet at Argenteuil*. Yale U. Pr. 1982 $45.00. ISBN 0-300-02577-7.
    A study of an important period in Monet's artistic life.
Wildenstein, Daniel. *Monet's Years at Giverny: Beyond Impressionism*. Abrams 1978
    $29.95. ISBN 0-8109-1336-4

MOORE, HENRY (SPENCER). 1898–1986

Born in Yorkshire, England, the sculptor Henry Moore was a dominant figure
in British art from the 1930s to the present. During World War II, he was unable
to sculpt and so instead sketched people in the London underground during
bombing raids. His career reached international prominence when he represented Britain at the 1948 Venice Biennale. Because many of his monumental
sculptures are displayed out of doors, he has a fame beyond that of most artists,
whose work can be seen only in museums. Throughout his long career, Moore
produced figural sculptures that seem to have a universal appeal. He was one of
the first English artists to be aware of sculpture outside the Western tradition.
He was one of the most successful public sculptors, and hundreds of his works
can be seen in parks and squares throughout the world. Among the most well
known are marble sculptures in Lincoln Center in New York City and UNESCO
headquarters in Paris.

BOOKS BY MOORE

Henry Moore: My Ideas, Inspiration, and Life as an Artist. (photographs by John
    Hedgecoe). Chronicle Bks. 1989 $25.00. ISBN 0-87701-391-8. A photographic essay.
Henry Moore on Sculpture. Da Capo 1992 $18.95. ISBN 0-306-80463-8. A collection of
    Moore's writings from many sources, with illustrations of his work.

BOOKS ABOUT MOORE

Lieberman, William S. *Henry Moore: 60 Years of His Art*. Thames Hudson 1983 $24.95.
    ISBN 0-500-23376-4. The catalog of an exhibition at the Metropolitan Museum of Art.
Mitchinson, David, and Julian Stallabrass. *Henry Moore*. Rizzoli Intl. 1992 $24.95. ISBN
    0-8478-1559-5. Mostly color illustrations.

O'KEEFFE, GEORGIA. 1887–1986

American artist Georgia O'Keeffe developed an intensely personal and
abstract style of painting. Born in Wisconsin, O'Keeffe was encouraged in art by
her mother, who saw that she had art lessons along with a well-rounded
education. O'Keeffe became famous with the help and patronage of world-
renowned photographer and gallery owner Alfred Stieglitz, whom she eventually married in 1924.

Although her early works depict scenes of New York City, O'Keeffe lived in
the Southwest for most of her life, and it was to that region that she looked for
the themes and motifs of her later work. In that work, she painted huge
canvases—their spaces beautifully filled with bleached bones, barren rolling
hills, desert blooms, adobe churches, and brightly colored close-ups of simple
flowers. Her work occupied a middle ground between abstraction and realism.

O'Keeffe's paintings are in many museums and private collections. Two of her
well-known works, *Cow's Skull, Red, White, and Blue* (1931) and *Sunflower,
New Mexico No. 2* (1934), can be seen at the Metropolitan Museum of Art in New
York City. Throughout her life, O'Keeffe insisted that her paintings needed no
analysis or interpretation to be understood and appreciated. When she died at
the age of 98, this self-sufficient woman was already a legend in the art world.

BOOK BY O'KEEFFE

A Woman on Paper. S & S Trade 1988 $24.45. ISBN 0-671-66431-X. Compiled from O'Keeffe's letters written to a close friend with whom she discussed her work.

BOOKS ABOUT O'KEEFFE

Berry, Michael. *Georgia O'Keeffe. American Women of Achievement Ser.* Chelsea Hse. 1989 $9.95. ISBN 0-7910-0420-1. An informative, easy-to-read biography of the artist.

Lisle, Laurie. *Portrait of an Artist: A Biography of Georgia O'Keeffe.* PB 1985 $5.99. ISBN 0-671-60040-0. The first full-length account of O'Keeffe's personal life as an artist and as the wife of Alfred Stieglitz.

Robinson, Roxana. *Georgia O'Keeffe: A Life.* HarpC 1989 $25.00. ISBN 0-06-015965-0. A detailed and moving story of O'Keeffe's life and work.

PALLADIO, ANDREA. 1508–1580

Palladio is one of the most influential architects in the history of architecture. He is known as the first professional architect, since he was trained to build and in fact pursued that career throughout his life. Palladio was born in Padua but moved to Vicenza to apprentice with a stonemason. There he built some of his greatest works. Like many artists of the Renaissance, he was a student of Latin literature and of the works of the Roman architect Vitruvius. He found a patron in Giangiorgio Trissino, who in 1545 took him to Rome, where Palladio was able to study the remains of ancient architecture. This led to his revival of Roman symmetrical planning, which is particularly evident in the several villas he built in the Veneto from 1550 onward and for which he is now famous. Among these are the Villa Rotonda outside Vicenza.

Palladio set forth his theories and achievements in his *Quattro Libri dell'Architettura* (*Four Books of Architecture*), which he published in 1570 and which has been republished many times throughout the world. It is one of the classic books of architecture.

BOOK BY PALLADIO

The Four Books of Architecture. 1570. Dover 1960 $13.95. ISBN 0-486-21308-0

BOOKS ABOUT PALLADIO

Ackerman, James S. *Palladio.* Viking Penguin rev. ed. 1974 $8.95. ISBN 0-14-020845-3. A classic.

Faber, Joseph, and Henry Hope Reed. *Palladio's Architecture and Its Influence: A Photographic Guide.* Dover 1980 $8.95. ISBN 0-486-23922-5. Introduces Palladio through discussion and photographs of existing work; explores his influence in England and America.

Puppi, Lionello. *Andrea Palladio: The Complete Works.* Rizzoli Intl. 1989 $35.00. ISBN 0-8478-1150-6. Catalogs works, including architectural drawings; scholarly discussion of basis of attribution.

PICASSO, PABLO. 1881–1973

Pablo Ruiz y Picasso, Spanish painter, graphic artist, and sculptor, is generally considered the most revolutionary, influential, and versatile artist of the twentieth century. He was born in Málaga, son of a painter, and studied in Barcelona. His extraordinary talent showed at an early age: Before he was 14, he had already produced a masterwork in the classic tradition. His early paintings (1901–04) of the so-called Blue Period (in which blues dominate the color scheme) deal with outcasts, beggars, sick children, and circus people. The *Old Guitarist* is the most famous of his Blue Period paintings. In Paris Picasso developed a lighter palette—the so-called Rose Period—which is exemplified in *The Boy with Horse*. In his so-called Negro Period (1907–09), he concerned himself with basic forms, revealing the influence of African art. During those same years, he turned to the incipient cubist movement. *Les Demoiselles d'Avignon*, in its semiabstract geometric forms, was a revolutionary step toward twentieth-century modernism, which he, together with Braque and MATISSE, really set in motion. Picasso went through the entire vocabulary of cubism, its analytical as well as its synthetic phase. After 1918 he was also hailed as an initiator of surrealism.

The horrors of the Spanish civil war affected Picasso deeply. With almost mythological power, his major work *Guernica* was inspired by the terror-bombing of the ancient capital of the Basques in northern Spain. Although the painting does not represent the event itself, it does evoke the agony and terror of war in general. The saturation bombing depicted in *Guernica* was the first demonstration of a technique later employed during World War II. *Night Fishing at Antibes* is another masterwork of that period. In his later years, Picasso experimented with ceramics and did highly original sculptures—including the famous *Goat*—as well as collages. He also produced a flood of drawings, lithographs, engravings, and stage designs. He remained creative to the last day of his life.

BOOKS BY PICASSO

Picasso Line Drawings and Prints. Dover 1982 $3.50. ISBN 0-486-24196-3. Selection of 44 works. Most reproductions are the same size as originals.

Picasso Lithographs: Sixty-One Works. Dover 1980 $3.95. ISBN 0-486-23949-7

Picasso's Vollard Suite. Trans. by Norbert Guterman. Thames Hudson 1985 $9.95. ISBN 0-500-27100-3

BOOKS ABOUT PICASSO

Arnheim, Rudolf. *The Genesis of a Painting: Picasso's Guernica*. U. CA Pr. 1980 repr. of 1962 ed. $47.50. ISBN 0-520-00037-0. A self-described "treasure hunt leading along a path to the creation of a most significant painting"; emphasizes the psychology of the artist.

Ashton, Dore. *Picasso on Art: A Selection of Views*. Da Capo 1988 $11.95. ISBN 0-306-80330-5. Despite Picasso's lifelong refusal to commit his views on art to paper, this work contains recollections of his remarks compiled posthumously by friends.

Barr, Alfred H. *Picasso: Fifty Years of his Art. Museum of Modern Art Publications in Repr. Ser.* Ayer repr. of 1955 ed. $26.00. ISBN 0-405-01519-4

Beardsley, John. *Pablo Picasso*. Abrams 1991 $18.95. ISBN 0-8109-3713-1

Berger, John. *The Success and Failure of Picasso*. Pantheon 1989 $11.00. ISBN 0-679-72272-6. Controversial examination of the effect that Picasso's fame and commercial success had on his work.

Bernadec, Marie-Louise. *The Picasso Museum, Paris: Paintings, Papiers Colles, Picture Reliefs, Sculptures, and Ceramics*. Abrams o.p. Selects 100 masterpieces from the museum and discusses them in the context of Picasso's life and stylistic development.

Gilot, Françoise. *Life with Picasso*. Doubleday 1989 $8.95. ISBN 0-385-26186-1. Written by one of Picasso's wives.

Hilton, Timothy. *Picasso. World of Art Ser.* Thames Hudson 1985 $12.95. ISBN 0-500-20144-7. Intended as a short critical introduction to the artist and his work.

Jaffe, Ludwig. *Picasso. Library of Great Painters Ser.* Abrams 1964 $49.50. ISBN 0-8109-0368-7. Mostly color plates with commentaries.

———. *Picasso. Master of Art Ser.* Abrams 1983 $22.95. ISBN 0-8109-1480-8. Concise edition of the above.

Leiris, Michel, ed. *Late Picasso: Paintings, Sculpture, Drawings, Prints, 1953–1972*. U. of Wash. Pr. 1988 $29.95. ISBN 0-295-96785-4. Catalog of an exhibition at the Tate Gallery of works from the last 20 years of the artist's life.

McCully, Marilyn, ed. *A Picasso Anthology: Documents, Criticism, Reminiscences*. Princeton U. Pr. 1982 $45.00. ISBN 0-691-04001-X

Oppler, Ellen, ed. *Picasso's Guernica: Illustrations, Introductory Essay, Documents, Poetry, Criticism, Analysis*. Critical Studies in Art History Ser. Norton 1988 $14.95. ISBN 0-393-95456-0

Palau i Fabre, Josep. *Picasso*. Rizzoli Intl. 1985 $22.50. ISBN 0-8478-0652-9. Contains color plates of 150 of Picasso's paintings.

Penrose, Roland. *Picasso: His Life and Works*. U. CA Pr. 1981 $13.95. ISBN 0-520-04207-7. Discusses Picasso's work in the context of his life. Contains minimal illustrations and assumes the reader knows what the works look like.

Podoksik, Anatoly. *Picasso*. Abrams 1990 $39.95. ISBN 0-8109-3705-0

Richardson, John. *A Life of Picasso: Volume 1: 1881–1906*. Random 1991 $44.50. ISBN 0-394-53192-2. The primary biography of Picasso.

Rubin, William, ed. *Pablo Picasso: A Retrospective*. Museum of Mod. Art 1980 $50.00. ISBN 0-87070-528-8. Produced in connection with a Museum of Modern Art retrospective. Arranged chronologically, the text explains contemporaneous events in the artist's life.

POLLOCK, JACKSON. 1912–1956

Jackson Pollock was born in Wyoming but eventually moved to New York, where he studied painting at the Art Student's League with the regionalist painter Thomas Hart Benton. During the Depression he worked on the Federal Arts Project, painting in the regionalist style of his teacher.

The drip style of painting that made Pollock famous did not emerge until the late 1940s. Then he abandoned the traditional painting easel and affixed his canvas to the floor or wall, pouring, dripping, or flinging paint onto its surface; hence, the term "gestural" or "action" painting. His flamboyant painting and lifestyle have made him a popular subject of biographers.

Books about Pollock

Cernuschi, Claude. *Jackson Pollock: Meaning and Significance*. HarpC 1992 $35.00. ISBN 0-06-430978-9. Rigorously examines the inner meaning of Pollack's work; assumes readers are familiar with the artist's work.

Frank, Elizabeth. *Jackson Pollock*. Abbeville Pr. 1983 $29.95. ISBN 0-06-430147-8. Introduces readers to Pollack's work; discusses only those works that are reproduced.

Frascina, Francis, ed. *Pollock and After: The Critical Debate*. HarpC 1985 $11.95. ISBN 0-06-430147-8. Pollock's critics debate the meaning of his work, its relevance to mass culture, and its political significance in cold war culture.

Landau, Ellen G. *Jackson Pollock*. Abrams 1989 $75.00. ISBN 0-8109-3702-6. Stunning reproductions of Pollack's work, including large reproductions of his major works.

Naifeh, Steven, and Greg W. Smith. *Jackson Pollock: An American Saga*. Crown Pub. Group 1989 $29.95. ISBN 0-517-56084-4

Solomon, Deborah. *Jackson Pollock: A Biography*. S & S Trade 1987 $19.95. ISBN 0-317-64593-5

RAPHAEL (Raffaello Sanzio). 1483–1520

Raphael was, with MICHELANGELO and LEONARDO DA VINCI, one of the three masters of the High Renaissance. He was also the youngest and died prematurely after a life of incredible creativity and accomplishment. The son of a painter, Giovanni Santi, his actual name was Raffaello Santi of Sanzio. He was trained in Florence but spent most of his short life in Rome. There he created his major works, famous for the harmony and elegance of their design. Above all, there are the frescoes for the papal apartments in the Vatican (*The Stanze*), which he painted at exactly the time Michelangelo was painting the Sistine Chapel (1508–12); among them are such masterpieces as the *School of Athens* and the *Disputà*. His oil painting, the *Sistine Madonna*, is justly famous. Raphael—in the Renaissance manner—was also an accomplished architect and, in his last years, architect-in-chief of St. Peter's.

BOOKS ABOUT RAPHAEL

Beck, James. *Raphael*. Abrams 1976 $49.50. ISBN 0-8109-0432-2. Beautifully produced book of the artist's work.

The Complete Paintings of Raphael. Abrams 1969 o.p. Comprehensive presentation of the artist's paintings.

The Complete Works of Raphael. Reynal 1969 o.p. Contains essays on Raphael's paintings, collaborators, drawings, sonnets, and life.

Crowe, Joseph A. *Raphael, His Life and Works*. Ayer 1972 repr. of 1885 ed. $48.00. ISBN 0-8369-6852-2

Golzio, Vincent. *Raphael: His Life, His Art, His Fortunes*. 2 vols. 1982 repr. of 1968 ed. $287.40. ISBN 0-89901-089-X

Joannides, Paul. *The Drawings of Raphael: With a Complete Catalog*. U. CA Pr. 1983 $129.95. ISBN 0-520-05087-8. Excellent collection of commentaries on all of Raphael's drawings.

Jones, Roger, and Nicholas Penny. *Raphael*. Yale U. Pr. 1987 $19.95. ISBN 0-300-04052-0. Scholarly presentation of the life and work of the artist.

Labella, Vincenzo. *Season of Giants 1492–1508: Michelangelo, Leonardo, Raphael*. Little 1990 $45.00. ISBN 0-316-85646-0. Examines each artist's life and work during the height of the Italian Renaissance.

Pope-Hennessy, John. *Raphael*. NYU Pr. 1970 $50.00. ISBN 0-8147-0476-X. Series of lectures given by the eminent art historian; includes quality reproductions.

REMBRANDT HARMENSZ VAN RIJN. 1606–1669

Rembrandt is the greatest painter of the Dutch School and one of the greatest painters of all time. With a glowing sense of color, he was often somber, with a tragic view of reality and the human condition and a wonderful eye for light and darkness. He was prodigiously creative: More than 600 paintings, more than 300 etchings (many of them masterpieces), and approximately 2,000 drawings (including many exquisite landscape sketches) have been counted. Biblical and historical subjects take up a large part of his work, but he was also a marvelous portrait painter, as we see in the portraits of his mother, his first and second wives, and his son, but above all in his searching self-portraits, done at various stages of his life—from the hopeful, lighthearted youth to the disillusioned but unflinching and deeply introspective old man. He completed more than 60 self-portraits—a record unique in the history of art.

Born in Leiden, in the Netherlands, Rembrandt moved to Amsterdam in 1631, where he spent the rest of his life. In his youth he loved luxury and the pleasures of life; later he became increasingly austere. Rembrandt was highly successful in his early years, but prevailing taste and his own style developed in very different directions. He died a poor and isolated man in 1669. The *Night Watch* and *The Anatomy Lesson of Dr. Tulp* (both in Amsterdam) are among his most famous paintings. Among the etchings, the *Hundred Guilder Print* stands out.

BOOKS ABOUT REMBRANDT

Alpers, Svetlana. *Rembrandt's Enterprise: The Studio and the Market*. U. Ch. Pr. 1988 $29.95. ISBN 0-226-01514-9. Examines the manner in which Rembrandt dealt with the commercial aspects of his life and his use of assistants and relationships with patrons.

Benesch, Otto. *Rembrandt*. Rizzoli Intl. 1990 $25.00. ISBN 0-8478-1216-2. A leading scholar distills the essence of aspects of Rembrandt, about whom he has written numerous volumes.

Clark, Kenneth. *An Introduction to Rembrandt*. HarpC 1979 $9.95. ISBN 0-06-430092-7. Based on a series of lectures given at the Metropolitan Museum of Modern Art.

Haak, Bob. *Rembrandt's Drawings*. Trans. by Elizabeth Willems-Treeman. Overlook Pr. 1977 o.p. A noted author discusses 94 (of 1,400 known surviving) drawings and advises readers on what can be learned from them.

Held, Julius. *Rembrandt Fecit: A Selection of Rembrandt's Etchings*. S. & F. Clark 1981 o.p. Selected etchings by a contemporary art historian who has written extensively on Rembrandt.

Le Bot, Marc. *Rembrandt*. Trans. by Marie-Helene Agueros. Crown Pub. Group 1991 $18.00. ISBN 0-517-58348-8. Mostly color plates.

Munz, Ludwig. *Rembrandt: Rembrandt Harmensz van Rijn*. Abrams 1984 $22.95. ISBN 0-8109-1594-4. Concise edition of the original 1967 book.

Rosenberg, Jakob. *Rembrandt, Life and Work*. Cornell Univ. Pr. 1980 repr. of 1964 ed. $18.95. ISBN 0-8014-9198-3. A classic among Rembrandt studies.

White, Christopher. *Rembrandt*. World of Art Series. Thames Hudson 1984 $11.95. ISBN 0-500-20-195-1. A good introduction to Rembrandt's life and art.

RENOIR, PIERRE AUGUSTE. 1841–1919

Pierre Auguste Renoir, together with MONET, was one of the two leading painters of the impressionist school. He was close to Monet, but he also was influenced by the realism of Courbet and the light palette of the rococo painters Watteau, Fragonard, and Boucher. The human figure—and human flesh—was one of his main interests, as it was also with MANET (but not with Monet). He preferred bright colors—pink, orange, red—and cheerful subjects. His output was amazing—nearly 6,000 pictures, many of them in U.S. collections. He achieved great success during his lifetime. His last years were spent in the south of France. Though crippled by arthritis in his last years, he continued to paint and even to produce some sculpture.

BOOKS ABOUT RENOIR

Gaunt, William. *Renoir*. Watson-Guptill 1989 $19.95. ISBN 0-8230-4536-6. Mostly color plates.

Monneret, Sophie. *Renoir*. Trans. by Emily Read. H. Holt & Co. 1990 $29.95. ISBN 0-8050-1359-9. An excellent and well-illustrated introduction to Renoir.

Pach, Walter. *Pierre Auguste Renoir*. Library of Great Painters Ser. Abrams 1950 $49.50. ISBN 0-8109-0446-2. Color plates with commentaries.

Renoir, Jean. *Renoir, My Father*. Lively Arts Ser. Trans. by Randolph and Dorothy Weaver. Mercury 1988 $9.95. ISBN 0-916515-39-7. The famous filmmaker son's recollection of his great father.

Stella, Joseph G. *The Graphic Work of Renoir: A Catalogue Raisonné*. J. C. Stella 1975 $40.00. ISBN 0-08-390168-X. Presents a category of work overshadowed by the artist's paintings; includes work produced in his final years.

White, Barbara Ehrlich. *Renoir, His Life, Art and Letters*. Abrams 1988 $34.95. ISBN 0-8109-8088-6. A well-illustrated biography.

REYNOLDS, SIR JOSHUA. 1723–1792

Sir Joshua Reynolds was the most influential and important painter of Georgian England, the first president of the Royal Academy, and, so to speak, the greatest establishment figure in English art. Born into a cultured family (unlike most artists of his day), he was a learned man, in touch with the leading literary figures of the time, SAMUEL JOHNSON (see Vol. 1) among them. He received thorough training in Italy (1750–52), where he studied the works of MICHELANGELO, RAPHAEL, and TITIAN. He thus became a confirmed neoclassicist, but some influences from the baroque style of RUBENS are also discernible. His *Discourses*, held at the Royal Academy and widely disseminated in print, are the most important documents of eighteenth-century classicism in art and exercised great influence.

As a painter, Reynolds excelled in portraiture. Many members of the high aristocracy of his time were painted by him in the grand manner, which he combined with subtlety and sensitivity. His technique was often faulty, and many of his pictures have cracked or lost much of their color. He was extraordinarily prolific until blindness struck him in his last year.

BOOKS BY REYNOLDS

Letters of Sir Joshua Reynolds. Ed. by Frederick W. Hilles. AMS Pr. repr. of 1929 ed. $23.00. ISBN 0-698-70796-2

Sir Joshua Reynolds: Discourses. Ed. by Pat Rogers. Viking Penguin 1992 $10.95. ISBN 0-14-043278-7. The artist discusses the work of famous predecessors, including many Italian Renaissance painters.

BOOKS ABOUT REYNOLDS

Penny, Nicholas, ed. *Reynolds.* Abrams 1986 $49.50. ISBN 0-8109-1565-0. The catalog of an exhibition held at the Royal Academy of Art, London.

Steegman, John. *Sir Joshua Reynolds.* Folcroft 1977 repr. of 1932 ed. o.p.

Waterhouse, Ellis. *Reynolds.* Praeger 1973 o.p. Introduction to Reynolds's life, with a collection of his portraits.

RICHARDSON, HENRY HOBSON. 1836–1886

Henry Hobson Richardson, the most influential American architect of the late nineteenth century, studied at Harvard University and then, like many of his American contemporaries, at the École des Beaux Arts in Paris (1859–62). However, he did not remain a Beaux-Arts man but developed a personal style of originality and power, based on Romanesque precedents: bold round arches, arcades, massive walls, often roughly rusticated, all with a very individual touch. The style—the so-called Richardsonian Romanesque, or simply Richardsonian—had enormous influence throughout the United States.

Richardson was aware of the practical and functional: His Marshall Field Warehouse in Chicago (now demolished) was, in effect, a totally modern storehouse. His great Trinity Church in Boston and his massive Allegheny Court House and Jail are among his most famous buildings. Richardson also designed libraries and railroad stations. He strongly influenced LOUIS HENRY SULLIVAN and even FRANK LLOYD WRIGHT, and pointed the way to the future in American architecture.

BOOKS ABOUT RICHARDSON

Hitchcock, Henry-Russell. *The Architecture of H. H. Richardson and His Time.* MIT Pr. 1966 $13.95. ISBN 0-262-58005-5. A good basic study.

Ochsner, Jeffrey Karl. *H. H. Richardson, Complete Architectural Works.* MIT Pr. 1982 $35.00. ISBN 0-262-65015-0. A complete catalog, necessary for any study of Richardson.

O'Gorman, James F. *H. H. Richardson: Architectural Forms for an American Society.* U. Ch. Pr. 1990 $12.95. ISBN 0-226-62070-0

Van Rensselaer, Mariana Griswold. *Henry Hobson Richardson and His Works.* Dover 1979 $9.95. ISBN 0-486-22320-5. Originally published in 1888, a summary of the architect's career by a contemporary.

RODIN, AUGUSTE. 1840–1917

Auguste Rodin, the most celebrated sculptor of the late nineteenth century, was born in Paris. He worked originally as a mason but soon devoted himself to sculpture. His great master was MICHELANGELO ("he freed me from academicism"). He was a supreme realist as well as a romantic; his first major work, *The Age of Bronze,* seemed so lifelike that he was even accused of having cast it from a living model (there are more than 150 recasts of it). Many of his sculptures are extremely popular and widely reproduced, such as *The Kiss, The Thinker,* and the haunting *Burghers of Calais.* One of his innovations was the torso or the fragment as a complete work of art. His main work is the vast *Gates of Hell.* Many of his works, or recasts of them, are in U.S. collections.

BOOKS ABOUT RODIN

Champigneulle, Bernard. *Rodin.* Trans. by J. Maxwell Brownjohn. *World of Art Ser.* Thames Hudson 1986 o.p. A general introduction to the life and work of the artist.
Grunfeld, Frederick V. *Rodin: A Biography.* H. Holt & Co. 1987 o.p. An illustrated account of the artist and his work.
Lampert, Catherine. *Rodin: Sculpture and Drawings.* Yale U. Pr. 1986 $24.95. ISBN 0-300-03832-1. An exhibition catalog.
Laurent, Monique. *Rodin.* Trans. by Emily Read. H. Holt & Co. 1990 $19.95. ISBN 0-8050-1252-4. A good overview, with many color plates.
Rilke, Rainer Maria. *Rodin.* Haskell 1974 $75.00. ISBN 0-8383-1913-0. The great German poet's recollection and appreciation of the master, as whose secretary he served.
Taillandier, Yvon. *Rodin.* Trans. by Anne Ross and A. Clarke. Crown Pub. Group 1988 $14.95. ISBN 0-517-08266-7. An overview of Rodin's life and work.
Tancock, John L. *The Sculpture of Auguste Rodin: The Collection of the Rodin Museum, Philadelphia.* Godine 1989 repr. of 1976 ed. $65.00. ISBN 0-87923-157-2. The catalog of one of the most important Rodin collections in the world.

RUBENS, PETER PAUL. 1577–1640

Peter Paul Rubens, Flemish baroque painter, son of a prominent Antwerp lawyer, was the most prolific, influential, and brilliant artist of his time. He was also a scholar, an entrepreneur, and a diplomat. He served in this last capacity in 1629, negotiating a peace between Spain and England. He spent several of his early years in Italy, where he learned much of his great art from the Italian Renaissance.

In 1608 Rubens settled in his hometown of Antwerp, where, assisted in his vast output by many assistants, he lived a sumptuous life. Great commissions came to him. The *Life of Maria Medici* (21 canvases, now in the Louvre) stands out, as do the ceilings at Whitehall in London. His style is exuberant, dramatic, and of an incomparable sureness of touch, whether depicting a female nude or a great historic event.

BOOKS ABOUT RUBENS

Burchard, Ludwig, comp. *Corpus Rubenianum Ludwig Burchard: An Illustrated Catalogue Raisonné of the Work of Peter Paul Rubens Based on the Material Assembled by the Late Dr. Ludwig Burchard in Twenty-Six Parts.* OUP 1968–1993. Pts. 4–6, 8, 10–15, 17, 20, 22, 25–26 o.p. Pt. 1 $95.00. ISBN 0-19-921012-8. Pt. 2 $175.00. ISBN 0-19-921011-X. Pt. 3 $95.00. ISBN 0-905203-64-X. Pt. 7 $95.00. ISBN 0-19-921032-2. Pt. 9 $95.00. ISBN 0-19-921015-2. Pt. 16 $95.00. ISBN 0-19-921017-9. Pt. 18 $95.00.

ISBN 0-19-921041-1. Pt. 19 $95.00. ISBN 0-19-921056-X. Pt. 21 $175.00. ISBN 0-19-921019-5. Pt. 23 $100.00. ISBN 0-905203-62-3. Pt. 24 $85.00. ISBN 0-19-921020-9. A monumental work, also containing scholarly monographs on individual works or groups of works by Rubens.

Downes, Kerry. *Rubens.* Hippocrene Bks. 1984 o.p.

Held, Julius S. *The Oil Sketches of Peter Paul Rubens: A Critical Catalogue.* 2 vols. Princeton U. Pr. 1980 $197.50. ISBN 0-691-03929-1

Scribner, Charles. *Peter Paul Rubens.* Abrams 1989 $22.95. ISBN 0-8109-1569-3. Mostly color plates with commentaries.

Warnke, Martin. *Peter Paul Rubens: Life and Work.* Trans. by Donna Pedini Simpson. Barrons 1980 $6.95. ISBN 0-8120-2101-0. A useful overview.

White, Christopher. *Peter Paul Rubens: Man and Artist.* Yale U. Pr. 1987 $70.00. ISBN 0-300-03778-3. A well-illustrated biography of Rubens presented as ". . . an embodiment of his times" (Preface).

SULLIVAN, LOUIS (HENRY). 1856–1924

Louis Henry Sullivan, American architect, was a key figure in the development of modern architecture; he is often called the father of the skyscraper. He was also an eloquent writer on the new style as he envisioned it.

Sullivan was born in Boston. He studied at the Massachusetts Institute of Technology and then briefly in Paris. He started his practice in Chicago, together with the architect Dankmar Adler. The massive Auditorium Building, innovative in the clarity and power of its design, is the chief building of the so-called Chicago School of Architecture and a memorial to his and Adler's noteworthy collaboration; they parted company in 1894. On his own, Sullivan had already designed one of the earliest masterpieces of skyscraper architecture in the United States, the Wainwright Building in St. Louis. His next great skyscraper design was the Guaranty Building in Buffalo.

Sullivan was a difficult and lonely man, beset by personal problems. In his later years, his practice dwindled, but he still created some buildings of great beauty, including many small banks in the Midwest, the Farmer's Bank at Owatonna, Minnesota, being the most famous. Sullivan was a master of ornament, although he aimed at clear forms and questioned the role of decoration. The famous slogan "form follows function," which he coined, has been variously interpreted, but it has become part of the vocabulary of modern architecture. FRANK LLOYD WRIGHT was Sullivan's assistant from 1887 to 1893 and considered him his *lieber meister* (dear master); he paid him eloquent tribute in his book *Genius and the Mobocracy.* Sullivan himself was a highly poetic and persuasive writer, above all in his *Kindergarten Chats* (1918) and his *Autobiography of an Idea* (1924).

BOOKS BY SULLIVAN

The Autobiography of an Idea. Dover 1956 repr. of 1924 ed. $7.95. ISBN 0-486-20281-X. The master's own story.

Kindergarten Chats. Dover 1980 $5.95. ISBN 0-486-23812-1. An imaginary discourse between the artist and a student concerning theoretical matters the student must consider before planning any structure.

Louis Sullivan: The Public Papers. Ed. by Robert Twombly. U. Ch. Pr. 1988 $29.95. ISBN 0-226-77996-3. A posthumously published compilation of Sullivan's views as expressed in letters to the editor and addresses to professional societies.

BOOKS ABOUT SULLIVAN

Morrison, Hugh. *Louis Sullivan, Prophet of Modern Architecture.* Norton 1962 repr. of 1935 ed. $8.95. ISBN 0-393-00116-4. The pioneer biography of a pioneer architect.

Sprague, Paul E. *The Drawings of Louis Henry Sullivan: A Catalogue of the Frank Lloyd Wright Collection at the Avery Architectural Library.* Princeton U. Pr. 1979 o.p.

Twombly, Robert C. *Louis Sullivan, His Life and Work.* U. Ch. Pr. 1987 $16.95. ISBN 0-226-82006-8. An exhaustive biography.

Weingarden, Lauren S. *Louis H. Sullivan: The Banks.* MIT Pr. 1987 $34.95. ISBN 0-262-23130-1. A well-illustrated study of some of Sullivan's most important buildings.

Wright, Frank L. *Genius and the Mobocracy.* Horizon Pr. 1971 o.p. Wright's eloquent tribute to his *lieber meister* (dear master).

TITIAN (Tiziano Vecelli). c.1487–1576

Titian was the greatest painter of the Venetian school of painting, which spanned the centuries from Bellini and Giorgione through Veronese and Tintoretto to Tiepolo. Titian represents the High Renaissance. In a shimmering, color-rich, sensuous style, he painted mythological, historical, religious, and erotic subjects—the whole range of the sixteenth-century imagination. He was also a portrait painter of rare psychological power and sympathy (his several portraits of the lonely and harassed emperor, Charles V, stand out as much as do his pictures of various fleshy Venetian beauties). The art of the 80-year-old Titian became mysterious and spiritual, much like the late paintings of REMBRANDT. Titian was much honored by his contemporaries during a long life, spent mostly in Venice.

BOOKS ABOUT TITIAN

All the Paintings of Titian. 4 vols. Ed. by Francesco Valcanover. Hawthorne Bks. 1964 o.p.

Biaderle, Susanna, and others, eds. *Titian.* TeNeues 1990 $85.00. ISBN 3-7913-1102-6. An excellent catalog of Titian's art, along with 16 essays on every aspect of his work.

Hope, Charles. *Titian.* HarpC 1980 o.p. Examines the stylistic development of the artist, with discussion of his larger works; stresses how his genius was nurtured by Venice.

Nash, Jane C. *Veiled Images: Titian's Mythological Paintings for Philip II.* Art Alliance 1986 $35.00. ISBN 0-87982-511-1. Analyzes the six paintings, each variations on the female nude, done for Philip II.

Rosand, David. *Titian.* Abrams 1978 o.p. Examines how innovative choice of canvas and brush type enabled the artist to create extraordinary effects.

———. *Titian: His World and His Legacy.* Col. U. Pr. 1982 o.p. Biography of Titian, a painter of the city of Venice and for the Holy Roman Empire; explores his sources for creative stimulation and his profound effect on Rubens.

Williams, Jay. *The World of Titian, c.1488–1576. Lib. of Art Ser.* Silver Burdett Pr. 1968 o.p. Part of the Time-Life Library of Art.

TURNER, JOSEPH MALLORD WILLIAM. 1775–1851

Joseph Mallord William Turner, together with CONSTABLE, was one of the two greatest English landscape painters and one of the greatest romantic artists of all time. He was also a major precursor of impressionism. Steam, breaking waves, fire, the luminosity of the air, and above all light itself, were his subject matter.

The son of a London barber, Turner showed a precocious talent and made an early success of his career, which enabled him to travel to France, Switzerland, and Italy. The Swiss Alps and the beauty of Venice nourished his vision. His enormous originality attracted criticism, but he found a powerful supporter in JOHN RUSKIN (see Vol. 1), who considered him the greatest of the "modern painters." He was freer in his composition than Constable, as he was in his impressionist technique and in his subject matter, which included such dramatic scenes as the famous *Shipwreck, Steam and Speed* and *The Snow-*

storm. He worked extensively for engravers and published a *Liber Studiorum* (1807–19) of his own landscape engravings, in defense, as it were, of his art.

The variety, spontaneity, and beauty of Turner's drawings and watercolor sketches are almost unequaled. There are no less than 20,000 of them. Personally, Turner was a hardheaded and taciturn man who became a recluse in his later years.

BOOK BY TURNER

Collected Correspondence of J.M.W. Turner with an Early Diary and a Memoir by George Jones. Ed. by John Gage. OUP 1980 o.p.

BOOKS ABOUT TURNER

Herrmann, Luke. *Turner: Paintings, Watercolours, Prints and Drawings*. Da Capo 1986 $22.95. ISBN 0-306-80270-8. Mostly illustrations, with a short introduction.
Reynolds, Graham. *Turner*. Thames Hudson 1985 $11.95. ISBN 0-500-20083-1
Selz, Jean. *Turner*. Crown Pub. Group 1984 $18.00. ISBN 0-517-52361-2. A well-illustrated summary.
Walker, John. *Joseph Mallord William Turner*. Library of Great Painters Ser. Abrams 1976 $49.50. ISBN 0-8109-0513-2. Mostly color plates with commentaries.
Wilton, Andrew. *Turner in His Time*. Abrams 1987 $49.50. ISBN 0-8109-1694-0. An important work by the curator of the Turner Collection of the Tate Gallery in London.

VAN GOGH, VINCENT. 1853–1890

Vincent Van Gogh was one of the great postimpressionist masters and, because of the power and accessibility of his work and the tragedy and dedication of his life, almost a legend as an artist. The son of a Dutch parson, he was largely self-taught. Ascetic and intensely spiritual, he viewed art as almost a religious vocation. He painted incessantly and left a vast volume of work but sold only one picture during his lifetime.

In 1888 Van Gogh went to Arles in search of the glowing sunlight, there breaking from the somber, earthbound realism of his early style to the brilliant colors, passionate thick brushstrokes, and incredible joyousness of his later style. Tragically, he became insane and shot himself in 1890. His letters to his brother Theo are a moving and fascinating account of his working processes and the agony and drama of his daily life.

BOOKS BY VAN GOGH

The Complete Letters of Vincent Van Gogh. Bulfinch Pr. 1979 repr. of 1958 ed. $125.00. ISBN 0-8212-0735-0
Dear Theo: The Autobiography of Vincent Van Gogh. Ed. by Irving Stone. NAL-Dutton 1969 $5.99. ISBN 0-451-16246-3
The Letters of Vincent Van Gogh. Ed. by Mark Roskill. Macmillan 1963 $10.95. ISBN 0-689-70167-5

BOOKS ABOUT VAN GOGH

Hammacher, A. M. *Van Goh: Twenty-Five Masterworks*. Abrams 1984 $14.95. ISBN 0-8109-2277-0. A critical look at 25 of the artist's best-known works; with illustrations.
Hammacher, A. M., and Renilde Hammacher. *Van Gogh*. Thames Hudson 1990 $24.95. ISBN 0-500-27603-X. Originally published as *Van Gogh, a Documentary Biography*. Presents Van Gogh's life through contemporary documents.
McQuillan, Melissa. *Van Gogh*. World of Art Ser. Thames Hudson 1989 $14.95. ISBN 0-500-20232-X. A well-illustrated biography.

Meier-Graefe, Julius. *Vincent Van Gogh: Biography*. Trans. by John Holroyd-Reece. Dover 1987 $4.95. ISBN 0-486-25253-1

Pickvance, Ronald. *Van Gogh in Saint-Remy and Auvers*. Abrams 1986 $18.95. ISBN 0-87099-477-8. Focuses on the last years of Van Gogh's life and the work he did in the asylum at Saint-Remy; includes introductory essays and many reproductions.

Schapiro, Meyer. *Vincent Van Gogh*. Masters of Art Ser. Abrams 1983 $22.95. ISBN 0-8109-1733-5. Contains mostly color plates with commentaries. A classic, informative study.

Stone, Irving. *Lust for Life*. Doubleday 1959 $17.95. ISBN 0-385-04270-1. A popular biography of the artist by a well-known American writer and novelist.

Sweetman, David. *Van Gogh: His Life and His Art*. Crown Pub. Group 1990 $30.00. ISBN 0-517-57406-3. Biography with a few black-and-white illustrations. Discusses Van Gogh in the context of nineteenth-century art and culture.

Uhde, Wilhelm. *Van Gogh*. Watson-Guptill 1990 $19.95. ISBN 0-8230-5585-X

Wolk, Johannes van der. *Vincent Van Gogh: Paintings and Drawings*. Rizzoli Intl. 1990 $90.00. ISBN 0-8478-1288-X. A monumental study.

VELAZQUEZ, DIEGO RODRIGUEZ DE SILVA. 1599–1660

Velazquez was the greatest painter of the Spanish Renaissance. Born in Seville, where he also worked in his early years, he became the court painter in Madrid in 1623. He remained in the service of Philip IV for the rest of his life, portraying his king in many psychologically searching and moving portraits. He visited Italy in 1629–31, but the roots of his art were firmly Spanish.

Court life was not Velazquez's only concern. Deeply human pictures of the humble and of street life are among his greatest; for example, *The Water Carrier of Seville* and *The Old Woman Cooking Eggs*. One of the outstanding historical paintings of all time is his *Surrender of Breda*. *Las Meninas* (*The Maids of Honor*), a court painting full of subtle allusions, is probably his best-known work. (Picasso later painted 44 variations on its theme.) Although his work was neglected in the eighteenth century, Velazquez exerted a strong influence on later nineteenth-century painting.

Books about Velazquez

Brown, Jonathan. *Velazquez, Painter and Courtier*. Yale U. Pr. 1986 $65.00. ISBN 0-300-03466-0. A well-illustrated examination of the life and works of Velazquez.

Dominguez Ortiz, Antonio, and Alfonso E. Perez Sanchez. *Velazquez*. Abrams 1989 $55.00. ISBN 0-8109-3906-1. The catalog of an exhibition held at the Metropolitan Museum of Art.

Serullaz, Maurice. *Velazquez*. Trans. by I. Mark Paris. Abrams 1987 $22.95. ISBN 0-8109-1729-7. Includes 48 high-quality color plates of Velazquez's masterpieces.

WARHOL, ANDY (Andrew Warhola). 1930?–1987

Born near Pittsburgh, Pennsylvania, of immigrant Czech parents, American artist Andy Warhol studied art at the Carnegie Institute in Pittsburgh. He then worked as a commercial artist in New York City. In the early 1960s, Warhol became the most famous pioneer of "pop art," which used comic books, advertisements, and consumer goods as subject matter. Warhol's colorful paintings of Campbell's soup can labels, boxes of Brillo pads, and celebrity icons such as Marilyn Monroe, became among the most recognizable examples of pop art. Warhol was also a filmmaker as well as a painter and graphic artist; his more memorable films include *Trash* (1969) and *Frankenstein* (1973). His studio, called "The Factory," became infamous as a locale for eccentrics and eccentric behavior, much of it associated with the New York drug scene. It was

Warhol who predicted that, "in the future, everyone will be famous for 15 minutes."

BOOKS BY WARHOL

The Andy Warhol Diaries. Ed. by Pat Hackett. Warner Bks. 1989 $29.95. ISBN 0-446-51426-8. Contains selections from daily diary tapes dictated by Warhol; published posthumously. Full of references to other celebrities.

The Philosophy of Andy Warhol: From A to B and Back Again. HarBraceJ 1990 $10.95. ISBN 0-15-672960-1. Contains autobiographical musings.

BOOKS ABOUT WARHOL

Bockris, Victor. *The Life and Death of Andy Warhol.* Bantam 1989 $21.95. ISBN 0-553-05708-1. Focuses on Warhol's glitzy, personal life rather than on his work.

Bourden, David. *Warhol.* Abrams 1989 $49.50. ISBN 0-8109-1761-0. Witty recollections of the artist's life; written by a friend of the artist.

Gidal, Peter. *Andy Warhol: Films and Paintings—The Factory Years.* Da Capo 1991 $14.95. ISBN 0-306-80456-5. Written by a young filmmaker who fervently believes Warhol brought life back to the art world.

McShine, Kynaston, ed. *Andy Warhol: A Retrospective.* Museum of Mod. Art 1991 $35.00. ISBN 0-87070-681-0. Contains critical essays and reproduces 460 works; published for an exhibition at the Metropolitan Museum of Modern Art.

Makos, Christopher. *Warhol.* NAL-Dutton 1990 $12.95. ISBN 0-452-26231-3

Ratcliff, Carter. *Andy Warhol. Modern Masters Ser.* Abbeville Pr. 1986 $19.95. ISBN 0-89659-385-1. Emphasizes the impenetrable quality of Warhol's work.

WREN, SIR CHRISTOPHER. 1632–1723

Sir Christopher Wren was the greatest English classical architect. Originally destined to be a scientist, Wren held the chair of astronomy at Oxford University before he was 30. SIR ISAAC NEWTON (see Vols. 4 and 5) considered him one of the best mathematicians of the day. Soon, however, he applied his untrained genius to architecture. His Sheldonian Theatre at Oxford is the work of a brilliant amateur. In 1665 Wren went to France to view architecture. Then the London fire of 1666 provided him with a great opportunity. For the restoration of the city, he produced a magnificent town plan with radiating streets—hardly the work of an amateur—and concerned himself with the rebuilding of 51 city churches and of the great St. Paul's Cathedral. The latter, with its vast dimensions and majestic dome, is one of his crowning achievements. Among numerous works, he built the library of Trinity College, Cambridge, a highly sophisticated design, and the great Greenwich Hospital. Order, grandeur, harmony, and a scientific ingenuity characterize Wren's buildings.

BOOKS ABOUT WREN

Bennett, James A. *The Mathematical Science of Christopher Wren.* Cambridge U. Pr. 1983 $39.95. ISBN 0-521-24608-3

Downes, Kerry. *The Architecture of Wren.* Universe 1982 o.p. The most authoritative and up-to-date treatment.

Furst, Viktor. *The Architecture of Sir Christopher Wren.* Somerset repr. of 1956 ed. $49.00. ISBN 0-686-01441-3

Gray, Ronald D. *Christopher Wren and St. Paul's Cathedral.* Cambridge U. Pr. 1980 $6.95. ISBN 0-521-21666-4

WRIGHT, FRANK LLOYD. 1867–1959

Wright is widely considered the greatest American architect and certainly one of the most influential. Throughout a career of nearly 70 years, he produced masterpiece after masterpiece, each different and boldly new and yet each with the unmistakable touch of Wright's genius in the treatment of material, the detailing, and the overall concept.

Born in Wisconsin of Welsh ancestry, Wright studied civil engineering at the University of Wisconsin and began his career in Chicago as chief assistant to LOUIS HENRY SULLIVAN, who influenced his early thinking on the American architect as harbinger of democracy and on the organic nature of the true architecture. Out of these ideas, Wright developed the so-called prairie house, of which the Robie House in Chicago and the Avery Coonley House in Riverdale, Illinois, are outstanding examples. In the "prairie-style," Wright used terraces and porches to allow the inside to flow easily outside. Movement within such houses is also open and free-floating from room to room and from layer to layer. Public buildings followed: the Larkin Administration Building in Buffalo (destroyed) and the Unity Temple in Oak Park, Illinois, the former probably the most original and seminal office building up to that time (1905). The Midway Gardens in Chicago and the Imperial Hotel in Tokyo (both gone) came next, winning Wright still greater acclaim.

Personal tragedy, misunderstanding, and neglect dogged Wright's middle years, but he prevailed, and in his later life gathered enormous success and fame. The masterworks of his mature years are the Johnson Wax Building in Racine, Wisconsin, and Fallingwater, Bear Run, Pennsylvania—with its bold cantilevered balconies over a running stream, probably the most admired and pictured private house in American architecture; then, toward the end of his life, the spiral design of the Guggenheim Museum in New York City. Wright's own houses, to which he joined architectural studios, are also noteworthy: Taliesin West was a true Shangri-la in the Arizona desert, to which he turned in order to escape the severe winters in Wisconsin, where he had built his extraordinary Taliesin East.

Wright was a prolific and highly outspoken writer, ever polemical, ever ready to propagate his ideas and himself. All of his books reflect a passionate dedication to his beliefs—in organic architecture, democracy, and creativity.

BOOKS BY WRIGHT

An Autobiography. Rprt. Serv. 1991 repr. of 1932 ed. $109.00. ISBN 0-7812-8431-7. His life and discussion of his buildings, with 20 pages of photographs.

Drawings and Plans of Frank Lloyd Wright: The Early Period (1893–1909). Dover 1983 repr. of 1910 ed. $9.95. ISBN 0-486-24457-1. ". . . [A] republication of the work originally published in 1910 by Ernst Wasmuth in Berlin under the title *Ausgefuhrte Bauten und Entwurfe von Frank Lloyd Wright*" (Preface).

Frank Lloyd Wright, the Guggenheim Correspondence. S. Ill. U. Pr. 1986 $29.95. ISBN 0-8093-1317-0. Contains a commentary by Bruce Brooks Pfeiffer.

The Future of Architecture. NAL-Dutton 1970 $11.95. ISBN 0-452-01018-7. A collection of his later major writings, beginning with the widely discussed "Conversation" (1953), in which he explains his aims and contributions. Includes several rare works originally published in separate editions.

The Letters Trilogy. CSU Pr. Fresno 1986 $39.00. ISBN 0-317-57114-1. This three-volume set consists of letters to apprentices, clients, and architects. Selected by Wright's disciple, Bruce Brooks Pfeiffer, with commentary by Pfeiffer.

Living City. NAL-Dutton 1970 $12.95. ISBN 0-452-01035-7. A lyrical and completely rewritten version of his *When Democracy Builds.*

The Natural House. NAL-Dutton 1970 $10.95. ISBN 0-452-00841-7. An infinite variety of houses for people of limited means; with practical comments and a restatement of Wright's principles and beliefs.

A Testament. Horizon Pr. o.p. Sets forth Wright's memories, ideas, and hopes for the future.

BOOKS ABOUT WRIGHT

Brooks, H. Allen. *Frank Lloyd Wright and the Prairie School.* Braziller 1984 $14.95. ISBN 0-8076-1084-4. Discusses Wright's early work (1900–19) during which he designed innovative residences; well-illustrated throughout.

———, ed. *Writings on Wright: Selected Comment on Frank Lloyd Wright.* MIT Pr. 1981 $12.95. ISBN 0-262-52086-9

Gill, Brendan. *Many Masks: A Life of Frank Lloyd Wright.* Ballantine 1988 $12.95. ISBN 0-345-35698-5. A good, readable biography.

Heinz, Thomas A. *Frank Lloyd Wright.* St. Martin 1982 $19.95. ISBN 0-312-30330-0. A color photographic overview.

———. *Frank Lloyd Wright. Architectural Monographs Ser. 18.* St. Martin 1992 $50.00. ISBN 0-312-07243-0. A pictorial survey emphasizing Wright's residences.

Hitchcock, Henry-Russell. *In the Nature of Materials, 1887–1941: The Buildings of Frank Lloyd Wright.* Da Capo 1975 repr. of 1947 ed. $19.95. ISBN 0-306-80019-5. The main book on the early works of Frank Lloyd Wright; still a basic document for any serious study.

Scully, Vincent. *Frank Lloyd Wright. The Masters of World Architecture Ser.* Braziller 1960 $10.95. ISBN 0-8076-0221-3. Mostly black-and-white illustrations, with an introduction by a famous critic.

Secrest, Meryle. *Frank Lloyd Wright.* Knopf 1992 $29.50. ISBN 0-394-56436-7. A magnificently detailed, nuanced, and dynamic work that explores the more scandalous aspects of Wright's life.

Twombly, Robert C. *Frank Lloyd Wright, His Life and His Architecture.* Wiley 1987 $29.95. ISBN 0-471-85797-1. Wright's life and work, including his apprenticeship with Sullivan; the "Prairie Years"; the founding of his Cooperative Communities; and the construction of great civic buildings and museums.

Wright, John Lloyd. *My Father, Frank Lloyd Wright.* Dover 1992 repr. of 1946 ed. $6.95. ISBN 0-486-26986-8. ". . . [A]n unabridged and slightly altered republication of the work originally published under the title *My Father Who Is on Earth*" (Preface).

CHAPTER 20

The Mass Media

Michael F. Keating

> What is to prevent a daily newspaper from being made the greatest organ of
> social life? . . . A newspaper can be made to take the lead . . . in the great
> movements of human thought and human civilization.
> — JAMES GORDON BENNETT, *New York Herald*

> This instrument can teach, it can illuminate; yes, and it can even inspire. But
> it can do so only to the extent that humans are determined to use it to those
> ends. Otherwise it is merely wires and lights in a box.
> —EDWARD R. MURROW

The mass media permeate our lives, bringing us everything from news to
entertainment to information about traffic, weather, and shopping goods.
Traditionally, speech and writing were the information media, but, over the last
century, these have been augmented—indeed, overtaken—by film and electrical and electronic channels of communication that reach tens of millions of
people all over the world.

"Mass media" is a collective term for television, radio, print, film, sound
recordings, advertising, and other vehicles of mass communication. In this
chapter we are concerned with journalism (both print and broadcast),
television and radio entertainment, and film—the media that have the largest
audiences and the greatest impact.

The mass media age began in the nineteenth century with the "penny press,"
newspapers that sold for a penny and tapped into popular taste with lurid stories
of crime, sex, and scandal alongside more serious reportage about the city, the
nation, and the world. The penny press reached its zenith with the *New York
World*, published by JOSEPH PULITZER beginning in 1887. It became the nation's
leading newspaper, attaining a circulation in the hundreds of thousands—a
mass audience for that time. Newspapers were partly supported by their
purchase price, but the more important source of financial support was
advertisers attracted by the mass market that the popular press could deliver.

The next mass medium to develop was motion pictures. Pioneered in the late
nineteenth century, movies were playing to vast audiences all over the world by
World War I. Silent film proved to be an international language; movies turned
out by Hollywood were understood by people everywhere. Even after the advent
of sound, American films retained their dominance because of Hollywood's
unmatched technical mastery and marketing skills. A major consequence of the
movies' universal appeal was the standardization of tastes in everything from
clothes and furnishings to romantic techniques and slang. Since Hollywood also
provided newsreels for mass distribution starting in 1927, journalism found a
new medium and a new way to appeal to large audiences.

Radio and film were the vibrant mass media of the period between World War I and World War II. Unlike movies, which were sustained by paid admissions to theaters, radio was supported solely by advertising. Companies paid for entertainment and news programming in return for the chance to broadcast messages about their products and services to the great numbers of people gathered about their home radio sets to listen to live music, comedy shows, and soap operas. Radio decisively altered the way in which news was delivered and perceived. For the first time in history, people could get the news as it was happening. This was especially exciting during World War II, as foreign correspondents broadcast news of battles going on, with bombs bursting in the background.

Then came television, the most powerful mass medium yet invented. Although the technology had been available in the 1920s, first the Depression and then World War II impeded commercial development. By the early 1950s, however, one-third of American homes had a television set; today virtually all do. It is the prevalent medium for entertainment, news, and all sorts of information, an unequaled cultural and political force in American life. Television has the ability to create a sense of urgency about events happening far away, which makes it a powerful tool for journalism. At the same time, it is capable of creating a sense of intimacy between viewer and subject, which makes it a powerful dramatic and confessional medium.

During the 1950s and 1960s, television programming was dominated by the three big networks—ABC, CBS, and NBC. Starting in the early 1970s, however, cable television expanded from a service to improve reception to a medium offering original entertainment, highly regarded news reporting, and shopping networks. Today more than half of national television reception is via cable.

The newest development in mass communications is interactive television. The term is a broad one that includes already existing shopping networks and two-way processing systems that produce information on color television screens, as well as projected interactive digital networks that will offer subscribers entertainment on demand, changing today's viewer into tomorrow's user.

When the technology of a medium changes, the content of that medium usually changes as well. The technology of fast presses and cheap paper that made it possible to print hundreds of thousands of copies of a newspaper daily changed *what* was printed; newspapers were transformed from leisurely presenters and interpreters of news to voracious gatherers of stories that were spewed out as quickly as possible. The technology of sound that allowed audiences to hear dialogue while watching images gave rise to a very different sort of film, one in which montage was replaced by more fluid editing. Cable and direct satellite broadcasting have made possible a vast array of offerings that the major networks could never provide with their single hookups, and in the process have splintered audiences so that today's mass audiences are relatively smaller than the mass audiences of a generation ago, or even a century ago.

With the twenty-first century nearly upon us, we are at the edge of radical developments in communications. The new electronic media—communications satellites, videocassettes, interactive videotext services, personal and home computers—are turning the mass media into something that will be less "mass" in the sense that the new audience fragmentation makes it less profitable to gear offerings to *everyone*. Yet the new media may actually be used by more people in many more ways.

REFERENCE WORKS

Anderson, Elliott, and Mary Kinzie, eds. *The Little Magazine in America: A Modern Documentary History*. Pushcart Pr. 1979 $35.00. ISBN 0-91366-04-9. Discusses the history of small magazines in the U.S. and talks about why so many of them fail.

Blode, Eleanor S., and James K. Bracken. *Communication and Mass Media: A Guide to the Reference Literature*. Libs. Unl. 1991 $40.00. ISBN 0-87287-810-4. Emphasizes the Anglo-American reference literature in the field, organized around reference genre rather than subject area.

Blum, Eleanor. *Basic Books in the Mass Media: An Annotated, Selected Booklist Covering General Communications, Book Publishing, Broadcasting, Film, Magazines, Newspapers, Advertising, Indexes, and Scholarly and Professional Periodicals*. U. of Ill. Pr. 1980 $34.95. ISBN 0-252-00814-6. Suggests research materials for the layperson and provides a bibliographic list for works relating to all aspects of mass media.

Blum, Eleanor, and Frances Wilhoit. *Mass Media Bibliography: An Annotated Guide to Books and Journals for Research and Reference*. U. of Ill. Pr. 1990 $49.95. ISBN 0-252-01706-4. Almost 2,000 entries for titles published from 1980 to 1987 dealing with theory, structure, and research as opposed to technique and methodology. Includes indexes.

Broadcasting and Cable Yearbook 1993. 2 vols. Bowker 1993 $159.95. ISBN 0-8352-3315-4. Published annually since 1935; the industry resource for latest information on radio, television, and cable.

DeFleur, Melvin, and Otto N. Larsen. *The Flow of Information: An Experiment in Mass Communication*. Transaction Pubs. 1986 $18.95. ISBN 0-88738-675-X. Searches for pathways and regularities in the process of message diffusion or communication through human social organizations.

DeFleur, Melvin, and Shearon Lowery. *Milestones in Mass Communications Research*. Longman 1988 $47.95. ISBN 0-8013-0039-8

De Vito, Joseph A. *The Communication Handbook: A Dictionary*. HarpC 1986 o.p. Definitions of more than 2,000 words and phrases plus essays on 100 terms.

Dominick, Joseph. *The Dynamics of Mass Communication*. McGraw 1990 $22.40. ISBN 0-07-017599-4. An up-do-date analysis of the theory, history, structure, economics, ethics, regulations, and social effects of all the media.

Gerbner, George, and Marsha Siefert, eds. *World Communications: A Handbook*. Longman 1984 $39.96. ISBN 0-582-28457-0. Collection of articles on issues related to international communication; with assessment of communication situations and policy statements on the same issues.

Gillmor, Donald M., and Jerome A. Barron. *Mass Communication Law: Cases and Comments*. West Pub. 1989 $58.25. ISBN 0-314-56267-2

Gitter, George, and Robert Grunin, eds. *Communications: A Guide to Information Sources*. Gale 1980 o.p. Provides an outline of the parameters of the scientific investigation of communication.

Gross, Lynne S. *The New Television Technologies*. Brown & Benchmark 1990. ISBN 0-697-05491-8. A history of technological events in television. Puts the events in the context of social and economic issues of the time.

Halpern, Jeanne W. *Computers and Composing: How the New Technologies Are Changing Writing*. S. Ill. U. Pr. 1984 $12.95. ISBN 0-8093-1146-1. Discusses the potentialities of computers and how they will change writing, learning, and teaching.

Hudson, Robert V. *Mass Media: A Chronological Encyclopedia of Television, Radio, Motion Pictures, Magazines, Newspapers, and Books in the United States*. Garland 1987 $70.00. ISBN 0-8240-8695-3. Brief summaries of significant events in history of mass media from 1638 to 1985; with indexes.

Joyce, William L., David Hall, Richard D. Brown, and John B. Hench. *Printing and Society in Early America*. Am. Antiquarian 1983 $37.50. ISBN 0-912296-55-0.

Lent, John A. *Bibliographic Guide to Caribbean Mass Communication*. Greenwood 1992 $59.95. ISBN 0-313-28210-2. International survey of 3,695 listings organized by region and subject subdivisions such as print media, radio and television, telecommunications, and public relations.

_____. *Global Guide to Media and Communications.* K. G. Saur 1987 $70.00. ISBN 3-598-10746-3. Selective list of books and articles relating to mass media. Arranged geographically and specifically omits U.S. listings.

Longley, Dennis, and Michael Shain, eds. *Dictionary of Information Technology.* OUP 1986 $29.95. ISBN 0-19-520519-7. This new edition shares the virtues of the first edition. Intended to satisfy the needs of experts encountering terms outside their own subspecialty. Emphasis on identifying acronyms and abbreviations.

McCavitt, William E. *Radio and Television: A Selected, Annotated Bibliography.* Supplement One: 1977–1981. Scarecrow 1982 $20.00. ISBN 0-8108-1556-7. Supplement Two: 1982–1986. Scarecrow 1989 $27.50. ISBN 0-8108-2158-3. Some 1,000 entries of subjects that include audience and ratings, biographies, law, new technologies, careers, foreign and international perspectives.

Obudho, Constance E., ed. *Human Nonverbal Behavior: An Annotated Bibliography.* Greenwood 1979 $29.95. ISBN 0-313-21094-2. Bibliography of articles and books about human nonverbal behavior written between 1940 and 1978.

Putnam, Linda L., and Michael E. Pacanowsky, eds. *Communication and Organizations: An Interpretive Approach.* Vol. 65 Sage 1983 $23.95. ISBN 0-8039-2110-1. Aims to define and explicate the tenets of a particular paradigm in organization communication—the interpretive approach.

Rosenberg, Jerry M. *Dictionary of Computers, Information, and Telecommunications.* Wiley 1987 $65.00. ISBN 0-471-85558-8. Comprises some 10,000 listings pertaining to all three information technologies. Includes abbreviations and cross-references and an English/Spanish/French glossary.

Shearer, Benjamin F., and Marilyn Huxford, eds. *Communications and Society: A Bibliography on Communications Technologies and Their Social Impact.* Greenwood 1983 $45.00. ISBN 0-313-23713-1

Snorgrass, J. William. *Blacks and Media: A Selected, Annotated Bibliography, 1962–1982.* U. Pr. Fla. 1985 $12.00. ISBN 0-8130-0810-7. Lists over 700 publications concerning blacks in four broad media categories: print, broadcast, advertising, and film.

Weik, Martin H. *Communications Standard Dictionary.* Van Nos. Reinhold 1988 $72.95. ISBN 0-442-20556-2

Weiner, Richard. *Webster's New World Dictionary of Media and Communications.* P-H 1990 $29.95. ISBN 0-13-969759-4. In addition to definitions, lists leading companies and professional associations.

GENERAL WORKS

Abel, Eli, ed. *What's News: The Media in American Society.* Transaction Pubs. 1981 $34.95. ISBN 0-87855-448-3. A good exploration of the news and its effects.

Bagdikian, Ben H. *The Media Monopoly.* Beacon Pr. 1993 $14.00. ISBN 0-8070-6157-3. A critical study of the trend toward monopoly in media ownership.

Barnouw, Erik, ed. *International Encyclopedia of Communications.* 4 vols. OUP 1989 $350.00. ISBN 0-19-504994-2. Published jointly by Oxford and the Annenberg School of Communications, with signed entries in alphabetical order, indexes, and bibliographies.

Blum, Eleanor. *Mass Media Bibliography: An Annotated Guide to Books and Journals for Research and Reference.* U. of Ill. Pr. 1990 $49.95. ISBN 0-252-01706-4. Almost 2,000 entries for works published from 1980 through 1987. Indexes included.

Butler, Matilda, and William Paisley, eds. *Women and the Mass Media: A Sourcebook for Research and Action.* Human Sci. Pr. 1980 $52.00. ISBN 0-87705-409-6. A source book of information on issues relating to women in the media, especially issues having to do with sexism.

Christians, Clifford C., and others. *Media Ethics: Cases and Moral Reasoning.* Longman 1991 $22.95. ISBN 0-8013-0650-7. Explores a wide spectrum of timely ethical issues, using commentaries and cases.

Codding, George A., Jr. *The International Telecommunication Union: An Experiment in International Cooperation. International Propaganda and Communications Ser.* Ayer 1972 repr. of 1952 ed. $27.50. ISBN 0-405-04744-4. A comprehensive look at the International Telecommunication Union from the point of view of its ability to adapt to changing technologies, the changing needs of states, and the changing international political environment.

Czitrom, Daniel J. *Media and the American Mind: From Morse to McLuhan.* U. of NC Pr. 1982 $10.95. ISBN 0-8078-4107-2. Study of the ways media have changed American society.

DeFleur, Melvin, and Sandra J. Ball-Rokeach. *Theories of Mass Communication.* Longman 1989 $24.95. ISBN 0-582-99870-0. Explores the theories of the effects of mass communication.

Diamond, Edwin, Norman Sandler, and Milton Mueller. *Telecommunications in Crisis: The First Amendment, Technology, and Deregulation.* Cato Inst. 1983 $6.00. ISBN 0-932790-39-9. Examines the Federal Communications Commission and the issue of the deregulation of telecommunication technology, with analysis of specific cases.

Dizard, Wilson P., Jr. *The Coming Information Age: An Overview of Technology, Economics, and Politics.* Longman 1989 $21.95. ISBN 0-8013-0305-2. A good interpretation of U.S. and world communications systems, offering an overview of technology, economics, and politics.

Dominick, Joseph. *The Dynamics of Mass Communication.* McGraw $22.84. ISBN 0-07-017559-4

Edelstein, Alex X., and others. *Communication and Culture.* Longman 1989 $39.95. ISBN 0-8013-0335-4

Feagans, Lynne, Catherine Garvey, and Roberta G. Koff. *The Origins and Growth of Communication.* Ablex Pub. 1984 $52.50. ISBN 0-89391-164-X. Collection of works about the origins and growth of interpersonal communication, primarily as related to child development.

Gerbner, George, and others. *The Global Media Debate: Its Rise, Fall and Renewal.* Ablex Pub. 1991 $32.50. ISBN 0-89391-791-5

Horwitz, Robert Britt. *The Irony of Regulatory Form: The Deregulation of American Telecommunications.* OUP 1991 repr. of 1988 ed. $17.95. ISBN 0-19-506994-4. History of telecommunications regulation and reform movements.

Hudson, Robert V. *Mass Media: A Chronological Encyclopedia of Television, Radio, Motion Pictures, Magazines, Newspapers, and Books in the United States.* Garland 1987 $70.00. ISBN 0-8240-8695-3. Brief summaries of significant events in mass media history from 1638 to 1985. Includes essay and indexes.

Hunt, Todd, and Brent Ruben. *Mass Communication: Producers and Consumers.* HarpC 1993 $37.50. ISBN 0-06-500052-8

Jamieson, Kathleen H., and Karlyn K. Campbell. *The Interplay of Influence: News, Advertising, Politics, and the Mass Media.* Wadsworth Pub. 1992. Price N/A ISBN 0-534-14106-4. Examines mass media and the implications of choices made by journalists, advertisers, and political activists.

McAnany, Emile, and Jorge Schnitman, eds. *Communication and Social Structure: Critical Studies in Mass Media Research.* Praeger Pubs. 1981 $37.95. ISBN 0-275-90679-5. Contributions by authors of diverse backgrounds, focusing on social structure and social change and their relationship to mass communications.

McQuail, Denis. *Media Performance: Mass Communication and the Public Interest.* Sage 1992 $65.00. ISBN 0-8039-8294-1. Considers technology, changing economic and political ideologies in a variety of countries and changing conceptions of print and electronic media in this far-reaching and important study.

Middleton, Kent R., and Bill F. Chamberlin. *The Law of Public Communication.* Longman 1991 $43.95. ISBN 0-8013-0449-0. Balanced coverage of the law as it pertains to all the media and their uses.

Mowlana, Hamid, and others, eds. *Triumph of the Image: The Media's War in the Persian Gulf—A Global Perspective*. Westview 1992 $55.00. ISBN 0-8133-1532-8. An exploration of the social, economic, and political context of media coverage in many countries, revealing a distorted image of the Gulf War.

Neuman, W. Russel. *The Future of the Mass Audience*. Cambridge U. Pr. 1992 $44.50. ISBN 0-521-41347-8. Thoughtful analysis of much of the traditional and recent research into the effect and future of the television and video industries.

Riggins, Stephen Harold, ed. *Ethnic Minority Media: An International Perspective*. Sage 1992 $42.95. ISBN 0-8039-4723-2. A worthy collection of case studies spanning a variety of ethnic minorities and countries.

Schiller, Herbert I. *Mass Communications and American Empire*. Westview 1992 $15.95. ISBN 0-8133-1440-2. An examination of the U.S. media's cultural power.

JOURNALISM

Journalism is the enterprise of collecting, selecting, and interpreting the news and presenting it to an audience through print (newspapers and magazines) or electronic (radio and television) media. Modern journalism traces its roots to the first regularly published newspapers that appeared in the early eighteenth century: the *Boston News-Letter* (1704) was the earliest true newspaper in the United States. The production of newspapers and magazines increased dramatically throughout the eighteenth and early nineteenth centuries, but it was advances in technology after the Civil War that made the low-cost mass-circulation newspaper and magazine possible.

A free press is the product of a democratic society that assumes it has the right to know about issues. Ever since the colonial press furthered the cause of American independence, an important segment of U.S. journalism has been associated with reforming crusades and investigative journalism. The heyday of print journalism was from the late nineteenth century to the middle of the twentieth century, when literacy rates were high and advertisers had few other outlets. Alongside the popular press, with its mix of gossip, scandal, and hard news served up in flamboyant prose, there existed a more sober press, with lengthy articles on serious subjects presented in sedate prose designed to appeal to a more educated audience. Magazines like HENRY LUCE's *Time* also flourished, providing a national perspective on issues.

Almost as soon as commercial radio started in 1920, there were regular news broadcasts. Most had formats modeled on newspapers, with reports, features, and editorials. More exciting was radio's live coverage of political conventions (in the days when presidential nominations really were decided at party conventions), famous trials, and faraway battles.

It was television, however, that had a revolutionary impact on journalism. It did not *tell* the news, like newspapers and radio; it *showed* it. Nightly and morning news programs on the three networks—CBS, NBC, and ABC—featured correspondents in Washington, D.C., around the country, and around the world who reported the news in front of, or as voices over, dramatic camera footage. People could now *see* brutal civil rights battles in the South, the assassination of President John F. Kennedy and the shooting of his assassin, the landing of an American astronaut on the moon, and the dive bombings and infantry assaults of the Vietnam War—often called the first "living-room war." They could watch presidential candidates debate one another and judge their demeanor as well as their words. The Watergate crisis unfolded before their eyes in often dramatic live hearings in the U.S. Senate and the House of

Representatives. Envisioned originally as a kind of headline service for people who would read the news "in full" in a daily newspaper, television gradually replaced the newspaper as people's regular source of information. Today the great majority of Americans get most or all of their news from television.

The major development in television journalism in recent years has been Cable News Network (CNN). Its 24-hour presence, global reach, and straightforward approach to reporting the news have made it the broadcast source that people around the world turn to for up-to-the-minute reportage. During the Persian Gulf War in 1991, CNN was used by both the Iraqi and the American governments to keep track of events and to communicate with each other. Just as network television news overtook print journalism during the 1960s and 1970s, CNN has been overtaking network news since the 1980s.

Where does the dominance of television leave print journalism? Newspapers today are struggling for survival in a society whose younger members never acquired the daily newspaper reading habit and whose older members are losing it. Many have been merging and diversifying by buying radio and television stations and cable outlets, the idea being to become all-around providers of information. Some combination of computer, television, and telephone technology will probably make even greater inroads into traditional newspaper journalism in the future. Still, print journalism is far from dead, for newspapers provide the kind of informed analysis and detailed comment that are largely absent from the electronic media. In fact, they are the primary developers of news, fielding more reporters, covering more subjects, and breaking more stories than electronic journalism.

Abramson, Phyllis Leslie. *Sob Sister Journalism*. Greenwood 1990 $37.95. ISBN 0-313-26513-5. The 1906 shooting of famous architect Stanford White by a jealous husband and the new kind of sentimental-sensationalist journalism it generated.

Adler, Renata. *Reckless Disregard: Westmoreland v. CBS et al.; Sharon v. Time*. Random 1988 $6.95. ISBN 0-394-75525-1. Two famous libel cases of the 1980s involving shoddy journalism.

Altschull, J. Herbert. *Agents of Power: The Role of the News Media in Human Affairs*. Longman 1984 $35.95. ISBN 0-582-28417-1. A provocative study of how the media act as proxies for the social, economic, and political leadership of society.

_____. *From Milton to McLuhan: The Ideas Behind American Journalism*. Longman 1990 $22.95. ISBN 0-582-28562-3. A brilliant examination of journalism's philosophical underpinnings.

Associated Press. *The Associated Press Stylebook and Libel Manual: The Journalist's Bible*. Addison-Wesley 1987 $10.53. ISBN 0-201-10433-4. An essential tool for journalists.

Belford, Barbara. *Brilliant Bylines: A Biographical Anthology of Notable Newspaperwomen in America*. Col. U. Pr. 1986 $49.50. ISBN 0-231-05496-3. A superb survey of American women journalists, with 24 profiles of reporters from the nineteenth century to the present.

Bernstein, Carl, and Bob Woodward. *All the President's Men*. S&S Trade 1987 $9.95. ISBN 0-671-64644-3. The well-known story of the Watergate investigation that helped set a new standard for investigative reporting.

Bliss, Edward, Jr. *Now the News: The Story of Broadcast Journalism*. Col. U. Pr. 1992 $19.95. ISBN 0-231-04403-8. An excellent history of broadcast journalism in the United States.

Bollinger, Lee C. *Images of a Free Press*. U. Ch. Pr. 1991 $22.50. ISBN 0-226-06348-8. An insightful work exploring the complex relationship between the First Amendment and the Supreme Court, the public, the press, and the democratic process.

Boyer, Peter J. *Who Killed CBS? The Undoing of America's Number-One News Network*. St. Martin 1989 $5.95. ISBN 0-312-91531-4. The definitive account of the troubles and cynicism that almost destroyed CBS.

Catledge, Turner. *My Life and The Times*. HarpC 1971 o.p.

Chandler, David L., and Mary V. Chandler. *The Binghams of Louisville: The Dark History Behind One of America's Great Fortunes*. 3 vols. Crown Pub. Group 1987 o.p. Revelations about a prominent newspaper publishing family whose quarrels destroyed their newspaper business.

Columbia University Graduate School of Journalism, ed. *Essential Liberty: First Amendment Battles for a Free Press*. Seven Locks Pr. 1992 $16.95. ISBN 0-929765-12-5. Personal reflections by prominent lawyers, journalists, and others in five landmark cases.

Cose, Ellis. *Inside America's Most Powerful Newspaper Empires—From the Newsrooms to the Boardrooms*. Morrow 1989 o.p.

Crouse, Timothy. *The Boys on the Bus: Riding with the Campaign Press Corps*. Ballantine 1986 $4.95. ISBN 0-345-34015-9. Behind-the-scenes coverage of the journalists who covered the 1972 presidential campaign—a classic.

Curry, Jane L. *Press Control Around the World*. Praeger Pubs. 1982 $39.95. ISBN 0-275-90775-9. An examination of the varieties of government controls on the press.

Dahlgreen, Peter, and Colin Sparks, eds. *Journalism and Popular Culture*. Sage 1992 $55.00. ISBN 0-8039-8670-X. An anthology of 11 essays, examining the historical origins of the division between "serious" journalism and its more populist relatives such as the tabloid press.

Edwards, Julia. *Women of the World: The Great Foreign Correspondents*. Ivy Books 1989 $3.95. ISBN 0-8041-0491-3. The saga of 140 years of women journalists covering great and catastrophic events, beginning with Margaret Fuller.

Ein, Marina Newmyer. *The Washington Black Book: The Directory to the Washington Press Corps*. Madison Bks. UPA 1988 $94.95. ISBN 0-8191-6878-5. A comprehensive guide to Washington journalists and bureaus.

Emery, Edwin, and Michael Emery. *The Press and America: An Interpretive History of the Mass Media*. P-H 1992 $59.00. ISBN 0-13-739277-X. An informative and standard textbook.

Epstein, Edward J. *News from Nowhere: Television and the News*. Random 1973 o.p. An exceptional critique of network news.

Filoreto, Carl, and Lynn Setzer. *Working in T.V. News: The Insider's Guide*. Mustang 1993 $12.95. ISBN 0-914457-50-0. A useful reference tool for television journalists.

Fischer, Heinz-Dietrich, ed. 3 vols. DeGruyter. Vol. 1 *Outstanding International Press Reporting: From the Consequences of World War I to the End of World War II 1928–1945*. 1984 $107.00. ISBN 3-11-008918-1. Vol. 2 *Pulitzer Prize-Winning Articles in Foreign Correspondence, 1946–1962: From the End of World War II to the Various Stations of the Cold War*. 1985 $106.00. ISBN 0-89925-026-2. Vol. 3 *Pulitzer Prize-Winning Articles in Foreign Correspondence, 1963–1977: From the Escalation of the Vietnam War to the East Asian Refugee Problems*. 1986 $85.50. ISBN 0-89925-027-0

Gans, Herbert. *Deciding What's News: A Study of CBS Evening News, NBC Nightly News, Newsweek and Time*. Vin. 1980 $10.95. ISBN 0-394-74354-7. A classic study of the role the mass media play in the workings of society.

Ghiglione, Loren. *The American Journalist: Paradox of the Press*. Lib. Congress 1990 $19.95. ISBN 0-8444-0701-1

Goldstein, Tom. *Killing the Messenger: One Hundred Years of Media Criticism*. Col. U. Pr. 1991 $15.50. ISBN 0-231-06603-1. A collection of 15 essays, speeches, and book excerpts published during the last century criticizing the press.

Goodwin, H. Eugene. *Groping for Ethics in Journalism*. Iowa St. U. Pr. 1987 $19.95. ISBN 0-8138-0819-7. Examines the current status of ethics in journalism and tries to present it in a way that will help journalists think through ethical problems.

Goulden, Joseph C. *Fit to Print: A.M. Rosenthal and His Times*. Carol Pub. Group 1988 $21.95. ISBN 0-8184-0474-4. A muckraking portrait of the rise of Abe Rosenthal and the story of his tenure as editor of *The New York Times*.

Graber, Doris. *Crime News and the Public*. Greenwood 1980 $75.00. ISBN 0-275-90491-1. Explores the impact that media images and audience images of the criminal justice process have on life in the U.S.

Halberstam, David. *The Powers That Be.* Doubleday 1986 $6.95. ISBN 0-19-505589-6. A major work on the emergence and influence of the mass media in America after World War II.

Herman, Edward, and Noam Chomsky. *Manufacturing Consent: The Political Economy of the Mass Media.* Pantheon 1988 $14.95. ISBN 0-679-72034-0. Explores the hypothesis that the news is structured by an underlying consensus of elites.

Hertsgaard, Mark. *On Bended Knee: The Press and the Reagan Presidency.* FS&G 1988 $22.50. ISBN 0-374-25197-5. A critique of the failure of the press to report the truth of what was happening during the Reagan administration and an exploration of the reasons for this failure. Based on some 175 interviews with top administration officials, senior journalists, and news executives.

Hosley, David H., and Gayle K. Yamada. *Hard News: Women in Broadcast Journalism.* Greenwood 1987 $42.95. ISBN 0-313-25477-X. A scholarly yet accessible history of the roles of women broadcast journalists from the 1920s to the present.

Jensen, Carl. *Censored: The Project Censored Yearbook, the News That Didn't Make the News—And Why.* Shelburne Pr. 1993 $12.95. ISBN 1-882680-00-6. An illuminating exposé of important events that did *not* make the news.

Kaniss, Phyllis. *Making Local News.* U. Ch. Pr. 1991 $24.95. ISBN 0-226-42347-6. A comprehensive look at local print and broadcast media whose premise is that Americans are as likely to form their opinions about government and business from information obtained through the local media, as they are from information obtained through national news sources.

Keeler, Robert F. *Newsday: A Candid History of the Respectable Tabloid.* Morrow 1990 o.p. The story of *Newsday*'s stormy rise to respectability as told by a member of its staff since 1971.

Kessler, Lauren. *The Dissident Press.* Sage 1984 $29.95. ISBN 0-8039-2086-5. Discusses the role of alternative journalism in American history, especially in relation to controversial issues.

Kluge, Pamela Hollie, ed. *Guide to Economics and Business Journalism.* Col. U. Pr. 1993 $39.50. ISBN 0-231-07072-1. A valuable guide for journalists.

Kluger, Richard. *The Paper: The Life and Death of the Herald Tribune.* Random 1989 $16.95. ISBN 0-394-75665-0. An excellent history of the famous New York daily newspaper from its heyday in the nineteenth century to its death in 1967.

Koch, Tom. *Fact and Context: The News as Myth.* Greenwood 1990 $45.00. ISBN 0-313-27268-9. Claims that journalism's form dictates news content and that reporters are dangerously reliant on official and bureaucratic sources.

Leapman, Michael. *Arrogant Aussie: The Rupert Murdoch Story.* Carol Pub. Group 1985 $14.95. ISBN 0-8184-0370-5. A portrait of the controversial head of a communications empire whose British and American newspapers exert tremendous social and political power.

Leonard, Thomas C. *The Power of the Press: The Birth of American Political Reporting.* OUP 1987 $25.00. ISBN 0-19-503719-7. A compelling book on the history of political reporting.

Levy, Leonard W. *Emergence of a Free Press.* OUP 1987 $9.95. ISBN 0-19-504240-9. An outstanding work on freedom of the press and free speech.

McKerns, Joseph P., ed. *Biographical Dictionary of American Journalism.* Greenwood 1989 $42.95. ISBN 0-313-23818-9. An excellent collection of biographical sketches of 500 important journalists from 1690 to the late 1980s.

Mahon, Gigi. *The Last Days of the New Yorker.* Mcgraw 1989 $18.95. ISBN 0-07-039635-3. An account of the 1985 sale of the magazine to S. I. Newhouse.

May, Antoinette. *Witness to War: A Biography of Marguerite Higgins.* Viking Penguin 1985 o.p. A biography of the Pulitzer Prize-winning overseas correspondent.

Merrill, John C. *The Imperative of Freedom: A Philosophy of Journalistic Autonomy.* Freedom Hse. 1980 $42.00. ISBN 0-932088-45-7. A philosophical study of journalism that considers journalists' everyday activities as well as journalistic objectivity, truth-seeking, and ethics.

Meyer, Karl E. *Pundits, Poets, and Wits: An Omnibus of American Newspaper Columns.*
OUP 1991 repr. of 1990 ed. $13.95. ISBN 0-19-507137-9. A wonderful collection
of newspaper columns by outstanding writers from Benjamin Franklin to Art
Buchwald.

Mickelson, Sig. *From Whistle Stop to Sound Bite: Four Decades of Politics and Television.*
Praeger Pubs. 1989 $42.95. ISBN 0-275-92351-7X. An excellent analysis of the
changes television has wrought on political campaigning, by a veteran broadcast
journalist.

Midgley, Leslie. *How Many Words Do You Want? An Insider's Stories of Print and
Television Journalism.* Carol Pub. Group 1989 $19.95. ISBN 1-55972-015-8. A wealth
of information by a renowned journalist.

Mills, Kay. *A Place in the News: From the Women's Pages to the Front Page.* Col. U. Pr.
1990 $39.50. ISBN 0-231-07416-6

Nimmo, Dan, and James E. Combs. *Nightly Horrors: Crisis Coverage on Television
Network News.* U. of Tenn. Pr. 1985 $32.50. ISBN 0-87049-443-0. Study of how the
three major U.S. television networks reported six major crises on the nightly news
from 1978 to 1982.

Noble, Gil. *Black Is the Color of My TV Tube.* Carol Pub. Group 1981 $12.00. ISBN 0-8184-
0297-0. Autobiography of an important African American reporter on a New York
City television station.

Parenti, Michael. *Inventing Reality: Politics and the Mass Media.* St. Martin 1985 $18.65.
ISBN 0-312-43474-X. A useful study of the press during the Reagan era.

Patner, Andrew. *I. F. Stone: A Portrait.* Doubleday 1990 $19.95. ISBN 0-385-41382-3.
A biography of the man who for some 60 years was America's most important radical
journalist.

Pickett, Calder. *Voices of the Past: Key Documents in the History of American Journalism.*
Macmillan 1977. ISBN 0-02-395790-5

Pizzigati, Sam, and Fred J. Solowey, eds. *The New Labor Press: Journalism for a Changing
Union Movement.* ILR Pr. 1992 $16.95. ISBN 0-87546-190-5. Contributors argue for
the importance of labor journalism in a media environment that generally neglects
labor issues. Special attention is given to the role of women and minorities in the
labor movement.

Porter, William E. *Assault on the Media: The Nixon Years.* U. of Mich. Pr. 1976 o.p.
Account of the efforts of government policy, from 1969 to 1974, to control the role of
the news media in the U.S.

Rather, Dan, and Mickey Hershkowitz. *The Camera Never Blinks: Adventures of a TV
Journalist.* Ballantine 1987 $4.95. ISBN 0-345-35363-3. Autobiography of the promi-
nent CBS anchor.

Reston, James. *Deadline: A Memoir.* Random 1991 $25.00. ISBN 0-394-58558-5. Fascinat-
ing memoirs of the Pulitzer Prize-winning journalist and *New York Times* editor.

Roberts, Chalmers M. *In the Shadow of Power: The Story of the Washington Post.* Ed. by
Jane Gold. Seven Locks Pr. 1989 $16.95. ISBN 0-932020-71-2. A history of the
Washington Post, its leaders, and its role in the nation's capital.

Robertson, Nan. *The Girls in the Balcony: Women, Men, and "The New York Times."*
Random 1992 $10.00. ISBN 0-449-90793-7. A reporter's view of women's struggle for
equal work and equal pay at a newspaper where, for many decades, only white males
were promoted to positions of influence. Includes sketches of careers of a number of
superior female journalists.

Ross, Ishbel. *Ladies of the Press: The Story of Women in Journalism by an Insider.* Ayer
1974 repr. of 1936 ed. $42.00. ISBN 0-405-06120-X

Salisbury, Harrison. *Journey for Our Times.* Carroll & Graf 1984 $10.95. ISBN 0-88184-
037-8. Account of his career by the long-time prominent foreign correspondent for
The New York Times.

Sanders, Marlene, and Marcia Rock. *Waiting for Prime Time: The Women of Television
News.* U. of Ill. Pr. 1988 $21.95. ISBN 0-252-01435-9. A behind-the-scenes look at
television news broadcasting from the 1950s to the present that focuses on the
challenges faced by television newswomen.

Scharff, Edward E. *Worldly Power: The Making of the Wall Street Journal.* NAL-Dutton 1987 $9.95. ISBN 0-317-56711-X. A history of the *Wall Street Journal*, with discussion about the power players and scandals that have surrounded it.

Schudson, Michael. *Discovering the News: A Social History of American Newspapers.* Basic 1981 $14.00. ISBN 0-465-01666-9. In which "Schudson sees news as a product packaged for consumers and sold for profit. Its market is society, and when society changes, news changes" (*Library Journal*).

Schwarzlose, Richard A. *Newspapers: A Reference Guide.* Greenwood 1987 $65.00. ISBN 0-313-23613-5. Valuable essays on the history and role of newspapers in America.

Sloan, David, ed. *American Journalism History: An Annotated Bibliography.* Greenwood 1989 $55.00. ISBN 0-313-26350-7. A useful bibliography beginning with U.S. colonial journalism and ending with contemporary times.

Sloan, David, et al, eds. *The Great Reporters: An Anthology of News Writing at Its Best.* Vision Pr. 1992 $18.95. ISBN 0-9630700-2-9. Eighteen stories by a variety of prize-winning reporters.

Smith, Hedrick, ed. *The Media and the Gulf War: The Press and Democracy in Wartime.* Seven Locks Pr. 1992 $24.95. ISBN 0-932020-99-2. An examination of how the media handled the Gulf War in the face of military censorship.

Smith, Jeffrey A. *Printers and Press Freedom: The Ideology of Early American Journalism.* OUP 1990 repr. of 1987 ed. $29.95. ISBN 0-19-505144-0. A scholarly historical account emphasizing that the major purpose of freedom of the press in the eighteenth century was to expose government misconduct.

Smolla, Rodney. *Suing the Press: Libel, the Media, and Power.* OUP 1986 $10.95. ISBN 0-19-505192-0. A study of trends in recent libel cases.

Steel, Ronald. *Walter Lippman and the American Century.* Random 1981 $15.95. ISBN 0-394-74731-3. An excellent portrait of an important journalist.

Stephens, Mitchell. *A History of News.* Viking Penguin 1989 $9.95. ISBN 0-14-009490-3. An impressive examination of the changing technology of communication from preliterate times to the present.

Talese, Gay. *The Kingdom and the Power.* Dell 1986 $6.95. ISBN 0-440-34525-1. Dated but still relevant story of intrigues and power struggles at *The New York Times*.

Tripp, Bernell. *Origins of the Black Press: New York, 1827–1847.* Vision Pr. 1992 $9.95. ISBN 0-9630700-1-0. The origin and motivation behind America's earliest African American newspapers.

Van Gerpen, Maurice, *Privileged Communication and the Press: The Citizen's Right to Know Versus the Law's Right to Confidential News Source Evidence.* Greenwood 1979 $45.00. ISBN 0-313-20523-X. A review of the issues surrounding confidentiality of news sources.

Wagner, Lilya. *Women War Correspondents of World War II.* Greenwood 1989 $42.95. ISBN 0-313-26287-X. In-depth analysis of the working conditions and lives of female correspondents in the war.

Walker, Martin. *Powers of the Press: Twelve of the World's Influential Newspapers.* Modan-Adama Bks. 1984 $12.95. ISBN 0-915361-10-8. Examines the power of 12 of the world's most influential newspapers and how each reflects its society.

White, Theodore. *In Search of History: A Personal Adventure.* Warner Bks. 1986 $7.95. ISBN 0-446-34657-8. Account of his career by the reporter who changed the course of presidential campaign reporting in the 1960s.

Winfield, Betty H., and Lois B. DeFleur. *The Edward R. Murrow Heritage: Challenge for the Future.* Iowa St. U. Pr. 1986 $19.95. ISBN 0-8138-1191-0. Deals with press performance within the larger sociopolitical milieu, as well as a number of standard dilemmas that plague the news-gathering process.

RADIO AND TELEVISION

We discussed radio and television as news purveyors earlier in this chapter. Here we are concerned with these media as entertainment and cultural forces.

Commercial radio started in 1920, and after a coast-to-coast hookup was made in 1924, the medium quickly gained a huge audience for its broadcasts of music and baseball games, comedy shows and dramas, soap operas and serials. President Franklin D. Roosevelt resourcefully used this intimate medium as a political tool in his "fireside chats." The 1930s and 1940s were the radio era; the great majority of American homes had a set and avidly followed stars like the comedian Jack Benny and the singer Bing Crosby.

Television took over as the home entertainment medium during the 1950s, in the beginning providing a mix much like radio's, but an entirely different experience because of the wedding of sight and sound. Television was black and white and live in the early days—variety shows like Ed Sullivan's *Toast of the Town* and comedy shows like Sid Caesar's *Your Show of Shows* were broadcast directly from studio to home—but taped shows and color became the norm during the 1960s and 1970s. Program content changed as well, as most production shifted to Hollywood, which turned out westerns like *Bonanza*, detective stories like *Kojak*, and miniseries like *Roots* and *The Winds of War*, as well as the situation comedies that have been a staple of television, from *I Love Lucy* to *Murphy Brown*.

Technology has always been the driving force in broadcasting. The development of satellite and cable television gave people many more choices than network television could offer. By 1993, 62 percent of American homes had cable, and the networks were rapidly losing viewers. Americans no longer all watched *I Love Lucy* on a weekday night; the new technologies made it possible to choose among sports, shopping, movie, religious, and other specialized networks, so the viewing audience became much more fragmented.

Today the race is on to develop digital interactive television that can be transmitted in computer codes. By merging two-way telephone network capabilities with the high-capacity information conduits of cable, it will be possible to create a 500-channel system that allows users to browse among a menu of offerings, from movies to video games to information services and consumer goods, and choose exactly what they want instantly. Also under development is a new standard of reception, high-definition television, that will provide a much clearer picture with truer color that will compare favorably with the rich images of film in a theater.

Arlen, Michael J. *Living-Room War*. Viking Penguin 1979 o.p. An analysis of how television coverage affected society's perceptions of the Vietnam War.

_____. *Thirty Seconds*. Viking Penguin 1981 $9.00. ISBN 0-14-005810-9. A superb account of the way television commercials were made in the late 1970s and early 1980s.

Auletta, Ken. *Three Blind Mice: How the Television Networks Lost Their Way*. Random 1991 $24.50. ISBN 0-394-56358-1. A behind-the-scenes look at the multibillion-dollar network television industry and its recent decline.

Bannerman, R. Leroy. *On a Note of Triumph: Norman Corwin and the Golden Years of Radio*. Carol Pub. Group 1986 $8.95. ISBN 0-8184-0512-0. A biography of the first writer admitted to the Radio Hall of Fame.

Barnouw, Erik. *A History of Broadcasting in the United States*. 3 vols. OUP Vol. 1 *A Tower in Babel: To 1933*. 1966 $50.00. ISBN 0-19-500474-4. Vol. 2 *The Golden Web: 1933 to 1953*. 1968 $50.00. ISBN 0-19-500475-2. Vol. 3 *The Image Empire: From 1950*. 1970 $50.00. ISBN 0-19-501259-3. The major work in the field.

_____. *The Sponsor: Notes on a Modern Potentate*. OUP 1978 $9.95. ISBN 0-19-502614-4. An excellent study of the economic structure and ideological impact of modern broadcasting.

————. *Tube of Plenty: The Evolution of American Television*. OUP 1990 $39.95. ISBN 0-19-506483-6. Excellent and lively synopsis of the history of American broadcasting by the leading historian of broadcasting.

Brown, Les. *Les Brown's Encyclopedia of Television*. Visible Ink Pr. 1992 $44.95. ISBN 0-8103-8871-5. A comprehensive guide to the entire television industry.

Busby, Linda J., and Donald L. Parker. *The Art and Science of Radio*. Allyn 1984 $44.00. ISBN 0-205-08049-9

Cantor, Muriel, and Joel M. Cantor. *Prime-Time Television: Content and Control*. Sage 1991 $29.95. ISBN 0-8039-3169-7. A useful introduction to a complex subject that is relatively free of jargon.

Comstock, George. *Television in America*. Sage 1991 $29.95. ISBN 0-8039-3338-X. Examines effects of television news on public attitudes.

Cross, Donna Woolfolk. *Media Speak: How Television Makes Up Your Mind*. NAL-Dutton 1984 $4.95. ISBN 0-451-62701-6. How television programming promotes establishment values.

Dominick, Joseph, and others. *Broadcasting—Cable and Beyond: An Introduction to Modern Electronic Media*. McGraw 2nd ed. 1992 $33.95. ISBN 0-07-017817-8. A useful exploration of the history, structure, economics, effects, programming, technology, and legal environment of electronic media.

Fornatale, Peter, and Joshua E. Mill. *Radio in the Television Age*. Overlook Pr. 1983 $22.50. ISBN 0-87951-106-0. A history of radio in the 1950s, 1960s, and 1970s.

Friendly, Fred W. *Due to Circumstances Beyond Our Control*. Vin. 1991 o.p. An engaging analysis of the workings of contemporary commercial television through a first-person account by the former president of CBS News.

Gianakos, Larry J. *Television Drama Series Programming: A Comprehensive Chronicle, 1980–82*. 2 vols. Scarecrow. Vol. 1 1983 $52.50. ISBN 0-8208-1626-1. Vol. 2 *1982–1984*. 1987 $69.50. ISBN 0-8108-1876-0. A complete list of television drama series programming, with episode titles, credits, and brief descriptions of each program.

Gitlin, Todd. *Inside Prime Time*. Pantheon 1985 $17.00. ISBN 0-394-73787-3. A thorough study of how prime-time shows get on the air and stay there.

Hammond, Charles M. *The Image Decade: Television Documentary, 1965–1975*. Hastings 1981 o.p. Deals with the art and practice of the television documentary in terms of concepts, programs, producers, reporters, and events.

Head, Sydney W. *Broadcasting in America*. HM 1991. Price N/A ISBN 0-395-54445-9. A comprehensive history.

Hill, George H., and Sylvia Hill. *Blacks on Television: A Selectively Annotated Bibliography*. Scarecrow 1985 $25.00. ISBN 0-8108-1774-8. Listing of black television personalities.

Hill, George H., and J. J. Johnson. *Black Radio in Los Angeles, Chicago, and New York: A Bibliography*. Daystar Co. Carson 1987 $8.00. ISBN 0-685-13858-5. A bibliography of the history of black radio, including a guide to the field's most influential pioneers, past and present.

Hoover, Stewart M. *The Electronic Giant: A Critique of Telecommunications from a Christian Perspective*. Bks. Demand 1982 $42.80. ISBN 0-317-55801-3

Inglis, Andrew F. *Behind the Tube: History of Broadcasting*. Focal Pr. 1990 $42.95. ISBN 0-240-80043-5. Maps the development of radio, television, and cable technology, covering the technical, personal, economic, and social aspect of this trajectory.

Iyengar, Shanto. *Is Anyone Responsible? How Television Frames Political Issues*. U. Ch. Pr. 1991 $19.95. ISBN 0-226-38854-9. An excellent study of television's impact on American politics.

Iyengar, Shanto, and Donald R. Kinder. *News That Matters: Television and American Opinion*. U. Ch. Pr. 1989 $19.95. ISBN 0-226-38856-5. How television newscasts affect public opinion.

Kaplan, E. Ann, ed. *Regarding Television: Critical Approaches*. Greenwood 1983 $42.95. ISBN 0-313-27009-0

Kellner, Douglas. *The Persian Gulf TV War*. Westview 1992 $19.95. ISBN 0-8133-1615-4. An attack on the myths, disinformation, and propaganda disseminated during the Gulf War.

Liebert, R. *The Early Window: The Effects of Television on Children and Youth*. Pergamon 2nd ed. 1982 $35.00. ISBN 0-08-027548-6. Examines the theories and research on television and its effect on children's attitudes, development, and behavior.

MacDonald, Fred J. *Blacks and White TV: Afro-Americans in Television Since 1948*. Nelson-Hall 1992 $18.95. ISBN 0-8304-1326-X

———. *One Nation under Television: The Rise and Decline of Network TV*. Nelson-Hall 1992 $19.95. ISBN 0-8304-1362-6. An authoritative history of network television.

McChesney, Robert W. *The Battle for the Control of U.S. Broadcasting, 1930–1935*. OUP 1993 $45.00. ISBN 0-19-507176-3

McCrohan, Donna. *Prime Time, Our Time: America's Life and Times through the Prism of Television*. Prima Pub. 1990 $19.95. ISBN 1-55958-005-4. Analyzes the two top-rated television programs for every year from 1950 to 1989.

Mitroff, Ian I., and Warren Bennis. *The Unreality Industry: The Deliberate Manufacturing of Falsehood and What It Is Doing to Our Lives*. Carol Pub. Group 1989 $17.95. ISBN 1-55972-014-X. A provocative exploration of the pervasive and dangerous effects of television on American culture.

Reed, Maxine K., and Robert M. Reed. *Career Opportunities in Television, Cable, and Video*. Facts on File 1990 $27.50. ISBN 0-8160-2318-2. Describes a hundred job opportunities in the fields of television, cable TV, and video, with information about job responsibilities, requirements, and qualifications.

Rose, Brian G., ed. *TV Genres: A Handbook and Reference Guide*. Greenwood 1985 $59.95. ISBN 0-313-23724-7. Nineteen formats of television programming, from documentary to game shows, are discussed in separate chapters.

Slater, Robert. *This . . . Is CBS: A Chronicle of 60 Years*. P-H 1988 o.p. A straightforward history of the network.

Spigel, Lynn. *Make Room for TV: Television and the Family Ideal in Postwar America*. U. Ch. Pr. 1992 $42.00. ISBN 0-226-76966-6. A provocative look at the way television became a mirror of America's dreams and fears.

Stempel, Tom. *Storytellers to the Nation: A History of American Television Writing*. Continuum 1992 $24.95. ISBN 0-8264-0562-2. A comprehensive and readable history of television writing from the 1940s to the present, based on in-depth interviews with over 40 television writers.

Terrace, Vincent. *Radio's Golden Years: The Encyclopedia of Radio Programs, 1930–1960*. A. S. Barnes 1981 o.p. A listing of 1,500 nationally broadcast network and syndicated old-time radio entertainment programs; includes photos.

———. *Encyclopedia of Television: Series, Pilots and Specials*. 3 vols. Zoetrope 1986 $39.95. ISBN 0-918432-69-3. Covers 1937 through 1984 in Vols. 1 and 2; Vol. 3 is an index.

West, Darrell M. *Air Wars: Television Advertising in Political Campaigns, 1952–1992*. CQ Pr. 1993 $17.95. ISBN 0-87187-756-2. A 40-year history of how candidates use television advertising to influence voters and win elections.

Williams, Huntington, III. *Beyond Control: The Rise and Fall of ABC*. Atheneum 1989 $19.95. ISBN 0-689-11818-X. An ABC insider's view of how the network rose to number one in the 1970s and how it was subsequently taken over.

CHRONOLOGY OF AUTHORS
(Journalism, Radio, and Television)

Pulitzer, Joseph. 1847–1911

Riis, Jacob A(ugust). 1849–1914

Tarbell, Ida. 1857–1944

Lippmann, Walter. 1889–1974

Luce, Henry R(obinson). 1898–1967

Paley, William S(amuel). 1901–1990

Liebling, A(bbott) J(oseph).
1904–1963
Murrow, Edward R(oscoe).
1908–1965

Salisbury, Harrison. 1908–1993
McLuhan, Marshall. 1911–1980
Cronkite, Walter. 1916–

CRONKITE, WALTER. 1916–

Regarded by the public as "the most trusted man in America" before he retired as anchor of the *CBS Evening News* in 1981, Walter Cronkite started out as a newspaperman, moved over to radio, and then shifted into television in the early days, becoming one of the pioneers who helped create television journalism.

Cronkite was born in St. Louis, Missouri, but grew up in Kansas City and Houston, Texas. He decided to become a reporter while still in high school, and in college worked part-time for the *Houston Post*, a paper he joined full-time after leaving the University of Texas. From 1940 to 1949, he reported for the United Press wire service. One of the first journalists accredited to cover World War II, Cronkite accompanied Allied forces on the Normandy invasion and the Battle of the Bulge. At the end of the war, he became UP's bureau chief in Moscow and then its chief correspondent at the Nuremburg war crimes trials.

After returning to the United States in 1948, he covered Washington, D.C., for a group of radio stations before joining CBS, where he remained for the rest of his career, first working on various news programs and then, in 1962, becoming anchor of the *CBS Evening News*. Over the years, Cronkite's assured professionalism in covering such important stories as the assassination of President John F. Kennedy, the moon landing of Apollo II (staying on the air 24 hours to do so), the Vietnam War, and the Watergate scandal won him numerous awards, including several Emmies, the Peabody Award (1962), the William A. White Journalism Award (1969), and the George Polk Award (1971), and gained him great credibility with the public. He twice visited Vietnam during the war, and, after the Tet offensive in 1968, candidly questioned the rationale for American involvement and the U.S. military's prospects for victory. It was said in Washington that, when Walter Cronkite turned against the war, so did the American people.

Cronkite has continued to work on special projects for CBS since his retirement. He has also spoken out against "soft journalism" in television—the expansion of feature stories at the expense of "hard news"—and become an advocate for hour-long network news broadcasts.

BOOKS BY CRONKITE

Challenges of Change Public Affairs Pr. 1971 o.p.
Eye on the World Cowles Pub. Co. 1971 o.p.
South by Southeast. (coauthored with Ray Ellis). Oxmoor Hse. 1983 $50.00. ISBN 0-8487-0539-4

LIEBLING, A(BBOTT) J(OSEPH). 1904–1963

A. J. Liebling was an urbane and prolific journalist whose style—incorporating first-person narrative, street talk, and exuberant metaphor—became a model for the New Journalism of the 1960s and later. Although he came from a genteel New York family, he was fascinated by the irreverent underworld all his life and made it his special subject.

After being expelled from Dartmouth College for refusing to attend chapel, Liebling graduated from Columbia University's Pulitzer School of Journalism in 1925 and then worked for various newspapers, including *The New York Times* (which fired him) and the *New York World*, before he found his métier at *The New Yorker* magazine in 1935. It was there that he developed his signature style and did his best work, writing about a wide range of subjects, from the city's characters to gastronomy to boxing to the London Blitz and the Normandy invasion. A born raconteur with a fertile imagination, Liebling carved out a territory between objective reporting and fiction, which so many other journalists have mined since. Yet he could also produce straight war reportage fine enough to merit receiving the Legion of Honor from a grateful France in 1952.

Starting in 1945, Liebling wrote a widely admired column for *The New Yorker* called "The Wayward Pressman," in which he criticized American journalism's priorities and performance; this was probably the first such column in U.S. journalism. During the 1950s and 1960s, he also wrote book reviews for *Esquire*. Besides his massive newspaper and magazine output, Liebling wrote about 20 books. He was married three times, the last time to the writer Jean Stafford.

BOOKS BY LIEBLING

Back Where I Come From. 1938. FS&G 1990 $10.95. ISBN 0-86547-425-7
Between Meals: An Appetite for Paris. 1962. FS&G 1986 $10.95. ISBN 0-86547-236-X
The Earl of Louisiana. 1961. La. State U. Pr. 1970 $9.95. ISBN 0-8071-0203-2. About Governor Earl Long, Huey Long's colorful but politically liberal brother.
The Honest Rainmaker: The Life and Times of Colonel John Stingo. FS&G repr. of 1953 ed. $9.95. ISBN 0-86547-396-X
The Road Back to Paris. Doubleday 1944 o.p.
The Sweet Science. Viking Penguin 1991 $9.95. ISBN 0-14-006191-6. Some of the best reporting on boxing ever written.
The Wayward Pressman. Doubleday 1947 o.p. Collection of Liebling's *New Yorker* columns about the press.

BOOK ABOUT LIEBLING

Sokolov, Raymond. *Wayward Reporter: The Life of A. J. Liebling.* Creative Arts Bk. 1980 $10.95. ISBN 0-916870-63-4

LIPPMANN, WALTER. 1889–1974

Walter Lippmann was a political journalist, moralist, and theorist with a lifelong interest in foreign affairs. Both in his public writings and private dealings, he counseled American presidents and foreign leaders for half a century. His work was informed by the idea that serious journalism should partake in both the discussion and the formulation of public policy.

This cosmopolitan intellectual who was perhaps the first true political columnist in America was born into a well-to-do New York family and traveled throughout Europe before entering Harvard University in 1906, where he was especially influenced by the philosopher-psychologist WILLIAM JAMES (see also Vol. 4) and the philosopher-poet GEORGE SANTAYANA (see Vol. 4). After graduating Phi Beta Kappa in 1910, he worked for the *Boston Common* but quit because he considered it politically naive. He next worked for *Everybody's Magazine*, where he soon became associate editor and established a reputation for progressive journalism. At the age of 24, he published his first book, *A Preface to Politics* (1913), which called for big government and strong political leadership to offset the power of big business.

With Herbert Crolly, Lippmann founded *The New Republic* in 1914, intending it as a progressive but pragmatic journal. President Woodrow Wilson was a regular reader of Lippmann's editorials, and, after World War I, Lippmann became an assistant to E. M. House, head of the U.S. Delegation at the Paris Peace Conference (1918–19), and reportedly had a strong influence on President Wilson's famous Fourteen Points.

Upon leaving government service, Lippmann joined the *New York World* and became director of its editorial page in 1924. After the *World* folded in 1931, he moved to Washington, D.C., and began to write a column called "Today and Tomorrow" for the *New York Herald Tribune*. Eventually the column was syndicated in 275 newspapers around the world and won Lippmann two Pulitzer Prizes (1958 and 1962), the Peabody Award (1962), and the National Institute of Arts and Letters Gold Medal (1965). In between his newspaper work, he wrote for magazines, including a biweekly column for *Newsweek*, and published a good many perceptive and influential books.

In his late years, Lippmann's politics became more conservative as he grew disillusioned with the course of American political and social life. Having hailed Lyndon Johnson as Franklin Roosevelt's successor, the president who would fulfill the New Deal in the Great Society, he watched, dismayed, as Johnson's presidency disintegrated under the weight of the unpopular war in Vietnam. Lippmann retired in failing health in 1974 and died later that year.

BOOKS BY LIPPMANN

Essays in the Public Philosophy. 1955. Transaction Pubs. 1989 $16.95. ISBN 0-88738-791-8
The Good Society. Little 1937 o.p.
A Preface to Morals. Macmillan 1929 o.p.
A Preface to Politics. Macmillan 1913 o.p. Applies Freudian psychological insights to problems of politics.
Public Opinion. 1922. Free Pr. 1965 $16.95. ISBN 0-02-919130-0. A great critical success when published and still considered a seminal work on mass communications.
The Stakes of Diplomacy. Holt 1915 o.p.
U.S. Foreign Policy. HarpC 1943 o.p.

BOOKS ABOUT LIPPMANN

Dam, Hari. *Intellectual Odyssey of Walter Lippmann.* Gordon Pr. 1973 $69.95. ISBN 0-87968-057-1
Luskin, John. *Lippmann, Liberty and the Press.* U. of Ala. Pr. 1972 o.p.
Steele, Ronald. *Walter Lippmann and the American Century.* Little 1980 o.p. An absorbing biography that emphasizes Lippmann's behind-the-scenes involvement with presidents and power brokers in helping to shape the policies and events he wrote about as a journalist.
Weingast, David Elliott. *Walter Lippmann: A Study in Personal Journalism.* Rutgers U. Pr. 1949 o.p. Concentrates on Lippmann's journalism and activities during the New Deal era.
Wright, Benjamin F. *Five Public Philosophies of Walter Lippmann.* U. of Tex. Pr. 1973 o.p. Critical assessment of Lippmann as a philosopher.

LUCE, HENRY R(OBINSON). 1898–1967

Henry R. Luce was a student at Yale University when he and Briton ("Brit") Hadden, both editors of the *Yale Daily News*, conceived of the idea of a magazine of news rewritten from the daily newspapers. Not long after, on March 3, 1923, they published the first issue of *Time* magazine. Luce was then only 23.

The facts of the news came from the daily newspapers. *Time* writers appropriated them without permission, summarized them, embellished them with novelistic flourishes, and produced a lively weekly digest of the news. The magazine turned its first profit in three years; by 1935 *Time* was making $2.2 million a year, Luce was rich, and his magazine was fashionable and influential. (Hadden had died at 31 from flu complications.)

Luce broke the twentieth-century journalistic canon that news should be presented objectively by unashamedly slanting it to conform to his conservative opinions. This practice was the subject of controversy throughout his life. The writer Merle Miller, who worked for *Time* for many years, once described the magazine this way in a public lecture: "It's edited brilliantly, is well written, but is dishonestly written. It is extremely unified in that every single story carries the slant of its editor, Henry Luce."

Luce had strong views and believed that "impartiality is often an impediment to truth." Born in China to American Protestant missionaries, he saw America's mission as a crusade to save the world, particularly from communism, and consciously used his magazine to advance this view with the American public and officials. Keeping dictatorial Chiang Kai-shek in power in China and the communists out was one of his most fervent crusades. The Vietnam War was another. Luce enjoyed his journal's influence: "*Time* is the most powerful publication in America," he wrote in a policy memo to his executives. *Time* writers who saw things differently either learned to accept revision of their work or left. It was hard to leave, however, because pay and perks were the best in the business.

Luce was a world traveler who mixed with heads of state, politicians, and diplomats, often passing on the substance of his conversations with them to his editors. His second wife, the editor and playwright Clare Boothe Luce, rose to prominence in national politics, serving as a congresswoman from Connecticut (1943–47) and as U.S. ambassador to Italy (1953–57).

Luce's superb editorial instincts made him the giant of magazine journalism in the twentieth century. He brought out three other highly successful magazines: the business magazine *Fortune* in 1930, the picture magazine *Life* in 1936, and the flashy *Sports Illustrated* in 1954. Where he created, others copied: *Time* gave rise to *Newsweek*, *Life* to *Look*, and *Sports Illustrated* to a number of imitators. The company he founded grew into one of the nation's leading media corporations. When Luce died, *Newsweek* put him on its cover and said: "There has been no one like him in the history of modern journalism."

BOOK BY LUCE

The Ideas of Henry Luce. (coauthored with John Knox Jessup). Atheneum 1969 o.p.
A collection of Luce's works showing his thoughts over a long period of time and on a wide range of topics.

BOOKS ABOUT LUCE

Baughman, James L. *Henry R. Luce and the Rise of the American News Media.* Macmillan 1987 $26.95. ISBN 0-8057-7755-5. Luce's life, both personal and professional.

Cort, David. *The Sin of Henry R. Luce: An Anatomy of Journalism.* Carol Pub. Group 1974 $12.50. ISBN 0-8184-0201-6. How Luce turned over his magazines to "executives" rather than to writers, by a Time Inc. editor.

Martin, Ralph G. *Henry and Clare: An Intimate Portrait of the Luces.* Putnam Pub. Group 1991 $24.95. ISBN 0-399-13652-5

MCLUHAN, (HERBERT) MARSHALL. 1911–1980

A poetry professor turned media theorist—or media guru, as some in the press called him at the time—Marshall McLuhan startled television watchers during the 1960s with the notion that the medium they were enthralled by was doing more than transmitting messages—it *was* the message: Its rapid-fire format, mixing programs and advertisements, conveyed as much as—or more than—any single broadcast element.

McLuhan grew up in the prairie country of the Canadian West and studied English at the University of Manitoba and Cambridge University. As television entered a period of huge growth during the 1950s, McLuhan, then a college professor, became interested in advertising. He thought of it as something to be taken seriously as a new culture form, beyond its obvious capability of selling products. That interest led to his increasing speculation about what media did to audiences.

In his unpredictable modern poetry classes at the University of Toronto, he spoke more and more of media. The students he taught were the television generation, the first to grow up with the medium. Many were fascinated by McLuhan's provocative observations that a medium of communication radically alters the experience being communicated. A society, he said, is shaped more by the style than by the content of its media. Thus, the linear, sequential style of printing established a linear, sequential style of thinking, in which one thing is considered after another in orderly fashion: it shaped a culture in which (objective) reason predominated and experience was isolated, compartmental- ized, and repeatable. In contrast, the low-density images of television, com- posed of a mosaic of light and dark dots, established a style of response in which it is necessary to unconsciously reconfigure the dots immediately in order to derive meaning from them; it has shaped a culture in which (subjective) emotion predominates and experience is holistic and unrepeatable. Since television (and the other electronic media) transcends space and time, the world is becoming a global village—a community in which distance and isolation are overcome. McLuhan was crisp and assured in his pronouncements and impatient with those who failed to grasp their import.

McLuhan's most famous saying, "the medium is the message," was explicated in the first chapter of his most successful book, *Understanding Media*, published in 1966 and still in print. It sold very well for a rather abstruse book and brought McLuhan widespread attention in intellectual circles. The media industry responded by seeking his advice and enthusiastically disseminating his ideas in magazines and on television. These ideas caused people to perceive their environment, particularly their media environment, in radically new ways. It was an unsettling experience for some, liberating for others.

Though McLuhan produced some useful insights, he was given to wild generalizations and flagrant exaggerations. Some thought him a charlatan, and he always felt himself an outcast at the university, at least partly because of his disdain for print culture and opposition to academic conventions. He never seemed quite as energetic after an operation in 1967 to remove a huge brain tumor, but he continued to work and teach until he suffered a stroke in 1979. He died a year later. Though today his writings are not discussed as much by the general public, his thesis is still considered valid and his ideas have become widely accepted.

BOOKS BY McLUHAN

The Global Village: Transformations in World Life and Media in the 21st Century.
(coauthored with Bruce R. Powers). OUP 1989 $29.95. ISBN 0-19-505444-X. A
prescient analysis of the global effects of modern mass media.
Gutenberg Galaxy: The Making of Typographic Man. U. of Toronto Pr. 1962 $19.95. ISBN
0-8020-6041-2. McLuhan's speculations on the effects of the alphabet and printing on
society; the first of his two key works.
The Mechanical Bride. Vanguard 1951 o.p.
The Medium Is the Message. S&S Trade 1966 $10.00. ISBN 0-671-68997-5
Understanding Media: The Extensions of Man. NAL-Dutton 1964 $4.95. ISBN 0-451-6246-
3. McLuhan's theories on how modern media extend the human senses; the second
of his two key works.

BOOKS ABOUT McLUHAN

Marchand, Philip. *Marshall McLuhan, the Medium and the Messenger.* Ticknor & Fields
1990 $11.70. ISBN 0-89919-947-X. A sympathetic and personal biography by a
former student of McLuhan's.
Sanderson, George, and Frank MacDonald, eds. *Marshall McLuhan: The Man and His
Message.* Fulcrum Pub. 1989 $17.95. ISBN 1-55591-035-1

MURROW, EDWARD R(OSCOE). 1908–1965

Edward R. Murrow's achievements as a pioneer of journalism in the new
media of radio and television continue to resonate in broadcasting today. His
legacy is particularly relevant to the debate within the television industry
between those who advocate making news broadcasts entertaining and those
who want to uphold the values of serious journalism.

Murrow was born in Greensboro, North Carolina, and grew up in Washington
state. His youthful travel for the National Student Foundation gave him an
internationalist outlook. He joined CBS in 1935, and four years later was
working in London as European news chief when World War II broke out. "I'm
standing on a rooftop looking out over London. . . ." So began Murrow's first
live radio coverage of the London Blitz. His dramatic and descriptive nightly
broadcasts "laid the dead of London at our doors," as poet ARCHIBALD MACLEISH
(see Vol. 1) said at a dinner honoring the 33-year-old Murrow when he returned
to America a star in late 1941.

Murrow had an admiring boss, WILLIAM S. PALEY, the founder of the Columbia
Broadcasting System (CBS). Together they made CBS the best news broadcaster
in America. Murrow's *See it Now* television broadcasts brought important
events into the living rooms of America. On one memorable occasion in 1954,
he attacked Joseph McCarthy, the Senate demagogue who was exploiting the
postwar fear of Communist subversives in high places.

Murrow's dark good looks framed in cigarette smoke and his evocative
phrasing made him a success in the hearts as well as the minds of his viewers.
Murrow the dignified newsman on *See it Now* represented the serious side of
broadcast journalism. But Murrow the star was the popular host of *Person to
Person*, a live interview show featuring celebrities in their homes—with a two-
way hookup between him and his subject.

As the audience for network television expanded, so did profits, and Paley and
Murrow grew apart. In a speech to broadcast journalists that Paley interpreted
as critical of him, Murrow said: "Television in the main is being used to distract,
delude, amuse, and insulate us. . . . This instrument can teach, it can illuminate;
yes, it can even inspire. But it can do so only to the extent that humans are

determined to use it to those ends. Otherwise, it is merely wires and lights in a box."

By 1961 the Murrow-Paley relationship had cooled, and Murrow's authority at the network had diminished along with his health, for lung cancer had stricken the famous smoker. When President John F. Kennedy offered him the directorship of the U.S. Information Agency that year, he accepted. His battle with lung cancer ended with his death in 1965.

When Murrow left CBS, the broadcast critic of *The New York Times* wrote: "To whatever extent television has found its voice of conscience, purpose and integrity, it was as much the doing of Edward R. Murrow as [of] any other single individual in one medium."

BOOKS BY MURROW

In Search of Light. (coauthored with Edward Bliss, Jr.). Knopf 1967 o.p. A selection of transcripts of Morrow's broadcasts from 1938 to 1961.

See It Now. (coauthored with Fred W. Friendly). S&S Trade 1955 o.p. Scripts of the famous television broadcasts.

This Is London. 1941. Schocken 1989 $8.95. ISBN 0-8052-0882-8. Excerpts from Murrow's World War II radio broadcasts from London. Edited and with an introduction by Elmer Davis.

BOOKS ABOUT MURROW

Lichello, Robert. *Edward R. Murrow: Broadcaster of Courage.* SamHar Pr. 1972 $2.50. ISBN 0-87157-004-1. Biography of the brilliant radio and television journalist, recounting how Murrow's unwillingness to be intimidated helped end the McCarthy era, a period in the early 1950s when Senator Joseph McCarthy spearheaded a series of punitive congressional investigations of suspected communists and sympathizers in public and private life.

Persico, Joseph. *Edward R. Murrow: An American Original.* McGraw 1989 $24.95. ISBN 0-07-049480-0. A definitive, well-written, biography of Murrow's career, his personal life, and the contradictions of his personality.

Sperber, A. M. *Murrow: His Life and Times.* Freundlich 1986 $25.00. ISBN 0-88191-008-2

PALEY, WILLIAM S(AMUEL). 1901–1990

William Paley heard radio for the first time on a crystal set in 1925. He was then 24 and working for his father's prosperous cigar-manufacturing company. The Paley family bought advertising time on the new medium and saw sales of their La Palina cigars increase tremendously as a result. In 1928 Paley became the owner of the struggling Columbia radio network. From this humble beginning, he built the Columbia Broadcasting System (CBS), branching out into television in the 1950s. CBS became a central player, first in radio, then in television. For years its chief rival was the National Broadcasting Company (NBC). The American Broadcasting Company (ABC) joined them later.

Bill Paley had a consummate feel for both the advertising possibilities of radio and television and the tastes of their audiences. Programming, he said, "must appeal to either the emotions or the self-interest [of the audience member], not merely to his intellect." His approach was hugely successful: CBS attracted enormous audiences, which enabled it to attract big-spending advertisers. While Paley concentrated on developing lowbrow popular programming, his deputy, Frank Stanton, and his star journalist, EDWARD R. MURROW, developed superior news, educational, and cultural programming, thereby giving CBS an image of class, so that it was called "the Tiffany network."

Paley lived the life of a socialite and art collector as well as businessman. He was married several times and was father and stepfather to four children. As he aged and network dominance of broadcasting declined, he lost or ceded (depending on the analysis) control of his empire to Laurence Tisch, chairman of the Loewes Corporation, and CBS went through a period of internal battling and retrenchment. But Paley was a strong leader and left the important legacy of using some of the huge profits of popular programming to support superior news programming.

Book by Paley

As It Happened: A Memoir. Doubleday 1979 o.p. Paley regretted writing this version of his life and intended to produce another one, but never did.

Book about Paley

Smith, Sally B. *In All His Glory: The Legendary Tycoon and His Brilliant Circle.* S&S Trade 1991 $15.00. ISBN 0-671-74917-X. Excellent biography of Paley, covering both his business career and his glamorous private life.

PULITZER, JOSEPH. 1847–1911

At a bankruptcy auction in 1878, Joseph Pulitzer, an immigrant from Hungary, bought the *St. Louis Dispatch* for $2,500. Three days later, he combined it with the *St. Louis Post* to create what would become one of America's leading newspapers—*The St. Louis Post-Dispatch*. His statement of policy read: "The *Post* and *Dispatch* will serve no party but the people, be no organ of Republicanism, but the organ of truth . . . will oppose all frauds and shams wherever and whatever they are, will advocate principles and ideas rather than prejudices and partisanship."

Five years later, this high-strung, intense man broke into the competitive news world of New York City by buying the *New York World*. Within a few years, the *World* broke every publishing record in America, increasing circulation from 15,000 to 250,000—the largest in the nation. It was the first mass-circulation daily, and it set the standard for the modern American newspaper.

Pulitzer achieved in the *World* a rare combination: lurid accounts of sex, scandal, and crime; brilliant and accurate reporting on the issues of the day; and a crusading and courageous editorial voice on behalf of workers, the poor, and immigrants. He initiated a daily sports section, emphasized illustrations, attracted women readers with stories of interest to them, argued labor's case for higher wages and better working conditions, and sent reporter Nellie Bly around the world in 72 days, besting the "record" set in Jules Verne's novel *Around the World in Eighty Days*. Cannons were fired in New York's Battery Park when she returned. Clearly, Pulitzer had the common touch.

What his critics called sensationalism he called stories "apt to be talked about." In 1884 he wrote in the *World*: "The daily journal is like the mirror—it reflects that which is before it. . . . Let those who are startled by it blame the people who are before the mirror, and not the mirror, which only reflects their features and actions." He was careful, however, not to go too far and his passion for accuracy was legendary. The only decorations in the *World's* newsroom were cards pasted on the walls at regular intervals exhorting: "Accuracy, Accuracy, Accuracy! Who? What? When? Where? How? The Facts—The Color—The Facts."

Pulitzer was stricken in mid-career by both blindness and a nervous disorder that made noise unbearable to him; the clink of a spoon at dinner would cause him to writhe in agony. He was forced to retire from active editorship of his papers in 1890 but maintained long-distance control until his death. Regarded by many as the leading American editor of modern times, he left a fortune of nearly $20 million at his death, one of the largest ever accumulated in the newspaper field. He was one of the first to view journalism as a profession; he endowed the Columbia University School of Journalism in 1915 in his will, and provided a fund for the annual Pulitzer Prizes in journalism, letters, and music.

BOOK BY PULITZER

Newsmen Speak: Journalists on Their Craft. (coauthored with Edmond D. Coblentz). Ayer 1954 $17.00. ISBN 0-8369-0318-8. Pulitzer's (and others') writings about journalism; Pulitzer never wrote much about himself.

BOOKS ABOUT PULITZER

Heaton, John L. *Story of a Page: Thirty Years in the Public Service in the Editorial Columns of the New York World Under the Editorship of J. Pulitzer.* 1913. Ayer 1970 $20.00. ISBN 0-405-01677-8

Ireland, Alleyne. *Adventure with a Genius: Recollections of Joseph Pulitzer.* Johnson Repr. 1969 repr. of 1937 ed. $24.00. ISBN 0-384-25945-6. Ireland's experiences as Pulitzer's secretary in the publisher's later years.

Rothmyer, Karen. *Winning Pulitzers: The Stories Behind Some of the Best News Coverage of Our Time.* Col. U. Pr. 1991 $29.00. ISBN 0-231-07028-4

Seitz, Don C. *Joseph Pulitzer, His Life and Letters.* 1924. AMS Pr. 1970 repr. of 1924 ed. $17.50. ISBN 0-404-05699-7. The experiences of Pulitzer as told by the man who led the *World* under his direction; a primary source.

RIIS, JACOB A(UGUST). 1849–1914

Jacob Riis was a crusading journalist-photographer whose exposés of the living and working conditions of the New York City poor during the late nineteenth century inspired that generation of American journalists known as the Muckrakers. He was uncompromising in his commitment to his work, regarding journalism as a noble profession in an era when few others did.

One of 16 children born to a part-time reporter in Ribe, Denmark, Riis emigrated to the United States as a young man and worked for a while as a carpenter. He got a job writing for the *South Brooklyn News* in 1874. For the next quarter of a century, he reported on "how the other half lives" for that paper, the *New York Tribune* (1877–88), and the *New York Evening Sun* (1888–99), documenting in prose and photograph the appalling slum life of New York's poor, the dreadful tenements in which they lived, the sweatshops where they and their children labored, the brutal crimes they committed and endured, and the police corruption that helped preserve these conditions. His harrowing portrayals of poverty and crime are classic works of photojournalism that influenced younger journalists and moved a future president, THEODORE ROOSEVELT, to vow to clean up New York when he became head of the city's police board.

Riis retired from active journalism toward the end of the century, becoming a popular lecturer and book writer. In *The Making of an American* (1901), a book still read today, he told the tale of his emigration and Americanization.

BOOKS BY RIIS

The Battle with the Slums. Patterson Smith 1969 repr. of 1902 ed. $14.00. ISBN 0-87585-077-4

Children of the Poor. Ayer 1971 repr. of 1892 ed. $23.50. ISBN 0-405-03124-6
Children of the Tenements. Ayer repr. of 1903 ed. $21.00. ISBN 0-8369-3565-9
How the Other Half Lives. Corner Hse. repr. of 1890 ed. $22.50. ISBN 0-87928-033-6
The Making of an American. Macmillan 1901 o.p. Story of the author's love for his
   adopted country, his first wife, and his fellow human beings.

BOOKS ABOUT RIIS

Alland, Alexander. *Jacob A. Riis: Photographer and Citizen.* Aperture 1993 $36.95. ISBN 0-
   89381-527-6
Ware, Louise. *Jacob A. Riis: Police Reporter, Reformer, Useful Citizen.* 1938. Ayer 1975
   $18.75. ISBN 0-8369-7173-6

SALISBURY, HARRISON. 1908–1993

Foreign correspondent par excellence, Harrison Salisbury reported on World
War II, Russia under JOSEPH STALIN and Khrushchev, Vietnam during the war,
China, and numerous other hot spots around the world. He also covered the
U.S. civil rights movement in the 1960s and inaugurated the op-ed page of *The
New York Times*, a paper he was associated with for much of his career.

Born into an intellectual family in Minneapolis, Salisbury got an early start in
his career. After graduating from high school two years early, he worked
intermittently as a reporter for the *Minneapolis Journal* while attending the
University of Minnesota. When he was expelled from the university because of
his crusading journalism, he joined United Press, and by 1934 was working in its
Washington, D.C., bureau. During World War II, he reported from England,
North Africa, and the Middle East, as well as Russia.

In 1949, Salisbury went to work for *The New York Times* as the paper's
Moscow correspondent. For the next six years, he got to know Russia and in
1955 wrote a series of articles on it that won him the Pulitzer Prize for
international reporting.

Salisbury joined the *Times* board in 1962 and became assistant managing
editor in 1964. Still he continued to make his journalistic forays abroad. From
December 12, 1966, to to January 7, 1967, he reported from Hanoi, North
Vietnam, the first American journalist to gain entrance to that country during
the Vietnam War. His dispatches earned him several awards, including the
Overseas Press Club's Asian Award, although the idea of an American reporting
from enemy territory upset many people in Washington and elsewhere. The
dispatches were soon turned into a book, *Behind the Lines—Hanoi* (1967).

Salisbury retired from the *Times* in 1973. He produced 23 books, several of
them dealing with social and political life in Russia under communism. He also
wrote two novels and two autobiographical books.

BOOKS BY SALISBURY

Behind the Lines—Hanoi. HarpC 1967 o.p. Account of the author's eye-opening trip to
   North Vietnam in the middle of the Vietnam War.
A Journey for Our Times. Carroll & Graf 1984 $10.95. ISBN 0-88184-037-8. Memoirs.
Russia on the Way. Macmillan 1946 o.p.
The Siege of Leningrad. HarpC o.p.
To Moscow—And Beyond. HarpC 1960 o.p.
Tiananmen Diary. Little 1989 $18.95. ISBN 0-316-80904-7. A firsthand account of the
   1989 student uprising in China and its brutal suppression, and why it happened the
   way it did.
Without Fear or Favor. NY Times 1980 o.p. A personal account of *Times* history during
   the period Salisbury worked there.

TARBELL, IDA. 1857–1944

"Muckraking" was not Ida Tarbell's description of her work; it was President THEODORE ROOSEVELT's. She and her fellow journalists who were exposing the predatory actions of turn-of-the-century American capitalists, Roosevelt said, were like the man with the muckrake in JOHN BUNYAN's (see Vol. 1) *Pilgrim's Progress* who fixed his gaze on cleaning mire when he might have looked up and seen the heavens.

Tarbell's exposés of the abuses of freewheeling capitalism, particularly the machinations of John D. Rockefeller and the Standard Oil Company, made her preeminent among the muckrakers. She was an inspiration to other journalists, who found much to rake—destructive trusts, child labor, political corruption, and abusive labor conditions.

Tarbell's relationship with the power of the big oil companies began in her childhood. Her father was an independent oilman, and she grew up in the Pennsylvania oilfields, where everything was slick with oil and smelled of it. Her father was the type of entrepreneur that Rockefeller was relentlessly driving out of business. As a result of her family's depressing struggle against big oil, Tarbell wrote, "There was born in me a hatred of privilege—of privilege of any sort."

Tarbell began her career in journalism at a newspaper published by the Chautauqua Assembly, a Christian adult education movement. In 1891 she moved to Paris, free-lanced for American journals, and wrote biographies of famous people that achieved great popularity. She returned to America at the invitation of Samuel McClure and began writing exposés for *McClure's Magazine*. Her fame rests on the series of articles she wrote over several years detailing Rockefeller's conspiracies to monopolize the oil business; these were later published as a book, *The History of the Standard Oil Company* (1904). In 1911 the Standard Oil Company trust was dissolved by the courts, at least partly as a result of Tarbell's work. Many of her other exposés of predatory competition eventually inspired regulatory laws.

Tarbell came of age at a time when women were struggling for independence and the vote. She was the only woman in her freshman class at Allegheny College, and from an early age she decided to avoid the confines of marriage. Yet she was ambivalent about feminism. Even as she reported on the exploitation of women, she extolled the virtues of the homemaker and often felt herself a failure for remaining unmarried all her life. She was writing a memoir she intended to call *Life After Eighty* when she died of pneumonia in 1944.

BOOK BY TARBELL

The History of the Standard Oil Company. 1904. Buccaneer Bks. 1987 $27.95. ISBN 0-89966-616-7. Tarbell's famous investigation of the Rockefeller trust.

BOOK ABOUT TARBELL

Brady, Kathleen. *Portrait of a Muckraker.* U. of Pittsburgh Pr. 1989 $12.95. ISBN 0-8229-5807-4. Definitive biography of Tarbell, covering both this complex woman and an important period in American history.

FILM

Film is the most modern and most popular of the arts. It was born a century ago when the Lumière brothers presented a 20-minute show with their Cinémarographe before an audience in Lyon, France. In the first decade of the twentieth century, France predominated in filmmaking, but America soon caught up, and, by the end of World War I, Hollywood had established a dominant position in world filmmaking that it has never since lost. From the silent era to talkies, color, wide screen, and now cable and video sales, Hollywood has had the financial and technical means and the acting and directorial talent to produce a steady stream of audience-pleasing films—and the marketing expertise to sell them to the masses at home and abroad.

The *auteur* theory, which recognizes the director as the primary creative force in filmmaking, originated among the French New Wave directors, particularly FRANÇOIS TRUFFAUT, and was popularized in this country chiefly by the film critic Andrew Sarris. Although film is patently a collaborative medium, requiring writers, performers, and a host of technicians to produce, it is the directors who most often have the opportunity to stamp their personal vision on a film. Traditionally, theirs is the last credit to appear on the screen, for they are the ones in charge of realizing a script: They tell the actors what to do and the camera operators what to shoot, and they usually supervise the editing of the film. Despite Hollywood's dominance, great directors have arisen elsewhere, from small European countries like Denmark (CARL DREYER) and Sweden (INGMAR BERGMAN) to the Soviet Union (which financed the films of SERGEI EISENSTEIN) to Asia (Japan's AKIRA KUROSAWA). Many have either written their own scripts or closely supervised the writing of them. Some have worked with actors chosen for them (the usual Hollywood practice), while others have used from film to film a band of players they have chosen themselves (more common in Europe). Some have been technical innovators; others have taken the technicalities of filmmaking for granted and used them to express a vision unlike that of any of their predecessors.

From the 1920s to the early 1950s, Americans were regular filmgoers and the big Hollywood studios flourished, turning out "screwball comedies," westerns, musicals, detective and adventure films, and spectacles. Then television claimed the audience's allegiance, and movie ticket sales dropped fairly steadily for years. A desperate Hollywood sold off its old films to the competition, inadvertently creating a new audience for films by JOHN HUSTON, HOWARD HAWKS, FRANK CAPRA, and others that are now regarded as classics.

Hollywood remains the source of most American films that attract crowds, but fewer films are being produced by the studio system. Independent filmmakers are the second major source of films, and they now have more ways to distribute their works to audiences: video sales and rentals, cable, and pay-per-view television.

General Reference and History

Acker, Ally. *Reel Women: Pioneers of the Cinema, 1896 to the Present.* Continuum 1991 $18.95. ISBN 0-8264-0579-7. A groundbreaking history of more than 100 important women in film.

Armour, Robert A. *Film: A Reference Guide.* Greenwood 1980 $42.95. ISBN 0-313-22241-X. A useful source.

Austin, Bruce A. *The Film Audience: An International Bibliography of Research.* Scarecrow 1983 $22.00. ISBN 0-8108-1622-9. An extensive study of types of film audiences.

Balio, Tino, ed. *United Artists: The Company Built by the Stars.* U. of Wis. Pr. 1976 $27.50. ISBN 0-299-06940-0. A complete and scholarly history of an important film company.

Barnouw, Erik. *Documentary: A History of the Non-Fiction Film*. OUP 1992 $10.95. ISBN 0-19-507898-5. An excellent introduction that identifies recent major films and trends.

Bogle, Donald. *Blacks in American Films and Television: An Encyclopedia*. Garland 1988 $60.00. ISBN 0-8240-8715-1. Concentrates on American films widely distributed, all made between 1919 and 1949, and black-oriented series and miniseries on television. Index included.

Bonadelia, Peter. *Italian Cinema: From Neorealism to the Present*. Continuum 1989 $17.95. ISBN 0-8264-0426-X. A classic, now revised, on Italian film and filmmakers.

Bordwell, David, and Kristin Thompson. *Film Art*. McGraw 4th ed. 1933 $22.42. ISBN 0-07-006446-6. An excellent text on the structure and processes that make film an art form.

Brady, Anna, and Carolyn N. Weiner, eds. *Union List of Film Periodicals: Holdings of Selected American Collections.* Greenwood 1984 $42.95. ISBN 0-313-23701-6. Explains access by subject and title and gives information on how to obtain specific issues through library visit or interlibrary loan.

Burch, Noel. *Life to Those Shadows*. U. CA Pr. 1990 $45.00. ISBN 0-520-07143-3. A personal history of early British, French, and American films.

Buss, Robin. *The French through Their Films*. Continuum 1988 $18.95. ISBN 0-8044-2089-0. How French society is depicted in the classics of French cinema.

Cowie, Peter, ed. *International Film Guide*. Blackwell Pubs. 1990 $115.95. ISBN 0-233-98503-4. An immensely useful, authoritative reference source.

Custen, George F. *Bio-Pics: How Hollywood Constructed Public History*. Rutgers U. Pr. 1992 $40.00. ISBN 0-8135-1754-0

Enser, A. G. *Filmed Books and Plays: A List of Books and Plays from Which Films Have Been Made, 1928–1986*. Ashgate Pub. Co. 1987 $59.95. ISBN 0-566-03564-2. A guide to the sources of many important films.

Flinn, Caryl. *Strains of Utopia: Gender, Nostalgia, and Hollywood Film Music*. Princeton U. Pr. 1992 $39.50. ISBN 0-691-04801-0. Extremely useful introduction to the uses of music (and other sound) in film.

Foreman, Alexa L. *Women in Motion*. Bowling Green Univ. 1983 $20.95. ISBN 0-87972-266-5. An interesting study of the roles women play in cinema.

Geduld, Harry M. *The Birth of the Talkies: From Edison to Jolson*. Bks. Demand 1975 $87.80. ISBN 0-8357-7273-X. An account of the invention of the technology necessary for talkies.

Gehring, Wes D. *Handbook of American Film Genres*. Greenwood 1988 $49.85. ISBN 0-313-24715-3. Scholarly essays on various genres (screwball comedy, western, etc.) with bibliographical overviews and notes. Index included.

Gomery, Douglas. *Shared Pleasures: A History of Movie Presentation in the United States*. U. of Wis. Pr. 1992 $40.00. ISBN 0-299-13210-2. Thorough and fascinating research on the economic history of the movie business from production and distribution to air-conditioning and popcorn.

Green, Stanley. *Encyclopedia of Musical Film*. OUP 1988 $15.95. ISBN 0-19-505421-0. A complete guide to this genre.

Halliwell, Leslie. *Filmgoer's and Video Viewer's Companion*. HarpC 1992 $50.00. ISBN 0-06-09639201. An up-to-date, informative guide to almost every movie likely to be on television or in the video store.

Katz, Ephraim. *The Film Encyclopedia*. Perigee 1990 $20.00. ISBN 0-06-09227-0. Bills itself as the most comprehensive one-volume encyclopedia of world film.

Kindem, Gorham, ed. *The American Movie Industry: The Business of Motion Pictures*. S. Ill. U. Pr. 1982 $29.95. ISBN 0-8093-1037-6. This thorough study of the business end of the industry ignores the glamour of filmmaking.

Kozloff, Sarah. *Invisible Storytellers: Voice-over Narration in American Fiction Film*. U. CA Pr. 1988 $14.00. ISBN 0-520-05861-5. The technique and effect of voice-over narration.

Langman, Larry. *Encyclopedia of American Film Comedy*. Garland 1987 $50.00. ISBN 0-8240-8496-9. A dictionary of comedy genres, characters, etc.

Luhr, William, ed. *World Cinema Since 1945: An Encyclopedic History.* Continuum 1987 $59.50. ISBN 0-8044-3078-0. The developments of the cinema from World War II through the 1980s, by 30 noted film critics and scholars.

Magill, Frank N., ed. *Magill Survey of Cinema.* 4 vols. Salem Pr. 1980 $200.00. ISBN 0-89356-225-4. Second Series 6 vols. 1981 $300.00. ISBN 0-89356-230-0. Synopses of the plots of a substantial number of the best-known films.

Maltin, Leonard, and others. *Leonard Maltin's Movie and Video Guide: 1993 Edition.* NAL-Dutton 1992 $17.00. ISBN 0-452-26857-5. Annual listing of all films, including those available for video rental, with short, pithy annotations. Modified actor/director index included.

Monaco, James. *Who's Who in American Film Now.* Zoetrope 1987 $19.95. ISBN 0-918432-62-6. A helpful guide.

Nash, Jay Robert, and Stanley Ross, eds. *The Motion Picture Guide.* 12 vols. Cinebooks 1987 $600.00. ISBN 0-933997-00-0. A ten-volume encyclopedia of motion pictures; includes synopses and anecdotal information, cast members, running times, etc.

Nowlan, Robert A. *Cinema Sequels and Remakes, 1903–1987.* McFarland & Co. 1989 $49.95. ISBN 0-89950-314-4. Alphabetical listing of all films with synopses. Includes index.

Niver, Kemp R. *The Early Motion Pictures: The Paper Print Collection in the Library of Congress.* Lib. Congress 1985 $24.00. ISBN 0-8444-0463-2. An authoritative study, including information on over 3,000 films released in the United States between 1894 and 1912.

O'Connor, John E., and Martin A. Jackson, eds. *American History/American Film: Interpreting the Hollywood Image.* Continuum 1988 $12.95. ISBN 0-8044-2672-4. An important analysis by 16 historians who use films from 1920 to 1986 to discuss American institutions, lifestyles, and values.

Oldham, Gabriella. *First Cut: Conversations with Film Editors.* U. CA Pr. 1992 $35.00. ISBN 0-520-07586-2. Interviews exploring how individual editors practice their craft.

Rawlence, Christopher. *The Missing Reel: The Untold Story of the Lost Inventor of Moving Pictures.* Viking Penguin 1992 $10.00. ISBN 0-14-015973-8. The mysterious disappearance of Augustin le Prince, the French inventor of the first motion picture camera and projector.

Reid, Mark A. *Redefining Black Film.* U. CA Pr. 1992 $30.00. ISBN 0-520-07901-9. An important reassessment of African American film history.

Sadoul, Georges. *Dictionary of Films.* Ed. and trans. by Peter Morris. U. CA Pr. 1972 $40.00. ISBN 0-520-01864-8. A guide to the world's most important films through 1970.

Schaefer, Dennis, and Larry Salvato. *Masters of Light: Conversations with Contemporary Cinematographers.* U. CA Pr. 1985 $14.00. ISBN 0-520-05336-2. Interviews with 15 cinematographers about their work.

Silver, Alain, and Elizabeth Ward. *Film Noir: An Encyclopedic Reference to the American Style.* Overlook Pr. 2nd ed. 1992 $19.95. ISBN 0-87951-479-5. Classic film reference to over 350 films, with illustrations.

Sullivan, Kaye. *Films for, by, and about Women.* Scarecrow 1985 $59.50. ISBN 0-8108-1766-7. A helpful guide to film studies from a female perspective.

Sussex, Elizabeth. *The Rise and Fall of the British Documentary: The Story of the Film Movement Founded by John Grierson.* U. CA Pr. 1976 $40.00. ISBN 0-520-02869-4. A good account of the history of the British documentary movement, based on interviews.

Talbot, Daniel, ed. *Film: An Anthology.* U. CA Pr. 1966 $10.95. ISBN 0-520-01251-8. A small treasure trove of classic articles on film.

Willis, John, ed. *Screen World.* Applause Theatre Bk. Pubs. 1992 $39.95. ISBN 1-55783-135-1. Lists domestic movies released in 1991, and gives information about box office stars and Oscar winners; includes photos.

Writers' Program (New York, NY). *The Film Index: A Bibliography.* Vol. 1 *Film as Art.* Arno Press 1988 $60.00. ISBN 0-527-29329-6. Vol. 2 *Film as Industry.* Kraus 1985 $95.00. ISBN 0-527-29334-2. Vol. 3 *Film in Society.* Kraus 1985 $85.00. ISBN 0-527-

29335-0. An exhaustive bibliography, compiled with the cooperation of the Museum of Modern Art (New York), of film literature and a guide to filmmakers and films from the days of silent cinema through 1986, with superb indexing.

Criticism and Theory

Andrew, Dudley. *Major Film Theories: An Introduction.* OUP 1976 $9.95. ISBN 0-19-501991-1. A helpful guide for newcomers to cinema theory.

Bazin, André. *What Is Cinema?* 2 vols. Trans. by Hugh Gray. U. CA Pr. 1967–71 $29.95 ea. ISBN 0-520-0091-9. A collection of classic and beautifully written essays by the most important film critic of his time.

Brownlow, Kevin. *Behind the Mask of Innocence: Sex, Violence, Prejudice, Crime: Films of Social Conscience in the Silent Era.* Knopf 1990 $50.00. ISBN 0-394-57747-7. America's most tragic face as shown in the silent era of films, from 1900–1920.

Bywater, Tim, and Thomas Sobchack. *Introduction to Film Criticism: Major Critical Approaches to Narrative Film.* Longman 1989 $23.95. ISBN 0-582-28606-9. A clear presentation of the seven principal techniques of criticism: journalistic, humanist, auteurist, genre, social science, historical, theoretical/ideological.

De Lauretis, Teresa. *Alice Doesn't: Feminism, Semiotics, Cinema.* Ind. U. Pr. 1987 $10.95. ISBN 0-253-20316-3. A ground-breaking and powerful feminist text.

Friedberg, Anne. *Window Shopping: Cinema and the Postmodern.* U. CA Pr. 1993 $28.00. ISBN 0-520-07916-7. An exploration of film and contemporary cultural theory that draws on the nineteenth-century visual experience.

Greenberg, Harvey Roy. *Screen Memories: Hollywood Cinema on the Psychoanalytic Couch.* Col. U. Pr. 1993 $29.50. ISBN 0-231-07286-4. An engaging psychoanalytic look at a wide range of films and film trends.

Hames, Peter. *The Czechoslovak New Wave.* U. CA Pr. 1985 $40.00. ISBN 0-520-04859-8. A look at the political role of several important Czech films of the late 1960s.

Kawin, Bruce. *How Movies Work.* U. CA Pr. 1987 $20.00. ISBN 0-520-07696-6. A complete and stunning analysis of how film works.

Lawrence, Amy. *Echo and Narcissus: Women's Voices in Classical Hollywood Cinema.* U. CA Pr. 1991 $42.50. ISBN 0-520-07071-2. A feminist examination of the representation of women in eight films.

Scharff, Stefan. *The Elements of Cinema: Toward a Theory of Cinesthetic Impact.* Col. U. Pr. 1982 $15.50. ISBN 0-231-05477-7. Examines uniquely cinematic elements of structure and casts light on the creative processes and aesthetic potential of filmmaking.

Sklar, Robert, and Charles Musser. *Resisting Images: Essays on Cinema and History.* Temple U. Pr. 1990 $44.95. ISBN 0-87722-738-1. A group of essays that raise questions about film history, historiography, and cultural theory.

Thurmin, Janet. *Celluloid Sisters: Women and Popular Cinema.* St. Martin 1992 $35.00. ISBN 0-312-07254-6. An examination of the representation of women in 18 British films between 1945 and 1965.

Traube, Elizabeth G. *Dreaming Identities: Class, Gender, and Generation in 1980's Hollywood Movies.* Westview 1992 $49.95. ISBN 0-8133-1313-9. A fascinating examination of the American frontier myth and the American dream in films of this period.

Wees, William C. *Light Moving in Time: Studies in the Visual Aesthetic of Avant-Garde Film.* U. CA Pr. 1992 $35.00. ISBN 0-520-07367-3. An intelligent and stimulating discussion of recent avant-garde films.

Directors

There are many film directors whose personal vision and style have generated films that are as distinct as the writing style of such authors as JANE AUSTEN (see Vol. 1) and JAMES JOYCE (see Vol. 1). The following books concern directors who are among the most important; there are, however, many significant directors who have not written books, published screenplays, or had books written about them. As a result, they are not included here.

Bock, Audrey. *Japanese Film Directors.* Kodansha 1985 $14.95. ISBN 0-87011-714-9. Studies of the work of Ozu, Kurosawa, Oshima, and Mizoguchi.

Bowman, Barbara. *Master Space: Film Images of Capra, Lubitsch, Sternberg and Wyler.* Greenwood 1992 $42.95. ISBN 0-313-28026-6. A compelling study of four early masters of film.

Chown, Jeffrey. *Hollywood Auteur: Francis Coppola.* Greenwood 1988 $45.00. ISBN 0-275-92910-8. An analysis of Coppola's personal filmmaking style.

Coppola, Eleanor. *On the Making of Apocalypse Now.* Limelight Edns. 1991 $14.95. ISBN 0-87910-150-4. The director's wife gives her version of the experience.

Corrigan, Timothy. *The Films of Werner Herzog.* Routledge Chapman & Hall 1986 $14.95. ISBN 0-416-41070-7. A collection of essays, written from a variety of perspectives, that focus on the merit of Herzog's work and its place in film history.

_____. *New German Film: The Displaced Image.* 1983 o.p. A collection of critical studies of films by directors Kluge, Fassbinder, Herzog, Wenders, Syberberg, and Schlondorff.

Cowie, Peter. *Coppola.* Macmillan 1990 $22.95. ISBN 0-684-19193-8. An interesting biography of an important American director.

Crist, Judith. *Take 22: Moviemakers on Moviemaking.* Continuum 1991 $14.95. ISBN 0-8264-0537-1. A discussion of the industry by 22 directors and actors.

Cumano, Ellen. *Film Forum: 35 Top Filmmakers Discuss Their Craft.* St. Martin 1985 $9.95. ISBN 0-312-28933-2. A worthwhile look at film techniques based on interviews.

Izod, John. *The Films of Nicolas Roeg: Myth and Mind.* St. Martin 1992 $39.95. ISBN 0-312-07904-4. A Jungian interpretation of the power of Roeg's films.

Kolker, Robert P. *Bernardo Bertolucci.* OUP 1985 $21.95. ISBN 0-19-520492-1. A perceptive study of the important Italian director and his films.

_____. *A Cinema of Loneliness: Penn, Kubrick, Scorsese, Spielberg, Altman.* OUP 1988 $16.95. ISBN 0-19-503390-7. An interesting look at themes that emerge in the films of several prominent American directors.

Lourdeaux, Lee. *Italian and Irish Filmmakers in America: Ford, Capra, Coppola, and Scorsese.* Temple U. Pr. 1990 $29.95. ISBN 0-87722-697-0. The impact of their ethnic cultures on four American directors.

MacDonald, Scott. *A Critical Cinema: Interviews with Independent Filmmakers.* U. CA Pr. 1988 $60.00. ISBN 0-520-05800-3. A collection of illuminating interviews.

_____. *A Critical Cinema 2: Interviews with Independent Filmmakers.* U. CA Pr. 1992 $48.00. ISBN 0-520-07917-5. An excellent sequel, with a new collection of interviews.

Madsen, Roy Paul. *Working Cinema: Learnings from the Masters.* Wadsworth Pub. 1990 ISBN 0-534-11880-1. On how cinema is made.

Mamet, David. *On Directing Film.* Viking Penguin 1997 $10.00. ISBN 0-14-012434-9. An intelligent look at every aspect of directing.

Monaco, James. *Alain Resnais.* OUP 1978 $22.50. ISBN 0-19-520037-3. An important book about this pivotal French New Wave director.

_____. *The New Wave: Truffaut, Godard, Chabrol, Rohmer, Rivette.* OUP 1986 $10.95. ISBN 0-19-502246-7. A film scholar's careful examination of the most important French directors associated with "The New Wave."

Robinson, Andrew. *Satyajit Ray: The Inner Eye.* U. CA Pr. 1990 $32.50. ISBN 0-520-06905-6. A comprehensive account of Ray's career by a man who spent much time with the director.

Sherman, Eric. *Directing the Film: Film Directors on Their Art.* Acrobat 1988 $14.95. ISBN 0-918226. Seventy-five directors discuss the complete process of filmmaking.

Singer, Michael, ed. *Film Directors: A Complete Guide*. Lone Eagle 1985 $59.50. ISBN 0-8108-1766-7. A list of film directors from all over the world, with information about their films and careers. Includes a few interviews.

Viano, Maurizio. *A Certain Realism: Making Use of Pasolini's Film Theory and Practice*. U. CA Pr. 1993 $38.00. ISBN 0-520-07854-3. An analysis of the films of the important postwar Italian filmmaker Pier Paolo Pasolini (1922–1975).

Zolotow, Maurice. *Billy Wilder in Hollywood*. Limelight Edns. 1988 $12.95. ISBN 0-87910-070-2. A study of the German-born filmmaker who produced some of the greatest American films.

CHRONOLOGY OF AUTHORS
(Film)

Cocteau, Jean. 1889–1963
Dreyer, Carl. 1889–1968
Lang, Fritz. 1890–1976
Renoir, Jean. 1894–1979
Hawks, Howard. 1896–1977
Capra, Frank. 1897–1991
Eisenstein, Sergei. 1898–1948
Buñuel, Luis. 1900–1983
Huston, John. 1906–1987
Visconti, Luchino. 1906–1976
Kurosawa, Akira. 1910–

Antonioni, Michelangelo. 1912–
Bergman, Ingmar. 1918–
Fellini, Federico. 1920–
Rohmer, Eric. 1920–
Kubrick, Stanley. 1928–
Godard, Jean-Luc. 1930–
Malle, Louis. 1932–
Truffaut, François. 1932–1984
Polanski, Roman. 1933–
Allen, Woody. 1935–
Fassbinder, Werner. 1946–1982

ALLEN, WOODY. 1935–

Woody Allen is one of those Hollywood rarities who writes, directs, and often stars in his own films. He began his career as a television comedy writer, and then switched to stand-up comedy, drawing his material from his own fantasies and insecurities. Many of his films are also autobiographical, either obliquely or directly, like *Annie Hall*, which won Academy Awards in 1977 for best director and best original screenplay. Allen's comedic vision of the guilt-ridden middle-class intellectual Jewish-American male becomes progressively more serious in his later films, such as *Manhattan* (1979), *Zelig* (1983), and *Hannah and Her Sisters* (1986).

BOOKS BY ALLEN

Four Films of Woody Allen. Random 1982 $20.00. ISBN 0-394-52443-8. Screenplays of *Annie Hall*, *Interiors*, *Manhattan*, and *Stardust Memories*.

Hannah and Her Sisters. Random 1986 $5.95. ISBN 0-394-74749-6. Screenplay of the film.

Three Films of Woody Allen. Random 1987 $16.00. ISBN 0-394-75304-6. Screenplays of *Zelig*, *Broadway Danny Rose*, and *The Purple Rose of Cairo*.

BOOKS ABOUT ALLEN

Altman, Mark. *A Woody Allen Encyclopedia*. Movie Pubs. Servs. 1991 $14.95. ISBN 1-55698-303-4. Everything you ever wanted to know about Woody Allen.

Benayoun, Robert. *The Films of Woody Allen*. Trans. by Alexander Walker. Crown Pub. Group o.p. An illustrated appraisal of Allen's films by a French film magazine editor.

Brode, Douglas. *Woody Allen: His Films and Career*. Carol Pub. Group 1987 $19.95. ISBN 0-8065-0950-7. A thorough, well-written biography and film analysis.

Hirsch, Foster. *Love, Sex, Death and the Meaning of Life: The Films of Woody Allen*. Limelight Edns. 1990 $12.95. ISBN 0-87910-143-1. Considers philosophical meanings of Allen's films.

Lax, Eric. *Woody Allen: A Biography*. Random 1992 $13.00. ISBN 0-679-73847-9. A biography written with the cooperation of the subject that takes Allen's life up to all but the most recent events of his highly publicized separation from the actress Mia Farrow and his custody battle for their three children.

McCann, Graham. *Woody Allen*. Blackwell Pubs. 1990 $24.95. ISBN 0-7956-063902-3. An evaluation of the director's career and films.

Pogel, Nancy. *Woody Allen*. Macmillan 1987 $22.95. ISBN 0-8057-9297-X. A fairly recent biography.

Wernblad, Annette. *Brooklyn Is Not Expanding: Woody Allen's Comic Universe*. Fairleigh Dickinson 1992 $29.50. ISBN 0-8386-3448-6. A superb study of Allen's humor and vision.

Yacowar, Maurice. *Loser Take All: The Comic Art of Woody Allen*. Continuum 1991 $14.95. ISBN 0-8264-0551-7. An excellent critique of Allen's work.

ANTONIONI, MICHELANGELO. 1912–

Michelangelo Antonioni of Italy graduated from the University of Bologna, studied cinema in Rome, and started out in films as a critic and screenwriter. When he made his first feature films in the 1950s, he broke away from the neorealism then in vogue in Italy and in a rigorously disciplined style explored the interior states of the isolated men and women in such films as *La Notte* (1960), *L'Eclipse* (1961), and *The Red Desert* (1964). Although his films are usually about the prosperous classes, his only social criticism is oblique. *L'Avventura* (1959), his sixth film, established his fame internationally as an original artist. His English-language films are *Blow-Up* (1966), set in mod London, and *Zabriskie Point* (1970), an apocalyptic vision of contemporary American youth and its politics. His last notable film is *The Passenger* (1975).

Books by Antonioni

The Passenger. Applause Theatre Bk. Pubs. 1986 $6.95. ISBN 0-936839-52-X. Screenplay.
That Bowling Alley on the Tiber: Tales of a Director. Trans. by William Arrowsmith. OUP 1987 $19.95. ISBN 0-19-504224-7. A collection of stories, sketches, and ideas for films.

Books about Antonioni

Lyons, Robert J. *Michelangelo Antonioni's Neo-Realism: A World View. Dissertations on Film Ser*. Ayer 1976 $17.00. ISBN 0-405-07618-5. A well-written study of Antonioni's earlier work.

Perry, Ted, and René Preto. *Michelangelo Antonioni's NeoRealism: A Guide to References and Resources*. Macmillan 1986 $50.00. ISBN 0-8161-8566-2. Thorough and helpful for understanding the director's work.

Rohdie, Sam. *Antonioni*. Ind. U. Pr. 1990 $49.95. ISBN 0-85170-274-0. A scholarly but fascinating examination of the director and his films, with illustrations.

BERGMAN, INGMAR. 1918–

Ingmar Bergman was born in Uppsala, Sweden, into a rigidly Lutheran family whose gloomy atmosphere and moral preoccupations had a profound effect on his temperament and art. After attending the University of Stockholm, he broke into cinema as a scriptwriter and then became a major figure among contemporary "complete filmmakers"—those who write, direct, and often produce their own films. He achieved international recognition with *Smiles of a Summer Night* (1955), a period comedy, followed by *The Seventh Seal* (1957) and *The Virgin Spring* (1959), somber allegories set in the Middle Ages. In these last two, and the contemporary *Through a Glass Darkly* (1961), *Winter Light* (1962), and *The Silence* (1963), Bergman's themes are the cosmic relationship between humanity and God and the awful aloneness of the individual. His later films are less metaphysical and more concerned with male-female relationships; especially notable is *Scenes from a Marriage* (1973), which was originally made for Swedish television but was later reissued in a shortened and more artistically successful version for cinema. Although Bergman has the reputation for making uncompromisingly bleak films, his range is actually much wider, encompassing the wry wit of *Wild Strawberries* (1957) and the delightful charm of *The Magic Flute* (1975), one of the best opera films ever made. After *Fannie and Alexander* (1982), he retired from filmmaking but continues to direct for the stage.

BOOKS BY BERGMAN

The Best Intentions. Little 1993 $22.95. ISBN 1-55978-207-9. In his first novel, Bergman re-creates the early years of his parents' marriage to investigate who his mother and father actually were.

A Film Trilogy: Through a Glass Darkly, The Communicants (Winter Light) and The Silence. M. Boyars Pubs. 1988 $9.95. ISBN 0-7145-0240-5. Three screenplays.

Four Screenplays of Ingmar Bergman: Smiles of a Summer Night; The Seventh Seal; Wild Strawberries; The Magician. S&S Trade 1989 $12.95. ISBN 0-671-67833-7. Screenplays of four of Bergman's major films.

The Magic Lantern: An Autobiography. Viking Penguin 1985 $19.95. ISBN 0-670-81911-5. A fascinating self-revelation.

The Marriage Scenarios. Pantheon 1988 $9.95. ISBN 0-679-72032-4. Includes *Scenes from a Marriage, Face to Face,* and *Autumn Sonata.*

Persona and Shame. Trans. by Keith Bradfield. M. Boyars Pubs. 1989 $10.95. ISBN 0-7145-0756-3. Two screenplays of important films that helped make Bergman famous.

BOOKS ABOUT BERGMAN

Bjorkman, Stig, and others. *Bergman on Bergman: Interviews with Ingmar Bergman.* S&S Trade 1975 $9.95. ISBN 0-671-22157-4. A self-portrait of the director emerges from this series of interviews he has given over the years.

Blake, R. A. *The Lutheran Milieu of the Films of Ingmar Bergman.* Ayer 1978 $26.50. ISBN 0-405-10751-X. A trenchant study of the religious bases of Bergman's earlier films.

Cohen, James. *Through a Lens Darkly.* D. I. Fine 1991 $19.95. ISBN 1-55611-260-2. Bergman's dark and often troubling vision of the human dilemma as portrayed in his films.

Cowie, Peter. *Ingmar Bergman: A Critical Biography.* 1982. Limelight Edns. 1992 $17.95. ISBN 0-87910-155-5. An updated, important biography and film analysis.

Donner, Jorn. *The Films of Ingmar Bergman.* Trans. by Holger Lundbergh. Dover 1972 $6.95. ISBN 0-486-20093-0. Perceptive study of the earlier films of Bergman.

Gado, Frank. *The Passion of Ingmar Bergman.* Duke 1986 $55.00. ISBN 0-8223-0586-0. A fine study of the forces that drive Bergman and his work.

Jones G. William. *Talking with Ingmar Bergman.* SMU Pr. 1983 $12.50. ISBN 0-87074-191-8. Lively interviews with the Swedish director.

Ketcham, Charles B. *The Influence of Existentialism on Ingmar Bergman: An Analysis of the Theological Ideas Shaping a Filmmaker's Art.* E. Mellen 1986 $99.95. ISBN 0-88946-556-8. An intelligent analysis of the philosophical and religious foundations of Bergman's art.

Lauder, Robert E. *God, Death, Art, and Love: The Philosophical Vision of Ingmar Bergman.* Paulist Pr. 1989 $11.95. ISBN 0-8091-3108-0. A sharply focused philosophical analysis of Bergman's philosophical landscape.

Manvell, Roger. *Ingmar Bergman: An Appreciation. Dissertations on Film Ser*. Ayer 1980
    $18.00. ISBN 0-405-12936-X. A useful study of many of Bergman's films.
Marker, Lise-Lone, and Frederick J. Marker. *Ingmar Bergman: A Life in the Theater*.
    Directors in Perspective Ser. Cambridge U. Pr. 1993 $59.95. ISBN 0-521-42082-2.
    A biography of Bergman, including his involvement with theater as well as film.
Mosley, Philip. *Ingmar Bergman: The Cinema as Mistress*. M. Boyars Pubs. 1984 $16.00.
    ISBN 0-7145-2644-4. Bergman's love affairs with film and the women in his films.
Mosley, Philip. *Ingmar Bergman: The Cinema as Mistress*. M. Boyars Pubs. 1986 $16.00.
    ISBN 0-7145-2804-8

BRAKHAGE, STAN. 1933–

[SEE Volume 1.]

BUÑUEL, LUIS. 1900–1983

The Spanish-born director Luis Buñuel made his first films with Salvador
Dali, whom he met among other surrealists at Madrid University in the 1920s.
Their first collaboration, *Un Chien Andalou* (1928), achieved notoriety for its
brutal but comic surreal images; the second, the equally notorious *L'Age d'Or*
(1930), is considered a masterpiece and a major key to Buñuel's later works.
Buñuel exiled himself from Franco's Spain in the 1930s, eventually settling in
Mexico. There he made a series of low-budget movies in relative obscurity until
he won the Cannes Film Festival director's prize for *Los Olvidados* (1950), an
unsparing portrait of street children in the slums of Mexico City. *Viridiana*
(1961), a tragicomedy with a lurid plot that is nonetheless a masterwork,
established him as a major presence on the European film scene. For the next
15 years, Buñuel directed several highly acclaimed films: *Belle de Jour* (1966),
Tristana (1970), *The Discreet Charm of the Bourgeoisie* (1972), *The Phantom of
Liberty* (1974). His work is a strange and compelling blend of the real and the
surreal, fatalism and anarchy; sexual liberation and dark repression.

BOOKS BY BUÑUEL

Belle de Jour. Faber & Faber 1988 $9.95. ISBN 0-571-12560-3. The screenplay.
The Exterminating Angel, Nazarin, and Los Olvidados. Faber & Faber 1988 $12.95. ISBN
    0-571-12575-1. Three screenplays.
L'Age d'Or and An Andalusian Dog. Faber & Faber 1989 $7.95. ISBN 0-571-12591-3. Two
    early screenplays by Buñuel.
My Last Sigh. Random 1984 $6.95. ISBN 0-394-72501-8. A lyrical and passionate
    autobiography.
Tristana. S&S Trade 1971 o.p. A screenplay.

BOOKS ABOUT BUÑUEL

Aranda, Francisco. *Luis Buñuel: A Critical Biography*. Ed. by David Robinson. Da Capo
    1976 repr. of 1975 ed. $35.00. ISBN 0-306-70754-3. A useful guide to the surrealist
    director's life and work.
Durgnat, Raymond. *Luis Buñuel*. U. CA Pr. 1978 $8.95. ISBN 0-520-03424-4. A splendid
    exploration of the complexities of Buñuel's themes and symbols.
Edwards, Gwynne. *The Discreet Art of Luis Buñuel: A Reading of His Films*. M. Boyars
    Pubs. 1983 $30.00. ISBN 0-7145-2754-8. A fine critique of Buñuel's important films.
Mellen, Joan, ed. *The World of Luis Buñuel: Essays in Criticism*. OUP 1978 o.p.
Sandro, Paul. *Diversions of Pleasure: Luis Buñuel and the Crises of Desire*. Ohio St. U. Pr.
    1988 $16.75. ISBN 0-8142-0439-2. A rigorous and stimulating analysis.
Williams, Linda. *Figures of Desire: A Theory and Analysis of Surrealist Film*. U. CA Pr. 1981
    $13.00. ISBN 0-520-07896-9. A fascinating analysis of Buñuel's *Un Chien Andalou*,
    L'Age d'Or, *Phantom of Liberty*, and *That Obscure Object of Desire*.

CAPRA, FRANK. 1897–1991

Born in Sicily, the Director Frank Capra immigrated to the United States with his family in 1903. Many of his films are idealistic, patriotic, and sentimental but glorious celebrations of American life and values. Throughout the 1930s Capra was Columbia Pictures' mainstay, the director who made Harry Cohn's studio a major force in Hollywood. His characteristic comic style—brisk pace, snappy dialogue, energetic love scenes—set a pattern that has been much imitated. He was a skilled director of actors, eliciting a populist sincerity that is still appealing. The Capra hero, epitomized by the protagonist in *Mr. Smith Goes to Washington* (1939), is a man of the people faced with tremendous challenges, which he overcomes through honesty, optimism, and sheer American stubbornness. Audiences loved his films, and Capra received three Academy Awards for best director: for *It Happened One Night* (1934), *Mr. Deeds Goes to Town* (1936), and *You Can't Take It with You* (1938). During World War II, Capra produced propaganda films for the U.S. Army and was awarded the Distinguished Service Medal for his "important influence on the morale of the Army." He returned to Hollywood to make the highly successful *It's a Wonderful Life* in 1946, but his career faltered in the 1950s and 1960s. He retired from film directing and wrote a popular autobiography detailing life among the movie stars and moguls.

BOOK BY CAPRA

The Name Above the Title: An Autobiography. 1971. Random 1985 $9.95. ISBN 0-394-71205-6. An exuberant autobiography that exhibits many of the winning characteristics of Capra's movies.

BOOKS ABOUT CAPRA

Carney, Ray. *American Vision: The Films of Frank Capra.* Cambridge U. Pr. 1986 $39.95. ISBN 0-521-32619-2. An incisive look at Capra's major films.

Levy, William T., and Victor Scherle. *The Films of Frank Capra.* Carol Pub. Group 1977 $16.95. ISBN 0-8065-0430-7. A discussion of each of the major films.

McBride, Joseph. *Frank Capra: The Catastrophe of Success.* S&S Trade 1992 $27.50. ISBN 0-671-73494-6. A fascinating critical biography covering parts of Capra's life that he omitted from his autobiography.

CHAPLIN, CHARLIE. 1889–1977

[SEE Volume 1.]

COCTEAU, JEAN. 1889–1963

Jean Cocteau was a leader of the Paris avant-garde of the 1920s and 1930s, and one of the most versatile writers of the twentieth century, producing poetry, plays, novels, screenplays, and criticism. He began his film career in a surrealistic mode, mixing dream and reality in *The Blood of a Poet* (1930). He expressed his personal vision in the poetical *Beauty and the Beast* (1945), based on Charles Perrault's fairy tale, and *Orphée* (1950), based on the Greek myth of Orpheus, as well as in the domestic drama *Les Parents Terribles* (1948). At the age of 70, he directed his own "last testament" in *Testament d'Orphée* (1960). Cocteau's demonstration of the poetry possible in film inspired a number of filmmakers who came after him in both the commercial and the underground cinema, although few have been able to combine artistic seriousness with sleight-of-hand and self-mockery as engagingly as he did.

BOOKS BY COCTEAU

Blood of a Poet and the Testament of Orpheus. M. Boyars Pubs. 1985 $7.95. ISBN 0-7145-0580-3. Two screenplays.

Diary of an Unknown. Paragon Hse. 1991 $12.95. ISBN 1-55778-466-3. A collection of semi-autobiographical essays in which Cocteau speaks intelligently on a wide range of subjects.

BOOKS ABOUT COCTEAU

Emboden, William A. *Visual Art of Jean Cocteau.* Abrams 1990 $49.50. ISBN 0-8109-3153-2. An illustrated study of Cocteau's painting.

Evans, Arthur B. *Jean Cocteau and His Films of Orphic Identity.* Art Alliance 1975 $27.50. ISBN 0-87982-001-X. The influence of Greek mythology, especially the Orpheus theme, on Cocteau's films.

Knapp, Bettina L. *Jean Cocteau.* Macmillan 1989 $24.95. ISBN 0-8057-8239-7. A useful biography of the playwright, filmmaker, and artist.

Lieberman, Nancy, and Julie Saul. *Jean Cocteau.* Gibbs Smith Pub. 1990 o.p. A short illustrated study of the writer and filmmaker.

Steegmuller, Francis. *Cocteau: A Biography.* Godine 1986 $15.95. ISBN 0-87923-606-X. A splendid biography by a master biographer.

_____. *Jean Cocteau, the Mimer and the Mask.* Godine 1992 $40.00. ISBN 0-87923-918-2. An excellent analysis of the many faces Cocteau showed in his work.

DISNEY, WALT(ER) ELIAS. 1901–1966

[SEE Volume 1.]

DREYER, CARL (THEODOR). 1889–1968

Carl Theodore Dreyer, a director who worked in France, Germany, Sweden, and Norway, as well as in his native Denmark, spanned the silent and sound eras of filmmaking. He was adopted, and only learned at 18 of his natural mother's tragic early death from an illegal operation, a revelation that affected him deeply and perhaps contributed to his film portraits of martyred women. His 1928 film *The Passion of Joan of Arc* is regarded as one of the greatest silent films ever made. Through the use of such techniques as uncut sequences, careful composition, and tight closeups, he illuminated the spiritual passion of the French saint burned as a heretic in the Middle Ages. In this film and in *Day of Wrath* (1943), a tale of medieval witch hunting, Dreyer's theme is the suffering born of intolerance and deliverance from evil through death. Dreyer made several other notable films, including the classic horror movie *Vampyr* (1932) and *The Word* (1955), a monumental story of spiritual and physical regeneration. His last film was *Gertrud* (1964).

BOOKS BY DREYER

Dreyer in Double Reflection: Carl Dreyer's Writings on Film. 1973. Da Capo 1991 $12.95. ISBN 0-306-80458-1. A valuable collection of essays by the director.

Four Screenplays. Boulevard 1970 $19.95. ISBN 0-91278-05-9

BOOKS ABOUT DREYER

Bordwell, David. *The Films of Carl Theodor Dreyer.* U. CA Pr. 1981 $42.50. ISBN 0-520-03987-4. A rigorous, formal analysis of his major films, with illustrations.

Carney, Raymond. *Speaking the Language of Desire: The Films of Carl Dreyer.* Cambridge U. Pr. 1989 $47.95. ISBN 0-521-37163-5. An in-depth analysis of Dreyer's art.

Helweg, Marianne. *Carl Dreyer.* Gordon Pr. 1979 $59.95. ISBN 0-8490-2880-9. A well-written biography.

Jensen, Jytte, ed. *The Films of Carl Theodor Dreyer*. Museum Mod. Art 1989 $9.95. ISBN 0-87070-305-6. An illustrated guide to Dreyer's films.

EISENSTEIN, SERGEI. 1898–1948

Potemkin, a silent film that appeared in 1925, was the great Russian film director's first brilliant "mass epic," originally commissioned just after the 1917 Russian Revolution to commemorate the 1905 anti-Czarist uprising. In it Eisenstein broke new ground in the cinema with his antinarrative technique of "shock-attraction," or dialectical, montage—a series of shots in which each pair being spliced gives rise to a collision of images, thereby creating a sharp impression, or synthesis, in the viewer's mind. Eisenstein (who had been an engineer before he became a film director) compared this technique to the series of explosions made by an internal combustion engine driving a vehicle forward—just so, the famous sequence of slaughter on the Odessa steps and the slow descent of a baby in its carriage through the carnage drives *Potemkin* forward. Dynamic cutting is again evident in *Ten Days That Shook the World* (1928), in which he uses slowly mounting sequences and fast cuts to depict the gathering storm of the Russian Revolution and its ultimate triumph.

Despite his glorification of the Russian Revolution and the new Soviet state, Eisenstein often found himself at odds with the Soviet government. For a while he even attempted to work in Hollywood, but he returned to Russia to make *Alexander Nevsky* (1938), his most popular film, and *Ivan the Terrible*, which he envisioned as a three-part epic. Part I (1944) was completed and released; Part II was withheld at first by the Soviet Film Trust and then later released; and Eisenstein died of a heart attack while working on Part III.

BOOKS BY EISENSTEIN

The Battleship Potemkin. Trans. by Gillon R. Atken. Faber & Faber. 1988 $9.95. ISBN 0-571-12559-X. The film's bound screenplay, with an introduction by the author and a bit of historical context. Includes photos.
The Film Form. 1948. HarBraceJ 1969 $8.95. ISBN 0-15-630920-3. Collection of essays that show key points in the development of Eisenstein's film theory and his analysis of the sound-film medium.
The Film Sense. 1942. HarBraceJ 1969 $8.95. ISBN 0-15-630935-1. Discusses his films in relation to a more expressive and profound medium that would appeal to all the senses, emotions, and intellect.
Immoral Memories: An Autobiography. HM 1983 $19.95. ISBN 0-395-33101-3. Looks back at his family and childhood and discusses how he became a filmmaker, as well as his philosophy of life and art.
Ivan the Terrible. Faber & Faber 1989 $14.95. ISBN 0-571-12586-7. The screenplay.
Non-Different Nature: Film and the Structure of Things. Cambridge U. Pr. 1988 $42.50. ISBN 0-521-32415-7. Reflections on film by the Russian director.
The Psychology of Composition. Trans. by Alan Upchurch. Heinemann Ed. 1989 $13.95. ISBN 0-413-19650-X. Compiled from several sources, Eisenstein's thoughts on the making of art. Originally planned to be part of a lecture series.
Selected Works. 2 vols. Ed. and trans. by Richard Taylor. Ind. U. Pr. Vol. 1 *Writing 1922–34*. 1987 $39.95. ISBN 0-253-35042-5. Vol. 2 *Towards a Theory of Montage 1937–40*. 1992 $70.00. ISBN 0-253-85170-2

BOOKS ABOUT EISENSTEIN

Leyda, Jay. *Kino: A History of the Russian and Soviet Film*. Princeton U. Pr. 1983 $19.95. ISBN 0-691-00346-7. Still a classic.
Montagu, Ivor. *With Eisenstein in Hollywood*. Intl. Pubs. Co. 1969 $1.95. ISBN 0-7178-0220-5. A memoir.

Nizhny, Vladimir. *Lessons with Eisenstein*. Da Capo 1979 $9.95. ISBN 0-306-80100-0. An interesting study by a student of Eisenstein.

Thompson, K. *Eisenstein's Ivan the Terrible: A Neoformalist Analysis*. Princeton U. Pr. 1981 $55.00. ISBN 0-691-06472-5. A theoretical study of one of Eisenstein's most famous films.

FASSBINDER, (RAINER) WERNER. 1946–1982

Werner Fassbinder, the German film director and actor, was prolific in his short life. Though he died at age 37, he had already directed 41 films in 13 years. He had also written, acted, and produced for the theater. Fassbinder's films, most of which were made with his own company of actors, are notable for the skepticism and irony with which they view the prosperous and corrupt German society that arose from the wreckage of World War II. Among his better-known works are *The Third Generation* (1979), about terrorists; *The Bitter Tears of Petra von Kant* (1972), which explores homosexuality (a recurrent theme in his work); and *Berlin Alexanderplatz* (1980), a searing descent into the lower-class and criminal worlds that was made for television.

BOOK BY FASSBINDER

The Marriage of Maria Braun. Ed. by Joyce Rheuben. Rutgers U. Pr. 1986 $30.00. ISBN 0-8135-1129-1. Discussion of the making of *The Marriage of Maria Braun*, with its history, script, cast, photos, and a collection of essays and reviews about the film.

BOOK ABOUT FASSBINDER

Katz, Robert. *Love Is Colder Than Death: The Life and Times of Rainer Werner Fassbinder*. Random 1987 $19.95. ISBN 0-394-53456-5. A somewhat gossipy biography of the director's stormy life.

FELLINI, FEDERICO. 1920–

Federico Fellini, the Italian film director and writer, is known for the extravagant personal style he developed early in his career, with its ornate visual effects, uninhibited sentiment, mischievous humor, and romantic fantasy. His collaboration with Roberto Rossellini on *Open City* (1945) brought him widespread critical acclaim in Italy. He first attracted attention abroad with *I Vitelloni* (1953) and *La Strada* (1955), which focuses on the poor in a deeply sensitive manner touched with poetry. The latter brought him international success, as did *La Dolce Vita* (1959), with its portrait of the rich and rootless in a decadent Rome, the autobiographical *8½* (1963), and the supple *Juliet of the Spirits* (1965), inspired by his actress-wife Giulietta Massina. Fellini's penchant for obsurity, his symbolism, and his sharp satire (of the church, for example) have made him controversial from time to time, but his imaginative impact is uncontested.

BOOK BY FELLINI

Comments on Film. Ed. by Giovanni Grazzini. CSU Pr. Fresno 1988 $11.95. ISBN 0-992201-15-0. The famous Italian director's ideas about filmmaking.

BOOKS ABOUT FELLINI

Alpert, Hollis. *Fellini: A Life*. Paragon Hse. 1987 $9.95. ISBN 1-5577-8-000-5. A fairly recent biography.

Benderson, Albert E. *Critical Approaches to Federico Fellini's "8½." Dissertations on Film Ser.* Ayer 1974 $15.00. ISBN 0-405-04877-7. A stimulating study of one of Fellini's most important films.

Burke, Frank. *Federico Fellini: "Variety Lights" to "La Dolce Vita." Filmmakers Ser.*
Macmillan 1984 $23.95. ISBN 0-8057-9300-3. A useful study of Fellini's earlier films.
Costello, Donald P. *Fellini's Road.* U. of Notre Dame Pr. $9.95. ISBN 0-268-00958-9.
A study of the thematic progression in Fellini's films.
Fava, Claudio G., and Aldo Vigano. *The Films of Federico Fellini.* Carol Pub. Group 1984
$19.95. ISBN 0-8065-0928-7. An illustrated guide to Fellini's major films through
1984.

FORD, JOHN. 1895–1973

[SEE Volume 1.]

GODARD, JEAN-LUC. 1930–

Jean-Luc Godard has often been hailed as the most influential and original
director of the 1960s. He was born in France, educated as a youth in
Switzerland, and returned to France to join the New Wave of filmmakers of the
late 1950s and early 1960s, who shattered the polite conventions of postwar
French cinema. In 1959 he made his directorial debut with *Breathless*, which
was admired for its innovative techniques, such as the jump cut, and became an
immediate international success. Sometimes criticized for his anarchistic use of
the medium, Godard made films in the 1960s that are fast-moving, choppy,
witty, informal—indeed, a wild collage of contrasting modes. His major films of
that decade are *Alphaville* (1965), *La Chinoise* (1967), and *Weekend* (1967).
Then, for a number of years, he devoted himself to making polemical leftist
films for very small audiences. Recently, however, Godard has been trying to
return to a more broad-based cinema.

BOOK BY GODARD

Breathless. Ed. by Dudley Andrew. Rutgers U. Pr. 1987 $13.00. ISBN 0-8135-1253-0.
Screenplay.

BOOKS ABOUT GODARD

Narboni, Jean, and Tom Milne, eds. *Godard on Godard.* Da Capo 1986 $11.95. ISBN 0-
306-80259-7. Paradoxical pronouncements by Godard.
Roud, Richard. *Godard.* Ind. U. Pr. 1970 o.p.

GRIFFITH, D(AVID) (LEWELYN) W(ARK). 1875–1948

[SEE Volume 1]

HAWKS, HOWARD. 1896–1977

Howard Hawks, an American producer, writer, and director, grew up in
California, studied engineering, and served in the Army Air Corps during World
War I. For 45 years he made movies in all of the standard Hollywood genres:
popular "screwball comedies" like *His Girl Friday* (1940) and *Bringing Up Baby*
(1938), westerns like *Red River* (1948) and *Rio Bravo* (1959), musicals like
Gentlemen Prefer Blondes (1953), gangster films like *Scarface* (1932), adventure
films like *To Have and Have Not* (1944), and private-eye melodramas like *The
Big Sleep* (1946). These were not run-of-the-mill movies, however, for Hawks
infused them with his own style and themes. He tended to use a symmetrical
structure and sparse dialogue, depending on concrete visual images to reveal
character in action. Although he worked with some of the best writers in
Hollywood (Ben Hecht, Jules Furthman, and WILLIAM FAULKNER [see Vol. 1], for
example), he allowed his actors to add or alter lines, believing that improvisation improved the verisimilitude of a film. Hawks received only one Academy

Award nomination in his career, for *Sergeant York* (1941), but he was given the Lifetime Achievement Award by the Academy in 1975.

BOOK BY HAWKS

Bringing Up Baby. Ed. by Gerald Mast. Rutgers U. Pr. 1988 $14.00. ISBN 0-8135-1341-3. Discusses the making of the 1938 film; includes the script, script variations, interviews, commentary, reviews, etc.

BOOKS ABOUT HAWKS

McBride, Joseph. *Hawks on Hawks.* U. CA Pr. 1982 $10.95. ISBN 0-520-04552-1. A series of interviews in which the director reflects on his career towards the end of his life.
Mast, Gerald. *Howard Hawks, Storyteller.* OUP 1982 $35.00. ISBN 0-19-503091-5. A useful biography.

HITCHCOCK, ALFRED. 1899–1980

[SEE Volume 1.]

HUSTON, JOHN. 1906–1987

The son of Walter Huston, the well-known movie actor, John Huston directed numerous Hollywood films, including such classics as *The Treasure of the Sierra Madre* (1948), for which he won an Oscar as best director, and *The Asphalt Jungle* (1950). He wrote the screenplays for many of them, including the quintessential hard-boiled detective movie *The Maltese Falcon* (1941), which was also his directorial debut.

Huston's protagonists are often either independent professionals whose tough exteriors hide a dedication to principle, like the detective in *The Maltese Falcon*, or losers whose obsession with a doomed quest leads to their destruction, like the three gold-seekers in *The Treasure of the Sierra Madre*. But, in his 46-year career, he would try his hand at almost everything, from the grand comedy of *The African Queen* (1952) to the shaggy dog tale *Beat the Devil* (1954), the offbeat western *The Misfits* (1961), the rather bloated epic *The Bible* (1966), and the medieval allegory *A Walk with Love and Death* (1970). As he aged, his films seemed to get deeper and better, starting with *The Man Who Would Be King* (1975) and continuing with *Wise Blood* (1979) and *Prizzi's Honor* (1985). His final work, *The Dead* (1987), is an exquisite film adaptation of the short story by JAMES JOYCE (see Vol. 1).

BOOKS BY HUSTON

Juarez. Ed. by Paul Vanderwood. U. of Wis. Pr. 1983 $9.95. ISBN 0-299-08744-1. The film's screenplay, with an introduction about the political context in which it was written, as well as notes about its production.
An Open Book. Ballantine o.p. Account of his life, including how he became a filmmaker and specifics about the making of several movies.

BOOKS ABOUT HUSTON

Grobel, Lawrence. *The Hustons.* Macmillan 1989 $24.95. ISBN 0-684-19019-2. A study of the acting and directing family, including Walter Huston, his son John, and John's children Anjelica and Tony.
Hammen, Scott. *John Huston.* Macmillan 1985 $22.95. ISBN 0-8057-9299-6. A biography and study of the films Huston made up to 1985.
Hart, Clive. *Joyce, Huston, and the Making of "The Dead."* Dufour 1989 $7.95. ISBN 0-86140-303-7. A fascinating look at the making of Huston's splendid final film based on the James Joyce story.

KUBRICK, STANLEY. 1928–

Stanley Kubrick was born in the Bronx, New York, and became a skilled photographer before he went into directing. He achieved fame with the fine antiwar film *Paths of Glory* in 1957, and his output since then has been extremely diversified. Through it all, however, runs a deep vein of pessimism. *Dr. Strangelove* (1964), *2001: A Space Odyssey* (1968), and *A Clockwork Orange* (1972) express his vision of an apocalyptic future, while *Spartacus* (1959) and *Barry Lyndon* (1975) reveal his dark view of futility in the past.

Kubrick has been able to work independently for most of his career, enjoying the rare right to make the final cuts of his films without studio interference. Some of his other notable films are *Lolita* (1954), based on VLADIMIR NABOKOV's (see Vol. 2) novel, and *Full Metal Jacket* (1987), about troops in the Vietnam War.

BOOK BY KUBRICK

Full Metal Jacket. Knopf o.p. The screenplay for Kubrick's Vietnam War movie.

BOOKS ABOUT KUBRICK

Kagan, Norman. *The Cinema of Stanley Kubrick.* Continuum 1989 $13.95. ISBN 0-8264-0422-7. A provocative, up-to-date study examining all of Kubrick's work.
Nelson, Thomas A. *Kubrick: Inside a Film Artist's Maze.* Ind. U. Pr. 1982 $39.95. ISBN 0-253-14648-8. A compelling analysis of Kubrick's films.

KUROSAWA, AKIRA. 1910–

Kurosawa generally is recognized as the best of the modern Japanese filmmakers. He was the first Japanese director to gain international recognition, partly because his storytelling technique is not culture-bound. *Rashomon* (1950), a story of rape and terror that is told from several different viewpoints, received first prize at the Venice Film Festival in 1951; the film's title has become synonymous with the concept of subjective truth expressed in widely varying versions of the same story. *The Seven Samurai* (1954), a humanistic tale of samurai risking their lives to defend a poor village, is another Kurosawa classic. Kurosawa has always been attracted to Western literature, and two of his most notable films are based on Shakespeare's plays: *Throne of Blood* (1957), a retelling of *Macbeth*, and *Ran* (1985), a masterly reinterpretation of *King Lear*.

BOOKS BY KUROSAWA

Ran. Shambhala o.p. Screenplay of Kurosawa's version of *King Lear.*
Something Like an Autobiography. Random 1983 $12.00. ISBN 0-394-71439-3. A collection of reminiscences.

BOOKS ABOUT KUROSAWA

Prince, Stephen. *The Warrior's Cinema: The Cinema of Akira Kurosawa.* Princeton U. Pr. 1991 $39.50. ISBN 0-691-03160-5. A thorough study of the director's films, showing the influence of Japanese culture on his artistic sensibility.
Richie, Donald. *The Films of Akira Kurosawa.* U. CA Pr. rev. ed. 1984 $15.95. ISBN 0-520-05191-2. The best study yet made of a film director's work, lavishly illustrated, with an excellent filmography.

LANG, FRITZ. 1890–1976

The German-born director Fritz Lang started in the film industry in Berlin in 1918 with his wife, who was a screenwriter. The most notable of Lang's films from this, his first German period, are *Destiny* (1921), *Metropolis* (1926), the melodrama *M* (1931) about a child murderer, and the two films about Lang's demonic creation Dr. Mabuse—*Dr. Mabuse, The Gambler* (1922) and *The Testament of Dr. Mabuse* (1933). He left Germany when Hitler, after whom Mabuse was patterned, confiscated the second Mabuse film. Lang went to Hollywood and made several films in the genre called *film noir*, a highly stylized type of crime film with shadowy photography, ominous atmosphere, malevolent characters, and an attitude of sang-froid: *Fury* (1936), *Man Hunt* (1941), *Scarlett Street* (1945), *Ministry of Fear* (1944), based on the GRAHAM GREENE (see Vol. 1) novel, and *The Big Heat* (1953) are examples. Among Lang's other American movies, *Rancho Notorious* (1951), stands out for the intense perversity of its vision of the western genre.

Lang left Hollywood in the mid-1950s because of his growing disputes with producers. He closed out his career in Germany with his third Mabuse film—*The Thousand Eyes of Dr. Mabuse* (1960).

BOOK BY LANG

Metropolis. Faber & Faber 1990 $9.95. ISBN 0-571-12601-4. The screenplay of his famous 1926 film.

BOOKS ABOUT LANG

Eisner, Lotte H. *Fritz Lang.* Da Capo 1986 $14.95. ISBN 0-306-80271-6. A complete and well-written biography.
Humphries, Reynold. *Fritz Lang: Genre and Representation in His American Films.* Johns Hopkins 1988 $32.00. ISBN 0-8018-3699-9. A stunning analysis of Lang's later work.
Jensen, Paul U. *The Cinema of Fritz Lang.* Ballantine 1988 o.p.
Kaplan, E. Ann. *Fritz Lang: A Film Guide.* Macmillan 1981 $55.00. ISBN 0-8161-8035-0. A helpful guide to each of the films.
Weinberg, Herman G. *Fritz Lang.* Gordon Pr. 1979 $250.00. ISBN 0-8490-2923-6. A fascinating study of the life and work of the film director.

LEE, SPIKE. 1957–

[SEE Volume 1.]

LUCAS, GEORGE WALTON, JR. 1944–

[SEE Volume 1.]

MALLE, LOUIS. 1932–

The most commercially successful of the New Wave French film directors of the 1950s is Louis Malle. He started directing in the early 1950s, but it was his 1958 erotic film *The Lovers* that gained him recognition. Since then he has continued to make films that offer surprising, and occasionally shocking, perspectives on conventional morality, such as *Murmur of the Heart* (1971), about mother-son incest, and the controversial *Pretty Baby* (1978), his first American film, which is set in a New Orleans brothel and features a child. His second American film, the critically acclaimed *Atlantic City* (1980), compassionately depicts the romance between an old man and a young woman. Other notable Malle films are *Lacombe, Lucien* (1973), *My Dinner with Andre* (1981), and *Au Revoir les Enfants* (1987), his account of children growing up in Nazi-occupied France. *Damage* (1992) is another shocking story of a father's obsessive love affair with his son's fiancée and the eventual destruction that results to all the characters.

BOOK BY MALLE

Au Revoir les Enfants. Trans. by Anselm Hollo. Grove Pr. 1988 $6.95. ISBN 0-8021-3114-X. Screenplay of Malle's important film about Jewish children in France during World War II.

POLANSKI, ROMAN. 1933–

The French-born Polish actor and director Roman Polanski survived one of the darkest events of the twentieth century, the Holocaust. At the age of 8, he was interned in a German concentration camp, where his mother died. He later attended the Polish Film School and, with his *film noir Knife in the Water* (1962), helped establish the reputation of Polish cinema abroad. Polanski's vision is of an unstable world of violence, sexual frustration, unconscious impulses, and destructive psychoses. *Repulsion* (1965), his first feature in the West, and the chilling *Rosemary's Baby* (1968), about satanic possession in New York City, marked him as a filmmaker who was unafraid to confront evil. He was forced to confront evil in his personal life once again when his wife, Sharon Tate, was brutally murdered in 1969 by the satanic Charles Manson cult in one of California's most sensational slayings. The horror of this experience informs his filmed version of Shakespeare's *Macbeth* (1972). Of his later films, *Chinatown* (1974), the story of a private investigator's discovery of twisted relationships in the wealthy family that has hired him, was well received, as was *Tess* (1981), Polanski's adaptation of THOMAS HARDY's (see Vol. 1) novel *Tess of the D'Urbervilles*.

BOOK BY POLANSKI

Knife in the Water: With Repulsion and Cul-de-Sac. Faber & Faber 1988 $12.95. ISBN 0-571-12590-5. Three screenplays.

BOOKS ABOUT POLANSKI

Ferranti, Philip. *Overcoming Our Obsessions*. ETC Pubns. 1979 $12.95. ISBN 0-88280-069-8. A study of Polanski's dark vision.

Wexman, Virginia W. *Roman Polanski*. Macmillan 1985 $21.95. ISBN 0-8057-9296-1. An interesting and well-written critical biography.

RENOIR, JEAN. 1894–1979

Second son of the French Impressionist painter PIERRE AUGUSTE RENOIR, Jean Renoir was one of the greatest of all filmmakers. In 1959 an international jury voted the antiwar film *The Grand Illusion* (1937) one of the 10 best films ever made. *The Rules of the Game* (1939) is also considered to be a masterpiece. The first of these films compassionately unfolds the relationships of French prisoners of war with each other and with their captors in a German prison camp during World War I, and the second indicts the love and hunting games of a society poised at the edge of World War II (its "rabbit hunt" sequence is justifiably famous).

Renoir was able to portray humanity in all of its fullness; he was sympathetic without being sentimental, realistic without sacrificing his humanism. He never sought to manipulate the audience's emotions, but with perfect lucidity he revealed the hidden meanings of situations. His films are noted for their perfect marriage of visual and narrative elements. Among his other notable films are *Boudu Saved from Drowning* (1932), *Toni* (1934), *La Bête Humaine* (1938), and *A Day in the Country* (1946). Renoir moved to the United States to escape the Nazi occupation of France in 1941 and became an American citizen. He made

The Southerner here in 1945 and received a special Oscar for Career Accomplishments in 1978.

BOOKS BY RENOIR

My Life and My Films. Da Capo 1991 $14.95. ISBN 0-306-80457-3. An excellent autobiography by the great French director.
Renoir on Renoir. Cambridge U. Pr. 1990 $54.95. ISBN 0-521-35151-0. Thematic interviews with Renoir, as well as his discussion of twenty of his films.

BOOKS ABOUT RENOIR

Bazin, André. *Jean Renoir*. Da Capo 1992 $14.95. ISBN 0-306-80465-4. An important study of this major filmmaker; considers both his life and his work.
Bertin, Celia. *Jean Renoir: A Life in Pictures*. Johns Hopkins 1991 $29.95. ISBN 0-8018-4184-4. A well-written, thorough study of his films.
Faulkner, Christopher. *The Social Cinema of Jean Renoir*. Princeton U. Pr. 1986 $35.00. ISBN 0-691-06673-6. An examination of Renoir's films from a sociological point of view.
Sesonske, Alexander. *Jean Renoir: The French Years 1924–1939*. HUP 1980 $13.95. ISBN 0-674-47360-4. A study of the period in which Renoir made his classic films.

ROHMER, ERIC. 1920–

The French filmmaker and writer Eric Rohmer began as an editor of the influential film journal *Les Cahiers du Cinéma*. His first feature film was *The Sign of the Lion* (1959). Considered one of the important New Wave directors, Rohmer is best known for a group of films he calls Six Moral Tales. Each examines the dilemma of a man who is on the brink of committing himself to one woman but discovers he is greatly attracted to another woman; in each film, the man returns to his original choice, who is his moral ideal. Though these works contain a great deal of dialogue, they retain their visual allure. The final three in the group—*My Night at Maud's* (1968), *Claire's Knee* (1970), and *Chloe in the Afternoon* (1972)—won Rohmer an international reputation. His recent works include a new cycle of films based on each of the four seasons.

BOOK BY ROHMER

Six Moral Tales. Continuum o.p. *My Night at Maud's*, *Claire's Knee*, and the rest of this cycle of moral tales, all in novelized form.

BOOK ABOUT ROHMER

Crisp, C. G. *Eric Rohmer: Realist and Moralist*. Ind. U. Pr. 1988 $29.95. ISBN 0-253-31908-0. An important examination of the philosophy behind Rohmer's films.

SIRK, DOUGLAS. 1900–1987

[SEE Volume 1.]

TRUFFAUT, FRANÇOIS. 1932–1984

François Truffaut was one of the principal figures in the French New Wave movement of the 1950s and early 1960s. As a young critic for the avant-garde film magazine *Les Cahiers du Cinéma*, he formulated the *politique des auteurs*—the idea that directors with a personal vision are the true authors of films, rather than conventional screenwriters or script-bound directors. An admirer of American films, Truffaut was much influenced by ALFRED HITCHCOCK (see Vol. 1). In several of his own films, Truffaut, who had an unhappy childhood and youth, portrayed a fictionalized version of himself, a character called Antoine

Doinel, to create personal cinema. The first of these films, which was also his first feature film, was *The Four Hundred Blows* (1959). It is still one of the most popular of his works. Other notable Truffaut films are *Shoot the Piano Player* (1960), the lyrical ménage à trois *Jules and Jim* (1961), the Academy Award-winning *Day for Night* (1973), *The Last Metro* (1980), and *The Woman Next Door* (1981).

BOOKS BY TRUFFAUT

Day for Night. Trans. by Sam Flores. Applause Theatre Bk. Pubs. 1974 o.p. Screenplay of Truffaut's "film within a film" in which he himself plays the director.
The Films in My Life. S&S Trade 1985 o.p. A collection of the director's essays and reviews.
The 400 Blows. Applause Theatre Bk. Pubs. 1986 $7.95. ISBN 0-936839-55-4. Screenplay of one of the early films that made Truffaut famous.
Hitchcock. Trans. by Helen G. Scott. S&S Trade 1985 $17.95. ISBN 0-671-60429-5. A very important collection of Truffaut's interviews of Hitchcock, providing much information on film technique.
Jules and Jim. Trans. by Nicholas Fry. S&S Trade 1968 o.p. The screenplay of Truffaut's early brilliant film about two close friends and the woman they both love.
The Last Metro. (coauthored with Suzanne Schiffman). Ed. by Mirella Affron and E. Rubenstein. Rutgers U. Pr. 1985 $11.00. ISBN 0-8135-1066-X. Screenplay of a film about the German Occupation.
Small Change. Trans. by Anselm Hollo. Applause Theatre Bk. Pubs. 1986 $6.95. ISBN 0-936839-51-1. Screenplay of Truffaut's film about a group of children.
The Story of Adèle H. Grove Pr. 1975 o.p. Truffaut's screenplay based on the life of Victor Hugo's daughter.
Truffaut by Truffaut. Abrams 1987 $29.95. ISBN 0-8109-1689-4. Some of Truffaut's writings, assembled to form a kind of autobiography, with splendid illustrations.

BOOKS ABOUT TRUFFAUT

Allen, Don. *Finally Truffaut*. Beaufort o.p. A useful guide to each of the director's films.
Insdorf, Annette. *François Truffaut*. Filmmakers Ser. G. K. Hall 1978 o.p. Looks at specific films to explore the thematic and stylistic concerns that emerge from Truffaut's work.
Walz, Eugene P. *François Truffaut: A Guide to References and Resources*. G. K. Hall 1982 o.p. A comprehensive list of sources relevant to all aspects of Truffaut and his work; includes a short biography.

VISCONTI, LUCHINO. 1906–1976

Visconti achieved worldwide fame as one of the triumvirate (with FELLINI and ANTONIONI) of great modern Italian directors. His art combines a deep social commitment with a colorful extreme realism. Notable films by Visconti include *La Terra Treme* (1947), *The Leopard* (1963), *The Damned* (1969), and *Death in Venice* (1971).

BOOKS BY VISCONTI

Luchino Visconti—Three Screenplays: White Nights, Rocco and His Brothers, The Job. Trans. by Judith Green. Garland 1985 $11.00. ISBN 0-8240-5784-8. The three bound screenplays, with a list of cast and crew. Includes photos.
Luchino Visconti—Two Screenplays: La Terra Treme, Senso. Trans. by Judith Green. Garland 1985 $11.00. ISBN 0-8240-5785-6. The two bound screenplays, with a list of cast and crew. Includes photos.

STERNBERG, JOSEF VON. 1894–1969

[SEE Volume 1.]

STROHEIM, ERICH VON. 1885–1957
[SEE Volume 1.]

WELLES, ORSON. 1915–1985
[SEE Volume 1.]

CHAPTER 21

Folklore, Humor, and Popular Culture

Harry Eiss

> The latest incarnation of Oedipus, the continued romance of Beauty and the Beast, stands this afternoon on the corner of 42nd Street and Fifth Avenue, waiting for the traffic light to change.
> —JOSEPH CAMPBELL, *The Complete Grimm's Fairy Tales*

Folklore crosses several traditional academic disciplines, in which it has often been considered to be the debris or lesser remains after the more important works are removed. This is partly due to folklore's own self-imposed definition as some "natural" form of expression coming from the "common people," especially those who are not highly trained in, or exposed to, the higher expressions or explanations of their culture.

However, such theorists as JEAN-JACQUES ROUSSEAU (See Vol. 2) and the writers of the resulting romantic movement helped to win respect for the truths supposedly inherent in "natural man," the human uncontaminated by culture, which was viewed as corrupt, or at least as blind to the truth. From the eighteenth century, a rapidly growing serious study of such lore, marked by a continual attempt to understand and classify it, finally resulted in a relatively new, unique discipline still young enough to be filled with energy and creative attempts to explain and define itself.

Once the romantic movement offered its theoretical support, folklore began in earnest. The BROTHERS GRIMM found the ideal literature that the romantic poets were attempting to write—a literature that dealt with nature in an honest language. Their collections of German folk tales sparked similar collecting across Europe. Peter Asbjornsen and Jorgen Moe were very important collectors in Norway, and they, in turn, influenced JOHN FRANCIS CAMPBELL, who developed an improved method for gathering the materials, as well as influenced others in England and across the Continent.

In 1864 the term "Folk-Lore" was coined by an Englishman, WILLIAM JOHN THOMS, to replace "popular antiquities," "popular literature," and other such vague and misleading phrases. The new term became the general heading for the study of the manners, customs, songs, stories, and beliefs of the common population, and the field began to establish itself. ANDREW LANG and JOSEPH JACOBS collected folk tales in England, Ireland, and Scotland, and developed new folklore theories, though, as the terminology was still being developed, their use of the term "fairy tale" resulted in more confusion than clarification.

When the British Folk-Lore Society was established in 1878 and the American Folk-Lore Society in 1888, an explosion of collecting followed. It soon became apparent that there were common motifs, stories, and characteristics to be found from widely divergent places and times; and the folklore scholars (generally, scholars from other, overlapping fields) began to put forth their theories. The Indo-European linguistic scholars held that the various tales came from a common language. A similar theory held that they came from a common locality, probably India. A third hypothesis held that folk tales were really just the debris of myths, either myths never completely developed or lesser stories surrounding the more important mythologies. Anthropologists suggested that the similarities in the stories were the result of similar minds and that they were, in fact, accurate recordings of the world views of early civilizations. Later, Freudians would suggest that these stories expressed or freed repressed sexual desires. Jungians would suggest that they expressed archetypal patterns (the collective unconscious of the race). Marxists would say that they expressed social and economic relationships. Feminists would hold that folk tales expressed and promoted a repressive patriarchal tradition. Recently, folklorists and other scholars have suggested that the very workings of the human mind can be understood by studying the structures and subjects of these tales.

JULIUS KROHN and his son KAARLE developed the most often employed "scientific" method of studying a folk tale through an examination of its history and geography in order to bring together all of its variations and trace its history. STITH THOMPSON developed the *Motif-Index of Folk-Literature*, a huge work based on the Krohns' theories.

In the early part of the twentieth century, some universities began to offer courses in folklore, mainly through anthropology departments. By mid-century, some colleges had begun to establish folklore as an undergraduate, and then as a graduate program of study. Stith Thompson led the way in the United States at Indiana University, which granted its first Ph.D. in folklore in 1953. Other universities, such as the University of California at Los Angeles, George Washington University, the University of Pennsylvania, and the University of Texas, also began offering doctoral programs.

In more recent years, other similar fields of study have gained support as viable areas of study. One of the most significant is the field of popular culture. In the early 1970s, the first program in the study of popular culture in the United States was established at Bowling Green State University under the leadership of Pat Browne and RAY BROWNE. This broad approach to understanding a culture applies strict scholarship to all aspects of a civilization, emphasizing the importance of what was traditionally called "lower" culture— that body of material beyond the scope of traditional academic disciplines. At the same time, the study of popular culture extends the definitions of *folklore* beyond literature, art, music, and dance into such areas as popular music, popular literature, such cultural experiences as the Vietnam War, and such unusual topics as tattoos. In 1970 the Popular Culture Association was formed; its goal was to study thoroughly and seriously all aspects of everyday culture worldwide. The founders were convinced that the vast body of material encompassed in print, television, comics, advertising, graphics, folk culture, entertainment, sports, and other activities and in other media reflect the ways of life of American and world cultures. The American Culture Association was founded in 1979 as a parallel organization, with the goal of applying the same types of study to North and South America, to the past and present, to the folk and the elite, as well as to popular culture. The Popular Culture Association has its own press that publishes several books a year on a variety of topics related to popular culture.

An area related to both folklore and popular culture is humor. Although humor has always been an important part of the human condition, only recently has it become separated as an important area of study. Early theories of humor tended to treat it as a unique phenomenon. More recent studies, however, have incorporated humor into larger categories of creativity involving the bringing together or synthesis of the familiar and the eternal. Thus, comedy and tragedy, laughter and tears, are all now considered a part of a continuum of the human mind. The groan that results from hearing a pun (which is often categorized as the lowest form of humor, while, at the same time, considered the ultimate basis upon which all humor rests) comes from the same place of recognition as the inspiration for creating scientific theories or works of art. Today, humor is dominated both by the influence of the mass media and the so-called black humor associated with a culture in rapid and violent transition.

Mythology is sometimes included in the study of folklore, sometimes studied separately or as part of other fields. While mythology and folklore both deal with primitive beliefs and superstitions, mythology does this in relation to gods and folklore in relation to human beings. Mythology is also essentially religious in origin, whereas folklore is non-religious. Recently, mythology has risen above the traditional view that it is simply the false beliefs of primitive peoples. JAMES G. FRAZER's work is an interesting crossroads in this development, suggesting the latter, yet laying the groundwork for our contemporary respect for myth. Certainly, the studies of classical Greek and Roman mythology and the work of Jungian psychologists, as brought together in the work of JOSEPH CAMPBELL (and the many post-Campbell mythologists, psychologists, feminists, Marxists, and so on who wish to reinterpret his views), have brought mythology into a central position in understanding the entire world of folklore. Since Campbell's first work, scholars have opened doors relating religion to the working of human thought, reaching toward an all-encompassing understanding of the human condition.

INTRODUCTORY WORKS: FOLKLORE AND MYTHOLOGY

The works in this section offer an introduction to the field of folklore and include histories of the subject, guides to folklore methodology, anthologies, textbooks, bibliographies, and encyclopedias. Reference works on single types of folklore, such as folk song or legend, will be found in the subsequent sections of this chapter. Similar materials concerning humor and popular culture are found in the appropriate sections later in this chapter.

General Works

Bett, Henry. *Nursery Rhymes and Tales: Their Origin and History.* Gordon Pr. 1972 $59.95. ISBN 0-8490-0743-7. Interesting discussion of the commonality of tale-telling for children among different countries and languages.

Bosma, Bette. *Fairy Tales, Fables, Legends, and Myths: Using Folk Literature in Your Classroom.* Tchrs. Coll. 1992 $15.95. ISBN 0-8077-3134-X. Practical teaching ideas for preschool through middle-school students.

Brunvand, Jan H. *Folklore: A Handbook for Study and Research.* St. Martin 1976 o.p. Written for college students, but useful to anyone interested in learning the history and methods of folklore and folklorists.

Clarkson, Atelia, and Gilbert B. Cross. *World Folktales: A Scribner Resource Collection.* Scribner 1984 $14.95. ISBN 0-684-17763-3

Coffin, Tristram P., and Hennig Cohen, eds. *Folklore in America.* Doubleday 1970 o.p. Draws from a wide range of folklore tradition brought to America through the world of games, riddles, songs, and stories.

Cox, George W. *An Introduction to the Science of Comparative Mythology and Folklore.* Gordon Pr. $59.95. ISBN 0-8490-0420-9. Still a useful analysis of mythology based on examination of Asian and European myths.

Dorson, Richard M. *America in Legend: Folklore from the Colonial Period to the Present.* Pantheon 1974 $17.95. ISBN 0-394-70926-8. Fully documented and written in a readable style that makes the book useful to professionals and to the general reader.

———. *American Folklore.* U. Ch. Pr. 1959. Surveys the field from colonial days to contemporary times; chapters cover regional folk cultures, immigrant folklore, African American folklore, and a gallery of folk heroes.

———. *Folklore and Fakelore: Essays toward a Discipline of Folk Studies.* HUP 1976 o.p. Moves from a theoretical to an in-depth examination of a series of vivid folk stories from Scotland to Michigan.

———, ed. *Folklore and Folklife: An Introduction.* U. Ch. Pr. 1982 $19.95. ISBN 0-226-15871-3. This book "maintains a professional, research-oriented tone and still manages to be exciting, readable, and filled with quaint and interesting facts" (*Library Journal*).

———. *Handbook of American Folklore.* Ind. U. Pr. 1983 $35.00. ISBN 0-253-32706-7. A monumental collection of essays by leading scholars that discusses the relationship between anthropology and literature in folklore. Introduction by W. Edson Richmond.

Dundes, Alan. *Interpreting Folklore.* Ind. U. Pr. 1980 $30.00. ISBN 0-253-14307-1. Thirteen essays by Dundes that offer interpretations of folklore terms, methods, and applications.

———. *The Study of Folklore.* P-H 1965 $21.95. ISBN 0-13-858944-5

Farrer, Claire R., ed. *Women and Folklore: Images and Genres.* Waveland Pr. 1986 repr. of 1975 ed. $8.50. ISBN 0-88133-227-5. Bold attempt to bring folklore tradition into current perspective with a discussion of women's role in folklore across time and diverse cultures.

Goldstein, Kenneth S. *A Guide for Field Workers in Folklore.* Gale 1964 $35.00. ISBN 1-55888-172-X. Preface by Hamish Henderson. The "first systematic guide to field collecting techniques published in the United States . . . serves as an introduction to the materials and problems of folklore collection and documentation for the beginner and the amateur . . ." (B. A. Botkin, *N.Y. Folklore Quarterly*).

Hartland, Edwin S. *Folklore: What Is It and What Is the Good of It.* AMS Pr. repr. of 1904 ed. $5.50. ISBN 0-404-53502-X

———. *Mythology and Folktales: Their Relation and Interpretation.* AMS Pr. repr. of 1900 ed. $5.50. ISBN 0-404-53507-0. Competent, brief, and basic delineation of myth and folklore written at the turn of the century.

Keightley, T. *Fairy Mythology.* M.S.G. Haskell Hse. 1969 repr. of 1850 ed. $75.00. ISBN 0-8383-0281-5

McKissack, Patricia C., and Ruthhilde Kronberg. *Piece of the Wind: And Other Stories to Tell.* HarpC 1990 $9.95. ISBN 0-06-064773-6. Collection of stories representing a large variety of cultures and traditions that stress the universality of human experience.

Metzger, Michael M., ed. *Fairy Tales as Ways of Knowing.* P. Lang Pubs. 1981 $33.25. ISBN 3-261-04883-2

Newall, Venetia J., ed. *Folklore Studies in the Twentieth Century: Proceedings of the Centenary Conference of the Folklore Society.* Rowman 1980 o.p. Composed of works by members of the leading British folklore society. Assumes a basic understanding of the issues in scholarly debates.

Olrik, Axel. *Principles for Oral Narrative Research.* Ind. U. Pr. 1992 $29.95. ISBN 0-253-34175-2. Comprehensive analysis of folklore and oral tradition.

Propp, Vladimir. *Theory and History of Folklore. Theory and History of Lit Ser.* U. of Minn. Pr. 1984 $15.95. ISBN 0-8166-1182-3. Introduction by Anatoly Liberman. Scholarly and detailed analysis of different schools of folklore theory. Provides valuable insight into the Russian folkloristic tradition for Western theorists.

Puhvel, Martin. *The Crossroads in Folklore and Myth*. P. Lang Pubs. 1989 $31.75. ISBN 0-8204-0839-5

Quimby, Ian M., and Scott T. Swank, eds. *Perspectives on American Folk Art*. Norton 1980 o.p. Ranges from practical to theoretical discussions; handsomely illustrated and highly readable.

Richmond, Winthrop E., ed. *Studies in Folklore: In Honor of Distinguished Service Professor Stith Thompson*. Greenwood 1972 repr. of 1957 ed. $15.00. ISBN 0-8371-6208-4. Collection of fascinating, in-depth analyses of original folk stories from Ireland to Denmark, dating back to the Middle Ages.

Rohrich, Lutz. *Folktales and Reality*. Ind. U. Pr. 1991 $39.95. ISBN 0-253-35028-X. Explore the complex relationships between folk tales and reality and argues for reevaluation of assumptions about folk narrative.

Spillman, Carolyn V., and Frances S. Goforth. *Guidebook to Folk Literature*. 1993 $24.95. ISBN 0-89774-747-X

Toelken, Barre. *The Dynamics of Folklore*. HM 1979 $39.95. ISBN 0-395-27068-5. Attractively illustrated, and clearly written; offers any reader a useful introduction to the subject and to the methods and concerns of modern folklorists.

Yoder, Don, ed. *American Folklife*. U. of Tex. Pr. 1976 $22.50. ISBN 0-292-70308-2. Includes 12 essays by Don Yoder and other major essayists in the field.

Reference Works

Ashliman, D. L. *A Guide to Folktales in the English Language*. Greenwood 1987 $45.00. ISBN 0-313-25961-5. Each entry gives a brief synopsis and indicates the tale's published title and collection in which it can be found.

Baughman, Ernest W. *Type and Motif Index of the Folktales of England and North America*. Mouton 1966 $75.00. ISBN 90-2790-046-9. Extensive cross-listing of North American and English folktale types and motifs; concludes that many were appropriated from England to North America.

Bronner, Simon J. *American Folk Art: A Guide to Sources. Reference Lib. of the Humanities*. Garland 1984 o.p. Explores a variety of theoretical folk art issues, with introductions and annotated references for each topic. Also includes references on where to find folk art collections and has several dozen detailed reproductions of folk art.

Daniels, Cora L., and C. M. Stevans, eds. *Encyclopedia of Superstitions, Folklore and the Occult Sciences of the World*. 3 vols. Omnigraphics Inc. 1993 $120.00. ISBN 1-55888-968-X. Good source of information about folk beliefs and practices that have not been studied as intensively as folk tales and folk songs.

Flanagan, Cathleen C., and John T. Flanagan. *American Folklore: A Bibliography, 1950–1974*. Scarecrow 1977 o.p. Lists many different forms of folk tales passed on through oral tradition. Mix of scholarly and more colloquial discussions of a broad range of indiginous and immigrant American folk traditions.

Folklife Sourcebook: A Directory of Folklife Resources in the United States and Canada. Ed. by Peter T. Bartis and Barbara C. Fertig. Lib. of Congress 1986 (*American Folklife Center*, no. 14) $10.00. ISBN 0-8444-0521-3

Jobes, Gertrude. *Dictionary of Mythology, Folklore and Symbols*. 3 vols. Scarecrow 1961 $99.50. ISBN 0-8108-2036-6. A good place to turn when puzzled by an unfamiliar name or type of folk tale.

Jones, Steven S. *Folklore and Literature in the U.S.: An Annotated Bibliography of Studies of Folklore in American Literature*. Ed. by Alan Dundes. *Folklore Bibliographies Ser.* Garland 1984 o.p. Trumpets the merits of the American folk tradition as the oral underpinning of American literature and the inspiration for many of the greatest works of American literature.

Leach, Maria, ed. *Funk and Wagnall's Standard Dictionary of Folklore, Mythology, and Legend*. HarpC 1984 $34.95. ISBN 0-06-250511-4. Compiled for both the general reader and the folklore specialist, this work contains definitions of terms, survey articles, brief biographies, accounts of museums, and so on, by distinguished authorities in the field.

Steinfirst, Susan. *Folklore and Folklife: A Guide to English Language Sources.* Garland 1992 $120.00. ISBN 0-8153-0068-9. General bibliographical survey.

Thomas, Northcote W. *Bibliography of Folklore, 1905–1907.* Kraus 1972 repr. of 1906 ed. $15.00. ISBN 0-8115-0526-X. Although the bibliography includes work published within a limited time span, the period was particularly rich in scholarship.

Thompson, Stith. *The Folktale.* U. CA Pr. 1977 $14.00. ISBN 0-520-03537-2. Guide to different types of folk tales, with extensive bibliographies. Dated, but still useful.

Yassif, Eli. *Jewish Folklore: An Annotated Bibliography.* Garland 1986 $35.00. ISBN 0-8240-9039-X. Covers publications from 1872–1980; mostly concerns studies of folklore, not folk-tale collections.

Ziegler, Elsie B. *Folklore: An Annotated Bibliography and Index to Single Editions.* Faxon 1973 $12.00. ISBN 0-87305-100-9. Annotated references by title, also cross-referenced with lists of illustrators, subjects, motifs, countries of origin, and types of folk stories.

FOLK SONG AND DANCE

The works listed in this section include general reference books on the subject of folk song and folk dance, as well as books on geographical and national collections of song and dance and critical studies of song and dance as a genre. Some U.S. regional and ethnic titles are included here, but see also the section "U.S. Regional and Ethnic Folklore," which includes "African American Folklore."

Banerji, P. *Aesthetics of Indian Folk Dance.* Humanities 1983 o.p. Explains the aesthetics of Indian folk dance.

Baring-Gould, Sabine. *A Garland of Country Song: English Folk Songs with Their Traditional Melodies.* Gordon Pr. 1974 $59.95. ISBN 0-8490-0211-7. Fifty songs (text and notes) compiled at the height of the British folk revival; by a clergyman who was dissatisfied with the contemporary material being provided to school children.

Bartok, Bela. *The Hungarian Folk Song.* Ed. by Benjamin Suchoff. Trans. by M. D. Calvocoressi. *Bartok Studies in Musicology.* State U. NY Pr. 1980 o.p. Scholarly examination of Hungarian folk music by a leading musicologist, who determined morphological elements by statistical analysis.

Benet, Sula. *Song, Dance, and Customs of Peasant Poland.* AMS Pr. repr. of 1951 ed. $26.00. ISBN 0-404-15906-0. Preface by Margaret Mead.

Blom, Jan B., and others, eds. *Norwegian Folk Music.* Col. U. Pr. 1981 o.p.

Brand, Oscar. *The Ballad Mongers: Rise of the Modern Folk Song.* Greenwood 1979 $45.00. ISBN 0-313-20555-8. "A lively, gossipy, informative off-the-cuff personal history of the folksong revival, its sources and popularity." (*N.Y. Folklore Quarterly*).

Breathnach, Breandan. *Folk Music and Dances of Ireland.* Dufour 1986 $12.95. ISBN 0-85342-509-4. Stresses the importance of the oral tradition to Irish music and warns that attempting to teach children from printed text could result in making children unable to play music in an accepted traditional style.

Buffington, Albert F. *Pennsylvania German Secular Folk Songs.* Penn. German Soc. 1974 $15.00. ISBN 0-911122-30-3. Prefaced with an explanation of background and methodology. Contains ninety-seven songs with tunes, German text, and English translation.

Causley, Charles, ed. *Modern Folk Ballads.* Pocket Poets Ser. Dufour 1968 $3.50. ISBN 0-8023-9043-9

Child, Francis J. *English and Scottish Popular Ballads.* 5 vols. Dover 1965 o.p. Child's aim was to include "every obtainable version of every extant English or Scottish ballad, with the fullest possible discussion of related songs or stories in the popular literature of all nations."

Christeson, R. P. *The Old Time Fiddler's Repertory: 245 Traditional Tunes.* U. of Mo. Pr. 1984 $19.95. ISBN 0-8262-0439-2. Songs collected from 33 fiddlers in 9 states over a period of 30 years. Songs are organized by category, such as waltz and quadrille.

Cohen, Anne B. *Poor Pearl, Poor Girl: The Murdered Girl Stereotype in Ballad and Newspaper.* Amer. Folklore Society Memoir Ser. Bks. Demand repr. of 1973 ed. $40.30. ISBN 0-7837-0089-X. An exhaustive study of ballads that were based on the murder and beheading of a pregnant woman from Greencastle, Indiana. A good example of a modern folklorist at work.

Cohen, Norm. *Long Steel Rail: The Railroad in American Folksong.* Music in Amer. Life Ser. U. of Ill. Pr. 1984 $18.95. ISBN 0-252-01145-7. "Cohen's narrative and interpretations, his discographical detail, the song texts and tune transcriptions, together with a variety of illustrative materials and extensive bibliography make this book an indispensable one for all scholars of railroad history and folklore as well as for those of blues and hillbilly music" (Ivan Tribe, *Journal of American Folklore*).

Cook, Harold E. *Shaker Music: A Manifestation of American Folk Culture.* Bucknell U. Pr. 1975 $30.00. ISBN 0-8387-7953-0. A fascinating account of the central role that music played in the Shaker religion and of the struggle of natural expression against regulation by the theorists.

Ferris, William, and Mary L. Hart, eds. *Folk Music and Modern Sound.* U. Pr. of Miss. 1981 $59.60. ISBN 0-8357-6837-6. Collection of essays on various types of American folk music. Examines the strengths and weaknesses of the way in which folk music is evolving.

Forucci, Samuel L. *A Folk Song History of America: America through Its Songs.* P-H 1984 o.p.

Fowke, Edith. *Lumbering Songs from the Northern Woods.* Amer. Folklore Society Memoir Ser. U. of Tex. Pr. 1970 o.p. Songs of lumbermen in Quebec and Ontario; collected in the field and transcribed with notes on the singers and the songs.

Gilbert, Cecile. *International Folk Dance at a Glance.* Burgess 1974 o.p. Step by step instructions for performing a variety of folk dances. Dances are graded by level of difficulty.

Glassie, Henry, and others. *Folksongs and Their Makers.* Bowling Green Univ. 1971 $6.00. ISBN 0-87972-006-9. Studies different folk composers in an attempt to reach conclusions about their relationship to the society in which they live.

Green, Archie. *Only a Miner: Studies in Recorded Coal Mining Songs.* Music in Amer. Life Ser. U. of Ill. Pr. 1972 $34.95. ISBN 0-252-00181-8. A rare amalgam of labor history, pop lore, American folk balladry, and hillbilly/blues discography.

Hague, Eleanor, comp. *Spanish-American Folk-Songs.* Kraus repr. of 1917 ed. $16.00. ISBN 0-527-01062-6. Ninety-five Spanish folk songs from California, Arizona, Mexico, Cuba, Puerto Rico, and Central and South America.

Hoff, Frank. *Song, Dance and Storytelling: Aspects of the Performing Arts in Japan.* Cornell East Asia Pgm. 1978 $8.00. ISBN 0-939657-15-5

Indiana University, Folklore Institute, Archives of Traditional Music. *A Catalog of Phonorecording of Music and Oral Data Held by the Archives of Traditional Music.* G. K. Hall 1976 o.p. Catalogues one of the richest collections of folk material in the country.

Isaku, Patia R. *Mountain Storm, Pine Breeze: Folk Song in Japan.* U. of Ariz. Pr. 1981 $12.95. ISBN 0-8165-0564-0. Very readable and does not assume prior knowledge of Japanese culture or familiarity with the music.

Jackson, George P. *Another Sheaf of White Spirituals.* Ed. by Kenneth S. Goldstein. *Publications in Folksong and Balladry Ser.* Folklorica Pr. 1982 repr. of 1952 ed. o.p. Contains 363 religious songs of rural white folks. Although the author held the now discredited view that black spirituals are derivative of white spirituals, this does not detract from the songs themselves. Preface by Dan Yoder.

Joukowsky, Anatol M. *The Teaching of Ethnic Dance.* Ayer 1980 repr. of 1965 ed. $22.00. ISBN 0-8369-9296-2. Presents 56 European folk dances, with step by step instructions. Compiled in the hope of preserving the dances before they die out as a living tradition.

Karpeles, Maud, and Cecil J. Sharp, eds. *Eighty Appalachian Folk Songs*. Faber & Faber 1983 o.p. Songs collected in Appalachia by two leading British folklorists. Karpeles, who literally wrote the book on folk fieldwork, contends that many of the songs have British roots.

Kennedy, Peter, ed. *Folksongs of Britain and Ireland*. Beekman Pubs. 1975 $44.95. ISBN 0-8464-2507-6. A guide to the living tradition of folk singing in Great Britain and Ireland. Contains 360 songs recorded in the field.

Kidson, Frank, and Mary Neal. *English Folk-Song and Dance*. 1915. Rowman 1972 o.p. Contrary to the views of most folklorists, Kidson expresses confidence that good folk songs have an indefinable quality that makes it nearly impossible for them to die out.

Lawless, Ray M. *Folksingers and Folksongs in America: A Handbook of Biography, Bibliography and Discography*. Greenwood 1981 repr. of 1965 ed. $65.00. ISBN 0-313-23104-4. An indispensable volume for libraries, this edition includes corrections, a supplement, new biographies, descriptions of books and magazines in the field, a selective list of records, and other material.

Leach, R., and R. Palmer, eds. *Folk Music in School*. Resources of Music Ser. Cambridge U. Pr. 1978 o.p. Discusses the development of folk music and the influence of historic events on music and vice versa. Includes numerous songs that illustrate points made in the text.

Lifton, Sarah. *Listener's Guide to Folk Music*. Facts on File 1983 o.p. An introduction to various types of American, British, and Irish folk music and a review of various records. The selection is that of a folk enthusiast rather than that of a scholar.

Lomax, Alan. *The Folk Songs of North America*. Doubleday 1975 $19.95. ISBN 0-385-03772-4. A collection of 377 songs, all with chord arrangements, 100 with piano arrangements. Songs represent the multiplicity of the American folk tradition.

———, ed. *The Folk Song Style and Culture*. Transaction Pubs. 1978 repr. of 1968 ed. $19.95. ISBN 0-385-03772-4. Divides the world into different cultural regions and analyzes the song styles, dance forms, and cantometrics of each region.

Malone, Bill C. *Country Music, U.S.A.: A Fifty Year History*. Amer. Folklore Society Memoir Ser. U. of Tex. Pr. 1985 $27.95. ISBN 0-292-71095-X. Very readable account of the development of folk music from the pre-commercial phase to modern Nashville.

Parsons, Kitty. *Gloucester Sea Ballads*. Fermata 1981 repr. of 1947 ed. $4.95. ISBN 0-939792-00-1

Pawlowska, Harriet. *Merrily We Sing: One Hundred Five Polish Folksongs*. Wayne St. U. Pr. 1961 $19.95. ISBN 0-8143-1753-7. Songs collected in the field in both Poland and in Polish-American communities. Both English and Polish texts are included; only music melodies are included.

Rubin, Ruth, ed. *A Treasury of Jewish Folksong*. Schocken 1976 o.p. A collection of 110 Yiddish and Hebrew songs. Includes English translations and annotations. With piano settings by Ruth Post and illustrations by T. Herzl Rome.

———, ed. *Voices of a People: The Story of Yiddish Folksong*. JPS Phila. 1979 repr. of 1973 ed. $8.95. ISBN 0-8276-0121-2. "Both a social history of Yiddish folk songs and a song-history of East European Jewry, from the Shtetl or small town of the Czarist Pale to U.S. and Palestinian immigration, the Soviet Union, Nazi concentration camps, and the Warsaw Ghetto." (*Folklore Quarterly*).

Sandberg, Larry, and Dick Weissman. *The Folk Music Sourcebook*. Knopf 1989 $16.95. ISBN 0-306-80360-7. Useful book for the folk musician. Covers a wide range of topics.

Sannella, Ted. *Balance and Swing: A Collection of Fifty-Five Squares, Contras and Triplets in the New England Tradition with Music for Each Dance*. Country Dance and Song 1990 $12.00. ISBN 0-685-35053-3

Seeger, Pete. *The Incompleat Folksinger*. S&S Trade 1972 o.p. An informal collection of writings by a leading folk artist. Includes commentary on political events, personal experiences, and other composers and performers.

Slobin, Mark, ed. *Old Jewish Folk Music: The Collections and Writings of Moshe Beregovski*. U. of Pa. Pr. 1982 o.p. Edits and translates the work of the great Russian Jewish folklorist. Contains more than 400 Yiddish songs, some folk poetry, and commentary on the cultural background in which these evolved.

Stambler, Irwin, and Grelun Landon. *The Encyclopedia of Folk, Country, and Western Music*. St. Martin 1983 o.p. Organized by names. Includes a short but comprehensive discussion.

Townsend, Jill. *Czech Song and Dance: Parts*. Beekman Pubs. 1990 $11.95. ISBN 0-8464-3341-9

——. *Czech Song and Dance: Score*. Beekman Pubs. 1990 $5.95. ISBN 0-8464-3340-0

Warner, Anne. *Traditional American Folk Songs from the Anne and Frank Warner Collection*. Syracuse U. Pr. 1984 $29.95. ISBN 0-8156-0185-9. Collector has selected approximately 200 songs from her collection of 1,000 songs recorded in North Carolina. Each song is accompanied by some information about the singer and origin of the song. With a foreword by Alan Lomax.

Wolfe, Charles K. *Kentucky Country: Folk and Country Music of Kentucky*. U. Pr. of Ky. 1982 $20.00. ISBN 0-8131-1468-3. Analyzes the evolution of country music in the context of regional history and culture.

FOLK TALE, LEGEND, AND MYTH

Folk tales, legends, and myths, although related to fiction, are derivations of actual events or efforts to explain events. In a sense, they are interpretations or perceptions of historical happenings. They thus provide information relating to the cultural history of a group or nation, enabling folklorists to study group attitudes and customs. Legends and myths are, in fact, the only source of information about groups of people who left no written records.

This section includes anthologies and critical studies of folk tales, legends, myths, and mythology in general, as well as works relating to individual countries; it includes a selected few U.S. ethnic titles (see the section "U.S. Regional and Ethnic Folklore" for additional references). The most complete series of folk tales remains the University of Chicago's *Folktales of the World Series*, edited by RICHARD M. DORSON. (See also Dorson's *Folktales Told around The World*.)

Abrahams, Roger D. *The Man-of-Words in the West Indies: Performance and the Emergence of Creole Culture*. Johns Hopkins 1983 $32.50. ISBN 0-898-2838-4. ". . . a significant volume of essays—significant because they show one man's development and refinement of a folkloristic theory . . . representative of the performance-centered school of folklorists . . . [which] touches the very core of the British West Indian cultural system and places West Indian creativity within a cultural and historical framework" (*Journal of American Folklore*).

Aiken, Riley. *Mexican Folktales from the Borderland*. SMU Pr. 1980 $12.95. ISBN 0-87074-175-6. Wonderful, vivid collection of stories drawn from the Mexican border culture of the 1930s.

Ainsworth, Catherine H. *Folktales of America*. 4 vols. Clyde Pr. 1981 $10.00 ea. ISBNs 0-933190-08-5, 0-933190-09-3, 0-933190-15-8, 0-933190-16-6. Short, funny American folk stories from the 1960s and 1970s ranging from cannibal tales to urban tales.

——. *Polish-American Folktales*. Clyde Pr. 1977 $10.00. ISBN 0-933190-04-2. Stories from the 1960s and 1970s that depict old traditions and superstitions brought into the United States through a Polish settlement in the Buffalo/Niagara Falls area called the Frontier.

Algarin, Joanne P. *Japanese Folk Literature: A Core Collection*. Bowker 1982 o.p. A comprehensive annotated bibliography of English-language sources of Japanese folk literature, with an introduction that discusses the historiography of Japanese folk literature.

Asbjornsen, Peter C., and Moe Jorgen. *Norwegian Folk Tales*. Pantheon 1982 $14.00. ISBN 0-394-71054-1. A compilation of existing folklore first published in 1852. Retold by the author in a manner that makes the works suitable to read to children. Illustrated by T. Kittelsen and Erik Werenskiold.

Bergeret, Annie, and Mabel Tennaille. *Tales from China*. World Folktale Lib. Silver Burdett Pr. o.p.

Bin Gorion, Micha J., and Emanuel Bin Gorion, eds. *Mimekor Yisrael: Classical Jewish Folktales*. Trans. by I. M. Lask. 3 vols. Ind. U. Pr. 1976 o.p. Powerful retelling of biblical Jewish tales and teachings, ranging from the allures of demonic forces to tales of slaves and kings.

Blair, Walter. *Tall Tale America: A Legendary History of Our Humorous Heroes*. U. Ch. Pr. 1987 $9.95. ISBN 0-226-05596-5

Bloomfield, Morton W., ed. *Allegory, Myth and Symbol*. HUP 1981 $32.50. ISBN 0-674-01640-8. Rigorous theoretical analysis of such topics as allegory contrasted with symbols and the effect of allegory on language.

Botkin, B. A., ed. *Treasury of American Folklore*. Outlet Bk. Co. 1989 $14.99. ISBN 0-517-67978-7. Stories, ballads, and traditions compiled from materials from the Federal Writers' Program. With a foreword by Carl Sandburg.

Briggs, Katherine M. *British Folktales*. Dorset Pr. 1989 $9.95. ISBN 0-88029-288-1. Author is both an important folklore scholar and a talented reteller of tales.

Buchan, David. *Scottish Tradition: A Collection of Scottish Folklore*. Routledge 1984 o.p. Contains many examples of folk narrative, folk song, folk sayings, and folk drama that treat universal folklore themes in a uniquely Scottish manner.

Cavendish, Richard, ed. *Legends of the World*. Outlet Bk. Co. 1989 $8.99. ISBN 0-517-68799-2. Contains 43 essays written by 34 experts. Illustrated by Eric Fraser. Touches on ancient folklore legends from all corners of the world; includes striking illustrations.

Coburn, Jewell R. *Encircled Kingdom: Legends and Folktales of Laos*. Burn Hart 1979 o.p.

Cocchiara, Giuseppe. *The History of Folklore in Europe*. Trans. by John N. McDaniel. Institute for the Study of Human Issues 1981 o.p. Traces the origins of European folklore and the influences of Asian and other cultures, ending with a section on recent trends. Includes a handy list of folklorists.

Curtin, Jeremiah. *Myths and Folktales of the Russians, Western Slavs, and Magyars*. Gordon Pr. 1977 o.p. Extensive collection of Eastern European folklore. Provides insight into the time-honored myths of various countries.

Danaher, Kevin. *Folktales of the Irish Countryside*. Irish Bks. Media 1982 repr. of 1976 ed. o.p.

Degh, Linda, ed. *Studies in East European Folk Narrative*. U. of Tex. Pr. 1978 o.p. Broad theoretical discussion of narrative folklore and in-depth methodological analysis of many different folklorists of Eastern Europe.

Delarue, Paul. *The Borzoi Book of French Folk Tales*. Folklore of the World Ser. Ayer 1980 $45.00. ISBN 0-405-13309-X. Captivating combination of supernatural, humorous, and animal stories with pen-and-ink illustrations. Abundant source of tales for bedtime storytelling.

Dobie, J. Frank. *I'll Tell You a Tale: An Anthology*. U. of Tex. Pr. 1981 $10.95. ISBN 0-292-73821-8. Tales by a leading Texas historian and folklorist who had a talent for making the material interesting to the general reader.

Domotor, Tekla. *Hungarian Folk Customs*. Ind. U. Pr. 1988 $85.00. ISBN 0-685-31467-7. Accounts of witch trials, werewolves, snakes, dragons, healers, and magical happenings. Helps "the discerning reader to realize the similarities among cultures with respect to folk beliefs" (*Choice*).

Dorson, Richard M. *Folktales Told around the World*. U. Ch. Pr. 1978 $22.95. ISBN 0-226-15874-8. Surprisingly, not well received by professional folklorists, but a wide-ranging and readable volume nonetheless.

Drower, Ethel A. *Folk Tales of Iraq*. AMS Pr. 1978 $30.50. ISBN 0-404-16165-0. Tales retold by a British woman living in Iraq in the 1930s. Tales are taken from all classes of people, from tribal villagers to cabinet ministers.

Druts, Yefim, and Alexei Gessler, eds. *Russian Gypsy Tales*. Trans. by James Riordan. Interlink Pub. 1992 $24.95. ISBN 1-56656-100-0. Thirty-six stories and woodblock-style prints.

El-Shamy, Hasan M., ed. *Folktales of Egypt. Folktales of the World Ser.* U. of Ch. Pr. 1982 $12.95. ISBN 0-226-20625-4. A vast amount of information pertaining to tale types and motifs with good suggestions for additional tale types. With a foreword by Richard M. Dorson.

Fowke, Edith. *Folklore of Canada*. Firefly Bks. Ltd. 1977 o.p. Includes a few examples of all folklore genres, "regardless of the worth, interest, or accuracy of available materials," and tries to "give equal representation to all parts of Canada. Only Manitoba and the Yukon Territory are left out entirely" (*Journal of American Folklore*).

Georges, Robert A. *Greek-American Folk Beliefs and Narratives: Survivals and Living Tradition*. Ed. by Richard M. Dorson. *Folklore of the World Ser.* Ayer 1980 $22.00. ISBN 0-405-13314-6. Based on fieldwork done in 1961–62. Includes the text of 54 stories, featuring motifs such as the "evil eye," legends of saints, and fairy tales.

Gilard, Hazel A. *A Giant Walked among Them*. Golden Quill 1977 o.p. "Half-tall" tales of Paul Bunyan.

Glassie, Henry. *Passing the Time in Ballymenone: Culture and History of an Ulster Community. Amer. Folklore Society Ser.* U. of Pa. Pr. 1982 $35.95. ISBN 0-8122-7823-2. "Through the tales, songs, fiddle and whistle tunes, house plans and decorations, daily labor, calendar and custom, belief and behavior . . . seeks the history and values of the community as perceived by its citizens. . . ." (*Journal of American Folklore*).

Gordon, Raoul, ed. *The Folklore of Puerto Rico*. Gordon Pr. 1976 $59.95. ISBN 0-8490-0179-X

Green, Lila. *Tales from Africa. World Folktale Lib.* Silver Burdett Pr. 1979 o.p. With illustrations by Jerry Pinkey.

———. *Tales from Hispanic Lands. World Folktale Lib.* Silver Burdett Pr. 1979 o.p. Illustrated by Donald Silverstein.

Greenway, John. *Tales from the United States. World Folktale Lib.* Silver Burdett Pr. 1979 o.p. Illustrated by Susan Perl.

Haggart, James A. *Stories of Lost Israel in Folklore*. Artisan Sales 1981 $5.00. ISBN 0-934666-08-3

Hall, Edwin S., Jr. *The Eskimo Storyteller: Folktales from Noatak, Alaska*. U. of Tenn. Pr. 1975 $37.50. ISBN 0-87049-603-4. A collection of 188 folk tales printed exactly as narrated by two elders of a Noatak village in northwestern Alaska.

Kightly, Charles. *The Folk Heroes of Britain*. Thames Hudson 1982 $19.95. ISBN 0-500-25083-0. Fascinating and detailed accounts of ancient battles and English and Scottish revolts of the Middle Ages. Beautiful photographs of the countryside and of artwork.

Klein, Barbro S. *Legends and Folk Beliefs in a Swedish American Community: A Study in Folklore and Acculturation*. Ed. by Richard M. Dorson. *Folklore of the World Ser.* 2 vols. Ayer 1980 $78.00. ISBN 0-405-13343-X. Focuses on folk legends and beliefs from the Swedish-American community of New Sweden, Maine. Based on interviews with 29 informants.

Kongas-Maranda, Elli Kaija. *Finnish American Folklore: Quantitative and Qualitative Analysis*. Ed. by Richard M. Dorson. *Folklore of the World Ser.* Ayer 1980 $51.50. ISBN 0-405-13319-7. Examines the folklore repertories of Finnish Americans. Based on extensive fieldwork.

Leach, Maria, and Jerome Fried, eds. *Funk and Wagnall's Standard Dictionary of Folklore, Mythology, and Legends*. HarpC 1984 $34.95. ISBN 0-06-250511-4

Leeming, David A. *The World of Myth: An Anthology*. OUP 1992 $13.95. ISBN 0-19-507475-0

Lindow, John. *Swedish Legends and Folktales.* U. CA Pr. 1978 $32.50. ISBN 0-520-03520-8. Vast array of short Swedish folk tales, some about superstitions and religion and others much like fairy tales, passed along verbally from the 1800s to the present. Provides informative and comparative commentaries on each folk tale.

Lowry, Shirley. *Familiar Mysteries: The Truth in Myth.* OUP 1981 $32.00. ISBN 0-19-502925-9. Simple, straightforward, and coherent account of myths, heroes, and the like. Easily accessible for the general reader.

Luthi, Max. *The European Folktale: Form and Nature.* Trans. by John D. Niles. *Translations in Folklore Studies Ser.* Ind. U. Pr. 1986 $7.95. ISBN 0-253-20393-7. Still an insightful and provocative interpretation.

Marshall, Sybil. *Everyman's Book of English Folktales.* Biblio Dist. 1981 o.p. Collection of lively folk tales with vivid narratives that flow together well as a body of work. Includes well-placed reproductions of wood engravings. With illustrations by John Lawrence.

Miller, Joseph C. *The African Past Speaks: Essays on Oral Tradition and History.* Shoe String 1980 o.p. Studies of the folkloric traditions of different African tribes from a historical and anthropological perspective.

Monteiro, Mariana. *Legends and Popular Tales of the Basque People.* Ayer repr. of 1887 ed. $15.00. ISBN 0-405-08796-9

Monter, William. *Ritual, Myth and Magic in Early Modern Europe.* Ohio U. Pr. 1984 o.p. Compact study of religious superstitions of the sixteenth century and the impact of the movement toward greater religious toleration in the seventeenth and eighteenth centuries.

Myles, Colette G., ed. *The Butterflies Carried Him Home and Other Indian Tales.* Artmans Pr. 1981 $4.95. ISBN 0-9605468-1-2. Illustrated by Yava Aarow.

Norton, Eloise S. *Folk Literature of the British Isles: Readings for Librarians, Teachers, and Those Who Work with Children and Young Adults.* Scarecrow 1978 o.p. Essays on the Anglo-Saxon folklore tradition and its passage from British into American culture.

Noy, Dov. *Studies in Jewish Folklore.* Ktav 1981 $25.00. ISBN 0-87068-802-2. Includes an incredible diversity of topics, with special emphasis on the cultural analysis of religious texts and the Sephardic folklore tradition.

Oinas, Felix J., ed. *Heroic Epic and Saga: An Introduction to the World's Great Folk Epics.* Bks. Demand repr. of 1978 ed. $99.60. ISBN 0-8357-3948-1. Fifteen essays that examine the major epics of the ancient Near East and ancient and medieval Europe to reveal the common source of formal literature and folklore.

Paredes, Americo, ed. *Folktales of Mexico. Folktales of the World Ser.* U. Ch. Pr. 1970 o.p. "... a welcome collection of Mexican folktales that still abound in oral literature ..." (Terrence Hansen, *Western Folklore*).

Pilling, Ann. *Realms of Gold: Myths and Legends from Around the World.* King Fisher Bks. 1993 $16.95. ISBN 1-85697-913-X. Contains 14 retellings from West Africa, the Pacific, Ancient Greece, China, and other treasuries. Profuse illustrations, colors, and design motifs by Kady Denton.

Robertson, R. MacDonald. *Selected Highland Folktales.* David & Charles 1977 o.p. A generous selection of Scottish folk tales.

Robinson, H. S., and K. Wilson. *The Encyclopedia of Myths and Legends of All Nations.* Ed. by Barbara L. Picard. Littlefield 1988 $11.95. ISBN 0-8226-0319-5

Segall, Jacob, ed. *Roumanian Folktales Retold from the Original.* Gordon Pr. 1977 $59.95. ISBN 0-8490-2544-3. A collection of Romanian oral stories.

Sheohmelian, O. *Three Apples from Heaven: Armenian Folk Tales.* Ed. by Arra Avakian and others. Trans. by O. Sheohmelian. Ararat Pr. 1982 $6.95. ISBN 0-933706-23-5. Delightful folk tales reminiscent of many American folk tales for children. Includes dynamic pen-and-ink illustrations. Illustrated by Adrina Zanazanian.

Slater, Candace. *Stories on a String: The Brazilian Literature de Cordel.* U. CA Pr. 1982 $45.00. ISBN 0-520-04154-2. Provides practical and personalized background on featured Brazilian authors and their stories. Works are given in the original Brazilian as well as English. Includes a glossary.

Slote, Bernice, ed. *Myth and Symbol: Critical Approaches and Applications.* Bks. Demand repr. of 1963 ed. $53.90. ISBN 0-317-58189-9. Selection of papers delivered by Northrop Frye, L. C. Knights, and others.

Smith, Alexander M. *Children of Wax: African Folk Tales.* Interlink Pub. 1991 $22.95. ISBN 0-940793-73-3. Twenty-seven stories collected in Matabeleland and Zimbabwe, rendered from the author's own transcriptions.

Stoddard, Florence J. *As Old as the Moon: Cuban Legends and Folklore of the Antillas.* Gordon Pr. 1976 $59.95. ISBN 0-8490-1457-3. Presents the myths of the Antillas and the Lucayas.

Strickland, Walter W. *Panslavonic Folklore.* AMS Pr. 1980 $25.00. ISBN 0-404-16166-9. A collection of Slavic, Russian, and Bulgarian folklore, with elucidative essays.

Thompson, Stith. *The Folktale.* AMS Pr. repr. of 1946 ed. $34.00. ISBN 0-404-15373-9. Includes two appendixes, "Important Works on the Folktale" and "Principal Collections of Folktales," as well as indexes of tale types and motifs.

————. *Motif-Index of Folk-Literature: A Classification of Narrative Elements in Folktales, Ballads, Myths, Fables, Medieval Romance, Exempla, Fabliaux, Jest-Books, and Local Legends.* 6 vols. Ind. U. Pr. 1955–58 $300.00. ISBN 0-253-33887-5. Comprehensively classifies the constituent elements of different kinds of traditional narrative.

Todd, Loreto. *Some Day Been Dey: West African Pidgin Folktale.* Routledge 1979 o.p. Twenty-eight pidgin tales from Cameroon, West Africa.

Toor, Frances. *Mexican Folkways.* Gordon Pr. 1976 $250.00. ISBN 0-8490-2235-5. Presents a composite picture of Mexican life by examining the history, economic life, religion, social organization, music, dance, and literature of the Mexican people.

Toth, Martin D. *Tales from Thailand: Folklore, Culture, and History.* C. E. Tuttle 1983 o.p. Retells 18 traditional Thai folk tales; briefly describes the history, geography, culture, and people of Thailand.

Van Duong, Quyen, and Jewell R. Coburn. *Beyond the East Wind: Legends and Folktales of Vietnam.* Burn Hart 1976 o.p. A collection of 10 traditional Vietnamese folk tales.

Wheeler, Post. *Tales from the Japanese Storytellers as Collected in the Ho Dan Zo.* Ed. by Harold G. Henderson. Tuttle 1974 o.p. Contains stories taken from the 10-volume *Ho-Dan-Zo* or *Treasury of Tales.*

Williamson, Duncan. *Tales of the Seal People: Scottish Folk Tales.* Interlink Pub. 1992 $24.95 ISBN 0-940793-99-7. Collection of 14 selkie tales from the Orkney and Shetland islands off the northern tip of Scotland. Stories that would otherwise require researching many indexes to locate are collected here in one volume.

Wolkstein, Diane, ed. *The Magic Orange Tree: And Other Haitian Folktales.* 1987 $14.95. ISBN 0-8052-0650-7. An assortment of Haitian folk tales, with comments on Haitian folklore.

Zeitlin, Steven J., Amy J. Kotkin, and Holly Cutting Baker. *A Celebration of American Family Folklore: Tales and Traditions from the Smithsonian Collection.* Smithsonian 1982 o.p. The first of its kind to be published; an excellent sourcebook for general readers and professionals prepared by the founders of the Family Folklore Program at the Smithsonian Institution.

U.S. REGIONAL AND ETHNIC FOLKLORE

Arranged by region—New England, Mid-Atlantic, South, Midwest, West—with additional sections on Native American Folklore and African American Folklore, this section includes titles relating to all aspects of the general subject: ballads and songs, folk tales, legends, riddles, haunts, superstitions, tall tales, ethnography, ethnomusicology, linguistics, humor, and more.

New England

Aldrich, Lawson. *The Cheechako: Facts, Fables and Recipes.* Down East 1982 o.p.

Beck, Jane C., ed. *Always in Season: Folk Art and Traditional Culture in Vermont*. Vt. Folklife Ctr. 1982 $14.95. ISBN 0-685-05821-2. A book form presentation of "Always in Season," Vermont's first folk art exhibition. With photographs by Eric Borg, a foreword by Ellen Lovell McCullock, and a preface by Elaine Eff.

Benes, Peter, ed. *Foodways in the Northeast*. Boston U. Pr. 1982 o.p. Essays on the preparation and serving of food in the Northeast, mainly in Massachusetts and mainly before 1800.

Botkin, Benjamin A. *Treasury of New England Folklore*. Outlet Bk. Co. 1989 $12.99. ISBN 0-517-67977-9. Concentrates on the living lore of New England; stresses its oral storytelling tradition.

Brown, Abram E. *Glimpses of Old New England Life: Legends of Old Bedford, Massachusetts*. Higginson Bk. Co. 1993 repr. of 1892 ed. $25.00. ISBN 0-8328-3132-8

Cahill, Robert E. *New England's Strange Sea Sagas. Collectible Class. Ser.* Chandler-Smith 1984 $3.95. ISBN 0-916787-04-4. One of his many collections of folk tales from New England.

Deindorfer, Robert G., ed. *America's One Hundred One Most High Falutin', Big Talkin' Knee Slappin', Golly Whoppers and Tall Tales: The Best of the Burlington Liars' Club*. Workman Pub. 1980 o.p.

Dorson, Richard M. *Jonathan Draws the Long Bow: New England Popular Tales and Legends*. Russell Pr. 1970 repr. of 1946 ed. o.p. A compendium of New England folk tales and legends assembled from little-known sources.

Drake, Samuel A. *Book of New England Legends and Folk Lore*. C. E. Tuttle 1971 repr. of 1884 ed. $14.95. ISBN 0-8048-0990-9

Flanders, Helen H., and George Brown. *Vermont Folksongs and Ballads*. 1931. Gale 1968 o.p. An assortment of folk songs and ballads from Vermont.

Flanders, Helen H., and Marguerite Olney, eds. *Ballads Migrant in New England. Granger Index Repr. Ser.* Ayer repr. of 1953 $17.00. ISBN 0-8369-6015-7. A collection of traditional New England ballads.

Gray, Roland P., ed. *Songs and Ballads of the Maine Lumberjacks*. Gale 1969 repr. of 1924 ed. o.p. Songs and ballads gathered by Gray in Maine.

Huntington, Gale. *Vineyard Tales*. Tashmoo 1980 $7.95. ISBN 0-932384-13-7

Jagendorf, Moritz A. *New England Bean Pot: American Folk Stories to Read and to Tell*. Vanguard 1978 o.p. For younger readers.

Kittredge, George L. *The Old Farmer and His Almanack*. Corner Hse. 1974 repr. of 1904 ed. $24.00. ISBN 0-87928-049-2. Develops topics addressed in the *Old Farmer's Almanac*.

——. *Witchcraft in Old and New England*. Atheneum 1972 repr. of 1929 ed. o.p. A treatise on witchcraft in pre-sixteenth-century England and New England.

Leland, Charles G. *The Algonquin Legends of New England*. Dover 1992 repr. of 1884 ed. $10.95. ISBN 0-486-26944-2. A selection of the myths, legends, and folklore of the North Eastern Algonquins.

Silitch, Clarissa M., ed. *The Old Farmer's Almanac Book of Old Fashioned Puzzles*. Yankee Pub. 1976 o.p.

Simmons, William S. *Spirit of the New England Tribes: Indian History and Folklore*. U. Pr. of New Eng. 1986 $16.95. ISBN 0-87451-372-3. Comprehensive collection of folklore narratives of three southern New England tribes.

Waugh, Charles G., Martin H. Greenberg, and Frank D. McSherry, Jr., eds. *Haunted New England*. Yankee Bks. 1988 $16.95. ISBN 0-89909-156-3

The Mid-Atlantic States

Ainsworth, Catherine H. *Legends of New York State. Folklore Bks.* Clyde Pr. 1983 $10.00. ISBN 0-933190-11-5. A collection of legends concerned with places, persons, and happenings in various parts of New York State from 1962 to 1978.

Bethke, Robert D. *Adirondack Voices: Woodsmen and Woods Lore*. U. of Ill. Pr. 1981 $19.95. ISBN 0-252-00829-4. "This book is a product of contemporary ways of thinking about folklore: it is about interaction, changing situations, and the many-sided potential for meaning that expressive forms have. . . . A lovely book . . . full of wonderful observation and fine detail" (*Journal of Amer. Folklore*).

Burrison, John A., ed. *Storytellers: Folktales and Legends from the South*. U. of Ga. Pr. 1990 $14.95. ISBN 0-8203-1267-3. Contains 250 authentic folk tales, rising out of a shared rural past and oral tradition, told in voices of African American, Anglo-Saxon, and Native American descent.

Cazden, Norman, and others. *Folk Songs of the Catskills*. State U. NY Pr. 1983 $49.50. ISBN 0-87395-582-X. Brings together 178 texts, including several recited examples, and accompanying tunes mainly from the farming, lumbering, and former rafting region of Delaware and Sullivan counties. Introduction by Pete Seeger.

Cohen, David S. *The Folklore and Folklife of New Jersey*. Rutgers U. Pr. 1983 $35.00. ISBN 0-8135-0964-5

Gardner, E. E. *Folklore from the Schoharie Hills, New York*. Ayer 1977 $29.00. ISBN 0-405-10094-9. A central New York classic.

Glimm, James Y. *Flatlanders and Ridgerunners: Folktales from the Mountains of Northern Pennsylvania*. U. of Pittsburgh Pr. 1983 $19.95. ISBN 0-8229-3471-X. A selection of oral folklore from northern Pennsylvania.

Hufford, Mary T. *Chaseworld: Foxhunting and Storytelling in New Jersey's Pine Barrens*. U. of Pa. Pr. 1992 $34.95. ISBN 0-8122-3132-5. Phenomenology of the working-class foxhunters of Southern New Jersey.

Jones, Louis C. *Three Eyes on the Past: Exploring New York State Folk Life*. Syracuse U. Pr. 1982 $13.95. ISBN 0-8156-0179-4. A "wonderfully informal but disjointed book . . . an excellent guide for any local historian [as well as] . . . folklore in the state of New York, embodying material drawn from his *Things That Go Bump in the Night* (1959) and essays that incorporate his abiding love for his native region" (*Choice*).

Kauffman, Henry J. *Pennsylvania Dutch American Folk Art*. Peter Smith rev. ed. $18.25. ISBN 0-8446-2354-7. An introduction to the folk art of the early German communities of Pennsylvania.

Kidd, Ronald. *On Top of Old Smoky: A Collection of Songs and Stories from Appalachia*. Ideals 1992 $13.95. ISBN 0-8249-8569-9. Written by a native of Appalachia. Three stories and eleven lyrics in dialect.

Korson, George G. *Black Rock Mining Folklore of the Pennsylvania Dutch*. Ayer 1979 $37.00. ISBN 0-405-10607-6. A selection of folklore from the early Dutch communities of Pennsylvania.

Leach, MacEdward, and Henry Glassie. *A Guide for Collectors of Oral Traditions and Folk Cultural Material in Pennsylvania*. Pa. Hist. & Mus. Commission 1973 $3.95. ISBN 0-911124-60-8

Levine, Gaynell S., ed. *Languages and Lore of the Long Island Indians*. Ginn Pr. 1981 o.p. Part of the Suffolk County Archaeological Association's series on Long Island's cultural past. Preface by James Truex.

Litchen, Frances. *Folk Art Motifs of Pennsylvania*. Dover 1976 $6.95. ISBN 0-486-23303-0

McMahon, William. *South Jersey Towns: History and Legend*. Rutgers U. Pr. 1990 repr. of 1973 ed. $11.95. ISBN 0-8135-0718-9. A fine assortment of little-known information and historical anecdotes about early southern New Jersey towns.

Pennsylvania Dutch Folklore. Applied Arts 1960 $3.00. ISBN 0-911410-02-3

Tall Tales of the Catskills. Purple Mnt. Pr. $12.50. ISBN 0-935796-24-X

Tantaquidgeon, Gladys. *Folk Medicine of the Delaware and Related Algonquin Indians*. Pa. Hist. & Mus. 1972 $7.50. ISBN 0-911124-70-5. Shows the curing practices, theories on disease, and plant lore of the Delaware Indians.

Thompson, Harold. *Body, Boots, and Britches*. Syracuse U. Pr. 1979 $14.95. ISBN 0-8156-0160-3. The best-known work by a pioneer folklorist, this is the beginning book for pleasurable examination of folklore in New York State. With an introduction by Thomas F. O'Donnell.

Thompson, Harold W. *New York State Folktales, Legends and Ballads*. Dover 1990 $9.95. ISBN 0-486-26563-3. Stories, legends, and ballads from New York State.

Welles, E. R., and J. P. Evans, *The Forgotten Legend of Sleepy Hollow, Rip Van Winkle, President Van Buren and Brom*. Learning Inc. 1984 $4.00. ISBN 0-913692-12-3

The South

Alvey, Gerald. *Kentucky Folklore*. U. Pr. of Ky. 1989 $4.50. ISBN 0-8131-0902-7. A series of folk tales from Kentucky.

Brown, Frank C. *The Frank C. Brown Collection of North Carolina Folklore*. Ed. by Newman I. White. 7 vols. Duke 1952–64 o.p. Contains games and rhymes, beliefs and customs, riddles, proverbs, tales, legends, folk ballads and songs, and superstitions of North Carolina.

Browne, Ray, ed. *A Night with the Hants and Other Alabama Experiences*. Bowling Green Univ. 1976 $17.95. ISBN 0-87972-075-1. A collection of 150 stories of the supernatural gathered from Alabama. Introduction by Carlos Drake.

Burrison, John A., ed. *Storytellers: Folktales and Legends from the South*. U. of Ga. Pr. 1990 $14.95. ISBN 0-8203-1267-3. A collection of more than 250 folk tales told in voices of African American, Anglo-Saxon, and Native American descent.

Carey, George. *A Faraway Time and Place: Lore of the Eastern Shore*. Ed. by Richard M. Dorson. *International Folklore Ser*. Ayer 1977 repr. of 1971 ed. $22.00. ISBN 0-405-10086-8. An impressive collection of stories from the white watermen in the region between the Nanticoke and Pocomoke Rivers on the lower eastern shore of the Chesapeake.

———. *Maryland Folklore*. Tidewater 1971 $12.95. ISBN 0-87033-396-8. "Perhaps the most important contribution of the book is the section on 'Urban and Modern Legends' . . . a good sampling of the grisly beliefs that reflect the anxieties of today's 'youth culture'" (*Journal of American Folklore*).

Carpenter, Cal. *The Walton War and Tales of the Great Smoky Mountains*. Copple 1980 o.p.

Chase, Richard. *American Folk Tales and Songs*. Dover 1971 $4.95. ISBN 0-486-22692-1. A classic collection, especially important for its songs.

———. *Jack Tales*. HM 1943 $13.45. ISBN 0-395-06694-8. Southern Appalachian versions of the 'Jack' cycle of folktales of the British-American trickster hero, the poor, unpromising, lazy, and often unscrupulous boy who wins out by his cleverness, sharpwittedness and luck . . ." (*N.Y. Folklore Quarterly*).

Clarke, Kenneth, and Mary Clarke. *The Harvest and the Reapers: Oral Traditions of Kentucky*. U. Pr. of Ky. 1974 $28.10. ISBN 0-685-23965-7. Covers the oral literary traditions of Kentucky.

Combs, Josiah H. *Folk Songs of the Southern United States*. Ed. by D. K. Wilgus. *Amer. Folklore Society Bibliographical and Special Ser*. U. of Tex. Pr. 1967 $15.95. ISBN 0-292-73692-4. From the original French *Folk Songs du Midi des Etats-Unis* and the English-language manuscript on which it was based. Includes music.

Cuthbert, John A. *West Virginia Folk Music*. West Va. U. Pr. 1982 $18.00. ISBN 0-937058-12-2. A source of information on recordings in the West Virginia and Regional History Collection.

Davis, Hubert J. *Myths and Legends of the Great Dismal Swamp*. Johnson Pub. 1981 o.p. Folklore from around the Dismal Swamp area of North Carolina and Virginia. With illustrations by Sarah Codd.

Fraser, Walter J., Jr., and Winfred B. Moore, Jr., eds. *The Southern Enigma: Essays on Race, Class, and Folk Culture. Contributions in Amer. History Ser*. Greenwood 1983 $42.95. ISBN 0-313-23640-2. An anthology of 15 essays selected from over 80 papers presented in April 1981 at the Citadel Conference on the South.

Gainer, Patrick W. *Witches, Ghosts and Signs: Folklore of the Southern Appalachians*. Seneca Bks. 1975. ISBN 0-89092-006-0. Contains Southern Appalachian folk tales.

Galbreath, Bob. *Tennessee Red Berry Tales*. Whites Creek Pr. 1986 $7.95. ISBN 0-961-6918-0-8

Gilmore, Robert K. *Ozark Baptizings, Hangings, and Other Diversions: Theatrical Folkways of Rural Missouri, 1885–1910*. U. of Okla. Pr. 1984 o.p. Covers a single generation (1885–1910) of Ozark history. Foreword by Robert Flanders.

Goehring, Eleanor E. *Tennessee Folk Culture: An Annotated Bibliography*. U. of Tenn. Pr. 1982 $39.60. ISBN 0-8357-6914-3. Excellent annotated bibliography of Tennessee folk culture that encompasses a large range of topics.

Harden, John. *Tar Heel Ghosts*. U. of NC Pr. 1980 $14.95. ISBN 0-8078-0660-9. A selection of ghost lore from North Carolina.

Hartsfield, Mariella G. *Tall Betsy and Dunce Baby: South Georgia Folktales*. U. of Ga. Pr. 1991 repr. of 1987 ed. $11.95. ISBN 0-8203-1332-7

Jones, Bessie, and Bess L. Hawes. *Step It Down: Games, Plays, Songs, and Stories from the Afro-American Heritage*. U. of Ga. Pr. 1987 repr. of 1972 ed. $12.95. ISBN 0-8203-0960-5

LaPin, Dierdre, and Louis Guida. *Hogs in the Bottoms: Family Folklore in Arkansas*. August Hse. 1982 o.p.

McNeil, W. K. *Southern Folk Ballads*. 2 vols. August Hse. 1987–88 $24.95 ea. ISBNs 0-87483-038-9, 0-87483-047-8. Introductory collection of familiar folk ballads along with song histories and singer biographies.

———. *Southern Mountain Folksongs*. August Hse. 1992 $24.95. ISBN 0-87483-284-5

Montell, William L. *Ghosts along the Cumberland: Deathlore in the Kentucky Foothills*. U. of Tenn. Pr. 1975 $12.95. ISBN 0-87049-535-6. A selection of death lore and ghost narratives from the foothills of south central Kentucky.

Randolph, Vance. *Ozark Folksongs*. Ed. by Norm Cohen. *Music in Amer. Life Ser.* U. of Ill. Pr. 1982 $49.95. ISBN 0-252-00815-4. Contains British ballads and songs, southern and western U.S. songs, humorous, play party, and religious songs. Contains an introduction by W. K. McNeil.

———. *Pissing in the Snow and Other Ozark Folktales*. U. of Ill. Pr. 1976 $8.95. ISBN 0-252-01364-6. ". . . a book of real significance for anyone interested at all in scatological lore." (*Journal of American Folklore*).

Randolph, Vance, and Gordon McCann. *Ozark Folklore: An Annotated Bibliography*. Vol. 2 U. of Mo. Pr. 1987 $40.00. ISBN 0-8262-0486-4. A compilation of authoritative annotations of approximately 1,600 books, articles, and manuscripts on Ozark folklore.

Rhyne, Nancy. *Tales of the South Carolina Low Country*. Blair 1982 $5.95. ISBN 0-89587-027-4. A collection of stories relating to the coastal area of South Carolina, with some passages written in Gullah.

Rosenbaum, Art, and Margo Rosenbaum. *Folk Visions and Voices: Traditional Music and Song in North Georgia*. U. of Ga. Pr. 1983 $29.95. ISBN 0-8203-0682-7. Foreword by Pete Seeger.

Williams, Thomas A. *Tales of the Tobacco Country*. Venture Pr. FL 1992 $14.95. ISBN 1-878853-05-8

The Midwest

Baker, Ronald L. *Hoosier Folk Legends*. Ind. U. Pr. 1982 $25.00. ISBN 0-253-32844-6. Contains numerous legends from Indiana.

Brewster, Paul G., ed. *Ballads and Songs of Indiana*. Ed. by Kenneth S. Goldstein and Winthrop E. Richmond. *Publications in Folksong and Balladry Ser.* Folklorica Pr. 1982 repr. of 1940 ed. o.p. One hundred ballads and folk songs gathered from southern Indiana.

Degh, Linda, ed. *Indiana Folklore: A Reader*. Ind. U. Pr. $25.00. ISBN 0-253-10986-8. A selection of articles reprinted from the *Journal of Indiana Folklore*.

Dewhurst, C. Kurt, and Yvonne R. Lockwood, eds. *Michigan Folklife Reader*. Mich. St. U. Pr. 1988 $30.00. ISBN 0-87013-259-8. An introduction to the wealth of folklore and folkways of Michigan.

Gard, Robert E., and L. G. Sorden. *Wisconsin Lore*. NorthWord 1971 $9.95. ISBN 0-942802-79-9. Contains hometown lore from Wisconsin.

Kane, Grace F. *Myths and Legends of the Mackinacs and the Lake Region*. Black Letter 1972 repr. of 1897 ed. $8.00. ISBN 0-912382-09-0. Native American tales obtained from other authors and from Native Americans of the Lake Region.

Koch, William E. *Folklore from Kansas: Customs, Beliefs, and Superstitions*. U. Pr. of KA 1980 $19.95. ISBN 0-7006-0244-5. Useful for a "researcher with a good deal of knowledge in the fields of customs, belief, and superstition." (*Journal of American Folklore*).

Laird, Charlton G. *Iowa Legends of Buried Treasures*. Foun. Bks. 1990 $8.95. ISBN 0-934988-23-4

Mittlefehldt, Pamela. *Minnesota Folklife: An Annotated Bibliography*. Ed. by I. Karon Sherarts. Minn. Hist. 1979 o.p. Preface by Ellen J. Stekert. An annotated bibliography of the folklore and folkways of Minnesota.

Neely, Charles. *Tales and Songs of Southern Illinois*. Crossfire Pr. 1978 repr. of 1938 ed. $18.95. ISBN 0-9623990-3-5. A collection of southern Illinois stories and songs.

Otto, Simon. *Walk in Peace: Legends and Stories of the Michigan Indians*. Grnd. Rpds. Intertribal 1992 $9.95. ISBN 0-9617707-5-9

Pound, Louise. *Nebraska Folklore*. Greenwood 1976 repr. of 1960 ed. $8.95. ISBN 0-8032-8724-0. Stories collected from Nebraska and edited by Pound shortly before her death.

Rosheim, David L. *Old Iowegian Legends*. Andromeda 1991 $12.95. ISBN 0-9502996-2-9

Sackett, S. J., and William E. Koch, eds. *Kansas Folklore*. Flint Hills $7.95. ISBN 0-318-35487-X

Stout, Earl J., ed. *Folklore from Iowa*. Amer. Folklore Society Memoir Ser. Kraus repr. of 1936 ed. $37.00. ISBN 0-527-01081-2. A selection of folk songs and beliefs of Iowa.

Thomas, Rosemary H. *It's Good to Tell You: French Folk Tales from Missouri*. U. of Mo. Pr. 1981 $28.00. ISBN 0-8262-0327-2. Twenty-one old French stories obtained mainly through "story meetings" held in Missouri.

Topinka, Rudy. *Walkin' and Talkin' Revisited*. Pine River WI 1989 $8.95. ISBN 0-9624616-0-1. Stories from the upper Midwest, including the Minnesota Iron Range and Wisconsin's lake country.

Welsch, Roger. *Shingling the Fog and Other Plains Lies*. U. of Nebr. Pr. 1980 $17.95. ISBN 0-8032-4709-5. [This book]. . . extends the collection and publication of the genre to include a sizable corpus of authentic tales from the Great Plains, primarily Nebraska; the abuses in this latest collection are of omission, and are certainly outweighed by the accurate depiction of the tall tale . . ." (*Journal of American Folklore*).

———, comp. *A Treasury of Nebraska Pioneer Folklore*. U. of Nebr. Pr. 1966 $12.95. ISBN 0-8032-9707-6. Compiled mainly from the 30 *Nebraska Folklore Pamphlets* prepared by the W.P.A. Writers Program from 1927 to 1940.

Wyman, Walker B. *Wisconsin Folklore*. U. Wisc.-River Falls Pr. 1981 $4.95. ISBN 0-686-27304-4

———. *Wolf and Bear Stories*. U. Wisc.-River Falls Pr. $3.00. ISBN 0-318-03969-9

The West

Abernathy, Francis E., ed. *Folk Art in Texas*. UNTX Pr. 1985 $35.00. ISBN 0-87074-210-8. Deals with Texan folk art that is mainly utilitarian.

———, ed. *Sonovagun Stew: A Folklore Misellany*. UNTX Pr. 1985 $21.95. ISBN 0-87074-211-6. Collection of folk tales from the Texas Folklore Society.

———, ed. *T for Texas: A State Full of Folklore*. E-Heart Pr. 1982 $15.95. ISBN 0-935014-03-9. Result of the Texas Folklore Society's efforts to preserve and present Texan folklore.

Anderson, Dorothy D. *Arizona Legends and Lore*. Golden West Pub. 1991 $5.95. ISBN 0-914846-55-8

Bauman, Richard, and Roger D. Abrahams, eds. *And Other Neighborly Names: Social Process and Cultural Image in Texas Folklore*. U. of Tex. Pr. 1981 $25.00. ISBN 0-292-70352-X. Focuses on the ways in which traditions arise and are maintained when diverse peoples come together by examining cojunto music, Gulf fisherman stories, and so forth.

Bratcher, James T. *Analytical Index to Publications of the Texas Folklore Society*. 36 vols. SMU Pr. 1973 $15.95 ea. ISBN 0-87074-135-7

Brett, Bill. *There Ain't No Such Animal and Other East Texas Tales.* Tex. A & M Univ. Pr. 1979 $12.95. ISBN 0-89096-068-2. A collection of tales from eastern Texas. Illustrated by Harvey Johnson.

Campa, Arthur L. *Sayings and Riddles in New Mexico.* Borgo Pr. 1982 $23.00. ISBN 0-89370-731-7

Cannon, Hal, ed. *Utah Folk Art: A Catalog of Material Culture.* Brigham 1980 o.p. An accompaniment to the Utah folk art exhibit shown throughout the state by the Utah Arts Council.

Dobie, J. Frank. *Coronado's Children: Tales of Lost and Buried Treasures of the Southwest.* U. of Tex. Pr. 1978 repr. of 1930 ed. $19.95. ISBN 0-292-71050-X. Stories, some dating back 450 years, about lost mines and buried treasure in the Southwest.

———. *The Longhorns.* U. of Tex. Pr. 1980 $11.95. ISBN 0-292-74627-X. Old Texan tales. Illustrated by Tom Lea.

———. *Tales of Old-Time Texas.* Little 1984 $11.95. ISBN 0-292-78069-9. Folklore of Texas and the Southwest.

———. *A Vaquero of the Brush Country.* U. of Tex. Pr. 1981 repr. of 1960 ed. $12.95. ISBN 0-292-78704-9. "Discusses the practices of the open range, characteristics of ranch people, the cowboy's belongings; includes tales of longhorns, razorbacks, mustangs and other range yarns, as well as authentic lore of the bloody border and the cattle trail" (*N.Y. Folklore Quarterly*).

———, ed. *Legends of Texas. Texas Folklore Society Publications.* 2 vols. SMU Pr. 1964 repr. of 1924 ed. $16.95. ISBN 0-87074-156-X. Legends assembled by Dobie from the state of Texas.

———, ed. *Texas and Southwestern Lore.* UNTX Pr. 1982 repr. of 1927 ed. $13.95. ISBN 0-87074-044-X

Garry, Jim. *This Ol'Drought Ain't Broke Us Yet (But We're All Bent Pretty Bad): Stories of the American West.* Crown Pub. Group 1992 $18.00. ISBN 0-517-58814-5. As much an oral history as folklore, this collection results from two decades of Garry's wanderings in pursuit of old-timers with stories to tell.

Helm, Mike. *Oregon's Ghosts and Monsters.* Rainy Day Oreg. 1983 $8.95. ISBN 0-931742-03-X

Judson, Katherine. *Myths and Legends of the Pacific Northwest. Shorey Indian Ser.* Shorey 1980 repr. of 1910 ed. $12.95. ISBN 0-8466-0147-8. An assortment of Native American folk tales mainly from Washington and Oregon.

Kilpatrick, Jack, and Anna Kilpatrick. *Friends of Thunder, Folktales of Oklahoma.* SMU Pr. 1977 repr. of 1964 ed. o.p. Cherokee tales and legends recorded and translated by the authors.

Lee, Hector. *Heroes, Villains, and Ghosts: Folklore of Old California.* Capra Pr. 1984 $23.00. ISBN 0-8095-4038-X. Legends drawn from California history; some based on real characters.

Lingenfelter, Richard E., and others, eds. *Songs of the American West.* U. CA Pr. 1968 o.p.

Maclean, Angus. *Cuentos: Based on the Folk Tales of the Spanish Californians.* Panorama West Pub. 1979. o.p. A series of legends, accumulated over a period of years, from California bandidos.

———. *Legends of the California Bandidos.* Bear Flag Bks. 1989 repr. of 1977 ed. $12.50. ISBN 0-939919-21-4

Nunis, and Harry Knill. *Tales of Mexican California.* Bellerophon Bks. 1992 $8.95. ISBN 0-88388-161-6

Paredes, Americo. *A Texas-Mexican Cancionero: Folksongs of the Lower Border.* U. of Ill. Pr. 1975 $11.95. ISBN 0-252-00894-4

Robb, John D. *Hispanic Folk Music of New Mexico and the Southwest: A Self-Portrait of the People.* U. of Okla. Pr. 1980 o.p.

Robe, Stanley. *Hispanic Folktales from New Mexico: Narratives from the R. D. Jameson Collection.* Bks. Demand repr. of 1977 ed. $58.50. ISBN 0-317-29029-0

Russell, Bert. *Calked Boots and Other Northwest Writings.* Lacon Pubs. 1979 $9.95. ISBN 0-930344-03-0

Schwartz, Henry. *Kit Carson's Long Walk and Other True Tales of Old San Diego.* Assn. of Creative Writers 1980 o.p.

Taylor, Lonn, and Ingrid Maar. *The American Cowboy.* HarpC 1983 o.p. Shows the real and fanciful aspects of an American phenomenon—the cowboy.

Thorp, N. Howard, ed. *Songs of the Cowboys.* U. of Nebr. Pr. 1984 repr. of 1908 ed. $20.00. ISBN 0-8032-4410-X. Twenty-three songs, reprinted in facsimile, with the original or reconstructed texts, variants, and tunes; includes historical and critical notes, a bibliography for each song, a lexicon, and a general bibliography.

Trimble, Marshall. *Arizona Adventure: Action Packed True Tales of Early Arizona.* Golden West 1982 $5.95. ISBN 0-914846-14-0. A collection of true stories that focus mainly on the cowboys of Arizona.

West, John O. *Mexican-American Folklore.* August Hse. 1988 $24.95. ISBN 0-87483-060-5. Focuses on the folk culture of the Southwest, incorporating Native American, African American, Asian, and European traditions in the melting pot that was the early West.

Native American Folklore

Bemister, Margaret. *Thirty Indian Legends of Canada.* Merrimack 1983 $9.95. ISBN 0-88894-025-4. A moving introduction to the heritage of Canada's native peoples.

Boatright, Mody C., ed. *The Sky Is My Tipi.* Texas Folklore Society Publications UNTX Pr. 1966 repr. of 1949 ed. $13.95. ISBN 0-87074-010-5. Kiowa-Apache tales gathered for publication by the Texas Folklore Society.

Boyer, L. Bryce. *Childhood and Folklore: A Psychoanalytic Study of Apache Personality.* Psychohistory Pr. 1979 $16.95. ISBN 0-914434-07-1. Written from a psychoanalytical approach, "generally clear and intelligible to the layman. . . . should serve as a model for future studies, but will be difficult to equal" (*Journal of American Folklore*).

Bright, William. *A Coyote Reader.* U. CA Pr. 1993 $30.00. ISBN 0-520-08061-0. Traces the legend of the coyote through North American history.

Choate, F. *The Indian Fairy Book: From the Original Legends.* Gordon Pr. 1977 $59.95. ISBN 0-8490-2053-0. Native American fairy tales chosen from stories collected by Henry R. Schoolcraft during the nineteenth century.

Clark, Ella E. *Indian Legends from the Northern Rockies. Civilization of the Amer. Indian Ser.* U. of Okla. Pr. 1977 repr. of 1966 ed. o.p. A selection of stories from 12 Native American tribes.

———. *Indian Legends of the Pacific Northwest.* U. CA Pr. 1953 $12.95. ISBN 0-520-00243-1. Contains Native American stories from the Pacific Northwest, a large number of which center around natural phenomena and geographical features of the Pacific Northwest.

Clements, William M., and Frances M. Malpezzi. *Native American Folklore, 1879–1979: An Annotated Bibliography.* Ohio U. Pr. 1984 $34.95. ISBN 0-8040-0831-0. A bibliography of more than 5,000 entries about Native Americans north of Mexico; includes narratives, songs, chants, prayers, formulas, orations, and proverbs and covers music, dance, games, and ceremonials.

Coffin, Tristram P., ed. *Indian Tales of North America: An Anthology for the Adult Reader. Amer. Folklore Society Bibliographical and Special Ser.* U. of Tex. Pr. 1961 o.p. An anthology of Native American lore from North America.

Cushing, Frank H. *Zuni Folk Tales.* Gordon Pr. 1977 $59.95. ISBN 0-8490-2858-2. Folk tales gathered by Cushing from the Zuni Pueblo people.

Eastman, Mary. *Dahcotah: Or, Life and Legends of the Sioux around Fort Snelling. Mid-Amer Frontier Ser.* Ayer 1975 repr. of 1849 ed. $24.50. ISBN 0-405-06861-1. Legends and tales gathered from the Sioux over a seven-year period. Contains a preface by C. M. Kirkland.

Erodes, Richard, and Alfonso Ortiz. *American Indian Myth and Legends.* Pantheon 1985 $17.00. ISBN 0-394-74018-1. Contains 166 legends from different native peoples of North America.

Gaddis, Vincent H. *Native American Myths* and *Mysteries.* Borderland Sciences 1991 repr. of 1976 ed. $12.95. ISBN 0-945685-10-6

Gossen, Gary H. *Chamulas in the World of the Sun: Time and Space in a Maya Oral Tradition.* Bks. Demand 1974 $107.80. ISBN 0-7837-1702-4. Offers a brilliant analysis of the cosmology, symbolism, and verbal behavior of the Chamula people of southern Mexico.

Grinnell, George B. *Blackfoot Lodge Tales: The Story of a Prairie People.* Corner Hse. 1972 repr. of 1892 ed. $21.50. ISBN 0-81928-030-1. A collection of Blackfoot oral literature.

Haile, Berard. *Navajo Coyote Tales: The Curly to Aheedliinii Version.* Amer. Tribal Religious Ser. Vol. 8. U. of Nebr. Pr. 1984 $20.00. ISBN 0-8032-2330-7

Jacobs, Melville. *Content and Style of an Oral Literature: Clackamas Chinook Myths and Tales.* U. Ch. Pr. 1959 o.p. Provides a method by which the oral literature of the now extinct Clackamas Chinook people can be understood.

Jagendorf, Moritz A. *Tales from the First Americans.* World Folktale Lib. Silver Burdett Pr. 1979 o.p. Illustrated by Jack Endewelt.

Malotki, Ekkehart, and Michael Lomatuway'ma. *Hopi Coyote Tales: Istutuwutsi.* Amer. Tribal Religious Ser. Vol. 9. U. of Nebr. Pr. 1984 $30.00. ISBN 0-8032-3088-5

Mayo, Gretchen W. *North American Indian Stories: More Earthmaker's Tales.* Walker & Co. 1990 $5.95. ISBN 0-8027-7344-3

Merriam, Alan P. *Ethnomusicology of the Flathead Indians.* Viking Fund Publications in Anthropology Ser. Aldine repr. of 1967 ed. o.p. ". . . an important work in the literature of primitive music . . . [providing] insight into Indian beliefs, social thought, customs, and intellectual responsiveness, and for the major contribution he makes towards the developing techniques of ethnomusicology" (*Library Journal*).

Newcomb, Franc J. *Navajo Folktales.* U. of NM Pr. 1991 repr. of 1967 ed. $11.95. ISBN 0-8263-1231-4. Includes a new foreword by Paul Zolbrod.

Norman, Howard, trans. *Where the Chill Came From: Cree Windigo Tales and Journeys: 1982.* North Point Pr. o.p. A collection of Windigo stories from the Cree.

Parker, Arthur C. *Seneca Myths and Folklore.* U. of Nebr. Pr. 1989 $13.95. ISBN 0-8032-8723-2

Pijoan, Teresa. *White Wolf Woman: And Other Native American Transformation Myths.* August Hse. 1992 $17.95. ISBN 0-87483-201-2. Forty transformation myths, providing a good introduction to the diverse spirit world of the continent's indigenous peoples.

Salomon, J. H. *The Book of Indian Crafts and Indian Lore.* Gordon Pr. 1977 $250.00. ISBN 0-8490-1531-6. Includes Native American tales of adventure told orally and written down by Salomon.

Sams, Jamie and Twylah Nitsch. *Other Council Fires Were Here Before Ours.* Harper SF 1991 $15.00. ISBN 0-06-250763-X. Sams and Nitsch, a Seneca Elder, relate the Seneca story of creation and the prophecies for the coming three ages. Much food for philosophical thought.

Schorer, C. E., ed. *Indian Tales of C. C. Trowbridge: Collected from Wyandots, Miamis and Shawanoes.* Green Oak Pr. 1985 $12.95. ISBN 0-931600-05-7. Native American tales originally collected by C. C. Trowbridge and edited by Schorer.

Shaw, Anna M. *Pima Indian Legends.* U. of Ariz. Pr. 1993 repr. of 1968 ed. $9.95. ISBN 0-8165-0186-6

Spencer, Katherine. *Reflections of Social Life in the Navaho Origin Myth.* Univ. of New Mexico Publications in Anthropology. AMS Pr. 1983 repr. of 1947 ed. $20.00. ISBN 0-404-15705-X. Focuses on descriptive and historical questions about the Navaho origin myth.

Talashoma, Herschel, and Ekkehart Malotki, eds. *Hopitutuwutsi-Hopi Tales: A Bilingual Collection of Hopi Indian Stories.* U. of Ariz. Pr. 1983 o.p. Hopi stories narrated by Talashoma and translated by Malotski.

Thompson, Stith, ed. *Tales of the North American Indians.* Ind. U. Pr. 1966 $12.95. ISBN 0-253-20019-1. Ninety-six tales arranged according to type, with "comparative notes, to show the extent of the distribution of each tale and each motif, [presented] . . . as to be obvious to the general reader" (Introduction).

Verlarde, Pablita. *Old Father Storyteller: Grandfather Stories of the Pueblo Native American Indians.* Clear Light 1993 repr. of 1989 ed. $14.95. ISBN 0-940666-24-3

Walker, James R. *Lakota Myth.* U. of Nebr. Pr. 1983 $35.00. ISBN 0-8032-4726-5

Williamson, Ray A., and Claire R. Farrer, eds. *Earth and Sky: Visions of the Cosmos in Native American Folklore.* U. of NM Pr. 1992 $32.50. ISBN 0-8263-1317-5. Essays on Native American starlore and its cultural uses and interpretations.

Wood, Marion. *Spirits, Heroes and Hunters from North American Indian Mythology.* P. Bedrick Bks. 1992 $22.50. ISBN 0-87226-903-5. Native American myths from North America gathered by the authors. Illustrated by John Sibbick.

African American Folklore

Abrahams, Roger D. *Deep Down in the Jungle: Negro Narrative Folklore from the Streets of Philadelphia.* Aldine 1970 $24.95. ISBN 0-202-01092-9. ". . . a selected body of obscene folk narrative collected in a single four-block Negro neighborhood in Philadelphia and consisting of playing the dozens, toasts, and jokes." (*N.Y. Folklore Quarterly*).

Allen, Ray. *Singing in the Spirit: African-American Sacred Quartets in New York City.* U. of Pa. Pr. 1991 $38.95. ISBN 0-8122-3050-7. Fills a need for information on this segment of the black "spiritual entertainment" tradition in music. Publication of the American Folklore Society.

Bascom, Willima. *African Folktales in the New World.* Ind. U. Pr. 1992 $35.00. ISBN 0-253-31128-4. Forward by Alan Dundes.

Bell, Michael J. *The World from Brown's Lounge: An Ethnography of Black Middle Class Play.* U. of Ill. Pr. 1983 $24.95. ISBN 0-252-00956-8. A "study of speech play among blacks who frequent a neighborhood bar in Philadelphia . . . provide[s] insight into . . . 'the aesthetics of ordinary experience'" (*Journal of American Folklore*).

Bonnefoy, Yves, ed. *American, African, and Old European Mythologies.* Trans. by Wendy Doniger and Geral Honigsblum. U. Ch. Pr. 1993 $25.00. ISBN 0-226-06457-3

Christensen, A. M. *Afro-American Folklore: Told round Cabin Fires on the Sea Islands of South Carolina.* Greenwood repr. of 1892 ed. $8.95. ISBN 0-8369-8802-7

Courlander, Harold. *Negro Folk Music, U.S.A.* Dover 1992 repr. of 1963 ed. $7.95. ISBN 0-486-27350-4

———. *A Treasury of African Folklore.* Crown Pub. Group 1975 o.p.

Dance, Daryl C. *Shuckin' and Jivin': Folklore from Contemporary Black Americans.* Ind. U. Pr. 1978 $35.00. ISBN 0-253-35220-7. ". . . [provides] evidence of the vitality, imagination, variety, and strength of the black folk tradition in America. . . . unexpurgated; all of the material is rendered in the language in which it is normally told, much of it obscene" (*Journal of American Folklore*).

Epstein, Dena J. *Sinful Tunes and Spirituals: Black Folk Music to the Civil War. Music in Amer. Life Ser.* U. of Ill. Pr. 1977 $16.95. ISBN 0-252-00875-8

Fry, Gladys-Marie. *Night Riders in Black Folk History.* U. of Ga. Pr. 1991 repr. of 1975 ed. $14.95. ISBN 0-8203-1338-6. Includes a new forward by Wm. Lynwood Montell.

Goss, Linda, and Marian E. Barnes, eds. *Talk That Talk: An Anthology of African-American Storytelling.* S&S Trade 1989 $12.95. ISBN 0-685-28304-6. Exceptional collection.

Hamilton, Virginia. *The People Could Fly: American Black Folktales.* Knopf 1993 $10.00. ISBN 0-679-84336-1. Widely praised anthology.

Hughes, Langston. *Book of Negro Humor.* Dodd 1965 $25.95. ISBN 0-89966-733-3. From African prototypes and memories of slavery to "The Jazz Folk" and "Harlem Jive," from work songs, sermons, and spirituals to songs, poetry, and prose "in the folk manner," the book explores the integral relationship between black folklore, life, and literature.

Hurston, Zora N. *Mules and Men.* Greenwood repr. of 1935 ed. $38.50. ISBN 0-8371-2000-4

Jackson, Bruce, ed. *The Negro and His Folklore in Nineteenth Century Periodicals. Amer. Folklore Society Bibliographic and Special Ser.* U. of Tex. Pr. 1977 repr. of 1967 ed. $14.50. ISBN 0-292-75510-4. ". . . brings into sharp focus the social and aesthetic values of Negro folklore as seen by white contemporaries from slavery to freedom." (*N.Y. Folklore Quarterly*).

Joyner, Charles. *Down by the Riverside: A South Carolina Slave Community. Blacks in the New World Ser.* U. of Ill. Pr. 1984 $29.95. ISBN 0-252-01058-2

Kebede, Ashenafi. *Roots of Black Music: The Vocal, Instrumental and Dance Heritage of Africa and Black America.* P-H 1982 o.p.

Klotman, Phyllis R., and others, eds. *Humanities through the Black Experience.* Kendall-Hunt 1977 $18.95. ISBN 0-8403-1631-3

Lester, Julius. *Black Folktales.* Grove-Atltic. 1991 $7.95. ISBN 0-8021-5052-7

Levine, Lawrence W. *Black Culture and Black Consciousness: Afro-American Folk Thought from Slavery to Freedom.* OUP 1977 $10.95. ISBN 0-19-502374-9

Livingston, Jane, and John Beardsley. *Black Folk Art in America, 1930–1980.* U. Pr. of Miss. 1982 $37.50. ISBN 0-87805-398-0

Norman, Floyd E. *Afro-Classic Folk Tales.* Vignette 1992 $9.95. ISBN 1-881368-00-9. Series of folk stories dating back to the days of American slavery.

Osofsky, Gilbert, ed. *Puttin' on Ole Massa: The Slave Narratives of Henry Bibb, William W. Brown, and Solomon Northrup.* HarpC 1969 o.p. By one of the first historians to realize that folkoristic sources were necessary for writing the history of peoples, white and black, who left no written record.

Owen, Mary A. *Voodoo Tales, as Told among the Negroes of the Southwest. Black Heritage Lib. Collection Ser.* Greenwood repr. of 1893 ed. $13.00. ISBN 0-8369-8754-3. With an introduction by C. G. Leland.

Puckett, N. Niles. *Folk Beliefs of the Southern Negro.* Patterson Smith 1968 repr. of 1926 ed. $22.00. ISBN 0-87585-022-7

Short, Sam. *Tis So: Negro Folk Tales.* Claitors 1972 $6.95. ISBN 0-87511-105-X

Skowronski, Joann. *Black Music in America: A Bibliography.* Scarecrow 1981 $45.00. ISBN 0-8108-1443-9

Smith, Michael P. *Spirit World: Pattern in the Expressive Folk Culture of Afro-American New Orleans.* New Orleans Urban 1984 $14.00. ISBN 0-9613133-0-7

Spalding, Henry D. *Encyclopedia of Black Folklore and Humor.* Jonathan David 1979 $14.95. ISBN 0-8246-0345-1. A collection of anecdotes, stories, songs, poems, proverbs, and superstitions, and a few recipes for soul food. With an introduction by J. Mason Brewer.

Szwed, John F., and Roger D. Abrahams. *Afro-American Folk Culture: An Annotated Bibliography of Materials from North, Central and South America and the West Indies.* 2 vols. Bks. Demand repr. of 1978 ed. $89.00–103.50 ea. ISBNs 0-8357-5244-5, 0-8357-5245-3

Talley, Thomas W. *Negro Folk Rhymes, Wise and Otherwise: A Study.* Folcroft 1980 repr. of 1922 ed. o.p.

Thomas, H. Nigel. *From Folklore to Fiction: A Study of Folk Heroes and Rituals in the Black American Novel.* Greewood 1988 $39.95. ISBN 0-313-26224-1. Explores the connection between African American folklore and African American literature.

Thompson, Rose. *Hush Child, Can't You Hear the Music.* Ed. by Charles Beaumont. *Brown Thrasher Original Ser.* U. of Ga. Pr. $14.95. ISBN 0-8203-0588-X

Waters, Donald J. *Strange Ways and Sweet Dreams: Afro-American Folklore from the Hampton Institute.* G. K. Hall 1983 $52.00. ISBN 0-8161-9022-4.

Whiting, Helen A. *Negro Folk Tales.* Assoc. Pubs. D. C. 1990 $4.25. ISBN 0-87498-006-2

MISCELLANEOUS AND APPLIED FOLKLORE

The application of folklore to other disciplines—history, literature, psychology, sociology, linguistics—is a major occupation of many present-day folklorists, and many of the titles in this selection deal with these applications. The titles deal with everyday life and the supernatural, including art and crafts, material culture, proverbs, riddles, beliefs, and customs, as well as with urban folklore, an emerging field of its own.

Baker, Donald. *Functions of Folk and Fairy Tales*. Assn. for Childhood Ed. 1981 $2.60. ISBN 0-87173-096-0

Baker, Margret. *Folklore of the Sea*. David & Charles 1979 o.p. "Beginning with the rituals surrounding shipbuilding itself, Baker sails along through the esoteric seas of phantom ships, strange seagoing custom, sea-serpents, and weather gods" (*Journal of American Folklore*).

Beck, Horace. *Folklore and the Sea*. Mystic Seaport 1973 $40.00. ISBN 0-8195-4063-3

Ben, Amos D., and K. Goldstein, eds. *Folklore: Performance and Communication. Approaches to Semiotics Ser.* Mouton 1975 o.p.

Bishop, Robert. *American Folk Sculpture*. NAL-Dutton 1983 o.p.

Bluestein, Gene, and Winfred Bernhard. *The Voice of the Folk: Folklore and American Literary Theory*. U. of Mass. Pr. 1972 o.p. A theoretical discussion of the relationship between folk literature and more traditional literary criticism, in which the "key literary figures are Emerson and Whitman . . . [drawing] upon Negro folksong (spirituals, blues, and jazz) and even the rock and roll music of the 1960s" (*Journal of American Folklore*).

Boatright, Mody C. *Folklore of the Oil Industry*. SMU Pr. 1984 $9.95. ISBN 0-87074-204-3

Botkin, B. A. *Sidewalks of America: Folklore, Legends, Sagas, Traditions, Customs, Songs, Stories, and Sayings of City Folk*. Greenwood 1976 repr. of 1954 ed. $59.50. ISBN 0-8371-9312-5

Brunvand, Jan H. *The Choking Doberman and Other "New" Urban Legends*. Norton 1984 $8.95. ISBN 0-393-30321-7

_____. *The Vanishing Hitchhiker: American Urban Legends and Their Meanings*. Norton 1982 $8.95. ISBN 0-393-95169-3. Effectively demonstrates the narrative process and established folkloristic techniques. "The text literally interweaves communication patterns and technological developments and so legitimizes American urban legends and their meanings." (*Journal of American Folklore*).

Cahill, Holger. *American Folk Art: The Art of the Common Man in America, 1750–1900. Museum of Modern Art Publications in Repr. Ser.* Ayer 1970 repr. of 1932 ed. $18.50. ISBN 0-405-01530-5

Camp, John. *Magic, Myth and Medicine*. Taplinger 1974 o.p.

Coffin, Tristram P. *Uncertain Glory: Folklore and the American Revolution*. Gale 1971 o.p.

Dickson, Paul, and Joseph Goulden. *There Are Alligators in Our Sewers and Other American Credos*. Delacorte 1983 o.p.

Dorson, Richard M. *American Folklore and the Historian*. U. Ch. Pr. 1971 o.p.

Dundes, Alan, and Carl R. Pagter. *When You're Up to Your Ass in Alligators: More Urban Folklore from the Paperwork Empire*. Wayne St. U. Pr. 1987 $34.95. ISBN 0-8143-1866-5. More "white-collar" folklore in the mode of *Work Hard and You Shall Be Rewarded*.

_____. *Work Hard and You Shall Be Rewarded: Urban Folklore from the Paperwork Empire*. Ind. U. Pr. 1978 $14.95. ISBN 0-8143-2432-0. A collection of expressions with annotations and interpretive comments that claims to be the first systematic book-length published collection of such material.

Eadie, John W. *Classical Traditions in Early America*. Trillium Pr. 1976 $10.00. ISBN 0-685-04941-8

Glassie, Henry. *All Silver and No Brass: An Irish Christmas Mumming*. U. of Pa. Pr. 1983 $16.95. ISBN 0-8122-1139-1. ". . . an honest presentation of how and why the folklorist practices his craft. . . . will be welcomed and appreciated by folklorists and general readers alike." (*Journal of American Folklore*).

_____. *Pattern in the Material Folk Culture of the Eastern United States. Amer. Folklore Society Ser.* U. of Pa. Pr. 1971 repr. of 1968 ed. $16.95. ISBN 0-8122-1013-1

Granger, Byrd H. *Motif Index for Lost Mines and Treasures, Applied to Redaction of Arizona Legends, and to Lost Mines and Treasure Legends Exterior to Arizona*. Bks. Demand repr. of 1977 ed. $72.10. ISBN 0-8357-8590-4

Hand, Wayland D. *Magical Medicine: The Folkloric Component of Folk Medicine in the Folk Belief, Custom, and Ritual of Non-Primitive Peoples.* U. CA Pr. 1981 $42.50. ISBN 0-520-04129-1

Herbert, S. *Child-Lore: A Study in Folklore and Psychology.* Gordon Pr. 1976 $59.95. ISBN 0-8490-1599-5

Herzfeld, Michael. *Ours Once More: Folklore Ideology, and the Making of Modern Greece.* U. of Tex. Pr. 1982 $10.00. ISBN 0-918618-32-0

Heuscher, Julius E. *A Psychiatric Study of Myths and Fairy Tales: Their Origin, Meaning and Usefulness.* C. C. Thomas 1974 $54.25. ISBN 0-398-02851-6

Hobsbawm, Eric, and Terence Ranger, eds. *The Invention of Tradition.* Cambridge U. Pr. 1983 $10.95. ISBN 0-521-43773-3

Hollis, Susan T., and others, eds. *Feminist Theory and the Study of Folklore.* U. of Ill. Pr. 1993. ISBN 0-252-02009-X

Jordan, Rosan A., and Susan J. Kalcik, eds. *Women's Folklore, Women's Culture.* U. of Pa. Pr. 1985 $19.95. ISBN 0-8122-1206-1

Knapp, Mary, and Herbert Knapp. *One Potato, Two Potato: The Secret Education of American Children.* Norton 1978 $7.95. ISBN 0-393-09039-6. A significant and extensive collection from children, mainly in the United States, that is "deserving of serious attention by educators, parents, and folklorists" (*Journal of American Folklore*).

Luthi, Max. *The Fairy Tale as Art Form and Portrait of Man.* Ind. U. Pr. 1985 $24.95. ISBN 0-253-32099-2

MacDonald, Margaret R., ed. *The Folklore of World Holidays.* Gale 1991 $80.00. ISBN 0-8103-7577-X. Explains the folklore surrounding 340 holidays in more than 150 countries.

McLerran, Jennifer, and Patrick McKee. *Old Age in Myth and Symbol: A Cultural Dictionary.* Greenwood 1991 $45.00. ISBN 0-313-27845-8. Resource for artists, writers, and behavioral scientists. Lists over 400 mythological and fictional characters associated with aging.

Marling, Karal A. *The Colossus of Roads: Myth and Symbol along the American Highway.* U. of Minn. Pr. 1984 $14.95. ISBN 0-8166-1303-6

Newall, Venetia. *An Egg at Easter: A Folklore Study.* Ind. U. Pr. 1989 $27.50. ISBN 0-253-31942-0. Study of the symbolism of eggs in many cultures and periods. Includes 24 color plates.

Propp, Vladimir. *Theory and History of Folklore.* U. of Minn. Pr. 1984 $15.95. ISBN 0-8166-1182-3

Renfro, Nancy, and Debbie Sullivan. *Puppets U.S.A.-Texas: Exploring Folklore, Music and Crafts with Puppets.* Renfro Studios 1985 $21.95. ISBN 0-685-10357-9

Rinzler, Carol A. *The Dictionary of Medical Folklore.* Ballantine 1980 $2.75. ISBN 0-345-28791-6

Scheub, Harold. *African Oral Narratives, Proverbs, Riddles, Poetry and Song: An Annotated Bibliography. Reference Publications Ser.* G. K. Hall 1977 o.p.

Schneiderman, Leo. *The Psychology of Myth, Folklore and Religion.* Nelson-Hall 1981 $28.95. ISBN 0-88229-659-0

Schoemaker, George H., ed. *Emergence of Folklore in Everyday Life: A Fieldguide and Sourcebook.* Trickster Pr. 1990 $9.95. ISBN 0-915305-03-8

Slobin, Mark. *Tenement Songs: The Popular Music of Jewish Immigrants. Music in Amer. Life Ser.* U. of Ill. Pr. 1982 $24.95. ISBN 0-252-00893-6. Shows the influence of folklore on related disciplines.

Taylor, Benjamin. *Storyology Essays in Folklore: Sea-Lore, and Plant-Lore.* Gordon Pr. 1976 $59.95. ISBN 0-8490-2693-8

Thomas, H. Nigel. *From Folklore to Fiction: A Study of Folk Heroes and Rituals in the Black American Novel.* Greenwood 1988 $45.00. ISBN 0-313-26224-1. Explores the connections between African American folklore and literature and the transposition of folk heroes and rituals at the hands of African American writers.

Using Folk Tales in Multicultural Education. U. of Conn. School of Education 1982 o.p. A slender pamphlet but the suggestions are sound.

Wernecke, Herbert H. *Christmas Customs around the World.* Westminster John Knox 1979 $8.99. ISBN 0-664-24258-8

Zipes, Jack. *Breaking the Magic Spell: Radical Theories of Folk and Fairy Tales.* U. of Tex. Pr. 1979 $15.00. ISBN 0-292-70725-8. ". . . deals mostly with the German Romantics in their social, political, and economic context, but [Zipes] also writes of other fringes of folklore." (*Journal of American Folklore*).

————. *The Trials and Tribulations of Little Red Riding Hood: Versions of the Tale in Socio-Cultural Context.* Greenwood 1983 $18.95. ISBN 0-89789-057-4. Presents the texts, with commentary, of the tale in a variety of versions—from France, Germany, England, the United States, and other countries.

FOLK AND POPULAR HUMOR

In a certain sense, no distinction exists between folk and popular humor. All humor is composed of discernible motifs and various basic situations. Folk humor, in its various forms, is of uncertain origin, is often vulgar, lives in the collective mind of segments of the public, and has been communicated through time by oral means. Popular humor is usually prepared by professionals and disseminated through the printed or electronic media. The two forms obviously blend. The following list includes samples and analyses of both types.

Allen, Woody. *Getting Even.* Random 1978 $7.00. ISBN 0-394-72640-5. An early collection of Allen's humorous discourses on life.

Anderson, John Q. *With the Bark On: Popular Humor of the Old South.* Bks. Demand repr. of 1967 ed. $94.30. ISBN 0-8357-3200-2

Asimov, Isaac. *Isaac Asimov's Treasury of Humor.* HM 1979 $8.95. ISBN 0-395-57226-6

Baker, Russell. *There's a Country in My Cellar: The Best of Russell Baker.* Morrow 1990 $20.95. ISBN 0-688-09598-4. More than 150 of Baker's cynical "Observer" columns that have appeared in the *N. Y. Times.*

Billington, Ray Allen. *Limericks Historical and Hysterical: Plagiarized, Arranged, Annotated and Some Written by Ray Allen Billington.* Norton 1981 o.p.

Boas, Guy. *An Anthology of Wit.* Arden Lib. 1977 repr. of 1934 ed. o.p.

Bombeck, Erma. *If Life Is a Bowl of Cherries.* Fawcett 1979 $3.95. ISBN 0-449-20839-7. Treasury of wit and wisdom that manages to hit everybody's funny bone.

————. *Motherhood: The Second Oldest Profession.* Dell 1984 $4.95. ISBN 0-440-15901-6. One of several books in print by a genuinely original wit and spokesperson for a maturing generation.

Bond, Simon. *One Hundred and One More Uses for a Dead Cat.* Crown Pub. Group 1982 $3.95. ISBN 0-517-54746-5

Brilliant, Ashleigh. *Be a Good Neighbor and Leave Me Alone.* Woodbridge Pr. 1992 $24.95. ISBN 0-88007-191-5. Engaging collection of essays, poems, and parodies by the popular author of the "Brilliant Thoughts" book series.

Buchwald, Art. *You Can Fool All of the People All the Time.* Fawcett 1986 $7.95. ISBN 0-449-90200-5. Satire aimed at those institutions—the Pentagon, the IRS, and the media, for example—who do succeed in fooling everybody.

Cohen, Hennig, and William B. Dillingham, eds. *Humor of the Old Southwest.* U. of Ga. Pr. 1975 repr. of 1964 ed. o.p.

Cohen, Stanley J., and Robert Wool. *How to Survive on Fifty Thousand to One Hundred Fifty Thousand Dollars a Year.* HM 1984 o.p.

Davies, John, ed. *Everyman's Book of Nonsense.* Biblio Dist. 1982 o.p. Foreword by Spike Milligan.

Dickson, Paul. *Jokes: Outrageous Bits, Atrocious Puns, and Ridiculous Routines for Those Who Love Jests.* Delacorte 1984 o.p. Illustrated by Don Addis.

Dodge, Robert K. *Early American Almanac Humor.* Bowling Green Univ. 1987 $26.95. ISBN 0-87972-393-9. Compilation of early-American humor that appeared in almanacs printed between 1776 and 1800.

Dorson, Richard M. *Man and Beast in American Comic Legend*. Bks. Demand repr. of 1983 ed. $54.90. ISBN 0-7837-3696-7. With an introduction by Alan Dundes and an afterword by Jeff Dorson. "The last work of the man who did more than anyone else to see folklore studies recognized as a legitimate field of study at American universities. . . . contains ten portraits of American legendary creatures. . . [and] portraits of eight legendary American liars." (*Choice*).

Downs, Robert B., ed. *Bear Went Over the Mountain: Tall Tales of American Animals*. Gale 1971 repr. of 1964 ed. $40.00. ISBN 0-55888-931-0. A spirited compilation of more than 63 lying, humorous, and fantastic tales of U.S. animals, arranged according to region, with the addition of animal-fable and shaggy-dog types.

Eastman, Max. *Enjoyment of Laughter*. Darby Pub. 1981 repr. of 1937 ed. o.p.

Elliot, Bob, and Ray Goulding. *From Approximately Coast to Coast: It's the Bob and Ray Show*. G. K. Hall o.p.

Ephron, Delia. *How to Eat Like a Child: And Other Lessons in Not Being a Grownup*. NAL-Dutton $3.95. ISBN 0-451-82181-5

Ervin, Sam J., Jr. *Humor of a Country Lawyer*. U. of NC Pr. 1983 $16.95. ISBN 0-8078-1566-7

Esar, Evan. *The Comic Encyclopedia*. Doubleday 1978 o.p.

————. *Twenty Thousand Quips and Quotes*. Doubleday 1968 o.p. A collection of single-sentence quips and quotes organized in 2,000 categories.

Fakih, Kimberly O. *The Literature of Delight: A Critical Guide to Humorous Books for Children*. Bowker 1993 $35.00. ISBN 0-8352-3027-9. Reference guide providing access to over 800 books, fiction and nonfiction, most published within the last decade.

Fisher, Seymour, and Rhoda L. Fisher. *Pretend the World Is Funny and Forever: A Psychological Analysis of Comedians, Clowns, and Actors*. Erlbaum 1981 $39.95. ISBN 0-89859-073-6

Gale, Steven H., ed. *Encyclopedia of American Humorists*. Garland 1987 $85.00. ISBN 0-8240-8644-9. Portraits of over 135 humorists, from Davy Crockett to Woody Allen.

Gruner, Charles R. *Understanding Laughter: The Workings of Wit and Humor*. Nelson-Hall 1978 $28.95. ISBN 0-88229-186-6

Holland, Norman N. *Laughing: A Psychology of Humor*. Cornell Univ. Pr. 1982 o.p. ". . . summarizes a tremendous amount of philosophy, physiology, anthropology, history, and psychology." (*Choice*).

Inge, M. Thomas. *The Frontier Humorists: Critical Views*. Shoe String 1975 $34.50. ISBN 0-208-01509-4

Keillor, Garrison. *Leaving Home: A Collection of Lake Wobegon Stories*. NAL-Dutton 1989 $4.95. ISBN 0-451-82197-1

Koon, George W., ed. *A Collection of Classic Southern Humor Fiction and Occasional Fact by Some of the South's Best Story Tellers*. Peachtree Pubs. 1984 $12.95. ISBN 0-931948-55-X

Kujoth, Jean S. *Subject Guide to Humor: Anecdotes, Facetiae and Satire from 365 Periodicals, 1968–74*. Scarecrow 1976 $25.00. ISBN 0-8108-0924-9

Legman, Gershon. *No Laughing Matter: An Analysis of Sexual Humor*. 2 vols. Ind. U. Pr. 1982 repr. of 1968 ed. $75.00. ISBN 0-253-34777-7. This first series, "the clean dirty jokes" to be followed by a second series of "the dirty dirty jokes."

————. *No Laughing Matter: Rationale of the Dirty Joke*. Breaking Point 1975 o.p. ". . . applies . . . heavily psychoanalytical theory and extreme Freudian approach to the deep feelings of hostility, guilt, and aggressiveness which lead a person to tell such jokes. . . . remains as a singular landmark in the study of erotic humor and should not be overlooked by any serious folklorist" (*Journal of American Folklore*).

Logue, Christopher. *Sweet and Sour: An Anthology of Comic Verse*. David & Charles 1983 o.p.

Loveland, Marion F. *America Laughs: A Sampler*. Collegium 1978 o.p.

Marc, David. *Comic Visions: Television Comedy and American Culture*. Routledge Chapman & Hall 1989 $39.95. ISBN 0-04-445284-5. Study of the situation comedy as a major exponent of the existing social order.

Meine, Franklin J. *Tall Tales of the Southwest.* Scholarly 1971 repr. of 1946 ed. $49.00. ISBN 0-7812-0188-8

Mintz, Lawrence E., ed. *Humor in America: A Research Guide to Genres and Topics.* Greenwood 1988 $55.00. ISBN 0-313-24551-7. Review of various sorts of humor (film, comic strip, etc.) or topics (racial, ethnic, political, etc.)

Moody, Raymond A., Jr. *Laugh after Laugh: The Healing Power of Humor.* Headwaters Pr. 1978 $7.95. ISBN 0-932428-07-X

Morris, Rosamund, ed. *Masterpieces of Humor.* Burn Hart 1983 o.p.

Rooney, Andy. *Not That You Asked . . .* Random 1989 $15.95. ISBN 0-394-57837-6. Humorous social criticism from the famed columnist and *60 Minutes* regular.

Shore, Sammy. *The Warmup: Life as a Warmup Comic.* Ed. by Pat Golbitz. Morrow 1984 o.p.

Spalding, Henry, ed. *Joys of Italian Humor and Folklore.* Jonathan David 1980 $16.95. ISBN 0-8246-0338-9

Truchtenberg, Stanley. *American Humorists, 1800–1950. Dictionary of Literary Biography Ser.* 2 vols. Gale 1982 $224.00. ISBN 0-8103-1147-X

Ziv, Avner, ed. *National Styles of Humor. Study of Popular Culture Ser.* Greenwood 1988 $55.00. ISBN 0-313-24992-X. Cross-cultural perspectives providing useful insight into the social and psychological differences of modern nations.

POPULAR CULTURE

Popular culture has been defined by RAY BROWNE, editor of the *Journal of Popular Culture* (founded in 1967), as "all aspects of the world we inhabit. . . . Our total life picture." It relates to the everyday world around us, what we do while awake, what we dream about when asleep. Popular culture today is usually disseminated by the mass media. Folklore is related to popular culture in that it reflects people's perceptions of their world and their place in it. It is part of the "popular literature" of a people. As a result of the close relationship of popular culture and folklore, many individuals work in both fields.

Allen, Irving I. *The City in Slang: New York Life and Popular Speech.* OUP 1993 $25.00. ISBN 0-19-507591-9. Approaches the study of popular slang from a historical rather than linguistic point of view.

Brantlinger, Patrick. *Bread and Circuses: Theories of Mass Culture as Social Decay.* Cornell Univ. Pr. 1983 $37.50. ISBN 0-8014-1598-5

Browne, Ray B., Marshall W. Fishwick, and Kevin Browne, eds. *Dominant Symbols in Popular Culture.* Bowling Green Univ. 1990 $40.95. ISBN 0-87972-481-1. Series of 19 essays addressing symbolism in such facets of popular culture as popular art, pornography, film, political cartoons, and advertising. Evaluates everything from movie theaters to car salesmen.

Browne, Ray B., and Pat Browne, eds. *Digging Into Popular Culture.* Bowling Green Univ. 1991 $34.95. ISBN 0-87972-521-4. Attempts to demonstrate how scholars of popular culture can employ such fields as anthropology and archaeology.

Cooper, B., and Wayne S. Haney. *Rock Music in American Popular Culture.* Haworth Pr. 1994. ISBN 1-56024-861-0

Cunningham, Patricia, and Susan Lob. *Dress and Popular Culture.* Bowling Green Univ. 1991 $39.95. ISBN 0-87972-507-9. Series of essays exploring the way dress and clothing reflects the popular material culture of a society.

Dahlgren, Peter, and Colin Sparks, eds. *Journalism and Popular Culture. Media, Culture and Society Ser.* Sage 1992 $55.00. ISBN 0-8039-8670-X. A series of 11 essays examining the division between "serious" journalism and its other subcultural genres.

Danna, Sammy R., ed. *Advertising and Popular Culture: Studies in Variety and Versatility.* Bowling Green Univ. 1992 $29.95. ISBN 0-87972-527-3

Donakowski, Conrad L. *A Muse for the Masses: Ritual and Music in an Age of Democratic Revolution, 1770–1870.* U. Ch. Pr. 1977 o.p. ". . . traces the development of the musical artist as propagandizer, as hero and as servant, and the development of music's use as decoration, communication and insulation in a way calculated to irritate the reader to further thought and study." (*Christian Century*).

Dorfman, Ariel. *The Empire's Old Clothes: What the Lone Ranger, Babar, and Other Innocent Heroes Do to Our Minds.* Trans. by Clark Hensen. Pantheon 1983 $14.45. ISBN 0-394-71486-5. A "commentary on the exploitation of Third World countries by industrialized, Western powers, and the role that children's literature (including comic-book characters like Donald Duck) plays in teaching children not to rebel and to become part of the consumer economy" (*Library Journal*).

Ewen, Stuart. *All Consuming Images: The Politics of Style in Contemporary Culture.* Basic 1988 $19.95. ISBN 0-465-00100-9. Discloses the process by which style has replaced substance in modern society.

Fishburn, Katherine. *Women in Popular Culture: A Reference Guide.* Amer. Popular Culture Ser. Greenwood 1982 $42.95. ISBN 0-313-22152-9. A history and bibliography of women in popular culture from colonial days to the present. Includes chapters on popular literature, magazines, film, television, advertising, and on theories of women in popular culture. In addition, appendixes list selected periodicals, bibliographies, a chronology of important dates, and research centers.

Fishwick, Marshall W. *Common Culture and the Great Tradition: The Case for Renewal. Contributions to the Study of Popular Culture Ser.* Greenwood 1982 $42.95. ISBN 0-313-23042-0

Fiske, John. *Understanding Popular Culture.* Routledge Chapman & Hall 1989 $39.95. ISBN 0-04-445438-4. Argues that popular culture has positive values and should not be denigrated as an act of hegemonic mass control.

Fraser, W. Hamish. *The Coming of the Mass Market, 1850–1914.* Shoe String 1981 o.p.

Geist, Christopher, and Jack Nachbar. *Popular Culture Reader.* Bowling Green Univ. 1983 $35.00. ISBN 0-87972-273-8

Geist, Christopher D., Ray B. Browne, Michael T. Marsden, and Carole Palmer, eds. *Directory of Popular Culture.* Oryx Pr. 1989 $50.00. ISBN 0-89774-351-2. Lists some 650 collections in the United States and Canada. Collections include television, fiction, popular humor, comics, toys, and advertising.

Goldbarth, Albert. *Popular Culture.* Ohio St. U. Pr. 1989 $19.95. ISBN 0-8142-0498-8. Explores the popular images of contemporary society.

Hoffman, Frank W. *Popular Culture and Libraries.* Shoe String 1984 o.p.

Inge, M. Thomas. *Comics As Culture.* U. Pr. of Miss. 1990 $32.50. ISBN 0-87805-407-3. Eleven lively essays illustrated with many examples of comic strip art.

———, ed. *Handbook on American Popular Culture.* 3 vols. Greenwood 1989 $165.00. ISBN 0-313-25406-0. Alphabetical arrangement of articles covering dance, fashion, musical theater, from "Advertising to Women." Includes indexes.

Jones, Steve. *Rock Formation: Music, Technology, and the Production of Culture.* Sage 1992 $29.95. ISBN 0-8039-4442-X. Detailed analysis of rock music and its impact on popular culture.

Landrum, Larry N., ed. *American Popular Culture: A Guide to Information Sources. Amer. Studies Information Guide* Gale 1982 $68.00. ISBN 0-8103-1260-3. Lists and annotates more than 2,000 information sources in the wide-ranging field of popular culture. Includes a cross-referenced, cross-indexed subject index and also a name index of both author and other personal name entries. Obligatory chapters on sports, games, music, dance, theater, and literature, as well as leisure, media, public art, advertising, and entertainment.

McSharry, Patra, and Roger Rosen, eds. *Coca Cola Culture: Icons of Pop.* Rosen Group 1993 $16.95. ISBN 0-8239-1593-X

Marc, David. *Comic Visions: Television Comedy and American Culture.* Routledge 1989 $39.95. ISBN 0-04-445284-5. Analyzes the role of the situation comedy in influencing our modern social order.

Mukerji, Chandra, and Michael Schudson, eds. *Rethinking Popular Culture: Contemporary Perspectives in Cultural Studies.* U. CA Pr. 1991 $49.95. ISBN 0-520-06892-0

Nachbar, Jack, and Kevin Lause. *Popular Culture: An Introductory Text.* Bowling Green Univ. 1992 $45.95. ISBN 0-87972-571-0. Methods and examples for studying the various genres of popular culture.

Schroeder, Fred E. *Five Thousand Years of Popular Culture: Popular Culture before Printing.* Bowling Green Univ. 1980 $18.95. ISBN 0-87972-147-2

_____. *Twentieth-Century Popular Culture in Museums and Libraries.* Bowling Green Univ. 1981 $31.00. ISBN 0-87972-162-6

Staples, Shirley. *Male Female Comedy Teams in American Vaudeville, 1865–1932.* Ed. by Bernard Beckerman. *Theater and Dramatic Studies* UMI Research 1984 o.p. Relates the origin and rise of vaudeville and the many individuals who took part. Shows, to some extent, the reflection of contemporary life in vaudeville routines.

Storey, John. *An Introductory Guide to Cultural Theory and Popular Culture.* U. of Ga. Pr. 1993 $30.00. ISBN 0-8203-1590-7

Thompson, E. P. *Customs in Common: Studies in Traditional Popular Culture.* New Press NY 1993 $15.95. ISBN 1-56584-074-7

Toll, Robert C. *The Entertainment Machine: American Show Business in the Twentieth Century.* OUP 1982 $35.00. ISBN 0-19-503081-8. Presents the "thesis that technology has created the changes in the popular styles of entertainment in America. . . . [and] discusses the difference between pleasing an audience directly and through an advertising sponsor" (*Library Journal*).

Wallace, Michele. *Black Popular Culture.* Ed. by Gina Dent. Bay Pr. $18.95. ISBN 0-941920-23-2

Warshow, Robert. *Immediate Experience: Movies, Comics, Theatre and Other Aspects of Popular Culture.* Atheneum 1970 o.p. Introduction by Lionel Trilling.

CHRONOLOGY OF AUTHORS

Grimm, Jacob, 1785–1863 and
   Grimm, Wilhelm. 1786–1859
Thoms, William John. 1803–1885
Campbell, John Francis of Islay.
   1822–1855
Child, Francis J(ames). 1825–1896
Krohn, Julius, 1835–1888 and
   Krohn, Kaarle. 1863–1933
Lang, Andrew. 1844–1912
Frazer, Sir James George. 1854–1941
Jacobs, Joseph. 1854–1916
Hamilton, Edith. 1867–1963

Rogers, Will. 1879–1935
Barbeau, Charles Marius. 1883–1969
Thompson, Stith. 1885–1976
Randolph, Vance. 1892–1980
Graves, Robert. 1895–1985
Campbell, Joseph. 1904–1986
Lomax, Alan. 1915–
Dorson, Richard M. 1916–1981
Opie, Peter, 1918–1982 and
   Opie, Iona. 1923–
Browne, Ray. 1922–

BARBEAU, CHARLES MARIUS. 1883–1969

Canada's most important folklorist, Charles Marius Barbeau was born at Ste. Marie-de-Beauce in Quebec. Educated at home by his parents until he was 12, he began training for the priesthood at age 14 but then went on to study law at Laval University in Quebec City. Later, as a Rhodes scholar at Oxford University, Barbeau became fascinated with anthropology, and upon his return to Canada he assumed a post at the newly formed National Museum in Ottawa, where he remained until the late 1960s.

Barbeau's most important contribution was as a collector of folk traditions. At the National Museum, he collected an enormous archive of traditional songs, texts, and artifacts, especially of French Canadian and native peoples. He worked tirelessly to preserve rural French Canadian folk traditions, which he believed reached back to medieval times. One native group he worked with extensively was the Tsimshian, in British Columbia. He recorded the tribe's traditional lore and helped preserve their legacy as the tribe entered the modern age.

Barbeau is also important as the founder of the Archives de Folklore at Laval and other folklore groups in Canada. He was very successful in bringing folklore to the Canadian public through his teaching, public lectures, and popular books. Before his death, Barbeau had received many honors, including being made a Companion of the Order of Canada.

BOOKS BY BARBEAU

Downfall of Temlaham. Macmillan 1928 o.p.
Folk Songs of French Canada. Yale U. Pr. 1925 o.p.
Indian Days in the Canadian Rockies. Macmillan 1923 o.p.
Quebec, Where Ancient France Lingers. Macmillan 1936 o.p.

BROWNE, RAY. 1922–

Ray Browne was born in Millport, Alabama, and was educated at the University of Alabama, Columbia University, and the University of California at Los Angeles. As founder of the Popular Culture Association (1970) and of the Department of Popular Culture at Bowling Green University, he is one of the most important figures in the field of popular culture in the United States today. Browne was an early advocate of applying serious study to popular culture. He has also played an important role in widening the definition of popular culture to include the study of artifacts and other material aspects of culture. He has authored, coauthored or edited a number of important works, including *Popular Culture and Curricula* (1969), *Popular Culture and the Expanding Consciousness* (1973), *Rituals and Ritualism in Popular Culture* (1980), *Symbiosis: Popular Culture and Other Fields* (1988), and *Digging Into Popular Culture* (1991). Browne has also served as editor of the *Journal of Popular Culture*, the *Journal of American Culture*, and the *Journal of Regional Cultures*. He is currently director of the Popular Press and chair of the Department of Popular Culture at Bowling Green University.

BOOKS BY BROWNE

Digging Into Popular Culture. Bowling Green Univ. 1991 $34.95. ISBN 0-87972- 521-4
Frontiers of American Culture. Purdue U. Pr. 1968 o.p.
Icons of Popular Culture. Bowling Green Univ. 1972 o.p.
Popular Culture and Curricula. Bowling Green Univ. 1970 $6.95. ISBN 0-87972-002-6
Popular Culture and the Expanding Consciousness. Wiley 1973 o.p.
The Popular Culture Explosion. W. C. Brown Pubs. 1972 o.p.
Rituals and Ritualism in Popular Culture. Bowling Green Univ. 1980 o.p.
Symbiosis: Popular Culture and Other Fields. Bowling Green Univ. 1988 $31.95. ISBN 0-87972-440-4

CAMPBELL, JOHN FRANCIS OF ISLAY. 1822–1855

G. W. Dasent, an English scholar of Norse antiquities, met JACOB GRIMM in Stockholm in 1840. He also knew the great Norwegian collectors Peter Asbjornsen and Jorgen Moe, who inspired him to translate important Norse folklore and mythology into English. This, in turn, led Dasent to urge his close friend John Campbell to do for the Gaelic-speaking people of the Scottish Highlands what the BROTHERS GRIMM had done for the German peasant.

Campbell was an energetic and intellectual man who came up with a way of collecting that transformed the entire field. He hired collectors expert in Gaelic and born in The Highlands and Western Isles to interview and record the local storytellers in their native dialects, recording their exact language (this would later lead to the use of tape recorders). Using this technique, he very quickly was able to collect a huge archive of tales. Eighty-six were printed in three volumes as *Popular Tales of the West Highlands* (1860–62), and a final note indicated that a total of 791 stories were in his possession. Furthermore, in a lengthy introduction, he indicated his methods in fine detail, offering a rough method for organizing the tales, and was careful to give scholarly indication of sources.

BOOKS BY JOHN CAMPBELL

More West Highland Tales. 2 vols. Trans. by John G. McKay. Ed by W. J. Watson. AMS Pr. repr. of 1940 ed. $90.00. ISBN 0-404-16070-0. Additional stories not included in first publication.
Popular Tales of the West Highlands, Orally Collected. Edinburgh 1860 o.p. The original collection.

CAMPBELL, JOSEPH. 1904–1986

Born in New York and educated at Columbia University and the Universities of Paris and Munich, Joseph Campbell is arguably the most important mythologist of the twentieth century. He has brought together the theories of CARL JUNG (see Vol. 5) and the stories of all cultures into a wide-ranging framework that encompasses psychology, theology, philosophy, and sociology. At the center rest Campbell's theories of the story of the hero, which he considered the most important archetype in human culture.

Drawing on a vast collection of the myths and spiritual expressions of the various civilizations of the world, Campbell has identified what he sees as the basic, underlying archetypal patterns that express humans' deepest understanding of life. These archetypal stories plunge into the dark unknowns, ultimately dealing with the central questions of life—where it began, how it began, what it is. As if that weren't enough, Campbell went on to offer a mythological center from which to live one's life.

The basic theories are first explained in *The Hero with a Thousand Faces* (1949) and then receive the detailed support of hundreds of collected stories in the four-volume *Masks of God.* Late in life, Campbell produced an excellent video series with Bill Moyers, centering on the hero's story but ranging across a wide array of subjects.

BOOKS BY JOSEPH CAMPBELL

The Hero's Journey: Joseph Campbell on his Life and Work. Ed. by Phil Cousineau. HarpC 1990 $24.95. ISBN 0-06-250102-X. A somewhat eclectic combination of biography and transcripts of Campbell discussing various theories.
The Hero with a Thousand Faces. Princeton U. Pr. 1990 $52.50. ISBN 0-691-09743-7. The seminal work for all who are interested in world mythology. Helps explain Campbell's basic philosophy.
The Masks of God. 4 vols. Viking Penguin 1991 $12.95–$13.00 ea. Vol. 1 *Primitive Mythology.* ISBN 0-14-019443-6. Vol. 2 *Oriental Mythology.* ISBN 0-14-019442-8. Vol. 3 *Occidental Mythology.* ISBN 0-14-019441-X. Vol. 4 *Creative Mythology.* ISBN 0-14-019440-1. Collections of stories that support Campbell's theories.

Myths to Live By. Bantam 1984 $5.95. ISBN 0-553-27088-5. Twelve essays taken from Campbell's lectures at The Great hall of The Cooper Union Forum between 1958–71, offering an easy introduction to his theories.

The Power of Myth. Doubleday 1988 $27.50. ISBN 0-385-24773-7. Transcript of Campbell's video series capturing the essence of his views. Coauthored with Bill Moyers.

BOOKS ABOUT JOSEPH CAMPBELL

Golden, Kenneth L., ed. *Uses of Comparative Mythology: Essays on the Work of Joseph Campbell*. Garland 1992 $45.00. ISBN 0-8240-7092-5. Seventeen critical essays. Topics include Freud and Jung as influences, romantic love and marriage, science-fiction and space-age myths.

Larson, Stephen, and Robin Larson. *A Fire in the Mind: The Life of Joseph Campbell*. Doubleday 1993 repr. of 1991 ed. $15.00. ISBN 0-385-26636-7. Reverent and monumental biography.

Maher, John, and Dennie Brigs, eds. *An Open Life: Joseph Campbell in Conversation with Michael Toms*. Larson Pubns. 1988 $9.95. ISBN 0-943914-47-7. Compilation of nine radio interviews taken from transcripts spanning a period of 10 years. A more conversational approach than Moyers's *The Power of Myth*.

Osbon, Diane, ed. *A Joseph Campbell Companion: Reflections on the Art of Living*. HarpC 1992 $20.00. ISBN 0-06-016718-1

Sartore, Richard L., ed. *Joseph Cambell on Myth and Mythology*. U. Pr. of Amer. 1993 $42.50. ISBN 0-8191-9080-2

CHILD, FRANCIS J(AMES). 1825–1896

American scholar, folklorist, and collector of ballads, Francis Child was born in Boston, Massachusetts, and educated at Harvard University. After graduating from Harvard, he studied for a time in Europe and then returned to the United States to teach at Harvard, eventually becoming professor of English there. Motivated by an interest in folklore, Child put together at the Harvard Library one of the largest folklore collections in existence at the time. Though a scholar of the British poets, notably EDMUND SPENSER (see Vol. 1) and GEOFFREY CHAUCER (see Vol. 1), Child is best known for his systematic study, collecting, and cataloging of folk ballads, particularly those of Scotland and England. He is noted for studying manuscript rather than printed versions of old ballads from these countries, and he studied and investigated ballads and stories in other languages that were related to the Scottish and English ballads. His first important work was *Four Old Plays* (1848). A subsequent eight-volume collection called *English and Scottish Ballads* (1857–58) eventually grew into his final and most ambitious collection, *The English and Scottish Popular Ballads* (1882–98). This work contains 305 ballads, many of which come from manuscript sources, and with all known versions of each ballad. It remains the most authoritative work on old English and Scottish ballads and folk songs. Child's teaching and collecting provided an important impetus for other scholars to gather ballads in the United States and elsewhere.

BOOK BY CHILD

English and Scottish Popular Ballads. 1882–98. 5 vols. Dover 1965 o.p.

DORSON, RICHARD M. 1916–1981

In 1957, Richard M. Dorson replaced STITH THOMPSON as the head of folklore studies at Indiana University, establishing himself as a major scholar and perhaps the foremost influence in the field. Dorson is often called the father of American folklore. In addition, he is given credit for bringing about an international or cross-cultural approach to the subject.

Dorson was editor of the *Journal of American Folklore* (1959–63), president of the American Folklore Society (1967–68), and author of numerous studies on the subject.

His textbook, *American Folklore* (1959), which employs a historical approach, was the first comprehensive study of the subject. In it he attempted to bring about what he calls a hemispheric theory, wherein the disciplines of both folklore and history are combined, stressing the intimate bonds between the culture of the folk and the history of the American experience. It is still recognized as a classic work.

BOOKS BY DORSON

American Folklore. U. Ch. Pr. 1961 $12.95. ISBN 0-226-15859-4

American Folklore and the Historian. Bks. Demand repr. of 1971 ed. $62.80. ISBN 0-8357-5369-7. Presents his theories of the subject, including his views of "fakelore."

British Folklorists: A History. U. Ch. Pr. 1969 $27.50. ISBN 0-226-15863-2. The only real historic overview of the field; well done.

Buying the Wind: Regional Folklore in the United States. U. Ch. Pr. 1972 $18.95. ISBN 0-226-15862-4. Excellent collection.

FRAZER, SIR JAMES GEORGE. 1854–1941

Coming from the world of British anthropological studies, James G. Frazer produced *The Golden Bough* (1890–1915), a mammoth 12-volume survey of world mythic and legendary themes. It was best known for T. S. ELIOT's (see Vol. 1) use of it in *The Waste Land* and for its promotion of supernatural influence on the folk beliefs and superstitions of primitive people and sympathetic magic.

He was born in Glasgow, Scotland, and attended Glasgow University, where he concentrated on the classics. He then continued his studies at Trinity College at Cambridge University, where he was elected a fellow in 1879. Except for a brief appointment as a professor of social anthropology at Liverpool University in 1907, he remained at Cambridge for the rest of his life.

Employing Sir Edward Taylor's comparative method, Frazer attempted to illuminate ancient rituals and myths by examining similar customs in contemporary indigenous peoples. Spending long hours in libraries, he gathered a great deal of information to support his views that magic gave rise to religion, which, in turn, gave rise to science—an evolutionary process. These views were extremely important to the late nineteenth century but have since come under attack as overly simplistic.

Frazer was possibly the most honored anthropologist of all time, knighted in 1914 and awarded the British Order of Merit in 1925.

BOOKS BY FRAZER

The Golden Bough. Macmillan 1985 $14.95. ISBN 0-02-095570-7. Manageable abridgement for the lay reader.

The Golden Bough. 13 vols. St. Martin 1969 repr. of 1890 ed. $450.00. ISBN 0-312-33215-7. The entire work. Including Part 1 *The Magic Art and the Evolution of Kings*. 2 vols. Part 2 *Taboo and the Perils of the Soul*. Part 3 *The Dying God*. Part 4 *Adonis, Attis, Osiris*. 2 vols. Part 5 *Spirits of the Corn and of the Wild*. 2 vols. Part 6 *The Scapegoat*. Part 7 *Blader the Beautiful; The Fire Festivals of Europe and the Doctrines of the Eternal Soul*. 2 vols. Part 9 *Aftermath: A Supplement*.

BOOKS ABOUT FRAZER

Ackerman, Robert. *J. G. Frazer: His Life and Work*. Cambridge U. Pr. 1987 $59.95. ISBN 0-521-34093-4. Recuperates Frazer as a first-rate classical scholar who forced the hidebound field to incorporate both the latest archaelogical discoveries and comparative perspectives from other civilizations.

————. *The Myth and Ritual School: An Introduction.* Garland 1990 $34.00. ISBN 0-8240-6249-3. Study of Frazer and the Cambridge ritualists.

Vickery, John B. *The Literary Impact of the Golden Bough.* Princeton U. Pr. 1973 $65.00. ISBN 0-691-06243-9. Traces the tremendous influence Frazer's compilation of images and customs had for twentieth-century modernist artists and writers.

GRAVES, ROBERT (VON RANKE). 1895–1985

A prolific writer, translator, and critic, Robert Graves was born in London to Alfred Perceval, an Irish poet, and Amalia (von Ranke) and educated at Charterhouse, a public school that was originally a monastery. Graves married Nancy Nicholson in 1918, with whom he had four children, Jenny, David, Catherine, and Samuel. Later he married Beryl Pritchard, with whom he had four additional children, William, Lucia, Juan, and Tomas.

Graves's career began in 1926 as a professor of English literature at Egyptian University in Cairo. In 1954 he was the Clarke Lecturer at Trinity College, Cambridge University. From 1961 to 1965, he was the professor of poetry at Oxford University. He also lectured in the United States in 1958 and 1966–67. He received numerous awards, including the James Tait Black Memorial Prize in 1935 for his historical novel *I, Claudius* (1934) and for the sequel, *Claudius, The God and His Wife Messalina* (1934); the Hawthronden Prize in 1935 for *I, Claudius*; and the Femina-Vie Heureuse Prize and the Stock Prize in 1939 for *Count Belisarius.* He also received the Russell Loines Memorial Fund Award in 1958, the Gold Medal of Poetry Society of America in 1959, the M.A., Oxford University in 1961, and the Queen's Gold Medal for Poetry in 1969.

His importance in folklore centers on his work with Greek and Roman mythology, which was published primarily during the late 1940s through early 1960s. This includes a novel, *The Golden Fleece* (1944), based on the legend of Jason and the Argonauts, and a major survey entitled *The Greek Myths* (1955). (For more on Graves, see Volume 1.)

BOOKS BY GRAVES

Good-bye to All That: An Autobiography. Peter Smith 1992 $19.50. ISBN 0-8446-6491-X. Written immediately after his marriage to Nancy Nicholson ended in 1929; a best-seller, this splendid work only covers his early life, including his experiences in World War I.

Greek Gods and Heroes. Dell 1965 $3.50. ISBN 0-440-93221-1. Very brief, clear outline of Greek mythology.

The Greek Myths. 2 vols. Viking Penguin 1955 Vol. 1 $4.95. ISBN 0-14-020508-X. Vol. 2 $4.95. ISBN 0-14-020509-8. Excellent survey of Greek mythology.

GRIMM, JACOB (LUDWIG KARL), 1785–1863 and GRIMM, WILHELM (KARL). 1786–1859

Born in Hanau in Hesse-Kassel, the German folklorists and philologists Jacob and Wilhelm Grimm were the most influential and popular collectors and the first to approach the folk tales from a scholarly perspective. The views of the romantic movement, which swept Europe while Napoleon was overthrowing the aristocracy in favor of a democracy, set the theoretical framework for scholars to embrace the common tales of the common people, those who were not corrupted by the aristocracy and the supposedly false and evil views of civilization.

While Napoleon was challenging Europe, the brothers Grimm were digging into manuscripts of the Middle Ages. Their popular book of fairy tales was but one small portion of this larger project. As their studies continued, the wars sweeping Europe continued to press other matters upon them. Jacob, who had visited the libraries of Paris in 1805 and learned to speak French, was appointed in 1808 auditor to the state council and superintendent of the private library of Jerome Buonoparte, the puppet king of Westphalia, thus freeing him from economic worries. Wilhelm was not as vigorous and forceful as Jacob, but he toiled endlessly over the collected stories, selecting them, piecing them together, and finding the exact language to convey the popular speech patterns he had heard.

The contemporary changes worried and depressed both brothers, and they sought consolation in the past, the traditions, and heritage of their culture. Their first collection appeared on Christmas of 1812. Although banned as a work of superstition in Vienna, it was received eagerly elsewhere as the unexpected masterpiece that the romantic movement had been seeking.

Volume Two was compiled mainly by Wilhelm, since Jacob was busy with his four-volume German grammar and two-volume history of the Germanic languages. It came out in January 1815, with a second edition issued in 1819, much enlarged and improved and containing an introduction by Wilhelm. A third volume—a work of commentary, containing additional matter, as well as a thoroughgoing comparative-historical study—appeared in 1822. This volume underwent revision for its final edition in 1856 and was later redone in five volumes by Johannes Bolte and Georg Polivka. Many editions of the Grimms' collection have been published over the years, including translations into many different languages. The first English translation was written by Edgar Taylor and illustrated by George Cruikshank in 1823; it was an immediate success. Its livelier, less scholarly format influenced the Grimms' 1825 edition.

The stories remain extremely popular today and have been translated into over 70 different languages. The complete collection listed below is but one of several, and there are many versions of the single tales available from various publishers and illustrated by some of the most important artists from each period.

BOOK BY THE GRIMM BROTHERS

The Complete Grimm's Fairy Tales. Ed. by James Stern. Trans. by Margaret Hunt. Pantheon 1976 $16.00. ISBN 0-394-70930-6. Contains commentary by Joseph Campbell.

BOOKS ABOUT THE GRIMM BROTHERS

Bettelheim, Bruno. *The Uses of Enchantment.* Knopf 1989 $11.00. ISBN 0-679-72393-5. A powerful defense of folk tales, using Grimm's tales as well as others, from a Freudian perspective.

Kamenetsky, Christa. *The Brothers Grimm and Their Critics: Folktales and the Quest for Meaning.* Ohio U. Pr. 1992 $45.00. ISBN 0-8214-1020-2. Sophisticated critical interpretations of the Grimms' collections.

Zipes, Jack. *Brothers Grimm: From Enchanted Forests to the Modern World.* Routledge 1989 $14.95. ISBN 0-415-90209-6. A Marxist perspective.

HAMILTON, EDITH. 1867–1963

Born in Dresden, Germany, to American parents—Montgomery and Gertrude Hamilton—Edith Hamilton was raised in Fort Wayne, Indiana. Hamilton began reading Latin at age 7, and her love of the classical ages continued throughout her life. After receiving her B.A. and M.A. in 1895 from Bryn Mawr College, she became headmistress of Bryn Mawr School in Baltimore, Maryland, a position she maintained from 1896 to 1922, when she became a full-time writer. She was also a member of the National Institute of Arts and Letters, the American Academy of Arts and Letters, and P.E.N. She received several honors, including the Mary E. Grant European fellow at the universities of Leipzig and Munich (1895–96), the National Achievement Award (1950), the Constance Lindsay Skinner Award (1958), and D. Litt. degrees from the University of Rochester (1949), the University of Pennsylvania (1953), and Yale University (1959). In 1957 she was named an honorary citizen of Athens, Greece.

Hamilton's importance in the field of folklore rests on her highly respected translations and interpretations of classical mythology, which are praised for their ability to bring the meanings and the entire world of classical Greece and Rome to life for the modern scholar as well as to the general reader. Among her most well-known works are *The Greek Way* (1930), *The Roman Way* (1932), and *Mythology: Timeless Tales of Gods and Heroes* (1940).

BOOKS BY HAMILTON

The Greek Way. 1930. Norton 1983 $4.95. ISBN 0-393-00230-6. Excellent scholarly interpretation of the classical Greek world.

Mythology: Timeless Tales of Gods and Heroes. NAL-Dutton 1989 $8.95. ISBN 0-452-00985-5. Highly respected distillation of mythology—mainly Greek, but some Norse—readily readable.

The Prophets of Israel. Norton 1936 o.p.

The Roman Way. 1932. Norton 1984 $3.95. ISBN 0-393-00232-2. Companion to *The Greek Way*, describing the Romans' way of life as presented in the works of Plautus, Virgil, and other important writers of the time.

JACOBS, JOSEPH. 1854–1916

While other collectors of English folk tales rewrote or left out the crude language of the originals, Joseph Jacobs brought the vigor of colloquial English into his folk tale collections, and such memorable phrases as *Fee-fi-fo-fum* and *chinny chin chin* remain the strength of his contributions.

Jacobs was born in Sydney, Australia, and emigrated to England to attend Cambridge University. His interests at Cambridge were very broad and included history, literature, anthropology, and philosophy. After graduating in 1876, he pursued a full and varied career, writing many essays for various periodicals including a famous series in 1882 on the Russian persecutions of the Jews. Jacobs also made his influence felt as a Jew by editing the first issues of *The Jewish Yearbook* (1896–99) and serving as president of the Jewish Historical Society. He also edited *The Jewish Encyclopedia* and, in this capacity, came to the United States in 1900, remaining here for the rest of his life. He later served as professor of English at the Jewish Theological Seminary in New York City.

Jacob's interest in folklore grew out of his studies in anthropology. From 1890 to 1893, he edited *Folk Lore*, a British journal on the subject. He also edited the *Arabian Nights* and AESOP's (see Vol. 2) *Fables* and produced a series of fairy tale books that placed him in a position much like that of his American contemporary, ANDREW LANG. These fairy tale collections were the result of regular research in folklore, literature, anthropology, and other fields, and they are, perhaps, the works for which he is best remembered today. Jacobs is praised for translating the preliterary experience of storytelling into literary form while maintaining the rhythms and "feel" of the storytellers of old. He is also noted as being the first writer to prepare folk tales specifically for an audience of children, thus avoiding the more pedantic approach of many other folklorists.

BOOKS BY JACOBS

Celtic Fairy Tales. 1891. Dover 1968 $5.95. ISBN 0-486-21826-0. Complete unabridged reprint; an excellent edition.

Celtic Fairy Tales. Amereon Ltd. repr. of 1891 ed. $18.95. ISBN 0-89190-078-0. Good complete reprint of the original.

English Fairy Tales. Dover repr. of 1890 ed. $5.95. ISBN 0-486-21818-X. An unabridged republication of the 3rd (1898) edition.

English Fairy Tales. Amereon Ltd. repr. of 1890 ed. $18.95. ISBN 0-89190-076-4. Good complete reprint.

The Fables of Aesop. 1894. Schocken 1966 $8.95. ISBN 0-8052-0138-6. Formatted for younger audience.

Indian Fairy Tales. Amereon Ltd. repr. of 1892 ed. $17.95. ISBN 0-89190-075-6. Good reprint of the original.

More Celtic Fairy Tales. Amereon Ltd. repr. of 1894 ed. $17.95. ISBN 0-89190-079-9. Good reprint of original.

More English Fairy Tales. Amereon Ltd. repr. of 1893 ed. $17.95. ISBN 0-89190-077-2. Good reprint of original.

KROHN, JULIUS, 1835–1888 and KROHN, KAARLE. 1863–1933

Julius Krohn and his son Kaarle set forth the historical-geographic method of comparative folk-tale research, known as the Finnish method, in *The Folklore Work Method* (1926). This approach involves listing literary texts of a single folk-tale chronologically and plotting the oral texts geographically. Variations are then reduced to outlines of important elements, and each element is examined for variations and patterns of distribution, finally allowing for a hypothetical "archetype" or original version. This extremely influencial method laid the basis for STITH THOMPSON's *Motif-Index of Folk-Literature* (1932–36), a huge catalog of folk-narrative elements.

BOOK BY THE KROHNS

Folklore Methodology: Formulated by Julius Krohn and Expanded by Nordic Researchers. Trans. by Roger L. Welsch. U. of Tex. Pr. 1971 $8.95. ISBN 0-292-72432-20. The major work expounding the theories.

LANG, ANDREW. 1844–1912

Andrew Lang's activities extended far beyond folklore. He was a historian, poet, journalist, translator, and anthropologist, in connection with his work on literary texts. Lang was born at Selkirk in Scotland and was educated at Edinburgh Academy, St. Andrews University, and Balliol College, Oxford University, becoming a fellow at Merton College. His poetry includes *Ballads and Lyrics of Old France* (1872), *Ballades in Blue China* (1880–81), and *Grass of Parnassus* (1888–92). His anthropology and his defense of the value of folklore as the basis of religion—his most influential work—is expressed in *Custom and Myth* (1884), *Myth, Ritual and Religion* (1887), and *The Making of Religion* (1898). He also translated HOMER (see Vol. 2) and critiqued JAMES G. FRAZER's views of mythology as expressed in *The Golden Bough*. He was considered a good historian, with a readable narrative style and knowledge of the original sources (e.g., *History of Scotland* [1900–7], *James VI and the Gowrie Mystery* [1902], and *Sir George Mackenzie* [1909]). In addition, he wrote some novels, not well thought of today; however, his critiques of contemporary novels are still highly regarded.

Lang's popularity was established with his collections of "Fairy" books, which were always titled with a color, such as *The Blue Fairy Book*. These books preserved and handed down many of the better-known folk tales from the time; however, his use of the term "fairy" to cover all kinds of folk tales continues to plague scholars, who generally distinguish between the terms "fairy" and "folk," judging fairy tales to be more of a fanciful creation and less grounded in cultural experiences, customs, and beliefs.

BOOKS BY LANG

The Blue Fairy Book. Dover 1965 $6.95. ISBN 0-486-21437-0. Contains 37 of the author's best-known stories taken from a variety of sources, including "Little Red Riding Hood" and "Hansel and Gretel."

The Brown Fairy Book. Dover $6.95. ISBN 0-486-21438-9. An entertaining assortment of adventures from all over the world, including stories from Persia, Australia, and India. Contains 32 stories, including "The Story of the Yara", and "Story of Wali Dâd the Simple-hearted."

The Crimson Fairy Book. Dover 1966. $6.95. ISBN 0-486-21799-X. A fascinating collection of 36 tales from many countries; a pleasant change from the well-worn classics. Among the stories included are "The Cottager and His Cat" and "Little Wildrose."

The Green Fairy Book. Dover 1965 $6.95. ISBN 0-486-21439-7. This third book in the series contains 42 tales from Spanish and Chinese traditions, the Grimm Brothers, and stories by Fénelon, Sébillot, Kletla, d'Aulnoy, and the Comte de Caylus. Included are such favorites as "The Three Little Pigs" and "The Blue Bird."

The Grey Fairy Book. Dover 1967 $6.95. ISBN 0-486-21791-4. The volume includes 35 strange and exotic stories from Greece, France, Africa, Germany, and Lithuania. Featured are stories about a donkey who turns into a prince and a spinning wheel that turns moss into silk.

The Lilac Fairy Book. Dover 1968 $6.95. ISBN 0-486-21907-0. Irish sources are featured in this 33-story collection of fairy tales, with other stories from India, Portugal, Brittany, and Scandanavia. Includes "The Brown Bear of Norway" and "The Winning of Olwen."

The Olive Fairy Book. Dover 1966 $5.95. ISBN 0-486-21908-9. Contains 29 unusual stories from Turkey, India, Denmark, Armenia, and the Sudan. Includes a story about a king who understands the language of animals and another about a green knight who is saved by a soup made from nine snakes.

The Orange Fairy Book. Dover 1968 $6.95. ISBN 0-486-21909-7. Delves into the oral traditions of Rhodesia, Uganda, and the Native American, and includes selections by Hans Christian Andersen ("The Ugly Duckling") and Madame d'Aulnoy ("The White Doe").

The Pink Fairy Book. Amereon Ltd. 1966 $21.95. ISBN 0-89190-080-2. An array of exotic locales are the source for this fairy-tale collection of 38 stories. Features "Uraschimataro and the Turtle" and "Katerina and Her Destiny."

The Red Fairy Book. Dover 1987 $6.95. ISBN 0-486-21673-X. In addition to such familiar favorites as "Jack and the Beanstalk" and "Rapunzel," this 37-story collection includes lesser-known tales from French, German, Danish, Russian, and Rumanian sources.

The Violet Fairy Book. Dover $6.95. ISBN 0-486-21675-6. Contains 35 strange and exotic tales from Japan, Serbia, Lithuania, Africa, Russia, and elsewhere. Includes a Japanese story about a magical dog called Schippeitaro that helps his master, and a Swahili tale about a youth who visits the King of the Snakes.

The Yellow Fairy Book. Dover $6.95. ISBN 0-486-21674-8. This 48-story collection of tales from across the globe includes such traditional favorites as "The Emperor's New

Clothes" and "The Nightingale." Also includes lesser-known tales of Native Americans and of Iceland.

LOMAX, ALAN. 1915–

Born in Austin, Texas, and educated at Harvard University, the University of Texas, and Columbia University, American folklorist Alan Lomax is one of the most dedicated and knowledgeable folk-music scholars of the twentieth century. Lomax became interested in collecting the recording folk songs through the work of his father, John Avery Lomax, a curator at the Library of Congress and a pioneer in the field of folk music. After college, he toured prisons in the South, recording folk song performances for the Archive of American Song of the Library of Congress. During his travels, he met the great blues singer Huddie Ledbetter ("Leadbelly"). Lomax later became responsible for introducing radio audiences to a number of folk and blues artists, including Woody Guthrie and Burl Ives. Between 1951 and 1958, he traveled throughout Europe, recording hundreds of folk songs in England, Scotland, Italy, and Spain. His most important work is, perhaps, *The Folk Songs of North America* (1959). He also published a number of works with his father, including *American Ballads and Folk Songs* (1934) and *Folk Song: USA* (1946). In addition to his work with folk songs, Lomax was very interested in the historical and social origins of jazz, and he wrote a notable biography of the early jazzman Ferdinand "Jelly Roll" Morton entitled *Mister Jelly Roll* (1950).

BOOKS BY LOMAX

American Ballads and Folk Songs. 1934. Rprt. Serv. 1993 repr. of 1934 ed. $75.00. ISBN 0-7812-5942-8. Coauthored with his father, John Avery Lomax.
Folk Song: USA. 1946. NAL-Dutton 1977 o.p.
The Folk Songs of North America. 1959. Doubleday 1975 $19.95. ISBN 0-385-03772-4
Mister Jelly Roll. 1950. Pantheon 1993 $15.00. ISBN 0-679-74064-3
Our Singing Country. 1938. Macmillan 1938 o.p.

OPIE, PETER, 1918–1982 and OPIE, IONA. 1923–

This husband-and-wife team are among the most thorough researchers and collectors of children's poetry and nursery rhymes, and their scholarship is recognized as the touchstone for all other discussions on the subject. The Opies' collaboration in the study of children's lore and literature resulted in an assemblage of early children's books, as well as collections of comics, toys, games, and educational aids. Their research has ranged from tracing the history of a medieval song to speaking with children about the games they play and the rhymes they recite.

Their *Oxford Dictionary of Nursery Rhymes* (1951), which took over seven years to compile, was, and remains, the central scholarship on traditional English nursery rhymes. It was followed by a number of other works including *The Oxford Nursery Rhyme Book* (1955), *The Lore and Language of School-children* (1959), a compilation of contemporary rhymes and corresponding games, and *Children's Games in Street and Playground* (1969), which was based on a survey of 10,000 children.

Iona was born in Colchester, England, to Sir Robert George and Olive Archibald, and obtained an M.A. from Oxford University in 1962. Peter was born in Cairo, Egypt, to Philip and Margaret Adams; he also obtained his M.A. from Oxford University in 1962. They were married in 1943 and had two children,

James and Robert Letitia. Peter died in 1982, but Iona continues to bring out new books.

BOOKS BY THE OPIES

A Dictionary of Superstitions. OUP 1989 $35.00. ISBN 0-19-211597-9. Produced by Iona with Moira Tatem after Peter's death; a scholarly style similar to that of the poetry collections.

The Lore and Language of Schoolchildren. OUP 1987 $10.95. ISBN 0-19-282059-1. Compiled from research about contemporary children.

A Nursery Companion. OUP 1980 $29.95. ISBN 0-19-212213-4. A collection of early eighteenth-century poetry, lesson books, and illustrations.

The Oxford Book of Narrative Verse. OUP 1989 $29.95. ISBN 0-19-214131-7. Excellent scholarly collection.

The Oxford Dictionary of Nursery Rhymes. OUP 1951 $47.50. ISBN 0-19-869111-4. The classic British collection.

The Oxford Nursery Rhyme Book. OUP 1955 $29.95. ISBN 0-19-869112-2. Sequel to the *Dictionary.*

RANDOLPH, VANCE. 1892–1980

Noted folklorist Vance Randolph was born in Pittsburg, Kansas. After attending college at Kansas State Teachers College, Clark University, and the University of Kansas, he worked as a staff writer for *Appeal to Reason,* as an assistant instructor in psychology at the University of Kansas, and as a scenario writer for MGM studios in California before devoting all of his time to freelance writing. Randolph is perhaps one of America's most prolific collectors of folk tales, and he is especially renowned for his study of the Ozarks and that region's ribald folk literature. Because of their bawdy nature, many collectors and compilers have passed over such tales from this region, but Randolph compiled many of them in a work entitled *Pissing in the Snow and Other Ozark Folk Tales* (1976). His regional specialization has led to a number of other works, including *The Ozarks: An American Survival of Primitive Society* (1931), *From an Ozark Mountain Holler: Stories of Ozark Mountain Folk* (1933), *Ozark Superstitions* (1947), and *Sticks in the Knapsack and Other Ozark Folk Tales* (1958). Regarding his work on the Ozarks, critics have said that Randolph "gives a sensitive portrayal of a fast-vanishing breed of people . . . [and] insight to a way of life that is rapidly passing" (*Choice*).

BOOKS BY RANDOLPH

From an Ozark Mountain Holler: Stories of Ozark Mountain Folk. 1933. Vanguard 1933 o.p.

The Ozarks: An American Survival of Primitive Society. 1931. Vanguard 1931 o.p.

Ozark Mountain Folks. 1932. Vanguard 1932 o.p.

Ozark Superstitions. 1947. Col. U. Pr. 1947 o.p.

Pissing in the Snow and Other Ozark Folk Tales. 1976 U. of Ill. Pr. 1976 $16.95. ISBN 0-252-01364-6

Sticks in the Knapsack and Other Ozark Folk Tales. 1958. Col. U. Pr. 1958 o.p.

ROGERS, WILL. 1879–1935

Born in Oolagah, Indian Territory (now Oklahoma), Will Rogers's parents were Clem Vann Rogers and Mary American Schrimsher, who were each one-quarter Cherokee, or true Native Americans. This parentage is quite appropriate because Rogers himself was the embodiment of the real people of America, the "average man." He was the last of the "crackerbox philosophers" to reach a national audience, and his words and reputation as the symbol of the "common man" and of common sense have continued to grow, even though his books and films are seldom read or watched today. He has, as it were, transcended himself to become a folk legend.

Rogers's rise from an Oklahoma cowboy to a world-famous humorist and philosopher is in itself a particularly American phenomenon. He began his career performing for Texas Jack's Wild West Show as a trick rider and roper. Later he performed for the Wirth Brothers Circus and then for the Mulhall Wild West Show. Eventually, he joined the Ziegfeld Follies as a regular, where he starred for 11 years.

By the 1920s Rogers had become a popular speaker. He had already published two books, *The Cowboy Philosopher on the Peace Conference* (1919) and *The Cowboy Philosopher on Prohibition* (1919), both of which are collections of miscellaneous writings featuring the humorous social and political commentary that would eventually make him famous. In 1926 he began writing a syndicated column for the *Saturday Evening Post*, which became extremely popular and continued until his death. During the 1920s he also moved to California and began making films for Hal Roach Studios, in which he played characteristically unassuming roles and made sage and witty remarks. He made his first talking picture, *They Had to See Paris*, in 1929, which established him as a film star.

Among Roger's other published collections of humor are *The Illiterate Digest* (1924), *Letters of a Self-Made Diplomat to His President* (1927), and *There's Not a Bathing Suit in Russia* (1927). An aviation enthusiast, Rogers died in a plane crash at Point Barrow, Alaska, in 1935 while flying with famous aviator Wiley Post. A selection of his writings, titled *The Autobiography of Will Rogers* (1949), was published posthumously.

Books by Rogers

The Autobiography of Will Rogers. Ed. by Donald Day. AMS Pr. repr. of 1949 ed. $39.50. ISBN 0-404-15293-7. A running commentary on United States history in Rogers's own words; filled with humor.

Convention Articles of Will Rogers. Ed. by Joseph A. Stout, Jr., and Peter C. Rollins. Okla. St. U. Pr. 1976 $10.50. ISBN 0-914956-08-6. A collection of humorous writings on a wide range of topics.

The Cowboy Philosopher on Prohibition. Ed. by Joseph A. Stout, Jr., and Peter C. Rollins. Okla. St. U. Pr. 1975 $6.95. ISBN 0-914956-05-1. More homespun humor.

The Cowboy Philosopher on the Peace Conference. Ed. by Joseph A. Stout, Jr., and Peter C. Rollins. Okla. St. U. Pr. 1975 $6.95. ISBN 0-914956-05-1. Rogers on world politics and other topics.

Either and Me or "Just Relax". Ed. by Joseph A. Stout, Jr. Okla. St. U. Pr. 1973 $8.95. ISBN 0-914956-01-9. Humorous writings on a wide range of topics.

How To Be Funny and Other Writings of Will Rogers. Ed. by Steven K. Gragert. Vol. 3 Okla. St. U. Pr. 1983 $10.95. ISBN 0-914956-04-3. Another disparate collection.

The Illiterate Digest. Ed. by Joseph A. Stout, Jr. Okla. St. U. Pr. 1974 $10.50. ISBN 0-914956-04-3. A collection of writings from the "common man's" point of view.

Letters of a Self-Made Diplomat to His President. Ed. by Joseph A. Stout, Jr., and Peter C. Rollins. Okla. St. U. Pr. 1977 $10.50. ISBN 0-914956-22-1. Humorous writings on politics.

More Letters of a Self-Made Diplomat. Ed. by Steven K. Gragert. Okla. St. U. Pr. 1982 $10.95. ISBN 0-9014956-22-1. More political humor.

Radio Broadcasts of Will Rogers. Ed. by Steven K. Gragert. Okla. St. U. Pr. 1983 $10.95. ISBN 0-914956-24-8. The homespun philosopher's radio work.

There's Not a Bathing Suit in Russia and Other Bare Facts. Ed. by Joseph A. Stout, Jr. Okla. St. U. Pr. 1973 $9.25. ISBN 0-914956-03-5. A collection of humorous writings on unrelated topics.

Will Rogers' Daily Telegrams: The Coolidge Years, 1926–1929. Vol. 1. Ed. by James M. Smallwood and Steven K. Gragert. Okla. St. U. Pr. 1978 $19.95. ISBN 0-914956-10-8. One of several chronological collections of Rogers's telegrams and weekly articles.

BOOKS ABOUT ROGERS

Alworth, E. Paul. *Will Rogers*. Twayne 1974 o.p. A short, basic introduction to Rogers, discussing him in the context of the "crackerbox" tradition of American humor.

Brown, William R. *Imagemaker: Will Rogers and the American Dream*. U. of Mo. Pr. 1978 o.p. Offers a somewhat overstated case for Rogers's influence on American thought.

Day, Donald. *Will Rogers: A Biography*. McKay 1962 o.p. Draws from Will Rogers's autobiography, which Day edited, relying heavily on Rogers's own words.

THOMPSON, STITH. 1885–1976

The son of a farmer, Stith Thompson was born near Bloomfield, Kentucky. In 1918 he married Louise Faust and they had two children, Dorothy and Marguerite. After receiving his Ph.D. from Harvard University in 1914, Thompson began his teaching career at the University of Texas at Austin, later teaching at Colorado College and then at the University of Maine. Finally, he went to Indiana University, where he established his prominence as a folklorist.

Thompson was instrumental in establishing folklore studies in the United States, legitimizing it as an academic discipline and placing it on a firm empirical foundation. In 1950 he organized an important international conference at Indiana University, bringing together world-renowned specialists to discuss aspects of the field in order to develop a historical perspective on folklore research. He also created a center for the study and research of folklore and for the training of folklore scholars at Indiana University. The University became the first in the United States to offer a doctoral program in folklore.

Using the historic-geographic methods developed earlier by JULIUS and KAARLE KROHN, Thompson translated Aarne's *Type-Index* and produced the *Motif-Index of Folk-Literature*, revising both in subsequent years. They remain the central indexes for the historical approach to folk tale study. Thompson gained international recognition for his writings, which were praised for both their scholarship and their style. It has been written of his work that "[it] is not dry, attenuated, dull, pedantic . . . for Mr. Thompson has . . . unspoiled direct appreciation of the zest and flavor of the best in traditional literature" (*N.Y. Times Book Review*).

BOOK BY THOMPSON

The Folktale. 1946. AMS Pr. repr. of 1946 ed. $34.00. ISBN 0-404-15373-9. A basic introduction to the subject.

Motif-Index of Folk-Literature, A Classification of Narrative Elements in Folk Tales, Ballads, Myths, Fables, Medieval Romances, Exempla, Fabliaux, Jest-Books, and Local Legends. 1932–37. 6 vols. Ind. U. Pr. 1955–58. $300.00. ISBN 0-253-33887-5. The major index in the field.

THOMS, WILLIAM JOHN. 1803–1885

William John Thoms initiated the term "Folk-Lore" into the study of "Popular Antiquities" or "Popular Literature" in a letter printed in the *Athenaeum*, August 22, 1846, and charted a course for its study. He envisioned reconstructing the ancient pagan mythology of Britain in the same fashion the BROTHERS GRIMM had done earlier in Germany. This was his central contribution to mythology and folklore but by no means his only one. In fact, while he supported himself as a clerk in the secretary's office at Chelsea Hospital (until

1845) and then as a clerk in the printed-paper office of the House of Lords (until 1863), he was a leading participant in antiquarian societies, elected a fellow of the Society of Antiquaries in 1838, and appointed secretary of the Camden Society the same year. He was also a council member of the Percy Society.

Thoms's main work as a literary antiquarian was as an editor, and it is important to note how strongly he advocated the need for careful scholarship in collecting folklore, always demanding exact dates, page references, and full titles for actual texts, rather than the vague allusions that had previously been common.

In addition to using the *Athenaeum* to launch folklore as a field of scholarship, Thoms continued to promote the field in *Notes and Queries*, which he founded in 1849, and for which he served as sole editor until 1872. Thoms also established a correspondence with George Laurence Gomme in the publication, beginning in 1876, which resulted in the formation of The Folk-Lore Society two years later.

BOOKS BY THOMS

Anecdotes and Traditions, Illustrative of Early English History and Literature and Derived from Manuscript Sources. AMS Pr. repr. of 1839 ed. $15.50. ISBN 0-404-50105-2. Interesting attempt to apply scholarship to unpublished manuscripts in the British Museum.

Early English Prose Romances. 3 vols. AMS Pr. 1972 repr. of 1858 ed. $120.00. ISBN 0-404-06470-1. Collections of stories from chapbooks.

CHAPTER 22

Travel and Exploration

Charles R. Goeldner

The world is a great book, of which they who never stir from home read only
a page.
—St. Augustine of Hippo, *Commentary on Psalm 45*

It is difficult to know if today's traveler differs markedly from those satirized in
Innocents Abroad (1869) by Mark Twain (see Vol. 1). Twain described the group
he accompanied around the world as passive viewers of selected stops on tours
and gullible listeners to the outrageous tales of tour guides. Although tourism is
not new, considerable evidence suggests that changes are in the wind as the
twenty-first century approaches. Probably the most obvious change lies in the
sheer increase in numbers of tourists, a phenomenon arising from a variety of
causes: Pictures taken from spacecraft and satellite communications make our
world seem smaller; jet travel puts world travel within the means of a greater
number of people; the expansion of businesses into worldwide enterprises
allows globe-trotting executives to combine business and pleasure; and news
coverage from all over the world makes far-flung places seem within reach. In
short, travel has become a prime goal for an increasing number of people,
ranging from the budget-minded student to the wealthy retiree.

Therefore, books provide information about historical aspects of different
locales, as well as advice on how to "see and enjoy" the best aspects of a
country. Some professional travelers glamorize their trips for the guidance of
the vacationer, while literary travelers write about their love for the places they
have visited. Some people seek adventure exploring the ocean in scuba diving,
in retracing historic routes, and in mountain climbing. There are those who,
like Thor Heyerdahl, Francis Chichester, Sir Edmund Hillary, Robert Falcon
Scott, and Jacques-Yves Cousteau, deliberately travel with only the basic
necessities of life in order to feel the challenge of pitting themselves against the
forces of nature.

Libraries and bookstores abound with travel guides. Names like Mobil,
Baedeker's, Berlitz, Michelin, Nagel, Fodor, Fielding, Let's Go, Insight, Lonely
Planet, Berkeley, and Frommer represent only a few of the countless number of
available travel guides. In the past, travel guides were meagerly illustrated and
encyclopedic in tone; today they are colorfully illustrated and engagingly
written. Those wishing assistance in selecting a travel guide can consult one of
two bibliographies to guidebooks. The first, by Greg Hayes (with Joan Wright),
is *Going Places: The Guide to Travel Guides*, and the second is Maggy Simony's
*The Traveler's Reading Guide: Ready-made Reading Lists for the Armchair
Traveler*. Both of these books are listed in the section "General Reference
Works." These guidebooks can easily be found in most libraries and bookstores.

Most of the references in this chapter deal with accounts of trips, adventures, and exploration. Because travel and tourism are a growing industry throughout the world, a brief list of references on the scholarly aspect of travel is also presented to provide a picture of the industry, its magnitude, and its impact.

SCHOLARLY REFERENCE WORKS

Dervaes, Claudine. *The Travel Dictionary*. Solitaire Pub. 1990 $12.95. ISBN 0-933143-16-8. Provides brief definitions for more than 2,800 terms. Includes country codes, airline codes, time-zone tables, and so on.

Gee, Chuck, James Makens, and Dexter Choy. *The Travel Industry*. Van Nos. Reinhold 1989 $39.95. ISBN 0-442-22825-2. Provides a comprehensive introduction to the rapidly growing, fast-changing tourism sector.

Gunn, Clare A. *Tourism Planning*. Taylor & Francis 1988 $32.00. ISBN 0-8448-111538-1. Describes opportunities for greater expansion of tourism on the state and regional scale without damage to delicate natural resources.

Heath, Ernie, and Geoffrey Wall. *Marketing Tourism Destinations*. Wiley 1992 $34.95. ISBN 0-471-54067. Intended to present guidelines for optimal planning, development, and marketing of tourism, particularly at regional and community levels.

Hecker, Helen. *Travel for the Disabled: A Handbook of Travel Resources and 500 Worldwide Access Guides*. Twin Peaks Pr. 1985 $9.95. ISBN 0-933261-00-4. Lists sources of information on all aspects of travel and services; includes a lengthy bibliography.

Jafari, Jafar, and others. *Bibliographies on Tourism and Related Subjects*. U. CO Busn. Res. Div. 1988 $25.00. ISBN 0-89478-007-7. A 73-page bibliography offering an annotated source book of bibliographies on tourism.

Khan, Mahmood, Michael Olsen, and Turgut Var, eds. *VNR's Encyclopedia of Hospitality and Tourism*. Van Nos. Reinhold 1993 $89.95. ISBN 0-442-00346-3. A reference volume with over 100 expert contributors, covering food-service management, hotel management, and travel and tourism.

Lundberg, Donald E. *The Tourist Business*. Van Nos. Reinhold 1989 $36.95. ISBN 0-442-23376-0. Explores the travel industry and covers travel modes, the role of tourist agents, why people travel, the economic and social impact of tourism, tourist-destination development, and travel research.

McIntosh, Robert W., and Charles R. Goeldner. *Tourism: Principles, Practices and Philosophies*. Wiley 1990 $39.95. ISBN 0-471-62255-9. A classic introduction to tourism, providing a broad global perspective, with emphasis on marketing planning and developing tourism, investigating the cultural, economic, sociological, and psychological aspects of tourism.

Mill, Robert Christie. *Tourism: The International Business*. P-H 1990 $36.00. ISBN 0-13-926296-2. Divided into four sections covering an overview of tourism, the development of tourism, the marketing of tourism, and the future of tourism.

Mill, Robert, and Alastair Morrison. *The Tourist System*. P-H 1992 $36.00. ISBN 0-13-925645-8. Presents a comprehensive systems view of tourism, stressing the interrelationships and interdependencies of its various elements.

Morrison, Alastair. *Hospitality and Travel Marketing*. Delmar 1989 $34.95. ISBN 0-8273-2938-5. Explains the basic concepts of hospitality marketing and emphasizes the eight *P*'s: product, people, packaging and programming, place, promotion, partnership, public relations, and pricing.

Pearce, Douglas. *Tourist Development*. Wiley 1989 $31.95. ISBN 0-582-01435-2. Gives a systematic overview of tourism development on a global basis.

Plog, Stanley. *Leisure Travel: Making It a Growth Market . . . Again!* Wiley 1991 $39.95. ISBN 0-471-52952-4. Shows how to develop new destinations that will maintain long-term allure, how to advertise and market more effectively, and how to match specific personality-based market segments.

Ritchie, J. R., and Donald Hawkins, eds. *World Travel and Tourism Review.* Annual. CAB Intl. Vol. 2 1992 $170.00. ISBN 0-85198771-0. Covers indicators, trends, and issues for 37 countries; provides market and industry trends; offers a special report on education, training, and human-resource issues.

Smith, Valene. *Hosts and Guests, The Anthropology of Tourism.* U. of Pa. Pr. 1989 $39.95. ISBN 0-8122-1280-0. A collection of 14 chapters on the role and cultural impact of tourism in various societies.

Waters, Somerset R. *Travel Industry World Yearbook: The Big Picture.* Annual. Child & Waters Inc. Vol. 36 1992 $79.00. ISBN 0-9611200-9-6. Presents a compact, up-to-date review of the latest events in the world of tourism.

Witt, Stephen, and Christine A. Witt. *Modeling and Forecasting Demand in Tourism.* Acad. Pr. 1991 $49.95. ISBN 0-12-760740-4. Compares the accuracy of seven forecasting methods applied to international-tourism-demand data.

Witt, Stephen, and Luiz Moutinho. *Tourism Marketing and Management Handbook.* P-H 1989 $100.00. ISBN 0-13-925885-4. An encyclopedia of tourism containing over 100 chapters and providing information on the most crucial issues in tourism marketing and management.

GENERAL REFERENCE WORKS

Adams, Percy G. *Travel Literature and the Evolution of the Novel.* Bks. Demand repr. of 1983 ed. $98.80. ISBN 0-8357-4290. ". . . especially illuminating on two traveler-novelists, Defoe and Smollett, and in his chapter on prose styles" (*Choice*).

———. *Travelers and Travel Liars, 1600–1800.* Dover 1962 o.p. About real accounts that contain untruths, armchair trips made to seem real, and the different impressions made when different people describe the same places or events.

Barry, Dave. *Dave Barry's Only Travel Guide You'll Ever Need.* Fawcett 1991 $9.95. ISBN 0-449-90759-7. "[By] one of the funniest people ever to tap tap on a PC. . . . a riot" (*The Philadelphia Inquirer*).

Barthelme, Donald. *Overnight to Many Distant Cities.* Contemporary Amer. Fiction Ser. Viking Penguin 1985 o.p. A collection of short stories that examine the modern urban landscape.

Blum, Ethel. *The Total Traveler by Ship: The Cruise Traveler's Handbook.* Hippocrene Bks. 1989 $14.95. ISBN 0-87052-426-7. Useful handbook of cruise-travel information.

Borders, Earl, Jr. *The Bus Trip Handbook.* Home Run Pr. 1985 $8.95. ISBN 0-917125-00-2.

Burns, Deborah, and Sarah May Clarkson. *Tips for the Savvy Traveler.* Storey Comm. Inc. 1990 $8.95. ISBN 0-345-7966-7. "Curious, sensible, and irreverent" (*Los Angeles Times*).

Carlson, Raymond, ed. *National Directory of Free Vacation and Travel Information.* Pilot Bks. 1984 o.p.

Clark, Merrian E., and Bonnie Wilson. *Ford's Freighter Travel Guide: 1980–81.* Fords Travel 1986 $7.95. ISBN 0-916486-42-7

Council on International Education Exchange. *Work, Study, Travel Abroad, 1992–1993.* St. Martin 1992 $12.95. ISBN 0-312-07128-0. Informative guide to jobs and study abroad.

Demko, George J., and others. *Why in the World.* Doubleday 1992 $10.00. ISBN 0-385-26629-4. ". . . takes the reader on a fascinating journey through the world of the new geography. . . . filled with maps, cartoons, and photographs; is rife with anecdotes" (Publisher's note).

Fraser, Keath, ed. *Bad Trips: A Sometimes Terrifying, Sometimes Hilarious Collection of Writing on the Perils of the Road.* Random 1991 $12.00. ISBN 0-679-72908-9. Includes riveting tales of danger and discomfort ranging from the Arabian desert to an urban wasteland to an ornate Southern California inn to a Colombian slaughter-house serving as a cocaine front.

Fussell, Paul. *Abroad: British Literary Traveling between the Wars*. OUP 1980 $10.95. ISBN 0-19-503068-0. "An elegy for the lost art of travel as opposed to today's tourism . . . a celebration of British writers who memorialized it—D. H. Lawrence, Graham Greene, Norman Douglas, Evelyn Waugh . . ." (Publisher's note).

Greene, Graham. *Reflections*. Viking Penguin 1990 $10.00. ISBN 0-14-012156-0. A collection of travel writing, essays, and reviews spanning nearly seven decades and showing Greene to have been "one of the shrewdest and kindest of men" (Paul Theroux, *Independent on Sunday*).

Guggenheim, Hans G. *Around the World in Eighty Ways*. St Martin 1988 $20.00. ISBN 0-317-43635-X

Halliburton, Richard. *Complete Book of Marvels*. Darby Pub. 1981 o.p. Descriptions and illustrations of many natural and human-made wonders of the Occident and the Orient in a classic work—includes the Golden Gate Bridge, Niagara Falls, Machu Picchu, Matterhorn, Colossus, Mt. Everest, Angkor, and others.

———. *The Royal Road to Romance*. Greenwood repr. of 1925 ed. $35.00. ISBN 0-8371-2412-3

Hayes, Greg, and Joan Wright. *Going Places: The Guide to Travel Guides*. Harvard Common Pr. 1988 $22.95. ISBN 1-55832-007-5. Distributed by R. R. Bowker, this book summarizes the better general and specialty travel guides that are available. Includes appendixes and indexes. Not truly comprehensive, but very useful.

Herbert, Anthony B. *The International Traveler's Security Handbook*. Hippocrene Bks. 1984 o.p. Details safety precautions to take while traveling abroad.

Herrmann, Paul. *The Great Age of Discovery*. Trans. by Arnold J. Pomerans. Greenwood 1974 repr. of 1958 ed. $35.00. ISBN 0-8371-7504-6. An unusual presentation, spanning five centuries, from Columbus to Livingstone in Africa.

Hindleu, Geoffrey. *Tourists, Travellers, and Pilgrims*. Hutchinson 1983 o.p. A tour of five centuries of European history as experienced by ambassadors, writers, and an assortment of odd travelers who recorded their impressions of the hazards and delights of traveling. Hindleu manages this integration of history seen through a wide variety of eyes with both charm and wit.

Huxley, Aldous. *Along the Road: Notes and Essays of a Tourist*. Ayer repr. of 1925 ed. $18.00. ISBN 0-8369-229-8. A collection of witty essays about Huxley's travel observations. Comments on various inevitable traveling phenomena.

Islands Magazine staff, eds. *Islands: A Treasury of Contemporary Travel Writing*. Capra Pr. 1992 $12.95. ISBN 0-88496-349-7. Twenty-nine island-hopping essays that span the globe: Herbert Gold on the Seychelles, Paul Theroux on remote islands of South Pacific, Pico Iyer on Cuba, Christopher Buckley on the Great Barrier Reef.

Jakle, John A. *The Tourist: Travel in Twentieth Century North America*. U. of Nebr. Pr. 1985 $29.95. ISBN 0-8032-2564-4. A fast-paced and thorough survey of the tourist industry in the United States and Canada and its development in this century.

Jenkins, Peter. *A Walk across America*. Fawcett 1983 $5.95. ISBN 0-49-20455-3. Author tells how he trained for a walk across America and what he learned about himself and others. Includes photos.

Jenkins, Peter, and Barbara Jenkins. *The Walk West: A Walk across America 2*. Morrow 1992 $12.00. ISBN 0-688-11271-4. "One heck of an adventure. . . . Peter and Barbara are a good couple to travel with whose enthusiasm is infectious. Their prose is crisp and full of humor" (*Washington Post*).

Keay, John. *Eccentric Travelers*. Putnam Pub. Group 1984 o.p. "Strange men and improbable journeys are the subjects of this collection of essays. There are seven travellers . . . including Manning in Tibet, Palgrave in Arabia, the naturalist Waterton in South America, and the blind Holman crossing Russia and Siberia in the winter" (*Library Journal*).

Leed, Eric J. *The Mind of the Traveler from Gilgamesh to Global Tourism*. Basic 1991 $15.00. ISBN 0-465-04619-3. "[Explores] the nature of the journey and the ways in which the mind of the traveler is transformed by what it encounters" (Helen Bevington).

MacCannell, Dean. *The Tourist: A New Theory of the Leisure Class.* Schocken 1989 $9.95. ISBN 0-8052-0895-X. A sociological study of tourists that examines the mind of the tourist in relation to modern civilization.

Melchett, Sonia. *Passionate Quests: Five Modern Women Travelers.* Faber & Faber 1991 $13.95. ISBN 0-571-12946-3. In which Dervla Murphy bicycles from England to India, Monica Kristensen treks to the South Pole, Clare Francis races across the Atlantic in a sailboat, Christina Dodwell rides through the mountains of Turkey, and Elaine Brook climbs Mt. Everest.

Mendel, Roberta. *A Survival Manual for the Independent Woman Traveler.* Pin Prick 1982 $12.95. ISBN 0-936424-06-0. A useful guide for women traveling alone.

Morris, Jan. *Locations.* OUP 1992 $19.95. ISBN 0-19-212996-1. A collection of 18 recent pieces with destinations as diverse as Chicago and Berlin, Canberra and Texas.

Mortimer, Charles G. *Travels of Charlie.* East Ridge Pr. 1975 $6.95. ISBN 0-914896-29-6. The former Chairman of the Board of General Foods tells how to enjoy retirement in this journal about his travels with his wife.

Naylor, Penelope. *The Woman's Guide to Business Travel.* Hearst Bks. 1981 o.p. Offers specific and practical advice about travel etiquette and practices for women business travelers.

Parry, J. H. *The Discovery of the Sea.* U. CA Pr. 1982 $12.95. ISBN 0-520-04237-9. ". . . describes the evolution of shipbuilding, navigation, geographical knowledge and trade and politics that made possible the voyages by European seafarers at the end of the fifteenth century and the beginning of the sixteenth [which] established beyond dispute that all the world's seas were connected" (Publisher's note).

Pletcher, Barbara A. *Travel Sense: A Guide for Business and Professional Women.* Kampmann 1980 o.p. Based largely on information gathered through interviews, this guide is geared toward such womens' concerns as diet and safety.

Portnoy, Sanford, and Joan Portnoy. *How to Take Great Trips with Your Kids.* Harvard Common Pr. 1984 $8.95. ISBN 0-916782-51-4. Practical advice about how to make traveling with kids easier, including tips about where to go, where to stay, and how to make travel plans with kids in mind.

Pratson, Frederick. *Consumer's Guide to Package Travel around the World.* Globe Pequot 1984 o.p. Provides information on package tours and tour companies.

Rosenthal, A. M., and P. Arthur Gelb, eds. *The Sophisticated Traveler: Winter, Love It or Leave It.* Random 1984 o.p. An uncommon guide to winter travel containing an array of travel writing by such authors as Joyce Carol Oates, Peter Benchley, John Updike, and William Buckley, Jr.

Rugoff, Milton, ed. *Great Travelers.* 2 vols. S&S Trade 1960 o.p. This handsomely produced and illustrated anthology provides a catholic variety of firsthand accounts, skillfully chosen and organized.

Savage, Michael D., and others. *How to Go around the World Overland.* Surf Trav. Pubns. 1984 $14.95. ISBN 0-915821-00-1. Information on how an independent traveler can go around the world on public transportation; discusses relevant issues such as insurance, reservations, and so on.

Sears, John F. *Sacred Places: American Tourist Attractions in the Nineteenth Century.* OUP 1989 $24.95. ISBN 0-19-505350-8. A book that "prompts us to reflect on our own motivations and responses as tourists and reveals why tourism was and still is such an important part of American life" (Publisher's note).

Simony, Maggy, ed. *The Traveler's Reading Guide: Ready-Made Reading Lists for the Armchair Traveler.* Facts on File 1987 $50.00. ISBN 0-8160-1244-X. Originally a three-volume paperback series, this revised, expanded edition "is intended to make it easier for armchair travelers, writers, teachers, travel professionals and the librarians who counsel them, to locate interesting background books, place-set novels and mysteries, travel memoirs, special guides, travel articles for the destination of choice" (Preface). Arrangement is geographical by continent or region, and then alphabetical by country or state.

Sinor, John. *Small Escapes under the Sun.* Alive Pubns. 1981 o.p. Guide to simple, out-of-the-way places.

Sobek's International Explorer's Society. *One Thousand Journeys to the Rivers, Lands and Seas of Seven Continents.* Crown Pub. Group 1984 o.p.

Sykes, Percy M. *A History of Exploration from the Earliest Times to the Present Day.* Greenwood 1976 repr. of 1949 ed. o.p. A survey of famous explorers and discoveries in all parts of the world. Includes some historical context.

Turner, A. C. *Traveller's Health Guide.* Bradt 1984 o.p.

Twain, Mark. *Innocents Abroad.* NAL-Dutton 1966 $4.95. ISBN 0-451-5202-7. An account of a steamship's pleasure excursion to Europe and the Holy Land; referred to by some as the new Pilgrim's Progress.

Yapp, Peter. *Traveller's Dictionary of Quotations.* Routledge 1985 $25.00. ISBN 0-415-02760-8. One thousand pages of who said what about where.

THE AMERICAS—NORTH AND SOUTH

Abbey, Edward. *Beyond the Wall: Essays from the Outside.* H. Holt & Co. 1984 o.p. This collection of 10 essays ranges from deserts of the Southwest and the Baja Peninsula of Mexico to the desertlike Arctic permafrost tundra of Alaska's Kongakut River.

Adams, Alice. *Mexico: Some Travels and Some Travelers There.* S & S Trade 1990 $10.00. ISBN 0-671-79277-6. In which "the narrative and descriptive talents of novelist Adams are evident in her Mexican travelogue, not only in depictions of spectacular landscapes and picturesque towns but in her portrayal of natives and tourists" (*Publishers Weekly*).

Audubon, John J. *Delineations of American Scenery and Character.* Amer. Environmental Studies Ayer 1970 repr. of 1926 ed. $24.50. ISBN 0-405-02655-2. A reprint of Audubon's travel essays as a collection; presents a picture of North American eastern frontier life, from 1808 to 1834, by a man who was as keen an observer of people as of wildlife.

Barth, Jack. *American Quest.* S & S Trade 1991 $8.95. ISBN 0-671-68240-7. The goofy quests of Jack Barth, which "include . . . re-creating the journey of *Easy Rider* and working in the world's largest McDonald's . . . for the Coca-Cola hotline, and at a multiplex movie theater" (*The Book Buyer's Advisor*).

Bemelmans, Ludwig. *The Donkey Inside.* Paragon Hse. 1990 repr. of 1968 ed. $10.95. ISBN 1-55778-343-8. Featuring a "whimsical zest for life . . . his feeling for animals, his humor and sense of beauty and shrewd observations are set down with an originality of expression and veracity of mood . . . not like anyone who has ever written about South America" (Publisher's note).

Beston, Henry. *The Outermost House: A Year of Life on the Great Beach of Cape Cod.* H. Holt & Co. repr. of 1928 ed. $9.95. ISBN 0-8050-1966-9. A classic of American nature writing, a chronicle of a solitary year spent on a Cape Cod beach: ". . . a colorful and ever-changing chronicle of movement that approaches the magnificent" (*Boston Transcript*).

Brower, Kenneth. *The Starship and the Canoe.* HarpC 1983 $11.00. ISBN 0-06-091030-5. The story of Freeman Dyson, the well-known quantum physicist, and his son, George, a strong conservationist; while Freeman Dyson was experimenting with the possibilities of atomic propulsion in connection with spacecraft, his son, George, was living in a tree house and working as a canoe maker in Canada.

Bryson, Bill. *The Lost Continent: Travels in Small Town America.* HarpC 1989 $11.00. ISBN 0-06-092008-4. "[As if] W. C. Fields [were] on a driving tour of thirty-eight American states. . ." (*Pittsburgh Press*).

Cahn, Robert, and Robert Glenn Ketchum. *American Photographers and the National Parks.* Viking Penguin 1981. "The work of 37 artists, these photographs comprise a record of the changing ways people have seen and used the parks. The pictures are arranged chronologically . . ." (*N.Y. Review of Books*).

Chaplin, Gordon. *Fever Coast Log: At Sea in Central America.* S & S Trade 1992 $11.00. ISBN 0-671-76729-1. In which, "With his lively companion Susan, he sets sail aboard his 35-foot motor-sailer *Lord Jim* for Belize, Guatemala, Honduras, Nicaragua, Costa Rica, and Panama" (Karin Buckley, author of *Panama: The Whole Story*).

Codrescu, Andrei. *Road Scholar: Coast to Coast Late in the Century*. Hyperion Conn. 1993 $19.95. ISBN 1-56282-878-9. By Romanian-born Codrescu, who moved to the United States in the 1960s and now appears on National Public Radio. Photographs by David Graham.

Cook, James H. *Fifty Years on the Old Frontier as Cowboy, Hunter, Guide, Scout, and Ranchman*. U. of Okla. Pr. 1992 $12.95. ISBN 0-8061-1761-3. This volume has been a favorite for its thoughtful perspective on the U.S. western frontier, as seen through the eyes of Captain James Cook, after he retired from the sea. His ranch in Nebraska was host to paleontologists, anthropologists, and others. Introduction by Charles King.

Cumming, William P., and others. *The Exploration of North America, 1630–1776*. Putnam Pub. Group 1974 o.p. "Extracts from journals, letters, and manuscripts compiled from the observations of explorers, missionaries, fur trappers, and others from 1630 until the period of the Revolution" (*Booklist*).

Duncan, Dayton. *Out West: American Journey along the Lewis and Clark Trail*. Viking Penguin 1988 $10.95. ISBN 0-14-008362-6. "An entertaining series of road adventures, paved with gems of history and lined with majestic conclusions about the development of the west" (*Boston Globe*).

Ford, Peter. *Around the Edge: A Journey among Pirates, Guerrillas, Former Cannibals, and Turtle Fisherman along the Miskito Coast*. Viking Penguin 1991 $22.95. ISBN 0-670-82827-0. "A fascinating portrait of the eastern Caribbean-influenced Central American coast" (Publisher's note).

Free Wheelin': A Solo Journey Across America. Ragged Mountain Pr. 1992 o.p. The true story of the author's bicycle journey across the northern half of the United States—5,400 miles and 17 states—from Sacramento to Bar Harbor.

Gold, Herbert. *Best Nightmare on Earth: A Life in Haiti*. S & S Trade 1991 $12.00. ISBN 0-671-75516-1. "Simply the best all-encompassing explanation of this contradictory and tragic Island that I have read" (*Playboy*).

Hall, B. C., and C. T. Wood. *Big Muddy: Down the Mississippi Through America's Heartland*. NAL-Dutton 1992 $23.00. ISBN 0-525-93476-6. A book that "Mark Twain would delight in . . . telling the dark side along with the good . . . true to the spirit of *Huck Finn* in their journey down the Mississippi" (Dee Brown, author of *Bury My Heart at Wounded Knee*).

Halsey, David. *Magnetic North: A Trek Across Canada from the Pacific to the Atlantic by Foot, Dogsled, and Canoe*. (coauthored with Diana Landau). Sierra 1990 $12.00. ISBN 0-87156-566-8. By a man whose "restless passion for adventure led him to tackle every danger the wilderness had to offer . . . an engrossing account of the two-year journey" (*Publishers Weekly*).

Harner, Michael J. *The Jivaro: People of the Sacred Waterfalls*. California Lib. Repr. Ser. U. CA Pr. 1983 $39.95. ISBN 0-520-05065-7. About a tribe in Ecuador.

Harris, Eddy L. *Mississippi Solo: A River Quest*. HarpC 1989 $10.00. ISBN 0-06-097247-5. Written in "a style to match the river—superbly paced, with fast chutes followed by deep contemplative pools . . . a stunning, accomplished debut" (Jonathan Raban, author of *Old Glory*).

Henfrey, Colin. *Manscapes: An American Journey*. Harvard Common Pr. 1973 o.p. "An English prose virtuoso's tour of the U.S. in the late 1960s presents often shocking, sometimes predictable, but always germane reactions to what has become of the contemporary American experience" (*Booklist*).

Johnson, Beth. *Yukon Wild: The Adventures of Four Women Who Paddled 2,000 Miles through America's Last Frontier*. Berkshire Hse. 1984 $11.95. ISBN 0-912944-78-1. Exciting account of women braving the wilds of the far north.

Kane, Joe. *Running the Amazon*. Random 1989 $9.95. ISBN 0-679-72902-X. Kane's account ". . . of the first expedition to travel the entirety of the world's longest river . . . a riveting adventure in the tradition of Joseph Conrad" (*N.Y. Times Book Review*).

Kirk, Ruth. *Exploring Washington's Past: A Road Guide to History*. (coauthored with Carmela Alexander). U. of Wash. Pr. 1990 $19.95. ISBN 0-295-96844-3. An indispensable guide for residents, tourists, and armchair travelers.

Kittredge, William, and Annick Smith, eds. *The Last Best Place: A Montana Anthology*. U. of Wash. Pr. 1992 $27.50. ISBN 0-295-96974-1. A Montana centennial book. A comprehensive history of the state as told by writers.

Lawlor, Eric. *In Bolivia: An Adventurous Odyssey Through the Americas' Least Known Nation*. Random 1989 $8.95. ISBN 0-394-75836-6. "... searches out the essence of the country ... and finds it not by talking to the men of power but to the victims of this power. ... *In Bolivia* is funny and terrible, sad and angry" (Moritz Thomsen).

Liebling, A. J. *Back Where I Came From*. N. Point Pr. 1989 repr. of 1938 ed. $10.95. ISBN 0-867547-425-7. Introduction by Philip Hamburger. "... a love letter to the City of New York. ... The sights, the sounds, the smells, the people, and ... the native manner of speaking" (Richard A. Lovett).

McGuire, Stryker. *Streets with No Names: A Journey into Central and South America*. Atlantic Monthly 1991 $21.95. ISBN 0-87113-433-0. By a man who "... understands Latin America, but more importantly, ... fell in love with it" (Jorge Castañeda, coauthor of *The U. S. and Mexico: The Limits of Friendship*).

Malcolm, Andrew H. *U. S. 1: America's Original Main Street*. St. Martin 1991 $29.95. ISBN 0-312-06480-2. A dryly humorous text that "often summons up the cranky and caustic ghost of H. L. Mencken as he takes us down the roadside of the nation's oldest highway. ... [Stretching] 2,467 miles from Maine to Florida ... metaphorically the story of America itself" (Publisher's note).

Meisch, Lynn. *A Traveler's Guide to El Dorado and the Inca Empire*. Penguin Handbooks Ser. Viking Penguin rev. ed. 1984 o.p. A very practical guidebook with sections on travel arrangements, food, clothing, border crossings, communications, history, and mythology. A must for anyone interested in following the old route to El Dorado.

Miller, Tom. *Trading with the Enemy: A Yankee Travels through Castro's Cuba*. Atheneum 1992 $24.00. ISBN 0-689-12094-X. This trip of more than seven months, producing "a vibrant, pungent, and rhythmic portrait of a land and a people ... too long shielded from American eyes" (Publisher's note).

Modzelewski, Michael. *Inside Passage*. HarpC 1991 $9.00. ISBN 0-06-092273-7. An "enthusiastic tale of his adventures on a wild northern island [that] will inspire dreamers and doers alike" (William L. Sullivan, author of *Listening for Coyote*).

Moon, William L. *Blue Highways: A Journey into America*. Fawcett 1984 o.p. From calendars to deluxe cafes, Cajun music, Trappist monks to hang-gliders, Moon took a circular trip around the United States and pictures what is gone and nearly gone from the United States, as well as presenting a wry, sophisticated view of what he saw.

Muir, John. *Travels in Alaska*. Rprt. Serv. 1991 repr. of 1915 ed. $89.00. ISBN 0-7812-6345-X. An explorer with a genuine love of the wilderness, the vanishing edge, Muir manages to capture Alaska in the 1800s better than any other writer.

O'Hanlon, Redmond. *In Trouble Again: A Journey Between The Orinoco and The Amazon*. Random 1988 $10.00. ISBN 0-679-72714-0. "... takes us into a heart of darkness infested with jaguars, assassin bugs, and piranha, a place where men are driven to murder over a bottle of ketchup ..." (Publisher's note).

Olson, Sigurd F. *Open Horizons*. Knopf 1969 o.p. "Sigurd Olson's beautifully written book (he has written five others on the Far North) [describes] his youth on a far-northern Wisconsin farm and the love of the lakes, forests and rivers that brought him back, after college, to learn the rugged life of a wilderness guide. Olson is a philosopher as well as a remarkable writer on nature. ... A spellbinder (*Publishers Weekly*).

Pern, Stephen. *The Great Divide: A Walk Through America Along the Continental Divide*. Viking Penguin 1989 $7.95. ISBN 0-13-009593-4. In which "Pern's foreignness gives him just the right perspective to snare the heart of America" (*Kirkus Review*).

Perrin, Noel. *Solo: Life with an Electric Car*. Norton 1992 $18.95. ISBN 0-393-03407-0. ". . . an engaging story of a pioneer in reverse, driving the Future back from California to New England" (Bill McKibben, author of *The End of Nature*).

Pindell, Terry. *Making Tracks: An American Rail Odyssey*. H. Holt & Co. 1990 $14.95. ISBN 0-8050-1740-2. By the man who, in 1988, set out to travel all 30,000 miles of America's remaining passenger lines.

Raban, Jonathan. *Hunting Mister Heartbreak: A Discovery of America*. HarpC 1991 $12.00. ISBN 0-06-098107-5. "The best book of travel ever written by an Englishman about the United States" (Jan Morris).

Spurr, Daniel. *Steered by the Falling Stars*. Intl. Marine 1992 $19.95. ISBN 0-87742-332-6. An account of "the author's life-changing voyage not only from Maine to Florida, but through the death and birth of children. . ." (John Barth).

Stanton, William. *The Great United States Exploring Expedition of 1838–1842*. U. CA Pr. 1975 o.p. ". . . a complex tale of political intrigue, adventure, shipwreck, personality conficts, professional jealousy—with some ludicrous episodes. . . . [The expedition] marked a turning point in American science, when gentlemen naturalists were replaced by professionals and specialists" (*Publishers Weekly*).

Stone, Roger D. *Dreams of Amazonia*. Viking Penguin 1993 $13.00. ISBN 0-14-017430-3. ". . . an up-to-date and documented account based on history, both human and natural" (*Scientific American*).

———. *The Voyage of the Sanderling: Exploring the Ecology of the Atlantic Coast from Maine to Rio*. Random 1989 $12.00. ISBN 0-679-73178-4. "More informative than a shelf full of environmental studies. . . . Must reading for anyone who cares about our vanishing coastlines" (William Warner, author of *Beautiful Swimmers*).

Sutton, Horace. *Travelers: The American Tourist from Stage Coach to Space Shuttle*. Morrow 1980 o.p. "Sutton approaches his subject with the enthusiasm of a busload of Rotarians at the Place Pigalle. His description of Americans on the road, whether to the watering holes of pre-Revolutionary New England or to the glamour spots of postwar southern France, are unfailingly witty and unflinchingly honest . . ." (*N.Y. Times Book Review*).

Taber, Sara Mansfield. *Dusk on the Campo: A Journey in Patagonia*. H. Holt & Co. 1991 $12.95. ISBN 0-8050-2092-6. "A revealing, candid look at a remote corner of the world" (*Publishers Weekly*).

Theroux, Paul. *The Old Patagonian Express: By Train through the Americas*. HM 1989 $9.70. ISBN 0-395-52105-X. An account of the author's travels and his discoveries about himself while riding the rails through South America.

Thoreau, Henry David. *The Maine Woods*. Buccaneer Bks. 1990 $21.95. ISBN 0-89966-653-1. "Originally published in 1864 . . . contains not only Thoreau's evocative renderings of the primitive forest but an impassioned protest against its despoilment in the name of commerce and sport" (Publisher's note).

Turner, Frederick. *A Border of Blue: Along the Gulf of Mexico from the Keys to the Yucatan*. H. Holt & Co. 1993 $23.00. ISBN 0-8050-2072-1. ". . . an absolutely brilliant delineation of place and time" (Jim Harrison, author of *Just Before Dark*).

Urrutia, Virginia. *Two Wheels and a Taxi: A Slightly Daft Adventure in the Andes*. Mountaineers 1987 $14.95. ISBN 0-89886-141-1. "An enchanting account of a feisty grandmother's journey by bicycle through Ecuador" (Donald J. Montague, South America Explorer's Club).

U.S. National Park Service. *Explorers and Settlers: Historic Places Commemorating the Early Exploration and Settlement of the United States*. Finch Pr. 1968 o.p. "Part 1 of the present volume covers in a fine narrative style the extension of European civilization into the New World. Part 2 is a splendid survey of historic sites and buildings, copiously illustrated" (*Library Journal*).

Waugh, Alec. *Love and the Caribbean: Tales, Characters, and Scenes of the West Indies*. Paragon Hse. 1986 repr. of 1958 ed. $12.95. ISBN 1-55778-351-9. By the experienced author of Caribbean travel tales.

White, Randy Wayne. *Batfishing in the Rainforest*. H. Holt & Co. 1991 $12.95. ISBN 0-8050-2229-5. ". . . not simply a wonderful writer, [but also] . . . a fishing guide of genius" (Paul Theroux).

Wright, Billie. *Four Seasons North: A Journal of Life in the Alaskan Wilderness*. Sierra 1991 $10.00. ISBN 0-87156-555-2. One of the best books about northern Alaska available, full of descriptions of the Brooks Range, the Nuamiut Eskimos, and so on.

Yardley, Jonathan. *States of Mind: A Personal Journey through the Mid-Atlantic States*. Random 1993 $23.00. ISBN 0-394-58911-4. ". . . visits the birthplaces of much of America's history and goes to the centers of much of its present. . . . and spends a lot of time . . . musing . . . about the modern world and its dubious delights" (Publisher's note).

Zwinger, Ann. *Run, River, Run: A Naturalist's Journey Down One of the Great Rivers of the West*. HarpC 1975 o.p. "Zwinger explored the Green River from its headwaters to its confluence with the Colorado, and her narrative is punctuated with quotations from earlier explorers, as well as with bits of information from a variety of disciplines (history, archaeology, botany . . .)" (*Library Journal*).

EUROPE

Bailey, Anthony. *A Walk Through Wales*. HarpC 1992 $23.00. ISBN 0-06-118003-3. By a man who "writes as naturally as he walks, and he is the last great walker" (John Updike).

Baker, Daisy. *More Travels in a Donkey Trap*. Intl. Spec. Bk. 1977 o.p. "The author describes her travels with a donkey and cart about the countryside of her cottage in Devon, England. She reminisces about the past as she remembers her childhood in the country, her period as between-maid to the bishop's daughters, her first love during the First World War, and her marriage" (Publisher's note).

Bowen, Elizabeth. *A Time in Rome*. Viking Penguin 1959 $9.95. ISBN 0-14-009584-5. "Bowen's account of a time spent in Rome between February and Easter . . . no ordinary guidebook but an evocation of a city—its history, its architecture and, above all, its atmosphere" (Publisher's note).

Bradley, David. *Lion Among Roses: A Memoir of Finland*. H. Holt & Co. 1965 o.p. "Penetrates heart and mind" (*Library Journal*).

Brett, David. *High Level: The Alps from End to End*. Trafalgar Sq. 1983 $24.95. ISBN 0-575-03202-2. Guide to the entire Alpine region of Europe.

Brodsky, Joseph. *Watermark*. FS&G 1992 $15.00. ISBN 0-374-14812-0. By the Nobel Prize winner and current Poet Laureate of the United States; "a curious, quirky, and brilliant picture of the physical and metaphysical life of the city of Venice" (Publisher's note).

Bryson, Bill. *Neither Here Nor There: Travels in Europe*. Avon 1992 $10.00. ISBN 0-380-71380-2. "Splendidly provocative . . . so hilarious and simultaneously honest that he's got to be, if not forgiven, at least excused for stepping on toes" (*Booklist*).

Burke, John. *A Traveller's History of Scotland*. Trafalgar Sq. 1990 $24.95. ISBN 0-7195-4840-3. ". . . a book for the thoughtful traveller . . . by an author who carries his research lightly and engagingly" (*The Scotsman*).

Connery, Donald S. *The Scandinavians*. S & S Trade 1972 o.p. Connery, "a free-lance writer, has done surprisingly well from limited sources and personal observations; he dwells too much on some popular notions of contemporary Scandinavia but dispels most myths about sex, suicides and sin" (*Library Journal*).

Daley, Robert. *Portraits of France*. Little 1991 $24.95. ISBN 0-316-17185-9. ". . . finds his stories in places where most . . . have not looked before . . . into what remains of the French concentration camps in the Pyrenees . . . of great men and small . . . of families . . . on Lourdes in the off-season" (Publisher's note).

Denham, H. M. *The Adriatic: A Sea Guide to Venice, the Italian Shore and the Dalmation Coast*. Norton 1977 o.p. "Unique and charming" (*Library Journal*).

————. *The Ionian Islands to Rhodes: A Sea Guide.* Norton 1976 $19.95. ISBN 0-393-03195

Durrell, Lawrence. *The Greek Islands.* Viking Penguin 1980 $14.95. ISBN 0-14-005661-0. One hundred outstanding color photos complement the writing, which describes sun-washed, history-laden islands. Evocative description—mythological, architectural, and archaeological details are woven with the author's personal reminiscences.

Fermor, Patrick L. *Roumeli: Travels in Northern Greece. Travel Lib.* Viking Penguin 1984 $7.95. ISBN 0-14-009509-7

Fussell, P. *Abroad: British Literary Traveling between the Wars.* OUP 1980 $25.00. ISBN 0-19-502767-1. "The English travel books of the 20s and 30s were . . . written in the Indian summer of what is now a dead form. Evelyn Waugh, Graham Greene, Norman Douglas, D. H. Lawrence, Robert Byron were the last masters of the art which was to be killed off by politics and the tourist industry" (*N.Y. Times Book Review*).

Gould, John. *Europe on a Saturday Night.* Down East 1979 repr. of 1968 ed. o.p. The entertaining travels of a Maine couple.

Hardyment, Christine. *Heidi's Alps: One Family's Search for Storybook Europe.* Atlantic Monthly 1987 $7.95. ISBN 0-87113-178-1. In which, with her four daughters, the author travels 4,000 miles to trace the roots of classics like Brinker's Holland, Andersen's Denmark, and Heidi's Alps.

Harrison, Barbara Grizzuti. *Italian Days.* Ticknor & Fields 1989 $12.95. ISBN 0-395-55131-5. ". . . a brilliant and beautiful work—superior in scope and spirituality to Luigi Barzini's famed *The Italians* of two decades ago. . . . Bravo!" (*Booklist*).

Hillaby, John. *A Walk through Britain.* HM 1978 o.p. The author's journey on foot from Land's End in southwestern Cornwall to John O'Groat's in northeastern Scotland during the spring and summer of 1966. "Hillaby's interest in and knowledge of natural life and prehistory give his book a lively theme and a distinctive flavor in which there is not a trace of the trite or commonplace. He also pleads convincingly for better conservation and recreation practices" (*Library Journal*).

Ingstad, Helge. *Westward to Vinland.* Trans. by Erik J. Friis. St. Martin 1969 o.p. Ingstad's account of Norse ruins in Newfoundland.

James, Henry. *Italian Hours.* HM 1987 repr. of 1909 ed. $12.95. ISBN 0-88001-147-5. Contains 22 essays written during James's trips to Italy in the 1870s—"A precise and personal account. . . . [that] lingers and resounds, remaining one of the greatest documents of travel . . ." (Publisher's note).

Kimbrough, Emily. *Floating Island.* Book & Tackle 1984 $15.00. ISBN 0-910258-15-5. An account of a 12-day barge trip by a group of Americans through the canals of central France.

Laxalt, Robert. *In a Hundred Graves: A Basque Portrait. Basque Bk. Ser.* U. of Nebr. Pr. 1972 $15.95. ISBN 0-87417-035-4. A first-person narrative about life in a small village in the Basque region of Spain. Has a philosophical tone that ponders questions about love, death, and life.

————. *Sweet Promised Land.* U. of Nev. Pr. 1989 $17.95. ISBN 0-87417-118-0. An old Nevada sheepherder returns to his native village in the Pyrenees for a visit.

Liberman, Alexander. *Greece, Gods, and Art.* Viking Penguin 1968 o.p. Introduction by Robert Graves; commentaries by Iris C. Love. This "does more to bring the reader close to ancient Greece than would a dozen weary jet flights and bus journeys. A superb technical and imaginative performance" (Lewis Mumford).

McCarthy, Mary. *The Stones of Florence.* HarBraceJ 1976 $49.95. ISBN 0-15-185079-8

————. *Venice Observed.* HarBraceJ 1963 $7.95. ISBN 0-15-693521-X. The novelist's brilliant pen explores past and present aspects of the Queen of the Adriatic.

McCracken, David. *Wordsworth and the Lake District: A Guide to the Poems and Their Places.* OUP 1985 o.p. ". . . outstandingly thorough . . . indispensable to the enthusiast" (*Times Literary Supplement*).

Margolies, Susanna, and Ginger Harmon. *Walking Europe from Top to Bottom: The Sierra Club Travel Guide to the Grande Randonnee Cinq (GR-5) through Holland, Belgium,*

Luxembourg, Switzerland, and France. Sierra 1986 $10.95. ISBN 0-87156-752-0. ". . . the first complete recreational guide to [a] popular hiking trail," passing through Van Gogh country, Flanders, the Alsace-Lorraine, the famous vineyards of the Moselle, and the Vosges and Jura Mountains (Publisher's note).

Mayle, Peter. *Acquired Tastes.* Bantam 1992 $25.00. ISBN 0553-09027-5. "[Featuring] the friendly eye and ear of a sympathetic foreigner to penetrate and then bring alive the unique and enduring . . . Provence" (Julia Child).

_____. *Toujours Provence.* Knopf 1991 $21.00. ISBN 0-679-40253-5. ". . . definitely what the *medecin* ordered for anyone homesick for southern France" (*The Washington Post Book World*).

_____. *A Year in Provence.* Random 1990 $10.00. ISBN 0-679-73114-8. Awarded British Book Awards "Best Travel Book of the Year."

Michener, James A. *Iberia: Spanish Travels and Reflections.* Random 1968 $29.95. ISBN 0-394-42982-6. "Michener unfolds a dazzling panorama of Spanish history, character, customs, and art; he discusses sex and bull-fighting, food and wine, picnics, pilgrimages, bird sanctuaries, cathedrals, museums, palaces. Scattered throughout are bright bits about fleabag hotels and delightful rogues" (*Saturday Review*).

Murray, William. *The Last Italian: Portrait of a People.* S&S Trade 1991 $10.00. ISBN 0-671-77999-0. ". . . delivers the Italy of today with all its petty politics, sordid scandals, and festering environmental and growth problems intact" (*Florida Times-Union*).

Newby, Eric. *Round Ireland in Low Gear.* Viking Penguin 1989 $9.95. ISBN 0-14-009588-8. By an author who, "like all fine travel writers, . . . is quirky, eccentric, independent of mind and attitude" (Thomas Flanagan, author of *The Tenants of Time*).

Niles, Bo. *A Window on Provence: One Summer's Sojourn into the Simple Life.* Viking Penguin 1990 $18.95. ISBN 0-670-82722-3. By an author who, "whether she is describing a trip to one of the nearby market towns, a visit to a tranquil monastery, or the lazy rhythms of daily life, [offers] prose . . . infused with the poetry and history of this splendid place" (Publisher's note).

Oakes, George W. *Turn Left at the Pub.* Congdon & Weed 1985 o.p. Offers walking tours of the English countryside; includes maps and information about various small towns.

Oakes, George W., and Alexander Chapman. *Turn Right at the Fountain.* H. Holt & Co. 4th rev. ed. 1981 o.p. Walking tours around 20 major European cities; includes brief historical notes about buildings and features along the routes.

Pillement, Georges. *Unknown Greece.* 2 vols. Intl. Pubns. Co. 1973 o.p. A guide to the less familiar regions of Greece. The author has written similar texts for France, Italy, Portugal, Sardinia and Corsica, Sicily, Spain, Turkey, and Yugoslavia.

Pritchett, V. S. *The Spanish Temper: Travels in Spain.* Ecco Pr. 1989 repr. of 1954 ed. $8.95. ISBN 0-88001-182-3. By a 30-year veteran of travel in Spain.

Raban, Jonathan. *Coasting: A Private Voyage.* Viking Penguin 1988 $7.95. ISBN 0-1401-0657-X. The story of a 3,000-mile voyage in 1982 around the British Isles. ". . . a glorious book, written with energy, wit, and a melancholy lyricism" (*Seattle Times/Seattle Post-Intelligence*).

Skelton, R. A. *The Vinland Map and the Tartar Relation.* Bks. Demand repr. of 1965 ed. $91.80. ISBN 0-8357-8365-0. Contains a reproduction of the map suggesting that the Norsemen discovered America about A.D. 1000. Foreword by Alexander O. Vietor.

Symons, Arthur. *Cities and Sea-Coasts and Islands.* Richard West 1978 repr. of 1918 ed. o.p. The author believes that one cannot write about an area or city unless it has aroused some intense emotion, whether love or hate. Each of the areas he covers has in some way moved him, and for this reason, he is able to provide an insight, a feeling of atmosphere, for those cities in Europe that he selected, which many other travel books lack.

Theroux, Paul. *The Kingdom by the Sea: A Journey around Great Britain.* PB 1990 $6.99. ISBN 0-671-70923-2. A chatty and detailed account of his travels around Great Britain; includes conversations with people he encounters.

Thublon, Colin. *Where Nights Are Longest: Travels by Car through Western Russia.* Random 1984 o.p. Account of a ten-week motor trip through the western Soviet Union in 1980. The author examines his fears and misconceptions about the country.

Toth, Susan Allen. *My Love Affair with England.* $18.00. Ballantine 1992 ISBN 0-345-37725-7. "Written clearly and with an understanding that far surpasses any feeling of condescension or superiority or general quaintness among the natives . . ." (M. F. K. Fisher).

Walker, Ian. *Zoo Station: Adventures in East and West Berlin.* Atlantic Monthly 1987 $7.95. ISBN 0-87113-197-8. Account in which "ideologies melt like freak snowfalls in May" (Publisher's note).

Walzer, Mary M. *A Travel Guide for the Disabled: Western Europe.* Van Nos. Reinhold 1982 o.p. The first comprehensive travel guide detailing how a disabled person can travel alone through Western Europe.

Williams, Niall, and Christine Breen. *O Come Ye Back to Ireland: Our First Year in County Clare.* Soho Press 1987 $9.95. ISBN 0-939149-22-2. The story of "a young American-Irish couple [who] give up New York to take up farming in the west of Ireland and find what has been a part of them since before they were born" (Publisher's note).

———. *The Pipes Are Calling: Our Jaunts Through Ireland.* Soho Press 1990 $9.95. ISBN 0-939149-52-4. A look at the "real" Ireland, with its farms and horse fairs, turf fires and thatched cottages, and sooty towns.

AFRICA, ASIA, AND OCEANIA

Alexander, Caroline. *One Dry Season: In the Footsteps of Mary Kingsley.* Random 1989 $10.95. ISBN 0-679-73189-X. By a rare female travel writer who wandered alone up the Ogooue River.

Alexander, Lamar. *Six Months Off: An American Family's Australian Adventure.* Morrow 1988 $9.95. ISBN 0-688-09510-0. ". . . a book for the American family: for hard-charging fathers, mothers, sons, and daughters who often run so fast that before they know it, they've lost each other. . . . an inspiration to all of us" (Peter Jenkins, author of *A Walk across America* and *Close Friends*).

Amantea, Carlos A. *The Blob that Ate Oaxaca and Other Travel Tales.* Mho & Mho 1992 $12.95. ISBN 0917320-32-8. One of the best examples of New Journalism travel writing—as told from the vantage point of a wheelchair.

Ames, Evelyn. *A Glimpse of Eden.* HM 1967 o.p. The experiences of the author and her husband photographing East African wildlife are the substance of this "poetic, moving and memorable book" (*Library Journal*).

Ash, Niema. *Flight of the Wind Horse: A Journey into Tibet.* Trafalgar Sq. 1990 $19.95. ISBN 0-7126-5397-X. "A wonderful portrait of Tibet today" (Glenn H. Mullin).

Bird, Isabella. *Six Months in Hawaii.* KPI Ltd. 1986 repr. of 1875 ed. $19.95. ISBN 0-7103-0232-0. "The story of an English lady who threw off her invalidism during a six months island journey and went on to become a daring and dashing world traveler" (Publisher's note).

Bock, Carl. *Temples and Elephants: Travels in Siam in 1881–1882.* OUP 1986 repr. of 1884 ed. $9.95. ISBN 0-19-58262X. ". . . restores to life the old Siam as seen through the eyes of a percipient European adventurer in the last quarter of the 19th Century" (Publisher's note).

Bouvier, Nicolas. *The Japanese Chronicles.* Mercury Hse. Inc. 1992 $19.95. ISBN 1-56279-008-0. Describes village festivals and the suburbs of Kyoto, retells Japanese myth and history, and reflects on Noh performances in rich, evocative prose.

Brewster, Barbara Marie. *Down Under All Over: A Love Affair with Australia.* Four Winds OR 1991 $14.95. ISBN 0-9628608-0-8. "From sheep farming to opal mines, from parading penguins to meditating monks, a magical Australia . . . [described] with an enthusiasm that is contagious" (Publisher's note).

Buruma, Ian. *God's Dust: A Modern Asian Journey*. FS&G 1989 $8.95. ISBN 0-374-52235-9. "Intelligent, humane, and entertaining" (James Fallows).

Candlin, Enid Saunders. *A Traveler's Tale: Memories of India*. Macmillan 1974 o.p. "The parameters of Eastern and Western civilization touch but do not mesh in this picture of the Indian sub-continent when British colonial rule ebbed in the aftermath of World War II" (*Booklist*).

Capstick, Peter Hathaway. *The African Adventurers: A Return to the Silent Places*. St. Martin 1992 $22.95. ISBN 0-312-07622-3. "Downright delightful. [Dead accurate about] . . . the bedrock levels of African history, tribal sociology, and appropriate sporting weapons, . . ." (Robert F. Jones, *Sports Illustrated*).

Chiang, Yee. *The Silent Traveller in Japan*. Norton 1972 o.p. "Japan and things Japanese as revealed by this distinguished Chinese scholar, artist and poet are experienced in a new dimension, for he sees them in relation to things Western and things Chinese" (Publisher's note).

Coedes, George. *Angkor*. OUP 1986 repr. of 1963 ed. $9.95. ISBN 0-19-638129-0. A book that ". . . few are likely to equal in scholarship and charm . . ." (Publisher's note).

Corn, Charles. *Distant Islands: Travels across Indonesia*. Viking Penguin 1991 $25.00. ISBN 0-670-82374-0. ". . . a rich, exotic galaxy [by an author who] is more pilgrim than jaded guide. . . . a book to inspire your dreaming!" (Martin Cruz Smith, author of *Gorky Park*).

Dalrymple, William. *In Xanadu: A Quest*. Random 1990 $9.95. ISBN 0-685-29462-5. Dalrymple's retracing of Marco Polo's route ". . . uncommonly satisfying. . . . [a blend of] history, danger, humour, architecture, people, hardships, politics" (*London Literary Review*).

Danziger, Nick. *Danziger's Travels Beyond Forbidden Frontiers*. Random 1987 $15.00. ISBN 0-679-73994. An account of the author's travels "without visas, disguised as an itinerant Muslim . . . on an 18-month journey beyond forbidden frontiers in Asia . . . [, describing] Afghan majahedeen, Uighar peasants, Tibetan lamas, and Chinese Communists" (Publisher's note).

Dedmon, Emmett. *China Journal*. Rand McNally 1973 o.p. "The author was one of the first American journalists to tour contemporary China. [He] shares his experiences and insights on this country's unique political and social organization" (Publisher's note).

Dickey, Christopher. *Expats: Travels in Arabia, from Tripoli to Teheran*. Atlantic Monthly 1990 $9.95. ISBN 0-887113-463-2. A unique version of the Middle East.

Doughty, Charles M. *Travels in Arabia Deserta*. 2 vols. Dover 1980 repr. of 1921 ed. $15.95 ea. ISBNs 0-486-23825-3, 0-486-23826-1. Introduction by T. E. Lawrence. ". . . a great record of adventure and travel (perhaps the greatest in one language)" (Publisher's note).

Edgar, Neal L., and Wendy Y. Ma, eds. *Travel in Asia: A Guide to Information Sources*. *Geography and Travel Information Guide Ser*. Gale 1982 o.p. Provides a host of useful information about traveling in Asia.

Farson, Negley. *Caucasian Journey*. Viking Penguin 1988 $6.95. ISBN 0-14-009581-0. "A classic that offers a 'last look at a lost world,' the Caucasus in 1929. . . . the land of wooden mosques and defunct monasteries on the Volga, of immense pine forests and spectacular mountain highways, of Mongol aristocrats, a tiny German enclave and fierce Tartars" (Publisher's note).

Frater, Alexander. *Chasing the Monsoon: A Modern Pilgrimage Through India*. H. Holt & Co. 1990 $12.95. ISBN 0-8050-2052-7. Following the monsoon from its "burst" on the beaches of Trivandrum, through Delhi and Calcutta, across Bangladesh, to its finale in Cherrapunji, the wettest place on earth; a "delightful . . . journey [of] pure pleasure" (*San Francisco Chronicle*).

Godden, Jon, and Rumer Godden. *Shiva's Pigeons: An Experience of India*. Viking Penguin 1972 o.p. "A fascinating and revealing document which . . . reflects and interreflects the ever-changing patterns of colors of an India where their spirits, like Shiva's pigeons, haunt the places they love" (Publisher's note).

Goodwin, Jason. *Time for Tea: Travels through China and India in Search of Tea*. Knopf 1990 $22.00. ISBN 0-394-57941-0. Following the serpentine paths of the historical tea trade from China to India to London; the writing, like good tea, ". . . has color, flavor, aroma, briskness, highlights, and a sort of bloom" (Nicholas Wollaston, *The Observer*).

Gorer, Geoffrey. *Bali and Angkor: A 1930s Pleasure Trip Looking at Life and Death*. OUP 1986 o.p. A vicarious adventure.

Hansen, Eric. *Stranger in the Forest: On Foot across Borneo*. Viking Penguin 1988 $14.00. ISBN 0-1400-95-86-1. An enchanting tale.

———. *Motoring with Mohammed: Journey to Yemen and the Red Sea*. Random 1991 $10.00. ISBN 0-679-73855-X. "Picaresque, beguiling, and great fun" (Diane Ackerman, *N.Y. Times*).

Harden, Blaine. *Africa: Dispatches from a Fragile Continent*. HM 1990 $10.95. ISBN 0-95-59746-3. Recipient of PEN's Martha Albrand Citation for first book of nonfiction, this work passionately evokes fabulous stories about the destruction of Africa at the end of the millenium.

Harris, Eddy L. *Native Stranger: A Black American's Journey into the Heart of Africa*. Random 1992 $12.00. ISBN 0-679-74232-8. "Magnificent . . . an adventurous travelogue, a lyrical love song to a continent and a political dissection of oppressive regimes . . . heartbreakingly beautiful [and] horrifying" (*Atlantic Journal-Constitution*).

Heller, Peter. *Set Free in China: Sojourns on the Edge*. Chelsea Green Pub. 1992 $18.85. ISBN 0-930031-53-9. In which the author mountain bikes into the lair of a jaguar hunter in Costa Rica, kayaks an unknown river in the High Pamirs, goes lobstering with a deranged fisherman off Cape Cod, and packs frozen fish in Sitka, Alaska.

Heminway, John. *No Man's Land*. Warner Bks. 1983 $9.95. ISBN 0-446-38793-2. "The best book I have ever read on Africa" (William F. Buckley, Jr.).

Horewitz, Tony. *Baghdad without a Map*. NAL-Dutton 1991 $10.00. ISBN 0-452-26745-5. "An irreverent travelogue through the Arab World, sort of a Charles Kuralt meets Hunter Thompson in Cairo, Baghdad and Beirut. . . . crammed with anecdotes and observations that tell volumes about Arab life" (*Buffalo News*).

Hudson, Mark. *Our Grandmother's Drums: A Portrait of Rural African Life and Culture*. H. Holt & Co. 1991 $13.95. ISBN 08050-1620-1. Winner of the Somerset Maugham Award and the Thomas Cook Award.

Huxley, Elspeth, ed. *Nine Faces of Kenya*. Viking Penguin 1990 $12.00. ISBN 0-1401-4985-6. Comprehensive and delightfully informative.

Hyland, Paul. *The Black Heart: A Voyage into Central Africa*. Paragon Hse. 1988 $10.95. ISBN 1-55778-323-3. ". . . draws past and present into a sensuous weft of shadow and glare, 'civilized' and 'primitive,' cruel and tender (*Times Literary Supplement*).

Iyer, Pico. *The Lady and the Monk*. Random 1992 $12.00. ISBN 0-679-73834-7. '. . . leads us into the cheerful land of the rising sun and finds there, instead, a strange and haunting island" (*Condé Nast Traveler*).

———. *Video Night in Kathmandu and Other Reports from the Not-so-far-East*. Random 1988 $13.00. ISBN 0-679-72216-5. "Some of the most polished travel writing to appear in a long time—always revealing, sometimes reflective, frequently riotous" (*Kirkus Review*).

Jenkins, Peter. *Across China*. Fawcett 1986 $5.95. ISBN 0-449-21546-7. ". . . a prism which reflects cultural differences and in which common human concerns converge" (*Baltimore Sun*).

Joris, Lieve. *Back to the Congo*. Trans. from 1987 Dutch ed. Atheneum 1992 $22.00. ISBN 0-689-12164-4. Retraces the steps of the author's late uncle, a Catholic missionary in the Belgium Congo.

Journey into China. Natl. Geo. 1984 $26.95. ISBN 0-87044-437-9. Quality photographs and descriptions.

Kane, Robert S. *Africa A to Z*. Doubleday 1972 o.p. This author has written many such guides, including *Asia A to Z* and *South Pacific A to Z*.

Kazantzakis, Nikos. *Japan-China: A Journal of Two Voyages to the Far East.* Trans. by George C. Papageotes. Creative Arts. Bk. 1982 $9.95. ISBN 0-916870-40-5. Epilogue by Helen Kazantzakis.

Kempe, Frederick. *Siberian Odyssey: Voyage into the Russian Soul.* Putnam Pub. Group 1992 $24.95. ISBN 0-399-13755-6. Portrays "a region and a people simultaneously changing and resisting change. . . . a captivating account" (Publisher's note).

Khosla, Jawaharlal. *Himalayan Circuit: A Journey in the Inner Himalayas.* OUP 1989 $10.95. ISBN 0-19-562418-1. ". . . ideal for all Himalayan travellers, particularly for those contemplating a trip to Spiti and Lahour. . . . or [for] . . . general readers who prefer the vicarious pleasure obtained by imagining the wonders of high altitude travel" (Publisher's note).

Latham, Aaron. *The Frozen Leopard: Hunting My Dark Heart in Africa.* S&S Trade 1991 $12.00. ISBN 0-671-79278-4. ". . . should be on the bedside table of every man in mid-life. The quest of a creative man in his mid-forties . . . for the [misplaced] magic of belief in himself . . ." (Gail Sheehy, author of *Passages* and *The Silent Passage*).

Lattimore, Owen, and Eleanor Lattimore. *Silks, Spices and Empire: Asia Seen through the Eyes of Its Discoverers.* Ed. by Evelyn S. Nef. Delacorte 1968 o.p. A fascinating anthology of writings collected by the noted orientalist and his wife.

Lawlor, Eric. *Looking for Asman: One Man's Travels through the Paradox of Modern Turkey.* Random 1993 $11.00. ISBN 0-679-73822-3. By an author with a "keen eye for telling details. . . . [who] sketches in a gallery of unforgettable portraits . . . a delightful travel memoir" (*Kirkus Review*).

Leighton, Ralph. *Tuva or Bust: Richard Feynman's Last Journey.* Viking Penguin 1992 $10.00. ISBN 0-14015614-3. The story of ten years in which the author and Feynman, a Nobel Prize-winning physicist and jazz drummer, followed a trail to remote Central Asia in search of Tuva.

Lessing, Doris. *African Laughter: Four Visits to Zimbabwe.* HarpC 1992 $25.00. ISBN 0-06-016854-4. ". . . evokes her childhood on an isolated farm in the bush. . . . [and] explores the often unexpected ways . . . [that] the past . . . survive[s]" (Publisher's note).

Lewis, Norman. *The Goddess in the Stones: Travels in India.* H. Holt & Co. 1991 $22.95. ISBN 0-8050-1959-6. Evokes an India off the beaten tracks, as rewarding today . . . as when first described by Caesar Fredericke in *Hakluyt's Voyages*.

McPhee, Colin. *A House in Bali.* OUP 1985 $8.95. ISBN 0-19-580448-1. ". . . a worthwhile period piece [giving] the reader an absorbing, thoughtful impression of life on the island forty years ago" (Publisher's note).

Matthiessen, Peter. *African Silence.* Random 1991 $10.00. ISBN 0-79-73102-4. Reveals a breathtaking knowledge of plants, animals, and people.

Moorhouse, Geoffrey. *On the Other Side: A Journey through Soviet Central Asia.* H. Holt & Co. 1990 $12.95. ISBN 0-8050-2108-6. Chronicles "the cruelty and conquest that have been the norm since the time of Alexander's armies" (*Washington Post Book World*).

Morris, Jan. *Hong Kong.* Random 1985 $8.95. ISBN 0-679-72486-9. "A wonderfully enlightened portrait—intelligent, insightful, lucid, up to the minute, and elegantly written" (Paul Theroux).

———. *Sydney.* Random 1992 $22.50. ISBN 0-394-55098-6. The ultimate portrait of Sydney, Australia's spiritual heart.

Mowat, Farley. *The Siberians.* Bantam 1989 $3.95. ISBN 0-553-24896-0. A report of two long visits this Canadian author made to Siberia in 1966 and 1969, in which he shows that Siberia has recently become a productive and modern country.

Mura, David. *Turning Japanese: Memoirs of a Sansei.* Doubleday 1991 $12.00. ISBN 0-385-42344-6. ". . . an intriguing perspective . . . [on] the New World quest for enlightenment from this ancient and ascendant culture, [by] . . . a *sansei*—a third-generation Japanese" (Publisher's note).

Murphy, Dervla. *Cameroon with Egbert.* Overlook Pr. 1990 $13.95. ISBN 0-879510476-0. ". . . a tart commentary on the local customs, history, and problems of contemporary Africa" (*Kirkus Review*).

————. *The Waiting Land: A Spell in Nepal.* Overlook Pr. 1989 $10.95. ISBN 0-87951-305-5. "The 'spell' of the subtitle refers to what the author feels and transmits to her readers, a spell conjured by the friendly, hardy people; their customs; and the unspeakable beauty of the country. Miss Murphy, a traveler who breaks all barriers of space, language, religion, food, comfort, and bacteria, writes with love, style, and wit" (*Library Journal*).

Newby, Eric. *A Short Walk in the Hindu Kush.* Viking Penguin 1987 $10.95. ISBN 0-14-009575-6. Like many other amateur mountaintop walkers, Newby had the ambition to be more than a tourist and to reach places where few Englishmen had been before. Introduction by Evelyn Waugh.

Perham, Margery. *African Apprenticeship: An Autobiographical Journey in Southern Africa.* 1929. Holmes & Meier 1974 o.p. "Here we see the beginning of her lifetime career and interest in Africa. . . . For all levels of libraries with an African interest" (*Choice*).

Pye-Smith, Charlie. *Travels in Nepal: The Sequestered Kingdom.* Viking Penguin 1990 $8.95. ISBN 0-14-009595-0. "Fast-paced and well balanced, mixing hard sociological facts with some lovely cameos of Nepal's remote corners" (*Daily Telegraph*).

Reynolds, Jim. *The Outer Path: Finding My Way in Tibet.* Fair Oaks CA 1992 $10.95. ISBN 0-933271-06-9. ". . . more than an adventure story. . . . during this trip, which he calls a journey of *dukkha* (suffering). . . . Reynolds made his final decision to devote his life to Buddhism" (Publisher's note).

Romero, Patricia W., ed. *Women's Voices on Africa: A Century of Travel Writings.* Wiener Pub. Inc. 1992 $14.95. ISBN 1-55876-048-2. Featuring "unique individuals ordinarily overlooked by African historians" (Robert O. Collins, author of many books on Africa and winner of the Jon Ben Snow Prize for the best book in British Studies).

Rotberg, Robert I. *Africa and Its Explorers: Motives, Methods and Impacts.* HUP 1970 o.p. Essays by nine Africanists on seven British and two German explorers of the nineteenth century—Barth, Livingstone, Burton, Speke, Baker, Rohlf, Stanley, Cameron, and Thomson.

Settle, Mary Lee. *Turkish Reflections: A Biography of a Place.* S & S Trade 1991 $10.00. ISBN 0-671-77997-4. "A diverting mixture of travelogue, history, polemic, and contemporary portrait" (*N.Y. Times Book Review*).

Severin, Timothy. *The African Adventure.* NAL-Dutton 1973 o.p. "The adventures of a variety of explorers, military men, missionaries and sportsmen as they encounter the huge African continent. . . . Severin examines the explorers' varying motives and personalities, basing his account on their numerous publications, covering several centuries and all parts of the continent" (*Library Journal*).

Shoumatoff, Alex. *In Southern Light: Trekking through Zaire and The Amazon.* Random 1990 $9.95. ISBN 0-679-73077-X. "An exotic and wonderful book" (Tracy Kidder).

Smith, Anthony. *Blind White Fish in Persia.* Viking Penguin 1990 repr. of 1953 ed. $8.95. ISBN 0-14-009596-9. "A book to rollick through, as the scientists themselves appear to have rollicked through Persia" (Jan Morris).

Spindel, Carol. *In the Shadow of the Sacred Grove.* Random 1989 $12.00. ISBN 0-6797-72214-9. ". . . like having one's ancestral home described by an unlikely outsider who has almost come to feel at home there" (Alice Walker).

Stevens, Stuart. *Malaria Dreams.* Atlantic Monthly 1989 $9.95. ISBN 0-87113-361-X. ". . . *The Heart of Darkness* starring the Marx Brothers" (*The San Diego Tribune*).

————. *Night Train to Turkistan: Modern Adventures Along China's Ancient Silk Road.* Atlantic Monthly 1988 $8.95. ISBN 0-87113-190-0. Retraces a 5,000-mile quest first made by Peter Fleming, an eccentric British travel writer in 1936—"A rare, high-spirited romp" (Publisher's note).

Swaan, Wim. *Japanese Lantern.* Taplinger 1970 o.p. A cultural guide in the form of essays.

Theroux, Paul. *The Great Railway Bazaar: By Train through Asia.* Ballantine 1981 $2.95. ISBN 0-345-30110-2. An account of a four-month railroad journey across Asia. "Perhaps not since Mark Twain's 'Following the Equator' (1897) have a wanderer's leisurely impressions been hammered into such wry, incisive mots. . . . By word and the seat of his pants Theroux has paid nostalgic homage to the pre-jet era, when men optimistically hoped to bind up the world with bands of steel" (*Time*).

Winchester, Simon. *Pacific Rising*. S & S Trade 1991 $14.00. ISBN 0-671-78004-2. "A marvelous tour de force. . . . sometimes hilarious, sometimes moving, always captivating travel adventures" (*Condé Nast Traveler*).

THE ARCTIC AND ANTARCTICA

Bass, Dick, and Frank Wells. *Seven Summits*. (coauthored with Rick Ridgeway). Warner Bks. 1986 $12.95. ISBN 0-446-38516-6. A story of conquest—of mountains, and of the authors—by themselves.

Berton, Pierre. *The Mysterious North: Encounters with the Canadian Frontier 1947–1954*. Firefly Bks. Ltd. 1989 repr. of 1956 ed. $14.95. ISBN 0-7710-1210-1. "Astonishingly comprehensive . . . thoroughly reliable . . . very entertainingly written" (*N.Y. Times Book Review*).

Bruder, Gerry. *Heroes of the Horizons: Flying Adventures of Alaska's Legendary Bush Pilots*. Alaska Northwest 1991 $12.95. ISBN 0-88240-363-X. Colorful firsthand accounts.

Counter, S. Allen. *North Pole Legacy: Black, White, and Eskimo*. U. of Mass. Pr. 1991 $24.95. ISBN 0-87023-736-5. Recounts the author's search for the sons of polar explorers Matthew Henson and Robert Peary and the effort to get recognition for fellow African American Henson's role in Arctic explorations.

Fisher, David E. *Across the Top of the World: To the North Pole by Sled, Balloon, Airplane, and Nuclear Icebreaker*. Random 1992 $25.00. ISBN 0-679-41116-X. An "eloquent, erudite, funny, informative story that brings to life the remarkable band of heroes, liars, visionaries, braggarts, and fools who attempted to sail, sled, or trek across the pole—and often died trying" (Barry H. Lopez).

Grossfeld, Stan. *The Whisper of Star: A Siberian Journey*. Globe Pequot 1988 o.p. Grossfeld's descriptions of what he experienced, both through the lens and through his encounters—a door to Siberia.

Kanint, Larry. *More Alaska Bear Tales*. Alaska Northwest 1989 $12.95. ISBN 0-88240-372-9. "From backyard to backcountry, from the gruesome to the educational, . . . vintage Alaska adventure" (Publisher's note).

Lopez, Barry H. *Arctic Dreams: Imagination and Desire in a Northern Landscape*. Macmillan 1986 $22.95. ISBN 0-684-18578-4. "Captures both the brevity and peril of this frozen land" (Publisher's note).

Millman, Lawrence. *Last Places: A Journey in the North*. HM 1990 $18.95. ISBN 0-685-45106-2. Explores ". . . that seldom visited swatch of globe from Norway to Newfoundland, including the Faeroe Islands; Iceland's volcanic Askja region; and the old Viking haunt of Igaliko, Greenland. . . . [showing] a canny gift for applying humor [and providing] a refreshing voice and a fine read" (*The National Geographic Traveler*).

Mowat, Farley, and David Blackwood. *The Wake of the Great Sealers*. Little 1974 o.p. The story of the Newfoundland men of the nineteenth and early twentieth centuries who set out in flimsy ships to hunt seals on the treacherous North Atlantic ice fields; lavishly illustrated.

Neatby, L. H. *Discovery in Russian and Siberian Waters*. Ohio U. Pr. 1973 o.p. "A most fascinating and well-written account of Arctic exploration beginning with the mid-19th century" (*Library Journal*).

Parfit, Michael. *South Light: A Journey to the Last Continent*. Ulverscroft 1992 $24.95. ISBN 0-7089-8627-7. A humorous and exceptionally well-told story.

Perkins, Robert. *Into the Great Solitude: An Arctic Journey*. Dell 1992 $5.99. ISBN 440-21244-8. Chronicles one man's 17 years of Arctic navigation.

Reader's Digest, eds. *Antarctica: The Extraordinary History of Man's Conquest of the Frozen Continent*. R. D. Assn. 1990 $32.95. ISBN 0-86438-167-0. Covers geography, a chronology of explorations, and many other topics.

Steger, Will, and Jon Bowermaster. *Crossing Antarctica.* Knopf 1992 $25.00. ISBN 0-394-58714-6. The story of the first crossing of Antarctica on foot.

Thayer, Helen. *Polar Dreams: The Heroic Saga of the First Solo Journey by a Woman and Her Dog to the Pole.* S & S Trade 1993 $22.00. ISBN 0-671-79386-1. "The enthralling story of a woman who at the age of 50 took an extraordinary journey that brought her to the edge of emotional and physical survival—an epic undertaking that few people of any age or sex could have achieved" (Sir Edmund Hillary, Foreword).

Wilson, Edward. *Diary of the Discovery Expedition to the Antarctic Regions, 1901–1904.* Ed. by Ann Savours. Humanities 1967 o.p. Foreword by the Duke of Edinburgh. "Edward Wilson, who died with Scott on their return from the South Pole in 1912, first visited the Antarctic some 10 years earlier, keeping a personal and detailed diary, describing the day-to-day work, and the adventures of the scientific expedition. The author, surgeon and scientist of the expedition, was himself a remarkable man, which becomes evident on reading this book. It is illustrated with 47 of Wilson's exquisite watercolors, numerous pencil sketches throughout the text and 5 maps" (*Library Journal*).

———. *Diary of the "Terra Nova" Expedition to the Antarctic: 1910–1912.* Ed. by H. R. King. Humanities 1972 o.p. "The tragic story of Scott's last expedition to the Antarctic . . . as seen through the eyes of Scott's second in command and scientific director" (*Library Journal*).

INDIVIDUAL TRAVELS AND EXPLOITS

Adamson, J. H., and H. F. Folland. *The Shepherd of the Ocean: Sir Walter Raleigh and His Times.* Gambit 1969 o.p. "Raleigh's story has probably never been better told" (Edward Wagenknecht).

Aebi, Tania. *Maiden Voyage.* Ballantine 1989 $5.95. ISBN 0-345-36876-2. "An exciting tale of an extraordinarily brave and romantic adventure" (Walter Cronkite).

Anderson, Charles R., ed. *Journal of a Cruise to the Pacific Ocean, 1842–1844, in the Frigate United States with Notes on Herman Melville.* AMS Pr. repr. of 1937 ed. $16.50. ISBN 0-404-00356-7

Audubon, Maria. *Audubon and His Journals.* 2 vols. Dover 1986 repr. of 1897 ed. $8.95. ISBN 0-486-25144-6. Zoological and other notes by Elliott Coves. "These rare journals, unavailable for many years, present[ing] the only complete, intimate portrait of John James Audubon" (Publisher's note).

The Best of Granta Travel. Viking Penguin 1991 $10.00. ISBN 0-14-014041-7. Thirty-five pieces selected from *Granta Magazine* travel writing, including pieces by Bryson, Chatwin, O'Hanlon, Rushdie, and Theroux.

Biennes, Ranulph. *To the Ends of the Earth: The Transglobe Expedition, the First Pole-to-Pole Circumnavigation of the Globe.* Arbor Hse. 1983 o.p. A born adventurer tells how his wife suggested the expedition and how it finally came about; provides a detailed account of the voyage.

Bombeck, Erma. *When You Look Like Your Passport Photo, It's Time to Go Home.* HarpC 1991 $5.99. ISBN 0-06-109981-3. "Scores direct hits on the funny bone" (Publisher's note).

Buckley, William F., Jr. *Atlantic High.* Little 1983 $17.95. ISBN 0-316-11440-5. The book is "filled with a variety of delectable morsels—anecdotes, yarns, jokes, reflections, discussions, and diary jottings, touching on everything that interests a small group of educated upper-middle-class men who are sailing together. . . . So much more than a book about a sailing trip" (*Book Review Digest*).

———. *Wind Fall: The End of the Affair.* Random 1992 $25.00. ISBN 0-679-40397-3. Photographs by Christopher Little. ". . . exhilarating reading for the years celebrating Columbus's first voyage" (Louis Auchincloss).

Callahan, Steven. *Adrift: Seventy-Six Days Lost at Sea.* Ballantine 1986 $5.95. ISBN 0-345-34083-3. "A tale of courage and determination in the face of almost insurmountable hardship" (*N.Y. Times Book Review*).

Champlain, Samuel De. *The Voyages and Explorations of Samuel De Champlain, 1604–1616.* 2 vols. AMS Pr. repr. of 1922 ed. $55.00. ISBN 0-404-54905-5. A narrative of the famous adventurer's voyages, including his thoughts on various countries and monarchs.

Clark, Miles. *High Endeavours: The Extraordinary Life and Adventures of Miles and Beryl Smeaton.* HarpC 1992 $14.00. ISBN 0-586-21699-5. "Both a love story and adventure story beyond compare" (Publisher's note).

Clark, Thurston. *Equator: A Journey.* Avon 1988 $9.95. ISBN 0-380-70855-8. ". . . includes both adventures and thought, social commentary and digressions into Equatorial exotica" (*N.Y. Times Book Review*).

Cott, Jonathan. *Wandering Ghost: The Odyssey of Lafcadio Hearn.* Kodansha 1990 $14.95. ISBN 4-77001-659-X. "A superb biography of one of the best American journalists . . . a bohemian and inveterate traveller" (*The Houston Post*).

Cousteau, Jacques, and Alexis Sivirine. *Jacques Cousteau's Calypso.* Abrams 1983 o.p. The volume focuses on the vessel itself, beginning in 1942 with its construction as a minesweeper for the British navy and continuing through many changes in its evolution into a modern research vessel. "Beautifully illustrated . . . a most attractive artistic production as well as a useful reference for those interested in the anatomy and equipment of ships, particularly research vessels" (*Choice*).

Dunlop, Bill, and Frank M. Drigotas, Jr. *One Man Alone across the Atlantic in a Nine-foot Boat.* Down East 1983 o.p. Exciting account of a solo transatlantic trip.

Faragher, John Mack. *The Life and Legend of an American Pioneer.* H. Holt & Co. 1992 $27.50. ISBN 0-8050-1603-1. Many voices revealing America's foremost frontier hero.

Feynman, Richard. *"Surely You're Joking Mr. Feynman!" Adventures of a Curious Character.* Bantam 1985 $12.95. ISBN 0-553-34668-7. "Quintessential Feynman— funny, brilliant, bawdy . . . enormously entertaining" (*The New Yorker*).

_____. *"What Do You Care What Other People Think?" Further Adventures of a Curious Character.* Bantam 1989 $12.95. ISBN 0-553-34784-5. "Funny, outrageous, egocentric, and . . . moving" (*The New Yorker*).

Fletcher, Colin. *The Complete Walker III.* Knopf 1984 $18.00. ISBN 0-394-72264-7

_____. *New Complete Walker.* Knopf 1974 o.p. A book for the stroller, the hiker, and the backpacker. Fletcher's *The Complete Walker* and its revised version (above) contain practical tips for the hiker and the backpacker, and backpacking-equipment analysis. In addition, the book is laced with thoughtful insights on the philosophy of walking.

Fremont, John Charles. *Report of the Exploring Expedition to the Rocky Mountains in the Year 1842: And to Oregon and North California in the Years 1843–44.* 1845. Rprt. Serv. 1992 repr. of 1843 ed. $75.00. ISBN 0-7812-2897-2. An actual formal, official report about Fremont's expeditions throughout the western United States. Includes maps and intricate sun charts.

Fussell, Paul. *Abroad: British Literary Traveling between the Wars.* OUP 1980 $10.95. ISBN 0-19-503068-0. "An elegy for the lost art of travel—as opposed to today's tourism. . . . and a celebration of the British writers who memorialized it—D. H. Lawrence, Graham Greene, Norman Douglas, Evelyn Waugh, and Robert Byron" (Publisher's note).

Graham, Robin L., and Derek Gill. *Dove.* HarpC repr. of 1972 ed. $14.95. ISBN 0-06-092047-5. The true story of a 16-year-old boy who sailed his 24-foot sloop around the world for five years and 33,000 miles to discover adventure and love.

Grant, George M. *Ocean to Ocean: Sandford Fleming's Expedition through Canada in 1872.* C. E. Tuttle 1967 o.p. "A stirring account of a small party's journey from Halifax in the east to Victoria in the west in search of a transcontinental railway route. A first-person story of the exhilarations and the hardships of the trip, it compares well with its nearest American counterpart, 'The Journals of Lewis and Clark'" (*N.Y. Times*).

Graves, Robert. *Lawrence and the Arabs.* Paragon Hse. 1991 repr. of 1927 ed. $14.95. ISBN 1-55778-338-1. "A brilliant and provocative volume" (*N.Y. Times*).

Hayes, Harold T. P. *The Dark Romance of Dian Fossey*. S & S Trade 1990 $10.95. ISBN 0-671-74231-0. "The best book yet to be written about Dian Fossey" (*Newsday*).

Huxley, Elspeth. *Out in the Midday Sun*. Viking Penguin 1985 $10.00. ISBN 0-14-009256-0. Africa between two world wars—". . . and what a Kenya it was" (*Financial Times*).

Johnson, William H. *The World's Discoverers: The Story of Bold Voyages by Brave Navigators during a Thousand Years*. Gordon Pr. 1977 $59.95. ISBN 0-8490-2847-7. Chronicles the lives and journeys of famous seafarers.

Kingsley, Mary. *Travels in West Africa: Congo Français, Corsico and Cameroons*. 1897. C. E. Tuttle 1987 $6.95. ISBN 0-460-87169-2. "This is one of the classic writings on African exploration. . . . Her explorations and account of her first two trips, in 1893 and 1895, were remarkable achievements. And, with far-reaching effects, her intelligent, humanitarian approach to the study of African culture demolished forever the concept of 'savage Africa' and its 'childlike natives'" (*Library Journal*).

Kingston, Maxine H. *The Woman Warrior*. S & S Trade 1989 $15.95. ISBN 0-671-69534-7. "Startling and important insights on American values in war and peace" (*San Francisco Chronicle*)

Kirkpatrick, Jane. *Homestead*. Word Inc. 1991 $10.99. ISBN 0-8499-3297-1. ". . . a moving adventure story of modern pioneers, full of courage, hard work, tender moments, and life-changing experiences" (Barbara Jenkins, coauthor of *The Walk West* and *The Road Unseen*).

Krakauer, Jon. *Eiger Dreams: Ventures Among Men and Mountains*. Dell 1990 $5.99. ISBN 0-440-20990-0. "Likely to please not only mountain maniacs but adventure buffs in general" (Publisher's note).

Kuralt, Charles. *A Life on the Road*. Ivy Books 1991 $5.99. ISBN 0-8041-0869-2. "A professional memoir of a gifted, good-humored and gracious man. . . . has the feel of good conversation on a long trip" (*N.Y. Times Book Review*).

Ledyard, John. *Journey through Russia and Siberia, 1787–1788: The Journal and Selected Letters*. Ed. by Stephen D. Watrous. U. of Wis. Pr. 1966 o.p. "John Ledyard was one of the most amazing explorers of all time. . . . he conceived the idea of journeying eastward across Europe and Siberia, thence shipping to Alaska and walking across North America to New York. This well-researched, ably edited book describes his journey almost to the Pacific Coast of Siberia, before Catherine the Great ordered him returned to Europe" (*Library Journal*).

Leslie, Edward E. *Desperate Journeys, Abandoned Souls: True Stories of Castaways and Other Survivors*. HM 1988 $11.95. ISBN 0-395-43608-7. ". . . reveals some dark truths about human nature, the limits of courage, and the fragility of life itself" (Sterling Seagrave).

Lovell, Mary S. *The Sound of Wings: The Life of Amelia Earhart*. St. Martin 1989 $12.95. ISBN 0-312-05160-3. "Has the expertise and understanding one would have expected from Lovell's excellent biography of Beryl Markham" (*New York*).

Montgomery, Sy. *Walking with the Great Apes: Jane Goodall, Dian Fossey, Birute Galdikas*. HM 1991 $9.95. ISBN 0-395-61156-3. ". . . brings us to a deep and compassionate understanding of these three modern shamans" (Farley Mowat).

Morris, Jan. *Journeys*. OUP 1985 $21.95. ISBN 0-19-503452-X. "Her latest journey takes her to . . . Vienna, Stockholm, Peking and Shanghai, Aberdeen in Scotland, Calcutta, and Wells, England. One of the 5 American stopovers is Las Vegas. . . . [She] may at times see more than is there, but a good travel writer has to. She may be the best we have" (*N.Y. Times Book Review*).

Mowat, Farley. *Woman in the Mists: The Story of Dian Fossey and the Mountain Gorillas of Africa*. Warner Bks. 1987 $10.95. ISBN 0-446-38720-7. "A rare gripping look at the tragically mingled destinies of a heroic, flawed woman and her beloved mountain gorillas . . ." (*N.Y. Times Book Review*).

Obregon, Mauricio. *Argonauts to Astronauts*. HarpC 1980 o.p. "The great explorers of the surface of the earth . . . are cited here for widening the horizons of the known world. . . ." [The author's] thesis is that with the space frontier we have come full circle. Astronauts are now the leading edge of knowledge and adventure that will open our world in much the same way that ancient explorers did theirs" (*School Library Journal*).

Pike, Zebulon Montgomery. *The Journals of Zebulon Montgomery Pike, with Letters and Related Documents.* Ed. by Donald Jackson. 2 vols. *Amer. Exploration and Travel Ser.* U. of Okla. Pr. 1966 o.p. Pike's journals of his difficult travels, reissued for the first time since 1895. Supplemented with maps and correspondence.

Rich, Doris L. *Amelia Earhart: A Biography.* Smithsonian 1989 $24.95. ISBN 0-87474-836-4. A *N.Y. Times* notable book of the year. ". . . a thoroughly researched yet eminently readable biography of a feminist before her time" (*Utne Reader*).

Roberts, David. *Great Exploration Hoaxes.* Ed. by Herbert Michaelman. Crown Pub. Group 1981 o.p.

———. *The Mountain of My Fear.* Vanguard 1968 o.p. The story of the first scaling of the western face of Alaska's Mount Huntington by four Harvard students in 1965.

Roth, Hal. *Two against Cape Horn.* Norton 1978 $10.95. ISBN 0-393-30259-8. First-person account of Roth and his wife sailing from California and around South America's Cape Horn; complete with the story of their shipwreck.

———. *Two on a Big Ocean.* Norton 1978 $24.95. ISBN 0-393-03216-7. "This book describes the 19 months the Roths spent circumnavigating the Pacific Ocean, from San Francisco to Tahiti and the South Seas, then to Japan, the sub-Arctic Aleutians and the mountainous Alaskan and Canadian coasts. In their 35-foot sailboat *Whisper*, they traveled 18,538 miles, called at 75 ports, made hundreds of new friends, and gained a new understanding of the sea and the people who live beside it" (Publisher's note).

Sayre, Woodrow Wilson. *Four against Everest.* P-H 1964 o.p. "Sayre's amazing ascent with three companions almost to the top of Everest was a tremendous test and magnificent achievement of the human spirit. With the sublime confidence of amateurs, without governmental permission or the help of Sherpas, and scorning oxygen as offensive to aesthetic principles and good sportsmanship, they faced unseen hazards but survived. . . . The chapter 'Why Men Climb' is a masterpiece" (*Library Journal*).

Speke, John H. *Journal of the Discovery of the Source of the Nile.* Biblio Dist. 1969 repr. of 1906 ed. o.p.

Steinbeck, John. *Travels with Charley in Search of America.* Viking Penguin 1980 $6.00. ISBN 0-14-005320-4. In late summer 1960, Steinbeck set out from Sag Harbor, New York, in a three-quarter-ton pickup truck with a small cabin built on it. He traveled over the face of America with his 10-year-old poodle of indifferent health named Charley.

Teilhard de Chardin, Pierre. *Letters from a Traveller.* Ed. by Claude Aragonnes. HarpC 1962 o.p. These are selections from letters written between 1923 and 1955 by Father Teilhard de Chardin, one of the world's leading paleontologists. His travels took him to China, Java, India, Ethiopia, South Africa, and the United States. A person of keen perception and spiritual insight, "He describes vividly the exotic lands where he searched for prehistoric man." Introductions by Julian Huxley, Pierre Leroy, S. J., and Claude Aragonnes.

Thomsen, Moritz. *The Saddest Pleasure: A Journey on Two Rivers.* Graywolf 1990 $9.95. ISBN 1-55597-124-5. Introduction by Paul Theroux. ". . . not just a report of a journey but a memoir, an autobiography, a confession, a foray into South America . . . a travel narrative . . . a summing up" (Paul Theroux).

Twain, Mark. *Following the Equator.* Ecco Pr. 1992 repr. of 1897 ed. $12.95. ISBN 0-88001-280-3. Focuses on "the personalities of the ship's crew and passengers, the poetry of Australian place names, and the success of women's suffrage in New Zealand.

Walker, Tom. *Denali Journal: A Thoughtful Look at Wildlife in Alaska's Majestic National Park.* Stackpole 1992 $16.95. ISBN 0-8117-2437-9. Enlightening photographs and candid comments in a unique journal format.

Wetzel, Betty. *After You Mark Twain: A Modern Journey Around the Equator.* Fulcrum Pub. 1990 $11.95. ISBN 1-55591-069-6. ". . . brings the reader much closer to the realities of the world as it is today in contrast to what it was in Twain's time" (Publisher's note).

Winchester, Simon. *The Sun Never Sets: Travels to the Remaining Outposts of the British Empire.* P-H 1985 $10.95. ISBN 0-13-877861-2. "A glorious book . . . unfailing entertainment . . ." (Jan Morris).

Zweig, Paul. *The Adventurer: The Fate of Adventure in the Western World.* Princeton U. Pr. 1981 repr. of 1974 ed. $37.50. ISBN 0-691-06451-2. Traces the history and literature of adventure travel, with portraits of famous adventurers. Analyzes the characteristics of adventurers.

CHRONOLOGY OF AUTHORS

Polo, Marco. 1254?–1324?
Columbus, Christopher. 1446–1506
Vespucci, Amerigo. 1451–1512
Hakluyt, Richard. 1552–1616
Cook, Captain James. 1728–1779
Clark, William. 1770–1838
Park, Mungo. 1771–1806
Lewis, Meriwether. 1774–1809
Borrow, George. 1803–1881
Kinglake, Alexander. 1809–1891
Livingstone, David. 1813–1873
Dana, Richard Henry, Jr. 1815–1882
Burton, Sir Richard. 1821–1890
Stanley, Sir Henry Morton.
    1841–1904
Slocum, Joshua. 1844–1909
Peary, Robert E(dwin). 1856–1920
Roosevelt, Theodore. 1858–1919
Scott, Robert Falcon. 1868–1912
Amundsen, Roald. 1872–1928
Stefansson, Vilhjalmur. 1879–1962
Freuchen, Peter. 1886–1957

Byrd, Richard E(velyn). 1888–1957
Lawrence, T(homas) E(dward).
    1888–1935
Morton, H(enry Canova) V(ollam).
    1892–1979
Stark, Freya. 1893–
Gunther, John. 1901–1970
Lindbergh, Charles A(ugustus).
    1902–1974
Snow, Edward. 1902–1982
Van der Post, Laurens. 1906–
Michener, James A(lbert). 1907–
Cousteau, Jacques-Yves. 1910–
Harrer, Heinrich. 1912–
Heyerdahl, Thor. 1914–
Hillary, Sir Edmund. 1919–
Matthiessen, Peter. 1927–
Aldrin, Edwin Eugene, Jr. 1930–
Theroux, Paul. 1941–
Ride, Sally. 1951–
Earle, Sylvia. 1955–

ALDRIN, EDWIN EUGENE (BUZZ), JR. 1930–

Edwin Aldrin was born in Montclair, New Jersey. After graduating from the U.S. Military Academy, he completed U.S. Air Force pilot training in 1952 and flew over 60 combat missions during the Korean War. In 1963 he was selected by NASA as an astronaut. He served as backup pilot of the *Gemini IX* and as pilot for *Gemini XII* in 1966. He was made backup command module pilot for *Apollo VIII* and lunar module pilot for *Apollo XI*, the most famous flight in space history, which landed on the moon July 20, 1969. Aldrin was the second man to walk on the moon; Neil Armstrong, the first man, beat Aldrin by just 15 minutes. He completed his Air Force career as commandant of the Aerospace Research Pilot School, retiring from the Air Force in 1972. Since then he has served as a consultant and has written two books. He holds the record of over 7 hours and 52 minutes outside a spacecraft in extra-vehicular activity.

BOOKS BY ALDRIN

Men from Earth: An Apollo Astronaut's Exciting Account of America's Space Program. (coauthored with Malcolm McConnell). Bantam 1989 $19.95. ISBN 0-553-05374-4.

"... provides a roaringly vivid view of the Spage Age right from the driver's seat ... as well as the fractious and sometimes petty battles among astronauts" (Charles Petit, *The San Francisco Examiner and Chronicle*).

Return to Earth. (coauthored with Wayne Warga). World 1973 o.p. "The troubled odyssey of a hero of technology who couldn't cope with earthly fame. . . . revealing autobiography of the 'second man' on the moon" (*Publishers Weekly*).

AMUNDSEN, ROALD (ENGELBRECHT GRAVNING). 1872–1928

Norwegian explorer Roald Amundsen was born in Borge, Norway. Although he studied medicine, he abandoned that career to pursue a life at sea. In 1897 he went to the Antarctic with a Belgian expedition. Their ship, the *Belgica*, became the first vessel to spend a winter in Antarctica. From 1902 to 1906, Amundsen explored the Northwest Passage, becoming the first person to navigate this waterway in both directions. In 1910 he set out to be the first person to reach the North Pole, but he was beaten there by ROBERT PEARY. As a result, he shifted his attention to the South Pole and became the first person to reach there—in December 11, 1911, the month before Captain ROBERT FALCON SCOTT. Amundsen disappeared in the Arctic in 1928 while searching by plane for his airship *Italia*, which had been missing. During his life, he wrote several books about his adventures, most notably his autobiography, *My Life as an Explorer* (1927).

BOOKS BY AMUNDSEN

My Life as an Explorer. 1927 o.p. The author's fascinating autobiography.
The Northwest Passage: Being the Record of a Voyage of Exploration of the Ship Gjoa, 1903–1907. 2 vols. AMS Pr. repr. of 1908 ed. $50.00. ISBN 0-404-11625-6. Amundsen's journals of his exploration of the Northwest Passage.

BOOKS ABOUT AMUNDSEN

Flaherty, Leo, and William Goetzmann. *Roald Amundsen and the Quest for the South Pole.* Chelsea Hse. 1993 $18.95. ISBN 0-7910-1308-1. Well-written account of Amundsen's South Pole expedition.

BORROW, GEORGE (HENRY). 1803–1881

Borrow was employed by the (Protestant) Bible Society to distribute bibles in Catholic Spain in 1835. He encountered much opposition and was on one occasion imprisoned for three weeks. The famous account of his experience has little to do with the Bible and much to do with the people, land, and perils of his journey. Borrow is as racy in his descriptions of places as of people. *Lavengro* (1851) and its sequel, *The Romany Rye* (1857), are like novels in their interest and excitement. They are stories of gypsies, rich in gypsy lore, superstitions, and customs. Borrow spent many years in close association with Spanish gypsies and translated the Gospel of St. Luke into their language. His linguistic abilities were remarkable; he gives much space to word derivations, particularly in *Lavengro*. His books abound in pugnacious passages; his attacks on SIR WALTER SCOTT (see Vol. 1), on prizefighters, and on "papists" are indicative of some of his sharp prejudices. He wrote marvelously, however, and those who admire him are devotees for life.

BOOKS BY BORROW

Lavengro: The Classic Account of Gypsy Life in Nineteenth Century England. 1851. Dover repr. of 1900 ed. $12.95. ISBN 0-486-26915-9
Works. Ed. by Clement Shorter. AMS Pr. repr. of 1961 ed. $300.00. ISBN 0-404-00970-0. Collection of writings, including many of his works on gypsies.

Romany Rye. 1857. OUP 1984 o.p.

BOOKS ABOUT BORROW

Collie, Michael. *George Borrow, Eccentric.* Cambridge U. Pr. 1983 o.p. ". . . has [used] . . . hitherto unpublished material [seeking to show that Borrow] . . . used religion, invented much of the material he presented as factual travel literature, and preserved a public facade to hide a disoriented personality" (*Choice*).

———, and Angus Fraser. *George Borrow: A Bibliographical Study.* Omnigraphics Inc. 1984 $70.00. ISBN 0-906795-24-9. Reprints 160 of the 316 pages in T. J. Wise's 1914 bibliography; provides short introductory essays to each section and clears up misinformation relating to Borrow's manuscripts.

BURTON, SIR RICHARD (FRANCIS). 1821–1890

Sir Richard Burton, the explorer, adventurer, translator, and student of Eastern sexual customs, was born in Torquay, England. He received a very irregular education, which included an expulsion from Oxford University. In 1842 Burton joined the East India Company and went to India, where he learned the Persian, Hindustani, Afghan, and Arabic languages. Orville Prescott has written: "One of the great explorers of the nineteenth century, Burton disguised himself as a Pathan dervish and doctor in order to penetrate the forbidden cities of Medina and Mecca. He was the first European to reach Harar, the religious capital of Somaliland. He was the discoverer of Lake Tanganyika and explored in the Congo, the Cameroons, Dahomey, and Brazil. He was a pioneer ethnologist and anthropologist. He was a linguist of dazzling ability, speaking 29 languages and 11 dialects. He wrote 43 books on his travels, 2 volumes of poetry, and translated (in addition to *The Arabian Nights*) 6 volumes of Portuguese literature, 2 of Latin poetry, and 4 of Neapolitan, African, and Hindu folklore" (*Saturday Review*).

Following a trip to America in 1860, Burton published an account of the Mormon settlement in Utah entitled *City of the Saints* (1861). His wife, Isabel Arundel, frequently traveled with him on such journeys. After Burton died in Trieste in 1890, she burned many of his journals, as well as the manuscript of an uncompleted work called *The Scented Garden Men's Hearts to Gladden.*

BOOKS BY BURTON

The Arabian Nights. Based on the Text of the Fourteenth-Century Syrian Manuscript. Ed. by Muhsin Mahdi. Trans. by Husain Haddawy. Norton 1990 o.p. The first serious English rendering in over a century.

The Arabian Nights: The Marvels and Wonders of the Thousand and One Nights. Trans. by Jack Zipes. NAL-Dutton 1991 $5.95. ISBN 0-451-2542-6. Adapted from Burton's unexpurgated edition. Reveals "tension between individual desire and social law . . . empower[ing] the oppressed . . . in ways they had thought were unimaginable" (Jack Zipes, Afterword).

The City of the Saints. AMS Pr. repr. of 1861 ed. $19.95. ISBN 0-87081-191-6. Burton's account of his overland journey in 1860 across America to the home of the Mormons in Salt Lake City.

The Erotic Traveler. Ed. by Edward Leigh. Putnam Pub. Group 1967 o.p. "Subtitled 'an astonishing exploration of bizarre sex rites and customs by the great adventurer,' this is sexual anthropology at its most exotic" (*Virginia Kirkus Service*).

First Footsteps in East Africa or, an Exploration of Harar. Dover 1987 repr. of 1894 ed. $11.95. ISBN 0-486-25475-5. "The epic tale of his remarkable expedition into . . . Harar remains one of the great adventure classics of all time" (Publisher's note).

Goa and the Blue Mountains: Or, Six Months of Sick Leave. U. CA Pr. 1991 repr. of 1851 ed. $40.00. ISBN 0-520-07610-9. ". . . the public debut of that astonishingly protean

Victorian. . . . explorer, soldier, consul . . . poet, translator, and prolific writer about the peoples and customs of alien lands" (Dane Kennedy, Introduction).

The Illustrated Kama Sutra, Ananga-Ranga and Perfumed Garden: The Classic Eastern Love Texts. Trans. by Burton and F. F. Arbuthnott. Inner Trad. 1991 $19.95. ISBN 0-89281-441-1

The Kama Sutra of Vatsyayama Now Complete and Unexpurgated. Ed. by W. S. Archer. Berkley Pub. 1966 repr. of 1883 ed. o.p. ". . . remains the best interpretation in English of an early Indian writer's treatment of the science and art of love" (W. S. Archer, Preface). Introduction by K. M. Panchkar.

The Lake Region of Central Africa: A Picture of Exploration. Scholarly 1972 repr. of 1860 ed. $95.00. ISBN 0-403-00492-X. Detailed descriptions of the geography, topography, and people of central Africa.

Mission to Gelele, King of Dahome. Ed. by C. W. Newbury. Greenwood 1966 o.p.

Perfumed Garden of Shagkh Nefzawi. Lightyear 1992 $21.95. ISBN 0-89968-296-0.

Personal Narrative of a Pilgrimage to Al-Madinah and Meccah. 2 vols. Dover 1964 repr. of 1893 ed. $9.95 ea. ISBNs 0-486-21217-3, 0-486-21218-1. ". . . a great classic of travel. . . . this matter-of-fact humor against a backdrop of constant hazard and possible exposure have delighted . . . readers over the last century" (Publisher's note).

Two Trips to Gorilla Land and the Cataracts of the Congo. 2 vols. Johnson Repr. repr. of 1876 ed. o.p. Additional accounts of his central African expeditions.

Wanderings in West Africa from Liverpool to Fernando Po. 2 vols. Johnson Repr. repr. of 1863 ed. $45.00. ISBN 0-384-06651-8

Zanzibar: City, Island, and Coast. 2 vols. Johnson Repr. repr. of 1872 ed. o.p. Detailed look at Zanzibar and its importance as a trading center between East Africa and the Arabic world.

BOOKS ABOUT BURTON

Brodie, Fawn M. *The Devil Drives: A Life of Sir Richard Burton.* Norton 1984 repr. of 1967 ed. $12.95. ISBN 0-393-30166-4. ". . . a first class biography of an exceptional man" (*N.Y. Times Book Review*).

McLynn, F. J. *Burton: Snow upon the Desert.* Trafalgar Sq. 1991 $34.95. ISBN 07195-4818-7. "A reconstruction of Burton's convoluted inner life . . . scholarly, well written, and compelling" (*Library Journal*).

Penzer, Norman M. *An Annotated Bibliography of Sir Richard Francis Burton.* B. Franklin repr. of 1923 ed. o.p. Useful reference source for materials by and about Burton.

Rice, Edward. *Captain Sir Richard Francis Burton: The Secret Agent Who Made the Pilgrimage to Mecca, Discovered the Kama Sutra, and Brought the Arabian Nights to the West.* HarpC 1991 $16.00. ISBN 0-06-097394-3. "A welcome biography of a man who refuses to be forgotten" (*Chicago Tribune*).

Sir Richard Burton's Travels in Arabia and Africa: Four Lectures from a Huntington Library Manuscript. Huntington Lib. 1990 o.p. Four lectures that discuss some of Burton's greatest accomplishments and his views on ethnology. Introduction by John Hayman.

BYRD, RICHARD E(VELYN). 1888–1957

Rear Admiral Byrd was a U.S. naval officer and aviator—the only person of his time who had flown over both poles and one of the first men to fly the Atlantic. During World War I, he was lieutenant commander of the U.S. air forces in Canada. *Skyward* (1928) tells of the first airplane flight made over the North Pole with Floyd Bennett in 1926. *Little America* (1930) is a detailed record of Byrd's flight over the South Pole. *Alone* (1938) is his remarkable tale of fortitude during his self-imposed isolation at Advance Base in the Antarctic in 1934. In the spring of 1947, Byrd returned from his fifth and largest polar expedition, the largest exploring expedition ever organized—13 ships staffed by 4,000 men, entirely naval in personnel.

"America's strategic concept of polar defense is an outgrowth of Admiral Byrd's five exploration ventures into the Arctic and Antarctic. . . . He was in over-all command of the Naval task force that, between 1955 and 1959, was to prepare, supply and maintain a series of scientific stations in Antarctica. . . . He was placed by President Eisenhower in charge of all Antarctic activities of the United States" (*N.Y. Times*).

Byrd received a special medal of the National Geographic Society from President Herbert Hoover in 1930, the Legion of Merit for "outstanding services" from President Franklin D. Roosevelt in 1945, and the Defense Department's Medal of Freedom in 1957. It is thought that he impaired his health seriously while on the 1933–34 expedition. He was buried with full military honors in the Arlington National Cemetery.

BOOKS BY BYRD

Alone. Island Pr. 1984 repr. of 1938 ed. o.p. Byrd's account of five months of isolation at Advance Base at the South Pole in 1934.

Antarctica: Accounts from Journals of Numerous Explorers. Marboro Bks. 1990 $24.95. ISBN 0-88029-506-6. Introduction by Charles Neider. Contains excerpts from Byrd's diaries and recollections, vividly recreating his five-month journey.

Discovery: The Story of the Second Byrd Antarctic Expedition. Rprt. Serv. 1991 repr. of 1935 ed. $79.00. ISBN 0-7812-8055-9

BOOKS ABOUT BYRD

Bernard, Raymond. *The Hollow Earth: The Greatest Geographical Discovery in History*. Carol Pub. Group 1991 $4.50. ISBN 0-8216-2507-1. Examines the significance of Byrd's polar expeditions.

———. *A Secret Meeting in Rome*. AMORC 1987 $6.95. ISBN 0-912057-48-36-6

Rodgers, Eugene. *Beyond the Barrier: The Story of Byrd's First Expedition to Antarctica*. Naval Inst. Pr. 1990 $24.95. ISBN 0-87021-022-X. "[a] demythologization . . . [and] well-researched account of his 1928 Antarctic expedition. . ." (*Library Journal*).

CLARK, WILLIAM. 1770–1838

[SEE LEWIS, MERIWETHER in this chapter.]

COLUMBUS, CHRISTOPHER (Cristoforo Colombo). 1446–1506

A man of imagination, dreams, and perseverance, Columbus, the Genoese, persuaded King Ferdinand and Queen Isabella of Spain to sponsor his search for the Orient through a Western route. Columbus made four voyages to the New World, always landing in the West Indies and believing he was very close to the "Island of Cipango" (Japan). Difficulties with his crew and with his native subjects led to his dismissal as Spanish governor of the islands, although King Ferdinand remained an admirer of his nautical prowess.

Fernando Colon (Ferdinand Columbus), his son, wrote *The Life of the Admiral Christopher Columbus*. "It is greatly to Ferdinand's credit as an honest biographer that, while trying to show what a hard, sad life his father led, he included so much evidence to suggest that Columbus enjoyed it" (*The New Yorker*).

The five-hundreth anniversary of Columbus's first trip to the Americas was celebrated in 1992. The approach of this anniversary prompted a renewed look at Columbus and his significance. As a result, there has been increased controversy about Columbus's role. Some continue to admire him as a visionary who expanded the horizons of Europe and helped usher in a new age. Others, however, view him as a despoiler of the New World who plundered its resources and destroyed the culture of its indigenous people. Elements of truth can be found in both views; it must be conceded, however, that Columbus was a great traveler and explorer.

BOOKS BY COLUMBUS

Christopher Columbus: His Life, His Works, His Remains, as Revealed by Original Printed and Manuscript Records. Ed. by John Boyd Thatcher. 3 vols. AMS Pr. 1967 repr. of 1903–04 ed. o.p.

Four Voyages to the New World. Trans. H. R. Major. Peter Smith $22.50. ISBN 0-8446-1883-7. Introduction by John E. Fagg. Columbus's journals of his voyages to America.

Letter to Rafael Sanchez. Johnson Repr. repr. of 1493 ed. o.p.

The Voyage of Christopher Columbus: Columbus's Own Journal of Discovery. Ed. and trans. by John Cummins. St. Martin 1992 $19.95. ISBN 0-312-07880-3. Log of Columbus's first journey to America supplemented by additional documented and biographical information.

BOOKS ABOUT COLUMBUS

Bowen, David, ed. *Columbus & The Crowns: Edited from William H. Prescott's History of the Reign of Ferdinand & Isabella.* Corona Pub. 1991 $15.95. ISBN 0-931722-82-9. More concise edition of William H. Prescott's three-volume work depicting Columbus's experiences.

Colon, Fernando. *The Life of Admiral Christopher Columbus by His Son Ferdinand.* Trans. by Benjamin Keen. Greenwood 1978 repr. of 1959 ed. $35.00. ISBN 0-313-20175-7. "The setting, the figures, and the actions of the drama of discovery emerge from these pages with an enthralling realism and immediacy" (*Preface*).

Dor-Ner, Zvi, and William Scheller. *Columbus and the Age of Discovery.* Morrow 1991 $34.49. ISBN 0-688-08545-8. Perhaps "the definitive book to emerge from the Columbus quincentenary. . . . The range of maps and the quality of scientific explanation alone reward close reading" (*The Christian Science Monitor*).

Flint, Valerie I. *The Imaginative Landscape of Christopher Columbus.* Princeton U. Pr. 1992 $24.95. ISBN 0-691-05681-1. A "distinctive scholarly study [that] analyzes in detail the admiral's knowledge of maps, sea lore, his known reading . . . which formed the certainty of his vision and . . . impelled him to success" (*Library Journal*).

Lopez, Barry Holstun. *Thamas D. Clark Lectures 1990: The Rediscovery of North America.* U. Pr. of Ky. 1990 o.p. "The most alluring item in the current Columbus backwash . . . also the lightest. . . . strings of . . . impeccable epiphanies [about losing] whole communities of peoples, plants, and animals because a handful of men wanted gold and silver. . ." (*San Francisco Review of Books*).

Morison, Samuel E. *Admiral of the Ocean Sea.* Atlantic Monthly 1941 $45.00. ISBN 0-316-58354-5. "A Pulitzer Prize winner. . . . written with the insight, energy, and authority that only someone who had himself sailed in Columbus's path . . . could master" (Publisher's note).

———. *Christopher Columbus, Mariner.* NAL-Dutton 1983 repr. of 1942 ed. $9.00. ISBN 0-452-00992-8. "Based on the definitive Pulitzer Prize-winning *Admiral of the Ocean Sea* . . . a stirring tale of early navigation, court politics, and unsurpassed adventure" (Publisher's note).

Paiewonsky, Michael. *Conquest of Eden, 1493–1515: The Other Voyages of Columbus: Puerto Rico, Hispaniola, Guadeloupe, The Virgin Islands.* Mapes Monde 1990 $38.50. ISBN 0-926330-03-9. ". . . a wonderfully illustrated essay. . . . much . . . from the reports and letters of Spanish participants in the conquest. . . . highlights Spanish lust for gold and destruction of native life . . . should be successful in whetting the appetites of non-specialists" (*Library Journal*).

Rouse, Irving. *The Tainos: Rise and Decline of the People Who Greeted Columbus.* Yale U. Pr. 1992 $25.00. ISBN 0-300-05181-6. A "masterpiece of the cultural/historical approach in archaeology . . . [based on] 35 years of research. . . . informative and accessible" (*Library Journal*).

Stannard, David E. *American Holocaust: Columbus and the Conquest of the New World.* OUP 1992 $25.00. ISBN 0-19-507581-1. Story of "the largest genocide in history. . . . though Stannard tends to gloss over violence and inter-tribal warfare in pre-Colonial America. . . . his is a carefully researched, well-written monograph" (*Library Journal*).

Taviani, Paolo. *Columbus: The Great Adventurer. His Life, His Times, and His Voyages.* Trans. by Luciano F. Farina and Marc A. Beckwith. Crown Pub. Group 1989 $20.00. ISBN 0-517-58474-3. "The best and most scholarly book I have read on Columbus's life" (Samuel Eliot Morison).

West, Delno C., and August Kling. *Columbus Quincentenary Series. The Libro de las profecias of Christopher Columbus.* U. Press Fla. 1991 $49.95. ISBN 0-8130-1054-3. A "superb edition and translation . . . intended primarily for scholars, but [its] introduction offers a concise biography of Columbus that highlights his spirituality and religious beliefs . . ." (*N.Y. Times Book Review*).

COOK, CAPTAIN JAMES. 1728–1779

Captain James Cook, one of Britain's greatest explorers, was born to a poor family in Yorkshire. After receiving only a limited education, he joined the British Navy and quickly moved up through the ranks, becoming captain of his own ship in 1759. Chosen to lead scientific expeditions to the Pacific and other areas, Captain Cook's voyages round the world resulted in the discovery of the Sandwich Islands and the eastern coast of Australia (New South Wales), as well as the gathering of other important geographical information. He was killed by natives in Hawaii in 1779. An obelisk was erected there in his memory in 1874. Cook's *Voyages* was written partly by himself and continued by Captain James King after Cook's death.

In a review of Cook's *Voyages, Library Journal* wrote, "It is not too easy at this distance to appreciate fully the impact which Cook's voyages had on the intellectual world of his day. In a period of acute international tension . . . the exploring ships went out, incidentally, with safe conducts from belligerents, and the published reports quickly translated into the principal languages aroused immense enthusiasm. . . . In many ways Cook's second voyage was the high point of his career as an explorer and scientist." In the fall of 1960, it was reported that a faded manuscript and logbook of Cook's first and second voyages were sold to a London bookseller for $148,400. In early 1969, an expeditionary party of the Academy of Natural Sciences of Philadelphia located some of Captain Cook's canons in waters ten fathoms deep off the coast of Australia.

BOOKS BY COOK

Authentic Narrative of a Voyage Performed by Captain Cook and Captain Clerke in His Majesty's Ships Resolution and Discovery during the Years 1776–1780: In Search of a North-West Passage between the Continents of Asia and America. 1782. Ed. by William Ellis. 2 vols. Da Capo 1969 o.p.

The Explorations of Captain James Cook in the Pacific, as Told by Selections of His Own Journals, 1768–1779. Ed. by A. Grenfell Price. Dover o.p. With an introduction by Percy G. Adams.

Journal of H. M. S. Endeavour, 1768–1771. Genesis Pr. 1977 o.p. Account of his Pacific voyage.

Voyages of Discovery. Ed. by John Barrow. Biblio Dist. 1976 o.p.

BOOKS ABOUT COOK

Beaglehole, J. C. *The Life of Captain James Cook.* Stanford U. Pr. 1974 o.p. ". . . may come to be regarded as definitive. . . . the bulk of the narrative is . . . devoted to the three great South Seas voyages (1768–1780). . . . [Cook emerges as] both loved and 'properly feared' by his men" (*Publishers Weekly*).

Joppien, Rudiger, and Bernard Smith. *The Art of Captain Cook's Voyages.* 3 vols. Yale U. Pr. Vol. 1 1985 $75.00. ISBN 0-300-03450-4. Vol. 2 1985 $75.00. ISBN 0-300-03451-2. Vol. 3 1988 $225.00. ISBN 0-300-04105-5. Brings together "all the images . . . made on Cook's voyages of discovery, now dispersed through the world. . . . an extraordinary experience to follow the artists as they confront what they had never seen before with slowly adapting eyes" (*N.Y. Times Book Review*). "Particular focus is upon the work of John Webber and William Ellis [whose] drawings and paintings are examined within their historical context and the particular episode of the voyage that stimulated their creation . . ." (*Choice*).

COUSTEAU, JACQUES-YVES. 1910–

French marine explorer, writer, and film producer, Cousteau has popularized the undersea world for people of all ages. In 1943 he was partially responsible for the invention of the Aqua-lung, making it possible to extend the duration of underwater swimming. After World War II, he persuaded the French naval minister to create a marine study center at Toulon. Several years of study dramatized the need for application research, so with a 25-million-franc gift, the ferry *Calypso* was purchased. Its voyage to the Red Sea resulted in a film that won the Grand Prix at the Paris documentary film festival. It was followed in 1956 by *The Silent World*, an Oscar winner. Ensuing explorations resulted in over 36 films. *The Undersea World of Jacques Cousteau* (1967) documented a scientific world cruise from the Red Sea through the Indian Ocean to the Pacific Ocean, as far north as Alaska. A 1972 television series filmed the expedition in the Antarctic and along the Chilean coast, and a 1975 archaeological expedition took Cousteau and his team to Greek waters. To date, the team has amassed 10 Emmy awards for documentary films for television. Cousteau has also written over 15 books, including a 20-volume encyclopedia, *The Ocean World of Jacques Cousteau*. He has produced numerous videotapes and has written a column, "Pulse of the Sea," for the *Saturday Review*, in addition to numerous articles for *National Geographic* magazine from 1952 to 1966.

In 1974, in order to arouse public opinion, he founded the Cousteau Society to preserve the oceans. He estimates that in his lifetime he has spent over seven years underwater, and that "during that time I have observed and studied closely, and with my own two eyes I have seen the oceans sicken."

BOOKS BY COUSTEAU

A Bill of Rights for Future Generations. Myrin Institute 1980 $1.50. ISBN 0-913098-29-9. Aimed at children, this discusses the ways of preserving the oceans for the future.

Cousteau's Great White Shark. (coauthored with Mose Richards). Abrams 1992 $39.95. ISBN 0-8109-3181-8. Highlights adventures of Cousteau's 40-person team's 2½-year investigation of the great white shark, with drawings and 120 color photographs.

Dolphins. Arrowood Pr. 1987 o.p.

Jacques Cousteau's Amazon Journey. (coauthored with Mose Richards). Abrams 1984 o.p. ". . . covers the entire Amazon basin from the mountains of Peru to the delta on the Atlantic . . . visually stunning and serious in its purpose of bringing forth important ecological concerns" (*Library Journal*).

Jacques Cousteau—Whales. (coauthored with Yves Paccalet). Abrams 1988 $24.98. ISBN 0-7924-4520-1. Confusing, untidy, and biased.

Jacques Cousteau's Calypso. (coauthored with Alexis Sivirine). Abrams 1983 o.p. A "volume . . . devoted . . . to the vessel itself [beginning] in 1942 when [it] was built in the U. S. as a minesweeper for the British Navy and continu[ing] through a multitude of changes as the ship evolved into a . . . modern research vessel" (*Choice*).

A Living Sea. (coauthored with James Dugan). Lyons & Burford 1988 $12.95. ISBN 0-941130-73-8. A sequel to *The Silent World* that shows Cousteau's role in the latest developments in sea exploration; displays his rare sensitivity for the sea and its creatures.

The Ocean World. Abrams 1985 $29.95. ISBN 0-8109-8068. Illustrated. Covers "every imaginable topic . . . from the chemistry of seawater and complex biology and behavior of sea creatures, to legends and stories inspired by the sea" (*The Christian Science Monitor*).

The Silent World. (coauthored with Frederick Dumas). Lyons & Burford 1987 repr. of 1953 ed. $13.95. ISBN 2-85089-227-X. Makes readers feel like eyewitnesses to undersea diving history.

Undersea Discoveries of Jacques-Yves Cousteau. 3 vols. Arrowood Pr. 1989 $49.98. ISBN 0-88486-017-5. Detailed look at many of Cousteau's discoveries.

BOOKS ABOUT COUSTEAU

Cousteau, Jean Michel. *California Reefs.* Chronicle Bks. 1991 $16.95. ISBN 0-877-01-7875. A beautiful book of underwater color photos taken along the California reefs. Text discusses the sea life of the area.

——. (coauthored with Mose Richards). *Cousteau's Papua New Guinea Journey.* Abrams 1989 o.p. "[Chronicles] in text and pictures, the Papua New Guinea where 'life changes . . . and life does not change at all'" (*National Geographic Traveler*).

Madsen, Axel. *Cousteau: An Unauthorized Biography.* Beaufort SC 1986 $17.95. ISBN 0-8253-0386-9. ". . . an engaging account of a man who . . . led the way in cinematic popularization of ocean ecology [but] too short to cover comprehensively such a long, fascinating life" (Susan Klimley, Columbia University Libraries).

Munson, Richard. *Cousteau: The Captain and his World.* Morrow 1989 o.p. ". . . written in exposé style . . . tries to show Cousteau as a showman remiss in protecting the environment" (Susan Kimley, Columbia University Libraries).

DANA, RICHARD HENRY, JR. 1815–1882

Two Years before the Mast (1840), the diary of what happened on the brig *Pilgrim* in its voyage around Cape Horn in 1834–36—a brig only 86 feet long and registering 180 tons—is a book so preeminent in the literature of the sea that England at one time gave a copy of it to every sailor in the Royal Navy.

The author "broke away from Harvard without a degree to become a common sailor," says Allan Nevins (*Saturday Review*). He had "a gift for close observation and character portrayal" and was "an appreciative student of nature," but wrote only one fascinating novel, although he tried others. Of the *Journal*, Nevins writes: "Robert F. Lucid, who presents the text with admirable care and illuminating annotations, remarks that Dana himself would emphatically agree that his journal does not rank with the diaries of BOSWELL [see Vol. 1] or PEPYS [see Vol. 1] as a document of self-revelation, but adds that it does reveal a great deal about the character of the man." Dana kept the journal from 1841 to 1860. Dana's *Autobiographical Sketch, 1814–1842* is a brief account of his first 27 years. One of his later activities was "helping to found the Free Soil Party and rescue runaway slaves" (Nevins).

BOOKS BY DANA

Collected Works. The Bucaneer and Other Poems. Poems and Prose Writings. Rprt. Serv. 1990 repr. of 1827 and 1833 eds. $75.00. ISBN 0-7812-2609-0

The Journal of Richard Henry Dana, Jr. Ed. by Robert F. Lucid. 3 vols. HUP 1968 o.p.

To Cuba and Back. Rprt. Serv. 1992 repr. of 1859 ed. $75.00. ISBN 0-7812-2615-5. A book that, "during Dana's lifetime . . . was as popular as his *Two Years before the Mast.* It became the standard guidebook for English-speaking travelers. . . . Now a historical curiosity, it is of interest primarily to students of Dana and of Cuban history and to devotees of older travel books . . ." (*Library Journal*).

Two Years before the Mast. NAL-Dutton 1964 $4.95. ISBN 0-451-52369-5. An account of Dana's two years as a common seaman on a brig rounding Cape Horn.

BOOKS ABOUT DANA

Adams, Charles F. *Richard Henry Dana.* 2 vols. Gale 1989 repr. of 1890 ed. o.p. The life of Dana, including excerpts from his writing. Discusses Dana's role in the Free Soil Movement and the Civil War, and his travels to Europe.

Shapiro, Samuel. *Richard Henry Dana, Jr.* Mich. St. U. Pr. 1961 $5.00. ISBN 0-87013-062-5. Scholarly biography of Dana.

EARLE, SYLVIA (ALICE). 1955–

Sylvia Earle can lay claim to the titles marine botanist, environmentalist, businesswoman, writer, and deep-sea explorer. Of them all, the last is perhaps the one that most captures the imagination. She has spent more than 6,000 hours (over seven months) underwater. In 1979 she attached herself to a submarine that took her, at times as fast as 100 feet per minute, to the ocean floor 1,250 feet below. Dressed in a "Jim suit," a futuristic concoction of plastic and metal armor, she made the deepest solo dive ever made without a cable connecting her to a support vessel at the surface. This daring dive is comparable to the NASA voyage to the moon 10 years before.

In 1984 Earle became the codesigner (with Graham Hawkes) of Deep Rover, a deep-sea submersible capable of exploring the midwaters of the ocean. Their company, Deep Ocean Technology, went on to develop a second-generation submersible, Deep Flight, that can speed through the ocean at depths of as much as 4,000 feet. Currently under development is Ocean Everest, expected to operate at a depth of up to 35,800 feet, which will take scientists to the deepest parts of the sea. Although the uses of submersibles are still largely scientific, Earle hopes that they might one day transport laypeople to the bottom of the sea. She feels that the "experience of flying through a dark ocean, of watching the lights of a luminescent creature flash all around us" might help us gain more respect for the largely unexplored ocean world.

In addition to the scientific work that led to her being appointed in 1990 as chief scientist of the National Oceanic and Atmospheric Administration (NOAA), Earle has worked tirelessly to educate the public. Working with Al Giddings, she coauthored a documentary film, *Gentle Giants of the Pacific,* which appeared on public television in 1980. In the same year, their book *Exploring the Deep Frontier* appeared. It includes a discussion of the "Jim dive."

Her most recent scientific and environmental work has been to assess the environmental damage caused by the Prince William Sound oil spill and the results of Iraq's destruction of some 400 oil wells during the 1991 Persian Gulf War.

BOOK BY EARLE

Exploring the Deep Frontier: The Adventure of Man in the Sea. Coauthored with Al Giddings. National Geog. 1980 $14.95. ISBN 0-87044-343-7. An authoritative, profusely illustrated work written in a graceful style with striking imagery.

FREUCHEN, PETER. 1886–1957

Danish explorer, journalist, and author, Peter Freuchen was born in Nykobing, Falster, Denmark, and studied at the University of Copenhagen. Freuchen made his first trip to the Arctic in 1906, joining the Knut Rasmussen expedition. Fascinated by the Arctic, he was a member of the famous Thule expeditions (1910–1925) in northwestern Greenland. He also served as governor of the Thule colony from 1913 to 1920. Off and on for more than two generations he lived, hunted, and traveled with the Inuit, understanding them better than any other man of his generation. His first wife was an Inuit, about whom he wrote in *Invalu, the Eskimo Wife* (1935).

Fliers en route from Fort Churchill to distant Arctic air bases can still trace their course by landmarks Freuchen first put on the map. He aided refugees from the Nazis during the late 1930s and was active in the Underground movement after Denmark was occupied and before his own escape to Sweden. In 1957 Freuchen won the Gold Medal of the International Benjamin Franklin Society for his "service to mankind in opening new frontiers."

BOOKS BY FREUCHEN

Arctic Adventure: My Life in the Frozen North. AMS Pr. repr. of 1935 ed. $32.50. ISBN 0-404-11638-8. An easy-to-read account of Freuchen's experience in the north, including some discussion of Eskimos.

Book of the Eskimos. Fawcett 1981 $3.95. ISBN 0-449-30038-2. An introduction to the Eskimos of Greenland, northern Canada, and Alaska. Uncovers some of the mystery of their religion, art, customs, and so on.

Ivalu, the Eskimo Wife. Trans. by Janos Jusztis and Edward P. Erich. AMS Pr. repr. of 1935 ed. $27.50. ISBN 0-404-11639-6

The Peter Freuchen Reader. Ed. and trans. by Dagmar Freuchen. S & S Trade 1965 o.p. Includes "selections from *Vagrant Viking, Book of the Seven Seas, Arctic Adventure,* and *Eskimo*, plus a few pieces translated from Danish . . . " (*Library Journal*).

Peter Freuchen's Book of the Seven Seas. S&S Trade 1966 o.p. Coauthored with David Loth.

GUNTHER, JOHN. 1901–1970

Born in Chicago, John Gunther began a career in journalism in 1922 as a reporter for the *Chicago Daily News*. A war correspondent during World War II, Gunther later devoted all his time to writing and is famous for his *Inside* books. Following his fourth visit to Russia in 1956, he presented important as well as trivial facts in *Inside Russia Today* (1958). "The greatest service Mr. Gunther has done is to bring Russia down to a level we can all understand and talk and argue about" (*N.Y. Times*). In 1958 he received the Geographic Society of Chicago Publication Award for his *Inside* books. Unfortunately, *Inside U.S.A.* (1951) is out of print.

Gunther wrote several biographies and a deeply moving account of the death of his young son of a brain tumor, *Death Be Not Proud* (1949). His *Procession* (1965) is a group of sketches of international political figures drawn from his *Inside* books and from articles. *Inside Australia* (1972), completed and edited by William Forbis, was published posthumously.

BOOKS BY GUNTHER

Death Be Not Proud: A Memoir. 1949. Borgo Pr. 1991 $20.00. ISBN 0-8095-9101-4

A Fragment of Autobiography: The Fun of Writing Inside Books. HarpC 1962 o.p. Lively and informative description of how he chose his topics, the preparations he made for his travels, the information he sought, and how he wrote his manuscripts.

Inside Africa. Ayer $45.25. ISBN 08369-8197-9

Inside Asia. Greenwood 1974 repr. of 1942 ed. $38.50. ISBN 0-8371-7825-8

Inside Europe Today. HarpC rev. ed. 1962 o.p. ". . . conscientious effort to interview some of the most important statesmen. . . . conspicuously successful with Adenauer and Macmillan. . . . a lot of pertinent observations and characteristic stories about many others, like de Gaulle, Salazar and Tito (*Library Journal*).

Inside South America. HarpC 1967 o.p. "Guntherization, as it must to all continents, has come again to South America, in another marvelous plum pudding of a book" (*N.Y. Times*).

John Gunther's Inside Australia. Completed and ed. by William Forbis. HarpC 1972 o.p. A vivid picture of Australia and New Zealand, including discussions of their topography, animals, cities, countryside, and politics.

BOOK ABOUT GUNTHER

Pridmore, Jay. *John Gunther: Inside Journalism.* Univ. Chi. Lib. 1990 $6.00. ISBN 0-943026-13-6. Biographical vignettes celebrating the life, career, and works of the famed journalist.

HAKLUYT, RICHARD. 1552–1616

Born in Herfordshire, English geographer and clergyman Richard Hakluyt devoted much of his life to preserving the records of all English voyages of discovery and promoting the advantages of exploring and settling North America.

While still a schoolboy, Hakluyt visited the law offices of his cousin and saw a large display of geographical materials. He immediately became fascinated with geography. In time he pursued this interest at Oxford University, where later he lectured on geography. Hakluyt was also ordained in the ministry, which enabled him to earn a living while indulging his passion for geography.

In 1582 Hakluyt published the first of his four major works, *Divers Voyages Touching the Discovery of America and the Islands Adjacent.* This work was, in part, propaganda for the English explorer Sir Humphrey Gilbert's doomed voyage to America the following year. Hakluyt next wrote an outline for colonial policy in America, stating some of the advantages of settlement and who should go. Ironically, this work, *The Discourse of Western Planting,* was not published until 1877. Nonetheless, Hakluyt was instrumental in reviving interest in the settlement of Virginia after the disappearance of the ill-fated Roanoke colony. He was one of the petitioners for the Virginia Company's 1606 grant that resulted in the Jamestown settlement. He also helped plan the East India Company, which colonized India.

Hakluyt's best-known work, *Principal Navigations, Voyages, Traffiques, and Discoveries of the English Nation,* first appeared in 1589, with a second edition published in 1599 and 1600. In 1846, the Hakluyt Society was founded, and it still continues today to publish narratives of early explorations, perpetuating his labors as well as his memory.

BOOKS BY HAKLUYT

Divers Voyages Touching the Discovery of America and the Islands Adjacent. 1582. Ye Galleon 1981 $12.00. ISBN 0-87770-242-X

Hakluyt's Voyages to the New World: A Selection. Ed. by David F. Hawke. Bobbs 1972 $3.40. ISBN 0-672-60887-1

Principal Navigations, Voyages, Traffiques and Discoveries of the English Nation. 12 vols. AMS Pr. repr. of 1905 ed. ISBN 0-404-03030-0. Letters and accounts concerning various voyages made by English explorers, primarily to Russia and Persia from 1052 to 1588.

Voyages and Discoveries. Ed. by Jack Beeching. Viking Penguin 1972 $7.95. ISBN 0-14-043073-3

Voyages and Documents. Ed. by Janet Hampden. OUP 1958 o.p.

BOOKS ABOUT HAKLUYT

Lynam, Edward. *Richard Hakluyt and His Successors.* Kraus repr. of 1946 ed. $21.00. ISBN 0-8115-0389-5. Interesting look at Hakluyt and his influence on later explorers.

Parks, George B. *Richard Hakluyt and the English Voyages.* Folcroft 1984 repr. of 1928 ed. o.p. Views Hakluyt as a contemporary historian in order to reveal the ideas and outlook of Elizabethan England.

HARRER, HEINRICH. 1912–

In 1939 Harrer was a member of the Nanga Parbat Expedition that was interned in India by the British at the outbreak of World War II. He escaped by way of Tibet, and during his seven years there, he was unofficial tutor to the Dalai Lama in Lhasa, whom he taught geography, arithmetic, and English. Harrer is an Austrian, and during his years at the College and University of Graz, he climbed hundreds of walls and ridges in the Alps, some for the first time.

BOOKS BY HARRER

Lost Lhasa: Heinrich Harrer's Tibet. Abrams 1992 $39.95. ISBN 0-8109-3560-0. Collection of photographs recording Harrer's excursion into Tibet between 1944 and 1950. With an introduction by Galen Rowell.

Seven Years in Tibet. J. P. Tarcher 1982 repr. of 1954 ed. $9.95. ISBN 0-87477-217-6. Account of the seven years Harrer spent in Tibet starting in 1943 after he escaped from an internment camp. Talks about his experiences as the tutor of the young Dalai Lama. With an introduction by Peter Fleming.

Tibet Is My Country. Trans. by Edward Fitzgerald. NAL-Dutton 1961 o.p. The oral autobiography of Thubten Jugme Norbu, brother of the Dalai Lama.

HEYERDAHL, THOR. 1914–

"This is an enthralling book," Hamilton Lasso wrote in *The New Yorker* of *Kon-Tiki* (1948), "and I don't think I can be very far off in calling it the most absorbing sea tale of our time." Heyerdahl, a Norwegian ethnologist, conceived the theory—not then accepted by other scientists—that Polynesia may have been originally settled by people who crossed the 4,100 miles of ocean from Peru in rafts made of balsa logs. *Kon-Tiki* is the story of how he and five others built the raft, as people of the Stone Age could build it, and traveled in it from Peru to a small island east of Tahiti—a "most fascinating description of intelligent courage."

Heyerdahl believes that he has at last solved the problem of how natives raised the great statues on Easter Island and has written a most absorbing account of it in *Aku-Aku* (1958). He has adduced further corroboration of his theory from the findings in *The Archaeology of Easter Island* (1961).

In the spring of 1969, Heyerdahl was engaged in a new experiment—planning to cross the Atlantic from Morocco to Yucatan in a 12-ton papyrus boat that he and others built themselves in the manner of the ancient Egyptians. In spite of general skepticism as to whether the boat, called the *Ra*, could make the journey without sinking when it became thoroughly water-soaked, Heyerdahl and six others set out in full confidence. They hoped to demonstrate that Egyptians might have made the journey in this manner 4,000 or 5,000 years ago and thus were the precursors of the Incas and Mayas. In July 1969, however, they were forced to abandon their attempt 600 miles short of their goal, near the

Virgin Islands, after a series of storms had crippled the *Ra*. They left it drifting in the hope that it might reach Barbados on its own. Their second attempt, in *Ra II*, was successful.

A subsequent journey in the reed-ship *Tigris* in 1977–78 was meant to show that such craft could maneuver against the wind and thus complete round-trip journeys through the ancient world via the Persian Gulf and Arabian Sea. Political conflicts in the region, however, led Heyerdahl and his crew to burn the *Tigris* in protest.

BOOKS BY HEYERDAHL

Aku-Aku. 1958. Ballantine 1974 o.p. Heyerdahl's account of his explorations on Easter Island.

The Archaeology of Easter Island: Reports of the Norwegian Archaeological Expedition to Easter Island and the East Pacific. Coauthored with Edwin L. Ferdon, Jr. U. of NM Pr. 1961 o.p. A superb work that gives full accounts of topography, climatology, flora and fauna, dwellings, artifacts, and, incidentally, the solution to several perplexing problems; intended for informed scientists and students of archaeology and anthropology, but with a wider appeal.

The Art of Easter Island. Doubleday 1976 o.p. Gives a history of the archeological excavations on Easter Island and the meaning of the art discovered. Includes photos.

Fatu-Hiva: Back to Nature on a Pacific Island. NAL-Dutton 1976 o.p. A "riveting escape book as well as a revealing, if unnecessarily preachy, essay on what white men have done to a once happy South Sea island, and how the island retaliated against a white couple attempting to settle there" (*N.Y. Times*).

Kon-Tiki: Across the Pacific by Raft. 1948. S&S Trade 1990 $4.95. ISBN 0-671-7652-8

The Maldive Mystery. Allen & Unwin 1986 o.p. An investigation into the pre-Islamic history of the Maldive Islands.

The Ra Expeditions. NAL-Dutton 1972 o.p.

BOOK ABOUT HEYERDAHL

Blassingame, Wyatt. *Thor Heyerdahl: Viking Scientist*. Lodestar 1979 o.p.

HILLARY, SIR EDMUND (PERCIVAL). 1919–

Sir Edmund Hillary, the New Zealand mountain climber and explorer, became one of the first two men to climb successfully to the top of Mount Everest, the tallest mountain in the world. He and his Sherpa guide, Tenzing Norkay, reached the top of Everest on May 29, 1953. Hillary wrote of this conquest in a chapter titled "Final Assault," found in *The Conquest of Everest* by Sir John Hunt. Queen Elizabeth knighted both of them during the coronation festivities of 1953. Before the Everest triumph, Hillary had written several books about his adventures on other famous expeditions, including several climbs of other Himalayan peaks.

In June 1960, Hillary announced that in the fall he would attempt an ascent of the 27,790-foot Malaka Peak in Nepal, about 20 miles east of Everest. He had two objectives: "first, to determine the effects of high altitude on climbers not equipped with oxygen equipment and, second, to make further efforts to track down the 'Abominable Snowman'" (*New York Times*). The results, which were negligible, are told in *High in the Thin Cold Air* (1962), which Hillary coauthored with Desmond Doig. This expedition did, however, establish a school at Khumjung, which made up for some of the other disappointments. In 1985 Hillary was named ambassador to India.

BOOKS BY HILLARY

The Crossing of Antarctica: The Commonwealth Trans-Antarctic Expedition 1955–1958. (coauthored with Vivian Fuchs). Greenwood repr. of 1959 ed. o.p. The story of their dangerous land crossing of Antarctica between November 1957 and March 1958.

From Ocean to Sky: Jet Boating. St. Mut. 1979 $85.00. ISBN 0-317-94144-5. Account of a trip from the mouth of the Ganges River upstream against the current to its source in the Himalaya mountains.

Nothing Venture, Nothing Win. Putnam Pub. Group 1975 o.p. Hillary's autobiography: ". . . an exciting adventure yarn, particularly when he's describing his early mountaineering exploits" (*Library Journal*).

BOOK ABOUT HILLARY

Kelly, Robert. *For Those in Peril: The Life and Times of Sir William Hillary Founder of the R.N.L.J.* St. Mut. 1979 o.p.

KINGLAKE, ALEXANDER (WILLIAM). 1809–1891

English historian Alexander Kinglake was born in Wilton House, near Taunton and was educated at Eton and Trinity College, Cambridge. A tour of the Far East in 1840 resulted in the publication of *Eōthen* (1844). *Eōthen* is a Greek word meaning "from the early dawn" or "from the East." *The Cambridge History of English Literature* regards this book as "perhaps the best book of travel in the English language." It consists of letters that Kinglake wrote home while making his extensive tour. He became the historian of the Crimea in 1863, writing the *History of the War in the Crimea* (1863–87), considered one of the finest historical works of the nineteenth century.

BOOKS BY KINGLAKE

Eōthen. 1844. Marlboro Pr. 1992 $11.95. ISBN 0-910395-82-9

The Invasion of the Crimea. 9 vols. AMS Pr. 1972 repr. of 1888 ed. $337.50. ISBN 0-404-03710-0. Detailed account of the Crimean conflict and its implications for subsequent history.

BOOK ABOUT KINGLAKE

Tuckwell, W. *A. W. Kinglake: A Biographical and Literary Study.* Richard West repr. of 1902 ed. o.p.

LAWRENCE, T(HOMAS) E(DWARD) (T. E. Shaw). 1888–1935

Born in Caernarvonshire in North Wales and educated at Oxford University, T. E. Lawrence was a soldier, author, archaeologist, traveler, and translator. After participating in archaeological expeditions in the Middle East from 1911 to 1914, he worked for British Army intelligence in North Africa during World War I. In 1916 he joined the Arab revolt against the Turks and became known as Lawrence of Arabia, the man who freed the Arabs from Turkish rule. The manuscript of his *The Seven Pillars of Wisdom* (1926) was lost when it had been two-thirds finished, and he rewrote the book from memory in 1919. Because it expressed certain personal and political opinions that Lawrence did not wish to publicize, it was offered for sale in 1926 in England at a prohibitive price. To ensure copyright in the United States, it was reprinted here by Doran (now Doubleday) and 10 copies were offered for sale at $20,000 each, a price "high enough to prevent their ever being sold." Doubleday then brought out a limited edition and a trade edition, substantially the same as the rare 1926 edition. *Revolt in the Desert* (1927) is an abridgment of *The Seven Pillars*, which the author made to pay the printing expenses of the original. *The Mint* (1955), an account of his service with the Royal Air Force, was published posthumously in an edition of 50 copies, 10 of which were offered for sale at a price of $500,000 each, to ensure no copies being sold. In 1950 a popular edition, in 1955 a limited edition, and in 1963 a paperback edition were published.

After World War I, Lawrence enlisted in the Royal Air Force as Private John Hume Ross; when his real identity was discovered, he transferred to the Royal Tank Corps under the name T. E. Shaw, a name he legally assumed in 1927. In 1937 Lawrence was killed when the motorbike given to him by GEORGE BERNARD SHAW (see Vol. 1) went out of control on an English country lane.

Earlier biographers, including Lowell Thomas and ROBERT GRAVES, were enthusiastic and laudatory of Lawrence. Twenty years after his death, Richard Aldington wrote *Lawrence of Arabia: A Biographical Enquiry*, which "set off a fury of charge and countercharge." But Lawrence's saga had become legend. In tribute to this adventurous, enigmatic genius, who shunned fame, wealth, and power, King George V wrote, "His name will live in history." Public interest in "the elusive, mysterious and complex young Irishman" who led the Arab revolt was revived by *Lawrence of Arabia*, 1962's most honored film.

In recent years the picture of Lawrence has changed again with the revelation of his illegitimacy, his readiness to embroider the truth, and other quirks and neuroses; but there were English witnesses to many of his accomplishments, and the disagreements among those who knew him have hindered efforts to discredit him in any definitive manner; even the Arabs view him with their Arab pride at stake. He remains enigmatic and eccentric, and is likely to be the subject of more research and many volumes before the truth about him is finally and fully understood.

BOOKS BY LAWRENCE

The Essential T. E. Lawrence: A Selection of his Finest Writings. OUP 1992 repr. of 1951 ed. $12.95. ISBN 0-19-282962-9. Preface by David Garnett. ". . . fulfills the dual role of being both an anthology and autobiography" (Malcolm Brown).

The Evolution of a Revolt: Early Postwar Writings of T. E. Lawrence. Ed. by Rodelle Weintraub. Penn. St. U. Pr. 1967 o.p. Newspaper and journal articles from 1918 to 1921.

The Mint. Norton 1963 o.p.

Revolt in the Desert. 1927. Transaction Pubs. 1990 $22.95. ISBN 1-85089-401-9

The Selected Letters. Ed. by Malcolm Brown. Paragon Hse. 1992 $16.95. ISBN 1-55778-518-X. Fascinating collection of over 300 letters to Mrs. George Bernard Shaw, printed here for the first time; many are inaccurate and printed in incomplete versions.

The Seven Pillars of Wisdom. 1926. Doubleday 1966 o.p.

BOOKS ABOUT LAWRENCE

Hart, B. H. *Lawrence of Arabia.* Da Capo 1989 repr. of 1934 ed. $13.95. ISBN 0-306-80354-2. A "rather dazzling analysis of Lawrence as strategist and tactician . . ." (*New York Times*).

Mack, John E. *A Prince of Our Disorder: The Life of T. E. Lawrence.* Little 1976 $14.95. ISBN 0-316-54229-6. "Takes us closer to the core of Lawrence than any previous biography" (*Time*).

Meyers, Jeffrey. *The Wounded Spirit: T. E. Lawrence's Seven Pillars of Wisdom.* St. Martin 1989 $35.00. ISBN 0-312-02721-4. Provides "succinct accounts of the Arab revolt . . . Lawrence's strange family background . . . and the fascinating story of his dealings with Arab notables and with confidants ranging from Winston Churchill to Mrs. Bernard Shaw" (*The Middle East Journal*).

Wilson, Jeremy. *Lawrence of Arabia. The Authorized Biography of T. E. Lawrence.* Macmillan 1992 $17.50. ISBN 0-02-082662-1. "Lawrence's monument" (Nigel Nicolson, *N.Y. Times Book Review*).

Yardley, Michael. *T. E. Lawrence: A Biography.* Madison Bks. UPA 1986 $19.95. ISBN 0-8128-3079-2. "Despite many irritating faults, a good and original book . . ." (Brian Holden Reid, *History*).

LEWIS, MERIWETHER, 1774–1809 and CLARK, WILLIAM. 1770–1838

The Lewis and Clark expedition was one of the earliest crossings of the United States. Eager to expand the country, President THOMAS JEFFERSON appointed Lewis, formerly his private secretary, to seek a Northwest passage to the Orient. Lewis and his partner, William Clark, were both seasoned soldiers, expert woodsmen, and boatmen. They both kept journals and so did 4 sergeants and 1 private in the party of 43 men. They started from St. Louis in 1804, heading up to the Missouri River, across the Rockies, and down to the Pacific coast at the mouth of the Columbia River. The Indian woman Sacajawea ("Bird Woman") gave them valuable help on the hazardous journey, which lasted 2 years, 4 months, and 10 days, and cost the U.S. government a total of $38,722.25. Lewis was the better educated of the two captains, and his account has more force, but Clark was a superb observer who wrote in an ingenious phonetic spelling of his own invention.

The official edition of the *Journals* did not appear until 1814, when they were edited in two volumes by Nicholas Biddle and Paul Allen. This text, a paraphrase of the journals, was used in various editions until 1904, when Reuben G. Thwaites edited an eight-volume edition, published in 1904–05. Many recent editions have followed the original text, making the journals available in all of their original freshness.

Early in 1960 it was announced in the *New York Times* that 67 notes written by Clark had been given by Frederick W. Beinecke of New York to the Yale University Library. "The documents, finger-smudged, blotted and blurred with cross-outs, list personal observations previously unknown to historians. . . . The documents, consisting of old letters, envelopes and scraps of paper, were the subject of an unusual legal fight. After the Clark notes were found in an attic in St. Paul, Minnesota, in 1952, the United States moved to obtain them. The Government contended the documents were part of the official records of Clark while he served the United States. The Federal Court of Appeals in St. Louis dismissed the suit on Jan. 23, 1958. The court test was closely watched by libraries, museums and the American Philosophical Society. Had the Government been upheld, the custody of similar historical documents would have been jeopardized. . . ."

Shortly after the end of the expedition, Lewis was appointed governor of the Territory of Upper Louisiana. When he at last took up his post, he was mysteriously killed—or took his own life—in the lonely wilderness.

BOOKS BY LEWIS AND CLARK

Atlas of the Lewis and Clark Expedition. Ed. by Gary E. Moulton. U. of Nebr. Pr. 1983 $125.00. ISBN 0-8032-2861-9. Interesting atlas of the expedition that should provide hours of satisfaction and enjoyment.

History of the Expedition under the Command of Captains Lewis and Clark. AMS Pr. repr. of 1922 ed. $85.00. ISBN 0-404-54920-9. Based on their detailed journals of the expedition from the Missouri River to the Pacific Northwest.

The History of the Lewis and Clark Expedition. Ed. by Elliott Coues. 3 vols. Dover repr. of 1893 ed. $9.95 ea. ISBNs 0-486-21268-8, 1-486-21269-6, 0-486-21270-X. Its copious footnotes make it "an indispensible reference . . . [and add] another dimension to the images of Lewis and Clark" (Paul Cutright).

The Journals of the Lewis and Clark Expedition. Ed. by Gary E. Moulton. 7 vols. U. of Nebr. Pr. 1991 $50.00 ea. Vol. 1 o.p. Vol. 2 ISBN 0-8032-2869-4. Vol. 3 ISBN 0-8032-2875-9. Vol. 4 ISBN 0-8032-2877-5. Vol. 5 ISBN 0-8032-2883-X. Vol. 6 ISBN 0-8032-2893-7. Vol. 7 ISBN 0-8032-2898-8. The definitive edition including all of the known journals.

BOOKS ABOUT LEWIS AND CLARK

Cutright, Paul R. *Lewis and Clark: Pioneering Naturalists.* U. of Nebr. Pr. 1989 $16.95. ISBN 0-8032-6334-1. A detailed study of the expedition's careful mapping, describing, and exploring of North American flora and fauna.

Lavender, David Sievert. *The Way to the Western Sea: Lewis and Clark across the Continent.* Doubleday 1990 $12.95. ISBN 0-385-41155-3. ". . . supersedes John Bakeless's Lewis & Clark. . . . a balanced, learned, and lively history. . ." (Gary E. Moulton, *The Journal of American History*).

Otfinoski, Steven. *Lewis and Clark: Leading America West.* Fawcett 1992 $4.00. ISBN 0-449-90398-2. Standard biography.

Ronda, James P. *Lewis and Clark among the Indians.* U. of Nebr. Pr. 1984 $9.95. ISBN 0-8032-8929-4. ". . . a sophisticated study of Indian–white relations. . . . [rigorous] approach to his sources . . . [interesting] narrative . . . [published] in footnote-sized type" (Bernard W. Sheehan, *The Journal of American History*).

LINDBERGH, CHARLES A(UGUSTUS), JR. 1902–1974

American aviator Charles Lindbergh was born in Detroit but grew up primarily in Minnesota with his mother. After working as an airmail pilot, he achieved world fame by making the first nonstop solo transatlantic flight from New York to Paris in May 1927. On the eve of World War II, Lindbergh advocated a policy of neutrality and opposed the entry of the United States into the war. Critical of U.S. foreign policy, some Americans accused him of being a Nazi sympathizer. After Pearl Harbor, he stopped his noninvolvement activity and served as a civilian adviser to the U.S. Army and Navy. Although a civilian, he also flew numerous combat missions in the Pacific. After the war, Lindbergh worked with Pan American Airways and the National Medical Center.

According to some critics, Lindbergh's autobiography, *The Spirit of St. Louis* (1953), is a magnificent book, an important historic document that reveals both a fascinating individual and a remarkable look at the nation and the fledgling aviation industry that would eventually become a great source of national strength and power. The book is the contemplative, almost hour-by-hour account of Lindbergh's famed transatlantic flight. In 1967, the *New York Times* celebrated the fortieth anniversary of Lindbergh's transatlantic flight by reprinting his original account as it appeared in that newspaper on May 23, 1927.

In the late 1960s, Lindbergh became involved in the conservation movement and campaigned for the protection of various endangered species. He also opposed the development of supersonic transport planes, because he believed that they would have a harmful effect on the earth's atmosphere. During his last years, Lindbergh was afflicted with incurable cancer, and he chose to spend his last days at his retreat on the Hawaiian island of Maui. He died there and was buried with private ceremonies in an unmarked grave.

BOOKS BY LINDBERGH

Boyhood on the Upper Mississippi: A Reminiscent Letter. Minn. Hist. 1972 $7.95. ISBN 0-87351-217-0. Recollections of his childhood life and activities on his Minnesota family farm.

The Spirit of St. Louis. Avon 1991 $33.95. ISBN 0-89966-793-7. This account of Lindbergh's historic flight and flying is very detailed and highly readable.

The Wartime Journals of Charles A. Lindbergh. HarBraceJ 1970 $19.95. ISBN 0-15-194625-6. Reveals Lindbergh's intuition and intellect as he responds to the war years.

We. Buccaneer Bks. 1991 $24.95. ISBN 0-89966-832-1. Lindbergh's account of his boyhood, his flight training, and his service as an airmail pilot as a prologue to his epic flight from New York to Paris.

BOOKS ABOUT LINDBERGH

Luckett, Perry D. *Charles A. Lindbergh: A Bio-Bibliography.* Greenwood 1986 $39.95. ISBN 0-313-23098-6. Essay on Lindbergh's life and his impact on science, aviation, and American popular culture. Includes a useful bibliography.

Miller, Francis T. *Lindbergh: His Story in Pictures.* Northstar Bks. 1989 $15.00. ISBN 0-910667-14-4

Milton, Joyce. *Loss of Eden: A Biography of Charles and Anne Morrow Lindbergh.* HarpC 1993 $25.00. ISBN 0-06-016503-0. ". . . makes the 1932 kidnapping of the couple's infant son the central moment in its narrative, the event that determined the future course of the Lindberghs' lives" (Publisher's note). Reveals the almost dysfunctional Morrow and Lindbergh families.

Newton, James. *Uncommon Friends: Life With Thomas Edison, Henry Ford, Harvey Firestone, Alexis Carrel, Charles Lindbergh.* HarBraceJ 1987 $19.95. ISBN 0-15-192753-7. Provides a rare glimpse of Lindbergh as a friend and family man. A worthwhile companion to more standard biographies.

Randolph, Blythe. *Charles Lindbergh.* Watts 1990 $13.95. ISBN 0-531-15150-6. Well-written portrait.

Thomas, W. Donald. *Lindbergh and Commercial Aviation: Pictorial Review of Colonel Lindbergh's Association with TAT, TWA, and PAA as Technical Advisor.* D. Thomas 1988 $16.00. ISBN 0-96186421-4

LIVINGSTONE, DAVID. 1813–1873

One of the most remarkable explorers of the nineteenth century, Livingstone sought first as a missionary and devout Christian to end the slave trade in Africa and then to locate the source of the Nile. In these attempts, he lost his wife, who caught a fever on an expedition in which she joined him. He discovered Victoria Falls and the lands between Nyasa and Tanganyika, encountering other hardships and tragedies in his double quest. He was apparently much beloved by Africans who knew him. He never abated in his efforts in their behalf. His association with SIR HENRY MORTON STANLEY is well known. The latter had been sent to find him by an American newspaper when Livingstone was feared lost; the formal approach of Stanley's first remark on finding him in a remote African village, "Dr. Livingstone, I presume," amused the world, and the greeting became a byword. Stanley was with Livingstone in northern Tanganyika when the latter died. *Missionary Travels* (1857) is essentially the contemporary record of Livingstone's two journeys to northwestern Rhodesia (now Zimbabwe) in 1851–53. These letters furnish "priceless source material not only for the student of religious history but for the anthropologist and sociologist. . . . Completely devoted to the cause of Christ, Livingstone was also a realist and a man of unusual intelligence" (*Library Journal*).

BOOKS BY LIVINGSTONE

The David Livingstone Family Letters. Ed. by Isaac Schapera. 2 vols. Greenwood 1975 repr. of 1959 ed. o.p.

Last Journals of David Livingstone in Central Africa from 1865 to His Death. Ed. by Horace
    Waller. 2 vols. Greenwood 1968 repr. of 1874 ed. o.p. Account of Livingstone's last
    years in Africa, including his final journal entries before his death.
*Livingstone's Africa: Perilous Adventures and Extensive Discoveries in the Interior of
    Africa. Black Heritage Lib. Collection Ser.* Ayer repr. of 1872 ed. o.p. Personal
    narrative, with the results of the Herald-Stanley expedition as furnished by Stanley.
Livingstone's Missionary Correspondence, 1841–1856. Ed. by Isaac Schapera. U. CA Pr.
    1961 o.p. A collection of letters, mostly to the Directors of the London Missionary
    Society, which detail his activities and views about missionaries and the slave trade.
Missionary Travels and Researches in South Africa. Select Bibliographies Repr. Ser. Ayer
    1972 repr. of 1857 ed. o.p.
*Narrative of an Expedition to the Zambesi and Its Tributaries: And of the Discovery of
    Lakes Shirwa and Nyasa, 1858–1864.* Johnson Repr. repr. of 1866 ed. o.p.
Some Letters from Livingstone, 1840–1872. Greenwood repr. of 1940 ed. o.p.
The Zambesi Expedition, 1858–1863. Ed. by J. P. Wallis. 2 vols. Humanities 1956 o.p.

BOOKS ABOUT LIVINGSTONE

Helly, Dorothy D. *Livingston's Legacy: Horace Waller and Victorian Mythmaking.* Ohio U.
    Pr. 1987 $18.95. ISBN 0-8214-0836-4. Explores at length how Waller's edits of
    Livingstone's original manuscripts affected the understanding of Livingstone.
Martelli, George. *Livingstone's River.* S & S Trade 1970 o.p. Interesting account of search
    for the source of the Nile.
Pachai, Bridglal, ed. *Livingstone, Man of Africa: Memorial Essays, 1873–1973.* Longman
    1973 o.p. A collection of essays by various scholars about Livingstone and his impact
    on Africa, especially concerning religion.
Stanley, Henry M. *How I Found Livingstone.* Greenwood repr. of 1913 ed. $35.00. ISBN 0-
    8371-1995-2. Stanley's own account of his search for Livingstone.

MATTHIESSEN, PETER. 1927–

Peter Matthiessen—novelist, travel writer, naturalist, and explorer—was born
in New York City. Matthiessen has participated in numerous anthropological
and natural-history expeditions around the world, including trips to Alaska,
Peru, Africa, New Guinea, Central America, and Nepal. As a travel writer, he is
known for the perceptive accounts of the people, wildlife, and places he has
encountered on these expeditions. Among his works are *The Cloud Forest*
(1961), about the Amazon rain forest; *Under the Mountain Wall* (1962), which
details the life of a tribe in New Guinea; and *The Snow Leopard* (1978), the
chronicle of a mountain trek through Nepal that won the National Book Award.
In his travels, Matthiessen is keenly aware of the effects of civilization on native
cultures and the environment. This concern is reflected in some of his novels,
such as *At Play in the Fields of the Lord* (1965) and *Far Tortuga* (1975).

BOOKS BY MATTHIESSEN

African Silences. Random 1992 $10.00. ISBN 0-679-73102-4. Provides a vivid, yet
    dismaying, picture of Africa's environment today.
At Play in the Fields of the Lord. 1965. Peter Smith 1992 $23.25. ISBN 0-8446-6636-X
The Cloud Forest. 1961. Peter Smith 1992 $19.50. ISBN 0-8446-6605-X
Far Tortuga. 1975. Random 1988 $13.00. ISBN 0-394-75667-3
Men's Lives: Surfmen and Baymen of the South Fork. 1986. Random 1988 $10.00. ISBN 0-
    394-75560-X. Keen look at commercial fishermen on the South Fork of Long Island,
    New York, and how their lives are changing because of modernization and
    increasing suburbanization.
The Snow Leopard. 1978. Viking Penguin 1987 $11.00. ISBN 0-14-010266-3
Under the Mountain Wall. 1962. Viking Penguin 1987 $10.00. ISBN 0-14-009548-9

MICHENER, JAMES A(LBERT). 1907–

Born in New York City and educated at Swarthmore College and the University of Northern Colorado, James Michener is known for novels that present panoramic views of different places. These works are based on comprehensive, in-depth research, and they include many facts about the places depicted. Michener embarked on his writing career at age 40. His first book, *Tales of the South Pacific* (1947), based on his experiences in the U.S. Navy during World War II, not only won the Pulitzer Prize, but also became the basis of the award-winning Rodgers and Hammerstein musical, *South Pacific*. Since then, he has written some 40 books, including international bestsellers *Sayonara* (1954), *The Bridges at Toko-Ri* (1953), *Hawaii* (1959), *The Source* (1965), *Iberia* (1968), *The Covenant* (1980), *Centennial* (1974), *Chesapeake* (1980), *Space* (1982), *Texas* (1985), *Alaska* (1988), and *Journey* (1990).

Michener has been honored with the Presidential Medal of Freedom, America's highest civilian award, and with an award from the President's Committee on the Arts and Humanities for his continuing commitment to art in America. In addition, he holds honorary doctorates in 5 fields from 30 leading universities. His devotion to education is evidenced by generous gifts to several colleges and universities, including the University of Iowa, Northern Colorado University, Swarthmore, and the University of Texas at Austin, which received $15 million from Michener in 1992.

BOOKS BY MICHENER

Alaska. Fawcett 1988 $6.95. ISBN 0-449-21726-4. Shows that "Mr. Michener is still, sentence for sentence, writing's fastest attention grabber" (*New York Times*).

The Bridges at Toko-ri. Fawcett 1953 $5.95. ISBN 0-449-20651-3. ". . . a story of action, ideas, and civilization's responsibilities" (*Saturday Review*).

The Caribbean. Fawcett 1989 $6.99. ISBN 0-449-21749-3. ". . . succeeds in presenting the Caribbean in its rich diversity. . . . will introduce a large audience to the Caribbean past" (*Cleveland Plain Dealer*).

Centennial. Random 1974 $40.00. ISBN 0-394-47970-X. According to Bill Marsano of the *Condé Nast Traveler*, superficial and overwritten.

Iberia. Fawcett 1968 $6.95. ISBN 0-449-20733-1. "One of the richest and most satisfying books about Spain in living memory" (*Saturday Review*).

Mexico. Random 1992 $25.00. ISBN 0-679-41649-8. ". . . vividly captures the sweep of Mexico's colorful history and teems with a multitude of unforgettable characters" (Publisher's note).

My Lost Mexico: The Making of a Novel. State House Pr. 1992 $24.95. ISBN 0-938349-93-7. ". . . makes history come alive in this engaging slice of Americana and Texas love . . ." (Publisher's note).

The Novel. Fawcett 1991 $5.99. ISBN 0-449-22143-1. ". . . an unveiling of a business that few of us see from the inside, and a revelation of some of Michener's private thoughts" (*The Philadelphia Inquirer*).

Poland. Random 1983 $16.95. ISBN 0-394-53189-2. An engrossing fictionalized depiction of Polish history from the thirteenth-century Tatar invasion to the twentieth-century Communist regime as it affects three Polish families representing nobility, gentry, and peasants.

Space. Fawcett 1982 $6.99. ISBN 0-449-20379-4. ". . . gives his readers an understanding of the men and women involved in . . . space" (*Washington Post*).

Tales of the South Pacific. Fawcett 1947 $5.95. ISBN 0-44920652-1

Texas. Fawcett 1985 $6.95. ISBN 0-449-21092-8. An epic blockbuster novel.

The World Is My Home: A Memoir. 1991. Random 1992 $25.00. ISBN 0-679-40134-2.
"Plain spoken, wise, and enormously sympathetic, . . . the real James Michener, a
man who can truly say, 'The world is my home'" (Publisher's note).

MORTON, H(ENRY CANOVA) V(OLLAM). 1892–1979

H. V. Morton began writing as an undergraduate in England. By the time he
was 19, he became assistant editor of the *Birmingham Gazette and Express.* Later
he joined the staff of the *Daily Mail* in London. Returning home from the British
army after World War I, he realized how little he actually knew his country. His
explorations led him to write a travel series later published by Dodd. He has
been called "perhaps the greatest living authority on the material being of the
British Isles—that is to say, on their landscape, buildings, monuments, customs
and history." As a devout churchman, he has also written several books on
biblical personages and places. He was an experienced and worldly traveler
who had a "unique talent for capturing the essence of lives long past."

BOOKS BY MORTON

H. V. Morton's Britain. Dodd 1969 o.p. Selections from his *In Search* books on England,
    Scotland, Ireland, and Wales.
I Saw Two Englands. Trafalgar Sq. 1990 $29.95. ISBN 0-413-62010-7. Discusses his views
    and impressions of pre-war England and his first glimpse of England at war. Includes
    photos.
In the Steps of the Master. Folcroft 1935 o.p. Account of his visits to ancient landmarks
    and localities connected with the birth of Christianity and a discussion of their
    significance.
A Traveller in Rome. Dodd 1984 o.p.
A Traveller in Southern Italy. Dodd 1969 o.p. "Well written, well illustrated and really a
    fine example of the bookmaker's art, . . . presents the whole of northern Italy with
    much skill" (*Library Journal*).

PARK, MUNGO. 1771–1806

Scottish explorer Mungo Park was born in Foulshiels on the Yarrow and
studied medicine at Edinburgh. In 1792 he was an assistant surgeon on an
expedition to Sumatra, and in 1795 his services were accepted by the African
Association. One of the earliest Europeans to explore Africa, Park discovered
the Niger River, and his explorations helped to map the interior of Africa. His
classic account of his adventures was originally published as *Travels in the
Interior Districts of Africa* (1799). On a second expedition to Africa in 1805, he
was lost, along with all of his companions, after being attacked by natives.

BOOKS BY PARK

Journal of a Mission to the Interior of Africa. Ayer o.p.
Travels in the Interior Districts of Africa. Ayer $15.00. ISBN 0-405-18974-5

BOOKS ABOUT PARK

Lupton, Kenneth. *Mungo Park: The African Traveler.* OUP 1979 o.p. The life of Park with
    excerpts from his journal put into historical context.
Thomson, Joseph. *Mungo Park and the Niger.* Argosy 1970 repr. of 1890 ed. o.p.
    Interesting account of Park's Niger expedition.

PEARY, ROBERT E(DWIN). 1856–1920

Robert E. Peary, the American who discovered the North Pole, first became
interested in Arctic exploration after a trip into the interior of Greenland in
1886. Later trips there funded by the Philadelphia Academy of Natural Sciences

proved that Greenland is an island and resulted in his account *Northward over the Great Ice* (1898).

Nearest the Pole (1907) tells of his Arctic trip when the "farthest north" record was set about 200 miles from the North Pole. On April 6, 1909, Peary finally reached the North Pole after a voyage in the specially built ship *Roosevelt* and a long trek over ice via dog sled. He was accompanied by an African American and four Inuits. *The North Pole*, published in 1910, is his account of that final trip. He retired from the U.S. Navy in 1911 with the rank of rear admiral but again served his country during World War I.

Dr. Frederick A. Cook, who had been ship's surgeon on one of Peary's earlier expeditions, claimed that he had discovered the North Pole earlier than Peary. However, Cook's claim was later proved false, and Congress, in 1911, formally recognized Peary as the discoverer of the North Pole. Peary's wife accompanied him on several trips, and his daughter was born in the Arctic—she is believed to be the first white child born north of the Arctic circle.

BOOKS BY PEARY

Nearest the Pole: A Narrative of the Polar Expedition of the Peary Arctic Club in the S.S. Roosevelt, 1905–1906. AMS Pr. repr. of 1907 ed. o.p.

The North Pole: Its Discovery in 1909 under the Auspices of the Peary Arctic Club. Dover 1986 $9.95. ISBN 0-486-25129-2

Northward over the Great Ice: A Narrative of Life and World among the Shores and upon the Interior Ice Cap of Northern Greenland in the Years 1886 and 1891–1897. 2 vols. AMS Pr. repr. of 1898 ed. o.p.

BOOKS ABOUT PEARY

Anderson, Madelyn K. *Robert E. Peary and the Fight for the North Pole.* Ed. by Iris Rosoff. Watts 1992 $13.95. ISBN 0-531-15246-4. Focuses on the conflicting claims of Peary and Frederick Cook.

Counter, S. Allen. *North Pole Legacy: Black, White, and Eskimo.* U. of Mass. Pr. 1991 $24.95. ISBN 0-87023-736-5. Tells of locating the half-Eskimo sons of explorers Matthew Henson and Robert Peary and helping them achieve their dream of visiting the United States.

Herbert, Wally. *Noose of Laurels.* Doubleday 1990 $12.95. ISBN 0-385-41355-6. ". . . writes knowledgeably about two of the most fascinating of the fakers: Robert E. Peary and Dr. Frederick Cook, archrivals in heroics and fraud. . . . a fascinating account of what might be called the psychopathology of exploration" (*Time*).

POLO, MARCO. 1254?–1324?

The Venetian traveler Marco Polo was one of the greatest European explorers of the Middle Ages. The record of his journey to Central Asia and China was the main source for European ideas about the Far East until the late nineteenth century.

Born in Venice, Marco Polo traveled to China as a merchant with his father and uncle in 1271. In 1275, after years of travel across central Asia, the Polos finally arrived in Shan-tu, the summer capital of Kublai Khan, the Mongol emperor of China. The emperor already knew the elder Polos from an earlier trip, and he welcomed them all with honor. Although it is not known for certain what the Polos did during their years in the Far East, it is believed that Marco Polo served as an envoy for Kublai Khan during some of that time. The Polos returned to Venice in 1295 after an absence of 24 years. According to legend, the travelers were not recognized on their return.

Sometime after his return, Marco Polo took part in a naval battle between the Italian states of Venice and Genoa and was taken prisoner by the Genoese. While in prison, he dictated the story of his wondrous experiences in Asia to a fellow prisoner. This manuscript was the famous travel narrative, *The Travels of Marco Polo* (c.1298). Written originally in French, the work was soon translated into many languages.

The Travels of Marco Polo is more a work of science than an autobiography or a travel book. It contains little of Polo's personality (only the prologue tells of Polo's life) or even of his adventures. Instead, it contains descriptions of land forms, animals, plants, customs, governments, and religions. Polo's account of amazing things and a technologically superior culture was met with disbelief by many of his contemporaries. Nonetheless, it stimulated interest in the Far East and trade with the cultures there. The book even inspired the Italian explorer CHRISTOPHER COLUMBUS, who sailed west in 1492 in search of the riches of the Far East. Until the late nineteenth century, Polo's description of parts of Central Asia were the only Western descriptions available.

BOOKS BY POLO

The Book of Sir Marco Polo, the Venetian, Concerning the Kingdoms & Marvels of the East. 3 vols. Ed. and trans. by Henry Yule. AMS Pr. repr. of 1920 ed. $245.00. ISBN 0-404-11540-3

The Travels of Marco Polo. Trans. by Ronald Latham. Abaris Bks. 1982 $35.00. ISBN 0-89835-058

Travels of Marco Polo. Ed. by T. Wright. Trans. by Edward Marsden. AMS Pr. repr. of 1854 ed. $41.50. ISBN 0-404-50023-4

Travels of Marco Polo. Harmony Raine 1982 $18.95. ISBN 0-89967-045-8

BOOKS ABOUT POLO

Hart, Henry H. *Marco Polo: Venetian Adventurer.* U. of Okla. Pr. 1967 o.p. Discusses the life of Marco Polo and includes illustrations, maps, and facsimiles of Polo's handwriting.

Komroff, Manuel, ed. *Contemporaries of Marco Polo.* Hippocrene Bks. 1990 $17.95. ISBN 0-88029-438-8. Travel records to eastern parts of the world by people such as William Rubrock, John of Pian de Carpini, and Friar Odoric.

———. *The Travels of Marco Polo.* Liveright 1982 $10.95. ISBN 0-87140-132-0

Olschki, Leonardo. *Marco Polo's Asia: An Introduction to His "Description of the World" called "Il Milione."* Trans. by John A. Scott. U. CA Pr. 1960 o.p.

Ross, E. Denison. *Marco Polo and His Books.* Folcroft repr. of 1934 ed. o.p.

Rugoff, Milton. *The Travels of Marco Polo.* New Amer. Pr. 1982 o.p.

RIDE, SALLY. 1951–

Rejecting Billie Jean King's advice to pursue a career in tennis, Sally Ride instead went on to take a doctorate in astrophysics at Stanford University. As she was finishing her dissertation, she read an advertisement in the campus newspaper that the National Aeronautics and Space Administration (NASA) was looking for young scientists to serve as mission specialists. Selected from a field of 8,000 applicants, she began training in 1978 and served as capsule communicator on the second and third shuttle missions in 1981 and 1982. As mission specialist and flight engineer of the seventh mission, in 1983, she participated in the deployment and recapture of a West German 3,300-pound space laboratory. This successful maneuver proved the ability of a shuttle crew to retrieve malfunctioning satellites, make onboard repairs, and return them to orbit.

Though much lauded as the first American woman in space and pressed to sign contracts for licenses to sell merchandise, Ride always refused. Her book *To Space and Back* (coauthored with Susan Okie), published in 1985, recounts highlights of her nine-year career as an astronaut.

Since 1989, she has served as director of the California Space Institute and professor of physics at the University of California at San Diego.

BOOK BY RIDE

To Space and Back. (coauthored with Susan Okie). Lothrop 1989 repr. of 1985 ed. $16.95. ISBN 0-688-06159-1. An engrossing account of a space journey; provides details of adjusting to weightlessness, preparing and eating meals, going to the bathroom, working on scientific projects, and other activities.

ROOSEVELT, THEODORE. 1858–1919 (NOBEL PRIZE 1906)

Vice President of the United States under William McKinley and the nation's twenty-sixth president, Theodore Roosevelt was born in New York City to wealthy socialite parents. After graduating from Harvard College in 1880, Roosevelt studied law at Columbia University and then entered politics, holding a number of appointive and elective posts.

Roosevelt gained national attention when he resigned his post in the Department of the Navy to fight in the Spanish-American War. As a lieutenant-colonel, he headed a cavalry regiment known as the "Rough Riders." Their charge up San Juan Hill enabled the Americans to take the city of Santiago. An aggressive man with strong opinions, Roosevelt became a thorn in the side of Republican leaders who tried to "bury" him politically in the position of vice president under William McKinley. McKinley's assassination in 1901, however, resurrected Roosevelt's political fortunes. As president, Roosevelt made good use of his "bully pulpit." Believing firmly that government should protect the people, he used his powers to that end, advocating reform, calling for the conservation of natural resources, and mediation in foreign affairs. For his efforts, he won the Nobel Peace Prize in 1906.

A prolific writer, Roosevelt wrote numerous essays, historical analyses, speeches, and letters. When writing of his many adventures (including big-game hunting in Africa), he vividly re-created the dangers and excitement of his wilderness trips. Roosevelt was also an ardent field naturalist and conservationist; during his administration he established the U.S. Forest Service and five new national parks. One of his best-known books, *Stories of the West*, provides an interesting look at the last American frontier region.

BOOKS BY THEODORE ROOSEVELT

African Game Trails. St. Martin 1988 $19.95. ISBN 0-312-02151-8. An engagingly written account of big-game hunting in Africa in the early 1900s.

Hunting Trips of a Ranchman. Regnery Gateway 1991 o.p. The American West described by one who knew it and loved it.

Outdoor Pastimes of an American Hunter. Stackpole 1990 repr. of 1905 ed. $16.95. ISBN 0-8117-3033-6. An account of different hunting trips that pictures an unexploited, turn-of-the-century American West.

The Rough Riders. Da Capo 1990 $12.95. ISBN 0-306-80405-0. Provides essential details about raising the regiment and its experiences in Cuba.

BOOKS ABOUT THEODORE ROOSEVELT

McCullough, David. *Mornings on Horseback: The Story of an Extraordinary Family, A Vanished Way of Life, and the Unique Child Who Became Theodore Roosevelt*. S&S

Trade 1982 $14.95. ISBN 0-671-44754-8. By a National Book Award-winning author who received the *Los Angeles Times* 1981 Book Prize for Biography for this ". . . fine account of Roosevelt's rise to manhood . . . [which] like its subject [is] full of irrepressible vitality" (*Denver Post*).

Miller, Nathan. *Theodore Roosevelt: A Life*. Morrow 1992 $27.50. ISBN 0-688-06784-0. "[Fills the need for a complete one-volume biography [that] . . . takes into account all the new sources and studies of Theodore Roosevelt that have appeared in recent decades . . ." (John Allen Gable, *The Bull Moose Years*).

Morris, Edmund. *The Rise of Theodore Roosevelt*. Ballantine 1986 $16.00. ISBN 0-345-33902-9. "Magnificent . . . told purely as a hard-riding adventure story, his life puts Buffalo Bill to shame. . . . one of those rare works that is both definitive for the period it covers and fascinating to read . . ." (*New York Times*).

Pringle, Henry. *Theodore Roosevelt*. HarBraceJ 1956 $12.95. ISBN 0-15-688943-9. A Pulitzer Prize biography. A book in which "through biographer Pringle you hear Roosevelt" (*Time*).

SCOTT, ROBERT FALCON. 1868–1912

After an initial expedition to Antarctica, the Briton Robert Scott reached the South Pole in 1912 only to find that the Norwegian explorer ROALD AMUNDSEN had beaten him by a month. Scott and his party perished in a blizzard on the return trip. It was not until the following spring that their bodies and scientific documents were recovered. The documents were published in two books that are valuable as records of scientific research and as human documents. *Scott's Last Expedition* (1913) is his own classic diary of the tragedy, together with scientific material gathered on the journey. "Captain Scott kept a precise diary of the bitter days of his last journey South. His hands and feet crippled by frostbite, his eyes and mind befuddled by Antarctic blizzard, he traveled on to final defeat—and, in a way, magnificent triumph. Coming to the South Pole area itself, Scott was overwhelmed to learn that he had been preceded by the Norwegian. He knew full well the shattering implications in terms of personal and national prestige. But, gentleman to the end, he dutifully picked up Amundsen's message to the world (left at the South Pole in case Amundsen did not make it home successfully), and this eventually was conveyed to the King of Norway as proof that the Norwegian had beaten the Briton. Scott's was an act that could have been performed only by a man of honor. It is on the return trip that Scott's diary reaches a poignancy seldom matched in exploration writing" (*Saturday Review*).

BOOKS BY SCOTT

Scott's Last Expedition: Captain Scott's Own Story. Transatlantic 1923 o.p. Introduction by Peter Scott.

The Voyage of the Discovery. 2 vols. Greenwood 1969 repr. of 1905 ed. o.p. Details about Scott's polar expeditions; expanded from his travel diaries.

BOOKS ABOUT SCOTT

Markham, Clements R. *Antarctic Obsession*. B & N Imports 1986 $48.25. ISBN 0-389-20847-7. "The book reveals a story which will be fascinating to polar enthusiasts, and indeed to many geographers too" (*Geography Journal*).

Sipra, Paul. *Roald Amudsen & Robert Scott: Race for the South Pole*. Childrens 1990 $26.00. ISBN 0-516-03056-6. Story of the Scott-Amundsen rivalry to be the first to reach the South Pole.

Wright, Charles S. *The Canadian with Scott. The Antarctic Diaries and Memoir of Charles S. Wright*. Ed. by Colin Bull and Pat F. Wright. Ohio St. U. Pr. 1992. ISBN 0-8142-0548-8

SLOCUM, JOSHUA. 1844–1909

Captain Joshua Slocum was born in Wilmot Township, Nova Scotia. An intrepid mariner, he has been called the Thoreau of the Sea. In 1886 Slocum set off for South America with his wife and two sons in a boat named *Aquidneck*. Wrecked on a sandbar along the Brazilian coast, he built a canoe from the wreckage and returned safely with his family. Slocum set out in April 1896 to sail around the world alone in a small sloop called *The Spray* that he had reclaimed from a derelict. The voyage took three years, two months, and two days. He told the story of this trip in *Sailing Alone Around the World*. He started out on another voyage on November 14, 1909, but he was never heard from again.

BOOKS BY SLOCUM

Sailing Alone Around the World. Sheridan 1991 repr. of 1954 ed. $14.95. ISBN 0-911378-0-0. Exciting story of the first man ever to sail around the world alone in his boat, *Spray*.
The Voyage of the Liberdade (and *Sailing Alone*). Macmillan 1970 o.p.
The Voyages of Joshua Slocum. Ed. by Walter Magnes Teller. Sheridan 1985 repr. of 1958 ed. $29.95. ISBN 0-911378-55-3. Includes all the published works, hitherto unpublished correspondence, a checklist, and a selected bibliography.

BOOKS ABOUT SLOCUM

Slocum, Victor. *Captain Joshua Slocum.* Sheridan 1993 $16.50. ISBN 0-924486-52-X. Well-written biography.
Teller, Walter M. *Joshua Slocum.* Rutgers U. Pr. 1971 o.p. Traces Slocum's life as a sailor. Based partly on talks with people who knew him, and includes actual correspondence and photos.

SNOW, EDWARD (ROWE). 1902–1982

Author, historian, and adventurer Edward Snow was born in Winthrop, Massachusetts. Descended from a long line of sea captains, he spent several years of his early life sailing around the world. A prolific writer, Snow wrote a number of books about New England and the sea, including such works as *The Islands of Boston Harbor* (1935), *Ghost, Gales, and Gold* (1972), and *Pirates, Shipwrecks, and Historic Chronicles* (1981). The *New York Times* called Snow "just about the best chronicler of the days of sail."

BOOKS BY SNOW

Ghost, Gales and Gold. Dodd 1972 o.p.
The Islands of Boston Harbor: 1630–1971. Dodd 1984 repr. of 1971 ed. o.p.
The Lighthouses of New England, 1716–1973. Dodd 1984 o.p.
Marine Mysteries and Dramatic Disasters of New England. Dodd 1976 o.p.
Pirates, Shipwrecks, and Historic Chronicles. Dodd 1981 o.p.
Supernatural Mysteries and Other Tales: New England to the Bermuda Triangle. Dodd 1974 o.p.

STANLEY, SIR HENRY MORTON. 1841–1904

Stanley was a U.S. traveler born in Wales, educated in the poorhouse, and adopted by a New Orleans merchant who gave him his name. He fought in the Confederate army and after the war became a newspaper correspondent. He was commissioned by the *New York Herald* to go in search of DAVID LIVINGSTONE in 1871.

Stanley based one of his most popular books, *Through the Dark Continent* (1878), on a series of diaries in which he recorded the progress of his expedition of 1874–77. He presented the day-to-day account of his journeys undertaken to discover the sources of the Nile and Congo rivers, his circumnavigation of Lakes Victoria and Tanganyika, and his dangerous trip down the Congo River to Boma.

BOOKS BY STANLEY

Autobiography. Ed. by Dorothy Stanley. Greenwood repr. of 1909 ed. o.p.

The Congo and the Founding of Its Free State. 2 vols. Scholarly repr. of 1885 ed. o.p. Account of his travels and stay in the Congo, with an eye toward encouraging British trade in Africa. Includes maps.

Coomassie and Magdala: The Story of Two British Campaigns in Africa. Select Bibliographies Repr. Ser. Ayer repr. of 1874 ed. $32.00. ISBN 0-8369-5816-0

How I Found Livingstone. Greenwood repr. of 1913 ed. $35.00. ISBN 0-8371-1995-2

My Early Travels and Adventures in America. Bks. Demand repr. of 1882 ed. $88.90. ISBN 0-7837-1836-5

My Kalulu, Prince, King, and Slave: A Story of Central Africa. Greenwood repr. of 1874 ed. o.p.

The Story of Emin's Rescue as Told in Stanley's Letters. Ed. by J. S. Keltie. Greenwood repr. of 1890 ed. o.p.

Through the Dark Continent, or The Sources of the Nile, around the Great Lakes of Equatorial Africa, and down the Livingstone River to the Atlantic Ocean. 1878. 2 vols. Dover 1988 $19.90. ISBNs 0-486-25667-7, 0-486-25668-5

BOOKS ABOUT STANLEY

Anstruther, Ian. *I Presume: H. M. Stanley's Triumph and Disaster.* A. Sutton Pub. 1989 $12.00. ISBN 0-86299-472-1. Focuses on Stanley as a Victorian and what his relationship with Dr. Livingstone meant to him.

Bierman, John. *Dark Safari: The Life behind the Legend of H. M. Stanley.* Knopf 1990 $24.95. ISBN 0-39458342-6. Reveals Stanley as a bully, a braggart, and a hypocrite, yet recognizes and celebrates his achievements.

Buel, James W. *Heroes of the Dark Continent.* Ayer repr. of 1889 ed. $32.75. ISBN 0-8369-8725-X

Farwell, Byron. *The Man Who Presumed: A Biography of Henry M. Stanley.* Norton 1989 $8.95. ISBN 0-393-30629-1. An easy-to-read biography; focuses primarily on his travels in Africa.

Kelsey, D. M. *Stanley's Story, or Through the Wilds of Africa.* Africa History Ser. Wolfe Pub. Co. 1988 $37.00. ISBN 0-935632-74-3

McLynn, Frank. *Stanley: The Making of an African Explorer.* Madson Bks. UPA 1990 $23.95. ISBN 0-8128-4008-9. A well-documented, balanced treatment of Stanley.

STARK, FREYA (MADELINE). 1893–1993

Freya Stark was brought up in northwestern Italy. After 1914 she became a wartime censor and then a nurse. She studied Arabic with a Capuchin monk in San Remo and after 1927 began wanderings into remote parts of the Middle East—alone, usually in poverty, and often ill. She was in the British government service, chiefly at Aden, Cairo, and Baghdad, from 1939 to 1945, and married S. H. Perowne in 1947. In 1952 she traveled about the western coast of Turkey looking at 55 ruined sites.

"Most of all she delighted in southern Arabia, but her passion for Persia comes out in clear, crisp descriptions. . . . For her light gleams from the ancient temples and the incense found in a Himyaritic tomb still smells sweetly" (*New York Times*). The *Atlantic* called her *Rome on the Euphrates* "an illuminating history of the Roman frontier in Asia Minor and the Middle East. The story sprawls across the events of eight centuries from west Africa from the Battle of Magnesia in 189 B.C. to the death of Justinian in 565 A.D. The author is not a professional historian, but she has worked through the basic sources with care, and she knows how to tell an interesting story." The *New Statesman* wrote: "Stark can astonish us no more. She has long been the first of contemporary English travel writers." Harold Nicolson said, "She has written the best travel books of her generation and her name will survive as an artist in prose."

BOOKS BY STARK

Alexander's Path. 1958. Overlook Pr. 1990 $17.95. ISBN 0-87951-309-8. Recreates ". . . the route that Alexander the Great . . . took. . . . An excellent and absorbing travel book that rewards the reader with its magical mingling of the ancient and the modern" (*Publishers Weekly*).

Ionia: A Quest. Transaction Pubs. 1990 $22.95. ISBN 1-805089-277-6. An account of Stark's travels along the coast of Turkey in 1952 before the intrusion of mass tourism.

The Journey's Echo. Ecco Pr. 1988 repr. of 1963 ed. $8.95. ISBN 0-88001-218-8. [This small anthology is both] ". . . a celebration of her past work and . . . the work to come. [One] who comes fresh to her is much to be envied [as he stumbles] upon prose so melodious, so energetic, and so spare" (*Foreword* by Lawrence Durrell).

The Valley of the Assassins: And Other Persian Travels. Transaction Pubs. 1985 $15.95. ISBN 1-85089-016-1. An account of several journeys into little-known regions of Persia.

Zodiac Arch. Transatlantic 1975 o.p. A collection of essays and remembrances of Stark's journeys, including her thoughts arising from these travels.

STEFANSSON, VILHJALMUR. 1879–1962

Stefansson, Canadian-born of Icelandic parentage and the last of the dog-sled explorers, spent many years in the Arctic. His books aim to combat popular misconceptions about the Far North. They show that it is a good place for colonization, that human life can be supported there on a diet of seal alone, and that it has possibilities for commercial usefulness. Stefansson's "findings changed man's prevailing concepts. By 'humanizing' the icy north, he became known as the man who robbed the Arctic Circle of all its terrors and most of its discomforts" (*Boston Globe*). As far back as 1915, he suggested the feat that the atom-powered *Nautilus* finally accomplished—submerging under the Arctic ice on the Pacific side and emerging, after two months, on the Atlantic side. The whole fascinating search for a northwest passage is told with scholarly authority in his *Northwest to Fortune* (1958). "Clearly and lovingly written, the book brings color and even warmth to regions which for so many of us have seemed wrapped in cold, fog, and ice" (*Christian Science Monitor*).

BOOKS BY STEFANSSON

Adventures in Error. Gale 1970 repr. of 1936 ed. o.p.

The Friendly Arctic: The Story of Five Years in Polar Regions. Greenwood repr. of 1943 ed. o.p.

Hunters of the Great North. AMS Pr. repr. of 1922 ed. $27.50. ISBN 0-404-11686-8

Iceland: The First American Republic. Greenwood 1971 repr. of 1939 ed. $38.50. ISBN 0-8371-5167-8. Preface by Theodore Roosevelt.

Northwest to Fortune. Greenwood 1974 repr. of 1958 ed. $45.00. ISBN 0-8371-5729-3

The Stefansson-Anderson Arctic Expedition of the American Museum of Natural History: Preliminary Ethnological Report. 1914. AMS Pr. repr. of 1919 ed. $42.50. ISBN 0-404-11688-4

Unsolved Mysteries of the Arctic. Press N. Amer. 1985 repr. of 1938 ed. $9.95. ISBN 0-938271-02-4. Introduction by Stephen Leacock.

BOOKS ABOUT STEFANSSON

Hunt, William R. *Stefansson: A Biography of Vilhjalaur, Canadian Arctic Explorer.* U. of Brit. Col. Pr. 1986 o.p. ". . . fast paced yet scholarly . . . the first balanced biography dealing with the often controversial Stefansson. . . . based . . . on previously unpublished documents" (*Choice*).

Le Bourdais, Donat M. *Stefansson: Ambassador of the North.* Bks. Demand $51.50. ISBN 0-7459-1307-5

THEROUX, PAUL (EDWARD). 1941–

Born in Medford, Massachusetts, Paul Theroux's writing reflects his relatively footloose life. Though known primarily as a travel writer, Theroux's literary output also includes novels, books for children, short stories, and poetry. His novels include *Picture Palace* (1978), which won the Whitbread Award; *The Mosquito Coast* (1981), which won the James Tait Black Award; *Saint Jack* (1973), filmed in 1979; and *Doctor Slaughter* (1984), filmed as *Half Moon Street* in 1987.

Although Theroux has also written general travel books and books about various modes of transport, his name is synonymous with the literature of train travel. He has remarked that "ever since childhood, when I lived within earshot of the Boston and Maine, I have seldom heard a train go by and not wished I was on it. Those whistles sing bewitchment; railways are irresistible bazaars." Theroux's 1975 best-seller, *The Great Railway Bazaar*, takes the reader through Asia. His second book about train travel, *The Old Patagonian Express* (1979), describes his trip from Boston to the tip of South America. His third contribution to the railway travel genre, *Riding the Iron Rooster: By Train Through China* (1989), won the Thomas Cook Prize for best literary travel book in 1989.

Theroux's leisure interest in rowing perhaps accounts in part for his latest book, *The Happy Isles of Oceania* (1992). He traveled to 51 islands and 1 continent by cargo ship, train, and collapsible kayak. He explored obscure coastal nooks, juts, and islets and included, according to an article in the *National Geographic Traveler*, ". . . summary lessons on the concept of South Sea paradises, cargo cults, cannibalism, privately owned islands, missionaries, THOR HEYERDAHL, diet, and colonialism."

BOOKS BY THEROUX

The Great Railway Bazaar. Ballantine 1981 $2.95. ISBN 0-345-30110-2. One of the few travel books to become a best-seller.

The Happy Isles of Oceania. Putnam Pub. Group 1992 $24.95. ISBN 0-399-13726-2

The Kingdom by the Sea: A Journey around Great Britain. PB 1990 repr. of 1983 ed. $6.99. ISBN 0-671-70923-2. ". . . filled with history, insights, landscape, epiphanies, meditations, celebrations, and laments . . ." (*New York Times*).

The Old Patagonian Express: By Train Through the Americas. HM 1989 $9.70. ISBN 0-395-52105-X. Makes Theroux's name synonymous with the literature of train travel.

Riding the Iron Rooster: By Train Through China. Outlet Bk. Co. 1991 $5.99. ISBN 0-517-03032-2. ". . . an opinionated, petty, and incomplete portrait [of China]" (*N. Y. Times Book Review*).

Sandstorms: Days and Nights in Arabia. Norton 1991 o.p. ". . . brimming with vivid sketches of life in a volatile, often contradictory, ever-intriguing culture" (*The Book Buyer's Advisor*).

To the Ends of the Earth. Random 1991 $23.00. ISBN 0-679-40246-2. Theroux's selection of his own travel writing, ". . . first class armchair traveling" (*Sunday Telegraph*).

VAN DER POST, LAURENS. 1906–

Colonel Laurens Van der Post, a British subject born in South Africa, has "spent most of his adult life with one foot in Africa and one in England." A soldier, explorer, traveler, and philosopher, he fought in World War II in Ethiopia, Syria, and the Far East. Since the war he has worked for the British government on a variety of missions throughout Africa. Van der Post's beautifully composed *Venture to the Interior* (1952) is much more than an account of the planned journey from London to Nyasaland in South Africa, the climbing of Mianje, and the exploration of Nyika. It catches the "unique and indefinable spirit of the ancient continent" and explores the interiors of people's minds. His *The Heart of the Hunter* (1961) points the way toward a rediscovery of the positive values of the wilderness in our own lives.

BOOKS BY VAN DER POST

A Far Off Place. HarBraceJ 1978 $10.95. ISBN 0-15-630198-9. A novel imbued with love of the land and studded with detail.

First Catch Your Eland. Ulverscroft 1982 $15.95. ISBN 0-7089-0868-3. "The author . . . has collected his thoughts about food as an expression of the various cultures of the African continent" (*N. Y. Times Book Review*).

The Heart of the Hunter. Transaction Pubs. 1986 $16.95. ISBN 1-85089-042-0. A study of the heart and soul of the African Bushmen that started in *The Lost World of the Kalahari*.

Journey into Russia. Island Pr. 1984 repr. of 1964 ed. $16.95. ISBN 0-933280-25-4. A simply written account of his travels throughout Russia, with some discussion of Russian history.

The Lost World of the Kalahari. Transaction Pubs. 1985 $15.95. ISBN 1-85089-007-2. An account of an expedition into the remote Kalahari Desert to study the few remaining communities of the Bushmen.

A Mantis Carol. Island Pr. 1975 o.p. Tells of the transmigration of a soul from the Kalamari to New York City with ". . . a beautiful command of language, an extraordinary psychological awareness, and a spellbinding ability to evoke the sights and sounds and moods of the African interior" (*Atlantic*).

Patterns of Renewal. Pendle Hill 1962 $3.00. ISBN 0-87574-121-5

Venture to the Interior. Transaction Pubs. 1987 repr. of 1952 ed. $18.95. ISBN 1-85089-157-5

A View of All the Russias. Morrow 1964 o.p. ". . . a fine piece of impressionistic writing, sensitive and perceptive, occasionally accurate but hardly the fare for the reader in search of information and insight" (*Library Journal*).

VESPUCCI, AMERIGO. 1451–1512

The Renaissance Florentine navigator Amerigo Vespucci, who explored the coast of America from Florida to the tip of South America, was the first to declare South America a continent rather than a series of islands, as was previously thought. Vespucci also measured the earth's circumference more accurately than anyone before him and devised a system for determining exact longitude.

Born into a noble family in Florence, Italy, Vespucci had an early interest in geography and navigation. He trained for a career in business, however, and was sent to Spain in 1492 as a representative of Florence's Medici family. While in Spain, Vespucci may have helped secure financing for the voyages of CHRISTOPHER COLUMBUS. His contact with Columbus and other explorers increased his interest in navigation, and he sought to make his own voyages of exploration.

Vespucci made two voyages to the West, the first in 1499–1500 for Spain and the second in 1501–1502 for Portugal. During these expeditions, he explored over 6,000 miles of coastline and determined that the lands Columbus discovered were not islands off the continent of Asia but were part of a "new world." Using his unique system of celestial navigation, Vespucci also correctly theorized that two oceans, rather than one, lay between the west coast of Europe and the east coast of Asia.

A letter allegedly written by Vespucci in 1504 claimed that he had made four voyages rather than two. However, this matter has been widely disputed, and no positive proof has been found to either prove or disprove the claim. In 1507 the German geographer Martin Waldseemüller published Vespucci's accounts of his voyages and suggested that the new lands to the West be named America in honor of the man who determined that they were new continents.

BOOK BY VESPUCCI

Letters and Other Documents Illustrative of His Career. Ed. and trans. by Clements R. Markham. *Hakluyt Society Ser.* B. Franklin repr. of 1894 ed. o.p.

BOOK ABOUT VESPUCCI

Alper, Ann Fitzpatrick. *Forgotten Voyager: The Story of Amerigo Vespucci.* Carolrhoda Bks. 1991 $11.95. ISBN 0-87614-442-3. Supports the work of Alberto Magnaghi, who studied early letters, and shows Vespucci's role in the discovery of the Americas.

Name Index

In addition to authors of books, this index includes the names of persons mentioned in introductory essays, section introductions, biographical profiles, general bibliographic entries, and "Books about" sections. Throughout, however, persons mentioned only in passing—to indicate friendships, relationships, and so on—are generally not indexed. Editors, translators, and compilers are not indexed unless there is no specific author given for the work in question. Writers of the introductions, forewords, afterwords, and similar parts of works are not indexed. The names of individuals who are represented by separate biographical profiles appear in boldface, as do the page numbers on which their profiles appear.

Title Index

Titles of all books discussed in *The Reader's Adviser* are indexed here, except broad generic titles such as "Complete Works," "Selections," "Poems," "Correspondence." Also omitted is any title written by a profiled author that also includes that author's full name or last name as part of the title, such as *The Collected Writings of John Maynard Keynes*. The only exception to this is Shakespeare (Volume 1), where *all* works by and about him are indexed. To locate all titles by and about a profiled author, the user should refer to the Name Index for the author's primary listing (given in boldface). In general, subtitles are omitted unless two or more works have the same main title, or the main title consists of an author's full or last name (e.g., *Maria Callas: The Woman Behind the Legend*). When two or more works by different authors have the same title, the authors' last names will appear in parentheses following the title.

Subject Index

This index provides detailed, multiple-approach access to the subject content of the volume. Arrangement is alphabetical. The names of profiled, main-entry authors are not included in this index; the reader is reminded to use the Name Index to locate these individuals. For additional information, the reader should refer to the detailed Table of Contents at the front of the volume.